CONSTITUTIONAL LAW

SEVENTH EDITION

By

John E. Nowak
David C. Baum Professor of Law Emeritus
University of Illinois

Ronald D. Rotunda
George Mason University Foundation Professor of Law
George Mason University School of Law

HORNBOOK SERIES®

THOMSON
™
WEST

Mat #40117044

Hornbook Series, *Westlaw*, and West Group are trademarks
registered in the U.S. Patent and Trademark Office.

COPYRIGHT © 1978, 1983, 1986, 1991, 1995 By WEST PUBLISHING CO.
COPYRIGHT © 2000 By WEST GROUP
© 2004 West, a Thomson business
      610 Opperman Drive
      P.O. Box 64526
      St. Paul, MN 55164–0526
      1–800–328–9352

ISBN 0–314–14452–8

 TEXT IS PRINTED ON 10% POST
CONSUMER RECYCLED PAPER

To my granddaughter, Julia: Happy First Birthday!—J.E.N.

To Ellen and Neil—R.D.R.

*

Preface to Seventh Edition

Many years have passed since we first signed an agreement with West Publishing to prepare a one volume treatise on constitutional law. We have been very pleased by the acceptance that the first six editions of this text have received from lawyers, judges, and scholars, as well as law students. The passage of time, and changes in constitutional doctrines that are the product of new Supreme Court decisions, have made it necessary for us to publish this new edition. We hope that this seventh edition of this reference text will be as well received by law students and professors as were the earlier editions.

A one volume text on constitutional law cannot serve both the needs of law students and the needs of all segments of the bench and bar. For that reason, in 1986 we published a multivolume *Treatise on Constitutional Law*, which is an expansion of this one volume treatise. We published the third edition of the multivolume *Treatise* in 1999. To distinguish this five volume *Treatise* from its single volume counterpart, the sequence of the authors' names is rotated on the *Treatise*, but the nature of the contributions and our editorial responsibilities has not been altered. Professors Nowak and Rotunda share equally the responsibility for the five volume *Treatise* and this one volume text.

In this text we provide analysis of the constitutional issues that are most studied and litigated today. As in earlier editions of this single volume book, we give little attention to issues that are not commonly studied in law school courses on constitutional law, such as court jurisdiction, conflict of laws, and criminal procedure. At appropriate points we refer the readers to our multivolume *Treatise* and to some other texts that examine those subjects. Many issues that we cover only briefly in this one volume work, including litigation problems under the Civil Rights Acts and problems of state and local taxation, are analyzed at length in our multivolume *Treatise*.

Because of space limitations in this edition, we have had to limit our references to secondary authorities, and to court decisions other than those of the United States Supreme Court. We hope that no scholar or judge will feel slighted by our failure to refer to his or her work in this one volume text. The five volume *Treatise* treats all of the subjects covered in this text with greater depth and with many more references to secondary authorities. The reader who uses this text as a starting point for a research project should refer to the multivolume *Treatise* for additional references on lower court decisions and secondary authorities.

The cut-off date for cases covered in this volume is March 1, 2004. We will publish periodic supplements to this text; we publish yearly pocket parts to the multivolume *Treatise*.

The number of persons to whom we are indebted has grown so large as to make it uneconomical for West Publishing Co. to print a complete listing of those who have played a role in the publication of the various editions of this text. Such a list would include not only all those persons mentioned in the preface to our first edition but also professors from across the country who have given us their reactions to the first six editions and suggestions for this edition. We are also grateful to the hundreds of judges who have written to us, commented upon, or cited our work. We also thank our students and staff who have contributed their efforts to this edition, particularly our secretaries, Jane Barton and Sally Cook. Professor Nowak would like to give special recognition to his faculty assistant, Mrs. Sally Cook, who has provided critical help in producing the manuscript, and in catching as many of Professor Nowak's grammatical errors as was humanly possible.

Our colleague, coauthor, and friend, J. Nelson Young, died before we began work on the third edition of this text. We still miss him. Nelson was responsible for our sections on state and local taxation, which now appear primarily in the multivolume *Treatise*. Nelson's contribution to the first two editions of this text, and the *Treatise*, was greater than a single chapter, however. When we were young professors beginning to work on the first edition, Nelson gave us not only knowledge about an area of constitutional law with which we were not familiar, but also an insight into the meaning of scholarship and collegiality. Although this edition does not contain Nelson's words, we hope that it reflects Nelson's view of legal scholarship.

J.E.N.
R.D.R.

March, 2004

Preface to First Edition

As has been often noted, it may be impossible to prepare a single volume treatise on Constitutional Law. To keep this volume within manageable size, we have had to exclude a variety of constitutional issues from consideration, and focus instead on selected areas of constitutional adjudication and decision-making. We have omitted most issues relating to jurisdiction, conflicts of laws, and criminal procedure; there are many fine texts which examine these specialized subject areas. In general, we have emphasized those areas of Constitutional Law which are most often studied and litigated today as well as those emerging issues that we believe will be of most importance in the years ahead. In the annual supplements to this edition we will include references to all constitutional opinions of the Supreme Court; these later developments, indeed, may alter the scope of our coverage in future editions. But for the present we have had to make subjective judgments concerning the areas that will be of most significance to students and scholars in the next several years.

Within each Chapter the reader will find subsections that differ in length and depth of treatment of particular issues—varying from summations of the Supreme Court's work to lengthy, analytical evaluations of the judicial process. We hope that each major section, when viewed as a unit, will give an accurate picture of what the Court has done and an evaluation of that work in terms of accepted scholarly critiques and our own analyses. We have endeavored to identify those portions of the text that emphasize our interpretive views of issues, as opposed to factual accounts of the work of the Court. In attempting to incorporate the political, historic and economic background of some of the more significant Court decisions, we have of necessity engaged in subjective evaluations and judgments.

It is far too late in the history of constitutional scholarship for the authors of a text such as this to claim full credit for the ideas presented in their work. In a very real sense we are indebted to all of those scholars whose works have gone before us and aided us in our own studies—from the late Professors Corwin and Thayer to the many outstanding scholars of today. In particular, we have been aided by the many excellent casebooks that are currently published for law school use; these texts have served all professors of Constitutional Law as important research resources as well as stimulating teaching tools. We have cited casebooks, texts and articles where we thought that those works would be of particular aid to the reader who refers to this book for study or research guidance; unfortunately, space requirements have limited our citations to secondary authorities.

We also gratefully acknowledge the invaluable suggestions of those professors who have commented upon drafts of our manuscript: Derrick A. Bell, Jr. of Harvard, Jesse H. Choper of the University of California at Berkeley, Martin H. Redish of Northwestern University, William W. Van Alstyne of Duke University, and our colleagues at the University of Illinois, Wayne R. LaFave and Peter H. Hay. Our indebtedness to all these scholars cannot be overstated. Their work is responsible for improvements to the text; responsibility for its failures remains with us alone (though each of us believes that the other two are at fault).

We also wish to express our thanks to the various students at the College who have aided us throughout the last three years with work ranging from research assignments to the drudgery of citation checking: Kimball Anderson, Karen Butler, Nancy J. Clawson, David Crumbaugh, David Finch, Judy Gross, Marianne Guerrini, Mary Hester-Tone, Robert Markowski, Gary Nelson, Judith Perlman, Frances E. Prell, Charles Salowitz, Patricia Smart, James Vroman and Ruth Wilcox. We express our appreciation to our secretaries, Kay Tresslar and Cynthia Utley, and those who assisted them—Beth Cobb, Patricia Estergard, Linda Graham, Patricia Love, and Judy Nowak.

A note on citation forms: To conserve space we have cited each Supreme Court case only to the official reporter; parallel citations to the Supreme Court Reporter and the Lawyers Edition may be found in the tables in the introductory pages of each bound volume of those reporters. We have cited recent cases to the Supreme Court reporter system when citations to the U.S. Reports were not available. The cut-off date for this volume is July 1, 1977. After initial citations and references to Bator, Mishkin, Shapiro and Wechsler, *Hart and Wechsler's The Federal Courts and the Federal System* (2d ed. 1973), we subsequently cite this excellent text only by its title. To make our cross references within sections easier to follow, we have generally used a separate numbering system for the footnotes in each subsection. Footnote cross references refer to the numbers within the same section; there are no cross references solely by footnote number to other portions of the text. We trust that these few peculiarities of our citation pattern will cause no inconvenience to the reader.

J.E.N.
R.D.R.
J.N.Y.

Champaign, Illinois
December, 1977

WESTLAW® Overview

Constitutional Law offers a detailed and comprehensive treatment of the basic rules, principles, and issues relating to constitutional law. To supplement the information contained in this book, you can access Westlaw, West's computer-assisted legal research service. Westlaw contains a broad array of legal resources, including case law, statutes, expert commentary, current developments, and various other types of information.

Learning how to use these materials effectively will enhance your legal research abilities. To help you coordinate the information in the book with your Westlaw research, this volume contains an appendix listing Westlaw databases, search techniques, and sample problems.

The instructions and features described in this Westlaw overview are based on accessing Westlaw via westlaw.com® at **www.westlaw.com**.

THE PUBLISHER

*

Summary of Contents

---

*

Table of Contents

CHAPTER 3.   SOURCES OF NATIONAL AUTHORITY

CHAPTER 4. THE FEDERAL COMMERCE POWER

CHAPTER 5. FEDERAL FISCAL POWERS

CHAPTER 6. INTERNATIONAL AFFAIRS

CHAPTER 17. FREEDOM OF RELIGION

APPENDICES

*

CONSTITUTIONAL LAW

*

Chapter 1

THE ORIGINS OF JUDICIAL REVIEW

§ 1.1 Introduction

The power of the Supreme Court to determine the constitutionality and, therefore, the validity of the acts of the other branches of government is firmly established as a basic component of the American system of Government. But it was not always so, and a major part of the Court's history has been its continuing effort to establish, maintain, and strengthen judicial power.

In a very real sense this entire treatise is an elaboration of the subject of this chapter, judicial review. Later chapters discuss the establishment and proper scope of judicial review in connection with a wide variety of subjects, ranging from the commerce clause to due process and the First Amendment. Here, we set out the early decisions establishing judicial review, coupled with an analysis of the historical debate and academic commentary.

§ 1.2 *Marbury v. Madison—* The Setting of the Case

The last years of the eighteenth century was a time of intense political rivalry for the new nation. The Federalist Party controlled the national government and did not hesitate to use its powers for partisan purposes, exemplified by the Sedition Act, which punished those who spoke out against President Adams or the Federalist Congress. The opposition responded with animosity towards the Federalists and the Federalist judges who enforced the Sedition Act against competing political parties.

In 1800, the Federalists lost power for a variety of reasons, including popular reaction against their use of the Sedition Act and the growing tensions with Great Britain.[1] Jefferson won the popular vote for the presidency but there was a tie vote between Jefferson and Aaron Burr in the electoral college. Jefferson was to be chosen President by the new House of Representatives.

Although the Federalists were facing the end of their era of power (the Federalists would never again win the White House), Adams remained President until the end of his term on March 4, 1801. In December 1800, Oliver Ellsworth, third Chief Justice of the United States, resigned his position on the Supreme Court. President Adams first sought to reappoint former Chief Justice John Jay to the Court, but Jay refused the appointment. Then Adams nominated John Marshall, his Secretary of State and a leading figure in the Federalist Party. On January 27, 1801, the lame duck Senate confirmed Marshall's nomination, and he became Chief Justice on February 4, 1801, only a month before Jefferson would take office. At President Adams' request, Marshall continued to serve as Secretary of State for the remainder of Adams' term.

In the last few weeks before Jefferson and the Republicans (sometimes also referred to as Democratic–Republicans, or Anti–Federalists) took office, the Federalists sought to maintain some of their power through continued control of an expanded federal judiciary. The Federalists passed the Circuit Court Act, which re-

§ 1.2

1. Robert McCloskey, The American Supreme Court at 37–38 (1960).

duced the number of Supreme Court Justices and eliminated the practice of having the Justices individually hold court in the circuits.[2] The Act also established sixteen new circuit courts and federal judgeships. President Adams quickly filled these new positions with federalist appointees, who received confirmation only two days before Jefferson was to take office, and who thus came to be known as the "midnight judges." But it was even later appointments that gave rise to the *Marbury* litigation.

On February 27, 1801, the holdover Federalist Congress authorized the appointment of 42 Justices of the peace to serve five-year terms in the District of Columbia and Alexandria.[3] President Adams appointed Federalists to these positions, and the Senate confirmed them on March 3, the day before the Republicans were to take office. The formal appointments were made by delivery of sealed commissions by the Secretary of State. John Marshall, as Secretary of State, executed and sought to deliver these commissions but, even though he had some assistance, there remained a few undelivered commissions that night.

Needless to say, the Republicans were not pleased by the prospect of these new Federalist judges taking office, and they took several steps to alter the situation. First, Jefferson's Secretary of State, James Madison, refused to deliver the remaining commissions for the Justices of the Peace. Second, the Republican Congress, after a debate on the wisdom and constitutionality of altering the judicial structure, repealed the Circuit Court Act in 1802, thus eliminating these judicial positions.[4]

William Marbury was one of the Justices of the peace whom Adams had appointed, but who had failed to receive his commission. Marbury sued the new Secretary of State, James

Madison, for delivery of his commission. He filed an original action in the Supreme Court seeking an order of mandamus to compel Madison to deliver the commission. He asserted jurisdiction under § 13 of the Judiciary Act of 1789, one of the first acts of that the new Congress, created by the new Constitution, had enacted.

Jefferson believed that a court could not order him to take such an action and so he instructed Madison to refuse to appear before the Supreme Court. The Court responded by issuing a rule to show cause as to why the mandamus should not issue and set the case for argument in the 1802 term. Congress was in the process of repealing the Circuit Court Act, and it rebuffed the Court by rescheduling the terms of the Supreme Court and eliminated part of the 1802 term of the Court.

Thus, when the Court began its 1803 term, it faced the issue of defining the judicial power in relation to the other branches of government. The Court avoided invalidating the repeal of the Circuit Court Act a week after it ruled it had no jurisdiction to entertain Marbury's action.[5] But, the decision in *Marbury* asserted judicial power to review the constitutionality of the actions of both the executive and legislative branches of the federal government.

Although the Republicans disputed this claim to power, the political opposition could not disobey the Court, for neither ruling actually ordered the Jeffersonians to do anything. Technically, Jefferson won; he had no order to defy because the Court did not order him or his Secretary of State to do anything. Had the Court reached another result in the case, the Republican Congress might well have considered impeaching the federalist Justices on the Supreme Court.[6] Instead, Marshall was able to establish the claim to judicial authority with-

2. Act of February 13, 1801, Ch. 4; 2 Stat. 89.

3. Act of February 27, 1801, Ch. 15; 2 Stat. 103.

4. Act of March 8, 1802, Ch. 8; 2 Stat. 132. For a history of the debate see 1 Charles Warren, The Supreme Court in United States History 204–22 (1932).

5. Stuart v. Laird, 5 U.S. (1 Cranch) 299, 2 L.Ed. 115 (1803). In this case the Court upheld part of the act but did not confront the most difficult issues. However, the

case is often cited as upholding the repeal act by implication.

6. Indeed the House of Representatives later did impeach Justice Chase, a leading and hated partisan Federalist, but the trial failed in the Senate. See, 1 Charles Warren, The Supreme Court in United States History 289–95 (1932).

out taking actions that would provoke immediate political reprisals. Jefferson won, and the Court cemented the theory that it has the power to declare laws unconstitutional.

§ 1.3 *Marbury v. Madison*—The Opinion of the Court

On February 24, 1803, Chief Justice Marshall delivered the opinion of the Court in *Marbury v. Madison*,[1] holding that Marbury had a right to his judicial commission, but that the Court would not enforce this right because the jurisdictional law under which he was suing was unconstitutional. In so doing, the Court found that the executive was subject to constitutional restraints that could be enforced by the judiciary. The Court also held that it could not grant a remedy because this original action was not within the jurisdiction that Article III fixed for the Court. Marshall interpreted a section of the Judiciary Act of 1789 as placing this action within its jurisdiction, but then found that this law conflicted with the Constitution and thus was invalid.

Marshall began his opinion by framing the case in terms of three issues. First, does Marbury had a right to the commission? Second, does the laws of the country established a remedy for the deprivation of the right? Third, can a mandamus be issued in an original action before the Supreme Court?[2]

Marshall first ruled that Marbury had a right to the commission once it was signed by the President and sealed by the Secretary of State. Based on the act of Congress authorizing the appointment of Justices of the Peace for the District of Columbia, the opinion ruled that the commission was a "vested legal right".[3]

The Court might have held that the right did not vest until delivery of the commission, thus avoiding the constitutional issues, but the Court instead stated that an irrevocable right accrued to the individual after the execution of the commission. The Court thus criticized the new administration and President Jefferson, who was Marshall's political adversary.

On the second issue, the opinion found that the "essence of civil liberty" required a legal remedy for a legal wrong. Because the government of the United States is one "of laws and not of men" it must grant a remedy for violation of vested legal rights.[4] Marshall did note that there would not be a judicial remedy for a wrong if the subject matter was political in nature or otherwise committed to the discretion of the executive.[5] In such instances the individual's remedy would have to be left to the political process. But, where individual rights depend on a duty established by law, there was a remedy that must be judicially enforced to protect the injured individual. This argument laid the basis for his conclusions in the next section concerning the scope of judicial review.

The crucial issue in the case thus became whether Marbury was entitled to the remedy for which he had applied to the Supreme Court. Marshall subdivided this issue into two further questions concerning the nature of the writ of mandamus and the power of the Court.

In examining the nature of the writ, the opinion asserted a judicial power to review the acts of the executive branch. Because the writ of mandamus is an order to an officer to take a specific action, Marshall inquired as to whether it could be used against officers of the executive branch. He recognized that the importance of the relationship between the President and the high executive officers, such as cabinet members, was one that should not be examined absent specific legal justification. Indeed, Marshall found two classes of executive acts that were not subject to judicial review. Where the action by the President or executive officers was in its nature "political" the matter was not one for judicial intervention.[6] Simi-

§ 1.3

1. 5 U.S. (1 Cranch) 137, 2 L.Ed. 60 (1803).

2. Note that Marshall asks last the question dealing with jurisdiction: does the Supreme Court have jurisdiction to issue mandamus in an original action.

3. 5 U.S. (1 Cranch) at 162.

4. 5 U.S. (1 Cranch) at 163.

5. 5 U.S. (1 Cranch) at 166.

6. This portion of *Marbury* portended the political question doctrine of Luther v. Borden, 48 U.S. (7 How.) 1, 12 L.Ed. 581 (1849) and its progeny.

larly, where the Constitution or federal law placed a subject matter within the sole discretion of the executive, it could not be reviewed by the Court. However, Marshall found that it was not the nature of the executive branch that limited judicial review but only the nature of the act: that is, the judiciary should not seek to review solely political or discretionary acts, but can review other acts of the executive branch.[7]

If the Constitution or federal law imposed some duty on the executive branch, the judiciary can enforce that duty. In such a case there is no intrusion into the power granted the President, but only an inquiry into the charge of a specific illegality.[8] Thus, Marshall established the basis for finding, first, that the actions of the executive branch are subject to review under both the Constitution and laws of the United States, and, second, that the federal judiciary can order the executive to comply with those principles.

This analysis left the question whether the mandamus against the executive should issue in this particular case. On this question, Marshall found a conflict between the Court's statutory jurisdiction and that fixed by Article III of the Constitution. Although he could have been interpreted Section 13 of the Judiciary Act of 1789[9] in a different manner, he ruled that it authorized original actions in the Supreme Court for writs of mandamus to officers

of the United States. Because the statute, as construed, provided for original actions, such as Marbury's action in this case, it violated Article III, which Marshall interpreted as limiting the original jurisdiction of the Supreme Court.[10]

The opinion concluded that Congress might have the power to alter the appellate jurisdiction of the Court, but Article III intended to fix the original jurisdiction. Thus, there was a clear conflict between the jurisdictional statute and the Constitution, leading Marshall to the essential question: whether a law that was in conflict with the Constitution is valid and whether the Supreme Court has the power to invalidate or, at least, disregard such a law.

Marshall claimed that the question of whether a federal statute contrary to constitutional provisions could be the law of the land was "not of an intricacy proportioned to its interest."[11] Marshall believed that the people of the nation had the right to establish binding, enforceable principles for the governing of society. While the people might have ratified a Constitution that created a government of general powers, they chose instead a Constitution that created one of defined and limited powers.

There could be, in Marshall's view, no middle ground between these types of government. That left the Court the choice either to declare

7. 5 U.S. (1 Cranch) at 170.

8. Id.

9. Act of September 24, 1789; Sec. 13; I Stat. 73, 80–81. The provision read:

"And be it further enacted, That the Supreme Court shall have exclusive jurisdiction of all controversies of a civil nature, where a state is a party, except between a state and its citizens; and except also between a state and citizens of other states, or aliens, in which latter case it shall have original but not exclusive jurisdiction. And shall have exclusively all such jurisdiction of suits or proceedings against ambassadors, or other public ministers, or their domestics, or domestic servants, as a court of law can have or exercise consistently with the law of nations; and original, but not exclusive jurisdiction of all suits brought by ambassadors, or other public ministers, or in which a consul, or vice consul, shall be a party. And the trial of issues of fact in the Supreme Court, in all actions at law against citizens of the United States, shall be by jury. The Supreme Court shall also have appellate jurisdiction from the circuit courts and courts of the several states, in the cases hereinafter

specially provided for; and shall have power to issue writs of prohibition to the district courts, when proceeding as courts of admiralty and maritime jurisdiction, and writs of mandamus, in cases warranted by the principles and usages of law, to any courts appointed, or persons holding office, under the authority of the United States."

Marshall could have interpreted this section to provide only a *remedy* of mandamus, assuming that the Court otherwise has jurisdiction.

10. U.S.Const. art. III reads in part:

"In all Cases affecting Ambassadors, other public Ministers and Consuls, and those in which a State shall be a Party, the supreme Court shall have original Jurisdiction. In all the other Cases before mentioned, the supreme Court shall have appellate Jurisdiction, both as to Law and Fact, with such Exceptions, and under such Regulations as the Congress shall make."

11. 5 U.S. (1 Cranch) at 176. Indeed the entire discussion of this point took less than two pages. 5 U.S. (1 Cranch) at 176–77.

the Constitution to be the superior and binding law, or to allow the legislature to be an entity of unlimited powers. The fact that the people chose a *written* Constitution with fundamental principles to bind the government in the future was evidence that the Constitution should be the superior and binding law. If the Constitution was the superior law, then an act repugnant to it must be invalid.

There remained the question of whether the Courts were obliged to follow the act of the legislature despite judges' view as to the statute's incompatibility with the Constitution. Marshall's argument for judicial review—the power of the courts to invalidate laws as unconstitutional—is deceptively simple. The essence of the argument is his first point, that "it is emphatically the province and duty of the judicial department to say what the law is."[12] Having previously recognized the Constitution as being the superior "law" in the nation, Marshall, with this statement, lays claim to the judiciary's final authority on matters of constitutional interpretation. It is this concept of the Constitution as law, and the judiciary as the institution with the *final* responsibility to interpret that law, that is the cornerstone of judicial review today.

Marshall advanced several other points in support of the judicial power to invalidate laws found to be in violation of the Constitution. Because the Court would be required to follow either the statute or the Constitution in a given case, an inability of the Court to reject the statute in favor of the Constitution would subvert "the very foundation" of a written Constitution.[13] The Constitutional text provided further support, for it extended the judicial power to "all cases arising under the Constitution."[14] Marshall reasoned that this jurisdictional power inevitably leads to the conclusion

that the framers of that provision must have been willing to allow the judiciary to use and interpret the Constitution in the cases arising under it.

Marshall cited several provisions that imposed specific limitations on the acts of government, such as the export tax clause,[15] the Bill of Attainder and *ex post facto* prohibitions,[16] and the establishment of requirements for proof of treason.[17] In cases that involve these provisions, Marshall argued, the framers of the Constitution must have contemplated that the courts would follow its terms rather than any contrary act of the legislature. He drew further support for this conclusion from the oath for the judges, which required them to support the Constitution.[18] To Marshall this required that the judges follow the Constitution rather than any subordinate law.

Marshall's argument closed as it began, with the concept of the Constitution as the superior law. He focused on the Supremacy Clause of Article VI the Constitution. That clause explicitly states that the Constitution is the supreme law of the land, and that the statutes and laws of the United States that are granted recognition are "those only which shall be made in *pursuance* of the Constitution."[19] Judges should only follow laws that are "in pursuance of the Constitution." Thus, he reasoned, the supreme law of the land must be the Constitution, and the Justices must follow it rather than any provisions of federal legislation that are inconsistent with the Constitution.

Accordingly, the Court denied Marbury his commission, because the Court held that it could not entertain an original action for mandamus inconsistent with its jurisdiction under Article III. To the extent that Section 13 of the

---

12.   5 U.S. (1 Cranch) at 177.

13.   5 U.S. (1 Cranch) at 178.

14.   U.S.Const. art. III, § 2.

15.   U.S.Const. art. I, § 9, cl. 5:

"No Tax or Duty shall be laid on Articles exported from any State."

16.   U.S.Const. art. I, § 9, cl. 3:

"No Bill of Attainder or ex post facto Law shall be passed."

17.   U.S.Const. art. III, § 3:

"Treason against the United States, shall consist only in levying War against, them or, in adhering to their Enemies, giving them Aid and Comfort. No Person shall be convicted of Treason unless on the Testimony of two Witnesses to the same overt Act, or on Confession in open Court."

18.   5 U.S. (1 Cranch) at 180.

19.   5 U.S. (1 Cranch) at 180 (emphasis in original).

Judiciary Act included a contrary provision it was unconstitutional and void.

§ 1.4 Notes on the *Marbury* Decision

(a) Criticisms of the *Marbury* Opinion

Marbury v. Madison has been the subject of continuing analysis and historical inquiry. Although the doctrine of judicial review is now firmly established, a recapitulation of the commentary concerning *Marbury* and its historical antecedents has more than historical interest. Theories concerning the proper scope of judicial actions under the Constitution often focus upon the legitimacy of the judiciary's claim to authority: commentators often argue that, to the extent that the authority for judicial review is weak, it should be exercised most sparingly.

In reviewing this material, one should remember the words of Justice Frankfurter:

The courage of *Marbury v. Madison* is not minimized by suggesting that its reasoning is not impeccable and that its conclusion, however wise, not inevitable. [S]ince Marshall's time and largely, I suspect, through the momentum of the experience which he initiated, his conclusion in *Marbury v. Madison* has been deemed by great English speaking Courts an indispensable, implied characteristic of a written Constitution.[1]

If we, today, see further, or more clearly, than Marshall did in his day, it is because we stand on the shoulders of this legal giant who came before us.

The criticisms of John Marshall's opinion in *Marbury v. Madison* fall into two general areas.[2] First, there is disapproval of the way in which Marshall strove to reach the conclusion concerning the constitutional authority of the Court over the other branches of government. Second, there is criticism of Marshall's arguments supporting judicial authority as merely bare assertions of authority rather than reasons justifying that authority.

It is certainly true that Marshall was eager to use this decision to establish a claim to the power of judicial review. The very fact that he heard the case (rather than disqualifying himself) demonstrated his view of its importance and his desire to use the decision on behalf of the judicial branch. Marshall did withdraw from a later decision concerning the Court's power over the acts of state courts when he had a direct financial interest in the decision,[3] but here his personal stake in the outcome was, perhaps, less clear. However, Marshall was the Secretary of State who did not deliver the disputed commission. If there were a trial, Marshall might have been called a witness, yet he did not disqualify himself. Normally a judge should not preside over a case if he is a relevant witness. The likelihood that this case might establish the foundation for future relationships between the authority of the three branches of government was such that Marshall was willing to disregard charges of partisanship and author the opinion himself.

Marshall clearly had opportunities to avoid the constitutional questions concerning both the executive and legislative acts. A ruling that Marbury lacked a right to the commission until delivery, or that the political process governed the remedy for refusals to honor appointments, would have avoided these issues.[4] Or, Marshall could have interpreted the

§ 1.4

1. Frankfurter, John Marshall and the Judicial Function, 69 Harv.L.Rev. 217, 219 (1955).

2. The historical criticisms of *Marbury* are analyzed and supplemented in Van Alstyne, A Critical Guide to Marbury v. Madison, 1969 Duke L.J. 1. We commend this excellent article, which contains a further bibliography, to those interested in more detailed and documented analytical treatment of the opinion. For one of the finest early pieces on the power of judicial review see Corwin, Marbury v. Madison and the Doctrine of Judicial Review, 12 Mich. L.Rev. 538 (1914).

3. See Martin v. Hunter's Lessee, 14 U.S. (1 Wheat.) 304, 4 L.Ed. 97 (1816). In *Marbury* Marshall was the

Secretary of State who originally was to have delivered the judicial appointment; therefore he might have been called as a witness.

4. The Court has since endorsed a wider power for the executive relating to appointments and discharges. See Myers v. United States, 272 U.S. 52, 47 S.Ct. 21, 71 L.Ed. 160 (1926); Humphrey's Executor v. United States, 295 U.S. 602, 55 S.Ct. 869, 79 L.Ed. 1611 (1935); Wiener v. United States, 357 U.S. 349, 78 S.Ct. 1275, 2 L.Ed.2d 1377 (1958); see also United States v. Smith, 286 U.S. 6, 47–48, 52 S.Ct. 475, 483, 76 L.Ed. 954 (1932); United States v. Le Baron, 60 U.S. (19 How.) 73, 15 L.Ed. 525 (1856). Van Alstyne, A Critical Guide to Marbury v. Madison, 1969 Duke L.J. 1, 10.

section of the Judiciary Act governing mandamus as establishing only a remedy, not jurisdiction. A construction that the Judiciary Act authorized mandamus only when jurisdiction was otherwise properly invoked would have avoided the ruling on the constitutionality of the statute.

Marshall's effort to reach the constitutional question is open to criticism under today's generally accepted principle that the Court should avoid ruling on a constitutional issue when a case can be decided on a narrower ground. However, this principle is the modern rule, only a general guide for Court action, and not an ironclad precept that has bound the Court at all times in its history. Even is modern times, when Justices believe that a constitutional decision is important for the protection of certain values, they have always felt free to decide the issue rather than to avoid it—provided the Court has jurisdiction.[5]

The extent to which one agrees with the conclusion that the Court should have the power to review the constitutionality of the acts of the federal government, determines, to a large measure, one's criticism of Marshall's reaching the constitutional issues in this case. He was correct in perceiving that this case offered the vehicle for laying claim to the power of judicial review while avoiding a direct confrontation with the other branches of government. Had Marshall avoided the constitutional issues in this case, he might not have received a similar opportunity to establish the basis of the judicial power. Whether he would have succeeded without deciding the case in this manner is a matter for conjecture, but the gamble was one that Marshall was unwilling to take. And it was part of Marshall's genius that he was able to persuade all the other members of the Court to join him.

Admittedly, Marshall's arguments concerning the relationship between the actions of the other branches of the federal government and the Constitution can be subdivided into a series of assertions, none of which inexorably leads to the conclusion that Marshall draws from them.[6] His discussion of judicial control of the powers of the executive is especially troublesome for its vagueness as to standards for the exercise of judicial power.

While Marshall makes it clear that the President is subject to specific legal restraints established either by statute or the Constitution, he does not further define the nature of the duties that are subject to judicial review. Instead, Marshall asserts an open-ended power to review executive actions based upon the principle that the executive can have no right to disregard a specific duty assigned to him by law. This general assertion of authority to review executive acts that gave rise to the greatest dispute at the time of *Marbury*. Over the years, several Presidents have, to varying degrees, disputed this judicial claim.[7] However, it was also this general principle that provided the Supreme Court, over one hundred and seventy years later, with a basis for holding that not even the President could disregard judicial subpoenas for evidence in ongoing criminal cases.[8]

Marshall's discussion of the constitutionality of legislative acts falls into two parts. First, Marshall found that a law that was not in conformity with constitutional principles could not be the law of the land. This proposition established the Constitution as a binding law superior to any other federal action.

One can question the individual reasons on which Marshall established this conclusion. The fact that the people established a govern-

---

5. See, e.g., Rescue Army v. Municipal Court, 331 U.S. 549, 67 S.Ct. 1409, 91 L.Ed. 1666 (1947).

6. Thus James Bradley Thayer admitted that Marshall's reasoning did not go beyond that earlier put forth by Hamilton and did not meet the most difficult questions concerning the nature of judicial power. J. Thayer, John Marshall, at 77–78 (1901).

7. Presidents Jefferson, Jackson, Lincoln, and Roosevelt disputed some aspects of the power when judicial rulings interfered with their implementation of federal

policy. For Presidential writings disputing the authoritativeness of Supreme Court decisions, see 1 Ronald D. Rotunda & John E. Nowak, Treatise on Constitutional Law: Substance and Procedure § 1.4 (West Pub. Co., 2d ed. 1992).

8. United States v. Nixon, 418 U.S. 683, 94 S.Ct. 3090, 41 L.Ed.2d 1039 (1974), certiorari denied 431 U.S. 933, 97 S.Ct. 2641, 53 L.Ed.2d 250 (1977), rehearing denied 433 U.S. 916, 97 S.Ct. 2992, 53 L.Ed.2d 1103 (1977).

ment of limited powers does not of necessity mean that they established a single document to control the actions of their own democratic process. It is at least possible that the legislature was to be guided by these principles, but that it was free to interpret them for itself, and not to have its acts overruled by the other branches of government. Marshall, however, sought to shore up the argument by finding that the essence of a written Constitution is that it is to be a fundamental and binding document. Once again, this conclusion is not necessarily true; other nations have employed written Constitutions as general principles of government but do not use the judicial departments to overrule acts by the other branches of the government.[9] Yet, despite these individual criticisms of the components of Marshall's opinion, the argument must stand or fall on his ultimate conclusion that the Constitution was intended to be law in its truest sense.

Second, having found that the Constitution was to be a form of law superior to legislation, Marshall went on to consider whether the judiciary must follow a law that was in conflict with the Constitution. He argued that the Constitution is "law," and it is the institutional responsibility of the judiciary to interpret law and apply the law that is superior in any conflict between the Constitution and legislation. However, this principle does not establish that the judiciary is the proper body to make the *final* determination of whether the statute is in fact so inconsistent with the provisions of the superior document that it is invalid.

He drew support for this position from a number of specific examples of cases that might involve a choice between following legislative acts or a very specific provision of the Constitution. If, for example, Congress passes a statute providing for the conviction of persons for treason on the testimony of less than two witnesses, the judges would be confronted with the question of whether to follow the Constitution or the statute in a trial for treason. But this choice involves no question of interpretation, for there is a clear conflict. What powers should the judiciary have when

the conflict is not a matter of mathematical certainly? Marshall does not discuss this question. Even Marshall's argument based on a clear violation of the Constitution does not necessarily support his conclusion that the judiciary can void the act of Congress. The court might only be able to refuse to apply the statute in the given case, where the Executive Branch comes to court and seeks the judiciary's aid in enforcing the statute.

Marshall found further support for judicial review because judges take an oath to support the Constitution. However, while this oath might give judges some support in choosing not to apply a specific act of Congress in a decision, it furnishes no claim to *superior* powers regarding constitutional interpretation, because the legislators and executive take similar oaths.

The supremacy clause of Article VI does not solve the problem, for it states only that federal laws are superior to state laws and state constitutions; it says nothing concerning the relationship between the Federal Judiciary and the co-equal branches of the Government: the Executive and Legislative Branches. Marshall's argument, that only laws made in pursuance of the Constitution are the supreme law of the land, assumes the point in dispute: who determines which statutes are not in pursuance of the Constitution? We are still left with the question of whether the judiciary, or Congress, or the President has the final determination of when a law is made in pursuance of the Constitution.

Although can divide and attack, Marshall's decision, it still stands as an impressive argument when taken as a whole. The Chief Justice, in this case, asserts that the Constitution is a superior form of law established by the direct will of society, and that judges must follow the law, including this higher law, in the course of deciding issues before them. This concept of judicial review and the role that courts must play is a unique American contribution to jurisprudence.

The concept of judicial review really rests upon three separate bases: (1) that the Consti-

9. See Mauro Cappelletti, Judicial Review in Comparative Perspective, 58 Calif.L.Rev. 1017 (1970).

tution binds all parts of the federal government, (2) that it is enforceable by the Court in actions before it, and (3) that the judiciary is charged with interpreting the Constitution in a unique manner so that its rulings are binding on all other departments of the government.[10] *Marbury* seeks to establish the first two of these principles and only implies the existence of the third. The first two principles are, in fact, both historically and logically easier to prove than the third.[11] But if a convincing case can be made that the Constitution is truly a binding law that is capable of being understood and interpreted as are other laws, then the claim to judicial superiority as the *final* interpreter becomes stronger.

In *Marbury*, Marshall admitted no arguments that would cast doubt on the first Corwin's two propositions. Marshall's opinion may be faulted for a failure to explore the concept of judicial authority to control the other branches of government and thereby to reflect upon doubts concerning the binding nature of the Constitution. However, there is a limit to how much weight one opinion should carry, and Marshall would explore these issues in later decisions.

In *McCulloch v. Maryland*,[12] Marshall laid claim to the judicial authority to bind all branches of government by constitutional interpretation. *McCulloch* treated the Constitution as a law capable of interpretation and of definition by the normal legal process. It also looks at the Constitution as a document of enduring principles requiring an independent judiciary to interpret and apply it throughout changing historical periods. Both Professor James Bradley Thayer and Justice Felix Frankfurter regarded *McCulloch* as Marshall's greatest opinion, because of its careful reasoning and its effect on the claim to judicial supremacy and the establishment of federal authority over the states.[13]

Marshall also explored and explained the concept of judicial supremacy and matters of constitutional interpretation in other decisions. In his opinions concerning the reviewability of actions of state government under the contract clause and the commerce clause, Marshall emphasized that the Constitution is a law that the judiciary has to interpret and enforce in order to maintain its supremacy. Throughout his thirty-four year tenure as Chief Justice of the United States, Marshall established the theoretical basis of judicial review with arguments both on and off the Court.[14] That Marshall did not accomplish this goal with a single opinion is hardly an indictment of his ability or contribution to the shaping of our legal history.

At he was ending his career, Marshall recognized, with dismay, that the Court had not yet secured its essential role in government. Professor Robert McCloskey observed:

> In his last years, Marshall was beset with misgivings about America's future, full of gloomy convictions that he had failed in his campaign to establish judicial sovereignty and to cement the bonds of national union. . . . Not even he, the architect-in-chief, realized how securely the cornerstones of American Constitutionalism had been laid. [I]f we can tolerate, as Marshall could not, a world of half certainty (and if we enjoyed, as he did not, the perspective of the future), we can see that his forebodings were excessive and his accomplishments greater than he knew. The doctrine of judicial sovereignty was still subject to occasional challenge in moments of stress . . . but surely the judicial monopoly, though imperfect, was very impressive. The nation, in general, thought of the Court as the principal authority and conceded its right to supervise the states in

10. Corwin, Marbury v. Madison and the Doctrine of Judicial Review, 12 Mich.L.Rev. 538, 552 (1914).

11. Corwin, Marbury v. Madison and the Doctrine of Judicial Review, 12 Mich.L.Rev. 538, 552 (1914).

12. 17 U.S. (4 Wheat.) 316, 4 L.Ed. 579 (1819).

13. James Bradley Thayer, John Marshall, at 68 (1901) as reprinted in Thayer, Holmes & Frankfurter, John Marshall (1967, Philip Kurland ed.); Felix Frankfurter, John

Marshall and the Judicial Function, 69 Harv.L.Rev. 217, 219 (1955).

14. Marshall defended the *McCulloch* decision and its reasoning in a series of newspaper articles published under the title "A Friend of the Constitution." See Gerald Gunther, ed., John Marshall's Defense of McCulloch v. Maryland (1969).

most matters.... America's devotion to the idea of fundamental law and the Court's ability to capitalize on opponents' errors had made sure of that.[15]

We know now that Marshall built better than he knew, and he laid the foundations for what has become the most powerful and admired judiciary in the world.[16]

(b) The Historical Antecedents of *Marbury*

A detailed examination of the possible historical basis for the claims to judicial review and the supremacy of judicial interpretations under the Constitution is of such intricacy and importance that it has been the subject of entire volumes and numerous articles.[17] Commentators dispute the extent to which the framers or ratifiers of the Constitution clearly intended to establish the Supreme Court as it developed as the final body to interpret the Constitution and control the acts of other branches of government. While it is true that many people expected some sort of judicial review, that does not mean that they foresaw the extent to which the judiciary would exercise judicial review in modern times. Professor Julius Goebel, after extensive historical research, concluded that there was indeed an historical basis for Chief Justice Marshall's claim to a judicial power to review the consti-

tutionality of the acts of other branches of government.[18] Others have disputed his conclusion; at a minimum, the claim can be made that the precedents for this principle prior to 1803 are not entirely clear.[19]

The historical data show that a number of the drafters of the Constitution accepted some form of judicial review and that some of the states, prior to the date of the *Marbury* decision, endorsed the concept. At its earliest stages judicial review was so undefined that debate over the exact contours of the original understanding of the concept can be virtually endless.

The concept of judicial review really includes three separate assertions: (1) the Constitution is meant to be the paramount law of the land; (2) the judiciary has some ability to interpret and apply the Constitution in cases before it; (3) the judicial interpretation is to be final and controlling over the views of the other branches of government.[20] Professor Edward S. Corwin, the noted Constitutional scholar of the early twentieth century, concluded that there is strong evidence for the first proposition, somewhat less strong (but still substantial) historical data supporting the second proposition, and historical data that is subject to conflicting interpretations as to the third principle.[21]

---

15. Robert McCloskey, The American Supreme Court at 77–79 (1960).

16. Rotunda, Exporting the American Bill of Rights: The Lesson from Romania, 1991 U. Ill. L. Rev. 1065 (1991); Rotunda, Eastern European Diary: Constitution–Building in the Former Soviet Union, 1 The Green Bag, 2d Series 163 (Winter 1998); William G. Ross, The Resilience of *Marbury v. Madison*: Why Judicial Review Has Survived So Many Attacks, 38 Wake Forest L. Rev. 733 (2003).

17. See e.g., Charles Beard, The Supreme Court and the Constitution (1912); Raoul Berger, Congress vs. The Supreme Court (1969); J. Goebel, 1 The Oliver Wendell Holmes Devise History of the Supreme Court of the United States—Antecedents and Beginnings to 1801 (1971); 1 A.A.L.S. Selected Essay on Constitutional Law, Chapter 1 (D. Maggs, Ed., 1938); Grey, Origins of the Unwritten Constitution: Fundamental Law in American Revolutionary Thought, 30 Stan.L.Rev. 843 (1978); Meigs, The American Doctrine of Judicial Power and Its Early Origin, 47 Am.L.Rev. 683 (1913); Nelson, Changing Conceptions of Judicial Review: The Evolution of Constitutional Theory in the States, 1790–1860, 120 U.Pa.L.Rev. 1166 (1972); Thayer, The Origin and Scope of the American Doctrine of Constitutional Law, 7 Harv.L.Rev. 1 (1893); Rotunda,

Original Intent, The View of the Framers, and the Role of the Ratifiers, 41 Vanderbilt Law Review 507 (1988).

18. J. Goebel, 1 The Oliver Wendell Holmes Devise History of the Supreme Court of the United States—Antecedents and Beginnings to 1801 (1971).

19. See 2 William W. Crosskey, Politics and the Constitution (1953) (attack on the concept of judicial review). Contra, R. Berger, Congress vs. The Supreme Court (1969); Hart, Book Review, 67 Harv.L.Rev. 1456 (1954). See also, Brinton Coxe, Judicial Power and Unconstitutional Legislation (1893); Charles A. Beard, The Supreme Court and the Constitution (1912); Edward S. Corwin, The Doctrine of Judicial Review (1914).

20. Corwin, Marbury v. Madison and the Doctrine of Judicial Review, 12 Mich.L.Rev. 538, 552 (1914).

21. Id. A problem in determining the "intent" of the drafters of the Constitution was created by the views of the drafters on the importance of "original intent." See, Powell, The Original Understanding of Original Intent, 98 Harv.L.Rev. 885 (1985); Rotunda, Original Intent, the View of the Framers, and the Role of the Ratifiers, 41 Vanderbilt L. Rev. 507 (1988).

Herein lies the essence of the debate over the historical basis for Chief Justice Marshall's ruling in *Marbury*. Today we understand "judicial review" as including not only the ability of the Supreme Court to interpret the Constitution but also its power to void the acts of other branches of government on this basis. The evidence supporting judicial review as we know it today was not clear in 1803, but this form of judicial authority was rapidly accepted following the *Marbury* decision.

Scholars who challenge the view that the concept of judicial review was publicly accepted by 1800 do admit that some form of judicial review seems to have been widely accepted throughout the states by 1820,[22] and that, by the time of the Civil War, the concept of the judiciary as the ultimate interpreter of the Constitution was generally accepted.[23] This continually expanding acceptance of the principle of judicial review may lead one to believe that there must have been some generally accepted core concept of judicial power at the time of *Marbury*. There are four main sources or precursors of judicial review in America.

The first major historical source was the English precedents for judicial review and the colonial experience. There is the widely quoted dictum of Lord Chief Justice Edward Coke, in *Dr. Bonham's Case*: "When an Act of Parliament is against common right and reason, the common law will control it and adjudge such Act to be void."[24] Although there is no solid historical basis for finding judicial review in British judicial practice, and Coke's language has several interpretations, Coke's audacious statement resounded through the ages.[25]

Some colonists may have understood the British system to include some form of judicial review because the English government, primarily through the Privy Council, had the power to review and void acts of the colonial legislatures that were found to be in violation of their charters or other English law.[26] However, this practice was a most limited one. On the other hand, even if there is no clear support for judicial review in the English-colonial experience, that is not the relevant issue. What is important to a search for the antecedents of *Marbury* is the understanding of the colonists concerning the English experience rather than the currently correct view of that history.

A second historical source for judicial review is the federal Constitutional Convention and the ratification process. This source offers the most fruitful support for the concept of judicial review. At the Convention almost every statement of a delegate that might be implied as reflecting on the subject of judicial review of the constitutionality of federal laws indicates an acceptance of it in some general form.[27] This evidence has led many scholars to conclude that the framers must have intended to create a new form of judicial review under the Constitution.[28] However, the undefined nature of the judicial power referred to during the Convention leaves the historical support for the *current* concept of judicial supremacy unclear.

The Federalist Papers, well read during the ratification process, also endorsed a concept of judicial review. Significantly, the Federalist Papers used arguments very close to those that Marshall used in *Marbury*, but the anti-

22. Nelson, Changing Conception of Judicial Review: The Evolution of Constitutional Theory in the States, 1790–1860, 120 U.Pa.L.Rev. 1166 (1972).

23. E. Corwin, Liberty Against Government (1948); Nelson, Changing Conception of Judicial Review: The Evolution of Constitutional Theory in the States, 1790–1860, 120 U.Pa.L.Rev. 1166 (1972).

24. Dr. Bonham's Case, 8 Coke Rep. 107, 116–121 (C.P. 1610). See, Plucknett, Bonham's Case and Judicial Review, 40 Harv.L.Rev. 30 (1926); Samuel Thorne, Dr. Bonham's Case, 54 L.Q.Rev. 543 (1938).

25. Catherine Drinker Bowen, The Lion and the Throne, 15 (1957).

26. J. Goebel, 1 The Oliver Wendell Holmes Devise History of the Supreme Court of the United States— Antecedents and Beginnings to 1801 (1971), at 50–83; But cf. Nelson, Changing Conceptions of Judicial Review: The Evolution of Constitutional Theory in the States, 1790–1860, 120 U.Pa.L.Rev. 1166, 1166–67 (1972).

27. J. Goebel, 1 The Oliver Wendell Holmes Devise History of the Supreme Court of the United States— Antecedents and Beginnings to 1801 (1971), at 196–251.

28. See Corwin, The Establishment of Judicial Review, 9 Mich.L.Rev. 102–25, 284–316 (1910–11).

federalists at the time disputed the extent of this power.[29]

The third area fruitful historical source is the experience in the state courts after the revolution. Between the time of the revolution and 1803, judicial decisions, or provisions in state constitutions in most of the states that had given any specific attention to the issue, adopted judicial review.[30] However, there was still opposition to this concept in a number of states prior to 1800.[31] If we do not limit our examination of the state courts to the period prior to 1803, the case for judicial review becomes much stronger. Between 1800 and 1820 the concept of judicial review in terms of whether to apply a statute in a given case had received widespread acceptance.

The Supreme Court of Pennsylvania was one of the most important courts of this era. While that court accepted the concept of judicial review, Justice Gibson of Pennsylvania (later Chief Justice of that court) attacked the historical and philosophical basis for judicial review and the decision in *Marbury*.[32] Eventually, Gibson came to believe that judicial review should be adopted out of necessity, if not historical accuracy.[33] His conversion illustrates the growth of support for judicial review.

The rapid acceptance of the doctrine in the states indicates that there may well have been a commonly shared, preexisting belief concerning the basic principle of judicial review. The people, it seems, were ready for judicial review, and that helps explain its affirmation and its growth following the Supreme Court's express adoption of this power.

A final historical source providing a legitimate basis for judicial review is found in the acts of the federal government following the establishment of the Constitution. The limited amount of data that exists indicate that there was an acceptance of the judicial review of legislation in some form. Individual Justices, when acting as Circuit Justices, refused to assume duties that they believed were beyond their constitutional authority.[34] Correspondence between the Court and President Washington showed that the Justices were concerned about the constitutionality of the Justices conducting trials in the circuits.[35] The Supreme Court, prior to *Marbury*, had upheld actions of the federal and state legislatures, in a way that indicated a belief that the Justices were free to disregard the acts should they find them to be in violation of the Constitution.[36] Yet, *Marbury* was the first Supreme Court opinion that expressly adopted the concept of judicial review.

During the pre-*Marbury* period, there is some evidence that Congress impliedly accepted the concept of judicial review. For example, the first Congress enacted the Judiciary Act of 1789, which grants jurisdiction to the Supreme Court to review the actions of state courts that

---

29. The Federalist Nos. 78 and 81 (Hamilton) (Modern Lib. ed. 1937). Marshall defended the concept of the Virginia convention, 3 J. Elliot, Debates in the Several States Conventions in the Adoption of the Federal Constitution at 553–4 (1836).

30. See J. Goebel, 1 The Oliver Wendell Holmes Devise History of the Supreme Court of the United States—Antecedents and Beginnings to 1801 (1971), at 125–42; Corwin, Marbury v. Madison and the Doctrine of Judicial Review (notes follow text) reprinted in, 1 A.A.L.S., Selected Essays in Constitutional Law at 171–72 (D. Maggs ed., 1938).

31. Nelson, Changing Conception of Judicial Review: The Evolution of Constitutional Theory in the States, 1790–1860, 120 U.Pa.L.Rev. 1166 (1972); Nelson, The Eighteenth Century Background of John Marshall's Constitutional Jurisprudence, 76 Mich.L.Rev. 893 (1978).

32. Eakin v. Raub, 51 Pa.Rep. (12 Sargent & Rawle) 330, 343 (1825).

33. Norris v. Clymer, 2 Pa. 277, 281 (1845).

34. See Case of Hayburn, 2 U.S. (2 Dall. 409) 408, 1 L.Ed. 436 (1792). Miller v. French, 530 U.S. 327, 120 S.Ct. 2246, 147 L.Ed.2d 326 (2000), explained that what was fatal in *Hayburn's Case* was that the law allowed the non-judicial branches to reopen a final judgment. In contrast, *prospective injunctive* relief is not "final" in the same way because it always remains subject to alteration due to changes in the underlying law. J. Goebel, 1 The Oliver Wendell Holmes Devise History of the Supreme Court of the United States: Antecedents and Beginnings to 1801 (1971), at chapters 9–17 and Appendix.

35. Several Justices sent a letter to President Washington; there was also individual correspondence between Chief Justice Jay and the President. See, H. Hart & H. Wechsler, The Federal Courts and the Federal System 68 (2d ed. 1973). The Court later upheld practice of Justices riding circuit in Stuart v. Laird, 5 U.S. (1 Cranch) 299, 2 L.Ed. 115 (1803).

36. Hylton v. United States, 3 U.S. (3 Dall.) 171, 1 L.Ed. 556 (1796); Calder v. Bull, 3 U.S. (3 Dall.) 386, 1 L.Ed. 648 (1798).

might concern constitutional issues, thus impliedly accepting a judicial power to review the constitutionality of state and federal laws.[37] In addition, when the Republican Congress debated whether to repeal the Circuit Court Act of 1801, which established the "Midnight Judges", some members of Congress expressed concern over the constitutionality of the action, though the bill did pass.[38] While neither incident confirms the claim to judicial review set out in *Marbury*, they offer some authority that the concept of judicial review was recognized as a plausible interpretation of the Constitution during this period.

(c) The Relationship Between *Marbury* and the Standards for Judicial Review

Most of the debate concerning judicial review centers on the appropriate role of a non-elected, judicial entity in a democracy. One's view of the judicial function in some measurement may relate to his or her view of the historical basis for Marshall's claim to judicial supremacy. If one does not believe that there is a solid basis for judicial review in the text or history of the Constitution, then one should accept the principle that the power of the Court to void the acts of other branches of government should be exercised rarely and then only out of absolute necessity. Thus, Judge Learned Hand felt that the power should be exercised only when absolutely necessary to prevent the democracy from overturning a clear and paramount constitutional principle.[39]

On the other hand, if one is convinced that the concept of judicial review has a solid historical basis, there is somewhat greater room

to embrace this power. In other words, if the ratifiers invited the judiciary to exercise judicial review, the judges should not be reluctant to accept the invitation. Thus, Professor Herbert Wechsler disagreed with Judge Hand, arguing that there was no doubt that the framers of the Constitution intended to create the power of judicial review. He therefore found a greater constitutional role for the judiciary.[40]

This historical view does not lead to a conclusion that the judiciary should overturn the acts of the government whenever judges disagree with the policy adopted by those acts. Professor Wechsler argued that the Court should only intervene against the will of democracy when the Justices could identify a clear and neutral principle that was not dependent upon their view of the equities of the given case or the practical policies behind governmental actions.[41] This concept of neutral principles, of limited, but legitimate, review over the acts of government forms the basis of the philosophy of judicial restraint whose well-known proponents have included Justice Felix Frankfurter,[42] Professor Alexander Bickel,[43] and others.[44]

Accepting the position that there is a clear historical basis for judicial supremacy in matters of constitutional interpretation may lead one to the conclusion that the Justices should be activist and should not be hesitant to strike down acts of other branches of government. This view went into disrepute when the Justices used their power to strike down a variety of economic and social welfare reform measures in the activists era between 1887 and 1937.[45] However, as the government has increasingly defined the scope of individual liber-

---

37. Act of Sept. 24, 1789; 1 Stat. 73; See 1 J. Goebel, The Oliver Wendell Holmes Devise History of the Supreme Court of the United States: Antecedents and Beginnings to 1801 (1971), at Chapter 11.

38. 1 C. Warren, The Supreme Court in United States History at 214–15 (1926).

39. L. Hand, The Bill of Rights 11–18 (1958).

40. Wechsler, Toward Neutral Principles of Constitutional Law, 73 Harv.L.Rev. 1, 3–5 (1959).

41. Id. See Greenawalt, The Enduring Significance of Neutral Principles, 78 Colum.L.Rev. 982 (1978); Rotunda, Judicial Biography and the Nature of Judicial Review, in R. Rotunda (ed.), Six Justices on Civil Rights (U. of Illinois Press 1983).

42. See Frankfurter, John Marshall and the Judicial Function 69 Harv.L.Rev. 217 (1955).

43. See A. Bickel, The Supreme Court and the Idea of Progress (1969).

44. See also, Thayer, The Origin and Scope of the American Doctrine of Constitutional Law, 7 Harv.L.Rev. 129 (1893); Wechsler, Toward Neutral Principles of Constitutional Law, 73 Harv.L.Rev. 1 (1959), and H. Wechsler, Principles' Politics and Fundamental Law (1961).

45. For an examination of these decisions see §§ 4.5–4.7, 11.2, 11.3, infra.

ty in society, other Justices, such as the late Justice William O. Douglas,[46] have reasserted the propriety of an active judiciary.

§ 1.5   Review of State Laws: The Early Cases

There are three decisions of particular importance that established federal judicial power over state laws. The first, *Fletcher v. Peck*,[1] is important because it was the earliest exercise of the Court's authority after it suffered a period of intense attack, 1803 and 1810.[2] After surviving these attacks, the Court, for the first time, invalidated a state law under the U.S. Constitution.[3]

Fletcher involved a Georgia statute that sought to annul earlier conveyances of land to private persons. An earlier, corrupt state legislature had authorized these conveyances, and the state now wished to cancel what seemed to be fraudulent acts. However, the land had since passed to a private good faith purchaser who sought the enforcement of his contract and ownership rights.

The Supreme Court construed the term "contract" to include an executed state contract or grant. The Court then held that the annulment was an impairment of the obligation of contract within the meaning of Article I. The repealing statute was, therefore, unconstitutional. It was immaterial that the state was the grantor, for the Court found no distinction between the obligation of contracts where the contract was between two individu-

als and where the contract was between the state and an individual.[4]

The second major early decision concerning federal judicial power is *Martin v. Hunter's Lessee*.[5] This case involved conflicting claims to land in the northern portion of Virginia.[6] Lord Fairfax was a former British national who had become a citizen of Virginia prior to his death. In 1781 he willed the extensive land he held in Virginia to his nephew in England, Denny Martin. Virginia later passed acts to confiscate the lands of those who had been British citizens or loyalists during the Revolutionary War. Virginia then granted a portion of Lord Fairfax's land to David Hunter. The stage was set for the litigation between the representatives of Martin and Hunter. The litigation spanned two decades and was complicated by a series of related actions.

Before he became a Justice, John Marshall, acting on behalf of the British representatives, had negotiated a compromise and personally purchased a large share of the land. His personal involvement and financial interests led him to recuse himself from deciding these cases when they came to the Court.

In connection with Marshall's compromise, the Virginia legislature adopted the 1796 Act of Compromise, but the U.S. Supreme Court did not mention this act in its original decision on the ownership of the land. The existence of that compromise, and the complicated transactions, make it unclear whether the "right"

---

46. See W. O. Douglas, The Right of the People (1958); W. O. Douglas, Go East, Young Man (1974). See also, Judge J. Skelly Wright's article, Professor Bickel, The Scholarly Tradition and the Supreme Court, 84 Harv. L.Rev. 769 (1971); Professor Charles Black, The People and the Court (1960). For further analysis, see our multivolume treatise on constitutional law, which discusses in more detail the secondary materials that represent different theories on the proper role of the Supreme Court in constitutional adjudication. See, Ronald D. Rotunda & John E. Nowak, Treatise on Constitutional Law: Substance and Procedure, Chapter 25 (West Group, 2d ed. 1999).

§ 1.5

1. 10 U.S. (6 Cranch) 87, 3 L.Ed. 162 (1810).

2. This included an attempt to impeach Justice Chase, a noted Federalist, that was successful in the House but failed in the Senate. During this period Marshall greatly

feared that the Court would lose its power and independence. See, R. McCloskey, The American Supreme Court 44–47 (1960).

3. The Court had earlier overridden state laws on the enforceability of state debts in federal courts in Chisholm v. Georgia, 2 U.S. (2 Dall.) 419, 1 L.Ed. 440 (1793) but this ruling was, in effect, "reversed" by the Eleventh Amendment. The Court had previously considered the constitutionality of state acts, thus indicating an early belief in the power, but it upheld the challenged act. See Calder v. Bull, 3 U.S. (3 Dall.) 386, 1 L.Ed. 648 (1798); Also the Court had enforced federal treaties; Clerke v. Harwood, 3 U.S. (3 Dall.) 342, 1 L.Ed. 628 (1797).

4. 10 U.S. (6 Cranch) at 139.

5. 14 U.S. (1 Wheat.) 304, 4 L.Ed. 97 (1816).

6. See, 4 Beveridge, The Life of John Marshall (1919); 1 C. Warren, The Supreme Court in United States History 442–53 (1922).

persons ever did receive the benefits of the property pursuant to the Supreme Court's mandate.[7] What is important today is that the Court enforced its decision on the constitutionality of state acts over the objections and contrary opinions of the state officials and judges.

Martin's representatives based their claim to the land on the anti-confiscation clauses of treaties between the United States and Great Britain. Hunter, and the State of Virginia, claimed that title had vested in Virginia prior to these treaties so that they were not applicable to his title. The highest court of Virginia, the Court of Appeals, had ruled for Hunter and the state, but in 1813 the Supreme Court of the United States found that the treaties secured title in Martin.[8]

Because state law is subordinate to federal treaties under the supremacy clause,[9] the case was returned to the Virginia courts for the entry of a judgment in favor of Martin's representatives and successors. The Virginia Court of Appeals refused to follow this order because it claimed that the case should have been decided differently on the basis of the compromise under state law.

The state court also stated that the U.S. Supreme Court could not constitutionally exercise jurisdiction over a state supreme court. The Virginia state court held section 25 of the Judiciary Act, which extended the appellate jurisdiction of the U.S. Supreme Court to state courts, was unconstitutional.[10]

This state court decision was a direct challenge to the authority of the national government in general, and the Supreme Court in

particular. Judge Spencer Roane of the Virginia, who led the Virginia Court, opposed the growth of power of the national government. He was also a long-time political foe of John Marshall.[11] Because Marshall was unable to respond for the Supreme Court, given his personal interests in the case, the responsibility passed to Justice Joseph Story, who wrote the opinion of the Court.[12]

Martin v. Hunter's Lessee[13] ruled that the Supreme Court had the jurisdiction and authority to review all state acts under the Constitution, laws and treaties of the United States. Writing for the Court, Story found that the Judiciary Act properly recognized the existence of appellate jurisdiction in the Supreme Court over actions in state courts.[14] Story explained that the supremacy clause of Article VI plainly indicates that the framers realized that federal issues might arise in state cases. The grant of jurisdiction to the Supreme Court in Article III over *all* cases within the judicial power of the United States was intended to include such decisions.

Virginia argued that it was a sovereign and that the U.S. Supreme Court could not restrict its judicial rulings. Story countered by noting that the people of the nation had chosen to limit state sovereignty when they established a Constitution that specifically restricted state acts in a variety of ways, such as the limitations included in Article I.[15] There was no reason to exempt actions of the state judiciary from these restrictions. Moreover, the lack of any exemption did not unduly impair the functions of the state judiciary because the su-

7. 1 C. Warren, The Supreme Court in U.S. History 450 (1922); 2 W. Crosskey, Politics and the Constitution 786 (1953).

8. Fairfax's Devisee v. Hunter's Lessee, 11 U.S. (7 Cranch) 603, 3 L.Ed. 453 (1813).

9. U.S. Const. art. VI, cl. 2.

10. Hunter v. Martin, devisees of Fairfax, 18 Va. (4 Munford) 1 (1815).

11. Note, Judge Spencer Roane of Virginia: Champion of States' Rights—Foe of John Marshall 66 Harv.L.Rev. 1242 (1953).

Warren, Legislative and Judicial Attacks on the Supreme Court of the United States—A History of the Twenty-fifth Section of the Judiciary Act, 47 Am.L.Rev. 1, 161,

(1913) notes: "Between 1789 and 1860 the courts of seven states denied the constitutional right of the United States Supreme Court to decide cases on writs of error to state courts...."

12. On Story, see, Rotunda & Nowak, Joseph Story: a Man for All Seasons, 1990 Journal of Supreme Court History: Yearbook of the Supreme Court Historical Society 17 (1990); Hoeflich & Rotunda, Simon Greafleaf on Desuetude and Judge–Made Law: An Unpublished Letter to Francis Lieber, 10 Const. Commentary 67 (1993), discussing Story's relationship with Greafleaf.

13. 14 U.S. (1 Wheat.) 304, 4 L.Ed. 97 (1816).

14. 14 U.S. (1 Wheat.) at 327–37.

15. 14 U.S. (1 Wheat.) at 324–25, 343–44.

premacy clause already required state judges to follow federal law.

Story concluded by asserting the Supreme Court's right and duty to be the single, final interpreter of federal law and the Constitution. A national government, whose parts are subject to a single Constitution, must include an entity to give a final interpretation to its laws. Moreover, state courts had to be subject to the rulings of the Supreme Court in federal issues so that the meaning and application of the laws, treaties and Constitution of the United States would have a uniform interpretation and application throughout the country.

Although the Court, in effect, rejected Virginia's claims of sovereignty, it did not consider the propriety of issuing a mandamus order against state judges. The Court merely held that the judgment of the Virginia Court of Appeals had to be reversed.[16]

Marshall had an opportunity to speak for the Court in asserting jurisdiction over state acts in another third case, *Cohens v. Commonwealth of Virginia*.[17] This case upheld the state prosecution of interstate sellers of lottery tickets, but in so doing established its authority to review state criminal proceedings. The decision came at a time when there were severe challenges to the Court from southern states fearing the growing national power.[18]

In *Cohens,* Virginia had prosecuted persons who sold lottery tickets in the state in violation of state law. The appellants claimed that the sales were permitted by a federal statute authorizing a lottery in the District of Columbia. Marshall held that the federal act did not protect these persons, but in the course of so deciding, he asserted federal authority to review state acts and criminal proceedings.

The Court ruled that the Eleventh Amendment was inapplicable in cases like this one (a criminal case) when state itself instituted suit. Most importantly, Marshall used *Cohens* to expound on the nature of the Constitution's control of state acts. Marshall explained that the Constitution was an original act of the people, which was apart from, and superior to, any concept of state sovereignty. To the extent that the people created a national power, the federal judiciary shared in it with the other branches of the federal government. Because the Constitution was created to be a paramount and enduring law, it would often require enforcement against outside challenges. In Marshall's opinion the federal courts were a proper institution for this purpose.

§ 1.6   Federal Judicial Review of State Laws

(a) Theory and Standards of Judicial Review

Once one accepts the basic concept of judicial review of federal laws, and rejects the notion that states are independent sovereigns, it is easy to justify federal judicial power to review the acts of state governments. Several roads all lead to the same conclusion.

First, let us look to legal history. During the Constitutional Convention, proponents of a strong central government argued that an extensive system of lower courts was necessary to protect federal interests. State's Right proponents *supported* federal judicial review of state courts as a way to undercut the argument that the U.S. Constitution had to mandate a lower court system. They argued that federal interests were adequately protected by the possibility of U.S. Supreme Court review of state court decisions.[1] The understanding

---

16. 14 U.S. (1 Wheat.) at 362. Justice Johnson joined the opinion only because it had not taken a position on the mandamus issue.

17. 19 U.S. (6 Wheat.) 264, 5 L.Ed. 257 (1821).

18. This had largely been a reaction to Marshall's opinion for the Court upholding federal law and limiting state power in McCulloch v. Maryland, 17 U.S. (4 Wheat.) 316, 4 L.Ed. 579 (1819), which is discussed in § 3.2, infra.

The Supreme Court did not issue its writ of mandamus to the Virginia Court of Appeals; the Supreme Court

apparently simply entered judgment. See Dodd, Chief Justice Marshall and Virginia 1813–21, 12 Am.Hist.Rev. 776, 779 (1907).

§ 1.6

1. P. Bator, P. Mishkin, D. Shapiro, H. Wechsler, Hart & Wechsler's The Federal Courts and the Federal System 11–12 (2d ed. 1973) [hereinafter cited as Hart & Wechsler].

that the U.S. Supreme Court has the power to review state courts accounts explains why the Constitution does not itself create lower federal courts (with complete federal question jurisdiction), but only authorizes Congress to create such lower courts and define their jurisdiction, as they may be needed over time. The Federalist Papers confirm this understanding,[2] and the first judiciary act expressly provided for such review.[3]

Second, the road of linguists leads us to the same destination. The most natural reading of Article III supports the conclusion that there is federal judicial power to review state courts on federal questions. After listing the types of cases to which the federal judicial power extends, Article III provides that, in a small class of cases, the U.S. Supreme Court would have original jurisdiction. "In *all other* cases before mentioned, the Supreme Court shall have appellate Jurisdiction, both as to Law and Fact, with such Exceptions, and under such Regulations as the Congress shall make".[4]

Third, if we take the route of legal precedent, we, once again, reach the same destination. The Court, in *Martin v. Hunter's Lessee*[5] speaking through Justice Story, reversed the Virginia Court of Appeals and ruled that it had the jurisdiction and authority to review all state acts under the Constitution, laws, and

treaties of the United States. Though Virginia argued that, as a sovereign, it could not be restricted by rulings of the U.S. Supreme Court,[6] Story decided that, when the people set up the central government, they chose to limit state sovereignty by establishing a Constitution that specifically restricted state acts in a variety of ways.[7]

Thus, the supremacy clause of Article VI of the U.S. Constitution specifically makes state law subordinate to the federal treaties and laws, as well as the Constitution.[8] That provision also charges state court judges with the duty of following the Constitution of the United States over state law whenever the two conflict. The framers would have taken an incomprehensible, inconsistent position if they had intended to have state judges review the constitutionality of state acts under the U.S. Constitution while denying a similar power to the Supreme Court in the appellate jurisdiction granted to it.[9] If nothing else, the supremacy clause strengthens the Court's claim to review state laws as a necessary way of declaring uniform principles of constitutional law.

Scholars and Justices have given almost universal acceptance these arguments, as well as those made in the early cases concerning the review of state laws.[10] Even Justice Holmes,

---

2. The Federalist Papers, No. 82 (Hamilton):

"[W]hat relation would subsist between the national and state courts in these instances of concurrent jurisdiction? I answer, that an appeal would certainly lie from the latter, to the supreme court of the United States. The constitution in direct terms, gives an appellate jurisdiction to the Supreme Court in all the enumerated cases of federal cognizance, in which it is not to have an original one; without a single expression to confine its operation to the inferior federal courts. The objects of the appeal, not the tribunals from which it is to be made, are alone contemplated."

3. Judiciary Act of 1789, § 25, 1 Stat. 73, 85.

4. U.S.Const. art. III, § 2, cl. 2 (emphasis added).

5. 14 U.S. (1 Wheat.) 304, 4 L.Ed. 97 (1816).

6. See Hunter v. Martin, Devisees of Fairfax, 18 Va. (4 Munf.) 1 (1814), affirmed 14 U.S. (1 Wheat.) 304, 4 L.Ed. 97 (1816). For example, Judge Cabell, who wrote one of the seriatim opinions, argued:

"But before one Court can dictate to another, the judgment it shall pronounce, it must bear, to that other the relation of an appellate Court. The term appellate, however, necessarily includes the idea of superiority. But one court cannot be correctly said to be superior to

another, unless both of them belong to the same sovereignty.... The Courts of the United States, therefore, belonging to one sovereignty, cannot be appellate courts in relation to the state courts, which belong to a different sovereignty—and of course, their commands or instructions impose no obligation.... It has been contended that the Constitution contemplated only the objects of appeal, and not the tribunals from which the appeal is to be taken; and intended to give the Supreme Court of the United States appellate jurisdiction in all the cases of federal cognizance. But this argument proves too much, and what is utterly inadmissible. It would give appellate jurisdiction, as well over the courts of England or France, as over the state courts...."

7. 14 U.S. (1 Wheat.) at 324–25, 343–44. See also, U.S. Const. art. I, § 7.

8. U.S.Const. art. VI, cl. 2.

9. This point can serve as a strong argument for a grant of judicial power to review federal as well as state acts. C. Black, The People and the Court, 23–25 (1960).

10. E.g., Fletcher v. Peck, 10 U.S. (6 Cranch) 87, 3 L.Ed. 162 (1810); Martin v. Hunter's Lessee, 14 U.S. (1 Wheat.) 304, 4 L.Ed. 97 (1816); Cohens v. Commonwealth of Virginia, 19 U.S. (6 Wheat.) 264, 5 L.Ed. 257 (1821).

who opposed active review of federal laws, found that the review of state acts was a necessary part of the federal judicial function.[11] Professor Thayer in his classic article on the nature of the judicial power in matters of constitutional law found no theoretical difficulty with the review of state acts.[12]

In addition to the establishment of the power of judicial review over the states, the Court also had to determine what standards to apply when reviewing such acts. A strong argument can be made for allowing the states greater freedom than the federal government when applying the provisions of the Bill of Rights to them, for those were originally drafted to restrict only the federal government.[13] On the other hand, to the extent that the concept of judicial restraint is based on democratic theory, there is less reason for the federal judiciary to defer to state governments. In such a situation the judiciary is confronted with the acts of a subsidiary unit of the federal system rather than those of a coordinate, elected branch of the national government.

Much of the modern theory of judicial restraint is based upon the work of Professor James Bradley Thayer. Interestingly, he did not advocate the use of greater restraint when federal courts reviewed state laws. Instead he argued that—

> when the question is whether State action be or not be conformable to the paramount constitution, the supreme law of the land, we have a different matter in hand. Fundamentally, it involves the allotment of power between the two governments,—where the line is to be drawn. True, the judiciary is still debating whether a legislature has

transgressed its limit; but the departments are not co-ordinate and the limit is at a different point. The judiciary now speaks as representing a paramount constitution and government, whose duty it is, in all its departments, to allow that constitution nothing less than its just and true interpretation; and having fixed this, to guard it against any inroads from without.[14]

In modern times, the Supreme Court holds the state and federal governments to identical standards when reviewing their acts under any constitutional guarantee applicable to both. This position is based on two principles. First, the provisions of the Constitution have a single meaning, which the judiciary is bound to respect and enforce. Second, the federal judiciary is acting as a non-democratic institution when it is reviewing either the acts of the state or federal governments.

This tenet of a single standard applies whether the constitutional provision involved is one of the provisions of the Bill of Rights that applies to the states[15] or a general guarantee such as due process or equal protection.[16] Indeed, this position has been accepted for so long that few remember Thayer's complete thesis, and, surprisingly, his article has been cited as authority for exercising greater restraint when reviewing state laws.[17]

(b) State Challenges

The most serious political challenges to the Court have come in the area of federal judicial authority over state acts. Prior to the Civil War there were recurring arguments that the individual states had the right to act free of federal constitutional restraints. As a result there were various political attempts to limit

---

11. Holmes once wrote: "I do not think the United States would come to an end if we lost our power to declare an Act of Congress void. I do think the Union would be imperiled if we could not make the declaration as to the laws of the several states." O. W. Holmes, Collected Legal Papers 295–96 (1920).

12. Thayer, The Origin and Scope of the American Doctrine of Constitutional Law, 7 Harv.L.Rev. 129, 154 (1893).

13. This position was advanced by the younger Justice Harlan. E.g. Williams v. Florida, 399 U.S. 78, 117, 90 S.Ct. 1893, 1914, 26 L.Ed.2d 446 (1970) (Harlan, J., concurring).

14. Thayer, The Origin and Scope of the American Doctrine of Constitutional Law, 7 Harv.L.Rev. 129, 154–55 (1893).

15. Malloy v. Hogan, 378 U.S. 1, 84 S.Ct. 1489, 12 L.Ed.2d 653 (1964).

16. United States v. Kras, 409 U.S. 434, 93 S.Ct. 631, 34 L.Ed.2d 626 (1973).

17. San Antonio Independent School District v. Rodriguez, 411 U.S. 1, 60, 93 S.Ct. 1278, 1310, 36 L.Ed.2d 16 (1973) (Stewart, J., concurring).

the Supreme Court's authority, ranging from alteration of its statutory jurisdiction to claims that a state could disregard its constitutional interpretation if it chose to "interpose" its sovereignty between the Court and the people of the state.[18] This interposition theory led to the argument that individual states had the power of "nullification"—the ability to disregard federal laws because the states were independent sovereigns. While this theory had strong support in individual southern states, it was never widespread and the Supreme Court exercised its authority in a manner that solidified its position over the states.[19]

After the Civil War, the power of the central government became firmly established and the arguments for states' rights disappeared, for a time, from the halls of Congress and most of the nation.[20] However, when the Court, in more recent years, began to enforce equal protection and other Constitutional rights, new challenges to the Court's authority arose.[21] These challenges are nothing more than political attempts to fight a concept now firmly established. The states have no power or right to disregard the Constitution or its enforcement by the federal judiciary. The Supreme Court reaffirmed this principle when it held that states could not deter the federal enforcement of desegregation orders regardless of their individual positions on the issue.[22]

Because these confrontations of Court authority involve no legitimate principle of constitutional law, we give them no extended treatment in this treatise, although we do note individual challenges if they are relevant to an historical explanation of an area of constitutional interpretation. To the extent that state officers choose to disregard federal rulings, they are subject to penalty under the contempt power and individual federal statutes. The executive branch may be called upon to enforce federal law in these instances.[23]

(c) State Court Review of State Laws

State courts may be called upon to review the constitutionality of either state or federal laws in the course of deciding issues in cases before them. When reviewing federal laws these courts must enforce federal laws over inconsistent state acts. If the state courts refuse to follow U.S. Supreme Court rulings, the Supreme Court can reverse. However, more difficult problems arise when state courts review state laws.

State courts are the final interpreters of state law even though their actions are reviewable under the federal constitution, treaties, or laws. The supreme court of a state is truly the highest court in terms of this body of law; it is not a "lower court," even in relation to the Supreme Court of the United States. It must follow the Supreme Court's rulings on the meaning of the Constitution of the United States or federal law, but it is free to interpret state laws or the state constitution in any way that does not violate principles of federal law.[24]

This power is an extremely important one, for it means that the state courts are always free to grant individuals more rights than those guaranteed by the Constitution, provid-

18. See Warren, Legislative and Judicial Attacks on the Supreme Court of the United States—A History of the Twenty–Fifth Section of the Judiciary Act, 47 Am.L.Rev. 1, 161 (1913).

19. R. McCloskey, The American Supreme Court, Chapters 3 & 4 (1960).

20. See Nowak, The Scope of Congressional Power to Create Causes of Action Against State Governments and the History of the Eleventh and Fourteenth Amendments, 75 Colum.L.Rev. 1413, 1460–64 (1975).

21. See Note, Interposition vs. Judicial Power—A Study of Ultimate Authority in Constitutional Questions, 1 Race Rel.L.Rep. 465 (1956); Comment, Jurisdiction of the Supreme Court to Issue Mandamus to a State Court, 20 Tex.L.Rev. 358 (1942); Corwin, National Power and State Interposition, 10 Mich.L.Rev. 535 (1912). Beatty,

State Court Evasion of United States Supreme Court Mandates During the Last Decade of the Warren Court, 6 Va.L.Rev. 260 (1972).

22. Cooper v. Aaron, 358 U.S. 1, 78 S.Ct. 1401, 3 L.Ed.2d 5 (1958); Bush v. Orleans Parish School Board, 364 U.S. 500, 81 S.Ct. 260, 5 L.Ed.2d 245 (1960), affirming 188 F.Supp. 916 (E.D.La.1960).

23. See Note, Enforcement of Court Orders—Federal Contempt Proceeding and Prevention of Obstruction, 2 Race Rel.L.Rep. 1051 (1957); Pollitt, Presidential Use of Troops to Execute the Laws: A Brief History, 36 N.C.L.Rev. 117 (1958).

24. Members of the Jamestown School Committee v. Schmidt, 122 R.I. 185, 405 A.2d 16, 18–19 (1979) (Bevilacqua, C. J.), citing Treatise; Thomas, J., citing Treatise in, Simms v. Oedekoven, 839 P.2d 381 (Wyo.1992).

ed it does so on the basis of state law.[25] The federal Constitution establishes minimum guarantees of rights. Granting additional liberties does not violate its provisions. Thus, if a state court rules that the death penalty is absolutely barred by the Eighth Amendment, the U.S. Supreme Court can overturn its ruling as contrary to Court interpretation of federal law.[26] But, if the state court based its decision on the state constitution, it cannot be overturned, for the Eighth Amendment only allows the states to execute people under certain circumstances—it does not require it. Thus, individual state courts, relying on their state constitutions, have taken actions that are not required by the Supreme Court, such as declaring sex classifications to be "suspect",[27] requiring equal financing of state schools,[28] or actively reviewing economic classifications.[29]

All of the federal principles we discuss in this treatise apply with full force to the ruling of state courts, because they are required to follow the Supreme Court's interpretation of the Constitution of the United States. Nevertheless, state courts are supreme in the interpretation of their own statutes and the state's own constitution, so they may interpret state law to grant more rights federal law guarantees (as long as they do not violate a valid federal law or treaty, or the U.S. Constitution).[30]

The state courts are in an appellate relationship to the U.S. Supreme Court but not in an appellate relationship to any lower federal courts. Because the state courts are not "lower courts," they are not required to follow the interpretation of lower federal courts, such as the Court of Appeals with jurisdiction over their state, even on matters relating to federal law.[31] The federal court orders are *res judicata* and binding to the particular parties before the court, but when a similar issue appears in a new state case, the state supreme court need only follow the rulings and interpretations of the Supreme Court of the United States.

If a state court issues rulings contrary to the lower federal court, it may be engaging in a futile action, because the federal court may be able to enforce its interpretation of federal law by the use of habeas corpus, or by the imposi-

---

25. See e.g., PruneYard Shopping Center v. Robins, 447 U.S. 74, 100 S.Ct. 2035, 64 L.Ed.2d 741 (1980), in which the Supreme Court upheld a state court decision interpreting the state constitution to protect the distribution of pamphlets and petitions at a private shopping center. Although the Supreme Court held that the First and Fourteenth Amendments did not prevent a private shopping center owner from prohibiting such activities on his property, the expansion of the rights of speech and association could be accomplished by interpretation of the state constitution.

26. The Supreme Court has overturned state judicial grants of rights where they were based on the state court's erroneous interpretation of the meaning of federal law. See, e.g., Lehnhausen v. Lake Shore Auto Parts, 410 U.S. 356, 93 S.Ct. 1001, 35 L.Ed.2d 351 (1973); see also Oregon v. Hass, 420 U.S. 714, 95 S.Ct. 1215, 43 L.Ed.2d 570 (1975).

When the Supreme Court reverses a state court decision that invalidated state law on the basis of an erroneous ruling or the meaning of the federal constitution, it normally notes that the state court remains free to review and invalidate the law at issue under the terms of the state constitution. See, e.g., Minnesota v. Clover Leaf Creamery Co., 449 U.S. 456, 461 n. 6, 101 S.Ct. 715, 722 n. 6, 66 L.Ed.2d 659 (1981) (overruling state court invalidation of commercial regulation under equal protection clause of the Fourteenth Amendment while allowing for independent review of the state law by the state courts under the state constitution).

27. Sail'er Inn, Inc. v. Kirby, 5 Cal.3d 1, 95 Cal.Rptr. 329, 485 P.2d 529 (1971); People v. Ellis, 57 Ill.2d 127, 311 N.E.2d 98 (1974).

28. Serrano v. Priest, 5 Cal.3d 584, 96 Cal.Rptr. 601, 487 P.2d 1241 (1971), appeal after remand 18 Cal.3d 728, 135 Cal.Rptr. 345, 557 P.2d 929 (1976), certiorari denied 432 U.S. 907, 97 S.Ct. 2951, 53 L.Ed.2d 1079 (1977), supplemented 20 Cal.3d 25, 141 Cal.Rptr. 315, 569 P.2d 1303 (1977); Robinson v. Cahill, 62 N.J. 473, 303 A.2d 273 (1973), on reargument 63 N.J. 196, 306 A.2d 65 (1973), certiorari denied 414 U.S. 976, 94 S.Ct. 292, 38 L.Ed.2d 219 (1973), on rehearing 69 N.J. 133, 351 A.2d 713 (1975).

29. Grace v. Howlett, 51 Ill.2d 478, 283 N.E.2d 474 (1972) (classification within no-fault insurance legislation); Hetherington, State Economic Regulation and Substantive Due Process of Law, 53 Nw.U.L.Rev. 13, 226 (1958).

30. Federal courts also have a role in interpreting state constitutions, when the issues come before them. For an analysis of this issue and an argument for a significant role for federal courts in interpreting state constitutions, see, Robert A. Shapiro, Polyphonic Federalism: State Constitutions in the Federal Courts, 87 Calif. L. Rev. 1409 (1999).

31. Similarly a federal district court is only bound to follow the interpretation of the Court of Appeals for its Circuit and one Court of Appeals is not bound to follow the reasoning or results of decision in other circuits. This may result in what is called a "split in the circuits" on a point of federal law. Only the Supreme Court can resolve this split in authority.

tion of a state-wide injunction against state officials. However, if the state supreme court believes that the lower federal court is in error as to the meaning of the Constitution, it may legitimately continue to hold an opposite interpretation so long as it does not interfere with a ruling of the federal court in a specific case. When such inconsistent rulings arise, it is common for the Supreme Court of the United States to exercise its appellate jurisdiction over a case involving the issue so that the matter can be finally resolved.[32]

32. One example was the continuing dispute between the Supreme Court of Maine and the Court of Appeals for the First Circuit and the District Court over the allocation of the burden of proof in manslaughter cases, a split that the Supreme Court finally resolved in Mullaney v. Wilbur, 421 U.S. 684, 95 S.Ct. 1881, 44 L.Ed.2d 508 (1975).

Chapter 2

FEDERAL JURISDICTION

§ 2.1 An Introduction to the Jurisdictional Framework of the Supreme Court

Article III Courts. The Supreme Court is the only federal court that the Constitution creates directly. Article III mandates that the judicial power be vested in "one Supreme Court." As to the inferior courts, the Constitution vests the judicial power only as Congress "may from time to time ordain and establish" such lower courts.[1]

The lower courts that Congress creates pursuant to its Article III powers are called Article III courts. Unlike Article I courts, the judges of Article III courts have the Constitution's guarantee of lifetime tenure, with no diminution of salary.[2]

Article III of the Constitution sets out the jurisdiction of all federal courts, which is limited in nature. Congress cannot expand federal jurisdiction beyond the contours set out in Article III. Federal courts can hear cases only because of the nature of the question, or the nature of the parties.

In other words, federal courts can hear cases "arising under" the Constitution, laws, and treaties of the United States (including admiralty cases). They can also hear cases because of the nature of the parties, that is, cases affecting ambassadors, other public ministers, and consuls, controversies to which the United States is a party, controversies between two or more states, between a state and citizens of another state, between citizens of different states, between citizens of the same state claiming lands under grants of different states, and between a state or its citizens and foreign states, citizens, or subjects.[3]

Article I Courts. In addition to creating these Article III courts, Congress also has the power, within certain limits, to create what are called *legislative courts* or Article I tribunals. These courts are tribunals that are inferior to the Supreme Court, but they are neither limited by, nor protected by, Article III.[4]

Article I tribunals are really akin to administrative agencies. The "judges" of Article I courts do not have any constitutionally guaranteed lifetime tenure and protection from salary diminution;[5] they are not governed by the case or controversy limitation of Article III[6] and thus may render advisory opinions.[7]

---

§ 2.1

1. U.S. Const. art. III, § 1.

2. Ronald D. Rotunda, A Few Modest Proposals to Reform the Law Governing Federal Judicial Salaries, 12 The Professional Lawyer 1 (A.B.A., Fall 2000).

3. U.S. Const. art. III, § 2, cl. 1.

4. U.S. Const. art. I, § 8, cl. 9. See, e.g., Marshall, C.J., in American Insurance Co. v. 356 Bales of Cotton, 26 U.S. (1 Pet.) 511, 546, 7 L.Ed. 242 (1828): "These courts [the superior courts of the territory of Florida, created by Congress], then, are not constitutional Courts, in which the judicial power conferred by the Constitution on the general government, can be deposited. They are incapable of receiving it. They are legislative Courts, created in virtue of the general right of sovereignty, which exists in the government, or in virtue of that clause, which enables Congress to make all needful rules and regulations, respecting the territory belonging to the United States."

5. E.g., Glidden Co. v. Zdanok, 370 U.S. 530, 533–34, 82 S.Ct. 1459, 1463, 8 L.Ed.2d 671 (1962), rehearing denied 371 U.S. 854, 83 S.Ct. 14, 9 L.Ed.2d 93 (1962) (plurality opinion of Harlan, J., joined by Brennan & Stewart, JJ.).

6. Glidden Co. v. Zdanok, 370 U.S. 530, 583, 82 S.Ct. 1459, 1490, 8 L.Ed.2d 671 (1962), rehearing denied 371 U.S. 854, 83 S.Ct. 14, 9 L.Ed.2d 93 (1962) (plurality opinion of Harlan, J.).

7. 370 U.S. at 579–83, 82 S.Ct. at 1487–1490 (plurality opinion of Harlan, J.).

To some extent these courts (e.g., territorial courts[8]) may receive business that Congress could have sent to an Article III court, but chose not to do so. Congress must have an appropriate reason to create Article I courts. It may not simply give any and all Article III business to an Article I court, or otherwise the very concept of a court protected and limited by Article III would have no meaning.[9]

At the present time, Article I courts include territorial courts, certain courts in the District of Columbia,[10] courts martial,[11] and legislative courts and administrative agencies that adjudicate "public rights."[12] Administrative law judges are Article I judges.

Supreme Court Jurisdiction. The Supreme Court has original jurisdiction, under Article III,[13] of all cases affecting ambassadors, other public ministers and consuls, and cases in which a state is a party. Congress cannot constitutionally expand this original jurisdiction.[14] Article III also gives the Court appellate jurisdiction of all the other cases within the limited jurisdiction of Article III, but this appellate jurisdiction is given "with such Exceptions, and under such Regulations as the Congress shall make."[15]

The Jurisdictional Framework. At the present time Congress has created thirteen judicial circuits, numbered one through eleven, plus the District of Columbia Circuit, plus the Court of Appeals for the Federal Circuit.[16] The Federal Circuit Court hears appeals from a final decision of the United States Claims Court, similar appeals from the federal district courts, the Court of International Trade, the Board of Patent Interferences, patent appeals from the federal district courts, and similar miscellaneous matters.[17] Cases heard in the federal court system normally are heard in district courts in one of these circuits.

From the district courts, the parties may appeal to the court of appeals for that circuit (or the Federal Circuit). The circuit normally sits in panels of three.

From there the parties may seek review in the Supreme Court, normally by way of certiorari (discretionary review); by way of appeal (obligatory review, at least in theory); or by certified questions. In 1988 Congress finally eliminated most of the Supreme Court's mandatory appellate jurisdiction, giving that Court a great deal of control over its own docket. The 1988 legislation converts almost all Supreme Court review to a discretionary, certiorari approach.[18]

In addition to this basic federal court system, Congress has sometimes established more specialized Article III courts. For example, it set up a special railroad court, composed of already sitting federal judges designated for part-time sitting on this court.[19]

Federal jurisdiction often raises not only statutory questions—when is a state decision

---

8. E.g., Ross v. McIntyre, 140 U.S. 453, 11 S.Ct. 897, 35 L.Ed. 581 (1891) (consular court); American Insurance Co. v. 356 Bales of Cotton, 26 U.S. (1 Pet.) 511, 7 L.Ed. 242 (1828) (superior court of the territory of Florida).

9. Northern Pipeline Const. Co. v. Marathon Pipe Line Co., 458 U.S. 50, 102 S.Ct. 2858, 73 L.Ed.2d 598 (1982), stayed 459 U.S. 813, 103 S.Ct. 199, 74 L.Ed.2d 160 (1982) (Opinion of Brennan, J., joined by Marshall, Blackmun & Stevens, JJ.) (violation of Art. III for non-Art. III judges to have the jurisdiction granted by § 241(a) of the Bankruptcy Act of 1978).

10. Palmore v. United States, 411 U.S. 389, 93 S.Ct. 1670, 36 L.Ed.2d 342 (1973).

11. Dynes v. Hoover, 61 U.S. (20 How.) 65, 79, 15 L.Ed. 838 (1858).

12. Den ex dem. Murray v. Hoboken Land & Improvement Co., 59 U.S. (18 How.) 272, 284, 15 L.Ed. 372 (1855); Atlas Roofing Co. v. Occupational Safety and Health Review Commission, 430 U.S. 442, 450, 97 S.Ct. 1261, 1266,

51 L.Ed.2d 464 (1977). *Atlas* defined "public rights" as, "e.g., cases in which the Government sues in its sovereign capacity to enforce public rights created by statutes within the power of Congress." 430 U.S. at 450, 97 S.Ct. at 1266.

13. U.S. Const. art. III, § 2, cl. 2.

14. Marbury v. Madison, 5 U.S. (1 Cranch) 137, 2 L.Ed. 60 (1803).

15. U.S. Const. art. III, § 2, cl. 2.

16. See, Federal Court Improvement Act of 1982, Pub.L. 97–164. See also, 28 U.S.C.A. §§ 41–48.

17. See 28 U.S.C.A. § 1295, "Jurisdiction of the United States Court of Appeals for the Federal Circuit."

18. See, Pub. L. 100–353, 102 Stat. at Large 662, revising 28 U.S.C.A. § 1257.

19. See 45 U.S.C.A. § 719; see Regional Rail Reorganization Act Cases, Blanchette v. Connecticut General Insurance Corp., 419 U.S. 102, 95 S.Ct. 335, 42 L.Ed.2d 320 (1974).

"final"; is the review by appeal or certiorari; and so on—but also constitutional questions. These constitutional questions occur because Article III allows Congress to grant federal courts only limited jurisdiction. For example, is the claim brought before the federal court a "case or controversy" within the meaning of Article III? If the case is brought on diversity grounds, are the parties really citizens of diverse states? In a diversity case, is the amount in controversy requirement of the diversity statute met by the plaintiff?

In addition to the statutory and constitutional questions that must be resolved prior to the court hearing the case on the merits, the Supreme Court has developed many rules of self restraint to avoid exercising its power to strike laws violative of the Constitution. In the remainder of this Chapter we shall consider these questions of constitutional jurisdiction, statutory jurisdiction, and self-imposed rules of restraint. We will also examine how the Court uses various doctrines, such as standing and ripeness, as tools to avoid reaching the merits. But first, let us turn to the long historical development that has led to the present jurisdictional framework of the Supreme Court.

§ 2.2 The Historical Development of the Jurisdictional Framework of the Supreme Court

While the framers of the Constitution readily accepted the notion that there should be a federal judiciary system,[1] the nature of that system was a subject of more than a little dispute. Article III of the Constitution declares that there shall be "one Supreme Court,"[2] yet the framers debated the nature of lower courts, and even the question of whether they should be created. Some of the framers wanted

no lower federal courts; others would provide only for lower federal courts of admiralty; some insisted that the Constitution require the establishment of lower federal courts; and others still would have granted Congress the power to create them with jurisdiction over all matters of general concern.[3]

The first sentence of Article III, section 1 reflects the resolution of the controversy:

The judicial Power of the United States, shall be vested in one Supreme Court, and in such inferior courts as the Congress *may* from time to time ordain and establish.[4]

Though the language is not without ambiguity, Congress, it would appear, was given discretion as to whether or not to establish lower federal courts.[5]

The question of whether Article III itself, or the due process clause of the Fifth Amendment, restricts congressional power over federal court jurisdiction is considered in more detail later in this Chapter.[6] In the meantime, it is important to keep the historical background of Article III in mind as one studies the development of federal jurisdiction.

The First Judiciary Act. A review of the history of federal jurisdictional statutes shows the continual expansion of federal jurisdiction, from its very narrow beginnings with until modern times. Let us start with the first Judiciary Act of 1789.[7]

This first Act was very important for several reasons: (1) it created a court organization that for nearly a century served the country substantially unchanged; (2) it created, under section 25 of the Act, a significant nationalizing influence by establishing Supreme Court review of state court decisions on federal questions; and (3) it established a system of lower

---

§ 2.2

1. Max Farrand, The Framing of the Constitution 79 (1913). See P. Hay & R. Rotunda, The United States Federal System: Legal Integration in the American Experience 12–26 (Giuffré, Milan 1982).

2. U.S.Const. art. III, § 1.

3. See generally H. Hart & H. Wechsler's The Federal Courts and the Federal System 11–12 (2d ed. 1973). See also, e.g., Martin Redish, Federal Courts: Cases, Comments and Questions 140–48 (1983).

4. U.S.Const. art. III, § 1 (emphasis added).

5. See, e.g., 1 M. Farrand, The Records of the Federal Convention 124–125 (1911) (remarks of Wilson and Madison on June 5, 1787: there is "a distinction between establishing such tribunals absolutely, and giving a discretion to the Legislature to establish or not establish them.")

6. See §§ 2.9, 2.10, infra.

7. 1 Stat. 73.

federal courts, which has been called its "transcendent achievement."[8]

The first Judiciary Act is also significant for what it did not do. Thus, it did not establish any general review in the Supreme Court of federal criminal cases.[9] In fact, it was not until 1889 that there was generally established direct appeals in federal criminal cases.[10] Before that, only the collateral attack of a writ of habeas corpus was previously available.[11] Similarly, although the first Act created diversity jurisdiction in the lower federal courts (with a jurisdictional amount of $500)[12] the Act did not provide for any general federal question jurisdiction in the lower federal courts. It was not until the Act of March 3, 1875[13] that Congress finally gave the lower courts basic jurisdiction, of cases arising under the Constitution, laws, or treaties of the United States.[14] It was not until 1914 that the Supreme Court was allowed to review state court decisions in which the state court had upheld the federal claim and held its own statute invalid.[15]

The original judiciary act also created circuit courts, but unlike the modern courts of appeal, these circuit courts had original jurisdiction as well as some appellate jurisdiction over the district courts.[16] Their own original jurisdiction in some matters was at times concurrent with, or exclusive of, the district courts.[17] The law also established three judicial circuits. Each circuit court originally consisted of one of the district judges within the circuit and two Supreme Court Justices.[18] The Justices objected to the rigors of riding circuit and, in correspondence to then President Washington, some even contended the requirement was unconstitutional.[19] However, when this issue actually came before the Court some years later, it upheld the constitutionality of the practice.[20]

The Midnight Judges Statute. In 1801, the Federalist Congress eliminated circuit riding, created sixteen new circuit judgeships, and authorized a greatly expanded jurisdictional authority.[21] Only a year later, the Jeffersonians repealed this so-called "Midnight Judges" statute,[22] amid a very lively debate as to the constitutionality of eliminating courts manned by life-tenured judges.[23] In 1869 Congress further reduced circuit riding by the Justices.[24]

The 1875 Reforms. In 1875 Congress finally conferred general federal question jurisdiction on the lower federal courts and expanded

---

8. F. Frankfurter & J. Landis, The Business of the Supreme Court: A Study in the Federal Judicial System 4 (1927). See also id. at 4–5: "No other English-speaking union (not to deal with nations nurtured in legal institutions radically different from our own) has a scheme of federal courts." (footnote omitted).

9. Judiciary Act of 1789, §§ 9, 11, 1 Stat. 73, 76–78. See also Judiciary Act of 1872, § 1, 17 Stat. 196.

10. In 1889 Congress granted the Supreme Court direct review of capital cases. Judiciary Act of 1889, § 6, 25 Stat. 656. The Evarts Act, § 5, 26 Stat. 827 expanded this review to all infamous crimes.

11. Ex parte Siebold, 100 U.S. (10 Otto) 371, 25 L.Ed. 717 (1880).

12. Act of 1789, § 11, 1 Stat. 73, 78.

13. 18 Stat. 470.

14. Excluding the short-lived Midnight Judges Statute of 1801, (also called the Circuit Courts Act), discussed below, which greatly expanded federal jurisdiction but which was repealed one year later. Act of 1801, § 11, 2 Stat. 92, repealed by Act of 1802, § 1, 2 Stat. 132.

This statutory phrase, "arising under" has been interpreted to be narrower in meaning than its analogous language in the Constitution. Compare Article III, § 2, cl. 1 and Osborn v. Bank of the United States, 22 U.S. (9 Wheat.) 738, 6 L.Ed. 204 (1824) (Marshall, C.J.) with, Romero v. International Terminal Operating Co., 358 U.S.

354, 379 n. 51, 79 S.Ct. 468, 484 n. 51, 3 L.Ed.2d 368 (1959).

15. Act of 1914, 38 Stat. 790.

16. Judiciary Act of 1789, §§ 21, 22, 1 Stat. 83–84.

17. Judiciary Act of 1789, §§ 9, 11, 12, 1 Stat. 73, 76, 78, 79. These circuit courts had "exclusive cognizance" of federal crimes except that they shared jurisdiction with the federal district courts over minor criminal matters.

18. Judiciary Act of 1789, § 4, 1 Stat. 73–74.

19. H. Hart & H. Wechsler, The Federal Courts and Federal System 68 (2d ed. 1973).

20. Stuart v. Laird, 5 U.S. (1 Cranch) 299, 309, 2 L.Ed. 115 (1803).

21. Judiciary Act of 1801, §§ 1–3, 7, 11, 2 Stat. 89–90, 92. See, F. Frankfurter & J. Landis, The Business of the Supreme Court 25 (1927).

22. Judiciary Act of 1802, § 1, 2 Stat. 132.

23. See F. Frankfurter & J. Landis, The Business of the Supreme Court 26–28 & n. 75 (1927).

A portion of this Repeal Act was upheld in Stuart v. Laird, 5 U.S. (1 Cranch) 299, 2 L.Ed. 115 (1803). See also, Van Alstyne, A Critical Guide to Marbury v. Madison, 1969 Duke L.J. 1, 5.

24. Judiciary Act of 1869, § 2, 16 Stat. 44.

their diversity jurisdiction.[25] This large expansion of jurisdictional authority in 1875, while not fully appreciated at the time, finally meant that the federal courts ceased to be tribunals restricted to assuring fair dealing between citizens of different states and, instead, became the primary adjudicator for vindicating every right secured by the Constitution, the laws, and treaties of the United States.[26]

The Evarts Act. The next significant change in federal jurisdiction came in 1891 with the Evarts Act,[27] named after Senator Evarts, a member of the Judiciary Committee.[28] This Act created the circuit courts of appeal and eliminated the limited appellate power of the old circuit courts. The new appellate courts could hear most of the appeals from the original cases brought in the old circuit or district courts. The Act also added additional circuit judgeships, and for the first time created a discretionary review system of certiorari in the Supreme Court.[29]

Within a few months the number of new cases docketed in the Supreme Court were greatly reduced: in 1890, 623 new cases had been docketed on the appeal docket; in 1892 the number had dropped to 275.[30] The old circuit courts, the existence of which were long difficult to justify, were finally eliminated in 1911 and district courts assumed their remaining original jurisdiction.[31]

The Judges Bill. In 1925 saw another important revision of the federal court system with the enactment of the Judges Bill.[32] This law, which a committee of Supreme Court Justices originally drafted (hence the name, "Judges Bill") drastically redistributed federal

judicial power.[33] The Judges Bill enlarged discretionary review and reduced mandatory appellate jurisdiction for a large class of cases.[34]

The 1948 Reforms. In 1948, with the codification and revision of the Judicial Code, the Circuit Courts of Appeal were renamed "United States Court of Appeal for the _____ Circuit," [e.g., "First Circuit"] and the name "District Court of the United States" was changed to "United States District Court for the _____ District" [e.g., "Northern District"].[35] The Act also established the District of Columbia Circuit in addition to ten other circuits, numbered one to ten, throughout the entire United States.[36] Within each of these circuits there is at least one district court and several district judges. Each state has at least one district court.

The 1982 Reforms. By 1982 the number of circuits had increased to thirteen, numbered one through eleven, plus the District of Columbia Circuit, and the Federal Circuit. Congress created the new Eleventh Circuit by dividing the Fifth Circuit. Congress established the Federal Circuit to handle appeals from the United States Claims Court, similar appeals from the federal district courts, patent appeals from federal district courts and from the Board of Patent Interferences, appeals from the Board of Patent Interferences, and similar miscellaneous matters.[37]

The Chief Justice now assigns one Supreme Court Justice to each circuit,[38] but the Justices no longer ride circuit.[39] The duties of a Circuit Justice include ruling on applications for stays of other court rulings and similar motions. By

---

25. Judiciary Act of 1875, 18 Stat. 470.

26. F. Frankfurter & J. Landis, The Business of the Supreme Court 65 (1927).

27. Judiciary Act of 1891, 26 Stat. 826.

28. F. Frankfurter & J. Landis, The Business of the Supreme Court 98 (1927).

29. Judiciary Act of 1891, §§ 1, 6, 26 Stat. 826, 828.

30. F. Frankfurter & J. Landis, The Business of the Supreme Court 102 (1927).

31. Judiciary Act of 1911, 36 Stat. 1087.

32. Judiciary Act of 1925, 43 Stat. 936.

33. F. Frankfurter & J. Landis, The Business of the Supreme Court 1 (1927).

34. American Const. Co. v. Jacksonville, T. & K. W. Ry. Co., 148 U.S. 372, 382, 13 S.Ct. 758, 762, 37 L.Ed. 486 (1893).

35. 28 U.S.C.A. §§ 43(a), 451.

36. 28 U.S.C.A. § 41.

37. See 28 U.S.C.A. § 1295, "Jurisdiction of the United States Court of Appeals for the Federal Circuit." See also 28 U.S.C.A. § 41.

38. 28 U.S.C.A. § 42.

39. The Justices do visit their circuit (typically to attend the annual meeting in each circuit), but they are more likely to travel by air than by horse.

Supreme Court rule, applications should be "addressed to the Justice allotted to the Circuit within which the case arises."[40] If the Circuit Justice denies the application, that fact will not prevent the litigant from renewing the matter before another Justice, though such forum-shopping is officially not favored unless the earlier denial has been without prejudice.[41]

The 1988 Supreme Court Docket Reforms. In 1988 Congress eliminated most of the mandatory appellate jurisdiction of the Supreme Court, giving that Court a great deal of control over its own docket. Supreme Court review is now almost always via a discretionary, certiorari approach.[42]

By this trial and error method of creating a national judiciary system, Congress over the last two hundred years has in general tended (a) to constantly broaden the jurisdiction of the lower federal courts, (b) to create a nationwide system of Courts of Appeal, which mainly operate to filter cases between the Supreme Court and the federal trial courts, and (c) to give the Supreme Court greater control over its own docket.[43]

§ 2.3 Original Jurisdiction

The basic statutes governing Supreme Court jurisdiction are found in title 28 of the U.S. Code. Section 1251 governs original jurisdiction and provides, in general, that the high court has original *and* exclusive jurisdiction of controversies between two or more states.[1] The Supreme Court must hear these cases.

The Supreme Court also has original, but not exclusive, jurisdiction of cases in which ambassadors or other public ministers or counsels or vice counsels of foreign states are parties; cases between the United States and a state; and cases brought by a state against citizens of another state or aliens. Because federal district courts may hear these cases as well, the Supreme Court rarely accepts original jurisdiction. Typically the Supreme Court refers cases within the original jurisdiction to a special master, who will receive evidence and prepare a record.[2] Original jurisdiction in practice accounts for but a small percentage of the Supreme Court caseload.

Although Congress, by statute, has always provided for the original jurisdiction of the Supreme Court, the Court has often stated in dictum that "the original jurisdiction of the Supreme Court is conferred not by Congress but by the Constitution itself. This jurisdiction is self-executing and needs no legislative implementation."[3]

California v. Arizona[4] raised the question of Congressional power to limit its original jurisdiction. California sought to invoke the Court's original jurisdiction in a suit to quiet title. California sued Arizona and the United States. Federal statutes provided that controversies between the United States and a state may be heard originally by the Supreme Court, and controversies between two or more states must be heard originally by the Supreme Court.[5] The United States, by statute, waived its sovereign immunity from suit in actions brought against it to quiet title to land, but a statute also provided that the federal district

---

40. Supreme Court Rule 43(4).

41. Supreme Court Rule 43(5). See Winters v. United States, 89 S.Ct. 57, 21 L.Ed.2d 80 (1968) (Douglas J., Circuit Justice). The Justice may refer the application for stay or bail to the full court. Supreme Court Rule 50(6).

42. Pub. L. 100–352, amending 28 U.S.C.A. § 1257.

43. See generally, Henry Friendly, Federal Jurisdiction: A General View (1973).

§ 2.3

1. The Supreme Court interprets section 1251(a) narrowly. Thus, political subdivisions of states are not states for purposes of this subsection. Illinois v. Milwaukee, 406 U.S. 91, 92 S.Ct. 1385, 31 L.Ed.2d 712 (1972). And cases within section 1251(b)(3) may be dismissed in the Court's judgment if there is another suitable forum when original jurisdiction to protect "the essential quality of the right asserted" is not "necessary for the State's protection." Massachusetts v. Missouri, 308 U.S. 1, 18, 60 S.Ct. 39, 43, 84 L.Ed. 3 (1939).

2. E.g., Mississippi v. Arkansas, 402 U.S. 926, 91 S.Ct. 1521, 28 L.Ed.2d 861 (1971); 402 U.S. 939, 91 S.Ct. 1601, 29 L.Ed.2d 108 (1971); 403 U.S. 951, 91 S.Ct. 2273, 29 L.Ed.2d 862 (1971); 411 U.S. 913, 93 S.Ct. 1539, 36 L.Ed.2d 305 (1973); 415 U.S. 289, 94 S.Ct. 1046, 39 L.Ed.2d 333 (1974); 415 U.S. at 302, 94 S.Ct. at 1052, 39 L.Ed.2d at 342 (1974).

3. California v. Arizona, 440 U.S. 59, 65, 99 S.Ct. 919, 923, 59 L.Ed.2d 144 (1979).

4. 440 U.S. 59, 99 S.Ct. 919, 59 L.Ed.2d 144 (1979).

5. 28 U.S.C.A. § 1251.

courts should have *exclusive* jurisdiction of such suits.[6] While the Court agreed that Congress could refuse to waive some or all of its sovereign immunity from suit in any court or all courts, *California v. Arizona* noted that, "once Congress has waived the Nation's sovereign immunity, it is far from clear that it can withdraw the constitutional jurisdiction of this Court over such suits."[7] The Supreme Court then avoided the constitutional question by construing the federal statute as excluding only state court jurisdiction over such cases and confining jurisdiction in those cases to the federal courts. Thus it allowed the suit to be brought originally in the Supreme Court.

§ 2.4   Appellate and Certiorari Jurisdiction

Under "direct appeal" the appellant can bypass the courts of appeal and have the Supreme Court directly hear the case. If review is by "appeal" the appellant will receive Supreme Court review, in theory, as of right.

6.   28 U.S.C.A. §§ 1346(f), 2409a.

7.   440 U.S. at 67, 99 S.Ct. at 923.

§ 2.4

1.   See, Title 28 U.S.C.A. § 1253. Direct appeals from decisions of three-judge courts.

In 1988, Congress repealed 28 U.S.C.A. § 1252, providing for direct appeals to the Supreme Court in a wider class of cases. This repeal was part of its efforts to give the Supreme Court greater control of its own docket by substituting discretionary review for mandatory review. See, Public Law 100–353, §§ 1, 7, 102 Stat. at Large 662, 664 (June 27, 1988).

2.   See 28 U.S.C.A. § 2281 (Injunction against enforcement of state statute; three-judge court required), and 28 U.S.C.A. § 2282 (Injunction against enforcement of federal statute; three judge court required), both repealed by Act of Aug. 12, 1976, Pub.L. 94–381, §§ 1 & 2, 90 Stat. 1119.

Federal law requires a three-judge district court "when otherwise required by Act of Congress, or when an action is filed challenging the constitutionality of the apportionment of congressional districts or the apportionment of any statewide legislative body." 28 U.S.C.A. § 2284(a), as amended by Act of Aug. 12, 1976, Pub.L. 94–381, § 3, 90 Stat. 1119.

3.   After the 1988 Amendments, § 1254 reads as follows:

§ 1254.   Courts of appeals; certiorari; certified questions

"Cases in the courts of appeals may be reviewed by the Supreme Court by the following methods:

Under "certiorari", review for the petitioner is discretionary.

Direct Appeal. Congress limited direct appeals in 1988, as part of its reform to give the Supreme Court much greater control over its own docket. The federal jurisdictional statute now give litigants the right of direct appeal from decisions of three-judge courts.[1] But modern federal statutes severely limits the use of three-judge court, so the number of such direct appeals is correspondingly reduced.[2]

Certiorari and Appeal.

After the 1988 statutory revisions, sections 1254[3] and 1257[4] grant the Supreme Court effective control of its docket.[5] The basic principle behind the 1988 reforms is that the Court itself, "in the light of the discretionary standards it has developed and is constantly refining and applying to new types of situations" is the—

best judge of what cases, out of the thousands put forward each year, are from the national standpoint the most deserving of a

"(1) By writ of certiorari granted upon the petition of any party to any civil or criminal case, before or after rendition of judgment or decree;

"(2) By certification at any time by a court of appeals of any question of law in any civil or criminal case as to which instructions are desired, and upon such certification the Supreme Court may give binding instructions or require the entire record to be sent up for decision of the entire matter in controversy."

4.   After the 1988 Amendments, § 1257 reads as follows:

§ 1257.   State courts; certiorari

"(a) Final judgments or decrees rendered by the highest court of a State in which a decision could be had, may be reviewed by the Supreme Court by writ of certiorari where the validity of a treaty or statute of the United States is drawn in question or where the validity of a statute of any State is drawn in question on the ground of its being repugnant to the Constitution, treaties, or laws of the United States, or where any title, right, privilege, or immunity is specially set up or claimed under the Constitution or the treaties or statutes of, or any commission held or authority exercised under, the United States.

"(b) For the purposes of this section, the term highest court of a State includes the District of Columbia Court of Appeals."

5.   The 1988 revisions do not appeal the provisions of 28 U.S.A. § 1253, requiring direct appeals to the Supreme Court from decisions of three judge courts.

hearing on the merits.[6]

As a result, virtually all review to the Supreme Court now occurs when the Supreme Court, in its discretion, decides to accept a case. The Court has almost complete control of its docket, with review by discretion, by certiorari.

Discretionary Review and Avoidance of Constitutional Issues. As a general principle, the Court often says that no Article III Court should reach a constitutional question prematurely, and courts should avoid deciding constitutional questions unnecessarily.[7] However, these general principles do not require the Supreme Court to deny certiorari in every case raising a novel constitutional question.[8] Rather, the lower federal court should not decide a question prematurely, and it should avoid deciding a constitutional issue unnecessarily. If the lower court has violated these principles, the Supreme Court may reverse on this procedural ground. If the lower court has not violated these principles, the Supreme Court has the discretion to grant the certiorari petition.

§ 2.5 Theoretical and Practical Differences Between Certiorari and Appeal

Even though the former distinction between certiorari and appeal is no longer of prime significance, it is still relevant to know the distinction to determine the significance of precedent, to know whether the Court denied certiorari in a case, or denied review when that review appeared to be obligatory.[1] In theory there was an important distinction between the discretionary review of certiorari and the obligatory review of appeal.

Certiorari. Under the Supreme Court's rules, a review on writ of certiorari is not a matter of right, but of sound judicial discretion, and the Court will grant it only where there are special and important reasons to do so.[2] Consequently, the Court need not explain its refusal to accept certiorari and one cannot deduce any decision on the merits or other precedential value from such denials.[3] The Court grants certiorari for the interest of the public, not merely for the interest of the parties. Thus, the Court will not ordinarily grant certiorari merely to achieve Justice in a particular case.[4]

The denial of certiorari technically means that fewer than four members of the Court, as a matter of their sound discretion, have voted to review a decision of the lower court.[5] Nonetheless, some members of the Court have frequently written lengthy dissents to denials of certiorari. Individual Justices have used their dissents to denial of certiorari to express their

---

6. Boskey & Gressman, The Supreme Court Bids Farewell to Mandatory Appeals, 121 F.R.D. 81, 99 (1988).

7. See §§ 2.13(d) & 2.13(g), infra.

8. Clinton v. Jones, 520 U.S. 681, 117 S.Ct. 1636, 1642, 137 L.Ed.2d 945 (1997).

§ 2.5

1. Not only did the relevant statutes allow some cases to be brought under either certiorari or appeal, but even under the section then dealing with appellate review from the state courts [see the former version of 28 U.S.C.A. § 1257(2)] a careful lawyer was able to make his case appear to be included as an appeal by drafting his pleadings to allege that the statute in question was invalid as applied to him. See Dahnke–Walker Milling Co. v. Bondurant, 257 U.S. 282, 42 S.Ct. 106, 66 L.Ed. 239 (1921).

2. Supreme Court Rules, Rule 10 (Jan. 1, 1990). The "character of reasons that will be considered," while not "controlling nor fully measuring the court's discretion" are listed in Rule 10.1.

"(a) When a United States court of appeals has rendered a decision in conflict with the decision of another United States court of appeals on the same matter; or has decided a federal question in a way in conflict with a

state court of last resort; or has so far departed from the accepted and usual course of judicial proceedings, or so far sanctioned such a departure by a lower court, as to call for an exercise of this Court's power of supervision.

"(b) When a state court of last resort has decided a federal question in a way in conflict with the decision of another state court of last resort or of a United States court of appeals.

"(c) When a state court or a United States court of appeals has decided an important question of federal law which has not been, but should be, settled by this Court, or has decided a federal question in a way in conflict with applicable decisions of this Court."

3. Maryland v. Baltimore Radio Show, 338 U.S. 912, 70 S.Ct. 252, 94 L.Ed. 562 (1950) (Frankfurter, J.).

4. Ticor Title Insurance Co. v. Brown, 511 U.S. 117, 122, 114 S.Ct. 1359, 1362, 128 L.Ed.2d 33 (1994) (per curiam).

5. Opinion of Frankfurter, J., respecting the denial of the petition for writ of certiorari in Maryland v. Baltimore Radio Show, 338 U.S. 912, 917, 70 S.Ct. 252, 254, 94 L.Ed. 562 (1950).

concern about the facts of the particular case, to reemphasize their earlier dissents, to urge reconsideration of a settled point, or to comment on the Court's workload.[6]

Other Justices have objected to these written dissents as "totally unnecessary," "the purest form of dicta," and "potentially misleading."[7] Yet, "it is just one of the facts of life that today every lower court does attach importance to denials and to presence or absence of dissents from denials, as judicial opinions and lawyers' arguments show."[8]

Appeal. When a party seeks review by appeal, the litigant, under the relevant statute, is invoking review as of right.[9] The Supreme Court rules require the appellant to file a jurisdictional statement,[10] which is similar to the petition for certiorari.[11] The appellee may, on the basis of these papers, file a motion to dismiss or affirm.[12] If there is a technical deficiency the Court may dismiss the appeal summarily on this procedural issue.[13]

It may also dismiss an appeal on the merits for *want of a substantial federal question*.[14] "Substantiality" is considered jurisdictional:

[A]lthough the validity of a law was formally drawn in question, it is our duty to decline jurisdiction whenever it appears that the constitutional question presented is not, and was not at the time of granting the writ, substantial in character.[15]

Thus, unlike certiorari, decisions to affirm summarily, and to dismiss for want of a substantial federal question are votes on the merits of a case[16] binding as precedent on the lower courts.[17] But, interestingly enough, this precedent is not as binding on the Supreme Court as would be one of its own more considered opinions.[18]

This distinction of precedential value accords with reality because, notwithstanding the important distinction in theory between certiorari and appeal, in fact the modern Supreme Court has failed to treat the two modes of review differently.:

[I]t has long since become impossible to defend the thesis that all the appeals which the Court dismisses on this ground [of lack of substantiality] are without substance. And any pretense that jurisdictional statements are concerned only with jurisdiction vanished when the Court began to affirm and even reverse judgments on the basis of

---

6. See Linzer, The Meaning of Certiorari Denials, 79 Colum.L.Rev. 1227 (1979).

7. Singleton v. Commissioner, 439 U.S. 940, 944, 99 S.Ct. 335, 338, 58 L.Ed.2d 335 (1978) (opinion of Stevens, J.) who was "puzzled" by the dissent's suggestion that certiorari may have been denied because the tax case was "devoid of glamour and emotion." 439 U.S. at 946, 99 S.Ct. at 339. Cf. Reproductive Services, Inc. v. Walker, 439 U.S. 1133, 99 S.Ct. 1057, 59 L.Ed.2d 96 (1979) (statement of Stevens, J.).

8. Brown v. Allen, 344 U.S. 443, 542–43, 73 S.Ct. 397, 428, 97 L.Ed. 469 (1953) (Jackson, J., concurring in the result).

9. E.g., Hart, Foreword: The Time Chart of the Justices, 73 Harv.L.Rev. 84, 88 (1959).

10. Supreme Court Rules, Rule 18.3.

11. See, Supreme Court Rules, Rule 14.

12. Supreme Court Rules, Rule 18.6.

13. Henry Hart, Foreword: The Time Chart of the Justices, 73 Harv.L.Rev. 84, 89 (1959).

14. Supreme Court Rules, Rule 18.10.

15. Zucht v. King, 260 U.S. 174, 176, 43 S.Ct. 24, 25, 67 L.Ed. 194 (1922) (Brandeis, J.).

16. Ohio ex rel. Eaton v. Price, 360 U.S. 246, 247, 79 S.Ct. 978, 979, 3 L.Ed.2d 1200 (1959) (Memorandum of Brennan, J.), lower court subsequently affirmed by equally divided Court, 364 U.S. 263, 80 S.Ct. 1463, 4 L.Ed.2d 1708 (1960), rehearing denied 364 U.S. 855, 81 S.Ct. 29, 5 L.Ed.2d 80 (1960).

17. Hicks v. Miranda, 422 U.S. 332, 344, 95 S.Ct. 2281, 2289, 45 L.Ed.2d 223 (1975). It is important to note that the summary affirmance by the Supreme Court affirms the judgment of the lower court only and not necessarily the reasoning by which it was reached. Mandel v. Bradley, 432 U.S. 173, 97 S.Ct. 2238, 53 L.Ed.2d 199 (1977) (per curiam), on remand 449 F.Supp. 983 (D.Md.1978).

Justice Tom Clark, when he was sitting by designation on a Fourth Circuit case, objected to the Supreme Court's statement in *Hicks*, that a dismissal for want of a substantial federal question is a decision on the merits. That view, he said, seems "to me to fly in the face of the long-established practice of the Court during the eighteen Terms in which I sat. During that time, appeals from state court decisions received treatment similar to that accorded petitions for certiorari and were given about the same precedential weight." Hogge v. Johnson, 526 F.2d 833, 836 (4th Cir.1975), (Clark, Justice, concurring) certiorari denied 428 U.S. 913, 96 S.Ct. 3228, 49 L.Ed.2d 1221 (1976).

18. Edelman v. Jordan, 415 U.S. 651, 671, 94 S.Ct. 1347, 1359, 39 L.Ed.2d 662 (1974), rehearing denied 416 U.S. 1000, 94 S.Ct. 2414, 40 L.Ed.2d 777 (1974), on remand 405 F.Supp. 802 (N.D.Ill.1975), reversed 551 F.2d 152 (7th Cir.1977).

them. Thus, the Court seems to have proceeded upon the view that a "right" of appeal not only does not include a right to be heard orally but does not include even a right to have the case considered upon plenary briefs. This view is hard enough to accept when it is the appellant who loses. But when the practice works to the prejudice of the appellee through a reversal on the jurisdictional papers, it seems impossible to reconcile with conventional conceptions of due process of law. In such cases the appellee, having had no adequate notice of the possibility, finds himself finally foreclosed without any real opportunity for argument at all.[19]

One former Supreme Court clerk reported that "jurisdictional statements and petitions for certiorari now stand on practically the same footing and upon the case made in the former, just as in the latter may depend the grant [or denial] of further hearing."[20] Professor Charles Alan Wright has cautioned that, although technically true, it is "seriously misleading" to think that appeal is a matter of right.[21] Several of the Justices have complained, as well, that the Court does not sufficiently distinguish the statutory differences between certiorari and appeal. It accepts certiorari in cases where the circumstances and importance of the issues do not warrant doing so, while issuing summary decisions and not granting a full appeal and when it should.[22]

Some commentators have defended the Supreme Court's discretionary treatment of its

review as a technique that is proper to use to avoid difficult constitutional decisions that, if decided, might legitimate unfortunate doctrine.[23] The desire to avoid difficult constitutional questions also helps explain the pressures on the Supreme Court to treat lightly summary affirmances, reversals, and—in particular—dismissals for want of a substantial federal question.

Needless to say, because the Supreme Court issuing summary decisions has almost complete control over its docket, it is correspondingly less necessary for it to resort to subterfuge in refusing to decide particular cases simply because the parties seek review.

Affirmance by an Equally Divided Court. Sometimes when the Court reviews a decision, it affirms by an equally divided Court. This type of affirmance is not entitled to precedential weight.[24] The decision only records the fact that the Supreme Court was equally divided and that the lower court decision stands. There is no reversal, for the Court issues no order.[25]

The Certiorari Pool. After Congress gave the Supreme Court almost complete control of its docket by broadening certiorari jurisdiction and virtually eliminating appeal as of right,[26] the question whether the Supreme Court had too much to do quickly faded into history. During the 1970s, the Court used to hear about four cases for each argument day; in the 1990s, two or three cases became the norm.

---

19. Henry Hart, Foreword: The Time Chart of the Justices, 73 Harv.L.Rev. 84, 89 n. 13 (1959).

20. Willey, Jurisdictional Statements on Appeals to the U.S. Supreme Court, 31 A.B.A.J. 239 (1945).

21. Charles Alan Wright, Law of Federal Courts, § 108 (4th ed. 1983).

22. See, e.g., Southern & Northern Overlying Carrier Chapters of the California Dump Truck Owners Association v. Public Utilities Commission, 434 U.S. 9, 98 S.Ct. 251, 54 L.Ed.2d 8 (1977) (Rehnquist, J., dissenting to per curiam dismissal of an appeal, without prejudice, from a state court, arguing that case should have been decided on the merits); Idaho Dept. of Employment v. Smith, 434 U.S. 100, 102, 98 S.Ct. 327, 328, 54 L.Ed.2d 324 (1977), on remand 100 Idaho 520, 602 P.2d 18 (1979) (Brennan, J., joined by Marshall, J., dissenting in part to per curiam summary reversal, arguing that certiorari should have been denied), id., 434 U.S. at 103–105, 98 S.Ct. at 329–330 (1977) (Stevens, J., dissenting in part to per curiam sum-

mary reversal arguing that certiorari should have been denied).

23. Alexander Bickel, The Least Dangerous Branch: The Supreme Court at the Bar of Politics 133–143, and passim (1962); Bickel, The Passive Virtues, 75 Harv.L.Rev. 40 (1961). Contra, e.g., Gerald Gunther, The Subtle Vices of the "Passive Virtues"—A Comment on Principle and Expediency in Judicial Review, 64 Colum.L.Rev. 1 (1964).

24. Neil v. Biggers, 409 U.S. 188, 192, 93 S.Ct. 375, 378, 34 L.Ed.2d 401 (1972); Etting v. Bank of the United States, 24 U.S. (11 Wheat.) 59, 78, 6 L.Ed. 419 (1826); The Antelope, 23 U.S. (10 Wheat.) 66, 6 L.Ed. 268 (1825).

25. The Antelope, 23 U.S. (10 Wheat.) 66, 126, 6 L.Ed. 268, 283 (1825); Durant v. Essex Co., 74 U.S. (7 Wall.) 107, 112, 19 L.Ed. 154 (1868).

26. See § 2.4, supra.

Some argument days were even canceled.[27]

Justice Brennan, who retired from the Court in 1990, was the last Justice who personally reviewed every petition.[28] By the 1990s, all of the Justices (except for Justice Stevens) used a "cert. pool"—the law clerks as a group divided up the certiorari petitions, with each clerk taking one and writing a "pool memo" summarizing the issues and recommending whether the Court should grant certiorari. All of the Justices (except for Justice Stevens) relied on the same pool memo. Justice Stevens did not join the pool, but divided the chore of sifting through the petitions with his law clerks. As a consequence of relying on law clerks, the Court sometimes takes cases that may be interesting because they involve Hollywood entertainers, but do not raise significant legal issues, while not taking cases that raise significant legal issues.[29]

§ 2.6 "Court Packing" and the Number of Justices on the Supreme Court

In a very real sense judicial review exists with the continual consent of the people, because the "political branches" control the high Court's membership, its size, the funds that Congress appropriates to it, its staff, the rules of procedure that govern it, and the agencies that enforce its will.[1] The sparse language of Article III does not guarantee, or even mention, these elements of the judicial structure. Particularly illustrative of this fact of life is the number of Justices on the Supreme Court.

Article III does not mention how many Justices compose the Supreme Court. The first Judiciary Act provided for a chief Justice and five associate Justices.[2] A few years later, the Act of 1801 provided that "after the next vacancy . . . [the Supreme Court] shall consist of five Justices only; that is to say, of one Chief Justice, and four associate Justices," but Congress repealed this entire act in 1802.[3] The Act of 1807 then increased the number of Associate Justices to six;[4] in 1837 the number of Associate Justices increased once again to eight,[5] and in 1864, to nine.[6]

Perhaps the total number on the Court might have remained at nine Associate Justices and one Chief, but Chief Justice Chase and his colleagues thought the Court too large and so informed Congress. Also about this time a vacancy occurred with the death of Justice Catron, and the Senate, rather than act on President Andrew Johnson's nomination, passed a bill reducing the number of Associate Justices to six, prohibiting any new appointments until two additional Associate Justice vacancies would occur, thus depriving Johnson of one actual and two potential nominees. A weak and reluctant Johnson signed the

---

27. Paul M. Barrett, Justices Duck Weighty Business Issues, Critics Charge, Wall Street Journal, Oct. 5, 1993, at B1, col. 1–4 (Midwest ed.).

28. Paul M. Barrett, Justices Duck Weighty Business Issues, Critics Charge, Wall Street Journal, Oct. 5, 1993, at B9, col. 1 (Midwest ed.).

29. Kenneth W. Starr, Trivial Pursuits at the Supreme Court, Wall Street Journal, Oct. 6, 1993, at A19, col. 3–6 (Midwest ed.); Kenneth W. Starr, Supreme Court Needs a Management Revolt, Wall Street Journal, Oct. 13, 1993, at A21, col. 4–6 (Midwest ed.); Arthur D. Hellman, The Shrunken Docket of the Rehnquist Court, 1996 Supreme Court Rev. 403.

Court Reform in the Circuit Courts. The federal Circuit Courts have also come under criticism. Often, oral argument and carefully reasoned opinions that are formally published are often the exception rather than the rule. See William M. Richman & William L. Reynolds, Elitism, Expediency, and the New Certiorari: Requiem for the Learned Hand Tradition, 81 Cornell L. Rev. 273, 275 (1996); William L. Reynolds & William M. Richman, Studying Deck Chairs on the Titanic, 81 Cornell L. Rev. 1290 (1997).

§ 2.6

1. Levy, Judicial Review, History, and Democracy: An Introduction in, Judicial Review and the Supreme Court 1, 12 (1967). On the Senate's efforts to use the confirmation process to determine the views of judicial nominees, see, e.g., Rotunda, The Confirmation Process for Supreme Court Justices in the Modern Era, 37 Emory L.J. 559 (1988); Fein, A Circumscribed Senate Confirmation Role, 102 Harv. L. Rev. 672 (1989); Jeffrey Shaman, Steven Lubet & James Alfini, Judicial Conduct and Ethics §§ 12.01 to 12.10 (1990); Rotunda, Innovations Disguised as Traditions: An Historical Review of the Supreme Court Nominations Process, 1995 U. Ill. L. Rev. 123 (1995).

2. Judiciary Act of 1789, § 1, 1 Stat. 73.

3. Judiciary Act of 1801, § 3, 2 Stat. 89, repealed, Judiciary Act of 1802, § 1, 2 Stat. 132.

4. Judiciary Act of 1807, § 5, 2 Stat. 420.

5. Judiciary Act of 1837, § 1, 5 Stat. 176.

6. Judiciary Act of 1864, § 2, 13 Stat. 4.

act.[7]

One new vacancy did occur during Johnson's term, leaving seven Associate Justices on the Court. In 1869, after the little-liked Johnson left and U.S. Grant became President, Congress passed a new statute setting the number of Associate Justices at eight, with one Chief Justice.[8]

President Grant and Efforts to Pack the Court. The change in circumstances gave President Grant two new appointments, one created by the new statute and one by the resignation of an Associate Justice. He announced these appointments a few hours after the Supreme Court held (five to three) that it was unconstitutional to apply the Legal Tender Acts to antecedent debts.[9] (Congress enacted the Legal Tender Acts during the Civil War and made United States notes legal tender for most debts, public and private.) The Justice who offered his resignation to Grant had joined the majority in this legal tender case. After Grant's appointments were confirmed by the Senate the newly enlarged court of nine Justices overruled the earlier legal tender decision, with the four members of the old majority in dissent.[10] Charges have been made and countered that Grant "packed" the Court.[11]

President Roosevelt and Efforts to Pack the Court. While the total number of Justices has remained at nine (including the Chief Justice), in 1937 President Franklin D. Roosevelt proposed to increase that number, also amid charges of court-packing. The President proposed to appoint an additional Justice for each Justice on the Court who had served at least ten years and had failed to retire within six months of reaching his 70th birthday. The maximum number of Justices on the Supreme Court would be set at 15. The proposal included new retirement privileges for Supreme Court Justices.[12] Roosevelt argued that new blood was needed on the Court and that the older Justices were less efficient. In reality, Roosevelt was reacting to the fact that a bare majority of unsympathetic Justices were often invalidating his legislative programs dealing with the economic depression.[13]

The great majority of the Congress, led by members of Roosevelt's own party, defeated the plan, would might have set an unfortunate precedent. The Congress did provide retirement benefits for Supreme Court Justices in a Judiciary Act passed in 1937,[14] which caused conservative Justice Van Devanter to resign in May of 1937. Also during the fight over the proposal, the Supreme Court appeared to change its position and upheld the validity of several important items of New Deal and state economic legislation.[15] This change was also caused in part by Justice Roberts who appeared to leave the conservative bloc and join

7. Judiciary Act of 1866, § 1, 14 Stat. 209. The President could fill no vacancy "until the number of Associate Justices shall be reduced to six."

8. Judiciary Act of 1869, § 1, 16 Stat. 44. During this period others urged that the Court be increased to 10, 18 and even 24. F. Frankfurter & J. Landis, The Business of the Supreme Court: A Study of the Federal Judicial System 49 n. 160 & 74–75 (1927); Rotunda, Predicting the Views of Supreme Court Nominees, 26 Trial 42 (Nov. 1990).

9. Hepburn v. Griswold, 75 U.S. (8 Wall.) 603, 19 L.Ed. 513 (1869).

10. Legal Tender Cases, 79 U.S. (12 Wall.) 457, 20 L.Ed. 287 (1871).

11. See, e.g., Ratner, Was the Supreme Court Packed by President Grant, 50 Pol.Sci.Q. 343 (1935); Fairman, Mr. Justice Bradley's Appointment to the Supreme Court and the Legal Tender Cases, 54 Harv.L.Rev. 977 (1941).

12. See H.R.Doc. No. 142, 75th Cong., 1st Sess. (1937).

13. For cases striking down New Deal legislation, see, e.g., Railroad Retirement Bd. v. Alton R.R., 295 U.S. 330,

55 S.Ct. 758, 79 L.Ed. 1468 (1935); A.L.A. Schechter Poultry Corp. v. United States, 295 U.S. 495, 55 S.Ct. 837, 79 L.Ed. 1570 (1935); United States v. Butler, 297 U.S. 1, 56 S.Ct. 312, 80 L.Ed. 477 (1936); Carter v. Carter Coal Co., 298 U.S. 238, 56 S.Ct. 855, 80 L.Ed. 1160 (1936).

14. Judiciary Act of 1937, 50 Stat. 24.

15. E.g., West Coast Hotel Co. v. Parrish, 300 U.S. 379, 57 S.Ct. 578, 81 L.Ed. 703 (1937) (state minimum wage law upheld), distinguishing Morehead v. New York ex rel. Tipaldo, 298 U.S. 587, 56 S.Ct. 918, 80 L.Ed. 1347 (1936) and overruling Adkins v. Children's Hosp., 261 U.S. 525, 43 S.Ct. 394, 67 L.Ed. 785 (1923). Chas. C. Steward Machine Co. v. Davis, 301 U.S. 548, 57 S.Ct. 883, 81 L.Ed. 1279 (1937) (Social Security tax upheld); Helvering v. Davis, 301 U.S. 619, 57 S.Ct. 904, 81 L.Ed. 1307 (1937) (Social Security payment of old age benefits upheld); NLRB v. Jones & Laughlin Steel Corp., 301 U.S. 1, 57 S.Ct. 615, 81 L.Ed. 893 (1937) (National Labor Relations Act of 1935 upheld); United States v. Darby, 312 U.S. 100, 61 S.Ct. 451, 85 L.Ed. 609 (1941) (Fair Labor Standards Act upheld), overruling Hammer v. Dagenhart, 247 U.S. 251, 38 S.Ct. 529, 62 L.Ed. 1101 (1918).

the liberal bloc.[16] In any event, Roosevelt lost the battle but appeared to have won the war.

Since then, members of both parties often charge that the President is trying to change the direction of the Court with each new appointment. In practice, Presidents have been unsuccessful because the Justices typically appear to be beholden to no one but history.[17]

§ 2.7 The "Rule of Four"

In deciding whether to accept a case for review, by either writ of certiorari or appeal, the Court uses what is often known as the "Rule of Four." This rule exists only through tradition, but it is a long one, and Congress probably had it in mind[1] when it approved the

Judges Bill[2] in 1925. If a party seeks review of a lower court decision, and four Justices would like to review it, the Court accepts the case for review.[3]

Even if only eight Justices consider a petition, four votes are still required to accept jurisdiction, but on "rare occasions, as when only six or seven Justices are eligible or available, the rule is sometimes but not invariably relaxed so as to permit the granting of certiorari on the vote of only three Justices—although Justice Douglas once stated flatly in an in-chambers opinion that 'three out of seven are not enough to grant a petition for certiorari.' "[4]

---

16. Justice Roberts and the Court Packing Plan.

Justice Roberts' decision to become the crucial fifth vote in West Coast Hotel Co. v. Parrish, 300 U.S. 379, 57 S.Ct. 578, 81 L.Ed. 703 (1937) (upholding state minimum wage law) and thus overrule Adkins v. Children's Hospital, 261 U.S. 525, 43 S.Ct. 394, 67 L.Ed. 785 (1923) was a surprise to his colleagues, and a switch in position from what it had been prior to the *Parrish* oral argument of December 16 and 17, 1936. When Roberts, in a "private chat," revealed his intention to uphold the state law to Chief Justice Hughes, the "Chief had almost hugged him." 2 M. Pusey, Charles Evans Hughes 757 (1951).

We do not know exactly when Roberts' conversion took place. Perhaps it took place during this private chat, or earlier. One biographer speculated: "it does not seem unreasonable to believe that in these early months of 1937, Hughes was laboring vigorously to bring his colleague to a view of the law more consonant with the undoubted drift of public opinion and with the social forces behind that opinion." D. Perkins, Charles Evans Hughes and American Democratic Statesmanship 181 (1956).

In any event, Roberts confirmed his change in position, on December 19, 1936, after the oral argument of December 16 and 17, 1938, *before* F.D.R's court packing plan was announced. Justice Stone, wrote his children on April 1, 1937 (just days after *Parrish* was released on March 29, 1937) that "Justice Roberts switched so the vote stood 5 to 4 in favor of validity." Mason, Harlan Fiske Stone and FDR's Court Plan, 61 Yale L.J. 791, 810 & n. 116.

Justice Roberts explained (in a memorandum that he gave to Felix Frankfurter, which Frankfurter revealed after Roberts' death), that Roberts voted for probable jurisdiction in *Parrish* because that case attacked the underpinnings of *Adkins*. But Roberts was not sure that he gave his reasons at the conference, when he voted for hearing *Parrish*. Roberts said that he heard "one of the brethren ask another, 'What is the matter with Roberts.' "Later, at the conference of December 19, 1936 (after oral argument in *Parrish*), Roberts voted with Hughes, Brandeis, and Cardozo. Stone then rejoined the Court on February 1, 1937 (after his illness). Roberts remembers: "I believe that the Parrish case was taken up at the conference on February 6, 1937, and Justice Stone

then voted for affirmance. The decision affirming the lower court was announced March 29, 1937. These facts make it evident that no action taken by the President in the interim had any causal relation to my action in Parrish." Felix Frankfurter, Mr. Justice Roberts, 204 U.Pa. L.Rev. 311, 314–15 (1955) (reprinting Roberts' Memorandum).

17. Ronald D. Rotunda, The Role of Ideology in Confirming Federal Court Judges, 15 Georgetown Journal of Legal Ethics 127 (2001).

§ 2.7

1. Leiman, The Rule of Four, 57 Colum.L.Rev. 975, 985 (1957). See also 81 Cong.Rec. 2814 (1937).

2. Act of 1925, 43 Stat. 936. Certiorari, or discretionary review, was created for the Supreme Court by the Evarts Act, 26 Stat. 826.

3. "The Court's practice, when considering a jurisdictional statement whereby a litigant attempts to invoke the Court's jurisdiction on appeal is quite similar to its well-known one on applications for writs of certiorari. That is, if four Justices or more are of opinion that the questions presented by the appeal should be fully briefed and argued orally, an order noting probable jurisdiction or postponing further consideration of the jurisdictional questions to a hearing on the merits is entered."

Ohio ex rel. Eaton v. Price, 360 U.S. 246, 246–247, 79 S.Ct. 978, 979, 3 L.Ed.2d 1200 (1959) (separate memorandum by Brennan, J.), lower court subsequently affirmed by equally divided Court, 364 U.S. 263, 80 S.Ct. 1463, 4 L.Ed.2d 1708 (1960), rehearing denied 364 U.S. 855, 81 S.Ct. 29, 5 L.Ed.2d 80 (1960). In this case the Court, by a vote of 4–4 noted probable jurisdiction of an appeal. Frankfurter, Clark, Harlan, and Whittaker, JJ., voted against probable jurisdiction because they believed the case turned on the same question as that decided by a 5–4 vote a short time earlier. Stewart, J., did not participate.

4. R. Stern and E. Gressman, Supreme Court Practice § 5.4 at 346 (5th ed. 1978), citing Pryor v. United States, 404 U.S. 1242, 1243, 92 S.Ct. 23, 24, 30 L.Ed.2d 156 (1971) (Douglas, Circuit Justice).

Justice Frankfurter opposed the rule of four as applied in Federal Employers' Liability Act cases. He objected to accepting a large number of these cases where the sole issue was the sufficiency of the evidence for submission to the jury.[5] There are cases where the Court, in several five to four opinions, has dismissed certiorari as improvidently granted, without elaborate discussion of the rule of four.[6]

§ 2.8   Tenure and Salary Protections

All of the federal judges appointed pursuant to Article III have lifetime tenure, and a constitutional guarantee that their salary "shall not be diminished during their Continuance in Office."[1] This clause is a specific means of ensuring the independence of the judiciary.[2]

Congress is not required to keep judicial salaries growing with inflation rates;[3] Congress may, in its discretion, increase the salaries of federal judges or refuse to increase them, so long as it does not reduce the nominal compensation of the judges. Congress can also nullify previously authorized increases in

judicial salaries *if* the Congressional nullification becomes law *before* the beginning of the fiscal year in which the previously authorized increase was to take effect.[4] Congress cannot repeal an increase in judicial salaries that takes effect under a formula previously set forth by statute, if the repealing act becomes law *after* the beginning of the fiscal year in which the increase took place.[5]

Article III judges also have lifetime tenure. They can be removed only by impeachment.[6] The purpose of this guarantee is to insulate "the individual judge from improper influences not only by other branches but by colleagues as well," in order to promote "judicial individualism."[7]

§ 2.9 *Ex Parte McCardle* and the Power of Congress to Limit the Jurisdiction of Federal Courts

Some commentators and courts often rely on the Supreme Court's post Civil War decision of *Ex parte McCardle*[1] as supporting a broad power of Congress to limit the jurisdiction of the

5. Rogers v. Missouri Pacific R. Co., 352 U.S. 500, 524, 77 S.Ct. 443, 459, 1 L.Ed.2d 493 (1957) (dissenting opinion).

6. E.g., NAACP v. Overstreet, 384 U.S. 118, 86 S.Ct. 1306, 16 L.Ed.2d 409 (1966), rehearing denied 384 U.S. 981, 86 S.Ct. 1857, 16 L.Ed.2d 692 (1966), a per curiam, 5–4 dismissal of the writ of certiorari as improvidently granted. There was no opinion for the majority, with a long dissent by Douglas, J., joined by Warren, C.J., Brennan and Fortas, JJ.

Cf. also, some of the War Crimes Cases, Milch v. United States, 332 U.S. 789, 68 S.Ct. 92, 92 L.Ed. 371 (1947) (motion for leave to file petition for writ of habeas corpus denied, 4–4); Everett v. Truman, 334 U.S. 824, 68 S.Ct. 1081, 92 L.Ed. 1753 (1948) (per curiam) (same; 4–4).

§ 2.8

1. U.S.Const. art. III, § 1. See United States v. Will, 449 U.S. 200, 101 S.Ct. 471, 66 L.Ed.2d 392 (1980) (federal statute unconstitutional to the extent that it purported to repeal judicial salary increase already in effect). See generally The Federalist Papers, No. 79 (Hamilton).

2. Rosenn, The Constitutional Guaranty Against Diminution of Judicial Compensation, 24 U.C.L.A.L.Rev. 308 (1976).

3. A number of federal judges filed suit in the Court of Claims to have their salaries raised on the claim that inflation reduced the real value of their salaries and, therefore, that the failure to raise their salaries violated both the compensation clause and the principle of separation of powers. The Court of Claims found no constitutional violation and the Supreme Court refused to review the decision. Atkins v. United States, 214 Ct.Cl. 186, 556 F.2d

1028 (1977), certiorari denied 434 U.S. 1009, 98 S.Ct. 718, 54 L.Ed.2d 751 (1978).

See discussion in, Ronald D. Rotunda, A Few Modest Proposals to Reform the Law Governing Federal Judicial Salaries, 12 The Professional Lawyer 1 (A.B.A., Fall 2000).

4. United States v. Will, 449 U.S. 200, 101 S.Ct. 471, 66 L.Ed.2d 392 (1980).

5. United States v. Will, 449 U.S. 200, 101 S.Ct. 471, 66 L.Ed.2d 392 (1980).

Federal judges, including Justices of the Supreme Court, are not disqualified from deciding cases under this compensation clause, because, under the common law "rule of necessity," the disqualification of all federal judges would leave this issue undecided, and the public interest and the independent judiciary unprotected. United States v. Will, 449 U.S. 200, 101 S.Ct. 471, 66 L.Ed.2d 392 (1980).

6. United States ex rel. Toth v. Quarles, 350 U.S. 11, 16, 76 S.Ct. 1, 3, 100 L.Ed. 8 (1955).

See also, The Federalist, No. 78 (Alexander Hamilton).

7. Northern Pipeline Const. Co. v. Marathon Pipe Line Co., 458 U.S. 50, 59 n. 10, 102 S.Ct. 2858, 2865 n. 10, 73 L.Ed.2d 598 (1982), stayed 459 U.S. 813, 103 S.Ct. 199, 74 L.Ed.2d 160 (1982) (Opinion of Brennan, J., joined by Marshall, Blackmun & Stevens, JJ.).

§ 2.9

1. 74 U.S. (7 Wall.) 506, 19 L.Ed. 264 (1869).

See, Van Alstyne, A Critical Guide to Ex Parte McCardle, 15 Ariz.L.Rev. 229 (1973).

This section discusses Congressional efforts to restrict the jurisdiction of the Supreme Court and lower federal

lower federal courts and the Supreme Court.[2] The case is a significant one and it is worth analyzing in detail.

Under the authority of the Reconstruction Acts, the military government had imprisoned McCardle, who then brought a habeas corpus action alleging that the Reconstruction legislation was unconstitutional. The lower court upheld the Act, and McCardle appealed under authority of the recently passed Act of February 5, 1867,[3] providing appeal to the Supreme Court from the circuit courts.[4]

After the Court had acknowledged jurisdiction in the case, but before it issued any decision on the merits, Congress withdrew the statutory right of appeal,[5] seeking to avoid a Supreme Court determination that the Reconstruction legislation was unconstitutional.[6] The Court complied with the withdrawal, dismissed the case for want of jurisdiction,[7] and remarked that while the appellate jurisdiction of the Supreme Court "is, strictly speaking, conferred by the Constitution ... it is conferred 'with such exceptions and under such regulations as Congress shall make' "[8] according to Article III, section 2, clause 2.

People have used *McCardle* to support unsuccessful efforts to assert extensive congressional power over the jurisdiction of the courts in order to control substantive results of court decisions in a variety of cases, for example, reapportionment,[9] subversive activities,[10] and school busing.[11]

This broad interpretation is troubling. If Congress can, in effect, overrule a constitutional decision by using its power over jurisdiction to control the substantive results of a case, to decision, then *Marbury v. Madison* is a lot less significant than most people think. For several reasons, it is not necessary to interpret *McCardle* in a way that gives *carte blanche* power to Congress.

First, it is noteworthy that *McCardle* explicitly recognized the limited nature of the statutory withdrawal that was involved in that case:

> Counsel seems to have supposed, if effect be given to the repealing act in question, that the whole appellate power of the court, in cases of habeas corpus, is denied. But this is an error. The act of 1868 does not except from the jurisdiction any cases but appeals from Circuit Courts under the act of 1867. It does not affect the jurisdiction which was previously exercised.[12]

The Court clarified the meaning of this statement several months later, in *Ex parte Yerger*,[13] where it held the repealing act at issue in *McCardle* did not affect its certiorari jurisdiction. The Court concluded that writs of habeas corpus and certiorari could revise the decision of the circuit court and free the prisoner from unlawful restraint.[14]

Yerger is important because it indicates that the limitation of the appellate jurisdiction in

---

courts. We should not forget that various authorities have urged Constitutional Amendments that would have similar effects, such as taking away federal jurisdiction over apportionment, or creating a new "Court of the Union" composed of all the state chief justices who could review and reverse all U.S. Supreme Court cases. For historical discussion, see William G. Ross, Attacks on the Warren Court by State Officials: A Case Study of Why Court-Curbing Movements Fail, 50 Buffalo L. Rev. 483 (2002).

2. E.g., National Mutual Insurance Co. v. Tidewater Transfer Co., 337 U.S. 582, 655, 69 S.Ct. 1173, 1199, 93 L.Ed. 1556 (1949) (Frankfurter, J., dissenting); Wechsler, The Courts and the Constitution, 65 Colum.L.Rev. 1001, 1005 (1965). See Elliott, Court–Curbing Proposals in Congress, 33 Notre Dame Lawyer 597 (1958).

3. Act of February 5, 1867, ch. 26, § 1, 14 Stat. 385.

4. See 74 U.S. (7 Wall.) at 508.

5. 74 U.S. (7 Wall.) at 508.

6. See C. Fairman, 6 The Oliver Wendell Holmes Devise History of the Supreme Court of the United States:

Reconstruction and Reunion 1864–88, pt. 1, at 433–514 (Paul Freund ed. 1971); Van Alstyne, A Critical Guide to Ex Parte McCardle, 15 Ariz.L.Rev. 229 (1973).

7. 74 U.S. (7 Wall.) at 515.

8. 74 U.S. (7 Wall.) at 512–13.

9. E.g., H.R. 11926, 88th Cong., 2d Sess. (1964).

10. E.g., S. 2646, 85th Cong., 1st Sess. (1957).

11. Rotunda, Congressional Power to Restrict the Jurisdiction of the Lower Federal Courts and the Problem of School Busing, 64 Georgetown L.J. 839 (1976).

12. 74 U.S. (7 Wall.) at 515.

13. 75 U.S. (8 Wall.) 85, 19 L.Ed. 332 (1869).

14. 75 U.S. (8 Wall.) at 103.

Under section 14 of the Judiciary Act of 1789, the Supreme Court and other courts could issue writs of habeas corpus and all other writs necessary in the aid of their respective jurisdictions. The writ of habeas corpus could not extend to prisoners unless they were in custody

McCardle, while important to Mr. McCardle, had little practical effect on similar cases because an alternative review was available. In the actual facts of *McCardle*, Congress was not withdrawing all jurisdiction from the lower federal courts and the Supreme Court. Rather, it was only withdrawing one avenue of appeal to the Supreme Court.

If Congress were to remove all appellate avenues to the Supreme Court, that would not give Congress the ability to use the power over jurisdiction to control the outcome of a case. It would only make the lower federal courts the final decision-makers; it would not oust the federal courts from their essential role in the constitutional plan of exercising judicial review.[15] In other words, even a wholesale removal of appellate jurisdiction—a fact situation much broader than that presented in *McCardle*—does not imply a congressional power to prevent all federal courts from exercising judicial review; it only implies a power to make lower federal courts the final decision makers. This latter power is not completely unusual. The original Judiciary Act of 1789, for example, did not provide for any direct review of federal criminal cases in the Supreme Court.[16] Even today, because of limited certiorari review, the federal Courts of Appeal are, de facto, the final decision makers in most cases.

It is also important that the jurisdictional limitation in *McCardle* was neutral. The denial of appeal to the Supreme Court applied to both the Government and a private party. If the Government had lost the habeas action below

(as it might lose it in a future case), the Government would, like Mr. McCardle, be denied an appellate remedy. The neutrality of a jurisdictional limitation helps to assure that congressional withdrawal will not be an attempt to alter the results of specific cases.

To emphasize the narrowness of its holding, *McCardle* distinguished that case from two state court decisions that it cited with approval, *State v. Fleming*[17] and *Dechastellux v. Fairchild.*[18] *McCardle* emphasized that its facts were not like the facts of these cases where the courts had struck down "the exercise of judicial power by the legislature, or of legislative interference with courts in the exercising of continuing jurisdiction."[19]

In *Fairchild,* the Pennsylvania Supreme Court invalidated a state law that granted a new trial to Fairchild, the unsuccessful defendant in a trespass suit. The court reasoned that the statute was an impermissible attempt by the legislature to exercise judicial power.[20] In *Fleming*, the state indicted defendant under an 1838 statute regulating the sale of liquor, but in 1846, while his prosecution was pending, the Tennessee legislature legalized such sales and provided that no one could be punished for violation of the earlier statute.[21] The Tennessee Supreme Court examined the 1846 statute carefully in the circumstances of that case, and held that it violated the Tennessee constitution because the legislature had no power to interfere with the judicial function.[22]

McCardle found that in *Fleming* and *Fairchild* the legislature had exercised judicial power by interfering with the courts' continuing jurisdiction. *McCardle* concluded that the

---

under color of the authority of the United States. See 75 U.S. (8 Wall.) at 96. *Marbury v. Madison* clarified that the power to issue writs of mandamus under section 13 of the Judiciary Act constitutes an exercise of appellate jurisdiction when exercised by the Supreme Court. See 5 U.S. (1 Cranch) 137, 147, 2 L.Ed. 60 (1803). Four years after *Marbury*, the Court similarly construed the provisions of section 14 relating to writs of habeas corpus and mandamus. Ex parte Bollman, 8 U.S. (4 Cranch) 75, 99–101, 2 L.Ed. 554 (1807).

15. Hart, The Power of Congress to Limit the Jurisdiction of Federal Courts: An Exercise in Dialectic, 66 Harv. L.Rev. 1362, 1365 (1953); Ratner, Congressional Power Over the Appellate Jurisdiction of the Supreme Court, 109 U.Pa.L.Rev. 157, 172 (1960); Ratner, Majoritarian Constraints on Judicial Review: Congressional Control of Supreme Court Jurisdiction, 27 Vill.L.Rev. 929 (1982).

16. Charles Alan Wright, Federal Courts § 1 (4th ed. 1983). The Supreme Court continued to exercise habeas jurisdiction, but that review is much narrower, limited to a lack of jurisdiction in the lower courts. This limitation forced the Court to expand the definition of lack of jurisdiction to include the situation where the criminal statute for violation of which the defendant was indicted was unconstitutional. Ex parte Siebold, 100 U.S. (10 Otto) 371, 25 L.Ed. 717 (1879).

17. 26 Tenn. (7 Humph.) 152 (1846).

18. 15 Pa. 18 (1850).

19. 74 U.S. (7 Wall.) at 514 (footnote omitted).

20. 15 Pa. at 20.

21. 26 Tenn. at 152–53.

22. 26 Tenn. at 154.

case it was deciding was different, because Congress had only exercised its constitutional power to make exceptions to the Court's appellate jurisdiction.[23] Congress was not using its power over jurisdiction to control the substantive results of a particular case.

Some commentators have argued that the historical evidence surrounding the exceptions clause of Article III, granting Congress power to regulate the Supreme Court's appellate jurisdiction, supports the view that the clause be read in light of the contemporary state practice to confine regulation basically to housekeeping matters and to certain proceedings where neither error nor certiorari traditionally had been available.[24] This proposition is controversial and historically inaccurate, for Congress has used its power over jurisdiction to effectuate results that are more significant than "housekeeping." For example, the Judiciary Act of 1789 did not provide for any general federal question in the federal courts, nor did it give federal courts direct appeals of criminal cases.[25]

Whatever the merits of this "housekeeping" argument, there is no evidence that the framers intended that the exceptions clause authorize Congress to control the results of particular cases. Analogously then, Congress may not use the power to restrict the federal courts' jurisdiction in order to control the results of particular cases and achieve the result forbidden by a proper interpretation of the exceptions clause.

A principle implied in Article III (and not refuted by *McCardle*) is that the guarantee of an independent federal judiciary limits the legislature in the exercise of its power to regulate

federal court jurisdiction. A post-*McCardle* decision, *United States v. Klein*,[26] directly supports this principle. *Klein* holds that Congress may not enact legislation to eliminate an area of jurisdiction in order to control the results in a particular case.

An 1863 statute allowed the recovery of land captured or abandoned during the Civil War if the claimant could prove that he had not aided the rebellion.[27] Klein, relying on this statute, sued in the Court of Claims to get his property back. Relying on an earlier Supreme Court decision that a presidential pardon proved conclusively that he had not assisted the rebellion,[28] Klein won his case in the Court of Claims.[29] The government appealed his to the Supreme Court, and while that appeal was pending, Congress, perhaps emboldened by recent victory in *McCardle,* passed a statute to reverse this result.

This new law, written in the guise of a jurisdictional statute, provided, first, that a presidential pardon would not support a claim for captured property. Second, acceptance without disclaimer of a pardon for participation in the rebellion was conclusive evidence that the claimant had aided the enemy. And, third, if the Court of Claims based its judgment in favor of the claimant of such a pardon, then the Supreme Court lacked jurisdiction on appeal.[30]

The Supreme Court declared this restriction of its jurisdiction unconstitutional. The Court agreed that Congress had the power under Article III to confer or withhold the right of appeal from Court of Claims decisions but held that Article III also requires that the judicial branch be independent of the legislative and

---

23. 74 U.S. (7 Wall.) at 514.

24. J. Goebel, 1 The Oliver Wendell Holmes Devise History of the Supreme Court of the United States: Antecedents and Beginnings to 1801, at 240 (P. Freund ed. 1971); Merry, Scope of the Supreme Court's Appellate Jurisdiction: Historical Basis, 47 Minn.L.Rev. 53 (1962).

25. Federal courts had no general federal question jurisdiction until 1875. See, Act of March 3, 1875, 18 Stat. at Large 470. Congress waited until 1889 to provide for direct appeals of federal criminal cases. Compare, Judiciary Act of 1789, §§ 9, 11, 1 Stat. at Large 73, 76–78, with Judiciary Act of 1889, § 6, 25 Stat. at Large 656; Evarts Act, § 5, 26 Stat. at Large 827.

26. 80 U.S. (13 Wall.) 128, 20 L.Ed. 519 (1871).

See generally, Young, Congressional Regulation of Federal Courts' Jurisdiction and Processes: United States v. Klein Revisited, 1981 Wis.L.Rev. 1189.

27. 80 U.S. (13 Wall.) at 138–39.

28. 80 U.S. (13 Wall.) at 143; see United States v. Padelford, 76 U.S. (9 Wall.) 531, 543, 19 L.Ed. 788 (1869).

29. 80 U.S. (13 Wall.) at 143.

30. 80 U.S. (13 Wall.) at 143–44. The statute also required the Court of Claims to dismiss actions of claimants with presidential pardons who had not previously disclaimed their participation in the rebellion. 80 U.S. (13 Wall.) at 143.

executive branches, and that requirement restricts Congressional power.[31] The Court found that the withdrawal of jurisdiction was only a means to deny to presidential pardons the effect that the Court previously had held them to have.[32] Such a denial of jurisdiction prescribes for the Court a rule for the decision of its cases. Thus, Congress had exceeded its power to regulate appellate jurisdiction and had passed the limit separating the legislative from the judicial branch.[33]

Klein strongly supports the contention that Congress must exercise its power to limit jurisdiction in a manner consistent with constitutional limitations and with the independence of the judiciary. Any jurisdictional limitation must be neutral; that is, Congress may not decide the merits of a case under the guise of limiting jurisdiction. Congress' power under the exceptions clause is subject, like any other congressional power, to the limitations that the Constitution imposes, including the restrictions of the Bill of Rights. Let us now consider, in more detail, the nature of these restrictions on Congress' power to restrict the jurisdiction of the federal courts.

§ 2.10 Due Process and Other Limitations on Congress's Jurisdictional Powers and a Survey of the Major Statutory Restrictions on Jurisdiction

Article III grants Congress the power to affect the jurisdiction of the lower federal

courts, but we should not be surprised that other parts of the Constitution limit that power. All other federal powers are subject to Constitutional limitations. For example, Congress has the right to define and punish piracy, but it cannot do so in a way that violates the Bill or Rights.[1] The power over federal court jurisdiction should be treated no differently.[2] Congress, in short, should not be able to exercise its power to create exceptions to federal jurisdiction that would violate the due process clause of the Fifth Amendment, or other Constitutional limits.[3]

For example, a law providing that federal courts have no jurisdiction in diversity cases where Catholics are plaintiffs should violate the First Amendment's free exercise clause. No one would seriously contend that a federal law that discriminated on religious belief should be exempt from the First Amendment simply because the law is found in title 28 of the United States Code (dealing with the jurisdiction of federal courts) rather than in another title.

Similarly, a law preventing federal courts from exercising jurisdiction in cases where the plaintiff alleges racial discrimination should

---

31. 80 U.S. (13 Wall.) at 145–47.

However, it is no violation of the separation of powers for Congress, by statute, to require the Government simply to waive one of its affirmative defenses. United States v. Sioux Nation, 448 U.S. 371, 100 S.Ct. 2716, 65 L.Ed.2d 844 (1980) (Congress by statute could waive res judicata effect of prior decision entered against Government).

32. 80 U.S. (13 Wall.) at 145.

33. 80 U.S. (13 Wall.) at 146–47.

§ 2.10

1. For example, although the Constitution gives Congress the power to punish piracies and felonies committed on the high seas, it limits that power by prohibiting ex post facto laws or bills of attainder. See U.S.Const. art. I, §§ 8, 9.

2. United States v. Bitty, 208 U.S. 393, 399–400, 28 S.Ct. 396, 397–398, 52 L.Ed. 543 (1908). Of course, Congress may eliminate statutorily-created rights simply by

repealing the statute. See Battaglia v. General Motors Corp., 169 F.2d 254, 257 (2d Cir.1948), certiorari denied 335 U.S. 887, 69 S.Ct. 236, 93 L.Ed. 425 (1948).

It should also be remembered that the state courts exist with their general jurisdiction to hear constitutional claims. These courts, under the Supremacy Clause, must implement the requirements of the Constitution. Yet the safety valve of the state courts' jurisdiction (assuming that Congress—if it could—does not purport to limit their jurisdiction) should not justify restrictions by the Congress on federal courts when those restrictions violate the due process clause or other such right. The possible exercise of checks on the abuse of power should not be used to justify the exercise of such abuses of power.

3. United States v. Bitty, 208 U.S. 393, 399–400, 28 S.Ct. 396, 397–398, 52 L.Ed. 543 (1908) (Harlan, J.): "What such exceptions and regulations should be it is for Congress, in its wisdom, to establish, having of course due regard to *all* the provisions of the Constitution." (emphasis added).

violate the equal protection component of due process.[4]

Concededly, one can find a lot of dictum in the case law that suggests that Congress' power over federal court jurisdiction is plenary. However, a careful survey of congressional limitations on the jurisdiction of the lower federal courts demonstrates that the Supreme Court will not uphold a statutory infringement of constitutional rights, even if that statute is written in the guise of a jurisdictional statute. If the dictum is read in context, it does not undercut this principle. The cases also show that courts do not construe ambiguous jurisdictional statutes in a way that infringes on constitutional rights.[5] Let us review this case law.

The Norris–LaGuardia Act. The Norris–LaGuardia Act,[6] perhaps the most famous example of congressional removal of jurisdiction, limits federal courts' power to issue an injunction or restraining order in a labor dispute.[7] If we consider this law carefully, we see that this withdrawal of equitable jurisdiction violates neither the Article III principles established in *United States v. Klein*[8] nor any constitutional rights. Although the restriction limits the relief that labor unions and employers may seek during a labor dispute, Congress may properly limit the courts' equitable jurisdiction if the limitation has some rational basis, because neither a union nor an employer is a suspect class.[9]

In upholding the Act's limitation, the Court spoke in broad terms and said that there "can be no question of the power of Congress thus to define and limit the jurisdiction of the inferior courts of the United States." However, the Court made this statement in the circumstance where a business does not have a constitutionally vested right to have a federal court issue an injunction in a case involving a labor dispute.[10] The Court, in upholding the law's jurisdictional limitation, specifically quoted and discussed section 7(e) of the Act. This section requires a federal court (before granting the claim for injunctive relief) to determine if the public officer charged with protecting a complainant's property is unable or unwilling to furnish adequate protection.

This provision supports the conclusion that the Act does not infringe on constitutional rights.[11] This section recognizes that there may be cases involving strikes where the state is acting in such a way that the strike will take the complainant's property. Due process forbids the state from taking property without just compensation. In such a case, and if, under this statute, the employer will suffer "substantial and irreparable injury," and if there is "no adequate remedy at law," then the inability of a court to order an injunction may violate due process. But section 7(e) avoids that result by protecting any right of an employer to due process of law before the uncompensated "taking" of property.[12] Hence, when read as a

---

4. Bolling v. Sharpe, 347 U.S. 497, 74 S.Ct. 693, 98 L.Ed. 884 (1954), supplemented 349 U.S. 294, 75 S.Ct. 753, 99 L.Ed. 1083 (1955); cf. Boddie v. Connecticut, 401 U.S. 371, 380–82, 91 S.Ct. 780, 787–88, 28 L.Ed.2d 113 (1971) (due process prohibits states from denying individuals seeking divorce access to the courts solely on the basis of inability to pay); Battaglia v. General Motors Corp., 169 F.2d 254, 257 (2d Cir.1948), certiorari denied 335 U.S. 887, 69 S.Ct. 236, 93 L.Ed. 425 (1948); cf. Youngstown Sheet & Tube Co. v. Sawyer (The Steel Seizure Case), 343 U.S. 579, 646, 72 S.Ct. 863, 875, 96 L.Ed. 1153 (1952) (Jackson, J., concurring) (Fifth Amendment gives a private right that limits governmental authority under Article I to execute the laws.)

5. Judges Harry T. Edwards and J. Skelly-Wright, citing Treatise in Bartlett v. Bowen, 816 F.2d 695, 703 n. 33, 705 n. 39 (D.C.Cir.1987).

6. 29 U.S.C.A. §§ 101–15.

7. 29 U.S.C.A. § 107.

8. 80 U.S. (13 Wall.) 128, 146–47, 20 L.Ed. 519 (1871). The Norris–LaGuardia Act requires a court to make find-

ings similar to those of an equity court before enjoining a labor dispute. The court must find that substantial and irreparable injury will occur without an injunction, that the balance of hardships favors the complainant, and that the complainant has no adequate remedy at law. Norris–LaGuardia Act §§ 7(b)–(d), 29 U.S.C.A. §§ 107(b)–(d).

9. See Lauf v. E. G. Shinner & Co., 303 U.S. 323, 330, 58 S.Ct. 578, 582, 82 L.Ed. 872 (1938).

10. See Lauf v. E. G. Shinner & Co., 303 U.S. 323, 330, 58 S.Ct. 578, 582, 82 L.Ed. 872 (1938).

11. See Norris–LaGuardia Act § 7(e), 29 U.S.C.A. § 107(e).

12. In fact, the Norris–LaGuardia Act serves to implement the First Amendment right to peaceful, noncoercive picketing. Cf. Thornhill v. Alabama, 310 U.S. 88, 102–03, 60 S.Ct. 736, 744–45, 84 L.Ed. 1093 (1940) (labor dispute is within area of free discussion protected by the Constitution).

whole, the restriction on jurisdiction is consistent with due process because a court is only precluded from issuing injunctions in those cases where refusing to issue an injunction will not deprive employers of any rights that are constitutionally guaranteed.

Yellow Dog Contracts. "Yellow dog" contracts are contracts where employees agree, as a condition of employment, not to become or remain a member of a labor union. Federal law precludes federal courts from enforcing these contracts.[13] As a substantive matter, the legislature may constitutionally forbid such contracts (unless one adopts the discarded theory of substantive due process).[14] Because, it violates no constitutional right if Congress prevents the federal courts from enforcing yellow dog contract, Congress may also preclude federal courts from having jurisdiction to grant of legal or equitable relief that supports the forbidden contracts. A limitation on federal jurisdiction to enforce such contracts restricts no constitutional right.

Firearms Registration. A convicted felon, sought relief from a firearms disability from the Bureau of Alcohol, Tobacco and Firearms, based on a statute that allows the Secretary of Treasury to grant such relief and grants judicial review of a denial of request. However, the Treasury Department returned the application unprocessed, because a separate appropriations law forbade the Treasury Department from spending any funds to investigate or act on such requests. Justice Thomas, for a unani-

mous Court, held that the agency's failure to act precluded court review, given the relevant language of the statute. No justice was troubled by this denial of judicial review.[15]

The Anti-Injunction Provisions of the Internal Revenue Code. The anti-injunction provisions of the Internal Revenue Code represent another limitation on federal jurisdiction.[16] The courts have upheld the Act's restriction on suits to restrain the assessment or collection of taxes, but only after finding that Congress has provided the injured taxpayer with other adequate remedies.[17] As Justice Brandeis pointed out in *Phillips v. Commissioner*,[18] "where only property rights are involved, mere postponement of the judicial enquiry is not a denial of due process, if the opportunity given for the ultimate judicial determination of the liability is adequate."[19]

Justice Brandeis' reasoning implies that a jurisdictional limitation in tax cases that deprived a person of property without due process of law would be improper. Consistent with this reading of the statute, federal courts have recognized that there may be an exception to the Act where a plaintiff has no other remedy.[20]

The Portal-to-Portal Cases. The portal-to-portal cases[21] provide an interesting example of constitutional limitations on congressional power over the jurisdiction of the lower federal courts. In the mid-1940s, the Supreme Court ruled that time spent by workers in

13. 29 U.S.C.A. § 103.

14. In the early part of the twentieth century, the Supreme Court had held that due process protects the employer's right to insist on "Yellow Dog" contracts. Coppage v. Kansas, 236 U.S. 1, 35 S.Ct. 240, 59 L.Ed. 441 (1915), and the Fifth Amendment, Adair v. United States, 208 U.S. 161, 28 S.Ct. 277, 52 L.Ed. 436 (1908). See also, Truax v. Corrigan, 257 U.S. 312, 42 S.Ct. 124, 66 L.Ed. 254 (1921). Since 1937, such cases are no longer good law and reflect discarded theories of substantive due process. See §§ 4.7, 4.8, 11.4.

15. United States v. Bean, 537 U.S. 71, 123 S.Ct. 584, 154 L.Ed.2d 483 (2002).

16. Int.Rev.Code of 1954, § 7421(a).

17. Bob Jones University v. Simon, 416 U.S. 725, 746, 94 S.Ct. 2038, 2050–51, 40 L.Ed.2d 496 (1974) (where judicial review available, injunction denied university suing to prevent revocation of its tax exempt status); Phillips v. Commissioner, 283 U.S. 589, 597–98, 51 S.Ct. 608, 611–12, 75 L.Ed. 1289 (1931) (summary procedure for collec-

tion of unpaid income and property taxes from transfer of property of taxpayer valid since transferee has two alternate methods of judicial review).

18. 283 U.S. 589, 51 S.Ct. 608, 75 L.Ed. 1289 (1931).

19. 283 U.S. at 596–97, 51 S.Ct. at 611.

20. See Note, Nontaxpayer Challenges to Internal Revenue Service Rulemaking: Constitutional and Statutory Barriers to Judicial Review, 63 Georgetown L.J. 1263, at 1286, 1288–89 (1975).

21. See Anderson v. Mt. Clemens Pottery Co., 328 U.S. 680, 66 S.Ct. 1187, 90 L.Ed. 1515 (1946); Jewell Ridge Coal Corp. v. Local No. 6167, 325 U.S. 161, 65 S.Ct. 1063, 89 L.Ed. 1534 (1945), rehearing denied 325 U.S. 897, 65 S.Ct. 1550, 89 L.Ed. 2007 (1945); Tennessee Coal, Iron & R. Co. v. Muscoda Local No. 123, 321 U.S. 590, 64 S.Ct. 698, 88 L.Ed. 949 (1944), rehearing denied 322 U.S. 771, 64 S.Ct. 1257, 88 L.Ed. 1596 (1944).

previously noncompensable work, such as underground travel in iron ore mines and similar incidental activities, was part of the work week compensable under the Fair Labor Standards Act.[22] This unexpected decision created immense retroactive liability for many businesses.[23] In an effort to eliminate this liability, Congress amended the statute to make such work noncompensable[24] and withdrew the jurisdiction of the courts to hear those cases that were presently pending or were to be brought under the old statute.[25]

Employees claimed that the jurisdictional limitation was unconstitutional, a taking of property without due process or just compensation. The Supreme Court never ruled on the question, but various lower courts did. All of the lower courts upheld the limitation, but several of them summarily dismissed the constitutional argument because the federal law was drafted as a jurisdictional limitation. The Second Circuit, in *Battaglia v. General Motors Corp.*,[26] carefully considered the constitutional problems presented by Congress' removal of jurisdiction.

Battaglia found that an Amendment of the Fair Labor Standards Act destroyed the plaintiffs' claim to overtime pay under the Act. However, there was no taking of property because the court held that the law only applies when no property rights had vested in the plaintiffs. Because the portal-to-portal Amendment did not constitute a taking of property,

the jurisdictional limitation therefore was valid: Congress' jurisdictional power had not been exercised to deprive any person of life, liberty, or property without just compensation.[27] By considering and rejecting this constitutional claim, this court of appeals explicitly recognized that congressional power over the jurisdiction of the courts is limited by the due process clause.

Battaglia, in effect, was deciding that there was no "vested" property right to overtime pay until the cause of action was reduced to judgment. The expectant property was not reduced to judgment if the case was still pending in the trial court, or if the time for appeal had not yet passed. When Congress eliminated the statutory right, it only eliminated the expectancy *prior* to the time that it would have been converted to a vested property right. Thus Congress, when it enacted the portal-to-portal act, did not distinguish any *vested* property right.

It is not generally realized that the normal statutory rule is that on appeal, the court applies the law that exists at the time of appeal, even if that law did not exist at the time of trial. The Supreme Court has recognized and applied this principle since at least the time of Chief Justice John Marshall.[28] Thus, when the Second Circuit in *Battaglia* applied the new portal-to-portal law, that application deprived no one of any *vested* property right or other constitutional right.[29] The

---

22. See Anderson v. Mt. Clemens Pottery Co., 328 U.S. 680, 690–93, 66 S.Ct. 1187, 1193–95, 90 L.Ed. 1515 (1946), rehearing denied 329 U.S. 822, 67 S.Ct. 25, 91 L.Ed. 699 (1946).

23. See D. Currie, Federal Courts: Cases and Materials 145–46 (1975).

24. Portal–to–Portal Act, ch. 52, 61 Stat. 84, as amended, 29 U.S.C.A. §§ 216, 251–62.

25. Portal–to–Portal Act, § 2(d), 29 U.S.C.A. § 252(d).

26. 169 F.2d 254 (2d Cir.1948), certiorari denied 335 U.S. 887, 69 S.Ct. 236, 93 L.Ed. 425 (1948).

27. 169 F.2d at 257. *Battaglia* held that the Portal–to–Portal Act did not encroach on the independent power of the judiciary, attempt to change previous Supreme Court decision, or impose a rule of decision that violated Article III or contradicted. While the Portal–to–Portal Act changed the Fair Labor Standards Act, it left private contractual rights enforceable in the courts except to the extent that they referred to the prior statutory law. See 169 F.2d at 261–62.

28. Application of New Statutes to Pending Cases. E.g., Hamm v. Rock Hill, 379 U.S. 306, 312, 85 S.Ct. 384, 389–90, 13 L.Ed.2d 300 (1964), rehearing denied 379 U.S. 995, 85 S.Ct. 698, 13 L.Ed.2d 614 (1965), quoting Chief Justice John Marshall in United States v. The Schooner Peggy, 5 U.S. (1 Cranch) 103, 110, 2 L.Ed. 49 (1801):

"[I]f subsequent to the judgment and before the decision of the appellate court, a law intervenes and positively changes the rule which governs, the [new] law must be obeyed. [T]he court must decide according to existing laws, and if it be necessary to set aside a judgment, rightful when rendered, but which cannot be affirmed but in violation of [present] law, [then] the judgment must be set aside."

29. Although Congress had imposed a jurisdiction limitation in the portal-to-portal statute, that limitation was actually irrelevant, because the law also took away claimants' expectancy. Claimants had lost no property right, because they only relied on a statute that no longer existed, a statute that had been repealed.

plaintiffs did not have a vested property right, only a cause of action based on a statute not repealed. They has a mere expectancy.

If there had been a *vested* property right—if, e.g., Congress had tried to eliminate a claim for back pay when the claimant had already reduced the cause of action into a money judgment and collected it—then Congress would be obligated to pay just compensation. Congress may not impose any jurisdictional limitation so as to avoid its obligation not to pay just compensation and its obligation not to take property without due process. That is the lesson of *Plaut v. Spendthrift Farm, Inc.*[30]

The seeds of *Plaut* were planted on June 20, 1991. That was when the Supreme Court held, in *Lampf, Pleva, Lipkind, Prupis & Petigrow v. Gilbertson*,[31] that litigation based on § 10(b) of the Securities Exchange Act and SEC Rule 10b–5 must be commenced within one year after discovery of the facts constituting the violation and within three years after the violation. Following *Lampf,* the trial court dismissed petitioners' claims in *Plaut* as untimely. Petitioners in *Plaut* filed no appeal and the judgment became final after 30 days. In December of 1991, the President signed a law that became § 27A of the Securities Exchange Act. Section 27A provided that if any § 10(b) suit started before and dismissed as time barred after June 19, 1991—the day before *Lampf* was decided—would have been timely but for *Lampf,* then the case was to be rein-

stated if a motion to do so was made no later than 60 days after December 19, 1991. After § 27A was enacted, the *Plaut* petitioners filed a motion to reinstate their action previously dismissed with prejudice.

Justice Scalia, for the Court, held that the law was unconstitutional: it violated the separation of powers because it retroactively commanded federal courts to reopen *final* judgments, in violation of *Marbury v. Madison. Plaut* acknowledged that, if a new law "makes clear that it is retroactive, an appellate court must apply that law in reviewing judgments still on appeal that were rendered before the law was enacted, and must alter the outcome accordingly."[32] However, that principle does not apply when the judgment is final. Section 27A is not like a law that provides that it applies "not only to proceedings brought after its enactment, but also to proceedings pending at the time of, or brought after, the decision [in a particular case]."[33]

Contrast *Miller v. French.*[34] In 1975, prison inmates at the Pendleton Correctional Facility filed a class action seeking injunctive relief regarding conditions of confinement. The district court granted the injunction, which remained in effect for many years. Twenty years later, Congress enacted the Prison Litigation Reform Act of 1995, which, among other things, sets a standard for entry and termination of prospective relief in civil actions objecting to prison conditions. One section of the

---

30. 514 U.S. 211, 115 S.Ct. 1447, 131 L.Ed.2d 328 (1995).

31. 501 U.S. 350, 111 S.Ct. 2773, 115 L.Ed.2d 321 (1991), rehearing denied 501 U.S. 1277, 112 S.Ct. 27, 115 L.Ed.2d 1109 (1991).

32. 514 U.S. at 226, 115 S.Ct. at 1457.

33. 514 U.S. at 235, 115 S.Ct. at 1461. Breyer, J., concurred in the judgment. He would only rule that "at least *sometimes* Congress lacks the power under Article I to reopen an otherwise closed court judgment." Stevens, J., joined by Ginsburg, J., dissented. They argued that Congress has the power to enact a law restoring rights that a large class of investors, reasonably and in good faith, thought that they had possessed prior to the Court's surprising and unexpected announcement in *Lampf.*

34. 530 U.S. 327, 120 S.Ct. 2246, 147 L.Ed.2d 326 (2000). Souter, J., joined by Ginsburg, J., filed an opinion concurring in part and dissenting in part. Breyer, J., joined by Stevens, J., filed a dissenting opinion.

Accord, Robertson v. Seattle Audubon Society, 503 U.S. 429, 112 S.Ct. 1407, 118 L.Ed.2d 73 (1992). Environmentalists filed lawsuits claiming that the timber harvesting would injure the spotted owl, an endangered species. In 1990, in response to this ongoing litigation, Congress enacted "the Northwest Timber Compromise," which applied only for a certain period of time and only to 13 national forests in areas known to contain the spotted owl. Subsection (b)(6)(A) stated that "Congress hereby determines and directs that management [of certain forests] according to subsections (b)(3) and (b)(5) . . . is adequate consideration for the purpose of meeting the statutory requirements that are the basis for [the litigation in two cases]." The law identified these two pending cases by name and caption number.

Thomas, J., speaking for a unanimous Court, held that § (b)(6)(A) did not violate Article III; it merely replaced the legal standards underlying these two cases. It did not direct any particular finding of fact or application of law to fact.

Act provided that a defendant or intervenor may move to terminate prospective relief under an existing injunction (like the one affecting Pendleton) that does not meet the standard of the Act. Another section stated that a court may not terminate such injunctive relief if it makes certain findings. Finally, another section (the automatic stay provision) provided that a motion to terminate such relief "shall operate as a stay" of that relief beginning 30 days after the motion is filed and ending when the court rules on the motion. This stay reflected the changed legal circumstances that prospective relief under the existing decree is no longer enforceable unless and until the court makes the findings required by the statute.

The lower courts ruled that the operation of the automatic stay provision violated due process and separation of powers, but Justice O'Connor, for the Court, reversed. Unlike *Plaut*, the automatic stay provision does not suspend or reopen a *final* judgment of an Article III court because prospective injunctive relief under a continuing, executory decree remains subject to alteration due to changes in the underlying law. When Congress changed the law underlying a judgment awarding relief, that relief is no longer enforceable to the extent that it is inconsistent with the new law. (If the judgment had awarded money damages in an action at law instead of a continuing injunction in an action in equity, then that judgment would be final and a later-enacted federal law could not affect plaintiff's right to those damages.)

Such continuing injunctions are "final" for purposes of appeal, but they are not the "last word of the judicial department" because they are subject to the court's continuing supervisory jurisdiction and may therefore be altered according to subsequent changes in the law. For the same reason, it is unlike *United States v. Klein*.[35]

The Selective Service Cases. Courts have traditionally exercised deferential review of selective service cases.[36] The Supreme Court has acknowledged constitutional issues concerning the congressional power to restrain federal court review of selective service cases, and it has interpreted the law to avoid these problems. It also has rejected a claim that Congress has no power to place some limits on federal jurisdiction in this area.

In *Oestereich v. Selective Service System*,[37] Justice Harlan, concurring, warned that it would raise serious constitutional problems to interpret section 10(b)(3) of the Selective Service Act,[38] which limits the courts' jurisdiction to review Selective Service decisions, as denying a registrant the opportunity to raise a constitutional issue in some competent forum.[39] To prevent the legislature from using the federal courts to accomplish unconstitutional ends, Congress's Article III power must be subject to the due process guarantees of the Fifth Amendment.[40]

The Federal Anti–Injunction Statute. The federal anti-injunction statute,[41] in general, forbids federal injunctions of state court proceedings. The cases upholding this law, when read carefully, do not support a broad

---

35. 80 U.S. (13 Wall.) 128, 146–47, 20 L.Ed. 519 (1871).

36. Compare Falbo v. United States, 320 U.S. 549, 554, 64 S.Ct. 346, 348, 88 L.Ed. 305 (1944), rehearing denied 321 U.S. 802, 64 S.Ct. 517, 88 L.Ed. 1089 (1944) (no judicial review of Selective Service Classification), with Estep v. United States, 327 U.S. 114, 119–20, 123–25, 66 S.Ct. 423, 425–27, 90 L.Ed. 567 (1946) (judicial review of Selective Service Classification after acceptance for induction permissible despite silence of Act.)

37. 393 U.S. 233, 89 S.Ct. 414, 21 L.Ed.2d 402 (1968).

38. Military Selective Service Act of 1967, § 10(b)(3), 50 U.S.C.A.App. § 460(b)(3).

39. 393 U.S. at 243 n. 6, 89 S.Ct. at 419 n. 6 (Harlan, J., concurring).

40. See also 114 Cong.Rec. 10888 (1968). Senator Tydings submitted opinions of legal scholars that a proposed bill eliminating federal review of the admission of confessions into evidence by state courts and federal habeas jurisdiction over state prisoners was arbitrary and would violate the equal protection guarantees included in the right to due process. 114 Cong.Rec. at 10888–97.

41. 28 U.S.C.A. § 2283 provides:

"A court of the United States may not grant an injunction to stay proceedings in a State court except as expressly authorized by Act of Congress, or where necessary in aid of its jurisdiction, or to protect or effectuate its judgments."

view of Congressional power over lower Federal Court jurisdiction.[42] The statute by its own terms exempts injunctions that are "expressly authorized by Act of Congress." The Supreme Court has held that section 1983 of title 42 is an "expressly authorized" exception. Section 1983 applies to state action and enforces and protects all rights secured by the Constitution. Thus, the anti-injunction act does not preclude federal courts from issuing injunction when they are necessary to protect rights secured by the Constitution.[43]

The Comity Restrictions. While section 1983 allows the injunctive remedy where appropriate in spite of the anti-injunction statute, federal courts must also resolve principles of equity, comity, and federalism before an injunction may issue.[44] The comity rules, however, are not used in a way that limits constitutional rights.

Younger v. Harris,[45] one of the leading cases construing the comity requirements, advises that generally no constitutional right is infringed by a statute forbidding injunctions of state proceedings because "the moving party has an adequate remedy at law and will not suffer irreparable injury if denied equitable relief."[46] However, comity considerations should not be applied to prevent the issuance of an injunction where it is necessary to prevent irreparable constitutional injury. In such a case, the remedy is necessary to preserve the right. The Court emphasized, quoting *Fenner v. Boykin*:[47]

> [W]hen absolutely necessary for protection of constitutional rights courts of the United States have power to enjoin state officers from instituting criminal actions. But this may not be done except under extraordinary circumstances where the danger of irreparable loss is both great and immediate.[48]

Thus the Court has allowed injunctions to issue if a state law is "flagrantly and patently violative of express constitutional prohibitions,"[49] or there is "bad faith, harassment, or any other unusual circumstance that would call for equitable relief."[50] *Younger*, though limiting the overly broad dictum in an earlier case,[51] approved the issuance of an injunction if the facts would indicate that equitable relief was necessary to prevent irreparable injury to constitutional rights.[52]

Congressional Efforts to Limit Judicial Review to Particular Tribunals. Another issue concerning Congressional power to control jurisdiction involves the power of Congress to require that challenges of regulatory action be restricted to certain courts and subject to

42. Mitchum v. Foster, 407 U.S. 225, 92 S.Ct. 2151, 32 L.Ed.2d 705 (1972); Amalgamated Clothing Workers v. Richman Bros., 348 U.S. 511, 75 S.Ct. 452, 99 L.Ed. 600 (1955); see also, Lynch v. Household Finance Corp., 405 U.S. 538, 92 S.Ct. 1113, 31 L.Ed.2d 424 (1972), rehearing denied 406 U.S. 911, 92 S.Ct. 1611, 31 L.Ed.2d 822 (1972), on remand 360 F.Supp. 720 (D.Conn.1973).

43. Mitchum v. Foster, 407 U.S. 225, 92 S.Ct. 2151, 32 L.Ed.2d 705 (1972).

44. 407 U.S. at 243, 92 S.Ct. at 2162.

See generally § 2.14(e), infra ("Abstention, Comity, and Federal Court Injunctions of State Court Proceedings").

45. 401 U.S. 37, 91 S.Ct. 746, 27 L.Ed.2d 669 (1971) (Black, J.). See, also, the companion cases of Samuels v. Mackell, 401 U.S. 66, 91 S.Ct. 764, 27 L.Ed.2d 688 (1971); Boyle v. Landry, 401 U.S. 77, 91 S.Ct. 758, 27 L.Ed.2d 696 (1971); Perez v. Ledesma, 401 U.S. 82, 91 S.Ct. 674, 27 L.Ed.2d 701 (1971); Dyson v. Stein, 401 U.S. 200, 91 S.Ct. 769, 27 L.Ed.2d 781 (1971); Byrne v. Karalexis, 401 U.S. 216, 91 S.Ct. 777, 27 L.Ed.2d 792 (1971).

46. 401 U.S. at 43–44, 91 S.Ct. at 750–51.

47. 271 U.S. 240, 46 S.Ct. 492, 70 L.Ed. 927 (1926).

48. 401 U.S. at 45, 91 S.Ct. at 751. (emphasis added).

49. 401 U.S. at 53, 91 S.Ct. at 755–56. See also, Mitchum v. Foster, 407 U.S. 225, 230, 92 S.Ct. 2151, 2155–56, 32 L.Ed.2d 705 (1972).

50. 401 U.S. at 54, 91 S.Ct. at 755. In Perez v. Ledesma, 401 U.S. 82, 85, 91 S.Ct. 674, 677, 27 L.Ed.2d 701 (1971) the Court stated:

"Only in cases of proven harassment or prosecutions undertaken by state officials in bad faith without hope of obtaining a valid conviction and perhaps in other extraordinary circumstances where irreparable injury can be shown is federal injunctive relief against pending state prosecutions appropriate."

51. Dombrowski v. Pfister, 380 U.S. 479, 85 S.Ct. 1116, 14 L.Ed.2d 22 (1965).

52. 401 U.S. at 47–49, 91 S.Ct. at 752–53.

See also, Pacific Telephone & Telegraph Co. v. Kuykendall, 265 U.S. 196, 204–05, 44 S.Ct. 553, 556, 68 L.Ed. 975 (1924) (Taft, C.J.) ("Under such circumstances [where the utility alleges confiscatory rates with no stay available under state law] comity yields to constitutional right, and the fact that the legislative fixing of rates has not been concluded will not prevent a federal court of equity from suspending the daily confiscation, if it finds the case to justify it.").

certain procedures. Although two World War II cases could be read to recognize an overly broad power to restrict jurisdiction, that interpretation is hardly compelled.

Lockerty v. Phillips[53] upheld a special statutory scheme set up during World War II to control inflation. The Emergency Price Control Act of 1942 created an Emergency Court of Appeals vested it with exclusive jurisdiction to determine the validity of any regulation, order, or price schedule issued under that Act. The litigants attacking price controls had to follow a specified procedure, and the Supreme Court could review judgments of the Emergency Court.[54]

Yakus v. United States[55] upheld the constitutionality of the provisions of the Emergency Price Control Act, which was construed to deprive litigants of the opportunity to attack the validity of a price regulation in a criminal prosecution violating the Act. The Court said broadly:

> Congress, through its power to define the jurisdiction of inferior courts and to create such courts for the exercise of the judicial power, could, *subject to other constitutional limitations*, create the Emergency Court of Appeals, give to it *exclusive* equity jurisdiction to determine the validity of price regulations prescribed by the Administrator, and *foreclose* any further or other consideration of the validity of a regulation as a defense to a prosecution for its violation.[56]

After *Yakus,* it was not entirely clear the extent to which Congress had power to prescribe certain procedures that, if not followed, would preclude one from attacking administrative regulations and orders. The Court suggested a narrow holding in other parts of its opinion, and it emphasized the special circumstances of wartime inflation.[57] The Court also noted that it was not deciding whether one charged with criminal violation of a duly promulgated regulation could assert a defense that the regulation was unconstitutional on its face. Nor did it decide whether a defendant charged and convicted of a regulation could be deprived of the defense that the regulation was invalid, if that person had been diligently seeking a determination of its validity pursuant to the statutory procedure.[58]

Later cases support the conclusion that one should not read *Yakus* too broadly. *Adamo Wrecking Co. v. United States*[59] illustrates that the Court, despite *Yakus*, will not readily interpret a Congressional statutory scheme to limit claims to specific courts in a way that raises constitutional problems.

The government indicted *Adamo* for violating a section of the Clean Air Act of 1970, which makes it a criminal offense to knowingly violate an "emission standard" promulgated by the Administrator of the EPA. Section 307(b) of the Clean Air Act allowed only a 30–day limitation period following promulgation for challenges to "any emission stan-

---

53. 319 U.S. 182, 63 S.Ct. 1019, 87 L.Ed. 1339 (1943).

54. 319 U.S. at 187–89, 63 S.Ct. at 1022–23.

55. 321 U.S. 414, 64 S.Ct. 660, 88 L.Ed. 834 (1944). The Court did not reach the issue of whether the Act, to the extent it prohibited all interlocutory relief by the Emergency Court, was unconstitutional.

56. 321 U.S. at 443, 64 S.Ct. at 676–77 (emphasis added).

57. 321 U.S. at 439, 64 S.Ct. at 674.

58. 321 U.S. at 446–47, 64 S.Ct. at 677–78.

59. 434 U.S. 275, 98 S.Ct. 566, 54 L.Ed.2d 538 (1978). See also, e.g., Califano v. Sanders, 430 U.S. 99, 109, 97 S.Ct. 980, 986, 51 L.Ed.2d 192 (1977).

Statutory limitations on judicial review. Franklin v. Massachusetts, 505 U.S. 788, 112 S.Ct. 2767, 120 L.Ed.2d 636 (1992) rejected Massachusetts' challenge to the method used to count federal employees serving overseas. The reallocation of these employees resulted in shift-

ing one representative from Massachusetts to Washington State. The state claimed that the executive branch decision to allocate military serving overseas to their "home of record" was arbitrary under the Administrative Procedure Act. The Court said that, even if executive action was not reviewable under the Administrative Procedure Act, the Court may still review the action to determine constitutionality. A fragmented Court then rejected the challenges on the merits.

Dalton v. Specter, 511 U.S. 462, 114 S.Ct. 1719, 128 L.Ed.2d 497 (1994) held that a claim that Pennsylvania Senator Arlen Specter and others brought, claiming that the President had exceeded his authority under a military base closings statute by accepting flawed recommendations from a Commission is not a constitutional claim that is subject to judicial review under *Franklin*. Plaintiffs are merely raising a statutory claim. It was proper for Congress to foreclose judicial review under a statute that commits discretion to the President. 511 U.S. at 477, 114 S.Ct. at 1728.

dard promulgated under section 112." All these challenges had to be filed in the District of Columbia Circuit. Further, any action of the Administration that could have been reviewed but was not, could not later be reviewed in a civil or criminal proceeding for enforcement.

Adamo Wrecking held that a defendant may assert that a regulation is not really an "emission standard" and thus not within section 112(c) as a defense in an enforcement proceeding: the 30 day limitations period would not bar this claim. The Court distinguished the statutory scheme of *Yakus*, which showed clear congressional intent to require all actions of the Price Administrator to be reviewed only in the Emergency Court of Appeals. That law differed substantially from the scheme of the Clean Air Act, which precludes review of only certain, limited, types of regulations of the EPA Administrator.[60] The Court said that the complexity of the Clean Air Act statutory scheme, which does not preclude review of most types of regulations, showed congressional intent to impose the more stringent penalties only on violators of "emissions standards." Because Congress did not intend to empower the Administrator to make a regulation an "emission standards" by his mere designation, the government was required to prove, in every prosecution, that the regulation violated was really an emission standard.[61] Underlying the Court's reasoning seems to have been a fear that precluding review would create potentially widespread liability for many small businesses.[62]

In a concurring opinion Justice Powell reached the question whether *Yakus* foreclosed a due process challenge to the Government's interpretation of the Clean Air Act. He noted that *Yakus* might be viewed as a special case limited to exercise of the war powers. Present day environmental concerns "are not comparable—in terms of an emergency justifying the short-cutting of normal due process rights—to the need for national mobilization in wartime of economic as well as military activity."[63]

Powell also emphasized that the Clean Air Act's 30–day limitation on judicial review would usually not afford adequate time for challenge to the regulations being promulgated. It would be "totally unrealistic" to believe that the many small businesses around the country, or more than a fraction of all persons and entities affected by these regulations, would have access to and knowledge of the Federal Registers and its daily publication of regulations. Thus, even if a lower court were to conclude that a regulation is an emission standard and that the preclusion provisions of section 307(b) apply, Powell understood the majority opinion to imply no view as to the constitutional validity of section 307(b) in the context of a criminal prosecution.[64]

Deportation of Illegal Aliens. In *Reno v. American–Arab Anti–Discrimination Committee*[65] resident aliens claimed that the defendants had targeted them for deportation, in violation of their rights under the First and Fifth Amendments, because they were affiliated with the Popular Front for the Liberation of Palestine. While the plaintiffs' suit was pending, Congress enacted a law restricting judicial review of the decision of the Attorney General's "decision or action" to "commence proceedings, adjudicate cases, or execute removal orders against any alien under this Act."[66] This new law deprived the federal courts of jurisdiction to grant any class-wide injunctive relief, but specified that this ban did not extend to individual cases.[67] The Court upheld this restriction, but only after finding that the jurisdictional limitation deprived no alien of any constitutional right.

The Court said broadly: "Our holding generally deprives deportable aliens of the defense

---

60. 434 U.S. at 279, 98 S.Ct. at 569–70.

61. 434 U.S. at 284, 98 S.Ct. at 572.

62. 434 U.S. at 282, n. 2, 98 S.Ct. at 572, n. 2.

63. 434 U.S. at 290, 98 S.Ct. at 575 (Powell, J., concurring).

64. 434 U.S. at 291, 98 S.Ct. at 576 (Powell, J., concurring).

65. 525 U.S. 471, 119 S.Ct. 936, 142 L.Ed.2d 940 (1999).

66. 8 U.S.C.A. § 1252(g).

67. 525 U.S. at 481–82, 119 S.Ct. at 942.

of selective prosecution."[68] The Court reached this conclusion in this case, even though there was "an admission by the Government that the alleged First Amendment activity was the basis for selecting the individuals for adverse action."[69]

Given this concession, the holding may first appear to be a very unusual one. But various reasons justified this opinion, which drew only one dissent.[70] The Court was dealing with a matter involving foreign policy. The Executive should not have to disclose to a court or the general public its "real" reasons for deeming nationals of a particular country a special threat. Moreover, for reasons of foreign policy, the President may simply wish to antagonize a particular foreign country by focusing on that country's nationals. Even if the President did disclose his real rationales, a court would be "ill equipped to determine their authenticity and utterly unable to assess their adequacy." The alien is not criminally prosecuted for an alleged act, only deported, which simply means that he is "being held to the terms under which he was admitted." His via may have expired, or the activity for which was his permitted residency has ended. In "all cases, deportation is necessary to bring to an end *an ongoing violation* of United States law."[71]

The restriction on jurisdiction did not deprive any illegal alien of a constitutional right because, when an alien's "continuing presence in this country is in violation of the immigration laws, the Government does not offend the Constitution by deporting him for the additional reason that it believes him to be a member of an organization that supports terrorist activity."[72]

The Court left open the opportunity to distinguish future cases: "To resolve the present controversy, we need not rule out the possibility of a rare case in which the alleged basis of discrimination is so outrageous that the foregoing considerations can be overcome."[73]

§ 2.11 The Eleventh Amendment

(a) Introduction and Historical Note

The Eleventh Amendment provides:

The Judicial power of the United States shall not be construed to extend to any suit in law or equity, commenced or prosecuted against one of the United States by Citizens of another State, or by Citizens or Subjects of any Foreign State.

This provision acts to bar suits brought against state governments in the federal courts.[1] It does not grant the states true immunity, for it does not exempt them from the restrictions of federal law; it only means that some types of suits against them must be initially brought in state rather than federal court, unless the state waives its Eleventh Amendment immunity.[2]

The Eleventh Amendment raises extremely important and complex issues. Court interpretations of the Amendment have involved both expansions and restrictions of the literal application of its wording. An in-depth consideration of this jurisdictional point may be found

---

68. 525 U.S. at 488 n. 10, 119 S.Ct. at 946, n. 10.

69. 525 U.S. at 488 n. 10, 119 S.Ct. at 946, n. 10.

70. Scalia, J., wrote the opinion of the Court. Only Souter, J., dissented. Ginsburg, J., filed an opinion concurring in part and in the judgment, joined by Breyer, J. as to Part I. Stevens, J., filed an opinion concurring in the judgment.

71. 525 U.S. at 491, 119 S.Ct. at 947 (emphasis in original).

72. 525 U.S. at 491–92, 119 S.Ct. at 947.

73. 525 U.S. at 491, 119 S.Ct. at 947.

§ 2.11

1. Churchill, J., in David Nursing Home v. Michigan Department of Social Services, 579 F.Supp. 285, 287 n. * (E.D.Mich.1984) called this section of the treatise an "ex-cellent discussion" of Eleventh Amendment limitations on federal court jurisdiction.

See San Diego Unified Port District v. Gianturco, 457 F.Supp. 283, 288 (S.D.Cal.1978) (Schwartz, C.J., quoting treatise), affirmed 651 F.2d 1306 (9th Cir.1981), certiorari denied 455 U.S. 1000, 102 S.Ct. 1631, 71 L.Ed.2d 866 (1982); Judge David V. O'Brien, citing Treatise, in Tonder v. M/V The Burkholder, 630 F.Supp. 691, 693 (D.V.I.1986).

2. Judge Levin H. Campbell, citing Treatise in Libby v. Marshall, 833 F.2d 402, 406 (1st Cir.1987).

elsewhere.[3] Here we present a brief sketch of the import of the Amendment as a part an understanding of federal jurisdiction.

Congress proposed, and the states ratified, the Eleventh Amendment as a reaction to the Supreme Court's decision in *Chisholm v. Georgia.*[4] Alexander Chisholm brought an original action against Georgia in the Supreme Court. Chisholm was the executor of the estate of a South Carolina decedent, Robert Farquar. During the revolutionary period, Farquar had delivered supplies to Georgia under a contract that remained unpaid at his death. Georgia never contested the debt but, instead, refused to appear on the grounds that the federal court had no jurisdiction over such a suit.

After delaying the case for a term so that Georgia might have fair notice of the Court's intention to proceed, the Supreme Court heard the plaintiff's counsel and reached a decision. By a vote of four to one the Court decided that it had jurisdiction in the case and entered a judgment by default against Georgia.[5] The Court had not yet begun the tradition of majority opinion for the Court (Chief Justice Marshall started that practice), so the Justices delivered individual opinions *seriatim.*

None of the Justices relied on a congressional grant of jurisdiction. The four voting together rested their decisions on a belief of a general power under Article III, and the view that states had only limited sovereignty in a national democracy. The one dissenting Justice refused to find any federal court jurisdiction over state governments absent specific con-

gressional authorization.[6] We know that the history of Article III simply does not resolve the issue of federal jurisdiction over debt actions against states.[7]

Congress proposed the Eleventh Amendment immediately after the *Chisholm* decision and the states ratified it in less than five years. The reasons for this reaction may have included popular opinion about the meaning of Article III; theoretical problems concerning the available judicial procedures against a sovereign, if subordinate, unit in the federal system; and a general fear of suits by Tory creditors.[8] While the individual state debts to British citizens and loyalists were not great, there were increasing tensions with Great Britain, and that created fear of debts arising from a new conflict as well as an animosity towards paying any such claims.[9]

Unfortunately, this historical background is of little help in resolving particular problems under the Amendment. The provision passed with such little debate that its history is silent on a great many issues. All that can be said with certainty is that the Amendment intended to bar federal jurisdiction in suits by noncitizens against a state for the payment of debts and damages for past actions absent specific congressional authorization of the federal cause of action. That is all that was necessary to reverse the *Chisholm* ruling. Judicial interpretation is left with the problem of resolving other questions, such as the application of the Eleventh Amendment to suits by citizens against their own state, the applica-

3. See, 1 Ronald D. Rotunda & John E. Nowak, Treatise on Constitutional Law: Substance and Procedure § 2.12 (West Group, 3d ed.1999); Nowak, The Scope of Congressional Power to Create Causes of Action Against State Governments and the History of the Eleventh and Fourteenth Amendments, 75 Colum.L.Rev. 1413 (1975).

4. 2 U.S. (2 Dall.) 419, 1 L.Ed. 440 (1793). *Chisholm* records the first use of the term, "politically correct." Justice Wilson said, in Chisholm v. Georgia, 2 U.S. (2 Dall.) 419, 462, 1 L.Ed. 440 (1793) (emphasis added): "The states, rather than the People, for whose sakes the States exist, are frequently the objects which attract and arrest our principal attention.... Sentiments and expressions of this inaccurate kind prevail in our common, even in our convivial, language. Is a toast asked? 'The United States,' instead of the 'People of the United States,' is the toast given. *This is not politically correct.*" James E. Pfander,

Where the Framers of the Constitution PC?, 11 Constitutional Commentary 13 (1994).

5. 2 U.S. (2 Dall.) at 479.

6. 2 U.S. (2 Dall.) at 432–35 (opinion of Iredell, J.). Justice Iredell was the only contrary vote but that the opinion was not labeled a "dissent."

7. Nowak, The Scope of Congressional Power to Create Causes of Action Against State Governments and the History of the Eleventh and Fourteenth Amendments, 75 Colum.L.Rev. 1413, 1422–30 (1975).

8. C. Warren, The Supreme Court in United States History 91–99 (1922).

9. Nowak, The Scope of Congressional Power to Create Causes of Action Against State Governments and the History of the Eleventh and Fourteenth Amendments, 75 Colum.L.Rev. 1413, 1433–41 (1975).

tion to actions to force a state to comply prospectively with federal law, and the status of congressional authorization of suits against states.

Chief Justice Marshall gave us the earliest interpretation of the Eleventh Amendment. In *Cohens v. Commonwealth of Virginia*,[10] Marshall indicated that the Amendment had no part in suits other than debt actions, and he held it inapplicable to suits that the state brought against a private individual, such as criminal proceedings. Later, in *Osborn v. Bank of the United States*,[11] Marshall stated that the Amendment was inapplicable whenever the state was not a party of record. These interpretations were to be narrowed in future years, but there was no other significant exploration of these issues until the 1880's. Thus Marshall's opinions are the only judicial exposition of the meaning of the Amendment at a time close to its adoption.

(b) An Outline of the Current Rules

Suits Brought in the Courts of Another State. The Eleventh Amendment prohibits federal courts from exercising jurisdiction over state governments in certain circumstances. It does not bar state courts from asserting jurisdiction over their own state government or over the government of another state.

In *Nevada v. Hall*,[12] the Court held that a suit brought in the courts of one state against another state did not violate the Eleventh Amendment, constitutional principles of federalism, or state comity. *Hall* involved California residents who were injured in an automobile accident in California when an employee of the University of Nevada, while on official business and driving an official Nevada vehicle, collided with their car. The California plaintiffs brought a tort suit in the California state court and named the state of Nevada as a party defendant. The California courts ruled that, as a matter of California law, the suit was proper. The Supreme Court upheld the

state judgment on the ground that the suit did not violate the Federal Constitution.

Justice Stevens, writing for the Court in *Hall*, concluded that traditional notions of sovereign immunity do not extend beyond a bar to suits against the sovereign in the sovereign's own courts. The framers of the Federal Constitution were concerned only with sovereign immunity involving suits brought against the states in federal courts. Nothing in the full faith and credit clause of the Constitution required California to give effect to Nevada's statutory provisions concerning its sovereign immunity, because Nevada's laws were in conflict with California's public policy to compensate resident motorists injured by accidents on California highways. Respect for the sovereign immunity of Nevada in California courts was merely a matter of comity and in no sense constitutionally required. However, Stevens did indicate that some constitutional constraints might be placed on the exercise of jurisdiction over a sister state if the court action posed a "substantial threat to our constitutional system of cooperative federalism."[13]

Federal Court Jurisdiction.

The Eleventh Amendment acts as a bar to federal jurisdiction over state governments, as such, when they are sued by anyone other than the federal government or another state.[14] The bar applies to all types of suits for damages or retroactive relief for past wrongs, but it is not an effective barrier that exempts the state from prospectively complying with federal law. The Eleventh Amendment did not repeal the supremacy clause.

As we shall see, if the Eleventh Amendment applies, the suit may be heard in federal court *if* the state consents. In spite of the Eleventh Amendment, Congress may create federal causes of action against states without their consent if such causes of action are necessary to enforce Constitutional rights, such as those

---

10. 19 U.S. (6 Wheat.) 264, 5 L.Ed. 257 (1821).

11. 22 U.S. (9 Wheat.) 738, 6 L.Ed. 204 (1824).

12. 440 U.S. 410, 99 S.Ct. 1182, 59 L.Ed.2d 416 (1979), rehearing denied 441 U.S. 917, 99 S.Ct. 2018, 60 L.Ed.2d 389 (1979).

13. 440 U.S. at 424 n. 24, 99 S.Ct. at 1190 n. 24.

14. Norris, J., quoting treatise, in Tennessee Department of Human Services v. U.S. Department of Education, 979 F.2d 1162, 1166 (6th Cir.1992).

in the Fourteenth Amendment.[15] Now, let us consider this points in more detail.

In resolving issues under the Eleventh Amendment one should ask five basic questions:

- (1) is the plaintiff one to whom the Amendment applies?
- (2) is the suit truly against the state?
- (3) is the suit seeking relief in a manner that is barred by the Amendment?
- (4) has the state waived its immunity?
- (5) is there a valid federal statute in the area that overrides the immunity?

Is the Plaintiff Within the Amendment?

First, one must determine if the plaintiff is subject to the jurisdictional bar. By its own terms the Amendment bars suits by citizens of other states or foreign nationals.[16] The Court held in *Hans v. Louisiana*[17] that the Amendment, by implication, also bars suits by citizens of a state suing their own state. Thus all private plaintiffs are subject to the Amendment.[18]

However, if the state brings an action against the private person, that suit does not come under the restrictions.[19] Similarly, a state may sue another state,[20] or the United States.[21] And the United States may sue a state, even if the purpose of the suit is to protect private individuals. Thus the Secretary of Labor of the United States may bring a federal suit against a state government to establish the rights of individual employees whose personal suit would be barred.[22]

The Eleventh Amendment also does not bar an award of money damages when one *state* sues another state in an original action brought before the U.S. Supreme Court. That Amendment applies, by its own terms, to suits by *citizens* against a state.[23]

---

15. Norris, J., quoting treatise, in Tennessee Department of Human Services v. U.S. Department of Education, 979 F.2d 1162, 1166 (6th Cir.1992).

16. See, e.g., Principality of Monaco v. State of Mississippi, 292 U.S. 313, 54 S.Ct. 745, 78 L.Ed. 1282 (1934); In re New York, 256 U.S. 490, 41 S.Ct. 588, 65 L.Ed. 1057 (1921); Fitts v. McGhee, 172 U.S. 516, 19 S.Ct. 269, 43 L.Ed. 535 (1899).

Collateral Order Doctrine. The protection of Eleventh Amendment is lessened if a court decision denying immunity cannot be appealed until after judgment in the trial court, because then the state entity loses the benefit of avoiding the costs and risks of discovery and trial. Thus states and state entities claiming to be arms of the state may take advantage of the collateral order doctrine and appeal, as a final order, the denial of a motion claiming Eleventh Amendment immunity. Puerto Rico Aqueduct & Sewer Authority v. Metcalf & Eddy, Inc., 506 U.S. 139, 113 S.Ct. 684, 121 L.Ed.2d 605 (1993), on remand 991 F.2d 935 (1st Cir.1993).

17. 134 U.S. 1, 10 S.Ct. 504, 33 L.Ed. 842 (1890).

18. See, Judge Ryskamp, citing Treatise, in Magula v. Broward General Medical Center, 742 F.Supp. 645, 646 (S.D.Fla.1990).

Indians. The Eleventh Amendment bars Indian tribes from suing states in federal court. Blatchford v. Native Village of Noatak and Circle Village, 501 U.S. 775, 111 S.Ct. 2578, 115 L.Ed.2d 686 (1991). Subsequently, Seminole Tribe of Florida v. Florida, 517 U.S. 44, 116 S.Ct. 1114, 134 L.Ed.2d 252 (1996), held that—even though the Commerce Clause gives Congress the right to regulate commerce "with the Indian Tribes"—Congress cannot constitutionally use the Commerce Clause to create private rights of action and abrogate the Eleventh Amendment immunity of the states.

19. Cohens v. Virginia, 19 U.S. (6 Wheat.) 264, 5 L.Ed. 257 (1821).

20. South Dakota v. North Carolina, 192 U.S. 286, 315–21, 24 S.Ct. 269, 274–77, 48 L.Ed. 448 (1904).

21. United States v. Mississippi, 380 U.S. 128, 140–41, 85 S.Ct. 808, 814–15, 13 L.Ed.2d 717 (1965), on remand 256 F.Supp. 344 (S.D.Miss.1966).

22. Employees of Dept. of Public Health & Welfare v. Missouri Dept. of Public Health & Welfare, 411 U.S. 279, 285–86, 93 S.Ct. 1614, 1618–19, 36 L.Ed.2d 251 (1973), superseded by statute/rule as stated in Carey v. White, 407 F.Supp. 121 (D.Del.1976). Cf. EEOC v. Wyoming, 460 U.S. 226, 103 S.Ct. 1054, 75 L.Ed.2d 18 (1983).

Once the suit has been instituted, the court may allow intervention. Thus, Arizona v. California, 460 U.S. 605, 103 S.Ct. 1382, 75 L.Ed.2d 318 (1983), a suit between two states to which the United States became a party, the Court allowed five Indian tribes, whose water rights were in controversy, to intervene. The Court held that there was no compromise of sovereign immunity because the tribes brought no new claims or issues against the states.

However, a suit is barred if a plaintiff state is merely acting as an agent to collect and distribute an amount that the defendant state owed to its citizens. New Hampshire v. Louisiana, 108 U.S. 76, 2 S.Ct. 176, 27 L.Ed. 656 (1883).

23. Maryland v. Louisiana, 451 U.S. 725, 745 n. 21, 101 S.Ct. 2114, 2128 n. 21, 68 L.Ed.2d 576 (1981); Texas v. New Mexico, 482 U.S. 124, 131, 107 S.Ct. 2279, 2285, 96 L.Ed.2d 105 (1987).

There may be difficulties in enforcing money judgments, so courts should be cautious; but typically states have (eventually) voluntarily respected and given effect to money damages awarded against them. Virginia v. West Virgi-

The "State" for Purposes of the Eleventh Amendment.

The second major issue concerns whether a "state" is being sued. Suit is barred only when the state government is the defendant. Agencies of the state come under this heading, but its political subdivisions do not. Thus suits in federal court against municipal corporations,[24] counties[25] and school boards[26] raise no Eleventh Amendment issue. An entity that is merely the instrumentality of state government shares its immunity, but an entity that is a politically independent unit enjoys no Eleventh Amendment protection.[27]

The fact that the federal government has agreed to indemnity a state instrumentality against the costs of litigation (including ad-

nia, 246 U.S. 565, 592, 38 S.Ct. 400, 402, 59 L.Ed. 1272 (1918).

Removal to Federal Court. If a case is filed in state court and can be removed to federal court, the fact that some of the claims may be barred by the Eleventh Amendment does not prohibit removal. While the federal court cannot hear the barred claim (unless the state waives the Eleventh Amendment), it may proceed to hear the non-barred claims. Wisconsin Department of Corrections v. Schacht, 524 U.S. 381, 118 S.Ct. 2047, 141 L.Ed.2d 364 (1998).

24. Maybanks v. Ingraham, 378 F.Supp. 913 (E.D.Pa. 1974); cf. Port of Seattle v. Oregon & Washington R. Co., 255 U.S. 56, 41 S.Ct. 237, 65 L.Ed. 500 (1921).

A municipal corporation is a person, as that term is used by 42 U.S.C.A. § 1983 so that it can be sued in either state or federal court for violating the federal rights of an individual. Monell v. Department of Social Services, 436 U.S. 658, 98 S.Ct. 2018, 56 L.Ed.2d 611 (1978), overruling part of Monroe v. Pape, 365 U.S. 167, 81 S.Ct. 473, 5 L.Ed.2d 492 (1961).

25. Lincoln County v. Luning, 133 U.S. 529, 10 S.Ct. 363, 33 L.Ed. 766 (1890).

26. Mt. Healthy City School District Bd. of Education v. Doyle, 429 U.S. 274, 97 S.Ct. 568, 50 L.Ed.2d 471 (1977), appeal after remand 670 F.2d 59 (6th Cir.1982).

Although the Governor appoints four of the five commissions of the St. Louis Board of Police Commissioners, it is not an "arm of the state" because the City of St. Louis was responsible for the Board's financial liabilities and the Board was not subject to state direction or state control in any other way. Thus it has no Eleventh Amendment immunity. Auer v. Robbins, 519 U.S. 452, 456 n. 1, 117 S.Ct. 905, 908–09 n. 1, 137 L.Ed.2d 79 (1997).

27. Compact Clause. In Lake Country Estates, Inc. v. Tahoe Regional Planning Agency, 440 U.S. 391, 99 S.Ct. 1171, 59 L.Ed.2d 401 (1979), on remand 474 F.Supp. 901 (D.Nev.1979) the Court by a 6 to 3 vote held that a defendant created by interstate compact agency was not immune from suit in federal court under the Eleventh

verse judgments) does not divest that state agency of Eleventh Amendment immunity.[28] The issue that is relevant in determining the Eleventh Amendment immunity is the entity's potential legal liability for judgments, not its ability to require a third party to reimburse it.

The basic catalyst behind the Eleventh Amendment is to prevent federal courts from issuing judgments that must be paid out of the state treasury. Thus, in determining whether an agency is entitled to share in the state's Eleventh Amendment immunity, the court should determine if the state is obligated to pay any of the agency's indebtedness. If the state has no legal obligation to bear the debts of the enterprise, then the Eleventh Amendment is not implicated.[29]

Amendment. 440 U.S. at 402–03, 99 S.Ct. at 1177–78. The Court did not conclude that all agencies created by inter-state compact would be subject to suit in federal court; the opinion merely found that the defendant agency, due to its composition, structure, and function, was a "political subdivision" of the states and not an "arm" of the states. 440 U.S. at 401–03, 99 S.Ct. at 1177–78. As such, the agency enjoyed no immunity from suit under the Eleventh Amendment. The Court also held that members of the defendant agency were absolutely immune from suit for actions taken in their legislative capacity. 440 U.S. at 402–06, 99 S.Ct. at 1177–78.

As a general rule, the Court presumes that any entity created pursuant to the Compact Clause, U.S. Const., Art. I, § 10, cl. 3., does not qualify for Eleventh Amendment immunity. In order for Eleventh Amendment immunity to attach, there must be "good reason" for the Court to believe that the states organized the entity so that it would have the states' Eleventh Amendment immunity, and that Congress concurred with that purpose. While there were indications that the states intended the Port Authority to have such immunity (in particular, the states had control over the powers and acts of the commissions of the Port Authority), other indications pointed the opposite way (in particular, the states lacked financial responsibility for the Port Authority).

28. Regents of the University of California v. Doe, 519 U.S. 425, 117 S.Ct. 900, 137 L.Ed.2d 55 (1997).

29. Hess v. Port Authority Trans–Hudson Corp., 513 U.S. 30, 51, 115 S.Ct. 394, 406, 130 L.Ed.2d 245 (1994). The Court there found, first, that there was no threat to the states' "dignity" when the separate entity was sued in federal court. Any entity created pursuant to the Compact Clause does not owe its existence to any one state. Second, no judgment would be satisfied from the state treasury, because neither state was legally or practically obligated to pay the debts of the separate entity called the Port Authority. Focusing on the financial issue is what the lower courts have been doing in this area for years. E.g., Jacinto-port Corp. v. Greater Baton Rouge Port Commission, 762 F.2d 435, 440 (5th Cir.1985), cert. denied 474 U.S. 1057,

Similarly, state officers may be sued in their *personal capacity* for damages in a federal action, because the amendment grants them no immunity from federal action even where they are acting in their official capacity.[30] However, if the suit actually requests that the officer be ordered to pay funds from the state treasury for wrongful acts of the state, or return property in the state's possession, the suit will be barred because the state is the real party in interest.[31]

In other words, if the plaintiff sued a state official in his or her "official capacity," that really is simply another way of pleading an action against the state, and is thus within the Eleventh Amendment.[32] However, a "personal capacity" suit seeks to impose individual, personal liability on the government officer for actions taken under color of state law, with the badge of state authority.[33] The Eleventh Amendment does not bar suits against state officers sued in their "individual capacity."[34]

There is no longer any requirement that the state be a named party of record. Thus, if a suit requests that the head of a state department of welfare be ordered to personally pay damages the suit is permissible, but if it requests an order requiring him to pay past due amounts from the state treasury it is barred.[35]

The one exception to the real party in interest rules arises in connection with the issue as to the nature of the relief sought, discussed next.

The Nature of the Relief Sought.

The third issue concerns the nature of relief sought in the federal action. Where the action is one for damages, past debts or retroactive relief of any type, it is barred whether it is brought in law, equity, or admiralty.[36] Thus federal suits at law for return of improperly collected state taxes are barred.[37] Similarly, when the Court of Appeals for the Seventh Circuit attempted to order the payment of illegally withheld welfare payments under an "equitable-restitution" theory, the Supreme Court reversed.[38]

The one exception to the amendment based on the form of action is that a private person may bring an equitable action to force state officers to comply with federal law in the future even though they will be required to spend state funds to so comply. The distinction had its genesis in *Ex parte Young*,[39] where the Court held that a state officer could be forbidden in a federal suit from enforcing state law. This holding was based on the legal fiction that the officer could not be given authority to violate federal law so that the suit was not

---

106 S.Ct. 797, 88 L.Ed.2d 774 (1986); Barket, Levy & Fine, Inc. v. St. Louis Thermal Energy Corp., 948 F.2d 1084, 1087 (8th Cir.1991), on remand 21 F.3d 237 (8th Cir. 1994); Bolden v. Southeastern Pennsylvania Transportation Authority, 953 F.2d 807, 818 (3d Cir.1991) (en banc), cert. denied 504 U.S. 943, 112 S.Ct. 2281, 119 L.Ed.2d 206 (1992); Metcalf & Eddy, Inc. v. Puerto Rico Aqueduct & Sewer Authority, 991 F.2d 935, 942–43 (1st Cir.1993); Baxter v. Vigo County School Corp., 26 F.3d 728, 732–33 (7th Cir.1994).

30. Scheuer v. Rhodes, 416 U.S. 232, 94 S.Ct. 1683, 40 L.Ed.2d 90 (1974), appeal after remand 570 F.2d 563 (6th Cir.1977), stay denied 434 U.S. 1335, 98 S.Ct. 29, 54 L.Ed.2d 47 (1977), certiorari denied 435 U.S. 924, 98 S.Ct. 1488, 55 L.Ed.2d 517 (1978).

31. Edelman v. Jordan, 415 U.S. 651, 94 S.Ct. 1347, 39 L.Ed.2d 662 (1974), rehearing denied 416 U.S. 1000, 94 S.Ct. 2414, 40 L.Ed.2d 777 (1974), on remand 405 F.Supp. 802 (N.D.Ill.1975), reversed 551 F.2d 152 (7th Cir.1977), on rehearing 563 F.2d 873 (1977), affirmed 440 U.S. 332, 99 S.Ct. 1139, 59 L.Ed.2d 358 (1979); In re Ayres, 123 U.S. 443, 8 S.Ct. 164, 31 L.Ed. 216 (1887).

32. Kentucky v. Graham, 473 U.S. 159, 105 S.Ct. 3099, 87 L.Ed.2d 114 (1985), on remand 791 F.2d 932 (6th Cir.1986).

33. Hafer v. Melo, 502 U.S. 21, 112 S.Ct. 358, 116 L.Ed.2d 301 (1991).

34. E.g., Hafer v. Melo, 502 U.S. 21, 112 S.Ct. 358, 116 L.Ed.2d 301 (1991).

35. Edelman v. Jordan, 415 U.S. 651, 94 S.Ct. 1347, 39 L.Ed.2d 662 (1974), rehearing denied 416 U.S. 1000, 94 S.Ct. 2414, 40 L.Ed.2d 777 (1974), on remand 405 F.Supp. 802 (N.D.Ill.1975), reversed 551 F.2d 152 (7th Cir.1977), on rehearing 563 F.2d 873 (1977), affirmed 440 U.S. 332, 99 S.Ct. 1139, 59 L.Ed.2d 358 (1979).

36. Concerning admiralty suits, see Ex parte Madrazzo, 32 U.S. (7 Pet.) 627, 8 L.Ed. 808 (1833); Platoro Ltd., Inc. v. Unidentified Remains of a Vessel, 508 F.2d 1113 (5th Cir.1975).

37. Ford Motor Co. v. Department of Treasury of the State of Indiana, 323 U.S. 459, 65 S.Ct. 347, 89 L.Ed. 389 (1945).

38. Edelman v. Jordan, 415 U.S. 651, 94 S.Ct. 1347, 39 L.Ed.2d 662 (1974), rehearing denied 416 U.S. 1000, 94 S.Ct. 2414, 40 L.Ed.2d 777 (1974), on remand 405 F.Supp. 802 (N.D.Ill.1975), reversed 551 F.2d 152 (7th Cir.1977), on rehearing 563 F.2d 873 (1977), affirmed 440 U.S. 332, 99 S.Ct. 1139, 59 L.Ed.2d 358 (1979).

39. 209 U.S. 123, 28 S.Ct. 441, 52 L.Ed. 714 (1908).

against the state authority itself.[40] Today the fiction is maintained to the extent that a state officer must be the named defendant in such a suit. Federal courts can issue prospective relief against state officials in order to enforce federal law, even if the relief may involve the official using state funds.[41]

Although the state is the real party in interest, the Eleventh Amendment was never intended to grant states the ability to subvert the supremacy clause by granting immunity to the states or their officials from judicial orders to comply with federal law.[42] Thus, in the same suit in which the Court struck the lower federal court's order to the state officer to pay *past*

due welfare checks, it upheld the order that forced him prospectively to disburse state payments in conformity with federal laws.[43]

Similarly the Supreme Court unanimously held that state officers could be subject to a federal cause of action, and ordered by a federal court, to force them to disburse state funds to institute educational programs in connection with a suit to desegregate public schools.[44] If state officials do not comply in good faith with the federal court order of prospective relief, the federal courts may impose monetary penalties upon either the particular state officers or the state itself.[45]

---

40. See Judge Garwood, citing this Treatise in American Bank and Trust Co. of Opelousas v. Dent, 982 F.2d 917, 921 n. 4 (5th Cir.1993).

41. Papasan v. Allain, 478 U.S. 265, 281, 106 S.Ct. 2932, 2942, 92 L.Ed.2d 209 (1986) (allegedly ongoing constitutional violation—the unequal distribution of the benefits of certain state school lands—is the type of continuing violation for which a remedy may be fashioned under *Ex parte Young*).

Yet this case does offer some basis for finding that states may waive their immunity by willfully engaging in federally regulated activities; the extent to which such activities constitute a waiver should also be determined by federal standards.

42. Ray v. Atlantic Richfield Co., 435 U.S. 151, 156–57 n. 6, 98 S.Ct. 988, 994 n. 6, 55 L.Ed.2d 179 (1978)(Eleventh Amendment does not bar suits in federal courts against state officials for the purpose of obtaining injunctive relief against the enforcement of unconstitutional state laws). John E. Nowak, The Scope of Congressional Power to Create Causes of Action Against State Governments and the History of the Eleventh and Fourteenth Amendments, 75 Colum.L.Rev. 1413, 1445–56, 1455–58 (1975).

43. Edelman v. Jordan, 415 U.S. 651, 94 S.Ct. 1347, 39 L.Ed.2d 662 (1974), rehearing denied 416 U.S. 1000, 94 S.Ct. 2414, 40 L.Ed.2d 777 (1974), on remand 405 F.Supp. 802 (N.D.Ill.1975), reversed 551 F.2d 152 (7th Cir.1977), on rehearing 563 F.2d 873 (1977), affirmed sub nom. Quern v. Jordan, 440 U.S. 332, 99 S.Ct. 1139, 59 L.Ed.2d 358 (1979). The doctrine was so well accepted by this time that the state did not contest the propriety of the injunction.

Notice Relief. Quern v. Jordan, 440 U.S. 332, 99 S.Ct. 1139, 59 L.Ed.2d 358 (1979) the held that the Eleventh Amendment did not bar federal court jurisdiction over a state government when the federal court ordered the state to notify specific persons that the state might have illegally withheld welfare payments owed to them and that they had a right to apply to a state agency for retroactive benefits. This type of "notice relief" is not prohibited by the Eleventh Amendment.

However, under the Eleventh Amendment, a federal court may not issue a declaratory judgment that state

officials violated federal law in the *past* when there is no ongoing violation of federal law. Such declaratory relief is really retroactive relief and therefore barred by the Eleventh Amendment. Similarly, a federal court cannot issue a "notice" to class members that state officials' past conduct violated federal law, because this "notice relief" is not ancillary to any valid prospective relief. Such notice relief would be useful only if it might be offered in state court proceedings as res judicata on the issue of liability, leaving to the state courts the job of computing damages. But then it would have much the same effect as a full-fledged award of damages or restitution by the federal court and the Eleventh Amendment prohibits that. Green v. Mansour, 474 U.S. 64, 106 S.Ct. 423, 88 L.Ed.2d 371 (1985), rehearing denied 474 U.S. 1111, 106 S.Ct. 900, 88 L.Ed.2d 933 (1986).

44. Milliken v. Bradley (Milliken II), 433 U.S. 267, 97 S.Ct. 2749, 53 L.Ed.2d 745 (1977), on remand 460 F.Supp. 299 (E.D.Mich.1978), remanded 620 F.2d 1143 (6th Cir. 1980), certiorari denied 449 U.S. 870, 101 S.Ct. 207, 66 L.Ed.2d 89 (1980).

Continuing Consequences of Past Actions. Breard v. Greene, 523 U.S. 371, 377–78, 118 S.Ct. 1352, 1356, 140 L.Ed.2d 529 (1998). In this case, state authorities violated consular notification provisions of the Vienna Convention by failing to notify the Paraguayan Consul of the state's arrest of a Paraguayan citizen. The Eleventh Amendment barred this suit by a foreign state against the Commonwealth of Virginia. Moreover, the Court added: "The failure to notify the Paraguayan Counsel occurred long ago and had no continuing effect." This case, therefore, is unlike Milliken v. Bradley, 433 U.S. 267, 97 S.Ct. 2749, 53 L.Ed.2d 745 (1977), which dealt with continuing consequences of past violations of federal rights.

45. See Hutto v. Finney, 437 U.S. 678, 98 S.Ct. 2565, 57 L.Ed.2d 522 (1978), rehearing denied 439 U.S. 1122, 99 S.Ct. 1035, 59 L.Ed.2d 83 (1979), holding that a federal district court was empowered to impose financial penalties, including attorneys fees, on state agencies when officials in those agencies have in bad faith failed to comply with orders of prospective or injunctive relief. As such awards serve only the purpose of a remedial fine similar to a civil contempt penalty, they are allowed as ancillary to the granting of the prospective relief.

If a plaintiff seeks a federal court order to state government officials to transfer to the plaintiff specifically identified pieces of property there will be an issue in the case regarding the applicability of the Eleventh Amendment. If the action is brought against the state government itself or if the plaintiff is merely seeking compensation from the state treasury based on a claim that the state has improperly taken funds from him or refused to pay money to him, the suit will be barred by the amendment.[46] However, if the plaintiff brings suit against the state officials and claims that the officials are acting unconstitutionally and beyond the scope of their authority by having in their possession specific pieces of property owned by the plaintiff, a federal court may be able to attach the property and adjudicate all parties' rights to the property in an *in rem* proceeding.[47]

This exception to the amendment's bar to federal court jurisdiction over state governments, allowing federal courts to order state officers to comply with federal law, does not open federal courts to all those who seek judgments against state governments that might be described as something other than "retroactive" relief. Federal courts are not allowed to adjudicate claims against state governments unless the cause of action falls into a specific category of actions which the Supreme Court has held not to be barred by the amendment. Thus, the executor of an estate could not use the Federal Interpleader Act, 28 U.S.C.A. § 1335, as a jurisdictional basis for forcing officials of two state governments to litigate in federal court the states' inconsistent claims of jurisdiction to tax the estate represented by the executor.[48]

This last point is important and occasionally overlooked:[49] the Eleventh Amendment does

---

46. Papasan v. Allain, 478 U.S. 265, 279–80, 106 S.Ct. 2932, 2941–42, 92 L.Ed.2d 209 (1986) (assuming that school land grants to Mississippi created binding trust, plaintiffs' claim seeking to force state officials to provide certain schools with proper trust income is retroactive monetary relief barred by Eleventh Amendment because the relief sought is the equivalent of money to take the place of the lost income from the corpus and the substitute for the lost corpus).

47. Florida Dept. of State v. Treasure Salvors, Inc., 458 U.S. 670, 102 S.Ct. 3304, 73 L.Ed.2d 1057 (1982), on remand 689 F.2d 1254 (5th Cir.1982).

In Rem Jurisdiction When the State Does Not Have Possession of the Res. Except for the fact that suits requesting return of specific items of property do not involve an extension of federal court jurisdiction over a state treasury, it is difficult to distinguish *Treasure Salvors* from cases where the Supreme Court has held that plaintiffs could not use a restitution theory to justify federal court jurisdiction over a cause of action if the plaintiff sought the return of money that the state allegedly had taken or withheld from him on an unconstitutional basis.

Treasure Salvors was a 5 to 4 decision with no majority opinion. Some lower courts may use *Treasure Salvors* to justify federal court jurisdiction over cases in which plaintiffs seek compensation from a state treasury for state interference with their property rights. See Florida Dept. of State v. Treasure Salvors, Inc., 458 U.S. 670, 102 S.Ct. 3304, 3323, 73 L.Ed.2d 1057 (1982) (White, J., concurring in part and dissenting in part, joined by Powell, Rehnquist and O'Connor, JJ.), on remand 689 F.2d 1254 (5th Cir. 1982). One should not read *Treasure Salvors* so broadly. The Court will not allow Congress to abrogate the Eleventh Amendment by a simple assertion that it is protecting procedural rights to just compensation. Florida Prepaid Postsecondary Education Expense Board v. College

Savings Bank, 527 U.S. 627, 119 S.Ct. 2199, 144 L.Ed.2d 575 (1999), discussed below.

California v. Deep Sea Research, Inc., 523 U.S. 491, 118 S.Ct. 1464, 140 L.Ed.2d 626 (1998) clarified and limited the scope of *Treasure Salvors*, Inc., as an earlier edition of the Treatise earlier predicted. In *Deep Sea Research, Inc.*, the respondent (DSR) located a ship in California's territorial waters. DSR sued in federal court seeking a resolution of its claims to the vessel. The State of California claimed that the Eleventh Amendment prevented the federal court from considering DRS's claim. The Court held that the Eleventh Amendment does not bar the jurisdiction of a federal court over an *in rem* admiralty jurisdiction *when* the res is not within the State's possession.

Unlike *Treasure Salvors*, *Deep Sea Research* asserts rights to a res that is not in the possession of the state. Assertions in *Treasure Salvors* that the Eleventh Amendment forbids a federal court from adjudicating any in rem action against the state are incorrect, for there should be a "more nuanced application of *Treasure Salvors* in the context of the federal courts' *in rem* admiralty jurisdiction." While the Eleventh Amendment bars federal jurisdiction over general title disputes relating to State property interests, "it does not necessarily follow that it applies to *in rem* admiralty actions, or that in such actions, federal courts may not exercise jurisdiction over property that the State does not actually possess." 523 U.S. at 506, 118 S.Ct. at 1473.

48. Cory v. White, 457 U.S. 85, 102 S.Ct. 2325, 72 L.Ed.2d 694 (1982), on remand 686 F.2d 225 (5th Cir. 1982).

49. Puerto Rico Aqueduct and Sewer Authority v. Metcalf & Eddy, Inc., 506 U.S. 139, 113 S.Ct. 684, 121 L.Ed.2d 605 (1993), reversing 945 F.2d 10 (1st Cir.1991), on remand to 991 F.2d 935 (1st Cir.1993).

not permit any suits in federal court against states and those agencies that are "arms of the State," regardless of the relief sought. The Eleventh Amendment is a bar to such suits, whether the relief sought is equitable or legal, prospective or retroactive, declaratory or injunctive. The exception in *Ex Parte Young* does not violate this basic principle because it only applies where the injunctive suit is against state *officials* and the action to be restrained is without authority of state law or contravenes the statutes or Constitution of the United States.[50]

The Supreme Court views the Eleventh Amendment as a bar to federal suits against state officials when the state is the real, substantial party in interest regardless of whether the suit seeks retroactive or injunctive relief. The *Ex parte Young* exception to this principle allows federal courts to hear suits against state officials if the suit seeks to force them to conform their conduct to *federal law*. That exception does not apply to suits that would seek to have federal judges order state officials to conform their conduct to *state* law. The Eleventh Amendment bars federal jurisdiction over suits that seek relief, whether prospective or retroactive, against state officials on the basis of state law and, similarly, bars jurisdiction over such claims that are brought as pendent claims in suits alleging federal causes of action.[51]

Waiver of Immunity.

Express Waiver. The fourth issue is whether the state has waived its Eleventh Amendment immunity for purposes of the particular suit. The Eleventh Amendment bar is not absolute and the state may consent to the suit in federal court. Although it is customary to refer to the Eleventh Amendment as a "jurisdictional bar," it is not jurisdictional in the same sense that Article III diversity jurisdiction is jurisdictional.[52] Parties cannot waive the requirement of being citizens from diverse states, but a state can waive its Eleventh Amendment immunity. The purpose of the Eleventh Amendment is to protect the state, and the state can waive that protection. The purpose of the jurisdictional limitations in Article III is to limit the federal courts, so parties cannot confer jurisdiction on a federal court by simply agreeing the submit to the court.

A waiver is typically defined as the *voluntary* relinquishment of a *known* right. Thus, in order for the state to waive it rights, its consent should be express. To constitute an express waiver the state must do more than merely allow suits to be brought in courts already having jurisdiction. The Supreme Court has read a state statutory provision permitting taxpayers to sue the state for tax

---

50. Worcester County Trust Co. v. Riley, 302 U.S. 292, 297, 58 S.Ct. 185, 187, 82 L.Ed. 268 (1937). See also Cory v. White, 457 U.S. 85, 91, 102 S.Ct. 2325, 2329, 72 L.Ed.2d 694 (1982), on remand 686 F.2d 225 (5th Cir.1982), holding that the Federal Interpleader Act, 28 U.S.C.A. § 1335, does not provide a jurisdictional basis to resolve inconsistent death tax claims by the officials of two states. The Eleventh Amendment bars injunctive suits to enjoin the state itself, even if plaintiff seeks no money judgment.

See also Idaho v. Coeur d'Alene Tribe of Idaho, 521 U.S. 261, 117 S.Ct. 2028, 138 L.Ed.2d 438 (1997). An Indian tribe filed suit in federal court claiming ownership in submerged lands, and seeking a declaratory judgment to that effect. A fragmented Supreme Court held that the Eleventh Amendment barred the tribe from suing Idaho in federal court. The Court reaffirmed the validity of *Ex Parte Young*, but ruled that it did not allow the tribe to sue for prospective injunctive and declaratory relief against various state officials because, in this "unusual" case involving "these particular and special circumstances," the tribe's suit was the "functional equivalent of a quiet title action, which implicates special sovereignty interests." Kennedy, J., announced the judgment of the

Court and delivered the opinion, part of which was the opinion of the Court (joined by Rehnquist, C.J., O'Connor, Scalia & Thomas, JJ., and part of which was a plurality opinion joined by Rehnquist, C.J., & O'Connor, J.)

51. Pennhurst State School & Hospital v. Halderman, 465 U.S. 89, 104 S.Ct. 900, 79 L.Ed.2d 67 (1984).

County of Oneida v. Oneida Indian Nation, 470 U.S. 226, 105 S.Ct. 1245, 84 L.Ed.2d 169 (1985), (in suit by Indian Tribe against a county, the county's cross-claim against the state government, which otherwise would be within a federal court's ancillary jurisdiction, cannot be heard in a federal district court because jurisdiction over the claim against the state government is barred by the Eleventh Amendment), rehearing denied 471 U.S. 1062, 105 S.Ct. 2173, 85 L.Ed.2d 491 (1985).

52. E.g., Insurance Corp. of Ireland v. Compagnie des Bauxites de Guinee, 456 U.S. 694, 702, 102 S.Ct. 2099, 2104, 72 L.Ed.2d 492 (1982), on remand to Compagnie Des Bauxites De Guinee v. Insurance Co. of North America, 554 F.Supp. 1080 (W.D.Pa.1983) (75–1567), judgment reversed by Compagnie des Bauxites de Guinee v. Insurance Co. of North Americaa, 724 F.2d 369 (3d Cir.1983).

refunds and a state constitutional provision allowing suits to be brought against the state "in such courts as shall be directed by law" to allow suits only in state courts.[53] But if the state clearly indicates that federal court suits against the state are generally permissible, or that an agency or corporation otherwise exempt may be sued in its own name, the waiver will stand.[54]

Implied Waivers. If a state does not wish to waive its immunity expressly, the Court will not imply a waiver merely because the state appeared in federal court.[55] The state's failure to plead immunity at the trial level also does not constitute a waiver, because the Court allows the State to raise the Eleventh Amendment as a bar on appeal.[56]

The Supreme Court initially embraced a doctrine of implied waiver of a state's sovereign immunity, but it no longer does so. The Court implied a waiver of state immunity in two major cases: the first of these may be read as only upholding the principle that interpretation of state waivers is a federal issue;[57] the second case did authorize implied waivers, and the Court explicitly overruled it in 1999.

In 1964 *Parden v. Terminal Ry. of Alabama State Docks Dept.*[58] did hold that there was an

53. Ford Motor Co. v. Department of Treasury of the State of Indiana, 323 U.S. 459, 65 S.Ct. 347, 89 L.Ed. 389 (1945) (tax refund suits); Atascadero State Hosp. v. Scanlon, 473 U.S. 234, 105 S.Ct. 3142, 87 L.Ed.2d 171 (1985) (state constitutional provision), rehearing denied 473 U.S. 926, 106 S.Ct. 18, 87 L.Ed.2d 696 (1985). See also Florida Dept. of Health and Rehabilitative Services v. Florida Nursing Home Association, 450 U.S. 147, 149–50, 101 S.Ct. 1032, 1033–35, 67 L.Ed.2d 132 (1981) (per curiam) (waiver of sovereign immunity for state agency does not constitute waiver of Eleventh Amendment immunity), rehearing denied 451 U.S. 933, 101 S.Ct. 2008, 68 L.Ed.2d 319 (1981), on remand 648 F.2d 241 (5th Cir.1981).

U.S. Department of Energy v. Ohio, 503 U.S. 607, 613–614, 112 S.Ct. 1627, 1632–33, 118 L.Ed.2d 255 (1992), on remand 965 F.2d 1401 (6th Cir.1992), holding that a waiver of the federal government's sovereign immunity must also be unequivocal, with such waivers strictly construed in favor of the sovereign.

Partial Waivers of Sovereign Immunity. This rule is not limited to the states. When the federal government waives sovereign immunity, the courts also strictly construe any partial waivers of sovereign immunity. E.g., Library of Congress v. Shaw, 478 U.S. 310, 318, 106 S.Ct. 2957, 2963, 92 L.Ed.2d 250 (1986); Ardestani v. Immigration & Naturalization Service, 502 U.S. 129, 112 S.Ct. 515, 116 L.Ed.2d 496 (1991).

54. Port Authority Trans–Hudson Corp. v. Feeney, 495 U.S. 299, 110 S.Ct. 1868, 109 L.Ed.2d 264 (1990). The Court held that the statutory consent to suit provision in the bi-state compact creating the Port Authority of New York and New Jersey was sufficient to waive any Eleventh Amendment immunity with respect to the Port of New York and New Jersey and its wholly owned railroad subsidiary. (The Court assumed, *arguendo* that the agency in question is a state agency entitled to the states' sovereign immunity.) Two provisions of the relevant Act persuaded the Court to reach this conclusion. One section provided that the states "consent to suit, actions or proceedings in any form or nature at law, in equity or otherwise . . . against the Port of New York Authority." Another section provided: "The foregoing consent is granted on the condition that venue in any suit, action or proceeding against the Port Authority shall be laid within a county or a judicial district, established by one of said States, *or by the United States,* and situated wholly or partially within the

Port of New York District." (emphasis added). This latter provision indicates that the state not only consent to suit, but that this consent extends to suits brought in federal court.

Federal Waivers. Compare, United States v. Nordic Village, Inc., 503 U.S. 30, 112 S.Ct. 1011, 117 L.Ed.2d 181 (1992), on remand 963 F.2d 118 (6th Cir.1992), holding that *federal* waivers of sovereign immunity must also be "unequivocally expressed," and should not normally be liberally construed. See also United States v. King, 395 U.S. 1, 4, 89 S.Ct. 1501, 1503, 23 L.Ed.2d 52 (1969); Holderman, J., citing Treatise in Cleveland v. Attorney Registration and Disciplinary Commission, 1996 WL 520857 at *2 (N.D.Ill.1996), aff'd sub nom. Skolnick v. Attorney Registration and Disciplinary Commission, 129 F.3d 119 (7th Cir.1997).

55. Clark v. Barnard, 108 U.S. 436, 2 S.Ct. 878, 27 L.Ed. 780 (1883).

56. Edelman v. Jordan, 415 U.S. 651, 94 S.Ct. 1347, 39 L.Ed.2d 662 (1974), rehearing denied 416 U.S. 1000, 94 S.Ct. 2414, 40 L.Ed.2d 777 (1974), on remand 405 F.Supp. 802 (N.D.Ill.1975), reversed 551 F.2d 152 (7th Cir.1977), on rehearing 563 F.2d 873 (1977), affirmed 440 U.S. 332, 99 S.Ct. 1139, 59 L.Ed.2d 358 (1979). The state may waive its immunity by appearing in federal court and stating through its counsel that it will consent to court orders awarding damages or other forms of retroactive relief to the plaintiff if its position on the merits of the litigation is rejected by the court. See Toll v. Moreno, 458 U.S. 1, 102 S.Ct. 2977, 73 L.Ed.2d 563 (1982).

57. Petty v. Tennessee–Missouri Bridge Commission, 359 U.S. 275, 79 S.Ct. 785, 3 L.Ed.2d 804 (1959). The Court found that a state waived its immunity from suit for actions relating to an agency created by an interstate compact. The Court found that a rather vague provision in the compact constituted a waiver of immunity. While the majority opinion is not clear on this point, it would appear only to hold that the terms of federally approved compacts are to be interpreted under federal law.

58. 377 U.S. 184, 84 S.Ct. 1207, 12 L.Ed.2d 233 (1964), rehearing denied 377 U.S. 1010, 84 S.Ct. 1903, 12 L.Ed.2d 1057 (1964), *overruled,* College Savings Bank v. Florida Prepaid Postsecondary Education Expense Board, 527 U.S. 666, 119 S.Ct. 2219, 144 L.Ed.2d 605 (1999).

implied waiver. In *Parden,* a state took over the operation of a railroad knowing that the Federal Government already regulated railroad liability extensively. The Court held that the state owned railroad was subject to federal employees' compensation laws and could be sued in a federal court by individuals claiming benefits under such laws. *Parden* treated the state's decision to operate the railroad as an implied waiver of immunity.[59]

Later cases undermined or cast doubt on *Parden,* leading to its eventual overruling. Even before the Supreme Court expressly overruled that decision, the Court was reluctant to find implied waivers and it never created a general rule that a state automatically waived its Eleventh Amendment immunity merely by operating a federally regulated enterprise. Moreover, in other cases the Court held that a state's waiver of its Eleventh Amendment rights should not be implied more

readily than any individual's waiver of personal constitutional rights.[60]

In addition, the post-*Parden* Court did not find implied waivers when Congress merely appeared to make a waiver a condition of receiving federal funds. The Court made clear that when Congress exercises its power under the spending power to attach conditions to the receipt of voluntarily accepted federal moneys, Congress may require a state to waive immunity in order to be eligible for federal funds, but a state's receipt of the funds will constitute a waiver only if Congress *clearly* required such a waiver and makes clear that it was explicitly granting a federal court right of action to individuals.[61] Neither the state's participation in a federal program in itself nor a concomitant agreement to obey federal law constitutes a waiver of Eleventh Amendment immunity.[62]

In *College Savings Bank v. Florida Prepaid Postsecondary Education Expense Board,*[63] the

59. Hilton v. South Carolina Public Railways Commission, 502 U.S. 197, 112 S.Ct. 560, 116 L.Ed.2d 560 (1991), on remand 307 S.C. 63, 413 S.E.2d 845 (1992). The Court reaffirmed *Parden.* In other words, the Federal Employers' Liability Act (FELA) creates a cause of action against a state-owned railroad, enforceable in state court. However, the Court reached this result as a matter of statutory construction and *stare decisis.* Cf. Port Authority Trans–Hudson Corp. v. Feeney, 495 U.S. 299, 110 S.Ct. 1868, 109 L.Ed.2d 264 (1990), where the Court assumed the applicability of the FELA to state-owned railroads.

60. The Court has held that waiver of this right by states should not be implied more readily than the waiver of any personal constitutional right, Edelman v. Jordan, 415 U.S. 651, 94 S.Ct. 1347, 39 L.Ed.2d 662 (1974), rehearing denied 416 U.S. 1000, 94 S.Ct. 2414, 40 L.Ed.2d 777 (1974), on remand 405 F.Supp. 802 (N.D.Ill.1975), reversed 551 F.2d 152 (7th Cir.1977), on rehearing 563 F.2d 873 (1977), affirmed 440 U.S. 332, 99 S.Ct. 1139, 59 L.Ed.2d 358 (1979).

61. Employees of the Dept. of Public Health and Welfare v. Department of Public Health and Welfare, Missouri, 411 U.S. 279, 93 S.Ct. 1614, 36 L.Ed.2d 251 (1973), superseded by statute/rule as stated in 407 F.Supp. 121 (D.Del.1976). In this case, Douglas, J., for the Court, held that a change in a federal statute did not indicate a Congressional purpose to sweep away the constitutional immunity of the states from suit in federal courts by a state's own citizens or citizens of other states.

See also, Edelman v. Jordan, 415 U.S. 651, 94 S.Ct. 1347, 39 L.Ed.2d 662 (1974), rehearing denied 416 U.S. 1000, 94 S.Ct. 2414, 40 L.Ed.2d 777 (1974), on remand 405 F.Supp. 802 (N.D.Ill.1975), reversed 551 F.2d 152 (7th Cir.1977), on rehearing 563 F.2d 873 (1977), affirmed 440 U.S. 332, 99 S.Ct. 1139, 59 L.Ed.2d 358 (1979).

62. These waiver principles formed the basis of the Court's ruling in Atascadero State Hospital v. Scanlon, 473 U.S. 234, 105 S.Ct. 3142, 87 L.Ed.2d 171 (1985), rehearing denied 473 U.S. 926, 106 S.Ct. 18, 87 L.Ed.2d 696 (1985) that a person who alleged that he was denied employment due to his physical handicap in a state program which received federal funds in violation of the Rehabilitation Act of 1973 could not bring suit against the state in a federal court to redress his injury from the violation of the Act. The majority opinion found that the federal court suit was barred by the Eleventh Amendment. Although Congress might require a waiver of Eleventh Amendment immunity for participation in a federally funded program, Congress must clearly state its intention to do so. The majority found that a State should not be deemed to have waived its immunity merely due to the receipt of federal funds. Congressional creation in the Rehabilitation Act of a cause of action for persons whose statutory rights are violated did not, according to the majority opinion, constitute a clear congressional attempt to abrogate the Eleventh Amendment bar to federal court suits against a state.

See also Florida Dept. of Health & Rehabilitative Services v. Florida Nursing Home Association, 450 U.S. 147, 150, 101 S.Ct. 1032, 1034–35, 67 L.Ed.2d 132 (1981) (per curiam), rehearing denied 451 U.S. 933, 101 S.Ct. 2008, 68 L.Ed.2d 319 (1981), on remand 648 F.2d 241 (5th Cir. 1981). Jenkins v. Massinga, 592 F.Supp. 480, 494 n. 12 (D.Md.1984) (Miller, J.), citing treatise.

63. 527 U.S. 666, 119 S.Ct. 2219, 144 L.Ed.2d 605 (1999), overruling Parden v. Terminal Ry. of Alabama State Docks Dept., 377 U.S. 184, 84 S.Ct. 1207, 12 L.Ed.2d 233 (1964), rehearing denied 377 U.S. 1010, 84 S.Ct. 1903, 12 L.Ed.2d 1057 (1964). In addition, *College Savings Bank* concluded that Congress could not use its powers under

Court concluded that its later decisions undermined any theory of implied or constructive waiver. It then explicitly overruled *Parden* and held that it will not imply a waiver of a State's Constitutional rights of sovereign immunity. Florida could waive its sovereign immunity for suit in federal court, if it did so explicitly and voluntarily. But, *College Savings Bank* continued, Florida did not waive it rights explicitly and, unless it does so, there is no waiver. This conclusion should not be surprising, given the fact that the Court has long defined a waiver as the "intentional relinquishment or abandonment of a known right or privilege."[64] In short, *College Savings Bank* held that neither the federal Trademark Remedy Clarification Act nor Florida's activities in interstate commerce constituted a valid waiver of Florida's sovereign immunity.

Federal Statutes that Abrogate a State's Eleventh Amendment Immunity. The fifth issue is whether federal statutes that grant specific jurisdiction to federal courts serve to abrogate the Eleventh Amendment.

Congressional Power Under the Fourteenth Amendment to Abrogate Eleventh Amendment Immunity. The Court has held that federal statutes, based upon the congressional power to enforce the Fourteenth Amendment are not subject to Eleventh Amendment jurisdictional rules.[65] This position is clearly supported by history.[66] The

Fourteenth Amendment, in short, limits the earlier-enacted Eleventh Amendment.

In *Hutto v. Finney,*[67] the Supreme Court found that the Civil Rights Attorney's Fees Awards Act of 1976[68] applies to state governments. Congress enacted this statute pursuant to its power to enforce the Fourteenth Amendment and so neither the Tenth nor the Eleventh Amendment stands as a barrier to awarding attorney's fees against state governments if they are otherwise able to be sued on the basis of a federal civil rights cause of action.[69] Indeed, a federal court may be able to award attorney's fees to a party who prevails on a statutory claim against the state which is pendant to a substantial constitutional claim against state officials.[70]

While the Court has been liberal in its construction of the Civil Rights Attorney's Fees Awards Act when states are otherwise suable in a federal court, it refused to create a general cause of action against state governments for the violation of federal rights because it has interpreted 42 U.S.C.A. § 1983 (which creates a cause of action against "persons" who deprive others of federally guaranteed rights) does not apply to state governments because they are not "persons" suable under that section.[71]

In *Quern v. Jordan*[72] the Court reaffirmed

---

section 5 of the Fourteenth Amendment to abrogate Florida's immunity from suit in federal court because one's right to be free from a competitor's false advertising is not "property" for purposes of section 1 the Fourteenth Amendment. See §§ 19.1 to 19.5.

64. Johnson v. Zerbst, 304 U.S. 458, 58 S.Ct. 1019, 82 L.Ed. 1461, 146 A.L.R. 357 (1938).

65. Fitzpatrick v. Bitzer, 427 U.S. 445, 96 S.Ct. 2666, 49 L.Ed.2d 614 (1976).

66. Nowak, The Scope of Congressional Power to Create Causes of Action Against State Governments and the History of the Eleventh and Fourteenth Amendments, 75 Colum.L.Rev. 1413 (1975).

67. 437 U.S. 678, 98 S.Ct. 2565, 57 L.Ed.2d 522 (1978), rehearing denied 439 U.S. 1122, 99 S.Ct. 1035, 59 L.Ed.2d 83 (1979).

68. 42 U.S.C.A. § 1988.

69. In Maine v. Thiboutot, 448 U.S. 1, 100 S.Ct. 2502, 65 L.Ed.2d 555 (1980) the Court allowed an award of attorney's fees against a state government to a party

prevailing on a federal, statutory, nonconstitutional claim under Section 1983 of the Civil Rights Act. The Court found that 42 U.S.C.A. § 1983 created a cause of action against persons who deprive others of any rights created by federal constitutional or statutory law. There was no Eleventh Amendment issue because the case had been brought in a state court. The Court was not required to determine in this case whether Section 1983 applied to state governments because the state did not appeal from the judgment against it.

70. Maher v. Gagne, 448 U.S. 122, 100 S.Ct. 2570, 65 L.Ed.2d 653 (1980). See also New York Gaslight Club, Inc. v. Carey, 447 U.S. 54, 100 S.Ct. 2024, 64 L.Ed.2d 723 (1980) (federal court action may be brought to recover an award of attorney's fees to the prevailing party in state administrative or judicial proceedings concerning federal civil rights. Congressional power under the Fourteenth Amendment overrides any possible state interest in denying attorney's fees awards in such cases).

71. See § 19.31, infra.

72. 440 U.S. 332, 99 S.Ct. 1139, 59 L.Ed.2d 358 (1979).

the holding of *Edelman v. Jordan*[73] that suits against states are permissible in federal court pursuant to § 1983 only to the extent that prospective, and not retrospective, relief is sought by naming a state official as the nominal defendant. Because the Eleventh Amendment does not bar suits seeking only prospective relief, such suits are proper under § 1983 when brought against state officials even though the state itself may be the real party in interest. The *Quern* Court held, however, that § 1983 did not manifest congressional intent to abrogate the states' Eleventh Amendment immunity from suit in federal court. Although the Court did not question congressional power to abrogate Eleventh Amendment immunity when legislating to implement the terms of the Fourteenth Amendment, the Court found that no intent to abrogate the immunity could be gleaned from the history of § 1983.[74]

The controversy in *Quern* resulted from the lower court ruling following the remand in *Edelman*. The district court had ruled that members of the *Edelman* plaintiff class were entitled to receive notice that they had been deprived of welfare benefits in violation of applicable law; the lower court therefore ordered the state to mail such notices together with notices of the availability of state process by which the injured welfare recipients could seek a remedy. The Seventh Circuit reversed the lower court because it found that the form of the notice purported to decide that the welfare recipients were in fact entitled to the lost benefits. However, the Seventh Circuit ruled that a notice that merely advised the class members that they might have a claim and that state process was available to them would constitute permissible prospective relief.[75] Thus the precise issue presented to the Supreme Court was only whether a federal court order mandating such notice violated the Eleventh Amendment bar to retrospective relief declared in *Edelman*.[76]

Justice Rehnquist's opinion for the Court repudiated any suggestion that cases decided subsequent to *Edelman* cast doubt on the validity of the *Edelman* precedent.[77] *Monell v. Department of Social Services*,[78] which had held that local governmental units were "persons" within the meaning of § 1983 and thus enjoyed no Eleventh Amendment immunity, was only a ruling on the applicability of the statute to local governmental units. Justice Rehnquist found that the legislative history of § 1983 was not sufficiently clear to warrant an inference that state immunity, an important attribute of state sovereignty, had been withdrawn for purposes of § 1983 suits. The majority opinion distinguished *Hutto v. Finney*[79] on the ground that the Civil Rights Attorney's Fees Awards Act had clearly been intended by Congress to override the states' Eleventh Amendment immunity with respect to attorney's fees in civil rights actions. Finally, Justice Rehnquist's opinion resolved the precise issue of *Quern* by finding that the method of notice proposed by the Seventh Circuit did not violate the ban on retrospective relief declared in *Edelman*.[80]

By strictly applying these principles, *Atascadero State Hospital v. Scanlon*[81] ruled that

---

73. 415 U.S. 651, 94 S.Ct. 1347, 39 L.Ed.2d 662 (1974), rehearing denied 416 U.S. 1000, 94 S.Ct. 2414, 40 L.Ed.2d 777 (1974), on remand 405 F.Supp. 802 (N.D.Ill.1975), reversed 551 F.2d 152 (7th Cir.1977), on rehearing 563 F.2d 873 (1977), affirmed 440 U.S. 332, 99 S.Ct. 1139, 59 L.Ed.2d 358 (1979), discussed at note 30, supra, and accompanying text.

74. Because the Court upheld the lower court's grant of prospective relief it was unnecessary to reach this issue but the majority did reach and decide the issue. Justices Brennan and Marshall refused to endorse the § 1983 ruling and Justice Brennan labeled it dicta. 440 U.S. at 349, 350, 99 S.Ct. at 1149–50 (Brennan, J., concurring); 440 U.S. at 366, 99 S.Ct. at 1158 (Marshall, J., concurring).

75. 440 U.S. at 336, 99 S.Ct. at 1142–43.

76. 440 U.S. at 334, 99 S.Ct. at 1141–42.

77. 440 U.S. at 338, 99 S.Ct. at 1143–44.

78. 436 U.S. 658, 98 S.Ct. 2018, 56 L.Ed.2d 611 (1978). The Supreme Court has held that municipalities are "persons" as that term is used by 42 U.S.C.A. § 1983. Monell v. Department of Social Services, 436 U.S. 658, 98 S.Ct. 2018, 56 L.Ed.2d 611 (1978) overruling on this point Monroe v. Pape, 365 U.S. 167, 81 S.Ct. 473, 5 L.Ed.2d 492 (1961).

79. 437 U.S. 678, 98 S.Ct. 2565, 57 L.Ed.2d 522 (1978), rehearing denied 439 U.S. 1122, 99 S.Ct. 1035, 59 L.Ed.2d 83 (1979).

80. 440 U.S. at 346–49, 99 S.Ct. at 1147–49.

81. 473 U.S. 234, 105 S.Ct. 3142, 87 L.Ed.2d 171 (1985), rehearing denied 473 U.S. 926, 106 S.Ct. 18, 87 L.Ed.2d 696 (1985).

the Rehabilitation Act did not give handicapped persons who had been wrongfully denied state employment a right to bring suit against the state in a federal court. This federal Act prohibits employment discrimination against handicapped persons by employers who are recipients of federal funds; the Act authorizes federal court suits by handicapped persons against recipients of federal funds who discriminate against such persons in their employment practices. The Act established a basis for federal court actions against recipients of federal aid other than state governments; federal suits brought by handicapped persons against a state government were barred by the Eleventh Amendment. The Court recognized that Congress could abrogate a state's Eleventh Amendment protection from federal suits, if Congress was exercising its power under the Fourteenth Amendment. However, the majority found that: "A general authorization for suit in a federal court is not the kind of unequivocal statutory language sufficient to abrogate the Eleventh Amendment. When Congress chooses to subject the states to federal jurisdiction it must do so specifically."[82]

Congress did speak clearly when it said, in the Age Discrimination in Employment Act (ADEA) that it was subjecting states to the provisions of the ADEA and abrogating their Eleventh Amendment immunity. Congress purported to act using its powers under section 5 of the Fourteenth Amendment to enforce section 1 of the Fourteenth Amendment. However, *Kimel v. Florida Board of Regents*[83] ruled that Congress could not constitutionally use section 5 in this manner because the abrogation exceeded federal power under section 5.[84]

Section 5 gives Congress the power to enforce section 1, not the power to define section 1 or determine what constitutes a violation of section 1. Age is not a suspect class under the equal protection clause and therefore laws that discriminate on the basis of age are constitutional if the classification is rational.[85] Thus, states may discrimination on the basis of age, by, for example, imposing mandatory retirement age on certain state employees.[86] There must be a congruence and proportionality between the injury Congress seeks to prevent or remedy and the means adopted to that end in order for a law enacted under section 5 to be valid. Congress cannot abrogate the states' Eleventh Amendment immunity merely by stating that it is enforcing the Fourteenth Amendment; the law must actually enforce (not redefine) section 1.[87]

Congressional Power to Abrogate Eleventh Amendment Immunity Under the Commerce Clause and Other Provisions

82. 473 U.S. at 246, 105 S.Ct. at 3149. Four justices dissented because they believed that the majority was using Eleventh Amendment language unjustifiably to protect state autonomy in the federal system rather than properly implementing congressional intention to make all recipients of federal funds refrain from discriminating against handicapped persons. The dissenting justices believed that the Eleventh Amendment should not bar a federal suit against a state by a person who is a resident of that state and, therefore, that Hans v. Louisiana, 134 U.S. 1, 10 S.Ct. 504, 33 L.Ed. 842 (1890) should be overruled.

See also County of Oneida v. Oneida Indian Nation, 470 U.S. 226, 105 S.Ct. 1245, 84 L.Ed.2d 169 (1985), rehearing denied 471 U.S. 1062, 105 S.Ct. 2173, 85 L.Ed.2d 491 (1985) where the Court held that (in a federal court suit against local governments by an Indian tribe) the Eleventh Amendment barred federal court ancillary jurisdiction over a cross-claim by the local governments against the state government. Justices Brennan and Marshall dissented in part based on their belief that the Eleventh Amendment should have no application to federal suits brought against a state government by residents of that (defendant) state. 470 U.S. at 254, 105 S.Ct. at 1262 (Brennan, J., dissenting, joined by Marshall, J.).

83. 528 U.S. 62, 120 S.Ct. 631, 145 L.Ed.2d 522 (2000).

84. This result was predicted in, Ronald D. Rotunda, The Americans with Disabilities Act, Bar Examinations, and the Constitution: A Balancing Act, 66 The Bar Examiner 6 (No. 3, August, 1997).

85. Gregory v. Ashcroft, 501 U.S. 452, 473, 111 S.Ct. 2395, 115 L.Ed.2d 410 (1991); Vance v. Bradley, 440 U.S. 93, 102–03 n. 20, 108–112, 99 S.Ct. 939, 59 L.Ed.2d 171 (1979); Massachusetts Bd. of Retirement v. Murgia, 427 U.S. 307, 317, 96 S.Ct. 2562, 49 L.Ed.2d 520 (1976) (per curiam).

86. Gregory v. Ashcroft, 501 U.S. 452, 473, 111 S.Ct. 2395, 2407–08, 115 L.Ed.2d 410 (1991)(Missouri Constitution's mandatory retirement provision for judges does not violate equal protection)

87. See also, College Savings Bank v. Florida Prepaid Postsecondary Education Expense Board, 527 U.S. 666, 119 S.Ct. 2219, 144 L.Ed.2d 605 (1999) (5 to 4) (Scalia, J., for the Court); Florida Prepaid Postsecondary Education Expense Board v. College Savings Bank, 527 U.S. 627, 119 S.Ct. 2199, 144 L.Ed.2d 575 (1999) (5 to 4) (Rehnquist, J., for the Court), both discussed below.

of the Constitution. Initially the Court suggested that Congress could use its powers found in the body of the Constitution in order to limit the application of the later-enacted Eleventh Amendment, but the Court has now rejected that position.

The road to that conclusion starts with *Welch v. Texas Department of Highways and Public Transportation,*[88] where a strongly divided Court ruled that the Eleventh Amendment prohibits admiralty suits against the state. However, the Court suggested that Congress, pursuant to its commerce clause power, could abrogate such Eleventh Amendment immunity if Congress expresses that intent in the statute itself, using *unmistakable* language, which it had not done in that case.

In *Pennsylvania v. Union Gas Co.,*[89] a fragmented Court adopted the proposition advanced in *Welch.* Justice Brennan, joined by Justices Marshall, Blackmun, and Stevens, ruled that, notwithstanding the Eleventh Amendment, Congress—when legislating pursuant to the commerce clause—has the authority to render states liable for money damages in federal court. These justices argued that the commerce clause gives plenary power to Congress. "The language of the Eleventh Amendment gives us no hint that it limits *congressional* authority; it refers only to 'the

judicial power' and forbids '*constru[ing]*' that power to extend to the enumerated suits— language plainly intended to rein in the judiciary, not Congress."[90]

Justice Scalia, joined by Chief Justice Rehnquist and Justice O'Connor (and in part by Justice Kennedy) concurred in part and dissented in part in *Union Gas.* In an extensive discussion, Scalia noted, among other things, that congressional power to act under section 5 of the Fourteenth Amendment (a provision "avowedly directed against the power of the States") does not justify "limitation of the principle embodied in the Eleventh Amendment through appeal to the antecedent provisions of the Constitution."[91] He argued that the commerce clause and other congressional powers enumerated in the body of the Constitution should not be construed to limit the later-enacted Eleventh Amendment; rather, the later-enacted Eleventh Amendment should be construed to limit earlier-enacted congressional powers. Otherwise, if the Article I commerce power allows Congress to abrogate the states' Eleventh Amendment immunity, "so do all the other Article I powers."[92]

Only seven years after the fragmented Court in *Union Gas*[93] concluded that Congress could use its commerce clause power to remove a state's Eleventh Amendment immunity, the

88. 483 U.S. 468, 107 S.Ct. 2941, 97 L.Ed.2d 389 (1987). There was no opinion of the Court.

89. 491 U.S. 1, 109 S.Ct. 2273, 105 L.Ed.2d 1 (1989), on remand 743 F.Supp. 1144 (E.D.Pa.1990).

Union Gas was overruled in, Seminole Tribe of Florida v. Florida, 517 U.S. 44, 116 S.Ct. 1114, 134 L.Ed.2d 252 (1996), discussed below.

90. 491 U.S. at 17, 109 S.Ct. at 2283 (emphasis in original). See also, Stevens, J., concurring, 491 U.S. at 23, 109 S.Ct. at 2286; White J., concurring, 491 U.S. at 57, 109 S.Ct. at 2295.

91. 491 U.S. at 41, 109 S.Ct. at 2302.

92. 491 U.S. at 39, 109 S.Ct. at 2301.

Justice O'Connor also filed a dissenting opinion.

Bankruptcy Powers. After *Union Gas,* a plurality of the Court (White, J., joined by Rehnquist, C.J. & O'Connor & Kennedy, JJ.), in Hoffman v. Connecticut Department of Income Maintenance, 492 U.S. 96, 109 S.Ct. 2818, 106 L.Ed.2d 76 (1989), concluded that Congress did not express a clear intention to use § 106(c) of the Bankruptcy

Code to abrogate the Eleventh Amendment immunity of the states, and that therefore § 106(c) does not authorize a bankruptcy court to issue a money judgment against a state that has not filed a proof of claim in the bankruptcy proceeding. Scalia, J., concurred in the judgment on the grounds that Congress has no power to abrogate Eleventh Amendment immunity, a question not addressed by the majority. Marshall, J., joined by Brennan, Blackmun, & Stevens, JJ., dissented, finding congressional intent to abrogate the state's Eleventh Amendment immunity to be "unmistakably clear." Stevens, J., joined by Blackmun, J., also filed a dissenting opinion.

Education of the Handicapped Act. In Dellmuth v. Muth, 491 U.S. 223, 109 S.Ct. 2397, 105 L.Ed.2d 181 (1989), on remand 884 F.2d 1384 (3d Cir.1989), the Court held that the Education of the Handicapped Act did not abrogate the state's Eleventh Amendment immunity because the Congress may abrogate a state's immunity only by making its intention unmistakably clear in the language of the statute.

93. Pennsylvania v. Union Gas Co., 491 U.S. 1, 109 S.Ct. 2273, 105 L.Ed.2d 1 (1989).

Court (five to four) explicitly overruled that decision in *Seminole Tribe of Florida v. Florida*.[94] Chief Justice Rehnquist wrote the opinion of the Court.

Seminole Tribe held that Congress cannot constitutionally use the Commerce Clause to create private rights of action and abrogate the Eleventh Amendment immunity of the states. The Eleventh Amendment prevents Congress from using the Commerce Clause to authorize private parties to file suits in federal court against unconsenting states, whether the relief sought is prospective injunctive relief or retroactive monetary relief.

Similarly, in *Florida Prepaid Postsecondary Education Expense Board v. College Savings Bank*,[95] the Court held that Congress may not validly abrogate Florida's Eleventh Amendment Immunity using its powers under the Patent Clause.[96] A patentee sued a state agency in federal court claiming that the state had infringed on its patent. Congress made clear in the relevant statute, the Patent Remedy Act, that it intended to revoke the states' Eleventh Amendment immunity. However, the law was still unconstitutional because it did not validly make such a revocation. Congress cannot use is powers under the Patent Clause to override the Eleventh Amendment anymore than it could use its powers under the commerce clause to override the Eleventh Amendment.[97]

Limits of Federal Power to Subject States to Suit in State Court.

The Eleventh Amendment, by its own terms, limits, the "Judicial power of the United States." It speaks to federal courts and says nothing about states being sued in their own state courts. In *Alden v. Maine*[98] the Court acknowledged that fact but, nonetheless, held that the sovereign immunity principles, which are derived from the structure of the Constitution, mean that Congressional powers under Article I do not include the power to subject nonconsenting States to private suits for damages in state courts. Just as Congress cannot force a state to be sued in federal court, Congress cannot force a state to be sued in its own court system. However, a state may explicitly consent to waive it sovereign immunity.

In *Alden*, state probation offices sued the State of Maine for violation of the overtime provisions of the Fair Labor Standards Act in federal district court. After the Supreme Court held that Congress could not use its commerce clause powers to take away a state's Eleventh Amendment sovereign immunity,[99] the federal district court dismissed the probation officers' suit, and they then filed the same action in state court in Maine. The Fair Labor Standards Act authorized such a suit in state court, but the state trial court dismissed on sovereign immunity grounds, because Maine had not consented to suit. The Maine Supreme Judicial Court affirmed. The U.S. Supreme Court, five to four, affirmed.[100]

---

94. 517 U.S. 44, 116 S.Ct. 1114, 134 L.Ed.2d 252 (1996). Rehnquist, C.J., was joined by O'Connor, Scalia, Kennedy, & Thomas, JJ. Stevens, J., filed a dissenting opinion. Souter, J., joined by Ginsburg & Breyer, JJ., filed another dissenting opinion.

95. 527 U.S. 627, 119 S.Ct. 2199, 144 L.Ed.2d 575 (1999).

96. U.S. Const., Art. I, § 8, cl. 8.

97. *Florida Prepaid Postsecondary* also ruled that section 5 of the Fourteenth Amendment, authorizing Congress to enact "appropriate legislation" to protect against deprivations of property without due process of law did not provide Congress with authority to abrogate the state's sovereign immunity. Stevens, J., joined by Souter, Ginsburg, & Breyer, JJ., filed a dissenting opinion. See §§ 19.1–19.5.

In a companion case, College Savings Bank v. Florida Prepaid Postsecondary Education Expense Board, 527 U.S. 666, 119 S.Ct. 2219, 144 L.Ed.2d 605 (1999), *overruling* Parden v. Terminal Ry. of Alabama State Docks Dept., 377 U.S. 184, 84 S.Ct. 1207, 12 L.Ed.2d 233 (1964), the Court ruled that it would not "imply" a waiver of a state's

sovereign immunity. In that case, the Court held that neither the Trademark Remedy Clarification Act nor Florida's activities in interstate commerce constituted a waiver of Florida's sovereign immunity.

98. 527 U.S. 706, 119 S.Ct. 2240, 144 L.Ed.2d 636(1999). *Alden* was decided the same day as two other federalism cases, Florida Prepaid Postsecondary Education Expense Board v. College Savings Bank, 527 U.S. 627, 119 S.Ct. 2199, 144 L.Ed.2d 575 (1999), and College Savings Bank v. Florida Prepaid Postsecondary Education Expense Board, 527 U.S. 666, 119 S.Ct. 2219, 144 L.Ed.2d 605 (1999).

99. Seminole Tribe of Florida v. Florida, 517 U.S. 44, 116 S.Ct. 1114, 134 L.Ed.2d 252 (1996).

100. Kennedy, J., joined by Rehnquist, C.J., O'Connor, Scalia, & Thomas, JJ., filed the opinion of the Court. Souter, J., filed a dissenting opinion, joined by Stevens, Ginsburg, & Breyer, JJ. He argued that the majority's conception of state sovereign immunity is neither true "to history nor to the structure of the Constitution," is "indefensible," and "probably [will be] fleeting."

The majority readily acknowledged that the text of the Eleventh Amendment did not control this case.[101] Instead, the Court held that "the powers delegated to Congress under Article I do not include the power to subject nonconsenting States to private suits for damages in state courts."[102] Later the Court reemphasized this point: "[W]e hold that the States retain immunity from private suit in their own courts, an immunity beyond the congressional power to abrogate by Article I legislation."[103]

The majority examined the debates surrounding the ratification of the Constitution and concluded that the states' sovereign immunity does not derive from the Eleventh Amendment and is not limited by the Eleventh Amendment. Instead, the states enjoyed this sovereign immunity *before* the ratification of the Constitution, and they retain this immunity today, "either literally or by virtue of their admission into the Union upon an equal footing with the other States."[104] Congress approved the Eleventh Amendment "not to change but to restore the original constitutional design."[105] As a matter of state dignity, the "immunity of a sovereign in its own courts have always been understood to be within the sole control of the sovereign itself."[106]

One must be careful not to read too much into *Alden*. Neither *Alden* nor other sovereignty immunity cases repeal the supremacy clause.[107] The case is an important one, but *Alden* also made clear that the state's constitutional privilege to assert its sovereign immunity in its own courts does not give a state the right to disregard the Constitution or a valid federal law. First, states may consent to suit in their own courts, just like the Federal Government does. In addition, this immunity belongs to the states themselves, but not to lesser entities within a state, such as municipalities.[108]

In addition, plaintiffs can continue to seek relief against state officers under *Ex parte Young*,[109] for injunctive or declaratory relief or for money damages when sued in their individual capacities.[110]

Also, a state's sovereign immunity does not prevent the Federal Government itself from instituting suing the state to enforce federal law. Under the Constitution, "the States consented to suits brought by other States or by the Federal Government."[111] The decision of the United States to sue Maine on behalf of the wronged employees, would have indicated that "the National Government must itself deem the case of specific importance to take

---

101. In earlier decisions, the Court had said that the Eleventh Amendment is inapplicable in state courts. E.g., Maine v. Thiboutot, 448 U.S. 1, 9, n. 7, 100 S.Ct. 2502, 2507, n. 7, 65 L.Ed.2d 555 (1980): "No Eleventh Amendment question is present, of course, where an action is brought in a state court since the Amendment, by its terms, restrains only '[t]he Judicial power of the United States.'"

Hilton v. South Carolina Public Railways Commission, 502 U.S. 197, 204–05, 112 S.Ct. 560, 564, 116 L.Ed.2d 560 (1991); Will v. Michigan Dept. of State Police, 491 U.S. 58, 63, 109 S.Ct. 2304, 2308, 105 L.Ed.2d 45 (1989); Atascadero State Hospital v. Scanlon, 473 U.S. 234, 239–40 n. 2, 105 S.Ct. 3142, 3146 n. 2, 87 L.Ed.2d 171 (1985).

See also, Nevada v. Hall, 440 U.S. 410, 418–21, 99 S.Ct. 1182, 1187–89, 59 L.Ed.2d 416 (1979). *Hall* distinguished a state's immunity from suit in federal court (which the U.S. Constitution does not allow) from its immunity from suit in the courts of other states (which the U.S. Constitution does allow). 440 U.S. at 420–21, 99 S.Ct. at 1188.

102. 527 U.S. at 712, 119 S.Ct. at 2246.

103. 527 U.S. at 754, 119 S.Ct. at 2266.

104. 527 U.S. at 713, 119 S.Ct. at 2247. On the "equal footing doctrine," see § 3.6.

105. 527 U.S. at 722, 119 S.Ct. at 2251.

106. 527 U.S. at 749, 119 S.Ct. at 2264.

107. In two other cases, decided the same day as *Alden*, the Court reaffirmed that section 5 of the Fourteenth Amendment gives Congress the power to create causes of action against the state to enforce the Fourteenth Amendment, but found that Congress did not properly exercise this power. College Savings Bank v. Florida Prepaid Postsecondary Education Expense Board, 527 U.S. 666, 119 S.Ct. 2219, 144 L.Ed.2d 605 (1999) (5 to 4) (Scalia, J., for the Court); Florida Prepaid Postsecondary Education Expense Board v. College Savings Bank, 527 U.S. 627, 119 S.Ct. 2199, 144 L.Ed.2d 575 (1999) (5 to 4) (Rehnquist, J., for the Court). See, Ronald D. Rotunda, The Implications of the New Commerce Clause Jurisprudence: An Evolutionary or Revolutionary Court?, 55 Arkansas Law Review 795 (2003).

108. 527 U.S. at 756, 119 S.Ct. at 2267.

109. 209 U.S. 123, 28 S.Ct. 441, 52 L.Ed. 714 (1908).

110. 527 U.S. at 757, 119 S.Ct. at 2267–68.

111. 527 U.S. at 755, 119 S.Ct. at 2267, citing Principality of Monaco v. Mississippi, 292 U.S. 313, 328–29, 54 S.Ct. 745, 750, 78 L.Ed. 1282 (1934).

against the State...."[112] Yet even though the Federal Government has "despite specific statutory authorization" to commence such a suit, it chose not to send even one Assistant U.S. Attorney to prosecute this litigation.[113]

Congress could enact a federal criminal statute that would apply to state actors, such as state prosecutors, state marshals, and so forth, that would impose severe criminal penalties for any state officials who violate federal statutes dealing with the overtime provisions at issue in *Alden*. Congress has ample tools at its disposal to ensure compliance with federal law, but it must respect the sovereignty of the states when using those tools.

Nothing in *Alden* alters the scope of federal power under the Civil War Amendments. As *Alden* specifically stated: "Congress may authorize private suits against nonconsenting States pursuant to its § 5 enforcement power" in order to protect those rights found within section 1 of the Fourteenth Amendment.[114] In addition, Congress can use its spending power to secure (to pay) the states to voluntarily consent to suit.[115]

§ 2.12 Case or Controversy and Related Doctrines

(a) Introduction

Article III, section 2 of the Constitution confines federal court jurisdiction to "cases" and "controversies."[1] In addition to its constitutional meaning, this requirement has also

prompted a nonconstitutional doctrine of judicial self-restraint, which is a significant, self-imposed limitation on judicial review.

(b) Advisory Opinions

Although the framers never accepted a proposal authorizing the President and the House and Senate to obtain advisory opinions from the Supreme Court,[2] the Justices, very early in the history of the Supreme Court, rendered advisory legal opinions in the form of letters to the executive.

As early as 1790, Chief Justice John Jay and a minority of the other Justices gave legal advice to President Washington. In response to his letter, they wrote that they thought the requirement of their riding circuit was unconstitutional.[3] Washington was apparently unmoved, the circuit riding continued, and when the practice was challenged in litigation over a decade later, the Court upheld circuit riding as justified by historical precedent. It did not refer to its earlier correspondence.[4]

Probably one of the most famous instances of letters to the President concerning the constitutionality of a practice was referred to in *Hayburn's Case*.[5] In a footnote to the opinion the court reporter cited letters that two circuit courts wrote to the President, objecting on constitutional grounds to the provisions of a particular statute.[6] The Court avoided any constitutional confrontation because Congress amended the statute prior to the decision, so the case was dismissed.[7] Nonetheless the case is significant for it reflected the view of several

---

112. 527 U.S. at 759–60, 119 S.Ct. at 2269.

113. 527 U.S. at 759, 119 S.Ct. at 2269, citing 29 U.S.C.A. § 216(c).

114. See §§ 19.1–19.5.

115. 527 U.S. at 755, 119 S.Ct. at 2267, citing South Dakota v. Dole, 483 U.S. 203, 107 S.Ct. 2793, 97 L.Ed.2d 171 (1987). See § 5.7.

§ 2.12

1. There is really no difference between "case" or "controversy" except that the latter may be narrower in meaning, including only civil cases. Aetna Life Insurance Co. v. Haworth, 300 U.S. 227, 239, 57 S.Ct. 461, 463, 81 L.Ed. 617 (1937).

2. I. M. Farrand, The Records of the Federal Convention at 1787, at 340–341 (1937).

3. H. Hart & H. Wechsler's The Federal Courts and the Federal System 68 (2d ed. 1973), citing 4 Am.Jurist 294 (1830); 2 J. Story, Commentaries on the Constitution

§ 1579 n. 1 (5th ed. Bigelow 1891). See also 1 C. Warren, The Supreme Court in United States History 108–111 (1926).

4. Stuart v. Laird, 5 U.S. (1 Cranch) 299, 309, 2 L.Ed. 115 (1803). For other examples of such unofficial letters, see generally, Westin, Out–of–Court Commentary by United States Supreme Court Justices, 1790–1962: Of Free Speech and Judicial Lockjaw, 62 Colum.L.Rev. 633 (1962).

5. 2 U.S. (2 Dall. 409) 408, 1 L.Ed. 436 (1792). Cf. Tutun v. United States, 270 U.S. 568, 46 S.Ct. 425, 70 L.Ed. 738 (1926). See Rotunda, Congressional Power to Restrict the Jurisdiction of the Lower Federal Courts and the Problem of School Busing, 64 Georgetown L.J. 839, 844–847 (1976).

6. 2 U.S. (2 Dall.) at 410–413 n. (a).

7. 2 U.S. (2 Dall.) at 410 & n. (a).

Justices who were refusing, on constitutional grounds, to execute a statute on Congress' terms over a decade before the Court decided *Marbury v. Madison.*[8]

One year after *Hayburn's Case*, there was an important exchange of correspondence between Chief Justice Jay and the Associate Justices and President Washington's Secretary of State, Thomas Jefferson. The Court's letter concluded that the federal courts may not constitutionally give advisory opinions:

> [T]he lines of separation [are] drawn by the Constitution between the three departments of the government. These being in certain respects checks upon each other, and our being judges in a court in the last resort, are considerations which afford strong arguments against the propriety of our extra-judicially deciding the questions [previously asked], especially as the power given by the Constitution to the President, of calling on the heads of departments for opinions [Art. II, § 2], seems to have been *purposely* as well as expressly united to the *executive* departments.[9]

The problem of advisory opinions and the case or controversy requirement formed the theoretical framework for *Muskrat v. United States.*[10] In 1902 Congress enacted a statute providing, as of a certain date, for a transfer of Cherokee property from tribal ownership to individual ownership by citizens of the Cherokee Nation. The statute also imposed certain restrictions on alienation of this land. Two later acts increased the number of Cherokees permitted to enroll, and increased the restrictions on alienation. Plaintiffs sued to have these subsequent statutes declared unconstitutional because they increased the number of Indians entitled to share in the final distribution of property. Other plaintiffs also sued to have the restraints on alienation removed.

Plaintiffs claimed that the restrictions on alienation and the increase in the number of enrollees constituted a taking of property without just compensation.

A special act of Congress authorized plaintiffs to institute suit in the Court of Claims to determine the validity of these acts "in so far as said acts . . . attempt to increase or extend the restrictions upon alienation, encumbrance, or the right to lease the allotments of lands . . . or to increase the number of persons entitled to share in the final distribution of lands and funds. . . ."[11] The state gave jurisdiction to the Court of Claims with a right of appeal in the Supreme Court. The United States, under the statutory scheme, was the party defendant, and if the plaintiffs were successful the statute authorized the government to pay the attorneys fees of the plaintiffs.

The Supreme Court reversed the Court of Claims and directed it to dismiss for want of jurisdiction. The government purported to be the defendant, but it had no interest in the outcome of this litigation. Plaintiffs do not "assert a property right as against the Government, or . . . demand compensation for alleged wrongs because of action upon its part."[12] The Court concluded that the jurisdictional act was merely an attempt to provide for a test in the Supreme Court of the validity of an act of Congress, without regard to the requirement of a case or controversy. That attempt was unconstitutional.

The power to declare a law unconstitutional exists only because the Court finds the law that one of the parties has relied on to be in conflict with "the fundamental law." In such a case, the Court rules the act unconstitutional because, in the course of deciding the actual controversy, it must choose the fundamental law over the statute. There is otherwise no

---

8. 5 U.S. (1 Cranch) 137, 2 L.Ed. 60 (1803). Subsequent cases have approved and relied on the footnote in *Hayburn's Case* as a correct interpretation of the Constitution. See Muskrat v. United States, 219 U.S. 346, 352–353, 31 S.Ct. 250, 252, 55 L.Ed. 246 (1911); United States v. Ferreira, 54 U.S. (13 How.) 40, 49–51, 14 L.Ed. 40 (1851).

9. See 3 H. Johnston, Correspondence and Public Papers of John Jay 486–489 (1891).

See generally, Judge Warren, citing Treatise in Ursida v. Milwaukee Crane and Services Co., 674 F.Supp. 278, 279 (E.D.Wis.1987).

10. 219 U.S. 346, 31 S.Ct. 250, 55 L.Ed. 246 (1911).

11. 219 U.S. at 350, 31 S.Ct. at 251.

12. 219 U.S. at 361, 31 S.Ct. at 255.

general power to revise actions of Congress.[13]

Part of the law in question in the *Muskrat* case—the restriction on alienation—was self-executing. If an Indian were to sell his land to a private party in violation of the alienation provisions, the case of the Indian versus the private person would create an appropriate case testing the constitutionality of the alienation provisions. The court might have to decide, for example, the claim of the Indian that the land should be returned if the sale was not valid. The private party could also seek a declaratory judgment that his title was valid, if a declaratory judgment procedure existed.

The section of the statute relating to the increasing of the Indian enrollments was not self-executing. Federal officers had to add to the list of enrollees. The Indians, in another case to which *Muskrat* specifically referred,[14] had already brought suit in a lower federal court to enjoin the Secretaries of Interior and Treasury from increasing the enrollments. The following year, that other case came to the Supreme Court for review, and the Court affirmed the lower court decision upholding the acts.[15] Jurisdiction should lie in that case because there was an actual controversy: parties injured by the action of government officials sought to enjoin those officials from carrying out statutorily mandated duties on the ground that the statute was unconstitutional.

The jurisdictional act that *Muskrat* invalidated was poorly drafted, justifying the Supreme Court's decision. The act only gave the Court jurisdiction to decide the constitutional issue. In a real case or controversy the Court

might never reach that issue: it might decide, for example, that the plaintiffs were not really Cherokee Indians, or go off on another, narrower ground. A more carefully written statute could have created the appropriate test case.[16] *Muskrat* shows that Congress cannot grant jurisdiction to give what is really an advisory opinion, even though the Court might reach the constitutional issue if an appropriate case presents it.

Declaratory Relief. We now know that coercive relief is not an essential element of the case or controversy requirement. That is, if there is an actual case or controversy, the court may issue only declaratory relief.[17] Thus the constitutionality of a declaratory judgment statute is now accepted.[18] A federal court may even issue prospective rulings, but, if it does, the relief must at least apply to the parties before it so that the opinion not be merely advisory.[19]

The Court of Claims, at the time of the *Muskrat* decision, was an Article I Court, not a Court created pursuant to Article III.[20] Article III does not bind Article I courts, so they may give advisory opinions. In fact, until the statute was changed and the Supreme Court held that the Court of Claims had become an Article III Court, the Court of Claims routinely fulfilled a congressional reference jurisdiction by rendering advisory opinions to Congress.[21]

The Supreme Court did not explain why it did not uphold the part of the *Muskrat* jurisdictional statute giving, in effect, the Court of Claims (at that time, an Article I court) the power to render an advisory opinion. The Su-

---

13. 219 U.S. at 361, 31 S.Ct. at 255.

14. "Nor can it make any difference that the petitioners had brought suits in the Supreme Court of the District of Columbia to enjoin the Secretary of Interior from carrying into effect the legislation subsequent to the act of July 1, 1902, which suits were pending when the jurisdictional act here involved was passed." 219 U.S. at 362, 31 S.Ct. at 256.

15. Gritts v. Fisher, 224 U.S. 640, 32 S.Ct. 580, 56 L.Ed. 928 (1912).

16. Cf. South Carolina v. Katzenbach, 383 U.S. 301, 335, 86 S.Ct. 803, 822, 15 L.Ed.2d 769 (1966) (test case procedure for testing the validity of the Voting Rights Act of 1965 upheld.)

17. See 28 U.S.C.A. §§ 2201–02 (Federal Declaratory Judgment Act) upheld in Aetna Life Insurance Co. of

Hartford, Conn. v. Haworth, 300 U.S. 227, 57 S.Ct. 461, 81 L.Ed. 617 (1937); See, Borchard, Declaratory Judgments (2d ed. 1941).

18. Aetna Life Insurance Co. v. Haworth, 300 U.S. 227, 239–240, 57 S.Ct. 461, 463–64, 81 L.Ed. 617 (1937).

19. E.g., Stovall v. Denno, 388 U.S. 293, 301, 87 S.Ct. 1967, 1972, 18 L.Ed.2d 1199 (1967).

20. Glidden Co. v. Zdanok, 370 U.S. 530, 82 S.Ct. 1459, 8 L.Ed.2d 671 (1962), rehearing denied 371 U.S. 854, 83 S.Ct. 14, 9 L.Ed.2d 93 (1962).

21. Glidden Co. v. Zdanok, 370 U.S. 530, 579–583, 82 S.Ct. 1459, 1487–90, 8 L.Ed.2d 671 (1962), rehearing denied 371 U.S. 854, 83 S.Ct. 14, 9 L.Ed.2d 93 (1962).

preme Court must have thought that the jurisdictional statute was not severable, that is, Congress did not want only the Court of Claims opinion as to the constitutionality of the statute; it wanted the Supreme Court's final judgment.

Objections to Advisory Opinions. While *Muskrat* reaffirmed the requirement of an actual case or controversy, it did not articulate some of the reasons justifying this limitation on the jurisdictional powers of Article III Courts. If we know the reasons for the rule, that should help us interpret and apply it. Several reasons are apparent.[22]

First, advisory opinions may not be binding on the parties. If the parties do not have to accept the advice that the Court gives, then its power is eroded. We have seen that when Chief Justice Jay and several associate Justices wrote President Washington contending that the requirement of riding circuit was unconstitutional, he was unpersuaded and the circuit riding continued. It can do the Court no good if parties get in the habit of not obeying it.

Advisory opinions also undermine the basic theory behind the adversary system. Suits for advisory opinions may more likely be collusive or the parties, anxious to obtain a certain advisory opinion, may be less likely to fully brief all of the relevant issues. Once again Jay's letter to Washington on riding circuit is instructive. When the actual issue came before the Court in concrete and real litigation, when the Court faced a precise case, it decided contrary to its earlier informal opinion.[23]

If the Court does not decide an issue until there is a genuine and real controversy before it, the Court might be able to avoid the constitutional issue entirely and decide the case on narrower grounds. Advisory opinions unnecessarily force the Court to reach out and decide complex constitutional issues. The jurisdictional statute in *Muskrat* prohibited this narrower alternative.

Recall that Chief Justice Marshall in *Marbury v. Madison*[24] emphasized that judicial review is a reluctant power, only used because the Court must exercise it in the course of deciding the litigation at hand. He said that the duty of the judicial department is to "say what the law is." If the Court looks to the law, it must look to all of it, including the written Constitution. Giving advisory opinions on matters of constitutional law is a far cry from a reluctant power, exercised only because the facts of the case force the Court to interpret and apply the Constitution.

The power to render such an advisory opinion is really a greater power than the reluctant judicial review that Marshall justified, because it increases the situations where the Court can exercise this significant power to intrude on the democratic process. The framers specifically rejected giving this power to Article III judges, because it is inappropriate for a democracy to give unelected judges the right to unnecessarily intrude themselves by freezing into Constitutional law their views, divorced from the need to decide any concrete case.[25]

Extrajudicial Duties by Federal Judges and the United States Sentencing Commission.

Article III judges have long served on nonjudicial, non-Article III commissions and engaged in non-Article III activities when not wearing their judicial hats. For example, John Jay, while our first Chief Justice, was ambassador to England. There he negotiated the Jay Treaty. When the Senate confirmed his nomination as ambassador it rejected a resolution condemning Jay's proposed extra-judicial ser-

---

22. See, Frankfurter, Advisory Opinions, 37 Harv. L.Rev. 1002 (1924). These reasons have not precluded some states from adopting the practice for their state courts, though they have sought to limit the power to avoid these objections. Comment, The State Advisory Opinion in Perspective, 44 Ford L.Rev. 81 (1975). Cf. Rotunda, The Public Interest Appellant: Limitations on the Right of Competent Parties to Settle Litigation Out of Court, 66 Nw.U.L.Rev. 199, 214–20 (1971).

23. Stuart v. Laird, 5 U.S. (1 Cranch) 299, 309, 2 L.Ed. 115 (1803).

24. 5 U.S. (1 Cranch) 137, 2 L.Ed. 60 (1803).

25. The framers did not accept a proposal to give the Supreme Court power to issue advisory opinions. 1 M. Farrand, The Records of the Federal Convention of 1787, at 340–41 (1937).

vice as "contrary to the spirit of the Constitution."[26]

Rule Making. In 1825, the Court held that Congress—enacting pursuant to the powers of the Necessary and Proper Clause—may confer rule making powers on federal judges.[27] For example, Congress may authorize federal judges to promulgate the Federal Rules of Civil Procedure.[28] Congress may also authorize the Supreme Court to establish rules of conduct for its own business and to promulgate rules of procedure for criminal cases or rules for lower federal courts in bankruptcy cases.[29] Similarly Congress may authorize the Supreme Court to revise the Federal Rules of Evidence.[30]

Sentencing Commission. In 1984 Congress enacted the Sentencing Reform Act,[31] in response to serious disparities among prison sentences by different judges operating in an indeterminate sentencing system. The Sentencing Reform Act created the United States Sentencing Commission, with seven voting members, at least three of whom must be Article III federal judges chosen from a list of six judges recommended by the Judicial Conference of the United States.[32] Congress authorized the Sentencing Commission to issue binding Sentencing Guidelines establishing a range of determinate sentences for all categories of federal offenses and for defendants according to various specific and detailed factors.

The Act, in effect, consolidated the power that had been exercised jointly by the sentencing judge and the Parole Commission to decide what punishment the convicted defendant should suffer. The Act stated that it rejected imprisonment as a means to promote rehabilitation. However, it acknowledged that punishment should serve retributive, educational, deterrent, and incapacitative goals.

The Act made all sentences determinative. The Sentencing Commission's "guidelines" are, in fact, binding on the courts. Although the trial judge has discretion to depart from the guidelines, the trial judge must find aggravating or mitigating factors, and give "the specific reason" for departing from the guidelines. There is limited appellate review of the sentence.

Mistretta v. United States[33] Court rejected multiple challenges to the constitutionality of the United States Sentencing Commission. Congress provided that at least three federal judges should serve on the Commission and share their commission authority with non-Article III judges. Petitioner claimed that Article III judges could not undertake such extrajudicial activities without violating the "case or controversy" requirements of Article III; that Congress had granted the Sentencing Commission excessive legislative discretion and thus violated the delegation of powers; that Congress violated the Separation of Powers; and that the power of the President *to remove* from the Commission any member for good cause, *including an Article III judge,* violated Article III and undermined the integrity of the Judicial Branch.

The Court concluded that the Sentencing Commission was an unusual hybrid, and that the various challenges to it were not entirely without difficulty, but that, in the end, the Commission should be held to be constitutional. In upholding the constitutionality of the Sentencing Commission, the Court said that the Constitution does not prevent Congress from some non-Article III duties to Article III

---

26. C. Warren, The Supreme Court in United States History 119 (rev. ed. 1926). See also, Jeffrey Shaman, Steven Lubet, & James Alfini, Judicial Conduct and Ethics § 9.04 (1990).

27. Wayman v. Southard, 23 U.S. (10 Wheat.) 1, 22, 6 L.Ed. 253 (1825) (Marshall, C.J., for the Court).

28. Sibbach v. Wilson & Co., 312 U.S. 1, 61 S.Ct. 422, 85 L.Ed. 479 (1941); Hanna v. Plumer, 380 U.S. 460, 85 S.Ct. 1136, 14 L.Ed.2d 8 (1965).

29. See, Kennedy, Some Comments About the Rules of Bankruptcy Procedure Under the Bankruptcy Reform Act, 85 Commercial Reform Act, 85 Commercial L. J. (1980).

30. E.g., Moore & Bendix, Congress, Evidence and Rulemaking, 84 Yale L.J. 9 (1974).

31. 18 U.S.C.A. § 3551 et seq. & 28 U.S.C.A. §§ 991–98. See, Senate Report No. 98–225 (1983), U.S. Code Cong. & Admin. News 3182 (1984).

32. See, 28 U.S.C.A. § 991(a).

33. 488 U.S. 361, 109 S.Ct. 647, 102 L.Ed.2d 714 (1989). The decision was eight to one.

judges. The constitutional question is whether the particular extrajudicial assignment "undermines the integrity of the Judicial Branch."[34]

Congress may delegate to the Judicial Branch nonadjudicatory functions that do not trench upon the prerogatives of another Branch and that are appropriate to the central mission of the Judiciary.... Because of their close relation to the central mission of the Judicial Branch, such extrajudicial activities are consonant with the integrity of the Branch and are not more appropriate for another Branch.[35]

The Court concluded that the President's removal power does not violate the Constitution. The President can remove members of the this Commission, including the judicial members, only for "good cause," such as neglect of duty or malfeasance in office. The President's removal power over the members of the Commission, including those members who are also Article III judges, does not authorize or diminish the status of Article III judges as judges. The President cannot affect either the tenure or compensation of Article III judges, even those who are also on the Commission.[36] Even if removed from the Commission, the Article III judges remain Article III judges. In short, this provision of the Sentencing Commission Act does not prevent the Judicial Branch from performing its constitutionally assigned function of fairly adjudicating cases and controversies.

The law creating the Sentencing Commission provided that it was "an independent commission in the judicial branch of the United States." This statutory proviso did not invalidate the law, but the reasoning of *Mistretta* suggests that this portion of its decision should not have much growing power. The judge's

unique role and experience in sentencing is not readily transferrable to other issues. *Mistretta*, for example, should not allow Congress to create a Commission (with Article III judges among it members), and charge this Commission to make rules governing what is "free speech" for purposes of the First Amendment. That should raise significant "case" or "controversy" questions.

Mistretta drew but one dissent, Justice Scalia, who filed a vigorous and strongly worded opinion. He concluded that what was wrong with the Sentencing Commission was not that there was a commingling between the branches but that Congress had created in the Commission a "new branch" of the Government, a "sort of junior-varsity Congress."[37] In his view, the agency that Congress created exercised no governmental powers other than the making of laws; the Commission is undemocratic because it is divorced from any responsibility for execution of the law or adjudication of private rights under the law.

Scalia foresaw Congressional creation of other, supposedly expert bodies, insulated from the political process: "How tempting to create an expert Medical Commission (mostly MDs with perhaps a few PhDs in moral philosophy) to dispose of such thorny 'no-win' political issues as the withholding of life-support systems in federally funded hospitals, or the use of fetal tissue for research."[38] Congress, he argued, should not be able to avoid its responsibilities, and the Court should not interpret the Constitution to allow the political branches to dodge their accountability.

(c) Mootness and Collusiveness

Article III Courts may not decide moot questions, only actual cases or controversies.

34. Mistretta v. United States, 488 U.S. 361, 402, 109 S.Ct. 647, 671, 102 L.Ed.2d 714 (1989).

35. Mistretta v. United States, 488 U.S. 361, 385–91, 109 S.Ct. 647, 663–64, 102 L.Ed.2d 714 (1989).

36. Commission members receive the salary of a court of appeals judge. Hence, if a district court judge were appointed to the Commission, he would receive an increase in salary, and if the President removed him from the Commission, that district court judge would receive a *decrease* in salary. The Court in *Mistretta* said: "We do not

address the hypothetical constitutional question whether, under the Compensation Clause of Article III, a district judge removed from the Commission must continue to be paid the higher salary." 488 U.S. at 411, n. 32, 109 S.Ct. at 674 n. 32.

37. 488 U.S. at 427, 109 S.Ct. at 683.

38. 488 U.S. at 421, 109 S.Ct. at 680 (Scalia, J., dissenting).

A justiciable controversy is thus distinguished from a difference or dispute of a hypothetical or abstract character; from one that is academic or moot. The controversy must be definite and concrete, touching the legal relations of parties having adverse legal interests. It must be a real and substantial controversy admitting of specific relief through a decree of a conclusive character, as distinguished from an opinion advising what the law would be upon a hypothetical state of facts.[39]

If the case is moot "there is no subject matter on which the judgment of the court's order can operate."[40]

While the Supreme Court has sometimes stated that mootness is a constitutional limitation,[41] it has at other times been willing to relax the mootness rule so that the requirement will not be so "rigid" as to prevent the review of important constitutional issues.[42] Mootness should therefore properly be regard-

ed as rooted in part in the constitutional limitation of the judicial power to cases and controversies, and in part rooted in a rule of self-restraint, a rule that the Court relax at times. In deciding mootness issues, the Court is not always clear when it is deciding based on self-restraint, or deciding based on the command of Article III.

A case may become moot for several reasons.[43] The controversy must normally exist at every stage of the proceeding, including the appellate stages.[44] Thus, a case that was not initially moot may become moot because the law has changed;[45] or, because defendant has paid moneys owed and no longer wishes to appeal, notwithstanding plaintiff's desire to obtain a higher court ruling.[46] A case may also become moot because allegedly wrongful behavior has passed, and could not reasonably be expected to recur;[47] or, because a challenged statute no longer can affect the litigant.

---

39. Aetna Life Insurance Co. v. Haworth, 300 U.S. 227, 240–241, 57 S.Ct. 461, 463–64, 81 L.Ed. 617 (1937).

40. Ex parte Baez, 177 U.S. 378, 390, 20 S.Ct. 673, 677, 44 L.Ed. 813 (1900). "Federal courts lack jurisdiction to decide moot cases because their constitutional authority extends only to actual cases or controversies."

41. E.g., St. Pierre v. United States, 319 U.S. 41, 42, 63 S.Ct. 910, 911, 87 L.Ed. 1199 (1943); Liner v. Jafco, Inc., 375 U.S. 301, 306 n. 3, 84 S.Ct. 391, 394 n. 3, 11 L.Ed.2d 347 (1964).

42. Roe v. Wade, 410 U.S. 113, 125, 93 S.Ct. 705, 713, 35 L.Ed.2d 147 (1973), rehearing denied 410 U.S. 959, 93 S.Ct. 1409, 35 L.Ed.2d 694 (1973). See Wirtz v. Glass Bottle Blowers Association, Local 153, 389 U.S. 463, 474, 88 S.Ct. 643, 649–50, 19 L.Ed.2d 705 (1968) (public interest in deciding issue helps prevent case from being moot), on remand to 405 F.2d 176 (3d Cir.1968).

43. See Judge H. Franklin Waters, citing Treatise in Gay and Lesbian Students Association v. Gohn, 656 F.Supp. 1045, 1049 (W.D.Ark.1987), reversed on other grounds 850 F.2d 361 (8th Cir.1988).

44. United States v. Munsingwear, Inc., 340 U.S. 36, 39, 71 S.Ct. 104, 106–07, 95 L.Ed. 36 (1950): "The established practice of the Court in dealing with a civil case from a court in the federal system which has become moot while on its way here or pending our decision on the merits is to reverse or vacate the judgment below and remand with a direction to dismiss." (footnote omitted, citing cases, and noting that as to federal civil cases "there are but few exceptions to this practice in recent years.")

Minnesota Public Interest Research Group v. Selective Service System, 747 F.2d 1204, 1205 (8th Cir.1984) (per curiam), citing treatise.

45. Normal Rule to Remand When Case Becomes Moot Because of Change in Legal Framework. See,

Lewis v. Continental Bank Corp., 494 U.S. 472, 110 S.Ct. 1249, 108 L.Ed.2d 400 (1990), hold that case that Illinois bank holding company brought attacking a Florida law became moot when Congress enacted changes to federal Bank Holding Company Act. The normal practice in such cases is not to vacate the judgment but to vacate and remand for further proceedings so that the parties may, if necessary, amend their pleadings or develop the record more fully.

United States v. Alaska S.S. Co., 253 U.S. 113, 40 S.Ct. 448, 64 L.Ed. 808 (1920) (pending appeal, Congress passed new law that makes the original case moot because it necessitates changes in the forms of bills of lading required by ICC; the form of these bills of lading was the subject matter of the original case).

Contrast Zablocki v. Redhail, 434 U.S. 374, 382, n. 9, 98 S.Ct. 673, 679 n. 9, 54 L.Ed.2d 618 (1978) (revision of state law under constitutional attack does not moot controversy because by its terms the new statute is to be enforced only if enforcement of the old statute is enjoined by court order).

46. E.g., California v. San Pablo & Tulare R.R., 149 U.S. 308, 313–314, 13 S.Ct. 876, 878, 37 L.Ed. 747 (1893) (any obligation of the railroad to pay to the State the sums sued for in the case together with interest, penalties, and costs, has been extinguished by the offer to pay and the deposit of the money in a bank; thus the case is moot).

47. SEC v. Medical Committee for Human Rights, 404 U.S. 403, 406, 92 S.Ct. 577, 579, 30 L.Ed.2d 560 (1972) (Dow Chemical Co. acquiesces in a request to include a shareholder's proposal for a corporate charter Amendment in Dow's proxy material, and the proposal receives less than 3% of the voting shareholder's support; Dow may thus exclude the proposal for a three-year period, and it is

For example, a law regulating rights of minors becomes moot when the complaining party, through lapse of time, is no longer within the age brackets governed by the statute;[48] or the party has died.[49]

Voluntary Cessation of Challenged Practice. To prevent either party from creating a technical mootness as a sham to deprive the Court of jurisdiction, the Court has created various exceptions to the doctrine. Thus, if a party voluntarily stops allegedly illegal conduct, that change does not make the case moot, if the defendant would be free to return to his old ways. Defendant must show that "there is no reasonable expectation that the wrong will be repeated."[50]

If the plaintiff challenges an action, and the defendant responds by stopping that action but then engaging in substantially similar action, the Court will not treat the case as moot. For example, when some general contractors challenged a city ordinance preferring minority owned businesses in awarding city contracts, the city repealed the ordinance and replaced it with another one. But the new law still disadvantaged the contractors, although to a lesser degree. The Court held that the case was not moot.[51]

Vacating Lower Court Judgements When They Become Moot on Appeal. If a case is brought in the *federal* system and then becomes moot on appeal, the Supreme Court practice is to vacate the appellate court judg-

---

extremely doubtful that at the end of that period the shareholders will resubmit the proposal and Dow will refuse it; thus, the decision of the Court of Appeals (overruling the arguments of the SEC) that it had jurisdiction to review the SEC's determination not to oppose Dow's initial refusal of the shareholders' proxy request is now moot).

48. Atherton Mills v. Johnston, 259 U.S. 13, 42 S.Ct. 422, 66 L.Ed. 814 (1922) (father and minor son sued on April 15, 1919, to enjoin corporation from firing son in order that the corporation could comply with the Child Labor Tax Act governing child labor between 14 and 16 years of age; the case was argued before the Supreme Court on December 10, 1919, and restored to the docket for reargument on June 6, 1921, reargued on March 7, 1922, and decided on May 15, 1922. "The lapse of time since the case was heard and decided in the District Court has brought the minor, whose employment was the subject-matter of the suit, to an age which is not within the ages affected by the act. The act, even if valid, can not affect him further." 259 U.S. at 15, 42 S.Ct. at 423).

Child Labor Tax Case. There is historical evidence that, in a case unencumbered by the mootness issue in *Atherton Mills*, Justice Brandeis (and perhaps a majority of the Court at this time) would have upheld the child labor laws later invalidated in Bailey v. Drexel Furniture Co. (The *Child Labor Tax Case*), 259 U.S. 20, 42 S.Ct. 449, 66 L.Ed. 817 (1922). Alexander Bickel, The Unpublished Opinions of Mr. Justice Brandeis: The Supreme Court at Work 2–10 (1957). Contra, Clyde Spillenger, Reading the Judicial Canon: Alexander Bickel and the Book of Brandeis, 79 J. of American History 125–51 (June 1922).

49. Durham v. United States, 401 U.S. 481, 91 S.Ct. 858, 28 L.Ed.2d 200 (1971) (per curiam): "death pending direct review of a criminal conviction abates not only the appeal but also all proceedings had in the prosecution from its inception." (401 U.S. at 483, 91 S.Ct. at 860, footnote omitted). Cat's Meow, Inc. v. City of New Orleans, 720 So.2d 1186, 1193 (La.1998), Knoll, J., for the Court, quoting Treatise.

50. United States v. W. T. Grant Co., 345 U.S. 629, 633, 73 S.Ct. 894, 897, 97 L.Ed. 1303 (1953), quoting

United States v. Aluminum Co. of America, 148 F.2d 416, 448 (2d Cir.1945).

A statement of the party that it would not be economical for them to engage in challenged activity, is not, standing alone, sufficient "to satisfy the heavy burden of persuasion which we have held rests upon those in appellees' shoes." United States v. Concentrated Phosphate Export Association, Inc., 393 U.S. 199, 203, 89 S.Ct. 361, 364, 21 L.Ed.2d 344 (1968). But if a party asks the court for an injunction in a case where the other party has voluntarily stopped engaging in the allegedly wrongful conduct, then the court, on grounds of equitable discretion, may, refuse to issue the requested injunction even if the case is not moot. See SEC v. Harwyn Indus. Corp., 326 F.Supp. 943 (S.D.N.Y.1971).

Mootness and Standing Compared. The defendant has the "formidable burden" of persuading the court that a case is moot because subsequent events make it "absolutely clear" that the alleged wrongful acts could not reasonably be expected to recur. In contrast, if plaintiff sues to force compliance, plaintiff has the burden to establish standing by showing that the defendant's allegedly wrongful behavior will occur or continue and that the threatened injury is impending. Friends of the Earth, Inc. v. Laidlaw Environmental Services (TOC), Inc., 528 U.S. 167, 120 S.Ct. 693, 145 L.Ed.2d 610 (2000). Adarand Constructors, Inc. v. Slater, 528 U.S. 216, 120 S.Ct. 722, 145 L.Ed.2d 650 (2000)(per curiam).

There "are circumstances in which the prospect that a defendant will engage in (or resume) harmful conduct may be too speculative to support standing but not too speculative to overcome mootness." Friends of the Earth, Inc. v. Laidlaw Environmental Services (TOC), Inc., 528 U.S. 167, 170, 120 S.Ct. 693, 698, 145 L.Ed.2d 610 (2000). See also, 528 U.S. 167, 170, 120 S.Ct. 693, 699, 145 L.Ed.2d 610 (2000).

51. Northeastern Florida Chapter of the Associated General Contractors of America v. City of Jacksonville, 508 U.S. 656, 113 S.Ct. 2297, 124 L.Ed.2d 586 (1993), on remand 997 F.2d 835 (11th Cir.1993).

ment and remand to the lower court with instructions to dismiss the complaint. The case then has no binding effect on the parties.[52]

However, if the case had been brought in the *state* system and is now before the U.S. Supreme Court, the situation is different, because Article III and federal rules of self restraint do not bind state courts and because the Supreme Court has no supervisory power over state courts. The state constitution may give its courts the power to issue advisory opinion. Thus, if the case, originally brought in state court, becomes moot on appeal, the Supreme Court held in *Doremus* that it cannot decide the case; it must normally dismiss the appeal, but it will not require the state court to vacate the judgement or dismiss the complaint.[53]

However, the U.S. Supreme Court will not treat the case from the state court as moot in the situation where state judgement causes "direct, specific, and concrete injury" to the parties who petition for review, assuming that otherwise the requisites of a case or controversy are met.[54] Even though the plaintiffs would not have had standing if they had brought their case in federal court, they brought their case in state court. The state court ruled in their favor and adverse to the defendants. That judgement, in effect, supplies the requisite injury (and injury to the defendants), which prevents the case from being premature or moot for federal purposes. Thus, we have a paradox: *Doremus* remains good law for plain-

tiffs who lack standing and lose in state court on the merits of their claim, but *Doremus* is not good law for plaintiffs who lack standing and prevail in the state courts on the merits of their federal claim.

Case Moot if Court Cannot Fashion Any Effective Relief. A federal case is moot if it is impossible for the court to fashion any effective relief. Federal courts under Article III may not declare principles of law that cannot affect the case before it. However, if the court can grant some type of meaningful relief, the case is not moot even if the court cannot return the parties to the status quo ante.

Consider *Church of Scientology v. United States.*[55] The Church opposed an IRS subpoena of audio tapes of conversations between Church officials and their lawyers. While the case was on appeal, the state court clerk delivered copies of the taps to the IRS. The Court of Appeals ruled that the case was moot, but a unanimous Supreme Court reversed. The court cannot erase all information that the IRS may have obtained by listening to the tapes, but "a court can fashion *some* from of meaningful relief. . . ."[56] It might offer partial relief by ordering the IRS to destroy or return all copies of the tapes in its possession.

Actions Capable of Repetition Yet Evading Review. Another exception to the general mootness rule concerns those cases that are "capable of repetition, yet evading

52. Deakins v. Monaghan, 484 U.S. 193, 199, 108 S.Ct. 523, 528, 98 L.Ed.2d 529 (1988).

53. Doremus v. Board of Education, 342 U.S. 429, 434–35, 72 S.Ct. 394, 397–98, 96 L.Ed. 475 (1952).

54. ASARCO, Inc. v. Kadish, 490 U.S. 605, 109 S.Ct. 2037, 104 L.Ed.2d 696 (1989). In *ASARCO* state taxpayers and a state teachers' association brought suit in Arizona state court arguing that a state statute governing mineral leases was unconstitutional because it was inconsistent with the federal laws that had originally granted those lands to Arizona. Although the Court was evenly divided on the question whether the plaintiffs would have met the federal requirements for standing if that had originally sued in federal court, the Court concluded that it could properly review the decision below. In this case the defendants-petitioners alleged that the Arizona state court judgment caused them concrete injury, and they invoked the authority of federal courts for the first time when they sought Supreme Court review. The Court agreed with the defendants-petitioners that the state court decision posed

a "serious and immediate threat" to the continuing validity of the mineral leases by its holding that they were granted under improper procedures and an invalid law. 490 U.S. at 617–37, 109 S.Ct. at 2045–56. Although the plaintiffs-respondents would not have had standing to commence this suit in federal court, it was the defendants-petitioners, not the plaintiffs-respondents, who were attempting to invoke the federal judicial power by seeking U.S. Supreme Court review. The Court refused to vacate the state court order, for to do that would be imposing federal requirements on a state court. Instead the Court decided the issue relating to the mineral leases. (The Supreme Court, on the merits, agreed with the Arizona state court and held that the mineral leases were in conflict with federal law and hence the leases were invalid.)

55. 506 U.S. 9, 113 S.Ct. 447, 121 L.Ed.2d 313 (1992), on remand 984 F.2d 988 (9th Cir.1993).

56. 506 U.S. at 12, 113 S.Ct. at 450 (emphasis in original).

review." A mere "physical or theoretical possibility" is not enough to meet the test of "capable of repetition, yet evading review," otherwise any matter of short duration would be reviewable. There must be a "reasonable expectation" or a "demonstrable probability" that "the same controversy will recur involving the *same* complaining party."[57]

Such cases may be divided into two main categories. In one, the challenged order is so short that it will normally expire before review may be had. Such cases include short sentences in criminal cases,[58] short term orders of agencies that usually will come up again,[59] short term injunctions that may be repeated,[60] and similar circumstances.

In the second category, the challenged order is not short term, but the factual circumstances appear to make the order moot by the time of appeal. Election cases illustrate this problem.[61] To beat the election clock, the Court may issue its decision as soon as possible prior to the election, with the opinion coming later.[62] Or, the Court may decide the issue after the election, if the issue is otherwise capable of repetition yet evading review.[63]

Collateral Consequences. Collateral consequences may prevent a case from being moot, even though some of the original relief requested may be moot.[64] A case is not moot as to the party defendant if another party paid the joint judgment rendered against them and then demanded a contribution from the other party. Then, the party "is still subject to a suit because of the original judgment as to its liability."[65]

57. Murphy v. Hunt, 455 U.S. 478, 482, 102 S.Ct. 1181, 1183, 71 L.Ed.2d 353 (1982) (per curiam) (emphasis added).

58. E.g., Sibron v. New York, 392 U.S. 40, 52–53, 88 S.Ct. 1889, 1897, 20 L.Ed.2d 917 (1968) (short sentence for "low visibility" minor offense).

See also Gannett Co., Inc. v. DePasquale, 443 U.S. 368, 377, 99 S.Ct. 2898, 2904, 61 L.Ed.2d 608 (1979) (a case is capable of repetition yet evading review if the challenged action—exclusion of reporters from pretrial hearing—is too short in its duration to be fully litigated prior to its cessation and there is reasonable expectation that the same complaining party would be subjected to the same action again).

59. E.g., Southern Pac. Terminal Co. v. Interstate Commerce Commission, 219 U.S. 498, 515, 31 S.Ct. 279, 283, 55 L.Ed. 310 (1911) (ICC rate order); SEC v. Sloan, 436 U.S. 103, 108, 98 S.Ct. 1702, 1706–07, 56 L.Ed.2d 148 (1978).

60. Carroll v. President and Commissioners of Princess Anne, 393 U.S. 175, 89 S.Ct. 347, 21 L.Ed.2d 325 (1968). After a white supremacist organization held a public rally, officials of Princess Anne and of Somerset County obtained an ex parte restraining order from local court to prevent the next planned rally, which therefore did not occur. A trial was held and a 10 month injunction was then issued. The state court of appeals reversed as to the 10 month order but affirmed the 10 day restraining order. The case is not moot as to that 10 day order because the petitioners "have sought to continue their activities ... and it appears that the decision of the Maryland Court of Appeals continues to play a substantial role in the response of officials to their activities." 393 U.S. at 178, 89 S.Ct. at 350 (footnote omitted).

61. Ely v. Klahr, 403 U.S. 108, 120–121, 91 S.Ct. 1803, 1809–10, 29 L.Ed.2d 352 (1971) (Douglas, J., concurring).

62. Ray v. Blair, 343 U.S. 154, 72 S.Ct. 598, 96 L.Ed. 852 (1952), opinion supplemented 343 U.S. 214, 72 S.Ct. 654, 96 L.Ed. 894 (1952), motion denied 72 S.Ct. 1034

(1952) (per curiam) (argued March 31, 1952; decided April 3, 1952; primary election to be held May 6, 1952. Mandate issued forthwith.) See also, Ray v. Blair, 343 U.S. 214, 216, 72 S.Ct. 654, 655, 96 L.Ed. 894 (1952).

63. E.g., Moore v. Ogilvie, 394 U.S. 814, 89 S.Ct. 1493, 23 L.Ed.2d 1 (1969). Plaintiffs, independent candidates for office of presidential and vice-presidential electors, objected to a state statute requiring nominating petitions to have at least 200 qualified signatures from each of the 50 counties, including the very sparsely settled counties. The election had passed by the time of Supreme Court review and it was urged that there was no possibility of granting relief to the plaintiffs. But the Court found that the burden placed on the nomination of "statewide offices remains and controls future elections, as long as Illinois maintains her present system as she has done since 1935." 394 U.S. at 816, 89 S.Ct. at 1494.

Cf. Hall v. Beals, 396 U.S. 45, 90 S.Ct. 200, 24 L.Ed.2d 214 (1969) (per curiam): objection to six month residency requirement in presidential election; by the time the case came to the Supreme Court plaintiffs had met the residency requirement, the election had been held, and the state legislature amended the statute to reduce the residency requirements to two months; held, case moot.

64. Judge Keith, citing Treatise in B & B Chemical Co., Inc. v. United States Environmental Protection Agency, 806 F.2d 987, 990 (11th Cir.1986); Cat's Meow, Inc. v. City of New Orleans, 720 So.2d 1186, 1196 (La.1998), Knoll, J., for the Court, citing Treatise.

65. Bank of Marin v. England, 385 U.S. 99, 101, 87 S.Ct. 274, 276, 17 L.Ed.2d 197 (1966). There was also remaining the issue of costs and respondents "sole financial interest" is protection against imposition of costs. The Court did not decide what would be the ruling as to mootness if costs alone were involved. 385 U.S. at 101, 87 S.Ct. at 276.

In *Powell v. McCormack*,[66] Congressman Powell's claim of improper exclusion from the House of Representatives was not mooted by his later seating, because there was a collateral consequence that a ruling would decide, the issue of his back pay remained.[67]

Even though the primary dispute has settled through the passage of time, if there are collateral consequences to one of the parties—even if they are quite minor—the controversy is not moot.[68]

Criminal Cases and Collateral Consequences. In criminal cases, the collateral consequences of a conviction serve to prevent mootness. Serving the sentence does not necessarily mean the case is moot. A criminal case is moot only if there is no possibility that any collateral consequences will be imposed because of the challenged conviction.[69]

A corollary to this principle is that the state may seek Supreme Court review of a lower court reversal of a criminal defendant's conviction, even if the defendant has already served his sentence. The case is not moot. If the conviction is allowed to stand, the state could impose collateral legal consequences on the defendant.[70]

***Roe, Super Tire, and DeFunis* Compared.** The complexities in this area are best understood by applying the general rules to several of the important cases in this area. First, *Roe v. Wade*.[71]

Roe challenged the constitutionality of Texas abortion legislation. Jane Roe, using a pseudonym, instituted the case in March of 1970, at a time when she alleged that she was unmarried, pregnant, and desired an abortion. She amended her complaint purporting to sue "on behalf of herself and all other women" similarly situated.[72] At the time of Roe's hearing in the district court several months later, on May 22, 1970, there was no evidence that she was then pregnant. By the time the Supreme Court heard the case, it was January 22, 1973; thus the appellee suggested "that

66. 395 U.S. 486, 89 S.Ct. 1944, 23 L.Ed.2d 491 (1969).

67. 395 U.S. at 495–500, 89 S.Ct. at 1950–53. Accord, Memphis Light, Gas, and Water Div. v. Craft, 436 U.S. 1, 8–9, 98 S.Ct. 1554, 1559–60, 56 L.Ed.2d 30 (1978) (plaintiffs claim for actual and punitive damages arising out of a power company's termination of services prevents the case from being mooted, even though plaintiffs no longer desire a hearing to resolve the dispute over their bills and there is no allegation of a present threat of termination of services).

68. Firefighters Local Union No. 1784 v. Stotts, 467 U.S. 561, 571, 104 S.Ct. 2576, 2584, 81 L.Ed.2d 483, 494 (1984), on remand 762 F.2d 1011 (6th Cir.1985). In this case the Supreme Court reviewed a lower court injunction that modified a Title VII consent decree that previously had established a remedy for a city's failure to hire and promote its employees in the fire department on a racially nondiscriminatory basis. A lower court had issued a preliminary injunction in 1981 requiring the city to lay off white rather than black employees in violation of the seniority agreement established between the city and the firefighters' union so that the laying off of the black "least-senior" employees would not result in reestablishing a segregated workforce. The white employees, who had taken lesser job positions with the city due to the injunction, or who were laid off, were soon offered their old positions back. They were offered their old jobs before the case reached the United States Supreme Court.

The Supreme Court found that the case was not moot because the terms of the injunction appeared to make it a continuing command to the city to lay off white workers in preference to black workers with less seniority in any future layoffs. Although the employees may only have been laid off or put in lesser paying positions for only one

month, a reversal of the lower court injunction would give them a claim for back pay because their demotions or layoffs were unjustified.

The Court concluded that a party could not invoke the jurisdiction of federal courts to obtain a modification of a consent decree or injunction and then "insulate" that ruling from review by the claim that the modification had only a minimal continuing adverse effect on other parties. The Court distinguished University of Texas v. Camenisch, 451 U.S. 390, 101 S.Ct. 1830, 68 L.Ed.2d 175 (1981), a case where an injunction had been issued but had expired prior to appellate review. In *Camenisch* the defendant was "in all respects restored to its pre-injunction status." 467 U.S. at 572 n. 6, 104 S.Ct. at 2585 n. 6, 81 L.Ed.2d at 495 n. 6.

69. Sibron v. New York, 392 U.S. 40, 57, 88 S.Ct. 1889, 1899–1900, 20 L.Ed.2d 917 (1968).

Evitts v. Lucey, 469 U.S. 387, 391 n. 4, 105 S.Ct. 830, 833 n. 4, 83 L.Ed.2d 821 (1985) (habeas petition of criminal defendant not moot; although the respondent was released and his civil rights restored, he was not pardoned and collateral consequences of his conviction remain—e.g., that the conviction could be used to impeach his testimony in a future proceeding, or that it could be used in a persistent felony prosecution).

70. Pennsylvania v. Mimms, 434 U.S. 106, 108 n. 3, 98 S.Ct. 330, 332 n. 3, 54 L.Ed.2d 331 (1977), on remand to 477 Pa. 553, 385 A.2d 334 (1978).

71. 410 U.S. 113, 93 S.Ct. 705, 35 L.Ed.2d 147 (1973), rehearing denied 410 U.S. 959, 93 S.Ct. 1409, 35 L.Ed.2d 694 (1973).

72. 410 U.S. at 120 & n. 4, 93 S.Ct. at 710 & n. 4.

Roe's case must now be moot because she and all other members of her class are no longer subject to any 1970 pregnancy."[73] But pregnancy is capable of repetition yet evading review if the litigation takes more than 9 months.

The Court rejected mootness, relying on the repetition exception to the mootness rule:

[W]hen ... pregnancy is a significant fact in the litigation, the normal 266–day human gestation period is so short that the pregnancy will come to term before the usual appellate process is complete. ... Our law should not be that rigid. Pregnancy often comes more than once to the same women, and in the general population, if man is to survive, it will always be with us. Pregnancy provides a classic justification for a conclusion of nonmootness. It truly could be "capable of repetition yet evading review."[74]

Therefor subsequent events did not moot the case.

The Court (five to four) reached a similar conclusion in *Super Tire Engineering Co. v. McCorkle.*[75] In New Jersey, where this case arose, employees were eligible for state welfare assistance even though they were engaged in an economic strike. After such a strike occurred, the employers sued for injunctive and declaratory relief against distribution of welfare payments to the strikers. Before the case was tried, the strike ended. The trial court rejected the union's contention that the case was moot and went on to decide the merits, holding that federal law did not prohibit the New Jersey practice.

The Supreme Court granted certiorari on the mootness issue after the Court of Appeals had held the case moot. The high court found that, as to the request for declaratory relief,

the case was not moot. "If we were to condition our review on the existence of an economic strike, this case most certainly would be the type presenting an issue 'capable of repetition, yet evading review.' "[76]

Seven days after the *McCorkle* decision, the Court issued a per curiam opinion in *DeFunis v. Odegaard.*[77] DeFunis had claimed that his denial of admission to a state law school constituted discrimination against him on account of his race. DeFunis was not a member of the various minority groups who were given preferential admissions.[78] DeFunis did not bring the case as a class action, and at the trial level, where he won his claim, the court ordered him admitted to the law school. When the case reached the state Supreme Court (where he lost), he was in his second year of law school. Then Justice Douglas, as Circuit Justice, stayed that judgment pending a final judgment by the Supreme Court. DeFunis was in his third year when the Court first considered his certiorari petition.

During oral argument the respondents indicated that DeFunis was now in his last quarter of his third year and that his registration would not be canceled "regardless of the outcome of this litigation."[79] Thus, a "determination by this Court of the legal issues tendered by the parties is no longer necessary to compel that result [of DeFunis' finishing school], and could not serve to prevent it."[80] The Supreme Court held that the case was moot.

Roe, Super Tire, and *DeFunis,* at first blush, do not appear to fit into a pattern. While the majority opinion in *DeFunis* cited *Roe,* none of the opinions in *DeFunis* even cited *Super Tire,* issued one week earlier. *Roe* itself might appear to suggest that the Court in *DeFunis* could have applied the "repetition" exception.

73. 410 U.S. at 124, 93 S.Ct. at 712.

74. 410 U.S. at 125, 93 S.Ct. at 713 (citations omitted).

75. 416 U.S. 115, 94 S.Ct. 1694, 40 L.Ed.2d 1 (1974), on remand to 412 F.Supp. 192 (D.N.J.1976), affirmed 550 F.2d 903 (3d Cir.1977), certiorari denied 434 U.S. 827, 98 S.Ct. 106, 54 L.Ed.2d 86 (1977), rehearing denied 434 U.S. 1025, 98 S.Ct. 753, 54 L.Ed.2d 773 (1978).

76. 416 U.S. at 125, 94 S.Ct. at 1700 (citations omitted).

77. 416 U.S. 312, 94 S.Ct. 1704, 40 L.Ed.2d 164 (1974), on remand to 84 Wn.2d 617, 529 P.2d 438 (1974) (per curiam).

78. The groups were Blacks, Chicanos, American Indians, and Filipinos, 416 U.S. at 320, 94 S.Ct. at 1708 (Douglas, J., dissenting).

79. 416 U.S. at 316 n. 3, 94 S.Ct. at 1705 n. 3. Compare 416 U.S. at 315 with 416 U.S. at 315 n. 2, 94 S.Ct. at 1705 n. 2.

80. 416 U.S. at 317, 94 S.Ct. at 1706.

Of the nine Justices participating in *DeFunis* and *Super Tire*, only Powell thought that both cases were moot.[81]

The Court did not carefully discuss the distinctions between these three cases, and several of the Justices did not think that they really were distinguishable. But they are. In *Roe* as in *Super Tire,* the issue is capable of repetition yet evading review as to the particular litigant. Jane Roe may get pregnant again, and once again desire to obtain an abortion. The union members in *Super Tire* may go on strike again, and once again ask for state welfare assistance. But Mr. DeFunis will, realistically, never again be subject to the state's allegedly discriminatory law school admission procedure. He was about to finish his third year of law school, and—as to him—the admissions issue was not capable of repetition.

The majority in *DeFunis* argued that it was irrelevant that mootness appeared to be created in part by the university. The case was moot, but not on the grounds that the university had merely voluntarily changed its ways and was free to go back to its old ways. The argument that "voluntary cessation of allegedly illegal conduct does not ... make the case moot"[82] was inapplicable, because the question of mootness was not a function of a unilateral change in admission procedure. DeFunis attacked those procedures, and if the defendant unilaterally changed them, it could always go back to its old ways, *unless* there were no reasonable expectation that the alleged wrong would be repeated.

The case was moot simply because litigation would no longer affect DeFunis' law school status.[83] This case was not one that was capable of repetition, yet evading review *as to* Mr. DeFunis personally.

DeFunis added a confusing comment, that there "is no reason to suppose that a subsequent case attacking those procedures will not come with relative speed to this Court, now that the Supreme Court of Washington has spoken."[84] But even that subsequent case should be moot, if the university lets in a new complaining student, and it becomes clear that new student will never again be subjected to the allegedly unconstitutional admissions procedure. One might think that a clever university could always avoid a constitutional decision by admitting those who sue. But that would not work, because word would eventually get around that an applicant's most successful ticket of admission is simply to file a complaint.

Four Justices dissented on the *DeFunis* mootness determination. "Any number of unexpected events—illness, economic necessity, even academic failure—might prevent [DeFunis'] graduation at the end of the term."[85] In addition the dissent argued that the public interest should require the Court to decide the case and end the issue.[86] But the majority regarded these "unexpected events" as simply conjectural, and not really realistic.

Mootness and Class Actions. If *DeFunis* had brought a class action, the case would not have been held moot. In *Sosna v. Iowa,*[87] decided the year after *DeFunis*, the Court explicitly held that, while there must be a live controversy at the time of Supreme Court review, the "controversy may exist, however, between a named defendant and a member of the class represented by the named plaintiff, even

---

81. While Justice Rehnquist dissented in *Roe* based on several arguments, none of them appear to have related to mootness. The closest Justice Rehnquist came to the mootness issue is an argument phrased more in terms of third party standing. 410 U.S. at 171–72, 93 S.Ct. at 736 (Rehnquist, J., dissenting).

82. 416 U.S. at 318, 94 S.Ct. at 1706 (quoting United States v. W. T. Grant Co., 345 U.S. 629, 632, 73 S.Ct. 894, 897, 97 L.Ed. 1303 (1953) and other cases).

83. The state law school could moot all future attacks on its preferential admissions program by simply admitting every student like DeFunis who objected to his exclusion. But there is an inner check that operates to prevent this method from being abused: disgruntled applicants will

quickly learn that the easiest law school admission ticket is the filing of a law suit.

84. 416 U.S. at 319, 94 S.Ct. at 1707.

85. 416 U.S. at 348, 94 S.Ct. at 1721 (Brennan, J., dissenting, joined by Douglas, White, and Marshall, JJ.). Mr. DeFunis did in fact graduate from law school.

86. 416 U.S. at 350, 94 S.Ct. at 1722 (Brennan, J., dissenting): "[W]e should not transform principles of avoidance of constitutional decisions into devices for side-stepping resolution of difficult cases."

87. 419 U.S. 393, 95 S.Ct. 553, 42 L.Ed.2d 532 (1975).

though the claim of the named plaintiff has become moot."[88]

Similarly, if the lower court erroneously denies class action certification, the mootness of the named plaintiff's personal claim does not moot the controversy because class certification, if granted by the appellate court, may be treated as related back to the original erroneous denial. Thus, in a class action the mootness of the named plaintiff's personal claim does not render the controversy moot if the class is certified either before or after the individual's personal claim is mooted.[89]

Feigned and Collusive Cases. In *United States v. Johnson*[90] one party sued another alleging that the rent he paid was in excess of the maximum allowed by federal regulation. The defendant moved to dismiss on the grounds that the Emergency Price Control Act, which authorized the rent regulation, was unconstitutional. The United States intervened and the trial court ruled on the merits that the Act was unconstitutional. The government then moved to reopen the case on the grounds that the suit was collusive, but the trial court refused. The Supreme Court reversed.

The record showed that plaintiff brought the suit under a fictitious name at the defendant's request. Defendant paid for and selected plaintiff's counsel, who never met plaintiff. Plaintiff never read the complaint, and defendant assured him that he would incur no expense in connection with the suit. In fact, plaintiff had no knowledge of the judgment he asked for, outside of reading about it in a local paper. Plaintiff had not even filed a brief on his behalf at the trial court. There was no claim,

however, that the original parties submitted any false or fictitious facts to the court. On this record, the case was held to be collusive and was dismissed.[91]

The parties may not submit cases on a stipulated statement of facts not in accordance with the actual facts.[92] Neither will the Court accept a case where the parties make a contract for the purposes of instituting a suit so that the parties may "procure the opinion of this court upon a question of law, in the decision of which they have a common interest opposed to that of other persons, who are not parties to this suit. . . ."[93] Thus, the Court would not accept a case where both sides argued and agreed that an anti-busing law was constitutional.[94]

The problem of a collusive suit was an issue in *United States v. Nixon*,[95] where President Nixon's counsel argued that the Court lacked jurisdiction to order the President to respond to a subpoena issued by the Special Prosecutor for presidential tapes and papers relating to a criminal prosecution. The President's lawyer argued that the matter was an intra-branch dispute between subordinate and superior offices within the Executive Branch.

The *Nixon* case was a criminal case brought in the name of the United States. Federal statutes gave the Attorney General the responsibility to conduct such litigation and to appoint subordinate officers to aid him. Pursuant to these statutory powers he issued regulations delegating authority to a Special Prosecutor "with unique authority and tenure."[96] Though the Attorney General could amend or revoke these regulations, he had not and, until he did,

---

88. 419 U.S. at 402, 95 S.Ct. at 559.

89. United States Parole Commission v. Geraghty, 445 U.S. 388, 100 S.Ct. 1202, 63 L.Ed.2d 479 (1980), on remand to 552 F.Supp. 276 (M.D.Pa.1982), affirmed 719 F.2d 1199 (3d Cir.1983), certiorari denied 465 U.S. 1103, 104 S.Ct. 1602, 80 L.Ed.2d 133 (1984) (plaintiff who filed class action challenging the validity of parole guidelines could continue his appeal of lower court ruling denying certification even though he had been released from prison while appeal was pending).

90. 319 U.S. 302, 63 S.Ct. 1075, 87 L.Ed. 1413 (1943) (per curiam).

91. 319 U.S. at 304–05, 63 S.Ct. at 1076–77.

92. Swift & Co. v. Hocking Valley Ry. Co., 243 U.S. 281, 37 S.Ct. 287, 61 L.Ed. 722 (1917).

93. Lord v. Veazie, 49 U.S. (8 How.) 251, 254, 12 L.Ed. 1067 (1850).

94. Moore v. Charlotte–Mecklenburg Bd. of Education, 402 U.S. 47, 91 S.Ct. 1292, 28 L.Ed.2d 590 (1971) (per curiam).

95. 418 U.S. 683, 94 S.Ct. 3090, 41 L.Ed.2d 1039 (1974), certiorari denied 431 U.S. 933, 97 S.Ct. 2641, 53 L.Ed.2d 250 (1977), rehearing denied 433 U.S. 916, 97 S.Ct. 2992, 53 L.Ed.2d 1103 (1977).

96. 418 U.S. at 694, 94 S.Ct. at 3100 (footnote omitted).

the United States was bound to respect them. "Moreover, the delegation of authority to the Special Prosecutor in this case is not an ordinary delegation by the Attorney General to a subordinate officer: with the authorization of the President, the Acting Attorney General provided in the regulation that the Special Prosecutor was not to be removed without the 'consensus' of eight designated leaders of Congress."[97] The Court concluded that there was a real case or controversy.

To be distinguished from collusive suits are cases where there is a default judgment,[98] or where the Solicitor General confesses error,[99] or a state's attorney confesses error,[100] or a party seeks naturalization and no one opposes the petition.[101] In all of these cases there is a real, not a feigned, case. The Court does not have to accept the Solicitor General's confession. In all these instances, there is no collusion, and the results of the court action has real and direct consequences operating on the parties before the court.

In spite of the general rule as to feigned cases, the Court at times has accepted cases where there was strong evidence the suit was collusive.[102] For example, the Court has accepted cases brought by stockholders seeking to prevent their corporation from complying with allegedly unconstitutional statutes. *Carter v. Carter Coal Co.*[103] upheld the right of stock-

holders to sue their corporation to prevent it from paying an allegedly unconstitutional tax.[104] Because neither the shareholders nor the corporation normally would want the Corporation to pay the tax, it would have been the better rule for the Court to have dismissed the case.[105]

(d) Ripeness, Prematurity, and Abstractness

Just as a case can be brought too late, and thereby be moot, it can be brought too early, and not yet be ripe for adjudication. Ripeness is an important enough requirement that federal courts may consider it on their own motion and dismiss a case as not yet ripe, even if it is the Court's prudential self-restraint rather the Article III requirement of a case or controversy that is the reason to find lack of ripeness.[106]

The purpose of the ripeness requirement is to avoid premature adjudication. Ripeness is designed to prevent the courts from entangling themselves in abstract disagreements over administrative policies that may never need to be decided. The ripeness rule also protects the agencies from judicial interference until an administrative decision has been formalized and its effects felt in a concrete way by the challenging parties.[107]

---

97. 418 U.S. at 696, 94 S.Ct. at 3102.

98. In re Metropolitan Ry. Receivership, 208 U.S. 90, 108, 28 S.Ct. 219, 223, 52 L.Ed. 403 (1908): "Jurisdiction does not depend on the fact that the defendant denies the existence of the claim made, or its amount or validity. If it were otherwise, then the Circuit Court would have no jurisdiction if the defendant simply admitted his liability and the amount thereof as claimed, although not paying or satisfying the debt."

99. Compare Young v. United States, 315 U.S. 257, 258–259, 62 S.Ct. 510, 511–12, 86 L.Ed. 832 (1942), with Casey v. United States, 343 U.S. 808, 72 S.Ct. 999, 96 L.Ed. 1317 (1952).

100. Sibron v. New York, 392 U.S. 40, 58–59, 88 S.Ct. 1889, 1900–01, 20 L.Ed.2d 917 (1968).

101. Tutun v. United States, 270 U.S. 568, 576–580, 46 S.Ct. 425, 426–28, 70 L.Ed. 738 (1926) (Brandeis, J.).

102. E.g., Fletcher v. Peck, 10 U.S. (6 Cranch) 87, 3 L.Ed. 162 (1810).

See A. Kelly & W. Harbison, The American Constitution: Its Origins and Development 276 (4th ed. 1970).

103. 298 U.S. 238, 56 S.Ct. 855, 80 L.Ed. 1160 (1936).

104. 298 U.S. at 286, 56 S.Ct. at 862.

105. Parties' Legal Theories Do Not Control the Court. If a claim is properly before the court, the parties do not have the power to limit the court to any particular legal theory. The court retains the power to identify and apply the proper construction of the governing laws even when the court ultimately concludes that the law does not govern because it is not in force. Kamen v. Kemper Financial Services, Inc., 500 U.S. 90, 99, 111 S.Ct. 1711, 1718, 114 L.Ed.2d 152 (1991), on remand 939 F.2d 458 (7th Cir.1991), cert. denied 502 U.S. 974, 112 S.Ct. 454, 116 L.Ed.2d 471 (1991).

106. Regional Rail Reorganization Act Cases, 419 U.S. 102, 138, 95 S.Ct. 335, 42 L.Ed.2d 320 (1974); Reno v. Catholic Social Services, Inc., 509 U.S. 43, 57, n. 18, 113 S.Ct. 2485, 125 L.Ed.2d 38 (1993); National Park Hospitality Association v. Department of Interior, 538 U.S. 803, 123 S.Ct. 2026, 155 L.Ed.2d 1017 (2003).

107. Abbott Laboratories v. Gardner, 387 U.S. 136, 148–149, 87 S.Ct. 1507, 18 L.Ed.2d 681 (1967); Ohio Forestry Association, Inc. v. Sierra Club, 523 U.S. 726, 732–733, 118 S.Ct. 1665, 140 L.Ed.2d 921 (1998).

While this general ripeness principle is not disputed, its application by the Supreme Court has resulted in a line of cases with seemingly inconsistent rulings. At least the grounds distinguishing them are sometimes too subtle for the commentators to appreciate.

A leading decision on the ripeness doctrine is *United Public Workers v. Mitchell*.[108] The plaintiffs sought declaratory relief and an injunction against the members of the United States Civil Service Commission to prevent enforcement of a sentence of the Hatch Act, which provided that "no officer or employee in the executive branch of the Federal Government ... shall take any active part in political management or in political campaigns."[109] The provision was challenged as unconstitutional for a variety of reasons, but only one plaintiff had actually violated the provision and the rules promulgated under it. As to the plaintiffs who had not been charged with violations, the Supreme Court found the issues not ripe for adjudication:

> Appellants want to engage in "political management and political campaigns" to persuade others to follow appellants' views by discussion, speeches, articles and other acts reasonably designed to secure the selection of appellants' political choices....

A hypothetical threat is not enough. We can only speculate as to the kinds of political activity the appellants desire to engage in or as to the contents of their proposed public statements or the circumstances of their publication.... Should the courts seek to expand

their power so as to bring under their jurisdiction ill-defined controversies over constitutional issues, they would become the organ of political theories.[110]

As to the plaintiff who had been charged with political activity, the Court did consider the constitutional issue "as defined" by the Commission's charges and proposed findings and plaintiff's admissions. The Court held that the plaintiff's particular activities could constitutionally be made the basis for disciplinary action.

Several policy considerations support the ripeness doctrine. Until the controversy becomes concrete and focused, it is difficult for the Court to evaluate the practical merits of the position of each party. This principle is particularly important for difficult issues. When the constitutional issues seem to be extremely close, the Court is more likely to demand a more concrete record, because it needs to know much more about the actual practices of enforcement, which the bare text of an unenforced statute does not show.[111]

Also, if a record is concrete rather than abstract in nature, the Court may find a way of interpreting the statute to avoid or minimize the constitutional issue. The statute may be interpreted to raise constitutional problems as applied to some issues and not to others. Or, evidence of the customary enforcement of the statute may justify a narrow interpretation of its scope. And, if the Court waits for an actual controversy, the whole constitutional

108. 330 U.S. 75, 67 S.Ct. 556, 91 L.Ed. 754 (1947).

See Wymbs v. Republican State Executive Committee of Florida, 719 F.2d 1072, 1086 (11th Cir.1983) (Tjoflat, J.) (citing this section of an earlier edition of this treatise).

109. 330 U.S. at 82, 67 S.Ct. at 560.

110. 330 U.S. at 89–91, 67 S.Ct. at 564–65.

See also, National Park Hospitality Association v. Department of Interior, 538 U.S. 803, 123 S.Ct. 2026, 155 L.Ed.2d 1017 (2003). The Contract Disputes Act of 1978 (CDA) established rules governing disputes arising out of certain government contracts. Later, Congress passed the National Parks Omnibus Management Act of 1998, which created a comprehensive concession management program for national parks. Then, the National Park Service issued implementing regulations including 36 CFR § 51.3, which purports to render the CDA inapplicable to concession contracts. The petitioner, a concessioners' association, challenged the validity of § 51.3. The lower courts reached

the merits but Thomas, J., for the Court, vacated and remanded, holding that the issue was not yet ripe because the respondents conceded that the Park Service has no delegated rule-making under the CDA. The Park Service's rule is not even an interpretative regulation, because the Park Service does not administer the CDA. The rule in question is no more than a general policy statement designed to inform the public of the Park Service's views on the applicability of the CDA. The validity of this regulation should await a concrete dispute about a particular concession contract.

111. Scharph, Judicial Review and the Political Question: A Functional Analysis, 75 Yale L.J. 517, 531–532 (1966) illustrating this point by a discussion of United Public Workers v. Mitchell, 330 U.S. 75, 67 S.Ct. 556, 91 L.Ed. 754 (1947) and Adler v. Board of Education, 342 U.S. 485, 72 S.Ct. 380, 96 L.Ed. 517 (1952).

problem may just be eliminated by later developments.

In *Adler v. Board of Education*[112] the majority upheld the constitutionality of a state law requiring the dismissal of any teacher who advocated or belonged to any organization advocating the overthrow of the government by force or violence. Black and Douglas dissented on the merits and would have invalidated the law.

Only Frankfurter dissented on the ripeness issue. It was no coincidence that Frankfurter was the only member of the Court who did not find the merits of the case as easy as the majority (who upheld the law) or the dissent (who would have invalidated the New York law). Frankfurter argued that the facts in this case "fall short of those found insufficient in the *Mitchell* case. These teachers do not allege that they have engaged in proscribed conduct or that they have any intention to do so. They do not suggest that they have been, or are, deterred from supporting causes or from joining organizations … except to say generally that the system complained of will have this effect on teachers as a group."[113]

Because Frankfurter thought that the issue was a close one, it was important for him to have a concrete situation, because he could envision circumstances where the law was invalid as applied, or valid at applied. For Frankfurter, the question for ripeness merged with and reflected his view of the merits. For Black and Douglas, ripeness or concreteness was not that important, because they could envision no circumstances where the law would be valid. The majority agreed with Black and Douglas that the case was concrete enough, but they could envision no circumstance where the law would be invalid.

Cramp v. Board of Public Instruction[114] involved a Florida statute that required every employee to take an oath that, inter alia, he had never lent "aid, support, advice or influence to the Communist party."[115] The plaintiff refused to take the oath but believed that he could truthfully do so if he understood its language. The Court found standing, and implicitly found ripeness, because:

> [T]he very vice of which he complains is that the language of the oath is so vague and indefinite that others could with reason interpret it differently. He argues, in other words, that he could unconstitutionally be subjected to all the risks of a criminal prosecution *despite* the sworn allegations as to his past conduct…. [116]

Citing *Mitchell* and *Adler*, the Court found "direct and serious" injury to the plaintiff.[117]

More recent cases have reaffirmed the basic principle of *Mitchell*, though the various fact situations involved show that no litmus tests can be applied here.[118] That result should not be surprising, because the Justices are less likely to think that the case is too abstract or premature when they think that the answer is easy.

Regulatory "Taking" of Property. Sometimes the plaintiff claims that a particular statutory scheme constitutes a "taking" of his or her property, even though the state does not actually possess the land. While the Court is reluctant to find that a regulatory taking has occurred, there are some regulations that are so extensive that they constitute a "taking" for which compensation must be paid.[119]

---

112. 342 U.S. 485, 72 S.Ct. 380, 96 L.Ed. 517 (1952). On the merits, *Adler* was later substantially rejected. See Keyishian v. Board of Regents, 385 U.S. 589, 593–595, 87 S.Ct. 675, 678–80, 17 L.Ed.2d 629 (1967).

113. 342 U.S. at 504, 72 S.Ct. at 390. See also, International Longshoremen's & Warehousemen's Union, Local 37 v. Boyd, 347 U.S. 222, 74 S.Ct. 447, 98 L.Ed. 650 (1954).

114. 368 U.S. 278, 82 S.Ct. 275, 7 L.Ed.2d 285 (1961), on remand to 137 So.2d 828 (Fla.1962).

115. 368 U.S. at 279, 82 S.Ct. at 276.

116. 368 U.S. at 284, 82 S.Ct. at 279 (emphasis in original).

117. 368 U.S. at 283, 82 S.Ct. at 278.

118. See 1 Ronald D. Rotunda & John E. Nowak, Treatise on Constitutional Law: Substance & Procedure § 2.13(a) (West Group, 3d ed.1999) for further analysis of the case law.

119. 2 Ronald D. Rotunda & John E. Nowak, Treatise on Constitutional Law: Substance and Procedure § 15.12(b) (West Group, 3d ed. 1999).

In *Yee v. City of Escondido*,[120] plaintiff alleged that a city ordinance imposing rent control amounted to the equivalent of a physical occupation, thus requiring that just compensation be paid. Because the plaintiff alleged that this ordinance, which provided for no compensation, was unconstitutional *on its face,* the Court agreed that the issue was ripe for adjudication. Similarly, if an agency regulating land use decides that a property owner's residential lot is ineligible for development, the claim of an unconstitutional regulatory taking is ripe for adjudication.[121]

In contrast, if the rent control ordinance in *Yee* were attacked *as applied,* or if the land use agency prohibiting further development still had some discretion to exercise (e.g., the power to grant a variance to the landowner), then the case would not be ripe until the government entity that implements the ordinance has reached a final decision regarding the application of the challenged regulation to the property at issue.[122]

This principle responds to the fact that some land use agencies have a high degree of discretion in softening the strictures of the general regulations that they administer. For example, the government entity might decide that the ordinance does not apply to the property, or, even if it did, it had the power to grant a variance, thereby making it unnecessary for the Court to reach the takings issue.[123]

The "takings clause" does not prevent the government from taking property; it merely requires that the government pay just compensation. If the state does not provide for just compensation and if the agency engaging in the alleged regulatory taking has no further discretion to exercise, then the takings claim is ripe.[124] However, if the state provides procedures so that the plaintiff could secure compensation, the "takings" claim is not ripe until plaintiff avails herself of those procedures, or until plaintiff shows that those procedures are inadequate. If the government provides a fair

120. 503 U.S. 519, 112 S.Ct. 1522, 118 L.Ed.2d 153 (1992). On the merits, the Court held that the rent control ordinance at issue in this case did not amount to the equivalent of a physical taking of the plaintiff's property (a mobile home park). See also Keystone Bituminous Coal Association v. DeBenedictis, 480 U.S. 470, 495, 107 S.Ct. 1232, 1247, 94 L.Ed.2d 472 (1987); Nollan v. California Coastal Commission, 483 U.S. 825, 834, 107 S.Ct. 3141, 3147, 97 L.Ed.2d 677 (1987).

121. Suitum v. Tahoe Regional Planning Agency, 520 U.S. 725, 117 S.Ct. 1659, 137 L.Ed.2d 980 (1997). The agency argued that the claim was not ripe for decision because the agency had granted the landowner so-called "Transfer Development Rights" (TDR). The agency argued that these TDRs were valuable because the landowner would have the right to sell these TRDs to third parties. However, while the TDRs may be relevant in determining if just compensation has been paid (the value of the TDRs may affect the amount of compensation that is owed), they do not affect the question of whether a regulatory taking has occurred. The land use agency in *Suitum* had no further discretion to exercise.

122. Agins v. City of Tiburon, 447 U.S. 255, 260, 100 S.Ct. 2138, 2141, 65 L.Ed.2d 106 (1980). In this case, the Court did not use the word "ripeness" but it spoke of the fact that the landowner (who challenged zoning ordinances that required approval for development) had not yet submitted a plan for development. If the landowner had done so, the board might have allowed the development, so the case was not yet "concrete" (a word that the Court did use).

See also Hodel v. Virginia Surface Mining and Reclamation Association, Inc., 452 U.S. 264, 297, 101 S.Ct. 2352, 2371, 69 L.Ed.2d 1 (1981); Williamson County Regional

Planning Commission v. Hamilton Bank, 473 U.S. 172, 186–97, 105 S.Ct. 3108, 3116–22, 87 L.Ed.2d 126 (1985), on remand 779 F.2d 50 (6th Cir.1985).

A court cannot decide if the "regulation goes 'too far' " (and thus amounts to a regulatory taking) "unless it knows how far the regulation goes." MacDonald, Sommer & Frates v. Yolo County, 477 U.S. 340, 348, 106 S.Ct. 2561, 2566, 91 L.Ed.2d 285 (1986).

123. With *Suitum*, contrast, Ohio Forestry Association v. Sierra Club, 523 U.S. 726, 118 S.Ct. 1665, 140 L.Ed.2d 921 (1998). The United States Forest Service, pursuant to the National Forest Management Act (NFMA), developed a Land and Resource Management Plan for a national forest in Ohio. This plan made logging in the forest more likely (it set logging goals, selected the areas suited to timber production, etc.), but it did not authorize cutting any trees. Before that happened, the Forest Service had to engage in other actions (propose a specific site and a specific harvesting method, make an environmental analysis, etc.). Breyer, J., for a unanimous Court, held that the challenge to the plan was not ripe for judicial review.

The Forestry Service's plan is not like an Environmental Impact Statement prepared pursuant to NEPA because NEPA (unlike the NFMA) guarantees a particular procedure, not a particular result. Thus, a person with standing who is injured by a failure to comply with the NEPA procedure may complain of that failure at the time the failure takes place, because the claim can never get any riper.

124. Williamson County Regional Planning Commission v. Hamilton Bank, 473 U.S. 172, 194–96, 105 S.Ct. 3108, 3120–22, 87 L.Ed.2d 126 (1985), on remand 779 F.2d 50 (6th Cir.1985).

and adequate procedure so that the plaintiff-property-owner can obtain just compensation, and if plaintiff uses that process and receives just compensation, then plaintiff has suffered no constitutional loss.[125]

Plaintiff has suffered a loss, and the state provides no reasonable, certain, and adequate provision for obtaining compensation, then the plaintiff's claim is ripe. Thus, the Court found a taking in *Palazzolo v. Rhode Island*.[126] The plaintiff was a prospective developer of wetlands property, and the local government continuously rejected applications to build on the property. A claim that a regulation has "taken" property is ripe when the landowner first follows "reasonable and necessary steps to allow regulatory agencies to exercise their full discretion in considering development plans for the property, including the opportunity to grant any variances or waivers allowed by law."[127] The reason behind this general rule is that the extent of the restriction on property is not yet known and the plaintiff has not established a regulatory taking until these ordinary processes have been followed. In *Palazzolo*, the state court had argued that there was doubt as to the extent of development that the Council would allow on the developer's parcel because of his failure to explore other uses for the property that would involve filling substantially less wetlands.[128] The Court rejected the state court's argument: "This is belied by the unequivocal nature of the wetland regulations at issue and by the Council's application of the regulations to the subject property."[129]

Postenactment transfer of title. The developer in *Palazzolo v. Rhode Island*[130] acquired the property *after* the regulations had been enacted, but that does prevent his takings claim, said Justice Kennedy, speaking for the Court. The state argued that the prospective developer had no reasonable investment-backed expectation that he could develop his property at the time that he bought it because the regulation pre-dated his purchase. The state's proposed rule regarding the postenactment transfer of title would absolve the state of its obligation to pay for property that it takes by putting an expiration date on the Takings Clause. "Future generations, too, have a right to challenge unreasonable limitations on the use and value of land."[131] In addition, the state's proposed rule does not take into account the effect on the owners at the time the law was originally enacted. The original owner may not survive the procedures to make the case ripe ("which, as this case demonstrates, will often take years").[132] Then, the new owner, under the state's theory, would be unable to sue.

(e) *Hayburn's Case* and the Requirement of Finality

The federal judiciary will not have its decision in a case frustrated by allowing the execu-

---

125. E.g., Regional Rail Reorganization Act Cases, 419 U.S. 102, 124–25, 95 S.Ct. 335, 349, 42 L.Ed.2d 320 (1974); Ruckelshaus v. Monsanto Co., 467 U.S. 986, 1013, 1018 n. 21, 104 S.Ct. 2862, 2878, 2881 n. 21, 81 L.Ed.2d 815 (1984).

Contrast, Lucas v. South Carolina Coastal Council, 505 U.S. 1003, 1009–15, 112 S.Ct. 2886, 2890–92, 120 L.Ed.2d 798 (1992), on remand 309 S.C. 424, 424 S.E.2d 484 (1992). The landowner claimed that there was a regulatory taking, which entitled him to just compensation. The Court agreed. In the course of reaching this decision, the Court noted that the state law had been amended to allow the landowner the right to ask for a special use permit. However, this change in the law did *not* render the landowner's claim unripe because the state supreme court had already issued a judgment on the merits of the claim rather than on the ripeness grounds. This judgment precluded the landowner from asserting any claim with respect to the alleged injury that occurred *prior* to the amendment of the statute allowing a variance procedure.

A *past* deprivation of property entitled the landowner to compensation. Even temporary deprivations of property

deserve compensation under the Takings Clause. First English Evangelical Lutheran Church v. County of Los Angeles, 482 U.S. 304, 107 S.Ct. 2378, 96 L.Ed.2d 250 (1987), on remand 210 Cal.App.3d 1353, 258 Cal.Rptr. 893 (1989), cert. denied 493 U.S. 1056, 110 S.Ct. 866, 107 L.Ed.2d 950 (1990).

126. 533 U.S. 606, 121 S.Ct. 2448, 150 L.Ed.2d 592 (2001).

127. 533 U.S. at 620–21, 121 S.Ct. at 2459.

128. The developer, among other things, wanted to fill in 11 of the property's 18 wetland acres to build a private beach club.

129. Palazzolo v. Rhode Island, 533 U.S. 606, 619, 121 S.Ct. 2448, 2458.

130. 533 U.S. 606, 121 S.Ct. 2448, 150 L.Ed.2d 592 (2001).

131. 533 U.S. at 609, 121 S.Ct. at 2453.

132. 533 U.S. at 609, 121 S.Ct. at 2453.

tive or legislative branches to revise, suspend, modify, or otherwise review it. Because of the principle of the separation of powers and the independence of the federal judiciary, the federal courts will not act as administrative agencies, or as an agent of the executive or legislative branches.[133]

The Supreme Court first spoke directly on the proper relationship between the legislature and the judiciary in *Hayburn's Case*[134] in 1792, shortly after adoption of the Constitution and enactment of the Judiciary Act of 1789.[135] *Hayburn's Case* concerned a statute authorizing federal and state courts to determine the propriety and amount of pensions for disabled veterans of the Revolutionary War.[136] The statute provided for the Secretary of War to review the court decision and transmit his opinion to Congress. If Congress agreed with the allowance and amount of the pension, it would appropriate the necessary funds. The Circuit Court for the District of Pennsylvania refused to consider William Hayburn's application for a pension under the statute, and the Attorney General sought a writ of mandamus in the Supreme Court.[137]

Prior to the decision, Congress amended the legislation to provide other relief for the pensioners, and the Supreme Court dismissed on grounds of mootness.[138] In a footnote to the dismissal, however, the reporter of decisions noted some of the views of the Justices on the constitutional division between the legislative and judicial functions.[139] He quoted Chief Justice Jay and Justice Cushing as Circuit Court

Justices, holding that, because the duties under the original pension act were not judicial, they could not perform them in their capacity as judges. They agreed, however, to perform the duties as commissioners while court was adjourned.

The footnote in *Hayburn's Case* also cited letters to the President from two circuit courts concerning the same statute. In 1792 the Circuit Court for the District of Pennsylvania, consisting of Supreme Court Justices Wilson and Blair and a district judge, had protested to the President that the statute was radically inconsistent with the independence of the judicial power that the Constitution vested in the courts. The Circuit Court for the District of North Carolina, including Associate Justice Iredell, also had written the President that no decision of any court of the United States could be liable to revision or suspension by the legislature because the Congress had no judicial power but impeachment.[140]

These five Justices were not speaking lightly. They were refusing, on constitutional grounds, to execute a statute according to Congress' terms over a decade *before* the Court decided *Marbury v. Madison*.[141]

Cases following *Hayburn's Case* further defined the boundaries between the legislative and judicial functions. *Gordon v. United States*[142] held that it had no jurisdiction to hear an appeal from a Court of Claims decision regarding damage done to petitioner by United

---

133. Johnston v. Cigna Corp., 14 F.3d 486, 495 (10th Cir.1993), quoting treatise; Levin, J., quoting Treatise, in Quinton v. General Motors Corp., 453 Mich. 63, 74, 551 N.W.2d 677, 682 (1996), rehearing denied, 453 Mich. 1205, 554 N.W.2d 12 (Mich.1996).

134. 2 U.S. (2 Dall. 409) 408, 1 L.Ed. 436 (1792).

See also, Humana Hospital Corp., Inc. v. Blankenbaker, 734 F.2d 328, 333 (7th Cir.1984) (Harlington Wood, J., for a unanimous court), citing this treatise.

135. See Hart & Wechsler, The Federal Courts and the Federal System (2d ed. 1973), at 1–23, 32–36.

136. See Act of March 23, 1792, ch. 11, 1 Stat. 243.

137. 2 U.S. (2 Dall.) at 409.

138. 2 U.S. (2 Dall.) at 410 & n. (a).

139. 2 U.S. (2 Dall.) at 410 n. (a) (quoting opinion of federal Circuit Court for the District of New York and

letters of Circuit Court Justices to the President). Subsequent cases approved and relied on the decisions reported in the margin of *Hayburn's Case* as a correct interpretation of the Constitution. See Muskrat v. United States, 219 U.S. 346, 352–53, 31 S.Ct. 250, 252, 55 L.Ed. 246 (1911); United States v. Ferreira, 54 U.S. (13 How.) 40, 49–51, 14 L.Ed. 40 (1851).

140. 2 U.S. (2 Dall.) at 410 n. (a). It was not until a year after *Hayburn's Case* that the Supreme Court concluded, in an exchange of correspondence with President Washington, that the federal courts may not constitutionally give advisory opinions. See H. Johnston, Correspondence and Public Papers of John Jay 486–89 (1891).

141. 5 U.S. (1 Cranch) 137, 2 L.Ed. 60 (1803).

142. 69 U.S. (2 Wall.) 561, 17 L.Ed. 921 (1864); see Gordon v. United States, Appendix I, 117 U.S. 697 (decided 1865, Opinion printed in Oct. Term, 1885).

States troops during the War of 1812.[143] Although the Court did not provide the reasons for its holding, in a draft opinion Chief Justice Taney argued that the Court of Claims was not exercising a judicial function because it did not have the power to enforce its decisions; it was dependent on the Secretary of the Treasury and Congress to estimate and appropriate funds to pay its judgments.[144] Taney reasoned that the award of a remedy is an essential part of the exercise of judicial power and that rendering a judgment and yet having the remedy subject to Congressional approval is not an exercise of Article III jurisdiction.[145]

Lending support to this reasoning is *Schneiderman v. United States*.[146] A naturalized citizen contested a federal district court's de novo determination under section 15 of the Naturalization Act of 1906 that his grant of citizenship from a naturalization court was invalid.[147] Although the full Court did not reach the issue, Justice Rutledge commented in a concurring opinion that Congress does not have authority both to confer jurisdiction and to nullify the effects of its exercise by other jurisdictional provisions in the same statute.[148]

The principle that Justice Rutledge raised reflects the constitutional independence of the judiciary and fosters the separation of powers

concept implicit in Article III. The full Court adopted this principle in *Chicago & Southern Air Lines, Inc. v. Waterman Steamship Corp.*,[149] which denied judicial review of an order of the Civil Aeronautics Board that was reviewable by the President. The Court concluded that such dual review would violate Article III.[150] The principle underlying *Hayburn's Case* and its progeny is that the Article III guarantee of an independent federal judiciary prevents the legislature and the executive from reviewing a judicial decision.[151]

In contrast, the situation if different if the court issues an injunctive decree instead of money damages, because injunctions are not final orders: courts may change the terms of an equitable decree to reflect changes in the circumstances, including a change in the underlying law. When Congress changes the law underlying a judgment awarding relief, that relief is no longer enforceable to the extent that it is inconsistent with the new law. If the judgment had awarded *money damages* in an action at law instead of a *continuing injunction* in an action in equity, then that judgment would be final and a later-enacted federal law could not affect plaintiff's right to those damages.[152]

---

143. 69 U.S. (2 Wall.) at 561.

144. Gordon v. United States, Appendix I, 117 U.S. 697, 698–99 (decided 1865, Opinion printed in Oct. Term, 1885) (draft opinion of Taney, C.J., published posthumously). This draft opinion is not found in the Lawyers' Edition.

145. 117 U.S. at 702.

146. 320 U.S. 118, 63 S.Ct. 1333, 87 L.Ed. 1796 (1943), rehearing denied 320 U.S. 807, 64 S.Ct. 24, 88 L.Ed. 488 (1943).

147. 320 U.S. at 120–22, 63 S.Ct. at 1334–35.

148. 320 U.S. at 168–69, 63 S.Ct. at 1357–58 (Rutledge, J., concurring).

149. 333 U.S. 103, 68 S.Ct. 431, 92 L.Ed. 568 (1948), mandate conformed 166 F.2d 1021 (5th Cir.1948).

150. 333 U.S. at 113–14, 68 S.Ct. at 437–38. In strong language, Justice Jackson observed that "[j]udgments within the powers vested in the courts by the Judiciary Article of the Constitution may not lawfully be revised, overturned or refused faith and credit by another Department of Government." 333 U.S. at 113, 68 S.Ct. at 437.

151. Reinhard, J., quoting North Penn Transfer, Inc. v. Duplex Products Inc., 1995 WL 57600, at *3 (N.D.Ill. 1995).

152. Miller v. French, 530 U.S. 327, 120 S.Ct. 2246, 147 L.Ed.2d 326 (2000). In 1975, prison inmates at the Pendleton Correctional Facility filed a class action seeking injunctive relief regarding conditions of confinement. The district court granted the injunction, which remained in effect. Twenty years later Congress enacted the Prison Litigation Reform Act of 1995, which, among other things, sets a standard for entry and termination of prospective relief in civil actions objecting to prison conditions. One section of the Act provides that a defendant or intervenor may move to terminate prospective relief under an existing injunction (like the one affecting Pendleton) that does not meet the standard of the Act. Another section states that a court may not terminate such injunctive relief if it makes certain findings. Finally, another section (the automatic stay provision) provides that a motion to terminate such relief "shall operate as a stay" of that relief beginning 30 days after the motion is filed and ending when the court rules on the motion. This stay reflects the changed legal circumstances that prospective relief under the existing decree is no longer enforceable unless and until the court makes the findings required by the statute.

The lower courts ruled that the operation of the automatic stay provision violated due process and separation of powers, but O'Connor, J., for the Court, reversed. Unlike *Hayburn's Case*, the automatic stay provision does not suspend or reopen a final judgment of an Article III court

(f) Standing

(1) Taxpayer and Citizen Standing

Justice Douglas has warned us that "Generalizations about standing to sue are largely worthless as such,"[153] and Professor Paul Freund has described the problem of standing as "among the most amorphous in the entire domain of public law."[154] While it may not be possible to explain all of the contours of this doctrine, an historical discussion of its development should prove useful.

The first important link in the standing chain is *Frothingham v. Mellon.*[155] Mrs. Frothingham challenged the constitutionality of a federal Maternity Act, which provided appropriations to the states if they would comply with its provisions. The intent of the Act was to reduce maternal and infant mortality. Plaintiff alleged that she was a taxpayer and in that capacity she was therefore injured because "the effect of the appropriations complained of will be to increase the burden of future taxation and thereby take her property without due process of law."[156]

The Court found this alleged injury unpersuasive. The Court distinguished the cases where a municipal taxpayer has been held to have standing to sue to object to alleged misuse of municipal moneys because in those situations, the Court claimed, the injury is "direct

and immediate"[157] and the situation "is not without some resemblance to that subsisting between stockholder and private corporation."[158] But a federal taxpayer's interest "is comparatively minute and indeterminable" and the effect of this case on future taxation is "remote."[159]

Frothingham also was concerned that granting standing to a federal taxpayer *qua* taxpayer would allow virtually anyone to challenge any federal act if its administration requires the outlay of money.[160] And virtually every piece of federal legislation requires the outlay of money. If the statute is administered, the administrators must be paid. It even costs money to publish the statute.

Frothingham rejected the plaintiff's theory and said that, for standing to exist, the party invoking judicial review—

> must be able to show not only that the statute is invalid but that he has sustained or is immediately in danger of sustaining some direct injury as the result of its enforcement, and not merely that he suffers in some indefinite way in common with people generally.[161]

There are several important effects and distinctions of *Frothingham* that should be noted. The opinion purported to distinguish federal review of claims of municipal taxpayers,[162] but

---

because "[p]rospective injunctive relief under a continuing, executory decree remains subject to alteration due to changes in the underlying law." When Congress changed the law underlying a judgment awarding relief, that relief is no longer enforceable to the extent that it is inconsistent with the new law. This injunction is a "final judgment" for purposes of appeal, but not the "last word of the judicial department" because it is subject to the court's continuing supervisory jurisdiction and may therefore be altered according to subsequent changes in the law. For the same reason, it is unlike *United States v. Klein.*

153. Association of Data Processing Service Organizations, Inc. v. Camp, 397 U.S. 150, 151, 90 S.Ct. 827, 829, 25 L.Ed.2d 184 (1970).

154. Hearings on S. 2097, before the Subcommittee on Constitutional Rights of the Senate Committee on the Judiciary, 89th Cong., 2d Sess., pt. 2 at 498 (1966).

155. 262 U.S. 447, 43 S.Ct. 597, 67 L.Ed. 1078 (1923). In *Massachusetts v. Mellon*, the Court denied the standing of Massachusetts to attack the constitutionality of the Maternity Act. The state did not have standing on its own behalf because the statute did not coerce the state to do anything. 262 U.S. at 480, 482, 43 S.Ct. at 598, 599.

Nothing could be done under the statute without the state's consent. The statute "simply extends an option which the State is free to accept or reject." 262 U.S. at 480, 43 S.Ct. at 598.

State as Parens Patriae. Neither can the state sue the federal government as representative of citizens of the state, for only the United States and not a state may be *parens patriae* as against the federal government. 262 U.S. at 485–486, 43 S.Ct. at 600–01. Cf. Texas v. I.C.C., 258 U.S. 158, 162, 42 S.Ct. 261, 262–63, 66 L.Ed. 531 (1922).

156. 262 U.S. at 486, 43 S.Ct. at 600.

157. 262 U.S. at 486, 43 S.Ct. at 600.

158. 262 U.S. at 487, 43 S.Ct. at 601.

159. 262 U.S. at 487, 43 S.Ct. at 601.

160. 262 U.S. at 487, 43 S.Ct. at 601.

161. 262 U.S. at 488, 43 S.Ct. at 601.

162. 262 U.S. at 486–87, 43 S.Ct. at 600–01.

Standing in Federal Court and Standing in State Court Compared. See, Doremus v. Board of Education, 342 U.S. 429, 72 S.Ct. 394, 96 L.Ed. 475 (1952). The Court

after *Flast,* discussed below, this distinction should not be valid. One's standing as a taxpayer in a federal court is not a function of whether the city, the state, or the federal government collects the taxes.

We should also realize that so-called taxpayer suits such as *Frothingham* really are not challenges to the taxing power but to the spending power. Such taxpayers do not really object to the taxes levied but to the uses to which they apply. If Mrs. Frothingham had won her suit, the judicial remedy would not affect her taxes. The court would have enjoined the federal expenditure, but that injunction would only affect an expenditure, the use to which federal money is applied, not the federal tax.[163]

A taxpayer, if successful on the merits in declaring an expenditure unconstitutional, would not have her taxation burden reduced, even minutely. Prohibiting an expenditure does not prohibit the taxation, for the two are not normally tied together. The federal government normally levies taxes without any limitation of purpose. An individual pays her income tax, for example, and the money collected becomes part of the government's general funds.[164] These taxes are not earmarked for special expenditures, so prohibiting one particular expenditure, or many expenditures, does not affect the tax.

Let us fantasize and assume that the federal government spends no tax money next year. That fact will not affect income taxes payments at all. Congress must enact a law to reduce income taxes, and Congress can enact such a law whether or not it reduces government expenditures. The federal income tax laws are separate from the federal government's laws authorizing expenditures, so an elimination of a general expenditure does not lower anyone's taxes.

Earmarked Taxes. Taxes that are *earmarked* for a certain purpose are, even under the *Frothingham* ruling, different. Taxpayers can challenge earmarked taxes in a variety of ways. A taxpayer may contest paying the earmarked tax because the purposes for which it is earmarked are alleged to be unconstitutional.[165] In that case, if the expenditure is invalid, a court may enjoin collection of the special tax earmarked for an invalid expenditure.

Taxpayers, as taxpayers, may also contest the assessment of their tax liability (as opposed to the expenditure of the money received by the Government)—by a suit for refund, in defense of civil suit brought by the Government, or in defense of a prosecution—on the grounds that, for example, the money taxed cannot constitutionally be taxed under the income tax Amendment to the Constitution,[166] or that reporting the income to be taxed violates the self-incrimination clause of the Fifth Amendment,[167] or that the tax is really a penalty in the guise of a tax,[168] or simply that the tax liability was incorrectly assessed under the statutory provisions.

The Court may not agree with the merits of the litigant's claim, but the litigant has stand-

---

dismissed an appeal: there is no standing for municipal taxpayers objecting to bible reading in public schools, *if* there is no allegation that the challenged activity adds any sum whatsoever to the cost of conducting school or is supported by a separate tax or any particular appropriation. *Doremus* distinguished *Everson* as a case where there was a "measurable appropriation or disbursement of school district funds occasioned solely by the activities complained of." 342 U.S. at 434, 72 S.Ct. at 397. The plaintiffs also had no standing to object to the bible reading as parents because, before the appeal was taken to the Supreme Court, the student had graduated and thus that aspect of the case was moot. 342 U.S. at 432, 72 S.Ct. at 396. The state court found standing, but standing in an Article III court is a federal question and does not depend on the party's standing in a state court. Cf. ASARCO Inc. v. Kadish, 490 U.S. 605, 109 S.Ct. 2037, 104 L.Ed.2d 696 (1989).

163. Flast v. Cohen, 392 U.S. 83, 118, 88 S.Ct. 1942, 1962, 20 L.Ed.2d 947 (1968) (Harlan, J., dissenting).

164. 392 U.S. at 118, 88 S.Ct. at 1962 (Harlan, J., dissenting).

165. Bailey v. Drexel Furniture Co., 259 U.S. 20, 42 S.Ct. 449, 66 L.Ed. 817 (1922) (challenge to payment of Child Labor Tax, challenge upheld as a penalty).

166. E.g., Eisner v. Macomber, 252 U.S. 189, 40 S.Ct. 189, 64 L.Ed. 521 (1920).

167. E.g., Marchetti v. United States, 390 U.S. 39, 48–61, 88 S.Ct. 697, 702–09, 19 L.Ed.2d 889 (1968).

168. E.g., Bailey v. Drexel Furniture Co., 259 U.S. 20, 42 S.Ct. 449, 66 L.Ed. 817 (1922).

ing to raise that claim, even under *Frothingham*.

Reaction to *Frothingham*. Many commentators attacked *Frothingham* as going too far in restricting taxpayer suits. It would appear not to allow standing to taxpayers who object to federal monies being used to construct a church of a particular religious denomination, in blatant disregard of the establishment clause of the First Amendment.[169] Thus, proposals have been made for a statutory modification of the *Frothingham* rule, with most commentators arguing that the decision rested primarily on policy grounds favoring judicial self-restraint and not on the constitutional requirements of an Article III case or controversy.[170]

***Flast v. Cohen* and its Progeny.** *Flast v. Cohen*[171] undertook a fresh examination of the limitations on standing to sue in a federal court and the application of those limitations to taxpayer suits. In *Flast*, federal taxpayers challenged, under the establishment clause, the expenditure of federal funds under the Elementary and Secondary Education Act of 1965 to finance teaching of reading, arithmetic, and other subjects in, and purchase of textbooks for use in, religious schools.

Flast first held that the rule of *Frothingham* was based on judicial self-restraint. It was not required by the Constitution, for "we find no absolute bar in Article III to suits by federal taxpayers challenging allegedly unconstitutional federal taxing and spending programs."[172] The Court, however, did not overrule *Frothingham*. Rather it established an important exception to its application:

> [I]n ruling on standing, it is both appropriate and necessary to look to the substantive

issues ... to determine whether there is a *logical nexus* between the status asserted and the claim sought to be adjudicated....

The nexus demanded of federal taxpayers has two aspects to it. *First* the taxpayer must establish a logical link between that status and the type of legislative enactment attacked. Thus, a taxpayer will be a proper party to allege the unconstitutionality *only of exercises of congressional power under the taxing and spending clause* of Art. I, § 8, of the Constitution. It will not be sufficient to allege an incidental expenditure of tax funds in the administration of an essentially regulatory statute.... *Secondly*, the taxpayer must establish a nexus between that status and the precise nature of the constitutional infringement alleged. Under this requirement, the taxpayer must show that the challenged enactment *exceeds specific constitutional limitations imposed upon the exercise of the congressional taxing and spending power* and not simply that the enactment is generally beyond the powers delegated to Congress by Art. I, § 8. When both nexuses are established, the litigant will have shown a taxpayer's stake in the outcome of the controversy and will be a proper and appropriate party to invoke a federal court's jurisdiction.[173]

The Court went on to explain that the *Flast* plaintiffs established both nexuses but Mrs. Frothingham had only met the first nexus. First, both the plaintiffs in *Flast* and in *Frothingham* complained of the exercise of the spending power under Article I, section 8. And, in both cases, the challenged program involved a substantial expenditure of funds, *not an incidental expenditure* of tax funds in the administration of an essentially regulatory statute.[174]

---

169. Flast v. Cohen, 392 U.S. 83, 98 n. 17, 88 S.Ct. 1942, 1951–52 n. 17, 20 L.Ed.2d 947 (1968).

170. See generally, Hearings on S. 2097, before the Subcommittee on Constitutional Rights of the Senate Judiciary Committee, 89th Cong., 2d Sess. (1966); Jaffe, Standing to Secure Judicial Review: Private Actions, 75 Harv.L.Rev. 255 (1961).

171. 392 U.S. 83, 94, 88 S.Ct. 1942, 1949, 20 L.Ed.2d 947 (1968).

172. 392 U.S. at 101, 88 S.Ct. at 1953.

173. 392 U.S. at 102–103, 88 S.Ct. at 1954 (emphasis added).

174. The *Flast* Court emphasized that the expenditure of funds must not be an incidental expenditure in the administration of an essentially regulatory statute. "This requirement," the Court said, "is consistent with the limitation imposed upon state—taxpayer standing in federal courts in Doremus v. Board of Education, 342 U.S. 429, 72 S.Ct. 394, 96 L.Ed. 475 (1952)." 392 U.S. at 102, 88 S.Ct. at 1954. *Doremus* is apparently still law after *Flast*. See Rebollo, J., dissenting, citing Treatise in, Asociacion de Maestros de Puerto Rico v. Torres, 1994 WL 780744, at *48 n. 17 (Puerto Rico 1994).

However, only the *Flast* taxpayer fulfilled the second requirement, that there must be a nexus between the status as a taxpayer and the precise nature of the constitutional infringement alleged. The Court reached this conclusion after it examined the history behind the establishment clause of the First Amendment and concluded that one of the "specific evils feared" was that the taxing and spending power would be used to favor one religion over another.[175] Thus, the challenged statute allegedly exceeded a specific constitutional limitation imposed on the taxing and spending power.

The basis of the challenge, unlike the *Frothingham* case, was not simply that the taxing and spending was generally beyond Congress' powers.[176] The plaintiffs in *Frothingham* relied on the Tenth Amendment. Under the *Flast* analysis, the Tenth Amendment is not a specific limit on the taxing and spending powers.

Justice Harlan, dissenting, agreed that there was no Article III barrier to plaintiffs' suit. He acknowledged that plaintiffs suing as representatives of the public interest, bereft of any personal or proprietary interest, are not constitutionally excluded from the federal courts,[177] but he believed that the Court should wait until Congress authorized such public actions, as it has done in the past.[178]

He feared that the Court's willingness to hear such public actions without a federal statute granting standing, "might well alter the allocation of authority among the three branches of the Federal Government."[179] The majority's limits to the public action plaintiff were not satisfactory, because the nexus test is not, "in any sense, a measurement of any plaintiff's interest in the outcome of any suit."[180] Harlan also was not persuaded that, even accepting the nexus tests, it could be shown historically that the establishment clause met the requirement of the second nexus.[181]

The *Flast* majority agreed that the establishment clause was a specific limitation to Congress' taxing and spending power. It offered no examples of what other types of constitutional provisions are specific limitations that grant standing to any taxpayer under the second nexus of the *Flast* test. Neither have later cases.

Thus, *United States v. Richardson*[182] held that taxpayers did not meet the *Flast* test and had no standing to challenge a statute for allegedly violating Article I, section 9, clause 7, of the Constitution, which requires that "a regular statement and Account of the Receipts and Expenditures of all public Money shall be published from time to time." Plaintiffs alleged that the challenged statute unconstitutionally allowed the Director of the CIA to avoid the requirement of public reporting of its public funds. Justice Powell, concurring in *Richardson,* found that Harlan's critique of the *Flast* nexus test "unanswerable" and predicted that the test's "lack of real meaning and of principled content . . . renders it likely that it will in time collapse of its own weight. . . ."[183]

The same day that the Court decided *Richardson,* it decided *Schlesinger v. Reservists Committee to Stop the War.*[184] The Court held that plaintiffs had no standing, either as taxpayers or as citizens generally, to challenge the membership of Members of Congress in the military reserve as being in violation of

---

175. 392 U.S. at 103, 88 S.Ct. at 1954.

176. 392 U.S. at 103–105, 88 S.Ct. at 1954–55.

177. 392 U.S. at 119–20, 88 S.Ct. at 1962–63 (Harlan, J., dissenting).

178. 392 U.S. at 131–32, 88 S.Ct. at 1968–69 (Harlan, J., dissenting). See, e.g., Oklahoma v. United States Civil Service Commission, 330 U.S. 127, 137–39, 67 S.Ct. 544, 550–52, 91 L.Ed. 794 (1947), where the Court found standing by a state because Congress had created such standing by statute.

179. 392 U.S. at 130, 88 S.Ct. at 1968 (Harlan, J., dissenting).

180. 392 U.S. at 121, 88 S.Ct. at 1964 (Harlan, J., dissenting).

181. 392 U.S. at 125, 88 S.Ct. at 1965–66.

182. 418 U.S. 166, 94 S.Ct. 2940, 41 L.Ed.2d 678 (1974). It was a five to four decision.

183. 418 U.S. at 183, 184, 94 S.Ct. at 2950 (Powell, J., concurring).

184. 418 U.S. 208, 94 S.Ct. 2925, 41 L.Ed.2d 706 (1974). The decision was by a vote of six to three.

Article 1, section 6, clause 2. This incompatibility clause provides that "no person holding any office under the United States, shall be a member of either house during his continuance in office." As to citizen standing, the Court found only "injury in the abstract."[185] As to taxpayer standing, the Court found that it did not exist because the plaintiffs below "did not challenge an enactment under art. I, § 8, but rather the action of the Executive Branch in permitting Members of Congress to maintain their reserve status."[186]

Similarly *Simon v. Eastern Kentucky Welfare Rights Organization*[187] denied standing to indigent plaintiffs to sue the Secretary of the Treasury on the theory that a Revenue Ruling was inconsistent with the Internal Revenue Code. Plaintiffs claimed that this Ruling (which granted favorable tax treatment to hospitals despite their refusal to give full service to indigents), injured them. They sought a requirement that all hospitals must serve indigents as a condition of favorable tax treatment. The Court found the allegations too speculative in the absence of any federal statute creating standing for such a class of plaintiffs. Justice Stewart's separate concurrence noted that "I cannot now imagine a case, at least outside the First Amendment area, where a person whose own tax liability was not affected ever could have standing to litigate the federal tax liability of someone else."[188]

The narrowness with which the Court has interpreted *Flast* is well illustrated by *Valley Forge Christian College v. Americans United for Separation of Church and State, Inc.*[189] The Secretary of Health, Education, and Welfare (now called the Secretary of Education) disposed of surplus federal property—in this instance, a 77 acre tract of real property—by giving it to the Valley Forge Christian College,

which would use it to train "men and women for Christian service as either ministers or laymen." The Secretary acted pursuant to a federal regulation, which implemented and helped effectuate a federal statute, which in turn was authorized by Article IV, section 3, clause 2 of the Constitution, which vests in Congress the power to "dispose of" and make "all needful Rules" regarding federal property.

Justice Rehnquist for the Court held, surprisingly, that the plaintiffs had failed the first prong of the *Flast* test. First, they "do not challenge the constitutionality of the Federal Property Administrative Services Act itself, but rather a particular Executive branch action arguably authorized by the Act;" thus the "source of their complaint is not a congressional action, but a decision by HEW to transfer a parcel of federal property." Second, said Rehnquist, "and perhaps redundantly," the property transfer was not pursuant to the taxing and spending clause but rather the property clause of Article IV, section 3.[190]

These arguments are unusual, because the source of the federal regulation was a federal statute. In addition, before the government could dispose of the property, it had to acquire and improve it, which required it to use it taxing and spending power.

The *Valley Forge* majority did not purport to overrule any prior cases, but the juxtaposition of that case with prior cases leads to surprising results. No one has standing to sue—that is, no one could be a plaintiff—to challenge the decision of the federal government to give a 77–acre plot of federal land to a Christian College with the self-described mission of training "leaders for church related ministries."

Yet the *Valley Forge* majority agreed that taxpayers would have standing to challenge

---

185. 418 U.S. at 217, 94 S.Ct. at 2930.

186. 418 U.S. at 228, 94 S.Ct. at 2935. See also Richardson v. Kennedy, 401 U.S. 901, 91 S.Ct. 868, 27 L.Ed.2d 800 (1971), affirming 313 F.Supp. 1282 (W.D.Pa.1970) (taxpayer has no standing, under the second nexus of the *Flast* test, to challenge Congressional salary increases under art. I, § 8).

187. 426 U.S. 26, 96 S.Ct. 1917, 48 L.Ed.2d 450 (1976).

188. 426 U.S. at 46, 96 S.Ct. at 1928 (Stewart, J., concurring).

189. 454 U.S. 464, 102 S.Ct. 752, 70 L.Ed.2d 700 (1982).

190. 454 U.S. at 479–480 & n. 15, 102 S.Ct. at 762 n. 15 (footnotes omitted). Brennan, J., joined by Marshall & Blackmun, JJ., filed a lengthy dissent; Stevens, J., also wrote a separate dissent.

federal financial aid to religious schools. The *Valley Forge* plaintiffs had no standing to sue because they were objecting to transfer of property pursuant to Article IV, section 3, cl. 2. Thus, Congress cannot give *money* to religious schools to aid their religious mission, but (because no one has standing), Congress can give away *property*.

Property can include personal property; it cannot be limited to real property; after all, Article IV refers to "Territory or *other* Property." The result then is that Congress cannot give money to religious schools to purchase educational tools, but it can buy the tools directly and give them to the religious schools. Congress cannot give money to religious schools to buy buildings, but Congress can give these schools the buildings themselves.

Perhaps Rehnquist, in *Valley Forge*, was simply stating that *Flast* would be limited precisely to its facts.

(2) Personal Standing, Nontaxpayer Suits and the Requirement of Injury in Fact

Whether a party has "alleged such a personal stake in the outcome of the controversy as to assure that concrete adverseness which sharpens the presentation of issues" is, we are told, "the gist" of the question of standing in Article III courts. It is, of course, a question of federal law.[191] In the taxpayer suits, the Court has attempted to formulate tests to determine when a taxpayer *qua* taxpayer has alleged such a personal stake in the outcome of a suit. In nontaxpayer actions, the determination of whether plaintiff has suffered something deemed to be an "injury" for purposes of the standing requirement has been the subject of much litigation and changing trends in the Supreme Court.[192]

The nexus requirement of taxpayer suits is not part of the constitutional requirements of standing outside the taxpayer context.[193] For personal standing, the plaintiff must establish, at a minimum, a "personal stake" in the outcome. This stake requires a two-fold showing: first, a "distinct and palpable injury" to the plaintiff, and second, a " 'fairly traceable' causal connection" between the claimed injury and the conduct that plaintiff challenges.[194] Plaintiff can meet the second prong of this requirement by showing that there is a "substantial likelihood" that the relief requested of the court will redress the claimed injury.[195]

Injury in Fact and Equal Protection. When a member of a group claims that the government has erected an allegedly unconstitutional barrier that makes it more difficult for her to obtain a benefit than it is for a member of another group, it is not necessary for the member of the first group to prove that she would have obtained the benefit "but for" the challenged government barrier. Plaintiff has standing because her real objection is the denial of equal treatment due to the imposition of the barrier; she is not actually objecting to the ultimate inability to obtain the benefit. Plaintiff is arguing that she should be considered equally, without the discriminatory barrier.

For example, in *Northeastern Florida Chapter of the Associated General Contractors of America v. City of Jacksonville*,[196] the plaintiff claimed that a city program that considers race and sex in the awarding of city contracts violates equal protection. The Court held that the plaintiff does not have to prove that, if the city contract program were invalidated, she

---

191. Baker v. Carr, 369 U.S. 186, 204, 82 S.Ct. 691, 703, 7 L.Ed.2d 663 (1962), on remand to 206 F.Supp. 341 (M.D.Tenn.1962); In the Matter of the Application of Northern States Power Co. for a Proposed Increase in Rates for Electric Service, 328 N.W.2d 852, 855 (S.D.1983) (Henderson, J., citing treatise).

192. Haden, C.J., quoting treatise in, West Virginia Pride, Inc. v. Wood County, West Virginia, 811 F.Supp. 1142, 1145 (S.D.W.Va.1993).

193. Duke Power Co. v. Carolina Environmental Study Group, Inc., 438 U.S. 59, 78–79, 98 S.Ct. 2620, 2633–34, 57 L.Ed.2d 595 (1978).

194. 438 U.S. at 72, 98 S.Ct. at 2630.

See People v. Smith, 420 Mich. 1, 49 n. 32, 360 N.W.2d 841, 863 n. 32 (1984) (Levin, J., dissenting) quoting this portion of the treatise.

195. 438 U.S. at 75 & n. 20, 98 S.Ct. at 2631 n. 20. See Young v. Klutznick, 652 F.2d 617, 629 (6th Cir.1981) (Keith, J., dissenting), citing an earlier edition of this treatise, certiorari denied 455 U.S. 939, 102 S.Ct. 1430, 71 L.Ed.2d 650 (1982).

196. 508 U.S. 656, 113 S.Ct. 2297, 2303 124 L.Ed.2d 586 (1993), on remand 997 F.2d 835 (11th Cir.1993).

would in fact have won the government contract. Plaintiff (in order to have standing) need only allege that she is able and ready to bid on city contracts and that a discriminatory policy prevents her from doing so on an equal basis. Once plaintiff alleges that, there is both injury in fact (the right to considered without the burden of allegedly invidious discrimination) and causality.[197] Plaintiff's injury in fact is the allegedly unequal treatment, not the ultimate inability to obtain the benefit.[198]

In *Northeastern Florida,* the Mexican–American Legal Defense and Education Fund, the American Civil Liberties Union, and other civil rights groups files amicus curiae briefs supporting the petitioner, which opposed the minority set-asides. Their position should not be surprising. Even though they disagreed with the petitioner on the merits, they wanted a rule of standing that would not be unrealistic. If the standing rule required the plaintiff to demonstrate that he or she would have been admitted but for the challenged program, then, in a future case, let us say one involving a school, if the school discriminated against many blacks in its admission policy, the only ones who would have standing would be those who should show that they specifically would have been admitted but for the racial discrimination. That would mean that many injured parties (those who want to compete on an equal footing) could obtain no relief.

The situation is different if the plaintiff is not alleging an imminent or on-going constitutional violation. Injunctive relief (where the plaintiff seeks forward-looking relief and complains about the inability to compete on an equal footing) is different from damages relief, where the plaintiffs seek to be made whole for damages they suffered. *Texas v. Lesage*[199] explained that if the plaintiff alleges no ongoing or imminent constitutional violation, then "the government's conclusive demonstration that it would have made the same decision absent the alleged discrimination precludes any finding of liability."[200] In *Lesage*, the plaintiff—"an African immigrant of Caucasian descent"—applied for admission to the University of Texas, which considered the race of the applicants, offered admission to at least one minority, and rejected Lesage along with about 90% of the other applicants. The Court held that the trial court was correct in granting summary judgment against Lesage and rejecting his retrospective claim for *damages* when the government proved that it would have made the same decision without the impermissible motive.

In contrast, if the plaintiff challenges an ongoing race-conscious admissions program or other race-based program, and seeks forward-looking relief, then *Florida Chapter* applies and the plaintiff need not show that he would have received the benefit in question if race had not been considered. The relevant injury is his or her "inability to compete on an equal footing."

Injury in Fact by Customers of Members of a Class Suffering Discrimination. Injury from a state's unconstitutional discrimination against interstate commerce does not end with members of the class against whom the state ultimately discriminates because *customers* of that class may also be injured. For example, a buyer of natural gas has standing to raise a commerce clause challenge to the exemption of local distribution companies from sales and use taxes imposed on the sellers of

---

197. E.g., Northeastern Florida Chapter of the Associated General Contractors of America v. City of Jacksonville, 508 U.S. 656, 666 & n. 5, 113 S.Ct. 2297, 2303 & n. 5, 124 L.Ed.2d 586 (1993), on remand 997 F.2d 835 (11th Cir.1993).

198. Quinn v. Millsap, 491 U.S. 95, 103, 109 S.Ct. 2324, 2329, 105 L.Ed.2d 74 (1989), on remand 785 S.W.2d 82 (Mo.1990).

Comparison with *Warth v. Seldin.* In *Warth,* 422 U.S. 490, 95 S.Ct. 2197, 45 L.Ed.2d 343 (1975), discussed later in this subsection, the Court found no standing. *Warth,* however, did not involve a claim that any discriminatory classification prevented the plaintiff from *applying* on an equal footing with other contenders for a state benefit. The *Warth* plaintiffs complained that the town officials refused to grant variances and permits. Their complaint was not that the plaintiffs could not compete equally; it was that they did not win.

199. 528 U.S. 18, 120 S.Ct. 467, 145 L.Ed.2d 347 (1999) (per curiam).

200. Texas v. Lesage, 528 U.S. 18, 21, 120 S.Ct. 467, 469.

natural gas. The buyer was not one of the sellers said to suffer discrimination under the challenged tax laws, but the buyer was a customer of the seller and thus suffered injury.[201] The customer was liable for payment for the tax and in all likelihood pays more for the gas it buys from out-of-state producers and marketers.

Similarly, an in-state stockholder has standing to challenge a state tax that is higher on stock from issuers with out-of-state operations than on stock from purely in-state operations.[202] And in-state milk dealers have standing to challenge a tax and subsidy scheme discriminating against out-of-state milk producers.[203]

The Role of Congress in Creating Standing. In general if plaintiff is protesting a claimed invasion of a generalized constitutional injury, the Court appears to be more reluctant to find standing—and thus create the need to dispose of a constitutional claim—than in cases where the plaintiff is arguably within the zone of interests protected by a federal statute, or a statute appears to grant

standing in the case. In other words, if Congress speaks, either explicitly or implicitly, the Court will accept Congress' decision to confer standing to litigate constitutional or statutory claims.

When Congress has acted, the requirements of Article III remain: "the plaintiff still must allege a distinct and palpable injury to himself, even if it is an injury shared by a large class of other possible litigants."[204] The injury-in-fact requirement is not satisfied by an "abstract, self-contained, noninstrumental 'right' to have the Executive observe the procedures required by law."[205] If plaintiff has only a generally available grievance about government and seeks relief that provides him no more benefit than the public at large, there is no injury in fact. On the other hand, Congress can often create standing by conferring a cash bounty on the victorious plaintiff. That would assure that plaintiff's relief gives him or her tangible benefit not available to the public at large.

If Congress has not spoken, the plaintiff alleging a constitutional injury must not only overcome the Article III standing require-

---

201. General Motors Corp. v. Tracy, 519 U.S. 278, 286, 117 S.Ct. 811, 818, 136 L.Ed.2d 761 (1997). Bacchus Imports, Ltd. v. Dias, 468 U.S. 263, 267, 104 S.Ct. 3049, 3053, 82 L.Ed.2d 200 (1984) (in-state liquor wholesalers have standing to challenge Hawaiian tax that exempts certain alcohols produced in-state; the wholesalers were hurt because the tax raised the price of their imported goods relative to the exempted in-state liquor).

202. Fulton Corp. v. Faulkner, 516 U.S. 325, 116 S.Ct. 848, 133 L.Ed.2d 796 (1996).

203. West Lynn Creamery, Inc. v. Healy, 512 U.S. 186, 114 S.Ct. 2205, 129 L.Ed.2d 157 (1994).

204. Simon v. Eastern Kentucky Welfare Rights Organization, 426 U.S. 26, 41 n. 22, 96 S.Ct. 1917, 1926 n. 22, 48 L.Ed.2d 450 (1976), quoting Warth v. Seldin, 422 U.S. 490, 501, 95 S.Ct. 2197, 2206, 45 L.Ed.2d 343 (1975).

205. Lujan v. Defenders of Wildlife, 504 U.S. 555, 601, 112 S.Ct. 2130, 2145, 119 L.Ed.2d 351 (1992).

Cf. Federal Election Commission v. Akins, 524 U.S. 11, 118 S.Ct. 1777, 141 L.Ed.2d 10 (1998). The Federal Election Campaign Act of 1971 ("FECA") imposed extensive record keeping and disclosure requirements on "political committees." Respondents who were voters with views often opposed to those of the American Israel Public Affairs Committee ("AIPAC")—petitioned the Federal Election Commission ("FEC") to treat the AIPAC as a "political committee." Justice Breyer for the Court (six to three) ruled that the Respondent-voters had standing to challenge the FEC's decision not to bring an enforcement

action against the AIPAC. The Court then remanded so that the lower court could determine if the AIPAC is a "political committee" in light of the new FEC regulations. The respondents have standing because, first, the relevant statute, the FECA, specifically provided that "[a]ny person" who believes that the FECA has been violated may file a complaint with the FEC, and "[a]ny party aggrieved" by an FEC order dismissing such a complaint may seek district court review of the dismissal. This alleged injury is an "injury in fact," because, although it is widely shared, it is concrete and particular. The "informational injury" is "directly related to voting, the most basic of political rights" and it is "fairly traceable" to the FEC decision to which the respondents complain. The courts can "redress" that injury, even though the FEC might then exercise its discretionary powers to reach the same result (*i.e.,* nonenforcement) for a different reason. While an agency's decision not to undertake an enforcement action is usually not subject to judicial review, this statute explicitly indicated to the contrary.

Scalia, J., joined by O'Connor & Thomas, JJ., dissented, arguing, first, that the statute should not be interpreted to allow a private party to bring an executive agency into court to compel its enforcement of the law against a third party, and second, that if the statute means that, it is unconstitutional because it transfers from the Executive to the courts the responsibility to "take Care that the Laws be faithfully executed." 524 U.S. at 37, 118 S.Ct. at 1792.

ments but also the judiciary's use of standing as a tool of judicial self-restraint.[206]

Standing and Nonconstitutional Cases.

Association of Data Processing Service Organizations v. Camp, and *Barlow v. Collins*[207] both decided the same day, illustrate the modern approach for nonconstitutional claims.

In *Association of Data Processing v. Camp* the Court, through Justice Douglas, held that the petitioners, who sold data processing services to businesses, had standing to challenge a ruling, by the Comptroller of the Currency, that allowed national banks to make data processing services available to other banks and bank customers. The petitioners claimed that this ruling was contrary to statutory prohibitions restricting the activities of national banks. Unlike *Flast*, the petitioners sued not as taxpayers but as competitors. To determine if these petitioners have standing, Douglas fashioned a two-part test.

First, the plaintiffs must allege that the challenged action has caused them "injury in fact, economic or otherwise."[208] Petitioners met this first test because, as competitors with banks, the ruling by the Comptroller threat-

ened them with loss of future profits. Secondly, the "question is whether the interest sought to be protected by the complainant is arguably within the zone of interests to be protected or regulated by the statute or constitutional guarantee in question."[209] The Court explicitly rejected a more limited test.[210]

The Zone of Interest Test. This "zone of interest test" is not supposed to be a trap for the unwary. Cases following *Association of Data Process* have treated the test as creating no particularly high burden; rather, the question is whether the entire statutory scheme (not merely the statute under which plaintiffs have sued) evidences an intent to *preclude* judicial review at the plaintiff's request.[211] The defendant has the burden of proving this intent to preclude review. As the Court later candidly admitted:

In cases where the plaintiff is not itself the subject of the contested regulatory action, the test denies a right of review if the plaintiff's interests are so marginally related to or inconsistent with the purposes implicit in the statute that it cannot reasonably be assumed that Congress intended to permit the suit. *The test is not meant to be especially demanding;* in particular, there need be no

---

206. Cf. Schlesinger v. Reservists Committee to Stop the War, 418 U.S. 208, 94 S.Ct. 2925, 41 L.Ed.2d 706 (1974).

Gladstone, Realtors v. Village of Bellwood, 441 U.S. 91, 99, 99 S.Ct. 1601, 1607–08, 60 L.Ed.2d 66 (1979) affirmed the distinction formulated in this paragraph between standing based solely on Article III (where plaintiff must satisfy both case or controversy requirements and prudential principles) and standing based on a statute (where Congress may expand standing to the full extent permitted by Article III without regard to prudential standing rules).

207. 397 U.S. 150, 90 S.Ct. 827, 25 L.Ed.2d 184 (1970); Barlow v. Collins, 397 U.S. 159, 90 S.Ct. 832, 25 L.Ed.2d 192 (1970).

See Young v. Klutznick, 652 F.2d 617, 629 (6th Cir. 1981), certiorari denied 455 U.S. 939, 102 S.Ct. 1430, 71 L.Ed.2d 650 (1982) (Keith, J., dissenting), citing this section of an earlier edition of this treatise.

208. Association of Data Processing Service Organizations v. Camp, 397 U.S. 150, 152, 90 S.Ct. 827, 829, 25 L.Ed.2d 184 (1970).

See generally, Nichol, Causation as a Standing Requirement: The Unprincipled Use of Judicial Restraint, 69 Ky.L.J. 185 (1981).

209. 397 U.S. at 153, 90 S.Ct. at 830.

210. 397 U.S. at 153, 90 S.Ct. at 830. The Court used the earlier, rejected test in Tennessee Elec. Power Co. v. Tennessee Valley Authority, 306 U.S. 118, 59 S.Ct. 366, 83 L.Ed. 543 (1939). In that case the Court denied competitors' standing to object to the T.V.A. operating allegedly in violation of the statutory plan. The Court then held injury in fact was not the test; rather, the right invaded must be a "legal right". See 306 U.S. at 137–139, 59 S.Ct. at 369–70.

211. See, e.g., Block v. Community Nutrition Institute, 467 U.S. 340, 348–51, 104 S.Ct. 2450, 2455–57, 81 L.Ed.2d 270 (1984), mandate conformed 742 F.2d 1472 (D.C.Cir. 1984). This case held that milk handlers have the right to seek judicial review of the Secretary of Agriculture's pricing orders under the Agricultural Marketing Agreement Act of 1937, but consumers do not have this right because allowing consumers to sue would disrupt the "complex and delicate administrative scheme." Also, the normal presumption of judicial review is overcome by the congressional intent to preclude judicial review. This intent is "fairly discernible in the statutory scheme."

indication of congressional purpose to benefit the would-be plaintiff.[212]

This zone of "interests" is not limited to economic interests any more than the "injury in fact" requirement includes only economic injury. The requisite injury may be aesthetic, conservational and recreational, economic, or reflect First Amendment values of free exercise and establishment.[213] One who is financially injured "may be a reliable private attorney general to litigate the issues of the public interest in the present case."[214] Presumably one suffering a noneconomic loss will also be a reliable private attorney general.[215]

In *Barlow v. Collins*,[216] the Court, again speaking through Justice Douglas, held that tenant farmers eligible for payments under a federal program had standing to contest the validity of a certain administrative regulation. After finding standing, the Court found, as it had earlier in *Data Processing*, that the statute, either expressly or impliedly, did not preclude judicial review of the Secretary of Agriculture's actions.[217]

Injury in Fact, Economic or Otherwise. Justice Brennan, joined by Justice White, concurred in the result and dissented in both *Data Processing* and *Barlow*. Brennan rejected the two step test and argued that the "first step is the only one that need be made to determine standing."[218] That is, if plaintiff alleges that a challenged action has caused him injury in fact, economic or otherwise, Brennan would find standing.[219]

Sierra Club v. Morton[220] emphasizes that the alleged injury is not limited to economic injury:

Aesthetic and environmental well-being, like economic well-being, are important ingredients of the quality of life in our society, and the fact that particular environmental interests are shared by the many rather than by the few does not make them less deserving of legal protection through the judicial process.[221]

Although embracing this broad state, the four to three majority in *Sierra Club* held that the plaintiffs did not have standing to contest a proposed development in the Mineral King Valley. The flaw was not a fatal one; there was only a pleading problem: the Sierra Club did not allege that it was among the injured.

The alleged injury [to the environment of the Mineral King Valley] will be felt directly only by those who use Mineral King and Sequoia National Park, and for whom the aesthetic and recreational values of the area will be lessened by the highway and ski resort. The Sierra Club failed to allege that it or its members would be effected in any of their activities or pastimes by the Disney development. Nowhere in the pleadings or affidavits did the Club state that its members use Mineral King for any purpose....[222]

In a footnote the Court explained that its decision does not bar the Sierra Club from amending its complaint to make the proper allegations to secure standing.[223] Once it secures standing, the plaintiff may assert the

---

212. Clarke v. Securities Industry Association, 479 U.S. 388, 399–400, 107 S.Ct. 750, 757, 93 L.Ed.2d 757 (1987) (footnote omitted) (emphasis added).

213. 397 U.S. at 154, 90 S.Ct. at 830, and cases cited therein.

214. 397 U.S. at 154, 90 S.Ct. at 830.

215. See also, Sierra Club v. Morton, 405 U.S. 727, 737 & 740 n. 15, 92 S.Ct. 1361, 1367–69 n. 15, 31 L.Ed.2d 636 (1972).

216. 397 U.S. 159, 90 S.Ct. 832, 25 L.Ed.2d 192 (1970). See also Douglas Oil Co. v. Petrol Stops Northwest, 441 U.S. 211, 218 n. 8, 99 S.Ct. 1667, 1672 n. 8, 60 L.Ed.2d 156 (1979), on remand to 605 F.2d 494 (9th Cir.1979) (defendants in a private antitrust action have standing under Article III to object to a court order releasing grand

jury transcripts to the plaintiffs, although the defendants had pled *nolo contendere*). Cf. Index Fund, Inc. v. Hagopian, 512 F.Supp. 1122, 1125–31 (S.D.N.Y.1981) (interpreting *Douglas Oil*).

217. 397 U.S. at 165, 90 S.Ct. at 837.

218. 397 U.S. at 168, 90 S.Ct. at 838 (Brennan J., concurring in the result and dissenting).

219. 397 U.S. at 172, 90 S.Ct. at 841 (Brennan J., concurring in the result and dissenting).

220. 405 U.S. 727, 92 S.Ct. 1361, 31 L.Ed.2d 636 (1972).

221. 405 U.S. at 734, 92 S.Ct. at 1366.

222. 405 U.S. at 735, 92 S.Ct. at 1366.

223. 405 U.S. at 735 n. 8, 92 S.Ct. at 1366 n. 8.

general public interest in its role as a private attorney general.[224]

Justice Douglas, in dissent, argued for an even broader view of standing. He said that the "critical question" of standing would be simpler and more in focus if the Court allowed environmental issues to be litigated before federal agencies or federal courts in the "name of the inanimate object about to be despoiled, defaced, or invaded by roads and bulldozers and where injury is the subject of public outrage."[225] The Court, however, has not given standing to trees or mountains. And, given the general view of standing that the Court adopted in *Sierra Club v. Morton*,[226] there will be no shortage of plaintiffs even if inanimate objects are not among them.

A case that probably represents "an all-time high in Supreme Court liberality on the subject of standing,"[227] is *United States v. Students Challenging Regulatory Agency Procedures (SCRAP)*.[228] SCRAP was an unincorporated association representing five law students who sought to enhance the quality of the environment. SCRAP protested the failure of the Interstate Commerce Commission to suspend a 2.5% surcharge on nearly all freight rates. SCRAP claimed standing because each of its members suffered economic, recreational, and aesthetic harm caused by the adverse environmental impact of the freight structure. Each of SCRAP's members, it was alleged, had to pay more for finished products because of this freight structure. The SCRAP members alleged that the increased freight rates adversely affected their use of the forests, rivers, streams, and so on. Moreover, they alleged, this modified rate structure made the air that the SCRAP members breathed more polluted. And, SCRAP alleged, each of its members has been forced to pay increased taxes because of the sums that

must be expended to dispose of otherwise reusable waste materials. The surcharge, SCRAP argued, was unlawful because the I.C.C. had failed to file a detailed environmental impact statement. SCRAP claimed that the 2.5% surcharge allegedly had an adverse impact on recycling and thus was a major federal action significantly affecting the environment.

The Court admitted that "all persons who utilize the scenic resources of the country, and indeed all who breath its air, could claim harm similar to that alleged by the environmental groups here." But, said the Court, "standing is not to be denied simply because many people suffer the same injury."[229] The majority thus found standing: "We cannot say on these pleadings that the appellees could not prove their allegations which, if proved, would place them squarely among those persons injured in fact by the Commission's action, and entitled under the clear impact of *Sierra Club* to seek review."[230] The Court specifically refused to limit standing to those "significantly" affected by agency action.

An "identifiable trifle" is enough,[231] but allegations must be more than an exercise in creative thinking. That point was made in *Lujan v. Defenders of Wildlife*,[232] which no standing in plaintiffs who objected to the Secretary of Interior's interpretation of the Endangered Species Act. The interpretation applied the Act only to actions that federal agencies take within the United States or on the high seas. The plaintiffs wanted the law to apply to actions that federal agencies fund in foreign nations. The Court rejected as "beyond all reason" plaintiffs' argument that anyone who sees Asian elephants in the Bronx Zoo can challenge a development pro-

---

224. 405 U.S. at 740 n. 15, 92 S.Ct. at 1369 n. 15.

225. 405 U.S. at 741, 92 S.Ct. at 1369 (Douglas, J., dissenting). See generally, C. Stone, Should Trees Have Standing (1974).

226. 405 U.S. 727, 92 S.Ct. 1361, 31 L.Ed.2d 636 (1972).

227. K. Davis, Administrative Law of the Seventies § 22.02–2 at 489 (1976).

228. 412 U.S. 669, 93 S.Ct. 2405, 37 L.Ed.2d 254 (1973).

229. 412 U.S. at 687, 93 S.Ct. at 2416.

230. 412 U.S. at 689–90, 93 S.Ct. at 2417.

231. 412 U.S. at 689 n. 14, 93 S.Ct. at 2417 n. 14, quoting Davis, Standing: Taxpayers and Others, 35 U.Chi. L.Rev. 601, 613 (1968).

232. 504 U.S. 555, 112 S.Ct. 2130, 119 L.Ed.2d 351 (1992).

ject in Sri Lanka that a federal agency funds in part.

Standing and Constitutional Cases. To such cases as *Sierra Club* and SCRAP must be compared cases involving constitutional issues. While SCRAP shows that the Article III threshold of case or controversy is very low indeed, it does not follow that the Court will always allow standing to plaintiffs who satisfy this minimum threshold and who seek to litigate constitutional claims. The policies of judicial restraint dictate a higher standard in some constitutional cases. A comparison of two such constitutional cases, *Trafficante v. Metropolitan Life Insurance Co.*[233] and *Warth v. Seldin*[234] will illustrate this distinction.

In *Trafficante* two tenants (one black and one white) of an apartment complex of 8,200 residents filed separate complaints with the Secretary of Housing and Urban Development under the Civil Rights Act of 1968. Each alleged that the owner of the complex had discriminated against nonwhites in the rental of housing. These two tenants alleged injury in that, among other things, they had lost the social benefits of living in an integrated community. While the unanimous Court found the legislative history of the 1968 Civil Rights Act "not too helpful,"[235] the Court found an Article III case or controversy and held that it could give vitality to the particular statutory section "only by a generous construction" that gives standing to sue to all those in the housing unit who are injured by racial discrimination in the management of those facilities within the coverage of the statute.[236]

In contrast, consider *Warth v. Seldin.*[237] Various organizations and residents in the Rochester, New York, metropolitan area brought an action against the town of Penfield, adjacent to

Rochester, and against members of Penfield's Zoning, Planning and Town Boards. Plaintiffs claimed that Penfield's Zoning Ordinance unconstitutionally excluded persons of low and moderate income from living in the town because of requirements such as lot size, setback, and floor area. In a lengthy opinion the majority ruled that none of the plaintiffs had standing.

The Court found no standing in the claims of plaintiffs who asserted injury as persons of low or moderate income and as members of racial or ethnic groups. These plaintiffs only alleged in conclusory terms that they had been personally injured: none had any present interest in any Penfield property; none was subject to the ordinance's strictures; none had ever been denied a variance or permit by the defendants. There was no evidence that proposed efforts of third parties to build low and moderate housing would have satisfied the plaintiffs' needs at prices they could afford. Their allegations suggested that "their inability to reside in Penfield is the consequence of the economics of the area housing market, rather than respondents' assertedly illegal acts."[238] Plaintiffs had not sufficiently alleged, with specific concreteness, that the challenged practices harmed them and that they would personally benefit in a tangible way if the Court were to intervene. The unsympathetic Court found that unadorned speculation is not enough to create standing.[239]

Some of the plaintiffs alleged standing as taxpayers of Rochester who claimed economic injury because Penfield's refusal to allow or facilitate construction of such low or moderate housing required Rochester to assume a greater burden. The majority also rejected this no-

233. 409 U.S. 205, 93 S.Ct. 364, 34 L.Ed.2d 415 (1972).

234. 422 U.S. 490, 95 S.Ct. 2197, 45 L.Ed.2d 343 (1975).

235. 409 U.S. at 210, 93 S.Ct. at 367.

236. 409 U.S. at 212, 93 S.Ct. at 368.

237. 422 U.S. 490, 95 S.Ct. 2197, 45 L.Ed.2d 343 (1975).

238. 422 U.S. at 506, 95 S.Ct. at 2209 (footnote omitted).

239. Contrast, Northeastern Florida Chapter of the Associated General Contractors of America v. City of Jack-

sonville, 508 U.S. 656, 113 S.Ct. 2297, 2303, 124 L.Ed.2d 586 (1993), on remand 997 F.2d 835 (11th Cir.1993). Plaintiffs in this case alleged that they were ready and able to bid on city contracts and that a discriminatory policy prevented them from being considered on an equal basis. If the court agreed with this claim, then plaintiffs would be awarded relief in the sense that they could bid on city contracts on an equal basis. Plaintiffs, given their claim, did not have to allege that their bids would be successful.

tion of standing and relied specifically on the lack of a Congressional statute that might create it. The only basis, the majority found, of the Rochester taxpayers' claim is that the Penfield ordinance violated the rights of third parties, persons of low and moderate income said to be excluded from Penfield. The prudential standing rule normally bars litigants from asserting the rights or legal interests of others. This "rule of judicial self-governance is subject to exceptions, the most prominent of which is that Congress may remove it by statute. Here, however, no statute expressly or by clear implication grants a right of action, and thus standing to seek relief, to persons in petitioners' position."[240]

One of the organizations claimed standing because 9% of its membership is composed of permanent residents of Penfield and these residents were denied the benefits of living in a racially and ethnically integrated community. The majority rejected this claim for standing and distinguished *Trafficante* because the plaintiffs there relied on the Civil Rights Act of 1968. Plaintiffs in *Warth* relied on the more general sections 1981, 1982, and 1983 of title 42.[241] The majority emphasized:

As we have observed above, Congress may create a statutory right or entitlement the

alleged deprivation of which can confer standing to sue even where the plaintiff would have suffered no judicially cognizable injury in the absence of statute. . . . No such statute is applicable here.[242]

Other plaintiffs were also found not to have standing on different grounds or not to have alleged the continued existence of a ripe controversy, with the result that no plaintiff was able to bring in the law suit.

Laird v. Tatum[243] dealt with plaintiffs who claimed allegedly illegal surveillance by the U.S. Army chilled them, in violation of the First Amendment. The Court held that they lacked sufficient standing to maintain the action. Plaintiffs were apparently insufficiently chilled. The plaintiffs probably felt more injury than the students in *SCRAP*. "But courts are more comfortable in protecting the environment than they are in restricting an espionage system."[244]

A statute could confer standing on plaintiffs in this case.[245] In *S. v. D.*,[246] for example, the Court held that a private citizen lacks a judicially cognizable interest in the prosecution or nonprosecution of another, but the majority specifically volunteered that a statute could cure this lack of standing.[247]

240. 422 U.S. at 509–10, 95 S.Ct. at 2211–12.

241. 422 U.S. at 493, 512–13, 95 S.Ct. at 2212–13.
When area residents and a village charged real estate brokers with "steering" prospective home buyers to different residential areas according to race, in violation of section 812 of the Fair Housing Act, Gladstone, Realtors v. Village of Bellwood, 441 U.S. 91, 99 S.Ct. 1601, 60 L.Ed.2d 66 (1979), held that Congress intended to the statute to grant standing as broadly Article III permits. The Court earlier interpreted section 810 of that Act in *Trafficante* in the same manner.
The Village of Bellwood had standing because it alleged that the racial steering manipulated the housing market in the Village and reduced its tax base. The individuals appeared before the trial court in two capacities. First, they acted as "testers" of defendants' practices, i.e., without intending to actually buy homes they pretended to be seeking homes to test the defendants. The plaintiffs did not press the claim of standing as testers before the Supreme Court, which did not decide that question. Second, plaintiffs sought standing as homeowners in the community at which the racial steering was directed. In that capacity the Court held that they had standing, but that two plaintiffs who did not reside in the target area lacked standing. 441 U.S. at 112 & n. 25, 99 S.Ct. at 1614 & n. 25.

Later, Havens Realty Corp. v. Coleman, 455 U.S. 363, 102 S.Ct. 1114, 71 L.Ed.2d 214 (1982) held that "testers," i.e., persons who pose as renters or purchasers for the purpose of gathering information of illegal racial steering, also have standing under this Act.

242. 422 U.S. at 513–14, 95 S.Ct. at 2212–13 citing S. v. D., 410 U.S. 614, 617, n. 3, 93 S.Ct. 1146, 1148 n. 3, 35 L.Ed.2d 536 (1973), and Trafficante v. Metropolitan Life Insurance Co., 409 U.S. 205, 212, 93 S.Ct. 364, 368, 34 L.Ed.2d 415 (1972).

243. 408 U.S. 1, 92 S.Ct. 2318, 33 L.Ed.2d 154 (1972), rehearing denied 409 U.S. 901, 93 S.Ct. 94, 34 L.Ed.2d 165 (1972).

244. Kenneth Davis, Administrative Law of the Seventies § 22.02–8, at 504 (1976).

245. Rotunda, Comment, 27 Harvard Law Bulletin 4 (Spring 1976).

246. 410 U.S. 614, 93 S.Ct. 1146, 35 L.Ed.2d 536 (1973).

247. 410 U.S. at 617 n. 3, 93 S.Ct. at 1148 n. 3. In Duke Power Co. v. Carolina Environmental Study Group, Inc., 438 U.S. 59, 79 n. 24, 98 S.Ct. 2620, 2633 n. 24, 57 L.Ed.2d 595 (1978), the Court said that in S. v. D., 410 U.S. 614, 93 S.Ct. 1146, 35 L.Ed.2d 536 (1973), the Court

The requirement that an individual be able to show an injury resulting from the governmental action in order to bring a constitutional challenge formed the basis for the Court's decision in *Allen v. Wright*.[248] The Court held that parents of black children attending public schools in districts undergoing desegregation did not have standing to require judicial review of the sufficiency of Internal Revenue Service standards that would deny tax exempt status to racially discriminatory private schools.

The diminution of the children's ability to receive an education in an integrated school was a "judicially cognizable injury," but standing was lacking because the injury was not "fairly traceable" to the challenged Internal Revenue Service conduct. The parents could not show that the IRS's allegedly illegal conduct caused their children's diminished ability to receive an education in a racially integrated school. The Court insisted that the parents must show that the Internal Revenue Service, by adopting stricter standards to withdraw tax exemptions from discriminatory schools, would make "an appreciable difference" in public school integration.[249]

Singleton v. Wulff[250] found that doctors have standing to raise their rights and the rights of their patients in challenging a state law forbidding Medicaid payments to be used for certain abortions. The Court appeared to emphasize the concrete commercial injury alleged. If the physicians prevail in their efforts to remove the Medicaid limitation of reimbursable abortions, they will benefit, for they will then receive payments for the abortions, and the state and the federal government will be out of pocket by the amount of the payments. "The

relationship between the parties is classically adverse, and there clearly exists between them a case or controversy in the constitutional sense."[251]

Related to these cases are those instances where plaintiffs allege that threatened governmental action will injure them in the near future. The Court is not entirely consistent when it finds that a threat is sufficient to confer standing and when it finds the threat insufficient.

O'Shea v. Littleton[252] found no Article III standing by plaintiffs (residents of Cairo, Illinois) who had brought a civil rights action against the State's Attorney, his investigator, the Police Commissioner, the county magistrate and an associate judge. Plaintiffs alleged that defendants, under color of law, engaged in a continuing violation of Constitutional rights in administering the criminal justice system by setting illegal bonds, imposing higher sentences on nonwhites, and requiring members of plaintiffs' class to pay for trial by jury. The majority found insufficient allegations of actual continuing injury.

Yet *Doe v. Bolton*[253] held that physicians, whom pregnant women consulted, had standing to contest the constitutionality of the state's abortion law—

despite the fact that the record does not disclose that any one of them has been prosecuted, or threatened with prosecution, for violation of the State's abortion statutes. The physician is one against whom these criminal statutes directly operate in the event he procures an abortion that does not meet the statutory exceptions and condi-

had denied standing "not because of the absence of a subject matter nexus between the injury asserted and the constitutional claim but instead because of the unlikelihood that the relief requested would redress appellant's claimed injury."

248. 468 U.S. 737, 104 S.Ct. 3315, 82 L.Ed.2d 556 (1984), rehearing denied 468 U.S. 1250, 105 S.Ct. 51, 82 L.Ed.2d 942 (1984).

249. The Court did not preclude the possibility that under different circumstances an individual could demonstrate that administrative actions by the Internal Revenue Service were frustrating the desegregation of public schools in a particular state or district.

250. 428 U.S. 106, 96 S.Ct. 2868, 49 L.Ed.2d 826 (1976), on remand to 538 F.2d 811 (8th Cir.1976).

251. 428 U.S. at 113, 96 S.Ct. at 2873.

252. 414 U.S. 488, 94 S.Ct. 669, 38 L.Ed.2d 674 (1974). See City of Los Angeles v. Lyons, 461 U.S. 95, 103 S.Ct. 1660, 75 L.Ed.2d 675 (1983) (lack of case or controversy to justify equitable relief); Ashcroft v. Mattis, 431 U.S. 171, 97 S.Ct. 1739, 52 L.Ed.2d 219 (1977) (per curiam), rehearing denied 433 U.S. 915, 97 S.Ct. 2990, 53 L.Ed.2d 1102 (1977).

253. 410 U.S. 179, 93 S.Ct. 739, 35 L.Ed.2d 201 (1973).

tions. The physician-appellants, therefore, assert a sufficiently direct threat of personal detriment. They should not be required to await and undergo a criminal prosecution as the sole means of seeking relief.[254]

What distinguishes *Doe* from *Tatum, O'Shea* and other such cases is not so much the reality of the threat—which was not dissimilar in all these cases—but the concreteness of the factual allegations, which were more precise in *Doe*. Also relevant is the nature of the relief sought, which required less judicial supervision and exertion of continual judicial power in *Doe* than in *Tatum* and *O'Shea*.

Generalized Interest in Enforcement of Law. While all citizens have an interest in having the government act according to law, this generalized interest, by itself, is insufficient to confer jurisdiction on a federal court. Similarly, a person cannot sue to force the state to prosecute another criminally because "a private citizen lacks a judicially cognizable interest in the prosecution or non-prosecution of another."[255] Thus, a doctor's interest in the enforcement of a state abortion law does not give him standing to appeal an order against the state holding the statute unconstitutional when the state has acquiesced in the lower court ruling of unconstitutionality.[256]

Standing Not Waivable. Standing must appear in the record.[257] The purpose of standing is to protect the courts and assure that they operate within Article III requirements. Because standing does not exist to protect the

parties, the parties cannot agree to waive standing. Even if the parties do not raise the issue, the court may raise it. If the trial court fails to raise the issue, the appellate court may raise it.[258]

Standing in Racial Gerrymandering Cases. *Gomillion v. Lightfoot*[259] invalidated an Alabama law that redefined the boundaries of the City Tuskegee, altering its shape from a square to an "uncouth" and "strangely irregular" twenty-eight-sided figure, with the result of removing from the city's boundaries all (except four to five) of its 400 black voters but not one single white voter or resident. The plaintiffs claimed that Act 140 was "a device to disenfranchise Negro citizens." The lower courts held that there was no cause of action, but Justice Frankfurter, for the Court, reversed, holding that the allegations are "a mathematical demonstration that the legislation is solely concerned with segregating white and colored voters," in violation of the Fifteenth Amendment. The Alabama law did not prevent blacks from voting; it prevented them from voting in Tuskegee because they were no longer residents of that city. The Court did not specifically discuss the question of standing on behalf of the plaintiffs (none of whom were residents of the newly formed boundaries of Tuskegee). The Court assumed that the plaintiffs were injured by racial gerrymandering, and neither the plaintiffs nor the defendant assumed otherwise.

---

254. 410 U.S. at 188, 93 S.Ct. at 745.

255. S. v. D. (also called, Linda R.S. v. Richard D.), 410 U.S. 614, 619, 93 S.Ct. 1146, 1149, 35 L.Ed.2d 536 (1973). See also, Bailey v. Patterson, 369 U.S. 31, 33, 82 S.Ct. 549, 551, 7 L.Ed.2d 512 (1962); Younger v. Harris, 401 U.S. 37, 42, 91 S.Ct. 746, 749, 27 L.Ed.2d 669 (1971); Leeke v. Timmerman, 454 U.S. 83, 102 S.Ct. 69, 70 L.Ed.2d 65 (1981), rehearing denied 454 U.S. 1165, 102 S.Ct. 1041, 71 L.Ed.2d 322 (1982); Sure–Tan, Inc. v. N.L.R.B., 467 U.S. 883, 104 S.Ct. 2803, 81 L.Ed.2d 732 (1984).

256. Diamond v. Charles, 476 U.S. 54, 106 S.Ct. 1697, 90 L.Ed.2d 48 (1986). See also, Bender v. Williamsport Area School District, 475 U.S. 534, 106 S.Ct. 1326, 89 L.Ed.2d 501 (1986), rehearing denied 476 U.S. 1132, 106 S.Ct. 2003, 90 L.Ed.2d 682 (1986) (one member of school board has no standing to appeal decision against school board when that member was never sued in his personal capacity).

257. FW/PBS, Inc. v. City of Dallas, 493 U.S. 215, 110 S.Ct. 596, 107 L.Ed.2d 603 (1990), on remand 896 F.2d

864 (5th Cir.1990). This case involved challenges to a licensing ordinance. While the city's attorney, at oral argument, conceded that "one or two" of the plaintiffs were denied licenses based on their criminal convictions, these representations were insufficient because the necessary factual predicate must appear in the record below.

258. E.g., FW/PBS, Inc. v. Dallas, 493 U.S. 215, 230–31, 110 S.Ct. 596, 607–08, 107 L.Ed.2d 603 (1990), on remand 896 F.2d 864 (5th Cir.1990); United States v. Hays, 515 U.S. 737, 742, 115 S.Ct. 2431, 2435, 132 L.Ed.2d 635 (1995), on remand 936 F.Supp. 360 (D.La.1996); Lewis v. Casey, 518 U.S. 343, 116 S.Ct. 2174, 135 L.Ed.2d 606 (1996), on remand 91 F.3d 1365 (9th Cir.1996).

259. 364 U.S. 339, 81 S.Ct. 125, 5 L.Ed.2d 110 (1960). Whittaker, J., concurring, argued that the decision should be rested on the Equal Protection Clause of the Fourteenth Amendment.

A quarter of a century later, *United States v. Hays*[260] turned to the standing issue. Plaintiffs claimed that Louisiana's congressional redistricting plan, called Act I, was an unconstitutional racial gerrymander in violation of the equal protection clause. Their claim's primary focus was on District 4, a "majority-minority district," that is, a district in which a majority of the population is a member of a specific minority group. However, the plaintiffs lived in District 5, not District 4. Justice O'Connor, for the *Hays* Court, held that plaintiffs lacked standing.

Hays did not distinguish or even discuss *Gomillion*. To have standing under *Hays*, a plaintiff must demonstrate "individualized harm," not a generalized grievance. *Hays* rejected the claim that everyone in the state has standing. The Court admitted that the burden of showing "individualized harm" may not be easily met in the racial gerrymandering context because it is often "difficult to discern why a particular citizen was put in one district or another." However, the Court announced, if a district is created solely to effectuate the perceived common interests of a particular racial group, then elected officials are more likely to represent the members of that group rather than their constituency as a whole. Therefore, a plaintiff who resides in the racially gerrymandered district has standing, but one who does not reside there, does not suffer these special harms, and must present "specific evidence" that he has personally suffered special injury. Thus, in general, only citizens who have standing are those who live in the district that is alleged to be racially gerrymandered.

This new rule of standing—which no member of the Court rejected—raises problems. For example, assume that the state creates a misshapen district that excludes all blacks. Assume, further, that no whites within the district object. Does that mean that the racial gerrymandering is immune from challenge based on standing? Recall that the plaintiffs in *Gomillion v. Lightfoot* were black citizens of Alabama who, at the time of suit, were no longer residents of the newly-redistricted Tuskegee. Though they were not residents of the redefined City, the Court did not suggest that there was any problem with their standing. However *Hays* points to the opposite conclusion. In a subsequent decision the Court reaffirmed *Hays* and added a caveat: The *Hays* rule "*absent specific evidence that he personally has been subjected to a racial classification.*"[261] The Court did not further define this exception.[262]

Democrats have generally supported the creation of racially gerrymandered election districts as a way of encouraging the election of black candidates. But isolating black voters in new districts has helped the Republicans running in the other districts, which became proportionally more white, as black voters were clustered into black districts.[263]

260. 515 U.S. 737, 115 S.Ct. 2431, 132 L.Ed.2d 635 (1995), on remand 936 F.Supp. 360 (D.La.1996). O'Connor, J., for the Court, said that the plaintiffs do not have standing because they "do not live in the district that is the primary focus of their racial gerrymandering claim...." 515 U.S. at 739, 115 S.Ct. at 2433. There were no dissents. Breyer, J., joined by Souter, J., filed a concurring opinion. Stevens, J., filed an opinion concurring in the result. Ginsburg, J., concurred in the judgment. There were no dissents.

261. Shaw v. Hunt, 517 U.S. 899, 903, 116 S.Ct. 1894, 1900, 135 L.Ed.2d 207 (1996), on remand from Shaw v. Reno, 509 U.S. 630, 113 S.Ct. 2816, 125 L.Ed.2d 511 (1993) (emphasis added). The two appellants who lived in District 12 had standing only with respect to that district. The Court found no suitable plaintiff for District 1 and therefore did not consider the challenge to that district.

262. Accord, Sinkfield v. Kelley, 531 U.S. 28, 121 S.Ct. 446, 148 L.Ed.2d 329 (2000). White Alabama voters sued, alleging that the state legislative districts violated the

Equal Protection Clause. The three-judge panel held that seven of the challenged majority-white districts were the product of unconstitutional racial gerrymandering. The Supreme Court, in a unanimous per curiam opinion, remanded with instructions to dismiss the complaint on the grounds that the plaintiffs lacked standing. "Like the appellees in *Hays*, they have neither alleged nor produced any evidence that any of them was assigned to his or her district as a direct result of having 'personally been subjected to a racial classification.' ... Appellees' suggestion thus boils down to the claim that an unconstitutional use of race in drawing the boundaries of majority-minority districts necessarily involves an unconstitutional use of race in drawing the boundaries of neighboring majority-white districts. We reject that argument."

263. In the South, dozens of Republicans received safer districts or were able to mount serious challenges on what had been solid Democratic turf. In the 1992 national election 23 Southern districts with white Democratic incumbents lost black constituents after redistricting. Demo-

Standing as a Decisional Tool to Avoid Deciding Difficult Cases. The cases discusses above indicate that, as a practical matter, the Court often uses the law of standing as a decisional tool to avoid disposing of difficult cases on the merits. As the merits of the constitutional issue are more perplexing, the Court is more likely to require the plaintiff to demonstrate that he or she is really hurt by the challenged active. The Court often requires more standing than in hard cases than might require in other, easier cases.

If Congress steps in and creates standing by statute, the Court is much more likely to decide the case on the merits. Congress then has, in effect, invited the Court to decide the issue, thus serving to justify the Court's exercise of judicial review. The only limit on Congress' power is that Congress cannot exceed the case or controversy requirements of Article III. But as we have seen in *United States v. SCRAP*[264] the Article III threshold of case on controversy can be very low indeed.

This view of the Court has been subjected to much criticism:

> Protecting against an excessive judicial role by using the law of standing is likely to mean for some cases not only providing that protection but also preventing judicial review that is needed in the interests of Justice. Therefore, the law of standing is the wrong tool to use for confining courts to a role that is appropriate for courts.[265]

Nonetheless, the Court often acts as if it is using standing as another tool for confining courts to a role that is appropriate for courts.[266]

(3) Third Party Standing

The general rules is that of the application of a statute to a litigant is constitutional, he will not be heard to attack the statute on the ground that impliedly it might also be taken as applying to other persons or other situations in which its application might be unconstitutional.[267] The basis for this rule of self restraint lies in prudential concerns. The Court desires to avoid constitutional questions and to assure that the most effective and concerned advocate attacking the statute is before the Court.[268] The Court is normally not interested in hearing how the statute, if creatively interpreted, could be applied in a way that makes that particular, and hypothetical, application unconstitutional.

However, in order to protect civil rights, this basic rule has several important exceptions that give third-parties standing to assert the rights of others not before the Court. In general, the Court will allow litigants to assert the rights of third parties after weighing the importance of the relationship between the litigant and the third party, the ability of the third party to vindicate his or her own rights, and the risk that the rights of third parties will be diluted if third party standing is not allowed.

Third Party Standing and the First Amendment. Before considering specific case applications of these exceptions, keep in mind that litigants also may challenge a statute as

---

crats also were hurt in the region's GOP districts, which lost an average of 43% of their black voters. Frisby, "Florida Race Shows How Democrats Were Hurt by Effort to Create Black–Dominated Districts," Wall St. Jrl., Oct. 25, 1994, at A20 (Midwest ed.).

264. 412 U.S. 669, 93 S.Ct. 2405, 37 L.Ed.2d 254 (1973).

265. K. Davis, Administrative Law of the Seventies § 22.21 at 523 (1976).

266. For example, City of Los Angeles v. Lyons, 461 U.S. 95, 103 S.Ct. 1660, 75 L.Ed.2d 675 (1983) ruled that an individual who sued police officers for damages based on an allegation that police had subjected him to a "choke hold" could not maintain an equitable action for injunctive relief against the City of Los Angeles Police Department for the purpose of limiting choke holds against

persons arrested for nonviolent crimes. The Court found that the case or controversy requirement was not satisfied. The plaintiff had failed to show more than a hypothetical chance that the controversy would reoccur *as to him*, and he could not allege or demonstrate that all Los Angeles police officers used choke holds in all arrests.

The basis for these Article III rulings was the belief that an individual in such a situation should be entitled only to damages and that the federal courts were not to be used as continuing monitors of state police forces.

267. United States v. Raines, 362 U.S. 17, 21, 80 S.Ct. 519, 522, 4 L.Ed.2d 524 (1960).

268. Duke Power Co. v. Carolina Environmental Study Group, Inc., 438 U.S. 59, 80, 98 S.Ct. 2620, 2634, 57 L.Ed.2d 595 (1978) (noting such prudential limits on third party standing).

overbroad and violative of free speech. In overbreadth cases, the litigant challenges a statute on its face because, it is argued, although a narrowly drawn statute could constitutionally prohibit the activity, the challenged statute is overbroad and appears to include activity that is constitutionally protected. The actual litigant before the Court in such cases is injured because the Court finds he or she has a right to be prosecuted only under a statute that is narrowly drawn.[269]

The Justices agree on no specific litmus test that determines when an individual may assert the rights of others not before the Court. The Court considers whether the party in the suit can properly frame the issues as well as making a judgment whether consideration of the issue is necessary to protect the rights of third parties:

> Where practical obstacles prevent a party from asserting rights on behalf of itself, for example, the Court has recognized the doctrine of *jus tertii* standing. In such a situation, the Court considers whether the third party has sufficient injury-in-fact to satisfy the Article III case or controversy requirement, and whether, *as a prudential matter*, the third party can reasonably be expected properly to frame the issues and present them with the necessary adversarial zeal.... Within the context of the First Amendment, the Court has enunciated other concerns that justify a lessening of prudential limitations on standing. Even where a First Amendment challenge could be brought by one actually engaged in protected activity, there is a possibility that, rather than risk punishment for his conduct in challenging the statute, he will refrain from engaging further in the protected activity. Society as a whole then would be the loser. Thus, when there is a danger of chilling free speech, the concern that constitutional adju-

dication be avoided whenever possible may be outweighed by society's interest in having the statute challenged.[270]

In the First Amendment area, prudential barriers are not quite as high.

Applying Third–Party Standing Rules. A leading case illustrating one of the exceptions to the basic third-party standing rule is *Barrows v. Jackson*.[271] Prior to *Barrows*, the Court in *Shelley v. Kraemer*[272] had held that, because of the equal protection clause, courts may not use injunctions to enforce racially restrictive covenants in real property. In *Barrows*, a co-covenantor did not seek an injunction but sued at law for damages against another co-covenantor (the white seller) who allegedly broke the agreement.

The Court held that the Fourteenth Amendment did not allow the co-covenantor to collect damages from the white seller. The Court discussed third-party standing and ruled that the white seller could assert the rights of the black purchaser. Unlike *Shelley*, "no non-Caucasian is before the Court claiming to have been denied his constitutional rights. May respondent, whom petitioners seek to coerce by an action to pay damages for her failure to honor her restrictive covenant, rely on the invasion of the rights of others in her defense to this action?"[273] The Court held that she could. She was in fact subject to possible injury, for she was sued for damages of nearly $12,000.[274] And, under the special circumstances of this case, if respondent could not raise the black person's rights, "it would be difficult if not impossible for the persons whose rights are asserted to present their grievance before any court."[275] Thus the Court created an exception to what it termed "only a rule of practice ... outweighed by the need to protect the fundamental rights which would be denied by per-

---

269. See § 20.08, infra.

270. Secretary of State v. Joseph H. Munson Co., Inc., 467 U.S. 947, 956, 104 S.Ct. 2839, 2847, 81 L.Ed.2d 786, 795–96 (1984) (emphasis added).

271. 346 U.S. 249, 73 S.Ct. 1031, 97 L.Ed. 1586 (1953), rehearing denied 346 U.S. 841, 74 S.Ct. 19, 98 L.Ed. 361 (1953).

272. 334 U.S. 1, 68 S.Ct. 836, 92 L.Ed. 1161 (1948).

273. 346 U.S. at 254–255, 73 S.Ct. at 1034.

274. 346 U.S. at 256, 73 S.Ct. at 1035.

275. 346 U.S. at 257, 73 S.Ct. at 1035.

mitting the damages action to be maintained."[276]

One wonders if *Barrows* really is an illustration of third party standing. Defendant was injured in fact. Plaintiff sued her and sought a hefty damage award. Moreover, if a black purchaser has an equal protection right to *buy* property from a willing white seller, without state interference,, should not a white seller have the same equal protection right to *sell* that property to a willing black purchaser? These rights are really two sides of the same coin.[277]

Whatever might have been the rationale of *Barrows*, its rule as to third party standing has continued. Thus, a medical doctor does not have third party standing to attack a state anti-contraceptive statute on the grounds that it prevents him giving his professional advice concerning the use of contraceptives to three patients whose condition of health might be endangered by child bearing.[278] But, if the person is convicted of prescribing, selling, or giving away contraceptives, he may raise, in the defense to that action the third-party rights of the recipients.[279] While the results in these two cases are completely different, the facts are indistinguishable. As far as the doctor is concerned, the restriction on medical practice is

same in both cases, although the one involves contraception and the other, abortion.[280]

This rule in contraceptive cases is also applied in obscenity cases. The mere private possession of obscene matter cannot constitutionally be made a crime.[281] However, there is no constitutional right to distribute or sell obscene materials, and those that do so cannot raise the rights of the recipients, who do have the constitutional right to privately possess obscene materials at home.[282]

In *Warth v. Seldin*[283] the Court refused third party standing to certain litigants attacking a town's zoning regulations. These litigant-taxpayers in Rochester, New York, claimed that the refusal of the town of Penfield to allow construction of low and moderate income housing raised the litigants' taxes because their town provided more such housing than it otherwise would.

Warth noted that these taxpayers were not themselves subject to the Penfield's ordinances. Nor did Penfield's laws preclude or adversely affect a relationship existing between them and the persons whose rights were allegedly violated. No other relationship (other than an incidental congruity of interests) ex-

---

276. 346 U.S. at 257, 73 S.Ct. at 1035.

277. Cf. Peters v. Kiff, 407 U.S. 493, 92 S.Ct. 2163, 33 L.Ed.2d 83 (1972), on remand to 491 F.2d 967 (5th Cir. 1974). The Supreme Court held that a white criminal defendant had standing to attack the verdict on the grounds that blacks were excluded from the grand jury and trial jury. But only three of the six Justices comprising the majority reasoned that the defendant was injured in fact by the exclusion, and therefore had direct standing. 407 U.S. at 500, 92 S.Ct. at 2167: "[T]he exclusion of a discernible class from jury service injures [all defendants] in that it destroys the possibility that the jury will reflect a representative cross section of the community." (Opinion by Marshall J., joined by Douglas and Stewart, JJ.). Cf. Phillips Petroleum Co. v. Shutts, 472 U.S. 797, 806, 105 S.Ct. 2965, 2971, 86 L.Ed.2d 628 (1985).

Subsequently, in McCleskey v. Kemp, 481 U.S. 279, 107 S.Ct. 1756, 95 L.Ed.2d 262 (1987), rehearing denied 482 U.S. 920, 107 S.Ct. 3199, 96 L.Ed.2d 686 (1987), the Court held that a black defendant who was sentenced to death for murdering a white victim has standing to argue that he was discriminated against on the grounds that statistically a black person killing a white person was much more likely to receive the death penalty than a white killing a white, a black killing a black, or a white killing a black. The black defendant was not really raising the rights of the victim or the rights of other defendants. Rather, he

was objecting to an irrational racial classification and an irrational exercise of governmental power that allegedly harmed him. 481 U.S. at 291 n. 8, 107 S.Ct. at 1766 n. 8. On the merits, the Court rejected the constitutional challenge.

278. Tileston v. Ullman, 318 U.S. 44, 63 S.Ct. 493, 87 L.Ed. 603 (1943) (per curiam). Cf. Doe v. Bolton, 410 U.S. 179, 188–189, 93 S.Ct. 739, 745–746, 35 L.Ed.2d 201 (1973), rehearing denied 410 U.S. 959, 93 S.Ct. 1410, 35 L.Ed.2d 694 (1973).

279. Eisenstadt v. Baird, 405 U.S. 438, 443–46, 92 S.Ct. 1029, 1033–35, 31 L.Ed.2d 349 (1972); see also Griswold v. Connecticut, 381 U.S. 479, 85 S.Ct. 1678, 14 L.Ed.2d 510 (1965).

280. K. Davis, Administrative Law in the Seventies § 22.06 at 516 (1976). See generally, K. Davis, Administrative Law Treatise § 22.06 (1958).

281. Stanley v. Georgia, 394 U.S. 557, 89 S.Ct. 1243, 22 L.Ed.2d 542 (1969), on remand to 225 Ga. 273, 167 S.E.2d 756 (1969).

282. United States v. Reidel, 402 U.S. 351, 91 S.Ct. 1410, 28 L.Ed.2d 813 (1971).

283. 422 U.S. 490, 508–10, 95 S.Ct. 2197, 2210–11, 45 L.Ed.2d 343 (1975).

isted between them and the excluded persons. Nor did the taxpayers show that the persons actually excluded from Penfield were somehow unable to claim their own rights in a proper case. The injury that the Rochester taxpayers complained of—increases in taxation—only occurred because of decisions made by the appropriate Rochester authorities. And they were not parties to the case.[284] Thus, the Court allowed no third party standing.[285]

Challenging the Racial or Sexual Composition of Juries. *Powers v. Ohio*[286] held that a criminal defendant, under the equal protection clause, may object to the prosecutor's use of peremptory challenges to exclude jurors based on their race, whether or not the defendant and the excluded juror are of the same race. In *Powers*, a white defendant on trial for aggravated murder objected to the state's use of peremptory challenges to remove seven black venire persons from the jury. The Court concluded that the criminal defendant suffered injury and had standing to raise the third-party equal protection claim of the excluded jurors.

Later, the Court held that *private* litigants in civil cases cannot constitutionally use peremptory challenges to exclude jurors based on their race.[287] Similarly, criminal defense counsel may not exclude jurors based on their race.[288] Attorneys may not use peremptory challenges to exclude jurors because of their sex.[289] White defendants have the standing to object to judges discriminating against blacks in the selection of grand jurors.[290] In all of these cases, the litigant can raise the rights of the juror.

Summary. In spite of the Court's attempts to set up tests to determine when the *Barrows* justification will allow third party standing and when it will not, no consistent rationale explains the case law.[291] The Court's confused pronouncements of the third party standing issue has sometimes resulted in extensive litigation prior to ever reaching the merits.

To the extent that the Court has created pitfalls for those seeking third party standing, its conclusions in this area conflict with the general loosening of procedural burdens in cases involving personal standing. Assuming that the litigant has suffered injury in fact from the challenged conduct, that the case is sufficiently concrete and ripe, and that prudential concerns do not dictate judicial self restraint, the Court should only forbid third party standing if it is persuaded that the party seeking standing will not be an adequate representative of the third parties whose interests he champions.[292] Some cases seem to follow these principles, but others do not.

(4) Standing by State Governments, Associations, and Congressmen

State Governments. A state may sue on behalf of its citizens as *parens patriae*, "to protect the general comfort, health, or property rights of its inhabitants threatened by the proposed or continued action of another State, by prayer for injunction...." But when a state joins the Union, it loses the power as a sovereign to present and enforce individual

---

284.　422 U.S. at 509, 95 S.Ct. at 2210.

285.　Cf. Schweiker v. Gray Panthers, 453 U.S. 34, 40 n. 8, 101 S.Ct. 2633, 2638 n. 8, 69 L.Ed.2d 460 (1981) (respondent, an organization dedicated to assisting the elderly, has standing to sue Secretary of Health and Human Services because respondent alleged and proved that some of its members are persons adversely affected by Secretary's Social Security regulations).

286.　499 U.S. 400, 111 S.Ct. 1364, 113 L.Ed.2d 411 (1991).

287.　Edmonson v. Leesville Concrete Co., Inc., 500 U.S. 614, 111 S.Ct. 2077, 114 L.Ed.2d 660 (1991), on remand 943 F.2d 551 (5th Cir.1991).

288.　Georgia v. McCollum, 505 U.S. 42, 112 S.Ct. 2348, 120 L.Ed.2d 33 (1992).

289.　J.E.B. v. Alabama, 511 U.S. 127, 114 S.Ct. 1419, 128 L.Ed.2d 89 (1994).

290.　In Campbell v. Louisiana, 523 U.S. 392, 118 S.Ct. 1419, 140 L.Ed.2d 551 (1998). In this case, a white criminal defendant (accused of killing another white man) had third party standing to object to a state judge's discrimination against black persons in the selection of grand jurors. Louisiana followed an unusual procedure, under which the judge chose the foreperson outside of the grand jury pool. The defendant has the standing to object to this allegedly racist appointment.

291.　K. Davis, Administrative Law in the Seventies § 22.06 at 518–19 (1976).

292.　Rohr, Fighting for the Rights of Others: The Troubled Law of Third Party Standing and Mootness in the Federal Courts, 35 U. Miami L.Rev. 393 (1981).

claims of its citizens as their trustee against a sister state.[293] Individual citizens, of course, can enforce their own claims against a state.

The state may also sue as *parens patriae* to protect its citizens from environmental damages,[294] because, in general, a state "may act as the representative of its citizens in original actions where the injury affects the general population of a state in a substantial way."[295] As Justice Holmes explained in *Georgia v. Tennessee Copper Co.*:[296]

> The State owns very little of the territory alleged to be affected, and the damage to it capable of estimate in money, possibly, at least, is small. This is a suit by a State for an injury to it in its capacity of *quasi*-sovereign. In that capacity the State has an interest independent of and behind the titles of its citizens, in all the earth and air within its domain. It has the last word as to whether its mountains shall be stripped of their forests and its inhabitants shall breathe pure air . . . . The alleged damage to the State as a private owner is merely a makeweight . . . .[297]

But a state cannot sue the federal government as representative of its citizens. In other words, a state may not be *parens patriae* as against the federal government.[298]

If a state is suing because it has suffered loss as a state, then it is suing *on its own behalf* and not under a *parens patriae* theory. Thus *Wyoming v. Oklahoma*[299] held that Wyo-

ming had standing to challenge Oklahoma legislation that required all Oklahoma coal-fired electric generating plants (including privately owned ones) producing power for sale in Oklahoma to burn at least 10% Oklahoma-mined coal. That law resulted in less mining of Wyoming coal, thus reducing the severance taxes that Wyoming received. The state did not claim merely a loss in *general* tax revenues. It lost specific tax revenues that "fairly can be traced" to the Oklahoma law. The Court found standing and then invalidated the law under the dormant commerce clause.

States do not have standing to sue the federal government or a federal agency merely because the state alleges that federal action injured the state's economy, thereby causing a decline in general tax revenues.[300] It that kind of general allegation were enough for standing, states could convert federal courts into a virtual "Council of Revision," reviewing any federal action that had economic consequences.

Similarly, states do not have standing if they cannot allege that the requested relief would satisfy its alleged harms. For example, a state does not have standing to challenge the accuracy of a reapportionment plan if there is no showing that the state would have received additional Representatives if the plan had used supposedly more accurate data.[301]

Associations. Associations of individuals have standing to invoke judicial protection of

---

293. North Dakota v. Minnesota, 263 U.S. 365, 375–76, 44 S.Ct. 138, 140, 68 L.Ed. 342 (1923); see New Hampshire v. Louisiana, 108 U.S. 76, 2 S.Ct. 176, 27 L.Ed. 656 (1883); Louisiana v. Texas, 176 U.S. 1, 16, 20 S.Ct. 251, 256, 44 L.Ed. 347 (1900). Maryland v. Louisiana, 451 U.S. 725, 736–39, 101 S.Ct. 2114, 2123–25, 68 L.Ed.2d 576 (1981).

294. E.g., Missouri v. Illinois, 180 U.S. 208, 21 S.Ct. 331, 45 L.Ed. 497 (1901).

295. Maryland v. Louisiana, 451 U.S. 725, 737, 101 S.Ct. 2114, 2124, 68 L.Ed.2d 576 (1981).

296. 206 U.S. 230, 27 S.Ct. 618, 51 L.Ed. 1038 (1907).

297. 206 U.S. at 237, 27 S.Ct. at 619.

298. Massachusetts v. Mellon, 262 U.S. 447, 485–86, 43 S.Ct. 597, 600–01, 67 L.Ed. 1078 (1923).

299. 502 U.S. 437, 112 S.Ct. 789, 117 L.Ed.2d 1 (1992).

300. E.g., Iowa ex rel. Miller v. Block, 771 F.2d 347 (8th Cir.1985), cert. denied 478 U.S. 1012, 106 S.Ct. 3313, 92 L.Ed.2d 725 (1986).

301. Franklin v. Massachusetts, 505 U.S. 788, 801–03, 112 S.Ct. 2767, 2776–77, 120 L.Ed.2d 636 (1992) (plurality opinion of O'Connor, J., joined by Rehnquist, C.J. & White & Thomas, JJ.). Department of Commerce v. United States House of Representatives, 525 U.S. 316, 119 S.Ct. 765, 142 L.Ed.2d 797 (1999). O'Connor, for a fragmented Court, held that several state residents had Article III standing because they showed that the use of statistical sampling would result in a loss of U.S. representatives from their state. In addition, there was intrastate vote dilution because states use the population numbers of the federal decennial census to redistrict state legislative districts. This vote dilution is injury in fact, is "fairly traceable" to the use of statistical sampling, and related to the requested relief—a permanent injunction against such sampling, which will redress the alleged injury.

The Court went on to hold that the Census Act prohibited the use of statistical sampling, either as a supplement or substitute to the traditional enumeration method for calculating the population for apportionment purposes.

the association *qua* association. In addition, associations may also assert the rights of its members as long as the challenged infractions adversely affect its members' associational ties.

In general, there is a three-prong test: the members of the association must otherwise have standing to sue; and the interests that the organization seeks to protect must be germane to the purposes of the organization; and neither the claim asserted nor the requested relief necessitates the participation of the individual members in the lawsuit.[302] The first two prongs are grounded in Article III and the third prong is a prudential requirement that Congress may abrogate by statute.[303]

Associations may also establish standing (even if they have no injury to themselves) as representative of the injury to their members, but the association must still allege the kind of injury that would satisfy the standing requirement had the individual members themselves brought suit.[304] As long as the nature of the claim and of the relief sought does not make the individual participation of each injured party indispensable to proper resolution of the cause, the association may be an appropriate representative of its members, entitled to invoke the court's jurisdiction.[305]

The standing of an association to sue on behalf of its members and assert their rights depends on the nature of the relief sought. It is easier for such an association to secure injunctive, declaratory, or some other form of prospective[306] relief because then, if the remedy is granted, it will benefit those members of the association who are actually injured.[307] This assurance does not exist if the remedy sought is money damages and if the association has not suffered damages *qua* association. If the damage claims are not common to the entire membership, nor shared by all in equal degree, an association does not have standing to sue for its members' damage claims. In these cases, any alleged injury will have been suffered by the individuals, and both the fact of injury and its degree require individualized proof.[308]

Standing of Government Officials. Government officials do have standing to object to the constitutionality of laws that they are required to enforce if their refusal to enforce could cause their removal from office, but their enforcement of the law might violate their oath to support the Constitution. When they have such a Hobson's choice they have alleged the requisite personal stake in the outcome of the litigation.[309]

---

302. Warth v. Seldin, 422 U.S. 490, 511, 95 S.Ct. 2197, 2211, 45 L.Ed.2d 343 (1975). Thus, in Hunt v. Washington State Apple Advertising Commission, 432 U.S. 333, 97 S.Ct. 2434, 53 L.Ed.2d 383 (1977), the Court upheld the standing of what was technically a state agency but actually a trade association to sue on behalf of its member apple growers to challenge the constitutionality of another state's law affecting apple growers.

303. United Food and Commercial Workers Union Local 751 v. Brown Group, Inc., 517 U.S. 544, 116 S.Ct. 1529, 134 L.Ed.2d 758 (1996). The Court held—without dissent—that a federal statute, the Worker Adjustment and Retraining Notification Act, granted the union the authority to sue seeking damages on behalf of its employee members and that it was constitutional for Congress to enact this broader rule of standing.

Before this decision, some federal courts had held that associations had third party standing to seek injunctions but never damages. National Association of Realtors v. National Real Estate Association, Inc., 894 F.2d 937, 941 (7th Cir.1990).

304. Warth v. Seldin, 422 U.S. 490, 511, 95 S.Ct. 2197, 2211–12, 45 L.Ed.2d 343 (1975); Sierra Club v. Morton, 405 U.S. 727, 734–41, 92 S.Ct. 1361, 1365–69, 31 L.Ed.2d 636 (1972); National Motor Freight Traffic Association v.

United States, 372 U.S. 246, 83 S.Ct. 688, 9 L.Ed.2d 709 (1963).

305. Warth v. Seldin, 422 U.S. 490, 511, 95 S.Ct. 2197, 2212, 45 L.Ed.2d 343 (1975).

306. E.g., National Motor Freight Traffic Association v. United States, 372 U.S. 246, 83 S.Ct. 688, 9 L.Ed.2d 709 (1963).

307. Warth v. Seldin, 422 U.S. 490, 515, 95 S.Ct. 2197, 2213, 45 L.Ed.2d 343 (1975).

308. 422 U.S. at 510–11, 95 S.Ct. at 2211–12.

309. Board of Education v. Allen, 392 U.S. 236, 241 n. 5, 88 S.Ct. 1923, 1925 n. 5, 20 L.Ed.2d 1060 (1968). Some lower courts have concluded that this portion of *Allen* has been overruled sub silentio by the Court's decisions in Schlesinger v. Reservists Committee to Stop the War, 418 U.S. 208, 94 S.Ct. 2925, 41 L.Ed.2d 706 (1974), and United States v. Richardson, 418 U.S. 166, 94 S.Ct. 2940, 41 L.Ed.2d 678 (1974), discussed in § 2.12(f)(1), supra. Other lower courts believe this *Allen* standing rule to remain good law. In City of South Lake Tahoe v. California Tahoe Regional Planning Agency, 449 U.S. 1039, 101 S.Ct. 619, 66 L.Ed.2d 502 (1980) the Court refused to decide the issue and denied certiorari. Justice White, joined by Justice Marshall, dissented and wrote a cogent opinion ex-

A different question is whether legislators have standing as legislators to sue over the enactment of bills. For many years, the Supreme Court avoided ruling on the matter[310] while some federal lower courts found standing in members of Congress *qua* member, while others have rejected this theory.[311]

In *Raines v. Byrd*,[312] the Court finally decided the question and denied standing to members of Congress *qua* member. Various member of Congress brought an action challenging the constitutionality of the Line Item Veto, which Congress had enacted in 1996.[313] The law in question authorized "Any Member of Congress" or any person adversely affected to sue to invalidate the law as unconstitutional, with an expedited appeal direct to the Supreme Court. The lower court in *Raines* found standing for the members of Congress, concluded that the case was ripe (although the President had not yet exercised any authority granted to him by the law), and then held that the line item veto law was unconstitutional.

Raines held that the individual members of Congress who were the plaintiffs (and voted against the line item veto law) did not have a sufficient personal stake in the dispute and did not allege a sufficient concrete injury to estab-lish the minimum standing required under Article III. The plaintiffs were not singled out for unfavorable or discriminatory treatment compared to other members of the House and Senate. While they claim that the line item veto law lessened congressional power, that is not a loss to which they are personally entitled (unlike a case where Congress refused to seat a Representative who was personally entitled to his seat).[314]

In this case, all the votes that plaintiffs have cast in Congress were counted and given effect. This case is not like *Coleman v. Miller*[315] where Kansas state legislators claimed that their votes (opposing ratification of the Child Labor Amendment to the U.S. Constitution) were nullified because the Kansas Lieutenant Governor broke a deadlock and voted, when he allegedly was not eligible to do so. *Coleman* only stands for the proposition that legislators whose votes would have been sufficient to defeat or enact a specific legislative action have standing to sue if that legislative action goes into effect (or is defeated) on the grounds that their votes were completely nullified.[316] But the plaintiffs in *Raines* voted for a specific bill and their votes were counted and given full effect.

plaining why the *Allen* standing rule is still good law. Legislators normally would not have standing under this theory because they do not normally enforce the law.

310. The issue was raised in the lower federal court but not decided by the Supreme Court in EPA v. Mink, 410 U.S. 73, 75 n. 2, 93 S.Ct. 827, 830 n. 2, 35 L.Ed.2d 119 (1973). See also Bowsher v. Synar, 478 U.S. 714, 722, 106 S.Ct. 3181, 3186, 92 L.Ed.2d 583 (1986).

311. E.g., Kennedy v. Sampson, 511 F.2d 430, 435–36 (D.C.Cir.1974) (standing upheld for Senator Kennedy seeking declaratory judgment that presidential pocket veto of a bill was ineffective); Holtzman v. Schlesinger, 484 F.2d 1307, 1315 (2d Cir.1973) (Congresswoman Holtzman does not have standing *qua* Congresswoman, to attack constitutionality of Indo–China war), certiorari denied 416 U.S. 936, 94 S.Ct. 1935, 40 L.Ed.2d 286 (1974).

312. 521 U.S. 811, 117 S.Ct. 2312, 138 L.Ed.2d 849 (1997). Souter, J., concurred in the judgment, joined by Ginsburg, J. Stevens, J. and Breyer, J., each filed dissenting opinions.

Later, Clinton v. City of New York, 524 U.S. 417, 118 S.Ct. 2091, 141 L.Ed.2d 393 (1998), allowed another challenge to the line item veto act. In this case, the President actually exercised the line item veto and the challengers sustained actual, concrete, and immediate injury as a result. The Court then went on to invalidate the Presidential line item veto as unconstitutional.

313. Pub. L. 104–130, 110 Stat. at Large 1200, codified at, 2 U.S.C.A. §§ 691 et seq. The Act itself does not use the term "veto." It authorizes the President to "cancel" certain spending and tax benefits, with the power of both Houses of Congress to override this cancellation.

314. In contrast, in Powell v. McCormack, 395 U.S. 486, 496, 512–14, 89 S.Ct. 1944, 1950–51, 1959–60, 23 L.Ed.2d 491 (1969), Powell alleged (and the Court found) that he had been singled out for unfavorable treatment and was unconstitutionally excluded from Congress and could not keep his seat although he had won the office.

315. 307 U.S. 433, 59 S.Ct. 972, 83 L.Ed. 1385 (1939). *Coleman* involved *state* lawmakers, a point that the *Raines* Court acknowledges. *Raines* suggests that other factors may distinguish *Colemen*. The Kansas Supreme Court had treated the Senators' interests in their votes as granting standing to decide the federal question. In addition, *Coleman* does not raise the separation of powers issues that are raised in cases involving Federal legislators. 521 U.S. at 824 n. 8, 117 S.Ct. at 2320 n. 8.

316. 521 U.S. at __ & n. 6, 117 S.Ct. at 2319 & n. 6. Accord, Bender v. Williamsport Area School District, 475 U.S. 534, 544–45 n. 7, 106 S.Ct. 1326, 1333 n. 7, 89 L.Ed.2d 501 (1986) (dicta).

The Line Item Veto Act passed notwithstanding their opposition. The institutional injury that plaintiffs alleged in *Raines* is not personal to the plaintiffs, is widely dispersed among all the legislators (unlike *Coleman*), and is wholly abstract.

(5) Standing and Equal Protection

Every challenge claiming that the law violates equal protection by being under inclusive raises a special standing issue. If a court invalidates the law, the state can respond either by extending the benefits equally to everyone, or denying the benefits equally to everyone.

If the person denied benefits sues, the state can argue that he has no standing because, if the state denies benefits to everyone, that person denied benefits will be no better off. If the person granted benefits sues, then the state can argue that he is not injured by the present law. In such circumstances the Supreme Court allows either party standing, otherwise under inclusive statutes would be immune from challenge.

The point is well illustrated in *Orr v. Orr*.[317] A divorced wife instituted contempt proceedings against her former husband for nonpayment of alimony. He asserted that the statutory scheme under which husbands but not wives could be required to pay alimony was unconstitutional. The husband failed to ask for alimony. If the state would respond by neutrally extending alimony to needy husbands as well as needy wives, Mr. Orr would still be obligated to pay the alimony to his former wife. The state therefore argued that Mr. Orr therefore had no standing, and that only a *needy* husband denied alimony could sue. But if the state would respond to a holding of unconstitutionality by neutrally denying alimony to everyone, then, under the state's theory, the needy husband would lack standing.

The Court concluded: "Because we have no way of knowing how the State will in fact respond, unless we are to hold that under inclusive statutes can never be challenged because *any* plaintiff's success can theoretically be thwarted, Mr. Orr must be held to have standing here."[318]

A person excluded from a class of persons receiving favorable governmental treatment may challenge the classification as a violation of equal protection even if invalidation of the classification would result in the elimination of benefits to all persons rather than the inclusion of others in the favored class. A rule that would prohibit members of a disfavored group from attacking classifications benefiting others because the plaintiff would never be included in the class would insulate unequal treatment from constitutional attack and perpetuate unconstitutional discrimination against members of a disfavored group.[319]

(g) The Duty to Avoid Constitutional Decisions

The doctrines related to advisory opinions, mootness, collusiveness, ripeness, prematurity and abstractness, standing, and other such rules of self-restraint are all functions of the general and basic judicial duty to avoid decisions of constitutional questions. This duty, in turn, draws support from Chief Justice Marshall's rationale of judicial review as a reluctant power exercised only because the Court must decide cases brought before it in conformity with the Constitution.[320]

There are also more pragmatic considerations for this policy of self-restraint. Judicial review is inconsistent with majority rule, and, because of the conflict between the judiciary and the democratic system, may result in popular disapproval of court action. The policy of

---

317. 440 U.S. 268, 99 S.Ct. 1102, 59 L.Ed.2d 306 (1979), on remand to 374 So.2d 895 (Ala.Civ.App.1979), writ denied 374 So.2d 898 (Ala.1979), appeal dismissed and certiorari denied 444 U.S. 1060, 100 S.Ct. 993, 62 L.Ed.2d 738 (1980).

318. 440 U.S. at 273, 99 S.Ct. at 1108 (emphasis in original). As the Court also noted by way of analogy, "There is no doubt that a state law imposing alimony obligations on blacks but not whites could be challenged by a black who was required to pay."

319. Heckler v. Mathews, 465 U.S. 728, 104 S.Ct. 1387, 79 L.Ed.2d 646 (1984).

320. Marbury v. Madison, 5 U.S. (1 Cranch) 137, 2 L.Ed. 60 (1803).

See Judge Tjoflat, citing Treatise in Thigpen v. Smith, 792 F.2d 1507, 1514 n. 12 (11th Cir.1986); Judge Dillin, citing Treatise in Laidlaw Acquisition Corp. v. Mayflower Group, Inc., 636 F.Supp. 1513, 1516 (S.D.Ind.1986).

a strict necessity in disposing of constitutional issues is a useful device that helps assure that judicial review does not take place gratuitously.[321] As Justice Rutledge frankly acknowledged in *Rescue Army v. Municipal Court:*[322]

> It is not without significance for the policy's validity that the periods when the power [to avoid a constitutional decision] has been exercised most readily and broadly have been the ones in which this Court and the institution of judicial review have had their stormiest experiences.[323]

In *Rescue Army,* Rutledge offered some of the important rationales for this policy, relying in part on Justice Brandeis' famous concurrence in *Ashwander v. Tennessee Valley Authority.*[324] Rutledge's opinion merits quotation at length. He explained that the Court has "developed, for its own governance in the cases confessedly within its jurisdiction, a series of rules under which it has avoided passing upon a large part of all the constitutional questions pressed upon it for decision." Thus, the Court should not decide constitutional issues affecting legislation in a friendly, nonadversary proceedings, or in advance of the necessity of deciding them, or in broader terms than are required by the precise facts to which the ruling is to be applied. If the record presents some other ground on which the case may be disposed of, the Court should seek that other ground. The Court should not decide a constitutional issue if the complaining party fails to show that he is injured by the statute's operation, or the party has availed himself of its benefits, or the Court can fairly construe the statute in a way that avoids the question.

To the more usual considerations of timeliness and maturity, of concreteness, definiteness, certainty, and of adversity of interests affected, are to be added in cases coming from state courts involving state legislation those arising when questions of construction, essentially matters of state law, remain unresolved or highly ambiguous. They include, of course, questions of incorporation by reference and severability.... Necessarily whether decision of the constitutional issue will be made must depend upon the degree to which uncertainty exists in these respects. And this inevitably will vary with particular causes and their varying presentations....[325]

Opinions often state that, when a law is challenged as unconstitutional, "this Court first ascertains whether the statute can be reasonably construed to avoid the constitutional difficulty."[326] Courts normally presume that statutes are constitutional. Illustrating this policy is the fact that some legislators may vote against a measure on the grounds of its unconstitutionality and later, when they become judges and are on the bench, they hold that the same law is constitutional. Though they may not have changed their personal viewpoint, they have exercised the self-restraint of the judiciary.[327]

---

321. Notwithstanding the Supreme Court's policy of strict necessity in deciding constitutional cases, the Court may limit the grant of review to certain questions presented, but its power to decide is not limited to the precise terms of the question presented. E.g., Procunier v. Navarette, 434 U.S. 555, 559–560, n. 6, 98 S.Ct. 855, 858 n. 6, 55 L.Ed.2d 24 (1978), on remand to 581 F.2d 202 (9th Cir. 1978) citing Blonder–Tongue Laboratories, Inc. v. University of Illinois Foundation, 402 U.S. 313, 320 n. 6, 91 S.Ct. 1434, 1438 n. 6, 28 L.Ed.2d 788 (1971), on remand to 334 F.Supp. 47 (N.D.Ill.1971), affirmed 465 F.2d 380 (7th Cir.1972), certiorari denied 409 U.S. 1061, 93 S.Ct. 559, 34 L.Ed.2d 513 (1972). See also, Hart & Wechsler's The Federal Courts and the Federal System 1599 (2d ed. 1973), and id. at 640 ("Are these practices consistent with the jurisdictional statute's provision for review of 'judgments or decrees', rather than issues?").

322. 331 U.S. 549, 67 S.Ct. 1409, 91 L.Ed. 1666 (1947). In re Contest of the Election for the Offices of Governor and Lieutenant Governor Held at the General Election on November 2, 1982, 93 Ill.2d 463, 496, 67 Ill.Dec. 131, 444 N.E.2d 170 (1983) (Ward, Goldenhersh, and Clark, JJ. dissenting, citing treatise).

323. 331 U.S. at 572 n. 38, 67 S.Ct. at 1421 n. 38.

324. 297 U.S. 288, 341–356, 56 S.Ct. 466, 480–87, 80 L.Ed. 688 (1936).

325. 331 U.S. at 568–574, 67 S.Ct. at 1419–22 (footnotes and case citations omitted).

326. Ellis v. Brotherhood of Ry., Airline & S.S. Clerks, 466 U.S. 435, 444, 104 S.Ct. 1883, 1890, 80 L.Ed.2d 428, 439 (1984), on remand to 736 F.2d 1340 (9th Cir.1984) citing Califano v. Yamasaki, 442 U.S. 682, 692–93, 99 S.Ct. 2545, 2553, 61 L.Ed.2d 176 (1979), on remand to 607 F.2d 329 (9th Cir.1979); Ashwander v. TVA, 297 U.S. 288, 347, 56 S.Ct. 466, 483, 80 L.Ed. 688 (1936) (concurring opinion).

327. Thayer, The Origin and Scope of the American Doctrine of Constitutional Law, 7 Harv.L.Rev. 129, 144 (1893).

§ 2.13   Adequate State Grounds and Federal Questions

(a) The General Rule

As a general rule, when the Supreme Court reviews a decision of a state court, it only reviews the federal questions, not the state law questions:

> The State courts are the appropriate tribunals, as this court has repeatedly held, for the decision of questions arising under this local law, whether statutory or otherwise. And it is not lightly to be presumed that Congress acted upon a principle which implies a distrust of their integrity or of their ability to construe those laws correctly.[1]

Hence, it is the general principle that the Court does not review state court judgments that rest on what are called *adequate and independent state grounds*. Justice Jackson has said that the reason for this rule is "so obvious" that it is rarely been thought to warrant statement. Its rationale, he explained, is—

> found in the partitioning of power between the state and federal judicial systems and in the limitations of our own jurisdiction. Our only power over state judgments is to correct them to the extent that they incorrectly adjudge federal rights. And our power is to correct wrong judgments, not to revise opinions. We are not permitted to render an advisory opinion, and if the same judgment would be rendered by the state court after

we corrected its views of federal laws, our review could amount to nothing more than an advisory opinion.[2]

This rationale is not entirely correct. There is historical evidence that Congress, in fact, did intend review of the whole case.[3] On occasion, the Supreme Court has said that it is unnecessary to determine if the rule is constitutionally based, because there is adequate statutory basis for the requirement.[4] Moreover, if the Supreme Court were to decide a federal issue when the state decision rested on an alternative adequate and independent state ground, the federal decision is more like a moot decision rather than an advisory one, because the case is a concrete controversy. While the Court has called mootness a constitutional requirement,[5] it has also been more willing to relax the requirement in the public interest, so that the law not be "that rigid."[6]

(b) Applications of the Rule

The intricacies of this rule of review of state court opinions are considered in detail elsewhere.[7] However, a summary of the basic elements of this rule is useful to appreciate some of the restrictions on Supreme Court review of state court decisions.

A state court may rule that a state law is repugnant to the state constitution, and also find, as an independent, alternative holding, that the state law violates the U.S. Constitution. In this case, there is no federal question

---

§ 2.13

1. Murdock v. City of Memphis, 87 U.S. (20 Wall.) 590, 626, 22 L.Ed. 429 (1874). An important issue in *Murdock* was whether the Judiciary Act of 1867, § 2, 14 Stat. 385, 386, which amended section 25 of the Judiciary Act of 1789, 1 Stat. 73, conferred on the Supreme Court the power to decide all of the questions presented by the state case that are necessary to its final judgment or decree; and not just the federal questions. The 1867 Amendment eliminated the clause of the 1789 Act that limited Supreme Court review to the federal questions. The Court decided that although the restrictive clause was not enacted Congress did not mean to confer such power. See generally, Note, The Untenable Nonfederal Ground in the Supreme Court, 74 Harv.L.Rev. 1375 (1961).

2. Herb v. Pitcairn, 324 U.S. 117, 125–126, 65 S.Ct. 459, 463, 89 L.Ed. 789 (1945) (emphasis added). See generally, M. Redish, Federal Jurisdiction: Tensions in the Allocation of Judicial Power 216–31 (1980); P. Hay & R. Rotunda, The United States Federal System: Legal Inte-

gration in the American Experience 203–18 (Giuffré, Milan 1982).

3. Charles Alan Wright, Law of Federal Courts § 107 (4th ed.1983): "Such a course seems wholly consistent with the temper of the times." See also 2 W. Crosskey, Politics and the Constitution in the History of the United States, 711–817 (1953).

4. Fay v. Noia, 372 U.S. 391, 430 n. 40, 83 S.Ct. 822, 844 n. 40, 9 L.Ed.2d 837 (1963) specifically referring to, but not accepting, Jackson, J.'s constitutional justification in Herb v. Pitcairn, 324 U.S. 117, 125–126, 65 S.Ct. 459, 462–63, 89 L.Ed. 789 (1945).

5. E.g., Liner v. Jafco, Inc., 375 U.S. 301, 84 S.Ct. 391, 11 L.Ed.2d 347 (1964).

6. Roe v. Wade, 410 U.S. 113, 125, 93 S.Ct. 705, 713, 35 L.Ed.2d 147 (1973), rehearing denied 410 U.S. 959, 93 S.Ct. 1409, 35 L.Ed.2d 694 (1973).

7. See generally Charles Alan Wright, Law of Federal Courts § 107 (4th ed. 1983).

for the Supreme Court to review. If the Supreme Court agrees with the state court interpretation of the U.S. Constitution, then it will affirm the state decision. And if the Supreme Court disagrees with the state court interpretation of the U.S. Constitution, it will still affirm the decision, because the U.S. Supreme Court cannot reverse the state court as to a decision resting on an interpretation of the state constitution.[8]

Similarly, there should be no federal review if the state court, though presented with a federal ground of decision, does not have to reach it, and chooses to base its decision only on the nonfederal ground.[9] For example, in the above hypothetical, assume that the state court holds that the state law violates the state constitution. The state court could have reached the federal ground but chose not to do so. Again, the general rule is that there should be no U.S. Supreme Court review. The state court is the final arbiter of what its own state constitution means. If the U.S. Supreme Court reaches out and decides the federal ground, that would not change the result in the case, because—whether the U.S. Supreme Court holds that the state law violates, or does not violate, the U.S. Constitution—the state court already invalidated the state law on state constitutional grounds.

If the state court holds the state law valid under both state and federal constitutional provisions, then the Supreme Court may review. In that case, if it disagreed with the state court's view of the federal constitution (or of the federal statute or of the treaty), the state decision would be reversed, regardless of the interpretation of the state law.

Now consider the situation where the state court holds that a statute violates both the state and U.S. Constitution, but the state court did not intend that its decision rest independently on the state ground. Assume, for example, that it said that the state free speech guarantee means exactly what the federal free speech guarantee means. If the state court interprets its state law ground to be as broad as the federal constitutional provision, then the Supreme Court may review the federal issue. Because the state court felt compelled, in construing its own law, to follow federal case law, the U.S. Supreme Court may review because the state court may have misapprehended federal law.[10] The state ground is not really "independent" of the federal ground. If the U.S. Supreme Court reverses and remands, the state court may change its interpretation of state law.

If the state court in fact decided the case on a federal ground, there can be Supreme Court review *even though* the state court ruling might have been decided on an adequate nonfederal ground.[11] For example, if a litigant claims that a state law violates the state and U.S. Constitution, the state court may hold that it violates the U.S. Constitution, and not bother to reach the state law ground. The U.S. Supreme Court can review, because, if it disagrees with the state court on the federal ground, the case will be reversed and remanded. The state court then will decide the state issue.

The Problem of Ambiguity. Sometimes the state ground of decision is unclear.[12] For example, the state court may strike a statute but the state court opinion may be ambiguous

8. E.g., Serrano v. Priest, 5 Cal.3d 584, 96 Cal.Rptr. 601, 487 P.2d 1241 (1971), appeal after remand 18 Cal.3d 728, 135 Cal.Rptr. 345, 557 P.2d 929 (1976), certiorari denied 432 U.S. 907, 97 S.Ct. 2951, 53 L.Ed.2d 1079 (1977), opinion supplemented 20 Cal.3d 25, 141 Cal.Rptr. 315, 569 P.2d 1303 (1977), Cf. Fox Film Corp. v. Muller, 296 U.S. 207, 56 S.Ct. 183, 80 L.Ed. 158 (1935).

9. E.g., Wood v. Chesborough, 228 U.S. 672, 33 S.Ct. 706, 57 L.Ed. 1018 (1913).

10. Delaware v. Prouse, 440 U.S. 648, 652–55, 99 S.Ct. 1391, 1395–97, 59 L.Ed.2d 660 (1979); South Dakota v. Neville, 459 U.S. 553, 556–57, 103 S.Ct. 916, 919 n. 5, 74 L.Ed.2d 748 (1983).

11. St. Louis, I. M. & Southern Ry. Co. v. McWhirter, 229 U.S. 265, 275–276, 33 S.Ct. 858, 862, 57 L.Ed. 1179 (1913). Orr v. Orr, 440 U.S. 268, 274–75, 99 S.Ct. 1102, 1109–10, 59 L.Ed.2d 306 (1979), on remand 374 So.2d 895 (Ala.Civ.App.1979), writ denied 374 So.2d 898 (Ala.1979), appeal dismissed, certiorari denied 444 U.S. 1060, 100 S.Ct. 993, 62 L.Ed.2d 738 (1980).

12. It is unclear in the case law if these criteria of "adequate" and "independent" are the same, alternative, or conjunctive. Note, The Untenable Nonfederal Ground in the Supreme Court, 74 Harv.L.Rev. 1374, 1381–1382 (1961).

as to its basis.[13] The decision may cite federal cases, reflect federal reasoning, or otherwise indicate its reliance on federal law.

When it is unclear whether the state court has relied only on state grounds, *Michigan v. Long*,[14] developed the following rule:

[If] a state court decision fairly appears to rest primarily on federal law, or to be interwoven with the federal law, and when the adequacy and independence of any possible state law ground is not clear from the face of the opinion, we will accept as the most reasonable explanation that the state court decided the case the way it did because it believed that federal law required it to do so. If a state court chooses merely to rely on federal precedents as it would on the precedents of all other jurisdictions, then it need only make clear by a plain statement in its judgment or opinion that the federal cases are being used only for the purpose of guidance, and do not themselves compel the result that the court has reached.... If the state court decision indicates clearly and expressly that it is alternatively based on bona fide separate, adequate, and independent grounds, we, of course, will not undertake to review the decision.[15]

The rule in *Long* solves the problem of what to do if the state decision is ambiguous. Instead of trying to divine in the state court tea leaves what the state court meant, and instead of delaying the litigation and remanding to state court for clarification, *Long* adopts a clear, bright line test. If the state court really intends the case to be decided on state law

grounds, it need only make its intention clear by a plain statement in its judgment.[16]

Justice O'Connor's opinion for the Court in *Michigan v. Long*[17] established an important principle of federalism: state courts should not bind states by imposing phantom federal restrictions. If a state court wishes to impose constitutional restrictions on the state, it may certainly do so, and if those restrictions are clearly based on the state constitution, the federal courts will not interfere. The state court has the right to go further in creating constitutional rights (based on the *state* Constitution) than a federal court would have gone (based on the U.S. Constitution).

If state courts are going to create and expand rights, they must take the responsibility for doing so and unambiguously decide the case on state law grounds. Power and responsibility go together like pepper and salt. Otherwise, state courts could, in effect, blame the federal Constitution for imposing what are really phantom constitutional restrictions on state government. In order to unleash the states from these phantom federal restrictions, the Supreme Court takes review of cases where state courts have created constitutional rights purportedly (or ambiguously) relying on the U.S. Constitution.[18]

State Law That Incorporates by Reference Federal Law. Sometimes a state law will incorporate a federal law by reference. The U.S. Supreme Court may review the state court decision in such circumstances, because the state court will be relying on federal law to

13. See Herb v. Pitcairn, 324 U.S. 117, 127, 65 S.Ct. 459, 464, 89 L.Ed. 789 (1945) ("it is not necessary to [the state court's] functions to make a sharp separation of the [state and federal questions on which] their discussion is often interlaced.")

14. 463 U.S. 1032, 103 S.Ct. 3469, 77 L.Ed.2d 1201 (1983), on remand 419 Mich. 636, 359 N.W.2d 194 (1984).

See O'Neill, The Good, the Bad, and the Burger Court: Victims' Rights and a New Model of Criminal Review, 75 J.Crim.L. & Criminology 363 (1984).

15. 463 U.S. at 1040–41, 103 S.Ct. at 3476, 77 L.Ed.2d at 1214. Uhler v. AFL–CIO, 468 U.S. 1310, 105 S.Ct. 5, 82 L.Ed.2d 896 (1984) (Rehnquist, Circuit Justice).

16. By way of footnote the Court warned that there may be circumstances in which clarification is necessary,

"and we will not be foreclosed from taking the appropriate action." 463 U.S. at 1041 n. 6, 103 S.Ct. at 3476 n. 6, 77 L.Ed.2d at 1214 n. 6.

17. 463 U.S. 1032, 103 S.Ct. 3469, 77 L.Ed.2d 1201 (1983), on remand 419 Mich. 636, 359 N.W.2d 194 (1984). The Tenth Amendment supports this conclusion.

18. New York v. Class, 475 U.S. 106, 106 S.Ct. 960, 89 L.Ed.2d 81 (1986), on remand 67 N.Y.2d 431, 503 N.Y.S.2d 313, 494 N.E.2d 444 (1986) (state court decision reversing weapons conviction did not rest on adequate and independent state ground where state court mentioned state Constitution only once (and then only in connection with the U.S. Constitution) and there was no plain statement that the decision rested on state grounds). See also, California v. Carney, 471 U.S. 386, 389 n. 1, 105 S.Ct. 2066, 2068 n. 1, 85 L.Ed.2d 406 (1985).

adjudicate rights. Usually the federal law is itself operative in the facts of the case. The Supreme Court may decide the federal question and remand to the state courts.[19] For example, state law may create a tort action for damages resulting from violation of a federal safety law. A state court decision involving the tort action may call for an interpretation of the federal law. The U.S. Supreme Court can review the federal issue.

State Procedural Law. The U.S. Supreme Court may not review a case if a decision on a state procedural ground prevents the state court from reaching the federal substantive issue. For example, the state court may have a consistent practice of declining to answer questions not reserved.[20] Or the state court may decide not to reach the substantive issue because of res judicata[21] or some other requirement of state law.[22] The state law procedural ground means that the state court never gets to the federal issue. Normally, the U.S. Supreme Court cannot get to the issue either.

But, there are some circumstances where the Supreme Court may review the state decision and overcome the state procedural hurdle.

Even though the claimed constitutional protection be denied on nonfederal grounds, it is the province of this Court to inquire whether the decision of the state court rests on a *fair or substantial* basis. If unsubstan-

tial, constitutional obligations may not be thus avoided.[23]

For example, U.S. Supreme Court review is not prevented by a novel procedural requirement that appears to be newly created by the state court in the very decision barring the litigant.[24] Similarly, a state court decision overruling its prior case law to bar the litigant's assertion of the federal right[25] will not prevent Supreme Court review.

When the resolution of the state procedural question depends on a federal constitutional ruling—e.g., whether a federal constitutional challenge was waived—then the state law prong of the state court holding is not independent of the federal law and the Supreme Court is not precluded from exercising jurisdiction.[26] As Justice Holmes explained, "Whatever springs the State may set for those who are endeavoring to assert rights that the State confers, the assertion of federal rights, when plainly and reasonably made, is not to be defeated under the name of local practice."[27]

Henry v. Mississippi[28] is an unusual case concerning the procedural rules that relate to foreclosing Supreme Court review. The state convicted Aaron Henry, a civil rights worker, of disturbing the peace by indecent proposals to, and offensive contact with, an 18 year-old hitchhiker. Under state law, the state needed corroborative evidence for conviction, and the only such evidence was the fruit of a search,

19. E.g., Moore v. Chesapeake & Ohio Ry. Co., 291 U.S. 205, 214, 54 S.Ct. 402, 405–06, 78 L.Ed. 755 (1934).

20. See Tileston v. Ullman, 318 U.S. 44, 63 S.Ct. 493, 87 L.Ed. 603 (1943). Cf. Webb v. Webb, 451 U.S. 493, 101 S.Ct. 1889, 68 L.Ed.2d 392 (1981) (where petitioner failed to raise her federal claim in the state courts, which failed to rule on the federal issue, the writ of certiorari dismissed for want of jurisdiction).

21. See Postal Telegraph Cable Co. v. City of Newport, 247 U.S. 464, 474–476, 38 S.Ct. 566, 570–71, 62 L.Ed. 1215 (1918).

However, the state court's decision to apply law of the case (as opposed to res judicata) is not a procedural hurdle foreclosing U.S. Supreme Court review. E.g., Pennsylvania v. Ritchie, 480 U.S. 39, 48 n. 7, 107 S.Ct. 989, 997 n. 7, 94 L.Ed.2d 40 (1987).

22. See, Edelman v. California, 344 U.S. 357, 358–359, 361, 73 S.Ct. 293, 294–95, 296, 97 L.Ed. 387 (1953) (denial of petitioner's motion rested on adequate state ground, his choice of the wrong remedy under local law.).

23. Lawrence v. State Tax Commission, 286 U.S. 276, 282, 52 S.Ct. 556, 558, 76 L.Ed. 1102 (1932) (emphasis added).

24. E.g., NAACP v. Alabama ex rel. Patterson, 357 U.S. 449, 457–58, 78 S.Ct. 1163, 1169–70, 2 L.Ed.2d 1488 (1958).

25. Brinkerhoff–Faris Trust & Savings Co. v. Hill, 281 U.S. 673, 678 & 682 n. 9, 50 S.Ct. 451, 453, 455 n. 9, 74 L.Ed. 1107 (1930).

26. Enterprise Irrigation District v. Farmers' Mutual Canal Co., 243 U.S. 157, 164, 37 S.Ct. 318, 320, 61 L.Ed. 644 (1917).

27. Davis v. Wechsler, 263 U.S. 22, 24, 44 S.Ct. 13, 14, 68 L.Ed. 143 (1923).

28. 379 U.S. 443, 85 S.Ct. 564, 13 L.Ed.2d 408 (1965), rehearing denied 380 U.S. 926, 85 S.Ct. 878, 13 L.Ed.2d 813 (1965), on remand 253 Miss. 263, 174 So.2d 348 (1965), motion denied 381 U.S. 908, 85 S.Ct. 1528, 14 L.Ed.2d 431 (1965), on remand 198 So.2d 213 (Miss.1967), reinstated 202 So.2d 40 (1967), certiorari denied 392 U.S. 931, 88 S.Ct. 2276, 20 L.Ed.2d 1389 (1968).

which the state supreme court had found to be illegal. The state supreme court reversed Henry's conviction, even though Henry's counsel had not made an objection to the introduction of the evidence at the time it was introduced. The state court excused Henry's counsel's failure to comply with Mississippi's contemporaneous objection rule because of what it called out-of-state counsel's unfamiliarity with local procedure. After this opinion the state filed a suggestion of error, explaining that Henry had also been represented by competent local counsel as well as out of state counsel. The state court then withdrew its opinion and filed a new one affirming the conviction.

The U.S. Supreme Court held that Henry's federal claims were not necessarily foreclosed by failure to comply with local procedure. Justice Brennan, for the majority, argued that "a litigant's procedural defaults in state proceedings do not prevent vindication of his federal rights unless the State's insistence on compliance with its procedural rule serves a legitimate state interest."[29] The Court found that the contemporaneous objection rule to the introduction of illegal evidence does serve a legitimate state interest but this purpose "may have been substantially served by petitioner's motion at the close of the State's evidence asking for a directed verdict because of the erroneous admission ..." of evidence.[30] Then the Court remanded to determine if petitioner's counsel *deliberately bypassed* the contemporaneous objection rule as part of trial strategy, in which case there really was a waiver of constitutional rights, and the State could insist on its procedural requirements.[31]

What *Henry* was apparently doing was to adopt a habeas corpus theory of waiver of constitutional rights in criminal cases, and then incorporate that habeas theory into a case under direct Supreme Court review. It was perhaps no accident that Justice Brennan, author of *Henry*, was also the author of the leading habeas case developing the waiver theory for collateral review.[32] *Henry* has not had any significant growth in the law, and it may be simply limited to its facts.[33]

Procedural requirements that are really federal in nature cannot be used to defeat Supreme Court review by a more restrictive state interpretation. Thus, a state court refusal to consider a federal claim on the grounds that it is moot will not prevent Supreme Court review, for the question of mootness in such circumstances is itself a question of federal law, which the Supreme Court must decide.[34]

State Substantive Law. In some cases the Supreme Court may review a state court decision because the state substantive law is interwoven with important federal interests. For example, normally what is a "contract" is a matter of state law, but the Constitution provides that no state shall impair "the Obligation of Contracts...."[35] So that the constitutional mandate may not become a dead letter, "we are bound to decide for ourselves whether a contract was made, what are its terms and conditions, and whether the State has, by later legislation, impaired its obligation. This involves an appraisal of the statutes of the State and the decisions of its courts."[36]

29. 379 U.S. at 447, 85 S.Ct. at 567.

30. 379 U.S. at 448, 85 S.Ct. at 568.

31. 379 U.S. at 450, 85 S.Ct. at 568–69.

32. Fay v. Noia, 372 U.S. 391, 439, 83 S.Ct. 822, 849, 9 L.Ed.2d 837 (1963). *Fay* was relied on in *Henry*, e.g., 379 U.S. 443 at 450, 452, 453, 85 S.Ct. 564 at 568–69, 569–70, 570–71.

On remand, the state court found waiver and reaffirmed his conviction. Henry v. State, 198 So.2d 213, 202 So.2d 40 (Miss.1967), certiorari denied 392 U.S. 931, 88 S.Ct. 2276, 20 L.Ed.2d 1389 (1968). See also 388 U.S. 901, 87 S.Ct. 2089, 18 L.Ed.2d 1342 (1967). Mr. Henry subsequently won his case when a federal district court, in a habeas corpus proceeding, found no waiver. Henry v. Williams, 299 F.Supp. 36 (N.D.Miss.1969).

33. Cf. Parker v. North Carolina, 397 U.S. 790, 90 S.Ct. 1458, 25 L.Ed.2d 785 (1970) (failure to follow state procedural rule that required objection to composition of grand jury before guilty plea is adequate state procedural ground of decision; *Henry* not cited). But see Camp v. Arkansas, 404 U.S. 69, 92 S.Ct. 307, 30 L.Ed.2d 223 (1971) (*Henry* cited and case reversed); Monger v. Florida, 405 U.S. 958, 962, 92 S.Ct. 1163, 1165–66, 31 L.Ed.2d 236 (1972) (*Henry* cited by dissenters urging reversal).

34. Liner v. Jafco, Inc., 375 U.S. 301, 304, 84 S.Ct. 391, 393–94, 11 L.Ed.2d 347 (1964).

35. U.S. Const. art. I, § 10.

36. Indiana ex rel. Anderson v. Brand, 303 U.S. 95, 100, 58 S.Ct. 443, 446, 82 L.Ed. 685 (1938) (footnote omitted), rehearing denied 303 U.S. 667, 58 S.Ct. 641, 82

Were the rule otherwise, a state court could preclude Supreme Court review of impairment of contract cases simply by claiming that, as a matter of state law, there never was a contract. Or a state could preclude review of a criminal case allegedly based on a forced confession by accepting the federal rule as to voluntariness but finding that, as a factual matter, the confession was not coerced.

§ 2.14   The Abstention Doctrine

(a) *Pullman* and the Origins of the Abstention Doctrine

The view that federal courts are under a duty to exercise their jurisdiction in every case where it was properly invoked is one that the courts followed for many years. As Chief Justice Marshall explained:

> [T]his Court will not take jurisdiction if it should not: but it is equally true, that it must take jurisdiction if it should.... We have no more right to decline the exercise of jurisdiction which is given, than to usurp that which is not given.[1]

In many older cases, the Court in fact, rejected requests for stays of its jurisdiction pending decision by the state courts.[2]

However, exercising federal jurisdiction can raise unnecessary constitutional problems when a plaintiff sues in federal court protesting state action and a decision as to the applicable interpretation of state law is relevant to the federal constitutional issue. Where state law is unclear, the federal court is faced with several unpleasant alternatives. The court can proceed and decide the state law question in such a way as to avoid the constitutional issue, but a state court may later disagree with the federal court's interpretation. Or, the federal court can apply the state law in such a way as to require a decision on constitutional grounds, but this alternative is not favored if there are nonconstitutional grounds for decision. Under either alternative, the federal rule as to the constitutionality of the state law is binding on state courts, but the state courts are still free to interpret the state law differently in a later case (except in the atypical case where the Supreme Court rules that no interpretation of the state law can save its unconstitutionality).

This situation has led to the creation of the "abstention doctrine". Under some circumstances, a federal court may abstain from exercising jurisdiction where the constitutional issue rests on an unsettled interpretation of state law. In these cases federal courts abstain from exercising jurisdiction otherwise conferred.

The leading abstention case is *Railroad Commission v. Pullman Co.*[3] Justice Frankfurter first identified and discussed the rule of abstention in this case.[4] The Pullman Company sought to enjoin enforcement of an order of

---

L.Ed. 1123 (1938), mandate conformed 214 Ind. 347, 13 N.E.2d 955 (1938).

It is sometimes unclear whether the federal court merely looks to the state law to assure itself that the state interpretation rests on a fair or substantial basis or whether there is a federal common law of, for example, "contract." Compare Demorest v. City Bank Farmers Trust Co., 321 U.S. 36, 42–43, 64 S.Ct. 384, 388–89, 88 L.Ed. 526 (1944) (Jackson, J.) (to determine what is a property right under state law the Supreme Court inquires whether the decision of the state court rests on a fair or substantial basis), with D'Oench, Duhme & Co. v. Federal Deposit Insurance Corp., 315 U.S. 447, 470, 62 S.Ct. 676, 685, 86 L.Ed. 956 (1942), rehearing denied 315 U.S. 830, 62 S.Ct. 910, 86 L.Ed. 1224 (1942) (Jackson, J., concurring) (the contract clause is "an example of the part the common law must play in our system").

§ 2.14

1. Cohens v. Virginia, 19 U.S. (6 Wheat.) 264, 404, 5 L.Ed. 257, 291 (1821).

2. See McClellan v. Carland, 217 U.S. 268, 30 S.Ct. 501, 54 L.Ed. 762 (1910); Chicot County v. Sherwood, 148 U.S. 529, 13 S.Ct. 695, 37 L.Ed. 546 (1893); Hyde v. Stone, 61 U.S. (20 How.) 170, 15 L.Ed. 874 (1857).

3. 312 U.S. 496, 61 S.Ct. 643, 85 L.Ed. 971 (1941).

4. In earlier cases the Court had in fact abstained but without any broad justification of doctrine. See Thompson v. Magnolia Petroleum Co., 309 U.S. 478, 60 S.Ct. 628, 84 L.Ed. 876 (1940) (federal court should defer to state court to determine state property law issue in bankruptcy proceeding); Pennsylvania v. Williams, 294 U.S. 176, 55 S.Ct. 380, 79 L.Ed. 841 (1935) (federal court, in a diversity case, should defer to state court to state administration of corporate assets by state officer; petition of Commonwealth of Pennsylvania granted); Langnes v. Green, 282 U.S. 531, 51 S.Ct. 243, 75 L.Ed. 520 (1931) (federal district court, in exercise of its discretion, should permit state court to proceed but retain a petition in its jurisdiction).

the Texas Railroad Commission requiring that a Pullman conductor be continuously in charge of any sleeping car operated in Texas. If the light traffic justified only one Pullman sleeper the railroads had, prior to this order, put only a porter in charge. This porter, in turn, was responsible to the train conductor. The Pullman porters, in those days, were black, and the conductors were white. The effect of the order then was to increase job opportunities for whites and decrease them for blacks.

An issue was whether Texas law authorized the Commission's order. If it did, the plaintiffs (including the black porters) charged violations of the equal protection, due process, and commerce clauses of the Constitution. The company and others had attacked the order by bringing an action in federal district court, which accepted jurisdiction and decided the necessary state law issues by holding that the Texas statutes did not allow the commission's order.

Justice Frankfurter, for the unanimous Court, reversed and remanded to the district court with directions to retain jurisdiction of the case pending determination of the state law question by the Texas courts. The Court instructed plaintiffs to bring state court proceedings with reasonable promptness. The district court, the high court said, should have abstained from exercising its jurisdiction.

The Court usually refers to *abstention* so we will use that term here, but it is more precise to speak of *Pullman deferral*, to emphasize that *Pullman* recognizes that federal courts should not *prematurely* resolve the constitutionality of a state statute.[5] The term *deferral* brings out more clearly the distinction between circumstances that require dismissal of

a suit and circumstances that require postponing consideration of its merits.

Pullman found the authority for its action in the wide discretion generally accorded a court of equity. A ruling on the constitutional question would involve a sensitive issue of state policy that should be avoided so long as there is another basis for adjudication.

A federal court ruling on the state law issue would be merely a prediction of the law, because the Supreme Court of Texas, the final authority on the matter, had not interpreted the scope of the statute. Such a forecast should be avoided, according to the Court, because "[t]he reign of law is hardly promoted if an unnecessary ruling of a federal court is thus supplanted by a controlling decision of a state court. The resources of equity are equal to an adjustment that will avoid the waste of a tentative decision as well as the friction of a premature constitutional adjudication."[6] The Court used the abstention doctrine to smooth relations between state and federal authority.

Later cases utilizing the abstention doctrine did not focus as heavily on the sensitivity of the state issue as did *Pullman*. The primary focus of the doctrine became the avoidance of unnecessary adjudication of a constitutional issue.[7] Justice Frankfurter classified the abstention doctrine as part of the principle that federal courts will determine a constitutional question only if there is no alternative basis on which the controversy can be decided.[8] By submitting the state issues to the state courts, it is possible that the resulting state construction will avoid the federal constitutional issue in whole or in part.

The abstention doctrine, particularly as applied outside of a *Pullman* factual situation, raises complicated issues that are considered in more detail elsewhere.[9] Here, we refer to

5. Growe v. Emison, 507 U.S. 25, 32 n. 1, 113 S.Ct. 1075, 1080 n. 1, 122 L.Ed.2d 388 (1993).

6. 312 U.S. at 500, 61 S.Ct. at 645.

7. See, e.g., City of Meridian v. Southern Bell Telephone & Telegraph Co., 358 U.S. 639, 79 S.Ct. 455, 3 L.Ed.2d 562 (1959); Shipman v. Du Pre, 339 U.S. 321, 70 S.Ct. 640, 94 L.Ed. 877 (1950). Cf. Moore v. Sims, 442 U.S. 415, 423–431, 99 S.Ct. 2371, 2377–81, 60 L.Ed.2d 994 (1979) (the fact that the challenge to a complex state statute is very broad-based is a factor militating in favor of

abstention, not against it, because of the opportunity in the state courts of a narrowing construction).

8. Burford v. Sun Oil Co., 319 U.S. 315, 338, 63 S.Ct. 1098, 1109–10, 87 L.Ed. 1424 (1943) (dissenting opinion), rehearing denied 320 U.S. 214, 63 S.Ct. 1442, 87 L.Ed. 1851 (1943).

9. E.g., 17 Charles Alan Wright, Arthur Miller & E. Cooper, Federal Practice and Procedure §§ 4241–4243. See also, 1 Ronald D. Rotunda & John E. Nowak, Treatise

the development of the *Pullman* doctrine to illustrate the significance of abstention as a tool to avoid constitutional issues, *viz.*, when should a federal court abstain from deciding a federal constitutional issue in cases that it has the jurisdiction to decide. Courts and commentators typically refer to the *Pullman* doctrine as *"Pullman* abstention." It is more accurate to call it *"Pullman* deferral" to emphasize that federal courts should not resolve the constitutionality of a state statute prematurely.[10] But, the term "abstention" is used to often that it is fruitless to insist on a change in vocabulary.

Given the reasons for *Pullman* abstention, its application would be inappropriate if any possible interpretation of the relevant state law would be unconstitutional[11] or if the state law is settled,[12] or if a state court ruling would not be helpful in a determination of the constitutional issue.[13] Even if there is no prior state court adjudication, abstention is also not appropriate where the meaning of the challenged statute is "pointedly clear."[14]

Pullman abstention also may be raised in a case where jurisdiction is grounded only on diversity and not on a federal question. This result may be a little surprising, because the

purpose of diversity is to have a federal court decide on state law questions. The Court has advised that the "presence of a federal basis for jurisdiction may raise the level of justification needed for abstention."[15]

Although the abstention doctrine was initially founded on the discretion vested in a court of equity,[16] the Court has applied it to actions at law as well.[17] In *Louisiana Power & Light Co. v. City of Thibodaux*,[18] the first decision authorizing abstention in a case at law, the Court acknowledged that prior cases were in equity, but "they did not apply a technical rule of equity procedure. They reflect a deeper policy derived from our federalism."[19]

The abstention doctrine may be applied in any type of case regarding state laws and is not limited solely to issues regarding property rights. *Harrison v. NAACP*[20] the ruled that abstention is applicable to cases involving civil rights. That case involved the interpretation of state's statutes that allegedly infringed on the plaintiff's civil rights. The Court, over a strong dissent, ordered abstention, indicating that the court should use the same criteria applied in any other case involving a constitutional ques-

---

on Constitutional Law: Substance & Procedure §§ 2.15(a)–2.15(f) (West Group, 3d ed.1999).

10. Growe v. Emison, 507 U.S. 25, 33 n. 1, 113 S.Ct. 1075, 1081 n. 1, 122 L.Ed.2d 388 (1993).

11. Harman v. Forssenius, 380 U.S. 528, 534–535, 85 S.Ct. 1177, 1181–82, 14 L.Ed.2d 50 (1965). Compare, Colautti v. Franklin, 439 U.S. 379, 392 n. 9, 99 S.Ct. 675, 684 n. 9, 58 L.Ed.2d 596 (1979) (abstention not argued by appellants nor is it appropriate given the extent of the vagueness of the challenged abortion statute for the court to abstain *sua sponte*), with, Anders v. Floyd, 440 U.S. 445, 99 S.Ct. 1200, 59 L.Ed.2d 442 (1979) (per curiam), rehearing denied 441 U.S. 928, 99 S.Ct. 2043, 60 L.Ed.2d 403 (1979) (possibility of abstention regarding abortion prosecution "suggested" by Supreme Court when state definition of viability is not clear [alternative constructions may obviate the constitutional difficulty] and criminal proceedings are pending in state court).

12. New Motor Vehicle Bd. v. Orrin W. Fox Co., 439 U.S. 96, 100 n. 3, 99 S.Ct. 403, 407 n. 3, 58 L.Ed.2d 361 (1978).

13. Public Utilities Commission of Ohio v. United Fuel Gas Co., 317 U.S. 456, 63 S.Ct. 369, 87 L.Ed. 396 (1943), rehearing denied 318 U.S. 798, 63 S.Ct. 557, 87 L.Ed. 1162 (1943).

14. Babbitt v. United Farm Workers Nat. Union, 442 U.S. 289, 297–312, 99 S.Ct. 2301, 2308–16, 60 L.Ed.2d 895 (1979) (no abstention as to challenged election procedures

because the statute is clear, but lower court should have abstained as to criminal penalty and consumer publicity provisions because statute is ambiguous and is reasonably susceptible of constructions that would obviate the constitutional problems).

15. Colorado River Water Conservation District v. United States, 424 U.S. 800, 815 n. 21, 96 S.Ct. 1236, 1245 n. 21, 47 L.Ed.2d 483 (1976), rehearing denied 426 U.S. 912, 96 S.Ct. 2239, 48 L.Ed.2d 839 (1976).

16. Meredith v. Winter Haven, 320 U.S. 228, 64 S.Ct. 7, 88 L.Ed. 9 (1943), mandate conformed 141 F.2d 348 (5th Cir.1944), rehearing denied 141 F.2d 1019 (5th Cir. 1944), certiorari denied 323 U.S. 738, 65 S.Ct. 43, 89 L.Ed. 592 (1944); Railroad Commission of Texas v. Pullman Co., 312 U.S. 496, 61 S.Ct. 643, 85 L.Ed. 971 (1941).

17. United Gas Pipe Line Co. v. Ideal Cement Co., 369 U.S. 134, 82 S.Ct. 676, 7 L.Ed.2d 623 (1962).

18. 360 U.S. 25, 79 S.Ct. 1070, 3 L.Ed.2d 1058 (1959), rehearing denied 360 U.S. 940, 79 S.Ct. 1442, 3 L.Ed.2d 1552 (1959).

19. 360 U.S. at 28, 79 S.Ct. at 1072. See also Clay v. Sun Insurance Office Ltd., 363 U.S. 207, 80 S.Ct. 1222, 4 L.Ed.2d 1170 (1960), on remand 319 F.2d 505 (5th Cir. 1963), this judgment of the 5th Circuit was later reversed in 377 U.S. 179, 84 S.Ct. 1197, 12 L.Ed.2d 229 (1964).

20. 360 U.S. 167, 79 S.Ct. 1025, 3 L.Ed.2d 1152 (1959).

tion that involved the interpretation of a state law.[21]

(b) Some Problems and Procedures of Abstention

The Problem of Delay. A major problem with the abstention is that forcing the parties to go to state court burdens the parties, increases the expenses of litigation, and delays the resolution of the case. The Supreme Court has not felt that such delay and inconvenience weigh too heavily when balanced against "the much larger issue as to the appropriate relationship between federal and state authorities functioning as a harmonious whole."[22] In the realities of an actual controversy, however, costs cannot be dismissed lightly.

Not only may the monetary expenditures of juggling between courts be high, but delay and inconvenience to individual litigants are real. In some abstention cases the parties move from court to court arguing procedural issues for years before ever reaching the merits.[23]

Only some Justices appear concerned with these delaying costs of abstention.[24]

The Procedures of *Pullman* Abstention. The problems of abstention as developed by the Courts are magnified by the procedural complexities surrounding its use. The federal court should abstain deciding the federal constitutional issue until the state court has had a chance to rule definitively on the interpretation of the state law in question, by a declaratory judgment action or otherwise. But the state court may decide that it cannot constitutionally give what to it is an advisory opinion.[25]

Some states have developed certification procedures, so that state law questions may be certified to the state supreme court,[26] but the great majority have not done so.[27] In some cases the state court will refuse to decide a certified question that is not considered ripe.[28] The state courts have no federal obligation to consider issues brought in this way, for they may refuse to adjudicate until a case comes to them in the normal manner.

---

21. The proposed Federal Jurisdiction Act of 1973 would reverse this result. See, S. 1876, 93d Cong., 1st Sess. (May 23, 1973). Section 1371(g) of the Proposed Federal Court Jurisdiction Act of 1973 provides:

> "This section ['abstention and stays in certain cases'] is inapplicable, and the district court shall proceed to judgment, in actions to redress the denial, under color of any State law, statute, ordinance, regulation, custom, or usage, of the right to vote or of the equal protection of the laws, if such denial is alleged to be on the basis of race, creed, color, sex, or national origin. This section is also inapplicable, and the district court shall proceed to judgment, in actions brought by the United States or an officer or agency thereof."

22. Chicago v. Fieldcrest Dairies, 316 U.S. 168, 172–73, 62 S.Ct. 986, 988, 86 L.Ed. 1355 (1942).

23. While the Court has argued that abstention does not "involve the abdication of federal jurisdiction, but only the postponement of its exercise...." Harrison v. NAACP, 360 U.S. 167, 177, 79 S.Ct. 1025, 1030–31, 3 L.Ed.2d 1152 (1959), that postponement can drag on for years. Charles Alan Wright, The Abstention Doctrine Reconsidered, 37 Tex.L.Rev. 815, 818 (1959).

E.g., Spector Motor Service, Inc. v. McLaughlin, 323 U.S. 101, 65 S.Ct. 152, 89 L.Ed. 101 (1944) and Spector Motor Service, Inc. v. O'Connor, 340 U.S. 602, 71 S.Ct. 508, 95 L.Ed. 573 (1951) (nearly seven years delay between decision requiring abstention and decision on merits); The *Spector* decision on the merits was later overruled in Complete Auto Transit, Inc. v. Brady, 430 U.S. 274, 97 S.Ct. 1076, 51 L.Ed.2d 326 (1977). United States v. Leiter Minerals, Inc., 381 U.S. 413, 85 S.Ct. 1575, 14

L.Ed.2d 692 (1965) (case dismissed as moot eight years after abstention required).

24. England v. Louisiana State Bd. of Medical Examiners, 375 U.S. 411, 423, 84 S.Ct. 461, 468–69, 11 L.Ed.2d 440 (1964), (Douglas, J., concurring); Clay v. Sun Insurance Office, 363 U.S. 207, 228, 80 S.Ct. 1222, 1234, 4 L.Ed.2d 1170 (1960) (Douglas, J., dissenting); and 363 U.S. at 224, 80 S.Ct. at 1226, 4 L.Ed.2d 1170 (Black, J., dissenting, joined by Warren, C.J., and Douglas, J.), on remand 319 F.2d 505 (5th Cir.1963); 5th Circuit judgment reversed in 377 U.S. 179, 84 S.Ct. 1197, 12 L.Ed.2d 229 (1964).

25. Compare United Services Life Insurance Co. v. Delaney, 328 F.2d 483 (5th Cir.1964), certiorari denied 377 U.S. 935, 84 S.Ct. 1335, 12 L.Ed.2d 298 (1964), rehearing denied 377 U.S. 973, 84 S.Ct. 1644, 12 L.Ed.2d 743 (1964) (ordering abstention), with, United Services Life Insurance Co. v. Delaney, 396 S.W.2d 855 (Tex.1965) (decision on state law in this abstention case denied because it would only be advisory opinion).

26. Florida first provided such a certification procedure, Fla.Stat.Ann., § 25.031, in 1945, and the Supreme Court approved of the practice. Lehman Brothers v. Schein, 416 U.S. 386, 94 S.Ct. 1741, 40 L.Ed.2d 215 (1974), on remand 519 F.2d 453 (2d Cir.1975); Zant v. Stephens, 456 U.S. 410, 416–17 & n. 4, 102 S.Ct. 1856, 1859 & n. 4, 72 L.Ed.2d 222 (1982).

27. Only a handful of states have a certification statute or rule of court. See generally Lillich & Mundy, Federal Court Certification of Doubtful State Law Questions, 18 U.C.L.A.L.Rev. 888 (1971).

28. In re Richards, 223 A.2d 827 (Me.1966).

Even when the state court does take the case, its procedural posture is intriguing and complex. Because the state courts have a duty to enforce and abide by the U.S. Constitution,[29] it would be improper for the state courts to construe the statute without considering it in light of the requirements of the federal Constitution.[30] After obtaining the authoritative state court judgment, the parties may return to the federal district court for the constitutional decision. Or the parties may seek U.S. Supreme Court review in the final state court decision. "Where, however, the party remitted to the state courts elects to seek a complete and final adjudication of his rights in the state courts, the District Court's reservation of jurisdiction is purely formal, and does not impair [Supreme Court] jurisdiction to review directly an otherwise final state court judgment."[31]

If the parties opt for Supreme Court review at this stage of the litigation, then they cannot later return to the district court after Supreme Court review or denial of a writ of certiorari. The Supreme Court has explicitly admitted that this discretionary review or even appellate review is an "inadequate substitute for the initial District Court determination" that plaintiff sought before the court invoked abstention.[32] This inadequate substitute applies not only to issues of law; "it is especially true as to issues of fact."[33]

The Supreme Court attempted to clarify the complexities of the abstention doctrine in *England v. Louisiana State Board of Medical Examiners*,[34] which outlined the procedural position litigants should take in an abstention case:

[I]f a party freely and without reservation submits his federal claims for decision by the state courts, litigates them there, and has them decided there, then—whether or not he seeks direct review of the state decision in this Court—he has elected to forgo his right to return to the District Court. . . .

We recognize that in the heat of litigation a party . . . denying the statute's applicability may be led not merely to state his federal constitutional claim but to argue it, for if he can persuade the state court that application of the statute to him would offend the Federal Constitution, he will ordinarily have persuaded it that the statute should not be construed as applicable to him. In addition, the parties cannot prevent the state court from rendering a decision on the federal question if it chooses to do so. . . . [A] party may readily forestall any conclusion that he has elected not to return to the District Court . . . by making on the state record the "reservation to the disposition of the entire case by the state courts" that we referred to [earlier]. That is, he may inform the state courts that he is exposing his federal claims there only for the purposes of complying with [the case law], and that he intends, should the state courts hold against him on the question of state law, to return to the District Court for disposition of his federal contentions.[35]

The Court emphasized that an explicit reservation is not indispensable to preserve the return to the state court: it must "clearly" appear that the litigant litigated his federal claims in the state courts.[36] *Either* party to the litigation may make this reservation.[37] One

29. Cf. Testa v. Katt, 330 U.S. 386, 67 S.Ct. 810, 91 L.Ed. 967 (1947).

30. Government & Civic Employees Organizing Committee, CIO v. Windsor, 353 U.S. 364, 366, 77 S.Ct. 838, 839, 1 L.Ed.2d 894 (1957).

31. NAACP v. Button, 371 U.S. 415, 427, 83 S.Ct. 328, 335, 9 L.Ed.2d 405 (1963).

32. England v. Louisiana State Bd. of Medical Examiners, 375 U.S. 411, 416, 84 S.Ct. 461, 465, 11 L.Ed.2d 440 (1964).

33. 375 U.S. at 416, 84 S.Ct. at 465.

34. 375 U.S. 411, 84 S.Ct. 461, 11 L.Ed.2d 440 (1964).

35. 375 U.S. at 419–421, 84 S.Ct. at 466–68.

36. 375 U.S. at 421, 84 S.Ct. at 467–68.

37. 375 U.S. at 422 n. 13, 84 S.Ct. at 468, n. 13. See also, Zablocki v. Redhail, 434 U.S. 374, 379–380 n. 5, 98 S.Ct. 673, 677–78 n. 5, 54 L.Ed.2d 618 (1978); Will v. Calvert Fire Insurance Co., 437 U.S. 655, 98 S.Ct. 2552, 57 L.Ed.2d 504 (1978) (opinion of Rehnquist, J., joined by Stewart, White, and Stevens, JJ. stating that if there is duplicative litigation in state and federal courts, the decision to defer to state courts is largely in the discretion of the federal district court even if matters of substantive federal law are involved), on remand 586 F.2d 12 (7th Cir.1978). See also 437 U.S. at 668, 98 S.Ct. at 2560 (Brennan, J., dissenting, joined by Burger, C.J., and Marshall & Powell, JJ.).

party's insistence on litigating the federal claim in state court waives his rights to return to federal court but not his opponent's rights.[38]

(c) The Abstention Doctrine After Frankfurter

The abstention doctrine received its greatest use during Justice Frankfurter's years on the Court. His retirement in 1962 left the doctrine a judicial orphan[39] for many years. The Court during the 1960's was far less amenable to use of abstention. In the first seven cases on abstention to reach the Court after Frankfurter's retirement, all were found to be improper for the exercise of abstention.[40] In four of these seven decisions the Court overruled lower court decisions to abstain.[41]

However, the decline of the abstention doctrine has not resulted in its disappearance. In 1975, in *Harris County Commissioners Court v. Moore*,[42] the Court, eight to one, reversed a three-judge district court and required abstention where the character of the federal right asserted and the availability of the relief sought turned in large part on unsettled state law.[43] The Court explained that "where the applicability of the statute is uncertain, abstention is often proper, while in the case where the vagueness claim goes to the obli-

gations imposed by the statute, it is not, since a single state construction often would not bring the challenged statute 'within the bounds of permissible constitutional certainty.' "[44]

Harris developed a test for when to apply abstention in cases where the allegedly uncertain state law is not a statute but the state constitution:

> [W]e [have] declined to order abstention where the federal due process claim was not complicated by an unresolved state-law question, even though plaintiffs might have sought relief under a similar provision of the state constitution. But where the challenged statute is part of an *integrated scheme* of related constitutional provisions, statutes, and regulations, and where the scheme as a whole calls for clarifying interpretation by the state courts, we have regularly required the district courts to abstain.[45]

This refusal to expand, in a wholesale manner, the abstention doctrine to cases where a claim might also be brought under the state *constitution* is very important. A contrary ruling could have turned abstention into a general requirement of judicial exhaustion. As the Court explicitly recognized in *Examining*

---

38.   375 U.S. at 422, n. 13, 84 S.Ct. at 468 n. 13.

39.   Note, Federal–Question Abstention: Justice Frankfurter's Doctrine in an Activist Era, 80 Harv.L. Rev. 604 (1967).

40.   Harman v. Forssenius, 380 U.S. 528, 85 S.Ct. 1177, 14 L.Ed.2d 50 (1965); Dombrowski v. Pfister, 380 U.S. 479, 85 S.Ct. 1116, 14 L.Ed.2d 22 (1965); Davis v. Mann, 377 U.S. 678, 84 S.Ct. 1441, 12 L.Ed.2d 609 (1964), on remand 238 F.Supp. 458 (E.D.Va.1964); Baggett v. Bullitt, 377 U.S. 360, 84 S.Ct. 1316, 12 L.Ed.2d 377 (1964); Hostetter v. Idlewild Bon Voyage Liquor Corp., 377 U.S. 324, 84 S.Ct. 1293, 12 L.Ed.2d 350 (1964); Griffin v. County School Bd., 377 U.S. 218, 84 S.Ct. 1226, 12 L.Ed.2d 256 (1964), motion granted 377 U.S. 950, 84 S.Ct. 1627, 12 L.Ed.2d 496 (1964); McNeese v. Board of Education, 373 U.S. 668, 83 S.Ct. 1433, 10 L.Ed.2d 622 (1963).

41.   Dombrowski v. Pfister, 380 U.S. 479, 85 S.Ct. 1116, 14 L.Ed.2d 22 (1965); Baggett v. Bullitt, 377 U.S. 360, 84 S.Ct. 1316, 12 L.Ed.2d 377 (1964); Griffin v. County School Bd., 377 U.S. 218, 84 S.Ct. 1226, 12 L.Ed.2d 256 (1964), motion granted 377 U.S. 950, 84 S.Ct. 1627, 12 L.Ed.2d 496 (1964); McNeese v. Board of Education, 373 U.S. 668, 83 S.Ct. 1433, 10 L.Ed.2d 622 (1963).

42.   420 U.S. 77, 95 S.Ct. 870, 43 L.Ed.2d 32 (1975). In this case plaintiffs, who were Justices of the peace and constables, challenged the constitutionality of a state law

relating to their removal from office prior to the end of their terms.

43.   420 U.S. at 88, 95 S.Ct. at 877.

See also, Zablocki v. Redhail, 434 U.S. 374, 379–380 n. 5, 98 S.Ct. 673, 677 n. 5, 54 L.Ed.2d 618, 626 n. 5 (1978); Will v. Calvert Fire Insurance Co., 437 U.S. 655, 98 S.Ct. 2552, 57 L.Ed.2d 504 (1978) (opinion of Rehnquist J., joined by Stewart, White, and Stevens, JJ. stating that if there is duplicative litigation in state and federal courts, the decision to defer to state courts is largely in the discretion of the federal district court even if matters of substantive federal law are involved); 437 U.S. at 669, 98 S.Ct. at 2560, 57 L.Ed.2d at 515 (Brennan J., dissenting joined by Burger C.J., and Marshall & Powell, JJ.), on remand 586 F.2d 12 (7th Cir.1978).

44.   420 U.S. at 86 n. 9, 95 S.Ct. at 876–77 n. 9, quoting Baggett v. Bullitt, 377 U.S. 360, 377–78, 84 S.Ct. 1316, 1326, 12 L.Ed.2d 377 (1964).

45.   420 U.S. at 84–85 n. 8, 95 S.Ct. at 876 n. 8 (emphasis added), citing Reetz v. Bozanich, 397 U.S. 82, 90 S.Ct. 788, 25 L.Ed.2d 68 (1970), and City of Meridian v. Southern Bell Telephone & Telegraph Co., 358 U.S. 639, 79 S.Ct. 455, 3 L.Ed.2d 562 (1959).

Board of Engineers v. Flores de Otero:[46]

Indeed, to hold that abstention is required because [a state statute] might conflict with [certain] broad and sweeping [state] constitutional provisions, would convert abstention from an exception into a general rule.[47]

The Court has reemphasized that "[a]bstention from the exercise of federal jurisdiction is the exception, not the rule."[48] The exceptional nature of abstention has confined its use to three general categories of circumstances: (1) cases presenting a federal constitutional issue that might be mooted or presented in a different posture by a state court determination of pertinent state law; (2) cases that present difficult questions of state law bearing on policy problems of substantial public import whose importance transcends the result in the case then at bar; and (3) cases where, absent bad faith, harassment, or a patently invalid state statute, the litigant invokes federal jurisdiction to restrain state criminal proceedings, or state nuisance proceedings (antecedent to a criminal prosecution) to close places exhibiting obscene films, or to restrain the collection of state taxes.[49]

(d) Abstention, Comity, and Federal Court Injunctions of State Court Proceedings—The Doctrine of "Our Federalism"

Related to the *Pullman* abstention doctrine and yet representing a distinct line of cases, is the question of when a federal court may grant a declaratory injunction or declaratory relief that relates to a threatened or pending state criminal prosecution. Such federal court intrusion into state proceedings is not favored because of what has been termed "Our Federalism," that is, a "sensitivity to the legitimate interests of both State and National Governments...."[50]

Several important distinctions between *Pullman* abstention and "Our Federalism" abstention are worth noting. In *Pullman* abstention, the question is whether the federal plaintiff should be forced to initiate a state proceeding that might not occur at all except by virtue of the abstention order. In the "Our Federalism" case, on the other hand, a state authorities have begun, or are about to begin, state proceeding, and the state wants the whole case to be litigated in that proceeding.[51]

Also, in a *Pullman* case, the federal court stays its own proceedings to allow the state court to rule on the state law issues. The Court postpones federal jurisdiction. In "Our Federalism" cases, the federal plaintiff seeks a stay of the state court proceeding (or threatened proceeding) so that the federal court can adjudicate the federal issue. If the federal court refuses to intervene, there is no federal court jurisdiction at all at this stage. If plaintiff is ultimately convicted he only has the chance of Supreme Court review or perhaps a habeas corpus claim in the lower federal courts.

Removal Cases Distinguished. The "Our Federalism" line of cases should also be distinguished from those cases where a civil action or criminal prosecution is commenced in state court and the state defendant seeks removal of the entire case to federal court (where it is still prosecuted by state officials but heard by a federal judge). Federal statutes provide for this type of removal because the state defendant is a federal officer, or member of the armed forces, or any person who is denied or cannot enforce in the state courts a right under any law providing for equal civil rights, or any person who is sued for doing any act under color of authority for any law providing for equal rights, or for refusing to do any act on

46. 426 U.S. 572, 96 S.Ct. 2264, 49 L.Ed.2d 65 (1976).

47. 426 U.S. at 598, 96 S.Ct. at 2279 (footnote omitted).

48. Colorado River Water Conservation District v. United States, 424 U.S. 800, 813, 96 S.Ct. 1236, 1244, 47 L.Ed.2d 483 (1976), rehearing denied 426 U.S. 912, 96 S.Ct. 2239, 48 L.Ed.2d 839 (1976).

49. 424 U.S. at 814–16, 96 S.Ct. at 1244–46.

50. Younger v. Harris, 401 U.S. 37, 44, 91 S.Ct. 746, 750, 27 L.Ed.2d 669 (1971).

51. H. Hart & H. Wechsler, The Federal Courts and the Federal System 1043 (2d ed. 1973).

the grounds that it would be inconsistent with such law.[52]

The case law and literature on "Our Federalism" is continually expanding[53] and we will not consider this subject in any detail here except to outline a few of the major considerations.

The Federal Anti–Injunction Statute. First, any federal injunction of a state court proceeding must pass the hurdle of the federal anti-injunction or comity statute.[54] This hurdle is not a high one because all constitutional claims against state action can be based in part on the constitutional cause of action created by the broadly worded section 1983 of title 42. The Supreme Court has held that section 1983 is an exception to the anti-injunction statute.[55] Thus, for all practical purposes, the bar to such injunctions lies not in statutory restrictions but in notions of judicial self-restraint, in comity, in "Our Federalism."

Pending and Non-pending Cases Distinguished. The comity rules of "Our Federalism" distinguish between "pending" and "not pending but threatened" proceedings. If the state proceedings are pending it is very difficult to obtain a federal court injunction. The federal plaintiff must show that the federal

injunction is necessary to prevent "irreparable injury" that is both "great and immediate."[56] A claim that the state prosecution chills First Amendment rights or is based on a statute unconstitutional on its face is insufficient to make the necessary showing of irreparable injury.[57] Plaintiff must show "bad faith, harassment, or any other unusual circumstance that would call for equitable relief."[58]

In deciding whether to issue declaratory relief in pending state prosecutions, courts must take into account the same equitable principles relevant to the propriety of an injunction.[59] If injunctive relief is inappropriate, declaratory relief should ordinarily be denied as well.

If the state prosecution is not pending but is merely threatened, plaintiff still must show a sufficiently immediate threat so as to confer standing.[60] If no state prosecution is pending, a federal plaintiff can secure declaratory relief if such a prosecution is threatened even though a showing of bad-faith enforcement or other special circumstances has not been made.[61]

Whether a federal injunction (as opposed to declaratory relief) would be allowed in such circumstances might appear to be a much

---

52. 28 U.S.C.A. §§ 1442, 1442a, 1443.

53. See, e.g., 1 Ronald D. Rotunda & John E. Nowak, Treatise on Constitutional Law: Substance and Procedure § 2.15(f) (West Group, 3d ed.1999).

54. 28 U.S.C.A. § 2283:

"A court of the United States may not grant an injunction to stay proceedings in a State court except as expressly authorized by Act of Congress, or where necessary in aid of its jurisdiction, or to protect or effectuate its judgments."

See Redish, The Anti–Injunction Statute Reconsidered, 44 U.Chi.L.Rev. 717 (1977); and, Mayton, Ersatz Federalism Under the Anti–Injunction Statute, 78 Colum.L.Rev. 330 (1978), which present a careful study of the anti-injunction statute, 28 U.S.C.A. § 2283.

State Court Injunctions of Federal Proceedings Distinguished. To be distinguished from federal court injunctions of state court proceedings are state court injunctions of federal court proceedings. It is not within the power of state courts, under the supremacy clause, to bar litigants from filing and prosecuting *in personam* actions in federal court. General Atomic Co. v. Felter, 434 U.S. 12, 98 S.Ct. 76, 54 L.Ed.2d 199 (1977) (per curiam).

55. Mitchum v. Foster, 407 U.S. 225, 92 S.Ct. 2151, 32 L.Ed.2d 705 (1972). As one commentator has noted, "it is difficult to imagine an instance in which such [injunctive]

relief could *not* be sought under § 1983 and in which § 2283 might therefore be a bar." H. Hart & H. Wechsler, The Federal Courts and the Federal System 1249 (2d ed. 1973) (emphasis in original; footnote omitted).

56. Younger v. Harris, 401 U.S. 37, 46, 91 S.Ct. 746, 751, 27 L.Ed.2d 669 (1971), quoting Fenner v. Boykin, 271 U.S. 240, 243, 46 S.Ct. 492, 493, 70 L.Ed. 927 (1926).

57. Younger v. Harris, 401 U.S. 37, 50–54, 91 S.Ct. 746, 753–55, 27 L.Ed.2d 669 (1971).

58. 401 U.S. at 54, 92 S.Ct. at 755.

59. Samuels v. Mackell, 401 U.S. 66, 91 S.Ct. 764, 27 L.Ed.2d 688 (1971); Cf. Great Lakes Dredge & Dock Co. v. Huffman, 319 U.S. 293, 63 S.Ct. 1070, 87 L.Ed. 1407 (1943).

60. Younger v. Harris, 401 U.S. at 42, 91 S.Ct. at 749–50.

61. Steffel v. Thompson, 415 U.S. 452, 94 S.Ct. 1209, 39 L.Ed.2d 505 (1974), mandate conformed 494 F.2d 691 (5th Cir.1974).

Cf. Patsy v. Board of Regents, 457 U.S. 496, 102 S.Ct. 2557, 73 L.Ed.2d 172 (1982), on remand 693 F.2d 558 (5th Cir.1982) (no exhaustion of state administrative remedies is required before bringing a suit under 42 U.S.C.A. § 1983).

more difficult issue given the distinctions the Supreme Court has drawn between the cases involving the less intrusive declaratory judgments versus the injunctive remedy,[62] but the Supreme Court has allowed injunctions when the state criminal prosecution is not pending.[63]

If state criminal proceedings are begun against the federal plaintiffs "after the federal complaint is filed but before any proceedings of substance on the merits have taken place in the federal court, the principles of *Younger v. Harris* [and Our Federalism] should apply in full force."[64]

The significance of the requirement that there be no *"proceedings of substance on the merits"* is substantially lessened because the Court has held that, if no state action is pending and the federal plaintiff is seeking declaratory relief, then the federal court may grant a preliminary injunction restraining the defendants from enforcing the disputed law until the end of the trial on the merits. The preliminary injunction should prevent a state from initiating a "proceeding of substance on the merits." In determining whether to issue such a preliminary injunction the trial court, as in other equitable actions, must find a sufficient showing of harm and likelihood of ultimate success on the merits.[65] At the end of this trial,

the court then may issue a declaratory judgment if the facts and law warrant.

State Civil Proceedings. These principles of "Our Federalism" apply to state civil proceedings if "the State is a party to the ... proceeding, and the proceeding is both in aid of and closely related to criminal statutes,"[66] as in a state civil action to abate the showing of an allegedly obscene movie as a nuisance, or a state contempt process.[67]

These principles also apply in federal suits seeking to enjoin executive branches of "an agency of state or local governments...."[68] However, federal courts give no deference based on "Our Federalism" to a state administrative board if it is incompetent by reason of bias to adjudicate the issues before it.[69]

A federal court should invoke "Our Federalism" and abstain from considering a challenge to the constitutionality of a state's attorney disciplinary rules if they are the subject of a pending state disciplinary proceeding.[70] Similarly, a federal court should abstain from a suit to enjoin (on free exercise grounds) the Ohio Civil Rights Commission from exercising jurisdiction over a sex discrimination claim brought by a discharged teacher against a private religious school.[71]

---

62. E.g., Steffel v. Thompson, 415 U.S. 452, 94 S.Ct. 1209, 39 L.Ed.2d 505 (1974), mandate conformed 494 F.2d 691 (5th Cir.1974).

63. Wooley v. Maynard, 430 U.S. 705, 707–711, 97 S.Ct. 1428, 1431–34, 51 L.Ed.2d 752 (1977) (threat of repeated prosecutions).

64. Hicks v. Miranda, 422 U.S. 332, 349, 95 S.Ct. 2281, 2292, 45 L.Ed.2d 223 (1975).

65. Doran v. Salem Inn, Inc., 422 U.S. 922, 95 S.Ct. 2561, 45 L.Ed.2d 648 (1975).

66. Huffman v. Pursue, Ltd., 420 U.S. 592, 604, 95 S.Ct. 1200, 1208, 43 L.Ed.2d 482 (1975), rehearing denied 421 U.S. 971, 95 S.Ct. 1969, 44 L.Ed.2d 463 (1975).

67. Id.; Juidice v. Vail, 430 U.S. 327, 97 S.Ct. 1211, 51 L.Ed.2d 376 (1977); See also Trainor v. Hernandez, 431 U.S. 434, 97 S.Ct. 1911, 52 L.Ed.2d 486 (1977) (principle of "Our Federalism" applies to civil attachment action brought by the state in its sovereign capacity), on remand 471 F.Supp. 516 (N.D.Ill.1978); Moore v. Sims, 442 U.S. 415, 99 S.Ct. 2371, 60 L.Ed.2d 994 (1979) (principle of "Our Federalism" applies to child abuse civil proceeding in which the state is a party).

68. Rizzo v. Goode, 423 U.S. 362, 380, 96 S.Ct. 598, 608, 46 L.Ed.2d 561 (1976) (43 U.S.C.A. § 1983 action against mayor of Philadelphia and other city officials).

69. Gibson v. Berryhill, 411 U.S. 564, 575–77, 93 S.Ct. 1689, 1696–97, 36 L.Ed.2d 488 (1973).

70. Middlesex County Ethics Committee v. Garden State Bar Association, 457 U.S. 423, 102 S.Ct. 2515, 73 L.Ed.2d 116 (1982), on remand 687 F.2d 801 (3d Cir.1982). The Court noted that state bar disciplinary hearings within the constitutionally prescribed jurisdiction of the state supreme court are "ongoing state judicial proceedings;" they implicate important state interests; and there is adequate opportunity in the state proceedings to raise the federal constitutional challenges. 457 U.S. at 434–35, 102 S.Ct. at 2522.

71. The school claimed that the investigation would violate its religious freedom; while the administrative proceedings were pending, the private school sued to enjoin the agency. "Our Federalism" required abstention. The state's interest in prohibiting sex discrimination was an important one, and the agency will give the private school adequate opportunity to raise its constitutional claim. Even if the state agency will not review the constitutional claim, the constitutional claim may be raised in a state court on judicial review. Ohio Civil Rights Commission v. Dayton Christian Schools, Inc., 477 U.S. 619, 106 S.Ct. 2718, 91 L.Ed.2d 512 (1986), on remand 802 F.2d 457 (6th Cir.1986).

The Supreme Court has even applied the principles of "Our Federalism" to an unusual civil case—Texaco sued Pennzoil in federal court to challenge a pending Texas state court judgment against it in excess of 11 billion dollars and to challenge the constitutionality of the application of Texas lien and appeal bond provisions requiring a bond in excess of 13 billion dollars. The state was not a party, but the Supreme Court emphasized that the state had an important interest to compel compliance with the judgment of its courts. Thus, federal courts should not interfere with the execution of state judgments when the federal plaintiff cannot meet its burden of showing that the state courts could not hear its constitutional claims.[72]

Res Judicata and Collateral Estoppel. A defendant's failure to appeal a state criminal conviction does not bar him from initiating a federal suit for prospective declaratory and injunctive relief, because the purpose of the federal suit is not to overturn the state criminal conviction but to preclude further prosecution under an allegedly unconstitutional state law. Plaintiff must, of course, show a genuine threat of future prosecutions.[73]

An important issue of the "Our Federalism" line of cases is the res judicata and collateral estopped effects of federal lower court decisions offering declaratory relief to particular federal plaintiffs.[74] For example, may a lower federal court issue an injunction against a pending state prosecution initiated against a federal plaintiff who had successfully secured declaratory relief? To what extent may other parties rely on the collateral estoppel effects of a lower federal court's declaratory judgment?

§ 2.15 Political Questions

(a) Introduction

The political question doctrine states that certain matters are really political in nature and best resolved by the body politic rather than suitable for judicial review. In a sense, it is misnomer. It should more properly be called the doctrine of nonjusticiability, that is, a holding that the subject matter is inappropriate for judicial consideration. The *White Primary Cases*,[1] the reapportionment decisions,[2] the steel seizure case,[3] and *United States v. Nixon*[4] are all cases involving "political" issues, but the Court rendered a decision. As Justice Jackson has noted, "all constitutional interpretations have political consequences."[5]

An important consequence of the political question doctrine is that it renders the govern-

---

72. Pennzoil Co. v. Texaco, Inc., 481 U.S. 1, 107 S.Ct. 1519, 95 L.Ed.2d 1 (1987).

Justice Powell's majority opinion surprisingly compared Pennzoil v. Texaco to Juidice v. Vail, 430 U.S. 327, 97 S.Ct. 1211, 51 L.Ed.2d 376 (1977) (federal court should abstain from adjudicating a challenge to a state's contempt process). The state's contempt process is closely related to its criminal system, and the state is, for all practical purposes, a party. Indeed, in Juidice v. Vail, the appellant, Juidice, was a Justice of the Dutchess County Court, whose contempt order required Vail to be arrested, jailed, and fined. 430 U.S. at 329–30, 97 S.Ct. at 1215. However, Powell in Pennzoil asserted otherwise:

"[*Juidice*] rests on the importance to the States of enforcing the orders and judgments of their clients. There is little difference between the State's interest in forcing persons to transfer property in response to a court's judgment and in forcing persons to response to the court's process on pain of contempt."

481 U.S. at 13, 107 S.Ct. at 1527.

73. Wooley v. Maynard, 430 U.S. 705, 710–712, 97 S.Ct. 1428, 1433–34, 51 L.Ed.2d 752 (1977).

74. See, e.g., Steffel v. Thompson, 415 U.S. 452, 470–71, 94 S.Ct. 1209, 1221–22, 39 L.Ed.2d 505 (1974); 415

U.S. at 477, 94 S.Ct. at 1224 (White, J., concurring); 415 U.S. at 482 n. 3, 94 S.Ct. at 1227 n. 3 (Rehnquist, J., concurring), mandate conformed 494 F.2d 691 (5th Cir. 1974).

§ 2.15

1. In these cases the Court opened up black participation in party primaries. E.g., Terry v. Adams, 345 U.S. 461, 73 S.Ct. 809, 97 L.Ed. 1152 (1953), rehearing denied 345 U.S. 1003, 73 S.Ct. 1128, 97 L.Ed. 1408 (1953).

2. E.g., Baker v. Carr, 369 U.S. 186, 82 S.Ct. 691, 7 L.Ed.2d 663 (1962), on remand 206 F.Supp. 341 (M.D.Tenn.1962); Reynolds v. Sims, 377 U.S. 533, 84 S.Ct. 1362, 12 L.Ed.2d 506 (1964), rehearing denied 379 U.S. 870, 85 S.Ct. 12, 13 L.Ed.2d 76 (1964).

3. Youngstown Sheet & Tube Co. v. Sawyer, 343 U.S. 579, 72 S.Ct. 863, 96 L.Ed. 1153 (1952).

4. 418 U.S. 683, 94 S.Ct. 3090, 41 L.Ed.2d 1039 (1974), rehearing denied 433 U.S. 916, 97 S.Ct. 2992, 53 L.Ed.2d 1103 (1977).

5. R. Jackson, The Supreme Court in the American System 56 (1955).

ment conduct immune from judicial review.[6] Unlike other restrictions on judicial review— doctrines such as case or controversy requirements, standing, ripeness and prematurity— all of which may be cured by different factual circumstances, a holding of nonjusticiability is absolute in its foreclosure of judicial scrutiny.

(b) The Leading Cases

An early and leading case developing the political question doctrine was *Luther v. Borden*,[7] an 1849 opinion by Chief Justice Taney. The case, in theory, was a simple action of trespass. Martin Luther sued Luther M. Borden and others, for breaking and entering plaintiff's house. The facts, however, made this case must more significant.

The defendants justified their actions on the grounds that they were agents of the state of Rhode Island and pursuant to military orders, broke into the house to search for and arrest plaintiff, who was engaging in insurrection against that state. The plaintiff retorted that this justification was invalid, because "before the acts complained of were committed, that government had been displaced and annulled by the people of Rhode Island, and that the plaintiff was engaged in supporting the lawful authority of the State, and the defendants themselves were in arms against it."[8] Thus, out of a simple trespass action, the Supreme Court was called on to determine which group represented the legitimate government of Rhode Island.

Chief Justice Taney turned to Article IV, section 4 of the United States Constitution, the guaranty clause:

The United States shall guarantee to every State in this union a Republican Form of Government, and shall protect each of them against Invasion; and on Application of the Legislature, or of the Executive (when the

Legislature cannot be convened) against domestic Violence.

Taney argued that the Constitution has treated the question of interference in the domestic concerns of a state "as political in nature," and placed the power in the hands of the federal government.[9] However, he added:

[I]t rests with congress to decide what government is the established one in a State. . . . And its decision is binding on every other department of the government, and could not be questioned in a judicial tribunal. . . .

After the President has acted and called out the militia [pursuant to authority granted by Act of Congress], is a Circuit Court of the United States authorized to inquire whether his decision was right? . . . . [I]t would [then] become the duty of the court (provided it came to the conclusion that the President had decided incorrectly) to discharge those who were arrested or detained by the troops in the service of the United States, or the government which the President was endeavoring to maintain.[10]

Thus, the question as to who represented the lawful government of Rhode Island was nonjusticiable. The guaranty clause is nonjusticiable.

The leading modern decision on the political question doctrine is *Baker v. Carr*.[11] It upheld the justiciability of legislative reapportionment. The case is considered in more detail below, in connection with other reapportionment decisions. Here it is important to outline the general theories and tests of political questions that *Baker* developed.

Baker reviewed in considerable detail the political question cases and concluded that it is the relationship between the judiciary and the

---

6. As Baker v. Carr, 369 U.S. 186, 209, 82 S.Ct. 691, 705–06, 7 L.Ed.2d 663 (1962), on remand 206 F.Supp. 341 (M.D.Tenn.1962) illustrated, a reapportionment case is nonjusticiable if brought under the guaranty clause but justiciable if brought under the equal protection clause.

7. 48 U.S. (7 How.) 1, 12 L.Ed. 581 (1849).

8. 48 U.S. (7 How.) at 35.

9. 48 U.S. (7 How.) at 42.

10. 48 U.S. (7 How.) at 42–43. Curiously, in dictum, the Court said that Congress "might, if they had deemed it most advisable to do so, have placed it in the power of a court to decide when the contingency had happened which required the federal government to interfere." 48 U.S. (7 How.) at 43. But this dictum has been largely forgotten.

11. 369 U.S. 186, 82 S.Ct. 691, 7 L.Ed.2d 663 (1962), on remand 206 F.Supp. 341 (M.D.Tenn.1962).

coordinate branches of the Federal Government, and not the federal judiciary's relationship to the states, that gives rise to the "political question."[12] To determine if, given that coordinate relationship, the doctrine should be invoked, the Court fashioned the following test:

> Prominent on the surface of any case held to involve a political question is found a textually demonstrable constitutional commitment of the issue to a coordinate political department; or a lack of judicially discoverable and manageable standards for resolving it; or the impossibility of deciding without an initial policy determination of a kind clearly for nonjudicial discretion; or the impossibility of a court's undertaking independent resolution without expressing lack of the respect due coordinate branches of government or an unusual need for unquestioning adherence to a political decision already made; or the potentiality of embarrassment from multifarious pronouncements by various departments on one question.[13]

The Court found that the guaranty clause cases involve the elements of a political question and thus are nonjusticiable. But those reasons for nonjusticiability have "nothing to do with their touching on matters of state governmental organization."[14] A reapportionment case is not foreclosed from judicial review if it is based on the equal protection clause rather than on the guaranty clause.[15]

Another leading case clarifying the political question standard is *Powell v. McCormack*.[16] After Congressman Adam Clayton Powell was elected to Congress in November of 1966, the 90th Congress refused to seat him. Powell sued to be seated, to receive back pay, and for a declaratory judgment that his exclusion was unconstitutional.

Before reaching the issue of justiciability, Chief Justice Warren, for the majority, held that the case not to be moot[17] nor precluded by the legislative immunity granted by the speech or debate clause.[18] Then the Court found that Powell was "excluded" from the 90th Congress rather than "expelled".

This last point is complex, but crucial to understanding the case. Article I, section 5, clause 2 governs expulsions and provides that each House "with the Concurrence of two-thirds" may expel a member. The respondents argued that the House could expel a member for any reason whatsoever.[19] The Court did not have to decide this argument, for it ruled that Powell would only be subject to expulsion if he had been allowed to take his seat and *then* required to surrender it.[20] Powell, the Court ruled, was "excluded." That is, the House did not permit him to take his seat and his oath of office.

Only a majority of the House is required for exclusion.[21] Although two-thirds voted against

---

12. 369 U.S. at 210, 82 S.Ct. at 706.

13. 369 U.S. at 217, 82 S.Ct. at 710.

14. 369 U.S. at 218, 82 S.Ct. at 710.

15. 369 U.S. at 237, 82 S.Ct. at 720.

16. 395 U.S. 486, 89 S.Ct. 1944, 23 L.Ed.2d 491 (1969).

17. Powell was reelected and was seated in the 91st Congress in January, 1969, long before the Supreme Court decision was issued on June 16, 1969. The majority held that Powell's claim for back salary prevented mootness. 395 U.S. at 496, 89 S.Ct. at 1950–51.

18. The Court held that the Speech or Debate Clause, art. I, § 6, was not a bar to the action:

"The purpose of th[is] protection afforded legislators is not to forestall judicial review of legislative action but to insure that legislators are not distracted from or hindered in the performance of their legislative tasks by being called into court to defend their actions. A legislator is no more or no less hindered or distracted by

litigation against a legislative *employee* calling into question the employee's affirmative action than he would be by a lawsuit questioning the employee's failure to act. Nor is the distraction or hindrance increased because the claim is for salary rather than damages, or because the litigation questions action taken by the employee within rather than without the House." (395 U.S. at 505, 89 S.Ct. at 1955–56.) (emphasis added).

The Court concluded that legislative employees who participate in unconstitutional activity are responsible for their acts even if the action against a Congressman would be barred by the Speech or Debate clause. But the Court also said that it was not deciding that the Speech or Debate clause would in fact bar an action solely against members of Congress where no agents participated and no other remedy was available. 395 U.S. at 506 n. 26, 89 S.Ct. at 1956, n. 26.

19. 395 U.S. at 507, 89 S.Ct. at 1956.

20. 395 U.S. at 507 n. 27, 89 S.Ct. at 1956 n. 27.

21. 395 U.S. at 492, 508, 89 S.Ct. at 1948–49.

Powell,[22] the Court did not find that it should judge the legality of his exclusion by the expulsion standard. The difference between calling the vote an exclusion rather than an expulsion was one of substance and not form for several reasons: (1) the House treated the vote as one of exclusion and not expulsion;[23] (2) while the law is unclear, the historical evidence and the belief of the House members was that expulsion cannot be applied for actions taken during a prior Congress,[24] which was Powell's case; and (3) some Congressmen expressed the view that they would have not voted to "expel" Powell though they did vote to "exclude" him.[25]

Then, applying *Baker v. Carr*,[26] the Court decided that, while the vote to expel Powell might not have been justiciable, the vote to exclude Powell was justiciable and was not a political question. Exclusion is governed by Art. I, § 5, cl. 1, which provides that each House is "the Judge of the Elections, Returns and Qualifications of its own Members. . . ." To determine if the Constitution provided a textual commitment to a coordinate branch of the federal government the Court said it had to interpret this clause. After examining the relevant historical materials the Court, in considering the House's power to discipline its members, ruled that the Constitution does not authorize the House "to *exclude* any person, duly elected by his constituents, who meets all the requirements for membership expressly prescribed in the Constitution."[27] The power to exclude, governed by a majority vote, is narrower than the power to expel, governed by

a two-thirds requirement. The Court concluded that the House was without power to discipline Powell by excluding him, because it was clear that he met the requirements of age, residence, and citizenship.

Because the petitions only sought declaratory relief it was unnecessary for the Court to express an opinion as to the appropriateness of coercive relief.[28] The Court thought it was an "inadmissible suggestion" that the House might disregard the Court's ruling.[29] Though the Court did not cite *Glidden Co. v. Zdanok*[30] at this point, it might well have done so.

Glidden ruled that the Court of Claims exercised Article III judicial power even though the Court of Claims or any federal court is impotent to enforce a money claim against the United States, which the Court of Claims may award.[31] The Supreme Court may also render a decision involving a money judgment between states,[32] though the Court cannot enforce that award. In private litigation, the Court may award money damages or injunctive relief even though that judgment cannot be enforced because the private litigant is judgment proof or subsequently escapes the jurisdiction of the Court.

Another particularly significant political question case is *United States v. Nixon*.[33] The Supreme Court affirmed the District Court decision ordering *in camera* examination of certain material including certain taped conversations, that the Watergate Special Prosecutor subpoenaed from President Nixon. The

---

22. 395 U.S. at 493, 89 S.Ct. at 1949.

23. 395 U.S. at 492, 508, 89 S.Ct. at 1948–49, 1957.

24. 395 U.S. at 508–510, 89 S.Ct. at 1957–58.

25. 395 U.S. at 511, 89 S.Ct. at 1959.

26. 369 U.S. 186, 217, 82 S.Ct. 691, 710, 7 L.Ed.2d 663 (1962), on remand 206 F.Supp. 341 (M.D.Tenn.1962).

27. 395 U.S. at 522, 89 S.Ct. at 1964. (emphasis in original; footnote omitted). It was all agreed that Powell met the requirements of age, residence, and citizenship required in Art. I, § 2, cl. 2. Nor were other standing qualifications in dispute. See also, 395 U.S. at 520 n. 41, 89 S.Ct. at 1963 n. 41.

28. 395 U.S. at 517, 550, 89 S.Ct. at 1961–62.

29. 395 U.S. at 549 n. 86, 89 S.Ct. at 1978, n. 86 citing McPherson v. Blacker, 146 U.S. 1, 24, 13 S.Ct. 3, 6, 36 L.Ed. 869 (1892).

30. 370 U.S. 530, 82 S.Ct. 1459, 8 L.Ed.2d 671 (1962), rehearing denied 371 U.S. 854, 83 S.Ct. 14, 9 L.Ed.2d 93 (1962).

31. Glidden Co. v. Zdanok, 370 U.S. 530, 568–572, 82 S.Ct. 1459, 1482–84, 8 L.Ed.2d 671 (1962), rehearing denied 371 U.S. 854, 83 S.Ct. 14, 9 L.Ed.2d 93 (1962) (Opinion of Harlan, J.). See also La Abra Silver Mining Co. v. United States, 175 U.S. 423, 461–462, 20 S.Ct. 168, 181–82, 44 L.Ed. 223 (1899).

32. South Dakota v. North Carolina, 192 U.S. 286, 318–321, 24 S.Ct. 269, 275–77, 48 L.Ed. 448 (1904).

33. 418 U.S. 683, 94 S.Ct. 3090, 41 L.Ed.2d 1039 (1974), certiorari denied 431 U.S. 933, 97 S.Ct. 2641, 53 L.Ed.2d 250 (1977), rehearing denied 433 U.S. 916, 97 S.Ct. 2992, 53 L.Ed.2d 1103 (1977).

unanimous opinion rejected the argument that a claim of executive privilege is a political question.

The controversy in *Nixon* was one the courts traditionally resolve: the production or non-production of certain specified evidence deemed by the prosecutor to be relevant to and admissible in a pending criminal case.[34] Such issues are traditionally justiciable and within the Article III power.[35] Enforcement of a subpoena duces tecum, of necessity, must be committed to the trial court's sound discretion.[36] While the Court should defer to other two branches, it cannot share its Article III judicial power with the Executive anymore than it could share in the Executive's veto power.[37] The issue of the applicability of executive privilege in these circumstances then is not committed to another branch of government but to the Court.

Given the broad exercise of judicial review expressed in *Baker, Powell,* and *Nixon,* the Political Question Doctrine, while still viable, does not appear to have extensive growing power. Let us turn to other important precedents in a few decided areas.

(c) A Few Decided Areas

The lengthy opinion in *Baker v. Carr*[38] discussed several of the questions that have been held to be political. It is useful to consider the cases discussed there as well as others in order to better illustrate the doctrine.

(1) Foreign Affairs and the War Making Power

Baker explicitly rejected the dictum, found in some earlier cases, that anything touching foreign affairs is immune from judicial review.[39] The fact that a matter relates to foreign policy or international affairs is certainly relevant, because of the need to avoid conflicting public postures or because of the nonjudicial discretion that lies with the executive or legislative branches. Thus a court will not usually decide if a treaty has been terminated, because on that issue, "governmental action ... must be regarded as of controlling importance," but if there has been no conclusive "governmental action" then a court can interpret the treaty and may find that it provides the answer.[40]

In connection with the Vietnam War the lower courts generally ruled that the issue of its legality was nonjusticiable, but the Supreme Court either denied certiorari or summarily affirmed, over the objection of several Justices who wanted full oral argument.[41] Given the sensitive problems of holding a war to be illegal, most issues relating to the constitutionality of a war may well be nonjusticiable. The effect of such a holding would be that,

34. 418 U.S. at 696–697, 94 S.Ct. at 3101–02.

35. 418 U.S. at 697, 94 S.Ct. at 3102.

36. 418 U.S. at 702, 94 S.Ct. at 3104.

37. 418 U.S. at 704, 94 S.Ct. at 3105–06.

38. 369 U.S. 186, 82 S.Ct. 691, 7 L.Ed.2d 663 (1962), on remand 206 F.Supp. 341 (M.D.Tenn.1962).

39. 369 U.S. at 211, 82 S.Ct. at 706–07.

40. 369 U.S. at 212, 82 S.Ct. at 707–08, comparing Terlinden v. Ames, 184 U.S. 270, 285, 22 S.Ct. 484, 490, 46 L.Ed. 534 (1902), with Society for the Propagation of the Gospel in Foreign Parts v. New Haven, 21 U.S. (8 Wheat.) 464, 492–495, 5 L.Ed. 662 (1823), and Clark v. Allen, 331 U.S. 503, 67 S.Ct. 1431, 91 L.Ed. 1633 (1947).

41. E.g., Atlee v. Laird, 347 F.Supp. 689 (E.D.Pa.1972) (3–judge court) (legality of Vietnam War nonjusticiable), affirmed summarily, sub nom. Atlee v. Richardson, 411 U.S. 911, 93 S.Ct. 1545, 36 L.Ed.2d 304 (1973) (Douglas, Brennan & Stewart, JJ. would note probable jurisdiction and set the case for oral argument); see also Holtzman v. Schlesinger, 484 F.2d 1307 (2d Cir.1973), certiorari denied 416 U.S. 936, 94 S.Ct. 1935, 40 L.Ed.2d 286 (1974) (Cambodian bombing nonjusticiable; stay granted by District

Court order enjoining the bombing); On the stay, see 414 U.S. 1304, 94 S.Ct. 1, 38 L.Ed.2d 18 (1973) (Marshall, Circuit Justice, in chambers, denying application to vacate stay of Court of Appeals order staying district court injunction of Cambodian bombing), and 414 U.S. 1316, 94 S.Ct. 8, 38 L.Ed.2d 28 (1973) (Douglas, Circuit Justice, in chambers, granting stay of Court of Appeals stay), and 414 U.S. 1321, 94 S.Ct. 11, 38 L.Ed.2d 33 (Marshall, Circuit Justice in chambers; stay of district court order granted; Burger, C.J., Brennan, Stewart, White, Blackmun, Powell & Rehnquist, JJ., agree).

See also, Mora v. McNamara, 389 U.S. 934, 88 S.Ct. 282, 19 L.Ed.2d 287 (1967), rehearing denied 389 U.S. 1025, 88 S.Ct. 584, 19 L.Ed.2d 675 (1967); Velvel v. Nixon, 396 U.S. 1042, 90 S.Ct. 684, 24 L.Ed.2d 686 (1970); McArthur v. Clifford, 393 U.S. 1002, 89 S.Ct. 487, 21 L.Ed.2d 466 (1968); Massachusetts v. Laird, 400 U.S. 886, 91 S.Ct. 128, 129, 27 L.Ed.2d 140 (1970), Douglas, J., dissenting to denial of certiorari; Mitchell v. Laird, 488 F.2d 611 (D.C.Cir.1973); Orlando v. Laird, 443 F.2d 1039 (2d Cir. 1971), certiorari denied 404 U.S. 869, 92 S.Ct. 94, 30 L.Ed.2d 113 (1971). Cf. Gilligan v. Morgan, 413 U.S. 1, 6–12, 93 S.Ct. 2440, 2443–47, 37 L.Ed.2d 407 (1973) (U.S. Const. art. I, § 8, cl. 16).

while only Congress can declare war, the President can make war, and Congress can authorize an undeclared war. That is, the decision whether or not war should formally be declared is a political question. The issue may be different if the President were to seek to make war over clear congressional opposition while Congress was not in session, so that even an argument of implicit congressional authorization could not be made.

It is also unclear if any soldier or other party could even have standing to raise the issue of an illegal war based on the alleged violation of the War Powers Resolution.[42] This Resolution was enacted over Presidential veto and concerns the division of war powers between Congress and the President.

(2) Amendments to the Constitution

The leading case in this area is *Coleman v. Miller*,[43] where plaintiffs included members of the Kansas Senate whose votes against ratification of a Constitutional Amendment had been overridden. They sued in state court to compel the Secretary of State to erase an endorsement on a resolution ratifying the proposed Child Labor Amendment and indicate instead that it "was not passed." They also asked the court to restrain the officers of the Senate and House from signing the resolution and the Kansas Secretary of State from authenticating it and delivering it to the Governor. The petitioners had three claims: (1) that the Lieutenant Governor could not cast the deciding vote in the Senate because he was not part of the "Legislature" within the meaning of Article V of the U.S. Constitution; (2) that Kansas could not ratify the Amendment because it had previously rejected it; and (3) that the Amendment could not be ratified because it was no longer viable, not having been ratified within a reasonable time.

Chief Justice Hughes' opinion for the Court held that the complaining senators had standing,[44] with Justices Frankfurter, Roberts, Black, and Douglas dissenting on this point.[45] The Court was equally divided on the issue of whether the Lieutenant Governor could cast the deciding vote on ratification, with the same four Justices arguing that this issue was nonjusticiable.[46]

Petitioners also argued that either a ratification or rejection of a proposed Amendment cannot later be changed. The Court held that the "question of the efficacy of ratifications by state legislatures, in the light of previous rejection or attempted withdrawal, should be regarded as a political question pertaining to the political departments, with the ultimate authority in the Congress in the exercise of its control over the promulgation of the adoption of the Amendment."[47] Congress, the Court said, could have enacted a statute relating to ratification after rejections (and rejections after ratification) but had not done so then.

Finally the petitioners argued that the proposed Amendment has been spent, was no longer viable, had lost its force, and could not be ratified because of the length of time—thirteen years—between its proposal and the Kansas ratification. Previously the Supreme Court had held that Congress may fix a reasonable time for ratification.[48] But Congress had not—and still has not—enacted any general statutory provisions governing the length of time. In the past, various proposed Amendments provided that they must be ratified within seven years.[49] But the proposed Child Labor Amendment did not include a time limit. At the time of *Coleman*, the average time to ratify an Amendment, excluding the first ten, had been three years, six months, and 25 days.[50]

---

42. Pub.L. 93–148, 87 Stat. 555, 50 U.S.C.A. §§ 1541–48.

43. 307 U.S. 433, 59 S.Ct. 972, 83 L.Ed. 1385 (1939).

44. 307 U.S. at 438, 59 S.Ct. at 975.

45. 307 U.S. at 460, 59 S.Ct. at 985 (Opinion of Frankfurter, J.).

46. 307 U.S. at 456, 59 S.Ct. at 983 (Black, J., concurring).

47. 307 U.S. at 450, 59 S.Ct. at 980.

48. Dillon v. Gloss, 256 U.S. 368, 41 S.Ct. 510, 65 L.Ed. 994 (1921).

49. See, e.g., U.S. Const., 18th amend., § 3; 20th amend., § 6; 21st amend., § 3; 22d amend., § 2.

50. 307 U.S. at 453, 59 S.Ct. at 981–82.

The Court acknowledged that, to the extent that economic, political, and social conditions relate to a proposed Amendment, make it nonviable, those factors change. Weighing those factors to determine viability was inappropriate for the judiciary. Thus, it concluded that the issue of a reasonable time "lies within congressional province." And that question should be "regarded as an open one for the consideration of the Congress when, in the presence of certified ratifications by three-fourths of the States, the time arrives for the promulgation of the adoption of the Amendment. Th[at] decision by the Congress ... of the question whether the Amendment had been adopted within a reasonable time would not be subject to review by the courts."[51]

Justice Butler dissented and would have held that more than a reasonable time had elapsed.[52]

The separate opinion of Justice Black joined by Frankfurter, Roberts, and Douglas stated: "Congress, possessing exclusive power over the amending process, cannot be bound by and is under no duty to accept the pronouncements upon that exclusive power by this Court or by the Kansas courts. Neither state nor federal courts can review that power."[53]

The problem of reconciling judicial review with majority rule adds another important reason why courts should be reluctant to make decisions on amending the Constitution, particularly decisions preventing Amendments. Congress proposed the Child Labor Amendment because of earlier Court decisions preventing adequate legislation in this area.

It is one thing for the Court to strike down the Child Labor Law as incompatible with its choice of constitutional values ... but it would seem to be quite a different matter if the Court could, by a narrow interpretation of the Amendment procedures, prevent the ratification of the Amendment which was intended to overrule [its earlier decisions].... [I]t is by no means inconceivable that an Amendment might be unconstitutional. But this seems to be one instance in which the Court cannot assume responsibility for saying "what the law is" without, at the same time, undermining the legitimacy of its power to say so.[54]

The Court is not entirely excluded from the Amendment process. The Court has upheld the power of Congress to fix a reasonable time for ratification and it has determined, where statutes required, when an Amendment has gone into effect.[55] But if statutes do not provide for a judicial role[56] and if the power of

---

51. 307 U.S. at 454, 59 S.Ct. at 982.

52. 307 U.S. at 470, 59 S.Ct. at 989–90 (Butler, J., dissenting).

53. 307 U.S. at 459, 59 S.Ct. at 984 (Black, J., concurring).

54. Scharpf, Judicial Review and the Political Question: A Functional Analysis, 75 Yale L.J. 517, 589 (1966). Cf. Rotunda & Safranek, An Essay on Term Limits and a Call for a Constitutional Convention, 80 Marquette Univ. L. Rev. 227 (1996).

In Leser v. Garnett, 258 U.S. 130, 42 S.Ct. 217, 66 L.Ed. 505 (1922) the Court upheld the constitutionality of the 19th Amendment, announcing that: "official notice to the Secretary [of State], duly authenticated, that [a state legislature] had [ratified a proposed Amendment] was conclusive upon him, and, being certified to by his proclamation, is conclusive upon the courts." 258 U.S. at 137, 42 S.Ct. at 218.

55. Dillon v. Gloss, 256 U.S. 368, 41 S.Ct. 510, 65 L.Ed. 994 (1921) (18th Amendment). See also Rhode Island v. Palmer (National Prohibition Cases), 253 U.S. 350, 386–388, 40 S.Ct. 486, 488–489, 64 L.Ed. 946 (1920) (18th Amendment case, holding, inter alia, that the two-thirds vote in each House of Congress required in proposing an Amendment is a vote of two-thirds of the members present, assuming a quorum, and not a two-thirds vote of the entire membership, present and absent); Hawke v. Smith, 253 U.S. 221, 40 S.Ct. 495, 64 L.Ed. 871 (1920) (18th Amendment case, holding that provision of state constitution requiring submission of ratification to referendum is unconstitutional under Article V of the Constitution); Hawke v. Smith, No. 2, 253 U.S. 231, 40 S.Ct. 498, 64 L.Ed. 877 (1920) (19th Amendment case, holding same as in Hawke v. Smith, No. 1); United States v. Sprague, 282 U.S. 716, 51 S.Ct. 220, 75 L.Ed. 640 (1931) (18th Amendment; Tenth Amendment does not limit power of Congress to choose ratification by legislature instead of convention); Hollingsworth v. Virginia, 3 U.S. (3 Dall.) 378, 381, 1 L.Ed. 644 (1798) (11th Amendment; President has nothing to do with the proposing or adoption of Amendment to the Constitution).

56. Under present law, it is the Administrator of the General Services Administration who is given statutory responsibility to publish his certificate that an Amendment "has been adopted, according to the provisions of the Constitution...." 1 U.S.C.A. § 106b.

The judicial role under this statute, and the extent to which the Administrator of the General Services Administration has any discretion to declare the ratification of a state (or a state's rescission of its earlier ratification) valid or invalid are unclear.

Congress to enact such statutes is not the matter in dispute, it may be the rule that all Amendment questions relating to the constitutionality of acts of Congress affecting the Amendment procedure should be regarded as political.[57]

(3) The Guaranty Clause

From *Luther v. Borden*[58] to the present, the Court has treated the guaranty clause of Article IV, section 7 as not a repository of "judicially manageable standards which a court could utilize independently in order to identify a State's lawful government."[59] Thus, a claim that a state initiative and referendum violates the guaranty clause is nonjusticiable.[60] Similarly, a claim that the state of Kentucky's procedure for determining the results of a contested election of Governor and Lieutenant Governor is not justiciable if brought under the guaranty clause.[61]

Some Justices in dissent have occasionally suggested that the guaranty clause ought not always to be regarded as nonjusticiable,[62] but the majority has never adopted that position.[63] The reapportionment cases themselves illustrate that a claim of reapportionment is nonjusticiable if brought under the guaranty clause but is justiciable if brought under the equal protection clause of the Fourteenth Amendment.

(4) Impeachment

Most commentators have thought that any impeachment proceeding, particularly a presidential impeachment, is a political question.[64] Certainly the language of the Constitution supports such a view. Article I, section 2 states that the House "shall have the sole power of Impeachment," and section 3 provides that the "Senate shall have the sole Power to try all Impeachments."

---

57. Compare Rotunda, Running Out of Time: Can the E.R.A. Be Saved, 64 A.B.A.J. 1507 (1978) (arguing in favor of the application of the political question doctrine), with Almond, id., 64 A.B.A.J. 1504 (1978) (arguing for opposing viewpoint).

One should distinguish the actions of states from the actions of Congress; the broad application of the political question doctrine to preclude courts from ruling on the constitutionality of acts of *Congress* affecting the Amendment process, does not necessarily imply that courts cannot review acts of the state. The state, unlike Congress, is not a coequal branch. See Uhler v. AFL–CIO, 468 U.S. 1310, 1312, 105 S.Ct. 5, 6, 82 L.Ed.2d 896, 898 (1984) (Rehnquist, Circuit Justice).

The Twenty–Seventh Amendment. On May 7, 1992, Michigan became the 38th state to ratify this Amendment, which Madison had proposed 203 years earlier. On December 19, 1789, Maryland was the first state to ratify this Amendment, which provides that a law "varying the compensation" of Senators and Representatives cannot take effect until "an election of Representatives shall have intervened." Various congressional leaders initially questioned the validity of this Amendment, which had laid dormant for many years. See William Van Alstyne, What Do You Think About the Twenty–Seventh Amendment?, 10 Const. Commentary 9 (1993).

The public strongly supported the Amendment and these congressional leaders did not try to stop it. The question of its dormancy may well be a political question. On May 19, 1992, the Archivist of the United States, after he received official notice of Michigan's ratification, declared the Amendment part of the Constitution, pursuant to his authority under 1 U.S.C.A. § 106b. Cf. Leser v. Garnett, 258 U.S. 130, 42 S.Ct. 217, 66 L.Ed. 505 (1922). The Court upheld the constitutionality of the 19th Amendment, announcing that: "official notice to the Secretary [of State], duly authenticated, that [a state legislature] had

[ratified a proposed Amendment] was conclusive upon him, and, being certified to by his proclamation, is conclusive upon the courts." 258 U.S. at 137, 42 S.Ct. at 218.

58. 48 U.S. (7 How.) 1, 12 L.Ed. 581 (1849).

59. Baker v. Carr, 369 U.S. 186, 223, 82 S.Ct. 691, 713, 7 L.Ed.2d 663 (1962), on remand 206 F.Supp. 341 (M.D.Tenn.1962).

60. Pacific States Telephone & Telegraph Co. v. Oregon, 223 U.S. 118, 32 S.Ct. 224, 56 L.Ed. 377 (1912).

61. Taylor v. Beckham, 178 U.S. 548, 20 S.Ct. 890, 44 L.Ed. 1187 (1900). See 178 U.S. at 581, 20 S.Ct. at 902 (Brewer & Brown, JJ., dissenting on 19th Amendment grounds), 178 U.S. at 585, 20 S.Ct. at 903 (Harlan, J., dissenting on 14th Amendment grounds).

62. See Fortson v. Morris, 385 U.S. 231, 249, 87 S.Ct. 446, 456, 17 L.Ed.2d 330 (1966), rehearing denied 385 U.S. 1021, 87 S.Ct. 719, 17 L.Ed.2d 560 (1967) (Fortas, J., dissenting, joined by Douglas, J., and Warren, C.J.); Baker v. Carr, 369 U.S. 186, 242 n. 2, 82 S.Ct. 691, 723 n. 2, 7 L.Ed.2d 663 (1962) (Douglas, J., concurring), on remand 206 F.Supp. 341 (M.D.Tenn.1962).

63. In, New York v. United States, 505 U.S. 144, 184–85, 112 S.Ct. 2408, 2433, 120 L.Ed.2d 120 (1992), on remand 978 F.2d 705 (2d Cir.1992), the Court raised the question whether the entire Guaranty Clause was always nonjusticiable, or whether it would be the better rule that the nature of the claim (rather than the nature of the clause under which it was brought) should determine whether the claim is justiciable.

64. E.g., Herbert Wechsler, Toward Neutral Principles of Constitutional Law, 73 Harv.L.Rev. 1, 8 (1959); Ronald D. Rotunda, An Essay on the Constitutional Parameters of Federal Impeachment, 76 Kentucky Law Review 707 (1988).

Because no statute sets out or otherwise defines impeachable offenses, the nature of the proceeding makes it difficult if not impossible for the Court to apply any judicial criteria for review. In fact any such statute—which would have to be passed with the input of the Senate—might be unconstitutional, for it would interfere with the House's *sole* power of Impeachment.[65]

The Chief Justice would be disqualified from setting on any hypothetical Supreme Court review of the impeachment of the President because the Constitution commands that he preside at the Senate trial.[66] Moreover, the potential for national confusion would be great if the Senate were to declare the presidential office vacant but the impeached President would refuse to leave, apply to the Supreme Court or a lower court for relief, and claim, for example, that some of the Senators who voted against him were prejudiced and should have disqualified themselves. Because the framers placed the sole power of impeachment in two *political* bodies—the House and Senate—it would certainly appear that such an issue remains a political question.

Yet some commentators have argued that at least some aspects of impeachment may be judicially reviewable.[67] The Supreme Court rejected the views of these commentators and adopted the theory of this treatise in *Nixon v. United States*.[68] The Nixon in this case was Judge Walter L. Nixon, the former Chief Judge of the District Court for the Southern District of Mississippi. He argued that the vote of the full Senate removing him from office (after he had been impeached by the House of Representatives) was unconstitutional, because the Senate used a *committee of Senators* to hear

evidence against him and to report that evidence to the full Senate. Senate Rule XI authorized this use of an impeachment committee. Chief Justice Rehnquist, for the Court, held that Nixon's claim was not justiciable.

A federal jury convicted Nixon of two counts of making false statements before a federal grand jury, which was investigating reports that Nixon had accepted a gratuity from a local Mississippi businessman in exchange for asking a local district attorney to halt the prosecution of the businessman's son. The Court of Appeals affirmed the conviction,[69] but Nixon refused to resign, so that he continued to collect his salary while serving his prison term. He, in fact, collected his salary until the Senate voted to remove him from office.[70]

The full trial did not occur on the Senate floor. Instead, the Senate's Rule XI Committee held four days of hearings and heard 10 witnesses, including Judge Nixon. This Committee presented the full Senate with a transcript of the proceeding, a report of the uncontested facts, and a report summarizing the evidence of the contested facts. Nixon was permitted to address the full Senate, which he did. Several Senators asked him questions and he responded. Any Senator could have attended the Rule XI hearing, or could watch videotapes of it. After the Senate voted to impeach by more than the necessary two-thirds majority, he sued for a declaratory judgment that his impeachment was void on the grounds that using the Rule XI Committee violated the Constitutional command of Article I, § 3, clause 6 that the Senate "try" all impeachments.

The Supreme Court held that this claim was nonjusticiable. The Court examined the histo-

---

65. Cf. Ritter v. United States, 84 Ct.Cl. 293 (1936), cert. denied 300 U.S. 668, 57 S.Ct. 513, 81 L.Ed. 875 (1937). In this case the court dismissed an action by former Judge Ritter, an impeached judge who sued for back pay, because the Senate has the *sole* power over impeachment.

66. U.S. Const. art. I, § 3, cl. 6.

67. R. Berger, Impeachment: The Constitutional Problems (1973). Contrast, Rotunda, An Essay on the Constitutional Parameters of Federal Impeachment, 76 Ky. L. J. 707, 728–32 (1987–1988).

68. 506 U.S. 224, 113 S.Ct. 732, 122 L.Ed.2d 1 (1993).

69. United States v. Nixon, 816 F.2d 1022 (5th Cir. 1987), rehearing denied 827 F.2d 1019 (1987).

70. See, H.R.Report No. 101–36, at p. 13 (1989). After this case, Congress enacted Public Law 101–659, 104 Stat. at Large 5124 (1990), which studied the issue of impeachment and recommended various reforms. It did not propose eliminating the Rule XI Committee. Rotunda, Impeachment Showdown: Congress vs. Judges, 16 Legal Times (of Washington, D.C.) 37 (Nov. 1, 1993). See also, Rotunda, Impeaching Federal Judges: Where Are We and Where Are We Going?, 72 Judicature: The Journal of the American Judicature Society 359 (1989).

ry, policy, and the language of the Constitution, the difficulty of fashioning relief, and the delay caused by judicial intervention. It Court concluded that the framers intended that the judiciary, and the Supreme Court in particular, should have no role in impeachments.

(5) Political Gerrymandering

Nearly a quarter of a century after *Baker v. Carr*[71] upheld the justiciability of lawsuits attacking malapportioned legislative districts, the Court in *Davis v. Bandemer*[72] (six to three) held that political gerrymandering cases are also justiciable under the equal protection clause. But the Court had no majority opinion on any other issue.

Plaintiffs claimed that Indiana's 1981 state apportionment of its upper and lower state house unconstitutionally diluted the votes of Indiana Democrats. A majority of the Court (with no majority opinion) rejected this claim, but a majority did agree that it was justiciable. As in *Baker,* which did not articulate a test to judge malapportionment, the Court did not articulate the standards to judge allegedly unconstitutional political gerrymandering. Justice White's plurality, joined by Justices Brennan, Marshall, and Blackmun, opted for a stricter standard than that proposed by the separate opinion of Justice Powell, joined by Justice Stevens—but these six judges could not even agree on the definition of unconstitutional political gerrymandering.[73]

Nonetheless, a majority of the Court announced its conclusion that political gerrymandering, like racial gerrymandering, is justiciable. The majority simply asserted that it could find no significant difference between *Bandemer* and other cases where the Court found justiciability.[74] A political group, rather than a racial group, was bringing the claim, but the majority did not think that factual difference affected the claim's justiciability. "That the characteristics of the complaining group are not immutable or that the group has not been subject to the same historical stigma may be relevant to the manner in which the case is adjudicated, but these differences do not justify a refusal to entertain the case."[75] However, individuals bring racial gerrymandering cases, because the equal protection clause protects "persons," not groups,[76] but the majority, like the plaintiffs, was more concerned with group rights.

Justice O'Connor, in response to the majority's conclusions, warned that the federal judiciary would find itself injected into heated partisan debates and that the nebulous standard for intervention would likely translate itself into proportional representation for political groups.[77] The lack of a workable standard, in fact, counsels against judicial intervention. After *Baker,* the Court developed the one person, one vote test because a more nebulous "arbitrary and capricious" test was unmanageable. The courts need a bright line when entering the political thicket in order to protect themselves from charges of judicial usurpation, but *Bandemer* offered no bright line, and the nature of the problem suggests that none may be possible.

71. 369 U.S. 186, 82 S.Ct. 691, 7 L.Ed.2d 663 (1962), on remand 206 F.Supp. 341 (M.D.Tenn.1962).

72. 478 U.S. 109, 106 S.Ct. 2797, 92 L.Ed.2d 85 (1986). O'Connor, J., joined by Burger, C.J., and Rehnquist, J., disagreed with the majority on this issue. 478 U.S. at 145, 106 S.Ct. at 2816.

73. Compare 478 U.S. at 138–39, 106 S.Ct. at 2813 (White, J., attacking Powell, J.'s definition of "gerrymandering"), with 478 U.S. at 164, 106 S.Ct. at 2827 (Powell, J., defining unconstitutional gerrymandering and gerrymandering when used "loosely").

74. See 478 U.S. at 118–19, 106 S.Ct. at 2803:

"We have also adjudicated claims that the configuration of single-member districts violated equal protection with respect to racial and ethnic minorities, although we have never struck down an apportionment plan because

of such a claim. See United Jewish Organizations of Williamsburgh, Inc. v. Carey, 430 U.S. 144, 97 S.Ct. 996, 51 L.Ed.2d 229 (1977); Wright v. Rockefeller, 376 U.S. 52, 84 S.Ct. 603, 11 L.Ed.2d 512 (1964)."

See also Gomillion v. Lightfoot, 364 U.S. 339, 81 S.Ct. 125, 5 L.Ed.2d 110 (1960) (racial gerrymandering of City of Tuskegee invalid under Fifteenth Amendment).

75. 478 U.S. at 125, 106 S.Ct. at 2806.

76. Shelley v. Kraemer, 334 U.S. 1, 11, 68 S.Ct. 836, 841, 92 L.Ed. 1161 (1948) (law that draws distinction on the basis of color unconstitutional even if whites and blacks are equally burdened). Buchanan v. Warley, 245 U.S. 60, 38 S.Ct. 16, 62 L.Ed. 149 (1917) (same).

77. 478 U.S. at 145, 106 S.Ct. at 2817 (O'Connor, J., joined by Burger, C.J., & Rehnquist, J., concurring in the judgment).

Political gerrymandering, unlike racial gerrymandering, is to some extent self-correcting. Every decade, after the new census, district lines are redrawn. It is often difficult to foresee, in 1991, what will be the political facts of life a decade later. People move. The same people, even if they do not move out of the district, change their political views and their party affiliation. Unlike racial gerrymandering, the make-up of the groups are often fluid. Race is immutable; political beliefs are not.

As the 1980's began, Indiana Republicans gerrymandered 10 congressional districts besides the state districts considered in *Bandemer*. They wanted to create seven "safe" Republican seats. By 1990, Democrats controlled eight of these 10 seats. The chief demographer of the Indiana School of Business noted, "Given the success of the 1980's, the Democrats ought to ask the Republicans to [draw the district lines] again."[78]

It is difficult to determine what will be the staying power of *Bandemer*. The membership of the Court, since its splintered decision, has changed, and the Court now may decide to breathe no new life into *Bandemer*. In one racial gerrymandering case, the Court remanded so that the lower court could determine if there was intentional racial gerrymandering (unconstitutional) or intentional political gerrymandering (constitutional).[79] The Court cited *Bandemer,* and merely noted that the Justices in that case "were not in agreement as to

the standards that would govern" a political gerrymandering claim.[80]

Apportionment of Congressional Districts Among the States. The Constitution provides that each state shall have at least one representative and that the number of representatives shall not exceed one for every 30,000 persons.[81] In addition, implicit in the Constitution, and the continuous historical practice is the requirement that congressional districts not cross state lines. So, apportionment of districts often results in *fractional remainders:* the fractional portion of the number that results when the state's total population is divided by the population of the ideal district must either be ignored or rounded to one whole Representative, because states are only represented by a whole number of legislators.

Over the years, Congress has tried various plans to deal with this problem. In 1941, Congress enacted a law that used the "equal portions" method. Montana objected because the use of this method, after the 1990 census, resulted in reducing its House delegation from two representatives to one. A unanimous Court held that Montana's claim were justiciable.[82] Montana's victory was short-lived, however, because the Court then turned to the merits, rejected Montana's claim, and held that Congress had broad discretion to enact the "equal portions" method.

In *Department of Commerce v. United States House of Representatives,*[83] various U.S.

78. Quoted in, Shribman, With Political Power Shifting South and West, Democrats Will Control Most of the Redistricting, Wall Street Journal, Nov. 29, 1990, at A16, col. 1, 3 (Midwest ed.).

79. Hunt v. Cromartie, 526 U.S. 541, 119 S.Ct. 1545, 143 L.Ed.2d 731 (1999) on remand 133 F.Supp.2d 407 (E.D.N.C. 2000), reversed sub nom. Easley v. Cromartie, 532 U.S. 234, 121 S.Ct. 1452, 149 L.Ed.2d 430 (2001). The appellants claimed that the state legislature intended to make a strong Democratic district, not to engage in *racial* gerrymandering (but to engage in *political* gerrymandering). Justice Thomas, for the Court, distinguished between unconstitutional racial gerrymandering and constitutional political gerrymandering:

"Our prior decisions have made clear that a jurisdiction may engage in constitutional political gerrymandering, even if it so happens that the most loyal Democrats happen to be black Democrats and even if the State were *conscious* of that fact."

526 U.S. at 551, 119 S.Ct. at 1551 (emphasis in original).

Stevens, J., joined by Souter, Ginsburg & Breyer, JJ., concurred in the judgment, and said of *Bandemer* that "bizarre configuration is the traditional hallmark of the political gerrymander."

526 U.S. at 555 n. 7, 119 S.Ct. at 1554.

80. 526 U.S. at 552 n. 7, 119 S.Ct. at 1551 n. 7.

81. U.S. Const. art. I, § 2, cl. 3.

82. United States Department of Commerce v. Montana, 503 U.S. 442, 112 S.Ct. 1415, 118 L.Ed.2d 87 (1992).

83. 525 U.S. 316, 119 S.Ct. 765, 142 L.Ed.2d 797 (1999). O'Connor delivered the Opinion of the Court, except for part III(B), which referred to the Congressional debates enacting the Census Act. Different justices joined different parts of her opinion.

residents sued federal agencies and officials objecting to their planned use of a statistical sampling during the next decennial census. Proponents of "sampling" (as opposed to an actual "counting" of people) claimed that it would address a problem of undercounting some groups of individuals. O'Connor, for a fragmented Court, held that several state residents had Article III standing because they showed that the use of statistical sampling would result in a loss of U.S. representatives from their state. In addition, there was intrastate vote dilution because states use the population numbers generated by the federal decennial census for redistricting state legislative districts. This vote dilution is injury in fact. Moreover, this injury is "fairly traceable" to the use of statistical sampling, and the requested relief—a permanent injunction against such sampling—will redress the alleged injury. The Court went on to hold that the Census Act prohibited the use of statistical sampling, either as a supplement or substitute to the traditional enumeration method for calculating the population for apportionment purposes.

(6) The Origination Clause

The Origination Clause requires that all bills for raising revenue "shall originate" in the House of Representatives.[84] In *United States v. Munoz–Flores*,[85] defendants claimed that a federal law that required courts to impose a monetary "special assessment" on a person convicted of a federal misdemeanor was unconstitutional because the law raised revenue, but it did not originate in the House. In this case the defendants claimed that the Senate was the first chamber to pass the assessment.

The Court held that the case was justiciable because none of the characteristics of *Baker v. Carr* applied. The Origination Clause is not a textually demonstrable commitment of the issue to Congress. A holding that the assessment statute violated the clause entails no more disrespect for Congress than the invalidation of any other law that Congress enacts. The Court, in short, should be able to engage in the prosaic judgment of creating judicially manageable standards to determine where a bill "originates" or if it is for "raising revenue."[86] On the merits, the Court ruled against the defendants.

(d) A Functional Test for Political Questions

Over the years various commentators have proposed different tests to justify and apply the political question doctrine. Professor Alexander Bickel argued:

> Such is the foundation, in both intellect and instinct, of the political-question doctrine: the Court's sense of lack of capacity, compounded in unequal parts of (a) the strangeness of the issue and its intractability to principled resolution; (b) the sheer momentousness of it, which tends to unbalance judicial judgment; (c) the anxiety, not so much that the judicial judgment will be ignored, as that perhaps it should but will not be; (d) finally ("in a mature democracy"), the inner vulnerability, the self-doubt of an institution which is electorally irresponsible and has no earth to draw strength from.[87]

Professor Louis Henkin proposed another analysis, viewing the doctrine as an "unnecessary, deceptive packaging of several established doctrines." It really consists of several propositions:

---

84. U.S. Const. art. I, § 7, cl. 1.

85. 495 U.S. 385, 110 S.Ct. 1964, 109 L.Ed.2d 384 (1990).

86. Turning to the merits, the Court found no violation of the clause. A statute that creates a particular federal program and raises revenue to support it as opposed to a statute that "raises revenue to support government generally" is not a bill for "raising revenue" within the meaning of the clause.

Scalia, J., concurred in the judgment. He argued that the Court should not undertake an independent investiga-

tion of where a law originated. The law in this case, when enacted, was designated "H.J.Res. 648," meaning "House Joint Resolution 648." The Court, he argued, should accept the congressional representation in this case. "This Court may thereby have the last word on what constitutes a bill for raising revenue [if the bill is designated, e.g., 'S.J.Res.'], and Congress the last word on where a particular bill has originated—which seems to me as it should be." 495 U.S. at 410, 110 S.Ct. at 1979.

87. A. Bickel, The Least Dangerous Branch 184 (1962).

1. The courts are bound to accept decisions by the political branches within their constitutional authority.

2. The courts will not find limitations or prohibitions on the powers of the political branches where the Constitution does not prescribe any.

3. Not all constitutional limitations or prohibitions imply rights and standing to object in favor of private parties.

4. The courts may refuse some (or all) remedies for want of equity.

5. In principle, finally, there might be constitutional provisions that can properly be interpreted as wholly or in part "self-monitoring" and not the subject of judicial review. (But the only one the courts have found is the "guarantee clause" as applied to challenges to state action, and even that interpretation was not inevitable.)[88]

Professor Scharpf considered the doctrine best explained in functional terms. The doctrine does not really represent the Court's unprincipled retreat from difficult cases or the lack of legal standards. Sometimes, he argued, the doctrine is justified because of the Court's inability to have access to information. This function is most clear in the cases affecting foreign relations, because the Court is generally hesitant to rely on its own understanding of the broader situation.[89] Thus, *United States v. Pink*[90] accepted the President's policy of recognizing a foreign government that was implied in the "Litvinov Assignment." The Court wished to avoid any interference with the President's attempt to deal with the problem of Russian debts as a political prerequisite for recognition. Scharpf argued that the Court should defer to "the prior decisions of another department within the latter's sphere of specific responsibility."[91]

The Court should be reluctant to apply the political question doctrine when questions of individual liberty are at stake. Individual liberty is within the Court's sphere of competence and there is less need to defer to the political branches. However, the Court's reluctance to apply the doctrine in the case of individual liberties finds its rational not in functional reasons, but for a normative reason: "where important individual rights are at stake, the doctrine will not be applied."[92] Thus it is unusual to apply the doctrine to the Bill of Rights.

88. Henkin, Is There a "Political Question" Doctrine? 85 Yale L.J. 597, 622–623 (1976) (footnote omitted).

89. Matthews, J., citing Treatise in State, Dept. of Natural Resources v. Tongass Conservation Society, 931 P.2d 1016, 1019 (Alaska 1997).

90. 315 U.S. 203, 62 S.Ct. 552, 86 L.Ed. 796 (1942).

91. Scharpf, 75 Yale L.J. 517, 573 (1966).

92. Scharpf, 75 Yale L.J. 517, 584 (1966).

Chapter 3

SOURCES OF NATIONAL AUTHORITY

§ 3.1 Introduction

In order to determine whether any action of the federal government complies with the U.S. Constitution, the Court must ascertain if the federal action meets two criteria. First, because the federal government is one of enumerated rather than inherent powers, the Court must decide if the action is pursuant to one of the powers that the Constitution grants to the federal government. The central government can act only to effectuate the powers specifically granted to it, rather than acting for the general welfare of the populace. Second, the Court must determine whether the action violates some specific check on federal power such as those contained in the Bill of Rights. These specific constitutional limitations restrict the federal government even if it is acting pursuant to one of its enumerated powers.

This two tier form of review should be contrasted with the way that federal courts review state laws. Because *state* constitutions, not the U.S. Constitution, are the source of state powers, it is not for federal courts to determine whether state acts are authorized by *state* law. Federal courts test only whether a state act violates some specific check on state power contained in the U.S. Constitution.[1] For the purposes of federal law, state governments (or their instrumentalities) are not creatures of limited powers. They have a general "police

power"—the power to protect the health, safety, welfare or morals of persons within their jurisdiction.

The different basis for review of federal laws relates to the formation of the federal government, and the creation of its powers in the Constitution. The federal government, and the ex-colonies, existed prior to the writing of the Constitution. With the Declaration of Independence and the war against Great Britain, the country became loosely aligned under the Articles of Confederation.[2] The Articles established a national government of very limited powers, which could not control the activities of the states, thereby allowing commercial problems.

During the Revolutionary period and its aftermath, the States enacted conflicting commercial regulations and established trade barriers to the movement of goods and services. These regulations so hampered both national and international commerce that there was a call for a convention to amend the Articles of Confederation to deal with this problem. It became apparent to the delegates attending the convention that a new form of government would be necessary to deal with these national commercial problems. Following this first meeting there was a convention—which we now know as the Constitutional Convention—to do much more than amend the Articles; rather, it created a new Constitution, with a stronger national government that could deal

---

§ 3.1

1. In the body of the Constitution, the main limitations on the states are in Article I, § 10, which prohibits states from entering into any treaties or alliances, from coining money, from impairing the obligation of contracts, etc. The Constitution, since the enactment of the Four-

teenth Amendment, also imposes substantial civil liberties limitations on the states.

2. The Articles were ratified on July 9, 1778. The text of the articles may be found in 5 R. Rotunda & J. Nowak, Treatise on Constitutional Law: Substance and Procedure, Appendix B (West Group, 3d ed. 1999).

with certain multi state problems.[3] This Convention, which began in May of 1787, produced our Constitution and the new federal government.

During the Convention, the Virginia delegation made several specific recommendations concerning the powers that should be granted the new federal government. Edmund Randolph submitted the Virginia proposals, which included a provision that authorized the national legislature "to legislate in all cases to which the separate States are incompetent, or in which the harmony of the United States may be interrupted by exercise of individual legislation." The Convention adopted this resolution while it rejected other resolutions that indicated more limited powers for the national legislature.[4] The Convention then sent its proposals to the Committee on Detail, and charged that Committee to draft specific constitutional provisions based on the proposals. The Committee's draft of the constitution contained an enumeration of powers for Congress that was very close to that contained in the final draft in Article I, section 8 of the Constitution. At no time did any delegate challenge the Committee's deviation from the language of the Randolph plan and the listing of specific powers for the federal government.

There was no significant debate on the concept of enumerated powers or on the seemingly sweeping powers that the commerce clause or the necessary and proper clause granted.

(In fact, the necessary and proper clause is sometimes called the "sweeping clause."[5]) The history and records of the Convention yield little evidence as to whether the delegates accepted these proposals because they thought that the national government should be strictly limited to a specific set of powers or because they assumed that this listing included the sweeping powers that the Randolph proposal had implied. During the ratification debates there was concern expressed over the national government's scope of powers, but while the debates were vigorous and the ratification process a difficult one, no clear picture emerges as to the general understanding of the powers of the national government.

During the ratification process there was a popular concern about the absence of a bill of rights for individual citizens, so supporters of the Constitution promised that the first Congress would propose such a bill.[6] Following ratification and the establishment of the federal government, the first Congress drafted a series of Amendments that were submitted to the states in September 1789.[7] Ten of these Amendments were accepted and ratified by December 15, 1791. These ten, or sometimes, the first eight, are now known as the Bill of Rights.[8] The first eight establish certain rights of individuals against infringement by the federal government. The Ninth Amendment recognizes that certain individual rights are retained by the people even though those rights

---

3. The resolution for a new convention to deal with commercial problems is reprinted in 1 H. Commanger, ed., Documents of American History 132 (5th ed. 1949). The 1780's was a period of intense regional conflict that laid the basis for increasing federal power that culminated in the formation of a stronger federal government under the Constitution. Note, The United States and the Articles of Confederation: Drifting Toward Anarchy or Inching Toward Commonwealth?, 88 Yale L.J. 142 (1978).

4. 1 Farrand, Records of Federal Convention of 1787, (1911) at 47, 53; Vol. 2, id. at 25–27, 181–82.

5. See, William Van Alstyne, The Role of Congress in Determining Incidental Powers of the President and of the Federal Courts: A Comment on the Horizontal Effects of "the Sweeping Clause," 36 Ohio St.L.J. 788 (1975).

6. See B. Schwartz, The Bill of Rights: A Documentary History (1971); Rotunda, Bicentennial Lessons from the Constitutional Convention of 1797, 21 Suffolk L.Rev. 589 (1987).

7. The states had offered approximately 124 Amendments. The first Congress, led by Madison, drafted the specific proposals. The House of Representatives passed seventeen Amendments. The Senate rejected two of these and combined the remaining into twelve proposed Amendments. Congressional Research Service, the Constitution of the United States of America—Analysis and Interpretation at 898–900 (92d Congress, 2d sess., Senate Doc. No. 92–82) (1972); H. Ames, The Proposed Amendments to the Constitution at 14, 184–85 (1896).

8. The two Amendments that were not ratified as a part of this Bill of Rights dealt with the apportionment of representatives to population and the compensation of members of Congress. In 1992, over two centuries later, a sufficient number of states ratified the Amendment dealing with compensation for Members of Congress. On May 13, 1992, the Archivist of the United States announced that, pursuant to 1 U.S.C.A. § 106b, he would accept this 27th Amendment as valid.

were not listed in the Constitution.[9] The Tenth Amendment indicates that the states and individual citizens retained powers that were not specifically granted to the new federal government.[10] The Ninth and Tenth Amendments, while hardly specific, seem to imply that the actions of the federal government are subject to limitations in the specification of its powers, and they also acknowledge the existence of certain individual rights.

Following the establishment of the federal government, the debate over its powers continued for many years. Federalists such as Hamilton advocated more federal legislation to control national problems. In contrast, the Republicans, also referred to as the Anti-federalists, led by Jefferson, opposed the increasing activity of the federal government as a usurpation of powers reserved to the states.

Prior to 1800, the Federalists enjoyed a period of virtually unchecked success. They passed legislation ranging from the establishment of the national judiciary to creation of a national bank to regulate monetary problems. They went so far as to pass sedition laws used to punish those whose political activities the Federalists claimed were harmful in some way to the national government.[11] Throughout this period Jefferson and the Republicans continued to advance the theory that the federal government had only those powers that were specifically listed in the Constitution and that those powers must be interpreted narrowly in order to avoid a violation of the rights of states and individual citizens.[12]

Many of the issues concerning the scope of national power during the first century of the country's existence were settled by the political branches of government rather than the judiciary.[13] But the Supreme Court was to play an important part in these debates and the framing of national power by its decision in *McCulloch v. Maryland*.[14] It is to that decision that we now turn.

§ 3.2 *McCulloch v. Maryland* and the Basis of Federal Power

In the landmark case of *McCulloch v. Maryland*[1] the Supreme Court interpreted the necessary and proper clause[2] to create implied powers and establish the legitimate role of the federal government in dealing with national problems. Prior to this decision the history of that clause had left the scope of federal authority unclear.[3] In the words of one historian, "there still remained a grave anxiety over the indeterminate language contained" in the nec-

---

9. "The enumeration in the Constitution, of certain rights, shall not be construed to deny or disparage others retained by the people." U.S.Const. Amend. IX.

10. "The powers not delegated to the United States by the Constitution, nor prohibited by it to the States, are reserved to the States respectively, or to the people." U.S.Const. Amend. X.

11. These laws are examined in connection with the First Amendment's guarantee of free speech in § 16.5, infra.

12. One of the most famous remarks of Jefferson on the attempts of the Federalists to expand national power concerned their attempt to grant a federal charter to a mining business. Jefferson wrote:

"I do not know whether it is understood that the Legislature of Jersey was incompetent to [do] this, or merely that we have concurrent legislation under the sweeping clause. Congress are authorized to defend the nation. Ships are necessary for defense; copper is necessary for ships; mines, necessary for copper; a company necessary to work the mines; and who can doubt this reasoning who has ever played at 'This is the House that Jack Built'? Under such a process of filiation of the necessities the sweeping clause makes clean work."

1 C. Warren, The Supreme Court in United States History 501 (Rev. ed. 1926) (footnote omitted).

13. In only two cases (or perhaps three cases) prior to the Civil War did the Court strike down federal legislation. The two major decisions are Marbury v. Madison, 5 U.S. (1 Cranch) 137, 2 L.Ed. 60 (1803), and Dred Scott v. Sanford, 60 U.S. (19 How.) 393, 15 L.Ed. 691 (1856). The Court also invalidates a third federal statute (or, at least interpreted in a very limited way because of Constitutional problems), in Hodgson v. Bowerbank, 9 U.S. (5 Cranch) 303, 3 L.Ed. 108 (1809). See Charles Wright, Federal Courts 26–27 n. 3 (4 ed. 1983).

14. 17 U.S. (4 Wheat.) 316, 4 L.Ed. 579 (1819).

§ 3.2

1. Id.

2. "Congress shall have the Power ... To make all Laws which shall be necessary and proper for carrying into Execution the foregoing Powers, and all other Powers vested by this Constitution in the Government of the United States, or in any Department or Officer thereof." U.S.Const. art. I, § 8.

3. See § 3.1 for a discussion of this clause during the Constitutional Convention, and the role of the Committee on Detail.

essary and proper clause.[4] This anxiety continued through the first federalist administrations as the new federal government embarked upon legislation touching a variety of state and local interests.

The Supreme Court had considered the meaning of that clause only once prior to *McCulloch*. In *United States v. Fisher*[5] the Court upheld federal legislation that gave priority to the payment of debts to the United States in settling the estates of insolvent debtors. The opinion, written by Chief Justice Marshall, asserted that "Congress must possess the choice of means, and must be empowered to use any means which are in fact conducive to the exercise of a power granted by the constitution."[6] A majority of the Court found the law to be clearly related to the financial powers of Congress but used no detailed analysis of those powers to justify the federal act.[7] Thus, when the Chief Justice examined the problem presented in *McCulloch*, he was writing on an essentially clean legal slate, even though the necessary and proper clause and the Bank of the United States had been the subject of widespread debate throughout the country.

McCulloch considered the ability of the federal government to charter the second Bank of the United States. The establishment of a national bank had been a great public controversy since the creation of the republic. Soon after the establishment of the federal government, Alexander Hamilton proposed the creation of a national bank to regulate currency and deal with national economic problems. This proposal caused the most serious dispute of a constitutional issue during President Washington's administration, because Jefferson and the Republicans protested that the establishment of this Bank would usurp state powers.[8] The Federalists, who were enjoying a period of widespread political support, were able to establish the Bank. However, it was only a limited success and its charter expired in 1811 without being renewed. By this time the Federalists

---

4. 1 C. Warren, The Supreme Court in United States History at 500 (Rev. ed. 1926).

5. 6 U.S. (2 Cranch) 358, 2 L.Ed. 304 (1805).

6. 6 U.S. (2 Cranch) at 396.

7. The only specific power of Congress referred to was the power "to pay the debt of the Union." 6 U.S. (2 Cranch) at 396. Art. I, § 8 provides for powers relating to currency and bankruptcy, which also could have been used to sustain this law.

The Constitutional Convention had rejected a motion to empower Congress to "grant charters of incorporation" and one may question the *McCulloch* holding in terms of this historical fact. Of course, the Convention may have rejected the motion on the grounds that Congress already had the power to grant charters of incorporation. Or, even if the Convention did not want Congress to have the power to grant charters of incorporation generally, this historical evidence does not mean that Congress was barred from granting charters to effectuate other enumerated powers, such as when the charter was necessary and proper to the effectuation of an enumerated power.

8. For a discussion of the political history and consequences of the bank and the Court's decision see 1 C. Warren, The Supreme Court in United States History 499–540 (Rev. ed. 1926).

Even after *McCulloch*, attacks on the Bank continued. For example, in Osborn v. Bank of the United States, 22 U.S. (9 Wheat.) 738, 6 L.Ed. 204 (1824), the Supreme Court, again speaking through Chief Justice Marshall, affirmed a lower court decision directing defendants to restore to the Bank the sum of $100,000. (The lower court decision as to the awarding of interest was reversed.) Osborn was the auditor of the state of Ohio and had proceeded against the Bank pursuant to an act of the state legislature entitled "an act to levy and collect a tax from all banks and individuals, and companies and associations of individuals, that may transact business in this state without being allowed to do so by the laws thereof." The Bank, under this act, pursued its operations contrary to the laws of the state.

In *Osborn* Marshall also proposed a very broad view of federal jurisdiction. He argued that constitutionally Congress may (and did, in the *Osborn* situation) extend federal jurisdiction to all cases where a title or right set up by a party may be defeated or sustained by a construction of the Constitution. The Bank was a creature of federal law; the Bank could make no contract, bring no suit, nor acquire any right unless authorized to do so by federal law. Thus, he argued, all issues involving the Bank arise under the laws and Constitution of the United States. Marshall readily admitted that the right of the Bank to sue may be settled law, and actually any lawsuit may revolve around a construction of a simple contract construed under state law, but to Marshall that made no difference. The original federal "question forms an original ingredient in every cause. Whether it be, in fact, relied on or not, in the defense, it is still a part of the cause, and may be relied on." 22 U.S. (9 Wheat.) at 824.

See also, the companion case of Bank of United States v. Planters' Bank of Georgia, 22 U.S. (9 Wheat.) 904, 6 L.Ed. 244 (1824).

Marshall's defense of *McCulloch* and of his broad view of federal jurisdiction took place not only in the case law but in the newspapers, under a pseudonym. See generally, G. Gunther, ed., John Marshall's Defense of McCulloch v. Maryland (1969).

had lost power and there was little interest in establishing a national bank. Only one year later this situation was dramatically changed, for the war against Great Britain brought new economic problems.

Following the War of 1812, the states seemed incapable of dealing with the monetary problems of a disrupted economy. Despite his Anti-federalist heritage, President Madison approved the establishment of a second Bank of the United States in 1816. Unfortunately, the Bank did not provide an answer to many of the economic ills. After a few years a very serious economic depression took place and people blamed the Bank's monetary practices for aggravating the situation. Also, it appeared that many of the branches were engaged in corrupt practices designed to profit those who controlled the Bank. Many of the states responded with attempts to limit the powers of the branches of the Bank located within their boundaries. It was a state action of this type that gave rise to *McCulloch*.

Maryland enacted a tax on the issuance of bank notes that was, in effect, a discriminatory tax on the national bank. The law required any bank that was not chartered by the state to pay a $15,000 per year state tax, or use certain "stamped" paper for its notes, which resulted in a 2% tax on those notes. Branches of the Bank of the United States continued to operate and issue bank notes in Maryland, but refused to comply with the statute. The state then brought an action for taxes and penalties against the cashier of the Bank, McCulloch. The Maryland Court of Appeals affirmed a judgment for the state, but the Supreme Court, speaking through Chief Justice Marshall, held the tax invalid.

In order to determine the validity of the Maryland tax, the Court had to determine the constitutionality of the national bank legislation. After all, if Congress could not establish such a bank, then the Maryland statute did not interfere with any legitimate federal authority. Maryland argued that the states did not surrender to the national government their ability to regulate banks because the Constitution gave the federal government only a limited amount of power; the states retained important sovereignty rights. Marshall and the Court rejected this "states' rights" argument and, in so doing, established the basis for federal supremacy.

The Chief Justice, in *McCulloch v. Maryland*,[9] deals with three distinct aspects of federal power. First, he established the principle that the federal government draws its authority directly from the people. Second, he interpreted the necessary and proper clause to allow Congress a wide scope of authority to implement the enumerated powers. Third, he concluded that state legislation (including state taxation) that might interfere with the exercise of these federal powers is invalid.

Marshall began by examining the general basis of authority for the federal government and the Constitution. The states had claimed that the Constitution emanated from their independent sovereignties and that the exercise of the federal power could not predominate over the states' claims to power. Marshall rejected this theory by stating that the federal government emanates directly from the people and not from the states.[10] Because the power is not derived from the states, they cannot limit the grant of power to Congress. Webster and Lincoln later reasserted the principle that national sovereignty comes from a direct popular base, and it became the "main tenets of American Nationalism."[11]

Marshall then turned to the question of how the Constitution, as the embodiment of federal powers, should be interpreted. He stressed the differences between a constitution and ordinary legislation: "Its nature, therefore, requires that only its great outlines should be marked, its important objects designated, and the minor ingredients which comprise those objects be deduced from the nature of the objects themselves."[12] This view justified broad judicial construction of the Constitution far

9.   17 U.S. (4 Wheat.) 316, 4 L.Ed. 579 (1819).

10.   17 U.S. (4 Wheat.) at 403–07.

11.   A. Kelly & W. Harbison, The American Constitution 289 (4th ed. 1970).

12.   17 U.S. (4 Wheat.) at 407.

beyond *Marbury v. Madison*,[13] the landmark case providing for federal judicial review of Congressional legislation.[14]

Marbury had invalidated a law that was in direct conflict with a constitutional provision. *McCulloch* went further and established the Constitution as a statement of binding principles that had the force of law but that could adapt to a changing society without continual alteration. Marshall implied the existence of wide ranging powers for the federal government in general, and the judiciary in particular, when he stated that "we must never forget that it is a *constitution* we are expounding."[15] *McCulloch* established the authority of the Court to engage in a more general interpretative function when determining the constitutionality of legislation.

The second major part of the opinion deals with the breadth of the powers that the federal government can exercise. Flexibility being essential, Marshall defined the broad standards within which federal laws must fall. He interpreted the grant of powers to Congress as allowing for the full effectuation of national goals. The necessary and proper clause, when combined with the specific grants of powers, evidenced the granting of broad powers to Congress. Congress' enumerated powers included the power to enact other legislation "necessary and proper for carrying into Execution the foregoing Powers, and all other Powers vested in this Constitution in the Government of the United States, or in any Department or Officer thereof."[16] Congress, in short, had a great deal of implied powers.

Marshall adopted what has become the classic test for the existence of federal power:

Let the end be legitimate, let it be within the scope of the constitution, and all means which are appropriate, which are plainly

adapted to that end, which are not prohibited, but consist with the letter and spirit of the constitution, are constitutional.[17]

Under this test federal acts are valid so long as they bear a reasonable relationship to an enumerated power of the government. Hence, Congress can create the second Bank of the United States because there is a reasonable connection between it and the enumerated Congressional powers to "lay and collect taxes; to borrow money; to regulate commerce; to declare and conduct a war; and to raise and support armies and navies."[18]

Using the same doctrine that Hamilton had used in support of the first Bank of the United States in 1791, Marshall derived implied federal powers from the principle that every legislature must have the appropriate means to carry out its powers. Because the framers intended the nation to endure, the federal government had to have the normal discretionary powers of a sovereign so that Congress could choose how to best effectuate national goals.

Marshall also relied on the structure of the Constitution. The necessary and proper clause followed the enumerated powers: the framers of the Constitution thus treated the necessary and proper clause as an additional power, another enumerated power. The placement of the clause indicated that the necessary and proper clause, rather than a limitation on the enumerated powers, was an express recognition of the need to provide additional law-making powers for the execution the other enumerated powers.

Marshall explained that the language of the necessary and power clause does not require Congress to use only means that were "absolutely" necessary to pursue an enumerated federal power. Another section of the Constitution uses the term "absolutely necessary,"[19]

13. 5 U.S. (1 Cranch) 137, 2 L.Ed. 60 (1803).

14. See Farber, The Supreme Court and the Rule of Law: Cooper v. Aaron Revisited, 1982 U.Ill.L.Rev. 387.

15. McCulloch v. Maryland, 17 U.S. (4 Wheat.) 316, 407, 4 L.Ed. 579 (1819) (emphasis added).

Because of the scope of power implied by this assertion, Justice Frankfurter thought it was the most important of the Court's statements of constitutional principle. Frank-

furter, John Marshall and the Judicial Function, 69 Harv. L.Rev. 217, 219 (1955).

16. U.S. Const., art. I, § 8, cl. 18.

17. 17 U.S. (4 Wheat.) at 421.

18. 17 U.S. (4 Wheat.) at 407.

19. U.S. Const., Art. I, § 10, cl. 2, allows a state to impose duties if they are "absolutely necessary for executing its inspection Laws. . . ."

but that phrase is not used in the necessary and proper clause. If the framers has meant to say "absolutely necessary," they would have done so, for they used that language in another clause. But it would be illogical to establish a nation with only very restricted powers.[20] Instead, the necessary and proper clause authorizes the federal government to select any reasonable means to effectuate the exercise of the enumerated powers.

The enumeration of powers in the Constitution limited the number of ends that the government could pursue and the Court advised that it would not add "great substantive and independent" powers to this list.[21] But where the government is pursuing a legitimate goal that relates to one of its enumerated powers, it has incidental, implied powers to accomplish its ends; implied powers could include very important powers of sufficient magnitude to deal with national problems.[22]

Whether a law met this test of reasonableness is a question of degree that the Court said Congress is better suited to answer. Thus, the Court would not void the law unless it were clear that it was designed for "the accomplishment of objects not intrusted to the government."[23]

In the third major portion of the opinion, Marshall held that the Maryland tax had to be stricken because it interfered with the exercise of a valid federal action. In all cases of conflict between federal and state laws, the Constitution established the supremacy of federal law.[24] States cannot possess incompatible powers that might be hostile to the federal actions.

In the final portion of the opinion, the Chief Justice said, broadly, that "the power to tax involves the power to destroy."[25] Thus, the state had no power to tax a valid federal

instrumentality, such as the National Bank, because such state taxation would subject the operations of the federal government to state control. Marshall implied a broad limitation on state taxing power, a limitation that the Court later expanded to cover state immunity from federal taxation. Eventually the Court rejected any broad doctrine of intergovernmental tax immunity.[26] However, the basic principle of *McCulloch,* dealing with doctrine of implied powers, remains valid today, as is the doctrine of federal supremacy, freeing the federal government of state regulation or taxation that would obstruct federal powers, whether enumerated or implied.

§ 3.3   Judicial Review and Federal Powers After *McCulloch*

A basic precept of the Constitution is that the federal government is one of enumerated powers and that it does not possess a general police power. In theory, at least, all federal actions must relate to a grant of power in the Constitution. In practice, the Supreme Court will accord the more democratic branches of the federal government great deference in their interpretation and implementation of those powers. The Court, under *McCulloch,* will review federal legislation only to see if it can be said to reasonably relate to an express grant of power. So long as it would be reasonable for Congress to view a problem as connected to one of the Constitution's grants of power, the law is valid, unless the Bill or Rights or other specific constitutional restrictions limit Congressional powers.

The Court was not always so lenient in reviewing the exercise of federal powers. During the period from the Civil War until 1937 the Justices guarded against the expansion of

---

20. 17 U.S. (4 Wheat.) at 413–16.

21. 17 U.S. (4 Wheat.) at 411.

22. While these were only "incidental" powers, Marshall was careful to note that they might include very important powers, and the fact that they were implied did not mean that they were "inferior." 17 U.S. (4 Wheat.) at 407–8.

23. 17 U.S. (4 Wheat.) at 423.

24. 17 U.S. (4 Wheat.) at 426.

25. 17 U.S. (4 Wheat.) at 427.

26. As Holmes, J., joined by Brandeis & Stone, JJ., dissenting, later noted: "The power to tax is not the power to destroy while this Court sits." Panhandle Oil Co. v. Mississippi ex rel. Knox, 277 U.S. 218, 223, 48 S.Ct. 451, 453, 72 L.Ed. 857 (1928). For an examination of the history of intergovernmental immunities and the limited ability of states to tax federal obligations and certain federal sources of revenue, see 2 R. Rotunda & J. Nowak, Treatise on Constitutional Law: Substance and Procedure § 13.9 (West Group, 3d ed. 1999).

federal power. This position reflected the Court's opinion that the Constitution protected individual liberty in the market place against government interference.[1] These Justices saw their function as protecting economic liberties from encroachment by legislative acts. During this period the Court also subjected state legislation to strict review under the due process and equal protection clauses of the Fourteenth Amendment.[2]

The Court subjected federal legislation to similar strict scrutiny, but the Court focused on the scope of Congressional power when reviewing federal laws, and construed the grants of power very narrowly. The majority of the pre–1937 Court believed that the Tenth Amendment put some forms of local activity beyond federal regulation. When Congress attempted to regulate business activities pursuant to its commerce power, the Court used the Tenth Amendment to demarcate the commerce power.[3]

The Court used the Tenth Amendment to define and limit the scope of many federal powers besides the commerce power. The pre–1937 Court used the Tenth Amendment to invalidate such varying pieces of legislation as arid land reclamation statutes[4] or penalties for racial discrimination in public accommodations.[5] The Court approved federal legislation only when a majority agreed that it was clearly related to a grant of power and that, in the Court's view, it impaired no legitimate state interest. Thus, the Court did uphold laws relating to the monetary system[6] or the dispen-

sation of electricity from federal dams.[7] It is interesting that during this period the Court, while reluctant to uphold federal power, did not use a narrow view of the necessary and proper clause to invalidate federal legislation. Instead, the Court advanced a broad view of the Tenth Amendment

This restrictive view of federal powers brought the Court into serious conflict with the administration of President Franklin Roosevelt. Following a series of cases in which the Court struck down New Deal legislation, F.D.R. proposed his now infamous Court Packing Plan.[8] In the meantime, at least one Justice became more lenient in how he reviewed the exercise of federal power and a new majority began to uphold federal legislation.[9] Shortly thereafter, several vacancies occurred on the Court and President Roosevelt appointed new Justices who would accord greater deference to the acts of the coordinate branches of government in the area of economic regulation.

Today the test for validity of a federal act is whether the Congress might reasonably find that the act relates to one of the federal powers.[10] If the act arguably relates to such an end, then it is valid so long as it does not violate a specific check on governmental action such as those contained in the Bill of Rights. We will see this position developed in terms of the federal commerce power in the next chapter, but the principle of *McCulloch* applies to all federal powers.[11] Thus, the Court grants deference to Congress in determining whether the reclamation of arid lands statutes relates

§ 3.3

1. See the sections on "substantive due process" from 1865–1900 and 1900–1937, §§ 11.2, 11.3, infra.

2. Id.

3. See §§ 4.4–4.7, 4.10(d), infra.

4. Kansas v. Colorado, 206 U.S. 46, 27 S.Ct. 655, 51 L.Ed. 956 (1907).

5. In re Civil Rights Cases, 109 U.S. 3, 3 S.Ct. 18, 27 L.Ed. 835 (1883), where Justice Bradley, a chief exponent of judicial control over legislation, specifically used Tenth Amendment principles to define and restrict congressional power under the subsequently enacted Fourteenth Amendment 109 U.S. at 14–15, 3 S.Ct. at 24.

6. Legal Tender Cases, 110 U.S. 421, 4 S.Ct. 122, 28 L.Ed. 204 (1884).

7. Ashwander v. Tennessee Valley Authority, 297 U.S. 288, 56 S.Ct. 466, 80 L.Ed. 688 (1936).

8. In February, 1937, President Roosevelt proposed legislation that would allow him to appoint a new Justice for each one on the Court who was over seventy years old. This would have allowed him to appoint six additional Justices to change the majority view in the Court.

9. See § 2.6, supra.

10. Weiner, J., dissenting in part, concurring in part, and dissenting in the result, citing Treatise, in United States v. Ardoin, 19 F.3d 177, 188 n. 37 (5th Cir.1994), cert. denied 513 U.S. 933, 115 S.Ct. 327, 130 L.Ed.2d 287 (1994).

11. See § 3.4, infra.

to federal powers[12] or whether civil rights statutes relate to the civil war Amendments.[13]

In assessing the federal government's power, it must be remembered that federal authority comes from several sources. For example, Article I, section 8, contains the basic, enumerated grants of congressional.[14] Article II deals with the powers and duties of the President.[15] Article III gives Congress the power to create lower federal courts, to make regulations concerning the jurisdiction of the Supreme Court, and to declare the punishment for treason.[16] The admiralty jurisdiction within Article III grants Congress powers relating to the judicial process beyond mere control of jurisdiction.[17] Article IV, section 1, gives Congress power to prescribe procedures for proving full faith and credit to the laws and court judgments of states.[18] Section 3 of Article IV grants Congress the power to admit new states to the Union,[19] and to regulate the territories and property of the United States.[20] This power is important because it allows the Federal gov-

ernment to act as a state or local government in relation to such property.[21] Several of the Amendments also specifically provide Congress with powers to enact legislation to effectuate their substantive provisions.[22]

There are also implied sources of federal authority, particularly relating to the conduct of foreign relations.[23] Because the United States cannot isolate itself from the rest of the world, the national government must be allowed to act in external affairs, and because the states have no individualized interest in external relations, the federal government has by implication an exclusive and general grant of power in this area.

The Regulation of the Armed Forces, Including State Militia. Several provisions of the Constitution vest in the federal government the power of national defense, including the power to create, maintain, and regulate armed forces for the United States. Article I gives Congress the power to provide for the

---

12. United States v. Gerlach Live Stock Co., 339 U.S. 725, 70 S.Ct. 955, 94 L.Ed. 1231 (1950).

13. Jones v. Alfred H. Mayer Co., 392 U.S. 409, 88 S.Ct. 2186, 20 L.Ed.2d 1189 (1968) (open housing statutes relate to Thirteenth Amendment); Katzenbach v. Morgan, 384 U.S. 641, 86 S.Ct. 1717, 16 L.Ed.2d 828 (1966) (voting rights statute relates to Fourteenth Amendment). The deference accorded congressional judgments in this area does not differ from the modern Court's review of other types of federal legislation.

14. See § 3.1, supra.

15. The powers of the President are discussed in Chapters 6–7.

16. For the complete text of Article III see the appendix. Section 1 grants congress power over the lower federal courts. Section 2 grants congress power to alter the jurisdiction of the Supreme Court. Section 3 defines Treason.

17. See, e.g., Panama R.R. v. Johnson, 264 U.S. 375, 44 S.Ct. 391, 68 L.Ed. 748 (1924) (Congress can create causes of action for injured seamen, and other maritime laws, based on article III grant of admiralty and maritime jurisdiction).

18. "Full Faith and Credit shall be given in each State to the public Acts, Records, and judicial Proceedings of every other State. And the Congress may by general Laws prescribe the Manner in which such Acts, Records and Proceedings shall be proved, and the Effect thereof." U.S.Const. art. IV, § 1.

19. "New States may be admitted by the Congress into this Union; but no new State shall be formed or erected within the Jurisdiction of any other State; nor any State be formed by the Junction of two or more States, or Parts

of States, without the Consent of the Legislatures of the States concerned as well as of the Congress." U.S.Const. art. IV, § 3, par. 1.

20. "The Congress shall have Power to dispose of and make all needful Rules and Regulations respecting the Territory of other Property belonging to the United States; and nothing in this Constitution shall be so construed as to Prejudice any Claims of the United States, or of any particular State." U.S.Const. art. IV, § 3, par. 2.

21. Berman v. Parker, 348 U.S. 26, 32, 75 S.Ct. 98, 102, 99 L.Ed. 27 (1954) (U.S. has "police power" as to the District of Columbia so that it may exercise powers of eminent domain not connected to another enumerated power.)

22. U.S.Const. Amend. 13, § 2 (abolition of slavery); Amend. 14, § 5 (citizenship and several forms of civil rights); Amend. 15, § 2 (prohibition of discrimination by race for voting); Amend. 16 (power to levy an income tax); Amend. 19, § 2 (prohibition of discrimination by sex for voting); Amend. 23, § 2 (representation for the District of Columbia); Amend. 24, § 2 (abolition of poll tax in federal elections); Amend. 26, § 2 (grant of franchise to citizens 18 yrs. of age or older). It should also be noted that Amendments 20 and 25 grant Congress a role in the selection, retention or replacement of the president or vice-president under certain circumstances.

23. Federal power in this area is examined more closely in Chapter 6.

See United States v. Curtiss–Wright Export Corp., 299 U.S. 304, 57 S.Ct. 216, 81 L.Ed. 255 (1936); Lofgren, United States v. Curtiss–Wright Export Corporation: An Historical Reassessment, 83 Yale L.J. 1 (1973).

defense of the United States,[24] to declare war,[25] to create and maintain land and naval military forces[26], and to regulate the armed forces,[27] and the militia (i.e., state National Guard units).[28] Article II designates the President as the Commander–in–Chief.[29] Article IV, in part, guarantees that the federal government shall protect the states against invasion and at least some types of domestic violence.[30] The necessary and proper clause allows Congress to make all regulations that it deems appropriate to carry out any of these various grants of power.[31] These federal powers provide the Congress with a set of powers that are often grouped together under the phrase, "The War Power."[32]

The supremacy of the federal government regarding foreign affairs and military regulations does not violate any constitutional right of state governments. Article I of the Constitution specifically prohibits state governments from maintaining their own armies in time of peace without the consent of Congress; states may engage in the military defense of their territory only when acting in conformity with federal statutes and the wording of Article I, section 10.[33]

The Supreme Court has repeatedly recognized the constitutional supremacy of the federal government over military affairs. For example, in the Nineteenth Century, the Supreme Court prohibited state courts from entertaining legal actions that would challenge the validity of a soldier's enlistment in the federal armed forces.[34] Early in the Twentieth Century, the Court upheld the power of the federal government to establish a system

---

24. Article I, § 8, clause 1 states: "The Congress shall have power to lay and collect Taxes, Duties, Imposts, and Excises, to pay the Debts and provide for the common Defense and general Welfare of the United States...."

25. Article I, § 8, clause 11 gives Congress the power "To declare War, grant Letters of Marque and Reprisal, and make Rules concerning Captures on Land and Water."

26. Article I, § 8, clause 12 gives Congress the power "to raise and support Armies, but no Appropriation of Money to that Use shall be for a longer Term than two Years." Clause 13 of Article I § 8 gives Congress the power: "to provide and maintain a Navy."

27. Article I, § 8, clause 14 gives Congress the power "to make Rules for the Government and Regulation of the land and naval Forces."

28. There are two militia clauses in Article I, § 8, although they are often referred to as a single "militia clause."

Article I, § 8, clause 15 gives Congress the power "To provide for calling forth the militia to execute the Laws of the Union, suppress Insurrections and repel Invasions." The three purposes listed in that clause are not the only reasons or purposes for which the federal government may call into federal service the national guard (militia) units of some or all states. See Perpich v. Department of Defense, 496 U.S. 334, 110 S.Ct. 2418, 110 L.Ed.2d 312 (1990) (the federal government is allowed to make members of the state militia members of the army of the United States; the President, pursuant to statute, may call into federal service a state national guard unit without the consent of the state's governor for purposes not listed in Article I § 8, clause 15.)

Clause 16 of Article I, § 8 gives Congress power to regulate the national guard or militia units of the states. Specifically, that clause gives Congress the power "To provide for organizing, arming, and disciplining, the Militia, and for governing such Part of them as may be employed in the Service of the United States, reserving to the States respectively, the Appointment of Officers and the Authority of training the Militia according to the discipline prescribed by Congress."

29. Article II, § 2, clause 1 states: "The President shall be Commander in Chief of the Army and Navy of the United States, and of the militia of the several States, when called into service of the United States...."

30. Article IV, § 4, clause 4, states: "The United States Shall guarantee to every state in this Union a Republican Form of Government, and shall protect each of them against Invasion; and on Application of the Legislature, or of the Executive (when the Legislature cannot be convened) against domestic violence."

The Supreme Court has not explained the nature of the guarantee given to states by this provision of the Constitution. See § 2.15 regarding "political questions."

31. Article I, § 8, clause 18 gives Congress the power "To make all Laws which shall be necessary and proper for carrying into Execution the foregoing Powers, and all other Powers vested by this Constitution in the Government of the United States, or any Department thereof."

32. See §§ 6.9–6.13 of this Treatise.

33. "No State shall, without the Consent of Congress, ... keep Troops, or Ships of War in time of Peace, enter into any Agreement or Compact with another State, or with a foreign Power or engage in War, unless actually invaded, or in such imminent Danger as will not admit of delay." U.S. Const. Article I, § 10, clause 3.

It is not clear whether a state has a right to have any independent, reserve military force (commonly called the militia or national guard). The Supreme Court has never had to reach that question, because Congress has never prohibited states from maintaining, at their own expense, a reserve military force (but not a standing army of the type prohibited by Article I).

34. Tarble's Case, 80 U.S. (13 Wall.) 397, 20 L.Ed. 597 (1871).

of involuntary conscription (a military "draft"), including conscription of members of a state national guard unit.[35]

In the mid-Twentieth Century, Congress enacted a federal statute that made everyone who enlisted in a state National Guard unit a member of the reserve National Guard of the United States; Congress also gave to the President the power to call state militia units into active federal service for training, or for other duty on behalf of the United States, without the consent of any state authority. *Perpich v. Department of Defense*[36] upheld the power of Congress and the President to federalize the state National Guard. In an opinion that contained an analysis similar to *McCulloch*'s analysis of the necessary and proper clause,[37] a unanimous Court held that the militia clauses did not limit Congress' powers to regulate state militia but, instead, gave the federal government full authority over state militia.[38]

As later Chapters indicate, there are limits placed on these powers—including the foreign affairs powers—by the separation of powers concept and the guarantees of individual liberties.[39] These limits, however, are no longer found in the language of the Tenth Amendment.

§ 3.4 Sources of Federal Power—Overview

The great bulk of the constitutional cases dealing with Congress' power to enact laws focus on only a few clauses in the Constitu-

tion, particularly the interstate commerce clause, and, more recently, section 5 of the Fourteenth Amendment. For that reason, this one volume work examines in depth only those sources of federal power.[1]

Our multi volume Treatise has expanded treatment of the topics covered here as well as other issues such as, e.g.: the admiralty power (both the ability of Congress to create substantive rules of admiralty and to create federal court jurisdiction regarding admiralty cases); the admission of states to the Union (including the "equal footing" doctrine regarding the equality of the states); the bankruptcy power; the federal power over copyrights and patents; the power to control the currency; federal "common law"; litigation between the states; the postal power; the property power (including the Article I property power, the status of the District of Columbia, and the Article IV property power); and the republican form of government clause as a source of federal power.[2]

The *McCulloch* analysis applies to the judicial examination of the scope of any congressional power. The necessary and proper clause of Article I, by its own terms, relates to every source of congressional power regardless of whether the power is listed in Article I.[3] The judiciary should be engaging in the same form of analysis, and with the same degree of deference to Congress, when it interprets the necessary and proper scope of Congressional authority to implement any federal power.

---

35. Selective Draft Law Cases, 245 U.S. 366, 38 S.Ct. 159, 62 L.Ed. 349 (1918).

36. 496 U.S. 334, 110 S.Ct. 2418, 110 L.Ed.2d 312 (1990).

37. McCulloch v. Maryland, 17 U.S. (4 Wheat.) 316, 4 L.Ed. 579 (1819). The *McCulloch* analysis is examined in § 3.2 of this Treatise.

38. Perpich v. Department of Defense, 496 U.S. 334, 348–51, 110 S.Ct. 2418, 2427–30, 110 L.Ed.2d 312 (1990).

39. The basic constitutional limitations on state and federal laws regulating aliens who seek admission into, or have been admitted into, this country are examined in §§ 14.11, 14.12 of this text. For an expanded examination of the constitutional principles governing immigration and naturalization, see, 5 R. Rotunda & J. Nowak, Treatise on Constitutional Law: Substance and Procedure, Chapter 22 (West Group, 3d ed. 1999). See also, Nowak & Rotunda, A

Comment on the Creation and Resolution of a "Nonproblem": Dames & Moore v. Regan, the Foreign Affairs Power, and the Role of the Court, 29 U.C.L.A.L.Rev. 1129 (1982).

§ 3.4

1. See Chapter 4 of this text regarding the commerce power and Chapter 15 regarding congressional enforcement of civil rights.

2. R. Rotunda & J. Nowak, Treatise on Constitutional Law: Substance and Procedure (West Group, 3d ed. 1999) (5 vols.). The listing of subjects mentioned are contained in §§ 3.4–3.11 of that treatise.

3. U.S. Const. art. I, § 8, cl. 18: "To make all laws which shall be necessary and proper for carrying into execution the foregoing powers, and all other powers vested by this Constitution in the government of the United States, or any department or officer thereof."

§ 3.5 The Separation of
Powers Principle

The modern concept of "separation of powers" has its origin in Western European struggles between legislative bodies and monarchs.[1] The English experience, in particular, formed the basis for the political beliefs most common in the American colonies. The continual shifting of power between the Monarch and Parliament led to the practical delineation of functions between the branches of English government that was the basis for John Locke's view of the proper division of powers.[2] But Montesquieu explained most convincingly the concept of separation of powers. His writings were well known throughout Eighteenth Century Western Europe and the American colonies. He persuasively argued that combining judicial, legislative or executive powers would create a system with an inherent tendency towards tyrannical actions.[3]

At the time of the American Revolution, the political leaders accepted the concept of separation of powers with virtual unanimity. Indeed, the constitutions of the early state governments sometimes referred to the principle specifically.[4] When the framers drafted the new federal Constitution, they divided the power of the federal government among three branches of government in a manner similar to Montesquieu's recommendations. But while the Constitution created separate executive, legislative, and judicial departments, it established no air tight compartmentalization of the branches. Instead, the drafters of the Constitution sought to establish a system of checks and balances to ensure the political independence of each branch and to prevent the accumulation of power in a single department.

Today we may not recognize that the system of "checks and balances" run counter to a strict separation of functions concept, but that was clearly realized at the time of the Revolution. While people sometimes refer to the three branches of the federal government as a three-layer cake, it is more accurate to think of it as a marble cake. For example, Congress enacts legislation, but the President can veto it, and Congress can override the veto. The judiciary is independent, but the President appoints the judges, who must be confirmed by the Senate.

Some opponents of the new Constitution charged that it did not sufficiently distinguish between the functions of each branch of government and thereby failed to follow the principle of separation of powers. James Madison answered this argument in *Federalist No. 47*, which explained that Montesquieu did not require a strict division of functions between the three branches of government. Madison defended the Constitution as having a sufficient division of functions between the three branches of government to avoid the consolidation of power in any one branch.[5]

The concept of separation of powers is not a legal litmus test and does not yield clear solutions to intra governmental disputes. As Professors Frankfurter and Landis warned:

> As a principle of statesmanship the practical demands of government preclude its doctrinaire application. [W]e are dealing with what Sir Henry Maine, following Madi-

§ 3.5

1. See, e.g., W. B. Gwyn, The Meaning of the Separation of Powers (Tulane Univ. 1965); M.J.C. Vile, Constitutionalism and the Separation of Powers (Clarendon Press 1967); Glennon, The Use of Custom in Resolving Separation of Powers Disputes, 64 Boston U.L.Rev. 109 (1984) (analysis that seeks to use history and governmental custom as a basis for resolving disputes between the political branches of government); Verkuil, Separation of Powers, the Rule of Law and the Idea of Independence, 30 Wm. & Mary L.Rev. 301 (1989); Shane, The Separation of Powers and the Rule of Law: The Virtues of "Seeing the Trees," 30 Wm. & Mary L.Rev. 375 (1989).

2. See, M.J.C. Vile, Constitutionalism and the Separation of Powers 64–67 (Clarendon Press 1967), discussing John Locke and his influential work, Second Treatise of

Government [An Essay Concerning the True Origin, Extent and End of Civil Government].

3. Montesquieu, The Spirit of the Laws, 151–52 (Nugent trans. 1949).

4. See, e.g., Constitution of Massachusetts—1780, Part the First, Art. XXX as reprinted in 5 W. Swindler, Sources and Documents of U.S. Constitutions 96 (Oceana Pub. 1975).

5. J. Madison, The Federalist, No. 47, The Meaning of the Maxim, Which Requires A Separation Of The Departments Of Power, Examined And Ascertained, in the Federalist Papers at 302–3 (new American Library Ed.1961). See also, B. Bailyn, The Ideological Origins of the American Revolution 55–93 (1967); A. Vanderbilt, The Doctrine of the Separation of Powers and Its Present–Day Significance 97–144 (1953).

son, calls a "political doctrine" and not a technical rule of law. Nor has it been treated by the Supreme Court as a technical legal doctrine. From the beginning that Court has refused to draw abstract, analytical lines of separation and has recognized the necessary area of interaction.[6]

This view of the separation of powers as a political doctrine, rather than a technical rule of law, is as true today as it was in 1924 when Frankfurter and Landis wrote. The Supreme Court has rejected the argument that would have it limit the activities of each branch of the federal government so that there would be no overlap or blending of functions,[7] but the Court has been cognizant of the principle when confronted with cases involving disputes between branches of the federal government.[8]

Because there is no fruitful rule or test that governs decisions relating to separation of powers, this treatise will not analyze "separation of powers cases" as a unit. Instead we have placed the cases that might arguably fall into such a category in the sections concerning

the central issue in each of those cases. Thus, the sections dealing with such issues as political questions, congressional vetoes, presidential powers, and executive privilege all refer to the separation of powers principle.[9]

§ 3.6 Term Limits

(a) Introduction

Term limits on executive branch officials are quite common on the state level. On the federal level, the U.S. Constitution, since 1951, has limited the President to two terms of office.[1] In the early 1990s, voters throughout the United States voted on proposals to extend these term limits to a broader assortment of officials. Term limit proponents were usually successful in passing referenda that limited state officials, both legislative and executive, and federal legislators (both Senate and House members).[2]

These voter initiatives responded to the concern that incumbents have advantages that make it difficult for nonincumbents to compete

---

6. Frankfurter & Landis, Power of Congress over Procedure in Criminal Contempts in "Inferior" Federal Courts—A Study in Separation of Powers, 37 Harv.L.Rev. 1010, 1012–14 (1924).

7. Nixon v. Administrator of General Services, 433 U.S. 425, 443, 97 S.Ct. 2777, 2790, 53 L.Ed.2d 867 (1977) stated:

"[United States v. Nixon] squarely rejected the argument that the Constitution contemplates a complete division of authority between the three branches.... Like the District Court, we therefore find that appellant's argument rests upon an 'archaic view of the separation of powers as requiring three outright departments of government.'"

See also, Powell v. McCormack, 395 U.S. 486, 89 S.Ct. 1944, 23 L.Ed.2d 491 (1969) (Court's decision on House refusal to seat Congressman does not violate separation of powers principle).

But see Industrial Union Dept., AFL–CIO v. American Petroleum Institute, 448 U.S. 607, 669, 100 S.Ct. 2844, 2877–78, 65 L.Ed.2d 1010 (1980) (Rehnquist, J, concurring in the judgment). Rehnquist, J., explicitly relied on John Locke to advocate a return to the pre–1937 view of the separation of powers principle that would have the Court invalidate delegations of legislative authority to executive agencies when a majority of the Justices concluded that the legislature had not sufficiently limited the power of the executive agency. While the Supreme Court, by a five to four vote, invalidated a health standard promulgated by the Occupational Safety and Health Administration limiting occupational exposure to benzene, the plurality opinion relied on the statutory basis that OSHA had failed to support its proposed standards with appropriate findings

of fact. Later, Justice Rehnquist convinced Chief Justice Burger that there should be active judicial review of congressional delegation to lawmaking power to regulatory agencies. See American Textile Mfrs. Institute, Inc. v. Donovan, 452 U.S. 490, 543, 101 S.Ct. 2478, 2507–08, 69 L.Ed.2d 185 (1981) (Rehnquist, J., dissenting, joined by Burger, C.J.).

See generally, Wood, J., citing Treatise in United States v. Neyens, 831 F.2d 156, 161 (7th Cir.1987); Johnson, J., citing Treatise in, Dillard v. Crenshaw County, 831 F.2d 246, 252 n. 15 (11th Cir.1987), on remand 679 F.Supp. 1546 (M.D.Ala.1988).

8. Professor Jesse Choper argued that the Supreme Court should rule separation of powers issues to be nonjusticiable. This proposal is a part of a scholarly examination of the role of the Supreme Court. J. Choper, Judicial Review and the National Political Process (1980). See also, Nowak, Book Review, 68 California L.Rev. 1223 (1980) (reviewing Choper).

9. To find the Court's treatment of the principle in a specific case, one need only identify the issue or case name in the index or case table found at the end of this treatise. Those interested in an examination of the various areas in which the principle is particularly relevant should consult the topic index under "separation of powers."

§ 3.6

1. U.S. Const. amend. 22.

2. E.g., Madigan, Washington State Term–Limit Fight in High Gear, Chicago Tribune, Nov. 3, 1991, at § 1, pp. 1, 4, col. 3–5.

for public office. Incumbents can prolong their cling to office through patronage, pork barrel projects, gerrymandering, name recognition, and voter inertia. Campaign finance reform, by limiting the expenditures of opponents to no more than the expenditures of the incumbents, also favors the sitting legislators. Incumbents also seek to use the legal system to make it more difficult for challengers to appear on the ballot, although the Supreme Court has invalidated the more obvious of this type of anti-incumbent legislation.[3] Thus, in general, turnover in the House of Representatives is usually less than turnover in the British House of Lords (where one serves until death) or the former Soviet Politburo. Of the 405 House incumbents who ran in 1990, 20% had no major party opponents, and 60% had opponents who raised less than half the amount of money that incumbents had raised. Common Cause, the citizens lobby group, found that only 23 of the House races in 1990 were truly competitive.[4] The 2000 census led to a new reapportionment, but that did not make the races more competitive.

(b) State Office Holders

Opponents of state term limit laws have claimed that such, as applied to *state* officials,

violate federal constitutional rights. The case law has rejected that argument For example, the West Virginia Supreme Court, in the course of upholding that state's law prohibiting its governor from seeking a third term, said that it found no U.S. Supreme Court case "even arguably on point holding a limitation on incumbent succession contrary to the Fourteenth Amendment...."[5]

In that case, the West Virginia Court applied its state constitutional term limit to the governor who already had been elected when the constitutional amendment was enacted, and had no problem with what the governor called a "retroactive" application of the new rule.[6] The U.S. Supreme Court dismissed the appeal in this case "for want of a substantial federal question."[7]

(c) Federal Legislators

A different question is whether the states can apply term limits to *federal* legislators, that is, the U.S. Representatives and Senators elected from the state in question.[8] Some people have suggested that no state can add to the qualifications already mentioned in the U.S. Constitution for the office in question.[9] Article

---

3. E.g., Bullock v. Carter, 405 U.S. 134, 92 S.Ct. 849, 31 L.Ed.2d 92 (1972), invalidating exorbitant filing fees.

4. Rotunda, No Impediment to Term Limits, The Washington Post, Feb. 13, 1993, at A31, col. 1. See also Rotunda, A Commentary on the Constitutionality of Term Limits, in The Politics and Law of Term Limits (Edward H. Crane & Roger Pilon, eds., Cato Institute, 1994).

5. State ex rel. Maloney v. McCartney, 159 W.Va. 513, 223 S.E.2d 607, 611, 612 (1976), appeal dismissed for want of a substantial federal question, sub nom. 425 U.S. 946, 96 S.Ct. 1689, 48 L.Ed.2d 190 (1976): "The universal authority is that restriction upon the succession of incumbents serves a rational public policy and that, while restrictions may deny qualified men an opportunity to serve, as a general rule the over-all health of the body politic is enhanced by limitations on continuous tenure."

See also, Legislature of California v. Eu, 54 Cal.3d 492, 286 Cal.Rptr. 283, 816 P.2d 1309 (1991), cert. denied 503 U.S. 919, 112 S.Ct. 1292, 117 L.Ed.2d 516 (1992). This constitutional amendment limited its governor, other elected state officials and state senators to two terms of four years; state assembly members were limited to three terms of two years. Once the prescribed maximum terms have expired, office holders are forever barred from running for the office. The state court did sever and invalidate (under the Impairment of Contracts Clause, U.S. Const. art. I, § 10, cl. 1) a provision that would have restricted vested pension rights of incumbent legislators.

6. 223 S.E.2d at 613–14.

7. Moore v. McCartney, 425 U.S. 946, 96 S.Ct. 1689, 48 L.Ed.2d 190 (1976). The Supreme Court even denied a stay of the judgment of the state court. Moore v. McCartney, 425 U.S. 927, 96 S.Ct. 1656, 48 L.Ed.2d 170 (1976).

8. Term Limits on the President. Sometimes commentators have wondered if a state could place term limits on the President, a question that may be moot after the enactment of the Twenty-second Amendment, limiting the President to two terms and after U.S. Term Limits, Inc. v. Thornton, 514 U.S. 779, 115 S.Ct. 1842, 131 L.Ed.2d 881 (1995), discussed below, forbidding state from imposing terms limits on federal legislators. Moreover, one should realize that the people do not directly elect the President; they vote for electors, who in turn elect the President.

So, the question becomes whether the state could place terms limits on presidential *electors*. Even if states could do that, it would not prevent an elector from voting for a particular presidential candidate. In other words, if a state could impose terms limits on presidential electors, that does not mean that it could impose term limits on the President.

9. If Article I, § 2, cl. 2 is read to say that age, U.S. citizenship, and state residency (but not, for example, residency within a district that the Congressman represents) can be the *only* qualifications for office, then that

I, section 2, clause 2 provides that a U.S. Representative must be at least 25 years old, a citizen of the United States at least seven years, and an inhabitant of the State from where he was chosen.

Some opponents of term limits have based their argument on the language of *Powell v. McCormack*,[10] where the Supreme Court ruled that it was unconstitutional for the House of Representatives to refuse to seat Adam Clayton Powell even though he had met the constitutional requirements of age (over 25), citizenship (U.S.), and residency (New York). *Powell* dealt with the limitations on what one House of Congress can do in the context of an *ad hoc* disciplinary proceeding. As Justice Douglas' separate opinion explained, the Court would not have interfered if the House of Representatives had expelled Powell under a different clause of the Constitution.[11] *Powell* only implies that the House of Representatives cannot use its limited power of exclusion to enforce term limit rules. Term limit legislation would

have to provide, explicitly or implicitly, for other methods of enforcement, such as limitations of ballot access.

When the nation was young, some states insisted that their representatives would be elected at large and not by district. To prohibit that practice, in 1842 Congress enacted a statute *requiring* states to impose a district qualification.[12] But this statute does not require that the candidates *reside* in the particular district.[13] Of course, it is possible for Representatives to be elected by district although they are not residents of the district, but that has not been the custom. However, one state court has declared a district residency requirement unconstitutional, on the grounds that it adds to the constitutional requirements.[14]

Respected commentators, like Justice Story, interpreted the Article I qualifications clause as not allowing states to require that the representative be an inhabitant "within any par-

---

section is inconsistent with other clauses of the Constitution that impose further qualifications for office. For example, when the Senate impeaches someone, it can impose a disqualification for U.S. Representative or Senator, as well as any other office of trust under the United States. Art. I, § 3, cl. 7. A cabinet member is similarly disqualified from becoming a member of Congress, even though he or she meets the minimum requirements of age, U.S. citizenship, and state residency. Art. I, § 6, cl. 2. Anyone who has taken oath to support the U.S. Constitution and then engaged in rebellion against the United States is similarly disqualified from office. Amendment 14, § 3. By a two-thirds vote in each House, Congress may remove this "rebellion disqualification."

10. 395 U.S. 486, 89 S.Ct. 1944, 23 L.Ed.2d 491 (1969).

11. 395 U.S. at 546 & n. 8, 89 S.Ct. at 1988 & n. 8 (Opinion of Douglas, J.).

12. Act of June 25, 1842, 5 Stat. at Large 491, § 2 (1842). For the legislative history, see Cong.Globe, 27th Cong., 2d Sess., App. 343, 493, 513 (1842).

The present law, which is substantially similar, may be found in 2 U.S.C.A. § 2c.

A state entitled to representation in the House by more than one Representative cannot have those Representatives chosen at large. States had tried to have at large elections in order to have a block of legislators who could then increase that state's influence in the House. That statute, however, did not require that Representatives reside in any particular district within the state, but only that the states elect Representatives by single-member districts. The legislative history indicates that Congress was not imposing a district residency requirement. See, e.g., Cong. Globe, 27th Cong., 2d Sess., 447–453, 471 (1842). See also id. at 318–19, 338, 380 (appendix).

See also Stephen J. Safranek, Term Limitations: Do the Winds of Change Blow Constitutional?, 26 Creighton L.Rev. 321 (1993); Stephen J. Safranek, The Constitutional Case for Term Limits: The Courts, the Congress and the Meaning of Federalism (U.S. Term Limits Foundation, 1993); Edward H. Crane & Roger Pilon, eds., The Politics and Law of Term Limits (Cato Institute, 1994); Daniel Hays Lowenstein, Are Congressional Term Limits Constitutional?, 18 Harv. J. of L. & Pub. Policy 1 (1994); Ronald D. Rotunda, The Constitution Lets States Impose Term Limits, Wall Street Journal, Nov. 30, 1994, at A21; Mark R. Killenbeck & Steve Sheppard, Another Such Victory?—Term Limits, Section 2 of the Fourteenth Amendment, and the Right to Representation, 45 Hastings L. J. 1121 (1994); Rotunda, Rethinking Term Limits for Federal Legislators in Light of the Structure of the Constitution, 73 Oregon Law Review 561 (1994).

13. Congress has not imposed a district *residency* qualification, it still has imposed a *district* qualification. In that sense, the congressional requirement that Congressmen be elected by district (even if they are not residents of that district) is in addition to the minimum qualifications of age, U.S. citizenship, and state residency, found in the qualifications clause of Article I, § 2, clause 2.

14. Hellmann v. Collier, 217 Md. 93, 141 A.2d 908 (1958) (per curiam). But see Williams v. Tucker, 382 F.Supp. 381, 388 (M.D.Pa.1974) (per curiam) (rejecting Art. I, "Qualifications" argument).

The *Hellmann* court noted that another jurisdiction, Maine, specifically required that its U.S. Representatives be residents of the district that they represented, but that requirement was not judicially challenged.

ticular district of the state, in which the member is chosen."[15] On the other hand, Justice Story admitted that other contemporary commentators did not share his view. Thus, President Jefferson concluded that the Constitution did not forbid the states from imposing additional qualifications to the office of senator or representative.[16] Jefferson argued that if it is the rule of interpretation that, when the Constitution "assumes a single power out of many," we "should consider it as assuming the whole," then the Constitution "would vest the general government with a mass of powers never contemplated."[17]

The federal requirement that states elect U.S. representatives by district may be seen as an additional qualification for office, although no court has so held. For example, assume that a state is divided into ten districts, each composed of two million residents and one million voters. Assume that in district number one, Candidate *A* (of Party No. 1) gets 499,000 votes, and loses to Candidate *B* (of Party No. 2) who gets 501,000 votes. Let us assume further that no candidate (winner or loser) in any of the other nine districts gets more than 499,000 votes. Perhaps, in the other districts, there were third party candidates or low voter turnout. Even though Candidate *A* received more votes than any other candidate in the state (except for Candidate *B*)—even though Candidate *A* was the second highest vote-getter in a field of at least 20 candidates, 10 of whom will become U.S. Representatives—Candidate *A* still is not elected as a U.S. Representative, because he or she did not meet the *additional qualification* of obtaining the votes

in the *right district*. That qualification is not found in Article I, § 2, clause 2. It is found in the federal statute requiring that Representatives be elected by district.

(d) The *Thornton* Decision and the Unconstitutionality of Term Limits Imposed on Federal Legislators

The Supreme Court considered the arguments discussed above and narrowly rejected the constitutionality of term limits on federal legislators in *U.S. Term Limits, Inc. v. Thornton*.[18] The Court held (5 to 4) that it is unconstitutional for states to impose term limits on federal legislators. Justice Stevens spoke for the majority (which included Kennedy, Souter, Ginsburg, and Breyer) and Justice Thomas spoke for the dissent (which included Rehnquist, O'Connor, and Scalia).

Justice Stevens acknowledged that *Powell* does not resolve the specific questions presented in this case,[19] because that case only held that the constitutional qualifications for congressional service are "fixed" in the sense that Congress may not add to them. But Congress did not add to qualifications in this case; rather, the state of Arkansas did. Stevens then examined the history behind the qualifications clauses and broadly held that there can be no additional qualifications added to those already provided for in Article I, dealing with age, citizenship, and residency. The framers intended, said Stevens, for the Constitution to be the exclusive source of qualifications of Members of Congress, and intended to divest the states of any power to impose additional qualifications.[20]

15. E.g., Joseph Story, Commentaries on the Constitution of the United States § 322 (R. Rotunda & J. Nowak, ed. 1987) (rejecting a requirement of district residency); Chancellor James Kent, 1 Commentaries on American Law 215–16 (1826).

16. See 2 Joseph Story, Commentaries on the Constitution, § 624 at 100 (1st ed. 1833), referring to and discussing Jefferson's arguments, and quoting 4 Correspondence of Thomas Jefferson 238–39.

17. 2 Joseph Story, Commentaries on the Constitution, § 624 at 100 (1st ed. 1833), quoting 4 Correspondence of Thomas Jefferson 239.

18. 514 U.S. 779, 115 S.Ct. 1842, 131 L.Ed.2d 881 (1995). After this decision, Ray Thornton, the Congressman who opposed term limits, announced that he would retire the following year, after he will have served a six-

year term in the House, beginning in 1990. "The people of Arkansas," he said, "have said that term limits are desired, and I will honor that." (Thornton also served a six-year term in the 1970s.)

Kathleen M. Sullivan, Dueling Sovereignties: U.S. Term Limits, Inc. v. Thornton, 109 Harv.L.Rev. 78 (1995); Ronald D. Rotunda & Steven Safranek, An Essay on Term Limits and a Call for a Constitutional Convention, 80 Marquette University Law Review 227 (1996).

19. 514 U.S. at 797, 115 S.Ct. at 1852.

20. 514 U.S. at 827, 115 S.Ct. at 1866.

Tenth Amendment. Justice Thomas' dissent concluded that the relevant history supports the power of the states to impose term limits on federal legislators. Thomas found that neither the qualifications clauses nor any other

However, the state constitutional provision at issue in *Thornton* did not prohibit candidates from serving more than a set number of terms. Rather, the state constitutional amendment imposed a ballot access requirement, not a permanent disqualification from office. It provided that the name of an otherwise-eligible candidate for Congress cannot appear on the general election ballot if that candidate has already served three terms in the House of Representatives or two terms in the Senate. However that candidate was still eligible for office.

During oral argument, counsel for the respondents agreed with Justice Scalia that the Arkansas law is not a "qualification." When asked by Justice Stevens whether the respondents conceded that the ballot access is not a qualification, he answered, "Yes," to which Stevens responded: "That's a major concession."[21] Consequently, Stevens, at the end of his opinion, did not simply invalidate the Arkansas law. First, he had to show that it was really a term limit law. Stevens said that the law was unconstitutional because it was "intended" to be a qualification.[22] "[W]e hold that

a state amendment is unconstitutional when it has the likely effect of handicapping a class of candidates and has the *sole purpose* of creating additional qualifications indirectly."[23]

Stevens also distinguished *Storer v. Brown.*[24] In *Storer,* the state precluded from the ballot anyone running for the House as an independent if that person had voted in a preceding party primary or had been registered with a political party within one year prior to the primary. The *Storer* Court rejected, as "wholly without merit" the argument that the California ballot access restriction violated the qualifications clauses.[25] Stevens said that *Storer* was inapplicable because, unlike that case, the Arkansas constitutional amendment is intended to be a qualification for office.

The Arkansas restriction on ballot access, unlike the ballot access restriction in *Storer v. Brown,* is a lifetime restriction. Souter, in oral argument, distinguished *Storer* on that basis.[26] Justice Thomas, in his dissent, replied that other ballot access laws (and even the Arkansas law) may not be intended to be lifetime restrictions.[27]

clause in the Constitution prohibits term limits: "The Constitution is simply silent on this question. And where the Constitution is silent, it raises no bar to action by the States or the people." 514 U.S. at 845, 115 S.Ct. at 1875 (Thomas, J., dissenting). Thus, the Tenth Amendment authorizes the states to impose term limits, because "the States can exercise all powers that the Constitution does not withhold from them." 514 U.S. at 848, 115 S.Ct. at 1876 (Thomas, J., dissenting). Thomas *did not* argue that the federal government can exercise only those powers expressly granted to it. On the contrary, he explicitly stated that the central government's powers can either be express or implied. 514 U.S. at 853, 115 S.Ct. at 1879 & n. 4 (Thomas, J., dissenting). See Ronald D. Rotunda, Cases Refine Definition of Federal Powers, 17 National Law Journal C9, C12 (July 31, 1995).

Stevens, J. responded that the power to impose additional qualifications on federal legislators was not one of "the powers retained by the pre-existing sovereign states," because the Tenth Amendment "could only 'reserve' that which existed before." 514 U.S. at 801, 115 S.Ct. at 1854. States could not impose restrictions on federal legislators before there was a federal legislature; hence, that power is not a reserved power. 514 U.S. at 803, 115 S.Ct. at 1855 ("With respect to setting qualifications for service in Congress, no such right existed before the Constitution was ratified.").

One should not read too much into Stevens' Tenth Amendment argument. The power to prosecute federal officials for trespass, or murder, or bribery, did not exist before the Constitution was ratified, because federal offi-

cials did not exist then. Yet, an F.B.I. agent or other executive branch official must still obey a constitutional state law. Even if Justice Stevens had agreed with Justice Thomas on the meaning and relevance of the Tenth Amendment, Stevens still would have concluded that state-imposed term limits are unconstitutional because he also concluded that the qualifications clause should be interpreted to preclude the states from imposing term limits.

21. 63 U.S. Law Week at 3453 (U.S. 12/13/94) (transcript of oral argument).

22. "In our view, Amendment 73 [the Arkansas ballot access provision] is an indirect attempt to accomplish what the Constitution prohibits Arkansas from accomplishing directly." 514 U.S. at 829, 115 S.Ct. at 1867.

23. 514 U.S. at 836, 115 S.Ct. at 1871 (emphasis added).

24. 415 U.S. 724, 94 S.Ct. 1274, 39 L.Ed.2d 714 (1974), rehearing denied 417 U.S. 926, 94 S.Ct. 2635, 41 L.Ed.2d 230 (1974).

25. 415 U.S. at 746 n. 16, 94 S.Ct. at 1287 n. 16.

26. See 63 U.S. Law Week at 3452 (U.S. 12/13/94) (transcript of oral argument).

27. 514 U.S. at 920, 115 S.Ct. at 1911: "I am not sure why the intent behind a law should affect our analysis under the Qualifications Clauses." But, if the intent behind the Arkansas law is key, then, in "reaching this conclusion at the summary judgment stage, however, the

After *Thornton*, supporters of term limits unsuccessfully lobbied for a constitutional amendment while also seeking to secure pledges by candidates that they will vote for and/or abide by term limits.[28] The Supreme Court dealt with one manifestation of this reaction in *Cook v. Gralike*.[29] In that case, Missouri voters adopted an amendment to their State Constitution designed to bring about a "Congressional Term Limits Amendment" to the U.S. Constitution. Among other things, Article VIII "instruct[s]" Missouri's Members of Congress to use all their powers to pass the federal amendment; prescribes that "DISREGARDED VOTERS' INSTRUCTION ON TERM LIMITS" be printed on ballots by the names of Members failing to take certain legislative acts in support of the proposed amendment; provides that "DECLINED TO PLEDGE TO SUPPORT TERM LIMITS" be printed by the names of nonincumbent candidates refusing to take a "Term Limit" pledge to perform those acts if elected; and directs the Missouri Secretary of State to determine and declare whether either statement should be printed by candidates' names. A nonincumbent House candidate sued to enjoin petitioner from implementing Article VIII on the ground it violated the Federal Constitution.

Stevens, J., for the Court,[30] held that the state constitutional amendment was unconstitutional because it was not a permissible exercise of the state's power to procedurally regulate the time, place, and manner of holding state elections for federal offices. The Court, argued, first, that Article VIII was not an exercise of any rights reserved by the Tenth Amendment because the federal offices at stake arose directly from the Constitution itself. "The federal Elections Clause[31] delegates to the States the power to regulate the Times, Places and Manner of holding Elections for Senators and Representatives."[32] No other constitutional provision gives the States authority over congressional elections, and the Tenth Amendment reserves no such authority.[33]

Missouri's Article VIII does not, said the Court, regulate the manner of elections: The "manner" of elections includes matters like "notices, registration, supervision of voting, protection of voters, prevention of fraud and corrupt practices, counting of votes, duties of inspectors and canvassers, and making and publication of election returns."[34] Instead, Ar-

---

majority has given short shrift to petitioners' contrary claim." Petitioners, if they were given an opportunity to present their evidence, would seek to show that the true intent behind the Arkansas law is to "level the playing field" for challengers and to compensate for the "congressional conferred advantages" that have "artificially inflated the pre-existing electoral chances of the covered candidates...." 514 U.S. at 921, 115 S.Ct. at 1911.

Intent of Laws that Encourage Term Limits. The "intent" argument raises interesting possibilities. If another state enacted a ballot access restriction like the kind imposed by Arkansas, could a lower court uphold the restriction if the court finds that its intent (unlike Arkansas's intent) is not to impose absolute term limits but only to level the playing field? What if the other state enacted a ballot access restriction that (unlike the Arkansas law) was not permanent. For example, the law would provide that a candidate for Senator could be on the ballot no more than two times out of every three. Someone who is not on the ballot could still run as a write-in candidate. This restriction on ballot access, like the ballot access restriction in *Storer v. Brown,* is not a lifetime restriction.

Alternatively, may a state provide (in an effort to level the playing field) that, if an incumbent Representative runs more than a given number of times in a row, then that candidate can remain on the ballot, *but* the Representative's political party must also nominate another candidate to run for the same office? For example, if Represen-

tative Jane Doe, a Republican, would seek yet another term, her name could appear on the ballot as the nominee of the Republican Party, but only if the Republican Party nominates another person who will also carry the Republican Party label.

28. See, e.g., Ronald D. Rotunda, The Aftermath of *Thornton,* 13 Constitutional Commentary (1996).

29. 531 U.S. 510, 121 S.Ct. 1029, 149 L.Ed.2d 44 (2001).

30. Stevens, J., wrote the opinion of the Court, joined by Scalia, Kennedy, Ginsburg, & Breyer, JJ., and in part by Souter & Thomas, JJ. Kennedy, J., filed a concurring opinion, Thomas, J., filed an opinion concurring in part and in the judgment, and Rehnquist, C.J., joined by O'Connor, J., filed an opinion concurring in the judgment.

31. U.S. Const. Art. 1, § 4, cl. 1: "The Times, Places and Manner of holding Elections for Senators and Representatives, shall be prescribed in each State by the Legislature thereof; but the Congress may at any time by Law make or alter such Regulations, except as to the Places of chusing Senators."

32. Art. I, § 4, cl. 1.

33. 531 U.S. 510, 511, 121 S.Ct. 1029, 1032, 149 L.Ed.2d 44.

34. 531 U.S. 510, 523–24, 121 S.Ct. 1029, 1038, 149 L.Ed.2d 44.

ticle VIII is "plainly designed to favor candidates who are willing to support the particular form of a term limits amendment set forth in its text and to disfavor those who either oppose term limits entirely or would prefer a different proposal." The labels "surely place their targets at a political disadvantage to unmarked candidates for congressional office."[35] The Court was concerned that rather than regulating the procedural mechanisms of elections, Article VIII attempted to "dictate electoral outcomes," a result it concluded was inconsistent with *Thornton.*[36]

The Court did not indicate if Missouri could require that a similar term limits notice be placed on ballots for *state* legislators, in an effort to encourage state legislators to propose a federal constitutional amendment imposing term limits. Because the Court based its conclusion that the state's rules did not govern the procedural mechanisms of *federal* elections, state rules governing election for *state* office should fare better, for the federal Elections Clause does not govern elections for state office.

35. 531 U.S. 510, 525–26, 121 S.Ct. 1029, 1039–40, 149 L.Ed.2d 44.

36. 531 U.S. 510, 526, 121 S.Ct. 1029, 1039, 149 L.Ed.2d 44.

Chapter 4

THE FEDERAL COMMERCE POWER

§ 4.1 Introduction: The Commerce Clause—Its Origins and Development

Article I, Section 8 of the Constitution provides in part that Congress shall have the power "To regulate Commerce with foreign Nations, and among the several States, and with the Indian Tribes."The brevity of this clause belies the fact that its interpretation has played a significant role in shaping the concepts of federalism and the permissible uses of national power throughout our history. The Constitution, at least in form, grant the federal government neither a general police power nor the inherent right to act on any subject matter in order to promote the health, safety or welfare of the people throughout the nation. But the framers did grant Congress a power to regulate commerce "among the several states."

This power over commerce might, depending on the definition of that seemingly non-technical word, include the power to promote the economic welfare of the citizens throughout the country. The grant of power also may be viewed as committing this subject matter to Congress and removing state power to deal with local matters that may be considered a part of the "commerce" described by this clause. Absent some further restriction upon the power, some people might use it to be the functional equivalent of a generalized "police power" because much of the activity that takes place within the country, and even within a single state, might be said to relate to

economic issues and problems. A broad reading of the clause would not only grant a sweeping power to the federal government but it would also restrict the ability of individual states to adopt laws that burden the types of commerce that were committed to the control of the federal government.

The history of the commerce clause adjudication is, in a very real sense, the history of federalism as well as the development of various doctrines supporting a broad federal power. It therefore becomes quite important to look at the treatment that the Supreme Court has given this clause throughout each stage in its history, even though we will also summarize the Court's current position in a single section.

This chapter first places in historical perspective the Court's interpretations of the commerce power. The early cases defining the commerce power demonstrate both the justices' historical and theoretical uncertainty in defining the scope of powers for the new national government. Next, we will examine the Court's attempt (from roughly the beginning of the Twentieth Century to 1937) to restrict the commerce power, primarily of a desire to protect the role of the states in the federal system than to hold the federal government to an original limited grant of power.

The concluding sections of this chapter, examine how the Supreme Court in the past half-century has developed what we will term modern commerce clause standards.[1] In those sections we will find that the Supreme Court

§ 4.1

1. See § 4.8, 4.9 for the development of modern commerce power standards.

has made a distinction between the scope of Congress's power to control private sector activities and the scope of Congress's power to regulate state and local governments.

The Supreme Court will give great deference to most, but not all, of the decisions of Congress regarding the regulation of private sector activities. The Court in the modern era will not invalidate a congressional regulation of persons, activities, or transactions that cross state lines so long as the congressional enactment does not violate a specific limitation on federal power, such as the Bill of Rights. Additionally, the Supreme Court will give great deference to a congressional determination that a single state activity has a substantial effect on commerce, and comes within the federal commerce power, if that activity is "commercial." However, the Supreme Court, in the 1990's, determined that congressional regulations of single state activities that are not commercial in character will only be upheld, as proper exercises of the federal commerce power, if there is a factual basis for finding that the single state activity has a substantial effect on interstate commerce.[2]

Federal regulations of state or local governments fall into two categories. First, Congress may try to directly order state or local governments to take legislative or executive actions. In the 1990's, a majority of the Justices ruled that these types of federal orders to state and local governments violated federalism principles. Second, Congress may make state and local governments subject to the terms of commerce power legislation that also regulates the activity of private sector persons or private sector corporations. As we will see in the last section of this chapter, the Supreme Court in the past quarter century has had great difficulty in determining what, if any, immunity state and local governments should be given from

federal laws that apply to both private sector and public sector activities.[3]

Before going on to an examination of the development of specific commerce clause tests and the modern rules, let us briefly discuss two related points.

First, the Court, historically, has not had any significant difficulties in upholding a plenary federal power over all forms of commercial regulations of foreign commerce and dealings with American Indians. That is because, as discussed below, those powers do not really interfere with state powers, and the Court (in the decades before 1937) was concerned with protecting states' rights over commerce, not with Indian rights or foreign rights. For the Court in the period prior to 1937, the issues under the commerce clause have centered on the ability of Congress to regulate commerce among the states.

Second, in order to put the Commerce Clause cases in perspective, we shall next examine some of the pre-constitutional commercial problems that gave rise to the grant of a national commerce power to Congress. This history, while not definitive, will indicate the range of options that the Court had before it early in its history and why it chose those options.

The remainder of this chapter will examine, chronologically, interstate commerce issues and principles that moved the Justices to define, contract, and extend the commerce power in particular ways during each major historical era.

§ 4.2 The Power to Regulate Commerce With Foreign Nations and Indian Tribes

Today the congressional power to regulate commerce among the states stands on an equal footing with its powers to regulate commerce relating to foreign nations or Indian tribes.[1]

---

2. The distinction between Congress's power to regulate "commercial" single state activities and Congress's power to regulate single state activities that are not "commercial" in character was established in United States v. Lopez, 514 U.S. 549, 115 S.Ct. 1624, 131 L.Ed.2d, 626 (1995).

3. See § 4.10(d).

§ 4.2

1. The License Cases, 46 U.S. (5 How.) 504, 578, 12 L.Ed. 256 (1847). But cf. Leisy v. Hardin, 135 U.S. 100, 10 S.Ct. 681, 34 L.Ed. 128 (1890); Pittsburgh & Southern Coal Co. v. Bates, 156 U.S. 577, 587, 15 S.Ct. 415, 419, 39 L.Ed. 538, 543–44 (1895).

But this state of affairs exists only because the Court has finally committed itself to deferring to congressional power to regulate interstate commerce in the same way that it has always recognized plenary powers to regulate the other two subjects. Even during periods when the Justices were debating whether to significantly restrict the congressional power to regulate intrastate activities under the commerce power, there was no serious advocacy of restrictions on the federal powers in these other areas.[2] The reason is quite simple: throughout the years, the Justices have never recognized any important or legitimate state interest in foreign affairs or dealings with American Indians. Thus, when the Court was seeking to reserve powers for the states under the Tenth Amendment, it had no cause to use that concept to restrict the federal powers in these areas.[3]

Commerce With Foreign Nations. The Court has always recognized a plenary power in Congress to deal with matters touching upon foreign relations or foreign trade. Indeed, as we note in Chapter 6, the federal powers in this area may constitute an exception to the normal requirement that the federal government justify its acts in terms of specific enumerated powers.

The history of the commerce clause and the shaping of the Constitution itself also endorse the finding of a broad Federal power in this area. As noted in the next section, one of the prime areas of commercial problems meant to be solved by the Constitution was the imposition of restrictions on imports and exports by the states. The Constitution specifically prohibits state government from imposing such duties without the consent of the national government.[4] The Article I section 10 listing of activities that are prohibited to the states primarily focuses upon matters touching upon their foreign trade or relations with foreign countries.[5] Thus it can be safely asserted that there was no constitutional recognition of any "reserved powers" of the states to act in these areas.

The Constitution as originally framed seems also to recognize a virtually unlimited power of Congress over commerce with foreign nations. The primary concern over congressional power in the international area came from the Southern states who feared that a broad power might be used to restrict the importation of slaves following the ratification of the Constitution. This possible use of the power was

2. Although the Constitution grants Congress the power to regulate foreign commerce and commerce among the states in parallel language, "there is evidence that the Founders intended the scope of the foreign commerce power to be the greater." Japan Line, Ltd. v. County of Los Angeles, 441 U.S. 434, 447, 99 S.Ct. 1813, 1821, 60 L.Ed.2d 336 (1979) (footnote omitted). See, e.g., Brolan v. United States, 236 U.S. 216, 222, 35 S.Ct. 285, 287, 59 L.Ed. 544 (1915).

An excellent example of the lack of debate is the Lottery Case (Champion v. Ames), 188 U.S. 321, 23 S.Ct. 321, 47 L.Ed. 492 (1903) in which the Court upheld the Congressional Act prohibiting the transport of lottery tickets into states that prohibited lotteries, over the dissents of four Justices. Yet these Justices indicated that they would not place restrictions on the power of Congress over international trade. 188 U.S. at 373–74, 23 S.Ct. at 333–34 (Fuller, C. J., dissenting, joined by Brewer, Shiras, and Peckham, JJ.). See also, United States v. Marigold, 50 U.S. (9 How.) 560, 13 L.Ed. 257 (1850).

3. See, e.g., Board of Trustees v. United States, 289 U.S. 48, 53 S.Ct. 509, 77 L.Ed. 1025 (1933) (protective tariffs); Weber v. Freed, 239 U.S. 325, 36 S.Ct. 131, 60 L.Ed. 308 (1915) (prohibition of importation of prize fight films); The Abby Dodge v. United States, 223 U.S. 166, 32 S.Ct. 310, 56 L.Ed. 390 (1912) (prohibition of sponges from Gulf of Mexico or waters off Florida construed as not

applicable within the States); Buttfield v. Stranahan, 192 U.S. 470, 24 S.Ct. 349, 48 L.Ed. 525 (1904) (prohibition of importation of certain types of tea).

4. U.S.Const. art. I, § 10, cl. 2.

5. "No State shall enter into any Treaty, Alliance, or Confederation; grant Letters of Marque and Reprisal; coin Money; emit Bills of Credit; make any Thing but gold and silver Coin a Tender in Payment of Debts; pass any Bill of Attainder, ex post facto Law, or Law impairing the Obligation of Contracts, or grant any Title of Nobility.

"No State shall, without the Consent of Congress lay any Imports or Duties on Imports or Exports, except what may be absolutely necessary for executing it's inspection Laws: and the net Produce of all Duties and Imposts, laid by any State on Imports or Exports, shall be for the Use of the Treasury of the United States; and all such Laws shall be subject to the Revision and Controul of the Congress.

"No State shall, without the Consent of Congress, lay any Duty of Tonnage, keep Troops, or Ships of War in time of Peace, enter into any Agreement of Compact with another State, or with a foreign Power, or engage in War, unless actually invaded, or in such imminent Danger as will not admit of delay."

U.S.Const. art. I, § 10.

eliminated by expressly prohibiting Congress from banning the importation of slaves until 1808.[6]

There were similar fears that so broad a power in Congress might result in certain states being favored in matters of foreign trade. Thus Section 9 of Article I insures that Congress will not tax exports or give preference to certain ports in matters of foreign trade.[7] It would seem clear from the document itself that the power to deal with foreign commerce was very precisely defined and is a plenary one within only the specific restrictions set by that document.

Commerce With American Indian Tribes. The Court has broadly upheld congressional power to regulate commerce with American Indian tribes on a unique rationale. The Court has continually recognized Indian tribes as constituting separate, though dependent, "sovereigns" within the nation. Part of the reason for the original designation of the Indians as such was the Court's desire to remove the states' ability to control or exploit the Indian tribes.[8] Thus the Court found that they were subject only to federal regulation because of their quasi-sovereign status.

The quasi-sovereign status of federally recognized Indian tribes meant that the national government had an inherent right to regulate Indian affairs.[9] The commerce clause provision regarding Indian tribes provided a textual basis for recognition of this power, but the Supreme Court almost certainly would have declared Indian affairs to be a subject for national, rather than local, regulation even if there were no reference to Indian tribes in the commerce clause.[10]

Indians and Equal Protection Analysis. There is an important distinction between governmental acts that classify persons for special treatment because of their Indian ancestry and the regulation of federally recognized Indian tribes. Laws that favor or disfavor persons because of their Indian ancestry should be considered suspect and subject to the most rigorous judicial scrutiny under the equal protection guarantee. However, congressional legislation or federal agency regulations regarding federally recognized Indian tribes and their members does not constitute a violation of the implied equal protection guarantee of the Fifth Amendment due process clause so long as the classification is "tied rationally to the fulfillment of Congress' unique obligation toward the Indians."[11]

---

6. U.S.Const. art. I, § 9, cl. 1; U.S.Const. art. V.

7. U.S.Const. art. I, § 9, cl. 6.

8. Cherokee Nation v. Georgia, 30 U.S. (5 Pet.) 1, 8 L.Ed. 25 (1831); Worcester v. Georgia, 31 U.S. (6 Pet.) 515, 8 L.Ed. 483 (1832). See Washburn, The Historical Context of American Indian Legal Problems, 40 Law & Contemporary Problems, 12 (1976); Ball, Constitution, Court, Indian Tribe, 1987 American Bar Foundation Research Journal 1.

9. When interpreting Congressional actions regulating Indian tribes, their property, and the scope of authority delegated to federal agencies or local governments over Indian affairs the Supreme Court has attempted to develop "canons of construction applicable in Indian law [that] are rooted in the unique trust relationship between the United States and the Indians." County of Oneida v. Oneida Indian Nation, 470 U.S. 226, 247, 105 S.Ct. 1245, 1258, 84 L.Ed.2d 169 (1985). See also Montana v. Blackfeet Tribe of Indians, 471 U.S. 759, 105 S.Ct. 2399, 2403, 85 L.Ed.2d 753 (1985). However "all aspects of Indian sovereignty are subject to defeasance by Congress." Escondido Mutual Water Co. v. La Jolla, Rincon, San Pasqual, Pauma, and Pala Bands of Mission Indians, 466 U.S. 765, 104 S.Ct. 2105, 2118, 80 L.Ed.2d 753 (1984), rehearing denied 467 U.S. 1267, 104 S.Ct. 3562, 82 L.Ed.2d 864 (1984).

The Legal Status of American Indian Tribes. A detailed examination of the legal status of American Indian tribes and their members is beyond the scope of this treatise. For citations to additional Supreme Court cases, and secondary authorities, on this point, see R. Rotunda & J. Nowak, Treatise on Constitutional Law: Substance and Procedure, vol. 1, § 4.2 (3rd ed. 1999, with annual supplements).

10. United States v. Kagama, 118 U.S. 375, 384, 6 S.Ct. 1109, 1114, 30 L.Ed. 228 (1886). Laurence, The Indian Commerce Clause, 23 Ariz.L.Rev. 204 (1981). For citations to additional Supreme Court cases, and secondary authorities, on this point, see R. Rotunda & J. Nowak, Treatise on Constitutional Law: Substance and Procedure, vol. 1, § 4.2 (3rd ed. 1999, with annual supplements).

11. Morton v. Mancari, 417 U.S. 535, 555, 94 S.Ct. 2474, 2485, 41 L.Ed.2d 290 (1974) (upholding employment preference for members of Indian tribes in Bureau of Indian Affairs); Washington v. Washington State Commercial Passenger Fishing Vessel Ass'n, 443 U.S. 658, 673 n. 20, 99 S.Ct. 3055, 3068 n. 20, 61 L.Ed.2d 823 (1979), opinion modified 444 U.S. 816, 100 S.Ct. 34, 62 L.Ed.2d 24 (1979), (interpreting federal treaties with certain Indian tribes to guarantee them a share of each run of anadromous fish in areas in the State of Washington and holding both that state laws limiting those rights were invalid and

The Supreme Court employs a mere rationality test when scrutinizing tribal classifications because such classifications are viewed as political rather than racial. Laws that give preferential employment or economic benefits to members of American Indian tribes may be upheld on this basis without consideration of whether they constitute a form of benign racial classification that might not otherwise survive scrutiny under the equal protection guarantee.[12] This rationality standard should not be used to justify legislation that imposes burdens upon persons because of their American Indian ancestry.[13]

The Application of the Bill of Rights to Indians. Commentators have questioned whether the unique constitutional status of members of American Indian tribes has benefitted tribal members.[14] The status of the tribes as quasi-sovereign entities has resulted in the Supreme Court refusal to apply the protections of the Bill of Rights to tribal regulations in the same manner as it has applied those provisions to the actions of local governments.[15] The extension of civil liberties protection to members of federally recognized tribes residing on tribal property has come about primarily by congressional action.[16]

The congressional power to pass laws limiting the use of tribal property or regulating the action of tribal members is subject to some constitutional restrictions. Although the Supreme Court has not made clear exactly which provisions of the Bill of Rights restrict congressional power in this area, it has held that the just compensation clause applies to the federal appropriation of tribal property.[17]

The authority of Indian tribes to govern their lands, and the people thereon, is subject to intrinsic limitations arising from the relationship of Indian tribes to the federal govern-

---

12. Morton v. Mancari, 417 U.S. 535, 94 S.Ct. 2474, 41 L.Ed.2d 290 (1974) (employment preference in Bureau of Indian Affairs upheld). See generally, Johnson & Crystal, Indians and Equal Protection, 54 Wash.L.Rev. 587 (1979).

13. In Washington v. Confederated Bands & Tribes of the Yakima Indian Nation, 439 U.S. 463, 99 S.Ct. 740, 58 L.Ed.2d 740 (1979), the Supreme Court held that a 1953 Act of Congress allows some states by legislative act to modify their jurisdiction so as to assume either full or partial jurisdiction over criminal offenses and civil causes of action regarding tribal Indians and Indian territories. The State of Washington had extended its criminal and civil jurisdiction over Indians and Indian territories except for eight subject matter areas that it would allow to remain within the jurisdiction of the Indian tribe unless the State was requested to assume full jurisdiction by the particular tribe. The Supreme Court found that this partial extension of jurisdiction and "checker board" jurisdictional pattern over Indian lands violated neither the federal statute nor the equal protection clause.

14. American Indians are full citizens of the United States, even though the federal government does retain significant authority to regulate activities on Indian reservations and to make classifications in federal laws relating to enrolled members of a recognized tribe. See, F. Cohen Handbook of Federal Indian Law (1982 ed.) 142–43 regarding the history of Indian citizenship under federal statutes. In Duro v. Reina, 495 U.S. 676, 110 S.Ct. 2053, 109 L.Ed.2d 693 (1990) the Supreme Court ruled that an Indian tribal court did not have jurisdiction over a criminal action committed on the reservation by an Indian who was a member of another tribe. The majority opinion in *Duro* stated: "We hesitate to adopt a view of tribal sovereignty that would single out another group of citizens, nonmember Indians, for trials by political bodies that do not include them. As full citizens, Indians share in the territorial and political sovereignty of the United States. The retained sovereignty of the tribe is but a recognition of certain additional authority the tribes maintain over Indians who consent to be tribal members." 495 U.S. at 693, 110 S.Ct. at 2063.

15. Proceedings in Indian tribal courts are not subjected to the Bill of Rights. Talton v. Mayes, 163 U.S. 376, 16 S.Ct. 986, 41 L.Ed. 196 (1896). Proceedings in the Indian courts are subjected to the terms of the Indian Civil Rights Act, 25 U.S.C.A. §§ 1301–1303. Thus, federal courts, on the basis of that Act, may review proceedings in tribal courts and grant habeas corpus to persons whose rights under the Act have been violated. For citations to additional Supreme Court cases on this point, see R. Rotunda & J. Nowak, Treatise on Constitutional Law: Substance and Procedure, vol. 1, § 4.2 (3rd ed. 1999, with annual supplements).

16. See, e.g., Indian Civil Rights Act, 25 U.S.C.A. § 1301 et seq.

17. United States v. Sioux Nation of Indians, 448 U.S. 371, 100 S.Ct. 2716, 65 L.Ed.2d 844 (1980) (although the taking of original title is not compensable, the government's acquisition of land held by an Indian tribe with recognized title to the land constitutes a compensable taking under the Fifth Amendment).

The question of whether an Indian tribe or a member of the tribe has a property interest based on federal statutes or treaties, and the question of whether such a property interest has been taken by a federal action, must be determined on a case-by-case basis. For citations to additional Supreme Court cases on this point, see R. Rotunda & J. Nowak, Treatise on Constitutional Law: Substance and Procedure, vol. 1, § 4.2 (3rd ed. 1999, with annual supplements).

that the granting of these preferential fishing rights to Indians did not violate the principles of equal protection).

ment. The primary limitations on tribal sovereignty relate to the transfer of land, external attributes of political sovereignty, and jurisdiction over non-Indians who are on Indian property. Although Congress has wide latitude in dealing with American Indians, the Supreme Court has held that tribal sovereignty is to be honored by federal courts to the extent that it does not conflict with federal statutes, federal treaties, or the overriding sovereignty of the United States.[18]

State Laws and Indian Tribes. State and local governments have no jurisdiction over Indian tribes unless they specifically have been granted such jurisdiction by Congress. The rights of tribal Indians under the statutes,

treaties, or Constitution of the United States are federal questions; federal law, as interpreted by the federal courts will supersede any conflicting state laws, regulations or court rulings.[19] The nature of the federal interest in Indian affairs, and the extent of federal regulation of American Indian tribes, has resulted in federal preemption of state regulations. State or local attempts to regulate the use of tribal property or the activities of individuals on tribal property often will be held invalid because of federal preemption.[20]

State jurisdiction over activity on Indian reservation lands located in the state is permitted only to the extent that it has been granted to the state by Congress.[21] Members of Indian

18. Extensions of tribal sovereignty often require congressional approval. The Supreme Court has found that the concept of inherent tribal sovereignty provides a basis for tribal regulation of tribal property and activities of tribe members while on tribal property. But the Supreme Court has stated that the "exercise of tribal power beyond what is necessary to protect tribal self-government or to control internal relations is inconsistent with the dependent status of the tribes, and so cannot survive without express congressional delegation." Montana v. United States, 450 U.S. 544, 564, 101 S.Ct. 1245, 1258, 67 L.Ed.2d 493 (1981), rehearing denied 452 U.S. 911, 101 S.Ct. 3042, 69 L.Ed.2d 414 (1981). Tribal sovereignty may be recognized as a basis for tribal regulation of activities of persons who are not members of the Indian tribe, but who are on tribal property, if the non-Indian persons have entered into a contract or lease providing for such control of their property or if the tribe's regulation of the conduct of non-Indians on certain "free lands" within the reservation is necessary to protect the "political integrity, the economic security, or the health or welfare of the tribe." Id. at 566, 101 S.Ct. at 1258.

Tribal Courts. Indian courts have only limited jurisdiction because the overriding sovereignty of the United States, as well as specific congressional enactments, limits the scope of tribal court powers. Oliphant v. Suquamish Indian Tribe, 435 U.S. 191, 98 S.Ct. 1011, 55 L.Ed.2d 209 (1978). For citations to additional Supreme Court cases, and secondary authorities, on this point, see R. Rotunda & J. Nowak, Treatise on Constitutional Law: Substance and Procedure, vol. 1, § 4.2 (3rd ed. 1999, with annual supplements).

19. Washington v. Washington State Commercial Passenger Fishing Vessel Ass'n, 443 U.S. 658, 99 S.Ct. 3055, 61 L.Ed.2d 823 (1979), opinion modified 444 U.S. 816, 100 S.Ct. 34, 62 L.Ed.2d 24 (1979) (state law as written or construed could not interfere with preferential fishing rights given Indian tribes by federal treaties).

Federal legislation may make Indian tribes subject to state jurisdiction. See, e.g., South Carolina v. Catawba Indian Tribe, Inc., 476 U.S. 498, 106 S.Ct. 2039, 90 L.Ed.2d 490 (1986), on remand 865 F.2d 1444 (4th Cir. 1989) (federal statutes explicitly redefine the relationship

between the federal government and specific Indian tribes; the federal statutes allow for application of state statute of limitations to a dispute regarding the possession of certain land). For citations to additional Supreme Court cases, and secondary authorities, on this point, see R. Rotunda & J. Nowak, Treatise on Constitutional Law: Substance and Procedure, vol. 1, § 4.2 (3rd ed. 1999, with annual supplements).

20. See, e.g., New Mexico v. Mescalero Apache Tribe, 462 U.S. 324, 103 S.Ct. 2378, 76 L.Ed.2d 611 (1983) (federally approved tribal ordinances regulating conditions under which both tribe members and nonmembers may hunt and fish preempted the application of New Mexico's laws).

Special Problems Regarding State Taxation. Some state taxes may be imposed on activities that take place on a reservation that involve persons who are not members of the Indian tribe. For example, states may require an Indian tribe to collect an excise (sales) tax on cigarettes sold by the tribe to non–Indian purchasers on an Indian reservation. See, California State Board of Equalization v. Chemehuevi Indian Tribe, 474 U.S. 9, 106 S.Ct. 289, 88 L.Ed.2d 9 (1985), rehearing denied 474 U.S. 1077, 106 S.Ct. 839, 88 L.Ed.2d 810 (1986); Washington v. Confederated Tribes of Colville Indian Reservation, 447 U.S. 134, 100 S.Ct. 2069, 65 L.Ed.2d 10 (1980), rehearing denied 448 U.S. 911, 101 S.Ct. 25, 65 L.Ed.2d 1172 (1980). The taxation of American Indian tribes is examined in R. Rotunda & J. Nowak Treatise on Constitutional Law: Substance and Procedure, vol. 2, § 13.11 (3rd ed. 1999, with annual supplements).

21. The Supreme Court often interprets federal statutes in a manner that minimizes the scope of state authority over the property or activities of American Indian tribes. Congress does have the authority to confer jurisdiction on states to regulate activities on tribal land. Assuming that the federal statute does not violate any constitutional restriction on federal power, a grant of authority from Congress to the state will be enforced by the Supreme Court. For example, the Supreme Court held that the Kansas Act, 18 U.S.C.A. § 3243 gave the State of Kansas jurisdiction over state criminal offenses on Indian

tribes may be subject to state or local regulation of their off-reservation activities if those local regulations do not conflict with federal regulations, legislation, treaties or constitutional provisions.[22]

In the remaining portions of this chapter we will examine the one federal commerce power that has been subject to differing types of restrictions during its history—the power to regulate commerce "among the states."

§ 4.3 A Brief History of the Commerce Clause

There was no debate in the Constitutional Convention over the enumeration of specific powers for the federal government following an initial, unsuccessful proposal to grant it a general "police" power.[1] One of the enumerated powers that was not specifically examined was the grant of power to Congress to regulate commerce "among the several States." Thus we have no direct history as to the meaning of the clause that could even arguably be called determinative of specific legal issues. Not only must we content ourselves with looking at the circumstances surrounding the calling of the Constitutional Convention and the ratification process, but we must note that this clause employs a concept, that of "commerce," that seems by its nature subject to differing definitions with the passing of time. Let us note some of the forces that gave rise to the calling of the convention and drafting of the clause

before moving on to the judicial interpretations of both the history and meaning of that provision.

There had been no significant commercial problems in the colonies prior to the Declaration of Independence, for Britain had controlled the trade between the colonies themselves as well as that with foreign nations. The acts of the colonial governments were subject to the review of the Privy Council, and the British Board of Trade supervised the general commercial transactions through the colonies.[2] Additionally all of the actions of the colonial governments and the forms of trade in which they engaged were at least formally subjected to the authority of the Secretary of State for the Southern Department. It was primarily the Board of Trade supervision over the trade of and the access to goods and services in each colony that eliminated economic conflict during the colonial period.

After the signing of the Declaration of Independence there was no central control over commercial transactions in the new states. The individual states were fearful of having their trade subjected to discriminatory restrictions either by states with conflicting commercial interests or a national government that might be controlled by such interests. Therefore when they formed a national government under the Articles of Confederation they granted the Continental Congress some pow-

reservations in the state. Federal courts retained jurisdiction over federal offenses committed on those reservations, but the state courts had jurisdiction to try persons for conduct on the reservation that violated state law. Negonsott v. Samuels, 507 U.S. 99, 113 S.Ct. 1119, 122 L.Ed.2d 457 (1993).

For citations to additional Supreme Court cases on this point, see R. Rotunda & J. Nowak, Treatise on Constitutional Law: Substance and Procedure, vol. 1 § 4.2 (3rd ed. 1999, with annual supplements).

22. Mescalero Apache Tribe v. Jones, 411 U.S. 145, 93 S.Ct. 1267, 36 L.Ed.2d 114 (1973) (upholding nondiscriminating state gross receipts tax as applied to business operated by Indian tribes on off-reservation land). At the close of the twentieth century, the concept of tribal immunity from state regulation and state taxation was endorsed by the Supreme Court on the basis of *stare decicis* principles. Kiowa Tribe of Oklahoma v. Manufacturing Technologies, Inc., 523 U.S. 751, 118 S.Ct. 1700, 140 L.Ed.2d 981 (1998) ruled that a Native American tribe had immunity from suit in state courts concerning promissory notes that

the tribe had signed. Justice Kennedy, writing for six Justices in *Kiowa Tribe*, noted that: "though the doctrine of tribal immunity is settled law and controls this case, we note that it developed almost by accident." 523 U.S. at 756, 118 S.Ct. at 1703. Although the basis for the development of tribal immunity in the earliest Supreme Court decisions may have been weak, Justice Kennedy's majority opinion found that the Supreme Court would continue to enforce the concept of tribal immunity that had been established in earlier cases because Congress had relied on the Court's decisions, and because Congress was in the best position to make determinations concerning the extent of tribal immunity. Justice Kennedy's majority opinion concluded: "In light of these concerns, we decline to revisit our case law, and choose to defer to Congress." 523 U.S. at 760, 118 S.Ct. at 1705.

§ 4.3

1. See § 3.1, supra.

2. A. Kelly & W. Harbison, The American Constitution, Its Origins and Development 50–54 (4th ed. 1970).

ers over national affairs but none over commerce between the new states. Not only did they fail to give Congress such a power but they restricted the Continental Congress' powers in foreign affairs by providing that no federal treaties might limit the individual states' powers over commerce and the taxation of imports and exports.[3]

The lack of a centralized authority over commerce and the conflicting economic interests of the new states led to what may best be described as economic chaos under the Articles of Confederation: the loss of a trade relationship with Great Britain; serious diminution of international trade with a resulting shortage of currency; and the coalition of local economic forces to protect their position in the now limited market place.

Individual states then began to set up trade barriers by imposing economic sanctions against competing products from other states as well as taxing trade passing through their state in order to gain a more solid economic position, further limiting the market place for goods and services.[4] New York and other states that controlled major foreign ports imposed taxes on incoming foreign commerce destined for the other states. In retaliation these states would tax goods brought in from other states at a rate so high as to foreclose access to their markets. The situation became such that many political leaders in the nation feared that the economic warfare would lead to a dissolution of the union and that "at a minimum" the powers of the Continental Congress to deal with commercial problems between the states had to be enhanced.[5] Thus there was a call for a convention to amend the powers of the national government under the Articles of Confederation so as to make it effective to deal with multistate problems.

When the delegates met to amend the Articles of Confederation, they quickly realized that the country needed an entirely new form of government to deal with national problems. Thus there was a call for a new convention, which we now know as the Constitutional Convention, to totally revise the powers of the national government.[6] This convention began in May of 1787 and produced the new federal government with its enumerated (but not debated) power to regulate commerce "among the states."

At the Constitutional Convention, several states expressed concern over the congressional power to regulate foreign commerce. The southern states feared control over this matter might lead to the prohibition of the importation of slaves to such an extent that they proposed limiting the national commercial powers. In the ensuing compromise the powers were not defined narrowly but the southern states received assurance in the Constitution that Congress would not bar the importation of slaves until 1808.[7] Several of the southern states also feared that the Northeast might control the Congress and thereby favor their trade centers and products at the expense of southern agricultural interests. These fears were overcome by the provisions of Section 9 of Article I, which guaranteed that no preference would be given to the ports of any state and which prohibited Congress from imposing any export taxes.[8]

The congressional power over international commerce was thus specifically defined by the convention, and there is no record of the power over commerce with the Indian tribes as a source of concern. But the power over internal commerce was both undefined and of great importance. Undoubtedly the Federalists intended Congress to have significant powers in this area but there are indications that some of the framers and ratifiers were opposed to

3. Articles of Confederation, art. IX, par. 1. The Articles are reprinted in Appendix B, of R. Rotunda & J. Nowak, Treatise on Constitutional Law: Substance and Procedure (3rd ed. 1999, with annual supplements).

4. See, A. Kelly & W. Harbison, The American Constitution 109 (4th ed. 1970); F. Broderick, The Origins of the Constitution 1776–1789, at 18 (1964); C. Heathcock, The United States Constitution in Perspective at 20 (1972).

5. Id.

6. The resolution for a new convention to deal with commercial problems is reprinted in 1 H. Commanger, Documents of American History 132 (5th ed. 1949).

7. U.S.Const. art. I, § 9, cl. 1; U.S.Const. art. V.

8. U.S.Const. art. I, § 9.

granting Congress such a wide power over commercial matters that it would remove all state autonomy in these areas.[9]

Thus the question of state power to enact regulations affecting interstate commerce, a question that was to be of the most frequent concern to the Court, did not have a legislative history that would be helpful to the Court. However, the Court could rely upon history to demonstrate two general concerns for the drafting of the Constitution in general and the commerce clause in particular: (1) the power must have been meant to put an end, either in itself or through federal legislation, to the trade barriers and tariffs that had led to the economic problems during the preceding period; and, (2) the national power must have been intended to be broad enough to deal with the type of economic problems of the nation as a unit. The experience under the Articles of Confederation showed that the individual states had literally no success in trying to deal with multistate economic problems. However, there was opposition to granting the federal government wide ranging power over local activities; extant historical materials give insufficient guidance as to how to reconcile concerns about national economic problems and state autonomy.[10]

As can be readily seen, this background has given the Court some themes to follow in its interpretation of the commerce clause but left for the Justices the task of analyzing the purpose and meaning of the commerce power in the federal system. It is to the Court's work in this area that we now turn.

§ 4.4 Judicial Interpretations of the Commerce Power Prior to 1888

In examining the interpretation of the commerce clause during this period, then Professor Felix Frankfurter commented: "Relatively little emerges up to the death of [Chief Justice] Waite in 1888, regarding the Court's attitude towards the commerce clause as an affirmative instrument for promoting 'commerce among the states.' The preoccupation [of earlier periods] is with the restrictive use of the clause."[1] And so it was, because Congress passed little commercial legislation during this period and the Supreme Court reviewed even less. No piece of federal commercial legislation was invalidated by the Court prior to the Civil War.[2] Indeed, the major review of Article I powers prior to the war was *McCulloch v. Maryland.*[3] But the Justices did reflect upon the scope of the national commerce power during this period in deciding cases concerning the validity of state laws under the "dormant" commerce clause.[4]

In *Gibbons v. Ogden*[5] Chief Justice Marshall examined the scope of both federal and state powers under the commerce clause. The opinion today ranks as one of the most important in history. In it Marshall laid the basis for later Justices to uphold a federal power to deal

---

9. Thus the Federalists felt called upon to answer charges that the scope of federal powers was so great as to endanger the autonomy of the states. See, e.g., The Federalist No. 45 (Madison), see also No. 11 (Hamilton), reprinted in, The Federalist Papers (New American Library Ed. 1961). For an examination of the conflicting economic forces that affected the framing of the Constitution, see generally, C. Beard, An Economic Interpretation of the Constitution of the United States (Rev. ed. 1960).

10. See M. Borden, The Antifederalist Papers (1965); C. Kenyon, The Antifederalists (1966), Note, The United States and the Articles of Confederation: Drifting Toward Anarchy or Inching Toward Commonwealth?, 88 Yale L.J. 142 (1978). See generally, Siler, J., citing Treatise in United States v. Wall, 92 F.3d 1444, 1446 n. 2 (6th Cir.1996).

§ 4.4

1. Felix Frankfurter, The Commerce Clause Under Marshall, Taney and Waite, at 7 (1964—first published 1937).

2. Only two federal acts were held unconstitutional during this period: see Marbury v. Madison, 5 U.S. (1 Cranch) 137, 2 L.Ed. 60 (1803) (part of Judiciary Act held unconstitutional grant of original jurisdiction); Dred Scott v. Sandford, 60 U.S. (19 How.) 393, 15 L.Ed. 691 (1857) (Missouri Compromise granting freedom to slaves in certain territories).

3. 17 U.S. (4 Wheat.) 316, 4 L.Ed. 579 (1819).

4. The development of standards to review these issues is examined in Chapter 8, infra.

5. 22 U.S. (9 Wheat.) 1, 6 L.Ed. 23 (1824). For a further discussion of *Gibbons* as it relates to state power over commerce, see Chapter 8, infra.

with national economic and social problems. But before that time would come, the Court would go through periods disregarding the basis of Marshall's ruling.

Gibbons concerned the granting of a steamboat monopoly to a private company. New York had granted the exclusive right to engage in steamboat navigation in the waters of New York to a partnership that had transferred the monopoly to Ogden. Gibbons began a competing service between New York and New Jersey. When Ogden sued Gibbons for encroachment on the monopoly, he defended by asserting that the state granted monopoly violated the commerce clause.

Instead of giving a definitive ruling on the scope of state powers under that clause, the Court found the monopoly invalid because it conflicted with a valid federal statute. Marshall's opinion held that the federal statute governing the licensing of ships granted those ships the right to engage in coastal trade and that the federal statute governed the issue because it was the supreme law of the land.[6]

In the course of the opinion, Marshall gave a broad reading to the powers of Congress under the commerce clause. Marshall defined commerce as "intercourse" and recognized that it extended into each state. Congress had the power to regulate "that commerce which concerns more states than one."[7] The federal power extended to commerce wherever it was present, and thus, "the power of Congress may be exercised within a state."[8]

The commerce power, in Marshall's opinion, was not to be restricted by the judiciary. His opinion for the majority of the Court found that the commerce power, "like all others vested in Congress, is complete in itself, may be exercised to its utmost extent, and acknowl-

edges no limitations other than are prescribed in the Constitution."[9] Marshall did state that some "internal" commerce of a state would be beyond the power of Congress to regulate.[10] According to Marshall's opinion for the Court, the only commercial activities that were immune from federal power, and reserved for state or local regulation, were those "which are completely within a State, which do not affect other States, and with which it is not necessary to interfere, for the purpose of executing some of the general powers of the government." Marshall thus described the "internal commerce of a state" as beyond the reach of federal power but simultaneously created a standard under which few commercial activities could be found to meet the definition of internal commerce.

It is, of course, impossible to assert with assurance whether Marshall would have favored or rejected a significant judicial role in circumscribing the scope of federal power and protecting state sovereignty. As Felix Frankfurter viewed the opinion:

> Marshall not merely rejected the Tenth Amendment as an active principle of limitation; he countered with his famous characterization of the powers of Congress, and of the commerce power in particular, as the possession of the unqualified authority of a unitary sovereign. He threw the full weight of his authority against the idea that, apart from specific restrictions in the Constitution, the very existence of the states operates as such a limitation. . . .[11]

Chief Justice Marshall had only two more opportunities to examine the meaning of the commerce clause prior to his death. Both of these cases focused on particular powers of the

---

6. 22 U.S. (9 Wheat.) at 210, 6 L.Ed. at 73.

7. 22 U.S. (9 Wheat.) at 189, 194.

8. 22 U.S. (9 Wheat.) at 195.

9. 22 U.S. (9 Wheat.) at 196.

10. 22 U.S. (9 Wheat.) at 194.

11. Felix Frankfurter, The Commerce Clause Under Marshall, Taney and Waite (1964—first published 1937) at 40; Marshall made the point thus, 22 U.S. (9 Wheat.) at 34:

"If, as has always been understood, the sovereignty of congress, though limited to specified objects, is plenary as to those objects, the power over commerce with foreign nations, and among the several States, is vested in congress as absolutely as it would be in a single government, having in its constitution the same restrictions on the exercise of the power as are found in the constitution of the United States."

states. In *Brown v. Maryland*[12] he invalidated a state statute that imposed a license fee or tax on wholesale importers. The tax was invalid for two reasons. First, it constituted a tax on international imports while they were still in their original package and before they became part of the "common mass" of property within the state. Therefore, it violated the constitutional prohibition against state duties on imports or exports.[13] Second, the tax conflicted with the commerce clause and the power of Congress to regulate and permit the sale of imports. Here Marshall described the power of Congress as the power to regulate commercial intercourse that reached into a state.[14] Once again Marshall was only describing a specific aspect of the power; he did not imply that the Court should limit the commerce power to protect state sovereignty.[15]

In *Willson v. Black–Bird Creek Marsh Co.*,[16] the Court upheld a Delaware statute that authorized the building of a dam across a navigable creek. Although this dam obstructed the passage of ships, including those with federal licenses, the Supreme Court in an opinion by Chief Justice Marshall, found the act consistent with the federal commerce power. He believed the act to be within the police power of the state to protect the public, which the state retained even after the ratification of the federal commerce clause. Also, he found that Congress did not intend to grant rights of passage over such creeks and, therefore, the state act did not conflict with an exercise of the federal power. However, Marshall's opinion did not indicate that he would have placed any restriction on the congressional power to

deal with this matter even though it involved a local "police power" issue.

Felix Frankfurter noted[17] that the concepts of commerce formulated in the Marshall opinions could lead to "obscuring formulas" for the proper exercise of both state and national powers. This confusion in fact took place over a long period of time and it was only after 1937 that the Court returned to Marshall's position. But from Marshall's death in 1835 until 1888, few restrictions were placed on the national commerce power.

Between 1837 and 1851, the Supreme Court reviewed several state acts under the commerce clause without formulating clear principles to govern the exercise of either state or national power. But there were statements in the decisions, even by supporters of Marshall's position, that indicated a sharp distinction between the types of commerce that could be regulated by Congress or the states.[18] In 1851 the Court decided *Cooley v. Board of Wardens*[19] and established the basic analysis of state power under the dormant commerce clause. The *Cooley* opinion established the concept of "selective exclusiveness" whereby commercial subjects requiring uniform national regulation could be regulated only by Congress, while subjects of local concern might be regulated to some extent by the states.[20] The opinion did not attempt to define the scope of federal power, but its division between "national" and "local" subjects would one day be used by Justices who sought to restrict federal power.

The Court under the leadership of Chief Justice Taney was more lenient in reviewing state legislation than the Marshall Court,[21] but

12. 25 U.S. (12 Wheat.) 419, 6 L.Ed. 678 (1827).

13. U.S.Const. art. I, § 10; The "original package" test for imports was abandoned in Michelin Tire Corp. v. Wages, 422 U.S. 1040, 95 S.Ct. 2652, 45 L.Ed.2d 692 (1975), judgment affirmed 423 U.S. 276, 96 S.Ct. 535, 46 L.Ed.2d 495 (1976), rehearing denied 424 U.S. 935, 96 S.Ct. 1151, 47 L.Ed.2d 344 (1976). The original package doctrine was not applied to state taxes on interstate commerce. Woodruff v. Parham, 75 U.S. (8 Wall.) 123, 19 L.Ed. 382 (1869).

14. 25 U.S. (12 Wheat.) at 446.

15. Marshall cited *Gibbons* and reiterated the concept that the power had "no limitations other than are prescribed by the constitution." 25 U.S. (12 Wheat.) at 446.

16. 27 U.S. (2 Pet.) 245, 7 L.Ed. 412 (1829).

17. Felix Frankfurter, The Commerce Clause Under Marshall, Taney and Waite (1964—first published 1937) at 31–32, 61–62.

18. Id.; see, e.g., the Passenger Cases, 48 U.S. (7 How.) 283, 400, 12 L.Ed. 702, 751 (1849) (opinion of McClean, J.).

19. 53 U.S. (12 How.) 299, 13 L.Ed. 996 (1851).

20. This case is examined in Chapter 8, infra.

21. See, e.g., Mayor, Aldermen and Commonalty of New York v. Miln, 36 U.S. (11 Pet.) 102, 9 L.Ed. 648 (1837); In fact, Chief Justice Taney never voted to strike down state legislation under the commerce clause. Felix Frankfurter, The Commerce Clause Under Marshall, Taney and Waite (1964—first published 1937) at 55.

the Court made no attempt to restrain federal commercial powers.[22] Indeed, there were indications during this period that the Court would have been willing to recognize sweeping federal powers under the commerce clause and Congress attempted extensive regulation. Taney seemed ready to defer to federal as well as state legislative judgments.[23] The Justices had little difficulty in upholding federal acts to prohibit trade in counterfeit money.[24] The Court also deferred to congressional judgment over commerce in the *Wheeling Bridge Cases*. In 1852, the Court invalidated Virginia statutes authorizing a bridge over the Ohio River that might interfere with commerce.[25] Congress then passed a federal law declaring the bridge to be lawful.[26] This statute was held by the Court to fall within the federal commerce power.[27]

Following the Civil War, the Supreme Court began to assert its authority to control the actions of the other branches of the federal government. During the Chief Justiceship of Salmon Chase from 1864 to 1873, eight federal statutes were held to be unconstitutional.[28]

The Court did not consider significant commercial issues until 1869. In that year, the Justices seemed ready to recognize wide federal powers when they held that Congress could pass a tax on state bank notes that would destroy their marketability.[29] But in the same year the Court upheld the state regulation of interstate insurance business because insurance contracts were not "articles of commerce."[30]

The year 1870 saw the Court temporarily staffed by Justices who were ready to restrict the federal power. In the first "legal tender case" the Court held that the Legal Tender Acts were unconstitutional as applied to preexisting debts.[31] In the same month the Court issued the first decision that held a federal commercial statute invalid because it exceeded the congressional power to regulate commerce. In *United States v. Dewitt*[32] the Supreme Court invalidated a federal statute that prohibited the sale of an illuminating petroleum product made of naphtha and oil if it was inflammable below certain fire test levels. Chief Justice Chase found this statute beyond any federal power because the commerce clause was "a virtual denial of any power to interfere with the internal trade and business of the separate states."[33]

Two new Justices were appointed to the Supreme Court at this time, and 1871 saw a shift back to deference toward the other branches of government. The Court quickly reversed the decision on the legality and application of the Legal Tender Acts.[34] The Court also gave a somewhat broader reading to the commerce clause. In *The Daniel Ball*[35] the Court upheld the application of a federal safe-

---

22. While Taney did not seek to control the commerce power generally, he did write the opinion invalidating the congressional act freeing slaves in certain territories, Dred Scott v. Sandford, 60 U.S. (19 How.) 393, 15 L.Ed. 691 (1857), and it appears that he would have also restricted the commerce power as to slavery issues, see Groves v. Slaughter, 40 U.S. (15 Pet.) 449, 10 L.Ed. 800 (1841); Felix Frankfurter, The Commerce Clause Under Marshall, Taney and Waite (1964—first published 1937) at 66–68.

23. Felix Frankfurter, The Commerce Clause Under Marshall, Taney and Waite (1964—first published 1937) at 65–73.

24. United States v. Marigold, 50 U.S. (9 How.) 560, 13 L.Ed. 257 (1850).

25. Pennsylvania v. Wheeling & Belmont Bridge Co., 54 U.S. (13 How.) 518, 14 L.Ed. 249 (1852).

26. Act of August 31, 1852 & 6, c. 111, 10 Stat. 110, 112.

27. Pennsylvania v. Wheeling & Belmont Bridge Co., 59 U.S. (18 How.) 421, 15 L.Ed. 435 (1856). See § 8.5, infra.

28. C. Fairman, 6 Oliver Wendell Holmes Devise History of the Supreme Court of the United States—Reconstruction and Reunion 1864–88, part one, at 1426 (1971).

29. Veazie Bank v. Fenno, 75 U.S. (8 Wall.) 533, 19 L.Ed. 482 (1869).

30. Paul v. Virginia, 75 U.S. (8 Wall.) 168, 19 L.Ed. 357 (1869). This decision was later overturned, United States v. South–Eastern Underwriters Ass'n, 322 U.S. 533, 64 S.Ct. 1162, 88 L.Ed. 1440 (1944), rehearing denied 323 U.S. 811, 65 S.Ct. 26, 89 L.Ed. 646 (1944).

31. Hepburn v. Griswold, 75 U.S. (8 Wall.) 603, 19 L.Ed. 513 (1870).

32. 76 U.S. (9 Wall.) 41, 19 L.Ed. 593 (1870).

33. 76 U.S. (9 Wall.) at 44.

34. Knox v. Lee (The Legal Tender Cases), 79 U.S. (12 Wall.) 457, 20 L.Ed. 287 (1871); see also Juilliard v. Greenman, 110 U.S. 421, 4 S.Ct. 122, 28 L.Ed. 204 (1884).

35. 77 U.S. (10 Wall.) 557, 19 L.Ed. 999 (1871).

ty regulation to a ship that operated solely on a river in Michigan. Because the ship was used for the intrastate part of an interstate journey—the ship was used for part of the transportation of goods moving from one state to another—it was an "instrumentality" of that commerce. Federal safety regulation of the Daniel Ball, a ship using the waterways of interstate commerce, was necessary because if the Daniel Ball was unsafe, that would affect other ships that were in fact making interstate journeys. The Court sustained the regulation without returning to the problem of purely "internal" trade. But the Justices in 1871 were still ready to protect the states to some degree from the power of the federal government; the Court held that certain federal taxes could not be applied to state payments to certain state officers.[36]

The last sixteen years in this period witnessed no real changes in the position of the Supreme Court. The Justices continued to strike down state legislation that would place significant burdens on interstate commercial transactions,[37] and the Court upheld what seemed already to be traditional exercises of the congressional power regarding the building of bridges,[38] legal tender,[39] or trade with Indians.[40] The Court also upheld the congressional power to license interstate communications agencies by striking down Florida's attempt to grant exclusive telegraph privileges within its borders.[41]

However, the Supreme Court did strike down one more piece of federal commercial legislation during this period. In *The Trade-Mark Cases*[42] the Court held that Congress exceeded its power under the commerce clause when it attempted to establish a trademark registration and regulation system that did not exempt commercial transactions occurring within a single state.[43]

As we turn to the next period in the history of the commerce clause, we can see that the Court in 1887 was relatively free to define the commerce power of Congress. Marshall's original position had been one of great deference to the Congress and of active promotion of national power. Under Taney the Court had given greater leeway to the states in the regulation of commerce and this line of cases helped to create the basis for an interstate/internal commerce dichotomy. Following the war, the Chase Court had asserted a new, independent control over the scope of federal powers and for the first time had struck down federal commercial legislation. Under Chief Justice Waite the Supreme Court allowed a fair range of congressional actions but again the Justices had invalidated some federal commercial legislation that regulated the internal commerce of the states. Although Waite believed in giving deference to other branches of both state and

---

36. Collector v. Day, 78 U.S. (11 Wall.) 113, 20 L.Ed. 122 (1871); see also, United States v. Baltimore & O. Railroad Co., 84 U.S. (17 Wall.) 322, 21 L.Ed. 597 (1873) (payment on certain municipal bonds exempted). For a discussion of the status of intergovernmental tax immunities today, see our multivolume treatise, 1 R. Rotunda & J. Nowak, Treatise on Constitutional Law: Substance and Procedure § 13.9 (3rd ed.1999, with annual supplements).

37. See, e.g., Welton v. Missouri, 91 U.S. (1 Otto) 275, 23 L.Ed. 347 (1876) (discriminatory tax invalid); Wabash, St. Louis & Pacific Ry. v. Illinois, 118 U.S. 557, 7 S.Ct. 4, 30 L.Ed. 244 (1886) (state regulation of interstate rates invalid).

38. Newport & Cincinnati Bridge Co. v. United States, 105 U.S. (15 Otto) 470, 26 L.Ed. 1143 (1882). See Felix Frankfurter, The Commerce Clause Under Marshall, Taney and Waite (1964—first published 1937), at 92–95.

39. Juilliard v. Greenman, 110 U.S. 421, 4 S.Ct. 122, 28 L.Ed. 204 (1884).

40. United States v. Forty–Three Gallons of Whisky, 108 U.S. 491, 2 S.Ct. 906, 27 L.Ed. 803 (1883).

41. Pensacola Telegraph Co. v. Western Union Telegraph Co., 96 U.S. (6 Otto) 1, 24 L.Ed. 708 (1878).

42. The Trade–Mark Cases (United States v. Steffens), 100 U.S. (10 Otto) 82, 25 L.Ed. 550 (1878).

43. The Court also held that this act was beyond the "patent and copyright" power of art. I, § 8, cl. 8. The effect of the decision was diminished in 1903, when the Court, per Justice Holmes, held that lithograph advertisements could be constitutionally copyrighted; Bleistein v. Donaldson Lithographing, 188 U.S. 239, 23 S.Ct. 298, 47 L.Ed. 460 (1903).

Later decisions concerning the regulation of advertising materials or labels under the copyright power have eliminated the import of this decision. It is thought that a modern Court might overturn this decision, but it is unlikely that it will have occasion to do so since virtually all business trademarks today are found to have a sufficient relationship to interstate commerce to be regulated under the theory of this decision. See 1 M. Nimmer, Nimmer on Copyright §§ 8.4, 9.1, 24 (multivolume treatise with annual supplementation).

federal governments,[44] the Court in the 1880's was moving toward more active control over the social and political policies of the other branches.[45] And the language finding "internal" commerce beyond the federal power would give these Justices a tool for restricting federal regulation of national, social, and economic conditions.[46]

§ 4.5 1888–1936: Summary

While this period began with a linguistic distinction between interstate commerce and the internal activities within a state, there were few restraints on federal power. In the first cases during this period, the distinction became stronger as the Court edged toward a concept of "dual federalism."[1] This concept involved the use of the Tenth Amendment to initially define and to limit the powers of Congress; under this theory the Tenth Amendment reserved the regulation of some activities for the states and federal power could only apply to other activities.

This dual federalism theory was the principle behind the Supreme Court's ruling that the antitrust acts did not apply to manufacturing combinations.[2] The production process was seen as an activity reserved for state regula-

tion and the Court required a "direct" connection to interstate commerce to place it under the federal power.

The Court tempered this use of the Tenth Amendment with the "stream" or "current" of commerce theory. Under this concept, Congress could regulate what seemed to be an intrastate activity if that activity was connected to the interstate movement of goods or services. Thus, stockyards could be subject to regulation because they were part of interstate commerce.[3] But this concept again was based on a finding of a "direct" connection to interstate commercial transactions.

In a very limited area, the Justices recognized that the economic impact of some activities might create a sufficient link with interstate commerce to subject them to federal regulation. The Supreme Court upheld the federal regulation of railroad rates and restricted state authority in this area because a majority of the Justices recognized that the local rate structures had a real effect on interstate transportation.[4] The Court agreed that the railroads were in need of national regulation, so federal railroad safety laws were also upheld.[5] But the Court did not extend the congressional power based on eco-

---

44. Felix Frankfurter, The Commerce Clause Under Marshall, Taney and Waite (1964—first published 1937), at 81–82.

45. It was during this period that the Court invalidated the Congressional act in The Civil Rights Cases, 109 U.S. 3, 3 S.Ct. 18, 27 L.Ed. 835 (1883). The concept of substantive due process was being debated at this time. See Munn v. Illinois, 94 U.S. (4 Otto) 113, 24 L.Ed. 77 (1876).

46. This linguistic distinction had become stronger over the years. In Coe v. Town of Errol, 116 U.S. 517, 6 S.Ct. 475, 29 L.Ed. 715 (1886), the Court held that logs cut and stored in New Hampshire for transport and sale in other states could be taxed by New Hampshire. The rationale of the decision was that the logs had not yet been put into commerce on the tax assessment day. The opinion seemed to use a sharp distinction between interstate commerce and local production or storage. For an in-depth analysis of state powers to tax items allegedly in interstate commerce, see Chapter 13 of our multivolume treatise, 1 R. Rotunda & J. Nowak, Treatise on Constitutional Law: Substance and Procedure, ch. 13 (3rd ed.1999).

§ 4.5

1. For an analysis the concept and its demise, see Corwin, The Passing of Dual Federalism, 36 Va.L.Rev. 1 (1950).

2. United States v. E. C. Knight Co., 156 U.S. 1, 15 S.Ct. 249, 39 L.Ed. 325 (1895).

3. Swift & Co. v. United States, 196 U.S. 375, 25 S.Ct. 276, 49 L.Ed. 518 (1905). See also Reid v. Colorado, 187 U.S. 137, 23 S.Ct. 92, 47 L.Ed. 108 (1902) (transportation of diseased livestock across state lines is subject to federal, not state, regulation).

4. The Shreveport Rate Case (Houston E. & W. Texas Ry. v. United States), 234 U.S. 342, 34 S.Ct. 833, 58 L.Ed. 1341 (1914); Wisconsin R.R. Com'n v. Chicago, B. & Q. R.R., 257 U.S. 563, 42 S.Ct. 232, 66 L.Ed. 371 (1922). For citations to other cases interpreting and applying the Shreveport Rate Case approach to determine the validity of federal regulations of commerce, see 1 R. Rotunda & J. Nowak, Treatise on Constitutional Law: Substance and Procedure § 4.5 (3rd ed.1999).

5. Southern Ry. Co. v. United States, 222 U.S. 20, 32 S.Ct. 2, 56 L.Ed. 72 (1911); Texas & Pac. Ry. v. Rigsby, 241 U.S. 33, 36 S.Ct. 482, 60 L.Ed. 874 (1916); United States v. Seaboard Air Line R.R., 361 U.S. 78, 80 S.Ct. 12, 4 L.Ed.2d 25 (1959).

nomic effects of intrastate activities beyond railroad regulation.

When persons or items traveled between two states, there could be no question that they constituted interstate commerce. Congress sometimes sought to set terms for the transportation of goods that in effect regulated activities within the states. These statutes were generally "police" regulations, including the prohibition against transporting women across state lines for certain immoral purposes or the interstate transportation of unwholesome food or drugs.

The Court at first upheld those regulations as a part of the federal commerce power, but the Justices restricted the power when Congress tried to regulate the employment conditions of children through such a statute.[6] The Supreme Court restricted congressional power over the interstate transport of goods to the regulation of activities that had a direct, harmful effect on interstate commerce.

These cases set the stage for the Supreme Court's battle against the New Deal legislation of the early 1930's. In a series of cases, the Court struck down major regulations of retirement systems, business practices, labor organizations, and agricultural production. A majority of the Justices viewed the Tenth Amendment as committing the regulation of such activities to the states. They interpreted the commerce clause in terms of what the Tenth Amendment left for federal regulation. Because these laws were not regulations of interstate transportation or the "stream" of commerce there would have to be a demonstrably "direct" connection between regulated activity and interstate commerce. The Justices independently reviewed the basis for the laws, and they refused to accept economic theories

that might show the effect of the activities on the national economy and commerce. Indeed, the Justices went so far as to strike down some regulations as improper delegations of national authority to regulatory agencies—a concept that has had no place in the cases before or after this short period.[7]

The Court placed similar restrictions on the taxing and spending powers of Congress. After having allowed Congress in the past to place prohibitory taxes on some items, the Court refused to allow a tax that would circumvent its commerce clause rulings by regulating the conditions of labor.[8] Similarly, the Court used the Tenth Amendment to restrict the congressional power to spend federal revenues. The Justices sought to stop Congress from buying compliance with federal regulation of single-state activities.[9] The taxing and spending powers are discussed in separate sections.[10]

It is interesting to note that during this period the Court gave a wide reading to powers of the federal government when the Justices did not think that federal regulation affected a subject reserved to the states by the Tenth Amendment. Thus, the Court upheld the taxing of firearms,[11] the federal nullification of gold clauses in contracts,[12] and the sale of electricity from federal dams.[13] These decisions emphasize how a combination of Tenth Amendment interpretation and the Justices' personal views of national economic policy shaped the decisions during this period. It must not be forgotten that this period coincides with the period when the same Justices controlled both state and federal economic and social welfare legislation with the doctrines of substantive due process and equal protection.

This period ends with President Roosevelt's court-packing plan. The President proposed to

---

6. Hammer v. Dagenhart (The Child Labor Case), 247 U.S. 251, 38 S.Ct. 529, 62 L.Ed. 1101 (1918) overruled by United States v. Darby, 312 U.S. 100, 61 S.Ct. 451, 85 L.Ed. 609 (1941).

7. Panama Refining Co. v. Ryan, 293 U.S. 388, 55 S.Ct. 241, 79 L.Ed. 446 (1935); A.L.A. Schechter Poultry Corp. v. United States, 295 U.S. 495, 55 S.Ct. 837, 79 L.Ed. 1570 (1935); cf. Sunshine Anthracite Coal Co. v. Adkins, 310 U.S. 381, 60 S.Ct. 907, 84 L.Ed. 1263 (1940).

8. The Child Labor Tax Case (Bailey v. Drexel Furniture Co.), 259 U.S. 20, 42 S.Ct. 449, 66 L.Ed. 817 (1922).

9. United States v. Butler, 297 U.S. 1, 56 S.Ct. 312, 80 L.Ed. 477 (1936).

10. See Chapter 5, infra.

11. Sonzinsky v. United States, 300 U.S. 506, 57 S.Ct. 554, 81 L.Ed. 772 (1937).

12. Norman v. Baltimore & O.R. Co., 294 U.S. 240, 55 S.Ct. 407, 79 L.Ed. 885 (1935).

13. Tennessee Electric Power Co. v. Tennessee Valley Authority, 306 U.S. 118, 59 S.Ct. 366, 83 L.Ed. 543 (1939).

alter the path of the Court by appointing a new Justice for each current Justice over 70 years of age. Congress refused to enact F.D.R.'s proposal; the Supreme Court did shift its position on these issues in 1937. Natural vacancies and the appointment process quickly solidified the new position.

§ 4.6   1888 to 1933

Two early cases from Iowa concerning the manufacture and sale of alcoholic beverages strengthened the distinction between intrastate activities and interstate commerce, although neither decision concerned the scope of federal power. In *Kidd v. Pearson*[1] the Supreme Court upheld an Iowa statute prohibiting the manufacture of intoxicating beverages within the state. The basis for this ruling was the Court's view that this activity could be regulated by the state because it was "manufacturing" and not "commerce."[2] Thus, in *Leisy v. Hardin*[3] the Supreme Court held that an Iowa ban on the importation of intoxicating beverages violated the commerce clause because it regulated an item of commerce before it became part of the general property within the state.[4]

These cases might still have led to a recognition of wide federal powers. Congress disagreed with the effect of the *Leisy* decision. A federal statute was enacted the same year that subjected liquors transported in interstate commerce to the laws of the state into which

they were shipped. The Supreme Court upheld this statute against the claim that it delegated federal powers to the states.[5] The opinion recognized that Congress had simply enacted a national commerce law with a rule of localized control. The statute did not allow any state to control another state's laws. Years later, Congress passed a statute prohibiting the transportation of such beverages into states that had laws against them. This act was also upheld by the Court.[6]

A related recognition of the congressional ability to share its power was *Field v. Clark*.[7] Here the Court upheld a tariff statute that allowed the president to suspend the free importation of some items if he found the tariffs of the origin countries "reciprocally unequal and unjust." The majority recognized that the statute did not give true legislative power to the President because it set sufficient standards to guide him. Of course, there was no Tenth Amendment concept of state interests for the majority in this case to protect.[8]

As the Supreme Court neared the turn of the century, the Justices evidenced a growing distaste for federal restrictions on business activities. Although the Court did not invalidate federal legislation, it restricted the scope of economic regulations. Thus, the Court held that the new Interstate Commerce Commission lacked statutory authority to issue subpoenas[9] or fix railroad rates.[10] These rulings

---

§ 4.6

1.   128 U.S. 1, 9 S.Ct. 6, 32 L.Ed. 346 (1888).

2.   "No distinction is more popular to the common mind, or more clearly expressed in economic and political literature, than that between manufacture and commerce." 128 U.S. at 20, 9 S.Ct. at 10.

3.   135 U.S. 100, 10 S.Ct. 681, 34 L.Ed. 128 (1890); see also Bowman v. Chicago & Northwestern Ry. Co., 125 U.S. 465, 8 S.Ct. 689, 31 L.Ed. 700 (1888).

4.   The case seemed to resurrect the interstate-original package concept expressed by Marshall in Brown v. Maryland, 25 U.S. (12 Wheat.) 419, 6 L.Ed. 678 (1827). However, the Court had held the concept inapplicable to interstate transactions in Woodruff v. Parham, 75 U.S. (8 Wall.) 123, 19 L.Ed. 382 (1869).

5.   Wilson Act, 26 Stat. 313, sustained in Wilkerson v. Rahrer, 140 U.S. 545, 11 S.Ct. 865, 35 L.Ed. 572 (1891). The Iowa statute in *Bowman* was upheld despite the Wilson Act in Rhodes v. Iowa, 170 U.S. 412, 18 S.Ct. 664, 42 L.Ed. 1088 (1898), because the Court interpreted the

statute not to subject liquor from other states to local authority until arrival in the hands of the person to whom consigned. See also Whitfield v. Ohio, 297 U.S. 431, 56 S.Ct. 532, 80 L.Ed. 778 (1936), in which the Court upheld a state law prohibiting the sale in open market of convict-made goods even if imported from other states and still in the original package.

See also § 8.5, infra.

6.   Webb–Kenyon Act, 37 Stat. 699, sustained in James Clark Distilling Co. v. Western Maryland R.R. Co., 242 U.S. 311, 37 S.Ct. 180, 61 L.Ed. 326 (1917).

7.   143 U.S. 649, 12 S.Ct. 495, 36 L.Ed. 294 (1892).

8.   U.S.Const. art. I, § 8 (Congress has power to regulate commerce with foreign nations). In a similar manner, the Court had no problem upholding the federal acts relating to the exclusion or deportation of Chinese nationals in Fong Yue Ting v. United States, 149 U.S. 698, 13 S.Ct. 1016, 37 L.Ed. 905 (1893).

9.   Counselman v. Hitchcock, 142 U.S. 547, 12 S.Ct. 195, 35 L.Ed. 1110 (1892).

10.   Cincinnati, N.O. & T.P.R. Co. v. Interstate Commerce Com'n, 162 U.S. 184, 16 S.Ct. 700, 40 L.Ed. 935

could be cured by new legislation. That was not true of the way the Court restricted the antitrust laws in *United States v. E. C. Knight Co.*[11]

In the *Knight* decision the majority held that the Sherman Antitrust Act could not be applied to a monopoly acquisition of sugar refineries. The majority found that regulation of "manufacture" was reserved to the states by the Tenth Amendment and, hence, beyond the commerce power. Nor could use of the statute be justified in this case under the theory that the monopoly might adversely affect interstate commerce because this market effect was only "indirect." The act was not struck but it was interpreted to exclude application to such manufacturing enterprises in order to avoid constitutional infirmities.[12]

The Supreme Court quickly eased its most restrictive interpretations of the antitrust acts. The Court held that the acts could be applied to agreements to fix prices by iron pipe manufacturing companies[13] and that joint control of competing parallel railways could be broken up.[14] The majority agreed that these practices had a sufficient connection to commerce. It should be noted that Justice Holmes dissented in the later case because he did not see how the Court could stop short of allowing Congress to regulate every individual activity under these theories.[15]

In 1905 Holmes created the "current" (or "stream" or "flow") of commerce metaphor. He wrote the opinion for a unanimous Court in *Swift & Co. v. United States*[16] upholding the application of the Sherman Act to an agreement of meat dealers concerning their bidding practices at the stockyards that would fix the price of meat. Although the stockyard activity took place within a single state, it was but a temporary stop in the interstate sale of cattle. It was, in Holmes' words, only an interruption in "a current of commerce among the States, and the purchase of the cattle is a part and incident of such commerce."[17] Thus, the physical relationship to interstate sales established that the activity was not one that should be reserved to a single state. It had a direct effect on commerce. However, the opinion could be interpreted in a restrictive manner because the test required tangible connections and direct relationships to commerce.

In the first few years of this century, the Court sustained the exercise of federal regulation or prohibition of items under the commerce and taxing powers. Taxes designed to prohibit sale of colored oleomargarine[18] and premiums given with tobacco[19] were upheld. In *"The Lottery Case" (Champion v. Ames),*[20] the Court upheld the Federal Lottery Act, which prohibited the interstate shipment of lottery tickets. The majority opinion by the elder Justice Harlan held that Congress had the power to prohibit as well as regulate interstate move-

---

(1896); Interstate Commerce Com'n v. Alabama Midland R. Co., 168 U.S. 144, 18 S.Ct. 45, 42 L.Ed. 414 (1897).

The authority of the Commission to pass upon the reasonableness of railroad rates was upheld in Interstate Commerce Com'n v. Brimson, 154 U.S. 447, 155 U.S. 3, 14 S.Ct. 1125, 15 S.Ct. 19, 38 L.Ed. 1047, 39 L.Ed. 49 (1894), as necessary and proper for the enforcement of the commerce power.

The powers of the Commission today are defined by the Transportation Acts (41 Stat. 474 and 54 Stat. 898), which "provide a completely integrated interstate regulatory system over motor, railroad, and water carriers." United States v. Pennsylvania R.R., 323 U.S. 612, 618–19, 65 S.Ct. 471, 475, 89 L.Ed. 499, 507–08 (1945).

11. (Sugar Trust Case), 156 U.S. 1, 15 S.Ct. 249, 39 L.Ed. 325 (1895).

12. See Hopkins v. United States, 171 U.S. 578, 19 S.Ct. 40, 43 L.Ed. 290 (1898); Anderson v. United States, 171 U.S. 604, 19 S.Ct. 50, 43 L.Ed. 300 (1898).

13. Addyston Pipe & Steel Co. v. United States, 175 U.S. 211, 20 S.Ct. 96, 44 L.Ed. 136 (1899).

14. Northern Securities Co. v. United States, 193 U.S. 197, 24 S.Ct. 436, 48 L.Ed. 679 (1904); See also United States v. Trans–Missouri Freight Ass'n, 166 U.S. 290, 17 S.Ct. 540, 41 L.Ed. 1007 (1897); United States v. Joint Traffic Ass'n, 171 U.S. 505, 19 S.Ct. 25, 43 L.Ed. 259 (1898).

15. Northern Securities Co. v. United States, 193 U.S. 197, 400, 24 S.Ct. 436, 468, 48 L.Ed. 679 (1904) (Holmes, J., dissenting).

16. 196 U.S. 375, 25 S.Ct. 276, 49 L.Ed. 518 (1905).

17. 196 U.S. at 398–99, 25 S.Ct. at 280.

18. In re Kollock, 165 U.S. 526, 17 S.Ct. 444, 41 L.Ed. 813 (1897).

19. Felsenheld v. United States, 186 U.S. 126, 22 S.Ct. 740, 46 L.Ed. 1085 (1902).

20. 188 U.S. 321, 23 S.Ct. 321, 47 L.Ed. 492 (1903).

ment or transportation. But it was clear that the majority agreed that lottery tickets were an "evil."[21] The Justices did not hold that Congress could exercise its regulatory power with a totally free hand.

The year 1905 marks the point at which a majority of the Justices had enough of what they considered to be unjustified tampering with the economic and social order.[22] In the next half dozen years these Justices struck down a wide variety of state and federal laws. The Supreme Court held invalid as beyond the commerce power the regulation of sales of intoxicants to Indians,[23] the quarantine of diseased animals,[24] imposition of liability on employers for employee injuries,[25] and the prohibition of harboring alien women.[26]

The Justices' special wrath was reserved for laws that interfered with employer-employee relationships. In 1905, the Court had stricken state maximum hour legislation under the due process clause in *Lochner v. People of New York*.[27] A similar fate awaited any employment regulation that the Justices felt was an unreasonable interference with the free market system.[28] In 1908, the Supreme Court for the first

time invalidated a federal statute solely on the basis of substantive due process. The Justices struck down a statute prohibiting railroads from firing employees for union membership.[29] When combined with a similar ruling concerning state regulations of employment contracts,[30] "yellow dog" (nonunion) contracts were constitutionally insulated from reform movements.

In 1908, the Court also began to apply the antitrust acts to labor[31] starting a series of cases in which the courts moved to stop union activities.[32] These cases resulted in the Norris–LaGuardia Act restriction of federal court jurisdiction in relation to such matters.[33] At the same time the Supreme Court restricted the impact of the antitrust laws on business when it held that only "unreasonable" restraints on trade were illegal.[34]

Beginning in 1911, the Supreme Court did evidence a greater tolerance for federal commercial regulation that the majority did not regard as unjustified regulations of labor. In the next several years the Court upheld the establishment of safety standards and regula-

---

21. 188 U.S. at 354, 23 S.Ct. at 326.

In the earlier case of Ex parte Rapier, 143 U.S. 110, 12 S.Ct. 374, 36 L.Ed. 93 (1892), the Court upheld an act excluding lottery tickets from the mails on the proposition that Congress had the power to refuse to allow facilities furnished by it to be used for distribution of matter deemed by Congress to be injurious to public morals.

22. In addition to the cases we have already examined, the Court had invalidated a federal income tax in Pollock v. Farmers' Loan & Trust Co., 157 U.S. 429, 15 S.Ct. 673, 39 L.Ed. 759 (1895). This decision resulted in the passage of the Sixteenth Amendment.

23. Matter of Heff, 197 U.S. 488, 25 S.Ct. 506, 49 L.Ed. 848 (1905), overruled in United States v. Nice, 241 U.S. 591, 36 S.Ct. 696, 60 L.Ed. 1192 (1916).

24. Illinois Central R. Co. v. McKendree, 203 U.S. 514, 27 S.Ct. 153, 51 L.Ed. 298 (1906).

25. The Employer's Liability Cases, 207 U.S. 463, 28 S.Ct. 141, 52 L.Ed. 297 (1908).

26. Keller v. United States, 213 U.S. 138, 29 S.Ct. 470, 53 L.Ed. 737 (1909).

27. 198 U.S. 45, 25 S.Ct. 539, 49 L.Ed. 937 (1905). See generally § 15.3, infra.

28. See, e.g., Hammer v. Dagenhart, 247 U.S. 251, 38 S.Ct. 529, 62 L.Ed. 1101 (1918) (child labor); Bailey v. Drexel Furniture Co., 259 U.S. 20, 42 S.Ct. 449, 66 L.Ed. 817 (1922) (child labor); Adkins v. Children's Hosp., 261 U.S. 525, 43 S.Ct. 394, 67 L.Ed. 785 (1923) (minimum

wage for women invalidated); Railroad Retirement Bd. v. Alton R. Co., 295 U.S. 330, 55 S.Ct. 758, 79 L.Ed. 1468 (1935) (pension for retired railroad workers); Southern Pac. Co. v. Jensen, 244 U.S. 205, 37 S.Ct. 524, 61 L.Ed. 1086 (1917) (workman's compensation).

29. Adair v. United States, 208 U.S. 161, 28 S.Ct. 277, 52 L.Ed. 436 (1908).

30. Coppage v. Kansas, 236 U.S. 1, 35 S.Ct. 240, 59 L.Ed. 441 (1915). But see Wilson v. New, 243 U.S. 332, 37 S.Ct. 298, 61 L.Ed. 755 (1917), in which the Court upheld a Congressional settlement of a threatened rail strike through wage and hour concessions in view of the existing national emergency.

31. Loewe v. Lawlor (The Danbury Hatters Case), 208 U.S. 274, 28 S.Ct. 301, 52 L.Ed. 488 (1908).

32. See, e.g. Duplex Printing Press Co. v. Deering, 254 U.S. 443, 41 S.Ct. 172, 65 L.Ed. 349 (1921) (printing); Coronado Coal Co. v. United Mine Workers, 268 U.S. 295, 45 S.Ct. 551, 69 L.Ed. 963 (1925) (mining); United States v. Brims, 272 U.S. 549, 47 S.Ct. 169, 71 L.Ed. 403 (1926) (carpenters); Bedford Cut Stone Co. v. Journeyman Stone Cutters' Ass'n, 274 U.S. 37, 47 S.Ct. 522, 71 L.Ed. 916 (1927) (stone cutters).

33. 29 U.S.C.A. §§ 101–115, limiting judicial power to issue injunctions; upheld in Lauf v. E. G. Shinner & Co., 303 U.S. 323, 58 S.Ct. 578, 82 L.Ed. 872 (1938).

34. United States v. E. C. Knight Co. (The Sugar Trust Case), 156 U.S. 1, 15 S.Ct. 249, 39 L.Ed. 325 (1895).

tion of hours for employees of railroads.[35] The Court also approved a restricted form of an employer's liability statute.[36]

After 1911, the Court sustained congressional actions that regulated the nature of items that could be shipped in interstate commerce in order to achieve "police power" ends. The Court upheld prohibition of impure or adulterated food and drugs[37] as well as retail labeling requirements for items that traveled through interstate commerce.[38] The Court reversed an earlier decision and held that Congress could restrict the sale of intoxicating beverages to Indians.[39] Additionally, the Court upheld the Mann Act, which prohibited the transportation of women across state lines for immoral purposes.[40] In 1918, however, the Court would once again step in to restrict labor regulation with which the Justices disagreed.

In *Hammer v. Dagenhart*[41] *("The Child Labor Case"),* the Court, by a five to four vote, invalidated a federal statute that prohibited the interstate shipment of goods coming from a mining or manufacturing establishment that employed children under certain ages.[42] The majority found the act to exceed the commerce power because it regulated the conditions of production. This subject matter was reserved for state regulation by the Tenth Amendment.

The government justified the law as necessary to eliminate unfair competition against products from states that prohibited child labor. The majority of the Supreme Court found that Congress had no power to equalize market conditions that were not a part of interstate commerce. The majority attempted to distinguish the earlier cases that allowed Con-

gress to prohibit or set the terms of interstate transportation of products. The opinion stated that the earlier prohibitions had all related to the elimination of a harmful item or commercial evil, but in the majority's view, there was nothing harmful about products made by children.

Writing for the dissenters, Holmes expounded an "embargo theory" of congressional power over the interstate transportation of people or products.[43] Holmes stated that the child labor regulation was clearly the regulation of commerce among the states and that the Court was wrong to invalidate it because of its effect or economic basis. He would not interpret the power of Congress in terms of its effect on the states. Thus, Congress could set any terms for the transport of items between the states.

In evaluating Holmes' theory, one must remember that he was not addressing a situation where the congressional prohibition of transport infringed a more specific guarantee of the Bill of Rights, such as the First Amendment. There is no indication that Holmes would have exempted the commerce power from more specific constitutional restraints. Rather, Holmes did not recognize the Tenth Amendment as a general limitation on the exercise of congressional control of commerce.

Congress sought to circumvent the *Child Labor* decision by levying an excise tax on anyone who employed child labor under the terms proscribed in the earlier regulation. The only difference between the two statutes was that this tax applied to businesses whether or

35. Baltimore & Ohio R. v. Interstate Commerce Com'n, 221 U.S. 612, 31 S.Ct. 621, 55 L.Ed. 878 (1911).

36. In re Second Employers' Liability Cases, 223 U.S. 1, 32 S.Ct. 169, 56 L.Ed. 327 (1912).

37. Hipolite Egg Co. v. United States, 220 U.S. 45, 31 S.Ct. 364, 55 L.Ed. 364 (1911).

38. McDermott v. Wisconsin, 228 U.S. 115, 33 S.Ct. 431, 57 L.Ed. 754 (1913); United States v. Sullivan, 332 U.S. 689, 68 S.Ct. 331, 92 L.Ed. 297 (1948).

39. United States v. Nice, 241 U.S. 591, 36 S.Ct. 696, 60 L.Ed. 1192 (1916), overruling Matter of Heff, 197 U.S. 488, 25 S.Ct. 506, 49 L.Ed. 848 (1905).

40. Hoke v. United States, 227 U.S. 308, 33 S.Ct. 281, 57 L.Ed. 523 (1913); also applied to noncommercial vice, Caminetti v. United States, 242 U.S. 470, 37 S.Ct. 192, 61

L.Ed. 442 (1917); Cleveland v. United States, 329 U.S. 14, 67 S.Ct. 13, 91 L.Ed. 12 (1946), rehearing denied 329 U.S. 830, 67 S.Ct. 361, 91 L.Ed. 704 (1946) (transportation of plural wives across state line by Mormon).

41. 247 U.S. 251, 38 S.Ct. 529, 62 L.Ed. 1101 (1918).

42. The statute required that for thirty days prior to the production, no child under sixteen be employed in a mine and no child under fourteen be employed in a manufacturing establishment. Additionally, it set maximum hours and days of work for children between fourteen and sixteen who were employed in factories.

43. 247 U.S. at 278, 38 S.Ct. at 533 (dissent).

not they shipped the goods in interstate commerce. In *The Child Labor Tax Case*,[44] the Court held that this tax was not a true tax but only a "penalty" for violation of a commercial regulation. As such, it was invalid under the prior decision because it exceeded the power of Congress and invaded the areas reserved for control by the states. The Court distinguished earlier cases that had allowed prohibitory taxes. "Incidental" regulatory motives could be tolerated, but there was some point "in the extension of the penalizing features of the so-called tax when it loses its character as such and becomes a mere penalty, with the characteristics of legislation and punishment."[45]

The *Child Labor Tax Case* cannot be distinguished in terms of its penalty or regulatory features from other prohibitory taxes that the Court had earlier upheld. The Court had upheld such taxes on tobacco premiums[46] and colored oleomargarine.[47] Only three years before the child labor decision, the Court upheld the Narcotic Drug Act tax.[48] That act required those who dispensed certain drugs to pay a $1 tax and to comply with very detailed regulations concerning the dispensation of drugs. The Court held that, as long as there was any relation to revenue, the tax could be upheld.

The real distinction between these cases and the *Child Labor Tax Case* was simply Congress' obvious attempt to circumvent the earlier child labor ruling. Once the Court had stricken the child labor regulations, it could

not uphold what it saw as a subversion of its ruling on the proper scope of federal and state authority. Even Holmes joined in the invalidation of this "tax."[49]

In a companion decision, the Court invalidated a tax on grain "futures" contracts.[50] The act levied a tax on grain, but it exempted contracts made through a board of trade whose practices had been approved by the Secretary of Agriculture. The Court quickly dispensed with this tax, holding that it was a penalty and a regulation that could not fit under the taxing power. However, this subject matter was not totally beyond the federal power; the next year the Supreme Court upheld the Grain Futures Act, which directly regulated these subjects.[51] The tax-penalty distinction ended after these cases.[52]

The Court also upheld a series of new federal commercial regulations. In *Stafford v. Wallace*[53] the Court found that Congress could subject meat stockyard dealers and commission men to regulation by the Secretary of Agriculture. The opinion by Chief Justice Taft was notable because it not only resurrected Holmes' current of commerce theory[54] but also implied that activities that had an economic effect on commerce could be regulated.[55] But the Court did not follow up on this concept until 1937.

Between 1922 and 1933, the Supreme Court did uphold several more federal commercial

44. (Bailey v. Drexel Furniture Co.), 259 U.S. 20, 42 S.Ct. 449, 66 L.Ed. 817 (1922).

45. 259 U.S. at 38, 42 S.Ct. at 451.

46. Felsenheld v. United States, 186 U.S. 126, 22 S.Ct. 740, 46 L.Ed. 1085 (1902).

47. In re Kollock, 165 U.S. 526, 17 S.Ct. 444, 41 L.Ed. 813 (1897).

48. United States v. Doremus, 249 U.S. 86, 39 S.Ct. 214, 63 L.Ed. 493 (1919).

49. Bailey v. Drexel Furniture Co., 259 U.S. 20, 42 S.Ct. 449, 66 L.Ed. 817 (1922). See, A. Bickel, The Unpublished Opinions of Mr. Justice Brandeis 3–4, 18–19 (1957).

50. Hill v. Wallace, 259 U.S. 44, 42 S.Ct. 453, 66 L.Ed. 822 (1922).

51. Chicago Bd. of Trade v. Olsen, 262 U.S. 1, 43 S.Ct. 470, 67 L.Ed. 839 (1923).

52. See United States v. Sanchez, 340 U.S. 42, 71 S.Ct. 108, 95 L.Ed. 47 (1950). See also United States v. Kahri-

ger, 345 U.S. 22, 73 S.Ct. 510, 97 L.Ed. 754 (1953), rehearing denied 345 U.S. 931, 73 S.Ct. 778, 97 L.Ed. 1360 (1953). The Supreme Court, since 1937, has not invalidated a federal statute on the basis that the statute was a "penalty" labeled a "tax," so long as the federal government had the power to regulate the penalized activity under the commerce clause. Nevertheless, the distinction between regulatory actions and penalties may still be of importance in the interpretation of federal statutes. Courts sometimes need to distinguish whether a state or federal "tax" is a civil regulation or a criminal penalty, for purposes of deciding whether the individual charged with violating the tax law is entitled to the procedural protections guaranteed to defendants in criminal cases. See § 13.9(a) of this Treatise, regarding the distinction between civil and criminal cases.

53. 258 U.S. 495, 42 S.Ct. 397, 66 L.Ed. 735 (1922).

54. See also Lemke v. Farmers' Grain Co., 258 U.S. 50, 42 S.Ct. 244, 66 L.Ed. 458 (1922); Minnesota v. Blasius, 290 U.S. 1, 54 S.Ct. 34, 78 L.Ed. 131 (1933).

55. 258 U.S. at 515–16, 42 S.Ct. at 401–02.

regulations. The period ended on a hopeful note as the Court upheld the regulation of railroad labor relations and railway workers unions because disruption in this field could affect interstate commerce.[56] The Court had previously upheld federal regulation of intrastate railroads because the Justices agreed that local railroad activities and rates had a close and substantial effect on interstate traffic.[57]

As we turn to the period of the New Deal, we can see several distinct lines of decisions regarding the commerce power. Under the *Shreveport Rate Case*,[58] Congress could regulate activities that had an economic effect on commerce among the states. The Court, however, did not apply this theory beyond the railroad regulation cases. The Court had also allowed the regulation of single-state activities that were a part of the stream or current of commerce, but this theory required a tangible connection of the activity to interstate commerce. The Court would allow other regulation of commerce only if the subject matter had a "direct" effect on interstate commercial transactions.

At the root of all these distinctions was the Court's use of the Tenth Amendment to reserve some subjects for state authority and its view that the federal power excepted those subjects. Even when Congress regulated the passage of goods or persons between states, the Court might block the regulation of these subjects under the Tenth Amendment.

§ 4.7   1933–36: The New Deal Crisis

The election of 1932 created a public mandate for a new approach to ending the economic depression that beset the country. Franklin D. Roosevelt had been elected president on the promise of a "new deal" and of immediate action. Congress cooperated by passing a wide variety of administrative proposals to alter economic conditions. However, the decisions of the Supreme Court over the previous fifty years indicated that the third branch of government might not acquiesce in the new federal approaches to economic problems.[1] From 1933 to 1937 the Court vacillated in the degree to which it controlled state economic regulations.[2] A majority of the Justices, however, continued to exercise strict control over the scope of federal legislation.

"Excessive Delegation" of Legislative Authority. In the first decision on New Deal legislation, the Court for the first time in history struck down a statute as an excessive delegation of legislative power to the executive branch. The National Industrial Recovery Act of 1933[3] [NIRA] had been designed to regulate competitive practices in hopes of increasing prices and improving the conditions of labor. The president was authorized by the Act to establish and enforce "codes of fair competition" for trades or industries. These codes were to be approved by industrial organizations or trade associations in each industry before the president adopted them. The Act also contained a specific provision allowing the president to prohibit the transportation of petroleum products produced in violation of state statutes, so-called "hot" oil.

In *Panama Refining Co. v. Ryan*,[4] the Supreme Court held that the Act was an excessive delegation of the legislative power to the executive because it did not set any standards for when the president should exercise his

56. Texas & New Orleans R. Co. v. Brotherhood of Ry. & S. S. Clerks, 281 U.S. 548, 50 S.Ct. 427, 74 L.Ed. 1034 (1930), Virginian Ry. Co. v. System Fed'n No. 40, 300 U.S. 515, 57 S.Ct. 592, 81 L.Ed. 789 (1937) (extending application of the Railway Labor Act to "back shop" employees repairing locomotives and cars).

57. The Shreveport Rate Case (Houston E. & W. Texas Ry. Co. v. United States), 234 U.S. 342, 34 S.Ct. 833, 58 L.Ed. 1341 (1914); Southern Ry. Co. v. United States, 222 U.S. 20, 32 S.Ct. 2, 56 L.Ed. 72 (1911); Wisconsin R.R. Com'n v. Chicago, B. & Q. R.R., 257 U.S. 563, 42 S.Ct. 232, 66 L.Ed. 371 (1922).

58. 234 U.S. 342, 34 S.Ct. 833, 58 L.Ed. 1341 (1914).

§ 4.7

1. See Stern, The Commerce Clause and the National Economy, 1933–1946, 59 Harv.L.Rev. 645 (1946).

2. See., e.g., Nebbia v. New York, 291 U.S. 502, 54 S.Ct. 505, 78 L.Ed. 940 (1934) (upholding price control on milk); Baldwin v. G. A. F. Seelig, Inc., 294 U.S. 511, 55 S.Ct. 497, 79 L.Ed. 1032 (1935) (invalidating certain provisions of law upheld in *Nebbia* because they touched interstate commerce).

3. 48 Stat. 195.

4. 293 U.S. 388, 55 S.Ct. 241, 79 L.Ed. 446 (1935).

discretionary power to prohibit shipment of these products. The Court did not reach the validity of the basic portion of the Act, the trade codes, at this time. But while the particular defect in this statute was easily remedied by legislative prohibition of all interstate shipments of "hot" oil,[5] the majority's use of the new delegation concept indicated that much New Deal legislation might meet with constitutional disapproval.

Restriction of the Commerce Power. In *Railroad Retirement Board v. Alton R. Co.,*[6] the Court, by a five to four vote, held that the Railroad Retirement Act of 1934 exceeded the commerce power. The Act required and regulated pension systems for railroad employees. The majority opinion distinguished earlier cases upholding the regulations of railroad employment conditions because those regulations related to safety or efficiency aspects of interstate commerce. Here the majority found the Act to be designed only to help "the social welfare of the worker, and therefore remote from any regulation of commerce."[7] The dissenting Justices would have accepted the congressional decision that there was a relationship between the financial well-being and morale of railroad employees and commerce,[8] but this relationship was not a sufficiently direct one in the view of the majority.

The NIRA was next declared to be invalid, this time by a unanimous vote. Pursuant to the code provisions already mentioned, a code of competition set for poultry dealers in and near New York City regulated the conditions and price of labor. In the "sick chicken cases," *A.L.A. Schechter Poultry Corp. v. United States,*[9] the Court invalidated the Act for two reasons: first, allowing the President to approve and adopt the trade codes constituted an excessive and unconstitutional delegation of power; and second, the act exceeded the scope of the federal commerce power.

The opinion was troublesome more for what it said than for what it did. The NIRA had proved to be an administrative disaster and the executive branch had already decided to allow the Act to expire without seeking its renewal.[10] The striking of the statute on a delegation theory also proved to be little problem because promulgating some standards could easily be done in legislation. Indeed the delegation concept died out after these cases and the Court has never again invalidated congressional actions on this ground.

However, the majority's discussion of the commerce power, in *Schechter Poultry*, showed the Court ready to strike down federal attempts to deal with the national problems of the 1930's. The majority opinion by Chief Justice Hughes found that the employment practices of a poultry business did not have a sufficiently "direct" connection to interstate commerce. The wages that employees engaged in "internal commerce" were paid or the hours they were required to work were subjects reserved for regulation by the States. The majority opinion flatly refused to find, in the national economic crisis, a basis for a federal power to deal with "internal" matters that only "indirectly" affected commerce.[11] Justices Cardozo and Stone, who usually dissented in such cases, concurred in the judgment, although they rejected the formal "directness" test.[12]

Any continuing hope that the Court would recognize a federal power to counteract the Depression came to an end in 1936.[13] In two

---

5. Hot Oil Act, 49 Stat. 30.

6. 295 U.S. 330, 55 S.Ct. 758, 79 L.Ed. 1468 (1935).

7. 295 U.S. at 368, 55 S.Ct. at 771. But see Railroad Retirement Bd. v. Duquesne Warehouse Co., 326 U.S. 446, 66 S.Ct. 238, 90 L.Ed. 192 (1946), wherein constitutionality of slightly different pension plan is apparently taken for granted.

8. 295 U.S. at 379, 55 S.Ct. at 775 (dissent).

9. 295 U.S. 495, 55 S.Ct. 837, 79 L.Ed. 1570 (1935). For a discussion of the *Schechter* opinion's weaknesses, see Stern, supra note 1 at 662.

10. Stern, supra note 1.

11. A.L.A. Schechter Poultry Corp. v. United States, 295 U.S. 495, 548, 55 S.Ct. 837, 851, 79 L.Ed. 1570 (1935).

12. 295 U.S. at 554, 55 S.Ct. at 853 (Cardozo, J., concurring).

13. United States v. Butler, 297 U.S. 1, 56 S.Ct. 312, 80 L.Ed. 477 (1936); Carter v. Carter Coal, 298 U.S. 238, 56 S.Ct. 855, 80 L.Ed. 1160 (1936). The Court also struck down as a penalty a federal tax on liquor dealers operating in states where selling liquor was illegal, United States v. Constantine, 296 U.S. 287, 56 S.Ct. 223, 80 L.Ed. 233 (1935).

decisions the majority made it clear that they would interpret federal powers in terms of the Tenth Amendment and reserve certain types of regulations as the exclusive province of the states.

In *United States v. Butler*[14] the Court invalidated the Agricultural Adjustment Act of 1933. The Act attempted to end depressed farm prices by authorizing the Secretary of Agriculture to make payments to farmers who agreed to reduce their acreage or production. The fund for the payments came from taxes on the processors of the commodities that were subject to these regulatory agreements. The government sought to defend the Act both as a tax and as a part of its power to spend for the "general welfare" of the country.

The majority opinion found it unnecessary to decide the precise scope of the taxing or spending powers because it found the Act to be in violation of the Tenth Amendment, regardless of the enumerated power on which it was arguably based. The Court found that the setting of the quantity and quality of agricultural production was a matter reserved to the state governments and, therefore, outside any of the enumerated powers of Article I. Nor could the government offer payments in return for compliance with these restrictions because that would constitute the purchase of submission to federal regulation of a subject reserved to the states.[15]

The most important decision of this period came in *Carter v. Carter Coal Co.*[16] when the Court struck down the Bituminous Coal Conservation Act of 1935. Under the Act, all coal producers were required to follow the maximum hour labor terms negotiated between miners and the producers of more than two-thirds of the annual national tonnage production for the preceding calendar year.[17] The minimum wages of employees were fixed in a similar manner, and there was a tax on the coal producers who did not comply with these restrictions. The Act also regulated coal prices, but the majority found it unnecessary to discuss this provision because it found the provision inseparable from the wage and hour requirements that it held invalid.

The majority held that the setting of requirements by private producers was an unconstitutional delegation of legislative power to private persons. This Act went beyond the earlier acts that had been stricken as improper delegations because it allowed competitors to set the regulations for other members of the industry. However, the Court treated the delegation point and instead focused on the national commerce power.

The majority opinion found that federal regulation of the wages and hours of employees involved in mining and production was outside the commerce power. The majority followed now typical Tenth Amendment analysis by holding that the relationships between employers and employees in all production occupations "is a purely local activity."[18] As such, the subject matter was reserved for the exclusive jurisdiction of the states unless it had a "direct" effect on interstate commerce. The majority believed that employment relationships had only an indirect effect on interstate commerce. The majority was simply unconvinced that labor relations had such a close relationship to interstate commerce that they should be removed from those subject matters reserved for the exercise of state power.

The *Carter* opinion showed that the Court was going to actively enforce its view of the Tenth Amendment against the national attempts to deal with the economic depression. The federal government would be precluded from controlling employer-employee relationships unless the Court changed its position.

Regulations of Some Local Activities Upheld. Even during this period the Court did not restrict federal power when there was no legitimate *state* interest at stake. Thus, the Court upheld federal legislation abrogating the gold clauses in contracts as a reasonable mea-

14. 297 U.S. 1, 56 S.Ct. 312, 80 L.Ed. 477 (1936).

15. 297 U.S. at 73, 56 S.Ct. at 322.

16. 298 U.S. 238, 56 S.Ct. 855, 80 L.Ed. 1160 (1936).

17. 298 U.S. at 283–84, 56 S.Ct. at 860–61; quoting 49 Stat. 991, Sec. 4, Part III, Subdiv. (g).

18. 298 U.S. at 304, 56 S.Ct. at 870.

sure to regulate the national currency.[19] The states had no Tenth Amendment interest in the regulation of the monetary system, so the Court had little problem in upholding this legislation. Similarly the Court upheld the establishment of a federal dam and the sale of hydroelectric power from that facility.[20] The Court was not going to prevent the Federal Government from competing with private businesses: the majority found no Tenth Amendment violation by the establishment of such a federal facility. Furthermore, the Court upheld a tax on firearms that was clearly designed to be a regulation of transactions in such items.[21] But the majority here found no constitutionally significant interest of either state governments or private persons in the absence of federal taxes or regulations concerning firearms and, therefore, the majority had no problem upholding this "tax." And in January of 1937, the Court upheld a congressional statute prohibiting the transportation of articles made by convict labor into states that had prohibited the sale of such goods.[22] In so doing, the Court recognized a broad power of Congress to set the terms of interstate transactions if it did not transgress any reserved powers of the states.

The Court, however, was not headed on a course of deference to legislative judgments concerning economic and social relationships. The country received a vivid reminder of this shortly after the *Carter* decision when the Court held that state laws establishing minimum wages for women violated the due process clause of the Fourteenth Amendment.[23] Despite the Court's favorable rulings on legislation whose purpose it thought was within the proper sphere of federal objectives, the majority had no intention of permitting legislation to alter what it considered to be the

constitutionally protected provinces of either state government or private business.

The Court Packing Plan. President Roosevelt was not one to accept what he saw as the Court's destruction of his economic and social programs. He did not make the Supreme Court rulings an issue during the 1936 campaign, but his overwhelming victory in that election constituted a mandate to pursue with even greater vigor his previous course of reform. In February of 1937 President Roosevelt unveiled his now famous "Court Packing Plan." The President asked for legislative authority to appoint an additional federal judge for each judge who was 70 years of age and had served on a court for at least ten years. There would be a maximum of 50 judges who might be appointed under the proposed legislation, with a total maximum of fifteen members on the Supreme Court of the United States. Had this plan been approved, there would actually have been fifteen Justices on the Court because six Justices were over 70 years of age in 1937.

The plan produced one of the greatest political controversies of the century.[24] The President and the staunch supporters of the New Deal legislation fought for the bill as a necessary way to allow social reforms and end the Depression. But the Court was ably defended by many persons, not the least of whom was Chief Justice Charles Evans Hughes. Indeed, the fight over the Court Packing plan helped bring into being the alliance between Republican members of Congress and conservative Democratic representatives from Southern states.

The plan was eventually defeated, in large measure because the Justices reformed themselves. Beginning in the spring of 1937 the

19. Norman v. Baltimore & O. Ry. Co., 294 U.S. 240, 55 S.Ct. 407, 79 L.Ed. 885 (1935). Although the Supreme Court held that Congress could abrogate gold clauses in private contracts, it held that the Congress could not constitutionally enact legislation that would terminate the express contractual obligation of the federal government to repay with gold rather than currency the holders of previously issued bonds. Perry v. United States, 294 U.S. 330, 55 S.Ct. 432, 79 L.Ed. 912 (1935).

20. Tennessee Electric Power Co. v. Tennessee Valley Authority, 306 U.S. 118, 59 S.Ct. 366, 83 L.Ed. 543 (1939).

21. Sonzinsky v. United States, 300 U.S. 506, 57 S.Ct. 554, 81 L.Ed. 772 (1937).

22. Kentucky Whip & Collar Co. v. Illinois Central R. Co., 299 U.S. 334, 57 S.Ct. 277, 81 L.Ed. 270 (1937).

23. Morehead v. People of New York ex rel. Tipaldo, 298 U.S. 587, 56 S.Ct. 918, 80 L.Ed. 1347 (1936).

24. See § 2.6, supra, for further discussion of the Court Packing plan.

Court began to defer to the other branches of government in matters of economics and social welfare.[25] No longer would the Court use substantive due process and equal protection to overturn laws that interfered with traditional views of economic freedom. The Court was willing to follow Chief Justice Marshall's advice and interpret the commerce clause as a plenary power without first considering what subject matters the Justices would wish reserved for state authority under the Tenth Amendment. While the full impact of the majority's change of position could not be appreciated for several years, it was immediately apparent that the Court would no longer threaten economic reforms.

Did the Court switch under pressure from President Roosevelt or because of realization of its proper role in reviewing economic and social legislation? It is easy to assume that the switch was a product of the Court Packing plan, but it must be remembered that the same period of time saw worsening of national economic conditions, including the outbreak of violent labor disputes. For whatever reasons, Justice Roberts began to vote more consistently to uphold both state and federal legislation. This switch was enough to form a new majority on the Court. In the next four years, President Roosevelt was able to appoint seven new Justices, all of whom were committed to the deferential approach towards federal commercial legislation.

§ 4.8   1937 to Present: Summary

The Supreme Court today interprets the commerce clause as a broad grant of power. The Tenth Amendment is no longer viewed as a reservation of certain subjects for state regulation. Once the Justices began to define the commerce power as an independent grant of

power rather than in terms of the Tenth Amendment, the production-commerce and direct-indirect distinctions soon passed away. The Court now will defer to the legislature's choice of economic rationale; the possible economic impact of an activity on commerce among the states will bring it within this power. Thus the old concepts of physical connection to commerce and the "current of commerce" theories have been discarded as inappropriate judicial restrictions on the commerce power. The Court has finally returned to Marshall's definition of commerce among the states as that which concerns more states than one. The Justices will defer to the legislative choices in this area and uphold laws if there is a rational basis upon which Congress could find a reasonable relation between its regulation and commerce.

Modern Commerce Power Tests. There are three ways that an item, person, or activity may come under the federal commerce power. First, Congress can set the regulations, conditions, or prohibitions regarding the permissibility of interstate travel or shipments if the law does not contravene a specific constitutional guarantee.[1] Second, the federal government may also regulate any activity, including "single state" activities, if the activity has a close and substantial relationship to, or effect on, commerce.[2] This relationship or effect may be based on economic relationships or economic impact. The activity may be subject to congressional power where it is one of a generic type of activities that have a cumulative effect on commerce. Third, Congress may regulate single-state activities that otherwise have no effect on commerce if the regulation is "necessary and proper" to regulating commerce or effectuating regulations relating to commerce.

25. West Coast Hotel Co. v. Parrish, 300 U.S. 379, 57 S.Ct. 578, 81 L.Ed. 703 (1937); NLRB v. Jones and Laughlin Steel Corp., 301 U.S. 1, 57 S.Ct. 615, 81 L.Ed. 893 (1937).

§ 4.8

1. For citations to many more of the Supreme Court's decisions upholding modern federal commerce power legislation in a wide variety of contexts, see the footnotes to 1 R. Rotunda & J. Nowak, Treatise on Constitutional Law: § 4.8 (3rd ed.1999, with annual supplements).

2. Clearly, the transmission of information interstate is a form of commerce. See, e.g., Federal Radio Com'n v. Nelson Bros. Bond & Mortgage Co., 289 U.S. 266, 53 S.Ct. 627, 77 L.Ed. 1166 (1933) (radio); Fisher's Blend Station v. Tax Com'n, 297 U.S. 650, 56 S.Ct. 608, 80 L.Ed. 956 (1936); New Jersey Bell Tel. Co. v. State Bd. of Taxes and Assessment, 280 U.S. 338, 50 S.Ct. 111, 74 L.Ed. 463 (1930) (telephone).

For a half-century the Court described the scope of the federal commerce power in terms of the standards set forth in the previous paragraph. Then, in 1995, the Supreme Court defined the scope of federal commerce clause power in a slightly different manner. In *United States v. Lopez*,[3] the Justices, by a five to four vote, invalidated a federal law that prohibited any person from carrying a firearm near any school by ruling that this law did not fall within the federal commerce power. Chief Justice Rehnquist, writing for the majority, described the scope of federal commerce powers as follows:

"We have identified three broad categories of activity that Congress may regulate under its commerce power ... First, Congress may regulate the use of the channels of interstate commerce ... Second, Congress is empowered to regulate and protect the instrumentalities of interstate commerce, or persons or things in interstate commerce, even though the threat may come only from intrastate activities ... Finally, Congress' commerce authority includes the power to regulate those activities having a substantial relation to interstate commerce ... i.e., those activities that substantially affect interstate commerce."[4]

The *Lopez* majority opinion divided the traditional first commerce clause standard (allowing Congress to regulate anything or anyone that crosses a state line) into two standards. Under the first standard, Congress can regulate the channels of interstate commerce. Under the second standard, Congress can regulate the instrumentalities of commerce or people or products that travel in interstate commerce.

The third commerce clause standard set forth in *Lopez* (regarding the regulation of single state activities that have a substantial effect on interstate commerce) is similar to the language of prior cases concerning the regulation of intrastate activities that have a close and substantial relationship to, or effect, on commerce.

Lopez modified the standard for determining the scope of the federal commerce power to regulate intrastate activity in two ways that may, or may not, prove to be important in the future. First, the majority ruled that Congress can regulate only single state activities that as a class have a *substantial* effect on interstate commerce.[5] Prior to *Lopez,* the opinions of the Supreme Court between 1937 and 1994 could have been read to allow Congress to regulate a class of intrastate activities that had only an insignificant, or trivial, effect on interstate commerce. Second, the *Lopez* majority found that the federal judiciary would give less deference to the congressional decision to regulate single state activity if the activity was not commercial in nature.[6] After *Lopez,* the judiciary should independently review the factual basis for determining the regulated single state activity had a substantial effect on interstate commerce, if the regulated activity is not commercial in nature.[7]

The majority in *Lopez* did not overturn any prior case. In fact, it cited with approval *Perez*

3. United States v. Lopez, 514 U.S. 549, 115 S.Ct. 1624, 131 L.Ed.2d 626 (1995). Justices Kennedy, O'Connor, and Thomas joined the majority opinion by Chief Justice Rehnquist and also filed concurring opinions. 514 U.S. at 567, 115 S.Ct. at 1634 (Kennedy, J., joined by O'Connor, J., concurring in the judgment and opinion of the Court); 514 U.S. at 583, 115 S.Ct. at 1642 (Thomas, J., concurring). Justices Stevens, Souter, Ginsburg and Breyer dissented in *Lopez,* 514 U.S. at 602, 115 S.Ct. at 1651 (Stevens, J., dissenting); 514 U.S. at 602, 115 S.Ct. at 1651 (Souter, J., dissenting); 514 U.S. at 614, 115 S.Ct. at 1657 (Breyer, J., joined by Stevens, Souter, and Ginsburg, JJ., dissenting).

4. United States v. Lopez, 514 U.S. 549, 557–59, 115 S.Ct. 1624, 1629–30, 131 L.Ed.2d 626 (1995).

5. 514 U.S. at 559, 115 S.Ct. at 1630.

6. 514 U.S. at 565, 115 S.Ct. at 1633.

7. Congress has authority under its commerce power to regulate, and make criminal, multistate activities, or activities that have a substantial effect on interstate commerce. Congress can increase the penalty for a criminal activity that is within the scope of the federal commerce power on the basis that a firearm was used in that activity. See generally, Muscarello v. United States, 524 U.S. 125 118 S.Ct. 1911, 141 L.Ed.2d 111 (1998) (the federal statute imposing a mandatory prison term on a person who "carries" a firearm during a "drug-trafficking crime" applies to a person who has a firearm in a vehicle, though not on his person, when committing a drug-trafficking offense) For additional rulings on this point, see the multivolume edition of this treatise. R. Rotunda & J. Nowak Treatise on Constitutional Law: Substance and Procedure (3rd ed. 1999).

v. United States,[8] where the Court upheld, under the commerce clause, a federal crime of extortionate credit transactions, that is, "loan sharking," even though the crime in this case did not cross any state lines and was "intrastate" activity. Yet that was a *commercial* crime, and the Court is willing aggregate data to show that it *affects* interstate commerce when the date aggregated is commercial in nature.

While one should not read too much into *Lopez*, one also should also not read too little into *Lopez*, for it was the first post–1937 case that found that an activity—possessing a gun near a school—did not "affect" interstate commerce. The majority explained, as discussed more fully below, that the non-commercial, the non-economic criminal nature of the conduct at issue was central to its decision. The Court made that clear in *United States v. Morrison*[9] when it invalidated a federal law that created a tort for the victims of "gender-motivated violence." The act was titled, "The Violence Against Women Act."[10]

In that case, Congress made numerous findings that gender-motivated violence imposes a serious impact on victims and their families, but the majority (5 to 4) concluded that those finding were irrelevant: the Court will not aggregate intra-state non-commercial activities (such as the gender-motivated violence, or violence in general) to determine if intra-state actions *affect* interstate commerce. But, the Court will aggregate inter-state commercial activities (such as loan-sharking or wheat grown to compete with wheat transported in interstate commerce) to determine that the intrastate commercial activities affect inter-state commerce. We may expect to find future cases

that raise the question if a particular activity is "commercial" in nature.

The modern Court easily finds an activity is subject to federal regulation under the Interstate Commerce Clause if the activity crosses a state line. In fact, it made that clear in *United States v. Robertson*,[11] unanimously decided within a week of *Lopez*. The Court said that if goods or people cross state lines, there is no need to apply the "affects" test, which only is necessary to define Congressional power over "purely intrastate commercial activities that have a substantial interstate affect".

When state or local governments engage in activities that are governed by federal statutes or regulations they may claim that either federalism principles or the Tenth Amendment exempt them from such federal laws. In the closing section of this Chapter, we will examine the Supreme Court decisions that have prohibited the federal government from directly ordering state or local governments to take legislative or regulatory actions and that have indicated that state and local governments have some immunity from federal commerce power regulations when Congress subjects states to laws that are not "generally applicable."[12]

The Modern Delegation of Power Doctrine—Delegations to States or the Executive Branch. Today, there is no significant "anti-delegation" principle that restricts the exercise of the commerce power. Congress may pass laws that allow states to independently regulate interstate commerce; such laws involve a federal adoption of varying structures for commerce rather than any unconstitutional delegation of the commerce power to the states.[13]

8. 402 U.S. 146, 91 S.Ct. 1357, 28 L.Ed.2d 686 (1971), upholding, Title II, 82 Stat. 159, 18 U.S.C.A. § 891 et seq.

9. 529 U.S. 598, 120 S.Ct. 1740, 146 L.Ed.2d 658 (2000). Rotunda, The Commerce Clause, the Political Question Doctrine, and Morrison, 18 Constitutional Commentary 319 (2001).

10. The official title of this law is appealing. Who, after all, could support violence against women? The law's alluring title might lead one to think that it offered special protections for women, but that would be incorrect. Instead, the only reference to "women" was in the title of the law. The substantive provision of § 13981 did not use

that word or any similar one. In effect, it merely created a federal tort that was more difficult to establish than an analogous state tort because it required the victim (whether male or female) to prove that the violence was motivated by animus based on sex.

11. 514 U.S. 669, 115 S.Ct. 1732, 131 L.Ed.2d 714 (1995)(per curiam).

12. See § 4.10, infra.

13. See § 8.5, infra. "When Congress so chooses, state actions which it plainly authorizes are invulnerable to constitutional attack under the commerce clause." Northeast Bancorp, Inc. v. Board of Governors, 472 U.S. 159,

The political process in modern times has resulted in federal control of wide variety of intrastate and multistate commercial matters; it has become impossible for the Congress to define with precision the scope and meaning of its commercial statutes. The past half century has witnessed increased congressional use of federal executive agencies to administer federal statutes and to promulgate regulations that effectuate legislative policies. The Congress may delegate both rulemaking and administrative functions to the executive branch or agencies it establishes.

Today the Supreme Court will allow Congress to share its legislative power with the executive branch by delegating aspects of that power to executive agencies. Such legislative delegations will be upheld unless Congress ab-

dicates one of its powers to the executive agency or fails to give legislative definition of the scope of the agency's power.[14]

If Congress were to grant a private group the power to control its competitors, in some instances there might be a procedural problem regarding whether the persons regulated were deprived of due process by being subject to the will of entities with interests contrary to theirs. However, this issue does not constitute an excessive delegation problem.[15]

Motive. If Congress is regulating an activity that may be deemed to come under the three-part test for the commerce power, the motive of Congress in passing the regulation is irrelevant. Thus Congress may exercise its commerce power for clearly noncommercial rea-

175, 105 S.Ct. 2545, 2554, 86 L.Ed.2d 112 (1985). See also, Whitman v. American Trucking Associations, 531 U.S. 457, 121 S.Ct. 903, 149 L.Ed.2d 1 (2001).

For further citations and analysis, see R. Rotunda & J. Nowak, Treatise on Constitutional Law: Substance and Procedure, vol. 1, § 4.8 (3rd ed. 1999, with annual supplements).

14. Delegation of Congressional Lawmaking Power. Between 1937 and 1999, no federal statute was held unconstitutional by the Supreme Court because of an excessive delegation of legislative power to an executive agency. The Court has focused on the need for statutory definition of agency power as both needed to avoid excessive delegation and a reason for upholding the delegation of power to agencies. The Supreme Court has sometimes invalidated particular agency regulations on the basis that the agency did not have legislative authorization to promulgate the regulation at issue. Hampton v. Mow Sun Wong, 426 U.S. 88, 96 S.Ct. 1895, 48 L.Ed.2d 495 (1976), on remand 435 F.Supp. 37 (D.Cal.1977). See, Kent v. Dulles, 357 U.S. 116, 78 S.Ct. 1113, 2 L.Ed.2d 1204 (1958) (construing narrowly a delegation of power to control passports so as to avoid First Amendment problems).

In Metropolitan Washington Airports Authority v. Citizens for the Abatement of Aircraft Noise, Inc., 501 U.S. 252, 111 S.Ct. 2298, 115 L.Ed.2d 236 (1991) the Court invalidated a federal statute that approved an agreement between Virginia and the District of Columbia to transfer authority over Washington National Airport and Dulles International Airport from the Department of Transportation to an Airports Authority insofar as the statute made the decisions of the Authority subject to the control of a "Board of Review" that was to be composed of nine members of Congress. If the statute was considered to be a grant of executive power, the separation of powers principle would not permit persons in Congress (on the Review Board) to exercise executive power. If the power of the Board of Review was considered to be an exercise of legislative power, the decisions made by the Board did not meet the bicameralism and presentment requirements for legislation set out in Article I, § 7.

In Bowsher v. Synar, 478 U.S. 714, 106 S.Ct. 3181, 92 L.Ed.2d 583 (1986) the Court invalidated a grant of power to the Comptroller General because the power was seen to be executive in nature and the Comptroller General could be dismissed from office by Congress through means other than the impeachment process. The *Bowsher* delegation violated the separation of powers principle by allowing Congress to control (through its ability to fire the person) an office holder who would be exercising executive branch powers.

Immigration and Naturalization Service v. Chadha, 462 U.S. 919, 103 S.Ct. 2764, 77 L.Ed.2d 317 (1983) invalidated a "legislative veto", by which Congress attempted to control actions of executive branch offices or agencies to which it had delegated authority, by finding that the legislative veto provision violated that bicameral requirement and the presentment requirement and the presentment requirement for the passing of legislation set forth in Article I and the separation of powers principle.

These decisions do not indicate a return to the approach taken in the mid–1930s by the Court regarding limitations on the ability of Congress to delegate rulemaking authority to executive agencies. Whenever a congressional delegation of rulemaking authority to an executive agency or department might be interpreted as having some limits, so that it does not constitute the total abdication of a federal legislative power by the Congress, the delegation will be upheld. For citations to additional Supreme Court cases, and secondary authorities, on this point, see R. Rotunda & J. Nowak, Treatise on Constitutional Law: Substance and Procedure, vol. 1 § 4.8 (3rd ed. 1999, with annual supplements).

15. Compare Eubank v. Richmond, 226 U.S. 137, 33 S.Ct. 76, 57 L.Ed. 156 (1912) (holding invalid a law that gave property owners power to set zoning regulations for neighboring property) with Eastlake v. Forest City Enterprises, Inc., 426 U.S. 668, 96 S.Ct. 2358, 49 L.Ed.2d 132 (1976), on remand 48 Ohio St.2d 47, 356 N.E.2d 499 (1976) (upholding system whereby zoning changes must be approved by voter referendum).

sons. The Court has upheld a wide variety of legislation under the commerce power including health regulations, criminal laws, and civil rights acts. If there is a rational basis for finding a sufficient relationship between the regulation and commerce under one of the three tests discussed above, the act is within the commerce power. If it does not violate a constitutional restriction or fundamental constitutional right the law must be upheld.

§ 4.9   Development of New Standards

The 1937 Decisions. In April of 1937, the Supreme Court, by a five to four vote, adopted an approach to defining the commerce power that was quite different from that of the previous period. The Court upheld the National Labor Relations Act and the labor board's orders against an employer's unfair interference with union activities in *NLRB v. Jones & Laughlin Steel Corp.*[1] The majority opinion found no fault in the Act, which by its terms regulated labor practices "affecting commerce."

The Act defined commerce in terms of transactions among states and "affecting commerce" as those practices or labor disputes that might burden or obstruct commerce. The case involved orders against practices in steel and iron works, but the Court rejected the production versus commerce distinction. This was most important for it meant that the Court would no longer define the commerce power in terms of Tenth Amendment reserved power concepts.

The steel company was a vertically integrated enterprise that operated in many states. Labor disruptions in its manufacturing component could affect commerce in several states. The majority, however, did not rest on a stream of commerce theory; it dismissed this phrase as only a metaphor to describe some

valid exercises of the commerce power.[2] The discussion of the power showed an institutional awareness of the economic needs of the nation; the decision stated that intrastate activities could be regulated if they had "a close and substantial relation to interstate commerce."[3] The opinion did not completely disregard the direct-indirect distinction; the case involved a large multistate corporation.

In a companion case the Court upheld the application of the National Labor Relations Act to a minor clothes manufacturer.[4] The opinion merely cited the facts that the enterprise shipped goods in interstate commerce and that a general strike in the industry in New York had severe effects on trade. This summary reliance on the *Jones & Laughlin* decision further confirmed a trend toward recognizing economic impact as a sufficient relationship to interstate commerce.

On May 24, 1937 the Supreme Court issued opinions on the tax and spending powers that showed the majority was committed to the economic effects approach.[5] In *Chas. C. Steward Machine Co. v. Davis*[6] the Court upheld the unemployment compensation tax and payment provisions of the Social Security Act. Under this system, employers received a credit for payments to state unemployment systems. A five-member majority held that this law was neither the regulation of activities beyond the federal powers nor an unconstitutional coercion of state government to enact such systems.

The opinion held that the national tax and spending powers were properly used to prevent the national economic consequences of unemployment and to eliminate the obstructions to state systems caused by the advantage of businesses in states without unemployment compensation taxes. The opinion rejected the

---

§ 4.9

1. 301 U.S. 1, 57 S.Ct. 615, 81 L.Ed. 893 (1937); Austin Road Co. v. Occupational Safety & Health Review Comm'n, 683 F.2d 905, 907 (5th Cir.1982) (Politz, J.), citing this section of an earlier edition of this treatise.

2. 301 U.S. at 36, 57 S.Ct. at 623–24.

3. 301 U.S. at 37, 57 S.Ct. at 624.

4. NLRB v. Friedman–Harry Marks Clothing Co., 301 U.S. 58, 57 S.Ct. 645, 81 L.Ed. 921 (1937).

For a decision finding a business not to fit within the meaning of "commerce" as delineated by the Fair Labor Standards Act, see Mitchell v. H. B. Zachry Co., 362 U.S. 310, 80 S.Ct. 739, 4 L.Ed.2d 753 (1960).

5. See Chapter 5, infra.

6. 301 U.S. 548, 57 S.Ct. 883, 81 L.Ed. 1279 (1937).

Tenth Amendment as a general limit upon the subjects of federal power.

In *Helvering v. Davis*[7] the Court upheld the old age benefits provision of the Social Security Act by a vote of seven to two. The Court was committed to recognizing at least federal taxing and spending powers of sufficient scope to deal with national economic problems.

Redefining the Role of the Court in Commerce Clause Cases. In the next two years the Supreme Court more clearly evidenced its rejection of the Tenth Amendment as a definitional limitation on federal powers. The Justices upheld laws that regulated employment relationships and single-state production activities. Among the acts upheld were regulation of tobacco warehouses to enforce production quotas,[8] product price-setting provisions,[9] and the application of the National Labor Relations Act to small production enterprises.[10]

In 1941 the Justices gave a more definite sign that economic impact was a basis for exercise of the commerce power, when they granted renewed deference to the congressional power to set the conditions for production of items that were the subject of multistate transactions. The Fair Labor Standards Act of 1936 prescribed the minimum wage and maximum hours for employees "engaged in [interstate] commerce or the production of goods for [interstate] commerce." The Act prohibited the interstate shipment of goods made in violation of these regulations and also imposed direct penalties on employers who violated the requirements.[11]

The Supreme Court in *United States v. Darby*[12] unanimously upheld both the terms of prohibition and direct regulation of wages and

hours. The opinion, by Justice Stone, first recognized Congress' plenary power to set the terms for interstate transportation. It made no difference that Congress was attempting to regulate production in this way because the "motive and purpose of a regulation of interstate commerce are matters for the legislative judgment upon the exercise of which the Constitution places no restriction and over which the Courts are given no control."[13] So long as Congress did not violate a specific check on its power such as the provisions of the Bill of Rights, it could set any terms for interstate transportation; that was clearly "commerce among the states." The Court would no longer use a reserved power view of the Tenth Amendment to place other restrictions on Congress. The only impediment to this interpretation was *Hammer v. Dagenhart*,[14] which the Court now overruled.[15]

The *Darby* opinion also upheld the direct regulation of the hours and wages of employees engaged in the production of goods for interstate shipment. The opinion found that Congress could regulate intrastate activities that "so affect interstate commerce or the exercise of the power of Congress over it."[16] The Court discarded the production-commerce distinction as well as the directness test and overruled *Carter Coal*.[17] Congress was free to set the terms of intrastate activities to protect or regulate interstate commerce. Congress could choose to protect commerce from competition by goods made under substandard labor conditions. Because competition was a sufficient economic tie to interstate commerce, it made no difference how small the individual

7. 301 U.S. 619, 57 S.Ct. 904, 81 L.Ed. 1307 (1937).

8. Mulford v. Smith, 307 U.S. 38, 59 S.Ct. 648, 83 L.Ed. 1092 (1939); Currin v. Wallace, 306 U.S. 1, 59 S.Ct. 379, 83 L.Ed. 441 (1939).

9. United States v. Rock Royal Co-op., Inc., 307 U.S. 533, 59 S.Ct. 993, 83 L.Ed. 1446 (1939) (milk); Sunshine Anthracite Coal Co. v. Adkins, 310 U.S. 381, 60 S.Ct. 907, 84 L.Ed. 1263 (1940) (coal).

10. NLRB v. Friedman–Harry Marks Clothing Co., 301 U.S. 58, 57 S.Ct. 645, 81 L.Ed. 921 (1937); NLRB v. Fruehauf Trailer Co., 301 U.S. 49, 57 S.Ct. 642, 81 L.Ed.

918 (1937); NLRB v. Fainblatt, 306 U.S. 601, 59 S.Ct. 668, 83 L.Ed. 1014 (1939).

11. 52 Stat. 1060, 29 U.S.C.A. § 200 et seq.

12. 312 U.S. 100, 61 S.Ct. 451, 85 L.Ed. 609 (1941).

13. 312 U.S. at 115, 61 S.Ct. at 457.

14. 247 U.S. 251, 38 S.Ct. 529, 62 L.Ed. 1101 (1918).

15. 312 U.S. at 116–17, 61 S.Ct. at 458–59.

16. 312 U.S. at 118, 61 S.Ct. at 459.

17. Carter v. Carter Coal Co., 298 U.S. 238, 56 S.Ct. 855, 80 L.Ed. 1160 (1936).

producer's share of shipments in commerce might be.[18]

The Court recognized that the Tenth Amendment did not serve as a basis for restricting the commerce power:

> Our conclusion is unaffected by the Tenth Amendment.... The Amendment states but a truism that all is retained which has not been surrendered. There is nothing in the history of its adoption to suggest that it was more than declaratory of the relationship between the national and state governments as it had been established by the Constitution before the Amendment or that its purpose was other than to allay fears that the new national government might seek to exercise powers not granted, and that the states might not be able to exercise fully their reserved powers.[19]

In *Darby*, the Court also upheld the requirement that employers who sold items for interstate commerce keep records of the hours and wages of all employees. Even if some employees worked solely on an intrastate product not directly affecting commerce, these regulations were necessary to full enforcement of the provision relating to employees who worked in production for interstate commerce.

The Supreme Court followed the theory that intrastate action could be regulated if the regulation was necessary to effectuate federal control of commerce among the states. In *United States v. Wrightwood Dairy Co.*[20] the Court upheld the application of federal milk regulations to milk that was produced and sold in a single state, because the failure to regulate them would interfere with congressional regulation of interstate commerce. The competition of unregulated intrastate milk would affect milk that crossed state lines, and that milk was federally regulated. The Court applied a necessary and proper clause analysis to find a Congressional power to regulate these intrastate activities.

In 1942, the Court completed the move to recognizing a plenary commerce power based on economic theory. It held that particular intrastate activities of a very small scale could be federally regulated if they might affect commerce when combined with similar small-scale activities. In *Wickard v. Filburn*[21] the Supreme Court held that a marketing quota legitimately could be applied to a farmer who grew a small amount of wheat, although the wheat was primarily to be consumed on his own farm with some to be sold locally.

The Court had no difficulty in upholding regulation of this farmer even though it would be difficult for him alone to affect interstate transactions. Total supply of wheat clearly affects market price, just as does the current demand for the product. The marketing quotas were designed to control the price of wheat. If many farmers raised wheat for home consumption, they would affect both the supply for interstate commerce and the demand for the product. The possibility of such an effect justified regulation of the individual farmer.[22]

The Court deferred to the legislative judgment concerning economic effects and the relationships between local activities and interstate commerce. It was not for the judiciary to restrict congressional power either by limiting the subject matter of the power or independently reviewing the "directness" of connections to commerce. The opinion explicitly returned to Chief Justice Marshall's broad definition of commerce in *Gibbons v. Ogden*.[23] The Court had come full circle and returned to the broad view of the commerce power that had existed for most of our history. Commerce was once again considered to be intercourse that affected more states than one.

Modern Commerce Clause Standards. After *Wickard*, the tests for proper exercise of the commerce power were settled. First, Congress could set the terms for the interstate transportation of persons, products, or ser-

18. United States v. Darby, 312 U.S. 100, 117, 61 S.Ct. 451, 458–59, 85 L.Ed. 609 (1941).

19. 312 U.S. at 123–24, 61 S.Ct. at 462.

20. 315 U.S. 110, 62 S.Ct. 523, 86 L.Ed. 726 (1942).

21. 317 U.S. 111, 63 S.Ct. 82, 87 L.Ed. 122 (1942).

22. Kirschbaum v. Walling, 316 U.S. 517, 62 S.Ct. 1116, 86 L.Ed. 1638 (1942) (recognizing that even minor transactions may have an effect on interstate commerce).

23. 317 U.S. at 120, 63 S.Ct. at 86–87, discussing and relying upon Gibbons v. Ogden, 22 U.S. (9 Wheat.) 1, 6 L.Ed. 23 (1824).

vices, even if this constituted prohibition or indirect regulation of single state activities. Second, Congress could regulate intrastate activities that had a close and substantial relationship to interstate commerce; this relationship could be established by congressional views of the economic effect of this type of activity. Third, Congress could regulate—under a combined commerce clause-necessary and proper clause analysis—intrastate activities in order to effectuate its regulation of interstate commerce.

The Court since 1938 has not restricted the scope of federal power to regulate private sector commercial activity even though the regulated activity might seem to be local in nature.[24] Thus, the Court has upheld the federal regulation of strip mining on land that was formerly used as farmland, even though the land was not a subject of interstate commerce.[25] In these cases the Justices reaffirmed the approach outlined in this section as they stated that: "A court may invalidate legislation enacted under the Commerce Clause only if it is clear that there is no rational basis for a congressional finding that the regulated activity affects interstate commerce, or that there is no reasonable connection between the regulatory means selected and the asserted ends."[26] Because it would not be irrational for Congress to conclude that use of land for strip mining

rather than farming could affect interstate commercial transactions relating to agricultural products or that the mines could create environmental hazards that might concern more than one state, the Court concluded that the federal regulation of such land use was valid. Because the Court has not significantly altered these approaches to reviewing commerce decisions, we will only outline the major decisions that complete the modern view.[27] We will then examine some special commerce problems in the next subsections.

Following these decisions the Court had no trouble in upholding federal legislation regulating interstate commerce in "intangibles" such as insurance contracts or securities issues. *United States v. South–Eastern Underwriters Association*[28] reversed decisions from the preceding periods and held that Congress could regulate interstate transactions in insurance.[29] The opinion stated that a business that concerned more than one state "is not deprived of its interstate character merely because it is built upon sales contracts which are local in nature."[30] Similarly, the Court upheld regulations of securities by the Securities Exchange Commission, including strict regulation of the entities that could control public utility shares.[31]

The Supreme Court has also continued to recognize a federal power to control the meth-

---

24. State and local governments may be immune from some types of federal regulation. Congress's power to control public sector activity is examined in § 4.10, infra. Rotunda, The Eleventh Amendment, *Garrett*, and Protection for Civil Rights, 53 Ala.L.Rev. 1183 (2002).

25. Hodel v. Virginia Surface Mining & Reclamation Ass'n, Inc., 452 U.S. 264, 101 S.Ct. 2352, 69 L.Ed.2d 1 (1981), judgment vacated 453 U.S. 901, 101 S.Ct. 3132, 69 L.Ed.2d 987 (1981); Hodel v. Indiana, 452 U.S. 314, 101 S.Ct. 2376, 69 L.Ed.2d 40 (1981). See generally § 4.10, infra.

26. Hodel v. Indiana, 452 U.S. 314, 325, 101 S.Ct. 2376, 2383–84, 69 L.Ed.2d 40 (1981).

27. The Supreme Court since 1936 has not restricted the congressional power to subject commercial activities to federal regulation. See note 24, supra. For citations to additional Supreme Court cases on this point, see R. Rotunda & J. Nowak, Treatise on Constitutional Law: Substance and Procedure, vol. 1, § 4.9 (3rd ed. 1999, with annual supplements). However, the Court has required plaintiffs alleging that a defendant's intrastate activity violates federal statutes to prove that the defendant's activity has the relationship to interstate commerce set

forth in the federal act as a condition of regulation. See Gulf Oil Corp. v. Copp Paving Co., Inc., 419 U.S. 186, 95 S.Ct. 392, 42 L.Ed.2d 378 (1974) (suit alleging anti-trust violations of Robinson–Patman Act and Clayton Act by producers of asphalt for highways dismissed due to plaintiff's failure to demonstrate requisite relationship between intrastate asphalt producer's activities and commerce as required by those statutes).

28. 322 U.S. 533, 64 S.Ct. 1162, 88 L.Ed. 1440 (1944), rehearing denied 323 U.S. 811, 65 S.Ct. 26, 89 L.Ed. 646 (1944).

29. Id., see Paul v. Virginia, 75 U.S. (8 Wall.) 168, 19 L.Ed. 357 (1869); New York Life Insurance Co. v. Deer Lodge County, 231 U.S. 495, 34 S.Ct. 167, 58 L.Ed. 332 (1913); Robertson v. California, 328 U.S. 440, 66 S.Ct. 1160, 90 L.Ed. 1366 (1946), rehearing denied 329 U.S. 818, 67 S.Ct. 25, 91 L.Ed. 697 (1946).

30. 322 U.S. at 547, 64 S.Ct. at 1170.

31. Electric Bond & Share Co. v. SEC, 303 U.S. 419, 58 S.Ct. 678, 82 L.Ed. 936 (1938); North American Co. v. SEC, 327 U.S. 686, 66 S.Ct. 785, 90 L.Ed. 945 (1946); American Power & Light Co. v. SEC, 329 U.S. 90, 67 S.Ct. 133, 91 L.Ed. 103 (1946).

ods of production and the sale of goods in interstate commerce. The Court has not deviated in later years from the ruling on the National Labor Relations Acts. It has upheld federal jurisdiction over employment relationships in single state enterprises that might arguably affect commerce.[32] And the Court has upheld the use of the antitrust laws against a wide variety of business practices that might affect commerce.[33]

In related cases, the Court has found that Congress can restrict the use of items follow-

ing their transportation in interstate commerce. Thus, the Court has upheld the provision of the Food, Drug, and Cosmetic Act that required precise labeling for the retail sale of items that have been a part of interstate commerce.[34] The Court rejected any possible "original package" limit on the commerce power and held that Congress could set the labeling requirements after shipment to assure that later sale did not undermine Congressional policies.[35] This concept of regulating items in commerce has also justified congressional police statutes, including one making it a crime

---

32. Howell Chevrolet Co. v. NLRB, 346 U.S. 482, 74 S.Ct. 214, 98 L.Ed. 215 (1953) (retail auto dealer part of manufacturer's distribution system); Plumbers, Steamfitters, Refrigeration, Petroleum Fitters, and Apprentices of Local 298 v. County of Door, 359 U.S. 354, 79 S.Ct. 844, 3 L.Ed.2d 872 (1959) (half of construction materials from outside state); NLRB v. Reliance Fuel Oil Corp., 371 U.S. 224, 83 S.Ct. 312, 9 L.Ed.2d 279 (1963) (retail distributor of fuel oil obtained oil from wholesaler who imported it from outside state).

33. See Goldfarb v. Virginia State Bar, 421 U.S. 773, 95 S.Ct. 2004, 44 L.Ed.2d 572 (1975), rehearing denied 423 U.S. 886, 96 S.Ct. 162, 46 L.Ed.2d 118 (1975) (attorney pricing agreements violate the Sherman Act); McLain v. Real Estate Bd., 444 U.S. 232, 100 S.Ct. 502, 62 L.Ed.2d 441 (1980), on remand 614 F.2d 535 (5th Cir.1980) (Sherman Act suit may be maintained against real estate brokers so long as jurisdictional requirement of connection to commerce is alleged and proved in the particular suit).

See Ronald D. Rotunda, Legal Ethics: The Lawyer's Deskbook on Professional Responsibility § 6–1.7 (ABA–West Group, 2nd ed. 2002) cf. Rotunda, Moving from Billable Hours to Fixed Fees: Task–Based Billing and Legal Ethics, 47 U. Kan.L.Rev. 801 (1999).

The Twenty–First Amendment. The Twenty-first-Amendment reserved for the states the power to restrict importation, sale, and local use of alcoholic beverages without being subject to the same type of commerce clause restraints as are applicable to state regulations of other commodities in interstate commerce. However, the Amendment did not exclude federal authority over interstate commerce involving alcoholic beverages or their production. California Retail Liquor Dealers Ass'n v. Midcal Aluminum, Inc., 445 U.S. 97, 100 S.Ct. 937, 63 L.Ed.2d 233 (1980) (Sherman Act applies to resale agreements between grape growers and wine merchants even though authorized by California state law; Twenty-first Amendment, granting control of local sale or use of alcoholic beverages to states does not preclude federal regulation).

South Dakota v. Dole, 483 U.S. 203, 107 S.Ct. 2793, 97 L.Ed.2d 171 (1987) upheld a federal statute that conditioned each state's receipt of its portion of federal highway funds on the adoption of a minimum drinking age of 21 years of age. A state that does not meet this condition loses five percent of the federal funds that it would otherwise be entitled to under federal highway grant programs.

Chief Justice Rehnquist wrote for seven members of the Court in finding that the condition was related to the

purposes of the federal grant (producing better and safe highway conditions) and that it did not compel the states to give up any area of sovereignty that had been reserved to them by the Tenth or Twenty-first Amendments. The Court did not determine in this case whether Congress could have directly imposed a national drinking age under its commerce clause power, as the majority found that the "encouragement to state action found in [the federal statute and its condition] is a valid use of the spending power."

In North Dakota v. United States, 495 U.S. 423, 110 S.Ct. 1986, 109 L.Ed.2d 420 (1990), the Court, without majority opinion, upheld two state liquor regulations as applied to the federal government. The first was a "reporting requirement" under which out-of-state liquor distributors had to report the volume of all liquor shipped in to the state, including liquor shipped to federal enclaves (such as military bases). The second was a "labeling requirement" under which out-of-state distributors had to label liquor bottles shipped directly to a federal enclave in a manner that would specify that the liquor was for consumption only within the federal enclave.

The Supreme Court unanimously upheld the reporting requirement; the Justices upheld the labeling requirement by a five to four vote. This case did not establish any new principles regarding the Twenty-first Amendment or intergovernmental immunity, but it involved significant disagreement between the Justices regarding the application of intergovernmental immunity principles established in previous cases.

Justice Stevens, writing for a four Justice plurality, found that the regulations: did not regulate the federal government directly; did not impose substantial burdens on the federal government that would interfere with any federal interest; and were not preempted. Justice Scalia wrote separately to explain why he believed the labeling requirement was valid.

34. United States v. Sullivan, 332 U.S. 689, 68 S.Ct. 331, 92 L.Ed. 297 (1948). But see Federal Trade Com'n. v. Bunte Bros., 312 U.S. 349, 61 S.Ct. 580, 85 L.Ed. 881 (1941).

35. United States v. Sullivan, 332 U.S. at 698, 68 S.Ct. at 336. The original package limitation is found in Lyng v. Michigan, 135 U.S. 161, 10 S.Ct. 725, 34 L.Ed. 150 (1890) (if in original packaging, part of interstate commerce and exempt from state tax); Schollenberger v. Pennsylvania,

for a convicted felon to possess a firearm that had ever been the subject of interstate commerce.[36]

Throughout our history the Court had consistently recognized a broad power to regulate navigable waterways under the commerce clause.[37] This power now includes the regulation of both navigable interstate waterways and streams that might be made navigable. When combined with the power to spend for the public welfare, the federal government has a complete power to regulate all waterways, build dams and establish projects to reclaim arid lands.[38]

Although Congress has plenary authority over navigable waters, if federal legislation or regulation deprives the owners of private waterways of significant property rights the federal government must compensate those owners for the taking of their property.[39]

Conclusion: Commerce Clause Standards at the Beginning of the Twenty-first Century

Between 1937 and 1995 the scope of the federal government's power to regulate interstate commerce could be described in terms of two standards.

First, the federal government could regulate activities, persons, products, or services state lines. Federal regulations regarding interstate transportation or interstate activities would be upheld even though they constituted indirect regulation of single state activities, so long as these federal regulations did not violate a specific check on the power of the federal government, such as the restrictions contained in § 9 of Article I or the Bill of Rights.

Second, Congress could regulate single state activities that had a close and substantial relationship to, or substantial effect on, interstate commerce. The federal government would be allowed to regulate those activities that had a substantial effect on interstate commerce. Additionally, under a combined necessary and proper clause and commerce clause analysis, the federal government could regulate single state activities in order to effectuate its regulation of interstate commerce.

During the period from 1937 to 1995, the Supreme Court majority gave great deference to Congressional decisions a single state activity could be regulated on the basis that the regulated activity had a substantial effect on multi-state economic concerns and interstate

---

171 U.S. 1, 18 S.Ct. 757, 43 L.Ed. 49 (1898) (state can't prohibit importation of oleomargarine if still in original package).

36. Barrett v. United States, 423 U.S. 212, 96 S.Ct. 498, 46 L.Ed.2d 450 (1976); cf. United States v. Bass, 404 U.S. 336, 92 S.Ct. 515, 30 L.Ed.2d 488 (1971). See also Perez v. United States, 402 U.S. 146, 91 S.Ct. 1357, 28 L.Ed.2d 686 (1971).

37. Congressional power to regulate all waterways includes the power to regulate interstate ferry rates, New York Central & Hudson River R. Co. v. Hudson County Bd. of Chosen Freeholders, 227 U.S. 248, 33 S.Ct. 269, 57 L.Ed. 499 (1913); tugboats towing cargo boats between points in one state, but through the waters of another state, Cornell Steamboat Co. v. United States, 321 U.S. 634, 64 S.Ct. 768, 88 L.Ed. 978 (1944), appeal dismissed 321 U.S. 632, 64 S.Ct. 776, 88 L.Ed. 975 (1944); services provided by those furnishing terminal facilities to a common carrier by water, California v. United States, 320 U.S. 577, 64 S.Ct. 352, 88 L.Ed. 322 (1944), rehearing denied 321 U.S. 802, 64 S.Ct. 516, 88 L.Ed. 1089 (1944); and numerous other activities of a truly maritime character, Providence & New York S.S. Co. v. Hill Mfg. Co., 109 U.S. 578, 3 S.Ct. 379, 27 L.Ed. 1038 (1883) (limitation of liability of ship owners); The Hamilton, 207 U.S. 398, 28 S.Ct. 133, 52 L.Ed. 264 (1907) (same); O'Donnell v. Great Lakes Dredge & Dock Co., 318 U.S. 36, 63 S.Ct. 488, 87 L.Ed. 596 (1943) (rights of seamen).

38. Pennsylvania v. Wheeling & Belmont Bridge Co., 59 U.S. (18 How.) 421, 15 L.Ed. 435 (1856); Gilman v. Philadelphia, 70 U.S. (3 Wall.) 713, 18 L.Ed. 96 (1866); Monongahela Navigation Co. v. United States, 148 U.S. 312, 13 S.Ct. 622, 37 L.Ed. 463 (1893); United States v. Chandler–Dunbar Water Power Co., 229 U.S. 53, 33 S.Ct. 667, 57 L.Ed. 1063 (1913); Arizona v. California, 283 U.S. 423, 51 S.Ct. 522, 75 L.Ed. 1154 (1931); United States v. Appalachian Electric Power Co., 311 U.S. 377, 61 S.Ct. 291, 85 L.Ed. 243 (1940), rehearing denied 312 U.S. 712, 61 S.Ct. 548, 85 L.Ed. 1143 (1941), petition denied 317 U.S. 594, 63 S.Ct. 67, 87 L.Ed. 487 (1942); Parkersburg & Ohio River Transportation Co. v. Parkersburg, 107 U.S. (17 Otto) 691, 2 S.Ct. 732, 27 L.Ed. 584 (1883); United States v. Rio Grande Dam and Irrigation Co., 174 U.S. 690, 19 S.Ct. 770, 43 L.Ed. 1136 (1899); Port of Seattle v. Oregon & Washington R. Co., 255 U.S. 56, 41 S.Ct. 237, 65 L.Ed. 500 (1921); Economy Light & Power Co. v. United States, 256 U.S. 113, 41 S.Ct. 409, 65 L.Ed. 847 (1921).

39. Kaiser Aetna v. United States, 444 U.S. 164, 100 S.Ct. 383, 62 L.Ed.2d 332 (1979); Vaughn v. Vermilion Corp., 444 U.S. 206, 100 S.Ct. 399, 62 L.Ed.2d 365 (1979), on remand 387 So.2d 698 (La.App.1980), lower court judgment reversed 397 So.2d 490 (La.1981). United States v. River Rouge Improvement Co., 269 U.S. 411, 46 S.Ct. 144, 70 L.Ed. 339 (1926); Henry Ford & Son v. Little Falls Fibre Co., 280 U.S. 369, 50 S.Ct. 140, 74 L.Ed. 483 (1930).

commerce. However, during those years, the Court was only examining the regulation of single state activities that were arguably commercial in nature.

In 1995, the Court examined the extent of congressional power to regulate single state non-commercial activities. In *United States v. Lopez*,[40] the Court (five to four) invalidated a federal statute that prohibited simply carrying firearms near any school in the United States. The statute was not within the scope of Congress's commerce clause power.

The Court ruled that this statute that was stricken in *Lopez* was not limited to a restriction on guns or persons that had crossed interstate lines prior to coming near the school. No facts were provided to the Supreme Court in *Lopez* on which a majority of the Justices could conclude that the appearance or "possession" of firearms near schools would have a substantial effect on interstate commerce.

Writing for the majority in *Lopez*, Chief Justice Rehnquist found that the federal judiciary should give less deference to congressional judgments that single state activities had a substantial effect on interstate commerce when those single state activities were not

commercial in nature.[41] Chief Justice Rehnquist's opinion stated: "We do not doubt that Congress has authority under the commerce clause to regulate numerous commercial activities that substantially affect interstate commerce and also affect the educational process. The authority, though broad, does not include the authority to regulate each and every aspect of local schools."[42]

The Chief Justice's opinion in *Lopez* indicated that the federal judiciary would continue to give great deference to a congressional determination that a class of single state commercial activities had a substantial effect on interstate commerce. The Chief Justice found that the judiciary should not give similar deference to a congressional determination that intrastate activities that were not commercial in nature had a substantial effect on interstate commerce. The *Lopez* majority considered the distinction between commercial and noncommercial single state activities to be a necessary one, even though Chief Justice Rehnquist's majority opinion recognized that a determination of whether an intrastate activity is commercial or noncommercial may in some cases result in legal uncertainty.[43]

---

40. United States v. Lopez, 514 U.S. 549, 115 S.Ct. 1624, 131 L.Ed.2d 626 (1995). This case was decided by a five to four vote of the Justices. Justices Kennedy, O'Connor, and Thomas joined the majority opinion by Chief Justice Rehnquist and also filed concurring opinions. 514 U.S. at 567, 115 S.Ct. at 1634 (Kennedy, J., joined by O'Connor, J., concurring in the judgment and opinion of the Court); 514 U.S. at 583, 115 S.Ct. at 1642 (Thomas, J., concurring). Justices Stevens, Souter, Ginsburg and Breyer dissented in *Lopez*. 514 U.S. at 602, 115 S.Ct. at 1651 (Stevens, J., dissenting); 514 U.S. at 603, 115 S.Ct. at 1651 (Souter, J., dissenting); 514 U.S. at 615, 115 S.Ct. at 1657 (Breyer, J., joined by Stevens, Souter, and Ginsburg, JJ., dissenting).

41. United States v. Lopez, 514 U.S. 549, 565, 115 S.Ct. 1624, 1633, 131 L.Ed.2d 626 (1995).

Congress retains authority under its commerce power to regulate, and make criminal, multi-state activities, or activities that have a substantial effect on commerce. Congress can increase the penalty for a criminal activity that is within the scope of the Federal Commerce Power, on the basis that a firearm was used in that activity. See generally, Bailey v. United States, 516 U.S. 137, 116 S.Ct. 501, 133 L.Ed.2d 472 (1995) (interpretation of federal statute criminalizing the use of a firearm during certain drug offenses, but finding that there was insufficient evidence to find that the defendants in the case had used a firearm, under the terms of the statute); Muscarello v.

United States, 524 U.S. 125, 118 S.Ct. 1911, 141 L.Ed.2d 111 (1998) (the federal statute imposing a mandatory prison term on a person who "carries" a firearm during a "drug-trafficking crime" applies to a person who has a firearm in a vehicle, though not on his person, when committing a drug-trafficking offense); Bryan v. United States, 524 U.S. 184, 118 S.Ct. 1939, 141 L.Ed.2d 197 (1998) (federal statute punishing anyone who "willfully" violates federal law by dealing in firearms without a federal license requires the government to prove that the defendant was aware that his conduct was unlawful, but does not require the government to prove that the defendant was aware of federal licensing requirements); Caron v. United States, 524 U.S. 308, 118 S.Ct. 2007, 141 L.Ed.2d 303 (1998) (a federal statute prohibiting a person convicted of a serious criminal offense in state court from possessing a firearm, unless the person's rights, including the right to carry arms, have been restored by local law, prohibits a convicted felon from having a gun regardless of the fact that he received a state law "restoration of rights" that allowed him to possess rifles, but restricted his ability to carry handguns).

42. 514 U.S. at 561, 115 S.Ct. at 1633. Ronald D. Rotunda, The Implications of the New Commerce Clause Jurisprudence: An Evolutionary or Revolutionary Court?, 55 Ark.L.Rev. 795 (2003).

43. United States v. Lopez, 514 U.S. 549, 565, 115 S.Ct. 1624, 1633, 131 L.Ed.2d 626 (1995).

The *Lopez* majority was concerned that judicial deference to congressional regulation of single state noncommercial activities would result in Congress's being able to turn the commerce power into a national police power.[44] In the view of the *Lopez* majority, allowing Congress to regulate guns near schools based on simply a rational argument that guns might affect the quality of education, an that in turn might affect interstate commerce would open the door to allowing Congress to regulate every aspect of education based solely on a rational argument that every aspect of school operations might effect the educational level of future workers in interstate commerce.

Chief Justice Rehnquist's majority opinion in *Lopez* ruled that there were three basis upon which Congress could regulate persons, things, or activities under its Article I power to regulate interstate commerce: "First, Congress may regulate the use of channels of interstate commerce ... Second, Congress is empowered to regulate and protect the instrumentalities of interstate commerce, or persons or things in interstate commerce, even though the threat may come only from intrastate activities ... Finally, Congress's commerce authority includes the power to regulate, those activities having a substantial relation to interstate commerce ... i.e., those activities that substantially affect interstate commerce."[45]

The Chief Justice's majority opinion in *Lopez* does not overturn any prior cases, and constitutes a complete endorsement of Congress's power to regulate all activities, persons, or products that cross state boundaries. So long as a federal regulation relates to interstate transactions or interstate transportation, the federal regulation would be justified under the first two branches of the *Lopez* description of the federal interstate commerce power.

Lopez also did not change the basis upon which the federal government could regulate single state activities. As was true in all of the cases since 1937, the Court held that Congress could regulate single state activities that had

a substantial affect on commerce. However, the Court created a distinction in *Lopez* regarding the degree of deference that the judiciary would give to Congress when determining whether a class of regulated single state activities had a substantial effect on interstate commerce. If the regulated single state activity is "commercial" in character, the Court will continue to give great deference to Congress. Federal regulations of single state commercial activities will enjoy a presumption of constitutionality, so that they will be upheld as being within the commerce power so long as there is any rational basis on which Congress could have concluded that the activities have a substantial affect on interstate commerce. Federal regulation of single state activities that are *not commercial* in character will not be upheld unless the federal government can demonstrate that there is a real factual basis (rather than a mere theoretical argument) for the conclusion that the single state activities, as a class, have a substantial effect on interstate commerce.

Lopez provided no specific guidance regarding the principles that the judiciary should use when determining whether a single state activity that was subject to federal regulation in fact was "commercial" or "non-commercial" in character. However, it did not overturn any prior law, it cited with approval *Wickard v. Filburn*,[46] and, in discussing the prior case law, it noted that all of the cases involved commercial activities. In *Wickard*, for example, Congress was trying to control the price of wheat (buying and selling wheat is commercial), and it needed to control home-grown and home-consumed wheat in order to truly control the price of all the wheat that was in interstate commerce. Home-grown wheat competed with interstate wheat.

The Court will allow Congress to regulate an activity that is within one state if it affects activities in other states, and if the activity is commercial. Merely "possessing" a gun near a school year (unlike, for example, buying a gun

44. 514 U.S. at 565–67, 115 S.Ct. at 1633–34.

45. 514 U.S. at 557–59, 115 S.Ct. at 1629–30. See Rotunda, The New States' Rights, the New Federalism,

the New Commerce Clause, and the Proposed New Abdication, 25 Okl.City L.Rev. 869 (2000).

46. 317 U.S. 111, 63 S.Ct. 82, 87 L.Ed. 122 (1942).

near a school year) is not commercial. Regulating the production of home-grown wheat in *Wickard* is the necessary and proper to regulating the price and supply of wheat that crossed state lines.

However, the Chief Justice's opinion in *Lopez* did not examine in detail the relationship of the necessary and proper clause to the commerce clause. The necessary and proper clause allows Congress to employ all means that are reasonably related to carrying out any federal power, including the commerce power.[47]

In the last quarter of the twentieth century, the Supreme Court was concerned with the extent to which federal statutes and regulations, which were justified under the commerce clause power of Congress, could be applied to state and local governments. In two cases, the Supreme Court ruled that the Tenth Amendment and principles of federalism prohibited the federal government from ordering a state or local government to take legislative or regulatory actions.[48]

In some cases, states and cities asked the judiciary to grant them a constitutional exemption from federal statutes and regulations that the federal government sought to justify under the Article I commerce power. Between 1976 and 1985, the Supreme Court briefly attempted to develop principles that would grant state or local governments limited immunity from federal laws that could be applied to private sector persons or businesses. In 1985 the Justices abandoned this approach and conclude that the Court would not set any significant limits on Congress' ability to impose "generally applicable" commercial regulations on state and local governments. The laws

are "generally applicable" when the regulations apply equally both public sector and private sector entities. For example, a minimum wage law that applies to all business in or affecting interstate commerce would govern both the minimum wage of state highway workers and private highway workers.[49]

In *Reno v. Condon*,[50] is another example of this principle. It held that the federal driver's Privacy Protection Act was within the scope of Congress's commerce power, and that it did not violate the Tenth Amendment. The Act prohibited *state governments* from disclosing information they receive from an individual who applies for a driver's license unless the individual driver consents to the disclosure or the disclosure falls within some specific exemptions from the ban, such as disclosures for law enforcement purposes. The Act also prohibited *private parties* who have received information concerning a driver from a state (pursuant to one of the exemptions in the Act) from disclosing the information about the driver except under certain circumstances.

Chief Justice Rehnquist, speaking for a unanimous Court, found that the information that the state received from drivers, which it would be turning over to private persons subject to the regulations in the Act, was obviously an item in interstate commerce. Thus, the Federal Act fell within the first two branches of the *Lopez* definition of the scope of the commerce power. Congress was regulating the channels of interstate commerce, and something in interstate commerce. It was unnecessary for the Court to consider whether the disclosure of drivers license information would have a substantial effect on interstate commerce.[51]

---

47. See Chapter 3, §§ 3.1–3.3, regarding the necessary and proper clause of Article I.

48. New York v. United States, 505 U.S. 144, 112 S.Ct. 2408, 120 L.Ed.2d 120 (1992) (Congress cannot order state to pass legislation regulating low-level radioactive waste or, in the alternative, to take ownership and possession of such waste); Printz v. United States, 521 U.S. 898, 117 S.Ct. 2365, 138 L.Ed.2d 914 (1997) (the federal government may not require state and local police officers to do "background checks" of persons who apply for firearm licenses). These cases are examined in § 4.10(d) of the Treatise.

49. The concluding section of this chapter analyzes the Court's decisions concerning the extent to which principles of federalism, and the Tenth Amendment, limit the scope of federal commerce legislation that can be made applicable to state and local governments. For example, Garcia v. San Antonio Metropolitan Transit Authority, 469 U.S. 528, 105 S.Ct. 1005, 83 L.Ed.2d 1016 (1985), overruled National League of Cities v. Usery, 426 U.S. 833, 96 S.Ct. 2465, 49 L.Ed.2d 245 (1976). These cases are examined in § 4.10(d) of the Treatise.

50. Reno v. Condon, 528 U.S. 141, 120 S.Ct. 666, 145 L.Ed.2d 587 (2000).

51. 528 U.S. at 148, 120 S.Ct. at 671.

Condon also unanimously ruled that the application of the Act to state agencies did not violate any Tenth Amendment principles because the states were being regulated with an otherwise valid commerce power law that applied to both private sector actors and public entities. The fact that states would have to spend money to comply with the federal Act, by setting up administrative systems for regulating disclosure of drivers license information, did not interfere with any aspect of state sovereignty that was protected by the Tenth Amendment.[52]

Later, the Court interpreted several statutes narrowly to avoid constitutional issues created by the *Lopez* line of cases.[53] But, the Court did not backtrack on *Lopez*, and later, in *United States v. Morrison*,[54] held (also, 5 to 4) that Congress could not make it a crime, under the commerce clause, to engage in sex-motived assaults. These issues are discussed below, in § 4.10(c).

§ 4.10   Refinement and Application of the New Standards

(a) Introduction

There are decisions in three subject areas— civil rights legislation, federal criminal laws concerning traditionally local crimes, and the regulation of activities of state governmental entities—that further refine general commerce clause principles. One must be aware of the approaches that the Court has taken in the review of the federal legislation in these areas in order to have a complete picture of current commerce clause analysis.

(b) Civil Rights Legislation

In 1964, the Supreme Court upheld the constitutionality of Title II of the Civil Rights Act.[1] This provision imposed penalties on anyone who deprived another person of equal enjoyment of places of public accommodation on the basis of the individual's race, color, religion, or national origin. The Act covered all but the smallest rooming houses or hotels, restaurants, entertainment centers, or other retail establishments that made use of products that had moved in interstate commerce or that had otherwise affected commerce.

The Court upheld the application of the restrictions to hotels in *Heart of Atlanta Motel Inc. v. United States*.[2] There were no congressional findings connected to the bill regarding the relationship between discriminatory practices in hotels and interstate commerce. However, the opinion found that there was no need for formalized congressional findings to support commerce power legislation because the Court does not treat Congress like it treats an administrative agency. Congress can properly collect information from outside the record of a congressional hearing; it can listen to the views of its constituents; it can respond to letters from voters. And, as a logical matter, the decision of motels to not serve blacks or

---

52. 528 U.S. at 149–50, 120 S.Ct. at 671–72. The scope of state immunity from federal laws is examined in § 4.10(d).

The fact that Congress may make a state government subject to regulation under the commerce power does not mean that the federal government may subject the states to suits by private persons if the state chooses to violate the federal regulation. For example, in Kimel v. Florida Board of Regents, 528 U.S. 62, 120 S.Ct. 631, 145 L.Ed.2d 522 (2000) the Supreme Court (5 to 4) held that state employees who had suffered age discrimination in violation of the age discrimination in employment act by their state government employer could not bring suit for money damages against the state, because such suits were barred by the Eleventh Amendment. For an examination of the scope of immunity from suits by private individuals that the Eleventh Amendment offers, see § 2.11 of this Treatise.

53. E.g, Jones v. United States, 529 U.S. 848, 120 S.Ct. 1904, 146 L.Ed.2d 902 (2000); Solid Waste Agency v.

United States Army Corps of Engineers, 531 U.S. 159, 121 S.Ct. 675, 148 L.Ed.2d 576 (2001).

54. 529 U.S. 598, 120 S.Ct. 1740, 146 L.Ed.2d 658 (2000).

§ 4.10

1. 78 Stat. 241, 42 U.S.C.A. § 2000 et seq.

Prior to 1964, the Supreme Court had established the power of Congress under the commerce clause to prohibit racial discrimination in the use of the channels of commerce. Mitchell v. United States, 313 U.S. 80, 61 S.Ct. 873, 85 L.Ed. 1201 (1941); Morgan v. Virginia, 328 U.S. 373, 66 S.Ct. 1050, 90 L.Ed. 1317 (1946); Henderson v. United States, 339 U.S. 816, 70 S.Ct. 843, 94 L.Ed. 1302 (1950); Boynton v. Virginia, 364 U.S. 454, 81 S.Ct. 182, 5 L.Ed.2d 206 (1960).

2. 379 U.S. 241, 85 S.Ct. 348, 13 L.Ed.2d 258 (1964). See also Daniel v. Paul, 395 U.S. 298, 89 S.Ct. 1697, 23 L.Ed.2d 318 (1969) (application of Title II to a public recreational facility).

other minorities, like the decision of restaurants not to serve blacks or other racial minorities, makes it much more difficult for these people to travel from state to state.

The Court stated that commerce power legislation would be upheld if there were any arguable connection between the regulation and commerce that touched more states than one. Congress' motive did not have to be commercial because the interstate commerce power was plenary. The opinion dictated the deference due Congress under the commerce power.

It stated the proper questions for judicial review:

> The only questions are: (1) whether Congress had a *rational basis* for finding that racial discrimination by motels affected commerce, and (2) if it had such a basis, whether the means it selected to eliminate that evil are reasonable and appropriate.[3]

The records of the congressional consideration of these bills was "replete with evidence" of the ways in which racial discrimination affected interstate travel by black persons.[4] The Court recognized, as it had done in the time of Chief Justice Marshall, that interstate transactions and transportation fell under the commerce power. Crossing state lines is classically treated as interstate commerce, at least since the *Lottery Act Cases*.[5] Congress can forbid the crossing of the state lines when it does not involve a commercial transaction—such as federal prohibition, found in the White Slave Traffic Act, of crossing state lines for debauchery and immoral purposes (noncommercial vice), as the Court held in the early part of the Twentieth Century.[6]

In *Katzenbach v. McClung*[7] the Court upheld the application of Title II of the Civil Rights Act to the now famous "Ollie's Barbeque," a family-owned restaurant in Birmingham, Alabama, located over a mile away from an inter-state highway or major method of transportation. The Act by its terms applied to any restaurant that either served interstate travelers or that served to intrastate patrons products of which a substantial portion had moved in interstate commerce.

No interstate travelers were served at the restaurant. However, Ollie's had purchased almost $70,000 worth of meat the previous year from a supplier who received it from out-of-state sources. This purchase both brought the restaurant under the terms of the Act and sustained a constitutional exercise of the commerce power over it. As a logical matter, if the restaurant would not serve interstate travelers, that also would *affect* interstate transportation because it would make it harder for all interstate travelers (whether or not members of a racial minority) to travel from state to state, because some restaurants would not serve interstate travelers.

Katzenbach v. McClung recognized that no direct congressional testimony clearly established a relationship between discrimination in such establishments and interstate commerce. However, a search for such detailed evidence would have been based on an erroneous view of the role of the Court in reviewing commerce power legislation. There could be no argument with the rationality of the theory that restricting the availability of food and public accommodations services to members of minority races had a restrictive effect upon their interstate travel. It made no difference that Ollie's Barbeque was quite small, for the *Wickard* principle already established that Congress could regulate what seemed to be trivial activities if, added together, they had, as an aggregate, a non-trivial affect on commerce.[8] There were additional bases for regulating the practices of Ollie's Barbeque based upon the affect of the discrimination on commerce and the regulations of goods that had passed across state lines.

---

3. 379 U.S. at 258–59, 85 S.Ct. at 358 (emphasis added).

4. 379 U.S. at 252–53, 85 S.Ct. at 355.

5. Champion v. Ames, 188 U.S. 321, 23 S.Ct. 321, 47 L.Ed. 492 (1903).

6. Caminetti v. United States, 242 U.S. 470, 37 S.Ct. 192, 61 L.Ed. 442 (1917).

7. 379 U.S. 294, 85 S.Ct. 377, 13 L.Ed.2d 290 (1964).

8. 379 U.S. at 301, 85 S.Ct. at 382, citing Wickard v. Filburn, 317 U.S. 111, 63 S.Ct. 82, 87 L.Ed. 122 (1942).

However, the Court did not formally abdicate its role in this area. Justice Black, concurring in *Heart of Atlanta Hotel*, said that "whether particular operations affect interstate commerce sufficiently to come under the constitutional power of Congress to regulate them is ultimately a judicial rather than a legislative question, and can be settled finally only by this Court."[9] In *Katzenbach v. McClung*, the Court agreed: "Of course, the mere fact that Congress has said when particular activity shall be deemed to affect commerce does not preclude further examination by this Court."[10] Yet, the Court was giving Congress deference on economic matters.[11] The question was simply whether Congress had a rational basis for finding a chosen regulatory scheme necessary for the protection of commerce.

(c) Federal Criminal Laws

Another area in which the Supreme Court has given increased deference to the legislature is its use of the commerce power to establish jurisdiction for federal criminal laws. Congress has the inherent power to establish criminal penalties for actions that interfere with any federal interest. Thus, Congress may establish crimes related to any action taken on federal lands under its property power,[12] activities relating to interstate communications under the postal power,[13] the evasion of tax statutes under the taxation power,[14] or the

violation of federal civil rights under the powers granted by certain Amendments to the Constitution.[15] The federal government may also place conditions on the use of federal money or activities taken with, or against, persons who have received federal grants.[16]

The commerce power also offers an independent basis for the enactment of federal criminal laws. The tests here are identical to those used to analyze the validity of any federal regulation under the commerce power. To be a proper subject for a commerce-based criminal statute, an activity must either relate to interstate transactions, have an effect on interstate commerce, or be an activity that is necessary and proper to regulate in order to effectuate the commerce power.

Perhaps the most far-reaching federal criminal statutes have related to the prohibition of interstate transportation incident to some other crime.[17] These include such well known statutes as the Mann Act, which outlaws the transportation of women for immoral purposes,[18] the Dyer Act, which punishes the interstate transportation of stolen vehicles,[19] and the Lindbergh Law, which punishes kidnapings that are related to interstate transportation or commerce.[20]

Congress, when establishing criminal statutes, may also make use of its power to regu-

9. Black, J., concurring, Heart of Atlanta Motel v. United States, 379 U.S. 241, 273, 85 S.Ct. 348, 366, 13 L.Ed.2d 258 (1964).

10. 379 U.S. 294, 303–04, 85 S.Ct. 377, 383, 13 L.Ed.2d 290 (1964).

11. 379 U.S. at 303–04, 85 S.Ct. at 383–84.

12. U.S. Const. art. IV, § 3, cl. 2. See, e.g., 18 U.S.C.A. §§ 3, 9a, 10a.

13. Ex parte Jackson, 96 U.S. (6 Otto) 727, 24 L.Ed. 877 (1878) (crime to circulate materials relating to lotteries). Public Clearing House v. Coyne, 194 U.S. 497, 24 S.Ct. 789, 48 L.Ed. 1092 (1904) (fraudulent orders); Roth v. United States, 354 U.S. 476, 77 S.Ct. 1304, 1 L.Ed.2d 1498 (1957), rehearing denied 355 U.S. 852, 78 S.Ct. 8, 2 L.Ed.2d 60 (1957), (mailing obscene matter).

14. 18 U.S.C.A. § 3045; 26 U.S.C.A. § 7201 et seq.

15. See, e.g., 18 U.S.C.A. §§ 241–245. The Congressional power to enforce civil rights is examined in Chapter 15.

16. For example, in Salinas v. United States, 522 U.S. 52, 118 S.Ct. 469, 139 L.Ed.2d 352 (1997), the Supreme Court ruled that the federal statute prohibiting bribing a

state or local government official, if that government entity had received more than $10,000 of federal money, did not require the federal government to prove that the bribery affected the use of federal funds. Justice Kennedy, writing for a unanimous Court in *Salinas,* avoided ruling on whether the federal grant to a state or local government would allow the federal government to have jurisdiction over every type of criminal activity that might involve the federal grant.

17. Rewis v. United States, 401 U.S. 808, 91 S.Ct. 1056, 28 L.Ed.2d 493 (1971) (conducting a gambling operation frequented by out-of-state bettors is not, without more, a violation of an act prohibiting interstate travel with intent to establish an illegal activity).

18. 18 U.S.C.A. § 2421. See Hoke v. United States, 227 U.S. 308, 33 S.Ct. 281, 57 L.Ed. 523 (1913).

19. 18 U.S.C.A. § 2312. See Brooks v. United States, 267 U.S. 432, 45 S.Ct. 345, 69 L.Ed. 699 (1925).

20. 18 U.S.C.A. § 1201. See Gooch v. United States, 297 U.S. 124, 56 S.Ct. 395, 80 L.Ed. 522 (1936).

late items that have passed in interstate commerce. Thus, Congress has made it a crime for a person who is convicted of a felony to receive or possess a firearm that was transported at any time in interstate commerce. The Supreme Court has not only upheld this statute but has applied it to a person who was not convicted of a felony until after he had received the firearm and long after it had been the subject of interstate commerce.[21]

The Supreme Court has given great, but not total, deference to Congress when reviewing criminal statutes enacted under the commerce power. The Court's deference to Congress is demonstrated in *Perez v. United States*.[22] In this case the Court upheld Title II of the Consumer Credit Protection Act, which makes a federal crime of extortionate credit transactions, an activity otherwise known as "loan sharking." The statute made it a crime to charge excessive rates of interest, or to use violence or the threat of violence to collect debts.

The Act did not require any specific connection between the transaction and interstate commerce to subject it to criminal penalties. However, the opening section of the Act included findings by Congress that organized crime was interstate in character and that a substantial part of the income of organized crime came from extortionate credit transactions. These findings also stated that extortionate credit transactions were carried out to a substantial extent in interstate commerce and that even where they were "purely intrastate in character, they nevertheless directly affect interstate and foreign commerce."

The defendant Perez had been found guilty of engaging in an extortionate credit transaction in his loans to a person in New York. All of the activities took place in the State of New York and there was no evidence that Perez was connected to organized crime or that he

had ever used the instrumentalities of commerce in connection with his loan sharking business. The Court, nonetheless, upheld his conviction under the commerce power. Justice Douglas, for the majority, found that it was rational for Congress to conclude that even intrastate loan sharking (a commercial activity) affected interstate commerce by altering property ownership on a massive scale and by financing criminal organizations that might operate in several states.

The opinion did note that although the Court gave deference to the Congressional findings, Congress did not need to make particular findings in order to support the statute.[23] The Court would have upheld the act as long as there was a rational argument for finding a connection between the regulated activity and commerce. It made no difference that the regulated activity was one of the traditional subject matters of local police power legislation. The Supreme Court would no longer interpret the congressional power in terms of subject areas reserved to the states by the Tenth Amendment.

Only Justice Stewart dissented in the *Perez* decision.[24] He stated that there were simply no facts upon which he could make a rational distinction between loan sharking and other local crimes. Because he could find no clear connection between intrastate loan sharking activities and interstate commercial problems, he would have held that the regulation of this local, intrastate crime was "reserved to the states under the Ninth and Tenth Amendments." But no other Justice was of the opinion that the Constitution required that the states be given primary jurisdiction over any subject matter—even traditional forms of local commercial crime.

Almost a quarter of a century after the *Perez* decision, the Supreme Court, without overrul-

---

21. Gun Control Act of 1968, 18 U.S.C.A. §§ 921–928. Barrett v. United States, 423 U.S. 212, 96 S.Ct. 498, 46 L.Ed.2d 450 (1976); Scarborough v. United States, 431 U.S. 563, 97 S.Ct. 1963, 52 L.Ed.2d 582 (1977). For citations to additional Supreme Court cases on this point, see R. Rotunda & J. Nowak, Treatise on Constitutional Law: Substance and Procedure, vol. 1, § 4.10 (3rd ed. 1999, with annual supplements).

22. 402 U.S. 146, 91 S.Ct. 1357, 28 L.Ed.2d 686 (1971), upholding, Title II, 82 Stat. 159, 18 U.S.C.A. § 891 et seq.

23. 402 U.S. at 155–56, 91 S.Ct. at 1362–63.

24. 402 U.S. at 157, 91 S.Ct. at 1363 (Stewart, J., dissenting).

ing *Perez,* limited the scope of Congress' power to make a single state activity a federal crime. In *United States v. Lopez,*[25] the Supreme Court, by a five to four vote, invalidated a federal statute that imposed criminal penalties on persons who "possessed" a firearm within one thousand feet of any school building. Writing for the majority in *Lopez,* Chief Justice Rehnquist ruled that the law exceeded the scope of congressional authority under the commerce clause.

One can read too much into *Lopez.* The Court did not overrule any prior case, and it cited with approval *Perez* and *Wickard v. Filburn.*[26] The statute at issue in *Lopez* was not limited to firearms or individuals that had crossed state lines; it was not limited to firearms that had been purchased in another state. It was not governing anything commercial in nature. The law simply forbade "possession" of a gun within 1000 feet of a school. The Federal Government, in the course of prosecuting Lopez, made no effort to. Yet, it is the fact that *Lopez* was the first U.S. Supreme Court decision since FDR.'s Court Packing Plan to find that something not in interstate commerce.

The Chief Justice's majority opinion in *Lopez* reaffirmed Congress' power, under the commerce clause, to regulate transactions, activities, persons, or products that cross state lines. Congress may also regulate intra-state *commercial* activities that have a substantial affect on interstate commerce. The Court distinguished *Wickard,* which it described as "perhaps the most far reaching example of

Commerce Clause authority over intrastate activity," as involving "*economic* activity" in a way that the *possession* of a gun in a school zone does not.[27] In *Wickard* the Government wanted to control the nationwide price of wheat, and it recognized that home grown wheat competed with, and had a substantial influence on, the price of wheat grown for sale.

The Court cited with approval *Perez,* but it noted that the law there forbade extortionate credit transactions and, that, the majority emphasized, is an *economic* crime, relating to commerce. In contrast, the law involved in *Lopez* is not "an essential part of a larger regulation of *economic* activity, in which the regulatory scheme could be undercut unless the intrastate activity were regulated."[28]

The statute in *Lopez* "has nothing to do with 'commerce' or any sort of economic enterprise, however broadly one might define those terms." It is not any "essential part of a larger regulation of economic activity, in which the regulatory scheme could be undercut unless the intrastate activity were regulated. It cannot, therefore, be sustained under our cases upholding regulations of activities that arise out of or are connected with a *commercial* transaction, which viewed in the aggregate, substantially affects interstate commerce."[29]

In a later case the Court again explained that. "a fair reading of *Lopez* shows that the *noneconomic,* criminal nature of the conduct at issue was central to our decision in that case."[30]

25. 514 U.S. 549, 115 S.Ct. 1624, 131 L.Ed.2d 626 (1995). Apparently Justice Scalia was the only member of the Court who could join the Chief Justice's majority opinion without adding any additional comments. Justices Kennedy, O'Connor, and Thomas joined the majority opinion by Chief Justice Rehnquist and also filed concurring opinions. 514 U.S. at 567, 115 S.Ct. at 1634 (Kennedy, J., joined by O'Connor, J., concurring in the judgment and opinion of the Court); 514 U.S. at 583, 115 S.Ct. at 1642 (Thomas, J., concurring). Justices Stevens, Souter, Ginsburg and Breyer dissented in *Lopez.* 514 U.S. at 602, 115 S.Ct. at 1651 (Stevens, J., dissenting); 514 U.S. at 603, 115 S.Ct. at 1651 (Souter, J., dissenting); 514 U.S. at 615, 115 S.Ct. at 1657 (Breyer, J., joined by Stevens, Souter, and Ginsburg, JJ., dissenting).

26. 317 U.S. 111, 63 S.Ct. 82, 87 L.Ed. 122 (1942).

27. 514 U.S. 549, 560, 115 S.Ct. 1624, 1630, 131 L.Ed.2d 626 (emphasis added). John C. Yoo, Sounds of Sovereignty: Defining Federalism in the 1990s, 32 Ind. L. Rev. 27 (1998).

28. 514 U.S. 549, 561, 115 S.Ct. 1624, 1631, 131 L.Ed.2d 626 (emphasis added). Ronald D. Rotunda, The Implications of the New Commerce Clause Jurisprudence: An Evolutionary or Revolutionary Court?, 55 Arkansas L. Rev. 795 (2003).

29. 514 U.S. 549, 560–61, 115 S.Ct. 1624, 1630–31, 131 L.Ed.2d 626 (emphasis added). Ronald D. Rotunda, The New States' Rights, the New Federalism, the New Commerce Clause, and the Proposed New Abdication, 25 Oklahoma City U. L. Rev. 869 (2000).

30. United States v. Morrison 529 U.S. 598, 610, 120 S.Ct. 1740, 1750, 146 L.Ed.2d 658 (2000).

The federal government in *Lopez* argued that the possession of firearms near schools might disrupt the educational process in the school and that disruption of the educational process would adversely affect the economy of the United States. However, the statute invalidated in *Lopez* did not contain any congressional findings as to the relationship of the regulated activity to interstate commerce. Moreover, *Lopez* stated that the Justices had to make an independent evaluation of the effect of the intrastate activity on interstate commerce. Indeed, even Justice Breyer's dissent, joined by Justices Stevens, Souter, and Ginsburg, conceded that: "we must judge this matter independently. '[S]imply because Congress may conclude that a particular activity substantially affects interstate commerce does not necessarily make it so.' "[31]

The simplest way to think of this case is that guns near schools are likely to cause crime near schools. That crime, like all crime, "affects" interstate commerce in that sense that almost everything affects interstate commerce. But, the *Lopez* Court said it will not use the aggregation doctrine, formulated in cases like *Wickard*, to aggregate *non-commercial intra*-state activities, although it will aggregate *commercial intra*-state activities. If the activities cross state lines (e.g., transportation of minors for immoral, non-commercial vice) all nine justices agree that Congress may regulate without regard to whether the activity prohibited is commercial.

Breyer's dissent in *Lopez* (which Stevens, Souter, and Ginsburg joined), rejected this test, but conceded that there are limits to the reach of the Commerce Clause, and that Congress could not, for example, "marriage, divorce, and child custody," or "any and all aspects of education."[32] This list is a little

unusual, for it includes matters that the federal government already regulates. Federal Government has a Cabinet-level Department of Education, and it already regulates many aspects of education. The Federal Government also regulates many aspects of child support.[33] Many people who have gone through divorce, as well as the federal and state judges who review the cases, realize that it is largely an economic dissolution; and much of the law surrounding it reflects these economic aspects. It is literally black letter law that even though federal courts do not grant divorces, federal statutes and case law already regulate a great deal of marriage, divorce, and child custody.[34]

Less than a week after *Lopez*, the Court decided *United States v. Robertson*.[35] The Government secured a conviction of Juan Robertson for various narcotics offenses and for violating a provision of the Racketeer Influenced and Corrupt Organizations Act ("RICO") by investing proceeds of his unlawful activities in an enterprise "engaged in, or the activities of which affect, interstate or foreign commerce." Robertson invested in a gold mine in Alaska. The Ninth Circuit reversed the RICO count because the Government had failed to introduce sufficient evidence that the gold mine was "engaged in or affect[ed] interstate commerce." A unanimous Supreme Court reversed. It was unnecessary to consider whether the activities of the gold mine "affected" interstate commerce because the "affects" test is necessary only to "define the extent of Congress' power over purely intrastate commercial activities that nonetheless have substantial interstate effects." In this case, there was proof of *inter*state activity: money, workers, and goods crossed state lines. That was the touchstone, the acid test, and every justice embraced it.[36]

31. 514 U.S. 549, 617, 115 S.Ct. 1624, 1658, 131 L.Ed.2d 626 (Breyer, J., dissenting).

32. 514 U.S. at 624, 115 S.Ct. at 1660 (Breyer, J., dissenting).

33. Bowen v. Gilliard, 483 U.S. 587, 107 S.Ct. 3008, 97 L.Ed.2d 485 (1987) (upholding the constitutionality of federal statutes governing the Aid to Families with Dependent Children ("AFDC") program). United States v. Faasse, 265 F.3d 475 (6th Cir. 2001) (upholding a criminal prosecution of the federal Child Support Recovery Act

("CSRA"), which was enacted pursuant to the Commerce power).

34. For a very succinct treatment of these issues and an excellent discussion of the more important federal statutes and case law, See Harry D. Krause, Family Law in a Nutshell 4–38, 263–67, 395–400 (3d ed. 1995).

35. 514 U.S. 669, 115 S.Ct. 1732, 131 L.Ed.2d 714 (1995) (per curiam).

36. Scarborough v. United States, 431 U.S. 563, 97 S.Ct. 1963, 52 L.Ed.2d 582 (1977), held that proof was

Congress can regulate crossing a state line, even if there is not "commercial" act, because of its power over interstate transportation. If there was no United States but only individual states, any of the states would have had the power to forbid importation or transportation of goods or services into its borders, even if the transportation was not a commercial act. With the formation of the union and the delegation of the commerce power to Congress, the Federal Government now has the power to forbid importation or transportation of goods or services across state lines, even if the transportation was not a commercial act.

After *Lopez,* it is very difficult for Congress to impose a federal criminal punishment in intra-state activity if is not commercial in character. The Court will not aggregate non-commercial, intra-state activity. *Lopez* did not overrule the *Perez* decision, but the crime in that case—loan sharking—was a commercial activity. The Court will continue to use the aggregation doctrine if the intra-state activity is commercial in character.

The theoretical argument that widespread intra-state crimes (which do not involve commercial activity) somehow affect commerce will not justify a federal criminal statute. However, Congress could tie in the crime with crossing a state line, even if those activities are not commercial.[37] In *United States v. Morrison*[38] the majority would not allow Congress to aggregate the affects of a non-commercial, intra-state act (a sexual assault), but it specifically approved[39] of lower courts[40] that accepted other parts of the same statute that prohibited, e.g., a person who "travels across a State line or enters or leaves Indian country with the intent to injure, harass, or intimidate that person's spouse or intimate partner."[41]

While the Court, after *Lopez,* will give great deference to Congress' regulation of single state activities that are commercial in nature (like the money lending activities regulated in *Perez*),[42] that deference does not apply if a regulated single state activity (like the possession of a firearm near a school) is noncommercial in nature.

required that a firearm previously traveled in interstate commerce to satisfy the required nexus between possession and commerce.

37. *Lopez* reaffirmed the traditional standards used to determine whether an activity came within the federal commerce power. The majority opinion found that Congress had the power, under the commerce clause, to regulate: (1) the channels of interstate commerce; (2) both the instrumentalities of interstate commerce and persons or things that traveled in interstate commerce; and (3) single-state activities that have a substantial relation to interstate commerce. United States v. Lopez, 514 U.S. 549, 557–59, 115 S.Ct. 1624, 1629–30, 131 L.Ed.2d 626 (1995).

The federal government may regulate firearms under its commerce power if its regulation fits within the commerce clause standards set out in *Lopez,* and so long as the regulation does not violate the Second Amendment. The Court has continued to uphold the federal statutes punishing the use of firearms connected with criminal activity that could be regulated under Congress's commerce powers. See, e.g., United States v. Rodriguez–Moreno, 526 U.S. 275, 119 S.Ct. 1239, 143 L.Ed.2d 388 (1999), w here Thomas, J., for the Court, held that a prosecution for carrying or using a firearm in relation to a crime of violence could be prosecuted in any federal district where the crime of violence was committed, even though the firearm was only used or carried by the defendant in a single district. In that case, the kidnaping progressed from Texas to New Jersey, New York, and then Maryland.

The Supreme Court has applied the federal statute prohibiting "carjacking" without specifically considering

the federal commerce power. The Carjacking Correction Act of 1996, amending the Violent Crime Control and Law Enforcement Act of 1994, refers to taking a motor vehicle "that has been transported, shipped, or received in interstate or foreign commerce." Because this federal statute regulates cars that have traveled in interstate commerce, the Court, when it interpreted the carjacking statute did not need to consider whether Congress would regulate local criminal activity under its commerce power. See, e.g., Holloway v. United States, 526 U.S. 1, 119 S.Ct. 966, 143 L.Ed.2d 1 (1999). On this issue, see 1 Ronald D. Rotunda & John E. Nowak, Treatise on Constitutional Law: Substance and Procedure, Chapter 4 (West Group, 3d. ed. 1999).

38. 529 U.S. 598, 120 S.Ct. 1740, 146 L.Ed.2d 658 (2000).

39. 529 U.S. 598, 613, 120 S.Ct. 1740, 1752, 146 L.Ed.2d 658.

40. United States v. Lankford, 196 F.3d 563, 571–572 (C.A.5 1999) (collecting cases).

41. 8 U.S.C. § 2261(a)(1).

42. Justices Kennedy and O'Connor, who joined Chief Justice Rehnquist's majority opinion, also wrote a concurring opinion to emphasize the limited nature of the Court's ruling. These Justices noted that the opinion did not have any effect on the congressional power to regulate single-state commercial activities. United States v. Lopez, 514 U.S. 549, 567, 573, 115 S.Ct. 1624, 1634, 1637, 131 L.Ed.2d 626 (1995) (Kennedy, J., joined by O'Connor, J., concurring).

United States v. Morrison[43] follows in the wake of *Lopez*. *Morrison* invalidated parts of the "Violence Against Women Act" on the grounds that sex-based assaults wholly within one state are not "commerce" under the interstate commerce clause. The Court was concerned that we would no longer have a government limited to enumerated powers (either express or implied) if non-commercial acts wholly within one state like violence (even violence based on animus towards one's sex) are enough to justify any federal action under the commerce clause.

Justice Breyer's dissent accepted the principle that there are limits to the reach of the commerce clause. He also acknowledged the important federalism issue at stake:

> "No one denies the importance of the Constitution's federalist principles. Its state/federal division of authority protects liberty-both by restricting the burdens that government can impose from a distance and by facilitating citizen participation in government that is closer to home."[44]

In *Morrison*, Congress made factual findings; but in the view of the Court, they were irrelevant to the constitutional analysis under the Commerce Clause. This is not a situation where the Court conducted its own hearing and rejected Congress' factual conclusions. Instead, the Court found the factual conclusions to be irrelevant, because the Court will not aggregate the affects of non-commercial activities (in this case, sex-motivated violence).

Crime affects national productivity; and, when one aggregates the costs of individual crimes, from murder to assaults (whether sex-motivated or not), one might conclude that they all affect commerce. Another way of rephrasing that argument is to assert that, in modern times, when we measure distances by time rather than miles—Los Angeles is only a few hours from Chicago—everything is "commerce among the states," and we no longer have a government of limited or enumerated powers. Under that theory, the Commerce Clause reaches every-thing, including bar room brawls. However, the Court has never accepted that argument in two centuries, and *all nine justices* explicitly rejected it in *Lopez*.

In *Morrison*, the four dissenters appeared to be moving away from their position in *Lopez*. Justice Souter's dissent (joined by Stevens, Ginsburg, and Breyer) argued that it was "the Founders' considered judgment that politics, not judicial review, should mediate between state and national interests as the strength and legislative jurisdiction of the National Government inevitably increased through the expected growth of the national economy."[45] Later, in a footnote he said acknowledged that the John Marshall and precedent did not suggest that "politics defines the commerce power." And then he added, "Nor do we," yet, at the end of the footnote he seems to reject what he just said, for he concludes that the question whether the federal government should regulate an activity even if the states have traditionally dealt with it, "should be a political choice and *only a political choice.*"[46]

The majority's distinction between commercial matters (where it will aggregate intrastate activity) and non-commercial matters (where it will not apply the aggregation theory) is important. In all the prior aggregation cases, the activities were, in some sense, "commercial" in the way that "possessing" a gun or committing a sexual assault is not a "commercial" act. However, future cases may raise questions as to exactly what is "commercial." For example, a simple mugging is "commercial" in the sense that money changes hands, which is the intent of the mugger. *Lopez* might allow Congress to reach that conduct under the Commerce Clause.

43. 529 U.S. 598, 120 S.Ct. 1740, 146 L.Ed.2d 658 (2000).

44. 529 U.S. 598, 655, 120 S.Ct. 1740, 1774, 146 L.Ed.2d 658 (Breyer, J., dissenting). Justice Stevens joined in the dissent. Justices Souter and Ginsburg joined only Part I–A of the Breyer dissent, and this quotation comes before Part I–A.

45. 529 U.S. 598, 647, 120 S.Ct. 1740, 1769–70, 146 L.Ed.2d 658 (footnote omitted) (Souter, J., dissenting).

46. 529 U.S. 598, 651 n. 19, 120 S.Ct. 1740, 1772 n. 19, 146 L.Ed.2d 658 (Souter, J., dissenting) (emphasis added).

(d) Regulation of State and Local Government Entities

(1) Federal Orders to State and Local Governments

In the 1990's the Supreme Court handed down a series of rulings that the federal government could not use its power over interstate commerce to require (or commandeer) state or local government to take legislative or executive actions to enforce federal rules. These decisions do not prevent the federal government from regulating interstate commerce, but they do prohibit the federal government from regulating the states' regulation of interstate commerce.

The federalism principle that prevents the federal government from ordering state or local government to take certain governmental actions does not grant state and local government immunity from federal regulation of commercial activity. Thus, a federal labor law regulating the wages paid to employees of any business in or affecting commerce could apply to state and local governments just as it would apply to private sector activities.[47] Similarly, a federal law regulating the disposal of waste products, such as atomic waste or chemically hazardous waste, that applied to private persons or corporations could be applied to state or local governments that disposed of such waste.[48] But the structure of "dual sovereignty" that the Tenth Amendment represents, under our constitutional structure of federalism, prohibits the federal government from using the Commerce power to conscript state instrumentalities as its agents.

The Court decided the first major case in this area in 1992. *New York v. United States*,[49] held that federal legislation could not order states to adopt state legislation that would set state standards for the disposal of low level radioactive waste nor could federal legislation order the states to take ownership of privately owned radioactive waste in their states.

In an attempt to deal with the multistate problems inherent in the creation and disposal of low level radioactive waste, Congress had taken three distinct steps, two of which *New York v. United States* upheld unanimously.

Congress' first provision involved its spending power and its commerce power. Congress allowed states that had adopted regulations regarding the storage and disposal of radioactive waste (or that had joined multistate compacts adopting such standards) to impose a charge on the disposal of such waste. This charge would provide funds for a federal grant program that, in turn, would provide assistance money to states that had storage sites for radioactive waste that complied with federal guidelines.

Justice O'Connor wrote for a unanimous Court in upholding this grant program, because Congress' powers under the commerce and spending clauses allowed it to condition grants to states that were fulfilling federal goals. Such grants did not violate any form of sovereignty protected by the Tenth Amendment or other federalism principles.[50]

Congress' second step towards getting states to deal with radioactive waste in a manner

---

47. Garcia v. San Antonio Metropolitan Transit Authority, 469 U.S. 528, 105 S.Ct. 1005, 83 L.Ed.2d 1016 (1985), rehearing denied 471 U.S. 1049, 105 S.Ct. 2041, 85 L.Ed.2d 340 (1985). This case is discussed in the next paragraphs of this subsection of the Treatise.

48. In New York v. United States, 505 U.S. 144, 112 S.Ct. 2408, 120 L.Ed.2d 120 (1992), on remand 978 F.2d 705 (2d Cir.1992), Justice O'Connor's majority opinion stated that Congress could directly regulate all disposal of radioactive nuclear waste under its commerce power, even though the ruling in the case prohibited Congress from ordering states to adopt state laws concerning environmental matters that meet congressional standards. 505 U.S. at 167, 173, 112 S.Ct. at 2424, 2427.

49. 505 U.S. 144, 112 S.Ct. 2408, 120 L.Ed.2d 120 (1992), on remand 978 F.2d 705 (2d Cir.1992).

50. 505 U.S. at 165, 169–72, 112 S.Ct. at 2423, 2425–27. Justices White, Blackmun, and Stevens dissented from the Court's ruling insofar as the Court prohibited Congress from requiring states to regulate radioactive waste or to join multistate compacts regarding this subject. These three Justices joined the Court's opinion insofar as it upheld the financial incentives for states to regulate radioactive waste and congressional actions enhancing the commerce power of states to bar radioactive waste under certain circumstances. New York v. United States, 505 U.S. 144, 188, 112 S.Ct. 2408, 2435, 120 L.Ed.2d 120 (1992) (White, J., joined by Blackmun and Stevens, JJ., concurring in part and dissenting in part); 505 U.S. at 210, 112 S.Ct. at 2446 (Stevens, J., concurring in part and dissenting in part).

that met Congress' standard involved a grant of commerce power to some states. The federal legislation gave states that adopted radioactive waste storage and disposal guidelines, or that entered multistate compacts for the disposal of radioactive waste consistent with federal guidelines, the authority to impose a discriminatory tax against, or to completely bar, the importation of radioactive waste from states that had not adopted storage and disposal programs or compacts consistent with federal guidelines.[51] Absent federal authorization, a state law banning the importation of out-of-state garbage or waste for disposal in local landfills would violate the commerce clause if the out-of-state waste did not represent a unique health hazard to the people of the state that enacted the tariff or trade barrier.[52]

Justice O'Connor found, also unanimously, that Congress could authorize the states to create such trade barriers. This exercise of Congress' commerce power would make the state law immune from any commerce power challenge.[53] The effect of these federal legislative provisions on states that had failed to adopt federal guidelines (and whose citizens and businesses, therefore, could not easily export their waste to other states) did not intrude on any element of sovereignty that was protected by federalism principles or the Tenth Amendment.

The only part of the federal program designed to guard against the hazards of low level radioactive waste that the Supreme Court invalidated was the so-called "take title provision" of the federal legislation. In the take title provision, Congress offered the states the "option" of either enacting state laws (through legislation or through joining a regional compact of states) that regulated the storage and disposal of radioactive waste in conformity with federal guidelines or, in the alternative, taking possession and ownership of all radioactive waste in the state (including all radioactive waste that had been produced by private persons or corporations in the state).

New York v. United States invalidated (6 to 3) the take title provision. Justice O'Connor for the majority, found that federal judges had a proper role in defining the limit of federal power over state and local governments due to the structure of the federal system established by our Constitution and the Tenth Amendment. The Tenth Amendment, she said, is a tautology. The real question is whether the Commerce Power, an enumerated power, authorizes the federal government to conscript the states to enact legislation that Congress orders the states to enact. Her conclusion is that the power of Congress to order a state to enact a law is a power the Constitution has not conferred on Congress and so it not part of it's commerce power.[54]

51. New York v. United States, 505 U.S. 144, 173, 112 S.Ct. 2408, 2427, 120 L.Ed.2d 120 (1992), on remand 978 F.2d 705 (2d Cir.1992). See also the dissenting opinions of Justices White and Stevens that were referred to in the previous footnote.

52. See, e.g., Chemical Waste Management, Inc. v. Hunt, 504 U.S. 334, 112 S.Ct. 2009, 119 L.Ed.2d 121 (1992) (invalidating a discriminatory fee imposed by a state on the disposal of hazardous waste from out-of-state sources); City of Philadelphia v. New Jersey, 437 U.S. 617, 98 S.Ct. 2531, 57 L.Ed.2d 475 (1978) (invalidating a trade barrier against the implication of out-of-state produced waste for disposal in privately owned landfills in the state).

53. "As a simple regulation, this provision [by which Congress allowed states that met federal guidelines to bar the importation of radioactive waste from states that did not meet federal standards] would be within the power of Congress to authorize the States to discriminate against interstate commerce." New York v. United States, 505 U.S. 144, 172, 112 S.Ct. 2408, 2427, 120 L.Ed.2d 120 (1992), on remand 978 F.2d 705 (2d Cir.1992).

54. She stated: "This limit [on congressional power over states] is not derived from the text of the Tenth Amendment itself, which, as we have discussed, is essentially a tautology ... the Tenth Amendment test directs us to determine, as in this case, whether an incident of state sovereignty is protected by a limitation on an Article I power ... it makes no difference whether one views the question at issue in this case as one of ascertaining the limits of the power delegated to the Federal Government under the affirmative provisions of the Constitution or one of discerning the core of sovereignty retained by the States under the Tenth Amendment." 505 U.S. at 156–58, 112 S.Ct. at 2418–2419.

The Court did not rule on the question of whether the republican form of government (the so-called guarantee clause) of Article IV, § 4 of the Constitution provided a basis for confining the federal power over state and local government because that issue would not affect the outcome of the case, given the Court's view of federalism and Tenth Amendment principles in this case. 505 U.S. at 182–184, 112 S.Ct. at 2432–2433.

Justice O'Connor's opinion recognized a wide scope of congressional power to regulate commerce. Congress could have directly regulated the disposal of radioactive waste.[55] However, Congress did not have the power "to regulate state governments' regulation of interstate commerce" because Congress could not simply "direct the States to provide for the disposal of radioactive waste."[56] Requiring the state to take possession and ownership of the radioactive waste was the same as requiring the state to use its legislative and executive powers. Thus, the portion of the take title provision that ordered noncomplying states to take ownership of radioactive waste was invalid.

If Congress wishes to regulate radioactive waste in a particular way, after *New York v. United States*, it can (1) regulate the activity directly (and take political accountability if members of the populace dislike the federal regulations); (2) reward states with monetary grants conditioned on achieving federal standards for the disposal of radioactive waste; and (3) strengthen the commerce powers of states that meet federal guidelines by allowing them to prohibit the importation of radioactive waste from states that do not meet federal safety guidelines.

New York v. United States is a very important decision. To an extent it places important limitations on the power of the federal government to impose unfunded mandates on states. But this ruling is also a very limited one that only prevents Congress from making the state

governments, or the subdivisions or branches thereof, instruments for the carrying out of congressional dictates.[57] The Court's decisions in this area are "modest countermeasures," that are "less like impassable roadblocks placed in Congress's pathway" and, in the words of Professor William Van Alstyne, more akin to "traffic bumps" that merely slow down legislative traffic.[58]

Printz v. United States[59] is the second major case in the wake of *New York v. United States*. In 1993, Congress passed, and the President signed, the "Brady Handgun Violence Prevention Act" [the Brady Act], which modified the Gun Control Act of 1968.[60] A key provision of the Brady Act required a background check, under certain circumstances, for persons attempting to purchase firearms. The Act required the Attorney General of the United States, by 1998, to set up a national system that would check the background of persons attempting to purchase a gun. However, for the period prior to the establishment of the national background check system, the Brady Act required the chief law enforcement officer (CLEO) in the jurisdiction in which the would-be purchaser of the gun resided, under most circumstances, to review a form filled out by the gun purchaser and determine whether the purchaser was within a group of persons who were prohibited by federal law from purchasing guns. Congress did not want to spend the money to pay for these background checks during this interim period (either by offering money to the states or hiring federal workers

---

55. "The Constitution permits both the Federal Government and the States to enact legislation regarding the disposal of low level radioactive waste. The Constitution enables the Federal Government to pre-empt state regulation contrary to federal interest and it permits the federal government to hold out incentives to the States as a means of encouraging them to adopt suggested regulatory schemes. It does not, however, authorize Congress to simply direct the States to provide for the disposal of radioactive waste generated within their borders." New York v. United States, 505 U.S. 144, 189, 112 S.Ct. 2408, 2435, 120 L.Ed.2d 120 (1992), on remand 978 F.2d 705 (2d Cir.1992).

56. 505 U.S. at 165, 188, 112 S.Ct. at 2423, 2435.

57. The majority opinion in the *New York* decision distinguished the cases in which congressional laws regulating private sector activities had been enforceable in state courts. The cases allowing Congress to require state

courts to enforce federal laws, in cases otherwise properly before the state courts, "involve no more than an application of the Supremacy Clause's provision that federal law shall be the supreme Law of the Land, enforceable in every State." New York v. United States, 505 U.S. 144, 177–78, 112 S.Ct. 2408, 2429–30, 120 L.Ed.2d 120 (1992) (internal quotation marks omitted), on remand 978 F.2d 705 (2d Cir.1992).

58. William Van Alstyne, When Can A State Be Sued?, 66 POPULAR GOV'T, Issue 3, at 44–47 (2001), text as at note 11.

59. 521 U.S. 898, 117 S.Ct. 2365, 138 L.Ed.2d 914 (1997).

60. Brady Handgun Violence Prevention Act, Pub. L. 103–159, 107 Stat. 536, amending in part, The Gun Control Act of 1968, 18 U.S.C.A. § 921 at et seq.

directly). Congress, instead, imposed what amounted to an unfunded mandate on state executive branch officials.

Printz v. United States[61] ruled (5 to 4) that the provision of the Brady Act violated the principles of federalism and the Tenth Amendment because it imposed administrative duties on state and local law enforcement officials to administer federal law. Justice Scalia's majority opinion rested *Printz*'s ruling on three principles that the majority found to exist. First, the history of the Constitution, and its Amendments, provided no evidence that Congress had been given authority to control the activities of state legislatures or executive legislative officials. Second, the federal system that the Constitution of 1787 created did not give the federal government the power to control state or local legislative or executive officers merely for the purpose of implementing federal law. Third, earlier decisions of the Court, including *New York v. United States*, "have made clear that the federal government may not compel the states to implement by legislation or executive action, federal regulatory programs."[62]

For the majority, the *Printz* case involved a simple application of the *New York v. United States* principle that Congress could not use its commerce power to order state or local governments to be the instruments of federal authority, or to make state governments subject to laws that were not "generally applicable." Justice Scalia found it unnecessary to address whether Congress could condition the monetary grants to state and local governments on legislative or executive actions.[63] The majority did not reach the question whether constitutional provisions limited the ability of the federal government to require state and local

governments to provide information to the federal government.

Justice O'Connor concurred, noting that *Printz* involved only an application of the principles of *New York v. United States*.[64] In addition, she noted the Court had left open important questions. For example, could Congress require local law enforcement officials to report cases of missing children to the Department of Justice. Perhaps the Court would allow these "purely ministerial reporting requirements," or Congress might justify then on the theory that it is variant of the spending power (states report missing children in exchange for having access to the nationwide data base of missing children).[65]

Justices Stevens, Souter, Ginsburg, and Breyer dissented in *Printz*.[66] They rejected the majority's historical evidence related to the drafting or ratification of the Constitution and the subsequent history. Justice Souter, who had voted with the majority in *New York v. United States*, dissented in *Printz*. In his dissenting opinion, he did not repudiate his earlier vote but argued that, based on a vague passage from *The Federalist Papers,* the federal government could require state and local executive officers to implement federal law, even if the federal government was prohibited from requiring state or local legislatures to enact legislation.[67] The majority's response was that the Constitution's supremacy clause does specifically require state *judges* to enforce federal law. Moreover, judges routinely enforce and interpret foreign laws (e.g., the law of Italy, if the choice of law rules call for applying Italian law to interpret or enforce a contract.) in the cases that they decide. But there is no just clause that allows Congress to treat state

---

61. 521 U.S. 898, 117 S.Ct. 2365, 138 L.Ed.2d 914 (1997).

62. 521 U.S. at 925, 117 S.Ct. at 2380.

63. 521 U.S. at 918–19, 117 S.Ct. at 2376. See § 5.7 of this Treatise regarding conditions on federal monetary grants.

64. Printz v. United States, 521 U.S. 898, 935–36, 117 S.Ct. 2365, 2385, 138 L.Ed.2d 914 (1997) (O'Connor, J., concurring).

65. Justice Thomas wrote a concurring opinion, not joined by any other Justices, in which he expressed his

desire to see the Supreme Court further restrict the federal government's authority under the commerce clause. 521 U.S. at 937, 117 S.Ct. at 2386 (Thomas, J., concurring).

66. Printz v. United States, 521 U.S. 898, 939, 117 S.Ct. 2365, 2386, 138 L.Ed.2d 914 (1997) (Stevens, J., joined by Souter, Ginsburg, and Breyer, JJ., dissenting).

67. 521 U.S. at 970, 117 S.Ct. at 2401 (Souter, J., dissenting). Souter also joined the dissent written by Justice Stevens.

officials or the state legislature as its enforcement arm.

Neither *New York v. United States* nor *Printz v. United States* called into question the *Garcia*, which had denied constitutional immunity to states or cities that suffered financial burdens when complying with federal commercial regulations that govern both private sector and public sector activities. The line of cases represented by *New York v. United States* and *Printz v. United States* should be understood as creating only a limited principle prohibiting Congress from using the Commerce Clause to order state or local governments to take legislative or regulatory actions or to require executive officials of those governments to implement federal regulatory programs.[68] Congress may use section 5 of the Fourteenth Amendment to enact laws that

impose burdens on states. It may also "bribe" the states by using its spending power. And, Congress may use the Commerce power to impose burdens on the states if the states are subject to "generally applicable" laws. In other words, Congress can set the minimum wage for all workers in or affecting interstate commerce, and the minimum wage will apply to state workers in or affecting interstate commerce. But Congress cannot simpler order states to pay their Governors a special minimum wage because that law would not be "generally applicable."

The federal government may subject states to commerce power regulations that are applied to both private sector businesses and public sector entities engaged in similar types of activities that are involved in interstate commerce.[69] In some instances compliance with those laws will require a state to change its administrative systems. Compliance with

68. New York v. United States, 505 U.S. 144, 160, 112 S.Ct. 2408, 2420, 120 L.Ed.2d 120 (1992): "This case presents no occasion to apply or revisit the holding of any of these cases [concerning the applicability of federal commercial regulations to state and local government activities], as this is not a case in which Congress has subjected a state to the same legislation applicable to private parties."

In the same term in which *Printz* was decided, the Supreme Court unanimously upheld the application of the Fair Labor Standards Act [FLSA] to a local police department in Auer v. Robbins, 519 U.S. 452, 117 S.Ct. 905, 137 L.Ed.2d 79 (1997). Because the local police board had not challenged the constitutionality of applying FLSA to local government activity, Justice Scalia, writing for the Court in *Auer,* considered only statutory questions concerning the wages and benefits due those police officers who had done over-time work.

In Pennsylvania Dept. of Corrections v. Yeskey, 524 U.S. 206, 118 S.Ct. 1952, 141 L.Ed.2d 215 (1998), the Court ruled that the Americans with Disabilities Act [ADA] applied to inmates in state prisons, and that Title II of the ADA prohibited a state from denying admission into a "boot camp" for first time offenders to a convicted person solely on the basis of his physical disability. Justice Scalia, writing for a unanimous Court in *Yeskey,* "assumed without deciding, that the plain statement rule [requiring Congress to be clear when regulating state or local governments] does govern the application of the ADA to the administration of state prisons." The Court ruled that the ADA clearly applied to state and local prisons. Justice Scalia noted that, because the issue had not been raised in the lower courts, the Supreme Court was not addressing the issue of "whether applications of the ADA to state prisons is a constitutional exercise of Congress's power under either the Commerce Clause ... or § 5 of the Fourteenth Amendment ..." 524 U.S. at 212, 118 S.Ct. at 1956 (internal citations omitted).

In Garcia v. San Antonio Metropolitan Transit Authority, 469 U.S. 528, 105 S.Ct. 1005, 83 L.Ed.2d 1016 (1985),

rehearing denied 471 U.S. 1049, 105 S.Ct. 2041, 85 L.Ed.2d 340 (1985) a majority of the Justices endorsed the position that states would rarely, if ever, have immunity from federal commercial regulations that apply equally to both private sector and public sector entities. *Garcia* is examined in the next paragraphs of this section of the Treatise.

69. Garcia v. San Antonio Metropolitan Transit Authority, 469 U.S. 528, 105 S.Ct. 1005, 83 L.Ed.2d 1016 (1985) overruled National League of Cities v. Usery, 426 U.S. 833, 96 S.Ct. 2465, 49 L.Ed.2d 245 (1976), on remand 429 F.Supp. 703 (D.D.C.1977). The majority in *Garcia* overruled earlier Supreme Court attempts to create an area of immunity from federal commercial regulation for state and local government. But two of the youngest Justices on the Court in *Garcia* dissented in that case and indicated they expected the Court, in the future, to provide some constitutional protection to state and local governments. 469 U.S. at 579, 105 S.Ct. at 1032 (Rehnquist, J., dissenting); 469 U.S. at 580, 105 S.Ct. at 1033 (O'Connor, J., dissenting). In 1992, Justice O'Connor wrote the majority opinion in which the Court found that there were federalism and Tenth Amendment principles that prohibited federal legislation ordering state governments to take state legislative or regulatory actions; Chief Justice Rehnquist joined the entirety of Justice O'Connor's opinion. New York v. United States, 505 U.S. 144, 112 S.Ct. 2408, 120 L.Ed.2d 120 (1992), on remand 978 F.2d 705 (2d Cir.1992). The only three Justices who were on the Court in 1992 who had also been in the majority in *Garcia,* dissented from the Court's ruling in the *New York* case insofar as it invalidated federal legislation forcing states to adopt state legislation concerning the disposal of radioactive waste. 505 U.S. at 188, 112 S.Ct. at 2435 (White, J., joined by Blackmun and Stevens, JJ., concurring in part and dissenting in part); 505 U.S. at 211, 112 S.Ct. at 2446 (Stevens, J., concurring in part and dissenting in part).

In Auer v. Robbins, 519 U.S. 452, 117 S.Ct. 905, 137 L.Ed.2d 79 (1997), the Supreme Court applied the Fair

such laws will not violate the principles established by the *New York* and *Printz* cases.

This principle is illustrated in *Reno v. Condon*.[70] The Court unanimously upheld the Federal Drivers Privacy Protection Act, which prohibited state governments from disclosing information they received in drivers license applications except under limited circumstances. The Act *also limited* the use of such information by private persons who received the information through one of the exemptions established in the Act. Chief Justice Rehnquist easily found that the drivers license information is an article in commerce, and that the Federal Act came within the scope of Congress's Article I commerce power. The state alleged that the Act violated the Tenth Amendment by requiring the state to adjust its administrative systems to deal with the disclosure of drivers license information in conformity with the Federal Act. The Chief Justice responded that this Federal Act "does not require the states in their sovereign capacity to regulate their own citizens. [The Act] regulates the states as owners of databases. It does not require the South Carolina legislature to enact any laws or regulations, and it does not require state officials to assist in the enforcement of federal statutes regulating private individuals."[71] The law applied to private parties as well as the state: neither could buy or sell the information if certain circumstances applied.

(2) State and Local Government Immunity from Federal Commerce Regulations

(i) Introduction and Summary

The previous subsection examined the Court's decisions that established a limited,

but significant, principle that prohibits the federal government from using the Commerce Clause to order the executive or legislative branches of state or local governments to take legislative, regulatory, or executive actions. We will now turn to the question of whether the Tenth Amendment or other federalism principles create doctrines that would provide states with a broader immunity from federal regulatory laws. We will first look at the brief flirtation the Court had with the idea of creating a principle and then concentrate on the Court's current position, which denies state and local governments a broad constitutional immunity from most, if not all, federal legislation.

The general principle now is that Congress can impose commercial regulations that also apply to states and their instrumentalities. Congress may impose generally applicable commercial rules on private entities and states or it, as a matter of policy, may exempt states from the normal rules that, for example, apply to overtime work, minimum wage, and so on. But Congress can use it commerce power to enact generally applicable laws (e.g., minimum wage laws) that apply to private workers in or affecting interstate commerce and state workers in or affecting interstate commerce.

The final portion of this subsection takes a detailed look at the ill-fated tests that the Supreme Court tried to create during the 1976 to 1985 time period, when a majority of the Justices attempted to establish workable standards that would give state and local governments limited immunity from the application of federal commercial regulations to them. The Court has now abandoned that effort, but it is useful to analyze it in order to see why the

---

Labor Standards Act [FLSA] requirements regarding overtime wages and benefits to a local police force. The Police Board, which had been sued by sergeants in the city police force for over-time benefits and pay in *Auer*, did not challenge the constitutionality of applying FLSA to the police. Justice Scalia, writing for a unanimous Court in *Auer*, upheld the claim of the police officers for additional over-time compensation, and noted that this case involved only questions of statutory interpretation. 519 U.S. at 457, 117 S.Ct. at 909.

70. Reno v. Condon, 528 U.S. 141, 120 S.Ct. 666, 145 L.Ed.2d 587 (2000).

71. 528 U.S. at 151, 120 S.Ct. at 672. The fact that Congress can subject state governments to commercial regulations that are applicable to both private sector and public sector commercial activities does not mean that Congress can make states subject to suits by private persons for the states violations of such laws. The Eleventh Amendment and federalism principles grant state governments some immunity from private suits brought against them by persons other than the federal government or the United States government. See § 2.11 of this Treatise.

Court rejected the caselaw it developed in the decade between 1976 and 1985.

Between 1976 and 1985, the Court attempted to limit the power of the federal government to subject state or local governments to federal commercial regulations. Even during this period, the Court did not restrict federal power to regulate private sector commercial activities merely because activities intrastate but affected interstate commerce. A majority of the Justices between 1976 and 1985, however, eventually developed this test to determine if state and local governments had immunity from the application of a federal commercial regulation to them; they were immune if the particular federal regulation: (1) addressed the "states as states;" (2) regulated attributes of state or local sovereignty; (3) directly impaired the ability of state or local governments to structure operations in areas of traditional functions; and (4) was not related to an overriding federal interest.

The problem, of course, is that this test is quite vague. What are, for example, "attributed of state sovereignty"? When does a regulation "directly impair" state functions and which functions are "traditional"?

Finally, in 1985, in *Garcia v. San Antonio Metropolitan Transit Authority*,[72] the Court overruled prior caselaw and held that neither the Tenth Amendment nor the structure of the federal system justified restriction of Congress' power to apply otherwise valid commercial regulations to state or local governments. The law in question was generally applicable: the state faced "nothing more than the same minimum-wage and overtime obligations that hundreds of thousands of other employers, public as well as private, have to meet."[73]

Garcia held open the possibility that the Justices would defend state governments against congressional actions that would eliminate the sovereignty that states must possess to be a member of the federal system. However, it is unlikely that the Court, so long as it remains true to the view of the judicial power set forth in *Garcia*, would invalidate any federal regulation of state or local governments that did not directly impair the territorial integrity of the state or constitute a direct command from the federal government to alter basic local government policies. After *Garcia*, state or local governments must persuade Congress rather than the Court that they should not be subject to general commerce power regulations when compliance with those regulations would impair their ability to structure and operate their governmental departments and carry out their governmental functions. Laws that apply to both public and private sector commercial activity are to be reviewed now only under the general test regarding the scope of the federal commerce power that was set forth previously in this chapter.[74]

The commerce power, like all other federal powers, is subject to the restrictions of the Bill of Rights and other fundamental constitutional guarantees. However, from 1936 until 1976, the Tenth Amendment did not impose any check. It was considered only a truism that said that a government of enumerated powers is limited to those powers, express or implied, and augmented by the necessary and proper clause. Because the Commerce Clause is an enumerated power, the Tenth Amendment simply did not apply. The theoretical basis for

72. 469 U.S. 528, 105 S.Ct. 1005, 83 L.Ed.2d 1016 (1985), rehearing denied 471 U.S. 1049, 105 S.Ct. 2041, 85 L.Ed.2d 340 (1985).

Responding to *Garcia,* Congress in November of 1985 enacted the Fair Labor Standards Amendments of 1985, Pub.L. 99–150, in order to 99 Stat. 787 (amending 29 U.S.C.A. § 207 et seq.), which authorized states, their political subdivisions, and interstate governmental agencies to provide compensatory time to their employees in lieu of overtime subject to certain conditions.

73. 469 U.S. 528, 554, 105 S.Ct. 1005, 1019, 83 L.Ed.2d 1016.

74. See §§ 4.8–4.10(c), supra.

This chapter examines whether there are federalism limits on the exercise of the federal commerce power. It is important to remember that federalism concerns may, or may not, play a part in the interpretation of other provisions of the Constitution. For example, the Supreme Court has never found that there was any significant federalism limitation on the exercise of federal powers regarding foreign affairs or the military. See § 3.4 of this Treatise. Similarly, the Supreme Court has never protected state or local governments from the federal laws regulating international commerce or the federal laws regulating of American Indian tribes. See § 4.2 of this Treatise.

the judicial refusal to enforce that Amendment seemed invincible by the end of this forty-year period.[75] The, from 1976 to 1985, the Tenth Amendment had bite. Since then, it is once again a truism—although the Court does now hold that the Commerce Clause does not give Congress the power to order the states to pass laws regulating commerce; the Commerce Clause "authorizes Congress to regulate interstate commerce directly; it does not authorize Congress to regulate state governments' regulation of interstate commerce."[76] In the same case the Court said that the Tenth Amendment "is essentially a tautology. Instead, the Tenth Amendment confirms that the power of the Federal Government is subject to limits that may, in a given instance, reserve power to the States."[77]

Between 1936 and 1976 the Court had several opportunities to review federal regulations of state activities. Each time it found them to be within the scope of the federal commerce power. Prior to 1968, the Court had upheld the application of statutes setting railroad safety, labor relations, and employer liability requirements for railroad companies owned by state governments.[78] Although at least one majority opinion had held that the states could not block the exercises of federal commercial power to a greater degree than private individuals,[79] the Court had not yet considered the application of federal regulations to employees in the purely governmental enterprises of the state.

In 1968, the Supreme Court considered the application of the federal minimum wage requirements to employees of state and local government institutions such as hospitals and schools. *Maryland v. Wirtz*,[80] upheld such an application of the statute with only two Justices dissenting.

In *Maryland v. Wirtz* there was no question that the regulation of the hours, conditions, and wages of laborers in enterprises affecting interstate commerce fell within the power of Congress. The sole issue was whether the Constitution carved out an exemption for the employment practices of state and local governments. The Court said no; the federal government could act to achieve the proper goals of its enumerated powers in a manner that might override important state interests. The majority opinion indicated that Congress could not engage in "the utter destruction of the state as a sovereign political entity"[81] but otherwise set no specific limits on the commerce power. Only Justices Douglas and Stewart, in dissent, would have held that the Tenth Amendment prohibited federal regulations that constituted an undue interference with the performance of sovereign or governmental functions of the state.[82]

In the 1970's, there were indications that the Supreme Court would establish a Tenth Amendment principle to protect state governmental entities from certain federal regulations.[83] The Court had not decided in *Wirtz*

---

75. See discussion in, 1 R. Rotunda & J. Nowak, Treatise on Constitutional Law: Substance and Procedure § 4.10 (3rd ed. 1999, with annual supplements).

76. New York v. United States, 505 U.S. 144, 166, 112 S.Ct. 2408, 2423, 120 L.Ed.2d 120 (1992).

77. New York v. United States, 505 U.S. 144, 157, 112 S.Ct. 2408, 2418, 120 L.Ed.2d 120 (1992).

78. United States v. California, 297 U.S. 175, 56 S.Ct. 421, 80 L.Ed. 567 (1936); California v. Taylor, 353 U.S. 553, 77 S.Ct. 1037, 1 L.Ed.2d 1034 (1957).

79. United States v. California, 297 U.S. 175, 184–85, 56 S.Ct. 421, 424, 80 L.Ed. 567 (1936).

80. 392 U.S. 183, 88 S.Ct. 2017, 20 L.Ed.2d 1020 (1968). *Wirtz* was overruled in part by National League of Cities v. Usery, 426 U.S. 833, 96 S.Ct. 2465, 49 L.Ed.2d 245 (1976); it was restored when the *National League of Cities* case was overruled by Garcia v. San Antonio Metro. Transit Authority, 469 U.S. 528, 105 S.Ct. 1005, 83

L.Ed.2d 1016 (1985), rehearing denied 471 U.S. 1049, 105 S.Ct. 2041, 85 L.Ed.2d 340 (1985).

Responding to *Garcia*, Congress in November of 1985 enacted the Fair Labor Standards Amendments of 1985, Pub.L. 99–150, in order to 99 Stat. 787 (amending 29 U.S.C.A. § 207 et seq.), which authorized states, their political subdivisions, and interstate governmental agencies to provide compensatory time to their employees in lieu of overtime subject to certain conditions.

81. 392 U.S. at 196, 88 S.Ct. at 2024.

82. 392 U.S. at 201, 88 S.Ct. at 2026 (Douglas & Stewart, JJ., dissenting).

83. There is little or no explanation for the shift in the Court's position regarding the judicially enforceable nature of the Tenth Amendment other than the political background and philosophy of the newly appointed Justices. The decisions of the 1970's, attacking the established principle of judicial deference to congressional decisions regarding federalism issues were joined only by

whether suits could be brought in federal court for individual recoveries for violations of the Fair Labor Standards Act by state-owned enterprises.[84] When the Court considered this issue in 1973, it held that the statute did not grant individuals a right to bring federal court actions to collect damages from the state. Justice Douglas, for the majority, was hesitant to find that Congress would by implication so severely damage the interests of state governments. In 1975, when the Court upheld the application of wage "freeze" legislation to state employees, the opinion indicated that it relied in part upon the emergency economic conditions in the nation to sustain the act.[85] The decision indicated that there might be some Tenth Amendment limitation upon the powers of the federal government to regulate state entities absent emergency conditions.[86] Then in 1976, the Court defined a new Tenth Amendment principle, which it would overrule in 1985.

Now, let us examine these decisions in detail.

(ii) The *National League of Cities* Decision

National League of Cities v. Usery (which the Court overruled in 1985),[87] held (five to four) that it was unconstitutional to apply the minimum wage and overtime pay provisions of the Fair Labor Standards Act to the employees of the state governments, even though they were in or affecting interstate commerce. The Court agreed with the Appellants' essential contention "that the 1974 amendments to the Act, while undoubtedly within the scope of the Commerce Clause," cannot constitutionally "be applied directly to the States and subdivisions of States as employers."[88] In so doing, the Court dismissed as "wrong" statements in earlier opinions that the states were not entitled to special exemptions from the exercise of the federal commerce power.[89] But the Court did not otherwise disturb basic commerce clause analysis.

It is important to recognize that the Court did not hold that the wages and hours of state employees were not commerce nor that they did not affect commerce. The opinion did not disturb the modern tests for finding relationships between intrastate activities and the commerce power. The Court also disdained any use of the Tenth Amendment to reserve subject areas of commerce for state regulation. The Court explicitly noted that Tenth Amendment principles would not limit the ability of the federal government to regulate the activities of *non*governmental entities or employees.[90]

When the federal government regulated intrastate commercial activities that *affected* commerce, it acted within its powers. It could regulate activities of the greatest local importance because all such activities were still subject to sovereignty of the federal as well as the state government. However, the opinion argued that the commerce power was limited not

---

Justices Blackmun, Powell, Rehnquist, Stewart (who was replaced by the even more states' rights oriented Justice O'Connor) and Chief Justice Burger. See Nowak, Foreword: Evaluating the Work of the New Libertarian Supreme Court, 7 Hastings Constitutional L.Q. 263 (1980); Nowak Resurrecting Realist Jurisprudence: The Political Bias of Burger Court Justices, 17 Suffolk U.L.Rev. 551 (1983). Justice Stevens urged the other Justices to avoid ad hoc decisionmaking on federalism issues so as to avoid the charge that constitutional law is nothing more than the exercise of the will of the individuals on the Court. See Florida Dept. of Health and Rehabilitative Services v. Florida Nursing Home Ass'n, 450 U.S. 147, 101 S.Ct. 1032, 67 L.Ed.2d 132 (1981) (Stevens, J., concurring, citing an earlier edition of this Treatise). By the turn of the century the Court moved towards active restriction of congressional power similar to the rulings of the late nineteenth century. See, Nowak, The Gang of Five and The Second Coming of an Anti–Reconstruction Court. 75 Notre Dame L. Rev. 1091 (2000).

84. 392 U.S. at 200, 88 S.Ct. at 2025–26.

85. Fry v. United States, 421 U.S. 542, 95 S.Ct. 1792, 44 L.Ed.2d 363 (1975), certiorari denied 421 U.S. 1014, 95 S.Ct. 2422, 44 L.Ed.2d 683 (1975).

86. 421 U.S. at 548, 95 S.Ct. at 1796.

87. 426 U.S. 833, 96 S.Ct. 2465, 49 L.Ed.2d 245 (1976), overruled by Garcia v. San Antonio Metropolitan Transit Authority, 469 U.S. 528, 105 S.Ct. 1005, 83 L.Ed.2d 1016 (1985).

88. National League of Cities v. Usery, 426 U.S. 833, 841, 96 S.Ct. 2465, 2469, 49 L.Ed.2d 245 (1976)(footnote omitted).

89. 426 U.S. at 855, 96 S.Ct. at 2476. The Court overruled, in part, Maryland v. Wirtz, 392 U.S. 183, 88 S.Ct. 2017, 20 L.Ed.2d 1020 (1968).

90. 426 U.S. at 841, 96 S.Ct. at 2469.

only by the specific guarantees and limitations of the Bill of Rights but also by the Tenth Amendment. The majority found no reason to distinguish the Tenth Amendment from the other Amendments and held that it should serve as a specific limitation upon the exercise of the commerce power just as might the First or Fifth Amendments.[91]

The majority concluded that the Tenth Amendment guaranteed that Congress would not abrogate a state's plenary authority over matters "essential" to the state's separate and independent existence.[92] This test is vague, and its application uncertain. Is it really "essential" for a state to pay its state employees less than the federal minimum wage? If the commerce clause does not allow the Federal Government to force states to pay their employees the minimum wage, does that mean that Congress similarly lacks power to prevent states from using child labor?

In *National League of Cities v. Usery*, Justice Rehnquist, for the majority, found that a local government or state's ability to determine its employees' wages was an "attribute" of state sovereignty that the Federal Government could not federalize. The federal wage regulation, Rehnquist said, could not apply to state or local governments because it impaired essential governmental activities by restricting the freedom of choice of local governments as to how to allocate local resources in carrying out traditional state and local governmental functions.

The majority opinion established no clear test for determining when a federal law so impaired the sovereignty of a state or local government that it could not be applied to those governmental units. Justice Blackmun provided the crucial fifth vote in the *National League of Cities* decision, filing a concurring opinion.[93] However, Justice Blackmun saw the decision as establishing only a "balancing test," which required the judiciary to deter-

mine whether a federal interest in commercial regulation was "demonstrably greater" than the state's claim for an exemption whenever a state alleged that the application of federal commercial regulations to it constituted an impairment of its sovereignty. He did not explain how to calibrate the scales or weigh the ingredients. How, for example, does a Court decide that minimum wages are not important enough to the federal government but environmental decisions are important enough? How does one weigh or compare apples to electricity?

The dissenters argued that the majority had gone beyond the proper role of the judiciary in our constitutional system.[94] They believed that the scope of federal power to regulate state governments should be decided by the democratic process, rather than by the courts. They claimed that neither constitutional text nor history supported the Court's ruling. Because the majority had failed to ground its ruling on a clear constitutional principle or objective test, the dissenters asserted that future rulings would be based on Justices' personal views of the proper balance of federal and state power rather than on legal standards.[95]

(iii) 1976–1985: The Aftermath of *National League of Cities*

Following *National League of Cities*, the Court embarked upon a period in which the Justices attempted to establish formal tests for the determination of when a federal law could or could not be applied to state and local governments consistently with the autonomy assured the states by the Tenth Amendment. In a series of cases, the Court established that a federal law would only be held to be an undue extension of the commerce power and inapplicable to state and local governments consistently with the Tenth Amendment if the federal law: (1) regulated "the states as states"; (2) addressed matters that were "indisputably attributes of state sovereignty"; (3)

---

91.   426 U.S. at 841–42, 96 S.Ct. at 2469–70.

92.   426 U.S. at 845, 96 S.Ct. at 2471.

93.   National League of Cities v. Usery, 426 U.S. 833, 856, 96 S.Ct. 2465, 2476, 49 L.Ed.2d 245 (1976) (Blackmun, J., concurring).

94.   National League of Cities v. Usery, 426 U.S. 833, 856, 96 S.Ct. 2465, 2476, 49 L.Ed.2d 245 (1976) (Brennan, J., joined by White, & Marshall, JJ., dissenting) 426 U.S. at 880, 96 S.Ct. at 2488 (Stevens, J., dissenting).

95.   Id. at 880, 96 S.Ct. at 2448 (Stevens, J., dissenting).

required state compliance with the federal law in a manner that directly impaired a state's ability to "structure integral operations in areas of traditional functions."[96] The Court also appeared to add a balancing test to this three-part test for the validity of a federal law. The Court several times mentioned that even if the application of a federal law to state and local governments met all three parts of the previously described test, the Court would uphold the law when the federal interests were sufficiently important to justify the impairment of state or local government autonomy.[97] It was unclear during this period whether the three-part test was a prelude to a judicial balancing of state and federal interests or whether the three-part test itself was a form of structuring a judicial balancing of national and local interests.[98]

96. See Hodel v. Virginia Surface Mining and Reclamation Association, 452 U.S. 264, 101 S.Ct. 2352, 69 L.Ed.2d 1 (1981); E.E.O.C. v. Wyoming, 460 U.S. 226, 103 S.Ct. 1054, 75 L.Ed.2d 18 (1983).

97. Hodel v. Virginia Surface Mining and Reclamation Association, Inc., 452 U.S. 264, 288 n. 29, 101 S.Ct. 2352, 2366 n. 29, 69 L.Ed.2d 1 (1981); United Transportation Union v. Long Island R. Co., 455 U.S. 678, 684 n. 9, 102 S.Ct. 1349, 1354 n. 9, 71 L.Ed.2d 547 (1982); Federal Energy Regulatory Com'n v. Mississippi, 456 U.S. 742, 763–64 n. 28, 102 S.Ct. 2126, 2139–40 n. 28, 72 L.Ed.2d 532 (1982), rehearing denied 458 U.S. 1131, 103 S.Ct. 15, 73 L.Ed.2d 1401 (1982).

98. In the case that overruled *National League of Cities*, the Justices found that there was a separate balancing test that followed the application of the three tests set forth in this paragraph. See Garcia v. San Antonio Metropolitan Transit Authority, 469 U.S. 528, 557, 105 S.Ct. 1005, 1021, 83 L.Ed.2d 1016 (1985) (Powell, J., joined by Burger, C.J., and Rehnquist & O'Connor, JJ., dissenting), rehearing denied 471 U.S. 1049, 105 S.Ct. 2041, 85 L.Ed.2d 340 (1985).

99. The Spending Power and the Tenth Amendment

The Supreme Court has found that the Tenth Amendment does not restrict the federal spending power to the same degree as it might restrict the federal power to regulate the activities of state and local governments.

In South Dakota v. Dole, 483 U.S. 203, 107 S.Ct. 2793, 97 L.Ed.2d 171 (1987) the Court upheld a federal statute that deprives a state of five percent of the federal funds to which it was otherwise entitled under certain federal highway grant programs if the state does not set a minimum age of 21 years for persons to be able to lawfully purchase alcoholic beverages in the state. Chief Justice Rehnquist, writing for seven members of the Court, found that the Tenth Amendment did not limit the conditions

What was clear is that lower court decisions were all over the map, and no Supreme Court decision between 1976 (when *National League of Cities* was born) and 1985 (when *National League of Cities* died), did the Supreme Court in fact rule that a federal law could not be applied to state or local governments because it interfered with the autonomy protected for them by the Tenth Amendment.

While *National League of Cities* held that the Tenth Amendment limited the Commerce Clause, that case also said that the Tenth Amendment did not limit the Spending Clause.[99] The Court did not explain but only announced this result. The Tenth Amendment also did not limit section 5 of the Fourteenth Amendment.[100] That result is easier to understand because the Fourteenth Amendment

that could be placed on federal grants to state and local governments, at least absent any proof that the condition on a federal grant constituted the type of compulsion against a state that might violate the Tenth Amendment. Other portions of the Bill of Rights, of course, might restrict federal grants; the Court noted that Congress could not condition a federal grant to states that would require them to take activities that would otherwise be unconstitutional (such as engaging in invidious discrimination). 483 U.S. at 208–11, 107 S.Ct. at 2797–98.

The Court also held that the condition did not violate the Twenty-first Amendment, which reserved some authority to the states regarding the regulation of the sale or use of alcoholic beverages within the state.

See also, Lawrence County v. Lead–Deadwood School District, 469 U.S. 256, 105 S.Ct. 695, 83 L.Ed.2d 635 (1985), on remand 367 N.W.2d 207 (S.D.1985) (federal law granting federal funds to local governments in lieu of payment of local taxes on federally owned property and allowing the local government to spend the money in any manner preempts state law that would limit the projects for which the local government could spend the money). Justices Rehnquist and Stevens dissented in *Lawrence County*; they would have interpreted the federal statute to allow the state governments to control local governmental use of the federal grant money. 469 U.S. at 272, 105 S.Ct. at 704 (Rehnquist, J., dissenting, joined by Stevens, J.), Justices Rehnquist and Stevens relied on Hunter v. Pittsburgh, 207 U.S. 161, 178, 28 S.Ct. 40, 46, 52 L.Ed. 151 (1907) in which the Supreme Court held that a state government could change the rights, powers, and existence of local governmental units.

100. "We express no view as to whether different results might obtain if Congress seeks to affect integral operations of state governments by exercising authority granted it under other sections of the Constitution such as the spending power, Art. I, s 8, cl. 1, or s 5 of the Fourteenth Amendment." National League of Cities v.

came into being after the Tenth Amendment, and the whole purpose of the Fourteenth Amendment was to impose new obligations on the states.

Later, the Supreme Court held that, notwithstanding *National League of Cities*, the Federal Government also could condition its preemption of the regulation of private sector activities in a way that required state governments to follow federal standards and procedures when regulating private commercial activities.[101] Under conditional preemption, the federal government can establish procedures and standards to be followed by state utility commissions when they establish rates for utility companies: if the states did not follow the federal guidelines, then the Federal Government would regulate the matter directly.[102]

The Court continued to whittled away at an expansive reading of *National League of Cities* when it held that the Tenth Amendment granted no immunity to states when they were exercising powers outside the areas of traditional government functions. This principle justified applying federal commercial regulations to state activities, such as the operation of railroads.[103] Of course, what is considered traditional today (running hospitals, schools, public transportation) was not traditional when the nation was not that much younger.

The Tenth Amendment tests used from 1976 to 1985 also allowed federal regulation of some state activities in areas that appeared to be traditional government functions, such as the operation of state park systems, when the regulation of employment or commercial practices by the state was not directly impaired by a federal regulation that made it more expensive for the states to perform the traditional government services.[104]

The lower courts had real problems trying to apply these vague tests and determining matters like, what is "traditional," or what is "essential."[105] Indeed, eight of the nine Justices during this time period considered the *National League of Cities* decision to be inconsistent with one or more of these later Supreme Court rulings.[106] In the later Supreme Court rulings, the four dissenters in *National League of Cities v. Usery* joined with Justice Blackmun, who had concurred in that decision, to limit the *National League of Cities* decision by upholding federal legislation.[107] Thus, as a practical matter, the validity of federal law was dependent during this period entirely on whether Justice Blackmun, the crucial vote to establishing a majority on this issue, would find that a federal law could or could not be applied to state and local governments through the use of his rather undefined balancing test. That is not a state of affairs that will lead to consistent rulings in the lower courts.

Usery, 426 U.S. 833, 852 n. 17, 96 S.Ct. 2465, 2474 n. 17, 49 L.Ed.2d 245 (1976).

101. Federal Energy Regulatory Com'n v. Mississippi, 456 U.S. 742, 102 S.Ct. 2126, 72 L.Ed.2d 532 (1982), rehearing denied 458 U.S. 1131, 103 S.Ct. 15, 73 L.Ed.2d 1401 (1982).

102. Id. See Rotunda, The Doctrine of Conditional Preemption and Other Limitations on Tenth Amendment Restrictions, 132 U.Pa.L.Rev. 289 (1984).

103. See United Transportation Union v. Long Island R. Co., 455 U.S. 678, 102 S.Ct. 1349, 71 L.Ed.2d 547 (1982).

104. In EEOC v. Wyoming, 460 U.S. 226, 103 S.Ct. 1054, 75 L.Ed.2d 18 (1983), the Court upheld the application of the federal Age Discrimination in Employment Act to state governments. The decision prevented states from discharging park employees and game wardens because of their age.

105. In Garcia v. San Antonio Metropolitan Transit Authority, 469 U.S. 528, 537–43, 105 S.Ct. 1005, 1010–13, 83 L.Ed.2d 1016 (1985), Justice Blackmun's majority opinion referred to the confused state of rulings in the lower

courts as an indication of the failure of the Tenth Amendment tests.

106. EEOC v. Wyoming, 460 U.S. 226, 244, 103 S.Ct. 1054, 1066, 75 L.Ed.2d 18 (1983) (Stevens, J., concurring).

107. Justices Brennan, Marshall, White and Stevens were consistent in their deference to Congress. Chief Justice Burger and Justices O'Connor, Powell and Rehnquist sought to limit congressional power over the states. In National League of Cities v. Usery, 426 U.S. 833, 96 S.Ct. 2465, 49 L.Ed.2d 245 (1976), Justice Rehnquist wrote a majority opinion joined by Justices Stewart, Blackmun, Powell and Chief Justice Burger. Justices Brennan, Marshall, Stevens, and White were in dissent. In FERC v. Mississippi, 456 U.S. 742, 102 S.Ct. 2126, 72 L.Ed.2d 532 (1982), Chief Justice Burger and Justices Powell, Rehnquist, and O'Connor (who replaced Stewart) were in dissent. Justices Brennan, Marshall, Stevens, and White had moved to the majority side by "acquiring" the vote of Justice Blackmun. In EEOC v. Wyoming, 460 U.S. 226, 103 S.Ct. 1054, 75 L.Ed.2d 18 (1983), the majority was composed of Justices Blackmun, Brennan, Marshall, Stevens and White; Chief Justice Burger and Justices O'Connor, Powell, and Rehnquist were in dissent.

Let us turn to some of the decisions leading to the overruling of *National League of Cities.*

The *Hodel* Decision. *Hodel v. Virginia Surface Mining and Reclamation Association, Inc.,*[108] upheld a federal statute controlling surface mining and replacing state control over the amount and conditions of such mining. In so doing the Court attempted to clarify the standard for the protection of state sovereignty previously established in *National League of Cities v. Usery.*[109]

The federal act at issue in *Hodel* empowered the Department of Interior to set standards for surface coal mining on "steep slopes" and the preservation of land or topsoil affected by such mining within each state. While a state could participate in the establishment of standards for mining within its jurisdiction, states were not required to act as enforcement agents for the federal government. However, once permanent standards were established, states could assume control over mining operations only if they adopted regulations approved by the Secretary of Interior. This federal action, in a sense, removed an element of state sovereignty by taking over the regulation of an activity that otherwise would have been within these states' jurisdiction, but the Supreme Court found that the Tenth Amendment did not invalidate this federal law. The federal law created a regulatory program that a state could adopt (if that program met federal minimum standards) or there would be a federal program for any state that chooses not to submit a program. Enforcement of the permanent programs rests either with the States (if they chose to participate) or with the Secretary of Energy as to nonparticipating States.

The majority opinion stated: "When Congress has determined that an activity affects interstate commerce, the courts need inquire only whether the finding is rational."[110] *Hodel* then reviewed the Tenth Amendment principle relied upon in the *National League of Cities* decision and found that three requirements must be satisfied for judicial invalidation of congressional commerce power legislation.[111] First, the federal statute must regulate "States as States." Second, the federal legislation must regulate "matters that are indisputably attributes of state sovereignty." Finally, the impact of compliance with the federal regulation must directly impair the state's ability "to structure integral operations in areas of traditional functions."

Hodel contrasted the regulation of "States as States," which required judicial scrutiny under the Tenth Amendment, to federal regulation of private individuals and businesses, who are also subject to state laws. Legislation merely regulating nongovernmental enterprises, the Court concluded, does not raise Tenth Amendment problems but is only tested under the rational basis test. The Tenth Amendment does not limit "congressional power to preempt or displace state regulation of *private* activities affecting interstate Commerce."[112] There were no dissents, and Rehnquist concurred in the judgment.

The *F.E.R.C.* Decision. In *Federal Energy Regulatory Commission v. Mississippi,*[113] the Justices (five to four) upheld the constitutionality of Titles I and III and Section 210 of Title II of the Public Utility Regulatory Policies Act of 1978, referred to by the Court as "PURPA" or, simply, "the Act."[114]

---

108. 452 U.S. 264, 101 S.Ct. 2352, 69 L.Ed.2d 1 (1981).

109. 426 U.S. 833, 96 S.Ct. 2465, 49 L.Ed.2d 245 (1976), overruled by Garcia v. San Antonio Metropolitan Transit Authority, 469 U.S. 528, 105 S.Ct. 1005, 83 L.Ed.2d 1016 (1985).

110. Hodel v. Virginia Surface Mining and Reclamation Ass'n, Inc., 452 U.S. 264, 277, 101 S.Ct. 2352, 2360, 69 L.Ed.2d 1 (1981).

111. 452 U.S. at 287–88, 101 S.Ct. at 2365–66.

112. 452 U.S. at 289–90, 101 S.Ct. at 2367 (emphasis added). See also Hodel v. Indiana, 452 U.S. 314, 101 S.Ct. 2376, 69 L.Ed.2d 40 (1981) (upholding "prime farmland" provisions of Surface Mining and Reclamation Control Act,

which limited mining on certain farmland and required the preservation of topsoil for farm usage in such areas).

113. 456 U.S. 742, 102 S.Ct. 2126, 72 L.Ed.2d 532 (1982), rehearing denied 458 U.S. 1131, 103 S.Ct. 15, 73 L.Ed.2d 1401 (1982). See, Rotunda, Usery in the Wake of Federal Energy Regulatory Commission v. Mississippi, 1 Const. Commentary 43 (1984); Rotunda, The Doctrine of Conditional Preemption and Other Limitations on Tenth Amendment Restrictions, 132 U.Pa.L.Rev. 289 (1984).

114. 16 U.S.C.A. §§ 2601–2645; 15 U.S.C.A. §§ 3201–3211; 16 U.S.C.A. § 324a–3.

PURPA had three features to which state governments objected.[115] First, the Act required each state agency with authority over public utilities to consider specific approaches for structuring utility rates and specific standards relating to the terms and conditions of public utility operations. Consideration of the federal standards was a condition for state regulation of public utilities: if the state failed to consider the federal standard, the Federal Government would impose its standards, occupy the field, and force the state to abandon regulation in this field. Second, the Act prescribed specific procedures to be followed by the state regulatory authorities or nonregulated utilities when considering the proposed standards. Third, the Act required the Federal Energy Regulatory Commission, FERC, after consultation with state regulatory authorities, to prescribe rules exempting certain cogeneration and small power facilities from state laws governing electric utilities and to issue such rules as necessary to "encourage cogeneration and small power production" and to require each state regulatory authority to implement the FERC rules regarding cogeneration and small power production facilities.

All of the Justices in *FERC v. Mississippi* found that the regulation of public utilities, even those that operated in a single state, was within the scope of congressional power under the commerce clause. The issue in *FERC v. Mississippi*, which created the division among the Justices related to the meaning and enforceability of the Tenth Amendment. Five Justices found that there was no violation of that Amendment in this case because Congress, in this instance, was only setting the conditions for the sharing of federal power with the states rather than interfering with the sovereignty of the states or traditional local government functions. Justice Blackmun's majority opinion began by explaining

that Congress could have entirely preempted the field of public utility regulation, a point that the dissenters did not dispute. Because the entire subject of public utilities regulation was within the federal commerce power, Congress could condition the ceding of this power to the states upon state agency consideration of federal interests. Thus, the provisions of the federal statute requiring state regulatory agencies to consider certain standards or rate structures were permissible.

The second feature of the Act—the setting of particular procedures by which the federally suggested standards were to be considered—also did not violate the Tenth Amendment. Blackmun reasoned that this feature only insured that the federal interest would be considered and did not require the state to exercise its sovereign authority in a particular manner by legislating on a subject in conformity with federal dictates, nor did it otherwise interfere with "attributes" of state sovereignty.

The third provision of the Act—requiring state regulatory authorities to implement FERC rules regarding cogeneration and small electric facilities—also did not violate the Tenth Amendment. The state commissions could implement this provision by "an undertaking to resolve disputes between qualifying facilities and electric utilities arising under [the Act]." The Supreme Court said that the statute-implementing regulations only required state authorities to adjudicate disputes arising under the statute.[116]

Justice Powell wrote a brief dissent objecting to the majority upholding the provision of the Act that prescribed exact procedures that state agencies must follow in considering the proposed federal standards.[117] Justice O'Connor, joined by Chief Justice Burger and Justice Rehnquist, filed a dissent arguing that Titles I

---

115. 456 U.S. at 746, 102 S.Ct. at 2130.

116. This type of dispute resolution was upheld by the Court on the basis of *Testa v. Katt.*, 330 U.S. 386, 67 S.Ct. 810, 91 L.Ed. 967 (1947). In *Testa* the Court had upheld a federal statute requiring state courts to adjudicate claims under a federal statute. The supremacy clause of the Constitution expressly recognized state courts as a means by which federal law would be enforced. The majority

opinion in *FERC v. Mississippi* did no greater damage to the scope of state and local authority by requiring agencies in states that had decided to regulate public utilities to adjudicate disputes within their jurisdiction than the Supreme Court in earlier years had done by requiring state courts to uphold and implement federal law.

117. 456 U.S. at 771, 102 S.Ct. at 2143.

and III of the Act were unconstitutional[118] because they interfered with attributes of state sovereignty and the ability of states to structure integral operations in areas of traditional government functions. In her view, the structure of the federal system, which she found implicit in the text of the Constitution and the Tenth Amendment, allows for complete preemption of commercial areas by the federal government but does not allow Congress to set conditions for the sharing of federal commercial power with the states when those conditions require state governmental entities to consider or implement federal standards in a manner dictated by federal law.

1983: *E.E.O.C. v. Wyoming.* The Supreme Court (five to four) upheld the application of the Age Discrimination in Employment Act to state and local governments in *Equal Employment Opportunity Commission (EEOC) v. Wyoming.*[119] Justice Brennan wrote the majority opinion and found that this ruling was technically consistent with the *National League of Cities, Hodel,* and *FERC* decisions.

Wyoming objected to being prohibited from discharging state park and game commission employees at age 55; the Act prohibited discrimination based on age against employees or potential employees between the ages of 40 and 70. In denying Wyoming's Tenth Amendment challenge, Brennan said that the state's claim of immunity must be subjected to the three-part test set forth in *Hodel* and that the conflicting state and federal interests would only have to be "balanced" if the federal regulation met all three tests.

Brennan readily conceded that the federal law prohibiting discrimination in employment based on age did regulate the "States as States," which was the first part of the three-part *Hodel* test. Whether the statute met the

second part of that test—regulating an "undoubted attribute of state sovereignty"—presented "significantly more difficulties" because "[p]recisely what is meant" by this phrase is "somewhat unclear" and "our subsequent cases applying the *National League of Cities* test have had little occasion to amplify on our understanding of the concept."[120] However, the majority did not have to explore the meaning of this amorphous concept because it held that the Age Discrimination Act did not meet the third prong of the *Hodel* test: it did not "'directly impair' the State's ability to 'structure integral operations in areas of traditional governmental functions.'"[121]

Justice Brennan rejected the state's claim that its mandatory retirement age of 55 was necessary to assure the physical preparedness of its game wardens. Under the federal law, Wyoming could meet this goal by proceeding in a more individualized manner and dismissing only those wardens who are not physically fit. Alternatively, under the federal act the state could keep its present policy if it could demonstrate that age is a bona fide occupational qualification for the job.[122]

Brennan argued that there was no reason to conclude that the federal law at issue would have any "wide-ranging threat to the structure of state governance." *National League of Cities* had concluded that imposing the federal minimum wage on state workers would significantly affect state decisions as to how to spend money for other vital programs. *EEOC v. Wyoming* refused to find that the Age Discrimination Act would have a similar result: the majority opinion indicated that not all federal commerce regulations that affected state resource allocation decisions would run afoul of

---

118. 456 U.S. at 775–76 n. 1, 102 S.Ct. at 2145 n. 1 (declining to determine the constitutionality of section 210).

119. 460 U.S. 226, 103 S.Ct. 1054, 75 L.Ed.2d 18 (1983). The decision ruled that the extension of The Age Discrimination in Employment Act of 1967, 81 Stat. 602, as amended, 29 U.S.C.A. § 621 et seq., was a valid exercise of the federal commerce power.

120. 460 U.S. at 238 n. 11, 103 S.Ct. at 1061 n. 11.

121. 460 U.S. at 239, 103 S.Ct. at 1062.

122. The Court noted that the limited intrusion on state sovereignty might be upheld even if the federal law were deemed to impair the state's ability to structure integral government operations. The overriding nature of the federal interest in preventing age discrimination in private sector and state employment was not negated by the fact that the Act did not apply to some federal government workers. EEOC v. Wyoming, 460 U.S. 226, 242 n. 17, 103 S.Ct. 1054, 1064 n. 17, 75 L.Ed.2d 18 (1983).

the Tenth Amendment.[123]

Justice Stevens, concurring opinion, noted that eight of the nine Justices believed that the *National League of Cities* and *EEOC* decisions were inconsistent; he advocated a direct overruling of *National League of Cities*.[124] The *EEOC* majority was composed of the four Justices who had dissented in the *National League of Cities* and Justice Blackmun.

Chief Justice Burger,, joined by Justices Powell, Rehnquist, and O'Connor dissented in *EEOC v. Wyoming*: "I have reexamined [the Constitution] and I fail to see where it grants to the national government the power to impose such strictures on the states either expressly or by implication."[125] Justice Powell dispensed with the Commerce Clause views of Chief Justice Marshall in a footnote,[126] and rejected the argument that the commerce power was a central concern to the drafters of the Constitution.[127]

The dissenters in *E.E.O.C. v Wyoming* also did not believe the Act could not be justified as an exercise of congressional power under section five of the Fourteenth Amendment.[128] The majority, having found the law to be a valid commerce power regulation, did not address the Fourteenth Amendment issue but implied

or at least suggested, that it would also uphold the Age Discrimination Act on that basis.[129]

Later, in 2000, when that issue came up directly, *Kimel v. Florida Board of Regents*[130] (5 to 4) held that the Eleventh Amendment barred a suit for damages and Congress could not used its powers under section five of the Fourteenth Amendment to abrogate the states' immunity under the Eleventh Amendment.

The Court had previously held that Congress could not override a state's Eleventh Amendment by use of its Article I powers.[131] Thus, the Age Discrimination Act could override the state's claim of sovereign immunity only if the Act was a proper exercise of the power granted to Congress by section 5 of the Fourteenth Amendment. *Kimel* ruled that the Age Discrimination Act was not valid Fourteenth Amendment legislation.[132] Thus, the Age Discrimination Act could not give state employees a right to sue the state. The Act applies to state and local governments, but state employees cannot receive damages when the state violates the Act and discriminates against them on the basis of their age.[133]

After *E.E.O.C. v. Wyoming*, the Tenth Amendment would not prevent federal regulation of some state activities in areas that

---

123. 460 U.S. at 240 n. 14, 241, 103 S.Ct. at 1062 n. 14, 1063. The majority stated that the examination of impact on state resource allocation decisions was to be "a more generalized inquiry, essentially legal rather than factual. . . ." 460 U.S. at 240, 103 S.Ct. at 1063.

124. EEOC v. Wyoming, 460 U.S. 226, 244, 103 S.Ct. 1054, 1066, 75 L.Ed.2d 18 (1983) (Stevens, J., concurring).

125. 460 U.S. 226, 251, 103 S.Ct. 1054, 1068, 75 L.Ed.2d 18 (1983) (Burger, C.J., joined by Powell, Rehnquist, & O'Connor, JJ., dissenting).

126. EEOC v. Wyoming, 460 U.S. 226, 269 n. 5, 103 S.Ct. 1054, 1077 n. 5, 75 L.Ed.2d 18 (1983) (Powell, J., dissenting, joined by O'Connor, J.). Powell believed that Marshall's opinion in Gibbons v. Ogden, 22 U.S. (9 Wheat.) 1, 6 L.Ed.23 (1824) concerning the scope of the commerce power was irrelevant to the decision of this case because Marshall's opinion was not concerned with issues of state sovereignty.

127. 460 U.S. at 267–68 nn. 2 & 3, 103 S.Ct at 1076–77 nn. 2 & 3 (Powell, J., dissenting).

128. EEOC v. Wyoming, 460 U.S. 226, 261–63, 103 S.Ct. 1054, 1072–75, 75 L.Ed.2d 18 (1983) (Burger, C.J., dissenting).

129. EEOC v. Wyoming, 460 U.S. 226, 244 n. 18, 103 S.Ct. 1054, 1064 n. 18, 75 L.Ed.2d 18 (1983).

130. Kimel v. Florida Board of Regents, 528 U.S. 62, 120 S.Ct. 631, 145 L.Ed.2d 522 (2000).

131. Seminole Tribe of Florida v. Florida, 517 U.S. 44, 116 S.Ct. 1114, 134 L.Ed.2d 252 (1996). See § 2.11.

132. The Court has ruled that Congress can override a state's Eleventh Amendment immunity by using its Fourteenth Amendment power. See § 2.11. The Court has also ruled that the Justices will independently decide whether a law that Congress declares was passed pursuant to its Fourteenth Amendment power is a valid exercise of the power granted to Congress by section 5 of that Amendment.

133. Kimel v. Florida Board of Regents, 528 U.S. 62, 78–91, 120 S.Ct. 631, 642–650, 145 L.Ed.2d 522 (2000). Four Justices dissented in *Kimel*, because they believed that "Congress's power to authorize federal remedies against state agencies that violate federal statutory obligations is coextensive with its power to impose those obligations on the states in the first place." 528 U.S. at 92, 93, 120 S.Ct. at 650, 651 (Stevens, J., joined by Souter, Ginsburg & Breyer, JJ., dissenting). See § 2.12 for further examination of this issue.

appeared to be "traditional" government functions, such as the operation of state park systems, simply because a federal regulation made it more expensive for the states to perform the traditional government services.[134] In addition, the Court held that federal commercial regulations could be applied to state activities like operating a railroad because they were not truly "governmental" in nature.[135] But the Court did not explicitly overrule *National League of Cities* until 1985. It is to that decision we now turn.

(iv) The Overruling of *National League of Cities*

In 1985, Justice Blackmun, who had joined the majority in *National League of Cities* now changed his mind and wrote the majority opinion in *Garcia v. San Antonio Metropolitan Transit Authority*,[136] which overruled the *National League of Cities* decision. The five person majority in this case was made up of the four dissenters in *National League of Cities* and Justice Blackmun, who had been voting with those four persons to uphold federal laws since 1976.

In *Garcia*, at issue was the application of the federal minimum wage and overtime provisions of the Fair Labor Standards Act (which the Court had found could not be applied to local police and highway departments in *National League of Cities*) to a municipally owned and operated mass transit system. The case was first argued on the issue of whether the operation of the buses and trains in a mass transit district should be considered a "traditional" government function and, therefore, exempt from wage regulation under *National League of Cities*, or like state-operated railroads, and not exempt.[137] Rather than deciding whether the operation of mass transit districts was—unlike the operation of a railroad—a traditional governmental function, the majority rejected the basic premise of *National League of Cities* and found that there was no principled role for the judiciary in granting to state and local governments an area of immunity from otherwise valid federal commerce power legislation that similarly governs private parties.

Justice Blackmun began by noting the difficulty that both the Supreme Court and lower courts had faced when trying to implement *National League of Cities*. Neither historical nor functional approaches had been able to provide a clear and principled basis for judicial determination of the scope of state powers that were immune from federal regulations.[138]

Justice Blackmun found that it was not the fault of specific tests or formulations of principles that had led court to seemingly inconsistent rulings, but a more basic error in *National League of Cities*.[139] He argued that political process that the structure of the Constitution established was the primary safeguard for state and local governments against legislation that impaired their ability to act as sovereigns. Justice Blackmun described how the workings

---

134. The Court did not limit other federal powers during the 1976–1985 era.

135. See United Transportation Union v. Long Island R. Co., 455 U.S. 678, 102 S.Ct. 1349, 71 L.Ed.2d 547 (1982).

136. 469 U.S. 528, 105 S.Ct. 1005, 83 L.Ed.2d 1016 (1985), rehearing denied 471 U.S. 1049, 105 S.Ct. 2041, 85 L.Ed.2d 340 (1985).

137. See United Transportation Union v. Long Island R. Co., 455 U.S. 678, 102 S.Ct. 1349, 71 L.Ed.2d 547 (1982).

138. 469 U.S. at 537–43, 105 S.Ct. at 1010–13.

139. For example, courts have held that regulating ambulance services, Gold Cross Ambulance v. City of Kansas City, 538 F.Supp. 956, 967–969 (W.D. Mo.1982), aff'd on other grounds, 705 F.2d 1005 (8th Cir. 1983), cert. denied, 471 U.S. 1003, 105 S.Ct. 1864, 85 L.Ed.2d 158 (1985); licensing automobile drivers, United States v. Best,

573 F.2d 1095, 1102–03 (9th Cir. 1978); operating a municipal airport, Amersbach v. City of Cleveland, 598 F.2d 1033, 1037–38 (6th Cir. 1979); performing solid waste disposal, Hybud Equipment Corp. v. City of Akron, 654 F.2d 1187, 1196 (6th Cir. 1981); and operating a highway authority, Molina-Estrada v. Puerto Rico Highway Authority, 680 F.2d 841, 845–846 (1st Cir.1982), *are protected* under *National League of Cities*. But other courts have held that regulation of traffic on public roads, Friends of the Earth v. Carey, 552 F.2d 25, 38 (2d Cir.), cert. denied, 434 U.S. 902, 98 S.Ct. 296, 54 L.Ed.2d 188 (1977); regulation of air transportation, Hughes Air Corp. v. Public Utilities Comm'n, 644 F.2d 1334, 1340–1341 (9th Cir. 1981); operation of a mental health facility, Williams v. Eastside Mental Health Center, Inc., 669 F.2d 671, 680–681 (1st Cir.), cert. denied, 459 U.S. 976, 103 S.Ct. 318, 74 L.Ed.2d 294 (1982); and provision of in-house domestic services for the aged and handicapped, Bonnette v. California Health and Welfare Agency, 704 F.2d 1465, 1472 (9th Cir. 1983), *are not protected.*

of the federal political process created restraints on undue federal interference with state and local governments.[140] The states have a meaningful role in the creation of federal legislation; although state legislatures no longer appoint senators, the states have a significant voice in congressional deliberations and influence upon the executive. Most importantly, voters in the state are not likely to return to office federal legislators whose actions they find to be destroying the ability of their state and local governments to provide them with basic governmental services.

Ultimately the question to be faced is whether the decisions of the country obtained through the political process regarding the relative scope of federal and state powers should be rejected when a majority of Justices believed that it contravenes their view of the proper balance of state and federal powers. Justice Blackmun concluded that there is no principled basis for the rejection of the decisions of the democratic process in this situation. Thus, the Court overruled *National League of Cities v. Usery*. There are neither historical, textural, nor functional reasons for judges to impose their decisions in this area against the will of the democratic process:

> the Framers chose to rely on a federal system in which special restraints on federal power over the States inhered principally in the workings of the National Government itself, rather than in discrete limitations on the objects of federal authority. State sovereign interests, then, are more properly protected by procedural safeguards inherent in

the structure of the federal system than by judicially created limitations on federal power.... We realize that changes in the structure of the Federal Government have taken place since 1789, not the least of which has been the substitution of popular election of Senators by the adoption of the Seventeenth Amendment in 1913, and that these changes may work to alter the influence of the States in the federal political process. Nonetheless, ... the fundamental limitation that the constitutional scheme imposes on the Commerce Clause to protect the "States as States" is one of process rather than one of result.[141]

Garcia rejected a judicial role in supervision of the scope of the federal commerce power as it was applied to state and local government activities. As Blackmun emphasized, the San Antonio Transit Authority "faces nothing more than *the same minimum-wage* and overtime obligations that hundreds of thousands of other employers, *public as well as private*, have to meet."[142]

Garcia left open the possibility that there was some role for the judiciary in protecting state governments from federal actions that truly eliminated their sovereignty. For example, *Garcia* noted that Article IV of the Constitution protects state governments from having their territory altered by the federal government; Article IV and the Tenth Amendment limit the scope of congressional power to order states to make certain basic governmental decisions, such as where each state may locate its capital.[143]

140. 469 U.S. at 551 n. 11, 105 S.Ct. at 1018 n. 11.

The political process, after *Garcia*, responded in the manner predicted by Justice Blackmun. Responding to *Garcia*, Congress in November of 1985 enacted the Fair Labor Standards Amendments of 1985, Pub.L. 99–150, in order to 99 Stat. 787 (amending 29 U.S.C.A. § 207 et seq.), which authorized states, their political subdivisions, and interstate governmental agencies to provide compensatory time to their employees in lieu of overtime subject to certain conditions.

141. 469 U.S. at 551–54, 105 S.Ct. at 1018–19 (footnotes omitted).

142. Garcia v. San Antonio Metropolitan Transit Authority, 469 U.S. 528, 554, 105 S.Ct. 1005, 1019 (1985) (emphasis added).

143. Section 3 of Article IV of the Constitution sets out the power of Congress to admit new states to the Union. "New States may be admitted by the Congress into this Union; but no new State shall be formed or erected within the Jurisdiction of any other State; nor any State be formed by the Junction of two or more States, or Parts of States, without the Consent of the Legislatures of the States concerned as well as of the Congress.".

Federal "Takings" of State Property

The property of state and local governments is protected by the takings clause of the Fifth Amendment, just as is property owned by all other persons. State and local governmental property, just as private property, may be taken by the federal government if the federal government pays just compensation to the owner. State and local governments are only entitled to the same compensation

However, other than, "rare exceptions, like the guarantee, in Article IV, § 3, of state territorial integrity, the Constitution does not carve out express elements of state sovereignty that Congress may not employ its delegated powers to displace."[144] This statement seems to reserve the power of the judiciary to intervene if Congress should ever take actions that, for example, eliminate the local functions of state and local governments in the federal system. The opinion gave no indication of what types of laws might contravene this rather undefined limitation on the federal power to regulate state and local governments. The Court would not deal with the hypothetical possibilities of congressional action that did truly eliminate the sovereign existence of state and local governments because no such legislation was before it. *Garcia* concluded that "these cases do not require us to identify or define what affirmative limits the constitutional structure might impose on federal action affecting the States under the Commerce Clause."[145]

Four Justices, in three separate opinions, dissented in *Garcia*. They attacked the majority's view of the role of the judiciary in the federal system and its overruling a Supreme Court decision rendered only nine years earlier. Justice Powell's dissent argued that the Court's overruling of *National League of Cities*, and its reaffirmation of *Maryland v. Wirtz*,[146] was improper because it rejected both the history that underlaying the formation of the Constitution, and the historic role of the

states in our federal system.[147] The dissenters, did not believe that the Court's acknowledgement that states might retain some area of sovereign power under the Constitution was meaningful since the majority opinion "does not identify even a single aspect of state authority that would remain when the Commerce Clause is invoked to justify federal regulation."[148]

Justice O'Connor joined Powell's opinion and wrote separately to emphasize her view that the intention of those who framed the Constitution, and the structure of our federal system, guaranteed a role as true sovereigns for state governments.[149] At earlier times in our history, she argued, the limited nature of national commercial concerns might have been such that the political process would guarantee that the federal government would not attempt to unduly restrict the states' freedom to make basic choices in areas of traditional governmental functions. O'Connor found both a historical and functional justification for judicial supervision of the extent to which the federal government could control *state* activities through commerce power legislation. She emphasized that the Court should not restrict the nature of federal power over *private* sector commercial activity. But she sought only to protect the role of the states as sovereigns in the federal system as the framers envisioned at the time of the framing of the Constitution.

---

as private persons for the federal taking of property. There is no constitutional requirement that the federal government pay for the cost of a substitute facility that is taken from the state; the state is only entitled to the market value of the property taken, just as a private owner would be, if that value is ascertainable. United States v. 50 Acres of Land, 469 U.S. 24, 105 S.Ct. 451, 83 L.Ed.2d 376 (1984).

144. 469 U.S. at 550, 105 S.Ct. at 1017, citing Coyle v. Smith, 221 U.S. 559, 31 S.Ct. 688, 55 L.Ed. 853 (1911) (Congress may not dictate location of state capital for state newly admitted to the Union).

Tenth Amendment—State Legislator's Claim to Immunity from Federal Prosecution. Even during the period when the Court was concerned with defining a Tenth Amendment limitation in the application of federal commerce power legislation to state and local governments, the Court held that the Tenth Amendment posed no barrier to the prosecution of state legislators who violated federal statutes. See United States v. Gillock, 445

U.S. 360, 100 S.Ct. 1185, 63 L.Ed.2d 454 (1980) (refusing to grant state privilege in federal criminal prosecutions for violations of federal statutes prohibiting bribe-taking and racketeering activity by officials).

145. Garcia v. San Antonio Metropolitan Transit Authority, 469 U.S. 528, 556, 105 S.Ct. 1005, 1020 (1985).

146. 392 U.S. 183, 88 S.Ct. 2017, 20 L.Ed.2d 1020 (1968), which *National League of Cities* had overruled.

147. Garcia v. San Antonio Metropolitan Transit Authority, 469 U.S. 528, 558, 105 S.Ct. 1005, 1021, 83 L.Ed.2d 1016 (1985), rehearing denied 471 U.S. 1049, 105 S.Ct. 2041, 85 L.Ed.2d 340 (1985) (Powell J., joined by Burger, C.J., and Rehnquist & O'Connor, JJ., dissenting).

148. 469 U.S. at 581, 105 S.Ct. at 1033.

149. Garcia v. San Antonio Metropolitan Transit Authority, 469 U.S. 528, 581, 105 S.Ct. 1005, 1033, 83 L.Ed.2d 1016 (1985), rehearing denied 471 U.S. 1049, 105 S.Ct. 2041, 85 L.Ed.2d 340 (1985) (O'Connor, J., joined by Powell & Rehnquist, JJ., dissenting).

Justice Rehnquist, who joined the dissents of both Justices Powell and O'Connor, also issued a brief dissent arguing that, while the exact nature of the test that should be established to impose some judicial restraint on the exercise of federal commercial power over state and local governments could be subject to debate, there was little doubt in his view that the Constitution imposed some limit on the federal exercise of powers over the states. He predicted that this federalism principle, which he had set out in *National League of Cities*, would "in time again command the support of a majority of this Court."[150]

The Court has not resurrected *National League of Cities*, but it has not entirely abdicated its role in this area. Starting in 1991, the Court held (again, 5 to 4), in *New York v. United States*,[151] that it was unconstitutional for Congress, under the Commerce Clause, to impose regulations on states if those regulations are imposed *only* on states.

In other words, Congress can subject the states to *generally applicable* laws under the Commerce Clause. It can, for example, impose a minimum wage on all employees in, or affecting, interstate commerce. But it does not have the power to impose special rules on the states; for example, it could not compel the states to pay their governors a special, federally mandated minimum wage. Nor could Congress require the states to enact legislation to deal with a problem that affects interstate commerce. Congress can use the Commerce Clause to regulate interstate commerce *directly*, but it lacks power to use the Commerce Clause to order the states to enact legislation that affects interstate commerce. This matter is discussed briefly in the next section as well as § 4.10(d)(1), above.

(v) Conclusion

National League of Cities (5 to 4) opened the door to judicial scrutiny of the reach of federal power over state and local governments. That decision, and the renewed interest of some Justices in protection of federalism principles they saw embodied in the Tenth Amendment, placed into doubt the validity of a wide variety of federal legislation that regulates or taxes the activities of state and local governments.[152]

---

150. 469 U.S. at 581, 105 S.Ct. at 1033 (Rehnquist, J., dissenting).

Chief Justice Rehnquist subsequently wrote a majority opinion for the Court in which he found that the Tenth Amendment would not restrict federal spending to the same degree as it might restrict federal commerce power regulations of state and local government activities. South Dakota v. Dole, 483 U.S. 203, 208, 107 S.Ct. 2793, 2797, 97 L.Ed.2d 171 (1987) (upholding conditions in federal statute that required a state to establish a minimum drinking age of 21 or else to forego receiving five percent of the federal funding that the state would otherwise be entitled to under certain federal highway grant programs).

Responding to *Garcia*, Congress in November of 1985 enacted the Fair Labor Standards Amendments of 1985, Pub.L. 99–150, in order to 99 Stat. 787 (amending 29 U.S.C.A. § 207 et seq.), which authorized states, their political subdivisions, and interstate governmental agencies to provide compensatory time to their employees in lieu of overtime subject to certain conditions.

151. 505 U.S. 144, 112 S.Ct. 2408, 120 L.Ed.2d 120 (1992), on remand 978 F.2d 705 (2d Cir.1992). See the beginning of this subsection [§ 4.10(d)(1)(a)] for a comparison of the *New York* decision and *Garcia*.

152. Possible Tenth Amendment Limitations on the Federal Taxing Power. The Supreme Court has virtually eliminated any "inter-governmental immunity" principle regarding Federal taxation. See R. Rotunda & J. Nowak, Treatise on Constitutional Law: Substance and Procedure, vol. 2, § 13.9 (3rd ed. 1999, with annual supplements). *National League of Cities* was not applied to

impose Tenth Amendment limitations upon the taxing power of the federal government.

Massachusetts v. United States, 435 U.S. 444, 98 S.Ct. 1153, 55 L.Ed.2d 403 (1978) held that there was no constitutional barrier to the federal government imposing an aviation "user tax" on state governments. This involved a flat fee registration tax on aircraft including those used by states solely for police activities. Justice Brennan, for the Court, held that the annual registration tax imposed on all civil aircraft that fly in the navigable airspace of the United States and that was imposed as part of a comprehensive program to recoup the costs of federal aviation programs from those using the national air system does not, as applied to an aircraft owned by a state and used by it exclusively for police functions, violate the implied immunity of a state government from federal taxation.

The portion of Justice Brennan's opinion indicating that the most recent Tenth Amendment rulings would not affect state tax immunity in any way was only a plurality, because only four members of the Court joined it. Indeed these were the same four Justices who had dissented in *National League of Cities*. Two other Justices (Powell and Stewart, JJ.) joined in the opinion to the extent that it established a particular test for determining when "user taxes" on state activities would be permissible. Rehnquist, J., and Burger, C.J., dissented on the point of whether the tax involved was a user tax; they would have required further proceedings to determine the nature, impact, and constitutionality of the tax. Justice Blackmun did not participate in the decision.

In 1985, in *Garcia v. San Antonio Metropolitan Transit Authority*,[153] the Court (5 to 4) overruled *National League of Cities*, when Justice Blackmun withdrew his support from that earlier case. "State sovereign interests, then, are more properly protected by procedural safeguards inherent in the structure of the federal system than by judicially created limitations on federal power." Justice Blackmun recognized that Congress theoretically might take an action that directly eliminated the ability of a state to function as a sovereign and that might require the Court to protect the state just as it would if Congress attempted to alter the territorial boundaries of this state without its consent.[154] However, this hypothetical possibility did not justify a restriction on the federal commerce power; the overruling of *National League of Cities* ended all of the formal tests developed during the 1976 to 1985 time period.

While the Supreme Court has now rejected all of the tests established during the 1976–1985 period, it will uphold the federal government's application of otherwise valid commercial regulations to the activities of state governments that *do not single out the states for special burdens*.

The Court may also interpret some federal statutes narrowly, to avoid constitutional issues, or to avoid other questions as to the limits on federal power to regulate states. For example, *Gregory v. Ashcroft*,[155] ruled that the federal Age Discrimination in Employment Act [ADEA] did not apply to state laws that require state judges to retire at a specified age. Justice O'Connor found that the ADEA should be interpreted narrowly in order to avoid serious constitutional questions concerning the scope of congressional power over the state governments.[156]

Gregory did not establish any constitutional restrictions on the scope of federal power. The majority opinion simply established a "plain statement rule" as a principle of statutory construction. Under the *plain statement rule*,

---

The Supreme Court has found that a provision of the Internal Revenue Code denying an exemption from federal income tax for interest earned on unregistered long-term state and local government bonds does not violate the Tenth Amendment. South Carolina v. Baker, 485 U.S. 505, 108 S.Ct. 1355, 99 L.Ed.2d 592 (1988), rehearing denied 486 U.S. 1062, 108 S.Ct. 2837, 100 L.Ed.2d 937 (1988). This decision may not establish the principle that the federal government is totally free to tax income produced for private individuals from state or local government bonds, even though *Baker* was decided by a seven to one vote of the Justices. Three concurring Justices in *Baker* indicated that they were not foreclosing the possibility that a federal taxation system that undercut the ability of state or local governments to raise revenue would be subject to some federalism restrictions. See, South Carolina v. Baker, 485 U.S. at 527, 108 S.Ct. at 1369 (Stevens, J., concurring); Id. at 527, 108 S.Ct. at 1369 (Scalia, J., concurring in part and concurring in the judgment); Id. at 527–29, 108 S.Ct. at 1369–70 (Rehnquist, C.J., concurring in the judgment). Justice Kennedy did not participate in the ruling; Justice O'Connor issued the only dissent in *Baker*.

153. 469 U.S. 528, 105 S.Ct. 1005, 83 L.Ed.2d 1016 (1985), rehearing denied 471 U.S. 1049, 105 S.Ct. 2041, 85 L.Ed.2d 340 (1985).

154. 469 U.S. at 556, 105 S.Ct. at 1020.

155. 501 U.S. 452, 111 S.Ct. 2395, 115 L.Ed.2d 410 (1991).

156. Gregory v. Ashcroft, 501 U.S. 452, 457–472, 111 S.Ct. 2395, 2399–2406, 115 L.Ed.2d 410 (1991) (majority opinion by O'Connor, J., joined by Rehnquist, C.J., and Scalia, Souter and Kennedy, JJ.). Seven of the Justices in

Gregory found that the ADEA did not apply to mandatory retirement laws that governed members of the judiciary, due to a provision of the ADEA that exempted from its coverage state employees at a policymaking level. Justices White and Stevens agreed with Justice O'Connor's conclusion regarding the scope of the ADEA but did not join her opinion; these two Justices did not imply that the Constitution, or its Amendments, would restrict congressional power to apply an anti-discrimination law to the selection or retention of members of the judiciary. Id. at 474, 111 S.Ct. at 2408 (White, J., joined by Stevens, J., concurring in part and concurring in the judgment).

The two dissenting Justices in *Gregory* would have found that the ADEA invalidated the mandatory judicial retirement provision of the state constitution and that the ADEA was a valid exercise of congressional power. 501 U.S. at 452, 111 S.Ct. at 2395 (Blackmun, J., joined by Marshall, J., dissenting).

In *Gregory*, the Court also examined the question of whether a state constitutional provision that required judges to retire at age 70 violated either the Age Discrimination in Employment Act [ADEA] or the equal protection clause of the Fourteenth Amendment. Justice O'Connor's majority opinion was joined by seven Justices insofar as she rejected the claim that the mandatory retirement provision violated the equal protection clause. Justice O'Connor's majority opinion found that the law should be subject only to the most deferential standard of review under the equal protection clause because it did not involve a fundamental right or a classification that was at all constitutionally suspect. See § 14.3 of this Treatise regarding equal protection standards of review in general and the *Gregory* decision in particular.

the Court will not interpret a federal statute in a manner that will interfere with essential state or local government functions unless Congress plainly states its intention to do so in the statute itself.[157] The plain statement rules, as a canon of statutory construction, does not undercut *Garcia.* Justice O'Connor noted that the *Garcia* decision was built on the concept that the primary protection for state and local government interests was the congressional process.[158] The Court cannot be sure that the interest of state and local governments had been considered in the congressional process unless Congress clearly stated its intention to regulate state or local governments. If federal judges interpreted an ambiguous federal statute so that the statute applied to essential functions of state and local governments, the state and local governments might have their autonomy impaired even though Congress had not intended to impose any significant burdens on state or local governments when it enacted the statute.

On another level, however, Justice O'Connor's opinion raises some of the concerns that underlie the *National League of Cities* rationale.[159] The majority stated that a federal stat-

ute that regulated a state's ability to control its judiciary would raise significant constitutional questions in terms of federalism principles that might be based upon the structure of the entire Constitution of 1787, the Article I Powers of Congress, the guarantee clause of Article IV, or the Tenth Amendment.[160]

In 1992, a majority of Justices created a very limited federalism restriction on congressional power over state and local governments. In *New York v. United States,*[161] the Supreme Court ruled that Congress could not use its Article I commerce power to order state governments to enact legislation on commercial matters nor could it order states to take whatever governmental steps might be necessary for the state to take possession of, and title to, property owned by people within the state. Specifically, the Court prohibited Congress from ordering states to take legislative or executive actions to regulate radioactive waste within the state. The majority believed that the Tenth Amendment, or federalism principles, preventing Congress from making the states the equivalent of mere federal agencies,

---

157. For Justice O'Connor's discussion of the federalism principles that give rise to this statutory interpretation principle, see Gregory v. Ashcroft, 501 U.S. 452, 457–472, 111 S.Ct. 2395, 2399–2406, 115 L.Ed.2d 410 (1991). The Supreme Court previously had established a similar plain statement rule for the interpretation of federal statutes that might abrogate a state's Eleventh Amendment immunity from federal trial court jurisdiction. Atascadero State Hospital v. Scanlon, 473 U.S. 234, 105 S.Ct. 3142, 87 L.Ed.2d 171 (1985), rehearing denied 473 U.S. 926, 106 S.Ct. 18, 87 L.Ed.2d 696 (1985). For an examination of Eleventh Amendment principles, see § 2.12 of this Treatise.

158. Gregory v. Ashcroft, 501 U.S. 452, 111 S.Ct. 2395, 2403, 115 L.Ed.2d 410 (1991): "Indeed, inasmuch as this Court in *Garcia* has left primarily to the political process the protection of states against intrusive exercises of Congress' commerce clause powers, we must be absolutely certain that Congress intended such an exercise."

159. None of the Justices who were in the majority in *Garcia* joined the portion of Justice O'Connor's opinion in *Gregory* that expressed reservation about whether the ADEA constitutionally could be applied to the retention of state judges. This portion of Justice O'Connor's opinion in *Gregory* was joined by Chief Justice Rehnquist, who had written the *National League of Cities* decision. Both Justice O'Connor and Chief Justice Rehnquist had dissented when the Court in *Garcia* overruled the *National League of Cities* decision. The part of Justice O'Connor's opinion in *Gregory* in which she expressed the view that the

narrow interpretation of the ADEA was necessary to avoid a serious constitutional question concerning the scope of federal power over state governments was joined by Justices Scalia, Souter and Kennedy, in addition to Chief Justice Rehnquist. Gregory v. Ashcroft, 501 U.S. 452, 457–472, 111 S.Ct. 2395, 2399–2406, 115 L.Ed.2d 410 (1991).

Justices White and Stevens, who had been in the majority in *Garcia,* concurred separately in *Gregory.* They believed that the statute should be interpreted in a manner that avoided applying its provisions to state judges even though they did not believe there was a constitutional barrier to a federal law that would eliminate age discrimination in the employment of members of a state judiciary. Gregory v. Ashcroft, 501 U.S. 452, 474, 111 S.Ct. 2395, 2408, 115 L.Ed.2d 410 (1991) (White, J., joined by Stevens, J., concurring in part and concurring in the judgment).

Justices Blackmun and Marshall, who had been in the majority in *Garcia,* dissented in *Gregory;* ADEA applied to the employment of state judges and the ADEA was a valid exercise of congressional power. Gregory v. Ashcroft, 501 U.S. 452, 485, 111 S.Ct. 2395, 2414, 115 L.Ed.2d 410 (1991) (Blackmun, J., joined by Marshall, J., dissenting).

160. Gregory v. Ashcroft, 501 U.S. 452, 457–472, 111 S.Ct. 2395, 2399–2404, 115 L.Ed.2d 410 (1991).

161. 505 U.S. 144, 112 S.Ct. 2408, 120 L.Ed.2d 120 (1992), on remand 978 F.2d 705 (2d Cir.1992). See the beginning of this subsection [§ 4.10(d)(1)(a)] for a comparison of the *New York* decision and *Garcia.*

whose decisions Congress controls.[162]

Yet, in this same decision, the Supreme Court upheld broad congressional power to directly regulate private sector activities that might have an effect on interstate commercial concerns.[163] The Court also upheld congressional use of the spending power to reward states that regulated commercial matters in a way that met federal guidelines.[164] Because of the narrow issue presented by the case, and the Court's limited ruling, the majority opinion in *New York v. United States* stated explicitly the present case presents "no occasion to apply or revisit the holdings of" *Garcia v. San Antonio Metropolitan Transit Authority*,[165] or similar cases, because "this is not a case in which Congress has subjected a State to the same legislation applicable to private parties."[166] Hence, there is no significant constitutional immunity for state and local governments from federal commercial legislation that applies with the same force to private sector and public sector activities that affect interstate commerce.[167]

A major decision in the wake of *New York v. United States* is *Printz v. United States*,[168]

where the Court, again 5 to 4, invalidated portions of the Brady Handgun Violence Prevention Act. Part of the Brady Act required state and local police departments, under certain circumstances, to review information contained in an application to purchase a firearm and to do a "background check" to determine whether the prospective purchaser was barred by federal law from purchasing the gun. Justice Scalia, for the majority, found that the same principles that prevented the federal government from requiring state and local governments to enact legislation, also prohibited the federal government from requiring state or local executive officers to implement federal law.[169] The majority opinion in *Printz*, like the majority opinion in *New York v. United States*, did not question the *Garcia* decision,[170] which recognized the power of the federal government to subject states to commercial regulations that are *equally applicable* to private sector and public sector activities.[171]

New York v. United States and *Printz* do not grant states immunity from regulations of commercial activities engaged in by both pri-

---

162. New York v. United States, 505 U.S. 144, 112 S.Ct. 2408, 120 L.Ed.2d 120 (1992), on remand 978 F.2d 705 (2d Cir.1992). Justice O'Connor's majority opinion found that the limits on congressional power could be based on either the Tenth Amendment or federalism principles that could be grounded in Article I. The majority opinion avoided ruling on the question of whether the guarantee clause of Article IV of the Constitution might present a basis for limiting federal powers over state governments that would not involve a political question. 505 U.S. at 183–84, 112 S.Ct. at 2432–33.

163. 505 U.S. at 169–73, 112 S.Ct. at 2425–27.

164. 505 U.S. at 173, 112 S.Ct. at 2427.

165. 469 U.S. 528, 105 S.Ct. 1005, 83 L.Ed.2d 1016 (1985), rehearing denied 471 U.S. 1049, 105 S.Ct. 2041, 85 L.Ed.2d 340 (1985).

166. New York v. U.S., 505 U.S. 144, 160, 112 S.Ct. 2408, 2420, 120 L.Ed.2d 120 (1992).

167. 505 U.S. at 160, 112 S.Ct. at 2420.

168. 521 U.S. 898, 117 S.Ct. 2365, 138 L.Ed.2d 914 (1997). Justices Stevens, Souter, Ginsburg, and Breyer dissented in *Printz*. 521 U.S. at 939, 117 S.Ct. at 2386 (Stevens, J., joined by Souter, Ginsburg, and Breyer, JJ., dissenting); 521 U.S. at 970, 117 S.Ct. at 2401 (Souter, J., dissenting); 521 U.S. at 2405, 117 S.Ct. at 977 (Breyer, J., joined by Stevens, J., dissenting).

169. 521 U.S. at 931–32, 117 S.Ct. at 2383.

170. Garcia v. San Antonio Metropolitan Transit Authority, 469 U.S. 528, 105 S.Ct. 1005, 83 L.Ed.2d 1016

(1985), rehearing denied 471 U.S. 1049, 105 S.Ct. 2041, 85 L.Ed.2d 340 (1985).

171. In *Printz*, Justice Scalia's majority opinion noted that the Court was not addressing questions concerning whether Congress could require states to provide information to the federal government or whether the federal government could condition federal funds on state legislative regulatory or executive action. Printz v. United States, 521 U.S. 898, 918, 117 S.Ct. 2365, 2376, 138 L.Ed.2d 914 (1997).

Justice O'Connor, who had written the majority opinion in New York v. United States wrote a concurring opinion in *Printz* to point out the narrowness of its holding. Printz v. United States, 521 U.S. 898, 935–36, 117 S.Ct. 2365, 2385, 138 L.Ed.2d 914 (1997) (O'Connor, J., concurring). Justice Thomas indirectly pointed out the narrowness of the majority opinion in his concurring opinion by suggesting that the majority should go further than it did in *Printz* and actually limit the federal power over private sector commercial activity and raising Second Amendment questions about federal regulation of firearms. 521 U.S. at 936–37, 117 S.Ct. at 2385 (Thomas, J., concurring). Justice Souter was the only Justice who believed that there was a constitutional distinction between the federal laws controlling state or local legislatures and federal laws to controlling state or local executive officers. Justice Souter was a part of the majority in *New York v. United States*, but he dissented in *Printz*. Printz v. United States, 521 U.S. 898, 970, 117 S.Ct. 2365, 2401, 138 L.Ed.2d 914 (1997) (Souter, J., dissenting).

vate sector businesses and public sector entities. Thus, in *Reno v. Condon*[172] the Court unanimously upheld the application of the Federal Drivers Privacy Protection Act to state governments. The Act prohibited state governments from disclosing information they received in drivers license applications except certain statutorily established reasons. The Act *also* prohibited *private persons* who received information from a state, in accordance with one of the statutory exceptions, from disclosing that information to other persons. Chief Justice Rehnquist, writing for the Court, ruled that the regulation of the information in drivers license data bases was the regulation of an activity that was part of interstate commerce. The law did not target state governments for special regulation, because of law applied to private sector entities that received drivers license information as well as to state governments. The federal law merely required the states to comply with a valid federal commerce power regulation and it did not require the states to take any legislative or regulatory actions, or to put their executive branch officials in the service of, or at the beck and call of, the federal government.[173]

---

172. Reno v. Condon, 528 U.S. 141, 120 S.Ct. 666, 145 L.Ed.2d 587 (2000).

173. 528 U.S. at 148–50 120 S.Ct. at 671–72. See § 4.10(d)(1) of this Treatise.

Chapter 5

FEDERAL FISCAL POWERS

§ 5.1 Introduction

Federal fiscal powers are comprehensive, and Congress exercises them in a way that exerts a controlling impact on the nation's economy. These powers, among the most important of those granted to the federal government, include the power to tax, the power to coin money and to borrow on the credit of the United States, and the power to spend. Each is discussed in the following sections.[1]

§ 5.2 General Scope of the Taxing Power

Express provisions of the Constitution grant broad powers of taxation to Congress.[1] Except for two specific limitations on the exercise of the power and one prohibition, the power to tax is plenary. The specific limitations on the exercise of the power to tax are these: (1) direct taxes and capitation taxes must be allocated among the states in proportion to population; and (2) all custom duties and excise taxes must be uniform throughout the United States. The single prohibition is that no duty shall be levied on exports from any state.[2] In addition, the due process clause of the Fifth Amendment operates as a general limitation on the exercise of the power to tax.

The Sixteenth Amendment, which permits imposition of a federal income tax without apportionment among the states, was necessitated by the five to four decision in *Pollock v. Farmers' Loan & Trust Co.*[3] Forty-two years later, with its decision in *New York ex rel. Cohn v. Graves,*[4] the Court in effect overruled

§ 5.1

1. See generally 1 R. Rotunda and J. Nowak, Treatise on Constitutional Law: Substance and Procedure §§ 5.1–5.11 (West Group, 3d ed.1999), for further discussion and analysis.

§ 5.2

1. The following Constitutional provisions directly relate to the substantive taxing powers granted to the federal government:

(a) *Article I, Section 2, clause 3:*

"Representatives and direct Taxes shall be apportioned among the several States which may be included within this Union, according to their respective Numbers. . . ."

(b) *Article I, Section 8, clause 1:*

"The Congress shall have Power To lay and collect Taxes, Duties, Imposts and Excises, to pay the Debts and provide for the common Defence and general Welfare of the United States; but all Duties, Imposts and Excises shall be uniform throughout the United States."

(c) *Article I, Section 9, clauses 4 and 5:*

"No Capitation, or other direct, Tax shall be laid, unless in Proportion to the Census or Enumeration herein before directed to be taken."

"No Tax or Duty shall be laid on Articles exported from any State."

(d) *Sixteenth Amendment:*

"The Congress shall have power to lay and collect taxes on incomes, from whatever source derived, without apportionment among the several States, and without regard to any census or enumeration."

2. United States v. IBM, 517 U.S. 843, 116 S.Ct. 1793, 135 L.Ed.2d 124 (1996) held that the Export Clause, Art. I, § 9, cl. 5, prohibits the Federal Government from imposing a generally applicable, nondiscriminatory federal tax on goods in export transit. Cases decided under either the dormant commerce clause or the Import–Export Clause (Art. I, § 10, cl. 2)—both of which limit *state* taxing power—do not govern the Export Clause. The dormant commerce, as *Complete Auto Transit* explained, only applies to state taxes that discriminate against interstate commerce, while the Export Clause denies Congress the power to tax exports at all.

3. 157 U.S. 429, 15 S.Ct. 673, 39 L.Ed. 759 (initial decision), 158 U.S. 601, 15 S.Ct. 912, 39 L.Ed. 1108 (decision on rehearing) (1895) (tax on income from real and personal property held invalid in the absence of apportionment).

4. 300 U.S. 308, 57 S.Ct. 466, 81 L.Ed. 666 (1937) (sustaining New York income tax on income derived by New York resident from New Jersey real estate).

Pollock and in so doing rendered the Sixteenth Amendment redundant.

§ 5.3　Direct versus Indirect Taxes

(a) Historical Background

Although the Constitutional grant of taxing power to the federal government is very broad, the dichotomy between direct and indirect taxes ultimately proved to be a stumbling block in the development of our present federal tax structure. Prior to the decision in *Pollock* in 1895, it had been the general consensus that the term "direct" tax employed in the Constitution embraced only taxes on land (real property) and poll or capitation taxes.

This understanding was firmly founded in at least three significant cases. The first was *Hylton v. United States,*[1] decided in the early years of the new Constitution. *Hylton* ruled that a federal tax on carriages was a duty or excise that was not subject to apportionment. The second case was *Veazie Bank v. Fenno,*[2] where the Court upheld (as an indirect tax) a prohibitory tax (duty) on the issuance and circulation of state bank notes. The third and most important was *Springer v. United States,*[3] in which the Court sustained the Civil War Income Tax Act as an excise or duty that was not subject to apportionment. In light of this existing precedent, the decision in *Pollock* came as a notable surprise.

Pollock held that the Income Tax Act of 1894 was a direct tax and thus unconstitutional and void, because it imposed a tax on income from real estate and personal property without apportionment.[4] However, it is important to note that in its decision on rehearing, the Court noted, with respect to taxes on the income of business and occupations:

We have considered the act only in respect of the tax on income derived from real estate, and from invested personal property, and have not commented on so much of it as bears on gains or profits from business, privileges, or employments, in view of the instances in which taxation on business, privileges, or employments has assumed the guise of an excise tax and been sustained as such.[5]

This exception to the basic decision was significant because the Court was making it clear that a tax on income from business and occupations was not a direct tax and thus could be subjected to taxation without the necessity of apportionment on the basis of population.

The story of the adoption of the Sixteenth Amendment, which reversed *Pollock*, is a fascinating chapter in American history. After the Populist movement produced the Income Tax Act of 1894, the Populists continued to gain momentum. In the campaign of 1908, the Democratic platform contained a plank supporting a constitutional Amendment to authorize an income tax. William Howard Taft, the Republican candidate, expressed his view that the country could have an income tax without a constitutional Amendment. In 1909, the pressure for an income tax culminated in a compromise with the addition of the Corporate Excise Tax of 1909 as an Amendment to the Payne–Aldrich Tariff Bill and the adoption of a joint resolution by the Senate and House of Representatives submitting the Sixteenth Amendment to the states for ratification. On February 25, 1913, the Secretary of State issued a proclamation declaring that the Amendment had been duly ratified.

§ 5.3

1. 3 U.S. (3 Dall.) 171, 1 L.Ed. 556 (1796) Justice Patterson, who had participated in the Constitutional Convention said, in his separate opinion: "I never entertained a doubt that the principal, I will not say the only objects, that the framers of the constitution contemplated as falling within the rule of apportionment [as a direct tax], were a capitation tax and a tax on land." 3 U.S. (3 Dall.) at 177.

2. 75 U.S. (8 Wall.) 533, 19 L.Ed. 482 (1869). The Court stated: "It may be rightly affirmed, therefore, that in the practical construction of the Constitution by Congress, direct taxes have been limited to taxes on land and

appurtenances, and taxes on polls, or capitation taxes." 75 U.S. (8 Wall.) at 544.

3. 102 U.S. (12 Otto) 586, 26 L.Ed. 253 (1880): "Our conclusions are, that *direct taxes*, within the meaning of the Constitution, are only capitation taxes, as expressed in that instrument, and taxes on real estate; and that the tax of which the plaintiff ... complains is within the category of an excise or duty." 102 U.S. (12 Otto) at 602.

4. The Court also held that under the doctrine of intergovernmental immunity the tax was invalid insofar as it applied to interest on state and municipal obligations.

5. 158 U.S. at 635, 15 S.Ct. at 920.

In the meantime, the Supreme Court sustained the Corporate Excise Tax Act of 1909 in *Flint v. Stone Tracy Co.*[6] The statute provided that every corporation "engaged in business in any state or territory" was required "to pay annually a special excise tax with respect to the carrying on or doing business" at the rate of one percent on all net income in excess of five thousand dollars. The constitutional challenge was based on *Pollock* and premised on the contention that the tax was invalid as an unapportioned direct tax because it applied to corporate income derived from real and personal property. In *Pollock*, the majority of the Court had concluded that a tax on income from property was the equivalent of a direct tax on the income-producing property itself.

Flint sustained the validity of the Corporation Excise Tax Act of 1909. It noted that the statute was structured "as a tax upon the doing of business in a corporate capacity" and that "the measure of the tax [was] ... income."[7] Having defined the structure of the tax, the Court considered whether a tax cast in such form, and computed on all income (including income derived from property) constituted a direct tax on real and personal property within the proscription of *Pollock*. The Court concluded that the rationale of *Pollock* was not controlling. First, *Pollock* itself had admitted that it did not bear "on gains or profits from business, privileges, or employments, in view of the instances in which taxation on business, privileges, or employments has assumed the guise of an excise tax and been sustained as such."[8] The Court also relied on *Knowlton v. Moore*,[9] sustaining a federal legacy tax as an excise on the transmission of property by inheritance, and *Spreckels Sug-*

ar Refining Co. v. McClain,[10] sustaining a special tax measured by gross receipts on the businesses of refining oil or sugar as an excise with respect to carrying on such businesses.

After reviewing several cases relating to state franchise taxes, the Court finally summarized its position with respect to the difference between the subject and the measure of a tax:

> [W]hen the sovereign authority has exercised the right to tax a legitimate subject of taxation as an exercise of a franchise or privilege, it is no objection that the measure of taxation is found in the income produced in part from property which of itself considered is non-taxable.[11]

Thus, the Court reasserted its adherence to the basic doctrine that, if the subject of a tax is within the taxing power, the measure of the tax is not a matter of judicial concern.

(b) Current Status of Direct versus Indirect Taxes

As indicated by *Flint v. Stone Tracy Co.*[12] and as confirmed by later decisions, the dichotomy between direct and indirect taxes is no longer a problem. The Court has held that the following taxes are indirect (excise) taxes and thus not direct taxes subject to the requirement of apportionment: federal legacy tax of 1898;[13] special federal tobacco tax of 1898;[14] special excise tax of 1898 imposed on the business of refining sugar and computed on gross annual receipts;[15] federal estate tax enacted in 1916;[16] and the federal gift tax of 1924.[17]

§ 5.4 Federal Taxing Power and Due Process

On occasion, but with rare success,[1] litigants have raised due process objections to federal tax provisions. In *Brushaber v. Union Pacific*

---

6. 220 U.S. 107, 31 S.Ct. 342, 55 L.Ed. 389 (1911).

7. 220 U.S. at 146, 31 S.Ct. at 347.

8. 220 U.S. at 148, 31 S.Ct. at 348.

9. 178 U.S. 41, 20 S.Ct. 747, 44 L.Ed. 969 (1900).

10. 192 U.S. 397, 24 S.Ct. 376, 48 L.Ed. 496 (1904).

11. 220 U.S. at 165, 3 S.Ct. at 354–55.

12. 220 U.S. 107, 31 S.Ct. 342, 55 L.Ed. 389 (1911).

13. Knowlton v. Moore, 178 U.S. 41, 20 S.Ct. 747, 44 L.Ed. 969 (1900).

14. Patton v. Brady, 184 U.S. 608, 22 S.Ct. 493, 46 L.Ed. 713 (1902).

15. Spreckels Sugar Refining Co. v. McClain, 192 U.S. 397, 24 S.Ct. 376, 48 L.Ed. 496 (1904).

16. New York Trust Co. v. Eisner, 256 U.S. 345, 41 S.Ct. 506, 65 L.Ed. 963 (1921).

17. Bromley v. McCaughn, 280 U.S. 124, 50 S.Ct. 46, 74 L.Ed. 226 (1929).

§ 5.4

1. In Nichols v. Coolidge, 274 U.S. 531, 47 S.Ct. 710, 71 L.Ed. 1184 (1927), the Court held that there was a violation of due process when the Government sought to tax, as part of the decedent's gross estate, a transfer of

R. Co.,[2] the first income tax (enacted in October, 1913, following ratification of the Sixteenth Amendment) was challenged on several due process grounds, including the fact that it was retroactive to March 1, 1913, and that it provided for graduated rates. The Court brushed aside these objections:

> So far as the due process clause of the Fifth Amendment is relied upon, it suffices to say that there is no basis for such reliance since it is equally well settled that such clause is not a limitation upon the taxing power conferred upon Congress by the Constitution; in other words, that the Constitution does not conflict with itself by conferring upon the one hand a taxing power and taking the same power away on the other by the limitations of the due process clause.[3]

In two subsequent income tax cases, the Court again refused to recognize the taxpayer's due process objections. The first was *Corliss v. Bowers*,[4] where the taxpayer challenged the provisions that taxed the income of revocable trusts to the settlor. The second was *Burnet v. Wells*,[5] where the taxpayer challenged the provisions for taxing the income of irrevocable life insurance trusts to the insured-settlor. *Corliss* concluded that it was reasonable to tax one on income that was subject to his unfettered control and that he was free to enjoy at any time he saw fit. And *Burnet* concluded that it was reasonable to tax the settlor on the income applied to maintain insurance policies on his own life for the benefit of family members because, in effect, he had reserved the income for his own peace of mind.[6]

§ 5.5 Federal Taxes as Regulatory Measures

Any tax, no matter the type, has an inevitable economic impact on business and commerce. This result is unavoidable, however desirable the ideal of a neutral tax system. Congress recognizes these fact of life, and sometimes, its real purpose is not to raise revenue but to produce a particular economic impact. Sometimes the tax is so high that it is prohibitory. Taxing certain activities heavily is a way to discourage those activities. In modern times, custom duties offer a classic example of a tax where the revenue gains may be secondary while the regulatory affects are primary.

Until the turn of the twentieth century, custom duties provided the major portion of federal revenues. Certain tariffs also protected American manufacturers against competition from foreign goods. Surprisingly, it was not until 1928 that the Court[1] explicitly sustained the validity of protective tariffs that tended to produce little or no revenue. The Court noted the historical background of our tariff policy going back to the first session of Congress and concluded that, whatever "we may think of the wisdom of a protection policy, we can not hold it unconstitutional."[2]

> So long as the motive of Congress and the effect of its legislative action are to secure revenue for the benefit of the general government, the existence of other motives in the selection of the subjects of taxes can not invalidate Congressional action.[3]

Earlier, *McCray v. United States*[4] had sustained a hefty federal excise tax of ten cents per pound imposed on the sale of colored oleomargarine. *McCray* portended the results in the protective tariff case. The Court rejected the argument that the margarine tax was prohibitory and therefore a violation of the due process provisions of the Fifth Amendment:

---

property that had been completed prior to the enactment of the federal estate tax in 1916.

2. 240 U.S. 1, 36 S.Ct. 236, 60 L.Ed. 493 (1916).

3. 240 U.S. at 24, 36 S.Ct. at 244. The Court also noted that retroactive provisions of the Civil War Income Tax had been sustained in Stockdale v. Atlantic Insurance Co., 87 U.S. (20 Wall.) 323, 22 L.Ed. 348 (1873).

4. 281 U.S. 376, 50 S.Ct. 336, 74 L.Ed. 916 (1930).

5. 289 U.S. 670, 53 S.Ct. 761, 77 L.Ed. 1439 (1933).

6. 289 U.S. at 680–81, 53 S.Ct. at 765.

§ 5.5

1. J. W. Hampton, Jr. & Co. v. United States, 276 U.S. 394, 48 S.Ct. 348, 72 L.Ed. 624 (1928).

2. 276 U.S. at 412, 48 S.Ct. at 353.

3. 276 U.S. at 412, 48 S.Ct. at 353.

4. 195 U.S. 27, 24 S.Ct. 769, 49 L.Ed. 78 (1904).

Since ... the taxing power conferred by the Constitution knows no limits except those expressly stated in that instrument, it must follow, if a tax be within the lawful power, the exertion of that power may not be judicially restrained because of the results to arise from its exercise.[5]

Once again, the Court said that it would be improper for the judicial branch to inquire into the underlying motives of the Congress irrespective of the purpose of the Act.

Although a federal tax *qua* tax may be an exercise of the taxing power, it may be invalid in light of specific constitutional limitations, such, for example, as the Fifth Amendment prohibition against self-incrimination.[6]

The Tenth Amendment, however, is not a specific limitation on the federal taxing power. Although *Bailey v. Drexel Furniture Co.*,[7] held that the federal government had violated the Tenth Amendment by infringing on the powers reserved to the state, in modern times the Court does not apply the Tenth Amendment in this manner. The Court treats the Tenth Amendment as a redundancy, only reserving to the states what the Constitution does not already give to the Federal Government, either expressly or by implication.

§ 5.6 The Power to Spend

The Constitutional power to spend is coupled with the power to tax and is cast in terms of the power to tax "and provide for the common Defense and general Welfare."[1] There have been no Court decisions directly involving the issue of the power to spend to provide for the "common Defense." However, the Court has considered the nature and extent of the power to spend for the general welfare.[2]

The leading case is *United States v. Butler*,[3] which provided, for the first time, an authoritative guide to the power to spend for the general welfare. The Court adopted a broad, Hamiltonian view of the spending power. The Court noted that the Constitution expressly gives Congress the power to tax for the general welfare. The funds collected will be spent. Taxes "can never accomplish the objects for which they were collected, unless the power to appropriate is as broad as the power to tax."[4] Hence, in the view of the Court, the "necessary implication from the terms of the grant is that the public funds may be appropriated 'to provide for the general welfare of the United States.'"[5] The decision merits quotation at length:

Since the foundation of the Nation, sharp differences of opinion have persisted as to the true interpretation of the phrase. Madison asserted it amounted to no more than a reference to the other powers enumerated in the subsequent clauses of the same section.... In this view the phrase is merely tautology, for taxation and appropriation are or may be necessary incidents of the exercise of any of the enumerated legislative powers. Hamilton, on the other hand, maintained the clause confers a power separate and distinct from those later enumerated, is not restricted in meaning by the grant of them, and Congress consequently has a substantive power to tax and to appropriate, limited only by the requirement that it shall be exercised to provide for the general welfare of the United States.... Mr. Justice Story,

5. 195 U.S. at 59, 24 S.Ct. at 778.

6. E.g., Marchetti v. United States, 390 U.S. 39, 88 S.Ct. 697, 19 L.Ed.2d 889 (1968).

7. 259 U.S. 20, 42 S.Ct. 449, 66 L.Ed. 817 (1922).

§ 5.6

1. U.S.Const. art. I. § 8, cl. 1. See generally, Roger Pilon, Freedom, Responsibility, and the Constitution: On Recovering Our Founding Principles, 68 Notre Dame L.Rev. 507, 530–33 (1993).

2. The dearth of decisions directly bearing on the power to spend is related to the general lack of taxpayer standing to sue to enjoin expenditure of federal funds.

Massachusetts v. Mellon, 262 U.S. 447, 43 S.Ct. 597, 67 L.Ed. 1078 (1923). Contrary to the state rule often applicable at the state and local level, taxpayer standing to sue in federal courts, is narrowly circumscribed except for alleged violation of the establishment clause of the First Amendment.

3. 297 U.S. 1, 56 S.Ct. 312, 80 L.Ed. 477 (1936). See also Helvering v. Davis, 301 U.S. 619, 640–41, 57 S.Ct. 904, 908–09, 81 L.Ed. 1307, 1314–15 (1937).

4. 297 U.S. at 65–66, 56 S.Ct. 312 at 319, 80 L.Ed. at 488 (footnotes omitted).

5. 297 U.S. at 65–66, 56 S.Ct. 312 at 319, 80 L.Ed. at 488 (footnotes omitted).

in his Commentaries, espouses the Hamiltonian position. [We] conclude that the reading advocated by Mr. Justice Story is the correct one. While therefore, the power to tax is not unlimited, its confines are set in the clause which confers it, and not in those of section 8 which bestow and define the legislative powers of the Congress. It results that the power of Congress to authorize expenditure of public moneys for public purposes is not limited by the direct grants of legislative power found in the Constitution.[6]

Although *Butler* provided a broad construction of the power to spend for the general welfare, it then, oddly enough, proceeded to hold the Agricultural Adjustment Act of 1933 to be a violation of the Tenth Amendment, an unconstitutional invasion of states' reserved powers. The following year, after the Court Packing Plan of 1937, the Court specifically rejected this Tenth Amendment limitation on the spending power.[7] Thus, *Butler* is good law as to its broad construction of the general welfare clause, but not as to its Tenth Amendment analysis.

Today the Supreme Court will not attempt to reserve areas of activity for the sole control of state governments. Thus federal spending programs will not be invalidated merely because they invade the "police power" of the states and influence local activities. The spending program will be upheld so long as its substantive provisions did not violate a specific check on the federal power.

The Tenth Amendment, in short, is not a specific check on Congress' power under the spending clause. If the states choose to accept the federal money, they must accept any federal strings that come attached to that money. "Requiring States to honor the obligations assumed as a condition of federal funding before recognizing their ownership of funds simply does not intrude on their sovereignty. The State chose to participate in the [particular federal] program and, as a condition of receiving the grant, freely gave its assurances that it would abide by the conditions of [the federal program]."[8]

A modern example of these principles is *Buckley v. Valeo*,[9] where the Court upheld the establishment of the Presidential Election Campaign Fund. Because the grant of public funds for presidential candidates did not violate any specific check on the federal power or limit any fundamental rights, the provisions were sustained under the rule stated in the *Butler* decision as an expenditure to promote the general welfare.

Similarly, *Oklahoma v. United States Civil Service Commission*[10] upheld Congressional Power to withhold federal highway funds from Oklahoma unless that state removed a *state* official who had engaged in certain political activities prohibited by the federal Hatch Act. "While the United States is not concerned with, and has no power to regulate, local political activities as such of state officials, it does have power to fix the terms on which its money allotments to states shall be dis-

---

6. 297 U.S. at 65–66, 56 S.Ct. 312 at 319, 80 L.Ed. at 488 (footnotes omitted).

7. Charles C. Steward Machine Co. v. Davis, 301 U.S. 548, 57 S.Ct. 883, 81 L.Ed. 1279 (1937); Helvering v. Davis, 301 U.S. 619, 57 S.Ct. 904, 81 L.Ed. 1307 (1937). These cases sustained the Social Security Act of 1935 as a proper exercise of federal authority that did not invade the province of the states under the Tenth Amendment.

8. Bell v. New Jersey, 461 U.S. 773, 790, 103 S.Ct. 2187, 2197, 76 L.Ed.2d 312, 326 (1983).

See, 1 R. Cappalli, Federal Grants and Cooperative Agreements § 1:09 (1982); Rotunda, Conditional Preemption and Other Limitations on Tenth Amendment Restrictions, 132 U.Pa.L.Rev. 289, 296–97, 314–15 (1984).

"The legitimacy of Congress' power to legislate under the spending power thus rests on whether the State voluntarily and knowingly accepts the terms of the 'contract.' "

Pennhurst State School and Hospital v. Halderman, 451 U.S. 1, 17, 101 S.Ct. 1531, 1539, 67 L.Ed.2d 694, 707 (1981), on remand 673 F.2d 647 (3d Cir.1982), motion to dismiss certiorari denied 463 U.S. 1251, 104 S.Ct. 45, 77 L.Ed.2d 1458 (1983). This is a rule of "statutory construction." 451 U.S. at 24, 101 S.Ct. at 1543, 67 L.Ed.2d at 712.

9. 424 U.S. 1, 90–91, 96 S.Ct. 612, 668–69, 46 L.Ed.2d 659, 728–29 (1976) (per curiam), mandate conformed 532 F.2d 187 (D.C.Cir.1976).

10. 330 U.S. 127, 67 S.Ct. 544, 91 L.Ed. 794 (1947). Cf. United Public Workers v. Mitchell, 330 U.S. 75, 67 S.Ct. 556, 91 L.Ed. 754 (1947).

See generally, P. Hay and R. Rotunda, The United States Federal System: Legal Integration in the American Experience 169–84 (Giuffré, Milan, 1982).

bursed."[11] Because Oklahoma accepted the federal highway funds, it must also accept the conditions attached to them: state officials must comply with the limitation on their political activities set out by the federal law.

In a host of cases, Congress uses its spending power to reward the states if they engage in certain activities, or withhold funds if they do not. Similarly, Congress uses its spending power to regulate the executive branch by denying funds for activities that Congress does not want to happen.[12]

The Four–Part Test to Measure the Spending Power

The Twenty–First Amendment & the Dole Case. *South Dakota v. Dole*[13] upheld the power of Congress to use the spending clause to withhold federal highway funds from states that allow the purchase or public possession of any alcoholic beverage by persons under twenty-one years of age. The Court rejected South Dakota's argument that section 2 of the Twenty-first Amendment gave the states complete control over whether to permit the sale or importation of liquor in its boundaries.

One would think that the most natural reading of the language of the second section of Twenty-first Amendment is that the section gives the states broad powers to *prohibit* the purchase or importation or sale of liquor within its jurisdiction, but says nothing about the power of the state to *allow* the purchase of liquor that Congress prohibits.[14] The Court, however, did not decide that issue. Its opinion was more narrow as regards the Twenty–First Amendment. The real significance of this case

is that it laid out a four-part test that applies in all spending clause cases when the party challenges the constitutionality of the legislation.

The Test in All Spending Clause Cases. Chief Justice Rehnquist, for the Court in *Dole*, acknowledged that the "spending power is of course not unlimited," but in this case, the federal legislation did not pass those limits. He distilled from the precedents a multi-part test.

First, the spending power must be in pursuit of the general welfare, which occurred here, "especially in light of the fact that 'the concept of welfare or the opposite is shaped by Congress....' "[15] *Second*, if Congress desires to condition the state's receipt of funds, it "must do so unambiguously," so the states can exercise their choice knowingly.[16] That too existed here. *Third* "our cases have suggested (without significant elaboration) that conditions on federal grants might be illegitimate if they are unrelated 'to the federal interest in particular national projects or Programs.' "[17] In this case, however, the Congressional condition is "directly related to one of the main purposes for which highway funds are expended—safe interstate travel." Congress had found that various drinking ages in different states "created particular incentives for young persons to combine their desire to drink with their ability to drive, and that this interstate problem required a national solution."[18] *Fourth*, the Court must determine whether any other Constitutional clause imposes an "independent bar" to spending power.

---

11. 330 U.S. at 143, 67 S.Ct. at 553–54, 91 L.Ed. at 806–07. Accord, Northern Virginia Regional Park Authority v. United States Civil Service Commission, 437 F.2d 1346 (4th Cir.1971), certiorari denied 403 U.S. 936, 91 S.Ct. 2254, 29 L.Ed.2d 717 (1971).

12. E.g., United States v. Bean, 537 U.S. 71, 123 S.Ct. 584, 154 L.Ed.2d 483 (2002). Bean, a convicted felon, sought relief from a firearms disability from the Bureau of Alcohol, Tobacco and Firearms, based on 18 U.S.C.A. § 922(c), which allows the Secretary of Treasury to grant such relief and grants judicial review of a denial of request. However, the Treasury Department returned the application unprocessed, because a separate appropriations law forbade the Treasury Department from spending any funds to investigate or act on such requests. Bean then filed suit in federal court and obtained relief. Thomas, J., for a unanimous Court, reversed, holding that the agen-

cy's failure to act precluded court review, given the relevant language of the statute. The Court was untroubled by this denial of judicial review.

13. 483 U.S. 203, 107 S.Ct. 2793, 97 L.Ed.2d 171 (1987).

14. U.S. Const. Amend. 21, § 2: "The transportation or importation into any State, Territory, or possession of the United States for delivery or use therein of intoxicating liquors, in violation of the laws thereof, is hereby prohibited."

15. 483 U.S. at 207, 209, 107 S.Ct. at 2796, 2797.

16. 483 U.S. at 207, 107 S.Ct. at 2796.

17. 483 U.S. at 207, 107 S.Ct. at 2796.

18. 483 U.S. at 209, 107 S.Ct. at 2797.

Independent Constitutional Bar. The fourth prong of the *Dole* test is crucial.[19] The Court concluded that the Twenty-first Amendment, like the Tenth Amendment, is not an *independent constitutional bar* to the federal government's conditional grant of funds. *Dole* interpreted *United States v. Butler* to hold "that the constitutional limitations on Congress exercising its spending power are less exacting than those on its authority to regulate directly."[20]

The Court explained what it meant by an "independent constitutional bar:"

[T]he "independent constitutional bar" limitation on the spending power is not, as petitioner suggests, a prohibition on the indirect achievement of objectives which Congress is not empowered to achieve directly. Instead, ... the power may not be used to induce the States to engage in activities that would themselves be unconstitutional. Thus, for example, a grant of federal funds conditioned on invidiously discriminatory state action or the infliction of cruel and unusual punishment would be an illegitimate exercise of the Congress' broad spending power. But no such claim can be or is made here. Were South Dakota to succumb to the blandishment offered by Congress and raise its drinking age to 21, the State's action in so doing would not violate the constitutional rights of anyone.

[I]n some circumstances the financial inducement offered by Congress might be so coercive as to pass the point at which pressure turns into compulsion. Here, however, Congress has directed only that a State desiring to establish a minimum drinking age lower than 21 lose a relatively small percentage [5%] of certain federal highway funds. Petitioner contends that the coercive nature of this program is evident from the degree of success it has achieved. We cannot conclude, however, that a conditional grant of federal money of this sort is unconstitutional simply by reason of its success in achieving the congressional objective.[21]

Dole reaffirmed *Stewart Machine*'s principle that motive or temptation is not equivalent to coercion: to conclude otherwise "is to plunge the law in endless difficulties." Thus, even if Congress might lack the power to impose a national minimum drinking age directly, we conclude that encouragement to state action found in [the federal law] is a valid use of the spending power.[22]

On the other hand, if federal legislation would violate the Bill of Rights or other Constitutional restriction, Congress cannot validly enact such legislation in the guise of the spending power. For example, Congress cannot suspend the Fourth Amendment and authorize the police to search a house without a warrant. Congress also cannot give money for low income housing on the condition that those who use the federally subsidized housing waive their Fourth Amendment rights.[23]

---

19. See, Rotunda, The Bar and the Legal Academy, in The Rule of Law in the Wake of Clinton 207, 217–19 (Roger Pilon, ed., Cato Institute 2000).

20. 483 U.S. at 209, 107 S.Ct. at 2797.

21. 483 U.S. at 211, 107 S.Ct. at 2798. See also, New York v. United States, 505 U.S. 144, 112 S.Ct. 2408, 120 L.Ed.2d 120 (1992), upholding federal monetary incentives designed to encourage states to implement a low level radioactive waste policy. The Court, however, invalidated a third provision that did not involve the federal spending power and simply imposed certain duties on the states.

22. 483 U.S. at 213, 107 S.Ct. at 2799.

Brennan dissented because he believed that the Twenty-first Amendment limited the spending power. O'Connor, the only other dissenter, believed that the federal law "is not a condition on spending reasonably related to the expenditure of federal funds and cannot be justified on that ground," but is an attempt to regulate the sale of liquor reserved to the states by section 2 of the Twenty-first Amendment.

23. Pratt v. Chicago Housing Authority, 848 F.Supp. 792 (N.D.Ill.1994); Rotunda, The Bar and the Legal Academy, in The Rule of Law in the Wake of Clinton 207, 217–19 (Roger Pilon, ed., Cato Institute 2000).

See, United States v. American Library Association., Inc., 539 U.S. 194, 123 S.Ct. 2297, 156 L.Ed.2d 221 (2003). A fractured Court, with no majority opinion, reversed the injunction and rejected the facial challenge to the Children's Internet Protection Act (CIPA), which requires libraries, as a condition of receiving federal funds, to install internet filters for children. These filters block obscene or pornographic images and to prevent minors from accessing material deemed harmful to them. Rehnquist, C.J., joined by O'Connor, Scalia & Thomas, JJ., concluded that the public libraries' use of internet filtering software does not violate their patrons' First Amendment rights, so CIPA does not induce libraries to violate the

§ 5.7 The Power to Borrow and Control the Currency

The grant of power to Congress to borrow is general and unlimited.[1] Exercise of the power to borrow is within the exclusive discretion of Congress and is considered in conjunction with the correlative power to coin money and regulate the value thereof.[2] The most significant aspect of the power to borrow and to coin money is the exercise of that power in the establishment of the national banking system,[3] the establishment of the federal reserve system with its control over the currency and money supply,[4] and the establishment of other federal credit facilities such as the federal land bank system.[5] The power to create a national banking system to implement the fiscal operations of the federal government includes the power to limit or to prohibit state taxation of such banks as instrumentalities of the federal government.[6]

Federal power with respect to the national banking system and control of the currency and coin includes the power to devalue the monetary unit. In 1933, during the Great Depression, Congress abolished the gold standard for our currency and, by Joint Resolution, invalidated the gold clauses in both private and public obligations. The resolution invalidating the gold clauses provided that every obligation that was by its terms payable in gold "shall be discharged upon payment, dollar for dollar, in any coin or currency that at the time of payment is legal tender for public and private debts." This action was sustained with

respect to private obligations in *Norman v. Baltimore & O.R. Co.*[7] as within the authority of Congress to regulate the currency and establish the monetary system of the country. Because Congress, in the exercise of its sovereign power over the currency, may alter or impair the rights of parties under private contracts, there is no deprivation of property without due process of law.

By contrast, *Perry v. United States*[8] held that the United States has no constitutional power to abrogate *its own* obligations incurred in the exercise of its power to borrow on the credit of the Government, and that it is liable for damages in the event of breach. The bondholder, holding a U.S. Government gold bond in the face amount of $10,000, contended that he was entitled to recover an amount in dollars equal to the current value of the former gold content of the United States dollar. If he had prevailed, he would have received $16,931. The Court acknowledged that the Government's repudiation of the gold clause in its bonds was unconstitutional, but it denied recovery on the ground that the bondholder had established no loss because he had received in legal tender the full face amount of the government obligation. A contrary decision would have resulted in an enrichment of the bondholder in the amount of $6,931.

An early historical illustration of the power of the federal government to control the value of the currency is found in *Veazie Bank v.*

Constitution, and is a valid exercise of Congress' spending power. Kennedy, J., concurring in the judgment, noted that the Government represents that a librarian will unblock filtered material or disable the Internet software filter without significant delay on an adult user's request, so "there is little to this case."

§ 5.7

1. U.S. Const. art. I, § 8, cl. 2 states: "The Congress shall have power ... to borrow Money on the credit of the United States...."

2. U.S. Const. art. I, § 8, cl. 5 reads: "The Congress shall have Power ... to coin Money, regulate the Value thereof, and of foreign Coin...."

3. McCulloch v. Maryland, 17 U.S. (4 Wheat.) 316, 4 L.Ed. 579 (1819) (state tax on national bank notes held invalid as a tax on an instrumentality of the federal government).

4. First Nat. Bank v. Fellows, 244 U.S. 416, 37 S.Ct. 734, 61 L.Ed. 1233 (1917) (sustaining the Federal Reserve Act).

5. Smith v. Kansas City Title & Trust Co., 255 U.S. 180, 41 S.Ct. 243, 65 L.Ed. 577 (1921) (sustaining the Federal Farm Loan Act).

6. Owensboro Nat. Bank v. Owensboro, 173 U.S. 664, 19 S.Ct. 537, 43 L.Ed. 850 (1899) (sustaining the power to limit taxation of national banks to taxes authorized by Congress). See First Agricultural Nat. Bank of Berkshire County v. State Tax Com'n, 392 U.S. 339, 88 S.Ct. 2173, 20 L.Ed.2d 1138 (1968) (holding invalid as unauthorized by Congress a state sales and use tax on purchases by a national bank of tangible personal property for its own use).

7. 294 U.S. 240, 55 S.Ct. 407, 79 L.Ed. 885 (1935).

8. 294 U.S. 330, 55 S.Ct. 432, 79 L.Ed. 912 (1935).

Fenno.[9] In this decision, the Court sustained a prohibitory ten percent tax on the issuance and circulation of state bank notes. The purpose of the prohibitory tax was to assure a stable national currency. Although the Court discussed at length the issue as to the difference between a direct and indirect tax, the decision was founded on the power of Congress to control the value of the currency.[10] As a corollary to *Veazie Bank*, the Court in the *Legal Tender Cases*[11] later recognized the constitutional authority of the Congress to provide that United States treasury notes shall constitute legal tender in the satisfaction of all obligations whether incurred before or after the enactment of the legislation.[12]

9. 75 U.S. (8 Wall.) 533, 19 L.Ed. 482 (1869).

10. 75 U.S. (8 Wall.) at 548–549.

11. 79 U.S. (12 Wall.) 457, 20 L.Ed. 287 (1870), overruling Hepburn v. Griswold, 75 U.S. (8 Wall.) 603, 19 L.Ed. 513 (1869).

12. Federal Regulations Preempt State Law. It should also be noted that Treasury Regulations governing the ownership of Government obligations are controlling for federal estate tax purposes irrespective of the nature of the interests in the property as determined by local law. United States v. Chandler, 410 U.S. 257, 93 S.Ct. 880, 35 L.Ed.2d 247 (1973) (registration of Government savings bonds in joint tenancy controls in determining decedent's gross estate even though decedent had delivered the bonds to the donee joint tenants as complete, irrevocable, inter vivos gifts).

Chapter 6

INTERNATIONAL AFFAIRS

§ 6.1 Introduction—The Role of the Three Branches of Government

The United States, in its capacity as a sovereign nation, must interact with other countries in the international realm, for the ability of a nation to conduct foreign relations is inherent in the concept of sovereignty.[1] Because specific constitutional references to foreign relations are sparse, much of the foreign affairs power has evolved from constitutionally implied powers and, perhaps, from extra-constitutional sources. Our effort to understand the constitutional sources of our foreign relations will begin with a study of the Constitutional text, and the roles that the Constitution envisions for the President, Congress and the courts in foreign affairs. We shall also examine the case law and historical tradition. Then we shall look more closely at specific areas of foreign affairs, the treaty power, executive agreements, and the war power.

§ 6.2 The Executive

Traditionally the President is responsible for conducting the foreign affairs of the United States.[1] Justice Sutherland, speaking for a unanimous Court, acknowledged this principle in the leading case of *United States v. Curtiss–Wright Export Corp.*:[2]

[T]he President alone has the power to speak or listen as a representative of the nation.... As Marshall said in his great argument of March 7, 1800, in the House of Representatives, "The President is the sole organ of the nation in its external relations, and its sole representative with foreign nations."[3]

Blackstone had earlier recognized the historical view that the executive predominates in foreign relations. In his influential *Commentaries*, Blackstone said: "What is done by the royal authority, with regard to foreign powers is the act of the whole nation."[4]

Interestingly, one cannot find such plenary executive power explicitly mentioned anywhere in the text of the Constitution. Nor will any examination of the affirmative grants of foreign affairs power in the Constitution reveal that the President is the "sole organ" of foreign relations.

Article II of the Constitution specifically enumerates the executive's foreign affairs. The President is empowered to make treaties, with a concurrence of two-thirds of the Senate, and to appoint ambassadors, public ministers and consuls with the Senate's advice and consent.[5] The Constitution also authorizes the chief executive, as the representative of the United States, to receive ambassadors and public min-

§ 6.1

1. See generally, 1 Ronald D. Rotunda & John E. Nowak, Treatise on Constitutional Law: Substance and Procedure §§ 6.1–6.16 (West Group, 3d ed.1999); Louis Henkin, Foreign Affairs and the Constitution 16 (1972).

§ 6.2

1. Louis Henkin, Foreign Affairs and The Constitution 37 (1972).

2. 299 U.S. 304, 57 S.Ct. 216, 81 L.Ed. 255 (1936).

3. 299 U.S. at 319, 57 S.Ct. at 220.

4. I, W. Blackstone, Commentaries 252 (Cooley ed. 1871).

5. U.S.Const. art. II, § 2.

isters.[6] The Commander–in–Chief power, constitutionally delegated to the President, also profoundly affects United States' international relations.[7] Although these provisions attest to the fact that the President has an active role in foreign affairs, the executive, over time, has gone far beyond these express grants in conducting international relations.

Hamilton's Rationale. From what sources, in addition to express Constitutional provisions, does the President receive his foreign affairs powers? Alexander Hamilton, in support of presidential supremacy in foreign affairs, published a series of articles in *The Gazette of the United States* supporting George Washington's "Proclamation of Neutrality," issued in 1793 after the outbreak of war between Great Britain and France. In these articles Hamilton, writing under the pseudonym of "Pacificus," argued that the first clause of Article II, providing that "the executive power shall be vested in a President of the United States. . . . " gave a general grant of power to the executive. He added that the specific grants of power in Article II, except when expressly limited, serve to interpret the general grant.

Hamilton concluded that any foreign affairs power (if not explicitly granted to Congress) devolves by implication to the President through the executive power clause.[8] He cited the President's power to recognize governments and terminate relations with foreign nations under the auspices of the constitutional provision authorizing the executive to receive foreign ambassadors and consuls.[9] Although treaties are subject to the advice and consent of the Senate, Hamilton believed that the President, by implication, is empowered to continue or suspend the treaty on his own initiative. Hamilton, a believer of strong executive power, warned that it was dangerous to restrict the executive's powers too severely.[10]

President Washington's Position. Implied Constitutional powers were recognized as early as George Washington's administration. Washington, by receiving "Citizen" Genet in accord with the Constitutional provisions allowing the President to receive foreign ambassadors and ministers, recognized the revolutionary government of France, and later, by demanding Genet's recall, ended diplomatic relations with France without consulting Congress.[11]

Washington also established historical precedent for limiting Congress's role in the area of treaty making. In 1789, he refused to comply with the Senate's request to see papers relevant to the negotiations involving an Indian Treaty. The executive's treaty negotiation powers were, Washington believed, exclusive.[12] The President alone is empowered to designate individuals to conduct foreign affairs negotiations and to determine what should be included in international agreements.[13]

The Supreme Court indirectly legitimized these extensions of the constitutional foreign affairs power in *Marbury v. Madison*,[14] where the Court stated that judicial review of conflicts between the executive and Congress over the foreign affairs power would be inappropriate as inherently political questions.[15]

Theories Based on the President's Role as "Commander–in–Chief" and His Duty to "Take Care" that "The Laws Be Faithfully Executed." One may extrapolate implied foreign affairs powers from the Commander–in–Chief clause and the Constitutional provision that the executive shall "take

6. U.S.Const. art. II, § 3.

7. U.S.Const. art. II, § 2.

8. Edward Corwin, The President: Office and Powers 179–81 (4th Rev.Ed.1957), citing from Alexander Hamilton, Works 76 (Hamilton, ed.).

9. U.S.Const. art. II, § 3.

10. See The Federalist Nos. 67, 70.

11. U.S.Const. art. II, § 3.

Edward Corwin and L. Koenig, The Presidency Today 30 (1956); Corwin, The President: Office and Powers 181–82 (4th Rev. Ed. 1957).

12. Corwin, The President: Office and Powers 181–83 (4th Rev. Ed. 1957).

13. Edward Corwin and L. Koenig, The Presidency Today 30 (1956); Corwin, The President: Office and Powers 31 (4th Rev. Ed. 1957).

14. 5 U.S. (1 Cranch) 137, 2 L.Ed. 60 (1803).

15. 5 U.S. (1 Cranch) at 166.

care" that "the laws be faithfully executed."[16] However, the extension of executive foreign affairs power on the basis of these two grants has not been as successful as Hamilton's claim to the presidential foreign affairs power premised on the "executive power clause."[17] Presidents have more typically relied on the clause empowering the executive to "take care" that laws are "faithfully executed" to justify executive action to insure that the United States faithfully adhere to its treaty provisions.[18]

Presidents have authorized forceful intervention in foreign conflicts under the auspices of "take care" clause, contending that the duty to see all laws are faithfully executed also encompasses international law. These assertions have, however, often been thought to be unpersuasive because it is generally understood that this clause applies to international law only to the extent it has been incorporated into the law of the United States in situations occurring either in situations within the United States or affecting American citizens or the government.[19]

The *Curtiss–Wright* Case. The Court acknowledged the unique role of the executive in *United States v. Curtiss–Wright Export Corp.*[20] The case involved a controversy surrounding a presidential Embargo Proclamation of May 28, 1934,[21] prohibiting the sale of arms to countries involved in the Chaco conflict in South America. Authorization for this declaration was granted in a joint congressional resolution passed earlier on the same day empowering the President to issue a proclamation limiting arms and ammunition sales to those involved

in the conflict.[22] Congress revoked the proclamation in November of 1935.[23]

The defendants, indicted in 1936 for conspiring to sell arms to Bolivia, challenged the joint resolution, claiming that it was an unconstitutional delegation of authority. At a time when the Court was hostile to delegations of power in the domestic sphere, the Court had no trouble upholding the resolution, finding the proclamation valid. Justice Sutherland, writing for the majority, addressed the special role of the President in international relations:

> [T]he federal power over external affairs in origin and essential character [is] different from that over internal affairs [and] ... participation in the exercise of the power is significantly limited. In this vast external realm ... the President alone has the power to speak or listen as a representative of the nation. He makes treaties with the advice and consent of the senate; but he alone negotiates.[24]

Sutherland also quoted with approval a statement that the Senate Committee on Foreign Relations had issued on February 1, 1816:

> The President is the Constitutional representative of the United States with regard to foreign nations. He manages our concerns with foreign nations.... The nature of transactions with foreign nations, moreover, requires caution and unity of design, and their success frequently depends on secrecy and dispatch.[25]

Sutherland concluded that it was important to realize that presidential authority to issue the proclamation came, not only from the joint resolution of Congress, but also from the "very

---

16. U.S.Const. art. II, § 3.

17. Louis Henkin, Foreign Affairs and The Constitution 42 (1972).

18. E.g., Louis Henkin, Foreign Affairs and The Constitution 54–55 (1972).

19. Louis Henkin, Foreign Affairs and The Constitution 55 (1972). For example, troops have been sent under presidential authority to Panama (1882), Cuba (1903), Haiti (1916), Korea (1950), Vietnam (1960's), Grenada (1980's), Panama (1989); Gulf War (1991); Haiti (1994); Bosnia and other countries in the Balkans (1994–2000) and other places. In over 200 instances the United States has employed its armed forces outside of this country for

the protection of its citizens or for national security purposes. Congressional Research Service, Instances of Use of United States Armed Forces Abroad, 1798 to 1983 (E. Collier ed. 1983).

20. 299 U.S. 304, 57 S.Ct. 216, 81 L.Ed. 255 (1936).

21. 48 Stat. 1744.

22. 48 Stat. 811.

23. 49 Stat. 3480.

24. 299 U.S. at 319, 57 S.Ct. at 220.

25. 299 U.S. at 319, 57 S.Ct. at 220 quoting U.S. Senate Reports, Committee on Foreign Relations vol. 8 at 24 (1816).

delicate, plenary and exclusive power of the President as the sole organ of the federal government in the field of international relations...." This power did not need to be based on an act of Congress, the Court said, although, the it added significantly, this power was "of course" to be exercised in subordination to express provisions of the Constitution.[26]

A pragmatic look at the international scene supported this view of the Constitutional framework. The President not Congress, has the better opportunity to know the conditions that prevail in foreign countries:

> He has his confidential sources of information. He has his agents in the form of diplomatic, consular and other officials. Secrecy in respect of information gathered by them may be highly necessary and the premature disclosure of it productive of harmful results.[27]

Although Sutherland depicts presidential predominance in foreign affairs, it should not be forgotten that, in that case, the President was acting *in accord with* congressional policy. Sutherland's broad language should be read in light of the facts with which he was faced. As Justice Jackson, in his concurrence in *The Steel Seizure Case*[28] noted, *Curtiss–Wright* was dealing with situations arising when the presidential actions are in harmony with an act of Congress, not when the President acts contrary to Congress.[29] The Jackson interpretation places a significant limitation on the theory of an unrestrained executive plenary foreign affairs powers.

The Court reaffirmed *Curtiss–Wright* when it refused to review an executive order concerning the involvement of United States citizens with foreign air transportation. The case was *Chicago and Southern Air Lines, Inc. v. Waterman Steamship Corp.*[30] The Civil Aeronautics Board, with the express approval of the President, granted an overseas air route to Chicago and Southern Air Lines and denied it to its rival, the Waterman Steamship Corporation. The proceedings were not challenged as to their regularity, but Waterman nonetheless sought review of the CAB decision as approved by the President. The Court recognized that Congress could delegate "very large grants of its power over foreign commerce to the President."[31] Also, the President possesses his own foreign affairs power.

Waterman found the President drew his powers from both sources. The Court (where the President was not acting in defiance of Congressional direction) reasoned:

> The President, both as Commander–in–Chief and as the Nation's organ for foreign affairs, has available intelligence services whose reports are not and ought not to be published to the world. It would be intolerable that courts, without the relevant information, should review and perhaps nullify actions of the Executive taken on information properly held secret.... [T]he very nature of executive decisions as to foreign policy is political, not judicial.[32]

Waterman therefore concluded (five to four) that whatever portion of the CAB order emanated from the President was not subject to judicial review. The CAB orders, before presidential approval, are premature and not subject to review. After such presidential approval, they "embody Presidential discretion as to political matters beyond the competence of the courts to adjudicate."[33]

---

26. United States v. Curtiss–Wright Export Corp., 299 U.S. 304, 320, 57 S.Ct. 216, 221, 81 L.Ed. 255 (1936).

See Nowak & Rotunda, A Comment on the Creation and Resolution of a "Non–Problem": Dames & Moore v. Regan, The Foreign Affairs Power, and the Rule of the Court, 29 U.C.L.A.L.Rev. 1129, 1149 (1982).

27. 299 U.S. at 320, 57 S.Ct. at 221.

28. Youngstown Sheet & Tube Co. v. Sawyer, 343 U.S. 579, 72 S.Ct. 863, 96 L.Ed. 1153 (1952).

29. 343 U.S. at 635–636 n. 2, 72 S.Ct. at 870–871 n. 2 (Jackson, J., concurring).

30. 333 U.S. 103, 68 S.Ct. 431, 92 L.Ed. 568 (1948) (Jackson, J., for the Court).

31. 333 U.S. at 109, 68 S.Ct. at 435.

32. 333 U.S. at 111, 68 S.Ct. at 436.

33. 333 U.S. at 114, 68 S.Ct. at 437. *Waterman* has been read not to preclude judicial review if the CAB's actions are beyond its powers, so that legally it could not place anything before the President. E.g., Pan American World Airways, Inc. v. CAB, 380 F.2d 770 (2d Cir.1967), affirmed by an equally divided Court, 391 U.S. 461, 88 S.Ct. 1715, 20 L.Ed.2d 748 (1968), rehearing denied 393 U.S. 957, 89 S.Ct. 370, 21 L.Ed.2d 369 (1968).

Thus, by constitutional exegesis, practical experience, and Congressional acquiescence, the executive has usually predominated the foreign affairs sphere, but this expansive international relations power is not plenary,[34] nor may it be exercised contrary to restrictions in the Constitution such as the Bill of Rights.

§ 6.3   Congress

There is a continual controversy between Congress and the executive as to the extent of each branch's foreign affairs power. The dispute centers on whether Congress and the President act as constitutional equals in this sphere or whether the executive initiates foreign policy, while Congress acts merely to implement the President's policy.[1] Supporters of Congress quickly recognized the importance of congressional participation in international affairs.

Madison's Rationale. In response to Alexander Hamilton's "Pacificus" articles supporting presidential supremacy in foreign affairs James Madison wrote a series of letters under the name of "Helvidius." Madison argued that Congress, not the President, was empowered to determine United States foreign policy. Hamilton, Madison argued, was attributing quasi-monarchical powers to the Executive branch reminiscent of the role of royalty in British foreign affairs.[2]

However one would resolve the Hamilton–Madison debate, the fact remains that Congress plays a vital role in the foreign affairs scenario. Success or failure of executive foreign policy depends, to a great extent, on the support of Congress. Congress received foreign affairs powers from express and implied constitutional grants.

There are specific Constitutional provisions granting Congress authority in foreign affairs matters. Article I, § 8 defines these powers broadly: "Congress shall have Power to provide for the common Defence,"[3] to regulate foreign commerce,[4] and to "define and punish Piracies and Felonies committed on the high Seas, and Offences against the law of Nations,"[5] to declare war, to make rules of war, grant letters of marque and reprisal,[6] and to raise, support and regulate an army and a navy.[7] Two-thirds of the Senate must consent to treaties before they are ratified. The Senate also is authorized to advise the President on the contents of the treaty.[8]

These express grants have been used extensively to validate congressionally exercise of foreign policy.

The Power Over Foreign Commerce. The commerce clause[9] legitimizes congressional legislation regulating United States foreign trade. With the increased importance of international business transactions in the world and national economies, foreign commerce has developed into a vital area of foreign affairs. Consequently, Congressional control of foreign commerce has a tremendous impact on the structure of United States foreign policy.[10]

Other Congressional Powers. Congress' power to declare war,[11] discussed later in this chapter, directly affects the executive's foreign

---

34. See Paust, Is the President Bound by the Supreme Law of the Land?—Foreign Affairs and National Security Reexamined, 9 Hastings Const.L.Q. 719 (1982).

§ 6.3

1. Edward Corwin, The President: Office and Powers (4th Rev.Ed.1957) at 184–85.

2. Edward Corwin, The President: Office and Powers (4th Rev.Ed.1957) at 180–82, citing 6 J. Madison, Writings 138 (Hunt, Ed.)

3. U.S.Const. art. I, § 8, cl. 1.

4. U.S.Const. art. I, § 8, cl. 3.

5. U.S.Const. art. I, § 8, cl. 10.

6. U.S.Const. art. I, § 8, cl. 11.

7. U.S.Const. art. I, § 8, cls. 12, 13.

8. U.S.Const. art. II, § 2.

9. U.S.Const. art. I, § 8, cl. 3. For a discussion of the exclusive nature of Congress's power to regulate foreign commerce see United States v. Guy W. Capps, Inc., 204 F.2d 655, 658 (4th Cir.1953), affirmed 348 U.S. 296, 75 S.Ct. 326, 99 L.Ed. 329 (1955), discussed below.

10. Japan Line, Ltd. v. County of Los Angeles, 441 U.S. 434, 99 S.Ct. 1813, 60 L.Ed.2d 336 (1979) (state tax on instrumentalities unconstitutional because such tax may subject foreign commerce to risk of multiple burdens and may impair federal uniformity in an area where federal uniformity is essential). Cf. Independent Warehouses v. Scheele, 134 N.J.L. 133, 137, 45 A.2d 703, 705 (1946), affirmed 331 U.S. 70, 67 S.Ct. 1062, 91 L.Ed. 1346 (1947); Gibbons v. Ogden, 22 U.S. (9 Wheat.) 1, 189–90, 6 L.Ed. 23 (1824).

11. U.S.Const. art. I, § 8, cl. 11.

affairs power. Other constitutional provisions give Congress the power to define and punish offenses against international law,[12] to punish international air piracy, to prohibit counterfeiting currency, and protect against foreign expropriations of the property of the United States or its citizens.[13] Through these provisions Congress creates binding foreign policy law.

Implied Congressional Powers. Congress has expanded its foreign affairs powers by reading implied grants to influence foreign policy. Article I, section 8 authorizes Congress:

> to make all Laws which shall be necessary and proper for carrying into the execution the . . . Powers vested by this Constitution in the Government of the United States or in any Department or Officer thereof.[14]

The necessary and proper clause can effectively check presidential foreign affairs power because the President relies on congressional legislation and appropriations to implement foreign affairs policy.

Thus Congress can stymie implementation of executive international policy by refusing to appropriate necessary funds.[15] Foreign aid programs depend on Congressional authorization as provided for in the spending power clause.[16] Congress, under the auspices of the postal power clause, has authorized international postal agreements.[17] These constitutionally implied foreign affairs powers provide a basis for many of the congressional actions that influence foreign policy.

Indeed, even if the Senate ratifies a treaty, if the treaty calls for money to be spent (to purchase a base, to fulfil a treaty obligation) that has not yet been appropriated, the House and Senate must pass a law to enact the necessary spending. The treaty itself cannot provide for the appropriation because the Constitution provides that all bills for raising revenue must originate in the House.[18]

Perez v. Brownell[19] held that Congress was acting within its foreign affairs power by providing, in the Nationality Act of 1940,[20] that any United States citizen voting in a foreign political election would lose his citizenship.[21] Justice Frankfurter, writing for the Court, asked:

> [W]hat is the source of power on which Congress must be assumed to have drawn? Although there is in the Constitution no specific grant to Congress of power to enact legislation for the effective regulation of foreign affairs, there can be no doubt of the existence of this power in the law-making organ of the nation. . . . [The] Government [must have] the powers indispensable to its functioning effectively in the company of sovereign nations. The Government must be able not only to deal affirmatively with foreign nations . . . [i]t must also be able to reduce to a minimum the frictions that are unavoidable in a world of sovereigns sensitive in matters touching their dignity and interests.[22]

The Court later *overruled* the precise holding of this case, but it did not cast doubt on the

---

12. U.S.Const. art. I, § 8, cl. 10.

13. E.g., 18 U.S.C.A. § 1651, 49 U.S.C.A. § 1472(i) (air piracy); United States v. Arjona, 120 U.S. 479, 484–88, 7 S.Ct. 628, 630–32, 30 L.Ed. 728 (1887) (Congress has the power to define and punish the offenses that disrupt harmonious foreign relations); The Hickenlooper Amendment, Foreign Assistance Act of 1961, § 620(e) as amended, 22 U.S.C.A. § 2370(e) (Congress authorizes the President to suspend foreign aid to any nation that has seized U.S. property or repudiated or nullified existing contracts with U.S. citizens or businesses when the foreign government fails to give full compensation for such acts within a reasonable time).

14. U.S.Const. art. I, § 8, cl. 18.

15. Louis Henkin, Foreign Affairs and the Constitution 76–79 (1972).

16. U.S.Const. art. I, § 8, cl. 1.

17. U.S.Const. art. I, § 8, cl. 7. See e.g. 39 U.S.C.A. §§ 505, 506. Louis Henkin, Foreign Affairs and the Constitution 77 (1972).

18. U.S.Const., art. I, § 7, cl. 1. Restatement of the Law of Foreign Relations of the United States, Third, § 111(4)(c) & Comment 6 (A.L.I.1987).

19. 356 U.S. 44, 78 S.Ct. 568, 2 L.Ed.2d 603 (1958).

20. 54 Stat. 1137 § 401 as amended Act of Sept. 27, 1944, 58 Stat. 746.

21. Perez v. Brownell, 356 U.S. 44, 62, 78 S.Ct. 568, 578, 2 L.Ed.2d 603 (1958), overruled in Afroyim v. Rusk, 387 U.S. 253, 87 S.Ct. 1660, 18 L.Ed.2d 757 (1967).

22. 356 U.S. at 57, 78 S.Ct. at 575.

principle that Congress can constitutionally legislate on such matters.[23]

The Court also legitimized Congressional involvement in foreign affairs in *Fong Yue Ting v. United States*:[24]

The United States are a sovereign and independent nation and are vested by the Constitution with the entire control of international relations and with all the powers of government necessary to maintain that control.... The Constitution ... speaks with no uncertain sound upon this subject.... The power ... being a power affecting international relations, is vested in the political departments of the government, and is to be regulated by treaty or by act of Congress.[25]

The United States, as a sovereign nation, possesses a "foreign affairs power" that is an inherent attribute of sovereignty.[26] Justice Sutherland, in *Curtiss–Wright*,[27] acknowledged that the foreign affairs power, arising from the sovereign status of the United States, expanded Congress' legislative authority in international relations matters.

Congress has used this broad foreign affairs power to justify a wide variety of legislation. Congress has promulgated alien immigration and registration laws on the strength of the foreign affairs power.[28] Congress may be able to compel United States citizens residing abroad to return to the United States for legal proceedings and to answer for conduct engaged in abroad.[29] It was presumably under this power that Congress authorized the Court to modify the act of state doctrine as recognized by the executive so that United States citizens may challenge some acts of foreign governments affecting them.[30] The extent of this congressional foreign affairs power is uncertain. Congress has not yet exercised this power as fully as the Supreme Court implies that it may.[31]

To What Extent Does the Constitution Follow the Flag: Does the Constitution Apply to the Territories? While Congress has the power to govern its territories, it is not always clear to what extent the Constitution follows the Flag, that is, to what extent the Constitution applies to territories that are acquired—but not incorporated—into the United States.[32] To what extent do Constitutional rights limit U.S. authority when it is exercised outside of American territory?

In the beginning of the twentieth century, the Court held that the requirement of uniformity of federal taxes did not apply to Puerto Rico.[33] The Court at that time saw the need to grant flexibility to Congress in administering its territories not previously subject to common law traditions.[34] However, the Court later

23. Perez v. Brownell, 356 U.S. 44, 78 S.Ct. 568, 2 L.Ed.2d 603 (1958), overruled in Afroyim v. Rusk, 387 U.S. 253, 87 S.Ct. 1660, 18 L.Ed.2d 757 (1967).

24. 149 U.S. 698, 13 S.Ct. 1016, 37 L.Ed. 905 (1893).

25. 149 U.S. at 711, 713, 13 S.Ct. at 1021–22.

26. E.g., Burnet v. Brooks, 288 U.S. 378, 396, 53 S.Ct. 457, 461–62, 77 L.Ed. 844 (1933).

27. United States v. Curtiss–Wright Export Corp., 299 U.S. 304, 318–19, 57 S.Ct. 216, 220–21, 81 L.Ed. 255 (1936).

28. The Chinese Exclusion Case, 130 U.S. 581, 9 S.Ct. 623, 32 L.Ed. 1068 (1889); Fong Yue Ting v. United States, 149 U.S. 698, 13 S.Ct. 1016, 37 L.Ed. 905 (1893).

29. Cf. Vance v. Bradley, 440 U.S. 93, 103–109, 99 S.Ct. 939, 946–49, 59 L.Ed.2d 171 (1979); Kinsella v. United States ex rel. Singleton, 361 U.S. 234, 245–46, 80 S.Ct. 297, 303–04, 4 L.Ed.2d 268 (1960).

30. Blackmer v. United States, 284 U.S. 421, 52 S.Ct. 252, 76 L.Ed. 375 (1932); Banco Nacional de Cuba v. Farr, 383 F.2d 166, 182 (2d Cir.1967), certiorari denied 390 U.S. 956, 88 S.Ct. 1038, 19 L.Ed.2d 1151 (1968), rehearing denied 390 U.S. 1037, 88 S.Ct. 1406, 20 L.Ed.2d 298 (1968).

31. Louis Henkin, Foreign Affairs and the Constitution 74–76 (1972); Louis Henkin, The Treaty Makers and the Law Makers: The Law of the Land and Foreign Relations, 107 U.Pa.L.Rev. 903, 922–23 (1959).

32. See generally, Sutherland, The Flag, The Constitution and International Agreements, 68 Harv.L.Rev. 1374 (1955); Green, Applicability of American Laws to Overseas Areas Controlled by the United States, 68 Harv.L.Rev. 781 (1955); Fairman, Some New Problems of the Constitution Following the Flag, 1 Stan.L.Rev. 587 (1949).

33. Downes v. Bidwell, 182 U.S. 244, 21 S.Ct. 770, 45 L.Ed. 1088 (1901) (Art. I, § 8, cl. 1 does not apply to Puerto Rico).

34. See, e.g., Hawaii v. Mankichi, 190 U.S. 197, 23 S.Ct. 787, 47 L.Ed. 1016 (1903) (right to indictment by grand jury and jury trial inapplicable in Hawaii); Dorr v. United States, 195 U.S. 138, 24 S.Ct. 808, 49 L.Ed. 128 (1904) (no constitutional requirement that territorial government of the Philippines provide jury trial in criminal cases); Ocampo v. United States, 234 U.S. 91, 34 S.Ct. 712, 58 L.Ed. 1231 (1914) (right to grand jury inapplicable in Philippines); Balzac v. Porto Rico, 258 U.S. 298, 42 S.Ct. 343, 66 L.Ed. 627 (1922) (no constitutional requirement of

held or otherwise indicated that other clauses of the Constitution do apply to Puerto Rico.[35]

Even if the Constitution does not apply directly, Congress may make constitutional provisions applicable to territories by statute. The Court will attach great weight to a legislative determination that a particular constitutional provision may practically and beneficially be applied in a territory. Thus *Torres v. Puerto Rico*[36] held that Congress' implicit determinations and long experience establish that the Fourth Amendment restrictions on search and seizure apply to Puerto Rico. The Court did not decide whether the Fourth Amendment applied directly or by operation of the Fourteenth Amendment.[37]

United States v. Verdugo–Urquidez[38] held that the Fourth Amendment does not apply to a search and seizure by United States agents of property located in a foreign country owned by a nonresident alien. In this case the United States Government obtained an arrest warrant for Verdugo–Urquidez, a Mexican citizen and resident, who was suspected of being the leader of a narcotics smuggling ring. Mexican authorities apprehended Verdugo–Urquidez, transported him to a United States Border Patrol Station in California, and then U.S.

Marshals arrested him and moved him to a correctional center. Later, U.S. Drug Enforcement Administration (DEA) agents, working with Mexican officials, searched Verdugo–Urquidez's Mexican residences and seized various documents related to alleged narcotics trafficking activities. Verdugo–Urquidez objected to the introduction of such evidence and moved to suppress it on the basis of the Fourth Amendment. The district court and Ninth Circuit granted the motion, but the Supreme Court reversed.

Verdugo–Urquidez distinguished the Fourth Amendment from the Fifth Amendment. The Fifth Amendment privilege against self-incrimination is a fundamental right of all criminal defendants. A Fifth Amendment violation occurs at trial if evidence is admitted in violation of the privilege against self-incrimination. In contrast, the Fourth Amendment prohibits "unreasonable searches and seizures" even if the evidence is not used at the trial; the violation of the Fourth Amendment is "fully accomplished" at the time of the unreasonable government intrusion.[39] Thus, if there were a Fourth Amendment violation, it occurred only in Mexico, where the U.S. Constitution does not apply.[40]

jury criminal cases in Porto Rico, which was not an incorporated territory of the United States even though its residents had been granted United States citizenship).

35. E.g., Balzac v. Porto Rico, 258 U.S. 298, 314, 42 S.Ct. 343, 349, 66 L.Ed. 627 (1922) (Court applies, without discussion, First Amendment in Puerto Rico); Calero–Toledo v. Pearson Yacht Leasing Co., 416 U.S. 663, 668–69 n. 5, 94 S.Ct. 2080, 2084 n. 5, 40 L.Ed.2d 452 (1974), rehearing denied 417 U.S. 977, 94 S.Ct. 3187, 41 L.Ed.2d 1148 (1974) (Court applies due process clause in Puerto Rico because " 'there cannot exist under the American flag any governmental authority untrammeled by the requirements of due process of law as guaranteed by the Constitution of the United States.' " quoting Magruder, C.J., in Mora v. Mejias, 206 F.2d 377, 382 (1st Cir.1953); Examining Bd. v. Flores de Otero, 426 U.S. 572, 599–601, 96 S.Ct. 2264, 2279–81, 49 L.Ed.2d 65 (1976) (equal protection guarantee applies to Puerto Rico); Califano v. Gautier Torres, 435 U.S. 1, 4 n. 6, 98 S.Ct. 906, 908 n. 6, 55 L.Ed.2d 65 (1978) (per curiam) (Court assumes without deciding that constitutional right to travel extends to Puerto Rico).

36. 442 U.S. 465, 470, 99 S.Ct. 2425, 2429, 61 L.Ed.2d 1 (1979). Cf., e.g., Best v. United States, 184 F.2d 131, 138 (1st Cir.1950), certiorari denied 340 U.S. 939, 71 S.Ct. 480, 95 L.Ed. 677 (1951), rehearing denied 341 U.S. 907, 71 S.Ct. 607, 95 L.Ed. 1345 (1951) (court assumes, "and we think it probably so," that Fourth Amendment extends to

protect U.S. citizens in foreign countries under occupation by our armed forces). See, Ronald D. Rotunda, The Chemical Weapons Treaty: Political and Constitutional Issues, 15 Constitutional Commentary 129 (1998).

37. Brennan, joined by Stewart, Marshall, and Blackmun concurred. They argued that the older cases restricting the applicability of constitutional guarantees in Puerto Rico and cited by the majority should not be given any expansion assuming their validity in modern times. 442 U.S. at 475, 99 S.Ct. at 2431–32. (Brennan, J., concurring). But see Chief Justice Burger's dictum in Haig v. Agee, 453 U.S. 280, 308, 101 S.Ct. 2766, 2782–83, 69 L.Ed.2d 640 (1981) ("Assuming, *arguendo*, that First Amendment protections reach beyond our national boundaries, ...").

38. 494 U.S. 259, 110 S.Ct. 1056, 108 L.Ed.2d 222 (1990).

39. United States v. Calandra, 414 U.S. 338, 354, 94 S.Ct. 613, 623, 38 L.Ed.2d 561 (1974); United States v. Verdugo–Urquidez, 494 U.S. 259, 264, 110 S.Ct. 1056, 1060, 108 L.Ed.2d 222 (1990).

40. Note that Johnson v. Eisentrager, 339 U.S. 763, 70 S.Ct. 936, 94 L.Ed. 1255 (1950) made clear that aliens are not entitled to Fifth Amendment rights outside of the sovereign territory of the United States. In *Eisentrager* the Court rejected this *extraterritorial* application of the

Verdugo–Urquidez concluded that the Fourth Amendment was not applicable. First, the phrase "the people" (also used in the First and Second Amendments, and to whom powers are reserved in the Ninth and Tenth Amendments) refers to a class of persons who are part of a national community. Second, the history of the Fourth Amendment also suggests that its purpose was to restrict searches and seizures by the United States occurring in domestic matters, not to restrain the federal government in any actions it might take against aliens outside of the United States. And, of course, if the United States had obtained a search warrant from a U.S. magistrate, that warrant would mean nothing in Mexico, where the search actually took place.

Aliens receive constitutional protections when they come within the territory of the United States *and* have developed substantial connections with the United States.[41] But Mr. Verdugo–Urquidez, a nonresident alien whose property subject to the search and seizure was in Mexico, was not in that category. If the Fourth Amendment applied to people like Mr. Verdugo–Urquidez, then aliens abroad, with no attachment to this country, could use American courts to bring damages claims against American foreign policy operations (such as those employed by the Armed Forces) conducted abroad or in foreign waters. Other foreign countries are not subject to such restraints, and the United States also should not be so subject.[42]

Fifth Amendment and did not allow enemy aliens arrested in China and imprisoned in Germany after World War II to secure habeas corpus relief on the grounds that their war crimes convictions violated the Fifth Amendment.

41. E.g., Kwong Hai Chew v. Colding, 344 U.S. 590, 596 n. 5, 73 S.Ct. 472, 477 n. 5, 97 L.Ed. 576 (1953); United States v. Verdugo–Urquidez, 494 U.S. 259, 271, 110 S.Ct. 1056, 1064, 108 L.Ed.2d 222 (1990).

42. See also, United States v. Alvarez–Machain, 504 U.S. 655, 112 S.Ct. 2188, 119 L.Ed.2d 441 (1992), on remand 971 F.2d 310 (9th Cir.1992), holding that a U.S. court may properly exercise jurisdiction over a defendant even though the U.S. government procured his presence before the court by forcible abduction in Mexico. The Court interpreted the extradition treaty with Mexico as not prohibiting abductions. See, Lea Brilmayer & Charles

§ 6.4 The Court

Although the executive and legislative branches of the federal government dominate United States foreign affairs, Supreme Court decisions also influence foreign policy. Specific constitutional provisions in Article III, § 2 indicate that the Court is in a position to wield substantial power in international affairs. Historically, however, the Court frequently defers to the judgment of Congress and the Executive when a conflict arises that may have an impact on foreign relations.

The Court's Jurisdiction. The Article III grant of judicial power to the federal courts extends to foreign affairs:

All Cases, in Law and Equity, arising under this Constitution, the Laws of the United States and Treaties made—or which shall be made under their authority;—to all cases affecting Ambassadors, other public Ministers and Consuls; ... to Controversies to which the United States shall be a Party, ... to Controversies ... between a State or Citizen thereof, and foreign States, Citizens or Subjects.... In all Cases affecting Ambassadors, other public Ministers and Consuls ... the Supreme Court shall have original jurisdiction.[1]

Thus, the Court exercises jurisdiction in cases involving foreign nations,[2] suits by United States citizens against aliens or foreign diplomats,[3] and suits to interpret and enforce treaty terms.[4] The Court also hears cases arising under the "Laws of the United States,"[5] which

Norchi, Federal Extraterritoriality and Fifth Amendment Due Process, 105 Harv.L.Rev. 1217 (1992).

§ 6.4

1. U.S.Const. art. III, § 2.

2. E.g., Banco Nacional de Cuba v. Sabbatino, 376 U.S. 398, 84 S.Ct. 923, 11 L.Ed.2d 804 (1964), on remand 272 F.Supp. 836 (S.D.N.Y.1965), judgment affirmed 383 F.2d 166 (2d Cir.1967), certiorari denied 390 U.S. 956, 88 S.Ct. 1038, 19 L.Ed.2d 1151 (1968), rehearing denied 390 U.S. 1037, 88 S.Ct. 1406, 20 L.Ed.2d 298 (1968).

3. 28 U.S.C.A. § 1251.

4. E.g., Terlinden v. Ames, 184 U.S. 270, 22 S.Ct. 484, 46 L.Ed. 534 (1902); Martin v. Hunter's Lessee, 14 U.S. (1 Wheat.) 304, 4 L.Ed. 97 (1816).

5. U.S.Const. art. III, § 2.

include all laws made in pursuance of the Constitution.[6]

Congress is constitutionally authorized to define and punish international law violations, thereby incorporating international law into United States law. The Constitution thus grants the Court jurisdiction over cases involving international law.[7] Consequently, the Court will occasionally address issues involving international law and will make pronouncements that affect both the structure of United States foreign policy and international law.

The Political Question Doctrine and Foreign Affairs. The Court hesitates to exercise any authority in the area of foreign affairs that would exceed the scope of these express constitutional grants. Although the Supreme Court is empowered to review acts of the legislature and executive to insure conformance with constitutional provisions, the political question doctrine is an important exception to this judicial review,[8] and demonstrates the Court's reluctance to take an active role in formulating foreign policy. As *Baker v. Carr*,[9] explained:

> Prominent on the surface of any case held to involve a political question is found a textually demonstrable constitutional commitment of the issue to a coordinate political department; ... or the potentiality of embarrassment from multifarious pronouncements by various departments on one question.[10]

The area of foreign affairs often fits squarely within the Court's definition of political questions:

There are sweeping statements to the effect that all questions touching foreign relations are political questions. Not only does resolution of such issues frequently turn on standards that defy judicial application, or involve the exercise of a discretion demonstrably committed to the executive or legislature; but many such questions uniquely demand single-voiced statement of the Government's views.[11]

Justice Brennan, in *Baker,* elaborated, citing *Oetjen v. Central Leather Co.*[12]

> The conduct of the foreign relations of our Government is committed by the Constitution to the Executive and Legislative—"the political"—Departments of the Government, and the propriety of what may be done in the exercise of this political power is not subject to judicial inquiry or decision.[13]

Baker indicated that there are some instances when the political question doctrine will not exempt foreign affairs issues from judicial review, but these exceptions are primarily limited to situations where the judiciary is acting in the absence of any conclusive action by the executive or Congress.[14]

In practice the Court employs the political question rationale to abstain from foreign affairs cases only infrequently. Typically, in order to maintain judicial independence and integrity, the Court refrains from reviewing executive and legislative action relating to foreign affairs by deciding that the political branches are acting within the scope of their

---

6. U.S.Const. art. VI.

7. U.S.Const. art. I, § 8. See The Paquete Habana, 175 U.S. 677, 700, 20 S.Ct. 290, 299, 44 L.Ed. 320 (1900).

8. Marbury v. Madison, 5 U.S. (1 Cranch) 137, 165–66, 2 L.Ed. 60 (1803) (discussion of judicial review).

9. 369 U.S. 186, 82 S.Ct. 691, 7 L.Ed.2d 663 (1962), on remand 206 F.Supp. 341 (M.D.Tenn.1962).

10. Baker v. Carr, 369 U.S. 186, 217, 82 S.Ct. 691, 710, 7 L.Ed.2d 663 (1962), on remand 206 F.Supp. 341 (M.D.Tenn.1962).

11. 369 U.S. at 211, 82 S.Ct. at 707. (footnotes omitted).

12. 246 U.S. 297, 302, 38 S.Ct. 309, 310–11, 62 L.Ed. 726 (1918).

13. 369 U.S. at 211 & n. 31, 82 S.Ct. at 707 n. 31.

14. Baker v. Carr, 369 U.S. 186, 212–13, 82 S.Ct. 691, 707–08, 7 L.Ed.2d 663 (1962), citing Terlinden v. Ames, 184 U.S. 270, 285, 22 S.Ct. 484, 490, 46 L.Ed. 534 (1902), on remand 206 F.Supp. 341 (M.D.Tenn.1962) (Court can construe a treaty to decide if it has been terminated in the absence of conclusive governmental action involving the treaty); The Three Friends, 166 U.S. 1, 63, 66, 17 S.Ct. 495, 503, 41 L.Ed. 897 (1897) (Court can construe executive declarations to determine if American neutrality standards have become operative); Ex parte Republic of Peru, 318 U.S. 578, 63 S.Ct. 793, 87 L.Ed. 1014 (1943) (Judicial action regarding immunity of foreign ship is permissible in absence of executive declaration).

constitutional authority.[15]

Interpreting International Law. The Supreme Court exercises considerable influence over foreign affairs legislation. The federal judiciary interprets laws, international law, executive agreements and treaties.[16] The Court affirmed its authority to construe international law in *The Paquete Habana*, where it said: "International law is a part of our law and must be ascertained and administered by the courts of Justice...."[17]

Federal Common Law and the Act of State Doctrine. The Court extended the scope of this "judicial legislation" in the foreign affairs area in the leading case of *Banco Nacional de Cuba v. Sabbatino*.[18] In that case, the Court established a doctrine that has a profound impact on United States foreign relations: it recognized "Federal common law" that is binding on the nation.[19]

The complex fact situation in *Sabbatino* involved a controversy between a United States commodity broker and the Cuban government over the title to Cuban sugar sold in New York. Banco Nacional, on behalf of the Cuban government, sued the commodity broker, Farr, Whitlock and Company, for conversion of bills of lading and the proceeds from the sale of the sugar. In defense, Farr, Whitlock argued that the proceeds belonged not to the Cuban government but to the Cuban sugar company owned primarily by residents of the United States. The Castro regime, Farr, Whitlock asserted, had illegally expropriated the property

of this American owned business in violation of international law. The Cuban government's title to the sugar was therefore invalid under international law.[20]

The lower courts held that Cuba had violated international law and ruled against Banco Nacional.[21] The Supreme Court reversed, relying on the "act of state" doctrine to bar judicial condemnation of Cuba's expropriation actions, even though the expropriation violated customary international law.[22] The act of state doctrine is not a rule that requires courts to abstain from deciding properly presented cases simply because their resolution may embarrass a foreign government. The doctrine only provides that the acts of foreign sovereigns *taken within their own jurisdiction* shall be deemed valid. The act of state doctrine "in its traditional formulation precludes the courts of this country from inquiring into the validity of the public acts a recognized foreign sovereign power committed within its own territory."[23]

Writing for the majority, Justice Harlan stated that failure to adhere to the act of state doctrine and give effect to the expropriation might interfere with or embarrass the executive branch's foreign affairs policy. The United States, arguing *amicus curiae*, urged that the Court reverse the lower courts on these same grounds.[24] In deciding to uphold the act of state doctrine, however, the Court was not arguing that it was bound to follow the directions of the executive branch. Harlan, protecting the judicial integrity of the Court, held that, although the act of state doctrine is not

---

15. See, e.g., Williams v. Suffolk Insurance Co., 38 U.S. (13 Pet.) 415, 420, 10 L.Ed. 226 (1839) (It is not within the Court's province to review actions of the executive done in accordance with its constitutional functions).

16. Louis Henkin, Foreign Affairs and the Constitution 216 (1972).

17. 175 U.S. 677, 700, 20 S.Ct. 290, 299, 44 L.Ed. 320 (1900).

18. 376 U.S. 398, 84 S.Ct. 923, 11 L.Ed.2d 804 (1964).

19. Louis Henkin, The Foreign Affairs Power of the Federal Courts: Sabbatino, 64 Colum.L.Rev. 805, 806 (1964).

20. Banco Nacional de Cuba v. Sabbatino, 376 U.S. 398, 401–08, 84 S.Ct. 923, 926–30, 11 L.Ed.2d 804 (1964).

21. Banco Nacional De Cuba v. Sabbatino, 193 F.Supp. 375 (S.D.N.Y.1961), affirmed 307 F.2d 845 (2d Cir.1962).

22. Banco Nacional de Cuba v. Sabbatino, 376 U.S. 398, 427–37, 84 S.Ct. 923, 939–45, 11 L.Ed.2d 804 (1964).

23. Banco Nacional de Cuba v. Sabbatino, 376 U.S. 398, 401, 84 S.Ct. 923, 926, 11 L.Ed.2d 804 (1964). See also, W.S. Kirkpatrick & Co., Inc. v. Environmental Tectonics Corp., International, 493 U.S. 400, 409, 110 S.Ct. 701, 707, 107 L.Ed.2d 816 (1990) (Act of State Doctrine not applicable to action alleging that competitor obtained military procurement contract from Nigerian government through bribery of Nigerian officials, because the federal court would not have to declare invalid the official acts of a foreign sovereign—even though findings sought by plaintiff would also support a finding that the contract was invalid under Nigerian law).

24. Banco Nacional de Cuba v. Sabbatino, 376 U.S. 398, 432–33, 84 S.Ct. 923, 942–43, 11 L.Ed.2d 804 (1964); see also Argument of Deputy Attorney General Katzenbach, 32 U.S.L.W. 3158 (U.S. Oct. 29, 1963).

within the text of the Constitution, the doctrine does have "constitutional underpinnings."[25] The scope of the doctrine "must be determined according to federal law."[26]

The Court established the act of state doctrine as federal common law and held that the federal judiciary will not examine expropriation acts of a recognized sovereign within its own territory in the absence of a treaty even if the taking violates customary international law.[27]

The Court's decision was made independently of congressional or executive directives. To that extent, its decision to uphold the act of state doctrine created foreign relations law. This exercise of judicial power does have important limits, even though the reference to "constitutional underpinnings" was somewhat less than crystal clear. While it may hint that the Court's definition was constitutional in origin and therefore Congress cannot change it, the language of the majority opinion suggests otherwise. Thus, immediately after the reference to "constitutional underpinnings" the Court stated: "It [the act of state doctrine] arises out of the basic relationships between branches of government in a system of separations of powers."[28] Later the Court stated:

[We] decide only that the Judicial Branch will not examine the validity of a taking of property within its own territory by a foreign sovereign government, extant and recognized by this country at the time of suit, *in the absence of* a treaty or other unambigu-

ous agreement regarding controlling legal principles, even if the complaint alleges that the taking violates customary international law.[29]

Sabbatino really exemplifies the creation of federal *common* law,[30] not federal *constitutional* law. The constitutional underpinnings of the act of state doctrine relate more to the separation of powers than to the constitutional origins of the doctrine. Thus, Congress can change the act of state doctrine and, by statute, require the courts to look to "customary international law."

Subsequent events supports this view of *Sabbatino.* Congress became concerned over the theories advocated in *Sabbatino.* Shortly after the Court handed this decision down, Congress effectively overruled the *Sabbatino* interpretation of the act of state doctrine by revising the Hickenlooper Amendment provisions regarding acts of states.[31] The Supreme Court subsequently denied certiorari in a case involving this legislation, *Banco Nacional de Cuba v. Farr,*[32] which was a suit arising out of the *Sabbatino* sugar transactions where the lower courts applied the new statute and not the *Sabbatino* decision.

In a later decision involving Cuban expropriation of United States citizen's property by the Cuban government, *First National City Bank v. Banco Nacional de Cuba,*[33] the divided Court deferred to the opinion of the executive branch in areas touching foreign affairs. Justice Rehnquist, writing for himself, Chief Justice Burg-

25. Banco Nacional de Cuba v. Sabbatino, 376 U.S. 398, 423, 84 S.Ct. 923, 938, 11 L.Ed.2d 804 (1964).

26. 376 U.S. at 427, 84 S.Ct. at 940 (footnote omitted).

27. 376 U.S. at 428, 84 S.Ct. at 940.

28. 376 U.S. at 423, 84 S.Ct. at 938.

29. 376 U.S. at 428, 84 S.Ct. at 940 (emphasis added).

30. See, e.g., Hay, Unification of Law in the United States: Uniform State Laws, Treaties and Judicially Declared Federal Common Law, in Legal Thought in the United States of America Under Contemporary Pressures: Reports from the United States of America on Topics of Major Concern as Established for the VIII Congress of the International Academy of Comparative Law 261, 280–81, 289 (J. Hazard & W. Wagner, eds. 1970).

31. 22 U.S.C.A. § 2370(e)(2); see also the divided Court opinion in First Nat. City Bank v. Banco Nacional de Cuba, 406 U.S. 759, 761–62, 92 S.Ct. 1808, 1810–11, 32

L.Ed.2d 466 (1972), rehearing denied 409 U.S. 897, 93 S.Ct. 92, 34 L.Ed.2d 155 (1972), on remand 478 F.2d 191 (2d Cir.1973) (plurality opinion of Rehnquist, J.).

Provisions of title 28 of the United States Code have been enacted (in October 21, 1976 to be effective 90 days after that) that also relate to the *Sabbatino* issue. See 28 U.S.C.A. § 1330 (Actions against foreign states); 28 U.S.C.A. Chapter 97 (Jurisdictional Immunities of Foreign States). See particularly 28 U.S.C.A. § 1605 of Chapter 97 (General exceptions to the jurisdictional immunity of a foreign state).

32. 243 F.Supp. 957 (S.D.N.Y.1965), affirmed 383 F.2d 166 (2d Cir.1967), certiorari denied 390 U.S. 956, 88 S.Ct. 1038, 19 L.Ed.2d 1151 (1968), rehearing denied 390 U.S. 1037, 88 S.Ct. 1406, 20 L.Ed.2d 298 (1968).

33. 406 U.S. 759, 92 S.Ct. 1808, 32 L.Ed.2d 466 (1972), rehearing denied 409 U.S. 897, 93 S.Ct. 92, 34 L.Ed.2d 155 (1972), on remand 478 F.2d 191 (2d Cir.1973).

er, and Justice White, acknowledged that the executive had advised the Court that the act of state doctrine should not be applied in the situation under consideration. His plurality opinion recognized, "the primacy of the Executive in . . . foreign relations," concluding:

> where the Executive Branch, . . . expressly represents to the Court that application of the act of state doctrine would not advance the interests of American foreign policy, that doctrine should not be applied by the courts.[34]

Not all of the members of the Court were in accord with the theory of judicial acquiescence to the executive and Congress in foreign affairs. The concurring opinion of Justice Powell and the dissent of Justice Brennan emphasized the importance of maintaining the integrity and independence of the judiciary.[35] Brennan was particularly adamant in his dissent, stressing that any decision should be made on the basis of constitutional authority and not upon recommendations of the executive.[36]

Relying on *Banco Nacional de Cuba v. Sabbatino*,[37] the Court has deferred to the political branch and held that "it is within the exclusive power of the Executive Branch to determine which nations are entitled to sue."[38] When it ruled that foreign nations are allowed to sue as "persons" within the meaning of the antitrust laws, and therefor allowed treble damages, the Court specifically referred to a letter from the Legal Adviser of the State Department indicating that it anticipated no

foreign policy problems from that holding.[39] Congress responded to this decision by amending the Clayton Act in order to eliminate, in general, the right of foreign governments to recover treble damages.[40]

§ 6.5 The Treaty Power

Constitutional provisions confer the treaty making power specifically on the President and the Senate. The Constitution empowers the President " . . . by and with the Advice and Consent of the Senate, to make treaties provided two thirds of the Senators present concur."[1] Other language expressly prohibits states from entering, in their own right, into treaties or alliances.[2] Treaties are proclaimed to be the supreme law of the land and binding upon states.[3] Federal judicial power, in addition, is constitutionally extended to encompass cases involving treaties made under the authority of the federal government.[4] Another constitutional directive relevant to the treaty power is the necessary and proper clause,[5] which enables Congress to enact all law needed to implement and enforce treaties.

§ 6.6 Limitations on the Treaty Power

The basic Constitutional provision is:

This Constitution, and the Laws of the United States which shall be made in Pursuance thereof; and all Treaties made, or which shall be made, under the Authority of the United States, shall be the supreme Law of the Land. . . .[1]

---

34. 406 U.S. at 767–68, 92 S.Ct. at 1813.

35. 406 U.S. at 773–76, 776–796, 92 S.Ct. at 1815–17, 1817–27.

36. 406 U.S. at 776–796, 92 S.Ct. at 1817–27.

37. 376 U.S. 398, 408–12, 84 S.Ct. 923, 929–32, 11 L.Ed.2d 804 (1964).

38. Pfizer, Inc. v. Government of India, 434 U.S. 308, 320, 98 S.Ct. 584, 591, 54 L.Ed.2d 563 (1978), rehearing denied 435 U.S. 910, 98 S.Ct. 1462, 55 L.Ed.2d 502 (1978). The Court also cited Jones v. United States, 137 U.S. 202, 11 S.Ct. 80, 34 L.Ed. 691 (1890) for this proposition.

39. Pfizer v. Government of India, 434 U.S. 308, 319 n. 20, 98 S.Ct. 584, 591 n. 20, 54 L.Ed.2d 563 (1978), rehearing denied 435 U.S. 910, 98 S.Ct. 1462, 55 L.Ed.2d 502 (1978).

The dissent objected to the reliance on this letter and argued that the decision as to whether foreign nations could sue should be left to Congress. 434 U.S. at 329 n. 3, 98 S.Ct. at 596 n. 3 (Burger, C.J., joined by Powell &

Rehnquist, JJ., dissenting); Pfizer v. Government of India, 434 U.S. 308, 331 n. 2, 98 S.Ct. 584, 597 n. 2, 54 L.Ed.2d 563 (1978), rehearing denied 435 U.S. 910, 98 S.Ct. 1462, 55 L.Ed.2d 502 (1978) (Powell J., dissenting).

40. See 15 U.S.C.A. § 15(b).

§ 6.5

1. U.S.Const. art. II, § 2, cl. 1.

2. U.S.Const. art. I, § 10, cl. 3; art. I, § 10, cl. 1.

3. U.S.Const. art. VI, cl. 2.

4. U.S.Const. art. III, § 2, cl. 1.

5. U.S.Const. art. I, § 8, cl. 18. See, Missouri v. Holland, 252 U.S. 416, 40 S.Ct. 382, 64 L.Ed. 641 (1920).

§ 6.6

1. U.S.Const. art. VI, cl. 2.

Justice Holmes suggested once that this clause meant that treaties were equal to the Constitution, even if they were not made in pursuance of it.[2] As a consequence the theory developed that treaties were not subject to any constitutional limitations.

This view is incorrect. As Justice Field stated, in often quoted dictum in *De Geofroy v. Riggs*,[3] the treaty power, like all other powers that the Constitution grants, is subject to constitutional limitations:

> That the treaty power of the United States extends to all proper subjects of negotiation between our government and the governments of other nations, is clear.... The treaty power, as expressed in the Constitution, is in terms unlimited except by those restraints which are found in that instrument against the action of the government or of its departments.... It would not be contended that it extends so far as to authorize what the Constitution forbids, or a change in the character of the government or in that of one of the States, or a cession of any portion of the territory of the latter, without its consent.... But with these exceptions, it is not perceived that there is any limit to the questions which can be adjusted touching any matter which is properly the subject of negotiation with a foreign country.[4]

Field was hardly a lone voice crying in the wilderness. Thus, Justice Black's opinion in *Reid v. Covert* made what is often considered the definitive pronouncement on this issue:[5]

> [N]o agreement with a foreign nation can confer power on the Congress, or on any other branch of Government, which is free from the restraints of the Constitution.[6]

Black concluded that Constitutional provisions limit the acts of the President, the joint actions of the President and the Senate, and consequently they limit the treaty power. Given these limitations on the scope of the treaty making power, unless treaties are contrary to the Constitution, they are equal in status to congressional legislation, and, as expressly provided in the text of the Constitution, the supreme law of the land.[7]

Treaties and the Tenth Amendment. The states have sometimes argued that the Tenth Amendment imposes additional limitations upon the treaty power. They claim that, under the Constitution, they retain control over certain matters, and the federal government cannot alter these reserved powers through treaties. The Court confronted this issue in *Hauenstein v. Lynham*.[8]

Hauenstein was a suit by the heirs of a Swiss citizen who died intestate owning prop-

---

2. See historical background discussed in, Nowak & Rotunda, A Comment on the Creation and Resolution of a "Non–Problem": Dames & Moore v. Regan, the Foreign Affairs Power, and the Role of the Courts, 29 U.C.L.A.L.Rev. 1129, 1134–55 (1982); Louis Henkin, Foreign Affairs and the Constitution 137 (1972).

See Missouri v. Holland, 252 U.S. 416, 433, 40 S.Ct. 382, 383, 64 L.Ed. 641 (1920) where Justice Holmes wrote: "Acts of Congress are the supreme law of the land only when made in pursuance of the Constitution, while treaties are declared to be so when made under the authority of the United States. It is open to question whether the authority of the United States means more than the formal acts prescribed to make the convention."

3.   133 U.S. 258, 10 S.Ct. 295, 33 L.Ed. 642 (1890).

4.   133 U.S. at 266–67, 10 S.Ct. at 296–97.

5.   354 U.S. 1, 77 S.Ct. 1222, 1 L.Ed.2d 1148 (1957). Black announced the judgment for the Court; his opinion was joined by only three other Justices (Warren, C.J., and Douglas and Brennan, JJ.), but none of the other Justices, either concurring or dissenting, questioned his analysis of Missouri v. Holland, 252 U.S. 416, 40 S.Ct. 382, 64 L.Ed.

641 (1920). There was no opinion for the Court. Whittaker took no part in the case; Frankfurter concurred in a separate opinion; Harlan also concurred in another separate opinion; and Clark, joined by Burton, dissented.

6.   354 U.S. at 16, 77 S.Ct. at 1230. See also, De Geofroy v. Riggs, 133 U.S. 258, 267, 10 S.Ct. 295, 297, 33 L.Ed. 642 (1890); Holden v. Joy, 84 U.S. (17 Wall.) 211, 242–43, 21 L.Ed. 523 (1872); The Cherokee Tobacco, 78 U.S. (11 Wall.) 616, 620–21, 20 L.Ed. 227 (1870); Doe ex dem. Clark v. Braden, 57 U.S. (16 How.) 635, 657, 14 L.Ed. 1090 (1853); New Orleans v. United States, 35 U.S. (10 Pet.) 662, 736, 9 L.Ed. 573 (1836).

7.   U.S.Const. art. II, § 2; Martin v. Hunter's Lessee, 14 U.S. (1 Wheat.) 304, 360, 4 L.Ed. 97 (1816); Foster & Elam v. Neilson, 27 U.S. (2 Pet.) 253, 314–315, 7 L.Ed. 415 (1829); Missouri v. Holland, 252 U.S. 416, 433, 40 S.Ct. 382, 383, 64 L.Ed. 641 (1920). See, Ronald D. Rotunda, The Chemical Weapons Treaty: Political and Constitutional Issues, 15 Constitutional Commentary 129 (1998). Cf. John C. Yoo, The New Sovereignty and the Old Constitution: The Chemical Weapons Convention and the Appointments Clause, 15 Constitutional Commentary 87 (1998).

8.   100 U.S. (10 Otto) 483, 25 L.Ed. 628 (1879).

erty in Virginia. The plaintiffs sought to recover the proceeds from the sale of the property by the local escheator. The heirs, invoking provisions of a treaty between the United States and Switzerland, prevailed over local law, which prevented such aliens from taking property by descent or inheritance. The Court held that treaties (like federal statutes) are the supreme law of the land and superior to the laws and constitutions of the individual states.[9] Treatise, like federal statutes and the U.S. Constitution, "are as much a part of the law of every State as its own local laws and Constitution."[10]

The landmark case of *Missouri v. Holland*[11] rejected any Tenth Amendment limitation on the federal treaty power. Initially, Congress enacted a statute to protect migratory birds in danger of extinction.[12] Lower courts invalidated this Act because they found that no specific constitutional provision empowered Congress to regulate matters of this nature.[13] (This was a time when the Court interpreted the interstate commerce clause narrowly.) Later, the United States concluded a treaty with Great Britain involving the same issues that the statute had covered. New statutes were passed to implement the treaty. In *Missouri v. Holland* the state brought a bill in equity to prevent the federal game warden from enforcing the Migratory Bird Treaty and the regulations made pursuant to it.

Missouri claimed that the treaty and new statutes interfered with its Tenth Amendment reserved rights and were therefore void. Justice Holmes, writing for the Court, concluded that the treaty and statutes did not interfere with rights reserved by states. The Tenth Amendment does not limit the treaty power because—

by Article II, § 2, the power to make treaties is delegated expressly, and by Article VI

treaties made under the authority of the United States, along with the Constitution and laws of the United States made in pursuance thereof, are declared the supreme law of the land. If the treaty is valid there can be no dispute about the validity of the statute under Article I, § 8 as a necessary and proper means to execute the powers of the Government.... It is said that a treaty cannot be valid if it infringes the Constitution, that there are limits ... to the treaty making power....[14]

Holmes then rejected the state's argument that the same constitutional limitations applying to acts of Congress should also apply to treaties. He reasoned:

An earlier act of Congress that attempted by itself and not in pursuance of a treaty to regulate the killing of migratory birds within the States had been held bad in the District Court.... *Acts of Congress are the supreme law of the land only when made in pursuance of the Constitution, while treaties are declared to be so when made under the authority of the United States.* It is open to question whether the authority of the United States means more than the formal acts prescribed to make the convention. We do not mean to imply that there are no qualifications to the treaty-making power; but they must be ascertained in a different way. It is obvious that there may be matters of the sharpest exigency for the national well being that an act of Congress could not deal with but that a treaty followed by such an act could....[15]

What Holmes must have meant is that, *before* the Treaty existed, the migratory bird act (assuming the correctness of the earlier decisions) did not implement any federal power. *After* the Treaty the migratory bird act did implement a federal power, the treaty power.

9.   100 U.S. (10 Otto) at 483–89.

10.   100 U.S. (10 Otto) at 490.

11.   252 U.S. 416, 40 S.Ct. 382, 64 L.Ed. 641 (1920).

12.   Act of March 4, 1913, C. 145, 37 Stat. 847.

13.   United States v. Shauver, 214 Fed. 154 (E.D.Ark. 1914); United States v. McCullagh, 221 Fed. 288 (D.Kan. 1915).

14.   Missouri v. Holland, 252 U.S. 416, 432, 40 S.Ct. 382, 383, 64 L.Ed. 641 (1920).

15.   252 U.S. at 432–33, 40 S.Ct. at 383 (emphasis added). See also Hay, Supranational Organizations and United States Constitutional Law, 6 Va.J. of Internat'l Law 195, 198 n. 10 (1966).

The provisions of the agreement did not contravene the Bill of Rights or any other constitutional provisions limiting congressional powers. Therefore, Holmes concluded, any limitation upon the treaty would have to be based upon the general terms of the Tenth Amendment. But the treaty power is specifically delegated to the federal governments and the Tenth Amendment only purports to apply to nondelegated powers. Thus the Tenth Amendment does not limit the treaty power.

Matters of national interest are best protected by national action Holmes reasoned. Because the problem of protecting migratory birds was national in scope, no one state could provide as complete a solution as the treaty and resulting statutes. Although Missouri could have regulated the birds in the absence of a treaty, treaties and accompanying statutes are binding throughout the nation and within the territory of a state. States exercise control over most of their internal activities but a treaty will override such power.

The Bricker Amendment. Efforts to limit federal treaty making power by constitutional Amendment have been unsuccessful.[16] During the 1950's, proponents of the Bricker Amendment campaigned for a legislative overruling of the *Missouri v. Holland* decision. These individuals were concerned that portions of Justice Holmes' dicta in *Missouri v. Holland* could be interpreted to mean that treaties were not subject to constitutional limitations as were acts of Congress.[17]

Senator Bricker led the effort in the early 1950's to enact the proposed Amendment, which would have provided that a treaty could become effective as internal law only through

legislation that would be valid in the absence of a treaty. The proponents feared not only that a treaty could enlarge federal power over the states, but that it could be self-enforcing.

A lower California state court decision increased these fears. That court held that a particular state land law was invalid because it conflicted with the United Nations Charter, which the state court found to be self-executing.[18] On appeal, the California Supreme Court found that the United Nations Charter was not self-executing, but then invalidated the state law on the basis of the equal Protection clause of the Fourteenth Amendment.[19]

Opponents of the Bricker Amendment argued that it would impair the foreign affairs power and that the fears of Bricker and others were simply not well founded. Much of the controversy over the Bricker Amendment centered on the dangers that the treaty power could erode states rights. But the framers intended that the treaty power would override state law. They provided that treaties would be the law of the land. Ultimately Congress rejected the Bricker Amendment as unnecessary, because Constitutional provisions and Supreme Court decisions already provided adequate restraints on federal power.[20]

The President's Power to Terminate Treaties. For a time, efforts to limit the treaty power focused on the President's authority to terminate treaties. If the Constitution requires a two-thirds vote of the Senate in order to ratify a treaty, the Constitution, it was argued, must also require a two-thirds vote before the President can abrogate a treaty. A fragmented Court rejected this claim in *Gold-*

---

16. S.J.Res. 1, 83d Cong., 1st Sess., 99 Cong.Rec. 6777 (1953).

17. 252 U.S. at 433, 40 S.Ct. at 383. Proponents of the Bricker Amendment were specifically concerned with Justice Holmes' statement, that "Acts of Congress are the supreme law of the land only when made in pursuance of the Constitution, while treaties are declared to be so when made under the authority of the United States," in Missouri v. Holland, 252 U.S. 416, 433, 40 S.Ct. 382, 383, 64 L.Ed. 641 (1920).

18. Sei Fujii v. State, 217 P.2d 481 (Cal.App.2d Dist. 1950).

19. Sei Fujii v. State, 38 Cal.2d 718, 242 P.2d 617 (1952).

20. See generally Louis Henkin, Foreign Affairs and the Constitution 146–47 (1972). See also, Lockwood, The United Nations Charter and United States Civil Rights Litigation: 1946–1955, 69 Iowa L.Rev. 901 (1984); Association of the Bar of the City of New York—Committee on Federal Legislation, The Risks of the 1956 Bricker Amendment 4–7 (1956).

water v. Carter.[21]

In that case, several Senators and others sued for declaratory and injunctive relief against President Carter after he announced that he planned to terminate the mutual defense treaty with Taiwan, the Republic of China. The President gave the one year notice that the termination clause of the treaty required. He also recognized the Peoples Republic of China (the Peking Government) rather than the Nationalist Government of Taiwan as the Government of China.

The Court, without opinion, granted certiorari and ordered the district court to dismiss the complaint. Justice Rehnquist, joined by Chief Justice Burger and Justices Stevens and Stewart, concurred in the judgment and filed a statement concluding that the "basic question presented by the petitioners in this case is political and therefore nonjusticiable because it involves the authority of the President in the conduct of our country's foreign relations and the extent to which the Senate or the Congress is authorized to negate the action of the President."[22]

Justice Brennan dissented and rejected the majority's view of the political question doctrine. However, he nonetheless would not question the presidential decision because it rested on the President's exclusive power to recognize foreign governments. The President abrogated the treaty with Taiwan because he recognized the Peking Government.

Only Justice Powell's concurrence rejected the political question doctrine, either as broadly held by Justice Rehnquist or as more narrowly held by Justice Brennan. Powell argued,

inexplicably, that there were judicially discoverable and manageable standards because decision in this case "only" required the Court to interpret the Constitution.[23] He did not tell us what these standards are. Nonetheless he concurred in the dismissal of the case because he thought that the issue was not yet "ripe" and would not be until Congress chose to "confront the President," and reached a "constitutional impasse."[24] He hinted that if the Senate would pass a resolution declaring that its approval was necessary for the termination of any mutual defense treaty and further declared that it intended the resolution to have retroactive effect, that might then make the case ripe. He appeared to be arguing that this case would become ripe if the Senate would ask for a judicial determination of its rights.

§ 6.7 Executory and Self–Executing Treaties

Although no provisions in the Constitution discuss the nature of a treaty, the Court has recognized that two types of treaties exist. Treaties may be either executory—that is, a ratified treaty that requires implementing legislation before it takes effect as domestic law—or self-executory—that is, a ratified treaty that takes effect as domestic law immediately upon ratification. *Foster v. Neilson*[1] held that state and federal courts should regard treaties as equivalent to an act of Congress whenever the treaty operates by itself without the aid of any federal statute to implement it:

> But when the terms of the stipulation import a contract, when either of the parties engages to perform a particular act, the treaty addresses itself to the political, not

21. 444 U.S. 996, 100 S.Ct. 533, 62 L.Ed.2d 428 (1979).

22. 444 U.S. at 1001, 100 S.Ct. at 536.

23. 444 U.S. at 999, 100 S.Ct. at 534–35. Cf. Roberts, J., in United States v. Butler, 297 U.S. 1, 62, 56 S.Ct. 312, 317–18, 80 L.Ed. 477 (1936):

"When an act of Congress is appropriately challenged in the courts as not conforming to the constitutional mandate the judicial branch of the Government has only one duty,—to lay the article of the Constitution which is invoked beside the statute which is challenged and to decide whether the latter squares with the former."

Powell also rejected the other tests, outlined in Baker v. Carr, 369 U.S. 186, 82 S.Ct. 691, 7 L.Ed.2d 663 (1962), on

remand 206 F.Supp. 341 (M.D.Tenn.1962) to determine whether there was a political question.

24. 444 U.S. at 998, 100 S.Ct. at 534.

Justice Marshall concurred in the dismissal but without any opinion. Justice Blackmun, joined by Justice White, did not reach the merits and would have set the case for oral argument and plenary consideration.

§ 6.7

1. 27 U.S. (2 Pet.) 253, 7 L.Ed. 415 (1829). Compare United States v. Percheman, 32 U.S. (7 Pet.) 51, 8 L.Ed. 604 (1833), where the Supreme Court held that the same treaty was self-executing, after examining the Spanish text and Spanish grammatical usage.

the judicial department; and the legislature must execute the contract before it can become a rule for the Court.[2]

Similarly, *Whitney v. Robertson*[3] acknowledged that executory treaties have no effect until the necessary legislation is enacted.

Thus, treaties are the "supreme law of the land," so a self-executing treaty, just like a statute, serves to override or preempt contrary state law.[4] But if the treaties are not self-executing, there must be implementing legislation before an American court can enforce the treaty as domestic law.

An international agreement of the United States is not "self-executing" if either, (1) the agreement itself states (or makes clear) that it will become effective as domestic law without the enactment of implementing legislation, or (2), the Senate when ratifying the treaty, or Congress by resolution, requires implementing legislation, or (3), if the Constitution itself requires implementing legislation.[5] As for requirement (3)—when the Constitution itself requires implementing legislation—it is generally thought that a treaty alone (one that the President has signed and the Senate has ratified) cannot appropriate money or impose a new tax or impose a new tariff (because the Constitution has a special clause providing that all revenue bills shall originate in the

House of Representatives).[6] Similarly, because the United States has no federal common law crimes,[7] it should require action by both Houses of Congress to create a crime, such as a crime punishing international genocide or piracy.[8] Because only Congress can "declare" a war, a treaty cannot itself declare way.[9] On the other hand, it is not uncommon for a treaty regulating foreign commerce to affect tariffs by including clauses that give "most-favored-nation" status to the signatories. But those treaties do *not* impose any new tariffs.

§ 6.8   Conflicts Between Treaties and Acts of Congress

While treaties as well as federal statutes are the supreme law of the land, the Constitution provides no explicit solution when a self-executing treaty conflict with acts of Congress.[1] *Whitney v. Robertson*[2] addressed this issue. The case involved a dispute arising between the United States and the Dominican Republic over the terms of a sugar trade treaty to which the two nations were parties.

Whitney stated that treaties and legislative acts are equal, both being the supreme law of the land. When the treaty and statute:

relate to the same subject, the courts will always endeavor to construe them so as to give effect to both, if that can be done with-

---

2.   27 U.S. (2 Pet.) at 314.

3.   124 U.S. 190, 194, 8 S.Ct. 456, 458, 31 L.Ed. 386 (1888).

4.   Constitutionally valid treaties, like constitutionally valid executive agreements, preempt inconsistent state law. American Insurance Association v. Garamendi, 539 U.S. ___, ___, 123 S.Ct. 2374, 2387, 156 L.Ed.2d 376 (2003).

5.   Restatement of the Law of Foreign Relations of the United States, Third, § 111(4)(c) (A.L.I.1987).

6.   U.S.Const. art. I, § 7, cl.1. See also, Restatement of the Law of Foreign Relations of the United States, Third, § 111(4)(c) & Comment i (A.L.I.1987).

On the other hand, Edwards v. Carter, 580 F.2d 1055 (D.C.Cir.1978), certiorari denied, 436 U.S. 907, 98 S.Ct. 2240, 56 L.Ed.2d 406 (1978) rejected a claim brought by members of the House of Representatives who sought to block transfer of federal property to a foreign nation through a self-executing treaty without a vote of the House. The Court of Appeals held that the property clause of the United States Constitution does not prohibit the

transfer of United States property to foreign nations through self-executing treaties. MacKinnon, C.J., dissented and filed a thoughtful opinion.

7.   United States v. Hudson, 11 U.S. (7 Cranch) 32, 3 L.Ed. 259 (1812)(no federal common law crimes).

8.   U.S.Const. art. I, § 8, cl. 10.United States v. Smith, 18 U.S. (5 Wheat.) 153, 5 L.Ed. 57 (1820) (Court upholds statute that punishes "piracy, as defined by the law of nations"). Restatement of the Law of Foreign Relations of the United States, Third, § 111(4)(c) & Comment i (A.L.I. 1987).

9.   U.S.Const. art. I, § 8, cl. 11; Restatement of the Law of Foreign Relations of the United States, Third, § 111(4)(c) & Comment i (A.L.I.1987).

§ 6.8

1.   U.S.Const. art. VI, cl. 2.

2.   124 U.S. 190, 8 S.Ct. 456, 31 L.Ed. 386 (1888). E.g., Rotunda, Roadblock to Mexico, The Washington Post, Sept. 21, 1993, at A19, col. 6.

out violating the language of either; but if the two are inconsistent, the one last in date will control the other.... [3]

Acts of Congress passed after the date of the treaty, the Court held, control over the treaty terms. Similarly, a self-executing treaty is valid as domestic law and takes precedence over a federal law enacted earlier. In short, the last expression of the sovereign will controls.

The *Chinese Exclusion Case*[4] held that an act excluding Chinese laborers from the United States was a constitutional exercise of legislative power even though it conflicted with an existing treaty. Because treaties are equivalent to acts of the legislature, they can, like statutes, be repealed or amended. The last expression of the sovereign will was the statute, which conflicted with the earlier enacted treaty.

However, as a rule of interpretation, the Court will not deem a treaty to be abrogated or modified by a later statute unless the Congressional purpose was clearly expressed.[5] The courts will not find that ambiguous congressional action has implicitly repealed a treaty. And *a fortiori*, legislative silence is insufficient to repeal a treaty.[6]

§ 6.9 Executive Agreements and Acts of Congress

International Agreements by Statute and Executive Agreement. The Constitution expressly provides that the President, "shall have Power, by and with the Advice and Consent of the Senate to make Treaties, provided that two thirds of the Senators present concur...."[1] This clause does not explicitly provide that it is the exclusive method of making international agreements, and neither historical practice nor the Supreme Court has interpreted the clause in this manner.

For example, it is not unusual for both Houses of Congress to enact (by simple majority) a statute or joint resolution that approves of an international agreement in lieu of ratification by two-thirds of the Senate.[2] While this conclusion may be initially surprising, historical tradition strongly supports it, and the commentators treat the question as no longer controversial.[3]

Presidents have also used Executive Agreements to make accords with foreign countries, without Senatorial approval.[4] These agreements, while they cannot be termed treaties because they lack the constitutional requirement of consent by the Senate, frequently cover the same subject matter as treaties.[5]

---

3. 124 U.S. at 194, 8 S.Ct. at 458. However, a treaty cannot change any Constitutional requirement that a power is within the exclusive mandate of Congress. For example, if a treaty provides that the United States will buy some foreign territory for $1 billion, ratification of the treaty does not have the effect of appropriating the money, because the Constitution requires the power to appropriate lies with both Houses of Congress, not just the Senate. E.g., Restatement of the Law of Foreign Relations of the United States, Third, § 111 & Comment *I* (A.L.I.1987).

4. Chae Chan Ping v. United States, 130 U.S. 581, 9 S.Ct. 623, 32 L.Ed. 1068 (1889).

5. Cook v. United States, 288 U.S. 102, 120, 53 S.Ct. 305, 311, 77 L.Ed. 641 (1933).

6. Weinberger v. Rossi, 456 U.S. 25, 32, 102 S.Ct. 1510, 1516, 71 L.Ed.2d 715 (1982); cf. Bacardi Corp. of America v. Domenech, 311 U.S. 150, 161–63, 61 S.Ct. 219, 225–26, 85 L.Ed. 98 (1940).

§ 6.9

1. U.S. Const. art. II, § 2, cl. 2.

2. See, e.g., B. Altman & Co. v. United States, 224 U.S. 583, 32 S.Ct. 593, 56 L.Ed. 894 (1912) treated a Congressional–Executive Agreement as a "treaty" within the meaning of a federal statute. Earlier, Von Cotzhausen v. Nazro, 107 U.S. 215, 2 S.Ct. 503, 27 L.Ed. 540 (1883) had

ruled that postal conventions have equal status with treaties.

The Trade Agreement Act of 1934 was an international agreement that was "ratified" as a statute passed by the House and Senate instead of being approved of as an international agreement. In fact, only a simple majority of the Senators approved of this international agreement. The vote was 57–33. See, 78 Cong. Rec. 10395 (1934). See also, Proclamation No. 2761A, 12 Fed. Reg. 8863 (1947) relating to American participation in the General Agreement on Tariffs and Trade (GATT).

3. E.g., Myers McDougal & Asher Lans, Treaties and Congressional–Executive or Presidential Agreements: Interchangeable Instruments of National Policy, 54 Yale L.J. 181 (Part I), & 534 (Part II) (1945); Louis Henkin, Foreign Affairs and the Constitution 173–201 (1972).

4. See, e.g., Weinberger v. Rossi, 456 U.S. 25, 30 n. 6, 102 S.Ct. 1510, 1514 n. 6, 71 L.Ed.2d 715 (1982).

5. The history and nature of executive agreements is discussed extensively in: McDougal and Lans, Treaties and Congressional–Executive or Presidential Agreements: Interchangeable Instruments of National Policy, 54 Yale L.J. 181 (Part I) & 534 (Part II) (1945), and Borchard, Treaties and Executive Agreements, A Reply, 54 Yale L.J. 616 (1945).

The Types of Executive Agreements. There are basically four types of executive agreements. First, the President may conclude an executive agreement based on exclusive presidential powers, such as the power as commander-in-chief of the armed forces pursuant to which he conducts military operations with our allies, or his power to receive foreign ambassadors and recognize foreign governments.[6] Second, the President may conclude an executive agreement in pursuance of an authorization contained in a prior treaty.[7] Third, the President may derive power to conclude an executive agreement from prior Congressional authorization. That is, the House and Senate together may delegate certain powers to the President, which he exercises together with his independent powers in the areas of foreign affairs.[8] Fourth, the President may obtain Congressional confirmation by both Houses of an agreement that the President has negotiated.[9]

The *Pink* Case. The Supreme Court discussed the status of the executive agreement in the leading case of the *United States v. Pink*.[10] That case involved a dispute over the title to the New York assets of a Russian insurance company. Russia had nationalized all her insurance companies in 1918 and 1919 by decrees intended to include the foreign assets of all Russian insurance businesses.[11] In 1933, President Roosevelt and the Soviet government concluded the Litvinov Assignment, an executive agreement whereby the United States agreed to recognize the Soviet Government. In return, the Soviet Union assigned (to the United States government) its interests in the assets of the Russian insurance company located in New York. This agreement was the first type of executive agreement discussed above: it was entered into pursuant to the President's constitutional authority to recognize foreign governments.

Under the terms of the executive agreement, the United States became entitled to the property; the rights of the United States were to be superior to the claims of the corporation and foreign creditors.[12] The Supreme Court found that the New York state court's policy not to recognize the Soviet government and the state's refusal to enforce the Litvinov Assignment ran counter to the executive agreement made by President Roosevelt in connection

---

6. Restatement of the Law, 2d, Foreign Relations of the United States, § 121 (1965). See id. at Comment *b*. A typical illustration:

"The President makes an agreement with state *A* whereby the United States will transfer to *A* a number of destroyers in exchange for the lease of areas for naval and air bases in certain territory of *A*. The agreement is valid under the President's powers as chief executive and commander-in-chief. Cf. Arrangement with Great Britain Respecting Naval and Air Bases, 54 Stat. 2405, E.A.S. No. 181, 3 Dept. State Bull. 199 (1940). Cf. 39 Opinions Atty.Gen. 484 (1940)."

Restatement of the Law, 2d, Foreign Relations of the United States (1965), § 121, at Comment *b*, Illustration 2. Accord, 19 Opinion of Attorney General 513 (1890) (Opinion of Solicitor General Taft); 39 Opinion of Attorney General 484 (1940) (transfer of overage destroyers for bases in United Kingdom); 40 Opinion of Attorney General 469 (1946).

It has been argued that the President's power to "faithfully execute" the laws, U.S.Const. art. II, § 3, furnishes the President additional and independent power as a basis for executive agreements. But this view is a minority one and is too open-ended to be acceptable.

7. See, e.g., Restatement of the Law, 2d, Foreign Relations Law of the United States, § 119, Comment *b*, Illustration 1:

"The United States and state A make a security treaty providing, among other things, that the two states may make administrative agreements governing the disposition of United States forces in A. Pursuant to that provision, the President of the United States makes an executive agreement defining jurisdiction over United States forces in A. The executive agreement is constitutional. Cf. Wilson v. Girard, 354 U.S. 524, 77 S.Ct. 1409, 1 L.Ed.2d 1544 (1957)."

8. See, e.g., Restatement of the Law, 2d, Foreign Relations of the United States (1965), at § 120, Comment *a*, Illustration 1:

"An act of Congress provides that when the President finds that existing duties or import restrictions of the United States or any foreign country are unduly burdening or restricting the foreign trade of the United States, he may enter into trade agreements with foreign governments and proclaim such modifications of existing duties and other import restrictions as may be necessary to carry out any such foreign trade agreement, provided that reductions or increases in any duty rate shall not exceed 50 per cent of any existing rate.... This agreement [of the President] is constitutional...."

9. See Restatement of the Law, 2d, Foreign Relations of the United States (1965), at § 120, Comment *b*.

10. 315 U.S. 203, 62 S.Ct. 552, 86 L.Ed. 796 (1942).

11. 315 U.S. at 210, 62 S.Ct. at 556.

12. 315 U.S. at 234, 62 S.Ct. at 567.

with his recognition of the Government of the U.S.S.R.[13] Thus, the state's refusal was invalid, because it conflicted with the executive agreement.

Justice Douglas, for the Court, noted that the Litvinov Assignment was an international compact, an executive agreement, which did not require Senate approval.[14] Citing *United States v. Curtiss–Wright Export Corp.*,[15] Douglas stated that the President is the "sole organ of the federal government" in foreign affairs.[16] Failure to find the Litvinov Assignment binding upon the United States and conclusive on the courts would usurp the function of the executive:

> A treaty is a "Law of the Land" under the supremacy clause ... of the Constitution. Such international compacts and agreements as the Litvinov Assignment have a similar dignity.[17]

Just as state law yields to treaties, Douglas indicated, so must provisions of the executive agreement prevail over state policy.[18] The Court found that the provisions of the Litvinov Assignment passing the vested Soviet right in the property to the United States must be recognized as valid by New York.[19]

Notice that the Executive Agreement in *Pink* preempted the inconsistent state law.

That preemption was explicit. Just like statutes, constitutionally Executive Agreements also preempt inconsistent state law even if the preemption is implicit.[20]

***Pink* and the Fifth Amendment.** The basic purpose of the Litvinov Assignment was to settle outstanding American claims against the U.S.S.R. at the same time that the United States agreed to recognize the Soviet Government. The U.S.S.R. assigned to the United States the U.S.S.R.'s interests in certain Russian properties expropriated by the Soviet Union but located outside of the U.S.S.R. The United States expected to use these assets to pay off claims by the United States and by United States citizens against the U.S.S.R. The existence of "unpaid claims against Russia and its nationals, which were held in this country, and which the Litvinov Assignment was intended to secure, had long been one impediment to resumption of friendly relations between these two great powers."[21]

The U.S.S.R., by decree, had intended to confiscate all of the assets of the First Russian Insurance Company. This decree was intended to have an extraterritorial effect and thus to include the New York branch.[22] However, if the U.S.S.R. assigned the assets of this branch to the United States, as the Litvinov Assign-

---

13. 315 U.S. at 231–32, 62 S.Ct. at 566–67. See also Moscow Fire Insurance Co. v. Bank of New York & Trust Co., 280 N.Y. 286, 20 N.E.2d 758 (1939), affirmed by an equally divided Court, sub nom., United States v. Moscow Fire Insurance Co., 309 U.S. 624, 60 S.Ct. 725, 84 L.Ed. 986 (1940) (New York Court of Appeals refused to recognize the superiority of the United States' claims on the basis of the Litvinov Assignment over the claims of others).

14. United States v. Pink, 315 U.S. 203, 229, 62 S.Ct. 552, 565, 86 L.Ed. 796 (1942). United States v. Belmont, 301 U.S. 324, 330, 57 S.Ct. 758, 760–61, 81 L.Ed. 1134 (1937).

15. 299 U.S. 304, 320, 57 S.Ct. 216, 221, 81 L.Ed. 255 (1936).

16. 315 U.S. at 229, 62 S.Ct. at 565.

17. 315 U.S. at 230, 62 S.Ct. at 565.

18. 315 U.S. at 230–31, 62 S.Ct. at 565–66.

19. 315 U.S. at 234, 62 S.Ct. at 567.

20. Constitutionally valid treaties preempt inconsistent state law. See. American Insurance Association v. Garamendi, 539 U.S. __, __, 123 S.Ct. 2374, 2387, 156 L.Ed.2d 376 (2003). Germany agreed to establish a foundation funded with 10 billion Deutsche Mark contributed

equally by Germany and German companies to compensate the companies' victims during the Nazi era. The U.S. President agreed that whenever a German company was sued on a Holocaust-era claim in an American court, the Government would: (1) submit a statement that it is in this country's foreign policy interests for the foundation to be the exclusive forum and remedy for such claims, and (2) try to persuade state and local governments to respect the foundation as the exclusive mechanism.

In *Garamendi*, Plaintiffs sought to enjoin the California Insurance Commissioner from enforcing a California statute requiring disclosure of information about Holocaust-era insurance policies. Souter, J., for the Court, held that California's Holocaust Victim Insurance Relief Act (HVIRA), and in particular a provision of the HVIRA requiring any insurer that did business in California and that sold insurance policies in Europe that were in effect during Holocaust-era to disclose certain information about those policies to the California Insurance Commissioner or risk losing its license, impermissibly interfered with the President's conduct of foreign affairs, and was preempted on that basis.

21. 315 U.S. at 225, 62 S.Ct. at 563.

22. 315 U.S. at 224, 62 S.Ct. at 562.

ment intended,[23] the United States might appear to be, in effect, confiscating property in violation of the Fifth Amendment protections of due process and just compensation. The United States might be seen to be taking advantage of foreign expropriations: if the United States could not itself confiscate an insurance company located in New York, the United States should not be able to use its assets. Thus, some contemporary commentators labeled *Pink* as proof that the Court would allow executive agreements to override unconstitutional takings of property.[24]

In fact, the Court, speaking through Justice Douglas, carefully noted that all the claims of domestic creditors and all claims arising out of the New York branch had already been paid.[25] Other creditors—who were not United States citizens and whose claims did not arise out of transactions with the New York branch—made claims on the one million dollars still held by the New York Superintendent of Insurance, who was distributing the remaining assets to claimants.[26] New York, as a matter of local law, had determined a priority for unsecured creditors.[27] The Supreme Court simply held, as a matter of federal law, that the United States, as a creditor, had priority over foreign creditors whose unsecured claims did not even arise out of transactions with the New York insurance company. Therefore, the Court concluded that the federal government had not unconstitutionally taken property and that the execu-

tive agreements did not otherwise violate the Bill of Rights.

If property had been taken, nothing in *Pink* suggests that just compensation is unavailable. Moreover, *Pink* did not imply that the President had unlimited power to enter into agreements that might have an unconstitutional effect on persons whether or not residing in the United States. *Pink* merely reaffirmed the President's ability to enter into agreements that would override state law, provided the agreement itself did not violate any provision of the Bill of Rights.[28]

The Iranian Assets Litigation. *Dames & Moore v. Regan*[29] illustrates the broad presidential power to settle foreign claims by use of executive agreements. Iranians seized the American Embassy in Tehran on November 4, 1980, and held the occupants hostage. President Carter, acting pursuant to his powers under the International Emergency Economic Powers Act, eventually issued a blocking order that froze all the Iranian Government assets subject to the jurisdiction of the United States. There followed lengthy negotiations and, eventually, Iran released the American hostages on January 20, 1981, after the United States and Iran signed an Agreement concerning the settlement of claims.

That Agreement required the United States to terminate all suits brought in the U.S. courts against Iran and to "nullify all attach-

---

23. 315 U.S. at 224, 62 S.Ct. at 562.

24. See, e.g., Jessup, Editorial Comment: The Litvinov Assignment and the Pink Case, 36 Am.J. Int'l L. 282, 282 (1942): "From the point of view of our constitutional law, the decision [in United States v. Pink] may well mark one of the most far-reaching inroads upon the protection which it was supposed the Fifth Amendment accorded to private property." (footnote omitted). Note, Effect of Soviet Recognition Upon Russian Confiscatory Decrees, 51 Yale L.J. 848, 853 (1942): "The logical result of the Court's position is that an international executive agreement according recognition may grant priority to anyone over anyone, ignoring 'due process' limitations on the exercise of the power." (footnote omitted). See also Finch, The Need to Restrain the Treaty–Making Power of the United States Within Constitutional Limits, 48 Am.J. Int'l L. 57, 67 (1954) (arguing that *Pink* sanctioned violations of the Fifth Amendment); Jessup, The Litvinov Assignment and the Belmont Case, 31 Am.J. Int'l L. 481, 483–84 (1937).

25. 315 U.S. at 211, 227, 62 S.Ct. at 556.

26. 315 U.S. at 211, 227, 62 S.Ct. at 556.

27. 315 U.S. at 211, 62 S.Ct. at 556.

28. See also United States v. Belmont, 301 U.S. 324, 57 S.Ct. 758, 81 L.Ed. 1134 (1937). Dicta in *Belmont* portended the result in *Pink*. The actual holding in *Belmont* was quite limited. The Court said only that the United States had a cause of action against the stake holders of the Russian funds. No adverse claimant to those funds was a party in the *Belmont* case. P. Hay & R. Rotunda, The United States Federal System: Legal Integration in the American Experience 56–60 (Giuffré Milan 1982).

29. 453 U.S. 654, 101 S.Ct. 2972, 69 L.Ed.2d 918 (1981). See Symposium: Dames & Moore v. Regan, 29 U.C.L.A.L.Rev. 977–1159 (1982); Nowak & Rotunda, A Comment on the Creation and Resolution of a "Non-Problem": Dames & Moore v. Regan, the Foreign Affairs Power, and the Role of the Court, 29 U.C.L.A.L.Rev. at 1129.

ments and judgments obtained therein, to prohibit all further litigation based on such
claims, and to bring about the termination of
such claims through binding arbitration" before an Iran–United States Claims Tribunal.[30]
President Carter, and later President Reagan,
signed a series of executive orders to implement this agreement. These orders purported
to nullify all attachments, liens, or other non-
Iranian interests in Iranian assets subject to
President Carter's November 14, 1979 freeze
of Iranian assets.

Petitioner sued for declaratory and injunctive relief against the enforcement of the Executive Orders and the Treasury Department's implementing regulations. They
claimed that enforcement was unconstitutional to the extent that it adversely affects petitioner's final judgment on a contract claim
against the Government of Iran and the Atomic Energy Organization of Iran, its execution
of that judgment in the state of Washington,
its prejudgment attachments, and its ability to
continue to litigate against the Iranian
banks.[31]

The Court, per Justice Rehnquist, upheld
the constitutionality of the Executive Orders
relying in large part on Justice Jackson's seminal analysis in *Youngstown Sheet & Tube Co.
v. Sawyer*.[32] The Court's opinion in *Dames &
Moore* was narrowly drafted and attentive to
the civil liberties implications. It held that, if
the President's freeze amounted to a taking of
property, the Government must provide just
compensation. This opinion provides no support for the proposition that the President has
inherent authority to sign an Executive Agreement that is inconsistent with any of the other
provisions of the Bill of Rights. On the contrary, the decision reaffirms the supremacy of
the Bill of Rights.[33]

The Court first concluded that Congress, by
statute, had explicitly authorized the President to nullify the post-freeze attachments and
to direct that the blocked Iranian assets be
transferred to the New York Federal Reserve
Bank and later to Iran.[34] The purpose of this
statute is to permit the President to maintain
the foreign assets at his disposal for use as a
"bargaining chip" when negotiating with a
hostile nation.[35]

In addition to the attachments of the Iranian assets there were the underlying claims
against Iran. The Court was unable to find any
explicit authority to suspend the claims pending in the U.S. Courts. However, while there
was no evidence of contrary congressional intent, there was evidence of legislative intent to
invite broad presidential action. There was
also a long history of congressional acquiescence of similar presidential conduct. "Crucial
to our decision today is the conclusion that
Congress has implicitly approved the practice
of claim settlement by executive agreement."[36]

The exercise of presidential power in this
case did not unconstitutionally divest the federal courts of jurisdiction, any more than a
finding of sovereign immunity divests the
courts of jurisdiction. Rather the President has
directed the federal courts to apply a different
rule of substantive law.[37]

Petitioner also charged that the suspension
of its claims constituted a taking of their property without just compensation. The Court
found this question was not ripe for review.
However the majority did find ripe the question whether petitioner would have a remedy
at law in the Court of Claims if in fact there
was a taking. And the Court held that, if there
were a taking, the Court of Claims would have

30. 453 U.S. at 665, 101 S.Ct. at 2979.

31. 453 U.S. at 667, 101 S.Ct. at 2980.

32. 343 U.S. 579, 634, 72 S.Ct. 863, 888, 96 L.Ed. 1153
(1952), cited, e.g., at 453 U.S. at 661–62, 674, 101 S.Ct. at
2977–78.

33. See 453 U.S. at 660–61, 688, 101 S.Ct. at 2976–77.

34. The Court relied on the "plain language" of the
International Emergency Economic Powers Act, 50
U.S.C.A. § 1702, its legislative history, and the legislative
history and cases interpreting the Trading with the Ene-

my Act, 50 U.S.C.A.App. § 5(b), from which was drawn
the pertinent language of § 1702.

35. 453 U.S. at 673, 101 S.Ct. at 2983.

36. 453 U.S. at 680, 101 S.Ct. at 2987. See also 453
U.S. at 679, n. 8, 101 S.Ct. at 2986, n. 8: "At least since
the case of the 'Wilmington Packet' in 1799, Presidents
have exercised the power to settle claims of United States
Nationals by executive agreement."

37. 453 U.S. at 684–85, 101 S.Ct. at 2989–90.

jurisdiction to provide compensation.[38]

When Executive Agreements Conflict with Federal Statutes. Although cases such as *United States v. Pink*,[39] and *Dames & Moore v. Regan*[40] indicate that executive agreements are as binding upon the nation as ratified treaties, questions still remain as to what extent an executive agreement is equivalent to a treaty. To what extent does an executive agreement override an earlier enacted federal statute? And when does a federal statute override an executive agreement promulgated earlier?

United States v. Guy W. Capps, Inc.[41] is a leading lower court decision discussing these issues. *Capps* involved an executive agreement between Canada and the United States regulating potato exports by Canada. This agreement was the third type of executive agreement discussed above.[42]

The Fourth Circuit stated:

[T]he executive agreement was void because it was not authorized by Congress and contravened provisions of a statute dealing with the very matter to which it related and [therefore] the contract relied on, which was

based on the executive agreement, was unenforceable in the courts of the United States for like reason.[43]

This executive agreement invalid because the Executive branch had not properly exercised those powers delegated to it by earlier federal statutes.[44]

Although the Supreme Court did not rule on this issue directly and affirmed *Capps* on other grounds,[45] *Capps* suggests that executive agreements might not be completely equal to treaties in all respects. The Restatement of the Law, (Second) Foreign Relations Law of the United States, has summarized the effect on domestic law of an executive agreement entered into pursuant to the President's constitutional authority, the first type of executive agreement described above:

(1) An executive agreement, is made by the United States without reference to a treaty or act of Congress, conforming to the [appropriate] constitutional limitations ... and manifesting an intention that it shall become effective as domestic law of the United States at the time it becomes binding on the United States.

38. 453 U.S. at 688–90, 101 S.Ct. at 2991–92. Stevens, J., concurred and would have held that the question as to the jurisdiction of the Court of Claims was not ripe. Powell, J., concurred and dissented in part. He would not have decided whether the President's nullification of the attachments represented a taking. The majority, in a footnote, had rejected petitioner's argument that although the President, when he froze assets, could have forbidden attachments, "once he allowed them the President permitted claimants to acquire property interests in their attachments." The Court, rather, concluded that "because of the President's authority to prevent or condition attachments, and because of the orders he issued to this effect, petitioner did not acquire any 'property' interest in its attachments of the sort that would support a constitutional claim for compensation." 453 U.S. at 674 n. 6, 101 S.Ct. at 2983–84, n. 6.

39. 315 U.S. 203, 62 S.Ct. 552, 86 L.Ed. 796 (1942).

40. 453 U.S. 654, 101 S.Ct. 2972, 69 L.Ed.2d 918 (1981).

41. 204 F.2d 655 (4th Cir.1953), affirmed on other grounds 348 U.S. 296, 75 S.Ct. 326, 99 L.Ed. 329 (1955). See Swearingen v. United States, 565 F.Supp. 1019, 1021 (D.Colo.1983) (Matsch, J.), citing this treatise.

42. The executive agreement was claimed to have derived its authority from prior Congressional authorization.

43. 204 F.2d at 658. The court also stated that no cause of action had been created by Congress for this type of injury. Id.

44. 204 F.2d at 658–59. The Circuit Court also said that the executive agreement is invalid because it affects foreign commerce and the President does not have the power to regulate interstate and foreign commerce because that power is vested in the Congress by the Constitution. This dictum is unpersuasive. The congressional power to regulate commerce power is not exclusive. See, e.g., Cooley v. Board of Wardens, 53 U.S. (12 How.) 299, 13 L.Ed. 996 (1851). "If the President cannot make agreements on any matter on which Congress could legislate, there could be no executive agreements with domestic legal consequences, since, we have seen, the legislative powers of Congress has few and far limits." Louis Henkin, Foreign Affairs and the Constitution 181 (1972).

45. United States v. Guy W. Capps, Inc., 204 F.2d 655, 658 (4th Cir.1953), affirmed on other grounds 348 U.S. 296, 75 S.Ct. 326, 99 L.Ed. 329 (1955). See also, Seery v. United States, 130 Ct.Cl. 481, 127 F.Supp. 601, 606 (Ct.Cl. 1955); American Bitumuls & Asphalt Co. v. United States, 37 Cust.Ct. 58, 146 F.Supp. 703, 708 (Cust.Ct.1956), reversed on other grounds 246 F.2d 270 (C.C.P.A.1957), certiorari denied 355 U.S. 883, 78 S.Ct. 150, 2 L.Ed.2d 113 (1957); Consumers Union of U.S., Inc. v. Rogers, 352 F.Supp. 1319 (D.D.C.1973).

(a) supersedes inconsistent provisions of the law of the several states, but

(b) does not supersede inconsistent provisions of earlier acts of Congress.[46]

The position of the Restatement, (Second)— that an executive agreement entered into by the President pursuant to his constitutional authority, the first type of agreement described above, does not supersede earlier acts of Congress—is not entirely correct *when* the President enters into an agreement pursuant to his *inherent* Presidential authority in the field of foreign relations.[47] The Reporter's Notes to the First Tentative Draft of the Restatement of the Law, Foreign Relations Law of the United States (Revised) rejects the position of the Restatement, (Second)[48] and the black letter of the Restatement (Revised) also does not adopt the view of the Restatement, (Second).[49]

In short, if the President has authority under the Constitution or otherwise to promulgate an executive order, and if that order is consistent with previously enacted federal law, then that executive agreement is also the supreme law of the land and must prevail over contrary state law; such an executive agreement should also prevail over earlier Congressional enactments *if* the President is, in fact, entering into an agreement pursuant to his exclusive presidential authority in the field of foreign relations. If the President's authority to promulgate an executive agreement does not derive from his exclusive presidential powers—if, for example, it does not derive from his power to recognize foreign governments or his power as commander-in-chief—then the executive agreement should not be able to override an earlier enacted federal statute.

§ 6.10 The Historical Development of the War Power

Constitutional language suggests that the President and Congress share the war power, the dominant authority being vested in the legislature. Congress declares war and has power to tax and finance expenditures necessary for defense. Congress determines the rules of warfare, is empowered to raise and support an army and navy and makes all laws necessary and proper for exercising the war power.[1] The President is the Commander–in–Chief of the armed forces.[2]

The Commander–in–Chief clause, read in concert with provisions vesting executive power in the President to see that the laws are faithfully executed and peace preserved, is read, as a matter of historical practice to authorize the President to use military force where required to protect national interests, unless Congress prohibits such action.[3] After all, the Constitution does not delegate to Congress the power to "conduct" war or to "make" war; it only delegates the power to "declare" war. While an early draft of the Committee on Detail gave Congress the power to "make" war, the framers substituted "declare" in the final draft.[4]

The nature of the executive and congressional war powers is the subject of a long debate—a debate that was initiated when the Constitution was written and continues to the present day. The framers, believing the power to declare war should be granted to the body most broadly representative of the people, vested the power to declare war in Congress.[5]

Alexander Hamilton writing on the executive's role in the *Federalist Papers* endorsed a limited Commander–in–Chief power.

46. Restatement of the Law, 2d, Foreign Relations Law of the United States, § 144(1) (1965).

47. Peter Hay & Ronald D. Rotunda, The United States Federal System: Legal Integration in the American Experience 59–60 (Giuffré, Milan 1982).

48. Tent.Draft No. 1, at 70 (Reporter's Notes to § 135) (April 1, 1980).

49. Tent.Draft No. 1, at 70 (Reporter's Notes to § 135) (April 1, 1980), at 64, § 135(1). See also, id. at 66, Comment (a).

§ 6.10

1. U.S.Const. art. 1, § 8.

2. U.S.Const. art. 2.

3. See Edward Corwin, The President: Office and Powers 134 (4th rev. ed. 1957).

4. 2 Max Farrand, The Records of the Federal Convention of 1787, at 313, 318–19 (Rev. ed. 1937).

5. C. Berdahl, War Powers of the Executive in the United States 79 (1921).

The President will have only the occasional command of such part of the militia of the nation as by legislative provision may be called into the actual service of the Union. [The Commander–in–Chief power] would amount to nothing more than the command and direction of the military and naval forces, as first general and admiral of the Confederacy.[6]

Hamilton believed the President was powerless to declare war and to raise armies.[7] However, he expressed fear that the war power would be construed to prohibit raising armies in peace time thereby preventing the nation from preparing to defend itself against future invasions.[8]

James Madison, sharing Hamilton's apprehension, suggested that the nation's interest in self preservation would prevail over any barriers that limited military preparations and precautions if there was no declared war.[9] Although the framers intended to place a constitutional check upon the President's power to involve the nation in war, they also wanted to be certain that the President had authority to mobilize military forces to repel sudden attacks.[10]

Historical Justifications for Presidential Military Interventions. Historically Presidents have justified their authorization of military intervention abroad without congressional approval on three basic theories: Self defense, neutrality and collective security.[11] First, Presidents have asserted they have power to order defensive military action in response to aggression without consulting Congress. The second theory, the neutrality theory, was developed as a justification for military intervention in foreign countries to protect United States nationals and property. The executive could send troops abroad for a limited security purpose but the troops were to be neutral as to any conflict in the foreign country. Third, presidential authorization of military intervention without prior congressional approval, has been justified as within the executive's power under collective security agreements such as the Organization of American States (O.A.S.), The North Atlantic Treaty Organization (N.A.T.O.) and the South East Asian Treaty Organization (S.E.A.T.O.).[12]

Self defense was the first theory used to justify expansion of executive war power. Hamilton, for example, strongly criticized President Jefferson's hesitation to take aggressive action against Tripoli without the consent of Congress after the Beys declared war against the United States. Hamilton wrote that no congressional approval was necessary for any defensive military action taken by the President as long as the United States was not the aggressor.[13]

Subsequent Presidents have relied on the self defense theory many times since Hamilton made this argument. For example, during the Mexican American War, Congress, after heated debate, upheld President Polk's orders authorizing the United States troops to attack first in self defense if the enemy crossed the Rio

---

6. A. Hamilton, The Federalist Papers, No. 69 at 417–18 (Rossiter ed. 1961).

7. A. Hamilton, The Federalist Papers, No. 69 at 418 (Rossiter ed. 1961).

8. A. Hamilton, The Federalist Papers, No. 25 at 162–67 (Rossiter ed. 1961).

9. J. Madison, The Federalist Papers, No. 41 at 256–64 (Rossiter ed. 1961).

10. 2 Max Farrand, The Records of the Federal Convention of 1787 at 313, 318–19 (rev. ed. 1937).

11. The "Pacificus" and "Helvidius" letters on the foreign affairs power also reflect the sentiments of Madison and Hamilton on the division of the war power between the President and Congress. Madison argued the foreign affairs power could be used to commit the nation

to a course of action leading to war. He concluded that, by virtue of the constitutional provision expressly granting Congress the power to declare war, the foreign affairs power must also be vested in Congress. Hamilton perceived the determination of the direction of foreign policy to be an inherently executive power although the implementation of such power depended upon subsequent acts of Congress. Edward Corwin The President: Office and Powers 177–81 (4th rev. ed. 1957).

12. The "Yale Paper"—Indochina: The Constitutional Crisis, 116 Cong.Rec. S 7117–S 7123 (May 13, 1970). See generally, Note, Congress, the President, and the Power to Commit Forces to Combat, 81 Harv.L.Rev. 1771, 1778–85 (1968).

13. A. Hamilton, Works of Alexander Hamilton 746–47 (J. Hamilton ed. 1851).

Grande into disputed territory.[14]

The Supreme Court specifically approved of this theory in the *Prize Cases*,[15] which arose during the Civil War. The Supreme Court found President Lincoln had the right to blockade southern states without a congressional declaration of war. Writing for a five to four majority, Justice Grier stated that the President has the power to determine if hostilities are sufficiently serious to compel him to act to suppress the belligerency or take defensive measures:

> [The President] has no power to initiate or declare a war either against a foreign nation or a domestic State. But by the Acts of Congress of February 28, 1795, and 3d of March, 1807, he is authorized to call out the military and naval forces of the United States in case of invasion by foreign nations, and to suppress insurrection against the government of a State or of the United States.
>
> If a war be made by invasion of a foreign nation, the President is not only authorized but bound to resist force by force. He does not initiate the war, but is bound to accept the challenge without waiting for any special legislative authority. And whether the hostile party be a foreign invader, or States organized in rebellion, it is none the less a war, although the declaration of it be "unilateral."[16]

The executive, the Court indicated, was also authorized to determine what degree of force should be used to respond to the conflict.[17]

Presidential actions in the twentieth century led to a steady erosion of the congressional war making power. Under the guise of the neutrality theory, Theodore Roosevelt sent troops to Panama in 1903. In reality, the troops fought the Colombian Army.[18] President Truman, without seeking Congressional authorization, ordered troops to South Korea to repel the North Korean invasion. Although Truman described involvement in Korea as a "police action," not a war, public opposition to the President's action developed as the nation became deeply involved in a major military conflict.[19] During the subsequent administration, President Eisenhower was careful to seek congressional approval prior to authorizing military involvement in Formosa and the Suez crisis.[20]

A modern trend has been for the President to secure general Congressional authorization to fall back upon in case the executive's power to authorize military intervention in foreign conflicts is later attacked. President Kennedy justified the adoption of the quarantine during the Cuban missile crisis on the basis of a joint Congressional resolution and the United States' O.A.S. collective security arrangement.[21]

President Johnson initially justified his decision to send the marines to the Dominican Republic under the neutrality theory, as necessary to protect United States' nationals. Later, in ordering American troops to Santo Domingo, he relied on the provisions of the Rio Treaty adopted pursuant to the O.A.S. Charter.[22] President Johnson relied upon the Commander–in–Chief clause and the Gulf of Tonkin Resolution to justify his authorization of

---

14. Act of May 13, 1846, ch. 16, 9 Stat. 9. Later, however, the House of Representatives amended a resolution of thanks to General Taylor to include language charging that Polk had unconstitutionally and unnecessarily involved the United States in a war. Note, Congress, the President, and the Power to Commit Forces to Combat, 81 Harv.L.Rev. 1771, 1780 n. 50 (1968).

15. 67 U.S. (2 Black) 635, 17 L.Ed. 459 (1862).

16. 67 U.S. at 668, 17 L.Ed. at 477.

17. 67 U.S. at 670, 17 L.Ed. at 477.

18. S. Bemis, A Diplomatic History of the United States 515–19 (4th ed. 1955).

19. R. Leckie, The Wars of America 850–58 (1968).

20. T. Bailey, A Diplomatic History of the American People 834–44 (6th ed. 1958).

21. See Presidential Proclamation No. 3504, 27 Fed. Reg. 10,401 (1962) where Kennedy justified the quarantine and accompanying, measures taken against Cuba and the Soviet Union on the basis of the joint resolution and a resolution passed by the Organization of American States authorizing the quarantine.

22. 2 A. Chayes, T. Ehrlich and A. Lowenfeld, International Legal Process 1179–82 (1969). Excellent accounts of the Dominican Republic Crisis are found in, N.Y. Times, Apr. 29, 1965, at 1, col. 8 and N.Y. Times, May 3, 1965, at 10, col. 1.

escalated military involvement in Viet Nam.[23]

President Reagan justified the 1983 American intervention in Grenada on three grounds: a confidential appeal from the Governor General of Grenada; a request for help from the Organization of Eastern Caribbean States, which relied on their collective defense treaty; and the need to protect approximately 1000 U.S. nationals on the island.[24]

From 1798 to 2000, there were over 200 cases where the President transferred arms or other war material abroad or actually sent troops, all without Congressional involvement.[25]

§ 6.11 Economic Regulations and the War Power

The power of the President and Congress to impose economic regulations in times of war provides insight into the nature and scope of the war power. In *Woods v. Cloyd W. Miller Co.*[1] the Supreme Court reversed the District Court, which had held that Congress' authority to regulate rent by virtue of the war power ended with the Presidential Proclamation terminating World War II hostilities.[2] The Supreme Court found that the war power sustained Title II of the Housing and Rent Act of 1947.

The Court relied on a passage from *Hamilton v. Kentucky Distilleries & Warehouse Co.*,[3] which had included in the war power the power "to remedy the evils which have arisen from

[the war's] rise and progress" and continues until the emergency has ended. Thus, cessation of hostilities is not necessarily the end of a war.[4] Because the power to wage war is the power to wage it successfully,[5] the context of a war or preparations for a war or its winding down may justify extensive legislative and executive power.[6]

The Steel Seizure Case. *Youngstown Sheet & Tube Co. v. Sawyer*[7] discussed the President's power to impose economic regulations under the Commander–in–Chief clause and other constitutional provisions. Apprehensive that an impending steel worker's strike would endanger national security, President Truman issued an executive order instructing Secretary of Commerce Sawyer to seize and operate many of the nation's steel mills.[8] Truman justified the executive order as valid under the constitutional and statutory power vested in him as President and Commander–in–Chief.

Pursuant to the President's order, the Secretary of Commerce seized the steel mills. Sawyer directed the presidents of the mills to operate their facilities in compliance with regulations that the Department of Commerce issued. Truman immediately informed Congress of these events, but the legislature failed to take any action.[9] Congress had previously enacted legislation for handling situations of this nature but, had expressly refused to authorize governmental seizure of property.[10]

23. Citing U.S. Dept. of State, The Legality of the United States Participation in the Defense of Viet Nam, 54 Dept. State Bull. 474, 484–85 (1966).

24. Riggs, The Grenada Intervention: A Legal Analysis, 109 Military L.Rev. 1, 2 (1985).

25. See, 1 Ronald D. Rotunda & John E. Nowak, Treatise on Constitutional Law: Substance and Procedure, at § 6.10 and Appendix following § 6.10 (West Pub. Co. 3d ed. 1999).

§ 6.11

1. 333 U.S. 138, 68 S.Ct. 421, 92 L.Ed. 596 (1948).

2. 333 U.S. at 140, 68 S.Ct. at 422.

3. 251 U.S. 146, 40 S.Ct. 106, 64 L.Ed. 194 (1919).

4. Woods v. Cloyd W. Miller Co., 333 U.S. 138, 141, 68 S.Ct. 421, 423, 92 L.Ed. 596 (1948).

5. E.g., United States v. Macintosh, 283 U.S. 605, 622, 51 S.Ct. 570, 574, 75 L.Ed. 1302 (1931); Home Building &

Loan Ass'n v. Blaisdell, 290 U.S. 398, 426, 54 S.Ct. 231, 235, 78 L.Ed. 413 (1934); Hirabayashi v. United States, 320 U.S. 81, 93, 63 S.Ct. 1375, 1382, 87 L.Ed. 1774 (1943). Thus the war power has been used to justify internment of Japanese–American citizens in World War II. See, e.g., Korematsu v. United States, 323 U.S. 214, 65 S.Ct. 193, 89 L.Ed. 194 (1944), rehearing denied 324 U.S. 885, 65 S.Ct. 674, 89 L.Ed. 1435 (1945). *Korematsu* should not be considered good law as to its specific result.

6. E.g., Louis Henkin, Foreign Affairs and the Constitution, 321 n. 15 (1973).

7. 343 U.S. 579, 72 S.Ct. 863, 96 L.Ed. 1153 (1952).

8. 343 U.S. at 583, 77 S.Ct. at 865. Executive Order 10340 April 8, 1952, 17 Fed.Reg. 3139 (1952).

9. 343 U.S. at 583, 77 S.Ct. at 865.

10. Corwin, The Steel Seizure Case: A Judicial Brick Without Straw, 53 Colum.L.Rev. 53, 55–56 (1953). Congress provided alternative solutions for similar problems in the Defense Production Act of 1950, 50 U.S.C.A.App.

The steel companies filed suit against Secretary of Commerce Sawyer in the district court praying for declaratory judgment and injunctive relief. The district court granted the plaintiffs a preliminary injunction, which the appellate court stayed. The Supreme Court, in an expedited proceeding, affirmed the district court's order in a six to three decision finding the executive's seizure order invalid.[11]

Justice Black wrote the opinion for the Court in which Justices Frankfurter, Douglas, Jackson and Burton concurred. Justice Clark concurred in the judgment of the Court. Black stated that the issue of the Constitutional validity of President Truman's order was ripe for determination.

The Court found that no express or implied statutory provision authorized the President's seizure order.[12] The Court rejected the argument that the order should be upheld as a valid exercise of the President's Commander-in-Chief power. In response to the government's contention that numerous cases have found military commanders entitled to broad powers, Black stated:

> Such cases need not concern us here. Even though "theater of war" be an expanding concept, we cannot with faithfulness to our constitutional system hold that the Commander in Chief of the Armed Forces has the ultimate power as such to take possession of private property in order to keep labor disputes from stopping production. This is a job for the Nation's law-makers, not for its military authorities.[13]

Black concluded that the executive power vested in the President by the Constitution, particularly his duty to see that the laws are faithfully executed, refuted the idea that the chief executive can make laws.[14] Congress has "exclusive constitutional authority to make laws necessary and proper to carry out the

powers vested by the Constitution" in the federal government.[15] The "necessary and proper" clause applies to Congress, not to the executive branch.

In his concurring opinion Justice Frankfurter indicated he was not drawing conclusions as to what powers the President would have had in the absence of legislation applicable to the seizure.[16] What was at issue was the President's authorization of the steel seizure after Congress had expressly refused to support this course of action.

> In formulating legislation for dealing with industrial conflicts, Congress could not more clearly and emphatically have withheld authority....[17]

Frankfurter warned, however:

> It is an inadmissibly narrow conception of American constitutional law to confine it to the words of the Constitution and disregard the gloss which life has written upon them. In short, a systematic, unbroken, executive practice, long pursued to the knowledge of the Congress and never before questioned ... may be treated as a gloss on "executive Power" vested in the President by § 1 of Art. II.[18]

Prior incidents of industrial seizures, Frankfurter concluded, did not indicate a past history of Congressional acquiescence of executive authority in this area.[19]

Justice Douglas stated in his concurring opinion that the branch of government with "the power to pay compensation for a seizure is the only one able to authorize a seizure or make lawful one that the President has effected. That seems to me to be the necessary result of the condemnation provision in the Fifth Amendment."[20]

§ 2071 (1952); The Labor Management Relations (Taft-Hartley) Act of 1947, 29 U.S.C.A. §§ 141–197 (1952); and the Selective Service Act of 1948, 50 U.S.C.A.App. §§ 451–462 (1952).

11. 343 U.S. at 584–86, 72 S.Ct. at 865–66.
12. 343 U.S. at 584–86, 72 S.Ct. at 865–66.
13. 343 U.S. at 587, 72 S.Ct. at 867.
14. 343 U.S. at 587, 72 S.Ct. at 867.
15. 343 U.S. at 588–89, 72 S.Ct. at 867.
16. 343 U.S. at 597, 72 S.Ct. at 890–91.
17. 343 U.S. at 602, 72 S.Ct. at 893.
18. 343 U.S. at 610–11, 72 S.Ct. at 897.
19. 343 U.S. at 613, 72 S.Ct. at 898.
20. 343 U.S. at 631–32, 72 S.Ct. at 887.

Justice Jackson's Three–Part Analysis.
Justice Jackson, in his separate concurrence, argued that the President's powers "are not fixed but fluctuate, depending upon their disjunction or conjunction with those of Congress."[21] The scope of the President's war powers, Jackson believed, depended upon the conditions existing at the time the executive asserted his authority. He developed a three part Twilight Zone analysis.

First, when the President's authority is at its maximum, if he acts pursuant to an express authorization of Congress.[22] If the President had seized the steel mills pursuant to Congressional grant of authority, the constitutional validity of his action would probably have been upheld.

Secondly, if the President acted:

in the absence of either a congressional grant or denial of authority, he can only rely upon his own independent powers, but there is a zone of twilight in which he and Congress may have concurrent authority, or in which its distribution is uncertain. Therefore, congressional inertia ... may sometimes ... enable, if not invite, measures on independent presidential responsibility.[23]

When, however, the President acts contrary to the express or implied will of Congress then the executive power falls to the third part of the analysis, an extremely low level, his "lowest ebb" of authority. The President can then:

rely only upon his own constitutional powers minus any constitutional powers of Congress over the matter. Courts can sustain exclu-

sive presidential control in such a case only by disabling the Congress from acting upon the subject. Presidential claim to a power at once so conclusive and preclusive must be scrutinized with caution.[24]

Jackson concluded that the steel seizure order was contrary to the will of Congress and, as a consequence, could only be upheld if such seizures were found to be within the power of the executive and beyond the scope of congressional authority.[25] The President's actions were not of that type.[26]

§ 6.12   The War Powers Resolution

The ability of the executive to deploy the military to foreign nations to fight in informal wars created a growing discontent with what many have regarded as the President's assumption of congressional war power during the Viet Nam conflict. To restore what has been argued to be the balance intended by the framers, Congress passed the War Powers Resolution over a presidential veto on November 7, 1973.

The War Powers Resolution restricts the executive's authority to involve the United States in foreign controversies without Congressional approval. Specific provisions of the Resolution, however, allow the President to send the military into combat without requesting authorization from Congress if the United States or one of its territories is attacked.[1]

The War Powers Resolution raises many interesting and unresolved questions. Is the Resolution binding? If it is, who has standing to sue claiming a violation of the provisions? No

---

21. 343 U.S. at 635, 72 S.Ct. at 870.

22. 343 U.S. at 635, 72 S.Ct. at 870.

23. 343 U.S. at 637, 72 S.Ct. at 871 (emphasis added).

24. 343 U.S. at 637–38, 72 S.Ct. at 871.

25. 343 U.S. at 640, 72 S.Ct. at 872–73.
The Court endorsed and applied Jackson's analysis in Dames & Moore v. Regan, 453 U.S. 654, 669, 101 S.Ct. 2972, 2981, 69 L.Ed.2d 918 (1981), but noted that "it is doubtless the case that executive action in any particular instance falls, not neatly in one of three pigeonholes, but rather at some point along a spectrum running from explicit congressional authorization to explicit congressional prohibition."

26. Justice Burton stated in his concurrence that the seizure order was repugnant to the separation of powers theory. In a concurring opinion, Justice Clark indicated

that although the President has extensive authority to act in times of national emergency this power is subject to limitations prescribed by Congress.

In the dissent, Justice Vinson, joined by Justices Reed and Minton, rationalized that the President was within the scope of his constitutional authority when he ordered the steel mills seized as an emergency situation existed.

§ 6.12

1. War Powers Resolution, 50 U.S.C.A. §§ 1541–48. Rotunda, *Fixing the War Powers Act*, The Heritage Lectures, No. 529 (The Heritage Foundation, 1995); Rotunda, The War Powers Act in Perspective, 2 Michigan Law & Policy Review 1 (1997).

specific language in the Resolution resolves the standing issue. Perhaps Justice Brennan's theory, expressed in the different context of other cases—that the only requirement for standing is injury in fact[2]—could provide a basis for military personnel sent abroad in violation of the resolution to sue the President.

If standing is found to exist, it may well be that judicial review of cases under this law is foreclosed by the doctrine of political questions.[3] The impact on foreign affairs of a judicial decision contrary to the President's military actions already underway may suggest that questions regarding provisions of the War Powers Resolution should be considered nonjusticiable and immune from judicial review as political questions.

Even if this War Powers Resolution were reviewable in litigation, its constitutionality may be subject to a presidential claim that the resolution improperly seeks to subtract from his inherent powers. However, in that case, the War Powers Resolution should still be relevant, for under Justice Jackson's analysis in the Steel Seizure case, the President's war powers should be at their lowest ebb: if he would act contrary to the War Powers Resolution, he would then have only his own powers minus any Constitutional powers of Congress to reduce his powers.

Legislative Veto. Even without raising the specter of inherent presidential powers, many commentators have concluded that section 5(c) of the War Powers Resolution is an unconstitutional legislative veto and therefore invalid in the wake of *Immigration and Naturaliza-*

tion Service v. Chadha.[4] Section 5(c) purports to allow Congress to force the President to withdraw U.S. armed forces engaged in hostilities outside the territorial United States. *Chadha* requires that action having "the purpose and effect of altering the legal rights, duties and relations of persons, including . . . Executive Branch officials,"[5] must be subjected to the possibility of presidential veto. But section 5(c) is not subject to a presidential veto. Adoption of a concurrent resolution under section 5(c) has the purpose and effect of altering the rights and duties of the President. Thus, *Chadha* invalidate the legislative veto provision in the War Powers Resolution.[6]

§ 6.13 Military Courts: An Introduction

Congress established military courts pursuant to its Article I power to make rules for the government and regulation of the land and naval forces and its power to make laws that are necessary and proper for implementing that power.[1]

During Wartime. During war or insurrection, military courts dispense Justice to both civilian and military transgressors. In wartime, even when civil courts continue to function and try nonmilitary crimes, enemy combatants may be tried by courts martial under the law of war,[2] whether the crimes were committed in a war zone or through entrance by stealth into a non-combatant zone.

The government can declare Martial law if, by reason of civil disturbance or invasion, the civil courts cannot function. During the period

---

2. See Association of Data Processing Service Organizations v. Camp, 397 U.S. 150, 90 S.Ct. 827, 25 L.Ed.2d 184 (1970) (Brennan, J., concurring); Barlow v. Collins, 397 U.S. 159, 90 S.Ct. 832, 25 L.Ed.2d 192 (1970) (Brennan, J., concurring).

3. See, Crockett v. Reagan, 720 F.2d 1355 (D.C.Cir. 1983), certiorari denied 467 U.S. 1251, 104 S.Ct. 3533, 82 L.Ed.2d 839 (1984), affirming 558 F.Supp. 893 (D.D.C. 1982) (holding that the issue whether a report is required to be submitted under § 4(a)(1) of the War Powers Resolution is a political question, at least in the context of El Salvador combat).

4. 462 U.S. 919, 103 S.Ct. 2764, 77 L.Ed.2d 317 (1983).

5. 462 U.S. at 952, 103 S.Ct. at 2784.

6. Glennon, The War Powers Resolution Ten Years Later: More Politics Than Law, 78 Am.J. of Internat'l L. 571, 577 (1984); Rotunda, Fixing the War Powers Act, The Heritage Lectures, No. 529 (The Heritage Foundation, 1995). On treason, see 1 Ronald D. Rotunda & John E. Nowak, Treatise on Constitutional Law: Substance and Procedure §§ 6.14–6.16 (West Group, 3d 1999).

§ 6.13

1. U.S.Const. art. I, § 8.

2. The law of war is a branch of international law that prescribes the rights and obligations of belligerents and other persons resident in a theater of war. For an explication of the law of war, see 2 Winthrop, Military Law and Precedents, The Law of War (2d ed.; 1920 reprint).

of martial law, all crimes are tried by courts martial. Martial law must end when civil courts can again function; court-martial under the law of war can occur at least until peace has been declared.

During Peacetime. During peacetime, military courts play the limited role of governing members of the armed forces. Although courts-martial may try members of the armed forces whether they are stationed within the United States or on foreign soil, these courts do not have jurisdiction to try those family members who accompany the servicemen, nor do they have jurisdiction to try civilian employees. Military courts have limited jurisdiction: they can try only persons who were members of the armed forces at the time of the offense charged; there is no requirement, however, that there be any "service connection" to the offense charged.[3] The Court reached that conclusion only after traveling down a long road.

The Supreme Court has severely limited the jurisdiction of courts-martial because courts-martial are established under Article I: they are not Article III courts.[4] Courts-martial do not have an independent judiciary with life tenure;[5] do not provide a jury of the accused's peers;[6] do not provide legal counsel for the accused in all non petty offenses;[7] and do not require indictment by grand jury.[8]

Article III courts, including the United States Supreme Court, did not have the power to directly review decisions of courts-martial until 1983, when Congress enacted the Military Justice Act of 1983.[9] Military prisoners may also petition Article III courts to grant a writ of habeas corpus, but review (in even collateral proceedings) is limited to ascertaining that the military court had jurisdiction and that it considered the defendant's claims. A civil court generally must abstain until the conclusion of the military trial before granting the writ of habeas corpus.

---

3. Solorio v. United States, 483 U.S. 435, 107 S.Ct. 2924, 97 L.Ed.2d 364 (1987), rehearing denied 483 U.S. 1056, 108 S.Ct. 30, 97 L.Ed.2d 819 (1987), overruling O'Callahan v. Parker, 395 U.S. 258, 89 S.Ct. 1683, 23 L.Ed.2d 291 (1969).

4. See Ronald D. Rotunda, Monitoring the Conversations of Prisoners, 13 The Professional Lawyer 1 (ABA, No. 3, 2002); Ronald D. Rotunda, No POWs: Unlawful Combatants, American Law, and the Geneva Convention, National Review Online, Jan. 29, 2002, http://www.nationalreview.com/comment/comment-rotunda012902.shtml

5. See, e.g., 10 U.S.C.A. § 826. The requirement of an independent judiciary is found in Article III of the Constitution and applies only to Article III courts.

6. See, e.g., 10 U.S.C.A. § 825.

7. Middendorf v. Henry, 425 U.S. 25, 96 S.Ct. 1281, 47 L.Ed.2d 556 (1976), on remand 536 F.2d 303 (9th Cir. 1976).

8. U.S.Const. amend. V; Ex parte Milligan, 71 U.S. (4 Wall.) 2, 18 L.Ed. 281 (1866).

9. P.L. 98–209 (Dec. 6, 1983). See 1 R. Rotunda & J. Nowak, Treatise on Constitutional Law: Substance and Procedure § 6.13(d) (West Group, 3d ed.1999).

Chapter 7

THE PRESIDENT AND CONGRESS

§ 7.1 Executive Privilege

(a) The Early Cases

The Constitution, while enumerating the President's powers and privileges, does not clearly spell out his amenability to service of process. In 1866, in *Mississippi v. Johnson,*[1] Attorney General Stanberry claimed presidential immunity and argued that the President is beyond legal process, analogizing that the President was the ultimate sovereign of the country and should enjoy the same type of privilege as European potentates.[2] Of course, our country had a revolution to rid ourselves of foreign potentates.

The Supreme Court dismissed the complaint on different grounds and carefully disavowed a decision based on a theory of total presidential immunity from process.[3] The Court distinguished judicial power to require the President to perform a single ministerial act from the power to control the President's exercise of broad constitutional discretion in carrying out his duties. The Court said that it had "no jurisdiction of a bill to enjoin the President in the performance of his official duties."[4] Despite the fact that Court never clearly reached the issue, some commentators broadly interpreted *Johnson* to mean that the President is immune from legal process when performing what he deems to be his constitutional duties.[5]

However, before *Johnson,* indeed, beginning with *Marbury v. Madison,*[6] the Court has always asserted power to determine and enforce constitutional and other legal obligations of executive branch officials, even when the alleged wrongs were done under the auspices of

---

§ 7.1

1. 71 U.S. (4 Wall.) 475, 18 L.Ed. 437 (1866). On the history of Presidents as witnesses, see Rotunda, Presidents and Ex–Presidents as Witnesses: A Brief Historical Footnote, 1975 U. of Ill.L.Forum 1. On presidential domestic power in general, see 1 R. Rotunda & J. Nowak, Treatise on Constitutional Law: Substance and Procedure §§ 7.1–7.5 (West Group, 3d ed. 1999).

Subpoenas of the President. Prior to the subpoena of a President upheld in United States v. Nixon, 418 U.S. 683, 94 S.Ct. 3090, 41 L.Ed.2d 1039 (1974), the courts only twice before issued a subpoena to a sitting President. The first was the subpoena issued to President Jefferson in United States v. Burr, 25 F.Cas. 30 (No. 14,692D) (C.C.Va. 1807); Chief Justice Marshall, sitting on circuit during the treason trial of Aaron Burr, was the trial judge. Burr intended to obtain a letter sent to Jefferson as well as various documents. The extent to which Jefferson complied is unclear. Jefferson withheld parts of the letter, and Marshall apparently accepted this withholding. The letter was not introduced in evidence. See Rhodes, What Really Happened to the Jefferson Subpoenas, 60 A.B.A.J. 52 (1974); Berger, The President, Congress, and the Courts, 83 Yale L.J. 1111 (1974).

On January 3, 1818, President Monroe became the second President to be served with a subpoena while in office. See Opinion of Attorney General Wirt, dated January 13, 1818, in the Records of the Judge Advocate General (Navy), Record Group 125, National Archives Building. A large part of the opinion is reprinted in 1 R. Rotunda & J. Nowak, Treatise on Constitutional Law: Substance and Procedure § 7.1(c) (West Group, 3d ed. 1999). This handwritten Opinion concluded that, in appropriate circumstances, it is proper to subpoena the President. President Clinton's subpoenas are discussed below.

2. 71 U.S. (4 Wall.) at 484.

3. 71 U.S. (4 Wall.) at 498.

4. 71 U.S. (4 Wall.) at 501. See also, Marbury v. Madison, 5 U.S. (1 Cranch) 137, 169–71, 2 L.Ed. 60, 71 (1803), which makes the same distinction.

5. See, e.g., C. Burdick, The Law of the American Constitution (1922) § 50, at 125–27; 3 W. Willoughby, The Constitutional Law of the United States (2d ed. 1929) §§ 979–80, at 1497–1500.

6. 5 U.S. (1 Cranch) 137, 2 L.Ed. 60 (1803).

presidential command.[7]

Youngstown Sheet & Tube Co. v. Sawyer[8] demonstrated the power of the courts to review the boundaries of executive action. The Court forced Secretary of Commerce Sawyer to return to their private owners the steel mills that he had seized on President Truman's order to terminate a wartime labor dispute. The Commerce Secretary was the nominal defendant, but President Truman was the real party in interest.

(b) The Watergate Tapes Case: *United States v. Nixon*

Though the courts have reviewed actions of executive officials since *Marbury*, in none of these early cases did litigants issue process directly against the President. *United States v. Nixon*,[9] one of the significant legal aftermaths of the famous Watergate break-in, put this issue squarely before the courts because President Nixon claimed that the secret tape recordings (which were subject to subpoena) were directly under his control and solely in his custody. Thus, when the Watergate Special Prosecutor wanted the tapes, he subpoenaed the President directly, rather than subpoena a nominal third party.

The legal issue began on March 1, 1974, when a grand jury sitting in the District of Columbia indicted seven of President Nixon's presidential aides and campaign staff for conspiracy to defraud the United States and to obstruct Justice. The grand jury named the President as an unindicted coconspirator. The Watergate Special Prosecutor moved the District Court to issue a subpoena *duces tecum*, requiring the President to produce certain memoranda, papers, and tapes that related to

specific meetings between the President and others. Nixon publicly released edited transcripts of 43 conversations, including edited portions of 20 conversations subject to the subpoena, but the President's attorneys moved to quash the subpoena for the *actual tapes* on the ground of executive privilege.[10]

The district court rejected the presidential arguments and ordered the tapes and documents to be delivered to the court on or before May 31. On May 24 the President asked the court of appeals for a writ of mandamus, seeking review of the lower court's action. The same day, the Special Prosecutor filed a petition in the Supreme Court for writ of certiorari before judgment. The Court granted the petition on May 31, 1974, the effect of which was to bypass the Court of Appeals and to bring the case immediately from the district court to the Supreme Court for review. The Supreme Court ordered that the subpoenaed material be produced forthwith, affirming the district court's denial of the President's motion to quash.

Chief Justice Burger,[11] for a unanimous Court, quickly disposed of the procedural issues by holding that the district court's order was "appealable" notwithstanding the finality requirement of the federal statute governing petitions for certiorari.[12] The Court also held that the specific procedural requirements for a subpoena *duces tecum* under the Federal Rules of Criminal Procedure, Rule 17(c), were met. Citing the Attorney General's regulations delegating unique authority and tenure to the Special Prosecutor, the Court concluded that sufficient adverseness existed to make the case

---

7. See also, Kendall v. United States ex rel. Stokes, 37 U.S. (12 Pet.) 524, 9 L.Ed. 1181 (1838); Land v. Dollar, 190 F.2d 623 (D.C.Cir.1951), vacated as moot 344 U.S. 806, 73 S.Ct. 8, 97 L.Ed. 628 (1952).

8. 343 U.S. 579, 72 S.Ct. 863, 96 L.Ed. 1153 (1952).

9. 418 U.S. 683, 94 S.Ct. 3090, 41 L.Ed.2d 1039 (1974), certiorari denied 431 U.S. 933, 97 S.Ct. 2641, 53 L.Ed.2d 250 (1977), rehearing denied 433 U.S. 916, 97 S.Ct. 2992, 53 L.Ed.2d 1103 (1977).

10. Subsequently, Nixon moved to expunge the grand jury's action naming him as an unindicted coconspirator.

11. Justice Rehnquist (who was a friend and worked with former Attorney General John Mitchell, one of the

indicted defendants) took no part in the consideration or decision of the case.

12. Court of appeals jurisdiction under 28 U.S.C.A. § 1291 encompasses only "final decisions of the district courts", but the Supreme Court noted that "[t]o require a President of the United States to place himself in the posture of disobeying an order of a court merely to trigger the procedural mechanism for review of the ruling would be unseemly, and would present an unnecessary occasion for constitutional confrontation between two branches of the Government." 418 U.S. at 691–92, 94 S.Ct. at 3099.

"justiciable" notwithstanding the "intra-branch" character of the dispute.[13]

The Court then addressed the key issue of executive privilege. The Court summarily rejected the President's first line of argument, that the separation of powers doctrine precludes judicial review of a presidential claim of privilege. Quoting the famous declaration in *Marbury v. Madison*[14] that it is the ultimate province and duty of the judiciary to decide what the law is, the Court noted that, "[a]ny other conclusion would be contrary to the basic concept of separation of powers and the checks and balances that flow from the scheme of tripartite government."[15]

President Nixon's second argument was that, as a matter of constitutional law, executive privilege prevails over the subpoena *duces tecum*. For the first time, the Supreme Court gave presidential executive privilege a stamp of approval, though it was a much narrower approval than President Nixon had wished.

The Court agreed that the President has a prima facie privilege to maintain the confidentiality of internal executive communications, because possible public dissemination of such communications could tend to inhibit frank discussion and advice in the decision-making process. The absence of an express constitutional provision was no bar to the assertion of such a privilege, because "[c]ertain powers and privileges flow from the nature of enumerated powers; the protection of the confidentiality of presidential communications has similar constitutional underpinnings."[16] To the extent that the presidential interest in confidentiality "relates to the effective discharge of a President's powers, it is constitutionally based."[17]

Although the Court recognized the need for executive privilege, the Court made it clear that such a privilege is not absolute and un-qualified. The prima facie privilege must yield to the higher claims of judicial process in any criminal case where either the prosecution or defense has demonstrated a need for the evidence subpoenaed, and the evidence would otherwise be admissible at trial.[18] The Court accorded "great deference" to the felt need of the President for complete objectivity and candor from his advisers. However, the Court reasoned:

> [W]hen the privilege depends solely on the broad, undifferentiated claim of public interest in the confidentiality of such conversations, a confrontation of other values arises. Absent a claim of need to protect *military, diplomatic, or sensitive national security secrets,* we find it difficult to accept the argument that even the very important interest in confidentiality of Presidential communications is significantly diminished by production of such material for *in camera* inspection with all the protection that a district court will be obliged to provide.[19]

In the next paragraph the Court stated that it would upset the constitutional balance to accept a generalized claim of confidentiality by the President in "nonmilitary and nondiplomatic discussions...." The Court gave no explanation why this time it eliminated any reference to "sensitive national security secrets." Several pages later the Supreme Court also referred to "military or diplomatic secrets,"[20] but did not mention the more open-ended category of national security.

Finally, the Court made it clear that it is for the judicial branch to decide the extent of the duty of the President and other executive officials to produce evidence. Even though it would accord "high respect to the representations made on behalf of the President,"[21] the Court would make the final determination.

---

13. 418 U.S. at 692–97, 94 S.Ct. at 3099–3102.

14. 5 U.S. (1 Cranch) 137, 177, 2 L.Ed. 60 (1803).

15. 418 U.S. at 704, 94 S.Ct. at 3106.

16. 418 U.S. at 705–06, 94 S.Ct. at 3106.

17. 418 U.S. at 711, 94 S.Ct. at 3109.

18. "The generalized assertion of privilege must yield to the demonstrated, specific need for evidence in a pending criminal trial." 418 U.S. at 713, 94 S.Ct. at 3110.

19. 418 U.S. at 706, 94 S.Ct. at 3107 (emphasis added).

20. 418 U.S. at 710, 94 S.Ct. at 3108.

21. 418 U.S. at 707, 94 S.Ct. at 3107, citing United States v. Burr, 25 F.Cas. 187, 190, 191–192 (No. 14,694) (C.C.Va.1807). On the Burr subpoena issued to President Jefferson by Chief Justice Marshall sitting on circuit during the treason trial of Aaron Burr, see Rotunda, Presidents and Ex–Presidents as Witnesses: A Brief Historical Footnote, 1975 U. of Ill.L.Forum 1, 4–5.

The Court, along with both parties to the litigation, accepted the notion that presidential communications are "presumptively privileged."[22] But the interest in confidentiality in this case was only generalized, and therefore there should be no high deference to the President.[23] Compulsory process to obtain evidence needed "either by the prosecution *or* the defense" is imperative to the function of the courts.[24] Thus, the President's generalized claim could not prevail over the "demonstrated, specific need for evidence in a pending criminal trial."[25]

The Court did slightly tip its hat to presidential concerns by ordering the trial court, in conducting its *in camera* examination, to excise all material not relevant and admissible.

Noncriminal Litigation. The Court explicitly did not consider the extent to which it would weigh and balance the interests in a noncriminal case involving the President's generalized interest in confidentiality. The *Nixon* decision leaves open how the Court would weight a generalized interest in confidentiality with the need for relevant evidence, in *civil* litigation or in a *congressional hearing*.

22. 418 U.S. at 708, 94 S.Ct. at 3108.

23. 418 U.S. at 711, 94 S.Ct. at 3109. The Court contrasted other cases that did grant high deference. Chicago & Southern Air Lines v. Waterman S.S. Corp., 333 U.S. 103, 111, 68 S.Ct. 431, 436, 92 L.Ed. 568 (1948) (foreign policy considerations; no claim of executive privilege); United States v. Reynolds, 345 U.S. 1, 10, 73 S.Ct. 528, 533, 97 L.Ed. 727 (1953) (military matters; claimant's demand for evidence in a Tort Claims Act case rejected).

24. 418 U.S. at 709, 94 S.Ct. at 3108 (emphasis added).

25. 418 U.S. at 713, 94 S.Ct. at 3110.

26. 418 U.S. at 712 n. 19, 94 S.Ct. at 3109 n. 19. One circuit court has, without much reasoning, concluded that it would not enforce a congressional subpoena for information because the court, after engaging in *ad hoc* balancing, determined the material was not needed that badly. Senate Select Committee on Presidential Campaign Activities v. Nixon, 498 F.2d 725 (D.C.Cir.1974). The D.C. Circuit purported to weigh the congressional interests, but did not bother to explain how it was calibrating the scales or valuing the importance of different interests.

27. Nixon. See, e.g., Nixon v. Fitzgerald, 457 U.S. 731, 735 n. 5, 102 S.Ct. 2690, 2694 n. 5, 73 L.Ed.2d 349, 354 n. 5 (1982) (referring to Nixon's deposition); Halperin v. Kissinger, 401 F.Supp. 272, 274 (D.D.C.1975) (Nixon's deposition ordered in Watergate-related action); Nixon v. Administrator of GSA, 408 F.Supp. 321 (D.D.C.1976) (Nixon's deposition required in case concerning ownership and custody of presidential materials). See also, N.Y. Times, Oct. 30, 1980, at 19, col. 1 (former President Nixon

The Court also did not consider the President's interest in preserving military or diplomatic secrets.[26] The Court will view itself as the arbiter of all inter-branch disputes over this issue and balance its view of the interest in confidentiality against its view of the need of the other branch of government to obtain evidence to effectuate its functions. However, the criminal process is unique in that the President, as chief executive officer, ultimately controls it. There is the added measure of unfairness in allowing the executive branch simultaneously to prosecute someone and then deny that party and the court relevant information, particularly when the secrecy of the information is not essential to legitimate executive interests.

Presidential Appearances in the Aftermath of *United States v. Nixon*. In the years following *United States v. Nixon*, various lower courts have approved subpoenas of Presidents or former Presidents, or those Presidents have appeared voluntarily in civil or criminal litigation or before congressional hearings.[27]

voluntarily testified at trial of former FBI officials accused of authorizing illegal break-in).

Ford. In United States v. Fromme, 405 F.Supp. 578 (E.D.Cal.1975) President Ford was compelled to testify by videotaped deposition at trial of Lynette "Squeaky" Fromme, who had attempted to assassinate Ford. In addition, while President, President Ford voluntarily appeared before a House subcommittee to answer questions that had been raised concerning his pardon of former President Nixon; and on September 15, 1988 Ford voluntarily appeared before a Senate Committee and testified about the War Powers Resolution, which he criticized as "impractical" and "unconstitutional".

Carter. During his presidency, President Carter gave videotaped testimony that was presented at the criminal trial of two Georgia state officials charged with gambling conspiracy, N.Y. Times, April 20, 1987, at 20, col. 5; two years later, President Carter provided videotaped testimony for a grand jury probing charges that Robert Vesco, a fugitive financier, had enlisted the White House to quash extradition proceedings against him, N.Y. Times, March 2, 1980, at 39, col. 1. Also while President, President Carter was interviewed under oath by the Counsel on Professional Responsibility pursuant to a Department of Justice order to investigate "for criminal, civil and administration purposes" any offenses resulting from his brother Billy Carter's relations with the Libyan Government. Inquiry into the Matter of Billy Carter and Libya, Hearings Before the Subcommittee to Investigate the Activities of Individuals Representing the Interests of Foreign Governments of

(c) The Presidential Recordings and Materials Preservation Act

Nixon v. Administrator of General Services Administration,[28] was a unique case that focused on a special federal statute dealing with executive privilege. After President Nixon resigned, Congress enacted the Presidential Recordings and Materials Preservation Act.[29] Title I of this Act directed the Administrator of the General Services Administration to take custody of former President Nixon's presidential papers and tape recordings; provide for their orderly processing and screening; return to the former President those items that were personal in nature; and establish the terms on which public might eventually have access for the remainder of the materials.

The former President brought suit attacking the constitutionality of the Act on a number of grounds, two of which are particularly relevant to this section. The Supreme Court upheld the Act and in so doing decided some important questions of separation of powers and executive privilege.

Separation of Powers. First the Court rejected the argument that the law violated principles of separation of powers. The executive branch, the Court argued, became a party to the Act's regulation when President Ford signed the bill into law; the new administration of President Carter supported the law; and the materials remained in the executive branch in the custody of a presidential appointee, the Administrator of the General Services Administration.

To determine whether a breach of the separation of powers exists, all of these facts are relevant because the "proper inquiry focuses on the extent to which [the Act] prevents the Executive Branch from accomplishing its constitutionally assigned functions."[30] The Court concluded that, on its face, the Act does not create undue disruption of the executive branch.

Taking of Property. Former President Nixon argued that the law, authorizing the Administrator of General Services to take custody of the Presidential papers and tape recordings, amounted to a taking of his property.

the Committee on the Judiciary, United States Senate, Ninety–Sixth Congress, Second Session, Serial No. 96–85, Volumes I and II (1981).

Reagan. United States v. Poindexter, 732 F.Supp. 142, 147 (D.D.C.1990) (citing Rotunda, Presidents and Ex–Presidents as Witnesses: A Brief Historical Footnote, 1975 U. of Ill. Law. Forum 1, 5 [1975]). In this case, the district court ordered videotaped deposition of former President Reagan, at the insistence of criminal defendant Poindexter; the former President testified on videotape, which was introduced in the trial, which was part of the series of trials prosecuted by the statutorily created Independent Counsel and growing out of the Iran–Contra affair.

Clinton. The Whitewater investigation, a failed land deal in Arkansas, led to the appointment of independent counsel Robert Fiske by Attorney General Janet Reno. Later, Congress reenacted the Independent Counsel statute, and a panel of the Washington, D.C. Court of Appeals appointed former Solicitor General Kenneth Starr as the new independent counsel. Both Fiske and Starr interviewed President Clinton and First Lady Hillary Rodham Clinton under oath, for several hours each on various distinct occasions on issues related to the criminal investigation of Whitewater and the couple's personal and campaign finances.

January 26, 1996, was the first time in history that a First Lady (Hillary Rodham Clinton) was forced to testify before a criminal grand jury. Subsequently, also in 1996, President Clinton became the first President in history who was forced to testify involuntarily—pursuant to court-ordered subpoena—in two criminal trials. In both cases

the President testified for the defense, and in both cases the testimony was videotaped. In the first case the jury found all of the defendants guilty; in the second case the jury was hung on some counts and acquitted on others. There was no retrial.

On August 17, 1998 President Clinton became the first sitting President in history to testify before a grand jury as a target. He was informed, prior to his testimony, that he was a target. The grand jury was investigating various matters, including perjury involving Monica Lewinsky, a former White House intern. When the grand jury subpoenaed the President, he initially resisted but then agreed to testify if the subpoena was withdrawn, if he could testify in the White House (with the grand jury linked by video), and if his lawyers could be present. The Independent Counsel agreed with these conditions. Later, the House of Representatives, which used a videotape of the Presidential grand jury testimony, voted to impeach President Clinton; there were an insufficient number of Senators voting to remove him from office. This was the first time that an elected President was impeached. President Andrew Johnson was the first non-elected President to be impeached. The Senate also did not remove Johnson from office.

For further discussion, see, 1 Ronald D. Rotunda & John E. Nowak, Treatise on Constitutional Law: Substance and Procedure § 7.1(c) (West Group, 3d ed. 1999).

28. 433 U.S. 425, 97 S.Ct. 2777, 53 L.Ed.2d 867 (1977).

29. Pub.L. No. 93–526, 44 U.S.C.A. § 2107.

30. 433 U.S. at 443, 97 S.Ct. at 2790.

The Court found it unnecessary and premature to decide who had "legal title" to the tapes and papers, for the Act provided that Nixon would receive just compensation if his economic interests were invaded.[31] If the papers and tapes were really his, Congress could still seize the property if it paid just compensation.[32]

The compensation issue dragged on for years. President Nixon, and later his estate initially sought more than $200 million in compensation for the thousands of secretly recorded tapes and presidential papers that the Government seized when he resigned in 1974. The Government initially offered to pay $2.2 million. Finally, the compensation issue was settled on June 13, 2000. After a lengthy trial in federal district court, the parties agreed to settle, and the Government agreed to compensate President Nixon's estate $18 million.[33]

Executive Privilege. Next the Court turned to the issue of executive privilege and decided several important questions. First the Court held that a former President could assert executive privilege. Although one need not be an incumbent to claim the benefit of the privilege, the Court found it significant that neither of the incumbent Presidents after President Nixon supported his claim. The fact that later Presidents disagreed with Nixon detracted from his claim that the Act intrudes into the executive function. Then the Court decided that the presidential privilege would exist only to those materials whose contents would fall within the narrow scope of the privilege recognized in *United States v. Nixon*,[34] where the subpoenaed information was sought by the Special Prosecutor in a criminal case.

The fact that the Act provided for the screening of materials persuaded the Court that there would be adequate safeguards to protect executive privilege. It is true that someone will be doing the screening and thus will be seeing the materials, but that intrusion is limited to personnel already in the executive branch and sensitive to executive concerns. Moreover, this limited intrusion has adequate justification: "the American people's ability to reconstruct and come to terms with their history [should not] be truncated by an analysis of Presidential privilege that focuses only on the needs of the present."[35]

Republication of Audio Tapes Produced at Trial. Various news organizations sought to copy Watergate tapes that had been introduced at the trial of the Watergate defendants. In *Nixon v. Warner Communications, Inc.*,[36] a divided Court held that neither common law, nor the First Amendment guarantee of free speech and press, nor the Sixth Amendment guarantee of a public trial gave the press the right to copy this evidence publicly received at the public trial. The majority specifically relied on the Presidential Recordings and Materials Preservation Act and held that it was a "decisive element"[37] that led the Court to the conclusion that the common law right of access to judicial records was inapplicable. The Administrator, under that Act, was free to design procedures for public access to the tape recordings. The Court also found inapplicable any First or Sixth Amendment rights of access.[38]

Four Justices dissented.[39] Justice Stevens' dissent caustically remarked:

---

31. Nixon v. Administrator of General Services 433 U.S. 425, 446 n. 8, 97 S.Ct. 2777, 2791 n. 8.

32. Folsom v. Marsh, 9 Fed. Cases No. 4,901 pp. 342, 347 (C.C.D.Mass.1841), where Justice Story held that, that no matter who has title, "from the nature of the public service, or the character of documents, embracing historical, military, or diplomatic information, it may be the right, and even the duty, of the government, to give them publicity, even against the will of the writers."

33. Ronald D. Rotunda, Modern Constitutional Law: Cases and Notes 365 (Thompson–West, 7th ed. 2003).

34. 418 U.S. 683, 94 S.Ct. 3090, 41 L.Ed.2d 1039 (1974).

35. 433 U.S. at 452–53, 97 S.Ct. at 2795 (footnote omitted).

36. 435 U.S. 589, 98 S.Ct. 1306, 55 L.Ed.2d 570 (1978).

37. 435 U.S. at 607, 98 S.Ct. at 1316, 55 L.Ed.2d at 585.

38. 435 U.S. at 608–11, 98 S.Ct. at 1317–19, 55 L.Ed.2d at 586–88.

39. Justice White, joined by Brennan, filed a dissenting opinion. Justice Marshall filed a dissenting opinion. And Justice Stevens filed a dissenting opinion.

Today the Court overturns the decisions of the District Court and the Court of Appeals by giving conclusive weight to the Presidential Recordings and Materials Preservation Act. That Act, far from requiring the District Court to suppress these tapes, manifests Congress' settled resolve "to provide as much public access to the materials as is physically possible as quickly as possible."

... For the Court now to rely on the Act as a basis for reversing the trial judge's considered judgment is ironic to put it mildly.[40]

§ 7.2   Absolute   Versus   Qualified Immunity From Civil Damage Claims Brought Against the President and Other Executive Officials

Like the Clinton Presidency a generation later, the Nixon Presidency spawned litigation and elaboration of the immunity attached to the President. Two important cases involving Nixon and his aides were decided the same day, *Nixon v. Fitzgerald*,[1] and *Harlow v. Fitzgerald*.[2] Fitzgerald was a management analyst for the Department of the Air Force; he was dismissed from his job after having "blown the whistle" in congressional hearings regarding cost overruns of the C–5A transport plane. The Air Force claimed that it terminated him as part of a reduction in force and not in retaliation for his embarrassing testimony.

After various congressional and Civil Service hearings[3] Fitzgerald sued President Nixon and various of his aides, including Butterfield, Harlow, and others. Fitzgerald relied on various statutes and the First Amendment to support his claim. The defendants claimed presidential immunity, and in *Fitzgerald*, the Court, speaking through Justice Powell, dealt with this question.

Presidential Damage Immunity. *Nixon v. Fitzgerald* quickly concluded that there were policies favoring some sort of immunity. The President "occupies a unique position in the constitutional scheme,"[4] diversion of his energies by concern with private lawsuits could raise risks to the functioning of government,[5] and the fragmentary historical evidence supports the notion of some presidential immunity,[6] but the "most compelling arguments" favoring presidential immunity arise from "the Constitution's separation of powers and the judiciary's historical understanding of that doctrine."[7]

The Court then held that "a former President of the United States is entitled to absolute immunity from damages liability predicated on his official acts. We consider this immunity a functionally mandated incident of the President's unique office, rooted in the constitutional tradition of the separation of powers and supported by our history."[8] This immunity from money damages is absolute, but it is *narrowly* limited to claims "predicated on his official acts."

The Court was writing on a slate where no federal statute governed the question. Thus the Court emphasized that this absolute civil damage immunity exists only in those cases where Congress has taken no "express legislative action to subject the President to civil liability for his official acts."[9]

The Court in the past has recognized an absolute immunity in other circumstances—e.g., the prosecutor when he files his indictment, a congressman when he makes a speech in Congress—but in those cases the Court has limited that immunity to performance of par-

---

40.   435 U.S. at 616–17, 98 S.Ct. at 1321–22, 55 L.Ed.2d at 591–92 (Stevens, J., dissenting) (footnotes and internal citation omitted).

§ 7.2

1.   457 U.S. 731, 102 S.Ct. 2690, 73 L.Ed.2d 349 (1982).

2.   457 U.S. 800, 102 S.Ct. 2727, 73 L.Ed.2d 396 (1982).

3.   The Civil Service Hearings Examiner concluded that Fitzgerald had been improperly terminated for "reasons purely personal" to him, but that the evidence did not

support a finding of retaliation. 457 U.S. at 738, 102 S.Ct. at 2696.

4.   457 U.S. at 749, 102 S.Ct. at 2702.

5.   457 U.S. at 751, 102 S.Ct. at 2703.

6.   457 U.S. at 751 n. 31, 102 S.Ct. at 2702 n. 31.

7.   457 U.S. at 752 n. 31, 102 S.Ct. at 2703 n. 31.

8.   457 U.S. at 749, 102 S.Ct. at 2701.

9.   457 U.S. at 748, 102 S.Ct. at 2701 (footnote omitted).

ticular functions of his office.[10] Absolute presidential immunity is not so limited: "we think it appropriate to recognize absolute Presidential immunity from damages liability for acts within the 'outer perimeter' of his official responsibility."[11]

The President has absolute immunity from money damage claims based on acts within the *outer perimeter* of his official responsibility. The reason that this immunity is broader than the absolute immunity of prosecutors and similar government agents (who have immunity limited to the performance of particular functions) is that the President is a different type of agent. The President, as the head of the Executive Branch, has a unique role in the constitutional system.

The reason for absolute immunity for civil monetary claims is *not* because the President is too busy to be bothered with lawsuits. *Fitzgerald* immunity only applies to *civil* suits; in a future Watergate, the President would have no immunity from possible criminal actions. Even in a civil suit, the immunity extends only to *money damage actions*; the President still has to contend with injunctive actions, even though he may claim that he is too busy to be bothered. Even then, the civil suit must arise out of action that is within the *outer perimeter*

of the President's *official* responsibility.[12] The purpose of immunity is simply to assure that the threat of money damages does not affect the President's exercise of his presidential discretion. The rationale of this immunity is not based on any theory that the President is like a medieval potentate, above the law and too busy to be bothered by it.[13]

Subsequently, *Clinton v. Jones*[14] emphasized the narrowness of the decision in *Nixon v. Fitzgerald*. The Supreme Court—without dissent—held that a private citizen could sue President Clinton for damages for an alleged sexual harassment committed while Clinton was governor of Arkansas. These alleged acts were not part of his official duties and were allegedly committed in his personal capacity. The plaintiff alleged that during the afternoon of May 8, 1991, during an official state conference held at the Excelsior Hotel in Little Rock, Arkansas, then Governor Clinton sent a state policeman to see the plaintiff, who was working as a state employee, staffing the registration desk. Plaintiff alleged that the state policeman asked her to leave her desk and to visit the Governor in a business suite at the hotel, where the Governor made "abhorrent" sexual advances that she vehemently rejected.[15]

10. 457 U.S. at 755–57, 758 n. 41, 102 S.Ct. at 2705, 2706 n. 41.

11. 457 U.S. at 755–57, 102 S.Ct. at 2705. See also, Rotunda, Paula Jones Day in Court, 17 Legal Times (of Washington, D.C.) 24, 27 (May 30, 1994); Rotunda, Is the President Above the Law?, Chicago Tribune, June 1, 1994, § 1, at 21, col. 3–4.

12. Recall that absolute immunity also protects every government prosecutor from *civil* suits that ask for *money* damages [as long as the civil suit arises out of the particular functions of his office (such as the decision to prosecute)]. The prosecutor's immunity is more limited than the President's only because it does not extend to actions within the *outer perimeter* of the prosecutor's official functions; the actions must lie within the particular functions of the prosecutor's office.

13. Justice White, joined by Brennan, Marshall, and Blackmun, JJ., dissented and would have given the President even less protection. They concluded that "the Court clothes the office of the President with sovereign immunity, placing it above the law." 457 U.S. at 767, 102 S.Ct. at 2711 (footnote omitted) (dissenting opinion). See also, 457 U.S. at 797, 102 S.Ct. at 2726 (Blackmun, J., joined by Brennan & Marshall, JJ.).

14. See Stevens, J., for the Court, citing Treatise, in Clinton v. Jones, 520 U.S. 681, 117 S.Ct. 1636, 137 L.Ed.2d 945 (1997).

While President Clinton's lawyer were arguing that the defense of the case would too time-consuming and would affect the President's ability to perform the responsibilities of the Presidency, President Clinton was making the opposite claim to the press. A veteran of the Clinton White House, who requested anonymity, said that of the President's decision to seek review of the *Jones* case in the Supreme Court: "The goal was to push it all off until after the election." Stuart Taylor, Jr., Crying Wolf at the High Court, Legal Times of Washington D.C., June 30, 1997, at 23, col. 1.

15. The Paula Jones Complaint, ¶ ¶ 18–22, alleged:

"18. Clinton then took Jones' hand and pulled her toward him, so that their bodies were in close proximity.

"19. Jones removed her hand from his and retreated several feet.

"20. However, Clinton approached Jones again. He said: 'I love the way your hair flows down your back' and 'I love your curves.' While saying these things, Clinton put his hand on Plaintiff's leg and started sliding it toward the hem of Plaintiff's culottes. Clinton also bent down to attempt to kiss Jones on the neck.

The Court went on to hold that the doctrine of separation of powers does not require a federal court to stay all private actions against a sitting President until he leaves office. It is "settled that the President is subject to judicial process in appropriate circumstances."[16] The President "errs by assuming that interactions between the Judicial Branch and the Executive Branch, *even quite burdensome interactions*, necessarily rise to the level of constitutionally forbidden impairment of the Executive's ability to perform its constitutionally mandated functions."[17]

Finally, *Clinton v. Jones* held that the District Court had abused its discretion in this case in deferring the trial until after the President left office. The judge, in appropriate cases, may require the plaintiff to submit to some delay, "not immoderate in extent and not oppressive in its consequences" to protect the public welfare.[18] But the lengthy delay that the trial court granted (deferring trial until after the President left office) was an abuse. During such a lengthy delay evidence could be lost, witnesses may forget, a party or witness could die.

Injunctions, Contempt of Court, and Other Remedies Against the President. The absolute immunity that *Nixon v. Fitzgerald* gives the President is narrow in scope,[19] because it only applies to suits contesting official actions when the remedy sought is a damage remedy against the President personally. The President is still liable, as an ordinary citizen or any federal judge for actions that are outside the pale of the immunity. Indeed, President Nixon's attorney, in the course of oral argument in *United States v. Nixon*[20] explicitly conceded that the President could be sued for non-presidential acts.[21] Later, *Nixon v. Fitzgerald* emphasized: "For the President, as for judges and prosecutors, absolute immunity merely precludes a particular private remedy for alleged misconduct in order to advance compelling public ends."[22]

Thus, the Court can enjoin Presidential acts; in addition, the President is subject to subpoena.[23] If the President disobeys a court order (even when sued in his personal capacity, in a private civil suit for damages) he is subject to contempt of court. In *Jones v. Clinton*,[24] the

"21. Jones exclaimed, 'What are you doing?' and escaped from Clinton's physical proximity by walking away from him. Jones tried to distract Clinton by chatting with him about his wife. Jones later took a seat at the end of the sofa nearest the door. Clinton asked Jones: 'Are you married?' She responded that she had a regular boyfriend. Clinton then approached the sofa and as he sat down he lowered his trousers and underwear exposing his erect penis and asked Jones to 'kiss it.'

"22. There were distinguishing characteristics in Clinton's genital area that were obvious to Jones."

16. 520 U.S. at 703, 117 S.Ct. at 1649. The courts already have tools to protect litigants from frivolous cases. See, e.g., Federal Rules of Civil Procedure, Rule 11, allowing courts to sanction litigants who bring frivolous cases.

17. 520 U.S. at 702, 117 S.Ct. at 1648 (emphasis added).

18. 520 U.S. at 706–07, 117 S.Ct. at 1650, quoting Landis v. North American Co., 299 U.S. 248, 254, 57 S.Ct. 163, 165–66, 81 L.Ed. 153 (1936).

19. 457 U.S. at 758, 102 S.Ct. at 2706.

20. United States v. Nixon, 418 U.S. 683, 94 S.Ct. 3090, 41 L.Ed.2d 1039 (1974).

21. Transcript of Oral Argument at 80 (July 8, 1964), United States v. Nixon, Nos. 73–1766, 73–1834. One of the justices asked:

"QUESTION: A president could be sued, couldn't he, for back taxes or penalties or what not?"

In response, Nixon attorney and White House Special Counsel James D. St. Clair said:

"MR. ST. CLAIR: Well, in questions of immunity I think individually he could be . . . I think the President could be sued for back taxes in his individual capacity. But in terms of his power to effect the responsibilities of his office, to protect the presidency from unwarranted intrusions into the confidentiality of his communications, that's not a personal matter."

22. 457 U.S. at 758, 102 S.Ct. at 2706 (footnotes omitted).

23. 457 U.S. at 754, 102 S.Ct. at 2704, citing Youngstown Sheet & Tube Co. v. Sawyer, 343 U.S. 579, 72 S.Ct. 863, 96 L.Ed. 1153 (1952), and United States v. Nixon, 418 U.S. 683, 94 S.Ct. 3090, 41 L.Ed.2d 1039 (1974) (in this case, the President was subpoenaed to turn over the secret audio tape). President Clinton, as discussed above, was subpoenaed to testify in two criminal cases.

24. Jones v. Clinton, 36 F.Supp.2d 1118 (E.D.Ark. 1999). During his deposition in this case, the President denied having a sexual relationship with Monica Lewinsky (who had been a federal employee in the White House). As a sanction for this false testimony, the trial court later held President Clinton in civil contempt and ordered him to pay plaintiff's reasonable attorney's fees and the trial court's expenses in traveling to Washington, D.C. "to preside over this tainted deposition." 36 F.Supp. 2d at 1132. The President did not contest the findings and paid $90,686 because of the civil contempt. See Linda Satter,

trial court did place President Clinton in contempt, and he had to pay a fine of nearly $100,000 because of his false testimony.[25] This case marked the first time that any court had ever held a President in contempt of court.[26]

Nixon v. Fitzgerald explicitly left open the possibility that Congress, by statute, could authorize private damage actions against the President for his official actions.[27] Even if that alternative is not constitutional, Congress should be able to authorize a damage action against the public purse. In other words, so that future Fitzgeralds would not be remediless, Congress should be able to authorize plaintiffs to sue the public treasury for out of pocket losses because of official Presidential action, in a lawsuit brought in the Claims Court or similar tribunal. Because the President would not have to pay damages out of his pocket, the damage remedy would not affect his the way he exercised his discretionary judgment any more than an injunctive remedy would.

The Qualified Immunity of Other Executive Officials. In *Harlow v. Fitzgerald*[28]— the companion case to *Nixon v. Fitzgerald*— the Court ruled that the scope of immunity for senior presidential aides and advisers was only qualified, not absolute. "For executive officials in general," said the Court, "qualified immunity represents the norm."[29]

Executive officials do not derive any absolute immunity from the President, unless the function that they are performing demands such immunity. The official claiming absolute immunity has the burden to demonstrate that the responsibilities of his office embrace such a sensitive function that he requires a total shield from liability and that he was performing such a function. Some Presidential "alter egos" could make such a showing of derivative immunity. For example, a claim to Presidential immunity would be strongest in foreign policy or national security, where the President could not discharge his "singularly vital mandate without delegating functions nearly as sensitive as his own."[30]

Earlier case law had stated that qualified immunity is not available if the official *"knew or reasonably should have known"* that his actions would violate the plaintiff's constitutional rights *"or if he took the action with malicious intention* to cause a deprivation of constitutional rights or other injury...."[31]

Court Lies Cost Clinton $90,686, Arkansas Democrat–Gazette, July 30, 1999, at p. 1. The trial court stated:

"Simply put, the President's deposition testimony regarding whether he had ever been alone with Ms. Lewinsky was intentionally false, and his statements regarding whether he had ever engaged in sexual relations with Ms. Lewinsky likewise were intentionally false, notwithstanding tortured definitions and interpretations of the term 'sexual relations.' "36 F.Supp. 2d at 1130 (footnote omitted)(emphasis added).

25. Jones v. Clinton, 36 F.Supp.2d 1118 (E.D.Ark. 1999).

Later, the Arkansas Supreme Court granted a private lawyer's mandamus action against the state disciplinary authority and ordered it to look into the complaint against "Arkansas licensed attorney William Jefferson Clinton, Arkansas Bar No. 73019". Hogue v. Neal, 340 Ark. 250, 12 S.W.3d 186 (2000) (per curiam). Thus, the President could also suffer legal discipline, such as suspension from the practice of law or disbarment.

26. See Franklin v. Massachusetts, 505 U.S. 788, 827, 112 S.Ct. 2767, 2787, 120 L.Ed.2d 636 (1992) (Scalia, J., concurring).

27. 457 U.S. at 748 & n. 27, 102 S.Ct. at 2701 & n. 27. Chief Justice Burger, in his concurring opinion, contended that Congress could not create any damage action against the President. 45 U.S. at 763–64 n. 7, 102 S.Ct. at 2709 n. 7 (Burger, C.J., concurring).

28. 457 U.S. 800, 102 S.Ct. 2727, 73 L.Ed.2d 396 (1982).

29. 457 U.S. at 807, 102 S.Ct. at 2733.

30. 457 U.S. at 812 n. 19, 102 S.Ct. at 2736 n. 19.

The Court also rejected any generalized absolute immunity derived from the President, although the Court had earlier recognized such immunity for congressional aides derived from the Senators' and Representatives' speech and debate immunity. 457 U.S. at 811, 102 S.Ct. at 2735. See Gravel v. United States, 408 U.S. 606, 92 S.Ct. 2614, 33 L.Ed.2d 583 (1972), rehearing denied 409 U.S. 902, 93 S.Ct. 98, 34 L.Ed.2d 165 (1972).

Chief Justice Burger's dissent would have given absolute immunity for the President's "alter ego" or "elbow aides" because these personal aides work more closely with the President on a daily basis than Cabinet officials or other executive officials do. 457 U.S. at 822, 102 S.Ct. at 2741. Brennan, J., joined by Marshall & Blackmun, JJ., filed an opinion concurring in the opinion of the Court. Rehnquist, J., also filed a short concurring opinion.

31. 457 U.S. at 815, 102 S.Ct. at 2737 (emphasis by the Court).

For qualified immunity under 42 U.S.C.A. § 1983, see 4 R. Rotunda & J. Nowak, Treatise on Constitutional Law: Substance and Procedure § 19.29 (West Group, 3d ed. 1999).

However this subjective element made it difficult for the trial courts to weed out insubstantial claims.

Therefore *Harlow* fashioned a new, more objective rule that would allow for summary judgment in appropriate cases:

> Reliance on the *objective reasonableness* of an official's conduct, as measured by reference to clearly established law, should avoid excessive disruption of government and permit the resolution of many insubstantial claims on summary judgment. On summary judgment, the judge appropriately may determine, not only the currently applicable law, but whether that law was clearly established at the time an action occurred. If the law at that time was not clearly established, an official could not reasonably be expected to anticipate subsequent legal developments, nor could he fairly be said to "know" that the law forbade conduct not previously identified as unlawful. Until this threshold immunity question is resolved, discovery should not be allowed. If the law was clearly established, the immunity defense ordinarily should fail, since a reasonably competent public official should know the law governing his conduct. Nevertheless, if the official pleading the defense claims extraordinary circumstances and can prove that he neither knew nor should have known of the relevant legal standard, the defense should be sustained. But again, the defense would turn primarily on objective factors. [B]are allegations of malice should not suffice to subject government officials either to the costs of trial or to the burdens of broad-reaching discovery. We therefore hold that government officials performing discretionary functions generally are shielded from liability for civil damages insofar as their conduct does not violate clearly established statutory or constitutional rights of which a reasonable person would have known.[32]

§ 7.3 The Pardoning Power

The Common Law Background. By the time of Henry VII's reign in England, the common law had developed the principle that the monarch was vested, absolutely and exclusively, with the power to pardon those accused or convicted of crime.[1] According to Lord Chief Justice Coke, the English King had great discretion and leeway in the exercise of this power; this pardon could be "either absolute, or under condition, exception, or qualification...."[2]

The idea of executive pardoning power was so firmly established in the common law that delegates to the Constitutional Convention adopted, with little debate, a clause granting the President the power of executive pardon. Article II § 2 of the Constitution gives the President "... Power to grant Reprieves and Pardons for Offences against the United States, except in Cases of Impeachment." Case law has now developed the extent of the power to pardon far beyond that recognized at common law.

American courts early accepted the notion of broad discretion in the use of the presidential. In *United States v. Wilson*[3], Chief Justice Marshall recognized that a pardon was an act of mercy, "an act of grace, proceeding from the power entrusted with the execution of the laws...."[4] For almost a full century after *Wilson* most courts adhered to this view of a pardon as the executive's personal act of mercy toward an individual.[5] Common law remained the basis for resolving questions concerning the reach of this "merciful" power.

Moving Beyond the Common Law. The Supreme Court ultimately abandoned the his-

---

32. 457 U.S. at 818–19, 817–18, 102 S.Ct. at 2739, 2738 (footnotes omitted) (emphasis added).

Presidential Impoundment. See, 1 R. Rotunda & J. Nowak, Treatise on Constitutional Law: Substance and Procedure § 7.4 (West Group, 3d ed. 1999).

§ 7.3

1. See Grupp, Some Historical Aspects of the Pardon in England, 7 Am.J.Legal History, 51, 55 (1963). See generally, A. S. Miller, Presidential Power in a Nutshell 307–13 (1977).

2. E. Coke, The Third Part of the Institutes of the Laws of England 233 (1817).

3. 32 U.S. (7 Pet.) 150, 8 L.Ed. 640 (1833).

4. 32 U.S. at 160.

5. See, e.g., Ex parte Garland, 71 U.S. (4 Wall.) 333, 380, 18 L.Ed. 366 (1866).

torical "act of grace" approach in *Biddle v. Perovich*,[6] which enunciated, for the first time, a theory of presidential pardon that went beyond simple adherence to common law precepts. The Court upheld a presidential commutation of sentence from death to life imprisonment even though the prisoner did not consent to the change in his sentence.

It is easy to appreciate the significance of *Biddle* by comparing it with an earlier case, *Burdick v. United States*,[7] which had held that acceptance of the pardon was essential and that a witness in a grand jury proceeding could refuse to accept a pardon and instead assert his privilege against self-incrimination. *Burdick* recognized that in some instances the stigma of a pardon would not be wanted and that one could therefore reject the "merciful" act. In *Biddle*, however, Justice Holmes' opinion for the Court made it clear that a pardon is an act for the public welfare, "not a private act of grace from an individual happening to possess power."[8] The Court recognized presidential power to impose "less severe" punishments for the public welfare and ruled that consent was not necessary in such a situation, because the prisoner "on no sound principle ought to have any voice in what the law should do for the welfare of the whole."[9]

In addition to changing the theoretical focus of the pardon power from a private act to one for the general welfare, *Biddle,* for the first time, refused to sanction a technical distinction between the power to pardon and the power to commute a sentence. Courts had previously viewed commutation as completely different forms of clemency.[10] The Court recognized that the President's power extends to

imposition of less severe punishments; where the substituted sentence is one generally recognized as being less hard, the President need not grant full pardon. The Court expanded the scope of the pardoning power to include commutation without the prisoner's consent, but it did not go so far as to hold that the President has unlimited freedom in substituting punishment.

Ex parte Garland[11] considered the effect of President Andrew Johnson's pardon of Garland for all offenses committed by him arising from his participation in the Civil War. Prior to the pardon, Congress had enacted a law providing that any individual who wished to practice law in the federal courts had to take an oath stating that he had never voluntarily borne arms against the United States or given aid to its enemies. Finding the Act to be unconstitutional as a bill of attainder, the Court held that the presidential pardon had relieved Garland from all penalties and disabilities, including the oath, for the named acts.

In speaking of the scope of the President's Constitutional pardoning power, the Court noted that "[i]t extends to every offence known to the law, and may be exercised at any time after its commission, either before legal proceedings are taken, or during their pendency, or after conviction and judgment."[12] A full pardon erases the act and its legal consequences so that "in the eye of the law the offender is as innocent as if he had never committed the offense" and restores the offender to "all his civil rights."[13]

Ex parte Grossman,[14] which held that the power extended not only to indictable crimes

6. 274 U.S. 480, 47 S.Ct. 664, 71 L.Ed. 1161 (1927).

7. 236 U.S. 79, 35 S.Ct. 267, 59 L.Ed. 476 (1915).

8. 274 U.S. at 486, 47 S.Ct. at 665.

9. 274 U.S. at 487, 47 S.Ct. at 666.

10. See, e.g., Ex parte Wells, 59 U.S. (18 How.) 307, 15 L.Ed. 421 (1855).

11. 71 U.S. (4 Wall.) 333, 18 L.Ed. 366 (1867).

12. 71 U.S. (4 Wall.) at 380. Note that while Congress cannot limit the presidential pardoning power, see also, United States v. Klein, 80 U.S. (13 Wall.) 128, 20 L.Ed. 519 (1872), Congress can enact amnesty statutes. The Laura, 114 U.S. 411, 414–17, 5 S.Ct. 881, 882–84, 29 L.Ed. 147 (1885).

13. 71 U.S. (4 Wall.) at 380.

Self–Incrimination. Acceptance of a pardon will take away one civil right of the offender—the privilege against self-incrimination. See Brown v. Walker, 161 U.S. 591, 598–99, 16 S.Ct. 644, 647–48, 40 L.Ed. 819 (1896).

14. 267 U.S. 87, 45 S.Ct. 332, 69 L.Ed. 527 (1925).

Civil Contempt. The Court did appear to distinguish criminal contempt (which a presidential pardon would reach) from civil contempt, which the pardon would not reach. 267 U.S. at 121–22, 45 S.Ct. at 337.

Contempt of Congress. A presidential pardon might not reach a contempt of Congress, based on separation of power concerns. E. Corwin, The President: Office and

but also to contempt of court. Other early decisions have made it clear that the pardoning power encompasses the capacity to remit fines and forfeitures;[15] to commute sentences;[16] to grant amnesty to specified classes or groups;[17] and to pardon conditionally as well as absolutely.[18]

The pardon power of Article II, § 2 power does have some limitations. *Knote v. United States*[19] noted that the pardon could not compensate the offender for personal injuries suffered by imprisonment, nor can a pardon affect any rights that have vested in others due to the judgment against the offender. *Knote* went on to point out:

> However large ... may be the power of pardon possessed by the President, and however extended may be its application, there is this limit to it, as there is to all his powers—it cannot touch moneys in the Treasury of the United States, except expressly authorized by act of Congress. The Constitution places this restriction upon the pardoning power.[20]

Schick v. Reed[21] affirmed the power of the President to attach conditions to grants of clemency. A divided Court[22] upheld the presidential commutation of a death sentence to life imprisonment conditioned on permanent ineligibility for parole, even where no statute provided for such a commuted sentence. *Schick* emphasized that the only limits that can be imposed on the presidential pardon power are those in the Constitution itself. To require the executive to substitute a punishment only if a statute already permitted it would place unauthorized congressional restrictions on the pardoning power.[23]

Schick continued the historical trend of the Supreme Court of extending the pardoning power beyond the scope of its English common-law counterpart, although *Schick* recognized that the President may not aggravate punishment.[24]

§ 7.4 The Congressional Power to Investigate

The investigatory power of Congress, buttressed by the sanction of contempt, is a very broad one. The Constitution nowhere expressly grants to either House of Congress a general power to investigate in aid of legislation, or in aid of overseeing the Executive Branch. However, the Supreme Court has long recognized that such a power is implied as an essential concomitant to Congress' legislative authority. It is a power that is "necessary and proper" to the exercise of other Congressional powers. Access to outside sources of information is essential to the legislative process, and the Courts have recognized that compulsory procedures are therefore required.

McGrain v. Daugherty,[1] is the leading case that gives explicit judicial recognition of the right of either House of Congress to put into

---

Powers 414 (4th rev. ed. 1957). Otherwise, the President could, in effect, preclude Congress from requiring his aides to testify. Even in this case, however, if the Congress sought to enforce the Contempt of Congress by using Article III courts rather than its own inherent power, the separation of powers concerns should not prevent the pardon. On Contempt of Congress, see § 7.5.

Presidential Self-pardon. There is some historical evidence that President Nixon thought that he could not pardon himself. President Ford pardoned him. See, Ronald D. Rotunda, True Significance of Clinton vs. Jones, Chicago Tribune, July 8, 1997, at 12, col. 1–6; Ronald D. Rotunda, Can a President Be Imprisoned?, 20 Legal Times (of Washington, D.C.) 22–23 (July 21, 1997).

15. Illinois Central R.R. v. Bosworth, 133 U.S. 92, 10 S.Ct. 231, 33 L.Ed. 550 (1890).

16. Armstrong v. United States, 80 U.S. (13 Wall.) 154, 20 L.Ed. 614 (1871).

17. United States v. Klein, 80 U.S. (13 Wall.) 128, 20 L.Ed. 519 (1871).

18. Ex parte William Wells, 59 U.S. (18 How.) 307, 15 L.Ed. 421 (1855).

19. 95 U.S. (5 Otto) 149, 24 L.Ed. 442 (1877).

20. 95 U.S. at 154.

21. 419 U.S. 256, 95 S.Ct. 379, 42 L.Ed.2d 430 (1974).

22. Burger, C.J., wrote the majority opinion; Marshall, J., joined by Douglas & Brennan, JJ., dissented.

23. 419 U.S. at 266–67, 95 S.Ct. at 385–86.

24. 419 U.S. at 267, 95 S.Ct. at 386.

§ 7.4

1. 273 U.S. 135, 47 S.Ct. 319, 71 L.Ed. 580 (1927). See also, Judge Charles R. Richey, citing Treatise in Universal Shipping Co., Inc. v. United States, 652 F.Supp. 668, 674 (D.D.C.1987).

See 1 R. Rotunda & J. Nowak, Treatise on Constitutional Law: Substance and Procedure §§ 8.1–8.5 (West Group, 3d ed. 1999).

contempt a witness who ignores its summons or refuses to answer its inquiries. *McGrain* upheld a Senate investigation of whether the Department of Justice was properly performing its duties. Although the Resolution did not expressly state that the investigation was in aid of legislation, the investigation was one on which legislation could be based.[2] Thus the Senate had the power to compel the attendance of witnesses to give information on the subject.

Congress also has an important investigative role in exercising its oversight function and exposing corruption. As Professor, and later President, Woodrow Wilson explained:

The informing function of Congress should be preferred even to its legislative function. The argument is not only that discussed and interrogated administration is the only pure and efficient administration, but more than that, that *the only really self-governing people is that people which discusses and interrogates its administration* . . . .[3]

Congress also has a right to compulsory process when it exercises its function of judging an election,[4] or determining if a member should be expelled.[5]

Congress' contempt powers in aid of its Article I functions has deep historical roots. The House of Representatives, first imposed contempt in late 1795 and early 1796, involving two defendants. The House itself tried, convicted, and imprisoned one defendant, Randall, of an attempt to corrupt two members of the House of Representatives. Thus the House did not need the aid of the courts. Randall remained as a prisoner of the House until January 13, 1796. The House discharged the other

defendant, Whitney, on January 5, 1796 because it found that the evidence against him was insufficient. Neither Randall nor Whitney had any appeal to the courts.[6]

The Randall and Whitney cases were an example of Congress using its *common law* power of contempt. There now exists also a *statutory* contempt procedure, using the process of the courts to try and sentence offenders.[7] It is to the issue of statutory contempt that we now turn.[8]

§ 7.5 The Development of Statutory Contempt

(a) The Statute

Because of the unclear limitations on nonstatutory contempt and because contempt trials are time consuming, in 1857 Congress enacted a statute providing for criminal process in the federal courts, with prescribed penalties for contempt of Congress.[1] This statute is supplementary to the nonstatutory power of Congress. It does not preempt the field.[2]

However, because Congress, by the use of that statute, seeks the aid of the federal courts, the courts require that every defendant prosecuted for a statutory violation be accorded all of the guarantees and safeguards that the law gives to every defendant in a federal criminal case—even though the defendant would not constitutionally have these right had Congress used its own common law power of contempt and not resorted to the courts.[3]

The federal statute providing for Contempt of Congress provides as follows:

2. 273 U.S. at 177–78, 47 S.Ct. at 329–30. See also Watkins v. United States, 354 U.S. 178, 187, 77 S.Ct. 1173, 1179, 1 L.Ed.2d 1273 (1957).

3. W. Wilson, Congressional Government 303–04 (1885) (emphasis added).

4. E.g., Barry v. United States ex rel. Cunningham, 279 U.S. 597, 49 S.Ct. 452, 73 L.Ed. 867 (1929) (investigation of senatorial election).

5. In re Chapman, 166 U.S. 661, 17 S.Ct. 677, 41 L.Ed. 1154 (1897).

6. Moreland, Congressional Investigations and Private Persons, 40 S.Calif.L.Rev. 189, 190 (1967).

7. 2 U.S.C.A. § 192.

8. On the Common Law Contempt Power of Congress, see 1 R. Rotunda & J. Nowak, Treatise on Constitutional Law: Substance and Procedure §§ 8.2–8.3 (West Group, 3d ed. 1999).

§ 7.5

1. 11 Stat. 155. The present day version of that statute is 2 U.S.C.A. § 192.

2. In re Chapman, 166 U.S. 661, 671–72, 17 S.Ct. 677, 681–82, 41 L.Ed. 1154 (1897).

3. E.g., Watkins v. United States, 354 U.S. 178, 206–208, 77 S.Ct. 1173, 1188–90, 1 L.Ed.2d 1273 (1957).

Every person who having been summoned as a witness by the authority of either House of Congress to give testimony or to produce papers upon any matter under inquiry before either House, or any joint committee established by a joint or concurrent resolution of the two Houses of Congress, or any committee of either House of Congress, willfully makes default, or who, having appeared, refuses to answer any question pertinent to the question under inquiry, shall be deemed guilty of a misdemeanor, punishable by a fine of not more than $1,000 nor less than $100 and imprisonment in a common jail for not less than one month nor more than twelve months.[4]

Congress has used this section extensively in recent years, especially since World War II. Consequently, the courts have considered it at length, and have identified four major elements of the crime:

- (a) the investigation during which the contempt occurred must be in aid of a valid legislative purpose;

- (b) the committee conducting the investigation must be authorized to conduct the particular inquiry in question;

- (c) the question that the witness refused an answer, or the papers that the committee required must be pertinent to the authorized inquiry; and,

- (d) the default must be willful.

(b) Legislative Purpose

The nature of the investigative power requires that each inquiry be based on a consti-

tutional grant of legislative authority. That power is, however, very broad:

It encompasses inquiries concerning the administration of existing laws as well as proposed or possibly needed statutes. It includes surveys of defects in our social, economic or political system for the purpose of enabling the Congress to remedy them. It comprehends probes into departments of the Federal Government to expose corruption, inefficiency or waste.[5]

Still, there is no power to expose the activities of individuals merely for the sake of exposure without justification in terms of functions of Congress; it is not the function of Congress to conduct legislative, show trials.[6] Congress may inquire into private affairs and compel their exposure, however, in pursuit of an independent legislative purpose.[7] Congress and its Committees do have the power "to inquire into and *publicize* corruption, maladministration or inefficiency in agencies of the Government."[8]

The existence of a valid legislative purpose is judged simply by whether the legislative body has jurisdiction over the subject matter of the investigation. The enabling resolution contains the grant and limitations of the committee's power.[9] The fact that a committee has reported no legislation at all as the result of an extended series of hearings does not negate a conclusion that the committee has a legislative purpose.[10]

Courts presume a legislative purpose when the subject matter of the investigation is within the jurisdiction of Congress.[11]

---

4. 2 U.S.C.A. § 192. See also 2 U.S.C.A. § 193 (Privilege of witnesses) and 2 U.S.C.A. § 194 (Certification of failure to testify; grand jury action failing to testify or produce records).

5. Watkins v. United States, 354 U.S. 178, 187, 77 S.Ct. 1173, 1179, 1 L.Ed.2d 1273 (1957). See also Barenblatt v. United States, 360 U.S. 109, 79 S.Ct. 1081, 3 L.Ed.2d 1115 (1959), rehearing denied 361 U.S. 854, 80 S.Ct. 40, 4 L.Ed.2d 93 (1959). See also, Lee v. Kelley, 99 F.R.D. 340, 343 n. 2 (D.D.C.1983), (Lewis, J.) citing this section of the treatise, order affirmed 747 F.2d 777 (D.C.Cir.1984).

6. Watkins v. United States, 354 U.S. 178, 200, 77 S.Ct. 1173, 1185–86, 1 L.Ed.2d 1273 (1957).

7. 354 U.S. at 200, 206, 77 S.Ct. at 1185–86, 1188–89.

8. 354 U.S. at 200 n. 33, 77 S.Ct. at 1185–86 n. 33, citing, inter alia, Landis, Constitutional Limitations on the Congressional Power of Investigation, 40 Harv.L.Rev. 153, 168–194 (1926).

9. United States v. Rumely, 345 U.S. 41, 44, 73 S.Ct. 543, 545, 97 L.Ed. 770 (1953).

10. Townsend v. United States, 95 F.2d 352, 355 (D.C.Cir.1938), certiorari denied 303 U.S. 664, 58 S.Ct. 830, 82 L.Ed. 1121 (1938).

11. McGrain v. Daugherty, 273 U.S. 135, 178, 47 S.Ct. 319, 330, 71 L.Ed. 580 (1927).

Motives Irrelevant. The defendant cannot rebut this presumption of legislative purpose by impugning the motives of individual Congressmen, for motive is irrelevant as long as the assembly's legislative purpose is in fact being served.[12] The Court will simply refuse to hear allegations that the ulterior motive of the investigators is not to aid legislation but to harass individuals for their political beliefs.[13]

If there is a legislative purpose, the permissible scope of the investigation may be as far reaching as the potential legislative function to which it is related.[14] It can encompass all matters necessary to the fulfillment of the legislative purpose.

(c) Authority of the Committee

A witness can be punished for refusal to testify before a Congressional committee only if that committee, and in turn its subcommittee, was authorized by its parent House or committee to conduct the investigation to which the testimony pertained. This requirement is an element of the pertinency requirement and therefore is jurisdictional.[15] A statute or special resolution can confer such authority. This authorization requirement is an element of the offense that the government must plead and prove.

Gojack v. United States[16] reversed a contempt citation because the government made no showing that the parent committee had delegated to its subcommittee, before whom the witness had appeared, the authority to make the inquiry. The full committee also had not specified the area of inquiry, as it own rules required. The authorization defines the subject of the inquiry and thus puts some limits on its scope. As *Gojack* explained: "The

jurisdiction of the courts cannot be invoked to impose criminal sanctions in aid of a roving commission. The subject of the inquiry of the specific body before which the alleged contempt occurred must be clear and certain."[17]

The requirement of committee authorization has two elements. First, the committee or subcommittee must be empowered to conduct the specific investigation undertaken. Second, the government must show that the inquiry, with respect to which the contempt occurred, was within the scope of the delegated authority.[18]

In the case of the House Un–American Activities Committee (HUAC), the Supreme Court has been willing to read the committee's authorizing resolution very broadly. Although *Watkins v. United States*[19] criticized the vagueness of the HUAC resolution and the ambiguity of its operative terms, the Court in *Barenblatt v. United States*[20] read *Watkins* narrowly and the HUAC authorizing resolution broadly.

Barenblatt involved a committee investigating alleged Communist infiltration into the field of education, including whether a former teaching fellow at the University of Michigan was then or had ever been a member of the Communist Party. Petitioner Barenblatt refused to answer the committee's questions on Party membership, objecting not on Fifth Amendment grounds, but rather disclaiming in general the right of the subcommittee to inquire into his "political" and "religious" beliefs or "other personal or private affairs" or "associational activities."

The Court affirmed Barenblatt's contempt conviction, rejected his contention that the subcommittee had no such powers of inquiry: "Just as legislation is often given meaning by

---

12. Barenblatt v. United States, 360 U.S. 109, 132–133, 79 S.Ct. 1081, 1096–97, 3 L.Ed.2d 1115 (1959), rehearing denied 361 U.S. 854, 80 S.Ct. 40, 4 L.Ed.2d 93 (1959); Watkins v. United States, 354 U.S. 178, 200, 77 S.Ct. 1173, 1185–86, 1 L.Ed.2d 1273 (1957).

13. Tenney v. Brandhove, 341 U.S. 367, 377–378, 71 S.Ct. 783, 788–89, 95 L.Ed. 1019 (1951), rehearing denied 342 U.S. 843, 72 S.Ct. 20, 96 L.Ed. 637 (1951).

14. Townsend v. United States, 95 F.2d 352, 361 (D.C.Cir.1938).

15. Watkins v. United States, 354 U.S. 178, 201, 206, 77 S.Ct. 1173, 1186, 1188–89, 1 L.Ed.2d 1273 (1957);

Gojack v. United States, 384 U.S. 702, 708, 86 S.Ct. 1689, 1693–94, 16 L.Ed.2d 870 (1966).

16. 384 U.S. 702, 705, 713–714, 86 S.Ct. 1689, 1692, 1696–97, 16 L.Ed.2d 870 (1966).

17. 384 U.S. at 715, 86 S.Ct. at 1697 (1966).

18. United States v. Lamont, 236 F.2d 312, 314 (2d Cir.1956). *Lamont* was relied on and approved of in Gojack v. United States, 384 U.S. 702, 714–715, 86 S.Ct. 1689, 1696–97, 16 L.Ed.2d 870 (1966).

19. 354 U.S. 178, 202, 77 S.Ct. 1173, 1186, 1 L.Ed.2d 1273 (1957).

20. 360 U.S. 109, 79 S.Ct. 1081, 3 L.Ed.2d 1115 (1959).

the gloss of legislative reports, administrative interpretation, and long usage, so the proper meaning of an authorization to a congressional committee is not to be derived alone from its abstract terms unrelated to the definite content furnished them by the course of congressional actions."[21] The committee's history persuaded the Court that its legislative authority to conduct the instant inquiry was "unassailable."[22]

In other areas, however, the courts have read authorizing resolutions narrowly, particularly where required to avoid the necessity of facing a constitutional question. Thus the Supreme Court has refused to find that the Senate Select Committee on Lobbying Activities was authorized to inquire into attempts to influence general public opinion through the publication and distribution of political books and pamphlets. The Court found that the subject was too remote from the authorized investigation to sustain the abridgement of the freedoms of speech and of the press that might be involved.[23]

(d) Pertinency

Closely related to the problem of the authority of the committee is the requirement that the questions asked be pertinent to the subject under inquiry. Pertinency is an explicit statutory requirement of the federal statute, which refers to a refusal to answer "any question pertinent to the question under inquiry...."[24] Because of the pertinency requirement, authorizations must be clear and specific.

Pertinency is an element of the offense, so the government must plead and prove it.[25] The

presumption of innocence of the accused in a criminal proceeding outweighs the presumption of regularity of Congressional activity.

The question must be pertinent to the particular subject under inquiry at any given time, and not merely the full investigative authority of the committee. The indictment must specify the question under congressional committee inquiry at the time of the defendant's alleged default.[26]

Pertinency and Relevance Distinguished. Pertinency is a broader concept than the concept of relevance in the law of evidence. Pertinency extends in its broadest reach to the entire field of inquiry that the legislative purpose permits.[27] It is a question of law that the court decides. A good faith mistake as to the law is not a defense for the defendant.[28]

It is the question and the possible answer that must be pertinent. The pertinence of the actual answer is immaterial.[29]

Because pertinency is an element of the offense, lower courts have held that the defense is not waived by a failure to object to a question on pertinency grounds,[30] but the Supreme Court has suggested to the contrary in dictum.[31]

Proving Pertinency. When a question is not clearly pertinent on its face, the government will be allowed to introduce extraneous evidence to establish pertinency.[32] There are generally five methods by which the government can show pertinency: (1) from the definition of the inquiry found in the authorizing resolution or statute; (2) from the opening

---

21. 360 U.S. at 117, 79 S.Ct. at 1088.

22. 360 U.S. at 122, 79 S.Ct. at 1091.

23. United States v. Rumely, 345 U.S. 41, 73 S.Ct. 543, 97 L.Ed. 770 (1953) (Frankfurter, J.).

24. 2 U.S.C.A. § 193.

25. Sinclair v. United States, 279 U.S. 263, 296–297, 49 S.Ct. 268, 272–73, 73 L.Ed. 692 (1929).

26. Russell v. United States, 369 U.S. 749, 771, 82 S.Ct. 1038, 1051, 8 L.Ed.2d 240 (1962).

27. United States v. Orman, 207 F.2d 148, 153 (3d Cir.1953).

28. Sinclair v. United States, 279 U.S. 263, 298–299, 49 S.Ct. 268, 273–74, 73 L.Ed. 692 (1929); Braden v. United States, 365 U.S. 431, 436, 81 S.Ct. 584, 587–88, 5

L.Ed.2d 653 (1961), rehearing denied 365 U.S. 890, 81 S.Ct. 1024, 6 L.Ed.2d 200 (1961).

29. United States v. Orman, 207 F.2d 148, 154 (3d Cir.1953).

30. United States v. Orman, 207 F.2d 148, 154 (3d Cir.1953); Bowers v. United States, 202 F.2d 447, 452 (D.C.Cir.1953).

31. Barenblatt v. United States, 360 U.S. 109, 123–25, 79 S.Ct. 1081, 1091–92, 3 L.Ed.2d 1115 (1959), rehearing denied 361 U.S. 854, 80 S.Ct. 40, 4 L.Ed.2d 93 (1959); Deutch v. United States, 367 U.S. 456, 472–73, 475, 81 S.Ct. 1587, 1595–96, 1597, 6 L.Ed.2d 963 (1961) (dissenting opinions).

32. Bowers v. United States, 202 F.2d 447, 450, 453 (D.C.Cir.1953).

remarks of the committee chairman; (3) from the nature of the proceeding; (4) from the question itself; and (5) from the response of the committee to a pertinency objection.[33]

Because statutory contempt is a criminal offense subject to the same due process safeguards as any other offense, the need to avoid unconstitutional vagueness requires that a witness must be able to know when he is violating the law. The committee must therefore make clear to the witness the pertinency of the question *before it compels him to answer*, at least so long as he makes an objection based on pertinency. Because the witness acts at his peril if he refuses to answer, he should be entitled to know, in advance, the subject of the inquiry to which the committee deems the question pertinent.

Watkins v. United States[34] explained that a witness is entitled to be informed of the relation of the question to the subject of the investigation with the same precision as the due process clause requires of statutes defining crimes.[35] Chief Justice Burger, while sitting on the District of Columbia Court of Appeals, interpreted *Watkins* as creating a reasonable man standard: it requires not that the witness in fact subjectively appreciate the pertinency of the question, but only that the government demonstrate with sufficient clarity that a reasonable man would have understood it.[36]

(e) Willfulness

Willful default is the fourth requirement of the statute, which the government must prove beyond a reasonable doubt.[37] Willfulness does not, however, require action with an evil mo-

tive or purpose. The statute only requires an intentional and deliberate act, one that is not the product of inadvertence or accident. It is not a defense that the witness acted in good faith.[38]

The statute encompasses all forms of intentional failure to testify: failing to appear, refusal to be sworn or to answer questions, and leaving the hearing before being excused.[39] The witness is, however, entitled to a clear ruling by the committee on his objections to their demands.[40] He must not be made to guess as to his legal position. The committee must make clear to him that it demands an answer notwithstanding his objection. The committee must also make clear the point at which the committee considers him to be in default.[41]

§ 7.6 First, Fourth, and Fifth Amendment Rights of Congressional Witnesses

(a) Fifth Amendment

A witness testifying before a Congressional committee has a Fifth Amendment right to refuse to incriminate herself.[1] The privilege is a personal one, however, and cannot be claimed on behalf of a corporation or in relation to documents kept in a representative capacity.[2] No particular form of words is necessary to invoke the Fifth Amendment privilege. All that is required is that the committee be able to understand the claim. "If an objection to a question is made in any language that a committee may reasonably be expected to understand as an attempt to invoke the privilege,

---

33. Watkins v. United States, 354 U.S. 178, 209–214, 77 S.Ct. 1173, 1190–93, 1 L.Ed.2d 1273 (1957).

34. 354 U.S. 178, 77 S.Ct. 1173, 1 L.Ed.2d 1273 (1957).

35. 354 U.S. at 208–209, 214–215, 77 S.Ct. at 1189–90, 1193–94.

36. Sacher v. United States, 252 F.2d 828, 835 (D.C.Cir.1958), reversed on other grounds 356 U.S. 576, 78 S.Ct. 842, 2 L.Ed.2d 987 (1958) (per curiam).

37. Quinn v. United States, 349 U.S. 155, 165, 75 S.Ct. 668, 674, 99 L.Ed. 964 (1955).

38. Sinclair v. United States, 279 U.S. 263, 298–299, 49 S.Ct. 268, 273, 73 L.Ed. 692 (1929).

39. Townsend v. United States, 95 F.2d 352, 358 (D.C.Cir.1938), certiorari denied 303 U.S. 664, 58 S.Ct. 830, 82 L.Ed. 1121 (1938).

40. See, United States v. Kamp, 102 F.Supp. 757, 759 (D.D.C.1952).

41. Quinn v. United States, 349 U.S. 155, 165–166, 75 S.Ct. 668, 675, 99 L.Ed. 964 (1955); Flaxer v. United States, 358 U.S. 147, 79 S.Ct. 191, 3 L.Ed.2d 183 (1958).

§ 7.6

1. Quinn v. United States, 349 U.S. 155, 162, 75 S.Ct. 668, 673, 99 L.Ed. 964 (1955).

2. McPhaul v. United States, 364 U.S. 372, 380, 81 S.Ct. 138, 143, 5 L.Ed.2d 136 (1960), rehearing denied 364 U.S. 925, 81 S.Ct. 282, 5 L.Ed.2d 264 (1960). Hale v. Henkel, 201 U.S. 43, 26 S.Ct. 370, 50 L.Ed. 652 (1906).

it must be respected both by the committee and by a court...."[3] The burden is then placed on the committee to inquire into objections that are unclear.[4]

Waiver. A witness waives the Fifth Amendment privilege unless it is invoked. The law does not allow partial waivers; that is, the witness cannot select the place to stop her testimony. Once she gives answers to incriminating questions, the privilege is waived as to other questions on the same subject, which can be refused only if they present a real danger of further incrimination. In fact, this waiver may occur even though the witness was not aware (until it was too late) that the right had been waived.[5]

The witness is not the sole judge of her claim.[6] The witness cannot use the privilege as a subterfuge to avoid answering innocent questions. A witness can claim the Fifth Amendment privilege only when there is a reasonable apprehension on the part of the witness that her answer would furnish evidence or reveal sources of evidence that could lead to her conviction for a criminal offense.[7] The committee may therefor ask her to explain her claim of reasonable apprehension, although the committee may not actually force her to disclose the information.[8] She need not disclose the incriminating facts in order to sustain her claim; it need only be evident that an answer or explanation of refusal to answer might result in injurious disclosures.[9]

Use Immunity. In Fifth Amendment privilege applies if a committee grants the witness immunity from prosecution.[10] The immunity

power of Congress, under the present statutory authority, is limited to offering only "use" immunity, not "transactional" immunity.[11] *Transactional immunity*, immunizes a witness from prosecution for the crime about which she is testifying. The narrower, *use immunity* only prohibits the use, in a criminal prosecution, of any information derived directly or indirectly from the testimony.[12]

A court has no discretion to deny an immunity request of the legislative branch where procedural prerequisites have been met.[13] In such a case, the duties of the court are purely ministerial, and "any attempted exercise of discretion on its part, either to deny the requests or to grant immunity with conditions, would be an assumption of power not possessed by the [court]."[14]

The function of the court in a statutory immunity request is first to determine whether the committee has complied with the established procedures. Then, the court should insure that Congress has constitutional jurisdiction over the inquiry area, that the particular agent of Congress has appropriate jurisdiction over the inquiry, and that the information sought is relevant to the matter under investigation.[15] The courts may not go beyond these inquiries to question the wisdom of granting immunity.

The court may not seek to condition, limit, or deny the immunity order on the grounds of prejudicial pretrial publicity. The court may not go beyond administering its own affairs and attempt to regulate proceedings before a

---

3. Quinn v. United States, 349 U.S. 155, 162–163, 75 S.Ct. 668, 673, 99 L.Ed. 964 (1955).

4. 349 U.S. at 162–164, 75 S.Ct. at 673–74.

5. Rogers v. United States, 340 U.S. 367, 370–374, 71 S.Ct. 438, 440–43, 95 L.Ed. 344 (1951), rehearing denied 341 U.S. 912, 71 S.Ct. 619, 95 L.Ed. 1348 (1951).

6. Hoffman v. United States, 341 U.S. 479, 71 S.Ct. 814, 95 L.Ed. 1118 (1951).

7. See Quinn v. United States, 349 U.S. 155, 162, 75 S.Ct. 668, 673, 99 L.Ed. 964 (1955).

8. E.g., United States v. Jaffe, 98 F.Supp. 191, 193–194 (D.D.C.1951).

9. Emspak v. United States, 349 U.S. 190, 198–199, 75 S.Ct. 687, 692–93, 99 L.Ed. 997 (1955).

10. See Kastigar v. United States, 406 U.S. 441, 453, 92 S.Ct. 1653, 1661, 32 L.Ed.2d 212 (1972), rehearing denied 408 U.S. 931, 92 S.Ct. 2478, 33 L.Ed.2d 345 (1972).

11. 18 U.S.C.A. §§ 6001, 6002, 6005.

12. Kastigar v. United States, 406 U.S. 441, 453, 92 S.Ct. 1653, 1661, 32 L.Ed.2d 212 (1972), rehearing denied 408 U.S. 931, 92 S.Ct. 2478, 33 L.Ed.2d 345 (1972).

13. Application of U.S. Senate Select Committee on Presidential Campaign Activities, 361 F.Supp. 1270 (D.D.C.1973) (Sirica, J.).

14. 361 F.Supp. at 1272.

15. 361 F.Supp. at 1278.

coordinate branch of government.[16]

(b) First Amendment

(1) Presence of Communications Media: The Congressional Right to Public Hearings

A witness does not ordinarily have a right to object to the presence of the communications media at a hearing.[17] *United States v. Orman*,[18] for example, rejected a claim that a witness before a congressional committee has a right to demand that certain information to which the witnessed testified must be withheld from the public. The witness claimed that the information did not aid the committee in its legislative purpose, but that issue is for legislative, not for judicial control.[19]

Other cases similarly acknowledge the right of a Committee to open the hearings to the public, for "a committee's legislative purpose may legitimately include the publication of information."[20] As *United States v. Hintz*[21] stated:

> This court has no power to impose upon Congress, a coordinate branch of our government, either a proscription against or a prescription for radio, television, movies or photographs. This court is of the opinion that the mere presence of such mechanisms at an investigative hearing does not infect the hearing with impropriety.[22]

Hintz specifically rejected any reading of the case law that would *per se* prevent the conviction of any witness who commits a contempt of Congress "while in the presence of spectators and the sensory apparatus which permits the nation to see and to hear."[23]

While there is no per se rule that prevents a contempt conviction when the congressional committee has televised hearings, there may be specific cases where this defense would be appropriate. *Hintz* said that it would allow the defendant a trial to argue to the jury that the conditions of testimony were not reasonably conducive to that clarity and accuracy to which defendant was normally capable.[24] A district court held that if the presence of TV cameras and reporters makes it impossible for the witness to testify in a calm, considered and truthful manner, then these special circumstances justify a refusal to testify.[25]

Continuances. If the publicity invoked by the congressional hearing interferes with a subsequent criminal trial on related matters, the court may grant a continuance of the criminal trial until the publicity abates or it might implement other techniques to safeguard the defendant's right to a fair trial. But the court may not interfere with the congressional hearing. It is "for the committee to decide whether considerations of public interest demanded at that time a full-dress public investigation...."[26]

(2) Limitations on the Congressional Power to Compel Reporter's Sources

Prosecutors and, at times, Congress have used the subpoena power to compel testimony and appearances by journalists. The press has responded by challenging the subpoenas, arguing that the First Amendment guarantee of freedom of the press should protect reporters from being compelled to disclose confidential sources of information.

In *Branzburg v. Hayes*,[27] the Supreme Court held (five to four) that the First Amendment affords newsmen no privilege, absolute or qualified, against appearing and testifying before a *grand jury*. Justice Powell, who supplied the crucial fifth vote, filed a brief concurring

---

16. 361 F.Supp. at 1280. See also Delaney v. United States, 199 F.2d 107, 114 (1st Cir.1952).

17. United States v. Hintz, 193 F.Supp. 325 (N.D.Ill. 1961).

18. 207 F.2d 148 (3d Cir.1953).

19. 207 F.2d at 159.

20. Application of U.S. Senate Select Committee on Presidential Campaign Activities, 361 F.Supp. 1270, 1281 (D.D.C.1973). See also Watkins v. United States, 354 U.S. 178, 200, 77 S.Ct. 1173, 1185–86, 1 L.Ed.2d 1273 (1957).

21. 193 F.Supp. 325 (N.D.Ill.1961).

22. 193 F.Supp. at 331–32.

23. 193 F.Supp. at 329.

24. 193 F.Supp. at 332.

25. United States v. Kleinman, 107 F.Supp. 407, 408 (D.D.C.1952).

26. Delaney v. United States, 199 F.2d 107, 114 (1st Cir.1952).

27. 408 U.S. 665, 92 S.Ct. 2646, 33 L.Ed.2d 626 (1972).

opinion suggesting that, on other facts, a First Amendment reporter's privilege might be appropriate: "[T]he courts will be available to newsmen under circumstances where legitimate First Amendment interests require protection."[28] Thus, the holding in *Branzburg*, especially in light of the fact that Justice Powell filed the crucial fifth vote, leaves open the issue of the reporter's privilege before a congressional hearing, as well as before an administrative hearing or civil case. *Branzburg* itself only dealt with the fact situation where a court seeks to compel a reporter to comply with a grand jury subpoena issued for a proper purpose in a criminal investigation.

(3) Free Speech and Association Limitations on Congressional Inquiry

In modern times the Court has focused on Congressional investigative powers based on the guarantees of the First Amendment, rather than on separation of power principles. A leading case illustrating this fact is *Watkins v. United States.*[29]

The *Watkins* Case. In *Watkins*, the House of Representatives had authorized the Un–American Activities Committee and its subcommittees to investigate alleged Communist activity.[30] HUAC subpoenaed Watkins, a trade-union official, to appear before one of the subcommittees after two witnesses linked him with the Communist Party during the Second World War. Watkins denied that he had ever been a Communist and testified freely about his personal activities and associations.[31] However, he refused to answer questions as to

whether he knew certain persons to have been past members of the Communist Party.

Watkins told the Committee: "I will answer any questions which this committee puts to me about myself. I will also answer questions about those persons whom I knew to be members of the Communist Party and whom I believe still are. I will not, however, answer any questions with respect to others with whom I associated in the past. I do not believe that any law in this country requires me to testify about persons who may in the past have been Communist Party members or otherwise engaged in Communist Party activity but who to my best knowledge and belief have long since removed themselves from the Communist movement."[32] He did not invoke his Fifth Amendment privilege against self-incrimination, but challenged both the power of the committee to ask such questions and the relevance of the questions to the duties of the committee.

The government indicted and convicted Watkins for statutory contempt of Congress.[33] A three-judge panel of the Court of Appeals for the District of Columbia reversed,[34] but, on rehearing en banc, the D.C. Circuit affirmed the conviction.[35] The Supreme Court reversed with only one dissent.

The Court admitted that the "power of the Congress to conduct investigations is inherent in the legislative process [and] is broad,"[36] but it reversed anyway. The Court found that neither the vague resolution of the House establishing the Committee nor the comments of the subcommittee chairman on the day of

---

28. 408 U.S. at 710, 92 S.Ct. at 2671.

29. 354 U.S. 178, 77 S.Ct. 1173, 1 L.Ed.2d 1273 (1957). Previously, several lower court cases had held that HUAC, the House Committee on Un–American Activities, was not violating the First Amendment in asking witnesses about Communist Party associations. Barsky v. United States, 167 F.2d 241 (D.C.Cir.1948), certiorari denied 334 U.S. 843, 68 S.Ct. 1511, 92 L.Ed. 1767 (1948), rehearing denied 339 U.S. 971, 70 S.Ct. 1001, 94 L.Ed. 1379 (1950); United States v. Josephson, 165 F.2d 82 (2d Cir.1947), certiorari denied 333 U.S. 838, 68 S.Ct. 609, 92 L.Ed. 1122 (1948), rehearing denied 333 U.S. 858, 68 S.Ct. 731, 92 L.Ed. 1138 (1948).

30. H.R. Res. No. 5, 83d Congress, 1st Session, 99 Cong.Rec. 15 (1953).

31. The Government, in its brief, admitted that: "A more complete and candid statement of his past political associations and activities ... can hardly be imagined." Brief for Respondent, pp. 59–60.

32. 354 U.S. at 185, 77 S.Ct. at 1178.

33. See 2 U.S.C.A. § 192, which proscribes refusal by a witness "to answer any question pertinent to the question under inquiry" by a congressional committee.

34. Watkins v. United States, 233 F.2d 681, 688 n. * (D.C.Cir.1956) (dissenting opinion).

35. Watkins v. United States, 233 F.2d 681 (D.C.Cir. 1956), reversed 354 U.S. 178, 77 S.Ct. 1173, 1 L.Ed.2d 1273 (1957).

36. 354 U.S. at 187, 77 S.Ct. at 1179.

questioning gave Watkins a sufficient indication of pertinence so that the defendant could know the conduct required of him.

However, Chief Justice Warren went beyond this narrow holding and, in broad dicta, announced principles that placed substantive limits on the congressional power to investigate. Although a broad power to investigate is inherent in the legislative process, each inquiry must be related to, and in furtherance of, a legitimate task of Congress. "[T]he First Amendment freedoms of speech, press, religion, or political belief and association" are thus protected in congressional investigations.[37] The Court said: "no doubt that there is no congressional power to expose for the sale of exposure. The public is, of course, entitled to be informed concerning the workings of its government. That cannot be inflated into a general power to expose where the predominant result can only be an invasion of the private rights of individuals. But a solution to our problem is not to be found in testing the motives of committee members...."[38]

Congressional Power to Publicize Governmental Corruption. In a footnote *Watkins* distinguished "the power of Congress to inquire into and publicize corruption, maladministration or inefficiency in agencies of the Government."[39] Thus, Congress may not delegate to its committees the power to question in protected areas of individual privacy unrelated to governmental inefficiency by resolutions so broad that they provide no standards for the questioners and no yardstick by which the courts can measure the need for information against the competing demands of individual freedom.

The *Sweezy* Decision. The same day that the Court decided *Watkins*, a plurality of the Court expanded that case's dictum about free speech rights in *Sweezy v. New Hampshire*.[40] *Sweezy* held invalid, under the Fourteenth Amendment, the contempt conviction of a guest lecturer at a state university who declined to testify to state authorities concerning his lecture and his associates.[41] Chief Justice Warren announced the judgment of the Court and delivered an opinion that Justices Black, Douglas, and Brennan joined.

Warren argued that questioning an unwilling witness about his prior expressions of political belief chills his exercise of the right of free speech and inhibits the expression of unorthodox opinion in the community. Such sanctions can be justified only if the questioning serves a countervailing state interest. In *Sweezy*, the delegation of authority to the attorney general, a one-man committee, had been in such broad terms that the legislature could not have determined a specific need for the information sought. Therefore, Warren did not reach the question of the state interest. "The lack of any indications that the [state] legislature wanted the information the Attorney General attempted to elicit from petitioner must be treated as the absence of authority."[42] The use of the contempt power violated the due process requirements of the Fourteenth Amendment by invading protected areas of speech in the absence of a legislation determination of public interest.

Barenblatt, and the Communist Party. Warren's views in *Watkins* and *Sweezy* did not bear fruit in *Barenblatt v. United States*,[43] decided two years later. This time Justice Harlan delivered the opinion of the Court, while War-

---

37. 354 U.S. at 188, 77 S.Ct. at 1179.

38. 354 U.S. at 200, 77 S.Ct. at 1185–86 (footnote omitted).

39. 354 U.S. at 200 n. 33, 77 S.Ct. at 1185 n. 33. See also Application of U.S. Senate Select Committee on Presidential Campaign Activities, 361 F.Supp. 1270, 1281 (D.D.C.1973).

40. 354 U.S. 234, 77 S.Ct. 1203, 1 L.Ed.2d 1311 (1957).

41. State law imposed various disabilities on "subversive persons" and "subversive organizations." N.H.Rev. Stat.Ann. 588:1–16. The legislature, by resolution, appointed the attorney general as a one-man legislative

committee to investigate violations of this law. Sweezy was summoned to appear; he answered some questions but was adjudged in contempt by a county court for refusal to answer questions about his speech or associates during the 1948 campaign. The state supreme court affirmed. Wyman v. Sweezy, 100 N.H. 103, 121 A.2d 783 (1956), reversed 354 U.S. 234, 77 S.Ct. 1203, 1 L.Ed.2d 1311 (1957).

42. 354 U.S. at 354, 77 S.Ct. at 1213.

43. 360 U.S. 109, 79 S.Ct. 1081, 3 L.Ed.2d 1115 (1959), rehearing denied 361 U.S. 854, 80 S.Ct. 40, 4 L.Ed.2d 93 (1959).

ren dissented with Black and Douglas. The *Barenblatt* majority actually found subcommittee authority to compel testimony about the witness' membership or part in the Communist Party and Communist infiltration into the field of education.[44] In fact, to establish authorization, the Court was willing to consider "the gloss of legislative reports, administrative interpretation, and long usage. . . ."[45] Unlike the facts in *Watkins*, the Court found that the questions in this case were pertinent to the authorized inquiry.[46]

In considering the First Amendment defense (the witness explicitly refused to rely on the Fifth Amendment)[47], the Court argued that where "First Amendment rights are asserted to bar governmental interrogation resolution of the issue always involves a balancing by the courts of the competing private and public interests at stake. . . ."[48] In balancing, the Court noted that the investigation was for a valid legislative purpose, that the Communist Party is not "an ordinary political party", and that thus "investigatory power in this domain is not to be denied Congress solely because the field of education is involved."[49] The Court then affirmed the conviction.

Uphaus and State Investigations. The same day that the Court decided *Barenblatt* it rejected, in *Uphaus v. Wyman*,[50] a First Amendment attack on a one-man legislative investigation by the New Hampshire Attorney General. The Court distinguished *Sweezy* because the academic and political freedoms discussed there were not present in *Uphaus*. In *Uphaus* the State Attorney General was investigating the allegedly subversive activities of World Fellowship Inc., which had a summer camp in New Hampshire. The Court accepted the state court finding that the legislature really desired an answer to the inquiries,[51] which sought the lists of names of all the people who had attended the camp during 1954 and 1955. The Attorney General had a valid reason to believe that the speakers and guests might be "subversive persons."[52] Warren, Black, and Douglas again dissented.[53]

Gibson and the NAACP. *Barenblatt* and *Uphaus* do not spell the end of the First Amendment role in legislative investigations in light of the later decision in *Gibson v. Florida Legislative Investigation Committee*.[54] The state legislative committee ordered the present of the Miami branch of the NAACP to bring with him the association's records identifying its members and contributors. The state claimed that it wanted to investigate the infiltration of Communists into various organizations. The president of the local NAACP told the committee that he would answer questions based on his own personal knowledge but not produce the requested papers. The Supreme Court reversed his contempt conviction.

The Court distinguished *Barenblatt* and other cases where the witness refused to answer questions about his own past or present membership in the Communist party. *Gibson* did not involve the Communist Party—

> it is not alleged Communists who are the witnesses before the Committee and it is not discovery of their membership in that party which is the object of the challenged inquiries. Rather it is the N.A.A.C.P. itself which is the subject of the investigation. . . .[55]

Unlike *Uphaus*, in *Gibson* there was "no semblance of such a nexus between the NAACP and subversive *activities* has been

---

44. 360 U.S. at 114–15, 79 S.Ct. at 1086–87.

45. 360 U.S. at 117, 79 S.Ct. at 1088.

46. 360 U.S. at 123–125, 79 S.Ct. at 1091–92.

47. 360 U.S. at 114, 79 S.Ct. at 1086.

48. 360 U.S. at 126, 79 S.Ct. at 1093.

49. 360 U.S. at 127–29, 79 S.Ct. at 1093–94.

50. 360 U.S. 72, 79 S.Ct. 1040, 3 L.Ed.2d 1090 (1959), rehearing denied 361 U.S. 856, 80 S.Ct. 40, 4 L.Ed.2d 95 (1959).

51. 360 U.S. at 77, 79 S.Ct. at 1044–45.

52. 360 U.S. at 79, 79 S.Ct. at 1045.

53. 360 U.S. at 82, 79 S.Ct. at 1047. Brennan, J. also dissented and in fact wrote this dissent.

54. 372 U.S. 539, 83 S.Ct. 889, 9 L.Ed.2d 929 (1963).

55. Gibson v. Florida Legislative Investigation Committee, 372 U.S. 539, 547, 83 S.Ct. 889, 894, 9 L.Ed.2d 929 (1963), mandate conformed to 153 So.2d 301 (Fla.1963). The Court emphasized that the NAACP is "a concededly legitimate and nonsubversive organization." 372 U.S. at 548, 83 S.Ct. at 895 (footnote omitted).

shown here.''[56] The Court then summarized the evidence and concluded that it disclosed no existence of ''any substantial relationship between the NAACP and subversive or Communist activities.''[57] The Court reversed the conviction.

***DeGregory* and Stale Investigations.** Several years later, the New Hampshire Attorney General was again before the Supreme Court. *DeGregory v. Attorney General*[58] reversed a contempt conviction of a witness who refused to answer questions about Communist activities prior to 1957. The Court concluded:

> [W]hatever justification may have supported such exposure in *Uphaus* is absent here; the staleness of both the basis for investigation and its subject matter makes indefensible such exposure of one's associational and political past—exposure which is objectionable and damaging in the extreme to one whose associations and political views do not command majority approval.[59]

The nature of the organization may be important in striking the apparently ad hoc balance between the First Amendment's associational interests and the legislature's investigative interests.[60]

(c) The Fourth Amendment

The Fourth Amendment's protections against unreasonable search and seizure applies to Congressional investigations[61] but the legislative subpoenas may be very broad in their inquiry and yet be upheld.[62] Criminal cases may not use any evidence improperly seized by congressional investigators.[63]

§ 7.7   The Speech and Debate Clause: An Introduction

Article I, section 6 of the Constitution,[1] known as the speech or debate clause, recognizes the need for protection of legislative independence in a governmental system of separation of powers, a theme long found in English law.

The language of this clause finds direct kinship in the English Bill of Rights of 1689. As the Court has explained:

> This formulation of 1689 was the culmination of a long struggle for parliamentary supremacy. Behind these simple phrases lies a history of conflict between the Commons and the Tudor and Stuart monarchs during which successive monarchs utilized the criminal and civil law to suppress and intimidate critical legislators. Since the Glorious Revolution in Britain, and throughout United States history, the privilege has been recognized as an important protection of the independence and integrity of the legislature.... In the American governmental structure the clause serves the additional function of reinforcing the separation of powers so deliberately established by the Founders.[2]

The clause provides protection of speech in Congress by making conduct of U.S. Senators or Representatives[3] engaged in legislative func-

---

56. 372 U.S. at 550, 83 S.Ct. at 895 (emphasis in original).

57. 372 U.S. at 554–55, 83 S.Ct. at 898.

58. 383 U.S. 825, 86 S.Ct. 1148, 16 L.Ed.2d 292 (1966).

59. 383 U.S. at 828–29, 83 S.Ct. at 1151. Cf. Doe v. McMillan, 412 U.S. 306, 93 S.Ct. 2018, 36 L.Ed.2d 912 (1973).

60. Cf. Shelton v. United States, 404 F.2d 1292 (D.C.Cir.1968), certiorari denied 393 U.S. 1024, 89 S.Ct. 634, 21 L.Ed.2d 568 (1969) (Ku Klux Klan investigation upheld).

61. Watkins v. United States, 354 U.S. 178, 188, 77 S.Ct. 1173, 1179–80, 1 L.Ed.2d 1273 (1957).

62. E.g., McPhaul v. United States, 364 U.S. 372, 81 S.Ct. 138, 5 L.Ed.2d 136 (1960), rehearing denied 364 U.S. 925, 81 S.Ct. 282, 5 L.Ed.2d 264 (1960).

63. Nelson v. United States, 208 F.2d 505 (D.C.Cir. 1953), certiorari denied 346 U.S. 827, 74 S.Ct. 48, 98 L.Ed. 352 (1953).

§ 7.7

1. ''[F]or any Speech or Debate in either House, they shall not be questioned in any other Place.'' U.S.Const. art. 1, § 6.

2. United States v. Johnson, 383 U.S. 169, 178, 86 S.Ct. 749, 754, 15 L.Ed.2d 681 (1966), certiorari denied 385 U.S. 846, 87 S.Ct. 44, 17 L.Ed.2d 77 (1966) (footnote omitted).

The English Bill of Rights of 1689 provided '' . . . That the freedom of speech and debates or proceedings in Parliament, ought not to be impeached or questioned in any court or place out of Parliament.'' 1 W. & M., Sess. 2, c. 2.

3. The speech or debate clause applies, by its own terms, only to federal legislators. Neither that clause nor

tions privileged against civil or criminal suit. That is not to say that there are no restraints on the conduct of federal legislators, for application of the privileges of the clause has been limited through narrow judicial interpretation. In addition, Congress itself has a certain amount of power, under Article 1, § 5, to regulate conduct of its members although in practice such regulation has been neither common nor consistent.

§ 7.8 Early Speech and Debate Case Law

The Supreme Court has written only a handful of decisions involving the construction, scope and interpretation of the speech or debate clause. The two earliest cases, *Kilbourn v. Thompson*[1] and *Tenney v. Brandhove*,[2] expressly adhered to a broad, liberal interpretation of the speech or debate clause. *Kilbourn* noted that the privilege should extend "to things generally done in a session of the House by one of its members in relation to the business before it."[3]

The *Kilbourn* Case. *Kilbourn* dealt with the question whether the House possessed a general contempt power, and what is the scope of the Congressional power to investigate. The scope of the speech or debate clause was a secondary issue.

In this case, the House was attempting to investigate the history and character of what was termed "the real estate pool" of the District of Columbia. The Jay Cooke Co. held a large portion of the pool when it went bank-

rupt, with the United States as one of its creditors. In the course of the House investigation, the committee investigating the scandal summoned (by a subpoena duces tecum) Hallett Kilbourn, a member of the Cooke Firm, to appear. Kilbourn appeared, answered some questions of the committee, but refused to answer others. He also refused to produce subpoenaed books or papers. As a result, a vote of the entire House cited him for contempt. Kilbourn sued for false imprisonment.

Later expansion of Congress' legitimate investigative role have made many of the Court's responses to the investigative issues questionable. However, Justices on all sides of the speech or debate controversy still cite the opinion with approval. *Kilbourn* held that, even though the investigation was outside the legitimate powers of Congress, the speech or debate clause protected the Congressmen who voted for the contempt from a civil suit for false imprisonment. However, the Sergeant-at-Arms, who had taken Kilbourn into custody pursuant to the congressional order, was not within the ambit of the clause and was therefore liable for damages.[4]

The Court's rationale in denying the privilege to the employees of Congress but upholding it for those giving them orders was unclear, and might have been based on the fact that the arrest was not a usual act in a legislative session. *Kilbourn* did not reach the issue of whether "there may ... be things done, in the one House or the other, of an extraordi-

---

federal common law provides any comparable protection to state legislators in federal prosecutions for bribery or other federal criminal prosecutions. United States v. Gillock, 445 U.S. 360, 100 S.Ct. 1185, 63 L.Ed.2d 454 (1980).

§ 7.8

1. 103 U.S. (13 Otto) 168, 26 L.Ed. 377 (1881).

2. 341 U.S. 367, 71 S.Ct. 783, 95 L.Ed. 1019 (1951), rehearing denied 342 U.S. 843, 72 S.Ct. 20, 96 L.Ed. 637 (1951).

3. 103 U.S. (13 Otto) at 204.

4. After the Court decided in favor of Kilbourn, the case went back to the District of Columbia court where Kilbourn eventually recovered a judgment of $20,000, which was paid by order of Congress with interest and the costs of suit. See In re Pacific Ry. Commission, 32 Fed. 241, 253 (C.C.N.D.Cal.1887). *Pacific Railway* applied *Kilbourn* and approved of it as a case that "will stand for all time as a bulwark against the invasion of the rights of the

citizen to protection in his private affairs against the unlimited scrutiny of investigation by a congressional committee." Id. Justice Field, sitting as circuit judge, wrote the opinion. The Supreme Court later cited this case with approval, in Sinclair v. United States, 279 U.S. 263, 292–93, 49 S.Ct. 268, 271–72, 73 L.Ed. 692 (1929).

See Hacker & Rotunda, Restrictions on Agency and Congressional Subpoenas Issued for an Improper Purpose, 4 Corp.L.Rev. 74 (1981), demonstrating that the gist of *Kilbourn* should still be good law: "Congress may not issue subpoenas nor use its investigatory powers for an improper purpose (i.e., for the ulterior purpose of aiding a private litigant), though it is not ousted of jurisdiction simply because its investigation incidentally may aid a private litigant." Id. at 78. See also, Landis, Constitutional Limitations on the Congressional Power of Investigation, 40 Harv.L.Rev. 153 (1926).

nary character, for which the members who take part in the act may be held legally responsible."[5]

Tenney and Immunity. *Tenney v. Brandhove*[6] offers a second possible rationale for the distinction between Congressmen and their aides. A former witness attempted to sue a state legislative committee by bringing a case under the Civil Rights Act. Though the Court based its decision on the interpretation of a federal statute in light of common law immunity, it surveyed and frequently referred to the speech or debate clause. The majority of the Court held that the committee was immune from suit, noting that the case would be different where "an official acting on behalf of the legislature" is sued.[7] The Court thus indicated that the clause's literal protection was only available to members of Congress.

The Speech and Debate Clause in the 1960's. Several significant constructions of the clause, usually in the form of dicta, are in three cases that dealt with the speech and debate clause during the 1960's—*United States v. Johnson*,[8] *Dombrowski v. Eastland*,[9] and *Powell v. McCormack*.[10]

The major theme linking these three more recent cases with the two earlier ones is that all—while espousing general principles of liberal interpretation of the clause—were far more narrow and restrictive in its actual application, particularly with regard to the liability of legislative aides for legislatively authorized activities. *Dombrowski* and *Powell*, like *Kilbourn*, declined to extend the immunity of the clause to the activities of legislative employees acting under the authority and direction of Congress or one of its committees.

In *Dombrowski*, plaintiffs alleged that the Chairman of a Senate subcommittee and that subcommittee's counsel conspired with Louisiana officials to violate the plaintiffs' Fourth Amendment rights. The Court found sufficient evidence against the counsel of the subcommittee to allow plaintiffs to go to trial. But the Court dismissed the complaint against Senator Eastland on grounds of the speech and debate clause:

> It is the purpose and office of the doctrine of legislative immunity, having its roots as it does in the Speech or Debate Clause . . . that legislators engaged "in the sphere of legitimate legislative activity," . . . should be protected not only from the consequences of litigation's results but also from the burden of defending themselves.[11]

In *Powell* the Court decided Congressman Powell's charge that the House unlawfully excluded him from taking his seat in the House of Representatives. The Court dismissed the action against House Speaker McCormack and other Congressmen, ruled for Powell on the merits, and held that the speech or debate clause was not a bar to Powell's action against the House employees, who were acting under House orders.[12]

Tenney had upheld the privilege as a bar against suit for members of a legislative committee but noted that the issue might have been different had the defendants been officials acting on behalf of the legislature rather than members of it.[13]

5.　103 U.S. (13 Otto) at 204.

6.　341 U.S. 367, 71 S.Ct. 783, 95 L.Ed. 1019 (1951), rehearing denied 342 U.S. 843, 72 S.Ct. 20, 96 L.Ed. 637 (1951).

7.　341 U.S. at 378, 71 S.Ct. at 789.

8.　383 U.S. 169, 86 S.Ct. 749, 15 L.Ed.2d 681 (1966), certiorari denied 385 U.S. 846, 87 S.Ct. 44, 17 L.Ed.2d 77 (1966).

9.　387 U.S. 82, 87 S.Ct. 1425, 18 L.Ed.2d 577 (1967) (per curiam).

10.　395 U.S. 486, 89 S.Ct. 1944, 23 L.Ed.2d 491 (1969).

11.　Dombrowski v. Eastland, 387 U.S. 82, 84–85, 87 S.Ct. 1425, 1427–28, 18 L.Ed.2d 577 (1967) (per curiam) quoting Tenney v. Brandhove, 341 U.S. 367, 376, 71 S.Ct.

783, 788, 95 L.Ed. 1019 (1951), rehearing denied 342 U.S. 843, 72 S.Ct. 20, 96 L.Ed. 637 (1951).

12.　Powell v. McCormack, 395 U.S. 486, 505–506, 89 S.Ct. 1944, 1955–56, 23 L.Ed.2d 491 (1969). In 395 U.S. at 506 n. 26, 89 S.Ct. at 1956 n. 26 the Court said it "need not decide whether under the Speech or Debate Clause petitioners would be entitled to maintain this action solely against members of Congress where no agents participated in the challenged action and no other remedy was available. Cf. Kilbourn v. Thompson, 103 U.S. (13 Otto) 168, 204–205, 26 L.Ed. 377 (1881)."

13.　341 U.S. at 377–78, 71 S.Ct. at 788–89.

Johnson held that the speech or debate clause covered a speech delivered by a Senator on the floor of Congress and the Senator's motivation for delivering it. Thus, the speech could not form the basis of a criminal charge of conspiracy to defraud the government. However, the Court went on to hold that the prosecution could still proceed with the conspiracy charge on the condition that the speech itself could not constitute an overt act. This limitation, the *Johnson* Court assumed, would purge the prosecution of all elements offensive to the speech or debate clause.[14]

In these cases, liberal rationales combined with narrow, restrictive holdings to make the precise scope of legislative privilege under the speech or debate clause unclear. None of these opinions, alone or in tandem, defined with any particularity the nature of legislative activity that would be protected by the clause.

§ 7.9 The Modern Speech and Debate Synthesis

The Speech and Debate Clause has two basic aspects. First, it provides a testimonial privilege. The person whom the Clause protects has a right not to be questioned about matters within the protection of the Clause. The Clause, after all, specifically states that the member "shall not be questioned in any other Place." Second, the Clause provides an immunity from liability. If a court, or the legislature, or the executive imposes liability, that certainly "questions" the Speech or Debate. The Clause immunizes the person from liability (either civilly or criminally) for matters within its protection.

In order to develop a test that explains the boundaries of the Clause's protection, the Court has focused on the Legislative–Political distinction.

The Legislative–Political Distinction. The Court has bypassed the broad dicta of earlier cases to take a narrow view of the activities of Congress protected by Article I, section 6. *United States v. Brewster*[1] held that the government could try Senator Daniel Brewster on a criminal charge of general application so long as the criminal case did not rest on legislative acts or the motives of the Senator in performing those acts. The Court distinguished between legislative acts that are "clearly a part of the legislative process—the *due* functioning of the process"[2] and activities that, while legitimate, are unprotected because they are essentially "political in nature."[3] The Court held that the speech or debate clause "does not prohibit inquiry into activities that are casually or incidentally related to legislative affairs but not a part of the legislative process itself."[4]

In the same session, *Gravel v. United States*[5] further developed the legislative-political distinction of *Brewster* by pointing out that acts do not become "legislative in nature" simply because members of Congress "generally perform [them] in their official capacity:"[6]

Legislative acts are not all-encompassing. The heart of the Clause is speech or debate in either House. Insofar as the Clause is construed to reach other matters, they must be an integral part of the deliberative and communicative processes by which Members participate in committee and House proceedings with respect to the consideration and passage or rejection of proposed legislation or with respect to other matters which the Constitution places within the jurisdiction of either House.[7]

Congressmen and Their Aides. *Gravel* expressly held that, for purposes of the speech or debate clause, a member of Congress and his assistant are treated as one in the perform-

---

14.   383 U.S. at 184–85, 86 S.Ct. at 757.

§ 7.9

1.   408 U.S. 501, 92 S.Ct. 2531, 33 L.Ed.2d 507 (1972). See, 1 R. Rotunda & J. Nowak, Treatise on Constitutional Law: Substance and Procedure § 8.8 (West Group, 3d ed. 1999).

2.   408 U.S. at 516, 92 S.Ct. at 2539 (emphasis in original).

3.   408 U.S. at 512, 92 S.Ct. at 2537.

4.   408 U.S. at 528, 92 S.Ct. at 2545.

5.   408 U.S. 606, 92 S.Ct. 2614, 33 L.Ed.2d 583 (1972), rehearing denied 409 U.S. 902, 93 S.Ct. 98, 34 L.Ed.2d 165 (1972).

6.   408 U.S. at 625, 92 S.Ct. at 2627.

7.   408 U.S. at 625, 92 S.Ct. at 2627.

ance of their legislative functions.[8] Any act that is protected by the clause if performed personally by a member of Congress is thus equally protected if performed by a legislative aide or assistant. The Court recognized that, in "view of the complexities of the modern legislative process," it is, as a practical matter, impossible for Members of Congress to perform their legislative tasks without the help of aides and assistants.[9]

Gravel and Earlier Case Law Distinguished. Applying these principles, the _Gravel_ Court held a Senator and his aide were immune from questioning by a grand jury concerning their investigatory acts in preparation for a subcommittee hearing, except insofar as those acts were criminal or related to third-party crime. This position did not reject the distinctions between employees and Congressmen found in the earlier cases, for the _Gravel_ Court carefully distinguished the previous holdings.

Gravel interpreted _Kilbourn_ as a case where the House resolution authorizing legislative arrest was immune from judicial review. "But the resolution was subject to judicial review insofar as its execution impinged on a citizen's rights as it did there. That the House could with impunity order an unconstitutional arrest afforded no protection for those who made the arrest."[10] Presumably if a congressman actually made the arrest in _Kilbourn,_ he would not be protected for that action, though he would be protected for voting for the arrest.

Gravel distinguished _Dombrowski_ as a case where the "record contained no evidence of the Senator's involvement in any activity that could result in liability . . . whereas the committee counsel was charged with conspiring with state officials to carry out an illegal seizure of records. . . ."[11]

And _Gravel_ interpreted _Powell_ as a case where the Court could afford relief against House aides seeking to implement invalid resolutions. As in _Kilbourn,_ the _Powell_ Court had noted that it did not reach the issue of the Congressmen's liability if they themselves would implement the resolution and no other remedy was available.[12]

Republication of Materials Not Protected. _Gravel_ made clear that the speech and debate clause did not protect any private _republication_ of materials that Congressmen or their aides had introduced and made public at a committee hearing. This ruling was a significant narrowing of the clause because it excluded from protection the informative function of Congress in publishing information for the benefit of constituents.

Gravel articulated the principle that before the privilege extends to matters beyond pure speech or debate in either House, "they must be an integral part of the deliberative and communicative processes by which Members participate in committee and House proceedings with respect to the consideration . . . of proposed legislation or with respect to other matters which the Constitution places within the jurisdiction of either House."[13] The extension of the privilege to matters that are not pure speech or debate will occur only when the protection afforded by the privilege is necessary to prevent indirect impairment of the deliberations of the House or Committee functions.

Helstoski and the Legislative–Political Distinction. _United States v. Helstoski_[14] clarified the legislative act-political act distinction. The government charged that a former congressman had, while a Member of Congress, accepted money in return for promising to introduce, and in fact introducing, private bills

---

8. The Court noted that congressional assistants must be treated as the Congressman's "alter ego." 408 U.S. at 616–17, 92 S.Ct. at 2622.

9. 408 U.S. at 616, 92 S.Ct. at 2622.

10. 408 U.S. at 618, 92 S.Ct. at 2623.

11. 408 U.S. at 619, 92 S.Ct. at 2624.

12. 408 U.S. at 620, 92 S.Ct. at 2624.

13. 408 U.S. at 625, 92 S.Ct. at 2627. But cf. Watkins v. United States, 354 U.S. 178, 200 n. 33, 77 S.Ct. 1173, 1185 n. 33, 1 L.Ed.2d 1273 (1957): The power of "Congress to inquire into and publicize corruption, maladministration or inefficiency in agencies of the Government . . . was the only kind of activity described by Woodrow Wilson . . . when he wrote: 'The informing function of Congress should be preferred even to its legislative function.'"

14. 442 U.S. 477, 99 S.Ct. 2432, 61 L.Ed.2d 12 (1979).

to suspend the application of the immigration laws. The government indicted Helstoski for violating a law that makes it a crime for a public official to corruptly ask for, or accept, anything of value in return for being influenced in the performance of official duties.

Promises Not Protected by the Privilege. The government argued that the speech or debate clause did not prohibit it from introducing references to past legislative acts because such references are essential to show the motive for taking money. Also, the government argued that exclusion of references to past acts is not logical because jurors, if they are told of promises to perform legislative acts, will want to know if the acts themselves were subsequently performed. Not telling them that will call the acts into question.

The majority rejected this reasoning and held that the speech or debate clause precludes any inquiry into acts that occur in the regular course of the legislative process and into the motivation for those acts. While such exclusion will make prosecution more difficult, "references to past legislative acts of a member cannot be admitted without undermining the values protected by the Clause."[15]

However, in an important concession to the government, the Court held that "[p]romises by a Member to perform an act *in the future* are not legislative acts."[16] Thus, the government may demonstrate corrupt promises. Even a promise to "deliver a speech, to vote, or to solicit other votes at some future date is not 'speech or debate.' Likewise, a *promise* to introduce a bill is not a legislative act."[17] Thus, the government may prosecute a Congressman for promising to vote a particular way on a bill, but it may not introduce the vote itself.

Individual Waiver. The Fifth Amendment is subject to implied waivers. Thus, the government argued that Helstoski had impliedly

waived the speech or debate clause privilege. The majority held that, assuming that it is possible for a congressman to waive the speech or debate privilege, such a waiver can only be found after explicit and unequivocal renunciation of the privilege, not found in this case.

Institutional Waiver. Some foreign countries recognize a privilege for legislators, and it is not uncommon for these countries to allow the legislative body to vote to strip a member of the immunity. Assuming that Congress could institutionally waive the privilege for its Members—a point raised but not decided in *Helstoski*—the Court held that the relevant statute does not constitute such a waiver.[18]

The Speech and Debate Clause, Civil Cases, and the Legislative–Political Distinction. The cases discussed above all deal with the scope of legislative immunity as applied to criminal cases. *Doe v. McMillan*[19] applied the speech or debate clause to civil litigation, and continued the distinction drawn in the earlier criminal cases between legislative and political acts.

In *McMillan*, parents of District of Columbia school children sued members of the House Committee on the District of Columbia, federal legislative employees of the Government Printing Office, and district school officials and employees seeking damages and declaratory and injunctive relief for alleged invasion of privacy resulting from public dissemination of a Committee report on the District of Columbia school system. This report identified, by name, students in highly derogatory contexts.[20] The Court held that the scope of the speech or debate clause clearly immunized members of Congress from liability for all of the acts on which the civil suit was based. The Court applied the "alter ego" test of *Gravel* to grant similar immunity to the committee staff, the

---

15. 442 U.S. at 491, 99 S.Ct. at 2440.

16. 442 U.S. at 489, 99 S.Ct. at 2439–40 (emphasis added).

17. 442 U.S. at 489, 99 S.Ct. at 2440 (emphasis in original).

18. 442 U.S. at 491–94, 99 S.Ct. at 2440–42, interpreting 18 U.S.C.A. § 201.

19. 412 U.S. 306, 93 S.Ct. 2018, 36 L.Ed.2d 912 (1973), motion for clarification of opinion denied 419 U.S. 1043, 95 S.Ct. 614, 42 L.Ed.2d 637 (1974).

20. Among other things, the report listed names of children as being frequent "class cutters", having failed examinations and for disciplinary problems. 412 U.S. at 308–09 and nn. 1–2, 93 S.Ct. at 2022–23 and nn. 1–2.

consultant and investigator introducing material at the committee hearings.

However, then the Court addressed the sole remaining issue in the case: whether the speech or debate clause affords absolute immunity from private suit to persons who, with authorization from Congress, distributed materials that allegedly infringed on the rights of individuals. The Court acknowledged the importance of informing the public of congressional activities, but felt that the act of informing the public was not always an essential part of legitimate legislative activity merely because authorized by Congress. To determine whether an act is immune, courts should apply the standard of *Gravel:* whether the act of informing the public is " 'an integral part of the deliberative and communicative processes by which Members participate in committee and House proceedings.' "[21]

The Court went on to hold that, in private suits such as this, the speech or debate clause affords no immunity to those who, at the direction of Congress, distribute actionable material to the general public. Thus, *Doe* upheld a cause of action against the public printer and superintendent of documents to the extent that they had printed excess copies of the report, that is, copies of the report for use other than internally by Congress.[22]

No Injunctions of Congressional Subpoenas. *Eastland v. United States Servicemen's Fund*[23] held that the federal courts may not enjoin the issuance of a subpoena by a congressional committee directing a bank to produce the bank records of an anti-war group, the USSF, which the committee was

investigating. Because the subpoena was directed to the bank and not to the USSF, the USSF was not in a position to assert its alleged constitutional claim by refusing to comply with the subpoena and then defending itself in a statutory contempt action.

The Court applied the immunity privilege despite allegations that the contribution lists subpoenaed were the equivalent of the membership lists of the anti-war group. The USSF argued that revealing these contribution lists would put First and Fifth Amendment rights in danger of irreparable harm. Chief Justice Burger's majority opinion simply accepted the government's argument of absolute congressional immunity and found that the Court had no power to review the subpoena.[24]

Defamatory Statements Outside the Legislative Chambers. *Hutchinson v. Proxmire*[25] elaborated on the legislative-political distinction and held that the speech or debate clause provides no absolute privilege from liability to civil plaintiffs for defamatory statements made outside the legislative chamber. Even though these statements would be "wholly immune" if made on the Senate floor,[26] or in a committee hearing (even if the hearing were held outside the chambers), even though the statements would be immune if published in a committee reports, their republication in a newsletter is not privileged.[27]

The Court conceded that the privilege applies when Congress informs itself by committee hearings and speeches on the floor; however, a congressman's individual transmittal of such information in order to inform the public "is not a part of the legislative function or the

21. 412 U.S. at 314, 93 S.Ct. at 2025, quoting Gravel v. United States, 408 U.S. at 625, 92 S.Ct. at 2627.

22. In Davis v. Passman, 442 U.S. 228, 235 n. 11, 99 S.Ct. 2264, 2272 n. 11, 60 L.Ed.2d 846 (1979) the Court noted the issue but intimated no view whether the speech or debate clause would shield a former Congressman from an implied civil damage brought by a former employee fired because of her sex.

23. 421 U.S. 491, 95 S.Ct. 1813, 44 L.Ed.2d 324 (1975), remanded and vacated 517 F.2d 825 (D.C.Cir.1975).

24. Joining Chief Justice Burger were Blackmun, Rehnquist, White & Powell. In a concurring opinion, Marshall, Brennan, and Stewart agreed that the facts of the instant case made no relief possible, but they suggested that a different procedure and/or different defendants

would provide a forum for asserting such constitutional claims. 421 U.S. at 513, 95 S.Ct. at 1826.

Douglas dissented, and would have ruled in favor of the Servicemen's Fund on the First Amendment issue. See, e.g., 421 U.S. at 518, 95 S.Ct. at 1829 (Douglas, J., dissenting): "[N]o regime of law that can rightfully claim that name may make trustees of ... vast powers immune from actions brought by people who have been wronged by official action."

25. 443 U.S. 111, 99 S.Ct. 2675, 61 L.Ed.2d 411 (1979).

26. 443 U.S. at 130, 99 S.Ct. at 2686.

27. 443 U.S. at 130–33, 99 S.Ct. at 2685–87.

deliberations that make up the legislative process."[28] Thus newsletters and press releases are not within the speech or debate privilege. Also, a congressman's "libelous remarks in ... follow up telephone calls to executive agencies and in radio and television interviews are not protected."[29]

In short, the traditional view of the speech or debate clause has come to mean that Congressional privilege, while important, is narrowly limited to essentially purely legislative tasks such as voting, preparation of internal reports, and debate. The Court has rejected criticisms from commentators,[30] and has refused to extend the protection of the clause to "political" activities of Congress, although these informative, mediating, and educational functions are now accepted as legitimate roles for legislators. Under the present test for the speech or debate clause, Congressmen and their aides are protected from suit only insofar as their actions are directly, essentially related to the legislative process.

§ 7.10 The Congressional Privilege From Arrest

Article I, section 6 of the Constitution creates the privilege from arrest clause:

> The Senators and Representatives ... shall in all Cases, except Treason, Felony and Breach of the Peace, be privileged from Arrest during their Attendance at the Session of their respective Houses and in going to and returning from the same. . . .

At the time of the drafting of the Constitution, arrest in *civil cases* was common.[1] The Court has interpreted this clause in light of this history. The privilege, thus, is limited to protecting Congressmen from a practice that is now obsolete.

Arrest is not the same as service of process. Thus the privilege does not protect a congressman from service of process in a civil case,[2] or in a criminal case.[3] Because the privilege is limited to civil suits, it affords no protection from arrest in any criminal case.[4] The Court has shown no interest in reading this clause more expansively,[5] and a broader reading is not consistent with the intent of the framers of the Constitution.

§ 7.11 The Appointment Process

Article II, section 2, clause 2 of the Constitution provides in part:

> "[The President] shall nominate, and by and with the Advice and Consent of the Senate, shall appoint Ambassadors, other public Ministers and Consuls, Judges of the Supreme Court, and all other Officers of the United States, whose Appointments are not herein otherwise provided for, and which shall be established by Law: but the Congress may by Law vest the Appointment of such inferior Officers, as they think proper, in the President alone, in the Courts of Law, or in the Heads of Departments."[1]

This appointment process is a practical working out of the doctrine of separation of powers,

---

28. 443 U.S. at 133, 99 S.Ct. at 2687 (footnote omitted.)

29. 443 U.S. at 121 n. 10, 99 S.Ct. at 2681 n. 10. Justice Stewart joined in all of the opinion except this footnote 10. 443 U.S. at 134, 99 S.Ct. at 2687–88.

30. See, e.g., Cella, The Doctrine of Legislative Privilege of Speech or Debate: The New Interpretation as a Threat to Legislative Coequality, 8 Suffolk L.Rev. 1019 (1974); Reinstein and Silverglate, Legislative Privilege and The Separation of Powers, 86 Harvard L.Rev. 1113 (1973).

§ 7.10

1. Long v. Ansell, 293 U.S. 76, 83, 55 S.Ct. 21, 22, 79 L.Ed. 208 (1934) (Brandeis, J.).

2. 293 U.S. at 82, 55 S.Ct. at 22.

3. United States v. Cooper, 4 U.S. (4 Dall.) 341, 1 L.Ed. 859 (C.C.D.Pa.1800).

4. Williamson v. United States, 207 U.S. 425, 435–446, 28 S.Ct. 163, 166, 52 L.Ed. 278 (1908) (extensive discussion of historical understanding).

5. Long v. Ansell, 293 U.S. 76, 82, 55 S.Ct. 21, 22, 79 L.Ed. 208 (1934): "Clause 1 defines the extent of the immunity. Its language is exact and leaves no room for a construction which would extend the privilege beyond the terms of the grant."

§ 7.11

1. U.S.Const. art. II, § 2, cl. 2. The rest of this clause concerns the treaty-making process.

See, State ex rel. Paluf v. Feneli, 69 Ohio St.3d 138, 142, 630 N.E.2d 708, 711 (1994), citing Treatise. See also, 2 R. Rotunda & J. Nowak, Treatise on Constitutional Law: Substance and Procedure §§ 9.1–9.18 (West Group, 3d ed. 1999).

with Congress establishing the federal offices[2] and the President (subject to Senate confirmation) choosing the officers.[3] The framers believed such a separation necessary because "the same persons should not both legislate and administer the laws."[4] The Constitutional Convention's consideration of the appointment clause sparked several debates and the final draft was probably a compromise, part of the framers' larger effort to balance power among the three branches of government.[5]

Primary Officers Versus Inferior Officers. The full appointment process, including Senate confirmation, does not apply to all appointments. The Constitution itself differentiates between two classes of officers.[6] Primary officers must be nominated by the President and confirmed by the Senate.[7] Congress has a choice, however, with respect to inferior officers, and can vest their appointment in the President, the courts of law, or in the heads of departments.[8]

In addition to these two classes, a third category of government appointees, "employees," is outside the constitutional appointment process altogether. As a pragmatic concession to the needs of the government bureaucracy,[9] employees are "lesser functionaries subor-

dinate to officers of the United States."[10] The appointment of an employee is not subject to constitutional rules regarding the appointment process.

An "Officer of the United States." Any appointee who exercises significant authority pursuant to the laws of the United States is an "officer of the United States," and must, therefore, be appointed in the manner proscribed by Article 2, § 2, clause 2.[11]

Thus, special trial judges of the tax court are "officers of the United States."[12] The President must appoint, and the Senate must confirm, all commissioned offices of the Armed Forces.[13] Every time the President appoints a commissioner officer to a higher rank, he or she receives another Presidential appointment and Senate confirmation.[14]

However, an officer does not need a new appointment and reconfirmation if the new duties are not that different from, are germane to, the original ones. For example, commissioned military officers who serve as military judges do not need reappointment because Congress may "increase the powers and duties of an existing office without thereby rendering it necessary that the incumbent be again nom-

---

2. This congressional power to create federal offices springs from the phrase "which shall be established by law."

3. See Buckley v. Valeo, 424 U.S. 1, 122–24, 96 S.Ct. 612, 684, 46 L.Ed.2d 659, 746–47 (1976), motion granted 424 U.S. 936, 96 S.Ct. 1153, 47 L.Ed.2d 727 (1976). See also Buckley, 424 U.S. at 271–74, 96 S.Ct. at 751–52, 46 L.Ed.2d at 831–33 (White, J., joining in part and dissenting in part).

4. Buckley, 424 U.S. at 272, 96 S.Ct. at 751, 46 L.Ed.2d at 831 (White, J., joining in part and dissenting in part). See also Springer v. Philippine Islands, 277 U.S. 189, 48 S.Ct. 480, 72 L.Ed. 845 (1928) (Congress may not control the enforcement of its laws by giving itself power to appoint who will execute the laws).

5. See Buckley, 424 U.S. at 129–31, 96 S.Ct. at 687–88, 46 L.Ed.2d at 750–52; Buckley, 424 U.S. at 271–74, 96 S.Ct. at 751–52, 46 L.Ed.2d at 831–33 (White, J., joining in part and dissenting in part).

6. United States v. Germaine, 99 U.S. (9 Otto) 508, 509–10, 25 L.Ed. 482, 483 (1879). See also, Morrison v. Olson, 487 U.S. 654, 670–77, 108 S.Ct. 2597, 2608–09, 101 L.Ed.2d 569 (1988) (special statute providing for the Attorney General to request a special panel of Article III judges, called the "Special Division", to appoint a special prosecutor or "Independent Counsel"; this Independent

Counsel is not a "head of a department" because she is subject to removal by a higher Executive Branch official for cause, and because the law grants to the Independent Counsel limited jurisdiction and limited duties).

7. Germaine, 99 U.S. (9 Otto) at 509–10, 25 L.Ed. at 483.

8. Germaine, 99 U.S. (9 Otto) at 509–10, 25 L.Ed. at 483.

9. See E. Corwin, The Constitution 177 (H. Chase & C. Ducat 14th ed. 1978). See also E. Corwin, The President 76 (Rev. 4th ed. 1957).

10. Buckley v. Valeo, 424 U.S. at 126, n. 162, 96 S.Ct. at 685, n. 162, 46 L.Ed.2d at 749, n. 162.

11. Buckley, 424 U.S. at 126, 96 S.Ct. at 685, 46 L.Ed.2d at 748.

See, e.g., Myers v. United States, 272 U.S. 52, 47 S.Ct. 21, 71 L.Ed. 160 (1926) (post master first class an officer); Ex parte Hennen, 38 U.S. (13 Pet.) 230, 10 L.Ed. 138 (1839) (clerk of a district court an officer).

12. Freytag v. Commissioner, 501 U.S. 868, 111 S.Ct. 2631, 115 L.Ed.2d 764 (1991).

13. 10 U.S.C.A. § 531.

14. 10 U.S.C.A. § 624.

inated and appointed."[15] While Congress could require reappointment by statute, reappointment is not constitutionally necessary because, in the military, military judges have no inherent judicial authority apart from the court martial to which they are assigned.

§ 7.12 Constitutional Restrictions on Congressional Appointment of Executive Officials

Recall that the U.S. Constitution specifically authorizes the President to appoint "all other Officers of the United States, whose Appointments are not herein otherwise provided for, and which shall be established by Law. . . ."[1] At no time, however, may the legislative branch exercise executive authority by retaining the power to appoint those who will execute its laws. Thus, *Springer v. Government of Philippine Islands*[2] held that the legislature of the Philippine Islands could not constitutionally provide for legislative appointment to executive agencies.

Buckley v. Valeo[3] reaffirmed this principle. The Supreme Court held that Congress had violated Article II in providing that the President *pro tempore* of the Senate and the Speaker of the House could appoint a majority of the voting members of the Federal Election Commission. *Buckley* involved a suit seeking a declaratory judgment that this portion of the Federal Election Campaign Act was unconstitutional and asking for an injunction against its enforcement.

The Court held that Congress had violated the appointments clause because neither of the legislative officers purportedly given the ap-

pointment power came within the terms "courts of law" or "heads of departments" as required by Article II. A "Head" of a Department is someone who is in the Executive Branch or "at least has some connection" with that Branch. Because they had not been appointed in accordance with the power granted the President under Article II to appoint "Officers of the United States," members of the Commission could not exercise the purely executive functions of administering the law.[4]

Congressional Powers to Set Qualifications of Appointees. While Congress may not appoint those who execute the laws, it may lay down qualifications of age, experience, and so on. Sometimes these qualifications significantly narrow the field of choice.[5] However, any Congressionally imposed qualifications must have a reasonable relation to the office. Otherwise, Congress would be, in effect, creating the appointing power in Congress, rather than in the President.[6]

Congress may, in short, create the office but may not appoint the officer. To distinguish between these two powers, the Court has developed a *germaneness* test. Congress may impose additional duties germane to an existing office without rendering it necessary that the incumbent be reappointed and reconfirmed.[7]

§ 7.13 Appointment Powers of the "Courts of Law"

The Constitution allows Congress the power to vest the appointment of inferior officers of the United States, "in the President alone, in the Courts of Law, or in the Heads of Depart-

---

15. Weiss v. United States, 510 U.S. 163, 114 S.Ct. 752, 127 L.Ed.2d 1 (1994).

§ 7.12

1. U.S.Const. art. II, § 2, cl. 2.

2. 277 U.S. 189, 48 S.Ct. 480, 72 L.Ed. 845 (1928).

3. 424 U.S. 1, 96 S.Ct. 612, 46 L.Ed.2d 659 (1976), motion granted 424 U.S. 936, 96 S.Ct. 1153, 47 L.Ed.2d 727 (1976) (per curiam).

4. Buckley v. Valeo, 424 U.S. 1, 109–13, 118–43, 96 S.Ct. 612, 677–80, 681–94, 46 L.Ed.2d 659, 739–41, 744–58 (1976), motion to extend stay granted 424 U.S. 936, 96 S.Ct. 1153, 47 L.Ed.2d 727 (1976) (per curiam).

5. See generally, Note, Power of Appointment to Public Office Under the Federal Constitution, 42 Harv.L.Rev.

426 (1929). See also, E. Corwin, The President: Office and Powers 1787–1957, at 363–65 (4th ed. 1957).

6. See, Myers v. United States, 272 U.S. 52, 96–97, 47 S.Ct. 21, 52, 71 L.Ed. 160 (1926).

7. E.g., Shoemaker v. United States, 147 U.S. 282, 13 S.Ct. 361, 37 L.Ed. 170 (1893), holding that Congress may create a Commission to supervise the development of a park in the District of Columbia and require that two members be the Chief of the Army and the Engineer Commissioner of the District of Columbia. The additional duties assigned to these commissioned officers were germane to their offices.

ments."[1]

The Watergate controversy led to the question of the propriety and constitutionality of the *judicial* appointment of a permanent (or temporary) Special Prosecutor to prosecute, in appropriate cases, governmental officials. There are only a few Supreme Court cases on this subject.[2]

In 1879, *Ex parte Siebold*[3] held that Congress could authorize the Circuit Courts to appoint election supervisors. *Siebold* read the Article II, section 2, clause 2 broadly, holding:

> [T]he duty [of the court] to appoint inferior officers, when required thereto by law, is a constitutional duty of the courts; and in the present case there is no such *incongruity* in the duty required as to excuse the courts from its performance, or to render their acts void.[4]

The "No Incongruity" Requirement. There are very few cases interpreting the *Siebold* requirement that the judicial appointment of inferior officers not be incongruous with the judicial function. The cases that have discussed the question do not interpret the "no incongruity" power so broadly that it places severe limits on the federal judicial appointment power. Thus, the Supreme Court has upheld the power of Congress to authorize the lower courts to appoint commissioners to handle extradition matters.[5]

The leading lower court decision is *Hobson v. Hansen*,[6] which required the District of Columbia district court to appoint the members of the District of Columbia Board of Education. The court read the *Siebold* requirement narrowly:

> The limitation ... is not an affirmative requirement that the duty of the officer be related to the administration of Justice. It is a negative requirement that the duty may not have "such incongruity" with the judicial function as would void the power sought to be conferred.[7]

The logic of the *Hobson* test finds support in historical tradition. Federal courts have long appointed defense counsel for indigent defendants. Though the President normally appoints the U.S. Attorney, federal courts—pursuant to federal law—may even appoint the U.S. Attorney if a vacancy occurs. This judicial appointee serves until the President fills that vacancy.[8]

While the limits of the "no incongruity" requirement may be unclear, no one would expect that it would be constitutional, for example, for Congress to authorize the Supreme Court to appoint the Secretary of State. The inability of the judiciary to appoint such an officer lies in the fact that the appointment is "incongruous." It may also lie in the fact that the Secretary of Defense is not an inferior officer but a head of a department.[9]

Independent Counsel and the Ethics in Government Act.

In *Morrison v. Olson*[10] the Supreme Court,

§ 7.13

1. U.S.Const. art. II, § 2, cl. 2.

2. E.g., The Final Report of the Select Committee on Presidential Campaign Activities, U.S. Senate, pursuant to S.Res. 60, Feb. 7, 1973, Report No. 93–981 (June 1974) at 96–100.

3. 100 U.S. (10 Otto) 371, 25 L.Ed. 717 (1879).

4. 100 U.S. (10 Otto) at 398 (emphasis added).

5. Rice v. Ames, 180 U.S. 371, 21 S.Ct. 406, 45 L.Ed. 577 (1901).

6. 265 F.Supp. 902 (D.D.C.1967).

7. 265 F.Supp. at 913 (alternative holding; see 265 F.Supp. at 911, relying also on U.S.Const. art. I, § 8, cl. 17).

8. United States v. Solomon, 216 F.Supp. 835 (S.D.N.Y.1963) (upholding constitutionality of what was then 28 U.S.C.A. § 506). The court, in dictum, suggested that an equally broad removal power could raise different issues. 216 F.Supp. at 843. In re Farrow, 3 Fed. 112 (C.C.N.D.Ga.1880) (judicial appointment of interim District Attorney upheld). Some state courts routinely appoint prosecutors. E.g., 51 Conn.Gen.Stats.Ann. § 175.

See also, Birch v. Steele, 165 Fed. 577 (5th Cir.1908) (court appointment of referees in bankruptcy upheld); Russell v. Thomas, 21 F.Cas. 58 (C.C.E.D.Pa.1874) (court appointment of U.S. Commissioners of insolvency upheld).

9. See U.S.Const. art. II, § 2, cl. 2.

10. 487 U.S. 654, 108 S.Ct. 2597, 101 L.Ed.2d 569 (1988).

See L. Fisher, Constitutional Conflicts Between Congress and the President (1985); Carter, The Independent Counsel Mess, 102 Harv.L.Rev. 105 (1988); Shane, Independent Policymaking and Presidential Power, 57 Geo. Wash. L.Rev. 596, 598–608 (1989); Rotunda, The Case

with one vigorous dissent,[11] upheld the Independent Counsel provisions of the Ethics in Government Act.[12] The provisions—an aftermath of the Watergate Crisis[13]—set up a procedure pursuant to which Congress could require the Attorney General to ask a panel of judges (called the "Special Division" by the Act) to appoint an "Independent Counsel" to investigate and, if appropriate, prosecute certain high-ranking officials for alleged violations of the federal criminal laws.

The Independent Counsel Law. The operation of the law involved in *Olson* is complex, and Chief Justice Rehnquist's opinion for the Court discusses it in great detail. In brief, if the Attorney General receives information that he determines is "sufficient to constitute grounds to investigate whether any person [covered by the Act] may have violated any Federal criminal law," then the Attorney General must conduct a preliminary investigation. After that investigation is completed or after 90 days (whatever comes first),[14] the Attorney General must report to what is called the Special Division, a panel of three Article III judges. If the Attorney General concludes that "there was no reasonable grounds to believe that further investigation is warranted," then he must so state to the Special Division. But if he determines that there exist "reasonable grounds to believe that further investigation is warranted," then he "shall apply" to the Special Division for the appointment of an "independent counsel."

If the Attorney General decides to ask the Special Division to appoint an Independent Counsel, then the Special Division "shall appoint an appropriate Independent Counsel and shall define that independent counsel's prosecutorial jurisdiction." The decision of the Attorney General whether to request, or whether not to request, the Special Division to appoint counsel *is not reviewable*. The statute explicitly so provides.[15] This point is a very important one that the Court emphasized more than once.[16] For example, Congressmen who are members of certain committees may request, but cannot require, the Attorney General to seek appointment of an Independent Counsel. In addition, the Act requires that the Independent Counsel "shall, except where not possible, comply with the written or other established policies of the Department of Justice respecting enforcement of the criminal laws."

Congress, of course, can impeach and remove the Independent Counsel.[17] Otherwise, only "personal action of the Attorney General" can result in removal, and then, "only for good cause, physical disability, mental incapacity, or any other condition that substantially impairs the performance of such Independent Counsel's duties."[18] If the Attorney General does remove the Independent Counsel, the Attorney General must report the reasons to the Special Division and to the Judiciary Committees of the House and Senate. The Independent Counsel can seek to obtain reinstatement or other appropriate relief by filing an action in the district court for the District of Columbia, but if she does, no judge of the Special Division can sit on that case.

The Independent Counsel's office is also terminated when she notifies the Attorney General that her investigation is complete, or when the Special Division, acting on its motion or at the suggestion of the Attorney General, concludes that the investigation is complete (or so substantially complete that the Department of Justice can complete the work).

Against Special Prosecutors, Wall St.Journal., Jan. 15, 1990, at A8, col. 4–6.

11. Justice Scalia dissented. Justice Kennedy took no part in the consideration or decision of this case.

12. 28 U.S.C.A. § 591 et seq.

13. See, The Final Report of the Select Committee on Presidential Campaign Activities, United States Senate, 93d Cong., 2d Session, Report 93–981 (1974).

14. See 28 U.S.C.A. § 592(c)(1).

15. 28 U.S.C.A. § 592(f).

16. E.g., 487 U.S. at 661 n. 4, 108 S.Ct. at 2603 n. 4. See also, 487 U.S. at 695, 108 S.Ct. at 2621:

"[U]nder the Act the Special Division has no power to appoint an independent counsel *sua sponte*; it may only do so upon the specific request of the Attorney General, and the courts are specifically prevented from reviewing the Attorney General's decision not to seek appointment, § 592(f)."

17. In addition to the Constitution so providing, the statute so provides as well. 28 U.S.C.A. § 596(a)(1).

18. 28 U.S.C.A. § 596(a)(1).

The Independent Counsel may send reports to Congress on her activities. She *must* inform the House of Representatives of any "credible information" that "may constitute grounds for an impeachment."[19]

The Appointments Clause. *Morrison v. Olson* decided, first, that the Act does not violate the Appointments Clause. The Independent Counsel is an "inferior office" within the meaning of that clause.[20] The Independent Counsel is not the "Head of a Department," for she is subject to removal by a higher Executive Branch official. The Independent Counsel has power to perform only certain, limited duties; and her office is limited in jurisdiction.[21]

The Court also rejected the argument that the Appointments Clause does not allow Congress to place the power to appoint an Independent Counsel outside the Executive Branch. The language, historical background and original intent behind the appointments clause did not support the argument of the appellees. In the past, the Court noted that federal courts have engaged in interim appointments of the U.S. Attorney,[22] and routinely appoint defense counsel.[23]

Restrictions on Supervisory Authority by Article III Judges. The appellees in *Morrison v. Olson* also argued that the Independent Counsel law violated the Article III "case" or "controversy" requirement. However, given that the appointments clause of Article II specifically authorizes the courts to exercised an appointment power, there can be no "case" or "controversy" problem.

Nor is there any violation of Article III because the Special Division has some discretion to define the nature and scope of the Independent Counsel's authority. Particularly when the office is temporary, it is "necessary and proper" for Congress to give power to the appointing authority to define the scope of the office as an incident to the appointments clause.

However, *Morrison v. Olson*, warned that Congress may not "give to the [Special] Division *unlimited* discretion to determine the Independent Counsel's jurisdiction."[24] The Special Divisions' power to define the Independent Counsel's jurisdiction must be "demonstrably related to the factual circumstances that gave rise to the Attorney General's investigation and request for the appointment of the Independent Counsel in the particular case."[25] The Special Division's power to define the Independent Counsel's jurisdiction is "incidental."

The Act also vests in the Special Division other powers that are not incident to the appointment power. Most of these powers are either passive (the power to receive the Independent Counsel's reports) or "essentially ministerial." Even when the Act authorizes the Special Division to exercise some judgment (the Special Division must determine whether the Attorney General has shown "good cause" to request an extension of the time period normally allowed for the preliminary investigation) the powers are still "essentially ministerial." Judges perform analogous functions all the time, such as the decision whether to

---

19.　28 U.S.C.A. § 595(c).

20.　U.S. Const. Art. II, § 2, cl. 2.

21.　487 U.S. at 671–72, 108 S.Ct. at 2608–09.

See also, United States v. Germaine, 99 U.S. (9 Otto) 508, 509–11, 25 L.Ed. 482 (1878); United States v. Eaton, 169 U.S. 331, 343, 18 S.Ct. 374, 379, 42 L.Ed. 767 (1898) (vice-counsel is a "subordinate officer"); Ex parte Siebold, 100 U.S. (10 Otto) 371, 379–80, 25 L.Ed. 717 (1879) (federal election supervisors are inferior officers); Go–Bart Importing Co. v. United States, 282 U.S. 344, 352–53, 51 S.Ct. 153, 156–57, 75 L.Ed. 374 (1931) (United States Commissioners, who have the power to institute certain prosecutions, are inferior officers); United States v. Nixon, 418 U.S. 683, 694 & n. 8, 696, 94 S.Ct. 3090, 3100 & n. 8, 3101, 41 L.Ed.2d 1039 (1974) (referring to the Watergate Special Prosecutor as a "subordinate officer").

22.　487 U.S. at 674–77, 108 S.Ct. at 2609–11.

See also, In re Hennen, 38 U.S. (13 Pet.) 230, 10 L.Ed. 138 (1839); Ex parte Siebold, 100 U.S. (10 Otto) 371, 397–98, 25 L.Ed. 717 (1879); Young v. United States ex rel. Vuitton et Fils S.A., 481 U.S. 787, 107 S.Ct. 2124, 95 L.Ed.2d 740 (1987). United States v. Solomon, 216 F.Supp. 835 (S.D.N.Y.1963).

23.　See, 18 U.S.C.A. § 3006A(b), authorizing such appointments.

24.　487 U.S. at 679, 108 S.Ct. at 2613 (emphasis in original).

25.　487 U.S. at 679, 108 S.Ct. at 2613 (footnote omitted).

extend a grand jury investigation, or whether to allow disclosure of matters occurring before a grand jury. The important conclusion is that the "Act simply does not give the [Special] Division the power to 'supervise' the Independent Counsel in the exercise of her investigative or prosecutorial authority."[26] It would violate the Constitution for Article III courts to exercise such executive supervision over prosecutors.

The Court specifically noted (and did not approve of) lower court cases involving Independent Counsel where the Special Division has given advisory opinions (e.g., purporting to exempt Independent Counsel from conflict of interest laws) or issued orders not directly authorized by the Act (e.g., ordering Independent Counsel to postpone an investigation until the completion of related state proceedings). The Court warned: not only does the Act not authorize such actions, but "the division's exercised of unauthorized powers risk the transgression of the constitutional limitations of Article III that we have just discussed."[27]

The Court was particularly troubled that the Act authorized the Special Division to terminate the office of Independent Counsel. This provision, on its face, does not authorize the Special Division to control the pace and depth of the Independent Counsel's investigation, but the Court acknowledged that this section of the law has not yet been tested in practice.

In order to save the statute from constitutional infirmities, the Court said that it had to interpret this provision narrowly. "The termination provisions of the Act do not give the Special Division anything approaching the power *to remove* the counsel while an investigation or court proceeding is still underway—this power is vested solely in the Attorney General."[28] Basically, the "termination" power must be construed to be only the power to

terminate when the Independent Counsel's job is "truly 'completed' "or so substantially completed that there is no further need for any continuing action by the Independent Counsel.[29] The Special Division, in short, should not use the termination power to supervise the Independent Counsel.[30]

Limitations on the Attorney General's Removal Powers. *Morrison v. Olson* concluded that the Act did not violate the principle of separation of powers. First, Congress has given itself no role in the removal process, unlike the scheme invalidated in *Bowsher v. Synar.*[31]

Second, the Court upheld the Act's provisions limiting the powers of the Attorney General (or the President) to remove the Independent Counsel. After canvassing the case law, the Court acknowledged that earlier cases had spoken of legislative restrictions over the removal of executive branch officials in terms of whether the office was "quasi-legislative" or "quasi-judicial"—

> but our present considered view is that the determination of whether the Constitution allows Congress to impose a "good cause"-type restriction on the President's power to remove an official cannot be made to turn on whether or not that official is classified as "purely executive." [T]he real question is whether the removal restrictions are of such a nature that they impede the President's ability to perform his constitutional duty, and the functions of the officials in question must be analyzed in that light.[32]

Some officials, the Court said, are so "purely executive" that the President must be able to remove them at will "if he is able to accomplish his constitutional role."[33] In this case, the Court said—

> we simply do not see how the President's need to control the exercise of [the indepen-

---

26. 487 U.S. at 681, 108 S.Ct. at 2613.

27. 487 U.S. at 684–85, 108 S.Ct. at 2615 (footnote omitted).

28. 487 U.S. at 682, 108 S.Ct. at 2614 (emphasis in original).

29. 487 U.S. at 654, 108 S.Ct. at 2614.

30. Butzner, J., concurring in part and dissenting in part, quoting Treatise, *In re* North, 10 F.3d 831, 837 (D.C.Cir.1993).

31. 478 U.S. 714, 730, 106 S.Ct. 3181, 3190–91, 92 L.Ed.2d 583 (1986).

32. 487 U.S. at 689, 691, 108 S.Ct. at 2618, 2619.

33. 487 U.S. at 690, 108 S.Ct. at 2618 (footnote omitted).

dent counsel's] discretion is so central to the functioning of the Executive Branch as to require as a matter of constitutional law that the counsel be terminable at will by the President.[34]

The Act did not "completely strip" the President of the power to remove the Independent Counsel. There could be removal if there was "cause;" hence, the removal restrictions did not prevent the President from engaging in the "faithful execution" of the laws.

Separation of Powers. Finally, the Court concluded that the Act, taken as a whole, did not violate the separation of powers. Congress, under the Act, is not increasing its powers at the expense of the Executive:

> [T]he Attorney General retains the power to remove the counsel for "good cause," a power that we have already concluded provides the Executive with substantial ability to ensure that the laws are "faithfully executed" by an independent counsel. [A]nd the Attorney General's decision not to request appointment if he finds "no reasonable grounds to believe that further investigation is warranted" is committed to his unreviewable discretion.[35]

Scalia's Dissent. Justice Scalia wrote a lengthy and vigorous dissent. He concluded by objecting to the majority's ad hoc approach. In such a case, the law is, "by definition, precisely what the majority thinks, taking all things into account, it ought to be. I prefer to rely upon the judgment of the wise men who constructed our system, and of the people who

approved it, and of two centuries of history that have shown it to be sound. Like it or not, that judgment says, quite plainly, that '[t]he executive Power shall be vested in a President of the United States.' "[36]

Policy Considerations. While *Morrison v. Olson* may decide the constitutional questions, various policy questions remain, which Congress will consider if it decides to amend the law, repeal it, or let it expire.[37] Commentators have attacked the independent prosecutor provisions on various grounds.

Some of the independent prosecutors have spent millions of dollars and months or years of time, out of proportion (some have argued) with any real or perceived wrongs.[38] Others have objected to tremendous resources used and time expended in investigations that produced no indictments. After *Morrison v. Olson* was decided, for example, the Independent Counsel, Alexia Morrison, simply dropped the 28 month investigation against Theodore B. Olson, a former Assistant Attorney General who had been accused of lying before a congressional subcommittee.[39]

The public Reports of the Independent Counsel raise further questions because they sometimes appear to criticize (indict by publication) the target of the probe, without ever giving that target a trial within which to defend the charges leveled against him or her.[40] The structure of the law raises additional problems because it appears to target an individual before the investigation has even begun—as if the Government were to advertise

---

34. 487 U.S. at 691–92, 108 S.Ct. at 2619 (footnote omitted).

35. 487 U.S. at 696, 108 S.Ct. at 2621.

36. 487 U.S. at 734, 108 S.Ct. at 2641 (Scalia, J., dissenting).

37. In 1992, Congress allowed the independent counsel law to expire. In 1994, after allegations surrounding President Clinton, Congress enacted a new independent counsel law. See, N.Y. Times, June 22, 1994, at 1, col. 1.

38. See, e.g., Special Prosecutors' Expensive: Justice Department Raps Probers' Lack of Fiscal Restraint, ABA Journal, Sept. 1, 1987, at 17. From May, 1986 to August, 1987, four Independent Counsel spent about 10% of the Department of Justice annual budget for the criminal division. By the end of 1993, Lawrence Walsh had spent, on the Iran–Contra investigation, more than $35 million by his estimate and more than $100 million in his critics'

estimate. Byron York, The Final (Pay) Days of Lawrence Walsh, Wall Street Journal, Aug. 11, 1993, at A10, at col. 3–6 (midwest ed.). By early 1994, Walsh issued his public report of this activities, which cost more than $40 million. Most of his convictions were reversed on appeal, and the General Accounting Office charged Mr. Walsh's office with violating various regulations designed to place limits on spending and travel allowances. Robert S. Bennet, How to Avoid Another Lawrence Walsh, Wall Street Journal, April 28, 1993, at A15 (midwest ed.); Mark J. Bredemeier, Lawrence Walsh's Final Abuse of Power, Wall Street Journal, Jan. 19, 1994, at A15 (midwest ed.).

39. E.g., Time Magazine, Sept. 5, 1988, at 84.

40. See Wood v. Hughes, 9 N.Y.2d 144, 212 N.Y.S.2d 33, 173 N.E.2d 21 (1961).

for people to investigate all facets of the life of Mr. or Ms. *X* in an effort to find something wrong.[41]

Due Process. The fact that the federal court may appoint an inferior officer and then decide on the merits some litigation regarding that officer does not necessarily create any per se due process problems.[42]

On the other hand, to say that there is no *per se* due process problems does not mean that there are no problems. Courts must be mindful of possible conflicts of interest. Thus, *Young v. United States ex rel. Vuitton et Fils S.A.*[43] held that a federal court may appoint a special private prosecutor to prosecute out-of-court contempt because of the special, unique nature of the offense.[44] However, if the court is forced to appoint a "private prosecutor," the court should not appoint to that position an attorney who is counsel for an interested party in the underlying civil litigation because to do so would place the private prosecutor in an improper conflict of interest position.[45] The private prosecutor must be disinterested.[46] In a

criminal contempt action the prosecutor (even if court-appointed) is supposed to represent the United States, not the private party who is the beneficiary of the court order that is claimed to have been violated.

Morrison v. Olson,[47] in upholding the constitutionality of the Independent Counsel law, concluded that when the lower court (called the "Special Division") exercised power under the law and appointed an Independent Counsel at the request of the Attorney General, there was no threat that the federal judiciary would not remain impartial and independent, because "the Special Division has no power to review any of the actions of the independent counsel or any of the actions of the Attorney General with respect to the counsel."[48]

Conclusion. The cases on the appointment power establish several general principles. The President has the power to appoint officers of the United States. Congress may not exercise the power to appoint those who execute the laws, but, as to "inferior officers," the federal courts share with the President the power of

---

41. Attorney General (and later Justice) Robert Jackson commented: "If the prosecutor is obliged to choose his case, it follows that he can choose his defendants. Therein is the most dangerous power of the prosecutor: that he will pick people that he thinks he should get, rather than cases that need to be prosecuted. With the law books filled with a great assortment of crimes, a prosecutor stands a fair chance of finding at least a technical violation of some act on the part of almost anyone. In such a case, it is not a question of discovering the commission of a crime and then looking for the man who has committed it, it is a question of picking the man and then searching the law books, or putting investigators to work, to pin some offense on him." R. Jackson, The Federal Prosecutor, Address Delivered at the Second Annual Conference of United States Attorneys, April 1, 1940.

42. As *Hobson v. Hansen*, 265 F.Supp. 902, 918 (D.D.C.1967) noted, even though federal judges appointed members of a school board—

"[The] official act of participating in the selection of [School] Board members does not in and of itself preclude on due process grounds the ability of the judge to decide fairly the merits of litigation challenging the validity of the performance by a Board member of his duties as such. If in a particular case such a challenge were made its soundness on due process grounds would depend on the circumstances bearing thereon and not on the mere fact that the judge had performed the duty reposed upon him by Congress...."

See also, United States v. Solomon, 216 F.Supp. 835, 843 (S.D.N.Y.1963).

43. 481 U.S. 787, 107 S.Ct. 2124, 95 L.Ed.2d 740 (1987). Cf. e.g., McCann v. New York Stock Exchange, 80

F.2d 211, 214 (2d Cir.1935), cert. denied 299 U.S. 603, 57 S.Ct. 233, 81 L.Ed. 444 (1936).

44. Contempt. Because courts must be able to punish disobedience to judicial orders so that they can vindicate their own authority without complete dependence on other branches, they cannot be at the mercy of another branch in deciding whether such proceedings should be initiated. 481 U.S. at 795, 107 S.Ct. at 2131. Congress may reasonably regulate such judicial power, but Congress cannot abrogate or render inoperative for all practical purposes the *inherent* power of courts to deal with contempt. Michaelson v. United States ex rel. Chicago, St. P., M. & O. Ry. Co., 266 U.S. 42, 65–66, 45 S.Ct. 18, 19–20, 69 L.Ed. 162 (1924). If a court is faced with a criminal contempt, it should ordinarily first request the U.S. Attorney to prosecute. If the U.S. Attorney denies the request, the court should then appoint a "private prosecutor." 481 U.S. at 801, 107 S.Ct. at 2134.

45. 481 U.S. at 802–15, 107 S.Ct. at 2135–2141.

Cf., e.g., People ex rel. Clancy v. Superior Court (Ebel), 39 Cal.3d 740, 218 Cal.Rptr. 24, 705 P.2d 347 (1985), cert. denied 479 U.S. 848, 107 S.Ct. 170, 93 L.Ed.2d 108 (1986) (contingency fee for prosecutor improper).

46. See generally, R. Rotunda, Professional Responsibility 149–51 (West Black Letter Series, 4th ed. 1995).

47. 487 U.S. 654, 108 S.Ct. 2597, 101 L.Ed.2d 569 (1988).

48. 487 U.S. at 683, 108 S.Ct. at 2615 (emphasis in original).

appointment. When the court appoints, the office may be unrelated to judicial administration but it should not be "incongruous" with the judicial function.

§ 7.14   The Removal Power

There is no express Constitutional clause dealing with a removal power (other than Congress' removal power in connection with impeachments). At least one framer of the Constitution, James Madison, felt it "absolutely necessary that the President should have the power of removing from office"[1] appointees to office. It is likely that the Constitutional Convention never formally discussed a presidential removal power.[2] However, such a power has long been assumed to arise from the grant of executive power under Article II, section 1 of the Constitution and the duty under Article II, section 3 to "take care that the Laws be faithfully executed."[3] Presidential control over purely executive functions would be seriously undermined by any efforts to limit this removal power.

The *Marbury* Dictum. Early judicial dictum on the removal power is found in *Marbury v. Madison.*[4] While Marbury had been appointed a Justice of the Peace for the District of Columbia shortly before the end of the administration of President John Adams, his commission was never delivered. Jefferson did not appreciate that Marbury and other federalist judges had been appointed in the "midnight hour" of the prior administration, so the new Secretary of State, James Madison, refused to deliver the commission.

Marbury went to the Supreme Court seeking mandamus to compel delivery. The Court denied the writ, holding that the Act of Congress

that purported to grant the Supreme Court original jurisdiction to issue mandamus was invalid because it conflicted with Article III of the Constitution. Writing the opinion for the Court, Chief Justice Marshall offered a narrow view of the executive's power of removal:

> [W]hen the officer is not removable at the will of the executive, the appointment is not revocable, and cannot be annulled: it has conferred legal rights which cannot be resumed....

> [A]s the law creating the office, gave the officer a right to hold for five years, independent of the executive, the appointment was not revocable, but vested in the officers legal rights, which are protected by the laws of his country.[5]

The holding of the case—that the Supreme Court lacked original jurisdiction in mandamus—was not dependent on the removal power; thus, Marshall's assertion that the President had no power to remove *Marbury* within the five year term of appointment was mere dictum. Indeed, as discussed more fully below, subsequent decisions of the Court did not follow Marshall's statement.[6] On its facts, *Marbury* is distinguished from the majority of cases involving presidential removal because it did not involve an executive office but a judicial office, in the local courts of Washington, D.C.

Removal by Heads of Departments. *United States v. Perkins,*[7] established that where Congress vests the power of appointment in some official other than the President,[8] it has the ability to regulate and restrict the manner of removing that appointee. *Perkins* involved a suit in the Court of Claims for lost wages by a naval cadet-engineer whom the

---

§ 7.14

1. Annals of Congress 387 (1789) [1789–1791]. See 2 R. Rotunda & J. Nowak, Treatise on Constitutional Law: Substance and Procedure § 9.10 (West Group, 3d ed. 1999).

2. See generally, M. Farrand, The Records of the Federal Convention (1911).

3. See, Myers v. United States, 272 U.S. 52, 164, 47 S.Ct. 21, 41, 71 L.Ed. 160 (1926).

4. 5 U.S. (1 Cranch) 137, 2 L.Ed. 60 (1803).

5. 5 U.S. (1 Cranch) at 162.

6. See, e.g. United States v. Smith, 286 U.S. 6, 47, 52 S.Ct. 475, 483, 76 L.Ed. 954 (1932) (completeness of appointment on signing of the commission); United States v. Le Baron, 60 U.S. (19 How.) 73, 15 L.Ed. 525 (1856); Parsons v. United States, 167 U.S. 324, 17 S.Ct. 880, 42 L.Ed. 185 (1897) (term of office). See also the cases on removal of officers discussed below.

7. 116 U.S. 483, 6 S.Ct. 449, 29 L.Ed. 700 (1886).

8. Pursuant to Article II, § 2 of the Constitution, Congress may by law vest the appointment of inferior officers in the heads of Departments.

Secretary of the Navy had discharged because his services were not required. Congress had provided that no officer could be dismissed from the armed services except by court-martial.

Invalidating Perkins' dismissal, the Court made it clear that "when Congress, by law, vests the appointment of inferior officers in the heads of Departments it may limit and restrict the power of removal as it deems best for the public interest."[9] Because *Perkins* was limited to removal by heads of Departments it did not reach the issue of whether Congress could place restrictions on the removal power of the President once it had vested him with a power of appointment over inferior officers.

***Myers* and the Removal of Executive Officials.** *Myers v. United States*[10] finally reached the key issue of Congressional restriction of the President's removal power. The Postmaster General, in an order issued by and sanctioned by the President, discharged Myers, a postmaster at Portland, Oregon. However, Congress had provided that the President could remove postmasters only "with the advice and consent of the Senate," and that, until so removed, they would hold office for four years.[11] President Wilson removed Myers without any attempt to secure Senate concurrence. The Court of Claims dismissed Myers' suit for lost pay because he had waited too long to sue. The Supreme Court affirmed on different grounds.

Chief Justice (and former President) William Howard Taft wrote the opinion for the Court, holding that "[t]he power to remove . . . is an incident of the power to appoint"[12]

and the Tenure of Office Act was unconstitutional insofar as it restricted the power of the President to remove officers he had appointed.[13] Contrasting the general grant of executive power contained in Article II of the Constitution with the specific grants of enumerated legislative powers found in Article I, the Court found that the fact that the Constitution placed no express limitation on the power of removal a "convincing indication that none was intended."[14] The Court relied heavily on its view of history as well as on the practical necessity of an unfettered removal power for the President to carry out the mandate of Article I to see that "the Laws be faithfully executed." The Court recognized that need for removal as a "disciplinary influence,"[15] because "as his [the President's] selection of administrative officers is essential to the execution of the laws by him, so must be his power of removing those for whom he cannot continue to be responsible."[16]

Three Justices dissented from *Myers'* holding of an absolute power of the President to remove. Justice McReynolds felt that an unlimited power of removal could only stem from clear language in the Constitution and should not be implied absent such language. Justice Brandeis noted that Senatorial approval in the removal of officials was a well established legislative practice and, lacking a judicial decision to the contrary, such a practice should be equivalent to judicial construction of the statute granting the appointment power to the President. The remaining dissenter, Justice Holmes, argued that where Congress creates a

---

9. 116 U.S. at 485, 6 S.Ct. at 450. Over a century later, the Court cited *Perkins* in Morrison v. Olson, 487 U.S. 654, 108 S.Ct. 2597, 101 L.Ed.2d 569 (1988), and quoted with approval the following language from *Perkins*:

"The constitutional authority in Congress to thus vest the appointment [of inferior officers in the heads of departments] implies authority to limit, restrict, and regulate the removal by such laws as Congress may enact in relation to the officers so appointed."

487 U.S. at 689, n. 27, 108 S.Ct. at 2618, n. 27, quoting United States v. Perkins, 116 U.S. 483, 485, 6 S.Ct. 449, 450, 29 L.Ed. 700 (1886).

10. 272 U.S. 52, 47 S.Ct. 21, 71 L.Ed. 160 (1926). See Van Alstyne, The Role of Congress in Determining Inci-

dental Powers of the President and of the Federal Courts: A Comment on the Horizontal Effect of "the Sweeping Clause," 36 Ohio St.L.J. 788, 800–09 (1975).

11. 19 Stat. 80 provided that: "[P]ostmasters of the first, second, and third classes may be removed by the President by and with the advice and consent of the Senate, and shall hold their offices for four years unless sooner removed according to law. . . ."

12. 272 U.S. at 161, 47 S.Ct. at 40.

13. 272 U.S. at 176, 47 S.Ct. at 45.

14. 272 U.S. at 128, 47 S.Ct. at 29.

15. 272 U.S. at 132, 47 S.Ct. at 30.

16. 272 U.S. at 117, 47 S.Ct. at 25.

position, and has the power to transfer the appointment power to an official other than the President, Congress clearly has the power to restrict the mode of removing the appointee.

Commentators severely criticized *Myers* for the suggestion that the President could remove quasi-judicial officers such as, members of independent regulatory agencies.[17] Read broadly, *Myers* would stand for the proposition that under the Constitution the President has unrestricted power to remove any official he had appointed, with the exception of federal judges.

***Humphrey's Executor* and *Wiener*.** Nine years after *Myers*, the Court in *Humphrey's Executor v. United States*[18] limited its broad language and reach. *Humphrey's Executor* held that the President cannot remove a member of an independent regulatory agency in violation of restrictions in the statutory framework. The Federal Trade Commission Act provided that the President could remove any commissioner from office only for "inefficiency, neglect of duty, or malfeasance in office."[19] President Roosevelt removed Humphrey from his position as a member of the Commission. Roosevelt candidly admitted that the removal was for policy reasons rather than for one of the causes enumerated in the statute. Humphrey's executor brought suit to cover his lost wages.

The *Humphrey* Court looked to the nature and function of the Federal Trade Commission and concluded that "its duties are neither political nor executive, but predominantly quasi-judicial and quasi-legislative."[20] Recognizing that the independence of the regulatory agencies could be severely curtailed by a presidential power to remove members at will, the Court held that, while *Myers* applied to all

purely executive officers, the Constitution does not grant the President unlimited removal power as to quasi-legislative or quasi-judicial officers, even where such hold office through presidential appointment.[21]

Wiener v. United States[22] further clarified the distinction made in the *Humphrey* case between purely executive officers and those whose duties extend to non-executive functions. *Wiener* held invalid President Eisenhower's dismissal of a Truman appointee to the War Claims Commission, *even though there was the absence* of an express congressional restriction on the President's power of removal. The Court built on *Humphrey's Executor,* which had held that the validity of statutory limitations on presidential removal powers turns on the question of whether the involved agencies included functions either partially legislative or judicial. *Wiener* emphasized the "sharp differentiation" setting apart "those who are part of the Executive establishment and those whose tasks require absolute freedom from Executive interference."[23]

While these cases limit the President's power to remove quasi-judicial and quasi-legislative officers, they still allowed the President the power to remove "purely executive" officers, who must be removable by the President at will if he is to be able to accomplish his constitutional role. However, as discussed below, when the Court upheld, in *Morrison v. Olson,*[24] the constitutionality of special legislation creating an "Independent Counsel" and providing that the Independent Counsel can be removed only for cause, the Court modified the prior law and allowed greater Congressional power to limit the removal of Executive Branch officials.

At this point in time, *Humphrey's Executor* and related cases gave the Executive Branch,

---

17. See the opinion of the Court, 272 U.S. at 135, 47 S.Ct. at 31. This implication led one commentator to call the decision a "menacing challenge to an administrative organization which represents years of planning and experimentation in meeting modern conditions." E. Corwin, The President's Removal Power under the Constitution, 68 (Nat'l Municipal League 1927).

18. 295 U.S. 602, 55 S.Ct. 869, 79 L.Ed. 1611 (1935).

19. 295 U.S. at 623, 55 S.Ct. at 872.

20. 295 U.S. at 624, 55 S.Ct. at 872.

21. 295 U.S. at 629, 55 S.Ct. at 874.

22. 357 U.S. 349, 78 S.Ct. 1275, 2 L.Ed.2d 1377 (1958).

23. 357 U.S. at 353, 78 S.Ct. at 1278.

24. 487 U.S. 654, 108 S.Ct. 2597, 101 L.Ed.2d 569 (1988). Contrast, Martin v. Tobin, 451 F.2d 1335 (9th Cir.1971), a pre-*Morrison* case.

in general, the power of summary dismissal over its employees, subject to two important exceptions. The first occurs in a *Perkins* situation where Congress has restricted or regulated the manner of removal. Secondly, where an executive department promulgates administrative regulations having the force and effect of law that establish procedures governing dismissal of employees, such regulations are binding on the official who prescribed them for so long as the regulation remains operative.[25] Following these principles, the Supreme Court has ruled that an executive department must follow its own administrative regulations governing employee discharge or the discharge will be deemed illegal.[26] The regulations of course may always be changed.

Removal of Executive Officials by Congress: The Gramm–Rudman–Hollings Act.

In *Bowsher v. Synar*[27] the Court held that powers vested in the Comptroller General under the Balanced Budget and Emergency Deficit Control Act (the Gramm–Rudman–Hollings Act) violated the rule that Congress can play no direct role in the execution of the laws. The Court emphasized that Congress cannot reserve for itself the power of removal (except by impeachment) of an officer charged with the execution of the laws.[28] The purpose of this law was to reduce the federal deficit, by requiring, in various circumstances, automatic reductions in federal expenditures. These automatic reductions were triggered by a complex procedure that began with a "report" of deficit estimates and budget reduction calculations. The Comptroller General would report his conclusions to the President, who, in turn, must issue a "sequestration" order mandating the spending reductions that the Comptroller specified.

The statutory scheme at issue in *Bowsher,* provided that Congress could remove the Comptroller General not only by impeachment but also by Joint Resolution. Thus Congress could remove this official for a variety of reasons, including inefficiency, neglect of duty, or malfeasance. The Gramm–Rudman–Hollings Act also gave the Comptroller various executive functions. His duties, the Court concluded, were not merely ministerial. When the Comptroller interpreted a federal law enacted to implement the legislative mandate to reduce the budget deficit, that is the very essence of "execution" of the law. Congress cannot grant to the Comptroller, an officer under its control, executive power, which is power that Congress does not possess:

> Under § 251, the Comptroller General must exercise judgment concerning facts that affect the application of the Act. He must also interpret the provisions of the Act to determine precisely what budgetary calculations are required. Decisions of that kind are typically made by officers charged with executing a statute.[29]

The Court went on to explain that the law contemplated that the Comptroller General would have the "ultimate authority" to determine the budget cuts to be made and the President would be required to carry out these commands. Thus the Court invalidated § 251 of the Gramm–Rudman–Hollings Act.

Congress responded to this decision by amending the law so that the Director of the Office of Management and Budget, an Executive Branch official, would issue the report that would trigger the application of the Gramm–Rudman–Hollings Act.[30] The Director of the Office of Management and Budget is supposed to give due regard to a report issued

---

25. The doctrine that the official prescribing such a regulation is bound by it stems from United States ex rel. Accardi v. Shaughnessy, 347 U.S. 260, 74 S.Ct. 499, 98 L.Ed. 681 (1954).

26. Service v. Dulles, 354 U.S. 363, 77 S.Ct. 1152, 1 L.Ed.2d 1403 (1957); Vitarelli v. Seaton, 359 U.S. 535, 79 S.Ct. 968, 3 L.Ed.2d 1012 (1959).

27. 478 U.S. 714, 106 S.Ct. 3181, 92 L.Ed.2d 583 (1986). See also, Myers v. United States, 272 U.S. 52, 114, 47 S.Ct. 21, 24, 71 L.Ed. 160 (1926).

28. 478 U.S. at 726, 106 S.Ct. at 3187–88. Cf. I.N.S. v. Chadha, 462 U.S. 919, 954–55, 103 S.Ct. 2764, 2786, 77 L.Ed.2d 317 (1983).

29. 478 U.S. at 733, 106 S.Ct. at 3191.

30. Public Law 100–119, 100 Stat. 754 (Sept. 20, 1987), amending, inter alia, 9 U.S.C.A. §§ 252(a)(1) & (a)(2).

earlier by the Director of the Congressional Budget Office.

President Reagan signed the law and stated that it did not preclude him or future Presidents from overseeing and directing the Director of the Office of Management and Budget. If the law were interpreted otherwise and required the President to follow the orders of one of his subordinates (in this case, the Director of the Office of Management and Budget), "it would plainly constitute an unconstitutional infringement of the President's authority as head of a unitary Executive Branch."[31]

Limitations on Executive Removal Powers after *Morrison v. Olson*. *Morrison v. Olson*,[32] in upholding the law providing for a special prosecutor or "Independent Counsel" to investigate and prosecute in certain cases involving officials within the Executive Branch, concluded that the Act did not violate the principle of separation of powers. The Independent Counsel Act provided that the Attorney General could only remove for cause. If the Attorney General does remove the Independent Counsel, the Attorney General must report the reasons to the Judiciary Committees of the House and Senate. In addition, the Attorney General must report the reasons to the panel of Article III judges who had appointed the Independent Counsel at the request of the Attorney General. This special panel is called the "Special Division" by the Act. The Independent Counsel can seek reinstatement by filing an action in the district court for the District of Columbia, but if she does, no judge who is on the Special Division can set on that case.

Though Congress placed limited on the power of the Attorney General to remove the Independent Counsel, Congress gave itself no role in the removal process, as it had tried to do in the scheme invalidated in *Bowsher v. Synar*.[33]

Because Congress could remove the Independent Counsel only through the impeachment process, it could not use the threat of removal as a way of trying to supervise the investigatory and prosecutorial (that is, executive) functions of the Independent Counsel.

The provisions limiting the Executive's powers to remove the Independent Counsel are constitutional. Although Court acknowledged that earlier cases had spoken of legislative restrictions over the removal of executive branch officials in terms of "quasi-legislative" or "quasi-judicial"—

[T]he real question is whether the removal restrictions are of such a nature that they impede the President's ability to perform his constitutional duty, and the functions of the officials in question must be analyzed in that light.[34]

While some officials, are so "purely executive" that the President must be able to remove them at will "if he is able to accomplish his constitutional role."[35] But the Independent's Counsel is not in that category.[36]

In addition, the Act did not completely strip the President of the power to remove the Independent Counsel, for there could be removal if there was "cause."

Removal of Article III Judges from Non–Article III Positions. *Mistretta v. United States*[37] upheld the constitutionality of the United States Sentencing Commission, a group that promulgated sentencing guidelines in criminal cases. The law provided that the Commission was "an independent commission in the judicial branch of the United States." The Court concluded that it was appropriate for Congress to delegate to this commission nonadjudicatory functions that do not intrude on the prerogatives of another branch and that

31. 23 Weekly Compilation of Presidential Documents 1091 (Oct. 5, 1987).

32. 487 U.S. 654, 108 S.Ct. 2597, 101 L.Ed.2d 569 (1988).

33. 478 U.S. 714, 730, 106 S.Ct. 3181, 3190–91, 92 L.Ed.2d 583 (1986).

34. 487 U.S. at 691, 108 S.Ct. at 2619.

35. 487 U.S. at 690, 108 S.Ct. at 2618 (footnote omitted).

36. 487 U.S. at 691–92, 108 S.Ct. at 2619 (footnote omitted).

37. 488 U.S. 361, 109 S.Ct. 647, 102 L.Ed.2d 714 (1989).

are appropriate to the central mission of the judiciary.

The President must appoint at least three of the members of the Commission from a list of six Article III judges whom the Judicial Conference of the United States recommends. Judges who are appointed to the Commission wear, in effect, two hats (an Article III judicial hat and an administrative hat), but not two hats at the same time. That is, those judges who are members of the Commission are members because the President appointed them. As members of the Commission they wield certain power, but that power is not Article III judicial power but administrative power derived from the enabling legislation.

The President can remove members of this Commission, including the judicial members, only for "good cause" such as neglect of duty or malfeasance in office. The Court concluded that this power to remove federal judges from the Commission does not violate the Constitution. The President's removal power over the members of the Commission, including those members who are also Article III judges, does not authorize or diminish the status of Article III judges as judges. The President cannot affect either the tenure or compensation of Article III judges, even those who are also on the Commission.[38] Even if an Article III judge is removed from the Commission, he remains an Article III judge. The Sentencing Commission Act does not prevent the Judicial Branch from performing its constitutionally assigned function of fairly adjudicating cases and controversies.

Conclusion. The removal power cases establish several general principles. First, purely executive officers appointed by the President are subject to a presidential removal power that may not constitutionally be limited by Congress, unless Congress has a good reason

to so limit the removal power. This test is admittedly vague, but that is the result of the holding of *Morrison v. Olson*. Second, Congress may similarly limit and regulate removal where it has vested the appointment power in some official other than the President. Third, after *Morrison v. Olson* Congress may limit the power of the President (or his delegate) to remove certain executive branch officials only for cause; the test is not whether the official is "quasi-legislative" or "quasi-judicial" but rather whether it is reasonable for Congress to restrict the Executive Branch's removal power.

The real question is whether the removal restrictions are of such a nature that they impede the President's ability to perform his constitutional duty, or whether the President's need to control the exercise of the discretion of the official in question is so central to the functioning of the Executive Branch that the official in question should be terminable at will by the President. Finally, where an executive department has established administrative regulations having the force and effect of law to govern employee dismissal, it may not remove any employee in a manner inconsistent with those regulations. The Government should abide by the rules and restrictions that it places on itself.

§ 7.15   Legislative Veto of Executive Branch Regulations and Actions

Congress, in an attempt to maintain more control over the President and over regulations promulgated by agencies of the federal government's executive branch, has in the past incorporated into legislation a provision known as the "legislative veto" or the "congressional veto." Congress sought by statute to give itself what the Constitution gives to the President.[1] Congress typically utilized veto provisions when granting the President or an

---

38. Commission members receive the salary of a court of appeals judge. Hence, if a district court judge were appointed to the Commission, he would receive an increase in salary, and if the President removed him from the Commission, that district court judge would receive a *decrease* in salary. The Court in *Mistretta* said:

"We do not address the hypothetical constitutional question whether, under the Compensation Clause of Article III, a district judge removed from the Commis-

sion must continue to be paid the higher salary." 488 U.S. at 411 n. 32, 109 S.Ct. at 674 n. 32.

§ 7.15

1. Rotunda, The Veto Power, in the Oxford Companion to the Supreme Court of the United States 896 (Oxford University Press, Kermit L. Hall, ed. 1992).

executive agency the power to promulgate regulations with the force of law. These provisions required the President or an agency official to present the proposed regulations to Congress, which retained a "right" to approve or disapprove any regulations before they take effect.

Such legislative veto provisions typically provided that a proposed regulation will become law after the expiration of a certain period of time, only if Congress does not affirmatively disapprove of the regulation in the meantime. Less frequently, the statute provided that a proposed regulation could become law only if Congress affirmatively approved it.[2] Both types of provisions established what congressional action is necessary. Sometimes the required action was action by both houses, or only one house, or perhaps just the action of one committee of one chamber.[3]

Since the early 1970's, Congress, with increasing frequency, retained veto rights when delegating powers to the executive and had utilized or attempted to utilize the congressional veto to reject agency regulations of public interest and controversy.[4] Commentators and litigants began challenging the use of the legislative veto as unconstitutional on several grounds: (1) that one-house veto provisions violate the sections of Article I of the Constitution requiring legislation to pass both chambers of Congress; (2) that legislative veto provisions violate the presentment clause of Article I requiring the presentment of legislation to the President for approval or veto; and (3) that legislative veto provisions generally

contravene the separation of powers doctrine implicit in Articles I, II and III.

The *Chadha* Decision. On June 23, 1983, the Supreme Court finally resolved the issue in *Immigration and Naturalization Service v. Chadha.*[5] In an unusually broad ruling, the Court held that the legislative veto provision contained in the Immigration and Nationality Act was unconstitutional. The *Chadha* holding requires that any "legislative veto" be passed as legislation by both chambers of Congress and presented to the President for approval or veto.

Justice White's strong dissent made clear the significance of *Chadha.* He stated: "Today the Court not only invalidates § 244(c)(2) of the Immigration and Nationality Act, but also sounds the death knell for nearly 200 other statutory provisions in which Congress has reserved a legislative veto."[6] He added that the "apparent sweep of the Court's decision today is regrettable" because it "appears to invalidate all legislative vetoes irrespective of form or subject ... to strike an entire class of statutes based on consideration of a somewhat atypical and more readily indictable exemplar of the class is irresponsible."[7]

Chadha was an alien in the United States on a nonimmigrant student visa. He overstayed his visa and was ordered to show cause why he should not be deported. Pursuant to section 244(a)(1) of the Immigration and Nationality Act, an immigration judge found that Chadha met the statutory requirements to have his deportation suspended. This suspension order, however, had to be submitted to Congress

---

2. See, 2 R. Rotunda & J. Nowak, Treatise on Constitutional Law: Substance and Procedure § 10.8 (West Group, 3d ed. 1999) for further analysis of the Legislative Veto.

On constitutional problems related to the enactment of federal legislation, and an analysis of how a bill becomes a law, see 2 R. Rotunda & J. Nowak, and J. Young, Treatise on Constitutional Law: Substance and Procedure §§ 10.1–10.9 (West Group, 3d ed. 1999).

3. B. Craig, The Legislative Veto: Congressional Control of Regulation 1–2 (1983).

4. In 1977, resolutions were submitted in both houses of Congress to veto the National Highway Traffic Safety Administration's passive restraint (air-bags) rule. Although the resolutions failed, the House was later successful in prohibiting use of any Department of Trans-

portation funds for air bags regulation. B. Craig, The Legislative Veto: Congressional Control of Regulation 116–17 (1983). In 1980, four sets of federal education regulations were successfully vetoed. Id. at 79. Also in 1980, the National Gas Policy Act of 1978, complementing the second phase of incremental pricing in natural gas deregulation, was successfully defeated by a one-house veto. Id. at 99. In 1982, the Federal Trade Commission's used car warranty rule was vetoed by both houses. Id. at 131–32.

5. 462 U.S. 919, 103 S.Ct. 2764, 77 L.Ed.2d 317 (1983).

6. 462 U.S. at 967, 103 S.Ct. at 2792, 77 L.Ed.2d at 355 (White, J. dissenting).

7. 462 U.S. at 974, 103 S.Ct. at 2796, 77 L.Ed.2d at 359 (White, J. dissenting).

under section 244(c)(1), and either chamber of Congress was given an opportunity to pass a resolution to overrule the executive branch and order that the alien be deported. The House of Representatives chose to exercise its section 244(c)(2) legislative veto power in Chadha's case and vetoed his suspension of deportation. This resolution was not treated as "legislation" and thus was not sent to the Senate or the President for approval.

The Supreme Court held (7 to 2) that the one-house veto provision of section 244(c)(2) violated the presentment clauses contained in clauses 2 and 3 of Article I, Section 7 of the Constitution, the bicameral requirement of Article I, Section 1 and Section 7, clause 2, and the implied separation of powers structure of Articles I, II and III. The Court found that the House's resolution ordering Chadha's deportation, although not legislative in form, supplanted congressional action through legislation and was legislative in character, purpose, and effect.[8]

Because the majority concluded that the legislative veto was really an act of legislation, *Chadha* ruled that it had to conform with the constitutional mandates of bicameral passage followed by presentment to the President. The congressional veto was not merely a "convenient short cut" that eliminated cumbersome and time consuming burdens. The legislative veto is efficient, but "the Framers ranked other values higher than efficiency," and they determined that federal legislation should be "a step-by-step, deliberate and deliberative process."[9] The Court emphasized that the checks and balances of the separation of powers system was the best way to preserve freedom; the duty to comply with explicit constitutional standards is more important than the desire to avoid delays.[10]

Whether or not legislative vetoes are efficient, they are bad policy, because it is harder for the special interests to capture the Department of Justice to Attorney General (the par-

ties involved in *Chadha* or an independent agency than for the special interest groups to capture a House or Senate Subcommittee), which tends to be the group to which the full House or Senate defer when exercising the legislative veto.

But the constitutional question is different than what is good or bad policy. On that issue, *Chadha* is written in a conclusory fashion. The Court tells us that a legislative veto is "legislation" and must be passed by both houses and signed by the President. Yet, when the Attorney General does that which the legislation at issue in *Chadha* authorized, then "he does not exercise 'legislative' power." He acts in "his presumptively Art. II capacity when he administers the Immigration and Nationality Act." It "might resemble 'legislative' action," but it is not "legislative action" and "is not subject to the approval of both Houses of Congress and the President for the reason that the Constitution does not so require."[11] The Court is announcing its holding, rather than explaining the reasoning that led to its holding.

If Congress can delegate law-making to independent agencies or to the Attorney General, can it delegate law-making to itself, or to one of its Houses, or to a committee or subcommittee? There are important differences in the delegation. If Congress delegates to an administrator (such as the Attorney General, as Congress did in *Chadha*), there is judicial review to make sure that there is no violation of other federal statutes (such as the Administrative Procedure Act), to make sure the administrator decided on the record (not on the basis, e.g., of ex parte contacts), that the all of the procedural niceties have been followed, and that there is a record that fairly supports the administrator's conclusions of law and fact. Granted, the courts give deference to the administrator, but the courts have various tools to overturn what the administrator did short of calling the action unconstitutional. Not so when Congress enacts a statute. Short of declaring the statute unconstitutional, or inter-

8.   462 U.S. at 952, 103 S.Ct. at 2784–85, 77 L.Ed.2d at 345.

9.   462 U.S. at 958–59, 103 S.Ct. at 2788, 77 L.Ed.2d at 349.

10.   See also, 462 U.S. at 957–58, 103 S.Ct. at 2787.

11.   I.N.S. v. Chadha, 462 U.S. 919, 954 n. 16, 103 S.Ct. 2764, 2785 n. 16, 77 L.Ed.2d 317.

preting the statute in a way to avoid constitutional problems, the courts have little control over Congressional statutes. The legislative veto is a lesser power (as Justice White argued in his dissent) but rather a greater power, for it allows Congress to micro manage the Executive without going through the burden of enacting legislation that must withstand a Presidential veto.

Severability. Though the congressional veto contained in section 244(c)(2) was unconstitutional, the Court held that it was severable from the remainder of the section. Thus, the Attorney General still had the authority to suspend Chadha's deportation under section 244(a)(1) and to report this action to Congress under section 244(c)(1). A presumption of severability arose from section 406 of the Act, which provided if any provision of the Act was held invalid, the remainder of the Act was not to be affected.

Additionally, the Court concluded that the provision was severable because, even after the Court severed the offending section, the Act was fully operative as a law. Without the one-house veto provision, Burger stated, the section would operate as a "report and wait" provision.[12] The deportation suspension order would then be reported to Congress, which could pass legislation barring its effectiveness

if it found it objectionable. This legislation would have to pass both houses and be subject to presidential veto. The Court had previously upheld such report and wait provisions in *Sibbach v. Wilson & Co.*[13]

The Post–*Chadha* Era. Two weeks after the *Chadha* decision, the Court upheld, in a memorandum decision, two lower court decisions invalidating the legislative veto provisions in the Natural Gas Policy Act of 1978 and the Federal Trade Commission Improvement Act of 1980.[14] This summary affirmation in fact extended the Court's previous decision in several respects. First, the separation of powers reasoning was applied for the first time to independent regulatory agencies.[15] Secondly, the legislative veto provision in the Federal Trade Commission Improvement Act, unlike that in *Chadha*, required the approval of both houses of Congress and thus met the bicameralism requirement (but not the presentment requirement) of Article I.[16] Finally, the Natural Gas Policy Act did not contain a severability clause, and thus there was the more difficult question of whether the veto provision could be severed from the rest of the Act.[17]

Chadha appears to require, on statutes containing legislative veto provisions, a case-by-case examination of whether the veto can be severed from the rest of the act.[18] Some legisla-

---

12. 462 U.S. at 935, nn. 8–9, 103 S.Ct. at 2776, nn. 8–9, 77 L.Ed.2d at 334, nn. 8–9. Justices Rehnquist and White objected to this severability conclusion, 462 U.S. at 1013, 103 S.Ct. at 2816, 77 L.Ed.2d at 384 (Rehnquist, J., dissenting).

13. 312 U.S. 1, 61 S.Ct. 422, 85 L.Ed. 479 (1941) (the statute provided that the Federal Rules of Civil Procedure "shall not take effect until they shall have been reported to Congress by the Attorney General at the beginning of a regular session thereof and until after the close of such session").

14. Consumer Energy v. Federal Energy Regulatory Commission, 673 F.2d 425 (D.C.Cir.1982), affirmed sub nom., Process Gas Consumers Group v. Consumer Energy Council of America, 463 U.S. 1216, 103 S.Ct. 3556, 77 L.Ed.2d 1402 (1983), rehearing denied 463 U.S. 1250, 104 S.Ct. 40, 77 L.Ed.2d 1457 (1983); Consumers Union of United States, Inc. v. Federal Trade Commission, 691 F.2d 575 (D.C.Cir.1982), affirmed sub nom., Process Gas Consumers Group v. Consumer Energy Council of America, 463 U.S. 1216, 103 S.Ct. 3556, 77 L.Ed.2d 1402 (1983), rehearing denied 463 U.S. 1250, 104 S.Ct. 40, 77 L.Ed.2d 1457 (1983).

Although a two-house veto provision would seem more defensible than the one-house veto—because the two-

house veto constitutes a rejection of the substantive rule by the entire Congress—the two-house veto also fails to allow the President the opportunity to veto the congressional action and force Congress to override that veto in order to make the congressional decision effective.

15. 463 U.S. at 1217, 103 S.Ct. at 3557–58, 77 L.Ed.2d at 1403 (White, J. dissenting to summary affirmance).

16. See U.S.Const. art. I, § 1, & art. I, § 7, cl. 2.

17. The Court of Appeals for the District of Columbia undertook an extensive examination of the legislative history of the Natural Gas Policy Act of 1978 and the legislative veto provision contained there. Without the benefit of a presumption, the court found that Congress would have enacted the incremental pricing without the veto provision. Consumer Energy, etc. v. Federal Energy Regulatory Commission, 673 F.2d 425, 444–45 (D.C.Cir. 1982), affirmed sub nom., Process Gas Consumers Group v. Consumer Energy Council of America, 463 U.S. 1216, 103 S.Ct. 3556, 77 L.Ed.2d 1402 (1983), rehearing denied 463 U.S. 1250, 104 S.Ct. 40, 77 L.Ed.2d 1457 (1983).

18. B. Craig, The Legislative Veto: Congressional Control of Regulation 143 (1983).

tive veto provisions have never been exercised and, thus, may never be subject to a judicial ruling *if* a congressional veto of a presidential or executive action is needed to avoid an advisory ruling.

Some litigants have played on the *Chadha* opinion when executive agencies threaten then with the enforcement of statutes that contain a legislative veto provision, even if the veto has not been exercised.[19] If the statute conferring enforcement or legislative power to the regulating agency contains a congressional veto clause, the alleged offender claims that the veto clause could not be severed from the remainder of the statute; the argument is that the mere presence of an unexercised veto automatically invalidates the entire statute. Thus, the litigant argues, because the entire statute would be invalid, the agency would lack authority to enforce the statute.

One district court accepted this argument *in toto*, holding that the entire Reorganization Act of 1977 was therefore unconstitutional.[20] In another case, also challenging the Equal Employment Opportunity Commission's authority, the Fifth Circuit found that the legislative veto provision in the Reorganization Act was unconstitutional but severable from the remainder of the Act.[21] These cases are interesting in that they portray how the constitutionality of a congressional veto provision may be challenged even though it has not been

exercised and even though the existence of the provision directly injures no party.

What is likely to happen in future cases where a law has a legislative veto is that Congress will henceforth not exercise it. The mere presence of an unexercised legislative veto provision in a statute may invalidate it, so Congress should reexamine such laws.

§ 7.16 President Line Item Veto

At the time of the Constitutional Convention, the term "line-item" veto did not exist because the problem of unrelated bills and riders did not then exist. Shortly before the Civil War, Congress first began the practice of attaching appropriations riders to bills.[1] Then, the term "rider" was developed, along with its corollary "line-item veto."[2]

In response to this development, Presidents, for many years, have proposed creating a line-item veto—that is, a power to veto a particular item (or line) in a federal appropriations bill without having to veto the entire bill.[3] Legislators often seek to amend essential legislation with their favorite projects, knowing that it will be difficult, if not impossible, for the President to veto the entire bill. Opponents of these techniques have urged the creation of a line-item veto, often in an effort to reduce pork barrel spending by giving the President more control over the appropriation process.[4]

19. E.g., Equal Employment Opportunity Commission v. Hernando Bank, Inc., 724 F.2d 1188 (5th Cir.1984); Equal Employment Opportunity Commission v. Allstate Insurance Company, 570 F.Supp. 1224 (S.D.Miss.1983), appeal dismissed for want of jurisdiction 467 U.S. 1232, 104 S.Ct. 3499, 82 L.Ed.2d 810 (1984), case remanded 740 F.2d 966 (5th Cir.1984).

20. Equal Employment Opportunity Commission v. Allstate Insurance Company, 570 F.Supp. 1224, 1229 (S.D.Miss.1983), ("a retained one-house veto is unconstitutional even when not exercised"), appeal dismissed 467 U.S. 1232, 104 S.Ct. 3499, 82 L.Ed.2d 810 (1984), case remanded 740 F.2d 966 (5th Cir.1984).

21. Equal Employment Opportunity Commission v. Hernando Bank, Inc., 724 F.2d 1188 (5th Cir.1984).

§ 7.16

1. Stephen Glazier, Reagan Already Has Line–Item Veto, Wall Street Journal, Dec. 4, 1987, at A14, col. 5 (midwest ed.); Sidak & Smith, Four Faces of the Item Veto: A Reply to Tribe and Kurland, 84 Northwestern U.L.Rev. 437 (1990); Ronald D. Rotunda, The Veto Power,

in The Oxford Companion to the Supreme Court of the United States 896 (Oxford University Press, Kermit L. Hall, ed. 1992).

2. Id. The Confederate Constitution thus gave President Jefferson Davis an explicit line-item veto because of the problems then current.

3. At least six Presidents before Reagan have proposed a line-item veto. See The Line–Item Veto, 41 Record of the Association of the Bar of the City of N.Y. 367 (1986); R. Ross & F. Schwengel, An Item–Veto for the President?, 12 Presidential Studies Quarterly 66, 71–72 (1982); J. Gregory Sidak & Thomas A. Smith, Why Did President Bush Repudiate the "Inherent" Line–Item Veto?, 9 Journal of Law & Politics 39 (1992);; Ronald D. Rotunda, Handed a Lesser Veto, 20 Legal Times (of Washington, D.C.) 27, 28 (May 26, 1997).

4. E.g., Ronald D. Rotunda, Line–Item Veto: Best Budget Fix?, 11 Legal Times (of Washington, D.C.) 15 (Mar. 27, 1989).

In the past Presidents sought to limit federal spending through use of presidential impoundment of funds, but Congress limited that power by statute.[5] The focus then shifted to the line-item veto as a device to control deficit spending. Most states have already given their governors line-item power.[6]

Congress could, of course, give the President a line-item veto by proposing a constitutional amendment subject to ratification by the states. The real issue is whether Congress could give the President a line-item veto by mere legislation, just as it now could authorize (or limit) presidential impoundment. For many years, the answer to this question was in constitutional limbo. When the Court finally decided the question, a majority held that Congress could not, by statute, grant the President a line-item veto.

Unconstitutionality of the Line Item Veto. In 1996, Congress enacted a statute granting the President line item veto.[7] President Clinton exercised the line item veto a number of times, and it was eventually tested in the Court. A divided Supreme Court invalidated the law in *Clinton v. City of New York.*[8]

The City of New York and others sued President Clinton, and others claiming that they had been injured by his decision to "cancel" a portion of a federal statute that waived the federal government's right to recoup certain funds from New York. Separately, owners of certain food refiners and processors sued, claiming that they had been injured by President Clinton's "cancellation" of a provision of a law that allowed them to defer recognition of capital gains. Justice Stevens, for the Court, then held that the Line Item Veto Act violated the presentment clause.[9]

Justice Stevens argued that the law's cancellation provisions amounted to the President amending "two Acts of Congress by repealing a portion of each,"[10] but his partial repeals did not conform to the requirements of the presentment clause. Stevens said that when the President exercises his veto of the whole bill, he returns it to Congress "*before* the bill becomes law." But, under the statute at issue, the "statutory cancellation occurs *after* the bill becomes law."[11] The constitutional silence on the issue of a line item veto, Stevens contended, should be treated as equivalent to an express constitutional prohibition.[12]

When Congress passed the Rules Enabling Act, it provided that the Supreme Court's enactment of the Rules of Procedure for the lower federal courts had the effect of overriding (cancelling?) prior Acts of Congress. The relevant language provided that "All laws in conflict with such rules shall be of no further force or effect after such rules have taken effect." The Court rule resulted in "repeal" of the inconsistent statute, a practice the Supreme Court upheld in 1941.[13] The Court has also upheld statutes where Congress delegates to the President the power to suspend (cancel?) statutes allowing importation of certain goods without paying import duties.[14]

---

5. See 1 Ronald D. Rotunda & John E. Nowak, Treatise on Constitutional Law: Substance & Procedure (West Group, 3d ed. 1999), at § 7.4. See also, Kendall v. United States ex rel. Stokes, 37 U.S. (12 Pet.) 524, 9 L.Ed. 1181 (1838); Train v. New York, 420 U.S. 35, 95 S.Ct. 839, 43 L.Ed.2d 1 (1975).

6. 41 Record of the Association of the Bar of the City of N.Y. 367, 371. The Confederacy granted a line-item veto power to President Jefferson Davis. Id. at 371.

7. 110 Stat. at Large 1200.

8. 524 U.S. 417, 118 S.Ct. 2091, 141 L.Ed.2d 393 (1998). Earlier the Court refused to rule on the question on jurisdictional grounds, because the plaintiffs (Members of Congress) did not allege a sufficiently concrete injury. Raines v. Byrd, 521 U.S. 811, 829–30, 117 S.Ct. 2312, 2322, 138 L.Ed.2d 849 (1997).

Cf. Ronald D. Rotunda, Handed a Lesser Veto, 20 Legal Times (of Washington, D.C.) 27, 28 (May 26, 1997).

9. Justices Scalia & O'Connor would have denied standing to some of the appellees and, on the merits, would have upheld the Line Item Veto statute as to those who had standing. He appreciated that the issue was really one of delegation of power, and this delegation was not outside the constitutional pale. Breyer, J., found standing and would have upheld the constitutionality of the Line Item Veto.

10. 524 U.S. at 438, 118 S.Ct. at 2103.

11. 524 U.S. 417, 118 S.Ct. 2091.

12. 528 U.S. at 439, 118 S.Ct. at 2103 (emphasis in original).

13. Sibbach v. Wilson & Co., 312 U.S. 1, 10, 61 S.Ct. 422, 425, 85 L.Ed. 479 (1941).

14. Field v. Clark, 143 U.S. 649, 12 S.Ct. 495, 36 L.Ed. 294 (1892).

But Justice Stevens was unpersuaded by these examples. He argued, for example, that when the President suspended an exemption under the the Tariff Act, "he was executing the policy that Congress embodied in the statute". In contrast, whenever the President cancels an item of new direct spending or a limited tax benefit he is rejecting the policy judgment made by Congress and relying on his own policy judgment.[15]

Although the sharply divided Court held that Congress cannot give the President a line item veto by statute, Congress could always decide to send to the President bills containing only individual items. Nongermane items would not be bundled together. Even germane items that are germane to each other could be cut into several separate bills, each subject to veto. For example, instead of enacting one highway bill, Congress could enact several highway bills, each covering a separate project.

However, if Congress were to decide to enact many small bills instead of a few large ones, it would lose the political leverage it now has in bargaining with the President. Individual Representatives and Senators would also lose a lot of the power they now have to bring home pork barrel projects to help their constituents. Consequently, we should not expect Congress to enact a series of small bills when one large bill is more likely to survive a Presidential veto threat.

Congress might also decide that, as a matter of convenience, it was treating many separate spending bills as one bill but then provide, in its rules of procedure or as a matter of legislative definition, that each nongermane provision is really a separate bill. In that case, the Court might allow the President to veto each "bill," because Congress defined the separate sections as different bills.

If there is no limit on the power of Congress to seek to veto-proof narrow legislation by attaching it as a rider to a bill, there can be serious erosion of executive powers. In theory, each Congress, which sits for two years, could determine, on the last day, that all its actions for that period would become part of one huge, omnibus bill. The earlier "bills" would be treated as part of this one giant bill. The President would then be faced with a Hobbesian choice, a "take it or leave it" proposition. The President could either veto two years of legislative work (including many bills favored by the President), and/or accept the entire "bill" and all the narrow pork barrel legislation that it contained.

---

15. Clinton v. City of New York, 524 U.S. 417, 444, 118 S.Ct. 2091, 2106, 141 L.Ed.2d 393 (footnote omitted).

Chapter 8

THE COMMERCE CLAUSE AND RESTRICTIONS ON STATE REGULATORY POWERS

§ 8.1 State Regulation Affecting Interstate Commerce— Introduction

The focus of this Chapter is on the question of what, if any, limitations the commerce clause places on state or local laws that relate to items or activities that have not been the subject of federal regulation. When the Supreme Court examines the compatibility of a state or local law with the commerce clause (on a subject regarding which Congress has not spoken) the Court may refer to its action as involving either "dormant commerce clause" principles or "negative commerce clause" principles. The phrase "dormant commerce clause" and the phrase "negative commerce clause" are functionally interchangeable. Both phrases embody the concept that the mere grant of a commerce power to Congress in Article I, § 8, by implication, places limits upon state or local laws regulating commerce.[1] When a state law regulates a commercial activity on which Congress has not spoken, the state is regulating an activity regarding which the commerce clause is dormant (in the sense that Congress has not brought to life its Article I, § 8 commerce power regarding the specific subject matter). The commerce clause of Article I, § 8 contains only an affirmative grant of power to Congress; it does not explicitly state any limitations on the extent of state or local legislation that regulates commerce. The negative aspect of the commerce clause is the principle, established by the Supreme Court, that the Article I grant of power to Congress, by implication, placed a limitation on state or local laws related to interstate commerce.

The Court might have interpreted the commerce clause to be an exclusive grant of power to Congress, so that states would not be able to enact any legislation that affected interstate commerce until Congress had given states such authority. Alternatively, the Supreme Court might have adopted a theory under which the commerce clause placed no limitations on state or local legislation. The Supreme Court took a middle course, between these two extremes. The Court decided that the judiciary was authorized to interpret the dormant commerce clause to invalidate certain types of state or local legislation, and that Congress had the power to approve state laws that otherwise would violate dormant commerce clause principles.

In this Chapter we are not concerned with state or local legislation that directly conflicts with federal law. The Constitution specifically

§ 8.1

1. U.S. Const. art. I § 8 cl.3. The definition of "commerce" in the commerce clause is the same regardless of whether the term is being used to justify federal control of an activity or to restrict state or local regulation of an activity. Philadelphia v. New Jersey, 437 U.S. 617, 623–24, 98 S.Ct. 2531, 57 L.Ed.2d 475, 481–82 (1978).

This chapter examines problems related to state and local government actions that affect interstate commerce.

State or local actions that affect international commerce are subject to additional constitutional restrictions. See §§ 4.2, 6.5–6.9.

For a more extensive analysis of all the principles that are touched upon in this Chapter, see the multi-volume version of this Treatise: R. Rotunda & J. Nowak, Treatise on Constitutional Law: Substance and Procedure, Chapters 3, 4, 6, 11, and 13 (West Group, 3d ed., 1999, with annual supplements).

grants power to Congress to regulate commerce, and as we have seen, the judiciary has given great deference to Congress when it exercises its commercial powers.[2] Any state or local law that conflicts with a valid federal law is invalid under the terms of the supremacy clause of Article VI of the Constitution.[3]

Congress may enact a law that expressly adopts or approves a specific type of state or local regulation affecting commerce. Federal legislation of this type will make such a state law immune from a commerce clause attack.[4] For example, a state statute regarding insurance companies that imposes special burdens on interstate insurance businesses might be held to violate the dormant commerce clause, if there was no federal legislation regarding the insurance industry.[5] If Congress enacts a law allowing states to regulate the insurance industry in a way that involves discrimination against out-of-state insurance companies, a state law that discriminates against out-of-state insurance corporations would no longer violate the commerce clause.[6] When the Court reviews federal legislation that allows states to regulate certain types of commerce, the Court is not reviewing the state law but, rather, the federal legislation. The federal legislation, in our example, clearly would fall within the commerce power of Congress because it involves the regulation of interstate commercial transactions. There is no requirement that the federal law help the national economy or inter-

state commerce. Approval of state laws that in any way affect, or even harm, interstate commerce comes within the power granted to Congress by the Article I, § 8 commerce clause.

The Supreme Court, since the time of John Marshall, consistently has found that judicial invalidation of some types of state or local laws is justified by the text of the Constitution, and democratic theory. Several reasons support the Supreme Court's decisions holding that there is a negative aspect of the commerce clause that limits state authority.

First, one of the key factors that led political leaders in the states to call for a meeting to revise the Articles of Confederation, which led to the eventual drafting of our Constitution, was economic competition between the states.[7] Under the Articles of Confederation, the federal government could not resolve economic disputes between states; states were free to create trade barriers against economic competition from other states. An initial meeting to revise the Articles of Confederation made it clear to the participating states that a new form of government had to be created if states were going to resolve their commercial conflicts. The inability of the states to resolve commercial conflicts under the Articles of Confederation provided the impetus for calling the convention that we now refer to as the Constitutional Convention. The Constitution of 1787 placed some specific limitations on

---

2. See Chapter 4 §§ 4.7–4.10, supra.

3. Thus, in Gibbons v. Ogden, 22 U.S. (9 Wheat) 1, 6 L.Ed.23 (1824). The Court invalidated a state law as being in conflict with a federal statute, although Chief Justice Marshall's opinion, *in dicta*, stated that the commerce clause itself would restrict some state control of commercial matters.

4. Congress "may adopt provisions of a state of any subject," Gibbons v. Ogden, 22 U.S. (9 Wheat.) 1, 207, 6 L.Ed. 23, 73 (1824). See also Pennsylvania v. Wheeling and Belmont Bridge Co., 59 U.S. (18 How.) 421, 15 L.Ed. 435 (1855) (Act of Congress declaring Wheeling Bridge to be a lawful structure is upheld even though the court had previously found that the bridge obstructed commerce). Wilkerson v. Rahrer, 140 U.S. 545 11 S.Ct. 865, 35 L.Ed. 572 (1891) (Congressional action may allow a state to regulate traffic in liquor that would otherwise be barred by the commerce clause, prior to the 18th and 21st Amendments). See § 8.5, Infra. "When Congress so chooses, state actions which it plainly authorizes are invulnerable to constitutional attack under the Commerce Clause."

Northeast Bancorp, Inc. v. Board of Governors, 472 U.S. 159, 175, 105 S.Ct. 2545, 2554, 86 L.Ed.2d 112 (1985).

5. See generally, Metropolitan Life Insurance Co. v. Ward, 470 U.S. 869, 105 S.Ct. 1676, 84 L.Ed.2d 751 (1985) (noting that a state law would have violated the commerce clause by discriminating against out of state insurance companies but for Congressional approval of state insurance authority; court rules that the state law violates the equal protection clause of the 14th Amendment).

6. United States v. South–Eastern Underwriters Association, 322 U.S. 533, 64 S.Ct. 1162, 88 L.Ed. 1440 (1944); Paul v. Virginia, 75 U.S. (8 Wall.) 168, 19 L.Ed. 357 (1869).

7. The resolution for a convention to examine commercial problems among the states under the Articles of Confederation is reprinted in 1 H. Commanger, Ed., Documents of American History 132 (5th Ed. 1949). See generally, note, the United States and the Articles of Confederation: Drifting Toward Anarchy or Inching Toward Commonwealth?, 88 Yale L.J. 142 (1978).

state powers regarding commerce, primarily in Article I, § 10 and Article IV.[8] Surprisingly, no text in the Constitution of 1787 specifically outlawed the type of tariffs and trade barriers that states had used during the Articles of Confederation era. Nevertheless, state tariffs and trade barriers would be eliminated by the Constitution if the affirmative grant of power to Congress was intended to deny states the power to create tariffs and trade barriers. It seems difficult to believe that the members of the Constitutional Convention, which was called, in part, to resolve interstate economic conflicts, had not intended to place some limitation on state actions that had been the source of interstate tension. Thus, judicial invalidation of state tariffs and trade barriers, pending consideration of such laws by Congress, seems to carry forth the original purpose of the Constitutional Convention.

Second, judicial invalidation of state laws under the commerce clause does not interfere with democratic processes in the same way as does the invalidation of state laws under most of the other provisions of the Constitution or its Amendments. When the judiciary invalidates state legislation under a provision of the Constitution other than the commerce clause, such as by finding that the state legislation violates the Fourteenth Amendment due process clause, the state cannot use that legislation, absent an amendment to the United States Constitution. Congress cannot give states the authority to disregard provisions of the Fourteenth Amendment. A state law that is held to violate due process cannot be resurrected by a congressional action. On the other hand, a constitutional amendment is not need-

ed to revise a state law that was held to violate the dormant commerce clause. When the Court holds that a state law violates the dormant commerce clause, Congress can effectively reverse that ruling by enacting federal legislation that approves that type of state law. For example, the Court held that a state law barring importation into the state of garbage from other states (for disposal in-state landfills) violated the dormant commerce clause.[9] If Congress passed a law giving that state, or all states, the power to ban the importation of garbage, the states could reserve local landfills for locally produced garbage.[10] Thus, Court actions invalidating state laws negative commerce clause principles are not truly incompatible with the democratic process. Rather, such judicial rulings may simply force consideration of multistate commercial problems by Congress.

Finally, Court actions enforcing dormant commerce clause principles recognize the realities of the democratic system. When state laws relate only to domestic (in-state) economic matters, and do not shift costs to out-of-state persons, all of the affected economic interests are represented in the state democratic system. When a state protects local economic interests by creating tariffs or trade barriers against out-of-state competition, it is attempting to enrich the local populace (who have a voice in the local democratic system) at the expense of out-of-state persons (who are not represented in the local democratic system). This aspect of the Court's dormant commerce clause rulings is sometimes said to reflect an "inner political check" theory.[11] The phrase

---

8. See Article I § 10 Clause 2, restricting tariffs on imports and exports and Article IV § 2 clause 1 protecting the privileges and immunities of citizens who commute into differing states. See the multi-volume version of this Treatise, R. Rotunda & J. Nowak Treatise on Constitutional Law: Substance and Procedure §§ 13.1, 13.2, 13.6 (3rd ed. 1999, with annual supplements) regarding the taxation of imports and exports. See, §§ 8.10, 9.16 of this text regarding the privileges and immunities clause of Article IV.

9. Philadelphia v. New Jersey, 437 U.S. 617, 98 S.Ct. 2531, 57 L.Ed.2d 475 (1978).

10. The Supreme Court in New York v. United States, 505 U.S. 144, 173, 112 S.Ct. 2408, 2427, 120 L.Ed.2d 120 (1992) upheld a federal law that gave certain states the

power to have discriminatory taxes on, or totally ban, low level radioactive waste that came from states that had not adopted radioactive waste treatment and disposal programs consistent with federal guidelines.

11. See generally, Ronald D. Rotunda, the Doctrine of the Inner Political Check, The Dormant Commerce Clause, and Federal Preemption, 53 Transportation Practitioner's Journal 263 (1986); Ronald D. Rotunda, Sheathing the Sword of Federal Preemption, 5 Const. Commentary 311 (1988).

"In applying this rule [regarding the negative implications of the commerce clause] the Court has often recognized that to the extent that the burden of state regulation falls on interests outside the state, it is unlikely to be alleviated by the operation of those political restraints

"inner political check" refers to the fact that all local persons affected by local legislation have the opportunity to participate in the democratic process that produces such legislation. Conversely, there is no political process designed to consider the interests of the out-of-state persons before the creation of state laws that shift costs to out-of-state persons through the establishment of tariffs and trade barriers.

To say that the Supreme Court has consistently upheld a judicial role in the examination of state laws under the dormant (or negative) commerce clause, is not to say that the Court has been able to develop clear standards for the judicial testing of state legislation under the dormant commerce clause. An important part of the problem in the development of dormant commerce clause principles relates to history. Until the mid twentieth century, the Supreme Court was not clear regarding how it was going to define the relationship between the commerce clause's affirmative grant of power to Congress in the commerce clause and the implied negative restrictions on states. Perhaps more importantly, the Supreme Court, throughout its history, has been confronted with two very different types of state or local laws that affect commerce: (1) state laws that operate as discrimination in the nature of a tariff for trade barrier against out-of-state competition; and (2) state laws regulating commerce in an even-handed manner that impose incidental burdens on interstate commerce.

The Court has almost always invalidated laws that it deemed to constitute discrimination against interstate commerce (in the sense that those laws operated as a tariff for trade barrier against out-of-state competitors or out-of-state consumers). Regardless of whether a state seeks to advantage local merchants or local consumers, barriers against interstate competition normally will be invalidated.

It would be misleading to say that all state laws that constitute "discrimination" are subject to rigorous scrutiny under the commerce clause. Rather, one must examine the type of discrimination that is established by a statute in order to know whether it will violate the commerce clause. The only type of discrimination that is subject to strict review under the commerce clause is discrimination that operates as a tariff or trade barrier against out-of-state interests.

There may be types of legislation concerning economic matters that discriminate on basis that do not involve in-state versus out-of-state distinctions. Two hypothetical laws about barbershops may illustrate this point. Assume that State A's law prohibits the ownership of barbershops in the state by any corporation; the law allows ownership of barbershops only by individual human beings. This barbershop law would involve discrimination against corporations, but it would not constitute discrimination in the nature of a tariff or trade barrier. A commerce clause challenge to the law would fail because both in-state and out-of-state corporations would be barred from owning a barbershop. A corporation that wanted to own a barbershop would have to challenge the discrimination under the equal protection clause of the Fourteenth Amendment.[12]

Assume that State B has a law that prohibits the ownership of barbershops by corporations that are domiciled outside of the state, and that allows ownership of barbershops by corporations that are domiciled in the state. State B's law would constitute discrimination in the nature of a tariff or trade barrier against out-of-state competition. This type of discrimination would be subject to a searching judicial inquiry under the commerce clause.

normally exerted when interest within the states are affected." Southern Pacific Co. v. Arizona, 325 U.S. 761, 767 n. 2, 65 S.Ct. 1515, 1519 n. 2, 89 L.Ed. 1915, 1923 n. 2 (1945) (internal citations omitted without indication).

12. This hypothetical is based on the Court's decision in Exxon Corp. v. Governor of Maryland, 437 U.S. 117, 98 S.Ct. 2207, 57 L.Ed.2d 91 (1978) in which the Supreme Court upheld a state law that prohibited the ownership of

retail gas stations by petroleum producers and refiners. The Court found that the law did not violate the equal protection clause by singling out producers and refiners of petroleum products for special burden; the Court found that the law did not violate the dormant commerce clause because it did not constitute discrimination in the nature of a tariff or trade barrier and did not impose a clearly excessive burden on interstate commerce.

The Court has long recognized that the purpose of the commerce clause was to eradicate interstate trade barriers, and to prohibit Balkanization of the Union in economic matters.

The Court has not been completely clear concerning the standard that is used to judge a state law that is deemed to be discrimination in the nature of a tariff or trade barrier. In several cases the Court has made statements similar to the following: "As we use the term here, 'discrimination' simply means differential treatment of in-state and out-of state economic interests that benefits the former and burdens the latter. If a restriction on commerce is discriminatory, it is virtually *per se* invalid ... [under that standard, such a statute] must be invalidated unless [the government] can show that it advances a legitimate local purpose that cannot be adequately served by reasonable nondiscriminatory alternatives."[13] The Court has sometimes said that such laws are subject to "rigorous scrutiny," although the Court has not compared that form of judicial review to the compelling interest test used in equal protection cases that involve racial classification.[14]

The Supreme Court's decisions concerning state laws that discriminate against out-of-state economic interests uniformly place the burden of proof on the state. The state government must demonstrate that such discrimination is truly necessary to achieve a legitimate interest apart from the enrichment of local economic interests. It might be easiest to summarize the Supreme Court cases by stating that: (1) any state or local law that involves discrimination in the nature of a tariff or trade

barrier against out-of-state economic interests will only be upheld if the state can prove that the discrimination in the law is necessary to promote a significant or important interest; and (2) that the economic enrichment of the local persons will not constitute a significant or important interest. Indeed, enrichment of local persons through the use of a discriminatory trade barrier should not be deemed a legitimate state goal.

The Court has only upheld discriminatory trade barriers when it has found that the state had proven that the trade barrier was necessary to protect the safety of the state's people, or the state's environment. Thus, the Court has invalidated state laws that prohibited the importation of privately owned, out-of-state garbage for disposal in privately owned landfills within the state.[15] Preserving the state's environment through restricting the growth of landfills would be a legitimate and, indeed, significant interest. However, out-of-state garbage is identical to in-state garbage, in terms of filling in-state landfills. Therefore, discrimination against out-of-state garbage is not necessary to promote a significant state interest. A state could ban importation into the state of a product that endangered the people of the state. For example, a state could ban all importation into the state of a type of fish if it could show: (1) that the out-of-state fish would be likely to carry diseases that could harm the state's environment; and (2) that there was no reasonably effective way to screen the fish, at the state's borders, in a manner that would protect the state's environment.[16]

13. Oregon Waste Systems v. Department of Environmental Quality, 511 U.S. 93, 99, 100–01, 14 S.Ct. 1345, 1350, 1351, 128 L.Ed.2d 13 (1994) (internal quotation marks omitted) in part quoting from Hughes v. Oklahoma, 441 U.S. 322, 99 S.Ct. 1727, 60 L.Ed.2d 250 (1979); New Energy Co. of Ind. v. Limbach, 486 U.S. 269, 278, 108 S.Ct. 1803, 1810, 100 L.Ed.2d 302 (1988).

14. C & A Carbone, Inc. v. Town of Clarkstown, 511 U.S. 383, 392, 144 S.Ct. 1677, 1683, 128 L.Ed.2d 399 (1994): "discrimination against interstate commerce in favor of local business or investment is per se invalid save in a narrow class of cases in which the municipality can demonstrate, under rigorous scrutiny, that it has no other means to advance a legitimate local interest." See § 18.3 regarding equal protection standards of review.

15. Philadelphia v. New Jersey, 437 U.S. 617, 98 S.Ct. 2531, 57 L.Ed.2d 475 (1978). See also Chemical Waste Management, Inc. v. Hunt, 504 U.S. 334, 112 S.Ct. 2009, 119 L.Ed.2d 121 (1992) (invalidating discriminatory fee imposed by a state on the disposal of hazardous waste from out-of-state sources).

16. In Maine v. Taylor, 477 U.S. 131, 106 S.Ct. 2440, 91 L.Ed.2d 110 (1986). The Supreme Court upheld a state statute that prohibited the importation into the state of live batefish based on the Court's finding that the State had demonstrated that there was no reasonably efficient way of screening live batefish for parasites that might harm the local live fish population. Compare with the Taylor decision, the Court's ruling in Hughes v. Oklahoma, 441 U.S. 322, 99 S.Ct. 1727, 60 L.Ed.2d 250 (1979) (invalidating a state law that prohibited taking certain fish

A law that is deemed to be discriminatory for commerce clause purposes is almost certainly going to be invalidated, by the judiciary, except in the rare case where a state trade barrier is truly necessary to protect health or safety interests. State laws that regulate commerce in a manner that does not involve discrimination of a tariff or trade barrier, on the other hand, rarely violate the commerce clause.

Some Justices have taken the position that courts are only justified in striking down state laws under the dormant commerce clause when the state law at issue constitutes a tariff or trade barrier against out-of-state competition.[17] These Justices do not believe that the judiciary should ever use the dormant commerce clause to invalidate a state law that does not constitute a tariff or trade barrier against out-of-state interests. However, a majority of Justices of the Supreme Court continue to take the position that the dormant commerce clause requires invalidation of state laws that impose certain types of burdens on interstate commerce, even when the state law

does not constitute discrimination against out-of-state interests.[18]

The Court has been less than clear in describing the standard it will use to review nondiscriminatory laws under the dormant commerce clause. Indeed, the Court's decisions reviewing nondiscriminatory forms of state legislation do not involve the consistent use of neoclassical economic analysis. While the Supreme Court will protect interstate commerce against certain types of burdens, the Court has never found that the Constitution prohibit all laws that impair efficient markets in the sense that economists would use that phrase.[19] Rather, a majority of justices has found that the affirmative grant of authority over commerce to Congress implies a negative principle that prohibits states from burdening commerce in ways that significantly and directly impede interstate commercial transactions. A state law that regulates commercial matters in an even handed matter, in the sense that it does not discriminate against out-of-state interests, may violate the dormant commerce clause if the law creates a burden on commerce cannot be justified by a legitimate local interest.

outside the state because the ban on the exportation of fish constituted a discriminatory trade barrier and was not necessary to promote a legitimate state interest).

17. See, e.g., Southern Pacific Co. v. Arizona, 325 U.S. 761, 784, 65 S.Ct. 1515, 1527, 89 L.Ed. 1915 (1945) (Black, J., dissenting); Id. at 795, 65 S.Ct. at 1532 (Douglass, J., dissenting); Camps Newfound–Owatonna, Inc. v. Town of Harrison, 520 U.S. 564, 595, 117 S.Ct. 1590, 1608, 137 L.Ed.2d 852 (1997) (Thomas, J., joined by Scalia, J., and, in part, by Rehnquist, C. J., dissenting).

18. For example, in Bendix Autolite Corp. v. Midwesco Enterprises, Inc., 486 U.S. 888 108 S.Ct. 2218, 100 L.Ed.2d 896 (1988) the Supreme Court invalidated a state statute of limitations that favored domestic corporations by an 8–1 vote of the Justices. The majority opinion by Justice Kennedy found that the state statute violated the commerce clause by engaging in an open balancing of the burdens imposed by the law on interstate commerce and foreign corporations against the degree to which the law promoted legitimate state benefits. Justice Kennedy's majority opinion endorsed the anti-discrimination principle, but, nevertheless, found that the Court would apply a balancing test in this case, which it deemed appropriate for laws that did not constitute discrimination in the nature of a terror for trade barrier. Justice Scalia concurred in the judgment in Bendix Autolite because he believed that the statute constituted an impermissible form of discrimination against interstate commerce, even though Justice Scalia did not believe the court would be justified in using a balancing test to examine the compati-

bility of non-discriminatory state laws with the dormant commerce clause. 486 U.S. at 895, 108 S.Ct. at 2223 (Scalia, J., concurring in the judgment).

19. A government subsidy to some persons who participate in market activities may have the effect of throwing off interstate or international market efficiency. See, Richard A. Posner, Economic Analysis of Law 309 (4th ed.) (1992); Dan T. Coenen, Business Subsidies and the Dormant Commerce Clause, 107 Yale L.J. 965 (1998); Christopher R. Drahozal, On Tariffs and Subsidies in Interstate Trade: A Legal and Economic Analysis, 74 Wash. U.L.Q. 1127, 1153 (1996). However, the Supreme Court has upheld at least some types of government subsidies to local businesses. For example, in Hughes v. Alexandria Scrap Corp., 426 U.S. 794, 96 S.Ct. 2488, 49 L.Ed.2d 220 (1976) the Supreme Court upheld a state program providing a monetary incentive for persons who reclaimed abandoned automobiles to do business with automobile scrap processors within the state. By a 5–4 vote of the Justices, the Court held that the State was acting as a "market participant" but that label did not explain the Court's tolerance of a government program that had the effect of throwing off market efficiency by influencing through government action the supply and demand for automobile scrap processing activity. The market participant language, as will be explained, Infra, was merely the Court's way of indicating that the provision of a direct subsidy to instate businesses did not constitute discrimination in the nature of a terror for trade barrier, nor would it be invalidated as an excessive burden on interstate commerce.

Throughout much of the nineteenth and twentieth centuries Supreme Court majority opinions often took the position that states cannot directly regulate interstate commercial transactions and that states may have nondiscriminatory laws that indirectly affect interstate commerce.[20] Despite the frequent appearance of direct versus indirect regulation of commerce language, the Court in the late twentieth century abandoned any commerce clause test that was based on whether a state law directly affected commerce. Since that time, the Court has not prohibited states from regulating economic activities in ways that have a direct effect on interstate commerce.

In the modern era, the Court has taken the position that a state or local law that regulates economic activities in a neutral manner (in the sense that it does not discriminate against out-of-state interests by creating a tariff or trade barrier) will be invalidated only if: (1) persons attacking the law can demonstrate that the state has no legitimate interest, or, perhaps, only a minuscule interest in creating the burden on interstate commerce; or (2) the state's interest can be completely achieved by regulations that placed a lesser burden on interstate commerce. In other words, the Court adopted a type of balancing test that favors the government for the review of nondiscriminatory laws under the dormant commerce clause.

Perhaps the best summary of the Court's approach to the examination of nondiscriminatory laws under the commerce clause was given in *Pike v. Bruce Church, Inc.*,[21] when the majority, stated:

> "Although the criteria for determining the validity of statues affecting interstate commerce have been variously stated, the general rule that emerges can be phrased as follows: where the statute regulates even handedly to effectuate a legitimate local public interest, and its effects on interstate commerce are only incidental, it will be upheld unless the burden imposed on such commerce is clearly excessive in relation to the putative local benefits. If a legitimate local purpose is found, then the question becomes one of degree. And the extent of the burden that will be tolerated will of course depend on the nature of the local interest involved, and on whether it could be promoted as well with a lesser impact on interstate activities. Occasionally the court has undertaken a balancing approach in resolving these issues, but more frequently it has spoken in terms of 'direct' and 'indirect' benefits and burdens."[22]

Pike, and the cases which have followed it, adopted a type of balancing test for the examination of nondiscriminatory laws that create incidental burdens on interstate commerce. Any balancing test necessarily involves ad-hoc decision making by the Justices. The Justices will evaluate the importance of the interests promoted by the state legislation, and the degree to which that interest is in fact promoted by the legislation. The Justices will then evaluate the qualitative and quantitative effects of the state regulation on interstate commerce. Finally, the Justices will compare the degree of burden on interstate commerce to the degree of local benefit produced by the legislation.

If the Justices did not give deference to state and local governments when applying this balancing test, the Justices would be merely second guessing the decisions of state and local rule makers concerning how legitimate local interests should be promoted. But the balancing test used in modern commerce clause cases does not allow the Justices free reign in making cost-benefit decisions concerning whether the promotion of a legitimate local interest is worth the cost imposed on interstate commerce. The balancing test used in dormant

---

20. More than 60 years ago, the late professor Noel T. Dowling explained why the Court's reliance on a direct versus indirect regulation of commerce distinction would prove to be unworkable. See, Dowling, Interstate Commerce and State Power, 27 VA. L. REV. 1 (1940). Over 30 years ago it was still possible for the Supreme Court to note that the Justices had most often referred to a direct

versus indirect test as the touchstone for negative commerce clause analysis. Pike v. Bruce Church, Inc., 397 U.S. 137, 142, 90 S.Ct. 844, 847, 25 L.Ed.2d 174 (1970).

21. Pike v. Bruce Church, Inc., 397 U.S. 137, 90 S.Ct. 844, 25 L.Ed.2d 174 (1970).

22. 397 U.S. at 142, 90 S.Ct. at 847.

commerce clause cases favors the government, as indicated by the quotation from the *Pike* majority opinion.

The commerce clause balancing test gives deference to the government in two ways. First, the burden of proof is placed on persons who challenge nondiscriminatory state laws under negative commerce clause principles. Second, the Court will uphold the state law unless it finds that the law places a clearly excessive burden on interstate commerce. The state is not required to prove that the social good produced by its law is worth the incidental cost it places on interstate commerce. Rather, the person attacking the law must demonstrate the public good produced by the law is so slight that the burden on interstate commerce should be considered truly excessive. The Court will not invalidate a state law merely because an economist might theoretically find that the cost of the state law to interstate commerce exceeds its benefit to local residents. The Court requires the person challenging a nondiscriminatory state law to prove that the burden on commerce is grossly excessive when compared to legitimate state interests. In other words, negative commerce clause principles will not be used to strike down a nondiscriminatory regulation of commerce merely because the Justices believe that the regulation creates a significant burden on interstate commerce. Instead, Justices will only strike such a law if they believe that the state's asserted legitimate local interest is promoted in only a negligible manner and that the burden on interstate commerce is truly excessive.

When the Court considers the constitutionality of a regulation of commerce that is nondiscriminatory in character, the Court does not always require the state to use the means with the least burden on commerce to achieve its legitimate interests, despite language to that effect in several cases.[23] The Court will require a state to use the means to achieve its goals that has the least burden on commerce if, but only if, persons attacking the law can demonstrate that the state could have achieved its goal with equal efficiency while

imposing a lesser burden on commerce than the burden created by the challenged state law.

A state will not be required to forgo complete attainment of important goals merely because the state law creates a burden on interstate commerce. For example, in *Minnesota v. Clover Leaf Creamery Co.,*[24] the Supreme Court upheld a Minnesota law that prohibited the sale of milk in plastic, non-refillable containers. This Minnesota law was nondiscriminatory, because it prohibited the sale of milk in plastic containers regardless of whether those containers, or the milk in them, were produced in the State of Minnesota or elsewhere. The Minnesota law placed a real burden on the interstate milk industry, because bottlers of milk in states where plastic non-refillable were permissible could not ship milk in plastic bottles into Minnesota. Although the Minnesota law burdened the interstate milk and milk packaging industries, the Minnesota law helped to protect the environment in Minnesota. Discarded plastic containers are not biodegradable; such containers create litter that lasts longer than discarded biodegradable materials. Nonbiodegradable plastic materials fill landfills longer, and make the disposal of waste products more difficult over time. There were many ways for Minnesota to protect its environment, and its landfills, other than prohibiting plastic non-refillable containers for the sale of milk. However, there was no other way for Minnesota to achieve the precise goal of reducing the amount of disposed plastic material in the state except by a prohibition of some plastic products, such as non-refillable plastic milk bottles. The parties challenging the Minnesota law were unable to convince a majority of the Justices that the burden on the interstate milk industry was clearly excessive when compared to the interest of a state in protecting its environment. The state was not required to use another means to protect its environment because other means, which would have imposed a lesser burden on the interstate commerce, would have been less ef-

23. See, e.g., Dean Milk Co. v. City of Madison, 340 U.S. 349, 354, 71 S.Ct. 295, 298, 95 L.Ed. 329 (1951).

24. Minnesota v. Clover Leaf Creamery Co., 449 U.S. 456, 101 S.Ct. 715, 66 L.Ed.2d 659 (1981).

fective in achieving the state's goal of reducing problems created by the disposal of plastic milk bottles.[25]

The Supreme Court has been hesitant to declare that a state law constitutes discrimination in the nature of a tariff or trade barrier if the challenged law, on its face, does not openly discriminate against out-of-state economic interests. The Court has not considered the purpose or motivation of legislators who voted for a law when determining whether that law constituted discrimination against out-of-state interests. Rather, the Court has looked only at the terms of the statute and its necessary effects.

In the previously discussed *Clover Leaf Creamery* case, the Supreme Court did not inquire into whether the Minnesota legislature had adopted the law prohibiting the sale of milk in non-refillable plastic containers in order to enrich local businesses that produced glass or cardboard containers. The Court did not inquire as to whether there were any plastic milk bottle businesses in Minnesota that were adversely affected by the law. Because the Minnesota law on its face regulated all milk bottles, regardless of where the bottles were created or filled, the Court did not apply the strict test of necessity used to examine laws that constitute discrimination in the nature of a tariff or trade barrier against out-of-state interests.[26]

Another example of the Court's refusal to consider legislative purpose is *Exxon v. Maryland*,[27] in which the Supreme Court upheld a state statute that prohibited the ownership of retail gas stations in the state by any person or business that also owned a petroleum refinery. The Supreme Court did not consider it relevant that no corporation or person domiciled in the State of Maryland owned a petroleum refinery. The Court refused to rule that the law was a discriminatory trade barrier, because the law, on its face, was a nondiscriminatory regulation of gas station ownership. The law discriminated against all businesses

that owned petroleum refineries, regardless of whether such a business was located in, or outside of, the State of Maryland. Because the Maryland law was seen as an even handed regulation of commerce it was subjected only to the balancing test, which, as we have noted, is tilted in favor of the state. The law did impose a burden on interstate gasoline sales. The law increased retail gasoline prices because it eliminated refinery owned gas stations, which often sold gasoline at the lowest prices. However, the people who would bear the primary economic burden of the Maryland law would be Maryland consumers. Local consumers no longer had access to gasoline stations owned by petroleum refining companies that would be able to offer gas at a lower price than independently owned gas stations. Maryland asserted that it's goal was to increase the degree of service to local shoppers for gasoline products by having local gasoline stations owned by persons who did not also own petroleum refineries. In the Court's view, the burden on commerce that might result from higher gasoline prices and lower sales of gasoline in Maryland was not grossly excessive when compared to the goal of the law.[28]

One of the few cases in which the Court found that a law constituted discrimination in the nature of a trade barrier, when the law did not contain discriminatory language on its face is *Hunt v. Washington State Apple Advertising Commission*.[29] In *Hunt* the Supreme Court invalidated a North Carolina law that required apples sold into the state to be marked only with the federal Department of Agriculture grade or marked as "not graded." Apples sold in North Carolina could be listed as being United States Department of Agriculture Grade A, regardless of whether the apples were produced in North Carolina or shipped into the state in closed containers. However, under the law, apples sold in North Carolina could not be marked as having met grading standards by an individual state, such as the State of Washington. The Supreme Court

---

25.　449 U.S. at 472–74, 101 S.Ct. at 728–29.

26.　Id.

27.　437 U.S. 117, 98 S.Ct. 2207, 57 L.Ed.2d 91 (1978).

28.　437 U.S. at 126–29, 98 S.Ct. at 2214–15.

29.　432 U.S. 333, 97 S.Ct. 2434, 53 L.Ed.2d 383 (1977).

found that the North Carolina law constituted discrimination in the nature of a tariff or trade barrier by removing a trade advantage from out-of-state apples. Washington apple growers, over time, had created a consumer preference for apples that received the Washington's highest grade. North Carolina's seemingly even handed regulation actually constituted a trade barrier by taking away the trade advantage gained by Washington State apples.

It is surprising that the Court did not simply use a balancing test to invalidate the North Carolina law in *Hunt*. North Carolina asserted that its law was designed to avoid consumer deception that might occur with conflicting types of grading standards used by different states. However, there was virtually no evidence in this litigation that consumers would be misled as to the quality of apples by the labeling of apples with Washington State grading standards in addition to the standards used by the United States Department of Agriculture. In contrast with the slight benefit to state consumers, the burden on interstate commerce created by the law was considerable. And, in the view of the Justices, discriminatory. The law removed the ability of producers of high quality apples of other states to identify to consumers in North Carolina that the apples they offered for sale were superior to those grown in North Carolina. The Court could have used the balancing test to strike the law. However, a majority of the Justices found that the North Carolina law was a discriminatory trade barrier.[30]

Most, if not all, of the cases in which the Supreme Court has invalidated a nondiscriminatory law with the balancing test involved fact situations where the Court might have ruled that the state law was a discriminatory trade barrier. For example, in *Dean Milk Company v. City of Madison*,[31] the Supreme Court found that a Madison, Wisconsin law prohibiting the sale in Madison of any milk that had not been packaged within the county in which Madison was located would violate the dormant commerce clause. Madison asserted that the law was needed so that local inspectors could insure that locally sold milk was bottled safely. The Court found that there were a variety of alternatives which would have imposed lesser burdens on commerce that would have guaranteed equally safe milk for consumers in Madison.[32] Had the Justices wanted to do so, they could have held that the law was nothing but an attempt to create a trade barrier against the exporting of milk packaging jobs outside of the local area in Wisconsin where milk was produced. Requiring the milk to be bottled near the city effectively prohibited milk supply businesses from creating bottling facilities outside of the State of Wisconsin, if these businesses wanted to have access to the Madison retail market. By using the balancing test, and stating that the city had failed to use the means with the least burden on commerce, the Court was able to invalidate the law without having to find that it was designed simply to create a trade barrier against competition for milk bottling jobs.[33]

Bibb v. Navajo Freight Lines, Inc.[34] provides another example of the Court using the balancing test as an alternative to finding that a law constituted a discriminatory trade barrier. In *Bibb* the Court found that an Illinois law requiring a certain type of contour mud flap for trucks in Illinois violated the commerce clause insofar as the law was to be applied to trucks that came into Illinois from other states. There was no safety advantage to the contour mudguards; evidence at trial showed that the types of mudguards used in other states actually might reduce traffic accidents. The type of mudguard required by the Illinois law was not required for trucks in any other states; the Illinois mudguards might well have presented traffic safety problems. Justice Black, who normally opposed the use of a balancing test, wrote for the Court in invalidating the Illinois law on the basis of the balancing test. The majority opinion found

30. 432 U.S. at 352–54, 97 S.Ct. at 2446–47.

31. 340 U.S. 349, 71 S.Ct. 295, 95 L.Ed. 329 (1951).

32. 340 U.S. at 354–56, 71 S.Ct. at 298–99.

33. Although the Court in Dean Milk did invalidate the law in terms of a balancing test, the majority opinion did note that the law had a discriminatory effect.

34. 359 U.S. 520, 79 S.Ct. 962, 3 L.Ed.2d 1003 (1959).

that the Illinois law produced no real safety benefit, and, that the law imposed a clearly excessive burden on interstate commerce, by requiring trucks of all other states, most of which required other types of mud flaps, from entering the state without switching to the type of mudguard required by the Illinois law. Because Justice Black's opinion used the balancing test, the majority did not have to inquire into whether the true purpose of the Illinois legislature was to create a barrier to competition. The Court's opinion did not mention the fact that one of the few contoured mudguard flap factories in the world was located in Illinois. By striking the law under the balancing test, the Court did not have to rule that Illinois legislators had attempted to discriminate against out-of-state truck parts in Illinois trucking markets.[35]

Some decisions of the Supreme Court may leave the reader wondering whether the Court was invalidating a state law under the dormant commerce clause because it constituted a discriminatory trade barrier or because the law, though nondiscriminatory, placed a grossly excessive burden on interstate commerce when compared to any possible legitimate local benefit produced by the law.

In two cases concerning state laws regulating the length of trucks the Justices wrote confusing opinions regarding the relationship between the anti-discrimination principle and the balancing test used to examine nondiscriminatory state laws. In 1978 the Supreme Court invalidated a Wisconsin law that barred trucks longer than 55 feet in length from operating on state highways; three years later the court invalidated an Iowa law banning the use of 65 foot long double trailers on its high-

ways. Despite the similar results in these cases, the Court rendered two very different types of opinions in these cases.

In *Raymond Motor Transportation, Inc. v. Rice*,[36] the Supreme Court invalidated Wisconsin regulations that implemented statutes banning trucks longer than 55 feet in length. The majority in *Raymond* ruled that the burden imposed on the interstate trucking industry by the truck length limit was grossly excessive when compared to alleged safety benefits produced by the Wisconsin law. There was a complete absence of evidence in the Wisconsin trial that 65 foot double trailers were any less safe than 55 foot trailers that were permitted by the regulations. Indeed, Wisconsin's sole witness had admitted that considerations of safety could not have been the basis for the law.[37] The Wisconsin law placed a major burden on interstate trucking industry, because the great majority of states allowed the use of so called double trailers that were 65 feet in length. Under the Wisconsin law, 65 foot length trucks, which were as safe as the shorter trucks permitted by Wisconsin, would not be able to pass through Wisconsin on an interstate trip. Because the complete absence of any evidence of a safety benefit produced by the law in *Raymond Motor Transport*, Justice Powell was able to write an opinion for a majority of the Justices in striking down the Wisconsin law under the balancing test.

Only three years after the decision on the Wisconsin law, the Supreme Court was unable to produce a majority opinion when the Justices invalidated an Iowa ban on 65 foot long double trailers. In *Kassel v. Consolidated Freightways Corporation of Delaware*[38] the Court examined a trial court record wherein

---

35. Justice Black's majority opinion employed the balancing test, to which he had objected in earlier cases, but he also noted the discriminatory impact of the law. Although the Illinois mudguard law did not discriminate against trucking companies from states outside of Illinois. It did have the effect of gaining a market advantage through regulation for a local Illinois business that produced contoured mudguards. This case may well be an example of how the Court could have used the anti-discrimination principle to invalidate every type of law that has been found to violate the balancing test used by the court to examine facially non-discriminatory laws under the commerce clause. For an examination of the theo-

ry that only the non-discrimination principle should be used by the justices to strike laws under the negative commerce clause. See Robert Sedler, the Negative Commerce Clause as a Restriction on State Regulation and Taxation: An Analysis in Terms of Constitutional Structure, 31 Wayne L. Rev. 885 (1986).

36. 434 U.S. 429, 98 S.Ct. 787, 54 L.Ed.2d 664 (1978).

37. 434 U.S. at 438 n. 11, 437–38, 98 S.Ct. at 792 n. 11, 791–92.

38. 450 U.S. 662, 101 S.Ct. 1309, 67 L.Ed.2d 580 (1981).

the State of Iowa had attempted to show that 65 foot long trailers were more likely to cause traffic safety problems than were shorter trucks. In *Consolidated Freightways* Justice Powell wrote for only a plurality, rather than a majority, of the Justices. The Powell plurality opinion found that the trucking industry had carried its burden of proving that the burden on commerce was clearly excessive and that Iowa had failed to rebut that showing with its evidentiary submissions regarding highway safety.[39] Two concurring Justices thought that the law should have been invalidated as being a discriminatory trade barrier, because the Iowa law contained exemptions that allowed the use of double trailers under some circumstances, most of which favored Iowa businesses.[40] The concurring Justices would have found that the purpose of the Iowa legislature was to create a trade barrier against competition for local Iowa trucking businesses from out-of-state trucking industries. The dissenting Justices in *Consolidated Freightways* thought that the plurality was right in finding that the Iowa law was not discriminatory.[41] The dissenters disagreed with the plurality because they believed the interstate trucking businesses, who challenged the Iowa law, had failed to show that the safety benefit produced by the truck length limitation was so slight that it was clearly outweighed by the burden on the trucking industry.

As our readers examine the cases presented in the problem areas examined throughout this Chapter, they should ask themselves whether the Court, when it has stricken a law under the balancing test, might have been concerned about whether the law constituted a discriminatory trade barrier even though the Court opinion was written in terms of applying a balancing test to a nondiscriminatory law.

The reader should also be aware that the Court may sometimes refer to a state commerce clause regulation that it invalidates as being an "extraterritorial regulation" or having an "extraterritorial effect." This language is not helpful analytically. The cases using extraterritorial regulation or extraterritorial effect terminology are cases in which the Court had difficulty in describing why it considered a law to constitute discrimination in the nature of a tariff or trade barrier. For example, in *Baldwin v. G. A. F. Seelig, Inc.*[42] The Court invalidated a New York law that required all milk dealers in the state to pay a certain minimum amount per gallon to milk producers, regardless of the location of the milk producer. The Court ruled that the law was invalid insofar as it was applied to milk that had been purchased in Vermont by New York milk dealers who wished to resell the milk in the State of New York. Justice Cardozo's majority opinion referred to the extraterritorial effect of the New York law, as if New York was truly concerned with the price paid at the point of sale in Vermont. Of course, New York had no interest in the sale of milk in Vermont. It would be hard to believe that those persons who created the New York law were concerned about the amount of money made by Vermont dairy farmers. The New York law was designed to prohibit bringing low priced milk into New York that would capture the market for milk sales from milk that was produced at higher prices by New York dairy farmers.[43] The New York law was simply a trade barrier.

Similarly, in cases regarding the pricing of alcohol, the Supreme Court invalidated state laws that prohibited wholesalers of alcohol beverages from selling those beverages in the state at a price higher than the lowest price offered by the liquor wholesaler to retailers in other states.[44] The Court, in each of these cases, referred to the extraterritorial effect of the law but, in each case, the Court simply

---

39. 450 U.S. at 671–72, 101 S.Ct. at 1317 (Judgment of the Court announced by Powell, J., in an opinion joined by White, Blackmun, and Stevens, J.J.).

40. 450 U.S. at 679, 101 S.Ct. at 1320 (Brennan, J., joined by Marshall, J., concurring in the judgment).

41. 450 U.S. at 687, 101 S.Ct. at 1325 (Rehnquist, J., joined by Burger, C.J., and Stewart, J., dissenting).

42. 294 U.S. 511, 55 S.Ct. 497, 79 L.Ed. 1032 (1935).

43. 294 U.S. at 521–22, 55 S.Ct. at 499–500.

44. Brown–Forman Distillers Corp. v. New York State Liquor Authority, 476 U.S. 573, 106 S.Ct. 2080, 90 L.Ed.2d 552 (1986); Healy v. Beer Institute, Inc., 491 U.S. 324, 109 S.Ct. 2491, 105 L.Ed.2d 275 (1989).

found that the law at issue created a discriminatory trade barrier. In the liquor pricing cases, states attempted to guarantee their local liquor retailers the lowest possible wholesale price by deterring local consumers from crossing state lines to purchase liquor in neighboring states. The states in both the milk pricing and liquor pricing cases were attempting to create a trade barrier against competition from out-of-state products (from low priced milk or low priced alcohol). If the Justices who wrote the opinions in these cases had not mentioned extraterritorial effect of these laws, and described the laws as barriers to competition, their opinions would have been easier to understand.

Perhaps the most confusing terminology in dormant commerce clause cases is the phrase "market participant." This phrase did not appear as a commerce clause standard in the Supreme Court opinions before the 1970s.[45] The phrase would not cause confusion for lower courts, and students, if the Supreme Court were clear regarding that the phrase market participant is merely a way of describing a principle that existed for many decades. The principle reflected in the market participant phrase is that a state may limit a direct subsidy to persons or businesses that are domiciled in the state.

Many people may call a direct subsidy a welfare benefit, but there is no category termed "welfare" in constitutional analysis. A direct subsidy may consist of money, products, or services that go directly from the government to an individual person or individual business. Thus, money or food given directly to economically impoverished persons constitutes a direct subsidy from government. [This type of direct subsidy is the one most commonly referred to as "welfare" by news media.] Money given by the government to farmers or businesses located in the state also constitutes a direct subsidy. [These business subsidies would constitute "welfare," if someone wanted to use that terminology.] If a person works directly for the state or city government the person is receiving a direct subsidy. [Thus, Professors at a state university could be described as receiving "welfare."]

There has never been a time in our history when the Supreme Court has ruled, under any provision of the Constitution, that a state that gives a direct subsidy to in-state persons must give a similar subsidy to persons who reside in other states. No state could afford to give free food to all of the economically poor persons in the state, if the state had to give an equal amount of food to people from all states who might come into the state merely to receive the free food and then return to their home state. No state could give free grade school education to children in the state if it had to provide an equal education to children from all neighboring states who might wish to have their parents transport them into the state during the day to go to school, and then transport them back to their home state in the evening.[46] The market participant phrase was created by the Court to describe why a state giving of economic subsidies to businesses domiciled in the state did not violate the commerce clause. The phrase was meant to separate the state as a subsidy provider from the state as a market regulator. It would have been better for those persons who have to analyze Supreme Court opinions if the Court had never used the phrase market participant and had merely stated that a state can limit direct subsidies to persons or entities who are domiciled in the state.[47]

---

45. Although the Court had earlier referred to states as receiving improper advantages by using regulatory power to enrich local businesses when it had invalidated laws under negative commerce clause principles. It seems not to have made a clear distinction between states as market regulators and market participants until its decision in Hughes v. Alexandria Scrap Corp., 426 U.S. 794, 96 S.Ct. 2488, 49 L.Ed.2d 220 (1976).

46. The Supreme Court upheld a state law requiring that an individual student be able to make a good faith declaration of in-state residency in order to receive a free grade school or high school education in Martinez v. Bynum, 461 U.S. 321, 103 S.Ct. 1838, 75 L.Ed.2d 879 (1983). In Martinez the Court considered the claim that the law violated the equal protection clause of the 14th Amendment. Nevertheless, the Court's opinion indicates that the law would not violate any provision of the Constitution so long as the state was merely requiring that the child be a good faith resident of the state as a condition of receiving the educational benefit.

47. In West Lynn Creamery, Inc. v. Healy, 512 U.S. 186, 114 S.Ct. 2205, 129 L.Ed.2d 157 (1994) the Supreme

The fact that a state is dispensing subsidies to in-state persons or in-state businesses will not allow it to place conditions on the use of those subsidies that constitute discrimination in the nature of a tariff or trade barrier, or that would violate another provision of the Constitution. For example, a state can require that all professors who work at a state university live within the state's boundaries.[48] However, the state cannot require university professors to spend their salaries only on in-state products.[49] The in-state spending requirement would be a barrier to competition that would violate the dormant commerce clause. As the reader examines cases in this Chapter that use the phrase market participant, the reader should ask whether those cases can be best explained by simply stating that the Constitution does not prohibit a state or city from giving of a direct subsidy only to persons or businesses who are domiciled in that state or city.

Giving subsidies to local businesses, such as local farms, might harm our nation's economy. For example, if a state were to give every dairy farmer in the state millions of dollars simply for operating an in-state dairy farm, in-state dairy farmers could sell their dairy products at incredibly low costs and capture the dairy product market from out-of-state farmers who were not receiving subsidies. Despite the effect on interstate markets, the subsidy to in-state

Court invalidated a state pricing order that imposed a tax on milk sold to in-state Massachusetts retailers, and then place the receipts of that tax into a fund that could only be used to subsidize Massachusetts dairy farmers. The majority opinion by Justice Stevens found that the law effectively discriminated against interstate commerce. Justice Stevens stated that the Court had "never squarely confronted the constitutionality of subsidies, and we need not do so now." 512 U.S. at 199 n. 15, 114 S.Ct. at 2241 n. 15. In a concurring opinion, Justice Scalia pointed out that the Court's prior cases indicated that a state grant of a subsidy out of a general fund, which would have been available for any state purpose, would have been permissible, in part because direct subsidies did not constitute the type of discrimination that was barred by the negative commerce clause. Nevertheless, Justice Scalia voted to invalidate the Massachusetts milk pricing order because the order operated tin the same way as would have a tax on out-of-state milk products only, which would have been a tariff that the judiciary had long found invalid under the dormant commerce clause. 512 U.S. at 207, 210–11, 114 S.Ct. at 2218, 2220–21 (Scalia, J., joined by Thomas, J., concurring in the judgment). See § 4.8, infra.

48. In McCarthy v. Philadelphia Civil Service Commission, 424 U.S. 645, 96 S.Ct. 1154, 47 L.Ed.2d 366 (1976) (per curiam) the Supreme Court rejected an equal challenge attack on a city law that required municipal workers to live within the city. Although the Court did not consider commerce clause issues in the McCarthy case, the Court's opinion indicated that nothing in the Constitution required the state to provide direct government employment to persons who were not residing within the city. The Court distinguished the McCarthy case in United Building and Construction Trades Council of Camden County and Vicinity v. Mayor and Council of the City of Camden, 465 U.S. 208, 104 S.Ct. 1020, 79 L.Ed.2d 249 (1984). In the United Building and Construction Trades Council case, the Court found that a city law requiring a private contractor to employ a minimum percentage of employees who were residents of the city appeared to violate the privileges and immunities clause of Article IV, although the Court remanded the case for a determination of whether the city could justify its preference for in-state residents. A city or state law requiring a preference in private sector employment constitutes a prima facia violation of Article IV, even though the state may be providing a subsidy to a private sector employer. See Hicklin v. Orbeck, 437 U.S. 518, 98 S.Ct. 2482, 57 L.Ed.2d 397 (1978). These Article IV cases distinguish private sector employment from true public sector employment. When the city or state employs a person directly, it is giving that person a direct subsidy, which would not be a violation of the Article IV privileges and immunities clause or the dormant commerce clause. See § 9.6 of this text for an examination of Article IV, privileges and immunities clause rulings.

49. In South–Central Timber Development, Inc. v. Wunnicke, 467 U.S. 82, 104 S.Ct. 2237, 81 L.Ed.2d 71 (1984). The Court invalidated a state law requiring purchasers of state-owned timber to have the timber partially processed within the state before they could ship it out of the state. There was no majority opinion in this case; only eight Justices participated in the case. The judgment of the court was announced in an opinion by Justice White, which was joined by Justices Brennan, Blackmun, and Stevens. They found that even if the state could have been found to be a market participant it did not have any right to impose "conditions downstream" in restricting how the recipient of state-owned timber (which was a direct subsidy) would be used after the timber was received by the private individual. Only two Justices, Justice Rehnquist and Justice O'Connor, dissented in the South–Central case. The remaining two justices who voted in the case believed that the case should be remanded for further factual findings. The South–Central case establishes the principle that once a subsidy is given to a private person by the government the state or local government may not prohibit that private person from taking the subsidy outside of the state, as in our example regarding in-state university professors and their salaries. The division of the justices in the South–Central case demonstrates the confusion that was brought into the analysis of subsidies after the Court determined that it should focus on whether a state was a market participant or market regulator, rather than merely examining whether any improper conditions were put on an otherwise valid subsidy from a state or local government to a private person.

dairy farmers would not be invalid under the dormant commerce clause.[50] Limiting a direct subsidy to in-state persons constitutes discrimination against out-of-state persons, but it is not the type of discrimination that is in the nature of a tariff or trade barrier that would be prohibited by the dormant commerce clause.

The Court's position that direct subsidies may be limited to in-state persons reflects the inner political check theory. Although interstate commerce is burdened when the state's subsidy creates market inefficiency, the primary people who bear the burden are the people of the state that is giving the subsidy. In our example, the money given to dairy farmers is money that could have been used for schools, roads, or other local interests. When a state is giving subsidies to in-state persons it is doing so at the cost to other persons who are in the state. The local political process is best suited to make a determination as to whether the subsidy is justified in terms of the promotion of legitimate local interests. Whether Congress could create legislation that would restrict state granted subsidies to businesses in manners that interfere with national markets is currently an open question.

A final confusing phrase that comes up in some commerce clause cases is the product of a mid nineteenth century case. The Court's decision in *Cooley v. Board of Wardens*[51] established the rule that states could not regulate those subject areas that require uniform national regulation. In *Cooley* the Supreme Court found that there were areas of commercial activity that were exclusively the province of Congress to regulate. The *Cooley* selective exclusivity test may still be a valid one, for the Court has never expressly disavowed the *Cooley* opinion. Nevertheless, the test established by *Cooley* is meaningless in the twenty-first

century. In the nineteenth century there may have been some commercial activities that required national uniformity, even though there was no federal legislation regarding those commercial activities. In the twenty-first century, it is hard to believe that there is any area of economic activity that would require uniform national regulation that has not already been subject to federal regulation of some type. In other words, the *Cooley* standard appears to be irrelevant to commerce clause analysis in the twenty-first century. However, the concept that some areas of commercial activity require uniform national regulation may play a part in the Supreme Court interpretation of federal statutes in preemption cases.[52] As we will see in the next Chapter, the Court is most likely to find that an unclear federal statute was meant, by implication, to preempt all state or local laws that relate to a subject area when the Justices believe that the regulated subject is one that requires nationally uniform regulation.[53]

The following sections of this Chapter are divided into problem areas that the Court has considered under negative commerce clause principles. The Court has not adopted separate constitutional standards for the different types of problems such as transportation regulation, the restriction of incoming goods, or restrictions on exports out of the state. These subtopics demonstrate how the Court has applied the principles that we have described in this introduction to different types of fact situations.

First, the Court, in almost all circumstances, will invalidate state or local laws that constitute discrimination in the nature of a tariff or trade barrier against out-of-state competition. Only when the state can prove that discrimination against out-of-state products or persons is truly necessary to promote a significant interest such as the health of the state's popu-

---

50. West Lynn Creamery, Inc. v. Healy, 512 U.S. 186, 207, 114 S.Ct. 2205, 2218, 129 L.Ed.2d 157 (1994) (Scalia, J., joined by Thomas, J., concurring in the judgment). See note 48, supra.

51. 53 U.S. (12 How.) 299, 13 L.Ed. 996 (1851).

52. See §§ 9.1–9.4 of this text regarding statutory and constitutional considerations in court interpretations of

federal statutes that are alleged to preempt state or local regulations.

53. Id. For citations to additional cases, including lower court cases, and secondary works on this topic see our multi-volume Treatise: R. Rotunda & J. Nowak, Treatise on Constitutional Law: Substance and Procedure Chapter 9 (3rd ed. 1999, with annual supplements).

lation will discrimination in the nature of a tariff or trade barrier be upheld. Second, the Court will only invalidate a nondiscriminatory state regulation of commercial activity if the persons challenging the state regulation can prove that the burden placed on interstate commerce by the regulation is grossly excessive when compared to any legitimate local interest promoted by the legislation. The examination of nondiscriminatory laws under the commerce clause will involve a balancing test that favors the government. Third, it is possible, though not likely, that the Court may find that some subject areas require national uniform regulation and that any state regulation of those commercial areas is automatically invalid under the test established in the *Cooley* decision. Finally, the Court will recognize that a state is free to limit direct subsidies to in-state persons or in-state businesses, even though that state will not be able to enrich local interests through the creation of tariffs and trade barriers.

§ 8.2   State Regulation Affecting Interstate Commerce—The *Gibbons* Case

In *Gibbons v. Ogden*,[1] under the forceful direction of Chief Justice Marshall, the Court enunciated a broad definition of commerce and embraced the supremacy of the common market concept, while acknowledging that there can be a category of concurrent regulation. This category, Marshall told us, supposedly emanated from what he called the state's "police powers."

New York had granted an exclusive steamboat operator's license to Livingston and Fulton, who had in turn had assigned it to Ogden. The highest court of New York State upheld an order enjoining Gibbons from operating a federally licensed steamboat in New York waters because that operation was inconsistent

with the monopoly that the state had granted to Ogden. Gibbons argued that the state monopoly interfered with his federally licensed steamboat, and violated the federal commerce power.

In assessing the scope of state power to regulate interstate commerce, Marshall spoke in broad terms. "Commerce" he said, is more than mere traffic. "[I]t is intercourse. It describes the commercial intercourse between nations and parts of nations...."[2] It includes navigation. "No sort of trade can be carried on between this country and any other to which this power does not extend."[3] The phrase "among the several States" means "intermingled with," for commerce among the states "cannot stop at the external boundary-line of each State, but may be introduced into the interior." These words, however, do not "comprehend commerce which is *completely internal* ... and which does not extend to or affect other States."[4] Thus Gibbons' vessel was in interstate commerce.

Then Marshall flirted with—but did not adopt—the idea that the power to regulate commerce among the states is exclusive. That is, Marshall did not adopt the argument that because Congress has power over interstate commerce, a state may not enact legislation that affects also interstate commerce.

On the other hand, Marshall clearly rejected Chancellor Kent's theory that states have free rein to enact legislation that affects interstate commerce, unless the state law conflicts with a federal statute. Those who believed that the states have a concurrent interstate commerce power, even though the federal government has it, argued from analogy that the federal government has a taxing power and yet the grant of that power to the federal government did not exclude the states from also exercising

---

§ 8.2

1.   22 U.S. (9 Wheat.) 1, 6 L.Ed. 23 (1824).
2.   22 U.S. (9 Wheat.) at 189.
3.   22 U.S. (9 Wheat.) at 193.
4.   22 U.S. (9 Wheat.) at 194 (emphasis added).

Completely Internal Commerce. What is "completely internal" has long been narrowly defined, for the com-

merce power extends to all matters that *affect* interstate commerce. Such is now the modern view and the early view. See, e.g., The Daniel Ball, 77 U.S. (10 Wall.) 557, 19 L.Ed. 999 (1871) (a vessel operating solely on a river within Michigan's borders is within the stream of interstate commerce). For a short period of time the Supreme Court rejected this broad view.

it. Marshall answered this argument by distinguishing the state power to tax from the state power to regulate commerce. State power to tax represented a necessary element for the state's very existence, he said. But, when a state regulates interstate commerce "it is exercising the very power that is granted to Congress, and is doing the very thing which Congress is authorized to do. There is no analogy, then, between the power of taxation and the power of regulating commerce."[5]

Proponents of Kent's theory also argued that the States have enacted inspection laws. These laws regulate commerce, but the Constitution specifically recognizes them.[6] Thus, they argued, that is evidence that the federal commerce power is not exclusive. Marshall admitted that the inspection laws may have "a remote and considerable influence on commerce" but he denied that they were really evidence of a commerce power. He claimed that their origin is not derived from any commerce power but from what is called the state's "police power:"

> [T]hat immense mass of legislation which embraces everything within the territory of a state not surrendered to a general government; all of which can be most advantageously exercised by the states themselves. Inspection laws, quarantine laws, health laws of every description, as well as laws for regulating the internal commerce of a State, and those which respect turnpike roads, ferries, etc., are component parts of this mass.[7]

Because New York's inspection laws and other such concededly valid laws derived—in Marshall's view—from the police powers, the enactment of such laws did not prove that New York had any power to enact legislation deriving from a commerce power.

The Police Power and the Origin-of-Power Question. The "police power" is nowhere mentioned in the Constitution but the term is frequently used, particularly in the commerce area. Marshall's inquiring into the derivation or source of the exercise of a power—whether it be the police power, the commerce power or some other power—has not been fruitful because of the difficulty of ascertaining the metaphysical origin of any given power. Marshall did not have the opportunity to develop the doctrine; and all we can be certain of is that the test did not prove to be a useful tool when turned over to others.[8] This "origin-of-power" question was not laid to rest however until *Cooley v. Board of Wardens*[9] discussed later in this section.

As we shall see in the development of the later case law, a state law may regulate health and safety and yet also regulate or affect commerce among the states. In general, if the regulation is more of a benefit to health and safety than it is a burden to interstate commerce, the Court will not strike down the state legislation. If it is more of a burden than a benefit, the Court will invalidate the state law. Later this Chapter shall examine some of the tests the Court has fashioned to determine how to weigh the burdens to interstate commerce and determine if they exceed the health and safety benefits that the state claims are promoted by its law.

After engaging in this metaphysical discussion of the origin of the exercise of health and safety rules affecting interstate commerce, Marshall turned to the argument that the commerce clause by its own terms exclusively gave to Congress the power to regulate commerce among the states. "There is great force in this argument" he said, "and the court is

---

5. 22 U.S. (9 Wheat.) at 199–200.

6. U.S.Const. art. I, § 10, cl. 2.

State inspection laws applied to goods brought into the state from outside the state are within the state police power when reasonable. E.g., Savage v. Jones, 225 U.S. 501, 32 S.Ct. 715, 56 L.Ed. 1182 (1912). However, inspection statutes that require the inspection of out-of-state (*but not in-state*) products are invalid. E.g., Voight v. Wright, 141 U.S. 62, 11 S.Ct. 855, 35 L.Ed. 638 (1891).

See also Minnesota v. Barber, 136 U.S. 313, 10 S.Ct. 862, 34 L.Ed. 455 (1890) (invalidation of state law requiring inspection of meat by local inspectors within twenty-four hours of slaughter because, in effect, it was a ban of meat from other states).

7. 22 U.S. (9 Wheat.) at 203.

8. See, F. Frankfurter, The Commerce Power Under Marshall, Taney and Waite 31–32, 61–62 (1964—first published 1937).

9. 53 U.S. (12 How.) 299, 13 L.Ed. 996 (1851).

not satisfied that has been refuted."[10] But Marshall did not decide this issue because, in this instance, Congress had acted, or more precisely—Marshall interpreted the federal act allowing a licensee to engage in coastal trade to be in conflict with the New York monopoly. Hence the state monopoly must fall. New York could not limit the scope of the federal license by creating a state monopoly over an interstate waterway that would render the federally-conferred license useless.

Right after this decision, competition in New York and the other states increased, causing the steamboat fare from New York to New Haven to be reduced from five to three dollars.[11] Removing the trade barrier among the states promoted interstate commerce, a result that is unsurprising. Removing state granted monopolies increases competition, which leads to reduced prices.

§ 8.3 State Regulation Affecting Interstate Commerce—Between *Gibbons v. Ogden* and *Cooley v. Board of Wardens*

Willson v. Black Bird Creek Marsh Co.[1] is an early post-*Gibbons* case that illustrates the problems inherent in the origin-of-power theory. State law had authorized the company's erection of a dam that, like the New York monopoly discussed in *Gibbons*, obstructed an interstate waterway. Willson's federally licensed ship broke the dam. The company successfully sued for damages in state court. Chief Justice Marshall, for the Court, affirmed, rejecting Willson's argument that the state law violated the commerce clause.

Marshall implied that the Delaware statute was not within the purview of the dormant commerce clause because it was plainly an example of the state's permissible regulation

of a local health and property matter. It is also noteworthy that the Delaware legislation resulted in a *nondiscriminatory* prohibition of all shipping, local as well as foreign, unlike the New York statute invalidated in *Gibbons*, which favored local shippers to the disadvantage of non-resident carriers. Nonetheless, contemporary observers viewed *Willson* as a retreat from the absolutist position of *Gibbons*. Marshall appeared to tacitly abandon the idea that a federal license conveyed to the holder an unrestricted right to travel in interstate commerce.

Willson was not the only decision, in the era between *Gibbons* and *Cooley v. Board of Wardens*[2] where the Court grappled with Marshall's origin-of-power theory. Subsequent decisions failed to formulate a satisfactory criteria for the test, and the members of the Court were unable to elicit majority support for any one position.

The "police power" theory formed the basis of *Mayor, Aldermen and Commonalty of New York v. Miln*,[3] upholding a New York statute requiring every shipmaster arriving in New York from any foreign country or other state of the union to report passenger identification information. Purportedly, the state measure functioned as a safety regulation protecting the local citizenry from the arrival of undesirables. Adhering to Marshall's description of state police power, Justice Barbour's opinion for the majority hastily dismissed any need to consider state power to regulate commerce. Once the Court announced that the New York statute was within the state police power, the Court summarily sustained the law as a proper regulation of the state's internal affairs.

The Court's ease in arriving at a conclusion was not necessarily an accurate reflection of the viability of the test.[4] Justice Thompson had written the first opinion for the Court, but

---

10. 22 U.S. (9 Wheat.) at 209.

11. 1 C. Warren, The Supreme Court in United States History 615 (Rev. ed. 1926).

§ 8.3

1. 27 U.S. (2 Pet.) 245, 7 L.Ed. 412 (1829). See generally, F. Frankfurter, The Commerce Power Under Marshall, Taney and Waite 27–34 (1964—first published 1937).

2. 53 U.S. (12 How.) 299, 13 L.Ed. 996 (1851).

3. 36 U.S. (11 Pet.) 102, 9 L.Ed. 648 (1837).

4. A statute requiring masters or owners of every vessel landing passengers from a foreign port to pay to the state $1.50 or provide a $300 bond for each passenger landed to indemnify the locality for expenses for relief or support was struck down in Henderson v. Mayor of New York, 92 U.S. (2 Otto) 259, 23 L.Ed. 543 (1876). The Court narrowly construed *Miln*:

his colleagues found that his approval of concurrent state power to regulate commerce was unacceptable. Justice Story dissented, not on the basis that the Court had applied the wrong standard, but because in his opinion the state statute constituted a regulation of commerce, and was, therefore, invalid. Interestingly, the same case had been argued at an earlier date[5] and Marshall, the author of the standard (who died between the first and second argument) then concurred with Story.

The Court remained impossibly divided over the issue of exclusive Congressional power in the decade between *Miln* and *Cooley*. In *The License Cases*[6] six Justices delivering separate opinions sustaining a state license requirement for the sale of imported liquor. In *The Passenger Cases*[7] eight Justices wrote separate opinions invalidating state legislation imposing a tax on alien passengers arriving from foreign ports.

Finally, stage was set for *Cooley v. Board of Wardens*,[8] where a majority of the Court agreed on one test that navigated between those who thought that the commerce power was always exclusive and those who thought that it never was.

§ 8.4 State Regulation Affecting Interstate Commerce—The *Cooley* Rule of Selective Exclusiveness

Cooley v. Board of Wardens[1] represents the culmination of the formative period of a search for an adequate standard for judicial review of state regulation of commerce in the absence of a federal law. This decision set the direction for commerce clause adjudication for almost the next 100 years. In *Cooley* the Court, speaking through Justice Benjamin Curtis—who resigned after the *Dred Scott* decision and later was counsel to President Andrew Johnson in his impeachment proceedings—upheld a Pennsylvania law requiring ships entering or leaving the Philadelphia port to engage a local pilot.

The state penalized Cooley for his failure to engage a local pilot. He challenged the law as an impermissible state regulation of interstate commerce. The Court distinguished between those subjects of commerce that demand a uniform rule throughout the country and those subjects that permit diversity of treatment in order to fulfill local needs. And it specifically rejected both extreme interpretations of the commerce clause; *i.e.*, either that congressional power was exclusive or that state regulation in the absence of congressional action could go unbridled.[2]

The *Cooley* doctrine looks to the nature of the subject of the challenged regulation as the crucial factor in determining its validity. The doctrine of selective exclusiveness states that, if the item is such that national uniformity is necessitated, then Congressional power is ex-

"Nothing is gained in the argument by calling it the police power. Very many statutes, when the authority on which their enactments rest is examined, may be referred to different sources of power, and supported equally well under any of them. A statute may at the same time be an exercise of the taxing power and of the power of eminent domain.... It must occur very often that the shading which marks the line between one class of legislation and the other is very nice, and not easily distinguishable.

"But, however difficult this may be, it is clear, from the nature of our complex form of government, that, whenever the statute of a State invades the domain of legislation which belongs exclusively to the Congress of the United States, it is void, no matter under what class of powers it may fall, or how closely allied to powers conceded to belong to the States." 92 U.S. at 271–72.

5. See C. Swisher, American Constitutional Development 196, 197 (2d ed. 1954).

6. 46 U.S. (5 How.) 504, 12 L.Ed. 256 (1847).

7. 48 U.S. (7 How.) 283, 12 L.Ed. 702 (1849). The Court used the commerce clause to strike other taxes on the carriage of persons. Henderson v. Mayor of New York, 92 U.S. (2 Otto) 259, 23 L.Ed. 543 (1875); Chy Lung v. Freeman, 92 U.S. (2 Otto) 275, 23 L.Ed. 550 (1875).

8. 53 U.S. (12 How.) 299, 13 L.Ed. 996 (1851).

§ 8.4

1. 53 U.S. (12 How.) 299, 13 L.Ed. 996 (1851). See also, Madsen, J., dissenting, citing Treatise, in State v. Thorne, 129 Wn.2d 736, 921 P.2d 514, 538 (1996).

2. McLean & Wayne, JJ., dissented. Daniel, J., concurred only in the judgment of the Court.

Justice McKinley did not participate in The *Cooley* opinion. See letter from Justice Curtis to George Ticknor, Feb. 29, 1852, quoted in J. Frank, Justice Daniel Dissenting: A Biography of Peter V. Daniel, 1784–1860, at 197, 313 (1964). We are indebted to Professor Charles Alan Wright for bringing this fact to our attention. The U.S. Reports at this time early in our nation's history did not always indicate if a Justice did not participate in a decision.

clusive. If, on the other hand, the item is matter of a peculiarly local concern (even though within the reach of the Congressional commerce clause power such as the Pennsylvania pilotage laws), allowing a diversity of treatment, then states may regulate the area, in the absence of congressional preemption.

While the *Cooley* Rule of Selective Exclusiveness is a major advance from the metaphysical origin-of-powers question, there were pitfalls in the *Cooley* doctrine as well. First, the decision supplies no litmus test to determine when is a subject appropriate for national, as opposed to local regulation. In *Cooley,* a federal statute indicated that Congress thought the matter did not mandate a nationally uniform regulation, but such statutes will not always exist.

Even if a matter is appropriate for diverse treatment, does that mean that all state laws are constitutional, even if they discriminate against the commerce from other states. Although a state might be regulating a local subject matter, the legislation could still be discriminatory in purpose or effect, thereby favoring residents over non-residents.

An important element of *Cooley* was that the Pennsylvania laws were in fact nondiscriminatory, falling with equal weight on Pennsylvania residents, although the Court did not focus on this issue. We shall see, in later cases, that the Court is more willing to sustain state regulations that equally burden local residents. When there is no discrimination against out-of-state citizens or residents, an inner political check operating within the state assures that the effects of the law will not be too harsh, for it will operate equally on the state citizens who enacted it.

§ 8.5 State Regulation Affecting Interstate Commerce: Federal Incorporation by Reference of State Laws

Cooley noted that the Congressional Act of 1789 specifically endorsed the continuation of

state regulation until Congress enacted other regulations. Interestingly, *Cooley* did not appear to hold the Act of 1789 binding, and decided the case as if there were no federal law on the scene that settled the issue by authorizing state pilotage laws, or at least authorizing nondiscriminatory state pilotage laws. Instead, the Court treats the federal law merely as evidence that Congress thought that the matter was appropriate for diverse treatment.

Justice Curtis raised the question of whether Congress could enact legislation adopting *future* state laws by incorporation, but he indicated that such action was not constitutional. Justice Curtis, we now know, was in error in equating Congressional adoption of future laws by incorporation as indistinguishable from Congress redelegating, back to the states, the power over interstate commerce.

We can best understand this point by looking at a few examples. Congress cannot delegate to Illinois the power to legislate federal pollution standards for the whole country. Then Congress would be abdicating interstate commerce control to one state to legislate for the nation. However, Congress can enact legislation prescribing that the federal pollution standard in each state shall be the same as the state standard. Then, Congress is not abdicating its authority but merely incorporating by reference future legislation. This type of "delegation" is appropriate because those having input into the political process creating the rule are also bound by it, assuring an inner political check.[1] Congress is incorporating state laws as they are now or are in the future:

> Rather than being a delegation by Congress of its legislative authority to the States, it is a deliberate continuing adoption by Congress [of laws] as shall have been already put in effect by the respective States for their own government.[2]

§ 8.5

1. E.g., United States v. Sharpnack, 355 U.S. 286, 78 S.Ct. 291, 2 L.Ed.2d 282 (1958).

Some old, poorly reasoned admiralty cases do not recognize this type of adoption. E.g., Knickerbocker Ice Co. v.

Stewart, 253 U.S. 149, 40 S.Ct. 438, 64 L.Ed. 834 (1920). Cf. Morrison, Worker's Compensation and the Maritime Law, 38 Yale L.J. 472 (1929).

2. United States v. Sharpnack, 355 U.S. 286, 294, 78 S.Ct. 291, 296, 2 L.Ed.2d 282 (1958).

Cases since *Cooley* support the view that courts interpret the need for uniformity in commercial regulation in the absence of Congressional action. Congress may reverse the Court's opinion of the need for uniformity by authorizing the invalidated state legislation. Consider *Leisy v. Hardin*.[3] In that case the Court invalidated, as a violation of the dormant commerce clause, an Iowa statute prohibiting the sale of intoxicating liquor in Iowa. Applying *Cooley,* the Court held that "transportation, purchase, sale and exchange of commodities is national in its character," and so "must be governed by a uniform system;" the absence of federal law indicates the congressional "will that such commerce shall be free and untrammeled."[4] The Court then invalidated Iowa statute.

Congress hastily reacted by enacting the Wilson Act[5] subjecting interstate liquor traffic to the laws of the state into which the liquor was imported. A unanimous Court upheld the Wilson Act in *Wilkerson v. Rahrer*.[6] The Court explained that the subsequent legislation did not represent Congressional delegation to the states of the federal power to regulate commerce, but rather a legitimate use of Congressional power under the commerce clause to authorize an acceptable form of state regulation.[7]

Conclusion. Since the time of Chief Justice Marshall, the Court has recognized that the commerce clause has a negative implication that restricts state laws that burden interstate commerce. When the Court strikes down a state or local regulatory act as inconsistent with the dormant commerce clause, it is interpreting the silence of Congress to hold that, in the absence of federal legislation, a state or local law may not create a trade barrier or imposes a discriminatory burden on interstate commerce.

Because the commerce clause is a grant of power to Congress, the final authority for determining the way in which interstate commerce is regulated belongs to Congress. When Congress passes a statute that allows states to have a commercial regulation that the Court had previously found to be inconsistent with the dormant commerce clause, Congress is not really reversing the Court's rule, for it is not stating that the state law was consistent with the dormant commerce clause. Rather Congress has now made the decision that the federal government should not regulate an area of commercial activity in a uniform way. Congress is, in effect, creating a federal rule for the regulation of the activity that allows for nonuniform or anticompetitive treatment by the states. There is no longer any need for the Court to interpret the dormant commerce clause—the silence of Congress—for Congress has now spoken.

Congress' power to regulate commerce includes the power to regulate commerce for anticompetitive purposes. When Congress approves state laws that regulate commerce in a manner that would not be permissible in the absence of congressional approval the Court is no longer reviewing the state law; it is reviewing a federal commercial regulation. The Court must uphold the federal statute so long as the activity that Congress has chosen to regulate (or to leave open for state regulation) is related to, or has an effect on, interstate commerce. There is no requirement that Congress regulates commerce in a way that promotes efficient rather than inefficient markets.

Nevertheless, Congressional approval of state or local laws that create trade barriers or otherwise regulate commerce in a manner that would not be permissible under dormant commerce clause principles creates inefficient markets and causes economic hardship to persons in some states through the shifting of economic burdens by states that seek to promote local

---

3.   135 U.S. 100, 10 S.Ct. 681, 34 L.Ed. 128 (1890).

4.   135 U.S. at 109–110, 10 S.Ct. at 684.

5.   26 Stat. 313.

6.   140 U.S. 545, 11 S.Ct. 865, 35 L.Ed. 572 (1891).

7.   E.g., Compare Pennsylvania v. Wheeling & Belmont Bridge Co., 54 U.S. (13 How.) 518, 14 L.Ed. 249 (1851)

(the Wheeling Bridge seriously obstructs navigation), with Pennsylvania v. Wheeling & Belmont Bridge Co., 59 U.S. (18 How.) 421, 15 L.Ed. 435 (1855) (an Act of Congress declaring the Wheeling Bridge to be a lawful structure and a post road is valid).

interests. For this reason, the Court will not find that Congress has removed state or local regulations from the limits of dormant commerce clause principles unless Congress has spoken clearly, or unless congressional intent to allow discriminatory state regulations of commerce is "unmistakably clear."[8] If Congress speaks clearly, the Court will accept that decision because it has built within it an inner political check. Because all segments of the country are represented in Congress, there is less danger that one state will be in a position to exploit the others.[9]

§ 8.6 State Regulation Affecting Interstate Commerce: The *Di Santo* Case

In the post-*Cooley* world, the Court recognized the states' concurrent power to regulate commerce in appropriate circumstances. While *Cooley* resolved the question of the exclusiveness of the commerce power, the Court still had to work out the test to determine the extent of permissible, concurrent state. Successive Courts invoked various verbal touchstones in an attempt to formulate a predictable dichotomy between permitted and invalid state exercise of regulatory power, but the absence of an adequate standard is evidenced by the plethora of cases that one cannot reconcile merely by applying the *Cooley* doctrine.[1]

In these decisions the Court finds that one factor is crucial: a legitimate state regulation must not burden interstate commerce, in either purpose or effect, unless the extent of that burden is outweighed by a legitimate

state objective that cannot be achieved in a less burdensome manner. The Court looks to the effect of the law and not merely its stated purpose in order to prevent states from easily avoiding the dormant commerce clause.

The mere fact that a state claims that its regulation is designed for health or safety purposes does not immunize that regulation under the commerce clause. Otherwise, states could avoid the restrictions of the dormant commerce clause by superficial changes in the language of the law. However, if the law operates in a nondiscriminatory manner, the Court is more willing to defer to the judgment of the state political process, because a nondiscriminatory regulation equally burdens those who were represented in that process that led to the regulation. State regulatory measures that fall equally on local residents are more likely to be sanctioned than parochial schemes that favor local citizens and disproportionately burden non-residents, for in the former situation an inner political check is operative that lessens the need for an active judicial review.

While the post-*Cooley* Court acknowledged discrimination against interstate commerce as one emerging test, the Court focuses on what where the supposed "direct" or "indirect" of the law. Thus, the Court had continuing difficulty with the practical application of the *Cooley* doctrine.

Di Santo v. Pennsylvania[2] was a typical case that neatly illustrates the problem. A Pennsylvania regulation required sellers of steamboat tickets to apply for and be granted a license. In

---

8. South–Central Timber Dev., Inc. v. Wunnicke, 467 U.S. 82, 91, 104 S.Ct. 2237, 2242, 81 L.Ed.2d 71 (1984), on remand 746 F.2d 1393 (9th Cir.1984), establishing requirement that Congressional intent be unmistakably clear. In this case, the mere fact that state policy regarding the use of resources taken from state lands mirrored Congressional policy with respect to similar resources taken from federal lands within the state did not constitute unmistakably clear approval of a state law that would have required persons purchasing timber from the state to process timber within the state before export.

In Hillside Dairy Inc. v. Lyons, ___ U.S. ___, 123 S.Ct. 2142, 156 L.Ed.2d 54 (2003). Plaintiffs brought a commerce clause and privileges and immunities clause challenge to California milk pricing regulations as they apply to out-of-state producers. Stevens, J., for the Court, held that Congress did not authorize California's pricing and

pooling regulations in a way that immunized them from commerce clause challenge. The Court also reinstated the producers' individual privilege and immunities clause claim even though the regulations did not, on its face, create classifications based on citizenship. The Court was unanimous, except that Thomas, J., dissented from the notion that there is such a thing as a dormant or negative Commerce Clause. See § 9.6 for additional cases concerning the Article IV privileges and immunities clause.

9. 467 U.S. at 91–92, 104 S.Ct. at 2242–43.

§ 8.6

1. See Brandeis J., joined by Holmes, J., dissenting, in Di Santo v. Pennsylvania, 273 U.S. 34, 43 & n. 4, 47 S.Ct. 267, 270–71 & n. 4, 71 L.Ed. 524 (1927).

2. 273 U.S. 34, 47 S.Ct. 267, 71 L.Ed. 524 (1927).

addition, the law charged the licensees an annual fee and subjected them to license revocation. The state claimed that the law protected local citizens from fraudulent acts.

The Court struck down the regulation as an unnecessary, burdensome interference with interstate commerce. It said that the law was not an "indirect" burden on commerce but a "direct" one, which the state could not justify as an exercise of the police power to prevent possible fraud. The Court said that, under *Cooley*, Congress has exclusive authority to regulate this commerce because the subject demands uniform treatment. Therefore, this state legislation is necessarily repugnant to the Congressional power.

Stone's Dissent in *Di Santo*. In his now famous dissent, Justice Stone departed from the majority's position and implored the Court to adopt a more appropriate standard for adjusting the conflicting claims of the federal government and the states.[3] Since *Cooley*, the Court's decisions had repeatedly acknowledged that the purpose of the commerce clause "was not to preclude all state regulation of commerce crossing state lines, but to prevent discrimination and the erection of barriers or obstacles to the free flow of commerce, interstate or foreign."[4]

To achieve this objective, Stone advocated a more realistic test, abandoning reliance on conclusory labels such as "direct" or "indirect." He shifted the focus from a metaphysical concern with "direct" burdens to a focus on burdens that discriminated against commerce from other states. Instead of rigid verbal formulae, the Court should use a more pragmatic test:

[T]he traditional test of the limit of state action by inquiring whether the interference with commerce is direct or indirect seems to me too mechanical, too uncertain in its application, and too remote from actualities, to be of value. In this making use of the expressions, "direct" and "indirect interference" with commerce, we are doing little more than using labels to describe a result rather than any trustworthy formula by which it is reached.

[I]t seems clear that those interferences not deemed forbidden are to be sustained, not because the effect on commerce is nominally indirect, but because a consideration of all the facts and circumstances, such as the nature of the regulation, its function, the character of the business involved and the actual effect on the flow of commerce, lead to the conclusion that the regulation concerns interests peculiarly local and does not infringe the national interest in maintaining the freedom of commerce across state lines.[5]

Years later, Professor Noel T. Dowling expanded Stone's ideas into an influential article,[6] which stressed that the Court should bring out into the open what it had really been attempting to do all along: "deliberately balancing national and local interest and making a choice as to which of the two *should* prevail."[7] Unless a federal law affirmatively consents to a state regulation affecting commerce, the courts should presume that Congress would invalidate any state action that constitutes "an unreasonable interference with national interests." This presumption is "rebuttable at the pleasure of Congress." If the state action falls short of such interference, it would prevail unless and until superseded or otherwise nullified by Congressional action.[8]

---

3. Prior to Stone's dissent in *Di Santo*, Black, Frankfurter and Douglas, JJ., dissenting in McCarroll v. Dixie Greyhound Lines, Inc., 309 U.S. 176, 183, 60 S.Ct. 504, 507, 84 L.Ed. 683, 688 (1940), rehearing denied 309 U.S. 696, 60 S.Ct. 610, 84 L.Ed. 1036 (1940), urged that the courts should not be in the business of drawing lines between the immunity of interstate commerce and the taxing power of the states. Instead, the courts should leave the task to Congress and state legislatures. Justice Black later repeated this view, but without success.

4. 273 U.S. at 43–44, 47 S.Ct. at 270–71.

5. 273 U.S. at 44, 47 S.Ct. at 271.

6. Dowling, Interstate Commerce and State Power, 27 Va.L.Rev. 1 (1940). Sedler, The Negative Commerce Clause as a Restriction on State Regulation and Taxation: An Analysis in Terms of Constitutional Structure, 31 Wayne L.Rev. 885, 968–99 (1986), challenges Dowling and persuasively argues that a nondiscrimination principle is the only defensible conceptual justification for the negative commerce clause.

7. 27 Va.L.Rev. at 21.

8. 27 Va.L.Rev. at 20.

The congressional will controls. If the Court sustains the state action as not discriminating or constituting an unreasonable burden on interstate commerce, and Congress concurs, no subsequent congressional action is required. If Congress concludes that the state action is undesirable, it retains the power to terminate its dormant state, and assert its will pursuant to its commerce clause power. Similarly, if the Court invalidates the state regulation, Congress can consequently resurrect the state law by expressing its consent to such state action.

The demise of formalistic tests and metaphysical attempts to interpret congressional silence has led to an era of more understandable rules.

§ 8.7 State Powers Over Transportation

A majority of the Court adopted the approach that Justice Stone had advocated in his *Di Santo* dissent in the early landmark case of *Southern Pacific Co. v. Arizona*.[1] Arizona charged Southern Pacific with violating a state Train Limit Law prohibiting trains with more than 14 passenger cars or 70 freight cars from operating within the state. Ostensibly, the state regulation was a safety measure.[2] Nonetheless, its practical effect was to impose a disproportionate burden on shippers who engaged in long hauls, as opposed to short hauls, and these long haul shippers were more likely to be using interstate as opposed to intrastate rail lines.

Stone, now Chief Justice, wrote the majority opinion. The trial court had found that the operation of long trains is standard practice through the United States; that approximately 93% of the Arizona freight traffic and 95% of the passenger traffic is interstate; that the train limit law required the Southern Pacific to haul over 30% more trains in Arizona. To comply with the Arizona train limit laws,

trains must either be broken up as they enter the border or conform to the lowest train limit restriction of all the states they travel through, thus allowing a state's train length regulations to have a substantial extraterritorial effect. Given the interstate nature of the train lines, "the Arizona law often controls the length of passenger trains all the way from Los Angeles to El Paso."[3]

In addition, the safety data presented at the trial was ambivalent at best. It turned out that the increased safety resulting from shorter trains was more than overcome by the added risks inherent in increasing the number of trains operating within the state. "The decisive question," the Court said, is whether in the these circumstances "the total effect of the law as a safety measure in reducing accidents and casualties is so slight or problematical as not to outweigh the national interest in keeping interstate commerce free from interferences which seriously impede it and subject it to local regulation which does not have a uniform effect on the interstate train journey which it interrupts."[4]

The majority agreed with the trial court that the Arizona law had no reasonable relation to safety, and found that the burdens on interstate commerce outweighed the state's equivocal evidence of safety. The majority weighed and evaluated the evidence. It did not accept the state's factual assertions of safety because the interests in interstate commerce are "not to be avoided by 'simply invoking the convenient apologetics of the police power.'"[5] The Court indicated by its language and actions that the test of "reasonableness" under the interstate commerce clause cases is much stricter than the modern test of "reasonableness" when the Court evaluates state or federal economic regulations challenged under the due process and equal protection cases.

---

§ 8.7

1. 325 U.S. 761, 65 S.Ct. 1515, 89 L.Ed. 1915 (1945).

2. Courts usually uphold state regulations furthering public safety, even though incidentally affecting interstate transportation, if there are no less restrictive alternatives. E.g., Minnesota Rate Cases, 230 U.S. 352, 33 S.Ct. 729, 57 L.Ed. 1511 (1913).

3. 325 U.S. at 774–75, 65 S.Ct. at 1523. (footnote omitted).

4. 325 U.S. at 775–76, 65 S.Ct. at 1523.

5. 325 U.S. at 780, 65 S.Ct. at 1525, quoting Kansas City Southern Ry. Co. v. Kaw Valley Drainage District, 233 U.S. 75, 79, 34 S.Ct. 564, 565, 58 L.Ed. 857 (1914).

Justices Douglas and Black dissented separately, accusing the majority of making the Court a "super-legislature." They contended that this case should be resolved in the political arena, not the judicial branch. In their opinions, the error was not that the Court had wrongly balanced the competing interests, but that the Court should not have engaged in a balancing inquiry at all.

The Court decided *Southern Pacific* in the wake of *South Carolina State Highway Department v. Barnwell Brothers, Inc.*[6] In that case a unanimous Court had sustained a South Carolina weight and width limitation for trucks operated within the state. Again Stone, then a Justice, wrote the opinion.

Barnwell upheld a South Carolina highway statute that prohibited trucks over 90 inches in width and with a loaded weight in excess of 20,000 pounds. All other states permitted the standard width of 96 inches and only four other states prescribed a gross weight as low as 20,000 pounds. Justice Stone emphasized that a state "may not, under the guise of regulation, discriminate against interstate commerce."[7] "[S]o long as the state action does not discriminate, the burden is one which the Constitution permits. . . ."[8] The commerce clause prohibits state legislation, nominally of local concern, that is really aimed at interstate commerce, or "by its necessary operation is a means of gaining a local benefit by throwing the attendant burdens on those without the state."[9]

But other language seems quite inconsistent with Chief Justice Stone's language in *Southern Pacific*. In *Barnwell,* Stone argued that it is for Congress and not the Court to decide to what extent "local interests should be required to yield to the national authority and interest."[10] "[C]ourts do not sit as legisla-

tures. . . ."[11] "Since the adoption of one weight or width regulation, rather than another, is a legislative not a judicial choice, its constitutionality is not to be determined by weighing in the judicial scales the merits of the legislative choice and rejecting it if the weight of evidence presented in court appears to favor a different standard."[12] "[C]ourts are not any the more entitled, because interstate commerce is affected, to substitute their own for the legislative judgment."[13]

While it is difficult to reconcile all of the language of these two cases, they are consistent in their results. In *Barnwell*, the evidence of the relationship between the state law and safety requirements was much stronger than the *Southern Pacific* case. In spite of the *Barnwell* language quoted above, the Court did in fact summarize and analyze the evidence of safety.[14] For example, 100 miles of South Carolina roads at the time were only 16 feet wide, too narrow for two 96 inch wide trucks. The Court also emphasized the local nature of the state highway system. While this reference to the local nature of state highways is not valid in modern times, it was convincing when *Barnwell* was decided in 1938. "Few subjects of state regulation are so peculiarly of local concern as in the use of state highways."[15] *Southern Pacific*, in distinguishing *Barnwell*, noted that the state's power over "its" highways is "far more extensive" than its control over railroads.[16] In 1938, that statement was true.

The Inner Political Check. It is also probably true that the political check operated more effectively in *Barnwell* than in *Southern Pacific*. While neither decision carefully articulates this rationale, the references in both cases to a *discriminatory* burden on interstate commerce supports the interpretation.[17]

6.   303 U.S. 177, 58 S.Ct. 510, 82 L.Ed. 734 (1938). Cardozo & Reed, JJ., did not participate.

7.   303 U.S. at 189, 58 S.Ct. at 515.

8.   303 U.S. at 189, 58 S.Ct. at 516.

9.   303 U.S. at 185–86, 58 S.Ct. at 514.

10.   303 U.S. at 190, 58 S.Ct. at 516.

11.   303 U.S. at 190, 58 S.Ct. at 516.

12.   303 U.S. at 191, 58 S.Ct. at 517.

13.   303 U.S. at 191, 58 S.Ct. at 517.

14.   303 U.S. at 191–196, 58 S.Ct. at 517–19.

15.   303 U.S. at 187, 58 S.Ct. at 515.

16.   325 U.S. at 783, 65 S.Ct. at 1527.

17.   South Carolina State Highway Department v. Barnwell Brothers, Inc., 303 U.S. 177, 185 n. 2, 58 S.Ct. 510, 513 n. 2, 82 L.Ed. 734, 738 n. 2 (1938) (internal citations omitted without indication):

"State regulations affecting interstate commerce, whose purpose or effect is to gain for those within the

The train length law involved in *Southern Pacific* probably burdens the long haul shipper more than the short haul shipper. The long haul shipper is more likely to be interstate and the short haul shipper is more likely to be intrastate. These intrastate shippers—feeling less of a burden of the state regulation—are less likely to use the political processes to urge the law's repeal. To the extent that the state regulation places a discriminatory burden on interstate commerce it works to the advantage of the competing, Arizona railroads. It is relatively easier for the short haul intrastate train to add freight or passenger cars to its engine as it crosses the state line. It can then compete effectively with its interstate rivals. But it is relatively harder for these interstate shippers to *split* a train and add an engine upon crossing the state line.

On the other hand, just as it is not cost effective for an interstate truck shipper to shift to a small truck when entering South Carolina, it is equally cost ineffective for the South Carolina trucker to shift to a larger truck when leaving his state; and if he does not shift, he suffers a competitive disadvantage because he does not have equivalent economies of scale of a larger truck. Because the burden of the South Carolina statute is not discriminatory against the interstate shipper, the South Carolina truckers have an incentive to change the law if it is not really warranted. That there is an inner political check and that it works is supported by the fact that the South Carolina state legislature, within three

months after the *Barnwell* decision, changed its law to expand its weight and width laws.[18]

An important factor in analyzing all cases attacking state regulation affecting interstate commerce is not only whether the burden on interstate commerce, as an absolute matter, is substantial, but whether the burden imposed on such commerce is discriminatory in favor of local concerns. To the extent that the burden is not discriminatory, there is room for operation of an inner political check that lessens the need for an active judicial review. When an inner political check is working, the Court is more likely to respect the state's own balancing of legitimate safety concerns with the national necessity for an efficient, uniform transportation system.[19]

If the state imposes a tariff on the importation of out-of-state goods, or charges a duty on goods that are transported across the state, Justice Stone's analysis would conclude that the burden of these tariffs or charges discriminate against intestate commerce. They are imposed on those people who live outside of the state and who therefore have no input into that state's political process. Yet economic theory teaches that the burdens of tariffs and similar trade barriers are also imposed on the people within the state—the consumers—who must pay to buy the goods or services because of the tariff or other charges. One should not read too much into that simple phrase, "inner political check." It is a tool of analysis, not a Rosetta Stone, and it should make one think of where the initial burden, or the most obvious burden, falls.

---

state an advantage at the expense of those without, or to burden those out of the state without any corresponding advantage to those within, have been thought to impinge upon the constitutional prohibition even though Congress has not acted.

"Underlying the stated rule has been the thought, often expressed in judicial opinion, that when the regulation is of such a character that its burden falls principally upon those without the state, legislative action is not likely to be subjected to those political restraints which are normally exerted on legislation where it affects adversely some interests within the state."

Southern Pacific Co. v. Arizona, 325 U.S. 761, 767 n. 2, 65 S.Ct. 1515, 1519 n. 2, 89 L.Ed. 1915, 1923 n. 2 (1945) (citations omitted without indication):

"In applying this rule the Court has often recognized that to the extent that the burden of state regulation

falls on interests outside the state, it is unlikely to be alleviated by the operation of those political restraints normally exerted when interests within the state are affected."

On the principle of the inner political check, see Rotunda, The Doctrine of the Inner Political Check, the Dormant Commerce Clause, and Federal Preemption, 53 Transportation Practitioners Journal 263 (1986); Rotunda, Sheathing the Sword of Federal Preemption, 5 Const. Commentary 311 (1988); Sidak & Woodward, Corporate Takeovers, and the Efficient Anonymity of Shareholders, 84 Nw.U.L.Rev. 1092 (1990).

18. South Carolina Acts No. 845 (1938).

19. John M. Walker, Jr., J., citing Treatise in, National Electric Manufactures Association v. Sorrell 272 F.3d 104, 109 (2d Cir. 2001).

The *Bibb* Case. *Bibb v. Navajo Freight Lines, Inc.*[20] invalidated an Illinois safety measure specifying contour mud flaps for trucks operated within its jurisdiction. The state's peculiar variation on mud flap design resulted in prohibiting interstate commerce operators from using a mud flap in Illinois, even though this mud flap was legal in 45 other states. In addition, the Illinois design was itself illegal in Arkansas, which required straight mud flaps. This multiplicity of standards retarded the free flow of interstate trucking unnecessarily.

The trial court found that the contour mud flap posed no safety advantage over the conventional or straight mud flap and there was evidence that it created new hazards by accumulating heat in the brake drum. The special mud flap design—because of the different and conflicting requirements of other jurisdictions—significantly interfered with interstate commerce. In language harking back to *Cooley*, the Court struck down the Illinois requirement:

> This is one of those cases—few in number—where local safety measures that are nondiscriminatory place an unconstitutional burden on interstate commerce. This conclusion is especially underlined by the deleterious effect which the Illinois law will have on the "interline" operation of interstate motor carriers. The conflict between the Arkansas regulation and the Illinois regulation also suggests that this regulation of mudguards is not one of those matters "admitting of diversity of treatment, according to the special requirements of local conditions"....[21]

Bibb noted that if the only issue were the interstate commerce carrier's cost of adjusting

to these new safety regulations, the Court would have sustained the law.[22] Apparently, the enhanced cost factor alone would not motivate the Court to strike down the train length regulation in *Southern Pacific*. Rather, it is the minimal evidence supportive of the safety rationale as contrasted with the onerous burden on the movement of interstate commerce that is decisive: the burdens on interstate commerce exceeded the benefits of local safety.

Full Train Crew and Other Transportation Cases. In a long line of cases the Supreme Court has upheld statutes requiring "full-crews" on railroad trains. This requirement, when nondiscriminatorily applied to intrastate, as well as interstate, trains, is sufficiently related to safety that the Court will not second-guess the legislature. As a factual matter, the added burden of adding crew members when the train crossed a border is not significant compared with the possible safety advantages.[23] It is also a burden that does not vary based on the whether the shipper is interstate or intrastate. It is as easy to add or subtract workers when crossing a state line.

Nearly a decade before *Brown v. Board of Education*[24] had integrated the schools, the Court, relying on the dormant commerce clause, held that Virginia could not require the segregation of white and black passengers on interstate motor traffic because "seating arrangements for the different races in interstate motor traffic require a single, uniform rule to promote and protect national travel."[25]

When the state denied certificates of convenience to interstate motor carriers on the grounds that the territory was already "ade-

---

20. 359 U.S. 520, 79 S.Ct. 962, 3 L.Ed.2d 1003 (1959).

21. 359 U.S. at 529, 79 S.Ct. at 967, quoting Hughes, C.J., in Sproles v. Binford, 286 U.S. 374, 390, 52 S.Ct. 581, 585, 76 L.Ed. 1167 (1932). See also, Ray v. Atlantic Richfield Co., 435 U.S. 151, 179, 98 S.Ct. 988, 1005, 55 L.Ed.2d 179 (1978).

22. 359 U.S. at 526, 79 S.Ct. at 966. See also Morris v. Duby, 274 U.S. 135, 144, 47 S.Ct. 548, 550, 71 L.Ed. 966 (1927) (statute setting maximum truck load upheld).

23. Brotherhood of Locomotive Firemen & Enginemen v. Chicago, Rock Island & Pacific R.R. Co., 393 U.S. 129, 89 S.Ct. 323, 21 L.Ed.2d 289 (1968), rehearing denied 393 U.S. 1045, 89 S.Ct. 610, 21 L.Ed.2d 598 (1969). See also, e.g., Brotherhood of Locomotive Engineers v. Chicago, R.I.

& P.R.R. Co., 382 U.S. 423, 438, 86 S.Ct. 594, 601–02, 15 L.Ed.2d 501 (1966), where Douglas, J., dissented on the grounds that the Federal Government had preempted such regulation. 382 U.S. at 438, 86 S.Ct. at 601–02.

24. 347 U.S. 483, 74 S.Ct. 686, 98 L.Ed. 873 (1954), supplemented 349 U.S. 294, 75 S.Ct. 753, 99 L.Ed. 1083 (1955).

25. Morgan v. Virginia, 328 U.S. 373, 386, 66 S.Ct. 1050, 1058, 90 L.Ed. 1317 (1946). Bob–Lo Excursion Co. v. Michigan, 333 U.S. 28, 68 S.Ct. 358, 92 L.Ed. 455 (1948) (commerce clause does not forbid state from applying its civil rights act to transportation company engaged in foreign commerce).

quately" served, the Court reversed.[26] In effect, the state was merely using the law to limit competition and burden the interstate shipper. But the state may deny such certificates for bona fide safety reasons, e.g., if adding a new carrier on a particular route that is already congested would cause valid safety problems.[27]

Summary. Commentators on the various problems and court tests in this area abound,[28] but perhaps the best summary of the law in this area is the Supreme Court's in *Pike v. Bruce Church, Inc.*[29]

Although the criteria for determining the validity of state statutes affecting interstate commerce have been variously stated, the general rule that emerges can be phrased as follows: Where the statute regulates evenhandedly to effectuate a legitimate local public interest, and its effects on interstate commerce are only incidental, it will be upheld unless the burden imposed on such commerce is clearly excessive in relation to the putative local benefits. If a legitimate local purpose is found, then the question becomes one of degree. And the extent of the burden that will be tolerated will of course depend on the nature of the local interest involved, and on whether it could be promoted as well with a lesser impact on interstate activities. Occasionally the Court has candidly undertaken a balancing approach in resolving these issues, but more frequently

it has spoken in terms of "direct" and "indirect" benefits and burdens.[30]

§ 8.8   Incoming Commerce

The Court no longer uses the so-called "original package" doctrine[1] as the definitive test to evaluate state regulatory power over products imported from out of state. The real question is whether the state legislation discriminates against interstate commerce, that is, whether the state law involves economic protectionism. If the statutory purpose or effect is to protect state producers from competitive interstate commerce, the parochial legislation is invalid. State laws affecting the national market, even justified under the guise of local health and safety concerns, are also invalid under the dormant commerce clause if there is a less burdensome, nondiscriminatory alternative.

The seminal case invalidating a state regulatory scheme that involved economic protectionism is *Baldwin v. G. A. F. Seelig, Inc.*[2] Justice Cardozo, writing for a unanimous court, rejected New York's efforts to rely on the original package doctrine or any direct/indirect burden distinction to justify its restriction of the sale of Vermont milk within New York's borders.

New York established minimum milk prices that dealers had to pay to producers. The Supreme Court had no problem with New York's minimum price laws as applied to prod-

---

26. Buck v. Kuykendall, 267 U.S. 307, 45 S.Ct. 324, 69 L.Ed. 623 (1925); Railroad Transfer Service, Inc. v. City of Chicago, 386 U.S. 351, 87 S.Ct. 1095, 18 L.Ed.2d 143 (1967); Lloyd A. Fry Roofing Co. v. Wood, 344 U.S. 157, 73 S.Ct. 204, 97 L.Ed. 168 (1952), rehearing denied 345 U.S. 913, 73 S.Ct. 638, 97 L.Ed. 1347 (1953) (merely requiring truckers to obtain permit does not amount to interference with commerce).

27. Bradley v. Public Utilities Commission, 289 U.S. 92, 53 S.Ct. 577, 77 L.Ed. 1053 (1933).

28. The classic books in this area include, F. Frankfurter. The Commerce Clause Under Marshall, Taney and Waite (1937); W. D. G. Ribble, State and National Power over Commerce (1937); B. Gavit, The Commerce Clause of the United States Constitution (1932). See also, Dowling, Interstate Commerce and State Power, 27 Va.L.Rev. 1 (1940); Dowling, Interstate Commerce and State Power—Revised Version, 47 Colum.L.Rev. 597 (1947).

29. 397 U.S. 137, 90 S.Ct. 844, 25 L.Ed.2d 174 (1970).

30. 397 U.S. at 142, 90 S.Ct. at 847 (case citations within quotation omitted without any special indications).

Walker, C.J., citing Treatise in National Elec. Mfrs. Ass'n v. Sorrell, 272 F.3d 104, 109 (2d Cir. 2001).

§ 8.8

1. Chief Justice Marshall created the original package doctrine in Brown v. Maryland, 25 U.S. (12 Wheat.) 419, 6 L.Ed. 678 (1827).

The Court has now interpreted *Brown*—in the context of a case dealing with the state's power to tax goods imported from foreign countries—to allow the state to levy nondiscriminatory and neutral taxes on foreign goods; i.e., a tax may be imposed without regard to the origin of the goods, and even if the goods taxed are in their original package. Michelin Tire Corp. v. Wages, 423 U.S. 276, 96 S.Ct. 535, 46 L.Ed.2d 495 (1976), rehearing denied 424 U.S. 935, 96 S.Ct. 1151, 47 L.Ed.2d 344 (1976), overruling Low v. Austin, 80 U.S. (13 Wall.) 29, 20 L.Ed. 517 (1871).

2. 294 U.S. 511, 55 S.Ct. 497, 79 L.Ed. 1032 (1935).

ucts originating within the state.[3] But New York milk dealers, in order to avoid paying the high milk prices in-state, preferred to buy their milk out-of-state. To keep the system unimpaired by competition from afar, the Act tried to extend its the protective prices to that part of the supply (about 30%) that came from other states. In other words, a New York milk dealer could not sell his milk within the state unless he had paid the milk producer (wherever the latter is located) whatever the dealer, under the state law, would have had to pay the New York producer. When Seelig bought its milk from a Vermont creamery at less than the New York set price, the New York Commission refused to license it to do business in New York. The New York procedure, in effect though not in name, imposed a tariff on the out of state milk. Even though the state collected no money, it artificially raised the price of out-of-state milk so that out-of-state purchasers could not underprice the local product.

No state has any power to project its legislation into another state by regulating the price to be paid in that other state for goods purchased there. Such a power, if allowed—

> will set a barrier to traffic between one state and another as effective as if customs duties, equal to the price differential, had been laid upon the thing transported.... [A] chief occasion of the commerce clauses was "the mutual jealousies and aggressions of the States, taking form in customs barriers and other economic retaliation." ... If New York, in order to promote the economic welfare of her farmers, may guard them against competition with the cheaper prices of Vermont, the door has been opened to rivalries and reprisals that were meant to be averted by subjecting commerce between the states to the power of the nation.[4]

The Court rejected the argument that the purpose of the New York law was to maintain an adequate supply of pure milk, the supply being put in jeopardy when the farmers of the state are unable to earn a living income. The Court correctly realized that this argument proves too much, for it would allow virtually all state trade barriers against other states. "The Constitution was framed under the dominion of a political philosophy less parochial in range. It was framed on the theory that the people of the several states must sink or swim together, and that in the long run prosperity and salvation are in union and not division."[5]

Baldwin invalidated a New York milk regulatory scheme that was an attempt to aid local milk producers by making more expensive the importation of milk from a sister state. In effect, the state imposed a wealth transfer to local producers directly financed by the out-of-state producers. There was no inner political check working within New York state to assure that the people of New York directly paid for this wealth transfer.

Tax Subsidies. The Court would have upheld the transfer of direct cash payments or tax subsidies (e.g., lower property tax assessments of dairy land) to New York milk producers (financed by the New York general taxpayer). An inner political check would assure that the people within the state, who directly paid for the subsidy, would weigh the costs and benefits. But when there is an attempt to shift the direct costs to out-of-state persons, this inner political check is not working as well and so there is a broader role for judicial review.

On the other hand, the Court will not uphold crude tax subsidies. For example, the state may not enact a crude tax subsidy scheme that taxes a given business and then subsidizes the in-state competitors with the money collected from the out of state competitors. There is no inner political check because those who pay the tax are out of state residents or companies with no real input into the taxing state's political processes. Any in-state taxpayers are won over to the tax because they

---

3. See Nebbia v. New York, 291 U.S. 502, 54 S.Ct. 505, 78 L.Ed. 940 (1934).

4. 294 U.S. at 521–22, 55 S.Ct. at 499–500. See also Polar Ice Cream & Creamery Co. v. Andrews, 375 U.S. 361, 84 S.Ct. 378, 11 L.Ed.2d 389 (1964).

5. 294 U.S. at 523, 55 S.Ct. at 500.

more than recoup their losses by a subsidy in the form of a rebate of the tax.

In *West Lynn Creamery, Inc. v. Healy*,[6] the Supreme Court invalidated a Massachusetts milk pricing order that imposed a special tax on all liquid milk sold to Massachusetts retailers that was placed into a specially earmarked state fund that subsidized Massachusetts dairy farmers. The Court found that the linking of the tax to the earmarked fund to subsidize farmers worked like an ordinary tariff, it effectively imposed additional costs on the purchase of out of state products. In a footnote the Court remarked that it was not "squarely" confronting the constitutionality of subsidies.[7] However, true subsidies that go to businesses or individuals from the general revenues of a state should not be invalidated under the dormant commerce clause.

In *West Lynn Creamery*, Justice Scalia wrote an opinion that sounded much like Professor Scalia explaining the problem to his students, during his days on law school faculties. Justice Scalia stated:

"There are at least four possible devices that would enable a state to produce the economic effect [the subsidy to local milk farmers] that Massachusetts has produced here: (1) a discriminatory tax upon the industry, imposing a higher liability on out-of state members than on their in-state competitors; (2) a tax upon the industry that is non-discriminatory in its assessment, but that has an exemption or credit for in-state members; (3) a non-discriminatory tax upon the industry, the revenues from which are placed into a segregated fund, which fund is disbursed as rebates or subsidies to in-state members of the industry (the situation at issue in this case); and, (4) with or without non-discriminatory taxation of the industry, a subsidy for the in-state members of the industry, funded from the state's general revenues. It is long settled that the first of

these methodologies is unconstitutional ... the second of them, exemption or credit against a neutral tax, is no different in principle from the first, and has likewise been held invalid ... the fourth methodology, application of a state subsidy from general revenues, is so far removed from what we have hitherto held to be unconstitutional, that prohibiting it must be regarded as an extension of our negative-commerce clause jurisprudence, and, therefore, to me, unacceptable ... the issue before us in the present case is whether the third of these methodologies must fall. Although the question is close, I conclude it would not be a principled point at which to disembark from a negative-commerce-clause train. The only difference between methodology (2) (discriminatory exemption from nondiscriminatory tax) and methodology (3) (discriminatory refund of a nondiscriminatory tax) is that the money is taken and returned rather than simply left with the favored in-state taxpayer in the first place. The difference between (3) and (4), on the other hand, is the difference between assisting in-state industry through non-discriminatory taxation and assisting in-state industry by other means. I would therefore allow a state to subsidize its domestic industry as long as it does so from non-discriminatory taxes that go to the state's general revenue fund."[8]

There are some important economic differences between tax subsidies and tariffs, even though both are economically inefficient and both negatively affect free trade and the free flow of goods and services. Although *West Lynn Creamery* does not make the point explicitly, it was implicit in the Court's acknowledgment that one could not rely on the "state's political processes" to prevent "legislative abuse" in the situation that existed in *West Lynn Creamery*. Pure subsidies are usual-

---

6. 512 U.S. 186, 114 S.Ct. 2205, 129 L.Ed.2d 157 (1994).

7. 512 U.S. at 199 n. 15, 114 S.Ct. at 2214 n. 15.

8. West Lynn Creamery, Inc. v. Healy, 512 U.S. 186, 207, 210–11, 114 S.Ct. 2205, 2218, 2220–21, 129 L.Ed.2d

157 (1994) (Scalia, J., joined by Thomas, J., concurring in the judgment) (internal quotation marks, internal citations, and internal paragraph divisions omitted).

ly more transparent to voters than tariffs; their economic affects are more obvious. In the case of tariffs the voter who is less economically sophisticated thinks that the party who is out-of-state is paying the tariff, while voters do know that it is they who must pay the taxes to raise the money that is given to the favored recipient in a tax subsidy situation.[9]

Compensating Use Taxes. *Baldwin* does not forbid a state from using its tax laws to subject interstate goods sold in its state to the same tax levied on intrastate goods sold in its state, i.e., a "compensatory use" tax. The tax laws in such a case are nondiscriminatory and are not used to compensate for natural competitive advantages of another state. Unlike the *Baldwin* situation, a "compensating use" tax does not smother competition but removes the artificial competitive disadvantage that the state's own tax laws would otherwise impose on products produced in the state; the state tax simply subjects imported goods to the same nondiscriminatory tax that in-state goods already have to pay.[10] Thus, *Henneford v. Silas Mason Co.*[11] approved a 2% sales tax on all retail sales within the state and a 2% compensating use tax on products used in the state on which a sales or use tax has not previously been paid.

Although the tax that *Henneford* upheld had a compensating feature, Justice Cardozo, for the Court, made clear that the Court was not ruling that this compensating aspect was a constitutional requirement. He explained:

> Yet a word of caution should be added here to avoid the chance of misconception. We have not meant to imply by anything said in this opinion that allowance of a credit for

other taxes paid to Washington made it mandatory that there should be a like allowance for taxes paid to other states. A state, for many purposes, is to be reckoned as a self-contained unit, which may frame it own system of burdens and exemptions without heeding systems elsewhere.[12]

In other words, State *A* ought to be able to impose, for example, a 2% sales tax on goods sold in State *A*, and also impose a 2% use tax on the first retail use of the good in that State. If the first retail user of the good has already paid the sales tax to State *A*, then State *A* may constitutionally grant a credit of 2%. But if the first retail user has not already paid a sales tax to State *A*, then State *A* may constitutionally insist on collecting its 2% use tax, even though this retail user has already paid a sales tax to State *B*, where this user had purchased the good.

It is not unconstitutional for State *A* to refuse to grant or take into account the taxes that this retail user had already paid to a different state. It is not State *A*'s fault that State *B* decided to levy a sales tax on that particular good. In addition, State *A* is not discriminating against interstate commerce when it grants a credit of 2% for the sales tax earlier paid to it, but does not grant any credit for the sales tax paid to State *B*; what State *A* is doing is merely the economic equivalent of imposing a 2% use tax, but collecting it earlier (and calling it a sales tax) as to goods purchased within the state.

States may not impose a use tax that is higher on goods purchased from out of state than the sales and use tax imposed on in-state goods.[13]

---

9. See, Dan T. Coenen, Business Subsidies and the Dormant Commerce Clause, 107 Yale L. J. 965 (1998);Christopher R. Drahozal, On Tariffs and Subsidies in Inter*state* Trade: A Legal and Economic Analysis, 74 Wash. U. L. Q. 1127, 1153 (1996).

10. See Brown, The Open Economy: Justice Frankfurter and the Position of the Judiciary, 67 Yale L.J. 219, 234–36 (1957).

11. 300 U.S. 577, 57 S.Ct. 524, 81 L.Ed. 814 (1937).

12. 300 U.S. at 587, 57 S.Ct. at 529. Cf. D.H. Holmes Company, Ltd. v. McNamara, 486 U.S. 24, 108 S.Ct. 1619, 100 L.Ed.2d 21 (1988), upholding the imposition of a Louisiana use tax on direct mail catalogues printed out-of-

state and mailed into Louisiana by a Louisiana corporation that operated department stores in Louisiana.

13. Associated Industries of Missouri v. Lohman, 511 U.S. 641, 114 S.Ct. 1815, 128 L.Ed.2d 639 (1994), where Thomas, J., for the Court, invalidated a statewide "additional use tax" on goods purchases from out of state but used, stored, or consumed within the state. The 1.5% use tax was in excess of the sales tax that some local jurisdictions imposed. The Court rejected Missouri's argument that the court should look at the statewide "average" tax. In South Central Bell Telephone Co. v. Alabama, 526 U.S. 160, 119 S.Ct. 1180, 143 L.Ed.2d 258 (1999) the Court ruled that an Alabama franchise tax, assessed in a discrim-

An argument can be made that a state would not have to give a credit against its use tax for sales taxes made in another state.[14] Though that argument would not be unreasonable, it seems clear a state with a compensating use tax that does not credit the taxpayer for a sales tax paid in another state (if the taxing state gives a credit against its use taxes for a sales tax paid on the purchase of an identical product in its state will have a difficult time in demonstrating that its tax does not discriminate against interstate commerce).[15]

The Least Restrictive Means Test. To avoid the *Baldwin* problem, some states have sought to draft more complex schemes that have more than a perfunctory reference to local health and safety interests. To deal with these situations the Court has developed a strict, active judicial review to assure that the legitimate safety measures can be accomplished by means imposing the least restrictive effects on interstate commerce.

This principle is well illustrated by *Dean Milk Co. v. City of Madison*.[16] A Madison ordinance made it illegal to sell pasteurized milk unless it had been processed and bottled at an approved pasteurization plant within a radius of five miles from the central square of Madison. The state court approved the five mile radius on the grounds that it promoted convenient, economical, and efficient plant inspection.

The Supreme Court invalidated the state law. First, it was unimpressed that Madison's law also excluded Wisconsin milk from outside the Madison area (i.e., some in-state milk) as well as interstate milk. The Court did not elaborate, but its principle should be clear. If a

locality could avoid the requirements of the dormant commerce clause by also discriminating against some in-state area, then it would be fairly easy to engage in economic discrimination. For example, each town in a state could discriminate against all interstate commerce and the commerce from other portions of the state. Or each half of the state could discriminate against all out-of-state goods and goods from the other half of the state. Under the theory of the city of Madison, the state as a whole would be accepting no out-of-state goods, but it would be able to avoid dormant commerce clause scrutiny merely because portions of the state would also be discriminating against other portions of the state.

Similarly the Court did not accept Madison's health rationale, for there were "reasonable nondiscriminatory alternatives, adequate to conserve legitimate local interests" that were available.[17] For example, if the city insisted that it was necessary for its own officials inspect distant milk sources, it could do so, and charge the actual and reasonable cost of such inspection to the importing producers and processors.[18]

The state does not have to use the means to promote its local interests that have the least burden on commerce if it is attempting to promote the health or welfare of its people, and if the use of laws with a lesser burden on commerce would place the health or welfare of its people at risk. In other words, when regulating to protect the health or welfare of its people, a state or local government only has to use the means with the least burden on commerce if the party challenging the state or local law can demonstrate that the state or

---

inatory manner on out-of-state corporations violated the dormant commerce clause. The different tax rates between foreign and domestic corporations did not offset differences in the tax rate. The tax was facially discriminatory against interstate commerce.

14. See generally, J. Nowak & Rotunda, Sales and Use Tax Credits, Discrimination Against Interstate Commerce, and the Useless Multiple Tax Concept. 20 U.C. Davis L.Rev. 273 (1987). For citations to additional cases, including lower court cases, and secondary works on this topic see our multi-volume Treatise: R. Rotunda & J. Nowak, Treatise on Constitutional Law: Substance and Procedure (3rd ed. 1999, with annual supplements).

15. Cf. Fulton Corp. v. Faulkner, 516 U.S. 325, 332–33, 116 S.Ct. 848, 854–55, 133 L.Ed.2d 796 (1996) (invalidating an "intangibles tax" that was deemed discriminatory; majority opinion explains that burden placed on a state that has a tax that appears to place an extra tax burden on interstate commerce.)

16. 340 U.S. 349, 71 S.Ct. 295, 95 L.Ed. 329 (1951).

17. 340 U.S. at 354, 71 S.Ct. at 298.

18. 340 U.S. at 356, 71 S.Ct. at 299.

local government could achieve exactly equal benefits through a law that would not place a great burden on commerce.

An unreasonable example may serve to illustrate this very reasonable position on the part of the Court. Let us assume that a state was regulating the quality of baby clothes, because it wanted children in the state to be clothed in material that was nonflammable. Our hypothetical state enacts a law (somewhat similar to the city law in the *Dean Milk* case) that prohibited anyone from selling clothes for babies or small toddlers unless it was packaged in the state. Businesses that package baby clothes in other states would attempt to show that the state could protect children within the state through alternative means such as by sending inspectors to baby clothes packaging facilities in other states. Let us assume that at the end of the litigation, the Court found that state's law requiring local packaging of baby clothes would insure that no child in the state was ever going to be severely burned or killed through accidental inflammation of the child's clothes; but that the state's law could be analyzed as imposing a multi-billion dollar burden on interstate commerce in children's clothing. If a court, at the end of the litigation finds that the alternatives offered by those challenging the law would result in the state facing the likelihood that one or two babies a year might be severely burned or killed from clothes that accidently caught fire, because the alternative means for inspecting clothes were not as good as the means used when the state could directly supervise local packaging of such clothes. The alternative means, that might or might not result in the loss of a baby's life every several years, would place a very small burden on the clothing industry. Under those circumstances, one can feel fairly certain that the state would not have to choose the means with the least burden on commerce. In other words, the state would not be required by the courts

to use alternative means to requiring local packaging of baby clothes, if the cost of using the means that created a lesser burden on commerce was the possibility that a child might be seriously injured in the future.

The State Reciprocity Requirements. The Court has looked with suspicion on state reciprocity agreements. In *Great Atlantic & Pacific Tea Co. v. Cottrell*[19] the challenged Mississippi law admitted interstate milk for sale only if the producing state had agreed to a reciprocal inspection standards agreement. Reaffirming the vitality of the *Baldwin* and *Dean Milk* standard, the Court refused to limit its inquiry because of the state's assertion of a need to regulate for legitimate health and safety reasons.

The Mississippi law was not really designed to promote health and safety. It permitted Louisiana milk to be admitted to Mississippi if Louisiana entered into a reciprocity agreement with Mississippi, even though Louisiana's standards were lower than Mississippi's. "The reciprocity clause thus disserves rather than promotes any higher Mississippi milk quality standards."[20] If it is the case that a state may insist that a sister state either sign a reciprocal agreement or be foreclosed from exporting its products to Mississippi, then such a rule would invite a multiplication of preferential and retaliatory trade barriers that are contrary to the purpose of the Commerce Clause.[21] Although Mississippi, ostensibly, sought to guarantee safe milk, the Court concluded that the substance of the regulatory scheme was contrived to protect Mississippi milk producers competing in foreign jurisdictions.[22]

The Commerce Clause and Privacy. When the alleged local benefit outweighs the degree of the state-imposed burden, states are not necessarily barred from restraining incoming interstate commerce. In *Breard v. Alexandria*[23] the Court upheld a municipal ordinance forbidding uninvited door-to-door solicitation.

---

19. 424 U.S. 366, 96 S.Ct. 923, 47 L.Ed.2d 55 (1976).

20. 424 U.S. at 375, 96 S.Ct. at 929–30.

21. 424 U.S. at 380, 96 S.Ct. at 932.

22. Accord, Sporhase v. Nebraska, 458 U.S. 941, 102 S.Ct. 3456, 73 L.Ed.2d 1254 (1982), on remand 213 Neb. 484, 329 N.W.2d 855 (1983) (reciprocity provision of state

statute regulating exportation of water is "explicit barrier to commerce").

23. 341 U.S. 622, 71 S.Ct. 920, 95 L.Ed. 1233 (1951), rehearing denied 342 U.S. 843, 72 S.Ct. 21, 96 L.Ed. 637 (1951).

The Court said that the local homeowner's right to privacy outweighed the economic burden even though "interstate commerce itself knocks on the local door."[24]

The Court gave greater deference to legislation designed to protect the privacy interests of the community than it would give local regulatory schemes revealing an attempt to preserve local prosperity at the expense of nonresidents. Our federalist system recognizes state power to reasonably regulate incoming commerce pursuant to legitimate local health and safety objectives, *but only* to the extent that the nondiscriminatory burden imposed on the national market place does not exceed the alleged local benefits.

Prohibition of Harmful Products. The Court's emphasis on nondiscrimination is important, because even products that are concededly harmful are still "commerce" and therefore subjected to standard commerce clause analysis. For example, if an article's worth in interstate commerce is "far outweighed" by the dangers in its movement—such as items that spread pestilence—then the state could prohibit its transportation across state lines.[25] In contrast, a state cannot prohibit the out of state importation of solid or liquid wastes in order to extend the life of landfill within the state and protect its environment. Such wastes are in commerce and protected by the commerce clause. The garbage dump owner is selling space, and the waste hauler is buying that space.

The state discriminated against out-of-state waste because it allowed *nonimported* wastes to be transported and buried within the state. A state cannot distinguish between in-state and out of state wastes by allowing the former but not the latter to be disposed of in landfill sites within the state, because a state cannot slow down or prohibit the flow of commerce in order to conserve for those within its borders privately-owned land fill.[26] What is really purchased in such cases is not the waste, but rather it is the landfill. States cannot prevent private landfill owners from selling portions of their landfill to out of state landfill users, any more than Wisconsin could prevent its dairy farmers from selling their cheese to out-of-state consumers.

If a state can demonstrate that it needs to keep a product out of the state in order to protect significant local interests, other than the economic well being of in-state persons or businesses, it may exclude the out-of-state products. For example, in *Maine v. Taylor*[27] the Supreme Court upheld a State of Maine statute that prohibited the importation of live bait fish into the State of Maine. The Court held that the findings of the trial court were not erroneous and that the State had adequately demonstrated that its law was reasonably designed to serve the legitimate purpose of protecting the local environment. At trial,

24. 341 U.S. at 636, 71 S.Ct. at 929.

25. Philadelphia v. New Jersey, 437 U.S. 617, 622, 98 S.Ct. 2531, 2534–35, 57 L.Ed.2d 475 (1978).

26. Philadelphia v. New Jersey, 437 U.S. 617, 98 S.Ct. 2531, 57 L.Ed.2d 475 (1978). See also, Chemical Waste Management, Inc. v. Hunt, 504 U.S. 334, 112 S.Ct. 2009, 119 L.Ed.2d 121 (1992), where the Court invalidated an Alabama law that imposed a hazardous waste disposal fee on hazardous wastes generated out of the state but disposed of within the state, at commercial (i.e., not state-owned) waste facilities. The fee did not apply to waste originating in Alabama. The state could not justify its rules based on any health or safety concerns, because these did not vary with the point of origin of the waste. Accord, Oregon Waste Systems, Inc. v. Department of Environmental Quality, 511 U.S. 93, 114 S.Ct. 1345, 128 L.Ed.2d 13 (1994), on remand 319 Or. 251, 876 P.2d 749 (1994).

C & A Carbone v. Town of Clarkstown, 511 U.S. 383, 114 S.Ct. 1677, 128 L.Ed.2d 399 (1994), on remand 208 A.D.2d 612, 617 N.Y.S.2d 482 (1994), where the Court invalidated a city ordinance that all nonhazardous solid waste generated or brought into the town must be processed at a particular transfer station, which charged above-market fees. The court held that the town may not use its regulatory powers to favor one or more local businesses by prohibiting patronage of out of state competitors.

It is a different situation if a state regulated all waste deposit in land fill areas, even if that rule affects interstate waste, if there is *no discrimination* against the interstate waste. See, e.g., Minnesota v. Clover Leaf Creamery Co., 449 U.S. 456, 101 S.Ct. 715, 66 L.Ed.2d 659 (1981), on remand 304 N.W.2d 915 (Minn.1981) (to conserve energy and resources Minnesota may ban retail sale of milk in plastic, nonrefillable containers; the statute does not discriminate against interstate commerce and the incidental burden on interstate commerce is not excessive in relation to the putative local benefits).

27. 477 U.S. 131, 106 S.Ct. 2440, 91 L.Ed.2d 110 (1986).

the state had shown that there was no economically reasonable way for the state to screen live bait fish for parasites that might be foreign to the State of Maine. The State, according to the majority, had demonstrated that non-native species of live fish, might disrupt the environment. The Supreme Court majority found that the trial court had not erred when it accepted the state's claim that it was not possible for the state to screen all live bait fish for possible parasites. Therefore, the law survived the difficult standard imposed on states for demonstrating the legitimacy of a tariff or a trade barrier.[28]

Commerce and the Twenty–First Amendment. To be distinguished from state power to regulate commerce in general is the state power to regulate commerce over *liquor*. Liquor is no longer treated like other products because of the Twenty–First Amendment, section two, which provides: "The transportation or importation into any State, Territory, or possession of the United States for delivery or use therein of intoxicating liquors, in violation of the laws thereof, is hereby prohibited."

The Twenty–First Amendment does not repeal the commerce clause as to state regulation of the importation or transportation of liquor, but it certainly affects it, and serves to give the state "wide latitude."[29] Thus a state may exact a license fee for the privilege of importing into that state liquor from another state,[30] although in the absence of the Twenty–First Amendment the dormant commerce clause would have forbade such an import fee.

Nonetheless, there are limits to the state's power. For example, a state cannot tax liquor imported into that state from a foreign country, in violation of the export import clause.[31] Even though the Twenty–First Amendment does impose some limits on the commerce clause, it does not impose those limit on the export import clause because there are foreign policy concerns that are present as to imports from abroad.

The state power over liquor does not insulate state regulations from the limitations of the Fourteenth Amendment.[32] It was not a purpose of the Twenty–First Amendment to limit the Bill of Rights. Also, notwithstanding the state's power to control the importation, sale, and distribution of liquor, Congress has the commerce clause power to prohibit resale price maintenance in violation of the Sherman Act.[33]

Even as to the commerce clause, the Twenty–First Amendment does not completely insulate state power for all judicial review. For example, New York may not constitutionally require every liquor distiller who sells liquor to wholesalers within that state to sell at a price that is no higher than the lowest price that the liquor distiller charged to wholesalers anywhere in the United States. This state law regulated out of state transactions in violation of the commerce clause.[34] The New York rule made it illegal for a distiller to reduce its price in other states during the period it is posted in New York, thus directly regulating commerce in other states. New York cannot constitution-

28. Justice Stevens was the only dissenter in *Taylor*; he noted that: "There is something fishy about this case. Maine is the only state in the union that blatantly discriminates against out of state bait fish by flatly prohibiting their importation." 477 U.S. at 152, 106 S.Ct. at 2454 (Stevens, J., dissenting).

29. Joseph E. Seagram & Sons, Inc. v. Hostetter, 384 U.S. 35, 42, 86 S.Ct. 1254, 1259, 16 L.Ed.2d 336 (1966).

30. State Board of Equalization v. Young's Market Co., 299 U.S. 59, 57 S.Ct. 77, 81 L.Ed. 38 (1936).

31. Department of Revenue v. James B. Beam Distilling Co., 377 U.S. 341, 84 S.Ct. 1247, 12 L.Ed.2d 362 (1964).

32. See, e.g., Craig v. Boren, 429 U.S. 190, 204–09, 97 S.Ct. 451, 460–63, 50 L.Ed.2d 397 (1976), rehearing denied 429 U.S. 1124, 97 S.Ct. 1161, 51 L.Ed.2d 574 (1977) (equal

protection); Wisconsin v. Constantineau, 400 U.S. 433, 436, 91 S.Ct. 507, 509–10, 27 L.Ed.2d 515 (1971) (due process). But cf. New York State Liquor Authority v. Bellanca, 452 U.S. 714, 101 S.Ct. 2599, 69 L.Ed.2d 357 (1981) (per curiam), on remand 54 N.Y.2d 228, 445 N.Y.S.2d 87, 429 N.E.2d 765 (1981), certiorari denied 456 U.S. 1006, 102 S.Ct. 2296, 73 L.Ed.2d 1300 (1982). See also, California v. LaRue, 409 U.S. 109, 93 S.Ct. 390, 34 L.Ed.2d 342 (1972), rehearing denied 410 U.S. 948, 93 S.Ct. 1351, 35 L.Ed.2d 615 (1973).

33. California Retail Liquor Dealers Ass'n v. Midcal Aluminum, Inc., 445 U.S. 97, 100 S.Ct. 937, 63 L.Ed.2d 233 (1980).

34. Brown–Forman Distillers Corp. v. New York State Liquor Authority, 476 U.S. 573, 106 S.Ct. 2080, 90 L.Ed.2d 552 (1986), on remand 68 N.Y.2d 794, 506 N.Y.S.2d 863, 498 N.E.2d 427 (1986).

ally require that distillers surrender whatever competitive advantages they may possess in other states,[35] and New York may not regulate the out of state transactions of distillers who sell in-state.[36]

South Dakota v. Dole[37] illustrates an important limitation on state power under the Twenty–First Amendment. *Dole* upheld a federal law that directed the Secretary of Transportation to withhold a percentage of highway funds from states "in which the purchase or public possession of any alcoholic beverage by a person who is less than twenty-one years of age is lawful." The Court upheld this federal law under Congress' spending power "even if Congress may not regulate drinking ages directly."[38] States can waive their Twenty–First Amendment powers, and thus they may accept federal grants on the condition that they exercise a waiver.

The Court, in each case challenged under the commerce clause, must carefully scrutinize the competing state and federal interests. The Court must determine whether a state law relating to the transportation, sale, or use of alcoholic beverages that would otherwise violate the commerce clause is so related to the central purpose of section two of the Twenty–First Amendment that it should be upheld despite its adverse effect on commerce or inconsistency with federal regulations.[39]

Summary. In general, if the state law does not discriminate on its face or as applied, the Court "tends to sustain the state action unless interference with commerce is clear and the local interest is not very substantial." If there is discrimination, then it must appear that there is no other reasonable method of safeguarding a legitimate local interest. If a state law has no other purpose than to favor local industry, this balancing of interest approach should not be used, because the purpose of the state regulation would be illegitimate.[40]

§ 8.9   Outgoing Commerce

The dormant commerce clause restricts states that seek to prevent home products from being exported into the national market. State statutes burdening the marketing of local products out-of-state are the equivalent of embargoes. Although embargoes *per se* are repugnant to a national common market, the Court recognizes that some state laws that affect the export of goods are legitimate when they represent the least burdensome alternative for achieving legitimate state goals and do not interfere with any federal law.

Consider *Parker v. Brown*.[1] Justice Stone, relying on his *Di Santo* dissent,[2] once again wrote the opinion for the Court. *Parker* sustained a California marketing scheme involving raisins. The Court held that a State may fix prices without violating either the dormant commerce clause or the federal antitrust laws.[3]

A California law required each raisin producer to deliver over two-thirds of his crop to a

35. See also, Baldwin v. G.A.F. Seelig, Inc., 294 U.S. 511, 528, 55 S.Ct. 497, 502, 79 L.Ed. 1032 (1935).

36. See also, Joseph E. Seagram & Sons, Inc. v. Hostetter, 384 U.S. 35, 86 S.Ct. 1254, 16 L.Ed.2d 336 (1966), rehearing denied 384 U.S. 967, 86 S.Ct. 1583, 16 L.Ed.2d 679 (1966).

37. 483 U.S. 203, 107 S.Ct. 2793, 97 L.Ed.2d 171 (1987).

38. South Dakota argued that section 2 of the Twenty–First Amendment gave it complete power to regulate the control, sale, or importation of alcohol. However, the most natural reading of section 2 says nothing about the power of the states to allow the importation of liquor that Congress prohibits. Rather, it seems only to grant the states broader power to prohibit the importation or sale of liquor within their boundaries.

39. Bacchus Imports, Ltd. v. Dias, 468 U.S. 263, 276, 104 S.Ct. 3049, 3058, 82 L.Ed.2d 200, 212 (1984) (invalidating state excise tax on sales of liquor insofar as the tax

exempted locally produced alcoholic beverages because the discriminatory taxation system constituted a violation of the commerce clause). The majority opinion stated: "state laws that constitute mere economic protectionism are therefore not entitled to the same deference as laws entitled to combat the perceived evils of an unrestricted traffic in liquor." 468 U.S. at 276, 104 S.Ct. at 3058, 82 L.Ed.2d at 212.

40. Stern, The Problems of Yesteryear—Commerce and Due Process, 4 Vand.L.Rev. 446, 458 (1951) (footnote omitted).

§ 8.9

1. 317 U.S. 341, 63 S.Ct. 307, 87 L.Ed. 315 (1943).

2. Di Santo v. Pennsylvania, 273 U.S. 34, 43, 47 S.Ct. 267, 270, 71 L.Ed. 524 (1927).

3. The Court also held that there was no antitrust violation in this instance because obeying state law cannot be construed as a conspiracy.

marketing control committee that, in effect, engaged in price fixing. The purpose of the is was to eradicate "injurious" price competition and stabilize raisin market. Between 90 and 95 percent of the raisins grown in California ultimately entered interstate or foreign commerce.

Justice Stone first applied a mechanical test: did the state impose its regulation *before* or *after* the raisins entered interstate commerce? Under this approach, the measure was within state power, because the regulation occurred *before* interstate commerce operation, but he acknowledged that courts should not be bound by such mechanical formulas. After all, the raisin regulations affected interstate commerce, and Congress could have preempted the state law. Citing *Di Santo*, Stone said that the real question was whether the local interests to be served outweighed the competing national interests.[4]

The Court held that the California law did not violate the Sherman Antitrust Act because the Court interpreted that law as not applying to a state. If all the raisin producers got together to set the price, that would be a violation of the antitrust laws. But here the producers were obeying a state law. The producers did not "conspire" with the state. Instead, the producers were merely obeying state law.

Turning to the specific facts of this case, the Court found that the state law did not violate the dormant commerce clause either. Stone noted the significance of the raisin industry in the California economy, where almost all of this nation's raisins are produced. He concluded that, on balance, the regulation should be sustained as a legitimate state attempt to deal with a peculiarly local problem that Congress did not specifically address. The California law restricted the flow of goods in interstate commerce, because the state law required price fixing. If there were no state price fixing, the prices would be lower, and more raisins would go to market. But Stone concluded that the there was no dormant commerce clause prob-

lem or violation of any federal law. In fact, his evaluation of federal law showed that Congress, itself, had recognized the distressed conditions of the agricultural production of the United States; the California program in fact supported (did not interfere with) this Congressional policy. Therefore, the state could legitimately fix the prices of goods within the state even though those commodities affected interstate commerce.

Milk Control Board v. Eisenberg Farm Products[5] upheld a Pennsylvania minimum price law affecting milk shipped in interstate commerce. The state law licensed milk dealers, and required them to pay a minimum price to milk producers in the state. A New York milk dealer challenged the law as an unconstitutional obstruction of interstate commerce to the extent that it applied to the purchase of Pennsylvania milk for resale outside of Pennsylvania.

Eisenberg was the converse of *Baldwin v. G. A. F. Seelig, Inc.*[6] where the state had tried to affect the price to be paid for milk in a sister state. The Court invalidate the *Baldwin* statute but upheld the *Eisenberg* regulatory scheme. The Court discussed several facts that it found important. First, the vast majority of the milk produced by local farmers was consumed within the state. Thus the law burdened local consumers equally, and there was some operation of an inner political check. Secondly, the sale itself took place in Pennsylvania, and for the Court to allow dealers to ignore the law if any of their milk was subject to interstate commerce operation would have nullified the efficacy of the state's entire price support program.

These reasons are less than persuasive. While the sale of milk physically took place within the state, the state regulation of the sale still *affected* interstate commerce. Milk dealers wanted to purchase the Pennsylvania milk and ship it out of state, but it was not

---

4. 317 U.S. at 362, 63 S.Ct. at 319, 87 L.Ed. at 332. See Terminal R. Ass'n v. Brotherhood of R.R. Trainmen, 318 U.S. 1, 8, 63 S.Ct. 420, 424, 87 L.Ed. 571, 578 (1943).

5. 306 U.S. 346, 59 S.Ct. 528, 83 L.Ed. 752 (1939), rehearing denied 306 U.S. 669, 59 S.Ct. 773, 83 L.Ed. 1063 (1939).

6. 294 U.S. 511, 55 S.Ct. 497, 79 L.Ed. 1032 (1935).

economical to do so if they had to pay the high price that the state law mandated.

While it was true that about 90% of the milk sold in Pennsylvania was consumed there as well,[7] that fact should not affect the power of the state to enact the law because the argument is circular. The state law set the price for milk purchased within the state; because this price was above the market price, it would not be profitable for milk dealers to purchase the Pennsylvania milk for export to other states. That is why most of the milk stayed in Pennsylvania. The situation is analogous to the State of Michigan mandating, by law, a high price of the retail sale of all Chevrolet cars, expressing surprise that so few Chevrolets were shipped to other states, and then using that fact to argue that the matter was an in-state, internal matter.

The Court's argument that upholding the entire regulatory scheme, including the effect on interstate commerce, is essential to the effectiveness of the state scheme is a bootstrap argument: if the state does not have the power to deal with a problem, the fact that it would like the power to deal with the problem does not grant the power.

However, the Court's weak arguments does not mean that the result of *Eisenberg* is wrong. More likely *Eisenberg* is justified on the theory that the Court was interpreting congressional silence under the dormant commerce clause to allow the state to solve what was perceived as essentially a local problem. The high in-state price supports meant that most of the milk would not leave the state because it was too expensive out of state. Meanwhile, the people of Pennsylvania were the ones who forced themselves to pay this high cost. In effect, the voters of the state decided to pay a subsidy to milk producers within the state. The state was not trying to set up some sort of de facto tariff. Instead, the

people of Pennsylvania were imposing the equivalent of a tax on themselves and giving the proceeds of that tax to the Pennsylvania milk producers. The state was engaging in price fixing, but, as the *Parker* case later decided, a state may engage in price-fixing within the state.[8]

Any local police power regulation that increases the cost of goods or services that might go into interstate commerce may be said to burden that commerce. However, where there is no discrimination and the effect on interstate commerce does not impair national interests, the Court will not strike the law.[9] The consumers within a state may decide to burden themselves with a state law mandating that they pay a price for milk that is higher than the market price. *Parker* interprets the dormant commerce clause to allow that.

In *Eisenberg* the state law did not discriminated against out of state residents, and the law involved an inner political check. *H. P. Hood and Sons v. Du Mond*[10] underscores the importance of these factors. New York refused to grant a Massachusetts milk distributor a license to operate a third milk receiving station in the state on the grounds that the additional diversion (the export) of New York milk to Massachusetts would impair the supply for the New York market. New York was, in effect, trying to keep milk within the state to keep its price low for New York consumers. What New York was doing was the economic equivalent of a tax on the export of milk. Only, instead of charging a certain amount to export each gallon of New York milk, the state was denying a license to a third milk receiving station because it would use that license to export. It was as if the state was saying, "You may export a certain amount of milk, and then no more. That's why we deny your license."

A narrowly divided Court (five to four) rejected the existence of state power to develop such a discriminatory plan:

7. 306 U.S. at 350, 59 S.Ct. at 530.

8. See, Cities Service Gas Co. v. Peerless Oil & Gas Co., 340 U.S. 179, 71 S.Ct. 215, 95 L.Ed. 190 (1950) (upholding a state order that required a pipeline company to pay rates for natural gas that were higher than prevailing rates; most of the gas would be shipped out of state, but the state rule coincided with federal policy).

9. Lone Star Gas Co. v. Texas, 304 U.S. 224, 58 S.Ct. 883, 82 L.Ed. 1304 (1938), rehearing denied 304 U.S. 590, 58 S.Ct. 1051, 82 L.Ed. 1549 (1938).

10. 336 U.S. 525, 69 S.Ct. 657, 93 L.Ed. 865 (1949), order denying license subsequently reversed 300 N.Y. 480, 88 N.E.2d 661 (1949).

May Michigan provide that automobiles cannot be taken out of that State until local dealers' demands are fully met? Would she not have every argument in the favor of such a statute that can be offered in support of New York's limiting sales of milk for out-of-state shipment to protect the economic interests of her competing dealers and local consumers?[11]

Justice Black, dissenting, argued that the majority had abandoned the *Cooley* approach and that the decision, therefore, would ultimately result in invalidating a wide range of state regulation. Contemporaneous commentators also criticized the decision as an unwarranted departure from the Court's earlier decisions in *Parker* and *Eisenberg*.[12]

Hood is not really a departure from the earlier cases. Unlike those other regulatory measures, the New York ad hoc licensing scheme in *Hood* discriminated against interstate commerce because the primary burden of the state action fell on non-residents, the people of Massachusetts who wanted to buy the milk exported from New York. In *Eisenberg* the state statute fixing a minimum price applied equally to in-state and out-of-state milk purchasers, but *Hood* imposed a classic trade barrier to the flow of goods to out of state buyers. Moreover, the persons burdened by such state action were individuals who had no representation in the state political process effecting them; it was this type of trade barrier that the commerce clause was drafted to eliminate. In *Parker* the Court found that the state

price fixing was consistent with federal statutes and policy, which had recognized California's problems, but there was no such evidence involving New York milk consumers. Under these circumstances, *Hood* correctly prohibited New York's embargo.

Occasionally, the Court still purports to use such conclusory tests as whether the state affect on interstate commerce is "incidental" and "indirect," or if the law affects the product "before or after interstate commerce operations occur." But the Court usually looks at what is really happening economically, and then applies Stone's balancing test. Each case turns on a weighing of all the relevant circumstances rather than the application of mechanical tests; that is, the Court grants the states some deference in dealing with genuine health and safety concerns, and rejects regulations that on their face, or as applied, discriminate against interstate commerce. The states may not use their regulatory powers to preserve a favored position for local industry.

While it is not easy to make all of these cases consistent, several illustrations may prove helpful. Let us now turn to them.

Embargoes to Promote Local Economic Objectives. The states may not burden the exportation of local products in order to enhance the reputation of local products,[13] retain domestic resources for local consumption,[14] insure local employment,[15] or keep a particular market open only to their own residents.[16]

---

11. 336 U.S. at 539, 69 S.Ct. at 665. Cf. Commonwealth Edison Co. v. Montana, 453 U.S. 609, 618, 101 S.Ct. 2946, 2953–54, 69 L.Ed.2d 884 (1981), rehearing denied 453 U.S. 927, 102 S.Ct. 889, 69 L.Ed.2d 1023 (1981), where the Court upheld a nondiscriminatory severance tax on coal mined in Montana. Although 90% of Montana coal is shipped to other states, "the Montana tax is computed at the same rate regardless of the final destination of the coal, and there is no suggestion here that the tax is administered in a manner that departs from this evenhanded formula."

12. See, e.g., Note, State Regulation of Interstate Commerce—Denial of License to Ship Milk Held Invalid, 37 Calif.L.Rev. 667 (1949).

13. Another example of the viability of Stone's balancing doctrine as applied to outgoing commerce is Pike v. Bruce Church, Inc., 397 U.S. 137, 90 S.Ct. 844, 25 L.Ed.2d 174 (1970). In a unanimous opinion the Court invalidated an Arizona law requiring that cantaloupes be packed with-

in the state. "[T]he State's tenuous interest in having the company's cantaloupes identified as originating in Arizona cannot constitutionally justify the requirement that the company build and operate an unneeded $200,000 packing plant in the State." 397 U.S. at 145, 90 S.Ct. at 849.

14. H. P. Hood & Sons v. Du Mond, 336 U.S. 525, 69 S.Ct. 657, 93 L.Ed. 865 (1949), order denying license subsequently reversed 300 N.Y. 480, 88 N.E.2d 661 (1949).

15. Foster–Fountain Packing Co. v. Haydel, 278 U.S. 1, 49 S.Ct. 1, 73 L.Ed. 147 (1928) (restrictions on shipping shrimp out of state struck down); Pike v. Bruce Church, Inc., 397 U.S. 137, 90 S.Ct. 844, 25 L.Ed.2d 174 (1970).

16. Toomer v. Witsell, 334 U.S. 385, 68 S.Ct. 1156, 92 L.Ed. 1460 (1948), rehearing denied 335 U.S. 837, 69 S.Ct. 12, 93 L.Ed. 389 (1948) (discriminatory license fee on nonresident shrimp travelers struck down as violation of Article IV privileges and immunities clause).

If the state does not impose an absolute barrier to the export of a local product, such as coal, the state still violates the dormant commerce clause if it requires an in-state industry to use a certain amount of the locally produced good. The state is simply using its regulatory power to favor a local industry and discriminate against interstate competition. Thus, *Wyoming v. Oklahoma*[17] used the dormant commerce clause to invalidate an Oklahoma law that required privately owned coal-fired electric generating plants to use at least 10% of Oklahoma-mined coal.

Embargoes of Natural Resources and Wild Game and Fish. In very early decisions, the Court upheld the states's regulation of the consumption of a state's natural resources, such as water.[18] In 1896, *Geer v. Connecticut*[19] upheld a state law that prohibited the export of game birds, even though hunters had lawfully killed the game birds within the state. Oddly enough, even the early cases prohibited a state from placing an embargo on natural gas.[20] Under the modern view of the dormant commerce clause, these water and game decisions allowing embargoes no longer are good law.

In 1979 *Hughes v. Oklahoma*[21] finally overruled *Geer v. Connecticut*.[22] The Court explicitly rejected the legal fiction that interstate commerce is not involved because the state "owns" all the wild animals within the state. The state can regulate fishing, but it does not

"own" the fish anymore than a wishful fisherman. Once the fisherman catches the minnows and reduces them to possession, he owns them, not the state. And when the state regulates, it must do so in a way that does not discriminate against interstate commerce.

Hughes invalidated an Oklahoma statute that provided that no natural minnows seined or procured within the state could be shipped outside of the state for sale. The statute on its face discriminated against interstate commerce of natural minnows by overtly blocking their export for sale. The law did not restrict what the modest fisherman could do with his catch as long as he did not sell them out of state. The Oklahoma law also did not limit the number of minnow that licensed minnow dealers could capture. (One might justify such a law for conservation reasons, but then, the law would not discriminate based on where the minnows went after they had been caught.) Once reduced to possession, the state allowed minnow dealers to process the fish for commercial purposes, so long *as the processing was within the state*. But, no one could take the fish out of state *for sale* to an out of state processor. The real purpose of the Oklahoma law was to favor in-state processing of minnows, in violation of the dormant commerce clause.[23]

While the state can conserve natural resources it must do so in a nondiscriminatory

---

17. 502 U.S. 437, 112 S.Ct. 789, 117 L.Ed.2d 1 (1992).

18. Hudson County Water Co. v. McCarter, 209 U.S. 349, 28 S.Ct. 529, 52 L.Ed. 828 (1908) (prohibition of transportation of water out of state upheld).

19. 161 U.S. 519, 16 S.Ct. 600, 40 L.Ed. 793 (1896) (prohibition against shipping game birds out of state upheld), overruled Hughes v. Oklahoma, 441 U.S. 322, 99 S.Ct. 1727, 60 L.Ed.2d 250 (1979); People of New York ex rel. Silz v. Hesterberg, 211 U.S. 31, 29 S.Ct. 10, 53 L.Ed. 75 (1908) (prohibition against possession of game out of season upheld, even if brought from outside state); Bayside Fish Flour Co. v. Gentry, 297 U.S. 422, 56 S.Ct. 513, 80 L.Ed. 772 (1936).

20. E.g., West v. Kansas Natural Gas Co., 221 U.S. 229, 31 S.Ct. 564, 55 L.Ed. 716 (1911).

21. 441 U.S. 322, 99 S.Ct. 1727, 60 L.Ed.2d 250 (1979), on remand 595 P.2d 1349 (Okl.Cr.App.1979). Cf. Baldwin v. Montana Fish and Game Commission, 436 U.S. 371, 385–86, 98 S.Ct. 1852, 1861, 56 L.Ed.2d 354 (1978): "States may not compel the confinement of the benefits of

their resources, even their wildlife, to their own people whenever such hoarding and confinement impedes interstate commerce." The Court did not decide *Baldwin* under the commerce clause but under the privileges and immunities clause of Article IV, § 2. The case rejected challenges to the differences in the cost (as between state residents and nonresidents) of the state hunting license fees because the licenses were needed to hunt Elk, a recreational sport.

22. 161 U.S. 519, 16 S.Ct. 600, 40 L.Ed. 793 (1896), overruled Hughes v. Oklahoma, 441 U.S. 322, 99 S.Ct. 1727, 60 L.Ed.2d 250 (1979).

23. Rehnquist, J., joined by Burger, C.J., dissented and claimed that the Oklahoma statute did not discriminate because the state law applied to state residents and non-residents alike. The law forbade both from exporting minnows for sale (for processing) out of state. However, while the law applied to both, the law was drafted to make sure that the processing was done in the state. Both residents and non-residents could sell the minnows, so long as they sold them in-state. The law discriminates against out of state processing.

fashion that recognizes that the relevant economic unit is the nation. Thus a state cannot prohibit the exportation of hydroelectric power that *private* facilities within the state produce, nor can it reserve for its own citizens the "economic benefit" of that hydroelectric energy.[24]

The Court has found that privately owned water is an article of commerce. Thus, if a state allows individuals to own groundwater (water taken from sub-land surface by means of piping) or water from lakes and streams, the government will have difficulty in keeping the private owner from sending that water out of the state. In *Sporhase v. Nebraska ex rel. Douglas*[25] the Court invalidated a state law that prohibited anyone from taking groundwater with a well or pit and sending it to another state unless they had a permit. The permit would only be issued if the amount of water taken was reasonable, did not hurt the ecology or the people of the state, and if the water was being sent to another state that allowed private owners of water to send their water to Nebraska. The Court in *Sporhase* found that the restrictions concerning only withdrawing a reasonable amount of water which was to protect the health and welfare of citizens was legitimate. However, the Court found that the barrier against exporting water constituted discrimination in the nature of a tariff or trade barrier that violated the dormant commerce clause. The Court found that the restriction requiring water be sent only to states that had a reciprocal water transfer provision simply a discriminatory means of allowing local residents to purchase water more cheaply than they could through a free national market. The state failed to justify its discriminatory trade barrier, in the view of the Court. The

majority opinion stated: "there is no evidence that this restriction [limiting water to states that would allow sales back to Nebraska] is narrowly tailored to the conservation and preservation rationale [advanced by the state] ... if it could be shown that the state as a whole suffers a water shortage, that the intrastate transportation of water from areas of abundance to areas of shortage is feasible regardless of distance, and that the importation of water from adjoining states would roughly compensate for any exportation to those states, then the conservation and preservation purpose might be credibly advanced for the reciprocity provision. A demonstrably arid state conceivably might be able to marshal evidence to establish a close means-end relationship between even a total ban on the exportation of water and a purpose to conserve and preserve water."[26] As Professor Robert Glennon has demonstrated, current property laws concerning the extraction and sale of groundwater may make the Supreme Court's hypotheticals real life situations in the future.[27]

The State as a Market Participant. When the state itself enters the market as a purchaser or seller of interstate commerce, nothing in the dormant commerce clause forbids it from restricting its own purchases or limiting its sales to its own citizens.[28] Such self-imposed restrictions are typically not economically efficient, but the state is not acting as a market regulator; it is a market participant. The state is not using its sovereign powers to regulate; rather, it is using the powers that any private person has over what it owns.

For example, a state may follow a policy of confining the sale of cement produced at a

---

24. New England Power Co. v. New Hampshire, 455 U.S. 331, 102 S.Ct. 1096, 71 L.Ed.2d 188 (1982). In Maine v. Taylor, 477 U.S. 131, 106 S.Ct. 2440, 91 L.Ed.2d 110 (1986) the Court upheld a state law prohibiting the importation of live bait fish into the state, based upon evidence that the state could not screen live bait fish for parasites that would harm the aquatic ecology of the state. This case is examined in § 8.8, supra.

25. 458 U.S. 941, 102 S.Ct. 3456, 73 L.Ed.2d 1254 (1982).

26. 458 U.S. at 958–959, 102 S.Ct. at 3465. Two Justices from Arizona dissented 458 U.S. at 960–965, 102 S.Ct. at 3466–3469 (Rehnquist, J., joined by O'Connor, J.,

dissenting). Perhaps Arizonans know best, as Professor Robert Glennon, who is referred to in the next footnote, teaches at the University of Arizona Law School.

27. Robert J. Glennon, Water Follies (2003).

28. Hughes v. Alexandria Scrap Corp., 426 U.S. 794, 810, 96 S.Ct. 2488, 2498, 49 L.Ed.2d 220 (1976) (5 to 4 decision holding that state bounty for scrap automobiles can favor scrap processors with an in-state plant). See generally, Belot, J., citing Treatise in Waste Connections of Kansas, Inc. v. City of Bel Aire, Kan., 191 F.Supp.2d 1238, 1245 (D.Kan.2002).

state owned cement plant solely to state residents.[29] What is really important is not that cement is the end-product of a complex process but that the state really owned the cement factory.[30] However, a state may not compel *privately owned* cement plants within the state to sell their products solely to state residents.[31] The state does not own the privately owned coal mine, and so, it cannot use its regulatory power to discriminate against out of state commerce.

When a state actually *owns* a business and favors its own citizens it is not violating the commerce clause because it is not using its regulatory powers. What the state is really doing is using its power of the purse to give money to some people within the state. In the state-owned cement plant, for example, what the state is doing when it limits the sale of its cement to its own residents is the economic equivalent of giving money to some of its citizens, those who buy cement. The state is simply engaging in a form of welfare.[32] It may be welfare for the rich or middle class, rather than for the poor, but the dormant commerce clause allows that.

The mere fact that a state owns a resource does not give it *carte blanche*, or total power, to allocate that resource in a way that discriminates against competition from out-of-state persons in local economic interests. Antitrust laws, for example, impose some limits in how the private owner of a resource can use or restrict that resource. The Constitution imposes somewhat analogous restrictions on what a state can do. For example, in our cement case, the state could not forbid the in-state purchas-

ers of cement from the state-owned cement plant from reselling that cement to out of state residents.

Some restrictions on the ability of out-of-state persons to engage in commercial activities may constitute a deprivation of the privileges of state citizenship that violates Article IV. Even if the Article IV privileges and immunities clause is inapplicable, the mere fact that the state is "participating" in the marketplace through the use of its financial or natural resources does not completely immunize its actions from review under the commerce clause.

When the state places regulations on the use of materials sold or distributed by the state, the courts must determine: (1), whether the regulation is one that results in the residents of the state bearing the cost for providing benefits to various persons within the state's jurisdiction or, (2), whether the regulation is an unconstitutional shifting of the cost for local benefits to out of state persons or interests by improper restrictions on competition.

The selling of state-owned resources to local residents at a lower price that the state charges to out of state interests is consistent with commerce clause principles because the state is acting as a "market participant"—that is, the residents of the state are bearing the cost of providing a welfare benefit to persons within the jurisdiction. When the state is bearing the cost of providing economic benefits, there is little reason for the Supreme Court to intervene, even though some inefficiency in the marketplace might be created, because the political process within the state should serve

---

29. Reeves, Inc. v. Stake, 447 U.S. 429, 100 S.Ct. 2271, 65 L.Ed.2d 244 (1980).

30. See McCready v. Virginia, 94 U.S. (4 Otto) 391, 395–96, 24 L.Ed. 248, 249 (1876):

"If Virginia had by law provided for the sale of its once vast public domain, and division of the proceeds among its own people, no one, we venture to say, would contend that the citizens of other States had a constitutional right to the enjoyment of this privilege of Virginia citizenship. Neither if, instead of selling, the State had appropriated the same property to be used as a common by its people for the purposes of agriculture, could the citizens of other States avail themselves of such a privilege."

31. See New England Power Co. v. New Hampshire, 455 U.S. 331, 102 S.Ct. 1096, 71 L.Ed.2d 188 (1982), holding that a state cannot prohibit a private power company from exporting locally generated hydroelectric power. The Court found unpersuasive the argument that the state "owned" the Connecticut River, which was used to generate the power. "This product is manufactured by a private corporation using privately-owned facilities." 455 U.S. at 339 n. 6, 102 S.Ct. at 1100 n. 6.

32. Cf. McCarthy v. Philadelphia Civil Service Commission, 424 U.S. 645, 96 S.Ct. 1154, 47 L.Ed.2d 366 (1976) (residence within a specific area can be a requirement of *public* employment); White v. Massachusetts Council of Construction Employers, Inc., 460 U.S. 204, 103 S.Ct. 1042, 75 L.Ed.2d 1 (1983).

as an inner political check on the state's decisions to participate in the marketplace.

Thus, if a state offers a company a cash bonus or tax exemption in exchange for the company locating a factory in the state, its action can be upheld because the state is bearing the cost of producing some economic benefits for people in the state. However, if the state seeks, by law, to force a company (not owned by the state) to keep its factory in the state or to force such a company to give employment preference to local residents, then the state law violates the commerce clause because it attempts to shift to out-of-state interests the cost of producing local economic benefits.

Sometimes it is not easy to tell whether a state's use or regulation of its natural or financial resources constitutes permissible distribution of welfare benefits through state "market participation" or the impermissible protection of local economic interests through commercial regulation that shifts costs to out-of-state interests. An example of the Court's "market participant" versus "market regulator" distinction is *South–Central Timber Development, Inc. v. Wunnicke.*[33]

South–Central Timber reviewed an Alaska statute that regulated the sale of state-owned timber. The statute commanded that all proposed contracts for sale of the timber contain a clause that required that the "primary manufacture" of the timber take place within the state of Alaska. The person or enterprise who successfully bid to purchase timber was required to process it within Alaska before shipping it out of the state by converting the logs into slabs or cants prior to export. The Court had little difficulty in finding that Congress had not approved of the Alaskan restriction on

processing state-owned timber.[34] Thus the Court faced a dormant commerce clause problem. The eight Justices who voted in this case could not agree whether the restriction violated the dormant commerce clause.

Four members of the Court found that the state requirement violated the commerce clause because the market-participant doctrine allows a State to impose burdens on commerce within the market in which it is a participant, but that doctrine allows it to go no further. "The State may not impose conditions, whether by statute, regulation, or contract, that have a substantial regulatory effect outside of that particular market."[35] The market, according to the plurality, had to be narrowly defined so that states would be allowed to subsidize the provisions of goods or benefits to their local residents but could not impose burdens on interstate commerce through contract restrictions that had a regulatory effect on multi-state or international markets.

The plurality found that it was irrelevant that the state could have directly supported its timber processing industry in other ways—by restricting sales to state residents; by operating its own processing business; or by direct subsidies to in-state processors. The plurality would not permit ownership of the commodity to allow what it called "downstream restrictions." The state cannot limit market activity even in natural resource that it owns *after* it sells them.[36]

Although the plurality noted that state restrictions on foreign commerce are "subjected to a more rigorous and searching scrutiny" than regulations of domestic commerce, the plurality's view of the limits of market participation would appear to apply equally to laws

---

33. 467 U.S. 82, 104 S.Ct. 2237, 81 L.Ed.2d 71 (1984), on remand 746 F.2d 1393 (9th Cir.1984).

34. "[F]or a state regulation to be removed from the reach of the dormant Commerce Clause, congressional intent must be unmistakably clear." South–Central Timber Dev., Inc. v. Wunnicke, 467 U.S. 82, 87–88, 91, 104 S.Ct. 2237, 2240, 2242, 81 L.Ed.2d 71 (1984), on remand 746 F.2d 1393 (9th Cir.1984).

35. South–Central Timber Dev., Inc. v. Wunnicke, 467 U.S. 82, 97, 104 S.Ct. 2237, 2245–46, 81 L.Ed.2d 71, 83 (1984) (footnote omitted), on remand 746 F.2d 1393 (9th

Cir.1984). Regarding the dormant commerce clause issue, Justice White wrote for a four-Justice plurality consisting of himself and Brennan, Blackmun, and Stevens.

36. Cf. A. D. Neale & D. G. Goyder, The Antitrust Laws of the United States of America: A Study of Competition Enforced by Law 249–87 (3d ed. 1980) (discussion of vertical restraints of trade including resale price maintenance). 3 P. Areeda & D. Turner, Antitrust Law: An Analysis of Antitrust Principles and Their Application ¶¶ 723–36 (1978).

that affect domestic as well as international commerce.[37]

Justices Rehnquist and O'Connor dissented in *South–Central Timber* because the state was acting as a market participant and, in terms of the economic realities of the situation, the state was "merely paying the buyer of the timber indirectly, by means of a reduced price, to hire Alaska residents to process the timber."[38] Because the state could have directly subsidized the local processing industry or directly paid the timber buyer to have the logs processed only if they were processed locally, Rehnquist and O'Connor did not believe that the state had improperly shifted cost to out-of-state persons or interests. The dissent was unconcerned about the post-sale restrictions. The plurality rejected the dissent's view of the economic effects of the law because they believed that the state was interfering with private marketplace decisions.

Also, if the state directly subsidized the local processing industry, or directly paid the timber buyer to process the logs in Alaska, it would be very clear to the Alaska voters exactly what is the cost of this subsidy. The state plan, which the Court invalidated, tried to hide this cost. *Wunnicke* did not prohibit Alaska from subsidizing its local timber processing industry; it just had to do it in a way that was not hidden from the democratic processes.

One Justice did not participate in the decision and two Justices would have remanded the case to the lower federal courts to determine whether the state was acting as a "market participant" and to determine whether the state's "primary manufacture" requirement was a substantial burden on interstate commerce under the traditional commerce clause test.[39]

Summary. If the state regulation, even under the guise of a legitimate goal, attempts to afford residents an economic advantage at the expense of a free-flowing national market, the countervailing national interest will override. Local economic measures are more likely to be upheld if there is no discriminatory purpose or effect. Justice Stewart, in *Pike v. Bruce Church, Inc.*,[40] summarized the modern standard, incorporating Stone's *Di Santo* dissent,[41] Dowling's theory,[42] and the Court's subsequent decisions:

> Where the state regulates even handedly to effectuate a legitimate local public interest, and its effects on interstate commerce are only incidental, it will be upheld unless the burden imposed on such commerce is clearly excessive in relation to the putative local benefits. If a legitimate local purpose is found, then the question becomes one of degree. And the extent of the burden that will be tolerated will of course depend on the nature of the local interest involved, and on whether it could be promoted as well with a lesser impact with interstate activities.[43]

§ 8.10 Personal Mobility

Because the definition of commerce includes the movement of persons, the Court has invoked the commerce clause to invalidate state regulations impairing the free mobility of citizens. The Court, however, has other arrows in its quiver, and it has also used these other constitutional provisions to protect the free movement of persons within our national common market. Indeed, the concept of personal mobility is part of the warp and woof of our constitutional system.

37. South–Central Timber Dev., Inc. v. Wunnicke, 467 U.S. 82, 100, 104 S.Ct. 2237, 2247, 81 L.Ed.2d 71 (1984), on remand 746 F.2d 1393 (9th Cir.1984) (plurality opinion).

38. South–Central Timber Dev., Inc. v. Wunnicke, 467 U.S. 82, 103, 104 S.Ct. 2237, 2248, 81 L.Ed.2d 71 (1984) (Rehnquist and O'Connor, JJ., dissenting), on remand 746 F.2d 1393 (9th Cir.1984).

39. Marshall, J., did not participate in the decision. Powell, J., joined by Burger, C.J., did not concur in Justice White's opinion regarding the dormant commerce clause

invalidation of the state legislation. 467 U.S. at 101, 104 S.Ct. at 2248 (Powell, J. and Burger, C.J., concurring in part and concurring in the judgment).

40. 397 U.S. 137, 90 S.Ct. 844, 25 L.Ed.2d 174 (1970).

41. Di Santo v. Pennsylvania, 273 U.S. 34, 44, 47 S.Ct. 267, 271, 71 L.Ed. 524 (1927).

42. Dowling, Interstate Commerce and State Power, 27 Va.L.Rev. 1 (1940).

43. 397 U.S. at 142, 90 S.Ct. at 847 (case citation within quotation omitted without indication).

In an early case, *Crandall v. Nevada*[1] made this important point as it struck down a state law imposing a capitation tax of one dollar on "every person leaving the state by any railroad, stage coach, or other vehicle engaged or employed in the business of transporting passengers for hire."[2] Justice Miller discussed the applicability of the commerce clause to the resolution of the question, but then held that it was unnecessary to resolve the issue on that ground because the right of the citizenry to enjoy unrestricted travel is inherent in the very fiber of a federal form of government.[3]

Justice Clifford agreed with the result, but argued that the Nevada Act should have been invalidated as inconsistent with congressional power under the commerce clause. Later, the Court adopted this reasoning in striking a California law making it a misdemeanor for any person knowingly to bring a non-resident indigent into the state. *Edwards v. California*[4] held that the state's attempt to bar the entry of indigent citizens was analogous to the economic barrier burdening the importation of milk products, invalidated in *Baldwin v. G. A. F. Seelig, Inc.*[5]

Edwards relied on the national common market theory of *Baldwin* to support the principle that, just as a state cannot shut its gates to the influx of competitive commodities, it also is prohibited from thwarting the influx of indigents. In order to maintain the existence of a national entity, the guarantee of unrestricted personal mobility is equivalent, if not superior to, the guarantee afforded commercial products. The majority rejected the contention that such state legislation could be justified as a valid exercise of the police power, noting that the statute's sole purpose was to burden interstate commerce by impeding the movement of people across state lines. The absence of an inner political check was an additional weakness inherent in the California statute; persons burdened by the state regulation, non-resident indigents, had no voice in the political process responsible for the enactment of the legislation.

Justice Douglas, concurring separately in *Edwards*, warned that relying on the commerce clause could dilute the right of personal mobility. Congress, after all, could authorize what would otherwise be a violation of the dormant commerce clause. Douglas argued that the right of persons to move from state to state is a fundamental right implicit in national citizenship. Therefore, in his view, it is incorporated in the privileges or immunities clause of the Fourteenth Amendment.[6] Moreover, argued Douglas, the right to travel is akin to the right to privacy; it is a "penumbra right" existing prior to, and independent of, the Fourteenth Amendment, emanating from the body of the Constitution itself and inuring to the benefit of all citizens.

Subsequent personal mobility decisions have incorporated both the majority's reluctance to enlarge the scope of the privileges and immunities doctrine and Justice Douglas' concern about relegating the protection of the right to travel solely to the commerce clause. Consequently, the Court has increasingly turned to equal protection as a preferential ground for

---

§ 8.10

1. 73 U.S. (6 Wall.) 35, 18 L.Ed. 745 (1867). Shapiro v. Thompson, 394 U.S. 618, 630 and n. 8, 89 S.Ct. 1322, 1329 and n. 8, 22 L.Ed.2d 600 (1969) noted it had "no occasion to ascribe the source of this right to travel interstate to a particular constitutional provision" but that past cases have grounded it on the commerce clause; the privileges and immunities clause of Art. IV, § 2, cl. 1, the privileges or immunities clause of the Fourteenth Amendment; and the due process clause of the Fifth Amendment.

2. 73 U.S. (6 Wall.) at 36, 18 L.Ed. at 745.

3. 73 U.S. (6 Wall.) at 44, 18 L.Ed. at 747.

Gloucester Ferry Company v. Pennsylvania, 114 U.S. 196, 203, 5 S.Ct. 826, 828, 29 L.Ed. 158, 162 (1885), flatly stated that "[c]ommerce among the States ... includes the transportation of persons," and is therefore not taxable by the states. See also, Gibbons v. Ogden, 22 U.S. (9 Wheat.) 1, 6 L.Ed. 23, (1824); Covington & Cincinnati Bridge Co. v. Kentucky, 154 U.S. 204, 14 S.Ct. 1087, 38 L.Ed. 962 (1894).

4. 314 U.S. 160, 62 S.Ct. 164, 86 L.Ed. 119 (1941).

5. 294 U.S. 511, 55 S.Ct. 497, 79 L.Ed. 1032 (1935).

6. Murphy & Black, JJ., joined Douglas. Justice Jackson, also concurring separately, preferred basing the decision on the privileges or immunities clause of the Fourteenth Amendment. He reminded the majority that the right to travel is not absolute; states may legitimately restrict the movement of fugitives from Justice or carriers of contagious disease for example. The California statute, however, erred, in his opinion, by enlisting property status as the criterion for determining the right to travel.

challenging state legislation that impinges the right to travel.[7]

In *Evansville–Vanderburgh Airport Authority District v. Delta Airlines,*[8] the Court sustained an Indiana law imposing a tax of one dollar on all commercial airline passengers. Although Justice Douglas argued, in dissent, that to sustain such a law required overruling *Crandall*, the majority specifically distinguished such nominal charges as constituting permissible reimbursement to the state for the cost of providing a public facility that in fact aids and advances transportation. Justice Brennan's opinion explained that the *Crandall* tax applied to persons traveling via *privately* owned facilities, such as the railroads, and therefore, was not analogous to a state-imposed charge limited to travelers benefiting from facilities provided for their use at state expense. The airport tax is like highway tolls. A charge "designed only to make the user of state-provided facilities pay a reasonable charge to help defray the costs of their construction and maintenance may constitutionally be imposed on interstate and domestic users alike."[9]

A tax imposed on those benefiting from state-provided transportation facilities is not an impermissible burden on interstate commerce, but an exit tax unrelated to a state-incurred expense is invalid. Also the one dollar tax in the *Delta Airlines* case is fairly nominal. The state cannot impose a tax on exiting, if that tax, unlike highway tolls or the *Delta Airlines* airline tax, is not proportional to the resources used in travel. A tax that really is a tax on exiting the state is the kind of tax that *Crandall* struck down.

The Article IV Privileges and Immunities Clause. The privileges and immunities clause of Article IV, section 2, protecting the

privileges of state citizenship and assuring that states do not discriminate against the citizens of other states, sometimes provides an appropriate basis for voiding restrictive state regulations. Historically, the Court has resisted acknowledging that provision as a broad source of individual rights.[10] It has been interpreted narrowly as a prohibition of local legislation that discriminates against non-residents.

The Court relied on this Article IV clause to invalidate a discriminatory licensing fee in *Toomer v. Witsell.*[11] South Carolina imposed a $2500 licensing fee on out-of-state shrimpers but only a $25 charge for residents. Ostensibly, the prohibitive charge was necessary to discourage excessive trawling, and thereby enhance the preservation of the state's shrimp supply. Although the Court recognized the goal as a legitimate state purpose, it rejected the means as an unreasonable remedy in violation of the privileges and immunities clause. The South Carolina restriction was directed only at nonresidents. Because trawlers follow migrating shrimp, and marginal sea fishing occurs off the coast of several Southern states, the statute inevitably invited retaliatory measures by neighboring jurisdictions. This was the exact situation that the framers of the Constitution intended the privileges and immunities clause to prevent.[12]

If a state or local law uses a residency or citizenship classification to allocate the ability to engage in an activity sufficiently fundamental to the preservation of interstate harmony to be protected by the clause (*e.g.*, employment on city projects, where the employees are working for the city), the Court must go on to determine whether there is a substantial, legitimate reason for the difference in treatment between local residents and out-of-state per-

---

7. See Shapiro v. Thompson, 394 U.S. 618, 89 S.Ct. 1322, 22 L.Ed.2d 600 (1969) and related cases.

8. 405 U.S. 707, 92 S.Ct. 1349, 31 L.Ed.2d 620 (1972), on remand 259 Ind. 464, 288 N.E.2d 136 (1972).

9. 405 U.S. at 714, 92 S.Ct. at 1354.

After *Evansville–Vanderburgh*, Congress enacted legislation to prohibit states and political subdivisions from imposing airport head taxes. 49 U.S.C.A. § 1513, the Federal Anti–Head Tax Act (AHTA).

10. However, Corfield v. Coryell, 6 F.Cas. 546 (C.C.E.D.Pa.1823) acknowledged the right to travel under the Art. IV privileges and immunities clause. For further discussion of the issues raised in that case, see § 9.6, infra, which discusses Article IV.

11. 334 U.S. 385, 68 S.Ct. 1156, 92 L.Ed. 1460 (1948), rehearing denied 335 U.S. 837, 69 S.Ct. 12, 93 L.Ed. 389 (1948).

12. See §§ 9.6, infra.

sons who wish to exercise that right or engage in the activity within the state. The commerce clause does not forbid this state discrimination because the state is acting as a market participant.[13]

However, the market participant theory does not automatically excuse the need for an inquiry under the Privileges and Immunities Clause of Article IV. In *United Building and Construction Trades Council v. Mayor and Council of Camden*[14] the court concluded that state and local governments are not absolutely prohibited from using local citizenship or residency classifications for purposes of hiring workers on city or state public works projects, *if* nonresidents in fact are shown to cause a particular harm to state or local interest. Then, they may be treated differently from local residents.[15] The Court went on to say that the state must demonstrate, by making a factual record at the trial, that there is a "substantial reason" for the difference in treatment between the local residents or citizen and nonresident.[16] Unfortunately, the Court did explain what that meant; it just remanded the case. It is an understatement to say that the standard of review in these cases is not clear.[17]

§ 8.11   State and Local Taxation

(a) Introduction

The federal commerce clause, as well as other limitations in the Constitution, such as the due process and equal protection clauses, place certain limits on the taxing powers of states and their subdivisions. We provide a detailed discussion and analysis of these issues elsewhere,[1] but here we will introduce some of them.

Dormant Commerce Clause. The Court measures a state or local tax against the dormant commerce clause in order to allow the state or locality to extract from interstate commerce a fair share of the expenses of state and local government, without unduly restricting the flow of interstate commerce. In *Complete Auto Transit, Inc. v. Brady,*[2] the Court fashioned the modern four-part test: a state or local tax is permissible under the dormant commerce clause if it is:

[1]   applied to an activity with a substantial nexus with the taxing State;

[2]   fairly apportioned (that is, the tax is internally and externally consistent);[3]

[3]   non-discriminatory against interstate commerce; and is

[4]   fairly related to the services provided by the State.[4]

Due Process. A state tax must also pass due process requirements. Due process limits the territorial reach of the state's power. There must be "minimum" contacts between the person, thing, or transaction taxed and the taxing state, and there must be "a rational relationship between the income attributed to that state and the intrastate values of the enterprise."[5]

The "substantial nexus" portion of the modern commerce clause test is similar to the due

---

13. White v. Massachusetts Council of Construction Employers, 460 U.S. 204, 103 S.Ct. 1042, 75 L.Ed.2d 1 (1983).

14. 465 U.S. 208, 104 S.Ct. 1020, 79 L.Ed.2d 249 (1984). (Rehnquist, J., for the Court).

15. United Building and Construction Trades Council v. Mayor and Council of Camden, 465 U.S. 208, 104 S.Ct. 1020, 79 L.Ed.2d 249 (1984).

16. United Building and Construction Trades Council v. Mayor and Council of Camden, 465 U.S. 208, 104 S.Ct. 1020, 79 L.Ed.2d 249 (1984).

17. See § 9.6 for additional cases concerning the Article IV privileges and immunities clause.

§ 8.11

1. See, Nowak & Rotunda, Sales and Use Tax Credits, Discrimination Against Interstate Commerce, and the Useless Multiple Tax Concept, 20 U.C. Davis L.Rev. 273 (1987); 2 Ronald D. Rotunda & John E. Nowak, Treatise on Constitutional Law. Substance and Procedure §§ 12.7, 13.1–13.11 (West Group 3d ed.1999).

2. 430 U.S. 274, 97 S.Ct. 1076, 51 L.Ed.2d 326 (1977).

3. Goldberg v. Sweet, 488 U.S. 252, 260, 109 S.Ct. 582, 588, 102 L.Ed.2d 607 (1989). Armco Inc. v. Hardesty, 467 U.S. 638, 644, 104 S.Ct. 2620, 2623, 81 L.Ed.2d 540 (1984).

4. 430 U.S. at 279, 97 S.Ct. at 1079, 51 L.Ed.2d at 331.

5. ASARCO Inc. v. Idaho State Tax Commission, 458 U.S. 307, 328, 102 S.Ct. 3103, 3109, 73 L.Ed.2d 787, 795 (1982).

process requirement except that the commerce clause test focuses on the burden on interstate commerce: while the commerce clause will require that the state or local tax be fairly apportioned in order to prevent an undue burden on interstate commerce, the due process clause requires state jurisdiction to tax.[6]

Equal Protection. State and local taxes must also face the hurdle of the equal protection clause, but this hurdle is normally not a very high one. The state or local tax must have a "rational basis" and not be "palpably arbitrary."[7] If the only purpose of a state tax is to promote in-state business and to discriminate

against businesses from other states, that purpose is impermissible and does not justify the imposition of discriminatory taxes. Such a tax will be invalidated under the equal protection clause.[8] Similarly, if a state, pursuant to its statutes and state Constitution, purports to subject all property to the same tax rate, but then engages in "intentional systematic undervaluation" of certain property, the property tax assessment scheme will violate equal protection, for it is not a rational scheme as measured by the state's own articulated purpose.[9]

Article IV Privileges and Immunities. The privileges and immunities clause of Article

---

6. If the Supreme Court placed all constitutional limitations on state taxation under the commerce clause, Congress would be free to write laws that effectively replace the Court rulings under its Article I commerce power. To the extent that the Court bases its rulings on the due process clause, its rulings can not be changed by congressional enactment, because the Congress (through the Fifth Amendment) is bound by due process principles (as are the states under the Fourteenth Amendment). In 2000, the Supreme Court used both the due process and commerce clauses to invalidate a state taxation system that gave a preference to in-state businesses by limiting the types of interest expense that could be deducted from state income taxes. In Hunt–Wesson, Inc. v. Franchise Tax Board of California, 528 U.S. 458, 120 S.Ct. 1022, 145 L.Ed.2d 974 (2000). the Court invalidated a state law that allowed a corporation (whether or not it was domiciled in the state) to take a deduction for interest expense only to the extent that the interest expense exceeds out-of-state income that the business received from an unrelated business activity. Justice Breyer, writing for a unanimous Court in *Hunt–Wesson*, found that the California tax code, in effect, assumed that all of the borrowing helped the non-related income, and, for that reason, indirectly resulted in assessing a tax upon part of the corporation's income that was produced by non-unitary business activity of a subsidiary corporation, according to the Supreme Court. On that basis the Court in *Hunt–Wesson* found that the limitation on the interest deduction violated both the due process and commerce clauses. "Because California's offset provision is not a reasonable allocation of expense deductions to the income that the expense generates, it constitutes impermissible taxation of income outside its jurisdictional reach. The provision therefore violates the due process and commerce clauses of the Constitution." 528 U.S. at 467, 120 S.Ct. at 1028.

Use taxes and mail order vendors and the Internet. Quill Corporation v. North Dakota, 504 U.S. 298, 112 S.Ct. 1904, 119 L.Ed.2d 91 (1992), on remand 487 N.W.2d 598 (N.D.1992), on rehearing 500 N.W.2d 196 (N.D.1993), cert. denied 510 U.S. 859, 114 S.Ct. 173, 126 L.Ed.2d 132 (1993). *Quill* involved mail order vendors engaged in continuous and widespread solicitation of business in the taxing state, but these vendors had no physical presence in the taxing state. A state law required these vendors to collect a use tax from their customers. *Quill* overruled

prior case law and explained that *due process* (which requires the taxpayer to have "minimum contacts" with the taxing state) does not require that mail order vendors have a physical presence in the taxing state. However, the *commerce clause* requires that a vendor have a "substantial nexus" with the taxing state. A mail order vendor, whose only contacts with the taxing state are by mail or common carrier, lacks this "substantial nexus."

Because only the commerce clause prohibits the states from requiring mail order houses from collecting use taxes, Congress is free to decide "whether, when, and to what extent the States may burden interstate mail-order concerns with a duty to collect use taxes." 504 U.S. at 318, 112 S.Ct. at 1916. Thus, Congress can either allow or prohibit states from taxing Internet sales.

7. Allied Stores of Ohio, Inc. v. Bowers, 358 U.S. 522, 526–28, 79 S.Ct. 437, 440–41, 3 L.Ed.2d 480 (1959) (State tax that discriminated against in-state businesses upheld.)

8. In rare circumstances, a state tax classification might violate equal protection. Compare Metropolitan Life Insurance Co. v. Ward, 470 U.S. 869, 105 S.Ct. 1676, 84 L.Ed.2d 751 (1985) (finding that state tax classification discriminating against out of state insurance companies might violate equal protection if state does not have a rational argument to support the classification other than favoring in-state businesses), with Fitzgerald v. Racing Association of Central Iowa, 539 U.S. 103, 123 S.Ct. 2156, 156 L.Ed.2d 97 (2003) (differing tax rates for slot machines on river boats as opposed to racetrack upheld). See § 13.7 and 18.3 regarding equal protection standards for the review of tax laws.

9. Allegheny Pittsburgh Coal Co. v. County Commission of Webster County, 488 U.S. 336, 109 S.Ct. 633, 102 L.Ed.2d 688 (1989). The Court in *Allegheny Pittsburgh* distinguished (and did not decide the validity of) California's tax assessment scheme. The Webster County scheme was an "aberrational enforcement policy," while the law in California was "generally applied." Although California has a similar policy that generally provides that property will be assessed at its 1975–76 value and reassessed only when transferred, that system is grounded on the belief that taxes should be based on the original cost of property and that the state should not tax unrealized paper gains in the value of property. In other words, California's tax

IV of the Constitution forbids state and local taxes discriminatory against out of state residents.[10]

Other Clauses. Other clauses of the Constitution also limit the taxing power. For example, we discuss elsewhere the First Amendment limits on taxes that discriminate against newspapers.[11]

(b) Goods Shipped in Interstate and Foreign Commerce

When Commerce Begins. Under both the commerce clause and the import-export clause, goods that have entered the stream of commerce, whether interstate or foreign, and whether as imports or exports, are immune from state and local taxation so long as the goods remain in the stream of commerce.[12] This principle effectuates the constitutional objective of protecting interstate and foreign commerce from both cumulative and discriminatory burdens of taxation that might otherwise result as a consequence of the movement of goods through more than one jurisdiction.

The initial question is whether the goods have entered the stream of commerce—i.e., has the "commerce" that gives rise to constitutional protection actually begun? If the owner is to transport the goods, he or she must have begun the actual transit of the goods in interstate or foreign commerce. If a common carrier is to transport the goods, possession of the goods must have been surrendered to the carrier for purposes of transit. Neither the intention to ship goods in interstate or foreign commerce, the assembling of goods, the packaging of goods, nor their warehousing is suffi-

cient to place the goods in the stream of commerce.

Coe v. Town of Errol[13] is the seminal case on this point. Logs had been cut from forests in New Hampshire and held on the banks of the Androscoggin River in New Hampshire, where there were to be floated down river at some later date to lumber mills in Maine. While held ready for shipment, New Hampshire assessed the property for general property tax purposes as of the regular assessment date in the same manner as other property in the state. The owners challenged the tax as violating both the commerce clause and the import-export clause on the ground that the goods were "in transit to market from one state to another."

The Court sustained the tax, reviewed a number of earlier cases, and stated the following test for determining whether goods have entered the stream of commerce:

> [G]oods do not cease to be part of the general mass of property in the state, subject, as such, to its jurisdiction, and to taxation in the usual way, until they have been shipped, or entered with a common carrier for transportation to another state, or have been started upon such transportation in a continuous route or journey.[14]

Coe did *not* decide that the logs were not in intrastate commerce or did not affect interstate commerce. *Coe* did not hold that the logs were beyond regulation of Congress. That question was not even before the Court. The question of when commerce has begun is simply a means to determine if the state tax law is nondiscriminatory. *Coe* simply held that the state tax did not violate the dormant com-

---

scheme furthered a rational state objective; Webster County's tax scheme was inconsistent with its stated objective. Subsequently, Nordlinger v. Hahn, 505 U.S. 1, 112 S.Ct. 2326, 120 L.Ed.2d 1 (1992) upheld the California tax scheme.

10. E.g., Ward v. Maryland, 79 U.S. (12 Wall.) 418, 430, 20 L.Ed. 449 (1870). See § 9.6 for additional cases concerning the Article IV privileges and immunities clause. For citations to additional cases, including lower court cases, and secondary works on this topic see our multi-volume Treatise: R. Rotunda & J. Nowak, Treatise on Constitutional Law: Substance and Procedure Chapters 12, 13 (3rd ed. 1999, with annual supplements).

11. § 16.22, infra. See, e.g., Minneapolis Star & Tribune Co. v. Minnesota Commissioner of Revenue, 460 U.S.

575, 103 S.Ct. 1365, 75 L.Ed.2d 295 (1983) (special use tax on cost of paper and ink in the production of periodic publications, but not on other business activity, violates First Amendment as applied to states through the Fourteenth Amendment), on remand 332 N.W.2d 914 (Minn. 1983).

12. Goods need only a minimal amount of interstate contact to enter the stream of commerce. Eureka Pipe Line Co. v. Hallanan, 257 U.S. 265, 42 S.Ct. 101, 66 L.Ed. 227 (1921) (state tax on oil intended primarily for out-of-state customers held invalid).

13. 116 U.S. 517, 6 S.Ct. 475, 29 L.Ed. 715 (1886).

14. 116 U.S. at 527, 6 S.Ct. at 478.

merce clause. The state tax was nondiscriminatory in that it applies to all goods; it taxed the logs in same manner as other property in the state.

Interruption of Commerce. Assuming that shipment of the goods has begun, there may be an interruption of the shipment of the goods prior to delivery at the ultimate market destination. If the interruption is for a purpose associated with, or is incidental to, the safe transportation of the property, the goods remain in the stream of commerce and enjoy constitutional tax immunity.[15] On the other hand, if the interruption in the shipment of the goods is for a separate business purpose unrelated to safe transportation of the goods, as for example, for processing or for holding the goods pending receipt of orders, the goods will be deemed to have been withdrawn from the stream of commerce. In that case, the property will be considered to have become a part of the taxable mass of goods in the jurisdiction in which movement of the goods has ceased.[16] The state can engage in the nondiscriminatory tax of such goods.

Termination of Commerce. The final issue for consideration is when the shipment of goods in interstate or foreign commerce has concluded. Generally, the carrier's delivery of the goods to the consignee purchaser or owner terminates the movement in interstate or foreign commerce and removes them from the protection of the commerce clause or the import-export clause.[17]

(c) Death Taxes

Jurisdictional concepts with respect to state death taxes parallel those that govern jurisdiction to impose general ad valorem property taxes. Tangible property, such as real property and permanently situated tangible personal property, have an exclusive tax situs in the state in which the property is located. *Intangibles*, on the other hand, have a potential multiple tax situs. Thus intangibles, like tangible personal property that is not permanently situated, are subject to multiple taxation under the general property tax. (It should be noted that the general adoption of reciprocal exemption statutes has reduced the potential for multiple death taxation.)

There are two complicating factors that relate to multiple death taxation of intangibles. The first is the fact that states apply different concepts in classifying certain property interests as tangible or intangible property. Second, because domicile provides a secure foundation for imposition of death taxes on intangibles, there may be circumstances in which more than one state claims to be the state of domicile of the decedent.[18]

(d) Income Taxes

Income Taxes on Individuals. Two leading cases, both decided in 1920, initially established the due process principles governing jurisdiction to impose state income taxes on individuals, residents and nonresidents. In *Maguire v. Trefry*,[19] a Massachusetts statute imposed a tax on the income received by a resident-beneficiary of a testamentary trust administered by a Philadelphia trust company. The trust income consisted of interest and dividends on securities comprising the trust corpus.

The taxpayer contended that the tax violated the due process requirements prescribed by *Union Refrigerator Transit Co. v. Kentucky*[20] because the law taxed property outside the jurisdiction of the state. In response, the Court

---

15. Champlain Realty Co. v. Brattleboro, 260 U.S. 366, 43 S.Ct. 146, 67 L.Ed. 309 (1922).

16. E.g., in American Steel & Wire Co. v. Speed, 192 U.S. 500, 24 S.Ct. 365, 48 L.Ed. 538 (1904), the taxpayer shipped wire and nails from its Illinois manufacturing plant to its warehouse in Tennessee. The taxpayer sorted and stored the goods in the Memphis warehouse prior to filling orders from its customers in southern states. The Court sustained a general property tax on the warehouse inventory on the ground that termination of shipment in Tennessee served a business purpose separate from the safe and convenient transportation of the goods.

17. Michelin Tire Corp. v. Wages, 423 U.S. 276, 96 S.Ct. 535, 46 L.Ed.2d 495 (1976), rehearing denied 424 U.S. 935, 96 S.Ct. 1151, 47 L.Ed.2d 344 (1976).

18. See, 2 Ronald D. Rotunda & John E. Nowak, Treatise on Constitutional Law: Substance and Procedure §§ 13.3(b)–13.3(f) (West Group, 3d ed.1999).

19. 253 U.S. 12, 40 S.Ct. 417, 64 L.Ed. 739 (1920).

20. 199 U.S. 194, 26 S.Ct. 36, 50 L.Ed. 150 (1905).

noted that "we are not dealing with the right to tax securities which have acquired a local situs [in another state], but are concerned with the right of the State to tax the [income of the] beneficiary of the trust at her residence, although the trust itself may be created and administered under the laws of another state."[21]

Maguire sustained the tax, and emphasized that the taxpayer was domiciled in the taxing state: "The beneficiary is domiciled in Massachusetts, has the protection of her laws, and there receives and holds the income from the trust property. We find nothing in the Fourteenth Amendment which prevents the taxation in Massachusetts of an interest of this character, thus owned and enjoyed by a resident of the states."[22] The Court drew an analogy to the property tax by observing that, in principle, imposition of an income tax on a taxpayer's out-of-state income does not differ from the imposition of an ad valorem property tax on a debt owed to the same taxpayer by an out-of-state debtor.

The second case, *Shaffer v. Carter*,[23] resolved the question whether a state may constitutionally impose an income tax on a nonresident citizen of another state on income earned in the taxing state. An Oklahoma statute imposed a general income tax on both residents and nonresidents and provided that the tax applied to "net income from all property owned, and of every business . . . carried on in this State by persons residing elsewhere." The taxpayer, a resident of Illinois, owned oil-producing land and operated oil and gas mining leases in Oklahoma.

The taxpayer contended that the tax violated due process, equal protection, and the privileges and immunities clause. The taxpayer primarily argued that the state lacked jurisdiction to tax the income of nonresidents even though the income was earned in and derived from the taxing state. The Court rejected this contention by emphasizing the benefits derived by the taxpayer under the laws of the taxing state. To be sure, the Oklahoma statute could result in double taxation if, for example, the state where the taxpayer was domiciled decided to tax the income that the taxpayer derived in Oklahoma. But the Constitution does not necessarily forbid double taxation. After all, both the state and federal governments may tax the same income.

Although it may have appeared that *Maguire* and *Shaffer* had fully resolved the issue as to state power to impose income taxes on individuals, another decision confirmed the power of a state to impose an income tax on out-of-state income of an individual residing and domiciled in the taxing state. In *People of New York ex rel. Cohn v. Graves*[24] the taxpayer resided in New York. During the tax years in question, the taxpayer (the beneficiary of a life estate under her husband's will) received rental income from real property located in New Jersey. Two of the executors resided in New Jersey and both the bond and mortgages were held for safekeeping in a New Jersey bank. The issue was whether New York had jurisdiction to tax the rentals and interest income derived from the New Jersey properties.

In reliance on *Pollock v. Farmers' Loan & Trust Co.*,[25] the taxpayer objected primarily on the ground that the tax was in substance and effect a tax on real estate and tangible property located outside of the state and therefore in violation of due process. The Court upheld the tax and distinguished between property taxes and income taxes,[26] emphasizing the benefits

---

21. 253 U.S. at 16, 40 S.Ct. at 418.

22. 253 U.S. at 17, 40 S.Ct. at 419.

23. 252 U.S. 37, 40 S.Ct. 221, 64 L.Ed. 445 (1920).

24. 300 U.S. 308, 57 S.Ct. 466, 81 L.Ed. 666 (1937).

25. 157 U.S. 429, 15 S.Ct. 673, 39 L.Ed. 759 (1895); 158 U.S. 601, 15 S.Ct. 912, 39 L.Ed. 1108 (1895). In *Pollock,* the Court held that an income tax on income produced by real and personal property was in effect a direct tax on the property itself. On this basis, *Pollock* invalidated the Income Tax Act of 1894 as violating Article I, § 2, cl. 3 and § 9, cl. 4, both of which require that all direct taxes shall be apportioned among the states according to population.

The decision in *Pollock* led ultimately to the adoption of the Sixteenth Amendment. Subsequently, the Court specifically overruled *Pollock* in South Carolina v. Baker, 485 U.S. 505, 108 S.Ct. 1355, 99 L.Ed.2d 592 (1988).

26. The Court acknowledged that New York could not impose a property tax on the New Jersey real estate but noted that "[T]he incidence of a tax on income differs from that on property. . . . The tax on each is predicated upon different governmental benefits; the protection of-

enjoyed by the taxpayer by reason of her status as a resident of the taxing state:

> That the receipt of income by a resident of the territory of a taxing sovereignty is a taxable event is universally recognized. Domicil itself affords a basis for such taxation. Enjoyment of the privileges of residence in the state and the attendant right to invoke the protection of its laws are inseparable from responsibility for sharing the costs of government.[27]

Cohn, by reaffirming the authority of a domiciliary state to tax all income of a resident individual irrespective of its source, effectively removed any lingering doubts that *Pollock* may have created.

Maguire, Shaffer, and *Cohn* established the constitutional power of a state to impose taxes on individuals whether or not domiciled there. In the case of individuals domiciled in the taxing state, domicile alone is sufficient to sustain the tax because the domiciliary enjoys personal benefits under the laws of the state. In the case of an individual who is neither domiciled in, nor resident of, the taxing state, an income tax on income earned in the taxing state is justified because the taxing state provides benefits by protecting the taxpayer's income-producing occupation, business, and property located within the state.

Income Taxes On Corporations. The same principles of due process that allow a jurisdiction to impose income taxes on individuals appear equally applicable to corporations. If a corporation is organized under the laws of the taxing state, it is taxable as a domiciliary corporation on all of its income whether derived from within or outside of the state of domicile. Under principles of due process, jurisdiction to tax all the income of a domestic corporation is particularly apropos because the taxpayer-corporation derives its very existence from the taxing state.[28] Similarly, a foreign corporation conducting business or owning income-producing property in the taxing state is taxable on the income derived from its business operations or property owned there because the taxing state provides benefits and protection.[29]

State taxes imposed on the income of corporations, like franchise taxes, must be reviewed under a four-part commerce clause test that was established in *Complete Auto Transit, Inc. v. Brady.*[30] The franchise taxes considered in earlier cases, if they were to be challenged again, would have to be reviewed in light of the *Complete Auto Transit* standards. The Supreme Court in *Complete Auto Transit* ruled that all state and local taxes, including franchise taxes, must: (1) apply only to activities that have a substantial nexus to the taxing state; (2) be fairly apportioned; (3) avoid discrimination against interstate commerce; and (4) be fairly related to services or benefits provided by the taxing jurisdiction.[31]

The most strictly enforced part of the *Complete Auto Transit* test is the principle that prohibits discrimination against interstate commerce. Any tax that appears to discriminate against out-of-state persons will be strictly scrutinized by the Court.[32] A state tax that appears to be discriminatory, in rare cases, might be upheld as a "compensatory tax" if the state proves that a tax is a precise way of equalizing the tax burden imposed on in-state persons by a similar tax.[33]

---

fered to the property in one state does not extend to the receipt and enjoyment of income from it in another." 300 U.S. at 314, 57 S.Ct. at 468.

27. 300 U.S. at 312–13, 57 S.Ct. at 467.

28. See Lawrence v. State Tax Commission, 286 U.S. 276, 52 S.Ct. 556, 76 L.Ed. 1102 (1932).

29. This basic principle is supported by Shaffer v. Carter, 252 U.S. 37, 40 S.Ct. 221, 64 L.Ed. 445 (1920) insofar as due process is concerned.

30. 430 U.S. 274, 97 S.Ct. 1076, 51 L.Ed.2d 326 (1977).

31. 430 U.S. at 279, 97 S.Ct. at 1079. State taxes that relate to international activities must survive the four-part test established in the *Complete Auto Transit* case, and additional commerce clause tests. In some instances, such taxes will also be reviewed under the import-export clause of Article I § 10. See § 13.1.

32. See, e.g., Oregon Waste Systems, Inc. v. Department of Environmental Quality, 511 U.S. 93, 114 S.Ct. 1345, 128 L.Ed.2d 13 (1994); Associated Industries of Missouri v. Lohman, 511 U.S. 641, 114 S.Ct. 1815, 128 L.Ed.2d 639 (1994).

33. See generally, Fulton Corp. v. Faulkner, 516 U.S. 325, 116 S.Ct. 848, 133 L.Ed.2d 796 (1996). The states have been able to impose a use tax on property brought into the state, when the use tax is complementary to a state sales tax and imposes an equal burden on persons

An example of a franchise tax that had no realistic opportunity of surviving commerce clause review is provided by the Alabama Franchise Tax that was invalidated by a unanimous Court in *South Central Bell Telephone Company v. Alabama*.[34]

An Alabama tax required each corporation that did business in the state to pay a tax that was based upon the firm's capital. The tax discriminated against out-of-state corporations through the methods that Alabama used to value of each firm's capital. Alabama allowed corporations that were domiciled in the state to control how their capital would be valued. Under Alabama statutes, the value of an in-state corporation was to be based on the par value of capital stock of the corporation. An in-state corporation would be able to set the par value of that stock at any level that it chose, so that it could lower the value of its capital for Alabama tax purposes. On the other hand, the value of corporations from outside of the State of Alabama, which did business in the state, had to be based on generally accepted accounting principles. Thus, out-of-state corporations lacked the ability to control the valuation of their capital and their liability to the Alabama Franchise Tax. Writing for a unanimous Court, Justice Breyer found that there was no justification for the discrimination against out-of-state corporations, because the franchise tax valuation system was not designed to insure that domestic and foreign corporations would

be subject to the same total tax burden on their business activity in Alabama.[35] Perhaps in recognition of the hopelessness of trying to justify a discriminatory tax, Alabama argued that the Supreme Court lacked jurisdiction in the case and, alternatively, that the Supreme Court should overrule all of its previous decisions that established the principle that state laws that discriminated against interstate commerce violated the commerce clause. Not surprisingly, the Court rejected those claims, and the Alabama Franchise Tax was invalidated.[36]

(e) State Taxes and Intergovernmental Immunity[37]

The genesis of the doctrine of intergovernmental immunity is *McCulloch v. Maryland*.[38] In that case, which invalidated a discriminatory state tax on the Bank of the United States, Chief Justice Marshall offered his broad slogan that "the power to tax involves the power to destroy."[39]

From this small beginning, the doctrine of intergovernmental immunity expanded during the following century to insulate direct government functions from taxation and also to insulate from taxation secondary or derivative transactions relating to the performance of governmental functions. The doctrine reached its zenith when it was extended to exempt the employees of the state and federal govern-

buying products from out-of-state and in-state. Henneford v. Silas Mason Co., 300 U.S. 577, 57 S.Ct. 524, 81 L.Ed. 814 (1937). See § 13.6 (b)(3) regarding use taxes.

34. 526 U.S. 160, 119 S.Ct. 1180, 143 L.Ed.2d 258 (1999).

35. 526 U.S. at 169, 119 S.Ct. at 1186.

36. Alabama argued that the Eleventh Amendment to the United States Constitution prohibited Supreme Court jurisdiction in this case; that argument was unanimously rejected by the Justices. South Central Bell Telephone Co. v. Alabama, 526 U.S. 160, 165, 119 S.Ct. 1180, 1184, 143 L.Ed.2d 258 (1999). The Justices were also unanimous in rejecting the state's argument that the state court decisions upholding the discriminatory tax rested on independent and adequate state grounds. 526 U.S. at 165–67, 119 S.Ct. at 1184–85. See Chapter Two regarding these federal jurisdiction issues. The majority opinion in *South Central Bell* found that the Court would not consider the argument that it should reconsider all commerce clause principles limiting state and local laws "because the State did

not make clear it intended to make this argument until it filed its brief on the merits." 526 U.S. at 171, 119 S.Ct. at 1186. In a concurring opinion, Justice O'Connor said that she saw no reason why the Supreme Court would want to reconsider "our well established body of negative commerce clause jurisprudence." 526 U.S. at 171, 119 S.Ct. at 1186–87. Justice Thomas, who joined the opinion of the Court, noted that he was only refusing to examine the commerce clause rulings of the Court because of the timing of the state's argument. 526 U.S. at 171, 119 S.Ct. at 1187 (Thomas, J., concurring).

37. For citations to additional cases, including lower court cases, and secondary works on this topic see our multi-volume Treatise: R. Rotunda & J. Nowak, Treatise on Constitutional Law: Substance and Procedure § 13.9 (3rd ed. 1999, with annual supplements).

38. 17 U.S. (4 Wheat.) 316, 4 L.Ed. 579 (1819). See, Rotunda, Intergovernmental Tax Immunity and Tax Free Municipals After *Garcia*, 57 U.Colo.L.Rev. 849 (1986).

39. 17 U.S. (4 Wheat.) at 431.

ments from income taxes imposed by the other,[40] and to exempt those leasing government lands.[41]

The early 1930's established some limits on the expansion of the doctrine, but reversal did not occur until the later years of that decade. In a brief span of sixteen months, the Court abruptly turned the tide in four cases, each involving an income tax.[42]

Paralleling the income tax cases, the same process of extension, and then limitation of the immunity doctrine occurred with respect to sales and use taxes. In reversing the extension of the doctrine (and in the absence of specific Congressional legislation), the Court concluded that a state sales tax affecting federal procurement contracts is permissible if the *legal incidence* of the tax falls on one other than the federal government, notwithstanding the fact that the economic burden may actually be borne by the federal fisc.[43]

Since *McCulloch v. Maryland,* it has been the established rule under the supremacy clause that property owned by the federal government is exempt from state and local property taxes,[44] *unless* Congress expressly permits such taxation or authorizes payments in lieu of taxation.[45]

Where the government leases its property to private persons for business or personal use, a question arises as to whether the immunity doctrine should bar local taxes on such use. In a series of cases decided in 1958, the Court held that lessees of government-owned manufacturing facilities are validly subject to nondiscriminatory property-use taxes on the value of the government facilities used for business purposes.[46] The nondiscriminatory property-user tax imposed on lessees of tax-exempt property merely served to equalize the tax burden relative to those who leased similar facilities from non-exempt owners.

Taxation of state or federal governmental functions by the other could, in some circumstances, violate the doctrine of intergovernmental immunity and disrupt our federal system. While the Court has abandoned any test based on artificial distinctions between what is called a "governmental" versus what is called a "proprietary" function,[47] the Court still recognizes that taxation of state or federal sovereignty would violate the doctrine of intergovernmental immunity, although taxation of other state functions is permitted. The test is whether the tax is destructive of state sovereignty.[48] For example, the following state activities have been held properly subject to federal taxation: the state sales of mineral wa-

40. Dobbins v. Commissioners of Erie County, 41 U.S. (16 Pet.) 435, 10 L.Ed. 1022 (1842) (state income tax on federal employee held unconstitutional); Collector v. Day, 78 U.S. (11 Wall.) 113, 20 L.Ed. 122 (1870) (federal income tax on state judge held unconstitutional). These decisions were premised on the rationale that an income tax on the salaries of the employees constituted a tax on the means by which each government exercised its powers.

41. Gillespie v. Oklahoma, 257 U.S. 501, 42 S.Ct. 171, 66 L.Ed. 338 (1922) (lessees of restricted Indian lands immune to state income taxes); Burnet v. Coronado Oil & Gas Co., 285 U.S. 393, 52 S.Ct. 443, 76 L.Ed. 815 (1932) (lessee of state school lands exempt from federal income taxes).

42. James v. Dravo Contracting Co., 302 U.S. 134, 58 S.Ct. 208, 82 L.Ed. 155 (1937); Helvering v. Gerhardt, 304 U.S. 405, 58 S.Ct. 969, 82 L.Ed. 1427 (1938), rehearing denied 305 U.S. 669, 59 S.Ct. 57, 83 L.Ed. 43 (1938); Graves v. New York ex rel. O'Keefe, 306 U.S. 466, 59 S.Ct. 595, 83 L.Ed. 927 (1939); Helvering v. Mountain Producers Corp., 303 U.S. 376, 58 S.Ct. 623, 82 L.Ed. 907 (1938).

43. Alabama v. King & Boozer, 314 U.S. 1, 62 S.Ct. 43, 86 L.Ed. 3 (1941). Accord, Curry v. United States, 314 U.S. 14, 62 S.Ct. 48, 86 L.Ed. 9 (1941). See also, United States v. New Mexico, 455 U.S. 720, 102 S.Ct. 1373, 71 L.Ed.2d 580 (1982).

44. E.g., Van Brocklin v. Anderson, 117 U.S. 151, 6 S.Ct. 670, 29 L.Ed. 845 (1886).

45. 117 U.S. at 175, 6 S.Ct. at 683.

46. United States v. Detroit, 355 U.S. 466, 78 S.Ct. 474, 2 L.Ed.2d 424 (1958); United States v. Muskegon, 355 U.S. 484, 78 S.Ct. 483, 2 L.Ed.2d 436 (1958).

47. Thus all of the Justices in New York v. United States, 326 U.S. 572, 66 S.Ct. 310, 90 L.Ed. 326 (1946) abandoned the governmental-proprietary distinction as unworkable. 326 U.S. at 583, 66 S.Ct. at 314–15 (opinion of Frankfurter, J., joined by Rutledge, J.); 326 U.S. at 586, 66 S.Ct. at 316 (Stone, C.J., concurring, joined by Reed, Murphy, & Burton, JJ.); 326 U.S. at 590–96, 66 S.Ct. at 318–20 (Douglas, J., dissenting, joined by Black, J.).

See also, Massachusetts v. United States, 435 U.S. 444, 457 & n. 14, 98 S.Ct. 1153, 1162 & n. 14, 55 L.Ed.2d 403, 414 & n. 14 (1978) (plurality opinion); Case v. Bowles, 327 U.S. 92, 101, 66 S.Ct. 438, 442, 90 L.Ed. 552 (1946).

48. Cf. Garcia v. San Antonio Metropolitan Transit Authority, 469 U.S. 528, 556, 105 S.Ct. 1005, 1020, 83 L.Ed.2d 1016, 1036 (1985), rehearing denied 471 U.S. 1049, 105 S.Ct. 2041, 85 L.Ed.2d 340 (1985).

ters;[49] sales of liquor in state-owned liquor stores;[50] state operations of a railroad;[51] and municipally operated parks and bathing beaches.[52]

The states do not have as broad a latitude in the taxation of federal activities, as the federal government has. For example, the courts have applied governmental immunity to invalidate a state tax on liquor sold to Government military installations.[53] Of course, Congress has the power to explicitly designate those functions of the federal government that may or may not be subjected to state taxation.[54]

The Overruling of *Pollock v. Farmers' Loan & Trust Co.* *Pollock v. Farmers' Loan & Trust Co.*[55] denied Congress the power to tax the interest on state or municipal bonds. The Court overruled that case nearly a century later, in *South Carolina v. Baker.*[56] Congress had codified the result in *Pollock,* but in 1982 (as part of tax reform) removed federal

income tax exemption of state or municipal bond interest *if* the bonds were issued in non-registered form. That is, bearer bonds are not tax exempt under federal law. South Carolina invoked the original jurisdiction of the Supreme Court, claiming that this new federal law violated the Tenth Amendment and principles of intergovernmental immunity.

Justice Brennan, for the Court, ruled that there was no Constitutional violation because there was no evidence that Congress deprived South Carolina of "any right to participate in the national political process" or that Congress "singled out" the State of South Carolina in a way that rendered it "politically isolated and powerless."[57] The Court then confirmed what many commentators had long argued,[58] "that subsequent case law has overruled the holding in *Pollock* that state bond interest is immune from a nondiscriminatory federal tax."[59]

---

49. New York v. United States, 326 U.S. 572, 66 S.Ct. 310, 90 L.Ed. 326 (1946).

50. Ohio v. Helvering, 292 U.S. 360, 54 S.Ct. 725, 78 L.Ed. 1307 (1934); South Carolina v. United States, 199 U.S. 437, 26 S.Ct. 110, 50 L.Ed. 261 (1905).

51. California v. Anglim, 37 F.Supp. 663 (N.D.Cal. 1941), affirmed 129 F.2d 455 (9th Cir.1942), certiorari denied 317 U.S. 669, 63 S.Ct. 74, 87 L.Ed. 537 (1942).

52. Wilmette Park District v. Campbell, 338 U.S. 411, 70 S.Ct. 195, 94 L.Ed. 205 (1949) (federal admissions tax).

53. United States v. State Tax Commission of Mississippi, 421 U.S. 599, 95 S.Ct. 1872, 44 L.Ed.2d 404 (1975).

54. Federal Land Bank of St. Paul v. Bismarck Lumber Co., 314 U.S. 95, 62 S.Ct. 1, 86 L.Ed. 65 (1941). See 12 U.S.C.A. § 548 (as amended by P.L. 91–156), which lifts the tax immunity previously available to national banks by providing that, for tax purposes, "a national bank shall be treated as a bank organized and existing under the laws of the State or other jurisdiction within which its principal office is located." Cf. Davis v. Michigan Department of Treasury, 489 U.S. 803, 109 S.Ct. 1500, 103 L.Ed.2d 891 (1989), holding that a federal statute and the principles of

intergovernmental immunity that it embodied invalidated a state discriminatory income tax that exempted the income of retired state and local government employees from taxation but taxed the retirement income of retired federal employees.

55. 157 U.S. 429, 583–84, 15 S.Ct. 673, 690, 39 L.Ed. 759 (1895).

56. 485 U.S. 505, 108 S.Ct. 1355, 99 L.Ed.2d 592 (1988).

57. 485 U.S. at 513, 108 S.Ct. at 1361, citing United States v. Carolene Products Co., 304 U.S. 144, 152 n. 4, 58 S.Ct. 778, 783 n. 4, 82 L.Ed. 1234 (1938).

58. E.g., Rotunda, Intergovernmental Tax Immunity and Tax Free Municipals After *Garcia,* 57 U.Colo.L.Rev. 849 (1986).

59. 485 U.S. at 524, 108 S.Ct. at 1367. O'Connor, J., filed the only dissent. Stevens, J., filed a concurring opinion; Scalia, J., concurred in part and in the judgment; Rehnquist, C.J., concurred in the judgment; and Kennedy, J., took no part in the consideration or decision of the case.

Chapter 9

FEDERAL REGULATION AND STATE AUTHORITY

§ 9.1 Federal Preemption: An Introduction

When Congress exercises a granted power, federal legislation may "preempt" or override concurrent state legislation. The supremacy clause[1] mandates that federal law overrides, *i.e.*, preempts, any state regulation where there is an actual conflict between the two sets of legislation. For example, if a federal statute forbids an act that state legislation requires, the federal law preempts the state law. Moreover, Congress, when enacting its statute, may specifically decide to "occupy the field" and expressly prohibit parallel state legislation.[2] Unfortunately, preemption questions seldom arise under such clear cut circumstances, because Congress does not always speak with a clear voice. Congress may *impliedly* occupy the field.

In recent years Congress had enacted legislation touching more and more areas that traditionally have been subject to state regulation. Often, state statutory schemes predated Congressional action. In initiating a new regulatory scheme, Congress seldom articulates a specific intent to preempt an entire field of regulation. Indeed, it is common for Congress to include a typical "savings clause" explicitly legitimizing concomitant state regulation,[3] but the scope of these saving clauses are sometimes unclear, so the judicial branch has shouldered the responsibility for discovering congressional intent and, if necessary, invalidating state laws that "impair federal superintendence of the field" and impermissibly interfere with the effectuation of Congressional objectives.[4] Preemption cases are really instances of statutory interpretation. Because courts are interpreting congressional intent, Congress, can always reverse the decisions by making clear its intent not to preempt (or to preempt) the field.[5]

The Court formulated the basic analytical standards for preemption decisions in the early leading cases of *Hines v. Davidowitz*,[6] and *Pennsylvania v. Nelson*,[7] discussed in the sec-

---

§ 9.1

1. U.S.Const. art. VI, cl. 2.

See 2 Ronald D. Rotunda & John E. Nowak, Treatise on Constitutional Law: Substance and Procedure §§ 12.1–12.7 (West Group, 3d ed. 1999); Rotunda, The Doctrine of the Inner Political Check, The Dormant Commerce Clause, and Federal Preemption, 53 Transportation Practitioners J. 263 (1986); Maxwell L. Stearns, A Beautiful Mend: A Game Theoretical Analysis of the Dormant Commerce Clause Doctrine, 45 Wm. & Mary L. Rev. 1 (2003).

2. Section 408 of Title IV of the Wholesome Meat Act, provided: "Marking, labeling, packaging, or ingredient requirements in addition to, or different than, those made under this chapter may not be imposed by any state...."

3. Securities Exchange Act of 1934, 15 U.S.C.A. § 78bb(a) instructs:

"... Nothing in this chapter shall affect the jurisdiction of the securities commissioner (or any agency or officer

performing like functions) of any State over any security or any person insofar as it does not conflict with the provisions of this chapter or the rules and regulations thereunder."

4. Hines v. Davidowitz, 312 U.S. 52, 61 S.Ct. 399, 85 L.Ed. 581 (1941). See also, Cologne, J., citing Treatise in, Partee v. San Diego Chargers Football Co., 128 Cal.App.3d 501, 180 Cal.Rptr. 416, 419 n. 3 (4th Dist.1982), later vacated 34 Cal.3d 378, 194 Cal.Rptr. 367, 668 P.2d 674 (1983).

5. E.g., Katz, J., quoting Treatise in, Barannikova v. Town of Greenwich, 229 Conn. 664, 682, 643 A.2d 251, 261 (1994).

6. 312 U.S. 52, 61 S.Ct. 399, 85 L.Ed. 581 (1941).

7. 350 U.S. 497, 76 S.Ct. 477, 100 L.Ed. 640 (1956), rehearing denied 351 U.S. 934, 76 S.Ct. 785, 100 L.Ed. 1462 (1956).

tion that follows. While one may outline succinctly the judicial criteria, there is no simplistic constitutional standard for applying the
preemption parameters in specific cases because of the diversity and complexity of preemption problems.[8]

Preemption decisions pervade the entire
range of federal regulation. The Court must
consider the federal law and its operation and
compare the state statute and its operation.
Of necessity, the nature of the problem of discovering congressional intent has resulted in
judicial ad hoc balancing. Therefore, one may
articulate the significant guideposts. It is difficult in this area—even more so than in others—to apply the rationale underlying a decision in one field to the problem in another
context.[9]

Despite the diversity of preemption problems, the underlying constitutional principles
have a common end: to avoid conflicting regulation of conduct by various official bodies that
might have some authority over the subject
matter.[10] Where there are no indicia of congressional intent the Court may have to balance the state and federal interests to achieve
this end.

§ 9.2   The Traditional Preemption Tests

In *Hines v. Davidowitz*[1] the Court held that
the Federal Alien Registration Act of 1940
precluded enforcement of Pennsylvania's Alien
Registration Act of 1939. The Court noted the
supremacy of national power in the general

field of foreign policy, and the sensitivity of
the relationship between the regulation of
aliens and the conduct of foreign affairs. It
concluded that Congressional enactment of
uniform national immigration laws "occupied"
the field so as to preempt state regulations
requiring the registration of aliens. Justice
Black, speaking for the majority, acknowledged that no rigid verbal formulae are *a
fortiori* determinative of displacement of concurrent state regulation. The test is whether,
under the circumstances of a particular case,
the state law "stands as an obstacle to the
accomplishment and execution of the full purposes and objectives of Congress."[2]

The Three–Part Test of *Pennsylvania v. Nelson*. In the following decade *Pennsylvania v.
Nelson*[3] elaborated the *Hines* rationale. Chief
Justice Warren enunciated a three-pronged inquiry to ascertain preemption: 1. pervasiveness of the federal regulatory scheme; 2. federal occupation of the field as necessitated by the
need for national uniformity; 3. the danger of
conflict between state laws and the administration of the federal program.[4]

Applying this three-part examination, the
Supreme Court held that federal anti-commu-
nist legislation superseded the state's Sedition
Act. Enforcing the state sedition laws might
lead to conflicts with federal laws because the
sporadic local prosecutions might obstruct federal undercover operations. Under the state
law, even private individuals could initiate a
prosecution, thus increasing the chance of in-

---

8. Justice Black cautioned in *Hines*: "But none of
these expressions provides an infallible constitutional test
or an exclusive constitutional yardstick. In the final analysis, there can be no one crystal clear distinctly marked
formula." 312 U.S. at 67, 61 S.Ct. at 404.

9. Hirsh, Toward a New View of Federal Preemption,
1972 U.Ill.L.F. 515. See, also, Note, Preemption as a
Preferential Ground: A New Canon of Construction, 12
Stan.L.Rev. 208 (1959).

10. Amalgamated Association of Street, Electric Ry. &
Motor Coach Employees v. Lockridge, 403 U.S. 274, 91
S.Ct. 1909, 29 L.Ed.2d 473 (1971), rehearing denied 404
U.S. 874, 92 S.Ct. 24, 30 L.Ed.2d 120 (1971), on remand to
94 Idaho 475, 491 P.2d 739 (1971).

§ 9.2

1. 312 U.S. 52, 61 S.Ct. 399, 85 L.Ed. 581 (1941). Cf.
DeCanas v. Bica, 424 U.S. 351, 96 S.Ct. 933, 47 L.Ed.2d 43
(1976).

2. 312 U.S. at 67, 61 S.Ct. at 404. Contrast, DeCanas v.
Bica, 424 U.S. 351, 96 S.Ct. 933, 47 L.Ed.2d 43 (1976),
where the Court upheld a state statutory scheme that the
Court determined aided federal policy. Federal law prohibited hiring certain aliens, and California law adopted federal standards in imposing criminal sanctions against employers who knowingly employ aliens who have no federal
right to employment within the country.

3. 350 U.S. 497, 76 S.Ct. 477, 100 L.Ed. 640 (1956),
rehearing denied 351 U.S. 934, 76 S.Ct. 785, 100 L.Ed.
1462 (1956).

4. 350 U.S. at 502–05, 76 S.Ct. at 480–82. See, Arraj,
J., citing Treatise in Rocky Mountain Airways, Inc. v.
County of Pitkin, 674 F.Supp. 312, 319 (D.Colo.1987).

terference with federal enforcement plans and undercover operations. The Court stressed that the need for national predominance mandated the conclusion that Congress intended to occupy the field. Federal regulation of seditious conduct preempted the state statute prohibiting seditious acts.

The progeny of *Hines* and *Nelson* have narrowed the scope of judicial inquiry to a determination of whether, under the particular facts of the case, the existence of the state regulatory scheme facilitates, or is detrimental to, the purposes and objectives of the federal statute. The Supreme Court has embarked on a case-by-case approach, examining state regulatory schemes under established principles of federal preemption.

For example, in *Geier v. American Honda Motor Co., Inc.*,[5] plaintiffs sued claiming that defendant designed the 1987 Honda Accord defectively because it lacked air bags. In 1984, the Federal Motor Vehicle Safety Standard allowed manufacturers for the 1987 model year to select from several passive restraint alternatives, including (but not limited to) airbags, in order to comply with safety rules. Justice Breyer, for the Court, held that this federal law preempted the common-law tort action because it was an obstacle to the accomplishment of the objectives of the federal standard.

The federal statute included an express preemption provision and a savings clause stating: "Compliance with" a federal safety standard "does not exempt any person from any liability under common law." This savings clause, said the Court, requires the express preemption provision to be read narrowly, to preempt only state statutes and regulations, because the clause assumes that there are

some significant number of common-law liability cases to save. However, this savings clause "does *not* bar the ordinary working of conflict preemption principles."[6] There can still be implied preemption. In this case, federal regulations preempt conflicting state tort actions. This "common-law 'no airbag' action" is one that "actually conflicts" with the federal standard. The history of the rule showed that the Department of Transportation deliberately sought variety, rejecting an "all airbag" standard for various reasons, including perceived public resistance. The 1984 standard consciously decided to gradually phase-in passive restraints, starting with a 10% requirement for 1987 model year vehicles. The tort action depends upon its claim that manufacturers had a duty to install an airbag when they manufactured the 1987 Honda Accord. But that requirement would have presented an obstacle to the variety and mix of devices that the federal regulation sought.

§ 9.3 Comparison of Preemption Cases With Commerce Power Cases

The Court's approach in determining the scope of federal preemption and the balancing of interests is similar to its approach in ascertaining unconstitutional burdens on interstate commerce. The courts tend to give greater deference to regulation that is traditionally parochial, *i.e.* health and safety measures.[1] Again, it must be emphasized that each case turns on its own facts.[2]

Thus, states, in an effort to favor local preferences,[3] may not regulate aviation in opposition to the national scheme, but they may require federally licensed seagoing vessels to meet local pollution standards.[4] The National Labor Relations Act does not preempt a union

---

5. 529 U.S. 861, 120 S.Ct. 1913, 146 L.Ed.2d 914 (2000).

6. 529 U.S. 861, 869, 120 S.Ct. 1913, 1919 (emphasis in original). Stevens, J., joined by Souter, Thomas, & Ginsburg, JJ. dissented, arguing that the federal rule merely set a minimum airbag standard.

§ 9.3

1. See, e.g., Andersen, J., citing Treatise in Inlandboatmen's Union of the Pacific v. Department of Transportation, 119 Wn.2d 697, 703, 836 P.2d 823, 829 (1992); Sweet,

J., citing Treatise in Bravman v. Baxter Healthcare Corp., 842 F.Supp. 747, 753 (S.D.N.Y.1994).

2. Cf. Michael H. Hoeflich & Ronald D. Rotunda, Simon Greenleaf on Desuetude and Judge–Made Law: An Unpublished Letter to Francis Lieber, 10 Constitutional Commentary 93 (1993).

3. Burbank v. Lockheed Air Terminal, Inc., 411 U.S. 624, 93 S.Ct. 1854, 36 L.Ed.2d 547 (1973).

4. Huron Portland Cement Co. v. Detroit, 362 U.S. 440, 80 S.Ct. 813, 4 L.Ed.2d 852 (1960).

member from filing a state tort action for intentional infliction of emotional distress against the union and union official, if the state tort is either unrelated to employment discrimination or a function of the particularly abusive manner in which the employment discrimination is accomplished; the tort may not be a function of the actual or threatened employment discrimination itself.[5]

States may not enact food labeling requirements that prohibit "reasonable variations" in accuracy if federal law allows such reasonable variations in accuracy. Federal regulators had decided that reasonable variations were appropriate because of moisture loss during distribution; given this federal judgment, the state law conflicts with the goal of the federal law, which is to facilitate value comparisons.[6]

Even under the same statutory scheme, preemption may apply to oust the state of regulatory authority in one area or over one issue, but not over another. In *Maurer v. Hamilton*[7] litigants challenged a Pennsylvania statute prohibiting the carrying of cars over truck cabs as conflicting with the Interstate Commerce Commission's national regulation of the field under the Motor Carrier Act of 1935. The Court ruled that the Interstate Commerce Commission's authority to issue safety regulations did not preempt the Pennsylvania statute, which was a weight and height regulation.

The Court deferred to state legislation where public safety and health are involved.[8]

Justice Black's opinion for the Court, in *Castle v. Hayes Freight Lines*[9] the following decade, struck down an Illinois law that suspended an interstate carrier's right to use Illinois highways for repeated violations of Illinois truck weight limits. The Court distinguished *Maurer because the ICC had exclusive power to regulate* which motor carriers could operate in interstate commerce. The Court concluded that the *Castle form of state regulation, unlike the situation in* Maurer, was not within the powers that the federal statute reserved to the states.

State laws that regulate activities in an area preempted by federal legislation are invalid under the supremacy clause because they conflict with federal law. If Congress may regulate an area of private sector activity through the legitimate use of any federal power, such as the federal tax or commerce powers, it may bar also state regulation of that activity by specifically preempting the area for federal action.[10]

§ 9.4 Modern Preemption Developments

In modern decisions the Supreme Court has refused either to presume or infer intent.[1] The Court has stated that it requires that Congress "manifest its intention clearly...."[2] However,

---

5. Farmer v. United Brotherhood of Carpenters & Joiners of America, Local 25, 430 U.S. 290, 97 S.Ct. 1056, 51 L.Ed.2d 338 (1977) (Court notes that inflexible application of rule of preemption in NLRA cases when state purports to regulate activities protected by section 7 of NLRA or unfair labor practices under section 8 of NLRA is to be avoided, especially where the state has a substantial interest at stake and that interest does not threaten undue interference with the federal regulatory scheme).

6. Jones v. Rath Packing Co., 430 U.S. 519, 97 S.Ct. 1305, 51 L.Ed.2d 604 (1977), rehearing denied 431 U.S. 925, 97 S.Ct. 2201, 53 L.Ed.2d 240 (1977).

7. 309 U.S. 598, 60 S.Ct. 726, 84 L.Ed. 969 (1940).

8. Congressional intent to supersede a state safety measure must be clearly manifested. H.P. Welch Co. v. New Hampshire, 306 U.S. 79, 85, 59 S.Ct. 438, 441, 83 L.Ed. 500, 505 (1939).

9. 348 U.S. 61, 75 S.Ct. 191, 99 L.Ed. 68 (1954). See also Service Storage & Transfer Co., Inc. v. Virginia, 359 U.S. 171, 79 S.Ct. 714, 3 L.Ed.2d 717 (1959).

10. See, e.g., Aloha Airlines, Inc. v. Director of Taxation, 464 U.S. 7, 104 S.Ct. 291, 78 L.Ed.2d 10 (1983),

where the Court held that a state tax on annual gross income of airlines operating within state was preempted by a federal statute *expressly* preempting gross receipt tax on such activities, even though the state titled its tax a property tax measured by gross receipts: " ... when a federal statute unambiguously forbids the States to impose a particular kind of tax on an industry affecting interstate commerce, courts need not look beyond the plain language of the federal statute to determine whether a state statute that imposes such a tax is preempted." 469 U.S. at 12, 104 S.Ct. at 294 (footnote omitted).

§ 9.4

1. New York State Dept. of Social Services v. Dublino, 413 U.S. 405, 93 S.Ct. 2507, 37 L.Ed.2d 688 (1973). See also, Bryant Radio Supply, Inc. v. Slane, 507 F.Supp. 1325, 1327 n. 2 (W.D.Va.1981) (Turk, D.J.), citing Treatise, affirmed 669 F.2d 921 (4th Cir.1982).

2. New York State Dept. of Social Services v. Dublino, 413 U.S. 405, 413, 93 S.Ct. 2507, 2513, 37 L.Ed.2d 688 (1973), quoting Schwartz v. Texas, 344 U.S. 199, 202–203, 73 S.Ct. 232, 235, 97 L.Ed. 231 (1952). See also Exxon

Congress need not manifest its intention by explicitly providing that the federal statute preempts the state law. Rather the Court seeks to find the intent of Congress.

Determining Intent. If this intent is not clear from the language of the statute—that is, if Congress did not explicitly provide that federal law does, or does not, preempt state law—, then Congress' intention may be clear from the pervasiveness of the federal scheme,[3] the need for uniformity,[4] or the danger of conflict between the enforcement of state laws and the administration of federal programs,[5] of the state law "stands as an obstacle to the accomplishment of the full purposes and objectives of Congress."[6] But absent persuasive reasons evidencing Congressional intent favoring preemption, the Court will not presume the invalidity of state regulations.[7]

An illustrative case is *New York State Department of Social Services v. Dublino.*[8] The Court sustained New York Work Rules that conditioned receipt of federal A.F.D.C. assis-

tance on an individual's fulfillment of an additional state requirement. In order to be eligible for federal assistance, the New York statute stipulated that individuals must accept employment. Justice Powell, for the Court, rejected the contention that the New York legislation was preempted due to federal pervasiveness in the field, and reiterated the presumption favoring the legitimacy of state legislation:

> If Congress is authorized to act in a field it should manifest its intention clearly. . . . The exercise of federal supremacy is not lightly to be presumed.[9]

The Supreme Court presumes that Congress does not intend to preempt state legislation unless there is an appropriate indication from the language or purposes of the federal action or regulation. Nonetheless, the Court may find part, or all, of a state law or other state action preempted because of the Court's interpretation of the intent or purpose of federal law.[10]

Corp. v. Governor of Maryland, 437 U.S. 117, 132, 98 S.Ct. 2207, 2217, 57 L.Ed.2d 91 (1978), rehearing denied 439 U.S. 884, 99 S.Ct. 232, 58 L.Ed.2d 200 (1978) ("This Court is generally reluctant to infer preemption. . . ."); Hisquierdo v. Hisquierdo, 439 U.S. 572, 581, 99 S.Ct. 802, 808, 59 L.Ed.2d 1 (1979) (the Court will not find that a state law dealing with family and family property law is preempted unless the state law does "major damage" to "clear and substantial" federal interests; "mere conflict" in the words of the two statutes does not imply federal preemption).

3. E.g., White Mountain Apache Tribe v. Bracker, 448 U.S. 136, 100 S.Ct. 2578, 65 L.Ed.2d 665 (1980) (state taxes as applied to commerce by non-Indians on an Indian reservation preempted by pervasive federal regulation); Local 926, International Union of Operating Engineers, AFL–CIO v. Jones, 460 U.S. 669, 103 S.Ct. 1453, 75 L.Ed.2d 368 (1983), on remand to 166 Ga.App. 723, 306 S.E.2d 99 (1983) (state tort action preempted by N.L.R.B.).

4. E.g., Jones v. Rath Packing Co., 430 U.S. 519, 97 S.Ct. 1305, 51 L.Ed.2d 604 (1977), rehearing denied 431 U.S. 925, 97 S.Ct. 2201, 53 L.Ed.2d 240 (1977).

5. E.g., Pennsylvania v. Nelson, 350 U.S. 497, 505–510, 76 S.Ct. 477, 481–84, 100 L.Ed. 640 (1956), rehearing denied 351 U.S. 934, 76 S.Ct. 785, 100 L.Ed. 1462 (1956). Wolfson, J., citing Treatise, in Stahl v. Village of Hoffman Estates, 296 Ill.App.3d 550, 230 Ill.Dec. 824, 694 N.E.2d 1102 (Ill.App.Ct.1998).

Preemption by Federal Agencies. The actions of federal agencies may preempt state law. When Congress gives an administrator or agency discretion to regulate a field of commercial activity the agency's decision to preempt state regulations should be upheld unless it is clear that Congress would *not* have sanctioned a preemp-

tion of state authority in the area regulated by the agency. See Fidelity Federal Savings and Loan Association v. de la Cuesta, 458 U.S. 141, 102 S.Ct. 3014, 73 L.Ed.2d 664 (1982).

6. Silkwood v. Kerr–McGee Corp., 464 U.S. 238, 104 S.Ct. 615, 78 L.Ed.2d 443 (1984), rehearing denied 465 U.S. 1074, 104 S.Ct. 1430, 79 L.Ed.2d 754 (1984), on remand 769 F.2d 1451 (10th Cir.1985).

7. E.g. Malone v. White Motor Corp., 435 U.S. 497, 98 S.Ct. 1185, 55 L.Ed.2d 443 (1978), on remand to 599 F.2d 283 (8th Cir.1979), affirmed 444 U.S. 911, 100 S.Ct. 223, 62 L.Ed.2d 166 (1979) (state statute relating to pensions not preempted by older federal law even though a new federal statute expressly provided for preemption).

8. 413 U.S. 405, 93 S.Ct. 2507, 37 L.Ed.2d 688 (1973).

9. 413 U.S. at 413, 93 S.Ct. at 2513.

Preemption in the European Union. In contrast, in the European Union, preemption of local law by European Union law is considered the norm; that is, when European Union law substantially regulates a subject matter, it is generally taken to preempt national legislation except in the cases in which European Union law provides for the contrary.

See A. Tizzano, Lo Svilluppo delle competenze materiali delle Comunit'a europee, 21 Revista di diritto europeo 139, 207–09 (1981); J.-V. Louis, Quelques réflexions sur la répartition des compétences entre la Communauté européene et ses Etats membres, 2 Revue d'Intégration Européenne 355, 364–70 (1979).

10. See, Cipollone v. Liggett Group, Inc., 505 U.S. 504, 112 S.Ct. 2608, 120 L.Ed.2d 407 (1992), where a splintered

The Court has summarized the basic principles as follows:

Absent explicit preemptive language, Congress' intent to supersede state law altogether may be found from a scheme of federal regulation so pervasive as to make reasonable the inference that Congress left no room [for the states] to supplement it, because the Act of Congress may touch a field in which the federal interest is so dominant that the federal system will be assumed to preclude enforcement of state laws on the same subject, or because the object sought to be obtained by federal law and the character of obligations imposed by it may reveal the same purpose.... Even where Congress has not entirely displaced state regulation in a specific area, state law is preempted to the extent that it actually conflicts with federal law. Such a conflict arises when compliance with both federal and state regulations is a physical impossibility, ... or where state law stands as an obstacle to the accomplishment and execution of the full purposes and objectives of Congress.[11]

Foreign Affairs. The fact that a state law touches foreign affairs does not automatically require preemption. Yet, that fact is hardly irrelevant. For example, in *Crosby v. National Foreign Trade Council*,[12] Justice Souter, for the Court, invalidated a Massachusetts law that barred state entities from buying goods or services from companies doing business with Burma. Three months later after the state enacted this law, Congress passed a law imposing various mandatory and conditional sanctions on Burma. The federal law authorized

the President to remove or modify sanctions if he certified Burma had made progress in civil rights, to impose new sanctions if he found repression, and to suspend sanctions in the interest of national security.

The federal law preempted state law and violated the Supremacy Clause because it frustrated federal statutory objectives. It was "implausible" that Congress would have gone to such lengths to empower the President if "it had been willing to compromise his effectiveness by deference to every provision of state statute or local ordinance that might, if enforced, blunt the consequences of discretionary Presidential action."[13] The federal law has no explicit preemption provision, but this failure "may reflect nothing more than the settled character of implied preemption doctrine."[14]

In *American Insurance Association v. Garamendi*,[15] illustrates the same principle, only this time it was an Executive Agreement instead of a federal statute that preempted state law. Various insurance companies and a trade association of insurance companies sought to enjoin the California Insurance Commissioner from enforcing a California statute requiring disclosure of information about Holocaust-era insurance policies. Again, Justice Souter, for the Court, held that California's Holocaust Victim Insurance Relief Act (HVIRA), and in particular a provision of the HVIRA requiring any insurer that did business in California and that sold insurance policies in Europe which were in effect during Holocaust-era to disclose certain information about those policies to the California Insurance Commissioner or risk losing its license, impermissibly interfered with

Court interpreted federal law to preempt some, but not all, state product liability suits against tobacco manufacturers after the effective date of a federal law (first enacted in 1965) mandating warning labels on cigarettes.

11. Pacific Gas & Electric Co. v. State Energy Resources Conservation & Dev. Commission, 461 U.S. 190, 203–04, 103 S.Ct. 1713, 1722, 75 L.Ed.2d 752 (1983) (California moratorium on nuclear plants not preempted by Atomic Energy Act in view of the economic purpose behind state regulation and the terms of the federal law) (internal quotations and citations omitted).

12. 530 U.S. 363, 120 S.Ct. 2288, 147 L.Ed.2d 352 (2000).

13. 530 U.S. 363, 376, 120 S.Ct. 2288, 2296 (footnote omitted).

14. Scalia, J., joined by Thomas, J., concurred in the judgment, and found it "perfectly obvious on the face of the statute" what Congress intended. The extensive discussion of legislative history tells future litigants that "even when a statute is clear on its face and its effects clear upon the record," they should turn to the legislative history for statements that may help (or harm) their case. This discussion is also wasteful: "it was not preordained, after all, that [the Court's opinion] was to be a 25–page essay." 530 U.S. 363, 390–91, 120 S.Ct. 2288, 2303–04 (Scalia, J., concurring in the judgment).

15. 539 U.S. ___, 123 S.Ct. 2374, 156 L.Ed.2d 376 (2003). Ginsburg, J., dissented and filed opinion, in which Stevens, Scalia, and Thomas, JJ., joined

the President's conduct of foreign affairs, and was therefore preempted. Souter conceded that the executive agreements at issue did not include any preemption clause, but there is a "sufficiently clear conflict to require finding preemption" based on the intent of the executive agreements and statements of high-level Executive Branch officials. HVIRA compromises " 'the very capacity of the President to speak for the Nation with one voice in dealing with other governments' to resolve claims against European companies arising out of World War II."[16]

§ 9.5   Interstate Compacts

(a) The Basic Definitions

Article I, section 10, clause 1, provides, inter alia, that:

No State shall enter into any Treaty, Alliance, or confederation. . . .

But clause 3 of that same section adds that:

No State shall, without the Consent of Congress, . . . enter into any Agreement or Compact with another State or with a Foreign Power. . . .

In *Holmes v. Jennison*,[1] Chief Justice Taney's plurality opinion tried to distinguish these two clauses:

In the first paragraph, the limitations are absolute and unconditional; in the second, the forbidden powers may be exercised with the consent of Congress. . . .

[T]he words "agreement," and "compact," cannot be construed as synonymous with one another; and still less can either of them be held to mean the same thing with the

word "treaty" in the preceding clause, into which the states are positively and unconditionally forbidden to enter; and which even the consent of Congress could not authorize.[2]

Taney went on to define "treaty" as "an instrument written and executed with the formalities customary among nations. . . ."[3] "Agreement" or "compact" are the more comprehensive terms.[4] An agreement need not even be in writing; it is merely "a verbal understanding to which both parties have assented, and upon which both are acting. . . ."[5] Because the framers "anxiously desired to cut off all connections or communication between a State and a foreign power" Taney defined "agreement" to "prohibit every agreement, written or verbal, formal or informal, positive or implied, by the mutual understanding of the parties."[6]

In 1893, in *Virginia v. Tennessee*[7] the Court, speaking through Justice Field, adopted a much narrower definition of "compact" or "agreement," but the two cases are not necessarily in conflict, for Taney's plurality opinion in *Holmes* was written in the context of a state agreeing with a foreign power, while Field's Court opinion in *Virginia v. Tennessee* was written in the context of an agreement between two states. Field said that congressional consent is not required as to those "many matters upon which different States may agree that can in no respect concern the United States".[8] Congressional consent, however, is required of any agreement tending to increase the political power of the States, which may

---

16.   539 U.S. at ___, 123 S.Ct. at 2392 (footnote omitted).

§ 9.5

1.   39 U.S. (14 Pet.) 540, 10 L.Ed. 579 (1840). On interstate compacts, see 2 Ronald D. Rotunda & John E. Nowak, Treatise on Constitutional Law: Substance and Procedure § 12.5 (West Group, 3d ed. 1999). Peter Hay & Ronald D. Rotunda, The United States Federal System: Legal Integration in the American Experience 185–95 (Giuffrè, Milan, 1982); Frankfurter and Landis, The Compact Clause of the Constitution—A Study in Interstate Adjustments, 34 Yale L.J. 685 (1925); F. Zimmerman and M. Wendell, Interstate Compacts Since 1925 (1951); F. Zim-

merman and M. Wendell, The Law and Use of Interstate Compacts (1961).

2.   39 U.S. (14 Pet.) at 570, 571, 10 L.Ed. at 594, 595.

3.   39 U.S. (14 Pet.) at 571, 10 L.Ed. at 595.

4.   In a later opinion the Court stated that a "compact" is merely more formal than an "agreement." Virginia v. Tennessee, 148 U.S. 503, 520, 13 S.Ct. 728, 734–35, 37 L.Ed. 537 (1893).

5.   39 U.S. (14 Pet.) at 572.

6.   39 U.S. (14 Pet.) at 572.

7.   148 U.S. 503, 13 S.Ct. 728, 37 L.Ed. 537 (1893).

8.   148 U.S. at 518, 13 S.Ct. at 734.

encroach on or interfere with the supremacy of the United States.

Justice Field offered several examples. If Virginia should come into possession and ownership of a small parcel of land in New York, and New York wished to purchase it as a site for a public building, no consent of Congress is necessary. Similarly, if Massachusetts wished to transport its exhibits to the World's Fair at Chicago by using the Erie Canal, the contract between the states could be made without the consent of Congress. But if two states would agree to change their boundary lines so that the states, or one of them, may increase political power or influence, consent of Congress is probably required.[9] However, state statutes that promote regional banking do not increase "political" power of the states within the region and thus do not affect our federal structure.[10]

(b) The Consent of Congress

The Constitution itself does not explain how Congress' consent to a compact is to be made, or when it is to be given.

How Consent Is Given. The Supreme Court early recognized that the mode or form of consent is to be left to the wisdom of Congress. Sometimes the consent may be implied from congressional legislation on the subject.[11] Thus when Congress consented to the separation of Kentucky from Virginia and the creation of Kentucky as a separate state, it must be taken to have consented to the compact by which the separation was made.[12] Congress may also place conditions on giving its consent.[13]

When Consent Is Made. Congressional consent will usually precede the compact, as, for example, a compact "to lay a duty of tonnage, to keep troops or ships of war in time of peace, or to engage in war."[14] Sometimes Congress has given its consent years before the proposed compact will have come into existence.[15] But if the compact relates to a matter that could not well be considered until its nature is fully developed, the consent may be subsequently given.[16]

(c) Supreme Court Interpretation of Interstate Compacts

The leading case on the power of the Supreme Court to interpret interstate compacts is *West Virginia ex rel. Dyer v. Sims.*[17] In 1940, Congress gave its consent to an eight State Compact entered into for purposes of controlling pollution in the Ohio River system. One of those states was West Virginia and a contro-

---

9. 148 U.S. at 518, 520, 13 S.Ct. at 734, 735. Thus United States Steel Corp. v. Multistate Tax Commission, 434 U.S. 452, 98 S.Ct. 799, 54 L.Ed.2d 682 (1978) held that it would not "circumscribe modes of interstate cooperation that do not enhance state power to the detriment of federal supremacy." 434 U.S. at 460, 98 S.Ct. at 806. See also 434 U.S. at 473, 98 S.Ct. at 812–13: "the test is whether the Compact enhances state power *quoad* the National Government."

10. See Northeast Bancorp, Inc. v. Board of Governors, 472 U.S. 159, 105 S.Ct. 2545, 86 L.Ed.2d 112 (1985).

11. Virginia v. West Virginia, 78 U.S. (11 Wall.) 39, 59–60, 20 L.Ed. 67, 72–73 (1870) (Act of Congress admitting West Virginia into the Union at the request of Virginia is a "clear and satisfactory" inference that Congress intended to consent to the admission of West Virginia with the contingent boundaries provided for in the statute of Virginia that prayed for West Virginia's admission, and in so doing it necessarily consented to the agreement of those States on the subject).

12. Green v. Biddle, 21 U.S. (8 Wheat.) 1, 85–87, 5 L.Ed. 547, 568–69 (1821).

13. See, e.g., Arizona v. California, 292 U.S. 341, 345, 54 S.Ct. 735, 736–37, 78 L.Ed. 1298 (1934) (Congressional approval of Colorado River Compact subject to certain limitations and conditions, the approval to be effective upon the ratification of the compact, as so modified, by the legislature of California and at least five of the other six states).

14. Virginia v. Tennessee, 148 U.S. 503, 521, 13 S.Ct. 728, 735, 37 L.Ed. 537 (1893). Cf. De Veau v. Braisted, 363 U.S. 144, 154, 80 S.Ct. 1146, 1152, 4 L.Ed.2d 1109 (1960) (Opinion of Frankfurter, J., joined by Clark, Whittaker, & Stewart, JJ.), rehearing denied 364 U.S. 856, 81 S.Ct. 30, 5 L.Ed.2d 80 (1960) (Congress expressly gave its consent to implementing legislation not formally part of the compact; "This provision in the consent by Congress to a compact is so extraordinary as to be unique in the history of compacts."). See also, Act of June 6, 1934, 48 Stat. at Large 909 (1934) (Congress consents in advance to agreements for the control of crime).

15. E.g., Cuyler v. Adams, 449 U.S. 433, 441 & n. 9, 101 S.Ct. 703, 708 & n. 9, 66 L.Ed.2d 641 (1981) (Congress, by enacting the Crime Control Consent Act of 1934, gave consent in advance to the Interstate Agreement on Detainers, initially drafted by the Council of State Governments in 1956).

16. Virginia v. Tennessee, 148 U.S. 503, 521, 13 S.Ct. 728, 735, 37 L.Ed. 537 (1893).

17. 341 U.S. 22, 71 S.Ct. 557, 95 L.Ed. 713 (1951).

versy arose within that State as to West Virginia's responsibilities under the Compact. The state auditor, Sims, refused to allow payment from the state treasury of a sum of money that the state legislature appropriated as its contribution to the expenses of the commission set up under the Compact.

The West Virginia Supreme Court upheld *Sims* and found the state act approving West Virginia's adherence to the Compact was unconstitutional under that *state's* Constitution because it delegated the state's police power to the federal government and to other states, and because it bound future state legislatures to make appropriations. Justice Frankfurter, for the Court, ruled that, just as the Supreme Court has the power to settle disputes between states where there is no compact, "it must have the final power to pass upon the meaning and validity of compacts."[18] Having said all that, Frankfurter appeared to construe *not* the Compact but the state constitution. Frankfurter quickly conceded that the state supreme court is, for state purposes, the ultimate tribunal for construing its state constitution. But, "we are free to examine determinations of law by State courts in the limited field where a compact brings in issue the rights of other States and the United States."[19] Frankfurter stated that it "is one of the axioms of modern government" that a state may delegate to an administrative body the power to make rules and decide cases.[20] Then he concluded: "the obligation of the State under the Compact is

not in conflict with Art. X, § 4 of the State Constitution."[21]

Justice Reed separately concurred and argued that the "interpretation of the meaning of the compact controls over a state's application of its own law through the Supremacy Clause and not by any implied federal power to construe state law."[22]

Justice Jackson, also separately concurred and forcefully rejected Frankfurter's analysis. Jackson relied on a federal estoppel theory:

West Virginia, for internal affairs, is free to interpret her own Constitution as she will. But if the compact system is to have vitality and integrity, she may not raise an issue of *ultra vires*, decide it, and release herself from an interstate obligation. The legal consequences which flow from the formal participation in a compact consented to by Congress is a federal question for this Court.[23]

Both the Reed and the Jackson analysis review and interpret the interstate Compact rather than the state constitution. The preferred analysis is that an interstate Compact is sufficiently federal so that all questions interpreting the Compact may be decided ultimately by the Supreme Court as a matter of federal common law.

Using the Compact Clause to Create Federal Questions. Subsequent cases follow the Jackson–Reed analysis. *Cuyler v. Adams*[24] held explicitly that "the construction of an

---

18.   341 U.S. at 28, 71 S.Ct. at 560.

19.   341 U.S. at 28, 71 S.Ct. at 560. See also, Murdock v. Memphis, 87 U.S. (20 Wall.) 590, 22 L.Ed. 429 (1874).

Note that *Murdock* was not decided on constitutional grounds. "It seems entirely plausible that Congress intended by eliminating [a restrictive proviso in 1867] to open the whole case for review by the Supreme Court, if there is a federal question in the case sufficient to take the case to the Supreme Court." C. Wright, Law of Federal Courts 543 (3d ed. 1976). But, with very few exceptions, federal courts consider state courts to speak with final authority on questions of state law.

20.   341 U.S. at 30, 71 S.Ct. at 561–62.

21.   341 U.S. at 32, 71 S.Ct. at 562–63.

22.   341 U.S. at 33, 71 S.Ct. at 563. (Reed, J., concurring).

23.   341 U.S. at 35, 71 S.Ct. at 564. (Jackson, J., concurring). Justice Black concurred without opinion. 341 U.S. at 32, 71 S.Ct. at 563.

Estoppel Theory. States may not "consent to," or be estopped from objecting to, an expansion of federal authority beyond what is enumerated in the Constitution. Thus, a state's prior support of a federal statute, or the state's prior benefit from that statute, does not preclude it from arguing that the federal statute is invalid because it unconstitutionally expands federal power. That a party has sought legislation does not estop the party from challenging that legislation in subsequent litigation. New York v. United States, 505 U.S. 144, 144, 112 S.Ct. 2408, 2432, 120 L.Ed.2d 120 (1992). In this case, New York never joined a regional compact governing radioactive waste, and therefore successfully challenged the federal law that required it to take title to the waste if it did not join a compact.

24.   449 U.S. 433, 101 S.Ct. 703, 66 L.Ed.2d 641 (1981).

interstate agreement sanctioned by Congress under the Compact Clause presents a federal question" because "congressional consent transforms an interstate compact within this Clause into a law of the United States. . . ."[25] The Court held that the construction of an agreement sanctioned by Congress presented a federal question even though the agreement, under the compact clause, did not *require* congressional consent, because the agreement would have been an appropriate subject for congressional legislation. The congressional consent thus *federalized* the interpretation of the interstate agreement. "[W]here Congress has authorized the States to enter into a cooperative agreement, and where the subject matter of that agreement is an appropriate subject for congressional legislation, the consent of Congress transforms the States' agreement into federal law under the Compact Clause."[26]

Compacts and the Scope of Judicial Relief. Congressional approval of a compact makes the compact a law of the United States and, as such, the compact may limit the scope of judicial relief that is available to the states that choose to become parties to the compact. Although changed circumstances may make the compact seemingly unfair to one of the parties to the compact, "unless the compact to which Congress has consented is somehow unconstitutional, no court may order relief inconsistent with its expressed terms."[27]

§ 9.6   Interstate Comity

Various sections of the Constitution, particularly sections 1 and 2 of Article IV, serve to insure comity and courtesy among the states. The primary purpose of Article IV "to help fuse into one Nation a collection of independent, sovereign states."[1]

The Articles of Confederation and Comity. The Articles of Confederation specifically referred to this idea of courtesy:

> The better to secure and perpetuate mutual friendship and intercourse among the people of the different States of this Union, the free inhabitants of each of these States, paupers, vagabonds and fugitives from Justice excepted, shall be entitled to all privileges and immunities of free citizens in the several States; and the people of each State shall have free ingress and regress to and from any other State. . . .[2]

Full Faith and Credit. Section 1 of Article IV provides for "full faith and credit" in each state of the public acts, records, and judicial proceedings of every other state. This clause, which gives Congress the authority to legislate in order to promote comity,[3] is normally considered in texts on Conflicts of Law or Choice of Law and is not analyzed here.[4]

The Fugitive From Justice Clause. Clause 2 of Section 2 is called the interstate rendition clause or fugitive from justice clause and places a duty on states to surrender fugi-

---

25. 449 U.S. at 438, 101 S.Ct. at 707.

26. 449 U.S. at 441, 101 S.Ct. at 708 (footnote omitted). In *Cuyler* the Interstate Agreement on Detainers did not demand congressional consent but it was an appropriate subject for congressional legislation under the commerce clause (Art. I, § 8, cl. 3) and the extradition clause (Art. IV, § 2, cl. 2). 449 U.S. at 442 & n. 10, 101 S.Ct. at 708–09 & n. 10. New York v. Hill, 528 U.S. 110, 120 S.Ct. 659, 145 L.Ed.2d 560 (2000) (the Interstate Agreement on Detainers, a congressionally sanctioned compact, is within the Compact Clause and therefore it is a federal law subject to federal construction).

27. Texas v. New Mexico, 462 U.S. 554, 564, 103 S.Ct. 2558, 2565, 77 L.Ed.2d 1, 12 (1983). The Court refused to follow the recommendation of special master that a United States Commissioner be allowed to vote to break tie votes between two states in a two-party compact when the two states could not agree to terms for fulfilling the compact's purposes. Other compacts allowed federal representatives to vote on commissions created by the compacts, or provid-

ed for federal arbitration. The Pecos River Compact clearly lacked such features.

§ 9.6

1. Toomer v. Witsell, 334 U.S. 385, 395, 68 S.Ct. 1156, 1162, 92 L.Ed. 1460 (1948), rehearing denied 335 U.S. 837, 69 S.Ct. 12, 93 L.Ed. 389 (1948). See 2 Ronald D. Rotunda & John E. Nowak, Treatise on Constitutional Law: Substance and Procedure §§ 12.6–12.7 (West Group, 3d ed. 1999).

2. Articles of Confederation, art. IV, cl. 1. Clause 2 of the Article dealt with the rendition of fugitives from Justice and Clause 3 is the ancestor of the modern full faith and credit clause.

3. There has not been a great amount of federal statutory law in area. See, 28 U.S.C.A. §§ 1738–1742.

4. See generally, Eugene Scoles & Peter Hay, Conflict of Laws (1982); Hay, International Versus Interstate Conflicts Law in the United States, 35 Rabels Zeitschrift 429 (1971).

tives from justice to their sister states.[5] For over one and one-quarter of a century—until it was overruled in part in 1987—the leading case in this area was *Commonwealth of Kentucky v. Dennison.*[6] Kentucky brought an original suit against Dennison, the Governor of Ohio, seeking a writ of mandamus to require Dennison to turn over a criminal fugitive who had violated Kentucky's laws by helping a slave to escape.

Chief Justice Taney that held the Court had jurisdiction, and that the words "treason, felony, or other crime" should be interpreted to "embrace every act forbidden and made punishable by a law of the State."[7] However, said Taney, the congressional statute implementing this clause, as well as the clause itself, imposed only a moral duty on the state to turn over fugitives from Justice:

> [T]he words "it shall be the duty" were not used as mandatory and compulsory, but as declaratory of the moral duty which this compact created.... The act does not pro-

vide any means to compel the execution of this duty. [S]uch a power would place every State under the control and dominion of the General Government, even in the administration of its internal concerns and reserved rights.... Congress may authorize a particular State officer to perform a particular duty; but if he declines to do so, it does not follow that he may be coerced, or punished for his refusal.[8]

The Court then unanimously rejected Kentucky's motion for mandamus.[9] Once the governor of the asylum state exercises his "moral duty" or discretion and grants extradition based on the demanding state's judicial determination that probable cause exists, the judiciary of the asylum state may make no further judicial inquiry on that issue.[10]

Dennison was written when the Civil War was at hand and federal power was at a low ebb. Cases since then have asserted and exercised federal judicial power to enjoin unconstitutional state actors.[11] *Dennison* also rested on

---

5. Fugitive Slave Clause. Clause 3 of the Section governs fugitives from labor, i.e., runaway slaves. The Civil War Amendments abolishing slavery have made this section obsolete.

Justice Story explained that this fugitive slave clause "contemplates the existence of a positive, unqualified right on the part of the owner of the slave, which no state law or regulation can in any way qualify, regulate, control or restrain. The slave is not to be discharged from service or labor, in consequence of any state law or regulation." Prigg v. Pennsylvania, 41 U.S. (16 Pet.) 539, 612, 10 L.Ed. 1060 (1842).

Earlier, in his *Commentaries on the Constitution* Story referred to this clause and stated:

> "[I]t cannot escape the attention of every intelligent reader, that many sacrifices of opinion and feeling are to be found made by the Eastern and Middle states to the peculiar interests of the south. This forms no just subject of complaint; but it should for ever repress the delusive and mischievous notion, that the south has not at all times had it full share of benefits from the Union."

Joseph Story, Commentaries on the Constitution of the United States § 952 (Originally published, 1833; R. Rotunda & J. Nowak edition, Carolina Academic Press 1987).

The Fugitive Slave Clause and Dred Scott. The existence of the Fugitive Slave Clause reinforces Justice Curtis's powerful dissent in *Dred Scott v. Sandford*, 60 U.S. (19 How.) 393, 15 L.Ed. 691 (1856) by making clear that slavery was purely a product of local law. Without the Fugitive Slave Clause, an escaped slave would cease to be a slave as soon as he entered the borders of a state that did not expressly recognize slavery as a matter of state

law. The fact that the framers believed that the Constitution needed the Fugitive Slave Clause means that they thought that there could not be a taking of property or any other Constitutional problem with having the slave relationship end when the slave entered into a federal territory.

In other words, it was the Fugitive Slave Clause—and not the Due Process Clause or other Constitutional provision, as the majority in *Dred Scott* claimed—that guaranteed that runaway slaves who escaped into free states would remain slaves in spite of the state law of the free states forbidding slavery. See, Gary Lawson & Guy Seidman, the Constitution of Empire (Yale University Press 2004).

6. 65 U.S. (24 How.) 66, 16 L.Ed. 717 (1860), overruled in part Puerto Rico v. Branstad, 483 U.S. 219, 107 S.Ct. 2802, 97 L.Ed.2d 187 (1987). See Ronald D. Rotunda & John E. Nowak, Joseph Story: A Man for All Seasons, 1990 Journal of Supreme Court History: Yearbook of the Supreme Court Historical Society 17 (1990).

7. 65 U.S. (24 How.) at 99, 16 L.Ed. at 726.

8. 65 U.S. (24 How.) at 107–08, 16 L.Ed. at 729. See 18 U.S.C.A. § 1073 (when illegal to flee state to avoid prosecution) and 18 U.S.C.A. § 3182 (duty of Governor to deliver interstate fugitives from Justice).

9. 65 U.S. (24 How.) at 110, 16 L.Ed. at 730.

10. Michigan v. Doran, 439 U.S. 282, 99 S.Ct. 530, 58 L.Ed.2d 521 (1978); Pacileo v. Walker, 449 U.S. 86, 101 S.Ct. 308, 66 L.Ed.2d 304 (1980) (per curiam).

11. E.g., Ex parte Young, 209 U.S. 123, 155–56, 28 S.Ct. 441, 452, 52 L.Ed. 714 (1908).

the principle of dual sovereignty—that the states and the central government are coequal sovereigns—but courts have long rejected that principle.[12] Consequently, in 1987, the Court, in *Puerto Rico v. Branstad*[13] overruled this "moral duty" portion of *Dennison*. Branstad held that federal courts may judicially enforce the extradition clause and order a state Governor to deliver up fugitives from Justice.

Branstad agreed with that part of *Dennison* that had held that the extradition clause creates a "mandatory duty" to deliver up fugitives if there is a proper demand.[14] Extradition is a summary procedure, offering no discretion to the asylum state. Neither the courts nor executive officials of the asylum state may inquire whether the crime charged was sufficient to withstand a generalized motion to dismiss or a common law demurrer.[15]

Thus, there are only four issues left open in deciding whether the fugitive must be delivered:

(a) whether the extradition documents on their face are in order; (b) whether the petitioner has been charged with a crime in the demanding state; (c) whether the petitioner is the person named in the request for extra-

dition; and (d) whether the petitioner is a fugitive from Justice.[16]

Other issues are irrelevant. It is, for example, irrelevant that the crime charged by the demanding state is not a crime in the asylum state.[17] *Branstad* then overruled the second part of *Dennison*. Now, federal courts have the authority under the Constitution to compel performance of the asylum state's *ministerial* duty of delivery of the fugitive.[18]

Fugitive from Justice Clause Not Self-Executing. The interstate rendition or extradition clause of Article IV is not self-executing; Congress must enact a statute in order to establish a procedure under which that clause will operate.[19] Enacting such a statute was one of the first orders of business when the nation was young: in 1793 Congress first enacted such a statute.[20]

Extradition from Territories. While the extradition clause itself only refers to states,[21] the statute enforcing this clause refers specifically to "State or Territory."[22] The Court has upheld the applicability of the extradition *statute* to a territory like Puerto Rico,[23] but noted that it has not specifically ruled on the power

12. E.g., FERC v. Mississippi, 456 U.S. 742, 761, 102 S.Ct. 2126, 2138, 72 L.Ed.2d 532 (1982), rehearing denied 458 U.S. 1131, 103 S.Ct. 15, 73 L.Ed.2d 1401 (1982).

13. 483 U.S. 219, 107 S.Ct. 2802, 97 L.Ed.2d 187 (1987).

14. 483 U.S. at 226, 107 S.Ct. at 2807. See also, Michigan v. Doran, 439 U.S. 282, 286, 99 S.Ct. 530, 534, 58 L.Ed.2d 521 (1978).

15. California v. Superior Court of California, 482 U.S. 400, 107 S.Ct. 2433, 96 L.Ed.2d 332 (1987) (Louisiana statutes properly charged father and grandfather with kidnaping the father's two children; California could *not* refuse to extradite the father and grandfather on its determinations that the affidavit forming the basis for the indictment was fraudulent and that the California custody decree had established the father as the lawful custodian of the children).

16. Michigan v. Doran, 439 U.S. 282, 284, 99 S.Ct. 530, 535, 58 L.Ed.2d 521 (1978). See also, Appleyard v. Massachusetts, 203 U.S. 222, 227, 27 S.Ct. 122, 123, 51 L.Ed. 161 (1906); Biddinger v. Commissioner of Police of City of New York, 245 U.S. 128, 132–33, 38 S.Ct. 41, 42, 62 L.Ed. 193 (1917).

17. Kentucky v. Dennison, 65 U.S. (24 How.) 66, 16 L.Ed. 717 (1860), overruled on other grounds, California v. Superior Court of California, 482 U.S. 400, 107 S.Ct. 2433, 96 L.Ed.2d 332 (1987). See also, New Mexico v. Reed, 524

U.S. 151, 118 S.Ct. 1860, 141 L.Ed.2d 131 (1998) (per curiam) (provision in the New Mexico Constitution could not prevail over the state's duty under the Extradition Clause) *Reed* also held that the Supreme Court of New Mexico was in error in allowing the extradition hearing to consider issues that cannot be heard in the asylum state, such as whether Ohio intended to revoke the fugitive's parole without due process, or whether Ohio intended to cause him physical harm, or whether the fugitive was not really a fugitive because he allegedly fled under duress.

18. Puerto Rico v. Branstad, 483 U.S. 219, 107 S.Ct. 2802, 97 L.Ed.2d 187 (1987).

19. E.g., Hyatt v. People of State of New York ex rel. Corkran, 188 U.S. 691, 708–09, 23 S.Ct. 456, 458, 47 L.Ed. 657 (1903).

20. The Extradition Act of 1793, 1 Stat. 302 (1793). The present statute can be found at: 18 U.S.C.A. § 3182.

21. U.S. Const. art. IV, § 2, cl. 2 ("A Person charged in any State ... the State from which he fled ... to the State having jurisdiction....").

22. 18 U.S.C.A. § 3182.

23. People of State of New York ex rel. Kopel v. Bingham, 211 U.S. 468, 29 S.Ct. 190, 53 L.Ed. 286 (1909); Puerto Rico v. Branstad, 483 U.S. 219, 230 & n. 5, 107 S.Ct. 2802, 2809 & n. 5, 97 L.Ed.2d 187 (1987).

of Congress to enact such a statute.[24] However, one would think that Congress would be empowered to enact such a statute, pursuant to its broad authority to make "all needful Rules and Regulations respecting the Territory or other Property belonging to the United States...."[25]

The Privileges and Immunities Clause of Article IV. Another major clause of Article IV dealing with comity is section 2, clause 1, also known as the comity clause or the privileges and immunities clause of Article IV: "The Citizens of each State shall be entitled to all Privileges and Immunities of Citizens in the several States." The terms "citizen" and "resident" are "essentially interchangeable" for "most cases" under this clause.[26]

The comity clause protects only United States citizens. Corporations may not advance a privileges and immunities clause claim: although a corporation as a legal entity may be considered a person, it is not a citizen for purposes of this clause.[27]

This clause, for the same reason, does not extend to alien residents of the United States because they are not United States citizens. However, a lawfully resident alien may receive very similar protection against unjust residency requirements or citizenship requirements from the equal protection clause. Durational residency requirements may also be challenged as violating the right to travel under either due process or equal protection clause guarantees,[28] or, in some cases, as violating the commerce clause.

While the Article IV privileges and immunities clause is written in terms of state citizenship guarantees, it applies to the citizenship or residency restrictions set up by local governments as well as the state. The Court will evaluate a municipal ordinance that establishes a city citizenship or residence requirement in the same manner as a state law, even though the municipal ordinance has the effect of burdening in-state as well as out-of-state residents. Otherwise it would be too easy for a state government or its instrumentalities to escape the requirement of Article IV. Each city of a state could impose residency requirements, which would end out excluding all out-of-state residents but only a fraction of in-state residence. And, taken as a whole, the cities would be excluding all out-of-state residents and no in-state residences. Also, in-state residents have the option of seeking redress at the polls, while out-of-state residents have no input into the political processes of other states. Thus, if a municipal ordinance creates a city residency requirement for the exercise of basic rights, a nonresident of the state may attack the clause under Article IV.[29]

The Judicial Test. When a state law establishes a state citizenship or state residency classification, the Court uses a two-step methodology for determining the compatibility of the law with the privileges and immunities clause of Article IV. First, the Court determines whether the benefit or activity constitutes one of the "privileges and immunities" protected by the clause. Second, the Court will determine if there is a substantial state inter-

---

24. Justice Scalia emphasized this point in his brief separate opinion concurring in part and concurring in the judgment. 483 U.S. at 231, 107 S.Ct. at 2810. He did not refer to the Government's broad power under the property clause of Article IV.

25. U.S. Const. art. IV, § 3, cl. 2.

26. Hicklin v. Orbeck, 437 U.S. 518, 524 n. 8, 98 S.Ct. 2482, 2486 n. 8, 57 L.Ed.2d 397 (1978).

27. Blake v. McClung, 172 U.S. 239, 19 S.Ct. 165, 43 L.Ed. 432 (1898).

See also Hemphill v. Orloff, 277 U.S. 537, 48 S.Ct. 577, 72 L.Ed. 978 (1928) (state trust denied protection of clause due to similarity to corporate form of organization).

Residency or citizenship requirements that adversely affect competition from out-of-state business entities may still be challenged as violations of the commerce clause

and the Fourteenth Amendment. The commerce clause is of particular importance in limiting barriers to out-of-state economic competition.

28. See generally, Shapiro v. Thompson, 394 U.S. 618, 89 S.Ct. 1322, 22 L.Ed.2d 600 (1969); Zobel v. Williams, 457 U.S. 55, 102 S.Ct. 2309, 72 L.Ed.2d 672 (1982).

29. United Building and Construction Trades Council v. Mayor and Council of Camden, 465 U.S. 208, 104 S.Ct. 1020, 79 L.Ed.2d 249 (1984), where the Court cited *The Slaughter–House Cases*, 83 U.S. (16 Wall.) 36, 21 L.Ed. 394 (1872), for the proposition that in-state residents have no claim under the Privileges and Immunities Clause, but they at least have the opportunity to seek redress at the polls.

est in the differing treatment of nonresidents. Reciting this test is easier than applying it.

Not all forms of benefits or activities fall within the protection of the clause. The Supreme Court often quotes the early nineteenth century opinion of Justice Washington for the proposition that the clause protects only "those privileges and immunities which are, in their nature, fundamental; which belong, of right, to the citizens of all free government; and which have, at all times, been enjoyed by the citizens of the several states which compose this Union...."[30]

The modern Court's determination that a right is sufficiently "fundamental" to be protected by privileges and immunities clause of Article IV should not be confused with a determination of whether an activity constitutes a fundamental right so as to require strict judicial scrutiny under the due process and equal protection clauses. For example, the regulation of conditions of employment is not considered a limitation of a fundamental right for due process and equal protection analysis, but the ability to engage in a private sector activity or employment is a fundamental right protected by the privileges and immunities clause.

Article IV case law states that the Court determines whether the restriction of a certain type of activity has a "bearing upon the vitality of the nation as a single entity" in determining whether the activity is one of the privileges and immunities protected by the clause.[31] Because *private* sector employment, like many other forms of commercial activity, is essential to the economic vitality of the nation, it is a

fundamental right for Article IV analysis.[32] In contrast, the states may create residency or citizenship requirements in relation to recreational activities, such as recreational hunting or fishing, because those activities are not deemed sufficiently fundamental to be considered Article IV privileges or immunities.[33]

True welfare benefits—giving goods or services directly to a group of recipients who have no inherent constitutional claim to them—may be restricted to state or city residents; but the state may not impose a *durational* residency requirement, which requires persons to maintain residency for a certain period of time before receipt of any welfare benefits: that would be a violation of the right to travel.[34]

A city requirement that city employees must be residents of the city does not violate the right to travel or the equal protection clause.[35] And, when the state or city requires that a certain percentage of all jobs on construction projects funded in whole or in part by city funds be filled by bona fide city residents there is no dormant commerce clause violation because the state or city is acting as a market participant.[36] On the other hand, the Court will evaluate, under Article IV, a state or city effort to bias *private* employment decisions by pressuring or requiring city contractors to favor the employment of state or city residents when the private contractors engage in public works projects funded in whole or in part by the city or state.[37]

All rights directly protected by the Constitution, such as First Amendment rights, or other

30. The statement was made by Justice Washington in a case where he sitting as circuit Justice. Corfield v. Coryell, 6 F.Cas. 546, 551 (No. 3,230) (C.C.Pa.1823).

31. Baldwin v. Montana Fish and Game Commission, 436 U.S. 371, 383, 98 S.Ct. 1852, 1860, 56 L.Ed.2d 354, 365 (1978).

32. United Building and Construction Trades Council v. Mayor and Council of Camden, 465 U.S. 208, 104 S.Ct. 1020, 79 L.Ed.2d 249 (1984).

33. Baldwin v. Montana Fish and Game Commission, 436 U.S. 371, 98 S.Ct. 1852, 56 L.Ed.2d 354 (1978).

34. United Building and Construction Trades Council v. Mayor and Council of Camden, 465 U.S. 208, 104 S.Ct. 1020, 79 L.Ed.2d 249 (1984). Scheindlin, District Judge, citing Treatise, in Lai v. New York City Government, 991 F.Supp. 362 (S.D.N.Y.1998).

35. McCarthy v. Philadelphia Civil Service Commission, 424 U.S. 645, 96 S.Ct. 1154, 47 L.Ed.2d 366 (1976) (per curiam) rejected an equal protection challenge to municipal residency requirements for municipal workers.

36. White v. Massachusetts Council of Construction Employers, Inc., 460 U.S. 204, 103 S.Ct. 1042, 75 L.Ed.2d 1 (1983). rejected a dormant commerce clause challenge to a city requirement that 50% of all jobs on construction projects funded in whole or in part by city funds be filled by bona fide city residents, because the city was acting as a market participant.

37. United Building and Construction Trades Council v. Mayor and Council of Camden, 465 U.S. 208, 219, 104 S.Ct. 1020, 1028, 79 L.Ed.2d 249, 259 (1984).

constitutional rights that the Court has been found to be fundamental for the purposes of due process and equal protection analysis, constitute privileges and immunities of citizenship. Thus, state or municipal laws that make local residency a requirement for the exercise of such rights are subject to the restraints of Article IV.[38]

While the Court has made clear that these local residency requirements are subject to restraint, it has been less clear in explaining how to determine when the residency requirement is invalid under Article IV, even though this residency requirement does not violate the dormant commerce clause or other constitutional provision. In *United Building and Construction Trades Council v. Mayor and Council of Camden*[39] the Court adopted a two-step methodology to judge a state or local law that imposes a residency or citizenship classification in order to allocate construction jobs on city projects. The Court first must decide if the discrimination against out of state residents is on a "matter of fundamental concern." *Camden* quickly concluded that the ability to seek employment with private construction companies working on projects funded with state or city dollars meets that test. However, the fact that "Camden is merely setting conditions on its expenditures for goods and services in the marketplace does not preclude the possibility that those conditions violate the Privileges and Immunities Clause."[40]

Thus the Court turned to the second part of its test. The Court explained that state and local governments are not absolutely prohibited from using local citizenship or residency classifications. Nonresidents may be treated differently from local residents when they in fact are shown to cause a particular harm to state or local interest—"to 'constitute a peculiar source of the evil at which the state statute is aimed' ".[41] How does not determine if the nonresidents are "a peculiar source of the evil"? The Court remanded for further proceedings, so the standard of review is not clear. The Court did say that the state must demonstrate through the making of a factual record at the trial courts that there is a "substantial reason" for the difference in treatment between the local residents or citizen and nonresident.[42] In reviewing the state's attempt to justify the discrimination, the Court must continue to bear in mind the purpose of the Article IV privileges and immunities clause to insure harmony between the residents of various states and the vitality of the nation as a single Union.

Commercial Fishing and Hunting. The modern cases interpreting the privileges and immunity clause of Article IV fall into several main groups. The first group deals with commercial rights and is well illustrated by the leading case of *Toomer v. Witsell.*[43] Several South Carolina statutes regulated commercial shrimp fishing within three miles of the coast of that state. No federal regulations governed any of the shrimp fishing extending from North Carolina to Florida. The regulations of the various states involved often aimed against non-resident fishing "have now irritated retaliation to the point that the fishery is effectively partitioned at the state lines...."[44] One of the challenged South Carolina laws required payment of a license fee of $25 for each shrimp

---

38. See Doe v. Bolton, 410 U.S. 179, 93 S.Ct. 739, 35 L.Ed.2d 201 (1973), rehearing denied 410 U.S. 959, 93 S.Ct. 1410, 35 L.Ed.2d 694 (1973) (invalidating residency requirement for women who sought abortions under terms of state law). *Doe* did not strike the statute merely because there was a residency requirement that allocated the ability to engage in a fundamental right, which was declared to exist in the companion case of Roe v. Wade, 410 U.S. 113, 93 S.Ct. 705, 35 L.Ed.2d 147 (1973), rehearing denied 410 U.S. 959, 93 S.Ct. 1409, 35 L.Ed.2d 694 (1973). *Doe* also found that the privileges and immunities clause of Article IV protected persons from residency requirements that restricted availability of medical services within a state.

39. 465 U.S. 208, 104 S.Ct. 1020, 79 L.Ed.2d 249, 259 (1984).

40. 465 U.S. 208, 220, 104 S.Ct. 1020, 1028–29, 79 L.Ed.2d 249.

41. United Building and Construction Trades Council v. Mayor and Council of Camden, 465 U.S. 208, 222, 104 S.Ct. 1020, 1029, 79 L.Ed.2d 249 (1984).

42. United Building and Construction Trades Council v. Mayor and Council of Camden, 465 U.S. 208, 104 S.Ct. 1020, 79 L.Ed.2d 249 (1984).

43. 334 U.S. 385, 68 S.Ct. 1156, 92 L.Ed. 1460 (1948), rehearing denied 335 U.S. 837, 69 S.Ct. 12, 93 L.Ed. 389 (1948).

44. 334 U.S. at 388, 68 S.Ct. at 1158.

boat owned by a resident and $2500 for each boat owned by a non-resident. That law was successfully challenged under the privileges and immunities clause of Article IV.

Chief Justice Vinson in *Toomer* explained that the test to determine a violation of the Article IV privileges and immunities clause is whether there are valid reasons for a state to make distinctions based on one's state citizenship and whether the degree of discrimination bears a "close relation" to these reasons.[45] This clause outlaws "classifications based on the fact of non-citizenship unless there is something to indicate that non-citizens constitute a peculiar source of the evil at which the statute is aimed."[46]

Vinson then noted that the South Carolina statute frankly and plainly discriminates against non-residents, that it serves to virtually exclude non-residents from South Carolina fishing waters, and that, even though the South Carolina statute is written in terms of residence rather than citizenship, it is still within the privileges and immunities clause.

Next, Vinson rejected the state's arguments based on need to conserve natural resources by carefully and actively scrutinizing the means used to achieve such an objective.[47]

The State finally argued that an unexpressed exception to the privileges and immunities clause of Article IV are *ferae naturae*; in other words, the State argued, that it was the trustee for its citizens who owned in common all of the fish and game within the State. The

Court acknowledged the existence of several older cases that supported this theory in dictum,[48] but there was only one case that actually upheld a State discriminating against citizens of other States in the area of commercial fishing or hunting where there was no persuasive independent justification for the discrimination.[49] That case, *McCready v. Virginia*,[50] was decided in 1876. *McCready* had upheld a state law prohibiting all non-Virginia citizens from planting oysters in the tidal waters of a Virginia river. The Court argued that the right of Virginians in Virginia waters is a property right similar to the planting of corn on state-owned land.

Toomer noted two important differences between it and *McCready*. First, the fish in *McCready* would remain in that state until removed by man. The fish in *Toomer* migrated from the water of other states and were in South Carolina only temporarily. The *Toomer* fish were, so to speak, in the stream of interstate commerce. Secondly, the *McCready* decision involved regulation of fishing in the inland waters but the *Toomer* case dealt with fishing in the marginal sea.

The Court refused to extend *McCready* and it struck the *Toomer* statute under the privileges and immunity clause. Perhaps equally as significant, the Court's opinion casts significant doubts on the reasoning and conclusions of *McCready*.

The majority noted that the ownership theory is "now generally regarded as a fiction

---

45. 334 U.S. at 396, 68 S.Ct. at 1162.

46. 334 U.S. at 398, 68 S.Ct. at 1163.

47. 334 U.S. at 398–99, 68 S.Ct. at 1163–64.

48. 334 U.S. at 400 n. 33, 68 S.Ct. at 1164 n. 33, citing *Geer v. Connecticut*, 161 U.S. 519, 16 S.Ct. 600, 40 L.Ed. 793 (1896). *Geer* was later overruled in *Hughes v. Oklahoma*, 441 U.S. 322, 99 S.Ct. 1727, 60 L.Ed.2d 250 (1979).

49. *Toomer* distinguished *Patsone v. Pennsylvania*, 232 U.S. 138, 34 S.Ct. 281, 58 L.Ed. 539 (1914) on the grounds that the state statute forbidding non-resident aliens from killing game or possessing firearms useful for that purpose found sufficient support in the record before the Court that it could not say that the Pennsylvania legislature was not warranted in assuming that resident aliens were the peculiar source of the evil the state sought to prevent. The state statute was found not to violate the Fourteenth Amendment. *Patsone* is an old case and, in

spite of *Toomer's* effort to distinguish it, it may not be good law under *Toomer's* analysis of the Article IV privileges and immunities clause.

Toomer also distinguished *Haavik v. Alaska Packers' Ass'n*, 263 U.S. 510, 44 S.Ct. 177, 68 L.Ed. 414 (1924). In that case the issue was the validity, under a Congressional statute, of a $5 fishing licensing fee imposed on nonresidents but not on residents by an Alaskan statute. *Toomer* correctly noted that the issue was not the state's tax powers but Congress'. Congress' power to authorize the tax was reasonably exercised in light of the fact that the fee was a reasonable contribution toward the protection that the local government gave nonresidents.

Later, *Mullaney v. Anderson*, 342 U.S. 415, 72 S.Ct. 428, 96 L.Ed. 458 (1952) invalidated an Alaskan licensing differential of $50 on non-resident fishermen and $5 on resident fishermen in territorial waters.

50. 94 U.S. (4 Otto) 391, 24 L.Ed. 248 (1876).

expressive in legal shorthand of the importance to its people that a State have power to preserve and regulate the exploitation of an important natural resource."[51] It cited with approval a case decided "only fifteen years after the *McCready* decision"[52] and pointedly noted that in that case the conservation statute upheld did not discriminate in favor of any state's citizens.[53] In a footnote it explained that the origin of the legal fiction laid in a confusion between the Roman concept of *imperium*, or governmental power to regulate, and *dominium* or ownership, and that the state power over fish and game was in origin only *imperium*.[54]

Thus the concept of "governmental power to regulate," in reality, simply restates the issue rather than answers it: does the state's power to regulate fish and game wholly within the state ever allow it under the privileges and immunities clause of Article IV to discriminate in favor of local commercial interests? The *Toomer* majority never completely answered this question, for it did not reverse *McCready*, only narrowed its holding. Yet one would think that under the modern view of the privileges and immunities clause, the modern view of the interstate commerce clause, and simple economic analysis, the Court should hold that while a state may—in the absence of preemptive federal authority—conserve its natural resources or exploit them, it may fashion neither policy with a view of discriminating against out-of-state residents or citizens. That, in fact, is what the Court concluded in *Hughes v. Oklahoma*,[55] discussed below.

Douglas v. Seacoast Products, Inc.[56] portended *Hughes*, although it was actually decided on federal preemption grounds: the majority held that Virginia statutes denying federally licensed ships owned by nonresidents of Virgi-

nia from fishing in the Virginia portion of Chesapeake Bay and prohibiting such ships owned by non-United States citizens from catching fish anywhere in Virginia denied licensees their federally granted rights to engage in fishing activities on the same terms as state residents. In the course of the majority opinion, the Court specifically rejected the theory of state ownership of fish and wildlife:

> A State does not stand in the same position as the owner of a private game preserve and it is pure fantasy to talk of "owning" wild fish, birds or animals. Neither the States nor the Federal Government, any more than a hopeful fisherman or hunter, have title to these creatures until they are reduced to possession by skillful capture.... The "ownership" language of [the older] cases ... must be understood as no more than a 19th-century legal fiction.... Under modern analysis, the question is simply whether the State has exercised its police power in conformity with the federal laws and Constitution.[57]

Hicklin v. Orbeck[58] followed in applied this test to invalidate the Alaska Hire Act under the Article IV privileges and immunities clause. The Court was unanimous. This Alaska law gave employment preference to Alaska residents over nonresidents for all oil and gas leases and other such agreements to which the state was a party. Alaska justified its action on the grounds that the state *owned* the oil and gas, and the Alaska Hire Act sought to leverage the state's power over its oil and gas.

The Court noted, first, that prior cases have held that such state discrimination against nonresidents seeking to pursue a trade, occupation, or common calling within the state violates this clause. Second, even if a state

---

51. 334 U.S. at 402, 68 S.Ct. at 1165 (footnote omitted).

52. 334 U.S. at 402, 68 S.Ct. at 1165.

53. 334 U.S. at 402 n. 35, 68 S.Ct. at 1165 n. 35, citing Manchester v. Massachusetts, 139 U.S. 240, 265, 11 S.Ct. 559, 565, 35 L.Ed. 159 (1891).

54. 334 U.S. at 402 n. 37, 68 S.Ct. at 1165 n. 37. Frankfurter, J., concurring, and joined by Jackson, J., would have read the privileges and immunities clause more narrowly and would have based the *Toomer* result

discussed here on the commerce clause. 334 U.S. at 407, 68 S.Ct. at 1167.

55. 441 U.S. 322, 99 S.Ct. 1727, 60 L.Ed.2d 250 (1979), overruling, Geer v. Connecticut, 161 U.S. 519, 16 S.Ct. 600, 40 L.Ed. 793 (1896).

56. 431 U.S. 265, 97 S.Ct. 1740, 52 L.Ed.2d 304 (1977).

57. 431 U.S. 265 at 284–85, 97 S.Ct. 1740 at 1751–52, 52 L.Ed.2d 304.

58. 437 U.S. 518, 98 S.Ct. 2482, 57 L.Ed.2d 397 (1978).

could seek to alleviate its unemployment problem by requiring such hiring preferences, the state's law could not withstand scrutiny under this clause because it was not sufficiently tailored to aid its intended beneficiaries. Finally, and most importantly, while Alaska's actual ownership of the oil and gas resources are a factor to be considered in judging the law, that ownership was insufficient to justify the pervasive discrimination. The "extensive reach" of the state law covered and extended to employers who had not connection "whatsoever" with the state's oil and gas. The law covered not only contractors and subcontractors but also suppliers of subcontractors. It sought to reach supplies who had no direct dealings with the state's oil or gas and never even set foot on state land. The Court rejected Alaska's efforts to leverage is oil and gas ownership to impose an "economic ripple effect" on all those who dealt, even indirectly or tangentially, with Alaskan oil and gas.[59]

Hughes v. Oklahoma,[60] followed in the wake of *Hicklin*. *Hughes* bluntly recognized that the "ownership" of wild game was a fiction and should not be recognized as justifying discrimination against out of state residents whether the challenge is brought either under the privileges and immunities clause or the commerce clause.[61] *Hughes* simply invalidated a state law

forbidding the transporting natural minnows (not hatchery-bred) out of state for sale.

Recreational Sport. The privileges and immunities clause protects nonresidents of a state who engage in commerce involving, for example, wild animals (or fish); in contrast, that clause is virtually inapplicable to nonresidents who hunt wild animals as *recreational* sport. *Baldwin v. Montana Fish and Game Commission*[62] created this distinction. A six to three majority upheld a Montana hunting license system—under which nonresidents were charged 7½ times more than residents for a hunting license entitling one to hunt Elk and other game[63]—against challenges that the system violated the privileges and immunities clause of Article IV and the equal protection clause of the Fourteenth Amendment.

Justice Blackmun for the majority stated that, while the "contours" of the privileges and immunities clause of Article IV "are not well developed",[64] it was nevertheless the law that States must treat its citizens and nonresidents equally only "with respect to those 'privileges' and 'immunities' bearing upon the vitality of the Nation as a single entity."[65] He concluded that it would be improper to link the right to hunt for sport with such things as the right to travel, the right to vote, and the

---

59. "Alaska Hire extends to employers who have no connection whatsoever with the State's oil and gas, perform no work on state land, have no contractual relationship with the State, and receive no payment from the State. The Act goes so far as to reach suppliers who provide goods or services to subcontractors who, in turn, perform work for contractors despite the fact that none of these employers may themselves have direct dealings with the State's oil and gas or ever set foot on state land." 437 U.S. at 530, 98 S.Ct. at 2489–90 (footnote omitted).

However, the mayor of Boston may require that all construction projects funded in whole or in part by city funds or funds that the city had the authority to administer should be performed by a work force consisting of at least 50% bona fide Boston residents because the city was acting as a market participant and the reach of its did not have the same extensive ripple effect of Alaska's rule. White v. Massachusetts Council of Construction Employers, Inc., 460 U.S. 204, 103 S.Ct. 1042, 75 L.Ed.2d 1 (1983). The Court distinguished *Hicklin* because in *White*, while the mayor's order affects contracts between public employers and their employees, "the mayor's executive order covers a discrete, identifiable class of economic activity in which the city is a major participant. Everyone affected by the order is, in a substantial if informal sense,

'working for the city.'" 460 U.S. at 211, n. 7, 103 S.Ct. at 1046, n. 7.

60. 441 U.S. 322, 99 S.Ct. 1727, 60 L.Ed.2d 250 (1979), on remand to 595 P.2d 1349 (Okl.Cr.1979).

61. 441 U.S. at 333, 99 S.Ct. at 1735. See e.g., Note, Hughes v. Oklahoma and Baldwin v. Fish and Game Commission: The Commerce Clause and State Control of Natural Resources, 66 Va.L.Rev. 1145 (1980).

62. 436 U.S. 371, 98 S.Ct. 1852, 56 L.Ed.2d 354 (1978).

63. If a Montana resident bought the same type of license it would cost him $30 versus $225 for the nonresident. If the resident wanted to hunt only Elk, his license was $9, but the nonresident still had to purchase a combination license for $225. 436 U.S. at 373, 98 S.Ct. at 1855.

64. 436 U.S. at 380, 98 S.Ct. at 1858 (footnote omitted).

65. 436 U.S. at 383, 98 S.Ct. at 1860. See also 436 U.S. at 387, 98 S.Ct. at 1862:

"With respect to such basic and essential activities, interference with which would frustrate the purposes of the formation of the Union, the States must treat residents and nonresidents without unnecessary distinctions."

right to pursue a calling. He distinguished *Toomer v. Witsell*[66] and other such cases as involving "commercial" licensing, but Elk hunting "in Montana is a recreation and a sport."[67]

However, the Court did not consider the fact that, while Elk hunters may be involved in a sport, the people who support them (such as guides, hunting lodges, equipment rental stores, etc.) are involved in a livelihood. These support services are in businesses that affects interstate commerce. These businesses are disproportionately in-state enterprises. Thus, to the extent that state hunting regulations hurt these businesses, the state is really hurting its own residents (more than the out-of-state hunters), and these residents have input into the state's political process, and can change these regulations if they wish.

Private Employment on Public Works Projects. The two step methodology used in reviewing Article IV privileges and immunities clause claims is exemplified by the Court's decision in *United Building and Construction Trades Council v. Mayor and Council of Camden.*[68] In this case the Court held that a city ordinance requiring that at least forty percent of the employees of contractors and subcontractors working on city construction projects be city residents was subject to the restriction of the privileges and immunities clause. Justice Rehnquist, writing for eight members of the Court, found that employment on public works projects was "sufficiently fundamental to the promotion of interstate harmony so as to fall within the purview" of Article IV.

Justice Rehnquist distinguished private sector employment funded through governmental

contracts from full time employment in the public sector. Although the Court did not rule that the privileges and immunities clause was totally inapplicable to full time public employment, the Court's reference to other cases upholding restrictions on public employment against equal protection and commerce clause attacks indicates that the Court is unlikely to invalidate city or state residency requirements for public sector employment under the privileges and immunities clause.[69] In contrast, restrictions on private sector commercial activity, even though the activity is undertaken on the basis of state contracts, must be subject to judicial review under Article IV to avoid the undercutting of the harmonious economic relationships between states.

Once the Court found that private sector employment fell within the protection of the clause, *United Building and Construction Trades Council* then turned to the second step of privileges and immunities clause analysis. Do the nonresidents, against whom the restriction is aimed, "constitute a particular source" of the social or economic evils sought to be avoided by the state, and is there a "substantial reason" for the difference in treatment between residents and nonresidents? The lower courts never reached this second step. They had assumed that the restrictions would be immune from attack under the privileges and immunities clause because similar restrictions had been held valid under the dormant commerce clause.[70]

Justice Rehnquist, for the majority, admitted that the commerce clause did not restrain the state acting as a market participant when it spent its own money to employ people. However, he said that the values protected by the

---

66. 334 U.S. 385, 68 S.Ct. 1156, 92 L.Ed. 1460 (1948), rehearing denied 335 U.S. 837, 69 S.Ct. 12, 93 L.Ed. 389 (1948).

67. 436 U.S. at 388, 98 S.Ct. at 1862.

68. 465 U.S. 208, 104 S.Ct. 1020, 79 L.Ed.2d 249 (1984).

69. 465 U.S. at 219, 104 S.Ct. at 1028 (1984). See McCarthy v. Philadelphia Civil Service Commission, 424 U.S. 645, 96 S.Ct. 1154, 47 L.Ed.2d 366 (1976) (per curiam).

70. The Court had upheld a city requirement that a minimum percentage of employees of a private contractor working on city funded construction projects be residents

of the state when the restriction was only challenged as a violation of the commerce clause in White v. Massachusetts Council of Construction Employers, 460 U.S. 204, 103 S.Ct. 1042, 75 L.Ed.2d 1 (1983). In *United Building and Construction Trades Council*, the Court stated: "Our decision in *White* turned on a distinction between the city acting as market participant and the city acting as market regulator ... but the distinction between market participant and market regulator relied upon in *White* to dispose of the commerce clause challenges is not dispositive in this context. The two clauses have different aims and set different standards for state conduct."

privileges and immunities clause are different, and they required courts to examine the factual basis for discrimination against nonresidents in these settings. The Court said that it could not complete the second step of the analysis because there was an insufficient factual record to determine whether there was a substantial, legitimate reason for guaranteeing that a minimum percentage of persons (whom the private contractors employed on governmentally funded projects) were residents of the funding governmental unit. The Court said that the government's ability to use its funds to help a state's residents and its local economy might be an important or even determinative factor in ruling on the permissibility of the law, but there still must be an independent judicial review of the need for cities and states to use its spending power to protect its local residents.

United Building and Construction Trades Council then remanded the case to the lower court without clarifying the issue further. The case does not appear to require a lower court to determine whether a specific city or state must justify its employment restriction based of its particular economic or unemployment problems. Such an individualized, city-by-city, or state-by-state, ruling would lead to *ad hoc* decisions with no predictable results. *United Building and Construction Trades Council* suggests that the Court will wait for a case where there is a concrete factual record examining the need of cities and states generally to protect the employment positions of the in-

state residents; the Court then may decide whether, under what circumstances, if any, cities or states are free to use residency restrictions in their construction contracts to ease unemployment of local residents.

The two step methodology that *United Building and Construction Trades Council* may provide little clarity. However, though the Court has not issued an exhaustive list of the rights or activities that will be considered so fundamental to interstate harmony as to fall within the privileges and immunities clause, it would seem clear that the ability to engage in private sector commercial activity is one of them.[71]

Access to the Courts and other Fundamental Rights. The privileges and immunities clause of Article IV protects the right of nonresidents to have access to the courts in each state. This clause also protects all rights deemed to be "fundamental" because they are expressly protected by the United States Constitution or any of its Amendments. And the clause protects all rights held to be fundamental rights for the purposes of due process and equal protection analysis.[72]

State and local governments will not be able to use either citizenship or residency requirements in relation to these rights unless the nonresident or noncitizen population restricted in its ability to engage in such activities (or in the exercise of such rights) constitutes a particular source of social or economic harm to the state, and the state can demonstrate that

---

71. No Preference for In–State Creditors. Although corporations are not, as such, protected by the privileges and immunities clause, so that the state may condition the ability of a foreign corporation to enter its territory to do business, the state may not grant preferences to in-state creditors ahead of out-of-state creditors in the administration of property of an insolvent corporation. Blake v. McClung, 172 U.S. 239, 19 S.Ct. 165, 43 L.Ed. 432 (1898). See also Henry L. Doherty and Co. v. Goodman, 294 U.S. 623, 55 S.Ct. 553, 79 L.Ed. 1097 (1935).

State and Local Tax. The state may not use its tax system to restrict out-of-state citizens and residents from coming into the state to compete in private sector commercial activity.

72. Creditors must have reasonable access to state courts but resident and nonresident classes of plaintiffs or defendants may provide a basis for technical distinctions in jurisdiction in the ability to use the courts. See Canadi-

an Northern Railway Co. v. Eggen, 252 U.S. 553, 40 S.Ct. 402, 64 L.Ed. 713 (1920). See also, New York v. O'Neill, 359 U.S. 1, 79 S.Ct. 564, 3 L.Ed.2d 585 (1959), on remand to 112 So.2d 837 (Fla.1959); Douglas v. New York, New Haven and Hartford R.R., 279 U.S. 377, 49 S.Ct. 355, 73 L.Ed. 747 (1929); Chambers v. Baltimore and Ohio R.R., 207 U.S. 142, 28 S.Ct. 34, 52 L.Ed. 143 (1907); Chemung Canal Bank v. Lowery, 93 U.S. (3 Otto) 72, 23 L.Ed. 806 (1876).

Thus the Court has upheld a Minnesota statute that applied the statute of limitations of the state where the cause of action arose unless the plaintiff is a Minnesota citizen and owned the cause of action ever since it accrued. The Court emphasized that plaintiff had delayed in asserting the claim and would have been barred in his home state. Canadian Northern Railway Co. v. Eggen, 252 U.S. 553, 40 S.Ct. 402, 64 L.Ed. 713 (1920).

there is substantial reason (rather than merely an economic preference for state or city residents) that justifies the classification.

The Practice of Law. In order for the Court to determine whether states may limit the ability to be a member of the bar to the residents of the state, the Court does not merely rely on its general statements that an attorney allowed to practice in one state has no inherent right to practice in another state's bar without meeting its entrance qualifications.[73] Instead, the Court first determines whether the ability to be a lawyer is a type of public sector commercial activity protected by the privileges and immunities clause, and then determines whether the state has a substantial interest in restricting admission to its bar to persons who are residents of the state.

The Court engaged in this more careful analysis in *Supreme Court of New Hampshire v. Piper,*[74] which held that the State Supreme Court rule limiting bar admission to state residents violated the privileges and immunities clause. Kathryn Piper was a resident of Vermont, living about 400 yards from the New Hampshire border. She was not allowed to be admitted to the bar in New Hampshire because she was not a resident of that state. She was otherwise qualified. So she sued the State Supreme Court, its five Justices and its Clerk, alleging that State Supreme Court Rule 42, which excluded nonresidents from the bar, violated the privileges and immunities clause of Article IV. *Piper* began its analysis by reasoning that the privileges and immunities clause "was intended to create a national economic union," and that one of the privileges it protected was the privilege of a citizen of State A doing business in State B on terms of substantial equality with the citizens of State B. While the state could provide for residency requirements that relate to it as a separate political community (like "the right to vote and the right to hold elective office") a lawyer is not an "officer" of the State in any political sense. Thus the practice of law is a "privilege" that Article IV protects.

Then the Court turned to the question of whether the State could nonetheless justify the discrimination against nonresidents because (i) there is a substantial reason for the difference in treatment; and (ii) the discrimination practiced against nonresidents bears a substantial relationship to the State's objective; and (iii) this discrimination could not be met by less restrictive means. The State asserted that nonresident members of the bar would be less likely: "(i) to become, and remain, familiar with local rules and procedures; (ii) to behave ethically; (iii) to be available for court proceedings [sometimes on short notice]; and (iv) to do pro bono and other work in the State." The Court found that none of the reasons met the test of "substantiality" and that the means chosen did not bear the necessary relationship to the State's objectives.[75] Ms. Piper got her license.

---

73. The Supreme Court, in Leis v. Flynt, 439 U.S. 438, 99 S.Ct. 698, 58 L.Ed.2d 717 (1979) (per curiam), rehearing denied 441 U.S. 956, 99 S.Ct. 2185, 60 L.Ed.2d 1060 (1979), held that an out-of-state lawyer who wished to appear pro hac vice for a case in a state court did not have an interest in representing a client in that particular case that was protected by the due process clause of the Fourteenth Amendment, so that no hearing need be accorded the lawyer before he or she was denied the ability to participate as a lawyer in that case.

While some dicta in that majority per curiam opinion might be taken to indicate that the Court would not have been sympathetic to a claim that out-of-state attorneys had a right protected by the privileges and immunities clause to appear in courts of another state, see 439 U.S. at 442 n. 4, 99 S.Ct. at 700 n. 4, 58 L.Ed.2d at 722 n. 4 (1979), the case did not rule on a privileges and immunities clause claim to become a member of the state bar without establishing residency in the state.

74. 470 U.S. 274, 105 S.Ct. 1272, 84 L.Ed.2d 205 (1985).

75. Accord, Sargus v. West Virginia Board of Law Examiners, 170 W.Va. 453, 294 S.E.2d 440 (1982); Noll v. Alaska Bar Association, 649 P.2d 241 (Alaska 1982); Gordon v. Committee on Character and Fitness, 48 N.Y.2d 266, 422 N.Y.S.2d 641, 397 N.E.2d 1309 (1979); Matter of Jadd, 391 Mass. 227, 461 N.E.2d 760 (1984).

Comity based on nonconstitutional grounds. The Supreme Court has also relied on nonconstitutional grounds to enforce comity within the nation. For example, Barnard v. Thorstenn, 489 U.S. 546, 109 S.Ct. 1294, 103 L.Ed.2d 559 (1989) invalidated an attorney residency rule that the federal district court for the Virgin Islands had imposed; it required attorneys who sought admission to the bar to intend to continue to reside and practice in the Virgin Islands. The Supreme Court invalidated this residence requirement under a federal law that made the Article IV privileges and immunities clause applicable to the Virgin Islands. In Frazier v. Heebe, 482 U.S. 641, 107 S.Ct. 2607, 96 L.Ed.2d 557 (1987), on remand 825 F.2d 89 (5th Cir.1987), Court exercised its inherent supervisory powers over the federal courts to hold that a federal district court may not require an applicant for admission to reside or maintain an office in the state where that court sits. Compare, Supreme Court of Virginia v. Friedman, 487 U.S. 59, 108 S.Ct. 2260, 101 L.Ed.2d 56 (1988), invalidating, on constitutional grounds, a permanent resident requirement for those who seek to be admitted to the Virginia bar on motion.

Chapter 10

INDIVIDUAL LIBERTIES—AN OVERVIEW

§ 10.1 Guarantees in the Original Text (Body) of the Constitution

The text of the Constitution contains three specific guarantees of individual rights which are rarely the subject of intensive constitutional study or litigation. Although they are examined elsewhere in this treatise one should note at the outset not only that these guarantees exist but also that they may apply differently to different governmental entities.

Article I, section 10 of the Constitution specifically prohibits a state legislature from impairing the obligation of contracts.[1] The terms of this provision only apply to the actions of a state legislature. The due process clause of the Fifth Amendment, however, would also bar any federal legislation which retroactively impaired the obligations of contract in a similar manner.[2]

The ex post facto clauses effectively eliminate the ability of either the federal or state governments to punish persons for actions which were not illegal when performed.[3] The federal government cannot enact any ex post facto criminal law because of the specific prohibitions against such provisions in Article I, section 9, paragraph 3. A similar prohibition is applied to the states under Article I, section 10, paragraph 1.

Another prohibited form of retroactive legislation is a law that imposes punishment on specific individuals. Such a law is known as a bill of attainder. Whether or not a legislature enacts a bill of attainder on the basis of a person's prior acts or on the basis of his political beliefs, the measure still is a legislative punishment that denies that person recourse to the courts. Consequently, the Constitution abolished bills of attainder.[4] The federal government is prohibited from enacting such bills by Article I, section 9, paragraph 3. A similar prohibition applicable to state governments is contained in Article I, section 10, paragraph 1.

§ 10.2 The Bill of Rights Provisions and Their Incorporation in the Fourteenth Amendment

The first ten Amendments to the Constitution are often called the Bill of Rights. These Amendments were submitted to the States by the first Congress in response to expressions of concern for guarantees of individual liberty that had been raised during the debates on the ratification of the Constitution. The Ninth and Tenth Amendments, however, usually are not considered as specific guarantees of individual liberties.[1] Thus sometimes only the

§ 10.1

1. "No State shall ... pass any ... Law impairing the Obligation of Contracts ...." U.S.Const. art. I, § 10. See § 11.8, infra.

2. "No person shall be ... deprived of life, liberty, or property, without due process of law...." U.S.Const. amend. 5. See § 11.8, infra.

3. "No Bill of Attainder or ex post facto Law shall be passed." U.S.Const. art. I, § 9.

"No State shall ... pass any Bill of Attainder, ex post facto Law...." U.S.Const. art. I, § 10. See § 11.9, infra.

4. U.S.Const. art. I, § 9. See §11.9(c), infra.

§ 10.2

1. "The enumeration in the Constitution, of certain rights, shall not be construed to deny or disparage others retained by the people." U.S.Const. amend. 9.

"Powers not delegated to the United States by the Constitution, nor prohibited by it to the States, are

first eight Amendments are referred to as the Bill of Rights.

In an early decision the Supreme Court ruled that these ten Amendments to the Constitution were not applicable to the states.[2] This holding was correct historically because the drafters of the Bill of Rights designed the Amendments as a check on the new national government. This judicially perceived intent of the drafters, however, limited the ability of the courts to control the substance of state law under the federal constitution.

After the passage of the Fourteenth Amendment the argument was made that this Amendment, through both its privileges and immunities clause and its due process clause, made the guarantees of the first ten Amendments applicable to the states. The Supreme Court, however, continually rejected this theory of total incorporation of the Bill of Rights into the Fourteenth Amendment. The Court, instead, adopted a theory of selective incorporation.

Selective Incorporation. Under this concept only those provisions of the Bill of Rights that the Court considers fundamental to the American system of law are applied to the states through the due process clause of the Fourteenth Amendment.[3] Therefore, the states cannot violate the first ten Amendments directly. They are only capable of violating those Amendments insofar as those provisions are incorporated into the Fourteenth Amendment and applied to the states. Thus, if a state were to abridge the freedom of speech, it would be abridging the First Amendment as applied to it through the Fourteenth Amendment. It would be technically incorrect to refer to the state as violating the First Amendment without noting its application to the state through the Fourteenth Amendment.

Knowing which of the Bill of Rights the Supreme Court has applied to the state governments is important when determining what specific constitutional limitations may be placed on a state. Under their own terms the Ninth and Tenth Amendments seem inapplicable to the states.

Of the first eight Amendments the Supreme Court has held explicitly that only three of the individual guarantees are inapplicable to the states. The three unincorporated guarantees are: (1) the Second Amendment guarantee of the right to bear arms;[4] (2) the Fifth Amend-

---

reserved to the States respectively, or to the People." U.S.Const. amend. 10.

For an expression of the view that at least the Ninth Amendment recognizes the existence of additional individual rights see, Griswold v. Connecticut, 381 U.S. 479, 486–99, 85 S.Ct. 1678, 1682–90, 14 L.Ed.2d 510 (1965) (Goldberg, J. concurring joined by Warren, C. J. & Brennan, J.).

2. Barron v. Mayor and City Council of Baltimore, 32 U.S. (7 Pet.) 243, 8 L.Ed. 672 (1833).

3. The most recent standard for incorporation of a provision into the Fourteenth Amendment is developed in Duncan v. Louisiana, 391 U.S. 145, 88 S.Ct. 1444, 20 L.Ed.2d 491 (1968), rehearing denied 392 U.S. 947, 88 S.Ct. 2270, 20 L.Ed.2d 1412 (1968). For a further examination of this issue see §§ 11.5–11.7, infra.

See generally, Dennis, J., dissenting, citing earlier edition of Treatise in Freeman v. City of Dallas, 242 F.3d 642, 665 n. 5 (5th Cir.2001); Thrash, J., citing earlier edition of Treatise in ABATE of Ga., Inc. v. Georgia, 137 F.Supp.2d 1349, 1353 n. 1 (N.D.Ga.2001); Nordyke v. King, 319 F.3d 1185, (9th Cir.2003, citing an earlier edition of this Treatise). Thornburg, J., citing Treatise, in Ryder v. Freeman, 918 F.Supp. 157, 160 (W.D.N.C.1996); Weinstein, J., citing Treatise, in Hamilton v. Accu–Tek, American Arms, Inc., 935 F.Supp. 1307 (E.D.N.Y.1996). Kennard, J., quoting Treatise in, People v. Bland, 10 Cal.4th 991, 43 Cal.Rptr.2d 77, 86, 898 P.2d 391, 400

(1995). See generally, Glenn Harlan Reynolds, a Critical Guide to The Second Amendment, 62 Tennessee L. Rev. 461 (1995); Werdegar, J., dissenting and citing Treatise in People v. Monge, 16 Cal.4th 826, 66 Cal.Rptr.2d 853, 941 P.2d 1121, 1152 (1997).

The Incorporation Controversy

See generally, Fairman, Does the Fourteenth Amendment Incorporate the Bill of Rights, 2 Stan.L.Rev. 5 (1949); Crosskey, Charles Fairman, "Legislative History," and the Constitutional Limits on State Authority, 22 U.Chi.L.Rev. 1 (1954). For citations to additional secondary authorities, see R. Rotunda & J. Nowak, Treatise on Constitutional Law: Substance and Procedure, § 14.2 (3rd ed.1999).

4. United States v. Cruikshank, 92 U.S. (2 Otto) 542, 553, 23 L.Ed. 588 (1876).

The Second Amendment. The Second Amendment states: "A well regulated Militia, being necessary to the security of a free State, the right of the people to keep and bear Arms, shall not be infringed."

The Supreme Court has not determined, at least not with any clarity, whether the Amendment protects only a right of state governments against federal interference with state militia and police forces or a right of individuals against the federal and state government which would restrict the ability of any governmental unit to prohibit the private possession of certain types of firearms.

ment clause guaranteeing criminal prosecution only on a grand jury indictment;[5] and (3) the Seventh Amendment guarantee of a jury trial in a civil case.[6]

Two provisions of the Bill of Rights have not been the subject of litigation which would establish their application to the states. The Third Amendment, which prohibits the quar-

In United States v. Miller, 307 U.S. 174, 59 S.Ct. 816, 83 L.Ed. 1206 (1939), the Court held that Congress could prohibit interstate transportation of (or ownership following interstate transportation of) certain types of firearms ("sawed off" shotguns). In Lewis v. United States, 445 U.S. 55, 100 S.Ct. 915, 63 L.Ed.2d 198 (1980), the Court upheld federal prohibition of gun ownership by convicted felons when the firearm had at any time been the subject of interstate commerce. In neither case was the Court presented with a total prohibition of firearms' ownership. Yet it must be noted that the *Miller* Court did state that Congress could prohibit gun ownership in a way that did not impair the state's ability to have a militia. *Miller* was cited for this principle in *Lewis*, 445 U.S. at 65 n. 8, 100 S.Ct. at 921 n. 8. However, the Court in *Miller* did not state unequivocally that either Congress or the States could ban all firearm ownership; it is arguable that some private ownership of guns of the type suitable for use in the militia in the eighteenth century was intended to be protected for all citizens by the persons who drafted or ratified the Amendment.

The Court in Presser v. Illinois, 116 U.S. 252, 6 S.Ct. 580, 29 L.Ed. 615 (1886), refused to incorporate the Second Amendment into the Fourteenth Amendment; the result of this case is that the Second Amendment at this time does not apply to state governments. However, the Court in *Presser* was examining only a state regulation of the use of firearms in public in a way that involved marching or simulated military activities. It remains arguable that a total prohibition of gun ownership by a state or local government should be considered a violation of a right fundamental to the form of liberty protected by the Fourteenth Amendment.

For citations to additional cases and secondary authorities see the multivolume edition of this treatise, R. Rotunda & J. Nowak, Treatise on Constitutional Law: Substance and Procedure § 14.2 (3rd ed. 1999, with annual supplements).

5. "No person shall be held to answer for a capital, or otherwise infamous crime, unless on a presentment or indictment of a Grand Jury . . . ." U.S.Const. amend. 5. Hurtado v. California, 110 U.S. 516, 4 S.Ct. 292, 28 L.Ed. 232 (1884).

6. "In a Suit at common law . . . the right of trial by jury shall be preserved. . . ." U.S.Const. amend. 7. Minneapolis & St. Louis R. Co. v. Bombolis, 241 U.S. 211, 36 S.Ct. 595, 60 L.Ed. 961 (1916); Melancon v. McKeithen, 345 F.Supp. 1025 (E.D.La.1972), affirmed 409 U.S. 943, 93 S.Ct. 289, 34 L.Ed.2d 214 (1972); Bringe v. Collins, 274 Md. 338, 335 A.2d 670 (1975), application denied 421 U.S. 983, 95 S.Ct. 1986, 44 L.Ed.2d 475 (1975). Continental Title Co. v. District Court, 645 P.2d 1310, 1316 n. 7 (Colo.1982), citing earlier edition of this treatise.

tering of soldiers in private houses, has not been interpreted or applied by the Supreme Court.[7] The Court has not determined whether the "excessive fine" provision of the Eighth Amendment is applicable to the states. However, because the provision seems logically intertwined with the other provisions of that Amendment, it may already have been impliedly made applicable to the states.[8]

7. "No soldier shall, in time of peace be quartered in any house, without the consent of the Owner, nor in a time of war, but in a manner to be prescribed by law." U.S.Const. amend. 3.

The Third Amendment. The United States Court of Appeals for the Second Circuit has found that the Third Amendment is a fundamental aspect of the right of privacy that is to be protected by due process clause of the Fourteenth Amendment. The court made this ruling in a case in which it held that prison correction officers, who were displaced from their living quarters in rented staff housing at a prison during a prison guard strike so that state military and law enforcement officers could occupy those premises and operate the prison, stated a prima facie claim of a violation of the Third Amendment and civil rights statutes. Englblom v. Carey, 677 F.2d 957 (2d Cir.1982). Thereafter, the District Court held that, even if there was a violation of the Third Amendment rights of the prison guards, the governor and state officers who acted to remove the guards from their homes had a "good faith defense" under the civil rights acts; the United States Court of Appeals upheld the dismissal of the suit on that basis. Englblom v. Carey, 572 F.Supp. 44 (S.D.N.Y. 1983), affirmed 724 F.2d 28 (2d Cir.1983).

8. "Excessive bail shall not be required, nor excessive fines imposed, nor cruel and unusual punishments inflicted." U.S. Const. amend. VIII.

The technical application of the provision may never be known since the primary problem in this area relates to the imprisoning of indigents for the failure to pay fines, and the Court has analyzed this under the equal protection clause, see, Tate v. Short, 401 U.S. 395, 91 S.Ct. 668, 28 L.Ed.2d 130 (1971), on remand 471 S.W.2d 404 (Tex. Crim.App.1971).

The Cruel and Unusual Punishment Clause. The cruel and unusual punishment provision is applicable to the states, see Louisiana ex rel. Francis v. Resweber, 329 U.S. 459, 67 S.Ct. 374, 91 L.Ed. 422 (1947); Robinson v. California, 370 U.S. 660, 82 S.Ct. 1417, 8 L.Ed.2d 758 (1962).

For an examination of the principles of the cruel and unusual punishment clause, see W. LaFave and A. Scott, Criminal Law, § 2.14(f) (1986) and sources cited therein. The basic due process and cruel and unusual punishment restrictions on the procedures used to impose the death penalty are mentioned in § 13.3 of this treatise.

The cruel and unusual punishment clause limits the state's ability to impose noncapital, as well as capital, punishments. A noncapital punishment extremely out of proportion to the gravity of the offense and to the sentences imposed on other persons for similar offenses may

The Eighth Amendment's prohibition of the imposition of excessive bail presents a different problem. No specific case exists in which the Court has ruled that this provision is applicable to the states. In a number of state cases, however, the Court has assumed that the clause is applicable.[9] Consequently, the provision for all practical purposes should be treated as incorporated into the Fourteenth Amendment.

Another specialized problem relates to the just compensation clause of the Fifth Amendment. The wording of the Amendment specifically requires the government to give just compensation for property taken for public use.[10] The due process clause of the Fourteenth Amendment, however, fails to contain this specific language, though it does prohibit the state governments from taking property without due process of law.[11]

The Fifth Amendment guarantee of just compensation technically has not been incorporated into the Fourteenth Amendment. Nevertheless, the Court has held that the Fourteenth Amendment due process guarantee provides the same safeguard against a state's taking of property without just compensation.[12] Thus, the rules that govern when a government may take property for public use and when it must pay just compensation to

private individuals when exercising its regulatory or eminent domain powers are identical under the two clauses.

The Ninth Amendment has not been used by the Supreme Court to define a set of rights which are protected from government regulation and, therefore, it cannot be said with certainty whether the Amendment would be applied to the states.[13]

§ 10.3   The Privileges and/or Immunities Clauses

Two clauses of the Constitution guarantee certain privileges to citizens against infringement by the state government. Article IV, section 2 requires that the citizens of each state receive all the "privileges and immunities" of citizens of other states.[1] Section 1 of the Fourteenth Amendment prohibits the states from making laws which would abridge "the privileges or immunities of citizens of the United States."[2] Despite the essentially similar wording of the two provisions they have widely differing applications.

The Article IV Privileges and Immunities Clause. This Article IV provision often is referred to as the comity clause. It prohibits any distinctions in law between citizens of a state and citizens of other states if those

---

be held to be a cruel and unusual punishment and void under the Eighth Amendment. See, Solem v. Helm, 463 U.S. 277, 103 S.Ct. 3001, 77 L.Ed.2d 637 (1983). Any punishment imposed upon persons for their "status" rather than their "actions" should be invalid under the Eighth Amendment. Compare *Robinson v. California* (cited above in this footnote) (a state may not impose a penalty on a person for being a drug addict if the person does not use illegal drugs within the jurisdiction) with Powell v. Texas, 392 U.S. 514, 88 S.Ct. 2145, 20 L.Ed.2d 1254 (1968), rehearing denied 393 U.S. 898, 89 S.Ct. 65, 21 L.Ed.2d 185 (1968) (a person may be found guilty of intoxication in a public place even though he is a chronic alcoholic; the individual is punished for the act of becoming intoxicated rather than for the status of being an alcoholic).

9. See, e.g., Schilb v. Kuebel, 404 U.S. 357, 365, 92 S.Ct. 479, 484–85, 30 L.Ed.2d 502 (1971), rehearing denied 405 U.S. 948, 92 S.Ct. 930, 30 L.Ed.2d 818 (1972).

10. "[N]or shall private property be taken for public use, without just compensation." U.S.Const. amend. 5.

11. "[N]or shall any State deprive any person of life, liberty, or property, without due process of law...." U.S.Const. amend. 14, § 1.

12. Chicago B. & Q.R. Co. v. Chicago, 166 U.S. 226, 17 S.Ct. 581, 41 L.Ed. 979 (1897).

Today the Supreme Court itself cites the *Chicago B & Q* decision as incorporating the takings clause into the Fourteenth Amendment, even though that decision does not refer to an incorporation issue. See Webb's Fabulous Pharmacies, Inc. v. Beckwith, 449 U.S. 155, 159, 101 S.Ct. 446, 450, 66 L.Ed.2d 358 (1980), on remand 394 So.2d 1009 (Fla.1981). The Amendment also bars the state's taking of property for private rather than public uses. Missouri Pacific Ry. Co. v. State of Nebraska ex rel. Board of Transportation, 164 U.S. 403, 17 S.Ct. 130, 41 L.Ed. 489 (1896).

13. The Ninth Amendment has not been the basis for Supreme Court invalidation of a state or federal law but it has been mentioned in Supreme Court opinions as a possible basis for justifying judicial definition of "fundamental rights." Regarding this subject, see § 11.7, infra.

§ 10.3

1. "The Citizen of each State shall be entitled to all Privileges and Immunities of Citizens in the several States." U.S.Const. art. IV, § 2.

2. U.S.Const. amend. 14, § 1.

distinctions are unreasonable. The clause is a specialized type of equal protection provision which guarantees that all classifications which burden persons because they are not citizens of the state must reasonably relate to legitimate state or local purposes.[3]

The Fourteenth Amendment Privileges or Immunities Clause. The privileges or immunities clause of the Fourteenth Amendment protects very few rights. The Supreme Court held that this clause neither incorporated any of the Bill of Rights nor protected all rights of individual citizens.[4] The Court, instead, decided that the provision only protected those rights peculiar to being a citizen of the federal government; it does not protect those rights which relate only to state citizenship. Therefore, the clause only refers to uniquely federal rights such as the right to petition Congress, the right to vote in federal elections, the right to interstate travel or commerce, the right to enter federal lands, or the rights of a citizen while in the custody of federal officers.[5]

The rights protected by the privileges or immunities clause of the Fourteenth Amendment cannot be terminated by a state or local government. However, that clause only protects uniquely federal rights, such as those referred to in *The Slaughter-House Cases*.[6] One of those uniquely federal rights is the right of a citizen of the United States who establishes residency in a state to be treated in a similar manner to long-time residents of the state. In *Saenz v. Roe*[7], the Supreme Court held that the privileges or immunities clause protected "the right of the newly arrived citizen to the same privileges and immunities enjoyed by other citizens of the same State."[8] For that reason, the *Saenz* Court held that

California could not give reduced welfare benefits to a newly arrived person who was a bona fide citizen of the State of California during the first year in which the person resided in California.

A state or local law that restricts civil liberties of individuals, or a class of individuals, will, almost certainly, survive review under the privileges or immunities clause of the Fourteenth Amendment if that law would survive review under the due process and equal protection clauses. The Supreme Court has not invalidated any restriction of civil liberties under the privileges or immunities clause, except for the Court's ruling in the *Saenz* case. In one case during the 1930's the Supreme Court found that a classification related to economic activity violated the privileges or immunities clause,[9] but that case was reversed by the Court five years later.[10]

The privileges or immunities clause of the Fourteenth Amendment has an importance beyond its limited use by the Supreme Court to review state or local legislation. This clause, when combined with Section 5 of the Fourteenth Amendment, may give Congress significant powers to prevent private individuals or government actors from impairing the exercise of federal rights by other persons.[11]

§ 10.4　Constitutional Constraints on Individual Actions

Almost all of the constitutional protections of individual rights and liberties restrict only the actions of governmental entities. For example, the Bill of Rights acts as a check only on the actions of the federal government. Moreover, the provisions of the body of the Constitution that protect individual rights are

---

3. See § 9.6, supra.

4. Slaughter-House Cases, 83 U.S. (16 Wall.) 36, 21 L.Ed. 394 (1873).

5. 83 U.S. (16 Wall.) at 79–81.

6. 83 U.S. (16 Wall.) 36, 21 L.Ed. 394 (1873). See notes 4, 5, and accompanying text, supra.

7. 526 U.S. 489, 119 S.Ct. 1518, 143 L.Ed.2d 689 (1999).

8. 526 U.S. at 502, 119 S.Ct. at 1526. The *Saenz* case is examined in § 14.38 of this Treatise in connection with

the right to travel that has been defined by the Supreme Court.

9. Colgate v. Harvey, 296 U.S. 404, 56 S.Ct. 252, 80 L.Ed. 299 (1935), overruled in Madden v. Kentucky, 309 U.S. 83, 60 S.Ct. 406, 84 L.Ed. 590 (1940).

10. Id.

11. United States v. Classic, 313 U.S. 299, 61 S.Ct. 1031, 85 L.Ed. 1368 (1941), rehearing denied 314 U.S. 707, 62 S.Ct. 51, 86 L.Ed. 565 (1941). The scope of Congressional power to protect civil rights is examined in Chapter 15 of this Treatise.

limited expressly in their application to actions of either the federal or state governments.[1] Finally, the Amendments to the Constitution which protect individual liberties only have been applied to the actions of the state or federal governments. The Civil War Amendments—thirteen, fourteen, and fifteen—contain the most important applications and the only significant exception to this principle.

The Thirteenth Amendment. The Thirteenth Amendment prohibits slavery and involuntary servitude within the United States.[2] No governmental action is required to violate the Thirteenth Amendment's proscription of slavery. The prohibition applies whether a private person or a government entity is seeking to enslave an individual. Nevertheless, the judiciary has hesitated in finding any given practice (short of actual slavery or peonage) to violate this Amendment absent some congressional guidance.

The Fourteenth Amendment. The terms of the Fourteenth Amendment only restrict the freedom of states to make certain types of laws or take certain actions.[3] Thus, traditional doctrine suggests that private individuals cannot violate the Amendment.

When dealing with problems about application of the Fourteenth Amendment, a checklist approach will facilitate the determination of whether a state has transgressed the strictures of the Amendment. Any official act of the state such as legislation, executive orders, or court decrees will always comprise state action. However, when a plaintiff complains about the actions of a seemingly private individual, an issue will arise as to the presence of "state action" related to the specific harm. First, courts will look for some formal connection between the individual and the government. Government employees generally will be held to be acting for the government unless their actions are clearly outside of both their formal authority and the de facto authority that their official position grants them.[4]

Although more complex questions will be analyzed in the chapter discussing state action, as a general rule courts usually will find a connection between a state and an individual if the state has provided significant aid to the individual or if it is fair to treat the individual as a partner or joint venturer with the state.[5] Additionally, a person will be subject to constitutional restraints if he has been allowed to perform an essential "state function."[6] Of course, all lesser governmental units such as county, city, or other local governments are considered to be a part of the state.

The Bill of Rights and the Fifteenth Amendment. When analyzing problems involving the federal government under the Bill of Rights or the Fifteenth Amendment, the analysis is identical to that used to determine whether a state government has acted under the Fourteenth Amendment.[7] Thus, all offi-

---

§ 10.4

1. See U.S. Const. art. I, §§ 9, 10.

2. "Neither slavery nor involuntary servitude, except as a punishment for crime whereof the party shall have been duly convicted, shall exist in the United States...." U.S. Const. amend. 13, § 1.

3. "*No State* shall make or enforce any law which shall abridge the privileges or immunities of citizens of the United States; *nor shall any State* deprive any person of life, liberty, or property without due process of law...." U.S. Const. amend. 14, § 1 (emphasis added). See Chapter 12 on State Action.

4. Griffin v. Maryland, 378 U.S. 130, 84 S.Ct. 1770, 12 L.Ed.2d 754 (1964); see also, Lombard v. Louisiana, 373 U.S. 267, 83 S.Ct. 1122, 10 L.Ed.2d 338 (1963).

5. See, e.g., Evans v. Newton, 382 U.S. 296, 86 S.Ct. 486, 15 L.Ed.2d 373 (1966); Burton v. Wilmington Parking Authority, 365 U.S. 715, 81 S.Ct. 856, 6 L.Ed.2d 45 (1961).

6. See, e.g., Marsh v. Alabama, 326 U.S. 501, 66 S.Ct. 276, 90 L.Ed. 265 (1946); Terry v. Adams, 345 U.S. 461, 73 S.Ct. 809, 97 L.Ed. 1152 (1953), rehearing denied 345 U.S. 1003, 73 S.Ct. 1128, 97 L.Ed. 1408 (1953).

7. In Columbia Broadcasting System, Inc. v. Democratic National Committee, 412 U.S. 94, 93 S.Ct. 2080, 36 L.Ed.2d 772 (1973) the Court determined that a privately owned broadcast station was not subject to First Amendment restrictions on its actions, because the Court found that the licensing and regulation of the private broadcaster by the federal government did not imbue the private broadcaster with "state action."

A government owned television station is subject to First Amendment limitations. Thus, in Arkansas Educational Television Commission v. Forbes, 523 U.S. 666, 118 S.Ct. 1633, 140 L.Ed.2d 875 (1998) the Supreme Court accepted the rulings of lower courts that a state owned public television broadcasting television station was subject to First and Fourteenth Amendment limitations. Nevertheless, the Court, in *Arkansas Educational Television*, ruled that the government owned station did not violate

cial acts of the Congress, the executive (including agency regulations), and the federal judiciary constitute governmental action for the purpose of the Bill of Rights or the Fifteenth Amendment. Similarly, the courts may find that individuals are so involved with the federal government, either through administrative or financial contacts, that these constitutional provisions also will limit their actions.

§ 10.5 Which Individuals Are Protected by the Constitutional Guarantees?

It is important to know that the wording and interpretation of several constitutional provisions limit the application of their specific guarantees to certain types of persons or entities. For example, the term "citizen" in Article III, which established the federal judiciary, includes corporations.[1] Therefore, suits involving corporations involve "citizens" for federal jurisdictional purposes.

The term "citizen", however, does not include either corporations or aliens under other provisions of the Constitution such as the definition of "citizen" in the Fourteenth Amendment.[2] Neither corporations nor aliens receive

the protection of the privileges or immunities clause of the Fourteenth Amendment or the comity clause of Article IV, because those clauses protect only citizens.[3]

The term "person" also has been interpreted to give varying protection to corporations. Under the Fifth Amendment's prohibition of compulsory self-incrimination, "person" fails to include corporations or other business entities.[4] Aliens within the United States, however, receive protection from self-incrimination under this provision. Both aliens and corporations are considered to be "persons" for the purposes of the due process clauses of the Fifth and Fourteenth Amendments and the equal protection clause of the Fourteenth Amendment.[5] Similarly, aliens and corporations are included within the protection of the Fourth Amendment which guarantees the right of the people to be free from unwarranted searches and seizures.[6]

The equal protection clause of the Fourteenth Amendment only requires that a state not practice unjustified discrimination in law against persons "within the jurisdiction" of the state.[7] Nevertheless, even persons not

---

the First Amendment when it excluded a candidate from a televised debate.

§ 10.5

1. "The judicial Power of the United States shall extend to all Cases, in Law and Equity, arising under the Constitution, the Laws of the United States, and Treaties made, or which shall be made, under their authority; …—between Citizens of different States …." U.S. Const. art. III, § 2. Louisville, Cincinnati & Charleston R. Co. v. Letson, 43 U.S. (2 How.) 497, 11 L.Ed. 353 (1844).

2. "All persons born or naturalized in the United States and subject to the jurisdiction thereof are citizens of the United States and of the State wherein they reside." U.S. Const. amend. 14, § 1.

3. As to the Fourteenth Amendment the first sentence of section 1 defines citizens of the United States and state citizens.

As to the protection of the comity clause—the interstate privileges and immunities clause of Article IV—see Blake v. McClung, 172 U.S. 239, 19 S.Ct. 165, 43 L.Ed. 432 (1898).

Corporations and aliens will not receive the protection of other Amendments which protect the right of citizens, such as the Fifteenth Amendment. Asbury Hosp. v. Cass County, 326 U.S. 207, 66 S.Ct. 61, 90 L.Ed. 6 (1945).

Regarding the scope of the Article IV privileges and immunities clause, see § 9.6, supra. Regarding discrimination against aliens, see §§ 14.11–14.13, infra.

4. Hale v. Henkel, 201 U.S. 43, 26 S.Ct. 370, 50 L.Ed. 652 (1906); United States v. White, 322 U.S. 694, 64 S.Ct. 1248, 88 L.Ed. 1542 (1944); Bellis v. United States, 417 U.S. 85, 94 S.Ct. 2179, 40 L.Ed.2d 678 (1974); see also Couch v. United States, 409 U.S. 322, 93 S.Ct. 611, 34 L.Ed.2d 548 (1973).

5. Santa Clara County v. Southern Pacific R.R., 118 U.S. 394, 6 S.Ct. 1132, 30 L.Ed. 118 (1886), (corporations); Truax v. Raich, 239 U.S. 33, 36 S.Ct. 7, 60 L.Ed. 131 (1915) (aliens); Plyler v. Doe, 457 U.S. 202, 102 S.Ct. 2382, 72 L.Ed.2d 786 (1982), rehearing denied 458 U.S. 1131, 103 S.Ct. 14, 73 L.Ed.2d 1401 (1982) (illegally resident aliens).

6. "The right of the people to be secure in their persons, houses, papers, and effects, against unreasonable searches and seizures, shall not be violated…." U.S. Const. amend. 4.

Silverthorne Lumber Co. v. United States, 251 U.S. 385, 40 S.Ct. 182, 64 L.Ed. 319 (1920) (corporations); United States v. Wong Quong Wong, 94 Fed. 832 (D.Vt.1899) (aliens); United States v. Toscanino, 500 F.2d 267 (2d Cir.1974), rehearing denied 504 F.2d 1380 (2d Cir.1974), on remand 398 F.Supp. 916 (D.N.Y.1975) (aliens).

7. Persons who are not citizens receive the protection of all of the civil liberties guarantees of the Constitution, and its Amendments, except for the privileges and immunity clauses. Corporations (and other organizations or associations) are excluded from the protection of the privileges and immunities clauses; these nonhuman "persons"

physically present in the state are protected by the clause because the Supreme Court has interpreted the provision to guarantee equal treatment under the law to all people who are subject to the law of a state.[8] Thus, anyone who is directly affected by a state law may challenge the law on the basis of the equal protection guarantee of the Fourteenth Amendment even though he is not physically present in the state at the time of the suit.

§ 10.6   Procedural Due Process Versus Substantive Review

(a) Introduction—Overview

When the Court reviews a law to determine its procedural fairness, it reviews the system of decision-making to determine whether or not a government entity has taken an individual's life, liberty, or property without the fair procedure or "due process" required by the Fifth and Fourteenth Amendments.[1] This type of review is easily justified because it involves no more than a judicial assessment of a decision-making process that has determined that a specific individual should suffer some burden. It may involve the review of the general fairness of a procedure authorized by legislation or merely the review of the fairness of a decision in an individual case. In either instance, little theoretical complaint exists about a court's active role in reviewing the fairness of a governmental decision-making process as the judiciary seems uniquely suited for such a task.

Procedural Review. It is important to realize that procedural review is limited in scope. Procedural due process guarantees only that there is a fair decision-making process before the government takes some action directly impairing a person's life, liberty or property. This aspect of the due process clauses does not protect against the use of arbitrary rules of law which are the basis of those proceedings. It is only necessary that a fair decision-making process be used; the ultimate rule to be enforced need not be a fair or just one.

For example, if a state legislature enacted a law which imposed the death penalty upon any person who had been found guilty of double parking an automobile after a determination of guilt through trial by jury and appellate review, the law would clearly comport with the *procedural* restrictions of the due process clauses. The law might violate the Eighth Amendment, as applied to the states by the

---

receive some, but not all, of the civil liberties protections in the Constitution and its Amendments.

The implied equal protection guarantee of the Fifth Amendment due process clause might impose some restrictions on Congress' ability to exclude lawfully resident aliens from statutory benefits, although the Supreme Court has not given close scrutiny to citizenship classifications in federal statutes. See § 14.11–14.13 regarding judicial review of classifications based on alienage. Classifications that discriminate against corporations are normally subject only to a rationality test under the due process clause of the Fifth Amendment and the due process and equal protection clauses of the Fourteenth Amendment. See § 14.3 regarding standards of review under the equal protection guarantee.

8. See Kentucky Finance Corp. v. Paramount Auto Exchange, 262 U.S. 544, 43 S.Ct. 636, 67 L.Ed. 1112 (1923).

§ 10.6

1. "No person shall be … deprived of life, liberty, or property, without due process of law…." U.S. Const. amend. 5.

"[N]or shall any State deprive any person of life, liberty, or property, without due process of Law…." U.S. Const. amend. 14, § 1.

See generally; Gladstone v. Bartlesville Independent School Dist. No. 30, 66 P.3d 442, 2003 OK 30 (Okla.2003, citing an earlier edition of this Treatise); Jackson, J., citing Treatise in Harksen v. Garratt, 29 F.Supp.2d 272, 279, 280 (E.D.Va.1998); Jackson, J. citing Treatise in Hall v. United States, 30 F.Supp.2d 883, 897 (E.D.Va.1998); Gillman, J. citing Treatise in U.S. v. Brandon, 158 F.3d 947, 956 (6th Cir.1998); Boudin, J., citing Treatise in Hasenfus v. LaJeunesse, 175 F.3d 68, 71 (1st Cir.1999); Trimble, J., citing this section of the Treatise in Merit v. Lynn, 848 F.Supp. 1266, 1270 (W.D.La.1994) and Tran v. Caplinger, 847 F.Supp. 469, 476 (W.D.La.1993); Slater, J., citing Treatise in, People v. Gloria Marion, 275 Ill.App.3d 494, 212 Ill.Dec. 117, 118, 656 N.E.2d 440, 441 (3 Dist. 1995); Madsen, J., (dissenting) citing Treatise, in State v. Manussier, 129 Wn.2d 652, 921 P.2d 473, 494 (1996), certiorari denied 520 U.S. 1201, 117 S.Ct. 1563, 137 L.Ed.2d 709 (1997). Thornburg, J., citing Treatise, in Ryder v. Freeman, 918 F.Supp. 157, 160 (W.D.N.C.1996), appeal dismissed and cause remanded 112 F.3d 510 (4th Cir.1996); H. Franklin Waters, District Judge, citing Treatise in Holt Bonding Co., Inc. v. Nichols, 988 F.Supp. 1232 (W.D.Ark.1997); Criswell, J., citing Treatise in People in Interest of E.I.C., 958 P.2d 511 (Colo.Ct.App.1998).

fourteenth, in that it constituted cruel and unusual punishment. Indeed the law might also violate the substantive guarantee of the due process clause of the Fourteenth Amendment insofar as it was an irrational and arbitrary abuse of the government's power to protect against traffic hazards. However, so long as the decision-making process by which the burden of the death penalty was handed out was a fair one the law could not be stricken on the basis of "procedural" due process.

Substantive Review. This brings us to the ability of the judiciary to review the substance of legislation. By "substantive review" we mean the judicial determination of the compatibility of the substance of a law or governmental action with the Constitution. The Court is concerned with the constitutionality of the underlying rule rather than with the fairness of the process by which the government applies the rule to an individual. Every form of review other than that involving procedural due process is a form of substantive review. For example, if the Court were to strike a law restricting the freedom of the press because it violated the First Amendment, the case would involve a form of substantive review by the Court. The Court would have determined that the substance or rule of the legislation was incompatible with the language of the Amendment.

Substantive review under specific Amendments or provisions of the Constitution has not met with intense intellectual criticism. Because the Constitution gives an indication through specific language that certain types of legislation or executive action are beyond the power of government, the ability of the judiciary to overrule state or federal law on the basis of specific textual provisions has not been challenged widely in the past century. The Court's ability to determine the constitutionality of state or federal laws or executive actions under the due process and equal protection clauses, however, is subject to much greater criticism.

The next chapter will examine the development of judicial control over state and federal legislation under the due process and equal protection clauses. The reader, however,

should appreciate how the Court can overrule a piece of legislation because the Court disagrees with its substance under a portion of the Constitution which speaks only of a process (or procedure) being due an individual. The concept the Court employs to control the substance of legislation under the due process clause is that certain types of lawmaking go beyond any proper sphere of governmental activity. In short, the Court views the act as incompatible with our democratic system of government and individual liberty. The judicial premise for this position is that any life, liberty, or property limited by such a law is taken without due process because the Constitution never granted the government the ability to pass such a law.

If the Court assumes that the government does not possess the power to pass legislation establishing the maximum number of hours for workers then the Court can hold that any law which would limit those hours must have been passed by an unconstitutional process. The measure would be void under the due process clause because no piece of legislation could limit the ability of employers or employees to set the terms of employment in a manner compatible with the Constitution. The importance of such a ruling is that it eliminates entirely the ability of the state or federal government to deal with a given type of problem.

Because the other branches of government theoretically are responsive to the people, this particular form of substantive review constitutes a judicial rejection of a democratic society's attempt to deal with its social problems. Although the effect of a substantive due process decision is readily apparent, the basis on which a court justifiably can reach such a decision has been a source of continuing controversy.

The Supreme Court used the substantive due process test to control a wide variety of legislation during the period from 1885 to 1937. During this period a majority of the Justices concluded that interference with certain types of economic liberty was not a permissible end of government and that the Court was free to determine what types of legislation rationally promoted legitimate economic goals. This role gave the Court the power of a "super legislature." If the Justices disagreed with any law, they could declare the measure unconstitutional because it failed to comport with their sense of the legitimate economic role of American government.

After 1937, however, a dramatic shift took place in the Court's manner of reviewing legislation under the due process clauses. The Court realized that nothing either in the language of the Constitution or in the basic judicial function gave federal judges a claim to superiority in determining the rationality of economic legislation. The Court, therefore, abandoned the role of an independent reviewer of "economic and social welfare" legislation under the due process clause. The Court no longer would overturn legislation under the due process guarantees unless the law had no rational argument supporting it. If the law can arguably be said to rationally relate to a legitimate goal of government, the Court will uphold the law even though the Justices might disagree with the wisdom of its provisions.

The Supreme Court continues to make an independent determination of the legitimacy of laws that affect the "fundamental rights." If legislation limits a fundamental right—a specific type of civil liberty as defined by the Court [2]—the Court will more carefully scrutinize the underlying factual basis for the legislation. The Court raises the standard that legislation must meet under the due process guarantees if the law regulates or limits a

fundamental civil liberty. The Court has said that such laws must be necessary to promote a compelling interest. If the Justices are not satisfied that the law is tailored to promote an end of government which is clearly more important than the limitation of the fundamental liberty, they will find the law violative of the due process clause. Unfortunately, many of the Supreme Court decisions involving fundamental rights are unclear regarding the standard used to review restrictions on fundamental rights.[3]

(b) The Mixing of Procedural & Substantive Issues in Some Administrative Cases

The rational relationship standard, referred to in the previous subsection, is easy to apply in cases involving a challenge to a legislative rule that governs all persons and in which no discretion is given to an administrator or administrative agency to interpret the rule in individual cases. For example, assume a school board establishes a rule that every public high school teacher must complete one college level course each academic year in order to retain his or her job in the public high school. If a teacher who does not wish to take such a course in order to retain his job challenges the requirement, the judiciary should defer to the school board and uphold the regulation because it has an arguably rational relationship to a legitimate interest of the state.[4] A court should not substitute its judgment for that of the school board by independently determining whether a person is a better teacher if he takes a college level course each year. If

---

2. These rights include the following: (1) First Amendment rights; (2) the right to engage in interstate travel; (3) the right to vote; (4) the right to fair proceedings before a deprivation of personal liberty (although this is somewhat unclear); (5) the right to privacy which includes some rights to freedom of choice in sexual matters; (6) the right to freedom of choice in marriage. This list may not be exclusive; for a discussion of the problems in this area, see §§ 11.5–11.7, infra.

The Supreme Court has held that states may charge "filing fees" for court actions. Nevertheless, states must waive a filing fee requirement for an economically poor individual when the filing fee would prevent the individual from exercising a fundamental constitutional right. Thus, because of the "basic importance" of the fundamental rights regarding marriage and child rearing, the Court in Boddie v. Connecticut, 401 U.S. 371, 91 S.Ct. 780, 28

L.Ed.2d 113 (1971) required a waiver of fees for indigent persons who were seeking a divorce. In M.L.B. v. S.L.J., 519 U.S. 102, 117 S.Ct. 555, 136 L.Ed.2d 473 (1996) the Court required the waiver of a transcript fee, as a condition to appeal, for an indigent woman whose parental rights had been terminated by a trial court.

See §§ 13.9, 13.10 regarding procedural fairness and the determination of family relationships. See § 14.28 regarding marriage and family rights.

3. See §§ 11.4, 14.3 regarding due process and equal protection standards.

4. See § 10.6(a) for an overview of the distinction between procedural due process and substantive due process; see § 11.4 regarding the standards of review used by the Supreme Court in substantive due process cases.

a teacher was informed that he was being fired for failing to take the required college course and he asserts that he in fact had completed the course requirement, a procedural due process issue would be raised by the factual dispute. The school board might be required to give him a hearing to determine whether or not he in fact had taken the course which was the condition of retaining his employment.[5]

A more difficult problem is presented in substantive due process terms when a rule-making body (a legislature or an administrative entity with rule-making capacity) delegates to a government agent or agency the power to make individualized determinations regarding the treatment of individual persons. In these cases there is no "rule" for courts to test with a substantive due process standard, although a court may be asked to review an administrative agency's or agent's decision on a substantive basis. For example, a school board may establish a policy requiring the principal of a public high school to evaluate the teaching performance of untenured high school teachers and to refrain from renewing the contract of any teacher who is found to be an inadequate classroom teacher. A teacher whose contract is not renewed on this basis may have a right to a fair process to explore the reasons why the principal has determined that his or her contract should not be renewed.[6] There may be no procedural issue in the case, however, because the principal has given an adequate hearing to the teacher whom the principal has decided not to reemploy. A court may be asked to review the substance of the principal's decision. The teacher who alleges that the principal abused his discretion by finding that the teacher was an inadequate or poor teacher is asking the court to engage in a form of substantive due process analysis. In this situation, the rationality standard is difficult to apply because there is no clear rule to be tested, except for the legislative decision that principals should have the power to fire poor or inadequate

teachers. The principal's decision is difficult for the judiciary to evaluate. Judges should not feel free to substitute their judgment regarding the quality of teachers for that of an administrative agent or agency who has been delegated power in this area. On the other hand, the teacher should not be subjected to arbitrary and capricious decisionmaking. It may be that the rationality standard can be adapted to this situation by requiring that the court which reviews the principal's decision determine only that there are some facts that could support the principal's decision and that the decision is not totally arbitrary and capricious. So long as there is some factual basis for the exercise of the principal's professional judgment, the judiciary should not overturn that judgment.

In several cases the Supreme Court has found that an individual's liberty or property interests were adequately protected by requiring that some government agent exercise professional judgment in determining how to treat the individual. In these cases the Court found that judges should not substitute their judgment for the judgment of an agency or agent to whom authority had been delegated by the government. These cases represent an attempt to adjust the substantive due process rationality standard to the problem of reviewing discretionary administrative authority.

In *Regents of the University of Michigan v. Ewing*,[7] the Justices unanimously upheld the decision of medical school faculty and administrators to dismiss a student from a combined undergraduate degree and medical degree program. To qualify for the final two years of the program, the student was required to pass a standardized examination. The student in the case earned the lowest score on the examination that had been recorded in the history of the combined degree program. Even though all other persons who previously had failed this examination had been given a chance to retake the examination, this student was dis-

---

5. See Chapter 13 regarding procedural due process principles.

6. For an analysis of the rights of public employees to procedural fairness see §§ 13.5(d), 13.9(c).

7. 474 U.S. 214, 106 S.Ct. 507, 88 L.Ed.2d 523 (1985).

missed from the program without the opportunity to retake the examination. Justice Stevens, writing for a unanimous Court, found that there was no significant procedural issue in this case because the student's dismissal had been reviewed in accordance with established school policies. The issue in the case was substantive: whether the basis for the faculty decision was a violation of the due process clause. Justice Stevens stated: "When judges are asked to review the substance of a genuinely academic decision, such as this one, they should show great respect for the faculty's professional judgment. Plainly, they may not override it unless it is such a substantial departure from accepted academic norms as to demonstrate that the person or committee responsible did not actually exercise professional judgment."

Department of Housing and Urban Development v. Rucker[8] involved issues of statutory interpretation, as well as due process issues. In *Rucker*, the Justices unanimously interpreted a federal statute in a way that authorized local public housing authorities to terminate the lease of any tenant if the tenant, a member of the tenant's household, or any of the tenant's guests had engaged in certain drug related activity.[9] The United States Court of Appeals for the Ninth Circuit had interpreted the same statute to prohibit eviction of tenants who did not know, and could not have known, that a member of their household or guest had engaged in the drug related activity. The Court of Appeals based its interpretation of the statute, in part, on the belief that allowing the eviction of tenants based on activities of other

persons would raise substantial constitutional issues. The Justices of the United States Supreme Court reversed the Court of Appeals because, in the Justices' view, the federal statute was both unambiguous and presented no significant constitutional issues. If the tenant of public housing had an entitlement interest in the lease, the tenant would be entitled to notice and a fair procedure prior to being evicted.[10] Chief Justice Rehnquist, writing for the Court in *Rucker*, explained that the tenants in these cases were given adequate notice, and the opportunity to contest the factual basis for their eviction at fair proceedings.[11] Thus, the only question in *Rucker* was a substantive one: could the government terminate a person's lease in public housing based on activity of a member of the person's household or a guest of the person, even though the person being evicted never knew of the drug related activity? The Justices had little trouble in finding that the answer to that question was: yes. The Supreme Court upheld the federal statute. The condition placed on continued occupation of public housing was related to the government's interest in being the landlord of safe public housing facilities.[12] The government was not imposing criminal penalties on persons for associating with other persons who were engaged in drug related activity; there was no substantial claim that the eviction violated the Eighth Amendment excessive fines clause.[13] Because the government was not penalizing the ability of the tenant to associate with other persons, but only regulating the use of public housing property, the government's

---

8. 535 U.S. 125, 122 S.Ct. 1230, 152 L.Ed.2d 258 (2002), on remand 304 F.3d 904 (9th Cir.2002).

9. Justice Breyer did not participate in the *Rucker* decision; Chief Justice Rehnquist delivered the opinion for eight members of the Court. There were no concurring or dissenting opinions in *Rucker*.

10. See §§ 13.5, 13.8 regarding the requirement that fair procedures be afforded to an individual before a government benefit is taken away if that benefit constitutes an entitlement or property for due process purposes.

11. Department of Housing and Urban Development v. Rucker, 535 U.S. 125, 135–36, 122 S.Ct. 1230, 1236, 152 L.Ed.2d 258 (2002).

12. Department of Housing and Urban Development v. Rucker, 535 U.S. 125, 135, 122 S.Ct. 1230, 1236, 152

L.Ed.2d 258 (2002). on remand 304 F.3d 904 (9th Cir. 2002): "the government is not attempting to criminally punish or civilly regulate respondent's [the evicted tenants] as members of the general populace. It is instead acting as a landlord of property that it owns, invoking a clause in a lease to which respondents have agreed and which Congress has expressly required. Scales [Scales v. United States, 367 U.S. 203, 81 S.Ct. 1469, 6 L.Ed.2d 782 (1961)] and Danaher [Southwestern Telegraph and Telephone Co. v. Danaher, 238 U.S. 482, 35 S.Ct. 886, 59 L.Ed. 1419 (1915)] casts no constitutional doubt on such actions."

13. 535 U.S. at 136 n. 6, 122 S.Ct. at 1236 n. 6.

actions did not infringe upon the First Amendment right of freedom of association.[14]

In *Youngberg v. Romeo*,[15] the Supreme Court considered the constitutional standards that should govern the treatment of involuntarily committed mentally retarded persons. The Court found that the due process clause established the substantive requirements that the government must provide safe conditions of confinement and freedom from unnecessary bodily restraints for these persons. The majority opinion by Justice Powell recognized that the substantive guarantee of due process would require the minimal training related to safety and freedom from unnecessary restraints. The opinion did not resolve the question of whether there was any general "right to treatment" beyond that needed to insure the individual's safety in the institution. The majority opinion indicated that the only substantive right beyond safety and freedom from unnecessary restraint was the right to have appropriate professional employees of the government institution make a professional judgment regarding the type of treatment that should be given to the individual. The majority opinion stated that: "the minimally adequate training required by the Constitution is such training as may be reasonable in light of [the individual's] liberty interests in safety and freedom from unreasonable restraints. In determining what is 'reasonable'—in this and in any case presenting a claim for training by a State—we emphasize that courts must show deference to the judgment exercised by a qualified professional ... the decision, if made by a professional, is presumptively valid; liability may be imposed only when the decision by the

professional is such a substantial departure from accepted professional judgment, practice, or standards as to demonstrate that the person responsible actually did not base the decision on such a judgment." [16]

In *Washington v. Harper*,[17] the Supreme Court separated procedural and substantive issues regarding the authority of prison administrators to give antipsychotic drugs to an inmate against his will. Nevertheless, the Court ruling resulted in an administrative entity receiving power to determine the real meaning of the substantive rule that it was to employ in each case. The prison regulations at issue in *Harper* allowed a special panel (consisting of a psychiatrist, a psychologist, and a prison official, all of whom were not involved in the inmate's diagnosis or treatment) to order the giving of antipsychotic medicine to a prisoner against his will, if the panel determined that the inmate was dangerous to himself or others and that the treatment was in the inmate's best medical interest. The Court approved both that substantive standard that was to be used by the panel and the prison procedures, which provided the inmate with notice, a hearing, and the possibility for judicial review. The Supreme Court's ruling will allow the medical-prison panel to clarify and, in effect, create the substantive rule (regarding the type of inmate who is dangerous and who should be treated with the drugs) as they apply the standard in each case (by determining that the inmate does, or does not, meet the standard).[18]

14. Department of Housing and Urban Development v. Rucker, 535 U.S. 125, 136 n. 6, 122 S.Ct. 1230, 1236 n. 6, 152 L.Ed.2d 258 (2002): "Lyng v. Automobile Workers, 485 U.S. 360, 108 S.Ct. 1184, 99 L.Ed.2d 380 (1988), forecloses respondent's claim that the eviction of unknowing tenants violates the First Amendment guarantee of freedom of association."

15. 457 U.S. 307, 102 S.Ct. 2452, 73 L.Ed.2d 28 (1982).

16. 457 U.S. at 322–23, 102 S.Ct. at 2461–62, 73 L.Ed.2d at 41–42 (footnotes omitted). See also Parham v. J.R., 442 U.S. 584, 99 S.Ct. 2493, 61 L.Ed.2d 101 (1979) (voluntary commitment of a child to a state-operated mental health care institution by his parents does not violate due process; due process requires only that the child have a "neutral fact finder" determine if the statuto-

ry criteria for commitment are met in the individual child's case).

17. 494 U.S. 210, 110 S.Ct. 1028, 108 L.Ed.2d 178 (1990).

18. Due process principles would be violated by criminally prosecuting a defendant who is not mentally competent to stand trial. Drope v. Missouri, 420 U.S. 162, 95 S.Ct. 896, 43 L.Ed.2d 103 (1975). In Cooper v. Oklahoma, 517 U.S. 348, 116 S.Ct. 1373, 134 L.Ed.2d 498 (1996), the Court ruled that a state violated the due process clause by requiring the defendant to prove by clear and convincing evidence that he or she was incompetent to stand trial. If a trial court finds that a defendant is not mentally competent to stand trial, it may also find that the administration of antipsychotic drugs to the defendant would make him competent to participate in his defense and to have a fair

In *Sell v. United States*[19] the Supreme Court ruled that, under limited circumstances, a trial court can order that medication should be given to a person held on a criminal charge for the sole purpose of making the individual mentally competent to stand trial. It would be a violation of procedural due process principles to try a person who was mentally incompetent, and could not help with his defense, because such a trial proceeding would be inherently unfair.[20] However, a defendant could receive a fair trial if he was medicated so that he could participate in his defense. The Court had previously ruled that individuals could be made to receive medication against their will to prevent them from being harmful to themselves or others.[21] If a person was already being medicated because of dangerousness, the person almost certainly would be in a condition that would allow him to stand trial. Prior to the *Sell* decision lower courts did not have a clear constitutional guideline for determining when a person who was not dangerous to himself or others, but who was not mentally competent to stand trial, could be forced to take medication solely so that the person could be prosecuted for an alleged crime.[22] The Supreme Court, in *Sell*, set substantive limits defining the standard that was to be used for determining when an individual could be given medical treatment against his will for the purpose of being able to stand a trial. The majority opinion in *Sell*, written by Justice Breyer, ruled that a trial court could order an individual to be medicated involuntarily for the purpose of being competent to stand trial only if the Court made its order following an examination of four factors. In order to issue such a ruling

the trial court would have to find that: (1) an important government interest was at stake (so that persons could not be involuntarily medicated simply to stand trial for very minor crimes); (2) that the medication would significantly further the important state interests (meaning that the drugs would be likely to make the defendant competent to participate in a trial that would be fair); (3) that the medication was necessary to further the important government interests; and (4) that the administration of the medicine was medically appropriate (so that the patient's best medical interests were adequately considered by the trial court).[23]

The *Sell* decision established the substantive due process standard to be used when determining whether a defendant could be involuntarily medicated solely for the purpose of standing trial. In each case where the government sought to have a defendant medicated against his will, that individual would be entitled, under procedural due process principles, to a fair process to determine whether the substantive standards were met in his case.

The Court had to separate substantive and procedural issues in two cases involving state laws requiring the registration of persons who had been convicted of certain sexual offenses.

In *Smith v. Doe*[24] the Supreme Court found that the Alaska Sex Offender Registration Act, which required every convicted sex offender and every convicted child kidnapper to register with the state so that information regarding him could be disseminated on a state-wide basis, did not constitute a criminal punishment. For that reason, the Act could be ap-

---

trial. In Riggins v. Nevada, 504 U.S. 127, 112 S.Ct. 1810, 118 L.Ed.2d 479 (1992), on remand 109 Nev. 966, 860 P.2d 705 (1993) the Supreme Court found that the administration of antipsychotic drugs to a defendant under certain circumstances constituted a deprivation of liberty that was protected by due process. For citations to additional cases on this point, see the multivolume edition of this Treatise: R. Rotunda & J. Nowak, Treatise on Constitutional Law: Substance and Procedure (3rd ed. 1999, with annual supplement).

19. ___ U.S. ___, 123 S.Ct. 2174, 156 L.Ed.2d 197 (2003).

20. See § 13.9 (a). Drope v. Missouri, 420 U.S. 162, 95 S.Ct. 896, 43 L.Ed.2d 103 (1975). See note 35, supra.

21. Washington v. Harper, 494 U.S. 210, 110 S.Ct. 1028, 108 L.Ed.2d 178 (1990); Riggins v. Nevada, 504 U.S. 127, 112 S.Ct. 1810, 118 L.Ed.2d 479 (1992).

22. Id.

23. Sell v. United States, ___ U.S. ___, ___, 123 S.Ct. 2174, 2184–85, 156 L.Ed.2d 197 (2003). Three Justices dissented in *Sell* because they believed that there was no final judgment that was appealable in this case under Court rules and that allowing for appeals from such interlocutory orders would disrupt the criminal justice process. ___ U.S. at ___, 123 S.Ct. at 2187 (Scalia, J., joined by O'Connor and Thomas, JJ., dissenting).

24. 538 U.S. 84, 123 S.Ct. 1140, 155 L.Ed.2d 164 (2003).

plied to persons who have been convicted of sex or kidnaping offenses before the date at which the Sex Offender Registration Act became law without violating the ex-post facto clause.[25] The Sex Offender Registration Act, by its terms, was a statute that did not involve criminal punishment and appeared to be a civil regulatory law, even though the Act imposed a duty to register on the regulated persons. Applying principles established in previous cases, the Court held that this formally civil law would not be deemed to be a criminal punishment unless the person making that claim could demonstrate by clear proof that the law had a punitive purpose and effect.[26]

The majority opinion in *Smith* found that the Sex Offender Registration Act was civil in nature because there was clearly a rational relationship between the the statute and a legitimate regulatory and (the protection of members of the public through awareness of their proximity to persons who had been convicted of the sex offenses).[27] An ex post facto clause challenge to a law is substantive in nature, because the challenge to the law relates to the rule established by the law. Once the majority in *Smith* determined that the law had a rational connection to a non-punitive

purpose, the Court, in effect, had found that the law did not violate substantive due process. However, as a formal matter, the Justices did not consider substantive due process claims apart from the ex post facto clause challenge to the law in *Smith*.[28]

Procedural due process principles require the government to give an individual a fair process if the government is going to deprive the person of a life, liberty or property interest, and if the individual whose interests are at stake has a factual dispute with the government.[29] Although a state law might give an individual a right to some type of fair process or hearing, simply to complain about the effect of a law on the individual, the due process clause of the Fourteenth Amendment does not give an individual a right to a hearing if the person admits that the law applies to him. In other words, once an individual admits that a law applies to him, he has no basis for a procedural due process claim because any fair procedure would, by his own admission, result in a finding that the law applies to him. The individual in such circumstances may make a substantive claim against the law by challenging the rule of law created by the statute or regulation.[30]

25. The ex post facto clause contained in Article I, § 9 applies to actions of the federal government. The ex post facto clause of Article I, § 10 applies to state and local governments. See § 11.9(b) of this Treatise for further examination of cases interpreting the ex post facto clauses.

26. The Court in Smith v. Doe, 538 U.S. 84, ___, 123 S.Ct. 1140, 1149, 155 L.Ed.2d 164 (2003) found that a wide variety of factors are relevant to a determination as to whether a law that appears to be a civil regulation on its face should be deemed as a matter of law to constitute a criminal statute imposing a criminal punishment. The majority relied heavily on factors set out in Kennedy v. Mendoza–Martinez, 372 U.S. 144, 168–69, 83 S.Ct. 554, 567–68, 9 L.Ed.2d 644 (1963) United States v. Ward, 448 U.S. 242, 100 S.Ct. 2636, 65 L.Ed.2d 742 (1980); Kansas v. Hendricks, 521 U.S. 346, 117 S.Ct. 2072, 138 L.Ed.2d 501 (1997).

27. Smith v. Doe, 538 U.S. 84, ___, 123 S.Ct. 1140, 1152–53, 155 L.Ed.2d 164 (2003). Justice Thomas concurred in the opinion and the judgment of the Court; he wished to reemphasize his position that there should not be any possible implementation base challenge to laws under the ex post facto clauses. ___ U.S. at ___, 123 S.Ct. at 1154 (Thomas, J., concurring). Justice Souter concurred only in the judgment of the Court; he rejected the ex-post-facto clause challenge with a less complicated consideration of factors than was used by the majority. ___ U.S. at ___, 123 S.Ct. at 1154 (Souter, J., concurring in the

judgment). Justice Stevens dissented in this case because he believed that a law could not be applied retroactively; he concurred in the judgment in a companion case decided on the same day (and discussed in the next sentences in this Treatise) because he believed that such laws could be applied prospectively without violation of the due process clause. ___ U.S. at ___, 123 S.Ct. at 1156 (Stevens, J., dissenting in *Smith* and concurring in the judgment in *Connecticut Department of Public Safety v. Doe*). Justices Ginsburg and Breyer dissented because they believe that the Sex Offender Registration Act was criminal in nature; they would not require "the clearest proof" that the statute was effectively a criminal statute despite the civil regulatory language in the statute. ___ U.S. at ___, 123 S.Ct. at 1159 (Ginsburg, J., joined by Breyer, J., dissenting).

28. See § 11.4 regarding standards of review used by the judiciary to examine substantive due process claims.

29. See Chapter 13 regarding procedural due process analysis.

30. This point has been clear for over a quarter century. See Dixon v. Love, 431 U.S. 105, 97 S.Ct. 1723, 52 L.Ed.2d 172 (1977) (no right to a hearing concerning suspension of a driver's license when the suspension is based on violations of traffic laws that had been previously established in separate court proceedings). See § 13.8 of this Treatise.

In *Connecticut Department of Public Safety v. Doe*[31] the Justices unanimously found that an individual did not have a right to a hearing to establish that he was not a sexually dangerous person. In *Connecticut Department of Public Safety* the individual was subject to the terms of a state sex offender registry law, which involved the state government distributing information about the person, to the public, because of his conviction for a sex related offense. The individual admitted that he had been convicted of the type of sex related offense that triggered the application of the sex offender registry law to him. Nevertheless, he claimed that he should be given a hearing to show that he was not dangerous. His procedural due process claim failed because he was not contesting the factual basis for the application of the law to him. In other words, he was only arguing that the law would hurt his reputation. Because he admitted that he had been convicted of the offense that triggered the registry law regulation, the Justices were unanimous in rejecting his procedural due process challenge to the law's application to him.[32]

The individual in the *Connecticut Department of Public Safety* case had not raised any equal protection or substantive due process claims. In a concurring opinion in which they cited another edition of this Treatise, Justices Souter and Ginsburg explained that, even after this decision, the individual could litigate the question of whether the law limited his liberty interest, in violation of substantive due process principles, or whether the classifications in the law, violated equal protection.[33]

(c) Separating Procedural & Substantive Issues in Prisoners' Rights Cases

The Supreme Court also focused on the difference between procedural and substantive due process when it upheld a variety of regulations pertaining to the confinement of pretrial detainees and convicted inmates of a federal correctional facility in New York City. In *Bell v. Wolfish*[34] the Court found that procedural

31. 538 U.S. 1, 123 S.Ct. 1160, 155 L.Ed.2d 98 (2003).

32. Justice Scalia joined the Court's opinion but wrote separately to emphasize his view that the enactment of the statute provided all of the process that was due an individual under the due process clause in these circumstances. Connecticut Department of Public Safety v. Doe, 538 U.S. 1, 8, 123 S.Ct. 1160, 1165 (Scalia, J., concurring). Justice Stevens concurred in the judgment in this case in an opinion that also served as the dissent in *Smith v. Doe* case which was decided the same day and which is discussed in the previous sentences in this section of the Treatise. *Smith v. Doe*, 538 U.S., 84, ___, 123 S.Ct. 1140, 1156, 155 L.Ed.2d 164 (2003) (Stevens, J., dissenting in *Smith v. Doe* and concurring in *Connecticut Department of Public Safety v. Doe*).

33. Justices Souter and Ginsburg, who concurred in the opinion of the Court, wrote an opinion to emphasize their view that sex registration laws might be challenged under substantive due process and equal principles. 538 U.S. at 8, 123 S.Ct. at 1165 (Souter, J., joined by Ginsburg, J., concurring). They also noted that: "The line drawn by the legislature between offenders who are sensibly considered eligible to seek discretionary relief from the courts and those who are not is, like all legislative choices affecting individual rights, open to challenge under the Equal Protection Clause. See, e.g. 3 R. Rotunda & J. Nowak, Treatise on Constitutional Law § 13.6 (3rd ed. (1999))...." 538 U.S. at 10, 123 S.Ct. at 1166 (Souter, J., joined by Ginsburg, J., concurring).

34. 441 U.S. 520, 99 S.Ct. 1861, 60 L.Ed.2d 447 (1979). Although the Court found that procedural due process would require a determination of guilt before punishment, it did not rule on whether a governmental objective other than insuring a defendant's presence at trial would constitutionally justify pretrial detention. Bell v. Wolfish, 441 U.S. 520, 534 n. 15, 99 S.Ct. 1861, 1871 n. 15, 60 L.Ed.2d 447, 465 n. 15 (1979).

In Schall v. Martin, 467 U.S. 253, 104 S.Ct. 2403, 81 L.Ed.2d 207 (1984), the Court upheld a system of pretrial detention for juveniles accused of crime and awaiting family court adjudication. In this case, the Court relied heavily on the state's interest in protecting the child as well as the state's interest in preventing harm to society caused by further criminal activity by persons awaiting trial. Thus, it is difficult to determine whether the case constitutes an endorsement of preventive detention prior to trial for adult offenders where the only state interest justifying detention is that of preventing additional criminal activity by the person arrested.

In Reno v. Flores, 507 U.S. 292, 113 S.Ct. 1439, 123 L.Ed.2d 1 (1993), on remand 992 F.2d 243 (9th Cir.1993) the Supreme Court upheld Justice Department regulations that required the detention of noncitizen juveniles who were being held for deportation proceedings if no parent, legal guardian, or relative was available to care for the children. These children were placed in facilities that were required to meet certain federal standards. The children would only be released into the custody of someone other than a guardian or close relative in exceptional circumstances. The Court found that the detention policy did not violate substantive due process rights because a child who was properly brought under the guardianship and custody of the state, even temporarily, did not have a fundamental right in being free from all forms of custody or being cared for in a noncustodial setting. In making this finding the Court in *Flores* relied on the statement in *Schall* that "juveniles, unlike adults, are always in some form of custody." Reno v. Flores, 507 U.S. 292, 301, 113 S.Ct.

due process would require fair procedures for determining guilt before someone could be punished, but that there was no general substantive due process right to have the government create the best possible conditions for the holding of persons awaiting trial.

The conditions at the facility in *Bell v. Wolfish* were challenged by persons who were being detained solely because they could not post bail and there were no less drastic means for insuring their presence at trial. The lower federal courts had overturned several practices of the federal facility including the assignment of two persons to rooms originally intended for single occupancy, the prohibition against receiving packages of food and personal items from outside the institution, the use of body cavity searches following contact visits, and the requirement that the pretrial detainees remain outside their rooms during routine searches or "shake-downs." The lower federal courts believed that they had a power to inquire into jail conditions because of a procedural due process right to fair treatment; the Supreme Court recognized that this case actually involved a substantive due process challenge to the government regulations.

The majority opinion, by Justice Rehnquist, determined that the correct standard was a determination of whether or not the specific condition could be considered "punishment of the detainee." [35] The Court thus found a distinction between measures which constituted punishment of the detainee and which therefore could not be imposed prior to a proper determination of guilt and reasonable regulatory restraints which could be imposed. Justice Rehnquist also stated that great deference should be paid to the decisions of prison officials because of their greater expertise in the assessment of interests in security and prison discipline. Federal courts were not entitled to inquire generally into whether or not government prison regulations are the least burdensome, or best, alternative for regulating the freedom of the detainees or prisoners. [36]

Based upon the approach for review of prison conditions set forth in *Bell v. Wolfish,* the Court later found that pretrial detainees did not have a constitutionally guaranteed right to "contact visits" (in which they could have physical contact with family members and friends who visited them) nor a right to observe "shake-down searches" of their cells by prison officials. Because there was no proof that the regulations prohibiting contact visits or allowing shake-down searches were enacted for punitive purposes, the Court said that the regulations should be upheld as long as they were reasonably related to a legitimate goal in the operation of the prison. Because of the deference to be accorded to prison administrators, the Court found that the lower courts had erred in overturning the prison administrators' decision that contact visits would jeopardize jail security absent an impractical set of administrative safeguards. The Court also held that shakedown searches outside the presence of the detainee were reasonably related to prison security concerns. [37]

When an inmate at a penal facility claims that he has been subjected to a special type of punishment, or unfavorable conditions to which other inmates have not been subjected, he raises a procedural due process issue in terms of the fairness of the administrative procedures by which he was selected for such

1439, 1447, 123 L.Ed.2d 1 (1993) on remand 992 F.2d 243 (9th Cir.1993), quoting Schall v. Martin, 467 U.S. 253, 265, 104 S.Ct. 2403, 2410, 81 L.Ed.2d 207 (1984). The *Flores* decision is examined in § 10.6 (e).

35. 441 U.S. at 535, 99 S.Ct. at 1872.

36. The Supreme Court, in *Bell v. Wolfish,* also upheld a restriction on prisoners, including detainees, that prohibited the receipt of hardbound books by detainees unless they came from a publisher or bookstore. The majority opinion noted that convicted prisoners do not forfeit all of their constitutional rights and that they retain some right to speech, religion, equal protection, and due process. However, the interest in prison discipline allowed for reasonable limitations on those rights, so long as the limitations were related to preserving internal order and discipline at the facility. The fact that prison officials could make a reasonable argument that items could be hidden in the hardbound book, and the difficulty of detecting those items justified the rule. Thus, the Court also approved the use of body cavity searches and shakedowns of inmate living areas outside of the presence of the detainee as reasonable under the circumstances; the majority opinion explicitly employed a balancing test to measure the privacy interest of the detainees against the interests in prison discipline.

37. Block v. Rutherford, 468 U.S. 576, 104 S.Ct. 3227, 82 L.Ed.2d 438 (1984).

punishment.[38] When the prisoner claims that the general conditions in the prison fall below constitutionally acceptable standards of decency, he is raising a substantive issue that can best be analyzed in terms of whether the prison conditions violate the principles of the cruel and unusual punishment clause, although the claim could also be categorized as a substantive due process issue. The Supreme Court has ruled that there is no simple test for determining when prison conditions fall below societal standards of decency from which the cruel and unusual punishment clause draws its meaning and which would also be relevant to reviewing substantive due process claims.[39]

In *Rhodes v. Chapman* [40] the Court held that the celling of two inmates in cells originally designed to house only one did not constitute cruel and unusual punishment because there was no evidence that the double celling of inmates in the particular prison examined by the Court inflicted "unnecessary or wanton pain or is grossly disproportionate to the severity of crimes warranting imprisonment." [41]

However, the Court indicated that federal judges are to "scrutinize claims of cruel and unusual confinement" in order to determine if conditions of confinement in other prisons amounted to cruel and unusual punishment. On the other hand, the majority also indicated that "courts cannot assume that state legislatures and prison officials are insensitive to the requirements of the Constitution or to the perplexing sociological problems of how best to achieve the goals of the penal function in the criminal justice system." [42]

In *Hudson v. Palmer* [43] the Supreme Court held that prisoners did not have a reasonable expectation of privacy in their prison cells so that the Fourth Amendment restriction on unreasonable searches and seizures would have no application to shakedowns or other searches of prisoner cells.[44] In so holding, the majority opinion by Chief Justice Burger noted that the ruling did not leave prisoners totally unprotected from searches which were only calculated harassment and totally unrelated to

38. §§ 13.4(b), 13.9(a), infra.

39. Compare Rhodes v. Chapman, 452 U.S. 337, 101 S.Ct. 2392, 69 L.Ed.2d 59 (1981) (finding that the housing of two inmates in a cell designed for a single inmate does not violate the cruel and unusual punishment clause) with Estelle v. Gamble, 429 U.S. 97, 97 S.Ct. 285, 50 L.Ed.2d 251 (1976), rehearing denied 429 U.S. 1066, 97 S.Ct. 798, 50 L.Ed.2d 785 (1977), (failure of prison authorities to provide for prison inmate's medical needs constitutes cruel and unusual punishment). Prison authorities (including guards) may be held liable for punitive as well as actual damages when a prisoner under their control has his Eighth Amendment rights violated. The prisoner must establish that the guard or prison official was reckless or acted in careless disregard or indifference to the inmate's safety. See, e.g., Smith v. Wade, 461 U.S. 30, 103 S.Ct. 1625, 75 L.Ed.2d 632 (1983). Thus a prisoner who is subjected to cruel and unusual punishment in violation of the Eighth Amendment may be able to bring a civil damage action against prison authorities under 42 U.S.C.A. § 1983. See also West v. Atkins, 487 U.S. 42, 108 S.Ct. 2250, 101 L.Ed.2d 40 (1988) (physician who was under contract with the government to provide medical services to prisoners at a state prison hospital on a part-time basis acted under color of law within the meaning of civil rights statute 42 U.S.C.A. § 1983 when he gave medical treatment to the prisoners). For citations to additional Supreme Court cases on this point, see R. Rotunda & J. Nowak, Treatise on Constitutional Law: Substance and Procedure, § 14.6 (3rd ed. 1999, with annual supplements).

40. 452 U.S. 337, 101 S.Ct. 2392, 69 L.Ed.2d 59 (1981).

41. 452 U.S. at 348, 101 S.Ct. at 2400.

42. 452 U.S. at 352, 101 S.Ct. at 2402. Justices who concurred in the judgment indicated even more willingness than the majority to examine the details of prison conditions to determine whether they violated our society's standards of human dignity. See Rhodes v. Chapman, 452 U.S. 337, 352, 101 S.Ct. 2392, 2402, 69 L.Ed.2d 59 (1981) (Brennan, J., joined by Blackmun and Stevens, J.J., concurring in the judgment); 452 U.S. at 368, 101 S.Ct. at 2410 (Blackmun, J., concurring in the judgment). Justice Marshall challenged the findings of both the majority and concurring Justices that the double-celling of inmates in the Ohio prison examined in the *Rhodes* litigation did not adversely affect the prisoners in a way which violated basic concepts of human dignity in our society. Rhodes v. Chapman, 452 U.S. 337, 369, 101 S.Ct. 2392, 2411, 69 L.Ed.2d 59 (1981) (Marshall, J., dissenting).

43. 468 U.S. 517, 104 S.Ct. 3194, 82 L.Ed.2d 393 (1984), on remand 744 F.2d 22 (4th Cir.1984).

44. The Court's decision regarding the applicability of the Fourth Amendment to prison cells and the possessions of prison inmates is substantive in nature and one that is not clearly required nor prohibited by the wording of the Fourth Amendment. Justice Stevens, writing for four Justices in dissent, explained how limited Fourth Amendment protection might have been given to prisoners. 468 U.S. at 542, 104 S.Ct. at 3208, 82 L.Ed.2d at 413 (Stevens, J., joined by Brennan, Marshall, and Blackmun, JJ., concurring in part and dissenting in part). For citations to additional Supreme Court cases, and secondary authorities, in this point, see R. Rotunda & J. Nowak, Treatise on Constitutional Law: Substance and Procedure, §§ 14.6, 17.9 (3rd ed. 1999, with annual supplements).

prison needs because the Eighth Amendment would stand as a protection against "cruel and unusual punishments" that might be involved in such cases and because there would have to be some type of adequate state tort or procedural remedies available to redress alleged destruction of the individual's property in order to comply with the restrictions of procedural due process.[45]

When analyzing a constitutional decision concerning the imposition of punishment for criminal activity, one must be cognizant of the distinction between substantive due process and procedural due process issues. The Court will actively examine whether or not an individual has received fair treatment in terms of the process of adjudication.[46] If a convicted defendant in a criminal case challenges the length or nature of the sentence he received, a reviewing court will determine whether the sentence violates the cruel and unusual punishment clause of the Eighth Amendment and whether the sentence is so arbitrary that it

violates due process principles. Apart from death penalty cases,[47] the Supreme Court has not established any strict limitations on the length of criminal sentences under either Eighth Amendment or due process principles.[48]

If a prison inmate brings suit challenging the conditions of his confinement, a court would use procedural due process principles to determine whether the individual was entitled to a hearing or process to determine whether he could be subjected to special disciplinary proceedings in the prison.[49] A court would use Eighth Amendment cruel and unusual punishment clause standards to determine whether the treatment of the prisoner was constitutionally impermissible.[50]

The Supreme Court has held that prison regulations restricting the fundamental constitutional rights of prisoners, such as the right of speech, marriage, or the free exercise of religion, will be upheld so long as the regulation at issue is reasonably related to a legitimate penological interest.[51] This standard of

---

45. 468 U.S. at 530, 104 S.Ct. at 3202, 82 L.Ed.2d at 405. The Supreme Court has held that the intentional infliction of harm on the person or property of a prisoner violates due process and that procedural due process principles require the state to grant a post-deprivation hearing to prisoners who allege intentional destruction of their liberty or property. Hudson v. Palmer, 468 U.S. 517, 104 S.Ct. 3194, 82 L.Ed.2d 393 (1984), on remand 744 F.2d 22 (4th Cir.1984). However, the Court has also held that injury to the person or property of a prisoner which is caused by the mere negligence of a prison employee does not violate the due process clause. Daniels v. Williams, 474 U.S. 327, 106 S.Ct. 662, 88 L.Ed.2d 662 (1986), overruling Parratt v. Taylor, 451 U.S. 527, 101 S.Ct. 1908, 68 L.Ed.2d 420 (1981). For citations and discussion of other cases regarding prisoners' rights, see §§ 13.4(b), 13.9(a), infra.

In Sacramento v. Lewis, 523 U.S. 833, 118 S.Ct. 1708, 140 L.Ed.2d 1043 (1998) the Court ruled that accidental death of a suspect which was the result of a collision between a motorcycle and a police car, did not violate the due process clause of the Fourteenth Amendment. The majority opinion in *Lewis* found that substantive due process principles, rather than Fourth or Eighth Amendment principles, would determine the constitutionality of many types of executive actions that caused harm to individuals. When due process, rather than Fourth Amendment or Eighth Amendment principles, govern the constitutionality of an executive action that harms individuals, the Court will use a "shocks the conscience" test to determine whether the challenged executive action is unconstitutional. The *Lewis* case is examined in § 10.6(f).

46. See Chapter 13, Procedural Due Process, for an examination of such issues.

47. Although this Treatise does not cover criminal procedure, some of the cases in which the Supreme Court has used the cruel and unusual punishment clause or the due process clauses to limit capital sentences are examined in § 13.3 because those cases examine basic due process principles.

48. The Supreme Court has not found that the Eighth Amendment cruel and unusual punishment clause, or the due process clause require the state to have sentences for each crime that are closely correlated to the nature and seriousness of each activity made criminal by the state. Even though the Supreme Court does not require a strict proportionality review of noncapital sentences, some noncapital sentences will violate the Eighth Amendment. For citations to additional Supreme Court cases on this point, see R. Rotunda & J. Nowak, Treatise on Constitutional Law: Substance and Procedure, ch. 17 (3rd ed. 1999, with annual supplements).

49. See, §§ 13.4, 13.8, 13.9(a) regarding challenges to condition of confinement and procedural due process issues in prisoners' rights cases.

50. For an examination of the principles used in cruel and unusual punishment clause analysis, see W. LaFave, Substantive Criminal Law, (2nd ed. 2003).

51. The Supreme Court first enunciated this test in Turner v. Safley, 482 U.S. 78, 107 S.Ct. 2254, 96 L.Ed.2d 64 (1987). In *Turner*, the Court applied this test to uphold a restriction on the ability of prisoners to send mail to other prison inmates because the particular regulation was related to prison safety and security; the regulation did not unnecessarily burden the First Amendment interests of prisoners. However, in *Turner* the Court used this standard to invalidate a prison regulation that prohib-

review requires a case-by-case analysis of whether a particular prison regulation, relates to legitimate penological interests, such as prison security or rehabilitation.[52] Such review must be distinguished from procedural due process review of prisoners' rights cases, where a court determines whether a prisoner is entitled to fair procedure before he is denied a liberty or property interest.[53]

In *Overton v. Bazzetta*[54] the Court found that certain prison regulations limiting visits between convicted inmates and persons from outside the prison did not violate First Amendment freedom of association, substantive due process, or the cruel and unusual punishment clause. In *Overton* the Court ruled only that the regulations at issue in the case were not invalid on their face. An individual prisoner who would lose visitation rights, or who would be subject to administrative segregation, under these regulations might have a procedural due process right to a fair process to determine whether the regulations were properly applied to him.[55]

At issue in *Overton* were a set of regulations governing visitation of prisoners in the State of Michigan Department of Corrections facilities. Except for a prisoner's attorneys or members of the clergy, a prisoner could only be visited by members of the prisoner's family

or a limited number of other individuals. A prisoner could not have a visitor under the age of 18, unless the individual child was related to the prisoner. A prisoner could not receive visits from his or her own child if the prisoner's parental rights regarding that child had been terminated. A prisoner could not receive visits from any former prisoners without prior approval of the correctional facility warden. Additionally, prisoners who had committed multiple substance abuse violations were not permitted to receive any visitors, other than attorneys or members of the clergy, for a period of up to two years. The *Overton* majority opinion, written by Justice Kennedy, stated that the Court was not ready to decide whether the conviction of an individual for a crime automatically terminated all associational rights of that individual that might be protected by the First Amendment freedom of association or substantive due process principles.[56] Justice Kennedy assumed that the regulations were significant limitations of a constitutional liberty interest of the prisoners. The majority opinion applied the standard that had previously been established by the Supreme Court for restrictions on fundamental rights of persons who had been convicted of crimes.[57] Under that standard, a prison regulation may limit the fundamental constitu-

---

ited marriages between inmates or between inmates and other persons, unless permission for the marriage was given by prison authorities on the basis of compelling circumstances. The Court found that the marriage prohibition did not promote legitimate security or rehabilitation concerns because there were a variety of alternative means of promoting those ends that would have regulated, but not virtually prohibited, the ability of prisoners to marry persons when the marriage presented no threat to penological interests.

52. For citations to additional cases, including lower court cases, and secondary works on this topic see our multi-volume Treatise: R. Rotunda & J. Nowak, Treatise on Constitutional Law: Substance and Procedure (3rd ed. 1999, with annual supplements).

53. See Chapter 13 regarding procedural due process.

54. ___ U.S. ___, 123 S.Ct. 2162, 156 L.Ed.2d 162 (2003).

55. See the preceding paragraphs in this section of the Treatise and § 13.4(b). Four Justices concurred in both the opinion of the Court and the judgment of the Court in *Overton* but they issued a separate opinion, written by Justice Stevens, to note that the Court, by approving the

limitation on visitation rights in this case, was not either lessening the standard for the substantive review of prison regulations nor in any way changing the Court's rulings concerning an individual prisoner's right to fair treatment if they were to be deprived of a liberty or property interest. Overton v. Bazzetta, ___ U.S. ___, ___, 123 S.Ct. 2162, 2170, 156 L.Ed.2d 162 (2003) (Stevens, J., joined by Souter, Ginsburg, and Breyer, JJ., concurring). Justice Stevens' concurring opinion in *Overton* referred back to an opinion that Justice Stevens had written regarding the procedural rights of prisoners who were subject to special forms of discipline when he was a Circuit Judge on the United States Court of Appeals for the Seventh Circuit. United States ex rel. Miller v. Twomey, 479 F.2d 701 (7th Cir. 1973).

56. Overton v. Bazzetta, ___ U.S. ___, ___, 123 S.Ct. 2162, 2167, 156 L.Ed.2d 162 (2003).

57. See Turner v. Safley, 482 U.S. 78, 89, 107 S.Ct. 2254, 96 L.Ed.2d 64 (1987); O'Lone v. Estate of Shabazz, 482 U.S. 342, 107 S.Ct. 2400, 96 L.Ed.2d 282 (1987). For citations to additional cases, and secondary works, on this topic see our multi-volume Treatise: R. Rotunda & J. Nowak, Treatise on Constitutional Law: Substance and Procedure (3rd ed. 1999, with annual supplements).

tional rights of prisoners so long as the regulation is rationally or reasonably related to legitimate penological interests. The majority opinion in *Overton* found that courts must consider four factors in determining whether a limitation placed on a constitutional right of prisoners meets this standard. In assessing prison regulations that restricted basic constitutional rights, courts must examine: "Whether the regulation has a valid, rational connection to a legitimate governmental interest; whether alternative meetings are open to inmates to exercise the asserted right; what impact and accommodation of the right would have on guards and inmates and prison resources; and whether there are ready alternatives to the regulation."[58]

The Court in *Overton* ruled that Michigan's regulations limiting visitation were rationally related to legitimate interests in prison security and the efficient operation of prisons. The majority opinion emphasized that prison regulations did not have to be the least restrictive means of promoting legitimate governmental interests: such regulations only had to be reasonably related to those interests. In assessing the restriction on all visitors for inmates who had engaged in two or more substance abuse violations, Justice Kennedy noted that the Court was not faced with a situation where the regulations, as written or as applied, were shown to establish a permanent ban on visitation rights in future litigation. An individual prisoner might challenge whether a permanent ban on his visitation rights violated substantive due process.[59]

(d) Separating Procedural & Substantive Issues in Punitive Damages Cases

Judicial review of punitive damage awards involves both substantive and procedural constitutional issues. Procedural due process principles require that a person be given a fair process for the deprivation of life, liberty, or property; these principles may require the establishment of procedures to limit the discretion of courts or juries that award punitive damages. When the Supreme Court uses the concept of substantive due process to examine a law, including a court ruling, it is determining whether the substantive rule of law is an unconstitutional limitation of life, liberty, or property interests; substantive due process principles might be used to place a limit on the size of punitive damage awards.

Prior to the 1990s, the Supreme Court had avoided ruling on the extent to which substantive due process and procedural due process principles limited the award of punitive damages in civil cases.[60] The Supreme Court has now ruled that the due process clause of the Fourteenth Amendment requires states to adopt procedures to ensure that punitive damage awards are made through a fair process that includes judicial review of jury awards. A majority of the Justices in the 1990s also endorsed the position that the due process clause authorizes review courts to impose a substantive limit on the amount of punitive damages. But the Justices did not provide any standards for determining when the amount of punitive damages might be so great as to violate the concept of substantive due process.

In *TXO Production Corporation v. Alliance*

---

58. Overton v. Bazzetta, ___ U.S. ___, ___, 123 S.Ct. 2162, 2168, 156 L.Ed.2d 162 (2003) (internal citation and internal quotation marks omitted), in part quoting from Turner v. Safley, 482 U.S. 78, 107 S.Ct. 2254, 96 L.Ed.2d 64 (1987).

59. The Supreme Court also ruled that the regulations did not violate the cruel and unusual punishment clause of the Eighth Amendment. Overton v. Bazzetta, ___ U.S. ___, ___, 123 S.Ct. 2162, 156 L.Ed.2d 162 (2003) (Part III of the majority opinion). Four Justices concurred in the opinion and the judgment of the Court, to emphasize the limited nature of the Court's ruling. ___ U.S. at ___, 123 S.Ct. at 2170 (Stevens, J., joined by Souter, Ginsburg, and Breyer, JJ., concurring). Two Justices concurred only in the judgment in *Overton*; they had a much narrower view of the constitutional rights that might survive conviction

for a crime than did either the majority or concurring Justices in *Overton*. ___ U.S. at ___, 123 S.Ct. at 2171 (Thomas, J., joined by Scalia, J., concurring in the judgment).

60. In Pacific Mutual Life Insurance Co. v. Haslip, 499 U.S. 1, 111 S.Ct. 1032, 113 L.Ed.2d 1 (1991) the Court held that the award of punitive damages in a civil case was not a per se violation of due process. In Browning–Ferris Industries of Vermont, Inc. v. Kelco Disposal, Inc., 492 U.S. 257, 109 S.Ct. 2909, 106 L.Ed.2d 219 (1989) the Court held that the award of punitive damages in a civil case did not violate the excessive fine provision of the Eighth Amendment, which applies to the states through the Fourteenth Amendment.

Resources Corporation,[61] a defendant claimed that a 10 million dollar punitive damage award violated substantive due process standards and that the procedures used in the trial court for awarding the punitive damages were so unfair that they violated procedural due process principles. The *TXO* case involved a suit for a declaratory judgment in which the TXO Corporation, which was eventually subjected to punitive damages, claimed certain oil and gas mineral rights. The Alliance Corporation defended its title to the mineral rights and counterclaimed for "slander of title," on the basis that the declaratory judgment action filed by the TXO Corporation had been undertaken in bad faith. On the basis of written submissions, the trial court ruled that the TXO Corporation had no claim to the oil and gas rights. Alliance's counterclaim for slander of title was tried before a jury; the jury awarded Alliance $19,000 in actual damages and 10 million dollars in punitive damages.

The Supreme Court, without a majority opinion, upheld the 10 million dollar punitive damage award in the *TXO* case. A majority of the Justices, in separate opinions, endorsed the use of substantive and procedural due process principles to limit punitive damage awards. Justice Stevens announced the judgment of the Court in a plurality opinion. In parts of the plurality opinion that was joined by Chief Justice Rehnquist and Justice Blackmun, Justice Stevens finding that the punitive damage award was not so grossly excessive as to violate substantive due process standards, because the jury, based on the evidence before it, might have concluded that the TXO Corporation had engaged in malicious and fraudulent actions in an attempt to gain millions of dollars of profit.[62] Justice Stevens was joined by Chief Justice Rehnquist and Justices Black-

mun and Kennedy in ruling that the procedures used in the lower court did not violate the due process clause, because the TXO Corporation had been given notice regarding the use of the potential for harm to the other corporation, and profit to itself, as a basis for punitive damages and because there were adequate review procedures in the state appellate courts.[63] While Justice Kennedy agreed with Justice Stevens' analysis of the procedural due process issues, he wrote separately to suggest that the Court should use a substantive due process standard that would uphold only those punitive damage awards that reflect a "rational concern" rather than "bias, passion, or prejudice."[64]

Justices Scalia and Thomas voted to uphold the award of punitive damages in the *TXO* case because they believed that the punitive damage award was a product of a fair trial and a fair damage assessment procedure. They concurred only in the judgment of the Court, rather than the plurality opinion, because Justices Scalia and Thomas did not believe that there should be any substantive due process limitation on the amount of punitive damages.[65]

Justices O'Connor, White and Souter dissented in *TXO.* The dissenters would have found that the 10 million dollar damage award was so excessive that it violated substantive due process standards. These three Justices also believed that the procedures used in the lower courts violated procedural due process principles because they were not sufficient to guard against grossly excessive damage.[66] The *TXO* case evidenced the fact that the Supreme Court was ready to use both substantive due process and procedural due process principles for punitive damage award cases. The four Justices who joined all, or part, of the plurality

61. 509 U.S. 443, 113 S.Ct. 2711, 125 L.Ed.2d 366 (1993).

62. 509 U.S. at 453–62, 113 S.Ct. at 2718–23 (judgment of the Court announced in an opinion by Stevens, J., joined by Rehnquist, C.J., and Blackmun, J.).

63. 509 U.S. at 462–64, 113 S.Ct. at 2723–24 (judgment of the Court announced in an opinion by Stevens, J., and joined in part iv of the opinion by Rehnquist, C.J., Blackmun, and Kennedy, JJ.).

64. TXO Production Corp. v. Alliance Resources Corp.; 509 U.S. 443, 467, 113 S.Ct. 2711, 2725, 125 L.Ed.2d 366 (1993) (Kennedy, J., concurring in part and concurring in the judgment).

65. 509 U.S. at 469, 113 S.Ct. at 2726 (Scalia, J., joined by Thomas, J., concurring in the judgment).

66. TXO Production Corp. v. Alliance Resources Corp., 509 U.S. 443, 473, 113 S.Ct. 2711, 2728, 125 L.Ed.2d 366 (1993) (O'Connor, J., joined by White, J., and, in part, Souter, J., dissenting).

opinion, and the three Justices who dissented, in *TXO* issued opinions that endorsed both a substantive due process and procedural due process limitation on punitive damages.

One year after the decision in *TXO,* Justice Stevens wrote the majority opinion in *Honda Motor Co., Ltd. v. Oberg,* [67] which overturned a punitive damage award and ruled that there were both substantive and procedural due process limitations on such awards. The defendant in this case manufactured and sold "three-wheeled all-terrain vehicles." The plaintiff, when driving one of the defendant's vehicles, had an accident in which he sustained severe injuries. In the Oregon courts, the plaintiff brought suit against the manufacturer on the theory that the vehicle was unreasonably dangerous in its design and that the defendant manufacturer knew, or should have known, of the danger to purchasers and users of the vehicle. At the conclusion of the trial, the jury found the manufacturer liable for over $900,000 in compensatory damages, but the jury reduced the compensatory damage amount by 20 percent (to an amount slightly over $735,000) because of contributory negligence on the part of the plaintiff. The jury also awarded the plaintiff $5 million in punitive damages. The state trial court, the intermediate state appellate court, and the Oregon Supreme Court upheld the award of punitive damages because there was some evidence to support the jury verdict. The Oregon Constitution specifically prohibited judicial review (at the trial or appellate court level) of the amount of punitive damages award "unless the court can affirmatively say there is no evidence to support the verdict." The defendant claimed that the restrictions placed on the judicial review of the $5 million punitive damage award denied the defendant due process of law because there was no judicial process in which the defendant could seek to have the award limited even if the courts agreed that the award was grossly excessive.

Justice Stevens' majority opinion in *Honda Motor Co.* ruled that the absence of judicial review of the fairness of the jury award of punitive damages violated procedural due process principles. Before he addressed the procedural due process issue, Justice Stevens, writing for a majority of the Court, endorsed the use of substantive due process for the judicial review of punitive damages awards. The majority opinion stated: "Our recent cases have recognized that the Constitution imposes a substantive limit on the size of damage awards ... although they failed to draw a mathematical bright line between the constitutionally acceptable and the constitutionally unacceptable ... in the case before us today we are not directly concerned with the character of the standard that will identify unconstitutionally excessive awards." [68]

When examining the procedural due process limits on the systems used for awarding punitive damages, Justice Stevens' opinion set forth a brief history of the common law practices for reviewing the size of damage awards in Great Britain and the United States. Although the majority opinion did not tie the history of punitive damage awards to the intention of persons who drafted and ratified the Fourteenth Amendment, Justice Stevens concluded that "both before and after the ratification of the Fourteenth Amendment, many American courts reviewed damages for partiality or passion and prejudice." [69] According to the majority, the state courts in every state except Oregon were able to review the size of damage awards. Justice Stevens concluded that: "Oregon's abrogation of a well-established common law protection against arbitrary deprivations of property raises a presumption that its procedures violate the due process clause." [70]

The ruling in *Honda Motor Co.* was not based merely on the presumption of unconstitutionality that arose from Oregon's deviation from the historic practices of Anglo–American courts. Justice Stevens explained that jury

67. 512 U.S. 415, 114 S.Ct. 2331, 129 L.Ed.2d 336 (1994).

68. 512 U.S. at 420, 114 S.Ct. at 2335 (internal citations and quotation marks omitted).

69. 512 U.S. at 424, 114 S.Ct. at 2337 (internal quotation marks omitted).

70. 512 U.S. at 428, 114 S.Ct. at 2339.

discretion regarding the amount of punitive damages created a danger that defendants would be arbitrarily deprived of property through excessive jury awards. Judicial review of jury awards was required as a procedural safeguard to guard against arbitrary and unjustified awards. Because Oregon provided no judicial review of the size of punitive damages, seven members of the United States Supreme Court voted to invalidate the system. But Justice Stevens' majority opinion did not explain the type of standards that would be used for evaluating the adequacy of judicial procedures for the review of punitive damages. And the majority opinion did not set forth standards for determining when a punitive damage award was so excessive that it should be held to violate substantive due process even if the trial and appellate courts had provided the defendant with fair procedures.[71]

In *BMW of North America, Inc. v. Gore*[72] the Supreme Court, for the first time, employed substantive due process principles to invalidate a state court award of punitive damages. In the state trial court the plaintiff, Dr. Gore, had proven that he had purchased a BMW automobile from a licensed BMW dealer based on representations that the car was a "new car." The plaintiff also proved that the dealer

and manufacturer of that car knew that the car had been damaged by weather, and had been repaired and repainted. In the trial court, a jury awarded the plaintiff four thousand dollars in compensatory damages and four million dollars in punitive damages. The state supreme court found the jury, to arrive at such a large punitive damage award, might have considered the number of similar sales in BMWs (of repaired vehicles as new vehicles) in all states, not merely the sales in Alabama. On that basis, the state supreme court ruled that the four million dollar punitive damage award was excessive and reduced the punitive damage award to two million dollars. The United States Supreme Court, by a five to four vote, reversed the Alabama Supreme Court and held that the two million dollar punitive damage award was so grossly excessive that it violated due process.

Justice Stevens' majority opinion in *Gore*, at certain points, seems to mix procedural due process and substantive due process issues. For example, Justice Stevens found that a critical flaw in the Alabama system for the awarding of damages was the failure to provide the defendant with adequate notice of the types of damages to which the defendant

71. When he concluded the portion of the majority opinion in which he found that the state's denial of judicial review of punitive damages awards violated due process, Justice Stevens added a footnote indicating that while the Court was not deciding what standard of review should be determined to judge the adequacy of judicial review of punitive damage awards that a proper standard might be equivalent to the standard that the Court used to determine whether there was a sufficient factual basis to justify a finding of guilt in a criminal case. Presumably Justice Stevens used this analogy only to indicate that a reviewing court should determine whether there were sufficient facts that might have justified the damage award for a reasonable trier of fact or jury. There is no indication that Justice Stevens meant to imply that there was any similarity in the review of the factual basis for a criminal conviction (where the finder of fact must find a defendant guilty beyond a reasonable doubt) and the standard of proof for the awarding of punitive damages. Honda Motor Co., Ltd. v. Oberg, 512 U.S. 415, 432 n. 10, 114 S.Ct. 2331, 2341 n. 10, 129 L.Ed.2d 336 (1994) (italics omitted).

Justice Scalia concurred in both the judgment of the Court and the majority opinion in the *Honda Motor Co.* case. He wrote separately to explain why he thought the denial of judicial review of jury imposed damage awards violated due process. But Justice Scalia did not explain

why he joined the majority opinion in its entirety, when the majority opinion clearly endorsed the use of substantive due process to limit the size of awards. Honda Motor Co., Ltd. v. Oberg, 512 U.S. 415, 434, 114 S.Ct. 2331, 2342, 129 L.Ed.2d 336 (1994) (Scalia, J., concurring). Justice Thomas, who had joined Justice Scalia's concurring opinion in the TXO case that rejected the use of substantive due process to review punitive damage awards, joined Justice Stevens' majority opinion in Honda Motor Co. without writing separate concurring opinion.

Only Justice Ginsburg and Chief Justice Rehnquist dissented in *Honda Motor Co.* These two Justices found that Oregon's procedures met procedural due process requirements because, in their view, prejudgment procedures, including the jury instructions, limited the degree of jury discretion. Because there was no claim that the damage award was so excessive as to violate substantive due process principles, the dissenters believed there was no basis for overturning the punitive damage award in this case. *Honda Motor Co., Ltd. v. Oberg,* 512 U.S. 415, 436, 114 S.Ct. 2331, 2343, 129 L.Ed.2d 336 (1994) (Ginsburg, J., joined by Rehnquist, C.J., dissenting).

72. 517 U.S. 559, 116 S.Ct. 1589, 134 L.Ed.2d 809 (1996), on remand 701 So.2d 507 (Ala.1997).

might be subject.[73] However, the majority opinion did not find that the defendant was unaware that it would have to contest the plaintiff's claims for both actual damages and punitive damages. If the defendant was made aware of the types of damages it might be ordered to pay by a trial court and jury, it could not have lacked notice. The majority did not find that the court process in Alabama had any procedural defects that denied the defendant a fair trial.

Justice Stevens employed substantive due process principles to limit the amount of the punitive damage award. The majority in *Gore* found that courts must examine the substantive basis of the punitive damage award to determine whether it was so excessive as to violate due process. If the damage award was not related to legitimate state interests, the award would violate due process. According to the majority, Alabama's only legitimate interests in awarding punitive damages were punishing the defendant for egregious unlawful conduct, and deterring it from future misconduct, within the state's borders. The majority opinion stated: "A state may not impose economic sanctions on violators of its laws with the intent of changing the tortfeasors lawful conduct in other states."[74]

The majority in *Gore* refused to establish a clear cut rule concerning the amount of punitive damages that could be awarded in a civil case. The majority opinion stated: "We are not prepared to draw a bright line marking the limits of a constitutionally acceptable punitive damage award."[75]

Justice Stevens' opinion in *Gore* set out a flexible three factor test for the assessment of whether a punitive damage award was so excessive that it violated due process. The majority opinion stated that courts must consider three key factors when examining the size of a punitive damage award. In determining whether an award was grossly excessive, the judiciary would have to examine: "the degree

of reprehensibility of [the conduct that formed the basis of the civil suit]; the disparity between the harm or potential harm suffered by [the injured party who was the plaintiff in the civil case] and [the plaintiff's] punitive damages award; and the difference between this remedy and the civil penalties authorized or imposed in comparable cases."[76]

The first of the three factors appears to be the key to judicial assessment of punitive damages. "The most important indicium of the reasonableness of a punitive damages award is the degree of reprehensibility of the defendant's conduct."[77] The degree of reprehensibility of the defendant's conduct did not seem great to the majority in *Gore,* in part because these Justices believed that the automobile company's failure to disclose the damage from weather to the vehicle would be entirely lawful in some states.

Justice Stevens' majority opinion in *Gore* also found that the second two factors favored the defendant. The majority believed that the relationship between the actual and punitive damages in this case was so disparate as to cause fairness concerns. Finally, the majority found that the availability of other methods for punishing misconduct by automobile manufacturers and dealers (such as civil and criminal penalties for deceptive trade practices) demonstrated that the large punitive damage award was not tailored to deterring illegal conduct within the state.

Justice Breyer wrote a concurring opinion for three of the five Justices in the majority in *Gore.* He emphasized the strong historical underpinnings for a judicial role in limiting the reasonableness of punitive damage awards.[78] Justice Breyer's concurrence appears to be a direct response to Justice Scalia's dissent.

Justice Scalia, joined by Justice Thomas in dissent, believed that there was no justification for the federal judiciary becoming the final determiners of what types of damages

---

73. 517 U.S. at 573, 116 S.Ct. at 1598.

74. 517 U.S. at 571, 116 S.Ct. at 1597.

75. 517 U.S. at 571, 116 S.Ct. at 1604.

76. 517 U.S. at 573–75, at 116 S.Ct. at 1598–99.

77. 517 U.S. at 575, 116 S.Ct. at 1599.

78. BMW of North America, Inc. v. Gore, 517 U.S. 559, 585, 116 S.Ct. 1589, 1604, 134 L.Ed.2d 809 (1996) (Breyer, J., joined by O'Connor and Souter, JJ., concurring).

could be awarded in state cases when the subject matter of the case involved no federal issue in itself.[79] Justice Scalia pointed out that the fairness of Alabama's court procedures had not been challenged by the defendant. The only basis for the majority's decision was substantive due process, despite references to procedural due process principles in parts of the majority opinion. According to the dissent, there was no basis in the text or history of the Fourteenth Amendment that justified federal courts using substantive due process to review the size of a punitive damage award.

Justice Ginsburg, joined by Chief Justice Rehnquist, dissented in *Gore* for two reasons. First, she believed that there was no historical justification for the Court creating substantive constitutional limits on punitive damages awards. Second, Justice Ginsburg believed that federal judicial review of such awards could not be justified on a practical basis.[80] Justice Ginsburg added an appendix to her decision demonstrating the state legislative activity in recent decades regarding punitive damages to demonstrate that there was no need for the federal judiciary to intervene in the democratic processes of the states in order to insure fairness in the awarding of punitive damages.[81]

It would be difficult to predict whether the Supreme Court, in the future, will engage in active review of the awards of punitive damages that have been approved by state courts. The typical case will involve a tort action of some type with no federal issue in the case apart from the size of the punitive damage award. If the state courts had established fair procedures for jury determination of punitive damages and the state judicial review of the

punitive damages, the only federal issue in these cases will be whether the punitive damages awarded in the civil action were so great as to violate due process. Justice Ginsburg, in dissent, pointed out that it would be impossible for the Supreme Court to review all state cases in which the defendant sought Supreme Court review of a state case on the basis of an allegedly excessive award of punitive damages.[82] However, the majority in *Gore* believed that using the standards created by the majority opinion in *Gore* would give guidance to lower courts, so that the Supreme Court should not have to consider many applications for certiorari where a case involved only an issue of the excessive amount of punitive damages.[83]

The Supreme Court has never expressly repudiated the plurality opinion, or result, in the *TXO Production Corporation* case.[84] However, it is difficult to believe that the Court, in the future, will uphold a punitive damage award that was as large a multiple of an actual damages award as that which was granted in the *TXO Production Corporation* case.

In *State Farm Mutual Automobile Insurance Company v. Campbell*[85] the Court held that an award of $145,000,000 in punitive damages, together with a $1,000,000 compensatory judgment award, violated substantive due process principles. The majority opinion in *State Farm*, written by Justice Kennedy, used the three factor analysis set out in *Gore*. Justice Kennedy found that in assessing punitive damages under substantive due process standards, all courts should "consider three guideposts: (1) the degree of reprehensibility of the defendant's misconduct; (2) the disparity between

---

79. BMW of North America, Inc. v. Gore, 517 U.S. 559, 597, 116 S.Ct. 1589, 1610, 134 L.Ed.2d 809 (1996). (Scalia, J., joined by Thomas, J., dissenting).

80. 517 U.S. at 605, 116 S.Ct. at 1614 (Ginsburg, J., joined by Rehnquist, C.J., dissenting).

81. 517 U.S. at 614–618, 116 S.Ct. at 1618–20 (appendix to dissenting opinion of Justice Ginsburg).

82. 517 U.S. at 561, 116 S.Ct. at 1592 (Ginsburg, J., joined by Rehnquist, C.J., dissenting).

83. BMW of North America, Inc. v. Gore, 517 U.S. 559, 586, n. 41, 116 S.Ct. 1589, 1604 n. 41, 134 L.Ed.2d 809 (1996). In Cooper Industries, Inc. v. Leatherman Tool Group, Inc. 532 U.S. 424, 121 S.Ct. 1678, 149 L.Ed.2d 674 (2001) the Supreme Court ruled that the United States

Court of Appeals should apply a de novo standard when it reviewed a district court interpretation of the constitutionality of a punitive damage award. The Court's ruling in *Cooper Industries* was based on due process principles. Therefore state appellate courts should grant de novo review of a state trial court determination of the constitutionality of punitive damages awards.

84. TXO Production Corporation v. Alliance Resources Corporation, 509 U.S. 443, 113 S.Ct. 2711, 125 L.Ed.2d 366 (1993).

85. 538 U.S. 408, 123 S.Ct. 1513, 155 L.Ed.2d 585 (2003).

the actual or potential harm suffered by the plaintiff and the punitive damages award; and (3) the difference between the punitive damages awarded by the jury and the civil penalties authorized or imposed in comparable cases."[86]

By a 6 to 3 vote, the Justices in *State Farm* ruled that an automobile liability insurer's alleged bad faith failure to settle within policy limits could not justify an award that was 145 times greater than the compensatory judgment. The majority found that the state courts in this case must have been including harm done in other states when considering the reprehensibility of the defendant's action. The majority opinion in *State Farm* reiterated the Court's position that the Justices would not set out a specific numerical guideline or limitation on the award of punitive damages. Nevertheless, Justice Kennedy's majority opinion stated: "Our jurisprudence and the principles it has now established demonstrate, however, that, in practice, few awards exceeding a single-digit ratio between punitive and compensatory damages, to a significant degree, will satisfy due process."[87] Thus, it appears that trial courts will have difficulty justifying any award of punitive damages that is more than 9 times greater than the amount of compensatory damages awarded in a case.[88]

(e) The DeShaney & Flores Cases—Two Children's Right Cases Made Easier by Separating Procedural & Substantive Issues

(1) The *DeShaney* Case. An example of the distinction between procedural due process and substantive due process guarantees is provided by the Supreme Court's decision in *DeShaney v. Winnebago County Department of*

Social Services.[89] In this case, a child who had been disabled as a result of being beaten by his father, who had custody of the child after a divorce, brought suit against a county department of social services alleging that the department had reason to know that he was being abused and did nothing to prevent the harm caused to him by his father. The social service caseworker who had been assigned to meet with the father and child had noted the evidence that provided her with a well-founded belief that someone in the household was abusing the child, and did nothing further to prevent the injury. The Supreme Court, by a six to three vote of the Justices, found that the child had not been deprived of life, liberty, or property without due process of law. The majority opinion by Chief Justice Rehnquist found that the only claim in the case was "one invoking the substantive rather than the procedural component of the due process clause." A procedural due process claim would have been raised if the child and his mother had attempted to show that state statutes gave the child an entitlement to receive protective services, that he was denied that entitlement, and that the state did not provide fair process to prevent or remedy his injury. But no such procedural claim had been made in the earlier stages of the litigation.[90] The child's claim in this case was that the state had an affirmative obligation to protect him and that its failure to meet that obligation was a violation of the due process clause. On the substantive issue, the majority opinion found that "a state's failure to protect an individual against private violence simply does not constitute a violation of the due process clause." If the state had taken custody of an individual, whether through a civil or criminal process, it would

86. ___ U.S. at ___, 123 S.Ct. at 1520, referring to BMW of North America, Inc. v. Gore, 517 U.S. 559, 573–75, 116 S.Ct. 1589, 1598–99, 134 L.Ed.2d 809 (1996).

87. State Farm Mutual Automobile Insurance Company v. Campbell, 538 U.S. 408, ___, 123 S.Ct. 1513, 1524, 155 L.Ed.2d 585 (2003).

88. In *State Farm Mutual Auto Insurance Company*, Justices Scalia, Thomas and Ginsburg each wrote a dissenting opinion to restate their views concerning the propriety of reviewing awards of punitive damages in state courts under substantive due process principles. ___ U.S. at ___, 123 S.Ct. at 1526 (Scalia, J., dissenting); ___ U.S.

at ___, 123 S.Ct. at 1526 (Thomas, J., dissenting); ___ U.S. at ___, 123 S.Ct. at 1527 (Ginsburg, J., dissenting).

89. 489 U.S. 189, 109 S.Ct. 998, 103 L.Ed.2d 249 (1989). The case was decided by a six to three vote of the Justices. 489 U.S. at 203, 109 S.Ct. at 1007 (Brennan, J., joined by Marshall and Blackmun, JJ., dissenting), 489 U.S. at 212, 109 S.Ct. at 1012 (Blackmun, J., dissenting).

90. The procedural due process argument was made for the first time in the Supreme Court of the United States and, for that reason, the Court refused to consider that claim. 489 U.S. at 195 n. 2, 109 S.Ct. at 1003 n. 2.

have some duty to assume responsibility for some level of protection for the individual's well-being.[91] If the state refused to provide protective services to a class of individuals because they were a disfavored minority, that class-based decision would violate the equal protection clause.[92]

(2) *Flores* and the Detention of Alien Juveniles.

In *Reno v. Flores,*[93] Justice Scalia wrote a majority opinion that made a clear distinction between substantive due process and procedural due process arguments and that upheld Immigration and Naturalization Service [INS] regulations regarding the detention of alien juveniles. Under the INS regulations, a juvenile who was taken into federal custody, and who was awaiting deportation proceedings, would be released to a parent, guardian, or adult relative who was in the United States and not in detention. Parents or legal guardians who were not in the United States could designate another person to take custody of their child, so long as the individual designated could properly care for the juvenile. A juvenile would be released to an adult who was not related to that juvenile only in "unusual and compelling circumstances" and in the discretion of INS officials. The juveniles who were kept in custody were kept in facilities that were to meet specific standards for the care and well-being of juveniles who were kept in detention. The Supreme Court found that these regulations were within the authority granted to the Attorney General, Department of Justice and the INS (which is a branch of the Justice Department) by federal statutes.

Justice Scalia's majority opinion in *Flores* described the issue of whether a child had a right to be freed from custody as being a substantive due process issue. Justice Scalia found that questions regarding whether the process used by the federal government to determine whether a specific child should remain in custody and be subject to deportation was fair, involved procedural due process issues.

On the substantive due process issue, the Supreme Court held that a child did not have a fundamental right to be free from custody whenever freedom from custody might be in the child's best interest. Justice Scalia noted that the case involved only facial challenges to the INS regulations and that claims that the conditions at the facilities for the custody of these children were substandard were not supported by evidence in the case. Justice Scalia stated children might often be seen as being "in custody," regardless of whether they were being subject to the control of their parents or an orphanage or a foster home or a facility such as that used in the deportation process. The majority opinion ruled that there was no basis in the Constitution for finding that a child had a fundamental right to be free from custody and/or a fundamental right to be treated by the government in a manner that was in the child's "best interests."

Justice Scalia's majority opinion found that recognition of the asserted rights would justify courts in requiring the government to prove that every child held in an orphanage could not have his interests better served elsewhere. If the Court made the best interests of the child standard a constitutional principle, a

---

91. DeShaney v. Winnebago County Department of Social Services, 489 U.S. 189, 195, 109 S.Ct. 998, 1004–1006, 103 L.Ed.2d 249 (1989). The Court noted that it was not examining a situation where a child had been removed "from free society" and placed in a state facility or a foster home operated by agents of the state. For that reason, the Court did not determine whether injury caused by foster parents would constitute a violation of the due process clause. 489 U.S. at 201 n. 9, 109 S.Ct. at 1006 n. 9. State responsibility for the safety of persons taken into custody as a part of the criminal process is based on both the due process clause and the Eighth Amendment prohibition of cruel and unusual punishment. See, Estelle v. Gamble, 429 U.S. 97, 97 S.Ct. 285, 50 L.Ed.2d 251 (1976). The government is also under a constitutional duty to provide some protection for the safety of persons it takes

into its custody outside of the criminal process. See Youngberg v. Romeo, 457 U.S. 307, 102 S.Ct. 2452, 73 L.Ed.2d 28 (1982). A city does not have a constitutional duty to train or warn its employees about known hazards in the workplace; the due process clause does not guarantee city employees a workplace that is free from unreasonable risks. Collins v. City of Harker Heights, 503 U.S. 115, 112 S.Ct. 1061, 117 L.Ed.2d 261 (1992).

92. DeShaney v. Winnebago County Department of Social Services, 489 U.S. 189, 197 n. 3, 109 S.Ct. 998, 1004 n. 3, 103 L.Ed.2d 249 (1989).

93. 507 U.S. 292, 113 S.Ct. 1439, 123 L.Ed.2d 1 (1993), on remand 992 F.2d 243 (9th Cir.1993).

court might rule that the government violated a child's fundamental rights by leaving him or her with his parents who were providing for him adequately even though he might have a better life if he were taken from his home and placed with another family.[94] For these reasons, the majority refused to rule that a child had a right to have the government make decisions in a child's best interests.

Because the regulation did not impair a fundamental right, or involve a class that receives special constitutional protection, the regulations would comply with substantive due process principles so long as there was a rational or reasonable connection between the regulation and a legitimate interest of government.[95] The INS regulation was upheld because the regulation was a reasonable way for the Jus-

tice Department to protect alien children while ensuring their appearance at deportation proceedings.

The children in *Flores* claimed that the INS regulations violated procedural due process principles for two reasons: (1) the INS was not making a case-by-case determination of the best interest of each child when it determined whether to retain a child in custody who had no parent or relative or named guardian in the United States and (2) alien children were allowed to waive their ability to have an immigration judge review the initial INS determination to commence a deportation proceeding and to retain the child in custody. Justice Scalia found that the first "procedural" argument was "just the substantive due process argument recast in procedural due

94. Reno v. Flores, 507 U.S. 292, 301–303, 113 S.Ct. 1439, 1447–1448, 123 L.Ed.2d 1 (1993): "If there exists a fundamental right to be released into what respondents inaccurately call a 'non-custodial setting' ... we see no reason why it would apply in the context of government custody incidentally acquired in the course of law enforcement. It would presumably apply to state custody over orphans and abandoned children as well, giving federal law and federal courts a major new role in the management of state orphanages.... The best interests of the child, a venerable phrase ... is a proper and feasible criterion for making the decision as to which of two parents will be accorded custody. It is not traditionally the sole criteria—much less the sole constitutional criteria for other, less narrowly channeled judgments involving children." (Internal citations and quotation marks omitted).

See Chapter 14, § 14.28, regarding the constitutional protection of family relationships, such as the parent-child relationship.

95. The substantive due process principle is quite similar to the equal protection principle and standards of review under the due process clauses of the Fifth and Fourteenth Amendments have a direct relationship to the standards of review and tests used under the equal protection clause of the Fourteenth Amendment. See § 14.3 of this Treatise. The Fourteenth Amendment equal protection clause applies only to state and local governments; it does not apply to the federal government due to its expressed terms. However, the due process clause of the Fifth Amendment, which applies to the federal government, has an implied equal protection guarantee that justifies federal courts in invalidating federal statutes that fail to meet certain equal protection standards. See § 14.1 of this Treatise.

In Reno v. Flores, 507 U.S. 292, 113 S.Ct. 1439, 123 L.Ed.2d 1 (1993), the majority opinion by Justice Scalia was clear in finding that the substantive rules established by the Justice Department regulations would receive only minimal judicial scrutiny because those rules did not in-

volve fundamental rights or suspect classification. However, Justice Scalia's majority opinion was not clear regarding the precise standard to be used in this case. When discussing why the Court rejected the substantive due process argument of the alien children (who believed that the INS program had to be narrowly tailored to prevent harm to children), Justice Scalia said: "But narrow tailoring is required only when fundamental rights are involved. The impairment of a lesser interest ... demands no more than a 'reasonable fit between the governmental purpose.'" Justice Scalia also said: "The INS regulation must still meet the (unexacting) standard of rationally advancing some legitimate government purpose."

The alien children also argued that the law violated the equal protection component of the Fifth Amendment by making improper classifications (1) between alien juveniles who were released (to relatives or guardians in the United States) and (2) by retaining custody of these alien juveniles when juveniles who were being held pending federal delinquency proceedings could be released to adults who were not related to those children. In concluding that both of these distinctions (between the children who would be released or kept in custody in deportation proceedings and between the treatment of juvenile aliens and juvenile citizens in delinquency proceedings) did not violate the equal protection guarantee of the Fifth Amendment, Justice Scalia stated no clear standard of review. Instead, his opinion simply stated: "The tradition of reposing custody in close relatives and legal guardians is in our view sufficient to support the former distinction (between groups of alien children who would or would not be released pending deportation); and a difference between citizens and aliens is adequate to support the latter (the distinction between children in delinquency proceedings and children in deportation proceedings)." These seemingly unclear or wavering statements regarding the precise standard of review are found in three consecutive paragraphs in Justice Scalia's majority opinion. 507 U.S. at 303–305, 113 S.Ct. at 1448–1449.

process terms." [96]   The first "procedural" argument was no more than an objection to the substantive rule established by the regulation whereby children were retained in the custody of the government if there was no parent, guardian, or relative to whom the child could be released.

The second procedural argument made by the alien children in *Flores* was based on procedural due process principles. This argument focused on the fairness of the procedures used to allow children to waive a statutory right to a hearing. The Supreme Court found that the regulations allowing the minors to waive their right to a hearing before an immigration judge did not violate due process because the waiver process was fundamentally fair. Under the regulations, a minor's waiver was revocable. The alien child could request a judicial redetermination of the custody decision at any time in the deportation process.[97]   At least some children were capable of making a knowing and intelligent waiver of the right to have their case viewed by an immigration judge. Because the regulations were being attacked on their face, there was no case before the Court involving a minor who alleged that he was unable to make a knowing and voluntary waiver.

(f) *Sacramento v. Lewis***—An Example of Problems Created by Unclear Judicial Attempts to Distinguish Procedural and Substantive Due Process Principles**

In *Sacramento v. Lewis*,[98] the Justices were unanimous in ruling that a person who was killed in a high-speed chase by a law enforce-

ment officer had not lost his life, liberty, or property in a manner that violated the due process clause of the Fourteenth Amendment. The *Lewis* decision in some ways clarifies, and in some ways clouds, the distinction between substantive due process and procedural due process issues. Additionally, the statements in Justice Souter's majority opinion in *Lewis* may lead to confusion concerning the meaning of the takings clause of the Fifth Amendment.

The *Lewis* case involved the death of a 16 year old boy, Philip Lewis, who was a passenger on a motorcycle being driven by an 18 year old friend of his. A police officer (a deputy sheriff of Sacramento County) observed the motorcycle traveling at a high speed. Through use of lights on his patrol car, and by other means, the police officer motioned the driver of the motorcycle to stop. The motorcycle operator sped away from the police officer; a high speed motorized chase ensued. Eventually, the motorcycle fell over during a turn. The driver of the motorcycle was thrown out of the way of the patrol car; Philip Lewis died as a result of being hit by the patrol car. Philip's parents brought suit against the County, the Sheriff's Department and the police officer claiming that their son's life was taken in violation of the due process clause. The Justices of the Supreme Court unanimously rejected that claim.

The *Lewis* majority opinion, written by Justice Souter, considered only the question of "the standard of culpability on the part of a law enforcement officer for violating substantive due process in a pursuit case."[99] Indeed, the Supreme Court may have been limited to

---

96.   Reno v. Flores, 507 U.S. 292, 308, 113 S.Ct. 1439, 1450, 123 L.Ed.2d 1 (1993), (Internal quotation marks omitted).

97.   Reno v. Flores, 507 U.S. 292, 309, 113 S.Ct. 1439, 1451, 123 L.Ed.2d 1 (1993), on remand 992 F.2d 243 (9th Cir.1993). Justices O'Connor and Souter joined the majority opinion, even though these two Justices wrote a concurring opinion in which they found that children had a "constitutionally protected interest and freedom from institutional confinement ... within the core of due process." These two Justices believed that the government regulation only had to be rationally connected to the government interests in preserving and promoting the welfare of the child. On the facts presented to the Court in this challenge to the regulations, they found no basis for invalidating the Justice Department regulations, 507

U.S. at 315, 318, 113 S.Ct. at 1454–1456 (O'Connor, J., joined by Souter, J., concurring). *Flores* was decided by a seven to two vote of the Justices. Justices Stevens and Blackmun dissented on the basis that the Justice Department regulations were not authorized by federal statute and that, even if they were, the regulations deprived alien children of liberty without due process of law by subjecting them to indefinite detention without any provision for individualized consideration of the child's best interest. Reno v. Flores, 507 U.S. 292, 318–47, 113 S.Ct. 1439, 1456–1471, 123 L.Ed.2d 1 (1993) (Stevens and Blackmun, JJ., dissenting).

98.   523 U.S. 833, 118 S.Ct. 1708, 140 L.Ed.2d 1043 (1998).

99.   523 U.S. at 839, 118 S.Ct. at 1713.

addressing this narrow question because of the way in which the Court had framed the grant of certiorari.[100] The Justice Souter majority opinion intentionally set aside questions concerning procedural due process and, perhaps unintentionally, set aside questions concerning takings clause issues. The majority opinion stated: "respondents [the parents of the deceased young man] do not argue that they were denied due process by virtue of the fact that California's post-deprivation procedures and rules of immunity have effectively denied them adequate opportunity to seek compensation for the state-occasioned deprivation of their son's life. We express no opinion here on the merits of such a claim ..., or on the adequacy of California's post-deprivation compensation scheme."[101]

In *Lewis*, the parents of the deceased young man brought suit against the government and the officer under the federal civil rights statute providing for damages for violation of federal rights to persons acting under color of law.[102] The Court considered only whether the county, the sheriff's department, and the police officer would be liable for a violation of substantive due process rights, without considering whether the family might be entitled to just compensation.

Despite the fact that the Justices ruled against the family of the deceased young man, the *Lewis* majority opinion constitutes a ringing endorsement of the use of substantive due process analysis, in general, and the application of substantive due process principles to executive action in particular. Justice Souter's

majority opinion ruled that the constitutionality of the police officer's action would be judged by substantive due process standards rather than being reviewed under the more "specific" constitutional provisions of the Fourth and Eighth Amendments[103] Justice Souter relied on early nineteenth century dicta, and a late nineteenth century ruling, as critical sources for establishing the proposition that due process had a substantive as well as a procedural component.[104] Indeed, the majority opinion involves a close parallel to the arguments made by Justice Chase in *Calder v. Bull*,[105] though the majority opinion made no reference to that case.

Justice Scalia, concurring only in the judgment of the Court, found that Justice Souter's majority opinion was little more than the type of substantive due process analysis advanced by Justice Souter in his separate opinion in the so-called "right-to-die" case, which had been rejected by the Court in 1997.[106] According to Justice Scalia: "Today, so to speak, the stone that the builders had rejected, has become the foundation-stone of our substantive-due process jurisprudence."[107] Nevertheless, Justice Souter's opinion in *Lewis* was joined by five other Justices.

Justice Souter's majority opinion in *Lewis* found that the "criteria to identify what is fatally arbitrary [a violation of substantive due process principles] differ depending on whether it [the government action being reviewed] is legislation, or a specific act of a government officer that is at issue."[108] In turning to a

---

100. Sacramento v. Lewis, 523 U.S. 833, 856, 118 S.Ct. 1708, 1721, 140 L.Ed.2d 1043 (1998) (Rehnquist, C.J., concurring in the opinion and judgment of the Court).

101. Sacramento v. Lewis, 523 U.S. 833, 840, n. 4, 118 S.Ct. 1708, 1714, n. 4, 140 L.Ed.2d 1043 (1998).

102. 42 U.S.C.A. § 1983. Justice Stevens would have decided the case based on the immunity of police officers from damage actions under 42 U.S.C.A. § 1983. Sacramento v. Lewis, 523 U.S. 833, 859, 118 S.Ct. 1708, 1723, 140 L.Ed.2d 1043 (1998) (Stevens, J., concurring in the judgment).

103. Sacramento v. Lewis, 523 U.S. 833, 845–46, 118 S.Ct. 1708, 1715–16, 140 L.Ed.2d 1043 (1998).

104. 523 U.S. at 845, 118 S.Ct. at 1716. In this portion of the opinion, Justice Souter referred to, and placed reliance on, Hurtado v. California, 110 U.S. 516, 527, 4

S.Ct. 111, 117, 28 L.Ed. 232 (1884), quoting Justice Johnson's opinion in Bank of Columbia v. Okely, 17 U.S. (4 Wheat.) 235–44, 4 L.Ed. 559 (1819).

105. 3 U.S. (3 Dall.) 386, 1 L.Ed. 648 (1798). See §§ 11.1, 11.2 of this Treatise.

106. County of Sacramento v. Lewis, 523 U.S. 833, 860, 118 S.Ct. 1708, 1723–24, 140 L.Ed.2d 1043 (1998) (Scalia, J., joined by Thomas, J., concurring in the judgment).

107. 523 U.S. at 861, 118 S.Ct. at 1724 (Scalia, J., joined by Thomas, J., concurring in the judgment). Justice Scalia referred to Washington v. Glucksberg, 521 U.S. 702, 117 S.Ct. 2258, 2267–69, 138 L.Ed.2d 772 (1997).

108. County of Sacramento v. Lewis, 523 U.S. 833, 846, 118 S.Ct. 1708, 1717, 140 L.Ed.2d 1043 (1998). The shocks the conscience standard had been developed by the

determination of how substantive due process principles would limit acts of government officers, Justice Souter found that "only the most egregious official conduct" would violate substantive due process principles.[109] The *Lewis* majority ruled that a "shocks the conscience" standard would determine whether executive action that harmed an individual violated due process.

According to Justice Souter, the shock the conscience test adopted by the majority, was not similar to any "traditional category of common-law fault."[110] The majority opinion described shock the conscience standard as reflecting a spectrum of due process limits on executive action. At one end of the spectrum was negligently inflicted harm, which never would meet the "shock the conscience" test so as to be a due process violation. "Liability for negligently inflicted harm is categorically beneath the threshold of constitutional due process."[111] At the other end of this due process spectrum was the intentional infliction of injury to persons or property by government officials. "Conduct intended to injure in some way, unjustifiable by any government interest, is the sort of official action most likely to rise to the conscience-shocking level."[112]

Cases in which injuries were caused to persons, or property, by government actors acting "with culpability falling within the middle range, following from something more than negligence, but less than intentional conduct, such as recklessness or gross negligence" would require case-by-case analysis to determine whether the activity violated the shock the conscience standard.[113] Thus, a governmental failure to protect individuals, or harm to individuals that was incidental to government activity, would require "an exact analysis of the circumstances before any abuse of a power is condemned as conscience-shocking."[114]

After finding that substantive due process principles imposed a shock the conscience standard on the activities of government officials, Justice Souter's majority opinion applied that standard to the actions of a police officer in pursuit of a suspect. The majority in *Lewis* found that "mid-level fault" had been the basis for establishing liability for "deliberate indifference" to the welfare of persons within control of the government when government officials had the "luxury" of being able to take time to make "unhurried judgments."[115] Because police in a high speed chase were pursuing an important government objective (the apprehension of a suspected criminal), and because they did not have time to weigh the possible consequences of specific acts taken in the chase, the *Lewis* majority refused to hold police officers, or their government employers, liable for harm caused to suspects in a police chase.[116]

The majority opinion in *Lewis* stated the Court's holding twice, and in slightly different terms each time. At the start of the opinion, Justice Souter said that the Court would "hold that in such circumstances [a high-speed chase] only a purpose to cause harm unrelated to the legitimate object of arrest will satisfy the element of arbitrary conduct, shocking to the conscience, necessary for a due process violation."[117] Near the end of the *Lewis* majority opinion, Justice Souter stated: "We hold that high-speed chases with no intent to harm suspects physically or to worsen their legal plight do not give rise to liability under the Fourteenth Amendment, redressable by an action under [42 U.S.C. § 1983]."[118]

Court in Rochin v. California, 342 U.S. 165, 72 S.Ct. 205, 96 L.Ed. 183 (1952) to control some types of police actions, before the time that the Court had made the Fourth Amendment restriction on searches and seizures applicable to the states. See, Nowak, Foreword: Due Process Methodology in the Postincorporation World, 70 Journal of Criminal Law and Criminology 397 (1980).

109. Sacramento v. Lewis, 523 U.S. 833, 846, 118 S.Ct. 1708, 1716, 140 L.Ed.2d 1043 (1998).

110. 523 U.S. at 848, 118 S.Ct. at 1717.

111. 523 U.S. at 849, 118 S.Ct. at 1718.

112. Id.

113. 523 U.S. at 849, 118 S.Ct. at 1718 (internal quotation marks & citations omitted).

114. 523 U.S. at 850, 118 S.Ct. at 1718–19.

115. 523 U.S. at 853, 118 S.Ct. at 1720.

116. 523 U.S. at 853, 118 S.Ct. at 1720–21.

117. Sacramento v. Lewis, 523 U.S. 833, 836, 118 S.Ct. 1708, 1711–12, 140 L.Ed.2d 1043, (1998).

118. 523 U.S. at 854, 118 S.Ct. at 1720 (internal citations omitted).

Neither of Justice Souter's summary statements regarding Court's holding in *Lewis* explains whether any constitutional violation might occur when the police in a high-speed chase act with gross negligence or recklessness and cause foreseeable harm to persons other than the suspects when the high-speed chase was not necessary to stop any eminent danger to the government or society. The wording of both "holdings" appears to relieve the government of all liability for harm to third parties during high-speed chases, even when the high-speed chase is a suspect for a traffic violation. However, it is important to note that the *Lewis* case involved harm to a suspect who was being pursued by the police. The Court had set aside the question of whether the state could use sovereign immunity to deny any compensation to any parties hurt in a police chase. Thus, the *Lewis* decision may not resolve most future cases in which involved innocent parties who were hurt by negligent, grossly negligent, or reckless police conduct in a high-speed chase of suspects for a non-violent crime.

It is possible that the greatest importance of the *Lewis* decision will not be its narrow holding regarding the liability of police officers for injuries to suspects in high-speed chase scenarios, but, rather, the majority opinion's endorsement of substantive due process analysis. On the day *Lewis* was decided, a clear majority of the Justices endorsed substantive due process analysis quite similar to that used during the first part of the twentieth century. Justice Souter's majority opinion in *Lewis* openly endorsed the use of a general inquiry into the history and traditions of our nation to determine the types of government actions that might violate substantive due process principles.

Although they noted their concern that the shock the conscience test might be quite difficult to apply; Justices Kennedy and O'Connor, in a concurring opinion stated "history and tradition are the starting point, but not the ending point of substantive due process inqui-

ry."[119] This statement is quite similar to statements made by Justices during the Warren Court era concerning the use of substantive due process in right-to-privacy cases.[120]

Despite the *Lewis* majority's narrowing of the issues it would consider, the question of whether there must be compensation for victims of government-inflicted injuries, may be the key issue in future cases of this type. The problem that will face lower courts, and which was not addressed in *Lewis*, can be demonstrated by what the authors of this Treatise term "the poor little Johnny hypothetical." In our hypothetical, little Johnny, an only child, is attending his first day of school. His mother and father are at home in their little house, which, unfortunately, happens to be quite close to a highway. A state police officer, in pursuit of a suspect, is driving his police car negligently, grossly negligently, or recklessly. Because of the negligent, grossly negligent, or reckless actions of the police officer, his squad car leaves the street, and hits the house of little Johnny's parents. Both of Johnny's parents are killed; the house catches fire and burns to the ground. Little Johnny has lost his parents, (his sole sources of support), and virtually all of the family economic resources (because his parents could not afford adequate insurance, and had very little equity in the property). Little Johnny finds a kindly attorney to bring suit against the state; the state admits the negligent, grossly negligent, or reckless conduct of the police officer. Nevertheless, the state refuses to pay any money to little Johnny on the basis of a state law that granted the state and local governments sovereign immunity. On these facts, would the state have taken little Johnny's property or liberty interests in violation of due process? Would the state have violated the taking of property clause, which applies to state and local governments thorough the due process clause of the Fourteenth Amendment? Is little Johnny, under these facts, entitled to some type of com-

119. County of Sacramento v. Lewis, 523 U.S. 833, 856–57, 118 S.Ct. 1708, 1721–23 140 L.Ed.2d 1043 (1998) (Kennedy, J. joined by O'Connor, J., concurring in the opinion and judgment of the Court).

120. See, e.g., Griswold v. Connecticut, 381 U.S. 479, 486, 85 S.Ct. 1678, 1682–83, 14 L.Ed.2d 510 (1965) (Goldberg, J. concurring).

pensation from the state? These are questions that were left unanswered in *Lewis*.

§ 10.7 The Equal Protection Clause

Analysis under the equal protection clause of the Fourteenth Amendment is identical to that used under the due process clauses. The only equal protection clause appears in the Fourteenth Amendment and it only applies to the states.[1] The Court, however, has interpreted the due process clause of the Fifth Amendment to test federal classifications under the same standard of review.[2] Thus, the Constitution may be said to contain an equal protection guarantee applicable to the federal government even though the Fourteenth Amendment cannot be applied to federal actions.

Review under both equal protection guarantees is always substantive in nature. The equal protection guarantees require the government to treat similarly situated individuals in a similar manner. They do not govern the process to be employed in decision-making but they do regulate the ability of the government to finally classify individuals as different in type, either for the purposes of dispensing governmental benefits or punishments.[3]

Under the due process clause the Court asks whether the legislation rationally relates to a legitimate end of government. The identical test exists under the equal protection clauses except that legislation reviewed under these guarantees always involves a classification. If a law burdens all persons equally when they exercise a specific right, then the courts will test the law under the due process clause. If, however, the law distinguishes between who may and who may not exercise a right, then

judicial review of the law falls under the equal protection guarantee because the issue now becomes whether the distinction between these persons is legitimate. The classification employed is the "means" used to achieve some end. Thus, the Court reviews the issue of whether the classification rationally relates to a legitimate end under the equal protection guarantees.

In the period from 1885 to 1937, the Supreme Court examined many economic legislative classifications to determine if the Justices agreed that those classifications were related to legitimate functions of an American government. This examination resulted in the striking of economic and general social legislation, although it was used less often than substantive review under the due process clauses.[4]

After 1937, however, the Court abandoned independent, nondeferential active review of legislation under the equal protection guarantees. Consequently, the Justices no longer will determine for themselves the legitimacy of classifications employed in general social welfare or economic legislation. If the classifications arguably relate to a legitimate function of government, the Court will sustain them under the equal protection guarantees.

If a classification is being tested under the rationality test it is the burden of the party attacking the law to show that there is no conceivable set of facts by which the legislative body could have rationally concluded that the classification was related to a legitimate government interest. The presumption of constitutionality given to laws that do not restrict fundamental rights or employ certain constitutionally suspect classifying traits is quite difficult to overcome. However, in a few cases, the

---

§ 10.7

1. The language of the clause refers only to the states. "[N]or shall any State . . . deny to any person within its jurisdiction the equal protection of the laws." U.S. Const. amend. 14, § 1.

2. Bolling v. Sharpe, 347 U.S. 497, 74 S.Ct. 693, 98 L.Ed. 884 (1954), opinion supplemented 349 U.S. 294, 75 S.Ct. 753, 99 L.Ed. 1083 (1955); United States v. Kras, 409 U.S. 434, 93 S.Ct. 631, 34 L.Ed.2d 626 (1973). There is dicta indicating that the Court will subject federal laws which burden aliens as a class to a more lenient standard of review because of unique federal interests in this area.

See, Nyquist v. Mauclet, 432 U.S. 1, 7 n. 8, 97 S.Ct. 2120, 2124 n. 8, 53 L.Ed.2d 63 (1977). The case is discussed in §§ 14.11–14.13 infra.

3. Duggan, J., citing Treatise in Dow v. Town of Effingham, 148 N.H. 121, 803 A.2d 1059, 1064 (2002); Cook, J., concurring in result, and dissenting in part, citing Treatise in, Ex Parte Melof, 735 So.2d 1172 (Ala.1999), cert.denied 528 U.S. 986, 120 S.Ct. 447, 145 L.Ed.2d 364 (1999).

4. R. McCloskey, The American Supreme Court 151 (1960).

Court has found that government classifications related to general economic or social welfare matters were so arbitrary or irrational that they violated the rationality test.[5]

The Supreme Court, in the modern era, has employed the equal protection guarantee to strike down a number of laws that created classifications related to exercising "fundamental rights."[6] If a law significantly impairs the ability of one class of persons to engage in such activities, the Court has often stated that the classification will be invalid unless the government can demonstrate that the classification is narrowly tailored to a compelling or overriding interest. However, in the last decades of the twentieth century, the Supreme Court upheld some government limitations on fundamental rights without stating a clear standard of review. The standard used by the Court when judging restrictions on fundamental rights is not entirely clear. However, it is clear that such laws will not enjoy a presumption of constitutionality; the Justices will independently determine whether the classification is constitutionally permissible. Because most of the fundamental rights cases in the modern era have been framed in terms of equal protection, rather than substantive due process, we will treat the fundamental rights cases in Chapter 14.

If a classification does not relate to a fundamental right the Court will grant the classification the presumption of constitutionality unless the classification was created through the use of certain traits that the Court has deemed to be "suspect" or "quasi-suspect."

Because of the Justices views of the history and purpose of the Fourteenth Amendment, laws that classify individuals on the basis of their status as a member of a racial minority or their national origin (ancestry) are viewed as "suspect," in that it is unlikely that a governmental use of such a classifying trait could be constitutionally permissible. The Court will not approve a governmental classification based on race or ancestry unless the government can demonstrate that the classification is truly necessary to promote a compelling government interest.[7]

An alienage classification is a law that treats people differently based on whether or not they are United States citizens The Court at times has referred to alienage classifications as being "suspect", although the Court has not invalidated all uses of alienage classifications. The Court has accorded a presumption of constitutionality to federal legislation that uses U.S. citizenship classifications but it has invalidated a variety of state laws that have employed similar classifications.[8]

The Court has developed a special standard of review for determining the constitutionality of classifications that are based on gender (sex) or illegitimacy (the trait of being born to parents who were not lawfully married). The Court will not grant such classifications of presumption of constitutionality, which would subject such classifications to the mere rationality test. The Court has not yet found that either sex or illegitimacy classifications are truly suspect; it has not yet applied strict judicial scrutiny and the compelling interest tests to such classifications. In the last quarter of the twentieth century, the Supreme Court developed a middle level standard of review—between rationality and the compelling interest test—for examining sex and illegitimacy classifications. When the government creates

---

5. See § 14.3 for an analysis of the standards of review used in judging the compatibility of government created classifications with the equal protection clause of the Fourteenth Amendment or the implied equal protection guarantee of the Fifth Amendment due process clause.

6. The Court's decision to declare a right "fundamental" involves substantive due process analysis; we will examine this point in §§ 11.5, 11.6. However, the government does not normally pass laws that attempt to take away a fundamental constitutional right from all persons. Rather, the cases that have involved impairments of fundamental rights have been ones in which the government has created a classification of persons who will not be

allowed to exercise the fundamental right on equal terms with other persons. For that reason most of the fundamental rights cases have been equal protection cases. The standard of review for equal protection cases is examined in § 14.3, and examination of specific rulings of the Court concerning fundamental rights are contained in §§ 14.26–14.46.

7. See §§ 14.5–14.10 regarding race and ancestry classifications.

8. See §§ 14.11–14.13 regarding alienage classifications.

such classifications it must be able to demonstrate that the classification is substantially related to an important government interest.[9]

If an individual believes that she has been treated by the government in an entirely different manner than all other similarly situated persons, she may bring an equal protection claim against the government even though she is, in a sense, only a "class of one."[10] In many, if not most, real-life cases, we would expect the government to have a rational argument for why the separate treatment of the individual was a reasonable method of promoting a legitimate governmental or societal interest. There may be circumstances under which the separate treatment of a single person would violate equal protection even under the rationality test. For example, let us assume that Susan Smith, the child of Sarah and Samuel Smith, is 6 years old and (under all state and local statutes) eligible for a free public education at her neighborhood public grade school. When Susan and her parents go to register her for the first grade, the school authorities refuse to register her; they will not allow her to attend the school. The school administration states: "We don't like the Smith family, and we don't want any Smith children in our public schools." Susan would have an equal protection claim against the governmental entity that operated the schools, which might or might not prevail after trial. If we assume that education is not a fundamental right, and that Susan was not excluded because of her race, gender, or status as a legitimate or illegitimate child, the Court would apply the rationality test to determine whether the denial of free public education to Susan violated the equal protection guarantee. Susan and her parents might be able to make a convincing argument that there is no possible legitimate interest that would justify singling out this child. Although the state would not have the burden of proof in this case, the Smith family should win, unless the government could rebut the Susan's argument by showing that the denial of education for Susan promoted a legitimate governmental interest. Were such a case to actually occur, the government should lose, under the equal protection clause, even though the Court was applying the classic form of minimal judicial scrutiny and the rationality test.[11]

---

9. Illegitimacy classifications are examined in §§ 14.14–14.19; gender classifications are examined in §§ 14.20–14.24.

10. In Village of Willowbrook v. Olech, 528 U.S. 562, 120 S.Ct. 1073, 145 L.Ed.2d 1060, (2000) (per curiam), the Court ruled that a woman could maintain an equal protection claim against a Village based on an allegation that the Village had demanded that she give the Village, in exchange for connection to the municipal water supply, a 33–foot easement on her property. All other similarly situated owners were required to give only a 15–foot easement to the Village in exchange for the municipal water supply connection. The majority opinion noted that the Court did not have to consider the subjective motives of the Village, because the Court had often recognized that an individual could bring an equal protection claim as a "class of one" by being treated differently from other similarly situated persons. Such a claim would be reviewed under the rationality test. Justice Breyer concurred in only the result in *Willowbrook*. Justice Breyer believed that the Court should focus on the fact that there was an allegation of an improper motive on the part of the governmental officials (a desire to harm the property owner because of other disputes with her); he wanted to reduce the possibility of persons bringing "run-of-the-mill zoning cases" to federal courts as constitutional claims.

11. See generally, Payne, D.J., quoting Treatise in McWaters v. Rick, 195 F.Supp.2d 781, 792 n. 10 (E.D.Va. 2002).

Chapter 11

SUBSTANTIVE DUE PROCESS

§ 11.1 Judicial Control of Legislation Prior to the Civil War

Almost since the beginning of the nation, the Justices of the Supreme Court have suggested that they had an inherent right to review the substance of legislation that either the Congress or state legislatures had enacted. Seventeenth and eighteenth century political theory had built on an earlier philosophical base in espousing the position that certain natural rights prevailed for all men and that a governmental body could not limit or impair these rights. In short, these rights existed in every society whether they arose from a social compact or from divine right. From this seventeenth and eighteenth century political thought grew the concept that a higher or natural law limited the restrictions on liberty that a temporal government could impose on an individual.

In the case of *Calder v. Bull*,[1] the Justices for the first time engaged in a debate concerning their ability to overrule legislation on the basis of natural law. In *Calder* the Court held that the Connecticut legislature had not violated the Constitution when it set aside a probate decree.[2] The case, however, is important for the opposing opinions of Justices Iredell and Chase, rather than for the precise issue or result of the litigation.

Justice Chase believed that the drafters of the constitutions of the federal and state governments intended to create governments of limited powers and that natural law, as well as the specific provisions of written constitutions, restricted and regulated governmental power.[3] He felt that the province of the judiciary was to ensure that the government did not violate the rights of the people under the natural law. Therefore, Justice Chase decided that the proper role of the Supreme Court was to invalidate legislation if the Justices believed that it interfered with rights that the natural law had vested in the people.

Justice Iredell, on the other hand, made a plea for what is now known as judicial restraint.[4] He contended that—even if natural law ought to prevail—no valid legal theory indicated that a court should have the power to enforce the natural law over the will of the people as that will was reflected by the other branches of government. He noted that the people had limited the acts of Congress and the states with specific constitutional checks;

---

§ 11.1

1. 3 U.S. (3 Dall.) 386, 1 L.Ed. 648 (1798).

2. 3 U.S. (3 Dall.) at 401, 1 L.Ed. at 654.

3. 3 U.S. (3 Dall.) at 386–88, 1 L.Ed. at 648–49. See, in particular, 3 U.S. (3 Dall.) at 388, 1 L.Ed. at 649: "An act of the Legislature (for I cannot call it a law) contrary to the great first principles of the social compact, cannot be considered a rightful exercise of legislative authority."

The Court in *Calder,* with the agreement of Justice Chase, ruled that the state law did not violate the ex post facto clause of Article I, section 9. Two hundred years after the *Calder* decision, Justice Thomas expressed the view that he would be "willing to reconsider *Calder* and

its progeny to determine whether a retroactive civil law that passes muster under our current takings clause jurisprudence is nonetheless unconstitutional under the ex post facto clause." Eastern Enterprises v. Apfel, 524 U.S. 498, 538, 118 S.Ct. 2131, 2154, 141 L.Ed.2d 451 (1998). (Thomas, J., concurring). No other Justice in the *Eastern Enterprises* case joined Justice Thomas's concurrence. In Eastern Enterprises the Court, without a majority opinion, invalidated a federal government action that would have required a corporation not currently engaged in the coal mining business to make payments into a fund that would provide health benefits for retired mine workers.

4. 3 U.S. (3 Dall.) at 398–400, 1 L.Ed. at 653–54.

if those specific checks were violated, the Court only would be enforcing democratic principles by declaring the legislation void. If the Court relied upon natural law to overturn legislative acts, the Justices not only would assume powers not granted them under the Constitution but also would disparage the democratic process. Thus, Justice Iredell believed that the courts had no role in enforcing natural law principles because enforcement of such principles would result in the subservience of the people to the individual views of the Justices.

In form, the Supreme Court has adopted the views of Justice Iredell and ruled that it only may invalidate acts of the legislative and executive branches of the federal and state governments on the basis of specific provisions of the Constitution. In substance, however, the beliefs of Justice Chase have prevailed as the Court continually has expanded its basis for reviewing the acts of other branches of government.

During the early years of the republic the Court refrained from overturning acts of the federal government. Indeed, the Court only held two acts of the federal government unconstitutional during the period from the Court's formation to the Civil War.[5]

Two reasons account for the Court's seeming acceptance of the actions of the other branches of the federal government during this period. First, the central mission of the Court during its early years—particularly under Chief Justice Marshall—was to build the federal system into a viable government. The rulings of the Court on the commerce power and necessary and proper clause helped to establish the federal power. Second, and more importantly, the new federal government made few attempts to limit the "natural" rights of liberty or property of individual citizens. The restrictions on the freedom to use property came from state rather than federal legislation.

In developing controls and checks over the state governments the federal judiciary moved slowly. The text of the Constitution and the Bill of Rights contain only a limited number of restraints on the actions of state governments. No matter how much individual Justices may have wanted to limit the authority of state governments on the basis of natural law, they realized that using natural law would be a difficult task. Strong arguments against the ability of any branch of the federal government to control state actions had been made by representatives of the states. Consequently, the Justices realized that they would need something more concrete than the natural law as the basis for their decisions if they voided state legislative or executive actions. The original Constitution, however, offered little basis for assuming control of state activities through a natural law formula.

The Bill of Rights might have provided a number of specific provisions for controlling the activities of state governments. The history of the Bill of Rights, however, clearly showed that the authors of the Amendments intended that they only apply to the federal government.

Anti-federalists had objected to the new Constitution because the document contained no specific guarantees that the new national government would not infringe on certain individual rights. The Federalists, on the other hand, had argued that no such enumeration was necessary because no power delegated to the natural government in the body of the Constitution would enable it to legitimately eliminate individual liberties. Indeed, the Federalists argued that listing protected rights would be dangerous because a government may interpret the enumeration of specific protected rights as an implied exclusion of those rights not so listed because of drafting or timing limitations. The Anti-federalists, however, sought and gained assurances that the

---

5. The first was the section of the Judiciary Act overturned in Marbury v. Madison, 5 U.S. (1 Cranch) 137, 2 L.Ed. 60 (1803).

The second was the Missouri Compromise which was held unconstitutional in Dred Scott v. Sandford, 60 U.S. (19 How.) 393, 15 L.Ed. 691 (1856). Actually the defendant's name in this case was misspelled; it should be "Sanford." C. Wright, Law of Federal Courts 249 n. 5 (3d ed. 1976), citing Latham, The Dred Scott Decision 26 (1968).

federal government, by Amendment to the Constitution, would guarantee certain individual liberties. This bargain resulted in the first Congress drafting the Bill of Rights. The ratification process for the ten Amendments went swiftly and they were ratified in 1791. The history of the Bill of Rights revealed the difficulty the Supreme Court would have had in suggesting that the Amendments were intended as a check on the powers of state governments. Indeed, the Court soon acknowledged that the Bill of Rights only limited the acts of the federal government.

In *Barron v. Mayor and City Council of Baltimore*[6] the Court confronted the question of whether or not the Fifth Amendment prohibition on taking private property for a public use without just compensation applied to state governments. Chief Justice Marshall answered that none of the first ten Amendments could apply to the state governments because the history of the Bill of Rights supported their application only to the activities of the newly formed central government.[7] Thus, limitations on state governments would have to exist either in natural law or in the specific portions of the text of the Constitution.

The original text of the Constitution contains some specific checks on the powers of state government. Article 1, section 10 of the Constitution limits the ability of state governments to take certain specific actions absolutely and it limits the states' ability to take other actions without the consent of Congress.[8] The prohibitions against bills of attainder[9] or *ex*

post facto laws[10] eliminated the ability of state governments to imprison people by legislative act, but these prohibitions had little to do with general police power legislation. Only a few of the Constitution's provisions served as a possible limit on the general types of police power legislation which might infringe individual liberties or vested property rights. Indeed, only the provision prohibiting the states from "impairing the obligation of contracts"[11] offered any hope for controlling legislation that eliminated vested property rights.

The Contract Clause. The Court used the contract clause in its attempt to gain some control over the substance of general police power legislation during the years prior to the Civil War. In 1810 Chief Justice Marshall wrote the opinion in *Fletcher v. Peck.*[12] In this decision the Chief Justice, with the approval of a unanimous Court, held that a state legislature could not rescind grants of land to original purchasers. So long as the original purchasers transferred the land to innocent third parties, the contract clause protected the original grant even though the original purchaser had bribed the members of the legislature to acquire the property initially.

Fletcher was one of the most important decisions in the history of the Court without regard to the contract clause issue. The Court had just survived many threats to its existence ranging from the wrath expressed by President Jefferson following the *Marbury* decision to the attempted impeachment of Justice Chase for partisan activities.[13] Having sur-

---

6. 32 U.S. (7 Pet.) 243, 8 L.Ed. 672 (1833). For references to historical materials concerning the ratification process and the call for a Bill of Rights, see § 3.1, 4.1–4.3, supra.

7. 32 U.S. (7 Pet.) at 249, 8 L.Ed. at 674–75.

8. "No State shall enter into any Treaty, Alliance, or Confederation; grant Letters of Marque and Reprisal; coin Money; emit Bills of Credit; make any thing but gold and silver coin a Tender in Payment of Debts; pass any Bill of Attainder, ex post facto Law, or Law impairing the Obligation of Contracts, or grant any Title of Nobility.

"No State shall, without the Consent of the Congress, lay any Imposts or Duties on Imports or Exports, except what may be absolutely necessary for executing its inspection Laws: and the net Produce of all Duties and Imposts, laid by any State on Imports or Exports, shall be for the Use of the Treasury of the United States; and

all such Laws shall be subject to the Revision and Controul of the Congress.

"No State shall, without the Consent of Congress, lay any Duty of Tonnage, keep Troops, or Ships of War in time of Peace, enter into any Agreement or Compact with another State, or with a foreign Power, or engage in War, unless actually invaded, or in such imminent Danger as will not admit of delay."

U.S.Const. art. I, § 10.

9. Id.

10. Id.

11. Id.

12. 10 U.S. (6 Cranch) 87, 3 L.Ed. 162 (1810).

13. See R. McCloskey, The American Supreme Court 44–53 (1960).

vived these challenges to its authority, the Marshall Court embarked on a main effort to control state legislation through the contract clause. Moreover, *Fletcher* was a rather adventuresome interpretation of the contract clause because the Court had to find that the clause applied to contracts made by the state as well as to state invalidation of private contracts. Furthermore, the Court was required to hold that grants of property rights by the state could be construed as contracts. Nevertheless, once he laid the groundwork for these positions in *Fletcher*, Marshall quickly enlarged upon these rulings so that they could become a basis for the control of state legislation.

In the famous case of *Trustees of Dartmouth College v. Woodward* [14] the Court confronted the question of whether a state legislature could control a college established by grant of the British Crown to publicly appointed trustees. Chief Justice Marshall held that the corporate charter was a contract within the meaning of the contract clause and that the state could not alter the charter materially without violating the prohibition of Article I.

Dartmouth College could have established a basis for controlling many forms of state legislation. The decision logically implied that all businesses or corporations chartered by the state had a right to use their property free of government regulation, because the limitation of the rights of the chartered business would violate the contract of the state. Indeed, Marshall apparently favored this reasoning because it would have fully protected vested property rights. The other Justices, however, were unwilling to extend the *Dartmouth* opinion this far. For example, in 1827, the Supreme Court upheld state bankruptcy laws that provided for the discharge of debts and held that the contract clause did not control prospective state interference with the use of property. [15]

The Doctrines of Vested Rights and the Police Power. The development of both natural law and the contract clause as protection for the individual against the actions of government was centered on the freedom to use property without government restriction. Professor Corwin, in his classic works on the nature of liberty in the American system, has called this "the doctrine of vested rights." [16] He stated that the general theme of the concept of vested rights "was that the effect of legislation on existing property rights was a primary test of its validity; for if these were essentially impaired then some clear constitutional justification must be found for the legislation or it must succumb to judicial condemnation." [17]

But at the same time that the judiciary was accepting the "doctrine of vested rights", another legal concept was developing which would oppose it. Political and judicial thought prior to the Civil War had begun to recognize the inherent need of governments to protect the safety and welfare of their citizens from the unrestrained liberty of some individuals. [18] This came to be known as the "police power" concept. This does not relate to any specialized power of government. Instead, the "police power" encompasses the inherent right of state and local governments to enact legislation protecting the health, safety, morals or general welfare of the people within their jurisdiction.

In 1837 the Court recognized that state and local governments had an inherent police power to protect the health, safety, welfare or morals of their people and that the reasonable exercise of the police power did not violate the contract clause. In *Proprietors of Charles River Bridge v. Proprietors of Warren Bridge* [19] the owners of a state-chartered toll bridge contended that the legislature could not authorize any competing bridges. The owners argued that any authorization of competing bridges would diminish the worth of their chartered

---

14. 17 U.S. (4 Wheat.) 518, 4 L.Ed. 629 (1819).

15. Ogden v. Saunders, 25 U.S. (12 Wheat.) 213, 6 L.Ed. 606 (1827); For an examination of this and other contract clause issues, see § 11.7, infra.

16. E. Corwin, Liberty Against Government 72 (1948).

17. Id.

18. E. Corwin, Liberty Against Government 88 (1948).

19. 36 U.S. (11 Pet.) 420, 9 L.Ed. 773 (1837).

monopoly. The Court held that, although it would construe the charter as a contract that bound the state, it would interpret the contract narrowly in favor of the state. The Justices here recognized the need of the legislature to act to provide for the welfare of its citizens. Consequently, the Court held that, whenever possible, it would interpret public grants and business charters so as to allow reasonable police power regulation. Thus, the contract clause was severely limited as a tool for controlling the substance of the state legislation. The clause would not become an important consideration again, because after the Civil War new means would exist to control the states through the Civil War Amendments.[20]

The Supremacy Clause and the Commerce Power. Other than the provisions of Article I, the Court had few bases for controlling state legislation prior to the Civil War. Any legislation of state or local governments that conflicted with federal legislation would be invalidated under the supremacy clause.[21] Pre-Civil War federal legislation, however, was limited in scope; consequently, the Court had little opportunity to find that state legislation was void because of a direct conflict with federal law or preempted by related, though not directly conflicting, federal acts.

The commerce clause provided the Court a method to control state legislation and, thus, to protect private property rights prior to the Civil War. The Court held that the commerce clause prohibited state legislation that would interfere unreasonably with the free flow of commerce between the states.[22] A broad interpretation of the clause was necessary not only to increase the scope of powers of the federal government but also to allow the federal judges to protect to some extent vested rights by controlling some state commercial legislation.

Substantive Due Process. A review of judicial control of the substance of legislation would be incomplete without some discussion of the philosophy of substantive due process.[23] Substantive due process theory began to develop before the Civil War. Both the English concept of due process of law and the early American legal theorists' idea of due process focused on the procedural feature of the concept. With the rise of natural rights philosophy, however, some theorists intimated that due process also should have a substantive content.

Under this theory, if a legislature passed any law which restricted vested rights or violated natural law, it exceeded all bounds of the social compact in restricting the freedom of some individuals. Therefore, some authorities reasoned that the legislature had denied due process of law to those individuals whose rights or liberties were limited by such legislation because the legislature had denied those deprived persons the guarantees of the basic social compact. Indeed, in several of the contract clause cases, the Marshall Court indicated that state laws which interfered with the free use of property by a chartered corporation violated not only the contract clause but also an inherent right of individuals to be free of legislation which interfered with vested property rights. The theory gained additional credence during this period because a number of state judiciaries held that laws that violated either natural law or vested rights philosophy were invalid under the due process clauses of state constitutions. The most famous federal and state pre-Civil War cases that indicated a judicial acceptance of substantive due process were rendered in 1856 and 1857.

The clearest use of substantive due process in the states occurred in the New York Court of Appeals decision in *Wynehamer v. People*.[24] The New York court held that a prohibition statute violated the state due process clause to

---

20. U.S.Const. amends. 13, 14, 15. The growth of judicial review following the Civil War is discussed in § 11.2, infra.

21. "This Constitution, and the Laws of the United States which shall be made in Pursuance thereof ... shall be the Supreme Law of the Land." U.S.Const. art. VI.

22. The development of the commerce clause is examined in Chapters 4, 8.

23. For a detailed study of this concept and its growth prior to the Civil War, see E. Corwin, Liberty Against Government 58–115 (1948).

24. 13 N.Y. (3 Kern.) 378 (1856).

the extent that it applied to liquor owned prior to the passage of the statute. Because the measure affected the vested rights of owners in their property (in this case the alcoholic beverages intended for further sale), the court held that the law's enactment was beyond any power given to the legislative body under the state's social compact with its citizens.

The federal decision invalidating a law as totally beyond the legislative power came in the case of *Dred Scott v. Sandford*.[25] Dred Scott had been taken as a slave into the state of Illinois and the northern part of the Louisiana Purchase territory. Not only had Illinois forbidden slavery, but the territory into which Scott's "owner" had taken him had been declared a free territory by the Missouri Compromise. Dred Scott sued his present owner and argued that, having been taken into free areas, he had been made a free man. In a decision which almost ended the concept of judicial supremacy, the Court ruled against Dred Scott.

The eight separate opinions filed in the case make the basis of the holding and the exact principle of the case unclear. Three reasons, however, do appear for the ruling. First, black slaves were not citizens of the United States. Second, the Supreme Court must respect the Missouri law declaring Scott a slave notwithstanding his previous entry into "free" area. Third, and most important for the growth of the concept of due process, the Missouri Compromise exceeded Congress' power. On this last rationale Chief Justice Taney suggested that the original Constitution had not given Congress any power to interfere with an "owner's" vested rights in his slaves. Thus, the Missouri Compromise was invalid because it deprived the owners of their rights without due process.

The decision, at a minimum, shows a pre-war willingness both to adopt substantive due process and the natural law philosophy of Justice Chase. However, Northern leaders saw the *Dred Scott* decision as a judicial attempt to protect the system of slavery and the reaction to the decision was violent. In light of this reaction, it is not surprising that the Court after the war sought to control state and federal legislation under specific provisions of the Constitution rather than the due process clauses. However, the concept of substantive due process, while slow to develop, would dominate constitutional adjudication during the next phase of the country's history.[26]

§ 11.2 The Growth of the Substantive Due Process Concept—1865 to 1900

The end of the Civil War prompted a great flurry of Congressional activity. Much of the legislation which Congress passed in the years immediately following the Civil War was designed to punish the southern states for their attempt to secede from the Union. Congress, however, did pass some measures intended to improve the plight of blacks in the South.

Although the Thirteenth Amendment forbidding involuntary servitude was ratified in 1865, the former slaves were unable to enjoy their new freedom. The southern states enacted "Black Codes" and other repressive measures to restrict the ability of blacks to enjoy and exercise their rights. To counteract these repressive measures Congress passed the Civil Rights Act of 1866.[1] The Act made all people born in the country citizens of the United States and gave to such citizens the same rights and "equal benefits of all laws and

---

25. 60 U.S. (19 How.) 393, 15 L.Ed. 691 (1856).

26. Professor Corwin concludes:

"In less than twenty years from the time of its rendition the crucial ruling in 'Wynehamer' was far on the way to being assimilated into the accepted constitutional law of the country. The 'due process' clause, which had been intended originally to consecrate a mode of procedure, had become a constitutional test of ever increasing reach of the substantive content of legislation. Thus was the doctrine of vested rights brought within the

constitutional fold, although without dominating it. For confronting it was the still-expanding concept of the police power."

E. Corwin, Liberty Against Government at 114–15 (1948).

§ 11.2

1. 14 Stat. 27 (1866); Cong. Globe, 39th Cong., 1st Sess. 1809, 1861 (1866).

proceedings for the security of person and property, as is enjoyed by white citizens...." [2]

As Congress was enacting the Civil Rights Act of 1866, it recognized the need to remove doubts about the constitutional ability of Congress to pass such legislation. Therefore, a week after Congress passed the Civil Rights Act a congressional committee submitted an early version of the Fourteenth Amendment for Congress' approval.[3] Finally, after several revisions Congress approved the present version of the Fourteenth Amendment and sent it to the states for ratification.[4] The ratification process for the Fourteenth Amendment was completed in 1868.

Unlike the Congress during the Civil War and the Reconstruction years, the Supreme Court at this time largely was inactive, exercising its power of judicial review infrequently, perhaps because of its reluctance to entangle itself in the passions and emotions which the War had aroused in the nation. Although the Court reviewed the Constitutionality of federal and state legislation only on a few occasions, it did void several state and federal measures that violated the provisions of the Constitution.[5]

On those occasions that the Court invalidated state and federal legislation, it used the specific language of the Constitution to strike the measures rather than concepts of natural law or fundamental rights. The Court relied on the Constitution's proscription of *ex post facto* laws and bills of attainder to void state legislation in *Cummings v. Missouri*[6] and *Ex parte Garland*.[7] In *United States v. Dewitt*[8] the Court struck federal legislation because it believed the commerce clause had not granted Congress the power to pass the legislation at issue. In short, the Court abandoned the con-

cept of natural law that had been referred to in some earlier decisions. Instead, the Court followed the advice of Justice Iredell to use the specific language and specific prohibitions of the Constitution to check the actions of the state and federal governments.

The Supreme Court's reluctance to give an expansive reading to the Constitution was exemplified dramatically in its first major attempt to interpret and apply the provisions of the new Fourteenth Amendment. The language of section one of the Amendment was broad and sweeping. The Amendment prevented any state from making and enforcing any measure that "shall abridge the privileges or immunities of citizens of the United States...." [9] Moreover, the Amendment adopted the due process language of the Fifth Amendment and made that language applicable to the states.[10] Finally, the Amendment mandated that no state shall "deny to any person within its jurisdiction the equal protection of the laws." [11] Although the Amendment's language was capable of a broad and expansive reading, the intent of the Congress that approved the Amendment was at best vague and ambiguous. Consequently, the Court was free to exercise discretion when it interpreted the language of the Fourteenth Amendment. At first the Court opted for a restrictive reading of the Amendment's provisions.

The *Slaughter–House Cases*[12] concerned a Louisiana law that prohibited livestock yards and slaughterhouses within New Orleans and the immediate area surrounding the city. The same statute, however, had an exception to its proscription which allowed the Crescent City Company to operate a slaughterhouse in a

---

2. 14 Stat. 27, § 1 (1866).

3. Fairman, Does the Fourteenth Amendment Incorporate the Bill of Rights?, 2 Stan.L.Rev. 5, 41 (1949).

4. Cong. Globe, 39th Cong., 1st Sess. 2545, 3042, 3149 (1866). For references to scholarly examinations of the history of the Civil War Amendments see our multivolume treatise. R. Rotunda & J. Nowak, Treatise on Constitutional Law: Substance and Procedure § 18.6 (3rd ed. 1999, with annual supplements).

5. B. F. Wright, The Growth of American Constitutional Law at 80–82 (1942) [hereinafter cited as Wright].

6. 71 U.S. (4 Wall.) 277, 18 L.Ed. 356 (1866).

7. 71 U.S. (4 Wall.) 333, 18 L.Ed. 366 (1866).

8. 76 U.S. (9 Wall.) 41, 19 L.Ed. 593 (1869).

9. U.S.Const. amend. 14, § 1.

10. "... nor shall any State deprive any person of life, liberty, or property, without due process of law...." Id.

11. Id.

12. 83 U.S. (16 Wall.) 36, 21 L.Ed. 394 (1872).

specified area of New Orleans. Butchers and others adversely affected brought an action to have the measure declared void, but the Louisiana state courts sustained the statute. The butchers appealed to the Supreme Court. The butchers contended that the Louisiana law violated both the Thirteenth and Fourteenth Amendments. Specifically, under the Fourteenth Amendment the butchers argued that the statute transgressed not only the Amendment's privileges and immunities clause, but also the Amendment's due process and equal protection clauses. The Court, however, rejected not only the Thirteenth Amendment argument, but also all three Fourteenth Amendment contentions.[13] The Court reasoned that the sole purpose behind the Thirteenth Amendment was to abolish slavery, and, therefore, the Amendment had no application to this case. The Court's reasons for rejecting the Fourteenth Amendment contentions, however, were more complex.

The majority opinion by Justice Miller focused on the first sentence of the Fourteenth Amendment, which declared that "[A]ll persons born ... in the United States ... are citizens of the United States and of the state wherein they reside."[14] The majority read this language to mean that two types of citizenship existed: state citizenship and national citizenship.[15] The second sentence of the Amendment, therefore, only prohibited states from making and enforcing laws that infringed on the privileges and immunities of national citizenship.

The Court listed some of the rights that it considered to be the privileges and immunities of United States citizenship. These rights included: the privilege to come to the seat of government to assert a claim; the right of free access to the country's seaports; the right to

travel to the government's subtreasuries, land offices, and courts; the right to assemble peaceably and petition for redress of grievances; the privilege of the writ of habeas corpus; the right to use the nation's navigable water; rights secured for citizens by national treaties; and the rights secured by the Thirteenth and Fifteenth Amendments and the other provisions of the Fourteenth Amendment.[16] The Louisiana statute that granted the legislatively created monopoly to the Crescent City Co. did not impair any of the privileges and immunities of the United States citizenship. Thus, the Court held that the butchers had no cause of action under the privileges and immunities clause of the Fourteenth Amendment.

The Court easily disposed of the butchers' contentions under the Fourteenth Amendment's due process and equal protection clauses. The Court decided that the due process provision only guaranteed that states would enact laws according to the dictates of procedural due process. Thus, the law did not deprive the butchers of their property or their rights without due process of law. In short, the due process clause of the Fourteenth Amendment did not guarantee the substantive fairness of laws passed by state legislatures. Moreover, the Court rejected the butchers' equal protection argument because it believed that the drafters of the Fourteenth Amendment only intended to protect blacks from discriminatory actions by a state.[17]

Justices Field, Justice Bradley and Swayne dissented.[18] Justice Field contended that the majority's reading of the Fourteenth Amendment's privileges and immunities clause rendered that clause useless. The dissenters argued that the Fourteenth Amendment did

13. 83 U.S. (16 Wall.) at 65–81.

14. U.S.Const. amend. 14, § 1.

15. 83 U.S. (16 Wall.) at 73–74, 21 L.Ed. at 407–08.

16. 83 U.S. (16 Wall.) at 79–80, 21 L.Ed. at 409–10. 126 years later, the Supreme Court would use this language as the basis for finding that the privileges or immunities clause of the Fourteenth Amendment created a right to travel that prohibited states from granting greater subsistence welfare benefits to long time residents than it granted to new residents of the state. See Saenz v. Roe,

526 U.S. 489, 119 S.Ct. 1518, 143 L.Ed.2d 689 (1999). See § 14.38 regarding the right to travel, and the *Saenz* decision.

17. 83 U.S. (16 Wall.) at 80–81, 21 L.Ed. at 410.

18. 83 U.S. (16 Wall.) at 83, 21 L.Ed. at 410 (Field, J., dissenting, joined by Chase, C.J. & Swayne & Bradley, JJ.); 83 U.S. (16 Wall.) at 111, 21 L.Ed. at 420 (Bradley, J., dissenting); see also 83 U.S. (16 Wall.) at 124, 21 L.Ed. at 424 (Swayne, J., dissenting).

guarantee equal protection of the laws to all persons in all the states.[19] They believed that the drafters of the Fourteenth Amendment did not intend to limit the application of the equal protection clause to black citizens. Moreover, these Justices believed that the Fourteenth Amendment protected the natural and inalienable rights of all citizens. In their view, the Amendment prevented states from enacting arbitrary laws that limited these natural rights.[20] Their opinions echoed somewhat the beliefs of Justice Chase on the philosophical limitations on governmental power.[21] A majority of the immediate post-Civil War Supreme Court, however, was not willing to read into the Fourteenth Amendment any substantive due process guarantee. Therefore, for the time being at least, the Court refused to accept the views of Bradley and Field. The economic and political realities of the late nineteenth century United States, however, soon would move the Court to accept the legal theories of the dissenting Justices.

The great industrial revolution the country experienced during the latter half of the nineteenth century had a profound influence on the growth of judicial review. The rapid growth of transportation and communication during this period led many states to attempt to regulate these industries.[22] As the states attempted to control industry, representatives of the regulated businesses would seek to have the state regulatory schemes declared unconstitutional.

Initially, the Supreme Court's reaction to these attempts to seek judicial invalidation of the state regulatory measures was restrained. The Court recognized that the states had a legitimate authority under their police powers to control business activity within their borders. The Court, between 1874 and 1896, would void a state regulatory measure only if the law violated a specific prohibition con-

tained in the Constitution or if the law interfered with interstate commerce.[23]

At the same time that the legal representatives of large businesses were pressing the Court to take a bold and affirmative stance to protect rapidly growing industries from government regulations, contemporary legal thought began actively to advocate a substantive interpretation of the due process clauses. Although the Court continued to defer to legislative judgments when it reviewed the constitutionality of state and federal laws, it began to suggest that certain limits existed that would control the legislative power.

The Court in *Munn v. Illinois*[24] gave an indication that the due process clause contained some implied and inherent restrictions on the police power of the states. Illinois had enacted laws regulating the rates of grain elevators. The grain elevator operators argued that the Illinois statutes violated not only the commerce clause but also the due process clause of the Fourteenth Amendment.

The Court rejected the commerce clause challenge because the statutes regulated businesses exclusively within the boundaries of the state. The Court also rejected the due process argument. The Court noted that a state could exercise its police power to control the use of property when it is necessary for the public good. The regulation of private property in this case was particularly appropriate because the operation of grain elevators was "affected with a public interest."[25] The Court even refused to evaluate the reasonableness of the established rates because the state legislature had the implied authority to establish maximum rates. The Court, however, qualified its approval of a state's use of its police power when it stated that "[u]ndoubtedly, in mere private contracts, relating to matters in which the public has no interest, what is reasonable must be judicially ascertained ... this is be-

---

19. 83 U.S. (16 Wall.) at 105–11, 21 L.Ed. at 418–20 (Field, J., dissenting, joined by Chase, C.J. & Swayne & Bradley, JJ.).

20. 83 U.S. (16 Wall.) at 106–11, 83 U.S. (16 Wall.) at 118–19.

21. See § 11.1, supra, for a review of the Chase "natural law" philosophy.

22. B. F. Wright, The Growth of American Constitutional Law 87 (1942).

23. Id. at 87–88.

24. 94 U.S. (4 Otto) 113, 24 L.Ed. 77 (1876).

25. 94 U.S. at 130, 24 L.Ed. at 85.

cause the legislature has no control over such a contract."[26]

The Court continued through 1886 to follow a policy of noninterference with legislative judgments.[27]

Finally, the Court explicitly stated in *Mugler v. Kansas*[28] that it would use substantive due process to determine the constitutionality of governmental regulatory measures. In *Mugler* the Court sustained a statute which prohibited the sale of alcoholic beverages. The Court recognized that the legislature could exercise its police powers once it determined what laws were needed to protect the public health, morals, and safety. At the same time, however, the *Mugler* Court stated that limits existed beyond which the legislature could not go. Moreover, the courts had the responsibility to determine whether the legislature had exceeded these limits. The *Mugler* Court decided that the judiciary must look to the substance of the laws to see if the legislature had surpassed its authority.[29]

The *Mugler* decision gave notice that the Court would begin evaluating the relationship of a law to its purported purposes. A statute had to have a substantial relation to the protection of the public health, morals, or safety before the Court would sustain the measure as a valid exercise of the state's police power.

In the year before the Court decided *Mugler*, it held, without discussion, that corporations were included under the term "persons" as that word was used in the Fourteenth Amendment.[30] Therefore, any protection of fundamental or natural rights that the Fourteenth Amendment offered was afforded to incorporated business entities as well as to people. The Court thus had laid the framework for using the Fourteenth Amendment as a broad

shield to protect industry from governmental regulation.[31]

In *Allgeyer v. Louisiana*,[32] the Supreme Court used the substantive due process framework already created to invalidate a state statute. This decision concerned a Louisiana statute which prohibited anyone from giving effect to marine insurance on any Louisiana property if the insurance company that issued the policy had not complied in all respects with Louisiana law. The state had convicted Allgeyer for violating the statute when he mailed a letter advising a New York insurance company about the shipment of some insured goods. The New York insurer was not registered to do business in Louisiana. The Supreme Court reversed the conviction and held that the statute violated the Fourteenth Amendment because it deprived the defendant of his liberty without due process of law.

The *Allgeyer* Court reasoned that the state of Louisiana had no jurisdiction over contracts made outside of the state with a foreign corporation. Although the Court primarily relied on this jurisdictional reasoning to void the law, it went on and extensively discussed the liberty of contract and the Fourteenth Amendment's protection of liberty interests. The *Allgeyer* Court reasoned that the "liberty" that the Fourteenth Amendment protected was a more extensive liberty than merely the right of a person to be free of physical restraints. The Fourteenth Amendment's due process clause also guaranteed that a person would be free to enjoy "all his faculties; to be free to use them in all lawful ways...."[33] To insure that a person could enjoy "all his faculties," the *Allgeyer* Court believed that the Fourteenth Amendment permitted a person to

---

26. 94 U.S. at 134, 24 L.Ed. at 87.

27. For references to additional cases, and secondary authorities, on this point see the multivolume edition of this Treatise: R. Rotunda & J. Nowak, Treatise on Constitutional Law: Substance and Procedure § 15.2 (3rd ed. 1999, with annual supplements).

28. 123 U.S. 623, 8 S.Ct. 273, 31 L.Ed. 205 (1887).

29. 123 U.S. at 661, 8 S.Ct. at 297.

30. Santa Clara County v. Southern Pacific R. Co., 118 U.S. 394, 6 S.Ct. 1132, 30 L.Ed. 118 (1886).

31. The Court first used this concept to strike a state law in Missouri Pacific R. Co. v. Nebraska, 164 U.S. 403, 17 S.Ct. 130, 41 L.Ed. 489 (1896). The Court there held that a law requiring railroads to allow privately owned grain elevators on their right of way denied the railroad company property without due process of law. There was no further exposition of the due process concept in the opinion.

32. 165 U.S. 578, 17 S.Ct. 427, 41 L.Ed. 832 (1897).

33. 165 U.S. at 589, 17 S.Ct. at 431.

seek any type of employment or to pursue any type of avocation, and, to facilitate this liberty, the Amendment protected the freedom of contract. The Louisiana statute deprived *Allgeyer* of his liberty to contract "which the state legislature had no right to prevent...."[34]

Summary. The Supreme Court during the last half of the nineteenth century had undergone a major philosophical transformation. The Court of the immediate post-Civil War years willingly deferred to the legislature's judgment on policy issues. The Court readily would recognize that the state's police powers gave the legislatures ample authority to impose regulatory schemes on the industries within their borders. The Court usually would invalidate these schemes only if they either violated a specific prohibition of the Constitution, or if they interfered with the federal government's power under the commerce clause. The Court, however, began slowly to abandon its non-interventionist philosophy. The economic, social, and intellectual thought of the late nineteenth century persuaded the Court that it must do more to protect business interests from encroaching governmental control. The idea of substantive due process became the most viable concept for the Court to adopt as a legal theory to protect industry from government regulation. By the turn of the century the Court had embraced the concept fully and was ready to use it as a rationale for striking legislation that attempted to restrain the freedom of businesses to contract.

§ 11.3 Substantive Due Process From 1900 to 1936

By the turn of the century, the Supreme Court had indicated its complete acceptance of the substantive due process doctrine. The dicta of *Allgeyer v. Louisiana*[1] revealed the Court's willingness to use the substantive due process doctrine to void any economic or social

legislation that the Court believed unreasonably infringed on the liberty to contract.

The substantive due process test could be easily stated: the government had to employ means (legislation) which bore some reasonable relation to a legitimate end. As the doctrine had developed, it held that any law which the Justices did not believe related to a legitimate end was void because government had no power to enact this limitation of liberty. Similarly, no matter how temperate the legislation might seem to others, it would be void if the Justices thought it related to some end which they considered beyond the proper role of government. Freedom in the marketplace and freedom to contract were viewed as liberties which were protected by the due process clause. Thus, the Justices would invalidate a law if they thought it restricted economic liberty in a way that was not reasonably related to a legitimate end. Because they did not view labor regulation, price control, or other economic measures as legitimate "ends" in themselves, only a limited amount of business regulation could pass this test. Only when the Justices were convinced that the regulation actually promoted public health, safety, or some other important "public interest" would they uphold the law. While the "test" might sound mild, independent judicial review of such legislation made the constitutionality of these laws dependent on the Justices' individual views. While many laws were invalidated on this basis, we will examine only a representative sample of the Court's actions during this period.

Although state legislatures were adopting a variety of methods to regulate businesses, one of the most popular state laws set the maximum number of hours that an employee could work in one week in a particular business. In 1898 the Supreme Court upheld a Utah statute that limited the hours men could work in mines and smelters.[2] After noting the extremely unsafe and unhealthy working condi-

---

34. 165 U.S. at 591, 17 S.Ct. at 432.

§ 11.3

1. 165 U.S. 578, 17 S.Ct. 427, 41 L.Ed. 832 (1897). See § 11.2, supra, for the development of the doctrine.

2. Holden v. Hardy, 169 U.S. 366, 18 S.Ct. 383, 42 L.Ed. 780 (1898).

tions of mines, the Court declared Utah's passage of the regulatory measure as a reasonable exercise of the state's police powers in relation to this type of occupation. Although the law limited the liberty of contract, the opinion sustained the Utah statute because it was a valid health law.[3] The Court, however, retained the authority under the substantive due process theory to invalidate any similar measure which the Court did not believe was a legitimate health measure.

The State of New York enacted a law that limited the number of hours a baker could work to only 60 hours a week or 10 hours a day. The issue of the constitutional validity of the New York statute came before the Court in the now infamous case of *Lochner v. New York*.[4] A majority of the Court held the law unconstitutional because it was an arbitrary and unnecessary interference with the liberty to contract between an employer and employee—a liberty protected by the Fourteenth Amendment. New York had infringed unreasonably on "the freedom of master and employee to contract with each other in relation to their employment."[5]

The *Lochner* majority found no legitimate purpose of government in regulating labor conditions or practices where the regulation was not a true health or safety measure. The Court rejected any suggestion that the New York law was a health measure. The majority refused to accept the argument that the legislature might rationally have taken these steps to protect the health of the workers. While the *Lochner* majority stated that it would not "substitut[e] the judgment of the court for that of the legislature,"[6] it also stated, in a more frank passage, that "[w]e do not believe in the soundness of the views which uphold this law."[7] Consequently, the provision, in the Court's view, was purely a piece of labor legislation and as such was an improper exercise of the state's police power.

Justice Holmes and Justice Harlan wrote dissents to the *Lochner* majority opinion.[8] Justice Holmes believed that the majority was imposing its own theory of a proper economic policy on the state of New York by invalidating this law. The Constitution, however, did not allow the Court to force a certain economic concept on the country. His remark that "[t]he Fourteenth Amendment does not enact Mr. Herbert Spencer's Social Statics"[9] has become one of the most famous in constitutional history. Holmes believed the founding fathers created a Constitution "for people of fundamentally differing views,"[10] and the Court should not void a law simply because a legislature enacted the measure to implement an economic policy the Justices do not believe proper. Justice Holmes stated that the Court should invalidate a law only when "a rational and fair man necessarily would admit that the statute proposed would infringe fundamental principles as they have been understood by the traditions of our people and our law."[11]

Justice Harlan's dissent followed a somewhat different analysis than Justice Holmes. Justice Harlan was willing to accept the New York statute as a valid health measure. He cited the evidence that supported the contention that limiting the number of hours bakers could work would protect the welfare of these workers whose health standard was below the national average.[12] Justice Harlan believed that as long as the statute arguably was a health measure the Court should sustain the law.

The majority and dissenting opinions in *Lochner* reveal the problem the Supreme Court experienced between 1900 and 1937. The state legislatures and the national government were enacting an ever-increasing amount of legislation that regulated the economic and social life of Americans. Many of the Supreme Court Justices believed they had an obligation

---

3. 169 U.S. at 393–98, 18 S.Ct. at 388–90.
4. 198 U.S. 45, 25 S.Ct. 539, 49 L.Ed. 937 (1905).
5. 198 U.S. at 64, 25 S.Ct. at 546.
6. 198 U.S. at 56–57, 25 S.Ct. at 543.
7. 198 U.S. at 61, 25 S.Ct. at 544.
8. 198 U.S. at 65, 74, 25 S.Ct. at 547.

9. 198 U.S. at 75, 25 S.Ct. at 546.
10. 198 U.S. at 76, 25 S.Ct. at 547.
11. Id.
12. 198 U.S. at 71, 25 S.Ct. at 549–50.

to protect the free enterprise system as it was embodied in the concept of laissez faire.[13] It must be stressed that their position resulted from their independent reading of the Constitution and the historic economic freedom of action in American life rather than from some arbitrary desire to protect big business. While they would uphold some laws which they felt were needed for health or safety, they were inclined to fully protect freedom of contract and liberty in the marketplace. Consequently, these Justices, as exemplified by the *Lochner* majority opinion, were willing to use not only the substantive due process concept, but also the commerce clause, the contract clause, and the equal protection clause to void those laws that they believed unreasonably infringed on free enterprise. At the same time, however, the Court had a tradition of judicial forbearance.[14] As the *Lochner* dissents indicated, the Court historically sustained legislation that arguably fell within the confines of constitutionality. Because this tension existed, the Court of the early twentieth century failed to follow a systematic and uniform approach to the legislation it reviewed.

Three years after *Lochner* the Court sustained state legislation that regulated the number of hours women could work. In *Muller v. Oregon*,[15] then attorney Louis D. Brandeis presented the Court with the now-famous "Brandeis brief," a brief that contained massive documentation—not only to legal precedent but also references to laws of other states and foreign countries; reports of European and American committees, inspectors of factories, commissioners of hygiene, and studies of

statistical bureaus—to justify the regulation of the work hours for women.[16]

Nine years after *Muller* the Court, without mentioning *Lochner*, sustained statutes that limited the work hours for men in certain industries.[17] Again, the supporters of the measure used a Brandeis brief to present the necessary documentation to justify the law. But the Court had not abandoned its use of substantive due process. The states had to be prepared to present sufficient evidence in support of legislation that controlled the hours of labor in order to convince the Court that the legislation was a proper exercise of the state's police power. If the states failed to justify adequately a particular labor regulation as an appropriate police power measure, the Supreme Court would invalidate the statute as violative of due process.

The Court not only relied on the due process clause as a standard to determine the constitutionality of labor or business legislation but also relied on the Fourteenth Amendment's equal protection clause.[18] The Court on several occasions also held state legislation that taxed certain businesses unconstitutional because the particular tax classifications denied businesses equal protection of the laws.[19] The Court's use of the equal protection clause to invalidate economic legislation that discriminated against certain industrial enterprises demonstrated the justices' view that economic freedom was as constitutionally significant as any civil liberty. The authors of the Fourteenth Amendment drafted the equal protection clause as a protective provision to shield

---

13. B. F. Wright, The Growth of American Constitutional Law 109–12 (1942) [Hereinafter cited as Wright]; R. G. McCloskey, The American Supreme Court 137–39 (1960) [Hereinafter cited as McCloskey].

14. McCloskey, supra note 13, at 138–39.

15. 208 U.S. 412, 28 S.Ct. 324, 52 L.Ed. 551 (1908).

16. The Brandeis Brief. Although called the "Brandeis Brief", the brief was primarily the work of Josephine Goldmark. On the use of the "Brandeis Brief," see generally, Bikle, Judicial Determination of Questions of Fact Affecting the Constitutional Validity of Legislative Action, 38 Harv.L.Rev. 6 (1924); Karst, Legislative Facts in Constitutional Litigation, 1960 Sup.Ct.Rev. 15; P. Freund, On Understanding the Supreme Court 86–91 (1949); A. T. Mason, Brandeis: A Free Man's Life 245–53 (1946); A. T.

Mason, Brandeis: Lawyer and Judge in the Modern State, Chapter 6 (1933).

17. Bunting v. Oregon, 243 U.S. 426, 37 S.Ct. 435, 61 L.Ed. 830 (1917).

18. See, e.g., Gulf, C. & S.F. Ry. Co. v. Ellis, 165 U.S. 150, 17 S.Ct. 255, 41 L.Ed. 666 (1897) (attorney's fees provisions for certain suits against railroads denies the railroads equal protection); Louisville Gas & Elec. Co. v. Coleman, 277 U.S. 32, 48 S.Ct. 423, 72 L.Ed. 770 (1928) (mortgage recording fee and tax classifications violate equal protection).

19. See, e.g., Quaker City Cab Co. v. Pennsylvania, 277 U.S. 389, 48 S.Ct. 553, 72 L.Ed. 927 (1928); Stewart Dry Goods Co. v. Lewis, 294 U.S. 550, 55 S.Ct. 525, 79 L.Ed. 1054 (1935).

blacks from laws that discriminated against them unfairly,[20] but the Court during this period found discrimination in favor of certain economic groups to be similarly objectionable.[21]

Often the Justices' concern over governmental intervention with business expressed itself in the Court's invalidation of legislation which regulated the relationship between employer and employee.[22] The Court, however, also voided some legislation which regulated the rates certain businesses could charge customers. The issue in many of these rate regulation cases was whether the regulated business was one "affected with a public interest." [23]

Beginning in 1923, however, the Court began to use the negative implications of the public interest concept to void legislative regulation. The Court decided a series of cases where it held various regulatory devices violative of the Fourteenth Amendment because the regulated businesses were not affected with a public interest.

Unless the business (1) resulted from a public grant or franchise, (2) was subject traditionally to regulation, or (3) "which though not public at their inception may be said to have risen to be such and have become subject in consequence to some government regulation," [24] the state could not regulate the business. The Court's guidelines to determine whether a state properly could regulate a business were of little help to the states. Those businesses which fell within the first two categories always had been subject to state supervision. The third category was the critical class of businesses, and the Court retained the power to determine subjectively the parameters of that class of businesses. The Court's approach to the public interest line of cases was as unprincipled as its application of the substantive due process doctrine and the commerce clause.

In *Nebbia v. New York*[25] the Court reversed the public interest line of cases. New York had established a regulatory board that had the authority to set minimum prices for the retail sale of milk. The Court sustained the legislation as a legitimate exercise of the state's police power. The petitioner contended that the milk industry was not a business affected with a public interest, and consequently, the state could not control the retail price of milk. The Court rejected the contention with the recognition that "there is no closed class or category of businesses affected with a public interest...." The *Nebbia* Court stated that the Court's function "is to determine in each case whether circumstances vindicate the challenged regulation as a reasonable exertion of governmental authority or condemn it as arbitrary or discriminatory." [26]

The opinion contained language that suggested that the Court's use of the substantive due process doctrine to invalidate economic or welfare legislation was at an end. The Court stated that "a state is free to adopt whatever economic policy may reasonably be deemed to promote public welfare, and to enforce that policy by legislation adopted to its purpose." [27] Moreover, the *Nebbia* Court observed that the courts did not have the authority either to establish an economic policy or to overrule the

---

20. For references to scholarly examinations of the history of the Civil War Amendments, see the multivolume edition of this Treatise: R. Rotunda & J. Nowak, Treatise on Constitutional Law: Substance and Procedure § 18.6 (3rd ed. 1999, with annual supplements).

21. For references to additional cases, and secondary authorities, on this point see the multivolume edition of this Treatise: R. Rotunda & J. Nowak, Treatise on Constitutional Law: Substance and Procedure §§ 15.2, 15.3.

22. See, e.g. Adair v. United States, 208 U.S. 161, 28 S.Ct. 277, 52 L.Ed. 436 (1908) (Court's invalidation of federal law prohibiting anti-union "yellow dog" employment contracts as violation of due process); Coppage v. Kansas, 236 U.S. 1, 35 S.Ct. 240, 59 L.Ed. 441 (1915) (state law prohibiting anti-union activity contracts held invalid as violation of due process).

23. See, e.g., Tyson & Bro.–United Theatre Ticket Offices v. Banton, 273 U.S. 418, 47 S.Ct. 426, 71 L.Ed. 718 (1927) (theater ticket sales regulation invalidated); Ribnik v. McBride, 277 U.S. 350, 48 S.Ct. 545, 72 L.Ed. 913 (1928) (employment agency practice and rate regulation invalid). The "public interest" issue concerned the Court majority whenever it reviewed new forms of business regulation. Wright, supra note 13, at 166.

24. Chas. Wolff Packing Co. v. Court of Industrial Relations, 262 U.S. 522, 535, 43 S.Ct. 630, 633, 67 L.Ed. 1103 (1923).

25. 291 U.S. 502, 54 S.Ct. 505, 78 L.Ed. 940 (1934).

26. 291 U.S. at 536, 54 S.Ct. at 515.

27. 291 U.S. at 537, 54 S.Ct. at 516.

legislative choice of an appropriate policy. The Court apparently had adopted Justice Holmes' *Lochner* dissent as the proper approach to economic legislation. The language of *Nebbia*, however, was deceiving because the Court continued to use the substantive due process concept to invalidate legislation.

Immediately after his election to his first term in office, President Roosevelt marshalled his support in Congress and persuaded Congress to enact his New Deal legislation designed to help the nation recover from the Great Depression.[28] The issue of the constitutionality of some of this legislation came before the Supreme Court between 1934 and 1936. With a remarkable series of decisions the Court invalidated many of the New Deal acts. The New Deal legislation presented to a majority of the Justices of the Court the greatest threat to their concept of free enterprise that they could imagine. Therefore, the Court used a narrow interpretation of the commerce clause to declare New Deal provisions unconstitutional.[29] The Court also refused to follow *Nebbia's* formulation of the Court's proper role when reviewing economic legislation under the due process clause.

Two years after *Nebbia* the Court declared unconstitutional another New York statute that had established a minimum wage for women. In *Morehead v. New York ex rel. Tipaldo*[30] the Court used the substantive due process doctrine much as it had before *Nebbia*. The minimum wage law violated the Fourteenth Amendment because it impaired the liberty to contract. The *Morehead* opinion's use of substantive due process was not unique. Nevertheless, the opinion is important because of its timing. The Court decided this case shortly after it invalidated much of President Roosevelt's New Deal legislation. Hence, the *Morehead* decision announced to the states, as the Court's decision on the New Deal legisla-

tion had announced to Congress, that the Court would continue to construe strictly the powers the government had to control business.

FDR's Court Packing Proposal. The Court's refusal to sustain much of the New Deal-type legislation of the early 1930's precipitated a constitutional crisis. The voters reelected Franklin Roosevelt to a second presidential term by an overwhelming margin in 1936.[31] The President interpreted his landslide margin of victory as a mandate from the people to do whatever was necessary to end the Depression. Before he could implement that mandate, however, he had to eliminate the Supreme Court as an obstacle to his programs. Therefore, Roosevelt proposed a plan whereby the President could appoint a new Justice if an incumbent Justice failed to retire when he reached seventy. Roosevelt wanted the opportunity to appoint Justices who would interpret the Constitution in a way that would allow the New Deal legislation to stand.

The President's plan confronted the Court with the most serious threat to its constitutional authority since the Court's inception. The President was proposing to "pack" the Court with his appointees largely because he disapproved of the Court's invalidation of his legislation. This plan threatened to destroy the concept of the Court as a neutral arbiter of constitutional issues. Congress debated the merits of the plan for almost six months. Ultimately Congress voted against the plan.[32] At this time the Court reversed its position and began to sustain much of the economic and labor legislation enacted by Congress and the states. The Court began to abandon its substantive due process review of economic and welfare legislation as well as broadening its interpretation of the federal commerce power.[33]

28. McCloskey, supra note 13, at 163.

29. See § 4.7, supra.

30. 298 U.S. 587, 56 S.Ct. 918, 80 L.Ed. 1347 (1936).

31. Wright, supra note 13, at 200–201.

32. Wright, supra note 13, at 202. See § 2.6.

33. Wright, supra note 13, at 203–08.

See particularly West Coast Hotel Co. v. Parrish, 300 U.S. 379, 57 S.Ct. 578, 81 L.Ed. 703 (1937): "What is this freedom? The Constitution does not speak of freedom of contract. It speaks of liberty and prohibits the deprivation of liberty without due process of law. In prohibiting that deprivation the Constitution does not recognize an absolute and uncontrollable liberty.... [R]egulation which is reasonable in relation to its subject and is

Civil Rights and *Lochner* Era Court.
Before turning to the modern era, we should mention that the Court during the first third of the twentieth century also started to apply the doctrine to the area of civil rights. Although the number of civil liberty cases the Court decided was small, the number increased as the years passed. The Supreme Court cases principally involved state statutes and the due process clause of the Fourteenth Amendment.

In *Buchanan v. Warley*[34] the Court voided a Louisville city ordinance that precluded blacks from moving into areas where the residents were primarily white. The ordinance violated the due process clause because it was an unwarranted interference with property rights. The Court felt constrained to use the due process clause to protect property rights in the civil rights area as it had done in the business area.[35]

Six years after *Buchanan* the Court began to expand the impact of substantive due process in the area of civil liberties. Nebraska had enacted a statute that prohibited teaching in any language other than English. In *Meyer v. Nebraska*[36] the Court declared the provision unconstitutional because it improperly infringed upon liberty to make educational decisions.[37]

Two years after *Meyer* the Court decided *Gitlow v. New York*.[38] Although the *Gitlow* Court sustained a conviction under the New York criminal anarchy statute, the ramification of the decision on civil liberties was profound. In *Gitlow* the Court assumed the Fourteenth Amendment's due process guarantee protected the freedom of speech. The *Gitlow* assumption implied that the Court had abandoned its earlier position that the Fourteenth Amendment's due process clause did not apply to the states the guarantees of the Bill of Rights.[39]

Finally, in 1931 the Court decided two cases that held that state statutes violated the due process clause because the provisions impaired the liberty of speech and press.[40] To an uncertain extent, then, the provisions of the Bill of Rights did apply to the states. Moreover, in a series of cases the Court decided that the states could not deny an individual a right to counsel nor could the state use forced confessions in criminal prosecutions.[41] Under the theory of due process, the Court began to incorporate into the Fourteenth Amendment some of the liberty guarantees of the first eight Amendments.

§ 11.4   Substantive Due Process Since 1937

Introduction. The history of the judicial use of substantive due process is linked closely

---

adopted in the interests of the community is due process." 300 U.S. at 391, 57 S.Ct. at 581–82. *West Coast Hotel* upheld a state minimum wage law for women and explicitly overruled Adkins v. Children's Hosp., 261 U.S. 525, 43 S.Ct. 394, 67 L.Ed. 785 (1923), which had declared that "freedom of contract is nevertheless the general rule and restraint the exception." 261 U.S. at 546, 43 S.Ct. at 397. *Adkins* had struck down a state minimum wage law for women. See also United States v. Darby, 312 U.S. 100, 61 S.Ct. 451, 85 L.Ed. 609 (1941) (wage and hour laws for men and women upheld).

34. 245 U.S. 60, 38 S.Ct. 16, 62 L.Ed. 149 (1917).

Professor Schmidt has presented substantial evidence to support the thesis that *Buchanan* should be understood as a judicial effort to restrict racially discriminatory legislation. Schmidt, Principle and Prejudice: The Supreme Court and Race in the Progressive Era, Part 1: The Heyday of Jim Crow, 82 Colum.L.Rev. 444 (1982).

The Supreme Court itself later stated that Buchanan v. Warley, 245 U.S. 60, 38 S.Ct. 16, 62 L.Ed. 149 (1917) is an example of Supreme Court rejection of efforts to justify racial classifications through acknowledgment of racial prejudice. See Palmore v. Sidoti, 466 U.S. 429, 104 S.Ct.

1879, 80 L.Ed.2d 421 (1984) (holding that societal prejudice against racially mixed marriages does not justify divesting natural mother of the custody of her child because of her remarriage to a person of a different race if she is otherwise a suitable guardian for the child).

35. McCloskey, supra note 13, at 171.

36. 262 U.S. 390, 43 S.Ct. 625, 67 L.Ed. 1042 (1923).

37. The Court also held that the state could not prohibit private schools, although the state could require them to meet secular educational standards. Pierce v. Society of Sisters, 268 U.S. 510, 45 S.Ct. 571, 69 L.Ed. 1070 (1925).

38. 268 U.S. 652, 45 S.Ct. 625, 69 L.Ed. 1138 (1925).

39. See Hurtado v. California, 110 U.S. 516, 4 S.Ct. 111, 28 L.Ed. 232 (1884).

40. Stromberg v. California, 283 U.S. 359, 51 S.Ct. 532, 75 L.Ed. 1117 (1931); Near v. Minnesota, 283 U.S. 697, 51 S.Ct. 625, 75 L.Ed. 1357 (1931).

41. Powell v. Alabama, 287 U.S. 45, 53 S.Ct. 55, 77 L.Ed. 158 (1932); Brown v. Mississippi, 297 U.S. 278, 56 S.Ct. 461, 80 L.Ed. 682 (1936).

to the judicial use of the equal protection doctrine. As explained elsewhere in this treatise,[1] courts use the concept of substantive due process to review the ability of government to restrict the freedom of action (regarding life, liberty, or property) of all persons. Equal protection analysis is applicable when the judiciary is called upon to review a governmentally established classification.[2] For example, if a state prohibited all persons from purchasing or using a certain drug or medicine, a challenge to that law would be based on substantive due process. The person who claimed that he should be able to purchase or use the drug would be alleging that the government prohibition violated the due process clause because the substance of the law (as opposed to the procedures used to enforce it) restricted the freedom of all persons in society without a constitutionally legitimate justification. However, if the state law allowed some persons (such as persons over the age of 29) to use the drug but denied other persons (those under the age of 30) the ability to use the drug, the law would be more properly analyzed under the equal protection guarantee. In such a case the person challenging the law (the person under 30 who wished to use the drug) would be requesting judicial review of the basis upon which the government determined that one classification of persons could receive the drug whereas other persons could not. In both substantive due process and equal protection cases, the judiciary is called upon to review the substance of a law and whether the law is constitutionally permissible. Thus, the substantive due process and equal protection guarantees involve complementary concepts.

In the period from 1890 to 1936 the Court relied primarily on due process analysis, rather than equal protection analysis, when reviewing economic and social welfare legislation. The reason why the Court frequently failed to focus on equal protection principles during this era is that there was no need for the Court to address equal protection issues once it found a substantive due process violation. For example, in *Lochner v. New York*,[3] the Supreme Court invalidated a legislative limit on the number of hours that could be worked by bakers. A majority of the Justices found that labor regulation to be a violation of substantive due process.[4] The majority viewed the regulation as a limitation on the right of every person to enter the baking profession and to work as many hours as he or she chose. The majority did not believe the regulation of bakers' working hours was in fact related to any legitimate interest of government. However, the majority opinion could have examined the law as an equal protection problem if the Justices had decided that the law involved a classification (bakers who were not allowed to work over a certain number of hours per day as opposed to workers in professions whose working hours were not so limited). If the Court had applied equal protection analysis, the Justices who were in the *Lochner* majority almost certainly would have found an equal protection violation because they would have believed that the classification did not relate to a legitimate end of government.

Since 1937 the Court has focused on equal protection, rather than substantive due process, in most cases involving challenges to governmental regulations in the area commonly referred to as "economic and social welfare" legislation. The reason for this fact is quite simple: most laws do not regulate all persons evenhandedly but, instead, involve classifications of persons. Regardless of whether a

---

§ 11.4

1. See §§ 10.6, 11.3. Among the cases citing this section of the Treatise are: Newville v. State, Dep't of Family Services, 267 Mont. 237, 883 P.2d 793 (1994) (Weber, J.); Freedman v. Longo, 1994 WL 469159, *5 (Del.Ch.1994) (Allen, C.); Feliciano v. City of Cleveland, 1992 WL 59128, *20 (N.D.Ohio 1992) (Aldrich, J.), judgment affirmed 988 F.2d 649 (6th Cir.1993), cert. denied 510 U.S. 826, 114 S.Ct. 90, 126 L.Ed.2d 57 (1993); Brock, C.J., citing Treatise, concurring in, Caspersen v. Town of Lyme, 139 N.H. 637, 661 A.2d 759, 766 (1995); Ransom, J., quoting Treatise, in, Garcia v. La Farge, 119 N.M. 532, 893 P.2d 428,

436 (1995); Becker, J., quoting Treatise in, Knight v. Tape, Inc., 935 F.2d 617, 627 (3d Cir.1991); Irenas, J., quoting Treatise in, Mannington Mills, Inc. v. Shinn, 877 F.Supp. 921, 933, 25 Envtl.L.Rep. 21,078 (D.N.J.1995); Smith, J., citing Treatise in, Lens Express, Inc. v. Ewald, 907 S.W.2d 64, 67 (Tex.App.—Austin 1995).

2. See §§ 10.7, 14.2, 14.3, 14.4.

3. 198 U.S. 45, 25 S.Ct. 539, 49 L.Ed. 937 (1905).

4. See § 11.3 for an analysis of the case.

court is employing substantive due process or equal protection analysis, it should use the same standards of review. If a law regulating all persons involves only matters of economics or social welfare, a court should defer to the legislature and uphold the law so long as it is rationally related to a legitimate interest of government. If a law involves a classification that relates only to matters of economics or social welfare, a court similarly should uphold the law so long as the classification is rationally related to a legitimate interest of government.

If a law regulates the exercise of a "fundamental right," a court should give less deference to the legislature and independently scrutinize the law or classification to determine that it has not improperly restricted a right explicitly (or implicitly—in the Supreme Court's view) given special protection by the Constitution or its Amendments.[5]

The determination of whether a right that is regulated by a law is a "fundamental right" is a substantive decision. The Supreme Court must determine whether the right is protected by the Constitution or its Amendments in a manner that will justify judicial review of a law with little or no deference to the governmental entity that created the law. Sometimes the Court determines that a right is a "fundamental right" even though the right is not expressly set forth in the Constitution or its Amendments (such as the right to privacy). In these cases the Court determines if the right should be protected as a part of the "liberty" that is protected by the due process clause of the Fourteenth Amendment (for review in state or local laws) or the due process clause of the Fifth Amendment (for review of a federal law).

Once the Supreme Court has determined that a right is a fundamental right, the Court may choose to review the law in a particular case under either due process or equal protection. If the Court views the law as one that regulates and restricts the ability of every person to exercise the fundamental right, it will

decide the case on the basis of the due process clause. If the Court determines that the law only restricts the ability of one classification of persons to exercise the fundamental right, the Court will decide the case with equal protection analysis.

Most fundamental rights cases since 1937 have involved Supreme Court rulings based upon equal protection rather than due process principles. The reason for this predominance of equal protection analysis in fundamental rights cases is not based upon any theoretical preference for equal protection analysis but, rather, on the fact that virtually all government laws regulating fundamental rights involve classifications. For example, laws regulating votings will enfranchise a class of persons or will give preferential voting rights to a particular group. Because these laws involve classifications, they are tested under equal protection rather than due process.[6] Because most fundamental rights cases in the modern era have involved equal protection analysis, we will defer examination of those rights and cases to Chapter 14. The one area of fundamental rights analysis that has involved many substantive due process rulings, as well as equal protection rulings, is the "right to privacy." The Supreme Court has seen some governmental regulations of sexual or reproductive rights as limiting the fundamental rights of all persons and, therefore, has used due process analysis in those cases. Analysis of right to privacy issues, along with the analysis of all other fundamental rights issues, is included in our equal protection chapter.[7]

The Supreme Court, in majority opinions that have not been overruled, has said that a law or classification that impairs a fundamental right is subject to "strict scrutiny" and that the law, or classification, must be necessary or narrowly tailored to promote a compelling or overriding interest. However, the Supreme Court has also decided some fundamental rights cases without stating what stan-

---

5. For an overview of fundamental rights analysis issues see §§ 11.7, 14.3.

6. Regarding voting rights issues see §§ 14.31–14.36.

7. Regarding the right to privacy see §§ 14.26–14.30.

dard or test the Court was using to determine the constitutionality of the law being challenged in the case.

In some equal protection cases, such as cases involving gender or illegitimacy classifications, the Supreme Court has used an "intermediate" standard of review, under which the Court will uphold the classification only if the government can demonstrate that the classification has a substantial relationship to an important interest.[8] This standard does not require the government to show that the classification promotes a compelling interest. However, the intermediate standard of review does not require great judicial deference to legislative decisionmaking, as does the rational relationship to a legitimate interest test. The Supreme Court may be using the intermediate standard in both substantive due process and equal protection cases that involve a regulation or impairment of fundamental constitutional rights. However, the Supreme Court has not formally adopted the intermediate standard as the test to be used in all fundamental rights cases. The standard of review for fundamental rights cases, under either the due process or equal protection clauses, remains unclear. Lower courts, and students of the Supreme Court's work, must examine the rulings regarding a specific fundamental right to determine for themselves what type of standard is actually being used in those cases.

This subsection contains a brief overview of the Court's approach to substantive due process analysis since 1937. In Chapter 14 we will analyze a number of additional cases to give the student a more complete understanding of the degree of judicial deference to legislative decisionmaking that has been established by the Supreme Court in the modern era.[9]

The Demise of the Old Substantive Due Process. During the first third of the century, the Supreme Court did not give any deference to the opinion of other branches of government regarding the legitimate ends of legislation or the proper means for achieving those ends.[10] A law would not be upheld unless a majority of the Justices were of the opinion that its end was within the proper scope of activities for an American governmental entity. Additionally, these Justices would not uphold a law unless they were of the opinion that the means employed to achieve even permissible ends were in fact reasonable.

Many of the Justices during this period were of the opinion that the government should not "arbitrarily" disrupt the free market economic system. But their rulings could not even be termed an economically consistent defense of laissez faire theories of economics. Instead, the Justices upheld laws which they personally agreed would be necessary to protect important social goals even though the legislation involved some restraint on commerce,[11] while they struck down as arbitrary legislation laws they considered to tamper unnecessarily with the free market system.[12] Thus, the independent review of legislation during this period resulted in an unprincipled control of social and economic legislation.[13]

Although the Supreme Court of the pre-1937 era relied on the commerce clause and the contract clause to void some economic legislation, the due process clause of the Fifth and Fourteenth Amendments and the equal protection clause provided the Court with the most useful and flexible concepts to promote and protect the economic scheme that the Justices

---

8. See § 14.3 for an overview of the test used by the Court in equal protection cases, including the intermediate test that is used in the gender classification and illegitimacy classification cases. For additional information and analysis regarding the creation of a fundamental right by the Court, which always involves a substantive decision, see §§ 11.5–11.7. For an examination of the basic differences between procedural due process, substantive due process, and equal protection analysis see §§ 10.6, 10.7.

9. See § 14.3.

10. See § 11.3, supra.

11. See, e.g. Muller v. Oregon, 208 U.S. 412, 28 S.Ct. 324, 52 L.Ed. 551 (1908), which was examined in § 11.3, supra.

12. See Lochner v. New York, 198 U.S. 45, 25 S.Ct. 539, 49 L.Ed. 937 (1905).

13. See Wright, The Growth of American Constitutional Law 204–26 (1967) [hereinafter cited as Wright]; R. McCloskey, The American Supreme Court 182–85 (1960) [hereinafter cited as McCloskey.]

believed was best for the country.[14] These clauses allowed the Justices to decide whether a regulatory program was reasonably related to a particular end, or whether a classification system was reasonably necessary for a certain economic objective. The Justices had complete discretion to determine the permissibility of economic and social welfare legislation. With the advent of the Great Depression, however, the economic beliefs of the majority of the Justices failed to comport with the economic programs of the "New Deal."[15] The two branches of the federal government began to work at odds with each other, and one branch would sooner or later have to yield to the other.[16]

In 1934 the Court decided *Nebbia v. New York*[17] and revealed, for the first time, a willingness to shift its thinking on economic substantive due process. In *Nebbia* the Court sustained a state regulatory scheme for milk because the regulations were reasonable in light of the desired end. The Court stated that "a state is free to adopt whatever economic policy may reasonably be deemed to promote public welfare."[18] The *Nebbia* opinion signaled the Court's possible abandonment of the traditional economic substantive due process thinking. The Court disclosed a willingness to defer to the legislative judgment on what was reasonable to promote the public welfare. The *Nebbia* decision, however, was followed with a series of cases where the Court applied traditional economic substantive due process concepts to void business regulations.[19] The final determination on whether the Court actually would change its approach to economic legislation was left to subsequent events.

The court-packing controversy of 1937 precipitated the permanent change in the Court's

application of the substantive due process concept. The Court's decisions of 1937 and the years immediately following revealed the Justices' total disenchantment with substantive due process as a constitutional theory that could protect property interests from government regulation and control. These decisions disclosed not only that the Court no longer believed that economic issues were of constitutional magnitude but also that the Justices were prepared to apply new and objective constitutional standards to test the constitutionality of economic legislation.[20]

The first significant sign of the demise of the Court's use of substantive due process in testing the constitutionality of economic legislation came in *West Coast Hotel Co. v. Parrish*.[21] In *Parrish* the Court sustained the constitutionality of the state of Washington's minimum wage law for women. The appellant, the owner of the hotel, alleged that the law violated substantive due process under the Fourteenth Amendment because it deprived him of the liberty of contract. The appellant's argument was reminiscent of the argument the Court accepted in *Adkins v. Children's Hospital*[22] in invalidating an identical law adopted for the District of Columbia. In *Parrish*, however, the Court rejected the substantive due process argument and labeled the *Adkins* decision "a departure from the true application of the principles governing the regulation by the State of the relation of employer and employed."[23]

The *Parrish* opinion marked the beginning of the end for judicial scrutiny of economic legislation under the concept of substantive due process. The Court had directly overruled a decision not only formulated during

---

14. McCloskey, supra note 13, at 182–84.

15. This conflict arose even more sharply in terms of judicial restrictions of the federal commerce powers. See § 4.7, supra.

16. The "court packing" plan of President Roosevelt is discussed in §§ 2.7, 11.3, supra.

17. 291 U.S. 502, 54 S.Ct. 505, 78 L.Ed. 940 (1934).

18. 291 U.S. at 537, 54 S.Ct. at 516.

19. See, Stewart Dry Goods Co. v. Lewis, 294 U.S. 550, 55 S.Ct. 525, 79 L.Ed. 1054 (1935) (tax classifications invalid); Morehead v. New York ex rel. Tipaldo, 298 U.S.

587, 56 S.Ct. 918, 80 L.Ed. 1347 (1936) (minimum wage law invalid). A similar approach was used under the commerce clause. Among these cases were some of the decisions by which "the Court tore great holes in the New Deal program of recovery legislation." McCloskey, supra note 13, at 165–66. See § 4.7, supra.

20. McCloskey, supra note 13, at 183–84.

21. 300 U.S. 379, 57 S.Ct. 578, 81 L.Ed. 703 (1937).

22. 261 U.S. 525, 43 S.Ct. 394, 67 L.Ed. 785 (1923).

23. 300 U.S. at 397, 57 S.Ct. at 584.

the zenith of the substantive due process concept but also decided firmly on substantive due process grounds.[24] The *Parrish* Court had sustained the Washington law as a legitimate exercise of the state's police power and discounted the statute's impact on the freedom of contract. Unlike the *Nebbia* opinion, the *Parrish* decision would not prove to be an isolated departure from the doctrine of substantive due process because the Court followed *Parrish* with a series of cases that reflected the discredit that had befallen economic substantive due process.

Footnote 4 of *Carolene Products*. A year after *Parrish* the Court decided *United States v. Carolene Products Co.*[25] The Congress had passed legislation that prohibited the interstate shipment of "filled" milk. The appellee contended that the legislation violated the Fifth Amendment's due process provision. The Court responded through Justice Stone that "where the legislative judgment is drawn in question, [the inquiry] must be restricted to the issue whether any state of facts either known or which could reasonably be assumed, affords support for [the legislation]."[26] The Court found sufficient facts in *Carolene Products* to support the finding of a rational basis for the measure. The legislative findings that filled milk was injurious to the public health revealed the congressional rationale behind the act.

Justice Stone, however, emphasized that even absent these legislative findings the Court would have sustained the legislation because "the existence of facts supporting the legislative judgment is to be presumed, for regulatory legislation affecting ordinary commercial transactions is not to be pronounced unconstitutional unless ... it is of such a character as to preclude the assumption that it rests on some rational basis...."[27] In the now famous "footnote 4," which he added at the end of this sentence, he gave reasons for the continued independent judicial review of some governmental actions:

4. There may be narrower scope for operation of the presumption of constitutionality when legislation appears on its face to be within a specific prohibition of the Constitution, such as those of the first ten Amendments, which are deemed equally specific when held to be embraced within the Fourteenth....

It is unnecessary to consider now whether legislation which restricts those political processes which can ordinarily be expected to bring about repeal of undesirable legislation, is to be subjected to more exacting judicial scrutiny under the general prohibitions of the Fourteenth Amendment than are most other types of legislation....

Nor need we enquire ... whether prejudice against discrete and insular minorities may be a special condition, which tends seriously to curtail the operation of those political processes ordinarily to be relied upon to protect minorities, and which may call for a correspondingly more searching judicial inquiry....[28]

Post–1937 Decisions and the Blending of Substantive Due Process and Equal Protection. When the Supreme Court reviews a law that restricts the liberty of all persons it will review the law under due process principles. When the Court reviews a law that classifies persons it will use equal protection principles. The due process clause of the Fourteenth Amendment restricts the actions of state and local governments. The due process clause of the Fifth Amendment restricts the actions of the federal government. The equal protection clause of the Fourteenth Amendment restricts the ability of state and local governments to classify persons. However, the equal protection clause of the Fourteenth Amendment does not apply to the federal government. The Supreme Court has held that the due process clause of the Fifth Amendment has an implied equal protection

---

24. Professor Wright viewed the Court's position in *Adkins* as "essentially that of the *Lochner* opinion." Wright, supra note 13, at 178.

25. 304 U.S. 144, 58 S.Ct. 778, 82 L.Ed. 1234 (1938).

26. 304 U.S. at 154, 58 S.Ct. at 784.

27. 304 U.S. at 152, 58 S.Ct. at 783.

28. 304 U.S. at 152–53 n. 4, 58 S.Ct. at 783–84.

guarantee that limits the ability of the federal government to classify persons for the allocation of benefits or burdens. As we will see in Chapter 14, the equal protection guarantee of the Fifth Amendment due process clause establishes principles that limit federal classifications that are virtually identical to the principles established by the equal protection clause of the Fourteenth Amendment (even though the Fifth Amendment equal protection guarantee is entirely independent from the Fourteenth Amendment).

Since 1937, the Supreme Court has required the judiciary to give great deference to federal, state and local law makers when reviewing economic and social welfare legislation under either due process or equal protection principles. Such legislation (or a classification in such legislation) is not to be overturned unless the law has no rational relationship to any legitimate interest of government. If the law (or the classification) has a rational relationship to a legitimate interest of government the law (or classification) will be upheld.

An economic or social welfare law will be subject to more rigorous standards of review under equal protection if the law employs a classification that receives special constitutional protection (such as gender or illegitimacy classifications or the "suspect classifications" of race, national origin, and alienage.) These cases are examined in Chapter 14.

If a law impairs a fundamental constitutional right it will be subject to independent judicial review. If the law limits the ability of all persons to exercise a fundamental right it will be tested under due process. If the law restricts in the ability of a class of persons to exercise a fundamental right, it will be tested under equal protection. Although the Supreme Court has often stated that a law (or a classification in a law) that impairs a funda-

mental right must be narrowly tailored to promote a compelling interest, the standard of review used in fundamental rights cases is unclear. Because the majority of modern fundamental rights cases involve equal protection rulings, the examination of fundamental rights cases will be deferred to Chapter 14.

Post–1937 Decisions Regarding Economic and Social Welfare Legislation. The exact dimension of the Court's deference to legislative economic judgments remained unclear after *Carolene Products*. The Court had suggested that it may consider the validity of the proffered rational basis for economic legislation. Subsequent Court decisions, however, disclosed that the judicial deference to the legislature's economic regulations was virtually complete.

In *Lincoln Federal Labor Union v. Northwestern Iron & Metal Co.*[29] the Court upheld the constitutionality of a state's "right-to-work" law. After noting the Court's rejection of the "Allgeyer–Lockner–Adair–Coppage constitutional doctrine,"[30] Justice Black stressed that the states have the authority to legislate against "injurious practices in their internal commercial and business affairs, so long as their laws do not run afoul of some specific federal constitutional prohibition, or of some valid federal law."[31]

Six years later in *Williamson v. Lee Optical of Oklahoma, Inc.*[32] the Court rejected the due process and equal protection arguments that the appellees made against the validity of an Oklahoma statute that restricted the ability of opticians to fit or duplicate eyeglasses. Not only was the Court unable to find a specific constitutional prohibition that the Oklahoma measure violated, but the Court was willing to conceive of possible reasons for the enactment that would furnish a rational basis for the law.[33] The *Williamson* opinion suggests that

29. 335 U.S. 525, 69 S.Ct. 251, 93 L.Ed. 212 (1949).

30. 335 U.S. at 535–36, 69 S.Ct. at 256.

31. 335 U.S. at 536, 69 S.Ct. at 257.

32. 348 U.S. 483, 75 S.Ct. 461, 99 L.Ed. 563 (1955).

33. Repeatedly throughout the opinion Justice Douglas rationalized some possible reasons for the Oklahoma statute: "[t]he legislature might conclude that to regulate [eyeglass lenses] effectively it would have to regulate [eye-

glass frames]. Or it might conclude that both sellers of frames and sellers of lenses were in a business where advertising should be limited or abolished in the public interest." 348 U.S. at 490, 75 S.Ct. at 466. Later he noted "it may be deemed important to effective regulation that the eye doctor be restricted to geographical location that reduce the temptations of commercialism."

348 U.S. at 490, 75 S.Ct. at 466.

the Court will not only presume that a legislature had a reasonable basis for enacting a particular economic measure, but also will hypothesize reasons for the law's enactment if the legislature fails to state explicitly the reasons behind its judgment. Consequently, anyone attempting to argue for the invalidation of a legislative economic enactment may have to discredit the Court's conceived reasons for the legislature's actions as well as the arguments of those who support the measure. The Court's turnabout from the *Lochner* era became complete with the *Williamson* decision.

Justice Black's opinion in *Ferguson v. Skrupa*[34] provides an appropriate epilogue for the demise of economic substantive due process. In sustaining a Kansas law that prohibited anyone from conducting the business of debt adjusting unless incident to the practice of law, the Court through Justice Black stated: "[W]e refuse to sit as a 'superlegislature to weigh the wisdom of legislation'.... Whether the legislature takes for its textbook Adam Smith, Herbert Spencer, Lord Keynes or some other is no concern of ours."[35] Justice Holmes's *Lochner* dissent had become the Court's standard.[36]

Another step in the Court's retreat from its position as guardian of the laissez faire concept of economics was taken when the Court decided that the equal protection clause did not guarantee that economic legislation would treat all businesses equally. In *Railway Express Agency v. New York*[37] the Court rejected a constitutional argument that a New York City ordinance violated the equal protection clause. The ordinance prevented owners of delivery vehicles from placing advertisements on the outside of their vehicles unless the

advertisement was for the owner's business. The appellant contended that the municipal regulation violated the equal protection clause because the proffered rationale for the ordinance, to reduce distractions for vehicle drivers and pedestrians, did not comport with the ordinance's classification. As long as the classification scheme "has relation to the purpose for which it is made and does not contain the kind of discrimination against which the equal protection clause affords protection"[38] the Court will sustain the regulation against arguments based on equal protection analysis. Because the classification had an arguable relation to the perceived goal of the legislation, the Court found that the ordinance violated no constitutional proscription.[39]

Morey v. Doud[40] is one of the rare instances in which the Supreme Court found that a law violated the equal protection rationality test.[41] *Morey* would be overruled almost twenty years later.[42] The Court's decision in *Morey*, and its later decision to overrule *Morey*, provide a useful background for consideration of the degree of deference that must be given to legislative rules or classifications in the area of economics or social welfare. The Court had decided several cases after *Railway Express Co.* that strongly suggested that it would defer to legislative judgment on economic matters even if those who opposed a business regulation raised equal protection arguments against the measure.[43] In short, the Court had implied that it would not use the equal protection clause to void economic regulations. In *Morey v. Doud*, however, the Court invalidated an Illinois statute because it violated the appellees' right to equal protection under the law.

---

34.   372 U.S. 726, 83 S.Ct. 1028, 10 L.Ed.2d 93 (1963).

35.   372 U.S. at 731–32, 83 S.Ct. at 1032 (footnotes omitted).

36.   See discussion of *Lochner* in § 11.3, supra.

37.   336 U.S. 106, 69 S.Ct. 463, 93 L.Ed. 533 (1949).

38.   336 U.S. at 110, 69 S.Ct. at 465.

39.   336 U.S. at 110, 69 S.Ct. at 465.

40.   354 U.S. 457, 77 S.Ct. 1344, 1 L.Ed.2d 1485 (1957), overruled in City of New Orleans v. Dukes, 427 U.S. 297, 306, 96 S.Ct. 2513, 2518, 49 L.Ed.2d 511 (1976).

41.   For an analysis of the Court's use of the "rationality" or "rational relationship" test to void several state or local laws under the equal protection clause see §14.3.

42.   City of New Orleans v. Dukes, 427 U.S. 297, 306, 96 S.Ct. 2513, 2518, 49 L.Ed.2d 511 (1976).

43.   Williamson v. Lee Optical of Oklahoma, Inc., 348 U.S. 483, 75 S.Ct. 461, 99 L.Ed. 563 (1955); Daniel v. Family Security Life Insurance Co., 336 U.S. 220, 69 S.Ct. 550, 93 L.Ed. 632 (1949); Kotch v. Board of River Port Pilot Com'rs, 330 U.S. 552, 67 S.Ct. 910, 91 L.Ed. 1093 (1947), (although decided before *Ry. Express Co.* it was reflective of the trend).

The statute in *Morey* required currency exchanges to meet certain requirements before the State Auditor could issue a license that would allow the exchange to conduct its business. The law specifically exempted from its requirements those who issued United States Post Office, American Express Company, or Western Union Telegraph Company money orders. The Court recognized that the purpose behind the regulation was "to afford the public *continuing* protection" [44] in its dealing with currency exchange. Moreover, the Court understood that the present characteristics of the American Express Company made unnecessary any regulation of the sale of that company's money orders. The Court, however, was concerned that the American Express Company would retain its exemption even if its present characteristics changed. In essence, the Act not only created advantages for a "closed class" of sellers but also only had "a remote relationship" between its purpose and its classification scheme. [45] Consequently, the Court concluded that the Illinois law violated the equal protection clause because a majority of the Justices believed that this closed class lacked even a rational basis.

Finally, in *City of New Orleans v. Dukes* [46] the Court declared that *Morey* was an erroneous decision and overruled it. The City of New Orleans had adopted an ordinance that prohibited pushcart vendors from selling their goods in the city's French Quarter. The law exempted from its prohibition those pushcart vendors who qualified under the ordinance's "grandfather" clause. Only two vendors qualified, and the respondent, who did not qualify under the "grandfather" clause, contended the ordinance violated the equal protection clause.

The Court rejected the contention after noting that the ordinance was purely an economic regulation. The Court reminded the respondent that it consistently had deferred to legislative determinations as to the desirability of a particular statutory classification. Any reliance on *Morey v. Doud* as a basis to invalidate the ordinance was mistaken. The Court explicitly overruled *Morey* and summarized its reaction to the equal protection argument when it stated that "the judiciary may not sit as a superlegislature to judge the wisdom or desirability of legislative policy determinations made in areas that neither affect fundamental rights nor proceed along suspect lines." [47]

Although the Supreme Court has never totally rejected a judicial role in the review of economic and social welfare legislation, it is rare that any law or classification would be held to violate substantive due process or equal protection principles under the rationality standard. In a few cases the Court has been confronted with situations where a legislative classification subjected out-of-state persons to discriminatory taxation [48] or where the state singled out a group, such as mentally retarded persons, for special burdens for no reason other than antipathy towards that group. [49] In these cases the Court invalidated the legislation under the equal protection rationality standard because the state could assert no interest to support the legislation other than a desire to discriminate against the disfavored group. Such laws violate equal protection because the desire to discriminate cannot in itself supply a justification for discriminatory classifications.

In sharp contrast to the Court's almost total abandonment of any real scrutiny of economic

44. 354 U.S. at 466, 77 S.Ct. at 1351 (emphasis in original).

45. 354 U.S. at 467, 469, 77 S.Ct. at 1351, 1352.

46. 427 U.S. 297, 306, 96 S.Ct. 2513, 2518, 49 L.Ed.2d 511 (1976).

47. 427 U.S. at 303, 96 S.Ct. at 2517.

48. See Metropolitan Life Insurance Co. v. Ward, 470 U.S. 869, 105 S.Ct. 1676, 84 L.Ed.2d 751 (1985); Williams v. Vermont, 472 U.S. 14, 105 S.Ct. 2465, 86 L.Ed.2d 11 (1985); Hooper v. Bernalillo County Assessor, 472 U.S. 612, 105 S.Ct. 2862, 86 L.Ed.2d 487 (1985). These cases are examined in § 14.3.

49. City of Cleburne v. Cleburne Living Center, 473 U.S. 432, 105 S.Ct. 3249, 87 L.Ed.2d 313 (1985) (Court invalidates a zoning ordinance to the extent that it excludes group homes occupied by mentally retarded persons and the government would allow group living arrangements for any other group of persons). See also, Romer v. Evans, 517 U.S. 620, 116 S.Ct. 1620, 134 L.Ed.2d 855 (1996) (Supreme Court invalidates an amendment to a state constitution that prohibited the state, or local legislatures within the state, from passing any law protecting persons from discrimination because of their sexual orientation). See §§ 14.3, 14.28, 14.30.

legislation under substantive due process or equal protection analysis is its increasingly strict examination of legislation and governmental actions that affect civil rights or liberties. Since 1937 the Court has deferred to the legislative judgment on economic matters but it has continued to emphasize that substantive due process analysis was available to protect an individual's civil rights.[50] The rights the Court has recognized as fundamental and deserving of significant judicial protection are most of the guarantees of the Bill of Rights,[51] the right to fairness in the criminal process, the right to privacy (including some freedom of choice in matters of marriage, sexual relations and child bearing), the right to travel, the right to vote, the freedom of association and some aspects of fairness in the adjudication of individual claims against the government (procedural due process rights).

Today the due process and equal protection guarantees are not significant restraints on the government's ability to act in matters of economics or social welfare. While due process still protects a person's liberty in society, only those liberties or rights of "fundamental" constitutional magnitude will be actively protected by the Supreme Court. Where no such right is restricted, the law need only rationally relate to any legitimate end of government. As long as there is any conceivable basis for finding such a rational relationship, the law will be upheld. Only when a law is a totally arbitrary deprivation of liberty will it violate the substantive due process guarantee.[52]

The equal protection clause governs the classification of persons for benefits or burdens by the government. While the clause applies only to state and local government, the due process clause of the Fifth Amendment restricts the federal government's ability to classify persons in a similar manner and so the Fifth Amendment creates another equal protection guarantee.[53] If the government classifies persons as to their ability to exercise fundamental rights, the Court will not give great deference to the legislative decision. In fundamental rights cases, the Court has often stated that the classification must be necessary or narrowly tailored to promote a compelling or overriding governmental interest. The meaning of that test is unclear; it may be that the Court is using an "intermediate test" in those cases that only requires the government to show that the law is substantially related to an important government interest.[54]

Even if the law does not involve a fundamental constitutional right, a law that burdens a classification of persons because of the "suspect" traits of race, national origin, or status as a resident alien, the Courts will engage in an independent review of the classification to determine if it is narrowly tailored to promote a compelling interest of government. Even when a law classifies persons in a manner that does not involve the exercise of fundamental rights, the Court will use an intermediate standard of review (less strict than the compelling interest test but less deferential than the rational relationship test) if the classification is based upon traits such as gender or illegitimacy. When the Court reviews a law that

50. See United States v. Carolene Products, 304 U.S. 144, 152–53 n. 4, 58 S.Ct. 778, 783–84 n. 4, 82 L.Ed. 1234 (1938). For a discussion of the Court's application of the substantive due process and equal protection theory to protect fundamental rights, see § 11.7, infra.

51. On this basis all of the first eight Amendments except for the Second, Third, and Seventh Amendments, and the grand jury clause of the Fifth Amendment, have been applied to the states. See § 11.6, infra.

52. The development of fundamental rights analysis represents a partial return to the judicial use of the due process clause to justify independent judicial review of laws that do not restrict rights or liberties which have explicit recognition in the text of the Constitution or its Amendments. For this reason the basic theoretical problem of judicial definition and protection of such rights is

noted in §§ 11.5–11.7, infra. Because most Supreme Court rulings finding unconstitutional infringements of fundamental rights have been based on the equal protection guarantee, detailed analysis of the Court's fundamental rights decision is deferred to Chapter 14.

53. See §§ 11.1–11.4, infra.

54. For an introduction to standards of review problems in equal protection cases see § 14.3. For further information regarding the relationship between fundamental constitutional rights analysis and equal protection analysis see §§ 11.5–11.7, 14.42. For rulings regarding specific fundamental rights see §§ 14.26–14.40. For further information regarding the similarities and differences between procedural due process principles, substantive due process principles, and equal protection principles see §§ 10.6, 10.7.

does not involve a fundamental constitutional right and does not classify persons on the basis of traits such as race, resident alien status, gender, or illegitimacy, the Supreme Court will give great deference to the decision of the legislature. The Court will uphold that type of law so long as the Justices can conceive of a basis for deciding that the classification is rationally related to a legitimate end of government.

We have come full circle with the concepts of substantive due process and equal protection in the area of general economic or social welfare legislation. Originally there was little active review of such legislation, because the judges realized that the federal courts should defer to the other branches of government unless laws were totally arbitrary deprivations of liberty. Slowly there emerged independent judicial control of all governmental policies under the guise of enforcing the due process guarantee. Today, the Justices have accepted the position that they are only to actively guard fundamental constitutional values and that they should allow other branches of government great latitude in dealing with issues of "economics and social welfare" which do not touch upon these values.

The Supreme Court, in majority opinions, employs the rational basis test in reviewing the substance of laws and regulations challenged under the due process or equal protection guarantees when the regulation does not involve a fundamental constitutional right, suspect classification or the characteristics of citizenship, gender, or illegitimacy. When the Court examines procedural due process claims it must employ independent judicial review of the fairness of an administrative or judicial system.[55] But when the Court examines substantive due process or equal protection claims, a majority of the Justices will uphold the challenged governmental act unless no reasonably conceivable set of facts could establish a rational relationship between the challenged regulation and a legitimate end of government.

A few Justices have indicated a desire to review the reasonableness of some economic or social welfare legislation but the strong presumption for validity of such statutes provided by the rational basis test has not been removed.[56] A majority of Justices continue to use the rational basis test to approve laws allocating welfare benefits,[57] restricting the use of property,[58] or regulating business or personal activity that does not involve a funda-

55. In Sacramento v. Lewis, 523 U.S. 833, 118 S.Ct. 1708, 140 L.Ed.2d 1043 (1998) the Justices ruled that the death of a suspect who was accidentally killed by a police patrol car in a high-speed chase of the motorcycle (on which the deceased person had been a passenger) did not violate substantive due process principles. The majority opinion in *Lewis* adopted "shock the conscience" studied for determining when actions of executive branch actors (such as police officers) would violate substantive due process principles. The Court in *Lewis* did not address taking of property issues or procedural due process issues. Nevertheless, harm cause to persons or property by actions of police officers may sometimes present taking of property issues, together with substantive and procedural issues. The *Lewis* decision is examined in § 10.6 of this Treatise. See §§ 10.6, 10.7, regarding the difference between procedural due process and substantive due process or equal protection. See also Chapter 13, Procedural Due Process, infra.

56. G.D. Searle & Co. v. Cohn, 455 U.S. 404, 102 S.Ct. 1137, 71 L.Ed.2d 250 (1982) (court rules that state statute tolling statute of limitations period against out-of-state corporation which does not have an officer located in the state for service of process does not violate equal protection; Justice Stevens in dissent would have found that the statute denied equal protection to these corporations). See § 14.3, infra.

57. See e.g., United States R.R. Retirement Bd. v. Fritz, 449 U.S. 166, 101 S.Ct. 453, 66 L.Ed.2d 368 (1980) (upholding congressional elimination of payment of dual retirement benefits to some employees who had engaged in both railroad and non-railroad employment on any basis that is not "patently arbitrary or irrational"); Schweiker v. Hogan, 457 U.S. 569, 102 S.Ct. 2597, 73 L.Ed.2d 227 (1982) (upholding Social Security Act classifications that provide for reimbursement of state providing Medicaid benefits to "medically needy" but exempting from program repayment for benefits to "categorically needy".) See §§ 14.3, 14.43.

58. See, Hodel v. Indiana, 452 U.S. 314, 101 S.Ct. 2376, 69 L.Ed.2d 40 (1981) (upholding the "prime farm land" provisions of the Surface Mining and Reclamation Control Act of 1977 against the claim that the restrictions on mining and certain farm land were arbitrary limitations of the use of property in select geographic areas). "Social and economic legislation like the Surface Mining Act that does not employ suspect classifications or impinge on fundamental rights must be upheld against equal protection attack when the legislative means are rationally related to a legitimate government purpose. Moreover such legislation carries with it a presumption of rationality that can only be overcome by a clear showing of arbitrariness and irrationality." 452 U.S. at 331, 101 S.Ct. at 2387 (citations omitted).

mental right.[59] Nevertheless, there is the possibility that those Justices who have demonstrated an unwillingness to accept government assertions of a theoretical or conceivable rational basis for legislation will be joined by new Supreme Court appointees who would also require the government to demonstrate a reasonable relationship between any governmental regulation of liberty or property and a constitutional end of government. Were that possibility to occur, the presumption of constitutionality for economic and social welfare legislation would disappear and the Court would return to the 1900–1936 approach to substantive due process and equal protection analysis.[60]

If the Supreme Court were to make an independent determination of the reasonableness of a law challenged under substantive due process, the Court would require government to make a factual demonstration that the challenged law promoted a legitimate end of government. The requirement that the government make a factual demonstration of the

reasonableness of its legislation would mirror the approach that the Court took from 1900 to 1936 to substantive due process and equal protection. Today, the Supreme Court most often describes the basic standard of review to be used in substantive due process and equal protection cases as one under which the courts will uphold a law so long as there is a "rational relationship" between the law and any "legitimate interest" of government. This form of judicial review gives great deference to legislature. Sometimes the Supreme Court describes this form of minimal judicial scrutiny as involving the determination of whether the law is reasonably related to a legitimate governmental interest. The Court now seems to equate a reasonableness standard with a true rationality standard. The Court employs a presumption of constitutionality for economic and social welfare legislation.[61] The Supreme Court will apply only minimal judicial review, commonly described as the rationality standard, to laws that do not regulate a fundamental right or involve a classification of persons

---

59. Thus the Supreme Court upheld a federal limitation on the liability of privately-owned nuclear power plants for accidents and resulting injuries at the plants. Since no fundamental rights were regulated by the statute, it was "a classic example of economic regulation" and was subject only to the minimum scrutiny rational basis test. Duke Power Co. v. Carolina Environmental Study Group, Inc., 438 U.S. 59, 98 S.Ct. 2620, 57 L.Ed.2d 595 (1978).

The Supreme Court upheld a state law which prohibited the ownership of retail gas stations by petroleum producers and refiners and which regulated their pricing practices. Exxon Corp. v. Governor of Maryland, 437 U.S. 117, 98 S.Ct. 2207, 57 L.Ed.2d 91 (1978). It took the Court only a single paragraph to dismiss the producers' argument that the law violated the principle of substantive due process; there was no problem in upholding these regulations under the rational relationship test. 437 U.S. at 125, 98 S.Ct. at 2213–14.

60. See § 14.3 for further analysis of the modern "rationality" or "rational relationship" standard in due process and equal protection cases.

Substantive Due Process and Administrative Rulings. It is sometimes difficult for courts to separate procedural due process and substantive due process issues when reviewing the action of an administrative entity with rule-making authority. This subject is considered in § 10.6.

61. In Reno v. Flores, 507 U.S. 292, 113 S.Ct. 1439, 123 L.Ed.2d 1 (1993), on remand 992 F.2d 243 (9th Cir.1993) the Justices, by a seven to two vote, upheld

Immigration and Naturalization Service regulations that kept alien minors in custody except in certain specified circumstances. The majority opinion by Justice Scalia rejected both substantive due process and equal protection attacks on the regulations. Justice Scalia found that juveniles had no fundamental right to be free of all forms of custody and thus the conditions of custody did not implicate any fundamental rights or interests of the juveniles. The Court in Flores refused to require that the government justify the law as being narrowly tailored to protect the best interest of the child. In three consecutive paragraphs, Justice Scalia described the standard of review differently. First, he found that the regulation would be upheld as long as there was a "reasonable fit between governmental purpose . . . and the means chosen to advance that purpose." He then found that the regulation would be upheld as long as it met "the (unexacting) standard of rationally advancing some legitimate government purpose." Finally, he rejected the claim that the classification of children kept in custody under federal law violated the implied equal protection guarantee of the Fifth Amendment due process clause because the "tradition of reposing custody in close relatives and legal guardians" and "the difference between citizens and aliens" was "adequate" to support the classification. 507 U.S. at 305, 113 S.Ct. at 1449.

Although Justice Scalia's majority opinion in Flores was unclear regarding the precise standard of review, Justice Scalia's opinion clearly refused to second guess the legislative and executive rule making processes. The Court in Flores would not strike down any rule or classification that was not truly arbitrary.

for whom special judicial protection is required.[62]

In *Lawrence v. Texas*,[63] the Supreme Court ruled that a state statute prohibiting consenting adults persons from engaging in same-sex sodomy violated the due process clause of the Fourteenth Amendment. Justice Kennedy wrote an opinion for five Justices in *Lawrence* that found the law invalid on the basis that the statute "furthers no legitimate state interest which can justify its intrusion into the personal and private life of the individual."[64] Justice O'Connor, who concurred in *Lawrence*, would have preferred to base the judgment of the Court on equal protection and make a ruling that the law banning only same-sex sodomy was designed solely to prosecute and persecute an unpopular group.[65] Only time will tell whether the *Lawrence* decision represents a truly ad-hoc judgment of the Court or whether the Court will return to *Locher*-era type of adjudication where the Justices will only approve laws where they believe that the end of the law, based on their personal values, justifies an intrusion on individual liberty.[66]

§ 11.5   A Note on the Meaning of "Liberty", Fundamental Constitutional Rights, and the Incorporation of the Bill of Rights

Even before the Court had decided *Marbury v. Madison*,[1] the Justices were debating the extent of their power to enforce natural law rights against the actions of other branches of government.[2] As previously noted, the philosophy that the Justices would overturn acts of other branches only to protect specific constitutional guarantees has been the formal guideline of the Supreme Court at every stage in its history. However, as we have seen in this chapter, the Court has continually sought to enforce those natural law rights which the Justices believed were essential in American society.

In the first four Sections of this Chapter, we saw the rise and fall of the concept of "substantive due process" as the means by which the judiciary would review the legitimacy of all types of legislative or regulatory actions. From the late 1890's through 1936, the Justices found that the due process clauses of the Fifth and Fourteenth Amendments justified invalidation of any law that a majority of the Justices thought was unreasonable.[3] During that era, any regulation of human activity that the Justices considered to be unreasonable, in the sense that it was not closely related to an interest that they believed to be legitimate, was invalidated as an unconstitutional intrusion on "liberty."

Beginning in 1937, the Court renounced the position that the courts were free to invalidate laws merely because the judges disagreed with the reasonableness of the law. In the modern era, the Court would uphold a law against the claim that it violated the due process or equal protection clauses so long as the law could, in some conceivable way, have a rational relationship to an end of government that was not clearly unconstitutional. Laws that did not substantially impair a fundamental constitutional right, or employ a constitutionally suspect classification, would enjoy a presumption of constitutionality. Those laws would not be invalidated unless the party attacking the law or classification could show that it had no

---

62. See § 14.3 of this Treatise regarding the judicial standards of review used under the equal protection guarantee.

63. Lawrence v. Texas ___ U.S. ___, 123 S.Ct. 2472, 156 L.Ed.2d 508 (2003).

64. ___ U.S. at ___, 123 S.Ct. at 2484.

65. ___ U.S. at ___, 123 S.Ct. at 2484–88 (O'Connor, J., concurring in the judgment).

66. The *Lawrence* case is examined in greater detail in § 14.28 of this Treatise. The dissenters in *Lawrence* were of the opinion that the majority's rationale for striking down the Texas anti-sodomy by homosexuals law mirrored

the reasoning of *Locher*-era cases. Lawrence v. Texas, ___ U.S. ___, 123 S.Ct. 2472, 2488, 156 L.Ed.2d 508 (2003) (Scalia, J., joined by Rehnquist, C.J., and Thomas, J., dissenting); ___ U.S. at ___, 123 S.Ct. at 2498 (Thomas, J., dissenting).

§ 11.5

1. 5 U.S. (1 Cranch) 137, 2 L.Ed. 60 (1803).

2. Calder v. Bull, 3 U.S. (3 Dall.) 386, 1 L.Ed. 648 (1798). See § 11.1, supra.

3. See §§ 11.2, 11.3.

possible rational relationship to any legitimate interest of government.[4]

During the modern era the Court will engage independent judicial review if the law substantially impairs a fundamental right or employs certain classifying traits that have special constitutional status (such as race, nationality, gender, or illegitimacy).[5] If a law does not employ a classification that would require independent judicial review, the Court will examine the law under the rationality test unless the law significantly impaired a fundamental constitutional right. If a law substantially impairs the exercise of a fundamental right by all persons the law will be reviewed under the due process clause. If the law restricts the exercise of a fundamental constitutional right by only a class of individuals, the law will be reviewed under the equal protection clause, or the implied equal protection guarantee of the Fifth Amendment due process clause.[6]

Although the Supreme Court has not been clear in defining the standard of review used in fundamental rights cases, it most commonly states that any significant impairment of a fundamental constitutional right will be invalid unless the government demonstrates that the law, or the classification, is narrowly tailored to promote a compelling or overriding interest.[7]

In order to avoid confusion in defining "liberty" and determining which rights should be "fundamental" it is important to remember the distinction between procedural due process and substantive review under the due process or equal protection clauses.[8] If an individual asserts that the government must provide him with some type of procedural safeguards before the government takes an interest from him, he must demonstrate that the interest constitutes life, liberty, or property.[9] For example, assume that a teacher asserts that he should be given a hearing before he is fired

from his job at a government operated school. The teacher will have to show his firing would deprive him of "liberty" or "property". The definition of "liberty" and "property" is central to procedural due process analysis.

There is no need to define life, property or liberty for substantive due process analysis, although some Supreme Court cases would lead a reader to believe the contrary. The fact that a government law or regulatory action restricts property or liberty does not automatically justify strict judicial scrutiny of the law. All laws might be said to restrict individual's use of property rights or personal liberty, in the sense of restricting which actions the individual can take in society. The laws regulating property or liberty that do not restrict the exercise of a fundamental right should be upheld unless the person attacking the law can overcome the presumption of constitutionality and demonstrate that the law is not rationally related to a legitimate interest.

Fundamental constitutional rights comprise a subset, or special part, of the concept of liberty. While all human activity may constitute liberty, only certain types of actions are fundamental constitutional rights. Perhaps this concept would have been easier to understand if the Court called these rights "fundamental constitutional liberties." When reading any of the Court's due process or equal protection cases the reader should remember that a determination that a regulated activity comes within the constitutional definition of liberty does not determine the manner in which the Court will review restrictions on that activity. Only significant impairments of fundamental constitutional rights will be subject to strict judicial scrutiny.

Two cases decided in early 1999 are examples of how confusion over the meaning of the word liberty has caused problems for the

---

4. See § 11.4, 14.3 regarding the standards of review used in substantive due process and equal protection cases.

5. See §§ 14.1–14.3.

6. See §§ 10.6, 10.7, for a discussion of the distinctions between procedural review and substantive review under the due process and equal protection clauses.

7. See note 4, supra.

8. See note 6, supra.

9. Procedural due process issues are examined in Chapter 13.

Court. In *Chicago v. Morales*[10] the Supreme Court invalidated a law that gave a police officer the authority to order individuals to disperse whenever the police officer believed the group of people who were gathered together in a public place involved one or more "street gang" members who were "loitering". Justice Stevens wrote for six Justices in finding that the law violated due process, because it was so vague that it allowed totally arbitrary and capricious enforcement by police officers. However, the portion of Justice Stevens's opinion that described the law as restricting "liberty" was joined only by three Justices. The dissenters attacked the majority, and the plurality opinion, for protecting an activity that they believed was not a fundamental constitutional right and was a constitutionally protected liberty interest.[11]

The *Morales* case did not require any fundamental rights analysis. In the portion of his opinion that was written for only three Justices, Justice Stevens noted that the Court was not ruling that the ability to stay on a sidewalk was a fundamental constitutional right.[12] Justice Stevens did not assert that the judiciary should closely scrutinize government laws regulating how many people could be on a sidewalk or the conditions on which people could walk down sidewalks in public places. Rather, the Stevens opinion, and the concurring Justices, merely found that the government could not make some form of human activity criminal without providing minimally adequate notice to individuals concerning the type of activity that would violate the law.[13] Just as every law must survive the minimal

rationality test, every criminal law must provide some notice to individuals concerning the conduct it makes criminal and provide some limitation of police discretion.[14]

In *Saenz v. Roe*[15] the Court invalidated a California law that gave lower welfare benefits to low income families during the first year of their residency in the state than the state gave to long-term residents. Instead of finding that the law violated the equal protection clause by creating a classification that substantially impaired the fundamental right to travel, Justice Stevens's opinion for a seven member majority found that the law violated the privileges or immunities clause of the Fourteenth Amendment.[16]

In prior cases, the Court had encountered problems in defining the constitutional basis for ruling that an individual's ability to establish residency in a new state was a fundamental constitutional right. Nevertheless, the Court had found that significant limitations of that right should be subject to independent judicial review and invalidated unless the regulations were narrowly tailored to a compelling interest. Although the Court had never before employed the privileges or immunities clause of the Fourteenth Amendment as a significant restriction on state or local legislation,[17] the majority opinion referred only to that clause as the basis for invalidation of the law in *Saenz*. It may be that a majority of the Justices in *Saenz* found it easier to resurrect the privileges or immunities clause of the Fourteenth Amendment than to explain the basis upon which the Justices would find that a right to travel was "fundamental."

10. 527 U.S. 41, 119 S.Ct. 1849, 144 L.Ed.2d 67 (1999).

11. 527 U.S. at 72–97, 119 S.Ct. at 1867–79 (Scalia, J., dissenting); 527 U.S. at 97–114, 119 S.Ct. at 1879–87 (Thomas, J., joined by Rehnquist, C.J., and Scalia, J., dissenting).

12. 527 U.S. at 53 n. 19, 64 n. 35, 119 S.Ct. at 1857 n. 19, 1863 n. 35 (opinion of Stevens, J., joined by Souter and Ginsburg, JJ.).

13. 527 U.S. at 50–61, 119 S.Ct. at 1856–1861 (opinion of Stevens, J., joined by Souter and Ginsburg, JJ.).

14. Chicago v. Morales, 527 U.S. 41, 119 S.Ct. 1849, 1861–62, 144 L.Ed.2d 67 (1999); 527 U.S. at 64–68, 119 S.Ct. at 1863–65 (O'Connor, J., joined by Breyer, J., concurring in part and concurring in the judgment); 527 U.S. at 68, 119 S.Ct. at 1865 (Kennedy, J., concurring in part

and concurring in the judgment); 527 U.S. at 68–72, 119 S.Ct. at 1865–67 (Breyer, J., concurring in part and concurring in the judgment).

15. 526 U.S. 489, 119 S.Ct. 1518, 143 L.Ed.2d 689 (1999). This case is examined more fully in § 14.38 of this Treatise.

16. The Supreme Court restricted the meaning of this clause in The Slaughter–House Cases, 83 U.S. (16 Wall.) 36, 21 L.Ed.394 (1873). Prior to 1999, the Court had used this clause in only one case, and then had overruled that case. Colgate v. Harvey, 296 U.S. 404, 56 S.Ct. 252, 80 L.Ed. 299 (1935) overruled in Madden v. Kentucky, 309 U.S. 83, 60 S.Ct. 406, 84 L.Ed. 590 (1940).

17. See § 14.38.

Most of the Court's rulings concerning fundamental rights have come in cases involving equal protection challenges to a law and, for that reason, are discussed in our Equal Protection Chapter.[18] In the next two Sections of this Chapter, we invite the reader to reflect on the relationship between the history of judicial review that we have examined in the first four Sections of this Chapter and two modern constitutional concepts: the judicial protection of fundamental constitutional rights, and the incorporation of the provisions of the Bill of Rights into the Fourteenth Amendment.

One fundamental right that has been protected primarily under the due process clauses is the right of a woman to choose to have an abortion without certain types of restrictions being imposed by governmental entities.[19] In one of the abortion cases decided in the 1990's, Justice O'Connor wrote for a majority of the Court when she found that the Justices would use similar analysis in determining whether the due process clause of the Fourteenth Amendment incorporated specific provisions of the Bill of Rights and in determining whether the concept of liberty in the Fourteenth Amendment gave special protection to a fundamental constitutional right.[20]

§ 11.6　Incorporation of the Bill of Rights

Prior to the Civil War the Court had held that the provisions of the Bill of Rights were not applicable to the activities of state and local governments.[1] However, it was not long after the passage of the Fourteenth Amendment before individuals claimed that the guarantees of individual rights contained in those Amendments were made applicable to the states by the Fourteenth Amendment. The Supreme Court rejected such contentions at first but the reasons for so doing may be found in decisions on other constitutional issues.

First, the Court had given a restrictive meaning to the privileges and immunities clause of the Fourteenth Amendment in one of its first decisions on the meaning of that Amendment.[2] This decision had the effect of eliminating the provision which was both historically and logically the one most likely to have been intended to include within its protections the guarantees of the Bill of Rights.[3] At the close of the twentieth century, the Supreme Court would find that the privileges or immunities clause of the Fourteenth Amendment protected one aspect of the "right to travel."[4] The Court, however, has not used that clause as the basis for protecting civil liberties generally, or for applying the Bill of Rights to the states.

The second reason for the Supreme Court's failure to closely analyze the incorporation issue during this period is that there was simply no need to do so. Because of the Court's expansive reading of the due process clause, the Justices were able to protect any form of individual freedom or natural law rights without resorting to a specific textual basis in the Constitution or the Bill of Rights. This fact is the key to understanding why the development of the so-called "incorporation" theory has come about relatively recently.

During the period from 1887 to 1934 the Supreme Court decided cases which restricted the activities of state and local governments on the basis of individual rights which were virtually identical to those protected by one or more

---

18.　See §§ 14.3, 14.26–14.41.

19.　See § 14.29 regarding the Supreme Court's rulings on abortion regulations.

20.　Planned Parenthood v. Casey, 505 U.S. 833, 846–48, 112 S.Ct. 2791, 2804–05, 120 L.Ed.2d 674 (1992). Part II of the majority opinion was joined by a majority of the Justices, although Justice O'Connor's analysis of abortion regulations was joined by only a plurality of the Justices. See § 14.29 for an examination of the *Casey* decision.

§ 11.6

1.　Barron v. Mayor and City Council of Baltimore, 32 U.S. (7 Pet.) 243, 8 L.Ed. 672 (1833).

2.　In re Slaughter–House Cases, 83 U.S. (16 Wall.) 36, 21 L.Ed. 394 (1872).

3.　See, J. tenBroek, Equal Under Law at 223 (enlarged edition 1965); J. James, The Framing of the Fourteenth Amendment, at 180 (1965).

4.　Saenz v. Roe, 526 U.S. 489, 119 S.Ct. 1518, 143 L.Ed.2d 689 (1999). The *Saenz* decision is examined in § 14.38.

of the first eight Amendments. However, in these cases the Court simply held that the state activity violated the due process clause because it arbitrarily limited the individual's interest in liberty.

Thus when the Court, under the general concept of due process, invalidated a state law which prohibited private religious schools, there was no need to resort to the religion clauses of the First Amendment.[5] Similarly, the Court struck down a state law prohibiting the teaching of foreign languages in private as well as public schools without relying on either the First Amendment or what today is known as the fundamental right of privacy.[6] Because of this approach, there was no clear focusing on whether specific provisions of the Bill of Rights were "incorporated" into the due process clause of the Fourteenth Amendment.

The Court during this period concentrated on whether specific interests deserved protection under the concept of "liberty." Some of the opinions are unclear as to whether the Court was focusing on only the Fourteenth Amendment or values reflected in other Amendments when it made a particular decision. The most notable example of such confusion (in terms of modern incorporation theories) is the decision of the Supreme Court concerning the just compensation clause of the Fifth Amendment.

In 1897 the Court decided that state and local governments were required to pay just compensation when they exercised their powers of eminent domain and took an individual's property for public use.[7] But the opinion of the Court, written by the elder Justice Harlan, did not state that the just compensation clause of the Fifth Amendment was applied to the states through the due process clause of the Fourteenth Amendment. Rather the decision only held that the due process clause protected individuals against having their property taken without just compensation. It was unnecessary for the opinion to reflect upon the issue of "incorporation," for the Justices felt quite secure in their ability to control all forms of state activities through the due process clause at this time.

As we near the close of the era of substantive due process, we find that the Court begins to concentrate its attention on whether specific guarantees of the Bill of Rights are made directly applicable to the states by the Fourteenth Amendment. These isolated decisions before 1937 seem to be the result of growing problems with the general concept of substantive due process; in addition, some particular cases were easier to analyze under the terms of one of the first ten Amendments. Thus, in 1925 we find the Court assuming that the free speech clause of the First Amendment was made applicable to the states by the due process clause in deciding a particular case.[8] In 1932 when the Supreme Court intervened to grant the defendants some protection in the now famous "Scottsboro Boys" case, the Justices found that at least some elements of the right to counsel under the Sixth Amendment were made applicable to local governments by the Fourteenth.[9]

However, the Court did not develop any consistent approach towards the concept of incorporation until after its denouncement of substantive due process. As late as 1934, the Supreme Court could reject the claims of religious conscientious objectors to attending state colleges with mandatory military training requirements by concentrating on whether the meaning of liberty included the right to enter-

5. Pierce v. Society of Sisters, 268 U.S. 510, 45 S.Ct. 571, 69 L.Ed. 1070 (1925).

6. Meyer v. Nebraska, 262 U.S. 390, 43 S.Ct. 625, 67 L.Ed. 1042 (1923).

7. Chicago, B. & Q.R. Co. v. City of Chicago, 166 U.S. 226, 17 S.Ct. 581, 41 L.Ed. 979 (1897).

8. Gitlow v. New York, 268 U.S. 652, 45 S.Ct. 625, 69 L.Ed. 1138 (1925).

9. Powell v. Alabama, 287 U.S. 45, 53 S.Ct. 55, 77 L.Ed. 158 (1932). The case involved charges of rape

against some black youths by a white woman and the circumstances of the trial were highly prejudicial to the defendants. *"The Scottsboro Boys."* On the Scottsboro Boys, see generally, D. Carter, Scottsboro: A Tragedy of the Old South (rev. ed. 1979); H. Patterson & E. Conrad, Scottsboro Boy (1950); C. Norris & S. Washington, The Last of the Scottsboro Boys: An Autography (1979). See also, Q. Reynolds, Courtroom (1950); G.B. Tindall, The Emergence of the New South, 1913–1945 (1967).

tain religious beliefs, rather than focusing on the First Amendment religion clauses.[10]

Many of the subject areas of the Bill of Rights were either not considered by the Supreme Court or were of a type that a majority of the Justices was not prepared to enforce prior to 1937. For example, the Court did not require the exclusion of a coerced confession by a defendant in a state criminal proceeding under the Fourteenth Amendment until 1936,[11] and the self-incrimination clause was not incorporated until 1964.[12] However, even federal defendants did not at this time receive significant protections in the criminal process. Until 1938 the Sixth Amendment right to counsel in federal courts meant only that a defendant would be able to have an attorney to represent him at certain points in the proceeding if he could afford to retain one.[13]

While the Supreme Court did decide a few particular issues concerning criminal procedure prior to this time, there were really no generally significant decisions in this area until the 1930's. For reasons that still remain unclear, the Court simply did not receive or decide cases involving these issues during this period.[14] Since most of the Bill of Rights are concerned with protections relating to the criminal justice system, there was little need to focus on incorporation problems.

In the last section we saw how the Supreme Court abandoned the use of the substantive due process concept as an active check on general economic or social welfare legislation. However, the Court did not indicate that it would retreat from enforcing specific constitutional guarantees or fundamental constitutional values against infringement by the other

branches of government. The majority of the Justices at this time only indicated that there was no inherent ability to overturn acts of the other branches of the government merely because they disagreed with the policy behind those acts.

But the Court was soon to point out that it would not hesitate to return to a strict form of review for acts that touched upon fundamental constitutional values.[15] The issue now became one of identifying what rights or values were of such a nature that they should be judicially enforced against the other branches of government. This question led the Supreme Court to consider which of the specific guarantees of the Bill of Rights were such fundamental rights. And so the Court began to focus on whether each of the guarantees was made applicable to the states by the Fourteenth Amendment. Today we phrase the issue as whether the provisions of the Bill of Rights are "incorporated" into the meaning of the word "liberty" so as to be protected by the due process clause of the Fourteenth Amendment and applied to the states.

Following 1936 the Supreme Court decided that some, but not all, of the Bill of Rights guarantees were applicable to the states. A few Justices, most notably Justice Black, argued that the history of the Fourteenth Amendment indicated that all of the Bill of Rights were to be made directly applicable to the states.[16] Other Justices, most notably Justice Frankfurter, argued that the concept of "liberty" was to have a judicially defined meaning which was not dependent upon the incorporation of specific guarantees of the Bill

---

10. Hamilton v. Regents of the University of California, 293 U.S. 245, 55 S.Ct. 197, 79 L.Ed. 343 (1934).

11. Brown v. Mississippi, 297 U.S. 278, 56 S.Ct. 461, 80 L.Ed. 682 (1936).

12. Malloy v. Hogan, 378 U.S. 1, 84 S.Ct. 1489, 12 L.Ed.2d 653 (1964). The earlier, contrary decisions were Twining v. New Jersey, 211 U.S. 78, 29 S.Ct. 14, 53 L.Ed. 97 (1908), and Adamson v. California, 332 U.S. 46, 67 S.Ct. 1672, 91 L.Ed. 1903 (1947).

13. Schaefer, Federalism and State Criminal Procedure, 70 Harv.L.Rev. 1 (1956). See Johnson v. Zerbst, 304 U.S. 458, 58 S.Ct. 1019, 82 L.Ed. 1461 (1938).

14. Schaefer, supra note 13, at 3–4.

15. United States v. Carolene Products Co., 304 U.S. 144, 152 n. 4, 58 S.Ct. 778, 783–84 n. 4, 82 L.Ed. 1234 (1938); Skinner v. Oklahoma, 316 U.S. 535, 62 S.Ct. 1110, 86 L.Ed. 1655 (1942).

16. See, e.g., Adamson v. California, 332 U.S. 46, 68, 67 S.Ct. 1672, 1684, 91 L.Ed. 1903 (1947) (Black, J., dissenting, joined by Douglas, J.). While Black would have incorporated all of these rights and no others, some Justices would have included those rights, plus implied fundamental rights. See 332 U.S. at 124, 67 S.Ct. at 1683–84 (Murphy, J., dissenting, joined by Rutledge, J.).

of Rights.[17]

Some of the cases concerning the question of whether a specific guarantee was incorporated into the due process clause contained classic debates over both the history of the Fourteenth Amendment and the role of the judiciary in enforcing natural law concepts of liberty.[18] Partially as a result of these judicial debates, scholars have labored over the question of whether the framers of the Fourteenth Amendment meant to incorporate the guarantees of the Bill of Rights into its provisions. The preponderance of historical evidence discovered by these scholars indicates that the drafters of the Amendment did not specifically intend to apply all of those provisions to the states.[19] However, a number of scholars, most notably Jacobus tenBroek, have isolated a concern of a number of drafters that a set of natural law values reflected in some of the Bill of Rights, as well as other sources, should have been made applicable to the states by the passage of the Fourteenth Amendment.[20]

The Supreme Court did follow an approach based on the historical view as well as the majority's view of the Court's role in reviewing acts of other branches of government. The Court settled upon the concept of "selective incorporation" whereby a provision of the Bill of Rights is made applicable to the states if the Justices are of the opinion that it was meant to protect a "fundamental" aspect of liberty.[21]

In the early cases the Court asked whether the specific Amendment was so fundamental that it could be said to be "implicit in the concept of ordered liberty," and "so rooted in the traditions and conscience of our people as to be as fundamental." [22]

Eventually the Supreme Court altered the test for whether a specific provision should be incorporated into the due process clause. In 1968, the Court held that the determination of whether the right to jury trial guaranteed by the Sixth Amendment was incorporated into the fourteenth depended on whether that guarantee was "fundamental to the American scheme of justice." [23] This new test meant that the Court would be willing to enforce values which the Justices saw as having a special importance in the development of individual liberty in American society, whether or not the value was one that was theoretically necessary in any system of democratic government.

The Provisions of the Bill of Rights Which Are Incorporated. Today virtually all the provisions of the Bill of Rights have been incorporated into the Fourteenth Amendment and made applicable to the states. Since 1934 there has been a steady process of judicial inclusion of provisions of the Bill of Rights into the Fourteenth Amendment. All of the provisions of the first Amendment concerning freedoms of religion,[24] speech,[25] press,[26] assem-

17. See, e.g., Adamson v. California, 332 U.S. 46, 59, 67 S.Ct. 1672, 1679, 91 L.Ed. 1903 (1947) (Frankfurter, J. concurring); Pointer v. Texas, 380 U.S. 400, 408, 85 S.Ct. 1065, 1070, 13 L.Ed.2d 923 (1965), (Harlan, J., concurring).

18. See, e.g., Adamson v. California, 332 U.S. 46, 67 S.Ct. 1672, 91 L.Ed. 1903 (1947), Pointer v. Texas, 380 U.S. 400, 85 S.Ct. 1065, 13 L.Ed.2d 923 (1965), Williams v. Florida, 399 U.S. 78, 90 S.Ct. 1893, 26 L.Ed.2d 446 (1970). See also, Rochin v. California, 342 U.S. 165, 72 S.Ct. 205, 96 L.Ed. 183 (1952).

19. See e.g. Fairman, Does the Fourteenth Amendment Incorporate the Bill of Rights?, 2 Stan.L.Rev. 5 (1949). For additional references to secondary authorities on this point see the multivolume edition of this Treatise: R. Rotunda & J. Nowak, Treatise on Constitutional Law: Substance and Procedure §§ 14.2, 15.6, 18.7 (3rd ed. 1999, with annual supplements).

20. See, J. tenBroek, Equal Law Under Law at 223 (enlarged edition 1965); See also J. James, The Framing of the Fourteenth Amendment (1965).

21. See generally, Henkin, "Selective Incorporation" in the Fourteenth Amendment, 73 Yale L.J. 74 (1963).

22. Palko v. Connecticut, 302 U.S. 319, 325, 58 S.Ct. 149, 152, 82 L.Ed. 288 (1937).

23. Duncan v. Louisiana, 391 U.S. 145, 148–9, 88 S.Ct. 1444, 1446–47, 20 L.Ed.2d 491 (1968).

24. Cantwell v. Connecticut, 310 U.S. 296, 60 S.Ct. 900, 84 L.Ed. 1213 (1940) (free exercise clause); Everson v. Board of Education, 330 U.S. 1, 67 S.Ct. 504, 91 L.Ed. 711 (1947) (establishment clause).

25. Gitlow v. New York, 268 U.S. 652, 666, 45 S.Ct. 625, 630, 69 L.Ed. 1138 (1925); Fiske v. Kansas, 274 U.S. 380, 47 S.Ct. 655, 71 L.Ed. 1108 (1927); Stromberg v. California, 283 U.S. 359, 51 S.Ct. 532, 75 L.Ed. 1117 (1931).

26. Near v. Minnesota, 283 U.S. 697, 701, 51 S.Ct. 625, 626, 75 L.Ed. 1357 (1931).

bly[27] and petition[28] have been held applicable to the states. The Second Amendment concerning the right to bear arms is not applicable to the states since it is perceived as primarily a guarantee that the federal government would not interfere with the state militia.[29] The Third Amendment, which prohibits the quartering of soldiers in private homes, has not been the subject of any constitutional litigation in the Supreme Court.[30]

The Fourth Amendment's regulation of searches and seizures has been held to be applicable to the police practices of state and local governments.[31] Of the guarantees of the Fifth Amendment, only the grand jury clause has been held not to be applicable to the states.[32] The Court has specifically incorporat-

ed both the double jeopardy and self-incrimination provisions of that Amendment.[33] The principles of the Fifth Amendment just compensation clause are applied to the states although it is unclear whether it is incorporated into the Fourteenth Amendment or whether the Amendment's due process clause merely has an identical meaning to that provision.[34] Each of several guarantees of the Sixth Amendment concerning rights in the criminal process has been held applicable to the states through the due process clause.[35] The Seventh Amendment right to jury trial in civil cases is not applicable to the states.[36]

The cruel and unusual punishment clause of the Eighth Amendment has been specifically made applicable to the states by the Supreme Court[37] and the excessive bail provision has

---

27. De Jonge v. Oregon, 299 U.S. 353, 57 S.Ct. 255, 81 L.Ed. 278 (1937).

28. 299 U.S. at 364, 365, 57 S.Ct. at 260, Hague v. CIO, 307 U.S. 496, 59 S.Ct. 954, 83 L.Ed. 1423 (1939); Bridges v. California, 314 U.S. 252, 62 S.Ct. 190, 86 L.Ed. 192 (1941).

29. Cf. United States v. Cruikshank, 92 U.S. (2 Otto) 542, 553, 23 L.Ed. 588 (1875); Presser v. Illinois, 116 U.S. 252, 265, 6 S.Ct. 580, 584, 29 L.Ed. 615 (1886); State v. Vlacil, 645 P.2d 677, 681 n. 1 (Utah 1982) (Oaks, J., concurring), citing earlier edition of this treatise; Eisele, J., citing Treatise in Ayers v. Norris, 43 F.Supp.2d 1039, 1048 (E.D.Ark.1999). For references to additional cases, and secondary authorities, on this point see the multivolume edition of this Treatise: R. Rotunda & J. Nowak, Treatise on Constitutional Law: Substance and Procedure §§ 14.2, 15.6 (3rd ed. 1999, with annual supplements).

30. The United States Court of Appeals for the Second Circuit has held that the Third Amendment is a fundamental aspect of the right of privacy protected by the due process clause of the Fourteenth Amendment. Thus prison correction officers, who were displaced from their living quarters in rented staff housing at a prison during a prison guard strike so that state military and law enforcement officers could occupy those premises and operate the prison, stated a prima facie claim of a violation of the Third Amendment and civil rights statutes. Engblom v. Carey, 677 F.2d 957 (2d Cir.1982). On remand the District Court held that, even if there was a violation of the Third Amendment rights of the prison guards, the governor and state officers who acted to remove the guards from their homes had a "good faith defense" under the civil rights acts; the United States Court of Appeals upheld the dismissal of the suit on that basis. Engblom v. Carey, 572 F.Supp. 44 (S.D.N.Y.1983), affirmed 724 F.2d 28 (2d Cir.1983).

31. Wolf v. Colorado, 338 U.S. 25, 69 S.Ct. 1359, 93 L.Ed. 1782 (1949); Mapp v. Ohio, 367 U.S. 643, 81 S.Ct. 1684, 6 L.Ed.2d 1081 (1961).

32. Hurtado v. California, 110 U.S. 516, 4 S.Ct. 111, 28 L.Ed. 232 (1884).

33. Benton v. Maryland, 395 U.S. 784, 89 S.Ct. 2056, 23 L.Ed.2d 707, (1969) (double jeopardy); Ashe v. Swenson, 397 U.S. 436, 90 S.Ct. 1189, 25 L.Ed.2d 469 (1970) (collateral estoppel); Malloy v. Hogan, 378 U.S. 1, 84 S.Ct. 1489, 12 L.Ed.2d 653 (1964) (self-incrimination); Griffin v. California, 380 U.S. 609, 85 S.Ct. 1229, 14 L.Ed.2d 106 (1965), (self-incrimination).

34. Chicago, B. & Q.R. Co. v. Chicago, 166 U.S. 226, 17 S.Ct. 581, 41 L.Ed. 979 (1897); Webb's Fabulous Pharmacies, Inc. v. Beckwith, 449 U.S. 155, 159, 101 S.Ct. 446, 66 L.Ed.2d 358 (1980).

35. Klopfer v. North Carolina, 386 U.S. 213, 87 S.Ct. 988, 18 L.Ed.2d 1 (1967) (speedy trial); In re Oliver, 333 U.S. 257, 68 S.Ct. 499, 92 L.Ed. 682 (1948) (public trial); Duncan v. Louisiana, 391 U.S. 145, 88 S.Ct. 1444, 20 L.Ed.2d 491 (1968) (jury trial); Irvin v. Dowd, 366 U.S. 717, 81 S.Ct. 1639, 6 L.Ed.2d 751 (1961) (impartial jury); In re Oliver, 333 U.S. 257, 68 S.Ct. 499, 92 L.Ed. 682 (1948) (notice); Pointer v. Texas, 380 U.S. 400, 85 S.Ct. 1065, 13 L.Ed.2d 923 (1965) (confrontation); Washington v. Texas, 388 U.S. 14, 87 S.Ct. 1920, 18 L.Ed.2d 1019 (1967) (compulsory process); Gideon v. Wainwright, 372 U.S. 335, 83 S.Ct. 792, 9 L.Ed.2d 799 (1963) (counsel).

36. Minneapolis & St. Louis R. Co. v. Bombolis, 241 U.S. 211, 36 S.Ct. 595, 60 L.Ed. 961 (1916).

For cases and secondary works regarding the Seventh Amendment guarantee of a right to a jury trial in civil cases in the federal courts, see R. Rotunda & J. Nowak, Treatise on Constitutional Law: Substance and Procedure §17.8 (3rd ed. 1999, with annual supplements).

37. Louisiana ex rel. Francis v. Resweber, 329 U.S. 459, 67 S.Ct. 374, 91 L.Ed. 422 (1947), rehearing denied 330 U.S. 853, 67 S.Ct. 673, 91 L.Ed. 1295 (1947); Robinson v. California, 370 U.S. 660, 82 S.Ct. 1417, 8 L.Ed.2d 758 (1962), rehearing denied 371 U.S. 905, 83 S.Ct. 202, 9 L.Ed.2d 166 (1962). For citations to additional Supreme Court cases, and secondary authorities, on this point, see R. Rotunda & J. Nowak, Treatise on Constitutional Law: Substance and Procedure, §§ 17.3, 17.4 (3rd ed. 1999, with annual supplements).

been made applicable by implication.[38] There are no cases concerning the applicability of the "excessive fine" provision of the Eighth Amendment to the states. It would seem to be applicable because it is intertwined with the other two and the Supreme Court has already regulated the imposition of fines on indigents through the equal protection clause of the Fourteenth Amendment.[39] Finally, the Ninth Amendment has not been the source of specific rights or rulings although some Justices would give it greater impact.[40] The Tenth Amendment, by its own terms, has no application to the states.

Some Justices have believed that, even if the Bill of Rights were applicable to the states, there was no need to hold state laws to the same standards under those Amendments.[41] However, a majority of the Justices have rejected this concept and held that when a provision of the Bill of Rights is made applicable to the states, it applies to state and local acts in the same manner as it does to federal actions.[42] Thus, rulings on the meaning of any incorporated provision of the Bill of Rights are of equal meaning for both federal and state laws.

This concept is sometimes known as the "bag and baggage" theory for it holds that when a provision of the Bill of Rights is made applicable to the states it is applied with all of its previous federal interpretation—it comes to the states, complete with its "bag and baggage." This doctrine squares with the philosophy of selective incorporation. When the Supreme Court holds a provision of the Bill of Rights applicable to the states, it does so because the Justices are of the opinion that it is a right which can be deemed "fundamental" to the American system of government. Accordingly, the Justices will not tolerate either federal or state activities which impair the right.[43]

§ 11.7 Fundamental Rights

Today the Justices of the Supreme Court will apply strict forms of review under the due process clauses and the equal protection clause to any governmental actions which limit the exercise of "fundamental" constitutional rights. These are rights which the Court recognizes as having a value so essential to individual liberty in our society that they justify the Justices reviewing the acts of other branches of government in a manner quite similar to the substantive due process approach of the pre-1937 period. Little more can be said to accurately describe the nature of a fundamental right, because fundamental rights analysis is simply no more than the modern recognition of the natural law concepts first espoused by Justice Chase in *Calder v. Bull*.[1]

38. See, Schilb v. Kuebel, 404 U.S. 357, 365, 92 S.Ct. 479, 484–85, 30 L.Ed.2d 502 (1971), rehearing denied 405 U.S. 948, 92 S.Ct. 930, 30 L.Ed.2d 818 (1972).

39. See, Tate v. Short, 401 U.S. 395, 91 S.Ct. 668, 28 L.Ed.2d 130 (1971), on remand 471 S.W.2d 404 (Tex.Cr. App.1971).

Revocation of a defendant's probation for failure to pay a fine, absent a determination that the defendant was responsible for the failure and that alternative forms of punishment are inadequate, will violate the principle of fundamental fairness protected by the due process and equal protection clauses. Bearden v. Georgia, 461 U.S. 660, 103 S.Ct. 2064, 76 L.Ed.2d 221 (1983), on remand 167 Ga.App. 334, 308 S.E.2d 63 (1983).

40. Griswold v. Connecticut, 381 U.S. 479, 85 S.Ct. 1678, 14 L.Ed.2d 510 (1965) (Goldberg, J., concurring); See, § 11.7, infra.

41. See, e.g., Malloy v. Hogan, 378 U.S. 1, 14, 84 S.Ct. 1489, 1497, 12 L.Ed.2d 653 (1964) (Harlan, J. dissenting); Benton v. Maryland, 395 U.S. 784, 808 n. 12, 89 S.Ct. 2056, 2070 n. 12, 23 L.Ed.2d 707 (1969) (Harlan, J., dissenting, citing opinions of Justice Stewart), on remand 8 Md.App. 388, 260 A.2d 86 (1969).

42. See e.g., Malloy v. Hogan, 378 U.S. 1, 84 S.Ct. 1489, 12 L.Ed.2d 653 (1964); Duncan v. Louisiana, 391 U.S. 145, 88 S.Ct. 1444, 20 L.Ed.2d 491 (1968); Baldwin v. New York, 399 U.S. 66, 90 S.Ct. 1886, 26 L.Ed.2d 437 (1970); Williams v. Florida, 399 U.S. 78, 90 S.Ct. 1893, 26 L.Ed.2d 446 (1970). For references to additional cases, and secondary authorities, on this point see the multivolume edition of this Treatise: R. Rotunda & J. Nowak, Treatise on Constitutional Law: Substance and Procedure §§ 15.7, 17.8 (3rd ed. 1999, with annual supplements).

43. The incorporation doctrine appears to have played a role in the judicial failure to address questions regarding the type of procedural fairness required by the due process clauses. See Nowak, Foreword: Due Process Methodology in the Postincorporation World, 70 Journal of Criminal Law & Criminology 397 (1980).

§ 11.7

1. 3 U.S. (3 Dall.) 386, 1 L.Ed. 648 (1798) (Opinion of Chase, J.). See § 11.1, supra, for a discussion of Chase's position.

See generally, Brown, District Judge, quoting Treatise in Doe v. S & S Consol. I.S.D., 149 F.Supp.2d 274, 285 n.

Despite claims to the contrary, there has never been a period of time wherein the Court did not actively enforce values which a majority of the Justices felt were essential in our society even though they had no specific textual basis in the Constitution. Indeed, some of the most noted "conservative" Justices advocated the use of a natural law analysis to select and protect the forms of liberty under the due process clause. Thus, it was that Justice Black could accuse Justice Frankfurter of assuming too great an authority by adoption of a natural law approach to constitutional issues rather than by making use of specific provisions of the Bill of Rights.[2] And it was the younger Justice Harlan who first advocated protecting a right of privacy which included the right of married persons to use contraceptive devices.[3] However, the use of a subjective natural law analysis under the due process and equal protection clauses did not work out well in the period between 1887 and 1937. When the Court rejected the substantive due process approach in 1937, it restricted the ability of the Justices to rely upon a natural law or openly subjective basis for defining liberty and individual constitutional rights.

It was not long after 1937 that the Court indicated that the Justices would still protect individual rights. In 1938 in *United States v. Carolene Products Co.*[4] the majority indicated that it might not follow the rejection of sub-

stantive due process in areas which touched upon specific constitutional guarantees or disadvantaged certain minority groups.[5] In 1942 the Supreme Court struck down a statute authorizing sterilization of some convicts because it arbitrarily classified persons in terms of a fundamental right.[6]

Thus, there was no real break in the use of a subjective test for finding individual rights and liberties following the 1937 renouncement of substantive due process as a control over economic and social welfare legislation. However, while the Justices have retained this power to protect individual rights, they were now deprived of the natural law-substantive due process language to describe the process by which they identified and enforced these fundamental rights. This has lead to confusing opinions when the Justices have attempted to give different justifications for actions that were simply a form of substantive due process.

A most notable example of this confusion is *Griswold v. Connecticut*[7] where the Court struck down a law which prohibited the use of contraceptives by married persons. The majority opinion by Justice Douglas found a fundamental "right to privacy" which was infringed by the law. He found this right in the "penumbras" of several guarantees of the Bill of Rights.[8] While Douglas managed to identify some arguably related provisions of the Bill of

---

14 (E.D.Tex.2001); Casellas, District Judge, citing earlier edition of Treatise in United States v. Acosta Martinez, 106 F.Supp.2d 311, 323 n. 39 (D.P.R.2000). Judge Schell, citing Treatise in Owens v. First City Nat. Bank of Beaumont, 714 F.Supp. 227, 232 (E.D.Tex.1989); Judge Lay, citing Treatise in Swenson v. Management Recruiters Intern., Inc., 858 F.2d 1304, 1306 (8th Cir.1988), cert. denied 493 U.S. 848, 110 S.Ct. 143, 107 L.Ed.2d 102 (1989); Selya, J., quoting Treatise in Vega–Rodriguez v. Puerto Rico Telephone Co., 110 F.3d 174, 182 (1st Cir.1997); Calchera v. Procarione, 805 F.Supp. 716, 718 (E.D.Wis. 1992) (Stadtmueller, J.) (citing Treatise); Provident Mutual Life Insurance Company of Philadelphia v. City of Atlanta, 864 F.Supp. 1274 (N.D.Ga.1994) (Hall, J.) (citing Treatise); Doe v. Taylor Independent School Dist., et al., 15 F.3d 443, 479 (5th Cir.1994) (Jolly and Davis, JJ.) (citing Treatise), cert. denied 513 U.S. 815, 115 S.Ct. 70, 130 L.Ed.2d 25 (1994); Payne, J., quoting Treatise in, Mandel v. Allen, 889 F.Supp. 857, 871 (E.D.Va.1995), affirmed 81 F.3d 478 (4th Cir.1996); Miner, Cir. J., citing Treatise, in Quill v. Vacco, 80 F.3d 716, 724 (2d Cir.1996); Kent, J., citing Treatise, in Fair v. City of Galveston, 915 F.Supp. 873, 878 (S.D.Tex.1996); Doucet, C.J., citing Trea-

tise, in Schulker v. Roberson, 676 So.2d 684, 687 (La.App. 1996). Drowota, J., citing Treatise, in Caldwell v. State, 917 S.W.2d 662 (Tenn.1996), rehearing denied (1996), cert. denied 519 U.S. 853, 117 S.Ct. 148, 136 L.Ed.2d 94 (1996); Heartfield, District Judge, citing Treatise in Ryans v. Gresham, 6 F.Supp. 2d 595 (E.D.Tex.1998).

2. Rochin v. California, 342 U.S. 165, 175–76, 72 S.Ct. 205, 211–12, 96 L.Ed. 183 (1952) (Black, J., concurring); Adamson v. California, 332 U.S. 46, 89–90, 67 S.Ct. 1672, 1695–96, 91 L.Ed. 1903 (1947) (Black, J., concurring).

3. Poe v. Ullman, 367 U.S. 497, 541–43, 550–54, 81 S.Ct. 1752, 1775, 1781, 6 L.Ed.2d 989 (1961) (Harlan, J., dissenting).

4. 304 U.S. 144, 58 S.Ct. 778, 82 L.Ed. 1234 (1938).

5. 304 U.S. at 152 n. 4, 58 S.Ct. at 783–84 n. 4. See also § 11.4, supra.

6. Skinner v. Oklahoma, 316 U.S. 535, 541, 62 S.Ct. 1110, 1113, 86 L.Ed. 1655 (1942).

7. 381 U.S. 479, 85 S.Ct. 1678, 14 L.Ed.2d 510 (1965).

8. 381 U.S. at 484, 85 S.Ct. at 1681.

Rights he gave no indication of how to search the shadows, or penumbras, of the Bill of Rights to find other fundamental guarantees.

Justice Goldberg, who concurred in the opinion, found that the right of privacy should be recognized without reliance on any specific guarantees of the Bill of Rights.[9] He found that the Ninth Amendment gave textual recognition to the fact that there were other values of equal importance to the specific provisions to the Bill of Rights even though they were not mentioned in the first Eight Amendments. While the Ninth Amendment did not directly create those rights, it authorized the Court to identify them and protect them against the acts of the other branches of government.[10] He attempted to give some objective guidelines to the search for these values by stating that the Court should rely on "the traditions and conscience" of the nation in determining what values were to be so protected.[11]

Only Justice Harlan was able to give a very clear basis for why he was recognizing the right to privacy as worthy of constitutional protection. As the Justice had said years before, in a dissenting opinion, he was willing to protect the right to privacy based on a natural law approach.[12] Harlan stood quite ready to defend the judicial function as selecting values which had a historical and philosophical right to be called fundamental and enforcing them against even the will of the majority. He did not advocate a return to the pre-1937 period, for there were very few rights that he would define as truly fundamental; Harlan did not advocate overturning laws merely because they offended his individual sense of reasonableness.[13]

Justice Black, who objected to this natural law approach to the definition of due process, dissented in *Griswold* because he found no clear basis for this right in the text of the Bill of Rights.[14]

The concept of fundamental rights remains vague today. All that can be said with certainty is that the Justices have selected a group of individual rights which do not have a specific textual basis in the Constitution or its Amendments and deemed them to be "fundamental." There can be no doubt that this judicial value selection must be based on the majority's deci-

9. Griswold v. Connecticut, 381 U.S. 479, 486, 85 S.Ct. 1678, 1682–83, 14 L.Ed.2d 510 (1965) (Goldberg, J., concurring).

10. The Ninth Amendment. Although the Ninth Amendment has not been used as the basis for defining rights of individuals and invalidating either federal or state laws, it has been mentioned as a possible basis for justifying judicial protection of rights not explicitly listed in the Constitution or other Amendments. References to the Amendment in the Supreme Court appear to be only in dicta or in opinions of individual Justices. See, e.g., Richmond Newspapers, Inc. v. Virginia, 448 U.S. 555, 579–80 n. 15, 100 S.Ct. 2814, 2828–29 n. 15, 65 L.Ed.2d 973 (1980) (plurality opinion by Burger, C.J.) justifying a judicial role in defining "fundamental rights not expressly guaranteed" and stating: "Madison's efforts, culminating in the Ninth Amendment, served to allay the fears of these who were concerned that expressing certain guarantees could be read as excluding others." The *Richmond Newspapers* decision, in the view of the plurality, ultimately was based on an implicit First Amendment right of the public to attend criminal trials.

See also, Roe v. Wade, 410 U.S. 113, 153, 93 S.Ct. 705, 727, 35 L.Ed.2d 147 (1973) (majority opinion mentions lower court reliance on Ninth Amendment as basis for a woman's right to an abortion but bases the right on the concept of liberty protected by the due process clauses); Roe v. Wade, 410 U.S. 113, 210, 93 S.Ct. 705, 757, 35 L.Ed.2d 147 (1973) (Douglas, J., concurring seeks to justi-

fy judicial protection of rights not expressly set forth in the Constitution or its Amendments although he states: "The Ninth Amendment obviously does not create federally enforceable rights.")

The Ninth Amendment (both as a source of rights and, alternatively, as a justification for judicial definition of "nontextual" fundamental rights) has been the subject of scholarly debate. See R. Rotunda & J. Nowak, Treatise on Constitutional Law: Substance and Procedure §§ 15.7, 18.30 (2nd ed. 1992).

11. 381 U.S. at 493, 85 S.Ct. at 1686, quoting Snyder v. Massachusetts, 291 U.S. 97, 54 S.Ct. 330, 78 L.Ed. 674 (1934).

12. Griswold v. Connecticut, 381 U.S. 479, 499, 85 S.Ct. 1678, 1690, 14 L.Ed.2d 510 (1965) (Harlan, J., concurring). Here he restated the views he expressed in Poe v. Ullman, 367 U.S. 497, 522, 81 S.Ct. 1752, 1766, 6 L.Ed.2d 989 (1961) (Harlan, J., dissenting).

13. Thus Harlan objected to the use of fundamental rights analysis to increase scrutiny under the equal protection guarantee. He thought it was used to increase judicial power to overturn policy judgments on issues the Court felt were of practical importance. See, Shapiro v. Thompson, 394 U.S. 618, 660–62, 89 S.Ct. 1322, 1345–46, 22 L.Ed.2d 600 (1969) (Harlan, J., dissenting).

14. Griswold v. Connecticut, 381 U.S. 479, 507, 85 S.Ct. 1678, 1694, 14 L.Ed.2d 510 (1965) (Black, J., dissenting).

sion to enforce some natural law rights against the acts of organized society.

There has been continual criticism of this approach throughout the history of the Court. Indeed, even Justice Harlan, who was willing to recognize the right to privacy through such an approach, strongly criticized the Court's use of fundamental rights analysis in protecting a wide variety of individual interests.[15] Similarly, commentators continue to reflect upon the legitimacy of the use of judicial power to protect values which have no basis in the constitutional text.[16] One group of scholars decry as illegitimate any judicial protection of values that are not identified in the text of the Constitution or its Amendments. Other scholars justify judicial protection of such values in terms of an historical or societal consensus on the nature of rights that should be placed beyond the power of the political process. A third group of scholars has confronted this problem of judicial value selection by examining the relationship of judicial decisionmaking to the values of the political process.

In *Bowers v. Hardwick*,[17] the Supreme Court refused to find any fundamental right in sexual activity between unmarried persons; it upheld a state statute that criminalized sodomy, even though punished actions only involved consenting adults in private. Justice White, writing for the majority, found that there was no basis for the judicial creation of a fundamental right that would protect homosexual activity from criminal sanction. Justice White ruled that the Court's earlier decisions defining a fundamental right to privacy, which in-

cluded rights regarding child-bearing, child-rearing, and family relationships, did not bear "any resemblance to the claimed constitutional right of homosexuals to engage in acts of sodomy." The majority did not believe that the right to engage in sodomy was "implicit in the concept of ordered liberty;" therefore, it was not a necessary part of the liberty protected by due process.[18] Nor, in the majority's opinion, was this right so "deeply rooted in this nation's history and tradition" that it should be judicially protected from the legislative process.[19]

Justice White equated the judicial creation of fundamental rights, at least when there was no clear authority for such a finding, and the Court's use of the due process clause to review economic and social welfare legislation in the 1900–1936 era. The majority opinion stated, "there should be, therefore, great resistance to expand the substantive reach of those clauses [the due process clauses of the Fifth and Fourteenth Amendments], particularly if it requires redefining the category of rights deemed to be fundamental. Otherwise, the judiciary necessarily takes to itself further authority to govern the country without expressed constitutional authority. The claimed right [to sexual activity between adults] pressed on us today falls far short of overcoming this resistance."[20] Finally, the Court concluded that the fact that the crime took place in the privacy of a home did not make it immune from legislative regulation and prosecution.[21]

---

15. See note 12 supra.

16. For citations to additional secondary works on this debate see R. Rotunda & J. Nowak, Treatise on Constitutional Law: Substance and Procedure § 15.7 (3rd ed. 1999, with annual supplements).

17. 478 U.S. 186, 106 S.Ct. 2841, 92 L.Ed.2d 140 (1986), rehearing denied 478 U.S. 1039, 107 S.Ct. 29, 92 L.Ed.2d 779 (1986).

18. 478 U.S. at 190, 106 S.Ct. at 2844, quoting in part Palko v. Connecticut, 302 U.S. 319, 325, 326, 58 S.Ct. 149, 151, 152, 82 L.Ed. 288 (1937) (using the concept of ordered liberty theory to determine which provisions of the Bill of Rights were incorporated into the concept of liberty protected by the Fourteenth Amendment).

19. 478 U.S. at 190, 106 S.Ct. at 2844, quoting in part Moore v. East Cleveland, 431 U.S. 494, 503, 97 S.Ct. 1932, 1937, 52 L.Ed.2d 531 (1977) (opinion of Powell, J.).

20. 478 U.S. at 194, 106 S.Ct. at 2846.

21. The Supreme Court did not reach the question whether the criminal penalty that in theory could be imposed upon a person for engaging in private, homosexual conduct under the statute would constitute cruel and unusual punishment under the Eighth Amendment. Bowers v. Hardwick, 478 U.S. 186, 196 n. 8, 106 S.Ct. 2841, 2846 n. 8, 92 L.Ed.2d 140 (1986), rehearing denied 478 U.S. 1039, 107 S.Ct. 29, 92 L.Ed.2d 779 (1986). This point was specifically noted in the concurring opinion of Justice Powell. 478 U.S. at 196–200, 106 S.Ct. at 2847–48 (Powell, J., concurring). The right to privacy is analyzed in §§ 14.26–14.30.

Four Justices dissented from *Bowers*.[22] The dissenters focused on the fact that sexual intimacy is valued by persons in a different way from other types of activity and, in their view, is a type of liberty interest that must be judicially protected from arbitrary limitation by a legislature. They did not believe that the state's assertion of a power and duty to act upon the moral beliefs of the majority of its citizens and to protect the moral tenure of its community with such laws could justify an infringement of this type of liberty.

In 2003, in *Lawrence v. Texas*[23] the Supreme Court overruled *Bowers* and ruled that a Texas law that prohibited sodomy between persons of the same sex violated the Fourteenth Amendment due process clause. The majority opinion in *Lawrence*, written by Justice Kennedy, did not find that sexual activity between unmarried persons was a fundamental right. Nevertheless, Justice Kennedy, writing for five Justices, invalidated any possible restrictions on private sexual activity between two consenting adults in private that did not cause physical or mental harm to either party.[24] Justice Kennedy found that there was no legitimate interest of government that would support a restriction on this type of activity.[25]

Justice O'Connor voted to invalidate the homosexual sodomy law on the basis that it was designed to harm a politically unpopular group[26] However, the majority chose to base its ruling on the due process clause and to strike the law under the rationality test. The dissenting Justices in *Lawrence* believed that the ruling in that case constituted a return to *Lochner*-era substantive due process adjudication.[27] Only time will tell whether the *Lawrence* decision was a limited ruling concerning a fundamental aspect of liberty or an indication that the Court was going to review all social and economic welfare laws under a true reasonableness test as it had once done in the early twentieth century.[28]

The list of rights which the Court has found to be fundamental, and, therefore, worthy of strict judicial scrutiny is not a long one. While there might be other ways to describe or divide these rights, they can be best understood as falling into six substantive categories (in addition to the fundamental guarantees of the Bill of Rights discussed in the previous section of this Chapter).

First, the freedom of association has been found to be a fundamental value which is implied by the First Amendment guarantees even though it has no specific textual recognition in that Amendment.[29] Second, the right to vote and to participate in the electoral process has been held to be a fundamental constitutional value which is reflected in several Amendments and given recognition as a form of "liberty" under the due process clauses.[30] Third, the Court has found a fundamental right to interstate travel; this right to travel has a long history of recognition as a right to personal mobility, a right derived from several provisions of the Constitution.[31] Fourth, the Court has implicitly recognized a right to fairness in the criminal process as a fundamental right although its "fundamental" nature has not been the subject of a specific decision.[32]

22. Bowers v. Hardwick, 478 U.S. 186, 199, 106 S.Ct. 2841, 2848, 92 L.Ed.2d 140 (1986) (Blackmun, J., joined by Brennan, Marshall, and Stevens, JJ., dissenting); 478 U.S. at 214, 106 S.Ct. at 2856 (Stevens, J., joined by Brennan and Marshall, JJ., dissenting).

23. ___ U.S. ___, 123 S.Ct. 2472, 156 L.Ed.2d 508 (2003).

24. ___ U.S. at ___, 123 S.Ct. at 2484.

25. ___ U.S. at ___, 123 S.Ct. at 2483–84.

26. ___ U.S. at ___, 123 S.Ct. at 2484, 2488 (O'Connor, J., concurring in the judgment).

27. ___ U.S. at ___, 123 S.Ct. at 2488 (Scalia, J., joined by Rehnquist, C.J., and Thomas, J., dissenting); ___ U.S. at ___, 123 S.Ct. at 2498 (Thomas, J., dissenting).

28. The *Lawrence* decision is analyzed in greater length in § 14.28 of this Treatise.

29. NAACP v. Alabama ex rel. Patterson, 357 U.S. 449, 460–61, 78 S.Ct. 1163, 1170–71, 2 L.Ed.2d 1488 (1958); Bates v. Little Rock, 361 U.S. 516, 522–23, 80 S.Ct. 412, 416–17, 4 L.Ed.2d 480 (1960).

30. Harper v. Virginia State Bd. of Elections, 383 U.S. 663, 86 S.Ct. 1079, 16 L.Ed.2d 169 (1966); Carrington v. Rash, 380 U.S. 89, 85 S.Ct. 775, 13 L.Ed.2d 675 (1965).

31. Shapiro v. Thompson, 394 U.S. 618, 89 S.Ct. 1322, 22 L.Ed.2d 600 (1969).

32. See, e.g., Douglas v. California, 372 U.S. 353, 83 S.Ct. 814, 9 L.Ed.2d 811 (1963) (right to counsel in first appeal); Mayer v. Chicago, 404 U.S. 189, 92 S.Ct. 410, 30 L.Ed.2d 372 (1971) (right to transcript in misdemeanor appeals); Bounds v. Smith, 430 U.S. 817, 97 S.Ct. 1491, 52 L.Ed.2d 72 (1977) (right to legal materials & access to courts).

Fifth, the Supreme Court has recognized that there is a right to fairness in procedures concerning individual claims against governmental deprivations of life, liberty, or property. Again, this right is not reflected in a specific decision but is, rather, an implied recognition of the fundamental nature of the due process clause in those decisions dealing with "procedural due process" rights.[33] Sixth, there is a fundamental right to privacy which includes various forms of freedom of choice in matters relating to the individual's personal life. This right to privacy has been held to include rights to freedom of choice in marital decisions,[34] child bearing,[35] child rearing[36] and some private, sexual activity.[37]

This list is not permanently exhaustive and the Court may alter it in years ahead.[38] Yet the subjective nature of the Supreme Court's decisions concerning the rights on this list should not give one a feeling of hopelessness in predicting the future actions of the Court. The prior rulings of the Court concerning these rights, and the long history of the judicial enforcement of natural law rights give a basis for anticipating that the Court will continue to honor these rights in the years ahead.

Conclusion. The basis upon which the Court declares an aspect of liberty to be a fundamental constitutional right remains vague today. All that can be said with certainty is that a majority of Supreme Court Justices, in a series of rulings spread across the last several decades, have selected a group of individual civil liberties which do not have a clear textual basis in the Constitution or its Amendments and declared those rights to be "fundamental." If the Court finds that a right is "fundamental" it will give independent judicial review to any law that constitutes a significant impairment of the fundamental right. If the law regulates or impairs the exercise of the fundamental right by all persons, the Court will use "substantive due process analysis" to review the constitutionality of the law. If the law creates a classification regarding the fundamental right, the Court will use equal protection analysis. In other words, if the law restricts the exercise of a fundamental right by some persons, but not others, the Court will consider the case to be an equal protection case. At this point, the reader may want to review the sections of Chapter 10 that discuss the difference between procedural and substantive due process and equal protection analysis and the introductory

33. The Court sometimes defines the nature of constitutional protection for a fundamental right as it rules on the procedures constitutionally mandated to avoid the unjustified deprivation of such rights in individual cases. See e.g., Youngberg v. Romeo, 457 U.S. 307, 102 S.Ct. 2452, 73 L.Ed.2d 28 (1982), (persons committed to state mental care institutions are constitutionally entitled to reasonably safe conditions of confinement and the exercise of professional judgment regarding their care that is not a substantial departure from generally accepted professional standards); Santosky v. Kramer, 455 U.S. 745, 102 S.Ct. 1388, 71 L.Ed.2d 599 (1982) (parental rights can only be terminated if state can prove allegations of parental unfitness by "clear and convincing evidence").

34. Boddie v. Connecticut, 401 U.S. 371, 91 S.Ct. 780, 28 L.Ed.2d 113 (1971); Loving v. Virginia, 388 U.S. 1, 12, 87 S.Ct. 1817, 1823, 18 L.Ed.2d 1010 (1967). Because of the fundamental constitutional nature of the relationship between parents and children, the Supreme Court ruled that a state, solely on the basis that she could not pay a mandatory fee for the preparation of a trial court record, could not deny an indigent woman an appeal from a trial court decision terminating her parental rights. M.L.B. v. S.L.J., 519 U.S. 102, 117 S.Ct. 555, 136 L.Ed.2d 473 (1996). The M.L.B. decision was, in part, based upon a series of earlier rulings establishing procedural due process safeguards when the government seeks to terminate

family relationships. See §§ 13.4, 13.8, 13.9, regarding procedural due process. The Court has held that marriage and relationships in traditional families are a part of the fundamental right to privacy for substantive due process and equal protection analysis. See § 14.28.

35. A claimed right to biological reproduction involves several particular rights, see §§ 14.26, 14.27, 14.30.

36. See, Pierce v. Society of Sisters, 268 U.S. 510, 535, 45 S.Ct. 571, 573–74, 69 L.Ed. 1070 (1925) (private education); Meyer v. Nebraska, 262 U.S. 390, 399, 43 S.Ct. 625, 626–27, 67 L.Ed. 1042 (1923); see also Prince v. Massachusetts, 321 U.S. 158, 166, 64 S.Ct. 438, 442, 88 L.Ed. 645 (1944). Today these particular decisions might be viewed as relating to certain First Amendment rights, but the Court cites them as establishing a fundamental right. See Carey v. Population Services International, 431 U.S. 678, 97 S.Ct. 2010, 52 L.Ed.2d 675 (1977).

37. Lawrence v. Texas __ U.S. __, 123 S.Ct. 2472, 156 L.Ed.2d 508 (2003). See § 14.28.

38. This difficulty is exacerbated by those cases in which the Supreme Court mixes procedural and substantive due process questions. See § 10.6. For references to scholarly examinations of the history of the Civil War Amendments see our multivolume treatise. R. Rotunda & J. Nowak, Treatise on Constitutional Law: Substance and Procedure § 18.6 (3rd ed. 1999).

sections of this Chapter, and Chapter 14, regarding the standards of review used in substantive due process and equal protection cases.

There has been little agreement on the Court or among scholars concerning the proper basis upon which the Justices should declare a right to be fundamental. There has been continual criticism of the protection of rights that do not have a clear basis in the text of the Constitution. Indeed, the younger Justice Harlan, who was willing to recognize the right to marital privacy, strongly criticized the Court's use of fundamental rights analysis in voting or interstate travel cases.[39]

When considering whether a right should be protected by the judiciary from infringement by legislative or regulatory actions, should the Justices consider one or more of the following: (1) the text of the Constitution and the "original intent" of the persons who drafted and ratified the constitutional provision at issue (such as the Fourteenth Amendment); (2) the history and traditions of our country both before and after the adoption of the Bill of Rights and the Fourteenth Amendment to determine whether the right is one for which our country has evidence they believe that it should be protected from legislative incursions; (3) political philosophy or moral philosophy in defining the group of natural law rights that must be respected by any just society, including our own.[40]

The *Griswold* and *Bowers* cases that were highlighted in this section of the Treatise are only two examples of the debate between the Justices concerning the proper basis for determining whether a right is a fundamental civil liberty. Based upon a consideration of the "history" and "traditions" of our country, the Supreme Court has ruled that the right to terminate one's life (i.e., commit suicide) is not a fundamental right, although a majority of the Justices have assumed that an individual has a right to refuse life-sustaining medical treatment.[41] Similar debate will be found in all of the cases concerning fundamental rights analysis. Those cases are examined in detail in Chapter 14, because most of the Supreme Court decisions concerning fundamental rights have involved equal protection analysis for the simple reason that the government rarely takes a fundamental right away from all persons but may in many instances restrict the ability of one classification of persons to exercise a fundamental right as easily or fully as other persons in society.

There has been a division among scholars concerning the legitimacy of the Court's interpretation of fundamental rights that mirrors the division of the Justices themselves. Each modern constitutional law casebook will have references to commentators who (1) decry as illegitimate any judicial protection of values that are not clearly identified by the text in original intent of those who drafted the Constitution; (2) who justify the judicial protection of certain fundamental rights in terms of

---

39. See Griswold v. Connecticut, 381 U.S. 479, 499, 85 S.Ct. 1678, 1690, 14 L.Ed.2d 510 (1965) (Harlan, J., concurring). In *Griswold,* Justice Harlan restated his views regarding the right of privacy for married couples that he had expressed previously in Poe v. Ullman, 367 U.S. 497, 522, 81 S.Ct. 1752, 1766, 6 L.Ed.2d 989 (1961) (Harlan, J., dissenting). Justice Harlan objected to the use of fundamental rights to increase judicial scrutiny of classifications under the equal protection guarantee because he thought fundamental rights analysis in equal protection cases was merely used to overturn legislative policy judgments. See, e.g., Shapiro v. Thompson, 394 U.S. 618, 660–62, 89 S.Ct. 1322, 1345–46, 22 L.Ed.2d 600 (1969) (Harlan, J., dissenting regarding recognition of a fundamental right to interstate travel that would place significant limits on durational residency requirements).

40. In order to justify finding that a right not mentioned in the Constitution is a fundamental right, a majority of the Justices must be convinced that the right is

implicit in the concept of ordered liberty or that it is protected by the nation's history and traditions. In Reno v. Flores, 507 U.S. 292, 113 S.Ct. 1439, 123 L.Ed.2d 1 (1993), the Court upheld Immigration and Naturalization Service regulations that required the detention of an alien minor awaiting deportation proceedings unless there were parents, guardians, or relatives of the child in the United States to whom the child could be released. The Court in *Flores* found that a minor did not have a fundamental right to be placed in a non-custodial setting or to have the government always make determinations in the "best interest" of the child. Because no fundamental right was impaired by the regulations, the Court required only that there be a rational relationship between the regulation and the legitimate government interests in taking care of alien children in a process that is designed to ensure their appearance at deportation proceedings.

41. See § 14.30 (c) regarding the "right to die" cases.

the history and traditions of our nation or our consensus on the nature of rights that should be placed beyond the power of the political process; (3) who believe that the Justices should define rights through a "process oriented analysis" by determining whether a specific civil liberty, such as the ability to vote, is best protected even in a democracy by an unelected judiciary rather than the political process; (4) who believe that fundamental rights problems should be examined on a case-by-case or right-by-right basis to determine whether there is a basis in moral philosophy or political philosophy for finding that the right must be protected by the judiciary. The multivolume edition of this Treatise includes references to the published works of many of the scholars who have entered this debate concerning the legitimacy of fundamental rights analysis. A student of constitutional law must assess for herself whether she believes that the Court's use of one or more of these bases for defining fundamental rights is legitimate in our constitutional democracy. A student or scholar will have no difficulty in finding references to scholars who have taken each of these positions.[42]

§ 11.8 The Contract Clause

(a) Introduction

The framers drafted the contract clause to prevent the states from enacting debtor relief laws. Under the leadership of Chief Justice John Marshall, however, the clause received an expansive reading. During the Marshall years the Court used the provision to invalidate statutes that retrospectively impaired almost any contractual obligation of private parties. The Court never used the clause to void laws that prospectively modified contractual obligations. Nevertheless, until the late nine-

teenth century the contract clause was the principal provision the Court used to void legislation that infringed on private property rights. Within the last 100 years, however, the Court rarely has relied on the clause as a reason to invalidate state legislation which retroactively affected contractual rights or obligations.

The Supreme Court has used the contract clause to restrict the ability of states to modify or alter public charters and contracts as well as private contracts. If a state is to retain the ability to modify a charter or public contract, it must explicitly so provide in the charter or in the enabling legislation. Moreover, if third parties' rights have accrued under the charter or public contract, the state may be unable to alter the contract even if it has made a general reservation to modify the contract. On the other hand, the contract clause will not prevent a state from altering its own contractual obligations that involve its inherent police powers. The Court has recognized that a state cannot bargain away its police power. If, however, the state commits itself to a financial obligation, the Court will review both the reasonableness and the necessity of any legislation that impairs that obligation. If the Court finds that the state law at issue is unnecessary and unreasonable in the way it alters the state's financial commitment, it may void the measure as violative of the contract clause.

(b) The Case Law

The contract clause of the Constitution prohibits the states from enacting any law that will impair "the Obligation of Contracts."[1] This prohibition, in general, prevents the states from passing any legislation that would alleviate the commitments of one party to a

---

42. References to many of these scholarly works are contained in the footnotes in Chapters 1, 15, 18, and 23 of R. Rotunda and J. Nowak, Treatise on Constitutional Law: Substance and Procedure (3rd ed. 1999, with annual supplements).

§ 11.8

1. U.S.Const. art. I, § 10: "No State shall ... pass any ... Law impairing the Obligation of Contracts." This clause does not apply to the federal government.

See generally, Smith v. Board of Trustees of Louisiana State Employees' Retirement System, 851 So.2d 1100 (La.

2003, citing this Treatise). Calvaruso, J., citing this section of the Treatise in Iffland v. Iffland, 155 Misc.2d 661, 664, 589 N.Y.S.2d 249, 251 (1992); Van Hoomissen, J., citing Treatise, in Oregon State Police Officers' Association v. State, 323 Or. 356, 364, 918 P.2d 765, 770 (1996); Nakayama, J., citing Treatise, in In re Herrick, 82 Hawai'i 329, 922 P.2d 942 (1996); John, J., citing Treatise in Miracle v. North Carolina Local Government Employees Retirement System, 124 N.C.App. 285, 477 S.E.2d 204, 209 (1996), review denied 345 N.C. 754, 485 S.E.2d 57 (199N.C.App7).

contract or make enforcement of the contract unreasonably difficult.[2]

The primary intent behind the drafting of the clause was to prohibit states from adopting laws that would interfere with the contractual arrangements between private citizens.[3] Specifically, the drafters intended to inhibit the ability of state legislatures to enact debtor relief laws.[4] Those who attended the Constitutional Convention recognized that banks and financiers required some assurance that their credit arrangements would not be abrogated by state legislatures. The drafters also realized that the country's economic growth depended in large measure on providing a stable environment for those who had money to invest or loan.[5] Therefore, as a means to help provide a stable economic environment, the draftsmen not only reserved in Congress the power to establish uniform bankruptcy laws[6] but also adopted the contract clause to restrict the power of the states to annul or void valid credit arrangements.

The Contract Clause and Chief Justice Marshall. Although the framers of the Constitution believed the contract clause would have limited application, John Marshall, as Chief Justice, saw the provision as a valuable weapon to protect property interests from unwarranted state regulation.[7] Three events that occurred before Marshall became Chief Justice helped color his view of the clause as a

shield to protect property owners from state regulation. First, in 1795, the circuit court for the district of Pennsylvania decided *Van-Horne's Lessee v. Dorrance*[8] in which it declared unconstitutional a Pennsylvania law that altered the title of disputed land because the statute violated the contract clause. This decision provided Marshall with valuable case authority to apply the contract clause to invalidate state statutes other than debtor relief laws.[9] Second, in 1798, the Supreme Court decided *Calder v. Bull*[10] and stated that the ex post facto clause[11] only applied to criminal legislation. With the ex post facto clause unavailable as a vehicle to void state civil legislation, the contract clause became a viable alternative as a means to protect property from retrospective legislation. Finally, the great Yazoo land scandal of the late 1790's presented Marshall, as Chief Justice, a prime opportunity to expound on the contract clause once the litigation that resulted from that scandal finally reached the Supreme Court in 1810, in the case of *Fletcher v. Peck*.[12]

In 1794 the Georgia legislature by statute granted thirty-five million acres of land to speculators for a purchase price of $500,000. When, however, the public learned of the widespread fraud and bribery that influenced the legislation, it demanded repeal of the statutory grant, and the Georgia legislature rescinded the legislation a year later.[13]

---

2. Edward S. Corwin's, The Constitution and What It Means Today 103 (Rev. ed. by H. Chase & C. Ducat 1973). See generally, B. Wright, The Contract Clause of the Constitution (1938); Hale, The Supreme Court and the Contract Clause, 57 Harv.L.Rev. 512, 621, 852 (1944) (three part article). For citations to additional secondary authorities, on this point, see R. Rotunda & J. Nowak, Treatise on Constitutional Law: Substance and Procedure, § 15.8 (3rd ed. 1999, with annual supplements).

For rules relating to federal government contracts, see § 11.9(a), infra.

3. B. Wright, The Growth of American Constitutional Law 41 (1967) [hereinafter cited as Wright].

4. Wright, supra note 3, at 64. See also Home Building & Loan Ass'n v. Blaisdell, 290 U.S. 398, 427–28, 54 S.Ct. 231, 235–36, 78 L.Ed. 413 (1934) (Hughes, C.J., discussing historical background of clause).

5. D. Smith, The Convention and the Constitution: The Political Ideas of the Founding Fathers 16–17 (1965).

6. U.S.Const. art. 1, § 8, cl. 4.

7. C. Magrath, Law and Politics in the New Republic—Yazoo: The Case of Fletcher v. Peck 70–71 (1966).

8. 2 U.S. (2 Dall.) 304, 319–20, 1 L.Ed. 391, 398 (1795) (C.C.D.Pa.1795).

9. C. Magrath, Law and Politics in the New Republic—Yazoo: The Case of Fletcher v. Peck 83 (1966).

10. 3 U.S. (3 Dall.) 386, 1 L.Ed. 648 (1798).

11. U.S.Const. art. I, § 10.

12. 10 U.S. (6 Cranch) 87, 3 L.Ed. 162 (1810).

13. C. Magrath, Law and Politics in the New Republic—Yazoo: The Case of Fletcher v. Peck 1–19 (1966).

The repealed legislation "was publicly and ceremoniously burned, the fire supplied from heaven (as legend has it) by means of a magnifying glass which concentrated the sun's rays into a flame. The [repealed] act was then expunged from all official State records." G. Haskins & H. Johnson, 2 The Oliver Wendell Holmes Devise History of the Supreme Court of the United States: Foundations of Power: John Marshall, 1801–15, at 340 (1981) (footnotes omitted).

See also Hagan, Fletcher v. Peck, 16 Ga.L.J. 1 (1927); C. H. Haskins, The Yazoo Land Companies, 6 Papers of the American Historical Association 61 (1891).

Peck had purchased some of the Georgia land from one of the original grantees and had resold the land to Fletcher. When Fletcher learned of the statutory repeal of the grant, he demanded rescission of the contract and his money back because of Peck's inability to convey good title. Peck, however, responded with the argument that he was a purchaser in due course and the rescinding act could not affect his title to the land.[14]

When *Fletcher v. Peck* came before the Supreme Court, Chief Justice Marshall may have been aware of the original limited intent behind the contract clause.[15] At the same time, however, he was also familiar with the position of Alexander Hamilton. Hamilton, like Marshall, was a leading Federalist, and he believed that Georgia's repeal of a land grant transferred for valuable consideration violated the prohibitions of the contract clause. Like Hamilton, Marshall believed the contract clause offered a valuable defense against reckless state legislatures which would interfere with established business and property interests.[16]

These countervailing considerations which Marshall entertained apparently worked at odds with each other while he was writing his opinion. Although Marshall's opinion in *Fletcher v. Peck* declared the rescinding statute unconstitutional, the constitutional basis for the opinion is somewhat uncertain. Some language in the decision implies that the Georgia statute violated the contract clause because the grant was in the nature of a contract.[17] Other language in the opinion, however, reflects Marshall's uncertainty on whether he could rest the entire decision on that clause. He states that the rescinding legislation violated not only general principles of society and government but also the concept of natural

law.[18] Therefore, whether the contract clause, by itself, would prohibit legislation that impaired the obligation of a state to a private party was unclear. Although *Fletcher v. Peck* was the Supreme Court's first decision that addressed the clause, subsequent Court decisions soon removed any uncertainty of whether the provision would prevent a state from avoiding its own obligations to a contract.

After *Fletcher v. Peck* the Court decided *New Jersey v. Wilson*[19] and *Dartmouth College v. Woodward*.[20] These cases removed any doubt that the contract clause would prohibit a state from abrogating agreements to which it was a party. In the *Wilson* case the New Jersey legislature enacted a statute that repealed a tax exemption which the colonial legislature had granted certain lands fifty years earlier. The Supreme Court invalidated the repealing measure as violative of the contract clause.[21]

In *Dartmouth College* the Court applied the clause to a statute that attempted to change the provisions of a charter issued to Dartmouth College.[22] The Court, through Chief Justice Marshall, stated without reservation or qualification that the clause applied to a state's obligation in a contract, that a charter was a contract, and that the covenants in the charter were invoidable even though the holders of the charter, the college trustees, had no beneficial interest in the instrument.[23] Although *Dartmouth College* involved a charitable and educational institution, the Court readily expanded the principles announced in the opinion to corporate charters issued for business purposes. Consequently, the decision protected industrial and financial corporations from much government regulation.[24]

Modification of Contracts Between Private Parties. The Supreme Court in *Fletch-*

14. C. Magrath, Law and Politics in the New Republic—Yazoo: The Case of Fletcher v. Peck 50–69 (1966).

15. C. Magrath, Law and Politics in the New Republic—Yazoo: The Case of Fletcher v. Peck 71 (1966).

16. B. Wright, The Contract Clause of the Constitution 42 (1938).

17. 10 U.S. (6 Cranch) at 136–37, 3 L.Ed. at 178.

18. 10 U.S. (6 Cranch) at 139, 3 L.Ed. at 178–79. On the uncertain foundation of the opinion, see B. Wright, The Contract Clause of the Constitution 42–43 (1938).

19. 11 U.S. (7 Cranch) 164, 3 L.Ed. 303 (1812).

20. 17 U.S. (4 Wheat.) 518, 4 L.Ed. 629 (1819).

21. 11 U.S. (7 Cranch) at 166–68.

22. See Wright, supra note 3, at 43.

23. 17 U.S. (4 Wheat.) at 651–52; see also R. McCloskey, The American Supreme Court at 73–75 (1960) [hereinafter cited as McCloskey].

24. Wright, supra note 3, at 44.

er v. Peck, Wilson, and *Dartmouth College* unquestionably had established that the contract clause would preclude states from passing legislation that would ameliorate the contractual commitments of a state to another party. Nevertheless, the original intent behind the provision was to inhibit the ability of states to enact debtor relief laws that would impair the contractual obligation of private parties. The Court, however, did not apply the clause to invalidate a debtor relief law until *Sturges v. Crowninshield,*[25] decided in the same year that the Court rendered the *Dartmouth College* opinion.

In *Sturges* the Court declared unconstitutional a New York insolvency law that discharged the obligations of debtors once they had surrendered their property. The principal constitutional defect of the law was its retroactive effect: the act released debtors from obligations assumed before the act's passage. The *Sturges* opinion, therefore, implied that the Court would sustain debtor relief legislation that had a prospective effect.

In *Ogden v. Saunders*[26] the Court expressly adopted the implication of *Sturges* and held a debtor relief law with prospective impact to be constitutional. Although Chief Justice Marshall contended that the contract clause prohibited states from enacting prospective debtor legislation, the majority of the Court disagreed, because they believed the framers of the Constitution clearly intended the clause to prohibit only retrospective legislation.

Chief Justice Marshall's inability to persuade the majority of the Court to adopt his view of the contract clause in *Ogden v. Saunders* was one of the few setbacks the Chief Justice suffered in his campaign to make that clause a shield to protect established property and business interests from unwarranted state intrusion. He had expanded the application of the provision beyond the original intent of the framers. The contract clause not only would inhibit states from impairing the obligation of contracts between private parties but also would prevent states from abrogating their own contractual commitments to private citizens. Under Marshall's leadership, the Court had declared that state grants and state charters were contracts and came under the protection of the contract clause. On the whole, the Chief Justice had succeeded in his efforts to make the clause a valuable provision to protect the "vested rights" of property holders and businessmen.

Modification of State Contracts—The Taney Court. The decisions the Court rendered during Chief Justice Taney's leadership adhered to the interpretations of the contract clause which the Marshall Court had formulated.[27] In several cases the Taney Court gave added definition and certainty to the scope of the contract clause. In *West River Bridge Co. v. Dix,*[28] for example, the Court emphasized that certain state powers were inalienable. Although the legislature in a corporate charter may promise not to exercise the power of eminent domain, the promise will fail to prevent the state from taking the property of the corporation with just compensation because the legislature never had the power to convey away the power of eminent domain.

The Court repeated the principle of *Dix* some thirty years later in *Stone v. Mississippi*[29] when it stated that the legislature cannot bargain away the public health and morals of the people. The legislature must allow the state to exercise its proper police powers. Moreover, the Supreme Court later extended the doctrine announced in *Dix* and stated that private parties who enter into a contract "may not estop the legislature from enacting laws for the public good." [30]

Modification of Remedies. In *Bronson v.*

---

25. 17 U.S. (4 Wheat.) 122, 4 L.Ed. 529 (1819).

26. 25 U.S. (12 Wheat.) 213, 6 L.Ed. 606 (1827).

27. McCloskey, supra not 23, 1t 81–85. For references to additional cases, and secondary authorities, on this point see the multivolume edition of this Treatise: R. Rotunda & J. Nowak, Treatise on Constitutional Law:

Substance and Procedure § 15.8 (3rd ed. 1999, with annual supplements).

28. 47 U.S. (6 How.) 507, 12 L.Ed. 535 (1848).

29. 101 U.S. (11 Otto) 814, 25 L.Ed. 1079 (1880).

30. Manigault v. Springs, 199 U.S. 473, 480, 26 S.Ct. 127, 130, 50 L.Ed. 274 (1905).

Kinzie[31] the Taney Court attempted to give added definition to the remedy-obligation distinction enunciated by the Marshall Court in *Sturges*. In *Sturges* the Supreme Court had conceded that although the contract clause precluded a state from adopting laws that impaired the obligation of contracts, the state may enact legislation that modifies the available remedies for the breach of a contract.[32] In *Bronson* the Court stated that the scope of allowable modifications of remedies under the clause depended on the reasonableness of those modifications and whether the modifying legislation affected substantial rights of the parties.[33] The Court's success, however, in defining the distinction between remedy and obligation is perhaps best reflected in Justice Cardozo's statement in *W. B. Worthen Co. v. Kavanaugh*.[34] Some ninety years after *Bronson*, Cardozo found that the distinction between obligation and remedy "is at times obscure." Nevertheless, highlighting the difference between the two concepts gave not only the Court but also state legislatures some flexibility in approving debtor relief statutes.

The Contract Clause From 1874 to the Turn of the Century. The Supreme Court from 1874 to 1898 used the clause in thirty-nine cases to invalidate state legislation.[35] At the same time, however, the Court had reached the end of the period of the expansive reading of the clause. During the latter part of the nineteenth century the provision lost its importance as the principal constitutional clause available to protect vested rights. Several developments help explain the diminished value of the contract clause as a defense for property interests.[36]

First, the states were reserving the right to amend or alter the charters they granted. If a state reserved the right to modify the terms of a charter either by a provision in the charter or by a general statutory scheme, a state could subsequently modify a granted charter without violating the contract clause. Therefore, states took advantage of this concession by passing the appropriate legislation or including the necessary charter provision.

Additionally, the rule that the Court would construe strictly the terms of any public grant prompted the states to write their grants carefully. Consequently, the states rarely would enact a statutory grant that would fail to give the state the necessary flexibility to pass legislation that may modify the previously issued public grant.

Finally, the Court began to rely on the doctrine of substantive due process to void legislation that would infringe on property or business interests. More often than not, any state legislation that impaired the obligation of contract would not only violate the contract clause but also would violate the Court's notions of economic substantive due process. The substantive due process doctrine gave the Court more discretion and flexibility than the contract clause in passing on the constitutionality of state legislation. Hence, if the Court had a choice, it would use substantive due process analysis rather than contract clause analysis to void state legislation.[37]

Twentieth Century Rulings—The *Blaisdell* Decision. During the Court's substantive due process era the contract clause faded in importance. When, however, the Great Depression came and states began to enact debtor relief legislation, the Court began to hear numerous cases where the opponents of the debtor relief measures relied on the clause to attack the constitutionality of the legislation. Earlier Supreme Courts had invalidated many of these laws if they had a retroactive effect. Nevertheless, in *Home Building & Loan Asso-*

---

31. 42 U.S. (1 How.) 311, 11 L.Ed. 143 (1843).

32. Sturges v. Crowninshield, 17 U.S. (4 Wheat.) 122, 200–01, 4 L.Ed. 529 (1819).

33. 42 U.S. (1 How.) at 315–17, 11 L.Ed. 143.

34. 295 U.S. 56, 60, 55 S.Ct. 555, 556, 79 L.Ed. 1298 (1935).

35. See Wright, supra note 3, at 96.

36. For references to additional cases, and secondary authorities, on this point see the multivolume edition of this Treatise: R. Rotunda & J. Nowak, Treatise on Constitutional Law: Substance and Procedure § 15.8 (3rd ed. 1999, with annual supplements).

37. See, e.g., Lochner v. New York, 198 U.S. 45, 25 S.Ct. 539, 49 L.Ed. 937 (1905). The concept of substantive due process is examined above, in §§ 11.1–11.4, supra.

ciation v. Blaisdell,[38] the Court sustained a debtor relief law despite its retrospective impact.

In 1933, Minnesota enacted a law that gave the state courts the authority to extend the redemption period after a foreclosure sale. However, before a court could approve an extension of the redemption period, it had to order the mortgagor to pay a reasonable part of the rental value of the property. The mortgagee in *Blaisdell* contended that the law violated the contract clause, but the Supreme Court rejected the contention.

The Court recognized the economy emergency that the country faced when Minnesota passed the Mortgage Moratorium Law of 1933.[39] Relying on the principle first announced in *West River Bridge Co. v. Dix*[40] and clarified in later cases, the Court stated that a state always retained a power to react to emergency situations and to protect the security of its people. Minnesota's adoption of this "Mortgage Moratorium" provision fell within this reserved power and, thus, did not violate the Constitution. The Court noted that the authority the mortgage law conferred was of limited duration and would not outlast the emergency it was designed to meet. These considerations underscored the reasonableness of the measure.

When the Court examined "emergency" debtor relief legislation which totally exempted major assets of debtors from creditors' claims or eliminated remedies for claims without protecting the creditors' rights, it found that such actions violated the contract clause.[41] Under *Blaisdell* the state could alter remedies for debts if the legislation reasonably related to a public purpose and protected the basic value of creditor claims; the states were not permitted to significantly impair the basis of creditors' accrued rights in order to improve the economic position of debtors.

The Contract Clause in The Modern Era. Although the Court did void a few state enactments as violative of the contract clause after the *Blaisdell* decision, it did sustain the great majority of state laws against attacks to their constitutionality under the contract clause. The Court's almost uniform refusal to use the clause to void legislation paralleled its abandonment of substantive due process analysis to void economic legislation. Perhaps the best example of the Court's reluctance to use the clause to invalidate state legislation is *El Paso v. Simmons*.[42]

In the facts of *El Paso*, Texas had sold land under contract for a small down payment. The purchaser could forfeit his right to the property by failing to make interest payments on the land, but could reinstate his claim to the land by paying in full the overdue interest as long as rights of third parties had not intervened. The reinstatement right had no time limit to its exercise. Some thirty years after the initial sale of the land Texas amended the statute governing the reinstatement right and placed a five-year limit on its exercise.[43]

Simmons contended that the amending legislation violated the contract clause. The Court, through Justice White, disagreed. Although Justice White was willing to assume that the statutory Amendment impaired the state's obligation under the land contracts, he was unwilling to declare the law unconstitutional. The rights that the amending legislation impaired were rights left unprotected by

---

38. 290 U.S. 398, 54 S.Ct. 231, 78 L.Ed. 413 (1934).

39. 290 U.S. at 424–30, 54 S.Ct. at 235–37.

40. 47 U.S. (6 How.) 507, 12 L.Ed. 535 (1848).

41. See, W. B. Worthen Co. v. Thomas, 292 U.S. 426, 54 S.Ct. 816, 78 L.Ed. 1344 (1934) (law exempting money for or from insurance premiums or benefits from creditors' claims held to violate the contract clause); W. B. Worthen Co. v. Kavanaugh, 295 U.S. 56, 55 S.Ct. 555, 79 L.Ed. 1298 (1935) (elimination of foreclosure remedies violates the contract clause when no money is paid to the creditor for

loss of possession and the debtor can only gain by continued default).

But see East New York Savings Bank v. Hahn, 326 U.S. 230, 66 S.Ct. 69, 90 L.Ed. 34 (1945) ("mortgage moratorium" legislation like that approved in *Blaisdell* upheld even though it was extended for over ten years; reasonable provision and consideration for creditor interests supported the Act).

42. 379 U.S. 497, 85 S.Ct. 577, 13 L.Ed.2d 446 (1965).

43. 379 U.S. at 500–01, 85 S.Ct. at 579–80.

the Constitution.[44] The unlimited reinstatement period had generated not only much land speculation but also much uncertainty over land titles. Justice White believed that the contract clause could not prevent the Texas legislature's ability to remedy this situation and to "restrict a party to those gains reasonably to be expected from the contract." [45] Therefore, although the law had modified a state's own contractual obligation, the Court sustained the measure as constitutional under the contract clause.

After the *El Paso* decision some commentators speculated that because of the recent history of the Court's application of the contract clause removal of the provision from the Constitution would not reduce the Constitution's effectiveness as a check on the arbitrary exercise of governmental power.[46] This speculation of the contract clause's complete demise, however, proved premature.

The *United States Trust Co.* Decision— Modification of Government Contracts. In *United States Trust Co. v. New Jersey*[47] the Court revived the clause and declared a New Jersey statute unconstitutional because the law impaired the state's contractual obligation to the bondholders of The Port Authority of New York and New Jersey.

In 1962 the New York and New Jersey legislature decided that the Port Authority should take over and subsidize a bankrupt passenger railroad line that serviced the New York City metropolitan area. To reassure the Port Authority bondholders that the Authority would not be asked in the future to take over mass transit deficit operations beyond the Authority's financial reserves, the two states agreed to limit the number of such operations the Authority would absorb. However, in 1974 New Jersey repealed the legislation that implemented the limitation agreement. The bondholders sought a declaratory judgment that the repealing legislation violated the contract clause because it reduced the financial security of their

bonds. The state responded that removing the limitation was necessary to permit the Port Authority to subsidize mass transportation programs for the New York City metropolitan area. The state highlighted the need for the repealing measure by relating it to the energy crisis of 1973 and to the air pollution problems faced by northern New Jersey.

The Court acknowledged that it traditionally had required more than a mere technical impairment of a contractual obligation before it would void a measure as violative of the contract clause. Moreover, the Court noted that it usually had deferred to the legislative judgment whenever a state had exercised its police power to impair retroactively the obligation of private contracts. In this case, however, the state was asking the Court to sustain a law that relieved the state of its *own* contractual obligation. Consequently, the Court believed that the customary deference to the legislative judgment was not in order, but on the contrary, that it should assess the necessity and reasonableness of the repealing legislation.[48]

In its assessment of the New Jersey enactment, the Court first noted that the state had obligated itself to a financial contract and had not bargained away one of its police powers. Therefore, the 1962 financial restrictions were valid when the state had entered into the contract. The Court then noted that—although mass transportation, energy conservation, and cleaning the environment are important goals—the state cannot refuse "to meet its legitimate financial obligation simply because it would prefer to spend the money to promote the public good rather than the private welfare of its creditors." [49] Because alternative means were available to promote these goals, the Court reasoned that the repealing measure was both unreasonable and unnecessary. Hence, the Court declared the New Jersey statute unconstitutional because it impaired the state's own obligation of contract

---

44. 379 U.S. at 509, 85 S.Ct. at 584.

45. 379 U.S. at 515, 85 S.Ct. at 587.

46. Edwin S. Corwin's The Constitution and What It Means Today 105 (Rev.ed. by H. Chase & C. Ducat, 1973).

47. 431 U.S. 1, 97 S.Ct. 1505, 52 L.Ed.2d 92 (1977).

48. 431 U.S. at 25–26, 97 S.Ct. at 1519–20.

49. 431 U.S. at 29, 97 S.Ct. at 1521.

without promoting an overriding police power interest.

The *Allied Structural Steel* Decision— Modification of Private Contracts. The Supreme Court in 1978 resurrected the contract clause as a vehicle for judicial review of state economic legislation that altered *private* contracts in *Allied Structural Steel Co. v. Spannaus*.[50] At issue in *Spannaus* was a Minnesota law which effectively increased the monetary obligations of companies which had a pre-existing pension plan for employees and which either terminated the plan or closed their business facility in Minnesota. The law required that employees who had worked for such a company for in excess of ten years be granted benefits upon termination or the closing of a plant regardless of the provisions of the employer's pension plan.

The majority opinion by Justice Stewart reviewed the past decisions of the Court concerning the contract clause and recognized the general principle that states could enact legislation which limited contractual rights when that legislation was enacted to protect a basic societal interest and was a reasonable and narrow means of protecting that interest. The majority opinion noted that, while this principle was not a very strict limit on the powers of

the states, the contract clause remained a meaningful part of the Constitution.

The majority found the Minnesota law in *Spannaus* to be a violation of the contract clause because of the following factors: (1) the impairment of contract caused by the law was "substantial";[51] (2) the plaintiff company had "relied heavily, and reasonably" on actuarial calculations as to the amount of funding necessary to sustain the projected payouts from the pension fund only to incur unexpected additional obligations as a result of the new law;[52] (3) the law was not necessary to remedy an "important and general social problem," but rather focused on a limited number of employers who "had in the past been sufficiently enlightened as voluntarily to agree to establish pension plans";[53] (4) the law was not a temporary measure to deal with an emergency situation,[54] and (5) the law regulated a field which the state had not previously sought to regulate.[55]

Although the above factors appear to limit the *Spannaus* decision, Justices Brennan, Marshall and White argued, in dissent, that the decision effected an unprecedented expansion of the meaning of the contract clause.[56] The dissenters stated that the majority disregarded the substantial remedial purpose of the

50. 438 U.S. 234, 98 S.Ct. 2716, 57 L.Ed.2d 727 (1978).

51. 438 U.S. at 244–45, 98 S.Ct. at 2722–23. The opinion noted that a minimal burden on contractual interests would require less stringent review and could be upheld more easily. 438 U.S. at 244–45, 98 S.Ct. at 2722–23.

See also Texaco, Inc. v. Short, 454 U.S. 516, 102 S.Ct. 781, 70 L.Ed.2d 738 (1982) (Statute providing for lapse of several mineral interest unused for 20 years constitutes permissible limitation of property interests and is not an unconstitutional impairment of contract rights.)

52. 438 U.S. at 246, 98 S.Ct. at 2723. The company had complied with all of its contractual pension fund obligations as well as all laws applicable to pension plans until this time. It was only the closing of the office that subjected the company to this law, which requires it to recalculate and pay out additional funds for the past ten years of pension plan contributions. The burden was so severe and the company's reliance so reasonable that the majority felt unable to presume the "necessity and reasonableness" of the law. Id.

53. 438 U.S. at 250, 98 S.Ct. at 2725. The fact that the law did not regulate other employers, who presented more serious problems in terms of failing to establish funds to provide for employee retirement, made the law so

narrow that it seemed to have little relation to solving a general social problem. Also, the Supreme Court, in a previous decision during the same Term, had held that Minnesota Act was not preempted by older Federal legislation but that it was preempted by recent Federal pension legislation that expressly provided for the preemption of such state laws. Malone v. White Motor Corp., 435 U.S. 497, 98 S.Ct. 1185, 55 L.Ed.2d 443 (1978), on remand 599 F.2d 283 (8th Cir.1979), judgment affirmed 444 U.S. 911, 100 S.Ct. 223, 62 L.Ed.2d 166 (1979). Thus, the effective time period and application of the act was so limited that it applied to only a small classification of employers.

54. 438 U.S. at 250, 98 S.Ct. at 2725. In this way the Court distinguished this legislation for the economic relief legislation upheld in Home Building & Loan Ass'n v. Blaisdell, 290 U.S. 398, 54 S.Ct. 231, 78 L.Ed. 413 (1934). When a law is a temporary means of dealing with an emergency, it is more likely to be upheld as a reasonable exercise of the police power that does not violate the contract clause.

55. 438 U.S. at 250, 98 S.Ct. at 2725.

56. Allied Structural Steel Co. v. Spannaus, 438 U.S. 234, 251, 98 S.Ct. 2716, 2726, 57 L.Ed.2d 727 (1978) (Brennan, J., dissenting, joined by Marshall & White, JJ.).

law. They would have accepted the state's purpose of protection of employees "within a few months of the 'vesting' of their rights" under a pension plan from unforeseen plant closings or unilateral termination of a plan by an employer.[57]

Justice Brennan, writing for the three dissenters, also argued that the majority had misinterpreted the scope of the contract clause. The dissenters felt that the clause could only be read to reach acts of a legislature which impair or abrogate existing contract rights, and could not be read to reach acts which merely increase existing contractual obligations. So construed, the contract clause would have no application to this legislation. The Brennan opinion would also uphold the law against a due process challenge because of its rational relationship to protecting pensions.[58]

Although *Spannaus* appears to be a limited holding hedged by a number of qualifying factors and tied closely to the facts before the Court, the dissent seems justified in viewing the case as an enlargement of the scope of the contract clause as it had been employed by the Court in recent years. The majority, however, was unwilling to follow an approach to contract clause adjudication that effectively would read the clause out of the Constitution. Thus,

the majority refused to give total deference to state legislative decisions concerning the need to alter contractual obligations or to rule that the clause did not apply to alteration of contract terms that merely increased contractual obligations. Those proposed limitations on judicial review, employed by the dissent, were not expressly adopted in the prior decisions of the Court and they would leave the Court with no meaningful role in enforcing the substantive principles of the contract clause. The majority opinion by Justice Stewart only held that a state was not free to severely alter contractual obligations or impair contractual rights unless the state could demonstrate that its legislation was a reasonable and narrow means of promoting important societal interests.

The Court followed the reasoning of *United States Trust Co.* and *Spannaus* when it upheld a state law placing a statutory ceiling on price increases which a natural gas supplier could charge a public utility under the escalator clause of a pre-existing contract. The Court held that to the extent that the law substantially impaired contract rights it was a narrowly tailored means of promoting the important state interest in protecting consumers from imbalance in market prices caused by federal deregulation.[59] Thus, the *Allied Structural*

---

57. 438 U.S. at 253, 98 S.Ct. at 2726. The pension plan that had been created by the plaintiff in the case provided, inter alia, for unilateral termination or modification of the plan by the employer, and gave no recourse to employees in the event of such actions. The plan also provided that there was to be no recourse against the employer if the employer failed to fund the plan adequately. See 438 U.S. at 237, 98 S.Ct. at 2719. In light of these facts and as noted by Justice Brennan, other common abuses of employee confidence by those employers who fail to inform their employees that their "pension plan" may not protect them, it seems that the majority might not have been justified in concluding that no "important or general" state interest was reasonably served by the Minnesota law. The majority, however, did realize that the question of reliance might "cut both ways," but the majority found that no showing was made in the case that any employees of plaintiff company had relied to their detriment on Allied's pension plan. 438 U.S. at 246 n. 18, 98 S.Ct. at 2723 n. 18. Given the limited nature and application of the law and the fact that the surcharged company appeared to have acted in good faith, the majority could not conclude that the Act was a reasonable means of protecting employees from abuse of pension plans programs so as to justify the serious retroactive burden placed on the company.

58. 438 U.S. at 255–64, 98 S.Ct. at 2727–32.

59. Energy Reserves Group, Inc. v. Kansas Power & Light Co., 459 U.S. 400, 103 S.Ct. 697, 74 L.Ed.2d 569 (1983). The Court found that the natural gas company's contractual rights were not substantially impaired as the contracting parties recognized the fact that their activities were and would be subject to wide ranging government regulation. To the extent that the relationship was substantially impaired the law promoted an overriding interest in consumer protection. 459 U.S. at 416, 103 S.Ct. at 708. "The threshold inquiry is whether the state law has, in fact, operated as a substantial impairment of a contractual relationship.... If the state regulation constitutes a substantial impairment, the state, in justification must have a significant and legitimate public purpose.... Once a legitimate public purpose is identified, the next inquiry is whether the adjustment of rights and responsibilities of contracting parties is based upon reasonable conditions and is of a character appropriate to the public purpose justifying the legislation's adoption." 459 U.S. at 411–12, 103 S.Ct. at 704–05 quoting in part the *United States Trust Co.* and *Spannaus* decisions discussed previously in this section (citations, quotation marks, and brackets within quotes omitted).

Steel Co. v. Spannaus decision represents only a refusal to abdicate the judicial role in the enforcement of the contract clause, rather than a return to the pre–1937 model of judicial protection of economic interests.

Although it affected preexisting contracts which allowed producers of oil and natural gas to pass on severance tax increases to their consumers, a law prohibiting the pass-through of severance taxes to wholesale or retail consumers is not merely an attempt to alter contract rights but, rather, a "generally applicable rule of conduct designed to advance a broad societal interest." [60] That "societal interest" would support regulation of prices of such commodities and allow states to require the sellers to absorb a tax increase rather than passing it through to their customers; the contract clause will not prohibit the incidental effect of such regulatory action on preexisting contracts.[61]

If legislation affects contracts but it does not substantially impair contract rights in a retroactive manner, there is no significant contracts clause question. If the legislation constitutes a substantial impairment of contracts, then the courts must determine whether the legislation is reasonably tailored to promote a significant and legitimate public purpose that justifies the impairment of the contractual obligation.

For example, in *Keystone Bituminous Coal Association v. DeBenedictis*,[62] the Supreme Court upheld a state statute that prohibited types of coal mining that would cause subsidence damage to a variety of publicly and privately owned properties. The statute was valid even though it prohibited the extraction of a fixed percentage of the coal owned by persons or corporations who held the "mineral estate" to the underground coal deposits and even though owners of the "surface estate" over these coal deposits had entered contracts with the coal owners waiving any claim for damages that might result from the removal of the coal.[63] The statute did not constitute a taking of property because it allowed owners of the mineral rights to engage in the profitable mining of coal.

The percentage of coal that was required to be left in the ground to support the surface estate did not unjustly reduce the investment-backed expectations of the owners of the mineral rights. The owners of the mineral estates alleged that the statute violated the contract clause insofar as it overrode the contractual waiver of liability for surface damage.

The Supreme Court held that the legislative requirement that a mine owner leave sufficient coal in the ground to avoid damage to surface property (or to repair or provide funds for the repair of any surface damage caused by the mine) constituted a substantial impairment of their contracts because the new legislatively imposed obligation was inconsistent with the damage waivers that had been a part of the contracts between surface owners and mineral owners.[64] The Court ruled that the

---

60. Exxon Corp. v. Eagerton, 462 U.S. 176, 192, 103 S.Ct. 2296, 2306, 76 L.Ed.2d 497, 511 (1983), quoting in part Allied Structural Steel Co. v. Spannaus, 438 U.S. 234, 249, 98 S.Ct. 2716, 2725, 57 L.Ed.2d 727, 739 (1978). In *Exxon*, the Court found that a state law prohibiting producers of oil or gas extracted from wells in the state from passing on the cost of a severance tax increase to purchasers did not violate the commerce clause. The *Allied Structural Steel Co.* and *United States Trust Co.* cases referred to in the previous paragraph of this section were distinguished as instances where the state statutes were specifically designed to affect previously executed contracts rather than setting a generally applicable rule of conduct with an incidental effect on preexisting contracts.

61. Exxon Corp. v. Eagerton, 462 U.S. 176, 194, 103 S.Ct. 2296, 2307, 76 L.Ed.2d 497, 512 (1983). See also Producers' Transp. Co. v. Railroad Com'n, 251 U.S. 228, 40 S.Ct. 131, 64 L.Ed. 239 (1920) (upholding state commission order setting rates that can be charged for transpor-

tation of oil by pipeline in manner that would override terms of preexisting contract).

62. 480 U.S. 470, 107 S.Ct. 1232, 94 L.Ed.2d 472 (1987).

63. The standards for determining when a governmental regulation of land use is a taking of property are considered in § 11.12 of this Treatise.

64. The Supreme Court in *Keystone Bituminous Coal Association* noted that most of the contracts that included waivers of any claim against the coal company from damage caused to surface property had been entered into over seventy years ago, by persons who no longer owned the surface property. The state courts had apparently held that the waiver provision "ran with the land" and bound subsequent owners of the surface property. Based on the assumption that the contractual waiver of liability was a perpetual covenant against subsequent owners, the Supreme Court found that contract rights were impaired by

impairment of contract rights did not constitute a violation of the contract clause because the legislature could determine that requiring coal companies to avoid or repair damage to surface property was reasonably tailored to deterring or repairing environmental damage caused by the activities of the miners. This legitimate societal interest justified adjustment of the rights and responsibilities of the parties to the mining contracts.

Conclusion—Private Contracts. The contract clause restricts the power of state or local governments to modify the obligations of parties to a private contract or to modify governmental obligations under a government contract with private parties. Although the Federal government is not subject to the contract clause, due process principles will place some limitations on the Federal government's power to enact legislation which has a retroactive effect on either private or governmental contracts.[65]

State and local governments are not absolutely prohibited from modifying the obligations in private or public contracts. In order to protect the health, safety, and welfare of its citizens, a state may enact legislation which impairs contracts under certain conditions. In determining whether a state law affecting an individual's ability to carry out obligations under contract is an improper impairment of contract, the court must go through a three step analytical process. First, the court must

ask whether the state law has "operated as a substantial impairment of a contractual relationship." A law which only operates prospectively to regulate the activities of all persons, but which makes carrying out of a contractual obligation difficult or impossible, may not be considered to be an impairment of contract. While the Supreme Court no longer follows a rigid distinction between laws that regulate only remedies to contracts and laws that regulate the substantive obligations of contracts, state legislation which is designed to alter contract remedies, rather than to directly alter the rights and responsibilities of parties to private contracts, may well constitute only an insignificant or insubstantial impairment of contract.[66]

If a state law does constitute a substantial impairment of rights and obligations in private contracts, the court, in the second step of its inquiry, must ask whether the state law is designed to promote a significant and legitimate public purpose. Legislation should not be designed merely to alter the position of the parties so as to favor parties with whom the government is in sympathy and who may be suffering some economic hardship by having to meet their obligations under existing contracts. There must be a significant and legitimate social purpose to support the legislative impairment of contracts.

In the third step of the inquiry, the court must determine whether the law adjusting the

---

the new statute requiring coal companies to avoid or repair damage to surface property caused by their mining activities. Keystone Bituminous Coal Association v. De-Benedictis, 480 U.S. 470, 504–05 nn. 31, 32, 107 S.Ct. 1232, 1252 nn. 31, 32, 94 L.Ed.2d 472 (1987).

65. The due process restrictions on other state laws and federal laws which retroactively effect contract obligations are examined in § 11.9(a), infra. In Eastern Enterprises v. Apfel, 524 U.S. 498, 118 S.Ct. 2131, 141 L.Ed.2d 451 (1998) the Court, by a five to four vote of the Justices, but without a majority opinion, invalidated a federal government action that would have required a corporation not currently engaged in the coal mining business to make payments into a fund that would provide health benefits for retired mine workers. Four of the five Justices who voted to invalidate the retroactive assessment on the corporation joined a plurality opinion written by Justice O'Connor, which refused to consider substantive due process principles. The plurality opinion found that the assessment against the corporation violated the Fifth Amendment prohibition against taking of property. Justice

Kennedy, in a concurring opinion that was not joined by any other Justice, found that the application of the 1992 Coal Act to the corporation under these circumstances violated substantive due process principles, because it was an "egregious" retroactive application of a law. 524 U.S. at 539, 118 S.Ct. at 2154 (Kennedy, J., concurring in the judgment and dissenting in part). The *Eastern Enterprises* case is examined in § 11.12 (a).

66. In General Motors Corp. v. Romein, 503 U.S. 181, 112 S.Ct. 1105, 117 L.Ed.2d 328 (1992) the Supreme Court stated that in contract clause decisions: "We first ask whether a change in state law operated as a substantial impairment of a contractual relationship.... this inquiry has three components: whether there is a contractual relationship, whether the change in law impairs that contractual relationship, and whether the impairment is substantial." 503 U.S. at 185, 112 S.Ct. at 1109. The Supreme Court, in the *General Motors* decision, found that there was no substantial impairment of employer-employee contracts when state legislation retroactively repudiated a state court interpretation of worker benefit statutes.

contract obligations and rights was a reasonable and narrowly tailored means of promoting the significant public purpose identified in step two of the inquiry rather than an unjustifiable attempt to merely change the obligation of parties to a private contract. This requires an analysis of the legislation in terms of whether it is a reasonable means to promote the public purpose.

Conclusion—Government Contracts. When a state passes legislation which modifies contracts of a governmental unit, the court should follow the same basic three step approach to analyze whether the law is invalid under the contract clause. First, the court should determine whether the law constitutes a substantial impairment of a contractual relationship. Again, there is no clear right-remedy distinction, but laws regulating only the form of remedies to enforce state obligations may, in many situations, constitute only an insubstantial impairment of the private party's contract rights. A court should determine whether the state had reserved the power to modify its contract at the time that it entered the contract with the private party. This retained right to modify the contract may come from a specific contract provision or a statute whose terms should be considered to be incorporated into the contract. Such a right of rescission may mean that state alteration of its contractual obligation is not a significant impairment of contract rights.[67]

If a state law substantially impairs a contractual obligation of the state to private parties, the court must ask, in the second step of its inquiry, whether the state law creating the impairment is justified by a significant, legitimate public purpose. The judiciary should find that the state cannot be obligated by contract to refrain from exercising any aspect of its police power that is necessary for the protection of the health and safety of its residents. However, state economic obligations should be enforced; courts will enforce the contract clause against states which merely seek to extricate themselves from an economic obligation to private parties by repudiating their contracts or any significant part of their contracts. In the final step of its analysis, the court should require that the method used by the state to advance the significant and legitimate public purpose not constitute an unnecessarily broad repudiation of its contract obligations to private persons.[68] As in the analysis of private contract problems, the court must determine if the law is narrowly tailored and reasonably necessary to promote the public interest.[69]

67. When a Statute Creates Contractual Rights. The courts should not rule that the government has entered into a contract with a private person or corporation unless it is clear that a governmental entity with authority to do so has contracted with the private party in a way that restricts the power of the government to act in the future. Governmental actions relating to the use of property or business activity normally will be regulatory and not contractual in nature. Thus modifications of the regulations of private businesses or property use should not constitute an impairment of contract in any sense.

For citations to additional cases, and secondary authorities on this point see the multivolume edition of the Treatise: R. Rotunda & J. Nowak, Treatise on Constitutional Law: Substance and Procedure § 15.8 (3rd ed. 1999, with annual supplements).

68. In United States v. Locke, 471 U.S. 84, 105 S.Ct. 1785, 85 L.Ed.2d 64 (1985) the Court upheld the constitutionality of a federal law that terminated the interests of holders of unpatented mining claims on federal lands who failed to comply with annual filing requirements. Although the law terminated otherwise valid claims to mining rights that existed before the statute's enactment, the law was upheld. The statute required that all such mining claims must be registered with the Bureau of Land Management within three years of the statute's enact-

ment; the statute also required a yearly filing "prior to December 31". Failure to comply with either of these filing requirements "shall be deemed conclusively to constitute an abandonment of the mining claim ... by the owner." The Supreme Court interpreted the statute to require the annual filing prior to December 31 and found that no specific evidence of intent to abandon the claim was necessary or relevant if the person failed to make a timely filing. The Court found that this was not unconstitutional retroactive legislation because it was designed to further a legitimate state interest through reasonable, if severe, means. There was no unconstitutional taking because: "regulation of property rights does not 'take' private property when an individual's reasonable, investment-backed expectations can continue to be realized as long as he complies with reasonable regulatory restrictions the legislature has imposed." 471 U.S. at 107, 105 S.Ct. at 1799. There was no unconstitutional irrebuttable presumption created by this law, because Congress was not presuming that a person actually intended to abandon the claim but was establishing a regulation that simply terminated all claim rights for failure to meet a reasonable regulation.

69. Municipal Bond Modification. If a municipal obligation is virtually worthless because the municipal authority is unable to meet its economic obligations, the

§ 11.9 Other Forms of Restrictions on Retroactive Legislation

(a) Due Process Limitations

A statute or law that attempts to establish the legal significance of transactions that have occurred before its enactment constitutes what is called "retroactive legislation." [1] The courts traditionally have opposed retroactive legislation not only because such legislation tends to create instability but also because the legislature can benefit or harm disfavored classes of citizens more easily with retrospective laws than it can with prospective laws. [2] The Constitution reflects this bias against retroactive statutes by prohibiting both the Congress and the states from enacting any ex post facto laws; [3] the contract clause of the Constitution also prevents the states from passing any legislation that impairs the obligations of contracts. [4]

Besides the explicit constitutional provisions against retroactive laws the Supreme Court has also used the due process clauses of the Fifth and Fourteenth Amendments to void certain legislation that has a retrospective impact. [5] The framers of the Fifth and Fourteenth Amendment due process clauses, however, did not specifically design those provisions to cover retroactive legislation. Therefore, unlike the contract or ex post facto clauses, the legislative history of the due process clauses fails to provide the Court with any special criteria to determine when retroactive legislation violates constitutional principles. Nevertheless, the cases where retroactive legislation is an issue fall into four main categories and the Court appears to treat each category differently. [6]

Court might uphold a state or local law drastically modifying the economic obligation of the municipality to private persons if the private parties were in fact being given fair value in cash or substitute obligations in exchange for the modification of the original municipal obligation. The Court in such an instance would have to find that the limited repudiation of the municipal economic obligation of private persons, such as bondholders, was a narrow and necessary means of promoting an important public interest. This alteration of bond obligations might be allowed if the state had not limited municipal taxing authority in a way that required the municipality to repudiate its contract obligation rather than use tax money to solve its financial problems. Compare Faitoute Iron & Steel Co. v. Asbury Park, 316 U.S. 502, 62 S.Ct. 1129, 86 L.Ed. 1629 (1942) (upholding a legislative plan that required the exchange of the bonds of an insolvent city for new bonds from the city in the same face amount but at a lower interest rate, and with a longer maturity date, because this constituted a limited way of assuring payment of unsecured municipal obligations when the municipality faced an economic emergency) with United States Trust Co. v. New Jersey, 431 U.S. 1, 97 S.Ct. 1505, 52 L.Ed.2d 92 (1977) (contract clause prohibits government from modifying its contract with bondholders by repealing statutory covenant not to use those revenues pledged as security for the bonds for any railroad facility which could not be certified as being self supporting because this repudiation of one of the obligations to bondholders was a substantial impairment of contract and was not a necessary means for promoting an important societal interest).

§ 11.9

1. Greenblatt, Judicial Limitations on Retroactive Civil Legislation, 51 Nw.U.L.Rev. 540, 544 (1956).

2. See, e.g., Dash v. Van Kleeck, 7 Johns. 477 (N.Y. 1811).

Federal statutes that impose retroactive liability on individuals or corporations might be found to violate the takings clause of the Fifth Amendment and the due process clause of the Fifth Amendment. See, Eastern Enterprises v. Apfel, 524 U.S. 498, 118 S.Ct. 2131, 141 L.Ed.2d 451 (1998). The *Eastern Enterprises* decision is examined in § 11.12 (a).

The Supreme Court has created a presumption against interpreting a federal statute in a way that would require retroactive application of the statute, unless such an application is clearly required by the terms of the statute. See, e.g., Hughes Aircraft Co. v. United States ex rel. Schumer, 520 U.S. 939, 117 S.Ct. 1871, 138 L.Ed.2d 135 (1997), on remand 119 F.3d 796 (9th Cir.1997); Landgraf v. U.S. I. Film Products, 511 U.S. 244, 114 S.Ct. 1483, 128 L.Ed.2d 229 (1994); Rivers v. Roadway Express, Inc., 511 U.S. 298, 114 S.Ct. 1510, 128 L.Ed.2d 274 (1994).

See also, Slawson, Constitutional and Legislative Considerations in Retroactive Lawmaking, 48 Calif.L.Rev. 216, 221 (1960); Hochman, The Supreme Court and the Constitutionality of Retroactive Legislation, 73 Harv.L.Rev. 692, 692–93 (1960) [hereinafter cited as Hochman].

3. U.S.Const. art. I, § 9, cl. 3, § 10, cl. 1.

4. U.S.Const. art. I, § 10. See, § 11.8, supra.

5. Hochman, supra note 2, at 693–94. The due process restrictions on retroactive legislation are not necessarily coextensive with the prohibition against impairment of contracts; the federal government may have more latitude to create retroactive legislation under the principles of the due process clause than states, which are regulated by the contract clause. See Pension Benefit Guaranty Corp. v. R. A. Gray and Co., 467 U.S. 717, 734, 104 S.Ct. 2709, 2720, 81 L.Ed.2d 601, 613 (1984); National Railroad Passenger Corp. v. Atchison, Topeka and Santa Fe Railway Co., 470 U.S. 451, 105 S.Ct. 1441, 84 L.Ed.2d 432 (1985).

6. Compare the categories listed in Slawson, Constitutional and Legislative Consideration in Retroactive Lawmaking, 48 Calif.L.Rev. 216, 238 (1960), with the three-part test of Hochman, supra note 2, at 697. Hochman's

The four categories of cases involving retroactive legislation under the due process clause are: (1) cases that involve emergency retroactive legislation;[7] (2) cases that challenge the constitutionality of curative statutes;[8] (3) cases that involve the constitutional merits of retroactive taxing legislation;[9] and (4) cases that contest the constitutionality of retroactive general legislation.[10] Although the constitutional criteria for determining when retroactive legislation will violate due process is unsettled, an analysis of each of these issues may help in predicting when a certain piece of legislation will infringe on the right to due process of law.

The Tests of The Due Process and Contract Clauses Compared. Although state legislation is subject to due process restrictions against retroactive legislation, it is unlikely that state legislation which does not violate the contract clause will violate the Fourteenth Amendment due process clause. For this reason most of the due process cases regarding retroactive legislation are federal cases because the federal government is not subject to the restrictions of the contract clause.

The Supreme Court has stated that the Fifth Amendment due process restrictions are not coextensive with the contract clause prohibitions on state regulations of preexisting contracts. It must be remembered that review of retroactive legislation under the due process clause is no more than a variety of judicial regulation of economic activity under the concept of the substantive due process. The only general principles which the Court has given us regarding the constitutionality of retroactive legislation under due process principles were summarized by the Court as follows:

. . . the strong deference accorded legislation in the field of national economic policy is no less applicable when that legislation is applied retroactively. Provided that the retroactive application of a statute is supported by a legitimate legislative purpose furthered by rational means, judgments about the wisdom of such legislation remain within the exclusive province of the legislative and executive branches. . . . [R]etroactive legislation does have to meet a burden not faced by legislation that has only future effects. . . . But that burden is met simply by showing that the retroactive application of the legislation is itself justified by a rational legislative purpose.[11]

Retroactive Emergency Legislation. If the constitutionality of retroactive emergency legislation is challenged, the Court usually will sustain the measure. A case that illustrates the judicial deference to emergency measures is *Lichter v. United States*.[12] Petitioner contested the constitutionality of the Renegotiation Act of 1942. This wartime measure allowed the War Department to renegotiate any contract it had with private citizens to prevent those citizens from realizing excessive profits from the government contract. The Act applied not only to contracts that arose after the law's enactment but it also applied to uncompleted contracts that the government entered into before the Act's passage. The petitioners challenged the retrospective impact of the measure under the Fifth Amendment.

In sustaining the Renegotiation Act the Court emphasized the history of the Act as a part of the nation's wartime posture. The Court suggested that Congress could have appropriated private enterprise and placed it into a governmental unit for wartime production.[13]

---

test for the constitutionality of retroactive legislation lists three major considerations: (1) the nature of the public interest involved; (2) the extent to which the statute modifies the pre-enactment right; and (3) the nature of the pre-enactment right. Id. These considerations, however, allow the Court to assess the weight of each factor. Even Hochman separates out certain types of legislation for specific discussion. 73 Harv.L.Rev. at 703–08.

7. See Hochman, supra note 2, at 698–99.

8. Slawson, Constitutional and Legislative Considerations in Retroactive Lawmaking, 48 Calif.L.Rev. 216, 238 (1960).

9. Id.

10. See Hochman, supra note 2, at 697–700, 715–17, 724–25.

11. These statements were made in Pension Benefit Guaranty Corp. v. R. A. Gray and Co., 467 U.S. 717, 730, 104 S.Ct. 2709, 2718, 81 L.Ed.2d 601, 611 (1984).

12. 334 U.S. 742, 68 S.Ct. 1294, 92 L.Ed. 1694 (1948).

13. 334 U.S. at 766–67, 68 S.Ct. at 1307–08.

Congress, however, by enacting this law did less and preserved private enterprise. Therefore, because Congress unquestionably had the power to act substantively in this area, the Court deferred to the legislative judgment on what was the best approach to restrain private enterprise in an emergency.

In most emergency situations the nature of the public interest involved is great.[14] In *Lichter* the Court recognized the need to prevent individuals from profiteering from wartime conditions. Consequently, if the constitutionality of emergency measures is questioned, the Court usually will sustain the legislation despite its retrospective effect. The nature of the public interest will outweigh the traditional reasons for viewing such legislation unfavorably. But the Supreme Court, will not always sustain emergency retroactive legislation, as illustrated by *Louisville Joint Stock Land Bank v. Radford.*[15]

In *Radford*, the Court invalidated an emergency depression measure because it substantially reduced the value of existing mortgages. Although the Court recognized the public interest of saving existing farms from mortgage foreclosure, the retrospective impact of the legislation deprived the mortgagees of the value of their mortgages without due process of law. However, two years later the Court upheld a federal statute modified in light of the *Radford* decision: the new statute gave the farmer normally a three-year stay of foreclosure rather than an absolute one; the property, though possessed by the debtor-farmer, was under the custody, supervision, and control of the court. If the debtor failed to pay the reasonable rental, or failed to comply with court orders, or it became evident that he could not reasonably rehabilitate himself financially within the three-year period, or if

the emergency ceased to exist, the court could terminate the stay and order a sale.[16]

Curative Statutes. The category of cases where the constitutionality of curative statutes is an issue presents another area where the Court will almost always sustain retroactive legislation. Curative statutes are those measures that will either ratify prior official conduct or make a remedial adjustment in an administrative scheme.[17]

The Court confronted and sustained a curative statute in *FHA v. The Darlington, Inc.*[18] Congress had authorized the Federal Housing Administration to insure mortgages on residential housing for veterans of World War II. The FHA had established a policy that housing mortgaged under the FHA program must be residential housing exclusively and not housing for transients. In 1954 the Congress ratified that policy by amending the Veterans Emergency Housing Act of 1946 with a provision that codified the FHA policy. The appellee had constructed an apartment building under the FHA program that contained some rentals for transients. When Congress adopted the 1954 Amendment, the appellee sought a declaratory judgment that the Amendment was unconstitutional if it applied to his building. He contended that a retrospective reading of the Amendment would violate his right to due process of law. The Court rejected his argument.

The Court in *Darlington* noted that the appellee was not penalized for anything done in the past. On the contrary, the Court found that the Act had only a prospective effect. Moreover, the Court stated that "federal regulation of future action based upon rights previously acquired by the person regulated is not prohibited by the Constitution. So long as the Constitution authorizes the subsequently enacted legislation, the fact that its provisions limit or interfere with previously acquired

14. Hochman, supra note 2, at 697–98.

15. 295 U.S. 555, 55 S.Ct. 854, 79 L.Ed. 1593 (1935).

16. Wright v. Vinton Branch of the Mountain Trust Bank, 300 U.S. 440, 57 S.Ct. 556, 81 L.Ed. 736 (1937). Cf. Home Building & Loan Ass'n v. Blaisdell, 290 U.S. 398, 54 S.Ct. 231, 78 L.Ed. 413 (1934).

17. Slawson, Constitutional and Legislative Considerations is Retroactive Lawmaking, 48 Calif.L.Rev. 216, 238–39 (1960).

18. 358 U.S. 84, 79 S.Ct. 141, 3 L.Ed.2d 132 (1958).

rights does not condemn it." [19]

Several reasons help explain the Court's willingness to sustain curative or remedial legislation. First, curative statutes often are the result of previous court decisions which overrule certain administrative conduct.[20] In these situations the legislature is only following a judicial suggestion on how to eliminate a defect in the existing statutory scheme and the curative legislation is simply correcting the statutory flaw. Second, the courts recognize a "strong public interest in the smooth functioning of the government."[21] Remedial statutes remove unintended flaws in existing legislation and help give full effect to the legislative intent behind the initial legislation.

The reasons for upholding curative legislation help explain the almost uniform rejection of the arguments against the constitutionality of the "Portal-to-Portal Pay Act of 1947." In *Anderson v. Mount Clemens Pottery Co.*[22] the Supreme Court gave an unexpected and expansive interpretation to the Fair Labor Standards Act. The Supreme Court interpretation exposed coal mine operators to a potential liability of over five billion dollars in claims of their employees. To remove this liability the Congress passed the Portal-to-Portal Act, which eliminated both the right to sue for the overtime pay claim at issue in *Anderson* and the jurisdiction of the courts to hear such claims. This retroactive measure not only cured a defect in the existing legislation that arose because of the Court's interpretation of

that legislation but it also gave full effect to the original congressional intent behind the Fair Labor Standards Act.[23] The courts which heard the arguments against the constitutionality of the Portal-to-Portal Act rejected those arguments because they realized that "the authority of the legislative body to validate voluntary transactions which at the time they were entered into were by statute invalid or illegal has been repeatedly upheld".[24]

Retroactive Tax Legislation. As noted in other sections of this Chapter, retroactive legislation may violate the ex post facto clauses or the contracts clause under limited circumstances.[25] The due process clauses of the Fifth Amendment and Fourteenth Amendments do not place significant restrictions on retroactive legislation. The Supreme Court, in a series of cases that spanned two-thirds of the twentieth century, established the principle that retroactive legislation will violate due process only if the legislation does not have a rational relationship to a legitimate government interest.

In 1927 and 1928, the Supreme Court invalidated retroactive applications of the newly enacted federal estate tax and federal gift tax without any clear statement of the test being used to determine the compatibility of retroactive tax laws with the due process clause of the Fifth Amendment. In 1927, the Supreme Court invalidated an application of the estate tax that altered the tax consequences of a transaction that had occurred a dozen years

---

19. 358 U.S. at 91, 79 S.Ct. at 146, quoting from Fleming v. Rhodes, 331 U.S. 100, 107, 67 S.Ct. 1140, 1144, 91 L.Ed. 1368 (1947).

20. Hochman, supra note 2, 73 Harv.L.Rev. at 704.

21. 73 Harv.L.Rev. at 705.

22. 328 U.S. 680, 66 S.Ct. 1187, 90 L.Ed. 1515 (1946). See also Jewell Ridge Coal Corp. v. Local No. 6167, 325 U.S. 161, 65 S.Ct. 1063, 89 L.Ed. 1534 (1945); Tennessee Coal, Iron & R. Co. v. Muscoda Local No. 123, 321 U.S. 590, 64 S.Ct. 698, 88 L.Ed. 949 (1944).

See generally, Morgan, The Portal-to-Portal Pay Case, in The Third Branch of Government: 8 Cases in Constitutional Politics 50–83 (C. Prickett & A. Westin eds. 1963), (1944).

23. Greenblatt, Judicial Limitations on Retroactive Civil Legislation, 51 Nw.U.L.Rev. 540, 556–57 (1956).

24. Seese v. Bethlehem Steel Co., 168 F.2d 58, 64 (4th Cir.1948); see also, Thomas v. Carnegie–Illinois Steel Corp., 174 F.2d 711 (3d Cir.1949); Battaglia v. General Motors Corp., 169 F.2d 254, 257 (2d Cir.1948), certiorari denied 335 U.S. 887, 69 S.Ct. 236, 93 L.Ed. 425 (1948).

The Supreme Court never accepted a case where the constitutionality of the Act was challenged; all the cases deciding the constitutionality of the Act were decided either in the lower federal courts or in the state courts. See Greenblatt, Judicial Limitations on Retroactive Civil Legislation, 51 Nw.U.L.Rev. 540, 551–61 (1956); Rotunda, Congressional Power to Restrict the Jurisdiction of the Lower Federal Courts and the Problem of School Busing, 64 Georgetown L.J. 839, 853–59 (1976).

25. See §§ 11.8, 11.9(b), 11.9(c) for examination of contracts clause, ex post facto clause, and bill of attainder clause issues.

before the new federal tax rule.[26] In 1928, the Court invalidated retroactive applications of the new gift tax.[27] A majority of the Justices in these cases found that retroactive applications of a new tax law to economic transactions that had been completed before the enactment of the law were so unreasonable as to violate due process. These rulings were made during an era when the Court used the concept of due process to strike down any law that the Justices believed was an unreasonable limitation on liberty or property rights.[28]

After 1937, the Supreme Court abandoned the use of substantive due process as a means of imposing a reasonableness requirement on all federal and state economic legislation.[29] The change in the Supreme Court's approach to substantive due process has been reflected in the Court's rulings concerning retroactive tax laws. In 1938, in *Welch v. Henry*,[30] the Supreme Court upheld a state tax law that was applied to corporate dividends received two years before the law was enacted. The majority opinion in *Welch* distinguished the Court's earlier rulings concerning gift and estate taxes on the basis that the taxpayer in each of those cases might have refrained from making the gift or bequest if the taxpayer had known that in the future there would be a new tax that would be applied to the transfer. In contrast, a taxpayer who was subject to a modified income tax simply had received income that became subject to a higher tax rate than the taxpayer anticipated.

The Supreme Court has little difficulty in upholding Amendments to income tax laws. Individuals should be on notice that all income may be subject to federal or state taxation at some future time. Income taxes are often modified, or tax rates increased, in order to meet revenue goals of governments. The legislative process is such that changes in the Internal Revenue Code are often considered by Congress for several months prior to their enactment. Statutes modifying the Internal Revenue Code often have a retroactive application of a year or less. The application of such tax changes to a prior tax year is rationally related to the legitimate government interest in raising revenue in accordance with current government economic policies.[31]

The *Welch* decision suggested that the Court might make a distinction between the retroactive application of income taxes and the retroactive application of estate and gift taxes. However, in later cases, the Supreme Court has not given different constitutional treatment to different types of tax legislation. In 1986, the Supreme Court, in *United States v. Hemme*,[32] upheld a statutory change to gift and estate tax deductions and credit provisions. The new tax law had the effect of retroactively denying a portion of an earlier gift tax exemption to persons who died after a certain date. This law involved a transition from separate estate and gift taxes to a unified tax. The change in the tax law was alleged to result in "double taxation" of some gratuitous transfers of wealth. However, the statute in reality only represented an increase in the tax rate on certain types of economic transactions. The Court in *Hemme* found that the due process clause did not bar the application of the higher tax rate, or the so-called "double taxation," for the estates of persons dying after a certain date. But the tax at issue in *Hemme* did not involve a congressional attempt to create and apply a higher tax rate to the estate of persons who had long since died. In other

---

26. Nichols v. Coolidge, 274 U.S. 531, 47 S.Ct. 710, 71 L.Ed. 1184 (1927).

27. Blodgett v. Holden, 275 U.S. 142, 48 S.Ct. 105, 72 L.Ed. 206 (1927); Untermyer v. Anderson, 276 U.S. 440, 48 S.Ct. 353, 72 L.Ed. 645 (1928).

28. For an examination of the rise and fall of substantive due process review of economic legislation see §§ 11.2, 11.3 of this Treatise.

29. See § 11.4 of this Treatise.

30. 305 U.S. 134, 59 S.Ct. 121, 83 L.Ed. 87 (1938).

31. United States v. Darusmont, 449 U.S. 292, 101 S.Ct. 549, 66 L.Ed.2d 513 (1981) (per curiam). The Su-

preme Court in *Darusmont* upheld the retroactive application of 1976 Amendments to the Internal Revenue Code minimum tax provisions to transactions made in the year prior to these Amendments. The Court's opinion stated: "The Court consistently has held that application of an income tax statute to the entire calendar in which the enactment took place does not per se violate the due process clause...." 305 U.S. at 297, 59 S.Ct. at 186.

32. 476 U.S. 558, 106 S.Ct. 2071, 90 L.Ed.2d 538 (1986).

words, Congress had not created a new tax that would be applied to the estates of persons who had died in earlier calendar years.[33]

In *United States v. Carlton*,[34] the Court upheld the application of a 1987 Amendment to the federal estate tax and, in so doing, ruled that all retroactive tax legislation should be subjected only to the rational relationship test regardless of whether the legislation involved estate, gift, or income taxes. The dispute in *Carlton* involved an estate tax deduction for the sale of stock to an employee stock ownership plan. In the Tax Reform Act of 1986, Congress created a special estate tax deduction for half of the proceeds of the sale to an employees' stock ownership plan of the securities of the business entity that employed the members of the plan. The decedent had died in 1985 but her estate tax return was not filed until the close of 1986. In December of 1986, the executor had purchased shares of a large corporation and sold those shares to the corporation's employee stock ownership plan in order to make use of the 1986 deduction. In December of 1987, the estate tax statute was modified so that the deduction would be granted only to the estates of taxpayers who before their death owned the securities which were later sold to the employee stock ownership plan. The Internal Revenue Service then disallowed the deduction for the 1986 transactions of the executor, which had been taken on behalf of the taxpayer who had died in 1985. In *Carlton,* the Justices unanimously upheld this retroactive application of the modified estate tax deduction.

Although the Supreme Court did not emphasize this point, it is important to note that the *Carlton* case did not involve the retroactive application of a wholly new tax to the estate of an individual who had died before the tax statute was enacted. The decedent taxpayer could not have altered her economic plans based upon the section of the estate tax at issue in *Carlton* because both the creation and modification of the estate tax deduction came after the time of her death.

Justice Blackmun wrote a majority opinion for six Justices in *Carlton* in which he stated that the constitutionality of a retroactive tax could not be determined under a formulation that limited "harsh and oppressive taxes." Rather, the majority ruled that retroactive tax legislation should be upheld so long as the legislation did not violate the "prohibition against arbitrary and irrational legislation that applies generally to enactments in this sphere of economic policy."[35] Justice Blackmun found that the lack of notice to the decedent taxpayer, and the executor's reliance on the earlier estate tax law, was not sufficient to find that the retroactive application of the modified estate tax deduction violated due process. Because Congress' purpose in modifying the tax was "neither illegitimate nor arbitrary," the Court upheld the retroactive application of the limitation on the estate tax deduction. The retroactive effect of the 1987 Amendment, which extended for only a little more than one year, was rationally related to

33. See also, United States v. Wells Fargo Bank, 485 U.S. 351, 108 S.Ct. 1179, 99 L.Ed.2d 368 (1988) in which the Supreme Court ruled that Congress had not exempted "project notes" issued by state and local government public agencies from the federal estate tax. The Court found that 1984 federal legislation, eliminating a purported estate tax exemption for such notes, only clarified prior law and did not constitute the retroactive application of an estate tax to previously tax exempt property.

34. 512 U.S. 26, 114 S.Ct. 2018, 129 L.Ed.2d 22 (1994).

35. 512 U.S. at 31, 114 S.Ct. at 2022 (internal quotation marks and citations omitted). The three Justices who concurred in the judgment of the Court, but did not join the majority opinion by Justice Blackmun, were Justices O'Connor, Scalia, and Thomas. Justice O'Connor wrote separately to express her belief that the application of a wholly new tax to a competed transaction might be so

unexpected and arbitrary as to violate the due process clauses. She disassociated herself from language in the majority opinion that seemed to indicate that there would be no realistic judicial review of retroactive tax legislation. United States v. Carlton, 512 U.S. 26, 34, 114 S.Ct. 2018, 2024, 129 L.Ed.2d 22 (1994) (O'Connor, J., concurring in the judgment). Justice Scalia, joined by Justice Thomas, wrote to express the view that the phrase "substantive due process" was meaningless and should not be used, under any circumstances, to justify the judicial creation of constitutional limits on state or federal legislation that were not grounded in specific language or history of the Constitution. These two Justices noted that the retroactive application of the tax in *Carlton* should have been held unconstitutional if substantive due process had any meaning at all. 512 U.S. at 39, 114 S.Ct. at 2026 (Scalia, J., joined by Thomas, J., concurring in the judgment).

Congress' attempt to modify the estate tax so that revenues would not be lessened by the granting of a deduction to those who had made "purely tax-motivated stock transfers." [36]

If a legislature creates a completely new tax, and retroactively applies that tax to economic transactions that occurred many years before the tax was enacted, the retroactive application of the new tax might violate due process. Such a retroactive tax might be ruled to have no relationship to any legitimate legislative purpose regarding revenue raising and economic policy. But there is little possibility that the Supreme Court will rule that any modern tax statute has the type of retroactive character that violates due process. Modern tax statutes are likely to be only variations or modifications of taxes that have been established at earlier times. The retroactive nature of a statutory modification of a prior tax law is likely to be limited to a period of less than several years. Proposed modifications of existing taxes are often considered by a legislature for months or years prior to the enactment of a tax modification statute. Legislatures often will design statutes modifying existing taxes to have some retroactive application in order to avoid having a rush of tax motivated economic transactions made by persons who desire to "beat" the new tax law which is being considered in the legislature. The retroactive modifications to existing taxes are likely to be found to be rationally related to legitimate government interests and, therefore, consistent with the limitations of the due process clauses of the Fifth and Fourteenth Amendments.

Retroactive General Legislation. The concepts of reasonable notice and reasonable expectations are important considerations for the Court when it considers the constitutional validity of general retroactive legislation. If the measure affects a remedy, the Court reasons that no one reasonably can expect a remedy to remain immune from legislative controls, and, consequently, it will sustain the retroactive legislation. However, there is no rigid distinction between "rights" and "remedies." Although modification of a remedy normally does not violate due process, if a governmental change to a contract remedy substantially impairs the value of a person's property it may be judicially reviewed under due process principles.

The Court's decision in *Chase Securities Corp. v. Donaldson*[37] reflects this reasoning. The plaintiff brought an action against the defendant based on an alleged violation of the Minnesota Blue Sky Law. The defendant pleaded the bar of the statute of limitations and on an appeal to the Minnesota Supreme Court he prevailed on that issue. During the process of retrial and appeal, however, the Minnesota legislature removed the statute of limitations for certain classes of blue sky cases. The plaintiff's case fit that category of cases affected by the Minnesota statute, and so the plaintiff reasserted his blue sky cause of action. The defendant contended that the amending legislation violated his right to due process of law.

On appeal to the Supreme Court the defendant presented his Fourteenth Amendment contention. The Court rejected the argument because it reasoned that a statute of limitations does not extinguish a right but only barred the remedy. The plaintiff always had the right to seek recovery from the defendant and the legislation only removed a bar to the remedy. The statute of limitations was a legislative creation and the legislature could remove the statute to allow plaintiffs to pursue their remedy.

The distinction between a right and a remedy, at times, can become hazy. The Court may base the distinction on some type of expectational interest. In cases involving the alteration of statute of limitations, the Court reasons that any reliance on a belief that the legislature will not alter a legislatively created procedural bar to a remedy is unreasonable and cannot rise to the status of a property right. Therefore, the Court will sustain legislation that modifies procedural rules because the expectational interest involved is minimal.

---

36. 512 U.S. at 32, 114 S.Ct. at 2023.

37. 325 U.S. 304, 65 S.Ct. 1137, 89 L.Ed. 1628 (1945).

The Court demonstrates great deference to the legislative judgment on procedural rules with retrospective effects.[38]

Some retrospective general legislation will directly affect property rights. In these cases the Court may demonstrate some reluctance to defer to the legislative judgment. In *Railroad Retirement Board v. Alton Railroad Co.*[39] Congress had adopted a law that required the railroads to establish a pension fund. The fund, however, would cover not only all currently employed workers but also those who had worked for the railroad within the year before Congress adopted the legislation. The Court, in a five to four decision, voided this legislation because of its retrospective impact. In this 1935 decision, the Court stated that the measure violated the due process clause of the Fifth Amendment because it "is not only retroactive in that it [imposes] new burdens [for] transactions long since past and closed; but as to some of the railroad companies it constitutes a naked appropriation of private property upon the basis of transactions with which the owners of property were never connected." The Court apparently found that the railroad operators' interests in receiving the benefits of completed labor had risen to a property right protected by the Fifth Amendment. It must be remembered that this decision was rendered in 1935, by Justices dedicated to the use of substantive due process and the constitutional protection of economic interests.

Although the Court has never overruled *Alton,* the decision in *Usery v. Turner Elkhorn Mining Co.*[40] severely narrowed its precedential importance. Congress had enacted legislation that provided benefits to mine workers who had contracted "black lung" disease. Congress placed some of the financial responsibility for the legislation on the coal mine oper-

ators. The operators contended that the law violated their right to due process of law because it required them to pay benefits to miners who had left mine employment before the effective date of the Act. The operators argued that the Act charged them with a liability that was completely unexpected.

The Court acknowledged that the operators may have been unaware of the danger of the disease. Moreover, the operators may have relied on the current state of the law that had failed to impose any liability on them. Therefore, the Court would not justify the legislation on any theory of deterrence or blameworthiness. Nevertheless, the Court believed the Act met the dictates of due process. Justice Marshall, writing for the Court, first noted that retroactive legislation is not unconstitutional simply "because it upsets otherwise settled expectations." He believed that this measure was justified as a rational method to spread the costs of the mine workers' disabilities to those who have benefitted from their labor. Justice Marshall was unwilling to weigh competing interests to assess the constitutionality of the legislation. He deferred to the legislative judgment and refused "to assess the wisdom of Congress' chosen scheme." The Court was satisfied "that the Act approaches the problem of cost-spreading rationally."[41]

The *Turner Elkhorn Mining* opinion suggests that the legislature generally may overcome the traditional bias against retrospective statutes as long as it rationally relates the legislation to a legitimate governmental purpose. If the legislation does have a rational relationship to a proper governmental end, the Court will uphold the retroactive law even though it may impair recognizable property rights.[42]

---

38. See generally, Gange Lumber Co. v. Rowley, 326 U.S. 295, 66 S.Ct. 125, 90 L.Ed. 85 (1945); Carpenter v. Wabash Ry. Co., 309 U.S. 23, 60 S.Ct. 416, 84 L.Ed. 558 (1940); Funkhouser v. J. B. Preston Co., 290 U.S. 163, 54 S.Ct. 134, 78 L.Ed. 243 (1933).

39. 295 U.S. 330, 55 S.Ct. 758, 79 L.Ed. 1468 (1935) (Roberts, J., for the Court). Hughes, C.J., joined by Brandeis, Stone, and Cardozo, JJ., dissented. 295 U.S. at 374–92, 55 S.Ct. at 773–80.

40. 428 U.S. 1, 96 S.Ct. 2882, 49 L.Ed.2d 752 (1976).

41. 428 U.S. at 19, 96 S.Ct. at 2894.

42. However, if the legislature wishes to destroy property rights retroactively, it should speak clearly. The Supreme Court may refuse to interpret federal statutes in a manner which would grant retroactive application to destroy property rights in order for the Court to avoid making the difficult decision of whether such destruction violates the due process clause. See, e.g., United States v. Security Industrial Bank, 459 U.S. 70, 103 S.Ct. 407, 74 L.Ed.2d 235 (1982), (Bankruptcy Reform Act of 1978 interpreted not to apply retroactively to destroy preexisting

When federal economic legislation restricts private contractual rights a court must determine whether the federal legislation in fact is altering substantive contractual rights in more than a minimal fashion, just as it would if the court was examining the alteration of contractual rights by state legislation under the contracts clause. However, when there is a substantial impairment of contract by federal legislation, and the law is reviewed under the Fifth Amendment due process clause rather than the contracts clause which applies to state legislation, a court will be more lenient in upholding the legislative impairment of contracts. The Supreme Court has stated the principle to be applied as follows:

> "When the contract is a private one, and when the impairing statute is a federal one, the next inquiry [after determining that there is a substantial impairment of contractual obligations] is especially limited, and the judicial scrutiny quite minimal. The party asserting a Fifth Amendment due process violation must overcome a presumption of constitutionality and establish that the legislature has acted in an arbitrary and irrational way."[43]

When the Government Modifies its Own Contractual Obligations. The Court has used a higher level of review to legislation that modifies the government's own contractual obligations than it does to federal legislation that alters or regulates private contracts. When the Court reviews legislation that modifies the government's obligation of contract, it will require more than a rational relationship between the modifying statutes and a governmental purpose before it will sustain the measure.[44]

In *Lynch v. United States*[45] the plaintiffs were beneficiaries of government insurance issued under the War Risk Insurance Act. The plaintiffs sought to recover amounts allegedly due under the insurance contract but the government resisted because Congress had repealed the law creating the insurance. The plaintiffs contended that the repealing measure violated their right to due process. The Supreme Court agreed. The Court stated that rights against the United States arising out of a valid contract receive protection from the Fifth Amendment. Therefore, Congress cannot annul these rights unless the action taken

property rights so as to avoid Fifth Amendment issue but indicating that there was "substantial doubt whether retroactive destruction of the appellees' [preexisting] liens in these cases comports with the Fifth Amendment").

For citations to additional Supreme Court cases on this point, see R. Rotunda & J. Nowak, Treatise on Constitutional Law: Substance and Procedure, § 15.9 (3rd ed. 1999, with annual supplements).

43. National Railroad Passenger Corp. v. Atchison, Topeka & Santa Fe Railway Co., 470 U.S. 451, 472, 105 S.Ct. 1441, 1455, 84 L.Ed.2d 432 (1985) quoting in part Pension Benefit Guaranty Corp. v. R.A. Gray & Co., 467 U.S. 717, 730, 104 S.Ct. 2709, 2718, 81 L.Ed.2d 601 (1984) and Usery v. Turner Elkhorn Mining Co., 428 U.S. 1, 15, 96 S.Ct. 2882, 2892, 49 L.Ed.2d 752 (1976).

In Eastern Enterprises v. Apfel, 524 U.S. 498, 118 S.Ct. 2131, 141 L.Ed.2d 451 (1998) the Court, by a five to four vote of the Justices, but without a majority opinion, invalidated a federal government action that would have required a corporation not currently engaged in the coal mining business to make payments into a fund that would provide health benefits for retired mine workers. Justice Kennedy, in a concurring opinion that was not joined by any other Justice, found that the application of the 1992 Coal Act to the corporation under these circumstances violated substantive due process principles, because it was an "egregious" retroactive application of a law. 524 U.S. at 539, 118 S.Ct. at 2154 (Kennedy, J., concurring in the

judgment and dissenting in part). The *Eastern Enterprises* case is examined in § 11.12 (a).

44. Determining When a Statute Creates Contractual Rights. The courts must be careful not to find that the government has entered into a contract with a private person or corporation unless it is clear that a governmental entity with authority to do so has contracted with the private party in a way that restricts the power of the government to act in the future. While each individual claim that a state or other governmental entity has entered into a contract with a private person or business must be assessed on its own facts, the Supreme Court has indicated that there is a presumption against finding that the government has contracted with private parties to restrict the freedom of future legislative bodies. Keefe v. Clark, 322 U.S. 393, 64 S.Ct. 1072, 88 L.Ed. 1346 (1944); Indiana ex rel. Anderson v. Brand, 303 U.S. 95, 58 S.Ct. 443, 82 L.Ed. 685 (1938); Dodge v. Board of Education, 302 U.S. 74, 58 S.Ct. 98, 82 L.Ed. 57 (1937). The Court found that this "presumption" that a state or local legislature did not intend to bind itself contractually, absent clear indication that a contractual relationship was created between the government and a private party, also applied to cases where federal governmental actions were challenged as violations of the due process clause. National Railroad Passenger Corp. v. Atchison, Topeka & Santa Fe Railway Co., 470 U.S. 451, 467, 105 S.Ct. 1441, 1452, 84 L.Ed.2d 432 (1985).

45. 292 U.S. 571, 54 S.Ct. 840, 78 L.Ed. 1434 (1934).

to void these rights "falls within the federal police power or some other paramount power." [46]

Summary. Much of the literature on retroactive legislation repeats the general proposition that the courts have a bias against such legislation. If, however, the constitutionality of emergency or curative retroactive statutes is challenged, the Supreme Court usually will sustain such legislation because of the overriding public interest that prompted the enactment of the emergency or remedial measure. Moreover, the Court will uphold a retroactive revenue measure either if it is a tax on income or if it is a transfer tax and the taxpayer reasonably could expect that the legislature would retrospectively tax such a transfer of property. Finally, the Court will sustain retroactive general legislation if the law is rationally related to a governmental purpose or if the retrospective law affects a remedy and not a right. On the other hand, the Court will closely review any federal legislation that impairs the government's own obligation of contract.

(b) The Ex Post Facto Clauses

The Constitution contains two *ex post facto* clauses: one that applies to the states[47] and one that applies to the federal government.[48] The clauses limit Congress and state legislatures when enacting penal laws that have a retrospective effect. An *ex post facto* law is a statute that imposes criminal liability on past transactions.[49] Early in its history the Supreme Court determined that the *ex post facto* clauses only prohibited the states and the federal government from passing *criminal or penal* measures that had a retroactive effect.[50]

In his opinion in *Calder v. Bull*,[51] Justice Chase described four types of laws that would clearly violate the *ex post facto* clauses; his description of these categories was still being relied upon by the Court at the close of the twentieth century.[52] Justice Chase described these four types of laws as follows:

---

46. 292 U.S. at 579, 54 S.Ct. at 843. See also, United States Trust Co. v. New Jersey, 431 U.S. 1, 25–26, 97 S.Ct. 1505, 1519, 52 L.Ed.2d 92, 112 (1977): "As with laws impairing the obligation of private contracts, an impairment may be constitutional if it is reasonable and necessary to serve an important public purpose. In applying this standard, however, complete deference to a legislative assessment of reasonableness and necessity is not appropriate because the State's self-interest is at stake." This reasoning should apply by analogy to due process cases.

See United States v. Locke, 471 U.S. 84, 105 S.Ct. 1785, 85 L.Ed.2d 64 (1985) (requiring owners of mining claims on federal lands to submit an annual filing or forfeit the claim is a reasonable property regulation and does not violate the due process clause).

47. U.S.Const. art. I, § 10, cl. 1: "No state shall ... pass any ... ex post facto law."

48. U.S.Const. art. I, § 9, cl. 3: "No ... ex post facto law shall be passed."

49. See, Ex parte Garland, 71 U.S. (4 Wall.) 333, 377, 18 L.Ed. 366 (1866). The ex post facto prohibitions do not invalidate civil legislation. See Watson v. Mercer, 33 U.S. (8 Pet.) 88, 110, 8 L.Ed. 876 (1834); Baltimore and Susquehanna Railroad Co. v. Nesbit, 51 U.S. (10 How.) 395, 401, 13 L.Ed. 469 (1850); Locke v. New Orleans, 71 U.S. (4 Wall.) 172, 18 L.Ed. 334 (1866); Orr v. Gilman, 183 U.S. 278, 285, 22 S.Ct. 213, 216, 46 L.Ed. 196 (1902); Kentucky Union Co. v. Kentucky, 219 U.S. 140, 31 S.Ct. 171, 55 L.Ed. 137 (1911); Bankers' Trust Co. v. Blodgett, 260 U.S. 647, 43 S.Ct. 233, 67 L.Ed. 439 (1923). See also Flemming v. Nestor, 363 U.S. 603, 80 S.Ct. 1367, 4 L.Ed.2d 1435 (1960).

The ex post facto law prohibitions apply only as a bar to legislation and not to judicial decisions. See Frank v.

Mangum, 237 U.S. 309, 35 S.Ct. 582, 59 L.Ed. 969 (1915); Ross v. Oregon, 227 U.S. 150, 33 S.Ct. 220, 57 L.Ed. 458 (1913). A broad judicial interpretation of a statute encompassing conduct not previously addressed by the statute, if applied retroactively, might constitute a violation of due process principles. See Bouie v. Columbia, 378 U.S. 347, 353, 84 S.Ct. 1697, 1702, 12 L.Ed.2d 894 (1964); Marks v. United States, 430 U.S. 188, 97 S.Ct. 990, 51 L.Ed.2d 260 (1977). But see Splawn v. California, 431 U.S. 595, 97 S.Ct. 1987, 52 L.Ed.2d 606 (1977); Ginzburg v. United States, 383 U.S. 463, 86 S.Ct. 942, 16 L.Ed.2d 31 (1966).

50. Calder v. Bull, 3 U.S. (3 Dall.) 386, 390, 397, 1 L.Ed. 648 (1798). At the close of the twentieth century, 200 years after the *Calder* decision, Justice Thomas expressed the view that he would be "willing to reconsider *Calder* and its progeny to determine whether a retroactive civil law that passes muster under our current takings clause jurisprudence is nonetheless unconstitutional under the ex post facto clause." Eastern Enterprises v. Apfel, 524 U.S. 498, 538, 118 S.Ct. 2131, 2154, 141 L.Ed.2d 451 (1998). (Thomas, J., concurring). No other Justice in the *Eastern Enterprises* case joined Justice Thomas's concurrence. The *Eastern Enterprises* case is examined in § 11.12 (a) of this Treatise.

51. 3 U.S. (3 Dall.) 386, 1 L.Ed. 648 (1798). See § 11.1 regarding the individual opinions of Justices Iredell and Chase in *Calder* and the continuing debate concerning the legitimacy of court invalidation of statutes for any reason that is not based on the text of the Constitution or its amendments.

52. For example, *Calder* was cited in the majority opinion in Lynce v. Mathis, 519 U.S. 433, 441 n. 13, 117 S.Ct. 891, 895, n. 13, 137 L.Ed.2d 63 (1997).

"1st. Every law that makes an action done before the passing of the law and which was innocent when done, criminal; and punishes such action. 2d. Every law that aggravates a crime, or makes it greater than it was, when committed. 3d. Every law that changes the punishment and inflicts a greater punishment, than the law annexed to the crime, when committed. 4th. Every law that alters the legal rules of evidence, and receives less, or different testimony, than the law required at the time of the commission of the offence, in order to convict the offender."[53]

In order to decide whether a law violates the *ex post facto* clauses, a court must determine whether the law constitutes a retroactive criminal penalty. Determining whether a law has increased punishment for a crime may be difficult. The Supreme Court has looked at objective factors to determine whether a law retroactively increases a criminal penalty, or imposes a criminal penalty for actions that were innocent when done. The Court has never resolved the question of whether a retroactive law affecting the criminal process (but which did not increase the penalty for an action taken prior to the new legislature) should be deemed to be a criminal penalty merely because the persons in the legislature who passed the law were motivated by a desire to punish individuals who had committed certain crimes.

If, at the time a defendant is convicted of a crime, statutes set a penalty with a statutory sentence reduction through "good-time credits", a later law rescinding the good-time credits that would have applied to the defendant's sentence (thereby increasing the actual amount of time that would have to be served towards a sentence before the possibility of

"early release") may constitute a violation of the *ex post facto* clauses. The effects of a statute rescinding the good time credits, rather than legislative intent, will be used by the judiciary to determine whether the statute violates the *ex post facto* clause.[54]

The typical retrospective law that will violate either *ex post facto* clause is a statute that imposes a criminal penalty for past conduct that was lawful when performed. Moreover, a law that imposes a harsher penalty or a potentially harsher penalty for unlawful conduct than existed before the passage of the law will also violate the *ex post facto* prohibition.[55] Even a statute altering penal provisions "accorded by the grace of the legislature" violates the *ex post facto* clause if the statute is both retrospective and harsher than the law in effect at the time of the offense. For example, in *Weaver v. Graham*,[56] the Supreme Court held that a Florida law which retrospectively reduced the good time credits available to a prisoner violated the *ex post facto* clause.

An *ex post facto* clause violation involves both a change to substantive law and the application of the changed law to a particular defendant. There are three types of *ex post facto* violations. First, the application of a statute to a defendant that would impose a criminal punishment on him for taking an act that was innocent (not punishable under the criminal law) when he took the act would violate the clause. Second, application to a defendant of a statute that increased the punishment for the crime the defendant committed (from the punishment that existed under the substantive law applicable to the defendant's crime at the time that he committed it) would violate the clause. Third, applying, to a

A law that retroactively takes away the availability of parole hearings that were guaranteed to prisoners at the time the defendant committed his crime may constitute a violation of the ex post facto clauses. For references to additional cases on this point, see the multivolume edition of this Treatise: R. Rotunda & J. Nowak, Treatise on Constitutional Law: Substance and Procedure § 15.9 (3rd ed. 1999, with annual supplements).

53. Calder v. Bull, 3 U.S. (3 Dall.) 386, 390, 1 L.Ed. 648 (1798) (emphasis deleted).

54. Lynce v. Mathis, 519 U.S. 433, 443, 117 S.Ct. 891, 897, 137 L.Ed.2d 63 (1997): "Whether such a purpose [a legislature passing bills for the purpose of increasing punishment of already convicted persons] alone would be a sufficient basis for concluding that a law violated the *Ex Post Facto Clause* when it actually had no such effect [the statute did not, in fact, increase the punishment of individuals retroactively] is a question the Court has never addressed."

55. Lindsey v. Washington, 301 U.S. 397, 57 S.Ct. 797, 81 L.Ed. 1182 (1937).

56. 450 U.S. 24, 101 S.Ct. 960, 67 L.Ed.2d 17 (1981).

defendant's case, a law that removed a defense to the crime that was available under the substantive law at the time that the defendant committed the crime would be an *ex post facto* clause violation.[57]

A mere change in the type of penalty, however, will not violate the provisions. If, for example, a state properly had imposed the death penalty on an individual, altering the form of capital punishment from death by hanging to death by electrocution would not violate the constitutional prohibition on *ex post facto* laws.[58] Moreover, the *ex post facto* clauses do not prevent the state legislatures or Congress from reducing either the harshness of a penalty or the scope of an existing penal statute.[59] Finally, a legislature can impose a penalty on a person for continuing once lawful conduct that the legislature has subsequently declared illegal.[60]

When Is a Law Penal for Ex Post Facto Purposes? An issue which often arises when a law is challenged under an *ex post facto* clause is whether the legislature has actually imposed a penalty for past conduct.[61] The Supreme Court labeled as punitive a post-Civil War law that required attorneys to take an oath before they could practice law in federal court.[62] The attorneys had to swear that they had not participated in the rebellion against the Union. The law was punitive because the taking of the oath had no relationship to the

professional duties of attorneys.[63] Hence, the Court found the law was penal in nature and applied to past conduct. The Court held that the law violated the *ex post facto* clause and was unconstitutional.[64]

On the other hand, laws that require deportation for past conduct,[65] or statutes that deny future privileges to convicted offenders because of their previous criminal activities, have been held not to impose penalties for past conduct.[66] Such measures do not violate the *ex post facto* prohibitions.

The Court has ruled that a statute designed to require the commitment of a person as a "sexually violent predator" was civil in nature, and that the statute could be applied to a prison inmate who was scheduled for release when the statute was enacted. In *Kansas v. Hendricks*[67] the Court held, as it had previously, that a state law allowing for the commitment of a person to a mental health care facility on the basis of the government proving, by clear and convincing evidence, that the individual was dangerous to himself or to others due to a mental disease, defect, or abnormality was not a criminal punishment.[68] The issue that divided the Justices in *Hendricks* related to the fact that the statute was being applied to a prison inmate who was scheduled for release when the statute was enacted. By a five to four vote, the Justices found that the

---

57. The Supreme Court uses this three pronged analysis when determining whether a particular application of a law to a defendant violates one of the *ex post facto* clauses. See, e.g., Collins v. Youngblood, 497 U.S. 37, 110 S.Ct. 2715, 111 L.Ed.2d 30 (1990); Beazell v. Ohio, 269 U.S. 167, 46 S.Ct. 68, 70 L.Ed. 216 (1925).

58. Malloy v. South Carolina, 237 U.S. 180, 35 S.Ct. 507, 59 L.Ed. 905 (1915).

59. Rooney v. North Dakota, 196 U.S. 319, 325, 25 S.Ct. 264, 265–66, 49 L.Ed. 494 (1905).

60. Samuels v. McCurdy, 267 U.S. 188, 45 S.Ct. 264, 69 L.Ed. 568 (1925).

61. See Flemming v. Nestor, 363 U.S. 603, 614–17, 80 S.Ct. 1367, 1374–76, 4 L.Ed.2d 1435 (1960) (deported alien's loss of Social Security benefits nonpunitive and valid).

62. Ex parte Garland, 71 U.S. (4 Wall.) 333, 18 L.Ed. 366 (1866).

63. See Cummings v. Missouri, 71 U.S. (4 Wall.) 277, 316, 18 L.Ed. 356 (1866) (companion case to Ex parte Garland).

64. Ex parte Garland, 71 U.S. (4 Wall.) 333, 381, 18 L.Ed. 366 (1866).

65. Marcello v. Bonds, 349 U.S. 302, 75 S.Ct. 757, 99 L.Ed. 1107 (1955).

66. See Hawker v. New York, 170 U.S. 189, 190, 18 S.Ct. 573, 574, 42 L.Ed. 1002 (1898) (physician barred from practicing medicine for a prior felony conviction); De Veau v. Braisted, 363 U.S. 144, 80 S.Ct. 1146, 4 L.Ed.2d 1109 (1960), rehearing denied 364 U.S. 856, 81 S.Ct. 30, 5 L.Ed.2d 80 (1960) (convicted felons' exclusion from employment as officers of waterfront union is neither a bill of attainder nor a violation of the ex post facto clause).

67. 521 U.S. 346, 117 S.Ct. 2072, 138 L.Ed.2d 501 (1997).

68. See, e.g., Addington v. Texas, 441 U.S. 418, 99 S.Ct. 1804, 60 L.Ed.2d 323 (1979); Foucha v. Louisiana, 504 U.S. 71, 112 S.Ct. 1780, 118 L.Ed.2d 437 (1992). The procedural due process requirements, concerning whether a commitment proceeding is fundamentally fair, are examined in §§ 13.4, 13.9 of this Treatise.

statute, and as written as applied to Mr. Hendricks, was not punitive in nature and that it did not increase his criminal penalty. Therefore, the Court ruled that the statute violated neither the *ex post facto* nor the double jeopardy clauses.[69]

Procedural Changes. Laws that alter rules of criminal procedure but do not affect the substantive rights of the defendant are not violative of the *ex post facto* clause even though the legislature makes the change during the process of the trial.[70] Laws, for example, that change the number of appellate judges[71] or enlarge the potential class of competent witnesses do not affect substantive rights and are constitutional.[72] Such laws do not impose an increased penalty for past conduct.[73]

The Supreme Court has held that a law which changed the procedures for imposition of the death penalty could be applied to a person whose crime predated the change. In *Dobbert v. Florida*[74] the defendant had been

---

69. Justice Thomas's majority opinion in *Hendricks* found that the definition used by the statute for describing persons who could be civilly committed for mental health care was not so arbitrary as to violate substantive due process standards. Because the majority ruled that the statute was not punitive in nature, it held that there could be no violation of the *ex post facto* or double jeopardy clauses in the application of the statute to the previously convicted defendant. Kansas v. Hendricks, 521 U.S. 346, 359–67, 117 S.Ct. 2072, 2081–85, 138 L.Ed.2d 501 (1997). Justice Kennedy pointed out that all nine Justices appeared to agree that the state could confine persons who were dangerous to themselves or others due to some type of mental disease or mental abnormality, and that the dispute in this case involved only whether the application of the statute to Mr. Hendricks was punitive in nature so as to violate the *ex post facto* clause. 521 U.S. at 371, 117 S.Ct. at 2087 (Kennedy, J., concurring). Four Justices believed that the statute as applied to the defendant in the case, who had been scheduled for release from prison when the statute was enacted, constituted an increase in his criminal sentence and a violation of the *ex post facto* clause. 521 U.S. at 371, 117 S.Ct. at 2087 (Breyer, J., joined by Stevens and Souter, JJ., and, in part, Ginsburg, J., dissenting).

In Seling v. Young, 531 U.S. 250, 121 S.Ct. 727, 148 L.Ed.2d 734 (2001), on remand 248 F.3d 1197 (9th Cir. 2001) the Supreme Court rejected an "as applied" challenge to a statute providing for the civil commitment of sexually dangerous predators, that was almost identical to the statute upheld in *Hendricks*. Eight Justices found that an act that was civil in nature could not be challenged as being a criminal punishment simply due to the way an individual who had been subject to civil commitment was treated by state authorities. Writing for seven Justices in *Seling*, Justice O'Connor stated that the determination of whether a statute was criminal or civil in nature must involve an examination of the (1) language of the statute, (2) the legislative history of the statute, and (3) the purpose and effect of the statute. If that analysis determined that the statutory commitment was civil in nature, the commitment of an individual to a mental health care facility, even if it was housed within a prison setting, did not subject the individual to double jeopardy (because he had already completed his sentence for a sex-related crime) or give rise to an ex-post facto claim (if the statute was written and applied to the individual after the date of his most recent sex-related crime). The majority opinion noted that an individual subject to civil commitment could still claim that the conditions of confinement were so

substandard as to violate substantive due process; the person could also claim that the procedures used to keep him committed to the mental health program violated procedural due process principles.

In Smith v. Doe, 538 U.S. 84, 123 S.Ct. 1140, 155 L.Ed.2d 164 (2003) the Supreme Court, by a 6 to 3 vote, found that a state sex offender registration law was civil in nature and that its application to persons who had been properly convicted of sex related offenses before the date of passage of the law did not violate the *ex post facto* clause of Article I, § 10.

In Connecticut Department of Public Safety v. Doe, 538 U.S. 1, 123 S.Ct. 1160, 155 L.Ed.2d 98 (2003) the Justices unanimously held that a sex offender registration law could be applied to an individual who had been properly convicted of sex related crimes without giving that individual an additional hearing to determine whether he was in fact, dangerous.

In a concurring opinion in *Connecticut Department of Public Safety* in which they cited this Treatise, Justices Souter and Ginsburg explained that, even after this decision, the individual could litigate the question of whether the law limited his liberty interest, in violation of substantive due process principles, or whether the classifications in the law, regarding which convicted criminals would be subject to the registry system, violated equal protection 538 U.S. at ___, 123 S.Ct. at 1165, 1166 (Souter, J., joined by Ginsburg, J., concurring).

70. See Duncan v. Missouri, 152 U.S. 377, 14 S.Ct. 570, 38 L.Ed. 485 (1894).

71. 152 U.S. at 382, 14 S.Ct. at 571–72.

72. Hopt v. Utah, 110 U.S. 574, 589, 4 S.Ct. 202, 209–10, 28 L.Ed. 262 (1884).

73. Neither the Congress nor state legislatures cannot evade the proscription of the *ex post facto* clauses by fashioning a civil statute out of what is basically a criminal measure. See, Burgess v. Salmon, 97 U.S. (7 Otto) 381, 24 L.Ed. 1104 (1878). However, when no substantive right is impaired, procedural changes are within the discretion of the legislature. See Portley v. Grossman, 444 U.S. 1311, 100 S.Ct. 714, 62 L.Ed.2d 723 (1980) (Opinion of Rehnquist, J., as Circuit Justice) (no ex post facto violation for the parole commission to apply current standards for parole rather than the standards in effect at the time of sentencing).

74. 432 U.S. 282, 97 S.Ct. 2290, 53 L.Ed.2d 344 (1977).

sentenced to death for murder in Florida. When the defendant committed the murder, Florida had a statute imposing the death sentence for that crime. However the state supreme court struck down the procedures for imposition of the sentence in accordance with prior decisions of the Supreme Court of the United States. Thereafter the state legislature passed a new statute for imposition of the penalty which met current constitutional standards. The defendant was sentenced under this statute and the Supreme Court of the United States upheld this sentence. The majority opinion reasoned that this new statute was only a change in procedure because the old statute had declared that murder was a capital offense, thus giving the defendant fair notice. Since the new statute made imposition of the penalty more difficult, the majority saw it as "ameliorative."

While the *Dobbert* majority thus made the decision fit within established doctrine, it seems difficult to dispute the dissent's argument that there was no valid means of imposing the death sentence in Florida when the defendant committed the crime.[75] The majority dismissed this argument summarily, but the point seems well taken because the ability to revise an invalid punishment and apply it to persons whose identities or characteristics are

already fixed and knowable by the law makers can be readily abused. The basic principle of the clauses would seem to deny a legislative power to design sentences for application to such persons. But this position was only recognized by the dissenters.

When a legislature changes procedures that apply to the sentencing of a convicted criminal between the date of the crime and the date of a defendant's sentencing, the courts must determine whether the statutory changes are truly procedural or whether they effectively increase the nature of the penalty for the previously committed crime. If the sentencing procedures change the nature of the punishment for the crime they cannot be applied to a defendant who committed the crime before the date when the statutory changes became effective.[76]

Recent Decisions. The second category of legislative actions that would constitute an *ex post facto* law set out by Justice Chase related to "every law that aggravates a crime or makes it greater than it was, when committed." Until the twenty-first century, it was unclear whether the extension of a statute of limitations for prosecution of a crime would constitute an increased punishment that

---

75. 432 U.S. at 303, 307, 97 S.Ct. at 2303, 2305 (Stevens, J., dissenting, joined by Brennan and Marshall, JJ.).

76. In Collins v. Youngblood, 497 U.S. 37, 110 S.Ct. 2715, 111 L.Ed.2d 30 (1990), the defendant had been convicted of aggravated sexual abuse. The jury, as the sentencing authority in the case, sentenced the defendant to life imprisonment and a fine of $10,000. After his conviction had been affirmed in the state courts, he applied for a state writ of habeas corpus. In that collateral attack on his conviction, he argued that state law did not authorize a jury to impose a monetary fine in addition to a term of imprisonment for the crime for which he had been convicted. He might have been entitled to a new trial, based on the state law that existed at the time of his criminal act and his original trial. However, after his conviction, the state had enacted a statute that allowed an appellate court to reform an improper verdict that assessed a punishment not authorized by law and to uphold a conviction after reforming such a verdict. Relying on that statute, the state appellate court reformed the verdict in the defendant's case by deleting the monetary punishment and upheld his conviction and jail sentence. The Supreme Court of the United States found that the statute, and the state's use of the statute in this case, did not constitute an *ex post facto* law. The law did not punish an act that was innocent when done. Nor did it increase the punishment for a crime after its commission. The law did

not deprive this defendant of any defense to the criminal charge that was available to him at the time when he committed the criminal act. The majority opinion in *Collins*, by Chief Justice Rehnquist, found that a legislature could not protect a law from the *ex post facto* clauses merely by labelling the law "procedural." Chief Justice Rehnquist found that courts had to make an independent determination as to whether a change in law changed the penalties for a crime, or the defenses available to a defendant, in a way that violated the *ex post facto* clause. The mere fact that the law disadvantaged a defendant by making it less likely that his conviction would be overturned did not, in itself, establish an *ex post facto* clause violation. If the law did increase the punishment for an offense (from the time when it was committed) or denied a defendant a defense that would have been available to him at the time he committed the crime, then the law would violate the *ex post facto* clause. In *Collins*, the Court overruled Kring v. Missouri, 107 U.S. 221, 2 S.Ct. 443, 27 L.Ed. 506 (1883) and overruled in part Thompson v. Utah, 170 U.S. 343, 18 S.Ct. 620, 42 L.Ed. 1061 (1898) because those decisions indicated that a law might violate the *ex post facto* clauses merely because the law made it easier to convict the defendant or to uphold a defendant's conviction.

would be invalid under Justice Chase's description of prohibited *ex post facto* clause legislation.

In *Stogner v. California*[77] the Supreme Court, by a 5 to 4 vote of the Justices, held that a law that was enacted after a previously applicable statute of limitations period had run for a criminal activity violated the *ex post facto* clause in Article I § 10 when the law was applied to a previously time-barred prosecution. The *Stogner* case involved a 1998 criminal statute that allowed for prosecution of sex-related crimes to children within one year of a victim's report to the police, even if the crime had been committed at a time when there was a specific statute of limitations that would have barred prosecution for the offense. Because of the new California law, which was enacted in 1998, the defendant was indicted for sex-related child abuse activities committed prior to 1974. At the time that the alleged crimes had been committed by the defendant, California had had a three year statute of limitations regarding the sex abuse crimes. United States Supreme Court, in an opinion by Justice Breyer, held that defendant could not be prosecuted for the crimes for which the statute of limitations had previously been expired without a violation of the *ex post facto* clause. Justice Breyer's majority opinion in *Stogner* did not rule on whether extensions of unexpired statutes of limitations would violate the *ex post facto* clause. Justice Breyer stated the Court's conclusion narrowly: "We conclude that a law enacted after expiration of a previously applicable limitations period violates the

ex post facto clause when it is applied to revive a previously time-barred prosecution."[78]

The fourth category of *ex post facto* law set forth by Justice Chase related to laws that altered the rules of evidence so that "less or different testimony" could be used to convict the defendant than were required at the time that the defendant committed the crime. Laws that merely change evidentiary rules, such as laws that increase the types of people who can be witnesses at a trial, would not constitute an *ex post facto* law because the law would neither increase the defendant's punishment nor lower the type or amount of evidence that could be used to establish the defendant's criminality. It is sometimes difficult to determine whether a law that nominally changes only evidentiary rules actually is a law that changed the quantum of proof necessary to convict a defendant, similar to a law that would remove a defense to the crime that was available under the substantive law at the time that the defendant committed the offense.

In *Carmell v. Texas*[79] the Court examined a case in which a man had been convicted of twenty criminal charges relating to his sexual assault and sexual abuse of his stepdaughter when she was between the ages of 12 to 16 years old. Prior to the defendant's trial, state law did not allow a person to be convicted of an alleged sexual offense against another person based on the uncorroborated testimony of the victim, unless the victim was younger than 14 years of age at the time of the offense. If

---

77. ___ U.S. ___, 123 S.Ct. 2446, 156 L.Ed.2d 544 (2003).

78. ___ U.S. at ___, 123 S.Ct. at 2461. Four Justices dissented in *Stogner* because they believed that majority's historical analysis of the *ex post facto* clauses and cases construing them were flawed. ___ U.S. at ___, 123 S.Ct. at 2461 (Kennedy, J., joined by Rehnquist, C.J., and Scalia and Thomas, JJ., dissenting).

The Supreme Court, in Garner v. Jones, 529 U.S. 244, 120 S.Ct. 1362, 146 L.Ed.2d 236 (2000) ruled that a statutory change that set the required time for parole hearings for persons incarcerated for life sentences to eight years, whereas the statutes had required consideration of parole for such persons every three years when the defendant committed his crime, did not in itself constitute an ex-post facto clause violation. The fact that the hearings were less frequent, and had fewer procedural safeguards (including the absence of formal hearings

where an attorney could be present), did not constitute a per se violation of the clause when applied to a defendant whose crime had been committed when statutes with more favorable parole hearing procedures were in effect. The Supreme Court found that, based on *Morales*, the ultimate inquiry was whether the new statute in its operation, and as applied to the defendant, "created a significant risk of increased punishment" and that the court of appeals and lower federal courts had failed to establish a record on which the Supreme Court could come to a final conclusion. Therefore, the case was remanded to the lower federal courts for a determination, in light of all facts in the case, of whether application of the law to the defendant would violate the ex-post facto clause. 529 U.S. at 256, 120 S.Ct. at 1371.

79. 529 U.S. 513, 120 S.Ct. 1620, 146 L.Ed.2d 577 (2000).

the victim was under 14 years of age at the time of the offense then the victim's testimony, alone, could convict the accused. Before a defendant's trial state law was amended to allow convictions for such crimes based solely on the uncorroborated statement of a victim who was under 18 years of age at the time that the alleged offense occurred. In the *Carmel* case, the defendant was convicted of fifteen counts in total. There was no ex-post facto issue regarding eleven of the counts, in part because six of the counts related to crimes that were committed when the victim was under 14 years of age and other counts involved offenses committed after the state law went into effect that allowed for conviction based on the uncorroborated testimony of a person over the age of 14 but under the age of 18. The issue in *Carmell* related to the fact that the defendant was convicted on four counts of sexually abusing the victim for acts that occurred when the child was 14 years of age or older and when the state evidentiary law would not have allowed conviction on those offenses based solely on the uncorroborated testimony of an alleged victim over 14 years of age.[80] By a 5 to 4 vote, the Supreme Court ruled that the defendant's conviction on those four counts of alleged sex-

ual abuse, based solely on the uncorroborated testimony of the victim, violated the ex-post facto clause. The Court described the statutory change as one that reduced the "minimum quantum of evidence necessary to sustain a conviction."[81] For that reason, the majority in *Carmell* ruled that the law could not be applied retroactively to an offense that had been committed when a higher quantum of evidence was required for conviction. The four dissenting Justices in *Carmell* believed that the law did not act so as to change the quantum of evidence necessary but, rather, merely allowed the testimony of a person between the ages of 14 and 18 to be considered credible.[82]

(c) Bills of Attainder

Traditionally, bills of attainder were legislative acts that imposed the death penalty without the usual judicial proceedings on persons allegedly guilty of serious crimes.[83] If the legislature imposed a lesser punishment than the death penalty, the measure was a bill of pains and penalties.[84] The Constitution contains two bills of attainder clauses—one that applies to the states [85] and one that applies to the federal government.[86] The Court has held that the provisions prohibit both bills of at-

---

80. In fact the victims testimony might have been considered corroborated however, that issue was not before the United States Supreme Court. 529 U.S. at 519 n. 4, 120 S.Ct. at 1626 n. 4.

81. 529 U.S. at 528, 120 S.Ct. at 1631.

82. Carmell v. Texas, 529 U.S. 513, 551, 120 S.Ct. 1620, 1643, 146 L.Ed.2d 577 (2000) (Ginsburg, J., joined by Rehnquist, C.J., and O'Connor and Kennedy, JJ., dissenting).

If a law is not retroactive, and does not increase punishment, it cannot be a violation of the ex-post facto clause. In Johnson v. United States, 529 U.S. 694, 120 S.Ct. 1795, 146 L.Ed.2d 727 (2000) the Court examined a situation in which a person had been given a maximum sentence of 25 months imprisonment and three years of "supervised release" for committing a federal crime. The individual was released early due to receiving "good-conduct credits", but seven months after his release he was arrested for other crimes. The original sentencing court reversed the person's supervised release and imposed an additional prison term of 18 months to be followed by another year of supervised release. The defendant claimed that it was a new statute that allowed the judge to add an additional period of supervised release to his sentence and that this application of the law violated the ex-post facto clause. The Supreme Court ruled that federal statutes at the time that the defendant committed the original crime, and at

the time he was originally sentenced, allowed district courts to impose additional terms of supervised release as well as additional months of incarceration for violating a condition on the defendant's original incarceration and supervised release. Thus, the federal law concerning his sentence, and the amount of time he would have to spend under supervised release, was the same both when he committed his original crime and when his original supervised release was revoked.

83. See generally, J. Story, Commentaries on the Constitution of the United States, § 1338 (1833); Berger, Bills of Attainder: A Study of Amendment by the Court, 63 Cornell L.Rev. 355 (1978); Ely, United States v. Lovett: Litigating the Separation of Powers, 10 Harv.C.R.–C.L.L.Rev. 1 (1975); Note, The Bounds of Legislative Specification: A Suggested Approach to the Bill of Attainder Clause, 72 Yale L.J. 330 (1962).

Because these cases involved the freedoms of speech and association, these cases are dealt with in §§ 16.41–16.44, infra.

84. J. Story, supra note 1.

85. U.S.Const. art. I, § 10, cl. 1: "No State shall . . . pass any Bill of Attainder."

86. U.S.Const. art. I, § 9, cl. 3: "No Bill of Attainder . . . shall be passed."

tainder and bills of pains and penalties.[87]

The bill of attainder provisions prohibit the state or federal legislatures from assuming judicial functions and conducting trials.[88] Consequently, the clauses proscribe any legislative act "no matter what [its] form, that appl[ies] either to named individuals or to easily ascertainable members of a group in such a way as to inflict *punishment* on them without a judicial trial."[89] This clause only protects individuals, not entities such as states.[90]

Because any legislative act which employs a classification might be said to burden or punish the class of persons who do not receive the benefits established by the legislation or who are disadvantaged by the classification, the Supreme Court has developed various tests to determine when the law inflicts prohibited punishment: the mere fact that a law imposes burdensome consequences does not mean that there is the forbidden "punishment." Rather the courts must determine first whether the law imposes a punishment "traditionally judged to be prohibited by the Bill of Attainder Clause."[91] Such historical punishments include "imprisonment, banishment, and the punitive confiscation of property by the sovereign, [and] a legislative enactment barring designated individuals or groups from participation in specified employments or vocations, a mode of punishment commonly employed against those legislatively banded as disloyal."[92]

Second, in addition to this historical test, the Court has developed a functional test: can the law reasonably be said to further nonpunitive goals, given the type and severity of the burdens imposed?[93] For example, a law is a bill of attainder if its purpose is to "purge the governing boards of labor unions of those whom Congress regards as guilty of subversive acts.…"[94]

Third, the Court looks to the legislative motivation: does the legislative record evidence a congressional intent to punish?[95] For purpose of this test the Court looks to the legislative record, floor debates, and so on. It also examines the features of the law under challenge to see if that law demonstrates any punitive interpretation.

Fourth, the Court finds it "often useful to inquire into the existence of less burdensome alternatives by which [the] legislature could have achieved its legitimate nonpunitive objectives."[96] The Court determines whether the legislative judgment is "rational and fairminded."[97]

The bill of attainder clauses do not replace equal protection analysis; they should be used only to invalidate legislative punishments.[98]

Legislation may validly establish criteria for employment or government benefits that adversely affect a limited class of individuals if the law is a nonpunitive establishment of standards relevant to a legitimate governmental

---

87. Cummings v. Missouri, 71 U.S. (4 Wall.) 277, 323, 18 L.Ed. 356 (1866). Cf. United States v. Brown, 381 U.S. 437, 85 S.Ct. 1707, 14 L.Ed.2d 484 (1965).

88. United States v. Brown, 381 U.S. 437, 85 S.Ct. 1707, 14 L.Ed.2d 484 (1965).

89. United States v. Lovett, 328 U.S. 303, 315, 66 S.Ct. 1073, 1079, 90 L.Ed. 1252 (1946) (emphasis added). See American Communications Ass'n, C.I.O. v. Douds, 339 U.S. 382, 70 S.Ct. 674, 94 L.Ed. 925 (1950) (punishment must be punitive rather than preventive).

90. State governments are not able to raise bill of attainder claims for themselves—because that clause does not protect states—or for their citizens—because the states are not parens patriae as against the federal government. See South Carolina v. Katzenbach, 383 U.S. 301, 324, 86 S.Ct. 803, 816, 15 L.Ed.2d 769 (1966).

91. Nixon v. Administrator of General Services, 433 U.S. 425, 475, 97 S.Ct. 2777, 2806, 53 L.Ed.2d 867, 911 (1977).

92. 433 U.S. at 474, 97 S.Ct. at 2806, 53 L.Ed.2d at 910–11.

93. 433 U.S. at 475, 97 S.Ct. at 2806, 53 L.Ed.2d at 911.

94. United States v. Brown, 381 U.S. 437, 460, 85 S.Ct. 1707, 1721, 14 L.Ed.2d 484 (1965).

95. 433 U.S. at 478, 97 S.Ct. at 2808, 53 L.Ed.2d at 913.

96. 433 U.S. at 482, 97 S.Ct. at 2810, 53 L.Ed.2d at 916.

97. Id.

98. Nixon v. Administrator of General Services, 433 U.S. 425, 471 & n. 33, 97 S.Ct. 2777, 2804 & n. 33, 53 L.Ed.2d 867, 909–09 & n. 33 (1977).

interest.[99] A bill of attainder is a legislatively declared punishment (often with a legislative finding of guilt regarding some crime or activity) for certain specific individuals. A bill of attainder may name the individuals or it may describe a class of persons subject to punishment because of specific conduct when in effect the description of that conduct operates to designate particular persons. If legislation denies a benefit or imposes a burden upon persons who have engaged in particular conduct, the law will be invalid as a bill of attainder if the law imposes "punishment" on those persons. The law will be upheld if it denies a benefit to individuals whose past conduct might reasonably be said to make them ineligible for the benefit. The legislature, in defining eligibility by conduct, may further a nonpunitive governmental interest. For example, if the legislature enacted a law stating that all doctors who had worked at a specific hospital would thereafter be ineligible to practice medicine, the law might be stricken as a bill of attainder. The conduct used to define the group relates merely to identifying persons for punishment rather than identifying any reasonable trait which would make someone unfit to practice medicine. However, if the legislature prohibited persons previously convicted of committing medical malpractice from continuing to practice medicine the legislation might be upheld as the establishment of nonpunitive licensing criteria. Thus, whenever the Court is confronted with the claim that legislation constitutes a bill of attainder, it must determine whether the designation of persons based on past conduct simply names individuals for

punishment or whether the designation promotes a *nonpunitive* goal based on reasonable criteria over which the individual has some control.[100]

The Supreme Court has used the prohibition against bills of attainder to void a congressional measure that prevented the payment of salaries to three named federal employees because the House of Representatives believed the three were subversives.[101] Similarly, the Court invalidated a law that declared unlawful the employment of a member of the Communist Party in a labor union.[102] The Court reasoned that the law impermissibly designated a class of persons (members of the Communist Party) for punishment.

The Court refused to declare unconstitutional a municipal ordinance that required municipal employees to take an oath that they were never members of the Communist Party or any similar organization that advocated the violent overthrow of the government.[103] The Court believed that the ordinance only established eligibility for employment.[104] Additionally, the Court sustained a state law that prevented convicted felons from holding a position with longshoremen's unions.[105] The Court observed that the prohibition was based on a judicial determination of culpability. The law did not create any further implications of the convicted felon's guilt. Therefore, the state legislature had imposed a penalty on an ascertainable class only after a court had established guilt. Hence, the law did not violate the prohibition against bills of attainder. Similarly, the termination of a deported alien's

---

99. For an example of a bill of attainder written under the guise of employment regulations, see Crain v. Mountain Home, 611 F.2d 726 (8th Cir.1979) (reduction of term and salary for city attorney).

100. Edwards, C.J., citing Treatise in BellSouth Corp. v. F.C.C., 162 F.3d 678, 688 (D.C.Cir.1998).

101. United States v. Lovett, 328 U.S. 303, 66 S.Ct. 1073, 90 L.Ed. 1252 (1946). Consider United States v. Robel, 389 U.S. 258, 88 S.Ct. 419, 19 L.Ed.2d 508 (1967) (where a similar statute making it unlawful for any member of a Communist action organization to be employed in a defense facility was held unconstitutional under the First Amendment with no mention made of the bill of attainder provisions).

102. United States v. Brown, 381 U.S. 437, 85 S.Ct. 1707, 14 L.Ed.2d 484 (1965).

103. Garner v. Board of Public Works of Los Angeles, 341 U.S. 716, 71 S.Ct. 909, 95 L.Ed. 1317 (1951). Cf. Konigsberg v. State Bar of Calif., 366 U.S. 36, 81 S.Ct. 997, 6 L.Ed.2d 105 (1961), rehearing denied 368 U.S. 869, 82 S.Ct. 21, 7 L.Ed.2d 69 (1961). Contrast these rulings with Supreme Court cases in the post-Civil War era, where statutes requiring persons to take an oath that they had never aided the Confederacy were held to be invalid bills of attainder. See Cummings v. Missouri, 71 U.S. (4 Wall.) 277, 18 L.Ed. 356 (1866); Klinger v. Missouri, 80 U.S. (13 Wall.) 257, 20 L.Ed. 635 (1871); Pierce v. Carskadon, 83 U.S. (16 Wall.) 234, 21 L.Ed. 276 (1872).

104. 341 U.S. at 722–23, 71 S.Ct. at 913–14.

105. De Veau v. Braisted, 363 U.S. 144, 80 S.Ct. 1146, 4 L.Ed.2d 1109 (1960) (plurality opinion).

social security benefits was not held to constitute a punitive measure.[106]

The Supreme Court sustained the Presidential Recordings and Materials Preservation Act,[107] which had been challenged by former President Nixon on the ground that it constituted a bill of attainder because it provided for governmental custody of only his presidential papers. In *Nixon v. Administrator of General Services,*[108] the Court ruled that the statute was not a bill of attainder within the historical meaning of that term because the law did not inflict punishment and was nonpunitive. The Act merely set the policy that historical materials should be preserved. Furthermore, the Act did not become a bill of attainder merely because it applied only to President Nixon, who was named in the Act. The Court held that the appellant, President Nixon, constituted a legitimate class of one because the papers of all other past Presidents were already safely housed in libraries.[109] The bill of attainder clause was not intended to be a variant of the equal protection clause; Congress constitutionally can legislate to burden some classes of individuals. To constitute a bill of attainder a law must both single out an individual or group for unfavorable treatment and impose "punishment" on that person or group.

In *Selective Service System v. Minnesota Public Interest Research Group,*[110] the Supreme Court upheld a federal statute which denied federal higher education financial assistance to male students who had failed to register for the draft. The Court, as a matter of statutory interpretation, held that the statute would al-

low male students to receive these federal benefits even though they registered more than thirty days after their eighteenth birthday, in violation of federal law requiring registration within that period.[111] Having found that the statute allowed late registration, the Court had little problem in finding that the statute was not a bill of attainder. The statute denied benefits to persons based on past conduct but the conduct did not merely define persons the legislature wished to punish, because the group disqualified for benefits was not defined "by irreversible acts committed by them."[112] Moreover, even if the statute were seen as defining a specific group for denial of a benefit, the statute, in the Court's view, still did not constitute a bill of attainder because it was not punitive in nature. Although the denial of federal educational benefits might be quite serious, "the severity of a sanction is not determinative of its character as punishment."

The majority opinion by Chief Justice Burger summarized the Court's rulings concerning determination of whether denial of a benefit to a discreet group of individuals constituted a punishment and attainder as follows:

> In deciding whether a statute inflicts forbidden punishment, we have recognized three necessary inquiries: (1) whether the challenged statute falls within the historical meaning of legislative punishment; (2) whether the statute, viewed in terms of the type and severity of burdens imposed, reasonably can be said to further nonpunitive legislative purposes; and (3) whether the

---

106. Flemming v. Nestor, 363 U.S. 603, 80 S.Ct. 1367, 4 L.Ed.2d 1435 (1960).

107. 44 U.S.C.A. § 2107.

108. 433 U.S. 425, 97 S.Ct. 2777, 53 L.Ed.2d 867 (1977).

109. 433 U.S. at 472–73, 97 S.Ct. at 2805.

110. 468 U.S. 841, 104 S.Ct. 3348, 82 L.Ed.2d 632 (1984).

111. The Court was ruling on a federal statute, § 1113 of the Department of Defense Authorization Act of 1983, which denied federal assistance under Title IV of the Higher Education Act of 1965 to male students between the ages of eighteen and twenty-six who had failed to register for the draft. The Military Selective Service Act had empowered the President to issue a proclamation requiring young men to register within thirty days of their

eighteenth birthday. The statutes, executive department proclamations, and the regulations implementing their terms are set forth at 468 U.S. at 845–47, 104 S.Ct. at 3351–52.

112. 468 U.S. at 849, 104 S.Ct. at 3353. The Court found this case distinguishable from post-Civil War cases in which the Court struck down statutes barring persons from professions unless they stated under oath that they had not aided the insurrection against the United States. Those oaths permanently disqualified persons from various professions on the basis of irreversible acts previously committed by them which were not punishable when committed. Cummings v. Missouri, 71 U.S. (4 Wall.) 277, 18 L.Ed. 356 (1867); Ex parte Garland, 71 U.S. (4 Wall.) 333, 18 L.Ed. 366 (1866).

legislative record evinces a congressional intent to punish.[113]

The Court found that the denial of educational benefits to those who fail to register for the draft did not constitute a punishment. Unlike imposition of a criminal sanction or denial of the ability to engage in a specific profession, the sanction was not equivalent to punishment historically associated with bills of attainder. The legislation reasonably furthered nonpunitive goals in limiting federal aid to those persons who "meet their responsibilities to the United States by registering with the Selective Service." The Court also found that "the legislative history provides convincing support" that Congress sought by this law to "promote compliance with the draft registration requirement and fairness in the allocation of scarce federal resources" rather than to inflict punishment.[114]

113. Selective Serv. System v. Minnesota Pub. Interest Research Group, 468 U.S. 841, 852–54, 104 S.Ct. 3348, 3355–56, 82 L.Ed.2d 632 (1984) (internal quotations and citations omitted).

114. The Court also decided that the statutory system, including administrative agency regulations requiring students to certify to their schools that they complied with the registration law as a condition for receiving the financial benefits, did not violate the Fifth Amendment because the registrant was not compelled to seek aid. The Court noted that the student could register late and obtain the aid without providing incriminating information to the school although more than thirty days had passed since the student's eighteenth birthday. The Court noted that it was not considering whether an individual who sought to register late would be subjected to an unconstitutional compulsion to give the government evidence that he had committed a crime by late registration. 468 U.S. at 858, 104 S.Ct. at 3358.

§ 11.10

1. J. Thayer, 1 Cases on Constitutional Law 952–53 (1895).

2. See generally, Lockett, Justice, citing Treatise in Deisher v. Kansas Dep't. of Transportation, 264 Kan. 762, 958 P.2d 656 (1998).

It is the "police power" that allows government to restrict individual freedom unless specifically forbidden by the Constitution. See E. Corwin, Liberty Against Government at 88, 173 (1948). It is an inherent power that the state governments possess but the federal government has such a power only in relation to federal property, such as the District of Columbia. As to the rest of the country, the federal government is one of enumerated powers with no express "police power". See Chapter 3.

Escheat. When real property is abandoned, and its owners cannot be located, the property reverts to the

§ 11.10   The Taking of Property Interests: Introduction

One of the powers of sovereign governments is the ability upon payment of adequate compensation, to take privately owned property.[1] This ability is called the power of eminent domain. Both the federal government and the individual state governments possess the power of eminent domain. Scholars and judges generally classify eminent domain as an incidental power and a means of fulfilling other governmental responsibilities.

The term "police power" is often used to define the panoply of governmental power. Throughout the rest of this treatise and in terms of the general principles of constitutional law, the term "police power" is used to designate the inherent power of government to take acts to promote the public health, safety, welfare or morals.[2] But in the area of eminent

ownership of the government through the process commonly referred to as escheat. When personal property, including intangible personal property, is abandoned, in the sense that its owners cannot be located, the property is also subject to appropriation by the governmental unit with jurisdiction over the property, a process that is sometimes termed escheat and sometimes termed an appropriation. These processes do not involve the taking of property from identified or identifiable owners. The Supreme Court has found that only the state with jurisdiction over the property may claim title through the escheat or appropriation principles. The right to real property that is subject to escheat belongs to the state in which the real property is located. The Supreme Court has been called upon in a series of cases to determine the appropriate state to claim the title to personal property under the escheat or appropriation principles. See, e.g., Delaware v. New York, 507 U.S. 490, 113 S.Ct. 1550, 123 L.Ed.2d 211 (1993); Pennsylvania v. New York, 407 U.S. 206, 92 S.Ct. 2075, 32 L.Ed.2d 693 (1972); Texas v. New Jersey, 379 U.S. 674, 85 S.Ct. 626, 13 L.Ed.2d 596 (1965).

Forfeitures of property to the government based on wrongdoing. The Supreme Court of the United States has long upheld the power of the government to seize and take title to property that has been used in the violation of "customs and revenue laws" and that has been used in connection with a crime or that has been used to commit "wrongs" to society or persons. However, the Court has not established clear constitutional guidelines regarding the government's ability to require the forfeiture of such property to the government.

In *United States v. Bajakajian*, 524 U.S. 321, 118 S.Ct. 2028, 141 L.Ed.2d 314 (1998), the Supreme Court created a framework for analyzing the compatibility of forfeitures with the excessive fines clause. The *Bajakajian* case involved an individual who failed to report to the federal government that he and his family were taking more than

domain cases and analysis, "police power" is used more narrowly to designate only the power of government to regulate the use of land and property without the payment of compensation. Authorities in the law of eminent domain view that power as distinct from such powers as the general police power and the power to tax.[3]

This section will trace the historical development of the constitutional law of eminent domain. It will also describe the case law currently governing the scope of the power of the state and federal governments to affect property interests without incurring any liability to compensate property owners. No single formula exists, however, to explain what one leading commentator has called the "crazy-quilt pattern of Supreme Court doctrine"[4] governing the use of eminent domain. This section, therefore, will discuss the broad issues that arise in the context of suits involving governmental acts affecting the use and possession of private property.

In analyzing the constitutional issues concerning the law of eminent domain, it is important to grasp the theoretical and historical underpinnings of the power. Section 11.11 therefore examines the nature of the power of eminent domain and the historical basis for the power and its limitations. That section also examines the sources of the power of eminent domain in the state and federal systems. Following that, we will discuss, in section 11.12 what scholars describe as the "taking" issue and the tests used by courts to determine whether a private property owner must be compensated for governmental interferences with his property interests. Then section 11.13 examines the "public use" limitation upon the exercise of eminent domain. We will conclude, in section 11.14, with brief notes on: (1) the rules used to determine what compensation is owing to a land owner whose property is "taken" by the exercise of eminent domain; and (2) the types of interests that can be appropriated by the government through the exercise of its eminent domain power.

$350,000 with them on a trip outside the United States. $357,000 in cash was found in the family's baggage as they were leaving the country. A federal statute prohibited anyone from transporting more than $10,000 in currency outside of the United States without filing a report with the federal government. Pursuant to that statute, the United States government brought suit against the individual seeking the forfeiture of the entire $357,000. By a five to four vote of the Justices, the Court held that the forfeiture of the total amount would violate the excessive fines clause of the Eighth Amendment. Justice Thomas, writing for the five member majority in *Bajakajian*, created a three-step framework for courts analyzing forfeitures under the Eighth Amendment excessive fines clause. First, a court must determine whether the forfeiture constitutes punishment for a criminal offense. Second, if the forfeiture appears to be a penalty, a court must determine whether the forfeiture was the type of forfeiture that was not subject to he excessive fines clause because the forfeiture was remedial in nature, or a forfeiture of the instrumentalities of crime, which historically had not been subject to the excessive fines clause. Third, if the forfeiture was a punishment, and not the type of forfeiture of exempted from excessive fine clause limitation the judiciary must determine whether the amount of the forfeiture was "of gross disproportionality" to the nature of the wrongdoing that triggered the forfeiture. For references to additional cases, and secondary authorities, on this point see the multivolume edition of this Treatise: R. Rotunda & J. Nowak, Treatise on Constitutional Law: Substance and Procedure § 15.10 (3rd ed. 1999, with annual supplements).

In Calero–Toledo v. Pearson Yacht Leasing Co., 416 U.S. 663, 94 S.Ct. 2080, 40 L.Ed.2d 452 (1974), rehearing

denied 417 U.S. 977, 94 S.Ct. 3187, 41 L.Ed.2d 1148 (1974) the Court upheld the seizure of property that might be moved prior to the time there could be a determination regarding whether the property could be constitutionally subject to forfeiture proceedings. The Court in *Calero–Toledo* recounted some of the history of the use of forfeiture laws in England and in the United States. In United States v. James Daniel Good Real Property, 510 U.S. 43, 114 S.Ct. 492, 126 L.Ed.2d 490 (1993) the Court ruled that the government must provide an individual with notice and some type of a hearing prior to seizing real property that might be subject to forfeiture because it was purchased with the proceeds of a crime. See §§ 13.8, 13.9 of this Treatise regarding the use of procedural due process principles to determine the fairness of procedures used in connection with government deprivations of property or liberty.

If the government proceeds against an individual's property in a civil forfeiture proceeding, the individual may claim that he is being subject to criminal proceedings that trigger all constitutional limitations on criminal trials. The Supreme Court has not ruled on the issue of whether all forfeiture proceedings are to be considered criminal trial proceedings. See footnote 1 in § 13.9 of this Treatise regarding the distinction between civil and criminal trials.

3. P. Nichols, The Power of Eminent Domain §§ 9–16 (1909).

4. Dunham, Griggs v. Allegheny County in Perspective: Thirty Years of Supreme Court Expropriation Law, 1962 Sup.Ct.Rev. 63.

§ 11.11 Limitations on the Exercise of Eminent Domain

The term "eminent domain" is said to have originated with Grotius, the seventeenth century legal scholar.[1] Grotius believed that the state possessed the power to take or destroy property for the benefit of the social unit,[2] but he believed that when the state so acted, it was obligated to compensate the injured property owner for his losses.[3] Blackstone, too, believed that society had no general power to take the private property of landowners, except on the payment of a reasonable price.[4] The just compensation clause of the Fifth Amendment to the Constitution was built upon this concept of a moral obligation to pay for governmental interference with private property.

The natural law philosophy that so greatly affected the development of American political and legal thought[5] also had an impact on the law of eminent domain. Early state court cases held that limitations on eminent domain existed independently of written constitutions.[6] The eminent domain clause of the Fifth Amendment, therefore, was not seen as creating a new legal restriction on the exercise of the power but rather as recognizing the existence of a principle of natural justice.[7] In the first half of the nineteenth century state courts applied this theory of natural law to

protect private property interests from state appropriations.[8]

No provision for the power of eminent domain appears in the federal Constitution.[9] The Supreme Court, however, has said that the power of eminent domain is an incident of federal sovereignty[10] and an "offspring of political necessity."[11] The Court has also noted that the Fifth Amendment's limitation on taking private property is a tacit recognition that the power to take private property exists.[12]

Because the federal government is a government of enumerated powers, it must be determined, when examining a specific federal use of the eminent domain power, whether the federal government possesses the constitutional power to take property for the proposed use. Because the power of eminent domain is an incidental power, it may be employed only when it is necessary and proper to the effectuation of one of the federal government's enumerated powers.[13] In general terms, therefore, the power of eminent domain may only be exercised by the federal government as a means of exercising one of its implied or enumerated powers.[14] Even if the exercise of eminent domain relates to an enumerated power, the Fifth Amendment also requires that private property be taken by the federal government only for a public use.[15]

§ 11.11

1. See, J. Thayer, 1 Cases on Constitutional Law 945 (1895).

2. See Grotius, De Jure Belli et Pacis lib. III. C. 20 VII 1 (1625), cited in J. Thayer, 1 Cases on Constitutional Law (1895). See also, Butler County Rural Water Dist. No. 8 v. Yates, 275 Kan. 291, 64 P.3d 357 (2003) (citing an earlier edition of this Treatise).

3. E. Freund, The Police Power 540 (1904).

4. Blackstone, 1 Blackstone's Commentaries 139 (Chitty Ed. 1829), cited in E. Freund, The Police Power 540 (1904).

5. See E. Corwin, Liberty Against Government (1948).

6. See Stoebuck, A General Theory of Eminent Domain, 47 Wash.L.Rev. 553, 555 (1972).

7. See Grant, The "Higher Law" Background of the Law of Eminent Domain, 6 Wisc.L.Rev. 67 (1931).

8. See, e.g. Gardner v. Village of Newburgh, 2 Johns. Ch. 162 (N.Y.Ch.1816).

9. Comment, State and Federal Power of Eminent Domain, 4 Geo.Wash.L.Rev. 130, 131 (1935).

10. United States v. Gettysburg Electric Ry. Co., 160 U.S. 668, 681, 16 S.Ct. 427, 429–30, 40 L.Ed. 576 (1896).

11. Bauman v. Ross, 167 U.S. 548, 574, 17 S.Ct. 966, 976, 42 L.Ed. 270 (1897).

12. United States v. Carmack, 329 U.S. 230, 241, 67 S.Ct. 252, 257, 91 L.Ed. 209 (1946).

13. P. Nichols, The Power of Eminent Domain 23 (1909); see Comment, The Public Use Limitation on Eminent Domain: An Advance Requiem, 58 Yale L.J. 599, 609–10 (1949).

14. Note, however, that the federal government possesses the full range of legislative powers over the District of Columbia, not merely those powers that the Constitution expressly confers. Shoemaker v. United States, 147 U.S. 282, 298–300, 13 S.Ct. 361, 390–91, 37 L.Ed. 170 (1893). See also the discussion of Berman v. Parker, 348 U.S. 26, 75 S.Ct. 98, 99 L.Ed. 27 (1954) in § 11.13, infra.

15. The public use limitation is examined in a later subsection. See § 11.13, infra.

The individual state governments, as political sovereigns, also possess the power of eminent domain. State constitutions now almost universally require that landowners be compensated when their property is taken by the state for a public use.[16] Only two of the original state constitutions adopted between 1776 and 1780, however, required that compensation be paid by the state when private property was taken for a public use.[17] Nevertheless, state courts applied doctrines of natural justice to require that such takings be made only for public uses[18] and only upon the payment of just compensation.[19]

Unlike the federal government, the state governments are not, for purposes of the federal Constitution, creatures of limited or enumerated powers. When examining a state exercise of eminent domain, therefore, it is not necessary, for federal Constitutional purposes, to determine whether the exercise of the power is necessary and incidental to the exercise of an express power. This exercise of the power will be valid so long as it does not violate any provision of the Constitution or its Amendments.

The Supreme Court, prior to the Civil War, held that the Fifth Amendment as part of the Bill of Rights did not apply to limit state interferences with private property.[20] In 1868 the Fourteenth Amendment was made part of the federal Constitution; its due process clause specifically protects property rights.[21] The Fourteenth Amendment, however, does not expressly require either that state "takings" of private property be for a public use or that the property owner receive just compensation for the loss.

In *Davidson v. New Orleans*[22] the Supreme Court stated that "it is not possible to hold that a party has, without due process of law, been deprived of his property, when, ... he has, by the laws of the State, a fair trial in a court of justice, according to the modes of proceeding applicable to such a case."[23] The Court in *Davidson* also noted that the just compensation clause of the Fifth Amendment was omitted from the Fourteenth Amendment.[24] At this early stage, therefore, it appears as though the Justices contemplated the due process clause as merely requiring that the state act with procedural fairness, with no requirement that state takings of private property be for a public use and only on payment of just compensation.

If indeed this was the Court's early view, it was short-lived. In two 1896 cases,[25] the Supreme Court held that the due process clause did require that land taken by the state be used for a public purpose. Finally, in 1897, in *Chicago, Burlington & Quincy R.R. Co. v. Chicago*,[26] the Court, in an opinion by the elder Justice Harlan, held that following prescribed procedure did not mean that the requirements of due process were met, for the clause regulated the "substance" as well as the form of such a taking.[27] The Court held that due process required both that the property be taken for a public use and that the owner of the property be compensated by the state for his loss.

---

16. Provisions limiting the exercise of the power of eminent domain appear in some form in every state constitution except that of North Carolina. The New Hampshire constitution states no requirement that the state provide compensation when it engages in a taking. P. Nichols, The Law of Eminent Domain (Rev. 3d ed. J. Schmar, ed.) (1976) § 1.3 at 79.

17. Grant, The "Higher Law" Background of the Law of Eminent Domain, 6 Wisc.L.Rev. 67, 69–70 (1931).

18. Lenhoff, Development of the Concept of Eminent Domain, 42 Colum.L.Rev. 596, 596–601 (1942).

19. Id.

20. See Barron v. Mayor and City Council of Baltimore, 32 U.S. (7 Pet.) 243, 250–51, 8 L.Ed. 672 (1833); West River Bridge Co. v. Dix, 47 U.S. (6 How.) 507, 532, 12 L.Ed. 535 (1848).

21. "(N)or shall any State deprive any person of life, liberty, or property without due process of law; ...." U.S.Const. Amend. 14, § 1.

22. 96 U.S. (6 Otto) 97, 24 L.Ed. 616 (1877).

23. 96 U.S. (6 Otto) at 105.

24. Id.

25. Fallbrook Irrigation District v. Bradley, 164 U.S. 112, 17 S.Ct. 56, 41 L.Ed. 369 (1896); Missouri Pac. Ry. Co. v. Nebraska, 164 U.S. 403, 17 S.Ct. 130, 41 L.Ed. 489 (1896).

26. 166 U.S. 226, 17 S.Ct. 581, 41 L.Ed. 979 (1897).

27. 166 U.S. at 234–35, 17 S.Ct. at 583–84.

Although some cases and commentators have viewed these Supreme Court decisions as incorporating the compensation clause into the Fourteenth Amendment, this view does not appear strictly correct. Rather the Court appears to have found independent public use and just compensation requirements inherent in the definition of due process. That the Court would find these limitations to exist in the concept of due process is easily understood when viewed in the light of the substantive due process doctrine prevalent at this time.[28] Today, the Supreme Court itself cites the *Chicago, Burlington & Quincy R.R. Co. v. Chicago* decision as incorporating the compensation clause into the Fourteenth Amendment.[29]

§ 11.12   The "Taking" Issue

(a) Introduction

The Fifth Amendment provides that private property may not be "taken" by the federal government without just compensation. The central issue in many eminent domain cases is whether the governmental interference amounts to a "taking". Although the concept of a taking may originally have contemplated only physical appropriation,[1] it is plain today that non-acquisitive governmental action may amount to a taking in a constitutional sense.[2] A "taking", therefore, may be found when governmental activity results in significant physical damage to property that impairs its use.[3] Although the state possesses the power to regulate property without payment of compensation, if the regulation goes too far, a taking may also be found.

Furthermore, a taking may occur as to an intangible property interest where the owner had a reasonable expectation that such property would not be used by the government and such expectation was impaired.[4]

28. See E. Freund, The Police Power 541 (1904). See also §§ 11.5–11.7, supra.

29. Webb's Fabulous Pharmacies, Inc. v. Beckwith, 449 U.S. 155, 159, 101 S.Ct. 446, 450, 66 L.Ed.2d 358 (1980) citing Chicago, Burlington & Quincy R.R. Co. v. Chicago, 166 U.S. 226, 17 S.Ct. 581, 41 L.Ed. 979 (1897). In *Webb's Fabulous Pharmacies,* the Supreme Court held that a Florida county's taking of the interest earned on an interpleader fund while such fund was temporarily held by the county court, in addition to a fee for the county's services for holding such fund, constituted a taking violative of the Fifth and Fourteenth Amendments.

§ 11.12

1. F. Bosselman, D. Callies, J. Banta, The Taking Issue 51 (1973).

2. See e.g. Pennsylvania Coal Co. v. Mahon, 260 U.S. 393, 43 S.Ct. 158, 67 L.Ed. 322 (1922); United States v. Causby, 328 U.S. 256, 66 S.Ct. 1062, 90 L.Ed. 1206 (1946), both discussed later in this section. See generally, Lenoir v. Porters Creek Watershed District, 586 F.2d 1081, 1093 (6th Cir.1978) (Engle, J., quoting an earlier edition of this work); Boudin, citing Treatise in National Education Association v. Retirement Board, 172 F.3d 22, 29 (1st Cir. 1999). Chin, J., citing Treatise in Kavanau v. Santa Monica Rent Control Board, 16 Cal.4th 761, 766, 66 Cal.Rptr.2d 672, 682, 941 P.2d 851, 861 (Cal. 1997); Sandstrom, J., quoting Treatise in, Southeast Cass Water Resource Dist. v. Burlington Northern R. Co., 527 N.W.2d 884, 898 (N.D.1995).

3. Pumpelly v. Green Bay & Mississippi Canal Co., 80 U.S. (13 Wall.) 166, 179–80, 20 L.Ed. 557 (1871).

4. In Phillips v. Washington Legal Foundation, 524 U.S. 156, 118 S.Ct. 1925, 141 L.Ed.2d 174 (1998) the Supreme Court declined to rule on whether a state law requiring funds held by attorneys for their clients be placed in a special interest bearing fund [with the fund's interest being used to provide legal services for low income persons] constituted a taking of property. A majority of the Court Justices in *Phillips* considered only the question of whether income interest generated by the money held in such accounts was the private property of attorney or the client whose funds the attorney held. The Court ruled that any interest generated by the placing of the money in the special fund was the property of the client, who owned the principal placed in the fund. Four Justices dissented in *Phillips,* because they believed that the Supreme Court should not decided the question of who owned the interest in property placed in the special fund, when the Court had not decided the question of whether a law requiring attorneys to place funds, which otherwise could not generate interest, into the special fund constituted a taking of property. 524 U.S. at 172, 118 S.Ct. at 1934 (Souter, J., joined by Stevens, Ginsburg, and Breyer, JJ., dissenting); 524 U.S. at 179, 118 S. Ct. at 1937 (Breyer, J., joined by Stevens, Souter, and Ginsburg, JJ., dissenting). In Brown v. Legal Foundation of Washington, 538 U.S. 216, 123 S.Ct. 1406, 155 L.Ed.2d 376 (2003) the Court, by a 5 to 4 vote, held: that state laws requiring the combination of small amounts of money held by attorneys or escrow agents for their clients (amounts so small that they would not have otherwise generated income), and requiring the transfer of that money to state funds used to subsidize legal services for low-income persons constituted a taking of property; that such a taking would unquestionably be for a public use; and that no compensation was owed to the owners of small funds that would otherwise not have generated monetary interest, because the monetary loss to such persons was in fact nothing (the amount owed to the owners of the small accounts was zero, because they had lost no monetary interest that they could have earned prior to the enactment of the statute).

Intangibles. Intangibles, such as trade secrets, and other nontraditional types of property may be protected by

Connolly v. Pension Benefit Guaranty Corporation,[5] upheld federal legislation that required an employer who was withdrawing from a multiemployer pension plan to pay a share of the plan's unfunded vested benefits even though this liability had not been established in the original pension plan trust agreement.[6] The Court held that this was not a taking of property but only a reasonable economic regulation, even though the law required the payment of money to a pension benefit system in order to help specific workers. The majority opinion by Justice White noted that many types of economic regulations result in economic costs being imposed on one class of persons or businesses and economic benefits being awarded to another group. However, these laws normally will not constitute a taking of property because they are really economic regulations in the public interest.[7]

In determining whether a regulation was taking of property, the majority opinion found that three factors were of particular importance: "(1) 'the economic impact of the regulation on the claimant [the person who was

required to pay money or whose property suffered a diminution in value]'; (2) 'the extent to which the regulation has interfered with distinct investment-backed expectations'; (3) 'the character of the governmental action.' "[8] Because the imposition of liability on employers withdrawing from the pension plans was not a direct government use or taking of property but only the establishment of a program that "adjusted the benefits and burdens of economic life to promote the common good," it was not a direct interference with property rights. The economic obligation imposed on a withdrawing employer was not necessarily "out of proportion to its experience with the plan." The Court also ruled that employers who participated in the pension plans should have been aware that pension plans would be subject to government regulation to protect employees. Thus, the pension plan regulation was not a taking of property. More important than the Court's specific ruling in *Connolly* is its indication that the three listed factors should be of concern in all cases wherein judges must determine whether an economic

---

the taking clause of the Fifth Amendment. The existence of the property right will be determined with reference to state law. Once it has been determined that a property interest exists in an intangible, the Court will inquire whether the holder of the interest had a reasonable investment-backed expectation that the property right would be protected. If the Court finds such a reasonable investment-backed expectation, the Court will determine whether governmental action impaired that expectation. If so, the Court will find that a compensable taking has occurred. See, e.g., Ruckelshaus v. Monsanto Co., 467 U.S. 986, 104 S.Ct. 2862, 81 L.Ed.2d 815 (1984).

Limits on Remedies. Legislative limitations on statutory or common law remedies for injuries may raise substantive due process, taking of property, and equal protection issues.

In Duke Power Co. v. Carolina Environmental Study Group, Inc., 438 U.S. 59, 98 S.Ct. 2620, 57 L.Ed.2d 595 (1978), the Court upheld the federal limitation on the liability of nuclear power plants for damages and injuries resulting from possible accidents or disasters at such plants against a due process clause challenge. A legislative limitation on a preexisting remedy would raise a question of whether the limitation is so arbitrary as to violate due process, limits the economic interests of a specific group so as to violate equal protection, or constitutes the termination of a preexisting property right in violation of the taking of property clause.

Welfare Payments. The statutory reduction of welfare benefits for a class of persons should not constitute a taking of property in most situations because such an

action is really a new decision regarding the amount of money that should be used for the welfare benefits, rather than a taking of a property interest. See, Bowen v. Gilliard, 483 U.S. 587, 107 S.Ct. 3008, 97 L.Ed.2d 485 (1987).

For citations to additional Supreme Court cases on these points, see R. Rotunda & J. Nowak, Treatise on Constitutional Law: Substance and Procedure, § 15.12 (3rd ed. 1999, with annual supplements).

5. 475 U.S. 211, 106 S.Ct. 1018, 89 L.Ed.2d 166 (1986).

6. The Supreme Court had previously upheld other retroactive aspects of the federal multiemployer pension plan regulations. See, Pension Benefit Guaranty Corp. v. R.A. Gray and Co., 467 U.S. 717, 104 S.Ct. 2709, 81 L.Ed.2d 601 (1984).

7. The Supreme Court has upheld a variety of retroactive legislative provisions that are designed to promote societal interest in a manner that does not unjustifiably shift social cost to a few individuals. See the discussion of Usery v. Turner Elkhorn Mining Co., 428 U.S. 1, 96 S.Ct. 2882, 49 L.Ed.2d 752 (1976) in § 15.9(a).

8. Connolly v. Pension Benefit Guaranty Corp., 475 U.S. 211, 225, 106 S.Ct. 1018, 1026, 89 L.Ed.2d 166 (1986) quoting Penn Central Transportation Co. v. New York, 438 U.S. 104, 124, 98 S.Ct. 2646, 2659, 57 L.Ed.2d 631 (1978), rehearing denied 439 U.S. 883, 99 S.Ct. 226, 58 L.Ed.2d 198 (1978).

regulation constitutes a taking of property.[9]

Uncertainty regarding the nature of interests that are protected by the takings clause. Near the close of the twentieth century, lower courts and commentators could not be certain as to whether the takings clause would be applicable to government actions that imposed financial costs on individuals but did not restrict the use of tangible or intangible property. This uncertainty was created by *Eastern Enterprises v. Apfel*,[10] in which the Supreme Court by a five to four vote of the Justices, and without a majority opinion, invalidated a monetary assessment on the prior owner of a coal mine that would have been used to fund medical benefits for some retired coal miners.

Between the 1940's and the late 1970's, negotiations between coal miners (through their union), the operators of coal mines, and representatives of the federal government resulted in the creation of a fund to provide health benefits to coal miners and their families. In the 1970's the "welfare and retirement fund" established by labor-management agreements specifically provided health benefits for retired miners and their families. A 1974 labor-management agreement was in part designed to comply with the Employment Retirement Income Security Act of 1974, which imposed monetary liabilities on employers withdrawing from multi-employer pension plan agreements.[11] Because of the economic instability of the welfare and retirement fund, the federal government enacted the Coal Industry Retiree Health Benefit Act of 1992 (the Coal Act),

which created a new multi-employer benefit plan, in part by merging the benefit plans from earlier labor-management agreements. The Coal Act financed the provision of benefits under the new plan by the assessment of premiums against coal operators that had signed the labor-management agreements that had established earlier benefit plans.[12]

On the basis of the Coal Act, the Commissioner of Social Security notified Eastern Enterprises that it was required to fund part of the plan due to the fact that Eastern had operated a coal mining business between 1947 and 1964 and signed earlier labor management agreements. Eastern Enterprises had formally stopped the operation of its coal mining business in 1963, when Eastern transferred its coal mining related operations to a wholly owned subsidiary. In 1987, Eastern sold its interests in the subsidiary. Although it was no longer operating any coal industry business, Eastern Enterprises was liable for some payments into the health and welfare fund, under the terms of the Coal Act, because of its prior involvement in the coal industry and its signing of earlier labor-management agreements. The monetary assessment imposed on Eastern Enterprises was based on its having once employed now retired coal miners who would be receiving benefits from the fund created by the Coal Act.

In *Eastern Enterprises v. Apfel* five Justices concluded that the monetary assessment on Eastern Enterprises violated the Fifth Amendment. However, these five Justices could not agree on which clause of the Fifth Amendment

---

9. The *Connolly* decision indicates that a court, in any taking of property case will have to assess both the nature and importance of the governmental interest and the nature and extent of the economic loss of the individual property owner or class of property owners. These general guidelines set out in *Connolly* will not provide a clear "test" for determining whether taking of property has taken place as a result of a governmental regulatory action.

In Concrete Pipe and Products of California v. Construction Laborers Pension Trust, 508 U.S. 602, 113 S.Ct. 2264, 124 L.Ed.2d 539 (1993) the Justices unanimously upheld an application of the Multiemployer Pension Plan Amendments Act that required an employer withdrawing from a multiemployer pension plan to make a monetary contribution to the plan even though very few, if any, of the employer's employees had vested rights in the pension

plan. The Court found that this legislation was not retroactive insofar as it was applied to this employer; the employer's due process argument against the statute was merely a substantive due process argument. Therefore, the law would be upheld as long as it was rationally related to any legitimate government interest.

10. 524 U.S. 498, 118 S.Ct. 2131, 141 L.Ed.2d 451 (1998).

11. Employment Retirement Security Act of 1974, 29 U.S.C. A. § 1001 Et. Seq.

12. The plurality opinion details the relationships between, and agreements among, the coal mine operators, the miners, and the federal government. Eastern Enterprises v. Apfel, 524 U.S. 498, 504–516, 118 S.Ct. 2131, 2137–42 141 L.Ed.2d 451 (1998).

was violated by the attempted assessment against Eastern Enterprises. Justice O'Connor, writing a plurality opinion for four members of the Court, found that the assessment against Eastern Enterprises violated the takings clause of the Fifth Amendment.[13] Justice Kennedy concurred in the judgment of the Court in *Eastern Enterprises*, but dissented from the plurality's takings clause analysis. He believed that the monetary assessment against Eastern Enterprises was the type of retroactive governmental action that violated the due process clause, even though it did not, in his view, involve a taking of property.[14]

The four dissenting Justices in *Eastern Enterprises* believed both that there was no basis for using the takings clause to determine the constitutionality of the assessment against Eastern Enterprises and that both the analysis in Justice Kennedy's concurring opinion, as well as the plurality opinion, was contrary to the Supreme Court's tradition of giving deference to the Congress concerning economic and social welfare legislation.[15]

The judgment of the Court in *Eastern Enterprises v. Apfel*[16] was announced in a plurality opinion by Justice O'Connor. Her plurality opinion was joined by Chief Justice Rehnquist and Justices Scalia and Thomas. The plurality opinion refused to address the question of whether the monetary assessment against the corporation violated substantive due process due to the alleged arbitrariness, or the retroactivity, of the assessment.[17] The plurality believed that this economic regulation constituted a taking of the corporation's property in violation of the Fifth Amendment. Justice

O'Connor recognized that the monetary assessment against the corporation did not involve either the government appropriation of property for its own use or the regulation of how the corporation could use its business property. However, she believed that earlier Supreme Court decisions established the principle that the type of "economic regulation such as the Coal Act may nonetheless effect a taking."[18] Recognizing that the case involved only a regulatory taking, Justice O'Connor found that Eastern Enterprises, the party attacking the government, faced a "substantial burden" in establishing that the regulatory action was so unfair as to constitute a taking of property.[19]

Justice O'Connor's plurality opinion analyzed the question of whether the monetary assessment constituted a taking of property by using the three factors set forth in *Connolly v. Pension Benefit Guaranty Corporation.*[20] The plurality described "the three factors that traditionally have informed our regulatory takings analysis,"[21] as being the economic impact of the regulation on the corporation, the extent to which the regulation interfered with the corporation's reasonable investment-backed expectations, and the nature of the government action. According to Justice O'Connor's plurality opinion, all three factors indicated that there was an unconstitutional taking of the corporation's property in this case. First, the plurality found that there was a severe economic impact on the corporation, because the corporation might be required to pay between $50 and $100 million in benefit payments under the terms of the Coal Act.

13. Eastern Enterprises v. Apfel, 524 U.S. 498, 118 S.Ct. 2131, 141 L.Ed.2d 451 (1998) (opinion of the Court announced by O'Connor, J., joined by Rehnquist, C.J., and Scalia and Thomas, JJ.). Justice Thomas also wrote a concurring opinion in which he questioned the Court's limitation of ex-post facto analysis to the imposition of criminal fines and punishments (a position which the Court had followed for 200 years). 524 U.S. at 538, 118 S.Ct. at 2154 (Thomas, J., concurring).

14. 524 U.S. at 539, 118 S.Ct. at 2154–60 (Kennedy, J., concurring in the judgment and dissenting in part).

15. 524 U.S. at 550, 118 S.Ct. at 2160 (Stevens, J., joined by Souter, Ginsburg, and Breyer, JJ., dissenting); 524 U.S. at 554, 118 S.Ct. at 2161 (Breyer, J., joined by Stevens, Souter, and Ginsburg, JJ., dissenting).

16. 524 U.S. 498, 118 S.Ct. 2131, 141 L.Ed.2d 451 (1998).

17. 524 U.S. at 536–37, 118 S.Ct. at 2153.

18. 524 U.S. at 522–23, 118 S.Ct. at 2146. The plurality opinion again made the point that earlier cases justified the analysis. 524 U.S. at 529–30, 118 S.Ct. at 2149.

19. 524 U.S. at 522–23, 118 S.Ct. at 2146.

20. 475 U.S. 211, 225, 106 S.Ct. 1018, 1026, 89 L.Ed.2d 166 (1986). See note 5, and accompanying text, supra.

21. Eastern Enterprises v. Apfel, 524 U.S. 498, 529–30, 118 S.Ct. 2131, 2149, 141 L.Ed.2d 451 (1998).

Second, the plurality found the Act substantially interfered with the corporation's reasonable investment backed expectations because the law was retroactive. The corporation had a reasonable expectation that it would not suffer a retroactive imposition of liability because "retroactivity is generally disfavored in the law."[22] Additionally, in the view of the plurality, reasonable investment backed expectations of the corporation were unfairly impaired because there was no significant connection between the current monetary assessment on Eastern Enterprises and its responsibility for health problems of former employees.[23]

Third, the government interest insofar as it was advanced by the imposition of retroactive liability was considered weak by the plurality. Justice O'Connor recognized that Congress could perceive a "grave problem" concerning the funding for retired coal miner's health benefits, and that Congress might have sought to remedy through a variety of legislative solutions. However, according to Justice O'Connor, a concern for the health of the miners did not justify Congress forcing an individual corporation "to bear the expense of lifetime health benefits for miners based on its activities decades before those benefits were promised."[24]

Justice Kennedy provided the fifth vote for invalidating the assessment of monetary liability on Eastern Enterprises for the provision of health benefits to retired mine workers.[25] Justice Kennedy refused to endorse the plurality's view that the imposition of liability constituted a taking of property because he believed that the takings clause analysis used by the plurality could be used to resurrect discredited substantive due process review of all economic regulation under another name. The only way to keep takings clause analysis in check, according to Justice Kennedy, was to insist that the takings clause be used only to review the use of property interests. As Justice Kennedy stated: "Until today, however, one constant limitation [on takings clause analysis] has been that in all of the cases where regulatory taking analysis has been employed, a specific property right or interest has been at stake."[26]

Although he dissented from the plurality's takings clause analysis, Justice Kennedy concurred in the judgment of the Court because he believed that the imposition of liability on Eastern Enterprises under the Coal Act was the type of retroactive legislation that violated the due process clause. Even when it was reviewing retroactive legislation, Justice Kennedy believed that the Court was required to give deference to Congress concerning the regulation of economic and social welfare matters. According to the Justice, retroactive economic regulation would be "invalidated on due process grounds only under the most egregious circumstances."[27] However, because of the amount of the liability retroactively imposed on Eastern Enterprises for acts that were not directly connected to its business activities, Justice Kennedy found that the "application of the Coal Act to Eastern would violate proper bounds of settled due process principles."[28]

Justices Stevens, Souter, Ginsburg, and Breyer dissented in *Eastern Enterprises*. Justice Stevens wrote a dissenting opinion for these four Justices in which he emphasized "the critical importance" of the expectation of both the miners and the mine operators [including Eastern and its subsidiary] at the time of their earlier labor-management agreements in assessing the reasonableness of the Congressional action requiring Eastern, and other

---

22. 524 U.S. at 532–34 118 S.Ct. at 2151.

23. 524 U.S. at 534–38, 118 S.Ct. at 2152–53. The plurality found that the absence of any relationship between the monetary assessment on Eastern Enterprises and responsibility for employee health problems made this case distinguishable from Usery v. Turner Elkhorn Mining Co. 428 U.S. 1, 96 S.Ct. 2882, 49 L.Ed.2d 752 (1976) in which the Court had upheld the provision of the black lung benefits act of 1972 that required coal mine operators to compensate coal miners, or their survivors, for health problems resulting from black lung disease caused by the miner's work in the coal industry.

24. Eastern Enterprises v. Apfel, 524 U.S. 498, 537, 118 S.Ct. 2131, 2153, 141 L.Ed.2d 451 (1998).

25. 524 U.S. at 539, 118 S.Ct. at 2154 (Kennedy, J., concurring in the judgment and dissenting in part).

26. 524 U.S. at 539–41, 118 S.Ct. at 2155 (Kennedy, J., concurring in the judgment and dissenting in part).

27. 524 U.S. at 548–49, 118 S.Ct. at 2159 (Kennedy, J., concurring in the judgment and dissenting in part).

28. 524 U.S. at 549–50, 118 S.Ct. at 2159–60 (Kennedy, J., concurring in the judgment and dissenting in part).

similarly situated companies, to provide a portion of the current funding for the health benefits for the miners.[29] Justice Breyer's dissent for these four Justices explained their view that prior Supreme Court decisions regarding the government's ability to use retroactive legislation did not require invalidation of the Coal Act assessment on Eastern Enterprises because the coal business activities of Eastern, and its subsidiary, meant that it was "not fundamentally unfair for Congress to impose upon Eastern liability for future health care costs of miners whom it long ago employed."[30]

(b) Property Use Regulations

The Early Cases. In *Pennsylvania Coal Co. v. Mahon*,[31] a state statute prohibited the mining of coal in such a way as to cause the subsidence of certain types of improved property. The issue before the Court was whether, through the exercise of its police power, the state could destroy the coal company's mining rights without compensation. The Supreme Court, per Justice Holmes, held that the rights of the coal company could not, consistent with due process, be so limited without payment of compensation.

Although the opinion noted that values incident to property could be reduced by noncompensable use regulation, Holmes stated that, "when [regulation] reaches a certain magnitude, in most if not in all cases, there must be an exercise of eminent domain and compensation to sustain the act."[32] Under this view, the police power and eminent domain exist in a continuum. Once regulation went so far, there was a "taking" and compensation had to be made to the injured land

owner. Here the Court found the extent of the regulation so great as to constitute a taking. "To make it commercially impracticable to mine certain coal has nearly the same effect for constitutional purposes as appropriating or destroying it."[33] In *Euclid v. Ambler Realty Co.*,[34] the Supreme Court dealt for the first time with the constitutionality of a comprehensive land use regulatory ordinance. In 1927 the Village Council of Euclid adopted a comprehensive zoning ordinance. The statute restricted the location of trades, industries, apartment houses, two-family houses, single-family houses and other land uses. The plan also regulated aspects of property use such as the size of lots and the size and heights of buildings.

The zoning ordinance was attacked on the ground that it deprived the property owner of liberty and property without due process of law, and that the use classifications deprived him of equal protection of law. The issue, as framed by the Court, was whether the owner was unconstitutionally deprived of property "by attempted regulations under the guise of the police power, which are unreasonable and confiscatory?"[35] The Court premised its holding by stating that, if valid, the ordinance, like all similar regulatory laws, would have to find its justification in the police power. The Court concluded that the statute was a valid police power regulation because there was a sufficient public interest in the segregation of incompatible land uses to justify the diminution of property values. The Court since *Euclid* has deferred to the zoning power against due process and equal protection challenges with few exceptions.[36]

29. Eastern Enterprises v. Apfel, 524 U.S. 498, 550, 118 S.Ct. 2131, 2160, 141 L.Ed.2d 451 (1998) (Stevens, J., joined by Souter, Ginsburg, and Breyer, JJ., dissenting).

30. 524 U.S. at 553, 118 S.Ct. at 2167 (Breyer, J., joined by Stevens, Souter, and Ginsburg, JJ., dissenting).

31. 260 U.S. 393, 43 S.Ct. 158, 67 L.Ed. 322 (1922).

32. 260 U.S. at 413, 43 S.Ct. at 159.

33. 260 U.S. at 414, 43 S.Ct. at 168.

The Supreme Court later determined that the Holmes majority opinion in *Pennsylvania Coal* only required the invalidation of a statute that unjustifiably shifted the cause of a private benefit from surface landowners to coal

companies, for the Supreme Court upheld a later Pennsylvania statute that restricted coal companies from removing a percentage of coal that would cause subsidence damage to a variety of public and privately owned properties. Keystone Bituminous Coal Association v. DeBenedictis, 480 U.S. 470, 107 S.Ct. 1232, 94 L.Ed.2d 472 (1987).

34. 272 U.S. 365, 47 S.Ct. 114, 71 L.Ed. 303 (1926).

35. 272 U.S. at 386, 47 S.Ct. at 118.

36. The Court has allowed a city to zone an area for "traditional" families, Village of Belle Terre v. Boraas, 416 U.S. 1, 94 S.Ct. 1536, 39 L.Ed.2d 797 (1974). In *Lawrence v. Texas*, ___ U.S. ___, 123 S.Ct. 2472, 156 L.Ed.2d 508 (2003) the Supreme Court invalidated a state law prohibit-

In two cases, considered shortly after *Euclid*, the Supreme Court held land use regulation invalid as a violation of the due process clause of the Fourteenth Amendment. In *Washington ex rel. Seattle Title Trust Co. v. Roberge*,[37] the Court struck down an ordinance that allowed for the issuance of use variances upon the two-thirds consent of surrounding landowners. The Court found the variance provision to be a due process violation because the surrounding landowners would be free to withhold consent for arbitrary and capricious reasons. However, there is no due process violation when exemptions from zoning requirements are granted only by a general referendum.[38]

In *Nectow v. Cambridge*,[39] the Supreme Court faced squarely the issue of the authority of local governments to regulate land use without payment of compensation. The Court found some outer limit to the power and struck down a Cambridge zoning ordinance on the ground that it deprived the plaintiff landowner of property without due process of law. The Court held that a zoning restriction "cannot be imposed if it does not bear a substantial relation to the public health, safety, morals or general welfare."[40] The Court, after reviewing the factual circumstances, found that regulation of the plaintiff's land was not necessary in order to promote the general welfare of the city's inhabitants. Under this very narrow view of the operation of a comprehensive zoning plan, the Court struck down the ordinance. The Court in *Nectow* did not dispute the legitimate nature of the zoning power; it only found that an individual landowner was denied due process when his land was arbitrarily classified.

Federal Judicial Review of Zoning Laws and Property Use Regulations as Takings of Property. After these early zoning cases the Supreme Court withdrew from the area for an extended period and allowed the state courts to develop rules governing the permissible scope of zoning regulation. In 1962, however, in *Goldblatt v. Town of Hempstead*,[41] the Court reexamined the constitutionality of zoning regulation and described an expansive power of local government to regulate land use. In *Goldblatt*, the landowner held a thirty-eight acre tract within the town of Hempstead. The land was used as a sand and gravel quarry and had been continuously so used since 1927. The town, having grown around the quarry, attempted through a series of ordinances to restrict the quarry's operation. In 1958, the town amended its zoning ordinance to prohibit any excavation below the water-line, which effectively prohibited continuance of the use to which the property had been devoted.

Emphasizing that there was a presumption that the statute was constitutional, the Court upheld the ordinance, finding "no indication that the prohibitory effect of the [ordinance was] sufficient to render it an unconstitutional taking...."[42] The Court, quoting *Lawton v. Steele*,[43] stated a two-part test to determine whether the statute was valid. First it must appear that "the interests of the public ... require such interference; and, second, that the means are reasonably necessary for the accomplishment of the purpose, and not unduly oppressive upon individuals."[44] After evaluating the nature of the menace caused by the quarry, the availability of less drastic steps,

---

ing same-sex sodomy, and, in so doing, brought into question the validity of zoning ordinances that restrict occupation of housing to traditional families. The *Lawrence* case is examined in § 14.28 of this Treatise. Zoning must not intrude upon the functioning of traditional families, see Moore v. East Cleveland, 431 U.S. 494, 97 S.Ct. 1932, 52 L.Ed.2d 531 (1977) (city cannot require family to subdivide and exclude blood relatives).

A city cannot exclude a group of persons from living together for no reason other than the fact that persons in the group are mentally retarded. Such an exclusion relates to no legitimate governmental interest. City of Cleburne v. Cleburne Living Center, 473 U.S. 432, 105 S.Ct. 3249, 87 L.Ed.2d 313 (1985).

37. 278 U.S. 116, 49 S.Ct. 50, 73 L.Ed. 210 (1928).

38. Eastlake v. Forest City Enterprises, Inc., 426 U.S. 668, 96 S.Ct. 2358, 49 L.Ed.2d 132 (1976).

39. 277 U.S. 183, 48 S.Ct. 447, 72 L.Ed. 842 (1928).

40. 277 U.S. at 188, 48 S.Ct. at 448.

41. 369 U.S. 590, 82 S.Ct. 987, 8 L.Ed.2d 130 (1962).

42. 369 U.S. at 594, 82 S.Ct. at 990.

43. 152 U.S. 133, 137, 14 S.Ct. 499, 501, 38 L.Ed. 385 (1894).

44. Goldblatt v. Town of Hempstead, 369 U.S. 590, 595, 82 S.Ct. 987, 990, 8 L.Ed.2d 130 (1962).

and the loss suffered by the landowner, the Court found the statute constitutional.

Only the most unusual and totally arbitrary zoning ordinance or property use regulation will require the granting of compensation to a property owner. So long as the zoning ordinance reasonably advances some arguable "police power" interest and does not literally transfer an existing property interest of the owner to the government or other parties, the zoning of property should not require compensation. Although the Justices may "balance" public and private interests in these cases, it is assumed that the public interest will prevail unless a property use regulation enriches the government or the public by regulations which terminate or eliminate the primary economic value of a property interest.[45]

Takings clause challenges to most types of government actions that result in a diminution of property values require judicial inquiry into the nature of the public interest that was advanced by the government action and the extent of economic loss that was placed upon the property owner. Two types of government actions constitute per se takings. In other words, there are two types of government actions that will be determined to be takings for which compensation is due regardless of the nature of the public interest that is advanced by those government actions. Under one of the per se rules established by the Court, any government action that denies the owner of land of all economically beneficial uses of the land is a compensable taking.[46] The second situation in which the Supreme Court will find that a government action is a per se taking involves the physical occupation of property by the government. This per se rule applies to a government action that allows persons other than the property owner to have permanent physical occupation of the property.[47]

Apart from the problem areas covered by the two per se rules, the Supreme Court has not provided clear standards for determining when government regulations of property use constitute a taking of property for which compensation is due. When the government regulates the use of property by all persons, or an entire class of property, the government regulatory action will be reviewed through an ad hoc inquiry into the nature of harm caused to the owners of property whose value has been diminished by the regulation and the social interests advanced by the regulation. It is unlikely that the judiciary will find that a general regulatory action is a taking of property unless the property owners can demonstrate that the regulation unjustly shifts social costs to them by greatly diminishing the value of their property without promoting legitimate social interests. When examining these types of general government regulations, the Supreme Court will give significant deference to the legislative entities that enact property use regulations.

When the government regulates only a specific piece of land, and does not regulate similar pieces of property within the jurisdiction, the owner of the regulated land may have an easier time in having the regulation declared to be a taking of property for which compensation is due.

The Supreme Court has not established a standard for the review of all government actions that might be described as "spot zoning" or "spot regulation." But the Court has established a standard for lower courts to use when reviewing a government conditioning the granting of a building permit on the property

---

45. The state may define ownership interests in real or personal property so that they terminate or lapse without paying compensation, at least when the termination is based upon the action of the owner. See, Texaco, Inc. v. Short, 454 U.S. 516, 102 S.Ct. 781, 70 L.Ed.2d 738 (1982) (state statute may deem as abandoned and lapsed several mineral interests upon failure of owner to use interest for 20 years or to file claim preventing lapse). For citations to additional Supreme Court cases, and secondary authorities, on this point, see R. Rotunda & J. Nowak, Treatise on Constitutional Law: Substance and Procedure, § 15.12 (3rd ed. 1999, with annual supplements).

46. Lucas v. South Carolina Coastal Council, 505 U.S. 1003, 112 S.Ct. 2886, 120 L.Ed.2d 798 (1992), on remand 309 S.C. 424, 424 S.E.2d 484 (1992).

47. See, e.g., Loretto v. Teleprompter Manhattan CATV Corp., 458 U.S. 419, 102 S.Ct. 3164, 73 L.Ed.2d 868 (1982), on remand 58 N.Y.2d 143, 459 N.Y.S.2d 743, 446 N.E.2d 428 (1983), reargument denied 59 N.Y.2d 761, 463 N.Y.S.2d 1030, 450 N.E.2d 254 (1983). The *Loretto* decision (and the per se rule for physical occupation cases) is examined in later paragraphs of this subsection of the Treatise.

owner's agreement to deed to the government the title to a part of the land or to open a part of the land to public use. When the government places such a condition on the granting of a building or development permit, the government must demonstrate that the condition is truly related to legitimate governmental interest. In such cases, the government must show that the harm caused to the property owner by having to give up the right to exclude other persons from a part of his property is "roughly proportional" to the harm that the new development will cause legitimate governmental interests.[48]

Eliminating the entire value of land—a per se taking. In *Lucas v. South Carolina Coastal Council*[49] the Supreme Court ruled that "when the owner of real property has been called to sacrifice *all* economically beneficial uses in the name of the common good, that is, to leave his property economically idle, he has suffered a taking."[50] If the value of real property is completely eliminated by governmental actions (regardless of whether those actions were called regulatory by the government), the government can only defend its action (as being something other than a taking) by showing that the owner had acquired title to the property subject to regulations that eliminated all of the economically beneficial uses for the property. "Where the State seeks to sustain regulation that deprives land of all economically beneficial use, we think it may resist compensation only if the logically antecedent inquiry into the nature of the owner's estate shows that the proscribed use interests were not part of his title to begin with."[51]

The Court did not need to make a specific ruling concerning the type of government action that might leave a land with no value in *Lucas*, because of the way the case was presented to the United States Supreme Court. The *Lucas* case involved a property owner who had purchased two residential lots in what was eventually deemed a coastal zone; government actions taken after the owner purchased the lots prohibited the construction of any occupiable improvements on the land and eliminated any development of the property. The lower courts had found that the property was rendered completely "valueless". The lower court finding concerning the regulations' effect of prohibiting any economically viable use of the property was not challenged in the United States Supreme Court.[52]

The United States Supreme Court in *Lucas,* also did not have to determine whether the property owner had taken title to the land subject to regulations that would have prohibited any beneficial use of the property. The state courts had not addressed that issue, but they would have to do so after the case was remanded.

The state supreme court had ruled that the total deprivation of value in the coastal land was not a taking of property because it believed that the act promoted an important societal interest (in protecting the coast line) and prevented the owner from using this land in a harmful manner (by altering the beauty and nature of the coast line). The United States Supreme Court ruled that states could not justify total deprivation of the value of land simply by declaring that any and all economically beneficial uses of the land were "harmful." The concept of harmful use might be helpful when determining whether a regulation that resulted in only a partial loss of value to a property owner was a taking, but the "noxious-use justification" could not justify eliminating the entire economic value of land without compensation.[53]

Because the state court had not attempted to determine whether all beneficial uses of property had been eliminated by statute, administrative action, or state common law prior to the time the individual took title to the coastal property, the Supreme Court of the United States did not have to make the final

---

48. This test was adopted in Dolan v. City of Tigard, 512 U.S. 374, 114 S.Ct. 2309, 129 L.Ed.2d 304 (1994).

49. 505 U.S. 1003, 112 S.Ct. 2886, 120 L.Ed.2d 798 (1992), on remand 309 S.C. 424, 424 S.E.2d 484 (1992).

50. 505 U.S. at 1018, 112 S.Ct. at 2895.

51. 505 U.S. at 1026, 112 S.Ct. at 2899.

52. 505 U.S. at 1022 n. 9, 112 S.Ct. at 2896 n. 9.

53. 505 U.S. at 1022–28, 112 S.Ct. at 2897–99.

determination concerning compensation for the individual landowner in *Lucas*. The Court's opinion indicates that it would be impossible for a state to avoid compensation unless the state could show that the individual took title to worthless land by showing that the individual had taken title to land that was already subject to state law restrictions that eliminated all beneficial use of the property. The Supreme Court stated that the "total taking inquiry" would normally involve an examination of state nuisance law, state common law, the uses of property by adjacent property owners, the history of the use of the property, the social value of the activity, and the nature of any harm that could be avoided by government actions short of a complete taking.[54] Nevertheless, it seems as if it will be difficult, if not impossible, for a state to demonstrate that state law had eliminated all beneficial uses of the land before the owner took title to it.

Lucas is an important, but limited, ruling. Three points, in particular, must be kept in mind when fitting *Lucas* into the analytical framework for the resolution of taking problems that have been established by the Supreme Court during the past century. First, *Lucas* establishes a per se rule that will require a finding of a taking of property when governmental actions result in the total loss of all economically beneficial use of real property. Second, the *Lucas* rule does not apply to the governmental regulations of personal property. The Supreme Court in *Lucas* stated that the state's "traditionally high degree of economic control over commercial dealings" left open the possibility that some regulations that prohibited sale or manufacture for sale of personal property might be upheld even if those regulations made the personal property totally valueless.[55] Third, the *Lucas* decision reinforces the judicial role in examining the question of when regulatory actions of government constitute a taking of property.

The per se rule established by the *Lucas* decision applies only when a government action results in the permanent loss of virtually all economically beneficial use of real property. If the government temporarily bans development of a parcel of land, whether by a statutory moratorium on development pending the revision of land use ordinances or a delay in the granting of a building permit, the government action does not constitute a total loss in the economic value of the land, and, therefore, that government action is not to be deemed a per se taking of property under *Lucas*. A temporary prohibition of land development should be examined under the multi-factor balancing test adopted by the Supreme Court in other land use regulation cases. When using the multi-factor balancing test, courts must consider the economic impact of the regulation, the diminution in investment-backed expectations of the property owner, and the nature of the government interest as well as the reasonableness of the regulation.

In *Tahoe–Sierra Preservation Council, Inc. v. Tahoe Regional Planning Agency*[56] the Supreme Court reviewed government actions that prohibited the development of parcels of land near Lake Tahoe for over thirty months. The landowners in the case wanted to develop property that was subject to the control of the Tahoe Regional Planning Council, which had been established by a multi-state compact.[57] Pursuant to that multi-state compact, the regulatory agency adopted two land use ordinances that imposed two moratoria on development of the land of the property owners. The moratoria were designed so that the agency could create a plan for allowing limited development of land in a way that would not result in degradation of the quality of Lake Tahoe itself. The two moratoria adopted by the agency resulted in there being a period of 32 months in which there could be no development of the land. Following that 32 month time period, litigation started by the State of

---

54. 505 U.S. at 1030, 112 S.Ct. at 2901.

55. Lucas v. South Carolina Coastal Council, 505 U.S. 1003, 1026–30, 112 S.Ct. 2886, 2899–2900, 120 L.Ed.2d 798 (1992).

56. 535 U.S. 302, 122 S.Ct. 1465, 152 L.Ed.2d 517 (2002).

57. 535 U.S. at 306–12, 122 S.Ct. at 1470–73 (part I of majority opinion).

California, one of the parties to the compact, further delayed land development.

In the *Tahoe–Sierra* case the United States Supreme Court considered only whether the 32 month ban on the development of the landowners property constituted a per se taking based upon the *Lucas* decision. Indeed, the question considered by the Court in *Tahoe–Sierra* was more narrow than the question of whether there had been a taking of property under the facts and circumstances of this case. The property owners had litigated the case based solely on the theory that a ban on property use, however temporary, should be considered a per se taking of property for which compensation was due. In the United States District Court, the property owners had lost their claim that the ban on development should be considered a taking of property even if there were no per se rule that required such compensation. The District Court had found that the multi-factor analysis established by earlier Supreme Court cases, including *Penn Central Transportation Company v. New York City*,[58] led to the conclusion that there was not a taking of property. The District Court had ruled that the purchasers' reasonable investment backed expectations were not seriously diminished by the temporary restriction on development. The landowners did not challenge that portion of the District Court's ruling. Therefore, the Supreme Court, in *Tahoe–Sierra*, did not rule on whether the facts of the case would have justified finding that there was a taking of property after an examination of the impact of the regulation on the reasonable investment backed expectations of the owners and the nature of the government interests.

Justice Stevens wrote for six Justices in *Tahoe–Sierra* in ruling that temporary bans on

development did not constitute a per se taking of property requiring compensation. Justice Stevens' majority opinion found that no prior Supreme Court decision required the establishment of such a per se rule.[59] *Lucas* held that a taking occurred when a total diminution of value of real property resulted from a permanent restriction on building development.[60] In *First English Evangelical Lutheran Church of Glendale v. County of Los Angeles*[61] the Supreme Court had held that if a government action constitutes a taking of property, that the government cannot simply rescind its regulation and avoid compensation. The Court in *First English Evangelical Lutheran Church* had assumed that a taking of property had occurred and ruled only that the government always must pay fair market value to a property owner who has lost property in a manner that constitutes a taking for purposes of the Fifth Amendment takings clause. The Court in *First English Evangelical Lutheran Church* did not rule that every temporary ban on government development was a taking, it only ruled that following a determination that a taking had occurred the government must owe compensation to the landowner if even if the government thereafter rescinds its regulation.[62]

The majority opinion in *Tahoe–Sierra*, found that an independent analysis of the history and purposes of the takings clause did not justify creation of a new per se rule that would require the government to pay compensation whenever there was a temporary ban on property use. Justice Stevens noted that requiring compensation for every delay in the development of property caused by government actions could not be justified in terms of principles of fairness. In the view of the majority, property owners must expect that a variety of government actions will result in their having

---

58. 438 U.S. 104, 98 S.Ct. 2646 57 L.Ed.2d 631 (1978), which is discussed in this section of the Treatise, set forth the variety of factors that a court may consider when determining whether a government regulation of property use is so unfair and unjust as to constitute a taking of property for Fifth and Fourteenth Amendment purposes.

59. Tahoe–Sierra Preservation Council, Inc. v. Tahoe Regional Planning Agency, 535 U.S. 302, 321–32, 122 S.Ct. 1465, 1478–1484, 152 L.Ed.2d 517 (2002).

60. Lucas v. South Carolina Coastal Council, 505 U.S. 1003, 112 S.Ct. 2886, 120 L.Ed.2d 798 (1992). The *Lucas* decision is discussed in earlier paragraphs of this section of the Treatise.

61. 482 U.S. 304, 107 S.Ct. 2378, 96 L.Ed.2d 250 (1987). See § 11.14 of this Treatise.

62. Tahoe–Sierra Preservation Council, Inc. v. Tahoe Regional Planning Agency, 535 U.S. 302, 328, 122 S.Ct. 1465, 1482, 152 L.Ed.2d 517 (2002).

to wait to develop property. Justice Stevens majority opinion emphasized that the Court was not ruling that temporary delays in the ability of a property owner to develop the property would never constitute a taking. Instead, the majority in *Tahoe–Sierra* ruled that temporary restrictions on property development should be subject into an inquiry into all of the relevant facts and circumstances in the particular case to determine whether "fairness and justice" required the judiciary to make a finding that the government action causing the delay constituted a taking of property for which compensation should be required under the Fifth Amendment takings clause.[63] When a court examines a challenge to a temporary ban on property development, that court should consider the economic impact of the ban on development on the investment-backed expectations of the property owners, the nature of the government's interest and the relationship of the temporary ban to the promotion of legitimate government interests.

The three dissenting Justices in *Tahoe–Sierra* believed that prior cases established the principle that a total ban on property development should be considered a taking.[64] However, the dissenting Justices did not advocate requiring the government to give property owners an economic windfall at society's expense whenever there was a delay in the granting of development rights. Both Justice Thomas's and Chief Justice Rehnquist's dissenting opinions emphasized that the amount of compensation should vary depending on the nature of the economic impact of the delay in development and the nature of the government's interest in each case.

Justice Stevens' majority opinion in *Tahoe–Sierra* described the ability to build on proper-

ty within a certain time period as merely one aspect of a parcel or bundle of rights that the owner had in the property. The majority opinion stated that a court should consider the value of the entire parcel of property when determining whether a taking of property had occurred for purposes of the balancing test.[65] Justice Thomas, in a dissent joined by Justice Scalia, pointed out that, in earlier cases, the Court had avoided ruling on whether courts must always consider a "parcel as a whole" when engaging in takings clause analysis prior to the date of the *Tahoe–Sierra* case.[66]

General Property Use Regulations. In *Agins v. Tiburon*,[67] the opinion of Justice Powell, for a unanimous Court, stated that the determination of whether property has been taken by a zoning ordinance requires a judicial weighing of private and public interest. *Agins* involved an "open space" zoning ordinance which required the owners of a five acre tract of land to build no more than five single-family residences on their property. Prior to the zoning the property owners might have been able to subdivide their land into smaller parcels and allow for the development of more single-family dwellings. However, the Supreme Court found that the government's interest in "assuring careful and orderly development of residential property with provision for open space areas" outweighed the property owner's interest in avoiding any diminution in the market value of their land. The Court engaged in a balancing of the public and private interest and concluded that: "It cannot be said that the impact of general land use regulations has denied the appellants the 'justice and fairness' guaranteed by the Fifth and Fourteenth Amendments."[68]

63. 535 U.S. at 334, 122 S.Ct. at 1485: "The ultimate constitutional question is whether the concepts of 'fairness and justice' that underlie the takings clause will be better served by one of these categorical rules or by a *Penn Central* inquiry into all of the relevant circumstances in particular cases."

64. Tahoe–Sierra Preservation Council, Inc. v. Tahoe Regional Planning Agency, 535 U.S. 302, 343, 122 S.Ct. 1465, 1490, 152 L.Ed.2d 517 (2002) (Rehnquist, C.J., joined by Scalia and Thomas, JJ., dissenting). 535 U.S. at 355, 122 S.Ct. at 1496 (Thomas, J., joined by Scalia, J., dissenting).

65. Tahoe–Sierra Preservation Council, Inc. v. Tahoe Regional Planning Agency, 535 U.S. 302, 330–31, 122 S.Ct. 1465, 1483–84, 152 L.Ed.2d 517 (2002).

66. 535 U.S. at 355, 122 S.Ct. at 1496 (Thomas, J., joined by Scalia, J., dissenting).

67. 447 U.S. 255, 100 S.Ct. 2138, 65 L.Ed.2d 106 (1980).

68. 447 U.S. at 262, 100 S.Ct. at 2142. See also Hodel v. Indiana, 452 U.S. 314, 101 S.Ct. 2376, 69 L.Ed.2d 40 (1981) (finding that "prime farmland" provisions of Surface Mining and Reclamation Control Act did not, on their

A zoning ordinance, or other property use regulation, will constitute a taking of property for which compensation is due, if the regulation unjustifiably shifts social costs to an individual property owner or a group of property owners. When a court upholds a zoning or property use statute "on its face", it is only holding that the statute does not constitute a per se taking of property from all persons whose property is regulated by the statute. A particular government statute regulating property use may not constitute a taking on its face but may still constitute a taking for which just compensation is due if the statute, as applied to an individual item of property or property owner, deprives a property owner of the value of the property.

In *Keystone Bituminous Coal Association v. DeBenedictis* [69] the Court held that a state statute and administrative regulatory system that required the owners of subsurface mineral rights to leave 50% of the coal in the ground below certain types of structures and surfaces was not a taking of property for which just compensation was due. Sixty-five years earlier, in *Pennsylvania Coal Co. v. Mahon*,[70] the Supreme Court had found that a statute that severely restricted the mining of coal by persons who own subsurface mining rights did constitute a taking of property. In the *Keystone* case, the Supreme Court ruled that Justice Holmes' opinion in *Pennsylvania Coal* was based on the premise that the original state statute served only the interest of climate owners of surface land and that the statute made it impractical to profitably mine coal. By a five to four vote, the Justices in the *Keystone* decision applied the modern balancing of interests test to determine whether the regulation constituted a taking of property. Under this approach, a court must examine the extent to which the regulation substantially advanced a legitimate state interest and the extent to which the regulation denies the prop-

erty owner an economically viable use of the property.

In *Keystone*, the majority found that the requirement that the mining operators leave a certain percentage of coal in the ground and take steps to prevent or repair damage to surface interests was designed to protect a wide variety of public and private uses of surface property. The statute was not merely a wealth transfer from the coal owners to the private owners of surface property rights. The mining restriction was not declared a taking on its face because it did not make the mining of coal impractical or in any sense unprofitable. Regardless of statutory restrictions, the technological state of the mining industry required a significant percentage of coal be left in the ground; the statute imposed, in the majority's view, only a slight and reasonable diminution in the value and investment-backed expectations of coal company operations. The Court was unwilling to find that a statute requiring a percentage of coal to be left in the ground was a physical appropriation of that coal; the majority examined the loss to the owners of the coal in terms of the diminution in the value of their mining business. The majority found that "our test for regulatory takings requires us to compare the value that has been taken from the property with the value that remains in the property . . .". Because the statute promoted a significant public interest, and resulted in only a slight diminution in value of mining operations, no taking was found.

However, the majority opinion in *Keystone* did not eliminate the possibility that an individual owner of subsurface coal rights might have his property taken. If an individual property owner could show that the application of the mining restriction to his property eliminated any economically viable use of the subsurface coal rights for that particular area, the Court might find that the property owner was owed just compensation by the government.[71]

face, deprive the property owner of economically beneficial use of his property without just compensation, even though the regulation restricted the amount, type, and profitability of mining operations).

69. 480 U.S. 470, 107 S.Ct. 1232, 94 L.Ed.2d 472 (1987).

70. 260 U.S. 393, 43 S.Ct. 158, 67 L.Ed. 322 (1922).

71. If the government appropriates property for its own use or for the use of the general public, the owner will

Landmark Zoning—The *Penn Central* Case. In *Penn Central Transportation Co. v. New York*,[72] the Supreme Court held that the New York City Landmarks Preservation Law might be employed, consistently with due process, to limit building rights in the vicinity of the historic Grand Central Station. The Court ruled that the limitation imposed by New York's Landmarks Preservation Commission did not constitute a "taking" or otherwise require exercise of the eminent domain power. Under the New York law, the Landmark Preservation Commission was empowered to designate property as a "landmark," and "landmark site," or a "historic district;" such designation was then approved by higher administrative authority in light of New York's overall zoning plan, and was ultimately subject to judicial review. Designation carried with it certain restrictions on the use of designated property, among which were that the owner must keep the property in "good repair," and that alterations of the external appearance of the property were subject to prior approval by the commission. Denial of approval was subject to judicial review. New York law also provided, however, for certain benefits to owners of property designated by the commission. Chief among these was the right of the owner to transfer unused development rights from restricted property to nearby property which had not been restricted by the commission. The effect of this allowance was to permit owners of both non-historic property and property designated as historic to exceed existing zoning regulations on the development of their non-historic property to the ex-

tent that development had been curtailed by the Landmark Law on their nearby historic property. This allowance was intended to mitigate much of the economic deprivation which would inevitably result from development restrictions on historic property.

In *Penn Central*, the Landmark Preservation Commission had denied Penn Central permission to build a multi-story office building above Grand Central Station. The Commission concluded that "to balance a 55–story office tower above a flamboyant Beaux–Arts facade seems nothing more than an aesthetic joke ...."[73] Rather than refrain from the endeavor and transfer its unused building rights to its other adjacent property, however, Penn Central sought review of the commission's decision.

The Supreme Court in *Penn Central* ruled that there had been no "taking" of property. A majority of the Justices found the regulations a reasonable means of promoting important general welfare interests in environmental control and historic preservation. The majority opinion found the existence of an allowance for transfer of development rights supportive of its determination of the law's reasonableness, but did not indicate that, absent such allowance, the restrictions imposed on Penn Central's property would have amounted to a "taking" for which compensation would be required.[74] The Court did, however, specifically note that the allowance of transfer rights mitigated the loss to owners of historic property, and was thus a factor both in the finding that the law itself was a reason-

---

be entitled to just compensation. The state might be able to totally destroy the value of some pieces of property if the government action is narrowly tailored to stop a public nuisance or the property is being used to engage in activity which the state can lawfully proscribe. Thus, the state might totally prohibit the use of a narcotic substance which was once lawful to hold and possess in the state, and it might require the complete elimination of property uses that created health hazards to the community. In each case, the type of actual taking (appropriation or regulation) is important in determining whether just compensation is due for only a slight diminution in value or whether the Court should engage in the balancing test used in the property use and zoning cases. Keystone Bituminous Coal Association v. DeBenedictis, 480 U.S. 470, 488 n. 18, 492 n. 22, 499 n. 27, 107 S.Ct. 1232, 1244 n. 18, 1246 n. 22, 1250 n. 27, 94 L.Ed.2d 472 (1987).

72. 438 U.S. 104, 98 S.Ct. 2646, 57 L.Ed.2d 631 (1978).

73. 438 U.S. at 117–18, 98 S.Ct. at 2656.

74. 438 U.S. at 137, 98 S.Ct. at 2666. The "adequate compensation" issue, as well as the taking issue, had been the focus of modern analysis of prospects for "transferable development right" (TDR) programs. See § 11.14, infra.

The dissenting Justices would have held that the restrictions on property use constituted a "taking" because those restrictions destroyed valuable property rights. The dissenting justices would not have reached the question of whether TDR's constituted adequate compensation; they would have remanded the case to the New York Court of Appeals for an initial determining of this issue. 438 U.S. at 151, 98 S.Ct. at 2673 (Rehnquist, J., dissenting, joined by Burger, C.J., & Stevens, J.).

able exercise of the police powers and in the finding that the magnitude of Penn Central's loss did not rise to the level of a "taking."[75]

The *Penn Central* case involved a type of "spot zoning," which is a term often used to describe a government regulation that is applicable only to one specific parcel of land. In the *Penn Central* case the government regulated a unique parcel of land in order to promote the public interest in the protection of a historic landmark. Because the owners of Grand Central Station, following the spot zoning, still received a reasonable return on their investment by developing and managing the property within the regulatory limits the Court in *Penn Central* was able to find that the spot zoning regulation did not constitute a taking of property.

A more difficult type of "spot regulation" problem is presented when a governmental entity conditions the granting of a building permit on the property owner's agreement to dedicate a portion of the property to public use. We will examine the conditional building permit problem after we examine the cases in which the Supreme Court has held that government actions that take away property owner's right to exclude other persons from the property are takings for which the government must pay just compensation.

Uncertainty Regarding Property Regulations and the Takings Clause at the Start of a New Millenium. At the start of the 21st Century the Supreme Court refused to give guidance to lower federal court and state court judges regarding two important questions regarding property use regulations and the just compensation clause. First, the Court left open the question of whether a land-use regulation that prohibited the owner of a plot of land from making any use of one portion of his land constituted a *per se* taking under principles established in *Lucas*.[76] Second, the Supreme Court was unclear regarding the extent to which a current property owner was entitled to just compensation for land use

regulations that existed at the time he purchased the property (and which might have constituted an unconstitutional taking of property from the prior owner of the land).

A hypothetical case. Let us assume that in 1970 Mr. Able, who was then 35 years old, purchased a 100 acre tract of land to fulfill his lifelong dream of owning his own farm. He made use of 80 of the acres of this land for his residence, farm buildings and crops that he grew and sold. 20 acres of the property was not usable for farming, because it was covered with water throughout much of the year. We will refer to the 20 acres that was not usable as "wetland."

We will also assume that, in 1980 the state government enacted a law that prohibits any development of land that is used as a habitat by certain types of birds. Such land is referred to as "wetland." This legislation allows a government established land use board to grant an owner of wetland permission to develop the wetland if the Board determines that the intended use of the land, for which the waiver is sought, would serve an overriding need.

In 1990, Mr. Able applied to the land use board [the Board] for permit to farm the final 20 acres of his land, which had been designated as a wetland area. Mr. Able waited until 1990 to apply for the permit, because this is the first time when it would be economically practical to drain the land and use it for farming. In 1990 Mr. Able's application was turned down by the Board. Mr. Able was advised by an attorney that he might be able to have the land use statute or the denial of his permit be declared an invalid taking of property without just compensation. Nevertheless, Mr. Able decided not to appeal from, or otherwise challenge, the ruling of the government board in court.

In the year 2000, Mr. Able decided to retire from farming and to sell his land. He sold the entire 100 acre tract to Ms. Baker, an entrepreneur who previously had successfully established several industrial parks and residential

---

75. Penn Central Transp. Co. v. New York, 438 U.S. 104, 115–16, 139, 98 S.Ct. 2646, 2654–55, 2666–67, 57 L.Ed.2d 631 (1978).

76. Lucas v. South Carolina Coastal Council, 505 U.S. 1003, 112 S.Ct. 2886, 120 L.Ed.2d 798 (1992).

developments. Mr. Able sold the property to Ms. Baker for $800,000. Indeed, the fair market value of the land, subject to the wetlands restrictions and assuming the 20 wetland acres could not be developed, was exactly $800,000. However, if the wetlands legislation were repealed, or if the Board would allow development of the 20 acres, the fair market value of the land would be $1,000,000.

In 2001, after purchasing the land for $800,000, Ms. Baker submitted a plan to the Board for development of the entire 100 acre tract of land as a business center. She asked for permission to fill in the 20 acres and to make the entire 100 acres a place where a variety of high technology (non-polluting) businesses might locate offices and research facilities. The types of uses that Ms. Baker plans for the land are entirely consistent with all state and local zoning laws, except for her intended use of the 20 acres of wetlands. In other words, Mrs. Baker could have developed a 20 acre business center. The Board turned down Ms. Baker's development plan by refusing to grant her a waiver for the development of the wetlands area. Ms. Baker chose not to submit a new plan for the use of the land. Instead, she brought suit against the government for taking her property by denying her the ability to fully develop the 100 acres.

Our Able–Baker hypothetical would present three questions that should be fairly easy to analyze. First, should Ms. Baker be able to challenge the denial of her plan as being an unconstitutional taking of property based on the permit denial alone? Second, if Ms. Baker can challenge the denial of the permit can she assert that the wetlands regulation (which applied to the land before she purchased it) took her property without just compensation or, in the alternative, did Mr. Able waive any such claim relating to the land (in the sense that he was the only person whose property was taken by the government action)? Third, if Ms. Bak-

er can assert that the wetlands regulation, and the denial of permit to her, constitute a taking of property, should the courts treat the government wetlands law as a law that eliminates the entire use of real property (the 20 acres) which would be a *per se* taking under *Lucas*[77] or, in the alternative, should a court analyze the issue in terms of the extent to which the regulation had diminished the value of the entire 100 acre tract of land?[78]

The *Palazzolo* Case. All of the above hypothetical questions were presented to the Supreme Court in *Palazzolo v. Rhode Island*.[79] In 1959, Mr. Palazzolo and some associates formed a corporation that purchased land. Eventually, Mr. Palazzolo, through payments to his partners, became the sole shareholder in the corporation. Most of the real property owned by the corporation was a salt marsh, which was subject to flooding at certain times of the year. Several times Mr. Palazzolo, and his corporation, attempted to develop the property, but the development plans were always turned down by government agencies prior to the time when the State of Rhode Island sought to protect certain coastal properties and wetlands. In the early 1970's Rhode Island created a government council with the responsibility of protecting certain coastal properties; that government council enacted regulations preventing the development of coastal wetlands, except under very limited circumstances.

In the late 1970's, Mr. Palazzolo's corporation's charter was revoked due to his failure to pay corporate taxes. When the corporate title was revoked, title to the marshland property passed to Mr. Palazzolo as an individual. In 1983 and in 1985 he applied for permission to fill 11 of the property's 18 wetland acres to build a private beach club. When his last permit application was denied, he brought suit in the state courts alleging that his property had been taken through the denial of his request

---

77. See notes 49–55, and accompanying text, supra.

78. Factors of particular importance involve an assessment of the economic impact of the regulation, the interference with investment-backed expectations and the nature of the government action. See, Connolly v. Pension Benefit Guaranty Corp., 475 U.S. 211, 225, 106 S.Ct. 1018,

1026, 89 L.Ed.2d 166 (1986); Penn Central Transportation Co. v. New York, 438 U.S. 104, 124, 98 S.Ct. 2646, 2659, 57 L.Ed.2d 631. See generally § 11.12(a).

79. 533 U.S. 606, 121 S.Ct. 2448, 150 L.Ed.2d 592 (2001).

to use the land. The Rhode Island State Supreme Court affirmed a lower court ruling against Mr. Palazzolo by finding that: his claim was not ripe; he had no right to challenge regulations that were enacted prior to 1978 when he took legal ownership of the property as an individual; and he could not assert a takings claim based on denial of 100% of the value of the wetlands acre because the regulation simply lowered the value of the entire tract of property.

It is somewhat surprising that the Supreme Court granted certiorari in the *Palazzolo* case, or did not dismiss the case as being one in which certiorari had been improvidently granted. The key difference between our hypothetical and the *Palazzolo* case is the clarity of the facts. In our hypothetical, we had two very distinct owners, Mr. Able and Ms. Baker. In the *Palazzolo* case there were two technically distinct owners, the corporation with one shareholder and the individual shareholder who took title to the property when the corporation ceased to exist. Nevertheless, in the *Palazzolo* case only the interests of one person, Mr. Palazzolo were at stake, both prior to and after the government regulations were enacted. For reasons known only to the Justices, the Court chose to decide the case as if there were two distinct owners: one that owned the land at the time the property regulation took effect (the corporation, which would be the equivalent of our Mr. Able); and one owner who purchased the land that had already been subject to the regulations and the refusal to allow usage of the wetlands area (Mr. Palazzolo in his personal capacity, who would be the equivalent of our Ms. Baker).

Justice Kennedy wrote the opinion of the Court in *Palazzolo*. His opinion was joined in its entirety by Chief Justice Rehnquist and Justices O'Connor, Scalia and Thomas. Justice Stevens concurred with the part of the Kennedy opinion regarding the ripeness issue [what we described as the first question in our hypo-

thetical], although he dissented on the merits of the case. Only the Chief Justice and Justice Thomas joined the Kennedy opinion without further comment. Justice O'Connor and Justice Scalia concurred in the majority opinion while offering separate views of how taking of property issues should be dealt with in the future.

Justice Kennedy's majority opinion in *Palazzolo* ruled that the taking of property issue were "ripe" for adjudication.[80] The ripeness issue centered on the fact that the property owner had not put forth a specific alternative use for the land, following the denial of his petition to develop the case. The government asserted that there was no ripe issue for adjudication, because there was no way to compare the value of his land after the denial of the permit to fill in the wetlands and the value of his land when it was merely subject to the wetland regulation. Six Justices, however, found that once Mr. Palazzolo's request for a permit to fill in the wetlands was denied by the government council, there was a distinct harm to the individual property owner who could then litigate the takings issue.[81]

Justice Ginsburg wrote a dissenting opinion that addressed only the ripeness issue.[82] She was joined by Justices Souter and Breyer in stating that any ruling on the taking of property claim was premature, because the owner could not show a specific harm that resulted from the denial of the permit. According to these dissenting Justices the owner could only show a specific harm if he had had a more specific plan for development of the property.

The Justices assumed that the corporation was sufficiently distinct from Mr. Palazzolo that it had to address the question of whether he could challenge the government regulation as a taking even though the regulation had occurred when the land was technically owned by the corporation. If the majority of the Justices had simply found that the corporation

---

80. The majority's analysis of the ripeness issue is contained in part II–A of the majority opinion by Justice Kennedy. 533 U.S. at 618–25, 121 S.Ct. at 2458–62.

81. Id. Ripeness issues are examined in § 2.13(d) of this Treatise.

82. Palazzolo v. Rhode Island, 533 U.S. 606, 644, 121 S.Ct. 2448, 2472, 150 L.Ed.2d 592 (2001) (Ginsburg, J., joined by Souter and Breyer, JJ., dissenting).

and individual landowner should be treated as one and the same, there would have been no issue concerning whether he could now raise the takings issue.

Justice Kennedy wrote for only five Justices in finding that the person who purchased land that was subject to prior property use regulations could challenge those regulations under the takings clause.[83] Justice Kennedy found that language in the *Lucas* opinion indicating that the government could defend against a takings claim by showing that the property owner purchased the property after it had been subjected to certain government regulations did not prohibit a new property owner from challenging these regulations.[84]

Justice Stevens dissented because he believed that the harm that occurred to the property at the time of the taking was personal to the individual (whether the individual was an actual human being or a legal entity such as a corporation) that owned the land at the time of the alleged regulatory taking.[85] In other words, in our hypothetical example, Justice Stevens would have found that Mr. Able could sue for the alleged taking of his property by the government regulation and permit denial. Under Justice Stevens' position, Ms. Baker could not have an injury from a government regulation, because she only purchased property that was 80% usable and she paid the fair market value for the property as subject to the regulation. Thus, if a court accepted Justice Stevens' view, it would rule that Ms. Baker suffered no injury from the government regulation, because the government never took her property.

As demonstrated by the separate opinions in *Palazzolo*, it appears that between six and eight of the Justices would agree that our hypothetical Ms. Baker could pay fair market value for land subject to regulation and then challenge the regulation as an improper taking of property. If Ms. Baker won that claim, she would have received a bargain, because she purchased the land at a lower value than it would have been worth if Mr. Able had himself sued the government under the takings clause.

Justice Stevens was the only Justice who asserted that a property owner should be completely barred from alleging that any property use regulations that had applied to the land prior to the time of his purchase constituted a taking of his property. Justice Ginsburg's dissent, joined by Justices Souter and Breyer, focused only on the ripeness issue, and did not foreclose the possibility that these Justices would, in the future, vote to allow a new prospect to challenge the property regulations that had been applicable to the property when she bought it.[86]

Justice O'Connor joined the majority opinion in *Palazzolo*. Nevertheless, she wrote separately to explain her belief that the fact that land was subject to regulation at the time of purchase was only one factor to consider when assessing a regulatory takings claim.[87] Justice Breyer dissented because he believed that the takings issue was not ripe for adjudication. Nevertheless, Justice Breyer stated that he "would agree with Justice O'Connor that the simple fact that a piece of property has changed hands (for example, by inheritance) does not always and automatically bar a takings claim. Here, for example, without suggesting that Palazzolo has any valid takings claim, I believe that his post-regulatory acquisition of the property (through automatic operation of law) by itself should not prove dispositive."[88]

Justice Scalia also joined the majority opinion in *Palazzolo*. In a separate opinion he stated that when a purchaser of land subject to property regulations is challenged those regulations as a taking of property, a court should

---

83. Palazzolo v. Rhode Island, 533 U.S. 606, 625–29, 121 S.Ct. 2448, 2462–64, 150 L.Ed.2d 592 (2001).

84. 533 U.S. at 629, 121 S.Ct. at 2464, distinguishing Lucas v. South Carolina Coastal Council, 505 U.S. 1003, 1029, 112 S.Ct. 2886, 2900, 120 L.Ed.2d 798 (1992).

85. Palazzolo v. Rhode Island, 533 U.S. 606, 636, 121 S.Ct. 2448, 2468, 150 L.Ed.2d 592 (2001) (Stevens, J., concurring in part and dissenting in part).

86. 533 U.S. at 644, 121 S.Ct. at 2472 (Ginsburg, J., joined by Souter and Breyer, JJ., dissenting).

87. 533 U.S. at 631, 121 S.Ct. at 2465 (O'Connor, J., concurring).

88. 533 U.S. at 653, 121 S.Ct. at 2477 (Breyer, J., dissenting).

give absolutely no weight to the fact that the land had been subject to the regulation prior to the time of purchase.[89] In such a situation, Justice Scalia asserted that the courts must allow the second owner [Ms. Baker in our hypothetical, and Mr. Palazzolo, in his personal capacity, in the real case] to receive an arguable windfall if the second owner was able to show that the regulation had constituted a taking of property when it was first applied to the land.

None of the Justices in *Palazzolo* considered the last issue that we set out in the hypothetical: whether the prohibition of any use of some part of a parcel of land should be analyzed as a *per se* taking under *Lucas,* or in the alternative, a diminution in the total value of the total parcel of land. Justice Kennedy's majority opinion in *Palazzolo* found that the Supreme Court did not need to address this issue because of the way in which the petition for certiorari had been worded. Justice Kennedy stated that addressing the issue of whether the individual was totally deprived of a distinct portion of land would require the Court to resolve a "difficult, persisting question...."[90] Justice Kennedy noted that some of the Supreme Court's decisions indicated that actions that removed one aspect of a land's value simply required that the impact of the regulatory action be measured against the value of the whole parcel of property, but that the Court had "at times expressed discomfort with the logic of this rule" because such a rule might allow for the total deprivation of the value of a distinct parcel of land.[91] Justice Kennedy's majority opinion omitted any reference to the easement cases, which established

the principal that changing the occupation rights to property would constitute a *per se* taking.[92] The property owner whose land becomes subject to wetlands regulation that prohibits any improvement of part of his land, when he challenges the regulation, asserts that the government has effectively taken an easement over a strip of his land. From the perspective of the property owner it is irrelevant that this easement allows for the use of the land by birds, rather than by human beings.

Justice Breyer noted that there should be no difference in the ability of an individual to make a claim regarding total deprivation of value simply by having structured transactions to isolate the portion of the land that was subject to the regulations.[93] Justice Breyer did not take a position on whether such wetlands or coastal protection legislation would constitute a taking of property. He simply indicated that in a case like our hypothetical, either Mr. Able should or should not receive compensation for making 20 acres of his land totally unusable. The takings clause determination should not rest in any way on whether Mr. Able brought the action while he owned the entire 100 acres, or whether he sold the 20 unusable acres to another person who would than bring the takings claim.

None of the Justices challenged the majority's conclusion that: "the case comes to us on the premise that the petitioner's entire parcel serves as the basis for his takings claim, and, so framed, the total deprivation [of the value of part of his land] argument fails."[94] Because the Justices found that Mr. Palazzolo had presented his case as one where the coastal and

---

89. 533 U.S. at 634, 121 S.Ct. at 2467 (Scalia, J., concurring).

90. Palazzolo v. Rhode Island, 533 U.S. 606, 631, 121 S.Ct. 2448, 2465, 150 L.Ed.2d 592 (2001).

91. Id. One year after the *Palazzolo* decision, the Supreme Court ruled that a temporary moratorium on the economic development of property was to be examined under the multi-factor *Penn Central* analysis. Tahoe–Sierra Preservation Council, Inc. v. Tahoe Regional Planning Agency, 535 U.S. 302, 122 S.Ct. 1465, 152 L.Ed.2d 517 (2002). Justice Stevens' majority opinion in *Tahoe–Sierra* stated that the nature of property interests in a parcel should not be considered separately for purposes of determining whether a temporary taking should be deemed to

be a per se violation of the takings clause. However, the *Tahoe–Sierra* case, like the *Palazzolo* case, did not require the Court to address the question of whether a complete prohibition of development of a discrete part of a parcel of land should be considered a per se taking of property.

92. See, e.g., Kaiser Aetna v. United States, 444 U.S. 164, 100 S.Ct. 383, 62 L.Ed.2d 332 (1979); Loretto v. Teleprompter Manhattan CATV Corp., 458 U.S. 419, 102 S.Ct. 3164, 73 L.Ed.2d 868 (1982).

93. 533 U.S. at 653, 121 S.Ct. at 2477 (Breyer, J., dissenting).

94. Palazzolo v. Rhode Island 533 U.S. 606, 631, 121 S.Ct. 2448, 2465, 150 L.Ed.2d 592 (2001).

wetlands regulation harmed the value of the entire parcel of land, his claim had to be assessed under the multi-factor analysis that stemmed from the decision in *Penn Central,* and cases following that decision.[95]

In her concurring opinion, Justice O'Connor found that the fact that an individual knew of the regulations prior to acquiring the land would play an important role in assessing the current owner's investment backed expectations.[96] According to Justice O'Connor that fact was an important factor, but only one factor, for courts to consider when determining whether fairness required compensation to the purchaser of a land subject to regulations that would have been found to be a taking if the regulations had been challenged by a prior owner. Justice Breyer agreed with Justice O'Connor's taking clause analysis.[97]

Justice Scalia, on the other hand, believed that the government should gain absolutely no benefit from the fact that property that is subjected to an unconstitutional regulation was transferred at a low price to a subsequent purchaser who challenged the regulation. In Justice Scalia's view, the "investment-backed expectations" of a current property owner include the assumed validity of a restriction that deprives the property of so much of its value as to be unconstitutional.[98]

Physical Occupations as Per Se Takings. Today the Court will allow governmental entities to regulate either real or personal property for the public good without the requirement of compensation so long as the action is not an unreasonable infringement of the rights of the private property owner. The government, however, is not free to transfer property rights from one group of owners to another or to take and use private property for the public good (1) unless the action is justified by emergency conditions, or (2) unless compensation is paid.

A permanent physical occupation of private property by the government or a government regulation which allows someone other than the property owner to have permanent physical occupation of a definable part of a piece of property should constitute a taking.[99] The government must pay compensation for such a taking of traditional property rights. However, in some cases, such as those which follow in this section, it may be difficult to determine when a transfer of property rights has taken place.[100]

The *Brown* Case—Tying Together Takings Clause Issues. In *Brown v. Legal Foundation of Washington*[101] the Justices were sharply divided in ruling on a variety of tak-

95. Penn Central Transportation Co. v. New York, 438 U.S. 104, 98 S.Ct. 2646, 57 L.Ed.2d 631 (1978). All of the cases that would be involved in a multi-faceted analysis of whether property use regulations constitute a taking of property are examined in subsections 11.12(a) and 11.12(b) of this Treatise.

96. Palazzolo v. Rhode Island, 533 U.S. 606, 631, 121 S.Ct. 2448, 2465, 150 L.Ed.2d 592 (2001) (O'Connor, J., concurring).

97. 533 U.S. at 653, 121 S.Ct. at 2477 (Breyer, J., dissenting).

98. 533 U.S. at 636, 121 S.Ct. at 2468 (Scalia, J., concurring).

99. Loretto v. Teleprompter Manhattan CATV Corp., 458 U.S. 419, 102 S.Ct. 3164, 73 L.Ed.2d 868 (1982), on remand 58 N.Y.2d 143, 459 N.Y.S.2d 743, 446 N.E.2d 428 (1983) (city ordinance requiring landlord building owner to allow installation of cable television receiver on apartment building and denying landlord the ability to demand payment in excess of $1 constitutes a compensable taking because the ordinance allowed for "permanent physical occupation" of a small part of the building).

100. Rent Control Statutes. In Yee v. City of Escondido, 503 U.S. 519, 112 S.Ct. 1522, 118 L.Ed.2d 153 (1992), the Supreme Court held that a rent control statute

applicable to mobile home parks did not constitute a physical occupation of the land owner's property. Thus, the rent control statute did not come under the so-called per se taking rule applied to government actions that involve physical invasions of property or government actions that require a landowner to submit to the occupation of his land. The Court did not rule on the question of whether the rent control statute at issue in *Yee* was a regulatory taking, because the Court believed that the claim was not ripe for review due to the fact that it had not been raised and fully explored in the lower courts.

The Supreme Court has upheld rent control and rent continuation statutes in light of congressional concerns over war time and post-war economic conditions. See Block v. Hirsh, 256 U.S. 135, 41 S.Ct. 458, 65 L.Ed. 865 (1921). See also Bowles v. Willingham, 321 U.S. 503, 64 S.Ct. 641, 88 L.Ed. 892 (1944). For citations to additional cases on this point, see R. Rotunda & J. Nowak, Treatise on Constitutional Law: Substance and Procedure, § 15.12 (3rd ed. 1999, with annual supplements).

101. 538 U.S. 216, 123 S.Ct. 1406, 155 L.Ed.2d 376 (2003).

ings clause issues. The *Brown* decision involved state regulation of the accounts held by attorneys and escrow services for clients, and the government's use of the interest on those funds. Attorneys often have to hold money for a client on a temporary basis. Rules of professional responsibility prohibit a attorney from co-mingling client funds with the attorney's own money. Sometimes, attorneys hold an amount of money for a client that is so large that the attorney will place the funds into an account with a financial institution that will generate monetary interest. That monetary interest, of course, belongs to the client.[102] Attorneys may hold money for clients in small amounts that would not generate interest, and these small amounts of money are normally placed in accounts that will not produce any monetary interest.

During the last part of the twentieth century every state, through legislation or a state supreme court rule, required attorneys to place all of the funds of their clients that would not otherwise generate monetary interest into single accounts of a type that would generate interest (because of the size of the account for the combined funds). The monetary interest that was created by funds held in such combined accounts would be considered the property of the clients whose funds were placed in the accounts.[103] nevertheless, each state required the attorneys to turn over the monetary interest from the fund with the combined small accounts to some type of government fund that would subsidize legal services for low-income persons.

Federal and state governments may take property for public use. Although the public use requirement has never been a significant one, the government taking of property, even with compensation, must be done to produce some type of social benefit. Justice Stevens wrote a majority opinion for five Justices in *Brown v. Legal Foundation of Washington*.[104] Justice Stevens' opinion, following an unbroken line of Supreme Court decisions, found that the public use requirement was satisfied so long as the taking of property, if any, was rationally related to promote any legitimate public interest.[105] The majority ruled that providing legal services for low-income persons was a legitimate, and, perhaps, compelling interest of government. Thus, any taking of property in this case would relate to a public use.[106]

A government regulation of property might constitute a taking of property if it diminishes the value of the property in an unfair and unjust manner.[107] The determination of whether a regulation constitutes a taking requires an examination of the nature of a government action that diminishes reasonable investment-backed expectations. That determination involves judicial consideration of a variety of factors that the Court has set out in cases following its landmark decision in the *Penn Central Transportation* case.[108] Justice Stevens' majority opinion in *Brown* found that the government regulation of trust accounts could not be found to be a taking of property under the factors following the "ad-hoc approach applied in *Penn Central Transportation* ... because [the owners of the money put into the combined accounts] had suffered neither an actual loss nor interference with any investment-backed expectations. . . . "[109]

102. The ownership issue had been settled in Phillips v. Washington Legal Foundation, 524 U.S. 156, 118 S.Ct. 1925, 141 L.Ed.2d 174 (1998).

103. The Court rules in statutes requiring these types of funds and the transfer of funds are collected in footnote 2 of the *Brown* decision. Brown v. Legal Foundation of Washington, 538 U.S. 216, 221 n. 2, 123 S.Ct. 1406, 1411–12 n. 2, 155 L.Ed.2d 376 (2003).

104. 538 U.S. 216, 123 S.Ct. 1406, 155 L.Ed.2d 376.

105. See § 11.13

106. Brown v. Legal Foundation of Washington, 538 U.S. 216, 232, 123 S.Ct. 1406, 1417, 155 L.Ed.2d 376 (2003): ". . . dramatic success of these programs in serving the compelling interests in providing legal services ... certainly qualifies [the program] as a 'public use' within the meaning of the Fifth Amendment."

107. Connolly v. Pension Benefit Guaranty Corp., 475 U.S. 211, 225, 106 S.Ct. 1018, 1026, 89 L.Ed.2d 166 (1986). The *Connoly* case is examined in § 11.12(a).

108. 438 U.S. 104, 124, 98 S.Ct. 2646, 2659, 57 L.Ed.2d 631 (1978). The *Penn Central* case is examined in § 11.12(d).

109. Brown v. Legal Foundation of Washington, 538 U.S. 216, 231, 123 S.Ct. 1416, 1418, 155 L.Ed.2d 376 (2003).

The government requirement that attorneys transfer the monetary interest on the combined small accounts to the fund for legal services was the equivalent of a direct government confiscation of that monetary interest. Therefore, Justice Stevens' majority opinion ruled that the required transfer of the interest income constituted a taking of property, based under the line of cases that found that government's physical occupation of property was a taking that required compensation.[110]

Because there was a taking of property, the owners of the property were owed just compensation. These persons were the beneficial owners of the small amounts of money held by an attorney who was required to place their money into an interest generating account with the funds of other clients. The Justices divided 5 to 4 over the question of what amount of compensation was owed to those persons.

The Supreme Court had long held that an amount owed to an individual whose property was taken by the government was to be based on the nature of the property owner's loss, rather than the value of the property after it was taken and used by the government.[111] For example, if the government took a piece of land that was worth $100,000 and then combined it with other land owned by the government, the value of the individual piece of land might have escalated from $100,000 to $1,000,000 [due to its now being a part of a large development]. However, the government would only owe $100,000 to the individual whose property was taken [the value of the property before it was taken by the government and converted to public use].

Applying the loss to the property owner concept in *Brown*, Justice Stevens' majority opinion found that no monetary compensation was due to the owners of small amounts of money that had been combined into accounts that generated the monetary interest that was transferred to the fund to subsidize legal services for low income persons. The owners of small amounts of money held by attorneys would not have received any interest prior to the state law allowing for the combination of funds into an interest bearing account. In other words, the net earnings for each client who had a small amount money that was being held by an attorney would have been zero before the enactment of the state statute. Therefore, the loss to each such person was, in the view of the majority, zero dollars; the amount of compensation they were to be paid also was zero.[112] If an individual client of an attorney had an account that was so large that it would have produced interest by being placed into a separate account, even prior to the legal services funding statute, the government would owe the interest amount to the property owner if it took that interest for a public use. However, the governmental taking of the monetary interest from the combined fund consisting of the small amounts of money held by attorneys (which would not have produced any income in individual accounts) required no compensation.[113]

Limitations on the Owner's Right to Exclude Others. *Kaiser Aetna v. United States* [114] held that the application of the federal navigational servitude to a lagoon on the island of Oahu constituted a taking for which

110. See § 11.14.

111. Brown v. Legal Foundation of Washington, 538 U.S. 216, 237–39, 123 S.Ct. 1406, 1420–21, 155 L.Ed.2d 376 (2003) (parts V and VI of the majority opinion).

112. Justice Scalia, writing for four Justices, believed that the Court's analysis of takings clause values and its analysis of the value to be paid to individuals once there is a taking of property was unprecedented as well as incorrect. 538 U.S. at 241, 123 S.Ct. at 1422 (Scalia, J., joined by Rehnquist, C.J., and Kennedy and Thomas, JJ., dissenting).

Justice Kennedy, in a dissent that was not joined by any other Justice, also believed that the use of the funds created by the pooling of small accounts for litigation

supporting the views of low-income clients might constitute a First Amendment freedom of association problem. 538 U.S. at 253, 123 S.Ct. at 1428 (Kennedy, J. dissenting).

113. Although Justice Stevens' majority opinion involved a rather straightforward application of the principles set forth in prior cases, and this Treatise, the majority opinion left open many issues. See generally, Ronald D. Rotunda, Found Money: IOLTA, Brown v. Legal Foundation of Washington, and the Taking of Property without the Payment of Compensation, 2002–2003 Cato Supreme Court Review 245.

114. 444 U.S. 164, 100 S.Ct. 383, 62 L.Ed.2d 332 (1979).

compensation was required. Historically, the pond in question was considered to be private property. It was leased, along with the surrounding land, to a resort and private housing developer. The developer converted the pond into a marina, and dug channels connecting it with a bay which allowed ships to travel from the lagoon into the bay and the ocean. The federal government claimed that the connection of the waterway to the bay made it a "navigable water" of the United States and therefore subject to regulation by the Corps of Engineers and open to public use.

The Supreme Court found that the lagoon was a navigable waterway and subject to regulation by the United States government and the Corps of Engineers acting under the commerce power. However, the government could not require the owners and lessees of the marina to allow the public free access without invoking the eminent domain power and paying them compensation. The Court held that although the government could have refused to allow connection of the lagoon to the bay or regulated use of the lagoon in any arguably reasonable manner, it could not simply convert private property into public property without paying just compensation.[115]

The state's removal of a property owner's right to exclude others under certain circumstances does not necessarily constitute a "taking" in the constitutional sense. In order to determine whether or not such a limitation of property rights constitutes a taking, a court

must consider the character of the government's action in terms of the degree to which it (1) promotes legitimate social goals, (2) diminishes the value of the private property owner's economic interest, and (3) interferes with reasonable expectations regarding the use of the property.

For example, in *PruneYard Shopping Center v. Robins*,[116] the United States Supreme Court upheld a decision of the California Supreme Court, which ruled that the California constitution prohibited the owners of private shopping centers from excluding persons who wish to engage in nondisruptive speech and petitioning activities. Although the state had thus eliminated part of the shopping center owner's right to exclude other persons, the owners did not suffer a taking in the constitutional sense because they could not demonstrate that an unchecked right to exclude others was a basic part of the economic value of the shopping center. The state court ruling was seen as a reasonable government regulation of the use of property normally open to members of the public and not a taking of property.[117]

Another example of the difficulty of determining when a legal restriction on a property owner's right to exclude others from using his property constitutes a taking is provided by the Supreme Court's decision in *Nollan v. California Coastal Commission*.[118] In this five to four decision, the Supreme Court found that a condition of a building reconstruction permit

---

115. 444 U.S. at 177–81, 100 S.Ct. at 391–94.

In Vaughn v. Vermilion Corp., 444 U.S. 206, 100 S.Ct. 399, 62 L.Ed.2d 365 (1979), the Court held that privately-owned canals connected with public waterways were not automatically open to general public use under the federal navigational servitude. Unless the government could show that the private canals had destroyed or diverted a pre-existing natural waterway, it would have to pay compensation to the canal owners whose private property was converted to a public waterway.

Not all actions taken by the federal government to enforce the federal navigational servitude and public access to waterways will be declared takings of property for which compensation is due. Government actions must be examined on a case-by-case basis to determine whether the government action at issue has taken or impaired a property interest in a manner that requires the granting of compensation. In United States v. Cherokee Nation of Oklahoma, 480 U.S. 700, 107 S.Ct. 1487, 94 L.Ed.2d 704

(1987), the Supreme Court found that no compensation was due to the Indian tribe that owned property rights in a river or riverbed when the federal government exercised its rights under the federal navigational servitude and made navigational improvements to the river.

116. 447 U.S. 74, 100 S.Ct. 2035, 64 L.Ed.2d 741 (1980).

117. The Court in *PruneYard Shopping Center* distinguished Kaiser Aetna v. United States, 444 U.S. 164, 100 S.Ct. 383, 62 L.Ed.2d 332 (1979), noted above at footnote 41, on the basis that the taking of the right of exclusivity from property held for private use in *Kaiser* went too far in interfering with "reasonable investment backed expectations," whereas the shopping center regulation was in the nature of a reasonable regulation of commercial functions. PruneYard Shopping Center v. Robins, 447 U.S. 74, 83–85, 100 S.Ct. 2035, 2041–43, 64 L.Ed.2d 741 (1980).

118. 483 U.S. 825, 107 S.Ct. 3141, 97 L.Ed.2d 677 (1987).

that required a public easement across beach property constituted a taking of property for which compensation was due. At issue in the case was a restriction placed on beachfront property in California. The owners wished to demolish a small building on the property and replace it with a larger structure. The Coastal Commission granted the construction permit on the condition that the owners allow the public to pass across the beach area of their property. This easement would allow members of the public to cross the private property when traveling between two public beach areas which were separated, in part, by the beachfront lot.

Although this point may be subject to some debate, it appears that the Court determined it was irrelevant whether the easement granted to the public ran from the street to the beach across the part of the property that abutted the house or merely across the beach portion of the property providing "lateral access" to the public beaches. The majority opinion by Justice Scalia found that there was no purpose supporting the required grant of a public easement, other than facilitating public travel across private property. This was not an illegitimate interest; the state could pursue it by condemning a portion of the land for the easement and paying just compensation to the property owner.[119]

Justice Scalia's opinion for the Court in *Nollan* stated, in dicta, that a zoning commission might condition a waiver of a zoning regulation regarding the size of buildings near a beach that would allow the construction of a new building blocking the public's view of the beach if the owner agreed to provide a limited public access area on the property for passersby to view the beach. In other words, since a limitation on the size of buildings for aesthetic purposes would be permissible (so long as it did not unreasonably diminish the economic value of the property), the limited granting of

access to the property for the purpose of providing the public the ability to see the beach should not be impermissible (unless the amount of required access constituted a substantial diminishment in the value of the property). However, the easement at issue in the *Nollan* case was not, in the view of the majority, related to preserving the aesthetic quality of the beachfront area or the public's ability to view the beach. The permit system in *Nollan* in effect created a continuous strip of publicly accessible beach by granting to the public the use of privately owned property.[120]

Conditional Development Permits—A Special Type of Spot Regulation. Most of the Supreme Court's decisions concerning whether a government property use regulation constitutes a taking of property have involved general regulations over all similarly situated property. One type of general regulation case involves a zoning law that defines and limits the types of property uses that will be allowed within an area of a city. Another type of general regulation case involves the regulation of all business entities of a certain type, such as coal mines. In these general regulation cases, the Court has given a great deal of deference to judgments made by legislatures or administrative entities.

When the government regulates a specific piece of real property, rather than regulating all similarly situated property within the jurisdiction, the government regulation is sometimes referred to as "spot zoning" or "spot regulation." In spot regulation cases there may be less reason than in general regulation cases for judicial deference to the legislative judgment. When the government regulates only a specific parcel of property, the individual property owner whose land is regulated cannot join with, or rely on, the owners of similar property to influence the government decisionmakers to give fair treatment to the

---

119. 483 U.S. at 831–34, 107 S.Ct. at 3145–46.

120. In dissent, Justice Brennan, joined by Justice Marshall attempted to demonstrate the ways in which the easement might be used to offset restricted visual and physical use of the public beaches by members of the public, occasioned by the increased development on the beachfront property. Nollan v. California Coastal Com-

mission, 483 U.S. 825, 840, 107 S.Ct. 3141, 3150, 97 L.Ed.2d 677 (1987) (Brennan, J., joined by Marshall, J., dissenting). Justices Blackmun and Stevens also dissented in Nollan, 483 U.S. at 863, 107 S.Ct. at 3162 (Blackmun, J., dissenting); 483 U.S. at 866, 107 S.Ct. at 3163 (Stevens, J., joined by Blackmun, J., dissenting).

economic interests of the land owner. Nevertheless, the Supreme Court has not established separate standards for the review of spot regulation. When the Supreme Court reviewed New York's spot rezoning of Grand Central Station in the *Penn Central Transportation Company* [121] case, it did not establish a special standard for government regulations of specific pieces of property. However, in *Penn Central*, the Court did not appear to be giving great deference to the local government's decision. Instead, the majority opinion seemed to give close examination to the question of whether the owners of Grand Central Station had suffered a loss in value to their property that was so severe that it could be said to be an unfair transfer of their economic interest to the public and a taking of their property. The fact that the owners appeared to be receiving a reasonable return on their investment seemed to be pivotal in the Court's decision that the regulation did not constitute a taking of property.

If a specific piece of property were regulated for the purpose of stopping the property owner from harming other persons it would be hard, if not impossible, for the property owner to show that the special regulation of his property constituted a taking. A government action prohibiting a property owner from engaging in activities that created a significant risk of harm to other persons should not be found to be a taking of property.[122] In such a circumstance, even a form of judicial review that gave no deference to the legislative or administrative decisionmaking authorities would result in a finding that the government had not unjustly extracted an economic benefit from the property owner. A government regulation that prohibits a property use that causes harm to the environmental or health interests of the populace should be reasonably related to legitimate government interest.

A government entity may require a property owner to receive a permit to develop real property or to improve the structures thereon. The governmental authority charged with the responsibility for operating the permit system may require the property owner to meet certain conditions in order to obtain a permit. Typical permit conditions require the property owner to demonstrate that the property development will be in accordance with all building regulations and environmental laws. Although a permit system conditions the ability of an individual to place improvements on property he owns, it will not result in a judicial finding that the regulation constitutes a taking so long as the permit conditions are reasonable regulations of property use. The Supreme Court has described a permit requirement that is conditioned upon compliance with laws of general applicability as follows: "[A] requirement that a person obtain a permit before engaging in a certain use of his or her property does not itself 'take' the property in any sense: after all, the very existence of a permit system implies that permission may be granted, leaving the landowner free to use the property as desired. Moreover, even if the permit is denied, there may be other viable uses available to the owner. Only when a permit is denied and the effect of the denial is to prevent 'economically viable' use of the land in question can it be said that a taking has occurred." [123]

When the government requires a property owner to get a permit in order to develop the land and imposes conditions on the granting of the permit that are not applicable to all similarly situated pieces of land within the jurisdiction, there should be a special concern as to whether the conditions on the permit constitute a taking. In this situation, the government is extracting a cost from a particular property owner that it is not imposed on other persons.

---

121. Penn Central Transportation Co. v. New York, 438 U.S. 104, 98 S.Ct. 2646, 57 L.Ed.2d 631 (1978).

122. For example, in Keystone Bituminous Coal Association v. DeBenedictis, 480 U.S. 470, 107 S.Ct. 1232, 94 L.Ed.2d 472 (1987) the Court upheld a regulatory system limiting the amount of coal that could be taken out of

subsurface excavation in order to protect structures and surfaces within the jurisdiction.

123. United States v. Riverside Bayview Homes, Inc., 474 U.S. 121, 127, 106 S.Ct. 455, 459, 88 L.Ed.2d 419 (1985) (upholding Corps of Engineers regulations regarding wetlands).

If the government conditions the granting of a development permit on the requirement that the property owner transfer the rights to a portion of the property to the government, or on the requirement that the property owner open the property to the public, the government must demonstrate that these conditions are reasonably related to legitimate public interests. If the government fails to justify the access condition, the government's conditional permit will be held to be a taking of property. As we have seen, a government law that would simply grant the public an easement to use a part of privately owned real property would be subject to the "per se rule" that forced changes in occupation rights constitute a taking for which just compensation is due. Making the individual give up her right to exclude others from her property in order to gain a development permit will be deemed to be an "unconstitutional condition" unless the government can demonstrate that the condition is reasonably related to promoting legitimate government ends.

In *Nollan v. California Coastal Commission*[124] the Court did not give a detailed explanation of the way in which the government might prove that requiring the property owner to open his property to public access might be a reasonable condition for a development permit. In that case, it was clear to a majority of the Justices that the government's attempt to secure a public easement across the beach had no possible relationship to any legitimate government interest.[125] Therefore, the majority in *Nollan* found that the government was simply trying to secure a public easement across a privately owned beach without having to pay the owner for that taking of property rights.

Dolan v. City of Tigard[126] established a standard for the review of a building permit condition requiring the dedication of privately owned land for public use. The property owner in *Dolan* owned a store with a gravel parking lot and that bordered a creek. The city had some problems with the creek overflowing in earlier years; it had adopted a drainage plan that involved improvements to the creek basin and recommendations that land immediately adjacent to the creek be used only as "greenways". The property owner sought a permit to increase the size of her store and to increase, and pave, the parking lot. She was informed that she would be denied this permit unless she met conditions that required her (1) to dedicate the portion of her property line immediately next to the creek for a greenway that could be used by the public, and (2) to dedicate a fifteen foot strip of land across her property for use as a pedestrian and bicycle pathway. The property owner claimed that these two conditions for her development permit constituted a taking of her property and could not be imposed upon her without just compensation.

By a five to four vote, *Dolan* ruled that the conditions imposed on the store owner constituted a taking of property. Those conditions would violate the takings clause unless the city paid just compensation to the property owner. The majority opinion in *Dolan*, written by Chief Justice Rehnquist, initially noted that the takings clause of the Fifth Amendment applied to the states through the Fourteenth Amendment due process clause and that imposing a condition on a building permit that was inconsistent with the takings clause would violate "the well-settled doctrine of unconstitutional conditions."[127]

---

124. 483 U.S. 825, 107 S.Ct. 3141, 97 L.Ed.2d 677 (1987).

125. 483 U.S. at 831–37, 107 S.Ct. at 3145–49.

126. 512 U.S. 374, 114 S.Ct. 2309, 129 L.Ed.2d 304 (1994).

127. Chief Justice Rehnquist recognized that the Court's earliest cases concerning whether state or local legislation constituted a taking of property were unclear regarding the incorporation of the takings clause into the Fourteenth Amendment. But the Chief Justice found that "there is no doubt that later cases have held that the Fourteenth Amendment does make the takings clause of

the Fifth Amendment applicable to the states" Dolan v. City of Tigard, 512 U.S. 374, 384 n. 5, 114 S.Ct. 2309, 2316 n. 5, 129 L.Ed.2d 304 (1994).

The Chief Justice in *Dolan* stated: "under the well-settled doctrine of 'unconstitutional conditions,' the government may not require a person to give up a constitutional right—here the right to receive just compensation when property is taken for a public use—in exchange for a discretionary benefit conferred by the government where the property sought has little or no relationship to the benefit." 512 U.S. at 374, 114 S.Ct. at 2309.

Chief Justice Rehnquist's majority opinion noted that state courts had taken three different approaches to reviewing these types of access conditions for building permits. Some states gave a great deal of deference to the governmental units employing such permit conditions and upheld the conditions if they had any arguably reasonable basis. Other state courts took the completely opposite position; these courts would invalidate such conditions unless the government could demonstrate that the condition was precisely tailored to meet specific social needs by mitigating harms caused by the building development for which the permit was requested. The majority opinion in *Dolan* endorsed a third approach, which was used by most state supreme courts. The Chief Justice described this approach as "an intermediate position, requiring [the governmental unit imposing the public use condition] to show a 'reasonable relationship' between the required dedication [of the land for public use] and the impact of the proposed development." [128] The majority stated that the intermediate test, which was used by most state courts, was the closer to the appropriate "federal constitutional norm" that either the highly deferential or very strict tests. Nevertheless, the majority did not wish to use the phrase "reasonable relationship" in the standard for takings clause issues, "because the term 'reasonable relationship' seems confusingly similar to the term 'rational basis' which describes the minimal level of scrutiny under the equal protection clause." [129] Instead, Chief Justice Rehnquist stated that the majority would adopt a "rough proportionality" test. The majority opinion concluded that "we think a term such as 'rough proportionality'

best encapsulates what we hold to be the requirement of the Fifth Amendment. No precise mathematical calculation is required, but [the governmental unit imposing the public use condition] must make some sort of individualized determination that the required dedication is related both in nature and extent to the impact of the development." [130]

The majority opinion in *Dolan* requires courts to go through a two-step process to determine whether a permit condition requiring dedication of private land for public use constitutes a taking of property. First a court must determine whether there is an "essential nexus" between the permit condition and a legitimate interest of government. Second, if such a nexus is found to exist, a court must determine whether there is rough proportionality between the condition requiring the property owner to dedicate a portion of the property to public use and the impact of the proposed development on governmental and social interests. [131] In making this determination a court is to place the burden on the government to demonstrate that there is a reasonable relationship, or "rough proportionality," between the permit condition and the nature of the proposed land development. [132]

Applying this two-step analysis, and the rough proportionality test, the Court in *Dolan* found that the conditions placed on the store owner's development permit constituted a taking of property. Thus, the conditions would be invalid unless the government provided the property owner with just compensation for the taking. Chief Justice Rehnquist's majority opinion found that the prevention of flood damage along the creek and the reduction of traffic congestion were legitimate interests

---

128. Dolan v. City of Tigard, 512 U.S. 374, 390, 114 S.Ct. 2309, 2319, 129 L.Ed.2d 304 (1994).

129. 512 U.S. at 389, 114 S.Ct. at 2319.

130. 512 U.S. at 374–75, 114 S.Ct. at 2311–12.

131. The Chief Justice's majority opinion in *Dolan* described the approach to the takings questions as follows: "We must first determine whether the essential nexus exists between the legitimate state interest and the permit condition exacted by the city ... if we find that a nexus exists, we must then decide the required degree of connection between the extractions [the conditions requiring dedication of the property for public use] and the projected impact of the proposed development." 512 U.S. at 386,

114 S.Ct. at 2317 (internal quotation marks and citations omitted).

132. "[I]n evaluating most generally applicable zoning regulations, the burden properly rests on the party challenging the regulation to prove that it constitutes an arbitrary regulation of property rights ... here, by contrast, the city made an adjudicative decision to condition [the property owner's] application for a building permit on an individual parcel. In this situation, the burden properly rests on the city." Dolan v. City of Tigard, 512 U.S. 374, 391 n. 8, 114 S.Ct. 2309, 2320 n. 8, 129 L.Ed.2d 304 (1994).

that arguably might be impaired by the property owner increasing the size of her store and parking lot. However, the majority ruled that the city had failed to demonstrate that requiring the property owner to dedicate a portion of her property to be a public greenway, which might be used by pedestrians, was related to the government interest in controlling flood damage along the creek. If the city had simply forbid the owner from building on the part of the property closest to the creek, without requiring that she make that public greenway available to public use, the condition might have been upheld as being reasonably related to the legitimate public interest in flood control. Requiring the property owner to open the greenway to the public was not proportional to, or reasonably related to, the effect of her proposed development on flood control within the city. The city had argued that the increase in the size of the store would result in increased traffic. But the Supreme Court found that "on the record before us, the city has not met its burden of demonstrating that the additional number of vehicle and bicycle trips generated by [the store owner's proposed development] reasonably relate to the city's requirement for a dedication of the pedestrian-bicycle pathway easement." [133]

So long as *Dolan* is not overruled, courts are not permitted to give great deference to the decision of a governmental unit to require a property owner to grant public access to the property as a condition for a building or development permit. Instead, the judiciary must independently determine whether the government interests asserted are legitimate ones and whether the access condition is reasonably related to those interests. To justify such a condition the government must demonstrate that the required dedication of private property for public use is "roughly proportional" to the adverse impact of the proposed development on legitimate public interests. [134]

The rough proportionality test is only to be used for determining the constitutionality of conditioning a building or development permit on the transfer of an easement or the right to occupy the property. The proportionality test is not appropriate for an examination of governmental regulations of property use. [135]

Utility Rate Regulation. Virtually all governmental entities that have conferred the right to be a legal monopoly on a utility company owned by private parties have regulated the utility's charges to its customers. The regulation of the amounts that utilities may bill for their services is a regulation of the

133. Dolan v. City of Tigard, 512 U.S. 374, 393, 114 S.Ct. 2309, 2321, 129 L.Ed.2d 304 (1994).

134. The *Dolan* case was decided by a five to four vote of the Justices. Justice Stevens dissented in an opinion that was joined by Justices Blackmun and Ginsburg. These three Justices found that the majority was engaging in nothing more than substantive due process analysis that had been rejected in other cases and that the majority had unjustifiably rejected the normal presumption of constitutionality for economic regulatory laws. Dolan v. City of Tigard, 512 U.S. 374, 395, 114 S.Ct. 2309, 2322, 129 L.Ed.2d 304 (1994) (Stevens, J., joined by Blackmun and Ginsburg, JJ., dissenting). Justice Souter believed that prior decisions of the Supreme Court required the government to show some nexus between the nature of the proposed development and a condition requiring public access to the property. Justice Souter dissented because he believed that prior cases did not require the government to produce clear evidence of the relationship between such a condition and the impact on those legitimate interests. Justice Souter stated: "I do not view this case as a suitable vehicle for taking the law beyond [the earlier takings clause decisions of the Court]." 512 U.S. at 411, 413, 114 S.Ct. at 2330, 2331 (Souter, J., dissenting).

135. In Monterey v. Del Monte Dunes at Monterey, Ltd., 526 U.S. 687, 119 S.Ct. 1624, 143 L.Ed.2d 882 (1999) the Court ruled that a developer who sued a city for

money damages, on the basis that the city had taken its property through wrongful denial of building permits, had a Seventh Amendment right to a jury trial on damages issues. The majority opinion, by Justice Kennedy, noted that the Court of Appeals, in a portion of its decision that was irrelevant to the outcome of the case, had assumed that the proportionality test should apply to land use regulations, and denials of building permits, even when there was no condition that the developer and landowner turnover part of the property to public use. Although the majority found that the issue was irrelevant to the Supreme Court's disposition of the case; Justice Kennedy noted: "Although in a general sense concerns for proportionality animate the takings clause ... we have not extended the rough proportionality test of *Dolan* beyond the special context of exactions—land-use decisions conditioning approval of development on the dedication of property to public use ... the rule applied in *Dolan* considers whether dedications demanded as conditions of development are proportional to the development's anticipated impacts. It was not designed to address, and is not readily applicable to, the much different questions arising where, as here, the landowner's challenge is based not on excessive exactions but on denial of development." 526 U.S. at 702, 119 S.Ct. at 1635.

property of the utility owners; if the government sets the utility's charges, and the rate of return on the owners' investment, at a level that is judicially determined to be unjust and confiscatory, the rate regulation would constitute a taking of the property of the utility. In *Duquesne Light Co. v. Barasch*,[136] Chief Justice Rehnquist wrote for eight Justices in upholding a state system of utility regulation; the majority opinion reviewed 90 years of Supreme Court cases concerning utility rate regulation.[137] In *Duquesne Light Co.* a Pennsylvania utility company asserted that the method used to determine the amount of its rates and rate increases constituted a taking of property because state law prohibited including in the rate base (the value of the utility that would be used for determining the rates and rate of return) the amount of money that the utility invested in initial stages of construction for four power plants that were cancelled prior to being put into use. Because the investments in these power plants were admitted to be "prudent" when the initial investments were made, the utility claimed that the method for calculating the rate of return was a violation of the principles of the takings clause because the state disregarded the historical cost of the utility. However, the utility did not claim that the rates that had been established by the State of Pennsylvania resulted in a total return on the utility's investment that was unjust or unreasonable. The Court found that the utility rate regulation would not constitute a taking of property so long as the rate of

return was not so unreasonable and unjust as to be considered "confiscatory."

Justice Rehnquist's majority opinion noted that the Supreme Court had examined utility regulations since late in the 19th century and had continuously followed the principle that state legislators, as well as state administrative entities, could limit utility charges and that limitations on those rates and charges would not be considered a taking of property unless the rates were so low as to be confiscatory.[138] Shortly after the Supreme Court began to examine utility rate regulations, in *Smyth v. Ames*,[139] the Court indicated that rates and charges should be set according to the present value of the assets employed by the utility, so as to determine whether the rate was reasonable by examining it as a return on the "fair value" of the utility. Justice Brandeis, in the 1920s, had noted the difficulty of attempting to establish the "fair value rule" as a constitutional requirement.[140] Justice Brandeis believed that the Constitution allowed utility rate regulations to be set with a system that would compare the utility's rate of return to the value of the capital that had been prudently invested in the utility throughout its history. The position advocated by Justice Brandeis, which is sometimes called the "prudent investment" or the "historical cost" principle, was eventually used by the Supreme Court in the 1940s. In *Federal Power Commission v. Hope Natural Gas Compa-*

136. 488 U.S. 299, 109 S.Ct. 609, 102 L.Ed.2d 646 (1989).

137. Justice Blackmun dissented on a jurisdictional issue, he did not make any comments upon the Chief Justice's examination of the taking of property issue. Duquesne Light Co. v. Barasch, 488 U.S. 299, 317, 109 S.Ct. 609, 621, 102 L.Ed.2d 646 (1989) (Blackmun, J., dissenting). Justice Scalia, joined by Justices White and O'Connor, joined the Chief Justice's opinion and also wrote a concurring opinion. 488 U.S. at 317, 109 S.Ct. at 620 (Scalia, J., joined by White and O'Connor, JJ., concurring).

138. Early Supreme Court opinions concerning utility rate regulation were written in terms of "due process of law", but those opinions are now understood as establishing principles identical to those inherent in the takings clause of the Fifth Amendment, which is now applicable to the states through the Fourteenth Amendment due process clause.

"The guiding principle has been that the constitution protects utilities from being limited to a charge for their property, serving the public which is so 'unjust' as to be confiscatory. Covington and Lexington Turnpike Road Co. v. Sandford, 164 U.S. 578, 597, 17 S.Ct. 198, 205–206, 41 L.Ed. 560 (1896) (a rate is too low if it is 'so unjust as to destroy the value of [the] property for all the purposes for which it was acquired,) and in so doing (practically deprive[s] the owner of property without due process of law')...." Duquesne Light Co. v. Barasch, 488 U.S. 299, 307–308, 109 S.Ct. 609, 615, 102 L.Ed.2d 646 (1989).

139. 169 U.S. 466, 18 S.Ct. 418, 42 L.Ed. 819 (1898).

140. Missouri ex rel. Southwestern Bell Telephone Co. v. Public Service Commission, 262 U.S. 276, 291–94, 43 S.Ct. 544, 547–548, 67 L.Ed. 981 (1923) (Brandeis, J., dissenting).

ny,[141] the Supreme Court found that the fair value rule, which had been previously adopted in *Smyth,* was not the only method for constitutionally setting utility rates and allowed state lawmakers to use the historical cost or prudent investment rule.

In *Duquesne Light Co.,* Chief Justice Rehnquist wrote for eight members of the Court in finding that no single formula for fixing utility rates was mandated by the Constitution.[142] So long as the utility's rate of return was not so unjust as to be confiscatory, it would not be invalidated due to the method by which the state law had set the rate structure. The Chief Justice noted that, if a utility company challenged a rate as being "confiscatory", an examination of the value of the company and the return upon prudent investments would be considerations in determining whether the rate was confiscatory.[143]

(c) Emergency Actions

A number of Supreme Court decisions have dealt with the conflicting rights and duties of the government and private landowners during times of emergency. Authorities have long stated that in time of extreme emergency, the government, if the need arises, may take or even destroy private property.[144] As a general rule, the Supreme Court has been reluctant, during the time of emergency, to find that the government need compensate the injured property owner.

Military actions taken in time of war are often found to be noncompensable emergency measures. In *United States v. Caltex, Inc.*[145] the Supreme Court found that the Army had not "taken" property which had been destroyed to prevent its capture by enemy forces.

The Army, in late 1941, destroyed the claimant's oil facilities in Manila as Japanese troops were entering the city. After the war, the owner of the facilities demanded compensation for all the property destroyed by the Army. The government agreed to pay for all the petroleum products used or destroyed but refused to pay for the destroyed terminal facilities. The Court, upholding the army's refusal, held that the destruction of private property during battle is a cost that must be borne by individual owners.[146]

Similarly, regulation to help the public purpose of solving an emergency will be upheld as noncompensable measures. Thus, in *United States v. Central Eureka Mining Co.,*[147] another case arising from government action during World War II, the Supreme Court refused to find that a War Production Board order requiring nonessential gold mines to cease operation amounted to a taking of the mines. The Court observed that the government had in no way taken physical possession of the affected mines,[148] and that the order was a reasonable means of conserving equipment needed to promote the war effort. "War, particularly in modern times," stated the Court, "demands the strict regulation of nearly all resources. It makes demands which otherwise would be insufferable."[149]

The Court reaffirmed these principles in *National Board of Young Men's Christian Associations v. United States.*[150] Here the Court denied compensation to a private landowner where looters in the Panama Canal Zone destroyed its building because American troops had taken shelter there. The Court, concluding that the presence of the troops in the area

141. 320 U.S. 591, 64 S.Ct. 281, 88 L.Ed. 333 (1944).

142. "[A]n otherwise reasonable rate is not subject to constitutional attack by questioning the theoretical consistency of the method that produced it." Duquesne Light Co. v. Barasch, 488 U.S. 299, 314, 109 S.Ct. 609, 619, 102 L.Ed.2d 646 (1989).

143. This point was emphasized by three concurring Justices. 488 U.S. at 310–311, 109 S.Ct. at 617. Id. at 317–318, 109 S.Ct. at 620–621 (Scalia, J., joined by White and O'Connor, JJ., concurring).

144. See, e.g., Comment, Land Use Regulation and the Concept of Takings in Nineteenth Century America, 40 U.Chi.L.Rev. 854, 860–61 (1973).

145. 344 U.S. 149, 73 S.Ct. 200, 97 L.Ed. 157 (1952).

146. 344 U.S. at 154–56, 73 S.Ct. at 202–04.

147. 357 U.S. 155, 78 S.Ct. 1097, 2 L.Ed.2d 1228 (1958), rehearing denied 358 U.S. 858, 79 S.Ct. 9, 3 L.Ed.2d 91 (1958).

148. 357 U.S. at 165–66, 78 S.Ct. at 1102–03.

149. 357 U.S. at 168, 78 S.Ct. at 1104.

150. 395 U.S. 85, 89 S.Ct. 1511, 23 L.Ed.2d 117 (1969).

had been for the landowner's benefit, found that "fairness and justice" did not require that the loss be compensated by the government and shifted to the public.[151] The Marines had not planned to take over the building but only sought its temporary use in an emergency; therefore there was no compensable taking.

The type of emergency situation that may enable the state to destroy property, without payment of compensation, is not limited to wartime conflict. *Miller v. Schoene*[152] involved the destruction by the State of Virginia of a large number of ornamental red cedar trees. The trees were infected with cedar rust, a disease that is highly dangerous to apple trees. The only effective means of controlling the disease is to destroy all infected red cedars growing within two miles of any apple orchards.

In *Schoene*, the Supreme Court held that the trees could be destroyed by the state without incurring any constitutional duty to compensate the injured landowner. The Court observed that apple production was an important agricultural activity in Virginia while the ornamental cedar trees had only minimal importance. The Supreme Court concluded that "[w]hen forced to such a choice, the state does not exceed its constitutional powers by deciding upon the destruction of one class of property in order to save another, which, in the judgment of the legislature, is of greater value to the public."[153] Like the zoning-property use decisions, this case comports with modern substantive due process analysis by allowing

the government to determine how to deal with societal problems without strict judicial review.

In *Dames & Moore v. Regan*[154] the Supreme Court upheld the validity of executive agreements suspending claims of United States citizens against the government of Iran in exchange for a return of our citizens who were being held hostage by that country.[155] In so doing the majority opinion by Justice Rehnquist found that the Presidential order nullifying attachments on Iranian assets and allowing a transfer of those assets out of the country did not constitute a compensable taking of property because the President had statutory authority to prevent or condition the allowance of such attachments so that those bringing claims against Iran did not have a property interest in the attachment.[156]

As a part of the agreement with Iran, the President suspended claims of United States citizens pending in United States courts and required their submission to a "claims tribunal." The Supreme Court refused to consider whether this suspension of claims constituted a compensable taking of property because all parties admitted that the issue was not ripe for review.[157] However, the Court found that persons whose claims were suspended by the Presidential order could bring an action in the Court of Claims to determine whether the suspension of their claim had resulted in an unconstitutional taking of property by executive action.[158]

---

151. 395 U.S. at 89–92, 89 S.Ct. at 1514–16.

152. 276 U.S. 272, 48 S.Ct. 246, 72 L.Ed. 568 (1928).

153. 276 U.S. at 279, 48 S.Ct. at 247.

154. 453 U.S. 654, 101 S.Ct. 2972, 69 L.Ed.2d 918 (1981).

155. The separation of powers aspects of this case are examined in Chapter 6, supra.

156. 453 U.S. at 674 n. 6, 101 S.Ct. at 2983–84 n. 6, Justice Powell was the only Justice who would have found that nullification of the attachments constituted a taking of property. He believed that the attachment entitling a creditor to resort to specific property for the satisfaction for a claim was a compensable property interest which could not be made less so through the executive order making the attachments conditional. 453 U.S. at 690, 101 S.Ct. at 2992 (Powell, J., concurring and dissenting in part).

157. Dames & Moore v. Regan, 453 U.S. 654, 689, 101 S.Ct. 2972, 2991–92, 69 L.Ed.2d 918 (1981).

158. 453 U.S. at 689–90, 101 S.Ct. at 2991–92. The Court was careful to note that, in finding that the President had power to settle claims against Iran it was not indicating that individual claimants did not have a "possible taking claim against the United States." 453 U.S. at 688, n. 14, 101 S.Ct. at 2991 n. 14.

In United States v. Sperry Corp., 493 U.S. 52, 110 S.Ct. 387, 107 L.Ed.2d 290 (1989), the Supreme Court found that a Department of Treasury Regulation requiring a deduction from each award given by the Iran–United States Claims Tribunal was not a taking of property but, rather, a constitutional user fee designed to reimburse the government for the establishment and operation of the Tribunal. The fact that the federal government had not set the user fee in a way that matched its costs did not result in a finding that the user fee violated the takings

(d) Impairment of Use

The taking issue can arise even when the government has neither destroyed nor regulated the use of private property. Where, as a result of some governmental activity, a landowner's use and enjoyment of his property is impaired, there may be a "taking" for which compensation is due.

The Constitution does not require the literal appropriation of property before there is a "taking". In *Pumpelly v. Green Bay & Mississippi Canal Co.*,[159] the Supreme Court of the United States was required to interpret the "taking" clause of a state constitution and it found that a serious interruption in the use of property might be the equivalent of a taking, so that the flooding of land by a government dam would be a "taking".[160] In *Bedford v. United States*,[161] however, the Court appeared to step back from the broad statements of *Pumpelly*. In this case the Court found noncompensable the backup of flood waters which was a consequential effect of government action. The opinion found that a distinction between damaging and taking must be observed for purposes of determining whether a constitutional requirement of compensation exists. The Court distinguished *Pumpelly* on the ground that the landowner in that case was directly injured by the dam project. In this case the government had only fortified the banks of a river to prevent flooding at a point distant from the plaintiff's land; the plaintiff was not directly injured by this act.

In this area the Court's rulings have an *ad hoc* quality because individual decisions are based on the degree of loss to the individual and the reasonableness of the government's actions in relation to the private property.

For example, in *Peabody v. United States*,[162] the Court faced the issue of whether the placement of a gun battery in the vicinity of the claimant's resort hotel amounted to a Fifth Amendment taking. The resort owners argued that the proximate location of the battery to the hotel property greatly impaired the land's recreational value for all practical purposes. The Supreme Court found no taking, but, in *dicta*, stated that if the government had installed the battery with the intent to practice at will over the hotel property, "with the intent of depriving the owner of its profitable use," such action would constitute an appropriation of property and would require compensation.[163]

Six years later, in *Portsmouth Harbor Land & Hotel Co. v. United States*,[164] the hotel owners again sought recovery as a result of additional firings of the battery. The Court rejected this second claim, refusing to infer an intent on the part of the government to create a servitude across the hotel's property. Three years later the same parties again sought recovery urging that the cumulative effect of subsequent firings had resulted in a taking.[165] The Court, per Justice Holmes, reversed the trial court's dismissal of the action, and, adopting the theory of *Peabody*, ordered that evidence be heard to determine whether the continued firings were sufficient to prove an intent to create a servitude over the hotel property.

In *United States v. Causby*,[166] the Supreme Court applied the rationale of the *Portsmouth Hotel* cases in determining whether frequent and regular flights of government planes over the plaintiffs' land had created an easement for the benefit of the government. The plaintiffs in this case owned a small chicken farm

---

clause. The deduction was a reasonable approximation of costs for the benefits supplied by the federal government to claimants; the deductions were not "so clearly excessive as to belie their purported character as user fees." 493 U.S. at 60, 62 n. 8, 110 S.Ct. at 394, 395 n. 8. The deduction was required by a federal statute that was enacted after the Tribunal had made the award to Sperry. The Supreme Court found that the legislation did not violate due process, even though it had a retroactive effect. The retroactive application of the legislation was justified by the legislative goal of requiring claimants to bear some of the costs for the Tribunal.

159. 80 U.S. (13 Wall.) 166, 20 L.Ed. 557 (1871).

160. 80 U.S. at 179–80.

161. 192 U.S. 217, 24 S.Ct. 238, 48 L.Ed. 414 (1904).

162. 231 U.S. 530, 34 S.Ct. 159, 58 L.Ed. 351 (1913).

163. 231 U.S. at 538, 34 S.Ct. at 160.

164. 250 U.S. 1, 39 S.Ct. 399, 63 L.Ed. 809 (1919).

165. Portsmouth Harbor Land and Hotel Co. v. United States, 260 U.S. 327, 43 S.Ct. 135, 67 L.Ed. 287 (1922).

166. 328 U.S. 256, 66 S.Ct. 1062, 90 L.Ed. 1206 (1946).

near an airport used by army and navy planes. The glide path of one of the airport runways passed directly over the property at a height of only 83 feet. The use of the runway greatly disturbed the occupants of the farm and also eventually forced the plaintiffs to give up their chicken business. The Supreme Court found that the frequent low altitude flights of government planes over the farm created an easement in the plaintiffs' land.[167] The Court held that the landowner was entitled to as much of the air space over his property as he had been reasonably using in connection with his land, and found that the government's use of this airspace resulted in the imposition of a servitude on the chicken farm.

If government agents or employees intentionally destroy or take a person's property, there should be no question that there has been a "taking" for which just compensation is due, although there may be questions in any given case regarding the adequacy of state administrative or judicial procedures for determining the amount of compensation.[168]

The Supreme Court added confusion to the taking of property concept when it ruled that mere negligence by government agents, which resulted in harm to a prisoner in a penal institution, did not constitute a taking of liberty without due process, even though state tort law and state sovereign immunity doctrines precluded any compensation for the prisoner.[169] In so doing, the Court reversed its earlier holding that a government agent's negligent

destruction of a prisoner's property could constitute a violation of due process.[170] In *Daniels v. Williams*,[171] the Court found that a state's tort law and sovereign immunity law could deny all compensation to an inmate of a penal institution who slipped on a pillow that a state employee negligently left on a stairway. In so ruling, the majority opinion by Justice Rehnquist stated: "We conclude that the due process clause is simply not implicated by a negligent act of an official causing unintended loss of or injury to life, liberty, or property." The Court in *Daniels* left open the question of whether any type of action by government agents short of an intentional destruction of property (such as the destruction of property though grossly negligent or reckless conduct) could constitute a taking of property.

If taken literally, the quoted statement from *Daniels* would mean that an individual had no constitutional right to just compensation when agents of the state negligently destroyed his property, regardless of the extent of loss or the nature of the state activity. For example, assume that a state employee negligently drove a truck filled with flammable liquids off the highway and crashed into a house, destroying the house and all persons therein. Could any surviving members of the family that owned the house be denied all compensation for the loss of their property and the lives of their family members due to a state sovereign immunity law? Literal application of the

---

167. 328 U.S. at 265, 66 S.Ct. at 1067–68. The Court later held that the establishment of a county owned airport next to residential property could constitute a taking if the flight and operation of the airport made the property unusable for residential purposes. Griggs v. Allegheny County, 369 U.S. 84, 82 S.Ct. 531, 7 L.Ed.2d 585 (1962), rehearing denied 369 U.S. 857, 82 S.Ct. 931, 8 L.Ed.2d 16 (1962).

168. See Hudson v. Palmer, 468 U.S. 517, 104 S.Ct. 3194, 82 L.Ed.2d 393 (1984), on remand 744 F.2d 22 (4th Cir.1984). Regarding the procedural due process issues inherent in such cases see §§ 13.4, 13.9. If government personnel assist a creditor in seizing the property of an alleged debtor, the joint activity of the government personnel and the creditor constitutes state action that makes both the government personnel's and the creditor's actions subject to the Fourth Amendment limitations and due process principles. In Soldal v. Cook County, 506 U.S. 56, 113 S.Ct. 538, 121 L.Ed.2d 450 (1992), the Justices unanimously ruled that deputy sheriffs and the owners of

a mobile home park violated the Fourth Amendment when the deputy sheriffs assisted the mobile home park owner in removing an alleged debtor's mobile home from its foundation, and towing it away from the mobile home park.

169. Daniels v. Williams, 474 U.S. 327, 106 S.Ct. 662, 88 L.Ed.2d 662 (1986) (due process clause is not violated by a state official's lack of due care in leaving a pillow on stairway that resulted in personal injury to a prisoner); Davidson v. Cannon, 474 U.S. 344, 106 S.Ct. 668, 88 L.Ed.2d 677 (1986) (the failure to protect an inmate from attack from fellow prisoners, though the result of the negligence of prison officials, did not violate the due process clause).

170. Parratt v. Taylor, 451 U.S. 527, 101 S.Ct. 1908, 68 L.Ed.2d 420 (1981), overruled by Daniels v. Williams, 474 U.S. 327, 106 S.Ct. 662, 88 L.Ed.2d 662 (1986).

171. 474 U.S. 327, 106 S.Ct. 662, 88 L.Ed.2d 662 (1986).

statement in *Daniels* would mean that a state doctrine of sovereign immunity could totally defeat any claim for just compensation in such a case. Perhaps the judiciary could avoid such a problem by finding that the government agent (in our hypothetical, the truck driver) had engaged in reckless or grossly negligent conduct. It would be better, in the authors' view, if the Supreme Court were to rule that the judiciary should use a case-by-case approach to determine whether the negligence of government employees had so unfairly shifted social costs (such as the cost for the societal benefit from the state agency that employed the truck driver) to an individual or a limited group of individuals (the property owners and family members in our hypothetical) that the unintended harm to the individual or group of individuals constituted a taking for which just compensation was required. This type of case-by-case approach would eliminate turning all minor tort suits into constitutional issues, while requiring just compensation for those persons who have been severely injured by negligent government actions. Such a construction of the prisoner's rights cases may be possible, because the Supreme Court in *Daniels* stated: "We need not rule out the possibility that there are other constitutional provi-

sions that would be violated by mere lack of care in order to hold, as we do, that such conduct [causing the minor injury to the prisoner in this case] does not implicate the due process clause of the Fourteenth Amendment."[172] The Court again avoided this taking of property question when it ruled executive actions that harm persons or property would be judged by a "shock the conscience" test.[173]

§ 11.13 The "Public Use" Limitation

The government is not entirely free to take a person's property whenever it is willing to compensate him. The individual may not wish to part with his property, and, under both the Fifth and Fourteenth Amendments, property may not be taken by the government, even upon payment of just compensation, unless the property is taken for a public use. Like the requirement that a landowner be compensated when his property is taken by the state, the "public use" limitation also has its roots in natural as well as constitutional law.[1] The early interpretation of this public use test was broadly viewed as properly exercisable for "the public good, the public necessity or the public utility".[2]

---

172. 474 U.S. at 334, 106 S.Ct. at 666.

The Supreme Court has held that the heirs of an individual who died when he was being chased by police at high speeds, and whose death was caused by running his automobile into a police road block (which consisted of a tractor trailer placed across a road shortly after a curve in the road), could bring suit against the government under 42 U.S.C.A. § 1983 based on the allegation that the death was caused by a seizure that violated the Fourth Amendment, which applies to state and local governments through the Fourteenth Amendment. Brower v. County of Inyo, 489 U.S. 593, 109 S.Ct. 1378, 103 L.Ed.2d 628 (1989). To maintain this action, the heirs would have to prove that the "seizure" was unreasonable and violated Fourth Amendment standards. The majority opinion, by Justice Scalia, stated that, for there to be a Fourth Amendment issue, the seizure must be an intentional termination of the individual's freedom. 489 U.S. at 597, 109 S.Ct. at 1381. (Thus, if a parked and unoccupied police car slips its brake and pins a passerby against the wall, it is likely that a tort has occurred, but not a violation of the Fourth Amendment in the majority's view). Four Justices, concurring in the judgement in *Brower*, believed that the statements of the majority regarding "unintentional" terminations of freedom of movement constituted only dicta and that the majority was unwise to discuss whether unintentional acts might or

might not violate the Fourth Amendment. 489 U.S. at 600, 109 S.Ct. at 1383 (Stevens, J., joined by Brennan, Marshall, and Blackmun, JJ., concurring in the judgment). Thus, it appears that the Fourth Amendment is not violated by unintentional, negligent actions of government officials.

173. In County of Sacramento v. Lewis, 523 U.S. 833, 118 S.Ct. 1708, 140 L.Ed.2d 1043 (1998) the Justices ruled that a suspect who was accidentally killed by a police patrol car in a high-speed chase of the motorcycle (on which the deceased person had been a passenger) did not lose his life in a manner that violated due process principles. The Court in *Lewis* did not address taking of property issues or procedural due process issues. Nevertheless, cases involving harm caused to persons or property by actions of police officers may sometimes present taking of property issues, together with substantive and procedural issues. See § 10.6 for further examination of the *Lewis* case and the mixing of procedural and substantive due process issues.

§ 11.13

1. Lenhoff, Development of the Concept of Eminent Domain, 42 Colum.L.Rev. 596, 598–99 (1942).

2. Comment, The Public Use Doctrine: "Advance Requiem" Revisited, 1959 Law and the Social Order 689, 689.

The broad interpretation of the public use limitation was abandoned in the later half of the nineteenth century, however, in order that the courts might better control the exercise of eminent domain by private enterprises to whom the power had been delegated.[3] The state courts developed, therefore, the "use by the public" test for determining when a public use existed. Under the "use by the public" test the public had to have a right to use or enjoy the property taken. Early in the twentieth century, however, the Supreme Court repudiated the narrow "use by the public" test[4] and returned to the broad public benefit test for determining when a use was public.

The leading modern case defining the scope of the public use limitation is the unanimous 1954 Supreme Court decision in *Berman v. Parker*.[5] This case involved the constitutionality of the 1945 District of Columbia Redevelopment Act. Under section 2 of that Act, Congress declared it the policy of the United States to eliminate all substandard housing in Washington, D.C. because such areas were "injurious to the public health, safety, morals, and welfare." The Act also created the District of Columbia Redevelopment Land Agency and granted that agency the power to assemble real property for the redevelopment of blighted areas of the city through the exercise of eminent domain. After assembling the necessary real estate, Congress authorized the Agency to lease or sell portions of the land to private parties upon an agreement that the purchasers would carry out the redevelopment plan.

The appellant in *Berman* held property within the redevelopment area upon which a department store was located. The appellants argued that their property could not constitutionally be taken for the project, first, because the property was commercial and not residential or slum housing, and second, because, by condemning the property for sale to a private agency for redevelopment, the land was being redeveloped for a private and not a public use as required by the Fifth Amendment. The Supreme Court, in an opinion by Justice Douglas, disagreed and upheld the use of the eminent domain power.

The opinion noted that Congress has a "police power" as to the city of Washington, D.C., which is equivalent to the police power of the individual states, to legislate as necessary for the health, safety and welfare of its residents. Congress was exercising this "police power" in *Berman*.[6] This use of the term "police power" by Justice Douglas did not indicate that the government could take property without compensation but only that the federal government is not of limited, enumerated powers when it legislates concerning the District of Columbia.

The significance of the *Berman* opinion is that it confirms that the public use limitation of the Fifth and Fourteenth Amendment is as expansive as a due process police power test.[7] The Court reaffirmed the rule that once the legislature has declared a condemnation to be for a public use, the role of the courts is an extremely narrow one.[8] The Court approved

---

3. Comment, The Public Use Limitation on Eminent Domain: An Advance Requiem, 58 Yale L.J. 599, 602–03 (1949).

4. See Mt. Vernon–Woodberry Cotton Duck Co. v. Alabama Interstate Power Co., 240 U.S. 30, 36 S.Ct. 234, 60 L.Ed. 507 (1916). See also Sachman, The Right to Condemn, 29 Albany L.Rev. 177, 183 (1965).

5. 348 U.S. 26, 75 S.Ct. 98, 99 L.Ed. 27 (1954).

6. 348 U.S. at 31, 75 S.Ct. at 101–02.

7. In Brown v. Legal Foundation of Washington, 538 U.S. 216, 123 S.Ct. 1406, 155 L.Ed.2d 376 (2003) the Court, by a 5 to 4 vote, held: that state laws requiring the combination of small amounts of money held by attorneys or escrow agents for their clients (amounts so small that they would not have otherwise generated income), and requiring the transfer of that money to state funds used to subsidize legal services for low-income persons constituted

a taking of property; that such a taking would unquestionably be for a public use; and that no compensation was owed to the owners of small funds that would otherwise not have generated monetary interest, because the monetary loss to such persons was in fact nothing (the amount owed to the owners of the small accounts was zero, because they had lost no monetary interest that they could have earned prior to the enactment of the statute).

8. Berman v. Parker, 348 U.S. 26, 32, 75 S.Ct. 98, 102, 99 L.Ed. 27 (1954). See also, Rindge Co. v. Los Angeles County, 262 U.S. 700, 709, 43 S.Ct. 689, 693, 67 L.Ed. 1186 (1923); Old Dominion Land Co. v. United States, 269 U.S. 55, 66, 46 S.Ct. 39, 40–41, 70 L.Ed. 162 (1925); and United States ex rel. Tennessee Valley Authority v. Welch, 327 U.S. 546, 551–52, 66 S.Ct. 715, 717–18, 90 L.Ed. 843 (1946).

the concept of area redevelopment by holding that property which, standing by itself, was innocuous could be taken as part of the overall plan.[9] As for the power of the legislature to condemn areas for the purpose of renovation, the Court stated that "[i]t is within the power of the legislature to determine that the community should be beautiful as well as healthy, spacious as well as clean, well-balanced as well as carefully patrolled."[10]

After *Berman*, the public use limitation is easily met whenever eminent domain is exercised by either the state or federal government as a means of realizing any object within its authority. For the state governments, and for the federal government when acting within federal territory, this means that eminent domain may be exercised whenever the purpose of the action is for the benefit of the health, safety and welfare of its citizens. For the actions of federal government concerning land within the states, this public use limitation is met whenever the object of the exercise bears any reasonable relationship to one of its implied or enumerated powers.

The Supreme Court followed the broad public benefit test of *Berman* in upholding the Hawaii Land Reform Act of 1967. The state legislature in Hawaii, through this Act, created a system for taking title and residential real property from lessors, and—after providing the lessors with just compensation—transfer-

ring title to the lessee of the property in order to reduce the concentration of land ownership in the state. In *Hawaii Housing Authority v. Midkiff*,[11] the Court found that this exercise of the eminent domain power was rationally related to the public purpose of correcting deficiencies in the real estate market and social problems attributed to land oligopoly. The fact that the property was transferred to private individuals did not invalidate the taking. The Court found that the public use requirement is "coterminous with the scope of a sovereign's police powers." This rule does not mean that a state can deprive an owner of the value of his land or take his property without just compensation or for a purely private reason. But, so long as the government is willing to pay fair market value for the property interest taken, the governmental act should be upheld whenever it is "rationally related to a conceivable public purpose...." The transfer of ownership in this case was not merely for the private benefit of the lessees but was rationally related to social and economic problems caused by the historic land oligopoly which had existed in Hawaii.[12]

§ 11.14   A Note on the Amount of Compensation and Compensable Property Interests

The Fifth and Fourteenth Amendments require that a person receive "just compensa-

---

9. Berman v. Parker, 348 U.S. 26, 35, 75 S.Ct. 98, 103–04, 99 L.Ed. 27 (1954).

10. 348 U.S. at 33, 75 S.Ct. at 102–03.

11. 467 U.S. 229, 104 S.Ct. 2321, 81 L.Ed.2d 186 (1984). In National Railroad Passenger Corp. v. Boston and Maine Corp., 503 U.S. 407, 112 S.Ct. 1394, 118 L.Ed.2d 52 (1992), on remand 976 F.2d 1444 (D.C.Cir. 1992) the Supreme Court upheld the decision of the Interstate Commerce Commission to condemn almost 50 miles of railroad track (for which it paid just compensation) even though the railroad track was taken by the government in order to give it to National Railroad Passenger Corp. (Amtrak—a private corporation created by Congress) and even though Amtrak subsequently conveyed the track property to another railroad. The Court found that the Interstate Commerce Commission acted within the scope of its statutory authority and ruled that there was no significant constitutional limitation on the ability of the agency to condemn the track that arose from the public use phrase in the Fifth Amendment takings clause. "We have held that the public use requirement of the Takings Clause is coterminous with the regulatory power, and that

the Court will not strike down a condemnation on the basis that it lacks public use so long as the taking is rationally related to a conceivable public purpose." 503 U.S. at 422, 112 S.Ct. at 1404 (internal quotation marks and citation omitted).

12. Justice O'Connor delivered an opinion for a unanimous court (Justice Marshall did not participate). Her opinion stated: "A purely private taking could not withstand the scrutiny of the public use requirement; it would serve no legitimate purpose of government and would thus be void. But no purely private taking is involved in this case. The Hawaii Legislature enacted its Land Reform Act not to benefit a particular class of identifiable individuals but to attack certain perceived evils of concentrated property ownership in Hawaii—a legitimate public purpose. Use of the condemnation power to achieve this purpose is not irrational. Since we assume for purposes of this appeal that the weighty demand of just compensation has been met, the requirements of the Fifth and Fourteenth Amendments have been satisfied." 467 U.S. at 243–245, 104 S.Ct. at 2331–32, 81 L.Ed.2d at 200.

tion" for property that has been taken by the state or federal government. The Supreme Court has said that the constitutional guarantee of just compensation is not a limitation on the power of eminent domain, but only a condition of its exercise.[1] In determining what is "just compensation" the courts have developed various standards of valuation.[2]

The most basic principle for determining the amount due an individual whose property has been taken is contained in the often-quoted statement by Justice Holmes that the test is "what has the owner lost, not what has the taker gained".[3] Thus determination of what the injured property owner has lost fixes the amount for which the state is liable. Here the courts normally look to the market value of the property that has been taken.[4] Moreover, in determining the market value of the land, the court will normally look to the value of the property as if land were applied to its "highest and best" use. The highest and best use of a piece of property is determined by the value of the property in light of its present and potential uses if those uses can be anticipated with reasonable certainty.[5]

The market value test is not, however, a definitive test. In *United States v. Fuller*,[6] the Supreme Court stated that the overall standard is governed by basic equitable principles of fairness. In *Fuller*, the Court held that the government as a condemnor was not required to pay for elements of the property's market value that the government had created by granting the landowner a revocable permit to graze his animals on adjoining Federal lands.[7]

When the Taking Occurs. Because the government may take property in several ways, it is not always easy to determine the point in time when the government took an individual's property. The fair market value of property must be determined on the date of the taking in order to compensate fully the owner in accordance with the guarantee of the just compensation clause. If there is a difference in value between the date of the taking and the date on which the government will tender payment, the individual will be entitled to interest on the value of the property from the date of the taking or a new valuation of the property if during the delay the value of the property changed materially.[8] Even when

§ 11.14

1. Long Island Water–Supply Co. v. Brooklyn, 166 U.S. 685, 689, 17 S.Ct. 718, 720, 41 L.Ed. 1165 (1897). See E. Freund, The Police Power 541 (1904) where the author concludes that the compensation requirement has always been an element of the exercise of eminent domain in civilized societies.

2. For an analysis of the compensation and valuation issue see, L. Orgel, Valuation Under the Law of Eminent Domain (2d ed.1953); Risinger, Direct Damages: The Lost Key to Constitutional Just Compensation When Business Premises Are Condemned, 15 Seaton Hall L.Rev. 483 (1985).

3. Boston Chamber of Commerce v. Boston, 217 U.S. 189, 195, 30 S.Ct. 459, 460, 54 L.Ed. 725 (1910).

4. Note, Valuation of Conrail Under the Fifth Amendment, 90 Harv.L.Rev. 596, 598 (1977).

5. Super–Power Co. v. Sommers, 352 Ill. 610, 618, 186 N.E. 476, 479 (1933).

6. 409 U.S. 488, 93 S.Ct. 801, 35 L.Ed.2d 16 (1973).

7. See also, United States ex rel. Tennessee Valley Authority v. Powelson, 319 U.S. 266, 63 S.Ct. 1047, 87 L.Ed. 1390 (1943), where the Supreme Court held that in condemning land the federal government need not take into consideration in valuing the property the loss of business opportunity dependent on the owner's privilege to use the state's power of eminent domain.

Appraisal Fees. In United States v. Bodcaw Co., 440 U.S. 202, 99 S.Ct. 1066, 59 L.Ed.2d 257 (1979) (per curiam) the Court unanimously held that appraisal fees incurred by the owner of land in connection with a condemnation proceeding were not constitutionally compensable interests in connection with the taking of land by the federal government. While a particular legislative body might grant such costs to property owners as a part of condemnation proceedings, the government was not required by the Constitution to reimburse these costs. The Court also held that such expenses were not to be repaid under applicable federal acts.

Replacement Cost. In keeping with the requirement that condemned land be paid for at market value, absent unusual circumstances, the Court, in United States v. 564.54 Acres of Land, 441 U.S. 506, 99 S.Ct. 1854, 60 L.Ed.2d 435 (1979), found that a private nonprofit organization whose recreational camp was condemned by the government, was not entitled to the replacement cost for the camp. In this case the replacement cost would have been higher than the market value because the reestablishment of the camp was subject to new regulations which had not applied to the first facility. The Court ruled that this case did not present a unique situation where there was no ascertainable market value for the property or where the use of market value would create manifest injustice to the owner.

8. Kirby Forest Industries, Inc. v. United States, 467 U.S. 1, 104 S.Ct. 2187, 81 L.Ed.2d 1 (1984).

the government seeks to secure title to the property through a judicial "condemnation" proceeding against the property, or through legislative action taking the property, it may be difficult to determine the exact date on which the taking occurred. Government actions prior to the formal transfer of title may have made the property virtually valueless to the individual. The Supreme Court has found that the same considerations used to determine whether a taking has resulted from government actions are to be considered in determining when the taking occurred. Thus, courts must determine the time at which the value of the property was so substantially reduced by the government's actions or announcement of intention to take title to the property that a taking occurred at that time.[9]

Inverse Condemnations. Particularly difficult problems arise when a property owner alleges that his property has been taken by the government by regulatory action or impairment of the value rather than by government agents physically taking possession of the property or court or legislative transfer of the title of the property to the government. In such situations, the property owner institutes an "inverse condemnation" suit against the government. The individual will be seeking a court determination that a taking of property has occurred so as to force the government to either pay just compensation to the property owner, cease the governmental actions, or rescind the governmental regulation that has caused the diminution of the value of the property and the taking.[10]

If an inverse condemnation proceeding results in a judicial determination that a governmental action or regulation has resulted in a taking of property, the government may seek to limit the property owner's remedy to invalidation of the government action which impaired the value of the property. Once it is determined that the government action constitutes a taking for which compensation is due, the government can choose to continue the action and pay fair market value for the permanent taking of the property. If the government chooses to end its action, a court must determine whether the governmental activity, which impaired the value of the property, constituted a taking of property for the time period between the initiation of the government action (or regulation) and the time when the government rescinded its action (at the conclusion of the inverse condemnation proceeding). If the court determines that there was a taking of property for that time period, and the government chooses not to exercise its eminent domain power and pay for a permanent taking of the property, the court must order appropriate just compensation for the temporary taking.[11]

---

9. The Court described the problem in Kirby Forest Industries, Inc. v. United States, 467 U.S. 1, 14, 104 S.Ct. 2187, 2196, 81 L.Ed.2d 1, 13 (1984), in the following way: "... while most burdens consequent upon government action undertaken in the public interest must be borne by individual landowners as concomitants of 'the advantage of living and doing business in a civilized community', some are so substantial and unforeseeable, and can so easily be identified and redistributed, that 'justice and fairness' require that they be borne by the public as a whole. These considerations are as applicable to the problem of determining when in a condemnation proceeding the taking occurs as they are to the problem of ascertaining whether a taking has been effected by a putative exercise of the police power." [Footnotes omitted].

10. See 6 P. Nichols, Eminent Domain § 25.41 (3d rev.ed.1984). The Supreme Court described the nature of inverse condemnation when it found that federal laws prohibited states from taking lands belonging to American Indians by any means other than formal judicial condemnation of the property; the purpose of the federal laws was to prohibit states from taking physical occupation of such land and forcing individuals or tribes to bring inverse condemnation suits for recovery of just compensation. See United States v. Clarke, 445 U.S. 253, 100 S.Ct. 1127, 63 L.Ed.2d 373 (1980).

11. After a series of cases in which the Court avoided ruling on the government's duty to pay for a temporary taking, the Supreme Court in First English Evangelical Lutheran Church of Glendale v. County of Los Angeles, Cal., 482 U.S. 304, 107 S.Ct. 2378, 96 L.Ed.2d 250 (1987) ruled that just compensation is required for temporary takings of property. The government will not have to pay as much compensation for a temporary taking as for a permanent taking because the owner, in a temporary taking case, will eventually have the full use of his property returned to him. In the *First English Evangelical Lutheran Church* case the Court assumed, without deciding, that a California property use regulation constituted a taking of property, and that the government would rescind its regulation rather than pay for a permanent taking. Chief Justice Rehnquist, writing for a six-Justice majority, found that a temporary regulatory taking, like a temporary physical appropriation of property by the government, would require compensation.

Related to determining the amount of compensation are issues concerning the interests that qualify as property for which any compensation is due. The power of eminent domain enables the government to take "property" for public uses and only requires compensation for such. When the federal government acts as the condemnor, or taker, of the property the issue of what may be taken and what must be paid for is a matter of federal law.[12] The Supreme Court, for example, has held that an Indian group had an insufficient interest in unrecognized Indian land to require that compensation be paid for divestiture of that interest.[13] The Court has held, however, that a lease interest is property and that an injured lessee had a property right requiring compensation.[14] In sum, the power of eminent domain extends to tangibles and intangibles,

including choses in action, contracts and charters.[15] As with the basic determination of value, this "test" combines traditional property law interests and equitable principles of fairness.

Transferable Development Rights. One of the most significant eminent domain issues to have arisen for several decades focuses on the compensation concept. In an effort to protect historical landmarks from destruction, a system termed "transferable development rights" has been developed. Under such a system, the owners of designated landmarks are given "rights" to exceed building height restrictions in their building zones as compensation for the decreased value of the building because of regulations which prohibit the modification of the landmark. Whether the system takes property or provides adequate compensation remains open to dispute.[16]

The Amount of Compensation and Compensable Property Interests. The *First English Evangelical Lutheran Church* decision only held that the government must pay compensation to a property owner after a regulation of property has been determined to be a violation of the takings clause. In such a situation the government cannot merely rescind its regulation; the government, under such circumstances, must pay the property owner the fair market value for the property owner's loss of use during the time when the regulatory taking was in effect. The *First English* decision did not rule that all temporary bans on property use constitute a taking for Fifth and Fourteenth Amendment purposes. In Tahoe–Sierra Preservation Council, Inc. v. Tahoe Regional Planning Agency, 535 U.S. 302, 122 S.Ct. 1465, 152 L.Ed.2d 517 (2002) the Court held that temporary bans on property development did not constitute a per se taking of property, and that the facts and circumstances of each case involving a temporary ban on property development would have to be examined to determine if a taking had occurred. The *Tahoe–Sierra* case is examined in § 11.12 of this Treatise.

When is Compensation to Be Paid? In Williamson County Regional Planning Commission v. Hamilton Bank of Johnson City, 473 U.S. 172, 105 S.Ct. 3108, 87 L.Ed.2d 126 (1985), on remand 779 F.2d 50 (6th Cir.1985), the Court held that the takings clause does not require that compensation be paid in advance of, or contemporaneously with, a taking of property. A state could provide a procedure for seeking just compensation that would require a property owner to file for compensation and which would preclude the owner from claiming that the just compensation clause had been violated, until the owner had followed the procedure and been denied just compensation. In making this ruling, the Court avoided ruling on the temporary regulatory takings problem it addressed in the *First English Evangelical Lutheran Church* decision.

When a state collects money from taxpayers with a tax that is unconstitutional under existing precedents of the United States Supreme Court, the state must provide

some type of relief to the taxpayer. However, the state procedure by which a taxpayer can challenge a tax statute does not have to precede the taxpayer's payment of the tax. McKesson v. Division of Alcoholic Beverages and Tobacco, 496 U.S. 18, 110 S.Ct. 2238, 110 L.Ed.2d 17 (1990).

For citations to additional Supreme Court cases, see our multivolume treatise: R. Rotunda & J. Nowak, Treatise on Constitutional Law § 15.14 (2nd ed. 1992, with annual supplements).

12. United States ex rel. Tennessee Valley Authority v. Powelson, 319 U.S. 266, 63 S.Ct. 1047, 87 L.Ed. 1390 (1943), mandate conformed 138 F.2d 343 (4th Cir.1943). See also, annot, 1 A.L.R.Fed. 479 (1969).

13. Tee–Hit–Ton Indians v. United States, 348 U.S. 272, 75 S.Ct. 313, 99 L.Ed. 314 (1955), rehearing denied 348 U.S. 965, 75 S.Ct. 521, 99 L.Ed. 753 (1955).

14. A. W. Duckett & Co. v. United States, 266 U.S. 149, 45 S.Ct. 38, 69 L.Ed. 216 (1924). See also Armstrong v. United States, 364 U.S. 40, 80 S.Ct. 1563, 4 L.Ed.2d 1554 (1960), on remand 152 Ct.Cl. 731, 287 F.2d 577 (1961) (materialmen's liens held to be a compensable interest).

15. City of Cincinnati v. Louisville & Nashville R. Co., 223 U.S. 390, 400, 32 S.Ct. 267, 268–69, 56 L.Ed. 481 (1912). The Court in *City of Cincinnati* also held that the constitutional limitation on any state law impairing the obligation of contracts was not intended to limit the exercise of eminent domain. Id.

16. The adequate compensation issue remains undecided. The Supreme Court upheld the use of the landmark preservation—transferable development rights (TDR) system to limit the alteration of the Grand Central Station in New York on the basis that this land use "regulation" did not constitute a "taking." Penn Central Transp. Co. v. New York, 438 U.S. 104, 98 S.Ct. 2646, 57

L.Ed.2d 631 (1978), rehearing denied 439 U.S. 883, 99 S.Ct. 226, 58 L.Ed.2d 198 (1978). The Justices, in *Penn Central*, did not examine the question of whether TDR's constituted adequate compensation for a taking. See § 11.12(b). In Suitum v. Tahoe Regional Planning Agency, 520 U.S. 725, 117 S.Ct. 1659, 137 L.Ed.2d 980 (1997), the Court ruled that a landowner's claim for compensation in a case involving transferrable development rights was ripe for a judicial determination. Because of the nature of the lower court rulings, the Supreme Court, in *Suitum*, did not rule on whether the government action constituted a taking.

Chapter 12

STATE ACTION

§ 12.1 Introduction *

(a) Central Theory

Most of the protections for individual rights and liberties contained in the Constitution and its Amendments apply only to the actions of governmental entities. The safeguards against deprivations of individual rights which are contained in the text of the Constitution specifically apply only to the activities of either the state or federal governments. Similarly, the Bill of Rights by its terms and necessary implications has been viewed only to limit the freedom of the government when dealing with individuals. Finally, the Amendments to the Constitution which protect individual liberties specifically address themselves to actions taken by the United States or a state. Only the Thirteenth Amendment, which abolishes the institution of slavery, is also directed to controlling the actions of private individuals. Thus whenever a suit is brought against private individuals on the basis that they have taken actions which have violated the civil or political rights of another, there is a question as to how the actions of the private individuals could be limited by these constitutional provisions. There must be a determination of whether defendant's actions constitute govern-

mental or "state" action of a type regulated by the appropriate constitutional provision.

In most forms of constitutional litigation there is no state action issue involved in the case. When a legislature, executive officer, or a court takes some official action against an individual, that action is subjected to review under the Constitution, for the official act of any governmental agency is direct governmental action and therefore subject to the restraints of the Constitution. The so called "state action" issue arises only when the person or entity alleged to have violated the Constitution is not acting on behalf of the government. In such a case the person alleged to have violated the constitutional provision will argue that he is incapable of violating the Constitution because he is not part of the government, giving rise to the state action issue.

It should be noted that actions of any governmental entity give rise to state action for the purposes of constitutional limitations. Any subdivision of a state, be it an administrative agency or an independent political subdivision, such as a city, represents government or state authority to a sufficient degree to invoke constitutional restrictions on its actions.[1]

§ 12.1

* Sections of this Chapter are derived in part from an article co-authored by one of the authors of this text. See Glennon and Nowak, A Functional Analysis of the Fourteenth Amendment "State Action" Requirement, 1976 Sup.Ct.Rev. 221. We express our thanks to Professor Robert J. Glennon, Jr., and to the editor of the Supreme Court Review, Professor Philip Kurland, for allowing us to make use of the article. See also, Rotunda, Runyon v. McCrary and the Mosaic of State Action, 67 Washington University L.Q. 47 (1989). For additional citations to secondary sources on this topic see, 3 R. Rotunda & J. Nowak,

Treatise on Constitutional Law: Substance and Procedure, Ch. 16 (3rd ed. 1999, with annual supplements).

1. The actions of, and processes used by, state and federal courts constitute "state action." For example, in M.L.B. v. S.L.J., 519 U.S. 102, 116 n. 8, 117 S.Ct. 555, 564 n. 8, 136 L.Ed.2d 473 (1996) the Court found that a civil proceeding in a state court initiated by a husband to terminate the parental rights of his former spouse, as a prelude to an adoption petition by his new spouse, involved "state action." In Santa Fe Independent School District v. Doe, 530 U.S. 290, 120 S.Ct. 2266, 147 L.Ed.2d 295 (2000) the Supreme Court found that a public school

The phrase "state action" is a misnomer because the issue arises in an identical manner when the federal government or its agents are involved in a case. If a person or agency is alleged to have violated some constitutional provision or civil rights statute directed at the federal government there will be an issue in the case as to whether the defendant has sufficient "federal government action" to be subjected to those limitations. However, all problems relating to the existence of government action—local, state or federal—which would subject an individual to constitutional restrictions come under the heading of "state action."

All of the cases involving a state action issue have an essentially similar fact pattern. In these cases one individual citizen (the "aggrieved party") feels that his freedoms or rights have been violated by the actions of another (the "alleged wrongdoer"). The aggrieved party, or some governmental agency acting on his behalf, claims that a violation of the Constitution has taken place by the other party's actions. In a very real sense the issue is simply which party's rights are of the greater constitutional significance. This question is answered by determining whether the challenged party's activities involve sufficient governmental action so that they are subjected to the values and limitations reflected in the Constitution and its Amendments.[2] If the Court

district policy that permitted public high school students to select one of their fellow students to lead a prayer at high school home football games violated the establishment clause. See Chapter 17, §§ 17.3, 17.5(c). Because the regulation was a government act, there was no state action issue in that case.

See generally, State v. Jones, 666 N.W.2d 142, (Iowa 2003, citing this Treatise); Wald, J., citing Treatise in, Alliance for Community Media v. FCC, 10 F.3d 812, 818 (D.C.Cir.1993) rehearing en banc granted, vacated 15 F.3d 186 (D.C.Cir.1994); Sharp, C.J., citing Treatise in, Ridlen v. Four County Counseling Center, 809 F.Supp. 1343, 1347 (N.D.Ind.1992); Mills, J., citing Treatise, in Stevens v. Umsted, 921 F.Supp. 530, 532 (C.D.Ill.1996); Brown, J., quoting Treatise, in Eggert v. Tuckerton Volunteer Fire Co. No. 1, 938 F.Supp. 1230 (D.N.J.1996); Bryant, J., (concurring) citing Treatise, in Kirsch v. Bowling Green State University, 1996 WL 284717 (Ohio App.1996); State ex rel. Howard v. Ferreri, 70 Ohio St.3d 587, 591, 639 N.E.2d 1189, 1193 (1994) (per curiam), citing Treatise.

2. A few cases may appear to differ from this fact pattern. In National Collegiate Athletic Association v. Tarkanian, 488 U.S. 179, 109 S.Ct. 454, 102 L.Ed.2d 469 (1988) the Supreme Court found that the National Collegiate Athletic Association's enforcement of its rules against the University of Nevada, Las Vegas did not involve state action that deprived a coach of due process, even though the NCAA's actions included an order to the university to "show cause" why it should not be punished by the Association if it did not remove the coach from all of his coaching duties at the university. The university's disciplinary action against the coach did involve state action. The question of whether the NCAA should be subject to the requirements of due process involved a determination of whether the NCAA performed a governmental function or whether the Association's actions were attributable to the state. In the dispute between the NCAA and the coach, the Court answered those questions in the negative and found that the NCAA did not have state action. The state actor in the case, the university, would be free to retain the coach and either withdraw from the Association or suffer additional sanctions against its sports programs.

In Brentwood Academy v. Tennessee Secondary School Athletic Association, 531 U.S. 288, 121 S.Ct. 924, 148

L.Ed.2d 807 (2001), a five Justice majority distinguished the *Tarkanian* decision, and ruled that an association of public and private schools that governed the high school athletic competition within a single state was so entwined with state government as to have "state action" for purposes of the Fourteenth Amendment and 42 U.S.C.A. § 1983. See, § 12.4(b).

In DeShaney v. Winnebago County Department of Social Services, 489 U.S. 189, 109 S.Ct. 998, 103 L.Ed.2d 249 (1989) the Supreme Court found that the governmental entity being sued did not violate the due process rights of the child when its social workers, who had been assigned to work with the child and his father and who had noted in their records the reasons why they believed the child was being abused, did nothing to prevent the child from suffering serious injury as a result of beatings from his father. This case did not involve a true state action issue because the child and his mother, the former wife of the father who beat the child, were not bringing suit on a constitutional basis against the father who caused the injury. They were suing the governmental entity itself. There is no question that the County Department of Social Services had state action and was subject to the due process clause. The Supreme Court found that there was no constitutional violation because the due process clause did not impose on the government a substantive duty to protect individuals from private harm, when the individual had not been in any sense taken into the custody or control of the government. The Court noted that the state might violate the equal protection clause if it selectively denied its protective services to "disfavored minorities." 489 U.S. at 197 n. 3, 109 S.Ct. at 1004 n. 3.

In Sacramento v. Lewis, 523 U.S. 833, 118 S.Ct. 1708, 140 L.Ed.2d 1043 (1998) the Supreme Court held that substantive due process principle established a "shock the conscience" standard for determining whether an executive action that caused incidental, but unintended, harm to individuals was unconstitutional. Justices Souter's majority opinion in *Lewis* referred to the *DeShaney* decision for the principle that the government had a duty to protect safety and well-being of persons who were taken under its custody. The *Lewis* majority ruled that police officers did not violate substantive due process principles

finds sufficient connections to the government it will declare that the aggrieved party's rights must prevail. In such a situation the aggrieved party has a constitutionally protected freedom of action which cannot be disregarded by the alleged wrongdoer. However, the Court may find that the alleged wrongdoer does not have sufficient contacts with the government to justify subjecting him to constitutional limitations. In that situation the alleged wrongdoer's rights will prevail and the aggrieved party will receive no relief from the federal courts. Here the activity is free from constitutional limitation and it will be allowed to continue until such time as it is made illegal under appropriate state or federal statutes.

The fact pattern described above also fits cases where it is an organization or association that is causing harm to other persons. If an organization or association of private persons excludes another person from the group because of the person's race, religion, sex, or sexual orientation the group will not have violated the First or Fourteenth Amendments unless that association has state action.[3] Local, state, or federal statutes might prohibit private associations from excluding persons because of characteristics such as race, religion, sex, or sexual orientation. An association of persons that is subject to such statutes (and forced to admit or accommodate persons that they did not want to accept) may challenge the application of the anti-discrimination law to their association on the basis of the First and Fourteenth Amendments. The statute making discrimination unlawful is an action of the government, and, therefore, constitutes state action. Thus, there will be no state action issue when a court examines the application of an anti-discrimination law to a private organi-

zation; the Court will have to determine whether the statute violates First or Fourteenth Amendment rights of the private association that does not want to comply with the statutory terms.[4]

While all state action cases arise in similar fact situations, they are brought on two distinct legal bases. The first type of suit is based solely on the provisions of the Constitution or a specific Amendment. In such a case the challenged party is alleged to have sufficient state action so that his activities directly violate the Constitution by limiting the rights of the aggrieved party. The second type of case is based upon a specific statute passed by the Congress pursuant to its powers to protect the principles of an Amendment to the Constitution. In the second type of case there are two issues: (1) whether the seemingly private party comes within the terms of the statute, and (2) whether Congress has the power to restrict the activities of private individuals in order to safeguard civil liberties.[5] The most important state action issues are involved in cases where the challenged activity is alleged to violate an Amendment to the Constitution or a general civil rights statute. In these cases the Court is presented with the question of how it is to determine when a private individual is to be subjected to constitutional limitations.

In the late 1980s and 1990s, Supreme Court majority opinions stated that a court should make two inquiries in determining whether a private actor who has harmed other persons acted with "state action." The Court said that it would determine first "whether the claimed constitutional deprivation [the harm caused to some private persons by the individual who is alleged to be acting with 'state

when they caused the accidental death of a suspect in a high-speed chase. The *Lewis* case is discussed in § 10.6.

3. Moose Lodge No. 107 v. Irvis, 407 U.S. 163, 92 S.Ct. 1965, 32 L.Ed.2d 627 (1972). See § 12.4(c).

4. Compare Roberts v. United States Jaycees, 468 U.S. 609, 104 S.Ct. 3244, 82 L.Ed.2d 462 (1984) (upholding application of state anti-discrimination statute to private, business related organization) with Boy Scouts of America v. Dale, 530 U.S. 640, 120 S.Ct. 2446, 147 L.Ed.2d 554 (2000) (finding that application of anti-discrimination law to Boy Scouts, so as to require the organization not to discriminate against Boy Scout leaders on the basis of

sexual orientation, violated the First Amendment freedom of association). Hurley v. Irish–American Gay, Lesbian, and Bisexual Group of Boston, 515 U.S. 557, 115 S.Ct. 2338, 132 L.Ed.2d 487 (1995) (private groups refusal to include persons in their parade because of sexual orientation did not involve state action; imposition of anti-discrimination law on the group organizing the parade would violate the First Amendment freedom of association). Freedom of association and freedom not to associate, cases are examined in Chapter 16, § 16.41.

5. Examination of this issue is included in Chapter 15.

action'] resulted from the exercise of a right or privilege having its source in state authority [or the authority of the federal government in a federal case] and, second, whether the private party charged with the deprivation could be described in all fairness as a state actor." [6]

In the first step of the analysis a court asks whether the private actor who caused the harm to another person was acting in conformity with the law of the jurisdiction when he caused the harm. That inquiry may well be of little practical importance in deciding any state action case. If a private actor is breaking the law of the jurisdiction when he harms another individual, it is unlikely that the private actor will be subject to a suit that centers on whether he had state action when he caused the harm. For example, when a burglar breaks into a house and takes away property, he is not subject to Fourth Amendment limitations on searches and seizures or Fifth Amendment restrictions on the taking of property, because his actions have absolutely no connection to the government. However, if the burglar broke into a house at the direction of state police, who wanted the burglar to seize

evidence for the government to use in a criminal investigation, the burglar would be acting with state action because he was in a conspiracy with, and acting at the direction of, the police.[7] Even though the burglar's actions in the latter situation would not be in conformity with state or local legislation, the burglar would be acting with state authority.

The second question asked by the Court (in its decisions in the 1980s and 1990s) melds the traditional "public function" and "entanglement" branches of state action analysis from earlier cases. In the second step of the analysis a court should determine whether the actions of the private actor can be described "in all fairness" as the acts of a person acting with state action. In making this determination, the Supreme Court said that a court should examine three factors: "[1] the extent to which the actor relies on governmental assistance and benefits.... [2] whether the actor is performing a traditional government function.... [3] and whether the injury caused is aggravated in a unique way by the incidence of government authority."[8]

---

6. Edmonson v. Leesville Concrete Co., Inc., 500 U.S. 614, 618–22, 111 S.Ct. 2077, 2082–83, 114 L.Ed.2d 660 (1991), citing, Lugar v. Edmondson Oil Co., 457 U.S. 922, 937–42, 102 S.Ct. 2744, 2753–56, 73 L.Ed.2d 482 (1982). See also, Georgia v. McCollum, 505 U.S. 42, 112 S.Ct. 2348, 120 L.Ed.2d 33 (1992).

7. Cases regarding conspiracies between government officials and private persons include: Screws v. United States, 325 U.S. 91, 65 S.Ct. 1031, 89 L.Ed. 1495 (1945) (applying a statute that required action "under color of any law" to punish private persons as well as government officials who had engaged in a conspiracy); Dennis v. Sparks, 449 U.S. 24, 101 S.Ct. 183, 66 L.Ed.2d 185 (1980) (conspiracy between government actors and private actors will give rise to state action in the activities of the private persons and make them subject to constitutional and statutory restrictions promised on state action, even if the government actor with whom they conspire has immunity). In Soldal v. Cook County, 506 U.S. 56, 60 n. 6, 113 S.Ct. 538, 543 n. 6, 121 L.Ed.2d 450 (1992) the Justices found that there was state action involved in the seizure of a debtor's mobile home because deputy sheriffs assisted the owner by protecting the owner's employees as they removed the trailer from the park even though the deputy sheriffs knew the owner had not secured a lawful eviction order against the mobile home owner.

See generally, Greenburg, J., quoting treatise in Mark v. Borough of Hatboro, 51 F.3d 1137, 1144 (3d Cir.1995), cert. denied 516 U.S. 858, 116 S.Ct. 165, 133 L.Ed.2d 107 (1995).

8. Edmonson v. Leesville Concrete Co., Inc., 500 U.S. 614, 620, 111 S.Ct. 2077, 2083, 114 L.Ed.2d 660 (1991). On remand 943 F.2d 551 (5th Cir.1991). In *Edmonson,* the Supreme Court found that a private litigant who used peremptory challenges in a civil case to exclude members of a racial minority from jury service would violate the equal protection guarantee of the due process clause of the Fifth Amendment (in a federal case) or the equal protection clause of the Fourteenth Amendment (in a state case).

The Supreme Court used similar analysis in Georgia v. McCollum, 505 U.S. 42, 112 S.Ct. 2348, 120 L.Ed.2d 33 (1992), on remand 262 Ga. 554, 422 S.E.2d 866 (1992) to find that a defendant's use of peremptory challenges in a criminal case to exclude persons from jury service because of their race would violate the equal protection clause of the Fourteenth Amendment. The Court in *McCollum* found that the defendant was exercising a right that had its source in state authority (the right to use peremptory challenges) in that the defendant could be described as a state actor regardless of his adversary nature to the state in the particular criminal proceeding. A party to a case (including a criminal defendant) must make use of the judicial system for assistance in excluding jurors. The selection of the jury was "a uniquely and constitutionally compelled government function." The Court also found that the harm to society, and minority race persons, through discriminatory use of jury challenges was the same regardless of whether the challenges were made by the prosecution or the defense. In J.E.B. v. Alabama ex rel. T.B. 511 U.S. 127, 114 S.Ct. 1419, 128 L.Ed.2d 89 (1994) the Supreme Court held that the intentional use of peremptory challenges by a government attorney to ex-

The second of the three factors listed by the Court in the second step of its analysis is merely traditional public function analysis, which we will examine in the next section of this chapter. The first and third factors are only some of the factors to consider when determining whether the totality of contacts between the government and a private person are such that it is fair, and constitutionally necessary, to restrict the actions of the private person with constitutional limitations. In later sections of this chapter we will examine the types of contacts between the government and a private actor that can be the basis for finding state action when the private actor is not performing a traditional government function.

Prior to the 1980s the Supreme Court did not use the two-step analysis outlined above for determining whether a private person or corporation was acting with "state action." Rather, the Court merely determined whether: (1) the private actor who caused the harm to another individual was performing a traditional government function (so that the private actor would automatically be acting with state action) or (2) whether the totality of facts and circumstances in the case connected the government to the private actor and harm in a way that made it fair to say that the private actor had acted with state action. The Supreme Court's decisions in the 1980s and 1990s that use the two-step approach described above did not change any of the Court's earlier state action rulings; we must understand the two-step inquiry in terms of all of the Court's state action decisions. For this reason, it is important to separate government function cases from all other types of state action cases.

A court, in making a state action determination, must first decide whether the private

actor was engaging in a traditional public function. A public function (sometimes called a "government function") is an activity that has been traditionally done by the government exclusively in our society.[9] If the government delegates the operation of a traditional public function to a private person or private organization that person or organization will be subject to constitutional limitation. For example, the Supreme Court has found that the operation of the election system is a traditional government function.[10] Thus, if the government would allow a private organization to operate the primary election system, the primary election system run by that organization would be subject to constitutional limitations on voting discrimination such as those that arise from the Fourteenth, Fifteenth, Nineteenth, and Twenty-sixth Amendments. Because the organization operating the actual election was performing a government function, we would find that the two state questions posed by the Supreme Court in the 1980s and 1990s cases should be answered "yes": (1) yes—the harm caused to individuals who were excluded from the election by the private organization was harm that had been the result of the organization exercising a right that it got from state authority [the right to control a traditional government function]; (2) yes—the private party could be described in all fairness as a state actor because they had accepted the responsibility for operating a traditional government function.

If a private actor who is alleged to have harmed persons by violating a constitutional provision was not performing a public function, a court must examine the totality of facts and circumstances in the case to determine whether the government has been involved with the private actor in a way that makes it

---

clude persons of one sex from a jury violated the equal protection clause. The *J.E.B.* litigation began with the government bringing a civil case on behalf of a woman in the state for child support payments from the father of her child. The government used nine of its ten peremptory challenges to exclude males from the jury. Because the facts of the *J.E.B.* case involved a state government attorney, the Court did not have to deal with issues concerning "state action."

9. Public function analysis is examined in § 12.2 of this chapter and the Court's rulings concerning the other factors to consider in a state action case are examined in the remaining sections of this chapter.

10. Terry v. Adams, 345 U.S. 461, 73 S.Ct. 809, 97 L.Ed. 1152 (1953), rehearing denied 345 U.S. 1003, 73 S.Ct. 1128, 97 L.Ed. 1408 (1953) this decision and other cases involving government functions are examined in § 12.2 of this Treatise.

fair to subject the private actor to constitutional limitations. If the court finds that the totality of facts and circumstances shows the government being involved in the harm caused to the victims of the private actor the court is likely to conclude that the private actor was acting with state action and violated the civil liberties of the victim. In other words, when a case does not involve a traditional government function, a court must simply look at the totality of facts and circumstances in determining whether: (1) the harm caused to the victim was somehow traceable to the private actor using a right granted to him by state law; and (2) whether the connection of the government to the private actor, and the harm caused by the private actor, is such that it is fair to subject the private actor's actions to constitutional restrictions.

In the later sections of this Chapter, we will examine the Supreme Court's rulings concerning state action in a variety of settings. Before we commence upon the inquiry into how the Supreme Court resolves modern state action problems, we must briefly examine the origins of the state action issue, which lie in the decisions of the Supreme Court in the latter half of the nineteenth century.

(b) Origins of the Problem

The issues concerning the applicability of constitutional restrictions and congressional legislation to private conduct did not rise until after the enactment of the Civil War Amendments. At the time of the proposal and ratification of the Thirteenth and Fourteenth Amendments, the Congress passed a wide ranging series of civil rights statutes designed to protect blacks against the actions of both state officials and private persons. In several cases between 1875 and 1882 the Supreme Court indicated that Congress was not empowered to regulate the conduct of private persons simply because that conduct might disadvantage blacks or other persons. In the two most important cases of the period the Court held

that federal criminal indictments under the Civil Rights Acts for participation in the lynchings of blacks were unconstitutional as applied to persons who had no connection to state governments and who were not interfering with uniquely federal rights such as the petitioning of Congress.[11] However the issue was not fully examined until 1883 in the *Civil Rights Cases.*[12]

The decision of the Supreme Court captioned the *Civil Rights Cases* concerned four criminal indictments and one civil action under Section 1 of the Civil Rights Act of 1875.[13] That Act established criminal and civil penalties against anyone who interfered with the "full and equal enjoyment" of public facilities and conveyances by persons because of their race. The five cases were brought against individuals and railroads who had excluded black persons from railroads, hotels and theaters because of their race. The Court reversed the indictments and the civil penalty, because a majority of the Justices found that these actions were immune from congressional legislation and the restrictions of the Fourteenth Amendment because they did not involve state action. Additionally, the Court held that the congressional acts could not be justified by the Thirteenth Amendment, as the Justices did not believe them to be related to abolition of slavery in the United States.

As to the Fourteenth Amendment issue, the Court's opinion was predicated upon the premise that the power of Congress to enforce the Amendment comprehended no legislation which did not deal with actions that constituted a violation of section 1 of the Amendment. The majority therefore examined what actions might constitute a violation of the guarantees of due process and equal protection under Section 1. The opinion found that the Amendment was only meant to guarantee the existence of certain rights in law. So long as neither the state government nor its agencies established the deprivation of rights nor authorized others

---

11. United States v. Cruikshank, 92 U.S. (2 Otto) 542, 23 L.Ed. 588 (1875); United States v. Harris, 106 U.S. (16 Otto) 629, 1 S.Ct. 601, 27 L.Ed. 290 (1883). See also, United States v. Reese, 92 U.S. (2 Otto) 214, 23 L.Ed. 563 (1875).

12. 109 U.S. 3, 3 S.Ct. 18, 27 L.Ed. 835 (1883).

13. Civil Rights Act of 1875, 18 Stat. 335, chap. 114.

to impair such rights the Justices could see no state violation of due process or equal protection of law.[14] In the view of these Justices the aggrieved person's rights remained in full force because, in theory, the state had not taken them away. The mere fact that private persons refused to allow black persons into public accommodations or public conveyances did not mean that the state had withdrawn the right of blacks to engage in such activities.[15] These actions by a private person or a corporation amounted to merely a private wrong which had no relationship to a deprivation of rights such as was prohibited by the Fourteenth Amendment.

Because the majority of Justices saw the harm to black persons as merely a conflict between private persons, they refused to allow the Congress to regulate these activities. The Court indicated that Congress' powers under section 5 of the Fourteenth Amendment could not extend beyond an enforcement of the basic provisions of Section 1 of the Amendment.[16]

The opinion of the Court in the *Civil Rights Cases* reflects two concerns as to congressional power. First, as the Amendment was directed only to the states, direct congressional regulation of private activities would be an unwarranted expansion of the federal power over individuals. Second, if Congress had a power to protect all rights against private deprivations it would allow the federal assumption of the functions of the state in a way which would violate principles inherent in the Tenth Amendment.

It is interesting to note that a majority of the Court used the Tenth Amendment to interpret both the applicability of the Fourteenth Amendment and the grant of power given to Congress by that Amendment.[17] This decision came at the time that Justices were

also beginning to restrict the scope of federal power under the commerce clause by using the Tenth Amendment to protect intrastate activities from federal regulation.[18] Additionally, it was during this period that the concept of substantive due process was gaining adherents on the Court.[19] The *Civil Rights Cases* can be seen then as another reflection of these Justices' antipathy towards government regulation of individual activities regardless of the basis of the legislation.

However, it should be noted that the Supreme Court recognized that Congress properly regulated the activities of private individuals when such regulation was based on a specific federal power such as those contained in section 8 of Article 1 of the Constitution.[20] Thus, the Justices laid the basis for recognition of congressional powers to protect uniquely federal rights against interference by private persons, a congressional power which would be recognized by the Court in the next century.[21]

The opinion in the *Civil Rights Cases* also reviewed the permissibility of these civil rights acts as an enforcement of the Thirteenth Amendment.[22] This question did not involve a state action issue, for that Amendment abolishes slavery and involuntary servitude in the United States regardless of whether those conditions are imposed by a government entity or private persons. However, for a law to be a valid enforcement mechanism for this Amendment it would have to relate to the abolition of the incidents of slavery.

The majority opinion stated that Congress had the right under this Amendment to "enact all necessary and proper laws for the obliteration and prevention of slavery with all its badges and incidents."[23] However, a majority of the Justices believed that they should inde-

---

14.   109 U.S. at 11, 3 S.Ct. at 21–22.

15.   109 U.S. at 17, 18, 3 S.Ct. at 25–26, 26–27.

16.   109 U.S. at 14, 15, 3 S.Ct. at 23, 24.

17.   109 U.S. at 15, 3 S.Ct. at 24.

18.   See §§ 4.5–4.7, supra.

19.   See §§ 11.2, 11.3, supra.

20.   In re Civil Rights Cases, 109 U.S. 3, 18, 3 S.Ct. 18, 26–27, 27 L.Ed. 835 (1883).

21.   See Griffin v. Breckenridge, 403 U.S. 88, 91 S.Ct. 1790, 29 L.Ed.2d 338 (1971). For an examination of the Congressional Power to enforce these Amendments see Chapter 15.

22.   109 U.S. at 20, 3 S.Ct. at 27–28.

23.   109 U.S. at 21, 3 S.Ct. at 28.

pendently determine whether the legislation in fact was related to the "badges and incidents" of slavery. Here the majority simply disagreed with the Congress. The Court refused to grant any real deference to the congressional acts, for that would allow the federal regulation of all private discriminations or wrongs against blacks. The Court took the position that Congress could only eliminate legal distinctions based upon slavery and that, once those distinctions had been eliminated, any further discrimination had to be dealt with under the Fourteenth Amendment.

Justice Harlan dissented in these cases.[24] In his opinion the Thirteenth Amendment eliminated not only the institution of slavery but the continuing distinctions based on race which resulted from the slavery experience. He found that Congress could enforce the rights of the blacks in relation to public accommodations, facilities, and conveyances since discriminations in those "public" or "quasi-public" functions was a continuing badge of servitude.[25] Additionally, he found that the Fourteenth Amendment authorized Congress to grant full protection to blacks against discrimination by private persons. He noted that the first sentence of the Fourteenth Amendment created a national citizenship which could be protected by congressional legislation. Thus, he found that protection from race discrimination was a basic civil right and part of citizenship in the United States which could be protected by Congress.[26]

There were three distinct holdings in the *Civil Rights Cases*. First, that the guarantees of civil liberties contained in the Fourteenth Amendment applied only to governmental or "state" actions. Second, that the Congress was only empowered by the Fourteenth Amend-

ment to regulate the activities which the Court independently would find to be a violation of section 1 of the Amendment. Third, that the Court would independently review congressional legislation under the Thirteenth Amendment to insure that it was designed to eliminate clear vestiges of slavery.

These three holdings have had varying degrees of acceptance by later Justices and the Court. The final holding relating to the Thirteenth Amendment has clearly been overruled, for the Court will no longer strictly review legislation based on the Thirteenth Amendment.[27] As to the second holding, relating to the power to regulate private activities, the position of the current Court is something less than clear.

Throughout much of the twentieth century the Court's position concerning whether Congress could regulate private activities under its Fourteenth Amendment power was unclear. The Court did hold that Congress could regulate private activities that infringed uniquely federal rights such as the right to travel or the right to vote in a federal election.[28] In 1966, six Justices indicated their belief that Congress could regulate private actions that would have constituted a denial of due process or equal protection if those actions had been undertaken by the state, but these Justices did not state that view in a majority opinion.[29] At the start of the twenty-first century, five Justices returned to the position taken by the Court in the late 1800s and ruled that Congress could not regulate or prohibit the actions of private persons merely because those actions would constitute a violation of equal protection if done by the state. In *United States v. Morri-*

24. 109 U.S. at 26, 3 S.Ct. at 32. (Harlan, J., dissenting).

25. 109 U.S. at 37–44, 3 S.Ct. at 40–46. (Harlan, J., dissenting).

26. 109 U.S. at 46–47, 3 S.Ct. at 46–48. (Harlan, J., dissenting).

27. Jones v. Alfred H. Mayer Co., 392 U.S. 409, 88 S.Ct. 2186, 20 L.Ed.2d 1189 (1968); Runyon v. McCrary, 427 U.S. 160, 96 S.Ct. 2586, 49 L.Ed.2d 415 (1976). For examination of Congressional power under the Thirteenth Amendment, see §§ 15.6–15.10 infra.

28. United States v. Classic, 313 U.S. 299, 61 S.Ct. 1031, 85 L.Ed. 1368, (1941), rehearing denied, 314 U.S. 707, 62 S.Ct. 51, 86 L.Ed. 565 (1941); United States v. Guest, 383 U.S. 745, 86 S.Ct. 1170, 16 L.Ed.2d 239 (1966).

29. Six concurring or concurring and dissenting Justices indicated such an opinion in United States v. Guest 383 U.S. 745, 86 S.Ct. 1170, 16 L.Ed.2d 239 (1966). 383 U.S. at 762, 86 S.Ct. at 1180 (Clark, J., concurring); 383 U.S. at 784, 86 S.Ct. at 1192 (Brennan, J., concurring in part). See §§ 15.2–15.5 of this Treatise.

son[30] the Court ruled that Congress did not have the power to give individuals a statutory right to be free from sexual assault by private persons, in part because a sexual attack by a private person did not involve state action.[31]

In 1997 the Supreme Court appeared to back away from the Court's twentieth century decisions that had recognized broad congressional power to protect civil rights and liberties. In *Boerne v. Flores*,[32] the Supreme Court invalidated a federal statute that attempted to expand the ability of people to be free from burdens placed on them by state or federal laws that interfered with their ability to follow their religious beliefs. Justices Kennedy's majority opinion in *Boerne* returned to the position, first announced in the *Civil Rights Cases*, that Congress could not expand the civil liberties protected through Section 1 of the Fourteenth Amendment (as defined by the Supreme Court) through its Section 5 power. At the time of the *Boerne* decision, it was unclear whether that decision would have any effect on Congress's Thirteenth Amendment power to prohibit racial discrimination.[33]

Finally, the first holding of the Court—that judges should not independently find violations of the Amendment absent state action—remains the position of the Supreme Court today. It is that issue which will concern us throughout most of this chapter. We will examine the bases on which the Court will find state action in the activities of a seemingly private person or entity.

The Court did not modify its strict position concerning state action until the 1940's, when the Justices began to find violations of the

Fourteenth Amendment even though the complained of activities were not formally linked to any action by state officials. From these early cases to the present, the Court has developed a series of theories by which it may be established that a private person is sufficiently tied to the activities of government so that his actions might violate certain constitutional provisions.

In each of these cases a private person (whom we may term the aggrieved party) claims that he has been deprived of some constitutionally guaranteed right by the activities of another seemingly private person (whom we may term the alleged wrongdoer). The Court must then determine whether the alleged wrongdoer has sufficient connection to the state to subject his or her activities to constitutional restrictions. If the Court determines that sufficient state action exists, it will order a remedy for the aggrieved party and the end of the practice of the alleged wrongdoer. If the Court finds that the alleged wrongdoer is not involved with state action, it will afford no remedy to the aggrieved party, who must continue to suffer whatever discrimination he has complained of. The remainder of this Chapter will deal with the basis upon which the Court may find state action in the activities of the alleged wrongdoer.

§ 12.2   The Public Function Concept

It is now clear that constitutional limitations on state activities restrict the manner in which governmental functions are conducted. If private persons are engaged in the exercise of governmental functions their activities are

---

30. 529 U.S. 598, 120 S.Ct. 1740, 146 L.Ed.2d 658 (2000). This case is examined in Chapters 4,15 of this Treatise.

31. United States v. Morrison, 529 U.S. 598, 616–26, 120 S.Ct. 1740, 1754–59, 146 L.Ed.2d 658 (2000). The majority also ruled that Congress did not have the power under the Article I commerce clause to grant such statutory rights to victims of sexual crimes. See § 4.9 of this Treatise. Four Justices dissented in *Morrison*. The opinion of Justice Souter stressed the position that prior Supreme Court cases required a finding that the Violence Against Women Act, which was the subject of the litigation, was within the Congress's Article I commerce clause power. 529 U.S. at 626, 120 S.Ct. at 1759 (Souter, J., joined by Stephens, Ginsburg, and Breyer, JJ., dissenting). Justice

Breyer's dissent also focused on the commerce clause question, but he did express doubts concerning the Court's use of state action analysis to limit Congress's power to enact Fourteenth Amendment legislation. The portion of his dissent that discussed Fourteenth Amendment principles was not joined by Justices Souter and Ginsburg. 529 U.S. at 655, 120 S.Ct. at 1774 (Breyer, J., joined by Stephens, J., and, in part, by Souter and Ginsburg, JJ., dissenting). The *Morrison* case is examined in § 4.9 and Chapter 15 of this Treatise.

32. 521 U.S. 507, 117 S.Ct. 2157, 138 L.Ed.2d 624 (1997), on remand 119 F.3d 341 (5th Cir.1997).

33. See, Chapter 15 of this Treatise regarding Congress's powers to enforce the Civil War Amendments.

subject to similar constitutional restrictions. The state cannot free itself from the limitations of the Constitution in the operation of its governmental functions merely by delegating certain functions to otherwise private individuals. If private actors assume the role of the state by engaging in these governmental functions then they subject themselves to the same limitations on their freedom of action as would be imposed upon the state itself. The functions of government which are subjected to these restraints are termed "public functions." But, while this theory is easily justified, it is very difficult to determine what activities should be deemed public functions and subjected to constitutional limitations.

The fact that a private person engages in an activity which could be performed by a state government will not in itself subject him to such limitations, for state governments could engage virtually in any activity. It is only those activities or functions which are traditionally associated with sovereign governments, and which are operated almost exclusively by governmental entities, which will be deemed public functions. Thus, the operation of election systems, the governance of cities and towns, and, perhaps, the operation of seemingly public facilities such as parks will be deemed public functions regulated by the Constitution. However, the mere operation of businesses which could be operated by a government will not be construed as a public function because that would involve a determination based on the practical importance of the activity rather than its relation to the function of the state. Thus, the operation of a public utility such as a power company is not a public function.[1] As the Court has given us only the most general guidelines to these determina-

tions, Jackson v. Met it is important to review the major decisions of the Court in this area.

The First Public Function Cases. The public function concept appears to have originated in a series of decisions relating to the applicability of the Fourteenth and Fifteenth Amendments to primary elections in Texas which were segregated by race.[2] As early as 1927 the Supreme Court held that the Texas state laws which excluded blacks from Democratic primaries violated the Fourteenth Amendment.[3] A few years later the Court held that granting political party committees the authority to determine who voted in the primary was similarly unconstitutional as these committees constituted the agents of the state.[4] However, in 1935 in the case of *Grovey v. Townsend*,[5] the Court held that a state political party convention which discriminated on the basis of race was not constitutionally invalid because there was no state action connected to it. However, this decision was overruled nine years later in *Smith v. Allwright*.[6]

In *Smith* the Supreme Court held that the white primary system which had been established by a state political party convention in Texas violated the Fifteenth Amendment. The basis for applying the Fifteenth Amendment to the primary system was that the election system and the fixing of qualifications for voters was a public function which was subjected to constitutional limitations regardless of who actually conducted the election. This decision had been foreshadowed in *United States v. Classic*.[7]

The *Classic* Court had upheld congressional regulation of primary elections on the basis that the electoral system was a unitary process which was entirely subject to the regulatory powers of Congress. In *Smith* the Justices found that the running of elections was an

§ 12.2

1. Jackson v. Metropolitan Edison Co., 419 U.S. 345, 95 S.Ct. 449, 42 L.Ed.2d 477 (1974). See generally, S.O.C., Inc. v. Mirage Casino–Hotel, 117 Nev. 403, 23 P.3d 243, 248 (2001) (Young, J. citing this section of the Treatise).

2. It should be remembered that Justice Harlan raised similar considerations in his examination of the rights protected by the Thirteenth Amendment. In re Civil Rights Cases, 109 U.S. 3, 37–44, 3 S.Ct. 18, 40–46, 27 L.Ed. 835 (1883) (Harlan, J., dissenting).

3. Nixon v. Herndon, 273 U.S. 536, 47 S.Ct. 446, 71 L.Ed. 759 (1927).

4. Nixon v. Condon, 286 U.S. 73, 52 S.Ct. 484, 76 L.Ed. 984 (1932).

5. 295 U.S. 45, 55 S.Ct. 622, 79 L.Ed. 1292 (1935).

6. 321 U.S. 649, 64 S.Ct. 757, 88 L.Ed. 987 (1944).

7. 313 U.S. 299, 61 S.Ct. 1031, 85 L.Ed. 1368 (1941).

essential state function, that the primary system was an integral part of the election process and that the delegation of this authority over the election system to the political party made it an agent of the state.

Following this decision state political parties attempted to retain their racially restrictive practices but these efforts met with little success. In *Terry v. Adams*[8] the Court reviewed a practice of the "Jay Bird Democratic Association" which was composed of supposedly voluntary clubs of white Democrats in Texas. These clubs held their own private elections of nominees who then ran in the Democratic primaries in Texas—usually unopposed. In this case the Supreme Court held that these pre-primary elections were subject to the restrictions of the Fifteenth Amendment even though there had been a "complete absence" of formal state connection to any of the activities of the political clubs. There was no majority opinion in this case but the Justices seemed to agree that the relationship between the club practices and electoral system constituted the delegation of a public function to this group so as to subject it to the Fifteenth Amendment.[9] Justice Frankfurter noted that while the state had taken no positive action it had abdicated its responsibility of insuring a racially neutral election system and that this abdication was the basis for subjecting the club to the restrictions of the Fifteenth Amendment.[10]

Perhaps the strongest use of the public function doctrine came in the case of *Marsh v. Alabama*.[11] This case involved a "company town" which was a privately owned area encompassing both residential and commercial districts. The Gulf Shipbuilding Corporation owned and governed this area but it had no formal ties to any state agency or authority. Agents of the corporation had ordered a Jeho-

vah's Witness to leave the privately owned business district and to refrain from distributing religious leaflets within the boundaries of the company town. If the order were valid it would have subjected the leafleter to conviction under state trespass laws for her refusal to leave the area or stop distributing literature. Unquestionably this town would have violated the First Amendment if it were an agency of the state attempting to suppress the distribution of the literature. Thus, the only issue in the case was the applicability of the First and Fourteenth Amendments to the conduct of the corporation that owned the town. A majority of the Justices, in an opinion by Justice Black, held that the company town was subjected to the limitations of the First and Fourteenth Amendments and that the individual had a right to distribute her leaflets within the town.

The Court relied on the fact that the state allowed private ownership of land and property to a degree which allowed this corporation to replace all of the functions and activities which would normally belong to a city. Because the privately owned business area served as the equivalent of a community shopping district in a normal city the First Amendment applied in full force to the activities which took place there. Perhaps the most revealing part of the opinion was the statement that, in the determining of the existence of a public function, the Court would "balance the constitutional rights of the owners of property against those of the people to enjoy freedom of press and religion."[12]

The public function concept appeared to include a wide range of activities when the Court decided *Evans v. Newton*.[13] This case involved the exclusion of members of racial minorities

8. 345 U.S. 461, 73 S.Ct. 809, 97 L.Ed. 1152 (1953).

9. 345 U.S. at 469, 73 S.Ct. at 813 (Black, J.); 345 U.S. at 484, 73 S.Ct. at 820–21 (Clark, J., concurring).

See generally, Chambers and Rotunda, Reform of the Presidential Nominating Conventions, 56 Va.L.Rev. 179, 194–96 (1970).

10. 345 U.S. at 477, 73 S.Ct. at 817 (Frankfurter, J., concurring).

See Pollak, Racial Discrimination and Judicial Integrity: A Reply to Professor Wechsler, 108 U.Pa.L.Rev. 1, 23

(1959): "[O]nly a state can conduct elections—especially so where the state is one in which, under the Constitution, a republican form of government is perpetually guaranteed." See also Rotunda, Constitutional and Statutory Restrictions on Political Parties in the Wake of Cousins v. Wigoda, 53 Texas L.Rev. 935, 952–957 (1975).

11. 326 U.S. 501, 66 S.Ct. 276, 90 L.Ed. 265 (1946).

12. 326 U.S. at 509, 66 S.Ct. at 280.

13. 382 U.S. 296, 86 S.Ct. 486, 15 L.Ed.2d 373 (1966).

from a park in Macon, Georgia. The park had been established in 1911 by testamentary trust in the will of Senator Bacon which required that the park be used only for white persons. The city had originally been the trustee and operator of the segregated park until the decision in *Brown v. Board of Education.*[14] The city then resigned as trustee and requested the appointment of private persons to take its place.

The Supreme Court held that the park could not be operated with the racial restriction even if the new trustees would have no connection to the city government. The decision of the Court seemed to center on the entanglement between the city government and the operation of the park. Indeed, this entanglement was a strong factor, for the city continued to offer certain maintenance assistance to the park even after the substitution of the private trustees. However, the opinion indicated that the park could not be operated on a racially restricted basis even if the city managed to sever all of its ties to the operation of the facilities. The majority opinion by Justice Douglas implied that the operation of the park was an essential municipal function which could not be delegated to private persons so as to avoid the restrictions of the Fourteenth Amendment.[15]

Following this decision the trust was terminated by the local state courts and the land reverted to the heirs of Senator Bacon. This reversion to the heirs—for uses other than a racially restrictive park—was upheld by the Supreme Court in *Evans v. Abney.*[16] A majority of the Court found that the application of property law which ended the trust and returned the land to the heirs did not violate the Constitution because it was not premised on any continuation of racial restrictions. This holding strengthens the theory that the operation of the public park on a racially restrictive basis violated the Fourteenth Amendment because it constituted a public function. Once

the land was being used for something other than a park it could be returned to the heirs. But as the public function concept has been narrowed in recent years, the case cannot at this time be taken to have established public amusement areas as public functions.

The Shopping Center Cases. The most interesting developments under the public function concept occurred in relation to privately owned shopping centers. In a series of three cases between 1968 and 1976 the Supreme Court wrestled with the problem of whether there was a right to go into the open areas of privately owned shopping centers to distribute information concerning public issues. In the final analysis the Court held that there were no First Amendment rights in these areas because the privately owned shopping centers did not constitute a public function and there was no state action which violated the Constitution. However, this result came about only after two totally conflicting decisions.

In *Amalgamated Food Employees Union v. Logan Valley Plaza*[17] a majority of the Justices held that striking laborers had a right to enter a private shopping area to picket a store with which they were having a labor dispute. The majority found that the shopping center was the functional equivalent of the company town involved in the *Marsh* case[18] so that no further contact between the state and the shopping center owners was necessary to establish the applicability of the First Amendment. Only a few years later the Court was confronted with a case involving antiwar demonstrators who wished to enter a private shopping center mall to distribute leaflets to patrons of the center. Here the Court found that there was no First Amendment right to engage in speech on privately owned property where that speech did not relate to the activities of the store owners on the property.[19] The majority opinion by Justice Powell attempted to distinguish the

---

14.   349 U.S. 294, 75 S.Ct. 753, 99 L.Ed. 1083 (1955).

15.   Evans v. Newton, 382 U.S. at 301–2, 86 S.Ct. at 489–90.

16.   396 U.S. 435, 90 S.Ct. 628, 24 L.Ed.2d 634 (1970).

17.   391 U.S. 308, 88 S.Ct. 1601, 20 L.Ed.2d 603 (1968).

18.   Marsh v. Alabama, 326 U.S. 501, 66 S.Ct. 276, 90 L.Ed. 265 (1946).

19.   Lloyd Corp., Limited v. Tanner, 407 U.S. 551, 92 S.Ct. 2219, 33 L.Ed.2d 131 (1972).

Amalgamated Food Employees case on the basis that the labor picketing had involved speech which was directly related to activities on the shopping center. However, the opinion was not clear as to why a difference in the content of the speech changed the determination of whether there was sufficient state action to invoke the protections of the First Amendment.

This uncertainty was clarified in *Hudgens v. National Labor Relations Board*[20] when the Court simply held that the First Amendment did not apply to privately owned shopping centers; the Court then explicitly overruled the *Amalgamated Food Employees* decision. The final position of the Court was that the operation of a shopping center, which was not part of a privately owned town, did not involve the assumption of a public function by private persons. So long as the state did not aid, command, or encourage the suppression of free speech, the First Amendment would not be violated by the actions of the shopping center owners. The majority held that the right to private property encompassed the right to exclude others in this manner. Only when the property was used as a city did it lose its private character. Thus, there would have to be some additional state involvement to establish state action.[21]

Public Function Analysis after 1974. The Supreme Court restricted the scope of public function analysis in *Jackson v. Metropolitan Edison Co.*[22] This case concerned the activity of a privately owned electric utility

and the applicability of the due process clause to its termination of services for individual customers. In this case a woman had her electrical service terminated without a final hearing to determine the status of her account with the company. She asserted that the utility company was required to give her notice and a hearing in the same manner as would a governmental agency which would terminate state benefits to her. The Court found no state action involved in the operation of this utility even though it was given virtually a monopoly status and licensed by the state.[23] The opinion found that there were insufficient contacts between the utility and the state to justify restricting its activities by constitutional limitation. As to the public function claim, the majority held that the fact that a state could have operated its own utilities did not make the activity of providing electric service a public function. Nor was the fact that these types of businesses might have a peculiar "public interest" enough to establish that the state was under an obligation to restrict them in conformity with constitutional guarantees.

The majority opinion in *Jackson* indicated that only those activities which were traditionally reserved to state authority or commonly associated with state sovereignty would be considered public functions. Thus, it would appear that few public functions will be found beyond those most essential services which are provided by governments and which have no direct counterpart in the private sector.[24] The

20.   424 U.S. 507, 96 S.Ct. 1029, 47 L.Ed.2d 196 (1976).

21.   In PruneYard Shopping Center v. Robins, 447 U.S. 74, 100 S.Ct. 2035, 64 L.Ed.2d 741 (1980), the Supreme Court held that its ruling in the *Hudgens* case did not preclude a state from granting protection to speech and associational activities at privately owned shopping centers. In *PruneYard Shopping Center* the United States Supreme Court affirmed a decision of the California Supreme Court holding that the California state constitution prohibited the use of trespass laws by shopping center owners to exclude peaceful distribution of literature and petitions on the mall area of a shopping center. The United States Supreme Court held that the state ruling did not constitute a taking of property from the shopping center owner; the state was free to expand its protection of civil liberties under its own constitution.

22.   419 U.S. 345, 95 S.Ct. 449, 42 L.Ed.2d 477 (1974).

23.   The Supreme Court later held that utility companies that are operated by government agencies are re-

quired to provide their customers with fair notice and billing review procedures prior to termination of service if state law provides for such termination only "for cause." Memphis Light, Gas and Water Division v. Craft, 436 U.S. 1, 98 S.Ct. 1554, 56 L.Ed.2d 30 (1978).

24.   It appears that the regulation of sports activities will not be regarded as a public function. San Francisco Arts and Athletics, Inc. v. United States Olympic Committee, 483 U.S. 522, 544, 107 S.Ct. 2971, 2985, 97 L.Ed.2d 427 (1987) (finding that the United States Olympic Committee, which is chartered by the United States government and which had the exclusive right to use the word, "Olympic", did not have state action when it denied some persons the ability to use the word "Olympic" to promote their own interest); National Collegiate Athletic Association v. Tarkanian, 488 U.S. 179, 198 n. 18, 109 S.Ct. 454, 465 n. 18, 102 L.Ed.2d 469 (1988) (finding that the NCAA did not have state action and, therefore, that its order to a university to show cause why it should not suffer penalties

electoral system and the operation of towns will constitute such functions while traditional business activities such as the operation of utilities or other regulated industries will not. A majority of the current Justices appear to believe that no private sector agency should be subjected to constitutional limitation of its autonomy unless it performs a delegated governmental function or is taking actions under the direction of state authorities.[25]

A majority of the Justices continued to employ restrictive definition of public functions as they approved a state law that allowed warehousemen to sell the property of their debtors. In *Flagg Brothers, Inc. v. Brooks*[26] the Supreme Court held that there was no state action in the sale of a debtor's goods by a warehouseman who had the goods in his possession and who had a lien on the goods for unpaid storage charges.[27] This was true even

though a state law, patterned after the Uniform Commercial Code, authorized such sales under certain circumstances. The majority opinion refused to examine whether the procedure specified in the law, or the actions of the warehousemen, violated the due process clause, because this "private" activity of the warehousemen was not subject to the restraints of the Fourteenth Amendment.

The majority opinion, by Justice Rehnquist, held that dispute resolution between debtors and creditors was not a public function so as to subject the debt collection practices of the creditor-warehouseman to constitutional constraints. Justice Rehnquist found that the two activities that the Court clearly has held to be public functions—operating towns and running elections—were undertaken by governmental entities to the exclusion of private actors.[28] The majority believed that the fact that

---

in terms of its ability to participate in NCAA sports activities if it did not remove a coach from his coaching duties did not deny due process to the coach). In the *Tarkanian* case, the Supreme Court indicated that the regulation of sports activities might constitute "state action", even if the regulation was done by an association of schools rather than the government itself, if the membership of the sports association "consisted entirely of institutions located within the same state, many of them public institutions created by the same sovereign." 488 U.S. at 193 n. 13, 109 S.Ct. at 462 n. 13.

Title IX of the Civil Rights Act prohibits sex discrimination in educational programs receiving federal financial assistance. 20 U.S.C.A. § 1681(a). In National Collegiate Athletic Association v. Smith, 525 U.S. 459, 119 S.Ct. 924, 142 L.Ed.2d 929 (1999), the Court ruled that the fact that the National Collegiate Athletic Association received dues from its members, who had received federal financial assistance, did not make the Association subject to the requirements of Title IX. The Court in *Smith* did not consider the claim that the NCAA should be subject to Title IX because recipients of federal financial aid (the member schools) were giving controlling authority over their programs to the NCAA, or the claim that the NCAA should be subject to Title IX because it received federal financial assistance through a federally funded sports program. Those claims had not been presented to the lower courts; the Supreme Court, in *Smith,* left those issues for initial consideration by the lower courts.

On February 22, 2000, the Supreme Court agreed to review a case in which the United States Court of Appeals had ruled that a statewide secondary high school athletic association did not have state action, so that the enforcement of its rules regarding recruiting of student-athletes, as applied to a private high school, was not subject to constitutional limitations. Brentwood Academy v. Tennessee Secondary School Athletic Association, 180 F.3d 758 (6th Cir.1999), cert. granted, 528 U.S. 1153, 120 S.Ct. 1156, 145 L.Ed.2d 1069 (2000).

25. The Court refused to impose due process limitations on the ability of a private school to discharge teachers or a private nursing home to discharge patients. In Rendell–Baker v. Kohn, 457 U.S. 830, 102 S.Ct. 2764, 73 L.Ed.2d 418 (1982) the Court found that a private school whose primary business was teaching students with educational or behavioral problems, and which received most of its funding from state sources, did not exercise state action when it discharged members of its staff.

In Blum v. Yaretsky, 457 U.S. 991, 102 S.Ct. 2777, 73 L.Ed.2d 534 (1982) the Court held that a nursing home did not exercise state action when it discharged or transferred patients, even though the home and the patients received state funds.

26. 436 U.S. 149, 98 S.Ct. 1729, 56 L.Ed.2d 185 (1978).

27. The charges resulted from the city marshall's arrangement for placement of Ms. Brooks household furnishings into the possession of a moving and storage company, Flagg Bros., following the eviction of Ms. Brooks and her family from her apartment in Mount Vernon, N.Y., 436 U.S. at 153, 98 S.Ct. at 1732. After a series of disputes between Ms. Brooks and Flagg Bros. concerning the amount of the moving and storage bill, Flagg Bros. threatened to sell her property pursuant to the New York Uniform Commercial Code § 7–210.

An almost identical situation involved a dispute between Ms. Jones and Flagg Bros. concerning the charges from storing her goods following her eviction from another Mount Vernon apartment. Ms. Jones paid her bill under threat of a sale. 436 U.S. at 154, 98 S.Ct. at 1732, n. 2, n. 3.

28. Flagg Bros., Inc. v. Brooks, 436 U.S. 149, 159, 160, 98 S.Ct. 1729, 1735, 56 L.Ed.2d 185 (1978) the portion of the opinion holding that there was no state encouragement of the sale is noted in § 12.3, infra.

an activity was traditionally within the province of government did not make it a public function; such functions exist only when there is a history of exclusive governmental activity of the type at issue.

This use of the exclusivity concept is consistent with recent state action decisions. However, the opinion left the concept of state action more unclear than ever. The majority opinion stated that the decision in *Flagg Brothers* did not affect prior rulings concerning the existence of state action in programs providing incidental aid to segregated schools.[29] Justice Rehnquist noted that activities such as "education, fire and police protection, and tax collection" might constitute public functions, although his opinion did not resolve these issues.[30] Indeed, the majority refused to rule that private control of debtor-creditor disputes could never constitute a public function or state action. "This is not to say that dispute resolution between creditors and debtors involves a category of human affairs that is never subject to constitutional constraints. We merely address the public function doctrine as respondents would apply it in this case."[31]

So long as the Supreme Court continues to employ a formal test for determining the presence of state action in a private person's activity, the opinions on public function concepts will never be more precise than Justice Rehnquist's majority opinion in *Flagg Brothers*. In an incisive dissent, Justice Stevens noted the inconsistency of the majority defining public functions in terms of a formal test for exclusivity while simultaneously admitting that some nonexclusive activities might be restrained by the Constitution.[32] Justice Stevens went to the

heart of the issue when he stated his belief that the power to order a resolution of debtor-creditor conflicts was precisely the type of power that involved the values of the due process clause.[33] He noted the danger of using a formal test for state action and that the majority's test logically should allow states to "recognize" the ability of a physically stronger disputant to take the property of the weaker person.[34] Justice Stevens noted that the line between public and private actions was not a clear one; he would have based the state action on the relevance of the constitutional value to the "private" activity.[35]

The majority opinion in *Flagg Brothers* asserted that: "Unlike the parade of horribles suggested by our Brother Stevens in dissent, this case does not involve state authorization of private breach of the peace."[36] But a state statute that "recognized" a right of the strong to take the property of the weak would not "encourage" their activity anymore than the warehouseman statute encouraged sales without specific procedural protections. The real difference between permitting the warehouseman's lien sale and legitimizing the forceful taking of property by physically strong creditors, or their employees, lies in the differing potential for creditor abuse of each practice and the differing value of the debtor's interest in avoiding lien sales or avoiding loss of his property to stronger persons.[37]

The difficulty of predicting the outcome of state action cases while the Supreme Court clings to its formal method of state action analysis is demonstrated by *Lugar v. Edmondson Oil Company*.[38] In *Lugar* the Supreme Court ruled that a debtor could challenge, as a violation of due process, the state

---

29. 436 U.S. at 163, 98 S.Ct. at 1737.

30. 436 U.S. at 163–164, 98 S.Ct. at 1737.

31. 436 U.S. at 162, n. 12, 98 S.Ct. at 1736–37, n. 12.

32. Flagg Bros., Inc. v. Brooks, 436 U.S. 149, 173 n. 10, 98 S.Ct. 1729, 1742 n. 10, 56 L.Ed.2d 185 (1978) (Stevens, J., dissenting, joined by White & Marshall, JJ.) (Justice Brennan did not participate in the decision).

33. 436 U.S. at 174–179, 98 S.Ct. at 1742–45 (Stevens, J., dissenting).

34. 436 U.S. at 170, 98 S.Ct. at 1740–41 (Stevens, J., dissenting).

35. 436 U.S. at 178, 98 S.Ct. at 1744–45 (Stevens, J., dissenting). As to the lack of a basis for formal distinctions between public and private activity, Justice Stevens cited, inter alia, the article upon which § 12.5, infra, is based. 436 U.S. at 178 n. 16, 98 S.Ct. at 1745 n. 16.

36. Flagg Bros., Inc. v. Brooks, 436 U.S. 149, 160 n. 9, 98 S.Ct. 1729, 1735 n. 9, 56 L.Ed.2d 185 (1978).

37. See § 12.1(a) regarding the terminology used by the Court in recent state action cases.

38. 457 U.S. 922, 102 S.Ct. 2744, 73 L.Ed.2d 482 (1982).

procedure by which a creditor secured a pre-trial writ of attachment against his property based upon the creditor's ex parte petition. The involvement of the state judicial system in the issuance of the writ, and the involvement of the county sheriff in the execution of the writ, distinguished the *Lugar* case from the *Flagg Brothers* creditor "self help" decision. Thus the debtor in *Lugar* could challenge the debt collection system whereas the debtor in *Flagg Brothers* could not.[39]

If police officers (or other government officials) assist a creditor in seizing the property of an alleged debtor, the joint action of the police and the creditor constitutes state action. The seizure of the alleged debtor's property through joint action of the creditor and police will violate due process and the Fourth Amendment if the seizure was not carried out with the procedural safeguards required for a constitutionally reasonable seizure of property.[40]

The seizure of the property of an alleged debtor is not a public function. If the creditor acts alone in seizing the property, the seizure does not involve state action. The involvement of the police department officers in the seizure gives rise to state action, so as to trigger due process and Fourth Amendment restrictions on both the police officers and the creditor.

The Supreme Court employed the exclusivity concept in *American Manufacturers Mutual Insurance Company v. Sullivan*,[41] as the Court held that the decision of a privately owned insurance company to withhold payment for medical bills to injured workers did not constitute state action. The majority opinion in *American Manufacturers Mutual Insurance*, written by Chief Justice Rehnquist, found that the state had not delegated a public function to the privately owned insurance companies. Prior to any workers' compensation laws, insurers had the ability to make their own determinations regarding withholding payments. Then the state enacted statutes that required insurers to pay disputed medical treatment for workers compensation claimants absent a ruling favorable to the insurance company by a state court judge. Finally, the state enacted statutes that insurance companies to withhold payments for medical services the company believed were unnecessary. The Chief Justice found that the fact that the state had for a time restricted an insurer's ability to withhold payments did not make the worker's compensation benefits payment system a public function. When the state statute allowed insurers to make decisions concerning whether or not to pay the medical bills of injured workers, the state was not engaging in "the delegation of a traditionally exclusive public function."[42]

State statutes allowed insurance companies to withhold payment for an injured worker's employee medical treatment on the basis that the medical treatment was not reasonable or necessary. When an injured worker challenged an insurance company's refusal to pay for medical treatment, the disputed claim had to be submitted to a review board that was created by state statute. The Court in *American Manufacturers Mutual Insurance* found that the state participation in the resolution of disputes between private insurers and worker compensation claimants did not imbue the private insurance company with state action.[43]

---

39. The distinction between *Lugar* and *Flagg* rests on the Court's recognition of state action when private parties act in concert with government officials. See § 12.3, infra.

40. Soldal v. Cook County, 506 U.S. 56, 60 n. 6, 113 S.Ct. 538, 543 n. 6, 121 L.Ed.2d 450 (1992). In *Soldal*, the Justices ruled that there was state action in the seizure of an alleged debtor's mobile home when the mobile home was removed from its foundation and towed away from a mobile home park by the park owner's employees who were supported by the actions of deputy sheriffs. The deputy sheriffs protected the park owner's employees even though they knew the owner had not secured a lawful eviction order against the mobile home owner. The Court of Appeals found that the actions of the deputy sheriffs and property owner established a conspiracy that gave rise to state action. Justice White, writing for a unanimous Court in *Soldal*, stated that the Supreme Court was "not inclined to review that holding."

41. 526 U.S. 40, 119 S.Ct. 977, 143 L.Ed.2d 130 (1999).

42. 526 U.S. at 57, 119 at S.Ct. at 988.

43. The majority in *American Manufacturers Mutual Insurance* found that neither the fact that the insurance corporations and the workers compensation system were regulated by the state nor the fact that the state had created and set standards for the review process involved the type of interaction that should make the insurance

The state statutes establishing the review procedures for disputed claims, and establishing a review board to conduct such reviews, involved state action. However, the Court found that the state statutory system for review of disputed claims did not violate the due process clause.[44]

The Jury Selection Cases. An attorney participating in jury selection is participating in a traditional public function. The Supreme Court in Edmonson v. Leesville Concrete Co., Inc., *Edmonson v. Leesville Concrete Co., Inc.,*[45] ruled that a private litigant would violate the equal protection guarantee if he used peremptory jury challenges to exclude persons from jury service because of their race. The Court in *Leesville Concrete* found that the defendant's actions were intertwined with the traditional function of the government in adjudicating civil cases and that the government was involved in the litigant's exclusion of minority race jurors to the extent that the government was allowing the use of peremptory challenges within the courtroom setting itself.[46]

In *Georgia v. McCollum,*[47] the Supreme Court held that the equal protection guarantee prohibited a defendant in a criminal case from using peremptory jury challenges to exclude persons from jury service because of their race. Although the defendant was the adversary of the state government in a criminal proceeding, the defendant's actions could be fairly termed to be the type of state action that should be subject to the restrictions of the equal protection clause for several reasons. First, the Court found that the harm caused to persons who were excluded from jury because of their race by a defendant's use of a peremptory challenge could be said to result from "the exercise of a right or privilege having its source in state authority" because the right to exercise jury challenges came from state law. Second, the Court found that the defendant could be fairly described as a "state actor" because the defendant relied on governmental assistance in order to cause the harm. The assistance of the court system was essential to a defendant's ability to exclude minority race persons from a jury. Third, the majority opinion in *McCollum* found that "the selection of the jury in a criminal case fulfills a unique and constitutionally compelled government function." Finally, the Court found that the harm caused to minority race persons and society by the operation of a racial discriminatory jury selection system was the same regardless of

company's decisions subject to Fourteenth Amendment limits. The Court rejected any implications from cases decided in the early 1960's that "joint participation" between a private actor and the government in all instances would make the private actor subject to constitutional limitations. 526 U.S. at 57–58, 119 S.Ct. at 988–89. See §§ 12.3, 12.4.

In *Manufacturers Mutual Insurance Company,* seven of the Justices agreed that there was no basis for finding that a private insurance company's decisions should be subject to Fourteenth Amendment limitations. The state action analysis of the Court is contained in Part II of the majority opinion by Chief Justice Rehnquist. American Manufacturers Mutual Insurance v. Sullivan, 526 U.S. 40, 119 S.Ct. 977, 985–89, 143 L.Ed.2d 130 (1999). Two concurring Justices agreed with the majority opinion's state action analysis, but questioned statements in the majority opinion concerning the due process standards that applied to state statutes regulating the resolution of disputes between workers' compensation claimants and insurance companies. 526 U.S. at 62, 119 S.Ct. at 991 (Breyer, J., joined by Souter, J., concurring in part and concurring in the judgment). Justice Ginsburg believed that the Court should not address the state action issue.

Justice Stevens believed that the state action issue was irrelevant, because he saw the case turning on the issue of whether the state procedures for the resolution of workers compensation disputes was fundamentally fair; be believed that the Court had failed to directly address that procedural due process issue. 526 U.S. at 60–62, 119 S.Ct. at 991–92 (Stevens, J., concurring in part and dissenting in part).

44. Chief Justice Rehnquist's majority opinion found that the persons making claims for payments of disputed medical bills did not have a property interest in those payments and, therefore, that the Court did not have to determine whether the procedures established for resolution of disputes between the injured workers and insurance companies were fundamentally fair. American Manufacturers Mutual Insurance Co. v. Sullivan, 526 U.S. 40, 57–60, 119 S.Ct. 977, 989–90, 143 L.Ed.2d 130 (1999).

The need to establish a liberty or property interest in order to establish a claim for procedural fairness in the resolution of disputes with government actors is examined in Chapter 13 of this Treatise.

45. 500 U.S. 614, 111 S.Ct. 2077, 114 L.Ed.2d 660 (1991).

46. See § 12.1 for an overview of the traditional examination of state action questions and the phrasing used by the Court for its state action tests in the *Lugar* and *Leesville Concrete* cases.

47. 505 U.S. 42, 112 S.Ct. 2348, 120 L.Ed.2d 33 (1992), on remand 262 Ga. 554, 422 S.E.2d 866 (1992).

whether the racial discrimination was the result of prosecutorial or defense actions.

It is possible to view the *Leesville Concrete* and *McCollum* cases as involving a multifaceted inquiry into the presence of state action in jury selection systems. However, it is also possible to look at these cases as ones in which the Court simply found that the jury selection system was an essential public function. If the government delegates a public function to private persons, the private persons who exercise that governmental power must do so within constitutional limitations. In other words, the *Leesville Concrete* and *McCollum* cases could be described as cases in which the Supreme Court found that (1) jury selection is a traditional government function to which several constitutional provisions, including the equal protection guarantee, apply and (2) a delegation of the public function to a private person cannot free the public function from constitutional limitations.[48]

Prisons. There are prisons in the United States that are owned and operated by private persons and private corporations. State or lo-

cal governments that do not have adequate prison facilities send prisoners to these private prisons; those prisoners are then housed at, and supervised by, the privately owned prison. The Supreme Court has reviewed a lower court decision applying civil rights statutes to guards employed at a privately owned prison but, in so doing, the Court noted that it was only presented with questions of statutory interpretation.[49] The Supreme Court has not yet decided whether the actions of employees of privately owned prisons qualify as "state action".

If the employees of a privately owned prison harm one of the prisoners, that prison employee, and the prison owner, should be subject to constitutional and statutory restrictions that apply to state action of a similar nature in a government operated prison. The operation of a prison should be deemed to be a public function by the judiciary, because, at, and after, the time the Fourteenth Amendment was ratified the operation of prisons has been performed almost exclusively by governmental entities. If the operation of a prison is a public

---

48. In J.E.B. v. Alabama ex rel. T.B., 511 U.S. 127, 114 S.Ct. 1419, 128 L.Ed.2d 89 (1994) the Supreme Court held that the intentional use of peremptory challenges by a government attorney to exclude persons of one sex from a jury violated the equal protection clause. See §§ 16.3, 18.23.

49. Richardson v. McKnight, 521 U.S. 399, 117 S.Ct. 2100, 138 L.Ed.2d 540 (1997). In *Richardson*, the Justices, by a five to four vote, ruled that prison guards employed by a private prison management company are not entitled to the same type of limited immunity from liability under 42 U.S.C.A. § 1983 that exists for government employed prison guards in government operated prisons. Justices Breyer's majority opinion noted that the Justices "have not addressed whether the defendants are liable under § 1983 even though they are employed by a private firm." When the Court refused to create an implied cause of action against corporations that operated a so-called halfway house for federal prisoners, the Justices appeared to assume that a private corporation that operated penal facilities acted with state action. The issue in Correctional Services Corporation v. Malesko, 534 U.S. 61, 122 S.Ct. 515, 151 L.Ed.2d 456 (2001) was whether an individual who was injured through alleged negligence of employees at a halfway house operated by a private corporation pursuant to a contract with the Federal Bureau of Prisons could sue the corporation, as well as its employees, directly under the Eighth Amendment. In Bivens v. Six Unknown Federal Narcotics Agents, 403 U.S. 388, 91 S.Ct. 1999, 29 L.Ed.2d 619 (1971), the Court created a cause of action for persons injured by unlawful searches by federal officers.

The Court extended the implied cause of action under the Bill of Rights to allow persons to bring suit against federal officers who injured persons in violation of the cruel and unusual punishment clause of the Eighth Amendment. Carlson v. Green, 446 U.S. 14, 100 S.Ct. 1468, 64 L.Ed.2d 15 (1980). In *Malesko* the Court ruled that there was no implied right of action against private corporations that engaged in allegedly unconstitutional activity while operating a federal correctional program. The lower courts had assumed that the private corporation was acting with governmental action and was subject to the Eighth Amendment; that ruling was not examined by the Supreme Court in the *Malesko* case. Chief Justice Rehnquist, writing for the majority in *Malesko*, assumed that private corporations operating such correctional facilities had government action. The majority opinion indicated that corporations operating correctional facilities pursuant to contract with state and local governments could be subject to liability under statutes that had a "color of law" requirement. The majority opinion stated that state prisoners "already enjoy a right of action against private correctional providers under 42 U.S.C. § 1983." 534 U.S. at 72 n. 5, 122 S.Ct. at 522 n. 5. The dissenting Justices in *Malesko* noted that the issue of whether the private corporation was subject to, and had violated, the Eighth Amendment cruel and unusual punishment clause was not at issue in this case. Thus, the Court did not have to address the question of whether the private corporation in fact was acting under color of federal law. Correctional Services Corporation v. Malesko, 534 U.S. 61, 75 n. 2, 122 S.Ct. 515, 524 n. 2, 151 L.Ed.2d 456 (2001) (Stevens, J., joined by Souter, Ginsburg, and Breyer, JJ., dissenting).

function, the delegation of that function to a private business entity should not free the private prison from constitutional limitations or statutes that would apply to a governmentally operated prison.

The conclusion that a prisoner who was harmed in a privately operated prison was harmed by "state action" flows from the method of analysis in the state action decisions of the 1990s. In the first prong of the analysis, a court should find that harm caused to the inmate by the private prison employees resulted from a right or privilege [the ability to operate a prison] that had its source in state authority. Second, it would seem fair to describe the administrators and employees of the private prison as "state actors," because they are entirely dependent upon state decisions in order to have prisoners to supervise. Third, the operation of a prison appears to be a function that the government must perform in some manner. Fourth, any harm caused to the inmate at the privately owned prison is, at least in part, attributable to the fact that the government chose to send that prisoner to the private prison, rather than to administer the prisoner's sentence of incarceration at a government operated prison.

§ 12.3 State Commandment or Encouragement of Private Activities

In other than the public function cases, the determination of state action is based on the relationship between government and the activities of the alleged wrongdoer. There is no formal test for the amount of contacts with government which will subject a private per-

son's activities to the restrictions of the Constitution. The one constant factor in the cases is the Justices' unwillingness to commit to any such test. The Court has stressed continually that it must determine on a case by case basis whether there is state action present by "sifting facts and weighing circumstances."[1] However, it is possible to isolate certain factors which have caused the Court to make a determination of state action in a particular activity. These factors will influence courts employing the two step approach to state action that we examined in § 12.1.

One category of cases are those where the aggrieved party claims that the wrongdoer has been commanded or encouraged by government to engage in the activity which has harmed the aggrieved party. In these cases the Court determines whether there is a sufficient nexus between the wrongdoer and the government by assessing the degree to which the government has commanded, encouraged or otherwise directed the complained of activity. Obviously the forms of state commandment or encouragement vary depending on the type of governmental entity which is alleged to have brought about the complained of activity. We will now examine the cases as they relate to encouragement of otherwise private activity by the legislative, executive, and judicial branches of government. Finally, we will note the effect of local customs in establishing and encouraging a practice.

Cases in which alleged wrongful activity is said to have a connection to state legislation present the widest scope of factual situations. In later sections we will examine variations of these problems based upon the legislative

§ 12.3

1. Burton v. Wilmington Parking Authority, 365 U.S. 715, 722, 81 S.Ct. 856, 860, 6 L.Ed.2d 45 (1961).

Skinner v. Railway Labor Executives' Association, 489 U.S. 602, 109 S.Ct. 1402, 103 L.Ed.2d 639 (1989) involved both legislative and administrative commandment and encouragement of private activities. In this case the Supreme Court upheld federal railroad regulations that required railroads to take blood and urine tests conducted for certain employees following specified types of train accidents. The regulations also authorized, but did not require, the private railroads to administer breath or urine tests to employees who violated certain identified safety rules. The Supreme Court found that the actions of the

private railroad were sufficiently connected to the federal government to subject the private railroad's drug testing policies and procedures to the restrictions of the Fourth Amendment. Although these drug testing policies and procedures were subject to constitutional review, the Court went on to find that the policies and procedures did not violate the Fourth Amendment because the infringement of employee privacy interests was justified by a "compelling interest". 489 U.S. at 633–634, 109 S.Ct. at 1421–22.

See generally, Graham, J., citing Treatise in CompuServe, Inc. v. Cyber Promotions, Inc., 962 F.Supp. 1015, 1026 (S.D.Ohio 1997).

granting of funds or special privileges to persons or entities which are alleged to have violated constitutional provisions. Our concern for the moment rests with legislation which commands or encourages a specific result which is alleged to violate the Constitution.

When state legislation commands a certain activity, or officially recognizes its legitimacy, there is no question but that state action is present whenever someone follows the guidelines of the statute. In such a situation the challenged activity must be taken to exist because the state legislature has commanded its occurrence and continuation. For example, if a state legislature commands that restaurants serve food on a racially segregated basis it is clear that the action of restaurant owners who discriminate between their patrons on the basis of race will constitute state action.[2]

Similarly state legislation may encourage an activity so as to give rise to state action in the activities of private persons. For example, state action will be found in a restaurant's racially restrictive practices where state legislation requires that restaurants serving members of minority races have separate toilet facilities for those persons.[3] The restaurant owner who refuses to serve members of a racial minority is restricted by constitutional provision because that decision must be held to be the result of the state legislation. To hold otherwise would allow the state to have helped establish or continue a practice without any effective remedy.

The state may also command or encourage the continuation of the alleged wrongdoing through its executive officers or agencies. Again the reason for this rule is that the alleged wrongdoing appears to be connected to activities of the state in such a way that it can be said to be the denial of rights by the state itself. How much encouragement or positive action by executive officials is necessary to invoke constitutional restrictions is, to say the least, unclear. It would appear that any significant encouragement of alleged wrongdoers to impair important rights of the aggrieved parties will be sufficient. Even though the complained of practice may not have resulted from the encouragement, the actions of the private wrongdoer will be subject to constitutional limitations.

For example, in *Lombard v. Louisiana*[4] the Supreme Court reversed the trespass convictions of sit-in demonstrators because the city officials, prior to the demonstration, had condemned sit-ins and stated that the city was prepared to enforce the law. These statements were taken to be official encouragement of store owners to use the state trespass laws in a discriminatory manner. However, it was not at all clear in this case whether the store owners had refused to serve the demonstrators or called the police because of the actions of the officials.

Even very strong encouragement by state officials might not result in a finding of state action where the challenged activities of private persons were themselves worthy of some constitutional deference. For example, assume that a mayor and sheriff encouraged the citizens of their town who were of a majority race to refuse to invite members of a racial minority to dinner. It would seem highly unlikely that the Supreme Court would find sufficient state action in members of the majority race refusing to invite minorities to their private dinner parties. The importance of private property and associational rights here would seem to require that no state action be found unless the racially discriminatory dinner invitations were solely the product of the official encouragement.

Even the judiciary may imbue the actions of private individuals with state action. When judges command private persons to take specific actions which would violate the Constitution if done by the State, state action will be present in the resulting harm to constitutionally recognized rights. The classic example of

2.   Peterson v. City of Greenville, 373 U.S. 244, 83 S.Ct. 1119, 10 L.Ed.2d 323 (1963).

3.   Robinson v. Florida, 378 U.S. 153, 84 S.Ct. 1693, 12 L.Ed.2d 771 (1964).

4.   373 U.S. 267, 83 S.Ct. 1122, 10 L.Ed.2d 338 (1963).

such a situation appeared in *Shelley v. Kraemer*.[5] In this case a white property owner attempted to sell his property to a member of a racial minority. This land was subject to a covenant which forbade sales to racial minorities; those persons with an interest in the restrictive covenant sued to restrain the current owner from violating the covenant by selling to a black.

The Supreme Court held that any court order which would enjoin the sale and enforce the covenant would violate the Fourteenth Amendment; the state court order would be a judicial command to the current owner—who is willing to sell to an equally willing buyer—to make a racial distinction in the sale of property. Such a command, interfering with a willing seller and a willing buyer, violates the Amendment.[6]

In a later case the Court also held that a white property owner who sold land to a member of a minority race could not be subject to monetary damages for the breach of a racially restrictive covenant.[7] While this damage suit would not involve a formal judicial order to discriminate on the basis of race it would be a state imposed penalty for refusal to discriminate. Such a state penalty is the functional equivalent of a command or encouragement to refuse to sell property to members of minority races. The judicial encouragement of racial discrimination is the state action which violates the Fourteenth Amendment.

The *Shelley* decision should not be taken as holding that any judicial decree which disadvantages members of a racial minority violates the Fourteenth Amendment. A court can uphold trespass convictions which are based on a private party's decision to refuse to open his home or other private property to members of a racial minority. If a home owner refuses to

allow persons into his home because of their race he is allowed to have that decision enforced by law enforcement officials and use of the trespass laws. In such a situation neither executive nor judicial action has prompted or required his decision to refuse to allow minority members onto his private property. As exclusivity is an attribute of private property, the owner may use the neutral trespass laws to enforce his decision so long as he has no other connection to state action.

A court may enforce racially neutral principles of property law even though a contrary ruling would be helpful to some members of a minority race. In *Evans v. Abney*[8] the Court allowed land to revert to the heirs of Senator Bacon, who had made a bequest of the land for the establishment of a public park that would be closed to members of racial minorities. While the city and the trustees were not allowed to conduct a racially restricted admissions policy for the park, the reverter of land to the heirs of the testator did not involve any continuing discrimination against black persons. Thus the application of the rules relating to failure of trust purpose and the reversion of land to a testator's heirs could be followed in this case.

Note that the principle of *Evans v. Abney* would not apply to a condition (or reverter clause) which would divest a property owner of the title to his property if he attempted to sell it to black persons. Such a clause would be the equivalent of monetary damages for failure to follow a restrictive covenant. When *Evans v. Newton*[9] and *Evans v. Abney* are read together it can be seen that the Court merely invalidated trusts for racially restrictive purposes which involved the activities of government or public functions.[10] Where grantors or testators

---

5.   334 U.S. 1, 68 S.Ct. 836, 92 L.Ed. 1161 (1948).

6.   See, Pollak, Racial Discrimination and Judicial Integrity: A Reply to Professor Wechsler, 108 U.Pa.L.Rev. 1, 13 (1959).

7.   Barrows v. Jackson, 346 U.S. 249, 73 S.Ct. 1031, 97 L.Ed. 1586 (1953).

8.   396 U.S. 435, 90 S.Ct. 628, 24 L.Ed.2d 634 (1970).

9.   382 U.S. 296, 86 S.Ct. 486, 15 L.Ed.2d 373 (1966).

10.   The Court has not passed on the validity of operating private trusts for allegedly unconstitutional purposes

apart from those in which there was a finding of government involvement or a public function. In Pennsylvania v. Board of Directors. of City Trusts, 353 U.S. 230, 77 S.Ct. 806, 1 L.Ed.2d 792 (1957) (per curiam) the Court found state involvement for a private trust to run a school for orphans on a racially restricted basis. Yet the Court refused to reconsider the legality of the school after both a finding by the state courts that private trustees could continue the school and a decision by a federal court that the substitution of trustees and continued operation of the school involved unconstitutional state action. In re Girard

attempt to establish such trusts in the future those provisions will be invalid *ab initio*. For already existing trusts of this type, such as the Macon Georgia park, the Court will declare an end to the discriminatory practices. The reverter in such a case will shift the use without penalizing those who would use land for racially neutral practices and without encouraging racial discrimination in the future.

Some Justices have taken the position that customs which had become so strong as to have the force of law might establish state action. For example, in a town with a strong custom of refusing to serve blacks in public facilities, a shop owner's refusal to serve blacks might be found to be the equivalent of state action violating the Fourteenth Amendment. However, a majority of the Justices have never held that custom alone would be sufficient to turn private activities into state action.

The Supreme Court avoided a decision on this issue in *Bell v. Maryland* [11] where a business owner refused to serve members of a minority race and had those persons prosecuted for trespass when they refused to leave his establishment. The Court as a whole avoided ruling on the merits by vacating the conviction and remanding the conviction for reconsideration in light of a new state law. An opinion by Justice Douglas, representing the views of three Justices, would have prohibited the discrimination by the restaurant owner because of the local custom of refusing to serve blacks. Justice Douglas indicated that he would not take such a position if the trespass conviction had related to the use of a private person's home,[12] but, where property was used for a semi-public function, Justice Douglas would subject the property owner's decisions to the restrictions of the Fourteenth Amendment. Justice Black, also representing two

other Justices, dissented and took a position opposite to Douglas.[13] He noted that any restriction of the property owner's scope of decision-making would go beyond all previous state action rulings. Justice Black indicated that private property rights should not be subjected to constitutional limitations absent some further connection to the government or its basic public functions.

A majority of the Court eventually followed Justice Black's position and refused to find that a private individual's or group's decision to exclude members of a racial minority constitutes state action violating the Fourteenth Amendment merely because it coincides with local custom. In *Moose Lodge Number 107 v. Irvis* [14] the Supreme Court held that there was insufficient state action connected with a private social club to review the club's racially restrictive policies. Because there was no official aid or encouragement of the club's decision to restrict its membership, it would not be subjected to constitutional restraint.

Both the majority and dissenting opinions in *Moose Lodge* focused on whether any real harm was done to members of a minority race by the existence of the segregated club. It is possible that the real difference between those who would or would not subject the lodge to constitutional restraint relates to their view of whether or not any harm was done to members of the minority race by its policies. But the decision appears to rest on a quantitative view of the existence of state action in the club's decisions. Absent some entanglement with the government, the Court will not find state action on the basis of a club's historic practices or the customs which might have given rise to those practices.

The existence of a state law which recognizes the legitimacy of an action taken by an

---

College Trusteeship, 391 Pa. 434, 138 A.2d 844 (1958), appeal dismissed and certiorari denied 357 U.S. 570, 78 S.Ct. 1383, 2 L.Ed.2d 1546 (1958), rehearing denied 358 U.S. 858, 79 S.Ct. 14, 3 L.Ed.2d 92 (1958) (per curiam); Pennsylvania v. Brown, 392 F.2d 120 (3d Cir.1968), certiorari denied 391 U.S. 921, 88 S.Ct. 1811, 20 L.Ed.2d 657 (1968). This problem is unlikely to rise again due to the Court's ruling on the scope of statutes passed pursuant to the Thirteenth Amendment, see §§ 12.4(c), 15.6–15.10, infra.

11. 378 U.S. 226, 84 S.Ct. 1814, 12 L.Ed.2d 822 (1964).

12. 378 U.S. at 253, 84 S.Ct. at 1829 (Douglas, J.).

13. 378 U.S. at 318, 84 S.Ct. at 1864 (Black, J., dissenting).

14. 407 U.S. 163, 92 S.Ct. 1965, 32 L.Ed.2d 627 (1972). See also § 12.4, infra.

otherwise private person will not give rise to "state action" being present in the private activity. To imbue an activity with state action there must be some non-neutral involvement of the state with the activity.[15] Thus, the Supreme Court has held that a law which allowed a warehouseman to sell property of another against which he had a lien did not involve state action in the sale.[16] This ruling was consistent with the Court's earlier decision that government approval of a privately owned utility company's rate policies and collection practices did not establish state action in the termination of customer services without a prior hearing by the utility.[17] Similarly, the Supreme Court ruled that the decision of a private insurance company to withhold payment for a workers' compensation claimant's medical bills did not constitute state action,

even though the insurance company was acting in accordance with state statutes that gave it the right to withhold such payments.[18]

These situations should be distinguished from those involving the de facto authorization of activities by public officers. When a public officer takes acts relating to his office those actions should be considered to be "state action" even if they exceed the scope of the officer's authority under the law of that jurisdiction. Thus, the Court has held that law enforcement officers who beat a prisoner to death did so under "color of law."[19]

Those who conspire with a government official to take action that deprives others of federal constitutional rights do so "under color of law" and are subject to a federal lawsuit even though the official is immune from civil liabili-

15. In Martinez v. California, 444 U.S. 277, 100 S.Ct. 553, 62 L.Ed.2d 481 (1980), the Court held that a state parole board was not liable under federal civil rights acts for the death of a young girl killed by a parolee, five months after his release because there was not state action connected to the death. This decision should not be understood as ruling that the decision of the parole board was not state action, but only that a parole board's failure to accurately assess the rehabilitation of prison inmates does not deprive other persons of any constitutionally protected interest, even if the parolee injures or kills those persons.

This interpretation of *Martinez* was adopted by the Court in DeShaney v. Winnebago County Department of Social Services, 489 U.S. 189, 109 S.Ct. 998, 103 L.Ed.2d 249 (1989). In *Deshaney,* the Supreme Court ruled that a governmental entity did not violate the due process clause when its social workers failed to intervene to protect a child from being beaten by his father. The Court found that there was no substantive right under the due process clause to governmental protection from harm caused by a private individual. In the course of rejecting the claim of a substantive right to government protection against private violence, the Court noted that *Martinez* was consistent with its ruling. 489 U.S. at 197 n. 4, 109 S.Ct. at 1004 n. 4.

In Sacramento v. Lewis, 523 U.S. 833, 118 S.Ct. 1708, 140 L.Ed.2d 1043 (1998) the Supreme Court held that substantive due process principle established a "shock the conscience" standard for determining whether an executive action that caused incidental, but unintended, harm to individuals was unconstitutional. Justices Souter's majority opinion in *Lewis* referred to the *DeShaney* decision for the principle that the government had a duty to protect safety and well-being of persons who were taken under its custody. The *Lewis* case is discussed in § 10.6 of this Treatise.

The state does have a substantive duty to protect the individuals in its custody from harm. See, e.g., Youngberg v. Romeo, 457 U.S. 307, 102 S.Ct. 2452, 73 L.Ed.2d 28

(1982) (due process clause requires the state to provide involuntarily committed mental patients with such services as are reasonably necessary to protect their safety); Estelle v. Gamble, 429 U.S. 97, 97 S.Ct. 285, 50 L.Ed.2d 251 (1976) (cruel and unusual punishment clause of the Eighth Amendment requires provision of adequate medical care to prisoners). For an examination of the interplay of the procedural and substantive components of the due process clause in these cases see § 10.6.

16. Flagg Bros., Inc. v. Brooks, 436 U.S. 149, 98 S.Ct. 1729, 56 L.Ed.2d 185 (1978). Due process principles will limit the ability of courts, which are government actors, to issue orders that impair the rights of a property owner. While creditor self-help may not involve state action, the attachment of an alleged debtor's property through government administrative or judicial systems involves state actions and must be subject to due process review. See generally, Connecticut v. Doehr, 501 U.S. 1, 111 S.Ct. 2105, 115 L.Ed.2d 1 (1991); Peralta v. Heights Medical Center, Inc., 485 U.S. 80, 108 S.Ct. 896, 99 L.Ed.2d 75 (1988); Lugar v. Edmondson Oil Co., Inc., 457 U.S. 922, 102 S.Ct. 2744, 73 L.Ed.2d 482 (1982). See §§ 13.8, 13.9 of this Treatise regarding due process limits on pre-trial creditor remedies.

17. Jackson v. Metropolitan Edison Co., 419 U.S. 345, 95 S.Ct. 449, 42 L.Ed.2d 477 (1974). The Court later held that similar customer service termination practices of government operated utility companies violated the due process clause. Memphis Light, Gas and Water Division v. Craft, 436 U.S. 1, 98 S.Ct. 1554, 56 L.Ed.2d 30 (1978).

18. American Manufacturers Mutual Insurance Co. v. Sullivan, 526 U.S. 40, 119 S.Ct. 977, 143 L.Ed.2d 130 (1999).

19. Screws v. United States, 325 U.S. 91, 65 S.Ct. 1031, 89 L.Ed. 1495 (1945) (interpreting and applying Congressional Act passed in pursuance of section 5 of the Fourteenth Amendment that used the phrase "under color of any law").

ty.[20] Similarly, when a private business hires an off duty police officer to act as a security guard, there is state action connected to his actions taken on behalf of the private business to the extent that he appears to the public to be exercising the authority of a police officer.[21]

These cases on de facto authorization of public officials' actions should be unaffected by the decisions regarding state "recognition" of otherwise private actions. Were it not for state action, the public official would not have the opportunity to abuse his authority, nor would he be able to represent to the public that his actions were authorized by the government. This fact distinguishes the de facto cases from the state recognition of many private "self-help" actions; the majority believes that self help remedies would exist to some extent even

if the state never recognized or authorized those actions.[22]

The distinction between recognition of private action and governmental authorization of activities by public officers was demonstrated by comparing two cases. In *Polk County v. Dodson*,[23] the Court held that a public defender did not act under color of state law when performing a lawyer's traditional functions as counsel to a defendant in a criminal proceeding. The public defender was serving an essentially private function, adversarial to and independent of the state.[24] She was not amenable to administrative direction in performing her duties for her client, but was required to exercise her own independent judgment on behalf of the client.[25] However, the Court noted that a public defender making hiring and firing decisions on behalf of the state may be a state actor.[26]

---

20. See Dennis v. Sparks, 449 U.S. 24, 101 S.Ct. 183, 66 L.Ed.2d 185 (1980) (those conspiring with a state judge to issue an illegal order were acting under color of law even though the judge was immune from liability.) Accord Tower v. Glover, 467 U.S. 914, 104 S.Ct. 2820, 81 L.Ed.2d 758 (1984).

In National Collegiate Athletic Association v. Tarkanian, 488 U.S. 179, 109 S.Ct. 454, 102 L.Ed.2d 469 (1988), the Supreme Court found that the actions of an association that included both private universities and state universities did not involve state action. The majority opinion, in this five to four decision, was written by Justice Stevens. The majority opinion, as well as the result in the case, cast no doubt on the continuing validity on the conspiracy cases, referred to in this footnote and the previous footnote. In the *National Collegiate Athletic Association* [NCAA] case, the issue was whether the NCAA violated the principles of due process when its committee ordered a member university, the University of Nevada, Las Vegas [UNLV], to show cause why penalties should not be imposed on it (such as suspension from the NCAA's basketball tournament) if it failed to suspend the coach from his athletic duties during a two year period when the school was on "probation" for NCAA rules violations. The majority opinion noted that the action of the university in suspending the coach would be state action regarding which the coach could properly raise due process issues. However, neither the coach nor UNLV was denied due process by the rules and rulings of the NCAA, which is a private association. The majority opinion noted that UNLV (the state university) had opposed the NCAA both in its disciplinary proceedings against the coach and in court actions brought by the coach against the NCAA. Although UNLV might fire the coach only due to its desire to remain a member of the NCAA, and to retain its ability to participate in NCAA events, UNLV never conspired with, or engaged in any kind of partnership or agreement with, the NCAA to punish the coach or to deny him a fundamentally fair procedure to determine whether he should be relieved of his coaching duties. The NCAA did

not act under "color of law", or with "state action", when it found that the university and the coach had violated the NCAA's rules and should be subject to disciplinary action in the Association (if the university chose to remain a member of the NCAA).

21. Griffin v. Maryland, 378 U.S. 130, 84 S.Ct. 1770, 12 L.Ed.2d 754 (1964).

22. Thus, the majority opinion in *Flagg Brothers*, which upheld the warehouseman's sale, indicated that the de facto authorization cases were correct but it did so by finding that Griffin v. Maryland, 378 U.S. 130, 84 S.Ct. 1770, 12 L.Ed.2d 754 (1964) was based on the finding that the police officer security guard "purported to exercise the authority of a deputy sheriff." Flagg Bros., Inc. v. Brooks, 436 U.S. 149, 163 n. 14, 98 S.Ct. 1729, 1737 n. 14, 56 L.Ed.2d 185 (1978), quoting Griffin v. Maryland, 378 U.S. 130, 135, 84 S.Ct. 1770, 1772, 12 L.Ed.2d 754 (1964).

23. 454 U.S. 312, 102 S.Ct. 445, 70 L.Ed.2d 509 (1981).

24. 454 U.S. at 318, 102 S.Ct. at 449–50.

25. 454 U.S. at 320, 102 S.Ct. at 450–51.

26. 454 U.S. at 324, 102 S.Ct. at 453 citing Branti v. Finkel, 445 U.S. 507, 100 S.Ct. 1287, 63 L.Ed.2d 574 (1980) (which held that the discharge of assistant public defenders was subject to First Amendment limitations).

Similarly, if a public defender conspires with public officials to violate the constitutional rights of the public defender's client, because of the conspiracy, the public defender may be found to have acted "under color of" state law and be subject to liability under section 1983 of the Civil Rights Act. Tower v. Glover, 467 U.S. 914, 104 S.Ct. 2820, 81 L.Ed.2d 758 (1984).

When the state employs a private physician to give medical services to prison inmates, it can not use that employment to avoid the state's Eighth Amendment responsibility to provide adequate medical treatment to persons whom it has incarcerated. The Supreme Court found

In contrast, the Supreme Court found that a private party was involved with state action in *Lugar v. Edmondson Oil Co., Inc.*[27] In *Lugar* an oil company sued an alleged debtor in Virginia state court and, pursuant to state law, obtained a prejudgment writ of attachment of some of the debtor's property. The prejudgment writ was executed by the county sheriff. In a five to four decision the Court held that the involvement of state officials in the prejudgment attachment process provided a state action basis for the debtor's claim that he had been deprived of property without due process.[28]

The Court set forth a two part test to determine if deprivation of a federal right may be fairly attributed to the state: "First, the deprivation must be caused by the exercise of some right or privilege created by the state, or by a rule of conduct imposed by the state, or by a person for whom the state is responsible.... Second, the party charged with the deprivation must be a person who may fairly be said to be a state actor [either] because he is a state official, or because he has acted together with or has obtained significant aid from state officials, or because his conduct is otherwise chargeable to the state."[29] *Lugar* satisfied this two part test. While the oil company's private misuse of a state statute could not be attributed to the state, the procedural scheme created by the statute was a product of state action. Second, the ex parte application of the oil company resulting in attachment of the property by the sheriff made the oil company a joint participant with state officials in the seizure of the property.

This second factor differentiates *Lugar* from *Flagg Brothers, Inc. v. Brooks*, according to a majority of the Justices. The debtor in *Lugar* was allowed to challenge the constitutionality of the state system of issuing prejudgment attachments because it involved judicial and executive officers of the state. The debtor could not challenge the decision of the creditor to employ the state statutory procedure because that was a decision of a private sector entity which was not commanded or encouraged by the government.[30]

The *Flagg Brothers* decision stands only for the proposition that a creditor who engages in true self-help does not violate constitutional provisions, such as the due process clause of the Fourteenth Amendment or the Fourth Amendment, that require "state action." If a creditor enlists the aid of police officers when he seizes the property of the alleged debtor, the seizure of the debtor's property will be subject to review under the Fourth Amendment restriction against unreasonable seizures of property and due process principles.[31] The joint creditor-police activity is similar to the type of conspiratorial activity between government officials and private persons that the Supreme Court has found to be state action that triggers the protections of the Bill of

---

that the actions of a physician who was employed on a part-time basis to provide medical services to inmates at a state prison hospital were actions taken under color of law within the meaning of civil rights statute 42 U.S.C.A. § 1983. West v. Atkins, 487 U.S. 42, 108 S.Ct. 2250, 101 L.Ed.2d 40 (1988).

27. 457 U.S. 922, 102 S.Ct. 2744, 73 L.Ed.2d 482 (1982).

28. The Court held that if the challenged conduct constitutes state action, that conduct is also action "under color of state law" and will support a suit under 42 U.S.C.A. § 1983, although all conduct satisfying the "under color of law" requirement may not meet the Fourteenth Amendment requirement of state action. 457 U.S. at 926–27, 102 S.Ct. at 2753.

"The ultimate issue in determining whether a person is subject to suit under § 1983 is the same question posed in cases arising under the Fourteenth Amendment: is the alleged infringement of federal rights fairly attributable to the state?" Rendell–Baker v. Kohn, 457 U.S. 830, 838, 102 S.Ct. 2764, 2770, 73 L.Ed.2d 418 (1982) citing Lugar v. Edmondson Oil Co., Inc., 457 U.S. 922, 938, 102 S.Ct. 2744, 2754, 73 L.Ed.2d 482 (1982).

29. 457 U.S. at 938–39, 102 S.Ct. at 2754.

30. 457 U.S. at 943, 102 S.Ct. at 2757.

31. In Soldal v. Cook County, 506 U.S. 56, 113 S.Ct. 538, 121 L.Ed.2d 450 (1992), Justice White wrote for a unanimous Court in ruling that the Fourth Amendment rights of an owner of a mobile home were violated when, without a properly issued writ of eviction, the owner of a mobile home park, with the assistance of the county sheriff's office, removed the person's mobile home from its foundation in the park, and towed it outside of the park. Justice White, in a footnote to his opinion for the Court, noted the Court of Appeals ruling concerning the state action principle and stated: "We are not inclined to review that holding." 506 U.S. at 60 n. 6, 113 S.Ct. at 543 n. 6.

Rights or the Fourteenth Amendment.[32]

A creditor's use of the courts to authorize the seizure of a debtor's property involves the combined action of government and private actors. In *Lugar v. Edmondson Oil Co., Inc.,*[33] the Court found that the creditor's use of a prejudgment writ of attachment gave rise to state action in the seizure of the alleged debtor's property. The creditor's use of a prejudgment attachment involves the use of judicial officers of the state, in securing the writ. In many instances, executive officers of the state will be involved when the creditor executes the writ.

The Supreme Court relied on *Lugar* in *Edmonson v. Leesville Concrete Co., Inc.*[34] to find that the equal protection guarantee prohibited a party in a private lawsuit from using peremptory challenges to exclude a person from a civil trial jury on the basis of the individual's race.[35] The Court had previously held that the equal protection guarantee prohibited government prosecutors from using peremptory challenges to prevent persons from serving on a jury due to their race.[36] The issue in *Leesville Concrete* was whether a private litigant was also subject to the equal protection guarantee when he used jury challenges. The Supreme Court decided that it should examine this issue

in two steps or inquiries. First, the Court asked whether the claimed harm to individuals who were excluded from jury service because of their race resulted from the exercises of a right that had a source in government authority.[37] The Court answered this question in the affirmative, because the private litigant would have no peremptory challenges if the law of the jurisdiction did not provide that right to the litigant. Peremptory challenges are created by federal law (for federal court cases) or by state law (for state court cases).

Justice Kennedy's majority opinion in *Leesville Concrete* stated that the second step of state action analysis involved an examination of whether the private litigant "could be described in all fairness as a state actor" when he used peremptory challenges on the basis of race. In making this determination, the Court indicated that it would consider several factors, including whether the actor is "performing a traditional government function" and "the extent to which the actor relies on government assistance and benefits ... and whether the injury caused is aggravated in a unique way by the incidence of government authority." The majority opinion found that the jury selection process was a traditional government function.[38] Even if the jury selec-

32. See notes 19, 20 in this section of the Treatise for cases where the Supreme Court has found that a conspiracy between private persons and government officials such as police officers gives rise to state action on the part of the private persons involved in the conspiracy.

33. 457 U.S. 922, 102 S.Ct. 2744, 73 L.Ed.2d 482 (1982). For an examination of the constitutional restrictions on the seizure of property from alleged debtors, see § 13.9(b) of this Treatise.

34. 500 U.S. 614, 111 S.Ct. 2077, 114 L.Ed.2d 660 (1991), on remand 943 F.2d 551 (5th Cir.1991).

35. *Leesville Concrete* involved a federal trial. The private litigant would be subject to the implied equal protection guarantee of the Fifth Amendment due process clause in this case; in a state case, the litigant would be subject to the equal protection clause of the Fourteenth Amendment. The majority opinion stated: "Recognizing the impropriety of racial bias in the courtroom, we hold the race-based exclusion violates the equal protection rights of the challenged juror. This case originated in a United States District Court, and we apply the equal protection component of the Fifth Amendment's due process clause." 500 U.S. at 615, 111 S.Ct. at 2080.

36. Batson v. Kentucky, 476 U.S. 79, 106 S.Ct. 1712, 90 L.Ed.2d 69 (1986).

37. In Edmonson v. Leesville Concrete Co., Inc., 500 U.S. 614, 618–22, 111 S.Ct. 2077, 2082–83, 114 L.Ed.2d 660 (1991), the Court based its analysis on the structure for analyzing state action cases that had been set forth in Lugar v. Edmondson Oil Co., 457 U.S. 922, 937–42, 102 S.Ct. 2744, 2753–56, 73 L.Ed.2d 482 (1982). The relationship of the language used in these two cases to more traditional views of the analysis used in state action cases is examined in § 12.1.

38. The dissent asserted that the jury selection process, unlike the trial process itself, could not be described as a government function for state action purposes since private parties have always been able to make private decisions concerning the tactics and standards they would use in the jury selection process. Edmonson v. Leesville Concrete Co., Inc., 500 U.S. 614, 631, 111 S.Ct. 2077, 2089, 114 L.Ed.2d 660 (1991) (O'Connor, J., joined by Rehnquist, C.J., and Scalia, J., dissenting), on remand 943 F.2d 551 (5th Cir.1991). Although the majority opinion by Justice Kennedy indicated that private litigants were involved with a traditional government function, the majority did not rely on the public function branch of state action alone but found the element of public function and civil trials to be an important factor in determining that the totality of facts and circumstances in the case make the decision that the private litigant's actions "could be

tion process could not be described as a traditional government function, the majority opinion ruled that there was state action in the private litigant's use of peremptory challenges because peremptory challenges were a benefit provided to the litigant by the government and because the harm caused to persons from the discriminatory use of jury challenge was exacerbated by the apparent government sanctioning of the discrimination by allowing it to take place in the courtroom.[39]

In *Georgia v. McCollum* [40] the Supreme Court ruled that the equal protection guarantee prohibited a defendant in a state criminal action from using peremptory challenges to exclude persons from the jury because of their race. Justice Blackmun's majority opinion in *McCollum* tracked the reasoning of *Leesville Concrete* in finding that there was sufficient state action in the criminal defendant's jury challenges so as to make the equal protection clause applicable to the defendant's actions. The majority in *McCollum* found that the harm caused to minority race persons, and society, from racially discriminatory jury selection practices "resulted from the exercise of a right (the defendant's right to a peremptory challenge) that had its source in state law." The Court also found that, despite his adversary relationship to the state government, the criminal case defendant could be fairly de-

scribed as a state actor because: (1) his use of peremptory challenges necessarily involved the assistance of the judicial system; (2) selection of a jury was a "unique and constitutionally compelled government function;" and (3) the injury caused to minority race persons and society by a racially discriminatory jury selection system was the same regardless of whether the racial discrimination was caused by prosecutors or defendants.[41]

§ 12.4　Mutual Contacts—Licensing, Symbiotic Relationships, Subsidies, and Other Entanglements

The remaining cases concerning the existence of state action relate to the number or type of contacts between government and the challenged practices or the alleged wrongdoer. Most decisions ordinarily included in this category actually focus on the granting of direct aid to the alleged wrongdoer, the governmental encouragement or ordering of the specific activities, or the delegation of public functions. All of these decisions must be evaluated in terms of the approach set out in § 12.1.

In a few cases the Court has found state action in an alleged wrongful practice simply on the basis of the entanglement between the government and private practice, but no specific test has emerged from these cases.[1] The

described in all fairness" as having the type of state action that should make the litigants subject to the equal protection guarantee.

39. The Court did not rule on whether the party challenging the use of peremptory challenges by the other litigant in this case had made out a prima facie case that the litigant had used peremptory challenges in a race-based manner. Edmonson v. Leesville Concrete Co., Inc., 500 U.S. 614, 629–33, 111 S.Ct. 2077, 2088–89, 114 L.Ed.2d 660 (1991), on remand 943 F.2d 551 (5th Cir. 1991). For an examination of how the Court has approached the question of whether a party has proven that prosecutors have used peremptory challenges in a racially discriminatory manner, see § 14.4.

40. 505 U.S. 42, 112 S.Ct. 2348, 120 L.Ed.2d 33 (1992), on remand 262 Ga. 554, 422 S.E.2d 866 (1992). For an overview of state action issues see § 16.1 of this Chapter. For an examination of the "public function" concept see § 12.2.

41. In J.E.B. v. Alabama ex rel. T.B., 511 U.S. 127, 114 S.Ct. 1419, 128 L.Ed.2d 89 (1994) the Supreme Court held that the intentional use of peremptory challenges by a government attorney to exclude persons of one sex from a jury violated the equal protection clause. The *J.E.B.*

litigation began with the government bringing a civil case on behalf of a woman in the state for child support payments from the father of her child. Because the facts of the *J.E.B.* case involved a state government attorney, the Court did not have to deal with issues concerning "state action."

§ 12.4

1. Several of these cases were examined in § 12.3, supra. Because the Supreme Court refuses to categorize its state action decisions, or even identify specific state action tests, there is necessary overlap between the sections of this chapter. Thus, cases involving actions undertaken by private persons acting in concert with government employees were examined in § 12.3, supra, but those cases could have been labeled "mutual contacts" cases and included in this section. The reader is encouraged to consider each decision examined in this section against the backdrop of all theories of state action examined in this Chapter. In Edmonson v. Leesville Concrete Co., Inc., 500 U.S. 614, 111 S.Ct. 2077, 114 L.Ed.2d 660 (1991), the Court found that the equal protection guarantee of the Fifth Amendment due process clause (in a federal civil trial) and the equal protection guarantee of the Fifth Amendment due process clause (in a federal civil right) and the equal

decisions merely hold that, on the facts presented by the individual case, the private wrongdoer should be subjected to constitutional restraints because of his relationship to government. It might be said that where there are sufficient contacts between a private individual and the government, then that the private individual takes on at least the appearance if not the actual authority of the state. Where the actions provide some tangible aid to both the alleged wrongdoer and the government, the two have come to be in a type of "symbiotic relationship." In such a situation the state and private individual have in effect become joint venturers even though they do not have any formalized agreements. Here the alleged wrongdoer's beneficial ties to the state justify subjecting his activities to constitutional limitations.

Cases involving determinations of state action based on the relationship between the private actor and government have fallen into three general categories: (1) cases where the private actor is subjected to extensive regulation by the government; (2) cases involving a wide range of physical and economic contacts between the actor and government; (3) cases where the government has provided some sort of direct aid or subsidy to the private actor.

Even if an entity has a relationship to the government that cuts across all three of these categories—it is licensed by the government, it has a wide range of economic relationships to the government, and it receives subsidies from the government—it is not necessarily an entity that should be treated like the government

and made subject to constitutional restrictions on its actions. In each case, the Court must determine whether the relationship between the entity and the government is such that the Constitution requires the imposition of restrictions on the actions of the otherwise private entity, so as to prevent the impairment of constitutionally protected values (such as values protected by the due process clause or the First Amendment).

In *San Francisco Arts & Athletics, Inc. v. United States Olympic Committee*,[2] the Supreme Court examined the constitutionality of federal statutes that granted the United States Olympic Committee exclusive use of the word "olympic" and certain olympic symbols and allowed it to prohibit other persons from using that word, or the olympic symbols, without its permission. The Supreme Court found that the granting of the exclusive right to use the word and olympic symbols to the United States Olympic Committee did not violate the First Amendment freedom of speech of those persons who wish to use the word to promote their own interests.[3]

The Court then addressed the question of whether the United States Olympic Committee had discriminated in its decisions regarding which persons or entities would be allowed to use the word "olympic" in a manner that would violate the equal protection component of the Fifth Amendment if the decisions had been made by an agency of the federal government.[4] The Supreme Court decided that the Fifth Amendment did not restrict the actions of the United States Olympic Committee, even

protection clause of the Fourteenth Amendment (in a state civil trial) would prohibit a private litigant from using peremptory challenges to jury members for the purpose of excluding persons from a jury because of the person's race. The Court based its ruling on several factors, including the fact that the race discrimination occurred within a courtroom and that the action was a part of a traditional state function in resolving disputes through civil litigation. The Court used the *Edmonson* analysis when it held that a defendant's exclusion of racial minority members from a jury in a criminal case constituted a violation of the equal protection clause. Georgia v. McCollum, 505 U.S. 42, 112 S.Ct. 2348, 120 L.Ed.2d 33 (1992), on remand 262 Ga. 554, 422 S.E.2d 866 (1992). See §§ 12.1, 12.2, 12.3 for an analysis of how these cases fit with the public function and state encouragement branches of state action analysis.

2. 483 U.S. 522, 107 S.Ct. 2971, 97 L.Ed.2d 427 (1987). As noted in footnote 1, many state action cases overlap several sections of this chapter.

3. The First Amendment aspects of this case are examined in Chapter 16.

4. The Court recognized that the Fifth Amendment due process clause includes an implied equal protection guarantee, even though it found that the United States Olympic Committee was not subject to this constitutional restriction. San Francisco Arts & Athletics, Inc. v. United States Olympic Committee, 483 U.S. 522, 542 n. 21, 107 S.Ct. 2971, 2984 n. 21, 97 L.Ed.2d 427 (1987). The Court has long held that the Fifth Amendment due process clause includes an implied equal protection guarantee, see §§ 14.1, 14.2.

though this corporation was chartered and regulated by the federal government, received some of its funds from direct grants from the federal government, and received an indirect subsidy through its right to exclusive use of the word "olympic" and olympic symbols. The Court found no involvement of the federal government in the individual decisions of the United States Olympic Committee to grant or withhold permission for the use of the olympic word or symbols by other persons or entities. The Olympic Committee, in the Court's view, was constitutionally indistinguishable from other private corporations that were chartered by the state or federal governments. Because it neither performed a governmental function nor had its decisions directly influenced by governmental actors, the Olympic Committee was not found to be the equivalent of a government agency.

(a) Licensing and Regulation

The fact that an otherwise private actor is regulated or licensed by a government agency will not make all of the actions of that person or business equivalent to actions of the government itself. The degree of entanglement between the government and a regulated industry is not an irrelevant fact. It may be easier to find state action in the business practices of a regulated entity than it would be of one with no formal contacts to the government. Indeed, it appeared for some time that the Court might subject some businesses to constitutional restraints merely because they received an important license from the state or because their business activities were extensively regulated. Such a position was not without some merit, for government licensing or regulation may give the appearance of an approval of the challenged action. However, the Supreme Court has refused to subject licensed entities or individuals to constitutional restraints merely because some of their activities or policies are regulated by the government.

In contrast, if the government regulation directly approved the challenged practice of the alleged wrongdoer, there is state action intertwined with that practice. This principle involves no more than the application of the "government encouragement" basis for finding state action discussed in the preceding section. When government commands, encourages, or actively approves a practice, that practice is subject to constitutional limitation. Where the government has not specifically approved the alleged wrongful activity the degree of regulation of the actor is only one factor to consider when assessing the presence of state action in the challenged activity.[5]

There are several cases which are of special significance to the state regulation or licensing theory for finding state action. *Public Utilities Commission v. Pollak*[6] involved a challenge to transit company's practice of broadcasting radio programs in its buses and street cars. The company was licensed to operate the buses in Washington, D.C., and, in the course of reviewing its activities, the Supreme Court seemed to find that the government's regulation of the company made it subject to constitutional restraints. However, the decision was unclear, because the Court held that the activity was compatible with the Constitution even if it constituted governmental action. The majority opinion may have only assumed *arguen-*

---

5. In Blum v. Yaretsky, 457 U.S. 991, 102 S.Ct. 2777, 73 L.Ed.2d 534 (1982) the Supreme Court rejected the argument that regulations imposing a range of penalties on nursing homes that fail to discharge or transfer patients whose continued stay is medically inappropriate dictate the decisions to discharge or transfer patients. Physicians make the decisions as to if a patient's care is medically necessary and those decisions ultimately turn on medical judgments made by private parties according to professional standards that are not established by the State. Adjustment in Medicaid benefit levels by the State in response to the discharge or transfer of a patient does not constitute approval or enforcement of that decision. For these reasons the Court refused to find state action in the discharge or transfer of patients; its decision left these

nursing home patients without any due process right to a hearing concerning their discharge.

In Rendell–Baker v. Kohn, 457 U.S. 830, 102 S.Ct. 2764, 73 L.Ed.2d 418 (1982) the Court held that although the state extensively regulated a private school for maladjusted students, the school's decisions to discharge several teachers were not compelled or even influenced by state regulations. The government regulation of the school's educational practices and funding of students attending the school were held to be unrelated to the private school's employment practices. Thus, the Court refused to find that the school's teachers had any due process right to a fair process regarding their discharge.

6. 343 U.S. 451, 72 S.Ct. 813, 96 L.Ed. 1068 (1952).

do the presence of state action in the practices of a regulated industry.[7] Twenty years passed before the Court again specifically considered whether state regulations or licensing gave rise to the state action.

In *Moose Lodge Number 107 v. Irvis*[8] the Court held that the activities of a private club were not subjected to constitutional restraint merely because it was given a liquor license by the city government. Although the granting of the license subjected the club to extensive regulation, there was, the Court said, no involvement of the city with the club's racially discriminatory policies. Additionally, the action of granting the license to the racially discriminatory club did not appear to burden anyone's ability to receive alcoholic beverages, although the total number of liquor licenses that could be granted was fixed by law. The majority opinion found no state action which encouraged the racially restrictive practices of the club or caused any detriment to members of minority races.

The Supreme Court next concluded that television and radio stations were not subjected to the restraints of the First Amendment because of their licensing and regulation by the federal government. In *Columbia Broadcasting System v. Democratic National Committee*,[9] antiwar groups challenged an individual station's refusals to accept editorial advertising as violative of the First Amendment. There was no majority opinion concerning the presence of government action in the activities of radio and television stations, because several of the Justices believed that the refusal to accept editorial advertising was

permissible even if it represented government action. However, three of the Justices indicated that there was no government action connected to the refusal, since the federal regulation of stations did not encourage or approve the challenged practice.[10] But the issue was left unclear as only two Justices found government action connected to these refusals which would violate the First Amendment.[11] The remaining Justices could assume the presence of some government action because they felt that allowing individual stations this editorial freedom did not violate the First Amendment.[12] Government owned broadcast stations are subject to First Amendment principles.[13] On the other hand, privately owned broadcast stations do not have sufficient state action to be subject to First Amendment limitations on their actions.

The Supreme Court held that extensive regulation of a business would not in itself subject all of its activities to constitutional restraint. In *Jackson v. Metropolitan Edison Co.*[14] the majority held that the actions of a public utility did not involve sufficient state action to subject it to constitutional restraint on the basis of its monopoly status and government regulation. In this case an electric company terminated service to a customer without having a final hearing to determine the status of the account or the customer's willingness to pay new charges.

The Court did not decide whether the customer would have been entitled to a hearing had the utility been a part of the governmental structure. Instead, a majority of the Justices

---

7. This point was emphasized in Jackson v. Metropolitan Edison Co., 419 U.S. 345, 356 n. 16, 95 S.Ct. 449, 456 n. 16, 42 L.Ed.2d 477 (1974).

8.   407 U.S. 163, 92 S.Ct. 1965, 32 L.Ed.2d 627 (1972).

9.   412 U.S. 94, 93 S.Ct. 2080, 36 L.Ed.2d 772 (1973).

10.   412 U.S. at 114–121, 93 S.Ct. at 2092–96, (Burger, C.J., joined by Stewart and Rehnquist, JJ.).

11.   412 U.S. at 172–181, 93 S.Ct. at 2121–26 (Brennan, J., dissenting, joined by Marshall, J.).

12.   412 U.S. at 147, 93 S.Ct. at 2108–09 (White, J., concurring); 412 U.S. at 148, 93 S.Ct. at 2109 (Blackmun, J., concurring, joined by Powell, J.).

13.   In Arkansas Educational Television Commission v. Forbes, 523 U.S. 666, 118 S.Ct. 1633, 140 L.Ed.2d 875 (1998) the Court reviewed the decision of a publicly owned

television station to exclude a candidate from a pre-election debate under First Amendment principles. In *Arkansas Educational Television*, all nine Justices accepted the finding of the lower court that a state owned public television broadcaster was subject to First and Fourteenth Amendment principles that might restrict its actions. A majority of the Justices in *Arkansas Educational Television* ruled that the exclusion of a candidate from a televised political debate would not violate the First Amendment so long as the decision of the government owned station was "a reasonable viewpoint-neutral exercise of journalistic discretion." 523 U.S. at 683, 118 S.Ct. at 1644.

14.   419 U.S. 345, 95 S.Ct. 449, 42 L.Ed.2d 477 (1974).

held that the termination of service by the utility would not be subject to constitutional review because it did not constitute state action. The majority found that the government licensing and regulation of the utility neither commanded, encouraged, nor sanctioned the termination practices of the company.[15] Even assuming the grant of a monopoly status to the utility company, the state had not been connected to the challenged practice. While the regulation and licensing disclosed certain continuing relationships between the company and the government, those relationships had nothing to do with the challenged activity in the view of the majority. Nor could the government and the utility be seen as joint venturers so that the utility could be subjected to constitutional restraint because of its "symbiotic relationship" to the government. Finally, the majority found that the provision of utility services did not constitute a "public function" as this did not relate to a sovereign function even though the state could operate a utility company.

In *American Manufacturers Mutual Insurance Company v. Sullivan*[16] the Supreme Court ruled that privately owned insurance companies that paid medical benefits to injured workers under a workers' compensation system that was regulated by the state did not have state action. Therefore, the decision of an insurance company to withhold payments for medical services requested by an injured worker, on the basis that the company did not believe the medical services were reasonable or necessary, was not subject to due process limitations.[17] Although the insurance companies were regulated by the state, and the system for resolving disputes between workers' compensation claimants and insurance companies was established by the state, the decisions of the private insurance company were neither commanded nor approved by the government. Thus, there was no "state action" in an insurance company's decision to withhold benefits claimed by an injured worker.[18]

(b) Multiple Contacts—Symbiotic Relationships

In many situations an alleged wrongdoer appears to have a variety of physical and economic contacts to the government even though it is not an agent of the government or part of a regulated industry. These multiple or joint contacts may so intertwine the private actor

---

15. 419 U.S. at 356–59, 95 S.Ct. at 456–58.

16. 526 U.S. 40, 119 S.Ct. 977, 143 L.Ed.2d 130 (1999).

17. State statutes established a review board to resolve disputes between workers compensation claimants and the private insurance corporations. These state statutes constituted state action; the statutes would be subject to constitutional limitation. The employees asserted that they had a right to prompt, fair procedures to determine whether their claims for compensation for medical treatment should be paid. The majority opinion ruled that a worker did not have a property interest in a claim for a medical payment that had never been found to be reasonable and necessary by an insurance company, or by the government. Therefore, the state was not required to provide prompt process for the resolution of disputes between the claimant and the insurance company. American Manufacturers Mutual Insurance Co. v. Sullivan, 526 U.S. 40, 58–60, 119 S.Ct. 977, 989–90, 143 L.Ed.2d 130 (1999). Justices Breyer and Souter agreed with the majority's state action analysis, but they believed that there might be circumstances under which an injured worker would have a property interest in his claim for compensation payments that would require any state established dispute resolution system to meet due process standards. 526 U.S. at 60–62, 119 S.Ct. at 991 (Breyer, J., joined by Souter, J., concurring in part and concurring in the judgment). Justice Ginsburg believed that due process did not require payments of medical bills within thirty days, as claimed by the workers in the case, although she believed that there might be circumstances that would require the state to establish fair procedures for disputes between claimants and insurance companies. Justice Ginsburg believed that the state action issue should not have been addressed in the case. 526 U.S. at 60–62, 119 S.Ct. at 990–91 (Ginsburg, J., concurring in part and concurring in the judgment). Justice Stevens believed that the state action issue was irrelevant to the decision; he believed that the majority had failed to address the due process issue of whether the procedures established for resolution of disputes between claimants and insurance companies was fundamentally fair. 526 U.S. at 62–64, 119 S.Ct. at 991–92 (Stevens, J., concurring in part and dissenting in part).

See Chapter 13 of this Treatise regarding the relationship between a determination of whether an interest claimed by an individual is "liberty" or "property" and the requirement that the government create fundamentally fair procedures for the resolution of fact disputes.

18. The majority opinion in American Manufacturers Mutual Insurance Co. v. Sullivan, 526 U.S. 40, 56, 119 S.Ct. 977, 988, 143 L.Ed.2d 130 (1999) also ruled that the state had not delegated a public function to the insurance corporations, because recognition of private insurance corporations' ability to withhold disputed payments did not involve the delegation of a "traditionally exclusive public function." See § 12.3 of this Treatise regarding public function analysis in state action decisions.

and the government that the private actor will be treated as a government agent. Of course, if the private actor was the agent or business partner of the government it would be subjected to constitutional restraints. However, even though there is no partnership, these contacts may give the appearance of government action. Where the private actor and government can be said to be in a "symbiotic relationship", the private actor will be subject to constitutional restraints.

This category is, in reality, a "catch all" which may have little, if any, substantive meaning. All that can be said with certainty is that some otherwise private actors have been found to have sufficient state action to subject them to constitutional restraints even though no single factor indicated that the government was responsible for their activities. In these cases a majority of the Justices simply found sufficient connections to hold the actor constitutionally accountable by "sifting the facts and weighing the circumstances."[19] Thus it may be said that when a private individual becomes so entangled with government policies that his actions appear to have the authorization of the state, it is likely that a majority of the Justices on the Supreme Court will find state action in his activities. During the decade of the 1960's three cases focused on these types of generalized relationships to establish state action.

In *Evans v. Newton*[20] the Supreme Court determined that the continued existence of a racially segregated park devised by Senator Bacon to the town of Macon, Georgia violated the Fourteenth Amendment. This park had been given to the city on the basis that it would serve only white persons and city trustees in fact had operated the park in a segregated manner. Once it was apparent that the

public park would have to be integrated, the city moved to have the public trustees replaced by private persons. However, even after the attempt to substitute private trustees, the city appeared to provide some services for the maintenance of the park's facilities.

The Supreme Court held that the park was so imbued with state action that even the private trustees could not run the park on a segregated basis. This decision was based on a number of factors such as the appearance of government approval of the restricted practices, the past and present aid given to the running of the park, and the public nature of land used as a park within a city. Since the city and the park had been so intertwined, the operation of the park could not be considered truly private or beyond the reach of the Constitution.

Following this decision the Georgia courts held that the land reverted to the heirs of Senator Bacon as the trust failed when the racially restrictive conditions could not be fulfilled; this action was affirmed by the Supreme Court.[21] The Supreme Court allowed the land to revert because there would be no continuing contact between the government and the future use of the property so long as its use as a public park was terminated and the government did not encourage its use in a segregated manner.

The classic "joint contact—symbiotic relationship" case is *Burton v. Wilmington Parking Authority*.[22] In this leading decision the Court held that a privately owned restaurant which leased space in a government parking facility could not refuse service to members of racial minorities. While the restaurant did not receive any direct aid from the government it benefited from its location within the govern-

---

19. Burton v. Wilmington Parking Authority, 365 U.S. 715, 722, 81 S.Ct. 856, 860, 6 L.Ed.2d 45 (1961).

The decisions examined in each section of this Chapter should not be viewed in isolation. Thus the "symbiotic relationship" cases must be compared to the "government subsidies" decisions examined in § 12.4(c), infra. The Supreme Court rejected the argument that a symbiotic relationship existed between a private school and the state in Rendell–Baker v. Kohn, 457 U.S. 830, 102 S.Ct. 2764, 73 L.Ed.2d 418 (1982). Although the school derived its income primarily from public sources and was extensively regulated by public authorities, the Court viewed the

school's fiscal relationship with the state as "... not different from that of many contractors performing services for the government." 457 U.S. at 843, 102 S.Ct. at 2772.

20. 382 U.S. 296, 86 S.Ct. 486, 15 L.Ed.2d 373 (1966).

21. Evans v. Abney, 396 U.S. 435, 90 S.Ct. 628, 24 L.Ed.2d 634 (1970), affirming 224 Ga. 826, 165 S.E.2d 160 (1968). See § 12.3, supra.

22. 365 U.S. 715, 81 S.Ct. 856, 6 L.Ed.2d 45 (1961).

ment facility. While there was no command or encouragement of its racially restrictive practices by the government, its location and status as a lessee of the government gave the appearance of government authorization of the practices. While the government and restaurant could not be termed joint venturers, they were in a "symbiotic relationship". The restaurant benefited from its location in the government facility and patronage by government workers. And to the extent the restaurant made improvements to the realty, it enjoyed the parking authority's tax exemption. The government benefited from convenience for its employees as well as the rental monies received.

The government to that extent benefited from the restaurant's policy of segregation. Although there was no single factor which indicated the presence of state action in the challenged practices, a majority of the Justices felt that the totality of the circumstances showed sufficient contacts to the government to subject the restaurant's activities to constitutional restraint. When the activities of the government and the private actor become so intertwined for their mutual benefit, the private party has no basis for complaint when his decisions are subjected to constitutional limitations in the same manner as those of the government.

The Supreme Court's decision in *Reitman v. Mulkey*[23] was the last of this trio of cases with generalized findings of state action. This case involved an Amendment to the constitution of the state of California which repealed open housing legislation and prevented the passage of similar legislation. A majority of the Justices on the Supreme Court of the United States held that this state Amendment would constitute state action connected to racially discriminatory housing and land transactions so as to violate the Fourteenth Amendment.

In traditional state action terms it might seem that the Amendment was invalid because it encouraged racial bias in land transactions. However the refusal to outlaw private discrimination on the basis of race in real estate activities cannot be taken as the encouragement of such activity. Such a position would mean that the state could never repeal legislation that protected rights which have a constitutional basis. Indeed, the majority conceded that it only engaged in such an assumption because the Supreme Court of California had held that in fact the Amendment would cause increased discriminatory practices.

A stronger rationale for *Reitman* was provided by Professor Charles Black who took the position that the same judgment could be reached without having to assume a hypothetical encouragement of racially restrictive land transactions resulting from the state Amendment.[24] He noted that the ultimate effect of California's constitutional provision was to establish a legal impediment to minority access to legislative remedies for their problems in the real estate market. Thus the Amendment could be considered the direct activity of a state to create a "super-majority" requirement for the passage of laws which would assist racial minorities. Before a city or the state could enact open housing legislation, the state constitution would have to be amended. So viewed the state Amendment would directly violate the Fourteenth Amendment because it restricted access to legislative remedies based on the race of those seeking legislative action.[25]

---

23.   387 U.S. 369, 87 S.Ct. 1627, 18 L.Ed.2d 830 (1967).

24.   Black, "State Action", Equal Protection, and California's Proposition 14, 81 Harv.L.Rev. 69 (1967).

25.   See also, Washington v. Seattle School District No. 1, 458 U.S. 457, 102 S.Ct. 3187, 73 L.Ed.2d 896 (1982) and Crawford v. Board of Education of the City of Los Angeles, 458 U.S. 527, 102 S.Ct. 3211, 73 L.Ed.2d 948 (1982).

In *Seattle School District No. 1*, the Supreme Court found unconstitutional a state statute, adopted through voter initiative, which effectively permitted mandatory assignment or transfer of students by local school boards for any reason except for the purpose of desegregating

schools. A five member majority held that the statute violated the equal protection clause because it used the racial nature of an issue to determine the governmental decisionmaking structure. Student assignment was left in the power of local school boards except when assignment related to desegregation. Assignment of students for desegregation purposes was removed from the power of local boards, and placed at the state level, thus imposing substantial and unique burdens on racial minorities seeking elimination of school segregation.

Seattle School District No. 1 was distinguished in *Crawford*, in which an eight member majority upheld a state constitutional Amendment providing that state courts

In *Romer v. Evans*,[26] the Supreme Court invalidated a state constitutional amendment that prohibited the state legislature, or any local legislature within the state, from passing any law that would prohibit discrimination against individuals in the state on the basis of their sexual orientation. The majority opinion in *Romer,* written by Justices Kennedy, followed the rationale set forth in Professor Black's article. Surprisingly, Professor Black's article was not cited in Justices Kennedy's majority opinion. Justices Kennedy's majority opinion ruled that the law establishing a class of persons who would be disabled from seeking legislative remedies for their problems (when all other persons could seek legislative remedies) created an arbitrary and invidious classification.

Under the state constitutional provision at issue in *Romer,* the state constitution would have to be amended before a city or state legislature could enact legislation protecting persons who were denied opportunities because of their sexual orientation. All persons other than homosexuals could lobby the state or city legislatures for legislative action that would enhance their ability to gain employment, housing, or other private sector benefits. Homosexuals did not comprise a constitutionally suspect classification; there was no fundamental right to engage in homosexual activity outside of marriage. Nevertheless, the Supreme Court ruled that the state constitutional amendment violated the equal protection clause because the restriction of access to legislative remedies for a class of persons was totally arbitrary.[27]

It must be remembered that in every state action case the question before the court will concern whether a seemingly private person or entity should be subject to the restrictions of the constitution and that this decision will be based on whether the conduct of that private person or entity, which allegedly has deprived a person of a constitutional right, can be attributed to governmental action. In *National Collegiate Athletic Association v. Tarkanian,*[28] the Supreme Court, by a five to four vote of the Justices, found that the National Collegiate Athletic Association [NCAA] could not have violated the due process rights of a basketball coach because it did not have state action so as to make it subject to the due process clause of the Fourteenth Amendment and statutes meant to enforce that constitutional provision. The NCAA had found that the coach and the basketball program of the University of Nevada, Las Vegas [UNLV] had violated the association's rules in a variety of ways. Consequently, the NCAA took certain disciplinary actions against the school, such as placing the school on probation, and ordering the school to "show cause" why it should not be subject to additional disciplinary sanctions (such as an increase in the number of years in which it would be excluded from the NCAA basketball tournament) unless it removed the coach from all coaching duties at the university during the period of time when the university was on NCAA probation. The fact that the

---

could not order mandatory assignment or transportation of students unless a federal court would do so to remedy a violation of the equal protection clause of the Fourteenth Amendment. Stressing that the Amendment did not embody a racial classification, the majority opinion held that the equal protection clause is not violated by the mere repeal of race-related legislation that was never required by the federal constitution. The state constitution did not allocate governmental or judicial power on the basis of a discriminatory principle, nor did it interfere with the school districts' obligation under state law to take steps to desegregate and their freedom to adopt reassignment and busing plans to effectuate desegregation.

For a further examination of these cases see § 14.9(a)(3)(f), infra.

26. 517 U.S. 620, 116 S.Ct. 1620, 134 L.Ed.2d 855 (1996). *Romer* was decided by a six to three vote. Justices Kennedy wrote the majority opinion; there were no con-

curring opinions. Three Justices dissented in an opinion written by Justices Scalia. 517 U.S. at 635, 116 S.Ct. at 1629 (Scalia, J., joined by Rehnquist, C.J., and Thomas, J., dissenting).

27. Professor Black's article is discussed in note 24, and accompanying text, supra. The Court in *Romer* did not question the continuing validity of Bowers v. Hardwick, 478 U.S. 186, 106 S.Ct. 2841, 92 L.Ed.2d 140 (1986), in which the Supreme Court had upheld a law making certain homosexual conduct criminal. In *Lawrence v. Texas,* ___ U.S. ___, 123 S.Ct. 2472, 156 L.Ed.2d 508 (2003), the Court overruled *Bowers* and invalidated a state law that prohibited sodomy performed between persons of the same sex. The *Lawrence* case is examined in § 14.28 of this Treatise.

28. 488 U.S. 179, 109 S.Ct. 454, 102 L.Ed.2d 469 (1988).

NCAA was made up of both private and state universities did not result in NCAA rules, or their enforcement by an NCAA committee, having the type of "state action" that would subject those rules and enforcement practices to constitutional restraints under the Fourteenth Amendment.

The Court has often found that when a private person engages in a conspiracy with government actors to deprive a person of federal rights that the conspiracy (and actions taken pursuant to it) involve state action by the government official and the private persons in the conspiracy.[29] However, in *Tarkanian* there was no conspiracy or agreement between the NCAA and the state university to deprive the coach of any federal right or take any action against him. The majority opinion noted that UNLV had supported the coach's position regarding his innocence and the unfairness of punishing him for what UNLV administrators believed were only alleged, but not proven, violations of NCAA regulations. UNLV had not delegated any power to the NCAA; UNLV was free to accept the coach's assertion of his innocence and refuse to take disciplinary action against him. The reason that UNLV chose to take actions against the coach was its desire to avoid having sanctions imposed upon it in its NCAA activities and its decision not to withdraw from the NCAA.

Even the Justices in the dissent found that there would be no state action in the decision of the NCAA to punish UNLV if the school chose not to discipline the coach, even if the NCAA action involved expelling UNLV from the Association.[30] The cost to the university from NCAA disciplinary actions, or withdrawal from the NCAA, might be very significant, due to the fact that it is difficult to operate a money making intercollegiate sports program if a school is not a part of the NCAA. Assuming that the NCAA is a "private monopolist", its actions regarding the university and the coach could not be properly termed "state action", because the actions of the association were not "fairly attributable to the state".[31] The coach would be free to argue to the university, or to any court that reviewed university disciplinary actions taken against him. If the university decided not to fire the coach, he would suffer no harm, even though the university might suffer significant harm due to the penalties placed upon it by the private association.[32]

29. See, e.g., Dennis v. Sparks, 449 U.S. 24, 101 S.Ct. 183, 66 L.Ed.2d 185 (1980); Tower v. Glover, 467 U.S. 914, 104 S.Ct. 2820, 81 L.Ed.2d 758 (1984). See also, Screws v. United States, 325 U.S. 91, 65 S.Ct. 1031, 89 L.Ed. 1495 (1945).

In Soldal v. Cook County, 506 U.S. 56, 60 n. 6, 113 S.Ct. 538, 543 n. 6, 121 L.Ed.2d 450 (1992) the Justices found that there was state action involved in the seizure of a debtor's mobile home when owner-manager of a mobile home park removed the debtor's mobile home from its foundation in the park and towed it out of the park. The deputy sheriffs assisted the owner by protecting the owner's employees as they removed the trailer from the park even though the deputy sheriffs knew the owner had not secured a lawful eviction order against the mobile home owner. The Court of Appeals in *Soldal* found that the actions of the deputy sheriffs and owner established a sufficient conspiracy to give rise to state action; the Supreme Court's opinion stated that the Justices were "not inclined to review that holding."

30. The four dissenting Justices believed that the decision of the university to suspend the coach, pursuant to its decision to follow the ruling of the NCAA, created the type of agreement that involves "state action" so that the rules and procedures used by the NCAA, as well as the state university, should comply with due process principles. However, these Justices found that "had UNLV refused to suspend Tarkanian, and the NCAA responded by imposing sanctions against UNLV, it would be hard indeed to find

any state action that harmed Tarkanian." National Collegiate Athletic Association v. Tarkanian, 488 U.S. 179, 199, 203, 109 S.Ct. 454, 466, 468, 102 L.Ed.2d 469 (1988) (White, J. dissenting, joined by Brennan, Marshall, and O'Connor, JJ.).

31. National Collegiate Athletic Association v. Tarkanian, 488 U.S. 179, 198, 109 S.Ct. 454, 465, 102 L.Ed.2d 469 (1988). "Even if we assumed that a private monopolist can impose its will on a state agency by a threatened refusal to deal with it, it does not follow that such a private party is acting under color of state law." 488 U.S. at 198–199, 109 S.Ct. at 465. "In the final analysis the question is whether 'the conduct allegedly causing the deprivation of a federal right [can] be fairly attributable to the state.'" 488 U.S. at 199, 109 S.Ct. at 465, quoting Lugar v. Edmondson Oil Co., 457 U.S. 922, 937, 102 S.Ct. 2744, 2753, 73 L.Ed.2d 482 (1982).

32. The majority opinion in National Collegiate Athletic Association v. Tarkanian noted that an athletic association that made rules that controlled the actions of government-operated schools probably would be held to involve state action "if the membership [of the association] consisted entirely of institutions located within the same state, many of them public institutions created by the same sovereign." 488 U.S. at 193 n. 13, 109 S.Ct. at 462 n. 13. In such a situation the association would have effectively taken the place of a state board of education or a state entity regulating the schools within the state; the

In *Brentwood Academy v. Tennessee Secondary School*[33] the Court followed *dicta* in the *Tarkanian* case[34] and ruled that an association, comprised of both public school and private school members, that governed high school athletics in a state had state action for the purposes of the Fourteenth Amendment and litigation under § 42 U.S.C.A. § 1983.

The *Brentwood Academy* case concerned the Tennessee Secondary School Athletic Association, which had incorporated under state law. The Association's members consisted of virtually all of the state's public high schools (approximately 290 state members) and 55 private schools. The employees of the Association were not employees of the state; the employees of the Association received their pay from the dues payed the association and money generated by association events. Nevertheless, the employees of the Association were part of the state government retirement system. Justice Souter wrote the majority opinion in *Brentwood Academy*; he noted that the public schools were represented in Association activities by public school employees who were acting within the scope of their duties. Between 1972 and 1996, the State Board of Education had a rule that expressly designated the Association as the supervisor of the junior and senior public high schools in the State of Tennessee. After 1996 the Board of Education changed its rules so as to simply "recognize" the value of intercollegiate athletics and the Association to member schools.

In 1997, a private academy that was a member of the Association was declared ineligible to compete in sports playoffs, placed on probation, and subject to a fine, because the Association Board found that the private academy had improperly sent recruiting materials to prospective student athletes. In *Brentwood Academy*, by a 5 to 4 vote of the Justices, the court ruled "that the Association's regulatory activity may and should be treated as state action owing to the pervasive entwinement of state school officials and the structure of the association...."[35] The majority opinion did not rule that the operation of the school athletic contests was a public function; Justice Souter noted that the state government itself had not encouraged or ordered the athletic association to punish the private school.[36] Because the case involved neither a public function nor a state commandment, Justice Souter stated: "State action may only be found if, though only if, there is such a close nexus between the state and the challenged action that seemingly private behavior may be fairly treated as that of the state itself."[37]

The majority in *Brentwood Academy* distinguished the *Tarkanian* case on the basis that the National Collegiate Athletic Association policies and rulings were not based on the action of a single state entity. The NCAA consisted of hundreds of member institutions, most of whom had no connection with the State of Nevada (which was going to discipline Coach Tarkanian because of NCAA sanctions). Justice Souter stated: "Since it was difficult to see the NCAA, not as a collective membership, but as surrogate for one State, we held the organizations' connection with Nevada too insubstantial to ground a state action claim."[38] In the *Brentwood Academy* case, however, the actions of the nominally private athletic association were intertwined in many ways with the state government.

Justice Thomas wrote a dissent in the *Brentwood Academy* case that was joined by Chief Justice Rehnquist and Justices Scalia and

---

delegation of that authority by a state government to control schools within it should constitute state action, even though the association of schools on a national level, an association who has a majority of private universities as its members, did not involve either a delegation of authority from a state government or a conspiracy between a state university and the National Association.

33. 531 U.S. 288, 121 S.Ct. 924, 148 L.Ed.2d 807 (2001).

34. The majority in *Brentwood Academy* referred to the portion of the *Tarkanian* decision that appears in note 29 supra.

35. Brentwood Academy v. Tennessee Secondary School Athletic Association, 531 U.S. 288, 289, 121 S.Ct. 924, 927, 148 L.Ed.2d 807 (2001).

36. 531 U.S. at 302, 121 S.Ct. at 934.

37. 531 U.S. at 295, 121 S.Ct. at 930.

38. 531 U.S. at 296, 121 S.Ct. at 931 (internal quotation marks and citations omitted).

Kennedy.[39] Justice Thomas stated: "We have never found state action based upon mere 'entwinement'. Until today, we have found a private organization's acts to constitute state action only when the organization performed a public function; was created, coerced, or encouraged by the government; or acted in a symbiotic relationship with the government." The dissent may have been correct in finding that prior cases had not used the word "entwinement." Nevertheless, the *Brentwood Academy* ruling seems to reflect whether many earlier state action cases in which the Supreme Court made a determination if a private organization was a state actor based upon the Justice's view of multiple contacts or symbiotic relationships.

The government is not under a constitutional duty to protect an individual from harm caused to him by other private individuals. However, in some circumstances the government's failure to protect an individual from private harm may result in an injury to the individual that is attributable to the state and that involves a substantive violation of a constitutional guarantee. In *DeShaney v. Winnebago County Department of Social Services* [40] the Supreme Court ruled that a governmental entity did not deny a child due process when its social workers failed to protect the child

from being abused by his father. The social worker had been assigned to work with the father and child, following indications that the child was being abused; the social worker noted evidence which provided her with a reasonable basis for concluding the child was being abused by the father. The Court found that the due process clause did not create for the child a substantive right to protection from harm caused to him by private individuals. However, the Supreme Court noted that when an individual was taken into the custody of the government the due process clause required the government to assume responsibility for the individual's safety.[41] Even if an individual was not taken into custody, a state would violate equal protection if it were to "selectively deny its services to certain disfavored minorities." [42]

DeShaney did not disturb previous rulings regarding the existence of state action in conspiracies between private and public actors to harm an individual.[43] For example, if a police officer were to release a prisoner from jail at a time and under circumstances that would allow private persons to harm the prisoner, the injuries caused to the prisoner would involve violations of due process and equal protection.[44] The conspiracy between the police offi-

39. Brentwood Academy v. Tennessee Secondary School Athletic Association, 531 U.S. 288, 304, 121 S.Ct. 924, 935, 148 L.Ed.2d 807 (2001) (Thomas, J., joined by Rehnquist, C.J., and Scalia and Kennedy, JJ., dissenting).

40. 489 U.S. 189, 109 S.Ct. 998, 103 L.Ed.2d 249 (1989).

41. See, e.g., Youngberg v. Romeo, 457 U.S. 307, 102 S.Ct. 2452, 73 L.Ed.2d 28 (1982) (due process requires the government to provide involuntarily committed mental patients with services necessary to protect their safety). The Eighth Amendment prohibition against cruel and unusual punishment also imposes duties on estate to protect the safety of persons whom it incarcerates. See, e.g., Estelle v. Gamble, 429 U.S. 97, 97 S.Ct. 285, 50 L.Ed.2d 251 (1976). In *DeShaney* there was no claim that the injured child had been taken into the custody or control of the state; the Court did not find it necessary to determine whether a child who had been placed in a foster home, and who was injured by the persons who had been designated as foster parents, would have a substantive claim to protection from harm under the due process clause. DeShaney v. Winnebago County Department of Social Services, 489 U.S. 189, 201 n. 9, 109 S.Ct. 998, 1006 n. 9, 103 L.Ed.2d 249 (1989). In Sacramento v. Lewis, 523 U.S. 833, 118 S.Ct. 1708, 140 L.Ed.2d 1043 (1998) the Supreme Court held that substantive due process principle estab-

lished a "shock the conscience" standard for determining whether an executive action that caused incidental, but unintended, harm to individuals was unconstitutional. Justices Souter's majority opinion in *Lewis* referred to the *DeShaney* decision for the principle that the government had a duty to protect safety and well-being of persons who were taken under its custody. The *Lewis* case is discussed in § 14.6 of this Treatise.

42. DeShaney v. Winnebago County Department of Social Services, 489 U.S. 189, 197 n. 3, 109 S.Ct. 998, 1004 n. 3, 103 L.Ed.2d 249 (1989).

43. Dennis v. Sparks, 449 U.S. 24, 101 S.Ct. 183, 66 L.Ed.2d 185 (1980); Tower v. Glover, 467 U.S. 914, 104 S.Ct. 2820, 81 L.Ed.2d 758 (1984).

44. Although the police officer in the example might be acting outside the scope of his official authority and duties, the exercise of de facto authority by the police officer should result in a finding that his activities involve state action. Screws v. United States, 325 U.S. 91, 65 S.Ct. 1031, 89 L.Ed. 1495 (1945) (applying statute that used the phrase "under color of any law" to similar actions). The conspiracy will involve a finding of state action on the part of the private persons who joined the conspiracy with the government actor even if the government actor has some immunity from liability. See, Dennis

cer and private individuals would involve an injury to the prisoner that was attributable to governmental action; the conspiracy would then involve state action on the part of both the private persons and the government member of the conspiracy. However, in *DeShaney*, as in *Tarkanian*, there was no conspiracy between government and private actors to cause harm to an individual.

If a government actor and a private person joined together to accomplish some specific goal, the private person, like the government actor, will be subject to constitutional limitations. However, the mere fact that a government agency and a private person can be seen as "joint participants" in an activity will not, in itself, be enough to subject the private person to constitutional limitations. Thus, the Supreme Court has ruled that the decisions of a government employed public defender, when representing an individual accused of a crime, did not involve state action that would subject the public defender's decisions to due process limitations.[45] Similarly, the Court held that the decision of a private insurance company to withhold payment to an injured worker did not involve state action that would make the decision of the private insurance company subject to due process limitations.[46] The fact that the public defender and the government, or the private insurance company and the government, could be described as being "joint participants" did not give rise to a finding of state action, because government actors did not conspire with the public defender or the insurance companies to cause harm to individuals in these cases.[47]

(c) Government Subsidies or Aid

The final set of joint contact cases involves public funding or other direct aid to persons who are alleged to violate the Constitution. In these cases the government is giving direct aid to a person whose activities would be held to violate the Constitution if they were engaged in by the government itself.

Two separate questions arise in such cases. First, does the granting of aid to a private party subject that person's activities to constitutional review? Second, even if the private activities are not subject to constitutional limitation, may the government continue to grant the private wrongdoer a subsidy?

For example, assume that an otherwise private school which discriminated on the basis of race receives a $5,000 yearly grant from the state. If a black student sues to gain admission to the school does the financial support by the state establish his right to entry under the Fourteenth Amendment? If the court finds that there is insufficient state action present in the school's activities to subject it to constitutional restraint, may the state continue to give that school cash subsidies? It should be noted that there is nothing that requires that these two questions be answered in the same manner, because the second question involves a government program rather than a limitation on the actions of private persons.

When the government provides some direct, specialized subsidy to an entity which impairs fundamental constitutional rights there can be no question but that the government aid program violates the Constitution. Regardless of whether the private party has a right to act free of constitutional restraints, it is clear that the government has no authority to provide specialized benefits to those who effectively burden the exercise of constitutional rights.

For example, the Supreme Court held that private clubs such as the Moose Lodge have a right—unless there is a law to the contrary—to exist as racially restrictive, private voluntary associations.[48] However, both before and

---

v. Sparks, 449 U.S. 24, 101 S.Ct. 183, 66 L.Ed.2d 185 (1980).

45. Polk County v. Dodson, 454 U.S. 312, 102 S.Ct. 445, 70 L.Ed.2d 509 (1981).

46. American Manufacturers Mutual Insurance Co. v. Sullivan, 526 U.S. 40, 119 S.Ct. 977, 143 L.Ed.2d 130 (1999).

47. See notes 39, 40. The Supreme Court in the *Polk County* and *American Manufacturers Mutual Insurance* cases found that neither the public defender nor the insurance company making workers compensation payments was exercising a traditional public function. See § 12.3 regarding public function analysis.

48. Moose Lodge Number 107 v. Irvis, 407 U.S. 163, 92 S.Ct. 1965, 32 L.Ed.2d 627 (1972).

after that decision, lower federal courts held that such clubs could not receive *specialized* tax exemptions which were the equivalent of a cash subsidy.[49] These clubs still can benefit from *generalized* government services such as police and fire protection or general tax exemptions. Regardless of their racially discriminatory acts they have a right to exist in the same manner as any other person or association—that is, such generalized government services do not constitute prohibited state action. However, they are not able to receive any specialized benefits as that would be the equivalent of government support for their racially restrictive practices.

The central question in determining the permissibility of state subsidies to those whose actions impair constitutionally recognized rights is whether the aid amounts to something more than generalized services. There is no quantitative test by which this can be determined and it is clear that qualitative factors must be taken into account. When the aid is provided to only a limited group, rather than all members of the public, it can be viewed as the equivalent of a direct subsidy to the alleged wrongdoer and the challenged practices. If the aid constitutes a subsidy to the wrongdoer then it will have to be terminated, for the government cannot aid a practice which would be in violation of the Constitution if undertaken directly by the government.

In assessing the quantity of aid and whether it provides support for the challenged activity it is clear that the Court will consider both the worth of the subsidized activity and the harm to constitutionally recognized rights. Thus, *Norwood v. Harrison*[50] invalidated the grant-

ing of books to students who attended racially discriminatory schools under a state law which provided free books to all students. The state aid was invalid even though the Court had previously upheld the granting of textbooks to children who attended religious schools under an identical statute.[51] While the form of state aid to each set of schools was identical, the Court found that the practice constituted an unconstitutional subsidy only insofar as it aided the racially restricted schools. While the sectarian schools represented the constitutionally recognized values of both free association and the free exercise of religion, the segregated schools represented no significant interest which could be accorded affirmative constitutional protection so as to sanction a disregard of the value of racial equality.[52]

Similarly, in *Gilmore v. City of Montgomery*,[53] the Supreme Court has held that a city could not grant exclusive use of public facilities to racially segregated groups even on a temporary basis because that would constitute a subsidy to the racially discriminatory practices. The Court did note that members of racially discriminatory groups might be allowed to use the public facilities along with others as this would constitute the provision of generalized public services rather than a subsidy to them.

The Supreme Court decisions in *Norwood*[54] and *Gilmore*[55] and the lower federal courts' decisions regarding the tax exempt status of racially discriminatory schools and fraternal organizations[56] make it appear as if the government may be prohibited from giving any special aid—such as exclusive use of public facilities or tax exempt status—to organiza-

---

49. See Pitts v. Department of Revenue, 333 F.Supp. 662 (E.D.Wis.1971) (three-judge district court); McGlotten v. Connally, 338 F.Supp. 448 (D.D.C.1972) (three-judge district court, opinion by Judge Bazelon); Falkenstein v. Department of Revenue, 350 F.Supp. 887 (D.Or.1972) (three-judge district court), appeal dismissed 409 U.S. 1099, 93 S.Ct. 907, 34 L.Ed.2d 681 (1973). Both decisions in *Falkenstein* came after the *Moose Lodge* decision.

50. 413 U.S. 455, 93 S.Ct. 2804, 37 L.Ed.2d 723 (1973).

51. Board of Education v. Allen, 392 U.S. 236, 88 S.Ct. 1923, 20 L.Ed.2d 1060 (1968).

52. Norwood v. Harrison, 413 U.S. at 467, 93 S.Ct. at 2811–12.

53. 417 U.S. 556, 94 S.Ct. 2416, 41 L.Ed.2d 304 (1974).

54. Norwood v. Harrison, 413 U.S. 455, 93 S.Ct. 2804, 37 L.Ed.2d 723 (1973).

55. Gilmore v. City of Montgomery, 417 U.S. 556, 94 S.Ct. 2416, 41 L.Ed.2d 304 (1974).

56. See Pitts v. Department of Revenue, 333 F.Supp. 662 (E.D.Wis.1971) (three-judge district court); McGlotten v. Connally, 338 F.Supp. 448 (D.D.C.1972) (three-judge district court, opinion by Judge Bazelon); Falkenstein v. Department of Revenue, 350 F.Supp. 887 (D.Or.1972) (three-judge district court), appeal dismissed 409 U.S. 1099, 93 S.Ct. 907, 34 L.Ed.2d 681 (1973). Both decisions in *Falkenstein* came after the *Moose Lodge* decision.

tions that discriminate on the basis of race. However, the Supreme Court avoided ruling on this specific issue in *Bob Jones University v. United States.*[57] In that case, the Court upheld the power of the Internal Revenue Service to deny tax exempt status to schools, including religious schools, which discriminated on the basis of race. Because the IRS had chosen to deny such schools an exemption, the Court did not have to rule on whether such an exemption would violate the equal protection guarantee of the Fifth Amendment due process clause.

This analysis brings us to the question of whether state aid to a private individual will subject that individual's actions to constitutional limitations. For example, if the state grants a yearly subsidy to a social club which discriminates on the basis of race, will that require the group to end its racially biased membership policies? The Supreme Court has never examined this question directly, although its opinions indicate that financial aid which is not given as a direct subsidy to the challenged practice will not subject the private practice to constitutional restraint.

For example, in *Jackson v. Metropolitan Edison Co.*[58] the public utility company certainly received some financial benefit from its licensing as the only electric company for the area. However, because this aid was not connected to the company's termination practices, those practices were not subjected to constitutional review. Similarly, the tax exempt status of the Moose Lodge and the granting of a liquor license to it might have resulted in some financial assistance to the club. But, because those forms of aid were not connected to its racially

restricted practices, it was not subjected to constitutional review. However both of those cases made clear that if the government had authorized the challenged practices, either through direct approval of them or granting subsidies for their continuance, then those practices would be subjected to constitutional restraint.

The distinction between authorization of challenged practices through the grant of subsidies for their continuance and government aid which is not a direct subsidy to the challenged practices have provided the basis for other Supreme Court decisions. In *Polk County v. Dodson,*[59] the Court held that a public defender's employment relationship with the state is insufficient to establish that she acts under color of state law when performing a lawyer's traditional functions as counsel to a defendant in a criminal proceeding. The public defender is not subject to administrative direction in performing her duties in the same sense as other state employees; she must exercise independent judgment on behalf of her client. The relationship of the public defender to her client was the same as that of any privately retained counsel and was unchanged by the state's employment of her.[60]

Similarly, in *Rendell–Baker v. Kohn,*[61] where the discharge of certain employees of a privately owned school was alleged to be state action, the Court held that the relationship between a private school and its teachers is not changed because the state pays the tuition of most students. "The school ... is not fundamentally different from many private corporations whose business depends primarily on contracts to build roads, bridges, dams, ships, or subma-

---

57. 461 U.S. 574, 103 S.Ct. 2017, 76 L.Ed.2d 157 (1983).

58. 419 U.S. 345, 95 S.Ct. 449, 42 L.Ed.2d 477 (1974).

59. 454 U.S. 312, 102 S.Ct. 445, 70 L.Ed.2d 509 (1981).

60. Indeed the State was required "to respect the professional independence of the public defender whom it engages." 454 U.S. at 321, 102 S.Ct. at 451 (footnote omitted).

In contrast, if a public defender conspires with public officials to violate the constitutional rights of the public defender's client, the public defender may be found to have acted "under color of" state law and be subject to liability under section 1983 of the Civil Rights Act on the

basis of the conspiracy. Tower v. Glover, 467 U.S. 914, 104 S.Ct. 2820, 81 L.Ed.2d 758 (1984).

If the state employs a physician to provide medical services to prisoners at a state prison hospital, that physician will be acting under color of law within the meaning of federal civil rights statute 42 U.S.C.A. § 1983. Thus, the physician's actions may violate the Eighth Amendment requirement that states provide some adequate medical care to those persons whom the state has incarcerated. See West v. Atkins, 487 U.S. 42, 108 S.Ct. 2250, 101 L.Ed.2d 40 (1988).

61. 457 U.S. 830, 102 S.Ct. 2764, 73 L.Ed.2d 418 (1982).

rines for the government. Acts of such private contractors do not become acts of the government by reason of their significant or even total engagement in performing public contracts."[62] Because the school's employment practices were not influenced by state regulation, or the government funding programs, the discharge of the teachers did not involve state action.

In other words, the current Justices do not believe that constitutional principles limit the autonomy of private persons or corporations simply because there is receipt of government funds. Further involvement between the private actor and government must be shown before these Justices will employ the Constitution to limit the decisions or actions of private entities. Thus, in *Blum v. Yaretsky* [63] the Court found that due process principles did not restrict a nursing home's freedom to discharge or transfer patients even though the home and patients received substantial government funding.[64]

It is possible that the most difficult state action issues concerning the granting of subsidies will not be resolved by the Supreme Court for two reasons. First, the most significant forms of aid to such institutions could be prohibited even though the actions of the private entities might not be subject to review.[65] This prohibition would have the effect of causing many of these private actors to change their practices so that they might continue to re-ceive specialized government subsidies. Second, the Supreme Court's interpretation of Section 1981 of the Civil Rights Act[66] makes it illegal for private schools and many other private businesses to discriminate between their students or customers on the basis of race.[67] Because the most significant problems are connected to racially discriminatory practices of private groups, this statutory interpretation may eliminate the need to address these state action issues. Section 1981 might force all "public" groups to refrain from discrimination on the basis of race and the Court may not have to confront the more difficult Fourteenth Amendment state action problems.

(d) The School Desegregation and Interdistrict Relief Cases

To date, the Supreme Court has found that only *de jure* segregation in public schools violates the Fourteenth Amendment.[68] While this is not often thought of as a state action determination, the *de facto-de jure* distinction presents a state action decision in pristine form. The Court has held that certain acts of commission by public officials are an indispensible prerequisite to finding that patterns of segregated attendance constitute a prohibited racial classification. The Court has simply made a decision that there is no state action connected to the racial separation which justifies a judicial change of the school attendance patterns absent positive acts of segregation by the government.

---

62. 457 U.S. at 841, 102 S.Ct. at 2771. The school whose employment practices were challenged in this case specialized in dealing with students who had educational or behavioral problems; public funds received for treating such students accounted for over 90% of the school's funding.

63. 457 U.S. 991, 102 S.Ct. 2777, 73 L.Ed.2d 534 (1982).

64. These patients suffered a diminution in medicaid benefits following discharge or transfer from the private nursing home. The majority opinion indicated that the Justices might have imposed due process restrictions on the discharge or transfer procedures if they had found that legislation commanded or influenced the discharge or transfer decisions. However, the majority found that the reduction in benefits was merely the incidental result of the decision of a private entity; the state's decision to lower patient benefits after discharge from the home was not contested in the case. Blum v. Yaretsky, 457 U.S. 991, 1005–10, 102 S.Ct. 2777, 2786–88, 73 L.Ed.2d 534 (1982).

65. The Supreme Court has held that the Internal Revenue Service was acting within its authority when it denied tax exempt status to schools, including religiously affiliated schools, which discriminated in admissions or educational policy on the basis of race. Bob Jones University v. United States, 461 U.S. 574, 103 S.Ct. 2017, 76 L.Ed.2d 157 (1983). See § 14.9(b), infra.

66. 42 U.S.C.A. § 1981.

67. Runyon v. McCrary, 427 U.S. 160, 96 S.Ct. 2586, 49 L.Ed.2d 415 (1976), appeal after remand 569 F.2d 1294 (4th Cir.1978), certiorari denied 439 U.S. 927, 99 S.Ct. 311, 58 L.Ed.2d 320 (1978). For an examination of the Congressional power to enforce the Civil War Amendments see Chapter 15.

68. See, Pasadena City Bd. of Education v. Spangler, 427 U.S. 424, 96 S.Ct. 2697, 49 L.Ed.2d 599 (1976), Milliken v. Bradley, 418 U.S. 717, 94 S.Ct. 3112, 41 L.Ed.2d 1069 (1974), Keyes v. School District No. 1, 413 U.S. 189, 93 S.Ct. 2686, 37 L.Ed.2d 548 (1973).

Individual Justices have stated that there is a duty for the state to provide integrated schools and that even *de facto* segregation violates the Constitution.[69] But a majority of the Court has so far refused to find that "one race" schools violate the Constitution where that condition did not result from some act of government connected to the educational system. Thus, segregation in city schools which is not traceable to "state action" is not remediable under the Fourteenth Amendment.

The use of a state action analysis in desegregation cases is most striking in those involving what is termed "interdistrict" relief. Although such a "multi-district" or "interdistrict" plan may be necessary to end the segregation of a central district or city, the Supreme Court will only allow such a remedy when the acts of governmental entities in every area subject to the court order have caused the segregated conditions.

Milliken v. Bradley[70] determined that interdistrict relief in the form of student reassignment and busing could not include students from school districts which were not found to have engaged in *de jure* segregation. The holding in *Milliken* was that, in the absence of positive acts designed to cause racial segregation, a school district is immune from interference by federal courts in the name of desegregation.[71] Of course, the state is always involved in segregated school districts, because the drawing of school district lines is subject to the power of the state government,[72] but this involvement is true of every type of *de facto* segregation, for it would always be within a state's prerogative to dismantle school districts within its boundaries and restructure them so as to create a truly integrated school system. Yet the Court has been reluctant to embrace such sweeping power, in part because the Justices have been unwilling to limit the property

and association rights of suburban residents unless their city governments were guilty of some active form of discrimination.

The Court will allow wide remedies to remedy segregation in a district where some government action has caused that condition. For example in *Keyes v. School District No. 1*;[73] the court-ordered, city-wide desegregation was based on the school officials' intentional segregation of one area. The Supreme Court upheld this order even though it placed a burden on residents in those areas previously unaffected by the school official's actions. As all of the areas were part of a single district they could be made to bear the responsibility of those officials who acted for the district.

This view of the school desegregation cases was reinforced by the Court's reasoning in another "interdistrict" relief case. In *Hills v. Gautreaux*[74] the Justices had to decide whether a federal court could order the Department of Housing and Urban Development (HUD) to locate public housing in the metropolitan area around Chicago, Illinois. In previous years the Chicago Housing Authority (CHA) had effectuated racial segregation in Chicago through its low-income housing site selection and tenant assignment practices. In federal court suits against CHA and HUD it was determined that HUD had violated the due process clause of the Fifth Amendment and the Civil Rights Act of 1964 by supporting the CHA practices. However, the district court refused to order HUD to do more than establish a city-wide desegregation plan.

The Seventh Circuit, in an opinion by Justice Tom Clark, held that a metropolitan plan was required to remedy effectively the racially discriminatory public housing system within the city.[75] His opinion found that in *Milliken*

---

69. See Keyes v. School District No. 1, 413 U.S. 189, 214, 93 S.Ct. 2686, 2700, 37 L.Ed.2d 548 (1973). (Opinion of Douglas, J.); 413 U.S. at 217, 93 S.Ct. at 2701 (Powell, J., concurring and dissenting); see also, Milliken v. Bradley, 418 U.S. 717, 793, 94 S.Ct. 3112, 3150–51, 41 L.Ed.2d 1069 (1974) (Marshall, J., dissenting).

70. 418 U.S. 717, 94 S.Ct. 3112, 41 L.Ed.2d 1069 (1974).

71. 418 U.S. at 718–20, 94 S.Ct. at 3114–15.

72. 418 U.S. at 793–807, 94 S.Ct. at 3150–58. (Marshall, J., dissenting).

73. 413 U.S. 189, 93 S.Ct. 2686, 37 L.Ed.2d 548 (1973).

74. 425 U.S. 284, 96 S.Ct. 1538, 47 L.Ed.2d 792 (1976).

75. Gautreaux v. Chicago Housing Authority, 503 F.2d 930, 936–939 (7th Cir.1974), affirmed sub nom. Hills v. Gautreaux, 425 U.S. 284, 96 S.Ct. 1538, 47 L.Ed.2d 792 (1976).

the Supreme Court had balanced the competing interests and had concluded that for equitable reasons the federal courts should not abridge political subdivisions in school desegregation suits. Clark reasoned that there was no equitable barrier to an interdistrict remedy since the interest of suburban residents in living in an area without public housing was less important than the interest in the educational experience of their children.

The Supreme Court affirmed this decision while rejecting its reasoning. In an opinion by Justice Stewart, the majority stated that *Milliken* imposed a basic limitation on the equity power of federal courts based on the concept that court-ordered remedies must be "commensurate with the constitutional violation to be repaired."[76] Of course, this argument in substance (if not form) does no more than reaffirm the *de facto-de jure* distinction as a state action problem. Thus, Stewart found that an interdistrict remedy could be ordered in this case since HUD had authority to act throughout the metropolitan area. He neglected to mention that, since HUD would be involved in all housing suits, in substance the Seventh Circuit was correct in finding *Milliken* inapplicable to such cases.

Perhaps realizing that the Supreme Court's formulation was a purely formal change in Justice Clark's reasoning, Justice Stewart characterized the decision on how far a court could go in ordering HUD to disregard local and suburban government as a "more substantial question."[77] Actually, it was the only question. Despite the federal action-commensurate remedy rhetoric, the case came down to

a question of how great a burden can be placed on a community which has not been directly implicated in a constitutional violation. The Court decided that HUD could operate under its statutory authority to place low income housing in suburban areas as long as the actual program did not undercut "the role of those governments in the federal housing assistance scheme."[78] A court order could place public housing in the suburbs as long as it did not violate the legitimate local interests in land use and city planning. The Court could claim a formal distinction between *Milliken* and *Gautreaux*, in that the former case required more direct action on local government units. However, it appears that the Court realized that in housing actions the rights of suburban property owners can be adequately protected without totally eliminating interdistrict remedies for violations of the rights of minority citizens in a large city. In school desegregation cases the interests of the suburban children and their parents will outweigh the need to fully integrate city schools.[79]

The 1995 ruling of the Supreme Court in *Missouri v. Jenkins*,[80] appears to confirm the foregoing analysis of *Milliken* and *Gautreaux*. The *Jenkins* litigation, which spanned almost 20 years, involved the desegregation of the Kansas City, Missouri School District. In the 1995 *Jenkins* decision, the Supreme Court reviewed two District Court orders. The first order required the state to fund salary increases for most of the staff of the Kansas City School District. The second order required the government to fund remedial "quality education" programs on a continuing basis. The Supreme Court, in an opinion by Chief Jus-

---

76. 425 U.S. at 294, 96 S.Ct. at 1545. This principle has been applied to single district cases as well; student transfer orders must be tailored to remedy the de jure segregation without undue burdens on students in the district. Dayton Bd. of Education v. Brinkman, 433 U.S. 406, 97 S.Ct. 2766, 53 L.Ed.2d 851 (1977).

77. 425 U.S. at 300, 96 S.Ct. at 1547.

78. 425 U.S. at 303, 96 S.Ct. at 1549.

79. For an examination of permissible judicial remedies for racially segregated school systems and state limitations on state remedies for de facto segregation in school systems, see § 14.9.

80. 515 U.S. 70, 115 S.Ct. 2038, 132 L.Ed.2d 63 (1995). Chief Justices Rehnquist wrote a majority opinion for Justices Scalia, O'Connor, Kennedy, and Thomas. Justices

Stevens, Souter, Ginsburg, and Breyer dissented. Justices O'Connor and Justices Thomas both joined the majority opinion and filed concurring opinions. 515 U.S. at 103, 115 S.Ct. at 2056 (O'Connor, J., concurring); 515 U.S. at 112, 115 S.Ct. at 2061 (Thomas, J., concurring). The four dissenting Justices believed that the Court had decided the interdistrict remedy question unnecessarily, because that question had not been clearly presented in the petition for certiorari and had not been fully briefed. The dissenters also believed that the ruling in the current *Jenkins* case was inconsistent with the Court's prior decisions concerning single-district and interdistrict remedies. 515 U.S. at 136, 115 S.Ct. at 2073 (Souter, J., joined by Stevens, Ginsburg, and Breyer, JJ., dissenting); 515 U.S. at 176, 115 S.Ct. at 2091 (Ginsburg, J., dissenting).

tices Rehnquist, overturned both of these District Court orders on the basis that the orders were not designed to cure de jure segregation within the Kansas City School District. Rather, each of the two orders constituted a type of multi-district remedy in that the orders were designed to make the Kansas City schools more attractive to majority race students from other school districts.

The majority opinion in *Jenkins* reaffirmed the power of the District Court to fashion

remedies that would effectively desegregate a school district that had been guilty of de jure segregation. However, the District Court was not authorized to create remedies that went beyond the scope of the intra-district violation identified in the litigation. The goal of integrating the city schools could not justify court orders that were aimed at influencing decisions of school children and parents outside of the school district that had been guilty of de jure segregation.[81]

81. Further analysis of the authority of federal courts to issue orders to implement desegregation rulings is contained in § 14.9 of this Treatise.

Chapter 13

PROCEDURAL DUE PROCESS—THE REQUIREMENT OF FAIR ADJUDICATIVE PROCEDURES

§ 13.1 Introduction

Both the Fifth and Fourteenth Amendments prohibit governmental actions which would deprive "any person of life, liberty or property without due process of law."[1] But due process has several quite distinct meanings.[2] As we have seen in Chapter Eleven, due process restricts the ways in which legislatures may limit individual freedom. This "substantive" due process may protect certain fundamental rights or void arbitrary limitations of individual freedom of action. Part of the substantive impact of the due process clause of the Fourteenth Amendment is the "incorporation" of certain guarantees in the Bill of Rights. Thus state legislatures cannot pass legislation which denies freedom of speech, for to do so would violate due process in that the liberty it protects includes the freedom of speech guaranteed by the First Amendment.

The due process clauses also have a procedural aspect in that they guarantee that each person shall be accorded a certain "process" if they are deprived of life, liberty, or property. When the power of the government is to be used against an individual, there is a right to a fair procedure to determine the basis for, and legality of, such action. But there is no general requirement that the government institute a procedure prior to taking acts which are unfavorable to some individuals. It is only when someone's "life, liberty or property" is to be impaired that the government owes him some type of process for the consideration of his interests. Today these concepts are being defined so as to exclude a variety of personal interests from their scope and protection even though earlier cases had recognized the phrase as virtually all-encompassing.

If life, liberty or property is at stake, the individual has a right to a fair procedure. The question then focuses on the nature of the "process" that is "due." In all instances the state must adhere to previously declared rules for adjudicating the claim or at least not deviate from them in a manner which is unfair to the individual against whom the action is to be taken. The government always has the obligation of providing a neutral decisionmaker—one who is not inherently biased against the

---

§ 13.1

1. "[N]or shall any person ... be deprived of life, liberty or property, without due process of law; U.S.Const. amend. V.

"[N]or shall any State deprive any person of life, liberty, or property without due process of law;" U.S.Const. amend. XIV.

2. See generally, Shattuck, The True Meaning of the Term "Liberty" in Those Clauses in the Federal and State

Constitutions Which Protect "Life, Liberty and Property," 4 Harv.L.Rev. 365 (1891); Smolla, The Re-emergence of the Right–Privilege Distinction in Constitutional Law: The Price of Protesting Too Much, 35 Stanford L.Rev. 69 (1982). For citations to additional secondary authorities, see R. Rotunda & J. Nowak, Treatise on Constitutional Law: Substance and Procedure, Chapter 17 (3rd ed. 1999, with annual supplements).

individual or who has personal interest in the outcome.

In instances where the person is to be deprived of his physical liberty for a substantial period of time, a trial is required. The criminal trial process must include all the safeguards of the Bill of Rights[3] as well as being a fair adjudicatory process. When the individual is to be penalized for some infraction of civil law through a judicial action, there is also the requirement that the trial process be a fair one although the Seventh Amendment's guarantee of a jury trial applies only to federal actions.[4] In a number of other circumstances the government may impair someone's "life, liberty or property" without a trial-type process. These situations involve the regulation of certain specific activities or the denial of some governmental benefits. There are some very specific rulings on the types of procedures that are necessary for the taking of physical property by creditors, but other required "processes" are decided in terms of what procedures are both necessary and affordable for proper resolution of certain types of claims.

In the first major section of the chapter we will examine what interests the Supreme Court has held to come within the scope of the terms "life," "liberty" or "property", for no process is required for government actions which do not deprive an individual of one of these three interests.

In the second major section we will examine the types of procedures which are due an individual when the government takes an action which deprives him of one of these interests.

§ 13.2 Deprivations of "Life, Liberty or Property" for Which Some Process Is Due

The due process clauses apply only if a government action will constitute the impairment of some individual's life, liberty, or property. Where government actions adversely affect an individual but do not constitute a denial of that individual's life, liberty or property, the government does not have to give the person any hearing or process whatsoever. One might assume (incorrectly as it turns out) that the phrase "life, liberty or property" was to include all aspects of an individual's life in society,[1] but the Supreme Court has given the phrase a more restrictive meaning. Since 1972, the Court has continually held that the government need not give someone a procedure to determine the fairness of how it has treated that individual unless its actions fall within distinct rulings as to the meaning of "life," "liberty," and "property."[2]

Erosion of the "Right–Privilege" Distinction. Earlier in the century there was a distinction in constitutional law between "rights" and "privileges." The government could not deny someone a "right" except for specific reasons which complied with constitutional standards. However an individual could be denied a "privilege" by the government for any reason and with no constitutional restrictions. For example, when a policeman lost his

---

3. Of the provisions of the Bill of Rights which relate to the investigation and adjudication of criminal charges, only the grand jury clause of the Fifth Amendment is not applicable to the states. Hurtado v. California, 110 U.S. 516, 4 S.Ct. 111, 28 L.Ed. 232 (1884). For an overview of the "incorporation" concept see § 10.2 and §§ 11.5–11.7, supra.

4. The Seventh Amendment has been held not to be applicable to the states. Minneapolis & St. Louis R. Co. v. Bombolis, 241 U.S. 211, 36 S.Ct. 595, 60 L.Ed. 961 (1916).

§ 13.2

1. Such a view would be pursued in a "literalist" position that the three terms are generic descriptions for all individual interests. For example, it is not uncommon for persons to refer to all matter as "animal, vegetable or mineral" with no intent to exclude fish, fruits or alloys. See generally, Hartz, J., quoting Treatise in United States

v. Buck, 281 F.3d 1336, 1345 (10th Cir.2002). Brown, J., citing this section of the Treatise in Frazier v. Garrison I.S.D., 980 F.2d 1514, 1528 (5th Cir.1993); Newblatt, J., citing Treatise in, Hilliard, as Guardian Conservator of Estate of Lee v. Walker's Party Store, Inc., 903 F.Supp. 1162, 1167 (E.D.Mich.1995); Norcott, J., citing Treatise, in State v. Patterson, 236 Conn. 561, 580, 674 A.2d 416, 425 (Conn.1996); Supreme Court of Iowa, citing Treatise in Sear v. Clayton County Zoning Board of Adjustment, 590 N.W.2d 512, 515 (Iowa 1999).

2. The first clear use of this approach was Board of Regents v. Roth, 408 U.S. 564, 92 S.Ct. 2701, 33 L.Ed.2d 548 (1972). For citations to additional Supreme Court cases, and secondary authorities, on this point, see R. Rotunda & J. Nowak, Treatise on Constitutional Law: Substance and Procedure, §§ 17.2, 17.5 (3rd ed. 1999, with annual supplements).

job for engaging in political activities, the Supreme Court of Massachusetts upheld the dismissal. As Justice Oliver Wendell Holmes noted: "The petitioner may have a constitutional right to talk politics, but he has no constitutional right to be a policeman."[3]

This rationale was followed by the Supreme Court in cases that upheld denials of occupational licenses for virtually any reason[4] and the placing of restrictions on who could attend state universities.[5] Because such things were mere "privileges" to which no one was entitled as of right, the state had virtually unlimited discretion in its methods of disbursing such benefits. But this view was at least formally ended as the Justices began to realize that, unless the government were required to accord fair treatment of individual interests that could not be termed "rights," there would be almost no check on the power of government to limit individual freedom in society.

The first significant development which eroded the right-privilege distinction was the concept of "unconstitutional conditions."[6] This doctrine recognizes that a state may not do indirectly what it is forbidden from doing directly. Thus, even "privileges" may not be denied for reasons which violate constitutional guarantees. The state cannot make the gaining or keeping of government benefits conditional upon the recipient's agreement to forego the exercise of constitutional rights. For example, a provision that government-subsidized housing would go only to those who agreed not to speak out against the foreign policy of the federal government would be an "unconstitutional condition"; although there may be no right to housing, the government cannot "buy up" First Amendment freedoms which it could not restrain directly.[7]

The right-privilege distinction was also undermined by substantive due process and equal protection cases that placed limits on the government's ability to arbitrarily restrict freedoms that were not explicit constitutional rights. The rationale for the distinction was laid to rest by Professor William Van Alstyne[8] who showed the "distinction" to be mere tautology—it meant that only rights had to be recognized by the state but rights were what the state had chosen to recognize. This "epigram" solved every problem by allowing the Court total freedom to choose a few rights to defend from some government actions. Clearly there needed to be a more logical rationale for the definition and protection of individual rights and freedom of action.

A basis for a new approach to these problems was offered by Charles Reich in his articles on "The New Property".[9] He noted that highly organized societies in which large numbers of persons were dependent on government "largess" or "privileges" resulted in the suppression of individual liberty. This result could be avoided by recognizing the individual's interest in government benefits as a "right" which could be protectable by procedural and substantive safeguards against arbitrary government action. Professor Reich believed that persons should be recognized as having a right to the forms of government benefits which they received, so as to attach constitutional safeguards to their allocation and termination. Reich used the term "entitlements" to designate these benefits as enforceable rights rather than mere privileges or

3. McAuliffe v. Mayor of New Bedford, 155 Mass. 216, 220, 29 N.E. 517 (1892) (per Holmes).

4. Barsky v. Board of Regents, 347 U.S. 442, 451, 74 S.Ct. 650, 655–56, 98 L.Ed. 829 (1954).

5. Hamilton v. Regents of University of California, 293 U.S. 245, 55 S.Ct. 197, 79 L.Ed. 343 (1934).

6. For the development of this concept, see, Hale, Unconstitutional Conditions and Constitutional Rights, 35 Colum L.Rev. 321 (1935); Note, Unconstitutional Conditions, 73 Harv.L.Rev. 1595 (1960); Sullivan, Unconstitutional Conditions, 102 Harv.L.Rev. 1413 (1989).

7. For citations to additional cases, and secondary authorities, see the multivolume edition of this treatise: R.

Rotunda & J. Nowak, Treatise On Constitutional Law: Substance and Procedure, Chapter 17 (3rd ed. 1999, with annual supplements).

8. Van Alstyne, The Demise of the Right–Privilege Distinction in Constitutional Law, 81 Harv.L.Rev. 1439 (1968).

9. Reich, The New Property, 73 Yale L.J. 733 (1964); Reich, Individual Rights and Social Welfare: The Emerging Legal Issues, 74 Yale L.J. 1245 (1965). It may be of interest to the reader to note Charles Reich's later, somewhat related, work: C. Reich, The Greening of America (1970).

gratitudes which could be denied or withheld as the government chose.[10]

For a short time it appeared as if the Supreme Court was going to truly end the right-privilege distinction and hold the government to certain standards of fairness in allocating public benefits. The Court never created any substantive rights to government subsistence payments, nor did the Justices ever require any general equality of treatment for poor persons, but in decisions on procedural due process, the Supreme Court seemed ready to require fair treatment of a wide variety of individual claims or interests. The Court required the government to grant persons a hearing before terminating such interests as welfare payments[11] or driver's licenses.[12] Thus, it appeared that the due process clause would insure fairness of treatment for all aspects of individual liberty and dispensation of government benefits even though it would not be a check on substantive policy decisions concerning wealth allocations. But this was not to be.

Judicial Definition of "Life, Liberty or Property." Since 1972 a majority of the Justices have chosen to take quite literally, and restrictively, the concept that due process applies only to "life, liberty or property." In recent years the decisions have narrowly construed these terms so that the government may take some actions adversely affecting people without having to give them any procedure to insure a fair treatment of their interests. Thus, as we shall see, the Court has allowed the government to injure someone's reputation or terminate his employment without a hearing since a majority of the Justices did not find "liberty" or "property" present in the facts of those individual cases. The majority has also allowed the states to define the scope of government benefits to which any individual is

"entitled," so that the state can insure that it has not created a property interest in government benefits which would require due process for their termination.

To a significant degree this trend has resurrected the discredited "right-privilege" distinction. While the Court has forsaken those terms, it now requires due process only for certain interests defined as life, liberty or property. The distinction is now between life, recognized liberty interests and property "entitlements" as opposed to unprotected interests or "mere expectations." Unless a government action deprives an individual of one of those interests, the Court will not require any "process" or hearing be given the individual who is adversely affected by the action.

When no life, liberty or property interest is at stake, a state is free to deny privileges to individuals without any hearing and, therefore, on an arbitrary basis. Thus, the Supreme Court summarily held, in a per curiam opinion, that out-of-state lawyers seeking to represent defendants in a state criminal proceeding were not entitled to any hearing as to whether or not they should be allowed to appear *pro hac vice*. In *Leis v. Flynt*,[13] the Court held that a lawyer has neither a liberty nor property interest in being admitted on a case-by-case basis to practice in a state in which he or she is not licensed and that there should be no inquiry into whether or not a state trial judge had been totally arbitrary in refusing to admit the attorneys to practice.

§ 13.3 Life

Definition of "Life". While the Supreme Court has never attempted to define the term "life", it has come very close to doing so in its decisions concerning the prohibition of voluntary abortions. In *Roe v. Wade*[1] the Court held that the term "person" in the Fourteenth

---

10. Reich, supra note 9, 74 Yale at 1256.

11. Goldberg v. Kelly, 397 U.S. 254, 90 S.Ct. 1011, 25 L.Ed.2d 287 (1970). This decision quoted from Charles Reich's article 397 U.S. at 262 n. 8, 90 S.Ct. at 1017 n. 8 quoting 74 Yale at 1255. The Court used the term "statutory entitlement" in the text but in 397 U.S. at 262 n. 8, 90 S.Ct. at 1017 n. 8 it quoted Reich and stated "It may be realistic today to regard welfare entitlements as more like 'property' than a 'gratuity.'"

12. Bell v. Burson, 402 U.S. 535, 91 S.Ct. 1586, 29 L.Ed.2d 90 (1971).

13. 439 U.S. 438, 99 S.Ct. 698, 58 L.Ed.2d 717 (1979).

§ 13.3

1. 410 U.S. 113, 93 S.Ct. 705, 35 L.Ed.2d 147 (1973).

Amendment does not apply to an unborn fetus. This conclusion was based on the majority's view of the use of the word "person" in various places in the Constitution; "in nearly all these instances the use of the word is such that it has application only postnatally."[2] When combined with the history of abortion practices prior to the adoption of the Fourteenth Amendment, this argument lead the Court to conclude that a fetus was not a constitutionally recognized person. Thus a fetus has no constitutional rights prior to birth, although a state may, if it chooses, restrict abortion practices to protect the fetus following its reaching a stage of "viability."[3]

Termination of Life. The Supreme Court has not dealt with the issue of when a person's life ends following a live birth.[4] Given the ability of medical doctors to sustain a person's life for extended periods following what otherwise would be a fatal occurrence of illness or injury, the procedural due process issue would arise if the government were to authorize the removal of life support systems where the patient has not made such a request. Where the patient wishes to have the life support system removed but the state refuses to allow the doctor to do so, there will be an issue concerning the right to freedom of choice or "personal privacy" somewhat related to the right involved in the abortion cases.[5] Where the refusal of medical treatment is based on the

patient's religious beliefs, there are also issues concerning the First Amendment guarantee of free exercise of religion.[6]

Relationship of Death Penalty Cases to Due Process Analysis. Detailed rules of criminal procedure, and the Court's rulings concerning the procedures that must be used for imposition of the death penalty, are beyond the scope of this Treatise. In this section we have cited only a few of the Court's decisions concerning the ability of government to impose the death penalty upon an individual for the commission of certain crimes and some basic restrictions on the processes used for selecting the individuals who will be subjected to the death penalty. Citations to all of the major Supreme Court decisions regarding death penalty procedures are contained in the footnotes in the multivolume edition of this Treatise.[7]

There are many serious legal as well as moral issues concerning when, if ever, the state should be allowed to take someone's life. The Supreme Court has held that the government may impose the death penalty on persons for certain crimes without violating either the due process clauses or the Eighth Amendment prohibition of cruel and unusual punishment.[8] To comport with the due process guarantee, statutory systems must allow for imposition of the death penalty only for the most serious criminal offenses[9] and only

---

2. 410 U.S. at 157, 93 S.Ct. at 729.

3. For an analysis of the issues concerning restrictions on abortions, see § 14.29, infra.

4. In Sacramento v. Lewis, 523 U.S. 833, 118 S.Ct. 1708, 140 L.Ed.2d 1043 (1998) the Justices ruled that a person who was accidentally killed by a police patrol car in a high-speed chase of a motorcycle on which the person had been a passenger did not lose his life in a manner that violated substantive due process principles. The Court in *Lewis* ruled that police actions that caused inadvertent and unintended harm to suspects did not violate due process principles unless the police actions violated a "shock the conscience" test. The *Lewis* decision is discussed in § 10.6 of this Treatise.

5. The question of whether substantive due process principles create a "right to die" is examined in § 14.30(c) of this Treatise.

6. See Chapter 17 on Freedom of Religion.

7. For citations to additional Supreme Court cases, and secondary authorities, on death penalty issues, see R. Rotunda & J. Nowak, Treatise on Constitutional Law:

Substance and Procedure, § 17.3 (3rd ed. 1999, with annual supplements).

8. See generally Maynard v. Cartwright, 486 U.S. 356, 108 S.Ct. 1853, 100 L.Ed.2d 372 (1988). For citations to additional cases, including lower court cases, and secondary works on this topic see our multi-volume Treatise: R. Rotunda & J. Nowak, Treatise on Constitutional Law: Substance and Procedure (3rd ed. 1999, with annual supplements).

9. See, Coker v. Georgia, 433 U.S. 584, 97 S.Ct. 2861, 53 L.Ed.2d 982 (1977) (death penalty may not be imposed for rape conviction because penalty is grossly disproportionate punishment for an offense that does not involve loss of life); Enmund v. Florida, 458 U.S. 782, 102 S.Ct. 3368, 73 L.Ed.2d 1140 (1982), on remand 439 So.2d 1383 (1983), appeal after remand 459 So.2d 1160 (1984), decision quashed 476 So.2d 165 (1985), (death penalty may not be imposed on a defendant convicted of felony murder if the defendant did not himself kill or intend that lethal force be used in the crime). The Court has invalidated a statute which imposed a mandatory death sentence for those who are found guilty of the murder of a police

where there is a fair system for sorting out those convicted criminals who shall die from those who will only be imprisoned.[10] Additionally, the exact procedures for selection of these persons must be such that they are not slanted "in favor" of the death penalty by devices such as exclusion of jurors who might not impose the penalty[11] or the way in which information regarding the propriety of imposing the death penalty is presented.[12]

While criminal procedure is not within the scope of this treatise, we must note the relationship between these decisions and other areas of procedural due process. In recent years the Supreme Court has increasingly recognized the ability of individual states to determine the scope of rights or liberties of people in their jurisdiction. So long as the government does not violate one of a few express or implied "fundamental rights," the Court will not protect the interests of individuals against the state.

Hence, the Court has refused to prohibit the use of the death penalty because a majority of the Justices found no textual basis for such a restriction. Additionally, the Court has required that the states follow only a minimal set of guidelines to establish a fair process and has left them very free to choose the manner of selecting those convicted defendants who shall be killed.[13] As Professor Charles Black has pointed out, the amount of discretionary features of the criminal justice system when combined with elements of pure chance make it impossible to determine whether any system for imposing the death penalty is minimally fair or evenhanded.[14]

But the current Court has not approached issues concerning the fairness of a procedural system through any comprehensive theory of value in individual liberty. Instead a majority of the Justices have looked to whether an individual was being deprived of a specific interest in life, liberty, or property by a process with what they might view as unreasonably few procedural safeguards for these interests. This majority of the Justices is satisfied

---

officer. Roberts v. Louisiana, 431 U.S. 633, 97 S.Ct. 1993, 52 L.Ed.2d 637 (1977).

Tison v. Arizona, 481 U.S. 137, 107 S.Ct. 1676, 95 L.Ed.2d 127 (1987), rehearing denied 482 U.S. 921, 107 S.Ct. 3201, 96 L.Ed.2d 688 (1987) (the Eighth Amendment does not prohibit imposition of the death penalty on a defendant whose participation in a felony resulted in a murder, if the record supports a finding that the defendant had an intention to kill or a mental state of "reckless disregard for human life implicit in knowingly engaging in criminal activities known to carry a grave risk of death").

10. The Constitution does not require that a jury, rather than a judge, impose a death penalty; a judge may sentence a defendant to death. See, Hildwin v. Florida, 490 U.S. 638, 109 S.Ct. 2055, 104 L.Ed.2d 728 (1989); Walton v. Arizona, 497 U.S. 639, 110 S.Ct. 3047, 111 L.Ed.2d 511 (1990); Lewis v. Jeffers, 497 U.S. 764, 110 S.Ct. 3092, 111 L.Ed.2d 606 (1990).

Regardless of whether a judge or jury is the sentencing authority, the sentencing hearing must meet the Eighth and Fourteenth Amendment standards including the requirement that the defendant have opportunity to present all relevant evidence. For citations to additional Supreme Court cases, and secondary authorities, on this point, and other death penalty issues, see R. Rotunda & J. Nowak, Treatise on Constitutional Law: Substance and Procedure, § 17.3 (3rd ed. 1999, with annual supplements).

11. Witherspoon v. Illinois, 391 U.S. 510, 88 S.Ct. 1770, 20 L.Ed.2d 776 (1968), rehearing denied 393 U.S. 898, 89 S.Ct. 67, 21 L.Ed.2d 186 (1968). The state may exclude a juror whose views on capital punishment "would prevent or substantially impair the performance of his

duties as a juror." Adams v. Texas, 448 U.S. 38, 45, 100 S.Ct. 2521, 2526, 65 L.Ed.2d 581 (1980), on remand 624 S.W.2d 568 (Tex.Cr.App.1981); Wainwright v. Witt, 469 U.S. 412, 420, 105 S.Ct. 844, 850, 83 L.Ed.2d 841 (1985). For citations to additional Supreme Court cases, and secondary authorities, on this point, and other death penalty issues, see R. Rotunda & J. Nowak, Treatise on Constitutional Law: Substance and Procedure, vol. 2 § 17.3 (2nd ed. 1992, with annual supplements).

12. See, e.g., Gardner v. Florida, 430 U.S. 349, 97 S.Ct. 1197, 51 L.Ed.2d 393 (1977) (death sentence cannot be based on material in presentence report that was not disclosed to the defendant); Lockett v. Ohio, 438 U.S. 586, 98 S.Ct. 2954, 57 L.Ed.2d 973 (1978) (plurality opinion by Burger, C.J., finding state system for imposing death sentences invalid insofar as it precluded consideration by the sentencing jury or judge of factors which the defendant wished to claim should be considered as mitigating circumstances). For citations to additional Supreme Court cases, and secondary authorities, on this point, and other death penalty issues, see R. Rotunda & J. Nowak, Treatise on Constitutional Law: Substance and Procedure, § 17.3 (3rd ed. 1999, with annual supplements).

13. For citations to Supreme Court cases, and secondary authorities, on this point, and other death penalty issues, see R. Rotunda & J. Nowak, Treatise on Constitutional Law: Substance and Procedure, § 17.3 (3rd ed. 1999, with annual supplements).

14. Black, Due Process for Death: Jurek v. Texas and Companion Cases, 26 Cath.L.Rev. 1 (1976). C. Black, Capital Punishment: The Inevitability of Caprice and Mistake (1974).

that their guidelines for fairness in selection of defendants for the death penalty is all that can be reasonably required of a state.[15] Their position that there is no specific basis for recognizing a wider interest in life thus correlates with the current approach to the due process issues which are examined in this chapter.

The Supreme Court has held that the Eighth Amendment prohibition of cruel and unusual punishment prevents the government from imposing the death penalty upon a prisoner who is presently insane; the government must provide a procedure that is designed to provide a fair hearing on the issue of a prisoner's insanity.[16]

In *Atkins v. Virginia*[17] the Supreme Court, by a 6 to 3 vote of the Justices, ruled that the Eighth Amendment cruel and unusual punishment clause, which applies to the states through the Fourteenth Amendment, prohibits government from imposing a death sentence on a person who is mentally retarded.[18] The *Atkins* decision superceded the Court's earlier

ruling in *Penry v. Lynaugh*[19] in which the Court had refused to prohibit executions of mentally retarded persons, but had required states to allow a defendant to present all mitigating evidence to a sentencing jury including evidence regarding mental capacity. The *Atkins* decision overruled the aspect of *Penry* that had allowed the execution of mentally retarded persons. However, the Court's ruling in *Penry* that a defendant must be allowed to present all information to a jury that might be considered mitigating evidence, including evidence regarding mental capacity and childhood abuse, was not altered by the *Atkins* decision.

The Court has also held that the Eighth and Fourteenth Amendments do not prohibit the imposition of the death penalty on a person who was under 18 years of age at the time that the individual committed the capital offense. The Court has approved the imposition of the death penalty for persons who committed murder at 16 or 17 years of age.[20]

15. **Due Process restrictions on clemency proceedings?** In Ohio Adult Parole Authority v. Woodard, 523 U.S. 272, 118 S.Ct. 1244, 140 L.Ed.2d 387 (1998) the Court rejected the claim of a prison inmate who was awaiting the death sentence that the State's procedure for reviewing his request for clemency from the governor violated due process principles. There was no majority opinion on the due process issue. For citations to additional Supreme Court cases, and secondary authorities, on this point, and other death penalty issues, see R. Rotunda & J. Nowak, Treatise on Constitutional Law: Substance and Procedure, § 17.3 (3rd ed. 1999, with annual supplements).

16. Ford v. Wainwright, 477 U.S. 399, 106 S.Ct. 2595, 91 L.Ed.2d 335 (1986) (majority opinion in part; plurality opinion in part). Due process principles would be violated by criminally prosecuting a defendant who is not mentally competent to stand trial. Drope v. Missouri, 420 U.S. 162, 95 S.Ct. 896, 43 L.Ed.2d 103 (1975). This principle should also prohibit forcing mentally incompetent defendants to participate in the sentencing phase of a prosecution for a capital offense. The state may make use of a presumption of competency, so that the counsel for the defendant will have to show the defendant's incompetency to stand trial. Medina v. California, 505 U.S. 437, 112 S.Ct. 2572, 120 L.Ed.2d 353 (1992), rehearing denied 505 U.S. 1244, 113 S.Ct. 19, 120 L.Ed.2d 946 (1992). For citations to additional cases on this point, see the multivolume edition of this treatise: R. Rotunda & J. Nowak, Treatise On Constitutional Law: Substance and Procedure § 17.3 (3rd ed. 1999, with annual supplements).

17. 536 U.S. 304, 122 S.Ct. 2242, 153 L.Ed.2d 335 (2002).

18. The Court in Atkins did not define mental retardation; the problem of defining mental retardation will be

left in the first instance to state courts as they attempt to apply the ruling of *Atkins*. Atkins v. Virginia, 536 U.S. 304, 317, 122 S.Ct. 2242, 2250, 153 L.Ed.2d 335 (2002). Chief Justice Rehnquist and Justices Scalia and Thomas dissented in Atkins. 536 U.S. at 321, 122 S.Ct. at 2252 (Rehnquist, C.J., and Scalia and Thomas, JJ., dissenting); 536 U.S. at 337, 122 S.Ct. at 2259 (Scalia, J., joined by Rehnquist, C.J., and Thomas, J. dissenting).

19. 492 U.S. 302, 109 S.Ct. 2934, 106 L.Ed.2d 256 (1989).

20. Stanford v. Kentucky, 492 U.S. 361, 109 S.Ct. 2969, 106 L.Ed.2d 306 (1989) (majority opinion in part and plurality opinion in part written by Justice Scalia). In Thompson v. Oklahoma, 487 U.S. 815, 108 S.Ct. 2687, 101 L.Ed.2d 702 (1988) the Supreme Court, without majority opinion, prohibited a state from executing a person who was 15 years old at the time he committed the offense. Justice O'Connor concurred in the judgments in both *Thompson* and *Stanford*.

In Johnson v. Texas, 509 U.S. 350, 113 S.Ct. 2658, 125 L.Ed.2d 290 (1993), rehearing denied 509 U.S. 941, 114 S.Ct. 15, 125 L.Ed.2d 767 (1993) the Court held that a set of instructions and questions presented to the jury in a capital case did not violate the Eighth and Fourteenth Amendments because they allowed the jury to give adequate consideration to the defendant's youth at the time of the murder. The defendant was 19 years old at the time of the murder and his attorneys argued on appeal that the special issue system used for instructing juries in Texas denied the defendant the ability to have the jury consider all aspects of his youth. In light of the facts of the case, the majority in *Johnson* concluded: "We decide that there is no reasonable likelihood that the jury would

§ 13.4 Liberty—Generally

(a) Introduction

One cannot ascribe a specific meaning to the term "liberty" for it may encompass any form of freedom of action or choice which is accorded constitutional recognition by the Court.[1] Indeed, it is the concept of liberty which is the primary limitation on the action of the states as regards individual rights. Liberty under the Fourteenth Amendment includes those provisions of the Bill of Rights which the Court deems to be "incorporated" into the due process clause as well as "fundamental rights" which are derived either from the concept of liberty or other constitutional values.[2] These constitute substantive prohibitions of government actions which would violate those rights.

The concept of liberty in the due process clauses is also the basis for the "substantive due process" requirement that legislation must relate to a legitimate end of government.[3] In their procedural aspect the due process clauses require that no individual be singled out for a deprivation of a constitutional liberty without a fair "process." One can focus on the procedural issue by asking what types of individual freedom of action (liberty) cannot be limited by the government except with a fair procedure to determine the basis for, and legality of, the limitation.

There are two distinct ways in which a person may be deprived of liberty. First, the government might deprive the person of his freedom of action by physically restraining him. Second, the government might limit someone's freedom of choice and action by making it impossible or illegal for that person to engage in certain types of activity. This last category can also be subdivided into two parts. The government might deny a person the ability to exercise a right with special constitutional protection (such as the right to free speech or the right to privacy); this restraint would constitute a clear deprivation of liberty. There are also cases where the government forecloses a form of freedom of action to an individual which does not have special constitutional status (such as the freedom to engage in a particular business activity). Thus we may subdivide "liberty" into three headings involving governmental restraints on (1) physical freedom, (2) the exercise of fundamental constitutional rights, and (3) other forms of freedom of choice or action.

(b) Physical Liberty

The essential guarantee of the due process clauses is that the government may not imprison or otherwise physically restrain a person except in accordance with fair procedures. The first due process clause is a part of the Fifth Amendment, which is primarily concerned with procedures used to convict someone of crime. But the due process guarantee has long been understood to go beyond the criminal justice system; it governs all government deprivations of liberty. Indeed the protection of physical liberty is the oldest and most widely recognized part of the guarantee.[4]

The initial requirement of due process is that there be some fair procedure for deter-

---

have found itself foreclosed from considering the relevant aspect of [the defendant's] youth."

For citations to additional Supreme Court cases, and secondary authorities, on this point, and other death penalty issues, see R. Rotunda & J. Nowak, Treatise on Constitutional Law: Substance and Procedure, § 17.3 (3rd ed. 1999, with annual supplements).

§ 13.4

1. See generally Monaghan, Of "Liberty" and "Property," 62 Cornell L.Rev. 405, 411–16 (1977); Ratner, The Function of the Due Process Clause, 116 U.Pa.L.Rev. 1048 (1968); Kadish, Methodology and Criteria in Due Process Adjudication—A Survey and Criticism, 66 Yale L.J. 319 (1957). For citations to additional secondary authorities, see the multivolume edition of this treatise: R. Rotunda & J. Nowak, Treatise On Constitutional Law: Substance and

Procedure §§ 17.1–17.6 (3rd ed. 1999, with annual supplements).

2. For an outline of the content of these guarantees, see Chapter 14 and §§ 11.5–11.7, supra.

3. The substantive due process restriction is examined in § 11.4, supra. The distinctions between substantive and procedural rulings are examined in §§ 10.6, 10.7, supra.

4. See, Hough, Due Process of Law—To–Day, 32 Harv. L.Rev. 218 (1918); Shattuck, The True Meaning of the Term "Liberty" in Those Clauses In the Federal and State Constitutions which Protect "Life, Liberty or Property," 4 Harv.L.Rev. 365 (1891). The concept can be traced back to chapter twenty-nine of the Magna Carta. See generally, E. Corwin, The "Higher Law" Background of American Constitutional Law 30–33 (1928).

mining whether an individual has lawfully been taken into custody by the government. While an individual may be arrested without prior judicial approval, such an arrest must be based on probable cause for the police to believe that the person has committed a crime.[5] If the arrest was in fact made without a warrant, the law enforcement authorities must make prompt application to a magistrate for a neutral determination that the arrest was made upon probable cause.[6] Custody of the person even then cannot continue except in conformity with the Eighth Amendment's prohibition of excessive bail.[7] The entire process leading towards the trial of a criminal charge must be undertaken in a timely manner in order to comply with the due process and speedy trial guarantees of the Bill of Rights.[8] The adjudicative process itself is governed by the specific guarantees of the Bill of Rights and an independent concept of fundamental fairness which is imposed by the due process clause. The reasonable doubt standard is derived from the due process clauses themselves and is the historical barrier to arbitrary deprivation of freedom in the criminal justice system.[9] The standard requires the government to prove, within a fair procedural framework, that a person is unquestionably guilty of the crime for which he is to be incarcerated. The standard also prohibits the use of any procedure which would shift to the accused the burden of proving his innocence as to any basic element of the criminal charge.[10]

Loss of Liberty Apart from a Criminal Conviction. The due process guarantee also applies to restraints on physical liberty which are imposed in noncriminal settings. While the required procedures may differ depending on the type of action, the government can never impose substantial physical restraints on an individual without establishing a procedure to determine the factual basis and legality of such actions. Thus a child may not be made a ward of the state and subjected to state custody unless the child first receives a fair procedure including a notice of any charges against him and the assistance of counsel.[11] Indeed, when juvenile proceedings are based on charges of alleged criminal activity, those charges must be proven beyond a reasonable doubt.[12]

A significant number of people are also deprived of their freedom of action by being involuntarily committed to state institutions for mental treatment. While the Court has

---

5. This requirement is part of the Fourth Amendment regulation of searches and seizures; it is incorporated into the term liberty and applied to the states through the due process clause of the Fourteenth Amendment. Mapp v. Ohio, 367 U.S. 643, 81 S.Ct. 1684, 6 L.Ed.2d 1081 (1961), rehearing denied 368 U.S. 871, 82 S.Ct. 23, 7 L.Ed.2d 72 (1961).

Interstate Extradition. Interstate extradition proceedings are governed by Article IV, § 2 of the Constitution. For citations to cases and statutes interpreting or implementing the interstate extradition clause, see R. Rotunda & J. Nowak, Treatise on Constitutional Law: Substance and Procedure, § 17.4 (3rd ed. 1999, with annual supplements).

6. Gerstein v. Pugh, 420 U.S. 103, 95 S.Ct. 854, 43 L.Ed.2d 54 (1975).

7. Stack v. Boyle, 342 U.S. 1, 72 S.Ct. 1, 96 L.Ed. 3 (1951). For citations to additional Supreme Court cases on this point, see R. Rotunda & J. Nowak, Treatise on Constitutional Law: Substance and Procedure, § 17.4 (3rd ed. 1999, with annual supplements).

8. Klopfer v. North Carolina, 386 U.S. 213, 87 S.Ct. 988, 18 L.Ed.2d 1 (1967).

9. In the Matter of Winship, 397 U.S. 358, 90 S.Ct. 1068, 25 L.Ed.2d 368 (1970). Jackson v. Virginia, 443 U.S. 307, 99 S.Ct. 2781, 61 L.Ed.2d 560 (1979).

For citations to additional Supreme Court cases, and secondary authorities, concerning the "presumption of innocence," see R. Rotunda & J. Nowak, Treatise on Constitutional Law: Substance and Procedure, §§ 17.4, 17.9 (3rd ed. 1999, with annual supplements).

10. Shifting the Burden of Proof. If the government formally shifts the burden of proof to the defendant regarding an essential element of the defense, it will violate due process, although the state may be able to require the defendant to bear the burden of proof regarding some affirmative defenses which are the equivalent of pleas of confession and avoidance. Compare Mullaney v. Wilbur, 421 U.S. 684, 95 S.Ct. 1881, 44 L.Ed.2d 508 (1975), with Patterson v. New York, 432 U.S. 197, 97 S.Ct. 2319, 53 L.Ed.2d 281 (1977). For citations to additional Supreme Court cases, on this point, see R. Rotunda & J. Nowak, Treatise on Constitutional Law: Substance and Procedure, §§ 17.3, 17.9 (3rd ed. 1999, with annual supplements).

11. Application of Gault, 387 U.S. 1, 87 S.Ct. 1428, 18 L.Ed.2d 527 (1967). The child need not be granted trial by jury or a public trial, McKeiver v. Pennsylvania, 403 U.S. 528, 91 S.Ct. 1976, 29 L.Ed.2d 647 (1971).

12. In the Matter of Winship, 397 U.S. 358, 90 S.Ct. 1068, 25 L.Ed.2d 368 (1970), mandate conformed to 27 N.Y.2d 728, 314 N.Y.S.2d 536, 262 N.E.2d 675 (1970).

not clearly defined the procedures required, it is clear that an adult cannot be committed for a treatment of "mental illness" unless there has been a fair procedure to determine that the person is dangerous to himself or others.[13]

In *Addington v. Texas*[14] the Supreme Court determined that an adult cannot be involuntarily committed to a psychiatric institution on a burden of proof that requires the state merely to show by a preponderance of the evidence that the person is dangerous to himself or another. Although the Court did not require a "beyond a reasonable doubt" standard, it held that trial courts must at least employ a "clear and convincing" evidence standard. Chief Justice Burger, writing for a unanimous Court, held that the societal and constitutional values placed on freedom from physical internment required adoption of a standard beyond the mere preponderance standard. However, the nature of commitment proceedings, which are non-punitive and concerned with issues upon which there is virtually never factual certainty, did not require states to adopt a "beyond a reasonable doubt" or "unequivocal proof" standard.[15]

The Supreme Court has not required states to provide similar due process safeguards for children who are committed to a mental health care facility by their parent or guardian. In *Parham v. J.R.*[16] the Court found that the voluntary commitment of a child to a state-operated mental health care institution by the child's parents, but over the child's objection, or by the state, if the child was a ward of the state, deprived the child of a liberty interest but that this deprivation did not require a pre-commitment adversarial hearing. The Supreme Court ruled that such a child was only entitled to have a "neutral fact finder" (such as a state-employed social worker or psychologist) determine if statutory criteria for commitment were met in the individual child's case. The Court did not determine whether the commitment of a child to a private institution by his or her parents constituted state action that deprived the child of a constitutionally protected liberty interest.[17]

The Supreme Court has found that juveniles have only a limited right to freedom from government custody. For that reason, the Supreme Court has upheld two types of detention programs for juveniles, without indicating whether similar detention programs for adults would meet constitutional standards. In *Schall v. Martin*[18] the Court upheld a pretrial detention system for juveniles who were accused of serious crimes, because the Court found that the detention program was non-punitive in nature and that the program protected both society and the well-being of the accused juvenile. In making that finding, the

---

13. O'Connor v. Donaldson, 422 U.S. 563, 95 S.Ct. 2486, 45 L.Ed.2d 396 (1975). See also State ex rel. Doe v. Madonna, 295 N.W.2d 356, 363 n. 9 (Minn.1980) (Kelly, J., quoting an earlier edition of this work). There must be some comparable safeguards between civil and criminal procedures for commitment. Jackson v. Indiana, 406 U.S. 715, 92 S.Ct. 1845, 32 L.Ed.2d 435 (1972), Humphrey v. Cady, 405 U.S. 504, 92 S.Ct. 1048, 31 L.Ed.2d 394 (1972). See note 1 in § 13.9 of this Treatise for further analysis of the distinction between civil trials and criminal trials. For citations to additional cases, including lower court cases, and secondary works on this topic see our multi-volume Treatise: R. Rotunda & J. Nowak, Treatise on Constitutional Law: Substance and Procedure (3rd ed. 1999, with annual supplements).

14. 441 U.S. 418, 99 S.Ct. 1804, 60 L.Ed.2d 323 (1979). This opinion was unanimous but Justice Powell did not participate in the decision.

15. If a defendant in a criminal case is acquitted on the basis of an insanity defense, he may be committed to a psychiatric facility even though the defense was established under the "preponderance of evidence" standard. Jones v. United States, 463 U.S. 354, 103 S.Ct. 3043, 77 L.Ed.2d 694 (1983). However, a defendant who is acquit-

ted on the basis of an insanity defense cannot be committed to a psychiatric facility absent evidence that he is mentally ill and dangerous to himself or others. Foucha v. Louisiana, 504 U.S. 71, 112 S.Ct. 1780, 118 L.Ed.2d 437 (1992). See § 13.9 of this Treatise for citations to additional cases regarding involuntary commitment.

16. 442 U.S. 584, 99 S.Ct. 2493, 61 L.Ed.2d 101 (1979). See also Secretary of Public Welfare of Pennsylvania v. Institutionalized Juveniles, 442 U.S. 640, 99 S.Ct. 2523, 61 L.Ed.2d 142 (1979).

17. It should be noted that the Supreme Court has in one case held that a state statute only recognizing the ability of private persons to help themselves does not create state action in the acts of those private persons. See Flagg Bros., Inc. v. Brooks, 436 U.S. 149, 98 S.Ct. 1729, 56 L.Ed.2d 185 (1978) (finding no state action in a warehouseman sale conducted without active state assistance but pursuant to a state statute). See §§ 12.2–12.4, 13.8, 13.9.

18. 467 U.S. 253, 104 S.Ct. 2403, 81 L.Ed.2d 207 (1984).

Court noted that "juveniles, unlike adults, are always in some form of custody," such as the custody of parents or school authorities.[19]

The Court relied on *Schall* when it upheld Immigration and Naturalization Service [INS] regulations regarding the custody of alien juveniles who were being held pending deportation proceedings. In *Reno v. Flores*[20] the Supreme Court upheld INS regulations that allowed for the release of alien juveniles awaiting deportation hearings only to relatives or guardians in the United States, except in the most unusual and compelling circumstances. The majority opinion, written by Justice Scalia, found a child did not have a fundamental right to be released into a noncustodial setting in all circumstances where noncustodial care would be in the child's "best interest." The *Flores* decision was based, in part, on the uncontested find-

ing that the government custodial program was not punitive in nature.[21]

In a decision which involved both substantive and procedural due process analysis the Supreme Court held that an involuntarily committed person had a substantive right to reasonably safe conditions of confinement and freedom from unnecessary bodily restraint.[22] However, the Court found that those rights would be sufficiently safeguarded if courts merely determine that "professional judgment was in fact exercised" in determining the degree of restraint imposed on the individual and that the judgment was not "a substantial departure from accepted professional judgment." The Court has avoided ruling on whether involuntarily committed persons have a constitutionally protected right to minimally adequate rehabilitative treatment.[23]

---

19. 467 U.S. at 265, 104 S.Ct. at 2410.

20. 507 U.S. 292, 113 S.Ct. 1439, 123 L.Ed.2d 1 (1993), on remand 992 F.2d 243 (9th Cir.1993).

21. In Reno v. Flores, 507 U.S. 292, 113 S.Ct. 1439, 123 L.Ed.2d 1 (1993), the INS regulation was attacked on its face, and not as applied to specific children. The majority did not believe that any significant evidence had been presented to show that the alien children who remained in custody were not being kept in facilities that met or exceeded standards established by the "Alien Minors Care Program of the Community Relation Service." Additionally, the majority found that there was no evidence that the INS regulations would unnecessarily lengthen the time that a child was held in custody pending deportation. The children's procedural arguments focused on the part of the regulations that allowed the children to waive their right to have an immigration judge review the initial determination of the child's deportability and the need to keep the child in custody. In *Flores* the majority found that many children would be capable of making a knowing and intelligent waiver of their rights and that the system did not violate due process standards. Because this case involved a challenge to the regulation on its face, there was no question as to whether a specific child was too young, ignorant, or immature to make an intelligent waiver of his rights. The regulation was upheld because the waiver system was not one that was inherently unfair to children in the deportation process. The regulation before the Court also allowed the child to revoke the waiver and receive a later judicial redetermination of the deportation and custody decisions. Reno v. Flores, 507 U.S. 292, 305–309, 113 S.Ct. 1439, 1449–1451, 123 L.Ed.2d 1 (1993), on remand 992 F.2d 243 (9th Cir.1993).

22. Youngberg v. Romeo, 457 U.S. 307, 102 S.Ct. 2452, 73 L.Ed.2d 28 (1982).

The duty to protect the safety and well-being of an arrested individual (who is in the custody of the government) is based upon the Eighth Amendment prohibition of

cruel and unusual punishment as well as the due process clause. See, Estelle v. Gamble, 429 U.S. 97, 97 S.Ct. 285, 50 L.Ed.2d 251 (1976). Cases regarding the interplay between the substantive and procedural rights of prisoners are examined in the remaining paragraphs of this section, section 13.9 of this Chapter, and section 10.6 of Chapter 10.

The duty of government to provide protection to persons taken into the custody or control of the government outside of the criminal process is based on the due process clause. The Supreme Court has found that the due process clause does not impose on governmental entities the duty to protect individuals who are not in custody from harm caused to them by private persons. See, DeShaney v. Winnebago County Department of Social Services, 489 U.S. 189, 109 S.Ct. 998, 103 L.Ed.2d 249 (1989) (a child's injuries that were the result of being beaten by his father were not injuries attributable to a violation of the due process clause, even though government social workers who worked with the family had reason to believe, and did believe, that the child was being abused and took no steps to stop that abuse).

23. Compare Youngberg v. Romeo, 457 U.S. 307, 102 S.Ct. 2452, 73 L.Ed.2d 28 (1982) (Blackmun, J., joined by Brennan & O'Connor, JJ., noting the unresolved and difficult nature of this substantive claim) with 457 U.S. at 329, 330, 102 S.Ct. at 2465 (Burger, C.J., concurring in the judgment asserting that there is no substantive right to training or rehabilitation).

The administration of antipsychotic drugs to a prison inmate, or the transfer of a prison inmate to a mental hospital, involves an impairment of liberty interest that was not taken away from the inmate by his conviction. Such liberty impairments must be accompanied by procedural safeguards. See, Vitek v. Jones, 445 U.S. 480, 100 S.Ct. 1254, 63 L.Ed.2d 552 (1980) (transfer from prison to prison hospital requires an administrative process that complies with due process principles); Washington v. Har-

Postincarceration Deprivations of Liberty—Prisoners' Rights Cases. In Chapter 10 we used the cases involving claims of prisoners that the conditions of their confinement violated due process to examine the distinction between procedural due process claims and substantive due process or equal protection claims.[24] Persons unclear on the distinction between procedural and substantive due process decisions should review that portion of Chapter 10 prior to focusing on the procedural issues raised in the prisoner's rights cases that are examined in this Chapter.

A court confronting a prisoner's rights claim will examine two questions. First, did the government action about which the prisoner is complaining involve an intentional deprivation of the individual's life, liberty, or property interests? If the court answers "yes" to this first question, will it go on to the second question? Second, was the person whose life, liberty, or property interest was taken by the government given a fundamentally fair procedure for determining whether applicable law justified the taking of that interest? In this section, we will examine the prisoner's rights cases to determine what kinds of interest a

prisoner might have that would require that he be given a fair hearing prior to depriving him of that interest. In a later section of this Chapter, we will examine the question of what type of procedure should be given to a prisoner if prison authorities are depriving him of a life, liberty, or property interest.[25]

Once a person has been incarcerated following a fair procedure, that does not completely terminate his or her right to liberty. Persons convicted of a crime may be placed on probation in lieu of being imprisoned or paroled from prison prior to the end of their maximum sentence. If the state seeks to revoke the probation or parole and place the convicted defendant in prison, it must give him a new hearing.[26] While this hearing need not have the safeguards of a criminal trial it must constitute a fair procedure for determining the basis for the revocation of parole or probation. The Court has held that taking away early release credit from a prisoner requires a fair procedure,[27] but it has also held that prisoners could be deprived of benefits by being transferred to a different corrections facility without a hearing.[28]

---

per, 494 U.S. 210, 110 S.Ct. 1028, 108 L.Ed.2d 178 (1990) (upholding a prison regulation regarding the administration of antipsychotic drugs to prisoners under both substantive due process and procedural due process principles). The procedural aspects of these cases are discussed §§ 13.4, 13.9 of this Treatise.

24. See Chapter 10, § 10.6 of this Treatise.

25. See § 13.9(a) of this Treatise.

26. Morrissey v. Brewer, 408 U.S. 471, 92 S.Ct. 2593, 33 L.Ed.2d 484 (1972) (parole); Gagnon v. Scarpelli, 411 U.S. 778, 93 S.Ct. 1756, 36 L.Ed.2d 656 (1973) (probation).

27. Wolff v. McDonnell, 418 U.S. 539, 94 S.Ct. 2963, 41 L.Ed.2d 935 (1974).

28. When a person has been convicted of a crime, he has received the best process which our society can afford to justify his liberty loss. A later transfer of the prisoner to differing conditions of confinement does not require a new process unless the new conditions may be said to be outside of the normal range of (or substantive constitutional limits on) the conditions of confinement. Thus, a prisoner who is transferred to a facility for mental treatment is entitled to a hearing. Vitek v. Jones, 445 U.S. 480, 100 S.Ct. 1254, 63 L.Ed.2d 552 (1980).

However, when a prisoner is placed in administrative segregation or transferred to a different penal facility, even one in another state, no new process is required because the transfer does not implicate a liberty interest

which was not adequately protected by the original criminal process and conviction. Montanye v. Haymes, 427 U.S. 236, 96 S.Ct. 2543, 49 L.Ed.2d 466 (1976), (transfer to different prison facility); Meachum v. Fano, 427 U.S. 215, 96 S.Ct. 2532, 49 L.Ed.2d 451 (1976) (transfer to maximum security prison); Howe v. Smith, 452 U.S. 473, 101 S.Ct. 2468, 69 L.Ed.2d 171 (1981) (state prisoner transferred to federal penal facility); Olim v. Wakinekona, 461 U.S. 238, 103 S.Ct. 1741, 75 L.Ed.2d 813 (1983) (state prisoner transferred from prison in Hawaii to maximum security prison in California).

In Sandin v. Conner, 515 U.S. 472, 115 S.Ct. 2293, 132 L.Ed.2d 418 (1995), the Court, by a 5 to 4 vote of the Justices, took the position, contrary to the approach taken by the Court in previous cases, that federal courts should not interpret or statutes relating to prisons, or prison regulations, in a way that gave prisoners an entitlement to any process beyond that required by the due process clause, unless the statute or regulation explicitly created such an entitlement. Although Chief Justice Rehnquist's majority opinion in *Sandin* stated that the Court was not overruling any previous decision, or the altering of due process principles, the *Sandin* decision made it difficult, if not impossible, for a prisoner to argue successfully that statutes, or prison regulations, gave him a right to some type of fair process beyond the minimum required by the due process clause. The authors are indebted to Professor Bennett L. Gershman, of The Pace University School of Law, for advising us of the importance of the *Sandin* decision for prisoner rights litigation. For citations to

In *Vitek v. Jones*,[29] the Supreme Court clarified its rulings concerning the treatment of prisoners when it held that an involuntary transfer of a prisoner to a mental hospital implicated a protected liberty interest and that due process was not satisfied by the mere certification of the need for such treatment by a state-designated physician or psychologist. The Court found the existence of a liberty interest in this case on two separate grounds. First, the state statutes at issue in this case gave rise to a legitimate expectation on the part of the prisoner that he would only be kept in normal prison facilities and not be transferred to a mental hospital for psychiatric treatment without an accurate determination of his need for that treatment. Secondly, the involuntary commitment to a mental hospital, unlike a transfer between normal correctional facilities, involved the loss of a liberty interest because it involved not only a greater degree of confinement but also the imposition of mandatory treatment and a realistic possibility of stigmatizing consequences for the defendant in the future. Because the transfer threatened a deprivation of the prisoner's protected liberty interest, he was entitled to "appropriate procedural safeguards against error."[30]

The administration of antipsychotic drugs to a prison inmate impairs a constitutionally protected liberty interest of the inmate that was not taken away by his criminal conviction.

Therefore, prison regulations regarding the administration of such drugs to a prison inmate without his consent must comply with both substantive and procedural due process principles.[31] In *Washington v. Harper*,[32] the Supreme Court upheld both the substantive and procedural aspects of a prison regulation that subjected certain inmates to involuntary treatment with such drugs. The regulation allowed prison authorities to administer the drugs to inmates who were dangerous to themselves or other persons if the treatment was in the inmate's medical interest. In the substantive due process portion of its ruling, the Court found that the regulation was reasonably related to legitimate penological interests.[33] The prison regulation at issue in *Harper* provided the inmate with notice and a hearing before a tribunal of medical professionals and prison authorities at which the inmate could challenge the initial decision to give him the drug treatment. The Court found that this hearing procedure complied with the fair process requirements of the due process clause.[34]

A convicted inmate of a penal institution does not have a constitutionally cognizable liberty or property interest in the possibility of receiving parole release before expiration of his prison sentence, but state law might create a specific entitlement to release under certain circumstances which would require some mini-

---

additional cases, including lower court cases, and secondary works on this topic see our multi-volume Treatise: R. Rotunda & J. Nowak, Treatise on Constitutional Law: Substance and Procedure (3rd ed. 1999, with annual supplements).

It is important to note that these decisions do not hold that "liberty," like "property", is to be defined only by reference to legislative or administrative actions rather than constitutional values. Rather, they hold that a prisoner's liberty has been taken with due process by our criminal justice system. Even after incarceration, a person may not be subjected to a form of punishment—such as beating or transference to a facility for psychiatric care—not normally expected in our penal system without due process. However, the prisoner has no interest protected by due process in the place or type of confinement so long as it comports with substantive standards of due process and the prohibition of cruel and unusual punishment. A state by statute or administrative regulation may commit itself to giving prisoners a fair proceeding to review their transfer. Such legislative or administrative action restores to the prisoner a measure of the liberty properly taken from him by his criminal conviction.

29. 445 U.S. 480, 100 S.Ct. 1254, 63 L.Ed.2d 552 (1980).

30. 445 U.S. at 495, 100 S.Ct. at 1265. The Court's rulings on the precise procedures to be afforded are noted in § 13.9(a), infra.

31. See § 10.6 regarding the distinctions between substantive due process and procedural due process issues.

32. 494 U.S. 210, 110 S.Ct. 1028, 108 L.Ed.2d 178 (1990).

33. In determining whether a prison regulation limits the constitutional rights possessed by all or some prisoners violates substantive due process or equal protection principles, the Supreme Court requires that the prison regulation be "reasonably related to legitimate penological interests." Turner v. Safley, 482 U.S. 78, 107 S.Ct. 2254, 96 L.Ed.2d 64 (1987). The Supreme Court ruled that this reasonableness test was the appropriate standard to use when determining whether the antipsychotic drug regulation violated any substantive rights of the prisoner. Washington v. Harper, 494 U.S. 210, 222, 110 S.Ct. 1028, 1037, 108 L.Ed.2d 178 (1990).

34. Washington v. Harper, 494 U.S. 210, 110 S.Ct. 1028, 1040–1044, 108 L.Ed.2d 178 (1990).

mal procedures to ensure fair decision-making by a parole board. The majority opinion, by Chief Justice Burger, in *Greenholtz v. Inmates of the Nebraska Penal and Correctional Complex* [35] found that the possibility of parole release under a generalized parole system constituted no more than the state holding out a possibility or hope of early release—"a hope which is not protected by due process." [36] Thus the majority distinguished its earlier application of due process principles to parole and probation revocations because those determinations involved termination, upon a finding of specific facts, of a state-granted, presently enjoyed, conditional liberty interest.

The State of Nebraska, whose parole system was challenged in *Greenholtz*, required by statute that the state parole board release an inmate eligible for parole unless the board found that parole should be denied for one of several specific statutory reasons. The Supreme Court found that this particular statute created a liberty interest entitled to "some measure of constitutional protection." But the majority opinion noted that this statute was unique and each state parole statute would have to be examined, on a case-by-case basis, to determine if it created similar entitlements.

The majority did not determine what particular procedural rights were necessary to protect this interest; the majority opinion merely found that the Nebraska Parole Board procedures were constitutionally sufficient. Justice Powell, who was of the opinion that all persons eligible for parole had a constitutionally protected liberty interest at stake in the proceedings, would have required more than a

one-day notice of the scheduled hearing to the prisoner so that the prisoner could prepare himself for the hearing. [37] However, the majority found no significant claim of prejudice to the prisoner resulting from the late notice procedure. [38]

Based upon the rationale of the *Greenholtz* decision, the Supreme Court ruled in *Connecticut Board of Pardons v. Dumschat* [39] that a prisoner serving a life sentence had no right to procedural fairness in the review of his request for commutation of his life sentence. Chief Justice Burger wrote for the majority in *Dumschat*, as he had in *Greenholtz*. The Chief Justice found that, absent a state-created entitlement to fair treatment in the review of his sentence, the due process clause imposed no procedural safeguards against arbitrary treatment of the defendant's request for commutation. The Court refused to find that the prisoner had a constitutionally cognizable interest at stake in the review of his sentence even though the review board commuted most of the life sentences which came before it.

Correctly analyzed, the ruling in this case is no more than a finding that the prisoner's liberty had been properly taken from him through the criminal trial-and-appeal process. The Court found that the prisoner had no right to a statement of reasons for the denial of his request because it amounted to nothing more than "an appeal for clemency." [40] However, some may mistakenly view the case as propounding the principle that "liberty" as well as "property" is only a creation of state law, a position which has no basis in prior

35. 442 U.S. 1, 99 S.Ct. 2100, 60 L.Ed.2d 668 (1979).

36. 442 U.S. at 11, 99 S.Ct. at 2105.

37. Justice Powell found the other aspects of the Nebraska hearing system to be a fair, sufficient process to protect the inmates' interests. 442 U.S. at 18–22, 99 S.Ct. at 2109–11, (Powell, J., concurring in part and dissenting in part).

38. Justices Marshall, Brennan and Stevens, in dissent, would have found that all those eligible for parole have a constitutionally protected liberty interest at stake in the proceeding. The dissenters would have required earlier notice to each prisoner regarding the time of his hearing, notice of the factors that the Board might consider regarding his parole, and a statement of the evidence relied upon by the Board, rather than a general statement

of reasons, whenever the Board denied parole. Greenholtz v. Inmates of the Nebraska Penal and Correctional Complex, 442 U.S. 1, 22, 99 S.Ct. 2100, 2111, 60 L.Ed.2d 668 (1979) (Marshall, J., concurring and dissenting, joined by Brennan & Stevens, JJ.)

39. 452 U.S. 458, 101 S.Ct. 2460, 69 L.Ed.2d 158 (1981).

40. 452 U.S. at 465, 101 S.Ct. at 2465. Similarly, in Jago v. Van Curen, 454 U.S. 14, 102 S.Ct. 31, 70 L.Ed.2d 13 (1981) the Court held that a parole board could rescind its decision to grant a prisoner parole without a hearing upon learning of the falsity of statements made to the board by the prisoner.

substantive or procedural due process rulings of the Supreme Court.[41]

These cases establish the principle that a prisoner has no liberty interest in release on parole that is protected by the due process clause unless the government (by statute or administrative regulation) creates such a liberty interest.[42] If such an interest is established by state law, then the due process clause will require the state to grant the individual a fair process for the determination of whether he should be released on parole.[43]

The somewhat confusing language of the *Dumshat* opinion contributed to the Supreme Court's inability to write a majority opinion describing the nature of an individual's interest in a clemency petition review process. In *Ohio Adult Parole Authority v. Woodard*,[44] the Supreme Court examined claims by a prisoner who had been sentenced to die. The prisoner's conviction had been affirmed on appeal; his claim for clemency from the Ohio governor had been denied. This prisoner, who was awaiting the death sentence, alleged that the Ohio system for consideration of clemency petitions violated the Fifth Amendment privilege against self-incrimination, because it effectively forced an individual seeking clemency to answer questions that might provide evidence of other crimes, and that the Ohio procedures

for executive review of clemency claims were so unfair as to violate due process principles.

In *Woodard*, Chief Justice Rehnquist wrote for a unanimous Court in ruling that the pressure an individual felt to answer questions as a part of a request for clemency did not constitute a violation of the Fifth Amendment prohibition against compelled self-incrimination.[45] By an eight to one vote, the Court found that the Ohio proceedings for consideration of clemency requests by persons subject to the death sentence did not violate due process principles. Nevertheless, there was no majority opinion in *Woodard*, on the procedural due process issue, because five Justices could not agree on how to describe an individual's interest in a clemency request proceedings.[46]

Chief Justice Rehnquist's opinion in *Woodard* was, in part, a plurality opinion. Writing for himself and Justices Scalia, Kennedy, and Thomas, the Chief Justice found that an individual did not have any interest at stake in the examination of his clemency petition that was protected by the due process clause.[47] The four Justice plurality opinion also found that the state of Ohio had not created any entitlement to fair treatment in clemency procedures supposed to make due process clause principles applicable to those proceedings.[48]

41. See note 28, supra.

42. See, Board of Pardons v. Allen, 482 U.S. 369, 107 S.Ct. 2415, 96 L.Ed.2d 303 (1987), in which the Supreme Court found that a state statute, which indicated that a Board "shall" release a prisoner under certain restrictions, created a liberty interest in parole release.

43. The process need not be a formal adversarial proceeding. The parole process, when a constitutionally protected liberty is involved, should be designed to provide for a fair consideration of the prisoner's claim for parole, although the pardon or parole board may be given a wide degree of discretion in making the ultimate judgment regarding the prisoners release. See generally, Greenholtz v. Inmates of Nebraska Penal and Correctional Complex, 442 U.S. 1, 99 S.Ct. 2100, 60 L.Ed.2d 668 (1979), on remand 602 F.2d 155 (8th Cir.1979).

44. 523 U.S. 272, 118 S.Ct. 1244 140 L.Ed.2d 387 (1998) (Parts I and III of the opinion, written by Chief Justice Rehnquist, are the majority opinion for the Court; part II of Chief Justice Rehnquist's opinion is a plurality opinion announcing the judgment of the Court).

45. 523 U.S. at 285–86, 118 S.Ct. at 1252. Justice Stevens, who was the sole dissenter in this case, noted his agreement with part III of Chief Justice Rehnquist's opinion, which rejected the prisoner's Fifth Amendment claim.

523 U.S. at 290, 118 S.Ct. at 1256 (Stevens, J., concurring in part, and dissenting in part).

46. Ohio Adult Parole Authority v. Woodard, 523 U.S. 272, 118 S.Ct. 1244, 1254, 140 L.Ed.2d 387 (1998) (Stevens, J., concurring in part and dissenting in part).

47. Ohio Adult Parole Authority v. Woodard, 523 U.S. 272, 279–81, 118 S.Ct. 1244, 1249–50, 140 L.Ed.2d 387 (1998) (opinion of Rehnquist, C.J., joined by Scalia, Kennedy, and Thomas, JJ.).

48. 523 U.S. at 281–82, 118 S.Ct. at 1250–51. The Chief Justice's opinion is somewhat unclear as to whether the plurality believed that Ohio created absolutely no interest in the clemency procedures that were protected by due process, or whether they believed that Ohio had established an entitlement in clemency petition review that merited some minimal procedural due process protection, which was provided by the Ohio statutes. The plurality opinion by Chief Justice Rehnquist also rejected the claim that under due process requirements should apply to clemency proceedings on the basis that these proceedings constituted another stage in the judicial appellate review system. 523 U.S. at 280–82, 118 S.Ct. at 1251–52 (opinion of Rehnquist, C.J., joined by Scalia, Kennedy, and Thomas, JJ.).

Justice O'Connor wrote a concurring opinion for four Justices in *Woodard*[49]; that was joined by Justices Souter, Ginsburg, and Breyer. These four Justices explicitly rejected "the suggestion and the principal opinion not, because clemency is committed to the discretion of the executor, the due process clause provides no constitutional safeguards...."[50]. Rather, Justice O'Connor asserted, a person convicted of a capital offense still had an interest in his life that was protected by the due process clause. Because the individual had been found guilty of an offense for which he could constitutionally be punished by death, the four concurring Justices found that only "some minimal procedural safeguards apply to clemency proceedings," and the Ohio procedures for review of clemency requests met procedural due process requirements.[51]

Justice Stevens dissented from the decision of the majority of not to remand the case to the District Court for an initial determination of whether the State of Ohio clemency petition review process met "the minimum requirements of due process."[52] He believed that the due process clause created a right to a fair review process for clemency petitions.

At the time *Woodard* was decided, there were five Justices who were ready to analyze the question of whether due process applied to clemency petition review procedures in a manner consistent with all prior decisions of the Supreme Court. Justice Stevens and the four Justices who joined in Justice O'Connor's concurrence agreed that a conviction for a crime, and a sentence of death, terminated some, but not all aspects of constitutionally protected "life" and "liberty" interests. Justice O'Connor's concurring opinion stated: "it is incorrect, by Justice Stevens' notes, to say that a

prisoner has been deprived of all interest in his life before his execution."[53] These five Justices could not produce on a majority opinion in *Woodard*, because the four concurring Justices believed that there was no need for a District Court review of Ohio procedures; they believed that those procedures clearly met procedural due process requirements. Justice Stevens, on the other hand, believed that the Court needed a better record in order to determine whether the Ohio procedures met minimum due process requirements.

Conclusion. It must be noted that any significant, even though temporary, physical restraint or punishment of a person constitutes a deprivation of liberty which requires some procedural safeguard. In *Ingraham v. Wright*[54] the Supreme Court upheld the use of corporal punishment for children by state school teachers so long as the state had some procedure to later determine the propriety of such actions and impose liability for any excessive use of force. But in so doing the majority opinion fully accepted the position that physical restraint constitutes a deprivation of liberty for which some process is due unless it would be of an extremely brief and *de minimis* nature.

The Supreme Court has ruled that the injury caused to the person or property of a prison inmate through the intentional action of a prison employee constitutes a taking of property or liberty. The state must provide post-deprivation procedure to determine the amount of fair compensation due the prisoner in such a case. Injury caused to a prisoner, or his property, through the mere negligence of a prison employee, however, does not constitute a violation of due process.[55] In these cases the

---

49. Ohio Adult Parole Authority v. Woodard, 523 U.S. 272, 288, 118 S.Ct. 1244, 1253, 140 L.Ed.2d 387 (1998) (O'Connor, J., joined by Souter, Ginsburg, and Breyer, JJ., concurring in part and concurring in judgment).

50. 523 U.S. at 288, 118 S.Ct. at 1253 (O'Connor, J., joined by Souter, Ginsburg, and Breyer, JJ., concurring in part and concurring in judgment).

51. 523 U.S. at 288–89, 118 S.Ct. at 1254 (O'Connor, J., joined by Souter, Ginsburg, and Breyer, JJ., concurring in part and concurring in the judgment).

52. Ohio Adult Parole Authority v. Woodard, 523 U.S. 272, 290, 118 S.Ct. 1244, 1257, 140 L.Ed.2d 387 (1998). (Stevens, J. concurring in part, and dissenting in part).

53. 523 U.S. at 288, 118 S.Ct. at 1254 (O'Connor, J. joined by Souter, Ginsburg and Breyer, JJ. concurring in part, and concurring in the judgment).

54. 430 U.S. 651, 97 S.Ct. 1401, 51 L.Ed.2d 711 (1977).

55. In Hudson v. Palmer, 468 U.S. 517, 104 S.Ct. 3194, 82 L.Ed.2d 393 (1984), on remand 744 F.2d 22 (4th Cir.1984), the Court found that a state would have to have a "meaningful post-deprivation remedy" to examine the

Court did not rule that a prisoner's person or property was not protected by due process but, rather, that the due process clauses were not violated by negligently caused (as opposed to intentionally inflicted) injury to the prisoner.

The Supreme Court has ruled that substantive due process principles establish a "shocks the conscience" standard for determining the constitutionality of many types of actions taken by executive officers, (such as police officers) that cause harm to persons or property. In so doing, the Court found that rulings concerning injuries to the property and person of prison inmates through unintentional actions of prison employees were applications of the substantive due process "shock the conscience" test, rather than true procedural due process rulings.[56]

The cases examined in this section involve the determination of when the procedural component of the due process clause requires prison authorities to create a fair procedure for determining that an inmate should be subject to some loss of liberty or property. The legitimacy of prison regulations that restrict the activities of all prisoners, or a specific class of prisoners in a penal facility, must be examined under substantive due process and equal protection principles.[57] The Supreme Court

has ruled that prison regulations that restrict the exercise of fundamental constitutional rights by prisoners should be upheld so long as the prison regulation is reasonably related to a legitimate penological interest.[58]

(c) Fundamental Constitutional Rights

Liberty includes the freedom of choice to engage in certain activities. When those activities have specific constitutional recognition, the liberty to engage in them is protected by the due process guarantee. In one sense it may be said that all activities or liberty have constitutional recognition because none is singled out for special limitations. But the government has broad powers to curtail individual freedom of action to promote the legitimate ends of society except where there is some specific constitutional limitation on its powers.

Since 1937 and the rejection of the old substantive due process, the Court will actively protect only "fundamental" constitutional rights.[59] These rights are those with textual recognition in the Constitution, or its Amendments, or values found to be implied because they are "fundamental" to freedom in American society, as reflected by history and the interpretation of the Supreme Court. The Court recognized the concept of fundamental

claim of a prisoner for compensation when that claim was based on an assertion that state employees had intentionally destroyed his personal property in the prison, including legal papers. In Daniels v. Williams, 474 U.S. 327, 106 S.Ct. 662, 88 L.Ed.2d 662 (1986), overruling Parratt v. Taylor, 451 U.S. 527, 101 S.Ct. 1908, 68 L.Ed.2d 420 (1981), the Court found that the due process clause was not violated by state tort law and a state doctrine of sovereign immunity that denied recovery to a prisoner for the injury caused him by slipping on a pillow that had been negligently placed on a staircase by a prison employee. In so ruling, the Court held that "the due process clause is simply not implicated by a negligent act of an official causing unintended loss of or injury to life, liberty, or property." Accord, Davidson v. Cannon, 474 U.S. 344, 106 S.Ct. 668, 88 L.Ed.2d 677 (1986) (due process clause was not violated by the negligent failure of prison employees to protect an inmate from being attacked by other inmates of a penal facility).

56. In Sacramento v. Lewis, 523 U.S. 833, 118 S.Ct., 1708, 140 L.Ed.2d 1043 (1998) the Justices unanimously refused to impose liability for a violation of substantive due process principles on police officers who inadvertently killed a young man who was a passenger on a motorcycle that the police officer was chasing at high speeds in a police control car. One Justice would have decided the case

on statutory principles regarding the immunity of law enforcement officers. Eight of the Justices found that the police did not violate substantive due process principles when they caused unintended harm to an individual whom they were pursuing as a part of a lawful attempt to make an arrest. The majority opinion in *Lewis*, found that no procedural issues were presented in the case. 523 U.S. at 840 n. 4, 118 S.Ct. at 1714 n. 4. The *Lewis* case is examined in § 10.6 of this Treatise.

57. For an examination of the differences between procedural due process review and substantive due process or equal protection review of legislation, see §§ 10.6, 10.7 of this Treatise.

58. Turner v. Safley, 482 U.S. 78, 107 S.Ct. 2254, 96 L.Ed.2d 64 (1987) (in *Turner* the Supreme Court enunciated this test and used it both to uphold prison regulations on the restriction of mailing privileges and to invalidate a prison regulation that prohibited prison inmates from entering a marriage relationship without the approval of the prison superintendent). For additional cases, see R. Rotunda & J. Nowak Treatise on Constitutional Law: Substance and Procedure, Chapters 14, 17 & 18 (1999, 3rd edition, with supplements).

59. See § 11.4, supra, on Substantive Due Process Since 1937.

rights when it incorporated most of the guarantees of the Bill of Rights into the due process clause of the Fourteenth Amendment and applied them to the states.[60] The most significant implied "fundamental" rights are the right to freedom of association, the right to interstate travel; the right to privacy (including some freedom of choice in marital, family, and sexual matters), and the right to vote.[61]

In their procedural aspects the due process clauses require that the government not restrict a specific individual's freedom to exercise a fundamental constitutional right without a process to determine the basis for the restriction. Thus, if a filmmaker is to be subjected to a licensing system to determine whether his film is obscene, the government must establish a prompt and fair procedure to determine its obscenity or allow him to show the film.[62] Whenever the government seeks to restrain speech, there must be a prompt procedure to determine whether the speech may be limited in conformity with First Amendment principles.[63]

The Supreme Court has not established specific rules regarding the nature of procedural safeguards that should be given to a governmental employee when the government discharges the employee for speech related activities. This problem area involves an intersection of First Amendment and procedural due process principles. In its First Amendment rulings, the Supreme Court has allowed the government to fire employees for speech

that is not related to an issue of public concern so long as the firing is not totally arbitrary.[64] The Court employs a balancing test to determine if the government may discharge an employee for speech that relates to an issue of public concern. The government will be allowed to discharge an employee for speech relating to public issues only when the government's interest as an employer outweighs the First Amendment values that would be promoted by allowing the employee's speech.[65]

When a government employee claims that he was fired for engaging in speech that was protected by the First Amendment, and the government agency which made the employment decision claims that the employee's speech related activities did not form any part of the decision to fire the employee, procedural due process principles may require the government to conduct a hearing to determine whether the employee's First Amendment activities were used as a basis for his discharge.[66] Supreme Court rulings indicate that a government employee must be able to establish a prima facie case that he was discharged for engaging in activity that was protected by the First Amendment in order have a due process right to a proceeding to determine the basis for the firing. The Supreme Court has not explained precisely how a discharged employee can meet his burden of showing that there is a factual basis for believing that he has been fired for activities protected by the First

---

60. For a listing of the decisions on "incorporation", see Chapter 10 and § 11.6.

61. For a note regarding the role of fundamental rights analysis today, see §§ 11.5–11.7, supra.

62. Freedman v. Maryland, 380 U.S. 51, 85 S.Ct. 734, 13 L.Ed.2d 649 (1965).

63. Blount v. Rizzi, 400 U.S. 410, 91 S.Ct. 423, 27 L.Ed.2d 498 (1971); Southeastern Promotions Ltd. v. Conrad, 420 U.S. 546, 95 S.Ct. 1239, 43 L.Ed.2d 448 (1975); See, Monaghan, First Amendment "Due Process," 83 Harv.L.Rev. 518 (1970).

64. Connick v. Myers, 461 U.S. 138, 103 S.Ct. 1684, 75 L.Ed.2d 708 (1983) (ruling, in part, that there should be only limited judicial review of government decisions to discharge employees for speech that was not related to an issue of public concern). If the government employee had a property interest or entitlement in her job, the employee would be titled to a fair procedure to resolve disputes

concerning the basis for her firing by procedural due process principles protecting property interests. See § 13.5(d).

65. First Amendment limitations on government policies restricting the speech and associational activities of government employees are examined in §§ 20.42, 20.52 of this Treatise. See, Rankin v. McPherson, 483 U.S. 378, 107 S.Ct. 2891, 97 L.Ed.2d 315 (1987) (statements of public employee in a private conversation concerning public issues could not be the basis for her discharge).

66. Givhan v. Western Line Consolidated School District, 439 U.S. 410, 99 S.Ct. 693, 58 L.Ed.2d 619 (1979) (finding that the First Amendment prohibited the firing of a teacher who objected to racially discriminatory school policies in private conversations); Pickering v. Board of Education, 391 U.S. 563, 88 S.Ct. 1731, 20 L.Ed.2d 811 (1968) (finding that the First Amendment prohibited the firing of a government teacher on the basis of a letter written to a local newspaper and published therein).

Amendment. Nor has the Court clearly described the government's burden in demonstrating that an unfavorable employment decision was not a punishment for protected speech. However, the Supreme Court has indicated that the burden it will place on the government to justify the firing may vary with the nature of the employee's expression.[67]

There may be instances in which the government and the discharged employee agree that the employee's speech at a given time and place was the basis for the employee's discharge, but the employee and government disagree as to what the employee said at that time and place. In such a situation, the government agency that discharged the employee will assert that the employee engaged in speech that was not protected by the First Amendment. The employee will claim that the government decisionmaker made a factual error concerning the nature of the employee's speech and that the speech activities engaged in by the employee, in fact, were activities for which the employee could not be fired consistently with the First Amendment.

In *Waters v. Churchill*,[68] the Court confronted a situation in which a nurse had been discharged from a government hospital for her speech on a certain day to another nurse. Several persons working at the hospital reported conflicting stories concerning the nature of the discharged nurse's speech. The Court of Appeals held that the government could only fire the employee for her speech if her speech, in fact, was such that it was not protected by

the First Amendment. The Supreme Court, by a seven to two vote, but without a majority opinion, overruled the Court of Appeals. It appears that the Supreme Court's ruling in the *Waters* case requires the government employer to act "reasonably" in attempting to determine the facts concerning an employee's speech before the government makes a decision to fire the employee for that speech. But, with no majority opinion, the case provides little guidance as to how to measure the reasonableness of the government's actions.

Justice O'Connor announced the judgment of the Court in *Waters* and wrote a plurality opinion in which she stated that there was no fixed set of procedures that the government must follow in determining the facts concerning an employee's speech before the government discharged the employee. The plurality opinion in *Waters* focused only on the nature of the First Amendment protections that should be given to government employees. Justice O'Connor's discussion of the First Amendment issue in *Waters* used language that normally would be used by a court when considering procedural due process issues. The reasonableness of the procedures used by the government, according to Justice O'Connor, would "turn on the particular context in which the question arises—on the cost of the procedure and the relative magnitude and constitutional significance of the risks it would decrease and increase."[69] In due process cases, the Court has determined that, when a liberty or property interest is at stake, the

---

67. Connick v. Myers, 461 U.S. 138, 103 S.Ct. 1684, 75 L.Ed.2d 708 (1983).

68. 511 U.S. 661, 114 S.Ct. 1878, 128 L.Ed.2d 686 (1994).

69. Waters v. Churchill, 511 U.S. 661, 671, 114 S.Ct. 1878, 1886, 128 L.Ed.2d 686 (1994) (O'Connor, J., announcing the judgment of the Court in an opinion joined by Rehnquist, C.J., and Souter, and Ginsburg, JJ.). Although he joined Justice O'Connor's plurality opinion, Justice Souter wrote a concurring opinion in which he emphasized that the Court's ruling required that the government takes reasonable steps to determine the basis for the firing and actually believe the facts that it used as the basis for the firing. 511 U.S. at 681, 114 S.Ct. at 1891 (Souter, J., concurring).

Justices Scalia, Kennedy, and Thomas joined only in the judgment of the Court in *Waters*. These three Justices

would place no significant procedural limitations on the government's ability to take disciplinary action against an employee who asserts that she was fired for engaging in activities protected by the First Amendment. Justice Scalia's concurring opinion emphasized the number of questions left open concerning the intersection of procedural and substantive rights of government employees by this decision. 511 U.S. at 685, 114 S.Ct. at 1893 (Scalia, J., joined by Kennedy and Thomas, JJ., concurring in the judgment).

Only Justices Stevens and Blackmun believed that the Court of Appeals had been correct in finding that a jury's ultimate determination of the facts should determine whether the speech engaged in by the employee could or could not serve as a basis for the employee's discharge under First Amendment and due process principles. 511 U.S. at 694, 114 S.Ct. at 1898 (Stevens, J., joined by Blackmun, J., dissenting).

judiciary will determine the adequacy of a procedure by examining (1) the importance of the individual's interest at stake, (2) the likelihood that more formalized procedures would avoid arbitrary or erroneous decisions by the government, and (3) the countervailing government interest (such as the efficiency of government administrative agencies).[70] Perhaps the Court will eventually use the due process clause to establish guidelines for resolving the issues presented in our firefighter hypothetical.

Termination of Family Relationships. Due process safeguards apply whenever the government seeks to burden an individual in the exercise of fundamental constitutional rights. The right to privacy includes a right to freedom of choice in marital and family decisions. Thus, when a state seeks to take a child away from its parents, the parents must be given a hearing to determine their fitness to retain the child. Because of the fundamental nature of the interest in family autonomy, the state must prove its allegation of parental unfitness by at least "clear and convincing" evidence.[71] This principle is valid even if the state seeks to take away an illegitimate child from its father. Due process requires that the

child and parent be granted a hearing and the equal protection guarantee prohibits discrimination against illegitimates.[72]

The Supreme Court in *Michael H. v. Gerald D.*[73] upheld a statute that established a presumption that a child born to a married woman was the child of the woman's husband. This presumption of legitimacy could be rebutted only in limited circumstances by the parties to the marriage; it could not be rebutted by a man who wished to establish that he was the father of the child born to a woman who was married to another man. There was no majority opinion in this case; the case leaves unclear the extent to which a state must give the biological father of a child the opportunity to establish a meaningful relationship with the child or, in the alternative, a hearing to determine whether he should be allowed to establish a relationship with the child. In *Michael H.*, Justice Scalia wrote for four Justices who believed that the male's asserted liberty interest in establishing relationship with the child was not a fundamental constitutional right that would require the opportunity for a meaningful hearing.[74] The four dissenting

---

70. This three-factor procedural due process analysis was first set out by the Court in Mathews v. Eldridge, 424 U.S. 319, 335, 96 S.Ct. 893, 903, 47 L.Ed.2d 18 (1976). This three-factor analysis, which is often referred to as a balancing test, is examined in the closing paragraphs of § 13.9 of this Treatise. The application of the *Matthews* three-factor analysis to a variety of due process problems is examined in § 13.9 of this Treatise.

71. Santosky v. Kramer, 455 U.S. 745, 102 S.Ct. 1388, 71 L.Ed.2d 599 (1982), on remand to 89 A.D.2d 738, 453 N.Y.S.2d 942 (1982), appeal denied 58 N.Y.2d 605, 459 N.Y.S.2d 1029, 445 N.E.2d 656 (1983). An indigent parent is not entitled to the services of state-paid counsel in such cases. Lassiter v. Department of Social Services, 452 U.S. 18, 101 S.Ct. 2153, 68 L.Ed.2d 640 (1981). The procedures required by these cases are examined further in § 13.8, infra.

A state may allow a mother seeking support from a putative father to prove paternity by a preponderance of the evidence. Rivera v. Minnich, 483 U.S. 574, 107 S.Ct. 3001, 97 L.Ed.2d 473 (1987). Unlike a proceeding that would terminate the parent-child relationship, the paternity suit does not seek to extinguish a fundamental right; a standard of proof beyond the preponderance of evidence standard is not required to protect the interest of the putative father.

The Court has left unclear whether the relationship between a foster child and foster parents will receive due

process protection. See Smith v. Organization of Foster Families for Equality and Reform, 431 U.S. 816, 97 S.Ct. 2094, 53 L.Ed.2d 14 (1977) (upholding system for removing children from foster homes but assuming *arguendo* that the foster parent-child interest was protected by due process, a point disputed in a concurring opinion by Justices Stewart and Rehnquist and Chief Justice Burger).

72. Stanley v. Illinois, 405 U.S. 645, 92 S.Ct. 1208, 31 L.Ed.2d 551 (1972). Due process also provides some procedural protection to a man charged in a paternity action with being the parent of an illegitimate child. See Little v. Streater, 452 U.S. 1, 101 S.Ct. 2202, 68 L.Ed.2d 627 (1981) (indigent has a right to state-paid blood test in paternity action initiated by, or at the order of, a government agency). See, § 13.8, infra.

73. 491 U.S. 110, 109 S.Ct. 2333, 105 L.Ed.2d 91 (1989).

74. 491 U.S. at 120–132, 109 S.Ct. at 2340–46 (the plurality opinion written by Justice Scalia is joined in its entirety by Chief Justice Rehnquist and joined in all but footnote 6 by Justices O'Connor and Kennedy). Justices O'Connor and Kennedy filed an opinion concurring in part in which they stated that footnote 6 of Justice Scalia's opinion established such a limited view of identifying liberty interest protected by the due process clause that it would be inconsistent with some earlier Supreme Court decisions regarding family and privacy rights. 491 U.S. at 131, 109 S.Ct. at 2346–47 (O'Connor, J., joined by Kennedy, J., concurring in part).

Justices in this case believed that a man who asserted biological parenthood of the child was asserting a liberty interest that was protected by the due process clause and that could not be denied without a hearing, or other fair process.[75]

In *Michael H.,* Justice Stevens concurred only in the judgment, which upheld the statute.[76] Justice Stevens agreed with the Scalia plurality that the state did not have an obligation to declare the biological father to be the "father" of the child born to the married woman. However, Justice Stevens disagreed with Justice Scalia's rejection of constitutional protection for the interest of the biological father. Justice Stevens was "willing to assume for the purpose of deciding this case" that the asserted right of the biological father was protected by due process. However, Justice Stevens believed that the state statutes did not prevent the biological father from bringing an action to show that he was a "person having an interest in the welfare of the child" so as to be allowed "reasonable visitation rights." Under Justice Stevens' reading of the statutes, the biological father was only denied the opportunity to establish his "fatherhood"; he would be given a hearing regarding whether he should have visitation rights and be able to establish a meaningful personal relationship with the child.

A majority of Justices on the Supreme Court might require a state to give a male asserting biological parenthood of a child some form of hearing to determine whether the father should be allowed visitation rights and opportunities to establish a relationship with the

child. However, in *Michael H.,* a majority of Justices on the Court ruled that a male has no right to a hearing to determine whether he should be declared the father of a child who was born to a woman who was married to another person.

In *M.L.B. v. S.L.J.,*[77] the Supreme Court ruled that a state's refusal to allow a woman to appeal from a trial court decision terminating her parental rights due to her inability to pay for a transcript of the trial court proceeding for the appeal violated both due process and equal protection. Court filing fees normally are upheld under due process and equal protection by use of the so-called presumption of constitutionality and the rationality test. Nevertheless, fees that make it impossible for an indigent person to exercise a fundamental constitutional right are subject to independent judicial review.[78] Because the majority in *M.L.B.* found that "choices about marriage, family life, and the upbringing of children are among associational rights this court has ranked as of basic importance in our society."[79] For that reason, the majority ruled that the judiciary must "inspect the character and intensity of the individual's interests at stake, on the one hand, and the state's justification for it exaction [of a fee as a prerequisite for an appeal from a termination of parental rights], on the other."[80] The state's interest in making its judicial system self-supporting might be legitimate, but it was not of sufficient importance to justify denying indigent persons the opportunity to appeal from termination of the parent-child interest.

75. Michael H. v. Gerald D., 491 U.S. 110, 137, 109 S.Ct. 2333, 2349, 105 L.Ed.2d 91 (1989) (Brennan, J., joined by Marshall and Blackmun, JJ., dissenting). 491 U.S. at 158, 109 S.Ct. at 2360 (White, J., joined by Brennan, J., dissenting).

76. Michael H. v. Gerald D., 491 U.S. 110, 133, 109 S.Ct. 2333, 2347, 105 L.Ed.2d 91 (1989) (Stevens, J., concurring in the judgment).

77. 519 U.S. 102, 117 S.Ct. 555, 136 L.Ed.2d 473 (1996).

78. 512 U.S. at 112, 117 S.Ct. at 562: "We have also recognized a narrow category of civil cases in which the state must provide access to its judicial process without regard to a party's ability to pay court fees." The majority opinion, in part, relied on Boddie v. Connecticut, 401 U.S. 371, 91 S.Ct. 780, 28 L.Ed.2d 113 (1971). See §§ 13.8,

14.28, 14.41, regarding *Boddie* and other decisions concerning family relationships.

79. M.L.B. v. S.L.J., 519 U.S. 102, 116, 117 S.Ct. 555, 564, 136 L.Ed.2d 473 (1996).

80. 519 U.S. at 120, 117 S.Ct. at 566. The *M.L.B.* case was decided by a six to three vote of the Justices. Justice Ginsburg wrote the majority opinion for five Justices. Justice Kennedy, who rested his decision entirely on procedural due process principles, concurred only in the judgment of the Court and not in the majority opinion. 519 U.S. at 128, 117 S.Ct. at 570 (Kennedy, J., concurring in the judgment). Chief Justice Rehnquist and Justices Scalia and Thomas were the dissenters in the *M.L.B.* case. 519 U.S. at 128, 117 S.Ct. at 570 (Rehnquist, C.J., dissenting); 519 U.S. at 128, 117 S.Ct. at 570 (Thomas, J., joined by Scalia, J., and, in part, by Rehnquist, C.J., dissenting).

The state also must make some process fairly available for persons to control the exercise of their freedom of choice in marital matters. Thus the state could not refuse to grant a divorce to those persons who were unable to pay court filing fees.[81] The due process clause requires the state to allow freedom of choice in marital matters and the equal protection clause prohibits an allocation of the freedom only to those who can pay for it.

Criminal Procedure Decisions. Similarly, the equal protection clause forbids imposing appellate fees or transcript costs on those persons convicted of crimes who cannot pay for those procedures as this relates to the protection of a fundamental constitutional right.[82] However, fees for a judicial process need not be waived for indigents when the process is not clearly necessary to the protection of a "fundamental" constitutional right.[83]

Citizenship. The Supreme Court has held that, in establishing loss of citizenship, the federal government must prove that an individual intended to surrender his or her United States citizenship, not just that he or she voluntarily acted in a manner declared by Congress to be sufficient to demonstrate a basis for expatriation.[84] However, the Court found that Congress could prescribe that the standard of proof in expatriation proceedings be a preponderance of the evidence because "expa-

triation proceedings are civil in nature and do not threaten a loss of liberty."[85]

Although inartfully phrased, this decision holds only that expatriation proceedings do not involve incarceration of the defendant and, therefore, do not require a greater standard of proof. This decision does not mean that loss of citizenship is unprotected by constitutional procedural requirements under either the citizenship clause of the Fourteenth Amendment or the due process clause of the Fifth Amendment.

(d) Other Rights or Liberties

While the Court has not defined the exact scope of the liberties which are protected by the due process clauses, it is clear that they go beyond mere physical restraint or fundamental constitutional rights. The clauses also guarantee that each individual will have some degree of freedom of choice and action in all important personal matters. The Court has stated that the term "denotes not merely freedom from bodily restraint but also the right of the individual to contract, to engage in any of the common occupations of life, to acquire useful knowledge, to marry, establish a home and bring up children, to worship God according to the dictates of his own conscience and generally to enjoy those privileges long recognized . . . as essential to the orderly pursuit of happiness by free men."[86] However, the Court was also careful to note that not all areas of

---

81. Boddie v. Connecticut, 401 U.S. 371, 91 S.Ct. 780, 28 L.Ed.2d 113 (1971). See also Zablocki v. Redhail, 434 U.S. 374, 98 S.Ct. 673, 54 L.Ed.2d 618 (1978) (invalidating as a violation of equal protection a state prohibition of marriage by persons who had not met financial obligation to pay alimony or child support arising from an earlier marriage and divorce).

82. Griffin v. Illinois, 351 U.S. 12, 76 S.Ct. 585, 100 L.Ed. 891 (1956). However, counsel need not be provided for indigents after their first appeal as of right. Ross v. Moffitt, 417 U.S. 600, 94 S.Ct. 2437, 41 L.Ed.2d 341 (1974).

An indigent criminal defendant only has right to appointed counsel in those cases wherein the defendant receives a punishment of imprisonment. Scott v. Illinois, 440 U.S. 367, 99 S.Ct. 1158, 59 L.Ed.2d 383 (1979). An indigent criminal defendant may be constitutionally convicted of a misdemeanor offense, without benefit of appointed counsel, if he was not imprisoned for the crime. For citations to additional Supreme Court cases, and secondary authorities, on this point, see R. Rotunda & J.

Nowak, Treatise on Constitutional Law: Substance and Procedure, §§ 17.4, 17.9 (3rd ed. 1999, with annual supplements).

83. United States v. Kras, 409 U.S. 434, 93 S.Ct. 631, 34 L.Ed.2d 626 (1973) (No right to waiver of fees for voluntary bankruptcy); Ortwein v. Schwab, 410 U.S. 656, 93 S.Ct. 1172, 35 L.Ed.2d 572 (1973) (No right to appellate review of welfare termination.) See § 13.10, infra, for a comment on these cases.

84. Vance v. Terrazas, 444 U.S. 252, 100 S.Ct. 540, 62 L.Ed.2d 461 (1980).

85. 444 U.S. at 266, 100 S.Ct. at 548. For citations to additional cases, and secondary authorities regarding immigration and naturalization, see the multivolume edition of this treatise: R. Rotunda & J. Nowak, Treatise On Constitutional Law: Substance and Procedure, Chapter 22 (3rd ed. 1999, with annual supplements).

86. Board of Regents v. Roth, 408 U.S. 564, 572, 92 S.Ct. 2701, 2706–07, 33 L.Ed.2d 548 (1972), quoting Meyer v. Nebraska, 262 U.S. 390, 43 S.Ct. 625, 67 L.Ed. 1042 (1923).

human activity could be described as "liberty" for constitutional terms and that individuals in some situations could be adversely affected by government without any substantive or procedural guarantees.[87]

It would appear that whenever the government takes an action which is designed to deprive an individual, or a limited group of individuals, of the freedom to engage in some significant area of human activity, some procedure to determine the factual basis and legality for such action being taken is required by the due process clause. The primary issues have arisen in terms of restrictions on employment, the granting or withholding of important occupational licenses, and injury to the reputation of an individual.

Professional Licenses. If the government terminates an individual's ability to engage in a profession, it must grant that individual a procedure to determine his fitness to be a member of the profession.[88] Thus if an agency with governmental authority seeks to revoke the professional status or license of a doctor or lawyer, it must accord that individual a fair hearing.

If the individual has been denied a license to engage in a profession, it is not clear whether he is entitled to a hearing if the denial is based on any factual matter which might be contested or clarified at a hearing. Some decisions concerning the right to "property" indicate

that no hearing may be due unless the person has already received a license which the government is seeking to revoke.[89] If this is true, the individual who has been denied an initial license would have to bring a judicial action to have the basis for the denial reviewed. But a loss of liberty should be involved where government actions foreclose a wide range of employment or professional opportunities. If the government denial of a license precludes one from gaining employment in both the public and private sectors, the individual should be granted a hearing to determine the basis of the government action.[90]

If someone seeks temporary admission to practice as a licensed professional in a state, state agencies are under no obligation to grant that person a hearing prior to denying him or her the opportunity to practice temporarily in the state, if state law has not created an "entitlement" to practice temporarily in the state. Thus, when a state court judge refused to allow attorneys, licensed only in other states, to appear *pro hac vice* in state court proceedings, there was no deprivation of property because there was no entitlement to engage in temporary practice under state law. The Supreme Court also found that the denial involved no deprivation of liberty because the attorneys' reputation and ability to practice law in other states, in which they were licensed, were not seriously damaged by the

87. 408 U.S. at 569–70, 575, 92 S.Ct. at 2705, 2708.

88. In re Ruffalo, 390 U.S. 544, 88 S.Ct. 1222, 20 L.Ed.2d 117 (1968), Dent v. West Virginia, 129 U.S. 114, 123, 9 S.Ct. 231, 233–34, 32 L.Ed. 623 (1889). Cf. Withrow v. Larkin, 421 U.S. 35, 95 S.Ct. 1456, 43 L.Ed.2d 712 (1975). Statutes defining the terms for retaining a professional license often use specific criteria for license suspension so that they may give an individual licensee a property interest or "entitlement" in the license. Thus, the New York licensing system for horse trainers created a property interest in licensed trainers that was protected by the due process clause. Barry v. Barchi, 443 U.S. 55, 99 S.Ct. 2642, 61 L.Ed.2d 365 (1979). See § 13.9(c), infra.

89. Board of Regents v. Roth, 408 U.S. 564, 576, 92 S.Ct. 2701, 2708–09, 33 L.Ed.2d 548 (1972).

90. On this point, note the concurring opinion of Justice Powell in Weinberger v. Hynson, Westcott & Dunning, Inc., 412 U.S. 609, 638, 93 S.Ct. 2469, 2487, 37 L.Ed.2d 207 (1973) (Powell, J., concurring). To constitute a deprivation of liberty, government action must result in a substantial restriction on an individual's ability to engage

in a significant area of human activity, such as the ability to continue as a member of a licensed profession. In Conn v. Gabbert, 526 U.S. 286, 119 S.Ct. 1292, 143 L.Ed.2d 399 (1999) the Court ruled that an attorney had not lost a liberty interest when he was stopped and searched, pursuant to a warrant, at the time that one of his clients was testifying before a grand jury. Taking away the attorney's ability to be available to his client, when his client was testifying before the grand jury, did not constitute the taking of a liberty interest that was protected by the due process clause. The attorney would have standing to complain that the search warrant was invalid and that the search and seizure violated the Fourth Amendment. The majority opinion noted that the grand jury witness did not have a constitutional right to have counsel present during the grand jury proceedings, under prior decision of the Supreme Court. The majority in Conn refused to reconsider the scope of a grand jury witness's rights, because the majority ruled that the attorney did not have standing to assert the due process rights of his client.

refusal.[91]

Government as Employer. When the government acts as an employer there are special issues regarding the existence of liberty and property rights in employment. If the individual employee has not been granted a term of guaranteed employment, absent removal for just cause, he will have no property right or entitlement to continued employment in that position.[92] Indeed, dismissal from a specific position does not amount to a loss of "liberty" because the Court has held that having one form of government employment foreclosed does not constitute a deprivation of freedom which is encompassed by that term.[93]

However, if in dismissing the employee, the government also forecloses the individual's possible employment in a wide range of activities in both the public and private sectors, this dismissal might constitute a deprivation of liberty sufficient to require that the individual be granted a fair hearing.[94] Additionally, if the termination appears to be based upon grounds which would violate the Constitution, the individual is entitled to a hearing to determine whether he is being dismissed for constitutionally improper reasons. When the employee can make a prima facie showing that he is being dismissed for exercising his right to freedom of speech as protected by the First Amendment, he will be entitled to a hearing to determine the basis for his termination.[95]

Driver Licenses. Whenever the government takes control of an important area of human activity, it must grant a hearing to those who are denied the right to engage in the activity. Because the government has taken control of who may drive automobiles on its highways, when it revokes someone's driver's license, that person is entitled to a hearing to determine the basis for the revocation.[96] However, when the revocation is based on prior judicial determinations of violations of traffic laws, no hearing will be required if there are no further factual issues to contest.[97] In that situation the person has already received the opportunity for full judicial hearings. Similarly, if the government revokes someone's license to engage in a commercial enterprise, it must grant him a hearing to determine any factual issues which relate to the basis for the revocation of the license.[98]

Freedom of Action Within the Community. Even where the government has not established a licensing system to regulate an activity, if it revokes someone's privilege to engage in an important area of activity it will be required to grant the individual a hearing. Thus, if the government singles out a person as a "drunkard"—a charge which, under state law, legally forecloses his ability to purchase alcoholic beverages, it will owe him a hearing to determine whether his liberty should be thus curtailed.[99] The government also must give a hearing to resident aliens who are to be deported as the ability to remain physically within the country is protected by the concept of liberty in the Fourteenth Amendment.[100]

---

91. Leis v. Flynt, 439 U.S. 438, 99 S.Ct. 698, 58 L.Ed.2d 717 (1979).

92. Board of Regents v. Roth, 408 U.S. 564, 92 S.Ct. 2701, 33 L.Ed.2d 548 (1972).

93. Board of Regents v. Roth, 408 U.S. 564, 92 S.Ct. 2701, 33 L.Ed.2d 548 (1972); cf. Cafeteria & Restaurant Workers Union, Local 473 v. McElroy, 367 U.S. 886, 81 S.Ct. 1743, 6 L.Ed.2d 1230 (1961).

94. However, this employee might receive no protection from the due process clause. See § 13.5(d).

95. See § 13.4(c), notes 67–69, supra.

96. Bell v. Burson, 402 U.S. 535, 91 S.Ct. 1586, 29 L.Ed.2d 90 (1971).

A driver may have his or her driver's license suspended for failure to take a drunk driving test under certain circumstances; see Mackey v. Montrym, 443 U.S. 1, 99 S.Ct. 2612, 61 L.Ed.2d 321 (1979). For citations to addi-

tional cases, and secondary authorities on this point, see the multivolume edition of this treatise: R. Rotunda & J. Nowak, Treatise on Constitutional Law: Substance and Procedure § 17.4 (3rd ed. 1999, with annual supplements).

97. Dixon v. Love, 431 U.S. 105, 97 S.Ct. 1723, 52 L.Ed.2d 172 (1977).

98. Weinberger v. Hynson, Westcott & Dunning, Inc., 412 U.S. 609, 638, 93 S.Ct. 2469, 2487, 37 L.Ed.2d 207 (1973) (Powell, J., concurring); cf. Dent v. West Virginia, 129 U.S. 114, 123, 9 S.Ct. 231, 233–34, 32 L.Ed. 623 (1889).

99. Wisconsin v. Constantineau, 400 U.S. 433, 91 S.Ct. 507, 27 L.Ed.2d 515 (1971).

100. Deportation. For citations to Supreme Court cases, and secondary authorities, regarding immigration, deportation, and exclusion, see R. Rotunda & J. Nowak, Treatise on Constitutional Law: Substance and Procedure, Ch. 22 (3rd ed. 1999, with annual supplements).

Personal Reputation. One of the most disputed aspects of liberty in recent years is the degree to which the due process clauses protect the interest of an individual in his reputation. Government actions which injure a person's reputation within the community do not constitute a *per se* deprivation of property or liberty so as to require that the person be granted a hearing prior to the government action.[101]

In *Paul v. Davis* [102] a sheriff had distributed to merchants listings of "active shoplifters." The plaintiff argued that listing him on the sheet violated due process because there was no hearing to determine whether in fact he had engaged in such activities and this resulted in an injury to his reputation.[103] The Supreme Court held that this did not constitute a violation of due process. The majority opinion held that mere injury to reputation alone was not a deprivation of "liberty".[104]

However, the majority opinion noted that the individual would have the right to sue the government officials who libeled him, in a state court, as a matter of state tort law. The ruling that mere injury to reputation does not constitute a deprivation of liberty thus may mean only that the injured person must be satisfied with a tort remedy which follows the defamatory action. If the State had no tort action for libel against such officials—If the State granted its public officials immunity to defame private citizens while otherwise recognizing defamation action—it would raise a much more serious question as to whether the State was depriving someone of liberty or property by allowing the government to damage his name with no hope of rectifying the

harm done. One of the Justices has indicated that he believes this "later process" is a better rationale for the opinion.[105] However, *Paul* seems to find that there is simply no impairment of liberty or property from an injury to one's reputation, although commentators have noted that leaving this important individual interest outside of the Constitution is a severe departure from earlier due process theory.[106]

If a government official distributes false information about a person, there might be a deprivation of liberty if the act results in the person's freedom of choice or action being seriously curtailed. If the damage to the person's reputation is so great that it will limit the individual's associational opportunities within a community or foreclose a wide range of employment to the individual, the act will constitute a deprivation of liberty. In *Paul*, the Supreme Court found there was no impairment of a constitutionally protected liberty or property interest even though, as commentators have noted, denying constitutional protection to a person's interest in his reputation appeared to be a departure from earlier due process theory. It is not clear whether harm to an individual's reputation by the government could ever constitute a liberty or property deprivation for the purposes of the due process clause. In *Goss v. Lopez*,[107] the Supreme Court ruled that disciplinary actions in a government school, which resulted in students being suspended from the school, constituted a deprivation of liberty interests, in part because the disciplinary charges and the suspension would damage the students' associational relationships with fellow students and their future educational and employment op-

---

101. Fletcher, J., citing Treatise in, Peloza v. Capistrano Unified School Dist., 37 F.3d 517, 523 (9th Cir.1994), cert. denied 515 U.S. 1173, 115 S.Ct. 2640, 132 L.Ed.2d 878 (1995).

102. 424 U.S. 693, 96 S.Ct. 1155, 47 L.Ed.2d 405 (1976).

103. The plaintiff had been arrested for shoplifting prior to the distribution of the circular but he had not yet gone to trial. His case was dismissed without a ruling as to his guilt or innocence.

104. 424 U.S. at 708–10, 96 S.Ct. at 1164–65.

105. Ingraham v. Wright, 430 U.S. 651, 97 S.Ct. 1401, 51 L.Ed.2d 711 (1977) (Stevens, J., dissenting).

106. Monaghan, Of "Liberty" and "Property," 62 Cornell L.Rev. 405, 532–34 (1977).

107. 419 U.S. 565, 95 S.Ct. 729, 42 L.Ed.2d 725 (1975). The Court has held that a medical student need not be given a hearing for an academic dismissal following notice and review of poor clinical work. In reaching this result, the Court assumed arguendo that the student had been deprived of "liberty." See Board of Curators v. Horowitz, 435 U.S. 78, 98 S.Ct. 948, 55 L.Ed.2d 124 (1978).

See also Carey v. Piphus, 435 U.S. 247, 98 S.Ct. 1042, 55 L.Ed.2d 252 (1978) wherein the Court held that a student was entitled to only nominal damages for a violation of his or her rights under *Goss*.

portunities. Based on *Goss,* one could argue that a person is entitled to some type of fair process from the government to prevent, or remedy, a government action that will harm the individual's reputation so severely that the person will lose a wide range of employment opportunities.[108] However, in *Siegert v. Gilley,*[109] the Supreme Court held that a discharged employee of the federal government stated no cause of action under the due process clause when he sued his former supervisor for writing a letter to a prospective employer that prevented him from being hired for the new job. The Supreme Court made this ruling even though the plaintiff in *Siegert* stated that the material in the government supervisor's letter was false and that the supervisor had made the statements maliciously.[110] Thus, it appears that a person's interest in his reputation may be totally unprotected by the due process clause.[111]

Conclusion. It would seem clear that liberty in its most general sense includes the ability of individuals to engage in freedom of action within a society and free choice as regards their personal lives. Of course, not every limitation of individual freedom constitutes a violation of "liberty" in a constitutional sense or requires that the government

grant the individual a hearing. When the government acts so as to regulate an area of human activity for all persons, the law will be tested under the substantive restrictions of the due process clause and the specific protections of the Constitution. But unless some specific fundamental constitutional right is involved the government will be able to regulate most areas of human activity. So long as the government does not classify persons in such a way as to violate the equal protection clause, it may also regulate certain classifications of persons.

But the government's ability to regulate or eliminate an area of activity for a general class does not mean that it should be able to single out individuals for special limitations of freedom of action without granting them some process to determine the basis for such an action. For example, while the state need not let anyone purchase alcohol, it cannot single out a specific individual for denial of the right to purchase alcohol without giving that individual a hearing to determine whether such an action is proper. This does not amount to a restriction on the substantive powers of the state to regulate activities within its jurisdiction, but only a recognition that when the state acts against a specific individual, it must

108. This is the implicit holding of Codd v. Velger, 429 U.S. 624, 97 S.Ct. 882, 51 L.Ed.2d 92 (1977) (per curiam); the Court held the individual was not entitled to a hearing because he did not claim the distributed information was false. The position seemed to be accepted that if the employee alleged that false information had injured him seriously, he would be entitled to a hearing. 429 U.S. at 638 n. 11, 97 S.Ct. at 889 n. 11. (Stevens, J., dissenting).

109. 500 U.S. 226, 111 S.Ct. 1789, 114 L.Ed.2d 277 (1991), rehearing denied 501 U.S. 1265, 111 S.Ct. 2920, 115 L.Ed.2d 1084 (1991).

110. The plaintiff in *Siegert* was a clinical Psychologist who had resigned his position at a government hospital in Washington, D.C. when he was threatened with being fired. He was denied permanent employment at a United States Army hospital in West Germany because of negative statements in a letter written to the hospital staff by his former supervisor at the D.C. hospital. Chief Justice Rehnquist's majority opinion in *Siegert* recognized that the plaintiff in *Paul* had not alleged that the government actor who harmed his reputation had malicious intent to do so, and explained that "our decision in *Paul v. Davis* did not turn, however, on the state of mind of the defendant but on the lack of any constitutional protection for the interest in reputation." Siegert v. Gilley, 500 U.S. 226, 233, 111 S.Ct. 1789, 1794, 114 L.Ed.2d 277 (1991),

rehearing denied 501 U.S. 1265, 111 S.Ct. 2920, 115 L.Ed.2d 1084 (1991).

111. In *Connecticut Department of Public Safety v. Doe,* 538 U.S. 1, 123 S.Ct. 1160, 155 L.Ed.2d 98 (2003) the Justices unanimously held that a sex offender registration law could be applied to an individual who had been properly convicted of sex related crimes without giving that individual an additional hearing to determine whether he was in fact, dangerous. In a concurring opinion in *Connecticut Department of Public Safety* in which they cited this Treatise, Justices Souter and Ginsburg explained that, even after this decision, the individual could litigate the question of whether the law limited his liberty interest, in violation of substantive due process principles, or whether the classifications in the law, regarding which convicted criminals would be subject to the registry system, violated equal protection. 538 U.S. at 9, 10, 123 S.Ct. at 1165, 1166 (Souter, J., joined by Ginsburg, J., concurring). In Smith v. Doe, 538 U.S. 84, 123 S.Ct. 1140, 155 L.Ed.2d 164 (2003) the Supreme Court, by a 6 to 3 vote, found that a state sex offender registration law was civil in nature and that its application to persons who had been properly convicted of sex related offenses before the date of passage of the law did not violate the ex post facto clause of Article I, § 10. These cases are examined in § 10.6 of this Treatise.

do so in a procedurally fair manner. However, the Court has not accepted the concept of a general right to freedom from arbitrary adjudicative procedures.[112]

§ 13.5   Property

(a) Introduction

In one sense all property is a creature of the state because each government is free to define or limit property rights. However, the ability of either the state or federal governments to limit rights in property is subject to constitutional limitations. There are substantive limitations—such as the First Amendment, the equal protection guarantee and the concept of substantive due process—which limit the ways in which government can define even the most general property rights. For example, the state government could not define or enforce rights in real property as contingent on the provision that the property not be turned over to a member of a racial minority, for this "definition" would violate the equal protection clause.[1] But within the few substantive guarantees of the Constitution, the government is free to define property rights as it chooses. There is still a procedural requirement that the government not deprive a person of any property unless it affords him "due process."

There are two basic questions concerning the procedural protection for property. First, when is the government depriving someone of property? Second, what constitutes "property"? The first question really is a state action issue: the due process clauses only protect against governmental, rather than private, deprivations of property. This state action issue is examined more fully in a separate chapter.[2] One should note here that, whenever the government enforces private claims to property of one person against another, it has acted to deprive someone of his property.[3] Thus the alleged debtor must be afforded some fair procedure to determine whether his property should be taken and transferred to the other party.

The most difficult issues relate to the definition of property. Certainly all of the traditional forms of real and personal property fall within this definition,[4] but a problem arises as to those governmental distributions which do not fit this classical concept of property ownership. Any recipient of government benefits or largess may be said to have no property right in the benefit because such a person has no traditionally recognized ownership interest in the largess. Under the old right-privilege distinction it would be easy to classify the interest of a recipient of welfare payments or a student's interest in receiving public education as an unprotected privilege. Because the government had no duty to create systems of welfare payments or education, its granting or withholding of such "privileges" was not restrained by constitutional guarantees during the era of this distinction.

As we have already noted, the right-privilege distinction has come to an end as both courts and commentators have realized that individuals should not be subjected to the unfettered discretion of government to withhold even "privileges." Such a rule would leave many individuals at the mercy of a bureaucratic system and threaten the liberties protected by the

---

112. See Wisconsin v. Constantineau, 400 U.S. 433, 91 S.Ct. 507, 27 L.Ed.2d 515 (1971).

§ 13.5

1. Shelley v. Kraemer, 334 U.S. 1, 68 S.Ct. 836, 92 L.Ed. 1161 (1948); Barrows v. Jackson, 346 U.S. 249, 73 S.Ct. 1031, 97 L.Ed. 1586 (1953), rehearing denied 346 U.S. 841, 74 S.Ct. 19, 98 L.Ed. 361 (1953).

2. See Chapter 12.

3. Sniadach v. Family Finance Corp., 395 U.S. 337, 89 S.Ct. 1820, 23 L.Ed.2d 349 (1969).

4. When dealing with the application of federal statutes to property interests, the Supreme Court will look to state law for a definition of the nature of the property interests held by an individual. The determination of whether the person's interest qualifies as "property" for federal purposes is a question that depends on the interpretation of federal law, or the United States Constitution, rather than on state law. See, e.g., United States v. Craft, 535 U.S. 274, 122 S.Ct. 1414, 152 L.Ed.2d 437 (2002) (federal tax lien could apply to property held by a husband and wife as tenants by the entirety even though only the husband was subject to the federal tax lien; Court explains the relationship of state law definition of property rights to the interpretation of federal statutes, which remains a federal question).

Bill of Rights.[5] When the government acts to dispense benefits, it must conform to the restrictions of the Constitution, which means that it may not deprive someone of an interest to which they are otherwise entitled without a procedure to determine the basis for the deprivation.[6]

The definition of property since the 1972 decision in *Board of Regents v. Roth*[7] has centered on the concept of "entitlement." The Court will recognize interests in government benefits as constitutional "property" if the person can be deemed to be "entitled" to them. Thus, the applicable federal, state or local law which governs the dispensation of the benefit must define the interest in such a way that the individual should continue to receive it under the terms of the law. This concept also seems to include a requirement that the person already has received the benefit or at least had a previously recognized claim of entitlement.[8]

A person has an entitlement-property interest in employment with the government if he has already received the position and applicable law guarantees him continued employ-

ment.[9] However, if the person has not yet been hired, he has no property right which requires a hearing on the refusal to initially employ him. Similarly, if one occupies a position that applicable law defines as terminable for any reason, that person can be discharged without the requirement of fair procedures.[10]

The concept of entitlement is meant to eliminate the requirement of hearings for those interests which are not statutory entitlements or are totally unlike traditional property. Unfortunately this analysis comes very close to the old right-privilege distinction, for states are allowed to define those interests that they will be required to protect under the due process clause. The requirement of present enjoyment also recognizes that the Constitution does not require a hearing for disappointed wishes or expectations but only for property entitlement. But this result leaves a person who must apply for even a highly defined system of general public benefits without procedural safeguards against totally arbitrary actions by government administrators. Again we see the specter of the right-privilege distinc-

---

5. See § 13.1.

6. Among the cases citing this section of the Treatise, or a corresponding section in the multivolume edition of this Treatise, are: Sullivan, C.J., quoting treatise, in Giaimo v. City of New Haven, 257 Conn. 481, 778 A.2d 33, 50 n. 13 (2001); Hollinger, J., citing Treatise, in Daniels v. Board of Curators, 51 S.W.3d 1, 6 (Mo.Ct.App.2001); Harper v. Secretary of Health and Human Services, 978 F.2d 260, 263 (6th Cir.1992) (per curiam); Brookpark Entertainment v. Taft, 951 F.2d 710, 714 (6th Cir.1991) (Guy, J.); Norris by Norris v. Board of Education of Greenwood, 797 F.Supp. 1452, 1469 (S.D.Ind.1992) (Tinder, J.); Owens v. New Britain General Hosp., 229 Conn. 592, 643 A.2d 233, 239 (1994) (Katz, J.); Montgomery, J., citing Treatise, in Board of Education of Carlsbad Municipal Schools v. Harrell, 118 N.M. 470, 477, 882 P.2d 511, 518, 94 Ed.Law Rep. 966 (1994); O'Scannlain, Circuit J., citing Treatise in Schneider v. California Dept. of Corrections, 151 F.3d 1194 (9th Cir.1998); Holderman, District Judge, citing Treatise in Smith v. McDonald, 1998 WL 259536 (N.D.Ill. 1998);Callahan, Chief J., citing Treatise in Packer v. Board of Educ. of Town of Thomaston, 246 Conn. 89, 717 A.2d 117 (1998); Kent, J., citing Treatise in, Gonzales v. Galveston Independent School Dist., 865 F.Supp. 1241, 1249, 95 Ed. Law Rep. 557 (S.D.Tex.1994); Bryant, J., (concurring) citing Treatise, in Kirsch v. Bowling Green State University, 1996 WL 284717, *11 (Ohio App.1996).

7. 408 U.S. 564, 92 S.Ct. 2701, 33 L.Ed.2d 548 (1972).

8. This "present enjoyment" concept is implied by some statements of the Court but it has not been the focus of a decision. Board of Regents v. Roth, 408 U.S. 564,

576, 92 S.Ct. 2701, 2708–09, 33 L.Ed.2d 548 (1972); Comment, Entitlement, Enjoyment and Due Process of Law, 1974 Duke L.J. 89, 101–02.

In Lyng v. Payne, 476 U.S. 926, 942, 106 S.Ct. 2333, 2343, 90 L.Ed.2d 921 (1986), rehearing denied 478 U.S. 1031, 107 S.Ct. 11, 92 L.Ed.2d 766 (1986), the Court cited *Walters* and noted that "[w]e have never held that applicants for benefits, as distinct from those already receiving them, have a legitimate claim of entitlement" protected by due process. A ruling on this issue was unnecessary in *Lyng*, however, because the Court found that, even if applicants for the government benefits at issue had an entitlement to those benefits, the notice about regulation of the benefits and benefit procedures, which was published in the Federal Register, satisfied due process. For citations to additional cases, including lower court cases, and secondary works on this topic see our multi-volume Treatise: R. Rotunda & J. Nowak, Treatise on Constitutional Law: Substance and Procedure (3rd ed. 1999, with annual supplements).

9. Perry v. Sindermann, 408 U.S. 593, 92 S.Ct. 2694, 33 L.Ed.2d 570 (1972). In *Perry* the applicable law was found to be administrative actions and a common law of tenure; see the subsection on employment which follows in this chapter.

10. Bishop v. Wood, 426 U.S. 341, 96 S.Ct. 2074, 48 L.Ed.2d 684 (1976).

tion, for the requirement of present enjoyment places virtually no procedural check on the government's initial decision to distribute benefits. However, it should be noted that the Supreme Court has not yet been confronted with a state which refuses to give any explanation or procedure to a person who is denied an initial allocation of a very important government benefit. For example, if a town refused to accept a particular child into its primary educational system, even though the child appeared to qualify under applicable law, it is difficult to believe that the concept of present enjoyment or entitlement would eliminate the requirement of a fair procedure to determine the basis for this action. It is possible that in such a case the Court would find that the definition of eligibility constituted a previous entitlement even though there was no actual receipt of the benefit prior to the request for a

hearing. However, the concept of present enjoyment is undefined at this time.[11]

Obviously, the distinction between "entitlements" and "expectancies" offers little guidance to those who need to solve problems relating to the meaning of property under the due process clauses. All that can be said with certainty is that the Supreme Court currently focuses on local law to determine if a person can be said to have a fair claim to a continuation of the government benefit. If a person has an entitlement to the benefit, he must receive a fair procedure to determine the basis for the government's withdrawal of the benefit. If he has no claim of entitlement under applicable law there need be no process at all. State law is critical to the determination of whether or not a person has a "property" or "entitlement" interest in a benefit he receives from the government. State law may indicate

---

11. In American Manufacturers Mutual Insurance Company v. Sullivan, 526 U.S. 40, 119 S.Ct. 977, 143 L.Ed.2d 130 (1999) the Supreme Court refused to place any constitutional restrictions on the decisions of private insurance corporations to refuse to make payments for medical bills to workers' compensation claimants, and the Court refused to establish any due process restrictions on the state created system for resolution of disputes between workers compensation claimants and those insurance corporations. Chief Justice Rehnquist wrote the majority opinion in *American Manufacturers Mutual Insurance Company.* He found that the decisions of private insurance companies to deny payment for medical bills that they believed were not reasonable and necessary were not decisions that involved "state action." Therefore, the insurance companies were not subject to constitutional limitations. 526 U.S. at 50–58, 119 S.Ct. at 985–89.

The state had created a system for resolution of a dispute between an individual who sought payment for a medical bill following an employment related injury and an insurance company that did not believe that the medical treatment was reasonable or necessary. This system involved the establishment of review boards that would make decisions concerning such disputes. In *American Manufacturers Mutual Insurance,* the individuals whose medical bills had not been paid asserted that due process guaranteed them the right to have their disputed claims resolved promptly and fairly. The Court employed the present enjoyment concept to completely eliminate any procedural due process protections for the workers who sought prompt and fair resolution of their disputes. Chief Justice Rehnquist's majority opinion found that, even though the injured workers had established their initial eligibility for medical treatment the injured workers had not yet established that a property interest in a particular medical treatment because neither the government nor the insurance company had ever found that the particular treatment was one to which they were entitled. Therefore, the majority ruled that the workers did not have a proper-

ty interest in payment of a specific medical treatment; the due process clause did not require the establishment of fair procedures for resolution of their claims. 526 U.S. at 53, 119 S.Ct. at 977.

Justice Ginsburg thought that the Court should not have addressed the state action issue in *American Manufacturers Mutual Insurance,* because she thought that due process would not require the state or the insurance companies to make a final determination regarding the payment of each requested medical bills within thirty days of receiving a claim for that bill. However, Justice Ginsburg believed that due process would require fair procedures for the resolution of claims for workers compensation. 526 U.S. at 60–62, 119 S.Ct. at 990–91. Justices Breyer and Souter agreed with the majority that the decisions of private insurance companies did not constitute state action, and that the individual claimants did not have a property interest in their claims for payments of bills. Nevertheless, these two Justices believed that there could be circumstances under which an individual workers' compensation claimant would have a property interest in his claims for medical payments based upon earlier payments from the insurance company for medical treatment of his injury. 526 U.S. at 62, 119 S.Ct. at 991 (Breyer, J., joined by Souter, J., concurring in part and concurring in the judgment). Justice Stevens believed that the state action issue was irrelevant to the question of whether due process required fair procedures for the resolution of disputes between workers compensation claimants and insurance companies; he also believed that the majority opinion in *American Manufacturers Mutual Insurance* had failed to address the question of whether the statutory system for resolution of such disputes was consistent with due process clause principles. 526 U.S. at 62–64, 119 S.Ct. at 991–92.

The state action issue is examined in Chapter 12 of this Treatise.

that a benefit previously granted to an individual, which it is now attempting to revoke, was not one protected by due process. However, the state cannot grant persons a right to a benefit that would be an "entitlement" for due process purposes and then, by statutory action or administrative ruling, give recipients fewer procedural safeguards for the termination of that benefit than would be required by a judicial analysis of due process principles. This is an important distinction. Local law provides the basis for the judiciary to determine whether an interest is protected by due process principles. If such an entitlement exists, the judiciary must determine independently of local law whether the procedures used by the state to terminate the entitlement meet the procedural requirements of due process.[12]

An individual who has a claim contract claim against a state or local government, will have received a fair process if the state allows the individual the opportunity to sue the state through the normal judicial process.[13]

There have been three particular problems in this area: (1) transfer of property in debt actions; (2) termination of government benefits; (3) government employment. In addition, an individual's interest in his or her reputation is reconsidered as a property interest.

(b) Debt Actions

Whenever property is taken from someone with the assistance of government officers, there is a deprivation of property. Thus, when the defendant in a lawsuit is ordered to pay money to a plaintiff, the defendant has been deprived of property. In such a situation, however, there is no denial of due process because the defendant received a fair process—the opportunity for a full trial.

A significant due process issue arises where the property in the possession of the alleged debtor is to be taken prior to trial. If, prior to trial, the government grants the plaintiff-creditor a writ of replevin, or otherwise assists in the transfer of property to the creditor, there is a deprivation of the debtor's property, requiring that the government establish a fair procedure to determine whether the creditor should receive the use of property and to insure that the debtor's interest in the property will be safeguarded pending the outcome of the litigation.[14] Even though the property of the defendant is only "frozen" prior to trial to insure that asset will be available to any later judgments, there is a deprivation of property.[15] Although the property itself has not been transferred, the debtor-defendant is deprived of its use. Such garnishments or attachments of debtor assets thus require a fair procedure to protect the interests of the debtor-defendant. The procedures required to safeguard these interests are examined in later sections of this Chapter.

It should be noted that many states have provisions in their commercial codes which legitimate private repossession of goods from debtors by creditors. While the private repossession constitutes a taking of a debtor's property, only "state action" is regulated by the due process clauses. A state's formal recognition of the "self-help" remedy has not been deemed sufficient to subject the self-help remedy to the restraints of the due process clause.[16]

12. Cleveland Board of Education v. Loudermill, 470 U.S. 532, 538–41, 105 S.Ct. 1487, 1491–93, 84 L.Ed.2d 494 (1985), on remand 763 F.2d 202 (6th Cir.1985). See also Davis v. Scherer, 468 U.S. 183, 192, 193 n. 10, n. 11, 104 S.Ct. 3012, 3019 n. 10 n. 11, 82 L.Ed.2d 139 (1984). See generally, Supreme Court of Connecticut citing Treatise in Packer v. Board of Education, 246 Conn. 89, 103, 717 A.2d 117, 127 (1998).

13. See Lujan v. G & G Fire Sprinklers, Inc., 532 U.S. 189, 121 S.Ct. 1446, 149 L.Ed.2d 391 (2001).

14. North Georgia Finishing v. Di–Chem, Inc., 419 U.S. 601, 95 S.Ct. 719, 42 L.Ed.2d 751 (1975).

15. Sniadach v. Family Finance Corp., 395 U.S. 337, 89 S.Ct. 1820, 23 L.Ed.2d 349 (1969).

16. See § 12.2. The Supreme Court upheld a state law, based on a provision of the Uniform Commercial Code, which allowed a warehouseman to sell the goods of another that were in his possession and against which he had a warehouseman's lien for storage charges. The majority opinion held that the law "allowing" the warehouseman-creditor to sell the goods did not give rise to "state action" in the sale. The majority opinion specifically noted that "this is not to say that dispute resolution between creditors and debtors involves a category of human affairs that is never subject to constitutional constraints." Flagg Bros., Inc. v. Brooks, 436 U.S. 149, 162 n. 12, 98 S.Ct. 1729, 1736–37 n. 12, 56 L.Ed.2d 185 (1978). Thus, the extent to which states may legitimize or recognize self-help remedies remains unclear. If government

(c) Government Benefits

This category includes all forms of benefits which the government dispenses to individuals. These benefits may be paid in cash (such as social security payments or farm subsidies) or distributed in kind (such as housing in publicly-owned facilities) or given in a hybrid form (such as food stamps, which constitute a subsidy for particular items). It should be remembered that even the most basic governmental services such as police protection or public primary education are forms of public welfare benefits.

Because the government is not under a duty to provide these benefits, they are sometimes referred to as government largess. But when the government distributes these benefits, it must do so in accordance with constitutional limitations. Thus, it cannot deny benefits to someone because he or she is a member of a racial minority for that would violate the equal protection guarantee.[17] Similarly, persons cannot be denied benefits because they engage in speech or associational activities which are protected by the First Amendment.[18] The Constitution may also restrain the government from making payments to some persons, such as religious societies[19] or groups that discriminate against others on the basis of race.[20] Where no fundamental constitutional principles are involved, the government has great latitude in its ability to select those to whom it will grant benefits.

Once the government has established a system of benefits, the due process clauses impose some requirement of fairness in the treatment of individual recipients of these goods or ser-vices. As Charles Reich has noted, the absence of recognition of individual "rights" in these benefits leaves the government with the power to undermine individual dignity and liberty through its dispensation of "privileges" to those dependent upon them.[21] Yet the Supreme Court has not required the government to establish fair procedures for the initial allocation of benefits. Although the Court has not resolved this issue, under the "entitlement" principle it would appear that a person has no property interest in a benefit unless he has previously been granted it by the government.[22]

A person receiving welfare payments, public housing, or public education will clearly lose an important interest if the government terminates his benefits. Yet the Supreme Court has refused to hold that prior receipt of benefits in itself gives one a right to a fair process to determine whether termination is proper. If the person's interest in the continuation of the benefit is categorized as a "mere expectancy", there is no loss of property which merits the protection of the due process clause. It is only when the person has a "claim of entitlement" that the interest rises to the level of constitutional property.[23]

Entitlement is determined by looking to applicable state or federal law regarding the disposition of the particular benefit. If the applicable law establishes criteria for continued receipt of the benefit which the individual appears to meet, he will have a claim of entitlement to continued benefits.[24] However, if applicable law creates no claim to future payments, the person has only an "ex-

---

personnel assist a creditor in seizing the property of an alleged debtor, the joint activity of the government personnel and the creditor constitutes state action that makes both the government personnel's and the creditor's actions subject to the Fourth Amendment limitations and due process principles. Soldal v. Cook County, 506 U.S. 56, 113 S.Ct. 538, 121 L.Ed.2d 450 (1992).

17. See §§ 14.5–14.10, infra.

18. See § 13.4, supra.

19. See Chapter 17.

20. See § 12.4 concerning state subsidies and "state action."

21. Reich, The New Property, 73 Yale L.J. 733 (1964); Reich, Individual Rights and Social Welfare: The Emerging Legal Issues, 74 Yale L.J. 1245 (1965).

22. See the discussion of this issue and citations in § 13.5(a), supra.

23. Board of Regents v. Roth, 408 U.S. 564, 92 S.Ct. 2701, 33 L.Ed.2d 548 (1972). See also City of Aurora v. Rhodes, 689 P.2d 603, 610 (Colo.1984) (citing an earlier edition of this treatise).

24. Goldberg v. Kelly, 397 U.S. 254, 90 S.Ct. 1011, 25 L.Ed.2d 287 (1970) (welfare payments); Goss v. Lopez, 419 U.S. 565, 95 S.Ct. 729, 42 L.Ed.2d 725 (1975) (school attendance).

pectancy" of continued benefits.[25] Under this theory a state may be allowed to eliminate the need for hearings to determine the basis for termination of benefits by establishing a system which clearly indicates that there is no right to continuation of benefits.

Because nursing home residents could establish no government-created entitlement to continued residence at a particular nursing home, the Supreme Court, in *O'Bannon v. Town Court Nursing Center*,[26] held that those residents had no right to a hearing before a government agency revoked the home's certification to receive payments from the Medicare and Medicaid programs. Decertification of a particular nursing home did not terminate a recipient's medical assistance but merely required him to find a different institution which would accept him and which was certified as qualified for the receipt of Medicare or Medicaid funds. While the residents of a particular nursing home might feel that they would be better treated at the former institution or that it would be difficult for them to find comparable care, they had no government-created entitlement to continued benefits at a particular nursing home that had been decertified. Only the owners of the nursing home had a right to be heard in the administrative process leading to the decertification.

The Supreme Court has found that state statutes granting an individual citizen welfare benefits create a sufficient entitlement in the continued receipt of public aid or housing payments to require a hearing to determine the

basis for termination of these benefits.[27] Similarly, the Court has held that when a state establishes a school system it must grant students a hearing regarding the fairness of dismissing or suspending them from the system.[28]

Government licenses are also a form of property insofar as they constitute an entitlement to engage in a valuable activity. Thus the government must have a fair procedure to determine whether driver's licenses[29] or occupational licenses[30] should be revoked. In all of these cases the government had established criteria for the receipt and continuation of the benefit which the individuals appeared to meet. As the individual had present enjoyment of the benefit and a claim of entitlement to its continuation under state law, he had a property interest which was protected by the due process clause.

In theory the government might be able to "reverse" the result of these cases by enacting a law which declares that individuals may have benefits (such as welfare payments, public schooling or occupational licenses) terminated for any reason by the government without any "process." However, such laws might well be susceptible to attack under the substantive due process and equal protection guarantees as totally arbitrary and invidious uses of governmental power. As to benefits, such as education or occupational licenses, there would be a further issue as to whether the government was in fact under a substantive duty to grant these items as "rights." Additionally, some terminations of benefits

25. Bishop v. Wood, 426 U.S. 341, 96 S.Ct. 2074, 48 L.Ed.2d 684 (1976) (government employment).

26. 447 U.S. 773, 100 S.Ct. 2467, 65 L.Ed.2d 506 (1980).

27. Goldberg v. Kelly, 397 U.S. 254, 90 S.Ct. 1011, 25 L.Ed.2d 287 (1970).

28. Goss v. Lopez, 419 U.S. 565, 95 S.Ct. 729, 42 L.Ed.2d 725 (1975). The *Goss* decision involved a student's dismissal from school for disciplinary reasons. That type of dismissal may affect both liberty and property interests of students. When a student is dismissed from an institution of higher education for academic reasons, a court will not require a complex hearing to determine the propriety of the academic dismissal. The Supreme Court has determined that judges should not review the decisions of academic authorities regarding academic dismissals other than to insure that appropriate officials

have exercised professional judgment regarding the dismissal. In these cases the Court has assumed arguendo that the student had a property interest in continued enrollment in the college or graduate program. See Board of Curators v. Horowitz, 435 U.S. 78, 98 S.Ct. 948, 55 L.Ed.2d 124 (1978); Regents of the University of Michigan v. Ewing, 474 U.S. 214, 106 S.Ct. 507, 88 L.Ed.2d 523 (1985). Regarding the process required to dismiss a student from school when the student has a liberty or property interest at stake in the dismissal proceeding, see § 13.9, infra.

29. Bell v. Burson, 402 U.S. 535, 91 S.Ct. 1586, 29 L.Ed.2d 90 (1971), mandate conformed to 124 Ga.App. 220, 183 S.E.2d 416 (1971).

30. In re Ruffalo, 390 U.S. 544, 88 S.Ct. 1222, 20 L.Ed.2d 117 (1968). See § 13.4(d) supra.

might also involve deprivations of liberty which would independently require a fair termination procedure.

At the current time it is difficult to predict how these issues would be resolved because the entitlement theory does not match the concept of property either to traditional property "rights" or to the importance of the interests to the individual.

(d) Government Employment

One form of government benefit to which the Supreme Court has strictly applied the entitlement theory is public employment.

If a person is hired for a government position which is clearly terminable at the will of his superiors, the employee does not have a property interest in the position which mandates a fair procedure for determining the basis for his termination. If the government gives the employee assurances of continual employment or dismissal for only specified reasons, then there must be a fair procedure to protect the employee's interests when the government seeks to discharge him from the position. This entitlement also may come from statutory law, formal contract terms, or the actions of a supervisory person with authority to establish terms of employment.

The dichotomy between a "claim of entitlement" to employment and a mere subjective expectancy of employment was brought out in the companion cases of *Board of Regents v. Roth* [31] and *Perry v. Sindermann*. [32] In *Roth* a teacher who was refused employment had only a one year contract and applicable state law left the retention of such persons in the total discretion of university officials. The majority opinion held that there was no claim of entitlement under local law and no deprivation of property which required a fair termination hearing. This case was the first use of the

entitlement concept to hold that some important individual interests could be excluded from the concept of "life, liberty or property." The college teacher in *Sindermann* had a similar lack of express rights under his contract, but in this case the college officials had previously indicated that he had a claim to reemployment under a "de facto" tenure program. The Court held that this gave him a sufficient claim of entitlement to require a hearing prior to the final decision not to renew his contract.

In *Arnett v. Kennedy* [33] the Court upheld the dismissal of a nonprobationary employee by the federal government without a pretermination hearing. Although there was no majority opinion, at least six Justices appeared to agree that the employee had an interest which could not be terminated without due process. The action of the Court seemed to be based on a majority view that pretermination review procedures and a post termination hearing constituted a sufficient procedure to safeguard this interest. [34]

But in *Bishop v. Wood* [35] the Court went further and held that the state could define the terms of what appeared to be permanent employment so as to eliminate the need for procedural safeguards for termination. Here an employee was terminated without any hearing under a law which appeared to deem him a "permanent employee" who could be dismissed only for failure to perform his work in a competent manner. The majority opinion deferred to the district court analysis of state law that the employee held his position at "the will and pleasure" of city officials. [36] The majority then held that the state was free to define the terms of employment so as to preclude claims of entitlement and procedural safeguards.

31. 408 U.S. 564, 92 S.Ct. 2701, 33 L.Ed.2d 548 (1972).

32. 408 U.S. 593, 92 S.Ct. 2694, 33 L.Ed.2d 570 (1972).

33. 416 U.S. 134, 94 S.Ct. 1633, 40 L.Ed.2d 15 (1974), rehearing denied 417 U.S. 977, 94 S.Ct. 3187, 41 L.Ed.2d 1148 (1974).

34. Arnett v. Kennedy, 416 U.S. 134, 171, 94 S.Ct. 1633, 1652, 40 L.Ed.2d 15 (White, J., concurring).

35. 426 U.S. 341, 96 S.Ct. 2074, 48 L.Ed.2d 684 (1976).

36. 426 U.S. at 345, 96 S.Ct. at 2078. The opinion of the district court on the meaning of North Carolina law was based on one opinion of the North Carolina Supreme Court which was not directly on point. The district judge had been affirmed by an equally divided vote of the Court of Appeals for the Fourth Circuit. Bishop v. Wood, 377 F.Supp. 501 (W.D.N.C.1973), affirmed 498 F.2d 1341 (4th Cir.1974).

The *Arnett* and *Bishop* cases establish the principle that the meaning of local law is critical to a determination of whether a government employee has an "entitlement" to her or his job that is protected by due process. However, state law cannot deny an employee who has an entitlement to her or his job the procedural safeguards against improper termination of employment that are guaranteed by due process. A state may define the procedures for terminating the employment of a government employee who has an entitlement to her job, only if the state procedures meet or exceed the minimum procedural safeguards required by due process. Thus, a state cannot by statute or regulation authorize the termination of employment for such employees without granting an employee a right to respond prior to the termination of her or his employment to the charges which are the basis of the job termination.[37]

It should be noted in closing that even those employees who lack any entitlement to continued employment cannot be discharged for reasons which in themselves violate the Constitution. Thus nontenured teachers cannot be fired because they have engaged in speech which is protected by the First Amendment.[38] However, a hearing will be required to determine the basis for the discharge of a nontenured teacher only where the individual can make a prima facie claim that he is being discharged for reasons which violated specific constitutional guarantees. Where the dismissal is based in part on the exercise of First Amendment rights, the dismissal will be upheld if the government can prove that the employee would have been discharged in any event for reasons unrelated to these activities.[39]

(e) Reputation Reconsidered as a Property Right

When the government acts so as to injure an individual's reputation, it will deprive that individual of his liberty if the damage is so severe as to significantly limit his associational or employment opportunities.[40] Only in those instances will the government be required to accord the individual some procedure to determine the basis and legality of its actions. In *Paul v. Davis*[41] the Supreme Court held that injury to one's reputation does not in itself constitute a deprivation of liberty or property.

In *Paul* a sheriff had distributed to local merchants a leaflet of "active shoplifters" which included the name and photograph of the plaintiff Davis. Davis had been arrested for shoplifting but his case later was dismissed without resolving the issue of his guilt. Davis brought an action in federal court against the sheriff for depriving him of liberty and property by failing to grant him a hearing before taking actions which injured his reputation. The Supreme Court held that Davis had not established a constitutionally cognizable loss of liberty or property, absent some further injury to his liberty.

The plaintiff in *Paul* could have brought a defamation suit against the sheriff in state court. State law did not grant the sheriff any privilege to defame; there was no general law of defamation to which state officials were exempt. There was a state procedure, a tort suit, available to remedy the deprivation of the individual's interest in his reputation, although the procedure followed, rather than preceded, the governmental act. Since that time, one Justice indicated that it was the finding of a sufficient, though delayed, process

---

37. Cleveland Board of Education v. Loudermill, 470 U.S. 532, 105 S.Ct. 1487, 84 L.Ed.2d 494 (1985). See § 13.9(c).

38. Board of Regents v. Roth, 408 U.S. 564, 575 n. 14, 92 S.Ct. 2701, 2708 n. 14, 33 L.Ed.2d 548 (1972).

39. Mount Healthy City School District Bd. of Education v. Doyle, 429 U.S. 274, 97 S.Ct. 568, 50 L.Ed.2d 471 (1977). The degree of burden placed on the government agency to demonstrate that the discharge decision was not a punishment of constitutionally protected speech may vary with the nature of the employee's expression. See,

Connick v. Myers, 461 U.S. 138, 103 S.Ct. 1684, 75 L.Ed.2d 708 (1983). See § 13.4(c) of this Treatise concerning the difficulty of determining when the government might be required to adopt a procedure designed to determine the facts concerning the employee's speech related activities before deciding to discharge the employee for her speech.

40. See § 13.4(c), supra.

41. 424 U.S. 693, 96 S.Ct. 1155, 47 L.Ed.2d 405 (1976).

to protect the reputation interest that justified denial of federal relief to the plaintiff in *Paul*.[42]

It is possible that a majority of the Justices in the 1970s would have found that the government was required to provide an individual whose reputation had been severely injured by government actions with some type of remedy, although the remedy might only have been the ability to bring tort suit against the government officials who harmed the person's reputation. However, that possibility may have been foreclosed by the Court's 1991 decision in *Siegert v. Gilley*.[43] The plaintiff in *Siegert*, was a former clinical psychologist at a federal government facility in Washington, D.C. He resigned from his position at that hospital after being threatened with job termination. Thereafter, he applied for a position with a United States Army hospital in West Germany. He was denied permanent employment at the Army hospital because of negative statements in a letter written to the United States Army hospital by his former supervisor at the government hospital. The plaintiff alleged that his former supervisor at the hospital had impaired his liberty and property interests by making defamatory statements that deprived him of the ability to engage in his profession. Chief Justice Rehnquist's majority opinion in *Siegert* ruled that plaintiff could not state any cause of action against the government or his former supervisor under the Fifth Amendment due process clause[44] regardless of whether the supervisor at the hospital had a malicious state of mind when he wrote the allegedly defamatory letter. The Chief Justice noted that the defendant in *Paul* had not acted mali-

ciously, but the Chief Justice explained that "our decision in *Paul v. Davis* did not turn, however, on the state of mind of the defendant, but on the lack of any constitutional protection for the interest in reputation."[45]

In *Connecticut Department of Public Safety v. Doe*[46], the Justices unanimously held that a sex offender registration law could be applied to an individual who had been properly convicted of sex related crimes without giving that individual an additional hearing to determine whether he was in fact, dangerous. In a concurring opinion in *Connecticut Department of Public Safety* in which they cited this Treatise, Justices Souter and Ginsburg explained that, even after this decision, the individual could litigate the question of whether the law limited his liberty interest, in violation of substantive due process principles, or whether the classifications in the law, regarding which convicted criminals would be subject to the registry system, violated equal protection.[47]

§ 13.6   Irrebuttable Presumptions— The "Non" Liberty or Property Due Process Requirement

In a few cases the Supreme Court has held that the government could not establish an "irrebuttable presumption" which classified people for a burden or benefit without determining the individual merit of their claims. These presumptions were said to violate due process because they deprived someone of a governmental benefit without any fair process. Thus the Court struck down a college tuition system which did not allow individuals a fair

---

42. Ingraham v. Wright, 430 U.S. 651, 700, 97 S.Ct. 1401, 1427, 51 L.Ed.2d 711 (1977) (Stevens, J., dissenting). Stevens, J. did not participate in the *Paul* decision.

43. 500 U.S. 226, 111 S.Ct. 1789, 114 L.Ed.2d 277 (1991), rehearing denied 501 U.S. 1265, 111 S.Ct. 2920, 115 L.Ed.2d 1084 (1991).

44. In *Siegert*, the plaintiff attempted to base his suit directly upon the Fifth Amendment rather than upon a specific federal civil rights statute. The Supreme Court has held that, under some circumstances, the Constitution or its Amendments will provide a basis for bringing a cause of action directly against the federal government. Bivens v. Six Unknown Named Agents Fed. Bureau of Narcotics, 403 U.S. 388, 91 S.Ct. 1999, 29 L.Ed.2d 619 (1971).

45. Siegert v. Gilley, 500 U.S. 226, 235, 111 S.Ct. 1789, 1795, 114 L.Ed.2d 277 (1991), rehearing denied 501 U.S. 1265, 111 S.Ct. 2920, 115 L.Ed.2d 1084 (1991).

46. 538 U.S. 1, 123 S.Ct. 1160, 155 L.Ed.2d 98 (2003)

47. 538 U.S. at 9, 10, 123 S.Ct. at 1165, 1166 (Souter, J., joined by Ginsburg, J., concurring). In Smith v. Doe, 538 U.S. 84, 123 S.Ct. 1140, 155 L.Ed.2d 164 (2003) the Supreme Court, by a 6 to 3 vote, found that a state sex offender registration law was civil in nature and that its application to persons who had been properly convicted of sex related offenses before the date of passage of the law did not violate the ex post facto clause of Article I, § 10. These cases are examined in § 10.6 of this Treatise.

chance to prove they were residents of a state.[1] Similarly, the Court struck down employment restrictions on pregnant teachers when the system made no individualized determination of their ability to continue working during their pregnancy.[2] Indeed, the Supreme Court engaged in one of its rare invalidations of a welfare payment qualification when it struck down a food stamp act provision which disqualified a large class of households without individualized determination as to their need.[3]

It now seems readily apparent that these cases actually rest on an equal protection rationale, for the objectionable portion of each law was the way in which it classified individuals.[4] It was the arbitrary classification by previous residency for tuition, by pregnancy for employment, or by income tax status for food stamps that was the impermissible basis of these laws.[5] In none of the cases would a "process" have saved the law because the procedure would only have determined whether an individual fit into one of these arbitrary classifications.[6] The Justices have consistent-

ly upheld classifications which were not invidious against charges that they constituted irrebuttable presumptions.[7]

For example, a state may ban all advertising on trucks which does not advertise the business interests of the truck owner. The classification between "owned" and "rented" advertising is sufficiently related to legitimate governmental concerns to pass review under the equal protection guarantee.[8] No hearing under the due process clause would be necessary unless a trucker who is fined for "rented" advertising claims his advertisement represented his own interests. To strike the law as an irrebuttable presumption against those who rented advertising space would be a resurrection of the now discredited theory of substantive due process as a check on economic or general welfare legislation.

While "irrebuttable presumption" analysis is not strictly a form of procedural due process it does highlight significant due process concerns. When the government dispenses benefits or burdens it should have some fair proce-

§ 13.6

1. Vlandis v. Kline, 412 U.S. 441, 93 S.Ct. 2230, 37 L.Ed.2d 63 (1973).

2. Cleveland Bd. of Education v. LaFleur, 414 U.S. 632, 94 S.Ct. 791, 39 L.Ed.2d 52 (1974). See also Turner v. Department of Employment Sec., 423 U.S. 44, 96 S.Ct. 249, 46 L.Ed.2d 181 (1975) holding that women could not be excluded from unemployment compensation because they were pregnant without an individualized determination of their ability to work.

3. United States Dept. of Agriculture v. Murry, 413 U.S. 508, 93 S.Ct. 2832, 37 L.Ed.2d 767 (1973).

4. Early academic commentary on this issue includes: Bezanson, Some Thoughts on the Emerging Irrebuttable Presumption Doctrine, 7 Ind.L.Rev. 644 (1974); Nowak, Realigning the Standards of Review Under the Equal Protection Guarantee—Prohibited, Neutral and Permissive Classifications, 62 Georgetown L.J. 1071, 1104–09 (1974).

5. Some Justices attempted to make this point when concurring in the irrebuttable presumption decisions. See, e.g., Vlandis v. Kline, 412 U.S. 441, 457–58, 93 S.Ct. 2230, 2238–39, 37 L.Ed.2d 63 (1973) (White, J., concurring); Cleveland Bd. of Education v. LaFleur, 414 U.S. 632, 651, 94 S.Ct. 791, 802, 39 L.Ed.2d 52 (1974) (Powell, J., concurring).

6. See also, Mourning v. Family Publications Service, Inc., 411 U.S. 356, 93 S.Ct. 1652, 36 L.Ed.2d 318 (1973) (upholding classification in Truth in Lending Act); Marshall v. United States, 414 U.S. 417, 94 S.Ct. 700, 38 L.Ed.2d 618 (1974) (upholding sentencing classification in

Narcotic Rehabilitation Act); Weinberger v. Salfi, 422 U.S. 749, 95 S.Ct. 2457, 45 L.Ed.2d 522 (1975) (upholding eligibility classifications of surviving spouses and stepchildren under Social Security Act based on the duration of their relationship to a deceased wage earner); Usery v. Turner Elkhorn Mining Co., 428 U.S. 1, 96 S.Ct. 2882, 49 L.Ed.2d 752 (1976) (upholding classifications in Federal Coal Mine Health and Safety Act); United States v. Locke, 471 U.S. 84, 105 S.Ct. 1785, 85 L.Ed.2d 64 (1985) (a federal statute terminating interests of owners of mining claims on federal land who failed to comply with annual filing requirements, which, under the statute, "shall be deemed conclusively to constitute an abandonment of the mining claim" does not constitute an irrebuttable presumption, even though proof of actual intention is irrelevant to abandonment of the claim, because the statute simply establishes a property regulation that terminates all claim rights for failure to meet a reasonable regulation).

7. See note 6, supra. The Court has avoided ruling on the continued vitality of irrebuttable presumption analysis. Lower federal courts had found a state policy denying in-state tuition status at the state university to resident nonimmigrant alien students violated due process, equal protection, and irrebuttable presumption principles. The Supreme Court in Toll v. Moreno, 458 U.S. 1, 102 S.Ct. 2977, 73 L.Ed.2d 563 (1982) held that the state policy conflicted with federal law and violated the supremacy clause and did not rule on the due process or equal protection claims.

8. Railway Express Agency v. New York, 336 U.S. 106, 69 S.Ct. 463, 93 L.Ed. 533 (1949).

dure for sorting out individual claims. This approach seems to support Professor Van Alstyne's call for recognition of a right to "freedom from arbitrary adjudicative procedures."[9] However, the Court since 1972 has found that a guarantee of procedural due process is only applicable where the government is held to deprive someone of "life, liberty, or property".[10]

By masking substantive decisions in procedural language, the Supreme Court, in the irrebuttable presumption cases, confused due process and equal protection analysis. Irrebuttable presumption analysis allowed the Court to overturn legislative decisions without having to justify the use of judicial power as would an open use of substantive due process or equal protection analysis. The use of irrebuttable presumption language was a conceptually confused, if not dishonest, method of justifying independent judicial review of legislative classifications. The declining use of irrebuttable presumption analysis may evidence increasing willingness of Justices to address directly the judicial role in reviewing legislatively created classifications.[11]

In *Michael H. v. Gerald D.*[12] the Supreme Court, without a majority opinion, upheld a state statute that established a presumption that a child born to a married woman was the legitimate child of the woman and her husband. This presumption could only be overcome, in limited circumstances, by either the wife or husband. The statutory presumption was attacked by a man who asserted that he was the biological father of a child born to a woman who was married to another man. Justice Scalia wrote for four members of the Court in finding that the statutory classification of the child as the offspring of the married husband and wife did not violate either substantive due process or procedural due process principles. Denying the male a hearing to establish paternity did not deprive the male of a constitutionally protected interest, because the rule of law used by the state to determine parenthood did not violate any provision of the Constitution. In other words, if the state can make the substantive decision that children born to a married couple are to be treated as the offspring of the two parties in the marriage, then there is simply nothing to have a hearing about. The assertion that the state had created an "irrebuttable presumption" was nothing more than an assertion that the substance of the state law should be rejected. Justice Stevens provided the fifth vote in this five to four decision; Justice Stevens believed that the statutory declaration of the husband as the father of the wife's child did not violate due process principles.[13] Justice Stevens believed that the state law at issue gave the male who was asserting biological parenthood of the child an opportunity to have a hearing on the issue of whether he should be allowed to visit the child even though the statute gave the male no hearing or opportunity to be declared the "father" of the child. Justice Stevens

9. Van Alstyne, Cracks in "The New Property": Adjudicative Due Process in the Administrative State, 62 Cornell L.Rev. 445, 487 (1977).

10. Perhaps the most amazing feature of this distinction is that Justice Stewart was the author of the majority opinion in Board of Regents v. Roth, 408 U.S. 564, 92 S.Ct. 2701, 33 L.Ed.2d 548 (1972) which was the first case to make such a distinction, and also the champion of the irrebuttable presumption analysis. See, Cleveland Bd. of Education v. LaFleur, 414 U.S. 632, 657, 94 S.Ct. 791, 804–05, 39 L.Ed.2d 52 (1974) (Rehnquist, J., dissenting) ("My Brother Stewart thereby enlists the Court in another quixotic engagement in his apparently unending war on irrebuttable presumptions.").

11. See cases cited in note 6 supra; see generally §§ 11.4, 14.3. See also National Potash Co. v. Property Tax Division, 101 N.M. 404, 683 P.2d 521, 524 (App.1984) (citing an earlier edition of the treatise); Commonwealth, Department of Transportation v. Slater, 75 Pa.Cmwlth. 310, 462 A.2d 870, 881 (1983) (citing an earlier edition of

this treatise); Parker, J., citing Treatise in Catlin v. Sobol, 93 F.3d 1112, 1118 (2d Cir.1996).

12. 491 U.S. 110, 109 S.Ct. 2333, 105 L.Ed.2d 91 (1989).

13. 491 U.S. at 133, 109 S.Ct. at 2347 (Stevens, J., concurring in the judgment).

Four Justices dissented in *Michael H.* Justices Brennan, Marshall and Blackmun believed that the law at issue violated both substantive and procedural due process principles. They believed that the conclusive presumption established by the statute impaired a liberty interest that was protected by the Constitution. Michael H. v. Gerald D., 491 U.S. 110, 133, 109 S.Ct. 2333, 2349, 105 L.Ed.2d 91 (1989) (Brennan, J., joined by Marshall and Blackmun, JJ., dissenting). Justice White also believed that the male had a liberty interest that could not be denied without fair process. 491 U.S. at 158, 109 S.Ct. at 2360 (White, J., joined by Brennan, J., dissenting).

believed that the only constitutionally protected interest that the male in this case might have would be the interest in establishing a personal relationship with the child and, therefore, that denial of any procedures by which the male would be declared to be the legal "father" of the child did not violate due process.

§ 13.7 What Process Is Due? The Procedures Required by the Due Process Clause—Introduction

When a person is deprived of life, liberty or property, there must be some process granted him in order to ensure that the action taken complies with the due process clauses. However, "process" is not a term with a clear definition and the nature of the procedure required to comply with the due process clause depends on many factors concerning the individual deprivation. Indeed the study of the required procedures has become splintered into several independent subject areas. Those who are interested in a detailed analysis of the procedures which are necessary to comply with due process in more specific terms are advised to consult one of the major reference works in the area of administrative law,[1] civil procedure[2] or criminal procedure.[3]

In this section we will outline the constitutional framework within which the Supreme Court must determine specific cases concerning the adequacy of procedures granted an individual prior to depriving him of life, liberty or property. Our discussion will be divided into three major parts: first, a brief statement of the general principles which the Court fol-

lows in determining the adequacy of any procedure; second, a look at the most significant decisions in terms of procedures required in three areas: deprivations of physical liberty, debtor-creditor relationships and termination of government benefits; and third, a note on access to judicial process.

§ 13.8 General Principles

The Supreme Court has tended to view its decisions on necessary procedures under the due process clause in an essentially utilitarian fashion. The Court has demonstrated a consistent belief that the adversary process is best designed to safeguard individual rights against arbitrary action by the government. The Justices determine the scope of trial-type procedures required for any particular deprivation by balancing the worth of the procedure to the individual against its cost to the society as a whole.

Professor Mashaw has exposed major flaws in the current approach of the Justices to these issues. Mashaw has argued that the Court should concern itself with safeguards other than adversary procedures because individual rights are often better protected by careful analysis of decision-making systems rather than new adversarial procedures.[1] He also has demonstrated why the Court's decisions in this area should follow an independent theory of due process values rather than the current utilitarian approach. The utilitarian balancing process often seems to degrade the nature of the rights and, in any event, seems one for which the judicial branch of government is not apparently well suited. Nevertheless, the Supreme Court continues to view the procedures required in terms of which additional adversary procedures should be engraft-

§ 13.7

1. See e.g., S. Breyer [Justice Breyer], R. Stewart, C. Sunstein & M. Spitzer, Administrative Law and Regulatory Policy (4th ed. 1999).

2. J. Moore, Moore's Federal Practice (2d ed.) (multivolume treatise with some differences in dates and coauthors of particular volumes); C. Wright, Federal Practice and Procedure (multi-volume treatise with some differences in dates and coauthors of particular volumes).

3. See, e.g., W. LaFave, J. Israel & N. King Criminal Procedure (1999 with annual supplements).

§ 13.8

1. Mashaw, The Management Side of Due Process: Some Theoretical and Litigation Notes on the Assurance of Accuracy, Fairness, and Timeliness in the Adjudication of Social Welfare Claims, 59 Cornell L.Rev. 772 (1974). For an insightful analysis of the adjudicative process and alternatives thereto, see Eisenberg, Participation, Responsiveness and the Consultative Process: An Essay for Lon Fuller, 92 Harv.L.Rev. 410 (1978).

ed on an administrative system and it makes this determination by a balancing process.[2]

Before examining the balancing test in operation, one should note the different elements of the adversary process which may be required as part of the "due process" which must be afforded to an individual when the government deprives him of life, liberty or property. The essential elements are: (1) adequate notice of the charges or basis for government action; (2) a neutral decision-maker; (3) an opportunity to make an oral presentation to the decision-maker; (4) an opportunity to present evidence or witnesses to the decision-maker; (5) a chance to confront and cross-examine witnesses or evidence to be used against the individual; (6) the right to have an attorney present the individual's case to the decision-maker; (7) a decision based on the record with a statement of reasons for the decision. Additionally there are six other procedural safeguards which tend to appear only in connection with criminal trials or formal judicial process of some type. Those are: (1) the right to compulsory process of witnesses; (2) a right to pre-trial discovery of evidence; (3) a public hearing; (4) a transcript of the proceedings; (5) a jury trial; (6) a burden of proof on the government greater than a preponderance of the evidence standard.

Need for Resolution of a Factual Dispute. The first decision which a court has to make on the due process issue is whether any procedure is required. There had been some indication that the Supreme Court might require some type of procedure to formalize decisions involving deprivations of life, liberty or property even though there were no factual issues to resolve. But the Court finally decid-

ed that there is no requirement of a procedure to determine the basis for an action which affects an individual where there are no factual issues in dispute. Thus the Court has held that a discharged government employee has no right to a procedure when he does not challenge the truthfulness of the facts upon which his discharge was based.[3] Similarly, the Court has held that there was no right to a hearing to determine whether property previously taken for delinquent taxes could be sold when there was no challenge to the original seizure of the property by the government.[4]

Cases also arise where the government makes a decision based upon facts which already have been determined through some adequate procedural system such as a trial. In these situations the individual will have no further right to a hearing if the disputed issues have already been resolved by adequate process. Thus the Court has held that there is no right to a hearing or other procedure in connection with a suspension or revocation of a person's automobile driver's license where the revocation is based on violations of traffic laws which were previously established through the judicial process.[5]

Rulemaking–Legislative Process. It is most common for the government to affect the life, liberty or property interest of a great number of people through its legislative functions. When the legislature passes a law which affects a general class of persons, those persons have all received procedural due process—the legislative process. The challenges to such laws must be based on their substantive compatibility with constitutional guaran-

---

2. Mashaw, The Supreme Court's Due Process Calculus for Administrative Adjudication in Mathews v. Eldridge: Three Factors in Search of a Theory of Value, 44 U.Chi.L.Rev. 28 (1976). See also, Redish & Marshall, Adjudicatory Independence and The Values of Procedural Due Process, 95 Yale L.J. 455 (1986).

3. Codd v. Velger, 429 U.S. 624, 97 S.Ct. 882, 51 L.Ed.2d 92 (1977) (per curiam).

4. Pearson v. Dodd, 429 U.S. 396, 97 S.Ct. 581, 50 L.Ed.2d 574 (1977).

5. Dixon v. Love, 431 U.S. 105, 97 S.Ct. 1723, 52 L.Ed.2d 172 (1977). Among the cases citing this section of the Treatise are: New York State Nat'l Org. for Women v. Pataki, 261 F.3d 156, 170 (2d Cir.2001), cert. denied 534

U.S. 1128, 122 S.Ct. 1066, 151 L.Ed.2d 969 (2002) (Walker, C.J.); Conopco, Inc. v. Roll Int'l, 231 F.3d 82, 88 (2d Cir.2000) (McLaughlin, J.); Supreme Court of California citing Treatise in Warden v. State Bar of California, 21 Cal.4th 628, 88 Cal.Rptr.2d 283, 291, 982 P.2d 154 (1999); Polozola, District Judge, citing Treatise in Summerchase Ltd. Partnership v. City of Gonzales, 970 F.Supp. 522, 536 n. 8 (M.D.La.1997). Motz, C.J., quoting Treatise in Knox v. Lanham, 895 F.Supp. 750, 759 (D.Md.1995); O'Scannlain, Circuit J., citing Treatise in Brewster v. Board of Educ. of Lynwood Unified School Dist., 149 F.3d 971 (9th Cir.1998); Acosta, District Judge, citing Treatise in Matos–Arroyo v. Diaz–Colon, 1997 WL 767280 (D.Puerto Rico 1997).

tees. Similarly, an administrative agency may make decisions that are of a legislative or general rulemaking character. When an agency promulgates generalized rules there is no constitutional right to a hearing for a specific individual. However when the agency makes rules that might be termed adjudicative in that they affect a very defined group of interests, then persons representing those interests should be granted some fair procedure to safeguard their life, liberty or property.

The line between rulemaking and adjudication is not at all clear and it may be that the Court will move towards requiring some type of hearing for those who are affected in any constitutionally cognizable way by even generalized agency rules. However, to date the Supreme Court has not required procedural safeguards of systemic fairness in this rulemaking or quasi-adjudicative process beyond those established in the Administrative Procedure Act.[6]

Specific Constitutional Limitations on the Adjudicatory Process. When the government is required to establish some procedure concerning individual deprivations of life, liberty or property, the scope of permissible procedures is sometimes limited by specific constitutional guarantees. This limitation applies to the criminal trial process, which is specifically regulated by the Bill of Rights.[7] The civil trial process is also regulated by special constitutional guarantees such as due process restrictions on court jurisdiction[8] and certain restraints on the enforcement of judgments arising from the full faith and credit clause.[9] Additionally the federal government is required to have jury trials for civil cases under the Seventh Amendment.[10] Yet Con-

6. Absent clear constitutional violations, the Administrative Procedure Act, 5 U.S.C.A. § 551 et seq. establishes the maximum procedural requirements for federal agency rulemaking. Reviewing courts may grant additional procedural rights regarding the rulemaking function of these agencies only if congressional authorization for such judicial review exists. In Vermont Yankee Nuclear Power Corp. v. Natural Resources Defense Council, Inc., 435 U.S. 519, 98 S.Ct. 1197, 55 L.Ed.2d 460 (1978), on remand to 685 F.2d 459 (D.C.Cir.1982), the Court unanimously (Justices Blackmun and Powell not participating) overturned a decision by the Court of Appeals for the District of Columbia that restricted the licensing of nuclear reactors by the Atomic Energy Commission. The Supreme Court opinion stated:

> "This is not to say necessarily that there are no circumstances which would ever justify a court in overturning agency action because of a failure to employ procedures beyond those required by statute. But such circumstances, if they exist, are extremely rare."

435 U.S. at 524, 98 S.Ct. at 1202.

7. For references, see § 13.7 notes 1 and 3 supra and §§ 13.4(b), 13.9(a).

8. Due Process Limitations on Court Jurisdiction. An examination of the technical basis upon which a court may exercise jurisdiction over a person or a corporation who resides outside of the physical boundaries of the jurisdiction (such as a state court attempt to exercise jurisdiction over an out-of-state person or corporation) is beyond the scope of this treatise. In § 17.8 of our multi-volume treatise, we note the relationship between rulings regarding limitations on court jurisdiction over nonresidents and the due process principles that require the government to follow a fundamentally fair process before taking a person's life, liberty, or property. See R. Rotunda & J. Nowak, Treatise on Constitutional Law: Substance and Procedure § 17.8 (3rd ed. 1999, with annual supplements).

9. Choice of Law—Conflict of Law Problems. There are many instances in which a state or federal court must determine whether the substantive law of one of several jurisdictions applies to resolve a case which involves a dispute between parties who reside in several different states. Rulings on these substantive choice of law problems have been only minimally affected by the due process principles set out in this chapter. Due process principles will restrict a state's ability to apply its law to a cause of action or occurrence that has no relation or contact with the state; the full faith and credit clause of Article IV may also restrict a state's choice of law by commanding a state to respect the sovereign interests of another state. For citations to Supreme Court cases, and secondary authorities, on this point, see R. Rotunda & J. Nowak, Treatise on Constitutional Law: Substance and Procedure, § 17.8 (3rd ed. 1999, with annual supplements).

10. The Seventh Amendment—Overview. The Seventh Amendment states: "In Suits at common law, where the value in controversy shall exceed twenty dollars, the right of trial by jury shall be preserved, and no fact tried by jury, shall be otherwise re-examined in any Court of the United States, than according to the rules of the common law." The Supreme Court has found that this is not a fundamental aspect of due process or the liberty protected by the due process clause of the Fourteenth Amendment so that it is not applicable to state court proceedings. Minneapolis and St. Louis R. Co. v. Bombolis, 241 U.S. 211, 36 S.Ct. 595, 60 L.Ed. 961 (1916).

Whether an individual in a federal court proceeding has a right to a trial by jury in a civil case, the court must determine not only whether the amount in controversy exceeds twenty dollars but also whether the issue to be resolved in the case is the type of issue which would have been submitted to jury determination at common law. For citations to additional Supreme Court cases, and secondary authorities, on this point, see R. Rotunda & J.

gress may establish new forms of public rights and actions that may be adjudicated by agencies without jury trials.[11] In this chapter we are only concerned with the requirements of due process as a general guarantee of fair procedure.

Right to a Fair Decisional Process and an Impartial Decisionmaker. The essential guarantee of the due process clause is that of fairness. The procedure must be fundamentally fair to the individual in the resolution of the factual and legal basis for government actions which deprive him of life, liberty or property. Due process only guarantees an individual a fundamentally fair procedure. Nothing in the Constitution, or its amendments, guarantees that an individual will have a process that is most likely to result in a favorable ruling for that individual. Neither substantive due process nor procedural due

process principles are violated when a government agency takes an adverse action against a government employee, for false statements the employee made during an investigation of misconduct within the agency.[12]

While different situations may entail different types of procedures, there is always the general requirement that the government process be fair and impartial. Therefore, there must be some type of neutral and detached decision-maker, be it a judge, hearing officer or agency. The Court has continually held that "a fair trial in a fair tribunal is a basic requirement of due process."[13] This requirement applies to agencies and government hearing officers as well as judges.[14]

The Supreme Court has strictly enforced this right and held that decision-makers are constitutionally unacceptable where they have

---

Nowak, Treatise on Constitutional Law: Substance and Procedure, § 17.8 (3rd ed. 1999, with annual supplements).

11. The Seventh Amendment—New Causes of Action. Congress can create statutory rights that are enforced by administrative or judicial tribunals. However, rights created by statutes often are enforced by actions in federal courts. Suits brought under the statute must be tried by a jury if the statute creates rights and remedies of a type that are closely analogous to those rights and remedies that would have been enforced in actions at "law" (rather than "equity") and would have required trial by jury in common law courts prior to 1791. However, it may be difficult in any given case to determine whether the newly created cause of action is one that involves fact issues that should be subjected to jury resolution at the demand of the parties. For citations to additional Supreme Court cases, and secondary authorities, on this point, see R. Rotunda & J. Nowak, Treatise on Constitutional Law: Substance and Procedure § 17.8 (3rd ed. 1999, with annual supplements).

12. LaChance v. Erickson, 522 U.S. 262, 118 S.Ct. 753, 139 L.Ed.2d 695 (1998). In *LaChance*, Chief Justice Rehnquist, writing for a unanimous Court, explained that neither the due process clause nor the self-incrimination clause provided a defense for an employee who gave false information to the government, although an employee under investigation could exercise Fifth Amendment right to remain silent, under appropriate circumstances. For citations to additional cases on this point, see the multivolume edition of this treatise: R. Rotunda & J. Nowak, Treatise On Constitutional Law: Substance and Procedure, § 17.8 (3rd ed. 1999, with annual supplements).

13. In re Murchison, 349 U.S. 133, 136, 75 S.Ct. 623, 625, 99 L.Ed. 942 (1955).

Other cases examining the fair tribunal requirement include: Aetna Life Insurance Co. v. Lavoie, 475 U.S. 813, 106 S.Ct. 1580, 89 L.Ed.2d 823 (1986), on remand 505

So.2d 1050 (Ala.1987); Gibson v. Berryhill, 411 U.S. 564, 93 S.Ct. 1689, 36 L.Ed.2d 488 (1973); Ward v. Monroeville, 409 U.S. 57, 93 S.Ct. 80, 34 L.Ed.2d 267 (1972); Tumey v. Ohio, 273 U.S. 510, 47 S.Ct. 437, 71 L.Ed. 749 (1927).

14. Withrow v. Larkin, 421 U.S. 35, 46, 95 S.Ct. 1456, 1464, 43 L.Ed.2d 712 (1975), on remand to 408 F.Supp. 969 (E.D.Wis.1975); Gibson v. Berryhill, 411 U.S. 564, 579, 93 S.Ct. 1689, 1698, 36 L.Ed.2d 488 (1973).

Absent a showing that the decisionmaker had a vested interest in the outcome of the proceeding it may be difficult to show that a decisionmaker had reason to favor one party, or to disfavor another party, in the proceeding. Statutes that require a judge to recuse himself or herself may, or may not, offer an easier basis for challenging a judge's participation in a case than does the due process fairness requirement. In Liteky v. United States, 510 U.S. 540, 114 S.Ct. 1147, 127 L.Ed.2d 474 (1994) the majority opinion by Justice Scalia interpreted a federal statute requiring a judge to disqualify himself or herself in proceedings "in which his impartiality might reasonably be questioned". Justice Scalia ruled that the statute provided only a very limited basis for considering extra judicial sources as grounds for requiring a judge to recuse himself under the statute. Thus, facts introduced concerning the conduct of the judge in prior proceedings involving the same parties or interests that might indicate some degree of favoritism or antagonism towards a party did not provide a sufficient basis for forcing the judge to withdraw from the case. In *Liteky*, Justice Kennedy wrote for four concurring Justices. The concurring Justices believed that, under the facts of the case, there was no reason for the district judge to disqualify himself but they also believed that Justice Scalia's majority opinion had construed the federal statute too narrowly. 510 U.S. at 556, 114 S.Ct. at 1158 (Kennedy, J., joined by Blackmun, Stevens, and Souter, JJ., concurring in the judgment).

a personal monetary interest in the outcome of the adjudication or where they are professional competitors of the individual.[15] The rule against biased decision-makers also serves to disqualify a judge in cases where that bias was solely the result of abuse or criticism from the parties appearing before him.[16] However the Court has held that a single hearing officer or agency may be given a combination of investigative and adjudicative functions. Thus the hearing officer could be charged with investigating and compiling facts in a case and making decisions based on those facts.[17] The fact that a government agency receives part of its funding from monetary penalties that it helps to assess does not necessarily make the agency a constitutionally unacceptable decision-maker. When no government official connected to the decision-making process personally profits from the decision, anyone challenging the process as inherently unfair would have to establish that the amount of agency funding traceable to the imposition of the civil penalty actually created an impermissible risk of bias in the decision-making process.[18]

One must also remember that the democratic process itself may be biased against an individual because a majority of the electorate may be biased, yet the system will still be upheld as "fair" within the meaning of due process. Thus the Court has upheld a requirement that zoning changes be subject to popular referendum, for that does no more than allow the general electorate to determine whether they wish to alter their laws.[19] Yet even this procedure cannot be used to disguise a system which subjects one to a determination of his rights by a group composed of his professional or commercial competitors. Thus the Supreme Court has held that the zoning of a tract of real property cannot be left to the discretionary voting of neighboring property owners with interests adverse to the individual property owner.[20]

Notice. In addition to the guarantee of an impartial decision-maker, due process requires

15. Gibson v. Berryhill, 411 U.S. 564, 579, 93 S.Ct. 1689, 1698, 36 L.Ed.2d 488 (1973); Ward v. Village of Monroeville, 409 U.S. 57, 93 S.Ct. 80, 34 L.Ed.2d 267 (1972); Tumey v. Ohio, 273 U.S. 510, 47 S.Ct. 437, 71 L.Ed. 749 (1927). For citations to additional decisions regarding this subject, see the multivolume edition of this treatise: R. Rotunda & J. Nowak, Treatise on Constitutional Law: Substance and Procedure (3rd ed. 1999, with annual supplements).

16. Taylor v. Hayes, 418 U.S. 488, 501–503, 94 S.Ct. 2697, 2704–06, 41 L.Ed.2d 897 (1974); Mayberry v. Penn., 400 U.S. 455, 91 S.Ct. 499, 27 L.Ed.2d 532 (1971); Pickering v. Board of Education, 391 U.S. 563, 568–69 n. 2, 88 S.Ct. 1731, 1735 n. 2, 20 L.Ed.2d 811 (1968); Cf. Ungar v. Sarafite, 376 U.S. 575, 584, 84 S.Ct. 841, 846–47, 11 L.Ed.2d 921 (1964).

17. Withrow v. Larkin, 421 U.S. 35, 95 S.Ct. 1456, 43 L.Ed.2d 712 (1975), on remand to 408 F.Supp. 969 (E.D.Wis.1975); Schweiker v. McClure, 456 U.S. 188, 102 S.Ct. 1665, 72 L.Ed.2d 1 (1982); see generally Rotunda, The Combination of Functions in Administrative Actions, 40 Ford.L.Rev. 101 (1971).

18. Marshall v. Jerrico, Inc., 446 U.S. 238, 100 S.Ct. 1610, 64 L.Ed.2d 182 (1980) (civil penalty provisions of Fair Labor Standards Act permissible even though the agency received partial reimbursement of its enforcement and administration expenses from the fines collected because there was no risk of personal bias by the agency decision-maker, who acted primarily as an investigator and prosecutor rather than an adjudicator).

If an initial factual determination in an administrative proceeding is made by a person who has both enforcement and factfinding duties, due process should require that the person whose rights were subject to that process be given

a *de novo* review by a truly neutral adjudicator. In Concrete Pipe and Products of California, Inc. v. Construction Laborers Pension Trust, 508 U.S. 602, 113 S.Ct. 2264, 124 L.Ed.2d 539 (1993) the Supreme Court upheld federal statutes that provided for the determination of the liability of an employer who was withdrawing from a multiemployer pension fund even though the initial assessment of liability was made by trustees of the pension fund who were appointed by unions that participated in the fund and by employers (most of whom would be continuing in the fund). The Court found that the possible lack of neutrality on the part of the trustees was offset by the fact that the statute provided for a *de novo* review of all decisions of the trustees by an arbitrator who was admittedly neutral and fair. The Court described the arbitrator review process as being the "first adjudication" of liability and found that the statutory system for determining liability, taken as a whole, met procedural due process standards. A statutory presumption favored determinations made by the plan sponsors, but the Court, in the *Concrete Pipe* case, ruled that the presumption did no more than place the burden of proof on the employer challenging the trustees' findings of liability (against the employer) to show that the initial assessment of liability was incorrect. Because the statutory presumption did not foreclose independent consideration of any issue by the arbitrator, the Court found that there was no due process violation.

19. Eastlake v. Forest City Enterprises, Inc., 426 U.S. 668, 96 S.Ct. 2358, 49 L.Ed.2d 132 (1976).

20. Washington ex rel. Seattle Title Trust Co. v. Roberge, 278 U.S. 116, 49 S.Ct. 50, 73 L.Ed. 210 (1928); Eubank v. Richmond, 226 U.S. 137, 33 S.Ct. 76, 57 L.Ed. 156 (1912).

the government to give notice to individuals of government actions which would deprive those individuals of a constitutionally protected life, liberty, or property interest. When individual interests are adversely affected by legislative action, there is no notice issue, because publication of a statute is normally considered to put all individuals on notice of a change in the law of a jurisdiction.[21] When a government agency or a court (even in a case where no government agency is a party) considers terminating or impairing an individual's constitutionally cognizable life, liberty, or property interest, notice must be given to the individual whose interest is at stake in the proceeding.

The form of the notice and the procedure for delivery or posting of the notice must be reasonably designed to insure that the interested parties in fact will learn of the proposed adjudicative action.[22] "An elementary and fundamental requirement of due process in any proceeding which is to be accorded finality is notice reasonably calculated, under all the circumstances, to appraise interested parties of the pendency of the action and afford them an opportunity to present their objections."[23]

Form of the Hearing or Process: The Balancing Test. If there is a deprivation of life, liberty or property which is based on disputed facts or issues, then the individual whose interests are affected must be granted a fair procedure before a fair decision-maker. However this principle does not mean that the individual has the right to a hearing before the action is taken or even to any personal hearing at any time. What is required is a procedure, not necessarily a hearing.

In many of the cases where the Court has found that there is a deprivation of life, liberty or property it has required that the affected individual be granted a personal hearing prior to the government action.[24] However, in some

---

21. Statutory Notice—Vagueness. Texaco, Inc. v. Short, 454 U.S. 516, 102 S.Ct. 781, 70 L.Ed.2d 738 (1982) (owners of mineral interests which lapsed under statute terminating undeveloped mineral interests were not entitled to notice beyond publication of the statute of the actions that they could have taken during two-year statutory grace period to avoid extinguishment of their interest). In determining whether a statute should be declared void for vagueness, the Supreme Court examines: (1) whether the law provides minimally adequate notice to individuals who might be prosecuted under the law; and (2) whether the law grants so much discretion to law enforcement authorities that it does not provide standards that will prevent totally arbitrary and discriminatory enforcement. See generally, Kolender v. Lawson, 461 U.S. 352, 103 S.Ct. 1855, 75 L.Ed.2d 903 (1983). In Chicago v. Morales, 527 U.S. 41, 119 S.Ct. 1849, 144 L.Ed.2d 67 (1999), the Court invalidated a city ordinance that prohibited "gang members" from "loitering" in any public place, in part because the state supreme court had ruled that the statute provided no limitation of police officer discretion. Although six Justices voted to invalidate the law in *Morales*, Justice Stevens wrote an opinion that was, in part, a majority opinion and, in part, a plurality opinion. A majority of the Justices agreed that the law was unconstitutionally vague because it did not establish minimal guidelines for law enforcement. 527 U.S. at 61–62, 119 S.Ct. at 1861–62. Justice Stevens wrote for only three Justices in finding that the statute would also be void for vagueness because it did not provide adequate notice to citizens regarding the types of activities that were made criminal by the statute. 527 U.S. at 50–56, 119 S.Ct. at 1856–59 (opinion of Stevens, J., joined by Souter and Ginsburg, JJ.).

For other cases regarding the adequacy of statutory notice see the footnotes to § 17.8 of our multivolume treatise. See R. Rotunda & J. Nowak, Treatise on Consti-

tutional Law: Substance and Procedure, § 17.8 (3rd ed. 1999, with annual supplements).

22. See, e.g., Greene v. Lindsey, 456 U.S. 444, 102 S.Ct. 1874, 72 L.Ed.2d 249 (1982) (posting notice of eviction action on door of apartment in public housing unit insufficient to meet due process standard); Memphis Light, Gas and Water Division v. Craft, 436 U.S. 1, 14, 98 S.Ct. 1554, 1562–63, 56 L.Ed.2d 30 (1978) (notice of possible termination of utility service by government operated utility did not meet due process standard for informing individual of opportunity to present objections to termination). For citations to other cases regarding the adequacy of notice given by a court or administrative agency, see R. Rotunda & J. Nowak, Treatise on Constitutional Law: Substance and Procedure, § 17.8 (3rd ed. 1999, with annual supplements). See generally, Parker, J., citing Treatise in Richmond Boro Gun Club, Inc. v. City of New York, 97 F.3d 681, 684 (2d Cir.1996).

23. Mullane v. Central Hanover Bank & Trust Co., 339 U.S. 306, 314, 70 S.Ct. 652, 657, 94 L.Ed. 865 (1950) (notice by newspaper publication of judicial action to settle accounts of trust fund was constitutionally sufficient notice for beneficiaries whose whereabouts could not be determined but violated due process because it was insufficient notice for known beneficiaries with ascertainable residence).

For citations to additional decisions regarding this subject, see the multivolume edition of this treatise: R. Rotunda & J. Nowak, Treatise on Constitutional Law: Substance and Procedure (3rd ed. 1999, with annual supplements).

24. See, e.g., Sniadach v. Family Finance Corp., 395 U.S. 337, 89 S.Ct. 1820, 23 L.Ed.2d 349 (1969); Bell v. Burson, 402 U.S. 535, 91 S.Ct. 1586, 29 L.Ed.2d 90 (1971), Goldberg v. Kelly, 397 U.S. 254, 90 S.Ct. 1011, 25 L.Ed.2d

cases the Court has held that hearings which take place after the government action will be sufficient process to comply with the guarantee.[25] And in a few cases the Court has held that due process was satisfied by a procedural safeguard which did not involve any personal hearing for the affected individual.[26]

The Court uses a balancing test to determine which procedures will be required. In *Mathews v. Eldridge* the Court stated that it will consider three factors in making this determination:

> First, the private interest that will be affected by the official action; second, the risk of an erroneous deprivation of such interest through the procedures used, and the probable value, if any, of additional or substitute procedural safeguards; and finally, the Government's interest, including the function involved and the fiscal and administrative burdens that the additional or substitute procedural requisites would entail.[27]

All courts must now employ the *Mathews v. Eldridge* balancing test to determine the type of procedures that are required by due process when a governmental action would deprive an individual of a constitutionally protected liberty or property interest.[28] On the side of the individual, a court must assess two factors: (1) the importance of the individual liberty or property interest at stake; (2) the extent to which the requested procedure may reduce the possibility of erroneous decision-making. On the other side of the "balance," the court must assess the governmental interest in avoiding the increased administrative and fiscal burdens which result from increased procedural requirements.

While this test may suit the purposes of the Supreme Court, one cannot accurately predict how any specific case will be decided by using this test for two reasons. First, because it is a "balancing test", it is impossible to predict the results unless one knows the personal value systems of those doing the balancing. Second, as Professor Mashaw has demonstrated, this

---

287 (1970) (terminating basic welfare benefits); Cf. Morrissey v. Brewer, 408 U.S. 471, 92 S.Ct. 2593, 33 L.Ed.2d 484 (1972) (preliminary hearing at place of arrest for parole violation). A pre-deprivation rather than post-deprivation process should be required wherever there is an established state procedure that would take a property interest; the state's interest in destruction of the property in such instances is minimal because the state designed system should be able to accommodate some procedure for consideration of the individual interest in the property prior to its deprivation. Logan v. Zimmerman Brush Co., 455 U.S. 422, 436, 102 S.Ct. 1148, 1158, 71 L.Ed.2d 265, 278 (1982).

25. See, e.g., North Georgia Finishing, Inc. v. Di-Chem, Inc., 419 U.S. 601, 95 S.Ct. 719, 42 L.Ed.2d 751 (1975) (attachment or replevin); Arnett v. Kennedy, 416 U.S. 134, 94 S.Ct. 1633, 40 L.Ed.2d 15 (1974), (termination of government employment); Mathews v. Eldridge, 424 U.S. 319, 96 S.Ct. 893, 47 L.Ed.2d 18 (1976) (termination of Social Security disability payments). Mackey v. Montrym, 443 U.S. 1, 99 S.Ct. 2612, 61 L.Ed.2d 321 (1979) (post-suspension hearing sufficient for suspending a person's driver's license for refusal to take a drunk driving test); Barry v. Barchi, 443 U.S. 55, 99 S.Ct. 2642, 61 L.Ed.2d 365 (1979) (post-suspension hearing for race horse trainer sufficient where suspension is based on detection of illegal drugs in the horse immediately after the race).

26. Ingraham v. Wright, 430 U.S. 651, 97 S.Ct. 1401, 51 L.Ed.2d 711 (1977) (possibility of tort suit sufficient to protect liberty interest of child who is subjected to physical punishment in school).

In Sacramento v. Lewis, 523 U.S. 833, 118 S.Ct. 1708, 140 L.Ed.2d 1043 (1998) the Justices ruled that the death of a suspect who was accidentally killed by a police patrol

car in a high-speed chase of the motorcycle (on which the deceased person had been a passenger) did not violate substantive due process principles. The Court in *Lewis* did not address taking of property issues or procedural due process issues. Nevertheless, harm cause to persons or property by actions of police officers may sometimes present taking of property issues, together with substantive and procedural issues. The *Lewis* case is examined in § 10.6 of this Treatise.

Supreme Court decisions regarding the circumstances under which the government only needs to provide a post-deprivation hearing or remedy for a liberty or property loss are examined at the end of § 13.9.

27. Mathews v. Eldridge, 424 U.S. 319, 335, 96 S.Ct. 893, 903, 47 L.Ed.2d 18 (1976).

28. Among the cases citing this section of the Treatise are: San Bernadino Community Hospital v. Workers' Compensation Appeals Board, 74 Cal.App.4th 928, 88 Cal. Rptr.2d 516, 522 (1999). Southwestern Bell Telephone Co. v. Oklahoma Corporation Commission, 873 P.2d 1001, 1016 (Okl.1994) (Opala, J., dissenting opinion), cert. denied 513 U.S. 869, 115 S.Ct. 191, 130 L.Ed.2d 123 (1994); In re Advisory From the Governor, 633 A.2d 664, 673 (R.I.1993) (per curiam); Schmit v. ITT Federal Elec. Int'l, 986 F.2d 1103, 1107 (7th Cir.1993) (Wood, J.); Chrysler Credit Corp. v. Cathey, 977 F.2d 447, 449 (8th Cir.1992) (per curiam); Buford v. Holladay, 791 F.Supp. 635, 643 (S.D.Miss.1992) (Barbour, C.J.); Weyerhaeuser v. Pierce County, 124 Wn.2d 26, 873 P.2d 498, 513 (1994) (Madsen, J., concurring in part and dissenting in part).

type of "intuitive functionalism" disregards a systematic pursuit of due process values.[29] Thus we can only advise individuals to reflect on these general principles and to examine the Supreme Court decisions on specific issues when attempting to predict how the current Justices will decide a new issue.

A court may need to employ the *Mathews v. Eldridge* balancing test in three areas of procedural due process rulings. First, a court should use the test to determine if an individual is entitled to a hearing prior to (rather than after) a governmental action which would deprive him of a liberty or property interest. The government should be able to act to advance important public interests even though it deprives someone of property or liberty without a prior hearing, so long as adequate post-deprivation process provides the individu-

al with a safeguard against arbitrary governmental actions.[30] The existence of a state court remedy may be sufficient process to protect individuals from improper deprivations of some liberty or property interests by state employees.[31] In addressing the first procedural due process issue, the Court starts from the premise that an individual should receive notice and some type of a hearing prior to any deprivation of life, liberty, or property by the government.[32] However, the Court has allowed the government to seize property, or temporarily deprive a person of liberty, prior to giving the individual a hearing in exceptional situations where an important governmental interest would be threatened by granting notice and a pre-deprivation hearing to the individual.[33]

---

29. Mashaw, supra note 2.

30. See notes 25, 26 supra.

The determination of whether an individual is entitled to a pre-deprivation hearing or a post-deprivation hearing is made by applying the Mathews v. Eldridge balancing test (examined in the text) to the particular type of property or liberty deprivation. See generally, Zinermon v. Burch, 494 U.S. 113, 110 S.Ct. 975, 108 L.Ed.2d 100 (1990) (the Supreme Court ruled that the *Mathew's* test is to be used in both property and liberty cases to determine whether a post-deprivation hearing complies with due process; the Court finds that an individual is normally entitled to a hearing prior to commitment to a state mental health care facility, although it did not rule that short-term, emergency admissions to such facilities, followed by a later hearing, would be unconstitutional). This topic is examined at the end of § 13.9.

See, e.g., Calero–Toledo v. Pearson Yacht Leasing Co., 416 U.S. 663, 94 S.Ct. 2080, 40 L.Ed.2d 452 (1974), (government seizure of ship used to transport contraband permissible without prior hearing).

31. See notes 25, 26 supra.

Post-deprivation process may be sufficient to remedy a deprivation of property interests that results from the unauthorized, intentional actions of government employees. The state cannot create a pre-deprivation administrative process to prevent such takings of property. A state law allowing a judicial remedy for such taking may preclude the finding of a violation of due process. Hudson v. Palmer, 468 U.S. 517, 104 S.Ct. 3194, 82 L.Ed.2d 393 (1984), on remand 744 F.2d 22 (4th Cir.1984), (prisoner's loss of property because of intentional action of prison officials does not violate due process if the state has an adequate post-deprivation remedy for the alleged destruction of property).

32. In United States v. James Daniel Good Property, 510 U.S. 43, 114 S.Ct. 492, 126 L.Ed.2d 490 (1993), the Court ruled that the United States government in a civil forfeiture case could not seize real property without

first granting the property owner notice and some type of a hearing. Writing for the five member majority, Justice Kennedy used the balancing test employed in Mathews v. Eldridge, 424 U.S. 319, 335, 96 S.Ct. 893, 903, 47 L.Ed.2d 18 (1976) (which is described in the previous paragraphs of this section of the Treatise) to determine whether the government was required to give a pre-deprivation hearing to an individual under these circumstances or whether a post-deprivation hearing would meet due process principles. The majority ruled that the government did not have a need to seize real property prior to a hearing. The majority distinguished Calero–Toledo v. Pearson Yacht Leasing Co., 416 U.S. 663, 94 S.Ct. 2080, 40 L.Ed.2d 452 (1974), in which the Court had upheld the seizure of personal property prior to a hearing on the basis that the government had an interest in preventing an individual from hiding or destroying personal property prior to forfeiture proceedings. The government did not need to seize real property without notice and a hearing in order to protect any important governmental interest.

33. In Los Angeles v. David, 538 U.S. 715, 123 S.Ct. 1895, 155 L.Ed.2d 946 (2003) (per curiam) the Justices unanimously held that a city did not violate due process by towing a car from a place where parking was forbidden and then having a 27 day delay before the individual who owned the car received a hearing to determine whether the money he paid to recover his car (as a fine for illegal parking and towing charges) should be returned to him (based on his allegation that trees obstructed the view of a no-parking sign). The Court in the *David* case relied on the three-factor balancing test established in Mathews v. Eldridge, 424 U.S. 319, 96 S.Ct. 893, 47 L.Ed.2d 18 (1976).

A five member majority ruled in United States v. James Daniel Good Real Property, 510 U.S. 43, 114 S.Ct. 492, 126 L.Ed.2d 490 (1993) that an individual was entitled to notice and a hearing prior to the time when the government seized the individual's real property, which the government asserted would be subject to forfeiture because illegal drugs had been found on the property. Justice

The adequacy of the notice given to a person whose liberty or property may be taken by the government is to be determined by this reasonableness test, rather than by use of the multi-factor balancing test that is used to determine the adequacy of the process that is to be afforded that individual.[34]

Second, whether the court decides that a pre-deprivation or post-deprivation hearing is required, it should employ the balancing test to determine the precise procedures to be employed at the hearing. These balancing test

rulings may cover the procedural spectrum from requiring only informal hearings[35] to requiring a full adversarial process.[36]

Third, if the court requires a formal adversarial process, it may use the balancing test to determine the standard of proof that the government must meet in order to justify the deprivation of the individual liberty or property interest in the individual case.[37]

The difficulty of predicting how the Supreme Court will employ the *Mathews* balancing test is demonstrated by its rulings in pa-

---

Kennedy's majority opinion stated: "We tolerate some exceptions to the general rule requiring pre-deprivation notice and a hearing but only in extraordinary situations where some valid governmental interest is at stake that justifies postponing the hearing until after the event." 510 U.S. at 53, 114 S.Ct. at 501 (internal quotation marks, and citations, omitted). In the *James Daniel Good Real Property* case, Judge Kennedy's majority opinion distinguished earlier decisions of the Supreme Court which the temporary seizure of real property when the government was collecting tax debts or other forms of debts to the United States or made seizures during wartime. Justice Kennedy's opinion found that those deprivations of property interests had been justified by government interests of greater significance than the interests involved in the government's attempting to take title to, or otherwise seize, residential property prior to a forfeiture proceeding.

For further analysis of the Court's use of the three factor balancing test to determine when a post-deprivation hearing is sufficient to protect liberty or property interests impaired by state actions, see § 13.9.

34. The due process requirement of adequate notice was clearly stated in Mullane v. Central Hanover Bank and Trust Co., 339 U.S. 306, 314, 70 S.Ct. 652, 657, 94 L.Ed. 865 (1950). See note 33, and accompanying text, supra. The multi-factor balancing test used to determine the timing and form of a process that must be given to an individual whose liberty or property is to be taken by the government was first set forth in Mathews v. Eldridge, 424 U.S. 319, 96 S.Ct. 893, 47 L.Ed.2d 18 (1976). In Dusenbery v. United States, 534 U.S. 161, 122 S.Ct. 694, 151 L.Ed.2d 597 (2002), the Supreme Court, by a 5 to 4 vote of the Justices, ruled that notice sent by mail, and placed in a newspaper, regarding the administrative forfeiture of money and property connected to an illegal drug business met due process standards. Writing for the majority, Chief Justice Rehnquist found that the reasonableness standard of *Mullane,* rather than the balancing test established by *Mathews,* should be used to determine whether the method of giving notice met due process standards. 534 U.S. at 167–68, 122 S.Ct. at 699. The four dissenting Justices in *Dusenbery* agreed that the *Mullane* reasonableness test should be used to determine whether the means of giving notice met due process standards. The dissenting Justices believed that the procedures at issue in that case did not constitute a reasonably reliable way of providing notice to a federal prisoner that his property was subject to forfeiture. Dusenbery v. United States, 534 U.S. 161, 173, 122 S.Ct. 694, 702, 151 L.Ed.2d 597 (2002)

(Ginsburg, J., joined by Stevens, Souter, and Breyer, JJ., dissenting).

35. For example, the Supreme Court employed the Mathews v. Eldridge, 424 U.S. 319, 96 S.Ct. 893, 47 L.Ed.2d 18 (1976), balancing test to determine the procedural safeguards due to termination of utility services.

In Memphis Light, Gas and Water Division v. Craft, 436 U.S. 1, 98 S.Ct. 1554, 56 L.Ed.2d 30 (1978), the Court found that the utility customer's interest in continued service and the "not insubstantial" risk of computer errors and erroneous service terminations outweighed the efficiency interests of the government utility. The Court tried to fashion a process that would not unduly lessen the efficiency, or significantly increase costs of the utility service. The majority opinion held that customers had to be provided with: (1) a pre-termination notice that advised them of the proposed termination and the availability of a procedure to consider complaints regarding erroneous billing, and (2) the opportunity for an "informal" pre-termination hearing before an employee who could review disputed bills and rectify errors.

36. Compare Goldberg v. Kelly, 397 U.S. 254, 90 S.Ct. 1011, 25 L.Ed.2d 287 (1970) (formal procedure required to terminate subsistence welfare benefits), with Mathews v. Eldridge, 424 U.S. 319, 96 S.Ct. 893, 47 L.Ed.2d 18 (1976) (adversarial process not required prior to termination of disability benefit).

37. Compare Addington v. Texas, 441 U.S. 418, 99 S.Ct. 1804, 60 L.Ed.2d 323 (1979), ("clear and convincing" evidence standard must be met when government seeks to commit adult to psychiatric care facility), with Parham v. J.R., 442 U.S. 584, 99 S.Ct. 2493, 61 L.Ed.2d 101 (1979) (no formal adversarial process required to safeguard child who is committed to psychiatric care facility by parent or guardian).

A state may choose to exceed due process minimum requirements when creating procedures to protect liberty or property interests. In Heller v. Doe, 509 U.S. 312, 113 S.Ct. 2637, 125 L.Ed.2d 257 (1993) the Supreme Court upheld state statutes that required the government to prove beyond a reasonable doubt that an individual should be committed to a mental health care facility on the basis of "mental illness", even though the state only required the government to prove by clear and convincing evidence that a person should be committed to a mental health care facility on the basis of "mental retardation."

rental rights cases. The importance of the parent-child relationship, in theory and fact, is such that the Court will strictly scrutinize the fairness of procedures used to establish or terminate that relationship.[38] A parent has a constitutionally protected interest in the relationship with his or her child so that the state must accord the parent a hearing before terminating that relationship.[39] However, because foster parents have a lesser interest in this relationship than do natural or adoptive parents, a less formal procedure may be used in removing children from foster homes.[40] The interest of the natural or adoptive parent is so great that the state must demonstrate by "clear and convincing evidence"—not merely a preponderance of the evidence—that statutory

criteria for termination of parental rights have been met in an individual case.[41] However, the interest of the parent is not so great, in the view of a majority of the Justices, to require the state to appoint an attorney for an indigent parent when the state institutes court proceedings to take a child from the parent.[42]

The Court has ruled that both due process and equal protection principles require a state to waive filing and transcript fees for an indigent parent. Filing and transcript fees cannot bar the parent from appealing a trial court decision that, if unchallenged, would permanently terminate the parent's relationship to her child.[43]

---

38. The Justices unanimously employed the Mathews v. Eldridge balancing test in Little v. Streater, 452 U.S. 1, 101 S.Ct. 2202, 68 L.Ed.2d 627 (1981) in finding that a state's refusal to pay the cost of a blood grouping test for an indigent defendant in a paternity action violated due process. The case was nominally a paternity action brought by the mother of an illegitimate child against the alleged father. Chief Justice Burger, in an opinion for a unanimous Court, found that the action should be treated as one brought by the government because state law compelled the woman to disclose the name of the "putative father under oath and to institute an action to establish the paternity" of the child because the child was a recipient of public aid. Indeed, the Court found that this proceeding had "quasi-criminal overtones." In this paternity proceeding the indigent defendant had requested that the state provide him with the funds or other means for a blood test of him and the child; the test was clearly effective evidence as it could exclude the possibility of paternity in many circumstances. The Court found that when an indigent was required to face the state as an adversary in a paternity proceeding, the state's refusal to provide him with the means to obtain blood test evidence denied him a fair opportunity to be heard.

39. Stanley v. Illinois, 405 U.S. 645, 92 S.Ct. 1208, 31 L.Ed.2d 551 (1972); Santosky v. Kramer, 455 U.S. 745, 102 S.Ct. 1388, 71 L.Ed.2d 599 (1982).

40. In Smith v. Organization of Foster Families for Equality and Reform, 431 U.S. 816, 97 S.Ct. 2094, 53 L.Ed.2d 14 (1977), the Court unanimously upheld a state procedure for removal of children from foster homes upon ten-days notice. There was a hearing at the request of the foster family equivalent to the more exacting requirements of past cases. The Court overturned the district court's ruling that the procedure should be automatic and include formal consultation of the child under the balancing test. Additionally, the Court upheld the use of more summary procedures where the child was with the foster family less than eighteen months. While the Justices were unanimous, it would have been difficult to predict with any assurance that: (1) the Justices could not agree on whether the foster parent-foster child relationship was a cognizable "liberty" interest, (2) that the district court was wrong in its particular objections to the procedures,

(3) that relationships of less than eighteen months required fewer procedural safeguards.

41. Santosky v. Kramer, 455 U.S. 745, 102 S.Ct. 1388, 71 L.Ed.2d 599 (1982).

A suit to establish paternity does not involve the potential impairment of a fundamental right in family relationships. The Supreme Court, in Rivera v. Minnich, 483 U.S. 574, 107 S.Ct. 3001, 97 L.Ed.2d 473 (1987) held that a state, consistent with the due process, could allow a mother or child seeking support from a putative father to establish paternity by a preponderance of the evidence. The putative father did not have any fundamental constitutional interest in avoiding financial obligations to his natural child; the paternity proceeding would be fair to both the putative father, and to the party seeking support, if a preponderance of the evidence standard was used.

42. In Lassiter v. Department of Social Services, 452 U.S. 18, 101 S.Ct. 2153, 68 L.Ed.2d 640 (1981), the Court refused to require the appointment of counsel for a woman who had her parental rights terminated by court action. The Court first found that its previous decisions under the Sixth and Fourteenth Amendments established "the presumption that an indigent litigant has a right to appointed counsel only when, if he loses, he may be deprived of his physical liberty." The majority opinion by Justice Stewart stated that the three elements of the balancing test would have to be weighed and then the Court would "set their net weight on the scales against the presumption" against the appointment of counsel.

The majority in *Lassiter* concluded that counsel would not be appointed in every parental termination proceeding because, despite the importance of the interest of the parent at stake in the proceeding, the state had "an urgent interest" in determining the best interest of the child. The appointment of counsel, according to the majority, would not necessarily add to either the fairness of the proceedings or a correct determination as to whether the interest of the child would be advanced by a termination of an individual's parental rights. The majority opinion indicated that trial court judges would have to make a case-by-case determination of whether the failure to appoint counsel for an indigent defendant in a child custody or parental status case would make the proceedings so fundamentally unfair as to violate due process.

43. In M.L.B. v. S.L.J., 519 U.S. 102, 117 S.Ct. 555, 136 L.Ed.2d 473 (1996), the Justices, by a six to three

We will now examine three major decisional areas: loss of physical liberty, enforcement of debtor-creditor relationships, and termination of government benefits.

§ 13.9 A Summary of the Major Decisional Areas

(a) Loss of Physical Liberty

Overview of Restrictions on the Criminal Process. Before an individual is subject-ed to punishment upon a criminal charge, he must receive a full trial in conformity with many constitutional safeguards or waive those rights. The primary restrictions on the criminal process are the result of the application of the principles of the Bill of Rights. The guarantees of the Fourth, Fifth, Sixth, and Eighth Amendments restrict the ways in which the government may investigate as well as prosecute someone for a criminal charge.[1] All of

vote, ruled that a state violated both due process and equal protection principles by refusing to waive a mandatory fee for preparation of a trial transcript as a condition of allowing a woman to appeal from a civil trial court decision terminating her parental rights. Justice Ginsburg, writing for five Justices in *M.L.B.*, ruled that the constitutional right inherent in the relationship of parents and children required the judiciary to scrutinize closely the state's justification for denying appellate process to parents who could not pay for preparation of a transcript for appeal. The state's interest in making the judicial process, in part, self-supporting was legitimate and would justify most filing fees, that interest could not justify eliminating a parent's ability to appeal a decision terminating the parent-child relationship. The system used by the state was fundamentally unfair, so that it violated due process, and created a classification between indigent parents and parents who could afford to pay for transcripts and filing fees that violated equal protection. Justice Kennedy concurred only in the judgment of the Court in *M.L.B.* because he wanted to base the decision solely on the procedural due process principles. M.L.B. v. S.L.J. 519 U.S. 102, 128, 117 S.Ct. 555, 570, 136 L.Ed.2d 473 (1996) (Kennedy, J., concurring in the judgment). Chief Justice Rehnquist, and Justices Scalia and Thomas would have allowed the state to deny the woman an appeal from the termination of her parental rights on the basis that she could not afford a transcript for the appeal. 519 U.S. at 128, 117 S.Ct. at 570 (Rehnquist, C.J., dissenting); 519 U.S. at 129, 117 S.Ct. at 570 (Thomas, J., joined by Scalia, J., and, in part, Rehnquist, C.J., dissenting).

§ 13.9

1. For examination of these topics, see W. LaFave, J. Israel & N. King, Criminal Procedure (multivolume treatise, 2nd ed., 1999 with supplements).

Judicial Proceedings—Criminal or Civil? When a legislature establishes a penalty for the violation of a legislative or administrative regulation a court may have to determine whether the penalty is a civil or criminal one. Only if a court determines that the penalty is a criminal one will the person or corporation charged with violation of the regulation be entitled to the protections of the Bill of Rights guarantees concerning a criminal prosecution. There is no precise standard which the Supreme Court employs to separate civil from criminal sanctions; the Justices will look at many factors surrounding the legisla-tive act including whether the sanction involves an affirmative disability or restraint, the history of the legislation, whether the behavior to which it applies is also a crime, and the possible ends promoted by the penalty.

In Smith v. Doe, 538 U.S. 84, 123 S.Ct. 1140, 155 L.Ed.2d 164 (2003) the Supreme Court, by a 6 to 3 vote, found that a state sex offender registration law was civil in nature and that its application to persons who had been properly convicted of sex related offenses before the date of passage of the law did not violate the ex post facto clause of Article I, § 10.

In Connecticut Department of Public Safety v. Doe, 538 U.S. 1, 123 S.Ct. 1160, 155 L.Ed.2d 98 (2003) the Justices unanimously held that a sex offender registration law could be applied to an individual who had been properly convicted of sex related crimes without giving that individual an additional hearing to determine whether he was in fact, dangerous. In a concurring opinion in *Connecticut Department of Public Safety* in which they cited this Treatise, Justices Souter and Ginsburg explained that, even after this decision, the individual could litigate the question of whether the law limited his liberty interest, in violation of substantive due process principles, or whether the classifications in the law, regarding which convicted criminals would be subject to the registry system, violated equal protection 538 U.S. at 10, 123 S.Ct. at 1165, 1166 (Souter, J., joined by Ginsburg, J., concurring). These cases are examined in § 10.6 of this Treatise.

In determining whether a proceeding is criminal for the purpose of the self-incrimination clause, a court must look to the statutory system to determine whether it is punitive in nature. A clearly punitive statutory system should be deemed to be a system that imposes a criminal sanction and subject to the procedural restrictions on criminal trials, despite the fact that a state has designated the system as civil in nature. This principle was recognized in Allen v. Illinois, 478 U.S. 364, 368, 106 S.Ct. 2988, 2992, 92 L.Ed.2d 296 (1986), although the Court, by a five to four vote, held that a state "sexually dangerous persons act," was civil in nature and, therefore, that the Fifth Amendment guarantee against compulsory self-incrimination did not apply to proceedings under that act which would result in commitment of a person.

In Department of Revenue v. Kurth Ranch, 511 U.S. 767, 114 S.Ct. 1937, 128 L.Ed.2d 767 (1994) the Supreme

these safeguards apply to the criminal process of state and local governments except for the grand jury requirement of the Fifth Amendment.[2] These specific guarantees include almost all of the procedural safeguards that were mentioned in our general discussion. Specifically, the Amendments require: (1) respect for individual rights to privacy and freedom from self-incrimination in the investigative process; (2) that the person not twice be placed in jeopardy for the same offense; (3) prompt processing of the charges; (4) that the trial of the charges be public; (5) that the charges be tried before an impartial jury; (6) fair notice of the charges and a chance to prepare a defense; (7) the right to confront and cross-examine witnesses; (8) compulsory process to obtain favorable witnesses and evidence; (9) the assistance of counsel; (10) that excessive bail not be used to keep the individual in custody prior to the termination of the prosecution; (11) that the punishment not be excessive or cruel.

Additionally, due process requires that all procedures be fundamentally fair. The process must always conform to the twin guarantees of an impartial determination of guilt or innocence[3] and respect for the dignity of the individual.[4] Perhaps the most important safeguard which is implied by the due process clause in criminal trials is the requirement that no one be found guilty of a criminal offense unless the charge has been proven by the government beyond a reasonable doubt.[5] Upon conviction, the defendant has a constitutionally protected expectation that he will only be deprived of his liberty to the extent allowed by statute and as determined by a sentencing agency, be it a judge or jury, properly exercising its discretion within the terms set by the legislature.[6]

The individual may forego these procedural protections by waiving his right to any specific safeguard. While the Supreme Court has always stated that waivers of rights must be "knowing and intelligent" to be binding upon the individual, there is no single standard for determining when the waiver of a right will be sufficient.[7]

The Court has adopted differing standards for determining the adequacy of an asserted waiver depending on the specific right involved in the case. The Court has required the government to warn defendants who are in custo-

Court ruled that a state dangerous drug tax was a criminal penalty, rather than a civil penalty, because it was not a remedy for damages or costs to the state. The tax could not be applied to the individuals in the *Kurth Ranch* case who had already been convicted of drug offenses in criminal proceedings because application of this tax statute to them would have violated the double jeopardy clause. For citations to additional Supreme Court cases, and secondary authorities, on this point, see R. Rotunda & J. Nowak, Treatise on Constitutional Law: Substance and Procedure § 17.9 (3rd ed. 1999, with annual supplements).

2. The grand jury clause has been held not to apply to the States. Hurtado v. California, 110 U.S. 516, 4 S.Ct. 111, 28 L.Ed. 232 (1884).

3. Mullaney v. Wilbur, 421 U.S. 684, 95 S.Ct. 1881, 44 L.Ed.2d 508 (1975) (reasonable doubt requirement); Tumey v. Ohio, 273 U.S. 510, 47 S.Ct. 437, 71 L.Ed. 749 (1927) (requirement of disinterested judge).

In Ake v. Oklahoma, 470 U.S. 68, 105 S.Ct. 1087, 84 L.Ed.2d 53 (1985) the Court held that a state must provide access to a psychiatrist to assist an indigent defendant if the defendant has made a preliminary showing that his sanity at the time of an alleged criminal offense will be a significant factor at his trial. This requirement should apply to the sentencing phase of a capital trial as well as the trial determination of guilt or innocence. There is some question as to whether this ruling applies only to a capital case. Id. at 87, 105 S.Ct. at 1098 (Burger, C.J., concurring in the judgment).

For citations to additional Supreme Court cases, and secondary authorities, on this point, see R. Rotunda & J.

Nowak, Treatise on Constitutional Law: Substance and Procedure, §§ 17.4(b), 17.9(a) (3rd ed. 1999, with annual supplements).

4. The due process clause has traditionally been used to regulate objectionable police methods on this basis without having to find a violation of more specific guarantees. See, e.g., Rochin v. California, 342 U.S. 165, 72 S.Ct. 205, 96 L.Ed. 183 (1952) (evidence gained from "stomach pumping" of the defendant held inadmissible); Turner v. Pennsylvania, 338 U.S. 62, 69 S.Ct. 1352, 93 L.Ed. 1810 (1949) (exclusion of coerced confession even if it met a "trustworthiness" test).

For citations to additional Supreme Court cases on this point, see R. Rotunda & J. Nowak, Treatise on Constitutional Law: Substance and Procedure §§ 17.4, 17.9 (3rd ed. 1999, with annual supplements).

5. Mullaney v. Wilbur, 421 U.S. 684, 95 S.Ct. 1881, 44 L.Ed.2d 508 (1975).

6. Hicks v. Oklahoma, 447 U.S. 343, 100 S.Ct. 2227, 65 L.Ed.2d 175 (1980) (improper instruction of a jury regarding the scope of its sentencing powers results in invalidation of the sentence imposed on a defendant even though the jury could have fixed the same sentence term under proper instructions).

7. See W. LaFave & J. Israel, Criminal Procedure (single volume treatise, 2nd ed., 1992); W. LaFave, J. Israel & N. King, Criminal Procedure (multivolume treatise, 2nd ed., 1999).

dy of their rights under the Fifth and Sixth Amendments prior to any asserted waiver of those rights by the individual.[8] The Court has held that any questioning of a defendant outside of the presence of his counsel after the initiation of adversarial proceedings will be held an automatic violation of the Sixth Amendment absent not only a warning but a most explicit waiver of that right.[9] On the other side of the scale, the Supreme Court has held that individuals may consent to searches of their persons or premises although they have not been advised of their rights by the investigative agencies or officers.[10]

When a defendant seeks pretrial suppression of statements or evidence which the government will seek to use against him at trial, his interest in the suppression hearing is of a lesser magnitude than his interest in the trial itself according to the Supreme Court. Therefore, the procedures used at a suppression hearing may be less elaborate than those accorded a defendant at his trial. In *United States v. Raddatz*,[11] the Supreme Court used the *Mathews v. Eldridge*[12] balancing test in

finding that the Federal Magistrates Act adequately protected a defendant's due process rights in a suppression hearing; the federal district judge was not required to personally rehear testimony submitted to a federal magistrate when the judge made a "de novo" determination of the admissibility of evidence.

Appellate Process. Once the criminal trial is over and the defendant has been found guilty, there is no inherent right to appeal. But, while the Court has stated that there is no right to an appellate process, the Justices have never been confronted, at least in modern times, with the situation where a state would not grant some review—either collateral or direct—of decisions which resulted in conviction of criminal charges.[13] Were such a case to arise, it is at least possible that the Court might hold that there is a right to the review of some portions of the original decision-making process wherein might lie serious errors of law or fact. The federal system of habeas corpus relief also serves some of the functions of an appellate system, at least as to jurisdic-

8. Miranda v. Arizona, 384 U.S. 436, 86 S.Ct. 1602, 16 L.Ed.2d 694 (1966), rehearing denied 385 U.S. 890, 87 S.Ct. 11, 17 L.Ed.2d 121 (1966); the requirement does not apply to noncustodial interviews, Beckwith v. United States, 425 U.S. 341, 96 S.Ct. 1612, 48 L.Ed.2d 1 (1976) (home interview by I.R.S. agents). For citations to additional Supreme Court cases, and secondary authorities, on this point, see R. Rotunda & J. Nowak, Treatise on Constitutional Law: Substance and Procedure, § 17.9 (3rd ed. 1999, with annual supplements).

9. Brewer v. Williams, 430 U.S. 387, 97 S.Ct. 1232, 51 L.Ed.2d 424 (1977), rehearing denied 431 U.S. 925, 97 S.Ct. 2200, 53 L.Ed.2d 240 (1977), on remand to 285 N.W.2d 248 (Iowa 1979), certiorari denied 446 U.S. 921, 100 S.Ct. 1859, 64 L.Ed.2d 277 (1980). See also United States v. Henry, 447 U.S. 264, 100 S.Ct. 2183, 65 L.Ed.2d 115 (1980) (defendant's incriminating statements made to paid informant confined in a prison cellblock with the defendant held inadmissible as being elicited from a defendant in violation of his Sixth Amendment right to counsel).

For citations to additional Supreme Court cases on this point, see R. Rotunda & J. Nowak, Treatise on Constitutional Law: Substance and Procedure, § 17.9(3rd ed. 1999, with annual supplements).

10. Schneckloth v. Bustamonte, 412 U.S. 218, 93 S.Ct. 2041, 36 L.Ed.2d 854 (1973).

11. 447 U.S. 667, 100 S.Ct. 2406, 65 L.Ed.2d 424 (1980), rehearing denied 448 U.S. 916, 101 S.Ct. 36, 65 L.Ed.2d 1179 (1980).

12. 424 U.S. 319, 96 S.Ct. 893, 47 L.Ed.2d 18 (1976).

13. See Ross v. Moffitt, 417 U.S. 600, 611, 94 S.Ct. 2437, 2444, 41 L.Ed.2d 341 (1974) (stating that due process does not require appellate process). Although the Supreme Court in United States v. Mendoza–Lopez, 481 U.S. 828, 107 S.Ct. 2148, 95 L.Ed.2d 772 (1987) did not find that there was a right to appeal in cases that resulted in a serious deprivation of liberty, it also created a right to challenge judicial or administrative actions in at least one area. At issue in *Mendoza–Lopez* was the validity of a law that provided that any alien who entered the United States after being deported under a specific statute was guilty of a felony. The individuals in the case had been deported after a hearing in which they waived their right to apply for a suspension of deportation or to appeal. Thereafter, they were arrested for attempting to enter the country. The Supreme Court found that due process required that they be allowed a "collateral challenge" to the use of a deportation proceeding as an element of their criminal offense when the deportation proceeding effectively eliminated the right to obtain judicial review of that proceeding. The Court's majority opinion written by Justice Marshall stated: "Our cases establish that where a determination made in an administrative proceeding is to play a critical role in the subsequent imposition of a criminal sanction, there must be some meaningful review of the administrative proceeding." 481 U.S. at 837–38, 107 S.Ct. at 2154.

For citations to additional Supreme Court cases on this point, see R. Rotunda & J. Nowak, Treatise on Constitutional Law: Substance and Procedure, § 17.9(a) (3rd ed. 1999, with annual supplements).

tional or constitutional defects in the criminal trial.

When a state does set up an appellate system, it must design that system to produce a fair review of the original trials of all persons. It may not establish a system which explicitly, or by its impact, affords fair appellate process only to those who can afford to pay for that process. Thus the state is required to waive filing fees and transcript reproduction costs for the appeals of indigent defendants.[14] Similarly, the state must provide defendants with the assistance of counsel for their first appeal as of right in order to insure that all classes of defendants receive a fair review of their trials.[15] However, the state need not provide counsel for indigent defendants who seek to attack their convictions in later discretionary appeals or collateral attacks,[16] because a majority of the Justices are of the opinion that the assistance of counsel at trial and on the first appeal of right insures an equality of treatment as to fundamental issues of law and fact. Apparently it is also the belief of a majority of the Justices that later appeals or collateral attack are not so significantly related to fairness as to require that indigent defendants be accorded completely equal access to them.

The Court has held that the right of access to the system of judicial review includes a right of persons to have legal research materi-

als.[17] Nor can the prison authorities preclude prisoners from assisting one another with the preparation of papers for judicial review of their convictions[18] or the filing of civil rights actions[19] if the state does not provide them with professional legal assistance. These rulings of right of access to currently established procedures may imply some duty of the state to establish systems of judicial review of criminal cases despite the language to the contrary in some decisions.

Parole or Probation Revocation. Following a criminal trial and conviction on a criminal charge, a person may be placed on conditional release from a penitentiary. The system known as probation allows one to forego serving his sentence of imprisonment so long as he meets certain conditions relating to his conduct. A person sentenced to serve a term of imprisonment may be allowed to leave prison prior to the expiration of his maximum term under a system of parole which also conditions continued release on certain standards of behavior. When the state seeks to revoke someone's continued right to parole or probation and place him in prison, it is depriving him of "liberty" within the terms of the due process clauses. However, this fact does not require the government to prove that the conditions of parole or probation have been violated in the same way that it had to prove the initial charge.[20]

---

14. Mayer v. Chicago, 404 U.S. 189, 92 S.Ct. 410, 30 L.Ed.2d 372 (1971).

15. Douglas v. California, 372 U.S. 353, 83 S.Ct. 814, 9 L.Ed.2d 811 (1963), rehearing denied 373 U.S. 905, 83 S.Ct. 1288, 10 L.Ed.2d 200 (1963).

For citations to additional Supreme Court cases, and secondary authorities, on this point, see R. Rotunda & J. Nowak, Treatise on Constitutional Law: Substance and Procedure, § 17.9 (3rd ed. 1999, with annual supplements).

16. Ross v. Moffitt, 417 U.S. 600, 94 S.Ct. 2437, 41 L.Ed.2d 341 (1974).

For citations to additional Supreme Court cases on this point, see R. Rotunda & J. Nowak, Treatise on Constitutional Law: Substance and Procedure, § 17.9 (3rd ed. 1999, with annual supplements).

17. Bounds v. Smith, 430 U.S. 817, 97 S.Ct. 1491, 52 L.Ed.2d 72 (1977).

In Strickland v. Washington, 466 U.S. 668, 104 S.Ct. 2052, 80 L.Ed.2d 674 (1984) the Supreme Court ruled that a court's review of a convicted defendant's claim that he received ineffective assistance of counsel, and thereby was

deprived of his Sixth and Fourteenth Amendment right to counsel, required an inquiry into whether counsel's performance was deficient and whether the defendant had suffered prejudice. In Lockhart v. Fretwell, 506 U.S. 364, 113 S.Ct. 838, 122 L.Ed.2d 180 (1993) the Supreme Court ruled that the failure of a defendant's court appointed attorney to raise an objection based upon a United States Court of Appeals ruling that was later overruled by the Court of Appeals—at a date following the defendant's conviction and the affirmance of his conviction by the state court—did not constitute ineffective assistance of counsel. The defendant's conviction and death sentence, in *Lockhart,* involved neither the unreliability nor unfairness that would be required to establish a Sixth or Fourteenth Amendment violation.

18. Johnson v. Avery, 393 U.S. 483, 89 S.Ct. 747, 21 L.Ed.2d 718 (1969).

19. Wolff v. McDonnell, 418 U.S. 539, 94 S.Ct. 2963, 41 L.Ed.2d 935 (1974).

20. Morrissey v. Brewer, 408 U.S. 471, 92 S.Ct. 2593, 33 L.Ed.2d 484 (1972) (parole); Gagnon v. Scarpelli, 411 U.S. 778, 93 S.Ct. 1756, 36 L.Ed.2d 656 (1973) (probation).

The procedures for revoking probation or parole must include: (1) notice of the claimed violation of parole or probation conditions; (2) disclosure of evidence to the defendant; (3) a personal hearing for the defendant; (4) the opportunity to present evidence on behalf of the defendant; (5) the right to confront and cross-examine witnesses against the defendant unless there is specific good cause for avoiding such a confrontation; (6) a written statement by the adjudicator as to the evidence relied on and the reason for revoking the parole or probation status. All of this must take place before a neutral hearing examiner or board.

The previously convicted defendant does not have an absolute right to counsel at either the probation or parole revocation hearing. Instead, the Court has held that the decision as to whether counsel must be allowed at the proceedings must be made on a case by case basis. There will be a need for counsel wherever the charges concerning the parole or probation violation are such that they could not adequately be defended against by the defendant alone.[21]

"Prisoners' Rights" Cases. An individual does not lose all of his constitutional rights by being imprisoned for commission of a crime. Specifically, if there are further signifi-cant deprivations of life, liberty, or property following imprisonment, the prisoner is entitled to a fair procedure to determine the basis for the deprivations. Because of the limited nature of a prisoner's constitutional rights, it is very difficult to determine when there is a constitutionally cognizable interest in life, liberty or property being denied a prisoner.[22] If prison officials impair the prisoner's interest in life, liberty, or property through their negligence, due process does not require a post-deprivation hearing or compensation for the prisoner. However, due process will require that a prisoner who is deprived of life, liberty, or property through the intentional action of prison authorities receive some type of fair post-deprivation hearing to determine whether he is entitled to compensation.[23]

In *Wolff v. McDonnell* [24] the Court held that where a state establishes a system of "good time credits" which reduce a defendant's time until possible parole, the state must accord the defendant a fair procedure prior to eliminating his good time credits. This hearing would not be an extensive one and would require only written notice of the violation, an opportunity for the convict to present evidence in his behalf and a written statement as to why the

---

For citations to additional cases, and secondary authorities, see the multivolume edition of this treatise: R. Rotunda & J. Nowak, Treatise On Constitutional Law: Substance and Procedure § 17.9 (3rd ed. 1999, with annual supplements).

21. Gagnon v. Scarpelli, 411 U.S. 778, 790, 93 S.Ct. 1756, 1763–64, 36 L.Ed.2d 656 (1973).

For citations to additional cases, and secondary authorities, see the multivolume edition of this treatise: R. Rotunda & J. Nowak, Treatise On Constitutional Law: Substance and Procedure § 17.9 (3rd ed. 1999, with annual supplements).

22. Prisoners' Rights cases are also examined in § 13.4, supra. The need to separate procedural due process and substantive due process issues in prisoner cases was examined in § 10.6. The Supreme Court has held that a prisoner's interest in a fair process to review his eligibility for parole is not protected by due process unless the state has by statute entitled him to a fair parole granting process. See Greenholtz v. Inmates of the Nebraska Penal and Correctional Complex, 442 U.S. 1, 99 S.Ct. 2100, 60 L.Ed.2d 668 (1979).

23. In Sacramento v. Lewis, 523 U.S. 833, 118 S.Ct. 1708, 140 L.Ed.2d 1043 (1998) the Court ruled that a young man's life had not been taken in violation of sub-stantive due process principles when he was accidentally killed by a police car that was chasing the motorcycle on which he was a passenger. The majority opinion in *Lewis* found that no procedural due process issues were presented by the case, because there was no challenge to the adequacy of state procedures for claiming compensation for the life of the young man (who was the son of the plaintiffs). The *Lewis* decision is examined in § 10.6 of this Treatise. The Supreme Court, in Hudson v. Palmer, 468 U.S. 517, 104 S.Ct. 3194, 82 L.Ed.2d 393 (1984), on remand 744 F.2d 22 (4th Cir.1984), ruled that the state must provide a post-deprivation remedy for a prisoner who alleges that his property was intentionally destroyed by prison authorities. In contrast, the Supreme Court held in Daniels v. Williams, 474 U.S. 327, 106 S.Ct. 662, 88 L.Ed.2d 662 (1986), overruling Parratt v. Taylor, 451 U.S. 527, 101 S.Ct. 1908, 68 L.Ed.2d 420 (1981), that due process was not violated when state tort law, and a state doctrine of sovereign immunity, denied recovery to an inmate for the injury he suffered by slipping on a pillow negligently placed on a stairway by a prison official. The Court in *Daniels* found that "the due process clause is simply not implicated by a negligent act of an official causing an unintended loss of injury to life, liberty, or property." Accord, Davidson v. Cannon, 474 U.S. 344, 106 S.Ct. 668, 88 L.Ed.2d 677 (1986).

24. 418 U.S. 539, 94 S.Ct. 2963, 41 L.Ed.2d 935 (1974).

disciplinary action is being taken.[25]

These procedural requirements will not apply to all prison disciplinary actions. The majority opinion in *Wolff* indicated that a prisoner would be entitled to a hearing whenever disciplinary actions were so serious as to cause a significant change in the individual's circumstances, such as the imposition of a punishment of solitary confinement.[26] However, the Court has held that prisoners could be transferred to "administrative segregation" or to prisons with less favorable conditions without any procedure.[27] These decisions might be taken to indicate that the degree of liberty which a prisoner enjoyed might be dependent solely upon state law but this position seems to conflict with established notions of the meaning of liberty.[28] In any event, it appears that the Supreme Court will only require a minimally fair procedure for the imposition of very severe and very formal disciplinary actions within a prison. Of course, in an emergency situation greater latitude would clearly be allowed to prison authorities to impose order and safe conditions in a prison without engaging in any formalized procedures.[29]

The Court has held that the mere possibility of receiving parole is not a liberty interest protected by the due process clauses and that even a state created entitlement of prisoners to receive parole under specific circumstances requires no more than informal hearings at which a parole board can receive a presentation by the prisoner.[30]

In *Vitek v. Jones*,[31] the Supreme Court held that an involuntary transfer of a prisoner to a mental hospital implicated a protected liberty interest and that due process was not satisfied by the mere certification of the need for such treatment by a state-designated physician or psychologist. The Court found that the transfer constituted a deprivation of liberty both because state statutes at issue in the case gave rise to a legitimate expectation on the part of the prisoner that he would only be kept in normal prison facilities and because this transfer involved a significantly greater degree of confinement, the imposition of mandatory treatment, and a realistic possibility of stigmatizing consequences for the defendant. The majority opinion by Justice White recognized that the state's interest in treating mentally ill patients was quite strong, but found that it was outweighed by the prisoner's interest in not being arbitrarily classified as mentally ill and subjected to treatment.

Five Justices in *Vitek* agreed that due process required: (1) notice to the prisoner of the

---

25. 418 U.S. at 563–72, 94 S.Ct. at 2978–82.

In *Wolff v. McDonnell* the Court stated that "the inmate facing disciplinary proceedings should be allowed to call witnesses and present documentary evidence in his defense when permitting him to do so will not be unduly hazardous to institutional safety or correctional goals," 418 U.S. at 566, 94 S.Ct. at 2979, 41 L.Ed.2d at 956. In *Baxter* the Court found that the calling of witnesses was "circumscribed" by the need to give some deference to institutional needs of prisons and the decisions of the officials of state prisons. As long as there was no evidence of a prison official abusing his discretion in refusing to call witnesses for the defendant at the disciplinary proceeding, there was no violation of due process. Baxter v. Palmigiano, 425 U.S. 308, 322–23, 96 S.Ct. 1551, 1560, 47 L.Ed.2d 810 (1976).

For citations to additional Supreme Court cases on this point, see R. Rotunda & J. Nowak, Treatise on Constitutional Law: Substance and Procedure, vol. 2 §§ 17.4(b), 17.9 (2nd ed. 1992, with annual supplements).

26. 418 U.S. at 571–72 n. 19, 94 S.Ct. at 2982 n. 19.

27. When a person has been convicted of a crime, he has received the best process which our society can afford to justify his liberty loss. A later transfer of the prisoner to differing conditions of confinement does not require a new process unless the new conditions may be said to be outside of the normal range of (or substantive constitutional limits on) the conditions of confinement. Due process requires some type of fair procedure before a state may subject a prisoner to some forms of punishment (such as beating or a transfer to a psychiatric care facility) that are not normally expected in our penal system. See Vitek v. Jones, 445 U.S. 480, 100 S.Ct. 1254, 63 L.Ed.2d 552 (1980); Smith v. Wade, 461 U.S. 30, 103 S.Ct. 1625, 75 L.Ed.2d 632 (1983). For citations to other prisoner's rights cases, see the footnotes in § 13.4(b), supra.

28. Id. The concept of liberty has historically been a federal issue, see § 13.4, supra. Meachum v. Fano, 427 U.S. 215, 230, 96 S.Ct. 2532, 2541, 49 L.Ed.2d 451 (1976), rehearing denied 429 U.S. 873, 97 S.Ct. 191, 50 L.Ed.2d 155 (1976) (Stevens, J., dissenting).

29. Regarding the nature of the process required for disciplinary proceedings, see note 25, supra.

30. Greenholtz v. Inmates of the Nebraska Penal and Correctional Complex, 442 U.S. 1, 99 S.Ct. 2100, 60 L.Ed.2d 668 (1979). This decision is examined in § 13.4, supra.

31. 445 U.S. 480, 100 S.Ct. 1254, 63 L.Ed.2d 552 (1980).

intended transfer and of his rights to contest that transfer; (2) time for the prisoner to prepare his arguments; (3) a hearing where the prisoner has the opportunity to be heard in person, to present evidence and witnesses, and to cross-examine state witnesses, except where good cause exists for limiting confrontation; (4) an independent decision-maker; (5) a written statement by the decision-maker detailing the evidence and rationale underlying a decision to transfer.

In *Washington v. Harper*[32] the Supreme Court upheld a prison regulation that authorized the administration of antipsychotic drugs to a prisoner without his consent. The Supreme Court found that the regulation was reasonably related to a legitimate penological interest and, for that reason, did not violate the substantive component of the due process clause.[33] Nevertheless, such a law had to be applied in accordance with the procedural protections provided by the due process clause. The prisoner retained a liberty interest, which was not taken away by his criminal conviction, that would be impaired by the administration of such drugs to him. The prison regulation examined in the *Harper* decision gave the prison inmate notice of the medical professional's intent to administer antipsychotic drugs to him, a hearing before a panel of medical professionals and prison officials who were not involved in the inmate's current treatment, a right to present evidence and to cross-examine persons at the hearing, and judicial review of the hearing committee's decision (if the prisoner filed a petition for judicial review with the trial courts in the state). The Supreme Court used the *Mathews v. Eldridge* balancing test[34] in determining whether these proce-

dures were sufficient to comply with procedural due process. The Court in *Harper* found that the government did not have to provide the prisoner with a hearing before a judge, rather than administrative panel. The Supreme Court found that the prison regulations provided the prisoner with a fair hearing, which was similar to the type of hearing a prison inmate would receive before being transferred to a mental health care facility. Therefore, the Court ruled that the regulation complied with the due process clause.

In *Sell v. United States*,[35] the Supreme Court ruled that a court could order a defendant who was not dangerous, to himself or others, to be involuntarily medicated for the sole purpose of making the defendant mentally competent to stand trial only if the trial court's order was based on a record that supported the trial judge in finding: (1) that important government interests were at stake; (2) that the medication would significantly further the important state interests; (3) the medication was necessary to further those important interests; and (4) that the administration of the medication, against the patient's wishes, was medically appropriate (in that it was in the best medical interests of the defendant and that the medication would allow the defendant to have a fair trial.)

Loss of Liberty Through Civil Process. When the state seeks to impose physical restraints of significant duration on a person it must afford him fair procedure to determine the basis and legality of such a deprivation of liberty, even when the nature of the state's action may be considered civil rather than criminal. When the state seeks to take custody of juveniles, it must accord the child a fair

32. 494 U.S. 210, 110 S.Ct. 1028, 108 L.Ed.2d 178 (1990).

33. 494 U.S. at 220–229, 110 S.Ct. at 1036–1040. The Supreme Court in *Harper* found that the substance of the rule at issue was only subject to a reasonableness standard. In prior prison regulation cases, the Supreme Court had held that a law restricting constitutionally protected rights of prison inmates only had to be reasonably related to legitimate penological interests. Turner v. Safley, 482 U.S. 78, 107 S.Ct. 2254, 96 L.Ed.2d 64 (1987). For an examination of the difference between procedural due

process and substantive due process issues and rulings, see § 10.6.

34. 424 U.S. 319, 335, 96 S.Ct. 893, 903, 47 L.Ed.2d 18 (1976). The Supreme Court in *Mathews* required courts to weigh several factors when determining the type of procedures that must be established in connection with the taking of a liberty or property interest by government. The *Mathews* test is examined in § 13.8.

35. 539 U.S. 166, 123 S.Ct. 2174, 156 L.Ed.2d 197 (2003). See § 10.6 regarding distinctions between substantive due process and procedural due process issues in prisoner's rights cases.

procedure.[36] This includes: (1) adequate notice of the charges; (2) a right to counsel; (3) the appointment of counsel for indigents; (4) the right to confrontation and cross-examination of witnesses and (5) the privilege against self-incrimination. Additionally, when the action is based upon a charge which would constitute a crime if committed by an adult, the state must prove its case beyond a reasonable doubt.[37] However, the state does not have to grant the juvenile either a jury trial or a public hearing.[38]

Pretrial Detention of Juveniles. In *Schall v. Martin*,[39] the Supreme Court upheld a limited form of pretrial detention for juveniles accused of serious crime.[40] The Court found that the state interest in "protecting both the community and the juvenile himself from the consequences of future criminal conduct is sufficient to justify such detention."[41] The majority opinion by Justice Rehnquist indicated that the Court would not uphold *punitive* measures taken toward children prior to an adjudication of guilt and delinquency. However, the child's liberty interest could be limited by a system which promoted safety for the community and protection for the child when the conditions of confinement were not punitive in nature. In this case, the child was not sent to a prison or facility where he would be exposed to adult criminals, and the detention was strictly limited in time prior to full adjudication of guilt through statutory limits on the detention and the provision for an expedited fact finding process.

Having found that the child's liberty interest could be limited by the state interest promoted by pretrial detention, the Court then used the balancing approach established by *Mathews v. Eldridge*[42] to determine whether the child was given sufficient procedural guarantees to guard against his liberty being taken without due process of law. The Court noted that "in some circumstances detention of a juvenile would not pass constitutional muster. But the validity of those detentions must be determined on a case-by-case basis." The system established by the statute at issue in *Schall* complied with the due process principles because it gave the juvenile notice, a right to an expedited hearing which included the right to be accompanied by his parent or guardian, the right to remain silent, and the right to counsel. These procedural guarantees were strengthened by the requirement of a probable cause hearing and the requirement of a written statement of findings regarding that issue and whether continued detention was necessary.

The Court noted that the appellees could identify no additional procedure which "would significantly improve the accuracy of the determination without unduly impinging on the achievement of legitimate state purposes." The Court upheld these procedures even though the judge was required to determine whether the child was likely to engage in other serious criminal conduct. The Court concluded that "from a legal point of view there is nothing inherently unattainable about a prediction of future criminal conduct."[43]

---

36. Application of Gault, 387 U.S. 1, 87 S.Ct. 1428, 18 L.Ed.2d 527 (1967).

37. In re Winship, 397 U.S. 358, 90 S.Ct. 1068, 25 L.Ed.2d 368 (1970).

38. McKeiver v. Pennsylvania, 403 U.S. 528, 91 S.Ct. 1976, 29 L.Ed.2d 647 (1971).

39. 467 U.S. 253, 104 S.Ct. 2403, 81 L.Ed.2d 207 (1984).

40. The Court noted that it was not considering the legitimacy of the part of the statute which allowed for detention of an accused juvenile offender prior to an initial appearance in family court. The Court only considered the ability of the state to detain the child prior to a full adjudicatory hearing regarding guilt in a case where the child did make an initial appearance before a family court judge and the judge determined that there was probable

cause to believe that the child had committed a serious crime and that the child might engage in other criminal conduct while awaiting trial if released. 467 U.S. at 257 n. 5, 104 S.Ct. at 2406 n. 5, 81 L.Ed.2d at 212–13, n. 5.

41. 467 U.S. at 264, 104 S.Ct. at 2410, 81 L.Ed.2d at 217. The Court noted that the "legitimate and compelling interest" in protecting the community from crime cannot be doubted. De Veau v. Braisted, 363 U.S. 144, 155, 80 S.Ct. 1146, 1152, 4 L.Ed.2d 1109 (1960). Id.

42. 424 U.S. 319, 335, 96 S.Ct. 893, 903, 47 L.Ed.2d 18 (1976). The balancing test established by that case for the determination of the adequacy of procedural safeguards when life, liberty, or property is being taken from an individual by the government is examined in § 13.8.

43. Schall v. Martin, 467 U.S. 253, 277, 104 S.Ct. 2403, 2417, 81 L.Ed.2d 207, 226 (1984). The Court referred here to its approval of determinations of the likelihood of

This case indicates that the Court may uphold a system of pretrial detention for adults accused of committing serious crimes if there is a statutory system which subjects the accused adult to nonpunitive conditions of confinement [44] and establishes procedures for a prompt determination of both probable cause to believe that the individual committed the crime and that the individual would be dangerous if released. Nonetheless, the issue regarding pretrial detention of adult offenders appears to remain open because the Court in *Schall* relied heavily on the limited nature of a child's liberty interest; that interest is modified by the role of parent, guardian, or the state, all of whom may act on behalf of the child's interest in ways which the child might oppose.

In *Reno v. Flores*,[45] the Court relied on *Schall* and upheld Immigration and Naturalization Service [INS] regulations regarding the custody of children pending deportation. Under the INS regulations an alien juvenile who was in custody pending deportation proceedings would be released to his parents, guardians, or relatives if such persons were in the United States and not in detention. If there was no guardian or relative in the United States who was able and qualified to take care of the child, the child would be kept in custody pending deportation proceedings. Children would be released to a person other than their relative or guardian, under the terms of the

INS regulations, only in the most "unusual and compelling" circumstances.

The majority opinion in *Flores*, written by Justice Scalia, found that there was no significant evidence that the children who were awaiting deportation proceedings were kept in custody that was not suitable for their care. The majority believed that the custodial facilities provided the detained alien children with adequate care. Justice Scalia stressed that the Court was only considering the validity of the INS regulations on their face. There was no claim in *Flores* that a specific child's case or care had been handled in a fundamentally unfair manner.

The Court in *Flores* separated substantive due process issues and procedural due process issues.[46] The majority opinion held that a child did not have a fundamental right to be placed in a "non-custodial setting" whenever that might be in the child's "best interest." [47] Justice Scalia then found that the substantive rule established by the regulations did not violate substantive due process principles because the INS rule was reasonably and rationally related to the government interests in providing proper care for the children and providing for their appearance at the deportation proceedings.

The children who were being held in custody claimed that each child had a procedural due process right to an individualized determination as to whether keeping the child in govern-

---

future criminal activity in Jurek v. Texas, 428 U.S. 262, 274–75, 96 S.Ct. 2950, 2957–58, 49 L.Ed.2d 929 (1976) (upholding death sentences imposed by juries considering future dangerousness as part of their deliberations); Greenholtz v. Inmates of Nebraska Penal and Correctional Complex, 442 U.S. 1, 9–10, 99 S.Ct. 2100, 2104–05, 60 L.Ed.2d 668 (1979), on remand to 602 F.2d 155 (8th Cir.1979) (consideration of board granting parole); Morrissey v. Brewer, 408 U.S. 471, 480, 92 S.Ct. 2593, 2599, 33 L.Ed.2d 484 (1972) (parole revocation). The Court also referred to lower court decisions predicting future criminal conduct as the basis for increased sentencing under federal statutes. 467 U.S. at 278 n. 30, 104 S.Ct. at 2417 n. 30, 81 L.Ed.2d at 226 n. 30.

44. The Court in *Schall v. Martin* noted that "in Bell v. Wolfish, 441 U.S. 520, 534 n. 15, 99 S.Ct. 1861, 1871 n. 15, 60 L.Ed.2d 447, 465 n. 15 (1979) we left open the question of whether any governmental objective other than ensuring a detainee's presence at trial may constitutionally justify pretrial detention." 467 U.S. at 264, 104 S.Ct. at 2410, 81 L.Ed.2d at 217. In *Bell*, the Court found

that due process would require fair procedures for determining guilt before a person could be subjected to punitive actions by the state but limited substantive judicial review regarding the physical condition of facilities where persons were held while they awaited trial.

45. 507 U.S. 292, 113 S.Ct. 1439, 123 L.Ed.2d 1 (1993), on remand 992 F.2d 243 (9th Cir.1993).

46. See § 10.6 of this Treatise regarding the distinction between procedural due process issues and substantive due process issues.

47. Reno v. Flores, 507 U.S. 292, 301–305, 113 S.Ct. 1439, 1447–49, 123 L.Ed.2d 1 (1993), on remand 992 F.2d 243 (9th Cir.1993). In this section of the opinion, Justice Scalia also ruled that the INS regulation regarding the release of alien juveniles complied with the implied equal protection guarantee of the Fifth Amendment due process clause. Because no fundamental right was limited by the regulations there was no need, in the view of the majority, to require the government to have a regulation that was narrowly tailored to promote the best interest of the child.

ment custody, or placing the child in the custody of a responsible adult who was not related to him, would be in his best interest. Justice Scalia found that this argument was merely an attempt to convert a substantive due process argument into a procedural due process argument. The majority rejected the claim for individualized procedures, as it had rejected the challenge to the substantive rule set out in the regulation, because children had no fundamental right to be placed in a noncustodial setting whenever it might be in their best interest.[48]

The alien juveniles made two other procedural claims in *Flores*. First, they claimed that the regulations created unnecessary delay, and unnecessary detention of children. Second, they claimed the regulation improperly allowed children to waive their statutory right to have an INS custody determination reviewed by an immigration judge.[49]

These two limited procedural attacks on the system for holding children in custody pending deportation proceedings were dispensed with in two paragraphs of the majority opinion. The majority first ruled that the Court would not invalidate the regulations on their face merely because of an allegation of unnecessary delay in the system when there was no evidence of such delay. Justice Scalia's majority opinion then found that many juveniles might be able to knowingly and intelligently waive their right to have review of the initial INS deportation process in custody determina-

tions.[50] The regulation made a minor's waiver of rights revocable, so that a minor who had waived his rights could change his mind and "request a judicial redetermination [of his custody and the initial deportation decision] at any time later in the deportation process."[51] The waiver process could not be found to be unfair to all detained alien juveniles. Any detained juvenile would still be free to litigate the question of whether the INS treatment of his particular case violated due process principles.

The Supreme Court in *Flores,* as in *Schall,* relied on the limited nature of a child's liberty interest. These cases may have only limited relevance to determining the validity of processes used to detain adults under similar circumstances.

Commitment for Mental Care. When the state seeks to commit someone for mental care on an involuntary basis, it must establish a fair procedure for determining that the individual is dangerous to himself or others due to a mental problem.[52]

The Supreme Court has not yet settled many issues concerning the number of procedural safeguards which must be accorded a person whom the state seeks to commit for mental care. The Court has held that the state must grant equivalent procedural safeguards to individuals whom it seeks to commit in civil proceedings and who have been found

---

48. "Respondents contend that this procedural system is unconstitutional because it does not require the service to determine in the case of each individual alien juvenile that detention in INS custody would better serve his interest than release to some other 'responsible adult.' This is just the 'substantive due process' argument recast in 'procedural due process' terms, and we reject it for the same reasons." Reno v. Flores, 507 U.S. 292, 307, 113 S.Ct. 1439, 1450, 123 L.Ed.2d 1 (1993), on remand 992 F.2d 243 (9th Cir.1993).

49. Reno v. Flores, 507 U.S. 292, 307–309, 113 S.Ct. 1439, 1450–1451, 123 L.Ed.2d 1 (1993), on remand 992 F.2d 243 (9th Cir.1993).

50. Reno v. Flores, 507 U.S. 292, 309, 113 S.Ct. 1439, 1451, 123 L.Ed.2d 1 (1993), on remand 992 F.2d 243 (9th Cir.1993): "We have held that juveniles are capable of 'knowingly and intelligently' waiving their right against self-incrimination in criminal cases. See Fare v. Michael C., 442 U.S. 707, 724–727, 99 S.Ct. 2560, 2571–2573, 61 L.Ed.2d 197 (1979); see also, United States v. Saucedo-

Velasquez, 843 F.2d 832, 835 (C.A.5 1988) (applying *Fare* to alien juvenile). The alleged right to redetermination of prehearing custody status in deportation cases is surely no more significant."

51. Reno v. Flores, 507 U.S. 292, 309, 113 S.Ct. 1439, 1451, 123 L.Ed.2d 1 (1993), on remand 992 F.2d 243 (9th Cir.1993).

52. O'Connor v. Donaldson, 422 U.S. 563, 95 S.Ct. 2486, 45 L.Ed.2d 396 (1975), on remand to 519 F.2d 59 (5th Cir.1975).

Due process principles would be violated by criminally prosecuting a defendant who is not mentally competent to stand trial. Drope v. Missouri, 420 U.S. 162, 95 S.Ct. 896, 43 L.Ed.2d 103 (1975). For citations to additional cases, and secondary authorities, see the multivolume edition of this treatise: R. Rotunda & J. Nowak, Treatise On Constitutional Law: Substance and Procedure § 17.9(a) (3rd ed. 1999, with annual supplements).

mentally incompetent in connection with criminal trials.[53]

The Supreme Court has allowed a state to make a distinction between "mentally ill" and "mentally retarded" persons in civil commit-

ment proceedings. In *Heller v. Doe*[54] the Supreme Court upheld Kentucky statutes that made it more difficult for the state to commit a person to a mental health care facility on the basis of mental illness rather than on the basis

---

53. Humphrey v. Cady, 405 U.S. 504, 92 S.Ct. 1048, 31 L.Ed.2d 394 (1972); Jackson v. Indiana, 406 U.S. 715, 92 S.Ct. 1845, 32 L.Ed.2d 435 (1972), McNeil v. Director, 407 U.S. 245, 92 S.Ct. 2083, 32 L.Ed.2d 719 (1972). However, a defendant acquitted of a criminal charge on the basis of an insanity defense may be committed to a psychiatric facility on that basis, even though the defense was established by a "preponderance of the evidence" rather than by "clear and convincing" evidence. Jones v. United States, 463 U.S. 354, 103 S.Ct. 3043, 77 L.Ed.2d 694 (1983).

The fact that a defendant was acquitted of a criminal charge on the basis of an insanity defense does not authorize the state to keep the defendant confined forever. In *Jones,* the Court noted that the individual would be "entitled to release when he has recovered his sanity or is no longer dangerous." Jones v. United States, 463 U.S. 354, 368, 103 S.Ct. 3043, 3052, 77 L.Ed.2d 694 (1983).

In Foucha v. Louisiana, 504 U.S. 71, 112 S.Ct. 1780, 118 L.Ed.2d 437 (1992) the Court held that a state violated due process by the continued commitment of a person who had been acquitted of a criminal charge based on an insanity defense after it was determined by state authorities that the individual was no longer suffering from mental illness. If the state wanted to keep that individual in confinement, the state would have to demonstrate by clear and convincing evidence that the defendant was mentally ill and dangerous. Justice White wrote a majority opinion in *Foucha* in which he found that the confinement of the individual after the basis for involuntary commitment had disappeared violated the due process clause of the Fourteenth Amendment. Justice White wrote for only four Justices when he expressed the opinion that the state had violated the equal protection clause by denying the protections of civil commitment proceedings to persons who had once been acquitted of a criminal act on the basis of an insanity defense but who had ceased to be mentally ill after their acquittal. However, there was no majority opinion as to whether the state system for involuntary commitment of persons acquitted of criminal charges on the basis of insanity violated the equal protection clause. 504 U.S. at 85–86, 112 S.Ct. at 1788–89 (portion III of the opinion of Justice White, which is joined by Justices Blackmun, Stevens, and Souter).

In Kansas v. Hendricks, 521 U.S. 346, 117 S.Ct. 2072, 138 L.Ed.2d 501 (1997) the Supreme Court upheld a statute that allowed for the civil commitment of a person as a "sexually violent predator" who would be dangerous to other persons because of a mental abnormality. There were no true procedural issues in the case, because the state provided the individual with more procedural safeguards than were required by the Supreme Court cases referred to in this Section of the Treatise. The Kansas statute at issue in *Hendricks* allowed for commitment of a person, as a sexually violent predator, only if the substantive standard for commitment was proven beyond a reasonable doubt at trial. The statute required the release of the individual after one year of commitment to the mental

health care facility, unless the government could again prove that the individual was dangerous to other persons due to a mental illness or mental abnormality. The Justices in *Hendricks* divided on the issue of whether the statute, as applied to a prison inmate who was scheduled to be released from prison when the statute was enacted, constituted a retroactive increase in the prisoner's penalty for his earlier crimes. By a five to four vote, the Court in *Hendricks* ruled that the statute as written and as applied to the individual in the case was not punitive in nature and did not violate the due process *ex post facto* or double jeopardy clauses. Justice Kennedy noted that all of the Justices seemed to agree that the state could confine persons who were dangerous to others due to a mental abnormality. Kansas v. Hendricks, 521 U.S. 346, 371, 117 S.Ct. 2072, 2087, 138 L.Ed.2d 501 (1997) (Kennedy, J., concurring) 521 U.S. at 371, 117 S.Ct. at 2087 (Breyer, J., joined by Stevens and Souter, JJ., and, in part, by Ginsburg, J., dissenting).

In Seling v. Young, 531 U.S. 250, 121 S.Ct. 727, 148 L.Ed.2d 734 (2001), on remand 248 F.3d 1197 (9th Cir. 2001), by 8 to 1 the Court ruled that a state statute similar to the one upheld in *Hendricks* cannot be challenged as being a criminal statute on an "as applied" basis. An "as applied" challenge would depend on the treatment of the individual who challenged the civil commitment as being criminal in nature. The majority opinion in *Seling* left open the question of whether conditions of confinement for all persons under a statute labeled civil in nature could result in a finding that the statute was in fact a criminal punishment. See note 1 in § 13.9 (a) for further cases examining the distinction between civil statutes and criminal punishments. In Kansas v. Crane, 534 U.S. 407, 122 S.Ct. 867, 151 L.Ed.2d 856 (2002) the Supreme Court ruled that an individual can be subject to involuntary commitment based upon the premise that he is dangerous to himself or others only if the government can prove that the individuals dangerousness is based upon some type of mental condition that results in "serious difficulty" in the individual controlling his dangerous behavior. The majority opinion in *Crane* explained that substantive due process required proof of a mental condition that resulted in serious difficulty in controlling behavior in order to prevent the government from using civil commitment proceedings (with their lesser procedural requirements) as an alternative to the criminal prosecution of individuals who had allegedly committed sexual offenses but whose actions were not based upon some mental condition that would justify involuntary commitment. The state must use the criminal law process when it seeks to punish someone for sex related criminal activity. The state cannot use involuntary commitment unless it can demonstrate that the individual's dangerous actions are based on mental conditions that present difficulty in the individual controlling his behavior in the future.

54. 509 U.S. 312, 113 S.Ct. 2637, 125 L.Ed.2d 257 (1993).

of mental retardation. The Kentucky statutes accomplished this end in two ways. First, the statutes created differing standards of proof for the commitment procedures. A state court would have to find by clear and convincing evidence that a person met mental retardation standards for involuntary commitment. A state court would have to find proof beyond a reasonable doubt that a person should be involuntarily committed for mental illness. Second, the statutes established procedural distinctions in these involuntary commitment proceedings. In commitment proceedings that were based upon alleged mental retardation, guardians and immediate family members of the defendant were allowed to participate as parties in the proceedings, which gave them a right to present evidence and to appeal from the trial court decision. Family members were not given such rights in commitment proceedings that were based on alleged mental illness.

The majority opinion in *Heller*, written by Justice Kennedy, first rejected equal protection attacks on these classifications. Justice Kennedy found no reason to overturn the legislative decision that the greater difficulty of determining mental illness, as opposed to mental retardation, and the more invasive treat-

ments for mental illness than for mental retardation justified giving greater substantive and procedural protections to persons who might be committed to a health care facility for treatment of mental illness.[55] The majority ruled that these classifications were rationally related to legitimate state interests in protecting individuals from erroneous decisions in the civil commitment process.

The majority in *Heller* also ruled that allowing guardians and immediate relatives to participate in commitment proceedings based on mental retardation did not violate procedural due process principles. Justice Kennedy employed the *Mathews v. Eldridge*[56] test in determining that the participation of family members in the civil commitment process would aid in the accurate determination of whether the defendant was mentally retarded and in need of commitment. The participation of these family members in the process might make it more likely that the person would be committed for care than if they were excluded from such proceedings. Because due process principles only protect the individual's interest in a fair proceeding, rather than an interest in favorable rulings, there was no due process violation.[57]

---

55. The Supreme Court in this case only required that these classifications have a rational relationship to a legitimate interest of government because all litigation in the lower court stages of this case had employed that standard of review. The persons attacking these classifications had not requested "heightened scrutiny" of the classification until they argued their case in the Supreme Court. For that reason the Court considered only whether these classifications met the rational basis standard. Heller v. Doe, 509 U.S. 312, 320, 113 S.Ct. 2637, 2642, 125 L.Ed.2d 257 (1993). The dissenting Justices in *Heller* agreed that the persons attacking the classification had failed to press their claim for heightened scrutiny in the lower courts. The dissenters believed that the distinctions between mentally retarded and mentally ill persons could not survive even rationality review. 509 U.S. at 333, 113 S.Ct. at 2650 (Souter, J., joined by Blackmun and Stevens, JJ., and, in part, by O'Connor, J., dissenting). 509 U.S. at 333, 113 S.Ct. at 2650 (O'Connor, J., concurring in the judgment in part and dissenting in part). Although he agreed with Justice Souter's dissent, Justice Blackmun also wrote separately to state his belief that classifications that discriminated against mentally retarded persons should be subject to heightened judicial review. 509 U.S. at 333D, 113 S.Ct. at 2650 (Blackmun, J., dissenting). See § 14.3 of this Treatise regarding the standards of review used in equal protection cases.

56. 424 U.S. 319, 335, 96 S.Ct. 893, 903, 47 L.Ed.2d 18 (1976). The *Mathews* test requires a consideration of the nature of the private interest at stake in the proceeding, the extent to which additional or different procedures might avoid the risk of erroneous deprivations, and the nature of the government interest in the proceeding. This test is examined in § 13.8 of this Treatise.

57. Heller v. Doe, 509 U.S. 312, 330, 113 S.Ct. 2637, 2648, 125 L.Ed.2d 257 (1993). "Even if parents, close family members, or legal guardians can be said in certain instances to have interests 'adverse to [those of] the person facing commitment' ... we simply do not understand how their participation as formal parties in the commencement proceedings increases 'the risk of an erroneous deprivation.'" 509 U.S. at 330, 113 S.Ct. at 2648 (internal citations omitted). The majority concluded: "Because allowing guardians and immediate family members to participate as parties in commitment proceedings increases the accuracy of those proceedings and implements the State's interest in providing family members a voice in the proceedings without undermining those interests of the individual protected by the Due Process Clause, these Kentucky statutes do not run afoul of due process." 509 U.S. at 332, 113 S.Ct. at 2649.

Although there may be circumstances that would justify the government detaining a person at a mental health care facility for a short time prior to a hearing, due process normally requires that an adult receive notice and a hearing prior to being involuntarily committed to a state mental health facility.[58]

In *Addington v. Texas*[59] the Supreme Court determined that an adult cannot be involuntarily committed to a psychiatric institution on a burden of proof that requires the state merely to show by a preponderance of the evidence that the person is dangerous to himself or another. Although the Court did not require a "beyond a reasonable doubt" standard, it held that trial courts must at least employ a "clear and convincing" evidence standard. Chief Justice Burger, writing for a unanimous Court, found that the societal, constitutional value placed on freedom from physical interment required adoption of a standard beyond the mere preponderance standard. However, the nature of commitment proceedings, which are nonpunitive and concerned with issues upon which there is virtually never factual certainty, did not require states to adopt a "beyond a reasonable doubt" or "unequivocal proof" standard.

The Supreme Court has held that minors who were admitted to state mental care institutions at the request of their parents, or by the order of governmental child care authorities if the minor was a ward of the state, were entitled to a fair review of their condition at the time of their admission, but not to an adjudicative or adversarial hearing. In *Parham v. J. R.*[60] a majority of the Justices held that such children, who were "voluntarily" committed by their parents or the state guardian, were entitled only to an admission screening procedure or inquiry by a "neutral fact finder" to determine if the statutory criteria for commitment to the mental health unit were met in the individual child's case. The inquiry may be conducted by a staff physician so long as the doctor is free to independently evaluate the child and refuse to commit the child if commitment is not justified. This inquiry must include a careful probing of the child's background as well as a personal interview with the child. The majority opinion employed the *Mathews v. Eldridge*[61] balancing test in determining that no quasi-formal hearing was required. The child has an important liberty interest at stake, but the state is free to recognize the interest of parental authority so long as it creates some procedural safeguard against completely arbitrary or erroneous commitments.

The Justices were unanimous in rejecting the assertion that the state should be required to have an adjudicative or adversarial hearing for the juvenile prior to the commitment to the mental institution.[62] The state had legitimate interests in recognizing parental authority, in providing health care for children by allocating more resources to treatment rather than administrative hearings, and removing procedur-

58. Zinerman v. Burch, 494 U.S. 113, 110 S.Ct. 975, 108 L.Ed.2d 100 (1990). In *Zinermon*, the individual did not receive any type of hearing concerning whether he should have been committed to the facility; he had been admitted to a state mental health care facility as a "voluntary patient". In his subsequent suit against the government, he alleged that the hospital employees knew, or should have known, that he was mentally ill and incapable of giving consent to a voluntary admission, and that he would not have met the statutory conditions for involuntary placement. The hospital employees did not use the procedures set up by state statutes for the short term emergency admission of a person when there was reason to believe that the person posed a danger to himself or others, was in need of treatment, and was mentally ill. The Court in *Zinermon* held only that the individual's complaint was sufficient to establish a due process violation if he could prove his allegations at trial. The Supreme Court did not examine the state's procedures for short-term emergency admissions or explain the circum-

stances under which an adult could be detained at a mental health care facility prior to a hearing.

59. 441 U.S. 418, 99 S.Ct. 1804, 60 L.Ed.2d 323 (1979). This opinion was unanimous but Mr. Justice Powell did not participate in the decision.

60. 442 U.S. 584, 99 S.Ct. 2493, 61 L.Ed.2d 101 (1979).

61. 424 U.S. 319, 96 S.Ct. 893, 47 L.Ed.2d 18 (1976).

62. Three Justices dissented to the rulings that gave no pre-admission hearing to wards of the state and only informal review procedures to juveniles after they had been hospitalized, but these Justices concurred in the ruling that children were entitled only to a neutral inquiry, and not an adjudicative hearing, prior to their commitment by their parents. Parham v. J. R., 442 U.S. 584, 625, 99 S.Ct. 2493, 2515, 61 L.Ed.2d 101 (1979) (Brennan, J., joined by Marshall and Stevens, JJ., concurring in part and dissenting in part).

al barriers that might deter parents acting in good faith from seeking care for children who needed treatment. All of the Justices recognized that a requirement of an adversarial hearing prior to the initial commitment would have been arguably applicable to any hospitalization or health care decision made by a parent over a child's objection.

Justices Brennan, Marshall, and Stevens dissented concerning the ability of the state to commit wards of the state to such facilities.[63] Although, as the dissent pointed out, the state in this situation did not have an interest in deferring to parental authority, and there was no individual guardian of the child's interest, a majority of the Justices refused to distinguish the interests of these wards of the state from the interests of children committed by their parents or individual guardians. The majority found no evidence that the decisions of state agencies to have children committed to mental health units were more likely to be arbitrary or erroneous than decisions made by parents.[64]

Brennan, Marshall, and Stevens also dissented from the majority's analysis of the process due a child once the child had been admitted to a state mental health care facility. Once the child was admitted to the facility, the dissent argued, there was no harmonious family unit for the state to defer to, and the child should be protected by an adjudicative hearing on the issue of whether the child should remain in the custody of the state at the mental health facility.[65] This is a strong argument as the child is clearly deprived of a significant constitutional freedom so long as he is kept in custody against his will. However, the majority refused to determine what type of post-

admission procedures would be required to safeguard the child's interest and held only that "the child's continuing need for commitment must be reviewed periodically by a similarly independent procedure."[66]

In a companion decision, *Secretary of Public Welfare of Pennsylvania v. Institutionalized Juveniles*,[67] the Court, by the same six to three vote, upheld a state statute which allowed for "voluntary" commitment of juveniles to such facilities by parents or guardians after examination by mental health professionals and which required review of the continuing need for commitment of the child every 30 days by hospital staff, but did not provide for any adjudicative hearings. While the Court found that the admission procedure was sufficient to meet due process standards, the majority was careful to note that it was not deciding what standards states had to meet for the periodic review of committed children.[68]

It should be noted that the Court did not decide what, if any, procedures were required to safeguard the interest of a child committed by his parents to a mental health care institution that was not operated by the state.[69] The majority noted that, so long as the hospital was a government institution, the individual child could bring a suit to determine if the standards and procedures had been properly applied to the child in his individual case.[70]

Conclusion. Whenever the government seeks to restrain someone physically, it is depriving him of a constitutionally significant liberty interest so long as the restraint is more than momentary. Where the physical restraint is of a very brief duration, lesser procedures may be required to determine the legitimacy of the action.

63. 442 U.S. at 625, 99 S.Ct. at 2515.

64. 442 U.S. at 618, 99 S.Ct. at 2512. The majority left open the issue of whether these wards were entitled to more formal post-admission review procedures. Id.

65. 442 U.S. at 633–37, 99 S.Ct. at 2519–22 (Brennan, Marshall & Stevens, JJ., concurring and dissenting).

66. Parham v. J. R., 442 U.S. 584, 605, 99 S.Ct. 2493, 2506, 61 L.Ed.2d 101 (1979) (footnote omitted).

67. 442 U.S. 640, 99 S.Ct. 2523, 61 L.Ed.2d 142 (1979).

68. 442 U.S. at 650 n. 9, 99 S.Ct. at 2528 n. 9.

69. The dissenting Justices in the 1979 cases would have found state action in a parent using a private hospital and they seem to have assumed that the other Justices

would have applied due process principles to safeguard the minor's interest in this "private" commitment situation even though the Justices in the majority might define those principles differently than the dissent. Secretary of Public Welfare v. Institutionalized Juveniles, 442 U.S. 640, 642, 99 S.Ct. 2523, 2524, 61 L.Ed.2d 142 (1979), (Brennan, J., dissenting joined by Marshall and Stevens, JJ.). See Chapter 12 regarding "State Action."

70. Parham v. J. R., 442 U.S. 584, 99 S.Ct. 2493, 61 L.Ed.2d 101 (1979); Secretary of Public Welfare v. Institutionalized Juveniles, 442 U.S. 640, 650 n. 9, 99 S.Ct. 2528 n. 9, 61 L.Ed.2d 142 (1979).

Thus when an individual is arrested by a police officer without an arrest warrant, the state must seek validation of the arrest from a judicial officer within a relatively short period of time.[71] This procedure will amount to no more than an ex parte determination of the officer's probable cause to arrest the defendant. While this procedure is very limited in its scope, it only authorizes the temporary detention of the defendant, who still has the safeguards of the speedy trial and excessive bail provisions to restrict the state's power to subject him to indefinite pretrial incarceration.[72]

Similarly, the Supreme Court has held that a public school student is deprived of liberty when he is subjected to physical punishment by school authorities.[73] However, the majority held that this liberty interest was adequately safeguarded by the creation of a cause of action in tort against teachers who exceeded their authority in imposing physical punishments on the child.[74]

(b) Enforcement of Debtor–Creditor Relationships

When a creditor uses government-enforced procedures to take the property of his alleged debtor, the debtor-defendant is deprived of a constitutionally significant interest in property. This deprivation exists whether the government transfers the property from the debtor to the creditor or merely prevents the debtor from using the property until the termination of the judicial proceeding instituted by the creditor. Of course, once the creditor has established her claim through a trial, the debtor has been accorded due process of law and the state may aid the creditor to enforce her judgment. However, the creditor may wish to have the property kept from the alleged debtor's use prior to trial in order to insure a recovery. When the government assists the creditor prior to trial, it must establish certain procedures to safeguard the interests of the alleged debtor.[75]

The government cannot garnish the wages of an alleged debtor without granting that individual the right to a hearing to determine whether there is a legitimate basis for keeping a portion of his wages from him. In *Sniadach v. Family Finance Corp.*[76] the Supreme Court held that garnishing a portion of a wage earner's salary to safeguard the interest of an alleged creditor was impermissible absent either a prior hearing for the debtor or an

---

71. Gerstein v. Pugh, 420 U.S. 103, 95 S.Ct. 854, 43 L.Ed.2d 54 (1975). For citations to additional Supreme Court cases on this point, see R. Rotunda & J. Nowak, Treatise on Constitutional Law: Substance and Procedure, vol. 2 § 17.9 (2nd ed. 1992, with annual supplements).

72. In Bell v. Wolfish, 441 U.S. 520, 99 S.Ct. 1861, 60 L.Ed.2d 447 (1979), the Supreme Court found that an individual could not be subjected to "punishment" without a finding of guilt, but ruled that the conditions of incarceration for pretrial detainees were not to be strictly regulated by federal courts if the detention was not considered punitive in nature. The case is discussed in § 11.6, supra. The Court in *Bell* left open the issue of whether an individual could be detained prior to trial for a reason other than insuring that individual's appearance at trial, such as detention to prevent additional criminal activity by the accused individual, 441 U.S. at 534 n. 15, 99 S.Ct. at 1871 n. 15.

See notes 39–40, 44–50, and accompanying text, supra.

73. Ingraham v. Wright, 430 U.S. 651, 672, 97 S.Ct. 1401, 1413, 51 L.Ed.2d 711 (1977).

74. 430 U.S. at 682, 97 S.Ct. at 1418.

75. If government personnel assist a creditor in seizing the property of an alleged debtor, the joint activity of the government personnel and the creditor constitutes state action that makes both the government personnel's and the creditor's actions subject to the Fourth Amendment limitations and due process principles. In Soldal v. Cook County, 506 U.S. 56, 113 S.Ct. 538, 121 L.Ed.2d 450 (1992), the Justices unanimously ruled that deputy sheriffs and the owners of a mobile home park violated the Fourth Amendment when the deputy sheriffs assisted the mobile home park owner in removing an alleged debtor's mobile home from its foundation, and towing it away from the mobile home park. In *Soldal,* the deputy sheriffs knew that the mobile home park owners did not have an eviction order and they knew, or should have known, that the eviction was unlawful under state law. The actions of the deputy sheriffs, in protecting the employees of the mobile home park so that the debtor could not defend his property triggered the protections of the Fourth Amendment prohibition against unreasonable seizures of property. This joint action of the deputy sheriffs and the creditor constituted state action that was subject to the Fourth and Fourteenth Amendments. A government assisted creditor remedy, which may involve the seizure of property will comply with the reasonableness requirement of the Fourth Amendment if the property is seized after the debtor has been accorded the procedural rights discussed in the following paragraphs.

76. 395 U.S. 337, 89 S.Ct. 1820, 23 L.Ed.2d 349 (1969).

extraordinary emergency situation which justified foregoing the hearing. The majority opinion did not explain what type of emergency situation might justify garnishing someone's wages without a hearing but, presumably, it would have to be one which would render the interest of the creditor virtually worthless before a hearing could be held. While the Court has made many conflicting statements about due process in the years since *Sniadach*, it has not withdrawn the strict requirement of a hearing prior to wage garnishments.[77]

In determining the type of process that must be provided to an individual in connection with a government termination of a liberty or property interest, the Court considers three factors: (1) the nature of the interest that will be impaired by the government action; (2) the extent to which formal procedures, or a specific procedure requested by the individual, might reduce the possibility of erroneous or otherwise improper decisions by the government; (3) and the governmental interest in the process and the burdens that additional or more complex procedures would impose on the government.[78] A consideration of these factors has led the Court to find that, absent some exigent circumstance, an individual should be provided with notice and a hearing prior to the time when a state court or administrative agency issues an order that would constitute a pretrial attachment of the individual's property. In *Connecticut v. Doehr*,[79] the Supreme Court invalidated a state statute that authorized the prejudgment attachment of real estate without notice and hearing prior to the attachment even though the statute conditioned the issuance of the attachment upon a showing that the person seeking the order had filed a court action against the property owner and that there were grounds to believe that the plaintiff would be likely to prevail at trial on the claim against the property owner. The Supreme Court found that prejudgment attachment orders constituted significant impairments of property interests and that there was a severe risk of erroneous deprivation in such prejudgment attachment processes because there was little assurance that the party seeking the order could prevail on the merits of a tort case. The statute at issue in *Doehr* provided the property owner with a hearing after the issuance of the attachment order. The Supreme Court found that there was no governmental or societal interest in having *ex parte* attachments that justified the harm that was caused to individuals by having their property interests frozen prior to the time when they received a hearing.[80] The Supreme

---

77. In Mathews v. Eldridge, 424 U.S. 319, 333–34, 96 S.Ct. 893, 902, 47 L.Ed.2d 18 (1976) the majority opinion by Justice Powell might be read because indicating that *Sniadach* did not impose such a clear requirement. Such a position would be clearly in error as the majority opinion in *Sniadach* stated: "absent notice and a prior hearing . . . this prejudgment garnishment procedure violates the fundamental principles of due process." Sniadach v. Family Finance Corp., 395 U.S. 337, 342, 89 S.Ct. 1820, 1823, 23 L.Ed.2d 349 (1969). One would hope that if the prior hearing requirement for wage garnishments is to be changed, the Justices will find a more principled way of doing this than simply misreading the *Sniadach* opinion. However the *Mathews* opinion may only have meant to indicate that *Sniadach* left the scope of the hearing unclear.

78. This three-part test has its origins in Mathews v. Eldridge, 424 U.S. 319, 96 S.Ct. 893, 47 L.Ed.2d 18 (1976). See § 13.8 of this Treatise. In *Mathews,* Justice Powell's majority opinion might be read to indicate that Sniadach did not impose a clear requirement that an individual receive notice and a hearing prior to the time that a court order for wage garnishment is issued. 424 U.S. at 333–34, 96 S.Ct. at 902. However, it is clear that the Sniadach Court was requiring a prior hearing as the majority opinion stated: "Absent notice and a prior hearing . . . this

prejudgment garnishment procedure violates the fundamental principles of due process." Sniadach v. Family Finance Corp., 395 U.S. 337, 342, 89 S.Ct. 1820, 1823, 23 L.Ed.2d 349 (1969).

79. 501 U.S. 1, 111 S.Ct. 2105, 115 L.Ed.2d 1 (1991).

80. The Supreme Court in *Doehr* noted that most states required pre-attachment hearings absent exigent circumstances. But Justice White, in a portion of his opinion that was joined by all of the Justices, stated; "We do not mean to imply that any given exigency requirement protects an attachment from constitutional attack. Nor do we suggest that the statutory measures we have surveyed are necessarily free of due process problems or other constitutional infirmities in general." The Supreme Court did not explain the types of exigent circumstances that might allow a state to provide for a pretrial attachment without a prior hearing.

Part of Justice White's opinion in *Doehr* was a plurality opinion in which he expressed the view that due process required a state to make the party seeking the attachment "to post a bond or other security" [in addition to giving notice and a hearing to the property owner-defendant prior to the attachment] if it was to allow such pretrial orders in situations where there was no emergency or exigency. Connecticut v. Doehr, 501 U.S. 1, 17, 111 S.Ct.

Court distinguished the cases in which it had found that a creditor who seeks a pretrial remedy to preserve assets of a debtor, on the basis of the nature of the creditor's interests and the likelihood that a written submission could demonstrate that the creditor would prevail at trial.[81]

A creditor may seek to have assets other than wages of an alleged debtor seized by the government to insure that there will be a source for recovery of later judgments against the debtor. Where the creditor has a specific interest in the property, he may seek return and use of the property prior to trial. These pre-judgment remedies against debtors include procedures such as replevin, attachment of assets and garnishment of property other than wages. For a time it appeared that the Supreme Court would always require a hearing prior to an attachment of the debtor's property; subsequently it appeared that the Court would allow creditors to regain such property with almost no procedural safeguards. In *Fuentes v. Shevin*[82] the Court, by a vote of four to three, indicated that there would be a requirement of a prior hearing in pre-judgment attachments or replevin just as there was for wage garnishments.

Only two years later the Court held, by a vote of five to four, that a state trial judge could order sequestration of personal property on the application of a creditor with very few safeguards, in *Mitchell v. W. T. Grant Co.*[83] Indeed, in *Mitchell* the dissenting Justices thought that *Fuentes* had been implicitly overruled.[84] But such was not the case and *Fuentes* was given renewed, if somewhat restricted, life in *North Georgia Finishing, Inc. v. Di–Chem, Inc.*[85] Here the Court, by a six to

three vote, invalidated a statute which allowed the creditor to garnish property of an alleged debtor with certain procedural safeguards but without a hearing prior to the garnishment or attachment of the debtor's assets.

In so doing, the majority in *Di–Chem* set four requirements for pre-judgment replevin, attachment or garnishment statutes which did not provide a prior hearing for the debtor. If the state gave the debtor a hearing prior to the attachment, it would have met the procedural due process requirement of even the strict *Sniadach* standard. Without such a prior hearing, the statute must have the following four features: (1) the creditor must post a bond to safeguard the interest of the debtor; (2) the creditor or someone with personal knowledge of the facts must file an affidavit which sets out a prima facie claim for prejudgment attachment of the property; (3) a neutral magistrate must determine that the affidavit is sufficient before issuing the writ of attachment or replevin; (4) there must be a provision for a reasonably prompt post-attachment hearing for the debtor.

Waiver of Debtor Rights. There are two exceptions to the general procedural due process requirements in commercial cases: waiver and emergency. It would seem that one can waive his rights to procedural due process in a commercial setting, but the proper basis for finding a waiver is not at all clear.

The Supreme Court has considered only one instance of a contractual waiver of due process rights in the commercial setting. In *D.H. Overmyer Co. v. Frick Co.*[86] the Court upheld a waiver of process clause which had been negotiated in a contract between two independent businesses. However, the Court did not indi-

---

2105, 2116, 115 L.Ed.2d 1 (1991) (White, J., joined by Marshall, Stevens, and O'Connor, JJ.).

81. The decision in *Doehr* does not appear to undercut the Court's rulings concerning the permissibility of a pretrial attachment order being issued in creditors' rights cases, so long as the pretrial remedy procedure established by a state complies with the bond, prima facie claim, neutral magistrate, and prompt post-attachment hearing requirements established by the cases that are examined in the next paragraphs of this section of the Treatise. The majority opinion in *Doehr* stated: "Disputes between debtors and creditors more readily lend themselves to accurate *ex parte* assessments of the merits [than assess-

ments of interest in tort actions, such as the assault and battery action which was the basis for the pretrial attachment in this case]." Connecticut v. Doehr, 501 U.S. 1, 16, 111 S.Ct. 2105, 2115, 115 L.Ed.2d 1 (1991).

82. 407 U.S. 67, 92 S.Ct. 1983, 32 L.Ed.2d 556 (1972).

83. 416 U.S. 600, 94 S.Ct. 1895, 40 L.Ed.2d 406 (1974).

84. 416 U.S. at 631, 94 S.Ct. at 1911–12 (Stewart, J., dissenting).

85. 419 U.S. 601, 95 S.Ct. 719, 42 L.Ed.2d 751 (1975).

86. 405 U.S. 174, 92 S.Ct. 775, 31 L.Ed.2d 124 (1972).

cate that it would be willing to uphold such waivers of process when it was unclear if the parties had truly bargained over the provision. Thus the validity of form contract provisions by which one party waives his rights to notice or process remains an open question.[87] If the Court were to apply the "knowing and intelligent" waiver standard of the criminal cases, it would be virtually impossible to uphold such provisions where the parties were of clearly unequal bargaining strength or where there was no real attempt to inform the debtor of the meaning of the provision.

Emergency Limitation of Due Process Rights. These requirements as to due process in the taking of property may also be modified by extraordinary or emergency conditions. Most states have provisions for pre-judgment sequestration or attachment of the assets of an alleged debtor where a creditor can make a prima facie claim that the assets are liable to be hidden or destroyed before the claim can be resolved by the trial process. These provisions would seem to be permissible so long as they are reasonably tailored to dealing with emergency situations rather than merely providing a form for creditors to avoid the pre-trial hearing process.

This theory was carried to its furthest extreme in *Calero–Toledo v. Pearson Yacht Leasing Co.*[88] when the Court upheld the government seizure of a ship used to transport contraband without a prior notice or hearing. The seizure was upheld because the majority saw it as serving a significant governmental interest in asserting jurisdiction over a moveable item of property against which it could

legitimately conduct forfeiture proceedings. The Court held that this was an "extraordinary situation in which postponement of notice and hearing until after seizure did not deny due process."[89]

The *Calero–Toledo* decision was clarified, and narrowed, in *United States v. James Daniel Good Real Property*[90] when the Court ruled that the federal government was required to give notice and some type of a hearing to the owner of real property before seizing the real property, which allegedly was subject to forfeiture proceedings. The federal government in the *James Daniel Good Real Property* case had sought to institute forfeiture proceedings against residential property on the basis that the owner of the property had been convicted of violating federal drug laws by keeping proscribed drugs on the property, which had resulted in the property owner being convicted of state crimes several years prior to the federal government's initiation of the forfeiture action. The federal government, in an ex parte proceeding, received a warrant from a federal magistrate that allowed seizure of the property; the final disposition of the property would be determined at a later adversary proceeding.

The Supreme Court, by a five to four vote, ruled that the government's use of an ex parte proceeding in these circumstances violated due process. Justice Kennedy's majority opinion in *James Daniel Good Real Property* examined the nature of the interests at stake, the need for adversary proceedings, and the nature of the government's interests.[91] The majority opinion found that the seizure of a home or other real property constituted a greater depri-

---

87. 405 U.S. at 188, 92 S.Ct. at 783; Swarb v. Lennox, 405 U.S. 191, 92 S.Ct. 767, 31 L.Ed.2d 138 (1972).

88. 416 U.S. 663, 94 S.Ct. 2080, 40 L.Ed.2d 452 (1974).

89. 416 U.S. at 680, 94 S.Ct. at 2090; see also 416 at 680 n. 15, 94 S.Ct. at 2090 n. 15, indicating that the Court was not assessing the sufficiency of the postseizure notice procedures.

Forfeitures of property to the government. The Supreme Court of the United States has long upheld the power of the government to seize and take title to property that has been used in the violation of "customs and revenue laws" and that has been used in connection with a crime or that has been used to commit "wrongs" to society or persons. However, the Supreme Court has not ruled on the issue of whether all forfeiture proceedings are to be considered criminal trial proceedings. See footnote 1

in § 13.9 of this Treatise regarding the distinction between civil and criminal trials. For citations to additional Supreme Court cases, and secondary authorities, on this point, see R. Rotunda & J. Nowak, Treatise on Constitutional Law: Substance and Procedure, § 17.9 (3rd ed. 1999, with annual supplements).

90. 510 U.S. 43, 114 S.Ct. 492, 126 L.Ed.2d 490 (1993).

91. United States v. James Daniel Good Real Property, 510 U.S. 43, 53, 114 S.Ct. 492, 501, 126 L.Ed.2d 490 (1993). These are the three factors which the Court has focused on in almost all cases concerning the type of process that is required by the due process clause since the Court's decision in Mathews v. Eldridge, 424 U.S. 319, 96 S.Ct. 893, 47 L.Ed.2d 18 (1976). The *Mathews* case is examined in § 13.8 of this Treatise.

vation of property interest than the seizure of personal property, that an ex parte warrant procedure did not sufficiently reduce the risk of erroneous determinations that the property could be seized, and that the federal government had no interest that outweighed the individual's interest in receiving a hearing prior to the seizure. Justice Kennedy distinguished *Calero–Toledo* on the basis that the government had to prevent personal property that might be subject to forfeiture proceedings from being hidden or destroyed. The government did not need to seize real property prior to granting the individual property owner notice and some type of hearing.[92]

Conclusion. The cases examined in this subsection concerned debt enforcement procedures that involved at least the formal use of courts or government personnel. In *Flagg Brothers, Inc. v. Brooks*,[93] the Supreme Court found that there was no "state action" connected with a sale of an alleged debtor's goods by a warehouseman when the sale did not involve use of a government agency. It remains to be seen whether the Court will allow states to enact laws that give creditors in a wide variety of circumstances the right to take the property of persons whom they allege to be

their debtors. The Court did not specify the extent to which a state may authorize creditor "self-help" remedies.[94]

The majority opinion in *Flagg Brothers* refused to determine whether there might ever be constitutional restraints on the "private" resolution of creditor-debtor conflicts.[95] One can only hope that the majority will articulate some limits on the mere "recognition" of self-help remedies and, thereby, prevent a state from freeing a wide variety of creditor-debtor conflict resolution procedures from constitutional values and restraints. As noted by Justice Stevens in his dissent in *Flagg Brothers*: "[T]he state power to order binding, nonconsensual resolution of a conflict between a debtor and a creditor is exactly the sort of power with which the Due Process Clause is concerned."[96] However, at the present time the Court will find sufficient "state action" in a creditor remedy only when the creditor employs the help of the judicial or executive branches of government to seize or attach the property of the alleged debtor.[97]

(c) Deprivations of Government Benefits

In the sections on liberty and property we saw a variety of situations in which the termi-

---

92. 510 U.S. at 52–59, 114 S.Ct. at 500–503. Justice Kennedy also distinguished the Court's earlier rulings that had allowed for seizure of property to enforce tax laws or other debts owed to the government in part on the basis that these cases, most of which were decided prior to 1950, were based upon the government need to collect revenue in order to provide basic governmental services. Justice Kennedy grouped these cases together with cases allowing seizures of property during wartime and seizures of contaminated food; he described these cases as instances in which the Court had allowed vital government interests to provide the basis for an exception of the general rule that an individual should be given notice and an opportunity to be heard prior to the time when the government deprives the individual of a liberty or property interest. United States v. James Daniel Good Real Property, 510 U.S. 43, 60–63, 114 S.Ct. 492, 504–05, 126 L.Ed.2d 490 (1993).

The dissenting Justices believed that an ex parte warrant procedure which complied with Fourth Amendment principles provided sufficient process to protect the property owner. United States v. James Daniel Good Real Property, 510 U.S. 43, 65, 114 S.Ct. 492, 507, 126 L.Ed.2d 490 (1993) (Rehnquist, C.J., joined by Scalia, J., and, in part, O'Connor, J., concurring in part and dissenting in part); 510 U.S. at 73, 114 S.Ct. at 511 (O'Connor, J., concurring in part and dissenting in part); 510 U.S. at 80,

114 S.Ct. at 515 (Thomas, J., concurring in part and dissenting in part).

93. 436 U.S. 149, 98 S.Ct. 1729, 56 L.Ed.2d 185 (1978).

94. If government personnel assist a creditor in seizing the property of an alleged debtor, the joint activity of the government personnel and the creditor constitutes state action that makes both the government personnel's and the creditor's actions subject to the Fourth Amendment limitations and due process principles. See note 74, supra.

95. Flagg Bros., Inc. v. Brooks, 436 U.S. 149, 162 n. 12, 98 S.Ct. 1729, 1736–37 n. 12, 56 L.Ed.2d 185 (1978).

96. 436 U.S. at 176, 98 S.Ct. at 1744 (Stevens, J., dissenting, joined by White and Marshall, JJ.). Justice Brennan did not participate in the decision.

97. In Lugar v. Edmondson Oil Co., 457 U.S. 922, 102 S.Ct. 2744, 73 L.Ed.2d 482 (1982) the Supreme Court ruled that a debtor stated cause of action for deprivation of property under color of law by alleging that private creditor used state procedures to perfect an attachment of the debtor's property which involved court issuance of writ of attachment that was executed by county sheriff. The debtor was challenging "state action" insofar as he claimed that the state statute and involvement of state officers in the attachment process deprived him of property without adequate procedural safeguards. See Chapter 12 regarding "state action."

nation of government benefits could be deemed a cognizable interest under the due process clauses. In these situations there is no uniformity as to the nature of the procedures required to give someone "due process." Instead the Justices will merely apply the general principles described in section 13.8 of this chapter.

The Justices use a balancing test to determine whether the individual interest merits a specific procedure in view of its cost to the government and society in general. Not surprisingly, this balancing process has yielded varying rules whereby some deprivations of government benefits can only be accomplished with very detailed hearings while others can be summarily terminated. A sampling of the major decisions in this area should give one a feeling for the way in which the current Justices are striking the balance.[98]

An interest which requires great procedural protection in the view of the Supreme Court is that of subsistence payments to indigent individuals. In *Goldberg v. Kelly*[99] the Court required a trial-type hearing before basic welfare benefits could be terminated. This case involved the termination of basic subsistence benefits and the Court found that the interest in those benefits was such that it could be likened to a property right.[100] While the majority opinion stated that a "quasi-judicial trial" would not be required,[101] it went on to hold that a pre-termination hearing must be granted, including such procedures that one could accurately describe it as a quasi-judicial trial.

The Court required that the welfare beneficiary be granted a hearing which included: (1) adequate notice; (2) an opportunity for oral argument to the adjudicator; (3) a chance to present evidence in his behalf; (4) an opportunity to confront any witnesses who are adverse to his claim; (5) an opportunity to cross-exam-

ine those witnesses; (6) disclosure of all evidence against him; (7) a right to have an attorney present his case; (8) a decision based solely on the evidence produced at the hearing; (9) that the decision-maker state the reasons for his determination and the evidence he relied on; and (10) that the decision-maker in fact be unbiased and impartial. The only basic administrative procedural requirements that the Court left out were the right to a complete record or comprehensive opinion, the assignment of counsel, and a formal finding of fact or opinion.[102] The guaranteed procedures come very close to an administrative trial and indicate the Court's belief that the full adversary process is necessary to protect an interest of this importance.

Lying in the middle range of interests, in terms of the procedural safeguards which they require, are terminations of important licenses or liberties. Two of the most important cases in this area involve the suspension of driving privileges and the suspension of students from school. In *Bell v. Burson*[103] the Court invalidated a statute which suspended the licenses of drivers involved in automobile accidents unless they furnished security to satisfy a judgment or gave proof of financial responsibility. The Court found that due process required a prior hearing to determine the probability of a judgment against an individual that would require proof of his financial responsibility. While the Court did not delineate all of the rights which would be involved in such a procedure, the opinion indicated that the procedures would be somewhat less than the administrative trial required in *Goldberg*. The Court later held that suspension of an individual's driver's license based on the number of times he has been convicted of traffic law violations does not require a hearing as there is no disputed issue of fact.[104]

98. For citations to additional cases, including lower court cases, and secondary works on this topic see our multi-volume Treatise: R. Rotunda & J. Nowak, Treatise on Constitutional Law: Substance and Procedure (3rd ed. 1999, with annual supplements).

99. 397 U.S. 254, 90 S.Ct. 1011, 25 L.Ed.2d 287 (1970).

100. 397 U.S. at 262 n. 8, 90 S.Ct. at 1017 n. 8, quoting Reich, Individual Rights and Social Welfare: The Emerging Legal Issues, 74 Yale L.J. 1245, 1255 (1965).

101. 397 U.S. at 266, 90 S.Ct. at 1020.

102. K. Davis, Administrative Law, Treatise 244 (2d Ed. 1979–80).

103. 402 U.S. 535, 91 S.Ct. 1586, 29 L.Ed.2d 90 (1971).

104. Dixon v. Love, 431 U.S. 105, 97 S.Ct. 1723, 52 L.Ed.2d 172 (1977).

In *Mackey v. Montrym* [105] the Court, by a five to four vote, upheld a state statute requiring the 90-day suspension of a person's driver's license for failure to take a chemical test or breath analysis test for usage of alcohol while driving a vehicle but allowing for prompt post-suspension administrative hearings. Those administrative hearings would determine three issues: (1) whether the police officer who requested the driver to take the test had reasonable grounds to believe that the driver was under the influence of intoxicating liquor; (2) whether the person was in fact arrested by the officer; (3) whether the person in fact refused to take the test. Applying the *Mathews v. Eldridge* [106] balancing test, the majority found that the individual's interest in a pre-suspension hearing to minimize the risk of erroneous deprivation of the driver's license for a 90 day period was outweighed by the governmental interest in protecting the safety of the populace through strict drunk driving penalties and prompt procedures for removing the drunk drivers from the highways. [107]

Also in the middle range of interests for due process protection are the interests of students who are suspended from public schools. In *Goss v. Lopez* [108] the Court held that high school students who were suspended for up to ten days were entitled to procedural protections against unfair or illegal suspensions. The applicable state law established an entitlement to attend school so as to create a consti-

tutional property interest. The suspension also was found to impinge upon the "liberty" of the students because it might limit their employment or associational opportunities.

The process that was required to safeguard these interests was less complex than the *Goldberg* administrative trial procedures. The majority opinion indicated that the procedure would require that the student be given some oral or written notice of the charges and an opportunity to explain his position to the school authorities. [109] The Court also noted that in situations that called for immediate action to establish discipline or order within a school, the school authorities could act prior to taking any procedures to safeguard the student interest. [110] Later the Court held that school authorities were free to impose physical discipline on children so long as there was some state law limitation of the authority to impose such punishments and the possibility of later judicial actions against teachers who exceeded their authority. [111]

The Supreme Court dealt with a number of procedural due process issues regarding the dismissal of students from institutions of higher education in *Board of Curators v. Horowitz*. [112] In this decision the Court upheld the dismissal of a student from a medical school, without a formal hearing, based on low evaluations of her clinical work. As a medical student, the plaintiff had been required to achieve satisfactory evaluations from faculty member

105. 443 U.S. 1, 99 S.Ct. 2612, 61 L.Ed.2d 321 (1979).

106. 424 U.S. 319, 96 S.Ct. 893, 47 L.Ed.2d 18 (1976).

107. The dissenting Justices believed that these state interests could be served by a prompt hearing on the issue of whether the driver had been intoxicated; this pretermination hearing could, in the view of the dissent, insure a fair determination of the ultimate issue while allowing for prompt removal of driving privileges from persons who had in fact used a vehicle while intoxicated. Mackey v. Montrym, 443 U.S. 1, 19, 99 S.Ct. 2612, 2621–22, 61 L.Ed.2d 321 (1979) (Stewart, J., dissenting, joined by Brennan, Marshall, and Stevens, JJ.).

For further analysis, see 2 R. Rotunda & J. Nowak, Treatise on Constitutional Law: Substance and Procedure § 17.9 (2d ed. 1992, with annual supplements).

108. 419 U.S. 565, 95 S.Ct. 729, 42 L.Ed.2d 725 (1975).

109. The opinion also noted that more severe deprivation such as longer suspensions might require more safeguards, Goss v. Lopez, 419 U.S. 565, 583, 95 S.Ct. 729,

740–41, 42 L.Ed.2d 725 (1975). In Carey v. Piphus, 435 U.S. 247, 98 S.Ct. 1042, 55 L.Ed.2d 252 (1978) the Supreme Court held that elementary and secondary school students who had been suspended from school without procedural due process were entitled to only nominal damages, absent proof of actual damages due to the constitutional deprivation. It should be noted that the Supreme Court, in Carey v. Piphus, did not have to determine whether the plaintiffs had asserted valid due process claims because the defendant school board failed to contest this issue. It was not clear whether the students adequately alleged that they wanted to contest some fact at the informal hearing which might have affected the decision regarding their suspensions. Thus, it is at least possible that some of the students were not deprived of procedural due process.

110. 419 U.S. at 582–83, 95 S.Ct. at 740–41.

111. Ingraham v. Wright, 430 U.S. 651, 97 S.Ct. 1401, 51 L.Ed.2d 711 (1977).

112. 435 U.S. 78, 98 S.Ct. 948, 55 L.Ed.2d 124 (1978).

doctors regarding her clinical performance in a variety of hospital departments. After a faculty doctor expressed dissatisfaction with her performance in the pediatrics department, a faculty-student council recommended that she be advanced to her second and final year on probationary status. She continued to receive unsatisfactory evaluations of her clinical performance and was notified of this fact by the Dean. Thereafter, the council recommended that she not be allowed to graduate and that she be dropped from school unless her performance greatly improved. The plaintiff was allowed to "appeal" from this recommendation by taking a set of oral and practical exams, which were reviewed by seven practicing physicians. Only two of those physicians thought that she should be allowed to graduate on schedule. Following further low evaluations of her clinical work, the council recommended that she not be allowed to re-enroll in the School of Medicine. This recommendation was approved by the Dean and a university provost after review of her academic record. All nine Justices agreed that there had been no deprivation of procedural due process rights in this case.

Because the plaintiff was given a fair procedure, if not a hearing, the Court found it unnecessary to decide whether this student had been denied a "liberty" or "property" interest. The majority opinion by Justice Rehnquist noted that it would be difficult to determine whether the student had been deprived of a significant liberty interest because it was not clear whether this action would significantly restrict her ability to pursue a medical education at another institution.

Assuming arguendo the existence of a liberty or property interest, the majority opinion found that the student had no right to a formal hearing at which she might challenge the basis for her dismissal. The opinion dis-

tinguished *Goss v. Lopez* on the ground that it involved a disciplinary procedure. An informal hearing in *Goss*, was necessary to allow a student to present his or her side of a disciplinary issue so as to diminish the possibility of wrongful suspensions. Although the severity of the deprivation might be greater in the academic dismissal situation, under the *Mathews v. Eldridge* balancing test fewer safeguards were required in *Board of Curators* because there was less chance of wrongful dismissal. All that was required was notice to the student and some form of fair procedure for evaluation and review of the student's academic record. The student in *Board of Curators* had received more than a minimally fair review of the facts upon which her dismissal was based.

The majority opinion noted that the school had followed all of the rules that it had previously established for such cases. The opinion stated that the failure to follow previously established rules would result in invalidation of a federal administrative action as a matter of federal administrative law,[113] but the opinion indicated that this was not a constitutional principle binding upon the states.[114] However, failure of an institution to follow its own established procedural rules might weigh in the determination of whether or not an individual had been treated in such an arbitrary manner as to constitute a violation of due process.

The majority opinion in *Board of Curators* also found that there was no violation of substantive due process in this case, even assuming that the judiciary could legitimately review standards for academic dismissals. So long as the announced basis for reviewing academic performance is arguably reasonable, the courts have no function in reviewing the substantive basis for dismissals under the due process clause unless those dismissals were shown to be clearly arbitrary or invidious.[115]

---

113. 435 U.S. at 92 n. 8, 98 S.Ct. at 956 n. 8. See Service v. Dulles, 354 U.S. 363, 77 S.Ct. 1152, 1 L.Ed.2d 1403 (1957); United States ex rel. Accardi v. Shaughnessy, 347 U.S. 260, 74 S.Ct. 499, 98 L.Ed. 681 (1954).

114. 435 U.S. at 92 n. 8, 98 S.Ct. at 956 n. 8.

115. Three dissenting Justices would have remanded the case to the lower court for further examination of the

substantive due process ruling. 435 U.S. at 97, 98 S.Ct. at 958–59. (Marshall, J., concurring and dissenting); 435 U.S. at 108, 98 S.Ct. at 964. (Blackmun & Brennan, JJ., concurring and dissenting).

In Regents of the University of Michigan v. Ewing, 474 U.S. 214, 106 S.Ct. 507, 88 L.Ed.2d 523 (1985), the Justices unanimously upheld the dismissal of a student from a

One of the interests which has received less procedural protection is the right to a continuation of disability or welfare payments under the Social Security Act. In *Mathews v. Eldridge* [116] the Court held that such benefits could be terminated under a system which accorded the individual no right to a hearing until after the termination of his benefits. Here the Court found that there were sufficient procedural safeguards other than a hearing to lessen the chances of improper terminations. A majority believed that the termination would be based on medical decisions concerning which written evidence would have been considered by the agency prior to the termination decision. The Court also felt that the interest in disability payments was not as significant as that in subsistence payments.[117] Finally the majority simply held that the benefits to the government and society in general from foregoing these administrative burdens outweighed the interests of the individual recipient of disability payments. While Professor Mashaw has shown that this type of utilitarian balancing process seems improper due to its focus on technique and disregard of due process of values,[118] a majority of the Justices seem committed to the *Mathews* balancing approach.

The Court employed the *Mathews* balancing approach to due process analysis as it upheld a ten dollar statutory limitation on the fee that could be paid to an attorney or agent who represents a veteran, or his or her family, seeking benefits for a service-connected disability before a hearing of a Veterans Administration board. In *Walters v. National Association of Radiation Survivors* [119] the Court found that Congress' goals in establishing the ten dollar limitation in the mid-nineteenth century, and retaining it since then, were a desire to save for each veteran the "entirety of the award" and a goal of keeping hearings informal and non-adversarial in nature. Both government interests were legitimate; the interest of reserving all benefits for the veterans was to be accorded "great weight" under the *Mathews* analysis. The majority opinion, by Justice Rehnquist, then balanced against these government interests the nature of the interest that would be affected by the official action and the probable value (in terms of a lessened risk of erroneous deprivations) of eliminating the maximum limit on attorney fees. The interest at stake in these proceedings was the interest of veterans, or their families, who were applying for service-related benefits or seeking to avoid a reduction or termination of their benefits.[120] Justice Rehnquist found that

---

six-year program of undergraduate and medical school studies that would have culminated in the award of an undergraduate degree and a medical degree. The Court assumed arguendo that the student had a substantive property right under the due process clause to continued enrollment and to be free from arbitrary dismissal. The student's dismissal was based on his extremely low score on a standardized examination. The Court found that the decision to dismiss the student from the program complied with both procedural and substantive due process principles.

116. 424 U.S. 319, 96 S.Ct. 893, 47 L.Ed.2d 18 (1976).

117. The Social Security Act authorizes the Department of Health, Education and Welfare to seek recoupment of overpayments to beneficiaries but it allows the individual beneficiaries to apply for reconsideration of whether an overpayment occurred over a waiver of the recoupment. In Califano v. Yamasaki, 442 U.S. 682, 99 S.Ct. 2545, 61 L.Ed.2d 176, (1979), the Supreme Court found that the recipient beneficiary need not be given a hearing concerning a request for reconsideration of whether an overpayment occurred but that the recipient was entitled to a "pre-recoupment hearing" when the recipient sought a waiver because, under the statute and regulations, the department would have to make a determination of whether the recipient was a person who had received

the overpayment "without fault" and from whom recoupment would defeat the purpose of the act by depriving the recipient of current income needed for living expenses. Written review of the payment records was a sufficiently fair process for determining whether overpayments occurred and therefore did not violate due process. The statute itself however required a pre-recoupment hearing for those seeking a waiver. The Court did not hold that due process would require such a hearing but its opinion indicated that this determination was one that could not be fairly made without some type of personal hearing.

See also Richardson v. Perales, 402 U.S. 389, 91 S.Ct. 1420, 28 L.Ed.2d 842 (1971) (written reports of physicians who examined the claimants were sufficient to support denials of disability benefits).

118. Mashaw, The Supreme Court's Due Process Calculus for Administrative Adjudication in Mathews v. Eldridge: Three Factors in Search of a Theory of Value, 44 U.Chi.L.Rev. 28 (1976).

119. 473 U.S. 305, 105 S.Ct. 3180, 87 L.Ed.2d 220 (1985).

120. The Supreme Court ruled only on the issue of whether those persons whose benefits were being terminated or reduced were entitled by due process to a fair hearing that would include a right to retain an attorney

these benefits, which were granted on the basis of whether a disability or death was service connected and not on the basis of need, "are more akin to the social security benefits involved in *Mathews* than they are to the welfare payments upon which the recipients in *Goldberg* depended for their daily subsistence."[121] Ready access to attorneys for veterans who were seeking to avoid termination or reduction of benefits was not essential to fair treatment. The majority found that those veterans who had represented themselves, or who had been represented by agents of veterans organizations or other non-attorneys, statistically fared nearly as well as those who were represented by attorneys. The hearing, at which the government was not represented by an attorney, was informal and procedurally simple so that the individual could fairly represent himself or obtain fair representation through an agent of a veterans organization.[122] Thus, the Court ruled that the limitation on the fee an individual could pay to an attorney for representation before the Veterans Administration did not violate due process.

The Court has also been fairly restrictive in its view of what procedures are necessary to

safeguard the interest of government employees who are discharged from their positions. As we have already noted, the Court will not find a significant property interest in government employment unless applicable law creates an entitlement or property right to the position. Nor will the Court find the deprivation of a liberty interest by the dismissal unless there is an injury to reputation so serious as to limit one's future associational or employment opportunities. But when such interests are involved, there must be fair procedures to determine the basis for the dismissal of the public employee. However, in *Arnett v. Kennedy*[123] the Court upheld the discharge of such an employee without a prior hearing where there were other procedures to review the decision to dismiss the employee. There was no majority opinion in this case, but there appeared to be a "working majority" who found that, at a minimum, there must be some pretermination review of the initial decision to dismiss the employee and a post-termination hearing which would take place before the employee was permanently deprived of the interest in the job.[124]

---

without regard to the statutory maximum. The Court did not consider whether the due process clause protected the interests of those persons who were first applying for benefits. The majority opinion noted that no case prior to this time had held that persons applying initially for governmental benefits had a property interest in those benefits that was protected by due process. Walters v. National Association of Radiation Survivors, 473 U.S. 305, 320 n. 8, 105 S.Ct. 3180, 3189 n. 8, 87 L.Ed.2d 220 (1985).

121. 473 U.S. at 333, 105 S.Ct. at 3195.

122. This case was decided by a vote of 6 to 3 among the Justices. Two of the six Justices who joined the majority opinion by Justice Rehnquist wrote separately to state their belief that, following this decision, individual veterans were free to claim that they must be allowed to pay an attorney more than ten dollars so that they could get an attorney for their individual case because, unlike most benefits cases, there were particular factors in their case that made it so complex that they required the assistance of an attorney in order to receive a fair hearing. Walters v. National Association of Radiation Survivors, 473 U.S. 305, 336–38, 105 S.Ct. 3180, 3197, 3198, 87 L.Ed.2d 220 (1985) (O'Connor, J., joined by Blackmun, J., concurring). The majority opinion was not clear on this point. As the two concurring Justices were necessary to the majority, however, lower courts might best be advised to consider claims of individual veterans for the ability to pay an attorney more than the ten dollar fee under the Mathews v. Eldridge balancing test, examined in § 13.8 of this treatise, to determine whether factors in a particular

case indicate that the individual veteran could not receive a fair hearing before the Veterans Administration without the assistance of an attorney.

In United States Department of Labor v. Triplett, 494 U.S. 715, 110 S.Ct. 1428, 108 L.Ed.2d 701 (1990), the Supreme Court upheld both the provision of the Black Lung Benefits Act of 1972 that prohibit attorneys' fees for representation of claimants except insofar as such fees are approved by the Department and the regulations providing for attorneys' fees to be paid by an employer, an insurer, or the Black Lung Disability Trust Fund under certain circumstances (and prohibiting attorney fees unless the fees were approved by the Department or a court). The majority opinion in *Triplett* reaffirmed the Court's decision in *Walters*. The majority in *Triplett* found that the Court did not have to reach the issue of whether the Black Lung Benefits Act violated due process, because there had been no showing that the Act, and Department's regulations, resulted in individual claimants being unable to obtain legal representation in Black Lung Benefits Act proceedings.

123. 416 U.S. 134, 94 S.Ct. 1633, 40 L.Ed.2d 15 (1974), rehearing denied 417 U.S. 977, 94 S.Ct. 3187, 41 L.Ed.2d 1148 (1974).

124. 416 U.S. at 171, 94 S.Ct. at 1652 (White, J., concurring). Professor Robert Rabin has argued that the most significant safeguard would be a reasoned explanation for the dismissal and that reduction in the number of other procedures required might lead the Court to recog-

In *Cleveland Board of Education v. Loudermill* [125] the Court found that a government employee who had an entitlement to his government position under local law could not be dismissed from that position without being given some opportunity to respond to charges that would form the basis for his job termination. In this case the government admitted that the employee had a property interest in his job. Local law provided for no pre-termination hearing for the individual but only a chance to have the job termination reviewed at a later date. The Supreme Court, in an opinion by Justice White, noted that state or local law was only relevant for determining whether the individual had an entitlement to his job. The opinion rejected the concept that states could limit the type of procedures necessary for job termination below that required by the due process clause by legislatively deciding that an employee was entitled to few procedural safeguards prior to the termination of his job. The Supreme Court in *Cleveland Board of Education* held that an employee is not entitled to a pre-termination "hearing" but only "an opportunity to respond" to charges against him prior to his job termination, followed by a post-termination hearing to review the decision of an informal or summary pre-termination process. The Court reached this conclusion by applying the *Mathews* three factor balancing approach. First, the Court found that the private interest in government employment, for a person who has an entitlement to his employment, was a "significant" interest. Second, the Court found that employment terminations often involve factual disputes or difficult questions regarding the appropriateness or necessity for a discharge from employment. A pre-termination opportunity to respond to charges would help to avoid erroneous or unjustified termination decisions. Finally, the Court found that the state interest in avoiding the cost and delay of pre-termination proceedings did not outweigh the employee's claim for fair treatment prior to the termination of this interest. However, the state's interests were sufficient for the Court to rule that "the pre-termination hearing, though necessary, need not be elaborate." If there was post-termination review of the termination decision, a government employee with an entitlement to his job could be fired following a pre-termination notice of the reasons for his discharge and a pre-termination opportunity to respond to those charges. Thus, the Court has given some pre-termination rights to government employees but it has not required the type of formal pre-termination proceedings for termination of employment that the Court has required for termination of subsistence welfare benefits. [126]

Post–Deprivation Hearings. There also seems to be an emerging concept that in some instances due process is fulfilled by a "post-deprivation" hearing or suit. This type of hearing would be in accordance with the utilitarian balancing test and might in fact result in a wider role for due process. It may be that the Court will be less fearful of recognizing a wide variety of interests as life, liberty or property if such recognition does not require universal government hearings prior to affecting those interests.

When someone's life, liberty or property interest is going to be taken by the government, procedural due process principles normally will require that the person receive notice and a hearing prior to the deprivation of the constitutionally protected interest. However, it is possible for a court using the *Mathews* balancing approach to determine that some types of deprivations of liberty or property can be justi-

---

nize greater interests in public employment. Rabin, Job Security and Due Process: Monitoring Administrative Discretion Through A Reasons Requirement, 44 U.Chi.L.Rev. 60 (1976). See § 13.5, supra, concerning rights to public employment.

125. 470 U.S. 532, 105 S.Ct. 1487, 84 L.Ed.2d 494 (1985), on remand 763 F.2d 202 (6th Cir.1985).

126. The Court avoided ruling on how soon a post-termination hearing must be held for a government em-

ployee who did not receive an elaborate pre-termination hearing but only notice and an opportunity to respond. Cleveland Board of Education v. Loudermill, 470 U.S. 532, 546–48, 105 S.Ct. 1487, 1496, 84 L.Ed.2d 494 (1985), on remand 763 F.2d 202 (6th Cir.1985).

The Court's ruling regarding the procedures necessary for termination of subsistence welfare benefits was Goldberg v. Kelly, 397 U.S. 254, 90 S.Ct. 1011, 25 L.Ed.2d 287 (1970).

fied without a pre-deprivation process, or with very informal or limited pre-deprivation procedures, if the individual whose interest is being taken by the government receives a subsequent (post-deprivation) process for review of the decision and possible restoration of that interest. It would be rare for a court to allow the government to take a person's liberty or property with no prior hearing of any type but a court may approve very informal pre-deprivation procedures if there is a more elaborate post-deprivation process available to protect the individual's interest.

As predicted in the first edition of this treatise[127], the Supreme Court in recent years has found that some liberty and property interests are adequately protected by procedures which take place after the governmental termination of that liberty or property interest. In these cases the Court rules that the insignificant nature of the individual liberty or property interest at stake, or the magnitude of the government's need to take action without administrative delay, justifies a government action temporarily depriving a person of a liberty in property interest until a "post-deprivation" hearing can be held. In a few cases the Court has ruled that the government need not initiate post-deprivation process because the individual's interest is adequately protected by state law which allows the individual to bring a state court action against the government agency or employees who allegedly wrongfully deprived him of a liberty or property interest.[128]

When the deprivation of life, liberty, or property is a severe one, and the risk of erroneous governmental action is substantial, the Supreme Court is not likely to find that post-deprivation judicial remedies constitute suffi-

cient process, absent emergency justification for the governmental action. Thus, a majority of the Justices found that government utility companies were required to establish a process for hearing customer billing disputes prior to termination of utility services. Both pre-deprivation and post-deprivation judicial remedies were rejected by the Court as insufficient to protect the individual's interest in avoiding wrongful termination of utility service.[129]

When the government acts to protect the public interest for harmful acts of individuals it may temporarily limit those arguably harmful actions. Based upon this rationale, the Court has upheld temporary suspension of a surface mining operation pending a review of allegations that the mine operator was violating environmental regulations.[130] Similarly, the Court has upheld a statutory system imposing a temporary suspension of a person's license to drive an automobile when that person refused to take a drunk driving test.[131] A majority of the Justices also found that a state did not have to give a pre-suspension hearing to a race horse trainer before suspending his license temporarily when one of his horses was found to have been drugged prior to a race, but that the state had to give the suspended trainer a prompt post-suspension hearing to verify the drug charge and to determine if the trainer was at fault.[132] In these cases the individual whose liberty or property was being temporarily limited had some ability to respond to charges, and talk to government decision-makers, prior to the initial government action as well as receiving a post-deprivation hearing. It will always be easier for a court to uphold a post-deprivation hearing system if the individual whose property or liberty is being limited is given some pre-deprivation

127. J. Nowak, R. Rotunda & J. Young, Constitutional Law 511 (1st ed. 1978).

128. The most significant decisions of this type are noted in the following paragraphs.

For an analysis of this trend and issues left unresolved by these decisions, see Smolla, The Displacement of Federal Due Process Claims by State Tort Remedies: Parratt v. Taylor and Logan v. Zimmerman Brush Co., 1982 U.Ill. L.Rev. 831; Brown, De–Federalizing Common Law Torts: Empathy For Parratt, Hudson, and Daniels, 28 Boston College L.Rev. 813 (1987).

129. Memphis Light, Gas and Water Division v. Craft, 436 U.S. 1, 98 S.Ct. 1554, 56 L.Ed.2d 30 (1978).

130. Hodel v. Virginia Surface Mining and Reclamation Ass'n, Inc., 452 U.S. 264, 101 S.Ct. 2352, 69 L.Ed.2d 1 (1981).

131. Mackey v. Montrym, 443 U.S. 1, 99 S.Ct. 2612, 61 L.Ed.2d 321 (1979).

132. Barry v. Barchi, 443 U.S. 55, 99 S.Ct. 2642, 61 L.Ed.2d 365 (1979).

opportunity to respond to charges against him or to communicate with the authority who will be making the initial decision to terminate the property or liberty interest.

When the Court finds both that the nature of the individual liberty or property at stake is minor and that the governmental interest in acting without unnecessary administrative delay is significant, it is likely to find a post-deprivation process sufficient to protect the asserted liberty or property interest. These lesser interests may be adequately safeguarded by state law giving the individual the right to bring a state court action against the government agency which deprived him of the interest. Such a system allows for judicial determination of whether the government acted lawfully or whether the individual has a right to a remedy for wrongful deprivation of his liberty or property interest.[133] Thus the Court found that a child who is subjected to physical punishment by a teacher in a state school was subjected to a loss of liberty, but that this liberty interest was adequately protected by state law allowing the child to seek a judicial remedy for excessive, unjustified infliction of physical harm by the teacher.[134]

The Supreme Court has ruled that the due process clause is not violated when negligent acts of prison officials or prison employees cause unintended injury to a prison inmate's person or property.[135] Thus, a state need not have any pre-deprivation or post-deprivation process to determine the extent or compensability of injuries caused to prison inmates through the negligent actions of state employ-

ees; state tort law or a state doctrine of sovereign immunity may bar recovery by the prisoner in such cases.[136] The Supreme Court has not determined whether an injury caused to an inmate by the gross negligence or recklessness of prison administrators or employees would constitute a violation of the due process clauses.[137] However, the Supreme Court has ruled that a prison employee's intentional impairment of the life, liberty, or property interest of a prison inmate is subject to due process clause restrictions.[138] When a prison inmate alleges that prison officials intentionally have deprived him of a constitutionally protected liberty or property interest, the state must provide fair procedure to determine the merits of his claim for compensation. Because these intentional deprivations of prisoners' rights by prison authorities are not authorized by the state, the state could not create any pre-deprivation process to protect the prisoners' rights. Thus, the state only will be required to have an established post-deprivation administrative or judicial procedure in which the prisoner can receive a fair assessment of his claim for compensation.

In *Hudson v. Palmer*,[139] the Court held that a state need only provide an adequate judicial or administrative post-deprivation remedy for an alleged intentional destruction of property by state employees. The Court in *Hudson* examined the claim of a prisoner who alleged that state employees had intentionally destroyed his property, including legal papers, during a shakedown search. The Court ruled

---

133. See Smolla, The Displacement of Federal Due Process Claims by State Tort Remedies: Parratt v. Taylor and Logan v. Zimmerman Brush Co., 1982 U.Ill.L.Rev. 831.

134. Ingraham v. Wright, 430 U.S. 651, 97 S.Ct. 1401, 51 L.Ed.2d 711 (1977).

135. Daniels v. Williams, 474 U.S. 327, 106 S.Ct. 662, 88 L.Ed.2d 662 (1986), overruling Parratt v. Taylor, 451 U.S. 527, 101 S.Ct. 1908, 68 L.Ed.2d 420 (1981).

136. Daniels v. Williams, 474 U.S. 327, 106 S.Ct. 662, 88 L.Ed.2d 662 (1986) (there is no denial of due process if a state doctrine of sovereign immunity bars a prisoner from recovering damages for injuries sustained because he slipped on a pillow that had been left on a stairway through the negligence of a sheriff's deputy); Davidson v. Cannon, 474 U.S. 344, 106 S.Ct. 668, 88 L.Ed.2d 677 (1986) (state statute protecting prison officials from liabili-

ty for injuries caused to one prisoner by another prisoner does not violate due process; prisoner is denied a remedy for injuries resulting from prison officials' negligent failure to protect him from attack by a fellow inmate even though the prisoner had attempted to alert prison officials of the danger to him).

137. Daniels v. Williams, 474 U.S. 327, 334 n. 3, 106 S.Ct. 662, 666 n. 3, 88 L.Ed.2d 662 (1986). Accord, Davidson v. Cannon, 474 U.S. 344, 106 S.Ct. 668, 88 L.Ed.2d 677 (1986).

138. Hudson v. Palmer, 468 U.S. 517, 104 S.Ct. 3194, 82 L.Ed.2d 393 (1984), on remand 744 F.2d 22 (4th Cir.1984). This case is examined in the next paragraph of this section.

139. 468 U.S. 517, 104 S.Ct. 3194, 82 L.Ed.2d 393 (1984), on remand 744 F.2d 22 (4th Cir.1984).

that the state would have to have a "meaning-ful post-deprivation remedy," although that state procedure need not be one that would compensate the individual as fully in monetary terms as a federal civil rights action. In find-ing that the state did not have to provide a pre-deprivation remedy, the Court focused on the reasons why some types of property depri-vations would only require after-the-fact ac-cess to judicial or administrative remedies. Takings of property "through random and un-authorized conduct" of state employees were unpredictable so that there could be no prac-tical system for pre-deprivation hearings in such situations. The inability of the state to control such conduct in advance and the na-ture of the taking of property were such that the state action regarding the property was not considered "complete until and unless it provides or refuses to provide a suitable post-deprivation remedy."[140]

In *Sacramento v. Lewis*[141], the Justices ruled that the death of a suspect who was acciden-tally killed by a police patrol car in a high-speed chase of the motorcycle (on which the deceased person had been a passenger) did not violate substantive due process principles. In so doing Justice Souter's majority opinion in *Lewis* described the *Hudson* decision as being one that was based on substantive due process, rather than procedural due process, principles. The Court in *Lewis* did not address taking of property issues or procedural due process is-sues. Nevertheless, future cases arising from harm caused to persons or property by actions of police officers may sometimes present tak-ing of property issues, and procedural due process issues together with substantive due process issues.[142]

In contrast to the ruling in *Hudson*, in *Lo-gan v. Zimmerman Brush Co.*,[143] the Court found that a state could not refuse to establish a pre-deprivation hearing procedure before

taking a property interest where the property deprivation is effected pursuant to a state stat-utory system. In *Logan* the Court unani-mously found that provisions of a state Fair Employment Practices Act violated procedural due process. The Act required that the com-plainant alleging that he had been improperly fired from his job because of his physical hand-icap must first file a charge with a state Em-ployment Practices Commission; before suit could be filed the Commission would have to hold a fact finding conference within 120 days of the filing of the claim. Although in the individual case before the Court the Commis-sion had admittedly failed to hold the fact finding conference through its own negligence, the state courts had ruled that the 120 day requirement was jurisdictional so that the complainant permanently lost the right to sue, due to the negligence of the Commission. The Supreme Court found that the statutory sys-tem created an entitlement to bring a fair employment practices suit; this entitlement was protected by the due process clause; and the possibility of suing the Commission for its negligence would not suffice as a remedy. In-stead, the state would have to allow the com-plainant to bring suit against the employer. The Court found that the post-deprivation remedy (the possibility of a negligence suit against the Commission) was insufficient to comply with due process because "unlike the complainant in *Parratt*, Logan is challenging not the Commission's error, but the 'estab-lished state procedure' that destroys his enti-tlement without according him proper proce-dural safeguards."[144]

Logan should not be taken as indicating that a state may never set up a statutory system which grants only a post-deprivation remedy to someone whose property rights have been taken. In *Logan*, the Court noted that its prior decisions "suggest that, absent 'the ne-

140. 468 U.S. at 533, 104 S.Ct. at 3204, 82 L.Ed.2d at 408.

141. 523 U.S. 833, 118 S.Ct. 1708, 140 L.Ed.2d 1043 (1998)

142. See § 10.6 for further examination of the *Lewis* case, and the mixing of procedural and substantive due process issues.

143. 455 U.S. 422, 102 S.Ct. 1148, 71 L.Ed.2d 265 (1982). This case also involved some confusion of sub-stantive and procedural issue. See §§10.6, 11.4.

144. 455 U.S. at 436, 102 S.Ct. at 1158, 71 L.Ed.2d at 278.

cessity of quick action by the State or the impracticality of providing any predeprivation process', a post-deprivation hearing here would be constitutionally inadequate. That is particularly true where, as here, the State's only post-termination process comes in the form of an independent tort action." [145]

In *Cleveland Board of Education v. Loudermill* [146] the Supreme Court held that a government employee who, under state law, had an entitlement to his job could not be terminated without any pre-termination process but only a post-termination review procedure. The Court employed the *Mathews* balancing approach and found that the state interest in avoiding the costs and delays of pre-termination process did not outweigh the significant individual interest in continued government employment and the value of pre-termination process for avoiding erroneous deprivations of that interest. The majority opinion, by Justice White, quoted statements from earlier Supreme Court opinions that indicated that the basic requirement of the due process clause is the opportunity for an individual to receive "notice and a hearing" before he is deprived of a constitutionally protected liberty or property interest. [147] Justice White's majority opinion in *Cleveland Board of Education* found that the pre-termination process for an individual need not be elaborate; the state need only give the employee a right to respond to charges against him. This type of process, according to the Court, could be "something less than a full evidentiary hearing." The post-termination process available to the employee minimized but did not eliminate the need for some type of pre-termination hearing in order to ensure fair treatment for the individual.

The *Cleveland Board of Education v. Loudermill* decision, like the *Logan* decision, does not hold that a state always must provide pre-deprivation hearings or procedures. In most circumstances procedural due process principles require the state to provide an individual with notice and a hearing before an impartial decision-maker prior to the deprivation of a life, liberty, or property interest. The government should be able to use an informal or limited form of pre-deprivation process, followed by a post-deprivation review of the government action, when the government need to act quickly or summarily is judicially determined to outweigh the individual interest in retaining the full extent of the liberty or property prior to final administrative resolution of the dispute between the individual and the government. There may be an even more limited group of cases wherein an individual is entitled to no pre-deprivation process because of the need of the government to act quickly or because there is no reasonable way for the government to establish a pre-deprivation administrative or judicial process to protect the type of interest at stake. [148]

In determining whether a post-deprivation administrative or judicial process is sufficient to protect property interests that would be taken by state action, the Court should not rigidly find that pre-deprivation hearings are always required when the taking is by statutory action or that post-deprivation process is always sufficient when the taking is through

---

145. 455 U.S. at 436, 102 S.Ct. at 1158, 71 L.Ed.2d at 278 (footnote omitted and internal citations omitted).

146. 470 U.S. 532, 105 S.Ct. 1487, 84 L.Ed.2d 494 (1985), on remand 763 F.2d 202 (6th Cir.1985).

147. 470 U.S. at 542, 105 S.Ct. at 1493 citing: Mullane v. Central Hanover Bank & Trust Co., 339 U.S. 306, 313, 70 S.Ct. 652, 656, 94 L.Ed. 865 (1950); Boddie v. Connecticut, 401 U.S. 371, 379, 91 S.Ct. 780, 786, 28 L.Ed.2d 113 (1971); Bell v. Burson, 402 U.S. 535, 542, 91 S.Ct. 1586, 1591, 29 L.Ed.2d 90 (1971); Board of Regents v. Roth, 408 U.S. 564, 569–70, 92 S.Ct. 2701, 2705, 33 L.Ed.2d 548 (1972); Perry v. Sindermann, 408 U.S. 593, 599, 92 S.Ct. 2694, 2698, 33 L.Ed.2d 570 (1972); Davis v. Scherer, 468 U.S. 183, 192, n. 10, 104 S.Ct. 3012, 3018, n. 10, 82 L.Ed.2d 139 (1984).

148. In the same term in which the Court decided Cleveland Board of Education v. Loudermill, the Court found that a state was not required to pay just compensation for taking of property prior to or contemporaneously with the taking. In Williamson County Regional Planning Commission v. Hamilton Bank, 473 U.S. 172, 105 S.Ct. 3108, 87 L.Ed.2d 126 (1985) the Court held that an individual's claim that his property had been taken without just compensation was not ripe, in part because the state had established a system for determining whether an individual had his property taken by zoning regulations and, if so, the nature of compensation which was due for the taking. The individual landowner had the ability to appear before zoning authorities prior to the decision to rezone his land and an ability to seek a variance from the zoning plan.

administrative action. Rather, the Court should apply the *Mathews v. Eldridge* analysis [149] that is used in other procedural due process settings to determine whether, given the nature of the liberty or property interest at stake, the precise form of post-deprivation process established by state law is fundamentally fair in that it adequately guards against arbitrary or unlawful taking of those interests. The Court must determine in each case: first, whether the ability to bring a judicial action for a review of the deprivation (or whether the judicial or administrative procedure designed specifically to review the possibility that there was an unlawful deprivation) would serve to deter unlawful or arbitrary deprivations; second, whether the state procedure was fundamentally fair to the individual; and third,

whether the state procedure had the potential to fully redress the injury to an individual whose deprivation was found to be improper.[150] The practicality of a pre-deprivation process in each case would have to be considered as well as the adequacy of the post-deprivation process established by state law.[151]

Zinermon v. Burch [152] provides an example of how the *Mathews* balancing test [153] applies to the question of whether a post-deprivation proceeding complies with due process. In *Zinermon*, the question before the Supreme Court was whether a former patient in a state mental care facility had stated a cause of action, under the due process clause, against state employees who admitted him to the mental health care facility as a "voluntary patient". The plaintiff alleged that he was not mentally

149. See the discussion of the balancing test employed by the Court for examination of procedural due process issues in § 13.8, supra.

150. The Supreme Court appeared to follow this method of analysis in Brock v. Roadway Express, Inc., 481 U.S. 252, 107 S.Ct. 1740, 95 L.Ed.2d 239 (1987) although the absence of a majority opinion in this case may limit its significance for determining the validity of post-deprivation process. At issue in the *Roadway Express* case were federal statutes and regulations that allowed the Secretary of Labor to order a motor carrier company to reinstate an employee who had been discharged for cause by the company. A federal statute prohibited the discharge of employees in the transportation industry if the discharge was in retaliation for the refusal to operate a motor vehicle that did not comply with certain safety standards or for filing complaints about the failure of the company to comply with such standards. The statute would have allowed the Secretary of Labor to conduct an initial investigation and order a temporary reinstatement of the employee based upon a finding of probable cause; the employer would, at its request, receive an evidentiary hearing and a final decision after the temporary reinstatement.

In *Roadway Express*, the Supreme Court ruled that the employer was entitled to notice and some process prior to the initial order to reinstate the employee, although the Court did not require an extensive hearing prior to the temporary reinstatement. The ruling of the case, was announced in a plurality opinion written by Justice Marshall.

151. In Federal Deposit Insurance Corporation v. Mallen, 486 U.S. 230, 108 S.Ct. 1780, 100 L.Ed.2d 265 (1988) the Supreme Court upheld federal statutes and regulations that allowed the Federal Deposit Insurance Corporation to suspend an officer or director of an insured bank if the officer was formally charged with a felony involving dishonesty or breach of trust. The Supreme Court found that the statute was not invalid on its face merely because it allowed for only a post-suspension hearing, which could take place up to 90 days following the suspension. The importance of the governmental interests in protecting

bank customer deposits and the public confidence in banks, coupled with the fact that a felony indictment provided some assurance that the suspension was not totally baseless, justified using a post-suspension, rather than pre-suspension, hearing process. In *Mallen* the Court ruled that the statute and regulations that gave the agency discretion as to whether to accept oral testimony at the post-suspension hearing were not invalid on their face. The Court also found that the suspended bank officer in this case had not offered any oral proof or testimony that would show that the regulation was fundamentally unfair and a violation of due process principles as applied in this case.

The Requirement of a Prompt Hearing. Whenever the government initiates a civil or criminal action against an individual, there may be issues concerning whether delay in bringing or concluding the action violated constitutional provisions. A claim that a criminal prosecution was not brought or prosecuted in a timely manner would raise issues that are primarily concerned with the interpretation of the speedy trial provision of the Sixth Amendment, although due process considerations may also be present in such situations. Civil proceedings prosecuted by the government also raise questions concerning whether the proceeding has been initiated and concluded in a timely manner. An unjustified delay may deny a person property or liberty without due process of law. For citations to Supreme Court cases, and secondary authorities, on this point, see R. Rotunda & J. Nowak, Treatise on Constitutional Law: Substance and Procedure, § 17.9 (3rd ed. 1999, with annual supplements).

152. 494 U.S. 113, 110 S.Ct. 975, 108 L.Ed.2d 100 (1990).

153. See Mathews v. Eldridge, 424 U.S. 319, 96 S.Ct. 893, 47 L.Ed.2d 18 (1976). For an examination of the basic principles established in *Mathews* for determining what type of process is required to protect an individual whose liberty or property interests are about to be, or have been, impaired by the government see § 13.8.

competent to sign admission forms at the time of his admission and that he did not meet the criteria for involuntary commitment to the facility. He also alleged that the state hospital employees who admitted him to the state facility knew, or should have known, that he could not make an informed choice as to whether to commit himself voluntarily. There were provisions in this state's law regarding state mental health care facilities that would have allowed for an emergency admission of a person through either administrative or court processes for a short period of time (up to 5 days) if the person appeared to be mentally ill, in need of mental health care, and likely to injure himself or others. State law provided for a judicial hearing for the indefinite involuntary commitment of an individual.

The plaintiff had been admitted to the mental hospital by agreeing to be a voluntary patient; he was afforded none of the procedures available under state law. He remained in the hospital for five months following his initial admission without receiving any hearing. The question in *Zinermon* was whether the plaintiff stated a cause of action under the due process clause, if all of the facts in his complaint were true.[154] The Court, by a vote of 5 to 4, found that the complaint did state a cause of action because the plaintiff's allegations, if true, would establish a violation of procedural due process principles. The majority opinion, written by Justice Blackmun, ruled that the *Mathews* analysis was to be used to determine whether a post-deprivation process was sufficient to comply with due process principles. The majority found that under some circumstances, that the impairment of liberty interests, like the impairment of property interests, would be permissible with only a post-deprivation process.

The majority opinion in *Zinermon* first ruled that the individual's interest in avoiding unjustified commitment was a significant liberty interest. Second, the Court found that the pre-deprivation process would provide a significant safe-guard against improper deprivations of that liberty interest.

Finally, the majority examined the government interests that might support denying an individual a pre-deprivation hearing. Justice Blackmun's opinion examined the question of whether the government employees' conduct (in admitting the individual through the "voluntary admission" rather than granting the statutory involuntary commitment process) was authorized by law. The third inquiry under *Mathews* (the inquiry into the government interest) only requires an examination of whether a pre-deprivation process was impractical and whether a post-deprivation process would adequately protect the individual liberty interests at stake. The majority found that providing the individual with a pre-deprivation process was practical, since state law provided a prompt process for the temporary placement of an individual in the state mental health care facility. If, as the plaintiff claimed in his complaint, the state hospital employees knew, or should have known, that he was incapable of giving consent to a voluntary admission, there was no reason why this individual was not provided with the statutory procedural safeguards for an involuntary temporary admission.

Justice O'Connor's dissent in *Zinermon*[155] contains confusing language concerning the standards to be used for determining when a post-deprivation process meets due process requirements. Justice O'Connor attacked the Court's reliance on *Mathews'* three-part analysis, even though prior Supreme Court decisions used the *Matthews* analysis to determine if a post-deprivation process complied with due process principles. Justice O'Connor could have argued that the *Mathews* tests, if properly applied, supported the conclusion that due

---

154. In *Zinermon*, the question before the Court was whether the individual's complaint, on its face, stated a cause of action under 42 U.S.C.A. § 1983. The basis for this § 1983 action was the allegation that state employees had denied the individual due process by failing to provide him with procedural safeguards prior to, or contemporane-

ous with, his commitment to the state mental health care facility.

155. Zinermon v. Burch, 494 U.S. 113, 138, 110 S.Ct. 975, 990, 108 L.Ed.2d 100 (1990) (O'Connor, J., dissenting, joined by Rehnquist, C.J., and Kennedy and Scalia, JJ.).

process did not require a pre-deprivation proceeding under the facts in this case.

The dissent's strongest argument was that the post-deprivation remedy provided by the state (the ability to sue the state hospital employees) for an improper voluntary admission, when viewed together with the involuntary admission procedures established state statutes, provided a fair process to each individual. Involuntary patients received pre-deprivation process; voluntary patients received a post-deprivation. The post-deprivation state process could redress individual deprivations of liberty. It would be impractical to require state hospital employees to challenge every individual's voluntary admission by having a hearing concerning whether the individual who wished to be admitted to the state hospital had the capacity to make an informed choice.

The majority in *Zinermon* did not seem to require a true pre-deprivation process for every person who was admitted to a state mental health care facility. The majority avoided ruling on whether the temporary admission provisions of the state law were constitutional. An individual might be temporarily admitted for examination at a state hospital with a prompt post-deprivation process. For example, if the employees whose actions were at issue in *Zinermon* had decided that plaintiff could not give voluntary consent, but that he was in need of mental health care and might pose a danger to himself or others, they could have admitted him to the hospital immediately, detained him for 48 hours based on the decision of a health care professional or for up to 5 days with a temporary court order, under the terms of their state's statutes. Nothing in *Zinermon* indicates that such a process is unconstitutional.

If the majority and dissent in *Zinermon* had focused on the third *Mathews* factor (whether the government interest justified some type of post-deprivation process) there would have been a clearer ruling as to whether the individual in the case was entitled to: (1) a formal

pre-deprivation process [which seems unlikely even after this case]; (2) an informal pre-deprivation process (screening by a health care professional at the hospital at the time of admission) and a formal post-deprivation process; or (3) an informal pre-deprivation process and a post-deprivation remedy that consisted only of the possibility of bringing suit against the hospital employees for abuse of discretion. The majority in *Zinermon* seemed to require the second alternative. The dissent argued for the third alternative.

The *Zinermon* opinions seem to bring further confusion to the question of when a post-deprivation process is sufficient to protect a liberty or property interest. The *Zinermon* decision, and all of the Court's post-deprivation cases, can best be understood by focusing on the three *Mathews* factors—the nature of the individual interest at stake, the worth of pre-deprivation proceedings to the individual, and the government interest in using only post-deprivation proceedings.

Four years after *Zinermon,* a majority of the Justices clearly endorsed the use of the three-factor *Mathews* balancing test for determining when a post-deprivation process would be sufficient to protect an individual's property interest. In *United States v. James Daniel Good Real Property,*[156] by a five to four vote of the Justices, the Court ruled that the federal government was required to give notice, and the opportunity for some type of a hearing, to the owner of real property before the government seized the property as a means of initiating forfeiture proceedings. Justice Kennedy's majority opinion stated that there was a "general rule requiring pre-deprivation notice and a hearing" but that there could be instances in which a post-deprivation process would comply with the procedural due process requirements of the Fifth or Fourteenth Amendments and that the Court would use "the three part inquiry set forth in *Mathews v. Eldridge*" to determine whether the government could seize real property without prior notice and a hearing.[157]

156.　510 U.S. 43, 114 S.Ct. 492, 126 L.Ed.2d 490 (1993).

157.　United States v. James Daniel Good Property, 510 U.S. 43, 53, 114 S.Ct. 492, 501, 126 L.Ed.2d 490

In the *James Daniel Good Real Property* case, the federal government was attempting to institute an in rem action in the United States District Court to forfeit an individual's house, and the four acres of land on which it was situated, because the property had been used in connection with the commission of a drug related crime. In 1985, state police officers had searched the home and uncovered a sizeable amount of marijuana and related paraphernalia. Later in 1984, the property owner plead guilty to a crime of promoting a harmful drug, which violated state law. The activity that provided the basis for the state conviction would have provided a factual basis for finding that the defendant violated federal drug laws. In 1989, the United States government instituted its action seeking forfeiture of the house and real property; the federal government initiated its action through a warrant authorizing the seizure of the property that was issued, in an ex parte proceeding, by a United States Magistrate.

In assessing the first *Mathews* factor—the importance of the private interest at stake— the majority opinion in *James Daniel Good Real Property* found that the seizure of a person's real property caused greater harm to the person than would the temporary loss of personal property. In analyzing the second *Mathews* factor—the need for pre-deprivation process—Justice Kennedy concluded that seizing real property without notice, and without an opportunity for the property owner to present his arguments to the government, "creates an unacceptable risk of error." Justice Kennedy then considered the third *Mathews* factor—the nature of the government's interest and whether it justified providing the property owner with only a post-deprivation process.

The majority held that there was no government interest that justified seizing real property as a means of initiating a civil forfeiture proceeding because under federal law the government could have initiated those proceedings without seizing the property.

Justice Kennedy distinguished *Calero–Toledo v. Pearson Yacht Leasing Co.,*[158] in which the Supreme Court had held that the government might make an ex parte seizure of personal property subject to civil forfeiture on the basis that personal property might be hidden or destroyed if the government had to notify the individual of its intent to seize the property and initiate civil forfeiture proceedings.[159] The majority opinion also distinguished cases in which the government was allowed to seize property during an emergency situation, such as war time seizure, on the basis that the protection of national security during war time or the protection of public health justified the seizure of property without prior notice and a hearing. Justice Kennedy's opinion was not very clear concerning the basis upon which the majority distinguished cases from the nineteenth century, and the first half of the twentieth century, that allowed the government to seize both personal and real property as a means of collecting federal tax delinquencies. Justice Kennedy referred to the view expressed by the Supreme Court in the earlier cases that the need to collect government debts or revenue was at that time vital to the operations of the government.[160]

The five member majority in *James Daniel Good Real Property* ruled that compliance with the Fourth Amendment procedures for seizing property in connection with a criminal trial was not sufficient to comply with due process

(1993) (internal citations and quotation marks omitted).

158. 416 U.S. 663, 94 S.Ct. 2080, 40 L.Ed.2d 452 (1974) (allowing seizure of a yacht subject to civil forfeiture without prior notice or a prior hearing).

159. 510 U.S. at 52–62, 114 S.Ct. at 500–504.

160. United States v. James Daniel Good Real Property, 510 U.S. 43, 59–62, 114 S.Ct. 492, 504–505, 126 L.Ed.2d 490 (1993):

"It is true that, in cases decided over a century ago, we permitted the ex parte seizure of real property when the government was collecting debts or revenue. See, e.g., Springer v. United States, 102 U.S. (12 Otto) 586, 593–

594, 26 L.Ed. 253 (1881); Murray's Lessee v. Hoboken Land and Improvement Co., 59 U.S. 272 (18 How.) 272, 15 L.Ed. 372 (1856). Without revisiting these cases, it suffices to say that their apparent rationale—like that for allowing summary seizures during war time, see Stoehr v. Wallace, 255 U.S. 239, 41 S.Ct. 293, 65 L.Ed. 604 (1921); Bowles v. Willingham, 321 U.S. 503, 64 S.Ct. 641, 88 L.Ed. 892 (1944), and seizure of contaminated foods see North American Cold Storage Co. v. Chicago, 211 U.S. 306, 29 S.Ct. 101, 53 L.Ed. 195 (1908)—was one of executive urgency."

limitations on the procedure that the government used to seize property in connection with a civil forfeiture process.[161] The four dissenting Justices believed that the Fourth Amendment warrant requirement was sufficient to protect the rights of the owner of property that was to be the subject of forfeiture proceeding when there had been a prior conviction involving using the property for illegal activities.[162] Perhaps, in the future, the four dissenting Justices will convince a new Justice to join them and reverse the *James Daniel Good Real Property* decision. But even if the Court's holding regarding civil forfeiture procedures does not withstand the test of time, the majority's use of the *Mathews* three-factor analysis to determine whether a post-deprivation hearing would be sufficient to protect liberty or property interests almost certainly will stand the test of time. For two decades a majority of the Justices have ruled that an individual should be given notice and an opportunity to be heard prior to a significant deprivation of a life, liberty, or property interest unless the Court, using the three-factor analysis, concludes that a post-deprivation process would provide fundamental fairness to the individual. In making this determination, the Court will consider (1) the importance of the life, liberty, or property interest being impaired, (2) the risk of erroneous deprivations of the interest absent prior notice and a prior hearing, and (3) the need of the government to act prior to a hearing in order to protect important governmental and societal interests.

In the late 1990s all of the Justices on the Supreme Court endorsed the use of the *Mathews* balancing approach for determining whether a post-deprivation process, rather than a pre-deprivation process, would satisfy due process requirements. In *Gilbert v. Homar*,[163] the Supreme Court Justices were unanimous in ruling that a security officer for a state university was not entitled to notice and a hearing prior being suspended from his job on his being charged with a violation of state drug laws. Mr. Homar, a police officer at a state university, was arrested on private property outside the university and charged with; with several felony crimes (including possession of, and intent to deliver, a banned substance). The charges were made through a complaint filed by the police; there was no grand jury indictment Following his being charged with the crimes, and without giving him a hearing prior to his suspension, the University suspended Mr. Homar, without pay.

In *Gilbert*, Justice Scalia wrote for a unanimous court in finding that Mr. Homar's temporary suspension without pay did not violate the due process clause. Based on the agreement of all the parties, the Court assumed that the university police officer, who could only have been dismissed from his position for "cause," had a property interest in his government employment. Justice Scalia applied the three-factor *Mathews* balancing approach to determine that the university police officer was not entitled to any type of pre-suspension notice or hearing. The first *Mathews* factor,

---

161. United States v. James Daniel Good Real Property, 510 U.S. 43, 50–52, 114 S.Ct. 492, 499–500, 126 L.Ed.2d 490 (1993). The Court also ruled in this case that federal courts could not dismiss a forfeiture action that had been filed within the five year statute of limitations for such actions on the basis that the government had not complied with certain other statutory timing rules concerning the reporting of violations of customs and drug laws that might make property subject to forfeiture. The portion of the opinion by Justice Kennedy concerning the inability of lower federal courts to dismiss forfeiture actions because of the failure to comply with "internal requirements relating to the timing of forfeitures" was written for a unanimous court. United States v. James Daniel Good Real Property, 510 U.S. 43, 61–67, 114 S.Ct. 492, 505–507, 126 L.Ed.2d 490 (1993).

162. The three dissenting opinions, issued by the four dissenting Justices in the *James Daniel Good Real Property* case each focused on a different aspect of the majority opinion. The dissenters seemed to agree that where an individual had been convicted of using real property as the location for criminal activity that an ex parte proceeding would meet Fourth Amendment requirements and due process requirements. United States v. James Daniel Good Real Property, 510 U.S. 43, 66, 114 S.Ct. 492, 507, 126 L.Ed.2d 490 (1993) (Rehnquist, C.J., joined by Scalia, J., and, in part, by O'Connor, J., concurring in part and dissenting in part); 510 U.S. at 73, 114 S.Ct. at 511 (O'Connor, J., concurring in part and dissenting in part); 510 U.S. at 81, 114 S.Ct. at 515 (Thomas, J., concurring in part and dissenting in part).

163. 520 U.S. 924, 117 S.Ct. 1807, 138 L.Ed.2d 120 (1997).

concerning the importance of the interest at stake, weighed in favor of the university because of the government action involved only a temporary suspension without pay, rather than a more serious deprivation of the property interest of the such as dismissal from his university position.[164] The second factor, concerning the risk of an erroneous deprivation without pre-suspension procedures, weighed heavily in favor of the state university, according to Justice Scalia. There was no need for a hearing prior to the suspension because the only issue at a hearing would have been the whether the employee had been formally charged with a felony. The employee admitted that he had been charged; that fact was easily verifiable by the university.[165] The third *Mathews* factor, concerning the government's interest, also weighed against the provision of a pre-suspension hearing for the university police officer. The Court's opinion stated that "the state has a significant interest in immediately suspending, when felony charges are filed against them, employees who occupy positions of great public trust and high public visibility, such as police officers."[166] Because the university could suspend the officer without a pre-deprivation hearing, the university could deny the individual monetary compensation during the period of his suspension.[167]

The Supreme Court, in *Gilbert,* assumed that the officer had a right to a post-deprivation hearing, in part because the charges against the police officer were dropped and, "once the charges were dropped the risk of an erroneous deprivation increased substantial-

ly."[168] However, the Court did not reach the question of what type of post-suspension might be required for the officer, or how soon the university might have been required to give the university police officer, a post-suspension. The lower courts had not addressed the question of the adequacy of post-suspension hearing process for the individual university employee. Therefore, the Supreme Court remanded the case to the lower courts for initial consideration of whether the defendant had been given an adequately prompt and adequately formal post-suspension hearing.

For breach of contract claims against a government entity, access to a court, for resolution of the claim, will constitute adequate due process.[169]

§ 13.10 The Right to Judicial Process— Access to the Courts

In the cases concerning "procedural due process" which we have examined, the issue has been whether the government must afford a hearing to a person whom it is about to deprive of life, liberty, or property. In these situations the government is either operating one of its own administrative systems or instituting judicial process against an individual. However, in some instances a person will want access to the judicial process whether or not he is about to be deprived of a constitutionally cognizable interest in life, liberty or property. This desire normally presents no problem, for individuals are free to file their suits and make use of the judicial process within the generally applicable rules of civil procedure. If state law

---

164. 520 U.S. at 932, 117 S.Ct. at 1813: "Unlike the employee [in Cleveland Board of Education v. Loudermill, 470 U.S. 532, 105 S.Ct. 1487, 84 L.Ed.2d 494 (1985)] who faced termination, respondent faced only a temporary suspension without pay. So long as the suspended employee receives a sufficiently prompt post-suspension hearing, the lost income relatively insubstantial...."

165. Gilbert v. Homar, 520 U.S. 924, 932, 117 S.Ct. 1807, 1813, 138 L.Ed.2d 120 (1997). The Court in *Gilbert* relied on F.D.I.C. v. Mallen, 486 U.S. 230, 108 S.Ct. 1780, 100 L.Ed.2d 265 (1988) (upholding suspension of a bank officer without a presuspension hearing following a criminal charge being filed against the bank officer).

166. Gilbert v. Homar, 520 U.S. 924, 932, 117 S.Ct. 1807, 1813, 138 L.Ed.2d 120 (1997).

167. 520 U.S. at 932, 117 S.Ct. at 1813: "[The suspended officer] contends that this interest [in suspending

employees in positions of public trusts that are charged with serious crimes] could have been accomplished by suspending him with pay until he had a hearing. We think, however, that the government does not have to give an employee charged with a felony a paid leave at taxpayer expense."

168. 520 U.S. at 934, 117 S.Ct. at 1814.

169. See also, Lujan v. G & G Fire Sprinklers, Inc., 532 U.S. 189, 121 S.Ct. 1446, 149 L.Ed.2d 391 (2001)(Court unanimously holds that a business with an arguable claim for breach of contract on the part of the government received due process by the state allowing the alleged aggrieved party to bring suit against the state through the normal judicial process for the resolution of contract claims).

allows persons to bring suit in state court to redress alleged grievances against public or private agencies, it cannot arbitrarily deny an individual the ability to use those judicial procedures. The arbitrary refusal to allow individuals to use the established state court process would seem to be invalid under even the most minimal due process or equal protection standards.[1]

In *Christopher v. Harbury*[2], the Supreme Court found that a woman had failed to state a cause of action against the federal government by alleging that federal officials had previously concealed information about the death of her husband, a foreign national, in a country outside of the United States. Justice Souter's opinion for the Court described prior cases regarding a right of access to courts as falling into two categories: "In the first are claims that systemic official action frustrates a plaintiff or plaintiff class in preparing and filing suits at the present time. Thus, in the prison-litigation cases, the relief sought may be a law library for a prisoner's use in preparing a case ... or a reader for an illiterate prisoner ... or simply a lawyer ... in denial-of-access cases challenging filing fees that poor plaintiffs cannot afford to pay, the object is an order requiring waiver of a fee to open the courthouse door for desired litigation, such as direct appeals or federal habeas petitions in criminal cases, or family law rights."[3]

A significant issue in terms of a right of access to courts arises when some individuals cannot pay the fees required by the government for the use of the courts. The Supreme Court has not held that there is any right to judicial process for an individual who seeks to use that process to his benefit. However, the state may not withhold this process when to do so would constitute the deprivation of a fundamental constitutional right. The government is also restrained by the equal protection guarantee in its granting of access to the judicial process. Filing fees are merely a way of allocating the judicial process to a certain class of plaintiffs—those who are willing and able to pay. The government may not impose filing fees which prohibit access to the courts by indigents when that would impair a fundamental constitutional right of the indigent or when the fees are so arbitrary that they invidiously exclude poor persons from the judicial process.

An example of filing fees which restrict a fundamental constitutional right are those imposed before married persons may receive a divorce. In *Boddie v. Connecticut*[4] the Supreme Court held that the filing fee requirement for divorce actions could not be applied to indigents who sought a divorce. The application of fees to indigent persons would effectively preclude them from exercising their constitutionally guaranteed right of freedom of choice in marital decisions.[5] Similarly, when the government attempts to impose prior restraints on the freedom of speech, it must not only grant access to the courts to challenge these restraints but it must also institute judicial proceedings against the would-be speakers so as to insure that there will be judicial review for the censorship system.[6] These pro-

§ 13.10

1. Logan v. Zimmerman Brush Co., 455 U.S. 422, 102 S.Ct. 1148, 71 L.Ed.2d 265 (1982). This case involved some confusion of substantive and procedural issues; it is examined in § 11.4, supra.

2. 536 U.S. 403, 122 S.Ct. 2179, 153 L.Ed.2d 413 (2002), on remand 44 Fed.Appx. 522 (Fed.Cir.2002).

3. 536 U.S. at 412–13, 122 S.Ct. at 2185. For insight into how the Court might employ the First Amendment to establish a right of access to courts, see Carol Rice Andrews, A Right of Access to Court Under the Petition Clause of the First Amendment: Defining the Right, 60 Ohio St. L. J. 558 (1999).

4. 401 U.S. 371, 91 S.Ct. 780, 28 L.Ed.2d 113 (1971). Woods v. Holy Cross Hosp., 591 F.2d 1164, 1173 n. 16 (5th Cir.1979) (Tjoflat, J., citing an earlier edition of this treatise).

5. In M.L.B. v. S.L.J., 519 U.S. 102, 117 S.Ct. 555, 136 L.Ed.2d 473 (1996) the Supreme Court ruled that a state violated both due process and equal protection principles by enforcing a rule that prohibited a woman from appealing from a trial court decision that would have totally terminated her parental rights solely because she was unable to pay for preparation of a trial transcript for the appeal. Justice Ginsburg, who wrote the majority opinion in *M.L.B.*, relied on the *Boddie* case when she noted that the Supreme Court had "recognized a narrow category of civil cases in which the state must provide access to its judicial processes without regard to a party's ability to pay court fees." 519 U.S. at 113, 117 S.Ct. at 562.

6. Freedman v. Maryland, 380 U.S. 51, 85 S.Ct. 734, 13 L.Ed.2d 649 (1965); Blount v. Rizzi, 400 U.S. 410, 91 S.Ct. 423, 27 L.Ed.2d 498 (1971); Southeastern Promotions

cedures are necessary to insure that problems of access to judicial review do not result in suppression of protected ideas.[7]

The Court has held that there is a right of access to courts for the purpose of reviewing individual claims in the criminal justice system. Through a series of decisions the Court has recognized that fairness in the criminal justice system is a fundamental right. Thus the state may not impose filing fees for appellate procedures on indigent defendants as that would deny them equal protection of the law.[8] Similarly, the indigent defendant must be provided with transcripts for appeal, or a suitable alternative, for denial of a transcript would effectively preclude his access to the appellate process.[9] The government is also required to provide counsel for indigent defendants in their first appeal as they would be denied equal protection of the law by a system which provided meaningful review only for those who could afford to retain an attorney.[10]

The Court has held that indigents do not have a right to state appointed counsel for discretionary review or collateral attack proceedings.[11] A majority of the Justices believed that the grant of counsel through the first appeal of right provided the defendant with

sufficient opportunity for meaningful review of his conviction. However, this holding does not allow the government to deny the indigent access to the courts for these proceedings. If the government does not provide counsel for the defendant, it cannot prohibit prisoners from assisting each other in the preparation of petitions for discretionary review procedures.[12] Indeed the Court has found that there is a right of access to the courts for the submission of civil rights actions following imprisonment.[13] In 1977 the Court explicitly recognized that defendants retained this "right of access" following their conviction and imprisonment when the Justices required the states to furnish prisoners with adequate legal research materials.[14]

Where access to the judicial process is not essential to the exercise of fundamental constitutional rights the state will be free to allocate access to the judicial machinery on any system or classification which is not totally arbitrary. Thus, filing fee requirements for such actions may be enforced so as to bar indigents from using the judicial process unless the fees are totally arbitrary.

In *United States v. Kras*[15] the Supreme Court held that access to the bankruptcy

---

Ltd. v. Conrad, 420 U.S. 546, 95 S.Ct. 1239, 43 L.Ed.2d 448 (1975).

7. Monaghan, First Amendment "Due Process," 83 Harv.L.Rev. 518 (1970).

8. Burns v. Ohio, 360 U.S. 252, 79 S.Ct. 1164, 3 L.Ed.2d 1209 (1959); Smith v. Bennett, 365 U.S. 708, 81 S.Ct. 895, 6 L.Ed.2d 39 (1961), on remand to 252 Iowa 976, 109 N.W.2d 703 (1961).

9. Griffin v. Illinois, 351 U.S. 12, 76 S.Ct. 585, 100 L.Ed. 891 (1956), rehearing denied 351 U.S. 958, 76 S.Ct. 844, 100 L.Ed. 1480 (1956); Long v. District Court, 385 U.S. 192, 87 S.Ct. 362, 17 L.Ed.2d 290 (1966); Mayer v. Chicago, 404 U.S. 189, 92 S.Ct. 410, 30 L.Ed.2d 372 (1971).

10. Douglas v. California, 372 U.S. 353, 83 S.Ct. 814, 9 L.Ed.2d 811 (1963), rehearing denied 373 U.S. 905, 83 S.Ct. 1288, 10 L.Ed.2d 200 (1963).

An indigent criminal defendant only has right to appointed counsel in those cases wherein the defendant receives a punishment of imprisonment. Scott v. Illinois, 440 U.S. 367, 99 S.Ct. 1158, 59 L.Ed.2d 383 (1979). For citations to additional Supreme Court cases, and secondary authorities, on this point, see R. Rotunda & J. Nowak, Treatise on Constitutional Law: Substance and Procedure, §§ 17.4, 17.9 (3rd ed. 1999, with annual supplements).

11. Ross v. Moffitt, 417 U.S. 600, 94 S.Ct. 2437, 41 L.Ed.2d 341 (1974).

See also, Pennsylvania v. Finley, 481 U.S. 551, 107 S.Ct. 1990, 95 L.Ed.2d 539 (1987), on remand 379 Pa.Super. 390, 550 A.2d 213 (1988) (because there is no equal protection or due process right to appointed counsel in a post-conviction proceeding, there is no due process or equal protection right to require extensive procedures to restrict the withdrawal of appointed counsel when that counsel discovers that the case is frivolous).

12. Johnson v. Avery, 393 U.S. 483, 89 S.Ct. 747, 21 L.Ed.2d 718 (1969).

13. Wolff v. McDonnell, 418 U.S. 539, 577–80, 94 S.Ct. 2963, 2985–86, 41 L.Ed.2d 935 (1974). Hudson v. Palmer, 468 U.S. 517, 522, 104 S.Ct. 3194, 3198, 82 L.Ed.2d 393 (1984), on remand 744 F.2d 22 (4th Cir.1984), cited *Wolff* and Johnson v. Avery, 393 U.S. 483, 89 S.Ct. 747, 21 L.Ed.2d 718 (1969) for the proposition that prisoners retain a right of access to courts: the due process clause of the Fourteenth Amendment does not require a predeprivation hearing where a state employee intentionally or negligently destroyed the property of a prison inmate, but due process is satisfied if a "meaningful postdeprivation remedy for the loss is available."

14. Bounds v. Smith, 430 U.S. 817, 97 S.Ct. 1491, 52 L.Ed.2d 72 (1977).

15. 409 U.S. 434, 93 S.Ct. 631, 34 L.Ed.2d 626 (1973).

courts could be denied those who were unable to pay the $50 filing fee for voluntary bankruptcy. Unlike divorce, bankruptcy is not the only method available for a debtor to adjust his legal relationship with his creditors. The debtor can settle his debts out of court. The Court justified its holding that, in effect, some people could be found too poor to go bankrupt by ruling that a congressional desire to make the bankruptcy system somewhat self supporting was a permissible justification for the fee. Because the bankruptcy process was not essential to the exercise of any fundamental constitutional right, Congress was free to allocate access to the system on such a basis without violating either the due process or equal protection guarantees.

Similarly, the Court has upheld a system which imposed $25 filing fees for appellate court review of welfare eligibility determinations, thereby effectively precluding indigent welfare recipients from receiving judicial review of the termination of their benefits.[16] While individuals whose welfare benefits were terminated were entitled to due process, that included only a fair initial hearing. As there is no fundamental constitutional right to welfare payments, the state could impose such filing fees on all persons. The Supreme Court, however, has never determined that legislatures are totally free to commit authority to make determinations over significant rights of individuals without providing for some system of appellate or judicial review. The Court's decision upholding the state procedural system which required a filing fee for appellate review of welfare eligibility determinations might be limited by the fact that the process did not involve fundamental rights and the administrative system met all requirements for procedural fairness. If fundamental constitutional

rights were at stake in an agency proceeding, or if an administrative body with authority over nonfundamental rights did not have its discretion limited by statute or regulations, it is possible that there may be a constitutional requirement that the state provide for administrative appellate review or judicial review of the agency's decisions. The Supreme Court avoided ruling on whether there was a right to judicial review of prison disciplinary proceedings, by finding that a state court ruling establishing such a right was based on state law. In so doing, the Court noted that: "the extent to which legislatures may commit to an administrative body the unreviewable authority to make determinations implicating fundamental rights is a difficult question of constitutional law."[17]

Filing fees for causes of actions which are not essential to the exercise of fundamental rights will still be invalidated if it can be shown that they are totally irrational and can serve no purpose other than to deter suits by poor persons. Thus, in *Lindsey v. Normet*[18] the Court invalidated a requirement that tenants who wish to appeal from summary eviction proceedings post appeal bonds in twice the amount that would be required to safeguard the interests of the landlord. This double bond requirement clearly served no purpose other than to deter appeals by low income tenants and it was stricken on this basis by the Court.[19]

The Supreme Court, in *Bankers Life and Casualty Company v. Crenshaw*,[20] upheld a state statute that imposed a 15% penalty against a person who appealed unsuccessfully from a money judgment. The Supreme Court distinguished this statute from the one at issue in *Lindsey;* it found that the penalty stat-

16. Ortwein v. Schwab, 410 U.S. 656, 93 S.Ct. 1172, 35 L.Ed.2d 572 (1973), (per curiam).

17. Superintendent v. Hill, 472 U.S. 445, 450, 105 S.Ct. 2768, 2771, 86 L.Ed.2d 356 (1985). The Court made this statement in a case in which it found that the Massachusetts Supreme Judicial Court had established a right of judicial review of prison disciplinary proceedings based on state law. The Court in this case also ruled that where "good time credits" constituted a protected liberty interest, the decision to revoke those credits must be supported by "some evidence" but that courts should affirm a disci-

plinary board's findings if there was any evidence in the record to support the determination. For citations to additional Supreme Court cases on this point, see R. Rotunda & J. Nowak, Treatise on Constitutional Law: Substance and Procedure, § 17.10 (2nd ed. 1992, with annual supplements).

18. 405 U.S. 56, 92 S.Ct. 862, 31 L.Ed.2d 36 (1972).

19. 405 U.S. at 74–79, 92 S.Ct. at 874–77.

20. 486 U.S. 71, 108 S.Ct. 1645, 100 L.Ed.2d 62 (1988).

ute in *Banker's Life* was not arbitrary and irrational. The penalty statute did not single out a narrow class of parties or defendants for discriminatory treatment. The 15% penalty applied to both plaintiffs and defendants and to all money judgments, as well as to a number of other types of judgments whose money value could be determined. There was a rational relationship between the 15% penalty on unsuccessful appeals and the statute's objective of deterring frivolous appeals. Unlike the statute struck down in *Lindsey,* the statute in *Banker's Life* was not likely to discourage nonfrivolous appeals, in the view of the Supreme Court.

Judicial review of punitive damages involves both substantive and procedural constitutional issues. Procedural due process principles require that a person be given a fair process for the deprivation of life, liberty, or property; these principles may require the establishment of procedures to limit the discretion of courts or juries that award punitive damages. When the Supreme Court uses the concept of substantive due process to examine a law, including a court ruling, it is determining whether the substantive rule of law is an unconstitutional limitation of life, liberty, or property interests; substantive due process principles might be used to place a limit on the size of punitive damage awards.[21]

However, the Court also held that the state was free to create a "summary" system for eviction of tenants after non-payment of rent and preclude defenses based on landlord breaches of duty to these tenants.[22] The summary action in such a situation was held to comply with both the due process and equal protection clauses because the Court found no fundamental constitutional liberties involved in such cases. The Supreme Court has continually allowed states to create laws which rationally further governmental purposes even though they burden poor persons so long as

they do not allocate the exercise of fundamental constitutional rights on the basis of wealth.[23]

In a series of cases the Supreme Court has held that the First Amendment freedom of association prohibits states from denying individuals the right to employ an attorney to represent their group interests.[24] These cases do not establish a First Amendment right of individuals to have access to the courts for the resolution of all grievances against the government or anyone else. The ability of an individual to have access to a judicial process should be determined by due process analysis, although the First Amendment should bar some governmental limitations on the ability of individuals to advance their common good through collective action. The question of whether an individual or group is receiving fair treatment from administrative or judicial entities is one that will be best focused on by courts if they employ due process analysis. In *Walters v. National Association of Radiation Survivors,*[25] the Court upheld a federal statutory limit of $10 on the amount that a veteran, or his or her family, could pay to an attorney for representing the veteran in a Veterans Administration board hearing to determine whether or not to terminate service related disability or death benefits. The Court found that the governmental interests in keeping the board proceedings informal and insuring that the entirety of an award to a veteran or his or her family would be used for the benefit of the family (rather than for the payment of attorney's fees) outweighed any interest the individual might have in being able to secure legal representation. The nonadversarial process established by the Veterans Administration was fundamentally fair and did not involve representation of the government by an attorney; the individual interest in retention of benefits was not so great as to require a trial-

---

21. See § 10.6 (d) regarding due process issues in punitive damages cases.

22. 405 U.S. at 64–69, 92 S.Ct. at 869–72.

23. See §§ 14.25, 14.42–14.46, infra.

24. United Mine Workers v. Illinois State Bar Association, 389 U.S. 217, 88 S.Ct. 353, 19 L.Ed.2d 426 (1967);

Brotherhood of Railroad Trainmen v. Virginia ex rel. Virginia State Bar, 377 U.S. 1, 84 S.Ct. 1113, 12 L.Ed.2d 89 (1964).

25. 473 U.S. 305, 105 S.Ct. 3180, 87 L.Ed.2d 220 (1985).

type hearing. After upholding the limitation on due process grounds, the majority opinion summarily rejected the veterans' separate First Amendment claim of a right to be represented by an attorney. The majority opinion by Justice Rehnquist stated: "the foregoing analysis of appellees' due process claim focused on substantially the same question—whether the process allows a claimant to make a meaningful presentation—and we concluded that appellees had such an opportunity under the present claims process, and that significant government interests favored the limitation on 'speech' that appellees attack. Under those circumstances appellees' First Amendment claim has no independent significance."[26]

26. 473 U.S. at 335, 105 S.Ct. at 3197.

Chapter 14

EQUAL PROTECTION

§ 14.1 Introduction to Equal Protection Analysis—Application to State and Federal Acts

The Fourteenth Amendment commands that no person shall be denied equal protection of the law by any state. This clause introduced a new concept into constitutional analysis by requiring that individuals be treated in a manner similar to others as an independent constitutional guarantee. There are similar concepts in the privileges and immunities clause of Article IV, and the commerce clause requirement that states not discriminate against interstate transactions, but these relate only to state treatment of certain specific matters. The equal protection guarantee, however, governs all governmental actions which classify individuals for different benefits or burdens under the law.

In recent years the equal protection guarantee has become the single most important concept in the Constitution for the protection of individual rights. As we have seen, substantive due process analysis was disclaimed after 1937 and the Justices today are not willing to

restrict the legislative ability to deal with a subject under that analysis. And the privileges or immunities clause of the Fourteenth Amendment has never been a meaningful vehicle for the judicial review of state actions,[1] although it may have been intended to be a primary safeguard of natural law rights by the drafters of the Amendment.[2]

Instead, the Court has increasingly focused upon the concept of equal protection to guarantee that all individuals are accorded fair treatment in the exercise of fundamental rights or the elimination of distinctions based on impermissible criteria. It was not that long ago that Justice Holmes could categorize the concept of equal protection as "the last resort of constitutional arguments."[3] However, the Court now recognizes that in some circumstances the review of legislative classifications is a permissible part of the judicial function, particularly since it entails only the requirement that the government either forego an action or include within it all persons of a similar position.[4]

§ 14.1

1. The meaning of the clause was restricted to protecting very limited "national" rights in In re Slaughter-House Cases, 83 U.S. (16 Wall.) 36, 21 L.Ed. 394 (1872). In one case the Court ruled that a state statute violated this clause, but it reversed the decision within a few years. See, Colgate v. Harvey, 296 U.S. 404, 56 S.Ct. 252, 80 L.Ed. 299 (1935), overruled in Madden v. Kentucky, 309 U.S. 83, 60 S.Ct. 406, 84 L.Ed. 590 (1940). In 1999, the Supreme Court ruled that the privileges or immunities clause of the Fourteenth Amendment protected one aspect of the "right to travel," and guaranteed that newly arrived citizens in a state would be treated in the same manner as long-time state citizens. Saenz v. Roe, 526 U.S. 489, 119 S.Ct. 1518, 143 L.Ed.2d 689 (1999). The *Saenz* decision, and the right to travel are examined in § 14.38. See also, Marti Navarro v. United States, 104 F.Supp.2d 96, 98 (D.P.R.2000, Laffitte, J., of Treatise); Judge Cle-

land, citing an earlier edition of this Treatise in Olympic Arms v. Magaw, 91 F.Supp.2d 1061, 1069 (E.D.Mich.2000), judgment affirmed 301 F.3d 384 (6th Cir.2002); Justice Sawaya, citing Treatise in Westerheide v. State, 767 So.2d 637, 654 (Fla.Ct.App.2000).

2. J. tenBroek, Equal Under Law 223 (Enlarged Edition 1965); cf. James, The Framing of the Fourteenth Amendment 180 (1965). See generally § 14.7, infra.

3. Buck v. Bell, 274 U.S. 200, 208, 47 S.Ct. 584, 585, 71 L.Ed. 1000 (1927).

4. Among the cases citing this section of the Treatise are: Kelly v. Municipal Court of Marion County, et al., 852 F.Supp. 724, 736 (S.D.Ind.1994) (Barker, C.J.); Phelps v. Phelps, 337 N.C. 344, 446 S.E.2d 17, 20 (1994) (Meyer, J.), rehearing denied 337 N.C. 807, 449 S.E.2d 750 (1994); Waters, C.J., quoting Treatise, in Callaghan v. Coberly, 927 F.Supp. 332, 334 (W.D.Ark.1996); Kelley v. Board of

The equal protection guarantee applies to both the state and federal governments although the restrictions have two totally distinct bases. The equal protection clause of the Fourteenth Amendment by its own terms applies only to state and local governments.[5] There is no equal protection clause that governs the actions of the federal government, and the Court has not attempted to make the clause itself applicable to federal acts. However, if the federal government classifies individuals in a way which would violate the equal protection clause, it will be held to contravene the due process clause of the Fifth Amendment. As we shall see in the following sections, the standards for validity under the implied equal protection guarantee of the Fifth Amendment due process clause and the equal

protection clause of the Fourteenth Amendment are almost identical.[6]

The difference in the method of analysis under the due process and equal protection guarantees relates only to whether or not the governmental act classifies persons. Whenever fundamental rights are limited, the laws will have to promote an overriding or compelling interest of government in order to be valid under either clause. When the governmental action relates only to matters of economics or general social welfare, the law need only rationally relate to a legitimate governmental purpose. If the law does not classify individuals, it will be subjected to the due process guarantee. However, if the means the law employs to achieve its end is the classification of persons for differing benefits or burdens, it

---

Trustees of University of Illinois, 832 F.Supp. 237, 242 (C.D.Ill.1993) (McDade, J.), affirmed 35 F.3d 265 (7th Cir.1994), cert. denied 513 U.S. 1128, 115 S.Ct. 938, 130 L.Ed.2d 883 (1995); Clark v. Joseph, 95 Ohio App.3d 207, 211, 642 N.E.2d 36, 39 (1994) (Dickinson, J.); Miner, Cir. J., citing Treatise in Quill v. Vacco, 80 F.3d 716, 725 (2d Cir.1996), cert. granted 518 U.S. 1055, 117 S.Ct. 36, 135 L.Ed.2d 1127 (1996); DiClerico, Jr., C.J., citing Treatise, in Cross v. Cunningham, 87 F.3d 586, 589 (1st Cir.1996); Thomas, J., citing Treatise in Garton v. State, 910 P.2d 1348, 1355 (Wyo.1996); Lohr, J., (dissenting/concurring) quoting Treatise, in People v. Black, 915 P.2d 1257, 1266 (Colo.1996), rehearing denied (1996); Pope, P.J., citing Treatise, in State v. Babel, 220 Ga.App. 130, 132, 469 S.E.2d 203, 205 (1996), reconsideration denied (1996), cert. denied (1996); Spindon, P.J., citing Treatise in Longview of St. Joseph v. City of St. Joseph, 918 S.W.2d 364, 371 (Mo.App.1996); Rosen, District J., citing Treatise in Kevorkian v. Thompson, 947 F.Supp. 1152, 1172 (E.D.Mich.1997); Freeman, J., citing Treatise in People v. Warren, 173 Ill.2d 348, 219 Ill.Dec. 533, 541, 671 N.E.2d 700, 708 (Ill. 1996); Albritton, J., citing Treatise in Baker v. City of Alexander City, 973 F.Supp. 1370 (M.D.Ala. 1997); Komives, Magistrate J., citing Treatise in Wall v. Cherrydale Farms, Inc., 9 F.Supp.2d 784 (E.D.Mich.1998); Duff, J., citing Treatise in Richardson v. Barr, 1994 WL 630817, *4 (N.D.Ill.1994); Kane, J., quoting Treatise in, Hassan v. Wright, 45 F.3d 1063, 1068 (7th Cir.1995), cert. denied 516 U.S. 842, 116 S.Ct. 128, 133 L.Ed.2d 77 (1995); Miller, J., quoting Treatise in, Miami Nation of Indians of Indiana, Inc. v. Babbitt, 887 F.Supp. 1158, 1176 (N.D.Ind. 1995); Nahra, J., quoting Treatise in, State Employment Relations Bd. v. City of Cleveland, 106 Ohio App.3d 128, 665 N.E.2d 693, 698 (1995); Neely, J., quoting Treatise in, Kyriazis v. University of West Virginia, 192 W.Va. 60, 67, 450 S.E.2d 649, 656, 95 Ed. Law Rep. 1102 (1994); Casebolt, J., citing Treatise in, People In Interest of C.G., 885 P.2d 355, 358 (Colo.App.1994); Crane v. Logli, No. 91 CV 20060, 1992 WL 70337, *2 (N.D.Ill.1992) (Reinhard, J.); Burch v. Sheffield-Sheffield Lake City School Dist. Bd. of Educ., No. 1:92CV2368, 1993 WL 414667, *5 (N.D.Ohio

1993) (Aldrich, J.); Kenneally v. Medical Bd. of California, 27 Cal.App.4th 489, 32 Cal.Rptr.2d 504, 507 (1994) (Grignon, J.); Godbold, Senior Cir.J., citing Treatise, in Shahar v. Bowers, 70 F.3d 1218, 1226 (11th Cir.1995), rehearing granted and opinion vacated 78 F.3d 499 (11th Cir.1996); Lohr, J., (dissenting, in part, and concurring, in part) citing Treatise, in People v. Black, 915 P.2d 1257, 1265 (Colo.1996), reh'g denied (1996); Dauphinot, J., concurring and dissenting, citing Treatise in Schleuter v. City of Fort Worth, 947 S.W.2d 920, 934 (Tex.App.1997); Gerrard, J., concurring and citing Treatise in State v. Champoux, 252 Neb. 769, 566 N.W.2d 763, 769 (Neb. 1997); Boudin, Circuit J., citing Treatise in Berthiaume v. Caron, 142 F.3d 12 (1st Cir.1998); Kinneary, District Judge, citing Treatise in Berridge v. Heiser, 993 F.Supp. 1136 (S.D.Ohio 1997); Albritton, District Judge, citing Treatise in Baker v. City of Alexander City, 973 F.Supp. 1370 (M.D.Ala.1997); Barker, Chief J., citing Treatise in Gillespie v. City of Indianapolis, 13 F.Supp.2d 811 (S.D.Ind.1998); Hall, J., citing Treatise in, Police Association of New Orleans v. City of New Orleans, 649 So.2d 951, 961 (La.1995); Abrahamson, J., citing Treatise in, Doering v. WEA Ins. Group, 193 Wis.2d 118, 532 N.W.2d 432, 436 n. 9 (1995). Flores, J., citing Treatise in Duarte v. Arizona ex rel. Lewis, 193 Ariz. 167, 169, 971 P.2d 214, 216 (Ariz.Ct.App.1998); Supreme Court of Montana, citing Treatise in Roosevelt v. Montana Department of Revenue, 293 Mont. 240, 975 P.2d 295, 303 (Montana 1999).

5. "No State shall . . .; nor deny to any person within its jurisdiction the equal protection of the laws." U.S.Const. amend. XIV, § 1.

6. See, e.g., Bolling v. Sharpe, 347 U.S. 497, 74 S.Ct. 693, 98 L.Ed. 884 (1954); Weinberger v. Wiesenfeld, 420 U.S. 636, 638 n. 2, 95 S.Ct. 1225, 1228 n. 2, 43 L.Ed.2d 514 (1975); Schlesinger v. Ballard, 419 U.S. 498, 500 n. 3, 95 S.Ct. 572, 574 n. 3, 42 L.Ed.2d 610 (1975). The Court may subject federal laws which burden aliens as a class to a more lenient standard of review because of unique federal interests in this area. See, §§ 14.11–14.13, infra.

will be tested under the equal protection guarantee.

If the classification does not meet the appropriate standard of review, then the legislation has failed to have a sufficient relationship to the required governmental purpose. A law which violates this concept also denies the individuals classified due process of law because the means employed by the government do not relate to a compelling to legitimate end of government. Thus, federal classifications in the area of fundamental rights or suspect classifications which do not promote a compelling governmental interest violate the due process clause.[7] Similarly, a federal law in the implied area of economics or social welfare which classifies persons will be upheld under the equal protection guarantee which is part of the due process clause so long as the law rationally relates to a legitimate governmental purpose.[8] Federal laws are therefore tested under the same standards as state laws and we will refer to both tests under the term "equal protection guarantee." It must be remembered, however, that classifications established by federal law are reviewed under the implied equal protection guarantee of the Fifth Amendment due process clause.

In the following two sections we will briefly introduce the basic concepts of classification and standards for judicial review that emanate from the equal protection guarantee.[9] For those seeking a more extensive introduction to the equal protection concept we strongly recommend the article "The Equal Protection of the Laws" by Joseph Tussman and Jacobus tenBroek.[10] Although written in 1949, that article contains a description of equal protection analysis that courts employ today.

§ 14.2 Government Classifications and the Concept of Equal Protection

The equal protection clause guarantees that similar individuals will be dealt with in a similar manner by the government. It does not reject the government's ability to classify persons or "draw lines" in the creation and application of laws, but it does guarantee that those classifications will not be based upon impermissible criteria or arbitrarily used to burden a group of individuals. If the government classification relates to a proper governmental purpose, then the classification will be upheld. Such a classification does not violate the guarantee when it distinguishes persons as "dissimilar" upon some permissible basis in order to advance the legitimate interests of society. Those who are treated less favorably by the legislation are not denied equal protection of the law because they are not similarly situated to those who receive the benefit of the legislative classification.

The equal protection guarantee has nothing to do with the determination of whether a specific individual is properly placed within a classification. Equal protection tests whether the classification is properly drawn. It is the guarantee of procedural due process that determines what process is necessary to find that an individual falls within or outside of a specific classification.[1] Equal protection deals with legislative line drawing; procedural due process deals with the adjudication of individual claims.

However, it is incorrect to say that equal protection has nothing to do with the application of a law. Some legislative acts will have,

7. See, e.g., Bolling v. Sharpe, 347 U.S. 497, 74 S.Ct. 693, 98 L.Ed. 884 (1954) (segregated schools in District of Columbia). The congruence of the equal protection guarantee of the Fifth Amendment due process clause and the Fourteenth Amendment equal protection clause was first clearly established in Bolling v. Sharpe, 347 U.S. 497, 74 S.Ct. 693, 98 L.Ed. 884 (1954). In the 1980s and early 1990s it was unclear whether the Court would apply the strict scrutiny test to examine federal classifications that involved a benign use of racial or ethnic traits (so-called affirmative action). In 1995, the Supreme Court ruled that strict judicial scrutiny (the compelling interest test) should be used to examine even benign uses of race classifications by the federal government. Adarand Constructors, Inc. v.

Pena, 515 U.S. 200, 115 S.Ct. 2097, 132 L.Ed.2d 158 (1995). The subject of benign racial classifications is examined in § 14.10 of this Treatise.

8. See, e.g., United States v. Kras, 409 U.S. 434, 93 S.Ct. 631, 34 L.Ed.2d 626 (1973) (bankruptcy fees and access to courts).

9. See §§ 14.2, 14.3, infra.

10. Tussman and tenBroek, The Equal Protection of the Laws, 37 Calif.L.Rev. 341 (1949).

§ 14.2

1. See §§ 13.7–13.9, supra.

by their own terms, a classification which is to be tested under the equal protection guarantee. The Court will then determine whether the law is valid "on its face." In some instances this judicial review will involve a further inquiry into the nature of the legislative classification and its purpose and effect. For example, a zoning ordinance may be found to constitute a racial classification if, but only if, it can be proven that the purpose and effect of the ordinance is the exclusion of members of a racial minority from a residential area.[2]

In other situations a law may have no impermissible classification by its own terms but it may be applied in such a way as to create a classification. Then the Court will test the law "in its application" to determine whether the classification established by administrative actions is permissible. For example, a law which eliminated the use of wooden buildings for hand laundries was found to constitute a racial classification in its administration when all Chinese persons owning such laundries were forced to give up their businesses while all non-oriental persons who had similar laundries were granted exemptions from the prohibition.[3] Again, it should be noted that, in these cases, equal protection is used to determine whether the classification established by the administrative acts is permissible and not whether a given individual falls within the terms of the classification.[4]

Equal protection is the guarantee that similar people will be dealt with in a similar manner.[5] In reviewing any classification it must be determined whether or not the persons classified by the law for different treatment are in fact "dissimilar." The question

relates to the bases upon which the government can distinguish between individuals in society. There is no requirement that government follow natural classifications and it may subdivide persons as it deems proper for the advancement of legitimate governmental purposes.

Conversely, classifications are not tested by whether or not the individuals are truly different in some absolute sense from those who receive different treatment. For example, it is undeniably true that men and women are biologically different. However that difference does not mean that gender-based classifications will be generally upheld, for most often there is no difference between men and women in terms of the promotion of a legitimate governmental end. Thus, sex cannot be the basis for determining whether an individual is able to be the executor of an estate[6] or mature enough to drink alcoholic beverages.[7]

Usually one must look to the end or purpose of the legislation in order to determine whether persons are similarly situated in terms of that governmental system.[8] The judiciary need not always review the permissibility of the legislative purpose, but it must decide what is the end of the legislation to be tested. Once a court has found an end of government which does not in itself violate the Constitution, it can analyze the way in which the government has classified persons in terms of that end.

Classifications can relate to government "ends" in any one of five ways,[9] any one of which may be determined to be constitutional or unconstitutional depending on the nature of

---

2. Arlington Heights v. Metropolitan Housing Development Corp., 429 U.S. 252, 97 S.Ct. 555, 50 L.Ed.2d 450 (1977).

3. Yick Wo v. Hopkins, 118 U.S. 356, 6 S.Ct. 1064, 30 L.Ed. 220 (1886).

4. The problems of "proving" the existence of a classification are examined in § 14.4, infra.

5. Souter, J., citing this Treatise in Connecticut Dept. of Public Safety v. Doe, 538 U.S. 1, 9, 123 S.Ct. 1160, 1165, 155 L.Ed.2d 98 (2003) (Souter, J., joined by Ginsburg, J.); see generally, Burnett, J., citing Treatise in In re Treatment and Care of Luckabaugh, 351 S.C. 122, 147, 568 S.E.2d 338, 351 (2002); Wiese, J., citing Treatise in, Alvin v. United States, 50 Fed. Cl. 295, 298 (2001); Laffite,

C.J., quoting Treatise in, Marti Navarro v. United States, 104 F.Supp.2d 96, 102 (D.P.R.2000); Mathias, J., quoting Treatise in, Phelps v. Sybinsky, 736 N.E.2d 809, 818 (Ind.Ct.App.2000). Tussman and tenBroek, The Equal Protection of the Laws, 37 Calif.L.Rev. 341 (1949).

6. Reed v. Reed, 404 U.S. 71, 92 S.Ct. 251, 30 L.Ed.2d 225 (1971).

7. Craig v. Boren, 429 U.S. 190, 97 S.Ct. 451, 50 L.Ed.2d 397 (1976).

8. Tussman and tenBroek, supra note 5 at 367.

9. For further analysis of these possible relationships, see Tussman and tenBroek, supra note 5.

the legislation in the specific case. First, the classification could be perfect in that it treats all similar persons in a similar manner. Second, the classification could be totally imperfect in that it selects exactly the wrong class for a burden or a benefit while excluding the class of persons who do relate to the legitimate purpose of the statute. Third, the classification can be under-inclusive in that it includes a small number of persons who fit the purpose of the statute but excludes some who are similarly situated. Fourth, the classification can be over-inclusive in that it treats in a similar manner not only those persons whose characteristics similarly relate to the purpose of the law but also some additional persons who do not share the legitimately distinguishing characteristic. Fifth, there can be a mixed relation of over- and under-inclusions. Some examples should help to clarify this breakdown of classifications.

The perfect classification involves the legislative use of a classifying trait which exactly fits the purpose of law and treats all similar people in a similar manner. On the other hand, a perfectly bad classification benefits a classification of persons who have no relationship to the legitimate purpose of the statute. Neither such relationship is likely to exist, for perfect line drawing, be it good or bad, is a rarity. We may best analyze classifications in terms of the difficult burden of trying to prove such a relationship.

For example, let us assume that a state government passes a law which allows men but not women to be bartenders. We will assume that the permissible purposes of the law are to have efficient bartenders and to avoid disturbances of the peace in establishments serving alcohol. The legislative classification would be perfect if it could be proven that all men would be good bartenders who would maintain discipline and that women bartenders always caused inefficient service or disturbances of the peace. The classification would be perfectly bad if it could be shown that all women made excellent bartenders but

that male bartenders always caused inefficiency or disturbances of the peace.

Under–Inclusive Laws. An under-inclusive classification contains all similarly situated people but excludes some people who are similar to them in terms of the purpose of the law.[10] To return to our bartender example, the law could be construed as an under-inclusive burden if it were found that no women would be good bartenders and that only some men would be good bartenders. In this situation all the women are similarly situated but a similar group of men is excluded from the imposition of the burden. The same law might be deemed an under-inclusive benefit if it could be shown that some women would not make good bartenders but that all men and some women would provide efficient and peaceful service. In this situation the law is under-inclusive because it fails to extend the benefit of a bartender's license to women who are similar in their abilities as bartenders to the men who receive the license.

Over–Inclusive Laws. A law may be said to be over-inclusive when the legislative classification includes all persons who are similarly situated in terms of the law plus an additional group of persons. In our bartender example the law could be construed as an over-inclusive burden if it could be proven that all men and some women made good bartenders but that a sub-group of women could not be efficient bartenders or gave rise to disturbances of the peace. The law would be over-inclusive because it burdened not only the group of women who would be bad bartenders but also those who would provide efficient service and avoid disturbances of the peace. Note that the same law might be construed as an over-inclusive benefit if it was shown that only a small group of men could give efficient bartender service and maintain the peace in these establishments. Were that the case, the law would be over-inclusive as a benefit measure because it gave the benefit of a bartenders license to not only qualified men but to all men.

10. Barnhorst v. Missouri State High School Activities Ass'n, 504 F.Supp. 449, 459 (W.D.Mo.1980) (Clark, D.J., quoting an earlier edition of this treatise).

Laws That Are Both Under– and Over– Inclusive. Many classifications can be said to be a mix of both over- and under-inclusions. The ease with which we could change labels by viewing the statute as one dispensing benefits or burdens in our bartenders example should highlight the fact that many classifications can have this mixed quality. Thus, in our bartenders example, it would be easiest to construe the statute as being both under- and over-inclusive, because some women and some men make good bartenders while some women and some men cannot give efficient service or control discipline within the establishments. In other words, we cannot identify the class of persons who will promote the end of the statute by the characteristic of gender. Thus, it can be said that men and women are similarly situated in terms of their abilities to be bartenders.[11]

It is important to analyze classifications in terms of their relationship to the legitimate purposes of the statute. This analysis will be the basis for determining whether the classification has a sufficient relationship to a proper governmental purpose so as to withstand a challenge under the equal protection guarantee. However, the labeling of a classification as over-inclusive or under-inclusive will not establish its compatibility with the equal protection clause.

It is sometimes said that under-inclusive burdens are not reviewed as strictly by the Court because those burdened by the classification are properly identified as deserving the burden or regulation[12] and that the legislature may seek to solve social problems "one step at a time."[13] As the foregoing examples should demonstrate, almost any classification can be alternatively analyzed as over or under-inclusive depending on one's view of the statutory

system and the facts developed in the course of a challenge to the statute. Very few classifications will be either a perfect promotion of an articulated governmental purpose or a clearly irrational mismatch of classifications with ends. The key factor in reviewing classifications is the degree of correlation between the means and the ends that is required by the judiciary and the extent to which the judiciary will analyze the permissible purposes of the legislation.

If under-inclusive classifications are usually upheld it is because they tend to appear in general as "economic" or "social welfare" regulations where the Court does not require the legislature to demonstrate a very close relationship between its classifications and the purposes of the statute. It was on this basis that the Supreme Court upheld a law which excluded some women from being bartenders in a case very close to our example.[14] Thus a key factor becomes the standard under which the Justices will review the permissibility of the government ends and the degree of relationship between the classification and these ends.

§ 14.3   An Introduction to Standards of Review Under the Equal Protection Guarantee

(a) Overview

As should be clear from the problem examined in the previous section, the degree to which a classification can be said to meet the equal protection guarantee depends on the purpose that one attributes to the legislative act and the determination of whether there is a sufficient degree of relationship between the asserted governmental end and the classification. It is rare that a classification is so

---

11. The Court in fact upheld a law which denied bartenders licenses to all women except the wives or daughters of male owners of bars. Goesaert v. Cleary, 335 U.S. 464, 69 S.Ct. 198, 93 L.Ed. 163 (1948).

The modern Court would not reaffirm *Goesaert* today. See Craig v. Boren, 429 U.S. 190, 210 n. 23, 97 S.Ct. 451, 463 n. 23, 50 L.Ed.2d 397 (1976). For an analysis of the varying degree of strictness with which the Court has reviewed sex-based classifications, see §§ 14.20–14.24, infra.

12. See, Developments in the Law Equal Protection, 82 Harv.L.Rev. 1065, 1084–86 (1969).

13. Williamson v. Lee Optical, 348 U.S. 483, 489, 75 S.Ct. 461, 465, 99 L.Ed. 563 (1955).

14. Goesaert v. Cleary, 335 U.S. 464, 69 S.Ct. 198, 93 L.Ed. 163 (1948). See §§ 14.20–14.24, infra. See also, Craig v. Boren, 429 U.S. 190, 210 n. 23, 97 S.Ct. 451, 463 n. 23, 50 L.Ed.2d 397 (1976) (disapproving *Goesaert* as improper gender-based classification).

artfully drawn that it can be said to promote perfectly any but the most peculiar or narrowly defined ends. Thus the ultimate conclusion as to whether a classification meets the equal protection guarantee in large measure depends upon the degree of independent review exercised by the judiciary over the legislative line-drawing in the establishment of the classification.

To the extent that the Court defers to the legislature's choice of goals or its determination of whether the classification relates to those goals, the Justices have in fact taken the position that it is the function of the legislature, rather than the judiciary, to make the equal protection determination as to the particular law. To the extent that the Justices independently determine whether the law has a purpose which conforms to the Constitution and whether the classification in fact relates to that purpose, the Justices are taking the position that the Court is able to assess these issues in a manner superior to, or at least different from, the determination of the legislature. Thus, the Court must decide whether it will engage in any realistic scrutiny of legislative classifications, and thereby assume the power to override democratic process, or whether, by deferring to that process, it will limit the concept of a unique judicial function.[1]

The Court's institutional decision as to the degree of unique judicial function and the amount of deference that should be paid to legislative policy decisions in equal protection issues has mirrored that made in terms of substantive due process. As we have seen in Chapter Eleven, the Court from 1887 to 1937 used both the equal protection and due process clauses to invalidate those forms of social welfare or economic legislation with which the Justices were in fundamental disagreement.[2] The Justices did not defer to legislative decisions but, instead, independently determined what ends the government might pursue in conformity with their view of the role of government in a free economy.

When the Court renounced the theory of substantive due process, it also rejected the claim to an institutional ability to determine the reasonableness of classifications when reviewing laws under the equal protection guarantee.[3] However, as we noted in Chapter Eleven, the Court did not at this time reject its function of protecting interests that the Justices believed were fundamental constitutional values.[4]

Thus, in the post 1937 period we have had a dichotomy between the judicial review of classifications employed in economic and general social welfare regulation and review of classifications that either touch upon fundamental constitutional values or use a criterion for classification which itself violates a fundamental constitutional value. Classifications of the first type will be upheld so long as they arguably relate to a legitimate function of government. Classifications of the second type, however, will be subjected to independent judicial review, which means that the Court will not give great deference to the legislature in those cases. When the Supreme Court examines the constitutionality of a governmental classification the methods of analysis the Justices use are referred to as equal protection "standards of review."

It is possible to rationalize all equal protection decisions as judicial determinations of whether the government has fairly classified persons and argue that there is only one equal protection standard of review. However, such an argument fails to recognize that the Supreme Court Justices perform quite different functions when they: (1) virtually prohibit governmental use of some classifications, (such as racial classifications); (2) independently examine the reasonableness and legitimacy of some classifications (such as gender classifications); and (3) presume that the use of some classifications is within the constitutional prerogative of the legislature (such as classifica-

---

§ 14.3

1. Tussman and tenBroek, The Equal Protection of the Laws, 37 Calif.L.Rev. 341, 366 (1949).

2. See § 11.3, supra.

3. See § 11.4, supra.

4. See §§ 11.4–11.7, supra.

tions relating to economic or social welfare matters).

There appear to be at least three standards of review that may be employed in equal protection decisions.

The Rational Relationship Test. The first standard of review is the rational relationship test which in Chapter 11 we saw developed for use in both equal protection and substantive due process issues in the post 1937 decisions of the Court. The Court will not grant any significant review of legislative decisions to classify persons in terms of general economic legislation. In this area the Justices have determined that they have no unique function to perform; they have no institutional capability to assess the scope of legitimate governmental ends in these areas or the reasonableness of classifications that is in any way superior to that of the legislature. Thus, if a classification is of this type the Court will ask only whether it is conceivable that the classification bears a rational relationship to an end of government which is not prohibited by the Constitution. So long as it is arguable that the other branch of government had such a basis for creating the classification a court should not invalidate the law.[5]

The Strict Scrutiny Test. The second type of review under the equal protection guarantee is generally referred to as "strict scrutiny". This test means that the Justices will not defer to the decision of the other branches of government but will instead independently determine the degree of relationship which the classification bears to a constitutionally compelling end. The Court will not accept every permissible government purpose as sufficient to support a classification under this test, but will instead require the government to show that it is pursuing a "compelling" or "overriding" end.

Even if the government can demonstrate such an end, the Court will not uphold the classification unless the Justices have independently reached the conclusion that the classification is necessary, or narrowly tailored, to promote that compelling interest. Although absolute necessity might not be required, the Justices will require the government to show a close relationship between the classification and promotion of a compelling or overriding interest. If the Justices are of the opinion that the classification need not be employed to achieve such an end, the law will be held to violate the equal protection guarantee.

Under the due process guarantee, the Court often employs the strict scrutiny compelling interest test in reviewing legislation which limits fundamental constitutional rights. However the Court will also use this standard of review under the equal protection guarantee in two categories of civil liberties cases: first, when the governmental act classifies people in terms of their ability to exercise a fundamental right; second, when the governmental classification distinguishes between persons, in terms of any right, upon some "suspect" basis.[6]

---

5. In Pennell v. City of San Jose, 485 U.S. 1, 108 S.Ct. 849, 99 L.Ed.2d 1 (1988) the Supreme Court upheld a rent control ordinance that allowed landlords to raise rents up to 8% but that gave tenants a right to object to rent increases beyond 8%. The Supreme Court found that the contention that the tenant hardship provision might constitute a taking of property by denying the property owner a reasonable return on his investment in the property was premature because there was no indication that any landlord had ever had a rent increase reduced below the figure that it would have been set at on the basis of the objective factors due to tenant hardship. The Court also rejected due process and equal protection attacks on this rent control statute. The majority opinion found that a state rent control regulation should be upheld under the due process clause so long as it was not "arbitrary, discriminatory, or demonstrably irrelevant to the policy the legislature is free to adopt." The ordinance would survive equal

protection so long as it was "rationally related to a legitimate state interest."

6. Justice Stone set forth the rationale for meaningful judicial review in these cases in 1938. United States v. Carolene Products Co., 304 U.S. 144, 152 n. 4, 58 S.Ct. 778, 783–84 n. 4, 82 L.Ed. 1234 (1938):

4. "There may be narrower scope for operation of the presumption of constitutionality when legislation appears on its face to be within a specific prohibition of the Constitution, such as those of the first Ten Amendments, which are deemed equally specific when held to be embraced within the Fourteenth....

"It is unnecessary to consider now whether legislation which restricts those political processes which can ordinarily be expected to bring about repeal of undesirable legislation, is to be subjected to more exacting judicial scrutiny under the general prohibitions of the Four-

Because equal protection problems involve classifications rather than the limitations of rights for all persons, the Court is sometimes called upon to exercise strict scrutiny of legislation because of the classifying traits employed by the legislature rather than the nature of the right touched upon by the legislative act. However, the Supreme Court will not strictly scrutinize all legislative classifications of persons for that would merely return to the pre-1937 general review of economic and social welfare legislation. The Court will only employ the strict scrutiny standard to review the legitimacy of classifications when they are based upon a trait which itself seems to contravene established constitutional principles so that any use of the classification may be deemed "suspect".[7]

Due to the Justices' views of the history and purpose of the Fourteenth Amendment, laws that classify persons on the basis of either their status as a member of a racial minority or on the basis of their national origin (ancestry) will be deemed suspect and subject to this strict standard of review.[8] Between 1980 and 1990, the Supreme Court appeared to use the intermediate standard to review the constitutionality of federal racial affirmative action programs.[9] During this time, the Court was using strict scrutiny (the compelling interest test) to review all state and local race classifications, regardless of whether they benefitted or harmed racial minorities.[10] In 1995, the Supreme Court ruled that the benign use of

racial classifications by the federal government had to be subjected to the strict scrutiny test and would not be upheld unless the racial classification was narrowly tailored to a compelling interest.[11]

The Court has also held that state or local laws which classify persons in terms of alienage, by treating resident aliens less favorably than citizens, will be deemed suspect and subject to this test. However, the test does not seem to be enforced quite as strictly in terms of the review of these classifications.[12]

The Intermediate Test. At the close of the 1960's it was still possible to do a detailed analysis of all Supreme Court equal protection decisions in terms of a "two-tiered" model involving recognition of only the two previously described standards of review.[13]

During the last third of the twentieth century, the Supreme Court adopted an intermediate standard of review that is not as difficult for the government to meet as the compelling interest test, but which involves far less deference to the legislature than does the rationality test. Under the intermediate standard of review, the Justices will not uphold a classification unless they find that the classification has a "substantial relationship" to an "important" government interest. The Supreme Court has used this intermediate standard of review in cases involving gender classifications and cases involving illegitimacy classifications.[14]

---

teenth Amendment than are most other types of legislation. . . .

"Nor need we enquire . . . whether prejudice against discrete and insular minorities may be a special condition, which tends seriously to curtail the operation of those political processes ordinarily to be relied upon to protect minorities, and which may call for a correspondingly more searching judicial inquiry. . . ."

7. The phrase originated in Toyosaburo Korematsu v. United States, 323 U.S. 214, 216, 65 S.Ct. 193, 194, 89 L.Ed. 194 (1944).

See, Brest, Foreword: In Defense of the Antidiscrimination Principle, 90 Harv.L.Rev. 1, 7 n. 35 (1976).

8. See, §§ 14.5–14.10, infra.

9. See Fullilove v. Klutznick, 448 U.S. 448, 100 S.Ct. 2758, 65 L.Ed.2d 902 (1980). Metro Broadcasting, Inc. v. Federal Communications Commission, 497 U.S. 547, 110 S.Ct. 2997, 111 L.Ed.2d 445 (1990), rehearing denied 497 U.S. 1050, 111 S.Ct. 15, 111 L.Ed.2d 829 (1990). In *Metro Broadcasting,* the Court specifically used the intermediate

standard of review but *Metro Broadcasting* was overruled by the Supreme Court in Adarand Constructors, Inc. v. Pena, 515 U.S. 200, 115 S.Ct. 2097, 132 L.Ed.2d 158 (1995). These cases are discussed in § 14.10 of this Treatise.

10. Richmond v. J.A. Croson Co., 488 U.S. 469, 109 S.Ct. 706, 102 L.Ed.2d 854 (1989).

11. Adarand Constructors, Inc. v. Pena, 515 U.S. 200, 115 S.Ct. 2097, 132 L.Ed.2d 158 (1995). See § 14.10.

12. See § 14.12, infra.

13. For citations to additional cases, including lower court cases see R. Rotunda & J. Nowak, Treatise on Constitutional Law: Substance and Procedure (1999, with supp.).

14. See §§ 14.20–14.24 regarding the judicial review of gender classifications. See §§ 14.14–14.19 regarding the review of illegitimacy classifications.

In one case the Justices appeared to use the intermediate standard of review to invalidate a state law that denied all government funded education, including grade school and high school education, to children who lived in the state but who could not demonstrate that they were in the United States lawfully.[15] However, the standard used by the Supreme Court in the undocumented children's case is not clearly stated in the majority opinion. The Supreme Court at times has described classifications based upon United States citizenship as "suspect" but has failed to employ the compelling interest test in some alienage cases.[16]

The Supreme Court in recent years appears to have altered the standard of review for laws regulating the exercise of fundamental constitutional rights.   The identification of a right as "fundamental" is a substantive decision unrelated to equal protection or technical standards of review.[17] The judicial review of a classification in a law regulating or restricting a fundamental right involves equal protection analysis. The Court in the 1960's and early 1970's indicated that laws making differentiations between persons exercising fundamental rights would be subject to strict judicial scrutiny and would not be upheld unless the government could demonstrate that it was necessary for it to use the classification in order to promote a compelling interest.[18]

Although some majority opinions continue to invoke strict scrutiny—compelling interest language in fundamental rights cases, it has been common for the Court to decide fundamental rights cases without stating a clear standard of review.[19] For example, the Court has found the right to vote to be fundamental but has in some cases upheld regulations of voting rights or the rights of candidates without requiring that the government formally demonstrate a compelling interest.[20] In those cases the Justices seem to exercise independent judicial review in order to insure that the regulation of the voting process reasonably promotes important ends (such as the governmental interest in running efficient and honest elections) and does not unreasonably restrict the voting rights of any class of individuals. This would appear to involve a middle-level standard of review which neither prohibits all regulation of the right to vote nor presumes that the government is free to limit voting rights as it would be under the traditional rational basis standard of review. The Court has ruled that any severe deprivation of voting rights is subject to the requirement that the state law be narrowly tailored to promote a compelling interest, but limited burdens on voters' rights might be justified by a variety of important interests.[21]

---

15. Plyler v. Doe, 457 U.S. 202, 102 S.Ct. 2382, 72 L.Ed.2d 786 (1982). This case is analyzed in § 14.13.

16. See §§ 14.11–14.13, infra.

17. This decision involves a judicial determination that the text or structure of the Constitution evidences the existence of a value that should be taken from the control of the political branches of government. The decision is one that can be best characterized as a substantive due process decision because it involves judicial protection of a substantive value and a limitation in the substance of laws or regulations which restrict that value or right. Most fundamental rights cases involve equal protection rulings because the cases involve review of laws which classify persons and impose differing restrictions on the ability of those classifications of person to exercise a fundamental right. See §§ 11.4–11.7, supra. For citations to secondary sources on this topic see, R. Rotunda & J. Nowak, Treatise on Constitutional Law: Substance and Procedure, vol. 3 § 18.3 (3rd ed. 1999, with annual supplements).

18. See, e.g., Loving v. Virginia, 388 U.S. 1, 87 S.Ct. 1817, 18 L.Ed.2d 1010 (1967) (marriage); Kramer v. Union Free School District, 395 U.S. 621, 89 S.Ct. 1886, 23 L.Ed.2d 583 (1969) (voting); Shapiro v. Thompson, 394

U.S. 618, 89 S.Ct. 1322, 22 L.Ed.2d 600 (1969) (interstate travel); Dunn v. Blumstein, 405 U.S. 330, 92 S.Ct. 995, 31 L.Ed.2d 274 (1972) (travel and voting).

19. See, e.g., Zablocki v. Redhail, 434 U.S. 374, 98 S.Ct. 673, 54 L.Ed.2d 618 (1978) (restrictions of marriage—examined in §§ 14.26–14.30, infra). Zobel v. Williams, 457 U.S. 55, 102 S.Ct. 2309, 72 L.Ed.2d 672 (1982) (right to travel—examined in §§ 14.37, 14.38, infra).

20. The voting and candidates' rights cases are examined in §§ 14.31–14.33, infra. See, e.g., Ball v. James, 451 U.S. 355, 101 S.Ct. 1811, 68 L.Ed.2d 150 (1981) (limitation on voting for election of limited purpose governmental unit upheld); Clements v. Fashing, 457 U.S. 957, 102 S.Ct. 2836, 73 L.Ed.2d 508 (1982) (limitation on candidacy for a governmental office of persons who hold a different public office upheld).

21. A clear example of the Court's use of a balancing test in voting rights cases is Burdick v. Takushi, 504 U.S. 428, 112 S.Ct. 2059, 119 L.Ed.2d 245 (1992) in which the Court upheld the State of Hawaii's prohibition on write-in voting. See § 14.31 of this Treatise regarding that case and basic voting rights issues.

It is possible that the Supreme Court is using a balancing test in fundamental rights cases that cannot be easily described in terms of one of the formal standards of review (the compelling interest test, the intermediate test, or the rationality test). If the Supreme Court were using a balancing approach in fundamental rights cases, it would first determine whether the right was fundamental by examining the concept of "liberty," which is a part of the due process clauses of the fifth and Fourteenth Amendments. If the right regulated by the state was deemed to be a fundamental aspect of liberty and, therefore, a fundamental right, the Court would balance the degree to which that right was impaired by the government regulation against the societal interests that were promoted by the government action. In other words, if a classification made it difficult for some group of people to exercise a fundamental right, the Court would weigh the burden on that group's fundamental right against the societal interests promoted by the law in which the classification was contained.

22. Planned Parenthood of Southeastern Pennsylvania v. Casey, 505 U.S. 833, 112 S.Ct. 2791, 120 L.Ed.2d 674 (1992), on remand 978 F.2d 74 (3d Cir.1992). Issues regarding abortions are examined in § 14.29 of this Treatise.

23. See §§ 14.37, 14.38, infra.

24. **Prisoners' Rights Cases.** The Supreme Court has established a separate standard of review for the judicial examination of laws or regulations that restrict the exercise of fundamental constitutional rights by prison inmates. The Court has found that such laws or regulations should be upheld so long as they are reasonably related to a legitimate penological interest. Turner v. Safley, 482 U.S. 78, 107 S.Ct. 2254, 96 L.Ed.2d 64 (1987). This standard of review involves a case-by-case analysis of whether the law in fact promotes legitimate penological interests; the existence of alternative means to promote the same interest may influence a court's decision on the legitimacy of such a regulation. For example, in Turner the Supreme Court invalidated a regulation that virtually prohibited all marriages between inmates or between inmates and persons who were not prisoners. Prisoners were not allowed to marry without the approval of prison authorities, which could be granted for compelling reasons. The Court found that there were a variety of alternative ways to promote the legitimate interests in prison security and rehabilitation without imposing a virtual prohibition of a prisoner's ability to enter a marriage relationship.

In *Turner*, the Supreme Court upheld a prison regulation that significantly restricted the ability of prisoners to mail information to each other because it found that the

The Court has come close to adopting a balancing approach in recent abortion rights cases. A plurality of the Justices have said that they will determine the constitutionality of an abortion regulation by inquiring as to whether the regulation imposes "an undue burden" on a woman's freedom of choice to have an abortion, which a majority of the Court agrees is a fundamental right.[22]

Similarly, the Supreme Court sometimes invokes the compelling interest test when it examines laws that restrict the ability of some persons to migrate from one state to another but in other cases it has upheld laws imposing some burden on the right to interstate travel without requiring that the government demonstrate that such laws were necessary to promote a compelling interest.[23]

The Court has adopted a special standard of review (which is a type of intermediate test) for the review of laws or regulations that restrict the rights of prisoners.[24]

Summary. As noted in the previous paragraphs, the Supreme Court has formally

regulation was a reasonable means of protecting prison security. See also, O'Lone v. Estate of Shabazz, 482 U.S. 342, 107 S.Ct. 2400, 96 L.Ed.2d 282 (1987), on remand 829 F.2d 32 (3d Cir.1987) (applying this standard and upholding a prison work regulation that interfered with a class of prisoners ability to attend religious services). In Shaw v. Murphy, 532 U.S. 223, 121 S.Ct. 1475, 149 L.Ed.2d 420 (2001). The Court employed the *Turner* standard to find that a prisoner does not have a First Amendment right to provide legal assistance to other inmates of a penal facility. See also Overton v. Bazzetta, 539 U.S. 126, 123 S.Ct. 2162, 156 L.Ed.2d 162 (2003) (Court employs the *Turner* standard to find that prison regulations excluding visits from certain collateral relatives and from children after parental rights have been terminated, and ban on all visitation for inmates with certain substance abuse violations in prison did not violate either substantive due process or the cruel and unusual punishment clause although Court leaves open the possibility that individual applications of a total ban on visitation might violate due process principles). See § 10.6 regarding the distinction between substantive due process and procedural due process issues in prisoner rights cases.

The Supreme Court applied this "reasonable relationship to a legitimate penological interest" standard in Thornburgh v. Abbott, 490 U.S. 401, 109 S.Ct. 1874, 104 L.Ed.2d 459 (1989) and upheld a federal bureau of prisons regulation that authorized prison wardens, pursuant to certain criteria, to prohibit prison inmates from receiving certain types of publications mailed to them. In this case, the Supreme Court overruled in part Procunier v. Martinez, 416 U.S. 396, 94 S.Ct. 1800, 40 L.Ed.2d 224 (1974) insofar as that decision would have applied a stricter

adopted three standards of review in equal protection cases.[25] The first standard is the "rational relationship" or "rational basis" test, which the Court uses when it finds no basis for giving truly independent examination to a government classification. This test gives a strong presumption of constitutionality to the governmental action; the Court only invalidates the law if it has no rational relationship to any legitimate interest of government.

The intermediate standard of review has been formally adopted for gender and illegitimacy cases. The Supreme Court used the intermediate standard in one federal racial affirmative action case, which was later overruled.[26] The Supreme Court appeared to use the intermediate standard in one case involving the denial of all public school education to children who could not prove that they were in this country lawfully, but the Court's opinion was not clear regarding the standard of review being used in that case.[27]

When the government uses a classification based on race or national origin the Supreme Court uses "strict scrutiny" and requires a classification to be necessary (narrowly tailored) to a compelling or overriding government interest.

A law that burdens the ability of all persons to exercise a fundamental right will be examined under substantive due process. A law that uses a classification that burdens or impairs the ability of only one class of persons who wished to exercise a fundamental constitutional right will be examined under equal protection. Because most government laws

regulating fundamental rights impose special burdens on one classification of persons (rather than imposing the regulation on all members of society) most of the fundamental rights cases are equal protection decisions. For that reason, they are examined in this Chapter. When the Court has used a formal test for the analysis for fundamental rights problems, it has most often stated that the law impairing the fundamental right must survive strict scrutiny and must be narrowly tailored to promote a compelling or overriding interest. However, in some cases, the Court has ruled on government regulations of fundamental rights without stating any clear standard of review.[28] It is possible that the Supreme Court is using the intermediate standard of review in fundamental rights cases but the Court has not adopted a standard of review that would tie together all of its fundamental rights decisions. The Supreme Court now openly uses a balancing approach in voting cases, although it has attempted to fit that approach together with its "compelling interest" test. The Court has ruled that any severe deprivation of voting rights is subject to the requirement that the state law be narrowly tailored to promote a compelling interest, but limited burdens on voters' rights might be justified by a variety of important interests.[29]

The Supreme Court has come close to stating that, in fundamental rights, cases it will use a balancing test or an intermediate form of review that would require the government to demonstrate that the restriction on the fundamental right was substantially related to an

standard to prison decisions regarding incoming publications as well as correspondence to prisoners. See § 10.6 regarding the difference between substantive due process and procedural due process in prisoners' rights cases. See generally, Baird, J., citing Treatise in, Dinkins v. State, 894 S.W.2d 330, 342 n. 10 (Tex.Crim.App.1995), cert. denied 516 U.S. 832, 116 S.Ct. 106, 133 L.Ed.2d 59 (1995).

25. For citations to additional cases, and secondary sources on this topic see, R. Rotunda & J. Nowak, Treatise on Constitutional Law: Substance and Procedure, vol. 3 § 18.3 (3rd ed. 1999, with annual supplements). See generally, Hoffner v. Johnson, 660 N.W.2d 909, (N.D. 2003, citing this Treatise); In re Treatment and Care of Luckabaugh, 351 S.C. 122, 568 S.E.2d 338 (S.C., 2002, citing this Treatise).

26. Metro Broadcasting, Inc. v. Federal Communications Commission, 497 U.S. 547, 110 S.Ct. 2997, 111

L.Ed.2d 445 (1990), rehearing denied 497 U.S. 1050, 111 S.Ct. 15, 111 L.Ed.2d 829 (1990), overruled in Adarand Constructors, Inc. v. Pena, 515 U.S. 200, 115 S.Ct. 2097, 132 L.Ed.2d 158 (1995). The subject of racial affirmative action is examined in § 14.10.

27. Plyler v. Doe, 457 U.S. 202, 102 S.Ct. 2382, 72 L.Ed.2d 786 (1982), rehearing denied 458 U.S. 1131, 103 S.Ct. 14, 73 L.Ed.2d 1401 (1982). See § 14.13.

28. See also §§ 10.7, 11.5–11.7

29. See, Burdick v. Takushi, 504 U.S. 428, 112 S.Ct. 2059, 119 L.Ed.2d 245 (1992) in which the Court upheld the State of Hawaii's prohibition on write-in voting. See § 14.31 of this Treatise regarding that case and basic voting rights issues; §§ 14.31–14.36 of this Treatise examine a variety of due process and equal protection issues related to elections.

important interest. Nevertheless, the court's majority opinions in fundamental rights cases continue to be unclear concerning, 1) the exact nature of the process that the Court uses to determine whether a right is fundamental, and 2) the method for analyzing whether an impairment of a fundamental right violates the due process or equal protection clauses.

(b) Is the Rationality Test Changing?

The rationality test used in cases that do not involve a fundamental right and wherein the Court does not find a classification of persons for whom there should be special judicial protection (such as racial, national origin, gender, or illegitimacy classifications). The rationality test is easy to state: the classification only has to have a rational relationship to any legitimate governmental interest in order to comply with the equal protection guarantee. However, the meaning of that test is not clear.

From 1937 to mid 1970s, it appeared that any classification would be upheld if it was subjected only to the rational relationship test. Whenever a majority of the Justices on the Supreme Court could find that conceivable set of facts that might establish a rational rela-

tionship between the classification and an arguably legitimate end of government the law would be upheld. The test was not totally meaningless, a classification that was totally arbitrary and that could have no rational relationship to a legitimate interest of government would be invalidated.

Some Justices indicated a desire to review the reasonableness of virtually all legislative classifications in a realistic manner, but they have been unable to remove the strong presumption of validity for classifications in the economic and social welfare area.[30] Thus, a majority of the Justices today continue to use the traditional rational basis test to approve classifications related to welfare benefits,[31] property use,[32] or business activity that does not involve a fundamental right.[33]

There is the possibility that the confusion over the nature of standards of review under the equal protection guarantee will contribute to a return to the pre-1937 approach to equal protection with Justices invoking rational basis language while independently scrutinizing the reasonableness of government classifications.[34] Those Justices who have demonstrated an unwillingness to ac-

---

30. See Schweiker v. Wilson, 450 U.S. 221, 101 S.Ct. 1074, 67 L.Ed.2d 186 (1981) (upholding Social Security Act classification giving reduced Medicaid benefits to persons institutionalized in certain public mental care institutions; Justice Powell, joined by Justices Brennan, Marshall and Stevens, in dissent, would engage in a review of the reasonableness of this classification). See also, F.C.C. v. Beach Communications, Inc., 508 U.S. 307, 320, 13 S.Ct. 2096, 2105, 124 L.Ed.2d 211 (1993) (Stevens, J., concurring).

For citations to additional Supreme Court cases on this point, see R. Rotunda & J. Nowak, Treatise on Constitutional Law: Substance and Procedure, vol. 3 § 18.3 (3rd ed. 1999, with annual supplements).

31. See, e.g., Lyng v. Castillo, 477 U.S. 635, 106 S.Ct. 2727, 91 L.Ed.2d 527 (1986) (Court upholds, under rational basis standard, a law that disadvantages in the distribution of food stamps nuclear families—parents, children, and siblings—and other persons who customarily purchase and prepare food together because Congress could rationally conclude that these types of households should enjoy economies of scale in the purchase and preparation of food). For citations to additional Supreme Court cases on this point, see R. Rotunda & J. Nowak, Treatise on Constitutional Law: Substance and Procedure, vol. 3 § 18.3 (3rd ed. 1999, with annual supplements).

32. See, Hodel v. Indiana, 452 U.S. 314, 101 S.Ct. 2376, 69 L.Ed.2d 40 (1981) (upholding the "prime farm land" provisions of the Surface Mining and Reclamation Control Act of 1977 against the claim that the restrictions

on mining and certain farm land were arbitrary limitations of the use of property in select geographic areas): "Social and economic legislation like the Surface Mining Act that does not employ suspect classifications or impinge on fundamental rights must be upheld against equal protection attack when the legislative means are rationally related to a legitimate government purpose. Moreover, such legislation carries with it a presumption of rationality that can only be overcome by a clear showing of arbitrariness and irrationality." 452 U.S. at 331, 101 S.Ct. at 2387. (citations omitted).

33. The Supreme Court upheld a state law which prohibited the ownership of retail gas stations by petroleum producers and refiners and which regulated their pricing practices in Exxon Corp. v. Governor of Maryland, 437 U.S. 117, 98 S.Ct. 2207, 57 L.Ed.2d 91 (1978), rehearing denied 439 U.S. 884, 99 S.Ct. 232, 58 L.Ed.2d 200 (1978). It took the Court only a single paragraph to dismiss the producers' argument that the law violated the principle of substantive due process; there was no problem in upholding these regulations under the rational relationship test. 437 U.S. at 125, 98 S.Ct. at 2213–14. For citations for additional Supreme Court cases on this point, see R. Rotunda & J. Nowak, Treatise on Constitutional Law: Substance and Procedure, vol. 3 § 18.3 (3rd ed. 1999, with annual supplements).

34. Confusion of Procedural and Substantive Issues. The confusion of procedural due process and equal protection issues in some cases has also contributed to the

cept government assertions of a theoretical rational basis for legislation will be joined by new Supreme Court appointees who would also require the government to demonstrate a reasonable relationship between any classification and a significant end of government. Were that possibility to occur, the presumption of constitutionality for economic and social welfare legislation and classifications would disappear.

In the last three decades of the twentieth century, the Supreme Court ruled that several laws violated the equal protection clauses because those laws created classifications that did not have a rational relationship to any legitimate interest of government. For example, the Court found that a city law that would have prohibited mentally retarded people from living together violated the rationality standard.[35] Similarly, the Court found that a state law that prohibited local legislative bodies from considering the enactment of laws that would protect persons against discrimination on the basis of their sexual orientation could not conceivably be related to any legitimate interest of government.[36] The Court has also invalidated some laws involving economic regulations on the basis that they could not meet the rationality test.[37]

The mere existence of the cases invalidating classifications under the rationality standard leads one to question whether the Supreme Court is slowly changing that standard, and returning to the approach the Supreme Court took between the late 1890s and 1937. The majority opinions of the Supreme Court continue to state that, when the Court is applying "minimal judicial scrutiny" (which is another way of describing the "rational basis" or "rationality" test), the Court will not second guess legislative judgments. It is possible that the Court is not changing the rationality standard and that the Court simply has found in some rare cases during the late twentieth century laws that establish classifications that were totally arbitrary and could not have any theoretical rational relationship to any legitimate interest of government.[38] In the next subsections of this section of the Treatise, we will examine some special problems that the Court confronted when applying the rationality standard in the late Twentieth Century. We must emphasize that the Court continues to state that the rationality test it is using does not involve any requirement that the government demonstrate that its law or classification is in fact reasonably related to any real and legitimate government interest. The Court today states that it will employ the traditional rational relationship test whenever a classification does not relate to a fundamental constitutional right, and does not employ the charac-

---

difficulty of identifying the proper standard of judicial review to be employed in equal protection decisions. When reviewing the permissibility of the procedures by which the government identifies a person for the granting or withholding of entitlements, the Justices must independently review the fairness of those procedures. However, when reviewing the legislative or regulatory classifications, the Court should grant a presumption of constitutionality to those classifications that do not touch upon a fundamental right nor employ racial, ethnic, citizenship, gender or legitimacy characteristics. See §§ 10.6, 10.7, supra.

35. Cleburne v. Cleburne Living Center, 473 U.S. 432, 105 S.Ct. 3249, 87 L.Ed.2d 313, 473 U.S. 432 (1985). This case is examined later in this section of the Treatise, and in §§ 14.30, 14.44.

36. Romer v. Evans, 517 U.S. 620, 116 S.Ct. 1620, 134 L.Ed.2d 855 (1996). This case is discussed in a later portion of this section of the Treatise, and in § 14.30.

37. Some of the other cases in which the Court invalidated a classification under the rationality test are: United States Department of Agriculture v. Moreno, 413 U.S. 528, 93 S.Ct. 2821, 37 L.Ed.2d 782 (1973). There are references

to this case in §§ 14.25, 14.28, 14.30, and 14.43 of this Treatise. Zobel v. Williams, 457 U.S. 55, 102 S.Ct. 2309, 72 L.Ed.2d 672 (1982). This case is examined in later portions of this section and in § 14.38. Allegheny Pittsburgh Coal v. County Commission, 488 U.S. 336, 109 S.Ct. 633, 102 L.Ed.2d 688. This case is examined in later portions of this section of the Treatise. For citations to additional cases and secondary authorities on these issues, see the multi-volume edition of this Treatise: R. Rotunda & J. Nowak, Treatise on Constitutional Law: Substance and Procedure, Chapter 18 (3rd ed. 1999, with annual supplements).

38. For example, in Dallas v. Stanglin, 490 U.S. 19, 109 S.Ct. 1591, 104 L.Ed.2d 18 (1989) the Supreme Court unanimously upheld a municipal ordinance that limited the use of certain dance halls to persons between the ages of 14 and 18. After finding that the law did not restrict the fundamental right of freedom of association, Chief Justice Rehnquist's opinion, for seven members of the Court, stated that under the rational basis test it was the burden of parties attacking the ordinance to demonstrate that there is no possible rational relationship between the classification and any legitimate interest of government, which included the government's interest in protecting minors from a variety of corrupting influences.

teristics of race, national origin, United States citizenship, sex, or legitimacy of birth to define a benefitted or burdened class of persons. When a law is subjected only to the rationality standard the law only has to be one that a rational legislative body could believe might promote a legitimate interest of government.[39]

It appears that the Court will only use the rational relationship test to invalidate laws that are wholly arbitrary and that cannot be justified by any rational argument that relates the classification to a legitimate state interest. While some laws may fail this test, in instances where a legislative entity has chosen to treat a classification of persons in a wholly arbitrary and invidious manner, there will be no independent judicial review of the factual basis for legislative decision making under this standard.

(c) Mandatory Retirement Laws—An Example of Rationality Review

The Court's decisions on mandatory retirement laws for government employees demon-

strate the strong presumption of constitutionally afforded a classification in the area of economics or social welfare. Such laws require all employees of a governmental unit to retire at a statutorily fixed age. These laws may result in many otherwise qualified people losing their employment and may not in fact promote efficiency in government. However, such laws have been upheld under the rational basis standard. There is no fundamental right to government employment. Classifications based on age are not treated as suspect or even deserving of the middle-level standard of review used in gender discrimination cases.[40] Thus, the Court used the deferential rational basis test in upholding these classifications.

In *Vance v. Bradley*[41] the Supreme Court, with only one dissent, upheld a requirement that participants in the foreign service retirement system[42] retire from their government positions at age 60. The plaintiff employees had alleged that the distinction between the mandatory retirement at age 60 for their job

---

39. Some of the Court's most recent statements concerning the nature of the rationality test appear at the end of this section of the Treatise.

40. Age classifications. The Supreme Court has not found that any form of heightened judicial scrutiny should be used when reviewing classifications that are based on age. The Court has upheld laws that have regulated the rights and liberties of children under the rationality standard (often described as "minimal scrutiny") when the classifications did not relate to a fundamental right. For example, in Reno v. Flores, 507 U.S. 292, 113 S.Ct. 1439, 123 L.Ed.2d 1 (1993), on remand 992 F.2d 243 (9th Cir.1993) the Court upheld Immigration and Naturalization Service regulations that denied release from government custody to an alien child awaiting deportation unless the child could be released in the care of a relative or guardian who was in the United States. The Court in *Flores* found that children did not have a fundamental right to be in a noncustodial setting or to have the government act in their best interest. Because no fundamental right was limited by the detention regulation, the regulation was tested under the rationality standards. The regulation was upheld because it had a reasonable and rational relation to the government interests in providing for proper care for the children and providing that they would appear at deportation proceedings. In Schall v. Martin, 467 U.S. 253, 104 S.Ct. 2403, 81 L.Ed.2d 207 (1984) the Court upheld a limited pretrial detention program for juveniles accused of serious crime. The Court found that the children would be kept in conditions that were nonpunitive in nature and that the program was designed (through a probable cause hearing and other procedural safeguards) to provide for the safety of the community while protecting the welfare of the juvenile.

Minors have the right to exercise some, but not all, fundamental rights in the same manner as do adults. The ability of a minor to receive abortion services without the consent of, or notification to, her parent or parents is considered in § 14.29 of this Treatise. The government and family interests in the protection of minors may also serve as a basis for limiting the First Amendment rights of minors. See §§ 16.60, 16.61 regarding the subject of obscenity and children. See § 17.9 regarding health and medical regulations, the treatment of children, and the free exercise clause of the First Amendment.

Congressional Action to Prohibit Age Discrimination. While the Court may not give significant protection to non-suspect classifications, it must be remembered that Congress may protect such groups through legislation. Age classifications are not suspect and, to date, they have not been subjected to any meaningful form of judicial review. However, Congress has made it unlawful for many employees to discriminate in employment practices or benefits for most employees between the ages of 40 and 70 because of their age. Age Discrimination in Employment Act, 29 U.S.C.A. § 621 et seq. For citations to additional Supreme Court cases, and secondary authorities, on this point, see R. Rotunda & J. Nowak, Treatise on Constitutional Law: Substance and Procedure, vol. 3 § 18.3 (3rd ed. 1992, with annual supplements).

41. 440 U.S. 93, 99 S.Ct. 939, 59 L.Ed.2d 171 (1979).

42. This retirement system and requirement applied to career foreign service officers, foreign service information and certain other career staff in the International Communications Agency.

classifications and the general federal requirement of retirement at age 70 for the federal Civil Service Retirement System personnel violated the equal protection component of the Fifth Amendment.

The Court, in an opinion by Justice White, found that the retirement classification should be tested by general equal protection principles,[43] but that it did not violate the equal protection guarantee. Although the parties agreed that the law should be tested under the traditional rational basis standard, Justice White's opinion stressed that the federal judiciary is not to review seriously those classifications that do not involve fundamental rights or suspect classifications:

> The Constitution presumes that, absent some reason to infer antipathy, even improvident decisions will eventually be rectified by the democratic process and that judicial intervention is generally unwarranted no matter how unwisely we may think a political branch has acted. Thus, we will not overturn such a statute unless the varying treatment of different groups or persons is so unrelated to the achievement of any combination of legitimate purposes that we can only conclude that the legislature's actions were irrational.[44]

The majority then applied the rational basis test, which had been employed in *Massachusetts Board of Retirement v. Murgia*[45] to uphold a mandatory retirement of state police officers at age 50, to the retirement classification. Although it appeared that the plaintiffs had abandoned their claim that the classification between those over and under age 60 was irrational, and only pressed the claim of discrimination between foreign service employees and civil service employees, the majority opinion made it clear that the rational relationship test was the only form of review justified for reviewing any aspect of this mandatory retirement program.[46]

The Supreme Court appeared to use the highly deferential rationality test in *Gregory v. Ashcroft*[47] to uphold a mandatory retirement provision for judges. Justice O'Connor, writing for the majority in *Gregory*, first found that the federal Age Discrimination in Employment Act did not apply to a state constitutional provision that required members of the state judiciary to retire at age 70. Justice O'Connor's majority opinion then examined the equal protection claim of state judges who were forced to retire at 70. The majority ruled that this age classification should be tested only in terms of whether the classification had a rational relationship to a legitimate interest of the state. Justice O'Connor's ma-

---

43. 440 U.S. at 94 n. 1, 99 S.Ct. at 941 n. 1. This point corresponds with the well established principle that the equal protection guarantee of the due process clause of the Fifth Amendment mirrors that of equal protection clause of the Fourteenth Amendment.

44. 440 U.S. at 97, 99 S.Ct. at 942–43. (footnote omitted).

45. 427 U.S. 307, 96 S.Ct. 2562, 49 L.Ed.2d 520 (1976).

46. The majority opinion repeatedly stressed that, while there were facts that supported the government's claims, it was not the responsibility of the government to justify the classification and that the lower courts had erred when they refused to accept a hypothetical rational basis for sustaining the Retirement Act and instead engaged in some realistic review of the classification. There was no reason to assume that Congress was rewarding "youth *qua* youth"; it was at least arguable that a significant percentage of people over age 60 might not perform their duties as foreign service officers as ably as those who were younger. It was the responsibility of those challenging the legislative classification to "convince the court that the legislative facts on which the classification is apparently based could not reasonably be conceived to be true by the governmental decisionmaker." Vance v. Bradley, 440

U.S. 93, 101, 111, 99 S.Ct. 939, 944–45, 949–50, 59 L.Ed.2d 171 (1979).

Justice Marshall, the only dissenter, argued that the Court should consider the age distinction, as well as the retirement system distinction, as a basis for engaging in some meaningful form of review of the classifications. Vance v. Bradley, 440 U.S. 93, 113, 99 S.Ct. 939, 950, 59 L.Ed.2d 171 (1979) (Marshall, J., dissenting).

While other members of the Court have at times joined Justice Marshall in seeking to use an intermediate form of review where it is required by the constitutionally significant nature of the rights effected or personal "status" basis of a classification, no other Justice was willing to engage in such wide ranging review of statutory employment criteria. Justice Marshall was also the only dissenter when the Court upheld the 50 year old retirement provision for a state police force. Massachusetts Bd. of Retirement v. Murgia, 427 U.S. 307, 317, 96 S.Ct. 2562, 2568–69, 49 L.Ed.2d 520 (1976). Justice Stevens did not participate in the Massachusetts decision but he joined the majority in *Vance*.

47. 501 U.S. 452, 111 S.Ct. 2395, 115 L.Ed.2d 410 (1991).

jority opinion found that the classification was rationally related to the state's interest in maintaining a competent judiciary, even though Justice O'Connor stated that "it is probably not true" that most judges suffer deterioration in performance at age 70 and that the generalization on which the classification was built "may not be true at all." It is not clear whether the *Gregory* opinion should be taken to mean that the rational relationship test will never be more than a mere rubber stamp for the use of generalizations by legislatures. Justice O'Connor's majority opinion also stated: "the people of Missouri have a legitimate, indeed compelling, interest in maintaining a judiciary fully capable of performing the demanding task that judges must perform". It may be that majority in *Gregory* gave extreme deference to the state because the classification related to an interest that was at the heart of state sovereignty.[48]

(d) Economic and Tax Classifications in the 1980s & 1990s.

In *Allegheny Pittsburgh Coal Co. v. County Commission,*[49] Chief Justice Rehnquist wrote for a unanimous Court in ruling that an assessment system used to value real property for tax purposes violated the equal protection clause. Chief Justice Rehnquist stated that a state could divide property into classification and impose differing tax burdens on those classifications of property "so long as those divisions and burdens are reasonable."[50] Under this lenient standard of review, most tax classifications would be upheld, because most tax classifications would arguably relate to some legitimate interest of the state. The Chief Justice's opinion cited with approval an earlier case that had upheld the imposition of a property tax on merchandise belonging to residents of the taxing state but exempting merchandise stored in the state by non-residents[51] and a case upholding a law imposing a property tax on personal property owned by corporations but exempting similar property owned by private individuals.[52]

In *Allegheny Pittsburgh Coal,* the Court examined a county assessor's practice of valuing real property at 50% of the price paid for it at the most recent sale of the property. The assessor would not revalue property except at the time at which it was sold. The complaining taxpayer in *Allegheny Pittsburgh Coal,* was a corporation that had purchased property in the county that had been valued by the assessor at the time of the recent sales. The assessor admitted that there was neighboring property similar to, if not identical to, the property owned by the complaining taxpayer that was valued much lower than the property of the taxpayer. The neighboring properties had not been the subject of a sale in recent times.

---

48. Justice O'Connor's equal protection analysis was contained in a portion of her opinion that was joined by seven Justices. These Justices found that the Age Discrimination in Employment Act did not apply to mandatory retirement laws that governed members of the state judiciary. Justice O'Connor wrote for five Justices in basing this statutory interpretation on a view of federalism principles and the need to avoid a constitutional question regarding whether Congress, under either the commerce clause or the Fourteenth Amendment, had the power to regulate the employment of state and local government officials who performed essential government functions. Gregory v. Ashcroft, 501 U.S. 452, 457–71, 111 S.Ct. 2395, 2399–2406, 115 L.Ed.2d 410 (1991). Two Justices used common principles of statutory interpretation to find that the Act did not apply to retirement laws regarding members of the state judiciary. These two Justices did not imply that the Constitution, or its Amendments, restricted Congress' power to apply an antidiscrimination law to the selection or retention of members of the judiciary. 501 U.S. at 474, 111 S.Ct. at 2408 (White, J., joined by Stevens, J., concurring in part, and concurring in the judgment). The two dissenting Justices in *Gregory* would have found that the Act invalidated the mandatory

retirement provision of state constitutions and that the Act was a valid exercise of congressional power. 501 U.S. at 485, 111 S.Ct. at 2414 (Blackmun, J., joined by Marshall, J., dissenting).

49. 488 U.S. 336, 109 S.Ct. 633, 102 L.Ed.2d 688 (1989).

50. 488 U.S. at 336, 109 S.Ct. at 638.

51. Allied Stores of Ohio, Inc. v. Bowers, 358 U.S. 522, 79 S.Ct. 437, 3 L.Ed.2d 480 (1959) (ruling that the exemption of merchandise or products belonging to a nonresident held in a storage warehouse did not violate the equal protection standard, which required tax classifications to have a rational basis and a fair and substantial relationship to the object of the tax legislation).

52. Lehnhausen v. Lake Shore Auto Parts Co., 410 U.S. 356, 93 S.Ct. 1001, 35 L.Ed.2d 351 (1973) (upholding tax system that imposed a tax on personal property owned by corporations and exempting identical personal property owned by individuals) overruling Quaker City Cab Co. v. Pennsylvania, 277 U.S. 389, 48 S.Ct. 553, 72 L.Ed. 927 (1928).

Resultingly, the complaining taxpayer's property had been assessed at a value of 8 to 35 times more than similar property in the county. Chief Justice Rehnquist's opinion found that the government's assessment of real property at 50% of the price paid at the recent sale did not violate the Constitution. The government was not required to make immediate adjustments of the values of all properties in the county to reflect market developments or to keep neighboring properties valued in a way that was equal to the property that had recently been the subject of a sales transaction. However, even the equal protection guarantee required the government to take some steps to achieve "the seasonable attainment of a rough equality in tax treatment of similarly situated property owners." [53]

The tax system reviewed in *Allegheny Pittsburgh Coal* was neither one that had only a "transitional delay" in adjusting assessed property values nor one that employed other means to give some rough equality of treatment to comparable properties. The assessor had refused to revalue the property of the complaining taxpayer so as to bring its valuation in line with the assessed values for neighboring properties. The state constitution guaranteed its citizens that taxes would be "equal and uniform" and that all property would be "taxed in proportion to its value." While the meaning of that provision of the state constitution would be left to the state courts, the existence of that state constitutional provision eliminated any argument by the assessor that the practice of valuing property only at its time of sale was the result of a legislative decision not to raise taxes on a property that increased value only due to inflation.[54] To the Justices of the Supreme Court, the county assessment system challenged in this case appeared to be only an "aberrational enforcement policy" that resulted in taxing similar pieces of property differently for no reason other than the assessor's refusal to take any steps to modify the inequality. So viewed, this tax assessment system was truly

arbitrary and capricious and its invalidation by the United States Supreme Court does not signal a return to the active review of tax classifications and economic regulations that existed in the first part of this century.

The Supreme Court later upheld a state constitutional provision that restricted reassessment of land for property taxation to times when the property was transferred or significantly changed for new construction. In so doing, the Court demonstrated the highly deferential nature of the rationality standard of review and strengthened the view that the Court's action in *Allegheny Pittsburgh Coal* was based on the complete arbitrariness of the administrative action at issue in that case. In *Nordlinger v. Hahn* [55], the Supreme Court upheld a provision of the California Constitution that was approved by a statewide ballot initiative commonly referred to as "Proposition 13." This state constitutional provision limited real estate property taxes to one percent of the property's full cash value, based on the 1975–76 assessment; assessments of property could be increased to reflect inflation at a rate that could not exceed two percent a year. The same constitutional provision allowed reassessment of the property (so that the property's value might be completely changed and revised upwards for tax assessment purposes) only when the piece of property was "purchased, newly constructed, or a change in ownership has occurred after the 1975 assessment."

The California constitutional provision contained two exceptions from the reassessment provision. These exceptions had the effect of freeing two types of post 1975 property transactions from triggering a property reassessment. The first exemption allowed the state legislature to give to homeowners over 55 years of age the ability to sell their principal residence, buy a new residence, and use the assessed value of their old residence as the assessed value of a replacement residence was of equal or lesser value. A second exemption allowed parents to transfer a principal resi-

---

53. Allegheny Pittsburgh Coal Co. v. County Commission, 488 U.S. 336, 344, 109 S.Ct. 633, 638, 102 L.Ed.2d 688 (1989).

54. 488 U.S. at 344 n. 4, 109 S.Ct. at 638 n. 4.

55. 505 U.S. 1, 112 S.Ct. 2326, 120 L.Ed.2d 1 (1992).

dence (and $1 million of other real property) to their children without the transfer constituting an event that would trigger a reassessment of the value of the property.

In *Nordlinger*, the United States Supreme Court found that the general limit on state taxation, which allowed reassessment only at the time of transfer or new construction, would comply with the constitutional guarantee of equal protection if it "rationally furthers a legitimate state interest." Under this test, the law would be upheld "so long as there is a plausible policy reason for the classification" and "the legislative facts on which the classification is apparently based rationally may have been considered to be true by the governmental decisionmaker." [56] The classification system was upheld because giving a tax assessment preference to long-time property owners avoided taxation of increased property values that were solely the result of inflation. This tax policy might encourage stable neighborhoods (by avoiding long time property owners having to sell their property at its new market value just to pay their tax assessments). Additionally, the state could honor the "reliance interest" of a person who purchased a piece of property with a low tax assessment who did not plan to pay higher taxes on the property if it only increased in value due to inflation.

The California tax assessment provisions had the effect of freezing property tax assessments for long-time owners of property. Such a tax system might have socially disadvantageous effects. These tax provisions might make it more difficult for younger persons to purchase homes and more difficult for new businesses that depend on ownership of property to compete in the marketplace. Long-time home owners and businesses who had owned their real estate for a long time would have the advantage of low property assessments and would not be contributing the same

amount of tax dollars for public services as would be the newer property owners.

The Supreme Court, in *Nordlinger*, did not make an independent judgment as to whether the tax assessment system, in fact, would promote the state's asserted interests because the taxation limits were at least arguably related to legitimate governmental interests. The Court distinguished *Allegheny Pittsburgh Coal* on the basis that all state law contradicted the claim of the county tax assessor that the state would allow a special tax assessment policy in order to protect long time owners of property. The *Allegheny Pittsburgh Coal* decision "was the rare case where the facts precluded any plausible inference that the reason for unequal assessment practice was to achieve the benefits" of a tax system designed to protect long time owners of property and their neighborhoods.[57] In other words, the facts in *Allegheny Pittsburgh Coal* demonstrated that the assessor's property valuation system was completely arbitrary. *Nordlinger* made it clear that it would uphold a tax classification so long as there was any rational argument that the classification related to a legitimate state interest.

Applying the highly deferential rationality standard of review, the Court in *Nordlinger* upheld the two exemptions from the reassessment of property that was transferred after 1975. The Supreme Court found that the people of the state might have believed "that older persons in general should not be discouraged from moving" by the danger of property tax reassessments. Thus, the exemption allowing persons over 55 to use their old property tax basis for their new home was arguably related to protecting senior persons. The Court also found that the people of the state, who provided an exemption from reassessment for property that was transferred between parents and children, "reasonably could

56. 505 U.S. at 10, 112 S.Ct. at 2332.

57. It should be noted that two of the Justices believed that the fact situations in the *Allegheny Pittsburgh Coal* case and the *Nordlinger* case were not distinguishable. Justice Thomas believed that the Court had gone too far in *Allegheny Pittsburgh Coal;* he would have preferred that the Court in *Nordlinger* overrule its earlier decision in *Allegheny Pittsburgh Coal.* Justice Stevens believed

that the correct result had been achieved in the *Allegheny Pittsburgh Coal* case and that that case required the invalidation of the tax classifications at issue in *Nordlinger.* See Nordlinger v. Hahn, 505 U.S. 1, 19, 112 S.Ct. 2326, 2336, 120 L.Ed.2d 1 (1992) (Thomas, J., concurring in part and concurring in the judgment); 505 U.S. at 27, 112 S.Ct. at 2341 (Stevens, J., dissenting).

have concluded that the interest of family and neighborhood continuity and stability" were furthered by such an exemption. The state almost certainly could not have proved that exemptions from reassessments for senior citizens or for parent-child property transfers promoted specific social ends. However, under the rationality standard of review, the state was not required to demonstrate that its classifications in fact promoted legitimate governmental interests. These classifications were upheld because the plaintiff who alleged that the exemption classifications violated equal protection "has not demonstrated that no rational bases lie for either of these exemptions." [58]

In *Metropolitan Life Insurance Co. v. Ward*[59] the Court held that a state law which imposed a higher tax on out-of-state insurance companies doing business in the state than was imposed on in-state insurance companies would violate equal protection if the law related to no state interest other than the desire to discriminate against competition for local businesses. The four dissenting Justices in *Metropolitan Life Insurance Co.* pointed out that the law conceivably was related to the state interest in protecting local consumers by fostering local insurance companies that would be more responsive to the consumer interests.[60] However, the majority opinion by Justice Powell found that the state had not attempted in the lower courts to advance any interest to support the statute other than the desire to improve the local economy at the expense of out-of-state companies, which was not a legitimate governmental interest.[61] The majority ruled only that, following a remand of the case to

the lower courts, the state would have to assert some plausible state interest apart from the desire to profit through discrimination against out-of-state competition. The statute might be upheld if it had a rational relationship to a legitimate interest.[62]

A legal classification relating to matters of economic and social welfare does not have to be truly reasonable in order to survive the rationality test. When such a classification, such as a classification in a tax law, might be said to rationally advance some legitimate interest of society, the courts will defer to the legislature and uphold the classification. For example, in *Fitzgerald v. Racing Association of Central Iowa*[63] the Justices unanimously upheld a state tax law that imposed a 36 percent tax on income from slot machines that were placed at racetracks, but only a 20 percent tax on income from slot machines placed on river boats. The Iowa Supreme Court in this case chose not to invalidate the tax classification on state law. Instead, the Iowa court ruled that the classification violated the equal protection clause of the Fourteenth Amendment, because the classification could not promote the general goal of the legislation of which it was a part and which (in total) was designed to help racetracks in the states from economic difficulties. The Justices of the Supreme Court of the United States unanimously reversed the state court. The United States Supreme Court, in an opinion by Justice Breyer, found that the fact that a provision in the law (such as the imposition of a higher tax rate on income from slot machines at racetracks) seemed inconsistent with the general purpose of the statute (such

---

58. Nordlinger v. Hahn, 505 U.S. 1, 16, 112 S.Ct. 2326, 2335, 120 L.Ed.2d 1 (1992). There was no plaintiff in the *Nordlinger* case who had standing to raise the argument that the tax assessment classifications significantly impaired the fundamental right to travel by deterring interstate migration; therefore, the Court did not examine the issue of whether the right to travel was implicated by the state's property tax classifications. 505 U.S. at 10, 112 S.Ct. at 2332.

59. 470 U.S. 869, 105 S.Ct. 1676, 84 L.Ed.2d 751 (1985).

60. 470 U.S. at 883, 105 S.Ct. at 1684 (O'Connor, J., joined by Brennan, Marshall, and Rehnquist, JJ., dissenting).

61. Metropolitan Life Insurance Co. v. Ward, 470 U.S. 869, 875 n. 5, 105 S.Ct. 1676, 1680 n. 5, 84 L.Ed.2d 751 (1985).

62. The Court in *Metropolitan Life Insurance Co.* found that the state interests in protecting local business or promoting local investment through discrimination against out-of-state companies were invalid purposes but remanded the case for a determination of whether other state purposes (which had not been properly raised before the lower courts) might support the statute. 470 U.S. at 875 n. 5, 883, 105 S.Ct. at 1680 n. 5, 1684.

63. Fitzgerald v. Racing Association of Central Iowa 539 U.S. 103, 123 S.Ct. 2156, 156 L.Ed.2d 97 (2003), reversing Racing Association of Central Iowa v. Fitzgerald, 648 N.W.2d 555 (Iowa, 2002).

as a statute designed to help racetrack owners) did not make the classification irrational. Writing for a unanimous Court, Justice Breyer stated that: "not every provision in the law must share a single objective."[64] Following that view Justice Breyer ruled that it was theoretically rational for a legislature to pass a law that helped racetracks while including a provision that disadvantaged racetracks in order to benefit other gambling interests in the states such as river boats.

Williams v. Vermont[65] involved a Vermont automobile use tax statute which exempted from payment of the tax Vermont residents who purchased an automobile in another state and paid a sales tax to the state in which they made the purchase but denied this exemption to a person moving into Vermont who was not a resident of Vermont when he made the purchase of the automobile and paid a sales tax in another state. The Supreme Court ruled that the law had no rational relationship to any legitimate purpose because it appeared to serve no purpose except to impose a higher tax on persons who were not residents of the state when they made an automobile purchase. The majority opinion concluded that "we can see no relevant difference between motor vehicle registrants who purchase their cars out-of-state while they were Vermont residents and those who only came to Vermont after buying a car elsewhere."[66] The dissenting Justices believed that the law might be conceivably

related to imposing a double tax only on a person who had used an automobile for a substantial amount of time in two separate states.[67] The majority did not find that the tax exemption for Vermont automobile purchasers was totally invalid, however, but only required the state to assert some reason that would support the law other than the desire to impose heavier taxes on out-of-state persons or new residents. The Court remanded the case to the lower courts for a determination of whether the statute might serve other legitimate state interest.[68]

It is important to note that in both *Metropolitan Life Insurance Co.* and *Williams* the Court was only demanding that the legislature be able to assert some plausible reason for the classification at issue other than the desire to discriminate against out-of-state persons or new residents. Even under the rationality test, the legislature is not entitled to pick out a group it disfavors, declare that group to be different, and then impose a special tax burden on the disfavored group. In both cases, the Supreme Court remanded the case to the lower courts to give the state an opportunity to assert that there was some basis for the law other than the desire to impose higher taxes on a disfavored group. If there was a rational argument that the law served some purpose other than the desire to discriminate against

64. 539 U.S. at ___, 123 S.Ct. at 2160.

65. 472 U.S. 14, 105 S.Ct. 2465, 86 L.Ed.2d 11 (1985).

66. A state resident was given credit for the sales tax paid in the other state if the other state (the state of purchase) in its tax legislation allowed a credit against its use tax for state residents who purchased a car in Vermont and paid a sales tax to the State of Vermont.

A typical use tax will allow a credit for sales taxes paid in another state. The Court has not determined whether, under the commerce clause, a state is required in all circumstances to grant a credit against its use tax for sales taxes paid in another state. The Court in *Williams* said: "we again put to one side the question of whether a state must in all circumstances credit sales or use taxes paid to another state against its own use taxes." 470 U.S. at 28, 105 S.Ct. at 2474. See § 13.6(b).

67. Williams v. Vermont, 472 U.S. 14, 30, 105 S.Ct. 2465, 2475, 86 L.Ed.2d 11 (1985) (Blackmun, J., joined by Rehnquist and O'Connor, JJ., dissenting). Justice Powell did not take part in the decision of this case; the case was decided by a five to three vote.

Justice Brennan concurred in the majority's opinion in *Williams* because he believed the law discriminated against persons in their right to freely migrate between the states. 472 U.S. at 30, 105 S.Ct. at 2475 (Brennan, J., concurring).

68. The state court had dismissed the complaint attacking the use tax on the basis that it did not present an equal protection claim which required further judicial investigation. The Supreme Court of the United States in *Williams* ruled only that the complaint should not have been dismissed for failure to state a cause of action because the classification appeared to violate the equal protection clause by discriminating against non-residents or new residents of the state. The Supreme Court stated that: "it is conceivable that, were a full record developed, it would turn out that in practice the statute does not operate in a discriminatory fashion." Williams v. Vermont, 472 U.S. 14, 28, 105 S.Ct. 2465, 2474, 86 L.Ed.2d 11 (1985).

those groups, the law could be upheld under the traditional rationality standard.

In the same Term that the Court decided *Metropolitan Life Insurance Co.* and *Williams,* it upheld a state law which prohibited the operation of a bank in the state by an out-of-state holding company that had its principal place of business outside of the geographic region in which the state was located. In so doing, the Justices indicated that a majority of the Justices still favored using the post-1937 deferential rationality test for the review of economic classifications. In *Northeast Bancorp, Inc. v. Board of Governors*[69] the Justices unanimously upheld state statutes that permitted an out-of-state bank holding company to acquire an in-state bank only if the holding company had as its principal place of business one of the New England states. The Court's opinion, by Justice Rehnquist, found that these laws did not violate the commerce clause because Congress had authorized states to create laws restricting the acquisition of in-state banks by out-of-state companies.[70] The classification did not violate the equal protection clause because it was conceivable that the law promoted legitimate state interests rooted in a concern for local control over the banking industry. Because the law was founded on concerns other than the simple desire to discriminate against out-of-state competition, the Court found that this restriction on regional banking met "the traditional rational basis for judging equal protection claims."[71]

The Supreme Court has taken the position that a state cannot deny benefits to new residents of the state if there is no reason for that denial other than the desire to give preferen-

tial treatment to old residents over new residents. In some circumstances the government may be able to require new residents to reside in the state for some period of time before receiving benefits to insure that the new entrant into the state is a bona fide resident or for the promotion of other important governmental interests.[72] However, the denial of benefits to new residents of the state must be based on some state goal other than the desire to discriminate against them. A law that denies benefits to new residents merely to give a preference to older residents will not survive the rationality test because the desire to discriminate against new residents is not a legitimate interest and, therefore, such a law would have no rational relationship to a legitimate governmental purpose.

In *Zobel v. Williams*[73] the Court invalidated an Alaska statute which distributed state money to local residents based upon the length of their residency in Alaska. Because the law awarded benefits retroactively it could not conceivably promote a state interest in inducing persons to move to the state. A state goal of simply rewarding citizens for past residency while denying similar treatment to new residents was not a legitimate state purpose in the Court's view.

Similarly, in *Hooper v. Bernalillo County Assessor,*[74] the Court invalidated a state property tax exemption limited to persons who were residents of the state before a specific date. In this case the state of New Mexico granted a property tax exemption to current residents who had been members of the armed services during the Vietnam War era and who

---

69. 472 U.S. 159, 105 S.Ct. 2545, 86 L.Ed.2d 112 (1985). Justice Powell did not participate in this decision; the eight voting Justices were unanimous in upholding this law.

70. 472 U.S. at 173–75, 105 S.Ct. at 2553–54. For discussion of the congressional ability to validate state legislation under the commerce clause see § 8.5.

The Court in *Northeast Bancorp* also found that these state statutes did not violate the compact clause of U.S. Const. art. I § 10. 472 U.S. at 175–77, 105 S.Ct. at 2554–55. See § 9.5.

71. Justice O'Connor wrote a concurring opinion to emphasize that the *Northeast Bancorp* ruling appeared to restrict the *Metropolitan Life Insurance Co.* decision to one

in which the Court invalidated the law solely because there appeared to be no possible justification for a law other than discrimination against out-of-state interests. This reading of the cases would allow states to have laws which promoted local institutions and economic interests responsive to local concerns. Northeast Bancorp, Inc. v. Board of Governors, 472 U.S. 159, 179, 105 S.Ct. 2545, 2556, 86 L.Ed.2d 112 (1985) (O'Connor, J., concurring).

72. For an analysis of the Court's rulings on the right to interstate travel see § 14.38.

73. 457 U.S. 55, 102 S.Ct. 2309, 72 L.Ed.2d 672 (1982).

74. 472 U.S. 612, 105 S.Ct. 2862, 86 L.Ed.2d 487 (1985).

were residents of New Mexico before May 8, 1976. The majority opinion found that welfare benefits could be limited to bona fide residents who had been veterans of the armed services because the distribution of welfare benefits based on that non-suspect classification might promote legitimate state interests in helping local persons in need of tax relief and rewarding persons for their service to our country. However, restricting the benefit to veterans who had been resident in the state before a specific date served no purpose other than to reserve the benefit for long-time residents, a goal which is not legitimate.[75]

(e) Classifications Designed to Harm Unpopular Groups: the Sexual Orientation and Mental Status Cases.

Legitimate ends of government do not involve singling out a class of citizens who are unpopular for special burdens in our society. It would seem difficult, if not impossible, to justify the establishment of a classification of persons who are prohibited from seeking help from local, state, or federal legislatures, because it would be difficult to conceive of any arguably legitimate interest in disadvantaging a group in the political process.

In *Romer v. Evans*,[76] the Supreme Court, by a six to three vote, invalidated a state constitutional amendment that prohibited the state legislature, and local legislative bodies in the state, from passing any legislation that would prohibit discrimination against individuals on the basis of their sexual orientation. The Supreme Court had previously ruled that homosexual activity was not a fundamental right.[77] The Court has not found homosexual persons to be a group of persons who require special constitutional protection. In *Romer*, Justice Kennedy's majority opinion stated that: "If a

law neither burdens a fundamental right nor targets a suspect class, we will uphold the legislative classification so long as it bears a rational relationship to some legitimate end. ... [the amendment prohibiting legislation that would help homosexual persons] fails, indeed defies even this conventional inquiry."[78]

The state in *Romer* argued that the constitutional amendment was designed to protect the associational freedom of landlords or employers who did not want to deal with homosexuals based on their religious or philosophical beliefs. The state also argued that it had a legitimate interest in preventing the city and state legislatures from adding homosexuality to antidiscrimination laws because expanding the scope of the antidiscrimination laws would drain state financial resources that otherwise could be used to fight discrimination against other groups (such as racial minorities or women). Only the three dissenting Justices believed that the constitutional amendment was rationally related to protecting those state interests.[79]

The majority in *Romer* found that the total prohibition of laws against discrimination on the basis of homosexuality was not rationally related to any legitimate interest. The amendment barred the group from seeking legislative help for their problems while it left all other groups free to seek to promote their interest (including their interest against discriminatory acts against them) by lobbying the appropriate local or state legislative entities. No other group in the state had to have the state constitution amended before it could seek legislative help for its problems. Only one group of persons who was selected solely because of their character traits, was prohibited from lobbying the legislature. The state was, in fact, punish-

---

75. The Justices, by a six to three vote, but without a majority opinion, invalidated a state civil service preference for veterans who had been residents of the state when they entered the military service but denied a similar preference to resident veterans who moved to the state after the time that they had entered the military. Attorney General of New York v. Soto–Lopez, 476 U.S. 898, 106 S.Ct. 2317, 90 L.Ed.2d 899 (1986), appeal after remand 840 F.2d 162 (2d Cir.1988).

76. 517 U.S. 620, 116 S.Ct. 1620, 134 L.Ed.2d 855 (1996).

77. Bowers v. Hardwick, 478 U.S. 186, 106 S.Ct. 2841, 92 L.Ed.2d 140 (1986). The *Bowers* decision is examined in § 14.30(a) of this Treatise.

78. Romer v. Evans, 517 U.S. 620, 631, 116 S.Ct. 1620, 1627, 134 L.Ed.2d 855 (1996).

79. Romer v. Evans, 517 U.S. 620, 635–52, 116 S.Ct. 1620, 1629–37, 134 L.Ed.2d 855 (1996) (Scalia, J., joined by Rehnquist, C.J., and Thomas, J., dissenting).

ing homosexuals in a way that was not related to any legitimate state interest. The Court's action in rejecting the state constitutional amendment did not give homosexuals a preferential treatment; the Court only placed homosexuals on an equal footing in terms of their ability, with everyone else, to take part in the political process.[80]

In *Lawrence v. Texas*[81] the Supreme Court by a 6 to 3 vote, invalidated a state law that prohibited same-sex sodomy. Justice Kennedy wrote for five Justices in finding that the law violated the due process clause. The majority opinion in *Lawrence*, written by Justice Kennedy, did not state that sexual activity outside of marriage was a fundamental right, even though the Justice Kennedy's majority opinion spent a great deal of time and space rejected the rationale as well as the holding of an earlier case regarding sexual conduct outside of marriage, which had focused on fundamental rights analysis.[82] Justice Kennedy's majority opinion in *Lawrence* ruled that no legitimate interest of government justified restrictions on private sexual activity performed between consenting adults in private, at least when both adults were voluntarily entering into a non-harmful sexual arrangement.[83] Justice Kennedy's majority opinion focused on the importance of sexual relationships as a form of basic liberty and it was surprising that the ruling did not simply hold that such activity was a fundamental right that was subject to independent judicial review. But the majority chose to base its ruling on the ra-

tionality test and the finding that there was no legitimate interest of government that justified this intrusion into liberty.

Justice O'Connor concurred in the judgment in *Lawrence*, she would have preferred to base the ruling on an equal protection rationale.[84] Justice O'Connor would have ruled that the law created a classification that was designed to harm a politically unpopular group but the majority chose to base its ruling on the due process clause.

The dissenting Justices in *Lawrence* feared that the majority's ruling would open the door to a wholesale judicial questioning, and a return to the *Lochner*-era form of adjudication.[85] Only time will tell whether the *Lawrence* decision is a narrow ruling concerning a specific aspect of liberty, so that the Court's ruling could be understood as applying a separate test only for restrictions on fundamental aspects of liberty, rather than being a return to a case by case judicial second guessing of legislative social policy judgments.[86]

When the federal government prohibits certain organizations that receive tax exempt income from using that tax exempt income to lobby the federal government for legislation, the federal government is not arbitrarily defining classifications of persons who cannot seek solutions of their problems from the federal legislature. The federal government has a legitimate interest in refusing to subsidize the lobbying through tax exemptions. The require-

80. Romer v. Evans, 517 U.S. 620, 633–35, 116 S.Ct. 1620, 1628–29, 134 L.Ed.2d 855 (1996): "It [the state constitutional amendment] identifies persons by a single trait and then denies them protection across the board. The resulting disqualification of a class of persons from the right to seek specific protection from the law is unprecedented in our jurisprudence." 517 U.S. at 635, 116 S.Ct. at 1629: "We must conclude that Amendment 2 classifies homosexuals not to further a proper legislative end but to make them unequal to everyone else. This Colorado cannot do. A state cannot so deem a class of persons a stranger to its laws."

The Court had previously invalidated state actions that required minority race groups to have the state constitution amended prior to having the local legislature pass a law that would protect them from invidious discrimination. Reitman v. Mulkey, 387 U.S. 369, 87 S.Ct. 1627, 18 L.Ed.2d 830 (1967). *Reitman* is examined in §§ 12.4(b) and 14.8.

See also, Washington v. Seattle School District No. 1, 458 U.S. 457, 102 S.Ct. 3187, 73 L.Ed.2d 896 (1982). This case is examined in § 14.9 of this Treatise.

81. Lawrence v. Texas, ___ U.S. ___, 123 S.Ct. 2472, 156 L.Ed.2d 508 (2003).

82. Bowers v. Hardwick, 478 U.S. 186, 106 S.Ct. 2841, 92 L.Ed.2d 140 (1986), overruled by Lawrence v. Texas, ___ U.S. ___, 123 S.Ct. 2472, 156 L.Ed.2d 508 (2003).

83. Lawrence v. Texas ___ U.S. ___, ___, 123 S.Ct. 2472, 2484, 156 L.Ed.2d 508 (2003).

84. ___ U.S. at ___, 123 S.Ct. at 2484–88 (O'Connor, J., concurring in the judgment).

85. ___ U.S. at ___, 123 S.Ct. at 2488 (Scalia, J., joined by Rehnquist, C.J., and Thomas, J., dissenting); ___ U.S. at ___, 123 S.Ct. at 2498 (Thomas, J., dissenting).

86. The *Lawrence* decision is examined in § 14.28 of this Treatise.

ment that tax exempt organizations use separate funds (that are not tax exempt) to finance their lobbying merely places those tax exempt organizations on an equal footing with other groups that seek to lobby the Congress.[87]

Although the rationality test used since 1937, as opposed to the reasonableness test of the 1900–1936 era, involves a very high degree of deference to the legislature, courts should strike down laws under the rationality test when it is clear that there is no purpose for a classification other than denying a benefit (even if it is not a fundamental right) to a group (even a non-suspect classification) when the denial of the benefit can serve no possible purpose other than the desire to discriminate against a group which is disfavored by the legislature.

In *City of Cleburne v. Cleburne Living Center*[88] the Justices unanimously invalidated a city zoning ordinance insofar as it prohibited the operation of a group home for the mentally retarded. The majority opinion by Justice White emphasized that the Court was not reviewing this law under any standard more strict than the rationality test. The majority opinion refused to find that legislative classifications that related to housing or classifications that treated mentally retarded persons

differently from other persons should be subjected to some form of truly independent judicial review. In so doing, the majority reaffirmed the Court's earlier decision upholding zoning ordinances that restricted residency to single families and restricted the number of persons who could live in a house based upon the size of the home. Those types of typical zoning statutes would be valid even though they had the effect of excluding group homes for retarded persons or for other unrelated individuals.[89]

The refusal of the Court in *City of Cleburne* to find that mentally retarded persons constituted a classification requiring special judicial protection meant that lower court judges were not justified by the equal protection clause in examining the reasonableness of classifications that give special treatment to such persons.[90] However, these laws would still have to be reviewed under the rationality test and should be invalidated if the state can assert no reason to justify the law other than a desire to discriminate against persons who were mentally retarded.

The Justices had no difficulty in invalidating the zoning regulation at issue in *Cleburne* because the denial of a permit for the group of mentally retarded persons to live together

---

87. See, Regan v. Taxation with Representation of Washington, 461 U.S. 540, 103 S.Ct. 1997, 76 L.Ed.2d 129 (1983), which is examined in § 20.11 of this Treatise.

88. 473 U.S. 432, 105 S.Ct. 3249, 87 L.Ed.2d 313 (1985).

89. The Court had upheld the constitutionality of an ordinance that restricted dwelling units to those occupied by a single family in Village of Belle Terre v. Boraas, 416 U.S. 1, 94 S.Ct. 1536, 39 L.Ed.2d 797 (1974). Although this issue was not before the Court, the Court in *City of Cleburne* referred with approval to a state court case which had upheld the constitutionality of a similar single family zoning ordinance even though it had the effect of excluding a group home for mentally retarded persons because the ordinance was supported by interests other than the desire to discriminate against the mentally retarded. City of Cleburne v. Cleburne Living Center, 473 U.S. 432, 440 n. 8, 105 S.Ct. 3249, 3254 n. 8, 87 L.Ed.2d 313 (1985) citing Macon Association for Retarded Citizens v. Macon–Bibb County Planning and Zoning Commission, 252 Ga. 484, 314 S.E.2d 218 (1984), dismissed for want of a substantial federal question 469 U.S. 802, 105 S.Ct. 57, 83 L.Ed.2d 8 (1984).

90. The majority opinion in *City of Cleburne* likened classifications based upon mental retardation to classifications based on age and referred to the Supreme Court's

decision in Massachusetts Board of Retirement v. Murgia, 427 U.S. 307, 96 S.Ct. 2562, 49 L.Ed.2d 520 (1976) refusing to allow lower courts to engage in independent judicial review of mandatory retirement laws. The majority opinion stated: "The lesson of *Murgia* is that where individuals in the group affected by a law have distinguishing characteristics relevant to interests the state has authority to implement, the courts have been very reluctant, as they should be in our federal system and with our respect for separation of powers, to closely scrutinize legislative choices as to whether, how and to what extent those interests should be pursued. In such cases, the equal protection clause requires only a rational means to serve a legitimate end." City of Cleburne v. Cleburne Living Center, 473 U.S. 432, 441, 105 S.Ct. 3249, 3255, 87 L.Ed.2d 313 (1985).

This refusal to extend the authority of courts to review legislation that classified persons by the status of being mentally retarded caused several Justices to dissent not from the ruling in this case but from the majority's refusal to provide for independent judicial review of all such legislation. Id. at 457, 105 S.Ct. at 3263 (Marshall, J., joined by Brennan and Blackmun, JJ., concurring in part and dissenting in part).

could not in any conceivable way promote any interest other than the desire to exclude mentally retarded persons from the city. The city zoning ordinance that authorized a denial of a "special use permit" for mentally retarded persons to live together in a group home in this case would have allowed an identical number of unrelated people to inhabit an identical house or apartment building if those persons were not mentally retarded. The city could not exclude mentally retarded persons based on an unsubstantiated fear or negative attitude about such persons. The desire to discriminate cannot constitute a legitimate end which then supports a discriminatory classification.[91]

91. The statute required a special permit for group homes for the mentally retarded, which was denied in this case. The majority concluded that: "requiring the permit in this case appears to us to rest on an irrational prejudice against the mentally retarded." 473 U.S. at 451, 105 S.Ct. at 3260.

92. 509 U.S. 312, 113 S.Ct. 2637, 125 L.Ed.2d 257 (1993).

93. In Addington v. Texas, 441 U.S. 418, 99 S.Ct. 1804, 60 L.Ed.2d 323 (1979) the Supreme Court held that an adult could not be committed to a psychiatric institution against his will on a mere preponderance of the evidence standard. But the Court rejected the argument that involuntary commitment should be allowed only on the basis of a "beyond a reasonable doubt" standard. Instead, the Court required the government to prove the elements necessary for involuntary commitments under a clear and convincing evidence standard. In *Heller* the majority opinion found that the state could exceed the minimum due process standard of proof, if it so chose, for one class of persons who were being involuntarily committed to mental health care facilities (persons who were committed on the basis of mental illness) without having to use the higher standard of proof in all commitment cases. The majority opinion in *Heller* specifically rejected the argument that increasing the standard of proof for the commitment of mentally ill persons violated the Court's earlier rulings regarding procedural due process issues. Heller v. Doe, 509 U.S. 312, 322 n. 1, 113 S.Ct. 2637, 2644 n. 1, 2648–49, 125 L.Ed.2d 257 (1993). In Kansas v. Hendricks, 521 U.S. 346, 117 S.Ct. 2072, 138 L.Ed.2d 501 (1997) the Supreme Court upheld a statute that allowed for the civil commitment of a person as a "sexually violent predator" who would be dangerous to other persons because of a mental abnormality. The case involved only substantive challenges to the standards used for defining the category of persons who could be involuntarily committed to a mental health care facility. There were no true procedural issues in the case, because the state provided the individual with more procedural safeguards than were required by earlier decisions of the United States Supreme Court. See §§ 17.4, 17.9 of this Treatise.

In Smith v. Doe, 538 U.S. 84, 123 S.Ct. 1140, 155 L.Ed.2d 164 (2003) the Supreme Court, by a 6 to 3 vote,

In *Heller v. Doe*,[92] the Court upheld classifications that distinguished mentally retarded persons from mentally ill persons. Kentucky statutes created substantive and procedural rules for the civil commitment of persons who were mentally retarded that were different from the rules used for commitment based upon mental illness. These state statutes required a court to refuse to order commitment of a person for mental retardation unless the moving party had demonstrated by clear and convincing evidence that the individual met the mental retardation commitment standard. This clear and convincing evidence standard complied with earlier procedural due process rulings of the United States Supreme Court.[93]

found that a state sex offender registration law was civil in nature and that its application to persons who had been properly convicted of sex related offenses before the date of passage of the law did not violate the ex post facto clause of Article I, § 10. In Connecticut Department of Public Safety v. Doe, 538 U.S. 1, 123 S.Ct. 1160, 155 L.Ed.2d 98 (2003) the Justices unanimously held that a sex offender registration law could be applied to an individual who had been properly convicted of sex related crimes without giving that individual an additional hearing to determine whether he was in fact, dangerous. In a concurring opinion in *Connecticut Department of Public Safety* in which they cited this Treatise, Justices Souter and Ginsburg explained that, even after this decision, the individual could litigate the question of whether the law limited his liberty interest, in violation of substantive due process principles, or whether the classifications in the law, regarding which convicted criminals would be subject to the registry system, violated equal protection 538 U.S. at 9, 10, 123 S.Ct. at 1165, 1166 (Souter, J., joined by Ginsburg, J., concurring).

These cases are examined in § 10.6 of this Treatise.

In Seling v. Young, 531 U.S. 250, 121 S.Ct. 727, 148 L.Ed.2d 734 (2001), on remand 248 F.3d 1197 (9th Cir. 2001) by 8 to 1 the Court ruled that a state statute similar to the one upheld in *Hendricks* cannot be challenged as being a criminal statute on an "as applied" basis. The majority opinion in *Seling* left open the question of whether conditions of confinement for all persons under a statute labeled civil in nature could result in a finding that the statute was in fact a criminal punishment. See § 13.9 (a) for further cases examining the distinction between civil statutes and criminal punishments.

In Kansas v. Crane, 534 U.S. 407, 122 S.Ct. 867, 151 L.Ed.2d 856 (2002) the Supreme Court ruled that an individual can be subject to involuntary commitment based upon the premise that he is dangerous to himself or others only if the government can prove that the individuals dangerousness is based upon some type of mental condition that results in "serious difficulty" in the individual controlling his dangerous behavior.

Kentucky required a court to refuse to commit a person to a mental health care facility on the basis of mental illness unless the moving party proved beyond a reasonable doubt that the person suffered from the types of mental illness standard that would justify commitment. The state allowed relatives and legal guardians of mentally retarded persons to participate as parties in proceedings to commit a person on the basis of mental retardation. However, the state did not allow relatives and guardians to participate as parties in proceedings to determine whether a person should be committed because he suffered from mental illness.

In *Heller* all of the Justices asserted that they were using only the rationality test to determine whether the statutory classifications, which created greater barriers to the commitment of someone due to mental illness than for the commitment of someone due to mental retardation, violated the equal protection clause. Justice Kennedy, writing for the majority in *Heller,* found that rational basis review, rather than some heightened form of judicial scrutiny, was required in this case because the parties attacking the classifications had not argued for a higher standard of review in any of the lower courts. Because these parties "press their heightened scrutiny argument for the first time in their merits brief in this Court" the majority refused to consider whether some form of judicial review more strict than the rational basis standard should be applied to the equal protection claims in this case.[94]

The Court in *Heller* ruled that the statutory distinctions in the two types of commitment proceedings could not be overturned under the rationality standard. Justice Kennedy described the great deference given the legislative bodies by the judiciary under this minimal form of judicial scrutiny. Justice Kennedy explained the rational basis standard as one that "does not require the State to place any

evidence in the records" to support its classifications. Under this standard "courts are compelled under rational-basis review to accept a legislature's generalizations even when there is an imperfect fit between means and ends."[95] Justice Kennedy concluded this discussion of the rationality standard by stating that "even the standard of rationality as we so often have defined it must find some footing in the realities of the subject addressed by the legislation."[96] This concluding statement seems inconsistent with his earlier description of the rational basis test being one in which any conceivable set of facts might justify the relationship of a classification to any arguably legitimate end of government. But Justice Kennedy did not give any further explanation of the standard of review used in this case.

The majority in *Heller* found that the State could provide a higher standard of proof for commitment on the basis of mental illness because of the greater difficulty in proving mental illness, as opposed to mental retardation. The state could justify its decision to allow relatives to be parties only in commitment proceedings regarding mental retardation because evidence of the defendant's family history could be more relevant and helpful to a court determination of whether the defendant was mentally retarded rather than to a court determination of whether the defendant was mentally ill. Justice Kennedy also found that the "prevailing methods of treatment for mentally retarded, as a general rule, are much less invasive than are those given to the mentally ill." For these reasons, in the view of the majority, the state could rationally conclude that it wished to have greater substantive and procedural safeguards against the possibly erroneous commitment of persons on the basis that they were mentally ill than it provided in mental retardation cases.

---

94. Heller v. Doe, 509 U.S. 312, 320, 113 S.Ct. 2637, 2642, 125 L.Ed.2d 257 (1993). The Americans with Disabilities Act of 1990, 104 Stat. 337, 42 U.S.C.A. § 12132 prohibits discrimination against persons with certain disabilities in the provision of public services. Nine years after the *Heller* decision the Justices, by a 6 to 3 vote, ruled that the Eighth Amendment cruel and unusual

punishment clause, which applies to the states through the Fourteenth Amendment, prohibited the execution of criminals who are mentally retarded. Atkins v. Virginia, 536 U.S. 304, 122 S.Ct. 2242, 153 L.Ed.2d 335 (2002).

95. 509 U.S. at 320, 113 S.Ct. at 2642–43.

96. 509 U.S. at 320, 113 S.Ct. at 2643.

Justice Souter, dissented in *Heller;* he wrote a dissenting opinion that was joined by Justices Blackmun and Stevens and, in part, by Justice O'Connor.[97] Justice Souter believed that using different standards for the commitment of mentally ill and mentally retarded persons was not rationally related to any legitimate state interest. Although the dissenting Justices asserted that they were reviewing these state classifications under the rationality test, these Justices appeared to make an independent determination of whether the difficulty of proving mental illness, as opposed to mental retardation, justified the state's different standards of proof and procedures. It is not clear whether the dissenting Justices believed that, at least in cases involving mental retardation, the rationality test should be converted into a standard by which the judiciary required the government to prove that its classifications in fact promoted specific government interests.[98]

(f) Conclusion: The Rationality Test Today.

Although all of the Supreme Court's recent majority opinions are consistent with the use of a true rationality test for the review of economic or social welfare legislation under the due process and equal protection clauses, it is possible that the Court is moving towards converting the rationality test into a "reasonableness" test similar to that employed during the 1900–1936 era. If the Justices on the Supreme Court today would explicitly adopt several distinct standards of review (such as a rationality standard, an intermediate *ad hoc* standard, and the strict scrutiny test) for analyzing substantive due process and equal pro-

tection problems, the Justices in each case would have to explain why a law was reviewed under a particular standard. Several Justices have argued that there should be no specific division of equal protection and substantive due process analysis in terms of specific tests or levels of scrutiny. These Justices favor an approach to due process and equal protection that would merge all equal protection and substantive due process analysis into a judicial assessment of the reasonableness of the law or classification at issue in each case. Although this type of generalized reasonableness approach may sound as if it does not involve great judicial control over legislative actions, it, in fact, was the standard used by the Court during the *Lochner* era.[99]

It is important to note that there may be no trend toward active review of economic and social welfare legislation. The Supreme Court, in majority opinions, continues to assert that it will only review economic and social welfare legislation (which does not involve a fundamental constitutional right or a classification that merits heightened judicial scrutiny) under the rational relationship standard.[100]

At the present time, the Supreme Court seems committed to upholding a true presumption of constitutionality in due process and equal protection cases that involves neither a fundamental right nor a classification of persons who receive independent judicial review (such as persons classified by race, national origin, alienage, gender, or illegitimacy). For example, in *Federal Communications Commission v. Beach Communications, Inc.,*[101] the Supreme Court unanimously upheld provi-

97. The dissenting Justices in *Heller* agreed that the rationality test should be used because that test had been used throughout the lower court litigation. 509 U.S. at 333, 113 S.Ct. at 2650 (O'Connor, J., concurring in part and dissenting in part). 509 U.S. at 333–49, 113 S.Ct. at 2650–58 (Souter, joined by Blackmun and Stevens, JJ., and, in part, by O'Connor, J., dissenting).

98. Although Justice Blackmun agreed with Justice Souter's dissenting opinion, he also issued a one paragraph dissenting statement to point out his "continuing adherence to the views that laws that discriminate against individuals with mental retardation ... or infringe upon fundamental rights ... are subject to heightened review." 509 U.S. at 333, 113 S.Ct. at 2650 (Blackmun, J., dissenting).

99. Lochner v. New York, 198 U.S. 45, 25 S.Ct. 539, 49 L.Ed. 937 (1905); see § 11.3.

100. Sullivan v. Stroop, 496 U.S. 478, 110 S.Ct. 2499, 110 L.Ed.2d 438 (1990) (upholding a classification created by federal statutes concerning family eligibility for Aid to Families with Dependent Children; the majority opinion by Chief Justice Rehnquist found that the classification would not violate the equal protection component of the Fifth Amendment due process clause "if any state of facts reasonably may be conceived to justify it.").

101. 508 U.S. 307, 113 S.Ct. 2096, 124 L.Ed.2d 211 (1993).

sions in the Federal Cable Communications Policy Act that exempted from regulation cable television facilities that serve one or more buildings under common ownership or management as long as the cable facility did not use public rights-of-way. The Act subjected to regulation similar types of cable television facilities that serve separately owned buildings. The distinction between the commonly owned and separately owned buildings was attacked as being a violation of the implied equal protection guarantee of the due process clause of the Fifth Amendment. Justice Thomas wrote for eight Justices in finding that the Court would uphold the classification as long as there was any conceivable set of facts that might provide a basis for concluding that the classification was rationally related to any legitimate interest of government.

The majority opinion in *Beach Communications* found that the judiciary should not make an independent examination of either the ends of the legislation, or the reasonableness of the classification, in this type of economic and social welfare case. Justice Thomas stated: "Those attacking the rationality of the legislative classification have the burden to negate every conceivable basis which might support it . . . moreover, because we never require a legislature to articulate its reasons for enacting a statute, it is entirely irrelevant for constitutional purposes whether the conceived reason for the challenged distinction actually motivated the legislature . . . in other words, a legislative choice is not subject to courtroom factfinding and may be based on rational speculation unsupported by evidence or empirical data." [102] Because it was at least arguable that cable television facilities serving commonly owned buildings did not require regulation, the Court upheld the federal statutory distinction.

In the *Beach Communications* case only Justice Stevens favored using a meaningful standard of review. Justice Stevens concurred in

the Court's judgment in *Beach Communications*, because he believed there was a sufficient basis in the facts and economic theory for Congress to make the statutory distinction between regulated and unregulated cable entities that was challenged in this case. However, Justice Stevens disagreed with the standard used by the majority, under which a classification would be upheld under "any reasonably conceivable state of facts." Justice Stevens found that "judicial review under the 'conceivable set of facts' test is tantamount to no review at all." [103]

Justice Stevens may be correct in finding that the rationality test used in *Beach Communications* does not provide independent judicial review of challenged legislation. However, the presumption of constitutionality established for such legislation during the past half century implies a rejection of independent judicial review of legislative decisions concerning economic and social welfare matters that involve neither groups with special constitutional protection nor fundamental constitutional rights. [104]

In some cases decided in the early 1990s, the Supreme Court failed to clearly specify the standard used to review classifications that involve neither fundamental rights nor classifications of persons receiving special judicial protection (such as classifications of persons defined by race, national origin, United States citizenship, legitimacy, or sex). Nevertheless, the Court appears to be committed to maintaining the presumption of constitutionality for such cases. In other words, the Court will uphold any classification that arguably has a rational relationship to any legitimate interest of government so long as the classification does not involve a fundamental right or separate persons because of their race, national origin, citizenship, legitimacy at birth, or sex.

Central State University v. American Association of University Professors [105] provides an

---

102. 508 U.S. at 315, 113 S.Ct. at 2102.

103. Federal Communications Commission v. Beach Communications, Inc., 508 U.S. 307, 320, 323 n. 3, 113 S.Ct. 2096, 2105, 2106 n. 3, 124 L.Ed.2d 211 (1993) (Stevens, J., concurring in the judgment).

104. For analysis on this point, references to additional cases and secondary authorities, see R. Rotunda & J.

Nowak, Treatise on Constitutional Law: Substance and Procedure § 18.3 (3rd ed. 1999, with annual supplements).

105. Central State University v. American Association of University Professors, 526 U.S. 124, 119 S.Ct. 1162, 143 L.Ed.2d 227 (1999) (per curiam).

example of the Court's use of the rationality standard near the close of the twentieth century. The Ohio legislature attempted to control the amount of time that professors at government owned and operated universities spent on teaching, as opposed to research or other activities. To achieve that end, Ohio enacted a statute that required the state's Board of Regents, and the state universities, to create standards for instructional workloads that should be met by faculty members at the state universities. The Ohio legislation required each state university to adopt faculty workload policies consistent with the standards that would be established by the Board of Regents. Earlier state statutes had allowed faculties to unionize; faculty workloads were a proper subject of collective bargaining under earlier state statutes. The new legislation made the workload standards operative despite any conflicting provisions in collective bargaining agreements and prohibited the state universities from engaging in collective bargaining regarding professorial teaching workloads.

The Ohio Supreme Court held that the statute, insofar as it created a class of state employees who could not engage in collective bargaining about their workloads, violated the concept of equal protection.[106] The Justices of the United States Supreme Court ruled that the classifications established by the Ohio statute requiring teaching workload standards for professors, and prohibiting collective bargaining over teacher workloads, did not violate the equal protection clause of the Fourteenth Amendment. The majority opinion in *Central State University* found that the classifications

would easily survive review under the equal protection clause rationality test. The Justices decided this case, and issued a *per curiam* opinion, without full briefing or oral arguments. The majority opinion stated: "We have repeatedly held that a classification neither involving fundamental rights nor proceeding along suspect lines ... cannot run afoul of the equal protection clause if there is a rational relationship between the disparity of treatment [the classifications created by the government] and some legitimate government purpose."[107]

The professors challenging the classification in *Central State University* asserted that the state had never produced any evidence showing that making teacher workloads the subject of collective bargaining would reduce the amount of classroom time that would be required from faculty members, or hurt faculty teaching performance. The United States Supreme Court noted that the government had no obligation to produce any evidence to justify a classification that was only subject to the rationality test. So long as a legislature could rationally conclude that making teacher workloads a subject of collective bargaining might interfere with its goal of improving teaching services at public universities, the classification had to be upheld. Only Justice Stevens, the sole dissenter in *Central State University*, believed that the judiciary should invalidate the classification if it found that there were no facts that would show that the classification was related to promoting legitimate state interests, such as the improvement of instruction at state universities.[108]

---

106. Although they agreed with the majority opinion concerning the rationality test, and its application to the Ohio statute, Justices Ginsburg and Breyer agreed with dissenting Justice Stevens that "A summary disposition is not a fit occasion for elaborate discussion of our rational basis standards of review." They also noted that "The Ohio Supreme Court is of course at liberty to resolve the matter under the Ohio Constitution." 526 U.S. at 129, 119 S.Ct. at 1164 (Ginsburg, J., joined by Breyer, J., concurring). The Ohio Supreme Court's opinion was not clear regarding whether the ruling was based on the state constitution or the equal protection clause of the Fourteenth Amendment to the United States Constitution. The Ohio Supreme Court would be free, both before and after the United States Supreme Court decision in this case, to invalidate the state classification under the state constitu-

tion. However, the Ohio Supreme Court could not give the equal protection clause of the Fourteenth Amendment a different meaning than the United States Supreme Court had given to it.

107. Central State University v. American Association of University Professors, 526 U.S. 124, 119 S.Ct. 1162, 1163, 143 L.Ed.2d 227 (1999) (per curiam) (internal citations and internal quotations omitted).

108. Justice Stevens dissented from the result in this case because he believed that the Court should not have decided the case without full briefing and oral argument, if at all. Because of the lack of clarity in the state court's decision, Justice Stevens would have allowed the Ohio Supreme Court decision to stand. Justice Stevens also noted that, although he was "not prepared to express an

If an individual believes that she has been treated by the government in an entirely different manner than all other similarly situated persons, she may bring an equal protection claim against the government even though she is, in a sense, only a "class of one." In many, if not most, real-life cases, we would expect the government to have a rational argument for why the separate treatment of the individual was a reasonable method of promoting a legitimate governmental or societal interest. There may be circumstances under which the separate treatment of a single person would violate equal protection even under the rationality test. For example, let us assume that Susan Smith, the child of Sarah and Samuel Smith, is 6 years old and (under all state and local statutes) eligible for a free public education at her neighborhood public grade school. When Susan and her parents go to register her for the first grade, the school authorities refuse to register her; they will not allow her to attend the school. The school administration states: "We don't like the Smith family, and we don't want any Smith children in our public schools." Susan would have an equal protection claim against the governmental entity that operated the schools, which might or might not prevail after trial. If we assume that education is not a fundamental right, and that Susan was not excluded because of her race, gender, or status as a legitimate or illegitimate child, the Court would apply the rationality test to determine whether the denial of free public education to Susan violated the equal protection guarantee. Susan and her parents might be able to make a convincing argument

that there is no possible legitimate interest that would justify singling out this child from school. Although the state would not have the burden of proof in this case, the Smith family should win unless the government could rebut the Susan's argument by showing that the denial of education for Susan promoted a legitimate governmental interest. Were such a case to actually occur, the government should lose, under the equal protection clause, even though the Court was applying the classic form of minimal judicial scrutiny and the rationality test.[109]

§ 14.4 Establishing and Testing Classifications of a Law—"On Its Face", in Its "Application", or in Its "Purpose and Effect"—The Problem of Statistics

As can be seen from the foregoing introductory sections, in order to subject a law to any form of review under the equal protection guarantee, one must be able to demonstrate that the law classifies persons in some manner. And even this first step will not be of much help to a person challenging the law for, as we have seen, a classification in the area of "economics or social welfare" will not be subjected to a very meaningful form of judicial review. Thus, the person challenging the law will need to show either that it classifies persons in terms of their ability to exercise a fundamental right or establishes a classification on the basis of race, national origin, alienage, illegitimacy, or gender.

---

opinion about the ultimate merits of the case," the statutory exclusion of teacher workloads from collective bargainings might violate the equal protection clause because prohibiting collective bargaining regarding workloads might not have any real relationship to teacher performance. Thus, it appears that Justice Stevens was ready to use a standard of review more strict than the rationality test. Central State University v. American Association of University Professors, 526 U.S. 124, 119 S.Ct. 1162, 1164–66, 143 L.Ed.2d 227 (1999) (Stevens, J., dissenting).

109. In Village of Willowbrook v. Olech, 528 U.S. 562, 120 S.Ct. 1073, 145 L.Ed.2d 1060, (2000) (per curiam) the Court ruled that a woman could maintain an equal protection claim against a Village based on an allegation that the Village had demanded that she give the Village, in exchange for connection to the municipal water supply, a 33–foot easement on her property. All other similarly

situated owners were required to give only a 15–foot easement to the Village in exchange for the municipal water supply connection. The majority opinion noted that the Court did not have to consider the subjective motives of the Village, because the Court had often recognized that an individual could bring an equal protection claim as a "class of one" by being treated differently from other similarly situated persons. Such a claim would be reviewed under the rationality test. Justice Breyer concurred in only the result in *Willowbrook*, he believed that the Court should focus on the fact that there was an allegation of an improper motive on the part of the governmental officials (a desire to harm the property owner because of other disputes with her) so as to reduce the possibility of persons bringing "run-of-the-mill zoning cases" to federal courts as claims of a denial of a constitutional right.

In the course of litigation, questions may often arise as to whether such a classification exists at all; if it does not the law will not be subjected to strict scrutiny. This issue may often involve difficult problems of proof and intricate statistical demonstrations. The details of those litigation problems are beyond the scope of this treatise but we do wish to introduce the basic concepts of how a court determines the existence of a classification.

A classification within a law can be established in one of three ways.[1] First, the law may establish the classification "on its face." This means that the law by its own terms classifies persons for different treatment. In such a case there is no problem of proof and the court can proceed to test the validity of the classification by the appropriate standard.

Second, the law may be tested in its "application." In these cases the law either shows no classification on its face or else indicates a classification which seems to be legitimate, but those persons challenging the legislation claim that the governmental officials who administer the law are applying it with different degrees of severity to different groups of persons who are described by some suspect trait. Here the challengers must establish that there is an administrative classification used to implement the law which merits some increased standard of review.

Finally, the law may contain no classification, or a neutral classification, and be applied evenhandedly. Nevertheless the law may be challenged as in reality constituting a device designed to impose different burdens on different classes of persons. If this claim can be proven the law will be reviewed as if it established such a classification on its face. However, because all laws are susceptible to having their impact analyzed in a variety of ways, it will be most difficult to establish this claim for the purpose of seeking strict judicial review of a legislative act.

The approach which the Court has taken on these issues over the years has not changed abruptly but many of its recent results may seem inconsistent with earlier decisions. One of the reasons for this apparent inconsistency is that the Supreme Court also reviews classifications under statutes which allow for easier proof as to the existence of discriminatory classifications than would be acceptable if the Court were only enforcing the equal protection guarantee. With this in mind, let us examine briefly the problems involved in establishing classifications based on the application or effect of a law.

Any law may be applied in a manner that creates a classification. For example, let us assume that it could be proven that a local police force only enforces an anti-littering ordinance against members of a minority race. This evidence would establish that the law as applied involved a racial classification so that enforcement of the law could be enjoined, at least until such a time as the authorities could

---

§ 14.4

1. For references to additional cases, and secondary authorities, see, 3 R. Rotunda & J. Nowak, Treatise on Constitutional Law: Substance and Procedure, vol. 3, § 18.4 (3rd ed. 1999, with annual supplements).

Among the cases citing this section of the Treatise are: Anderson, J., citing Treatise in State v. Frazier, 649 N.W.2d 828, 833–34 (Minn.2002); Patterson, J., citing Treatise in, Aida Renta Trust v. Dept. of Revenue, 197 Ariz. 222, 3 P.3d 1142, 1157 (App.2000); Supreme Court of Montana, citing Treatise in Roosevelt v. Montana Department of Revenue, 293 Mont. 240, 975 P.2d 295, 303 (1999); Justice Neuman, citing Treatise in In re Detention of Williams, 628 N.W.2d 447, 452 (Iowa 2001); Justice Baird, citing earlier edition of Treatise in Stewart v. State, 13 S.W.3d 127 (Tex.App.2000); Justice Croskey, citing Treatise in City of Los Angeles v. Superior Court (Brandon), 84 Cal.App.4th 767, 101 Cal.Rptr.2d 156, 164 n. 7 (2000); Greenwalt v. Ram Restaurant Corp. of Wyoming,

71 P.3d 717 (Wyo.2003; citing an earlier edition of this Treatise); State v. Frazier, 649 N.W.2d 828 (Minn.2002, citing this Treatise). Marcus, J., citing Treatise in, State v. Baxley, 656 So.2d 973, 978 n. 11 (La.1995); Comer, et al. v. Kemp, 37 F.3d 775 (2d Cir.1994) (Oakes, J.); Wellmaker v. Dahill, 836 F.Supp. 1375, 1385 (N.D.Ohio 1993) (Bell, J.); Ameritech Corp. v. United States, No. 93 C 6642, 1994 WL 142864, *7 (N.D.Ill.1994) (Grady, J.); Orange Lake Associates, Inc. v. Kirkpatrick, 21 F.3d 1214, 1225–1226 (2d Cir.1994) (Oakes, J.); People v. Wegielnik, 152 Ill.2d 418, 178 Ill.Dec. 693, 698, 605 N.E.2d 487, 492 (1992) (Miller, C.J.); Dauphinot, J., concurring and dissenting, and citing Treatise, in Schleuter v. City of Fort Worth, 947 S.W.2d 920, 934 (Tex.App.1997); McDade, District Judge, citing Treatise in Hamlyn v. Rock Island County Metro. Mass Transit Dist., 986 F.Supp. 1126 (C.D.Ill.1997); Ransom, J., citing Treatise in, Garcia v. La Farge, 119 N.M. 532, 893 P.2d 428, 433–34 (1995).

show that there would be no further discriminatory application.[2]

The first and leading case in this area is *Yick Wo v. Hopkins*[3] where the Court held unconstitutional the enforcement of a San Francisco ordinance banning the operation of hand laundries in wooden buildings. It was demonstrated in that case that the vast majority of such laundries were owned and operated by Chinese residents of the city, but the Court did not rest its ruling on the direct impact of the statute. It was also demonstrated that all non-oriental launderers who had applied for an exemption from the statute had received one, while no Chinese applicant had been granted an exemption. This discriminatory application of the law constituted a racial classification which had to be invalidated.

The decisions of the Supreme Court make it easier to prove that a government impermissibly classifies persons in the administration of neutral laws than to prove that a seemingly neutral law has an impermissible discriminatory effect. The reason is a relatively simple one: the administrative discretionary selection process deserves less deference than rule-making for society's benefit, whether that rule-making is done by a legislative body or administrative agency. What is being tested in the application cases is the administrative selection of persons for a burden or benefit.

The problem of proof in showing that the actions have been taken with a discriminatory purpose is far less than proving the intent of a legislative body. For example, in *Washington v. Davis*[4] the Supreme Court held that the fact that a criterion for government employment, such as a written objective test, has a greater degree of impact on one race than another does not in itself constitute purposeful discrimination. However, in the *Davis* case the Court noted that there was no challenge to the individual selection of police officers for government employment. To the extent that those officials who hired police officers were allowed to use subjective criterion, statistical proof as to the result of how they exercised their hiring discretion would be extremely relevant; such proof might establish a prima facie case that they were in fact employing racial criteria which were not expressed in the statute.

Similarly, when the Court upheld a zoning ordinance against the challenge that its effect was racially disproportionate, the opinion noted that an opposite result would be reached if there were proof that the city had granted exemptions from the zoning restrictions on a racially discriminatory basis.[5]

Throughout its decisions in cases concerning the existence of classifications, the Court has held that statistical proof is usually relevant but rarely determinative. The problem to be

2. There may be cases in which it is alleged that a refusal to provide state services to a group of persons constitutes a violation of equal protection. If the statute creating the system for the delivery of the service (such as a statute creating a department of social welfare services or a police department) does not create a classification of recipients, or if the classification system in the statute does not violate equal protection on its face (because there is no trait used in the classification which might violate the Constitution), persons challenging the state's delivery of services on equal protection grounds will need to show that the statute was applied in a manner that involved the use of an unconstitutional classification. In DeShaney v. Winnebago County Department of Social Services, 489 U.S. 189, 109 S.Ct. 998, 103 L.Ed.2d 249 (1989), the Supreme Court found that the due process clause did not impose on the government a duty to protect a child from his father, who was physically abusing him, even though the government had assigned a social worker to work with the father and the social worker had recorded a variety of events and circumstances that made the social worker believe that the father was abusing the child. The Court found that due process did not require the government to

protect an individual but the majority opinion noted that the equal protection clause would be violated if the government were to "selectively deny its protective services to certain disfavored minorities." 489 U.S. at 197 n. 3, 109 S.Ct. at 1004 n. 3. Equal protection should prohibit a prosecutor or police department from using a person's race or ethnic ancestry as the basis for deciding whether to arrest or prosecute a person who broke the law. Nevertheless, on the basis of statistical proof alone, it is difficult to establish that a prosecutor has engaged in unconstitutional selective enforcement of a facially race neutral law. For references to cases on this point see the multi-volume edition of this Treatise: R. Rotunda & J. Nowak, Treatise on Constitutional Law: Substance and Procedure § 18.4 (3rd ed. 1999, with annual supplements).

3.   118 U.S. 356, 6 S.Ct. 1064, 30 L.Ed. 220 (1886).

4.   426 U.S. 229, 96 S.Ct. 2040, 48 L.Ed.2d 597 (1976).

5.   Arlington Heights v. Metropolitan Housing Development Corp., 429 U.S. 252, 267, 97 S.Ct. 555, 565–67, 50 L.Ed.2d 450 (1977), on remand 558 F.2d 1283 (7th Cir. 1977).

confronted is whether the decision-maker is employing some form of suspect criterion and thereby establishing a classification within the law or in its application. Where the statistical proof is overwhelming, it may be sufficient to establish a prima facie case.

Proof by statistics is especially useful when one is challenging an individual selection or application process; there the criterion is subjective and unknowable to all those except the officials charged with the enforcement or application of the law. It is less difficult to inquire into their motivation, for there is no need to pay them the deference that the judiciary should afford either an independent branch of government or an administrative agency when it is acting in a rule-making capacity. However, to the extent that the Court finds some independent societal value in the discretionary system it will be more hesitant to employ statistical proof to establish a prima facie case of discrimination. This factor is demonstrated quite clearly by the jury selection cases.

The Court has long held that it is unconstitutional to exclude members of racial minorities, or to allow only for their disproportionately low representation, on either grand juries or petit juries in criminal cases.[6] Following this ruling, states have enacted a variety of measures for selecting jurors which have been challenged and overturned by the Court as constituting racial classifications. In these cases the Court has continually allowed statistics to establish a prima facie case of discrimination whenever there was a sta-

tistically significant underrepresentation of minority members on juries or the panels from which juries were selected. It is clearly established that no individual has a right to have his particular grand jury or petit jury reflect the racial composition of the community,[7] but it is equally clear that there must be an equal opportunity for such persons to serve on juries.[8]

The reason for the Court's use of statistics in the jury selection cases is that the challenged procedures have included some form of subjective selection process by judicial or executive officials. Procedures using juror selectors or allowing officials to select jurors from lists which made them consciously aware of the individual's race were stricken when the statistics showed racially disproportionate results.[9] So too, the use and review of questionnaires or other qualifications for jury service has been overturned when the statistics indicated that the selectors were using their discretion in a racially discriminatory manner.[10]

However, when the selection process did not involve any subjective elements but only the random selection of persons from tax lists the Court did not overturn the law because of its statistical impact.[11] In that situation there was no subjective discretion to test and the challenge constituted one to the terms of the law in its necessary effect rather than its application. Similarly, a jury selection procedure will not be stricken "on its face" because it grants officials some discretion, for the law is valid unless there is a prima facie statistical

6. Strauder v. West Virginia, 100 U.S. (10 Otto) 303, 25 L.Ed. 664 (1879); Norris v. Alabama, 294 U.S. 587, 55 S.Ct. 579, 79 L.Ed. 1074 (1935); Avery v. Georgia, 345 U.S. 559, 73 S.Ct. 891, 97 L.Ed. 1244 (1953).

7. See, Akins v. Texas, 325 U.S. 398, 65 S.Ct. 1276, 89 L.Ed. 1692 (1945).

8. A prosecutor's use of peremptory challenges to exclude racial minority members from a jury violates the equal protection clause even though the Sixth Amendment right to a jury trial does not prevent either side in a criminal case from excluding cognizable groups from a jury. Compare Batson v. Kentucky, 476 U.S. 79, 106 S.Ct. 1712, 90 L.Ed.2d 69 (1986) (purposeful exclusion of black persons from petit jury for the trial of a black defendant violates equal protection clause), with Holland v. Illinois, 493 U.S. 474, 110 S.Ct. 803, 107 L.Ed.2d 905 (1990) (the

Sixth Amendment's "fair cross-section" requirement for juries does not prevent either side in a criminal case from using peremptory challenges to eliminate cognizable racial groups from the petit jury which is finally impaneled).

9. Whitus v. Georgia, 385 U.S. 545, 87 S.Ct. 643, 17 L.Ed.2d 599 (1967).

10. See, e.g., Castaneda v. Partida, 430 U.S. 482, 97 S.Ct. 1272, 51 L.Ed.2d 498 (1977); Alexander v. Louisiana, 405 U.S. 625, 92 S.Ct. 1221, 31 L.Ed.2d 536 (1972); Cassell v. Texas, 339 U.S. 282, 70 S.Ct. 629, 94 L.Ed. 839 (1950); Hill v. Texas, 316 U.S. 400, 62 S.Ct. 1159, 86 L.Ed. 1559 (1942); cf. Eubanks v. Louisiana, 356 U.S. 584, 78 S.Ct. 970, 2 L.Ed.2d 991 (1958).

11. Brown v. Allen, 344 U.S. 443, 73 S.Ct. 397, 97 L.Ed. 469 (1953).

demonstration that it is being applied in a discriminatory manner.[12]

The Supreme Court had long held that exclusion of members of identifiable racial minorities from petit juries, as well as grand juries, violates the equal protection clause.[13] Nevertheless, *Swain v. Alabama*,[14] ruled that a prima facie case of racial minority exclusion from petit juries through prosecutorial peremptory challenges could only be demonstrated by showing that the prosecutors in the jurisdiction had consistently excluded members of a particular race from jury service in a series of cases. The decision in *Swain* was contrary to the approach the Court had taken in the grand jury selection cases, where the Court allowed persons alleging an equal protection violation to show a prima facie case of intentional discrimination through the use of statistical evidence of exclusion and an analysis of the systems used for grand juror selection.[15] Thus, in 1986, the Supreme Court overruled *Swain* in *Batson v. Kentucky*.[16] The Court has now made an individual's burden in establishing that a prosecutor's use of peremptory challenges constituted purposeful race discrimination identical to the burden an individual must meet for proving purposeful racial discrimination in any type of government action that does not involve an explicit use of racial criteria.

When "discriminatory purpose" is in issue, the Supreme Court has long held that statistical evidence of the adverse impact of a law or administrative action on identifiable racial minorities is relevant evidence that should be considered by the judiciary. However, statistical evidence will rarely be sufficient in itself to prove discriminatory purpose. The Court in *Batson* found that a defendant could prove unconstitutional racial discrimination in the selection of petit juries in either of two ways. First, the defendant could demonstrate that members of his identifiable racial group had been excluded from juries through a systematic practice existing over an extended period of time; proof of that type of systematic exclusion would raise the inference of purposeful discrimination and shift the burden of proof to the state. Alternatively, the defendant could attempt to prove a prima facie case of discrimination in the selection of his *particular* petit jury, without attempting to prove a long continued practice of using peremptory challenges to exclude members of his race from jury panels.

If the defendant attempts to prove that the prosecutor's use of peremptory challenges in the defendant's particular case involved racial discrimination, the defendant must establish that (1) he is a member of a "cognizable racial group," (2) the prosecutor in fact "exercised peremptory challenges to remove" members of the defendant's race from the jury, and (3) "these facts and any other relevant circumstances raise an inference that the prosecutor used the practice to exclude the veniremen from the petit jury on account of their race." The *Batson* opinion stated that the defendant was "entitled to rely" on the fact that the peremptory challenge system allows a prosecu-

12. Statistical evidence of systematic exclusion of identifiable racial minority members from the grand jury may shift the burden to the state to disprove the prima facie demonstration of discrimination. If the defendant has proven that there was purposeful exclusion of potential grand jurors because of their race, his conviction will be overturned; racial discrimination in the selection of the grand jury is not subject to "harmless error" analysis. Vasquez v. Hillery, 474 U.S. 254, 106 S.Ct. 617, 88 L.Ed.2d 598 (1986). See also, United States v. Bass, 536 U.S. 862, 122 S.Ct. 2389, 153 L.Ed.2d 769 (2002) (per curiam) (Supreme Court unanimously overturns lower federal court ruling that allowed a defendant's motion for discovery regarding allegation of selective prosecution based upon nationwide statistics regarding race of persons charged with death penalty offenses by the federal government; defendant's showing failed to indicate disparity

about charges brought against defendants who were similarly situated to the defendant in this case).

For references to additional cases, see, R. Rotunda & J. Nowak, Treatise on Constitutional Law: Substance and Procedure, vol. 3, § 18.4 (3rd ed. 1999, with annual supplements).

13. See, e.g., Strauder v. West Virginia, 100 U.S. (10 Otto) 303, 25 L.Ed. 664 (1879); Avery v. Georgia, 345 U.S. 559, 73 S.Ct. 891, 97 L.Ed. 1244 (1953); Castaneda v. Partida, 430 U.S. 482, 97 S.Ct. 1272, 51 L.Ed.2d 498 (1977).

14. 380 U.S. 202, 85 S.Ct. 824, 13 L.Ed.2d 759 (1965), overruled in Batson v. Kentucky, 476 U.S. 79, 106 S.Ct. 1712, 90 L.Ed.2d 69 (1986).

15. See footnotes 6–12 supra.

16. 476 U.S. 79, 106 S.Ct. 1712, 90 L.Ed.2d 69 (1986).

tor who wishes to discriminate on the basis of race to use his peremptory challenges in that manner. The Court did not explain whether there would be any cases in which statistics alone would present a prima facie case of racial discrimination or whether a defendant would always need to have some nonstatistical evidence pointing to the existence of purposeful racial discrimination by the prosecutor.[17] The majority opinion stated that "the trial court should consider all relevant circumstances," when determining whether the prosecutor had used peremptory challenges in a racially discriminatory manner.[18]

Mayor of Philadelphia v. Educational Equality League[19] upheld a mayor's practices in selecting persons for a nominating panel for the school board despite the fact that statistical analysis indicated that blacks were continually underrepresented on this panel. It found that the "simplistic percentage comparisons" used by the lower court did not have any "real meaning" in this case.[20] A chief executive officer's ability to choose persons for administrative positions of importance is a function that the Court felt should be deferred to by the judiciary. Thus it would not restrict the mayor's power absent clear proof of discrimination beyond statistical impact.

The most difficult problem regarding classifications is proving that a properly enacted law or agency regulation which is neutral on its face, and in its application, nevertheless constitutes a purposeful device to classify persons on a suspect criterion. In these cases the Court is confronted by decision-making entities to whom it feels it owes some deference. The problems of proof are initially greater than in the cases of proving discriminatory application because of the general principle against inquiring into the "motives" of proper rule-making or legislative authorities. In only rare cases would the direct testimony of members of the agency or legislative body be admitted, due both to problems of separation of powers and the announced principle against searching inquiries into legislative motives.[21] The most extensive problems concerning an agency have occurred in connection with school desegregation cases but even there the Court has required objective proof that school board policies were designed to create a segregated school system.[22]

It is not easy to establish the proper role of the Court in this area. In these cases the Court is not merely determining whether the law has differing impact upon different racial groups. Nor is the test solely one of legislative "motive" in the sense of looking into the sub-

17. Because *Batson* makes it easier for the defendants to demonstrate an equal protection violation in the selection of their juries and employs a standard that could not have been anticipated following the *Swain* decision, the Supreme Court has held that the *Batson* decision is not fully retroactive. In Allen v. Hardy, 478 U.S. 255, 106 S.Ct. 2878, 92 L.Ed.2d 199 (1986) (per curiam) the Court held that *Batson* would not be applied retroactively to collateral review of convictions that became final before the *Batson* opinion was announced. For further analysis on this point, see R. Rotunda & J. Nowak, Treatise on Constitutional Law: Substance and Procedure § 18.4 (3rd ed. 1999, with annual supplements).

18. A prosecutor may be able to rebut a defendant's prima facie case of race-based exclusion of jurors. If the prosecutor can explain his use of peremptory challenges against persons who were members of a minority race in race-neutral terms, the court may find that the prosecutor had not engaged in purposeful racial discrimination. The Supreme Court has not given precise guidelines to lower courts regarding how they should determine whether a prosecutor has violated the equal protection guarantee through the use of peremptory challenges.

For references to additional cases, on this point see the multi-volume edition of this Treatise: R. Rotunda & J.

Nowak, Treatise on Constitutional Law: Substance & Procedure § 18.4 (3rd ed. 1999, with annual supplements).

19. 415 U.S. 605, 94 S.Ct. 1323, 39 L.Ed.2d 630 (1974).

20. 415 U.S. at 620, 94 S.Ct. at 1333. This attitude was also evidenced in Carter v. Jury Com'n, 396 U.S. 320, 90 S.Ct. 518, 24 L.Ed.2d 549 (1970) where the Court indicated it would not strike the mere grant of discretion to the executive absent such proof.

21. The Court has taken the position that only the most extreme circumstances might allow for the use of legislators' testimony, which it recognized as a possibility. See, Arlington Heights v. Metropolitan Housing Development Corp., 429 U.S. 252, 268 n. 18, 270 n. 20, 97 S.Ct. 555, 565 n. 18, 566 n. 20, 50 L.Ed.2d 450 (1977); Citizens to Preserve Overton Park, Inc. v. Volpe, 401 U.S. 402, 420, 91 S.Ct. 814, 825–26, 28 L.Ed.2d 136 (1971); See also Mayor of Philadelphia v. Educational Equality League, 415 U.S. 605, 618–9, 94 S.Ct. 1323, 1332–33, 39 L.Ed.2d 630 (1974); The origin of this position has been traced by the Court to Fletcher v. Peck, 10 U.S. (6 Cranch) 87, 130–31, 3 L.Ed. 162 (1810).

22. These cases are examined in § 14.9(a)(2)(a), infra.

jective intent of individual legislators. That would not only raise severe problems of separation of powers in specific cases, it would also overturn many acts which might have come out of a non-discriminatory democratic process merely because some of the people voting for the acts were prejudiced.

On the other hand, the Court cannot allow all laws to stand unchallenged when they may constitute devices used by another branch of government to subvert the equal protection guarantee. Thus, the Supreme Court is faced with a most difficult problem in these cases.[23]

The Court has attempted to take a middle road. It gives significant deference to other branches of government while searching all sources outside of inquiries into particular legislator's motives to determine if a law constitutes a purposeful device for discriminatory treatment. Three sources may be used to establish such a conclusion: (1) the differing practical or statistical impact upon certain classifications of persons; (2) the general history concerning the problems which the legislative or administrative rule seeks to solve; (3) the history of the passage or enactment of the legislation or agency rule.[24]

For some time it had been thought that statistics alone would prove the existence of such classifications, but this belief was built upon the theory used in cases under specific civil rights statutes. The Court has determined that some statutes allow for easier proof of discriminatory classifications when applicable.[25] When enforcing the general equal protection guarantee, the Court will not allow legislative or administrative rules to be overturned on the basis of statistics alone unless the statistical proof is so great that it estab-

lishes a clear and convincing case that the legislation had to be adopted for a discriminatory purpose.[26]

However the Court will allow for other proof of discrimination and when it is convinced that the background of the legislative decision or its particular history shows discriminatory purpose, it will strike down the law. Here the Court has said that it will only require the showing of the entry of discriminatory considerations as a motive for the action—not necessarily the sole or dominant motive of the decision-making body.

The way in which the Court looks at proof of discriminatory purpose in legislation may be demonstrated by decisions concerning literacy tests for voting. The Court struck down the use of a literacy test where it exempted all persons who had qualified to vote at an earlier time. The reason for this ruling was that the "grandfather clause" related to a period when blacks were excluded from voting within the state so that it had the effect of imposing the test upon all blacks but on only a small fraction of white voters.[27]

Following this case, the state enacted a registration requirement which also gave preferential treatment to those previously registered and the Court invalidated this requirement as well.[28] When viewed against the background of racial discrimination within the state, the Court could easily reach the conclusion that these requirements constituted a racial classification.

However, the Court later upheld a literacy test after the state supreme court had independently stricken down the "grandfather clause" so that the law would be applied

---

23. For references to additional cases, and secondary authorities, on this point see the multi-volume edition of this Treatise: R. Rotunda & J. Nowak, Treatise on Constitutional Law: Substance and Procedure § 18.4 (West Group, 3rd ed. 1999, with annual supplements).

24. Arlington Heights v. Metropolitan Housing Development Corp., 429 U.S. 252, 266–68, 97 S.Ct. 555, 563–65, 50 L.Ed.2d 450 (1977).

25. See, e.g. Griggs v. Duke Power Co., 401 U.S. 424, 91 S.Ct. 849, 28 L.Ed.2d 158 (1971); Dothard v. Rawlinson, 433 U.S. 321, 97 S.Ct. 2720, 53 L.Ed.2d 786 (1977).

26. Arlington Heights v. Metropolitan Housing Development Corp., 429 U.S. 252, 266 n. 12, 97 S.Ct. 555, 563 n. 12, 50 L.Ed.2d 450 (1977).

27. Guinn v. United States, 238 U.S. 347, 35 S.Ct. 926, 59 L.Ed. 1340 (1915).

28. Lane v. Wilson, 307 U.S. 268, 59 S.Ct. 872, 83 L.Ed. 1281 (1939).

equally to persons of all races.[29] The Court held that there was no basis on the record for finding that the law would be applied in a discriminatory manner. The fact that members of one racial group might be disproportionally affected by the law was not enough to overturn the otherwise valid decision to require some demonstrated ability, in terms of literacy, in order to exercise the franchise.

In its rulings on the constitutionality of laws creating a districting map for elections, the Supreme Court has also distinguished laws that employ racial criteria on their face from race neutral laws that have an adverse effect on one racial group. If an election law, or any other law, has a race classification on its face, the law will be invalid unless the government can prove that the racial classification is narrowly tailored to promote a compelling interest. If a law is racially neutral on its face, the persons challenging the law as being a racial classification that violates equal protection must show that the law was created or maintained for a racially discriminatory purpose. The court will apply the compelling interest test to a law that is neutral on its face only if the court finds a racially discriminatory purpose.

In rare instances, the Court will find that a law that does not mention race is a law that constitutes racial discrimination "on its face" because the law (though race neutral in its language) cannot be explained except in terms of race. In other words, if a law that does not mention race can be explained only as being (1) an irrational act of government or (2) a law designed to use race to allocate benefits or burdens, the law will constitute a racial classification on its face. For example, in *Gomillion v. Lightfoot* [30] the Supreme Court held that a law altering a town's boundaries constituted racial discrimination on its face so that no racially discriminatory purpose inquiry had to be undertaken in the case. The law in *Gomillion* altered the shape of a town so that the

town would have 25 sides and a separation of black voters from white voters. The law removed black voters from the city; the newly designed 25 sided town would have a permanent white majority. There was no need for evidence of the background of racial discrimination in this political unit because there could be no reason for the odd reshaping of the town except for racial discrimination.

Shaw v. Reno [31] involved a finding that a legislative district map that promoted the interests of minority race voters constituted racial discrimination on its face. In *Shaw,* the Court, by a five to four vote of the Justices, held that North Carolina's map for the election of members to the House of Representatives of the United States constituted intentional racial discrimination and, therefore, that the law had to be narrowly tailored to promote a compelling governmental interest.

The dispute in *Shaw* arose, in part, from the interplay of state and federal law. Most of the counties in North Carolina are covered by § 5 of the Voting Rights Act. Under § 5 of the Voting Rights Act, certain areas in the United States are precluded from changing any voting laws without the approval of the Attorney General of the United States or the United States District Court in the District of Columbia. The Attorney General and the District Court can deny such a jurisdiction the ability to change its voting laws if the proposed change would have the effect of denying the right to vote to persons because of their race.[32] The North Carolina legislature created a congressional districting map following a new census and the allocation of an additional seat in the United States House of Representatives to North Carolina. The Attorney General of the United States posed an objection to the new districting plan because the new plan created only one district where it was likely that minority race voters would be able to determine the results of an election. Given the popula-

29. Lassiter v. Northampton County Bd. of Elections, 360 U.S. 45, 79 S.Ct. 985, 3 L.Ed.2d 1072 (1959).

30. 364 U.S. 339, 81 S.Ct. 125, 5 L.Ed.2d 110 (1960).

31. Shaw v. Reno, 509 U.S. 630, 113 S.Ct. 2816, 125 L.Ed.2d 511 (1993).

32. Section 5 of the Voting Rights Act of 1965 is codified in 42 U.S.C.A. § 1973c. See § 15.11 of this Treatise regarding congressional enforcement of the Fifteenth Amendment.

tion in North Carolina, it was the opinion of the Attorney General that there should be two districts wherein "Black and Native American voting strength" would predominate, in order to avoid the dilution of the voting strength of racial minorities in the state.

After the Attorney General objected to its first map, the North Carolina legislature revised the congressional district map. The final North Carolina map created two congressional districts that would have a majority of African–American voters in the district. One of these two districts (District 12) was 160 miles long and, according to the Supreme Court, "for much of its length, no wider than the I–85 corridor [a highway in the state]." In *Shaw* a majority of the Supreme Court found that District 12 could not be explained in any terms other than race. Therefore, the district map had to be considered as having a racial classification on its face. The majority made this finding even though the voters who objected to the new congressional district plan in North Carolina did not claim that the voting strength of white voters had been unconstitutionally diluted.[33]

Writing for the majority in *Shaw,* Justice O'Connor found that "no inquiry into legislative purpose is necessary when the racial classification appears on the face of the statute . . . [or in] those 'rare' statutes that, although race neutral, are, on their face unexplainable on grounds other than race." [34] If the State had given consideration to a variety of factors, including race, when drawing the district lines,

the districting law might have been explainable on grounds other than race. For example, if the state had created compact districts that followed political subdivision lines, but that created districts where minority race voters were virtually certain to be able to elect the representative to Congress, there might have been no finding of intentional discrimination. If there was no finding of race discrimination on the face of the statute, the plaintiff would be required to show discriminatory purpose.

The majority in *Shaw* found that the state's use of race as the only criteria for at least one district had to be subject to strict judicial scrutiny. Therefore, the law had to meet the compelling interest test, even though the districting law was designed to help the interest of racial minorities.[35]

The majority in *Shaw* remanded the case for an initial determination by the lower courts as to whether the plan could be justified in terms of a compelling interest. The Supreme Court did not indicate whether North Carolina's history of racial discrimination against minority race voters in earlier decades, might give rise to a remedial interest that would support the creation of the congressional district that favored minority race voters.[36]

The dissenters in *Shaw* noted that the prior cases in which the Supreme Court had found that a law that did not use racial terms constituted racial discrimination on its face involved laws wherein a racial group was denied some benefit, such as the right to vote.[37] But the

33. Shaw v. Reno, 509 U.S. 630, 642, 113 S.Ct. 2816, 2824, 125 L.Ed.2d 511 (1993).

34. 509 U.S. at 642–44, 113 S.Ct. at 2824–25.

35. In Shaw v. Reno, 509 U.S. 630, 113 S.Ct. 2816, 125 L.Ed.2d 511 (1993) Justice O'Connor, who wrote the majority opinion, distinguished the Supreme Court's earlier decision in United Jewish Organizations v. Carey, 430 U.S. 144, 97 S.Ct. 996, 51 L.Ed.2d 229 (1977) in which the Supreme Court ruled that legislative districts drawn so as to protect the voting power of racial minorities did not violate equal protection. Justice O'Connor, in *Shaw,* found that the plaintiffs in the *United Jewish Organizations* case had failed to claim that the districting map was "so highly irregular that it rationally could be understood only as an effort to segregate voters by race." 509 U.S. at 651, 113 S.Ct. at 2829. Justice O'Connor's majority opinion in *Shaw* found that the Supreme Court in the *United Jewish Organizations* case had not been presented with a

claim that required the Court to find racial classification on the face of the statute to which strict scrutiny and the compelling interest test had to be applied.

36. 509 U.S. at 653–58, 113 S.Ct. at 2830–32.

37. The four dissenters in *Shaw* focused on the fact that the districting map that was subject to strict scrutiny by the Supreme Court complied with the one person, one vote principle, was not alleged to deny white voters ballots and was not alleged to dilute the voting strength of white voters. In other words, in the view of the dissenters, the law did not present any injury to the white plaintiffs that constituted a cognizable constitutional claim. Shaw v. Reno, 509 U.S. 630, 658, 113 S.Ct. 2816, 2834, 125 L.Ed.2d 511 (1993) (White, J., joined by Blackmun and Stevens, JJ., dissenting); 509 U.S. at 675, 113 S.Ct. at 2843 (Blackmun, J., dissenting); 509 U.S. at 675, 113 S.Ct. at 2843 (Stevens, J., dissenting); 509 U.S. at 679, 113 S.Ct. at 2845 (Souter, J., dissenting).

majority believed that, because there could be no doubt that race was the only criteria used in the creation of some legislative districts in North Carolina, the congressional map had to comply with the compelling interest test.

The Court in *Miller v. Johnson*[38] may have expanded the *Shaw* ruling. In *Miller,* the Court, by a five to four vote, invalidated a Georgia congressional redistricting plan because one of the congressional districts was created for the sole purpose of insuring minority race representation and strengthening minority race voting power. The district at issue had been created by the Georgia legislature in response to the United States Department of Justice's refusal to clear a state redistricting plan under the Voting Rights Act. The original districting plans submitted to the Justice Department included two districts in which minority race voters would constitute a majority of the voters in the district. The Georgia congressional district at issue in *Miller* had been created for the purpose of strengthening minority race representation and giving minority race voters the power to control elections in a third congressional district. The additional legislative district that was designed by the Georgia legislature to have a predominance of minority race voters was not as bizarre in shape as the North Carolina district that had been at issue in *Shaw.* The majority opinion in *Miller,* written by Justice Kennedy, ruled that the Georgia plan constituted a racial classification on its face, even though the statutes creating the districts did not use racial terms and there was no proof that majority race persons were having their voting power diluted through the racial gerrymandering.

Justice Kennedy found that a bizarre shape for a legislative district was not a prerequisite for finding that a voting district was race based. The *Miller* majority wanted to "make clear that parties alleging that a state has assigned voters on the basis of race are neither confined in their proof to evidence regarding the district's geometry and make-up nor required to make a threshold showing of bizarreness."[39] Justice Kennedy stated that a lower court should determine, on the basis of all of the evidence before it, whether the legislature's purpose in creating a legislative district was based upon the race of voters. According to the majority in *Miller:* "The plaintiff's burden [when challenging a legislative district on the basis of racial gerrymandering] is to show, either through circumstantial evidence of a district's shape and demographics or more direct evidence going to legislative purpose, that race was the predominant factor motivating the legislature's decision to place a significant number of voters within or without a particular district."[40]

Justice O'Connor, who had written the majority opinion in *Shaw,* concurred in both the opinion and judgment of the Court in *Miller.* She also wrote separately to state that "the standard would be no different if a legislature had drawn the boundaries to favor some other ethnic group; certainly this standard does not treat efforts to create majority-minority districts less favorably than similar efforts on behalf of other groups."[41]

In *Shaw v. Hunt (Shaw II)*[42] the Court held that the State of North Carolina was unable to

---

See §§ 14.10, 14.31, 14.32 of this Treatise for an examination of the Supreme Court's decisions concerning racial affirmation action and racial discrimination in the voting process.

38. 515 U.S. 900, 115 S.Ct. 2475, 132 L.Ed.2d 762 (1995), on remand 922 F.Supp. 1552 (D.Ga.1995). Justice Kennedy wrote a majority opinion that was joined by Chief Justice Rehnquist and Justices O'Connor, Scalia, and Thomas. Justice O'Connor also wrote a concurring opinion. 515 U.S. at 928, 115 S.Ct. at 2497 (O'Connor, J., concurring). Justices Stevens, Souter, Ginsburg, and Breyer dissented in *Miller,* 515 U.S. at 928, 115 S.Ct. at 2497 (Stevens, J., dissenting); 515 U.S. at 932, 115 S.Ct. at 2499 (Ginsburg, J., joined by Stevens and Breyer, JJ., and, in part, by Souter, J., dissenting).

39. Miller v. Johnson 515 U.S. 900, 915, 115 S.Ct. 2475, 2488, 132 L.Ed.2d 762 (1995), on remand 922 F.Supp. 1552 (D.Ga.1995).

40. 515 U.S. at 915, 115 S.Ct. at 2488.

41. 515 U.S. at 928, 115 S.Ct. at 2497 (O'Connor, J., concurring).

42. 517 U.S. 899, 116 S.Ct. 1894, 135 L.Ed.2d 207 (1996). *Shaw II* also involved rulings concerning the standing of individuals to attack districts as being improperly based on race; the majority found that voters who lived in a district alleged to involve unconstitutional racial gerrymandering had standing to raise such an argument while voters in other districts did not. 517 U.S. at 901–03, 116 S.Ct. at 1899–1900.

justify the race-based districting that had been the subject of the Court's earlier decision in *Shaw v. Reno (Shaw I)*.[43] After the Supreme Court decision in *Shaw I,* the lower federal court ruled that in North Carolina legislative districts created to strengthen minority race representation were constitutional, because the districts were necessary to further the compelling interest of the state in complying with §§ 2 and 5 of the Voting Rights Act. In *Shaw II,* the Supreme Court, by a five to four vote, overturned the district court and ruled that the North Carolina districts were not narrowly tailored to a compelling state interest.

Chief Justice Rehnquist's majority opinion in *Shaw II* reaffirmed the standards that had been used in *Miller* for determining whether a legislative districting plan constituted a racial classification. The Chief Justice stated that a legislative district would be subject to the compelling interest test only if the persons attacking the districting plan had demonstrated that race was "the predominant factor" in the creation of the legislative district.[44]

In *Shaw II,* the majority ruled that the evidence in the case proved that the North Carolina districts were created primarily to advance the interests of certain voters because of their race. Therefore, Chief Justice Rehnquist subjected the racial classification to the strict scrutiny and the compelling interest test. The majority ruled that the districts were not truly necessary or narrowly tailored to promote a compelling interest in the correction of prior racial discrimination.[45]

The Chief Justice's majority opinion in *Shaw II* left open the question of whether the Court, in the future, might uphold a state's creation of legislative districts in which a majority of the voters would be minority race persons solely to comply with § 2 or § 5 of the Voting Rights Act. The Chief Justice found that § 5 of the Voting Rights Act did not require maximization of minority race voting power, or the creation of districts on the basis of race in order to increase minority race representation in a legislature. Chief Justice Rehnquist assumed, for the purposes of the *Shaw II* case only, that compliance with § 2 of the Voting Rights Act would be a compelling interest for a state. Nevertheless, the majority ruled that the districts created to increase the voting power of minority race voters in North Carolina were not narrowly tailored to avoiding violation of § 2 of the Voting Rights Act, because the state was unable to demonstrate that the districts were a narrowly tailored means of avoiding the intentional dilution of the voting power of racial minorities.[46]

Justices Stevens, Souter, Ginsburg and Breyer dissented in *Shaw II,* in part because they believed that race was not the predominant factor in the creation of the North Carolina congressional districts. In the view of the dissenting Justices, the evidence before the district court demonstrated only that race was only one of the factors considered by the legislature along with a variety of traditional legislative concerns including the protecting of certain districts for specific legislators or parties. The dissenters also believed that these districts should be upheld because they were tailored to correct past discrimination against minority race voters and to avoid current violations of the Voting Rights Act.[47]

Both the majority and dissenting opinions in *Shaw II* indicated that legislative consideration of race along with a variety of traditional factors when creating legislative districts (such as creating contiguous and compact districts or creating districts that would reflect historical interest of regions of a state) would not be

---

43. Shaw v. Reno (Shaw I), 509 U.S. 630, 113 S.Ct. 2816, 125 L.Ed.2d 511 (1993).

44. Shaw v. Hunt (Shaw II), 517 U.S. 899, 903, 116 S.Ct. 1894, 1900, 135 L.Ed.2d 207 (1996).

45. 517 U.S. at 909, 116 S.Ct. at 1903.

46. 517 U.S. at 914–16, 116 S.Ct. at 1905–1906.

47. Shaw v. Hunt (Shaw II), 517 U.S. 899, 918, 116 S.Ct. 1894, 1907, 135 L.Ed.2d 207 (1996) (Stevens, J.,

joined in part by Ginsburg and Breyer, JJ., dissenting). Justice Souter's dissent in *Shaw II* merely made a reference to his dissent in *Vera,* which was decided the same day as *Shaw II,* 517 U.S. at 951, 116 S.Ct. at 1923 (Souter, J., joined by Ginsburg and Breyer, JJ., dissenting) referring to Bush v. Vera, 517 U.S. 952, 1044, 116 S.Ct. 1941, 1997, 135 L.Ed.2d 248 (1996) (Souter, J., joined by Ginsburg and Breyer, JJ., dissenting).

subject to the compelling interest test. The compelling interest test would only be employed if the persons attacking the creation of a legislative district could demonstrate that racial considerations had been the predominant factor in creating the legislative district.

The Court's decision in *Shaw II* appeared to show that a majority of the Justices would use the *Miller* standard when determining whether a legislative district had to meet the strict scrutiny test, and be narrowly tailored to a compelling state interest. Nevertheless, on the same day that *Shaw II* was decided, the Court decided *Bush v. Vera* and, in so doing, demonstrated that there was very little agreement on the Court about the meaning of *Miller.*[48] The *Vera* decision showed that the Justices were hopelessly split concerning whether a district created to have a majority of voters who were minority race persons might ever be upheld. In *Vera,* the Justices, by a five to four vote, invalidated three districts in a state congressional districting plan. Justice O'Connor announced the judgment of the Court in a plurality opinion that was joined only by Chief Justice Rehnquist and Justice Kennedy. Despite their agreement on the plurality opinion Justice O'Connor and Justice Kennedy each wrote a concurring opinion, that was not joined by any other Justice.

Justice O'Connor's plurality opinion, in *Vera,* stated that "strict scrutiny does not apply merely because redistricting is performed with consciousness of race ... for strict scrutiny to apply the plaintiff must prove that other,

legitimate districting principles were subordinated to race ... [so that race was] the predominant factor dominating ... 'the creation of the legislative district.' "[49] According to the plurality, that evidence presented to the district court, including the testimony of state officials, demonstrated that the districts were created for the predominant reason of guaranteeing representation to minority race persons. Therefore, the districts would be invalid unless the state could demonstrate that the districts were necessary to promote a compelling interest.

In her plurality opinion, Justice O'Connor found the intentional creation of a race-based district could only be justified as a remedial measure if the state demonstrated first that it was remedying "specific identified discrimination" and, second, that the creation of the legislative district was "necessary" for the correction of the earlier violation of the Constitution or Voting Rights Act.[50] The state failed to meet those standards according to the plurality opinion. Therefore, the districts violated the equal protection clause because the districts were not narrowly tailored to promote the compelling interest in remedying past discrimination.

In addition to her plurality opinion in *Vera,* Justice O'Connor wrote a concurring opinion in which she expressed the view that a state would have a compelling interest in avoiding a violation of § 2 of the Voting Rights Act, which prohibits intentional dilution of the voting power of racial groups.[51] Justice O'Connor,

48. Bush v. Vera, 517 U.S. 952, 116 S.Ct. 1941, 135 L.Ed.2d 248 (1996). The judgment of the Court was announced in an opinion by Justice O'Connor that was joined by Chief Justice Rehnquist and Justice Kennedy. Justice O'Connor and Justice Kennedy also wrote separate concurring opinions, and neither of their concurring opinions was joined by any other Justice. 517 U.S. at 990, 116 S.Ct. at 1968 (O'Connor, J., concurring); 517 U.S. at 996, 116 S.Ct. at 1971 (Kennedy, J., concurring). In *Vera,* Justices Thomas and Scalia concurred only in the judgment, of the Court. 517 U.S. at 998, 116 S.Ct. at 1972 (Thomas, J., joined by Scalia, J., concurring in the judgment). Justices Ginsburg and Breyer did not write separately but they joined both of the dissenting opinions, which were written by Justice Stevens and Justice Souter. However, Justice Stevens and Justice Souter did not join each other's dissenting opinions. Bush v. Vera, 517 U.S. 952, 1002, 116 S.Ct. 1941, 1974, 135 L.Ed.2d 248 (1996)

(Stevens, J., joined by Ginsburg and Breyer, JJ., dissenting); 517 U.S. at 1044, 116 S.Ct. at 1997 (Souter, J., joined by Ginsburg and Breyer, JJ., dissenting).

Chief Justice Rehnquist, who had written the majority opinion in *Shaw II* did not write a separate opinion in *Vera.*

49. Bush v. Vera, 517 U.S. 952, 957–59, 116 S.Ct. 1941, 1951–52, 135 L.Ed.2d 248 (1996) (plurality opinion by O'Connor, J., joined by Rehnquist, C.J., and Kennedy, J.).

50. 517 U.S. at 980–82, 116 S.Ct. at 1962–63 (plurality opinion by O'Connor, J., joined by Rehnquist, C.J., and Kennedy, J.).

51. Bush v. Vera, 517 U.S. 952, 990, 116 S.Ct. 1941, 1968, 135 L.Ed.2d 248 (1996) (opinion of O'Connor, J., concurring).

in her separate opinion, reaffirmed the position that legislative districts in which minority race persons were a majority of the voters would not have to meet the compelling interest test if the state simply considered race, along with other traditional criteria in the creation of the districts.[52]

Justice Kennedy, who had joined Justice O'Connor's plurality opinion, did not join Justice O'Connor's concurring opinion in *Vera.* In a concurring opinion of his own, Justice Kennedy stated that he did not believe that any statements in the plurality opinion "foreordains that one race be the majority in a certain number of districts or a certain part of the state."[53] It is not clear whether Justice Kennedy would ever find that race conscious legislative districts might be upheld under a standard less demanding than the strict scrutiny test.

Justices Thomas and Scalia concurred only in the judgment in *Vera.*[54] They believe that any consideration of race in the creation of a legislative district required that the district be subject to strict scrutiny. These two Justices will not vote to uphold any legislative district that has been created with any race consideration, unless the legislature creating the district can demonstrate that the district was necessary to correct identified unconstitutional discrimination against racial minorities.

Justices Stevens and Souter wrote dissenting opinions in *Shaw II* and *Vera,* each of which was joined by Justices Ginsburg and Breyer.[55] Both dissents took the position that not all consideration of race in legislative districting should be subjected to the strict scrutiny test. Justice Stevens would have used the *Miller* standard to find that race had not been

the predominant goal in the creation of Texas districts.[56] He also believed that to the extent race was considered it was narrowly tailored to correcting past discriminatory practices. Justice Souter emphasized the fact that no injury to majority race voters had occurred in *Shaw I, Shaw II,* or *Vera.*[57]

In *Shaw I* and *Miller,* the Supreme Court made it quite easy for majority race voters to show that a legislative districting plan that strengthened minority race voting power was invalid on its face. In the 1990s, the Supreme Court made it difficult for minority race plaintiffs to show that a legislative districting plan that diluted minority race voting power violated the Fourteenth or Fifteenth Amendments or the Voting Rights Act. Justices would assert that the Supreme Court used the same standards when considering challenges to legislative districting plans that were brought by white voters and by minority race voters.[58] Nevertheless, the litigation that resulted in the Supreme Court decisions in *Miller v. Johnson*[59] and *Abrams v. Johnson*[60] provides an example of the apparent difference between the majority's approach to legislative district plans that helped minority voters rather than white voters.

The *Abrams* case involved the same districting problems litigation that had resulted in the Supreme Court's 1995 decision in the *Miller.* Prior to 1995, the Georgia legislature adopted a plan establishing the district lines for election of representatives from Georgia to the United States House of Representatives. The original congressional districting map drawn by the Georgia legislature included two congressional districts that were likely to elect minority race representatives. The Attorney General refused to approve the plan under § 5

---

52. 517 U.S. at 987, 116 S.Ct. at 1965 (O'Connor, J., concurring).

53. 517 U.S. at 996, 116 S.Ct. at 1971 (Kennedy, J., concurring).

54. Bush v. Vera, 517 U.S. 952, 998, 116 S.Ct. 1941, 1972, 135 L.Ed.2d 248 (1996) (Thomas, J., joined by Scalia, J., concurring in the judgment).

55. See the references to the dissenting opinions in notes 47, 48, supra.

56. 517 U.S. at 1002, 116 S.Ct. at 1974 (Stevens, J., joined by Ginsburg and Breyer, JJ., dissenting).

57. Bush v. Vera, 517 U.S. 952, 1044, 116 S.Ct. 1941, 1997, 135 L.Ed.2d 248 (1996) (Souter, J., joined by Ginsburg and Breyer, JJ., dissenting).

58. See, e.g., Miller v. Johnson, 515 U.S. 900, 928, 115 S.Ct. 2475, 2497, 132 L.Ed.2d 762 (1995) (O'Connor, J., concurring).

59. 515 U.S. 900, 115 S.Ct. 2475, 132 L.Ed.2d 762 (1995).

60. 521 U.S. 74, 117 S.Ct. 1925, 138 L.Ed.2d 285 (1997).

of the Voting Rights Act. Instead of challenging the Attorney General's decision in the United States District Court in the District of Columbia, the Georgia legislature adopted a new districting plan with three congressional districts that would be controlled by minority race voters. White voters then challenged the plan of the United States District Court in Georgia. The United States Supreme Court, in *Miller*, ruled that the final Georgia congressional districting plan, with three minority race controlled congressional district, violated the equal protection clauses and remanded the case to the United States District Court in Georgia.[61] The District Court, in the next round of litigation, adopted a congressional district map for Georgia in which there was only one congressional district in which a majority of the voters would be minority race persons. The plan adopted by the District Court gave less voting power to minority race persons than had that had been the original districting plan adopted by the Georgia legislature, which the Attorney General had refused to approve under section 5 of the Voting Rights Act.

Minority race voters, in *Abrams*, claimed that the plan adopted by the District Court was not within the power of the court because (1) the court ordered plan failed to follow the original intention of the Georgia legislature to create at least two districts with minority race representation, and (2) the statistics for the new districting plan showed that it diluted voting power of minority race voters in a way that violated the Fourteenth and Fifteenth Amendments, and § 2 of the Voting Rights Act. The United States Supreme Court ruled that the District Court had not exceeded its remedial power and upheld the plan adopted by the District Court.

Justice Kennedy, writing for a five member majority in *Abrams*, ruled that the District

Court had in fact followed the true intent of the Georgia legislature.[62] The majority arrived at this conclusion by finding that the first congressional district map adopted by the Georgia legislature did not reflect the true intent of the legislature, because the plan with two districts in which minority voters would control the election, were only created with a view to submitting the plan for "preclearance" to the Justice Department under § 5 of the Voting Rights Act. The plan adopted by the District Court, with only one minority race district, did not violate the Constitution because there had been no proof of racially discriminatory purpose in adopting the plan.[63] Additionally, Justice Kennedy's majority opinion stated that the District Court's congressional plan did not violate § 2 of the Voting Rights Act because the "black population was not sufficiently compact" for the creation of more than one voting district.

The four dissenting Justices in *Abrams*[64] pointed out that the districting plan that had been invalidated in *Miller*, which provided for three minority race districts, did not dilute the voting power of white persons. The map for congressional districts that had been adopted District Court, and approved by the majority, would result in minimal representation of minority race persons in the Georgia congressional delegation.

The principles that govern the determination of whether a legislative district involves a racial classification, which would then be subject to the compelling interest test, are fairly simple. However, the application of those principles to a specific fact situation can be extremely difficult.

The litigation following the Supreme Court's invalidation of North Carolina's 12th Congressional District, in the *Shaw I* and *Shaw II*

61. Miller v. Johnson, 515 U.S. 900, 115 S.Ct. 2475, 132 L.Ed.2d 762 (1995).

62. Abrams v. Johnson, 521 U.S. 74, 117 S.Ct. 1925, 138 L.Ed.2d 285 (1997).

63. The Court was not presented with a discriminatory purpose claim. The only constitutional objection to the District court ordered plan was whether the districts in that plan violated the one person, one vote principle. The

majority ruled that the population deviation between districts was within the limits set in earlier Supreme Court decisions Abrams v. Johnson, 521 U.S. 74, 97–99, 117 S.Ct. 1925, 1939–40, 138 L.Ed.2d 285 (1997).

64. Abrams v. Johnson, 521 U.S. 74, 103, 117 S.Ct. 1925, 1943, 138 L.Ed.2d 285 (1997) (Breyer, J., joined by Stevens, Souter, and Ginsburg, JJ., dissenting).

cases,[65] presents an example of the difficulty that can arise when applying the racial classification in discriminatory purpose concepts. Following *Shaw II,* North Carolina created a new districting plan for its congressional districts. District 12, which had been invalidated in *Shaw II,* was modified in significant ways. The new District 12 had become smaller but it still had a fairly odd shape. Once again, District 12 was challenged by white voters who alleged that the District constituted a racial classification even though the new District 12 had slightly under 50% minority race voters. A three judge District Court ruled that the shape of the district and the high percentage of minority race voters justified a finding that District 12 still constituted a racial classification, which should not withstand strict judicial review. For that reason, the District Court granted summary judgment for the persons attacking the new districting plan and issued an injunction preventing the new congressional districting plan from going into effect.

In *Hunt v. Cromartie*[66] the Justices unanimously held that the District Court had committed error when it granted the challenger's motion for a summary judgment without a trial. Despite their unanimity in overruling the District Court, the Justices split 5 to 4 in terms of their assessment of the facts that had been before the District Court and the possibility that those facts, after a trial, might establish a basis for invalidation of the new congressional districting plan.

The majority opinion in *Cromartie,* written by Justice Thomas, set out the basic principles concerning racial classifications. When the government explicitly uses race in a statute, there is no need for judicial inquiry into legislative purpose, because a racial classification appears on the face of the statute. When a law that does not mention race is attacked as being a racial classification, the persons challenging the law bear the burden of proving

that the law was motivated by a racial purpose, which they might do by showing that it was impossible to explain classifications created by the law on any ground other than race. Persons challenging a facially neutral classification on the basis of race could use direct or circumstantial evidence, or some combination thereof, to carry their burden of proof. If a legislative districting plan was facially neutral, a court should only find that a legislative district was a race classification, "if race was the predominant factor in motivating the legislature's districting decision."[67] Justice Thomas found that the difficult nature of examining legislative purpose would mean that summary judgment in favor of someone attacking a facially neutral districting plan on the basis of race would rarely be appropriate, although he noted that there might be a rare case in which summary judgment could be justified on the basis of "uncontroverted evidence and reasonable inferences".[68]

None of these basic principles set forth in Justice Thomas's majority opinion were challenged by four Justices who concurred only in the judgment in *Cromartie.*[69] The differences between the majority opinion and the concurring Justices related to the assessment of the facts in the case.

Justice Thomas's opinion stated that the majority would not address the question of whether the parties challenging the districting plan could show racial motivation in the creation of District 12. Nevertheless, the majority opinion noted that the challengers had submitted evidence concerning ways in which the 12th District did not comply with typical districting criteria. Justice Thomas also noted that the challengers had presented evidence showing that District 12 was drawn in a way that included areas with a high proportion of minority race residents while it excluded areas close to the center of the district that had a majority of registered democrat voters who

65. The issue of whether legislatures may ever use race as a factor in creating legislative districts is examined in § 14.10(c) of this Treatise.

66. Hunt v. Cromartie, 526 U.S. 541, 119 S.Ct. 1545, 143 L.Ed.2d 731 (1999).

67. 526 U.S. at 547, 119 S.Ct. at 1549.

68. 526 U.S. at 553, 119 S.Ct. at 1552.

69. 526 U.S. at 555–57, 119 S.Ct. at 1554–55 (Stevens, J., joined by Souter, Ginsburg, and Breyer, JJ., concurring in the judgment).

were not minority race persons. On that basis, Justice Thomas's majority opinion stated that the evidence that had been presented to the District Court "tends to support an inference that the state drew its district lines with an impermissible racial motive" rather than being the function of traditional districting criteria, such as the protection of the incumbent political party.[70] Nevertheless, the majority ruled that there were factual issues that needed to be resolved at trial, because "the legislature's motivation is itself a factual question,"[71] and because the government had presented evidence, including testimony of state legislators, that the legislative districts were drawn to preserve the political balance in the state's congressional delegation.

Justice Stevens wrote for four Justices who concurred only in the judgment of the Court in *Cromartie*.[72] The concurring Justices believed that the configuration of District 12, when analyzed in light of the actual voting patterns of persons in that area of North Carolina, demonstrated that it was most likely that District 12 was drawn for the purpose of protecting incumbent legislators and preserving political balance between the parties. The concurring Justices thought that there was no need to consider whether the evidence even raised an inference regarding improper motive on the part of the legislators, "because we do not have before us the question of whether the District Court erred in denying the state's motion for summary judgment."[73] That statement indicates that the concurring Justices might have ruled that the challenge to District 12 should have been summarily dismissed, if that issue had been brought before the Court.

The Supreme Court in *Hunt I* remanded the litigation to the three-judge court. The three judge district court then held a trial in which it took testimony regarding the establishment of the new Congressional District 12 for North Carolina. That testimony included an expert on behalf of the plaintiff (who asserted that the data showed that District 12 boundaries must have been based on racial, rather than political, considerations), and an expert for the state (who asserted that the data showed that it was most likely that political factors, rather than racial considerations, established the basis for the creation of the District 12 boundaries). After examining the evidence, the three judges ruled, by a 2–1 vote, that District 12 had indeed been created for the purpose of insuring a majority representation by racial minority voters and, therefore, that it was a racial classification that would violate the equal protection clause.

In 2001, in *Hunt v. Cromartie [Hunt II]*,[74] the United States Supreme Court, by a 5 to 4 vote, overruled the district court. In *Hunt II*, the Supreme Court ruled that the district court should have found that the plaintiffs had failed to demonstrate that racial considerations, rather than political considerations, were the predominant motivating factor for the state legislature's creation of District 12. Therefore, according to the Supreme Court, District 12 did not involve unconstitutional racial classification.

In *Hunt II*, Justice Breyer wrote a majority opinion that was joined by Justices Stevens, O'Connor, Ginsburg, and Breyer. In *Hunt I*, four of those Justices, had indicated that they would vote to uphold the constitutionality of

70. Hunt v. Cromartie, 526 U.S. 541, 119 S.Ct. 1545, 1550, 143 L.Ed.2d 731 (1999). The majority opinion by Justice Thomas noted that some types of political gerrymandering might be constitutionally permissible although he did not explain that point; he noted that the Court had not set standards for determining what types of political gerrymandering would be constitutionally permissible. 526 U.S. at 552 n. 7, 119 S.Ct. at 1551 n. 7.

71. Justice Thomas' majority opinion found that the mere fact that minority race persons constituted a majority of voters in a congressional district would not, without further evidence, prove that the creation of the district was motivated by race. If there was evidence showing "a high correlation between race and party preference," there

would be a fact issue regarding whether the district boundaries were drawn for racial or political purposes. 526 U.S. at 552, 119 S.Ct. at 1551.

72. Hunt v. Cromartie, 526 U.S. 541, 119 S.Ct. 1545, 1554, 143 L.Ed.2d 731 (1999) (Stevens, J., joined by Souter, Ginsburg, and Breyer, JJ., concurring in the judgment).

73. 526 U.S. at 557, 119 S.Ct. at 1555 (Stevens, J., joined by Souter, Ginsburg, and Breyer, JJ., concurring in the judgment).

74. Hunt v. Cromartie [*Hunt II*], 532 U.S. 234, 121 S.Ct. 1452, 149 L.Ed.2d 430 (2001).

District 12. Justice O'Connor had joined Justice Thomas's opinion in *Hunt I*, because she believed that there needed to be full consideration of all evidence concerning the creation of District 12 in order to make a determination of whether that congressional district constituted a racial classification. Once all of the evidence had been presented in court, Justice O'Connor, along with the four other Justices in the *Hunt II* majority, believed that District 12 had not been proven to be a racial classification.[75]

The majority opinion in *Hunt II* did not establish any new principles of constitutional law. Nevertheless, the majority opinion demonstrated the difficulty that any court will have in determining whether a legislative district with a majority of minority race persons should be treated as a racial classification.

After giving the factual background of the case, Justice Breyer's majority opinion in *Hunt II* emphasized the basic principle. That a person challenging a legislative district as being a race-based classification has the burden of proving that race was the predominant motivating factor in the creation of the district.[76] According to the majority opinion in *Hunt II*, four principles must be considered by any court that has to determine whether a person challenging a legislative district as race based met the burden of proof.

First, a legislative district with a majority of minority race voters (often called a majority-minority district) is not a *per se* racial classification.[77] A court should only rule that a legislative district is race-based if the court is convinced that the state or local entity responsible for creation of the legislative district was primarily motivated by racial considerations. In other words, if a court determines that race

was merely one of several factors that resulted in the creation of boundaries for a specific legislative district, it should not find that that district was race-based.

Second, when a Court examines a question of whether a legislative district is race based it must clearly place the burden of proof on the persons who are attacking the constitutionality of the district. The majority opinion in *Hunt II* adopted a position first set forth by Justice O'Connor in finding that the burden of proof on those who attacked a district as being a race-based would be a "demanding one."[78] The majority opinion in *Hunt II* did not formally adopt a clear and convincing evidence standard as the burden of proof. Nevertheless, the Supreme Court's close examination of the evidence in *Hunt II* shows that any court should not rule that a legislative district is race-based unless that court is convinced that racial considerations were the motivating factor, and not merely one of several factors, considered by those who drew legislative boundaries. Justice Breyer explained that the creation of legislative districts "ordinarily falls within a legislature's sphere of confidence," and that judicial review of legislative maps called for "caution [in a case wherein] the state has articulated a legitimate political explanation for its districting decision, and the voting population is one in which race and political affiliation are highly correlated."[79]

Third, some element of partisan political gerrymandering is constitutional and may provide a legitimate reason for creating a legislative district. In one previous case, the Supreme Court indicated, without a majority opinion, that political gerrymandering, would violate the First and Fourteenth Amendments if the

---

75. Justice O'Connor did not write a separate opinion in these cases. If a plaintiff demonstrates that a legislative district was in fact created for the purpose of separating persons (into and outside of the district) by race then the district constitutes a racial classification. Justice O'Connor had written previous opinions examining the basis for finding that a district was in fact race-based and examining the question of whether such a district could ever be found to be narrowly tailored to a compelling interest. Those cases are examined in this section of the Treatise. The question of whether a legislative district that was race-based could survive the compelling interest test is also examined in § 14.10(b)(4) of this Treatise.

76. This analysis is set forth in Part II of Justice Breyer's opinion. Hunt v. Cromartie [*Hunt II*], 532 U.S. 234, 241–43, 121 S.Ct. 1452, 1458–59, 149 L.Ed.2d 430 (2001).

77. 532 U.S. at 241, 256, 121 S.Ct. at 1458, 1466 (parts II and IV of the majority opinion).

78. 532 U.S. at 241, 121 S.Ct. at 1458, in part quoting, Miller v. Johnson, 515 U.S. 900, 928, 115 S.Ct. 2475, 2494, 132 L.Ed.2d 762 (1995) (O'Connor, J., concurring).

79. Hunt v. Cromartie [*Hunt II*], 532 U.S. 234, 241, 121 S.Ct. 1452, 1458, 149 L.Ed.2d 430 (2001).

gerrymandered legislative map virtually ended the political influence of persons who believed in one political party.[80] All of the Justices in *Hunt II*, both in the majority and the dissent, appeared to take the position that legislative districts drawn for political purposes normally would be constitutional, at least so long as those legislative districts complied with other constitutional principles, such as the one-person, one-vote principle.[81] The majority in *Hunt* found that the district court should have accepted the state's argument that the creation of District 12 was based on concerns about party affiliation and party voting, rather than race.[82] The majority's conclusion could not have been possible if creating a legislative district based upon political affiliation considerations was per se unconstitutional. The dissent in *Hunt II*, written by Justice Thomas, was written on the premise that districting based on political affiliation would have been constitutional. Nevertheless, the dissenting Justices believed that the district court had not made a clearly erroneous finding when it held that the district was based on racial considerations rather than political considerations.[83]

Fourth, an appellate court reviewing a trial court finding that a legislative district constituted a racial classification should conduct an independent search of the entire factual record, but should only overrule the trial court if the trial court's findings were clearly erroneous.[84] Because *Hunt* litigation (like most litigation challenging the constitutionality of congressional districts or districts for statewide legislative bodies) began in a three-judge federal district court, the district court's findings were appealable only to the United States Supreme Court. Because the United States Supreme Court did not have an intermediate appellate court decision to rely upon, the Justice engaged in an extensive review of the district court findings. The Supreme Court in *Hunt II* overruled the district court because a majority of the Justices believed that the district court findings were clearly erroneous.

Justice Breyer's majority opinion in *Hunt II* ruled that the district court had committed clear error when it found that the plaintiffs had met the burden of proof in establishing that Congressional District 12 was based on race rather than political considerations. The majority opinion in *Hunt II* found that "the issue in this case is evidentiary."[85] In its review of the district court record, the majority found that the district court should have examined the actual voting behavior of persons in the state, rather than merely voter registration, in determining whether the district was created for political, rather than racial, reasons. The majority also found that the district court had given too much weight to the plaintiff's expert and some isolated statements by state legislators concerning the creation of the district. Additionally, the United States Supreme Court majority found that the district court had attached too little weight to the State's expert, who testified that there were significant factual data showing that the creation of the odd-shaped district would be a reasonable way of promoting certain political goals.

80. Davis v. Bandemer, 478 U.S. 109, 106 S.Ct. 2797, 92 L.Ed.2d 85 (1986). See § 14.36 (e) of this Treatise for an examination of that decision.

81. Hunt v. Cromartie [*Hunt II*], 532 U.S. 234, 258, 121 S.Ct. 1452, 1470, 149 L.Ed.2d 430 (2001) (Thomas, J., joined by Rehnquist, C.J., and Scalia and Kennedy, JJ., dissenting).

82. "The basic question is whether the legislature drew District 12's boundaries because of race rather than because of political behavior (coupled with traditional, non-racial districting considerations)." Hunt v. Cromartie [*Hunt II*], 532 U.S. 234, 258, 121 S.Ct. 1452, 1466, 149 L.Ed.2d 430 (2001) (part IV of majority opinion).

83. 532 U.S. at 258, 121 S.Ct. at 1470 (Thomas, J., joined by Rehnquist, C.J., Scalia and Kennedy, JJ., dissenting).

84. Hunt v. Cromartie, 532 U.S. 234, 242–43, 121 S.Ct. 1452, 1458–59, 149 L.Ed.2d 430 (2001) (part II of majority opinion).

85. 532 U.S. at 256, 121 S.Ct. at 1466: "We can put the matter more generally as follows: in a case such as this one, where majority-minority districts (or the approximate equivalent) are at issue and where racial identification correlates highly with political affiliation, the party attacking the legislatively drawn boundaries must show at least that the legislature could have achieved its legitimate political objectives in alternative ways that are comparably consistent with traditional districting principles. That party must also show that those districting alternatives would have brought about significantly greater racial balance. Appellees failed to make any such showing here. We conclude that the district court's contrary findings are clearly erroneous."

The dissenting Justices in *Hunt II* believed that the evidence before the district court provided a reasonable basis for the district court finding that race was the determining factor for the creation of District 12.[86] Writing for the four dissenters, Justice Thomas admitted that it might be possible to construct hypothetical scenarios in which a district such as District 12 could have been created for political, rather than racial, reasons. Because the dissenting Justices believed that there was a factual basis for finding that this specific district had its boundaries drawn primarily for racial reasons, these Justices did not believe any reviewing court, including the Supreme Court, should find that the district court's ruling was clearly erroneous.

The Court has refused to overturn legislative districting which complies with the one-person, one-vote principle because the particular districting plan has a disproportionate effect on racial minorities.[87] Where the statistical proof is supplemented with other evidence of discrimination on the part of those engaged in the districting, the Court will overturn a plan that otherwise complies with the one-person, one-vote principle unless the state can demonstrate that the plan in fact was not created for a discriminatory purpose.[88]

Even an at-large voting system may be held to violate equal protection if it is created or maintained to dilute the voting power of racial minorities. Statistical proof of an electoral system's adverse impact on the voting power of minority citizens will be relevant but not determinative in such a case. The plaintiff attacking the at-large system must prove that it was created or maintained for a racially discriminatory purpose. Thus, in *Mobile v. Bolden*[89] the Supreme Court refused to invalidate a city commission system whereby all three members of the city's governing body were elected at-large. Although no black person had ever been elected to the city commission, there was no proof that the electoral system was maintained for a racially discriminatory purpose.

Conversely, in *Rogers v. Lodge*,[90] the Supreme Court approved federal district court and court of appeals rulings invalidating an at-large election system for a rural county's board of commissioners. The Supreme Court found that the lower courts had correctly determined that the electoral system could only be invalidated upon a showing of discriminatory purpose. Although black persons were a majority of the population, the at-large system examined in *Rogers* had prevented black representation on the county board. The statistical evidence in *Rogers* was supported by other facts showing that elected officials in the coun-

---

86. 532 U.S. at 259, 121 S.Ct. at 1471 (Thomas, J., joined by Rehnquist, C.J., and Scalia and Kennedy, JJ., dissenting).

87. Whitcomb v. Chavis, 403 U.S. 124, 91 S.Ct. 1858, 29 L.Ed.2d 363 (1971).

88. White v. Regester, 412 U.S. 755, 93 S.Ct. 2332, 37 L.Ed.2d 314 (1973).

89. 446 U.S. 55, 100 S.Ct. 1490, 64 L.Ed.2d 47 (1980).

After Mobile v. Bolden, 446 U.S. 55, 100 S.Ct. 1490, 64 L.Ed.2d 47 (1980), Congress amended section two of the Voting Rights Act to ease the burden of a plaintiff in proving the existence of racial discrimination in a voting law or standard.

Section 2 of the Voting Rights Act, as amended, has been interpreted by the Supreme Court to require the plaintiff to make a prima facie showing that a challenged election system results in the dilution of the voting power of a racial minority. If the plaintiff makes a prima facie demonstration of racial discrimination through vote dilution, the government must rebut the plaintiff's case. The court must consider the totality of the evidence in determining whether there has been a dilution in the voting

power of a minority racial group that would violate § 2 of the Voting Rights Act.

In Thornburg v. Gingles, 478 U.S. 30, 106 S.Ct. 2752, 92 L.Ed.2d 25 (1986) the Supreme Court established three conditions that must be met for a plaintiff to make a prima facie case of racial discrimination through the dilution of the voting power of a racial minority. First, the plaintiff must show that the minority group would be sufficiently large and geographically compact, so that the racial group might have constituted a majority in a legislative electoral district. Second, the plaintiff must show that the minority group is "politically cohesive." Finally, the plaintiff must prove that the white voters in the area (and in the challenged legislative districts) are sufficiently likely to vote as a bloc so as to enable the majority to defeat the minority's candidates. 478 U.S. at 50–51, 106 S.Ct. at 2766–2767.

For further analysis of this issue, and references to additional cases, see 3 R. Rotunda & J. Nowak, Treatise on Constitutional Law: Substance and Procedure § 18.4 (3rd ed. 1999), (with annual supplements).

90. 458 U.S. 613, 102 S.Ct. 3272, 73 L.Ed.2d 1012 (1982).

ty had been insensitive to the needs of the black community and had maintained the at-large voting system for the purpose of minimizing the voting strength of black persons.

The Supreme Court has also tried to walk a middle ground in two cases dealing with the termination of municipal services.[91] In *Griffin v. Prince Edward County School Board*[92] the Court found that the closing of local schools constituted a racially discriminatory act which justified a judicial order to reopen those schools. In this case the governmental decision followed a desegregation order and there was evidence that the local government then offered aid to private schools which discriminated on the basis of race.

However, the Court in *Palmer v. Thompson*[93] allowed a city to close its public pools after a judicial desegregation order. The city maintained that the pools could no longer be operated safely or economically and the Court found no independent proof of discriminatory purpose on the part of the city authorities. It was true in this case that the closing of the pools would have a greater impact on blacks than whites for there were private pools which served only whites, but there was no proof that the city aided the establishment or maintenance of those pools.

The Court has continued to follow this middle ground by finding that statistical proof alone will not be sufficient to establish that an otherwise neutral law constitutes a racial classification unless the statistical proof is overwhelming or there is some other evidence of discriminatory purpose. Thus the Court has upheld a referendum procedure for allowing low income housing into an area[94] but overturned a referendum system which was re-

quired to authorize the implementation of open housing or desegregation ordinances.[95] Similarly, the Court refused to find that the provision of a lower percentage funding to a welfare program for Aid to Families with Dependent Children as compared to those programs for the Aged, Blind or Disabled constituted racial discrimination merely because the differing statistical impacts upon racial groups.[96]

The Court was also confronted with classification problems by employment cases under Title VII of the Civil Rights Act.[97] In those cases it found that statistical proof that employment criterion excluded a disproportionately high percentage of racial minority members constituted a prima facie case of racial discrimination. In the leading case of *Griggs v. Duke Power Co.*[98] the Court held that a violation of the Act could be established for the requirements of a high school diploma and intelligence tests simply because they had a disproportionate impact on racial minority job applicants.

As the Court continued to enforce this rule, hopes were raised that it would find violations of the equal protection guarantee upon a similar statistical basis.[99] However, such hopeful predictions overlooked the fact that in Title VII cases the Court is enforcing a decision of the federal legislature to totally eliminate racial discrimination in public and private employment to which the statute applies. Thus there was no need for a policy of deference to employment decisions or criteria under the terms of such statutes.

When the Supreme Court returned to issues under the equal protection guarantee, however, it continued to hold that statistical proof of

---

91. This issue is also considered in § 14.9, infra.

92. 377 U.S. 218, 84 S.Ct. 1226, 12 L.Ed.2d 256 (1964), motion granted 377 U.S. 950, 84 S.Ct. 1627, 12 L.Ed.2d 496 (1964).

93. 403 U.S. 217, 91 S.Ct. 1940, 29 L.Ed.2d 438 (1971).

94. James v. Valtierra, 402 U.S. 137, 91 S.Ct. 1331, 28 L.Ed.2d 678 (1971) (statistical proof not sufficient).

95. Hunter v. Erickson, 393 U.S. 385, 89 S.Ct. 557, 21 L.Ed.2d 616 (1969). Here the Court considered the discriminatory impact so clear that it constituted a racial classification "in its face." See also Reitman v. Mulkey,

387 U.S. 369, 87 S.Ct. 1627, 18 L.Ed.2d 830 (1967). The Court has employed similar analysis in examining the constitutionality of voter approved Amendments to state laws which restrict the transferring or "busing" of students. See § 14.9, infra.

96. Jefferson v. Hackney, 406 U.S. 535, 92 S.Ct. 1724, 32 L.Ed.2d 285 (1972).

97. 42 U.S.C.A. § 2000e–2(a).

98. 401 U.S. 424, 91 S.Ct. 849, 28 L.Ed.2d 158 (1971).

99. See, e.g., Albemarle Paper Co. v. Moody, 422 U.S. 405, 95 S.Ct. 2362, 45 L.Ed.2d 280 (1975).

differing impact upon racial groups would not be sufficient to establish a racial classification absent some other proof that the law was adopted for a racially discriminatory purpose. Thus, in *Washington v. Davis* [100] the Court found that the District of Columbia did not violate the equal protection guarantee by employing a form of intelligence test for prospective police officers. The Court noted that there was no accusation that those selecting the officers had used their discretion to eliminate members of racial minorities but only that the otherwise neutral test had a disproportionate impact on blacks. In conformity with its earlier constitutional decisions, the Court found that this evidence was insufficient to establish a prima facie case of racial discrimination. If the challengers to the test could establish some other proof of racially discriminatory purpose either from the general background of employment conditions or the history of the process which resulted in the establishment of the test, then they might prevail, but not otherwise. [101]

The next year, the Court upheld a suburban zoning plan which eliminated multi-family housing and the decision of city authorities not to grant an exemption from that zoning plan for a multi-family project which would have dramatically increased the percentage of minority residents in the city. [102] The Court noted that there was no proof that the city had granted exemptions from the zoning plan on a discriminatory basis; the ultimate question was whether the adoption and enforcement of the zoning plan constituted a purposeful device to exclude black persons. [103] While the

statistical proof was significant, many types of zoning plans have been adopted for totally race neutral reasons which might also have such a disproportionate impact. Since there was no proof in this case that the law had been adopted for a discriminatory purpose, either from the history of the town or the process which resulted in the plan, the city's actions were upheld.

In *Personnel Administrator of Massachusetts v. Feeney* [104] the Supreme Court, by a vote of seven to two, upheld a state statute granting a strict, lifetime preference for state civil service employment to veterans of American military service. There was no doubt that the preference had a severe disparate impact upon women; of the one quarter of the Massachusetts population who were veterans over 98% were male. The lower court had found that the Massachusetts preference was not established, either at its inception in 1896 or in later Amendments, as a means for preferring males generally; yet the lower court and the plaintiffs had claimed that the absolute preference was so serious a burden on women that legislators must have appreciated that they were disfavoring women as a class.

The Supreme Court, in an opinion by Justice Stewart, noted that the degree of burden placed upon a class was not relevant to determining the nature of the classification or whether the legislature had engaged in invidious gender classification; the legislature was not free to impose even minor invidious discriminations against women but it need not forego valid non-discriminatory laws because

100. 426 U.S. 229, 96 S.Ct. 2040, 48 L.Ed.2d 597 (1976).

101. The Court found the record also indicated a sufficient relationship between the test and employment qualification that it would be upheld under statutory standards as well. 426 U.S. at 250–52, 96 S.Ct. at 2052–54.

102. Arlington Heights v. Metropolitan Housing Development Corp., 429 U.S. 252, 97 S.Ct. 555, 50 L.Ed.2d 450 (1977).

103. 429 U.S. at 265, 97 S.Ct. at 563.

Following the remand of the decision in *Arlington Heights*, the Court of Appeals found that the racially disparate impact might show a violation of the Fair Housing Act, 42 U.S.C.A. § 3601 et seq.; the Supreme Court declined to review this decision. Metropolitan Housing Development Corp. v. Village of Arlington Heights, 558

F.2d 1283 (7th Cir.1977), cert. denied 434 U.S. 1025, 98 S.Ct. 752, 54 L.Ed.2d 772 (1978). In Cuyahoga Falls v. Buckeye Community Hope Foundation, 538 U.S. 188, 123 S.Ct. 1389, 155 L.Ed.2d 349 (2003) the Justices unanimously rejected a variety of equal protection and due process challenges to a city administrator's refusal to issue a building permit for low income housing pending a state court determination of the validity of a voter referendum to repeal the ordinance that authorized the building of a low-income housing complex. The *Cuyahoga Falls* case is discussed in § 14.44 of this Treatise.

104. 442 U.S. 256, 99 S.Ct. 2282, 60 L.Ed.2d 870 (1979), on remand 475 F.Supp. 109 (D.Mass.1979), judgment affirmed 445 U.S. 901, 100 S.Ct. 1075, 63 L.Ed.2d 317 (1980).

of the impact of those laws.[105]　The majority recognized that the legislation was non-neutral, in the sense that it preferred the class of veterans over the class of non-veterans, but the purpose of the law demonstrably was to prefer veterans over non-veterans; there was no proof that the laws were ever enacted for the purpose of preferring men over women. Mere appreciation by the legislature of the fact that the veterans preference would have adverse consequences for women as a class did not make the legislative act purposefully discriminatory.　To establish that a law neutral on its face is in fact one based on a specific classification meriting increased judicial scrutiny, those challenging the law must demonstrate "that the decision-maker, in this case a state legislature, selected or reaffirmed a particular course of action at least in part 'because of', not merely 'in spite of' its adverse effects upon an identifiable group."[106]　It was clear to the majority that the history of the veterans preference legislation in Massachusetts showed that the preference was enacted to reward and aid all veterans, male or female, and not to purposely prefer men over women in government employment.　Thus the legislation was a non-invidious, neutral classification that was upheld against an equal protection challenge.

These cases did not indicate that the Court was stepping back from its historic position concerning the ways in which subjective decisions were tested when laws were challenged as establishing classifications in their application.　In the same term that the Court upheld the Arlington Heights zoning plan, it struck down a system for juror selection on the basis of statistical proof showing a vastly disproportionate impact on members of racial minorities from a subjective selection process.[107]　The Court found a prima facie case that the discretion of the jury selectors had been used in a discriminatory manner and this evidence would prove a racial classification absent contrary proof by the state.

The Supreme Court applied the principles discussed in this section as the Justices unanimously invalidated a provision of the Alabama Constitution which disenfranchised persons convicted of a variety of crimes including any crime that involved "moral turpitude."　In *Hunter v. Underwood*,[108] the Court, in an opinion by Justice Rehnquist, held that the Court of Appeals, which had invalidated this law, had correctly found that the persons attacking the law were required to show that the intent to disenfranchise persons because of their race was the purpose of the state constitutional convention that adopted this voting qualification.　Justice Rehnquist noted that it was often more difficult to demonstrate discriminatory purpose when a law was adopted by a large body, such as a legislative chamber or state constitutional convention, than when a law or regulation was adopted by a small legislative body or administrative agency.[109]　After a person attacking a law as the establishment of an unconstitutional classification in its impact or effect establishes that the legislative body that adopted the law had a discriminatory purpose, the burden shifts to the state to show that the law would have been adopted regardless of that discriminatory purpose for other, constitutionally permissible, reasons.[110]　In *Hunter*,

105.　442 U.S. at 279, 99 S.Ct. at 2296.

106.　442 U.S. at 281, 99 S.Ct. at 2297 (footnote omitted).　In the accompanying footnote to this statement the majority indicated that the consequences of a law might be relevant to proving discriminatory purpose though the statistical impact in itself would not establish the classification or purpose.　442 U.S. at 279 n. 25, 99 S.Ct. at 2296 n. 25.

107.　Castaneda v. Partida, 430 U.S. 482, 97 S.Ct. 1272, 51 L.Ed.2d 498 (1977).

108.　471 U.S. 222, 105 S.Ct. 1916, 85 L.Ed.2d 222 (1985).　Justice Rehnquist wrote for a unanimous Court of eight Justices; as Justice Powell did not participate in this decision.

109.　471 U.S. at 228, 105 S.Ct. at 1920.　The Supreme Court noted the difficulty in assessing the motivation of large legislative bodies as it referred to the special problem of inquiring into congressional motives that was examined in United States v. O'Brien, 391 U.S. 367, 383–84, 88 S.Ct. 1673, 1682–83, 20 L.Ed.2d 672 (1968), in which the Court had refused to find a congressional motivation to punish speech in the enactment of a law that required males to carry military draft registration cards.

110.　Regarding shifting the burden of proof to require a state to show that the same governmental decision would have been made regardless of the consideration of the impermissible purpose, once a person attacking the law had shown that the legislature considered a constitutionally impermissible factor in passing the legislation, the

the Court found that statistical proof that the state definition of crimes involving "moral turpitude" disenfranchised a significantly greater percentage of black voters than white voters was relevant evidence. However, the statistical proof of adverse impact on black persons was not the sole basis for a finding of discriminatory purpose in this case. Justice Rehnquist found that the Court of Appeals was correct in its assessment of the records of the 1901 state convention, in which "zeal for white supremacy ran rampant," and the testimony of historians who had given the trial court their assessment of the historical background of the adoption of the voter disqualification provision.

The state in *Hunter* had argued that the 1901 state convention had sought to exclude both poor white persons and all black persons from voting through the adoption of the crimes of moral turpitude provision. Justice Rehnquist found that the Court did not have to assess the legitimacy of a variety of motives that might have played a part in the enactment of this constitutional provision because he found that it was clear that, despite any additional purposes the law might have, the desire to discriminate against black persons was "beyond peradventure ... a 'but for' motivation for the enactment" of the provision.[111] Regardless of whether state officials since 1901 have had different motivations for maintaining the law, the law had been adopted for an unconstitutional purpose and "continues to this day to have that effect." Thus, the voter

disqualification law violated the equal protection clause, regardless of the motivation of current Alabama governmental officials.[112]

Similarly, the Court has not diminished the protection accorded individuals by the civil rights legislation in its recent rulings. In the same term in which the Supreme Court refused to invalidate an at-large electoral system under the Fourteenth or Fifteenth Amendment because of a plaintiff's failure to prove discriminatory purpose,[113] the Court ruled that Congress *by statute* could bar changes in local electoral systems that had the effect of diluting the voting power of racial minorities without a showing of discriminatory purpose.[114]

The Court upheld the use of seniority systems which might have had the effect of continuing discrimination which occurred before the Civil Rights Act because it found these to be authorized under the terms of the Act unless the seniority systems were clearly proven to have been adopted for the specific purpose of establishing racially discriminatory benefit systems.[115]

However, the Court strictly enforced the basic anti-discrimination portions of Title VII when it found that statistical proof alone constituted a sufficient basis for finding a prima facie case that a city school system had discriminated on the basis of race in the hiring of teachers.[116] Similarly, the Court struck down, as violation of the Act, height and weight qualifications for prison guards; it found them to constitute sex discrimination because of

Supreme Court in *Hunter* referred to Arlington Heights v. Metropolitan Housing Development Corp., 429 U.S. 252, 270 n. 21, 97 S.Ct. 555, 556 n. 21, 50 L.Ed.2d 450 (1977), and Mt. Healthy City School District Board of Education v. Doyle, 429 U.S. 274, 287, 97 S.Ct. 568, 576, 50 L.Ed.2d 471 (1977). Hunter v. Underwood, 471 U.S. 222, 232–33, 105 S.Ct. 1916, 1922–23, 85 L.Ed.2d 222 (1985).

111. Hunter v. Underwood, 471 U.S. 222, 232, 105 S.Ct. 1916, 1922, 85 L.Ed.2d 222 (1985).

112. 471 U.S. at 233, 105 S.Ct. at 1923.

113. Mobile v. Bolden, 446 U.S. 55, 100 S.Ct. 1490, 64 L.Ed.2d 47 (1980).

114. Rome v. United States, 446 U.S. 156, 100 S.Ct. 1548, 64 L.Ed.2d 119 (1980).

See also, City of Pleasant Grove v. United States, 479 U.S. 462, 107 S.Ct. 794, 93 L.Ed.2d 866 (1987).

After Mobile v. Bolden, 446 U.S. 55, 100 S.Ct. 1490, 64 L.Ed.2d 47 (1980), Congress amended section two of the Voting Rights Act to ease the burden of a plaintiff in proving the existence of racial discrimination in a voting law or standard. For references to additional cases, and secondary authorities on this point, see the multi-volume edition of this Treatise: R. Rotunda & J. Nowak, Treatise on Constitutional Law: Substance and Procedure §§ 18.4, 19.11, 19.12 (3rd ed. 1999, with annual supplements).

115. International Brotherhood of Teamsters v. United States, 431 U.S. 324, 97 S.Ct. 1843, 52 L.Ed.2d 396 (1977).

116. Hazelwood School District v. United States, 433 U.S. 299, 97 S.Ct. 2736, 53 L.Ed.2d 768 (1977).

their effect.[117] These rulings will always be open to criticism because they are by their nature *ad hoc*; they must be made on the basis of individual records and evidence before the Court.

When the Supreme Court examines a claim that a defendant has violated a federal civil rights statute because of the allegedly racially or sexually discriminatory impact of the defendant's actions, the Court confronts the discriminatory effect versus discriminatory purpose issue. However, in statutory cases the issue is resolved by examining the purpose of the statute at issue and the intention of Congress in passing the statute. The Court has found that an employer's use of hiring or promotion tests that have an adverse impact on women or racial minorities is presumptively invalid under Title VII of the Civil Rights Acts passed in 1964,[118] but that statutes passed in 1866 to prevent racial discrimination against black persons in property or contract opportunities are only violated by actions undertaken with a discriminatory purpose.[119] Congress can outlaw those practices which have a discriminatory impact on women or minorities, but the Court will follow the discriminatory purpose analysis in the absence of such statutory action.

In *McCleskey v. Kemp,*[120] the Supreme Court refused to invalidate either the death penalty for a black defendant or the state's death penalty system on the basis of statistics show-

ing that a black defendant convicted of killing a white person was more likely to receive the death penalty than was a white defendant convicted of killing a black person. This case was decided by a five to four vote, with Justice Powell, who is no longer a member of the Court, writing the majority opinion. Regardless of whether the Court in future years will change the result in this type of case, the case demonstrates the difficulty in proving discriminatory purpose.

On behalf of the defendant in *McCleskey,* there was submitted to all appropriate courts a statistical study performed by several professors that involved a sophisticated statistical analysis of death penalty cases in the state. The study took into account over 200 variables; the statistical evidence in this case was very strong. Black defendants convicted of killing white victims were statistically much more likely to be subject to the death penalty than were other types of convicted homicide defendants. Nevertheless, the Supreme Court found that the evidence was insufficient in itself to show that the death penalty statute had been applied on a racially discriminatory basis or enacted for a racially discriminatory purpose. In order to show that the law was applied to him in a racially discriminatory manner, the defendant would be required to make a prima facie case that the jury had imposed the death penalty on him at least in

---

117. Dothard v. Rawlinson, 433 U.S. 321, 97 S.Ct. 2720, 53 L.Ed.2d 786 (1977).

118. Compare, Watson v. Fort Worth Bank and Trust, 487 U.S. 977, 108 S.Ct. 2777, 101 L.Ed.2d 827 (1988) (statistical proof and disparate impact analysis may establish a prima facie case of discrimination that violates Title VII even when the challenged employment practices are subjective or discretionary in nature; employer may rebut the prima facie case by producing evidence that the employer had legitimate, nondiscriminatory reasons for establishing and using the employment practice); with, Wards Cove Packing Co., Inc. v. Atonio, 490 U.S. 642, 109 S.Ct. 2115, 104 L.Ed.2d 733 (1989) (a prima facie case of racial discrimination under Title VII is not made by a comparison of the racial composition of an employers employees in skilled and unskilled positions; the statistical comparison should be between the racial composition of the jobs at issue and the racial composition of a qualified labor pool for those jobs; statistical disparity must be related to one or more of the employer's employment practices). For references to additional cases and second-

ary authorities, see 3 R. Rotunda & J. Nowak, Treatise on Constitutional Law: Substance and Procedure § 18.4 (3rd ed. 1999, with annual supplements).

119. General Building Contractors Ass'n, Inc. v. Pennsylvania, 458 U.S. 375, 102 S.Ct. 3141, 73 L.Ed.2d 835 (1982) (proof of discriminatory intent is required to establish a violation of 42 U.S.C.A. § 1981, enacted in 1866 and based on Congress' Thirteenth Amendment power, which guarantees to all persons the same contract rights as those "enjoyed by white citizens").

See also, Memphis v. Greene, 451 U.S. 100, 101 S.Ct. 1584, 67 L.Ed.2d 769 (1981), rehearing denied 452 U.S. 955, 101 S.Ct. 3100, 69 L.Ed.2d 965 (1981) (closing of street passing through white neighborhood and going into neighborhood with a predominantly black population does not violate 42 U.S.C.A. § 1982 granting all citizens those property rights "enjoyed by white citizens").

120. 481 U.S. 279, 107 S.Ct. 1756, 95 L.Ed.2d 262 (1987), rehearing denied 482 U.S. 920, 107 S.Ct. 3199, 96 L.Ed.2d 686 (1987).

part because of his race. Statistics alone would not establish a prima facie of racial discrimination.

The defendant in *McCleskey* also attempted to use the statistical study to prove that the state's statutory system for imposition of the death penalty violated both the equal protection clause and the Eighth Amendment. Justice Powell's majority opinion stated that, for the equal protection claim to prevail, the defendant "would have to prove that the Georgia legislature enacted or maintained the death penalty statute *because of* an anticipated racially discriminatory effect."[121] As in prior cases regarding legislative intent, the Court found that statistical evidence would not be sufficient in itself to prove discriminatory purpose. The majority also ruled that the creation of a sentencing system that left discretion to a jury met due process and Eighth Amendment standards, at least so long as the state limited the jury's discretion to cases in which the Court had found that the crime at issue could constitutionally justify the imposition of the death penalty and the procedures for submission of information to the jury met the fairness standards established in prior decisions.[122]

The Court's treatment of statistics as a form of proof which is of great worth in the Civil Rights Act cases, somewhat less in the discriminatory application cases, and very little in the "effect" cases is certainly open to criticism from those who desire a single standard for testing the impact of all rules that might have differing effects on racial or sexual classifications of persons.

§ 14.5 Classifications Based on Race or National Origin: Introduction

Today the equal protection clause of the Fourteenth Amendment mandates that no governmental entity shall burden persons, or deny a benefit to them, because they are members of a racial minority. After many years of indifference to the use of racial classifications,

the Supreme Court has in the last forty years enforced the constitutional principle of racial equality. Of course, there was no such principle prior to the Civil War when slavery existed with constitutional and Supreme Court sanction. Following the War the Thirteenth, Fourteenth and Fifteenth Amendments were passed as part of an effort to grant by constitutional decree equal rights to black persons. Although it appeared at the outset as though the Supreme Court might strongly enforce the equal protection guarantee, the Court endorsed racial segregation of public facilities and functions, other than overt discrimination in jury selection, by accepting the concept of "separate but equal."

Following 1930 the Court began to evidence a growing distaste for having to place a constitutional imprimatur on racial discrimination. In the mid 1940's, the Court upheld the wartime restrictions on persons of Japanese ancestry but indicated that classifications based on race or national origin would not be consistent with constitutional principles absent the most important justification. Finally the Supreme Court began to enforce the concept of equal protection by forbidding the establishment of separate educational facilities for blacks. Thereafter the Court was to strike down every form of government action that discriminated against members of a minority race or segregated public facilities by race.

Classifications based on race or national origin have been held to be "suspect," that is, the Justices will use "strict scrutiny" to determine whether the law is invidious. The use of these classifications will be invalid unless they are necessary to promote a "compelling" or "overriding" interest of government. Burdening someone because of his national origin or status as a member of a racial minority runs counter to the most fundamental concept of equal protection. To legitimate such a classification the end of the governmental action would have to outweigh the basic values of the

---

121. McCleskey v. Kemp, 481 U.S. 279, 297, 107 S.Ct. 1756, 1769, 95 L.Ed.2d 262 (1987), rehearing denied 482 U.S. 920, 107 S.Ct. 3199, 96 L.Ed.2d 686 (1987) (emphasis in original).

122. Some of the cases regarding due process and Eighth Amendment limitations on the discretion of a sentencing jury in a capital case are examined in § 17.3 of this Treatise.

Amendment. For this reason no such classification has been upheld since 1945 when the Supreme Court accepted the argument that the classification at issue would burden racial minorities. However, the Court has not held that all government acts must be race-neutral (or "color-blind") and we do not yet know whether the government may use racial classifications to grant special benefits to members of minority races except where the classification is used to remedy proven discrimination.

When we use the term "national origin" in this text, we are referring to ancestry or ethnicity, rather than citizenship. For example, if the mother one of the coauthors of this book had been denied benefits when she first came to this country, from Italy, because she was not yet a United States citizen, her claim against the government would be one based on an alienage classification (which is a classification that awards burdens or benefits based on United States citizenship)[1]. If, after she became a United States citizen, she was denied a government benefit because she had come from Italy, her claim against the government would be one based on "national origin." If in the year 2000, the government were to deny the coauthors of this book some benefit because they had ancestors from Italy, the authors would bring an equal protection claim against the government based on national origin or ancestry. The Supreme Court has treated claims of discrimination based on national origin or ancestry in a manner identical to how it treats racial discrimination claims. Thus, in our example, when the authors brought suit against the government, because of the denial of benefits to them that was based on their Italian heritage, the Court would not need to decide whether the classification should be called a racial classification or

an ancestry classification. It would apply strict judicial scrutiny, and the compelling interest test, to their case. Since the middle of the twentieth century the Court has not found that any classification based on ancestry or national origin should be treated differently than a racial classification.[2]

We stress the term "governmental action" for the equal protection guarantee extends to all governmental acts. The Fourteenth Amendment applies to any state, including all subdivisions or local governments within a state. The due process clause of the Fifth Amendment imposes a similar equal protection guarantee upon the federal government. The Court has held that any classification which would violate the equal protection clause when done by the federal government is an arbitrary and invidious use of power which constitutes an independent violation of the due process clause of the Fifth Amendment.

The actions of persons with no connection to any governmental entity are not subject to either the Fifth or Fourteenth Amendments. A discussion of the relationships to government that subject someone to constitutional constraint is contained in Chapter Twelve, on state action.

What follows is a development of these principles and a study of their application. While the section on classification is complete in itself, the following section, on the problems of implementing integration, provides additional insight into the principles of racial equality. The section on affirmative action and benign classifications examines the arguments relating to a most important but unresolved undecided issue.

---

§ 14.5

1. For an examination of the standards used to determine the compatibility of alienage classifications with the equal protection guarantees of the Fifth and Fourteenth Amendments, see §§ 14.11–14.13. By the way, the person in the hypothetical would have been Evelyn Bucci, the mother of Professor Nowak. The rest of the hypothetical will involve both of the coauthors, because both Professors Nowak and Rotunda are of Italian ancestry.

2. In Rice v. Cayetano, 528 U.S. 495, 120 S.Ct. 1044, 145 L.Ed.2d 1007 (2000) the Supreme Court held that the

Fifteenth Amendment prohibited Hawaii from limiting the vote for members of a board that administered programs to benefit "Native Hawaiians" or "Hawaiians" (groups defined by ancestry) to persons who were native Hawaiians or Hawaiians. The Court found that this law constituted an ancestry classification and that, at least in this instance, (as in many other Supreme Court cases) "Ancestry can be a proxy for race. It is that proxy here." 528 U.S. at 513, 120 S.Ct. at 1055. See § 14.10 (c) regarding the use of racial classifications to assist the voting power of minority race persons.

§ 14.6   Racial Discrimination Prior to the Civil War

Prior to the Civil War there was no constitutional safeguard against depriving persons of rights or privileges because of their race, the inevitable position of a system which legitimized slavery.[1]

There was some sentiment in colonial America for total abolition of slavery. During the period under which the states followed the Articles of Confederation, slavery was prohibited in the territories by the Northwest Ordinance.[2] At the constitutional convention the various sectional groups approached the problem of slavery as an economic and political one. The northern delegates were not ready to risk their economic and political unification with the south over the slavery issue. The southern representatives sought some assurances that the new federal government would not take steps to abolish slavery in their states. Eventually the convention agreed that the federal government should not be able to limit the importation of slaves for a period of time and that southern slaveholders should have full recognition of their right to hold slaves. Thus Article I forbade Congress to restrict the slave trade prior to 1808[3] and Article V prohibited Amendments which would remove this restriction.[4] The rights of slaveholders were recognized in the fugitive slave clause of Article IV.[5]

No branch of the new federal government moved to curtail slavery within the states following the formation of the union. The second Congress passed the "fugitive slave act" which established the slaveowners' rights to the return of slaves who escaped into free states.[6] The Supreme Court of the United States upheld and enforced the act as a proper implementation of the slave clause of Article IV.[7] The Court struck down state laws that punished those who "kidnapped" fugitive slaves in free states as conflicting with the federal policy[8] and upheld state laws that punished those who harbored fugitive slaves.[9]

The Supreme Court also proved unhelpful to former slaves who asserted that they had become free. The Court generally ruled in favor of the slaveholders who asserted that the individuals making the claim had not been freed according to the laws of the appropriate jurisdiction.[10] Individuals seeking to establish that they had been freed from slavery were dependent upon local courts to enforce their rights.

In the north, states systematically began

---

§ 14.6

1. For a more complete treatment of this period see Derrick Bell, Race, Racism and American Law (2d ed. 1980). For citations to additional secondary authorities, see the multi-volume edition of this treatise: R. Rotunda & J. Nowak, Treatise on Constitutional Law: Substance and Procedure, Chapter 18 (3rd ed.1999, with annual supplements).

2. The Northwest Ordinance of July 13, 1787, is reprinted in our multi-volume treatise, R. Rotunda, & J. Nowak, Treatise on Constitutional Law: Substance and Procedure, vol. 5, App. C (3rd ed. 1999, with annual supplements).

3. The provision allowed for taxation but not prohibition. U.S.Const. art. I, § 9, cl. 1:

"The Migration or Importation of Such Persons as any of the States now existing shall think proper to admit, shall not be prohibited by the Congress prior to the Year One thousand eight hundred and eight, but a Tax or duty may be imposed on such Importation, not exceeding ten dollars for each Person."

4. U.S.Const. art. V:

"... Provided that no Amendment which may be made prior to the Year One thousand eight hundred and eight shall in any Manner affect the first and fourth clauses in the Ninth Section of the first Article."

5. U.S.Const. art. IV, § 2, cl. 3:

"No Person held to Service or Labour in one State, under the Laws thereof, escaping into another, shall, in Consequence of any Law or Regulation therein, be discharged from such Service or Labour, but shall be delivered up on Claim of the Party to whom such Service or Labour may be due."

6. Act of Feb. 12, 1793, 1 Stat. 302.

7. Jones v. Van Zandt, 46 U.S. (5 How.) 215, 12 L.Ed. 122 (1847); Ableman v. Booth, 62 U.S. (21 How.) 506, 16 L.Ed. 169 (1858).

8. Prigg v. Pennsylvania, 41 U.S. (16 Pet.) 539, 10 L.Ed. 1060 (1842).

9. Moore v. Illinois, 55 U.S. (14 How.) 13, 17, 14 L.Ed. 306 (1852).

10. See, e.g., Queen v. Hepburn, 11 U.S. (7 Cranch) 290, 3 L.Ed. 348 (1813); Scott v. Ben, 10 U.S. (6 Cranch) 3, 3 L.Ed. 135 (1810); but see, McCutchen v. Marshall, 33 U.S. (8 Pet.) 220, 8 L.Ed. 923 (1834); see generally, Roper, In Quest of Judicial Objectivity: The Marshall Court and the Legitimation of Slavery, 21 Stan.L.Rev. 532 (1969).

eliminating slavery within their jurisdictions.[11] If a slave became subject to the jurisdiction of a free state for a sufficient period of time, he would become free according to the laws of that state. Until approximately 1830 most state courts applied a rule of "reasonableness" to determine whether a slave had remained in a free state long enough to become free.[12] Northern states would not declare slaves free if they were brought into free territory for only a short time, while southern states would honor the free status of slaves emancipated this way.[13]

As the rivalry between the free and slave states intensified, the rule of reasonableness and judicial cooperation came to an end.[14] Northern states would declare a slave free even though that person had been in the state only a short time, while southern states would refuse to honor the free status of former slaves who returned to slave states. The abolitionist movement and the southern defense of slavery simply could not be reconciled by local legal systems, and the need for some sort of federal action intensified.

The federal government moved to limit the slave trade after the constitutional prohibition in Article I expired.[15] The restriction on the importation of slaves was enforced by the Supreme Court in an attempt to greatly restrict the slave trade.[16] Yet the Court was unwilling

to move to strike down the slave trading practices. Justice Johnson, as a Circuit Justice, struck down a state law regulating and enslaving free blacks incident to slave trade regulation as invalid under the commerce clause,[17] but the Court as a whole only pronounced dicta against the immorality of slavery while refusing to limit slavery beyond the statutory trade restrictions.[18] However, it is interesting to note that the Supreme Court recognized that foreign black Africans were free persons who had, and retained, individual rights if they were brought into this country in violation of the congressional restriction of slave trade.[19]

Some protection was given to those blacks unlawfully brought into the country, but free blacks were not given rights against racial discrimination. The Supreme Court had no conception of a right of free blacks to equal protection of the laws. In the southern states not only was there unequal treatment of blacks, but white abolitionists who traveled into slave territory were unlikely to receive the protection of the southern legal authorities.[20] The North provided no more meaningful protection for free blacks against unequal distribution of rights based on race.[21] Indeed it was the Supreme Court of Massachusetts that created the concept of "separate but equal" when it upheld a separate school system for black

---

11. L. Litwack, North of Slavery 3–20 (1961); D. A. Zilversmit, The First Emancipation: The Abolition of Slavery in the North (1967); D. Bell, Race, Racism and American Law § 1.3 (2d ed. 1980).

12. Note, American Slavery and the Conflict of Laws, 71 Colum.L.Rev. 74 (1971).

13. During this period at least some southern courts also enforced the prohibition of slavery contained in the Northwest Ordinance, supra note 2, by declaring free those who had become subject to the jurisdiction of the territory. Merry v. Chexnaider, 8 Martin (N.S.) 699, 5 La.Ann. part 3 at 224, (La.1830); Forsyth v. Nash, 4 Martin (O.S.) 385, 1 La.Ann. part 4 at 117 (La.1816).

14. Note, American Slavery and the Conflict of Laws, 71 Colum.L.Rev. 74, 92–8 (1971).

15. 2 Stat. 426 (Act of March 2, 1807, to be effective on January 1, 1808); 3 Stat. 450; 3 Stat. 600.

16. See, e.g., The Josefa Segunda, 18 U.S. (5 Wheat.) 338, 5 L.Ed. 104 (1820).

17. Elkison v. Deliesseline, 8 F.Cas. 493 (No. 4366) (C.C.S.C.1823). (Johnson sitting as Circuit Justice).

18. The Antelope, 23 U.S. (10 Wheat.) 66, 6 L.Ed. 268 (1825) (dicta that slave trade had to be authorized by statute as it was contrary to national law). See Roper, In Quest of Judicial Objectivity: The Marshall Court and the Legitimation of Slavery, 21 Stan.L.Rev. 532 (1969).

19. The Amistad, 40 U.S. (15 Pet.) 518, 10 L.Ed. 826 (1841). The Court here set free a group of black Africans who had revolted against their captain on a Spanish schooner and landed in the United States. The Court recognized these persons as kidnapped free persons. The case was argued for the Africans by former president John Quincy Adams, who was a part of the abolitionist effort.

20. For a recounting of the history of attacks on the abolitionists and their response see, J. tenBroek, Equal Under Law 35–40 (1965).

21. D. Bell, Race, Racism and American Law § 1.3 (2d ed. 1980); L. Litwack, North of Slavery (1961); L. Greene, The Negro in Colonial New England (1942). Some "free" states actually prohibited the immigration of black persons into the states. See, e.g., Nelson v. People, 33 Ill. 390 (1864).

students.[22] In some states only blacks could be slaves.[23] In others, all blacks were presumed to be slaves.[24]

The move to abolish slavery steadily gained momentum following the turn of the century. The American Anti-Slavery Society was founded in 1833 and thereafter the abolitionist movement became a more potent political force. As the abolitionists had little hope of limiting or ending slavery by local legislation in the south, they turned to the national government to advance this cause.

A battle ensued in Congress over not only congressional power to limit slavery but also over the whole scope of federal power under the Constitution. At first the abolitionists sought only an end to slavery in federally held areas such as the District of Columbia. Eventually they sought the total abolition of slavery by Congressional act. These pressures were resisted by southern representatives whose position changed from arguing the tacit recognition of slavery in the Constitution to asserting the right of individual states to refuse to follow or "nullify" federal laws.[25]

In 1820 Congress had found a temporary solution in the Missouri Compromise.[26] This compromise did not change the balance of power or the slavery system within the country, but it avoided battles over the admission of new states by dividing them into "free" and "slave" states. Following 1820 the political struggle had intensified and the constitutionality of congressional action affecting slavery was in doubt. Arguments over slavery, congressional power, nullification and possible secession were inexorably linked. Indeed it can be fairly said that, by the time the Supreme Court spoke on these issues, the country was

in the midst of a constitutional as well as a political crisis.

In 1857, in its only attempt to constitutionally resolve the slavery conflict, the Court displayed an amazing lack of moral or political wisdom. At issue in *Dred Scott v. Sandford*[27] was the effect of state and federal laws granting freedom and citizenship to former slaves. Scott had been taken as a slave by his owner into Illinois, a free state, and an area of the Louisiana Purchase territory which had been made a free territory under the Missouri Compromise. Upon returning to Missouri, Scott sued his owner in federal court to establish his freedom.

The Supreme Court could have avoided the most difficult issues by finding that the federal court was bound to follow Missouri law, under which Scott was still considered a slave or even that proper diversity jurisdiction was not present.[28] But, perhaps, due to the fact that at least one dissenting Justice intended to defend the Missouri Compromise and the Congressional power to free slaves, a six member majority of the Court went far beyond the basic issues in resolving Scott's claim.[29]

There were eight separate opinions which covered over 200 pages of the U.S. Reports, but it is the majority opinion by Chief Justice Taney which was, and is, the center of controversy. The opinion by Taney found that neither black slaves nor their descendants could be considered citizens of the United States or persons who received any individual rights under the Constitution. This conclusion was based on the majority's historical and legal perception of blacks as persons of an inherently inferior position in society. In the view of the majority, no state could alter the status of slaves or their descendants by granting them

---

22. Roberts v. City of Boston, 59 Mass. (5 Cush.) 198 (1849).

23. Gaines v. Ann, 17 Tex. 211 (1856). Contra, State v. Van Waggoner, 6 N.J.Law (1 Halst.) 374 (1797); See also Scott v. Raub, 88 Va. 721, 14 S.E. 178 (1891).

24. Forsyth v. Nash, 4 Martin (O.S.) 385, 1 La.Ann. part 4 at 117 (La.1816).

25. An excellent history of the times in terms of conflicting political theories is J. tenBroek, Equal Under Law (1965) (first published as "The Antislavery Origins of the Fourteenth Amendment").

26. 3 Stat. 545–48.

27. 60 U.S. (19 How.) 393, 15 L.Ed. 691 (1856).

28. Such a course had been followed six years earlier in Strader v. Graham, 51 U.S. (10 How.) 82, 13 L.Ed. 337 (1850).

29. It may well have resulted from a combination of the possible dissent and the majority's belief in its own ability to save the country from a major social conflict. R. McCloskey, The American Supreme Court 92–95 (1960).

citizenship. The majority opinion even went beyond these assertions to hold that Congress could not grant citizenship to these persons. The Missouri Compromise was held unconstitutional; the majority found that Congress was without power to grant citizenship to slaves or their descendants, based on the majority's view that the original Constitution and Bill of Rights by implication precluded any possibility of constitutional protection for black slaves or their descendants. The opinion implied that any congressional action to emancipate slaves would violate the substantive due process protections for a slaveholder and his interest in his "property."

Taney's majority opinion in *Dred Scott* may well have been based on an honest and fairly objective view of the attitudes of some of the founders of the country, but the majority could not be excused from using its interpretative powers to reach out and protect the morally reprehensible practice of slavery from reform through the democratic process. The opinion was greeted with unmitigated wrath from every segment of the United States except the slave holding states, causing the Court to lose both its moral authority and political base until after the Civil War, when it slowly began

to reassert its power and align itself with national economic interests.[30]

Prior to the Civil War the Court showed no interest as an institution in limiting slavery or racial discrimination. It would take the Civil War Amendments to establish some basis for black citizenship and constitutional rights for members of racial minorities. In later years both the Court and country have tried to excise the *Dred Scott* decision from our legal heritage. As Professor Derrick Bell has summarized:

> The understandable desire on the part of the legal profession to finally erase what Chief Justice Charles Evans Hughes called the Court's "self-inflicted wound" has resulted in the Dred Scott case being the most frequently overturned decision in history. The final demise of Dred Scott has been attributed to the following: (1) the Civil War—"The law of the case was lost in the maelstrom which engulfed North and South," A. Blaustein and C. Ferguson, Desegregation and the Law 85 (1957); (2) the Thirteenth Amendment, according to The Civil Rights Cases, 109 U.S. 3, 3 S.Ct. 18, 27 L.Ed. 835(1883); (3) the Fourteenth Amendment, by H. Horowitz and K. Karst, Law, Lawyers and Social Change 102 (1969); (4)

---

30. See, Robert McCloskey, The American Supreme Court 95–97:

"The tempest of malediction that burst over the judges seems to have stunned them; far from extinguishing the slavery controversy, they had fanned its flames and had, moreover, deeply endangered the security of the judicial arm of government. No such vilification as this had been heard even in the wrathful days following the Alien and Sedition Acts. . . .

"The extent of that tragedy is revealed by the peculiar transvaluation of values that took place in connection with the case of *Ableman v. Booth* in 1859. Ableman, a Milwaukee editor, had assisted a fugitive slave to escape from federal custody, and was therefore arrested for violation of the national Fugitive Slave Law. The Wisconsin Supreme Court ordered him released on a writ of habeas corpus, and the order was obeyed. However, the national government then appealed to the Supreme Court of the United States, which held that the state courts had no business to interfere with the conduct of federal law and that the Fugitive Slave Law was constitutional.

"Now the first point was of course the very keystone of the Supreme Court's jurisdictional arch; this was the principle for which Marshall has fought so shrewdly and

effectively. If the national government and its judicial arm can operate only by the leave of the several states, the nation is not a nation and the Supreme Court is not a supreme court. Yet the decision was violently attacked, the state was urged to resist, the cry that the Court had no power thus to overrule a state was heard, not only in Wisconsin, but throughout the North.

"This was the doctrine of nullification, familiar since the Virginia and Kentucky resolutions of 1798–99, reenergized by the mordant genius of Calhoun in 1832, and now becoming an article of faith below the Mason-Dixon line. That it should be invoked by a northern state as a challenge to the Court is a measure of the witless inconsistency of some Northern opinion but is also a measure of judicial bankruptcy. The Court's effective existence depended on acceptance of the principle of national authority, and there was no hope that this principle would be entertained in the South one minute after an anti-slavery opinion was rendered. The judicial constituency had always been drawn from those who had a stake in nationalism, and in 1859 that meant the North. But the monumental indiscretion of *Dred Scott* had forfeited Northern allegiance. For the first time in its history, the Court seemed almost friendless (for the fair-weather friendship of the South provided very cold comfort)."

all three Civil War Amendments, by former Chief Justice Earl Warren: E. Warren, A Republic If You Can Keep It, 46 (1972); (5) *Brown v. Board of Education*, ... (1954), ... by Judge John Minor Wisdom in *United States v. Jefferson County Board of Education*, 372 F.2d 836, 873 (5th Cir.1966); and (6) *Jones v. Mayer Co.*, ... (1968) ... by Larsen, The New Law of Race Relations, 1969 Wis.L.Rev. 470, 486.[31]

§ 14.7　The Civil War Amendments and Racial Discrimination—An Introductory Note

The Civil War changed the basic features of the Constitution just as it altered the country's political and social structure. Three Amendments to the Constitution were proposed after the war and were ratified by 1870. These three Amendments—the Thirteenth, Fourteenth, and Fifteenth—are often referred to as the Civil War Amendments because they are the direct outgrowth of the war and its political aftermath. As the Amendments are closely tied to the earlier abolitionist movement and the post war struggle concerning the rights of freed blacks, we shall briefly review these Amendments prior to continuing our discussion of racial classifications.

The Thirteenth Amendment, proposed by Congress and ratified by the states in 1865, consists of two sections.[1] The first section prohibits "slavery" and "involuntary servitude" throughout the United States or its territories. This prohibition applies to all persons subject to the jurisdiction of the United States and is not dependent on the existence of government action. It proscribes such practices even where they are imposed by individuals with no connection to any governmental entity. The only exception is that made by section one for the punishment of properly convicted criminals. Section two of the Amendment grants Congress the power to make laws to enforce the Amendment.

The Fourteenth Amendment, proposed by Congress in 1866 and ratified in 1868, has five sections dealing with separate issues.[2] Section

---

31. Derrick Bell, Race, Racism and American Laws at 21–22 (1st ed. 1973).

§ 14.7

1. U.S.Const. amend. XIII:

"Section 1. Neither slavery nor involuntary servitude, except as a punishment for crime whereof the party shall have been duly convicted, shall exist within the United States, or any place subject to their jurisdiction.

"Section 2. Congress shall have power to enforce this article by appropriate legislation."

2. U.S.Const. amend. XIV:

"Section 1. All persons born or naturalized in the United States, and subject to the jurisdiction thereof, are citizens of the United States and of the State wherein they reside. No State shall make or enforce any law which shall abridge the privileges or immunities of citizens of the United States; nor shall any State deprive any person of life, liberty, or property, without due process of law; nor deny to any person within its jurisdiction the equal protection of the laws.

"Section 2. Representatives shall be apportioned among the several States according to their respective numbers, counting the whole number of persons in each State, excluding Indians not taxed. But when the right to vote at any election for the choice of electors for President and Vice President of the United States, Representatives in Congress, the Executive and Judicial officers of a State, or the members of the Legislature thereof, is denied to any of the male inhabitants of such State, being twenty-one years of age, and citizens of the United States, or in any way abridged, except for participation in rebellion, or other crime, the basis of representation therein shall be reduced in the proportion which the number of such male citizens shall bear to the whole number of male citizens twenty-one years of age in such State.

"Section 3. No person shall be a Senator or Representative in Congress, or elector of President and Vice President, or hold any office, civil or military, under the United States, or under any State, who having previously taken an oath, as a member of Congress, or as an officer of the United States, or as a member of any State legislature, or as an executive or judicial officer of any State, to support the Constitution of the United States, shall have engaged in insurrection or rebellion against the same, or given aid or comfort to the enemies thereof. But Congress may by a vote of two-thirds of each House, remove such disability.

"Section 4. The validity of the public debt of the United States, authorized by law, including debts incurred for payment of pensions and bounties for services in suppressing insurrection or rebellion, shall not be questioned. But neither the United States nor any State shall assume or pay any debt or obligation incurred in aid of insurrection or rebellion against the United States, or any claim for the loss or emancipation of any slave; but all such debts, obligations and claims shall be held illegal and void.

"Section 5. The Congress shall have power to enforce, by appropriate legislation, the provisions of this article."

one is the provision that has been the source of most "civil rights" rulings by the Supreme Court. This section consists of two sentences containing a total of four clauses. Sentence one grants citizenship to everyone "born or naturalized in the United States, and subject to the jurisdiction thereof...." The three clauses of sentence two grant important individual rights, but they secure these rights only against interference by the states. Thus sentence two appears to be inapplicable to the actions of private persons or the federal government. The first clause of sentence two prohibits the states from abridging "the privileges or immunities of citizens of the United States." The second clause mirrors the language of the Fifth Amendment due process clause and prohibits the states from depriving anyone of "life, liberty or property, without due process of law." The last clause of section one contains the only equal protection clause in the Constitution, and it prohibits the states from depriving anyone of "the equal protection of the laws."

Section 2 of the Fourteenth Amendment altered the regulation of the electoral franchise in two ways. First, blacks were counted as full citizens for purposes of representation in the Congress by replacing the provisions of Article I Section 2 which counted only three-fifths of "all other persons" (meaning slaves—a term the Constitution's drafters avoided). Second, representation in the federal Congress would be reduced for those states which denied any adult male citizen the right to vote except for "participation in rebellion, or other crime...." In these ways the drafters of the Amendment hoped to encourage the states to grant universal male suffrage without direct federal action.

Sections three and four of the Fourteenth Amendment relate to political problems of the period. Section three bars from federal office, except by vote of Congress, any previous government office holder who participated in a

rebellion or gave aid to the enemies of the United States. Section four insulates the government debt, including the Union war debt, from legal attack. It also insures that the federal government would never pay any of the Confederate debt.

Section five of the Fourteenth Amendment gives Congress the power to enforce the Amendment.

The Fifteenth Amendment,[3] proposed by Congress is 1869 and ratified in 1870, enfranchised blacks by prohibiting both the state and federal governments from denying anyone the right to vote "on account of race, color, or previous condition of servitude." Section two of the Amendment grants enforcement powers to Congress.

As we saw in the previous section, slavery and racial discrimination were given constitutional protection prior to the Civil War. Although there were many economic or political influences that took part in causing the war, the Northern Abolitionists and their goals of abolishing slavery and providing for the freed blacks were of critical importance in the shaping of postwar history.

While the three Amendments were not part of a preconceived legislative "package" or plan, they represent the natural progression of the abolitionist goals as these goals were represented in Congress by the "Radical Republicans." Each of the Amendments can be traced in part to particular political considerations, but most of the leading Republican members of Congress were confirmed abolitionists. The desire to secure freedom and safety, if not social equality, for freed black persons was shared by a large part of the population, at least in the North.

During this period, there were times in which the people of the northern states seemed to want all reconstruction issues to end and the southern states to be "readmitted" to the Union. Indeed, the continued

---

3. U.S.Const. amend. XV:

"Section 1. The right of citizens of the United States to vote shall not be denied or abridged by the United States or by any State on account of race, color, or previous condition of servitude.

"Section 2. The Congress shall have power to enforce this article by appropriate legislation."

discrimination against black persons in the northern states gives one cause to doubt the popular strength of the abolitionist movement after the war. Yet the continued mistreatment of freed blacks in the South resulted in renewed Northern dedication to the abolitionists' goals. Thus, following a period of seemingly lessening Northern interest, we find the Fifteenth Amendment being ratified in 1870 and the major civil rights act being passed in 1871.

The history of these Amendments, and the use of history to justify modern judicial rulings, has been the subject of extensive scholarly debate. In the multi-volume edition of this treatise, we give an overview of history of these Amendments and references to some of the scholarly examinations of that history.[4]

Congress realized that the passage of the Amendments alone would not secure equality for blacks or stop the atrocities committed against them. As news of lynchings and other violent acts against blacks reached Washington, northern congressmen sought legislation to stop these practices. This resulted in the Civil Rights Act of 1871 which was known at the time as the "Ku Klux Klan Act."[5] The Act was designed to civilly and criminally punish those who acted to deprive others of their civil rights. The total Act granted sweeping presidential powers to use the armed forces to enforce its provisions and even to suspend the right to habeas corpus when necessary to restore order to areas dominated by violent organizations. Although these provisions were the focus of most of the debate in Congress, the most important section was to be the civil penalty provision. Now usually referred to as simply "section 1983",[6] it provides the cause of action and general basis for federal courts to protect individual civil rights.[7]

We now turn back to a history of the constitutional decisions concerning racial discrimination. These sections deal with the impact of the Fourteenth Amendment equal protection clause and the Fifth Amendment due process clause. The Thirteenth and Fifteenth Amendments have been the subject of only limited rulings and their primary impact has been in connection with federal legislation. They will be examined in connection with the congressional power to enforce the Civil War Amendments.[8]

§ 14.8 Classifications Based on Race or National Origin Following the Civil War

(a) Introduction

The problem of racial classification is most easily analyzed as an equal protection issue. The Fourteenth Amendment prohibits states from denying any person the "equal protection of the laws."[1] Whenever any governmental entity classifies persons by their race for dispensation of benefits or burdens, it probably has violated the equal protection clause, which requires that similar persons be dealt with in a similar manner.[2] Therefore, it must be determined when, if ever, the government may rule that a person is "dissimilar" from others for the purpose of a law because of that person's race.

---

4. For references to scholarly works analyzing the history of the Fourteenth Amendment see our multi-volume treatise, R. Rotunda & J. Nowak, Treatise on Constitutional Law: Substance and Procedure §18.6 (3rd ed. 1999, with annual supplements).

5. Act of April 20; 17 Stat. 13 (1871).

6. 42 U.S.C.A. §1983 (From Act April 20, c. 22, §1, 17 Stat. 13 (1871)): "Every person who, under color of any statute, ordinance, regulation, custom, or usage, of any State or Territory, subjects, or causes to be subjected, any citizen of the United States or other person within the jurisdiction thereof to the deprivation of any rights, privileges or immunities secured by the Constitution and laws, shall be liable to the party injured in an action at law, suit in equity, or other proper proceeding for redress."

7. The judicial interpretation of 42 U.S.C.A. §1983 is examined in Chapter 19 of our multi-volume treatise, R. Rotunda & J. Nowak, Treatise on Constitutional Law: Substance and Procedure, ch. 19 (3rd ed. 1999, with annual supplements).

8. The constitutional basis for congressional enforcement of civil rights is examined in Chapter 15 of this text.

§ 14.8

1. U.S.Const. amend. XIV.

2. For an overview of basic equal protection-classification analysis see § 14.2, supra.

The Supreme Court has considered race and national origin classifications together for they both involve the government's treatment of persons on the basis of their ethnic ancestry rather than individual actions. Classifications based on alienage—the status of not being a citizen—relate to the personal attributes of citizenship rather than ancestry alone and they are dealt with in a separate section.[3]

Today classifications based on race or national origin are "suspect;" courts will make an independent inquiry to determine whether they should be stricken as "invidious" discrimination.[4] Such classifications are permissible only if they are necessary to promote a compelling or overriding interest of government. This conclusion requires a judicial finding that the use of the classification is so important as to outweigh the central purpose of the Amendment. But this present position of the Court was not easily arrived at: the Court went through a long period of allowing the use of racial classifications, especially for segregating public facilities.

The sections which immediately follow deal with the development of standards for the permissibility of explicit classifications based on race or national origin which are used by any branch of the government, including both state and federal governments. Although the federal government is not subject to the Four-teenth Amendment, the due process clause of the Fifth Amendment has been interpreted to encompass an equal protection guarantee.[5]

The Thirteenth Amendment has not served as a significant prohibition of racial discrimination absent congressional action. The Amendment prohibits "slavery" or "involuntary servitude" throughout the United States or any territory under its jurisdiction.

The Supreme Court acknowledged shortly after the ratification of the Amendment that it prohibited systems of peonage as well as the type of slavery that existed prior to the Civil War.[6] Only a few years later the Court found that racial discrimination by private persons did not violate the Amendment because it did not involve imposition of the incidents of slavery upon those against whom the discriminatory actions were taken nor did it involve a slavery or peonage system.[7] By ruling that "mere discriminations on account of race or color were not regarded as badges of slavery,"[8] the Court restricted the application of section one of the Thirteenth Amendment to a prohibition of peonage or slavery. However, in the next century the Supreme Court would rule that Congress has the power under section two of the Amendment to outlaw by statute almost any form of racial discrimination even though section one of the Amendment did not in itself outlaw such discrimination.[9]

---

3. See §§ 14.11–14.13, infra.

4. For an overview of classification analysis see §§ 14.1–14.4, supra.

5. Bolling v. Sharpe, 347 U.S. 497, 74 S.Ct. 693, 98 L.Ed. 884 (1954), opinion supplemented 349 U.S. 294, 75 S.Ct. 753, 99 L.Ed. 1083 (1955); Weinberger v. Wiesenfeld, 420 U.S. 636, 638 n. 2, 95 S.Ct. 1225, 1228 n. 2, 43 L.Ed.2d 514 (1975); Schlesinger v. Ballard, 419 U.S. 498, 500 n. 3, 95 S.Ct. 572, 42 L.Ed.2d 610 (1975), rehearing denied 420 U.S. 966, 95 S.Ct. 1363, 43 L.Ed.2d 446 (1975).

6. In re Slaughter–House Cases, 83 U.S. (16 Wall.) 36, 21 L.Ed. 394 (1872).

7. In re Civil Rights Cases, 109 U.S. 3, 20–25, 3 S.Ct. 18, 27–32, 27 L.Ed. 835 (1883).

8. 109 U.S. at 25, 3 S.Ct. at 31–32.

9. Jones v. Alfred H. Mayer Co., 392 U.S. 409, 88 S.Ct. 2186, 20 L.Ed.2d 1189 (1968); Runyon v. McCrary, 427 U.S. 160, 96 S.Ct. 2586, 49 L.Ed.2d 415 (1976), appeal after remand 569 F.2d 1294 (4th Cir.1978), certiorari denied 439 U.S. 927, 99 S.Ct. 311, 58 L.Ed.2d 320 (1978). The power of Congress to expand the scope of the Thirteenth Amendment is examined in Chapter 15, infra.

In order to prove that an individual has violated 18 U.S.C.A. §§ 241, 1584, by taking part in a conspiracy to deny someone the Thirteenth Amendment right to be free from involuntary servitude, the government must show that the involuntary servitude involved (1) threatened or actual physical force, or (2) threatened or actual physical coercion or coercion through law. See, United States v. Kozminski, 487 U.S. 931, 108 S.Ct. 2751, 101 L.Ed.2d 788 (1988). (Court finds that Congress did not intend to give to the judiciary the ability to define involuntary servitude through case-by-case adjudication; although factors relating to psychological coercion might be relevant evidence regarding involuntary servitude, juries must be instructed

The Court has enforced the Thirteenth Amendment's prohibition of slavery or peonage.[10] A state may force individuals to perform duties traditionally demanded of citizens by government such as military service, jury duty, or work during imprisonment.[11] Similarly, the state may enforce labor contracts[12] but it may not compel a person to work for another to repay a debt or place a person into forced labor or prison for failure to pay a debt.[13]

In a previous section of this chapter we dealt with the problem of determining when a law which appears neutral on its face might be found in fact to be a racial classification due to its necessary statistical impact.[14] In a separate chapter we examine the problem of determining when the actions of seemingly private persons may be found to have sufficient "state action" to subject them to constitutional limitations such as the equal protection guarantee.[15]

(b) The First Cases—Institutional Uncertainty

Shortly after the ratification of the Fourteenth Amendment, the Court decided *Strauder v. West Virginia.*[16] In this case, the Justices invalidated a state statute excluding blacks from juries because it violated the equal protection clause. A West Virginia statute provided that only white male citizens were eligible to serve on juries and the Court had to consider whether the defendant, a black citizen, had the right to trial by a jury selected without discrimination against persons of his race or color.

As the Court specifically noted, the question was not whether he had the right to have persons of his own race serve on the jury but, rather, whether the law might exclude all blacks solely because of their race or color. With two dissents the Court held this to be a violation of the Fourteenth Amendment. This

---

in such cases that involuntary servitude involves the use or threatened use of physical coercion or coercion through law).

10. For analysis of the Court's peonage decisions at a pivotal historical period in the development of legal protection for racial minorities see Schmidt, Principle and Prejudice: The Supreme Court and Race in the Progressive Era, Part 2: The Peonage Cases, 82 Colum.L.Rev. 646 (1982).

11. **The Thirteenth Amendment:** See Butler v. Perry, 240 U.S. 328, 36 S.Ct. 258, 60 L.Ed. 672 (1916), which stated:

"[The Thirteenth Amendment] certainly was not intended to interdict enforcement of those duties which individuals owe to the State, such as services to the army, militia, on the jury, etc." 240 U.S. at 333, 36 S.Ct. at 259–60.

In *Butler* the Court upheld a state statute requiring able-bodied males between 21 and 45 years of age to work on public roads for a certain time. A state "has inherent power to require every able-bodied man within its jurisdiction to labor for a reasonable time on public roads near his residence without direct compensation." 240 U.S. at 330, 36 S.Ct. at 258.

The military draft laws in effect requiring labor by soldiers and conscientious objectors have also been upheld. Arver v. United States, 245 U.S. 366, 390, 38 S.Ct. 159, 165, 62 L.Ed. 349 (1918).

12. See International Union v. Wisconsin Employment Relations Bd., 336 U.S. 245, 69 S.Ct. 516, 93 L.Ed. 651 (1949) (injunctions issued in labor disputes preventing interference with business activity do not violate the Thirteenth Amendment).

See also Robertson v. Baldwin, 165 U.S. 275, 17 S.Ct. 326, 41 L.Ed. 715 (1897) (labor contract of seamen enforced). The *Robertson* case may be of little precedential value because it is based on nineteenth century social and legal views of the unique obligation of sailors to their employer. 165 U.S. at 282–3, 17 S.Ct. at 329–30.

13. "The state may impose involuntary servitude as a punishment for crime, but it may not compel one man to labor for another in payment of a debt, by punishing him as a criminal if he does not perform the service or pay the debt." Bailey v. Alabama, 219 U.S. 219, 244, 31 S.Ct. 145, 152, 55 L.Ed. 191 (1911).

Similarly, the state may not "indirectly" reach this result "by creating a statutory presumption which upon proof of no other fact [than failure or refusal to serve without paying his debt] exposes him to conviction and punishment." 219 U.S. at 244, 31 S.Ct. at 153.

See also, United States v. Reynolds, 235 U.S. 133, 35 S.Ct. 86, 59 L.Ed. 162 (1914) (holding invalid a state law system allowing a "surety" to collect his debt for payment of a debtor's fine in the form of court approved labor); Taylor v. Georgia, 315 U.S. 25, 62 S.Ct. 415, 86 L.Ed. 615 (1942) (holding invalid a statute which in effect established a presumption that a defendant committed a criminal fraud by non-payment of a debt); Pollock v. Williams, 322 U.S. 4, 64 S.Ct. 792, 88 L.Ed. 1095 (1944) (same).

A few lower courts enforced the Thirteenth Amendment prohibition even before these Supreme Court decisions. See Peonage Cases, 123 Fed. 671 (M.D.Ala.1903). The federal "Anti-Peonage Act" was enacted in 1864 and is codified in 42 U.S.C.A. § 1994.

14. See § 14.4, supra.

15. See Chapter 12.

16. 100 U.S. (10 Otto) 303, 25 L.Ed. 664 (1879).

violation justified the removal of the case to federal court.[17]

In reaching these results, the majority opinion examined the conditions which had led to the passage of the Fourteenth Amendment. The opinion described the Fourteenth Amendment as one of a series of constitutional provisions with a common purpose, namely, securing to blacks "all the civil rights that the superior race may enjoy." Federal protection was necessary because it was recognized that the states might attempt to perpetuate the distinctions between the races. In the opinion of the majority, blacks as a race were unprepared or unable to take an equal place in post Civil War society. Thus they were in need of federal protection and, accordingly, the Fourteenth Amendment was adopted.[18]

The opinion next discussed the meaning and the effect of the Amendment. The Court found that laws must be the same for all persons, black or white, and prohibited discrimination against blacks because of their color. The prohibitory language of the Amendment contained a necessary implication of a right for blacks—the right to be exempt from unfriendly legislation, to be exempt from legal discriminations, "implying inferiority in civil society, lessening the security of their enjoyment of the rights which others enjoy," and "which are a step toward reducing them to the condition of a subject race."[19] The majority found the exclusion from juries to be a proscribed discrimination because it expressly denied blacks the right to serve as jurors because of their color. However, the Court would not strike down a conviction where a black defendant had been tried before an all white jury if blacks were not excluded from jury service.[20]

The next major decision involved statutes proscribing interracial marriages or providing stricter punishment for fornication or adultery when the partners were of different races. Such statutes had become numerous in this country.[21] In *Pace v. Alabama*,[22] the Court upheld an Alabama statute which provided for more severe penalties for adultery and fornication if the couple were composed of a white and a black than if the two members were of the same race. If both partners were of the same race, the punishment for the first such offense was a fine of not less than $100 and a possible sentence of not more than six months imprisonment. On the other hand, the penalty for adultery, fornication, or marriage where one partner was white and other black was a sentence of not less than two years imprisonment.

The statute was upheld because, in the unanimous view of the Justices, it applied to both races equally. If both partners were of the same race, whether white or black, one penalty was imposed. If the partners were of different races, the same sentence applied to both. Any discrimination was not between races but between offenses. While the marriage portion of the statute was not relevant to the *Pace* case, the Court there seemed to approve that provision. The Court did not directly rule on interracial marriage prohibitions until 1967, when it invalidated all such laws.[23] Until that time *Pace* stood as authority for such laws, although *Pace* and its reasoning had been explicitly overruled earlier in *McLaughlin v. Florida*.[24]

---

17. Justices Clifford and Field dissented without opinion. Congressional power to enforce the Amendment is discussed in § 15.2, infra.

18. 100 U.S. (10 Otto) at 306.

19. 100 U.S. (10 Otto) at 307–08.

20. Virginia v. Rives, 100 U.S. (10 Otto) 313, 25 L.Ed. 667 (1879).

21. D. Bell, Race, Racism and American Law, chapter 2 (2 ed. 1980); Applebaum, Miscegenation Statutes: A Constitutional and Social Problem, 53 Georgetown L.J. 49 (1964).

22. 106 U.S. (16 Otto) 583, 1 S.Ct. 637, 27 L.Ed. 207 (1883).

23. Loving v. Virginia, 388 U.S. 1, 87 S.Ct. 1817, 18 L.Ed.2d 1010 (1967).

24. 379 U.S. 184, 189–90, 85 S.Ct. 283, 286–87, 13 L.Ed.2d 222 (1964). The Court, however, did not reach the question of the constitutionality of laws against interracial marriage. 379 U.S. at 195, 85 S.Ct. at 290. See text at notes 97 & 98 infra.

The Supreme Court refused to adjudicate and denied certiorari to a miscegenation case shortly after its decision in Brown v. Board of Education, 347 U.S. 483, 74 S.Ct. 686, 98 L.Ed. 873 (1954). Jackson v. State, 37 Ala.App. 519, 72 So.2d 114 (1954), certiorari denied sub nom., Jackson v. Alabama, 348 U.S. 888, 75 S.Ct. 210, 99 L.Ed. 698 (1954). See also, Naim v. Naim, 350 U.S. 891, 76

In 1883, the Court struck down certain federal civil rights legislation as beyond the power granted Congress by the Civil War Amendments. In the *Civil Rights Cases*[25] the Court held that Congress could not impose sanctions against private persons for interfering with the civil liberties of others. In the opinion of a majority of the Justices, the Thirteenth Amendment prohibited only the direct badges or incidents of slavery and could not be used to remedy private discrimination. The Fourteenth Amendment, in their opinion, could only be violated by "state action" and not by the acts of private individuals. The majority limited congressional power to remedy that which the Justices felt would violate the Amendments and thus struck down the legislation.

Justice Harlan dissented because he saw these Amendments as granting a full panoply of civil liberties to blacks and empowering Congress to fully protect their rights.[26] The decision is discussed in greater detail in the section on state action,[27] but it should be noted here as evidencing the tendency of the Court during this period to refrain from fully protecting the rights of black citizens.

In 1886 the Supreme Court again announced a prohibition of explicit racial discrimination. In *Yick Wo v. Hopkins*,[28] the Court held that an ordinance could not be enforced where its application was designed to burden one race. A San Francisco ordinance prohibited the operation of laundries in wooden buildings without the consent of a board of supervisors. The defendant and all other Chinese persons had been denied permission to operate such laundries, while all non-Chinese persons operating laundries in wooden buildings were given permission to do so. This

application of the law was found to constitute explicit racial discrimination which violated the Fourteenth Amendment.[29] The Court found that these facts established "an administration directed so exclusively against a particular class of persons as to warrant and require the conclusion, that, whatever may have been the intent of the ordinances as adopted, they are applied ... with a mind so unequal and oppressive as to amount to a practical denial by the State of [equal protection]."[30] No reason for the discrimination could be shown other than hostility against the Chinese. Therefore, the ordinance could not be enforced.

(c) 1896–1954: The "Separate but Equal" Doctrine and Its Limitation

During the period from 1896 to 1954 there existed a concept known as "separate but equal." Under this "principle," persons of minority races could be given separate services or treatment so long as it was equal to that provided for whites. Of course this amounted to no more than the Court giving racial discrimination a constitutional imprimatur. Although the concept has been totally rejected since 1954, these rulings are still important. It is only against the background of these decisions that one can understand the basis for recent decisions and the degree to which the Supreme Court as an institution has helped, or failed to help, establish the rights of racial minorities.

The separate but equal concept made its first appearance in a pre-Civil War decision of the Massachusetts Supreme Court. In *Roberts v. City of Boston*,[31] suit was brought on behalf of a black child who was denied admission to the elementary school nearest her home because it was an all-white school. The applica-

S.Ct. 151, 100 L.Ed. 784 (1955), motion denied 350 U.S. 985, 76 S.Ct. 472, 100 L.Ed. 852 (1956), and Naim v. Naim, 350 U.S. 985, 76 S.Ct. 472, 100 L.Ed. 852 (1956) (denial of appeal from Supreme Court of Virginia, affirming annulment of marriage as violating Virginia's miscegenation statute), discussed in H. Hart & H. Wechsler, The Federal Courts and the Federal System 660–62 (2d ed. 1973).

25. 109 U.S. 3, 3 S.Ct. 18, 27 L.Ed. 835 (1883).

26. 109 U.S. 3, 26, 3 S.Ct. 18, 32, 27 L.Ed. 835 (1883) (Harlan, J., dissenting).

27. See § 12.1, supra.

28. 118 U.S. 356, 6 S.Ct. 1064, 30 L.Ed. 220 (1886).

29. The problems of proving racially biased application of laws or racially disproportionate impact is discussed in § 14.4, supra.

30. 118 U.S. at 373, 6 S.Ct. at 1072–73.

31. 59 Mass. (5 Cush.) 198 (1849).

ble statutes did not mention race or color restrictions, providing simply that each child was to attend the school nearest to his or her residence unless special provisions were made. Nevertheless, the Massachusetts court held that she could be required to attend a school established for blacks although it was further from her home because it was in all other respects "equal". That court noted that there was no tradition of local schools in Boston and that a child's education would not be hurt by having to travel across Boston to go to school. It was more than a century before this position was rejected.[32]

The Supreme Court skirted the separate but equal issue until 1896[33] when the Court adopted the doctrine in *Plessy v. Ferguson.*[34] A Louisiana statute required that all railway companies provide "equal but separate accommodations" for black and white passengers, imposing criminal penalties for violations by railway officials. Plessy, who alleged his ancestry was seven-eighths Caucasian and one-eighth African, attempted to use the coach for whites. The Louisiana Supreme Court denied his request for a writ of prohibition against the judge who was to try him for a violation of the statute. The Supreme Court of the United States affirmed the denial of the writ and held that the statute was not violative of the Fourteenth Amendment.

The majority in *Plessy* summarily dismissed any Thirteenth Amendment claim. The opinion simply held that the Amendment was meant to insure only the basic legal equality of blacks as was necessary to the abolition of involuntary servitude. The majority at this time refused to add any judicial restrictions on classification by race under that Amendment.

The Fourteenth Amendment's equal protection clause did not present much more of a barrier to such practices. The majority of the Justices fully adopted the separate but equal doctrine: "The object of the Amendment was undoubtedly to enforce the absolute equality of the two races before the law, but in the nature of things, it could not have been intended to abolish distinctions based upon color, or to enforce social, as distinguished from political equality, or a commingling of the two races upon terms unsatisfactory to either."[35] Laws requiring racial separation, according to the Court, did not necessarily imply the inferiority of either race and had been recognized to be within the police power of a state. The Court then referred to the custom of separate schools and the Massachusetts decision in *Roberts.*

The Court went on to define the nature of the power to afford black persons separate but equal treatment. The majority held that persons could be legally classified and treated in such a manner because of their race when the classifying law was a reasonable exercise of the police power. This meant that such laws must be reasonable, good faith attempts to promote

---

32. The same arguments accepted by the Massachusetts court were rejected in Brown v. Board of Education, 347 U.S. 483, 74 S.Ct. 686, 98 L.Ed. 873 (1954).

33. Questions of "separate but equal" accommodations had risen in earlier cases in other contexts. Congress agreed to allow a railroad to pass through the District of Columbia, but required that "no person shall be excluded from the cars on account of color." The Court, construing this statute in Washington A & G R Railroad Co. v. Brown, 84 U.S. (17 Wall.) 445, 21 L.Ed. 675 (1873), ruled that it meant that blacks must be permitted to travel on the same cars with whites; the requirement was not satisfied by the provision of separate cars for blacks, even upon a showing that the cars were equal to the cars provided whites and the cars sometimes were used exclusively for whites.

The constitutionality of statutes requiring separate but equal accommodations had also risen in two cases prior to *Plessy*, but in a very different context—the provisions were challenged by the railroads as being a burden on interstate commerce. In Hall v. De Cuir, 95 U.S. (5 Otto)

485, 24 L.Ed. 547 (1877) the Court invalidated the statutory requirement, stating that although the requirement was applicable only within the state, the train would be required to carry extra cars and therefore would be affected outside the state as well, and thus create a direct burden on interstate commerce.

In Louisville, New Orleans and Texas Ry. Co. v. Mississippi, 133 U.S. 587, 10 S.Ct. 348, 33 L.Ed. 784 (1890), the Court upheld a similar statute finding it was applicable only to intrastate commerce and therefore imposed no direct burden upon interstate commerce.

34. 163 U.S. 537, 16 S.Ct. 1138, 41 L.Ed. 256 (1896). For an excellent in depth examination of the philosophy of Justice Brown, who wrote the opinion, and the social theories which might have given rise to this opinion, see, Glennon, Justice Henry Billings Brown: Values in Tension, 44 U.Colo.L.Rev. 553 (1973).

35. 163 U.S. at 543–44, 16 S.Ct. at 544.

the public good and not be designed to oppress a particular class.

The question in any particular case, according to the *Plessy* majority, was whether the statute was reasonable. The Court recognized the great discretion in the legislature. In determining reasonableness, the legislature might look to established usages, customs, and traditions of the people and act with a view to the promotion of their comfort and the preservation of public peace and good order. Under the reasonableness standard, the majority refused to say that a statutory authorization or requirement of separate accommodations was unreasonable or obnoxious to the Fourteenth Amendment.

The majority found both that the enforced separation of the races did not mark the black race with a badge of inferiority and that social prejudice could not be overcome by law. The opinion stated that "if the two races are to meet upon terms of social equality, it must be the result of natural affinities, a mutual appreciation of each other's methods and a voluntary consent of individuals."[36]

Only Justice Harlan dissented in *Plessy*.[37] He viewed the Civil War Amendments as together removing "the race line from our governmental systems."[38] In the opinion of Harlan, the Constitution was now "color-blind"[39] so that government could not use a person's color to determine his rights. It should be noted that Justice Harlan was speaking to a system that he saw as designed to protect "a dominant race—a superior class of citizens",[40] while imposing a "badge of servitude"[41] on others. Thus it is not completely certain how Justice Harlan would have enforced his color-blind principle in a case involving affirmative government action to aid members of minority

races.[42] However, Justice Harlan was an accurate prophet when he viewed the *Plessy* separate but equal doctrine as one which "will, in time prove to be quite as pernicious as the decision made by this tribunal in the Dred Scott Case."[43]

Although the separate but equal doctrine in *Plessy* applied only to accommodations on public conveyances, it was used to uphold widespread segregation in public schools and other state institutions and statutory requirements of segregation in privately-owned business. The Court did not fully reconsider the validity of the separate but equal doctrine again until 1954. Prior to that time, the Supreme Court decided a number of issues within the framework of that doctrine, many of them in the context of education.

In *Cumming v. Board of Education*[44] the Court did not seriously attempt to enforce the "equal" requirement of the separate but equal doctrine. In this case, a local school board was allowed to close down the black high school for "purely economic reasons" and convert the school to a primary school for a larger number of black children. The Court, per Justice Harlan, considered only the question whether the white high school should be closed until equal provisions were made for blacks. The Court decided that such an action would only deprive whites of education without providing anything for blacks, and therefore, upheld the action.

The Court continued to uphold statutes requiring segregation of blacks by private enterprises. Thus, in *Berea College v. Kentucky*,[45] the Supreme Court upheld a fine imposed by Kentucky upon a private college because white and black students were taught together. The

---

36. 163 U.S. at 551, 16 S.Ct. at 1143.

37. Plessy v. Ferguson, 163 U.S. 537, 552, 16 S.Ct. 1138, 1144, 41 L.Ed. 256 (1896) (Harlan, J., dissenting). Justice Brewer did not participate in the decision.

38. 163 U.S. at 555, 16 S.Ct. at 1145.

39. 163 U.S. at 559, 16 S.Ct. at 1146.

40. 163 U.S. at 560, 16 S.Ct. at 1147.

41. 163 U.S. at 562, 16 S.Ct. at 1147.

42. The "affirmative action" issue is discussed in § 14.10 infra.

43. 163 U.S. at 559, 16 S.Ct. at 1146. (Harlan, J. dissenting). See generally, T. Alexander Aleinikoff, Re-Reading Justice Harlan's Dissent in Plessy v. Ferguson: Freedom, Antiracism and Citizenship, 1992 U.Ill. L. Forum 961; Gabriel J. Chin, The *Plessy* Myth: Justice Harlan and the Chinese Cases, 82 Iowa Law Review 151 (1996).

44. 175 U.S. 528, 20 S.Ct. 197, 44 L.Ed. 262 (1899).

45. 211 U.S. 45, 29 S.Ct. 33, 53 L.Ed. 81 (1908).

act under which the school had been incorporated reserved to the legislature the right to repeal any charter or alter it in any way which did not substantially impair the object of the grant. In the opinion of the Court, the requirement that members of different races be taught at different times or in different places did not impair the object of educating those attending the college and, accordingly, was valid.

McCabe v. Atchison, T. & S.F. Ry. Co.[46] upheld a statute that required "separate but equal accommodations" on trains. However, the opinion indicated that a company which provided a dining car for whites also had to provide a dining car for blacks even if there was not a sufficient volume of black traffic to support the cost of a separate dining room.

The Justices were willing to strike segregation laws when they could not accept the separation as incident to a valid police power end. Accordingly, the Court in *Buchanan v. Warley*[47] unanimously struck down a law entitled "An ordinance to prevent conflict and ill-feeling between the white and colored races in the city of Louisville, and to preserve the public peace and promote the general welfare, by making reasonable provisions, requiring, as far as practicable, the use of separate blocks, for residences, and places of assembly by white and colored people respectively." The ordinance prohibited a black from moving into a neighborhood which was predominantly white at the time the ordinance was passed and vice versa.

The ordinance was held invalid under the due process clause of the Fourteenth Amendment because it arbitrarily eliminated the right to acquire, use, and dispose of property. The Court distinguished this case from *Plessy* and *Berea* because in those cases blacks were

not deprived of transportation or education; they were merely required to conform to "reasonable rules" concerning the separation of races. In this case, however, the statute effectively deprived persons of the right to acquire land in a neighborhood predominated by members of the other race or to dispose of their property to a member of the race which was not predominant.

It always has appeared to the authors of this treatise that *Buchanan* can only be explained by the desire of Supreme Court Justices during this era to protect property rights, given the fact that these Justices did not otherwise strive to promote the goals of racial equality or desegregation.[48]

In *Gong Lum v. Rice*[49] the separate but equal doctrine was also implicitly accepted in the context of public education. Suit was brought on behalf of child of Chinese ancestry who was an American citizen but who was denied admission to a school established for whites in Mississippi. The Court found the only issue to be whether a Chinese child was denied equal protection when she was classified as "colored" and, therefore, only entitled to attend the school for nonwhites. The Court referred to other state and federal cases upholding segregation and then stated that although the cases referred only to whites and blacks, "we cannot think that the question is any different, or that any different result can be reached, assuming the cases cited to be rightly decided, where the issue is as between white pupils and the pupils of the yellow race."[50] Therefore, the Court unanimously found there was no violation of the Fourteenth Amendment.

Following 1930, there was a series of cases in which the Court, without re-examining the separate but equal doctrine, found that the

---

46. 235 U.S. 151, 35 S.Ct. 69, 59 L.Ed. 169 (1914).

47. 245 U.S. 60, 38 S.Ct. 16, 62 L.Ed. 149 (1917).

48. The Supreme Court itself acknowledged that Buchanan v. Warley, 245 U.S. 60, 38 S.Ct. 16, 62 L.Ed. 149 (1917) is an example of Supreme Court rejection of justifying racial classifications through acknowledgment of racial prejudice. See Palmore v. Sidoti, 466 U.S. 429, 104 S.Ct. 1879, 80 L.Ed.2d 421 (1984) (holding that societal prejudice against racially mixed marriages does not justify divesting natural mother of the custody of her child be-

cause of her remarriage to a person of a different race if she is otherwise a suitable guardian for the child). For references to secondary authorities on this point, see the multi-volume edition of this Treatise: R. Rotunda & J. Nowak, Treatise on Constitutional Law: Substance and Procedure § 18.8 (3rd ed. 1999, with annual supplements).

49. 275 U.S. 78, 48 S.Ct. 91, 72 L.Ed. 172 (1927).

50. 275 U.S. at 87, 48 S.Ct. at 94.

black plaintiffs were entitled to relief because they had not in fact been offered "equal" educational opportunities. In the first of these cases, *Missouri ex rel. Gaines v. Canada*,[51] an admittedly qualified black applicant to the state law school was denied entrance solely because of his color. Because there was no law school for blacks in Missouri, the state sought to fulfill its obligation to provide blacks an education that was "substantially equal" to the education provided whites by paying plaintiff's tuition at a comparable out-of-state school that did admit blacks. The Court, however, found that this procedure did not satisfy the state's duty—the question was not whether the legal education a black could receive at the out-of-state school was equal to the legal education received at the Missouri school, but what opportunities Missouri provided for whites, but not blacks, solely on the basis of color.

In subsequent cases, the Court began to examine intangible as well as tangible factors in determining if the educational opportunities offered to blacks were equal. In *Sweatt v. Painter*,[52] the petitioner again was a black who was seeking admission to a law school and who was turned down solely on the basis of race. The trial court recognized that this situation was a denial of equal protection, but instead of ordering the school to admit petitioner, it continued the case to allow the state to supply substantially equal facilities. A school for blacks was established while petitioner's appeal was pending and as a result the case was remanded. The trial court found the new school for blacks was "substantially equivalent", and petitioner, therefore, was not entitled to be admitted to the law school for whites. This decision was reversed by the Supreme Court.

The Court expressly reserved the question of the validity of the separate but equal doctrine, holding that the newly established law school was not substantially equal. The white law school had a better faculty, a better offering of courses, a better library, and a wider range of

activities than the law school established for blacks. Furthermore, the white school possessed those qualities which are immeasurable but make a superior law school, e.g., reputation of the faculty, position and influence of alumni.

In *McLaurin v. Oklahoma State Regents for Higher Education*,[53] decided the same day, a different facet of the question was presented— whether a state after admitting a black graduate student to its university might afford him different treatment because of his race. McLaurin had been admitted to a previously all-white school after a court ruling at an earlier stage of the litigation. However, he was admitted upon a specially segregated basis. He was required to sit at a desk in a classroom anteroom behind a railing with a sign "for colored's only", to sit at a designated desk on the mezzanine floor of the library and to eat at a different time and at a specified table in the cafeteria. During the course of litigation, the requirements were changed so that he was allowed a seat in the classroom but in a special row for black students, was assigned a desk on the main floor of the library, and was allowed to eat at the same time as the white students but still at a specified table.

The Court held that such state-approved restrictions based on race produced inequality in educational opportunities that violated even the separate but equal test. The restrictions impaired and inhibited "his ability to study, to engage in discussions, and exchange views with other students, and in general, to learn his profession."[54] As in *Sweatt*, the Court relied on intangible factors in making its determination that blacks were not being offered equal educational opportunities. The Court agreed that McLaurin might still have been set apart in the absence of state-approved restrictions but held that to be immaterial. There was a vast difference—a constitutional difference—between a state-imposed prohibition of the intellectual commingling of students and

51. 305 U.S. 337, 59 S.Ct. 232, 83 L.Ed. 208 (1938).

52. 339 U.S. 629, 70 S.Ct. 848, 94 L.Ed. 1114 (1950).

53. 339 U.S. 637, 70 S.Ct. 851, 94 L.Ed. 1149 (1950).

54. 339 U.S. at 641, 70 S.Ct. at 853.

the voluntary refusal of individuals to commingle socially.

(d) The Modern Position on Racial Restrictions

(1) The World War II Japanese Restriction Cases—A Turning Point for "Suspect Classifications". Out of a fear of espionage by Japanese persons in the United States or an invasion by Japanese military, severe restrictions were placed on the rights of persons of Japanese ancestry during World War II. In our Western states Japanese persons, whether aliens or citizens, were subject to detention in guarded camps whether or not they were as individuals at all likely to engage in disloyal acts. These actions were taken with the unanimous concurrence of the various branches of government. As a security measure, President Roosevelt issued an executive order authorizing military commanders to exclude persons from vast areas.[55] Congress then made it a federal crime to violate military orders made pursuant to this authority.[56]

Beginning in March 1942 an appropriate army general issued a series of such orders for "Military Area No. 1"—the Pacific coast states. These included a curfew which kept Japanese persons in their residences all night and required the movement of Japanese persons from certain areas to inland "relocation centers". In a series of three cases in 1943 and 1944, the Supreme Court upheld the curfew and the temporary relocation and temporary detention practices, while invalidating the indefinite detention of admittedly loyal persons as beyond the scope of the executive order.

It is obvious that the result in these cases does not represent a favorable "turning point"

in the treatment of persons by their race or national origin. However, in the course of these opinions a majority of the Justices indicated that such restrictions were contrary to the basic purpose of the Civil War Amendments and constitutionally disfavored even when employed by the federal government. Only the majority's belief in the need of the executive to have a wide scope of powers during wartime resulted in the actions being upheld. When combined with the position of the dissenters, the opinion indicated that the Justices were ready to revise the constitutional doctrines concerning the permissibility of racial restrictions. This change in judicial perspective could be seen in the stricter application of the last separate but equal cases that we have examined. Indeed, these cases stand today as the last decisions upholding classifications burdening minority races and the only such cases which have not been at least implicitly overruled.[57]

Two of the opinions are of little importance beyond the impact of the result reached in the individual cases. In *Hirabayashi v. United States*[58] the Court upheld the 8 p.m. to 6 a.m. curfew requirement as within the discretion granted the executive to wage war. In *Ex parte Endo*[59] the Court held that President Roosevelt's executive order did not authorize the continued detention of Japanese persons following an initial evacuation and determination of their loyalty. This opinion did indicate that the Justices would have stricken such an order as being beyond any reasonable exercise of war powers, but the decision was based on the president's order.

The decision in the third case, *Korematsu v.*

---

55. Executive Order 9066; 7 Fed.Reg. 1407 (Feb. 19, 1942).

56. Public Law 77–503; 56 Stat. 173 (Act of March 21, 1942).

57. The Court has summarily approved the keeping of government records that included racial information kept to further race-neutral goals. See Hamm v. Virginia State Bd. of Elections, 230 F.Supp. 156 (E.D.Va.1964), affirmed per curiam sub nom. Tancil v. Woolls, 379 U.S. 19, 85 S.Ct. 157, 13 L.Ed.2d 91 (1964) (invalidating the keeping of separate lists of voters and taxpayers by race but

permitting the state to require that the race of a husband and wife be identified in a divorce decree).

Classifications burdening minority races could be termed "prohibited" in order to clarify equal protection theory. Nowak, Realigning the Standards of Review Under the Equal Protection Guarantee—Prohibited, Neutral and Permissive Classifications, 62 Georgetown L.J. 1071 (1974).

58. 320 U.S. 81, 63 S.Ct. 1375, 87 L.Ed. 1774 (1943).

59. 323 U.S. 283, 65 S.Ct. 208, 89 L.Ed. 243 (1944).

United States,[60] was the start of a revolution in constitutional analysis of equal protection issues. In this case the Court upheld, by a six to three vote, the temporary exclusion and detention of persons of Japanese ancestry. The opinion gave great deference to the combined war powers of the president and Congress as these detentions far exceeded anything necessary to protect the country.[61]

The dissenting Justices would not have tolerated any but the most necessary restrictions to promote the war effort. Indeed, the three dissenting opinions remain as classic statements against the false security which results from using war powers to burden minorities.[62] The majority opinion agreed with the dissent as to the general unconstitutionality of imposing burdens on a person because of his race but these Justices felt that the needs of the nation, as perceived at the start of the war, justified these measures.

The majority opinion by Justice Black established the basis for a new constitutional standard of review of race classifications:

It should be noted, to begin with, that all legal restrictions which curtail the civil rights of a single racial group are immediately suspect. That is not to say that all such restrictions are unconstitutional. It is to say that courts must subject them to the most rigid scrutiny. Pressing public necessity may sometimes justify the existence of such restrictions; racial antagonism never can.[63]

This opinion thus established three points for future analysis of classifications based on race or national origin. First, these classifications were "suspect" which meant, at a minimum, that they were likely to be based on an impermissible purpose. Second, these classifications were to be subject to independent judicial review—"rigid scrutiny."[64] Third, such classifications would be invalid if based on racial antagonism and upheld only if they were based on "public necessity."[65] From this opinion came the concepts of "strict judicial scrutiny" and the requirement that some restric-

60. 323 U.S. 214, 65 S.Ct. 193, 89 L.Ed. 194 (1944).

61. For an examination of the War Power see Chapter 6, supra.

See generally, P. Irons, Justice at War: The Story of the Japanese American Internment Cases (1983); J. tenBroek, E. Barnhart & F. Matson, Prejudice, War and the Constitution 325–26 (1968); Dembiz, Racial Discrimination and the Military Judgment, 45 Colum.L.Rev. 175 (1945); Rostow, The Japanese-American Cases—A Disaster, 54 Yale L.J. 489 (1945); M. Grodzins, Americans Betrayed (1949); Morris, Justice, War, and the Japanese-American Evacuation and Internment, 59 Wash.L.Rev. 843 (1984).

In Korematsu v. United States, 323 U.S. 214, 235, 65 S.Ct. 193, 202, 89 L.Ed. 194 (1944), Justice Murphy's dissent described the situation regarding the Japanese-American internment as "one of the most sweeping and complete deprivations of constitutional rights in the history of this nation." Murphy was later vindicated. In 1980 Congress enacted Pub.L. No. 96–317 (1980), section 2 of which established a Commission to investigate this episode. The Commission concluded that "there was substantial credible evidence, known at the time, from governmental agencies indicating that the claimed ground of military necessity was defective and did not warrant the exclusion and detention of ethnic Japanese." Because of "race prejudice, war hysteria, and a failure of political leadership" there was a "grave injustice" which was done "to American citizens and resident aliens of Japanese ancestry who, without individual review or any probative evidence against them, were excluded, removed and detained by the United States during World War II." See, Personal Justice Denied: Report of the Commission on Wartime Relocation and Internment of Civilians 18 (1982).

62. 323 U.S. at 225–33, 65 S.Ct. at 198–201. (Roberts, J., dissenting); 323 U.S. at 233–42, 65 S.Ct. at 201–06 (Murphy, J., dissenting); 323 U.S. at 242–48, 65 S.Ct. at 206–08. (Jackson, J., dissenting).

63. Korematsu v. United States, 323 U.S. 214, 216, 65 S.Ct. 193, 194, 89 L.Ed. 194 (1944).

64. Justice Black's personal intentions when he used the word "suspect" are not clear, see, Brest, Foreword: In Defense of the Antidiscrimination Principle, 90 Harv. L.Rev. 1, 7 n. 35 (1976).

While Justice Black may have meant to advance only an initial theory of independent judicial review, the continual invalidation of statutes under this standard has led Professor Gunther to aptly describe it as "strict in theory and fatal in fact." Gunther, Foreword: In Search of Evolving Doctrine on a Changing Court: A Model for a Newer Equal Protection, 86 Harv.L.Rev. 1, 8 (1972).

65. In fact no such "necessities" have been found, see note 57 supra.

It may be possible for government agencies to use a racial classification in dealing with an emergency situation when separation of persons by race is demonstrably necessary to promote an end which the government is obligated to pursue—such as the protection of the lives of those persons in its custody. Thus, Justice Black was of the opinion that prison authorities could separate persons by race in order to stop an outbreak of disorder based on racial conflict in the prison. Lee v. Washington, 390 U.S. 333, 334, 88 S.Ct. 994, 994–95, 19 L.Ed.2d 1212 (1968) (Black, J., concurring).

tions on liberty must be necessary to promote "compelling" or "overriding" interests.[66]

(2) The Rejection of Separate but Equal and Establishment of Racial Equality as a Constitutional Principle. Overview. The final period of Court rulings concerning racial discrimination can be rather confusing unless one has some appreciation of the current position of the Court. As we have seen, by the late 1940's the Justices had deemed classification based on race or national origin to be suspect and subject to strict review under the equal protection guarantee. In the early 1950's the Court ended the concept of separate but equal, although this doctrine was not finally eradicated until a series of summary rulings had stricken down every manner of state enforced segregation. During this period the Court also held that the due process clause of the Fifth Amendment would be violated whenever the federal government used invidious classifications. Thus, the federal government was subjected to an equal protection guarantee even though the equal protection clause of the Fourteenth Amendment could only apply to the states.[67] In the 1960's the Court at last began to enforce the concept of racial equality by striking down government actions which burdened members of minority races in addition to those which required segregation of public facilities.

By the end of the 1960's it was clear that the Court had finally accepted what seemed to be the correct original position: that the government could not classify persons by race to impose a burden on, or deny benefits to, members of minority races. However the Court has not yet definitively decided the next classification question in this area—whether the government may have "affirmative action" programs which classify persons by race in order to grant some remedial preferences to members of minority races.[68]

The Supreme Court has examined a number of racial discrimination issues which are analyzed in other sections of this text. First, while legal segregation was declared invalid in the 1950's, the problem of remedying official segregation, especially in schools, remains. This issue is the focus of the next section.[69] Second, during the 1960's the Supreme Court protected those persons publicly protesting racial discrimination by enforcing their First Amendment rights in a variety of settings. These cases are examined in our Chapter on Freedom of Speech.[70] Third, the Court has had to settle a variety of issues concerning seemingly private racial discrimination which might have some connection to government action. These problems are dealt with in our Chapter on State Action.[71] Fourth, the Court has resolved some specific issues concerning the Thirteenth and Fifteenth Amendments. Since virtually all of these cases had to do with the application of federal laws prohibiting racial discrimination, they are dealt with in our section on congressional power to enforce the Civil War Amendments.[72] These cases are extremely important for the broad interpretation given these statutes has resulted in the statutory prohibition of many forms of overt private racial discrimination.[73]

With this overview in mind, we can now turn to the period from 1954 to the present to examine the basic racial-equal protection issue: When may the government classify persons for different treatment because of their race or national origins? Not surprisingly, the cases begin with the first school desegregation decision.

The *Brown* Decision. In 1954, the Court in *Brown v. Board of Education*[74], for the first

---

66. For an overview of the different standards of review see § 14.3, supra.

67. For a description of the relationship between the two clauses see § 14.1, supra.

68. The arguments for and against such programs are discussed in § 14.10, infra. See generally, John E. Nowak, The Rise and Fall of Supreme Court Concern for Racial Minorities, 36 William & Mary L. Rev. 345 (1995).

69. See § 14.9, infra.

70. See § 16.47, infra.

71. See Chapter 12.

72. See Chapter 15.

73. See the discussion of these matters in §§ 12.1, 12.4, supra, and Chapter 15, infra.

74. 347 U.S. 483, 74 S.Ct. 686, 98 L.Ed. 873 (1954), supplemented by Brown v. Board of Education, 349 U.S. 294, 75 S.Ct. 753, 99 L.Ed. 1083 (1955).

time since *Plessy*, fully examined the validity of the separate but equal doctrine. The Court did not expressly overrule *Plessy*, but held simply that the separate but equal doctrine had no place in education. *Brown* involved four consolidated cases focusing on the permissibility of local governments conducting school systems which segregated students by race. In each case blacks sought admission to public schools on a nonsegregated basis and in each the state court based its decision upon the separate but equal doctrine. The plaintiffs challenged the validity of the doctrine, arguing that segregated schools were not "equal" and could not be "equal."

The case was briefed and argued at two successive terms of Court. The reargument before the Supreme Court centered largely around the circumstances surrounding the adoption of the Fourteenth Amendment and the intentions of its framers. Because it was a constitutional Amendment rather than a statute that the Court was interpreting, the search for the intent of the framers had two facets: whether the drafters contemplated that the Amendment would immediately abolish segregation in public schools and, if not, whether the Amendment was to embody a principle that would allow Congress or the judiciary to abolish segregation in the future.[75]

The Court in *Brown* found that the legislative history was inconclusive at best.[76] The conflicting statements of the drafters gave little guidance as to the anticipated effect of the principles of equality on future generations. Indications that they did not expect segregation to end seemed to relate to their predictions of what in fact would happen in society and were clouded by the limited nature of public school systems. Thus the Court could honestly deem history inconclusive and interpret the principles of the Amendment as they should apply to modern society.[77]

The Court in *Brown* next traced the development of the separate but equal doctrine. Cases decided shortly after the adoption of the Amendment construed it as a prohibition of all state-imposed discrimination against blacks. In 1896, the separate but equal doctrine appeared in the Court in the field of transportation. American courts have since that time labored with the doctrine. As we have seen, the Court had grown increasingly uneasy about the doctrine. Because recent cases had found inequality in challenged practices, there had been no necessity to reexamine the doctrine in order to grant the requested relief.

Here the question was directly presented. The record showed that the schools were equalized or being equalized with respect to the buildings, curricula, qualifications and salaries of teachers, and other tangibles. The decision, therefore, could not turn on measurable inequalities; it was necessary to look to the effects of segregation itself. Having previously determined history to be inconclusive, the Court gave no more thought to the past but instead looked only to the present. The opinion noted that the Court could not "turn the clock back to 1868 when the Amendment was adopted, or even to 1896 when *Plessy v. Ferguson* was written."[78] It stated the question presented as: "Does segregation of children in public schools solely on the basis of race, even though the physical facilities and other 'tangible' factors may be equal, deprive the children of the minority group of equal educational opportunities?"[79] The Justices unanimously found that it did and, in so doing, sounded the death knell for legally enforced segregation.

The Court, however, did not explicitly overrule *Plessy* or hold the separate but equal doctrine unconstitutional. Instead, it limited its holding to the conclusion "that in the field of public education the doctrine of 'separate but equal' has no place."[80] The opinion referred to the earlier recognition in *Sweatt* and

75. Bickel, The Original Understanding and the Segregation Decision, 69 Harv.L.Rev. 1, 59 (1955).

76. 347 U.S. at 489, 74 S.Ct. at 688–89.

77. Bickel, supra note 75 at 59–65.

78. Brown v. Board of Education, 347 U.S. 483, 492, 74 S.Ct. 686, 690–91, 98 L.Ed. 873 (1954), supplemented 349 U.S. 294, 75 S.Ct. 753, 99 L.Ed. 1083 (1955).

79. 347 U.S. at 493, 74 S.Ct. at 691.

80. 347 U.S. at 495, 74 S.Ct. at 692.

McLaurin that intangibles played a considerable role in the value educational opportunities offered. Although all tangibles such as faculty, books, or buildings were "equal", a difference in "intangibles" such as separation would render a school unequal. To separate black children "from others of similar age and qualifications solely because of their race generates a feeling of inferiority as to their status in the community that may affect their hearts and minds in a way unlikely ever to be undone."[81]

The Court stated that this finding was "amply supported by modern authority" and in a footnote cited findings of sociologists, anthropologists, psychologists, and psychiatrists who had done work in race relations.[82] The reliance on social science data and limited approach of the opinion were later subject to criticism.[83] The Court, however, evidently sought to reduce public hostility by presenting only a limited ruling supported by some factual evidence. The rulings which followed *Brown* made clear what we take for granted today—no governmental entity may segregate or burden people because of their race or national origin.

Denials of Equal Protection by the Federal Government. On the same day, the Court invalidated segregation of public schools in the District of Columbia in *Bolling v. Sharpe.*[84] Because the equal protection clause of the Fourteenth Amendment, upon which the decision in *Brown* was based, is inapplica-

ble to the federal government, the precise legal question differed from that of *Brown*. The issue was whether racial segregation violated the due process clause of the Fifth Amendment.

Although "liberty" had not been defined with precision, it included educational opportunities. Because no sufficient governmental objective could be shown which required segregation of schools, such segregation imposed upon blacks a burden that constituted a deprivation of their liberty. Racial segregation constituted an impermissible means of accomplishing even legitimate government goals. Thus the practice violated the due process clause. In view of *Brown*, it was unthinkable that the Constitution would impose a lesser burden on the federal government. Today it is accepted that the due process clause imposes an equal protection guarantee on the federal government.[85]

Post-*Brown* Rulings. Although *Brown* technically invalidated the separate but equal doctrine only as applied to education, a series of Court decisions soon came down which indicated the invalidity of that doctrine in other areas as well: public beaches and bathhouses,[86] municipal golf courses,[87] buses,[88] parks,[89] public parks and golf courses,[90] athletic contests,[91] airport restaurants,[92] courtroom seating,[93] and municipal auditoriums.[94] These decisions were short, per curiam opinions which

---

81. 347 U.S. at 494, 74 S.Ct. at 691. (the Court here is quoting from lower court rulings).

82. 347 U.S. at 494 n. 11, 74 S.Ct. at 692 n. 11.

83. Compare, Wechsler, Toward Neutral Principles of Constitutional Law, 73 Harv.L.Rev. 1 (1959), with, Pollak, Racial Discrimination and Judicial Integrity: A Reply to Professor Wechsler, 108 U.Pa.L.Rev. 1 (1959) and Black, The Lawfulness of the Segregation Decisions, 69 Yale L.J. 421 (1960).

For additional analysis, see 3 R. Rotunda & J. Nowak, Treatise on Constitutional Law: Substance and Procedure § 18.8 (3rd ed. 1999, with annual supplements).

84. 347 U.S. 497, 74 S.Ct. 693, 98 L.Ed. 884 (1954), opinion supplemented 349 U.S. 294, 75 S.Ct. 753, 99 L.Ed. 1083 (1955).

85. Weinberger v. Wiesenfeld, 420 U.S. 636, 638 n. 2, 95 S.Ct. 1225, 1228 n. 2, 43 L.Ed.2d 514 (1975); Schlesinger v. Ballard, 419 U.S. 498, 500 n. 3, 95 S.Ct. 572, 574 n. 3, 42 L.Ed.2d 610 (1975).

86. Mayor of Baltimore v. Dawson, 350 U.S. 877, 76 S.Ct. 133, 100 L.Ed. 774 (1955).

87. Holmes v. City of Atlanta, 350 U.S. 879, 76 S.Ct. 141, 100 L.Ed. 776 (1955).

88. Gayle v. Browder, 352 U.S. 903, 77 S.Ct. 145, 1 L.Ed.2d 114 (1956), rehearing denied 352 U.S. 950, 77 S.Ct. 323, 1 L.Ed.2d 245 (1956).

89. Muir v. Louisville Park Theatrical Ass'n, 347 U.S. 971, 74 S.Ct. 783, 98 L.Ed. 1112 (1954).

90. New Orleans City Park Improvement Ass'n v. Detiege, 358 U.S. 54, 79 S.Ct. 99, 3 L.Ed.2d 46 (1958).

91. State Athletic Com'n v. Dorsey, 359 U.S. 533, 79 S.Ct. 1137, 3 L.Ed.2d 1028 (1959).

92. Turner v. City of Memphis, 369 U.S. 350, 82 S.Ct. 805, 7 L.Ed.2d 762 (1962).

93. Johnson v. Virginia, 373 U.S. 61, 83 S.Ct. 1053, 10 L.Ed.2d 195 (1963).

94. Schiro v. Bynum, 375 U.S. 395, 84 S.Ct. 452, 11 L.Ed.2d 412 (1964).

often only cited *Brown*. Thus, through *Brown* and these subsequent cases the entire separate but equal doctrine was invalidated, requiring that classifications be subject to "strict scrutiny" and prohibited.[95]

In 1964 the Court also rejected the limited view of equal protection which had allowed the use of racial classifications to determine whether certain activity was criminal so long as the same sanctions were given members of each race.[96] In *McLaughlin v. Florida*[97] a statute prohibiting a white person and black person from living together or occupying the same room at night was found violative of the equal protection clause because such behavior between persons of the same race was not proscribed. The Court in *McLaughlin* stated that, while statutory classifications normally would be upheld if they were not totally arbitrary, when the classification was drawn on the basis of race the legislature was without its normally wide discretion. The statute would be upheld only if the state were able to show an overriding purpose requiring proscription of the specified conduct when engaged in by members of different races but not when engaged in by persons of the same race. Because no such purpose could be shown, the statute was invalid.

Justices Douglas and Stewart concurred in the Court's opinion in *McLaughlin* but objected to the implication that it might be possible for a state to show an overriding purpose which would validate such a statute.[98] In the view of these Justices, any statute which made the color of the actor the test for whether his conduct was criminal was an invidious discrimination and per se unconstitutional.

It was not until 1967 that the Supreme Court held antimiscegenation statutes, which existed in many states, unconstitutional.[99] In *Loving v. Virginia*[100] the Court ruled that an antimiscegenation statute violated both the equal protection and due process clauses. The Court rejected the notion that the mere "equal application" of a statute containing a racial classification was enough to remove the classification from the Fourteenth Amendment's proscription of racial classifications. While some weight was to be given statements made at the time of passage of the Amendment about miscegenation, historical sources were inconclusive and insufficient to resolve the problem.

The purpose of the Fourteenth Amendment was clearly to remove invidious racial classifications. There was no question that the Virginia statute, by proscribing behavior if the couple were of different races which was accepted if they were of the same race, was based on an invidious racial classification and therefore invalid. The fact that it "burdened" members of both races was irrelevant as it used a person's race to determine his right to marry

---

95. Although the Court would grant a local jurisdiction time to provide for gradual desegregation of its schools, there was no reason to delay desegregation of other facilities because desegregation of those facilities did not involve the complicated educational policy issues associated with transfer of students and desegregation of schools. Thus, there should have been no delay in desegregation of city parks and other facilities of that type. The Court eventually had to specifically hold that public antagonism toward desegregation of such facilities was not a compelling reason for delaying the implementation of the constitutional prohibition of segregation in publicly owned or operated recreational facilities. Watson v. Memphis, 373 U.S. 526, 83 S.Ct. 1314, 10 L.Ed.2d 529 (1963).

See generally, Bell, Foreword: The Civil Rights Chronicles, 99 Harv. 4 (1985).

96. During this period the Supreme Court unaccountably refused to consider the appeal of one accused of violating a miscegenation statute, although this refusal was arguably based on the procedural posture of the decision below. Naim v. Naim, 197 Va. 80, 87 S.E.2d 749 (1955), vacated 350 U.S. 891, 76 S.Ct. 151, 100 L.Ed. 784

(1955), on remand 197 Va. 734, 90 S.E.2d 849 (1956), appeal dismissed 350 U.S. 985, 76 S.Ct. 472, 100 L.Ed. 852 (1956).

97. 379 U.S. 184, 85 S.Ct. 283, 13 L.Ed.2d 222 (1964).

98. 379 U.S. at 198, 85 S.Ct. at 291. (Stewart and Douglas, JJ., concurring).

99. For the history and application of such laws, see D. Bell, Race, Racism and American Law, Chapter 2 (2 ed. 1980).

At the time of this Supreme Court decision such statutes were found in fifteen states: Alabama, Alaska, Arkansas, Florida, Georgia, Kentucky, Louisiana, Mississippi, Missouri, North Carolina, Oklahoma, South Carolina, Tennessee, Texas, and West Virginia. They had been outlawed within 15 years in 14 other states: Arizona, California, Colorado, Idaho, Indiana, Maryland, Montana, Nebraska, Nevada, North Dakota, Oregon, South Dakota, Utah, and Wyoming. Loving v. Virginia, 388 U.S. 1, 6 n. 5, 87 S.Ct. 1817, 1820–21 n. 5, 18 L.Ed.2d 1010 (1967).

100. 388 U.S. 1, 87 S.Ct. 1817, 18 L.Ed.2d 1010 (1967).

another. The statute also had an obvious stigmatizing effect on blacks, implying they were inferior and must be kept separate. Additionally, this statute suffered from the vice of arbitrarily limiting the freedom to marry.[101]

Since the early 1960's the Court has consistently invalidated explicit governmental discrimination against minorities. Even before this period, the Supreme Court in a number of decisions reaffirmed its holding in *Strauder* that blacks may not be excluded from jury service.[102] In *Carter v. Jury Commission of Greene County*,[103] the Court found that black citizens who were qualified to be jurors, as well as black defendants tried by juries from which blacks had been excluded, had standing to challenge the exclusion. The Court will find a violation of these rights where statistics on jury service in a jurisdiction give rise to an inference of racial discrimination, unless the evidence of racial imbalance is clearly rebutted by the government.[104]

In matters relating to the integration of public facilities and services, the Court has come to the position that no continued racial discrimination will be constitutionally tolerated.[105] This rule has the effect of prohibiting

most forms of official racial discrimination. Additionally, the application of federal civil rights statutes to persons who refuse to contract with others because of their race[106] also evidences the modern Supreme Court's position that racial discrimination is incompatible with essential constitutional values.

The constitutional prohibition against burdening members of racial minorities in election systems has also been the focus of a series of Supreme Court decisions. Where a governmental unit discriminates by race in the granting of voting rights it will violate the Fifteenth Amendment as well as the equal protection guarantee.[107] Going beyond such obvious discrimination, the Court has also prohibited attempts to use the electoral system to discriminate against racial minorities. For example, the Court struck down a system whereby the race of each candidate for elective office was noted on the ballot, as this requirement was certain to support and facilitate, if not induce, racial prejudice.[108]

Similarly, requiring racial minorities to take their problems to public referenda rather than to the normal legislative process will also vio-

101. Because the right to marry was a protected right and the statute interfered with the exercise of that right, the due process clause was violated. See the discussion of right to privacy in §§ 14.26–14.29, infra.

102. Virginia v. Rives, 100 U.S. (10 Otto) 313, 25 L.Ed. 667 (1879); Neal v. Delaware, 103 U.S. (13 Otto) 370, 26 L.Ed. 567 (1880); Bush v. Kentucky, 107 U.S. 110, 1 S.Ct. 625, 27 L.Ed. 354 (1883); Gibson v. Mississippi, 162 U.S. 565, 16 S.Ct. 904, 40 L.Ed. 1075 (1896).

103. 396 U.S. 320, 90 S.Ct. 518, 24 L.Ed.2d 549 (1970). The Court, however, denied relief on the particular facts.

104. Castaneda v. Partida, 430 U.S. 482, 97 S.Ct. 1272, 51 L.Ed.2d 498 (1977). On proving the discrimination in such cases, see § 14.4, supra. For references to additional cases on this point, see 2 R. Rotunda & J. Nowak, Treatise on Constitutional Law: Substance and Procedure §§ 18.4, 18.8 (2nd ed. 1992, with annual supplements).

105. The tolerance of racial discrimination while government proceeded to integrate schools "with all deliberate speed" has ended. Alexander v. Holmes County Bd. of Education, 396 U.S. 19, 90 S.Ct. 29, 24 L.Ed.2d 19 (1969), rehearing denied 396 U.S. 976, 90 S.Ct. 437, 24 L.Ed.2d 447 (1969). The Court's impatience with the states' desegregation efforts became evident as early as 1963, when the Court found no reason for delay in the integration of public recreational facilities. Watson v. City of Memphis, 373 U.S. 526, 83 S.Ct. 1314, 10 L.Ed.2d 529 (1963).

106. See, e.g., Runyon v. McCrary, 427 U.S. 160, 96 S.Ct. 2586, 49 L.Ed.2d 415 (1976), appeal after remand 569 F.2d 1294 (4th Cir.1978), certiorari denied 439 U.S. 927, 99 S.Ct. 311, 58 L.Ed.2d 320 (1978); Jones v. Alfred H. Mayer Co., 392 U.S. 409, 88 S.Ct. 2186, 20 L.Ed.2d 1189 (1968). These statutes and cases are discussed in Chapter 15, infra. The societal interest in ending invidious discrimination on the basis of gender or race is sufficient to override the associational freedom of those persons who would wish to discriminate on such basis. See § 16.41, infra.

107. This rule applies even if the state attempts to freeze out minority participation by having "private" elections which exclude members of minority races. For a discussion of these "White Primary" cases, see § 12.2 supra, and § 14.33, infra.

In Hunter v. Underwood, 471 U.S. 222, 105 S.Ct. 1916, 85 L.Ed.2d 222 (1985) the Supreme Court invalidated a provision of the Alabama Constitution, adopted at a state constitutional convention in 1901, that disenfranchised persons convicted of crimes "involving moral turpitude". The Court found that this provision was adopted in 1901 for the purpose of discriminating against black persons in the voting system and continued to have that effect. See § 14.4, supra.

108. Anderson v. Martin, 375 U.S. 399, 84 S.Ct. 454, 11 L.Ed.2d 430 (1964).

late equal protection. In *Reitman v. Mulkey*[109] the Court struck down a California constitutional provision which would have prohibited open housing statutes because it would have encouraged racial discrimination and prevented minorities from seeking the help of the legislature to remedy their specific problems.[110]

In *Hunter v. Erickson*,[111] after the enactment of a fair housing ordinance, the voters amended the city charter to provide that no ordinance dealing with racial, religious, or ancestral discrimination in housing could be implemented without the approval of a majority of the voters. The Court held the provision invalid, finding it was a violation of the equal protection guarantee. It contained "an explicitly racial classification" by disadvantaging persons who would benefit from the prohibition of racial, religious, or ancestral discrimination, i.e., minority groups.

Similarly, the Supreme Court has invalidated a state law, enacted through a voter initiative, which effectively prohibited local school boards from transferring students to achieve racial integration but allowed the school boards the ability to transfer students between schools for many other reasons.[112] Relying on *Hunter*, the Court ruled that this restriction of school board powers was an invalid allocation of governmental power and benefits based on racial criteria.[113]

Racial Discrimination and Voting. Just as governmental units cannot lock minorities out of the political process, they may not seek to dilute the voting power of members of racial minorities. There is no constitutional violation if such persons are underrepresented statistically in the governing bodies because their candidates fail to attract the support of a majority of voters.[114] But if the electoral districts are "gerrymandered" to dilute the voting power of racial minorities, the districting system is invalid even if it otherwise represents perfect compliance with "one person-one vote" principles.[115]

---

109. 387 U.S. 369, 87 S.Ct. 1627, 18 L.Ed.2d 830 (1967). This case is analyzed in § 12.4(b), supra.

110. Black, Foreword, "State Action", Equal Protection, and California's Proposition 14, 81 Harv.L.Rev. 69, 82 (1967): A state may not place "in the way of the racial minority's attaining its political goal any barriers which, within the state's political system taken as a whole, are especially difficult of surmounting, by comparison with those barriers that normally stand in the way of those who wish to use political processes to get what they want." The theory advanced by Professor Black, prohibiting imposing barriers to use of the political process on a defined group of persons, was later used to invalidate a state constitutional provision that prohibited the state legislature or any local legislature in the state from passing laws that barred discrimination against persons on the basis of their sexual orientation. Romer v. Evans, 517 U.S. 620, 116 S.Ct. 1620, 134 L.Ed.2d 855 (1996). In part based on *Romer*, the Supreme Court in *Lawrence v. Texas* ___ U.S. ___, 123 S.Ct. 2472, 156 L.Ed.2d 508 (2003) invalidated a law prohibiting sodomy when performed between persons of the same sex. The *Lawrence* decision is examined in § 14.28 of this Treatise.

111. 393 U.S. 385, 89 S.Ct. 557, 21 L.Ed.2d 616 (1969).

112. Washington v. Seattle School District, 458 U.S. 457, 102 S.Ct. 3187, 73 L.Ed.2d 896 (1982).

113. Id. The Court upheld, however, an Amendment to a state constitution which prohibited state courts from transferring or busing students to different schools unless such an order was necessary to remedy a violation of federal law. Crawford v. Los Angeles Bd. of Education, 458 U.S. 527, 102 S.Ct. 3211, 73 L.Ed.2d 948 (1982). These cases are contrasted in § 14.9(a)(3)(f), infra.

114. Whitcomb v. Chavis, 403 U.S. 124, 91 S.Ct. 1858, 29 L.Ed.2d 363 (1971).

115. White v. Regester, 412 U.S. 755, 93 S.Ct. 2332, 37 L.Ed.2d 314 (1973). Compare, Mobile v. Bolden, 446 U.S. 55, 100 S.Ct. 1490, 64 L.Ed.2d 47 (1980) (at-large voting system for county board is not invalid merely because racial minorities are not represented on board), with, Rogers v. Lodge, 458 U.S. 613, 102 S.Ct. 3272, 73 L.Ed.2d 1012 (1982) (at-large voting system violates equal protection when maintained for the purpose of diluting racial minority voting power). See § 14.4, supra.

After Mobile v. Bolden, 446 U.S. 55, 100 S.Ct. 1490, 64 L.Ed.2d 47 (1980), on remand 542 F.Supp. 1050 (S.D.Ala. 1982), Congress amended section two of the Voting Rights Act to ease the burden of a plaintiff in proving the existence of racial discrimination in a voting law or standard.

Section 2 of the Voting Rights Act, as amended in 1982 [42 U.S.C.A. § 1973] has been interpreted by the Supreme Court to require the plaintiff to make a prima facie showing that a challenged election system results in the dilution of the voting power of a racial minority. If the plaintiff makes a prima facie demonstration of racial discrimination through vote dilution, the government must rebut the plaintiff's case. The court must consider the totality of the evidence in determining whether there has been a dilution in the voting power of a minority racial group that would violate § 2 of the Voting Rights Act.

For further analysis, and references to additional cases, see R. Rotunda & J. Nowak, Treatise on Constitutional Law: Substance and Procedure §§ 18.4, 18.10, 19.11 (3rd ed. 1999, with annual supplements).

The use of racial classification in election laws is subject to strict scrutiny under both the Fourteenth Amendment equal protection clause and the Fifteenth Amendment.[116] If a legislative body were to pass a law that disenfranchised persons because of their race, that law would violate both the Fourteenth and Fifteenth Amendments. If a law does not employ a racial classification on its face, a court will find the law to be a racial classification only if the persons attacking the law can show that the law was created or maintained for a racially discriminatory purpose.[117] If the law is based on a discriminatory purpose it will be treated as a race classification and it will be invalidated unless the government can demonstrate that the law is narrowly tailored to promote a compelling interest.

When a legislative body draws a districting map for the purpose of creating districts from which persons will be elected to office, persons attacking the districting map may allege that the map is based on racial classifications. If the districting map on its face employed a racial classification (by openly segregating people into different electoral districts because of their race) the law would be subject to strict judicial scrutiny and the compelling interest test. If the drawing of district lines could be explained by the legislature in terms of nonracial factors (such as a desire to fully comply with the one person, one vote principle while creating compact and contiguous legislative districts) the persons attacking the law would have to prove a discriminatory purpose on the part of the legislature. Realistically, it would only be possible to prove such a discriminatory

purpose if the plaintiffs could show that the district lines were drawn for the purpose of making it difficult for persons of a certain race to control the outcome of elections.[118]

A law that does not use racial language might still be found to be a law that involves a racial classification "on its face", if the law cannot be explained in any terms other than race. In other words, if a law can only be understood as being one that is entirely irrational or in the alternative, as being based upon a desire to differentiate citizens by race, the law will be deemed to be one that involves a racial classification on its face. This concept was the basis of the Court's ruling in cases such as *Reitman* and *Hunter*.[119]

It is important to remember that establishing the existence of a racial classification in a law is only the first step in the constitutional analysis. Following the definition of the racial classification, the court must determine whether the racial classification can be justified as being necessary to promote a compelling interest, which would override one of the central purposes of the Fourteenth Amendment equal protection clause and, in voting laws, a central purpose of the Fifteenth Amendment.

If the law employs a racial classification that harms members of the minority, it is clear that the state law would be invalid. There would never be a compelling interest in excluding minority race persons from the political process or in intentionally diluting their voting strength. For example, *Gomillion v. Light-*

---

116. The Supreme Court has used the Fifteenth Amendment as the basis for its rulings when there has been a clear use of a racial classification to deny voting rights to minority race members. See, e.g., Gomillion v. Lightfoot, 364 U.S. 339, 81 S.Ct. 125, 5 L.Ed.2d 110 (1960). Rice v. Cayetano, 528 U.S. 495, 120 S.Ct. 1044, 145 L.Ed.2d 1007 (2000). See § 14.10(c). The Court tends to use the equal protection clause of the Fourteenth Amendment, or federal statutes, when invalidating laws that are proven to have a racially discriminatory purpose to dilute the voting power of members of racial minorities. See, e.g., Rogers v. Lodge, 458 U.S. 613, 102 S.Ct. 3272, 73 L.Ed.2d 1012 (1982). A litigant attacking an election law on the basis of racial discrimination should assert that the election law at issue violates both the Fourteenth Amendment equal protection clause and the Fifteenth Amend-

ment. If a federal law were being attacked on the basis of an alleged racial classification, the litigant would have to attack the law under the Fifteenth Amendment and the implied equal protection guarantee of the Fifth Amendment due process clause.

117. See § 14.4 of this Treatise regarding the proof of discriminatory purpose.

118. See footnotes 114, 115, and accompanying text in this subsection of the Treatise.

119. See footnotes 109–113, and accompanying text, in this subsection of the Treatise discussing Reitman v. Mulkey, 387 U.S. 369, 87 S.Ct. 1627, 18 L.Ed.2d 830 (1967) and Hunter v. Erickson, 393 U.S. 385, 89 S.Ct. 557, 21 L.Ed.2d 616 (1969).

foot [120] found that a state legislature violated the Fourteenth Amendment by redefining the boundaries of the city in a manner that excluded minority race voters from the city. When the old and new city boundary maps were compared there could be no rational explanation for the law other than the desire to exclude minority race voters from having significant power in the city election. Therefore, *Gomillion* found that the law involved a racial classification on its face and that the law was invalid. [121]

If an electoral law is designed to assist minority race voters, the constitutionality of the law may be more difficult to determine. The federal, state, and local governments can act to eliminate racial discrimination in voting systems. Such discrimination would constitute violations of the Fourteenth and Fifteenth Amendments; the government has a compelling interest in stopping unconstitutional racial discrimination. [122]

The Supreme Court has made it clear that Congress has some power to eliminate electoral practices in both the federal and state election systems that might have the effect of denying persons the right to vote, or diluting their voting power, because of their race even though the prohibited electoral practice might not have been found to constitute violations of the Fourteenth or Fifteenth Amendments in themselves. For example, based upon the congressional finding that literacy tests had been used in a racially discriminatory manner, Congress has the power to prohibit the use of literacy tests in all elections in the United States. Congress has this power even though the Supreme Court had never found that a state's literacy requirement, as a condition of a

right to vote, was a per se violation of the Fourteenth and Fifteenth Amendments. [123] The Supreme Court also has upheld a federal statute that requires certain areas of the country, which had extremely low registration percentages for minority race voters in previous decades, to have any change in their voting laws approved by the Attorney General of the United States or the federal court in the District of Columbia to ensure that any change in their voting laws did not have the effect of diluting the voting power of minority race persons. [124]

Can Congress or a state government go beyond the mere protection of minority race voters' right to vote and take steps to guarantee that minority race voters will be able to control the outcome of some elections of representatives to city, state, or federal legislative bodies? That question currently has no clear answer. We will examine that question in a separate section of this chapter. [125]

Conclusion. Racial classifications that burden members of a minority race or ethnic group, or which have a stigmatizing effect because of differing governmental treatment of persons because of their race, run contrary to the fundamental goal of racial equality which the Supreme Court has come to recognize as a core value of both the equal protection clause of the Fourteenth Amendment and the equal protection component of the Fifth Amendment due process clause. The Court in recent years has stressed that such classifications require that the government demonstrate both a compelling interest and that the classification is truly necessary to the promotion of that interest. In *Palmore v. Sidoti* [126] the Supreme

---

120. 364 U.S. 339, 81 S.Ct. 125, 5 L.Ed.2d 110 (1960).

121. Because *Gomillion* found racial discrimination on the face of this statute relating to the distribution of the right to vote it found that the law violated the Fifteenth Amendment. Today, there is a question as to whether the Fifteenth Amendment applies to claims that the voting power of a minority racial group has been "diluted". It may be that in such "dilution" cases the Court will examine the claim that the law is racially discriminatory in terms of the Fourteenth Amendment equal protection clause and relevant federal statutes rather than under the Fifteenth Amendment itself. See footnote 115.

122. See generally, Rome v. United States, 446 U.S. 156, 100 S.Ct. 1548, 64 L.Ed.2d 119 (1980); Oregon v.

Mitchell, 400 U.S. 112, 131–34, 91 S.Ct. 260, 268–69, 27 L.Ed.2d 272 (1970).

123. South Carolina v. Katzenbach, 383 U.S. 301, 317, 86 S.Ct. 803, 813, 15 L.Ed.2d 769 (1966); Oregon v. Mitchell, 400 U.S. 112, 131–34, 91 S.Ct. 260, 268–69, 27 L.Ed.2d 272 (1970).

124. South Carolina v. Katzenbach, 383 U.S. 301, 86 S.Ct. 803, 15 L.Ed.2d 769 (1966).

125. See § 18.10, infra.

126. 466 U.S. 429, 104 S.Ct. 1879, 80 L.Ed.2d 421 (1984), appeal after remand 472 So.2d 843 (Fla.App.1985).

Court invoked this test as the Justices unanimously held that a state court could not remove an infant child from the custody of its natural mother, otherwise found to be an appropriate person to have custody, simply because she had married a person of a different race.

The Court recognized that racial and ethnic prejudices might affect the couple and the mother's child from a previous marriage but held that "the reality of private biases and the possible injury they might inflict" were not permissible considerations for removal of the child from the custody of the mother. Because "[c]lassifying persons according to their race is more likely to reflect racial prejudice than legitimate public concerns" it is necessary to have "the most exacting scrutiny" in order to insure that a classification of this type was justified by a compelling interest and was indeed necessary to the accomplishment of that interest. Under this test, it is difficult to hypothesize what circumstances would ever justify a state in using a racial classification to burden members of minority races or ethnic groups; these classifications are highly likely to reflect racial prejudice, or may be seen to stigmatize one race or ethnic group, or give effect to social prejudice against racial integration.[127]

Although racial considerations may not be used to burden members of minority races, the government appears to have some right to know the racial impact of its actions. Thus, it would appear that the government can compile racial information so long as it is not used to burden anyone because of his race.[128] At least it is clear that some compilation of racial statistics will be required when issues of racial discrimination in public services are litigated. Although statistics on racial impact do not decide substantive issues regarding discrimination, the information is relevant to determine government purposes.[129]

Finally, we have an open question as to the permissibility of racial classifications which burden members of a majority race in order to benefit members of a minority. Should these "affirmative action" programs be subjected to the compelling interest test and stricken? This issue is the subject of a later section.[130] Before addressing that issue we will examine the implementation of the desegregation rulings.

§ 14.9 Implementation of the Desegregation Decisions

(a) Desegregation of the Schools

(1) The Rise and Fall of "All Deliberate Speed".

In 1954 the Court decided *Brown v. Board of Education* (*Brown I*)[1] which held that

127. It is not possible to anticipate every possible argument the government may make to justify such classifications, but the Court's refusal (since the World War II Japanese internment cases) to uphold any racial classification which burdens minority members or appears to have a stigmatizing effect would lead one to believe that few governmental interests, other than a possible interest in protection of human life, could justify any use of such classifications. It may be possible for the government to use racial classification on a temporary basis in an emergency situation, at least when separations of persons by race is demonstrably necessary to promote safety. Justice Black was of the opinion that prison authorities could separate persons by race in order to stop an outbreak of disorder based on racial conflict in the prison. Lee v. Washington, 390 U.S. 333, 334, 88 S.Ct. 994, 995, 19 L.Ed.2d 1212, 1214 (1968) (Black, J., concurring).

128. The Court has summarily approved the keeping of government records which included racial information kept to further race-neutral goals. See Hamm v. Virginia State Bd. of Elections, 230 F.Supp. 156 (E.D.Va.1964), affirmed per curiam sub nom. Tancil v. Woolls, 379 U.S. 19, 85 S.Ct. 157, 13 L.Ed.2d 91 (1964) (invalidating the keeping of separate lists of voters and taxpayers by race

but permitting the state to require that the race of a husband and wife be identified in a divorce decree).

129. The use of statistics to prove discrimination is examined in § 14.4, supra.

130. See § 14.10, infra. For references to additional cases, and secondary authorities, on this point see the multi-volume edition of this Treatise: R. Rotunda & J. Nowak, Treatise on Constitutional Law: Substance and Procedure §§ 18.4, 18.8, 18.10 (3rd ed. with annual supplements).

§ 14.9

1. 347 U.S. 483, 74 S.Ct. 686, 98 L.Ed. 873 (1954); Bolling v. Sharpe, 347 U.S. 497, 74 S.Ct. 693, 98 L.Ed. 884 (1954) (Federal segregation of public schools is denial of due process). The Court in these decisions fashioned no immediate relief, setting the question of relief for reargument. An invitation to submit briefs to aid in the formulation of decrees was extended to the Attorney General of the United States and the attorney generals of all states which by law required or permitted segregation. 347 U.S. at 495–496, 74 S.Ct. at 692–93.

segregated school systems violated the equal protection guarantee. But that decision postponed any ruling as to the relief to be granted in the cases. The Court heard new arguments concerning the proper scope of its decree in the next term. In *Brown v. Board of Education (Brown II)*[2] the Supreme Court addressed the question of the manner in which relief should be accorded black students who previously had been found to have been denied equal protection of the laws due to the segregation of public schools.

Generally when a court finds there has been a constitutional violation, it will order an immediate end to the unconstitutional practice. In *Brown II*, however, because of the complexities the Court anticipated would occur nationwide in the transition to a system of public education freed of racial discrimination, the Court required only that school authorities dismantle segregated school systems with "all deliberate speed."[3] A "prompt and reasonable start toward full compliance"[4] was required. Once such a start had been made, school authorities might be permitted additional time to comply if "necessary in the public interest" and "consistent with good faith compliance at the earliest practicable date."[5]

This decision was in part predicated on faith in state and lower federal courts, which, because of their proximity to local conditions, were best suited to perform the duty of insuring good faith implementation of the decision.[6]

The lower courts, like the school authorities, were given no specific guidelines. They were to be guided by equitable principles, which traditionally had been characterized by practical flexibility and facility for balancing public and private needs.[7] Unfortunately, local courts were not able to measure up to this task.

The decision was met with massive resistance in the states with official segregation. Their tactics included inaction, defiance by political leaders, and vigorous defensive action in the legislatures, including attempts to punish civil rights attorneys.[8] The resistance was typified by the occurrences in Little Rock, Arkansas, in 1957 which resulted in an important Court decision regarding these tactics. School authorities developed a plan for desegregation, but the legislature engaged in a program to perpetuate racial segregation.[9] When the governor sent state troops to prevent blacks from entering the previously white high school, he was enjoined from further interference by a federal court.[10] To enforce the constitutional ruling, federal troops were sent to allow the blacks to attend the schools. School authorities requested postponement of their desegregation plan because they believed that the extreme public hostility caused by the actions of the governor and the legislature made it impossible to maintain a sound education program with the black students in attendance.

---

2. 349 U.S. 294, 75 S.Ct. 753, 99 L.Ed. 1083 (1955).

3. 349 U.S. at 301, 75 S.Ct. at 757. See generally, B. Schwartz, Super Chief: Earl Warren and His Supreme Court—A Judicial Biography 121–29 (unabridged ed. 1983).

4. 349 U.S. at 300, 75 S.Ct. at 756.

5. Id.

6. 349 U.S. at 299, 75 S.Ct. at 755–56.

7. 349 U.S. at 300, 75 S.Ct. at 756.

8. Virginia enacted a new rule aimed at civil rights attorneys which would have disbarred those who represented organizations with "no pecuniary interest" in litigation. The statute was stricken on First Amendment grounds in NAACP v. Button, 371 U.S. 415, 83 S.Ct. 328, 9 L.Ed.2d 405 (1963). The issues are examined in depth in Bell, Serving Two Masters: Integration Ideals and Client Interests in School Desegregation Litigation, 85 Yale L.J. 470, 493–505 (1976). For references to state laws and secondary authorities, on this point see the multi-

volume edition of this Treatise: R. Rotunda & J. Nowak, Treatise on Constitutional Law: Substance and Procedure § 18.9 (3rd ed. 1999, with annual supplements).

For a discussion of tactics adopted by states in an attempt to avoid desegregation, see § 14.9(a)(3), infra.

9. An amendment to the state constitution was passed, commanding the General Assembly to oppose "in every constitutional manner the un-constitutional desegregation decisions of May 17, 1954 and May 31, 1955 of the United States Supreme Court." Ark.Const. amend. 44. Pursuant to the Amendment, the General Assembly enacted a pupil assignment law, Ark.Stats. §§ 80–1519 to 80–1524, a law relieving school children from compulsory attendance at racially mixed schools, Ark.Stats. § 8–1525, and a law enacting a State Sovereignty Commission, Ark.Stats. §§ 6–801 to 6–824.

10. Aaron v. Cooper, 156 F.Supp. 220 (E.D.Ark.1957), affirmed sub nom., Faubus v. United States, 254 F.2d 797 (8th Cir.1958), certiorari denied 358 U.S. 829, 79 S.Ct. 49, 3 L.Ed.2d 68 (1958).

In *Cooper v. Aaron*,[11] the Court denied the city any additional time to comply with the ruling. The opinion was headed by the names of all nine Justices of the Court to emphasize the strength of the ruling that was to "unanimously reaffirm" the holding in *Brown*.[12] The Court accepted without reservation the assertions that the school board had acted in good faith and that the educational process of all students would suffer if the prevailing conditions of the previous year continued but stated that the rights of black children were not to be sacrificed to violence and disorder engendered by the actions of state officials. *Brown* could not be nullified either "openly and directly by state legislators or state executive or judicial officers" or "indirectly by them through evasive schemes for segregation whether attempted 'ingeniously or ingenuously.' "[13]

Many school districts persisted in the use of dilatory practices to avoid complete desegregation.[14] As time passed and no appreciable progress toward integration was made, the Court manifested its impatience.[15] In 1963, the Court noted that "the context in which we must interpret and apply this language to plans for desegregation has been significantly altered."[16] The following year in *Griffin v.*

Prince Edward County Board of Education,[17] the Court stated "the time for mere deliberate speed had run out;"[18] black children who had been denied admission to public schools on the basis of race were entitled to quick and effective relief. In 1968, in *Green v. County School Board*,[19] the Court restated the need for prompt adoption and effectuation of a plan that would actually disestablish a dual system. *Brown II* had recognized that the dismantling of a segregated school system was complex and would thus require time, but school boards were nevertheless charged with the affirmative duty to take the necessary steps to eliminate racial discrimination. The Court stated further that "[t]he burden on a school board today is to come forward with a plan that promises realistically to work, and promises realistically to work now."[20]

By 1969, the Supreme Court was no longer willing to tolerate delay. Reviewing a Fifth Circuit decision granting more time for the desegregation of a public school system, the Court ruled: "the Court of Appeals should have denied all motions for additional time because continued operation of segregated schools under a standard of allowing 'all deliberate speed' for desegregation is no longer

11. 358 U.S. 1, 78 S.Ct. 1401, 3 L.Ed.2d 5 (1958).

12. For an examination of the voting patterns of the Justices in the cases that formed the basis for the Court's action in *Cooper v. Aaron*, see Hutchinson, Unanimity and Desegregation: Decisionmaking in the Supreme Court, 1948–1958, 68 Georgetown L.J. 1 (1979).

13. 358 U.S. at 17, 78 S.Ct. at 1409. The Supreme Court found that its earlier rulings on desegregation were "the supreme law of the land" and bound all state officials. 358 U.S. at 18, 78 S.Ct. at 1410.

14. The Court, for eight years after *Brown*, refused to review cases questioning the validity of pupil placement regulations or the appropriateness of applying the doctrine of exhaustion of administrative remedies to frustrate suits challenging segregated school systems. D. Bell, Race, Racism and American Law 458 (1973); Covington v. Edwards, 264 F.2d 780 (4th Cir.1959), certiorari denied 361 U.S. 840, 80 S.Ct. 78, 4 L.Ed.2d 79 (1959); Carson v. Warlick, 238 F.2d 724 (4th Cir.1956), certiorari denied 353 U.S. 910, 77 S.Ct. 665, 1 L.Ed.2d 664 (1957); Hood v. Board of Trustees, 232 F.2d 626 (4th Cir.1956), certiorari denied 352 U.S. 870, 77 S.Ct. 95, 1 L.Ed.2d 76 (1956); Shuttlesworth v. Birmingham Bd. of Education, 162 F.Supp. 372 (N.D.Ala.1958), affirmed 358 U.S. 101, 79 S.Ct. 221, 3 L.Ed.2d 145 (1958).

15. In 1963, the Court ruled that the doctrine requiring exhaustion of administrative remedies before relief could be sought in a federal court was not applicable in school desegregation cases. McNeese v. Board of Education, 373 U.S. 668, 83 S.Ct. 1433, 10 L.Ed.2d 622 (1963).

In the same term the Court invalidated a transfer policy which allowed students assigned to a school where their race was in the minority to transfer to a school where their race was in the majority because the policy's inevitable effect was the perpetuation of school segregation. Goss v. Board of Education, 373 U.S. 683, 83 S.Ct. 1405, 10 L.Ed.2d 632 (1963).

16. Goss v. Board of Education, 373 U.S. 683, 689, 83 S.Ct. 1405, 1409, 10 L.Ed.2d 632 (1963). See also Watson v. City of Memphis, 373 U.S. 526, 83 S.Ct. 1314, 10 L.Ed.2d 529 (1963) (in addressing the desegregation of public recreational facilities, the Court specifically noted that public antagonism toward desegregation of such facilities was not a compelling reason for delaying integration).

17. 377 U.S. 218, 84 S.Ct. 1226, 12 L.Ed.2d 256 (1964), motion granted 377 U.S. 950, 84 S.Ct. 1627, 12 L.Ed.2d 496 (1964). The case is discussed more fully in § 14.9(a)(3), infra.

18. 377 U.S. at 234, 84 S.Ct. at 1235.

19. 391 U.S. 430, 88 S.Ct. 1689, 20 L.Ed.2d 716 (1968).

20. 391 U.S. at 439, 88 S.Ct. at 1694.

constitutionally permissible. Under explicit holdings of this Court the obligation of every school district is to terminate dual systems at once and to operate now and hereafter only unitary schools."[21] Acknowledging the Court's holding, the Fifth Circuit nevertheless permitted a semester delay in the implementation of a court order to desegregate because the order was issued in the middle of the school year. The Supreme Court summarily reversed in a per curiam opinion.[22] Two concurring Justices thought that the time between a finding of noncompliance and the effective date of the remedy, including any judicial review, should not exceed eight weeks.[23] Four other Justices thought that even that delay would be too long.[24]

Once there has been a showing of deliberate segregation of schools, school authorities must develop a plan which will provide immediate relief. State legislatures and governors will not be allowed to hinder the implementation of desegregation plans.[25] The courts are empowered to act if school authorities fail to discharge their duties or if state officials thwart desegregation.

However, despite these rulings, many black children are still denied their right to equal educational opportunities. School boards rarely take action to desegregate schools except under the threat of a court order.[26] Courts can order desegregation only if there has been a showing of purposeful segregation.[27] Another problem is that orders for the integration of city schools often lead to "white flight" from a city, which leads to increasingly black public schools, which in turn reduces the likelihood of political support for education—which leaves black children disadvantaged, as before.[28]

Professor Bell has noted that the economic and political realities of urban America may mean that earnest implementation of the desegregation principle can actually hurt the educational opportunities afforded black children.[29] This result may be corrected by litigation designed to protect or upgrade educational quality,[30] but given the restrained judicial attitude towards educational issues, success in litigation may be very difficult to accomplish.[31]

All desegregation suits proceed through three stages. First, it must be shown that the

21. Alexander v. Holmes County Bd. of Education, 396 U.S. 19, 20, 90 S.Ct. 29, 24 L.Ed.2d 19 (1969) (per curiam).

22. Singleton v. Jackson Municipal Separate School District, 419 F.2d 1211, 1216 (5th Cir.1969) (per curiam), reversed sub nom., Carter v. West Feliciana Parish School Bd., 396 U.S. 290, 90 S.Ct. 608, 24 L.Ed.2d 477 (1970) (per curiam).

23. 396 U.S. at 291–93, 90 S.Ct. at 608–10. (Harlan & White, JJ., concurring).

24. 396 U.S. at 293, 90 S.Ct. at 610 (opinion of Black, Douglas, Brennan, & Marshall, JJ.); cf. Dowell v. Board of Education, 396 U.S. 269, 271, 90 S.Ct. 415, 416, 24 L.Ed.2d 414 (1969) (desegregation should not be stayed pending appeal).

See, Rotunda, Congressional Power to Restrict the Jurisdiction of the Lower Federal Courts and the Problem of School Busing, 64 Georgetown L.J. 839, 864–66 (1976).

25. North Carolina State Bd. of Education v. Swann, 402 U.S. 43, 46, 91 S.Ct. 1284, 1286, 28 L.Ed.2d 586 (1971), (unanimous Court invalidated state statute banning involuntary bussing); Cooper v. Aaron, 358 U.S. 1, 78 S.Ct. 1401, 3 L.Ed.2d 5 (1958).

26. For further analysis of the Supreme Court's desegregation rulings see Wilkinson, The Supreme Court and Southern School Desegregation, 1955–70: A History and Analysis, 64 Va.L.Rev. 485 (1978). Jones, Strategies for Completing the Job of School Integration, 19 How.L.J. 82 (1975).

For additional citations to secondary sources on this topic see, R. Rotunda & J. Nowak, Treatise on Constitutional Law: Substance and Procedure, vol. 3 § 18.9 (3rd Ed. 1999, with annual supplements).

27. See Keyes v. School District No. 1, 413 U.S. 189, 93 S.Ct. 2686, 37 L.Ed.2d 548 (1973), rehearing denied 414 U.S. 883, 94 S.Ct. 27, 38 L.Ed.2d 131 (1973).

28. Abramowitz and Jackson, Desegregation: Where Do We Go From Here?, 19 How.L.J. 92, 93 (1975).

29. Bell, Serving Two Masters: Integration Ideals and Client Interests In School Desegregation Litigation, 85 Yale L.J. 470 (1976).

30. "Correspondence", 86 Yale L.J. 378–384 (1976) (letter of Nathaniel Jones, general counsel for N.A.A.C.P. Special Contribution Fund Concerning Professor Bell's article; reply by Professor Bell).

31. On this issue see, e.g., § 14.45, infra. San Antonio Independent School District v. Rodriguez, 411 U.S. 1, 93 S.Ct. 1278, 36 L.Ed.2d 16 (1973), rehearing denied 411 U.S. 959, 93 S.Ct. 1919, 36 L.Ed.2d 418 (1973).

The Court has held that federal courts could order remedial and compensatory education programs as part of a school desegregation decree. Milliken v. Bradley, (Milliken II), 433 U.S. 267, 97 S.Ct. 2749, 53 L.Ed.2d 745 (1977), on remand 460 F.Supp. 299 (E.D.Mich.1978).

See § 14.9(a)(4), infra.

school system is subject to *Brown* because it has engaged in purposeful or de jure segregation. Second, the school system or state is given the opportunity to devise a plan for ending the segregation system and creating an integrated one. Finally, if the state will not devise a plan, the court must issue orders to integrate the school system. The remainder of this section will discuss the schools subject to the integration principle, the permissibility of certain state acts in relation to integration and, finally, the scope of federal court power to act if the state or city refuses to fully correct its segregated school system.

(2) Institutions Subject to the Desegregation Principle

(a) The De Jure-De Facto Distinction. Neither *Brown I* nor later decisions of the Supreme Court require all public schools to be racially integrated. Rather, the decisions require that public schools not be racially segregated. School systems which have not been segregated by law need not take steps to integrate their school system even though their individual schools have racially unbalanced student populations. However, if a school district has operated a racially segregated system, it must entirely eradicate that practice by integrating its schools. These historical differences are the core of the de jure-de facto distinction.

De jure ("by law") segregation is racial separation which is the product of some purposeful act by government authorities. De facto ("by the facts") segregation occurs because of housing and migration patterns and is unconnected to any purposeful governmental action to racially segregate schools. If a school system involves de jure segregation, it violates the equal protection guarantee; the courts will intervene if necessary to remedy this situation. But if a school district has become unintentionally (de facto) segregated, there is no constitutional violation and the courts will not intervene.

In the South where it was easy to show schools had been segregated by law, desegregation orders were issued and compliance slowly followed. In the North and West, however, where there were no express statutory provisions authorizing segregation of schools, blacks faced the difficult task of showing purposeful discrimination in school assignments even where segregation resulted from discriminatory housing practices or gerrymandering of school districts. As a result, in 1970 in the South only 39.4% of black students attended predominantly minority schools, while in northern and western states the figure was 57.6%.[32]

Today a central issue in school desegregation suits is whether the school system constitutes de jure rather than de facto segregation. Mere statistics showing an imbalance between the racial make-up of individual schools will not in itself be sufficient, for such an imbalance could have arisen unintentionally from housing and migration patterns. The Supreme Court has held that de jure segregation is only present when there has been "segregative purpose or intent" and government action to maintain segregated schools.[33] Unfortunately the Court has not clarified the way in which "purposeful" segregation may be proven. Some clarity is added by the Court's opinions on the use of statistics to prove the existence of racial classifications by the disproportionate impact of other types of laws. In those cases the Court has indicated that only in the most rare case will statistical proof be so overwhelming as to prove discrimination from the evenhanded application of a seemingly race-neutral law.[34] Instead, some additional proof of discrimination is needed.[35]

Proving Discriminatory Purpose. There are three possible ways to prove a discriminatory purpose, although the Supreme Court has yet to clearly choose one of them. First, the Court could require proof of the

---

32. J. Barron and C. Dienes, Constitutional Law: Principles and Policy 622 (1st ed. 1975).

33. Keyes v. School District No. 1, 413 U.S. 189, 208, 93 S.Ct. 2686, 2697, 37 L.Ed.2d 548 (1973).

34. See § 14.4.

35. Id. For the pronouncement of the general rule, see Washington v. Davis, 426 U.S. 229, 96 S.Ct. 2040, 48 L.Ed.2d 597 (1976).

subjective motive to discriminate on the part of individual legislators or school board members. This alternative seems unlikely as the Court has, in other areas, continued to adhere to the position that "motivation" of legislators is irrelevant.[36] However, the purpose versus motivation distinction makes little sense in school board inquiries because there is less reason to respect the decision-making process as one would respect the decision-making process of a primary branch of government. But this theory would mean that educational policies would stand or fall on the subjective intent of those who adopted them rather than on the educational worth of the policies.

A second approach to the problem would be to view school districts as having purposeful segregation whenever the school board practices can objectively be said to have encouraged or maintained segregation in the system. This alternative has the advantage of avoiding vague inquiries into the motives of school board members, but it is a most imprecise tool to determine purpose. If it were applied strictly it could end the de jure-de facto distinction because a wide variety of practices might be found (using statistical hindsight) to have maintained racial segregation even though the policies appeared to be race-neutral to those who adopted them. In any event, it focuses the inquiry on statistics to the exclusion of all else, a result which recent cases on statistical proof attempt to avoid.[37]

A third approach to determine purpose has been advocated by a law review commentator[38] and some lower courts.[39] This approach is a hybrid of the two other methods. The third position would allow objective criteria of school board policies to establish a prima facie case of purposeful segregation; this case could be disproved by the school board showing that the policies were adopted for race-neutral educational reasons. Accurately labeled an "institutional intent" test,[40] it exposes the basis for the adoption of school board policies. When objective criteria show that the policies encouraged or maintained segregation, a presumption of unconstitutional segregation acts is permissible. If the governmental entity (normally the school board) that adopted the school policy can show that it was the most efficient way for achieving race-neutral educational goals, the presumption is rebutted. If the school board cannot do this, it is fair to conclude that the policies were adopted for segregative (as opposed to irrational or unknown) purposes. A similar approach to discovering racial discrimination in the calling of jurors has worked well and been approved by the Supreme Court in that context.[41] Thus, it seems that this approach is the one most likely to be adopted by the Court. But the issue remains unsettled. We will discuss the most important decisions of the Court on this issue before turning to our next subject.

In 1973 in *Keyes v. School District No. 1,*[42] the Court for the first time considered a charge of racially discriminatory behavior against a school system in a large metropolitan area outside the South. The Denver school district had never operated under a constitutional or statutory provision that explicitly required or permitted racial segregation in the public schools. However, there was proof that at least some of the schools had been used to isolate blacks and Hispanic-Americans. The

36. For an examination of this problem, see § 14.4, supra.

37. Arlington Heights v. Metropolitan Housing Development Corp., 429 U.S. 252, 97 S.Ct. 555, 50 L.Ed.2d 450 (1977); Washington v. Davis, 426 U.S. 229, 96 S.Ct. 2040, 48 L.Ed.2d 597 (1976).

38. Note, Reading the Mind of the School Board: Segregative Intent and the De Facto/De Jure Distinction, 86 Yale L.J. 317 (1976).

39. Oliver v. Michigan State Bd. of Education, 508 F.2d 178 (6th Cir.1974), certiorari denied 421 U.S. 963, 95 S.Ct. 1950, 44 L.Ed.2d 449 (1975); see also United States v. School District of Omaha, 521 F.2d 530 (8th Cir.1975),

certiorari denied 423 U.S. 946, 96 S.Ct. 361, 46 L.Ed.2d 280 (1975); Amos v. Board of School Directors, 408 F.Supp. 765 (E.D.Wis.1976), motion denied 408 F.Supp. 825 (1976).

40. See Note, Reading the Mind of the School Board: Segregative Intent and the De Facto/De Jure Distinction, 86 Yale L.J. 317 (1976). The Note writer describes how to employ the test to determine institutional intent. Of course, courts might adopt a different manner of applying the test while still agreeing with the basic concept.

41. See, e.g., Castaneda v. Partida, 430 U.S. 482, 97 S.Ct. 1272, 51 L.Ed.2d 498 (1977).

42. 413 U.S. 189, 93 S.Ct. 2686, 37 L.Ed.2d 548 (1973).

Court adopted the de jure-de facto analysis and held that there was a constitutional violation to the extent there was "segregative purpose or intent" in school board actions.

The Court first discussed the method of defining a "segregated school." Because the Court found Hispanic-Americans and blacks suffer identical discrimination in treatment when compared to whites, schools with a combined predominance of blacks and Hispanic-Americans may be considered "segregated" schools.[43] The majority opinion then went on to find that government-designed segregation as to a substantial portion of the school system could not be viewed in isolation from the rest of the district. If plaintiffs prove that school authorities have carried out a systematic program of segregation affecting a substantial portion of the students, schools, teachers, and facilities within the school system, it is logical to assume there is a predicate for a finding of the existence of a dual school system.[44] Normally, racially discriminatory actions will have an impact beyond the particular schools. However, it is possible that the school board might be able to show that the segregated portion did not directly affect the other schools.

The Court noted that even if the board were able to prove this contention, the finding of intentional segregation on the part of the school board in one portion of the school system is highly relevant to the question of the board's intent with respect to other segregated schools in the system. A "finding of intentionally segregative school board actions in a meaningful portion of a school system, as in this case, creates a presumption that other segregated schooling within the system is not adventitious."[45] Such a finding establishes a prima facie case of unlawful segregation and

shifts the burden to school authorities to prove that other segregated schools are not also the result of deliberate racial discrimination. In discharging this burden, the school board must do more than simply offer some allegedly logical, racially neutral explanation for their actions. They must produce proof sufficient to support a finding that segregative intent was not among the motivating factors for their actions. If segregative intent has been shown, the board can rebut the prima facie case only by showing that past discriminatory acts did not create or contribute to the current segregated condition of the schools.[46]

Justices Powell and Douglas each filed separate opinions, stating that the de jure-de facto distinction is no longer viable. Justice Douglas would have required a remedy for de facto segregation in recognition of the fact that many state policies contribute to neighborhood segregation.[47] Justice Powell argued that the courts could not resolve problems of subjective intent to determine the existence of constitutionally impermissible segregation. He proposed a new standard: "where segregated public schools exist within a school district to a substantial degree, there is a prima facie case that the duly constituted public authorities [are] sufficiently responsible to warrant imposing upon them a nationally applicable burden to demonstrate they nevertheless are operating a genuinely integrated system."[48] But, unlike Douglas, he moved to an objective criterion to determine responsibility rather than suggest the elimination of all segregation.[49]

Inter-District Integration Problems. The de jure-de facto distinction was strengthened when the Court held that suburbs with de facto segregation could not be ordered to integrate with a neighboring system involving de jure segregation. In *Milliken v. Bradley*[50]

---

43. 413 U.S. at 198, 93 S.Ct. at 2692.

44. 413 U.S. at 201, 93 S.Ct. at 2694.

45. 413 U.S. at 208, 93 S.Ct. at 2699.

46. 413 U.S. at 211, 93 S.Ct. at 2698–99.

47. Keyes v. School District No. 1, 413 U.S. 189, 214–17, 93 S.Ct. 2686, 2700–02, 37 L.Ed.2d 548 (1973) (opinion of Douglas, J.).

48. 413 U.S. at 224, 93 S.Ct. at 2705. (Powell, J., concurring and dissenting).

49. Justice Powell has reemphasized his view that court-ordered remedial measures to establish integration in a school system should not exceed the degree to which there was objective proof of segregation. Austin Independent School District v. United States, 429 U.S. 990, 991–95, 97 S.Ct. 517, 517–518, 50 L.Ed.2d 603 (1976).

50. 418 U.S. 717, 94 S.Ct. 3112, 41 L.Ed.2d 1069 (1974).

the question, as phrased by the Court, was "whether a federal court may impose a multi-district, areawide remedy to a single-district de jure segregation problem absent any finding that the other included school districts have failed to operate unitary school systems within their district, absent any claim or finding that the boundary lines of any affected school district were established with the purpose of fostering racial segregation in public schools, absent any finding that the included districts committed acts which effected segregation within the other districts, and absent a meaningful opportunity for the included neighborhood school districts to present evidence or be heard on the propriety of a multidistrict remedy or on the question of constitutional violation by those neighboring districts."[51] As indicated by the manner in which the opinion stated the question, the answer of the majority was no.

In the *Milliken* case, the Detroit public schools were found to be unlawfully segregated. The federal district court found that the plans proposed for the desegregation of Detroit would only make the Detroit system even more clearly a one-race system, with the suburban schools becoming the white school system. The district court, therefore, adopted a metropolitan plan, in which fifty-three Detroit suburbs were included in the "desegregation area." The Supreme Court of the United States, however, found it impermissible for the lower court to decree inter-district relief simply to produce areawide integrated schools.

According to the majority opinion, school district lines are not sacrosanct, but local autonomy in education is of great importance. In determining the validity of a court decree

requiring cross-district or inter-district consolidation in order to remedy segregation found in one district, the Court stated that the controlling principle is that the scope of the remedy must be determined by the extent and the nature of the constitutional violation. "Before the boundaries of separate and autonomous school districts may be set aside by consolidating the separate units for remedial purposes or by imposing a cross-district remedy, it must first be shown that there has been a constitutional violation within one district that produces a significant segregative effect in another district."[52] Thus, inter-district relief would be appropriate where it is shown either that the racially discriminatory acts of one district affected an adjacent district or where district lines have been drawn according to race. To order such relief absent such a showing would be impermissible.

Four of the Justices dissented.[53] Although their opinions differed in part, they all believed that once there has been a finding of state-imposed segregation, it becomes the duty of the state to remove all traces of racial segregation. Here, black students were denied the only effective relief because of administrative inconvenience and undue regard for school district lines. They would have held that the constitutional rights of black students were too fundamental to be abridged on such grounds. The school district decision remains undisturbed, but the Court has approved inter-district housing remedies for racial segregation in public housing under limited circumstances.[54]

School Districts With Continuing or Recurring Segregation. In *Pasadena City Board of Education v. Spangler*[55] the Supreme

---

51. 418 U.S. at 721–22, 94 S.Ct. at 3116.

52. 418 U.S. at 744–45, 94 S.Ct. at 3127.

53. Milliken v. Bradley, 418 U.S. 717, 757, 94 S.Ct. 3112, 3133, 41 L.Ed.2d 1069 (1974) (Douglas, J., dissenting); 418 U.S. at 762, 94 S.Ct. at 3136 (White, J., dissenting); 418 U.S. at 781, 94 S.Ct. at 3145 (Marshall, J., dissenting). Justice Brennan joined in the dissent of Justices White and Marshall.

54. Hills v. Gautreaux, 425 U.S. 284, 96 S.Ct. 1538, 47 L.Ed.2d 792 (1976). This case is discussed in § 12.4(d), supra, and § 14.9(b), infra.

55. 423 U.S. 1335, 96 S.Ct. 416, 46 L.Ed.2d 364 (1975).

Following the remand of this case, the district judge entered an order deleting the provision of his earlier order that had required annual readjustment of attendance zones to prohibit schools with a majority of minority race students. The district judge also prohibited the school board from making further changes in the method of student assignment. Members of the school board then sought to have a writ of mandamus issue to the district court because they believed that statements made by the judge would continue to pose a continuing no "school with a majority of minority students" requirement on the school district. Justice Rehnquist, sitting as a Circuit Justice, denied their application for a stay order. Justice

Court invalidated the district court's requirement as a part of a desegregation plan that the composition of the student body of particular schools fit a certain ratio every year. Because the system involved de jure segregation, the initial use of a statistical goal for racial integration was proper, but once a racially neutral school system had been established the lower court exceeded its authority in requiring annual readjustment to racial balance. Later changes in racial mixture were not caused by segregative acts of school or state authorities and, therefore, the new racial imbalance constituted only de facto segregation.[56]

This decision evidences some movement by the Justices of the Supreme Court to make the de facto-de jure distinction more important and more objective. Similarly, the Court has summarily remanded a lower court decision on segregation for lower court consideration of whether there was sufficient evidence of purposeful school segregation.[57] In remanding the case, several Justices indicated their view that remedies designed to promote school integration could not exceed the scope of purposeful segregation that had been established at trial.[58] Such an approach would make the finding of de jure discrimination more important than ever before.

In recent years the Justices appear to be attempting to employ an "institutional intent" approach for identifying de jure racial segregation while tailoring the scope of the judicial remedies to correction of the identified segregation. The institutional intent test, described above, allows for the objective identification of purposely discriminatory acts by school boards in order to identify de jure segregation in the absence of explicit racial classifications in city or state laws. However, this test does not justify the imposition of integration orders upon school districts that have a racial imbalance in their schools due only to de facto segregation.

While statistical proof of racial disparity in schools will not in itself establish unconstitutional segregation, proof that a school board has been aware of serious racial imbalance in its schools and that it has knowingly adopted policies that have been designed to maintain or exacerbate the racial imbalance will give rise to an inference of purposeful discrimination on the part of the school board:

> Proof of purposeful and effective maintenance of a body of separate black schools in a substantial part of the system itself is prima facie proof of a dual school system and supports a finding to this effect absent sufficient contrary proof by the [school] Board....[59]

The school board's recognition of the foreseeable effects of its actions on the racial imbalance in the schools is one element of proof of purposeful discrimination, and the establishment of purposeful discrimination as to one area of school board activity or one part of the school system will give rise to an inference of system wide discrimination. However, these inferences only shift the burden to the state or local government to demonstrate that the

---

Rehnquist believed that the district court order in fact eliminated the "no majority" continual reassignment provision. Vetterli v. United States District Court, 435 U.S. 1304, 98 S.Ct. 1219, 55 L.Ed.2d 751 (1978) (Rehnquist, Circuit Justice).

56. After the effects of de jure discrimination have been eliminated as far as practicable, the remedial order should be terminated. Board of Educ. v. Dowell, 498 U.S. 237, 111 S.Ct. 630, 112 L.Ed.2d 715 (1991).

A district court has authority to relinquish in stages its supervision of a school district that had been found to have de jure segregation. As the district court finds that portions of the school system have been integrated, and the effects of past segregation eliminated, it may relinquish supervision over those aspects of the school system in which desegregation has been achieved. Thus, a district court, with a proper factual basis and findings on the record, could relinquish supervision over the student as-

signments in a school district after it found that the effects of prior segregation in the school district student assignments had been eliminated even though that court would retain supervision of other aspects of the school district's program (such as teacher assignments and resource allocations) until it found that those aspects of the program had been cured of the effects of prior segregation. Freeman v. Pitts, 503 U.S. 467, 112 S.Ct. 1430, 118 L.Ed.2d 108 (1992), on remand 979 F.2d 1472 (11th Cir. 1992).

57. Austin Independent School District v. United States, 429 U.S. 990, 97 S.Ct. 517, 50 L.Ed.2d 603 (1976).

58. 429 U.S. at 991 97 S.Ct. at 517. (Opinion of Powell, J., joined by Burger, C.J., and Rehnquist, J.).

59. Columbus Bd. of Education v. Penick, 443 U.S. 449, 458, 99 S.Ct. 2941, 2946–47, 61 L.Ed.2d 666 (1979).

school board policies were intended to promote important educational objectives and did not constitute purposeful discrimination.

In two highly publicized but relatively simple cases, the Court upheld lower court findings that two cities in Ohio had engaged in purposeful discrimination in their school districts and that their refusal to remedy past discrimination was a violation of the constitutional obligation to dismantle de jure segregated school systems and to avoid any action that would impede the disestablishment of such an unconstitutional system. By a vote of seven to two, the Court upheld a District Court and Court of Appeals finding that the schools in Columbus, Ohio had been purposely discriminating against black students and intentionally maintaining a dual school system through the early 1950's and that, after the Supreme Court's initial rulings that such systems violated the Fourteenth Amendment, the Columbus school board had not only failed to dismantle its dual school system but also had intentionally adopted policies such as the establishment of optional attendance zones and boundary changes that maintained and increased the system wide segregation.[60]

By a five to four vote the Court also found that the Court of Appeals for the Sixth Circuit had been correct in ordering system wide desegregation plans for the school district of Dayton, Ohio.[61] There was little doubt that Dayton had maintained a dual school system through the early 1950's, and both the District Court and Court of Appeals had found that the Dayton school board had violated the Fourteenth Amendment in the past. There was a closer division of the Justices in this case,

however, because there was less proof that the school board's actions had been designed to maintain a dual school system throughout the school district.

The District Court had found that the constitutional violation was limited to a few schools within the district, but the Court of Appeals had found that the school board had not effectively rebutted the inference of area-wide discrimination that arose once there was proof of purposeful discrimination as to some schools in the district.

A majority of the Justices of the Supreme Court agreed with the Court of Appeals because, "given intentionally segregated schools in 1954", the school board had an obligation to dismantle the dual system and to refrain from taking "any action that would impede the process of disestablishing the dual system." Because "the board has never seriously contended that it fulfilled its affirmative duty or heavy burden of explaining its failure to do so," the majority of the Justices found that the Court of Appeals was justified in finding that the board had purposefully maintained a dual school system throughout the district. The fact that the original decisions resulting in the segregated system may have occurred over 20 years ago did not relieve the board from its duty of undoing the segregative effect, which it simply exacerbated by its continual refusal, in over a quarter of a century, to integrate its previously segregated school system.[62]

When ruling on whether a governmental unit has met its obligation to end racial discrimination in government programs outside of the educational area, the Supreme Court

---

60. Columbus Bd. of Education v. Penick, 443 U.S. 449, 99 S.Ct. 2941, 61 L.Ed.2d 666 (1979). Justice White wrote a majority opinion in this case, joined by Justices Brennan, Marshall, Blackmun, and Stevens.

Justice Stewart, joined by Chief Justice Burger, filed an opinion concurring in the judgment as to this case but dissenting as to the judgment in the companion case from Dayton, Ohio case. 443 U.S. at 469, 99 S.Ct. at 2952. Dayton Bd. of Education v. Brinkman, 443 U.S. 526, 99 S.Ct. 2971, 61 L.Ed.2d 720 (1979).

Justices Powell and Rehnquist dissented, for they felt that the Court's use of inferences to shift burdens of proof to the school board had the effect of justifying remedies for de facto segregation. If a state university system was

segregated by law (through statutes or other purposeful discrimination) in the past the state is under the obligation to eliminate the effects of racial discrimination, but it may be difficult to determine if or when a state has accomplished that goal. See § 14.9(a)(2)(c) of this Treatise.

61. Dayton Bd. of Education v. Brinkman, 443 U.S. 526, 99 S.Ct. 2971, 61 L.Ed.2d 720 (1979).

62. If a state university system was segregated by law (through statutes or other purposeful discrimination) in the past the state is under the obligation to eliminate the effects of racial discrimination, but it may be difficult to determine if or when a state has accomplished that goal. See § 14.9(a)(2)(c).

has refused to require the government to eliminate the continuing effects of prior government segregation. In *Bazemore v. Friday,*[63] the Court found that state sponsored 4–H Clubs and Homemaker Clubs complied with equal protection principles by ending the prior practice of assigning students to separate all-white and all-black clubs. Justice White, writing for five Justices, stated: "The mere continued existence of single race clubs does not make out a constitutional violation ... [e]ven if the service [the state agency] in effect assigned blacks and whites to separate clubs prior to 1965, it did not do so after that time. While school children must go to school, there is no compulsion to join 4–H or Homemaker Clubs, and while school boards customarily have the power to create school attendance areas and otherwise designate the school that particular students may attend, there is no statutory or regulatory authority to deny a young person the right to join any club he or she wishes to join ... [o]ur cases requiring parks and the like to be desegregated lend no support for requiring more than what has been done [ending the discriminatory assignment and practices by the state] in this case."

(b) The Desegregation Principle and Private Schools. Private schools which segregate on the basis of race do not violate the Constitution unless they have sufficient contacts with the state or the federal government to allow description of their acts as "state action," because the equal protection clause of the Fourteenth Amendment applies only to the states and the due process clause of the Fifth Amendment applies only to the federal government. Thus, private segregated schools present a classic "state action" issue and under traditional analysis, they are not subject to constitutional restraint absent further contacts with the government.[64] However, the government may not give any aid to these schools because that would constitute government support for and facilitation of racial segregation. Therefore, these schools could be put to an election between receiving assistance from the government and maintaining the segregative practices.

Although these schools do not violate the Constitution, they are illegal under federal civil rights statutes insofar as they refuse to contract with persons on the basis of the person's race. The major issue now is whether the government must permit the existence of (and perhaps offer neutral educational benefits to) religious schools that segregate because of the principles of their religion. The few decisions of the Supreme Court concerning private school segregation sharpen these issues.

The Supreme Court has invalidated all attempts to aid segregative schools that exceed generalized governmental services such as police and fire protection. In several cases the Court affirmed lower court decisions which enjoined states from making tuition grants to students attending segregated schools.[65] In

---

63. 478 U.S. 385, 106 S.Ct. 3000, 92 L.Ed.2d 315 (1986) (per curiam), on remand 848 F.2d 476 (4th Cir. 1988). This case involved a highly unusual method of explaining the Court's decision. The ruling of the Court on all of the issues in the case was given in a short per curiam decision. The explanation for the Court's rulings regarding the application of federal civil rights statutes to possible continuing salary disparities between white and black workers in this case was explained by Justice Brennan in an opinion that was titled "Justice Brennan, joined by all other Members of the Court, concurring in part." The ruling regarding the constitutionality of the state's decision to allow voluntary membership practices for 4–H and Homemaker Clubs, even though they may have been segregated through official practices prior to 1965, was explained in an opinion titled "Justice White, with whom the Chief Justice, Justice Powell, Justice Rehnquist, and Justice O'Connor joined, concurring." 478 U.S. at 407, 106 S.Ct. at 3012. Justices Brennan, Marshall, Blackmun, and Stevens dissented from the ruling that neither the Fourteenth Amendment nor civil rights statutes required

any affirmative efforts to desegregate the once segregated clubs. 478 U.S. at 409, 106 S.Ct. at 3013 (Brennan, J., joined by Marshall, Blackmun, & Stevens, JJ., dissenting in part).

64. See § 12.1, supra.

It might have been argued that education was a public function and, therefore, that all accredited schools embodied state action. However the cases in this area leave little doubt that the Court would not accept such an argument. See § 12.2, supra.

65. Norwood v. Harrison, 413 U.S. 455, 463 n. 6, 93 S.Ct. 2804, 2810 n. 6, 37 L.Ed.2d 723 (1973). The Court lists the following decisions in its note 6: Brown v. South Carolina State Bd. of Education, 296 F.Supp. 199 (D.S.C. 1968), affirmed per curiam 393 U.S. 222, 89 S.Ct. 449, 21 L.Ed.2d 391 (1968); Poindexter v. Louisiana Financial Assistance Com'n, 275 F.Supp. 833 (E.D.La.1967), affirmed per curiam 389 U.S. 571, 88 S.Ct. 693, 19 L.Ed.2d 780 (1968). See Wallace v. United States, 389 U.S. 215,

Norwood v. Harrison [66] the Court held that a state could not lend textbooks to students at such schools even though the program was identical to one under which the Court had allowed textbooks to go to students of religious schools.[67] The Court held that state aid to racially discriminatory schools was not permissible even where the aid and the discrimination were not tied together. The state could give limited assistance to children at parochial schools because of the constitutionally recognized value in the free exercise of religion. However, there is no constitutionally significant value or support for racial discrimination.

The Supreme Court clarified the state aid issue when it held that racially discriminatory schools could not be allowed to reserve public recreational facilities for temporary exclusive use. In *Gilmore v. Montgomery* [68] the Court found that this connection constituted aid to the racially discriminatory entity. A majority of the Justices did not decide whether the nonexclusive use of public recreational facilities by such groups was also prohibited. If the use amounted to an informal use of the facilities with other persons on a desegregated basis, it might be viewed as no more than a generalized service such as police and fire protection. Yet there was no decision on this point, and four Justices indicated that they would not allow any use of public facilities

that was part of the segregated school program or that otherwise aided the school.[69]

Another form of aid to segregated schools comes from tax exemptions. Lower federal courts had invalidated any exemptions which could be viewed as specific aid (such as tax exempt status) rather than as a generalized grant to all persons (such as depreciation deductions).[70] Such a decision would seem to cast doubt on state property tax exclusions for such groups.[71] Although property tax exemptions for churches have been upheld, under the rationale of *Norwood,* this aid should be classified as specific aid which may be granted to insure religious freedom but not to allow racially segregative practices. The Internal Revenue Service agreed with this position and ruled that racially discriminatory entities would not receive tax exempt status. This IRS ruling was upheld by the Supreme Court because the refusal to extend aid to religious schools which discriminate by race constitutes the neutral enforcement of a secular constitutional value rather than the imposition of a burden on a religious organization because of its beliefs.[72]

The Supreme Court decisions in *Norwood* [73] and *Gilmore* [74] and the lower federal courts' decisions regarding the tax exempt status of racially discriminatory schools and fraternal organizations [75] make it appear as if the government may be prohibited from giving any

---

88 S.Ct. 415, 19 L.Ed.2d 422 (1967), affirming Lee v. Macon County Bd. of Education, 267 F.Supp. 458, 475 (M.D.Ala.1967).

Mississippi's tuition grant programs were invalidated in Coffey v. State Educational Finance Com'n, S.D.Miss., C.A. No. 2906, decided Sept. 2, 1970 (unreported). The latter case involved a statute which provided for tuition loans rather than tuition grants. See Green v. Connally, 330 F.Supp. 1150 (D.D.C.1971), affirmed sub nom. Coit v. Green, 404 U.S. 997, 92 S.Ct. 564, 30 L.Ed.2d 550 (1971).

66. 413 U.S. 455, 93 S.Ct. 2804, 37 L.Ed.2d 723 (1973).

67. Board of Education v. Allen, 392 U.S. 236, 88 S.Ct. 1923, 20 L.Ed.2d 1060 (1968).

68. 417 U.S. 556, 94 S.Ct. 2416, 41 L.Ed.2d 304 (1974).

69. 417 U.S. at 576, 94 S.Ct. at 2430 (Marshall, J., concurring); 417 U.S. at 577, 94 S.Ct. at 2430 (Brennan, J., concurring); 417 U.S. at 581, 94 S.Ct. at 2429 (White and Douglas JJ., concurring).

70. McGlotten v. Connally, 338 F.Supp. 448 (D.D.C. 1972) (three judge court per Bazelon, C.J.); Green v. Connally, 330 F.Supp. 1150 (D.D.C.1971) (three judge

court per Leventhal, J.), affirmed sub nom., Coit v. Green, 404 U.S. 997, 92 S.Ct. 564, 30 L.Ed.2d 550 (1971).

71. See Pitts v. Department of Revenue, 333 F.Supp. 662 (E.D.Wis.1971) (three judge court); Falkenstein v. Department of Revenue, 350 F.Supp. 887 (D.Or.1972) (three judge court), appeal dismissed 409 U.S. 1099, 93 S.Ct. 907, 34 L.Ed.2d 681 (1973).

72. Bob Jones University v. United States, 461 U.S. 574, 103 S.Ct. 2017, 76 L.Ed.2d 157 (1983). Earlier litigation concerning this issue was dismissed because it was brought in a manner which violated the tax injunction statutes. Bob Jones University v. Simon, 416 U.S. 725, 94 S.Ct. 2038, 40 L.Ed.2d 496 (1974).

73. Norwood v. Harrison, 413 U.S. 455, 93 S.Ct. 2804, 37 L.Ed.2d 723 (1973), on remand 382 F.Supp. 921 (N.D.Miss.1974), opinion supplemented 410 F.Supp. 133 (1976), appeal dismissed 563 F.2d 722 (5th Cir.1977).

74. Gilmore v. City of Montgomery, 417 U.S. 556, 94 S.Ct. 2416, 41 L.Ed.2d 304 (1974).

75. See supra notes 69–70.

special aid, such as exclusive use of public facilities or tax exempt status, to organizations that discriminate on the basis of race. However, the Supreme Court avoided ruling on this specific issue in *Bob Jones University v. United States*.[76] In that case, the Court held that the Internal Revenue Service was empowered by Congress to deny tax exempt status to schools, including religious schools, that discriminated on the basis of race. Because the IRS had chosen to deny such schools an exemption, the Court did not have to rule on whether such an exemption would violate the equal protection guarantee of the Fifth Amendment due process clause.

The existence of racially discriminatory schools may now be coming to an end since the Supreme Court has upheld the application of civil rights statutes prohibiting racial discrimination to them. In 1976, in *Runyon v. McCrary*,[77] it held that a private school that excluded children because of their race violated 42 U.S.C.A. § 1981, the Civil Rights Act. This statute declares that all persons shall have the same right to contract as white persons. The statute was passed pursuant to congressional power granted by the Thirteenth Amendment and was to be applied to the actions of private persons or groups.

The Court dismissed challenges to the validity of applying the statute to private schools, as past cases had established beyond peradventure that the Civil War Amendments did not recognize any associational-privacy right to segregate in public dealings or contracts. The Court did not explicitly decide whether a school which did not offer its services to all whites but only to an "invited" group would come under the terms of the statute, though the Court implied that § 1981 would not cover that situation.

Additionally, there is a question as to the application of the statute to religious schools that segregated because of principles of their religion. This question is more serious than the tax exemption issue for it would end the existence of these schools by government rule. The Court reserved this question for the future.[78] It may be that the religion clauses of the First Amendment require the government to tolerate the existence of such schools while the equal protection clause of the Fourteenth Amendment requires the government to refrain from giving them any aid. Yet if these schools have any significant impact on the desegregation of other schools, it may be that the Civil War Amendments will authorize the total prohibition of these racially discriminatory practices.

(c) Colleges and Universities. The deliberate speed concept was never applicable to state universities. The desegregation of higher education had begun prior to *Brown* in a series of Court decisions in which findings that educational facilities and opportunities afforded blacks were not equal resulted in the mandate of immediate admission of black students to previously white universities and law schools on a nonsegregated basis.[79]

Following *Brown II*, some efforts were made to use the deliberate speed formula to slow

---

76. 461 U.S. 574, 103 S.Ct. 2017, 76 L.Ed.2d 157 (1983).

77. 427 U.S. 160, 96 S.Ct. 2586, 49 L.Ed.2d 415 (1976), appeal after remand 569 F.2d 1294 (4th Cir.1978), certiorari denied 439 U.S. 927, 99 S.Ct. 311, 58 L.Ed.2d 320 (1978).

78. 427 U.S. at 167 n. 6, 96 S.Ct. at 2593. The societal interest in ending racial or gender discrimination is sufficiently important to allow governmental entities to curtail the associational, interests of persons who wish to discriminate on such basis in public activities or contracts. See generally, Roberts v. United States Jaycees, 468 U.S. 609, 104 S.Ct. 3244, 82 L.Ed.2d 462 (1984); Hishon v. King & Spalding, 467 U.S. 69, 104 S.Ct. 2229, 81 L.Ed.2d 59 (1984) finding that the interest in gender discrimination was sufficient to justify a limitation of associational interests, at least regarding economic associations and discuss-

ing the basis for limiting such freedom in order to end these types of discrimination. The Supreme Court has found that the application of anti-discrimination laws to some private groups violates the freedom of association when such application would impair the First Amendment freedom of association without being narrowly tailored to a compelling interest. See, e.g., Boy Scouts of America v. Dale, 530 U.S. 640, 120 S.Ct. 2446, 147 L.Ed.2d 554 (2000). In none of these cases did the Court find that application of the law prohibiting racial discrimination violated the First Amendment freedom of association. For a discussion of these cases see § 16.41.

79. Sweatt v. Painter, 339 U.S. 629, 70 S.Ct. 848, 94 L.Ed. 1114 (1950), McLaurin v. Oklahoma State Regents, 339 U.S. 637, 70 S.Ct. 851, 94 L.Ed. 1149 (1950).

down integration.[80] The Supreme Court rejected all such attempts, stating that qualified blacks seeking to enter colleges, graduate or professional schools were entitled to prompt relief.[81] In regard to private colleges and universities, the statutory prohibition of discriminatory admission practices by private schools, discussed in the previous section, will apply. The problem regarding religiously affiliated colleges will remain.

Determining whether a state that had de jure racial discrimination in its state university systems had taken sufficient actions to eliminate the vestiges of past racial discrimination should not be difficult for courts in most cases. Courts normally would take the same approach to remedying past discrimination in state universities as in state grade school and high school cases. Because state universities do not involve attendance zones similar to those used for public grade schools and high schools, dismantling a segregated university system may be easier than dismantling a segregated public school system. In some states, the task of remedying unconstitutional race discrimination in higher education may be very difficult because some of those states had created colleges for minority race students that are now termed "historically black colleges." Some historically black colleges are state universities that are excellent educational institutions.

In *United States v. Fordice*,[82] the Supreme Court took a limited step towards clarifying the approaches that state officials and courts should take in the desegregating of state university systems that had given rise to historically black state colleges. *Fordice*, examined the state university system of the State of Mississippi. The state university system in Mississippi had been run on a racially segregated basis, by way of statutes and purposeful discriminatory administrative actions, through most, if not all, of the 1960s. In the 1970s, responding to actions of the United States

Department of Health, Education and Welfare, the state board with authority for the state university system submitted plans for compliance with the constitutional desegregation principle and federal statutes. The lawsuit that resulted in the Supreme Court case was begun in 1975; plaintiffs claimed that the state had maintained the racially segregated school system by allowing its effects to continue. They claimed that the state colleges that once had been officially for white students only remained an institution with very few minority students. The state colleges that had once been for minority students only remained as schools with primarily minority race students. By the end of the 1980s, the plaintiffs and defendants were still in disagreement regarding whether the state had ever dismantled its prior de jure racially segregated university system.

The lower federal courts ruled that Mississippi's financial and educational policies since the late 1970s were racially neutral (including the student admission policies at the state universities) and that the state had met its obligation to dismantle its racially segregated university system. The United States Supreme Court disagreed with the lower courts. In *Fordice*, Justice White wrote a majority opinion for eight Justices. Justice White found that state university systems were under the same obligation to eliminate the effects of de jure segregation as public grade schools and high schools. Mere elimination of prior segregation, and ending racially discriminatory policies, did not meet this obligation. Justice White's majority opinion noted that all of the Supreme Court's decisions since the early 1950s "established that a state does discharge its constitutional obligations until it eradicates policies and practices traceable to its prior de jure dual system that continue to foster segregation."

Some racially segregated practices of states (in areas outside of education) could be remed-

80. E.g., Board of Supervisors of Louisiana State University v. Tureaud, 225 F.2d 434 (5th Cir.1955), certiorari denied, 351 U.S. 924, 76 S.Ct. 780, 100 L.Ed. 1454 (1956).

81. Florida ex rel. Hawkins v. Board of Control, 350 U.S. 413, 76 S.Ct. 464, 100 L.Ed. 486 (1956).

82. 505 U.S. 717, 112 S.Ct. 2727, 120 L.Ed.2d 575 (1992).

ied merely by a court ordering a state to cease its racial segregation. Thus, a court could end racial segregation regarding physical facilities such as parks or hospitals by simply ordering an end to racially discriminatory practices. In *Bazemore v. Friday* [83] the Supreme Court had held that certain state sponsored clubs for young people (4–H Clubs and Homemaker Clubs) that had racially segregated policies in the past could comply with equal protection principles simply by ending prior racially discriminatory practices and adopting race neutral policies. *Fordice* distinguished *Bazemore.* Justice White's majority opinion held that the lower federal courts, in the educational segregation cases, must determine whether the adoption of race neutral policies has eliminated the effects of segregation or whether the current policies perpetuate a racially segregated system.

In *Fordice* Justice White stated:

"If the State perpetuates policies and practices traceable to its prior system that continue to have segregative effects—whether by influencing student enrollment decisions or by fostering segregation in other facets of the university system—and such policies are without sound educational justification and can be practicably eliminated, the state has not satisfied its burden of proving that it has dismantled its prior system. Such policies run afoul of the Equal Protection Clause, even though the State has abolished the legal requirement that whites and blacks be educated separately and has established racially neutral policies not animated by a discriminatory purpose." [84]

The majority opinion went on to find that the State of Mississippi's current admissions policies (which required higher test scores for state universities that happened to be historically white institutions) and the widespread duplication of educational programs at historically white and black colleges appeared to perpetuate the effects of past discrimination. The Supreme Court noted that the lower fed-

eral courts, after the case was remanded, should examine the basic question of whether all eight of the state's higher educational institutions had to be continued in operation. If the continuation of all eight schools was a perpetuation of the prior racially discriminatory system, the courts would have to consider whether one or more of the schools should be closed or merged. If the courts fully adopted the standards used in public school desegregation cases when examining state university systems, it might be that there could be no justification for the continuation of some state universities that operated with racially neutral admissions policies but continued to be institutions that served almost solely racial minority students. On the other hand, it might be that the interest in providing an educational atmosphere conducive to minority race students at a historically black college might at the current time (rather than at the time the institution was started) be designed to advance the educational interests of minority race students.

Justice Thomas, who concurred in the opinion and judgment of the Court in *Fordice,* stated:

"We do not foreclose the possibility that there exists 'sound educational justification' from maintaining historically black colleges as such. Despite the shameful history of state-enforced segregation, these institutions have survived and flourished ... think it undisputable that these institutions have succeeded in part because of their distinctive history and traditions ... obviously, a state cannot maintain such traditions by closing particular institutions, historically white or historically black, to particular racial groups. However, it hardly follows that a state cannot operate a diverse assortment of institutions—including historically black institutions—open to all on a race-neutral basis, but with established traditions and pro-

83. 478 U.S. 385, 386–88, 106 S.Ct. 3000, 3002–03, 92 L.Ed.2d 315 (1986) (per curiam), on remand 848 F.2d 476 (4th Cir.1988). See § 14.9(b) of this Treatise regarding "desegregation of other facilities."

84. United States v. Fordice, 505 U.S. 717, 730, 112 S.Ct. 2727, 2737, 120 L.Ed.2d 575 (1992), on remand 970 F.2d 1378 (5th Cir.1992).

grams that might disproportionally appeal to one race or another." [85]

In *Fordice,* the Court only had to rule that the lower federal courts were in error when they accepted the adoption of race neutral policies by the state university system as the equivalent of dismantling the former segregated system of public universities in Mississippi. However, near the end of the majority opinion, Justice White stated:

"If we understand private petitioners to press us to order the upgrading of [the historically black state universities in Mississippi] solely so that they can be publicly financed, exclusively black enclaves by private choice, we reject that request. The state provides these facilities for all its citizens and it has not met its burden under *Brown* to take affirmative steps to dismantle its prior de jure system when it perpetuates a separate, but 'more equal' one. Whether such an increase in funding is necessary to achieve a full dismantlement under standards we have outlined [requiring the state to make sure that student choices regarding which state institutions to apply to and attend were truly free of the effects of past segregation] is a different question, and one that must be addressed on remand." [86]

Thus, it would seem that the principles employed in school segregation cases during the past 40 years would require states to dismantle racially discriminatory state university system as fully as they would dismantle racial segregation in a public grade school or high school system. Whether some historically black state universities and colleges will be able to retain their educational character, as

indicated by Justice Thomas' concurrence, is a question that must await future cases.

(3) State School Programs Relating to Desegregation. As discussed briefly above, in connection with massive resistance, school authorities and state legislatures often adopted measures in an attempt to evade compliance with the principle of *Brown.* When faced with desegregation orders, some authorities reacted by closing public schools and giving financial support to private schools; others attempted to form new school districts. In other cases, school authorities superficially indicated compliance with the desegregation mandate but adopted desegregation plans which did not effectively integrate schools. These included freedom-of-choice plans or grade-a-year plans. In recent years, state legislatures have attempted to evade *Brown* through the passage of "antibusing" statutes. The Supreme Court has invalidated all of the above methods when used in an attempt to perpetuate segregated school systems.

(a) Grade-A-Year Plans. The grade-a-year plan, under which one school grade was desegregated per year, was a method commonly used in the desegregation of Southern schools. However, after the Supreme Court held that the time for mere deliberate speed had run out,[87] the Court invalidated a grade-a-year plan because the plan was too slow. In *Rogers v. Paul*[88] the Court was confronted with a school board which adopted such a plan, beginning with the first grade in 1957. Thus, in 1966 the 10th, 11th, and 12th grades remained segregated by law. The Court in a per curiam decision reversed the lower court's denial of the request by black high school students for immediate integration. The Court

---

85. 505 U.S. at 744, 112 S.Ct. at 2744, 2746 (Thomas, J., concurring).

86. United States v. Fordice, 505 U.S. 717, 742, 112 S.Ct. 2727, 2743, 120 L.Ed.2d 575 (1992). O'Connor, J., joined the opinion of the Court and wrote a concurring opinion that seemed to endorse full implementation of all the public school desegregation cases in the university setting. 505 U.S. at 742, 112 S.Ct. at 2743 (O'Connor, J., concurring). Scalia, J., wrote an opinion agreeing that Mississippi had to remove all racial discrimination in its school system and that Mississippi's current use of admission test requirements needed further review by the lower courts, but he rejected any rule that would require all

state segregated universities to demonstrate compliance with equal protection in the same ways as public school systems (the result of such a rule would be that historically black institutions would be eliminated by court orders). 505 U.S. at 748, 112 S.Ct. at 2746 (Scalia, J., concurring in part and dissenting in part).

87. Griffin v. County School Board of Prince Edward County, 377 U.S. 218, 84 S.Ct. 1226, 12 L.Ed.2d 256 (1964), motion granted 377 U.S. 950, 84 S.Ct. 1627, 12 L.Ed.2d 496 (1964).

88. 382 U.S. 198, 86 S.Ct. 358, 15 L.Ed.2d 265 (1965).

again noted that delays were no longer tolerable. Clearly such tactics could not be used to evade a constitutional mandate any longer.

(b) Freedom-of-Choice Plans. Some school authorities in districts with official segregation adopted free transfer or freedom-of-choice plans which gave the student some voice in deciding which school he would attend. In 1963, the Court invalidated a transfer policy that allowed students assigned to a school where their race was in the minority to transfer to a school where their race was in the majority because its inevitable effect was the perpetuation of school segregation.[89]

Five years later, in *Green v. County School Board*[90] the question before the Court was whether the school board's adoption of a freedom-of-choice plan that permitted a student to choose his own public school constituted adequate compliance with the board's responsibilities, as stated in *Brown*, "to achieve a system of determining admission to the public schools on a nonracial basis."[91] The Supreme Court invalidated the plan.

Pursuant to state statute, a segregated school system had been established and had been perpetuated by the formation of a board to assign children to segregated schools. After being enrolled in a school, a child could request reassignment, but as of 1964, no pupil ever applied for admission to a school maintained for the other race. In 1965, following the initiation of this suit, the school board adopted the freedom-of-choice plan in order to desegregate the schools and remain eligible for federal financial aid. Under the plan, first and eighth graders were to choose a school. Pupils in other grades could annually choose a school, but if they did not, they simply remained assigned to the school they were attending.

The Court stated that "in the context of the state-imposed segregated pattern of long standing, the fact that in 1965 the Board opened the doors of the former 'white' school to Negro children and of the 'Negro' school to white children merely begins, not ends, our inquiry whether the Board has taken steps adequate to abolish its dual, segregated system."[92] The Court then examined the plan to see whether it realistically could be expected to provide immediate relief. Here, no white had enrolled at any black school, and 85% of the black students continued to attend all-black schools. The Board, therefore, was required to present an effective desegregation plan.

The Court in *Green* did not hold that the freedom-of-choice plan could not be adopted, but, rather, that in desegregating a school system such a plan might be of use under some circumstances. However, if there were reasonable alternatives available which would provide for speedier, more effective desegregation of schools, a freedom-of-choice plan was clearly unacceptable.

As indicated by *Green*, freedom-of-choice plans seldom achieved the desegregation required by *Brown*. Whites did not choose to attend black schools, and blacks were often discouraged from electing white schools because they feared retaliation or exertion of undue pressure by school officials; other times they were simply deterred by poverty. Where they did elect white schools, they were often targets of violence.[93] In *Raney v. Board of Education*,[94] a companion case to *Green*, the Court found that a freedom-of-choice plan was inadequate when blacks seeking admission to the white school were denied entrance because of overcrowding. In a third case, the Court struck down a free transfer plan that had not significantly affected the racial composition of segregated schools. The duty of school authorities who have run a de jure segregated system is to integrate the system, not to maintain the status quo created by prior official segregation.[95]

---

89. Goss v. Board of Education, 373 U.S. 683, 83 S.Ct. 1405, 10 L.Ed.2d 632 (1963).

90. 391 U.S. 430, 88 S.Ct. 1689, 20 L.Ed.2d 716 (1968).

91. 391 U.S. at 431–32, 88 S.Ct. at 1691.

92. 391 U.S. at 437, 88 S.Ct. at 1694.

93. 391 U.S. at 440, n. 5, 88 S.Ct. at 1695, n. 5.

94. 391 U.S. 443, 88 S.Ct. 1697, 20 L.Ed.2d 727 (1968).

95. Monroe v. Board of Com'rs, 391 U.S. 450, 88 S.Ct. 1700, 20 L.Ed.2d 733 (1968).

The Supreme Court, however, has refused to require government entities to eliminate the effects of past governmental segregation outside of the educational area. It appears that the government may comply with the equal protection principle by merely ending segregative practices in other types of government programs.[96]

(c) Closing Public Schools. Another tactic employed to avoid desegregation of schools was to close public schools and to give financial support to private segregated schools. For example, when the Prince Edward County School Board was ordered in 1959 to take "immediate steps" beginning in September toward desegregation, the public schools simply did not open in the fall; instead private schools were established for whites. Most of the financial support of these private schools was in the form of indirect state and county tuition grants available for all students who attended private nonsectarian schools or in the form of private contributions prompted by the creation of a property tax exemption.

In *Griffin v. County School Board of Prince Edward County*,[97] the Court affirmed that the closing of the Prince Edward County public schools was a denial of equal protection to black students. This decision is correct, as the record clearly indicated that the state and county financially supported the private discriminatory schools; all other Virginia counties maintained public schools; and the only purpose for closing the public schools was to avoid desegregation.

Because of the need for immediate relief, the Court upheld the district court's order that the payment of local tuition grants, the allowance of tax exemptions, and the processing of applications for state grants be suspended as long as the public schools remained closed. The Supreme Court also indicated that the district court could order appropriate local authorities to reopen and to support financially the public schools.[98]

(d) Creation of New School Districts. School authorities sometimes redesigned or established new school districts surprisingly soon after being ordered to desegregate a de jure segregated district. In 1972, in *Wright v. City Council of Emporia*[99] and *United States v. Scotland Neck City Board of Education*,[100] the Court forbade the creation by local authorities of new school districts which would adversely affect the effectiveness of an earlier desegregation order.

In *Wright*, a five to four majority upheld an injunction prohibiting subdivision of a school district based on the impact of such an action. The City of Emporia, Virginia and the county had entered a contractual agreement by which the county would continue to provide public schooling to Emporia residents along with others, with Emporia sharing the costs. The lower court found de jure segregation; therefore, Emporia and the county were ordered to have a desegregated school system. Two weeks after the desegregation decree was entered, Emporia began its plans to operate its own unitary school system. Because Emporia had long been part of the de jure segregated county school system and had decided to withdraw only after the issuance of the desegregation decree, a showing of an independent constitutional violation did not have to be made. The proposal for the new school system was to be judged by the standard stated in freedom-of-choice plan decisions; it would be found inval-

---

96. See, Bazemore v. Friday, 478 U.S. 385, 106 S.Ct. 3000, 92 L.Ed.2d 315 (1986) (per curiam), on remand 848 F.2d 476 (4th Cir.1988), in which the Court found that a state agriculture extension service previously operating segregated 4–H and Homemaker Clubs complied with equal protection by ending practices that established or encouraged segregated clubs, even though the voluntary choices of persons joining those clubs resulted in some clubs continuing to be all-white or all-black. The ruling was issued in a short per curiam opinion; the rationale for the decision was given by Justice White in a concurring opinion. 478 U.S. at 407–09, 106 S.Ct. at 3012–13 (White, J., joined by Burger, C.J., and Powell, Rehnquist, and

O'Connor, JJ., concurring). Justice White stated: "however sound *Green* may have been in the context of public schools, it has no application in this wholly different milieu."

97. 377 U.S. 218, 84 S.Ct. 1226, 12 L.Ed.2d 256 (1964), motion granted 377 U.S. 950, 84 S.Ct. 1627, 12 L.Ed.2d 496 (1964).

98. 377 U.S. at 233–4, 84 S.Ct. at 1234–35.

99. 407 U.S. 451, 92 S.Ct. 2196, 33 L.Ed.2d 51 (1972).

100. 407 U.S. 484, 92 S.Ct. 2214, 33 L.Ed.2d 75 (1972).

id if it hindered rather than furthered school desegregation. The finding of the district court, that the establishment of the new school system would deprive blacks living in the county of their right to desegregated public schooling, was supported by adequate evidence, including *inter alia* the resulting racial disparity between the city and county schools, the timing of Emporia's action, and the superior quality of the previously white schools located in the city compared to the outlying black schools. Thus, Emporia could not now create a new district, claim that it involved only de facto segregation, and avoid the desegregation ruling.

The four dissenting Justices[101] agreed with the principles stated by the majority but disagreed with the findings of fact. Chief Justice Burger summarized their position when he stated that the city should have a right to terminate its own system unless there were a clearer showing that it would frustrate the dismantling of the dual school system.[102]

In *Scotland Neck* the Supreme Court unanimously upheld the District Court's decision to enjoin the carving out of a new school district from a larger district which had been ordered to desegregate. The majority here simply relied upon the holding in *Wright*. The four Justices dissenting in *Wright* filed a concurring opinion to explain why they distinguished *Wright* and *Scotland Neck*.[103] Here, the operation of a separate school system would preclude meaningful desegregation. Additionally, Emporia had been accepting its responsibility as an independent governmental entity to provide independent education whereas this change was clearly motivated by desire to avoid desegregation.

(e) Legislative Modifications of Federal Desegregation Remedies. The transferring of students to achieve integration of schools has met with public disapproval. But if legislatures respond to public pressure with "anti-busing" statutes, the courts must respond by striking them down. In *North Carolina State Board of Education v. Swann*[104] the Supreme Court affirmed the lower court decision striking a North Carolina statute that forbade the school assignment of any student on the basis of race or for the purpose of creating a racial balance in the schools and forbade the use of busing for such purpose. Under the Fourteenth Amendment and the supremacy clause of Article VI, the States may not interfere with federal remedies for constitutional violations.[105]

There have been a variety of proposals before the Congress to restrict the authority of federal courts to remedy racial segregation in public school systems. Congress did pass legislation providing for the stay of busing orders pending appeal[106] and setting forth a priority of remedies which indicated that the transportation of students should be used only as a last resort.[107] But these statutes did not limit the authority of federal courts to issue orders calling for the redistricting of schools or transportation of students in order to correct de jure segregation.[108] Congress has not approved legislative proposals to restrict federal court authority to remedy a racially segregated school system which had been judicially determined

---

101. Justices Burger, Blackmun, Powell, and Rehnquist dissented. 407 U.S. at 471, 92 S.Ct. at 2207.

102. 407 U.S. at 471–72, 92 S.Ct. at 2207–08 (Burger, C.J., dissenting).

103. 407 U.S. at 491, 92 S.Ct. at 2218 (Burger, C.J., concurring).

104. 402 U.S. 43, 91 S.Ct. 1284, 28 L.Ed.2d 586 (1971).

105. Cf. New York v. Cathedral Academy, 434 U.S. 125, 130, 98 S.Ct. 340, 344, 54 L.Ed.2d 346 (1977), where the majority opinion stated that a state legislature may not "effectively modify a federal court's injunction whenever a balancing of constitutional equities might conceivably have justified the court's granting similar relief in the first place."

106. Education Amendments Act of 1972, Pub.L. No. 92–318 § 803, 82 Stat. 235. See generally, Hearings on Proposed Amendments to the Constitution and Legislation Relating to Transportation and Assignment of Public School Pupils, Before Subcommittee No. 5 of the House Committee on the Judiciary, 92d Cong., 2d Sess. (1972).

107. Education Amendments Act of 1974, Pub.L. 93–380, 88 Stat. 484.

108. This interpretation of the statute was the position of Justice Powell. See Drummond v. Acree, 409 U.S. 1228, 93 S.Ct. 18, 34 L.Ed.2d 33 (1972) (opinion of Justice Powell as Circuit Justice) denying stay in Acree v. County Bd. of Education, 458 F.2d 486 (5th Cir.1972), certiorari denied 409 U.S. 1006, 93 S.Ct. 431, 34 L.Ed.2d 299 (1972).

to be in violation of the Fourteenth Amendment.[109]

(f) Modification of State Remedies. In two states, voters expressed their dissatisfaction with the busing of students pursuant to state law by enacting legislation limiting remedies available for desegregating schools. However, because of the different methods employed to limit the transfer of students to achieve integration, only one state's action was upheld.

In Washington, voters adopted, through a statewide initiative, a statute which effectively permitted assignment and transfer of students for all purposes except for the purpose of integration of schools.[110] The Supreme Court in *Washington v. Seattle School District No. 1* [111] held that the statute was a violation of the equal protection clause of the Fourteenth Amendment because it did not allocate governmental power on the basis of any general principle, but instead "... uses the racial nature of an issue to define the governmental decision-making structure, and thus imposes substantial and unique burdens on racial minorities."[112] Rejecting the state's argument that the legislation had no racial overtones, the Court saw the statute as removing the authority to address a racial problem, and that problem only, from the local school board and placing it in the hands of the state legislature. This restructuring of governmental power places special, impermissible burdens on minority interests, because those seeking integration of Washington schools must now seek relief from the statewide electorate or the state legislature, a new and remote level of government.

In California voters adopted a state constitutional Amendment providing that state courts cannot order mandatory student assignment or transportation unless a federal court would do so to remedy a violation of the equal protection clause of the Fourteenth Amendment. In *Crawford v. Board of Education*,[113] the Supreme Court upheld the Amendment, rejecting the argument that the mere repeal of race related legislation embodies a presumptively invalid racial classification. The Court refused to see the Amendment as allocating governmental or judicial power on the basis of a discriminatory principle. Having gone beyond the requirements of the Fourteenth Amendment, California was free to return to the standard of the federal Constitution. The Court saw the Amendment as removing simply one means of achieving integrated schools because under California law, the local school districts still retain the obligation to alleviate segregation regardless of cause and they remain free to adopt busing plans to effectuate desegregation.

Justice Powell, writing the majority opinion in *Crawford* and a dissenting opinion in *Seattle*, viewed the two decisions as incompatible.[114] Crucial distinctions, however, underlie the two holdings. The Washington statute embodied an explicit racial classification in that it reallocated decision-making authority in such a way as to make it more difficult for minority groups than other community members to obtain legislation in their interest. By singling out minorities for particularly disadvantageous treatment within the political process, the statute did more than the California constitutional Amendment, which merely repealed the right to invoke a state judicial busing remedy heretofore available. Though the California Amendment, like the Washington statute, may make it more difficult to achieve school integration, it does not do so by altering

---

109. For an examination of this issue see §§ 2.9, 2.10, supra.

110. The statute allowed busing for racial purposes in one circumstances: it did not "prevent any court of competent jurisdiction from adjudicating constitutional issues relating to the public schools." Wash.Rev. Code § 28A.26.060 (1981). Washington v. Seattle School District No. 1, 458 U.S. 457, 102 S.Ct. 3187, 3191, 73 L.Ed.2d 896 (1982).

111. 458 U.S. 457, 102 S.Ct. 3187, 73 L.Ed.2d 896 (1982).

112. 458 U.S. at 470. 102 S.Ct. at 3195.

113. 458 U.S. 527, 102 S.Ct. 3211, 73 L.Ed.2d 948 (1982).

114. Washington v. Seattle School District No. 1, 458 U.S. 457, 102 S.Ct. 3187, 3204, 73 L.Ed.2d 896 (1982) (Powell, J., dissenting, joined by Burger, C.J., Rehnquist and O'Connor, JJ.).

the political process in such a way as to burden minority interests.[115]

Also underlying the *Crawford* holding is a concern over limiting a state's authority to deal with racial problems. To hold that the mere repeal of race related legislation is unconstitutional would imply that such legislation could never be repealed and discourage the states from experimenting with legislation designed to improve race relations.[116] Further, the people of the state, as the final authority over their state constitution, have the right to determine the nature of the judicially enforceable desegregation obligation under their constitution.[117] To define that obligation in terms of the principles of the Fourteenth Amendment does not violate that Amendment.

(4) Federal Court Remedial Powers. When, in the years following *Brown*, little progress was made toward the desegregation of schools, the Supreme Court stated the need for immediate relief but said little about what form this relief should take. The result was confusion. The problems encountered by judges of the lower federal courts made clear their need for guidance from the Supreme Court as to the scope of federal court powers to dismantle de jure segregated school systems. Therefore, in 1971, in *Swann v. Charlotte–Mecklenburg Board of Education*[118] the Court discussed in more precise terms the scope of the duty of school authorities and district courts to fashion an end to racially segregated school systems.

A federal court is not empowered to take any action or to require the school authorities to take any action until there has been a showing of de jure segregation. The Court has preserved the de jure-de facto distinction. Only if there is a showing of purposeful discrimination in a substantial portion of a school district is there a presumption of intentional discrimination in the rest of the district. The presumption can be rebutted only by showing that no such intent existed.[119]

Even when the Court finds there has been purposeful discrimination, school authorities will be given the opportunity to submit a plan for desegregation. Only when the school authorities are found to be engaged in de jure segregation and also fail to submit an adequate desegregation plan does the district court have the authority to order specific steps to desegregate the schools.

The Court in *Swann* first discussed the responsibilities of school authorities in regard to nonstudent remedies. The existing policy and practices with regard to faculty, staff, transportation, extracurricular activities, and facilities are among the most important indicia of a segregated school system. If it is possible to identify a school as a white school or a black school by the racial composition of the faculty and staff, the quality of the school buildings or equipment, or the organization of sport activities, a prima facie case of an equal protection violation is established.[120]

---

115. See the concurring opinion of Justice Blackmun, joined by Justice Brennan, in Crawford v. Board of Education, 458 U.S. at 547, 102 S.Ct. at 3222–23. A state constitutional amendment that prohibited local legislatures from passing laws that protected people against discrimination on the basis of race was invalidated in Reitman v. Mulkey, 387 U.S. 369, 87 S.Ct. 1627, 18 L.Ed.2d 830 (1967). See §§ 12.4(b), 14.8, for further discussion of *Reitman*. A state constitutional amendment prohibiting any local or state legislature within the state from passing laws that prohibited discrimination against persons on the basis of their sexual orientation was invalidated in Romer v. Evans, 517 U.S. 620, 116 S.Ct. 1620, 134 L.Ed.2d 855 (1996). In part based on *Romer*, the Supreme Court in *Lawrence v. Texas* ___ U.S. ___, 123 S.Ct. 2472, 156 L.Ed.2d 508 (2003) invalidated a law prohibiting sodomy when performed between persons of the same sex. The *Lawrence* decision is examined in § 14.28 of this Treatise.

116. See 458 U.S. at 540, 102 S.Ct. at 3219.

117. The right of each state to determine what its constitution means, as long as it meets the minimum guarantees of the federal Constitution, is the basis of each state's power to expand its constitutional protection of individual rights beyond those established by the federal Constitution. See § 1.6, supra.

118. 402 U.S. 1, 91 S.Ct. 1267, 28 L.Ed.2d 554 (1971), rehearing denied 403 U.S. 912, 91 S.Ct. 2200, 29 L.Ed.2d 689 (1971).

119. Keyes v. School District No. 1, 413 U.S. 189, 93 S.Ct. 2686, 37 L.Ed.2d 548 (1973). See generally, L. Graglia, Disaster by Decree (1976) for criticism and analysis of this case and similar decisions.

120. Swann v. Charlotte–Mecklenburg Bd. of Education, 402 U.S. 1, 18, 91 S.Ct. 1267, 1277, 28 L.Ed.2d 554 (1971).

When there has been a violation of equal protection the first duty of school authorities is to eliminate all invidious racial discriminations. The action should be immediate with respect to transportation, supporting personnel, extracurricular activities, maintenance of buildings and distribution of equipment.[121] Faculty assignment and the construction of new schools offer easy, flexible ways to achieve integration. The Court, therefore, upheld the district court's use of a fixed ratio in making faculty assignments to achieve an initial degree of desegregation and correction of the de jure segregation. Because the location of school buildings may determine the racial composition of individual schools, particular care must be given by school authorities and courts to prevent the use of future school construction and abandonment to perpetuate or re-establish the dual system.[122]

The Court then turned its attention to the question of remedies for the de jure racial segregation of students. Where such practices have existed they must be terminated and a nondiscriminatory school system must be established. Here the school authorities are given an opportunity to correct the system by presenting an effective plan for desegregation. As already discussed, grade-a-year plans, freedom-of-choice plans, or other preferred "remedies" that do not truly reverse the segregation are inadequate. In such situations, the district court is forced to use student remedies.

The Court in *Swann* discussed the extent to which attendance zones may be remedially altered by district courts. The redesign of school districts and attendance zones has been one of the tools most frequently used by both school planners and courts to eliminate dual systems. As an interim measure such zoning, including the creation of attendance zones neither compact nor contiguous, is within the remedial powers of a court.[123] If all things are equal, students should be assigned to the school closest their homes. But the Court emphasized that all things are not equal in a

deliberately segregated school system; the students formerly segregated must be mixed to desegregate the system. Although the remedy may be administratively awkward or burdensome for some students, some reasonable amount of inconvenience or burden cannot be avoided in the transition from segregation to integration. In determining the validity of a particular attendance plan the lower court should make its decision in light of the objective sought and its knowledge of local conditions. Reasonable decrees will meet with the approval of the Supreme Court.

The Court also discussed busing, which has been an important tool for the desegregation of schools. If, as in *Swann*, the assignment of students to the schools nearest their homes would not effectively dismantle the segregated school system, the court may order the assignment of some students to schools at a distance which requires the provision of some transportation for students. Because of the infinite variety of local problems and conditions, the Supreme Court did not set rigid guidelines in *Swann*. It simply stated that neither the time nor the distance involved should be so great as to risk the health of the children or to significantly impinge on the educational process.[124] The age of the children is probably the primary factor for the courts to consider in determining the limits on travel time.[125] Very young children are not to be assigned to schools far from their homes. Older children such as those in high school can ride buses to school with little impact on their education.

There is little else to the busing problem. Where a school district has engaged in de jure segregation and has refused to submit an effective plan to end segregation, the district court must fashion for them a remedial decree to end segregation. The district judge's only other option would be to violate his oath to support the Constitution by simply allowing a school district to refuse to comply with the requirements of the Fourteenth Amendment, as interpreted by the Supreme Court.

---

121. Id.

122. 402 U.S. at 20–21, 91 S.Ct. at 1278–79.

123. 402 U.S. at 27–28, 91 S.Ct. at 1281–82.

124. 402 U.S. at 30–31, 91 S.Ct. at 1282–83.

125. Id.

The district court may decree that some students be assigned to schools other than those closest to their home in order to desegregate the student bodies of the schools. If the reassignment is beyond normal walking distance for a child, the court may order the school district to provide transportation for the students. Often this reassignment has been linked in public debate to some concept of "statistical ratios" being imposed by judges. However, as discussed in a previous section, statistical imbalance alone will not establish de jure segregation, though the extent to which children are reassigned to eliminate segregation does involve the use to statistics as explained in *Swann*.

The Court has upheld the use of an initial statistical ratio for faculty assignment. The Supreme Court also found that the limited use of mathematical ratios in student assignment was valid, especially if the school board fails to submit an effective plan. But there is no requirement that every school reflect the racial composition of the school system as a whole.[126] Indeed, the Court ruled in *Swann* that there was no absolute requirement that every one-race school be eliminated. Schools whose students are all, or virtually all, of the same race would require close scrutiny, but their existence alone is not a sufficient indication of a segregated system.

Because the goal is to end de jure segregation, school and judicial authorities would necessarily be concerned with the elimination of such schools. Yet, federal courts cannot require schools to maintain a certain racial balance but, instead, must tailor their decrees to provide a reasonable remedy. A district court should not require an annual adjustment in the student ratios in the absence of a showing that the shift in racial balance was the result of purposeful discrimination.[127] The court ordered remedy should be terminated when the effects of de jure discrimination have been eliminated.[128]

A federal court may find that a school district had de jure discrimination, and that was subject to a court remedial order, had eliminated the effects of de jure discrimination in part, but not all, of its policies and practices. Such a finding would justify the court in rescinding the part of its remedial order that dealt with aspects of the school system wherein all effects of de jure discrimination had been eliminated. In *Freeman v. Pitts*,[129] the Supreme Court found that a federal district court had authority to rescind its remedial order over a racially segregated school district in incremental stages. Thus, the court might relinquish judicial control over the assignment of students to particular schools in the school district (based on findings that all aspects of racial discrimination in the student assignments had been eliminated) while it retained court supervision over other aspects of the school district programs (such as the assignment of faculty members to particular schools, and the allocation of resources that would determine the quality of education at particular schools) where the court found that the vestiges of past de jure discrimination had not been eliminated.

The Scope of a Remedial Order—Inter-District Remedies. The final, and most im-

---

126. Swann v. Charlotte–Mecklenburg Bd. of Education, 402 U.S. 1, 24–25, 91 S.Ct. 1267, 1280–81, 28 L.Ed.2d 554 (1971).

127. Pasadena City Bd. of Education v. Spangler, 427 U.S. 424, 96 S.Ct. 2697, 49 L.Ed.2d 599 (1976).

128. Board of Education v. Dowell, 498 U.S. 237, 111 S.Ct. 630, 112 L.Ed.2d 715 (1991).

129. 503 U.S. 467, 112 S.Ct. 1430, 118 L.Ed.2d 108 (1992), on remand 979 F.2d 1472 (11th Cir.1992). The majority opinion by Justice Kennedy in this case dealt with the issues presented in a straight forward manner and merely found that district courts had the power, with proper factual findings, to retain supervision over some aspects of the racially segregated school district while rescinding court control over aspects of the school system where full compliance with the desegregation principle had been met. The concurring opinions, however, demonstrate that it is possible to put various types of spin on this opinion, either by viewing it as an opinion that endorses the termination of remedial orders at as early a date as possible consistent with the Supreme Court's desegregation rulings or whether it is an opinion that endorses the concept that a federal court should not terminate any aspects of remedial orders until the court is sure that the school district had eliminated all effects of its past discrimination from the educational policies that might be at issue. Compare id. 503 U.S. at 500, 112 S.Ct. at 1450 (Scalia, J., concurring) and 503 U.S. at 507, 112 S.Ct. at 1454 (Souter, J., concurring), with 503 U.S. at 509, 112 S.Ct. at 1455 (Blackmun, J., joined by Stevens and O'Connor, JJ., concurring in the judgment).

portant, limit on federal court remedial powers arose in *Milliken v. Bradley.*[130] A majority in that case prohibited district courts from fashioning remedies that included more than one school district absent any finding that the other included school districts have failed to operate unitary, integrated school systems or that the boundary lines of the affected school districts were established with the purpose of fostering racial segregation.

The Supreme Court followed these previously agreed upon principles in two unanimous decisions on school desegregation orders. In *Milliken v. Bradley (Milliken II),*[131] the Court held that a federal district court could order the State of Michigan to pay a share of the cost of compensatory and remedial educational programs. These programs were found necessary to correct the effects of past de jure discrimination in the establishment and maintenance of the Detroit school system for which the State had some responsibility. The order violated neither the Tenth nor Eleventh Amendments since the order required prospective compliance with the requirements of the Fourteenth Amendment.

In the second case, the Court remanded for reconsideration and clarification, a case wherein a district judge had ordered a wide ranging student transfer plan for a seemingly minor occurrence of segregation in a school district. In *Dayton Bd. of Education v. Brinkman,*[132] the Court unanimously held that, if the evidence in the record supported a finding of segregation throughout the school system, the judge might be able to order system-wide busing if it did not impair educational interests. If the segregation in fact occurred only in a part of

the system, the remedy must be limited to that area.

Following the remand of the *Dayton* case, the district court found that there was a violation of the Constitution as to only a limited number of schools in the district, but the court of appeals reversed and found that the proof of purposeful discrimination as to a selected group of schools gave rise to an inference of area wide discrimination and that the school board had failed to meet its burden of showing that it had not engaged in area wide discrimination.

The Supreme Court upheld the court of appeals and found clear proof that the Dayton school board had intentionally discriminated against black students and operated segregated schools in 1954, that the board had never taken any action to dismantle its dual school system, and that the board had simply refused to attempt to integrate the school system which had been admittedly segregated in the past.[133] The clear establishment of a continuing violation as to a few schools gave rise to an inference of area wide discrimination, and the school board was unable to demonstrate that the inference was unjustified; it did not show that its policies had been clearly designed to achieve important educational goals rather than to maintain the segregated school system.[134]

Court Orders Requiring the Enactment of Legislation to Implement a Desegregation Decree. After a federal court has found that a school district has engaged in unconstitutional racial segregation, and that it has

---

130. 418 U.S. 717, 94 S.Ct. 3112, 41 L.Ed.2d 1069 (1974), discussed in text at n. 49, supra.

131. 433 U.S. 267, 97 S.Ct. 2749, 53 L.Ed.2d 745 (1977).

132. 433 U.S. 406, 97 S.Ct. 2766, 53 L.Ed.2d 851 (1977).

133. Dayton Bd. of Education v. Brinkman, 443 U.S. 526, 99 S.Ct. 2971, 61 L.Ed.2d 720 (1979).

134. The Supreme Court has avoided ruling on the details of desegregation plans adopted by lower federal courts since the 1979 Ohio cases. See, e.g., Delaware State Bd. of Education v. Evans, 447 U.S. 916, 100 S.Ct. 3004, 64 L.Ed.2d 865 (1980) (Rehnquist, Stewart, and Powell, JJ., dissenting to denial of certiorari).

The Supreme Court declined to review a case where a district court order to remedy school segregation involved student reassignment beyond the boundaries of an individual city. However, in this case the lower courts had found evidence of purposeful segregation in the establishment of attendance zones within a system that included a variety of municipalities. Cleveland Bd. of Education v. Reed, 445 U.S. 935, 100 S.Ct. 1329, 63 L.Ed.2d 770 (1980), (Rehnquist, J., joined by Burger, C.J., and Powell, J., dissenting to denial of certiorari) on remand 500 F.Supp. 404 (N.D.Ohio 1980), judgment affirmed 662 F.2d 1219 (6th Cir.1981), certiorari denied 455 U.S. 1018, 102 S.Ct. 1713, 72 L.Ed.2d 135 (1982).

failed to remedy that segregation, the court will issue an order directing the school district to take appropriate actions to end the segregation in the school system and to eliminate the effects of the unconstitutional segregation. The Supreme Court has approved lower court orders requiring cities and school districts to provide appropriate educational resources to school systems, and to individual schools, in order to end the effects of unconstitutional racial discrimination.[135] The state government, as well as a city or school district, will be required to provide resources for the implementation of a school desegregation decree, if the federal court finds that the state government bears responsibility, in whole or in part, for the creation or maintenance of the racially segregated school system.[136]

If a unit of local government, such as a city, refuses to implement the federal district court's desegregation decree, the district court may hold the city in contempt of court, and

impose monetary fines on the city.[137] If a local government asserts that it lacks the monetary resources to comply with the remedial order, the federal district court may order local taxing authorities to provide the financial resources for implementation of the desegregation decree. However, a federal district court should not itself order an increase in local or state taxes. The district court should, instead, order the appropriate taxing body (most commonly a city or a school district) to increase its tax levy in a manner sufficient to fund the actions required by the remedial order. If state statutes prevent a local taxing district from increasing its tax levy in the manner required to fund the remedial order, the district court may enjoin the state from enforcing its statutes. Such court action is necessary to ensure that the local school district will comply with the command of the Fourteenth Amendment to remedy the effects of its prior unconstitutional racial discrimination.[138]

135. For example, in Swann v. Charlotte–Mecklenburg Board of Education, 402 U.S. 1, 18, 91 S.Ct. 1267, 1277, 28 L.Ed.2d 554 (1971), examined previously in this section, the Supreme Court approved lower court orders requiring a school district to distribute personnel, equipment, and financial support for extra-curricular activities programs at individual schools so as to eliminate the effects of the unconstitutional racial discrimination.

136. See, e.g., Milliken v. Bradley (Milliken II), 433 U.S. 267, 97 S.Ct. 2749, 53 L.Ed.2d 745 (1977) (State of Michigan required to pay a share of cost for remedying racial discrimination in the Detroit school system, due to state responsibility regarding the creation and maintenance of de jure racial discrimination); Missouri v. Jenkins, 495 U.S. 33, 110 S.Ct. 1651, 109 L.Ed.2d 31 (1990) (federal district court order requiring both a city and state to provide funds for the implementation of a desegregation remedy which included improvements in the quality of curriculum, library and other resources for several schools in the district was upheld; the district court should not increase local school district taxes to fund the remedial order but it could order the school board to raise the tax rate in a manner appropriate to funding the steps required to remedy the de jure segregation).

137. In Spallone v. United States, 493 U.S. 265, 110 S.Ct. 625, 107 L.Ed.2d 644 (1990), the Supreme Court overturned a district court order that held members of a city council in contempt of court. *Spallone* involved the aftermath of a suit that had been brought against the City of Yonkers, New York in which it was alleged that the city was liable for intentionally enhancing and promoting residential segregation in violation of civil rights statutes and the equal protection clause of the Fourteenth Amendment. The city had entered into a consent decree to settle that lawsuit. The consent decree required the city to adopt an "affordable housing ordinance" that would regulate the

construction of multi-family housing so as to include a specified number or percentage of subsidized housing units in new multi-family housing developments. Although the city had approved the consent decree, the city council, by a four to three vote of the council members, failed to enact the required ordinance. The district court then held both the city and individual council persons in contempt for failure to comply with the consent decree; the district court would have imposed monetary fines on both the city itself and the city council persons. The Supreme Court found that the district court order was improper insofar as it imposed contempt of court sanctions against individual council members for the failure to vote in favor of the ordinance. This ruling was based on equitable considerations; the Supreme Court did not rule that the Constitution prevented such orders in all cases.

138. In Missouri v. Jenkins, 495 U.S. 33, 110 S.Ct. 1651, 109 L.Ed.2d 31 (1990), the Supreme Court, by a five to four vote of the Justices, held that a district court should not have issued an order directly increasing the tax rate for a local school district in order to fund a remedial order in a desegregation case. The majority opinion stated that the district court could issue an order to the local taxing body (in this case, the local school district) requiring it to increase the tax rate in an amount necessary to fund the remedial order. Justice White, writing for a majority of the Court, in *Jenkins,* held that the district court order was improper insofar as it had directly raised the tax levy for the local school district. However, the majority found that the district court "could have authorized or required KCMSD [the Kansas City, Missouri School District] to levy property taxes at a rate adequate to fund the desegregation remedy and could have enjoined the operation of state laws that would have prevented KCMSD from exercising this power." 495 U.S. at 51, 110 S.Ct. at 1663. The majority found that an order to the

It is important to keep in mind that the underlying issue in cases wherein the district court has ordered the enactment of legislation (including tax increases) is whether the initial remedial order issued by the district court was proper. If the initial district court order was narrowly tailored to correct prior unconstitutional racial segregation (in accordance with the principles established by the Supreme Court) then the district court has the power to force the city and state governments to provide the resources to implement its desegregation order.

Federal courts have broad authority to fashion remedies for the correction of de jure racial segregation in a school system. Nevertheless, a federal court may not issue orders that are designed to affect more than one school district, if there was no finding that multiple school districts were involved in the unconstitutional racial segregation. These points were reaffirmed by the Supreme Court's 1995 ruling in *Missouri v. Jenkins*,[139] when the Court reviewed the continuing efforts of the United States District Court to implement remedial orders designed to integrate the Kansas City, Missouri schools. In litigation that spanned almost 20 years, the District Courts had fashioned a variety of remedies to attempt to remove the effects of de jure racial segregation in the Kansas City schools.[140] During the years that had passed since the start of the *Jenkins* litigation, many white families had left the school district; it was becoming increasingly difficult for the federal courts to fashion remedies aimed solely at Kansas City that would create a racially integrated city school system in that city.

In its 1995 decision, the Supreme Court ruled that the District Court exceeded its authority when it issued two orders. These orders had been issued by the District Court to increase the quality of the Kansas City schools in order to influence majority race school children in neighboring school districts to transfer into the Kansas City schools. The first order required the government to increase the salaries of most of the teaching and non-instructional staff of the school district. The second order required the government to fund "quality education" programs on a continuing basis.

By a five to four vote, the Justices in *Jenkins* ruled that the two District Court's orders were invalid because the orders constituted an inter-district remedy, which was not tailored to correct the de jure segregation that had existed in the Kansas City schools. In the original litigation, the lower federal courts had only found that the Kansas City School District had engaged in de jure racial segregation. The District Court found that any of the neighboring school districts were involved in this violation of the Fourteenth Amendment. Therefore, the court orders in the case had to be tailored eliminating the vestiges of prior de jure segregation within the Kansas City School District. The Supreme Court, in an opinion by Chief Justice Rehnquist, found that the two orders contested in this case were adopted to implement an inter-district goal (influencing white students to leave other school districts and enter the Kansas City school system) and could not be justified as being tailored to correction of the intra-district violation that had been identified in this litigation.[141]

school district to raise taxes involved less intrusion into local government than a court order setting a new tax rate. The majority found that there was no constitutional barrier to a judicial order requiring a unit of local government to increase a local property tax in order to fund a narrowly tailored remedy for a Fourteenth Amendment violation.

Justice Kennedy, joined by Chief Justice Rehnquist and Justices O'Connor and Scalia, concurred in the judgment in *Jenkins* insofar as the Court overturned the district court order that directly increased the tax rate. These four Justices, however, challenged the majority opinion insofar as it permitted a federal court to order a state or local government to increase tax rates. These Justices viewed the majority opinion's description of the powers of

the federal judiciary as "broad dictum" that resulted in an unjustified "expansion of power in the federal judiciary." 495 U.S. at 58, 110 S.Ct. at 1667 (Kennedy, J., joined by Rehnquist, C.J., and O'Connor and Scalia, JJ., concurring in part and concurring in the judgment).

139. 515 U.S. 70, 115 S.Ct. 2038, 132 L.Ed.2d 63 (1995).

140. The United States Supreme Court, in 1990, had examined other orders of the District Court in this litigation. See note 138, supra.

141. Missouri v. Jenkins, 515 U.S. 70, 91, 115 S.Ct. 2038, 2051, 132 L.Ed.2d 63 (1995). This case was decided by a five to four vote of the Justices. Chief Justice Rehnquist wrote a majority opinion for Justices Scalia, O'Con-

(b) Desegregation of Other Facilities

Although the Supreme Court delayed implementation of public school desegregation, it did order an immediate end to state-imposed racial segregation in other public facilities. In the decade following *Brown I*, primarily in a series of per curiam decisions, the Court invalidated the segregation of public beaches and bathhouses,[142] golf courses,[143] buses,[144] parks,[145] athletic contests,[146] public restaurants,[147] auditoriums,[148] and courtroom seating.[149] The lower courts followed suit[150] so that where racial segregation was found in contexts other than public education, immediate relief was ordered so long as state action was found. However, many of the public facilities that excluded or segregated blacks were privately owned and, therefore, not subject to the restrictions of the equal protection clause.

Further desegregation of public facilities was required after the enactment of the Civil Rights Act of 1964, which prohibits racial discrimination in "establishments affecting interstate commerce or supported in their activities by State action as places of public accommoda-

tion, lodgings, facilities principally engaged in selling food for consumption on the premises, gasoline stations [and] places of exhibition or entertainments."[151] The Act was upheld by the Court as an exercise of congressional power to regulate interstate commerce.[152] Similarly, the Court has upheld and applied statutes passed pursuant to the Congressional power under the Thirteenth Amendment to eliminate racial discrimination in property sales and business contracts.[153]

The closing of public facilities and the reopening of privately-owned facilities in their stead has also occurred in other contexts besides schools as in the *Griffin v. Prince Edward County Board of Education* case discussed above. In *Palmer v. Thompson* [154] the Court faced the issue of the constitutionality of shutting down city pools allegedly in response to a court decree that pools could not be racially segregated. The Court affirmed the lower court's decision that closing the pools did not violate the equal protection clause. The city was under no affirmative duty to operate any swimming pools. Although one pool previous-

nor, Kennedy, and Thomas. Justices Stevens, Souter, Ginsburg, and Breyer dissented. Justice O'Connor and Justice Thomas both joined the majority opinion and filed concurring opinions. 515 U.S. at 102, 115 S.Ct. at 2056 (O'Connor, J., concurring); 515 U.S. at 112, 115 S.Ct. at 2061 (Thomas, J., concurring). The four dissenting Justices believed that the Court had decided the inter-district remedy question unnecessarily, because that question had not been clearly presented in the petition for certiorari and had not been fully briefed. The dissenters also believed that the ruling in the current *Jenkins* case was inconsistent with the Court's prior decisions concerning single-district and inter-district remedies. 515 U.S. at 137, 115 S.Ct. at 2073 (Souter, J., joined by Stevens, Ginsburg, and Breyer, JJ., dissenting); 515 U.S. at 175, 115 S.Ct. at 2091 (Ginsburg, J., dissenting).

142. Mayor of Baltimore City v. Dawson, 350 U.S. 877, 76 S.Ct. 133, 100 L.Ed. 774 (1955) (per curiam).

143. Holmes v. City of Atlanta, 350 U.S. 879, 76 S.Ct. 141, 100 L.Ed. 776 (1955) (per curiam). New Orleans City Park Improvement Ass'n v. Detiege, 358 U.S. 54, 79 S.Ct. 99, 3 L.Ed.2d 46 (1958) (per curiam).

144. Gayle v. Browder, 352 U.S. 903, 77 S.Ct. 145, 1 L.Ed.2d 114 (1956) (per curiam).

145. Muir v. Louisville Park Theatrical Ass'n, 347 U.S. 971, 74 S.Ct. 783, 98 L.Ed. 1112 (1954) (per curiam); New Orleans City Park Improvement Ass'n v. Detiege, 358 U.S. 54, 79 S.Ct. 99, 3 L.Ed.2d 46 (1958) (per curiam).

146. State Athletic Com'n v. Dorsey, 359 U.S. 533, 79 S.Ct. 1137, 3 L.Ed.2d 1028 (1959) (per curiam).

147. Turner v. City of Memphis, 369 U.S. 350, 82 S.Ct. 805, 7 L.Ed.2d 762 (1962).

148. Schiro v. Bynum, 375 U.S. 395, 84 S.Ct. 452, 11 L.Ed.2d 412 (1964) (per curiam).

149. Johnson v. Virginia, 373 U.S. 61, 83 S.Ct. 1053, 10 L.Ed.2d 195 (1963).

150. D. Bell, Race, Racism and American Law, 208–15 (1st ed. 1973); see also D. Bell, Race, Racism and American Law Ch. 3, (2d ed. 1980).

151. 42 U.S.C.A. § 2000a(b).

152. Heart of Atlanta Motel, Inc. v. United States, 379 U.S. 241, 85 S.Ct. 348, 13 L.Ed.2d 258 (1964); Katzenbach v. McClung, 379 U.S. 294, 85 S.Ct. 377, 13 L.Ed.2d 290 (1964).

153. Runyon v. McCrary, 427 U.S. 160, 96 S.Ct. 2586, 49 L.Ed.2d 415 (1976), appeal after remand 569 F.2d 1294 (4th Cir.1978), certiorari denied 439 U.S. 927, 99 S.Ct. 311, 58 L.Ed.2d 320 (1978); Jones v. Alfred H. Mayer Co., 392 U.S. 409, 88 S.Ct. 2186, 20 L.Ed.2d 1189 (1968). The societal interest in ending racial or gender discrimination is sufficiently important to allow the state to curtail the associational interests of persons who wish to discriminate on such basis in public economic associations. See generally, Roberts v. United States Jaycees, 468 U.S. 609, 104 S.Ct. 3244, 82 L.Ed.2d 462 (1984); Hishon v. King & Spalding, 467 U.S. 69, 104 S.Ct. 2229, 81 L.Ed.2d 59 (1984).

154. 403 U.S. 217, 91 S.Ct. 1940, 29 L.Ed.2d 438 (1971).

ly leased from the YMCA by the city apparently was being run by that organization for whites only and another pool previously owned by the city was owned and operated by a predominantly black college, there was no evidence to show the city was directly or indirectly involved in the funding or operation of either pool. The majority would not examine the motivation of the legislators.[155] The dissenting Justices in *Palmer*, disagreed with the assertion that it was impermissible to find invidious purpose on the evidence in the case. The closing came only after a desegregation order and the dissent believed the ruling came dangerously close to allowing a town to evade the mandate of the Fourteenth Amendment.[156]

Interdistrict relief problems have also arisen apart from school integration. In *Hills v. Gautreaux*[157] the question before the Court was the appropriateness of interdistrict relief in the context of public housing. The Court distinguished this case from *Milliken v. Bradley*[158] and held that district court should have considered the possibility of ordering a metropolitan area remedy.

In 1969 summary judgment was entered against the Chicago Housing Authority (CHA) on the basis of uncontradicted evidence showing that it had selected public housing sites and had made tenant assignments on the basis of race. CHA was accordingly directed to locate its new family public housing in predominantly white neighborhoods. Summary judgment was also entered against the U.S. Department of Housing and Urban Development (HUD) for its violation of the Fifth Amendment and Civil Rights Act of 1964 by assisting the CHA discriminatory actions. In formulating a remedy, the district court reject-

ed a plan for metropolitan relief, finding that there had been no proof of separate racially discriminatory acts in the suburbs of Chicago into which the public housing might be placed.[159] The United States Court of Appeals for the Seventh Circuit reversed and remanded the case for the adoption of a "comprehensive area plan."[160]

The Supreme Court rejected HUD's contentions that *Milliken* barred the adoption of a metropolitan area plan and found that the district court had the authority to order remedial action by HUD outside the city limits. HUD, unlike the suburban school districts in *Milliken*, had been found to have violated the Constitution, thereby providing the necessary predicate for the entry of a remedial order against HUD.[161] Following the finding of a constitutional violation, the district court has broad authority to provide for an effective remedy. Nothing in *Milliken* suggested the federal courts lack the authority to order parties guilty of unconstitutional behavior to undertake remedial efforts beyond the boundaries of the city where the violation occurred. Rather, they lacked the authority to interfere with the operations of governmental units that had not been implicated in any wrongdoing.

The Court then turned to the contention that the order would impermissibly interfere with local governments and suburban housing authorities by requiring HUD to "ignore the safeguards of local autonomy and local political processes."[162] The Court found that no such interference would result from the remedy in this situation. In contrast to the *Milliken* desegregation order, a metropolitan relief order would not consolidate or restructure lo-

---

155. On the problem of establishing classifications which do not openly appear in government acts and the question of legislative purpose see § 14.4, supra.

156. 403 U.S. at 231, 91 S.Ct. at 1948 (Douglas, J., dissenting); 403 U.S. at 240, 91 S.Ct. at 1952 (White, J., dissenting); 403 U.S. at 271, 91 S.Ct. at 1968 (Marshall J., dissenting). Justice Brennan joined in the dissent of Justices White and Marshall.

157. 425 U.S. 284, 96 S.Ct. 1538, 47 L.Ed.2d 792 (1976).

158. 418 U.S. 717, 94 S.Ct. 3112, 41 L.Ed.2d 1069 (1974). The distinction between the cases is also considered in § 12.4(d), supra.

159. Gautreaux v. Romney, 363 F.Supp. 690 (N.D.Ill. 1973), judgment reversed 503 F.2d 930 (7th Cir.1974).

160. Gautreaux v. Chicago Housing Authority, 503 F.2d 930 (7th Cir.1974) (opinion per Clark, J.), judgment affirmed 425 U.S. 284, 96 S.Ct. 1538, 47 L.Ed.2d 792 (1976).

161. Hills v. Gautreaux, 425 U.S. 284, 297–300, 96 S.Ct. 1538, 1546–48, 47 L.Ed.2d 792 (1976).

162. 425 U.S. at 300, 96 S.Ct. at 1548.

cal political units; the decree would have the same effect as a discretionary decision by HUD to offer alternatives to the segregated Chicago public housing system created by CHA and HUD. The case was therefore remanded to the district court for further consideration of the appropriateness of metropolitan area relief in the specific case.

§ 14.10 Benign Racial Classifications— Affirmative Action Programs

(a) Overview

(1) Introduction. In the previous sections of this chapter we saw that the Supreme Court had held that racial classifications that discriminate against racial minorities are inherently "suspect" and subject to "strict scrutiny". Such a classification will be upheld only if it is necessary to promote a "compelling" interest.[1] In 1989, a majority of Supreme Court Justices found that a racial classification used by the government for "affirmative action" purposes (a classification designed to aid members of racial minorities) should also be subject to strict judicial scrutiny and invalidated unless it is narrowly tailored to promote a compelling governmental interest.[2]

In 1995, the Supreme Court ruled that any federal law that created a racial classification, regardless of whether the classification benefitted or burdened minority race persons, would be subjected to strict judicial scrutiny, and would not be upheld unless the government could demonstrate that the racial classification was necessary to promote a compelling interest.[3]

Federal law may not shield a racial classification in a state law from strict judicial scrutiny. In *Shaw v. Reno*[4] the Supreme Court found that state legislation establishing two districts for the election of representatives to the United States House of Representatives in which minority race persons would constitute a majority of the voters involved racial discrimination on its face. These two districts had been created by the state legislature after the United States Attorney General had objected to an earlier districting map, on the basis of the federal Voting Rights Act, because the state's earlier map would have allowed minority race voters to control the outcome of only one congressional election. The Supreme Court ruled that the second map, which virtually guaranteed the election of two minority race representatives, was a racial classification that must be subjected to the compelling interest test.[5] However, the Supreme Court in *Shaw* did not rule on the constitutionality of the districting map because the lower courts had not examined the question of whether the districts could be justified as being narrowly tailored to promote a compelling interest.[6]

In *Richmond v. J.A. Croson Co.,*[7] the Court invalidated a city's plan for increasing the number of minority owned businesses who were awarded city construction contracts. In *J.A. Croson*, Justice O'Connor wrote an opinion that was in part a majority opinion and in part a plurality opinion. When Justice O'Connor's opinion, which was joined in all parts by Chief Justice Rehnquist and Justice White, is read together with the concurring opinions of

---

§ 14.10

1. See § 14.8(d). See generally, John E. Nowak, The Rise and Fall of Supreme Court Concern for Racial Minorities, 36 William & Mary L.Rev. 345 (1995).

2. Richmond v. J.A. Croson Co., 488 U.S. 469, 109 S.Ct. 706, 102 L.Ed.2d 854 (1989).

3. Adarand Constructors, Inc. v. Pena, 515 U.S. 200, 115 S.Ct. 2097, 132 L.Ed.2d 158 (1995), overruling Metro Broadcasting, Inc. v. Federal Communications Commission, 497 U.S. 547, 110 S.Ct. 2997, 111 L.Ed.2d 445 (1990), rehearing denied 497 U.S. 1050, 111 S.Ct. 15, 111 L.Ed.2d 829 (1990).

See also, Boudin, Circuit J., citing Treatise in Raso v. Lago, 135 F.3d 11 (1st Cir.1998).

4. 509 U.S. 630, 113 S.Ct. 2816, 125 L.Ed.2d 511 (1993).

5. For an examination of the *Shaw* finding that the map included racial discrimination "on its face", so that the persons attacking the map did not have to prove that it was based on a racially discriminatory purpose, see §§ 14.3, 14.8.

6. We will defer consideration of the asserted compelling interests in *Shaw* until § 14.10(c), after we have examined the Court's earlier opinions as to the types of interests that might support benign racial classifications.

7. 488 U.S. 469, 109 S.Ct. 706, 102 L.Ed.2d 854 (1989).

Justices Kennedy[8] and Scalia,[9] a majority of Justices found that the strict scrutiny-compelling interest test should be applied to affirmative action classifications based on race.

While it is clear that a majority of Justices will use the strict scrutiny-compelling interest test in state and local government racial affirmative action cases, the meaning of that test is not entirely clear. In the *J.A. Croson* case, the Court examined a Richmond ordinance that created a plan for awarding city funded construction contracts. As a part of that plan, 30% of the dollar amount of each city funded construction contract had to be awarded by the prime contractor to subcontractor businesses that were owned by members of racial minorities. Richmond alleged that this plan was remedial in nature, because a very low percentage of construction related businesses in the Richmond area and in the nation are owned by minority race persons. A majority of the Justices found that correcting "societal discrimination" was not a compelling interest that would justify the use of a racial classification.[10] If a state or local government attempts to defend its use of a racial classification on the basis that the classification is "remedial", the governmental entity must be able to show that the racial classification is narrowly tailored to correct past discrimination by the governmental entity itself or by private sector entities within its jurisdiction.

Fourteen years after *J.A.Croson*, Justice O'Connor would write a majority opinion finding that, at least in some contexts, the creation of a racially diverse student body in institutions of higher education (post-secondary education) would be a compelling interest and that race-conscious admissions policies that were narrowly tailored to that interest would be upheld.[11]

Federal Laws. Between 1990 and 1995, the Supreme Court allowed lower courts to review federal laws that employed benign racial classifications with less than strict judicial scrutiny. In 1995 the Court ruled that any federal racial classification would violate the implied equal protection of the Fifth Amendment due process clause unless the government could demonstrate that the classification was necessary to promote a compelling interest.

In *Metro Broadcasting, Inc. v. Federal Communications Commission*[12] the Supreme Court, by a five to four vote, held that a federal statute that used race in a benign, affirmative action classification, or a regulation of a federal agency that used a racial affirmative action policy that was mandated by Congress, would be upheld as long as the racial affirmative action classification had a substantial relationship to an important interest that was within the powers of Congress.

The Court upheld two minority preference policies used by the Federal Communications Commission in *Metro Broadcasting*. The Court ruled that the equal protection component of the Fifth Amendment due process clause did not require strict scrutiny of either of the FCC policies. The majority opinion, written by

---

8. 488 U.S. at 518, 109 S.Ct. at 734 (Kennedy, J., concurring in part and concurring in the judgment).

9. 488 U.S. at 520, 109 S.Ct. at 735 (Scalia, J., concurring in the judgment). Justice Stevens concurred without endorsing the use of any formal test or standard of review. Richmond v. J.A. Croson Co., 488 U.S. 469, 511, 109 S.Ct. 706, 730, 102 L.Ed.2d 854 (1989) (Stevens, J., concurring in part and concurring in the judgment). The dissent recognized that "Today, for the first time, a majority of this Court has adopted strict scrutiny as its standard of Equal Protection Clause review of race-conscious remedial measures." 488 U.S. at 552, 109 S.Ct. at 752 (Marshall, J., joined by Brennan and Blackmun, JJ., dissenting).

10. Justice O'Connor wrote for five Justices in Grutter v. Bollinger, 539 U.S. 306, 123 S.Ct. 2325, 156 L.Ed.2d 304 (2003) in upholding the race conscious admissions policy of the University of Michigan Law School by finding that the admissions policy of the law school was narrowly tailored

to a compelling interest in creating a racially diverse student body in the law school. Justice O'Connor joined the majority opinion in Gratz v. Bollinger, 539 U.S. 244, 123 S.Ct. 2411 (2003), which invalidated the University of Michigan's admissions policy for undergraduate students, because she agreed with the other Justices in the *Gratz* majority that the undergraduate admissions system was not tailored to the compelling interest in creating a racially diverse student body. These cases are discussed, infra, in § 14.10(b)(2).

11. Richmond v. J.A. Croson Co., 488 U.S. 469, 498–507, 109 S.Ct. 706, 723–28, 102 L.Ed.2d 854 (1989) (this portion of Justice O'Connor's opinion is a majority opinion, which is joined by Chief Justice Rehnquist and Justices Kennedy, Stevens, and White).

12. 497 U.S. 547, 110 S.Ct. 2997, 111 L.Ed.2d 445 (1990).

Justice Brennan, found that both FCC policies had a substantial relationship to the legitimate federal interest in promoting diversity in entertainment and news programming.

In 1995, the *Metro Broadcasting* decision was overruled, when Justice Thomas joined the four Justices who had dissented in *Metro Broadcasting*. In *Adarand Constructors, Inc. v. Pena*,[13] the Court, by a five to four vote, ruled that the implied equal protection guarantee of the Fifth Amendment due process clause established standards for federal racial classifications that were identical to the standards of review imposed on state classifications by the equal protection clause of the Fourteenth Amendment. The *Adarand* majority found that neither state nor federal racial classifications should be upheld unless they were narrowly tailored to promote a compelling interest. However, Justice O'Connor's majority opinion in *Adarand* stated that the Court's use of strict scrutiny in racial affirmative action cases did not eliminate the possibility that a state or federal racial affirmative action program might be upheld in a future case.[14]

Quota Issues. In judging the constitutionality of affirmative action programs, a distinction must be drawn between two basic forms of affirmative action. A quota may be set reserving a specific number of places for minority members and a specific number for nonminority members. Alternatively, separate standards may be set giving preferential treatment to minority members without the use of a quota.

Quota programs are difficult, if not impossible, to defend. When the government distributes benefits under a strict quota system, it totally disregards individual circumstances and also burdens members of minority races. For example, if a government housing project consists of 100 units to be assigned 50% to white families and 50% to black families, the fifty-first black family to apply will be denied housing because of its race even if there are housing units available. This system disregards both the need for benefits and the availability of government benefits. The fact that the program burdens both white and black persons should be irrelevant given past decisions of the Supreme Court.[15] Nonetheless in the 1970s lower federal courts upheld such a system on the basis that the quotas prevented "white flight" and maintained integrated public housing.[16] Yet a majority race member's dislike of living near a large number of minority persons hardly seems to be a sufficient reason for refusing to extend benefits to a black person. Indeed, this use of the quota system stands integration on its head; it becomes a tool for limiting the rights of minorities by accepting the bias of members of the majority race.[17]

---

13. 515 U.S. 200, 115 S.Ct. 2097, 132 L.Ed.2d 158 (1995), overruling Metro Broadcasting, Inc. v. Federal Communications Commission, 497 U.S. 547, 110 S.Ct. 2997, 111 L.Ed.2d 445 (1990), rehearing denied 497 U.S. 1050, 111 S.Ct. 15, 111 L.Ed.2d 829 (1990).

14. Justice O'Connor announced the judgment of the Court in Adarand Constructors, Inc. v. Pena, 515 U.S. 200, 115 S.Ct. 2097, 132 L.Ed.2d 158 (1995) in an opinion that was, in part, a majority opinion and, in part, a plurality opinion. Only Justice Kennedy joined Part III–C of the opinion in which Justice O'Connor explained the reasons why the concept of stare decisis should not prevent the court from overruling the *Metro Broadcasting* decision. Her opinion was a majority opinion insofar as it overruled *Metro Broadcasting* and established the strict scrutiny (compelling interest) test as the proper standard to be used for federal racial affirmative action laws. In part III–D of her opinion, which was written for a majority of the Justices, Justice O'Connor stated that "we wish to dispel the notion that strict scrutiny is strict in theory, but fatal in fact." 515 U.S. at 235, 115 S.Ct. at 2117 (internal quotation marks and citation omitted). Justice Scalia and Justice Thomas wrote separately to explain their views

that it would be virtually impossible for the government to meet the compelling interest test and to use racial classifications. Id. at 237, 115 S.Ct. at 2118 (Scalia, J., concurring in part and concurring in the judgment); Id. at 239, 115 S.Ct. at 2119 (Thomas, J., concurring in part and concurring in the judgment). Perhaps, in a future case, Justice O'Connor will join the *Adarand* dissenters and uphold a racial affirmative action program that (in her view) is narrowly tailored to a compelling interest.

15. Loving v. Virginia, 388 U.S. 1, 87 S.Ct. 1817, 18 L.Ed.2d 1010 (1967) (striking miscegenation statute though state argued it limited the marital rights of both black and white persons).

16. See, Otero v. New York City Housing Authority, 484 F.2d 1122 (2d Cir.1973).

17. The Supreme Court's decision in Cooper v. Aaron, 358 U.S. 1, 78 S.Ct. 1401, 3 L.Ed.2d 5 (1958) held that violent reaction of white persons could not justify a delay in integrating schools. Indeed, Plessy v. Ferguson, 163 U.S. 537, 16 S.Ct. 1138, 41 L.Ed. 256 (1896) was based in part on the belief that white persons would react violently if they had to ride a train with blacks and that the state

In *Richmond v. J.A. Croson Company*,[18] a majority of Justices found that a state or local government's affirmative or benign use of race had to be subject to strict judicial scrutiny and justified by a compelling government interest. A true "quota system", under which the government allocates welfare benefits, such as housing units, on racial criteria for no purpose other than to achieve a racial mix in the recipient population would be difficult to justify under the strict scrutiny approach. In order to justify the use of a racial quota, a court would have to find that the goal of integration, even in the absence of proof of prior discrimination, was so compelling as to justify denying benefits to some people (including some minority race persons) solely because of their race.

It is doubtful that even a federal law establishing an affirmative action racial classification would be upheld if the law used a racial quota system, which fixed the share of benefits that would be allocated to different groups of persons by race. *Metro Broadcasting, Inc. v. Federal Communications Commission*[19] found that federal laws that employed a racial classification for affirmative action purposes should be upheld so long as the classification had a substantial relationship to an important interest within the authority of Congress. Any possibility that the Supreme Court would uphold a true quota system for awarding benefits to members of racial minorities was ended by

Adarand Constructors, Inc. v. Pena,[20] which overruled *Metro Broadcasting*. The Court in *Adarand* ruled a federal racial classification would not be upheld unless the classification was narrowly tailored to promote a compelling interest, regardless of whether the federal law benefitted or burdened minority race persons. No fixed quota system should be able to survive a compelling interest test.

When a program gives members of minority races preferential treatment, such as guaranteeing them a minimum (but not fixed) share of benefits, the problem becomes more complex. Here the goals of racial equality for the minority and integration both seem to be effectively promoted by the affirmative action program. The issue is whether the use of a racial classification is prohibited because the Constitution prohibits limiting the opportunities of anyone on the basis of his race.

(2) Involuntary Affirmative Action—Remedying Proven Racial Discrimination.

The Supreme Court has ruled that the use of racial classifications by school authorities to implement the desegregation of an intentionally segregated school system is not only constitutionally permissible but mandated by the Fourteenth Amendment.[21] Similarly, in the field of employment, giving preference to qual-

---

could grant "separate but equal" facilities to blacks to avoid this. Since the rejection of *Plessy*, one is surprised to find a federal court raising "white flight" to a constitutional consideration. See also, United States v. Scotland Neck City Bd. of Education, 407 U.S. 484, 491, 92 S.Ct. 2214, 2218, 33 L.Ed.2d 75 (1972) (fear of white flight "cannot ... be accepted as a reason for achieving anything less than complete uprooting of the dual public school system.").

In other contexts the Supreme Court consistently has rejected majority racial prejudice as a justification for racial classifications. See, e.g., Palmore v. Sidoti, 466 U.S. 429, 104 S.Ct. 1879, 80 L.Ed.2d 421 (1984), appeal after remand 472 So.2d 843 (Fla.App.1985) (social prejudice against racially mixed couples cannot justify racial classification, which removes a child from the custody of its mother who is otherwise an appropriate person to be the child's guardian); Watson v. City of Memphis, 373 U.S. 526, 83 S.Ct. 1314, 10 L.Ed.2d 529 (1963) (community hostility to desegregation of city parks cannot justify delaying integration of parks and other recreational facilities); see also Wright v. Georgia, 373 U.S. 284, 83 S.Ct. 1240, 10 L.Ed.2d 349 (1963), mandate conformed 219 Ga.

125, 131 S.E.2d 851 (1963) (in holding that breach of the peace statute did not provide adequate notice to black persons playing basketball in a park that their conduct was prohibited, the Court found that the possibility of disorder could not justify exclusion of black persons from a public place they otherwise had a constitutional right to use; the Court based its ruling on the equal protection clause).

18. 488 U.S. 469, 109 S.Ct. 706, 102 L.Ed.2d 854 (1989).

19. 497 U.S. 547, 110 S.Ct. 2997, 111 L.Ed.2d 445 (1990).

20. 515 U.S. 200, 115 S.Ct. 2097, 132 L.Ed.2d 158 (1995), overruling Metro Broadcasting v. Federal Communications Commission, 497 U.S. 547, 110 S.Ct. 2997, 111 L.Ed.2d 445 (1990), rehearing denied 497 U.S. 1050, 111 S.Ct. 15, 111 L.Ed.2d 829 (1990).

21. See Swann v. Charlotte–Mecklenburg Bd. of Education, 402 U.S. 1, 91 S.Ct. 1267, 28 L.Ed.2d 554 (1971), rehearing denied 403 U.S. 912, 91 S.Ct. 2201, 29 L.Ed.2d 689 (1971); O'Neil, Racial Preference and Higher Education: The Larger Context, 60 Va.L.Rev. 917, 928 (1974).

ified minority employees to remedy past discriminatory practices has been judicially approved. While the Court has not upheld using minimum quotas for hiring new employees where past discrimination is found, it has upheld other remedial practices under the civil rights acts.[22]

The judiciary may issue decrees that use race-cognizant remedies to correct discrimination against members of a racial minority, if that prior discrimination has been proven in court. However, neither the judiciary nor any other governmental entity has an open-ended power to use racial classifications by merely asserting that its use of race is "remedial." The identification of the prior illegal or unconstitutional race discrimination only justifies a race-conscious remedial order that is narrowly tailored to correct the past discrimination.[23]

In a case that involved only statutory issues, *Local No. 93, International Association of Firefighters v. Cleveland,*[24] the Court held that § 706(g) of Title VII of the Civil Rights Act [25] did not preclude a federal court from entering a consent decree that required an employer to promote minority race employees in order to meet integration requirements established by the decree. In this case, a city had agreed to a consent decree with an organization of black and hispanic firefighters. The consent decree required the city's fire department to divide a

new set of promotions between minority and nonminority fire fighters. Because only ten minority members qualified under other criteria for promotion to fifty-two upper-level positions, the decree required that all ten would be promoted. Justice Brennan wrote for six members of the Court in finding that the provision of Title VII that appeared to place some limits on the remedial authority of a federal court in employment discrimination cases did not apply to consent decrees.[26] However, the majority opinion did not reach the question whether other provisions of the federal Civil Rights Acts would prevent a court from enforcing the consent decree if the decree established a mandatory quota for the promotion of minority race members who had not been the victims of discrimination on the basis of race. Additionally, the Court did not reach the question of whether the equal protection component of the Fifth Amendment restricted the power of federal courts to enforce consent decrees establishing affirmative action hiring or promotion quotas.[27]

United Steelworkers of America v. Weber [28] held that voluntary affirmative action programs by private employers are permissible. The *Local No. 93, International Association of Firefighters* decision indicates that at least one provision of the Civil Rights Acts will not bar the use of consent decrees by public or private

---

22. In United Steelworkers of America v. Weber, 443 U.S. 193, 99 S.Ct. 2721, 61 L.Ed.2d 480 (1979), on remand 611 F.2d 132 (5th Cir.1980), the Court held that Title VII of the Civil Rights Acts did not prohibit the voluntary use of affirmative action programs by private employers.

For references to additional cases, and secondary authorities, on this point see the multi-volume edition of this Treatise: R. Rotunda & J. Nowak, Treatise on Constitutional Law: Substance and Procedure § 18.10 (3rd ed. 1999, with annual supplements).

23. The Supreme Court has not set clear standards for determining when, if ever, a state may use racial classifications in election laws that are designed to help increase minority race representation in legislative bodies. See § 18.10(b)(4) of this Treatise.

24. 478 U.S. 501, 106 S.Ct. 3063, 92 L.Ed.2d 405 (1986).

25. The statute at issue was § 706(g) of Title VII of the Civil Rights Act of 1964, as amended, 42 U.S.C.A. § 2000e–5(g).

26. The decision in this case did not resolve the question of what, if any, limits § 706(g) placed on the courts'

authority to create and enforce orders designed to remedy proven discrimination by employers or unions. 478 U.S. at 515 n. 7, 106 S.Ct. at 3072 n. 7. Procedural issues regarding employment discrimination lawsuits and consent decrees are beyond the scope of this Treatise. For citations to additional Supreme Court cases, and secondary authorities, on this point, see R. Rotunda & J. Nowak, Treatise on Constitutional Law: Substance and Procedure, vol. 3, § 18.10 (3rd ed. 1999, with annual supplements).

27. The majority opinion in *Local No. 93, International Association of Firefighters* concluded, "The only issue before us is whether § 706(g) barred the district court from approving this consent decree. We hold that it did not. Therefore, the judgment of the Court of Appeals is affirmed." In her concurring opinion Justice O'Connor clarified the issues left open by the decision. Local No. 93, International Association of Firefighters v. Cleveland, 478 U.S. 501, 530, 106 S.Ct. 3063, 3080, 92 L.Ed.2d 405 (1986) (O'Connor, J., concurring).

28. 443 U.S. 193, 99 S.Ct. 2721, 61 L.Ed.2d 480 (1979), on remand 611 F.2d 132 (5th Cir.1980) (discussed in this section).

employers,[29] however, the scope of federal court authority to enter and enforce consent decrees remains unclear.

A second 1986 decision of the Court involved both statutory and constitutional questions regarding the permissible scope of federal court remedies for proven acts of illegal racial discrimination. In *Local 28 of the Sheet Metal Workers' International Association v. E.E.O.C.,*[30] the Court examined an order of a federal district court, which had been approved by the court of appeals, that required a union to engage in various activities to remedy proven discrimination against nonwhite persons who had applied for union membership in the past. In upholding the decision of the lower federal courts, Justice Brennan announced the judgment of the Court in an opinion that was, in part, a majority opinion and, in part, a plurality opinion. Justice Brennan wrote for a majority of the Justices in finding that the lower courts properly decided that the union had engaged in racially discriminatory practices in violation of Title VII of the Civil Rights Act of 1964, that a fine against the union was a proper remedy for the union's failure to follow the remedial order, and that use of the money produced by the contempt fine to establish a fund to be used to increase nonwhite membership in the apprenticeship program of the union was permissible.[31]

Five Justices, in *Local 28 of the Sheet Metal Workers,* voted to uphold the portion of the district court's remedial order that established a 29% nonwhite membership goal for the union, although there was no majority opinion regarding the legality or constitutionality of this part of the remedial order. Brennan's

opinion for four members of the Court does not clearly indicate whether he considered the district court's order to establish a fixed minimum nonwhite membership quota for the union. The order could be considered as only setting a goal to remedy past discrimination—a goal that might be modified if circumstances indicated that the goal could not be reasonably achieved. The plurality opinion believed that federal statutes permitted a court order granting preferential hiring and promotion benefits to individuals who were not actual victims of racial discrimination if such an order was reasonably necessary to remedy serious violations of the federal statutes prohibiting racial discrimination in employment practices. Justice Brennan's plurality opinion also found that the judicial order did not violate the Fifth Amendment equal protection component because "the relief ordered in this case passes even the most rigorous test—it is narrowly tailored to further the Government's compelling interest in remedying past discrimination." [32]

Justice Powell concurred in only part of Justice Brennan's plurality opinion in *Local 28 of the Sheet Metal Workers.* He agreed that, under appropriate circumstances, the judiciary could require preferential hiring goals that would benefit persons who were not actual victims of discrimination by a union or employer.[33] Because the union charged with racial discrimination in this case had been the subject of state and federal attempts to remedying its racially discriminatory membership practices since 1964, Justice Powell found that this case involved the type of egregious violation of Title VII that established a basis for

---

29. Justices White and Rehnquist dissented from the Court's ruling that federal courts could enter the type of consent decree involved in this case. However, they differed in their interpretation of those Civil Rights Act provisions that arguably restricted federal court authority to enter consent decrees for violations of federal civil rights statutes. Compare Local No. 93, International Association of Firefighters v. Cleveland, 478 U.S. 501, 531, 106 S.Ct. 3063, 3081, 92 L.Ed.2d 405 (1986) (White, J., dissenting), with 478 U.S. at 535, 106 S.Ct. at 3082 (Rehnquist, J., joined by Burger, C.J., dissenting).

30. 478 U.S. 421, 106 S.Ct. 3019, 92 L.Ed.2d 344 (1986).

31. One portion of Justice Brennan's opinion that was joined by a majority of the Court was the final portion of his opinion, in which he summarized the votes of the Justices in this case that resulted in the Court's ruling. 478 U.S. at 482, 106 S.Ct. at 3054. We would recommend reading that summary of the case prior to reading the individual opinions of the Justices in *Local 28 of the Sheet Metal Workers.*

32. Local 28 of the Sheet Metal Workers' International Association v. E.E.O.C., 478 U.S. 421, 481, 106 S.Ct. 3019, 3053, 92 L.Ed.2d 344 (1986) (plurality opinion by Brennan, J., joined by Marshall, Blackmun, and Stevens, JJ.).

33. 478 U.S. at 483, 106 S.Ct. at 3054–57 (Powell, J., concurring in part and concurring in the judgment).

such an order. He found a compelling governmental interest in the elimination of these Civil Rights Act violations and he determined that the order in the individual case was narrowly tailored to promote that goal.

The dissenting opinions of Justices O'Connor and White in *Local 28 of the Sheet Metal Workers* were based in part on the belief that the membership goal used in the remedial order was, in fact, an attempt by the lower courts to establish an inflexible goal that required the union to admit into membership a minimum percentage of racial minority members.[34]

The statutory interpretation decisions of the Supreme Court statutory cases did not resolve the constitutional issues concerning government programs that give preferential treatment to members of a racial minority.[35] If a government entity is found to have discriminated against members of racial minorities in the past, a narrowly tailored court order to remedy that discrimination will be upheld. A majority of the Court found that federal civil rights statutes allow for "preferential" relief in employment discrimination cases that benefit minority race members who are not the actual victims of discrimination by a specific employer or union. Whether or not one considers the disestablishment of a racially discriminatory practice to be a form of "affirmative action," a narrowly tailored court order to achieve that goal should survive even the strict scrutiny test because it will be a narrowly tailored means of promoting the compelling government interest in the elimination of illegal or unconstitutional racial discrimination.

If a government entity is found to have engaged in purposeful discrimination against members of racial minorities, a Court may be required to adopt a remedy that seems quite similar to an affirmative action program. Such a remedy should be upheld if it is narrowly tailored to correct the prior de jure discrimination. For example, in the cases in which the Supreme Court has addressed the need to correct de jure segregation in public school systems, it has upheld lower court orders that have assigned teachers or students to schools, based upon the race of those teachers or students, in order to establish a desegregated school system.[36]

United States v. Paradise [37] upheld a district court order that set a numerical goal for the promotion of black troopers in a state police department. The government agency that was the focus of this decision was the Alabama Department of Public Safety; the first district court order finding systematic exclusion of blacks from employment or promotion in the Department had been issued in 1972. In 1983, the district court found that the selection and promotion procedures of the department continued to have an adverse impact on black persons, despite virtually continuous litigation and attempts at court monitoring of the hiring and promotion practices of the Department. The district court then entered an order that required the promotion of one black person for every white person promoted in the department (to a specific rank), if there were qualified black candidates for the position, if the rank to which the persons were being promoted had fewer than 25% black persons, and if the Department failed to provide the district court with an adequate alternative promotion plan. Although the district court order in *Paradise* was upheld by only a vote of five to four and there was no majority opinion for the Supreme Court, the Justices appeared

---

34. O'Connor and White dissented based upon a common belief that the membership quota was not a remedy authorized by Congress for Title VII violations, though they differed somewhat in their assessment of the scope of permissible Title VII relief. Compare, Local 28 of the Sheet Metal Workers' International Association v. E.E.O.C., 478 U.S. 421, 489, 106 S.Ct. 3019, 3057, 92 L.Ed.2d 344 (1986) (O'Connor, J., concurring in part and dissenting in part), with 478 U.S. at 499, 106 S.Ct. at 3062 (White, J., dissenting).

35. For references to additional cases, and secondary authorities, on this point see the multi-volume edition of

this Treatise: R. Rotunda & J. Nowak, Treatise on Constitutional Law: Substance and Procedure § 18.10 (3rd ed. 1999, with annual supplements).

36. The school desegregation cases are examined in § 14.9 of this Treatise.

37. 480 U.S. 149, 107 S.Ct. 1053, 94 L.Ed.2d 203 (1987) (judgment announced in a plurality opinion by Brennan, J., joined by Marshall, Blackmun, and Powell, JJ.).

to be unanimous in accepting the proposition that a narrowly tailored order to correct past governmental racial discrimination is not truly an affirmative action program or, in the alternative, that a judicial order of that type will be considered as necessary to promote a compelling or overriding government interest.

Justice Brennan announced the judgment of the Court in *Paradise* in a plurality opinion for four Justices.[38] Justice Brennan stated that the Court did not have to address the appropriate constitutional analysis for true affirmative action programs because "we conclude that the relief ordered survives even strict scrutiny analysis." According to the Brennan plurality, "the government unquestionably has a compelling interest in remedying past and present discrimination by a state actor." Justice Brennan found that the refusal of the Department to eliminate the effects of its past de jure discrimination against black persons, and its continuing use of hiring and promotion systems that disadvantaged black persons, justified the use of percentage goals for promotions in this case.[39]

Justice Stevens, who concurred only in the judgment in *Paradise,* not only accepted the position that remedying past government discrimination was a compelling interest but

found that the Supreme Court should not require that judicial remedies for proven de jure discrimination be necessary to achieve a compelling interest.[40] He found that Supreme Court's school desegregation cases established the principle that lower courts had a reasonable degree of flexibility in fashioning remedies for proven government discrimination.

The four dissenting Justices in *Paradise* did not challenge Justice Brennan's statement that the remedying of past government discrimination was a compelling interest that would justify a judicial order setting hiring or promotion goals in some cases. The dissenting Justices found that the use of a racial quota in this case was not demonstrably necessary to correct the past discrimination and that the district court should have considered alternatives to the use of hiring and promotion quotas.[41]

As the preceding cases demonstrate, a court may use or adopt a race-conscious remedy to correct illegal or unconstitutional racial discrimination that was proven in court. When the judiciary remedies past illegal or unconstitutional discrimination, the issue is whether the remedial action taken by the court, or adopted by the court through the approval of a consent decree,[42] is narrowly tailored to pro-

---

38. Id.

39. Although Justice Powell joined Justice Brennan's opinion, he also wrote separately to explain why he believed that the history of litigation in this case justified the numerical remedy for the proven racial discrimination in the state police force. 480 U.S. at 186, 107 S.Ct. at 1074 (Powell, J., concurring).

40. United States v. Paradise, 480 U.S. 149, 189, 107 S.Ct. 1053, 1076, 94 L.Ed.2d 203 (1987) (Stevens, J., concurring in the judgment).

41. Although she employed the compelling interest standard, Justice O'Connor, writing for three Justices in dissent in *Paradise,* did not find that lower courts were prohibited in all cases from using statistical quotas as a means of remedying past governmental discrimination. She stated:

"If a district court order that is imposed after no evident consideration of the available alternatives can survive strict scrutiny as narrowly tailored, the requirement that a racial classification can be 'narrowly tailored' for a compelling purpose has lost most of its meaning ... because the district court did not even consider available alternatives to a one-for-one promotion quota, and because these alternatives would have successfully compelled the Department to comply with the consent decrees, I must

respectfully dissent." 480 U.S. at 196, 201, 107 S.Ct. at 1080, 1082 (O'Connor, J., joined by Rehnquist, C.J., and Scalia, J., dissenting).

Justice White's dissent in *Paradise* consisted entirely of the following statement:

"Agreeing with much of what Justice O'Connor has written in this case, I find it hopefully evident that the district court exceeded its equitable powers in devising a remedy in this case. I therefore dissent from the judgment of affirmance." 480 U.S. at 196, 107 S.Ct. at 1080 (White, J., dissenting).

42. Some of the cases examined earlier in this section involved a court adopting a remedy that had been agreed upon by a plaintiff and defendant in a suit in which the plaintiff had alleged that the defendant (usually in a defendant's employment policies) had engaged in illegal or unconstitutional discrimination against racial minorities (or women). The judicial adoption of such a "consent decree," which employs a race conscious plan to benefit members of a minority race (or women) can be challenged by those persons (usually majority race or male current employees or applicants for employment) who are disadvantaged by the consent decree. For citations to additional cases, including lower court cases, and secondary works on this topic see our multi-volume Treatise: R. Rotunda & J.

mote the compelling interest in correcting the illegal or unconstitutional discrimination against members of a minority race.

Firefighters Local Union No. 1784 v. Stotts [43] overturned lower court orders which had required a city to lay off white workers during a period of budgetary restriction before laying off black workers who were more recently hired and who would otherwise have been laid off first under the terms of a seniority system agreed to by the city and the union. The decision did not establish any constitutional principles regarding affirmative action programs because the city had not voluntarily agreed to promote black workers in preference to white workers or to fire white workers before black workers.

The majority opinion in *Firefighters* was careful to note that the Court was not addressing the question of whether a city, as a public employer, could voluntarily adopt an affirmative action program which granted preferential employment rights to persons based on race.[44] The Court held only that Title VII allowed employers to use a seniority system that had an adverse impact on the employment of minority race employees absent proof that the system was designed to discriminate against such workers and was not a bona fide seniority system.[45]

In this case the city had earlier agreed to a "consent decree" following a suit brought against it under Title VII by black persons who claimed that they had been discriminated against in the hiring and promotion decisions of the city on the basis of race. The Court noted that, while the consent decree modified the hiring and promotion practices of the city, the city had never admitted that it engaged in intentional discrimination against persons because of their race, nor was there any finding that the city had intentionally discriminated in its hiring and promotion or layoff practices.[46] The Court endorsed a principle established in earlier cases that when an individual proves that an employer has followed a "pattern or practice" of discriminatory employment policies that adversely affect black applicants or employees, the plaintiff is not to be awarded a preference in employment or seniority ahead of non-minority persons, unless the individual plaintiff can show that he was specifically denied employment, promotion, or seniority through an illegal racially discriminatory practice.

The Court also held that federal courts had no inherent power to modify a Title VII consent decree so as to protect a racial balance in the work force of an employer following layoffs undertaken for nondiscriminatory purposes. The Court explained that Title VII prohibited court orders to employers to violate the terms of a bona fide seniority system which had been agreed to by employers and the employees' union for purposes other than discrimination

---

Nowak, Treatise on Constitutional Law: Substance and Procedure (3rd ed. 1999, with annual supplements).

43. 467 U.S. 561, 104 S.Ct. 2576, 81 L.Ed.2d 483 (1984), on remand 762 F.2d 1011 (6th Cir.1985).

44. If the city had voluntarily undertaken an affirmative action program that would have laid off white workers in preference to black workers in order to maintain an integrated work force, the Court would have been confronted with both a statutory and constitutional issue. The Court would have had to decide whether *public* sector employers have the same freedom to voluntarily adopt affirmative action plans as was given *private* sector employers in United Steelworkers v. Weber, 443 U.S. 193, 99 S.Ct. 2721, 61 L.Ed.2d 480 (1979), on remand 611 F.2d 132 (5th Cir.1980).

The Court would also have had to address the question of whether use of an affirmative action system of this type would violate the Fourteenth Amendment equal protection principle, because the employer (the city) would be estab-

lishing a racial preference through state action. Thus, even if a state employer might be granted the same freedom to adopt affirmative action plans as private employers under Title VII, the state employer would still be creating a racial classification that would be subject to the restrictions of the equal protection clause, restrictions which have not yet been clearly defined.

45. The Court earlier established the principle that bona fide seniority systems are protected by Title VII and an individual would have to demonstrate that he had personally been the victim of a discriminatory practice to be awarded competitive seniority in International Brotherhood of Teamsters v. United States, 431 U.S. 324, 97 S.Ct. 1843, 52 L.Ed.2d 396 (1977), appeal after remand 659 F.2d 690 (5th Cir.1981); Franks v. Bowman Transportation Co., 424 U.S. 747, 96 S.Ct. 1251, 47 L.Ed.2d 444 (1976).

46. Firefighters Local Union No. 1784 v. Stotts, 467 U.S. 561, 583 n. 16, 104 S.Ct. 2576, 2590 n. 16, 81 L.Ed.2d 483, 501, n. 16 (1984), on remand 762 F.2d 1011 (6th Cir.1985).

against minority employees.[47] Because there was no demonstration of an intention to discriminate on the part of the city, the Court did not have to address the scope of lower court authority to correct findings of intentional discrimination, under either Title VII or other civil rights acts.[48]

(3) Voluntary Affirmative Action Programs—Statutory Rulings.

The Supreme Court has ruled that Title VII of the Civil Rights Acts, which literally forbids race discrimination in private employment, did not prohibit an employer from adopting a voluntary affirmative action program. By a five to two vote, in *United Steelworkers of America v. Weber* [49] the Court interpreted Title VII to permit such programs, voluntarily adopted by employers or bargained for by employers and unions, because the Congress which adopted the statute was demonstrably concerned with discrimination against members of minority races, there was no evidence that Congress would have prohibited these programs, and the statute only stated that it did not "require" such programs, thus leaving open the possibility of voluntary programs. But the majority opinion in *Weber* was careful to note that the case did not involve a challenge to an affirmative action program undertaken with state action so that there was no need to consider the constitutionality of such programs. In *Weber* the Court held only that Title VII did not prohibit employers or unions from seeking to remedy racial imbalances in traditionally segregated job categories.

In *Johnson v. Transportation Agency, Santa Clara County, California,* [50] the Supreme Court upheld the legality of a county transportation agency's affirmative action plan, which gave a preference in hiring to women and members of racial minorities. The particular focus of the litigation had been on the promotion of women to positions where they had been underrepresented in the view of the government agency, but the majority opinion by Justice Brennan discussed the cases regarding the legality of affirmative action programs for both women and minorities. No constitutional issue was addressed in this case, even though the affirmative action plan was adopted by a government agency, because no constitutional issues had been raised in the lower court litigation. Justice Brennan wrote for a majority in finding that the prior cases of the Supreme Court, established the principle that Title VII of the Civil Rights Act did not prohibit an employer from undertaking a voluntary affirmative action program for women and minorities to attain a balanced work force, at least so long as the plan did not arbitrarily burden male or members of majority races. The Brennan majority did not explain what types of voluntary programs might be so arbitrary in the treatment of males or majority race members that they would violate Title VII. Justice Brennan did state that Title VII did not impose restrictions on affirmative action programs that were identical to the restrictions imposed by the equal protection guarantee on governmental affirmative action programs.[51] Thus, it appears that the Court will allow employers a fairly wide degree of latitude under current federal statutes, to adopt affirmative action programs where ethnicity or sex is considered as a factor, when evaluating otherwise quali-

---

47. 467 U.S. at 575, 104 S.Ct. at 2586, 81 L.Ed.2d at 497: "[A]s our cases have made clear ... Title VII protects bona fide seniority systems, and it is inappropriate to deny an innocent employee the benefits of his seniority in order to provide a remedy in a pattern or practice suit such as this."

48. For citations to additional cases, including lower court cases, and secondary works on this topic see our multi-volume Treatise: R. Rotunda & J. Nowak, Treatise on Constitutional Law: Substance and Procedure (3rd ed. 1999, with annual supplements).

49. 443 U.S. 193, 99 S.Ct. 2721, 61 L.Ed.2d 480 (1979), on remand 611 F.2d 132 (5th Cir.1980). This case was decided by a 5 to 2 vote. The majority opinion in *Weber*

was written by Justice Brennan. Justice Blackmun concurred in both the opinion and result, but he added a separate statement as well. Justices Powell and Stevens did not participate in the decision. Only the Chief Justice and Justice Rehnquist dissented in *Weber*. It is interesting to note that Justice Stewart voted with Justice Brennan in *Weber* and with Justice Stevens in *Bakke,* thus reflecting his own judgment as to the proper statutory interpretation of Title VI (in *Bakke*) and Title VII (in *Weber*).

50. 480 U.S. 616, 107 S.Ct. 1442, 94 L.Ed.2d 615 (1987).

51. 480 U.S. at 636, 107 S.Ct. at 1454.

fied candidates for jobs, in order to attain a racially or sexually integrated work force.[52]

(4) Voluntary Remedial Measures— Constitutional Issues. A difficult question arises where there has been no finding of de jure segregation and such remedial measures are undertaken voluntarily. The Supreme Court has suggested that a school board does have the authority to use racial classifications to produce a mixed student body which reflects society.[53] Voluntary measures to end de facto school segregation in elementary and high schools by use of racial classifications and integration programs have been upheld consistently by both federal and state courts.[54] These situations may be differentiated from preferential admissions to professional schools because all students are provided with a public education and no one has a right to attend segregated schools. However, some students may suffer because they are no longer able to attend the best schools, but schools should be relatively equal within a school district unless the authorities have engaged in other discriminatory acts. The differences between the

schools should not determine the resolution of the constitutional issue. It has been argued that it would be anomalous to require remedial measures where there has been a showing of explicit government discrimination but not to permit such measures to be voluntarily undertaken where there had been de facto segregation.[55]

The Supreme Court has approved the use of compensatory or benign classifications in several cases that did not involve racial classifications. The Court has upheld an affirmative action classification for members of Indian tribes, but this decision was based on the unique relationship of Indians to the federal government.[56] The Court has also upheld some financial aid benefits for women but required equal benefits for men where the program was not reasonably related to compensation for previous discrimination against women.[57]

In a few narrow rulings prior to 1989, the Court upheld or invalidated affirmative action

---

52. *Johnson* was decided by a six to three vote of the Justices. Justice O'Connor concurred only in the judgment; she wrote separately to explain why she believed that both Title VII and the equal protection clause allowed a limited amount of discretion to employers in establishing hiring goals for women and minorities but did not allow for what she considered to be the improper shifting of burdens to males or members of the majority race for the maintenance of an integrated work force. 480 U.S. at 647, 107 S.Ct. at 1460 (O'Connor, concurring in the judgment). For citations to additional cases, including lower court cases, and secondary works on this topic see our multivolume Treatise: R. Rotunda & J. Nowak, Treatise on Constitutional Law: Substance and Procedure (3rd ed. 1999, with annual supplements).

53. The Court stated in Swann v. Charlotte–Mecklenburg Bd. of Education, 402 U.S. 1, 16, 91 S.Ct. 1267, 1276, 28 L.Ed.2d 554 (1971), rehearing denied 403 U.S. 912, 91 S.Ct. 2201, 29 L.Ed.2d 689 (1971):

"School authorities are traditionally charged with broad power to formulate and implement educational policy and might well conclude, for example, that in order to prepare students to live in a pluralistic society each school should have a prescribed ratio of Negro to white students reflecting the proportion for the district as a whole. To do this as an educational policy is within the broad discretionary power of the school authorities; absent a finding of a constitutional violation, however, that would not be within the authority of a federal court."

54. When state agencies or courts engage in the transferring or busing of students to achieve a racially balanced

school system which is not mandated by the Fourteenth Amendment, state law may be amended to end that action if, but only if, the state does so without employing a racial classification. Compare, Washington v. Seattle School District, 458 U.S. 457, 102 S.Ct. 3187, 73 L.Ed.2d 896 (1982), with, Crawford v. Board of Education of Los Angeles, 458 U.S. 527, 102 S.Ct. 3211, 73 L.Ed.2d 948 (1982).

55. For citations to secondary sources on this topic see, R. Rotunda & J. Nowak, Treatise on Constitutional Law: Substance and Procedure, vol. 3 § 18.10 (3rd ed. 1999, with annual supplements).

56. Morton v. Mancari, 417 U.S. 535, 94 S.Ct. 2474, 41 L.Ed.2d 290 (1974) (preferential hiring of members of federally recognized American Indian Tribes for Bureau of Indian Affairs positions). See § 4.2, supra. In Rice v. Cayetano, 528 U.S. 495, 120 S.Ct. 1044, 145 L.Ed.2d 1007 (2000) the Court ruled that the *Morton* decision was not relevant to determining whether Hawaii could use an ancestry classification for an election. See § 14.10(c).

For an excellent analysis of equal protection issues involving American Indian classifications see, Johnson & Crystal, Indians and Equal Protection, 54 U.Wash.L.Rev. 587 (1979).

57. Compare Califano v. Webster, 430 U.S. 313, 97 S.Ct. 1192, 51 L.Ed.2d 360 (1977) (Social Security benefits increase valid); Kahn v. Shevin, 416 U.S. 351, 94 S.Ct. 1734, 40 L.Ed.2d 189 (1974) (tax benefit for widows valid); with Califano v. Goldfarb, 430 U.S. 199, 97 S.Ct. 1021, 51 L.Ed.2d 270 (1977) (requiring only males to prove dependency on deceased wage earner for social security benefits invalid). See §§ 14.20–14.24, infra.

programs without addressing the basic constitutional issue of the standard of review that should be employed to determine the compatibility of a benign racial classification with the equal protection guarantee.[58] The Court was unable to produce an opinion on this issue which had the support of a majority of the Justices, until cases decided in 1989 and 1990.

State and Local Laws. In *Richmond v. J.A. Croson Company* [59], which is examined in greater detail in the next subsection of this Chapter, the Supreme Court invalidated a city plan that required prime contractors of city awarded construction projects to subcontract at least 30% of the dollar amount of the contract to one or more minority owned subcontractor businesses. Justice O'Connor announced the judgment of the Court in an opinion that was, in part, a plurality opinion and, in part, a majority opinion. Justice O'Connor's opinion, together with the opinions of concurring Justices, marks the first time that a majority of the Court agreed that classifications that were designed to assist members of minority racial groups should be tested under the strict scrutiny-compelling interest test.[60]

A majority of Justices in *J.A. Croson* found that a remedial goal would support some race

based classifications. However, in order to justify the use of race classification in terms of a remedial goal, the state or city must identify public or private sector discrimination that occurred within its jurisdiction and demonstrate that it is now attempting to remedy that discrimination. The government does not have a compelling interest in remedying "societal discrimination" against members of racial minorities.[61] The mere identification of prior governmental or private sector discrimination within its jurisdiction will not give the state or city an open-ended power to use race based classifications. The Court will demand that the remedial plan adopted by the city or state be narrowly tailored to correct the identified past discrimination.

Prior to the decision in *J.A. Croson*, the Supreme Court had dealt with two cases regarding racial preferences in education. In *Regents of the University of California v. Bakke* [62] the Court, without a majority opinion, ruled on the legality of affirmative action racial preferences in higher education admission programs. The *Bakke* decision turned on the applicability and meaning of Title VI of the Civil Rights Act [63], which prohibits discrimination in federally funded programs. While a

---

58. Regents of the University of California v. Bakke, 438 U.S. 265, 98 S.Ct. 2733, 57 L.Ed.2d 750 (1978) (medical school affirmative action program found to violate federal statute); United Steelworkers of America v. Weber, 443 U.S. 193, 99 S.Ct. 2721, 61 L.Ed.2d 480 (1979), on remand 611 F.2d 132 (5th Cir.1980) (Title VII of Civil Rights Acts does not prohibit private employees from voluntarily using an affirmative action employment program); Fullilove v. Klutznick, 448 U.S. 448, 100 S.Ct. 2758, 65 L.Ed.2d 902 (1980) (federal public works statute setting aside contract funds for businesses owned by members of minority races upheld) overruled by Adarand Constructors, Inc. v. Pena, 515 U.S. 200, 115 S.Ct. 2097, 132 L.Ed.2d 158 (1995); Wygant v. Jackson Board of Education, 476 U.S. 267, 106 S.Ct. 1842, 90 L.Ed.2d 260 (1986), rehearing denied 478 U.S. 1014, 106 S.Ct. 3320, 92 L.Ed.2d 728 (1986) (invalidating a school board and teacher union agreement that resulted in the school board laying off nonminority teachers with less seniority than minority race teachers who were not laid off).

59. 488 U.S. 469, 109 S.Ct. 706, 102 L.Ed.2d 854 (1989).

60. Richmond v. J.A. Croson Co., 488 U.S. 469, 518, 109 S.Ct. 706, 734, 102 L.Ed.2d 854 (1989) (Kennedy, J., concurring in part and concurring in the judgment); 488 U.S. at 520, 109 S.Ct. at 735 (Scalia, J., concurring in the

judgment); Justice Stevens concurred without endorsing the use of any formal test or standard of review. Richmond v. J.A. Croson, 488 U.S. 469, 510, 109 S.Ct. 706, 730, 102 L.Ed.2d 854 (1989) (Stevens, J., concurring in part and concurring in the judgment). The dissent recognized that "Today, for the first time, a majority of the Court has adopted strict scrutiny as its standard of Equal Protection Clause review of race-conscious remedial measures." 488 U.S. at 551, 109 S.Ct. at 752 (Marshall, J., joined by Brennan and Blackmun, JJ., dissenting).

61. Richmond v. J.A. Croson Co., 488 U.S. 469, 497–508, 109 S.Ct. 706, 723–28, 102 L.Ed.2d 854 (1989) (this portion of Justice O'Connor's opinion is a majority opinion, which is joined by Chief Justice Rehnquist and Justices Kennedy, Stevens, and White).

62. 438 U.S. 265, 98 S.Ct. 2733, 57 L.Ed.2d 750 (1978).

63. 42 U.S.C.A. § 2000d et seq. The statute is referred to as "Title VI" because that was the designation of the relevant provisions in the Civil Rights Act of 1964. 78 Stat. 252, Pub.L. 88–352, Title VI, § 601 et seq. (July 2, 1964). This statute governs the operation of "any program or activity receiving Federal financial assistance" and prohibits racial discrimination in such programs. Thus, the judgment of the Court on the Title VI issue applies to any such program; the application of the statute is not limited to programs involving "state action."

five member majority voted to invalidate the specific affirmative action program that was before the Court in *Bakke* there was no majority opinion regarding the basis for that ruling. Five Justices voted to recognize the validity of some race conscious admission programs in higher education but could not resolve the issue of what standards should be used to determine the constitutionality of a benign or affirmative action racial classification.

In *Wygant v. Jackson Board of Education*,[64] the Supreme Court, without a majority opinion, invalidated a system for laying off teachers employed by a school board. The school board had laid off white teachers from their jobs before laying off black teachers for the sole purpose of maintaining a racially integrated faculty. Justice O'Connor wrote a concurring opinion in *Wygant* indicating that a majority of Justices might uphold a school board program that considered race in the hiring of teachers so as to create a racially diverse faculty in the schools within the school board's jurisdiction.[65] The Court in *Wygant,* as in *Bakke,* did not resolve the issue of what standard should be applied to determine whether a state or local governmental program designed to aid members of a minority race violated the equal protection clause.

In 2003, the Supreme Court used the strict scrutiny-compelling interest test (which had been adopted for the review of racial classifications in state and local laws in the *J.A.Croson* case) to review the University of Michigan's admissions policies for its undergraduate studies program and its law school. Employing this test, the Justices upheld the University of Michigan's admissions policy for its law school, but invalidated that University's admissions

policy for its undergraduate program. The Court ruled that the interest in creating a diverse student body could, at least in some situations, be a compelling interest, but that a race conscious admissions policy would withstand judicial scrutiny only if it was narrowly tailored to that compelling interest.[66]

Prior to 1995, the Supreme Court made two rulings concerning a state legislature's use of racial considerations to help insure that minority race persons are able to elect some representatives to a legislative body. But the Court, in these decisions, has not set forth standards for determining when, if ever, a legislature may overtly use racial considerations in order to enhance the voting power of racial minorities. In *United Jewish Organizations v. Carey,*[67] the Supreme Court, without a majority opinion, rejected an equal protection attack against New York legislation that established legislative districts that were designed to insure that minority race persons represented a majority of the voters. The New York districting legislation did not, on its face, use racial criteria as the basis for the creation of the districts. These legislative districts could be described as ones that were designed to be compact districts that complied with the one person one vote rule while avoiding the dilution of the voting power of racial minorities.

In *Shaw v. Reno* [68] the Supreme Court found that North Carolina legislation creating districts for the election of representatives to the United States Congress employed a racial classification on its face. For that reason, the majority ruled that the creation of districts that could be explained only in terms of racial criteria would violate the equal protection clause unless the districts were narrowly tai-

---

64. 476 U.S. 267, 106 S.Ct. 1842, 90 L.Ed.2d 260 (1986). The case is analyzed in the subsection of this chapter.

65. 476 U.S. at 285, 106 S.Ct. at 1853 (O'Connor, J., concurring in part and concurring in the judgment).

66. Justice O'Connor wrote for five Justices in finding that the Law School's admissions policy, though being cognizant of racial factors, was narrowly tailored to a compelling interest. Grutter v. Bollinger, 539 U.S. 306, 123 S.Ct. 2325, 156 L.Ed.2d 304 (2003). On the same day that *Grutter* was decided, Justice O'Connor joined a majority opinion written by Chief Justice Rehnquist that found that the University of Michigan's use of a system designed

to give a distinct numerical advantage (in terms of calculating an admissions score) for racial factors on the basis that the numerical advantage system was not narrowly tailored to a compelling interest and, therefore, failed to meet the strict scrutiny standard. Gratz v. Bollinger, 539 U.S. 244, 123 S.Ct. 2411, 156 L.Ed.2d 257 (2003). The diversity in education cases [the *Bakke, Wygant,* and *Bollinger* cases] are examined, infra, in § 14.10(b)(2).

67. 430 U.S. 144, 97 S.Ct. 996, 51 L.Ed.2d 229 (1977).

68. 509 U.S. 630, 113 S.Ct. 2816, 125 L.Ed.2d 511 (1993).

lored to further a compelling governmental interest.[69] However, the Court in *Shaw* did not rule on the question of whether these legislative districts were narrowly tailored to a compelling interest because that question had not been addressed by the lower court. We will examine the subject of race conscious legislative districting at the end of this section.[70]

Federal Laws. For the first half of the 1990s, it appeared that the Supreme Court would not subject federal racial affirmative action laws to strict judicial scrutiny. Then, in 1995, the Supreme Court ruled that any federal law employing a racial classification would violate the implied equal protection guarantee of the Fifth Amendment due process clause unless the government could demonstrate that the racial classification was narrowly tailored to promote a compelling interest.[71]

In *Metro Broadcasting, Inc. v. Federal Communications Commission*,[72] the Supreme Court by a five to four vote of the Justices, held that a benign affirmative action racial classification that was established by a federal statute, or in a federal agency regulation that was mandated by Congress, would not violate the equal protection principle so long as the classification had a substantial relationship to an important interest within the power of Congress.

Justice Brennan wrote the majority opinion in *Metro Broadcasting;* he distinguished the ruling in *J.A. Croson* by finding that the equal protection component of the Fifth Amendment due process clause did not require the judiciary to use the compelling interest standard that was required for review of state or local government racial classifications under the equal protection clause of the Fourteenth Amendment. The *Metro Broadcasting* decision allowed Congress to use a racial classification that is benign, in the sense that it affirmative-

ly aids members of a minority race, so long as the classification can be found and have a "substantial relationship" to a federal interest that the Court deems "important."

In *Metro Broadcasting* the Court found that two FCC policies that gave an advantage to minority race persons or minority owned businesses in securing a license to operate a radio or television station were substantially related to the federal interest in promoting diversity in broadcast programs. The Court found that the promotion of diversity in the broadcast industry and in broadcast programming was an important interest. Justice Brennan's majority opinion appeared to give a significant amount of deference to congressional decision-making when in finding that the Communications Commission policies, which had been mandated by Congress, were "substantially related" to the in program diversity.

In 1995 Justice Thomas, who was not on the Court at the time *Metro Broadcasting* was decided, joined the four *Metro Broadcasting* dissenters to overrule that decision. In *Adarand Constructors, Inc. v. Pena*,[73] the Supreme Court ruled that any federal racial classification, including a benign racial classification in an affirmative action law, had to be subject to strict judicial scrutiny. Such a classification would not be upheld unless the federal government could demonstrate that the classification was narrowly tailored to promote a compelling governmental interest. We will examine the *Adarand* decision, and earlier decisions concerning federal racial affirmative action programs, after we have examined the Supreme Court decisions regarding state and local racial affirmative action programs.[74]

Legislative Districts. In *United Jewish Organizations v. Carey*,[75] the Supreme Court, without a majority opinion, rejected an equal

69. Shaw v. Reno, 509 U.S. 630, 649, 113 S.Ct. 2816, 2828, 2832, 125 L.Ed.2d 511 (1993).

70. See § 18.10(c).

71. Adarand Constructors, Inc. v. Pena, 515 U.S. 200, 115 S.Ct. 2097, 132 L.Ed.2d 158 (1995), overruling Metro Broadcasting, Inc. v. Federal Communications Commission, 497 U.S. 547, 110 S.Ct. 2997, 111 L.Ed.2d 445 (1990).

72. 497 U.S. 547, 110 S.Ct. 2997, 111 L.Ed.2d 445 (1990).

73. 515 U.S. 200, 115 S.Ct. 2097, 132 L.Ed.2d 158 (1995), overruling, Metro Broadcasting, Inc. v. Federal Communications Commission, 497 U.S. 547, 110 S.Ct. 2997, 111 L.Ed.2d 445 (1990), rehearing denied 497 U.S. 1050, 111 S.Ct. 15, 111 L.Ed.2d 829 (1990).

74. See § 14.10(b)(3).

75. 430 U.S. 144, 97 S.Ct. 996, 51 L.Ed.2d 229 (1977).

protection attack against New York legislation that established legislative districts that were designed to insure that minority race persons represented a majority of the voters. The New York districting legislation did not, on its face, use racial criteria as the basis for the creation of the districts. These legislative districts could be described as ones that were designed to be compact districts that complied with the one person one vote rule while avoiding the dilution of the voting power of racial minorities.

In *Shaw v. Reno (Shaw I)*[76] the Supreme Court found that North Carolina legislation creating districts for the election of representatives to the United States Congress employed a racial classification on its face. The districting map at issue in *Shaw I* was enacted by North Carolina after the Attorney General of the United States had refused to give approval to the earlier districting map. It was the Attorney General's opinion that the state's first plan for congressional districts would hurt minority race representation because it created only one district where minority race voters would be a majority of the voters.[77] A majority of the Justices in *Shaw I* found that at least one district in the final map could be explained only as an attempt to create a district for minority race voters that would produce the election of minority race representatives. For that reason, the majority ruled that the North Carolina districting plan on its face involved a racial classification that required close judicial scrutiny and that would only be upheld if it was narrowly tailored to a compelling interest. Justice O'Connor, writing for the majority in *Shaw I*, stated that the use of race on the face of a legislative districting plan conveyed the message to voters, and to elected representatives, that persons of each racial group were of only one set of viewpoints and

interests and that different racial groups had few, if any, common interests. For that reason, the majority ruled that the creation of districts that could be explained only in terms of racial criteria would violate the equal protection clause unless the districts were narrowly tailored to further a compelling governmental interest.[78] However, the Court in *Shaw I* did not rule on the question of whether these legislative districts were narrowly tailored to a compelling interest because that question had not been addressed by the lower court. At the end of this section, we will examine the questions of (1) whether there are any circumstances under which some consideration of race in the creation of a legislative district that has a majority of minority race voters will not be subject to strict judicial scrutiny; and (2) when, if ever, a legislative district drawn to aid minority race voters will be deemed narrowly tailored to a compelling interest.[79]

(b) Supreme Court Decisions

(1) The *J.A. Croson* decision and an overview of the Supreme Court's rulings regarding state and local governments' racial affirmative action programs.

A governmental entity that has not previously been found guilty of illegal or unconstitutional racial discrimination may employ a race based classification to benefit members of a minority race. Such an affirmative action program is subject to review under the equal protection clause of the Fourteenth Amendment (for a state or local governmental program) or the equal protection component of the Fifth Amendment due process clause (for a program of the federal government).

In 1989, in *Richmond v. J.A. Croson Company*,[80] a majority of the Justices found that a racial classification in an affirmative action

76. 509 U.S. 630, 113 S.Ct. 2816, 125 L.Ed.2d 511 (1993), on remand 861 F.Supp. 408 (E.D.N.C.1994).

77. The Attorney General in both cases was exercising power under § 5 of the Voting Rights Act, which requires certain states and local governments in the United States to get "preclearance" of any changes in their voting laws from the Attorney General of the United States or the United States District Court for the District of Columbia. These provisions of federal law have been upheld by the United States Supreme Court, see South Carolina v. Katzenbach, 383 U.S. 301, 86 S.Ct. 803, 15 L.Ed.2d 769

(1966); Allen v. State Board of Elections, 393 U.S. 544, 89 S.Ct. 817, 22 L.Ed.2d 1 (1969).

78. Shaw v. Reno, 509 U.S. 630, 649, 656, 113 S.Ct. 2816, 2828, 2832, 125 L.Ed.2d 511 (1993), on remand 861 F.Supp. 408 (E.D.N.C.1994).

79. See § 14.10(c).

80. 488 U.S. 469, 109 S.Ct. 706, 102 L.Ed.2d 854 (1989).

program must be reviewed with "strict scrutiny" and such a classification, like racial classifications that burden minorities, will be upheld only if it can be shown to be necessary (or narrowly tailored) to the promotion of a compelling interest.

In *J.A. Croson,* the Supreme Court examined and invalidated a plan adopted by the City of Richmond for awarding city construction contracts. The plan required the primary contractor on a city awarded construction contract to subcontract at least 30% of the amount of the contract to subcontractor businesses that were owned by members of certain minority racial groups. The minority groups were identified in the statute as persons who are "black, Spanish-speaking, Orientals, Indians, Eskimos, or Aleutes." The plan allowed a prime contractor to seek a waiver of the 30% requirement in "exceptional circumstances" (when the 30% minimum could not reasonably be fulfilled).

Six Justices voted to invalidate Richmond's affirmative action plan. The judgment of the Court in *J.A. Croson* was announced in an opinion by Justice O'Connor that was, in part, a majority opinion and, in part, a plurality opinion. When the portion of Justice O'Connor's opinion regarding the standards of review, which was joined by Chief Justice Rehnquist and Justice White, is combined with the concurring opinions of Justice Kennedy [81] and Justice Scalia,[82] it can be seen that five Justices voted to subject all racial classifications, including those classifications that appear in affirmative action programs, to the strict scrutiny-compelling interest standard. Of the six Justices who voted to invalidate the law, only Justice Stevens found it unnecessary to address the standard of review question.[83] Jus-

tice Marshall, in a dissent joined by Justices Brennan and Blackmun, noted that this case marked the first time that a majority of the Court voted to employ the strict scrutiny-compelling interest standard to the review of racial classifications that aided members of a racial minority.[84]

While it seems clear that the *J.A. Croson* decision effectively adopted a strict scrutiny-compelling interest standard for state and local racial affirmative action cases, the decision leaves open several questions.

In *J.A. Croson,* the City of Richmond asserted that its affirmative action plan for minority owned businesses was designed to remedy past discrimination against minorities in construction businesses. A majority of the Justices found that a state or local governmental entity only had a compelling interest in remedying past discrimination if the governmental entity could identify past discrimination against a racial minority within its jurisdiction.[85] Cities and states may not justify a racial affirmative action plan on the basis that they are correcting "societal discrimination." In other words, a city must identify past governmental or private sector discrimination within the city in order to create a plan that seeks to remedy that discrimination. A state affirmative action program would have to be justified by the state identifying governmental or private sector discrimination within the state. The affirmative action program of either a state or local government must be narrowly tailored to correct the identified discrimination.

What type of proof is required to identify past discrimination? The Supreme Court in *J.A. Croson* did not make clear how a lower court should determine if a city or state gov-

81. 488 U.S. at 518, 109 S.Ct. at 734 (Kennedy, J., concurring in part and concurring in the judgment).

82. 488 U.S. at 520, 109 S.Ct. at 735 (Scalia, J., concurring in the judgment).

83. Justice Stevens concurred without endorsing the use of any formal test or standard of review. Richmond v. J.A. Croson Co., 488 U.S. 469, 511, 109 S.Ct. 706, 730, 102 L.Ed.2d 854 (1989) (Stevens, J., concurring in part and concurring in the judgment).

84. "Today, for the first time, a majority of the Court has adopted strict scrutiny as its standard of Equal Pro-

tection Clause review of race-conscious remedial measures." 488 U.S. at 551, 109 S.Ct. at 752 (Marshall, J., joined by Brennan and Blackmun, JJ., dissenting). See generally, Highsmith, J., citing this section of the Treatise in Peightal v. Metropolitan Dade County, 815 F.Supp. 1454, 1462 (S.D.Fla.1993).

85. Richmond v. J.A. Croson Co., 488 U.S. 469, 497–508, 109 S.Ct. 706, 723–28, 102 L.Ed.2d 854 (1989) (this portion of Justice O'Connor's opinion is a majority opinion that is joined by Chief Justice Rehnquist and Justices Kennedy, Stevens, and White).

ernment has established a factual basis for showing prior governmental or private sector discrimination that might justify an affirmative action plan. A majority of the Justices found that the statistics showing that, in Richmond, there was a very low percentage of construction business owners or subcontractors who were members of a minority race was not sufficient to show racial discrimination within construction industry in the city. If the Court allowed a statistical showing of under-representation of minority races in a job category or business activity to prove past illegal or unconstitutional discrimination, the ruling might allow state and local governments to use affirmative action racial classifications whenever the government chose, because minority race persons may be underrepresented in many jobs or businesses due to the effects of societal discrimination against members of racial minorities.

Justice O'Connor's opinion in *J.A. Croson* was, in part, a plurality opinion and, in part, a majority opinion. In a portion of Justice O'Connor's opinion which was a majority opinion (a part joined by Justices White, Kennedy, and Stevens as well as Chief Justice Rehnquist) she appears to set out conflicting approaches to the use of statistics for identifying past racial discrimination. Justice O'Connor states that the disparity between the number of minority businesses that had received city construction contracts or subcontracts in previous years and the percent of minority race members in the city population would not demonstrate identifiable racial discrimination against minority race members in the construction business.[86] In this portion of the opinion, Justice O'Connor also stated that the city, and the district court which had upheld the city's plan had wrongly relied on evidence that minority owned businesses were statistically under-represented in a local contractors' association. The disparity between the number of minority owned construction businesses and minority participation in the contractors' association, (like the disparity between the percentage of city residents who were mem-

bers of a minority race and the percentage of construction contracts that were awarded to minority race members) could be attributable to a variety of reasons, including generalized societal discrimination against minorities. These statistics did not identify past illegal or unconstitutional racial discrimination against minority owned construction businesses or against minority race persons who desired to establish a business that might be eligible to receive city construction contracts. When Justice O'Connor discussed the need to identify past private or public sector discrimination against minority businesses, she cited cases in which the Supreme Court had examined the use of statistical evidence to establish a prima facie case of employment discrimination. Her citations to those cases may mean that a court should examine the evidence put forward by the city or state to justify its affirmative action program in terms of whether that evidence would be sufficient to establish a prima facie case of identified discrimination if the case had been brought under a civil rights statute.

In a portion of her opinion that was a majority opinion, Justice O'Connor noted that the low representation of minority owned businesses in an association of contractors who did business with the city might help an individual city in a particular case to show past private sector discrimination. Justice O'Connor stated: "For low minority representation in these associations [groups of contractors in a city who often dealt with city contracts] to be relevant, the city would have to link it to the number of local MBEs [Minority Business Enterprises] eligible for membership. If the statistical disparity between eligible MBEs and MBE membership [in the trade association] were great enough an inference of discriminatory exclusion would arise. In such a case the city would have a compelling interest in preventing its tax dollars from assisting these organizations and maintaining a racially segregated construction market."[87] In other words, if the city can make a prima facie case of past private or public sector discrimination

---

86. Richmond v. J.A. Croson Co., 488 U.S. 469, 501, 109 S.Ct. 706, 725, 102 L.Ed.2d 854 (1989).

87. 488 U.S. at 503, 109 S.Ct. at 726.

against minority owned businesses of a certain type, the city has a compelling interest in creating a program to correct that racial discrimination. If the racial discrimination related to businesses to whom the city awards contracts, the city could adopt an affirmative action plan that was narrowly tailored to ensure that future city contracts would be awarded to a racially diverse group of contractors or subcontractors.

Even if city or state can identify prior illegal or unconstitutional discrimination within its boundaries, the affirmative action plan adopted by the governmental entity must be narrowly tailored to correct the identified discrimination. The Supreme Court in *J.A. Croson* found that, even if Richmond had identified past discrimination against minority owned construction businesses in the city, its use of a 30% quota for subcontracts to minority owned businesses, which provided for only limited waivers from the quota system, showed that the plan was not narrowly tailored to the correction of prior discrimination.[88]

In a portion of her opinion that was joined by Chief Justice Rehnquist, and Justices White and Kennedy, Justice O'Connor stated: "nothing we say today precludes a state or local entity from taking action to rectify the effects of identified discrimination within its jurisdiction."[89] According to the plurality, to justify a plan for awarding construction contracts or subcontracts in a manner that preferred businesses owned by minority race members, a city might be able to rely on "an inference of discriminatory exclusion" that would arise from a "significant statistical disparity" between the number of qualified minority contractors in the city and the number of minority contractors who had been employed by the jurisdiction in prior years. "In the extreme case [Justice O'Connor's plurality opinion concluded], some form of narrowly tailored racial

preference might be necessary to break down patterns of deliberate exclusion."[90]

In *J.A. Croson,* the Supreme Court created a framework for determining the constitutionality of racial affirmative action programs that are "remedial" in nature. However, in that case, the Court did not tell us whether there are other interests that would be sufficiently "compelling" to justify a racial classification that favored members of a minority race.

In two cases decided prior to *J.A. Croson,* it appeared that the government's interest in creating racial and ethnic diversity in the faculties of all state operated schools, and in the faculty and student bodies of state operated universities and professional schools, might allow the government to take cognizance of a person's race, so long as the government did not establish a "racial quota" and did not stigmatize any member of any racial group.

In *Regents of the University v. Bakke*[91] the Supreme Court invalidated a state medical school admissions program that set aside places in an entering class for members of racial minorities in order to ensure that there would be a certain minimum number of racial minority persons in each entering class. Although the case was decided without a majority opinion and was based on a federal civil rights statute, the *Bakke* decision appeared to allow university and professional school admissions officers, or admission committees, to consider an applicant's race for the purpose of ensuring racial diversity in the student body if, but only if, the admissions system promoted diversity without using racial quotas and without imposing burdens on individuals because of their race.

Wygant v. Jackson Board of Education[92] invalidated a school board's action that laid off white teachers from their jobs, before laying off black teachers, for the purpose of maintaining a racially integrated faculty. There was

---

88. 488 U.S. at 507–10, 109 S.Ct. at 728–29.

89. Richmond v. J.A. Croson Co., 488 U.S. 469, 508, 109 S.Ct. 706, 729, 102 L.Ed.2d 854 (1989) (O'Connor, J., joined by Rehnquist, C.J., and White and Kennedy, JJ.).

90. 488 U.S. at 508, 109 S.Ct. at 729 (O'Connor, J., joined by Rehnquist, C.J., and White and Kennedy, JJ.).

91. 438 U.S. 265, 98 S.Ct. 2733, 57 L.Ed.2d 750 (1978).

92. 476 U.S. 267, 106 S.Ct. 1842, 90 L.Ed.2d 260 (1986).

no majority opinion in *Wygant.* The concurring opinion by Justice O'Connor indicated that a majority of Justices might uphold a governmental program of hiring (rather than firing) teachers that took cognizance of the race of an applicant for a teaching position in order to have a racially diverse faculty in grade schools and high schools within the school board's jurisdiction.[93]

For fourteen years following *J.A. Croson,* lower courts were left with no guidance regarding whether they should use the form of analysis adopted by Justice Powell in his plurality opinions in *Bakke* and *Wygant* when reviewing race conscious admissions policies of educational institutions. In 2003, in a majority opinion written by Justice O'Connor, the Supreme Court adopted Justice Powell's analytical framework, and ruled that the University of Michigan Law School's race conscious admissions policy was narrowly tailored to a compelling interest.[94] On the same day in 2003, Justice O'Connor joined a majority opinion written by Chief Justice Rehnquist which ruled that the race conscious admissions policy employed by the University of Michigan for its undergraduate studies program was not narrowly tailored to a compelling interest.[95] We will review the Court's decisions concerning racial diversity in education in the next subsection of this Chapter.

(2) Race conscious government policies designed to promote educational diversity—The Bakke, Wygant & Bollinger decisions.

In a quarter-century (from 1978 to 2003), the Supreme Court decided four cases concerning government policies that were designed to create racial diversity in schools. This era be-

gan with *Regents of the University v. Bakke,*[96] a case in which Justice Powell, in part of his opinion that was not joined by any other Justice, set forth an analytical framework for determining the constitutionality of admissions programs for higher education. The era ended on a day in 2003 when, in two separate cases, a majority of the Rehnquist Court Justices: adopted Justice Powell's analysis; upheld a race conscious admissions program for the University of Michigan Law School; and invalidated the University of Michigan's policy for admitting students to its undergraduate studies program.[97] The 2003 decisions concerning the University of Michigan would leave unresolved questions concerning the creation or maintenance of racial diversity in primary and secondary school faculties, which the Court had dealt with in *Wygant v. Jackson Board of Education.*[98]

In the following paragraphs, we will examine Justice Powell's opinion in *Bakke* at greater length than the Court's 2003 decisions, because the Court in 2003 established constitutional principles primarily through reference to the position taken by Justice Powell, in 1978, in his opinion in the *Bakke* case.

Regents of the University v. Bakke.[99] Allan Bakke had been denied admission to the Medical School of the University of California at Davis [hereinafter referred to as Davis] in both 1973 and 1974 because the admissions committee did not believe that his qualifications justified admitting him under the general admissions program, even though his academic qualifications were substantially equivalent to those of other students being admitted under the program at that time. However, during each of those years Davis operated a special

---

93. Wygant v. Jackson Board of Education, 476 U.S. 267, 287, 106 S.Ct. 1842, 1853, 90 L.Ed.2d 260 (1986) (O'Connor, J., concurring in part and concurring in the judgment).

94. Grutter v. Bollinger, 539 U.S. 306, 123 S.Ct. 2325, 156 L.Ed.2d 304 (2003). See § 14.10(b)(2), infra.

95. Gratz v. Bollinger, 539 U.S. 244, 123 S.Ct. 2411, 156 L.Ed.2d 257 (2003). See § 14.10(b)(2), infra.

96. 438 U.S. 265, 98 S.Ct. 2733, 57 L.Ed.2d 750 (1978).

97. By a 5 to 4 vote, the Supreme Court upheld the University of Michigan's Law School program, by finding that it was narrowly tailored to a compelling interest in

diversity, in Grutter v. Bollinger, 539 U.S. 306, 123 S.Ct. 2325, 156 L.Ed.2d 304 (2003). On the same day that the *Grutter* case was decided, Chief Justice Rehnquist wrote a majority opinion that invalidated the University of Michigan's admission policy for its undergraduate program. Gratz v. Bollinger, 539 U.S. 244, 123 S.Ct. 2411, 156 L.Ed.2d 257 (2003).

98. 476 U.S. 267, 106 S.Ct. 1842, 90 L.Ed.2d 260, rehearing denied 478 U.S. 1014, 106 S.Ct. 3320, 92 L.Ed.2d 728 (1986).

99. 438 U.S. 265, 98 S.Ct. 2733, 57 L.Ed.2d 750 (1978).

admissions program to consider the applications of candidates who asked to be considered as "economically and/or educationally disadvantaged," or as members of a "minority group."

Under the Davis program, membership in certain racial or ethnic minorities—Afro-American, Mexican–American, Asian, or American Indian—qualified one for consideration under the special admissions program. Bakke was not a member of the specified racial minority groups and, therefore, was not eligible for consideration for admission under the special admissions program. Since a certain number of places in the class were reserved for these minority or disadvantaged students, Bakke contended that the refusal to admit him was the result of the special admissions program.[100]

Bakke brought suit in state court alleging that the Davis special admissions program caused him injury by effectively excluding him from the freshman medical classes during 1973 and 1974 and that the Davis program violated the constitution of the state of California, Title VI of the Federal Civil Rights Act of 1964, and the equal protection clause of the Fourteenth Amendment to the United States Constitution. The state trial court found that the Davis program violated all three provi-

sions, but held that Bakke was not entitled to a judgment in his favor because he could not demonstrate that he would have been admitted to Medical School if the special admissions program had not been in operation.

The Supreme Court of California reversed the holding of the state trial court; it ruled that the trial court erred by requiring Bakke to demonstrate that he would have been admitted but for the special admissions program.[101] The Davis Medical School did not challenge this ruling of the California Supreme Court and, therefore, there was no issue concerning Bakke's ability to demonstrate that he was injured by the special admissions program in the case as it was presented to the Supreme Court of the United States.[102]

The Supreme Court of California avoided ruling on either the state constitutional issue or the applicability of Title VI of the Civil Rights Act to the Davis program. That court held that the Davis admissions program violated the equal protection clause of the Fourteenth Amendment because that Amendment, in the view of a majority of the state court Justices, meant that the government could not take cognizance of race in dispensing governmental benefits. The state supreme court therefore ordered the admission of Mr. Bakke to the Medical School.[103]

100. Bakke applied late in 1973, and would perhaps have gained admission in that year had it not been for this fact. See 438 U.S. at 276–77, 98 S.Ct. at 2741–42 (Opinion of Powell, J.). In 1974 Bakke applied early. In that year he also possessed academic credentials above the average of persons admitted in 1974 to the medical school at Davis under the regular admissions program. See 438 U.S. at 276–77 n. 7, 98 S.Ct. at 2741 n. 7.

101. Bakke v. Regents of University of California, 18 Cal.3d 34, 132 Cal.Rptr. 680, 553 P.2d 1152 (1976), judgment affirmed in part, reversed in part 438 U.S. 265, 98 S.Ct. 2733, 57 L.Ed.2d 750 (1978).

102. This point was noted by Justice Powell, 438 U.S. at 280 n. 13, 98 S.Ct. at 2743 n. 13, and by Justice Stevens, 438 U.S. at 410, 98 S.Ct. at 2809. Justice Powell indicated that Bakke had standing due to his exclusion from consideration for the special admissions program. 438 U.S. at 280, n. 14, 98 S.Ct. at 2743 n. 14.

103. Some of the Justices of the United States Supreme Court disagreed as to the scope of the California Supreme Court decision and the precise question upon which they were compelled to rule. Justice Powell maintained that the California decision invalidated the Davis program because it took account of race and asserted that the California court had held that all educational admis-

sions programs had to operate on a colorblind basis. 438 U.S. at 1318, 98 S.Ct. at 2762–63 (Opinion of Powell, J.). Justice Powell was correct in his characterization of the California opinion. See Bakke v. Regents of the University of California, 18 Cal.3d 34, 54–56, 132 Cal.Rptr. 680, 683, 694, 553 P.2d 1152, 1155, 1166 (1976), judgment affirmed in part, reversed in part 438 U.S. 265, 98 S.Ct. 2733, 57 L.Ed.2d 750 (1978). Justice Powell believed both that the Davis program was illegal and that Davis and other institutions could employ some race conscious programs. Therefore Justice Powell had to vote to reverse the part of the judgment of the California Supreme Court that prohibited race conscious programs even though he voted to affirm the order of the California court that required Davis to accept Mr. Bakke and to refrain from using its present special admissions program.

Justice Stevens speaking for the other four members of the United States Supreme Court who voted to affirm the California Supreme Court, stated that the California court had ordered only the admission of Mr. Bakke to the Davis Medical School and that there was no outstanding order prohibiting race conscious programs on a constitutional basis. 438 U.S. at 409–410, 98 S.Ct. at 2808–09 (opinion of Stevens, J., joined by Burger, C.J., & Rehnquist & Stewart, JJ.).

The Justices of the Supreme Court of the United States affirmed the decision of the California Supreme Court; however, they came as close to being evenly divided as they could with all nine Justices voting on the legality of the Davis program. Four of the Justices—Chief Justice Burger and Justices Stewart, Rehnquist, and Stevens—concluded that the Davis program violated Title VI of the Federal Civil Rights Act.[104] They found that the application of Title VI to the admissions program made it unnecessary to reach any constitutional issue. Four Justices—Justices Brennan, White, Marshall and Blackmun—were of the opinion that Title VI was meant to bar only such racial discrimination as was prohibited by the Fourteenth Amendment and that the Davis program did not violate either the equal protection clause or Title VI.[105] Thus, the ruling of the case turned on the vote of Justice Powell, even though his analysis of the issues was not supported by a majority of Justices.

Justice Powell found that the equal protection clause and, therefore, Title VI, required invalidation of the Davis program. But Justice Powell was of the opinion that neither provision would require the invalidation of all race conscious affirmative action programs. He therefore voted with the group of four Justices who ruled only on the Title VI issue to the extent of finding the Davis program a violation of Title VI and ordering Davis to accept Mr. Bakke into the medical school. However, Justice Powell voted to reverse the California decision insofar as it required state governmental units to avoid all consideration of race in affirmative action programs. Only two portions of Justice Powell's opinion were

joined by four other Justices: the statement of facts and the paragraph in which he stated that not all racial classifications were invalidated by the Fourteenth Amendment.[106] Nevertheless, he cast the fifth vote that resulted in the affirmance of the order that required Davis to accept Mr. Bakke while allowing it and other educational institutions to make some use of race conscious admissions criteria.

Thus, the *Bakke* decision means that an admissions program of an institution receiving federal funds that uses clear, strict racial preferences, such as that of the Davis Medical School, will be held to violate Title VI of the Civil Rights Act because five Justices would find it to be a Title VI violation, although for differing reasons. A program of admissions to institutions of higher education that allows admissions officers to consider race as an affirmative factor without using clear racial preferences will be held to violate neither the equal protection clause nor Title VI because a different alignment of five Justices would vote to uphold such programs. In *Bakke,* five Justices, with no majority opinion, did vote for the proposition that Title VI bars only such racial discrimination as would violate the equal protection clause if it involved state action.

Bakke left many important issues regarding racial preferences unsettled. There was no ruling on the constitutionality of any affirmative action program other than those relating to admission to higher education. The Court did not determine whether other federal civil rights acts can, or do, mandate or restrict the use of such benign classifications; the statutory ruling involved only Title VI.[107]

The four Justices who voted to reverse the California Supreme Court in total did not have to enter this procedural debate because they simply would have reversed the decision of the California Supreme Court regardless of how its judgment might be described.

104. 438 U.S. at 421, 98 S.Ct. at 2815 (Stevens, Rehnquist, Stewart, JJ., & Burger, C.J., concurring in the judgment in part and dissenting in part).

105. 438 U.S. at 325, 98 S.Ct. at 2766 (Brennan, Marshall, Blackmun & White, JJ., concurring in the judgment in part and dissenting in part).

106. 438 U.S. at 271–84, 320, 98 S.Ct. at 2738–45, 2763–64 (Opinion of Powell, J.).

107. Indeed, the Court did not decide whether Title VI creates a private cause of action that would allow persons, other than Mr. Bakke, to bring suit for either monetary or injunctive relief from educational institutions that employ programs similar to that used at the Davis Medical School. Four members of the Court—Justices Powell, Brennan, Marshall and Blackmun—appeared to assume a private cause of action under Title VI in order to find Title VI protection equivalent to that of the Fourteenth Amendment, and ultimately to address the constitutional issue. See 438 U.S. at 284, 98 S.Ct. at 2745 (Opinion of Powell, J.); 438 U.S. at 328, 98 S.Ct. at 2767–68 (Opinion of Brennan, Marshall, White & Blackmun, JJ. concurring in part and dissenting in part). Four members of the Court apparently found the existence of such a private cause of

The Supreme Court, in *Bakke*, ruled only that the Davis program violated Title VI. It did not hold that the Davis program violated the equal protection clause. It is important to note that the Court also did not establish the constitutional standards to be employed in reviewing benign or affirmative action race classifications. Four of the five Justices who reached the constitutional issue would have used an intermediate standard of review for affirmative action classifications.[108] Justice Powell was the only Justice reaching the constitutional issue who would have subjected all race conscious affirmative action programs to strict judicial scrutiny and the most exacting test of constitutionality.[109] Four Justices ruled only that Congress could and did require that recipients of federal funds dispense the benefits of programs employing those funds on a purely "colorblind" basis.[110]

Justice Powell found that all racial classifications are inherently suspect and subject to the strictest judicial scrutiny. Justice Powell

also found that there was no difference between setting racial quotas and establishing "goals" of minority representation; in so doing the Justice was taking the position that he would subject any use of racial criteria to the most strict equal protection test.[111] Justice Powell argued that application of the strictest equal protection test to racial and ethnic classifications was required by the "constitutional and demographic history" of the country. He concluded that it was "far too late to argue that the guarantee of equal protection to all persons permits the recognition of special wards entitled to a degree of protection greater than that accorded others." [112]

In reaching the conclusion that all racial and ethnic classifications should be subjected to the most exacting scrutiny, Justice Powell distinguished three groups of prior Supreme Court decisions. First, he found that the school desegregation cases were not relevant to the affirmative action decision because they involved only remedies designed to redress

---

action under Title VI. See 438 U.S. at 420, 98 S.Ct. at 2814 (Stevens, J., joined by Burger, C.J., & Rehnquist & Stewart, JJ., concurring in the judgment in part and dissenting in part). In a separate opinion Justice White expressly found no private cause of action under Title VI. See 438 U.S. at 379–380, 98 S.Ct. at 2793–94 (Separate opinion of White, J.). In Cannon v. University of Chicago, 441 U.S. 677, 99 S.Ct. 1946, 60 L.Ed.2d 560 (1979), on remand 605 F.2d 560 (7th Cir.1979) the Supreme Court held that an implied cause of action existed under Title IX, which would allow a woman allegedly discriminated against by sex in the admission process of a medical school receiving federal funds to seek a remedy against the school in federal court. The Court reasoned in part that Title IX, which forbids discrimination on the basis of sex by educational programs that are federally funded, was patterned on Title VI and that Congress was aware when it passed Title IX that several federal courts had found an implied private cause of action under Title VI. Although the Court in *Cannon* technically did not resolve the question of whether there would be a similar implied cause of action under Title VI, the majority opinion strongly indicates that a majority of the Justices agree that Title VI, as well as Title IX, gives rise to an individual cause of action. Justices White, Blackmun, and Powell dissented in *Cannon*.

108. 438 U.S. at 355–62, 98 S.Ct. at 2781–85 (Brennan, Marshall, White & Blackmun, JJ., concurring in part and dissenting in part).

109. 438 U.S. at 287–305, 98 S.Ct. at 2746–56 (Powell, J.). The position of Justice White on the applicable standard of review is not entirely clear in *Bakke*. On the one hand, White joined that portion of Justice Powell's opinion which calls for exacting strict scrutiny. See 438 U.S. at

387 n. 7, 98 S.Ct. at 2797 n. 7 (Separate Opinion of White, J.). On the other hand, Justice White specifically stated that he joined the views of the Brennan, Marshall, White and Blackmun opinion on "the equal protection issue." 438 U.S. at 387, 98 S.Ct. at 2797 (Separate opinion of White, J.). It would appear that Justice White believes that any affirmative action program that is truly benign and meets the Brennan tests will also satisfy the proper strict scrutiny standard.

110. In Fullilove v. Klutznick, 448 U.S. 448, 100 S.Ct. 2758, 65 L.Ed.2d 902 (1980) Justices Stewart, Rehnquist and Stevens took strict positions against the use of racial classifications for affirmative action purposes, while Chief Justice Burger refused to commit to a specific standard for the review of such programs. There is still no majority position regarding the appropriate standard of review for the benign use of racial classifications for affirmative action programs. The *Fullilove* case is examined following the examination of the opinions of individual Justices in *Bakke*.

111. 438 U.S. at 287–299, 98 S.Ct. at 2746–53. It was in Part III–A of his opinion that Justice Powell concluded that the "quota"—"goal" distinction was irrelevant and that all such racial classifications were subject to the strict scrutiny test. Justice White stated that he joined Part III–A of the Powell opinion, even though he also joined in all of Justice Brennan's opinion. 438 U.S. at 387, n. 7, 98 S.Ct. at 2797, n. 7 (Separate Opinion of White, J.); Justice White did not join in any of Justice Powell's explanation of the standard or Powell's analysis of the statutory or equal protection issues. No other Justice joined Part III–A of the Powell opinion.

112. 438 U.S. at 295, 98 S.Ct. at 2750–51 (Powell, J.).

specific constitutional violations.[113] Second, the employment discrimination cases decided under Title VII of the Civil Rights Acts were not relevant because the affirmative action remedies were ordered in such cases only after a judicial or administrative finding of discrimination against a racial minority in a particular business or industry.[114] Third, he found that the use of less than the most strict standard in gender-based classification cases was irrelevant to the race affirmative action question.[115] The special societal and constitutional history of race discrimination in America made racial classification qualitatively different. Additionally the greater judicial ability to deal with gender-based classifications, which involve only two possible groups, justified the greater allowance of their use for remedial purposes by government units.

Justice Powell applied his strict scrutiny-compelling interest test to the Davis program and found it wanting. In order to test the Davis program he examined each of the asserted purposes of the state and school. First, the school could not assert as a legitimate purpose the attainment of a minimum specified percentage of a particular racial or ethnic group in the class; in Justice Powell's view, that purpose would be "facially invalid." [116] Second, the Justice recognized that the state had a legitimate interest in eliminating the effects of "identified discrimination," but he found that this end would only support programs that were judicially, legislatively, or administratively found to be necessary to remedy violations of the constitution or statutes which had been passed to promote constitutional purposes.[117] Because the University could not claim any ability, or any state granted authority, to make findings of particular discrimination in its or other educational programs, the University's special admissions program could not be held to further the governmental interest in ending the effect of prior acts of racial discrimination.

---

113. 438 U.S. at 300–01, 98 S.Ct. at 2753–54 (Powell, J.).

114. 438 U.S. at 301, 98 S.Ct. at 2754.

Justice Powell also stated that no other decision of the Supreme Court regarding any civil rights legislation mandated the approval of racial classification under less than a strict scrutiny standard. He found that Lau v. Nichols, 414 U.S. 563, 94 S.Ct. 786, 39 L.Ed.2d 1 (1974), which on the basis of Title VI, had required a city to provide remedial English instruction for students of oriental ancestry, was based both on the Court's deference to an agency decision that prior practices had had the effect of subjecting individuals to discrimination on the basis of their national origin, and the Court's recognition that the program did not result in denial of benefits to members of any other racial or ethnic group. Similarly, Justice Powell found that United Jewish Organizations v. Carey, 430 U.S. 144, 97 S.Ct. 996, 51 L.Ed.2d 229 (1977), in which the Court had approved the use of race-conscious criteria in creating voting districts, was irrelevant because it was based on an administrative finding that the measures were necessary to improve the ability of previously disadvantaged racial groups to participate in the voting process, and because the creation of such districts did not deny any person their right to vote in any meaningful matter.

Justice Powell's view of the *United Jewish Organizations* case might be supported by the Supreme Court's later decision in Shaw v. Reno, 509 U.S. 630, 113 S.Ct. 2816, 125 L.Ed.2d 511 (1993). In *Shaw* a majority of the Justices found that state legislation establishing districts for the election of members of the United States House of Representatives that employed racial criteria for the purpose of insuring the representation of minority race groups was subject to the compelling interest test. The Court in *Shaw* remanded the case for an initial determina-

tion by the lower courts as to whether the plan was narrowly tailored to promote a compelling government interest. The basis upon which the Court found that the districting plan in *Shaw* constituted racial discrimination on its face is examined in §§ 14.4, 14.8 of this Treatise.

115. 438 U.S. at 302–03, 98 S.Ct. at 2754–55 (Powell, J.). Justice Powell also found that the cases regarding congressional treatment of American Indians were inapposite because of the unique relationship between the government and Indian tribes. 438 U.S. at 304 n. 42, 98 S.Ct. at 2755 n. 42 [on the unique nature of American Indian classifications see § 4.2, supra].

116. 438 U.S. at 307, 98 S.Ct. at 2757 (Powell, J.).

117. 438 U.S. at 307–10, 98 S.Ct. at 2757–59 (Powell, J.). Justice Powell indicates in his footnote 44 that the statistically demonstrated "disparate impact" of an employment practice or job qualification is not sufficient in itself to establish a violation of Title VII of the Civil Rights Acts. Proof of such disparate impact does establish a prima facie case of such discrimination and it will suffice as the basis for a finding of a Title VII violation if the employer whose employment practice is challenged cannot show that the practice is not discriminatory but, instead, is justified by business necessity or relationship to job performance. Carefully read, Justice Powell's footnote only indicates that courts do not order remedies for Title VII violation until all evidence in a case is considered and the court concludes that the challenged practice in fact violates Title VII.

Justice Powell also noted that the University had been unable to demonstrate that the special admissions program was necessary to evaluate minority applicants due to some inherent cultural bias in grading or testing procedures. 438 U.S. at 306 n. 43, 98 S.Ct. at 2756–57 n. 43.

Third, Justice Powell found that the program was not a reasonably necessary way of improving health care for communities that currently did not receive adequate medical services. Even assuming that in some situations an interest in health care might be compelling, he found that there was no proof that the Davis program would in fact substantially increase the number of doctors or the quality of health care available to economically deprived citizens.[118]

Fourth, Justice Powell found that the attainment of a "diverse student body" would be a compelling interest under some circumstances; it was on this basis that he would approve some of the race-conscious admissions programs that had been employed by universities other than Davis.

Justice Powell found that the attainment of a diverse student body related to "academic freedom," which in turn was related to the guarantees of the First Amendment.[119] Because Justice Powell believed that this interest embodied a value of independent constitutional importance, he would consider it compelling under some circumstances.

In graduate and professional schools, as well as undergraduate colleges, a faculty could attempt to insure that students and teachers would be exposed to a wide variety of diverse social and political interests. The use of racial or ethnic classifications, whether described as "goals," quotas or something else, did not further this goal, however, because it set aside places in the class for persons solely on this basis, without regard to whether the acceptance or rejection of specific individuals on the basis of their race was promoting true diversity within the university. "The diversity that furthers a compelling state interest encompasses a far broader array of qualifications and characteristics of which racial or ethnic origin is but a single though important element."[120]

Thus, Justice Powell found that strict racial "track" programs for admission, no matter how many special groups they might include, did not further a compelling interest. Instead, if a university wished to assert this "compelling interest" to justify its admissions program, it would have to establish an admissions procedure that would consider all facets of an applicant's background when that applicant was considered for admission on the basis of particular personal characteristics, or for the attainment of diversity in the student body. In attaining this diversity the educational institution, in Justice Powell's opinion, may consider or give positive weight to virtually any personal characteristic of the applicant. "An otherwise qualified medical student with a particular background—whether it be ethnic, geographic, *culturally advantaged or disadvantaged*—may bring to a professional school of medicine experiences, outlooks and ideas that enrich the training of its student body and better equip its graduates to render with understanding their vital service to humanity."[121]

Justice Powell did not limit consideration of these personal factors only to granting a "plus" because an individual was a member of a racial or disadvantaged minority rather than an educationally advantaged member of a racial majority. Indeed, his statement regarding "cultural advantage or disadvantage," and his statement that "the weight attributed to a particular quality may vary from year to year depending upon the 'mix' both of the student body and the applicants for the incoming class,"[122] make it appear that Justice Powell would allow a university to give a "plus" to economically advantaged *white* students over minorities once it had a sufficient "mix" of minority members. While it seems hard to believe that the Justice meant to approve of systems that subtly disadvantaged a minority member because of his or her race, the opinion provides little basis for limiting this use of the "diversity" goal.

---

118. 438 U.S. at 311, 98 S.Ct. at 2759 (Powell, J.).

119. 438 U.S. at 311–314, 98 S.Ct. at 2759–61 (Powell, J.).

120. 438 U.S. at 315, 98 S.Ct. at 2761 (Powell, J.).

121. 438 U.S. at 314, 98 S.Ct. at 2760 (Powell, J.) (emphasis added).

122. 438 U.S. at 318, 98 S.Ct. at 2762 (Powell, J.).

Justice Powell noted that some persons claimed that such discretionary programs could be a subtle means of employing a racial preference. Yet Justice Powell found that there would be no "facial infirmity" in such programs and that the Court, in his opinion, would not allow such an admissions program to be challenged on the basis of its disparate impact on persons of similar races because "good faith would be presumed" in the absence of a showing of a discriminatory purpose.

Justice Powell concluded that affirmative action programs would be constitutional if they followed the race consciousness approach without the use of predetermined racial classifications preferences, quotas, or goals. For this reason he voted with Justice Brennan and the other Justices who would have upheld the Davis program in total, but he did so only to the extent of reversing the California Supreme Court ruling that race could never be considered in educational admissions programs. The only portion of Justice Powell's opinion concerning the constitutionality of racial classifications that received five votes was the following paragraph:

> In enjoining petitioner from ever considering the race of any applicant, however, the courts below failed to recognize that the State has a substantial interest that legitimately may be served by a properly devised admissions program involving the competi-

tive consideration of race and ethnic origin. For this reason, so much of the California court's judgment as enjoins petitioner from any consideration of the race of any applicant must be reversed.[123]

Justices Brennan, White, Marshall and Blackmun voted to uphold the Davis program under both Title VI and the equal protection clause. They joined Justice Powell to form a majority in holding that some affirmative action programs are both constitutional and legal under Title VI, but they differed from Justice Powell in that they would have found that the Davis program, or ones employing similar racial goals or preferences, met the relevant constitutional and statutory standards. These four Justices joined in an opinion written by Justice Brennan, although each of the other three Justices added additional comments in separate concurring opinions.[124]

Justice Brennan noted that he and the three Justices who joined in his opinion agreed with Justice Powell only to the extent of finding that neither the Fourteenth Amendment nor Title VI prohibited the use of race in an affirmative action setting; Justice Brennan's opinion would establish criteria for legality and constitutionality quite different from those set forth by Justice Powell.

For two reasons Justice Brennan believed that classifications which burden white persons incident to remedial programs should be subjected to a standard of review similar to

---

123. 438 U.S. at 320, 98 S.Ct. at 2763 (Powell, J.).

124. Regents of The University of California v. Bakke, 438 U.S. at 324, 98 S.Ct. at 2765 (1978) (Brennan, Marshall, White & Blackmun, JJ., concurring in the judgment in part and dissenting in part); 438 U.S. at 379, 98 S.Ct. at 2794 (Separate Opinion of White, J.); 438 U.S. at 387, 98 S.Ct. at 2797 (Separate Opinion of Marshall, J.); 438 U.S. at 402, 98 S.Ct. at 2805 (Separate Opinion of Blackmun, J.).

Justice White, in his separate opinion, examined only whether Title VI implicitly created a private right of action.

Justice Marshall's separate opinion emphasized the history of racial discrimination both in the nation at large and in the decisions of the Supreme Court. He noted the pervasive historic discrimination against Blacks by both society at large and the government; for him the continuing impact of this discrimination justified affirmative action programs. 438 U.S. at 387–402, 98 S.Ct. at 2797–2805 (Separate Opinion of Marshall, J.).

Justice Blackmun added several important points in his separate opinion concerning the justification for the use of the judicial power to approve affirmative action programs and the lack of similar justification for judicial disapproval of affirmative action programs. He noted that the Davis program might only be "barely" constitutional but that, because it met Justice Brennan's two-pronged test, it should be upheld. Blackmun concluded his opinion by citing Chief Justice Marshall's statement, justifying the Court's use of wide interpretative powers, that "we must never forget, that it is a constitution that we are expounding." Justice Blackmun believed that the Court has the institutional responsibility to avoid interpreting the Fourteenth Amendment and the concept of equal protection in a manner that would inhibit the attainment of true racial equality. 438 U.S. at 402–408, 98 S.Ct. at 2805–08 (separate opinion of Blackmun, J.) quoting M'Culloch v. Maryland, 17 U.S. (4 Wheat.) 316, 407, 4 L.Ed. 579 (1819) (Opinion by Marshall, C.J.).

that employed in the gender and illegitimacy cases. First, such classifications might often be used to "stereotype and stigmatize" a small, powerless segment of individuals. Second, these racial classifications, like gender and illegitimacy classifications, were based on "immutable characteristics which its possessors are powerless to escape or set aside."

Brennan would describe laws that burden members of racial minorities because of their racial status as ones that "stigmatize" that group and are not truly benign. Such laws must be subjected to the strict scrutiny—compelling interest test that Professor Gunther had described as "fatal in fact." [125] However, when a government program could be described as "benign" to racial minorities, it would be subjected to a form of intermediate standard of review that allows for independent judicial evaluation of both the importance of the articulated purposes of the program and whether there was a real and substantial relationship between the means employed and that purpose. To be a valid benign racial classification program, in the view of these four Justices, a program must: (1) be justified by an articulated purpose of demonstrably sufficient importance to justify burdening members of the racial majority, and (2) be substantially related to that purpose to avoid stigmatizing any racial group or singling out powerless persons to bear the burden of the program.

After finding Davis' remedial purpose to be sufficient to meet the first part of the two part test, Justice Brennan's plurality opinion then went on to determine whether the program met "the second prong of our test—whether the Davis program stigmatizes any discrete group or individual and whether race is reasonably used in light of the program's objective." [126] The four Justices who joined this opinion found that the Davis program met this test and, therefore, that it comported with the equal protection guarantee.

Justice Stevens wrote an opinion joined by Chief Justice Burger and Justices Stewart and Rehnquist. [127] These four Justices found it unnecessary to address the constitutional issue in *Bakke* because both Davis' special admissions program and, therefore, the exclusion of Mr. Bakke from medical school violated Title VI. [128]

Justice Stevens concluded that Section 601 of the Civil Rights Act of 1964 required complete racial neutrality, or "colorblindness," by all administrators of programs accepting federal funds. He found that the "plain language of the statute" required this result absent clear legislative history indicating an intent to give the words a meaning other than their normal ordinary reading. [129]

The result of the division of the Justices in *Bakke* was that even though five members of the Supreme Court of the United States ruled that some affirmative action programs are constitutional and legal under Title VI, only those racial affirmative action programs in federally funded colleges that meet the Powell criteria will be upheld. The *Bakke* ruling made it appear that the interest in educational diversity could support some use of racial classifications but there was no majority opinion and that point remains unclear.

---

125. 438 U.S. at 361–62, 98 S.Ct. at 2784–85 quoting Gunther, Foreword: In Search of Evolving Doctrine on a Changing Court: A Model for a Newer Equal Protection, 86 Harv.L.Rev. 1, 8 (1972). Justice Brennan cited to Professor Gunther's article concerning equal protection standards of review wherein he refers to the strict scrutiny standard "strict in theory and fatal in fact."

126. 438 U.S. at 373–374, 98 S.Ct. at 2791.

127. 438 U.S. at 408–21, 98 S.Ct. at 2808–15 (Stevens, Stewart, Rehnquist, JJ., & Burger, C.J., concurring in part and dissenting in part).

128. 438 U.S. at 411, 98 S.Ct. at 2809–10. Justice Stevens first noted that the case was an individual's suit, not a class action, and found the distinction significant because the trial court's order and the California Supreme Court's reversal thereof could be read narrowly. Justice

Stevens argued that the California Supreme Court had only ordered the individual plaintiff admitted to medical school, and not ordered all state agencies or all schools to stop considering race when processing applications for educational or other benefits. These Justices believed that Title VI itself precluded any race-conscious admissions program; therefore, for this plurality, the Title VI ground for affirming the California Supreme Court's decision obviated any need to reach the constitutional issues. "It is ... perfectly clear that the question whether race can ever be used as a factor in an admissions decision is not an issue in this case, and that discussion of that issue is inappropriate."

129. 438 U.S. at 412–13, 98 S.Ct. at 2810.

In *Richmond v. J.A. Croson Co.,*[130] the Supreme Court ruled that a state or local government could not use a racial affirmative action classification unless the classification was narrowly tailored to promote a compelling interest. A racial classification could only be justified as narrowly tailored to promote the compelling interest of remedying racial segregation or discrimination if the state or local governmental entity could show that its affirmative action racial classification was narrowly tailored to correct past discrimination by that governmental entity itself or by private sector persons entities within its jurisdiction. The opinion of Justice O'Connor in *J.A. Croson,* which was in part a plurality opinion and in part a majority opinion, did not explain which, if any, government goals other than remedying identified past discrimination would be sufficiently compelling to justify the use of a racial affirmative action classification.

The ruling in *Bakke* has not been overruled. We will examine the impact of the *J.A. Croson* decision on *Bakke,* after an examination of the *Wygant* decision.

The *Wygant* Decision—Maintenance of a Racially Integrated Faculty. In *Wygant v. Jackson Board of Education,*[131] the Supreme Court invalidated an attempt by a local school board to maintain a racially integrated faculty, at a time when the school board had to reduce the number of faculty members that it employed, through the means of laying off white teachers before laying off black teachers with less seniority. There was no majority opinion issued by the Court; specific Justices espoused a variety of positions regarding the proper

standard of review to be employed by the judiciary when determining whether racial affirmative action programs complied with the equal protection guarantee.

All of the Justices voting in *Wygant* seem to agree that the problem presented to the Court had its roots in community racial tension on a variety of topics, including education. In 1972, negotiations between the Jackson Board of Education and the teachers' union, which objected to changes in the seniority system for faculty benefits and job protection, resulted in the addition of a layoff provision to the collective bargaining agreement between the Board and the union. This agreement provided that, if it was necessary to lay off teachers, layoffs would be done on a seniority basis (the last hired would be the first laid off) "except that at no time will there be a greater percentage of minority personnel laid off than the current percentage of minority personnel employed at the time of the layoff." In other words, layoffs would be made proportionally among nonminority and minority teachers so that layoffs would not result in increasing the disparity between the percentages of minority and nonminority faculty members. This system resulted in the layoff of some nonminority teachers with more seniority than some minority teachers who were not laid off.

The federal district court and court of appeals had upheld the proportional layoff agreement. The basis for the lower court rulings upholding the legality and constitutionality of the proportional layoff agreement was the subject of some dispute between Justices on the Supreme Court.[132]

---

130. 488 U.S. 469, 109 S.Ct. 706, 102 L.Ed.2d 854 (1989).

131. 476 U.S. 267, 106 S.Ct. 1842, 90 L.Ed.2d 260 (1986), rehearing denied 478 U.S. 1014, 106 S.Ct. 3320, 92 L.Ed.2d 728 (1986).

132. A majority of Justices appear to have agreed that a race conscious remedy can be used to insure correction of an illegal or unconstitutional use of race. See Local 28 of the Sheet Metal Workers' International Association v. E.E.O.C., 478 U.S. 421, 481, 106 S.Ct. 3019, 3053, 92 L.Ed.2d 344 (1986) (plurality opinion by Brennan, J.); 478 U.S. at 483, 106 S.Ct. at 3054 (Powell, J., concurring in part and concurring in the judgment).

There was a dispute in *Wygant* over whether the proceedings in the lower federal courts, and earlier proceed-

ings in the state courts, provided a sufficient basis for rejecting the school board's claim before the Supreme Court of the United States that the layoff provision was designed to remedy prior racial discrimination by the school board. Justice Powell's plurality opinion found that asserting past government discrimination as a justification for a remedial program required evidentiary support and that the prior court proceedings in this case did not provide any basis for such a conclusion. Wygant v. Jackson Board of Education, 476 U.S. 267, 278 n. 5, 106 S.Ct. 1842, 1848–49, 1849 n. 5, 90 L.Ed.2d 260 (1986), rehearing denied 478 U.S. 1014, 106 S.Ct. 3320, 92 L.Ed.2d 728 (1986) (plurality opinion by Powell, J.).

Justices Marshall, Brennan, and Blackmun dissented in *Wygant*. They filed an opinion stating that the district

The Supreme Court of the United States, by a five to four vote, held that the layoff of nonminority race teachers solely because of the race of the individual teachers violated the equal protection clause of the Fourteenth Amendment. However, there was no majority opinion regarding this ruling.[133] Even the four Justices who dissented could not agree on a single standard of review.[134] Therefore, we need to examine the opinions issued by individual Justices or groups of Justices in this case to understand the standards of review that are being employed to review voluntary affirmative action programs.

Justice O'Connor argued, in a concurrence, that there appeared to be agreement among virtually all members of the Court that a public employer may take some affirmative steps to insure an integrated work force even though a particular affirmative action program would be invalid if a majority of Justices believe that it is not precisely tailored to promote an interest that they believe justifies imposing some not "disproportionate" burden on nonminority members.[135]

Justice Powell wrote the plurality opinion announcing the judgment of the Court in *Wygant*. Powell's opinion was joined by Chief Justice Burger and Justice Rehnquist and, in part, by Justice O'Connor.[136] Powell's plurality opinion found that a racial classification, regardless of whether it aided or burdened the members of a minority racial group, would be invalid unless it was narrowly tailored to promote a compelling interest. This formulation is similar to the position Powell had taken in earlier affirmative action cases and is quite close to the formulation used in cases examining racial classifications that burden members of minority races, although the compelling interest test is often stated in terms of whether a law is "necessary" to promote a compelling or overriding government interest.[137] Justice Powell found that a goal of remedying societal discrimination would not in itself be sufficient to support this racial classification.

Justice Powell did not exclude the possibility that maintaining a diverse and racially integrated faculty could be found to be a compelling interest. Regardless of the legitimacy or compelling nature of that interest, Justice Powell's plurality opinion found that a layoff plan that imposed the burden of achieving racial equality on particular nonminority individuals, (who were to be laid off or fired despite their seniority) was not narrowly tailored to the promotion of that interest. He noted that "[o]ther, less intrusive means of accomplishing similar purposes—such as the adop-

court, because of its ruling on the legal issues in the case, did not have occasion to develop a full record regarding whether there had been prior governmental discrimination in the hiring of teachers. They believed the Supreme Court should remand the case "to develop a factual record adequate to resolve the serious issue" of whether the action of the school board was related to the compelling interest of remedying prior government discrimination. 476 U.S. at 295, 106 S.Ct. at 1858 (Marshall, J., joined by Brennan, and Blackmun, JJ., dissenting).

133. The references for the separate opinions of the Justices who voted in the majority are as follows: Wygant v. Jackson Board of Education, 476 U.S. 267, 106 S.Ct. 1842, 90 L.Ed.2d 260 (1986), rehearing denied 478 U.S. 1014, 106 S.Ct. 3320, 92 L.Ed.2d 728 (1986) (Powell, J., announces the opinion of the Court and delivers an opinion joined by Burger, J., and Rehnquist, J., and joined in parts I, II, III–A, III–B, and V by O'Connor, J.); 476 U.S. at 284, 106 S.Ct. at 1852 (O'Connor, J., concurring in part and concurring in the judgment); 476 U.S. at 294, 106 S.Ct. at 1857, (White, J., concurring in the judgment).

134. 476 U.S. at 295, 106 S.Ct. at 1858 (Marshall, J., joined by Brennan and Blackmun, JJ., dissenting), 476 U.S. at 313, 106 S.Ct. at 1867 (Stevens, J., dissenting).

135. 476 U.S. at 287, 106 S.Ct. at 1853, 1854 (O'Connor, J., concurring): "Ultimately, the Court is at least in accord in believing that a public employer, consistent with the Constitution, may undertake an affirmative action program which is designed to further a legitimate remedial purpose and which implements that purpose by means that do not impose disproportionate harm on the interest, or unnecessarily trammel the rights, of innocent individuals directly and adversely affected by a racial plan's racial preference."

136. Justice Powell's opinion was joined in total only by Chief Justice Burger and Justice Rehnquist. See footnote 122, supra.

137. Justice Powell, in his *Wygant* plurality opinion, cited the works of a number of scholars for the proposition that the "narrowly tailored" language involves an independent judicial assessment of whether the means used by the government, in this case a racial classification, has a close "fit" with the end that would justify the particular type of law or classification (a compelling interest in the racial classification). 476 U.S. at 280 nn. 6, 7, 106 S.Ct. at 1850 nn. 6, 7.

tion of hiring goals—are available." [138]

Prior decisions of the Supreme Court, including opinions by Justice Powell, provided a basis for finding that a race conscious remedy can be used to correct governmental racial discrimination. The Jackson School Board asserted that its layoff program was designed to correct past governmental discrimination against minority race applicants for faculty positions. But Justice Powell's plurality opinion found that there was no evidentiary support for the assertion that the remedial program was adopted to correct past governmental discrimination. The plurality believed that "evidentiary support for the conclusion that remedial action is warranted" was required in order to assure that governmental entities would not merely assert fictitious past discrimination as a basis for justifying racial preferences that otherwise would be invalid under the equal protection clause. [139]

Justice O'Connor concurred in part of Justice Powell's plurality opinion and in the judgment. She agreed with Powell that racial classifications should be narrowly tailored to promote a compelling interest, although she stated that "the distinction between a compelling and an important government purpose may be a negligible one." [140] She wrote separately to note that a governmental practice designed to achieve and maintain an integrated faculty for a school district might be upheld if the governmental action was narrowly tailored to further that goal and did not impose a disproportionate harm on nonminority members. Anyone seeking to employ Justice O'Connor's opinion in other cases, however, would be advised to read her opinion closely. Her opinion does not specify the extent to which the implementation of hiring goals will be constitutionally permissible in the absence of some proof of past employment discrimination by the government agency.

Justice White concurred in the judgment in *Wygant*, but he did not set out a legal standard of review for racial discrimination or affirmative action case. Indeed, his concurring opinion did not cite any prior decision of the Court. [141] Thus, his opinion cannot be evaluated in terms of traditional standards of review. Justice White asserted that "[w]hatever the legitimacy of hiring goals or quotas may be," the discharge of some persons to favor or make room for others on the basis of race could not be consistent with the principles of the equal protection clause.

The separate opinions of the five member *Wygant* majority do not appear to adopt the position that attempts by government entities to achieve and maintain an integrated governmental work force are *per se* unconstitutional under the equal protection clause. Some affirmative action programs by government employers that do not involve the discharge of nonminority members or a disregard for the merit of nonminority applicants for government positions may yet be approved by a majority of the Justices.

Justice Marshall wrote a dissenting opinion in *Wygant* that was joined by Justices Brennan and Blackmun. [142] These Justices believed that remedial use of race should be permissible under the equal protection clause if the remedial program or affirmative action program in the individual case is substantially related to the achievement of important government objectives. The maintenance of a racially integrated faculty and the correction of societal discrimination against persons who have strived to be members of the teaching profession would justify, in their view, a program that was substantially and reasonably related to achieving those ends. Because the agreement that provided the basis for the layoffs was negotiated between the union and the school board, Justice Marshall found little basis for finding that it was not, in fact, narrowly

138. 476 U.S. at 283, 106 S.Ct. at 1852 (plurality opinion by Powell, J.).

139. 476 U.S. at 276, 106 S.Ct. at 1848 (plurality opinion by Powell, J.).

140. 476 U.S. at 285, 106 S.Ct. at 1853 (O'Connor, J., concurring in part and concurring in the judgment).

141. 476 U.S. at 294, 106 S.Ct. at 1857 (White, J., concurring in the judgment).

142. 476 U.S. at 295, 106 S.Ct. at 1858 (Marshall, J., joined by Brennan and Blackmun, JJ., dissenting).

tailored to maintain the degree of integration in the faculty that was related to important educational and remedial objectives. Additionally, these dissenting Justices believed that the entire case should have been remanded to the lower federal courts for a further determination of whether there was a factual basis for the Board's assertion that the program was designed to remedy past governmental discrimination.

Perhaps the most interesting opinion in *Wygant* was delivered by Justice Stevens, in dissent.[143] For those persons who must attempt to apply *Wygant* to other cases, his decision may be of little importance. It was not joined by any other Justice; it does not state any clear standard of review. What is interesting is that Justice Stevens' dissenting opinion appears to be built on the theory that there need not be a clear standard of review for racial affirmative action programs and that case-by-case adjudication should be able to determine those few instances in which the use of race by the government may be permissible. He believes that the equal protection clause "absolutely prohibits the use of race in many governmental contexts" because race in most contexts will be unrelated to any truly legitimate public purpose. Nevertheless, Stevens found that "race is not always irrelevant to sound governmental decisionmaking" and that a school board could conclude "that an integrated faculty will be able to provide benefits to the student body that could not be provided by an all white, or nearly all white faculty." That educational purpose would not justify the use of a race conscious remedy in all instances. Rather, Justice Stevens found that there must be an additional inquiry into "the procedures that were used to adopt and implement" the race conscious remedy and "an evaluation of the nature of the harm" to nonminority persons that resulted from the race conscious program. In Stevens' view, there

was no basis for judicial invalidation of the layoff compromise. It had been designed to achieve a legitimate educational objective through a process that involved participation by the disadvantaged individuals (through the negotiations by the teachers union); the harm to the individual laid off teachers was not based on "any lack of respect for their race, or blind habit and stereotype."

Diversity in Education—A Compelling Interest After All. In *Richmond v. J.A. Croson Co.,*[144] the Court held that state and local governments could only use a racial classification, even if it was a classification that benefitted minority race persons, if the classification was narrowly tailored to promote a compelling interest. Justice O'Connor wrote an opinion in *J.A. Croson* that was, in part, a majority opinion and, in part, a plurality opinion. The fact situation in *J.A. Croson* only required the Court to determine whether a city plan, giving a preference in the awarding of city contracts to minority owned businesses, was narrowly tailored to correct past discrimination against minority race persons in that city. Justice O'Connor had no need to, and did not, explain what governmental interests, if any, other than the remedying of identified past discrimination against minorities might be sufficiently "compelling" to justify a state or local government's racial affirmative action program.

In the quarter century between 1978 and 2003, lower courts were left with virtually no guidance regarding how they should assess the constitutionality of the university's consideration of race in an admissions process. No other Justice had joined Justice Powell's constitutional analysis in *Bakke*; the Court's decisions concerning racial affirmative action in the 1990s might lead lower courts to believe that Justice Powell's views concerning the permissibility of some types of race conscious admissions programs could be disregarded.[145]

143. 476 U.S. at 313, 106 S.Ct. at 1867 (Stevens, J., dissenting).

144. 488 U.S. 469, 109 S.Ct. 706, 102 L.Ed.2d 854 (1989).

145. Based on the view of how lower courts should interpret plurality opinions (cases decided with opinion by

the Supreme Court in which there was no majority opinion or in which there was a partial majority opinion and partial plurality opinion) set out in Marks v. United States, 430 U.S. 188, 97 S.Ct. 990, 51 L.Ed.2d 260 (1977) it would have been possible to view Justice Powell's plurality opinion in Regents of the University v. Bakke, 438 U.S. 265, 98 S.Ct. 2733, 57 L.Ed.2d 750 (1978) as setting

2003, Justice Powell's views in *Bakke* would become established as the law of the land, when five Justices in *Grutter v. Bollinger*[146] employed Justice Powell's views and upheld the University of Michigan's Law School's race conscious admissions policy. The *Grutter* ruling would be a narrow one; it would be difficult for state universities to establish race conscious admissions programs that would comply with the Powell standards, as they were understood by a majority of the Justices in 2003. On the same day that *Grutter* was decided, the Court, in *Gratz v. Bollinger*,[147] invalidated the University of Michigan's policies governing the admission of students to its undergraduate programs.

In *Grutter v. Bollinger*[148] Justice O'Connor wrote the majority opinion for five Justices. Some of the five Justices in the majority wrote concurring opinions; but all of the concurring Justices joined Justice O'Connor's majority opinion in *Grutter*.[149] As one might expect, the majority opinion began with a description of the system used by the University of Michigan Law School for its admissions program and the lower court litigation.[150] As described in the majority opinion, the law school's admission system did not guarantee admission to the Law School for anyone based on their numerical scores on a standardized test or their numerical grade point average in an undergraduate or graduate degree program. Instead, according to the Law School and the majority opinion, the law school individually evaluated each applicant in an effort to find a truly diverse student body for the purpose of having

a "critical mass" of persons from under represented minority races and from persons with various points of view so that the Law School could best train future leaders in society, as well as future attorneys.

Justice O'Connor recognized that some statements in majority, plurality, and concurring opinions since *Bakke* might have lead lower courts to believe that diversity in education was not a compelling interest. Her majority opinion found that it was unnecessary "[to] decide whether Justice Powell's opinion [had been] binding" because the Court majority in *Grutter* had decided independently "[to] endorse Justice Powell's view that student body diversity is a compelling state interest that can justify the use of race in university admissions."[151]

Having found that diversity in education was a compelling governmental interest, the majority opinion went on to consider whether the University of Michigan's Law School was narrowly tailored to promote that compelling interest. The majority opinion, like the four dissenting Justices in *Grutter*, found that the use of race in admissions, to any extent, constituted a racial classification that had to be reviewed under "strict scrutiny" and that "this means that such classifications are constitutional only if they are narrowly tailored to further compelling governmental interest."[152] However, the majority found that this test was not "fatal" and that "context matters when reviewing race-based governmental action."[153]

---

forth guidelines that should be used by lower courts when litigating the constitutionality of race conscious programs in education. Cases of the Supreme Court between 1978 and 2003, raise questions in the minds of lower court judges concerning the position of the Supreme Court concerning what, in this text, we have referred to as "voluntary remedial measures." An overview of those cases is contained in § 14.10(a)(4). In Grutter v. Bollinger 539 U.S. 306, ___, 123 S.Ct. 2325, 2335, 156 L.Ed.2d 304 (2003) Justice O'Connor's majority opinion noted that the Supreme Court had granted certiorari in these cases "to resolve this agreement among the Courts of Appeals on a question of national importance: whether diversity is a compelling interest that can justify the narrowly tailored use of race in selecting applicants for admission to public universities."

146. Grutter v. Bollinger, 539 U.S. 306, 123 S.Ct. 2325, 156 L.Ed.2d 304 (2003).

147. Gratz v. Bollinger, 539 U.S. 244, 123 S.Ct. 2411, 156 L.Ed.2d 257 (2003).

148. Grutter v. Bollinger, 539 U.S. 306, 123 S.Ct. 2325, 156 L.Ed.2d 304 (2003).

149. 539 U.S. at ___, 123 S.Ct. at 2347 (Ginsburg, J., joined by Breyer, J., concurring).

150. Grutter v. Bollinger, 539 U.S. 306, ___, 123 S.Ct. 2325, 2331–32, 2341–47, 156 L.Ed.2d 304 (2003) Part I A and Part III B of the majority (opinion by Justice O'Connor).

151. 539 U.S. at ___, 123 S.Ct. at 2337.

152. 539 U.S. at ___, 123 S.Ct. at 2337–38.

153. 539 U.S. at ___, 123 S.Ct. at 2338.

Although the majority opinion found that some deference or latitude had to be given to educational decision makers, Justice O'Connor stated that the dissenting Justices in *Grutter* were wrong when they accused the majority of abandoning the Court's historic position of strictly scrutinizing [taking a very close look at] any race-based classification that the government claimed was narrowly tailored to advance a compelling interest.[154] Once again Justice O'Connor's majority opinion in *Grutter* tracked the reasoning of Justice Powell in *Bakke*. The *Grutter* majority opinion found that the University of Michigan Law School did not use a quota system, made a truly individualized consideration of each application, and did not set aside any seats simply for minority race persons. The fact that Law School officials had stated that the faculty wanted a "critical mass" of minority race students did not make the program invalid. On this point, Justice O'Connor noted that Michigan's Law School admissions policy was similar to a Harvard admissions program, which had employed minimum goals for minority admissions, that received favorable comments from Justice Powell in *Bakke*.

The majority in *Grutter* recognized that the Law School had not examined every race neutral alternative method of achieving student body diversity, but the majority found that the "narrow tailoring [requirement of the strict scrutiny test] does not require exhaustion of every conceivable race-neutral alternative."[155]

Near the close of Justice O'Connor's opinion, she stated that race based policies designed to achieve a compelling interest, including racial diversity in institutions of higher education, should be limited in time in order to qualify under the narrow tailoring requirement of the strict scrutiny standard. In her majority opinion Justice O'Connor stated "we

expect that 25 years from now, the use of racial preferences will no longer be necessary to further the interest approved today."[156] Two of the concurring Justices believe that this statement in the majority opinion did not place a 25 year time limit on the use of a race conscious admissions program, but only expressed the hope that a future generation would not need to use race based policies to achieve true equal opportunity.[157] At least some of the dissenting Justices believed that the majority opinion placed a 25 year time limit on the University of Michigan's Law School admissions program.[158]

Four Justices joined in the dissent that was written by Chief Justice Rehnquist in *Grutter*.[159] The Chief Justice found that the use of race conscious decisionmaking in government might be allowed in some circumstances; the Chief Justice did not specifically endorse or reject the majority's conclusion that diversity in education might be a compelling interest and under certain circumstances would support a race conscious admissions policy for a state operated institution of higher learning. The Chief Justice believed that the majority had failed to truly scrutinize the University of Michigan's Law School admissions program because a close scrutiny of that program would demonstrate, that the law school was in fact operating an admissions policy that simply set aside some places for minority race applicants by giving those applicants admission based solely upon their race. The dissenters believed that the majority had not used a true strict scrutiny test, because the majority had not demanded that the government show that its Law School admissions policy was necessary to promote a compelling interest. Chief Justice Rehnquist set out facts regarding the University of Michigan's Law School's admissions from the years 1995 through 2000 to demon-

154. 539 U.S. at ___, ___, 123 S.Ct. at 2341, 2343.

155. 539 U.S. at ___, 123 S.Ct. at 2344.

156. 539 U.S. at ___, 123 S.Ct. at 2347 (this statement is made in the last sentence of Part III of the majority opinion).

157. Grutter v. Bollinger, 539 U.S. 306, ___, 123 S.Ct. 2325, 2347–48, 156 L.Ed.2d 304 (2003) (Ginsburg, J., joined by Breyer, J., concurring).

158. 539 U.S. at ___, 123 S.Ct. at 2365 (Thomas, J., joined as to Parts I–VII by Scalia, J., concurring, in part, and dissenting, in part).

159. Grutter v. Bollinger, 539 U.S. 306, ___, 123 S.Ct. 2325, 2365, 156 L.Ed.2d 304 (2003) (Rehnquist, C.J., joined by Scalia, Kennedy, and Thomas, JJ., dissenting).

strate why the dissenters believed that the Law School in fact was operating a program that set quotas based on race.[160] A true quota system could not truly be considered to be narrowly tailored to a compelling interest.

Justice Kennedy wrote a dissent in *Grutter* that was not joined by any other Justice, in part indicated agreement with Justice Powell's method of analysis in *Bakke*.[161] In *Grutter* Justice Kennedy took the position that a university's admissions policy that had numerical goals for enrollment of minority race students could never be considered narrowly tailored to a compelling interest. Surprisingly, Justice Kennedy disregarded the statements in the majority opinion that pointed out that Justice Powell had stated that he would vote to approve a program such as that used by the Harvard undergraduate admissions program in the mid–1970s, which established goals for the admission of minority race students.

Justices Scalia and Thomas, in their two dissenting opinions, asserted that the University of Michigan was using a quota system that could not be considered to be narrowly tailored to a compelling interest.[162] The only difference between the Scalia and Thomas dissenting opinions appears to be Justice Thomas's acceptance of the fact that the Justices, perhaps to follow the principle of stare decisis, would have to consider diversity in education to be a com-

pelling interest that might support some types of race conscious admissions policies for state operated institutions of higher education.[163]

On the same day that the Court upheld the University of Michigan's Law School admissions policy, the Supreme Court, in *Gratz v. Bollinger*,[164] invalidated the admissions policy used by the University of Michigan for students seeking admittance to its undergraduate degree programs.[165] The University of Michigan's undergraduate admissions policy was invalidated by a 6 to 3 vote of the Justices; Chief Justice Rehnquist wrote a majority opinion for five Justices in *Gratz*.[166]

The *Gratz* case had taken an unusual route to the Supreme Court. Jennifer Gratz and Patrick Hamacher had been denied admission to the liberal arts college at the University of Michigan. Ms. Gratz had enrolled at the University of Michigan at Dearborn and graduated from that school. Mr. Hamacher had enrolled at Michigan State University; he had graduated from that school, although he indicated that he had intended to transfer to the University of Michigan if his challenge to their undergraduate admissions program been successful. During the course of the litigation in the District Court, the University of Michigan had changed its admissions guidelines; all of the university admissions policies had a distinct

---

160. 539 U.S. at ___, 123 S.Ct. at 2368–69 (tables 1, 2, and 3 in the dissenting opinion of Rehnquist, C.J., joined by Scalia, Kennedy, and Thomas, JJ., dissenting).

161. 539 U.S. at ___, 123 S.Ct. at 2370–74 (Kennedy, J., dissenting).

162. 539 U.S. at ___, 123 S.Ct. at 2348–50 (Scalia, J., joined by Thomas, J., concurring, in part, and dissenting, in part); 539 U.S. at ___, 123 S.Ct. 2350–65 (Thomas, J., joined as to Parts I–VII by Scalia, J., concurring in part and dissenting in part).

163. Justice Scalia stated that he was joining in Parts I–VII of Justice Thomas's opinion; Justice Thomas's opinion consisted only of Parts I–VII. However, after some asterisks near the end of Part VII of Justice Thomas' dissent, there was a paragraph in which indicated acceptance of the fact that the majority's opinion would stand for a 25 year period. Perhaps it is that final paragraph of Justice Thomas' dissent, opinion that Justice Scalia did not care to join.

164. Gratz v. Bollinger, 539 U.S. 244, 123 S.Ct. 2411, 156 L.Ed.2d 257 (2003).

165. The Supreme Court had previously held that if an admissions policy violated the Fourteenth Amendment

equal protection clause it would also violate Title VI of the Civil Rights Statutes and 42 U.S.C. § 1981. The majority opinion in *Gratz* thus concluded: "We conclude, therefore [for the reasons set out in the majority opinion], that because the University's use of race in its current freshman admissions policy is not narrowly tailored to achieve respondents [the University] asserted compelling interest in diversity, the admissions policy violates the equal protection clause of the Fourteenth Amendment. We further find that the admissions policy also violates Title VI and 42 U.S.C. § 1981." 539 U.S. at ___, 123 S.Ct. at 2340.

166. Justice O'Connor was one of the five Justices who joined the opinion of the Court but she wrote a separate concurring opinion; Justice Breyer joined Justice O'Connor's analysis but did not join the majority opinion. Gratz v. Bollinger, 539 U.S. 244, ___, n. ___, 123 S.Ct. 2411, 2431, n. ___, 156 L.Ed.2d 257 (2003) (O'Connor, J., concurring; footnote reference to Breyer, J., joining the concurring opinion except for the sentence indicating Justice O'Connor's agreement with the majority opinion). 539 U.S. at ___, 123 S.Ct. at 2433–34 (Breyer, J., concurring in the judgment).

preference to racial minorities. Beginning with the 1998 academic year the University used a point score system with a maximum of 150 points. That system each member of certain racial minorities received an automatic 20 points simply based on their being a part of that racial or ethnic group. No other factor unrelated to test scores or grade point averages received nearly as many points.

The United States District Court that heard the challenge to granted Ms. Gratz and Mr. Hamacher the ability to be representatives of a class challenging the University of Michigan's undergraduate admissions policy. The District Court, in ruling on motions for summary judgment, ruled that the admissions policy the University of Michigan from 1995 through 1998 (which employed distinct admissions criteria for each student based upon the student's racial or ethnic status) was unconstitutional, but that the admissions program used by the University in 1999 and 2000, (which used the point system), did not violate equal protection. While this case was on appeal to the United States Court of Appeals for the Sixth Circuit, the Supreme Court of the United States granted certiorari to a Sixth Circuit ruling concerning the University of Michigan's Law School admissions policy. The United States Supreme Court granted certiorari to the parties in the *Gratz* case even though the Court of Appeals had not ruled on the case, so that the Justices could consider all of the current challenges to University of Michigan race based admissions policies.[167]

After finding that the plaintiffs had standing to challenge the University's undergraduate admissions policy,[168] the Chief Justice's majority opinion in *Gratz* turned to the constitutionality of the University's undergraduate admissions policy. The majority did not question the District Court's ruling that the system of admissions used by the University of Michigan through 1998, which involved totally separate consideration of applications by racial groups, was unconstitutional. The majority in *Gratz* focused on the most recent version of the University's undergraduate admissions system, which awarded 20 points towards an admissions score for students based simply upon their membership in certain racial or ethnic minorities.

Without endorsing the ruling in *Grutter*, from which he had dissented, the Chief Justice, in his majority opinion in *Gratz*, stated that the argument that educational diversity could never be a compelling interest had been rejected by the Court in *Grutter*.[169]

Having assumed that the interest in educational diversity was a compelling interest, the Chief Justice's majority opinion in *Gratz v. Bollinger* looked at the relationship of the University of Michigan's undergraduate admissions scoring system and found that its admissions policy was not narrowly tailored to a compelling interest in racial diversity. Therefore, the majority found that the current admissions policy violated the equal protection clause of the Fourteenth Amendment, and related statutes.[170]

In *Gratz*, Chief Justice Rehnquist referred to Justice Powell's opinion in the *Bakke* case to explain why the current University of Michigan's undergraduate admissions policy could not be considered narrowly tailored to promote racial diversity. Chief Justice Rehnquist found

---

167. Gratz v. Bollinger, 539 U.S. 244, ___, 123 S.Ct. 2411, 2417–22, 156 L.Ed.2d 257 (2003) (Part I of majority opinion, which contains a description of the history of the litigation and the University's admissions policy).

168. 539 U.S. at ___, 123 S.Ct. at 2422–2426 (Part IIA of the majority opinion, which contains the Court's analysis of, and ruling on, the standing of the petitioners to litigate the constitutionality and legality of the University's admissions process). Two Justices dissented regarding the issue of the petitioner's standing. 539 U.S. at ___, 123 S.Ct. at 2434 (Stevens, J., joined by Souter, J., dissenting); 539 U.S. at ___, 123 S.Ct. at 2438–42 (Souter, J., joined in part by Ginsburg, J., dissenting; Justice Ginsburg did not join Part I of the opinion by Justice Souter, which dis-

cussed the issue of Article III standing). The subject of standing to litigate a constitutional issue is examined in Chapter 2 of this Treatise.

169. 539 U.S. at ___, 123 S.Ct. at 2426–27, referring to Grutter v. Bollinger, 539 U.S. 306, 123 S.Ct. 2325, 2338–2341, 156 L.Ed.2d 304 (2003).

170. Gratz v. Bollinger, 539 U.S. 244, ___ n. 23, 123 S.Ct. 2411, 2430 n. 23, 156 L.Ed.2d 257 (2003) (concluding paragraph of majority opinion, and footnote thereto, explains that the majority's ruling concerning the invalidity of the program under equal protection also involves a ruling that the program violates Title VI of the Civil Rights Acts and 42 U.S.C. § 1981).

that as Justice Powell had claimed, the equal protection clause demanded, that each individual application be given individualized consideration. Race could not be used as an automatic basis for admission if a program were to have any possibility of being considered narrowly tailored to promote educational diversity in a college or university. According to the majority in *Gratz*, the University of Michigan system did not provide individualized consideration of each student, even though there was the possibility that some students who were not members of a minority race might be considered for admission if their score was below the normal point score for admitted students. The applications of students who were not members of designated racial minorities, under the University of Michigan program, would not receive individualized consideration until after most of the decisions regarding admissions had been made by the University. In contrast to other applicants, members of racial minorities were automatically been given 20 points towards the minimum score needed for admission; virtually every student in the designated minority group who met absolute minimum standards for the University of Michigan would be given automatic admission.[171] Students who were not members of a designated racial minority group would not receive automatic admission to the University of Michigan merely because they met minimum admissions standards. Rather, the students in the racial groups that were not favored by the University of Michigan would have to have test scores, grade point averages from their high school, and points awarded for other factors (such as state of residency, alumni relationships or personal achievement) that would raise their admissions score close to, or over, 100 points. A minority race student whose grades and test scores were at the minimally acceptable level, would have a point score near, or over, 100 points once they were given the automatic 20

points for being a member of a racial or ethnic group favored by the University of Michigan for diversity purposes.[172]

The Chief Justice's majority opinion in *Gratz*, recognized that it might be difficult, if not impossible, for a large university such as the University of Michigan to give truly individualized consideration to each of the thousands of applications that it receives for its undergraduate program. The majority opinion stated that "the fact that the implementation of a program capable of providing individualized consideration might present administrative challenges does not render constitutional an otherwise problematic system."[173] For that reason, the majority ruled that the University of Michigan's system of awarding automatic points to members of minority races for the purposes of meeting scores needed for admission could not be considered necessary or narrowly tailored to promoting educational diversity. The admissions polices failed the strict scrutiny test, because the system was not narrowly tailored to a compelling interest.

Justice O'Connor, who had authored the majority opinion in *Grutter* upholding the Law School's admissions policy, wrote an opinion concurring in both the judgment and opinion of the Court in *Gratz*, which invalidated the University's undergraduate admissions policy.[174] Justice Breyer joined the entirety of Justice O'Connor's concurring opinion except for the last sentence of her opinion (the sentence that stated Justice O'Connor's concurrence in Chief Justice Rehnquist's opinion). Justice O'Connor thought that her analysis was entirely consistent with the majority opinion. Justice Breyer agreed entirely with Justice O'Connor's analysis, but he thought that her analysis was inconsistent with the majority opinion that was written by Chief Justice Rehnquist.[175]

---

171. 539 U.S. at ___, 123 S.Ct. at 2425, 3429–30.

172. 539 U.S. at ___, 123 S.Ct. at 2419–20.

173. 539 U.S. at ___, 123 S.Ct. at 2430.

174. Gratz v. Bollinger, 539 U.S. 244, 123 S.Ct. 2411, 2431, 156 L.Ed.2d 257 (2003) (O'Connor, J., concurring in the opinion and the judgment of the Court joined by

Breyer, J., as to all but the last sentence of her opinion which joined the opinion of the Court).

175. 539 U.S. at ___, 123 S.Ct. at 2433–34 (Breyer, J., concurring in the judgment and explaining his joining part of Justice O'Connor's concurring opinion and part of Justice Ginsburg's dissenting opinion).

Justice O'Connor based her vote to invalidate the University of Michigan's undergraduate admissions policy on the basis that the mechanical assignment of a great number of points towards an admissions score merely for membership in a racial minority was not tailored to achieve racial diversity. Instead, according to Justice O'Connor, the Michigan undergraduate admission system was nothing more than a quota system or a set aside of some places in the class for minority race students.[176]

Justice Thomas concurred in the judgment and opinion of the Court; he wrote an opinion in *Gratz* to emphasize his view that "a state's use of racial discrimination in higher education admissions is categorically prohibited by the equal protection clause."[177] His brief concurring opinion in *Gratz* referred to his dissenting opinion in *Grutter,* in which he relied on the statement of the first Justice Harlan that the Constitution should be "color-blind."[178]

Justice Ginsburg dissented in *Gratz* in an opinion that was joined by Justice Souter and, in part, by Justice Breyer.[179] Justice Breyer agreed with Justice Ginsburg to the extent that she found government programs that were designed to undo the harmful effects of a

racial caste system that existed for much of our country's history would comply with equal protection principles.[180] Justice Ginsburg, joined only by Justice Souter, would have ruled that the undergraduate admissions policy was narrowly tailored to remedying the effects of racial discrimination in our society by the creation of a diverse student body. She believed that the University of Michigan system was of necessity somewhat mechanical because of the great number of applications for admissions to an undergraduate program that would be received by a high quality state operated institution in a large state.[181] Justice Ginsburg noted that the University of Michigan did not save a particular number of places in the class for minority race persons; the University was honestly striving to achieve diversity, rather than using a system that involved some quick look at the thousands of applications received by the University and then operated as a way of granting preferences to some racial groups. Chief Justice Rehnquist, in the majority opinion in *Gratz,* accused Justice Ginsburg of taking the position that the Court should alter constitutional principles merely to allow large universities to achieve diversity.[182] Justice Ginsburg responded that she did not believe the Constitution should be

176. 539 U.S. at ___, 123 S.Ct. at 2431–33 (O'Connor, J., joined in part by Breyer, J., concurring).

177. 539 U.S. at ___, 123 S.Ct. at 2433 (Thomas, J., concurring).

178. Grutter v. Bollinger, 539 U.S. 306, ___, ___, 123 S.Ct. 2325, 2350, 2365, 156 L.Ed.2d 304 (2003) (Thomas, J., joined, in part, by Scalia, J., concurring, in part, and dissenting, in part) referring to Plessy v. Ferguson, 163 U.S. 537, 559, 16 S.Ct. 1138, 41 L.Ed. 256 (1896). (Harlan, J., dissenting).

Interestingly, Justice Thomas's use of Justice Harlan's opinion was not challenged by the dissenting opinions in *Gratz.* Justice Ginsburg in *Gratz* referred to the need to rectify the caste system that had existed in this country for many generations. Gratz v. Bollinger, 539 U.S. 244, ___, 123 S.Ct. 2411, 2442–45, 156 L.Ed.2d 257 (2003) (Ginsburg, J., joined by Souter, J., and as to this part of her opinion, joined by Breyer, J., dissenting). The first Justice Harlan had used the "color blind" phrase only once in his opinion; he had emphasized the need to eliminate the race-based caste system in our society. It is difficult to know how the first Justice Harlan would have considered racial affirmative action programs, because it is difficult to believe he could have conceived of a society that would have taken positive steps to assist African-American persons such as Robert Harlan (who was either

the half brother or the cousin of the first Justice Harlan, depending on which side of the family you believed). See generally Tinsley V. Yarborough, Judicial Enigma: The First Justice Harlan (Oxford University Press 1995); T. Alexander Aleinikoff, Re-reading Justice Harlan's Dissent in Plessy v. Ferguson: Freedom, Anti–Racism and Citizenship, 1992 U.Ill. Rev. 961.

179. Gratz v. Bollinger, 539 U.S. 244, ___, 123 S.Ct. 2411, 2442, 156 L.Ed.2d 257 (2003) Ginsburg, J., (joined by Souter, J., and as to Part I of her opinion by Breyer, J., dissenting).

180. Justice Breyer agreed with Justice Ginsburg's analysis of the compelling nature of the governmental interest in remedying past societal discrimination against minority race persons; Justice Breyer believed that the University of Michigan undergraduate admissions policy was invalid because of its mechanical assignment of benefits by race. 539 U.S. at ___, 123 S.Ct. at 2433–34 (Breyer, J., concurring in the judgment).

181. 539 U.S. at ___, 123 S.Ct. at 2445–46 (Ginsburg, J., joined by Souter, J., dissenting; Part II of Justice Ginsburg's dissenting opinion, which was not joined by Justice Breyer).

182. Gratz v. Bollinger, 539 U.S. 244, ___ n. 22, 123 S.Ct. 2411, 2430 n. 22, 156 L.Ed.2d 257 (2003).

altered by the Court based on the needs of large universities but, rather, that "the Constitution, properly interpreted," would allow the government to openly attach importance to racial factors to eliminate the results of past societal and governmental discrimination, so as to allow our country to put behind it the effects of a long history of racial inequality.[183]

Justice Souter wrote a dissenting opinion in which he stated his belief that parties in the case did not have standing to litigate the constitutionality of the University of Michigan's undergraduate admissions policy; and that, if the majority reached the merits of the case, the University of Michigan's policy should be deemed to be narrowly tailored to the compelling interest in racial diversity.[184] Justice Ginsburg joined Part II of Justice Souter's opinion, which dealt with the constitutionality of the University of Michigan's admissions policy; she did not join part I of his opinion, which dealt with the issue of standing.[185] Justice Souter thought that the record in this case, which had never been reviewed by the Court of Appeals, did not justify the Court finding that the program did not give individualized consideration to all applicants. He believed that the record, though unclear, lent credence to the University's claim that it attempted to give individualized consideration to virtually all of the applicants who were anything more

than minimally qualified for admission to the University. Chief Justice Rehnquist, in the majority opinion, simply rejected Justice Souter's view of the record; the majority in *Gratz* found that there was no real individualized consideration of applicants in the University of Michigan system that offset the automatic grant of a preferential score to minority race applicants.[186]

Justice Stevens, in an opinion joined by Justice Souter, took the position that the Court should dismiss the case as not being within the Article III jurisdiction of federal courts because the plaintiffs in the case did not have a personal stake in the outcome that should give them standing to litigate the constitutionality of the University of Michigan's admissions policies.[187] Justice Stevens refused to comment on the merits of the claim that the University of Michigan's undergraduate admissions policy violated the equal protection clause. Justice Stevens' position concerning the use of race conscious policies to promote racial diversity and to eliminate the effects of society's history of discrimination against racial minorities remains unclear.[188]

After the Court's decisions in 2003, lower courts received a little more guidance than they previously had regarding how to review the constitutionality of race conscious pro-

183. 539 U.S. at ___ n. 11, 123 S.Ct. at 2446 n. 11 (Ginsburg, J., joined by Souter, J., dissenting).

184. 539 U.S. at ___, 123 S.Ct. at 2438–42 (Souter, J., joined in part by Ginsburg, J., dissenting). Justice Souter's analysis of the issue of Article III standing is contained in Part I of his dissenting opinion, which was not joined by Justice Ginsburg or any other Justice. 539 U.S. at ___, 123 S.Ct. at 2439 (Souter, J., dissenting).

185. Justice Souter's analysis of the University of Michigan's admission system, and his belief that there was an insufficient record for finding that the system violated equal protection was contained in Part II of his dissenting opinion, which was joined by Justice Ginsburg. 539 U.S. at ___, 123 S.Ct. at 2439–42 (Souter, J., joined by Ginsburg, J., dissenting).

186. Gratz v. Bollinger, 539 U.S. 244, ___, nn. 20, 21, 123 S.Ct. 2411, 2429–30 nn. 20, 21, 156 L.Ed.2d 257 (2003).

187. 539 U.S. at ___, 123 S. Ct. at 2434 (Stevens, J., joined by Souter, J., dissenting).

188. Justice Stevens joined Justice O'Connor's majority opinion in Grutter v. Bollinger, 539 U.S. 306, 123 S.Ct.

2325, 156 L.Ed.2d 304 (2003). Justice Stevens in *Grutter* did not explain how the University of Michigan program, which he voted to uphold, differed from the University of California Medical School admissions program, which he had voted to invalidate in Regents of the University v. Bakke, 438 U.S. 265, 408–21, 98 S.Ct. 2733, 2808–15, 57 L.Ed.2d 750 (1978) (Stevens, Stewart, Rehnquist, JJ., and Burger, C.J., concurring in part and dissenting in part). In *Bakke*, Justice Stevens had found that Title VI of the Civil Rights Act required complete racial neutrality. The majority opinion in *Grutter* found that the University of Michigan's Law School admissions policy complied with Title VI and 42 U.S.C. § 1981. 539 U.S. at ___, 123 S.Ct. at 2347 (Part IV of majority opinion written by Justice O'Connor, which was joined by Justice Stevens). Justice Stevens' most direct explanation of his views concerning the use of race in an educational setting may be contained in his separate opinion in Wygant v. Jackson Board of Education, 476 U.S. 267, 313, 106 S.Ct. 1842, 1867, 90 L.Ed.2d 260 (1986) (Stevens, J., dissenting). The reader is advised to pay careful attention to the shifting nature of Justice Stevens' votes in cases concerning racial affirmative action programs adopted by the federal government, which are examined in § 14.10(b)(3) of this Treatise.

grams in government operated schools that were allegedly designed to achieve racial diversity. Only Justices Kennedy and Scalia joined the Chief Justice's opinion in *Gratz* without writing separate opinions. Justice Scalia predicted that the Court left the lower courts with no guidance in this area and that the Court's 2003 decisions would simply be the catalyst that would start a new era of litigation concerning the constitutionality of such educational policies.[189]

The Supreme Court did provide lower courts with the answer to at least one question: could the achievement of racial diversity in colleges, universities, and professional schools be a compelling interest? The Court's answer, in 2003, was: yes. When lower courts review challenges to race conscious admissions policies of those types of educational institutions, the lower courts will no longer need to struggle with the question of whether or not the government is asserting a compelling interest. Rather, the lower courts can focus their attention solely on the question of whether a particular institution's admissions policy is narrowly tailored to the compelling interest in racial diversity. By tracking Justice Powell's analysis in *Bakke*, Justice O'Connor's opinion in *Grutter,* and the Chief Justices'opinion in *Gratz*, provide some guidance to lower courts assessing the narrow tailoring issue. Lower courts now know that it is the University's obligation to demonstrate that individualized consideration is given to all of the persons in the applicant pool and that there can be no setting aside of some places in the class for members of minority races whether that set aside is done through quotas, or systems that are effectively mechanical in nature in their granting of preferences to members of minority race groups. Unless the Supreme Court in 2003 had been ready to totally invalidate all attempts in education to achieve racial diversity that involved race conscious decision making, there was no alternative to a future of case-by-case litigation concerning

whether each challenged school's policies in fact involved individualized consideration of applicants so that the policies can be deemed narrowly tailored to the compelling interest in racial diversity in higher education.

The 2003 cases left open some many questions. For example, the 2003 cases did not explain whether Justice Powell's views in *Wygant*[190] would also be followed by the current group of Justices. Justice Powell's plurality opinion in *Wygant* indicated that primary and secondary schools might take some steps to create a racially diverse faculty, but that schools could not use a formula-based approach to achieve racial balance in their faculties. The Court in *Grutter* and *Gratz* did not explain whether the achievement of racial diversity in faculties, at any level of education, would constitute a compelling governmental interest.

The 2003 cases concerned only education and, therefore, the majority opinions in these cases did not give any clear indication as to whether the government could seek to achieve racial diversity outside of the educational arena. The 2003 cases did not modify other Supreme Court decisions concerning government programs designed to encourage the creation of minority race owned businesses that would participate in government funded projects, or government employment policies designed to achieve a racially diverse public sector work force. These issues are examined in other sections of this Chapter.[191]

(3) Federal Affirmative Action Programs—The *Adarand, Metro Broadcasting,* and *Fullilove* Decisions.

The *Adarand* Decision—The "Final Word" on Federal Racial Affirmative Action? The Supreme Court has examined the constitutionality of federal racial affirmative action plans in three cases. In *Fullilove v. Klutznick*,[192] the Court, in 1980, upheld a federal law that gave a preference to minority

---

189. Grutter v. Bollinger, 539 U.S. 306, __, 123 S.Ct. 2325, 2348, 156 L.Ed.2d, 304 (2003) (Scalia, J., joined by Thomas, J., concurring, in part, and dissenting, in part).

190. Wygant v. Jackson Board of Education, 476 U.S. 267, 106 S.Ct. 1842, 90 L.Ed.2d 260 (1986).

191. See § 14.10(a)(1)–(3); 14.10(b)(3); 14.10(b)(4).

192. 448 U.S. 448, 100 S.Ct. 2758, 65 L.Ed.2d 902 (1980).

race businesses in securing contracts for federal public works projects. However, the Court in *Fullilove* did not issue a majority opinion; the standards used by the Court, and the reasons why the law was upheld, were unclear. In 1990, the Court in *Metro Broadcasting, Inc. v. Federal Communications Commission*,[193] by a five to four vote of the Justices, ruled that federal racial affirmative action programs would be upheld so long as the benign racial classification had a substantial relationship to an important interest. Using that standard, the Court upheld preferential treatment for certain race minority persons in the awarding of television and radio broadcast licenses. Five years later, the Supreme Court overruled the *Metro Broadcasting* decision. In *Adarand Constructors, Inc. v. Pena*,[194] the Supreme Court, by a five to four vote, made two rulings that were inconsistent with the *Metro Broadcasting* decision.[195] First, the Court in *Adarand* held that the equal protection component of the Fifth Amendment due process clause required the Court to use the same standards when reviewing federal racial classifications that it used to review state or local classifications under the equal protection clause of the Fourteenth Amendment. Second, the *Adarand* majority held that any law using a racial classification (including the benign use of a racial classification in a federal affirmative action program) would be invalid unless the government could demonstrate that the classification was narrowly tailored to promote a compelling interest.

In *Adarand*, the Supreme Court examined, but did not make a final ruling regarding, the preference for minority race contractors that was a part of the Small Business Act. The plaintiff was a subcontractor who had bid to

do guard rail work for a prime contractor who had been awarded a contract for work on a public highway construction project in Colorado. Although this subcontractor submitted the low bid to the prime contractor, this subcontractor was not granted the contract, which was given to construction firms owned by minority race persons. Federal law gave additional compensation to prime contractors (such as the contractor that was awarded the prime contract for the highway construction) if the prime contractor hired subcontractors that were certified as small businesses that were controlled by "socially and economically disadvantaged individuals."[196] Federal statutes, and agency regulations, created a presumption that members of certain racial minority groups were socially and economically disadvantaged, so that businesses owned by members of these minority races had an advantage in bidding for contracts on public works projects. The Court of Appeals, using the principles set forth in the *Metro Broadcasting* decision, had upheld this presumption on the basis that, this federal program was substantially related to an important interest in creating racial diversity in the construction business that received public contracts. The Supreme Court found that the Court of Appeals had used the wrong standard of review for determining the constitutionality of the racial classification. A majority of the Court in *Adarand* overruled *Metro Broadcasting* and held that a federal racial classification need be narrowly tailored to promote a compelling interest.

In *Adarand*, Justice O'Connor announced the judgment of the Court and delivered an opinion that was, in part, a majority opinion and, in part, a plurality opinion. In the portions of her opinion that were written for a

---

193. 497 U.S. 547, 110 S.Ct. 2997, 111 L.Ed.2d 445 (1990), rehearing denied 497 U.S. 1050, 111 S.Ct. 15, 111 L.Ed.2d 829 (1990).

194. 515 U.S. 200, 115 S.Ct. 2097, 132 L.Ed.2d 158 (1995).

195. "We hold today that all racial classifications, imposed by whatever federal, state, or local government actor, must be analyzed by a reviewing court under strict scrutiny. In other words, such classifications are constitutional only if they are narrowly tailored means that further compelling interest. To the extent that *Metro Broad-*

casting is inconsistent with that holding, it is overruled." Adarand Constructors, Inc. v. Pena, 515 U.S. 200, 227, 115 S.Ct. 2097, 2113, 132 L.Ed.2d 158 (1995).

196. This presumption and preference for members of racial minorities was contained in portions of the Small Business Act, 15 U.S.C.A. §§ 631, 637, 644. The federal statutes and agency rulings that created the preference are examined in part I of Justice O'Connor's majority opinion in Adarand Constructors, Inc. v. Pena, 515 U.S. 200, 205–209, 115 S.Ct. 2097, 2102–2104, 132 L.Ed.2d 158 (1995).

majority, Justice O'Connor found that the preference created for subcontracting businesses owned by members of minority races created a racial classification that disadvantaged contracting businesses owned by members of racial or ethnic groups that had not been deemed to be presumptively disadvantaged by federal statutes and federal agency regulations. The majority ruled that any government classification that was based on race had to be subjected to strict judicial scrutiny and would be invalid unless the classification was narrowly tailored to a compelling governmental interest.[197] Justice O'Connor stated that the same reasons that had led the Court in the *J.A. Croson* decision[198] to rule that state governments must meet the compelling interest standard when using benign racial classifications mandated the Court to use strict judicial scrutiny when reviewing federal classifications.[199] In other words, Justice O'Connor's majority opinion in *Adarand* relied on, and reaffirmed, the position set out by Justice O'Connor in *J.A. Croson.*

Although a majority of the Justices in *Adarand* ruled that the federal affirmative action program had to be subjected to strict judicial scrutiny, the Court did not rule on whether the federal statutes and agency regulations that gave a preference to minority race contractors would survive that standard of review. Two of the five Justices in the *Adarand* majority took the position that the government would never have a compelling interest in using racial classifications to remove the effects of generalized racial discrimination. Justice Scalia stated that he would never vote to uphold a racial classification that the government

attempted to justify in terms of making up for past racial discrimination.[200] Justice Thomas also indicated that he would never vote to uphold benign racial classifications because, despite the "good intentions" that might give rise to racial affirmative action programs, the Constitution prohibited the government from making distinctions based on race.[201] However, both Justice Scalia and Justice Thomas joined the part of Justice O'Connor's majority opinion in which she stated that the majority "wish[ed] to dispel the notion that strict scrutiny is strict in theory but fatal in fact ... when race-based action is necessary to further a compelling interest, such action is within constitutional constraints if it satisfies the narrow tailoring test this Court has set out in previous cases."[202]

In *Adarand,* Justice O'Connor found that the Court need not consider whether the program for benefitting minority race construction businesses that was upheld in *Fullilove v. Klutznick*[203] could survive strict judicial scrutiny. Nevertheless, her opinion in *Adarand* relied on Justice Powell's opinion in *Fullilove.*[204] Justice Powell had used the compelling interest test and voted to uphold the preference for racial minority businesses in *Fullilove.*[205]

The *Adarand* decision settles some questions and leaves others open. The Court has settled, at least temporarily, the standard of review to be used by the judiciary when reviewing a federal racial affirmative action programs. All racial classifications, including benign racial classifications in federal racial affirmative action programs, must be narrowly tailored to serve a compelling governmental

197. Adarand Constructors, Inc. v. Pena, 515 U.S. 200, 227, 115 S.Ct. 2097, 2113, 132 L.Ed.2d 158 (1995).

198. Richmond v. J.A. Croson Co., 488 U.S. 469, 109 S.Ct. 706, 102 L.Ed.2d 854 (1989). This decision is examined later in this section of the Treatise.

199. Adarand Constructors, Inc. v. Pena, 515 U.S. 200, 221–227, 115 S.Ct. 2097, 2110–2113, 132 L.Ed.2d 158 (1995).

200. Adarand Constructors, Inc. v. Pena, 515 U.S. 200, 237, 115 S.Ct. 2097, 2118, 132 L.Ed.2d 158 (1995) (Scalia, J., concurring in part and concurring in the judgment).

201. 515 U.S. at 239, 115 S.Ct. at 2119 (Thomas, J., concurring in part and concurring in the judgment).

202. 515 U.S. at 235, 115 S.Ct. at 2117.

203. Fullilove v. Klutznick, 448 U.S. 448, 100 S.Ct. 2758, 65 L.Ed.2d 902 (1980).

204. Justice O'Connor, in part V D of her opinion, stated that: "Our action today makes explicit what Justice Powell thought implicit in the *Fullilove* lead opinion ... but we need not decide today whether the program upheld in *Fullilove* would survive strict scrutiny as our more recent cases have defined it." Adarand Constructors, Inc. v. Pena, 515 U.S. 200, 235, 115 S.Ct. 2097, 2117, 132 L.Ed.2d 158 (1995).

205. Fullilove v. Klutznick, 448 U.S. 448, 496, 100 S.Ct. 2758, 2783, 65 L.Ed.2d 902 (1980) (Powell, J., concurring).

interest. The Court left open the question of what, if any, governmental interests might be deemed "compelling." Justices Scalia and Thomas will not vote to uphold any use of racial classification for benign purposes. Nevertheless, if any of the members of the *Adarand* majority believed that a racial affirmative action program, challenged in a later case, was narrowly tailored to a compelling interest, that Justice could join the four *Adarand* dissenters to uphold that racial affirmative action program.[206]

We will turn to the *Fullilove* decision, which was not overruled in *Adarand*. After we examine *Fullilove*, we will then examine the *Metro Broadcasting* decision, which was decided by a five to four vote of the Justices, and which was overruled in *Adarand*.

The *Fullilove* Decision. In *Fullilove v. Klutznick*[207] the Supreme Court upheld the constitutionality of the minority business enterprise provision of the Public Works Employment Act.[208] This provision required 10% of the amount of every federal public works project grant be expended for work done by minority business enterprises. The statute defines such businesses as ones in which a majority of the equity interest is owned by "citizens of the United States who are Negroes, Spanish-speaking, Orientals, Indians, Eskimos, [or] Aleuts."[209]

While the federal program was upheld in this case, and all nine of the Justices voted on the constitutionality of this affirmative action program, no single theory concerning the constitutionality of affirmative action programs commanded the votes of more than three Justices. The Court seemed to split evenly between three different methods of analysis.

First, Chief Justice Burger, in an opinion joined by Justices White and Powell, found the Act to be a permissible use of the federal power to eliminate or redress discrimination in federal contract practices without ever specifying a test for the constitutionality of such programs. Although the Chief Justice refused to employ a specific test in his opinion, Justice Powell, while concurring in the Chief Justice's opinion, found that the federal program could be upheld under a compelling interest test.

Second, Justice Marshall, in an opinion joined by Justices Brennan and Blackmun, advocated the use of a test which would require remedial racial classifications to be substantially related to an important governmental objective.

Finally, Justices Stewart, Rehnquist, and Stevens dissented and opposed the use of racial classifications for the granting of government benefits, although Justice Stevens was unwilling to vote for an absolute prohibition of classifications based upon race.

Several factors indicate that the *Fullilove* case will not serve as a guide for future constitutional decisions concerning affirmative ac-

---

206. Justices Stevens, Souter, Ginsburg, and Breyer dissented in *Adarand*. Adarand Constructors, Inc. v. Pena, 515 U.S. 200, 242, 115 S.Ct. 2097, 2120, 132 L.Ed.2d 158 (1995) (Stevens, J., joined by Ginsburg, J., dissenting); 515 U.S. at 264, 115 S.Ct. at 2131 (Souter, joined by Ginsburg and Breyer, JJ., dissenting); 515 U.S. at 270, 115 S.Ct. at 2134 (Ginsburg, J., joined by Breyer, J., dissenting).

207. 448 U.S. 448, 100 S.Ct. 2758, 65 L.Ed.2d 902 (1980).

208. Public Works Employment Act of 1977, Pub.L. 95–28, 91 Stat. 116. The statute amended the Local Public Works Capital Development and Investment Act of 1976, Pub.L. 94–369, 90 Stat. 999. The statute states in relevant part:

"Except to the extent that the Secretary determines otherwise, no grant shall be made under this Act for any local public works project unless the applicant gives satisfactory assurance to the Secretary [of Commerce] that at least 10 per centum of the amount of each grant shall be expended for minority business enterprises. For purposes of this paragraph, the term 'minority business enterprise'

means a business at least 50 per centum of which is owned by minority group members or, in case of a publicly owned business, at least 51 per centum of the stock of which is owned by minority group members. For the purposes of the preceding sentence minority group members are citizens of the United States who are Negroes, Spanish-speaking, Orientals, Indians, Eskimos, and Aleuts."

209. The Economic Development Administration (EDA), a part of the commerce department charged with administration of the public works grant program, issued guidelines which set standards for determining when a business enterprise qualified as a minority business enterprise. As a part of these regulations the EDA defined the six minorities that were to receive a preference in terms of the geographic or ethnic origin of an individual. Relevant portions of the guidelines are quoted in the Appendix to the opinion of Chief Justice Burger, Fullilove v. Klutznick, 448 U.S. 448, 492, 100 S.Ct. 2758, 2782, 65 L.Ed.2d 902 (1980) (Appendix to opinion of Burger, C.J.).

tion. First, the case concerned a unique federal program that could be rationalized as a congressionally created remedy for past discrimination in public works projects against minority-owned enterprises. Second, the fact that Justice White joined the opinion of the Chief Justice rather than that of Justice Marshall seems to have reduced from four to three the number of Justices who are committed to the use of an intermediate standard of review for affirmative action programs. Third, Justice Stewart's retirement from the Court lessens the number of Justices who have committed to a position that would find most if not all affirmative action programs invalid. Finally, while three Justices appeared willing to uphold most affirmative action programs and three would have invalidated almost all such programs, the three Justices whose votes will decide the outcome of future affirmative action cases were less than clear on the standards which they will employ in those cases.

Chief Justice Burger took a curious path in coming to the conclusion that the public works set-aside program was valid.[210] The Chief Justice decided that the analysis must proceed "in two steps." First, he would inquire "whether the *objectives* of this legislation are within the power of Congress" and, if so, "whether the limited use of racial and ethnic criteria, in the context presented, is a constitutionally permissible *means* for achieving the congressional objectives."[211] This approach deviates from traditional equal protection analysis under any standard of review because the Chief Justice totally fails to tell us whether his assessment of the "objectives" of the legislation is only to determine whether they are legitimate and not prohibited by the Constitution or whether the ends will be independently evaluated by the Court to determine if they are sufficiently important or compelling to justify the use of a racial classification. No standard was set forth by the Chief Justice for determining the relationship between the means employed by

Congress and promotion of the congressional goals.

The Chief Justice had little problem in determining that the goals of the congressional action were within the federal power. The Chief Justice's conclusion that public works projects could be funded by the federal government under the commerce and spending powers was hardly a startling decision.

The Chief Justice also focused on the power of Congress under section 5 of the Fourteenth Amendment "to regulate procurement practices of state and local grantees of federal funds." The Chief Justice's opinion was unclear on this issue. At some points in the opinion he seemed to conclude that Congress has the power under the Fourteenth Amendment to take affirmative steps to aid members of racial or ethnic minorities to achieve social or economic equality. At other points he appeared only willing to rule that Congress could, and had, determined that minority owned businesses had been subject to unconstitutional and illegal discrimination in federal procurement programs in the past and that affirmative steps needed to be taken to remedy such prior discrimination. If the Chief Justice was indicating agreement with the first position one might expect him to vote to uphold a wide variety of affirmative action programs, at least if they were enacted by the Congress. If he was only indicating that the federal government could move to correct its own past discriminatory practices his opinion was indeed a narrow one.

When the Chief Justice looked at the means which Congress used to accomplish "these plainly constitutional objectives" he, in a single paragraph, indicated that the Court must pay significant deference to the congressional choice of means to promote its goals but that there had to be "careful judicial evaluation" to ensure racial or ethnic criteria were not used in an unconstitutional manner.[212] At this point in his opinion Chief Justice Burger de-

---

210. Fullilove v. Klutznick, 448 U.S. 448, 100 S.Ct. 2758, 65 L.Ed.2d 902 (1980) (Burger, C.J., announcing judgment of the Court in an opinion joined by White and Powell, JJ.).

211. 448 U.S. at 473, 100 S.Ct. at 2772, (emphasis in original).

212. 448 U.S. at 478–82, 100 S.Ct. at 2774–77.

scribed the congressional action as "remedial," perhaps to indicate that the goal Congress was pursuing was the undoing of the effect of past racial discrimination in federal public works projects.

Chief Justice Burger specifically rejected "the contention that in the remedial context the Congress must act in a wholly 'colorblind' fashion." [213] This is the most significant passage in the Chief Justice's opinion because, for the first time, we are assured that there are not five Justices who would vote to strike out virtually all benign racial classifications. However, the statement is of limited importance because Burger justified the congressional use of race in this manner by likening the Act to a decree by a court which formulated a remedy for proven unconstitutional racial discrimination.

The Chief Justice did indicate that Congress was to have a reasonable degree of latitude to frame its remedial statute so that a minor amount of over-inclusiveness or under-inclusiveness in the granting of the benefit should not make it invalid. Yet the Chief Justice was not willing to endorse a congressional power to use racial classifications whenever Congress wished to remedy the effects of past discrimination. Instead, the Chief Justice noted that the program before the Court was reasonably tailored to promote a remedial objective.[214] Those who sought to take advantage of the minority preference by the creation of "front entities" could be identified and eliminated from participation by administrative agencies. Waivers could be granted to public works grantees who could show that their best efforts could not produce 10% minority firm participation; the 10% target was not a rigid quota but a means of assuring fair treatment of minority business enterprises. The program, therefore, was not a strict racial quota or preference, in the view of the Chief Justice.

In conclusion the Chief Justice stated that "[t]his opinion does not adopt, either expressly or implicitly, the formulas of analysis articulated in such cases as *University of California Regents v. Bakke*." [215]

Justice Powell joined in the opinion of Chief Justice Burger but he wrote a concurrence to note that he "would place greater emphasis than the Chief Justice on the need to articulate judicial standards of review in conventional terms." [216] In other words, Justice Powell realized that Chief Justice Burger's opinion failed to put the Supreme Court's ruling into the framework of equal protection analysis.

Justice Powell applied the compelling interest test, as he had done in *Bakke*.[217] While racial preference could never constitute a compelling state interest, the remedying of identified discrimination by a government body competent to make a finding of discrimination could be a compelling interest. Justice Powell found that Congress had the authority under the commerce power, as well as under the Civil War Amendments, to identify and remedy the continuing effects of racially discriminatory practices.[218] Congress thus survived the "ends" test and Justice Powell required only that the means employed by Congress be "reasonable remedies to advance the compelling state interest in repairing the effects of discrimination." [219]

Justice Powell placed special emphasis on the enforcement clauses of the Thirteenth and Fourteenth Amendments; he would give Congress some latitude in the employment of a race conscious remedy for discrimination, although he would review state affirmative action programs more strictly. Justice Powell required a showing that the federal program was reasonable and did not shift the burden

---

213. 448 U.S. at 482–84, 100 S.Ct. at 2776–78.

214. 448 U.S. at 486, 100 S.Ct. at 2778–79.

215. 448 U.S. at 492, 100 S.Ct. at 2781.

216. Fullilove v. Klutznick, 448 U.S. 448, 495, 100 S.Ct. 2758, 2783, 65 L.Ed.2d 902 (1980) (Powell, J., concurring).

217. Regents of the University of California v. Bakke, 438 U.S. 265, 98 S.Ct. 2733, 57 L.Ed.2d 750 (1978) (Powell, J.).

218. Fullilove v. Klutznick, 448 U.S. 448, 502, 100 S.Ct. 2758, 2787, 65 L.Ed.2d 902 (1980) (Powell, J., concurring).

219. 448 U.S. at 510, 100 S.Ct. at 2791 (Powell, J., concurring).

for the remedy of racial discrimination to innocent third parties in an unreasonable manner.

Justice Marshall, in a concurring opinion joined by Justices Brennan and Blackmun, advocated the use of an intermediate standard of review, between the deferential rationality test and the insurmountable strict scrutiny standard.[220] Justices Marshall, Brennan, and Blackmun, endorsed the use of a strict scrutiny standard for determining the validity of laws which burden members of racial or ethnic minorities because they stigmatize members of the minority in a way that is contrary to the fundamental principles of equal protection. Even laws that are defended as benign racial classifications should be examined with more than the deferential rational basis standard of review for they may be easily misused, either to mask discrimination against a racial minority or to burden another politically powerless segment of society. For these reasons the concurring Justices found that "the proper inquiry is whether racial classifications designed to further remedial purposes serve important governmental objectives and are substantially related to achievement of those objectives." [221] Under this standard the validity of the public works law was "not even a close one." The purpose of remedying the effects of past racial discrimination against minority-owned businesses was clearly an important one and the program was a reasonable method of insuring an end to the harshest effects of past discrimination in this area.

Justices Stewart and Rehnquist, in dissent, took the position that the guarantee of equal protection inherent in the due process clause of the Fifth Amendment and the equal protection clause of the Fourteenth Amendment prohibited any governmental entity from using race as the basis for allocating benefits or burdens.[222] "Under our Constitution, any official action that treats a person differently on account of his race or ethnic origin is inherently suspect and presumptively invalid." [223] These Justices found that the history of the Fourteenth Amendment, and the philosophic premises of past Supreme Court decisions invalidating racial classifications, precluded the use of racial criteria to assign benefits or burdens in our society. The most fundamental value of an equal protection guarantee was undercut by such laws; the framers of the Fourteenth Amendment had seen the effects of governmental definitions of race and ethnicity.

The Act before the Court in *Fullilove* involved the categorization of persons by race with accompanying regulations establishing the criteria for inclusion of persons into racial groupings. This division of society along racial lines was antithetical to the equal protection guarantee in the view of Justices Stewart and Rehnquist. However, they would approve the limited use of racial classifications by a court formulating a specific remedy for a proven violation of a law prohibiting racial discrimination. Judicial formulation of such specific remedies does not involve the division of society along racial lines.

Justice Stevens was unwilling to join Justices Stewart and Rehnquist but he took a position against racial classifications nearly as strict.[224] Justice Stevens found that "[r]acial characteristics may serve to define a group of persons who have suffered a special wrong and who, therefore, are entitled to special reparations." [225] He might allow narrowly tailored laws to give reparations to specific groups against whom the government has committed a demonstrable wrong in the past, such as American Indians or some segment of Black citizens. However Justice Stevens would not allow Congress to use racial criteria to remedy

220. Fullilove v. Klutznick, 448 U.S. 448, 517, 100 S.Ct. 2758, 2794, 65 L.Ed.2d 902 (1980) (Marshall, J., joined by Brennan and Blackmun, JJ., concurring in the judgment).

221. 448 U.S. at 518, 100 S.Ct. at 2795.

222. Fullilove v. Klutznick, 448 U.S. 448, 522, 100 S.Ct. 2758, 2797, 65 L.Ed.2d 902 (1980) (Stewart, J., joined by Rehnquist, J., dissenting).

223. Id.

224. Fullilove v. Klutznick, 448 U.S. 448, 532, 100 S.Ct. 2758, 2803, 65 L.Ed.2d 902 (1980) (Stevens, J., dissenting).

225. 448 U.S. at 537, 100 S.Ct. at 2805.

the effects of societal discrimination against members of racial minorities.

There was insufficient proof for Stevens that any specific minority business enterprise in the past was denied access to public contracts and that the federal program was a means of remedying such specific acts of discrimination rather than the granting of a general preference by race. Justice Stevens required such an exact matching of remedial programs to demonstrations of specific instances of past discrimination that it is difficult to envision what types of programs for the benefit of racial minorities could survive his searching form of judicial review.[226]

The *Metro Broadcasting* Decision: The 1990–95 Standard of Review. *Metro Broadcasting, Inc. v. Federal Communications Commission*[227] upheld two Federal Communications Commission [FCC] policies that had been designed to increase the number of radio and television stations that were owned by members of minority racial groups. These two policies had been initiated by the FCC; Congress, in appropriations legislation, required the FCC to maintain these policies.

The first policy, the "comparative proceedings policy", required the FCC to consider minority race ownership, and minority race participation in station management, as a "plus" when considering completing applications to receive a license to operate a new radio or television station. When several individuals or groups apply for a license to operate a new radio or television broadcast station on a specific frequency, the FCC policies require consideration of factors such as: diversifica-

tion of mass media communications industry, full time participation in station operation and management by the ownership group, the proposed programming for the new station, the past broadcast record, if any, of the applicants, the most efficient use of the broadcast frequency and the general character of the applicants. In addition to consideration of those factors, this new comparative proceedings policy required the FCC to consider minority ownership to be a "plus" for an applicant if, but only if, a minority race owner would be actively participating in the day to day management of the station (if that applicant were awarded the license).

The second FCC policy, known as the "distress sale policy," provided a special means by which minority race persons, or minority owned businesses, might acquire a license to operate an existing radio or television station. Normally, the FCC would prohibit a broadcast licensee from assigning or transferring the license after the licensee's qualifications to continue to hold that broadcast license had been called into question. The normal FCC policy would prohibit assignment or transfer of the license until the FCC conducted a hearing in which it would consider the qualifications of the licensee and the use of the license to date. If the FCC found that the license should be revoked the current station owner would have no license to sell. The distress sale policy allowed a broadcaster whose license had been questioned, and who was facing a revocation or renewal application hearing, to transfer the broadcast license if, but only if, the transfer was to a minority race person or a minority

---

226. The strictness of his approach may best be captured in the following statements indicating his belief that the program was not a narrowly tailored means for redressing past discrimination.

"Even if we assume that each of the six racial subclasses [receiving a preference from the statutes] has suffered its own special injury at some time in our history, surely it does not necessarily follow that each of those subclasses suffered harm of identical magnitude. Although 'the Negro was dragged to this country in chains to be sold in slavery,' *Bakke* opinion of Marshall, J., [citation omitted], the 'Spanish-speaking' subclass came voluntarily, frequently without invitation, and the Indians, the Eskimos and the Aleuts had an opportunity to exploit America's resources before most American citizens arrived. There is no reason to assume, and

nothing in the legislative history suggests, much less demonstrates, that each of these subclasses is equally entitled to reparations from the United States Government." 448 U.S. at 537, 100 S.Ct. at 2805 (Stevens, J., dissenting).

This passage by Justice Stevens ended with the following inexplicable footnote: "8. Ironically, the Aleuts appear to have been ruthlessly exploited at some point in their history by Russian fur traders. See The New Columbia Encyclopedia, p. 59." 448 U.S. at 538, n. 8, 100 S.Ct. at 2805 n. 8 (Stevens, J., dissenting).

227. 497 U.S. 547, 110 S.Ct. 2997, 111 L.Ed.2d 445 (1990) overruled by Adarand Constructors, Inc. v. Pena, 515 U.S. 200, 115 S.Ct. 2097, 132 L.Ed.2d 158 (1995).

enterprise (a business entity with minority race ownership, as determined by the FCC). The minority person or business that had purchased the station and license would have to meet the FCC's basic qualifications for owners.

The Supreme Court, by a five to four vote of the Justices, upheld both of the FCC policies. Justice Brennan wrote the majority opinion in *Metro Broadcasting*. Justice Stevens joined Justice Brennan's opinion and wrote a concurring opinion.[228] Justice O'Connor wrote a dissenting opinion, which was joined by Chief Justice Rehnquist and Justices Scalia and Kennedy.[229] In addition to joining Justice O'Connor's dissent, Justice Kennedy filed a dissenting opinion that Justice Scalia joined.[230]

Both the majority and dissenting opinions agreed that the case did not require the Court to define the scope of congressional power under § 5 of the Fourteenth Amendment.[231] The FCC policies had not been defended in terms of a congressional attempt to remedy any state, local governmental, or private sector racial discrimination. The congressional regulation of the broadcast industry, and FCC regulations that were enacted within the scope of authority delegated to the FCC by Congress, were justified by Congress' Article I powers, particularly the federal commerce power. There was no doubt that regulation of the broadcast industry is within the commerce power of Congress, as is the regulation of virtually any type of activity that might affect economic interests in more than one state.[232] Thus, the only issue in *Metro Broadcasting* was whether the equal protection component of the Fifth Amendment due process clause should be interpreted to invalidate either or

both of the FCC racial affirmative action policies.

The most important aspect of *Metro Broadcasting* was the adoption, in the majority opinion, of the intermediate standard of review for determining the validity of a racial classification that had been mandated by Congress to benefit minority race persons. The majority opinion by Justice Brennan ruled that a racial classification that benefitted members of a minority race that was a part of a federal statute, or which was part of a federal agency regulation that had been mandated by Congress, would be upheld so long as that affirmative action racial classification bore a substantial relationship to an important interest within the power of Congress.[233]

Justice Stevens, in his concurring opinion, described the majority approach as if it were consistent with the views that he expressed in earlier cases. Justice Stevens will vote to uphold a racial classification if, but only if, the government has proven that the law "falls within the extremely narrow category of government decisions for which racial or ethnic heritage may provide a racial basis for deferential treatment [in terms of an unquestionably legitimate end of government]."[234] Justice Stevens also joined the majority opinion that clearly adopted a standard of review requiring the federal affirmative action racial classification to be "substantially related to an important interest."

The majority opinion found that the interest test, which had been adopted in *Richmond v. J.A. Croson Co.*[235] for reviewing state or local affirmative action classifications under the equal protection clause, should not be used to determine whether a federal government ra-

---

228. 497 U.S. at 601, 110 S.Ct. at 3028, (Stevens, J., concurring).

229. 497 U.S. at 602, 110 S.Ct. at 3028 (O'Connor, J., joined by Rehnquist, C.J., and Scalia and Kennedy, JJ., dissenting).

230. 497 U.S. at 631, 110 S.Ct. at 3044 (Kennedy, J., joined by Scalia, J., dissenting).

231. Metro Broadcasting, Inc. v. Federal Communications Commission, 497 U.S. 547, 564–65, 110 S.Ct. 2997, 3008–09, 111 L.Ed.2d 445 (1990). 497 U.S. at 605–6, 110 S.Ct. at 3030 (O'Connor, J., joined by Rehnquist, C.J., and Scalia and Kennedy, JJ., dissenting).

232. See Chapter 4 regarding the scope of the federal commerce power.

233. Metro Broadcasting, Inc. v. Federal Communications Commission, 497 U.S. 547, 564–65, 110 S.Ct. 2997, 3008–09, 111 L.Ed.2d 445 (1990).

234. 497 U.S. at 601, 110 S.Ct. at 3028 (Stevens, J., concurring).

235. 488 U.S. 469, 109 S.Ct. 706, 102 L.Ed.2d 854 (1989).

cial affirmative action classification violated the equal protection component of the Fifth Amendment due process clause.[236]

The implied equal protection guarantee of the Fifth Amendment due process clause is independent from the equal protection guarantee of the Fourteenth Amendment's equal protection clause. However, since 1954, the Supreme Court had consistently ruled that the equal protection component of the Fifth Amendment due process clause established restrictions on the federal classifications that were virtually identical to the restrictions that the equal protection clause of the Fourteenth Amendment placed upon state or local governments.[237]

The majority opinion in *Metro Broadcasting* justified the use of a less rigorous standard for reviewing federal, rather than state or local, racial affirmative action classification on two basis. The majority did not believe that the national legislature was susceptible to the same types of pressures to simply award benefits to racial factions as was a state or local legislature.[238] Justice Brennan's majority opinion also relied on *Fullilove*.[239] Although there was no majority opinion in *Fullilove*, five of the six Justices who voted to uphold the federal affirmative action program in *Fullilove* did not subject the federal classification to strict judicial scrutiny and the compelling interest test.

Justice O'Connor's dissenting opinion in *Metro Broadcasting*, which was joined by three other Justices, found that the federal government's use of race should be subject to the strict scrutiny approach adopted in *J.A. Croson*.[240] However, Justice O'Connor said that "the Court has repeatedly indicated that the reach of the equal protection guarantee of the Fifth Amendment is co-extensive with that of the Fourteenth."[241]

Justice O'Connor's dissent found that the *Fullilove* decision was not inconsistent with the view that a racial classification in a federal affirmative action program should only be upheld if it was narrowly tailored to a compelling interest. The dissent believed that the statute at issue in *Fullilove* might be upheld as an exercise of Congress' power under § 5 of the Fourteenth Amendment.[242] Thus, the federal set aside program in *Fullilove* could be upheld as a narrowly tailored means of correcting racial discrimination in the awarding of government construction contracts.

Justice Brennan's majority opinion in *Metro Broadcasting* found that the interest in promoting diversity in the programming of radio and television stations was an important interest. The majority found that both FCC policies were substantially related to this interest and that the policies did not stigmatize or stereotype persons by race. Justice Brennan's

236. Metro Broadcasting, Inc. v. Federal Communications Commission, 497 U.S. 547, 565, 110 S.Ct. 2997, 3009, 111 L.Ed.2d 445 (1990).

237. See, Bolling v. Sharpe, 347 U.S. 497, 74 S.Ct. 693, 98 L.Ed. 884(1954) opinion supplemented 349 U.S. 294, 75 S.Ct. 753, 99 L.Ed. 1083 (1955) (finding that the operation of the public school system in the District of Columbia was intentionally segregated by race and, therefore, violated the equal protection component of the Fifth Amendment due process clause). See § 14.3 regarding equal protection standards of review. The one area in which the Court has more strictly controlled the use of state and local classifications is the ability of the federal or state government to use classifications that are based upon United States citizenship. See § 14.12.

238. Metro Broadcasting, Inc. v. Federal Communications Commission, 497 U.S. 547, 565–66, 110 S.Ct. 2997, 3009, 111 L.Ed.2d 445 (1990).

239. 497 U.S. at 565, 110 S.Ct. at 3009: "*Croson* cannot be read to undermine our decision in *Fullilove*."

240. 497 U.S. at 602, 110 S.Ct. at 3028 (O'Connor, J., joined by Rehnquist, C.J., and Scalia and Kennedy, JJ.,

dissenting). One year earlier the Supreme Court had found that the compelling interest test was to be applied to a state or local benign, affirmative action racial classification. Richmond v. J.A. Croson Co., 488 U.S. 469, 109 S.Ct. 706, 102 L.Ed.2d 854 (1989). (Justice O'Connor announced the judgment of the Court in an opinion that was, in part, a plurality opinion and, in part, a majority opinion.)

241. Metro Broadcasting, Inc. v. Federal Communications Commission, 497 U.S. 547, 604, 110 S.Ct. 2997, 3030, 111 L.Ed.2d 445 (1990) (O'Connor, J., joined by Rehnquist, C.J., and Scalia and Kennedy, JJ., dissenting).

242. The dissent found that "*Fullilove* concerned an exercise of Congress' powers under § 5 of the Fourteenth Amendment" and that "even if *Fullilove* applied outside a remedial exercise of Congress' § 5 power, it would not support today's adoption of the intermediate standard of review." 497 U.S. at 606, 608, 110 S.Ct. at 3031, 3032. (O'Connor, J., joined by Rehnquist, C.J., and Scalia and Kennedy, JJ., dissenting).

opinion seemed to give significant deference to the initial decision of the FCC to employ these racial classifications and the decision of Congress to mandate that those classifications be used to promote diversity in broadcast programs. Justice Brennan described a history of failure on the part of prior FCC regulations to promote both entertainment and information programming that would serve people of all races. It is hard to tell from the majority opinion whether the majority made an independent determination that the FCC policies were substantially related to an important interest even though the majority opinion found a "host of empirical evidence" to support the FCC policies.[243]

The dissenting opinion by Justice O'Connor challenged the majority on the application of the intermediate standard, as well as on the question of whether the compelling interest test should be used to review the FCC policies.[244] The dissenters believed that the federal government could not prove that the FCC policies were designed to promote diversity in broadcasting by any means other than racial stereotyping.

It was not surprising that the dissenters found that the interest in promoting diversity of broadcast was not sufficient to support a racial classification. Justice O'Connor's dissent went further than merely rejecting the broadcast diversity interest. Her dissent said: "Under the appropriate standard, strict scrutiny, only a compelling interest may support the Government's use of racial classifications. Modern equal protection doctrine has recognized only one such interest: remedying the

effects of racial discrimination."[245] Does this statement show that the interest in promoting diversity in education would never be sufficiently compelling to justify any type of racial affirmative action classification in the view of the four dissenting Justices?

In *J.A. Croson*, Justice O'Connor had not explicitly excluded the possibility that a racial affirmative action program that did not set numerical goals or quotas based on race, and that was used to increase racial diversity in the student body or faculty of government operated schools, might be constitutional. Perhaps Justice O'Connor's dissent in *Metro Broadcasting* was only meant to indicate that the government could not distribute benefits purely along racial lines for any reason other than remedying identified illegal or unconstitutional discrimination. So interpreted, Justice O'Connor's dissent in *Metro Broadcasting* might allow for consideration of race in the admission of students state owned university or in the hiring of faculty for a public school so long as the state university or public school was not simply dividing the benefits (positions in the student body or employment as a faculty member) through the use of racial quotas or numerical goals.

Justice Kennedy's dissent in *Metro Broadcasting*[246] echoed his concurring opinion in *J.A. Croson*.[247] He found that the equal protection component of the Fifth Amendment due process clause, and the equal protection clause of the Fourteenth Amendment, should prohibit any governmental unit from using racial classifications unless they were truly

---

243. "Although all station owners are guided to some extent by market demand in their programming decisions, Congress and the Commission have determined that there may be important differences between the broadcasting practices of minority owners and those of their nonminority counterparts. This judgment—and the conclusion that there is a nexus between minority ownership and broadcasting diversity—is corroborated by a host of empirical evidence." Metro Broadcasting, Inc. v. Federal Communications Commission, 497 U.S. 547, 580, 110 S.Ct. 2997, 3017, 111 L.Ed.2d 445 (1990) (footnote omitted).

244. "Our traditional equal protection doctrine requires, in addition to a compelling state interest, that the government chose a means necessary to accomplish and narrowly tailored to further the asserted interest. ... the Court instead finds the racial classifications to be 'sub-

stantially related' to achieving the government's interest. The FCC's policies fail even this requirement." 497 U.S. at 617, 110 S.Ct. at 3036–7 (O'Connor, J., joined by Rehnquist, C.J., and Scalia and Kennedy, JJ., dissenting).

245. 497 U.S. at 612, 110 S.Ct. at 3034 (O'Connor, J., joined by Rehnquist, C.J., and Scalia and Kennedy, JJ., dissenting).

246. Metro Broadcasting, Inc. v. Federal Communications Commission, 497 U.S. 547, 631, 110 S.Ct. 2997, 3044, 111 L.Ed.2d 445 (1990) (Kennedy, J., joined by Scalia, J., dissenting).

247. Richmond v. J.A. Croson Co., 488 U.S. 469, 518, 109 S.Ct. 706, 734, 102 L.Ed.2d 854 (1989) (Kennedy, J., concurring in part and concurring in the judgment).

necessary to promote an interest that the government could not disregard—the remedying of identified discrimination. Justice Kennedy believes that "strict scrutiny is the surest test the Court has yet devised for holding true to the constitutional command of racial equality." [248]

The *Metro Broadcasting* decision, and the use of an intermediate standard to review federal racial affirmative action programs, would survive for only a few years.

In 1995, Justice Thomas joined the dissenters in *Metro Broadcasting*—Chief Justice Rehnquist and Justices O'Connor, Scalia, and Kennedy—in overruling the *Metro Broadcasting* decision. In *Adarand Constructors, Inc. v. Pena,*[249] the Court ruled that any other use of a racial classification by a governmental entity, including a federal racial affirmative action program, had to be subject to strict judicial scrutiny. After *Adarand,* no racial classification can be upheld unless it is narrowly tailored to promote a compelling governmental interest.[250] At least for the time being, a racial affirmative action program mandated by Congress will violate the equal protection component of the Fifth Amendment due process clause unless the government can demonstrate that the racial affirmative action program is narrowly tailored to promote a compelling interest. *Adarand* was decided by a five to four vote of the Justices.[251] If the dissenting Justices in *Adarand* were joined by a new Justice

who believed that congressional power to protect the interest of racial minorities should be given special deference by the Court, we might see the Court in the future overrule *Adarand* and turn back to the principles it had espoused in the *Metro Broadcasting* decision.

The Supreme Court has yet to clarify whether the decision in *Adarand* limited the result in *Fullilove* or whether Department of Transportation programs favoring minority race businesses are now invalid.[252]

(c) Race Conscious Legislative Districting and the Compelling Interest Test

The Supreme Court has not set clear standards regarding the extent to which governmental entities may act to improve the voting power of racial minorities. The Court's rulings in this area can be best understood by breaking the topic down into three categories.

First, the government may act to correct specific unconstitutional or illegal acts of voting discrimination against minority race voters. If a voting regulation in a specific governmental unit is found to be racially discriminatory on its face, or maintained for a racially discriminatory purpose, the Court will apply the compelling interest test and invalidate the law. A trial court in such a case should fashion a remedy that is narrowly tailored to correct the racial discrimination that was proven in the case.[253] That

---

248. Metro Broadcasting, Inc. v. Federal Communications Commission, 497 U.S. 547, 634, 110 S.Ct. 2997, 3045, 111 L.Ed.2d 445 (1990) (Kennedy, J., joined by Scalia, J., dissenting).

249. 515 U.S. 200, 115 S.Ct. 2097, 132 L.Ed.2d 158 (1995).

250. 515 U.S. at 227, 115 S.Ct. at 2113.

251. Justice O'Connor, in part V D of her opinion, stated that: "Our action today makes explicit what Justice Powell thought implicit in the *Fullilove* lead opinion … but we need not decide today whether the program upheld in *Fullilove* would survive strict scrutiny as our more recent cases have defined it." Adarand Constructors, Inc. v. Pena, 515 U.S. 200, 235, 115 S.Ct. 2097, 2117, 132 L.Ed.2d 158 (1995).

252. The Court avoided these issues in Adarand Constructors, Inc. v. Mineta, 534 U.S. 103, 122 S.Ct. 511, 151 L.Ed.2d 489 (2001) (dismissing certiorari as improvidently granted). After the decision in the original *Adarand* case [*Adarand I*] the United States Court of Appeals for the

Tenth Circuit found that the facts of the case made the case moot but this decision was revered summarily by the United States Supreme Court. Adarand Constructors, Inc. v. Slater, 169 F.3d 292 (10th Cir.1999), reversed and remanded by Adarand Constructors, Inc. v. Slater 528 U.S. 216, 120 S.Ct. 722, 145 L.Ed.2d 650 (2000) (per curiam) [*Adarand II*]. After the remand in *Adarand II*, the Court of Appeals found that persons attacking the federal program lacked standing and that the Department of Transportation program survived strict scrutiny. After granting certiorari in *Adarand II*, the United States Supreme Court, with a per curiam opinion, dismissed the case with no ruling on the merits. Because a change in the procedural posture of the case meant that the Court would have to examine some federal race-based programs that had not been examined by the lower federal courts, the Court dismissed the writ of certiorari and did not rule on the merits of the case.

253. See, e.g., Rogers v. Lodge, 458 U.S. 613, 102 S.Ct. 3272, 73 L.Ed.2d 1012 (1982), rehearing denied 459 U.S. 899, 103 S.Ct. 198, 74 L.Ed.2d 160 (finding that an at-

type of judicial remedy is narrowly tailored to the compelling governmental interest in stopping identified illegal or unconstitutional racial discrimination in voting practices.

Second, Congress has some power to regulate state and local elections for the purpose of promoting equality in electoral laws and eliminating racial discrimination, although the extent of this power is not clear. Congress has the power to make illegal, and penalize, state and local voting practices that would be ruled unconstitutional by the Supreme Court. The Court has also recognized that Congress has power to eliminate racially discriminatory voting practices that have never been held to be violations of equal protection by the Supreme Court because of Congress' greater factfinding ability. Thus, Congress has been able to eliminate the use of literacy tests as a condition of voting even though the Supreme Court never found that literacy tests constituted a per se violation of equal protection.[254] Congress also has the authority to protect minority race voters by requiring state and local governments, under certain conditions, to have any change in their voting laws approved by either the Attorney General of the United States or the United States District Court for the District of Columbia.[255]

Third, the Supreme Court has not issued a clear ruling concerning whether state governments, or Congress, may use a racial classification that is designed to help minority race voters increase their voting power by creating

electoral districts where minority race voters would control election results.

The Supreme Court may follow the approach used in its cases regarding racial affirmative action in the education area, which were decided without majority opinions,[256] by allowing the government to give some consideration to the interest of racial minorities as it enacts voting laws while subjecting any clear use of benign racial classifications to the compelling interest tests.

When a city or state creates districts for the purpose of electing representatives some affirmative consideration may be given to protecting the voting strength of minority racial groups together with other traditional considerations in drawing district lines (such as creating continuous or compact districts or following traditional political subdivision lines). In *United Jewish Organizations v. Carey*,[257] the Supreme Court, without a majority opinion, upheld New York's creation of several districts in which minority race voters would be a majority of the voters in the district. The Court rejected an attack on this plan that was brought by members of a Hasidic community that was split between two districts. While there was no majority opinion, it appears that a majority of the Justices upheld the New York districting plan because they believed that it was not meant to stigmatize, or dilute the voting power of, any racial or ethnic group.

In *Shaw v. Reno (Shaw I)*[258] the Supreme Court held that North Carolina legislation creating districts for the election of representa-

---

large electoral system for the election of County Board of Commissioners violates equal protection because it is maintained for a racially discriminatory purpose); Gomillion v. Lightfoot, 364 U.S. 339, 81 S.Ct. 125, 5 L.Ed.2d 110 (1960) (finding that legislation changing the area and shape of a town was unconstitutional and could not stand because it excluded minority race voters in the city and constituted racial discrimination on its face). See § 14.4 of this Treatise regarding the need to prove a racially discriminatory purpose when a racial classification does not appear on the face of the statute, as a condition for finding unconstitutional racial discrimination and justifying a judicial remedy therefor.

254. See South Carolina v. Katzenbach, 383 U.S. 301, 86 S.Ct. 803, 15 L.Ed.2d 769 (1966); Oregon v. Mitchell, 400 U.S. 112, 91 S.Ct. 260, 27 L.Ed.2d 272 (1970). See Chapter 15 of this Treatise regarding the congressional enforcement of the Fifteenth Amendment.

255. See, City of Rome v. United States, 446 U.S. 156, 100 S.Ct. 1548, 64 L.Ed.2d 119 (1980); United States v. Board of Commissioners, 435 U.S. 110, 98 S.Ct. 965, 55 L.Ed.2d 148 (1978). For references to additional cases, and secondary authorities, on this point see the multi-volume edition of this Treatise: R. Rotunda & J. Nowak, Treatise on Constitutional Law: Substance and Procedure §§ 18.10 (b) 4, 19.11, 19.12.

256. See, Regents of the University v. Bakke, 438 U.S. 265, 98 S.Ct. 2733, 57 L.Ed.2d 750 (1978); Wygant v. Jackson Board of Education, 476 U.S. 267, 106 S.Ct. 1842, 90 L.Ed.2d 260 (1986), rehearing denied 478 U.S. 1014, 106 S.Ct. 3320, 92 L.Ed.2d 728 (1986). These cases are examined in § 18.10(b)(2).

257. 430 U.S. 144, 97 S.Ct. 996, 51 L.Ed.2d 229 (1977).

258. 509 U.S. 630, 113 S.Ct. 2816, 125 L.Ed.2d 511 (1993).

tives to the United States Congress used racial criteria "on its face" and, for that reason, that this legislation must be subject to strict judicial scrutiny and the compelling interest test. North Carolina had its number of representatives to the House of Representatives of the United States increased by Congress following a national census. The state legislature adopted an initial plan creating new congressional districts that had to be submitted to the Attorney General of the United States, because North Carolina was subject to the administrative preclearance procedures of the Voting Rights Act. The Attorney General objected to North Carolina's initial plan because only one of the twelve congressional districts in that plan appeared to be one in which minority race voters would control the election of a representative to Congress, despite the fact that 22 percent of the North Carolina population was comprised of racial minorities.

North Carolina chose not to challenge the Attorney General's decision. Instead, the North Carolina legislature adopted a new districting plan that created two districts in which minority race voters would be the majority of the district and control the district elections for congressional representatives. The Attorney General did not object to the second districting plan. The final North Carolina congressional districting plan was challenged in the federal courts in North Carolina by persons who claimed that the new plan involved unconstitutional racial discrimination in favor of minority race persons.

By a five to four vote the Justices in *Shaw* found that the final districting plan involved a racial classification on its face, although the Court did not rule on the question of whether the use of race by North Carolina was narrowly tailored to promote a compelling interest. Justice O'Connor wrote the majority opinion in *Shaw*. The majority ruled that the plaintiffs did not have to show a discriminatory purpose in the creation of this legislation, because the odd shape of the districts that were

meant to protect minority race voters demonstrated that the legislation on its face employed racial criteria. Justice O'Connor then found that the law had to be subjected to the compelling interest test as it involved a state use of a racial classification.[259]

The Supreme Court in *Shaw* did not rule on the question of whether the districts that were designed to protect minority race voters could be upheld under the compelling interest test because the lower federal court had not considered that question. The Supreme Court remanded the case to the district court for an initial consideration of this question. The district court had dismissed the challenges to the state districting plan on the basis that the plaintiffs had failed to demonstrate that the legislature had used a racial classification that should be subjected to the compelling interest test.

Although Justice O'Connor's majority opinion stated that the Court was not ruling on whether the districting plan met the compelling interest test, Justice O'Connor discussed North Carolina's arguments in favor of upholding its final districting plan, which included two districts that were created to protect minority race interests.

North Carolina claimed that it needed to create the two districts in order to insure that the voting power of racial minorities was not weakened by the creation of new congressional districts following the most recent census. North Carolina argued that the two districts were created to comply with the "nonretrogression" principle under the federal Voting Rights Act. Justice O'Connor recognized that the Voting Rights Act might require the creation of reapportionment plans that avoided the dilution of minority race voting power. But she noted that the Court had never ruled that the Voting Rights Act, or the nonretrogression principle, justified the use of race as the sole or primary criterion in creating electoral districts. Justice O'Connor stated: "In-

---

259. See § 14.4 of this Treatise regarding the distinction between testing a law on its face and testing it due to the racially discriminatory purpose of the governmental entity that created or applied the law. The portion of the

Shaw opinion that found that the North Carolina legislation constituted racial discrimination on its face is examined in § 14.4 of this Treatise.

deed, the Voting Rights Act and our case law make clear that a reapportionment plan that satisfies § 5 [of the Act] still may be enjoined as unconstitutional. ... a reapportionment plan would not be narrowly tailored to the goal of avoiding retrogression if the state went beyond what was reasonably necessary to avoid retrogression." [260]

North Carolina also claimed that it needed to use racial criteria as the sole criteria for creating at least one, and possibly two, voting districts with a majority of minority race voters in order to avoid violations of the Voting Rights Act by the intentional dilution of minority race voting power. The Supreme Court did not rule on this claim. But Justice O'Connor's opinion noted that the persons attacking the plan argued: "that the state's black population is too dispersed to support two geographically compact majority-black districts"; that elections in recent years in North Carolina showed that there was no racial block voting that hurt minority race interests; and "that if § 2 [of the Voting Rights Act] did require the adoption of North Carolina's revised plan, § 2 is to that extent unconstitutional." Justice O'Connor concluded this portion of her opinion by stating: "These arguments were not developed below and the issues remain open for consideration on remand." [261]

North Carolina argued that the creation of the minority race districts was "the most precise way—the only effective way—to overcome the effects of racially polarized voting." Justice O'Connor responded with the following statement: "The question also need not be decided at this stage of the litigation. We note, however, that only three Justices in [the *United Jewish Organizations* case] were prepared to say that states have a significant interest in minimizing the consequences of

racial bloc voting apart from the requirements of the Voting Rights Act." [262]

The Supreme Court in *Shaw* did not rule on the question of whether the North Carolina districting plan could be upheld under the compelling interest test. Nevertheless, Justice O'Connor's majority opinion may be read as indicating that a majority of the Justices would only allow the use of racial criteria to help minority race voters if that racial classification was necessary to remedy identified prior acts of unconstitutional discrimination against minority race voters in the jurisdiction. But the *United Jewish Organizations* case, and Justice O'Connor's description of that case in *Shaw* indicate that the Court might allow a legislature that is engaged in reapportionment to consider the need to protect the voting power of racial minorities together with other traditional considerations in reapportionment systems (such as creating compact or contiguous districts).

In 1995 the Court in *Miller v. Johnson*,[263] by a five to four vote, invalidated a Georgia congressional districting plan insofar as that plan created one congressional district that was based on race. The Georgia plan at issue in *Miller* was the third congressional districting plan that Georgia had created following a census that had resulted in Georgia receiving an additional seat in the United States House of Representatives. Georgia was subject to § 5 of the Voting Rights Act; the Justice Department had the power to review and reject any changes in that state's voting laws, to insure that the changes did not hurt minority race voters. The Justice Department had taken the position that two previous Georgia plans, which created only two congressional districts that would clearly be controlled by minority race voters, were inadequate to meet the requirements of the Voting Rights Act. The Georgia legislature then created a plan with

260. Shaw v. Reno, 509 U.S. 630, 654, 113 S.Ct. 2816, 2831, 125 L.Ed.2d 511 (1993).

261. 509 U.S. at 654, 113 S.Ct. at 2831.

262. 509 U.S. at 656, 113 S.Ct. at 2832.

263. 515 U.S. 900, 115 S.Ct. 2475, 132 L.Ed.2d 762 (1995). The *Miller* case was decided by a five to four vote of the Justices. Justice Kennedy wrote a majority opinion that was joined by Chief Justice Rehnquist and Justices

O'Connor, Scalia, Kennedy and Thomas. Justice O'Connor also submitted a concurring opinion. 515 U.S. at 928, 115 S.Ct. at 2497 (O'Connor, J., concurring). Justices Stevens, Souter, Ginsburg, and Breyer dissented in *Miller*. 515 U.S. at 928, 115 S.Ct. at 2497 (Stevens, J., dissenting); 515 U.S. at 932, 115 S.Ct. at 2499 (Ginsburg, J., joined by Stevens and Breyer, JJ., and, in part, by Souter, J., dissenting).

three congressional districts that would be controlled by minority race voters. In *Miller*, the Supreme Court, in an opinion by Justice Kennedy, ruled: (1) that the creation of the district for the purpose of allowing minority race persons to control the outcome of the election was a race-based classification that must be subject to strict judicial scrutiny; and (2) that Georgia's desire to satisfy the Justice Department's requirements was not a compelling interest that would justify the plan.

The congressional district that was created by the Georgia legislature to gain Justice Department approval did not have a bizarre shape, as did the district at issue in *Shaw I*. Justice Kennedy's majority opinion ruled that a court did not have to find that a legislative district had a bizarre shape as a prerequisite to finding that the district was based upon race. The majority opinion stated that "parties alleging that a State has assigned voters on the basis of race are neither confined in their proof to evidence regarding a district's geometry and make-up nor required to make a threshold showing of bizarreness".[264] A plaintiff attacking a district plan as being race-based would have to show "either through circumstantial evidence of a district's shape and demographics or more direct evidence going to legislative purpose, that race was the predominant factor motivating" the creation of the legislative district's boundaries.[265]

In *Miller*, as in *Shaw I*, the Supreme Court held that a legislative district based on race would be invalidated unless the government could demonstrate that the district was narrowly tailored to achieve a compelling interest. According to the *Miller* majority, the fact that the Justice Department demanded that the state create a certain number of districts that would be controlled by minority race voters could not serve as a compelling interest that would justify race-based districting. Justice

Kennedy stated: "Whether or not, in some cases compliance with the Voting Rights Act, standing alone, can provide a compelling interest independent of any interest in remedying past discrimination, it cannot do so here.... we do not accept the contention that the state has a compelling interest in complying with whatever preclearance mandates the Justice Department issues."[266]

The Court in *Miller* ruled that the Voting Rights Act did not give the Justice Department the right to demand that a certain number of legislative districts be controlled by racial minority voters, at least when the creation of such districts was not required to remedy an identified instance of past discrimination against minority race voters. The *Shaw I* and *Miller* decisions left open two important voting rights questions: (1) the amount of proof that will be required to establish that a legislature used race as the basis for creating legislative districts; and (2) what, if any, kind of showing by the government would demonstrate that a race-based district was narrowly tailored to promote a compelling interest.

Some of the questions left open by *Shaw I* and *Miller* were addressed, but not answered, by the Court in two 1996 cases.

In *Shaw v. Hunt (Shaw II)*,[267] the Supreme Court reexamined the districts that had been considered in *Shaw I*. By a five to four vote, the Court in *Shaw II* ruled that the North Carolina districts had to be considered rational classifications. The *Shaw II* majority opinion, written by Chief Justice Rehnquist, ruled that persons who lived within the district had met the *Miller* standard by proving that race was the predominant reason for the creation of the districts.[268] Therefore, the districts were subject to strict judicial scrutiny; the districts

---

264. Miller v. Johnson, 515 U.S. 900, 915, 115 S.Ct. 2475, 2488, 132 L.Ed.2d 762 (1995).

265. 515 U.S. at 915, 115 S.Ct. at 2488.

266. 515 U.S. at 919–921, 115 S.Ct. at 2490–91.

267. Shaw v. Hunt (Shaw II), 517 U.S. 899, 116 S.Ct. 1894, 135 L.Ed.2d 207 (1996). *Shaw II* also involved issues concerning the standing of individuals to attack districts as being improperly based on race. For citations to addi-

tional cases, including lower court cases, and secondary works on this topic see our multi-volume Treatise: R. Rotunda & J. Nowak, Treatise on Constitutional Law: Substance and Procedure (3rd ed. 1999, with annual supplements).

268. Shaw v. Hunt (Shaw II), 517 U.S. 899, 903, 116 S.Ct. 1894, 1900, 135 L.Ed.2d 207, (1996).

would not be upheld unless they were narrowly tailored to a compelling interest.

The federal district court, following the remand in *Shaw I,* had found that the districts were narrowly tailored to the compelling interest in remedying past racial discrimination. That lower court finding was overruled in *Shaw II.* Chief Justice Rehnquist's majority opinion found that the government would have a compelling interest in correcting identified unconstitutional discrimination against minority race voters. However, the majority opinion stated the government did not have a compelling interest in the correction of societal discrimination against minority race persons that may have resulted in minority race persons not having an effective voice in the political process.[269]

According to the *Shaw II* majority, the state could not merely assert that there had been government discrimination against minority race voters in the past on the basis of data showing underrepresentation of minority race persons as voters or legislators. The lack of minority race voting power in the state might simply be the result of societal discrimination.[270] The state would have to present significant evidence demonstrating a specific identified governmental discrimination against minority race voters and the state would have to prove that the new legislative district, which guaranteed minority race control of the district election outcomes, was narrowly tailored to correct the prior constitutional violation.[271]

The Chief Justice assumed without deciding that a state might have a compelling interest in creating legislative districts that would not violate § 2 of the Voting Rights Act by diluting the voting power of racial groups. The majority opinion left open the question of whether § 5 of the Voting Rights Act, requiring certain

jurisdictions to have changes in their legislative districting maps cleared by the Department of Justice, could provide a compelling interest that might justify the creation of legislative districts that aided minority race members.

In *Shaw II,* the majority ruled that the districts created by North Carolina were not narrowly tailored to avoiding violations of the Voting Rights Act and were not narrowly tailored to correcting identified specific instances of past governmental discrimination against minority race persons.[272] Thus, the majority in *Shaw II* was able to avoid any detailed explanation of when, if ever, there would be a compelling interest that would justify the creation of a legislative district in which minority race voters were a majority of the voters in the district.

The Chief Justice's opinion in *Shaw II,* at first glance, seems to answer questions left open by *Shaw I* and *Miller.* First, the persons who were alleging that a legislative district was a racial classification have the burden of proving that race was the predominant motivating factor in the drawing of the district lines not merely considered together with other factors when the district was created. Second, once a showing of race-based districting had been made, the government must demonstrate that the district in which the minority race voters were given majority control was narrowly tailored to correct past government discrimination against that minority racial group. However, on the same day that *Shaw II* was decided, the five Justices who joined the *Shaw II* majority opinion demonstrated that they were hopelessly divided over the meaning of the principles set out in Chief Justice Rehnquist's *Shaw II* opinion.

In *Bush v. Vera,*[273] the Court by a five to four vote, but without a majority opinion, invalidat-

269. 517 U.S. at 910, 116 S.Ct. at 1903.

270. Id.

271. 517 U.S. at 910, 116 S.Ct. at 1903.

272. 517 U.S. at 914–16, 116 S.Ct. at 1905–1906.

273. Bush v. Vera, 517 U.S. 952, 116 S.Ct. 1941, 135 L.Ed.2d 248 (1996). The judgment of the Court was announced in an opinion by Justice O'Connor that was joined by Chief Justice Rehnquist and Justice Kennedy.

Justice O'Connor and Justice Kennedy also wrote separate concurring opinions; neither of their concurring opinions was joined by any other Justice. 517 U.S. at 990, 116 S.Ct. at 1968 (O'Connor, J., concurring); 517 U.S. at 996, 116 S.Ct. at 1971 (Kennedy, J., concurring). In *Vera,* Justices Thomas and Scalia concurred only in the judgment of the Court. 517 U.S. at 998, 116 S.Ct. at 1972 (Thomas, J., joined by Scalia, J., concurring in the judgment). Justices Ginsburg and Breyer did not write separately but they

ed three congressional districts that had been created by the State of Texas. The Texas congressional delegation had been increased as the result of the most recent census. The Texas legislature had created three districts in which minority race voters would be a majority of the voters in the district. The State of Texas took this action, at least in part, to comply with § 2 and § 5 of the Voting Rights Act.

The five Justices who agreed that the districts were invalid were unable to agree on how the *Miller* standard should be applied for determining whether a district was race-based. Justice O'Connor announced the judgment of the Court in an opinion that was joined by Chief Justice Rehnquist and Justice Kennedy. In the plurality opinion, Justice O'Connor stated that the plaintiffs had the burden of demonstrating, that race was the predominant factor in the legislature's drawing the district lines and that other traditional districting factors, such as the creation of compact districts or districts that followed local government lines, had been disregarded.[274] According to the plurality opinion, the strict scrutiny standard would not apply to districts where the legislature had considered race so as to protect minority race voting power, together with other traditional factors considered by legislative groups drawing district maps.

Though he had joined the plurality opinion in *Vera*, Justice Kennedy wrote a separate opinion in which he stated that he was not ready to make a ruling on whether legislative consideration of race in the drawing of a district's boundaries should be subject to strict judicial scrutiny when race was not the predominant factor for drawing boundaries.[275] Justices Thomas and Scalia concurred only in the judgment in *Vera*, because they believe that any use of race by a governmental entity drawing legislative district lines should automatically be subject to strict judicial scrutiny and should not be upheld unless it was narrowly tailored to a compelling interest.[276]

In *Vera*, Justice O'Connor was the only member of the majority to express the view that a state had a compelling interest in avoiding violating § 2 of the Voting Rights Act.[277] That section of the Voting Rights Act prohibits states from impairing the voting strength of minority race persons; that section can be violated by the allegedly unintentional dilution of minority race voting power through the division of minority race voters in a compact area into several districts. The other four Justices in the five member majority have not committed to finding that a state's desire to avoid violating the Voting Rights Act would be a compelling interest that would justify race-based districting.

Justices Stevens and Souter wrote dissenting opinions in the *Shaw II* and *Vera* cases that were joined by Justices Ginsburg and Breyer.[278] The dissenters argued that there is no constitutional basis for the judiciary to invalidate legislative decisions designed to pro-

joined both of the dissenting opinions, which were written by Justice Stevens and Justice Souter. However, Justice Stevens and Justice Souter did not join each other's dissenting opinions. Bush v. Vera, 517 U.S. 952, 1002, 116 S.Ct. 1941, 1974, 135 L.Ed.2d 248 (1996) (Stevens, J., joined by Ginsburg and Breyer, JJ., dissenting); 517 U.S. at 1044, 116 S.Ct. at 1997 (Souter, J., joined by Ginsburg and Breyer, JJ., dissenting).

Chief Justice Rehnquist, who had written the majority opinion in *Shaw II*, did not write a separate opinion in *Vera*.

274. Bush v. Vera, 517 U.S. 952, 957–59, 116 S.Ct. 1941, 1951–52, 135 L.Ed.2d 248 (1996) (plurality opinion by O'Connor, J., joined by Rehnquist, C.J., and Kennedy, J.).

275. 517 U.S. at 996, 116 S.Ct. at 1971 (Kennedy, J., concurring).

276. Bush v. Vera, 517 U.S. 952, 998, 116 S.Ct. 1941, 1972, 135 L.Ed.2d 248 (1996) (Thomas, J., joined by Scalia, J., concurring in the judgment).

277. Bush v. Vera, 517 U.S. 952, 990, 116 S.Ct. 1941, 1968, 135 L.Ed.2d 248 (1996) (opinion of O'Connor, J., concurring).

278. Shaw v. Hunt (Shaw II), 517 U.S. 899, 918, 116 S.Ct. 1894, 1907, 135 L.Ed.2d 207 (1996) (Stevens, J., joined in part by Ginsburg and Breyer, JJ., dissenting). Bush v. Vera, 517 U.S. 952, 1002, 116 S.Ct. 1941, 1974, 135 L.Ed.2d 248 (1996) (Stevens, J., joined by Ginsburg and Breyer, JJ., dissenting).

Justice Souter's dissent in *Shaw II* merely made a reference to his dissent in *Vera*, which was decided the same day as *Shaw II*. Shaw II, 517 U.S. at 951, 116 S.Ct. at 1923 (Souter, J., joined by Ginsburg and Breyer, JJ., dissenting) referring to Bush v. Vera, 517 U.S. 952, 1044, 116 S.Ct. 1941, 1997, 135 L.Ed.2d 248 (1996) (Souter, J., joined by Ginsburg and Breyer, JJ., dissenting).

tect minority racial groups, at least when the strengthening of minority race voting power was accomplished without the dilution of majority race voting power. In the North Carolina and Texas cases, minority race persons were not over-represented following the alleged racial gerrymandering. In each case, the districts that protected minority race voting power merely insured that minority race persons would be represented in number close to, but not exceeding, their proportion of the voter population.

The Supreme Court has not explained whether there are any circumstances that will justify the government intentionally creating a voting district to strengthen the voting power of minority race persons. The Court should uphold a state or local legislative district map designed to increase the likelihood that a district election would will be controlled by minority race voters if that was the only method by which the government could correct identified illegal or unconstitutional discrimination against minority race voters in prior years. Proving that the new district was narrowly tailored to correct past unconstitutional or illegal racial discrimination would be very difficult. It seems unlikely, so long as the membership of the Court remains the same as it was in the mid 1990s, that compliance with the Voting Rights Act might be a compelling interest that would support the creation of legislative districts drawn for the primary purpose of assuring control of district elections by minority race voters.[279] At the close of the century, the Justices had provided little guidance to

lower federal courts regarding how those courts should assess statistical and circumstantial evidence when determining if a legislative district was race-based.[280]

The cases we have examined in this subsection involved attempts by the government to strengthen minority race voting power by designing legislative districts that were likely to be controlled by minority race voters. In none of these cases did the government simply limit voting in the election to persons of a certain race. If the government were to granted the right to vote in an election only to certain persons, based on the race or ancestry of those persons, or if the government excluded persons from receiving a ballot because of their race or ancestry, the governmental action would violate the Fifteenth Amendment.

In *Rice v. Cayetano*,[281] the Supreme Court invalidated a provision of the State of Hawaii's Constitution that allowed only persons who were "Native Hawaiians" or "Hawaiians" to vote for the trustees of a trust fund that was dedicated to helping persons of Hawaiian ancestry. The terms "Native Hawaiians" and "Hawaiians," as used in the state constitution, referred to persons who lived in Hawaii, were United States citizens, and who had certain ancestral ties to persons who had resided in Hawaii at a much earlier time. The Supreme Court, by a seven to two vote of the Justices, ruled that prohibiting persons from voting in the elections for the trustees simply because they were not of a certain ancestry was a

---

279. For further analysis of the Court's rulings concerning the scope of Congress's power to protect the right to vote under the Fourteenth and Fifteenth Amendment, see the multi-volume edition of this Treatise, R. Rotunda & J. Nowak Treatise on Constitutional Law: Substance and Procedure, Chapter 19 (3rd ed. 1999, with annual supplements).

280. The Supreme Court has established the principle that parties attacking a voting district on the basis that the district was created for racial reasons have the burden of proving that racial considerations were the primary motivation for the legislature's drawing of the boundaries of the challenged legislative district. However, that standard is difficult to apply for any court because it requires close examination of the evidence concerning whether race was only one factor considered in the creation of the legislative district boundaries or whether the racial considerations were so predominant in the districting process

that the district itself should be considered as a racial classification. Compare Hunt v. Cromartie [*Hunt I*] 526 U.S. 541, 119 S.Ct. 1545, 143 L.Ed.2d 731 (1999) (Justices unanimously find the three-judge district court should not have entered summary judgment against the government in a case involving an allegation of race-conscious districting), with Hunt v. Cromartie [*Hunt II*], 532 U.S. 234, 121 S.Ct. 1452, 149 L.Ed.2d 430 (2001) (by a 5 to 4 vote, the Court overturns a district court finding that the district involved in the *Hunt I* litigation was race-based; the Supreme Court majority finds that the evidence concerning the creation of the district made the trial court's finding of a race-based district a "clearly erroneous finding"). The *Hunt I* and *Hunt II* cases are examined in § 14.4 of this Treatise.

281. Rice v. Cayetano, 528 U.S. 495, 120 S.Ct. 1044, 145 L.Ed.2d 1007 (2000).

racial classification that violated the terms of the Fifteenth Amendment. Justice Kennedy's majority opinion found that Hawaii could not justify its law in terms of previous Supreme Court cases that had allowed Congress to create classifications that benefitted members of recognized native American Indian tribes and that, by implication, allowed tribal elections to be limited to members of the tribe. Justice Kennedy, writing for five Justices, said that the tribal elections of Native American Indian tribes involved "the internal affairs of a quasi-sovereign."[282] The state agency in Hawaii that operated the trust fund was simply a unit of government whose actions had some impact on all of the people of the state. The Court was not confronted with the issue of whether the Hawaiian trust fund that benefitted only persons of Hawaiian or Native Hawaiian ancestry was a benign racial classification that was compatible with the equal protection clause.[283]

Only Justices Stevens and Ginsburg dissented in *Rice*. Those two Justices believed that earlier Supreme Court decisions recognizing the power of the federal government to grant benefits to members of Native American tribes, and the right of tribes to self-determination, required the Court to uphold the State's limitation of the right to vote for the trustees of the fund to help Native Hawaiians and Hawaiians.[284]

§ 14.11 General Status of Aliens—Citizenship, Immigration, Deportation, Naturalization, and Expatriation [1]

Many types of laws or executive actions may distinguish between citizens of the United States and noncitizens. Such actions raise the question of the constitutionality of classifications based on "alienage", the status of being a noncitizen. Aliens do not receive the protection of constitutional guarantees that by their terms apply only to "citizens."[2] However,

---

282. 528 U.S. at 520, 120 S.Ct. at 1059. The Court was primarily distinguishing the ruling in Morton v. Mancari, 417 U.S. 535, 94 S.Ct. 2474, 41 L.Ed.2d 290 (1974). Justices Breyer and Souter concurred in the result in the case. They disagreed with the majority opinion only insofar as they thought the majority did not have to describe the cases involving the rights of Native Americans and members of Native American tribes with "so vague a concept as 'quasi-sovereign' ... rather [in the view of the dissent] we should reject—efforts to justify its rules through analogy to a trust for an Indian tribe because the record makes clear that (1) there is no 'trust' for Native Hawaiians here, and (2) OHA's [the agency's] electorate, as defined in the statute, does not sufficiently resemble an Indian tribe." 528 U.S. at 522, 120 S.Ct. at 1060. (Breyer, J., joined by Souter, J., concurring in the result).

283. The majority noted that the person attacking the voting system had not attacked the constitutionality of the underlying programs to benefit persons of certain ancestry or the existence of the government agency designed to administer those programs. For that reason, the Court decided only the Fifteenth Amendment question, and assumed, for the purpose of deciding this case, that the State of Hawaii program to benefit persons of certain ancestry was constitutionally valid. Rice v. Cayetano, 528 U.S. 495, 509–11, 522, 120 S.Ct. 1044, 1053–54, 1060, 145 L.Ed.2d 1007 (2000).

284. 528 U.S. at 526, 120 S.Ct. at 1062 (Stevens, J., joined in part by Ginsburg, J., dissenting). Justice Ginsburg joined only the portion of Justice Stevens' dissent regarding the power of Congress to deal with Native Americans and the relationship of that power to the voting system at issue in this case. Justice Ginsburg did not join the portions of Justice Stevens dissent in which he stated that there was a clear distinction between ancestry and race classifications and that the Hawaii voting system

would not have violated the Fifteenth Amendment even if one disregarded the cases concerning the power of the federal government to assist members of native American tribes. 528 U.S. at 574, 120 S.Ct. at 1073 (Ginsburg, J., dissenting).

§ 14.11

1. This section is intended to provide the reader with an overview that will be of assistance to the reader when examining the problems analyzed in § 14.12. For citations to additional Supreme Court cases, and secondary authorities, on this point, see R. Rotunda & J. Nowak, Treatise on Constitutional Law: Substance and Procedure, vol. 3, §§ 18.11, 18.13, vol. 5, ch. 22 (3rd ed. 1999, with annual supplements).

2. Aliens would not be entitled to protection under the privileges or immunities clause of section 1 of the Fourteenth Amendment, which provides that "No State shall make or enforce any law which shall abridge the privileges or immunities of citizens of the United States."

Furthermore, the validity of citizenship as a prerequisite of voting is impliedly recognized by the constitutional guarantees of the Fifteenth and Nineteenth Amendments that the right of citizens to vote would not be denied or abridged on the basis of race or sex and by Supreme Court opinions. E.g. Sugarman v. Dougall, 413 U.S. 634, 649, 93 S.Ct. 2842, 2851, 37 L.Ed.2d 853 (1973).

The Constitution expressly makes citizenship a requirement to hold the office of representative, senator, or president. Article II Section 2 makes citizenship for seven years a requirement for representative. Article II Section 3 requires senators to have been citizens nine years. Article II Section 1 requires that the President be a natural born citizen (or a citizen when the Constitution was adopted).

aliens are protected by those provisions which refer to "persons."[3] Thus, they receive the protection of the Bill of Rights, including the Fifth Amendment due process clause, and the Fourteenth Amendment due process and equal protection clauses.[4]

Citizenship is defined and conferred by section one of the Fourteenth Amendment which states: "All persons born or naturalized in the United States, and subject to the jurisdiction thereof, are citizens of the United States and of the State wherein they reside."

The Congressional ability to set standards for naturalization of aliens has never been significantly limited by the Court.[5] But the Fourteenth Amendment grant of citizenship contains no provision for termination of citizenship. Thus problems have arisen as to expatriation—the termination of a person's

citizenship. Voluntary expatriation is permissible so that a person may renounce his citizenship.[6]

The Court, however, has stricken several congressional attempts to provide for involuntary termination of citizenship. Thus, the Court has held that persons could not be deprived of their citizenship because of refusal to serve in the armed forces or for voting in a foreign election.[7] However, there may still be a question as to whether Congress might by statute require a person to elect to reject his citizenship for an act totally opposed to that status, such as service in the armed forces of a nation at war with the United States. While the Court has taken the position that Congress was without power to deprive a person of citizenship since the Fourteenth Amendment was meant to be an irrevocable grant of citi-

3. Yick Wo v. Hopkins, 118 U.S. 356, 6 S.Ct. 1064, 30 L.Ed. 220 (1886).

4. Wong Wing v. United States, 163 U.S. 228, 238, 16 S.Ct. 977, 41 L.Ed. 140 (1896) (due process clause of Fifth Amendment applicable to aliens); Yick Wo v. Hopkins, 118 U.S. 356, 6 S.Ct. 1064, 30 L.Ed. 220 (1886).

5. The Supreme Court has upheld federal statutes that granted citizenship at birth to a child born outside of the United States to a United States citizen male and a non-citizen female who were not married to each other only upon the fulfillment of certain conditions by the United States citizen father. These statutes granted immediate citizenship at birth to a child born outside of the United States to a United States citizen female and a non-citizen male who were not married to each other. The statutes also grant automatic citizenship to a child at birth who is born to a U.S. citizen (whether male or female) and a non-citizen who were married to each other at the time of the child's birth.

In Miller v. Albright, 523 U.S. 420, 118 S.Ct. 1428, 140 L.Ed.2d 575 (1998) the Court, without a majority opinion refused to invalidate the preference for legitimate children over illegitimate children or the preference for children born to non-citizen mothers as opposed to non-citizen fathers while they were outside of the United States and not married to the other parent. The Court in *Miller*, albeit without a majority opinion, appeared to uphold the classification based on legitimacy without considering the gender classification inherent in this naturalization system. See § 14.18, infra.

In Tuan Anh Nguyen v. Immigration and Naturalization Service, 533 U.S. 53, 121 S.Ct. 2053, 150 L.Ed.2d 115 (2001) the Court upheld both the gender and legitimacy classifications in these naturalization statutes. The majority opinion, written by Justice Kennedy, ruled that these classifications were substantially related to important government interests in: assuring the biological relationship in fact existed between the person asserting paternity and

the person receiving naturalization; and in creating an opportunity for those persons to develop a meaningful parent-child relationship. Because the statutes met the standard for gender and illegitimacy classifications, Justice Kennedy found that the Court did not need to consider whether it should give special deference to congressional use of illegitimacy or gender traits in immigration and naturalization matters, or whether the Supreme Court had the power to grant citizenship under terms not clearly established by Congress. 533 U.S. at 71–73, 121 S.Ct. at 2059, 2065–66. See §§ 14.18, 14.23.

6. "By the Act of July 27, 1868 [15 Stat.L. 223, chap. 249] Congress declared that 'the right of expatriation is a natural and inherent right of all people.' Expatriation is the voluntary renunciation or abandonment of nationality and allegiance." Perkins v. Elg, 307 U.S. 325, 334, 59 S.Ct. 884, 889, 83 L.Ed. 1320 (1939). The Act has since been repealed and the right of expatriation is covered by 8 U.S.C.A. §§ 1482, 1483.

See also Kennedy v. Mendoza–Martinez, 372 U.S. 144, 159 n. 11, 83 S.Ct. 554, 563 n. 11, 9 L.Ed.2d 644 (1963) where Court states there is no disagreement that citizenship may be voluntarily relinquished either expressly or by conduct.

7. Kennedy v. Mendoza-Martinez, 372 U.S. 144, 83 S.Ct. 554, 9 L.Ed.2d 644 (1963) (expatriation of one who departed from or remained outside the United States in time of War or during a period of national emergency for the purpose of evading military service found unconstitutional); Trop v. Dulles, 356 U.S. 86, 78 S.Ct. 590, 2 L.Ed.2d 630 (1958) (expatriation for desertion of military services during war held unconstitutional as applied to native born citizen); Afroyim v. Rusk, 387 U.S. 253, 87 S.Ct. 1660, 18 L.Ed.2d 757 (1967) (expatriation of citizen for voting in foreign election found unconstitutional) overruling Perez v. Brownell, 356 U.S. 44, 78 S.Ct. 568, 2 L.Ed.2d 603 (1958).

zenship to certain persons,[8] it might be argued that at some point a person's actions might constitute voluntary expatriation.[9]

In *Vance v. Terrazas*,[10] the Court held that an individual cannot be deprived of his United States citizenship unless the government demonstrates not only that he *voluntarily* took an action which Congress has deemed to be expatriating, but also that he *intended to renounce* his citizenship when he took that action. The government, however, need only prove the elements of voluntariness and specific intent by a preponderance of the evidence.

A five member majority of the Court also upheld the statutory presumption that any person who committed an act of expatriation listed by Congress did so voluntarily. However, this presumption was upheld only insofar as it could be used to demonstrate the voluntariness of the action; it could not be used to establish intent to relinquish citizenship.

In this case, a young man born with dual citizenship in the United States and Mexico had applied for a certificate of Mexican nationality. In so doing, he had sworn allegiance to that government and had stated that he was renouncing citizenship in all other governments, including the United States. The Court found that the declaration of allegiance to the Mexican government did not in itself establish a basis for expatriation despite a statute to that effect.[11] The young man, however, would be deprived of his United States citizenship if the Secretary of State could demonstrate that the oath was taken voluntarily and with an actual intent to relinquish citizenship. The Secretary would be helped in meeting this burden by the statutory presumption of voluntariness, but there would have to be some other basis for showing intent.

A person who has not been born in this country may become a naturalized citizen if he or she complies with the conditions for naturalization set by Congress.[12] Following naturalization in this country the naturalized citizen is not subject to involuntary expatriation to any greater extent than a natural born citizen with one exception; if the person engages in fraud or misrepresentation in the naturalization process later discovery of the fraud will annul the grant of citizenship.[13]

Congress may also attach reasonable conditions to the original grant of citizenship under which the person might later be divested of

---

8. Afroyim v. Rusk, 387 U.S. 253, 87 S.Ct. 1660, 18 L.Ed.2d 757 (1967).

9. See, e.g., Chief Justice Warren's dissent in Perez v. Brownell, 356 U.S. at 68–69, 78 S.Ct. at 581–82 (1958), with which the *Afroyim* majority declared its agreement. *Afroyim* overruled *Perez*.

10. 444 U.S. 252, 100 S.Ct. 540, 62 L.Ed.2d 461 (1980), rehearing denied 445 U.S. 920, 100 S.Ct. 1285, 63 L.Ed.2d 606 (1980), on remand 494 F.Supp. 1017 (N.D.Ill.1980), judgment affirmed 653 F.2d 285 (7th Cir.1981).

11. 8 U.S.C.A. § 1481(a)(2).

12. The Constitution vests Congress with the power "to establish an Uniform Rule of Naturalization." Art. I, § 8, cl. 4. The Supreme Court has given Congress great latitude in selecting the appropriate conditions. United States v. Macintosh, 283 U.S. 605, 615, 51 S.Ct. 570, 571–72, 75 L.Ed. 1302 (1931);

Congress has provided by statute that the right to become a citizen may not be denied on the basis of race, sex, or marital status. § 311, 66 Stat. 239, 8 U.S.C.A. § 1422. The right will be denied where, for example, a person is or has been a member of an organization advocating the violent overthrow of the government. § 313(a) and (c), 66 Stat. 240, 8 U.S.C.A. § 1424(a) and (c). "Good moral character" is prerequisite, § 316(a)(3), 66 Stat. 242, 8 U.S.C.A. § 1427(a)(3).

13. § 340(a), 66 Stat. 260, 8 U.S.C.A. § 1451(a). Proof of fraud or misrepresentation may be proved and result in

loss of citizenship at any time regardless of how long ago person became a citizen. Costello v. United States, 365 U.S. 265, 81 S.Ct. 534, 5 L.Ed.2d 551 (1961) (27 years); Polites v. United States, 364 U.S. 426, 81 S.Ct. 202, 5 L.Ed.2d 173 (1960) (10 years); Knauer v. United States, 328 U.S. 654, 66 S.Ct. 1304, 90 L.Ed. 1500 (1946), rehearing denied 329 U.S. 818, 67 S.Ct. 25, 91 L.Ed. 697 (1946) (6 years).

However, absent fraud, Congress cannot take away citizenship of one born in the United States or naturalized in the United States. Schneider v. Rusk, 377 U.S. 163, 84 S.Ct. 1187, 12 L.Ed.2d 218 (1964). (Court struck provision that naturalized citizen lost his citizenship if he resided continuously for three years in the country of which he was formerly a national or in which he was born.)

In Fedorenko v. United States, 449 U.S. 490, 101 S.Ct. 737, 66 L.Ed.2d 686 (1981), the Supreme Court upheld the denaturalization of a person who was proven to have given false and incomplete information on his visa application and, therefore, to have "illegally procured" his naturalization. The person had failed to disclose facts concerning his service as a concentration camp guard which made him ineligible for a visa; the federal courts had no "equitable discretion" to refrain from entering a judgment of denaturalization.

citizenship, *if* the person is naturalized *outside* of the United States. Thus, in *Rogers v. Bellei*[14] the Court upheld the requirement for children born abroad with only one parent of United States citizenship that they later spend five continuous years in the United States between the ages of 14 and 28 in order to retain United States citizenship. Since these persons were not born in the United States or finally naturalized there, they were not granted citizenship by the first sentence of section one of the Fourteenth Amendment. Congress could grant the conditional citizenship just as it could have refused to make any grant of citizenship until they fulfilled the residence requirement.[15]

Congress also has a virtually unrestricted power to set the terms for alien immigration[16] and this power may be delegated in part to the executive.[17] The immigration acts have set conditions and quotas for entry into this country.[18] For many years, Congress set quotas for immigration based on nationality[19] and, despite the racial-national origin classification, the law was never seriously questioned.[20] The executive branch also has been given the authority to exclude individual aliens whom are either unqualified for immigration or who may present some moral or social danger.[21] The individuals who are refused entry have not been given a constitutional right to a hearing to determine the basis for their exclusion.[22] Indeed the Supreme Court once upheld the refusal to grant a hearing to an alien who sought re-entry to the country after an absence, even though no other country would accept this person.[23] This decision may now be constitutionally infirm, even though it has never been overruled. In any event, it does demonstrate the historic refusal of the Court to review immigration decisions. The Supreme Court has been able to avoid ruling on

---

14. 401 U.S. 815, 91 S.Ct. 1060, 28 L.Ed.2d 499 (1971).

15. Justices Black, Brennan, Douglas, and Marshall dissented. But see, Schneider v. Rusk, 377 U.S. 163, 84 S.Ct. 1187, 12 L.Ed.2d 218 (1964).

16. Congress does not derive its power to regulate immigration from a specific constitutional grant. It is simply regarded as a power inherent to a sovereignty. See Chinese Exclusion Case, 130 U.S. 581, 9 S.Ct. 623, 32 L.Ed. 1068 (1889). For a further discussion of Congressional authority and foreign affairs, see L. Henkin, Foreign Affairs and the Constitution (1972). See note 1, supra.

17. U.S. ex rel. Knauff v. Shaughnessy, 338 U.S. 537, 543, 70 S.Ct. 309, 312–13, 94 L.Ed. 317 (1950).

18. For citations to additional cases, and secondary sources on this topic, see R. Rotunda & J. Nowak, Treatise on Constitutional Law: Substance and Procedure, vol. 3, §§ 18.11, 18.13, vol. 5, ch. 22 (3rd ed. 1999, with annual supplements).

19. The first Congressional act limiting immigration on the basis of race or nationality was the Chinese Exclusion Act of 1882, Act of May 6, 1882, 22 Stat. 58, which remained in effect until 1943. In 1924 Congress set up the national origin quota system, Act of May 26, 1924, 43 Stat. 153, which remained in effect until 1965. Act of October 3, 1965, P.L. 89–236, 79 Stat. 911, 8 U.S.C.A § 1152(a) now prohibits the use of race, national origin, sex, place of birth, or place of residence to determine the eligibility of an alien to immigrate.

20. See Ozawa v. United States, 260 U.S. 178, 43 S.Ct. 65, 67 L.Ed. 199 (1922); United States v. Bhagat Singh Thind, 261 U.S. 204, 43 S.Ct. 338, 67 L.Ed. 616 (1923); Toyota v. United States, 268 U.S. 402, 45 S.Ct. 563, 69 L.Ed. 1016 (1925); Morrison v. California, 291 U.S. 82, 54 S.Ct. 281, 78 L.Ed. 664 (1934). The Court refused to review the only case in which the constitutional issue was raised and rejected, Kharaiti Ram Samras v. United States, 125 F.2d 879 (9th Cir.1942), certiorari denied 317 U.S. 634, 63 S.Ct. 34, 87 L.Ed. 511 (1942).

21. 8 U.S.C.A. §§ 1103, 1104. See note 18, supra.

22. For aliens who have never been naturalized nor acquired residence in the United States, the decision of an executive or administrative officer, acting within the powers conferred by Congress is due process. United States v. Ju Toy, 198 U.S. 253, 263, 25 S.Ct. 644, 646, 49 L.Ed. 1040 (1905).

A citizen of the United States or a permanent resident alien who makes a trip abroad is denied a constitutionally protected interest when the government seeks to exclude him from returning to the country. It would appear that the citizen who wishes to return to the country always has a claim that he has lost liberty in such a situation. The alien who was lawfully resident in the United States before his trip abroad has a claim that he had a statutory entitlement to residence which was denied him by the government when it prevented him from reentering the country. If the resident alien's absence from the country was extended he may lose his entitlement. When the absence was brief he should be entitled to some type of a due process hearing, in the nature of a deportation hearing, to determine the reasonableness of prohibiting him from reentering the country. The cases finding that an alien seeking initial admission to the United States has no constitutional rights regarding his application do not bar the granting of a hearing to either the citizen or lawfully resident alien who has been temporarily absent from the country and wishes to return. See, Landon v. Plasencia, 459 U.S. 21, 103 S.Ct. 321, 74 L.Ed.2d 21 (1982).

23. Shaughnessy v. United States ex rel. Mezei, 345 U.S. 206, 73 S.Ct. 625, 97 L.Ed. 956 (1953), see note 22, supra.

the continuing validity of earlier decisions that failed to place any significant constitutional restrictions on the ability of the executive to exclude or detain persons who were seeking initial admittance into the country by finding that current federal statutes and regulations established limitations on executive agency discretion.[24]

The congressional power to regulate immigration and naturalization includes the power to regulate the behavior of aliens who are in this country.[25] Pursuant to statute, aliens may be deported for a variety of activities deemed harmful to this country.[26] These conditions will be upheld as within the power of Congress because the Court defers to the legislature in such matters. But the resident alien will have a right to a hearing prior to the

deportation.[27] The hearing will determine whether the person is an alien or a citizen, and, if he is an alien, whether the conditions for continuing residence have been violated. While the procedural aspects of the due process clause requires this hearing to establish the basis for the deportation, an alien who has violated the statutes or conditions of entry has no right to continued residence in this country.

The Court has extended the protection of the Fourteenth Amendment equal protection clause to illegally resident aliens but, in so doing, it did not impliedly limit the power of the federal government to exclude or deport such persons.[28] Thus, when we examine the rights of an alien in this country we are really looking primarily at the rights of lawful resi-

---

24. For example, in Jean v. Nelson, 472 U.S. 846, 105 S.Ct. 2992, 86 L.Ed.2d 664 (1985) the Supreme Court found that current Immigration and Naturalization Service regulations prohibited consideration of the race or national origin of persons who were seeking initial admittance into the country and who were being detained prior to their admission. Officials were to make decisions regarding the temporary parole of such persons into the country on an individualized basis and without consideration to race or national origin. This ruling avoided a constitutional ruling on whether Haitian detainees who had not been paroled into the United States, and who had been held in custody since their arrival in this country, had been denied due process. A constitutional ruling would have required reexamination of cases such as Shaughnessy v. United States ex rel. Mezei, 345 U.S. 206, 73 S.Ct. 625, 97 L.Ed. 956 (1953).

For citations to additional Supreme Court cases, and secondary authorities, on this point, see R. Rotunda & J. Nowak, Treatise on Constitutional Law: Substance and Procedure, vol. 3, §§ 18.11, 18.13, and vol. 5, Ch. 22 (3rd ed. 1999, with annual supplements).

25. Aliens who enter the United States illegally may be subject to prosecution under federal criminal statutes as well as to deportation. See generally, Almendarez–Torres v. United States, 523 U.S. 224, 118 S.Ct. 1219, 140 L.Ed.2d 350 (1998) (upholding federal statute providing for a sentence of up to 20 years in prison for illegally entering the country after deportation that followed a conviction of a felony; the government was not required to charge, in the indictment, that the defendant had been convicted of a felony prior to the deportation because that fact was a sentencing factor, rather than an element of the crime).

26. 8 U.S.C.A. § 1251. Reasons for deportation include non-compliance with eligibility requirements for entrance, a conviction of a crime of moral turpitude within five years after entry, and membership in proscribed organizations. The latter provision was upheld as to aliens who had become members of the communist party before

the law was established. See Harisiades v. Shaughnessy, 342 U.S. 580, 72 S.Ct. 512, 96 L.Ed. 586 (1952), rehearing denied 343 U.S. 936, 72 S.Ct. 767, 96 L.Ed. 1344 (1952) (interpreting and upholding predecessor section, 54 Stat. 670, 8 U.S.C.A. § 137).

27. 8 U.S.C.A. § 1252(b). A person arrested and held for deportation who claims to be a citizen is entitled to his day in court. Ng Fung Ho v. White, 259 U.S. 276, 281, 42 S.Ct. 492, 494, 66 L.Ed. 938 (1922). In Zadvydas v. Davis, 533 U.S. 678, 121 S.Ct. 2491, 150 L.Ed.2d 653(2001) the Supreme Court interpreted federal statutes so as to impose a reasonable time limitation on the period of time that the federal government could hold a person in detention following an order of deportation. The majority opinion in *Zadvydas*, written by Justice Breyer, found that in order to avoid serious constitutional questions about the statute, the statute should be interpreted in a manner that did not give the Justice Department the power to have indefinite detention of a person within the United States The majority opinion distinguished Shaughnessy v. United States ex rel. Mezei, 345 U.S. 206, 73 S.Ct. 625, 97 L.Ed. 956 (1953), which had allowed the federal government to detain a person indefinitely prior to the individual's admission into the United States. Justice Breyer's majority opinion in *Zadvydas* found *Mezei* distinguishable on the basis that the person in that case had not been admitted to the United States. Justice Breyer noted that every person was within the United States, regardless of whether he or she was in the country legally, received the protection of the due process clause of the Fifth Amendment. Zadvydas v. Davis, 533 U.S. 678, 692–93, 121 S.Ct. 2491, 2500–2501, 150 L.Ed.2d 653 (2001). For citations to additional Supreme Court cases, and secondary authorities, on this point, see R. Rotunda & J. Nowak, Treatise on Constitutional Law: Substance and Procedure, vol. 3, § 18.12, vol. 5, ch. 22 (3rd ed. 1999, with annual supplements).

28. Plyler v. Doe, 457 U.S. 202, 102 S.Ct. 2382, 72 L.Ed.2d 786 (1982). This case is examined in § 14.13, infra.

dent aliens apart from questions of immigration, deportation, or naturalization. The ability of the government to treat resident aliens differently from citizens depends on the degree to which alienage is relevant to legitimate goals of government programs. It is this problem of classification and discrimination which is the subject of the next subsection.

§ 14.12   Classifications Based on Alienage

(a) Overview

Aliens are persons, so they receive the protection of the due process clauses and the equal protection clause.[1] It should be noted that, while the equal protection clause does not apply to the federal government, the Fifth Amendment's due process clause guarantees equal protection in the application of federal law.[2] State classifications which treat aliens differently on the basis of that status are reviewed under the equal protection clause of the Fourteenth Amendment while federal acts are subject to the due process clause of the Fifth Amendment.

The equal protection guarantee requires that the government treat similar persons in a similar manner. When testing a classification based upon alienage the issue is whether the status of being a United States citizen differentiates persons in terms of a proper governmental purpose. If not, it should be invalidated as an arbitrary refusal to accord equal treatment to lawfully resident persons who are not citizens. The Supreme Court has refused to enunciate a single test to be used when determining the compatibility of alienage classifications with the equal protection guarantee of the Fourteenth Amendment equal protection clause or the Fifth Amendment due process clause.

All of the Court's decisions since 1970 on this issue would appear to be consistent if the Court were using an intermediate standard of review—between the traditional rational basis test and the strict compelling interest test—which required the government to demonstrate that a citizenship classification bore a reasonable and substantial relationship to an important government interest.[3]

Since state and local governments have no interest in foreign affairs, their use of alienage classifications would have to be reasonably justified by a significant local interest. Thus, state laws prohibiting aliens from voting or holding important government positions could be upheld as related to the important local interest in the self-governance process. However, state laws imposing United States citizenship restrictions on eligibility for welfare payments or the practice of a profession would not in most instances be reasonable ways of promoting an important local interest.

Federal laws employing citizenship classifications would almost always be upheld under a substantial relationship to an important interest standard. The federal interest in international affairs, as well as the federal power over immigration and naturalization, should justify the use of alienage classifications. So long as a federal alienage classification was not a totally arbitrary means of disfavoring lawfully resident aliens, the classification would be upheld. Such rulings would assure the federal government freedom to pursue national goals without simultaneously granting the government a virtually unchecked power to make use of arbitrary and invidious classifications burdening noncitizens. Unfortunately, the Court has chosen not to analyze all alienage classifications in terms of a single standard of review. Instead, the Court has divided alienage cases into three categories.

First, when state of local laws classify persons on the basis of United States citizenship for the purpose of distributing economic benefits, or limiting the opportunity to engage in

---

§ 14.12

1. Wong Wing v. United States, 163 U.S. 228, 238, 16 S.Ct. 977, 41 L.Ed. 140 (1896) (due process clause of Fifth Amendment); Yick Wo v. Hopkins, 118 U.S. 356, 6 S.Ct. 1064, 30 L.Ed. 220 (1886) (equal protection).

2. Bolling v. Sharpe, 347 U.S. 497, 74 S.Ct. 693, 98 L.Ed. 884 (1954), opinion supplemented by Brown v. Board of Education, 349 U.S. 294, 75 S.Ct. 753, 99 L.Ed. 1083 (1955). See §§ 14.1, 14.3, supra.

3. See § 14.3, supra.

private sector economic activity, the law will be subjected to strict judicial scrutiny. In this situation, the Court recognizes that classifications based on alienage should be deemed "suspect" and upheld only if necessary to promote a compelling or overriding interest.[4] Until recently, the Court upheld alienage classifications whenever the Justices believed that the state had a "special public interest" in granting privileges only to citizens. Now that the Court has subjected these economic citizenship classifications to strict scrutiny, the state must demonstrate a compelling purpose for treating aliens in a less favorable manner than citizens. This test will be quite difficult for the state to meet because in almost all instances the lawfully resident noncitizen is subject to federal and state taxation just as is the resident citizen. The lawfully resident alien is not reasonably distinguishable from the citizen in terms of legitimate, nondiscriminatory economic goals of the state.

Second, an alienage classification created by state or local law which relates to allocating power or positions in the political process will be upheld under the traditional rational basis test. The state clearly has a legitimate interest in reserving positions in the self-governance process for United States citizens. The state need not allow noncitizens the right to vote or hold elective office. Indeed, it appears that the state need not allow the noncitizen to hold an important governmental position of any type.[5] The Supreme Court has created a "political function" exception to the strict scrutiny of state alienage regulations so that local governments may require citizenship as a condition of obtaining a government position "intimately related to the process of democrat-

ic self-government.'"[6] If a government position is related to the self-governance process, involves a significant policy-making function, or requires the exercise of important discretionary power over citizens, the state or local government may reserve that position for a United States citizen. However, states may not use a United States citizenship classification to exclude lawfully resident aliens from employment in government positions which are purely functionary and are not related to the interest in self-governance.[7]

The trait of being an United States citizen does define a class of persons, in the view of the Court, who have a special affiliation to both the federal and state governments and, therefore, who may be given a priority for employment in governmental positions that are related to the self-governance process and involve the exercise of important powers in our democratic system. A political, as opposed to economic, alienage classification will be upheld so long as it is rationally related to the state interest in preserving the governmental process for citizens. Even in the political area, a state may not be totally arbitrary in its use of the alienage classification.[8]

If the alienage classification does not relate to this self-governance interest, the state classification will be tested under the strict scrutiny standard. It must be remembered that states may not pursue foreign policy objectives; state classifications must relate to a legitimate local interest. Additionally, states will not be allowed to intrude into the foreign relations interests of the United States and any state law regulating aliens which might interfere with federal policy in this area will be

---

4. See, e.g., Graham v. Richardson, 403 U.S. 365, 91 S.Ct. 1848, 29 L.Ed.2d 534 (1971); Application of Griffiths, 413 U.S. 717, 93 S.Ct. 2851, 37 L.Ed.2d 910 (1973). These cases are examined in § 14.12(b), infra.

5. See, e.g., Ambach v. Norwick, 441 U.S. 68, 99 S.Ct. 1589, 60 L.Ed.2d 49 (1979); Cabell v. Chavez-Salido, 454 U.S. 432, 102 S.Ct. 735, 70 L.Ed.2d 677 (1982). These cases are examined in § 14.12(b), infra.

6. Bernal v. Fainter, 467 U.S. 216, 219, 104 S.Ct. 2312, 2316, 81 L.Ed.2d 175, 180 (1984), on remand 737 F.2d 495 (5th Cir.1984).

7. In Bernal v. Fainter, 467 U.S. 216, 104 S.Ct. 2312, 81 L.Ed.2d 175 (1984), the Supreme Court held that a

Texas statute requiring a notary public to be a United States citizen violated the equal protection clause because the position was essentially clerical and ministerial. Therefore the position did not involve the type of "responsibilities that go to the heart of representative government." For that reason, the classification was reviewed under the strict scrutiny test to determine whether it was narrowly tailored or necessary to promote a compelling governmental interest; the statute advanced no compelling interest to support such a classification.

8. See, Sugarman v. Dougall, 413 U.S. 634, 93 S.Ct. 2842, 37 L.Ed.2d 853 (1973) (total exclusion of noncitizens from state civil service position held invalid).

held void under the supremacy clause or preempted by federal law.[9]

Third, alienage classifications created by federal law will be subjected to only the rational basis standard of review. Although the Court has not been clear in identifying the proper standard of review to be employed in these cases, it would appear that the federal government may use a citizenship classification so long as it is arguably related to a federal interest.[10] Although some judicial opinions read as if every federal alienage classification will be upheld, a federal alienage classification should be invalid if it is an arbitrary and invidious classification designed only to burden a disfavored group of persons. Most, if not all, federal alienage classifications would be upheld under any standard of review other than the strictest form of the compelling interest test.

The proper differentiation between federal and state laws in this area is not in terms of the standard of review to be employed, but in the nature of the governmental interest which justifies the classification. The federal government has an important interest in foreign affairs and foreign relations. The federal government should be allowed to classify persons by their citizenship when that classification is arguably related to foreign policy interests. Such interests include the manner in which our citizens might be treated in other countries, bargaining power with other governments, national security, or simply the image which the nation wishes to present to the world. However, if the federal government does not appear to be pursuing such ends, it should not be allowed the freedom to engage

in invidious classification of aliens and such a federal action should be invalidated as a totally arbitrary imposition of burdens on a group of persons whom the federal government has allowed to remain in this country.

(b) Supreme Court Decisions Before 1970

In *Yick Wo v. Hopkins*[11] the Supreme Court held that aliens are "persons" so as to enjoy the protection of the equal protection clause. The case involved a challenge to the licensing system for laundries in San Francisco. It was found that the system had been used to deny licenses to resident Chinese aliens. The application of the law violated the Fourteenth Amendment as the distinction was based on "no reason ... except hostility to the race and nationality to which petitioners belong."[12] But the Court was not clear as to what other "reasons" might support an alienage classification.[13]

In the period from the *Yick Wo* decision until 1948, aliens were not accorded very significant constitutional protection. Aliens could be treated differently than citizens when the alienage status made them dissimilar for some legitimate reason. Had the Supreme Court been willing to strictly review legislation to determine if alienage was in fact being used as an arbitrary classification aliens might have received equal protection of the law. But the Court allowed aliens to be treated in a less favorable manner whenever the alienage classification related to a "special public interest". The special public interest doctrine permitted alienage classifications except where the state had no interest of any significance other than a mere hostility toward aliens.[14] If no public

---

9. See, e.g., Toll v. Moreno, 458 U.S. 1, 102 S.Ct. 2977, 73 L.Ed.2d 563 (1982) (state university regulated denying "in-state" tuition status to nonimmigrant aliens with federal visa for employees of international organizations violated supremacy clause of Article VI by interfering with federal policy); Hines v. Davidowitz, 312 U.S. 52, 61 S.Ct. 399, 85 L.Ed. 581 (1941) (state law regarding registration of aliens is preempted by federal law). State power in this area may be expanded when the state assists in the fulfillment of federal policy. See De Canas v. Bica, 424 U.S. 351, 96 S.Ct. 933, 47 L.Ed.2d 43 (1976).

10. See, Mathews v. Diaz, 426 U.S. 67, 96 S.Ct. 1883, 48 L.Ed.2d 478 (1976). See § 14.12(b), infra.

11. 118 U.S. 356, 6 S.Ct. 1064, 30 L.Ed. 220 (1886).

12. 118 U.S. at 374, 6 S.Ct. at 1073.

13. The reader must remember that insofar as a classification is deemed to be based on the "race" or "national origin" of the persons classified, rather than their citizenship, it will be deemed "suspect" and subject to strict judicial scrutiny under the compelling interest test. See §§ 14.5–14.10, supra.

14. The Court at the time upheld licensing statutes which prohibited issuance to aliens, thereby closing them out of many occupations. E.g., Ohio ex rel. Clarke v. Deckebach, 274 U.S. 392, 47 S.Ct. 630, 71 L.Ed. 1115 (1927).

interest could be shown in the classification, it would be a violation of the equal protection clause.[15] The restriction on aliens fell into three main categories: use of natural resources, ownership of land, and employment.

During this period the Court recognized a "special public interest" in the preservation of natural resources, both animal and mineral. Aliens could be forbidden from taking possession of these resources for their benefit as the state had a significant legitimate interest in reserving use of these resources for its citizens. Thus aliens were prohibited from various activities relating to natural resources including the killing of wild game[16] or the planting and taking of shellfish.[17]

These results were compatible with the Court's general deference to the state interest in natural resources during this period. At this time the Court also allowed the states to reserve the use of natural resources for its own citizens to the detriment of citizens of other states as well as aliens.[18]

Laws prohibiting the ownership of land by aliens were also upheld by the Supreme Court. The state interest in regulating the use of its territory was considered a "special public interest." The Court found that aliens were distinguishable as to land ownership and use for reasons other than hostility to race. The Court took this position in *Terrace v. Thompson*[19] and rejected the argument that such laws were based on hostility to persons of certain races or nationality.

This was a very significant holding since persons from Oriental nations were not then eligible for citizenship under federal statutes; upholding these classifications allowed the western states to prohibit Chinese and Japanese persons from owning and using land in any significant manner. Thus when the Court upheld a California statute prohibiting the use of land by "ineligible" aliens it, in effect, sanctioned a racial classification.[20]

Because there was a special public interest in prohibiting the ownership of lands by ineligible aliens the Court also allowed the states to prohibit the indirect control of lands by aliens. Similarly, laws prohibiting food crop contracts with aliens[21] or the transfer to aliens of shares of a land owning corporation were also upheld.[22] The Court upheld statutes under which land would escheat to the state if the owner attempted to convey it to an alien.[23]

Finally, in 1948, the Supreme Court indicated that statutes restricting land ownership by aliens might be invalid. In *Oyama v. California*[24] the Court struck down a state presumption that land transfers to citizens which were paid for by an ineligible alien were an illegal attempt to transfer property to that alien. Here the state sought to take land which was conveyed to the citizen son of an ineligible alien because the alien father paid the consideration. The Supreme Court held that the presumption and escheat of the property denied the citizen son equal protection of laws

---

15. In Truax v. Raich, 239 U.S. 33, 36 S.Ct. 7, 60 L.Ed. 131 (1915), the Court struck a statute requiring Arizona employers with more than five employees to hire eighty per cent qualified voters or native-born citizens. The provision was invalid because it was directed to private persons and did not pertain in any way to the protection of the public domain. Where statutes requiring that citizens be hired were limited to "public works," they were upheld. Heim v. McCall, 239 U.S. 175, 36 S.Ct. 78, 60 L.Ed. 206 (1915); Crane v. People of New York, 239 U.S. 195, 36 S.Ct. 85, 60 L.Ed. 218 (1915).

16. Patsone v. Pennsylvania, 232 U.S. 138, 34 S.Ct. 281, 58 L.Ed. 539 (1914).

17. McCready v. Virginia, 94 U.S. (4 Otto) 391, 24 L.Ed. 248 (1876).

18. See McCready v. Virginia, 94 U.S. (4 Otto) 391, 24 L.Ed. 248 (1876).

19. 263 U.S. 197, 44 S.Ct. 15, 68 L.Ed. 255 (1923).

20. Porterfield v. Webb, 263 U.S. 225, 44 S.Ct. 21, 68 L.Ed. 278 (1923). The statute in question was similar to that found in *Terrace* except that instead of the total exclusion of aliens, only "ineligible" aliens were unable to own land. The Court in *Terrace* had rejected the argument that because pursuant to the congressional act only free whites and Africans could become citizens, the Act invidiously discriminated against Orientals; any naturalization classification made by Congress was presumed to be reasonable. In *Porterfield*, the Court simply relied upon *Terrace*.

21. Webb v. O'Brien, 263 U.S. 313, 44 S.Ct. 112, 68 L.Ed. 318 (1923).

22. Frick v. Webb, 263 U.S. 326, 44 S.Ct. 115, 68 L.Ed. 323 (1923).

23. See Cockrill v. California, 268 U.S. 258, 45 S.Ct. 490, 69 L.Ed. 944 (1925).

24. 332 U.S. 633, 68 S.Ct. 269, 92 L.Ed. 249 (1948).

but the opinion also cast doubt on the validity of land laws based on alienage.

In 1948, the Court eroded the "special interest" theory in *Takahashi v. Fish & Game Commission*.[25] Takahashi was a resident Japanese alien who was ineligible for citizenship under federal law, which excluded certain national and racial groups from naturalization. He had held a fishing license in California for over 25 years prior to World War II. Following the evacuation of all Japanese from the area, California amended the statute which had previously authorized the issuance of commercial fishing licenses to all qualified persons. The statute prohibited issuance to any "person ineligible for citizenship." Takahashi, on his return, was unable to get a license solely because of his ineligibility for citizenship and, therefore, he was no longer able to make his living by fishing in the ocean.

The Supreme Court of California upheld the statute on the basis of the state's proprietary interest in the fish.[26] The question presented was whether California could constitutionally "use this federally created racial ineligibility for citizenship as a basis for barring Takahashi from earning his living as a commercial fisherman in the ocean waters off the coast of California."[27]

The United States Supreme Court found it could not. The fact that the United States regulated immigration and naturalization on the basis of racial classifications did not mean the state could adopt such classifications to prevent an alien from earning a living in the same manner as citizens. The states do not have the broad power the federal government has to regulate the admission and naturalization of aliens; they may not add or subtract from the conditions imposed by Congress. State laws which impose discriminatory burdens on the entrance or residence of aliens are therefore invalid.

The Court found it unnecessary to resolve whether the motivation for the statute was a desire to conserve fish or to discriminate against the Japanese, simply analyzing the statute in terms of the former. The power of the state to apply its laws exclusively to its alien inhabitants, particularly certain racial groups, is limited by the Fourteenth Amendment. The Court was unable to find that the "special public interest" on which California relied provided support for the state ban on Takahashi's commercial fishing. The Court stated "to whatever extent the fish in the three-mile belt off California may be 'capable of ownership' by California, we think that 'ownership' is inadequate to justify California in excluding any or all aliens who are lawful residents of the state from making a living by fishing in the ocean off its shore while permitting all others to do so."[28]

(c) Supreme Court Decisions After 1970

It was not until recent decades that the Court again ruled on the validity of state classifications based on alienage under the equal protection clause. In *Graham v. Richardson*[29] the Court held that the equal protection clause prevented a state from conditioning welfare benefits either upon the possession of United States citizenship or residence in this country for a specified number of years. The opinion noted that prior decisions had equated classifications based on alienage with those based on race or national origin and declared that such classifications are inherently suspect and subject to close judicial scrutiny. The classification would only be valid if it was necessary to promote a compelling state interest.

The state sought to justify the restrictions on the basis of a "special public interest" in favoring its own citizens over aliens in the distribution of limited resources such as welfare benefits. The Court noted that it had previously upheld statutes upon such grounds, but that the decision in *Takahashi* had cast doubt on the continuing validity of the special public-interest doctrine in all contexts. The

25. 334 U.S. 410, 68 S.Ct. 1138, 92 L.Ed. 1478 (1948).

26. Takahashi v. Fish & Game Commission, 30 Cal.2d 719, 185 P.2d 805 (1947), reversed and remanded 334 U.S. 410, 68 S.Ct. 1138, 92 L.Ed. 1478 (1948).

27. 334 U.S. at 412, 68 S.Ct. at 1139.

28. 334 U.S. at 421, 68 S.Ct. at 1143–44.

29. 403 U.S. 365, 91 S.Ct. 1848, 29 L.Ed.2d 534 (1971).

Court stated further: "whatever may be the contemporary vitality of the special public-interest doctrine in other contexts after *Takahashi*, we conclude that a state's desire to preserve limited welfare benefits for its own citizens is inadequate to justify Pennsylvania's making noncitizens ineligible for public assistance, and Arizona's restricting benefits to citizens and long time resident aliens."[30]

The special public interest doctrine had been heavily grounded in the notion that whatever is a privilege, rather than a right, may be dependent upon citizenship; this distinction between rights and privileges no longer exists. Absent the special public-interest doctrine, there was no compelling reason for the classification. The Court had held in *Shapiro v. Thompson*[31] that fiscal integrity was not a "compelling interest" and the same conclusion was true here. Although, unlike *Shapiro*, no fundamental right was invoked in this case, the use of a suspect classification required application of the compelling interest test. The justification of limiting expenses was especially inappropriate where the class discriminated against was aliens who also pay taxes and may have lived and worked in the state for many years.

The Court in *Graham* also held the statute invalid because it interfered with the exclusive exercise of the federal government's control of aliens. Congress has broad powers to determine who may enter and reside in this country and Congress has not barred any aliens who become indigent after entry into the country. Thus the opinion found that "state laws that restrict the eligibility of aliens for welfare benefits merely because of their alienage conflict with these overriding national policies in an area constitutionally entrusted to Federal Government."[32]

The Court went further in requiring only narrow uses of alienage classifications in *Application of Griffiths*.[33] In this case, the Court invalidated a state court requirement of citizenship for admission to the bar. The majority opinion stated that, because alienage is a suspect classification, the classification must promote a substantial state interest. The opinion equated the term "substantial," "overriding" and "compelling" in describing the type of state end that would justify such a classification.

The state asserted that a person's citizenship affected his or her ability to fulfill the responsibilities of an attorney, but the state could not prove the truth of this assertion. The Court found it did not denigrate lawyers' high responsibilities to observe that their duties hardly involve matters of high state policy or acts of such unique responsibility so as to entrust them only to citizens. The possibility that some resident aliens are unsuited to the practice of law cannot be a justification for a wholesale ban. Since the state could not demonstrate that the classification was a narrow means of promoting a compelling or "substantial" end, the rule was invalid.

While the Court has been quite strict in recent years in prohibiting the use of alienage classifications in the economic area, it has allowed the states much wider latitude to use alienage classifications which are related to the self-governance process. When the government claims that an alienage classification serves political goals, the Court must determine whether the classification is so overinclusive or underinclusive that the claim should not be believed. When the state uses such a classification to exclude noncitizens from holding government employment, the Court should ask whether the positions from which the noncitizens are excluded relate to the self-governance process.

In *Sugarman v. Dougall*,[34] the Supreme Court invalidated a law making citizenship a requirement for any position in the competitive class of a state civil service system. The

---

30. 403 U.S. at 374, 91 S.Ct. at 1853.

31. 394 U.S. 618, 89 S.Ct. 1322, 22 L.Ed.2d 600 (1969). The Court invalidated a state residency requirement which had to be met by persons wishing to receive welfare benefits. The preservation of fiscal integrity was not a

sufficient justification to inhibit the exercise of the right of interstate travel.

32. 403 U.S. at 378, 91 S.Ct. at 1855.

33. 413 U.S. 717, 93 S.Ct. 2851, 37 L.Ed.2d 910 (1973).

34. 413 U.S. 634, 93 S.Ct. 2842, 37 L.Ed.2d 853 (1973).

competitive class included all positions for which it was practicable to determine merit by a competitive exam and reach various positions in nearly the full range of governmental services. The state asserted that its goal was to employ only persons with undivided loyalty, but this prohibition was applicable to many positions whose function had no relationship to the loyalty, or citizenship, of the individual excluded.

Because the Court exercises some form of realistic judicial scrutiny in determining whether an alienage classification is related to legitimate political ends, this classification could not withstand analysis. The state showed no need to require citizenship for all government positions other than simple economic preference for its citizens. The state also could not justify the statute on the grounds that it desired long-time employees; it offered no proof that aliens were a poorer risk in this regard than were citizens of another state within the Union. The sweeping prohibition on the employment of aliens in the public sector appeared so broad as not to be reasonably tailored to promote a legitimate interest in reserving the political process for members of the political community. It appeared only to grant an arbitrary economic preference to residents of the state who were also United States citizens.

The Court noted that its holding was a narrow one: it did *not* hold that "on the basis of individualized determination, an alien may not be refused, or discharged from, public employment, even on the basis of noncitizenship, if the refusal to hire, or the discharge rests on legitimate state interests that relate to qualifications for a particular position or to the characteristics of the employee."[35] Nor did the Court hold that a state may not, in an appropriately defined class of positions, require citizenship as a valid qualification for employment. In later cases, the Court upheld laws which reserved positions in state governmental agencies for citizens.

The Self-Governance or Political Function Exception to Strict Scrutiny. In *Foley v. Connelie*,[36] the Supreme Court upheld, by a six to three vote, a state law which excluded aliens from appointment as members of the state police force. The majority opinion by Chief Justice Burger stated that the earlier cases "generally reflect a close scrutiny" of alienage classifications, at least when they are used by state governments, but that the Supreme Court "never suggested that such legislation is inherently invalid, nor ... held that all limitations on aliens are suspect."[37] Of course, this statement is incorrect to the extent that it would deny that alienage classifications have been held to be "suspect." The statement is correct to the extent that prior cases make it clear that alienage classifications are not to be reviewed as strictly as the suspect classifications of race or national origin.

The majority opinion noted that the Court has recognized that obtaining the status of a citizen is a significant act because many rights relating to self-government may be properly reserved to citizens. In this way Chief Justice Burger is able to harmonize the substance of prior cases even though prior opinions use inconsistent language. Prior cases have recognized that reasonable alienage classification may be employed to pursue substantial state interests, such as that of self-governance, although prior "strict scrutiny" language has clouded these rulings. The majority in *Foley* believed that the great discretion granted police officers made individual officers important components of the system of government. Thus, the majority concluded that these positions could be reserved for those who have a right to participate in the governance process.

In his concurrence, Justice Blackmun, the author of the majority opinions in *Graham v. Richardson* and *Nyquist v. Mauclet*, found that the law could be upheld even though alienage classifications had been deemed to be inherently "suspect" and subject to close scrutiny.[38] Justice Blackmun found that, when a state is

35. 413 U.S. at 646–7, 93 S.Ct. at 2850.

36. 435 U.S. 291, 98 S.Ct. 1067, 55 L.Ed.2d 287 (1978).

37. 435 U.S. at 294, 98 S.Ct. at 1070.

38. 435 U.S. at 300–301, 98 S.Ct. at 1073 (Blackmun, J., concurring).

pursuing goals related to self-governance, the use of citizenship classifications need only be shown to have some rational relationship to the interest in preserving the political community.

Justice Marshall, in a dissent joined by Justices Brennan and Stevens, was of the opinion that a compelling interest test should be used to review alienage classifications, but that the statute had to be invalidated so long as any form of review above the most minimal was employed. Justice Marshall stated that officers below a policy-making level in the police department were involved in the application of public policy rather than the formulation of policies relating to self-governance. Thus, there was no permissible basis upon which to exclude all aliens because these classifications did not promote any interest relating to self-governance.[39]

The dissenting opinion of Justice Stevens, joined by Justice Brennan, found that there was no group characteristic of aliens that would serve as a permissible classifying trait for their total exclusion from employment in the state police department.[40] Justice Stevens stated that in a representative democracy neither the police nor the military has broad policy-making responsibilities, and, therefore, that the qualifying traits would have to be job related. Justice Stevens pointed out that the Court in *Elrod v. Burns*[41] had held that most public employees were protected from patronage discharges because such dismissals would punish them for their political beliefs. Thus, the refusal to allow aliens to hold non-policy-making positions could not be treated as a permissible means of dispensing rewards for voting or participation in the political system.[42]

In recent years, the Supreme Court sought, perhaps unsuccessfully, to add some framework to its alienage decisions of the 1970's. By a five to four vote, in *Ambach v. Norwick*,[43] the Court upheld a state law prohibiting the employment as a teacher, in any publicly operated grade school or high school, of any person who was not a citizen of the United States unless that person had manifested an intention to apply for citizenship or was not yet eligible for citizenship. The majority opinion by Justice Powell admitted that the decisions of the Supreme Court regarding alienage classifications "have not formed an unwavering line over the years." Powell noted the history of the public interest doctrine and its rejection in recent years, and he attempted to avoid any resurrection of that doctrine even though the majority was upholding an alienage classification.

Justice Powell's majority opinion cited with approval the earlier cases of the 1970's finding alienage classifications to be "inherently suspect" and rejecting the general public interest doctrine. However, the majority opinion went on to find that a state alienage classification would be judged by a rational basis test when the classification related to a state function that was "bound up with the operation of the State as a governmental entity."[44] The Court had long recognized that only citizens had a right to participate in the voting and self-governance processes; the majority noted that the Constitution itself reserved the right to direct participation in the governance process to citizens and made citizenship a meaningful distinction. The majority would apply a rational basis standard if the state could assert the promotion of a "governmental function" as the basis for the classification.

39. Foley v. Connelie, 435 U.S. 291, 303 n. 1, 98 S.Ct. 1067, 1074 n. 1, 55 L.Ed.2d 287 (1978) (Marshall, J., dissenting).

40. 435 U.S. at 308, 98 S.Ct. at 1077 (Stevens, J., dissenting).

41. 427 U.S. 347, 96 S.Ct. 2673, 49 L.Ed.2d 547 (1976).

42. Justice Stevens also noted that there should be some similarity between the non-policy making class of jobs that were protected from patronage firing by the *Elrod* decision and that classification of jobs from which aliens could not be excluded. He noted it would be

impermissible to dismiss a citizen state police officer on the basis of his political affiliation because under *Elrod* this would not be considered a high policy making position. Nevertheless, after *Foley*, aliens could be excluded from being employed in the same positions on the rationale that the jobs were high ranking, policy making positions.

43. 441 U.S. 68, 99 S.Ct. 1589, 60 L.Ed.2d 49 (1979).

44. 441 U.S. at 73, 74, 99 S.Ct. at 1593.

Thus, there were two issues to be considered: first, whether public school teachers were a part of a governmental function; second, whether the classification rationally related to that function. The majority found that the role of teachers in publicly funded and operated grade schools and high schools constituted a significant governmental function. Teachers in these schools were employed, in part, to prepare young persons for participation in the governance process as citizens. Public school teachers were also to foster and preserve many societal values, including those relating to self-governance. The majority found that standardization of teaching materials would not fulfill this important role because teachers served as a "role model" of persons involved in the American democratic system.

Having found that teachers were a part of a government function the majority upheld the alienage classification as rationally related to the promotion of a self-governance, or governmental, function. For the majority this distinguished the teacher and police officer cases from the earlier cases finding that aliens could not be excluded from becoming licensed attorneys or engineers. The attorney and engineer positions were not positions of government employment and the exclusions of aliens from those professions, therefore, was not related to a governmental function.[45] The majority noted that the state had not attempted to bar aliens from positions as teachers in public institutions of higher education or from any teaching positions in private schools.[46] It would be most difficult to uphold the bar of aliens as teachers in private schools, if they met educational requirements, because those teachers are not public employees and those schools do not perform the same government function as do publicly operated schools.

Justice Blackmun, author of the early alienage decisions of the 1970's, wrote a dissenting opinion that was joined by Justices Brennan,

Marshall, and Stevens.[47] The dissent examined the classification in a more traditional manner. It employed a realistic standard of review to determine whether the alienage characteristic was a demonstrably reasonable way of determining that the burdened class was not similar to the benefited class. The dissent found nothing in the role of high school teachers that involved them in the creation or execution of significant public policy. There was nothing in the characteristic of being a lawfully resident alien that made one less able to be a grade school or high school teacher of most basic subjects.

Justice Blackmun pointed out that the New York statutory scheme itself failed to promote any significant purposes for three reasons: (1) it contained an exception for persons ineligible to be United States citizens; (2) its exclusion was not related to whether the failure to apply for citizenship related to the individual fitness to teach; (3) the scheme would prefer a less qualified candidate as teacher over a better candidate if the poorer teacher were a United States citizen and the better candidate a resident alien. Indeed, it appeared that the classification was merely one of a general list of positions denied to aliens by the State of New York after World War I.

Although the dissenters may have been correct in finding the restriction unreasonable; a majority of the Justices rejected the dissenter's claim that it was "logically impossible" to differentiate this case from those striking the exclusion of aliens from practice as attorneys or engineers. The majority opinion found that the dissenters "missed the point" by failing to ask first if the public employment position were a part of a governmental (in the sense of self-governance) function.[48] An affirmative answer to that question, for the majority, allows the state to use any classification that will pass a rational basis test.

---

45. 441 U.S. at 76 n. 6, 99 S.Ct. at 1594 n. 6.

46. 441 U.S. at 70 n. 1, 3, 99 S.Ct. at 1591 n. 1, 3.

47. Ambach v. Norwick, 441 U.S. 68, 81, 99 S.Ct. 1589, 1597, 60 L.Ed.2d 49 (1979) (Blackmun, J., dissenting, joined by Brennan, Marshall, and Stevens, JJ.). Justice

Blackmun wrote the majority opinions in *Graham* and *Sugarman.*

48. Ambach v. Norwick, 441 U.S. 68, 76 n. 6, 99 S.Ct. 1589, 1594 n. 6, 60 L.Ed.2d 49 (1979).

It now appears that state governments cannot employ alienage classifications in a burdensome manner in their police power regulations or their granting of social welfare benefits but they will receive greater latitude in excluding aliens from public employment as well as from direct participation in the governance process. While the states will not be allowed to have a blanket exclusion of aliens from public employment, they will be able to exclude aliens from positions that are part of a governmental function.

The Supreme Court appears to require a judicial determination of whether a state or local law requiring United States citizenship for government employment is reasonably related to the government's interest in allocating power in our democratic system of governance. However, the Court also appears to give a significant degree of deference to the decision of legislative bodies. The Court upheld the ability of states to require that a person be a citizen of the United States to be a "peace officer" even though the state defined that term so that it included a wide variety of persons employed in the criminal justice process. Thus in *Cabell v. Chavez–Salido*,[49] the Supreme Court held that the California statutory requirement that peace officers be citizens was not unconstitutional and that it could be applied to exclude lawfully resident aliens from holding positions as deputy state probation officers. After reviewing the decisions noted previously in this section, the majority opinion by Justice White stated, "while not retreating from the position that restrictions on lawfully resident aliens that primarily affect economic interest are subject to heightened judicial scrutiny ... we have concluded that strict scrutiny is out of place when the restriction primarily serves a political function."[50]

The majority found that aliens could be excluded from the governmental process because

this was not the arbitrary imposition of burdens on a disfavored class but "a necessary consequence of the community's process of political self-definition."[51] When the state excluded persons from exercising political power or holding government offices its action was not initially subject to strict judicial scrutiny.

"[A] claim that a particular restriction on legally resident aliens serves political and noneconomic goals is to be evaluated in a two-step process. First, the specificity of the classification will be examined: a classification that is substantially over or underinclusive tends to undercut the governmental claim that the classification serves political ends.... Second, even if the classification is sufficiently tailored, it may be applied in the particular case only to 'persons holding state elective or important nonelective executive, legislative, and judicial positions,' those officers who 'participate directly in the formulation, operation, or review of broad public policy' and hence 'perform functions that go to the heart of representative government.' "[52]

The Court found that the exclusion of citizens from the position of deputy probation officer met these tests. The general law enforcement character of all peace officers, including probation officers, resulted in the Court finding that the exclusion was "sufficiently tailored" to the legitimate political purpose of limiting the exercise of important governmental powers to members of the political community.

Justice Blackmun dissented in *Cabell*. He and three other Justices believed that the exclusion of aliens from the position of deputy probation officer could not withstand any realistic form of judicial review.[53] It was their belief that the exclusion "stemmed solely from state parochialism and hostility towards for-

49.   454 U.S. 432, 102 S.Ct. 735, 70 L.Ed.2d 677 (1982).

50.   454 U.S. at 437–39, 102 S.Ct. at 738–40.

51.   454 U.S. at 439–41, 102 S.Ct. at 739–41.

52.   Cabell v. Chavez–Salido, 454 U.S. 432, 439–41, 102 S.Ct. 735, 739–41, 70 L.Ed.2d 677 (1982) in part quoting

Sugarman v. Dougall, 413 U.S. 634, 93 S.Ct. 2842, 37 L.Ed.2d 853 (1973).

53.   Cabell v. Chavez–Salido, 454 U.S. 432, 447–49, 102 S.Ct. 735, 743–44, 70 L.Ed.2d 677 (1982) (Blackmun, J., dissenting, joined by Brennan, Marshall & Stevens, JJ.).

eigners."[54] Nevertheless, a majority of the Justices refused to subject the classification to rigorous judicial scrutiny once they believed that it was tailored to serve legitimate political ends. A majority of Supreme Court Justices will continue to apply these "strict scrutiny" tests to determine whether state or local laws employing an alienage classification violate the equal protection clause when the classification does not relate to allocating power in the democratic system. Lawfully resident aliens are protected by the equal protection clause but have no representation in the political process. Therefore the Court will uphold classifications which burden these persons only if they are narrowly tailored to promote a compelling state interest.

There is an exception to the general principle that state and local laws employing alienage classifications will be subject to strict scrutiny. "This exception has been labelled the 'political function' exception and applies to laws that exclude aliens from positions intimately related to the process of democratic self-government."[55] The state may exclude noncitizens not only from elected government positions but also from those positions which are related to the democratic process, involve a significant policy-making function, or require the exercise of important discretionary governmental powers over citizens. If the alienage classification relates to self-governance or to positions that go to "the heart of representative government" the classification will be upheld with a deferential standard of review. If the classification does not relate to the self-governance process and, therefore, does not come under the political function exception, it will be subjected to strict scrutiny and invalidated unless it is narrowly tailored to promote a compelling state interest.[56]

Federal Laws. The Supreme Court has employed a lenient standard of review when examining federal laws which employ citizenship classifications. The Court has not clarified the standard of review to be employed when examining federal alienage classifications but it seems apparent that most, if not all, such classifications will be upheld under any but the strictest form of judicial review. Because of the important nature of the federal interest in foreign affairs and foreign relations, as well as the federal power to regulate immigration and naturalization, the Court will defer to the Congress and uphold alienage classifications so long as they are not clearly an arbitrary and invidious imposition of burdens upon a politically powerless group.

In *Mathews v. Diaz*[57] the Court held Congress could condition an alien's eligibility for participation in a federal medical insurance program on continuous residence in the United States for a five-year period. The Court found that Congress had no duty to give all aliens the full benefits of citizens. The opinion noted that illegal or temporary resident aliens could present no substantial claims. The question was whether Congress could impose a durational residency requirement in order to define who was eligible for the benefits. Because some line had to be drawn, the opinion held it reasonable for Congress to make an alien's eligibility for benefits depend on the "character and the duration of his residence." The determination of precisely where to fix the line for eligibility was for Congress, as any cutoff would produce some apparently arbitrary consequences for those falling slightly short of the requirement.

While the *Diaz* case makes it clear that the federal government may use alienage classifi-

---

54. 454 U.S. at 461–63, 102 S.Ct. at 750–51.

55. Bernal v. Fainter, 467 U.S. 216, 220, 104 S.Ct. 2312, 2316, 81 L.Ed.2d 175, 180 (1984), on remand 737 F.2d 495 (5th Cir.1984).

56. In Bernal v. Fainter, 467 U.S. 216, 104 S.Ct. 2312, 81 L.Ed.2d 175 (1984), on remand 737 F.2d 495 (5th Cir.1984), the Supreme Court held that a Texas statute requiring a notary public to be a United States citizen violated the equal protection clause. Justice Marshall wrote a majority opinion for eight members of the Court in which he found that the Court must apply the strict

scrutiny test to this alienage classification and determine whether it is the least restrictive means available to promote a compelling state interest. The majority opinion refused to apply the political function exception. The Justices found that the functions of a notary were essentially clerical and ministerial and, therefore, did not involve the type of responsibilities that go "to the heart of representative government" which would justify a classification based on United States citizenship.

57. 426 U.S. 67, 96 S.Ct. 1883, 48 L.Ed.2d 478 (1976).

cations to a greater degree than classifications based on the other suspect criteria of race or national origin, this decision is not inconsistent with recent alienage cases. Classifications based on race, national origin or alienage are "suspect", for they are highly likely to be used to arbitrarily disadvantage these groups. The history of the Civil War Amendments and post-war racial discrimination justify a judicially imposed prohibition against using race and national origin to disfavor these minorities.

However, aliens bear a relationship to this country which is in fact different from that of citizens. They have yet to establish a permanent commitment to this country and they retain the obligations and benefits of citizenship in another nation. Another nation continues to have a legitimate interest in their treatment by this government.

These factors may distinguish them, for some government programs, for nonarbitrary (nonprejudiced) reasons from citizens. These differences, however, relate only to national citizenship. The states have no interest in regulating aliens and their legitimate local interests do not relate to national citizenship. Thus, the states will rarely be able to show that they need to distinguish between aliens and citizens to promote substantial state interests.[58] States may restrict the employment of those who are not lawful residents of the United States.[59]

Only the federal government may conduct foreign relations activities; therefore, it alone has a need to distinguish between citizens and aliens. Since the treatment of aliens is intertwined with our relations with foreign nations, distinguishing aliens and citizens does not demonstrate prejudice against aliens or an arbitrary treatment of them. Thus the federal government has a "substantial" or "compelling" interest in the conduct of foreign rela-

tions and it may make reasonable use of alienage classifications to promote those ends.[60]

Because the national treatment of aliens is interwoven with foreign policy the Supreme Court will grant Congress some deference in its use of alienage classifications even though they are suspect. Where, as in *Mathews*, the classification appears to relate to national policy and is not based on a prejudice against aliens the Court will uphold the classification. However, even the federal government cannot make free use of alienage classifications which do not relate to foreign policy.

Thus, in *Hampton v. Mow Sun Wong*[61] the Court held unconstitutional a regulation of the United States Civil Service Commission barring resident aliens from employment in the competitive federal civil service. The majority struck down the regulation because it was unclear whether the classification was to promote foreign policy or only employment efficiency. If the purpose were to promote foreign policy, it should be valid, although the majority did not decide this issue. The majority also did not invalidate the regulation as an unconstitutional delegation of authority from Congress, reserving the question of congressional power to authorize the classification. Instead, the majority opinion for the Court only held that the regulation appeared to exceed the actual grant of authority from Congress to the Commission.

The Congress could have given the agency some role in pursuing foreign policy through employment regulation but it did not appear to have done so in the past. Thus, the agency might be exceeding its powers by making such a decision. If Congress in fact had not granted it such a power, the regulation would have to be judged merely in terms of employment efficiency and it would be invalid under *Sugarman*.

After *Hampton*, the Congress could establish the employment restriction on its own and the

---

58. Thus, Puerto Rico could not restrict the practice of engineering by aliens. Examining Bd. of Engineers, Architects & Surveyors v. Flores de Otero, 426 U.S. 572, 96 S.Ct. 2264, 49 L.Ed.2d 65 (1976).

59. DeCanas v. Bica, 424 U.S. 351, 96 S.Ct. 933, 47 L.Ed.2d 43 (1976).

60. For a further discussion of constitutional issues in foreign affairs, see generally, L. Henkin, Foreign Affairs and the Constitution (1972).

61. 426 U.S. 88, 96 S.Ct. 1895, 48 L.Ed.2d 495 (1976), on remand 435 F.Supp. 37 (N.D.Cal.1977).

Supreme Court would assume that it was to promote foreign policy, since the Court would assume that the Congress was basing the law on its full power in the area. If Congress actually delegated the authority to the Commission to make such restrictions based on foreign policy considerations, the Court would review the regulation as an act of Congress. While the Court reserved the question, the regulation would not be stricken if it appeared to be related to national policy other than the arbitrary treatment or exploitation of aliens. But where the Civil Service Commission did not appear to consider foreign policy or even to be empowered to pursue such policy, the statute was invalidated.[62]

The Supreme Court attempted to clarify the constitutional status of resident aliens in *Nyquist v. Mauclet*.[63] In this case the Court invalidated a state law which granted aid for higher education to citizens and resident aliens who were or would be applying for citizenship. By a six to three vote the Court found no compelling state interest in encouraging citizenship or limiting general programs to those who determine its policy.

The most important point of the decision is not the result of the case, which is in complete conformity with earlier rulings, but a statement in the majority opinion, written by Justice Blackmun, that "classifications by a state that are based on alienage are inherently suspect and subject to close judicial scrutiny."[64] In an accompanying footnote to this statement Justice Blackmun stated that the Court used "relaxed scrutiny" in upholding the federal welfare requirements in *Diaz* because "Congress, as an aspect of its broad power over immigration and naturalization, enjoys rights to distinguish among aliens that are not shared by the states."[65]

The decision in *Nyquist v. Mauclet* has the distinction of leaving this area even more unclear than it was before that decision. The use of two totally different tests (strict scrutiny-compelling interest versus great deference-rational basis) for federal and state laws under the equal protection guarantee seems both analytically and historically unsound.[66] Not only is this contrary to the long development of uniform standards of review, it would allow the federal government to engage in the arbitrary and discriminatory treatment of aliens.

It seems unlikely that such a result was intended to be achieved with what appears to be the most casual dictum in a footnote. The footnote does not mention any of the cases stating the principle of congruence of standards of review under the equal protection guarantees. Nor does it note that the Congressional power to create general classifications for nonsensitive employment was not deferred to in *Hampton* as the Court expressly reserved the question in that case. Thus it may be that the dictum here was only intended to establish that there was a clear basis for a realistic review of state law in this case regardless of what the ultimate conclusions might be on the review of federal alienage classifications. To the extent this is true, it leaves untouched our earlier analysis.

As we have seen, the Court employs different standards of review for different types of alienage cases.[67] When a state or local government distributes economic benefits on the basis of United States citizenship, the classification will be deemed "suspect" and subject to heightened judicial scrutiny and some form of the compelling interest test. When the state seeks to allocate political power, including the opportunity to hold important government positions, it will be able to do so whenever a majority of the Justices believe that the law is

---

62. After this decision President Ford, by executive order, barred most resident aliens from employment in the competitive federal civil service. See Executive Order 11935, 41 Fed.Reg. 37301 (Sept. 2, 1976). On remand the trial court upheld the validity of the executive order. Mow Sun Wong v. Hampton, 435 F.Supp. 37, 42–46 (N.D.Cal.1977).

63. 432 U.S. 1, 97 S.Ct. 2120, 53 L.Ed.2d 63 (1977).

64. 432 U.S. at 7 n. 8, 97 S.Ct. at 2124 n. 8.

65. 432 U.S. at 7 n. 8, 97 S.Ct. at 2124 n. 8.

66. The development of congruence of standards is examined in Karst, The Fifth Amendment's Guarantee of Equal Protection, 55 N.C.L.Rev. 541 (1977).

67. Sam, J., quoting Treatise in, United States v. Phetchanphone, 863 F.Supp. 1543, 1547 (D.Utah 1994).

reasonably tailored to further a legitimate political end.   When the federal government employs an alienage classification, the Court will invoke only the rational basis test and defer to Congressional judgment over the dispensation of either economic benefits or political rights on the basis of citizenship.   The cases could be made consistent by recognition of an intermediate standard of review for alienage cases but the split among the Justices concerning the proper judicial role in reviewing alienage classifications may mean that this area will remain one of great theoretical confusion.

§ 14.13 Classifications Burdening Illegal Aliens, or Undocumented Persons

Congress has virtually plenary power to define the class of persons (other than citizens of the United States) who may lawfully reside in this country.   A person who is born in the United States, and subject to the jurisdiction thereof, is a U.S. citizen at birth, due to the first sentence of the Fourteenth Amendment. Congress has no constitutional authority to take away the citizenship of any anyone who is a citizen under the terms of the Fourteenth Amendment.[1] A person may be a U.S. citizen, because she was born in the U.S., although she lacks documents that would prove the place of her birth and, therefore, her citizenship. Such a person is not an illegally or unlawfully resident alien. Rather, she is a citizen of the United States. For the sake of legal accuracy, and not for so-called "political correctness" reasons, such a person should be referred to as an "undocumented person," rather than as an illegal or unlawful alien.

The Court has long held that all persons within the country are protected by the due process guarantee; any person within the jurisdiction of the United States is entitled to a fair process to determine whether he may be deported from, or prohibited from returning to, the United States for violation of a federal statute or regulation.[2]   The Court has not yet imposed any substantive restrictions on the ability of Congress to define the class of persons who may lawfully reside in the country or the ability of Congress to disfavor unlawfully resident persons in the distribution of federal benefits.

In 1982, the Justices, by a five to four vote, for the first time extended the scope of the equal protection clause of the Fourteenth Amendment to give *unlawfully* resident aliens limited protection from state or local laws which arbitrarily denied them benefits or imposed burdens upon them.[3]   In so doing, the Court employed a middle level standard of review by which it required the state to demonstrate that a classification burdening the children of illegal aliens in fact furthered a substantial goal of the state.   The Court indicated that states might be given greater leeway in burdening unlawfully resident aliens when they were acting pursuant to authority given them by the federal government or promoting an articulable federal policy.   Indeed, the Court did not prohibit states from taking other actions which give preferential treatment to citizens and lawfully resident aliens in the dispensation of governmental benefits.

Because of the limited nature of the Court's ruling it is difficult to predict at this time the nature of the equal protection guarantee which will limit the ability of state and local governments to differentiate between lawfully resident aliens, unlawfully resident aliens, and undocumented persons.

In *Plyler v. Doe,*[4] the Court held that a Texas statute which withheld from local school districts any state funds for the education of children who were not "legally admitted" into the United States, and which authorized local school districts to deny enrollment in their

---

§ 14.13

1.   See § 14.11, supra. For citations to additional cases, including lower court cases, and secondary works on this topic, see our multi-volume Treatise: R. Rotunda & J. Nowak, Treatise on Constitutional Law: Substance and Procedure Chapter 22 (3rd ed. 1999, with annual supplements).

2.   See § 14.11, supra.

3.   Plyler v. Doe, 457 U.S. 202, 102 S.Ct. 2382, 72 L.Ed.2d 786 (1982).

4.   457 U.S. 202, 102 S.Ct. 2382, 72 L.Ed.2d 786 (1982).

schools to children who were not "legally admitted" to the United States, violated the equal protection clause of the Fourteenth Amendment. The State of Texas had argued that the equal protection clause was not applicable to this law and that it only protected those persons lawfully within the state.

The majority opinion by Justice Brennan totally rejected that argument. There was nothing in the history of the Fourteenth Amendment or its language which indicated that the scope of the equal protection clause was meant to be narrower than that of due process. The Fourteenth Amendment reads in relevant part: "No state shall ... deny to any person within its jurisdiction the equal protection of the laws." Justice Brennan found no reason not to apply the equal protection clause literally; the majority ruled that laws which gave unequal treatment to unlawfully resident aliens were subject to some form of judicial review under the terms of the equal protection clause.

The majority opinion by Justice Brennan focused on the precise problem before the Court and did not make a sweeping ruling on the nature of rights that must be granted to illegal aliens. Brennan noted that the state had made powerful arguments that it should be allowed to withhold its benefits from those persons whose very presence in the state was the result of their own unlawful conduct. However, in this case, the state was denying its benefits to the children who had been brought into the country illegally. "Even if the state found it expedient to control the conduct of adults by acting against their children, legislation directing the onus of a parent's misconduct against his children does not comport with fundamental conceptions of justice."[5]

The Court refused to recognize illegal aliens as a suspect class, which would have required that laws burdening this class of persons be subject to strict judicial scrutiny.[6] The majority opinion also refused to find that all laws burdening illegal aliens should be subject to a meaningful form of judicial review, such as were laws that employed gender or illegitimacy classifications, because the status of being an undocumented alien was not "an absolutely immutable characteristic since it is the product of conscious, indeed unlawful, action."[7] The fact that the Texas law at issue was directed against the children of those persons who entered the country illegally required, in the majority's view, some realistic examination of whether it was arbitrary to penalize these children for the actions of their parents.

In examining the permissibility of excluding the illegally resident children from public education, the Court noted that education is not a right specifically granted by the Constitution, nor a right which in the past has been found by the Supreme Court to be a fundamental constitutional right.[8] Thus, there was no basis for subjecting the law to strict scrutiny and requiring a compelling state interest to justify the exclusion of these children. However, the importance of education to a person's ability to function in society, and the fact that denial of all educational benefits to these children would result in their being deprived of any opportunity to advance their personal or economic interests on the basis of individual merit, led the majority to the conclusion that the Court should not simply defer to the state decision to deny an education to these children.

The federal government might exclude or deport these children,[9] but the state was not

---

5.   457 U.S. at 218–20, 102 S.Ct. at 2395–96.

6.   457 U.S. at 219 n. 19, 102 S.Ct. at 2396 n. 19.

7.   457 U.S. at 218–22, 102 S.Ct. at 2395–98.

8.   457 U.S. at 220–22, 102 S.Ct. at 2396–98.

9.   **The detention of children who are allegedly in the country unlawfully.** In Reno v. Flores, 507 U.S. 292, 113 S.Ct. 1439, 123 L.Ed.2d 1 (1993), on remand 992 F.2d 243 (9th Cir.1993) the Court upheld Immigration and Naturalization Service [INS] regulations that required the federal government to retain custody of alien children who

were being held pending deportation proceedings in almost all instances when there were no relatives or guardians in the United States to whom the children could be released. The majority opinion, written by Justice Scalia, found that the INS regulations did not violate the substantive or procedural guarantees of the due process clause of the Fifth Amendment or the implied equal protection guarantee of the due process clause of the Fifth Amendment. The children held in custody argued that the government regulations must be narrowly tailored to serve the best interest of a child and that the government must release a

entitled to a strong presumption of constitutionality for a law which would impose "a lifetime hardship on a discrete class of children not accountable for their disabling status."[10] For this reason, the Court found that laws which disfavored the children of undocumented aliens should be subjected to some form of realistic judicial review and "the discrimination contained in § 21.031 [the statute at issue] can hardly be considered rational unless it furthers some substantial goal of the state."[11]

In examining the state law under this realistic but less than strict form of judicial scrutiny, Justice Brennan's majority opinion initially noted that the state action was not taken pursuant to a federal mandate. The state's authority might be expanded when it was pursuing a clearly articulated federal policy and assisting Congress with the pursuit of important federal interests.[12] However, the majority found no indication that Congress had intended to allow aliens to remain within the country illegally and have the children of these aliens be subjected to arbitrary burdens.

The majority then noted that the state might in some circumstances have an interest in employing a classification which disfavored illegal aliens when that classification would limit serious economic effects of sudden shifts in population. But the state could not demonstrate that its denial of services to the children of illegal aliens was a reasonable disincentive to illegal entry into the state as the dominant incentive for illegal immigration appeared to be the availability of employment rather than free education. Nor could the state demon-

strate that the exclusion of the children of illegal aliens would improve the quality of public education because the legality of the residency of a child was not related to the cost which that child imposed upon the state by going to school. A child who is not fluent in English imposed the same burden on a public school system regardless of whether he was lawfully or unlawfully resident within the state. Indeed, the state could not demonstrate that the children of unlawfully resident aliens were less likely than other children to remain within the boundaries of the state because the state did not structure its education system based on the assurance that any child, whether or not he or she was a citizen, would employ his education for the good of the state by remaining within the state.

Chief Justice Burger in a dissent joined by Justices White, Rehnquist, and O'Connor, found no reason to engage in realistic judicial review of laws which burdened illegal aliens generally or their children in particular. "Once it is conceded—as the court does—that illegal aliens are not a suspect class, and that education is not a fundamental right, our inquiry should focus on and be limited to whether the legislative classification at issue bears a rational relationship to a legitimate purpose."[13]

After noting that the burden on the children was not insubstantial, Chief Justice Burger indicated that denying them education "is not a choice I would make were I a legislator."[14] Nevertheless, the Chief Justice found no reason to give any protection from the arbitrary

---

child into the custody of nonrelatives when the best interest of the child would be served by such a release. The majority opinion found that children did not have a fundamental right to be placed in a noncustodial setting or a right to have the government make decisions in "the best interest of the child." Because there was no fundamental right involved in this case, Justice Scalia's majority opinion found that there only had to be a "reasonable fit" between the regulation and legitimate government interest. The majority opinion stated that regulation had to meet "the (unexacting) standard of rationally advancing some legitimate government purpose." 507 U.S. at 305, 113 S.Ct. at 1449. The regulations were upheld because they were rationally related to the government purposes in securing the appearance of the children in the deportation proceedings while providing them with adequate care.

10. Plyler v. Doe, 457 U.S. 202, 223, 102 S.Ct. 2382, 2398, 72 L.Ed.2d 786 (1982).

11. Id., 457 U.S. at 222–24, 102 S.Ct. at 2397–99.

12. 457 U.S. at 225, 102 S.Ct. at 2399. The opinion made reference to De Canas v. Bica, 424 U.S. 351, 96 S.Ct. 933, 47 L.Ed.2d 43 (1976) wherein the Court had upheld state legislation requiring employers to hire lawfully resident persons in part because it reflected a similar federal policy.

13. Plyler v. Doe, 457 U.S. 202, 247–49, 102 S.Ct. 2382, 2410–12, 72 L.Ed.2d 786 (1982), (Burger, C.J., dissenting, joined by White, Rehnquist & O'Connor, JJ.).

14. 457 U.S. at 250–52, 102 S.Ct. at 2212–14 (Burger, C.J., dissenting).

denial of benefits and imposition of burdens on these children. In the view of the dissent it was not unconstitutional to deny any opportunity for an education to these children because it was not irrational for a state to conclude that it did not have the responsibility to provide benefits for persons whose presence in the country was illegal.

The closeness of the vote in *Plyler* and the narrowness of the ruling, striking down only a law which denied an education to the children of illegal aliens, make it difficult to predict the nature of the equal protection guarantee that will be defined in future cases involving the rights of illegal aliens.[15]

§ 14.14 Illegitimacy Classifications: Introduction

An illegitimate child is one whose parents were not lawfully married to each other at the time of his birth.[1] Some statutes have accorded more favorable treatment to legitimate children than to illegitimate children, particularly

when dispensing benefits following the death or disability of one of the children's parents. Although legitimacy classifications have not been held to be among those classifications that are deemed "suspect", they do receive a meaningful review under the equal protection guarantee. The compelling interest test has not been applied to these classifications, but the Justices will independently review the basis of these classifications to determine if they reasonably advance a legitimate government purpose. The Court has stated that "imposing disabilities on the illegitimate child is contrary to the basic concept of our system that legal burdens should bear some relationship to individual responsibility or wrongdoing."[2]

The governmental use of a classification that is based on the status of a person having been "legitimate" or "illegitimate" at birth will be upheld only if the classification is substantially related to an important government interest. This standard of intermediate scrutiny, which falls between the rational relationship test and

---

15. Three of the Justices who joined the Brennan majority opinion found it necessary to add concurring opinions. Justice Marshall noted that he remained committed to the view that laws denying educational benefits to a class of persons should be subjected to some realistic form of judicial review even though such laws might not be subjected to the traditional strict scrutiny or compelling interest test. Plyler v. Doe, 457 U.S. 202, 230–32, 102 S.Ct. 2382, 2402–03, 72 L.Ed.2d 786 (1982), (Marshall, J., concurring).

Justices Blackmun and Powell had voted in San Antonio Independent School District v. Rodriguez, 411 U.S. 1, 93 S.Ct. 1278, 36 L.Ed.2d 16 (1973), to employ only the traditional rational basis test in cases in which a state classified persons for the dispensation of educational benefits along lines that were not suspect. Justices Blackmun and Powell concurred in *Plyler* because they thought that realistic review of the Texas law was necessitated by the fact that it did not merely allocate different amounts of educational benefits to different classes of persons but in fact excluded a class of children from any opportunity to receive public education. The decision of the state to subject a class of children to a type of permanent disadvantage in society through the denial of any opportunity for state funded education had to be subject to meaningful judicial review. Plyler v. Doe, 457 U.S. 202, 230–32, 102 S.Ct. 2382, 2402–03, 72 L.Ed.2d 786 (1982), (Blackmun, J., concurring); 457 U.S. at 235–37, 103 S.Ct. at 2404–05 (Powell, J., concurring).

The Supreme Court, by an eight to one vote, upheld a state statute which permitted a school district to deny tuition free education to a child who lived apart from his parent or lawful guardian if the child's presence in the school district was "for the primary purpose" of attending

school in the district. Martinez v. Bynum, 461 U.S. 321, 103 S.Ct. 1838, 75 L.Ed.2d 879 (1983). "A bona fide residence requirement, appropriately defined and uniformly applied, furthers the substantial state interest in assuring that services provided for its residents are enjoyed only by residents." 461 U.S. at 328, 103 S.Ct. at 1842. The majority opinion found that this residence requirement did not violate the equal protection clause because it was not based on a suspect classification and it did not limit the exercise of a fundamental right. The Court noted that public education was not such a right. 461 U.S. at 328, n. 7, 103 S.Ct. at 1842–43, n. 7. *Martinez* held that the statute at issue was a bona fide residence requirement because it provided free education for all children who resided in the school district with the intent to remain in the district indefinitely. The Court did not pass upon the residency claim of the child in this case, a United States citizen whose parents were non-resident aliens living in Mexico. See 461 U.S. at 333, 103 S.Ct. at 1845 (Brennan, J., concurring). Only Justice Marshall would have invalidated the residency requirement on its face. 461 U.S. at 334, 103 S.Ct. at 1845–54 (Marshall, J., dissenting).

§ 14.14

1. For an examination of the status of illegitimacy and related legal issues, see, H. Krause, Illegitimacy: Law and Social Policy (1971); H. Krause, Family Law in a Nutshell, Chapter 11 (2 ed. 1986). For additional citations to secondary sources on this topic, see R. Rotunda & J. Nowak, Treatise on Constitutional Law: Substance and Procedure, vol. 3, §§ 18.14–18.19 (3rd ed. 1999, with annual supplements).

2. Weber v. Aetna Casualty & Surety Co., 406 U.S. 164, 175, 92 S.Ct. 1400, 1407, 31 L.Ed.2d 768 (1972).

the strict scrutiny test in terms of the strictness of the judicial review of classification, was not formally adopted for illegitimacy classifications until 1988.[3] Nevertheless, the Supreme Court's pre–1988 decisions are consistent with this form of intermediate standard of review.

Classifications that distinguish illegitimate from legitimate children may be upheld if the Court finds that they advance permissible government purposes and are not burdens placed on the illegitimate child because of his status. Neither state nor federal laws may use these classifications to punish the parent's behavior for giving birth to an illegitimate child. Nor can illegitimate children be burdened on the theory that unfavorable treatment of them will encourage legitimate family relationships.[4] Legitimacy classifications created for impermissible reasons constitute the arbitrary burdening of the child or his parents rather than mere regulation of activities that the state has a right to proscribe.

The state may not disadvantage illegitimate children in the dispensation of government benefits, or of property rights from their parents, merely because the problem of proving parentage may be difficult.[5] Statutes must include procedures to resolve questions of parentage; difficulties of proof may not be used as a barrier to the rights of illegitimate children. But the government need not give all children an equal presumption of a support or dependency relationship to their parents if that classification is not based on the status of illegitimacy.

Governmental benefit systems designed to give support to those children dependent upon a parent who is deceased or disabled may presume dependency for legitimate children and certain classes of illegitimates who have a relationship to the parent that indicates a support obligation from the parent to the child. This classification will be valid even though it excludes from the presumption some classes of illegitimate children. However, to survive scrutiny under the reasonable basis test, the classification must be narrowly drawn to identify those with a likelihood of dependency upon the parent, and it must grant a presumption of dependency to illegitimate children whose personal circumstances indicate that they have been acknowledged or supported by the parent. Furthermore, these laws should also permit other illegitimate children to prove their actual entitlement to benefits because of their continuing relationship to the parent, even though they do not have a presumption of dependency.[6]

The Supreme Court now requires, in cases involving an illegitimacy classification, that the government demonstrate that the classification is substantially related to an important state interest.[7]

Because the decisions on illegitimacy have been made under a "middle level" scrutiny test for validity of classifications, they have a certain *ad hoc* quality. The Court's rulings on the permissibility of a classification depends in part on the Justices' view of the purpose of the classification and whether it is used to invidiously burden illegitimate children. The ad hoc nature of the Court's rulings was demonstrated in three cases, decided in the 1978–79 term, which involved combined illegitimacy

---

3. This standard of review was formally adopted by Justice O'Connor when she wrote for a unanimous Court in Clark v. Jeter, 486 U.S. 456, 461, 108 S.Ct. 1910, 1914, 100 L.Ed.2d 465 (1988). In *Clark* the Court invalidated a six-year statute of limitations for paternity actions by illegitimate children; in earlier cases the Court had consistently invalidated statutes of limitations on child support actions that treated illegitimate children less favorably than legitimate children. See § 14.19, infra. See generally, Dennis, J., citing Treatise in, Pace v. State Through Louisiana State Employees Retirement System, 648 So.2d 1302, 1306, 18 Employee Benefits Cas. 2833 (La.1995); Levin, J., (dissenting), citing Treatise, in Frame v. Nehls, 452 Mich. 171, 207, 550 N.W.2d 739, 755 (1996). Whit-

beck, J., dissenting and citing Treatise in, Crego v. Coleman, 591 N.W.2d 277, 287 n. 12 (Mich.App.Ct.1999).

4. Trimble v. Gordon, 430 U.S. 762, 97 S.Ct. 1459, 52 L.Ed.2d 31 (1977). See also Mills v. Habluetzel, 456 U.S. 91, 99–101 n. 8, 102 S.Ct. 1549, 1554–55 n. 8, 71 L.Ed.2d 770 (1982). But cf. Parham v. Hughes, 441 U.S. 347, 353, 99 S.Ct. 1742, 1746, 60 L.Ed.2d 269 (1979).

5. Gomez v. Perez, 409 U.S. 535, 93 S.Ct. 872, 35 L.Ed.2d 56 (1973).

6. Mathews v. Lucas, 427 U.S. 495, 96 S.Ct. 2755, 49 L.Ed.2d 651 (1976).

7. Clark v. Jeter, 486 U.S. 456, 108 S.Ct. 1910, 100 L.Ed.2d 465 (1988). See § 14.19, infra.

and gender classifications.[8] All of the cases were divided by five to four votes and there was a majority opinion in only one case.[9]

It is helpful to note the range of results in the illegitimacy decisions before going on to examine them individually. Statutes granting causes of action for wrongful death cannot deny a right of recovery to either illegitimate children or to their mothers.[10] The Court has held that such actions should be unrelated to the fact of illegitimacy and should depend upon the continuing relationship between the child and the mother. However, fathers of illegitimates may be prohibited from suing for the wrongful death of an illegitimate child unless the father has legitimated or formally acknowledged the child during the child's lifetime.[11]

Neither the Social Security System[12] nor state worker's compensation provisions may deny benefits to all illegitimate children.[13] Such laws must be based upon the relationship between the child and the parent and cannot arbitrarily exclude all illegitimates because of the status of their birth. If a state grants legitimate children a right of support from either their mothers or their fathers, it must grant similar support rights to illegitimates who can prove their parentage.[14] The fact that it will be difficult for the state to create

systems for proving parentage will not excuse it from its obligation of treating illegitimates in a fair manner.[15]

For a time the Court held that illegitimate children could be treated less favorably than legitimate children in the property distribution from the estate of a male parent who died without a will.[16] The Court then adopted the position that illegitimate children cannot be arbitrarily excluded from inheriting from either their mother or their father, even though allowing inheritance rights to illegitimates will raise problems of proof of parentage.[17] However, the Court upheld a state law that excluded illegitimates from inheriting from their fathers unless they had been found, in a judicial proceeding, to be the children of the decedent father during his lifetime.[18]

State and local laws that classify persons are subject to analysis under the equal protection clause of the Fourteenth Amendment; federal classifications are examined in terms of the implied equal protection guarantee of the Fifth Amendment due process clause. The Supreme Court appears to have employed the intermediate standard of review when examining classifications based on gender or legitimacy and both state and federal laws with one possible

8. Lalli v. Lalli, 439 U.S. 259, 99 S.Ct. 518, 58 L.Ed.2d 503 (1978); Parham v. Hughes, 441 U.S. 347, 99 S.Ct. 1742, 60 L.Ed.2d 269 (1979); Caban v. Mohammed, 441 U.S. 380, 99 S.Ct. 1760, 60 L.Ed.2d 297 (1979), on remand 47 N.Y.2d 880, 419 N.Y.S.2d 74, 392 N.E.2d 1257 (1979). Although the opinions in these cases discussed the constitutionality of gender classifications more than illegitimacy classifications, we shall examine these cases together in this section because the decisions also illuminate the Court's position on the constitutional worth of asserted state interests in illegitimate children, the status of those children, and the permissible distinctions between maternal and paternal relationships to illegitimate children.

9. Caban v. Mohammed, 441 U.S. 380, 99 S.Ct. 1760, 60 L.Ed.2d 297 (1979). See also Orr v. Orr, 440 U.S. 268, 99 S.Ct. 1102, 59 L.Ed.2d 306 (1979), on remand 374 So.2d 895 (Ala.Civ.App.1979), invalidating a state law allowing only for alimony payments from husbands to wives upon the dissolution of marriages. For a further examination of this case, see §§ 14.20–14.24, infra.

10. Levy v. Louisiana, 391 U.S. 68, 88 S.Ct. 1509, 20 L.Ed.2d 436 (1968); Glona v. American Guarantee & Liability Insurance Co., 391 U.S. 73, 88 S.Ct. 1515, 20 L.Ed.2d 441 (1968).

11. Parham v. Hughes, 441 U.S. 347, 99 S.Ct. 1742, 60 L.Ed.2d 269 (1979).

12. Jimenez v. Weinberger, 417 U.S. 628, 94 S.Ct. 2496, 41 L.Ed.2d 363 (1974).

13. Weber v. Aetna Casualty & Surety Co., 406 U.S. 164, 92 S.Ct. 1400, 31 L.Ed.2d 768 (1972).

14. Gomez v. Perez, 409 U.S. 535, 93 S.Ct. 872, 35 L.Ed.2d 56 (1973). See also Mills v. Habluetzel, 456 U.S. 91, 102 S.Ct. 1549, 71 L.Ed.2d 770 (1982).

15. Trimble v. Gordon, 430 U.S. 762, 97 S.Ct. 1459, 52 L.Ed.2d 31 (1977).

16. Labine v. Vincent, 401 U.S. 532, 91 S.Ct. 1017, 28 L.Ed.2d 288 (1971).

17. Trimble v. Gordon, 430 U.S. 762, 97 S.Ct. 1459, 52 L.Ed.2d 31 (1977).

The Supreme Court applied the decision in *Trimble* to an estate of a father who died several months before the date of the *Trimble* decision. Reed v. Campbell, 476 U.S. 852, 106 S.Ct. 2234, 90 L.Ed.2d 858 (1986), rehearing denied 478 U.S. 1031, 107 S.Ct. 11, 92 L.Ed.2d 766 (1986); see § 14.16.

18. Lalli v. Lalli, 439 U.S. 259, 99 S.Ct. 518, 58 L.Ed.2d 503 (1978).

exception: federal immigration and naturalization laws.

The Supreme Court has upheld the federal immigration laws that placed special restrictions on the ability of a United States citizen father, as opposed to a United States citizen mother, to receive an immigration preference for an illegitimate child who was born in another country.[19] The Court has also upheld federal naturalization laws that require the United States citizen father of a child born out of wedlock to take certain steps prior to the child's receiving citizenship, while the same statutes granted immediate citizenship to a child born out of wedlock to a United States citizen mother who was outside the country.[20] The Court found the gender and illegitimacy classifications established by these immigration laws were related to establishing that the male United States citizen was in fact the parent of the child. The dissenting Justices in these cases pointed out that the generalized classifications were difficult to describe as being substantially related to an important government interest.[21]

As a formal matter, we must accept the Court's ruling that these classifications were substantially related to an important interest. Nevertheless, one should not assume that the Court would be so lenient when examining gender or illegitimacy classifications in areas unrelated to immigration and naturalization.[22]

The Court has looked with disfavor upon laws based on an arbitrary view of the worthiness of the parents of illegitimate children or family units containing illegitimate children to receive governmental benefits or equal treatment of laws relating to family matters. Households cannot be disqualified from receiving benefits because they contain illegitimate children.[23] However, the Court held that a Social Security Act provision which restricted surviving parent benefits to persons who have been lawfully married to a deceased wage earner prior to the wage earner's death did not discriminate against illegitimates.[24] States may not presume that the father of an illegitimate child is unfit to take custody of the child but must allow fathers some opportunity to retain custody following the death of the child's mother.[25] Similarly, the Court overturned a statute that required the consent of the mother but not the father of illegitimate children prior to their adoption, at least insofar as the statute excluded the known or ascertainable fathers of older children.[26]

§ 14.15 Illegitimacy Classifications: Wrongful Death Actions

In a series of decisions since 1968 the Court has employed a standard of review that must

19. Fiallo v. Bell, 430 U.S. 787, 97 S.Ct. 1473, 52 L.Ed.2d 50 (1977).

20. Tuan Anh Nguyen v. Immigration and Naturalization Service, 533 U.S. 53, 121 S.Ct. 2053, 150 L.Ed.2d 115 (2001). The Court had earlier issued a ruling, without a majority opinion, that had the effect of upholding the illegitimacy and gender classifications in the statutes that were explicitly approved in *Tuan Anh Nguyen*. Miller v. Albright, 523 U.S. 420, 118 S.Ct. 1428, 140 L.Ed.2d 575(1998). For further analysis of these cases, see §§ 14.18, 14.23 of this chapter.

21. Tuan Anh Nguyen v. Immigration and Naturalization Service, 533 U.S. 53, 73, 121 S.Ct. 2053, 2066, 150 L.Ed.2d 115 (2001) (O'Connor, J., joined by Souter, Ginsburg, and Breyer, JJ., dissenting). Some Justices on the Court, whose votes were necessary to form majorities in these cases, did not believe that the Court had power to second guess congressional determinations regarding naturalization laws. 533 U.S. at 73, 121 S.Ct. at 2066 (Scalia, J., joined by Thomas, J., concurring); Miller v. Albright, 523 U.S. 420, 452, 118 S.Ct. 1428, 1446, 140 L.Ed.2d 575 (1998) (Scalia, J., joined by Thomas, J., concurring in the judgment).

22. For an analysis of constitutional issues related to naturalization and citizenship, see the multi-volume edition of this Treatise: R. Rotunda & J. Nowak, Treatise on Constitutional Law: Substance and Procedure, Vol. 5, Ch. 22 (3rd ed. 1999, with annual supplements).

23. New Jersey Welfare Rights Organization v. Cahill, 411 U.S. 619, 93 S.Ct. 1700, 36 L.Ed.2d 543 (1973).

24. Califano v. Boles, 443 U.S. 282, 99 S.Ct. 2767, 61 L.Ed.2d 541 (1979).

See also, Bowen v. Owens, 476 U.S. 340, 106 S.Ct. 1881, 90 L.Ed.2d 316 (1986) (Court upholds now superseded provision of Social Security Act that granted survivors benefits to wage earner's widowed spouse who remarried after age sixty but denied benefits to an otherwise similarly situated divorced widowed spouse who remarried after age sixty; the provision was reviewed only under the rational relationship standard).

25. Stanley v. Illinois, 405 U.S. 645, 92 S.Ct. 1208, 31 L.Ed.2d 551 (1972).

26. Caban v. Mohammed, 441 U.S. 380, 99 S.Ct. 1760, 60 L.Ed.2d 297 (1979).

be implied from its rulings. In that year the Court, in *Levy v. Louisiana*,[1] overturned a state statute denying recovery to an illegitimate child for the wrongful death of his mother. The majority opinion first noted that illegitimate children were persons entitled to the full protection of the equal protection guarantee. The general rule that states could not invidiously discriminate against a particular class of people was of special importance because the classifications involved intimate family relationships and basic civil rights. The Court indicated that it would be sensitive to misuse of these classifications because they touched upon such relationships and were burdens based on religious or philosophical views of the worth of illegitimates or their parents.

In this case, the Louisiana wrongful death statute denied to a child the right to sue for the death of his parent merely because he had been born out of wedlock. The right to sue was not based upon past support by the parent or continuing relationships with the parent but solely upon the fact of legitimacy. The United States Supreme Court held that the legitimacy of one's birth had no relationship, rational or otherwise, to the wrong inflicted upon the mother, which is the basis for wrongful death suits. The opinion stated that "it is invidious to discriminate against [illegitimate children] when no action, conduct, or demeanor of theirs is possibly relevant to the harm that was done the mother."[2]

A companion case, *Glona v. American Guarantee & Liability Insurance Co.*,[3] refused to allow the state of Louisiana to deny an illegitimate child's mother the right to bring suit for the child's death. Employing an analysis similar to *Levy*, the Court held that the state had no rational basis to believe that denying recovery to mothers of illegitimates would tend to reduce illegitimate births. The disability had no causal relationship to the earlier actions or to any continuing wrongdoing by the mother. The opinion acknowledged that false claims of motherhood might arise following the death of children but held that these problems would not excuse the state's invidious classification.

Justices Harlan, Black, and Stewart dissented in *Levy* and *Glona*.[4] The dissent noted that wrongful death was a statutory rather than common law cause of action and argued that the legislatures could draw almost any line for the allocation of this benefit.

In *Parham v. Hughes*,[5] the Supreme Court upheld a Georgia statute which allowed the father of an illegitimate child to sue for the wrongful death of that child only if the mother of the child was deceased and the father had legitimated the child before the child's death. While the Justices examined this law in terms of sex discrimination rather than as an illegitimacy classification, none of the five Justices in the majority talked about the generalized gender discrimination in the Georgia statutes which prohibited any father from suing for the wrongful death of the child if the mother was alive. For a majority of the Justices, the case focused solely on the requirement that the father legitimate the child before its death to be entitled to sue.

Justice Stewart wrote a plurality opinion for four members of the Court.[6] He treated the law, in part, as one which did not classify either by an illegitimacy or gender trait and, in part, as one that survived whatever the appropriate test might be for such classifications. The plurality opinion noted that state laws are generally entitled to a strong pre-

---

§ 14.15

1. 391 U.S. 68, 88 S.Ct. 1509, 20 L.Ed.2d 436 (1968).

2. 391 U.S. at 72, 88 S.Ct. at 1511.

3. 391 U.S. 73, 88 S.Ct. 1515, 20 L.Ed.2d 441 (1968).

4. Glona v. American Guarantee & Liability Insurance Co., 391 U.S. 73, 76, 88 S.Ct. 1515, 1517, 20 L.Ed.2d 441 (1968). (dissent applying to both *Levy* and *Glona*).

5. 441 U.S. 347, 99 S.Ct. 1742, 60 L.Ed.2d 269 (1979).

6. The Stewart opinion was joined by the Chief Justice and Justices Rehnquist and Stevens.

It is interesting to note that Justices Blackmun and Stevens switched sides between *Parham* and Lalli v. Lalli, 439 U.S. 259, 99 S.Ct. 518, 58 L.Ed.2d 503 (1978) which is examined in § 14.16 infra. Apparently, Justice Stevens found the *Lalli* distinction arbitrary and the *Parham* one reasonable, while Justice Blackmun would defer to the state interest in regulating intestate succession but realistically review the *Parham* distinction. However, neither Justice explained his position in these decisions.

sumption of validity and would be stricken only if they "bear no rational relationship to a permissible state objective." But the opinion stated that not all such classifications or statutes were "entitled to the same presumption of validity"; that presumption would be undermined by the use of suspect classifications or "other immutable human attributes." [7]

The plurality opinion then found that the classification was not an invidious one based on illegitimacy or gender, which would require increased scrutiny, but the opinion also seemed to employ a realistic standard for reviewing whether or not the classification was permissible. The plurality endorsed the *Weber v. Aetna Casualty & Surety Co.*[8] position that classifications based on illegitimacy at birth appeared contrary to a principle requiring that burdensome classifications bear some relationship to individual responsibility, but the opinion also stated that fathers of illegitimates who had not legitimized their children were "responsible for fostering an illegitimate child and for failing to change its status." [9]

The plurality opinion in *Parham* also found that the law was not one invidiously based on gender. Although the opinion recognized that a state was not free to make overbroad generalizations involving sex classifications, it stated that "in cases where men and women are not similarly situated, however, and a statutory classification is realistically based upon the differences in their situations, this Court has upheld its validity." [10] Justice Stewart then found that the fathers and mothers of illegitimate children were not similarly situated; only the father had to, or could, legitimate a child under Georgia statutes. Because the mothers of illegitimates were readily identifiable, and more directly responsible for the care of a child immediately following its birth, it was reasonable to establish separate standards

for when fathers might be entitled to recover for the death of the illegitimate child.

Having found that the classification was not invidiously based on illegitimacy or gender, the plurality readily accepted the assertion that the goals of the statute were promoted by the classification. Only the mothers of illegitimate children had a right to sue for the wrongful death of the child. A majority of the Justices appear to believe that the distinction between mothers and fathers of illegitimates is demonstrably related to the important state goals of encouraging the legitimization of illegitimate children and guarding against spurious claims relating to paternity.

In a concurring opinion, Justice Powell mirrored much of the analysis used by the plurality but did so with a clearer statement of the appropriate standard of review for gender-based classifications.[11] He applied the intermediate standard of review adopted in *Craig v. Boren*[12] for reviewing gender classifications. Those classifications must "serve important governmental objectives and must be substantially related to the achievement of those objectives." But Justice Powell found that this statute was a realistic and reasonable way of achieving the state interest in avoiding problems of proof of paternity after the death of the child as well as encouraging the legitimization of illegitimate children.

Justice White, writing for four Justices in dissent, also employed the *Craig v. Boren* standard.[13] The dissenters found that the statute reflected only one facet of a generalized assumption about the difference in the relationships between fathers and mothers and their children: the statute denied recovery to any father so long as the mother of the child was alive.

---

7.   441 U.S. at 351, 99 S.Ct. at 1745.

8.   406 U.S. 164, 92 S.Ct. 1400, 31 L.Ed.2d 768 (1972).

9.   441 U.S. at 353, 99 S.Ct. at 1746.

10.   441 U.S. at 354, 99 S.Ct. at 1747.

11.   Parham v. Hughes, 441 U.S. 347, 359, 99 S.Ct. 1742, 1749, 60 L.Ed.2d 269 (1979) (Powell, J., concurring).

12.   429 U.S. 190, 97 S.Ct. 451, 50 L.Ed.2d 397 (1976).

See generally, Bremer, M.J., citing Treatise in, Pargo v. Elliott, 894 F.Supp. 1243, 1262 (S.D.Iowa 1995), affirmed 69 F.3d 280 (8th Cir.1995); Howell, C.J., citing Treatise, in Freeman v. Freeman, 323 S.C. 95, 473 S.E.2d 467, 473 (App.1996).

13.   Parham v. Hughes, 441 U.S. 347, 361, 99 S.Ct. 1742, 1750, 60 L.Ed.2d 269 (1979) (White, J., dissenting, joined by Brennan, Marshall, and Blackmun, JJ.).

Justice White found no important state interest that was advanced by the distinction between the fathers and mothers of illegitimate children for three reasons. First, the end of promoting family unity or establishing standards of morality through the placing of burdens on illegitimates or their parents at the time of death was irrational, and rejected in previous decisions. Second, the goal of avoiding problems of proof in paternity cases could be met by more narrow and less burdensome means than a total bar on suits by fathers of illegitimates. The state was free, in the view of the dissent, to require specific forms of proof of paternity in order to meet these problems. Third, the assertion that in all cases fathers who failed to legitimate their children suffered no real loss upon the death of the child was totally unreasonable; the state could set standards for reducing or denying recovery to parents who in fact had little or no interest in the lives of their children while they were alive. There was no basis or need for the generalized assumption that no father of an illegitimate ever had a relationship with his child equal to that of a mother.

§ 14.16 Illegitimacy Classifications: Government Benefits, Inheritance, and Support Rights

The Supreme Court, in *Labine v. Vincent*,[1] had upheld a law which allowed illegitimate children to receive equal treatment in the intestate distribution of their father's estate only if they had been formally acknowledged by the father during his life. The majority apparently based the entire decision upon deference to the states' right to regulate property distributions after the death of a citizen. However, the opinion is almost indecipherable. It applies the equal protection analysis only in a footnote[2] and spends the entire text on a discussion of why these laws should be beyond the reach of the equal protection guarantee, a position with no support in any case prior to or following this one. The opinion may have

turned on the fact that the state-created barrier to inheritance was not insurmountable; the illegitimate child could have been acknowledged by his parent or left property in a valid will.[3] The four dissenting Justices argued that it was not rational to disfavor children in intestate distributions; it was an arbitrary burden based on status and an attempt to punish them because of the illegitimacy of their birth.[4]

This case existed for six years as the one case in which the Court had upheld a burden based solely on a social view of the status of illegitimates. In the years after *Labine* the composition of the Court changed, and the majority returned to equal protection analysis. In *Weber v. Aetna Casualty & Surety Co.*,[5] the Court invalidated a Louisiana workers' compensation law that granted full recovery for injury to parents by legitimate and acknowledged illegitimate children but limited benefits to unacknowledged illegitimates. The Court held that when unacknowledged children had been dependent upon the injured parent, there was no basis for denying them full benefits.

The majority opinion distinguished *Labine* as being based on a deference to the states' power over property distribution. However, the Court's discussion, in *Weber*, of illegitimacy classifications thoroughly undercut the result in *Labine*. The majority opinion by Justice Powell explained that these classifications touched upon fundamental personal interests and that they appeared to run contrary to basic concepts of fairness. The opinion stated that the Court would exercise a "stricter scrutiny" over these classifications. It did not hold them to be suspect classifications subject to the most exacting tests.[6] Instead, the opinion held that in these situations "the essential inquiry [is] however, inevitably, a dual one: What legitimate state interest does the classification promote? What fundamental personal

---

§ 14.16

1. 401 U.S. 532, 91 S.Ct. 1017, 28 L.Ed.2d 288 (1971).
2. 401 U.S. at 536, n. 6, 91 S.Ct. at 1019, n. 6.
3. 401 U.S. at 538, 91 S.Ct. at 1020–21.

4. 401 U.S. at 541, 91 S.Ct. at 1022.
5. 406 U.S. 164, 92 S.Ct. 1400, 31 L.Ed.2d 768 (1972).
6. 406 U.S. at 172, 92 S.Ct. at 1405.

rights might the classification endanger?"[7] Here the law did not rationally promote legitimate state concerns because the state could not use later punishment of these persons to discourage illicit relationships in the future nor did this constitute a scheme to distinguish between those children dependent upon a wage earner and those not dependent. The personal rights involved were extremely sensitive because they involved family relationships and punishments of children who were not responsible for their status at birth.

In *Gomez v. Perez*,[8] the Court held that Texas could not deny illegitimate children the right to financial support from their natural fathers when this right was given to legitimate children. Without explaining the standard which it employed, the opinion held that the legislature could not permissibly decide to give parental support only to legitimate children. The opinion admitted that enforcement of support rights for illegitimates would be more difficult because of the problems of resolving complex factual questions of paternity. The Court decided, however, that the state could not justify on the ground of difficulty of birth the creation of "an impenetrable barrier that works to shield otherwise invidious discrimination."[9]

In response to *Gomez*, Texas enacted a statute establishing procedures to be followed in a paternity suit to identify the natural father of an illegitimate child for purposes of obtaining support. The state required that the suit be brought before the child was one year old, or it was barred. *In Mills v. Habluetzel*[10] the Su-

preme Court held that the one-year period denied illegitimate children equal protection of law.

Equal protection, the Court held, requires first that the period for obtaining support must be of sufficient duration to present "a reasonable opportunity for those with an interest in such children to assert claims on their behalf," and, second, that "any time limitation placed on that opportunity must be substantially related to the state's interest in avoiding the litigation of stale or fraudulent claims."[11] Problems of proving paternity may justify greater restrictions on support suits by illegitimate children than on those by legitimate children,[12] but the support opportunity provided to illegitimate children "must be more than illusory."[13] The Court later employed the "substantially related to a legitimate interest" test when the Justices unanimously invalidated a state law which required a support or paternity action to be filed against the father of an illegitimate child before the child was two years old.[14]

The Supreme Court invalidated several other laws burdening illegitimates. In *New Jersey Welfare Rights Organization v. Cahill*,[15] the Court invalidated a program providing welfare to low-income family units consisting of married couples with either natural or adopted children. The opinion held that the states could not deny benefits to family units simply because they contained illegitimate children. The effect of the statute was to punish illegitimate children by denying benefits to them and their families. The Court

---

7. 406 U.S. at 173, 92 S.Ct. at 1405.

8. 409 U.S. 535, 93 S.Ct. 872, 35 L.Ed.2d 56 (1973).

9. 409 U.S. at 538, 93 S.Ct. at 875.

10. 456 U.S. 91, 102 S.Ct. 1549, 71 L.Ed.2d 770 (1982).

11. 456 U.S. at 99–101, 102 S.Ct. at 1555.

12. 456 U.S. at 95–99, 102 S.Ct. at 1552–56. Texas allows legitimate children to sue their natural father for support at any time until the age of eighteen. 456 U.S. at 99–101, 102 S.Ct. at 1555–56.

13. 456 U.S. at 95–97, 102 S.Ct. at 1552–53.

14. Pickett v. Brown, 462 U.S. 1, 103 S.Ct. 2199, 76 L.Ed.2d 372 (1983). The law did not provide a reasonable opportunity for children to bring support claims. The Court's opinion found that the two-year limitation, which provided exceptions only for acknowledged children or

children likely to become "a public charge," was not substantially related to preventing the litigation of stale or fraudulent claims.

15. 411 U.S. 619, 93 S.Ct. 1700, 36 L.Ed.2d 543 (1973). See also Davis v. Richardson, 342 F.Supp. 588 (D.Conn. 1972), affirmed 409 U.S. 1069, 93 S.Ct. 678, 34 L.Ed.2d 659 (1972); Griffin v. Richardson, 346 F.Supp. 1226 (D.Md.1972), affirmed 409 U.S. 1069, 93 S.Ct. 689, 34 L.Ed.2d 660 (1972). These cases, which were affirmed by the Supreme Court, held a provision of the Social Security Act unconstitutional because it tended to disfavor illegitimates by allowing them to receive benefits only if favored classes did not qualify for full benefits. Both lower courts applied the strict scrutiny-compelling state interest test in reviewing the statute.

concluded that there was not an acceptable justification for distinguishing between legitimates and illegitimates when the purpose of the benefits should be to support needy persons rather than single out a class of children as unworthy because of their status at birth.

Similarly, in *Jimenez v. Weinberger*,[16] the Court invalidated a provision of the federal Social Security Act barring recovery by illegitimate children born after the onset of the worker's disability. These children were not distinguishable in terms of the purpose of the law, which was aimed at supporting disabled workers or their dependents. The law violated the equal protection component of the Fifth Amendment due process clause. There was no legitimate governmental interest, compelling or otherwise, which was related to dispensing support benefits on the basis of a child's status at birth. The Court found it unnecessary to determine whether illegitimacy classifications were suspect. It found the laws constitutionally invalid under the equal protection guarantees using a lesser test.[17]

In 1976 the Supreme Court held that the Social Security Act could condition the eligibility for survivor's benefits of certain illegitimate children upon a showing that the deceased wage earner was both the child's parent and was supporting the child at the time of his death. In *Mathews v. Lucas*,[18] the Court examined under the Fifth Amendment equal protection guarantee the permissibility of a law which granted a presumption of dependency to legitimate children and illegitimates who were entitled to inherit from the decedent under state law. Other illegitimate children were allowed to establish their dependency upon the deceased wage earner and to collect survivor's benefits, but they had to produce evidence of their dependency.

The *Mathews* Court upheld the law because it found that the reduction in administrative problems and expense in avoiding a proof of dependency requirement for all children could support this classification. The classification was not strictly a division between legitimate and illegitimate children because those illegitimate children whose circumstances indicated that the children were dependent on the wage earner were treated in a manner similar to legitimate children. Illegitimate children were entitled to a presumption of dependency if they could inherit personal property from the parent under state law, if their parents had ever gone through a purported marriage ceremony or had acknowledged the children, if they had been decreed by a court to be the wage earner's children, or if the wage earner had ever been ordered by a court to support the children. Thus, only a small group of illegitimate children were not entitled to a presumption of dependency upon the death of their parents. Furthermore, the remaining children were allowed to prove their dependency, in which case they would be qualified for benefits. The law was upheld because it was not an attempt to burden illegitimate children but only a narrow way of easing administrative problems for the establishment of dependency.[19]

Lucas did not indicate a change in the Court's analysis of illegitimacy classifications as was shown by the decision in *Trimble v. Gordon*.[20] *Trimble* involved a challenge to an Illinois statute which allowed illegitimate children to inherit by intestate succession from the estates of their mothers but not their fathers. The state supreme court had sustained the law on the authority of *Labine*; the United States Supreme Court held the law unconstitutional.

---

16. 417 U.S. 628, 94 S.Ct. 2496, 41 L.Ed.2d 363 (1974).

17. 417 U.S. at 632–34, 94 S.Ct. at 2498–99.

18. 427 U.S. 495, 96 S.Ct. 2755, 49 L.Ed.2d 651 (1976).

19. See also United States v. Clark, 445 U.S. 23, 100 S.Ct. 895, 63 L.Ed.2d 171 (1980) holding that Civil Service Retirement Act provision 5 U.S.C.A. § 8341 (which automatically grants survivors' benefits to the legitimate children of a federal service employee, but allows "recognized natural" children to qualify only if they lived with the

employee in a family relationship), requires payment of benefits to an employee's illegitimate child who had once lived with him, but who no longer lived with the employee at the time of his death. The Court construed the statute to avoid the constitutional question of whether a narrower grant of benefits to illegitimate children is an impermissible illegitimacy classification.

20. 430 U.S. 762, 97 S.Ct. 1459, 52 L.Ed.2d 31 (1977).

The majority opinion by Justice Powell in *Trimble* held that the Illinois act was not a reasonable way of promoting any legitimate governmental purpose. Nothing but conjecture suggested that such burdens upon illegitimates would promote legitimate family relationships or influence the actions of unmarried persons. Nor could the theory that intestate succession laws were "statutory wills" support the law because the possibility that many citizens would disfavor their illegitimate children upon death could not justify a total barrier to inheritance by illegitimates. Nor could the fact the father might leave these children property by will save the law; it still constituted a differentiation between children based solely upon their legitimacy.[21] The Court did not overrule *Labine* and indicated that, if in nothing else, the Louisiana statute was different because it had created different subclasses of illegitimates with different rights.

In *Lalli v. Lalli*,[22] the Supreme Court distinguished *Trimble* and upheld a requirement that in order for an illegitimate child to qualify as an heir of his or her father, and share in the intestate estate of the father, the child had to receive "an order of filiation declaring paternity" from a court of "competent jurisdiction" during the father's life. The proceeding, in which the illegitimate child received a judicial declaration of paternity of the alleged father prior to the death of the father, could have been initiated by the child, the child's mother, or the father during his lifetime.

The plurality opinion by Justice Powell used a realistic form of review that might be described as a middle level equal protection test, even though Powell did not state the test with particularity. The plurality opinion noted that classifications based on illegitimacy were not subject to strict scrutiny but that "they nevertheless are invalid under the Fourteenth

Amendment if they are not related to a permissible state interest." The plurality also referred to the state interests in the case as "important" and "articulated." *Lalli* demonstrates that a majority of the Justices favor some form of realistic scrutiny of whether the use of an illegitimacy classification relates to a significant, in the sense of articulated and not impermissible, state interest. However, the precise nature of the test is unclear since four of the seven Justices who employed realistic scrutiny dissented in this case.

The Powell plurality opinion in *Lalli* distinguished New York's requirement of a judicial finding of paternity from the Illinois statute in *Trimble v. Gordon* which had excluded an illegitimate child from the father's estate unless the child was legitimated through the intermarriage of the natural parents and the father's acknowledgement of paternity. The requirement of intermarriage was an arbitrary and unreasonable means of attempting to encourage legitimate family relationships by burdening illegitimate children. The plurality found that the New York paternity order requirement was demonstrably related to the state interest in the orderly disposition of property and the accurate determination of paternity suits. While evidence regarding the actual purpose of the legislature was unclear, the law did not appear to be designed to penalize illegitimates as a class; there was some legislative history indicating that the law had been designed to treat illegitimate children in an equitable manner while insuring efficient and accurate proceedings for the establishment of paternity.[23]

The plurality recognized that there might be other legitimate ways of providing for inheritance by illegitimates that would promote the state's interest, but the plurality did not re-

---

21. 430 U.S. at 775, 97 S.Ct. at 1467–68.

22. 439 U.S. 259, 99 S.Ct. 518, 58 L.Ed.2d 503 (1978). Justice Powell announced the judgment in an opinion joined only by the Chief Justice and Justice Stewart.

Justices Rehnquist and Blackmun concurred in the judgment but would have employed a significantly less strict standard to test the classification than did the Powell plurality. They would defer totally to the state interest in determining the system of devolution of proper-

ty from its citizens who die without a will and overturn Trimble v. Gordon, 439 U.S. at 276, 99 S.Ct. at 528 (Rehnquist, J., concurring), 439 U.S. at 276, 277, 99 S.Ct. at 529 (Blackmun, J., concurring).

23. Lalli v. Lalli, 439 U.S. 259, 268–272, 99 S.Ct. 518, 524–27, 58 L.Ed.2d 503 (1978). The plurality noted and relied upon the work of a state commission that had examined the need for revision of the state intestacy laws regarding illegitimates.

quire the legislature to achieve its ends through the means least burdensome on illegitimates as a class. The Justices in the plurality believed that a requirement only of acknowledgement during the father's life would not provide the same degree of proof and certainty for the determination of heirs and avoidance of spurious paternity claims as would the New York judicial order requirement. Thus, in the view of the plurality, the requirement was "substantially related to the important state interest the statute is intended to promote." [24] *Lalli* did not consider whether the New York statutes established impermissible gender discrimination by allowing illegitimates to be heirs of their mothers without a declaration of maternity while requiring a judicial declaration of paternity for them to be intestate heirs of their natural fathers.

Justice Brennan, in a dissent joined by Justices White, Marshall and Stevens, employed a degree of scrutiny or equal protection test greater than the rational basis test but less than the strict scrutiny-compelling interest standards. [25] Although the dissent did not specify the precise test that should be used to review the legitimacy classifications, it examined the importance of the ends asserted by the state and the relationship between those ends and the classification. Justice Brennan found that the state goals of avoiding spurious paternity claims and the efficient identification of heirs could be achieved substantially by the "less drastic means" of requiring illegitimates to prove their paternity by a higher standard of proof following the death of the father or by accepting some forms of acknowledgement in lieu of a judicial declaration of paternity.

The Supreme Court requires realistic, independent judicial review of death benefit or inheritance classifications that are based upon

a child's legitimacy. In *Reed v. Campbell,*[26] the Supreme Court ruled that *Trimble v. Gordon,*[27] which had invalidated the denial of all inheritance rights to illegitimate children upon the death of their father, was applicable to the estate settlement of a man who had died four months prior to the Court's decision in *Trimble.* Justice Stevens, writing for a unanimous Court, found that *Reed* was not a case deciding the retroactivity of *Trimble,* although it obviously has the effect of making *Trimble* somewhat retroactive. Instead, Stevens found that *Reed* was a case involving the question of whether special burdens could be imposed upon illegitimate children who wish to inherit from their fathers.

Justice Stevens stated that the prior decisions of the Supreme Court "have unambiguously concluded that a State may not justify discriminatory treatment of illegitimates in order to express disapproval of their parents' misconduct, [but the Court also has] recognized that there is a permissible basis for some distinctions made in part on the basis of illegitimacy; specifically, we have upheld statutory provisions that have an evident and substantial relationship to the State's interest in providing for the orderly and just distribution of a decedent's property at death." [28] After an estate has been finally distributed, "the interest in finality may provide an additional, valid justification for barring the belated assertion of claims" even though the barred claims might be meritorious. [29] It is the state's obligation to show that a classification based upon legitimacy has some reasonable and substantial relationship to a legitimate governmental interest so the judiciary can be assured that the classification is not a means of arbitrarily burdening illegitimate children. The state was not able to demonstrate any legitimate interest in denying inheritance rights to the child in *Reed.*

24. 439 U.S. at 275, 276, 99 S.Ct. at 528–29.

25. Lalli v. Lalli, 439 U.S. 259, 277–278, 99 S.Ct. 518, 529–30, 58 L.Ed.2d 503 (1978) (Brennan, J., dissenting, joined by White, Marshall, & Stevens, JJ.).

26. 476 U.S. 852, 106 S.Ct. 2234, 90 L.Ed.2d 858 (1986), rehearing denied 478 U.S. 1031, 107 S.Ct. 11, 92 L.Ed.2d 766 (1986).

27. 430 U.S. 762, 97 S.Ct. 1459, 52 L.Ed.2d 31 (1977). The ruling in *Trimble* is discussed, and distinguished from the Court's ruling in Lalli v. Lalli, 439 U.S. 259, 99 S.Ct. 518, 58 L.Ed.2d 503 (1978).

28. Reed v. Campbell, 476 U.S. 852, 854–855, 106 S.Ct. 2234, 2237, 90 L.Ed.2d 858 (1986), rehearing denied 478 U.S. 1031, 107 S.Ct. 11, 92 L.Ed.2d 766 (1986).

29. Id.

§ 14.17 Illegitimacy Classifications: Adoption Problems

The Court has recognized that the fathers of illegitimates are entitled to some constitutional protection of their relationship to the child even though they have not married the mother of the child. In *Stanley v. Illinois*,[1] the Court invalidated a statute which denied the father of illegitimate children a hearing prior to their adoption by another person. In this case the father had lived with the mother and the illegitimate children until the mother's death. At that time, the state sought to remove the children from the custody of the father without making an individual determination of the fitness of the father to retain custody. The Court held that the state denied the father his due process right to a determination of his fitness and a continuation of his relationship with the children. Just as there is no reason to arbitrarily burden the illegitimate child in his relationship to his parents, there is no basis for presuming that such fathers are unfit to retain custody of their children.

Caban v. Mohammed[2] invalidated a New York law that required the consent of the mother of an illegitimate child prior to its adoption but which did not give equal consent rights to the father of the child. The majority found that the law constituted an impermissible form of gender-based discrimination between the parents of illegitimate children, although the majority did not reach the question of whether such discrimination would be allowed when the father of the child was not readily ascertainable or during the period when the child was in its infancy.

Under the New York statutes, a legitimate child could not be adopted over the objection of either its mother or father unless the parent had abandoned the child or otherwise been judicially determined to be incompetent to care for the child. The mothers of illegitimate children were treated like the parents of legitimates; the natural father of an illegitimate child had only the right to protest adoption

proceedings involving his child. If the natural father exercised his right to object, then the trial court would determine whether the would-be adoptive parents were qualified to care for the child, whereas the mother's objection would block the adoption under any circumstances.

The majority opinion adopted the intermediate standard of review which requires that gender-based classifications bear a "substantial relation to some important state interest."[3] Employing this test, the majority rejected the two bases which the state asserted for the classification. First, the majority found that maternal and paternal relationships to illegitimates were not so inherently different as to justify the conclusion that all mothers of illegitimates had a more significant interest in the well-being of the child than did any father. Second, while recognizing the importance of the interest in promoting the adoption and legitimization of these children, the majority found that the means used to promote adoption were unreasonable because there was no demonstration that fathers were more likely than mothers to object to adoptions for reasons that did not involve the well being of the children. Nor was there proof that the difficulty in locating fathers would interfere with the adoption of children beyond the infancy stage. The majority did not consider whether a statute could be drafted that would grant adoption consent rights to only the mothers of illegitimates when the father could not be easily ascertained or when the child was to be adopted during the "infancy stage." The majority merely held that the "undifferentiated distinction between unwed mothers and unwed fathers, applicable in all circumstances where adoption of a child of theirs is at issue, does not bear a substantial relationship to the State's asserted interest."[4]

Although the Court has not settled the rights of fathers of illegitimate children to gain initial custody of the children, *Caban* and *Stanley* indicate that fathers of illegitimate

§ 14.17

1. 405 U.S. 645, 92 S.Ct. 1208, 31 L.Ed.2d 551 (1972).
2. 441 U.S. 380, 99 S.Ct. 1760, 60 L.Ed.2d 297 (1979).

3. 441 U.S. at 388, 99 S.Ct. at 1765–66.
4. 441 U.S. at 394, 99 S.Ct. at 1769 (footnote omitted).

children should be given notice and a hearing before the child can be adopted by another person, at least where the natural father can be located and identified without unreasonably complicated or expensive administrative systems.[5] However, a father who fails to take any steps toward acknowledgment of his paternity and does not seek to establish a relation-

5. Parental Rights of Fathers of Illegitimate Children.

The Supreme Court has not clearly ruled on whether a male who asserts that he is the parent of a child has a fundamental constitutional right to establish a personal relationship with the child so that the state could not grant preferential custody rights over the child to the biological mother, rather than the biological father, of the child. The cases referred to in this section examine some specific problems concerning the establishment of parent-child relationships or the distinctions between custodial rights of mothers and fathers of an illegitimate child.

The Supreme Court upheld a state statute which established a presumption that a child born to a woman who was lawfully married was the child of her husband but it did so without a majority opinion and in a manner that left unclear whether the interest of a male who asserted that he was the biological parent of the child born to a woman who was married to another man would receive any constitutional protection. In Michael H. v. Gerald D., 491 U.S. 110, 109 S.Ct. 2333, 105 L.Ed.2d 91 (1989) (judgment of the Court announced in an opinion by Scalia, J., joined by Rehnquist, C.J., and, in part, by O'Connor and Kennedy, JJ.) Justices Scalia, O'Connor, and Kennedy, and Chief Justice Rehnquist found that a male had no constitutionally protected interest in establishing a relationship with a child born to a woman who was married to another man, regardless of whether he could prove that he was the biological parent of the child. Justice Stevens, who concurred in the judgment, found that the male had no constitutionally protected interest in being declared the "father" of a child born to a married couple but assumed for purposes of the case that the male in this situation had a constitutionally protected liberty interest in establishing a personal relationship with the child. Justice Stevens found that interest was sufficiently protected by a related state statute that allowed any person who had an interest in the well-being of a child to seek a court judgment that the individual should be allowed visitation rights. Four dissenting Justices believed that the putative father in this case, like the putative fathers of illegitimacy cases where the woman was not married to another man, had a constitutionally protected liberty interest in his relationship with the child. 491 U.S. at 136, 109 S.Ct. at 2349 (Brennan, J., joined by Marshall and Blackmun, JJ., dissenting). 491 U.S. at 157, 109 S.Ct. at 2360 (White, J., joined by Brennan, J., dissenting).

In Lehr v. Robertson, 463 U.S. 248, 103 S.Ct. 2985, 77 L.Ed.2d 614 (1983), the Supreme Court held that the state was not required by due process or equal protection to provide notice and a hearing to the putative father of a two year old illegitimate child when the father had never sought to establish a substantial relationship with, or accept responsibility for, the child. In Lehr the state allowed a man who claimed to be the father of an illegitimate child to file a statement to that effect in the "puta-

ship with his illegitimate child can be denied a right to veto the adoption of that child even though a veto power is granted to other parents.[6]

The dissenting Justices in Caban did not employ a significantly different standard of review than the majority, but they reached an opposite conclusion on the ultimate issue in

tive father registry"; that registration would guarantee that the man received notice of future adoption proceedings. Due process did not require a more extensive system to identify or notify fathers who had never claimed responsibility for the child; equal protection did not require that such fathers be granted rights equal to those who had established a substantial custodial, legal, or financial relationship with the child.

See also, Rothstein v. Lutheran Social Services, 405 U.S. 1051, 92 S.Ct. 1488, 31 L.Ed.2d 786 (1972), on remand 59 Wis.2d 1, 207 N.W.2d 826 (1973), appeal after remand 68 Wis.2d 36, 227 N.W.2d 643 (1975), summarily vacating 47 Wis.2d 420, 178 N.W.2d 56 (1970); Vanderlaan v. Vanderlaan, summarily vacating 126 Ill.App.2d 410, 262 N.E.2d 717 (1970), judgment vacated 405 U.S. 1051, 92 S.Ct. 1488, 31 L.Ed.2d 787 (1972).

6. Quilloin v. Walcott, 434 U.S. 246, 98 S.Ct. 549, 54 L.Ed.2d 511 (1978). The Supreme Court unanimously rejected the claim of the natural father of an illegitimate child who sought to veto the adoption of that child by the husband of the natural mother. The Court's opinion in Quilloin by Justice Marshall recognized that parent-child relationships received significant protection under the due process and the equal protection clauses. However, there was no violation of the natural father's procedural due process rights since his petition to stop the adoption and formally acknowledge the child was rejected only after a full hearing and a determination that the adoption would be in the "best interest of the child." Thus, there was no violation of the Stanley requirement that the father be afforded some form of fair procedure.

The Court found that even if the "best interest of the child" standard might be challengeable in other situations, it was a permissible basis for determining whether to allow a child to be adopted over the objections of a parent (such as the natural father in this case) who had never sought actual nor legal custody of his child prior to the time when the child was to be adopted. The statutes reviewed in Quilloin granted fathers of legitimate children an absolute veto power over adoptions of those children. The father of a legitimate child retained this right until he specifically surrendered his rights in the child, abandoned the child, or had his rights terminated by a court for cause. The Supreme Court found no violation of equal protection in denying a similar veto power to fathers who had never sought custody of, nor taken significant responsibility for, the child in question. The fact that married fathers of legitimate children, at least for some period of time, had legal custody and responsibility for those children was a permissible basis to distinguish their rights from those of persons such as the unmarried father in this case.

the case due to their assessment of the importance of facilitating adoptions.[7] Given the state interest in promoting adoptions and relationship of the mother to the child, the dissenting Justices believed it was permissible to give a veto/consent right to the mother alone.

Although Justices Stewart and Stevens were writing in dissent, they did note several important points that are critical to an understanding of the majority opinion. First, it is not at all clear whether this decision will have a retroactive effect; given the reasonableness of reliance on the previous adoption processes, it would seem unconscionable to call into question untold numbers of completed adoptions. Second, the problem of questioning mothers of newborns to ascertain the male parentage of newborns may constitute a basis for distinguishing between mothers and fathers when the adoption concerns an infant, a point not reached by the majority. Third, not even the dissenters would appear to endorse a principle that would distinguish between the legal status of mothers and fathers of legitimate children. Indeed, there is no indication that any of the Justices would allow for termination of parental rights in relationship to a legitimate child absent a finding of unfitness on the part of the parent.

§ 14.18 Illegitimacy Classifications: Immigration

In *Fiallo v. Bell*,[1] the Supreme Court held that the federal government could grant special preferences in immigration which excluded the illegitimate children of foreign national fathers seeking their admission. Under these laws legitimate children of either male or female parents, or the illegitimate children of a foreign national mother seeking admission to this country, were not subject to certain immigration quotas. However, these quotas applied to the illegitimate children of fathers

seeking admission to this country. The Court was not in this case indicating that illegitimacy classifications were subject to only traditional standards of review, or that the Fifth Amendment included a lesser equal protection guarantee. Rather, the federal government has a strong interest in setting standards for immigration and naturalization which the Court has always respected. This decision comports with decisions deferring to the legislative power over immigration and naturalization.[2]

In *Fiallo*, the Court did not engage in separate analysis of the gender basis of the classification that favored foreign national mothers over foreign national fathers separately from the illegitimacy basis of the classification, which placed special restrictions on the ability of parents to bring to this country children who were born out of wedlock. Two decades after *Fiallo*, the Court examined both illegitimacy and gender based classifications in United States naturalization statutes.

In *Miller v. Albright*,[3] the Court examined federal statutes that granted citizenship to children who were born outside of the United States to U.S. citizen parents. Under federal statutes challenged in the *Miller* litigation, a child born outside of the United States to a married couple that included one or two United States citizens, was automatically granted U.S. citizenship at birth. Different treatment was given to illegitimate children born outside of the United States who had only one U.S. citizen parent.

Under these statutes, a child born outside of the United States to an unmarried father and mother, only one of whom was a U.S. citizen, would receive citizenship "as of the date of birth" if the child's mother was a United States citizen. If the father of the illegitimate child was born outside the United States a United States citizen, and his mother was a

7. Caban v. Mohammed, 441 U.S. 380, 395, 99 S.Ct. 1760, 1769–70, 60 L.Ed.2d 297 (1979), (Stewart, J., dissenting). 441 U.S. at 401, 99 S.Ct. at 1773 (Stevens, J., dissenting, joined by Burger, C.J., and Rehnquist, J.)

§ 14.18
1. 430 U.S. 787, 97 S.Ct. 1473, 52 L.Ed.2d 50 (1977).

2. See § 14.11. For citations to additional Supreme Court cases, and secondary authorities, see R. Rotunda & J. Nowak, Treatise on Constitutional Law: Substance and Procedure, vol. 4, Ch. 22 (2nd ed. 1992, with annual supplements).

3. 523 U.S. 420, 118 S.Ct. 1428, 140 L.Ed.2d 575 (1998).

foreign national, the child would retroactively receive citizenship at birth if, but only if, the father took certain actions to acknowledge the child before the child's eighteenth birthday[4]

These statutory classifications were challenged in *Miller* by a woman who had been born in 1970 outside the United States to a non-citizen mother and a U.S. citizen father. She had not received "acknowledgment" of her status as his child from her father until she was eighteen years old, and for that reason, her petition for U.S. citizenship had been denied by the Secretary of State. She alleged that the naturalization law denied equal protection of the law to both to her father and herself. As a result of the Court's ruling in *Miller v. Albright* the statutory system for naturalization survived judicial review for the time being. There was no majority opinion for the Court in *Miller*; the Justices divided their votes in a way that makes it appear that the Court would continue to uphold the illegitimacy classifications in naturalization laws while bringing into question the continued validity of the gender classification in naturalization laws.

Justice Stevens announced the judgment of the Court in *Miller* in an opinion that was joined only by Chief Justice Rehnquist.[5] These two Justices did not separate the illegitimacy and gender aspects of the naturalization law. Justice Stevens found that the creation of special rules regarding the granting of citizenship to a child born out of wedlock to a United States citizen father and a national of another country was related to government interests in avoiding fraudulent claims of paternity, and fostering family relationships between fathers and children. Justice's Stevens opinion was unclear regarding the standard that he and Chief Justice Rehnquist were using to evaluate the classifications. At one point, the Stevens' opinion stated, that these two Justices found that the classification is "neither arbitrary nor invidious". At another point in the opinion, Justice Stevens explained that the government interests that supported the statute are "important" and that the statute was "well-tailored" to serve those important government interests.[6]

Justices Scalia and Thomas also voted to uphold the naturalization law in *Miller* without separating the gender and illegitimacy aspects of these naturalization statutes. Those two Justices believed that the judicial had no authority to invalidate naturalization laws in a way that would grant citizenship to an individual who did not meet the explicit statutory requirements for naturalized citizenship.[7] Thus, they did not discuss the compatibility of the gender and illegitimacy classification with the equal protection guarantee.

Justices O'Connor and Kennedy cast the deciding votes in *Miller*; they provided the fifth and sixth votes against Ms. Miller's challenges to the naturalization law.[8] In an opinion joined only by Justice Kennedy, Justice O'Connor refused to take a position regarding the constitutionality of the gender-based classification that separated the treatment of illegitimate children born to U.S. citizen mothers as opposed to illegitimate children born to U.S. citizen fathers outside of the United States. Justices O'Connor and Kennedy believed that Ms. Miller did not have "standing" to raise the rights of her biological father. For that reason, they refused to address the issue of whether the classification violated the equal protection component of the Fifth Amendment due process clause on the basis of a gender-based classification. Justices O'Connor and Kennedy found that Ms. Miller could only challenge the

---

4. The statutory requirements for the granting of citizenship to children born outside of the United States to only one parent who was a United States citizen were contained in U.S. C. A. § 1401, 1409. The details of the statutes were set out in the plurality opinion of Justice Stevens. 523 U.S. at 429 n. 6, 430 n. 7, 118 S. Ct. at 1435, n. 6, n. 7.

5. 523 U.S. 420, 118 S.Ct. 1428, 140 L.Ed.2d 575 (1998) (opinion of the Court announced by Stevens, J., in an opinion joined by Rehnquist, C.J.).

6. 523 U.S. at 436–40, 118 S. Ct. at 1438–40 (Stevens, J. joined by Rehnquist, C.J.).

7. 523 U.S. 420, 118 S.Ct. 1428, 1446, 140 L.Ed.2d 575 (1998). (Scalia, J., joined by Thomas, J., concurring in the judgment).

8. 523 U.S. at 444, 118 S. Ct. at 1442 (O'Connor, J., joined by Kennedy, J. concurring in the judgment).

statute under a "rational basis" standard and that the separate treatment of illegitimate children under these statutes was rationally related to legitimate governmental interests.[9]

The opinion written by Justice O'Connor in *Miller* is difficult to interpret, apart from her clear rejection of the woman's standing to raise the gender-based classification. Justice O'Connor previously had written an opinion for a unanimous Court finding that illegitimacy based classifications should be subject to the same standard as gender based classifications.[10] That standard requires the government to demonstrate that an illegitimacy or gender based classification has a substantial relationship to an important governmental interest.[11] Nevertheless, Justice O'Connor made no reference to that standard of review in her *Miller* opinion. Perhaps Justice O'Connor's opinion in *Miller* was based on the belief that there was no separate illegitimacy classification claim presented by the case, because the only challenge had been to the treatment of illegitimate children born to U.S. citizen fathers, as opposed to U.S. citizen mothers. Perhaps Justice O'Connor meant to take the position that illegitimacy classifications in immigration and naturalization laws would not be subject to the same type of intermediate scrutiny that would be applied to illegitimacy classifications in federal or state laws regarding domestic matters. Unfortunately, Justice O'Connor's opinion in *Miller* did not clearly state a position on the proper standard of review to be used by the judiciary when examining a legitimacy based classification in federal statutes.

The three Justices in *Miller* who used the Court's previously adopted standard for the judicial review of gender classifications voted to invalidate the statute. In two opinions, Justices Ginsburg and Breyer, joined by Justice Souter, explained why the gender classification could not be upheld under any form of independent judicial review.[12] In the view of the dissenters, the history of gender classifications in our country's immigration and naturalization laws, and the lack of a need for separate treatment of paternity, as opposed to maternity, claims in immigration cases meant that the preference for children born to U.S. citizen mothers was not substantially related to any important government interest.

In 2001, the Supreme Court examined the same federal statutes that had been at issue in the *Miller* case 3 years earlier. In *Tuan Anh Nguyen v. Immigration and Naturalization Service*[13] Justice Kennedy wrote for six Justices in upholding the statutes that granted immediate statutory citizenship to a child born abroad to married parents, at least one of whom was a United States citizen, and to children who were born outside of the United States to a U.S. citizen mother. Those statutes did not grant citizenship to a child born outside of the United States to a non-citizen mother and a U.S. citizen father. The majority upheld the explicit gender classification in the statute, and assumed that the legitimacy classification issue either had been settled by *Miller* or that upholding the gender classification automatically meant that the illegitimacy classification was also valid.

Justice Kennedy's majority opinion in *Tuan Anh Ngugen* ruled that the gender classification (which made it more difficult for a male, as opposed to a female, United States citizen to obtain U.S. citizenship for a child born out of wedlock in another country) met the intermediate standard of review that had been previously used in gender and illegitimacy cases. The majority found that the classification requiring fathers to take certain steps to establish paternity and citizenship for the child before the child realized a certain age was

---

9. 523 U.S. at 449–51, 118 S. Ct. at 1445–46 (O'Connor, J., joined by Kennedy, J., concurring in the judgment).

10. Clark v. Jeter, 486 U.S. 456, 108 S.Ct., 1910, 100 L.Ed.2d 465 (1988).

11. See § 14.19, 14.23 of this Treatise.

12. 523 U.S. 420, 460, 118 S.Ct. 1428, 1449, 140 L.Ed.2d 575 (1998). (Ginsburg, J., joined by Souter and Breyer, JJ., dissenting); 523 U.S. at 471, 118 S.Ct. at 1455 (Breyer, J. joined by Souter and Ginsburg, JJ., dissenting). See § 14.23 of the Treatise regarding the standards of review for gender based classifications.

13. 533 U.S. 53, 121 S.Ct. 2053, 150 L.Ed.2d 115 (2001). 533 U.S. at 71–73, 121 S.Ct. at 2059, 2065–66.

substantially related to two important government interests: insuring that the child was in fact the biological child of the U.S. citizen father; and guaranteeing that the father had taken actions to create the opportunity for the father and child to have a true parent child relationship before the child became an adult.

Because the majority in *Tuan Anh Nguyen* found that these classifications were substantially related to important government interests (thus meeting the intermediate standard of review), Justice Kennedy stated that whether the Court would not consider whether a lesser standard, such as the rationality test, should be used to review illegitimacy or gender classifications in immigration and naturalization laws. The dissent in *Tuan Anh Nguyen* pointed out that there were many ways to establish paternity that were at least as accurate as making the father take certain legal steps before a child's 18th or 21st birthday.[14] In fact, the father in the *Tuan Anh Nguyen* case had brought his child back to the United States prior to the child's sixth birthday and had demonstrated paternity, after the child was an adult, through a DNA test.

While Justice Kennedy's majority opinion in *Tuan Anh Nguyen* was correct in stating that the substantial relationship to an important interest test did not require the government to adopt the means that was most narrowly tailored or necessary to achieve its interest, the majority did not seem to apply any form of independent judicial review when it was examining whether Congress had any realistic need to use the illegitimacy and sex preferences in the immigration and naturalization laws. Despite statements in the *Miller* plurality opinion and the *Tuan Anh Nguyen* majority opinions, the Court in these cases did not appear to

apply the intermediate standard of review in a meaningful way. Rather than assuming that the Court in 2001 was watering down the meaning of the intermediate standard for equal protection, it would be best to assume that the majority found that the intermediate standard was not in part to avoid the questions of whether there was any legitimate basis upon which a court could grant United States citizenship to a person who had not met the letter of congressional naturalization statutes.[15]

§ 14.19   Illegitimacy Classifications: Conclusion

Prior to the illegitimacy-gender cases decided in the 1978–79 Term, the Supreme Court had quite consistently invalidated laws which discriminated against illegitimate children or their parents. Illegitimacy classifications which were upheld by the Supreme Court were narrowly drawn to promote legitimate governmental interests and did not stand as impenetrable barriers to obtaining benefits.[1]

The illegitimacy-gender cases, however, allowed legislatures to erect some classifications which could deprive an illegitimate child, or his or her father, of benefits due to failure to comply with legal requirements even where there was a continuing relationship between the parent and child. Perhaps these decisions can be made consistent with prior cases upon the assumption that the Supreme Court will guard against the arbitrary use of gender or illegitimacy classifications, while attempting to allow legislatures to deal with significant social problems through the use of such classifications when they are not based on stereotypes. Yet the decisions are difficult to analyze because of the alignments of different Justices

---

14.   533 U.S. at 73, 121 S.Ct. at 2066 (O'Connor, J., joined by Souter, Ginsburg, and Breyer, JJ., dissenting).

15.   Justice Kennedy's majority opinion did not take a position on the degree of deference that should be given to Congress concerning immigration and naturalization powers or whether the Court could have granted citizenship to the person challenging the law if the Court had found the classification in the statute was invalid. Tuan Anh Nguyen v. Immigration and Naturalization Service, 533 U.S. 53, 71, 121 S.Ct. 2053, 2065, 150 L.Ed.2d 115 (2001). Justices Scalia and Thomas joined the majority opinion in *Tuan Anh Nguyen* but wrote a separate paragraph to restate

their view, first expressed in *Miller*, that the Court could not provide citizenship to a person who was not born in the United States and did not meet the exact letter of the statutes created by Congress. 533 U.S. at 73, 121 S.Ct. at 2066 (Scalia, J., joined by Thomas, J., concurring).

§ 14.19

1.   See Reed v. Campbell, 476 U.S. 852, 106 S.Ct. 2234, 90 L.Ed.2d 858 (1986), rehearing denied 478 U.S. 1031, 107 S.Ct. 11, 92 L.Ed.2d 766 (1986), which is examined in § 14.16.

that brought about the particular result in each case.

Between 1968 and 1988, the Court reviewed classifications based on illegitimacy in a meaningful way, even though the Court was not clear concerning the standard of review being applied in such cases. A majority of the Justices consistently required the government to demonstrate that the classification was not an arbitrary burden on illegitimate children or their parents. This type of review involved neither great deference to the legislature, which would virtually permit all but the most invidious classifications, nor strict judicial scrutiny, which would require the government to justify the classification in terms of a compelling or overriding interest.

In 1988 the Court formally adopted an intermediate standard of review for the review of classifications based on illegitimacy.[2] Under this intermediate standard of review, a classification will be invalid unless the government demonstrates that the classification has a substantial relationship to an important government interest. This standard had been formally adopted for gender classifications some years earlier.[3] The Court's decisions in illegitimacy and gender cases have an ad hoc quality, because the application of an intermediate standard of review depends on the judicial assessment of the facts in an individual case and an assessment of whether the particular classification truly promotes an important government interest.[4]

The Court will invalidate state laws that place unnecessary roadblocks to proof of paternity. For example, under the state statute at issue in *Mills v. Habluetzel*,[5] the failure of an illegitimate child (with his guardian) to file a paternity suit within the first year of the child's life resulted in the illegitimate being forever barred from the right to sue his natural father for support. In that case, the Court also required that restrictions relating to illegitimacy must be substantially related to a legitimate state interest.[6] The Court rejected the state assertion that legitimacy classifications promoted the continuation of the institutions of family and marriage; the Court repeated that imposing disabilities on the illegitimate child is contrary to the basic principle of our law that burdens should bear some relationship to individual responsibility or wrongdoing.[7] However, this unanimous judgment of the Court was made in the context of a strict and substantial restriction on the rights of illegitimates to obtain parental support. Restrictions of lesser magnitude on the rights of an illegitimate child to seek support from his or her natural father may result in a divided Court upholding or striking a particular illegitimacy classification based on the Justices' differing views of the purpose and effect of the restriction.

Following *Mills*, the Justices were unanimous in invalidating a two-year statute of limitations on paternity actions brought by illegitimate children[8] and a six-year statute

2. Clark v. Jeter, 486 U.S. 456, 108 S.Ct. 1910, 100 L.Ed.2d 465 (1988). In *Clark*, Justice O'Connor wrote for a unanimous court in finding that a state's six-year statute of limitations on support actions by illegitimate children was invalid because it did not treat illegitimate children as favorably as legitimate children who sued a parent for support; the distinction between legitimate and illegitimate children was not substantially related to an important interest, such as the interest in avoiding stale or fraudulent claims being brought in the courts. Justice O'Connor's opinion formally adopted the intermediate standard of review for illegitimacy cases, which had been used in gender classification cases and which requires a classification to be "substantially related to an important governmental objective." 486 U.S. at 461, 108 S.Ct. at 1914.

3. For a review of the development and application of the intermediate scrutiny test in gender classification cases, see §§ 14.22, 14.23 of this Treatise.

4. For an overview of standards of review under the equal protection guarantee, see § 14.3 of this Treatise.

5. 456 U.S. 91, 102 S.Ct. 1549, 71 L.Ed.2d 770 (1982).

6. 456 U.S. at 97–99, 102 S.Ct. at 1553–55.

7. 456 U.S. at 99–101 n. 8, 102 S.Ct. at 1554–56 n. 8.

8. In Pickett v. Brown, 462 U.S. 1, 103 S.Ct. 2199, 76 L.Ed.2d 372 (1983), Justice Brennan wrote for a unanimous Court in holding invalid a state law that required a support action to be filed against the father of an illegitimate child before the child was two years old. The law did not provide a reasonable opportunity for the illegitimate child to bring support claims. Justice Brennan's opinion identified the standard of review as one requiring illegitimacy classifications to be "substantially related to a legitimate interest". Justice Brennan found that the two year limitation, which provided exceptions only for acknowledged children or children likely to become "a public charge", was not substantially related to preventing the litigation of stale or fraudulent claims.

of limitations on paternity actions by such children.[9] These statute of limitations classifications, in the view of the Court, were not substantially related to the important governmental objective of avoiding stale or fraudulent claims in the courts. The distinction in these statutes of limitations between support cases brought by legitimate children and those brought by illegitimate children could not withstand any form of judicial review beyond the most deferential rational relationship test. The Court's opinions in these cases establish the principle that any law that burdens a classification of persons solely because of the status of being illegitimate will be upheld only if the government can demonstrate that the use of the illegitimacy classification is substantially related to an important government interest.[10]

§ 14.20 Gender Classifications: Introduction

Men and women were not originally considered to stand as equals before the law. The married woman in particular was subject to severe legal disabilities at common law.[1] The passage of the Fourteenth Amendment had no immediate effect upon the use of sex-based classifications. States continued to pass, and courts continued to uphold, legislation which reflected traditional beliefs of sex-defined roles and provided distinct treatment for men and women, notably in regard to employment opportunities and jury duty.

The earliest challenge to unequal treatment of women arose under the privileges and immunities clause of the Fourteenth Amendment. These challenges were unsuccessful chiefly because of the narrow construction given to this phrase by the Supreme Court. The clause was construed to encompass only those privileges or immunities which resulted from national, as opposed to state, citizenship.[2]

Similarly, the Court originally gave the equal protection clause a very narrow interpretation which indicated that it would not provide any support for equal rights for women. Discussing the scope of the clause, the Court, in 1872, stated that it very much doubted "whether any action of a state not directly by way of discrimination against the [N]egro as a class, or on account of their race, will ever be held to come within the purview of this provision."[3]

Although the equal protection clause was soon found to apply to other arbitrary classifications besides race, prior to 1971 sex-based classifications were treated exactly as were general economic regulations. When the Court was taking an active role in the evaluation of economic regulation under substantive due process, it took a correspondingly active role in the evaluation of statutes which treated women differently from men. The Court generally upheld these statutes because it agreed with the legislatures that it was necessary to give women special treatment; however, where the Court found special treatment was not needed, it struck the legislation. Following the repudiation of substantive due process,[4] the Court treated all economic and social welfare legislation—including all sex-based classifications—with great judicial deference. The Court engaged in independent judicial review only when a fundamental right or suspect class was involved.

---

9. In Clark v. Jeter, 486 U.S. 456, 108 S.Ct. 1910, 100 L.Ed.2d 465 (1988), Justice O'Connor wrote for a unanimous Court in holding invalid a state law that required a support (paternity) action to be filed against the father of an illegitimate child before the illegitimate was six years old when other state statutes allowed a legitimate child to seek support from his or her parents at any time. The primary importance of the *Clark* was not the ruling, which merely followed prior decisions of the Supreme Court regarding the use of an arbitrary statute of limitations to burden illegitimate children, but Justice O'Connor's opinion, which found that illegitimacy classifications should be subject to the same "intermediate scrutiny" as classifications based on sex.

10. Id.

§ 14.20

1. The married woman would for example lack the legal capacity to contract or convey property. She could also not be held criminally responsible for an act done at her husband's direction.

2. Slaughter–House Cases, 83 U.S. (16 Wall.) 36, 21 L.Ed. 394 (1872).

3. Slaughter-House Cases, 83 U.S. at 81.

4. See § 11.4, supra.

In 1971, in *Reed v. Reed*,[5] the Supreme Court broke from this tradition and engaged in the independent judicial review of a statute which discriminated between persons on the basis of sex, without declaring sex to be a suspect classification. It soon became clear that the Court would no longer treat sex-based classifications with the judicial deference given economic regulations; however, it became equally clear that such classifications are not subject to the "strict scrutiny" given to truly suspect classifications such as those based upon race. For a five year period, the Court struggled with the appropriate standard or review to be applied in gender-based discriminations.

In 1976, *Craig v. Boren* [6] defined an intermediate level of review for the examination of sex-based classifications. "To withstand constitutional challenge, classifications by gender must serve important governmental objectives and must be substantially related to achievement of those objectives." [7] This "substantial relationship to an important interest" standard has been applied by a majority in the sex discrimination cases following *Craig*. In the

cases since *Craig*, the Justices have often been divided on the meaning of the *Craig* standard and the degree of freedom that will be allowed the government to employ sex-based classifications.

The Court has invalidated statutory provisions that entitled women workers to less benefits for their family than their male counterparts.[8] Preferential treatment for women has been upheld where it is compensatory for past discrimination against women as a class,[9] but not when it unreasonably denied benefits to men.[10] The Court has also invalidated age-sex differentials in the context of entitlement to support payments[11] and in the sale of alcoholic beverages.[12] But the Court has upheld sex-based classifications when a majority of the Justices believed that the classification reasonably advanced a state interest that the majority found to be significant. Thus, the Court has upheld differentiations between the rights of mothers and fathers of illegitimate children to bring a wrongful death action following the death of the child,[13] a statutory rape law that punished only adult men who had sexual inter-

---

5. 404 U.S. 71, 92 S.Ct. 251, 30 L.Ed.2d 225 (1971).

6. 429 U.S. 190, 97 S.Ct. 451, 50 L.Ed.2d 397 (1976).

7. 429 U.S. at 197, 97 S.Ct. at 457.

8. Frontiero v. Richardson, 411 U.S. 677, 93 S.Ct. 1764, 36 L.Ed.2d 583 (1973); Weinberger v. Wiesenfeld, 420 U.S. 636, 95 S.Ct. 1225, 43 L.Ed.2d 514 (1975); Wengler v. Druggists Mutual Insurance Co., 446 U.S. 142, 100 S.Ct. 1540, 64 L.Ed.2d 107 (1980).

9. Kahn v. Shevin, 416 U.S. 351, 94 S.Ct. 1734, 40 L.Ed.2d 189 (1974); Califano v. Webster, 430 U.S. 313, 97 S.Ct. 1192, 51 L.Ed.2d 360 (1977).

10. Califano v. Goldfarb, 430 U.S. 199, 97 S.Ct. 1021, 51 L.Ed.2d 270 (1977); Wengler v. Druggists Mutual Insurance Co., 446 U.S. 142, 100 S.Ct. 1540, 64 L.Ed.2d 107 (1980), on remand 601 S.W.2d 8 (Mo.1980).

Although the Supreme Court has consistently invalidated those provisions of governmental pension or benefit systems which require husbands or widowers (but not wives or widows) to prove dependency upon a worker or deceased worker in order to receive benefits, the Court has upheld the use of such a classification on a temporary basis to relieve demonstrable economic hardship suffered by female spouses. Thus, after the Supreme Court had invalidated the gender-based classification in the spousal benefit provisions of the Social Security Act in Califano v. Goldfarb, 430 U.S. 199, 97 S.Ct. 1021, 51 L.Ed.2d 270 (1977), Congress repealed the improper dependency requirement that made husbands or widowers (but not wives or widows) of retired or deceased workers demon-

strate dependency on the wage-earning wives in order to receive spousal benefits. However, because elimination of the dependency test would increase the number of persons entitled to spousal benefits and could create a severe fiscal problem for the social security system, Congress established a "pension offset" provision. This offset required a reduction in spousal benefits to any individual by the amount of money that that individual received from certain federal or state government pensions. Congress exempted from the pension offset requirement (until December 1982) those spouses who would have qualified for unreduced benefits under the Act as it was in effect in 1977, before the Supreme Court's ruling in *Goldfarb*. This exemption had the effect of extending for a five-year period the gender-based classification in the old social security system. The Supreme Court in Heckler v. Mathews, 465 U.S. 728, 104 S.Ct. 1387, 79 L.Ed.2d 646 (1984), upheld this classification under the intermediate standard of review, which requires the gender-based classification to be substantially related to the achievement of an important governmental interest. See §14.23, infra.

11. Stanton v. Stanton, 421 U.S. 7, 95 S.Ct. 1373, 43 L.Ed.2d 688 (1975), on remand 552 P.2d 112 (Utah 1976), state court decision after remand vacated 429 U.S. 501, 97 S.Ct. 717, 50 L.Ed.2d 723 (1977).

12. Craig v. Boren, 429 U.S. 190, 97 S.Ct. 451, 50 L.Ed.2d 397 (1976).

13. Parham v. Hughes, 441 U.S. 347, 99 S.Ct. 1742, 60 L.Ed.2d 269 (1979).

course with a child of the opposite sex,[14] and the exemption of women from military draft registration.[15]

The exclusion of insurance payments for costs related to pregnancy from employee benefits has been found not to constitute a classification by sex and upheld by a majority of the Justices,[16] even though overly restrictive maternity leave regulations and ineligibility for unemployment benefits based upon pregnancy status were found to be violative of due process.[17] While the Court has invalidated a state law that prohibited men from attending a state operated nursing school, it is not clear that a majority would find "separate but equal" male-only and female-only state-funded schools to violate the equal protection guarantee.

These rulings lead one to believe that the Court's decisions in this area are *ad hoc* decisions dependent on whether the Justices believe that a law is based on a sexual stereotype or was intended to promote a significant governmental interest. Perhaps it is inevitable that Court decisions will have an ad hoc quality to them whenever judges employ an intermediate standard of review that requires them

to examine the asserted governmental interests and the relationship of the law to those interests. It is important to remember, however, that the Court continues to employ the substantial relationship to an important state interest standard when reviewing governmental classifications that are based on sex.[18]

The Supreme Court has continued to apply the intermediate standard of review in gender cases, despite statements in recent opinions noting that the Court has not made a ruling on whether gender classifications might ever be considered to be a suspect classification.[19] The Supreme Court has left open the possibility that, in the future, gender classifications will be considered to be suspect classifications and subject to strict judicial scrutiny. If the Supreme Court ruled that gender classifications were suspect classifications, the government would be required to prove that any intentional use of a gender classification was narrowly tailored to promote a compelling interest.

The intermediate standard, employed by majority opinions in gender classification cases beginning in 1976, requires the government to demonstrate that a classification has a sub-

---

14. Michael M. v. Superior Court, 450 U.S. 464, 101 S.Ct. 1200, 67 L.Ed.2d 437 (1981).

15. Rostker v. Goldberg, 453 U.S. 57, 101 S.Ct. 2646, 69 L.Ed.2d 478 (1981).

16. Geduldig v. Aiello, 417 U.S. 484, 94 S.Ct. 2485, 41 L.Ed.2d 256 (1974).

17. Cleveland Bd. of Education v. LaFleur, 414 U.S. 632, 94 S.Ct. 791, 39 L.Ed.2d 52 (1974); Turner v. Department of Employment, 423 U.S. 44, 96 S.Ct. 249, 46 L.Ed.2d 181 (1975).

18. It may be that "equal" treatment of workers is inherently unequal if the employer or the government does not take into account the employment difficulties faced by pregnant women. Differing governmental treatment of persons based upon biological differences between the genders, however, could mask governmental acts that would disadvantage women. For references to cases, and secondary authorities, on this point see the multi-volume edition of this Treatise: R. Rotunda & J. Nowak, Treatise on Constitutional Law: Substance and Procedure §§ 14.3, 14.20 (3rd ed. 1999, with annual supplements).

19. In J.E.B. v. Alabama ex rel. T.B., 511 U.S. 127, 114 S.Ct. 1419, 128 L.Ed.2d 89 (1994), the Supreme Court ruled that a government attorney's use of preemptory challenges to exclude members of one sex from the jury violated the equal protection clause. Justice Blackmun's

majority opinion in *J.E.B.* noted that the Court did not have to address the question of what standard of review was appropriate in gender cases and that the Court had not excluded the possibility of gender becoming a suspect classification. 511 U.S. at 137 n. 6, 114 S.Ct. at 1425 n. 6.

In Harris v. Forklift Systems, 510 U.S. 17, 114 S.Ct. 367, 126 L.Ed.2d 295 (1993) the Supreme Court ruled that an employer would be in violation of Title VII of the Civil Rights Act if the employer's employees created an abusive or hostile work environment for women. Justice Ginsburg wrote a concurring opinion in *Forklift Systems* in which she stated that there "remains an open question whether classifications based on gender are inherently suspect." 510 U.S. at 26, 114 S.Ct. at 373 (Ginsburg, J., concurring) (internal quotations and citations omitted).

In 1998, the Justices were unable to agree on the standard of review that should be applied to a gender classification in a naturalization law. In Miller v. Albright, 523 U.S. 420, 118 S.Ct. 1428 140 L.Ed.2d 575 (1998) the Supreme Court, without a majority opinion, refused to invalidate a federal statute that granted citizenship at birth to an illegitimate child born outside of the United States to a U.S. citizen mother and a non-citizen, but granted citizenship for an illegitimate child born outside of the United States to a U.S. citizen father and a non-citizen mother only if the father complied with statutory conditions. The *Miller* case is examined in § 14.23.

stantial relationship to an important interest.[20] As an alternative to declaring gender classifications to be suspect, the Court might modify the intermediate standard of review used in gender classification cases.

In *Mississippi University for Women v. Hogan*,[21] the Supreme Court found that a state violated the equal protection clause by having a state nursing school that was opened only to women students. The majority opinion, by Justice O'Connor, ruled that the government had failed to prove that the sex classification (limiting the school to women students) was substantially related to important governmental objectives. Because the government failed to meet that standard of review, Justice O'Connor found it unnecessary to decide whether gender classification should be subject to strict judicial scrutiny and the compelling interest test.[22]

In *United States v. Virginia*[23] the Supreme Court ruled that a state's creation, and continued operation, of a university [the Virginia Military Institute] for male students only violated the equal protection clause. [Hereinafter this case will be referred to as the V.M.I. case.] Justice Ginsburg wrote a majority for six Justices in the V.M.I. case; Chief Justice Rehnquist concurred only in the judgment of the Court.[24] Justice Scalia dissented in the V.M.I. case.[25] Justice Thomas did not participate in the case.

Justice Ginsburg, in the V.M.I. case, referred to the intermediate standard of review

as the minimum standard that would be applied in a gender classification case. The majority opinion stated that the government "must show at least that the [challenged] classification serves important governmental objectives and that the discriminatory means employed are substantially related to those objectives."[26] At more than one place in the majority opinion, Justice Ginsburg stated that the government in a gender discrimination case must offer "exceedingly persuasive" proof that the different treatment of men and women was justified.[27] The government would have the burden of proving that there was a real difference between men and women that related to the government's objective.[28] The majority ruled that the state had failed to prove that the educational opportunities offered at the Virginia Military Institute campus could not be achieved if the school admitted female as well as male students.

Chief Justice Rehnquist, who at one time had opposed the use of the intermediate standard for gender cases, concurred only in the judgment in the V.M.I. case.[29] The Chief Justice believed that the substantial relationship to an important governmental interest test, which had been used in gender cases by the Supreme Court from 1976 to 1996, was a clearer standard than the "exceedingly persuasive justification" standard referred to in parts of the majority opinion.[30] No other Justice joined the Chief Justice's concurrence in the V.M.I. case.

20. This standard was first used in Craig v. Boren, 429 U.S. 190, 97 S.Ct. 451, 50 L.Ed.2d 397 (1976). See §§ 14.22, 14.23 of this Treatise.

21. 458 U.S. 718, 724 n. 9, 102 S.Ct. 3331, 3336 n. 9, 73 L.Ed.2d 1090 (1982).

22. 458 U.S. at 724, n. 9, 102 S.Ct. at 3336, n. 9.

23. 518 U.S. 515, 116 S.Ct. 2264, 135 L.Ed.2d 735 (1996).

24. 518 U.S. at 556, 116 S.Ct. at 2287 (Rehnquist, C.J., concurring in the judgment).

25. 518 U.S. at 564, 116 S.Ct. at 2291 (Scalia, J., dissenting).

26. United States v. Virginia, 518 U.S. 515, 116 S.Ct. 2264, 2275, 135 L.Ed.2d 735 (1996).

27. 518 U.S. at 529, 531, 556, 116 S.Ct. at 2274, 2275, 2287. The "exceedingly persuasive justification" phrase had been used in Justice Marshall's majority opinion in

Kirchberg v. Feenstra, 450 U.S. 455, 461, 101 S.Ct. 1195, 1199, 67 L.Ed.2d 428 (1981).

28. 518 U.S. at 533, 116 S.Ct. at 2276.

29. United States v. Virginia, 518 U.S. 515, 556, 116 S.Ct. 2264, 2287, 135 L.Ed.2d 735 (1996) (Rehnquist, C.J., concurring in the judgment). Then Justice Rehnquist had opposed using a standard other than the rationality standard for gender classifications in cases such as Craig v. Boren, 429 U.S. 190, 217, 97 S.Ct. 451, 467, 50 L.Ed.2d 397 (1976) (Rehnquist, J., dissenting) and Frontiero v. Richardson, 411 U.S. 677, 691, 93 S.Ct. 1764, 1773, 36 L.Ed.2d 583 (1973) (Rehnquist, J., dissenting). See also, Weinberger v. Wiesenfeld, 420 U.S. 636, 655, 95 S.Ct. 1225, 1236–37, 43 L.Ed.2d 514 (1975) (Rehnquist, J., concurring).

30. United States v. Virginia, 518 U.S. 515, 558, 116 S.Ct. 2264, 2288, 135 L.Ed.2d 735 (1996) (Rehnquist, C.J., concurring in the judgment). See note 27, supra.

Justice Scalia, dissenting in the V.M.I. case, believed that the majority, in fact, had not used the intermediate standard of review.[31] He believed the state had an important interest in providing military oriented college education and that the creation of one sex colleges was substantially related to that end.[32] Justice Scalia asserted that, under the intermediate standard, the Court should have allowed Virginia to provide single sex military education for males at one school and some similar alternative education for females at a separate school. No other Justice joined Justice Scalia's view that the Virginia Military Institute's one sex policy could have been upheld under the intermediate standard.

Chief Justice Rehnquist's concurrence and Justice Scalia's dissent both asserted that the majority was not using the substantial relationship to an important interest test that had been used during the previous twenty years in gender classification cases. Justice Ginsburg's majority opinion in the V.M.I. case might be signaling a change in, and strengthening of, the intermediate standard in gender classification cases.

§ 14.21 Gender Classifications: Cases Prior to *Reed v. Reed*

Bradwell v. Illinois,[1] in 1873, was the first case in which the constitutionality of different treatment for men and women was challenged. Relying upon the privileges and immunities clause of the Fourteenth Amendment, Bradwell challenged the refusal of the Illinois Su-

preme Court to grant her a license to practice law solely because she was a woman. On appeal to the United States Supreme Court, Bradwell maintained that she was entitled to a license to practice because the Fourteenth Amendment "opens to every citizen of the United States, male or female, black or white, married or single, the honorable professions as well as the simple enjoyments of life."[2] The Supreme Court rejected this argument, affirming the state court decision with but one dissent.[3] Earlier that Term, the Court had held that the privileges and immunities clause protected only those privileges and immunities which were the result of United States citizenship.[4] The concurring Justices upheld the different treatment of women because it was mandated by "the law of the creator."[5] Job opportunities for women were necessarily more limited than for men; women were not suited for occupations with highly special qualifications and responsibilities. The "paramount destiny and mission of womanhood are to fulfill the noble and benign offices of wife and mother." The views quoted here were representative of the attitudes women met when they attempted to challenge sex-based classifications.

The Court in two cases following *Bradwell* upheld the denial of these rights to women.[6] Subsequent Supreme Court decisions have forbidden arbitrary denial of admission to state bars[7] and the passage of the Nineteenth Amendment in 1920 extended to women the right to vote.

---

31. United States v. Virginia, 518 U.S. 515, 564, 116 S.Ct. 2264, 2291, 2293–94, 135 L.Ed.2d 735 (1996) (Scalia, J., dissenting).

32. This analysis appears in part II of Justice Scalia's dissenting opinion in the V.M.I. case. 518 U.S. at 568–75, 116 S.Ct. at 2293–96 (Scalia, J., dissenting).

§ 14.21

1. 83 U.S. (16 Wall.) 130, 21 L.Ed. 442 (1872).

2. 83 U.S. at 137 (1873), argument of Mr. Matthew Hall Carpenter for the plaintiff-in-error.

3. Chief Justice Chase, the lone dissenter, filed no opinion.

4. Slaughter–House Cases, 83 U.S. (16 Wall.) 36, 21 L.Ed. 394 (1872). The privileges and immunities clause of Article IV § 2 was inapplicable because Bradwell was an Illinois citizen.

5. Although the method of communication between the Creator and the judge was never disclosed, "divine ordinance" was a dominant theme in justifying sex classifications. R. Ginsburg, Constitutional Aspects of Sex-Based Discrimination (1974).

6. In re Lockwood, 154 U.S. 116, 14 S.Ct. 1082, 38 L.Ed. 929 (1894) (Woman admitted to bars of Supreme Court and District of Columbia could be denied admission to state bar of Virginia); Minor v. Happersett, 88 U.S. (21 Wall.) 162, 22 L.Ed. 627 (1874) (Statute limiting right to vote to men).

7. Application of Griffiths, 413 U.S. 717, 93 S.Ct. 2851, 37 L.Ed.2d 910 (1973), on remand 165 Conn. 807, 309 A.2d 689 (1973) (aliens). The issue has not arisen in recent years in regard to women.

Prior to 1937, the Court took an active role in the review of economic regulation.[8] During this period a majority of the Justices engaged in an independent review of the reasonableness and legitimacy of sex-based classifications just as they did for other forms of legislation. As a result of independent judicial review, the Court held in *Lochner v. New York*[9] that a state law setting maximum hours for bakers was invalid because it was not a legitimate exercise of police power and, in the Court's view, an unnecessary regulation which interfered with an individual's liberty to contract.

However, three years later *Muller v. Oregon*[10] upheld a statute prohibiting the employment of women "in any mechanical establishment, or factory, or laundry for more than ten hours a day." The Court rejected the argument of the defendant, a male laundry operator charged with violating the statute, that *Lochner* was controlling. That position incorrectly "assume[d] that the difference between the sexes [did] not justify a different rule respecting a restriction of the hours of labor."[11]

After stating the right to contract was not absolute but subject to reasonable restrictions, the majority opinion engaged in an extended discussion of the differences between men and women which justified the special legislation. That a woman's physical structure and her performance of maternal functions rendered her less capable of prolonged toil was a widespread belief as well as a proposition supported by medical testimony.[12] "[A]nd as healthy mothers are essential to vigorous off-

spring, the physical well-being of a woman becomes an object of public interest and care in order to preserve the strength and vigor of the race."[13]

Although the Court continued to uphold similar legislation prescribing maximum hours for women,[14] it did not uphold all laws designed to protect women workers. The Justices determined for themselves whether such treatment was a reasonable means of promoting legitimate state goals. Where the Court was in disagreement with the legislature, the statute was invalid. In *Adkins v. Children's Hospital*[15] the Court found the setting of minimum wages for women was a violation of due process, because it restricted the liberty to contract and there was no showing of a need for women to be treated differently in that regard.

However, in 1937, the Court, giving great deference to the legislative judgment, upheld a minimum wage standard for women and reversed *Adkins*.[16] Four years later the Court upheld federal maximum hours and minimum wage requirements for both men and women.[17]

The Supreme Court in 1937 retreated from its active role and began to treat economic regulations with great deference.[18] The Court employed independent judicial review only where a statutory provision affected a "fundamental right" or contained a classification by a "suspect class" such as race, a category which did not and still does not include sex. Classifications based on sex, therefore, were treated with the same deference given economic legis-

---

8. For a discussion of the Court's role prior to 1937, see § 11.3, supra.

9. 198 U.S. 45, 25 S.Ct. 539, 49 L.Ed. 937 (1905).

10. 208 U.S. 412, 28 S.Ct. 324, 52 L.Ed. 551 (1908).

11. 208 U.S. at 419, 28 S.Ct. at 325.

12. In a footnote the Court referred to the brief of those who sought to uphold the law (now known as the "Brandeis brief" but which was primarily the work of Josephine Goldmark) which contained citations to state and foreign laws restricting hours of labor and extracts of over 90 reports of detrimental effects of long working hours upon women. 208 U.S. at 419 n. 1, 28 S.Ct. at 325 n. 1.

13. 208 U.S. at 421, 28 S.Ct. at 326–27.

14. Bosley v. McLaughlin, 236 U.S. 385, 35 S.Ct. 345, 59 L.Ed. 632 (1915); Miller v. Wilson, 236 U.S. 373, 35 S.Ct. 342, 59 L.Ed. 628 (1915); Hawley v. Walker, 232

U.S. 718, 34 S.Ct. 479, 58 L.Ed. 813 (1914); Riley v. Massachusetts, 232 U.S. 671, 34 S.Ct. 469, 58 L.Ed. 788 (1914).

15. 261 U.S. 525, 43 S.Ct. 394, 67 L.Ed. 785 (1923). *Adkins* was reaffirmed in Morehead v. New York ex rel. Tipaldo, 298 U.S. 587, 56 S.Ct. 918, 80 L.Ed. 1347 (1936). See § 11.3, supra.

16. West Coast Hotel Co. v. Parrish, 300 U.S. 379, 57 S.Ct. 578, 81 L.Ed. 703 (1937).

17. United States v. Darby, 312 U.S. 100, 61 S.Ct. 451, 85 L.Ed. 609 (1941).

18. For a discussion of the Court's retreat and its post-1937 treatment of economic legislation, see §§ 11.4–11.7, 14.3, supra.

lation and were upheld if they rationally related to a legitimate goal of the legislature.

An example of post-1937 judicial deference to the use of sex-based classifications is *Goesaert v. Cleary*.[19] In this case the Court upheld a Michigan statute which provided that no female would be licensed as a bartender unless she was the wife or daughter of the male owner of a licensed liquor establishment. The statute was challenged as being violative of equal protection because it discriminated between the wives and daughters of owners and the wives and daughters of nonowners. The majority began with the proposition that Michigan could bar all women from being bartenders. The issue of total exclusion was not addressed by the dissent and even the plaintiff centered her argument on the exception for wives and daughters of male owners rather than on the general exclusion.[20]

The question addressed by the majority, therefore, was whether, in view of the general prohibition of women bartenders, the state could make an exception in favor of the wives and daughters of bar owners. The majority opinion found that bartending by women might "in the allowable legislative judgment" create the need for preventive measures against moral and social problems. The majority would defer to the legislative belief that for a defined class of women other factors reduced these problems so that different treatment could be accorded them. As long as the belief in the distinction was "entertainable"— not totally irrational—the classification did not violate the equal protection clause. The Court did not question whether this rationale was supportable in fact.

When freed of the need to defer to legislative or executive judgments, the Court showed some awareness of the claim to sexual equality. In *United States v. Dege*[21] the Court reject-

ed the argument that a husband and wife were incapable of conspiracy. Such an immunity would require one of two assumptions: either that responsibility of both for joint participation in crime would cause marital disharmony or that the wife must be presumed to act under the coercive influence of her husband and, therefore, could never be a willing participant. "The former assumption is unnourished by sense; the latter implies a view of American womanhood offensive to the ethos of our society."[22] The latter would also require the disregard of the "vast change in the status of women—the extension of her rights and correlative duties."[23]

A year later, in *Hoyt v. Florida*,[24] the Court upheld statutory provisions which made males eligible for jury duty unless they requested an exemption but granted females an exemption unless they waived it and registered their desire to be placed on the jury list. The Court declined the invitation to consider the continuing validity of earlier dictum to the effect that a state may constitutionally confine jury duty to males. This case presented the narrower issue of the validity of the exemption of women. The relevant inquiry was whether the exemption itself was based upon a reasonable classification.[25]

Hoyt found that "despite the enlightened emancipation of women from the restrictions and protections of bygone years, and their entry into many parts of community life formerly considered to be reserved to men, woman is still regarded as the center of the home and family life."[26] The Court could not say that "it is constitutionally impermissible for a state, acting in pursuit of its general welfare, to conclude that a woman should be relieved from the civic duty of jury service unless she herself determines that such service is consistent with her own special responsibilities."[27] The state might have exempted only those

---

19. 335 U.S. 464, 69 S.Ct. 198, 93 L.Ed. 163 (1948).

20. R. Ginsburg, Constitutional Aspects of Sex-Based Discrimination 24 (1974).

21. 364 U.S. 51, 80 S.Ct. 1589, 4 L.Ed.2d 1563 (1960).

22. 364 U.S. at 53, 80 S.Ct. at 1591.

23. 364 U.S. at 54, 80 S.Ct. at 1591.

24. 368 U.S. 57, 82 S.Ct. 159, 7 L.Ed.2d 118 (1961).

25. Chief Justice Warren and Justices Douglas and Black concurred, finding that the statute did not discriminate on the basis of sex. 368 U.S. at 69, 82 S.Ct. at 166–67.

26. 368 U.S. at 61–62, 82 S.Ct. at 162–63.

27. 368 U.S. at 62, 82 S.Ct. at 162–63.

women with family responsibilities, but it was not irrational for a state to decide on a broad exemption, if it found such an exemption more administratively feasible. *Hoyt* gave great deference to the state but it would be overruled following the Court's decision to give meaningful review to sex-based classifications.[28]

§ 14.22 Gender Classifications: Definition of a Standard—From *Reed v. Reed* to *Craig v. Boren*

It must be remembered that prior to 1971 the Supreme Court had always reviewed sex-based classifications under the equal protection clause in the same manner that it reviewed purely economic classifications. In 1971, in *Reed v. Reed*,[1] the Supreme Court for the first time offered realistic protection against sex discrimination under the equal protection guarantee. *Reed* involved a challenge to an Idaho statute which established a scheme for the selection of the administrator of an intestate estate. Under the statute eligible persons were grouped into eleven categories by their relationship to the decedent and the categories were ranked in an order which was to be determinative if it was necessary to select between two competing applicants. The challenged portion of the statute provided that if it was necessary to select between two competing applicants in the same category the male was to be preferred over the female. As construed by the Idaho Supreme Court, the statutory preference for males was mandatory and was to be given effect without regard to individual qualifications.

The Supreme Court of the United States unanimously held that the arbitrary preference for males could not withstand constitutional attack. The opinion did not find sex classifications to be "suspect" and there was

no direct challenge to a legislature's power to classify persons by gender. But the opinion impliedly challenged the power to provide different treatment of persons on the basis of their sex when that was unrelated to the legitimate objective of a statute. "A classification must be reasonable, not arbitrary and must rest upon some ground of difference having a fair and substantial relation to that object of the legislation, so that all persons similarly circumstanced shall be treated alike."[2]

The question thus presented in *Reed* was whether the difference in the sex of the administrator had a rational relationship to some permissible objective of the statute. While the objective of reducing the workload by eliminating one class of contests is not without some legitimacy, the crucial question is whether the preference of males advances that objective in a manner consistent with the command of the equal protection clause. The Court's conclusion was that it did not. "To give a mandatory preference to members of either sex over members of the other, merely to accomplish the elimination of hearings on the merits, is to make the very kind of arbitrary legislative choice forbidden by the Equal Protection Clause of the Fourteenth Amendment; and whatever may be said as to the positive values of avoiding intrafamily controversy, the choice in this context may not lawfully be mandated solely on the basis of sex."[3]

This test was not the traditional rational relation test applied by the Court in *Goesaert* and *Hoyt*. Under the rationality test used in those cases, the statute could have been found to be related to a permissible purpose similar to the administrative convenience purpose of the statute in *Hoyt*. It would have been easier and less costly for the probate courts to choose administrators if one class of claimants (wom-

---

28. The Supreme Court distinguished *Hoyt* when it ruled that the jury trial provision of the Sixth Amendment meant that women could not be excluded from jury service, Taylor v. Louisiana, 419 U.S. 522, 95 S.Ct. 692, 42 L.Ed.2d 690 (1975). In J.E.B. v. Alabama ex rel. T.B., 511 U.S. 127, 134 n. 5, 114 S.Ct. 1419, 1424 n. 5, 128 L.Ed.2d 89 (1994) the Court ruled that the use of peremptory challenges by a government attorney to exclude persons of one sex from the jury would violate the equal protection clause; the majority opinion in *J.E.B.* stated that *Taylor*

had effectively overruled *Hoyt*. These cases are discussed in §§ 14.22, 14.23.

§ 14.22

1. 404 U.S. 71, 92 S.Ct. 251, 30 L.Ed.2d 225 (1971), mandate conformed 94 Idaho 542, 493 P.2d 701 (1972).

2. 404 U.S. at 76, 92 S.Ct. at 254, quoting F.S. Royster Guano Co. v. Virginia, 253 U.S. 412, 415, 40 S.Ct. 560, 561, 64 L.Ed. 989 (1920).

3. 404 U.S. at 76–77, 92 S.Ct. at 254.

en) were eliminated. The Court, however, found that the manner by which the objective was to be accomplished was arbitrary. Clearly the statute was not designed to pick the most competent administrators unless it was based on a theory that women were not as capable as men to administer the estate; the Court's refusal to defer to the use of such an assumption allowed it to find the classification arbitrary. The Court determined that the state's interest in judicial efficiency was less important than the interest of women in equal treatment with respect to the purpose of choosing qualified administrators of decedents' estates.

In the five years following *Reed*, the Court considered a variety of sex-based classifications without agreement among the Justices on the appropriate standard of review.[4] A majority of the Justices were committed to independently reviewing the reasonableness of these classifications but could not agree on a standard of review between the traditionally weak rational basis test and the almost insurmountable "strict scrutiny" or "compelling interest" test. Cases decided during this five-year period are instructive both in terms of giving one a basis for predicting the outcome of future cases and for help in understanding that different Justices may be employing quite differing tests for the legitimacy of gender classifications even though they assert in their opinions to be applying a test agreed upon by a majority of the Justices.

In the term following *Reed* the Court in *Frontiero v. Richardson*[5] faced a question concerning the rights of a female member of the uniformed services to claim her spouse as a "dependent" for the purposes of obtaining increased quarters allowances and medical and dental benefits. A serviceman could automati-

cally claim his wife as a dependent without regard to whether she was in fact dependent upon him; a servicewoman was required to show her husband was in fact dependent upon her for over half of his support. The question before the Court was whether this difference in treatment constituted a violation of the due process clause of the Fifth Amendment.[6] With one dissent,[7] the Court found it was.

Justice Brennan, in a plurality opinion, stated that sex was a suspect class, finding implicit support in the unanimous decision in *Reed*. Brennan reached this decision after examining the history and nature of discrimination against women. However, this view of sex as a suspect class never gained the support of a majority of Justices voting in a single case. Furthermore, later opinions show that although Justices Douglas and White joined in the Brennan opinion even they did not actually mean that sex was a suspect class in the same way as racial classifications. The concurring Justices found that such a declaration was unnecessary to reach a decision in this case and that the Court should await the outcome of the proposed Equal Rights Amendment before ruling on the suspect class issue.

After concluding sex was a suspect class, Justice Brennan engaged in a discussion of the rationale behind the statutory provision. The only justification offered by the government for the differential treatment was administrative convenience. Congress might have found it easier to conclusively presume wives were dependent, but require proof that a servicewoman's husband was in fact dependent. However, no concrete evidence was introduced which showed that the government did in fact save money. The government's explanation failed to convince the Court that there were

---

4. For references to additional cases, and secondary authorities, on this point see the multi-volume edition of this Treatise: R. Rotunda & J. Nowak, Treatise on Constitutional Law: Substance and Procedure §§ 18.20—18.24 (3rd ed. 1999, with annual supplements).

5. 411 U.S. 677, 93 S.Ct. 1764, 36 L.Ed.2d 583 (1973).

6. While the Fifth Amendment contains no equal protection clause as the Fourteenth Amendment does, it has been recognized that a classification may be so arbitrary as to be a denial of due process. E.g., Bolling v. Sharpe, 347 U.S. 497, 74 S.Ct. 693, 98 L.Ed. 884 (1954).

The Court has held that gender discrimination by the federal government or its agents gives rise to a cause of action under the due process clause of the Fifth Amendment. See Davis v. Passman, 442 U.S. 228, 99 S.Ct. 2264, 60 L.Ed.2d 846 (1979).

7. Justice Rehnquist dissented. Frontiero v. Richardson, 411 U.S. 677, 691, 93 S.Ct. 1764, 1773, 36 L.Ed.2d 583 (1973) (Rehnquist, J., dissenting).

sufficient grounds upon which to base the classification. As in *Reed*, the legislative judgment was no longer treated with great judicial deference; the Justices asked for proof that the classification actually achieved legitimate legislative goals.

In *Kahn v. Shevin*[8] a widower brought suit claiming denial of equal protection of the laws because a Florida statute allowed widows a $500 property tax exemption but provided no analogous exemption for widowers. The Court believed that the financial difficulties confronting a surviving wife exceed those facing a husband. Whether due to overt discrimination or the socialization process of a male dominated culture, she was more likely to be subject to an inhospitable job market. The difference in treatment therefore bore a sufficient relation to the legislative objective as required by *Reed*.

Justices Brennan and Marshall dissented because the governmental purpose could be served equally well by a more narrowly drafted statute. Consistent with their statement in *Frontiero* that sex was a suspect class, these Justices found that gender-based classifications could not stand merely because they promoted legitimate governmental interests. The exemption, in their opinion, was plainly over-inclusive and should have been limited to widows needing financial assistance.

In *Schlesinger v. Ballard*[9] a male Naval line officer who after nine years of active service was passed over for promotion and consequently discharged, as required by statute, unsuccessfully claimed his discharge constituted unconstitutional discrimination because women were not discharged for lack of promotion until they had been in the Navy for thirteen years. The Court distinguished the provision from those in *Reed* and *Frontiero* in two respects. First, the differential treatment involved here was not based on an overbroad generalization as in those cases, but rather on the fact that promotion opportunities for male and female line officers differed (due to the exclusion of women from all combat and most sea duty) which might have led Congress to rationally believe that women line officers had less opportunity for promotion. Secondly, the purpose of the classification is a flow of promotion commensurate with the Navy's current needs, not mere administrative convenience.

The dissenting Justices found nothing in the legislative history to support the majority's suggestion that different treatment might have been provided to compensate women for "disadvantages visited upon them by the Navy." Furthermore, they found "quite troublesome the notion that a gender-based difference in treatment can be justified by another, broader, gender-based difference in treatment imposed directly and currently by the Navy itself."[10] The need for a correct flow of promotions could not be used to justify the distinct treatment given male and female line officers. The issue should be not whether the discharge policy promoted a legitimate or compelling state interest, but whether the differences in treatment accorded men and women could be justified.

In 1975, in *Taylor v. Louisiana*[11] the Court ruled that the practice of automatically exempting a woman from jury duty unless she waived her exemption violated a defendant's Sixth Amendment right. The exemption operated to virtually exclude women from jury venires and thus denied a criminal defendant his Sixth Amendment right to have a jury drawn from a fair cross-section of society. It was no longer tenable to suggest that jury duty would be a hardship for all women or that women could not be spared from their other duties.[12] Almost 20 years after the *Tay-*

---

8. 416 U.S. 351, 94 S.Ct. 1734, 40 L.Ed.2d 189 (1974).

9. 419 U.S. 498, 95 S.Ct. 572, 42 L.Ed.2d 610 (1975).

10. 419 U.S. at 511 n. 1, 95 S.Ct. at 579 n. 1 (1975) (dissenting opinion).

11. 419 U.S. 522, 95 S.Ct. 692, 42 L.Ed.2d 690 (1975).

12. In *Duren v. Missouri*, 439 U.S. 357, 99 S.Ct. 664, 58 L.Ed.2d 579 (1979), the Court held that a statute granting all women an exemption from jury duty upon their request also violated a defendant's Sixth Amendment right to a jury drawn from a fair cross section of the community. The exclusion of any or all women upon request could not be justified by a desire to allow some persons to stay home to meet their family responsibilities; the exception was both under and over inclusive in terms of that end. But the majority opinion, by Justice White, indicated that a precisely drawn exemption for persons that was based on individual hardship, incapacity, or other

lor decision, the Supreme Court held the intentional exclusion of persons from a jury solely because of their gender would violate equal protection principles.[13]

In *Weinberger v. Wiesenfeld*[14] the Supreme Court struck statutory provisions that conferred payments based on the earnings of a deceased husband and father upon his widow and minor children but which conferred payments based on the earnings of a deceased wife and mother only upon her minor children. While the statute could clearly have been regarded as discrimination against widowers who received no benefits, the basis of the Court's decision was the discriminatory effect upon women workers who received less protection for their survivors. The Court found the distinction between men and women was indistinguishable from the distinction invalidated in *Frontiero* because both rested upon the assumption that the earnings of male workers were vital to a family while those of female workers were not.[15]

Stanton v. Stanton[16] for the first time addressed age-sex differentials. In *Stanton* the statute in question provided that females reached majority at 18 and males at 21. As a result, the appellee had discontinued support payments ordered by the divorce decree for his daughter when she reached 18. The state court upheld the statute despite the equal protection challenge, finding that the classification had a reasonable basis in the belief that males were to provide the primary support of a home and, therefore, should receive an education. The Supreme Court reversed, relying

on *Reed*. The differences between genders did not warrant the statutory distinction in the appellee's obligation to support them. The place of women was no longer solely the home; an education was equally important for females. The Court found that "under any test—compelling state interest, or rational basis, or something in between" the different ages for reaching majority in the context of child support could not survive an equal protection attack.[17]

The Supreme Court also invalidated an Oklahoma law which permitted the sale of 3.2% beer for off-premises consumption to women at age eighteen but required males to be twenty-one in *Craig v. Boren*.[18] The Court began with the statement that previous cases had established the principle that to withstand constitutional challenge, classifications by gender must serve important governmental objectives and must be substantially related to the achievement of those objectives. A majority of the Justices now had agreed upon a specific definition for the intermediate level of review applied in gender discrimination cases.

Indeed, the Court's agreement on a standard of review was much more important than the holding in *Craig*. Under almost any form of realistic judicial review, the classification examined in *Craig* could not withstand analysis. The Court accepted traffic safety as the goal of the legislation, but found the statistical evidence could not support a conclusion that the classification reasonably served to achieve that objective. The relationship between traffic safety and the gender classification was too

---

important reasons, including the fulfillment of family responsibilities, would survive the requirement that the state demonstrate that the exemption classification serve a significant state interest.

13. J.E.B. v. Alabama ex rel. T.B., 511 U.S. 127, 114 S.Ct. 1419, 128 L.Ed.2d 89 (1994). The Court ruled in *J.E.B.* that the equal protection clause was violated by a government attorney's use of peremptory challenges to exclude men from a jury solely because of their sex.

14. 420 U.S. 636, 95 S.Ct. 1225, 43 L.Ed.2d 514 (1975).

The Supreme Court later upheld the restriction of "mothers insurance benefits", extended to fathers in *Wiesenfeld*, to those mothers or fathers of a deceased wage earner's child who had been married to the deceased wage earner prior to his or her death. Califano v. Boles, 443 U.S. 282, 99 S.Ct. 2767, 61 L.Ed.2d 541 (1979).

15. Justice Rehnquist concurred, for he found it irrational "to distinguish between mothers and fathers when the sole question [was] whether a child of a deceased contributing worker should have the opportunity to receive the full time attention for the only parent remaining to it." 420 U.S. at 655, 95 S.Ct. at 1236–37 (Rehnquist, J., concurring).

16. 421 U.S. 7, 95 S.Ct. 1373, 43 L.Ed.2d 688 (1975), lower court opinion after remand 552 P.2d 112 (Utah 1976) lower court opinion vacated 429 U.S. 501, 97 S.Ct. 717, 50 L.Ed.2d 723 (1977) (per curiam).

17. 421 U.S. at 17, 95 S.Ct. at 1379.

18. 429 U.S. 190, 97 S.Ct. 451, 50 L.Ed.2d 397 (1976).

tenuous. While it might be true that more teenage males were involved in car accidents than females, and that more teenage males were arrested for driving while intoxicated than were teenage females, there was no evidence that would substantiate the claim that a person's gender made him or her more or less likely to become a drunken driver. The classification was based upon a stereotype perception of teenage males and females. It was not substantially related to the important state interest in traffic safety.

§ 14.23   Gender Classifications: Decisions Under the Intermediate Standard of Review

After 1976, a majority of the Justices in each case involving gender discrimination have asserted that they are applying the substantial relationship to an important interest test. However, the meaning of this test is less than clear. As would be true of any intermediate standard of review, the test is one which neither prohibits the use of all gender classifications nor one which requires the Justices to defer to legislative decisions. Thus, each Justice may independently evaluate the importance of the interest which the government asserts to justify the gender classification and the reasonableness of the relationship between the gender classification and that interest. The Court's decisions appear to be *ad hoc* judgments based upon Justices' perceptions of the gender classification at issue in each case.

The major emphasis of the post-*Craig* cases has been the elimination of governmental classifications that arbitrarily burden one gender in terms of economic rights. Such laws are almost always viewed as based upon little more than sexual stereotypes. When the government employs a gender classification which

does not allocate economic rights, the Court has a difficult time analyzing the constitutionality of that gender classification.

Benign Classifications. Not all laws which allocate economic rights on the basis of gender will be invalid. Those laws which appear to the Justices to be a reasonable means of compensating women as a class for past economic discrimination will be upheld. Thus, the Court was unanimous in upholding a now superceded provision of the Social Security Act which allowed women to compute their benefits with a more favorable formula relating the past earnings than could be used by men at retirement.[1] Giving women some preference on a scale for retirement benefits which was keyed to earnings was reasonable because it compensated for the fact that discrimination in the employment market might have kept an undefinable class of women from achieving their highest potential in terms of earnings and contributions to the Social Security System.

Conversely, the Court will strike down laws giving preference to women in the economic area if the Justices believe that those laws are not reasonable means of compensating for past discrimination against women as a class. Thus, the Court struck down a provision of the Social Security System that required male, but not female, spouses of deceased wage earners to prove actual dependency in order to receive survivor's benefits.[2]

Marital Property—Alimony. In *Orr v. Orr*,[3] the Supreme Court employed the substantial relationship to an important governmental interest standard as it struck down a state law which provided that the state courts could grant alimony payments only from hus-

§ 14.23

1. Califano v. Webster, 430 U.S. 313, 97 S.Ct. 1192, 51 L.Ed.2d 360 (1977). The Court also upheld a provision of the Act that provided greater secondary benefits for a woman married to a retired wage earner than for divorced spouse of wage earner. Mathews v. De Castro, 429 U.S. 181, 97 S.Ct. 431, 50 L.Ed.2d 389 (1976).

2. Califano v. Goldfarb, 430 U.S. 199, 97 S.Ct. 1021, 51 L.Ed.2d 270 (1977).

In Heckler v. Mathews, 465 U.S. 728, 104 S.Ct. 1387, 79 L.Ed.2d 646 (1984), the Court upheld this classification

under the intermediate standard of review. Justice Brennan wrote for a unanimous Court in finding that the temporary extension of a gender-based classification was substantially related to the important governmental interest in protecting a group of women who retired before or shortly after revision of the Social Security Act from economic injury caused by their reasonable reliance on the terms of the statute as it existed in January 1977.

3. 440 U.S. 268, 99 S.Ct. 1102, 59 L.Ed.2d 306 (1979).

bands to wives and never from wives to husbands. The majority opinion, by Justice Brennan, rejected the permissibility of any goal of the state related to insuring that the husband was allocated primary responsibility for the family; the Court has consistently rejected any state interest in keeping men in a role of primary responsibility in the family.

The majority opinion did note that there were two possible objectives for such laws that might be considered sufficiently important to support a gender based classification: providing help for needy spouses and compensating women for past economic discrimination. However, the majority found that the law was impermissible because the classification did not substantially promote either important governmental interest. Indeed, the majority opinion noted that the Court did not have to engage in an analysis that would require the Justices to determine if this gender based classification was a "sufficiently accurate proxy" for need, or for compensating women as a class for past societal discrimination, because the Alabama system in fact could not promote either purpose.

Alabama, like virtually all other states, required an individualized court hearing at which the parties' financial circumstances were examined before the court entered an alimony order. Because the state required individualized hearings there was no demonstrable need to use the gender based classification as a proxy for need or as compensation for past discrimination. It would cost the state nothing to determine, at that hearing, whether the woman was financially secure and the husband in need of financial support. As there was no state goal that could not be achieved by applying a sex neutral rule at the hearing, the statutory classification was invalid.

Family Welfare Systems. The Court also employed the substantial relationship-impor-

tant interest test in *Califano v. Westcott*[4] to invalidate a gender based classification used to allocate benefits to families with dependent children. The Social Security Act system of aid to families with dependent children provided benefits to families with children deprived of parental financial support because of the unemployment of the father only; no benefits were paid when support was lost due to the unemployment of the child's mother. Although the government claimed that there was no "gender bias" in the statute because it always affected a family unit with a male and a female parent and one or more children, the Justices unanimously found that the law discriminated against mothers who in fact were the primary economic providers for their families. The classification was invalid under the equal protection component of the Fifth Amendment because it did not substantially advance the government interests in identifying children in need of support or reducing the unemployed father's incentive to desert his family, which had been encouraged by earlier federal aid programs.

In *Westcott* the Court concluded that the program should be extended to all families where a parent was unemployed. Although the decision as to extension of benefits or termination of the program is a nonconstitutional one, as invalidating the statute also would eliminate the unconstitutional classification, a majority of the Justices concluded that the congressional objective of providing for needy children and families would be best effectuated by extension of benefits in this case.[5]

Worker Dependents' Benefits. The middle level standard of review should allow the Court to analyze clearly the validity of gender-based discrimination. For example, in *Wengler v. Druggists Mut. Ins. Co.*[6] the Court held, by an eight to one vote, that a state worker's

---

4. 443 U.S. 76, 99 S.Ct. 2655, 61 L.Ed.2d 382 (1979).

5. Four Justices concurred in the finding that the classification was unconstitutional but dissented as to the extension of benefits ruling; they would have invalidated the unemployed parent aid provisions on the basis that Congress had never intended to pay benefits based on the unemployment of the child's mother. Califano v. West-

cott, 443 U.S. 76, 93, 99 S.Ct. 2655, 2665, 61 L.Ed.2d 382 (1979) (Powell, J., concurring and dissenting, joined by Burger, C.J., and Stewart and Rehnquist, JJ.). Of course, Congress has the choice of continuing the program on a gender neutral basis or terminating this aid program.

6. 446 U.S. 142, 100 S.Ct. 1540, 64 L.Ed.2d 107 (1980).

compensation law which provided death benefits (upon the work-related death of a spouse) to a widower only if he was mentally or physically incapacitated or could prove actual dependence on his wife's earnings, but automatically granted such benefits to a widow, was unconstitutional. The Court found that the statute discriminated against both men and women. The Court has consistently used a middle level standard of review in cases where discrimination is said to exist against working women because lesser benefits are granted to their spouses or dependents than are granted to the spouses or dependents of their male counterparts. Justice Stevens, in a concurring opinion, thought that the statute only discriminated against men, but he believed that the statute should still be subjected to the middle level standard of review.[7]

The majority opinion stated that, "[h]owever the discrimination is described in this case, our precedents require that gender-based discriminations must serve important governmental objectives and that the discriminatory means employed must be substantially related to the achievement of those objectives."[8] Providing benefits for needy spouses of deceased workers was deemed to be an important government objective, but that objective could have been achieved in a non-discriminatory manner by giving benefits only to widows and widowers who could demonstrate need. The state made only a generalized claim of administrative convenience for employing the classification, asserting that it might result in the savings of dollars that could then be used to pay benefits. The Court stated that "[i]t may be that there are levels of administrative convenience that will justify discriminations that are subject to heightened scrutiny under the equal protection clause, but the requisite showing has not been made here by the mere claim that it would be inconvenient to individualize determinations about widows as well as widowers."[9]

It seems difficult to believe that a showing of administrative convenience will ever be found sufficient to support a gender-based discrimination because the state could always be charged with finding some way to determine need as regards beneficiaries and challenged worker's compensation systems and doing so in a manner that would not seriously deplete the resources available for paying benefits under those systems. In *Wengler* the Supreme Court remanded the case to the state supreme court for a determination as to whether the classification should be made equal by granting benefits to all widows and widowers automatically or by requiring proof of dependency or need from all widows and widowers following the work-related death of their spouses.

Property Rights—Control of Marital Property. Laws which allocate property or economic rights on the basis of gender should be invalidated under the intermediate level of review. *Kirchberg v. Feenstra*[10] invalidated a Louisiana statute that gave a husband, as "head and master" of the family, the unilateral right to dispose of property jointly owned with his wife without her consent. Because neither the state nor the husband who was a party to the case could identify any important state interest which was in fact promoted by such a law, this granting of special rights to men violated the equal protection clause. Louisiana statutes allowed a wife to take steps to protect her property interest and avoid some of the discriminatory impact of the statute, but this fact could not save the gender-based classification because the degree of burden placed upon women is irrelevant when the gender-based classification fails to serve any important governmental objective.

Parental Rights—Illegitimacy Cases. The Court has had a great deal of difficulty in analyzing the constitutionality of a gender classification when the classification at issue did not allocate property or economic rights. While the Court in these cases also applies the substantial relationship to an important inter-

---

7. 446 U.S. at 152–55, 100 S.Ct. at 1546–47, (Stevens, J., concurring).

8. 446 U.S. at 148–50, 100 S.Ct. at 1544–45.

9. 446 U.S. at 152–54, 100 S.Ct. at 1546–47. See footnote 2, supra.

10. 450 U.S. 455, 101 S.Ct. 1195, 67 L.Ed.2d 428 (1981).

est test, the outcomes of the cases vary with the judicial assessment of the asserted governmental interests.

In two cases that involved combined gender and illegitimacy classifications[11] the Court applied this standard in differentiating between the rights and duties of fathers and mothers of illegitimate children.[12] The Justices, by a five to four vote, invalidated a state law which granted a veto power over the adoption of such children to all mothers but no fathers because the state failed to show that such discrimination was necessary to achieve important interests in the facilitation of adoptions of illegitimates.[13] By a five to four vote, but without a majority opinion, the Court approved the denial of a right to sue for the wrongful death of an illegitimate to a father, but not a mother, if the father had failed to acknowledge the child during its life; the interest in determining paternity before the death of the child, as well as encouraging the legitimization of these children, supported such a distinction.[14] In a related illegitimacy case the Court upheld the exclusion of illegitimates from the intestate estates of their decedent fathers if they failed to get a judicial order of paternity before the death of the father; the difference in the difficulty of proving paternity, as opposed to maternity, justified the state's desire to have such suits settled before the death of the father.[15]

These decisions seem to reflect the opinions of a majority of the Justices concerning the importance of state interests in illegitimate children more than they reflect a majority view of the proper degree of scrutiny for gender based classifications.

Combined Illegitimacy and Gender Classifications in Immigration and Naturalization Laws. In 1977, only one year after the adoption of the intermediate standard of review for gender classifications,[16] the Supreme Court upheld combined illegitimacy and gender classifications in federal immigration law. In *Fiallo v. Bell*,[17] the Court upheld federal statutes that granted an immigration preference to the illegitimate children of foreign national women who were lawfully living in the United States that was denied to the children of a foreign national father who was lawfully living in the United States. Under the immigration laws in force at the time of the *Fiallo* litigation, any permanent lawful resident parent could bring her or his legitimate child, who resided in another country, to the United States without that child being subject to certain immigration quotas. A permanent lawful resident foreign national woman was also allowed to have her illegitimate child come to the United States without being subject to immigration quotas. However, a lawfully resident foreign national father could not bring his child to the United States unless the child's admission fit within the quota limits for immigrants from the country where the illegitimate child resided.

The majority opinion in *Fiallo* did not examine the government's use of a gender basis separately from its use of the illegitimacy basis for this classification in this immigration preference law. Rather, the majority simply stated that the Supreme Court traditionally had given great deference to Congressional decisions

---

11. These cases are examined in detail in §§ 14.14–14.19, supra.

The Supreme Court has not clearly ruled on whether a male who asserts that he is the parent of a child has a fundamental constitutional right to establish a personal relationship with the child so that the state could not grant preferential custody rights over the child to the biological mother, rather than the biological father, of the child. See § 14.17, supra. The cases referred to in this section examine some specific problems concerning the establishment of parent-child relationships or the distinctions between custodial rights of mothers and fathers of an illegitimate child.

12. Caban v. Mohammed, 441 U.S. 380, 99 S.Ct. 1760, 60 L.Ed.2d 297 (1979); Parham v. Hughes, 441 U.S. 347, 99 S.Ct. 1742, 60 L.Ed.2d 269 (1979).

13. Caban v. Mohammed, 441 U.S. 380, 99 S.Ct. 1760, 60 L.Ed.2d 297 (1979).

14. Parham v. Hughes, 441 U.S. 347, 99 S.Ct. 1742, 60 L.Ed.2d 269 (1979).

15. Lalli v. Lalli, 439 U.S. 259, 99 S.Ct. 518, 58 L.Ed.2d 503 (1978).

16. Craig v. Boren, 429 U.S. 190, 97 S.Ct. 451, 50 L.Ed.2d 397 (1976). *See* § 14.22 regarding the development of the intermediate standard.

17. Fiallo v. Bell, 430 U.S. 787, 97 S.Ct. 1473, 52 L.Ed.2d 50 (1977).

concerning immigration and that the Justices were "no more inclined to reconsider this line of cases" than they had been in prior years.[18]

The majority opinion in *Fiallo,* written by Justice Powell, appears to find that the statute's use of a combined illegitimacy and gender classification was related to the government interest in avoiding fraud, because a foreign national father in the United States might be able to easily fraudulently claim that many children were his illegitimate children so that they could avoid United States Immigration preferences.[19] However Justice Powell was unclear concerning which standard of review should be applied to gender classifications in immigration and naturalization laws. The majority opinion's lack of clarity might be attributable to several reasons. First, the Supreme Court throughout our history, has given great deference to Congress in immigration naturalization laws. Second, the intermediate standard of review, had been adopted only one year prior to the *Fiallo* case, and the Justices may have been unwilling to explore the meaning of the intermediate standard for the first time in an immigration setting. Third, the Court had not adopted a clear standard of review for illegitimacy classifications in 1977. Additionally, the Justices may have believed that the fact that they struck a state inheritance law that discriminated against illegitimate children, setting on the same day that they decided *Fiallo,*[20] demonstrated that they would continue to engage in independent judicial review of classifications that were based on the legitimacy/classification so long as the classification was not within federal immigration or naturalization laws. Despite all of the ways in which we can recast *Fiallo* in terms of today's equal

protection standards, the *Fiallo* majority opinion seems to reject all basis for independent review of illegitimacy and gender classifications in immigration laws. The majority's refusal to subject the law to any meaningful form of judicial review was challenged only by Justices Marshall, Brennan, and White, who dissented in *Fiallo.*[21]

Two decades after *Fiallo,* the Justices appeared to be hopelessly divided concerning the appropriate standard of review that should be used to determine the compatibility of classifications in federal naturalization statutes with the equal protection component of the Fifth Amendment due process clause. In *Miller v. Albright,*[22] the Court, without a majority opinion, avoided ruling on the constitutionality of a gender classification in a naturalization statute, while the Justices upheld the use of the illegitimacy trait for establishing classification. The law at issue in *Miller* created the basis upon which a child born out of the United States to a U.S. citizen and a non-citizen, who were not married to each other, could become a citizen of the United States.[23] Under the federal law, an illegitimate child born to an unmarried American citizen female outside the country received citizenship at birth so long as the mother had one year of continuous residence in the United States. A child born out of wedlock to a U.S. citizen father and a non-citizen woman outside of the country would receive citizenship that related back to the date of birth if, but only if, the father had resided in the United States for at least 2 years after the age of 14 and if the father took

---

18.   430 U.S. at 793 n. 4, 97 S. Ct. at 1478 n. 4.

19.   In Clark v. Jeter, 486 U.S. 456, 108 S.Ct. 1910, 100 L.Ed.2d 465 (1988). Justice O'Connor wrote for a unanimous Court in finding that classifications based on legitimacy should be invalidated unless they were "substantially related to an important governmental objective." 486 U.S. at 461, 108 S. Ct. at 1914. For an examination of the development of an intermediate standard of review for illegitimacy cases, see §§ 14.14–14.19.

20.   Trimble v. Gordon, 430 U.S. 762, 97 S.Ct. 1459, 52 L.Ed.2d 31 (1977). See § 18.16 of this treatise.

21.   Fiallo v. Bell, 430 U.S. 787, 800, 97 S.Ct. 1473, 1482, 52 L.Ed.2d 50 (1977) (Marshall, J. joined by Bren-

nan, J., dissenting); 430 U.S. at 816, 97 S. Ct. at 1490 (White, J., dissenting).

22.   523 U.S. 420, 118 S.Ct. 1428, 140 L.Ed.2d 575 (1998).

23.   The statutes establishing the conditions for granting citizenship to the child borne of one United States parent born outside of the United States were codified in 8 U.S. § 1401, 1408, 1409. These statutory provisions are set forth in the plurality opinion of Justice Stevens; § 1409 provided the acknowledgment requirements which were at issue in *Miller.* 523 U.S. at 434–36, 118 S. Ct. at 1435 (Stevens, J., joined by Rehnquist, C.J., announcing the judgment of the Court).

several steps to acknowledge the child's eighteenth birthday.[24]

The *Miller* litigation involved a woman who was born in the Philippines to a non-U.S. citizen mother; she did not receive the acknowledgment of her father until after she was 18 years old. Because Ms. Miller had not been "acknowledged" by her father prior to the time she was 18, the Secretary of State refused her citizenship request. Ms. Miller claimed that the distinction between illegitimate children born to a U.S. citizen mother, and those with a U.S. citizen father denied violated the equal protection principle of the due process clause of the Fifth Amendment.

In *Miller v. Albright*, seven Justices believed that Ms. Miller could raise the issue of discrimination against U.S. citizen fathers, as opposed to U.S. citizen mothers, as well as discrimination against a certain classification of illegitimate children, to which she belonged (the class of children whose fathers were U.S. citizens and who had not received acknowledgment prior to their 18th birthday). Five Justices considered the constitutionality of the gender classification in a meaningful way; three of these five Justices voted to invalidate the statutory distinction between illegitimate children born to United States citizen mothers and those born to United States citizen fathers. Nevertheless, the Supreme Court did not invalidate the classification in the naturalization law in *Miller* because of the division of the Justices' votes on both jurisdictional issues and equal protection claims.

Justice Stevens announced the judgment of the Court in *Miller*, in an opinion that was only joined by Chief Justice Rehnquist.[25] These two Justices found that the young woman could raise the gender discrimination issue as well as issues concerning discrimination against her class of illegitimate children. Jus-

tice Stevens and the Chief Justice were unclear regarding the standard that they were applying to these classifications. At one point in the opinion, Justice Stevens states that the classification would be upheld because it is "neither arbitrary nor invidious."[26] At another point in his opinion, Justice Stevens appears to use the substantial relationship to an important interest test that had been adopted for both gender and illegitimacy classifications in prior Supreme Court cases concerning issues unrelated to immigration or naturalization. Justice Stevens stated that the government's interest in avoiding fraud "insuring reliable proof of a biological relationship" of the parent and child was "an important governmental objective."[27] The Stevens opinion also found that the government had important interests in "encouraging the development of a healthy relationship between the citizen parent and the child, while the child is a minor and the related interest in fostering ties between the foreign born child and the United States."[28] Justice Stevens and the Chief Justice asserted that the statute was "well-tailored" to accomplish those interests that they believed were both legitimate and important. Thus, Stevens–Rehnquist opinion could be interpreted as applying the met the intermediate standard of review.

Justices Ginsburg, Souter and Breyer dissented in *Miller v. Albright*, because they believed that the portion of the law that placed additional requirements on a father's ability to pass on citizenship to his illegitimate child born in another country could not survive any meaningful form of judicial review. In the view of the three dissenters, the equal protection guarantee required that mothers and fathers be given the same ability to pass on citizenship to their children. Justice Ginsburg's dissent

---

24. None of the Justices in *Miller* examined the provision of 8 U.S.C.A. § 1409 that requires the father of an illegitimate child to provide in writing that he would give financial support to the person until child was 18 years of age. Justice Stevens noted that this provision of the statute, which had no companion financial support requirement for female parents of illegitimate children, being considered by the Supreme Court in this case. 523 U.S. at 434–37, 118 S. Ct. at 1435–36 (Stevens, J., joined by Rehnquist, C.J.).

25. Miller v. Albright, 523 U.S. 420, 118 S.Ct. 1428, 140 L.Ed.2d 575 (1998) (opinion of Stevens, J., joined by Rehnquist, C.J., announcing the judgment of the Court).

26. 523 U.S. at 432, 118 S. Ct. at 1432 (Stevens, J., joined by Rehnquist, C.J.).

27. 523 U.S. at 436, 118 S. Ct. at 1438 (Stevens, J., joined by Rehnquist, C.J.).

28. 523 U.S. at 439–40 118 S. Ct. at 1439 (Stevens, J., joined by Rehnquist, C.J.).

explained how gender based classifications in immigration and naturalization preferences had been based on nothing more than stereotypes of males and females.[29] Justice Breyer's dissent reviewed the gender based classification under the standard of review used all gender classification cases since 1976. The intermediate standard of review required distinction between males and females "to further important government objectives, and the discriminatory means employed must be substantially related to the achievement of those objectives."[30] The dissenting Justices believed that modern scientific means of establishing genetic relationships (between parents and children) eliminated the need of the government to have special documentation requirements for paternity claims. The dissenters, on that basis, concluded that the requirement that the acknowledgment take place before the 18th birthday of the illegitimate child was not substantially related to any important government interest.[31]

With the five Justices who reached the gender discrimination claim dividing in the manner described above, the decision in *Miller* turned on the votes of four Justices who refused to give independent judicial review to Ms. Miller's gender discrimination claim. Two of these Justices, Justices Scalia and Thomas, refused to review of the classifications in the naturalization law because of they believe that the Court had no power to invalidate a portion of a naturalization law in a manner that would give United States citizenship to any person who did not completely fulfill the requirements created by Congress.[32]

Justice O'Connor wrote an opinion concurring only in the judgment of the Court; her

opinion was joined only by Justice Kennedy. These two Justices believed that Ms. Miller, who claimed citizenship through her U.S. citizen father, did not have "standing" to litigate the claim that the naturalization laws had an unconstitutional classification based on the gender of U.S. citizen males and U.S. citizen females.[33] For that reason, these Justices O'Connor and Kennedy considered only the claim of the woman that the laws' creation of a special class of illegitimate children that had to receive acknowledgments of paternity in order to gain citizenship was unconstitutional. Putting aside the gender discrimination issue, Justice O'Connor's opinion found that Ms. Miller's attack on the specialized legitimacy classification "triggers only rational basis scrutiny, and [the statute] is sustainable under that statute."[34]

Three years after the *Miller* decision, the Court examined the gender discrimination in the laws regarding the granting of citizenship to a child born outside of the United States, to one United States citizen who was not married to the other parent of the child in question. When the Court confronted that gender discrimination issue, we learned that Justices O'Connor and Kennedy in fact had opposing views concerning the equal protection issue they had avoided in *Miller*.

Tuan Anh Nguyen v. Immigration and Naturalization Service[35] involved a citizenship question that arose during deportation proceedings. In 1969, Joseph Boulais, who was a United States citizen working in Vietnam for a private corporation, fathered a child with a woman who was a Vietnamese citizen. In 1975, Mr. Boulais brought the child, Tuan Anh Ngu-

---

29. Miller v. Albright, 523 U.S. 420, 118 S.Ct. 1428, 1449–55, 140 L.Ed.2d 575 (1998) (Ginsburg, joined by Souter, and Breyer, JJ., dissenting).

30. 523 U.S. at 481, 118 S. Ct. at 1460. (Breyer, J., joined by Souter, and Ginsburg, JJ., dissenting) (internal quotation and internal citation omitted).

31. Justice Breyer's dissent emphasized that elimination of the distinctions between males and females would still leave standing the statutory requirement that a U.S. citizen parent—whether male or female—provide clear and convincing evidence of a biological relationship to a child in order for that child to receive United States citizenship if the child was born outside the United States.

523 U.S. at 471, 118 S.Ct. at 1455 (Breyer, J., joined by Souter and Ginsburg, JJ., dissenting).

32. Miller v. Albright, 523 U.S. 420, 118 S.Ct. 1428, 1446–49, 140 L.Ed.2d 575 (1998) (Scalia, J., joined by Thomas, J., concurring in the judgment).

33. 523 U.S. at 445, 118 S.Ct. at 1442 (O'Connor, J., joined by Kennedy, J., concurring in the judgment).

34. 523 U.S. at 452, 118 S.Ct. at 1446 (O'Connor, J. joined by Kennedy, J., dissenting).

35. 533 U.S. 53, 121 S.Ct. 2053, 150 L.Ed.2d 115(2001).

yen, to the United States. Mr. Boulais did not technically legitimate the child, acknowledge the paternity in writing and under oath, or establish paternity through the ruling of a competent court before the child was 18. When Nguyen was 22, he was convicted, based on a guilty plea, of two crimes that would have made him deportable. It was not until Nguyen's appeal of a deportation order that Mr. Boulais obtained a DNA test showing that Nguyen was his child; he then received a state court order establishing paternity. Because these actions were not completed until Nguyen was 28 years old, Nguyen did not have citizenship under the terms of the federal statutes.

In other words, the statutory system granted immediate citizenship to the child of a U.S. citizen woman who gave birth to a child outside of the United States and who was not married, so long as the woman and the child met certain requirements concerning residency in the United States.[36] Nguyen would have been a citizen of the United States if his one U.S. citizen parent had been a female. Mr. Boulais and Mr. Nguyen both appealed from a ruling of the Board of Immigration Appeals that rejected Nguyen's claim to United States citizenship.

Five Justices in *Tuan Anh Nguyen* ruled that the gender classification in the statute did not violate the equal protection guarantee of the Fifth Amendment due process clause. Justice Kennedy's majority opinion stated that the Court was using the intermediate protection standard that had been used in other gender classification cases, and was requiring the government classification to be substantially related to important governmental interests. Therefore, according to Justice Kennedy, the Court did not have to consider either whether Congress should be given special deference regarding immigration and naturaliza-

tion classifications, or whether a court could have granted citizenship to someone who did not meet the statutory standards, if those standards were invalidated.

The majority in *Tuan Anh Nguyen* rejected any claim that the gender classification "did not withstand conventional equal protection scrutiny."[37] In other words, Justice Kennedy's opinion asserted that the majority had applied the identical intermediate standard of review used in all other gender classification cases during the past quarter century. The majority ruled that the gender classification in the naturalization statute was substantially related to two important government interests. First, Justice Kennedy found that the law was tailored to "assuring that a biological parent-child relationship exists."[38] According to the majority, the United States citizen mother status of a child for immigration and naturalization purposes would be easily verifiable at birth, whereas other standards would be needed to determine that the alleged U.S. citizen father who claimed eligibility for citizenship was in fact the parent of the child. The persons challenging the law had claimed that the law was not substantially related to that interest because other means, such as DNA testing, could establish paternity as easily, and with greater certainty, than the statutory legitimization or affirmation requirements. The majority rejected that argument. Justice Kennedy stated that the Constitution did not require Congress to choose one particular method for requiring fathers to establish paternity and that such requirements would not solve any gender classification problems because the paternity tests would still only be required of one gender. According to the majority, the need to assure the biological relationship would result in Congress at least requiring fathers, but not mothers, of children to take DNA tests, and

---

36. Statutes applicable in both the *Miller* and *Tuan Anh Nguyen* cases granted statutory citizenship to children born outside of the United States only if their U.S. citizen parent or parents had resided within the United States for a certain period of time. These requirements were met by the parents in both cases. See Chapter 22 for analysis of other cases concerning the requirements for immigration or citizenship.

37. Tuan Anh Nguyen v. Immigration and Naturalization Service, 533 U.S. 53, 71, 121 S.Ct. 2053, 2065, 150 L.Ed.2d 115 (2001). Justice Kennedy's opinion was joined by Chief Justice Rehnquist and Justices Stevens, Scalia, and Thomas. Justices Scalia and Thomas filed a separate opinion concurring in both the opinion and the judgment of the Court. 533 U.S. at 73, 121 S.Ct. at 2066 (Scalia, J., joined by Thomas, J., concurring).

38. 533 U.S. at 61, 121 S.Ct. at 2060.

that a gender classification would necessarily appear in the statutory system. Justice Kennedy stated: "the use of gender-specific terms takes into account a biological difference between the parents. The differential treatment is inherent in a sensible statutory scheme, given the unique relationship of the mother to the event of birth."[39]

Second, Justice Kennedy also found that the government had an important interest in ensuring that the United States citizen parent and the child born out of wedlock in another country had the opportunity to have a meaningful relationship before the child was an adult. The majority opinion admitted that the statutory scheme making the father take certain steps before the child was 18 or 21 would not guarantee that the United States citizen father would in fact establish a personal relationship with the child. According to the majority, however, the law was sufficiently tailored to that end so as to survive the substantial relationship to an important interest standard.[40]

Justice O'Connor wrote for the four dissenting Justices in *Tuan Anh Nguyen v. Immigration and Naturalization Service*.[41] The dissent emphasized that the rulings in all recent gender classification cases had clearly required the government to bear the burden of proof in demonstrating that a gender based classification was substantially related to the achievement of an important governmental interest. Prior cases had required government to demonstrate an exceedingly persuasive justification for the law, which meant that "the existence of comparable or superior sex-neutral alternatives [to the gender classification in the

law] was a powerful reason to reject a sex-based classification."[42] The dissenting Justices believed that the majority had completely disregarded the Court's prior emphasis of the government's burden of proof by allowing the government to simply choose a sex-based alternative for establishing parenthood of a child born out of wedlock outside of the United States when there were other sex-neutral alternatives for demonstrating that such a child was in fact the biological child of a United States citizen.

The cases involving combined illegitimacy and gender classifications in immigration and naturalization laws should not be seen as or changing the intermediate standard of review used under the equal protection guarantee of the Fifth Amendment that is normally used to review gender or illegitimacy classifications in federal statutes or regulations. Although the majority in *Tuan Anh Nguyen* claimed that it was using the "conventional" standard, Justice Kennedy was writing for a majority, rather than a plurality, of Justices only because he obtained the votes of Justices Scalia and Thomas, who clearly stated their view that "the Court lacks power to provide relief of the sort requested in this suit–namely conferral of citizenship on a basis other than that prescribed by Congress."[43] In cases involving gender discrimination in areas other than immigration and naturalization laws, Justices Kennedy and Stevens have voted to require the government to demonstrate with an exceedingly persuasive justification when the government asserted that a gender-based classification in fact was substantially related to an important governmental interest[44] It ap-

39. 533 U.S. at 63, 121 S.Ct. at 2061.

40. Justice Kennedy, in part III–C of the majority opinion stated that "the obligation [the statute] imposes with respect to acquisition of citizenship by the child of a citizen father is minimal" and that if such a child [has substantial ties to the United States that child can] seek citizenship in his or her own right, rather than via reliance on ties to a citizen-parent. And that this option was not available to the person in this case "due to the serious nature of his criminal offenses [rather than to] an equal protection denial or to any supposed rigidity or harshness in the citizenship laws." 533 U.S. at 69–71, 121 S.Ct. at 2064–65.

41. 533 U.S. 53, 73, 121 S.Ct. 2053, 2066, 150 L.Ed.2d 115 (2001) (O'Connor, J., joined by Souter, Ginsburg, and Breyer, JJ., dissenting).

42. 533 U.S. at 80, 121 S.Ct. at 2070 (O'Connor, J., joined by Souter, Ginsburg, and Breyer, JJ., dissenting).

43. 533 U.S. at 73, 121 S.Ct. at 2066 (Scalia, J., joined by Thomas, J., concurring). These two Justices had taken the same position 3 years earlier. Miller v. Albright, 523 U.S. 420, 452, 118 S.Ct. 1428, 1446–49, 140 L.Ed.2d 575 (1998) (Scalia, J., joined by Thomas, J., concurring in the judgment).

44. An example of the use of the intermediate standard of review, which requires independent review of the

pears that the Court in fact was applying a very deferential standard of review in these immigration and naturalization cases, rather than applying an intermediate equal protection standard that would have required independent judicial review of congressional judgments in this area.

Statutory Rape. In *Michael M. v. Superior Court*,[45] the Supreme Court, without a majority opinion, upheld California's "statutory rape" law which defined as unlawful sexual intercourse "an act of sexual intercourse accomplished with a female not the wife of a perpetrator, where the female is under the age of 18 years." Although the statute provided only for the punishment of males who engaged in sexual intercourse with minor females and not for females who engaged in sexual activity with minor males, the Court did not overturn the statute.

Justice Rehnquist, writing for four members of the Court, found that the state had an important interest in preventing illegitimate pregnancies and that the gender-based classification was sufficiently related to that end "[b]ecause virtually all of the significant harmful and inescapably identifiable consequences of teenage pregnancy fall on the young female."[46]

Justice Stewart, in a concurring opinion, noted that there was a variety of statutes in California which made unlawful various types of sexual activity with both males and females below specified ages; the statutory rape law was merely the imposition of an additional sanction which promoted the state's interest in avoiding illegitimate teenage pregnancies

and the unique harm caused by them to young females.[47]

Justice Blackmun, concurring in the judgment, applied the substantial relationship-important state interest test. He believed that the law was valid because it substantially promoted the interest in the avoidance of illegitimate teenage pregnancies.[48]

Justice Brennan, in a dissent joined by Justices White and Marshall, believed that the Court had either not applied or misapplied the intermediate standard of review.[49]

Military Service—The Selective Service Case. The Supreme Court upheld the constitutionality of the military selective service act, which exempted women from the draft registration process, in *Rostker v. Goldberg*.[50] The majority opinion, by Justice Rehnquist, stated that the Court should accord Congress great deference when reviewing laws having to do with the establishment or regulation of the military, but went on to find that the gender-based classification would survive scrutiny under the substantial relationship-important interest test.

The majority ruled "the government's interest in raising and supporting armies" was an important governmental interest. The majority opinion found that Congress could conclude that men and women, because of the combat restrictions on women, were not similarly situated for purposes of a draft or registration for a draft. For this reason the congressional decision to authorize only the registration of men did not violate the equal protection component of the Fifth Amendment due process clause. The majority found that "the exemption of women from registration is not only sufficient-

---

basis for the legislation and the question of whether the government has met its burden of proof, is United States v. Virginia, 518 U.S. 515, 116 S.Ct. 2264, 135 L.Ed.2d 735 (1996). Both Justices Stevens and Kennedy join Justice Ginsburg's majority opinion in the *Virginia* case, which is examined in this section of the Treatise.

45. 450 U.S. 464, 101 S.Ct. 1200, 67 L.Ed.2d 437 (1981).

46. 450 U.S. at 476, 101 S.Ct. at 1208 (Rehnquist, J., joined by Burger, C.J., and Stewart and Powell, JJ.).

47. 450 U.S. at 476–77, 101 S.Ct. at 1208–09 (Stewart, J., concurring).

48. 450 U.S. at 482, 101 S.Ct. at 1211 (Blackmun, J., concurring in the judgment).

49. Michael M. v. Superior Court, 450 U.S. 464, 488, 101 S.Ct. 1200, 1213, 67 L.Ed.2d 437 (1981) (Brennan, J., joined by White and Marshall, JJ., dissenting). Justice Stevens dissented because he found the law not only unreasonable but irrational in its total failure to provide for punishment of females who engage in sexual intercourse with young men, particularly when the age of the persons engaged in the sexual intercourse might be quite close or identical. 450 U.S. at 496, 101 S.Ct. at 1218 (Stevens, J., dissenting).

50. 453 U.S. 57, 101 S.Ct. 2646, 69 L.Ed.2d 478 (1981).

ly but closely related to Congress' purpose in authorizing registration." [51]

Educational Programs. The uncertain meaning of the intermediate standard of review employed in gender discrimination cases was demonstrated in *Mississippi University for Women v. Hogan.*[52] Mr. Hogan was a registered nurse in Mississippi who did not hold a baccalaureate degree in nursing. He applied for admission to the Mississippi University for Women [MUW] School of Nursing, which offered a four-year baccalaureate program in nursing and a graduate program. Although Mr. Hogan was otherwise qualified for admission, he was denied admission to the school of nursing solely because of his sex. Mississippi statutes, which included the charter of the university, limited the enrollment at Mississippi University for Women to women. The exclusion of males from the state nursing school was invalidated by only a five to four vote. Indeed, the majority opinion left open the question of whether the Mississippi University for Women could deny admission to men because of their sex to schools within the university other than the school of nursing.

Justice O'Connor wrote for the majority in *Mississippi University for Women.* The majority opinion, like those since 1976, stated that the classification would only be upheld if it served important governmental objectives and if the classification was substantially related to the achievement of those objectives. "That this statute discriminates against males rather than against females does not exempt it from scrutiny or reduce the standard of review." [53]

Mississippi justified the single sex admissions policy on the basis that it compensated for discrimination against women. However, the fact that women were not under-represented in the field of nursing undercut the reasonableness of the state's argument. Indeed, "rather than compensate for discriminatory barriers faced by women, MUW's policy of excluding males from admission to the school of nursing tends to perpetuate the stereotyped view of nursing as an exclusively woman's job." [54]

The majority was unwilling to take a broad position against the dispensation of educational benefits by gender. Justice O'Connor's opinion, in a footnote, stated: "we decline to address the question of whether MUW's admissions policy, as applied to males seeking admission to schools other than the school of nursing, violates the Fourteenth Amendment." [55] It might be that one or more Justices in the five member majority would view the limiting of admissions to other schools in the university, or other types of state supported schools, to one gender as being a permissible means of compensating for past discrimination against persons of one gender or to achieve some other asserted governmental interest in the education process.

Four Justices dissented in *Mississippi University for Women.* They believed that the fact that the state offered some coeducational nursing programs at other state schools justified limiting this nursing program or that the entire university to a single gender.[56]

---

51. 453 U.S. at 77, 97 S.Ct. at 2658. Three Justices dissented because they believed the government failed to show that there was a need to draft only combat troops, or that there was a need to draft men for noncombatant as well as combat positions, while exempting females from any need to register for or be subject to a draft for noncombatant military positions. 453 U.S. at 83, 101 S.Ct. at 2661, (White, J., joined by Brennan, J., dissenting); 453 U.S. at 86, 101 S.Ct. at 2662 (Marshall, J., joined by Brennan, J., dissenting).

52. 458 U.S. 718, 102 S.Ct. 3331, 73 L.Ed.2d 1090 (1982).

53. 458 U.S. at 724, 102 S.Ct. at 3336.

54. 458 U.S. at 730, 102 S.Ct. at 3339.

55. 458 U.S. at 723 n. 7, 102 S.Ct. at 3335 n. 7.

56. Chief Justice Burger, dissented separately in his words: "to emphasize that the Court's holding today is limited to the context of a professional nursing school ... it suggests that a state might well be justified in maintaining, for example, the option of an all-women's business school or liberal arts program." Mississippi University for Women v. Hogan, 458 U.S. 718, 734, 102 S.Ct. 3331, 3341, 73 L.Ed.2d 1090 (1982) (Burger, C.J., dissenting). Justice Blackmun, in dissent, stated: "I hope that we do not lose all values that some think are worthwhile (and are not based on differences of race or religion) and regulate ourselves to needless conformity." 458 U.S. at 735, 102 S.Ct. at 3342 (Blackmun, J., dissenting). Justice Powell believed that the majority's opinion would lead inevitably to prohibiting states from providing one gender schools. 458 U.S. at 735, 102 S.Ct. at 3342 (Powell, J., dissenting, joined by Rehnquist, J.).

Fourteen years after the *Mississippi University for Women* case, in *United States v. Virginia*,[57] the Supreme Court ruled that a male-only state college [the Virginia Military Institute] violated the equal protection clause. [Hereinafter, this case will be referred to as the V.M.I. case.] Justice Ginsburg wrote a majority opinion for six of the seven Justices who voted against the State of Virginia in the V.M.I. case. Chief Justice Rehnquist concurred only in the judgment of the Court.[58] Justice Scalia dissented in the V.M.I. case.[59] Justice Thomas did not participate in the case.

Justice Ginsburg's majority opinion in the V.M.I. case noted that the Supreme Court had not yet equated gender classifications "for all purposes, to classifications based on race or national origin."[60] The majority ruled that Virginia had failed to meet the intermediate standard of review, which required invalidation of a law unless the government could demonstrate that the gender classification was substantially related to an important interest. Because the state case was unable to meet the intermediate standard in the V.M.I. case, the majority did not have to address the question of whether gender classifications in education should be reviewed with strict judicial scrutiny, and invalidated if they were not narrowly tailored to a compelling interest.

Some language in Justice Ginsburg's majority opinion made the intermediate standard seem more difficult for the government to meet than it had been in the 1970s and 80s. The majority opinion stated:

"To summarize the Court's current directions for cases of official classification based on gender: focusing on the differential treatment or denial of opportunity for which relief is sought, the reviewing Court must determine whether the proffered justi-

fication is exceedingly persuasive. The burden of justification is demanding and it rests entirely on the state ... the state must show at least that the [challenged] classification serves important governmental objectives and that the discriminatory means employed are substantially related to those objectives.... The justification must be genuine, not hypothesized or invented *post hoc* in response to litigation. And it must not rely on overbroad generalizations about the different talents, capacities, or preferences of males and females."[61]

The intermediate standard of review allows for ad hoc decisionmaking by the Justices. When employing the intermediate standard, the Justices must make a case-by-case evaluation of the evidence that the government has presented in its attempt to demonstrate that there is a distinction between males and females that is not based on stereotypes and that substantially relates to an important governmental interest. Justice Ginsburg's opinion in the V.M.I. case is instructive concerning the government's burden of proof and the types of justifications that can be used by governmental entity in a gender classification case. Justice Ginsburg's majority opinion in the V.M.I. case described the government's burden in a gender classification case in the following terms:

"The heightened review standard our precedent establishes does not make sex a proscribed classification. Suppose inherent differences are no longer accepted as a ground for race or national original classifications.... Physical differences between men and women, however, are enduring ... Inherent differences between men and women are enduring: the two sexes are not fungible.... [gender classification based on alleged differences between men and women

57. 518 U.S. 515, 116 S.Ct. 2264, 135 L.Ed.2d 735 (1996).

58. 518 U.S. at 556, 116 S.Ct. at 2287 (Rehnquist, C.J., concurring in the judgment).

59. 518 U.S. at 564, 116 S.Ct. at 2291 (Scalia, J., dissenting).

60. United States v. Virginia, 518 U.S. 515, 531, 116 S.Ct. 2264, 2275, 135 L.Ed.2d 735 (1996). The question of whether a gender classification should, under some cir-

cumstances, be subject to the compelling interest test had been left open in Mississippi University for Women v. Hogan, 458 U.S. 718, 724 n. 9, 102 S.Ct. 3331, 3336 n. 9, 73 L.Ed.2d 1090 (1982) and J.E.B. v. Alabama ex rel. T.B., 511 U.S. 127, 136 n. 6, 114 S.Ct. 1419, 1425 n. 6, 128 L.Ed.2d 89 (1994).

61. United States v. Virginia, 518 U.S. 515, 531, 116 S.Ct. 2264, 2275, 135 L.Ed.2d 735 (1996).

may not be used] for denigration of the members of either sex or for artificial constraints on an individual's opportunity. Sex classifications may be used to compensate women for particular economic disabilities . . . [and] to advance full development of the talent and capacities of our Nation's people. But such classifications may not be used . . . to create or perpetuate the legal, social, and economic inferiority of women."[62]

This portion of Justice Ginsburg's opinion indicates that any governmental entity will have a difficult burden in demonstrating that a gender classification is based upon real differences between men and women rather than stereotypes or traditions. The history of discrimination against women in our society may provide a constitutionally sufficient basis for benign (or so-called affirmative action) classifications that aid women. A benign gender classification would have to be tailored to remedying past social or governmental discrimination against women in order to be upheld as being substantially related to an important interest.

Justice Ginsburg found that the State of Virginia had failed to provide any real proof that any important educational goal would be jeopardized by the admission of women into the Virginia Military Institute. The Virginia Military Institute did not exclusively prepare its students for a military career; the vast majority of V.M.I. graduates in recent decades did not become career military officers. Even if the Virginia Military Institute had provided only military education, the ability of the United States service academies to have both male and female students showed that no education-

al goal of V.M.I. was threatened. The majority ruled that Virginia had totally failed to show any "exceedingly persuasive justification for excluding women from the citizen-soldier training afforded by V.M.I."[63]

As an alternative to admitting female students to the Virginia Military Institute, the State of Virginia sought to provide specialized "leadership" education for women by creating, and paying for, the "Virginia Women's Institute for Leadership," an educational program that would be provided at a private college for women. Six of the seven Justices voting on the V.M.I. case found that this alternative educational program did not give female students the same types of education and career advantages that the Virginia Military Institute provided for male students.[64]

Chief Justice Rehnquist concurred in the judgment of the Court, because he found that the Virginia Military Institute provided educational benefits to men in Virginia that were not provided to women. Chief Justice Rehnquist, who had once opposed the use of an intermediate standard of review in gender classification cases, wanted to require the state to demonstrate that the gender classification was substantially related to an important interest.[65] He believed that the majority's requirement that the government have an "exceedingly persuasive justification" for a gender classification altered the intermediate standard of review.[66]

Justice Scalia, the sole dissenter in the V.M.I. case, believed that the majority opinion had altered the intermediate standard by making it extremely difficult for the government to

---

62. 518 U.S. at 531–33, 116 S.Ct. at 2275–76.

63. 518 U.S. at 533, 116 S.Ct. at 2276.

64. 518 U.S. at 556, 116 S.Ct. at 2287. Chief Justice Rehnquist based his decision on the fact that Virginia had not provided equal educational benefits to the male and female students. United States v. Virginia, 518 U.S. 515, 556, 564, 116 S.Ct. 2264, 2287, 2291, 135 L.Ed.2d 735 (1996) (Rehnquist, C.J., concurring in the judgment).

65. United States v. Virginia, 518 U.S. 515, 556, 116 S.Ct. 2264, 2287, 135 L.Ed.2d 735 (1996) (Rehnquist, C.J., concurring in the judgment). Then Justice Rehnquist had opposed using a standard other than the rationality standard for gender classifications in cases such as Craig v. Boren, 429 U.S. 190, 217, 97 S.Ct. 451, 467, 50 L.Ed.2d 397 (1976) (Rehnquist, J., dissenting) and Frontiero v.

Richardson, 411 U.S. 677, 691, 93 S.Ct. 1764, 1773, 36 L.Ed.2d 583 (1973) (Rehnquist, J., dissenting). See also, Weinberger v. Wiesenfeld, 420 U.S. 636, 655, 95 S.Ct. 1225, 1236–37, 43 L.Ed.2d 514 (1975) (Rehnquist, J., concurring).

66. 518 U.S. at 558, 116 S.Ct. at 2288, (Rehnquist, C.J., concurring in the judgment). The exceedingly persuasive justification language appeared at several places in Justice Ginsburg's majority opinion. United States v. Virginia, 518 U.S. 515, 529, 531, 556, 116 S.Ct. 2264, 2274, 2275, 2287, 135 L.Ed.2d 735 (1996). That phrase had been used in Justice Marshall's majority opinion in Kirchberg v. Feenstra, 450 U.S. 455, 461, 101 S.Ct. 1195, 1199, 67 L.Ed.2d 428 (1981).

provide exceedingly persuasive proof that might justify gender classification.[67] However, most of Justice Scalia's dissent was focused on attacking the Court's interference with what Justice Scalia believes are educational and social policies that should be left within the decisionmaking powers of state and local governments. Justice Scalia asserted that there was no basis for the creation of the principles in the majority opinion that would make it impossible for states to have single sex schools and impossible for states to provide any type of significant financial or tangible aid to single sex schools.[68]

The Supreme Court has not yet ruled on whether any governmental entity might provide some type of "separate but equal" elementary or high school courses for male and female students. There may be stronger arguments in support of one sex elementary or high schools, or some one sex courses in elementary or high schools, than the arguments put forth by the State of Virginia to justify its one sex college. The Chief Justice, in his concurring opinion, left open the question of whether educational benefits from single sex education might allow the government to create equal, but separate, single sex schools.[69] Justice Ginsburg's majority opinion also leaves that question open,[70] although her majority opinion will make it difficult for the government to meet its burden of proof under the intermediate standard. After the V.M.I. case, a government entity attempting to provide one sex schools at the grade school, high school or college level will have to provide an "exceedingly pervasive justification" for the separate but equal educational program. It will be the government's burden to prove that its one sex educational program is substantially related to an important educational interest. Such a burden will be difficult, if not impossible, for the government to meet.

Conclusion. The adoption of the substantial relationship to an important governmental interest standard by a majority of the Justices has settled, at least formally, the issue of the proper definition of a middle level standard of review for gender classifications. However, that standard of review is such that it allows Justices to base their votes upon individual perceptions of the reasonableness of a gender classification and the governmental interest asserted in each case. Were our country to adopt a constitutional Amendment prohibiting gender discrimination by governmental agencies, the Court would have to employ some form of strict scrutiny or compelling interest test under that Amendment which would limit the ability of individual judges to argue for the legitimacy of gender classifications based upon their personal perceptions of the reasonableness of allocating rights by gender.[71]

Absent the adoption of such an Amendment, it appears that the Court will continue to apply the middle level standard of review and it will be difficult to predict the degree of protection that will be given to persons against

---

67. United States v. Virginia, 518 U.S. 515, 564, 116 S.Ct. 2264, 2291, 135 L.Ed.2d 735 (1996) (Scalia, J., dissenting). Justice Thomas did not participate in the case.

68. Justice Scalia found that the Court's analysis would mean that the state would always lose when it attempted to justify single sex education where women were excluded from any program. Justice Scalia stated: "the only hope for state assisted single-sex private schools is that the Court will not apply in the future the principles of law that it has applied today." 518 U.S. at 585, 116 S.Ct. at 2307 (Scalia, J., dissenting).

69. United States v. Virginia, 518 U.S. 515, 564, 116 S.Ct. 2264, 2291, 135 L.Ed.2d 735 (1996) (Rehnquist, C.J., concurring in the judgment).

70. United States v. Virginia, 518 U.S. 515, 534 n. 7, 116 S.Ct. 2264, 2276 n. 7, 135 L.Ed.2d 735 (1996).

71. The proposed Equal Rights Amendment, which failed to win ratification, read as follows:

Section 1. Equality of rights under the Law shall not be denied or abridged by the United States or by any state on account of sex.

Section 2. The Congress shall have the power to enforce, by appropriate legislation, the provisions of this article.

Section 3. The Amendment shall take effect two years after the date of ratification.

The possible impact of this Amendment on constitutional analysis of gender classifications was noted in J. Nowak, R. Rotunda & J. Young, Constitutional Law 618 (1st ed. 1978). In that text, we also noted the progress of the proposed Amendment through the ratification process. See id. at App. C, and 1982 Supplement to the first edition at Appendix C. For additional citations to secondary sources on this topic, see R. Rotunda & J. Nowak, Treatise on Constitutional Law: Substance and Procedure, vol. 3, § 18.23 (3rd ed. 1999, with annual supplements).

the arbitrary assignment of rights and benefits in society on the basis of gender.

In *J.E.B. v. Alabama ex rel. T.B.*[72] the Supreme Court ruled that the intentional use of peremptory challenges to exclude men from a jury would violate the equal protection clause. In the *J.E.B.* case an attorney for the government prosecuted a civil child support case on behalf of the mother of a minor child. There was no significant state action issue in this case because the attorney was a government employee acting on behalf of the government. The Court had previously ruled that the use of peremptory challenges to exclude members of a racial group from juries by governmental attorneys, or by privately employed attorneys, would violate the equal protection clause.[73]

If there is no state action, gender discrimination by private persons or associations is not unconstitutional under the Fourteenth Amendment.[74] However, by statute the legislature may restrict the freedom of such groups to engage in gender discrimination in their public activities.[75]

Additionally, it must be remembered that the review of gender-based classifications may still be complicated by issues concerning whether a law, neutral on its face, constitutes gender discrimination.[76]

§ 14.24 Gender Classifications: Pregnancy Classifications and Irrebuttable Presumptions

In *Cleveland Board of Education v. LaFleur*[1] the Supreme Court ruled that mandatory maternity leaves for teachers violated due process. Under the Cleveland rule, a pregnant teacher had to take a maternity leave beginning five months before the expected birth of her child and could not return without a doctor's certificate of physical fitness or until the semester which began after her child had reached the age of three months. A Virginia rule, which was challenged in a companion case, required a woman to leave four months before the expected birth, but guaranteed her re-employment the first day of the school year after she had received a doctor's certificate of physical fitness and could assure the school that child care would not interfere with her teaching.

The mandatory maternity leave provisions involved in these cases placed a heavy burden on a woman's exercise of her freedom of personal choice in matters of marriage and family life, a fundamental right. The question was whether there was a state interest sufficient to justify the rules. The firm cut-off dates were claimed to be necessary to maintain the continuity of classroom instruction.

The Court recognized this purpose was a significant and legitimate educational goal, but found that the arbitrary cut-off date bore no rational relationship to the promotion of that goal as long as the school received substantial advance notice. Requiring women to leave at a later date would serve the same purpose while imposing a lesser burden. Furthermore, because pregnancies fell at different times of

72. 511 U.S. 127, 114 S.Ct. 1419, 128 L.Ed.2d 89 (1994).

73. Batson v. Kentucky, 476 U.S. 79, 106 S.Ct. 1712, 90 L.Ed.2d 69 (1986) (prosecutor's use of challenge in criminal case); Edmonson v. Leesville Concrete Co., 500 U.S. 614, 111 S.Ct. 2077, 114 L.Ed.2d 660 (1991) (attorney's use of challenges in civil case); Georgia v. McCollum, 505 U.S. 42, 112 S.Ct. 2348, 120 L.Ed.2d 33 (1992) (defense attorney in criminal case). These state action decisions are examined in Chapter 12 of this Treatise.

74. See generally § 12.1, supra.

75. See, e.g., Hishon v. King & Spalding, 467 U.S. 69, 104 S.Ct. 2229, 81 L.Ed.2d 59 (1984) (Congressional action prohibiting employment discrimination on the basis of gender may be validly applied to law firm's decisions regarding employment or promotion of attorneys); Roberts v. United States Jaycees, 468 U.S. 609, 104 S.Ct.

3244, 82 L.Ed.2d 462 (1984) (state may prohibit organization engaged in both commercial and expressive activity from discriminating in membership decisions on the basis of gender). The interest in ending invidious discrimination on the basis of gender or race justifies a limitation of the freedom of association of such nonintimate groups. For citations to additional Supreme Court cases, and secondary authorities, on this point, see R. Rotunda & J. Nowak, Treatise on Constitutional Law: Substance and Procedure, vol. 3, § 18.23 (3rd ed. 1999, with annual supplements).

76. This issue was examined as the Court upheld a state employment preference for veterans. See Personnel Administrator of Massachusetts v. Feeney, 442 U.S. 256, 99 S.Ct. 2282, 60 L.Ed.2d 870 (1979). See § 14.4, supra.

§ 14.24

1. 414 U.S. 632, 94 S.Ct. 791, 39 L.Ed.2d 52 (1974).

the school year, the cut-off date often hindered rather than promoted continuity as in the present case where the teachers were required to leave shortly before the end of the term. Nor could the arbitrary cut-off date be justified by the necessity of keeping physically unfit teachers out of the classroom. The Court found that this reason was a legitimate purpose and it would assume arguendo that some pregnant teachers became unfit to teach during the latter stages of pregnancy. However, this rationale could not justify the "irrebuttable" presumption that every pregnant teacher reaching the fifth or sixth month of pregnancy was physically incapable of teaching.

Finding that the firm cut-off dates were invalid, the Court turned to the evaluation of the provisions regarding the return to teaching. The Court noted there was no serious challenge made to the medical requirement of an individual determination of the teacher's health or to the requirement of waiting for a new term following birth before resumption of teaching duties. However, the Court could find no reasonable justification for requiring that the woman's child be older than three months before she could return. The age of the child was entirely unrelated to the continuity of education and the medical certificate served to protect the school interest. Thus, this requirement was also a violation of due process.

Relying on *LaFleur*, the Court in a per curiam decision invalidated a statutory provision which declared a pregnant woman ineligible for employment benefits from twelve weeks before the expected birth until six weeks after birth.[2] The presumption of incapacity and unavailability for employment was found to be virtually identical to the presumption invalidated in *LaFleur*. In both these cases, the provisions were invalidated not because they

were a denial of equal protection but because they constituted "irrebuttable presumptions." The relationship between this due process rationale and equal protection is examined in other sections of this text.[3]

In *Geduldig v. Aiello*[4] the Court rejected the claim that a California disability insurance system which covered all disabilities of a prescribed duration[5] with the sole exception of disabilities resulting from normal pregnancy resulted in an invidious discrimination under the equal protection clause. The program might rightfully exclude some risks and the exclusion of pregnancy served a legitimate interest in keeping costs low. The majority rejected the contention that this exclusion was a sex-based classification, stating there was no evidence that the selection of risks which were covered harmed any definable group. There were no risks from which men were protected that women were not and vice versa.

Justices Brennan, Marshall, and Douglas dissented. The program paid for disabilities regardless of whether they were costly, voluntary, as with cosmetic surgery, unique to one sex such as prostatectomies or hemophilia, or statistically more likely to occur to one race, such as sickle-cell anemia, or the result of a preexisting condition. Despite this otherwise broad coverage, the program denied compensation for disabilities suffered in connection with "normal pregnancy", disabilities unique to women. Women suffering such disabilities had equivalent medical and economic needs as persons suffering from disabilities covered by the program. The dissent therefore would have found that the sex-based discrimination violated the equal protection clause.

A suit attacking a similar provision under Title VII[6] was equally unsuccessful.[7] Relying on *Geduldig* the Court stated that the exclu-

---

2. Turner v. Department of Employment Sec., 423 U.S. 44, 96 S.Ct. 249, 46 L.Ed.2d 181 (1975) (per curiam).

3. See § 13.6; see generally §§ 10.6, 10.7.

4. 417 U.S. 484, 94 S.Ct. 2485, 41 L.Ed.2d 256 (1974).

5. Statute excluded coverage for disabilities lasting less than 8 days or greater than 26 weeks. There was also an exception mentioned for drug addicts, sexual psychopaths and dipsomania—these exclusions however were not strictly adhered to.

6. Suit was brought under § 703(a) "It shall be an unlawful employment practice for an employer (1) . . . or otherwise to discriminate against any individual with respect to his compensation, terms, conditions, or privileges of employment, because of such individual's race, color, religion, sex, or national origin" 42 U.S.C.A. § 2000e–z.

7. General Electric Co. v. Gilbert, 429 U.S. 125, 97 S.Ct. 401, 50 L.Ed.2d 343 (1976).

sion of pregnancy from a disability benefits plan providing general coverage was not a gender-based distinction. A prima facie case of discrimination could admittedly have been established by showing that the effect of the "facially neutral" plan was discriminatory against a protected class, but the Court found no attempt had been made to show this effect in this case. In a later decision the Court found that Title VII did prohibit the use of pregnancy classifications or regulations that imposed a substantial burden on women employees.[8] Congress has amended Title VII so that discriminatory treatment of employees on the basis of pregnancy is now prohibited by statute.[9]

§ 14.25   Classifications Based on Wealth

The constitutional protection for classifications burdening poor persons, sometimes called wealth classifications, can be described as nothing more than the protection given to any other classification of persons or business entities which are described by criterion which the Court does not regard to be suspect. The Court will uphold legislative actions which burden poor persons as a class under the equal protection or due process guarantee if the actions have any rational relationship to a legitimate end of government. So long as these laws do not involve the allocation of fundamental rights, the Court will consider them to be regulations concerning economic and social welfare policy. As such, these laws have no relationship to values with constitutional recognition so as to merit active judicial review under the strict scrutiny-compelling interest standard. It is apparently the view of the majority of the Justices that there is nothing in the judicial function which makes them institutionally capable of deciding economic policy as to the allocation of income and wealth through the review of legislative classifications. However, the Justices will actively review those classifications which burden the exercise of fundamental rights even when such classifications are based upon wealth.

The Supreme Court has consistently held that the government is not permitted to restrict the ability to engage in fundamental constitutional rights on the basis of individual wealth.[1] However, the Court has held that the state need not subsidize the financing of abortions for women who lack the economic resources to obtain an abortion during the first two trimesters of their pregnancy. This distinction is based upon the Court's view that the right to privacy concerning abortions involves only the absence of express governmental limitations on the abortion decision and that the failure to subsidize these practices constitutes no more than a policy choice not to give increased wealth or welfare benefits to a class of people who are not described by any suspect trait.[2]

---

8. The next year the Court held that an employer's practice of taking away accumulated seniority from women who had to take mandatory pregnancy leave constituted a form of sex discrimination prohibited by Title VII. Nashville Gas Co. v. Satty, 434 U.S. 136, 98 S.Ct. 347, 54 L.Ed.2d 356 (1977). In that case the Supreme Court found that the substantial burden imposed on women by this practice rendered it a form of sex discrimination. This was true even though the same statistical impact analysis would not establish as a form of sex discrimination the employer's failure to grant insurance or sick leave pay benefits to pregnant employees. The Court remanded the case for a determination of whether the particular employer's sick pay policy was a mere pretext for invidious sex discrimination barred by Title VII. Later changes to the federal statute, Title VII, would require invalidation of discriminatory sick pay policies related to pregnancy, see note 9.

9. Pub.L. 95–555, 92 Stat. 2076 (1978) added Section 701(k) to Title VII proscribing as sex discrimination discriminatory treatment based on pregnancy or childbirth. For citations to additional Supreme Court cases, and secondary authorities, on this point, see R. Rotunda & J. Nowak, Treatise on Constitutional Law: Substance and Procedure, vol. 3, §§ 18.23, 18.24 (3rd ed. 1999, with annual supplements).

§ 14.25

1. See, e.g., Douglas v. California, 372 U.S. 353, 83 S.Ct. 814, 9 L.Ed.2d 811 (1963) (counsel in first appeal for criminal conviction); Harper v. Virginia State Bd. of Elections, 383 U.S. 663, 86 S.Ct. 1079, 16 L.Ed.2d 169 (1966) (invalidation of tax as prerequisite to voting in state elections); Boddie v. Connecticut, 401 U.S. 371, 91 S.Ct. 780, 28 L.Ed.2d 113 (1971) (filing fees for divorce cannot bar indigent). For citations to additional cases, including lower court cases, and secondary works on this topic see our multi-volume Treatise: R. Rotunda & J. Nowak, Treatise on Constitutional Law: Substance and Procedure (3rd ed. 1999, with annual supplements).

2. See Maher v. Roe, 432 U.S. 464, 97 S.Ct. 2376, 53 L.Ed.2d 484 (1977); Poelker v. Doe, 432 U.S. 519, 97 S.Ct. 2391, 53 L.Ed.2d 528 (1977); Beal v. Doe, 432 U.S. 438, 97 S.Ct. 2366, 53 L.Ed.2d 464 (1977); Harris v. McRae, 448

In a series of decisions in the 1960's concerning rights to fair treatment in the criminal process,[3] voting rights,[4] and ability to engage in interstate travel,[5] opinions of the Supreme Court had indicated that classifications which burden the poor were to be reviewed under an increased standard of review as suspect classifications. However, the Court had not yet squarely faced a law which burdened a class of persons who lacked financial resources for the allocation of benefits which had no other constitutional recognition. In *Dandridge v. Williams*[6] the Court reviewed a statute which set a formula for the provision of aid to families with dependent children that in effect did not offer any benefits for children born to families over a certain size. Since the Court has never recognized the interest of an individual in government subsistence benefits as a fundamental constitutional interest, there was no fundamental right present in this case. The majority opinion then upheld the law under a rational relationship test, finding an arguable basis for relating the classification to the state interest in economy and the provision of certain families.

This result was reached over the strong dissent of Justice Marshall who argued that classifications which burden poor persons in the ability to obtain the basic necessities for functioning in society should be judged by some meaningful standard of review even if they were not subjected to the compelling interest test.[7] However, the majority found no basis for distinguishing this law from any other economic regulation since all such measures to some extent involved the reallocation of resources or wealth. Thus, the majority found that these regulations constituted "economic and social welfare" legislation which merited only the traditional standard of review.[8]

This position has been consistently followed by the Court; it has held that there was no basis for using any form of strict scrutiny, or increased standard of review, to test legislation which burdens classifications of poor persons in the receipt of other forms of welfare benefits,[9] public housing,[10] or access to the judicial process when no fundamental right is involved.[11]

The Court again explicitly confronted the contention that some forms of wealth classifications should be held to be suspect in *San Antonio Independent School District v. Rodriguez*.[12] In that case the Court upheld the constitutionality of a property tax system that financed primary and secondary education in

---

U.S. 297, 100 S.Ct. 2671, 65 L.Ed.2d 784 (1980); Williams v. Zbaraz, 448 U.S. 358, 100 S.Ct. 2694, 65 L.Ed.2d 831 (1980).

3. See, e.g., Douglas v. California, 372 U.S. 353, 83 S.Ct. 814, 9 L.Ed.2d 811 (1963).

4. Harper v. Virginia State Bd. of Elections, 383 U.S. 663, 86 S.Ct. 1079, 16 L.Ed.2d 169 (1966).

5. Shapiro v. Thompson, 394 U.S. 618, 89 S.Ct. 1322, 22 L.Ed.2d 600 (1969).

6. 397 U.S. 471, 90 S.Ct. 1153, 25 L.Ed.2d 491 (1970).

7. 397 U.S. at 508, 90 S.Ct. at 1173 (Marshall, J., dissenting).

8. 397 U.S. at 485, 90 S.Ct. at 1161.

9. See, e.g., Schweiker v. Wilson, 450 U.S. 221, 101 S.Ct. 1074, 67 L.Ed.2d 186 (1981); Jefferson v. Hackney, 406 U.S. 535, 92 S.Ct. 1724, 32 L.Ed.2d 285 (1972). But cf., United States Dept. of Agriculture v. Moreno, 413 U.S. 528, 93 S.Ct. 2821, 37 L.Ed.2d 782 (1973) (unrelated household members exclusion of food stamp act held to violate rationality test).

Compare United States Dept. of Agriculture v. Murry, 413 U.S. 508, 93 S.Ct. 2832, 37 L.Ed.2d 767 (1973) (food stamp act exclusion of households based on previous status of individual member invalidated as an irrebuttable presumption), with Lyng v. Castillo, 477 U.S. 635, 106

S.Ct. 2727, 91 L.Ed.2d 527 (1986) (upholding a classification for the dispensation of federal food stamp benefits that gave lesser benefits to a household comprised of parents, children, and siblings—as opposed to households composed of more distant relatives—on the basis that it was not irrational to conclude that traditional family households might realize economies of scale in the customary preparation of group meals). See also, Bowen v. Gilliard, 483 U.S. 587, 107 S.Ct. 3008, 97 L.Ed.2d 485 (1987) (upholding statute that effectively reduced the amount of benefits under the Aid to Families With Dependent Children program for certain families by redefining the nature of the family unit, and family unit income, that determined the level of benefits for a family).

10. James v. Valtierra, 402 U.S. 137, 91 S.Ct. 1331, 28 L.Ed.2d 678 (1971), see also Lindsey v. Normet, 405 U.S. 56, 92 S.Ct. 862, 31 L.Ed.2d 36 (1972); Arlington Heights v. Metropolitan Housing Development Corp., 429 U.S. 252, 97 S.Ct. 555, 50 L.Ed.2d 450 (1977).

11. United States v. Kras, 409 U.S. 434, 93 S.Ct. 631, 34 L.Ed.2d 626 (1973) (bankruptcy fee); Ortwein v. Schwab, 410 U.S. 656, 93 S.Ct. 1172, 35 L.Ed.2d 572 (1973) (filing fee to appeal from decision to terminate welfare benefits).

12. 411 U.S. 1, 93 S.Ct. 1278, 36 L.Ed.2d 16 (1973).

school districts in a manner that created large differences in the amount of money spent on the education of individual children. The Court found nothing in the allocation of educational opportunities based on the wealth of the district in which a child resided that furnished a constitutionally cognizable basis for close judicial supervision of legislative policies in this area. In so doing the opinion noted that in no case had the Court ever engaged in an active standard of review solely because the law burdened poor persons in the allocation of benefits which could not be deemed to be fundamental constitutional rights.[13]

The Court has held that governmental entities may not take actions which limit the capabilities of a class of persons to engage in the exercise of fundamental constitutional rights because of their lack of economic resources. In this area the Court has a separate basis for engaging in the active review of the actions of other branches of government: these laws burden interests which the Court has found to be of such a value as to merit special protection against arbitrary limitations. The state may be free to allocate economic benefits on any economic policy it chooses but the fact that these rights are of fundamental constitutional magnitude means that they cannot be given only to those who can afford to pay for them.[14]

Thus the Court has held that indigents must be granted equal access to all the aspects of the criminal process that are basic to the fair determination of their guilt or innocence.[15] However, once the state has fulfilled this duty by granting them the opportunity for a fair trial and access to the initial appellate process, there is no requirement that the state go further and level all economic distinctions by continuing to provide counsel for the individual throughout successive appeals or collateral attacks.[16]

In a decision concerning the right to vote, the Court has held that any form of voter taxes is an impermissible way to limit access to the ballot.[17] The right of an individual to stand for elective office is also part of that fundamental right. The state may impose filing fees on candidates who can afford to pay them, for this is a reasonable means of determining which candidates are seriously interested in running for office, but the same filing fees cannot be applied to a person without the funds to pay them; otherwise the right to run for elective office would be allocated on the basis of individual financial resources.[18] Similarly the state cannot establish residency requirements for government benefits when that would penalize the right to interstate travel for poor persons.[19] And where access to the courts is necessary to protect one of these fundamental rights the process may not bar litigants because of their inability to pay filing fees.[20]

---

13. 411 U.S. at 28, 93 S.Ct. at 1293–94. The Court has held that a state may not arbitrarily deny all access to education to a class of children. See, Plyler v. Doe, 457 U.S. 202, 102 S.Ct. 2382, 72 L.Ed.2d 786 (1982) (invalidating statute denying education to children of illegal aliens).

14. See §§ 14.29(b)(4), 14.31–14.33, 14.37, 14.38, infra.

15. See, e.g., Smith v. Bennett, 365 U.S. 708, 81 S.Ct. 895, 6 L.Ed.2d 39 (1961) (filing fees may not bar collateral attack); Douglas v. California, 372 U.S. 353, 83 S.Ct. 814, 9 L.Ed.2d 811 (1963) (counsel in first appeal); Mayer v. Chicago, 404 U.S. 189, 92 S.Ct. 410, 30 L.Ed.2d 372 (1971) (transcript fees). For references to additional cases, and secondary authorities, on this point see the multi-volume edition of this Treatise: R. Rotunda & J. Nowak, Treatise on Constitutional Law: Substance and Procedure §§ 18.25, 18.41 (3rd ed. 1999, with annual supplements).

16. Ross v. Moffitt, 417 U.S. 600, 94 S.Ct. 2437, 41 L.Ed.2d 341 (1974). For citations to additional Supreme Court cases, and secondary authorities, on this point, see R. Rotunda & J. Nowak, Treatise on Constitutional Law:

Substance and Procedure, § 17.9 (3rd ed. 1999, with annual supplements).

17. Harper v. Virginia State Bd. of Elections, 383 U.S. 663, 86 S.Ct. 1079, 16 L.Ed.2d 169 (1966) (State and local fees). Poll taxes for federal elections are proscribed by the Twenty-Fourth Amendment. U.S.Const. amend. XXIV.

18. Lubin v. Panish, 415 U.S. 709, 94 S.Ct. 1315, 39 L.Ed.2d 702 (1974); Bullock v. Carter, 405 U.S. 134, 92 S.Ct. 849, 31 L.Ed.2d 92 (1972).

19. Shapiro v. Thompson, 394 U.S. 618, 89 S.Ct. 1322, 22 L.Ed.2d 600 (1969); Memorial Hosp. v. Maricopa County, 415 U.S. 250, 94 S.Ct. 1076, 39 L.Ed.2d 306 (1974).

20. Boddie v. Connecticut, 401 U.S. 371, 91 S.Ct. 780, 28 L.Ed.2d 113 (1971) (divorce); Smith v. Bennett, 365 U.S. 708, 81 S.Ct. 895, 6 L.Ed.2d 39 (1961) (collateral attack on criminal conviction). Thus, the Supreme Court has held that a state must waive otherwise mandatory filing fees for indigent persons seeking a divorce. Boddie v. Connecticut, 401 U.S. 371, 91 S.Ct. 780, 28 L.Ed.2d 113 (1971). Similarly, the Court has held that a state could not

It should be noted that the issue in fundamental rights cases is whether the individual statute constitutes a limitation of the fundamental right that violates the Constitution and not whether it is fair or unfair to poor persons. The law may be invalidated as a violation of the fundamental constitutional right even though it seeks to level wealth distinctions in the exercise of the right rather than to create them. Thus in *Buckley v. Valeo*[21] the Court invalidated limits on campaign spending by candidates for public office as an unconstitutional burden on the right to freedom of speech. While the legislation was in part designed to equalize the ability to run for office between persons of differing wealth status, the majority found no interest of a sufficiently compelling magnitude to justify the limitation on the First Amendment right to free speech.

The Court has ruled that states need not subsidize abortions during the first two trimesters of pregnancy for women who are unable to pay for those abortions. The majority opinions in these cases construed a woman's right to an abortion, as protected by the constitutionally fundamental value of privacy, to entail only a freedom from direct government restraints on her ability to choose to have an abortion.[22] Thus, the majority considered the legislature's policy to encourage childbirth by providing benefits for childbirth procedures and other maternity requirements, but not for abortions, as a permissible social welfare measure. To the majority this limitation amounted to nothing more than the refusal to offer to increase the income position of persons who wished to enjoy a benefit available in the private sector which they could not afford given the other allocations of their resources. This classification did not burden the fundamental right and did not merit any increased standard of review. The majority opinion noted that wealth classifications have never been granted the protection of a standard of review above the rationality test.[23]

The dissenting opinions in these cases pointed out that this decision did not seem to correlate with the many instances in which the Court had invalidated state burdens on the exercise of fundamental rights by poor persons.[24] The differences between the majority and the dissent are truly irreconcilable, for these Justices have totally different views of the Court's role in insuring free exercise of fundamental rights by persons of extremely limited economic resources. The view of the dissent is that the state is not only required to respect the exercise of fundamental rights but also to facilitate their exercise within its existing wealth and income reallocation systems. The majority views the duty of the state only in terms of an inability to create barriers to the exercise of those rights.

In those instances where the state controls the means necessary to the exercise of the

---

deny a woman an appeal from a trial court decision permanently terminating her parental rights (terminating her right to have a relationship with her children) solely on the basis that she could not afford to pay for a transcript of the trial court record. M.L.B. v. S.L.J., 519 U.S. 102, 117 S.Ct. 555, 136 L.Ed.2d 473 (1996). The Court has also ruled that the government must waive filing fees for candidates who are indigent and cannot afford to pay the filing fee otherwise required to appear as a candidate on the election ballot. See § 14.32.

21. 424 U.S. 1, 96 S.Ct. 612, 46 L.Ed.2d 659 (1976). See Chapter 16, regarding election regulations and the freedom of speech.

22. Harris v. McRae, 448 U.S. 297, 100 S.Ct. 2671, 65 L.Ed.2d 784 (1980)(limitation on payments for abortions under Social Security-Medicaid program upheld); Williams v. Zbaraz, 448 U.S. 358, 100 S.Ct. 2694, 65 L.Ed.2d 831 (1980) (Federal statutes do not require payment for abortions).

See also, Maher v. Roe, 432 U.S. 464, 97 S.Ct. 2376, 53 L.Ed.2d 484 (1977) (payments for nontherapeutic abortions may be denied poor women); Beal v. Doe, 432 U.S. 438, 97 S.Ct. 2366, 53 L.Ed.2d 464 (1977) (Social Security Act does not require such payments); Poelker v. Doe, 432 U.S. 519, 97 S.Ct. 2391, 53 L.Ed.2d 528 (1977) (City hospital may provide free child birth assistance without providing corresponding services for nontherapeutic abortions).

These decisions are examined in § 14.29, infra.

23. See, Maher v. Roe, 432 U.S. 464, 471, 97 S.Ct. 2376, 2381, 53 L.Ed.2d 484 (1977); Harris v. McRae, 448 U.S. 297, 323, 100 S.Ct. 2671, 2694, 65 L.Ed.2d 784 (1980), rehearing denied 448 U.S. 917, 101 S.Ct. 39, 65 L.Ed.2d 1180 (1980).

24. See, Harris v. McRae, 448 U.S. 297, 329, 100 S.Ct. 2671, 2694, 65 L.Ed.2d 784 (1980) (Brennan, J., dissenting, joined by Marshall & Blackmun, JJ.); 448 U.S. at 337, 100 S.Ct. at 2706 (Marshall, J., dissenting); 448 U.S. at 348, 100 S.Ct. at 2711 (Blackmun, J., dissenting). See also, 448 U.S. at 349, 100 S.Ct. at 2712 (Stevens, J., dissenting).

right, or to their protection through litigation, the majority will engage in some redistribution of economic benefits by allowing indigent persons free access to those governmental "benefits." However, it is the view of the majority that the state is not required to equalize the ability to exercise fundamental rights in the private sector for persons of differing wealth classifications. To this extent the case may be seen as consistent with the decision refusing to engage in a meaningful review of welfare programs. Any denial of a welfare benefit to class of poor persons can be said to make them less able to exercise a variety of fundamental rights in society by decreasing their total resources.[25]

§ 14.26　The Right to Privacy: Introduction

The "right to privacy" has varied meanings. In the common law of torts, the right encompasses a freedom from intrusion by others into privately owned areas as well as freedom from disclosures of information about an individual's private life.[1] The phrase also has several meanings in terms of constitutional analysis. The oldest constitutional right to privacy is that protected by the Fourth Amendment's restriction on governmental searches and seizures. The First Amendment has been held to protect some rights to privacy in speech or association.[2] The Court has also confronted the tort right to privacy in determining when suit may be brought against a person whose speech has invaded the privacy of another.[3]

But in terms of due process and equal protection the "right to privacy" has come to mean a right to engage in certain highly personal activities. More specifically, it currently relates to certain rights of freedom of choice in marital, sexual, and reproductive matters. Even this definition may be too broad, for the Court still has not recognized any general right to engage in sexual activities that are done in private. Instead, the Justices have acknowledged the existence of a "right" and defined it by very specific application to laws relating to reproduction, contraception, abortion, and marriage.[4]

This general constitutional right to privacy may have had its inception in an article written in 1890 by Samuel Warren and Louis D. Brandeis.[5] The article attacked intrusions by newspapers into the private affairs of individuals and advocated the protection of the "inviolate personality" of each person. In contemporary terms Warren and Brandeis were advocating protection, under the law of torts, for dissemination or use of facts relating to an individual's private life. They did not consider the problem of government intrusion into the "inviolate personality" of each individual, but they did help to establish recognition in American legal thought that each person had a cognizable legal interest in a private life, both physical and emotional.

Later, as a Justice of the Supreme Court, Brandeis would advocate a wide reading of the Fourth Amendment in order to insure that government did not intrude into the "privacy of the individual." While Justice Brandeis did not foresee the issue of government restrictions or decision-making in private matters, he laid the basis for the modern right when he recognized a right to protection of one's private life from government intrusion or "the right to be alone—the most comprehensive of

---

25. For citations to secondary sources on this topic, see R. Rotunda & J. Nowak, Treatise on Constitutional Law: Substance and Procedure, vol. 3, § 18.25 (3rd ed. 1999, with annual supplements).

§ 14.26

1. For the leading original analysis of this concept, see Warren & Brandeis. The Right to Privacy, 4 Harv.L.Rev. 193 (1890). See generally, David D. Meyer, Lochner Redeemed: Family Privacy After Troxel and Carhart, 48 UCLA L. Rev. 1125 (2001).

2. See §§ 16.41–16.47, infra.

3. E.g., Gertz v. Robert Welch, Inc., 418 U.S. 323, 94 S.Ct. 2997, 41 L.Ed.2d 789 (1974); Cox Broadcasting

Corp. v. Cohn, 420 U.S. 469, 95 S.Ct. 1029, 43 L.Ed.2d 328 (1975). See also §§ 16.32–16.36, infra.

4. See generally, Lucas, C.J., citing this section of the Treatise in Hill, et al. v. National Collegiate Athletic Association, 7 Cal.4th 1, 26 Cal.Rptr.2d 834, 851, 865 P.2d 633, 650 (1994); State ex rel. Thomas v. Ohio State Univ., 71 Ohio St.3d 245, 248, 643 N.E.2d 126, 129, 96 Ed.Law Rep. 237, 23 Media L.Rep. 1856 (1994) (per curiam), citing Treatise.

5. Warren & Brandeis, The Right of Privacy, 4 Harv. L.Rev. 193 (1890).

rights and the right most valued by civilized man." [6]

During the first part of this century the Supreme Court held that the liberty protected by the due process clause included the freedom to make decisions which did not adversely affect legitimate state interests. In *Meyer v. Nebraska*[7] the Court invalidated a statute which prohibited all grade schools from teaching subjects in any language other than English. In *Pierce v. Society of Sisters*[8] a statute which required students to attend public rather than private schools was found repugnant to the due process clause of the Fourteenth Amendment. In each case the majority found that the law restricted individual freedom without any relation to a valid public interest. Freedom of choice regarding an individual's personal life was recognized as constitutionally protected.

These decisions may only have reflected the attitude of the Court towards government regulation during the apex of "substantive due process."[9] While these decisions might today be grounded on the First Amendment, their existence is important to the growth of the right to privacy. If nothing else, they show a historical recognition of a right to private decision-making regarding family matters as inherent in the concept of liberty.

§ 14.27 Sterilization and Contraception

The development of the contemporary concept of a constitutionally protected "right of privacy" in sexual matters can be traced to the Supreme Court's decision in *Skinner v. Oklahoma*.[1] On the basis of the equal protection clause, the Court held unconstitutional a statute which authorized the sterilization of persons previously convicted and sentenced to imprisonment two or more times of crimes "amounting of felonies of moral turpitude" in the state. Under the statute persons convicted of "offenses arising out of the violation of

the prohibitory laws, revenue acts, embezzlement, or political offenses" were excepted from sterilization. A person was subjected to sterilization only if her or his crimes were classified (perhaps arbitrarily) as ones involving moral turpitude. Under this system grand larceny was deemed to be such a crime while embezzlement was not. Thus a person convicted three times of larceny could be subjected to sterilization while the embezzler was free from the risk of sterilization no matter how often he committed the crime or how large a sum of money he appropriated.

The Court did not "stop to point out all the inequities of the Act," but instead rested the decision upon the artificiality of the distinction drawn between larceny and embezzlement, crimes of intrinsically the same nature. Despite the broad police powers of the state, this classification violated the equal protection clause because it could not withstand the scrutiny to which the fundamental nature of the right involved demanded it be subjected. The Court noted that the Act dealt with "one of the basic civil rights of man. ... Marriage and procreation [were] fundamental to the very existence and survival of the race".[2] In the Court's view this required strict scrutiny of the classification for "[w]hen the law [laid] an unequal hand on those who [had] committed intrinsically the same quality of offense and sterilize[d] one and not the other, it [made] as invidious a discrimination as if it had selected a particular race or nationality for oppressive treatment."[3] In this way the Court went beyond traditional rational relationship standard of review.

This rationale was to have two important ramifications. First, it established the basis for "fundamental rights" analysis under the due process and equal protection guarantees by finding that some rights deserved special judicial protection from the majoritarian pro-

---

6. See his dissenting opinion in Olmstead v. United States, 277 U.S. 438, 478, 48 S.Ct. 564, 572, 72 L.Ed. 944 (1928).

7. 262 U.S. 390, 43 S.Ct. 625, 67 L.Ed. 1042 (1923).

8. 268 U.S. 510, 45 S.Ct. 571, 69 L.Ed. 1070 (1925).

9. See §§ 11.1–11.3, supra.

§ 14.27

1. 316 U.S. 535, 62 S.Ct. 1110, 86 L.Ed. 1655 (1942).

2. 316 U.S. at 541, 62 S.Ct. at 1113.

3. 316 U.S. at 541, 62 S.Ct. at 1113.

cess. Second, while the opinion never mentioned a "right of privacy" relating to sexual matters, it established interests in marriage or procreation as ones of special constitutional significance.

It should be noted that the Supreme Court has not ruled that involuntary sterilization is *per se* unconstitutional. *Skinner* was an equal protection ruling in which the Court held that classifications of persons who were sterilized would be subjected to strict scrutiny. This holding therefore does not establish a constitutional prohibition of all such statutes. Previously, in *Buck v. Bell*,[4] the Court had upheld a sterilization statute, in an opinion by Justice Holmes, stating that the legislature was the branch of government most suited to defining the necessity of these procedures. However, this decision came prior to the use of the fundamental rights—strict scrutiny analysis. Because the statute would now be viewed as an interference with the fundamental right of privacy (the freedom of choice regarding the individual's ability to reproduce) it could only be justified by a compelling governmental interest.

Some lower courts have allowed states to order sterilization of mentally retarded persons both in criminal and civil proceedings.[5] But it is doubtful that the Supreme Court would follow *Buck v. Bell* today. If the Justices can find no compelling interest to justify the prohibition of abortions, any state interest in sterilization should be held insufficient to impair this fundamental right.

The right to privacy was given its first exposition by Justice Harlan in his dissent in *Poe v. Ullman*.[6] The majority did not reach the merits and held that the challenges to Connecticut statutes prohibiting the use of contraceptive devices, and the giving of medical advice on

the use of such devices, did not present a justiciable controversy as there was no apparent intent by state officials to enforce these statutes. Justice Harlan dissented on this issue; he saw the statute and its possible enforcement as imposing a burden on the plaintiffs. More importantly, he reached the merits of their claims and found that application of the statute to married persons would violate the due process clause because the regulation invaded marital "privacy." In his opinion, the statute intruded upon "the most intimate details of the marital relation" and prosecution under the statutes would require disclosure of those relationships.

In *Griswold v. Connecticut*,[7] the Court held the same Connecticut statutes invalid because they restricted the right of married persons to use contraceptive devices. The appellants in this case, a doctor and executive of the Planned Parenthood League, were convicted for giving information and medical advice to married persons concerning means of preventing conception.

The majority opinion by Justice Douglas found that the statute impermissibly limited the right of privacy of married persons. The law violated the due process clause because it deprived these married persons of the liberty protected by this fundamental right.

There was some confusion caused by Douglas' attempt to find a specific textual basis for a "right of privacy" that would include the right of married persons to use contraceptives, but it should be realized that this confusion was not the sole fault of the Douglas opinion, for the Court continued to formally reject the substantive due process decisions of the first part of the century.[8] Thus, Douglas was

---

4. 274 U.S. 200, 47 S.Ct. 584, 71 L.Ed. 1000 (1927).

See also Stump v. Sparkman, 435 U.S. 349, 98 S.Ct. 1099, 55 L.Ed.2d 331 (1978), where the Supreme Court held that state judges were immune from suits under the Civil Rights Acts for acts done in their official capacity. The case involved the unjustified granting of an order to sterilize a fifteen year old female.

5. See, e.g., In re Cavitt, 182 Neb. 712, 157 N.W.2d 171 (1968), appeal dismissed sub nom., Cavitt v. Nebraska, 396 U.S. 996, 90 S.Ct. 543, 24 L.Ed.2d 490 (1970).

The relevant cases are collected in annot., 53 A.L.R.3d 960; annot., 74 A.L.R.3d 1210; annot., 74 A.L.R.3d 1224.

6. 367 U.S. 497, 522, 81 S.Ct. 1752, 1766, 6 L.Ed.2d 989 (1961) (Harlan, J., dissenting).

7. 381 U.S. 479, 85 S.Ct. 1678, 14 L.Ed.2d 510 (1965).

8. § 11.4, supra.

forced to repudiate *Lochner v. New York*[9] and state that the Supreme Court "did not sit as a super-legislature." [10] Yet he had to justify the decision of the Court to invalidate this law on the basis that it infringed the general area of liberty. It was too close—in terms of decisional, if not calendar, time—to the period of substantive due process to admit that the Supreme Court had to protect some individual rights against government intrusion in much the same manner as the Court had done in *Lochner*. The difference was, of course, in the nature of the right to be protected and the role of the Court as the proper entity to define and protect the right. But at this time Douglas had to create a more specific right and relate it to the text of the Constitution in order to formally differentiate this decision from earlier uses of substantive due process.

In order to justify the decision as one mandated by specific constitutional principles, the majority opinion created a new "right to privacy." Justice Douglas found that the "penumbras" and "emanations" of several guarantees of the Bill of Rights established this right to privacy. The right of parents to send their children to parochial schools[11] and the freedom of private schools from excessive restrictions[12] evidenced special values in the liberty to make personal decisions free of governmental restrictions. Indeed, the entire freedom of association was implied from the express guarantees of the First Amendment. This Amendment included a right to privacy, as the government could force disclosure of association or speech only in the most limited circumstances. The Fourth and Fifth Amendments also reflected sources for individual privacy and freedom from government demands for information. Thus the opinion found that a right to privacy existed within the bases for these express rights.

It is fair to say that the right of privacy was created in *Griswold*: no specific, Court-defined right to engage in private acts had existed

before this decision. But the opinion was nonetheless correct in finding that the values of privacy, including freedom from government intrusion with private thoughts, association, and liberty, had long been part of American legal philosophy. These values indeed had been the basis for the arguments of Brandeis and the earlier opinions cited by Justice Douglas.

The Douglas opinion turned these historical values into a specific guarantee to help justify the Court's enforcing the values against a legislative decision. The Connecticut legislature banned the use of contraceptives by married persons, which contravened the established values of privacy in three ways: (1) it regulated a personal marital relationship without an identifiable, legitimate reason; (2) it gave government the right to inquire into these private marital relationships; (3) prosecution under the statutes would often require husbands and wives to testify to the intimate details of their relationship.

Separate concurring opinions brought forward reasons for judicial protection of these privacy values against legislative or executive actions. Justice Goldberg took the position that it was the function of the Court to defend certain fundamental rights under the due process clause even though these rights were not expressed in the first eight Amendments. Goldberg was of the opinion that the Ninth Amendment evinced the historic belief that certain fundamental rights could not be restricted by the government even though it did not create specific rights. The Court should look to the "tradition and [collective] conscience of our people" [13] to determine if a right was fundamental and one which should be judicially protected from infringement by other branches of government. There was no doubt that "marital privacy" was such a right because there were clear historic values in freedom of choice in marital relationships. As

---

9. 198 U.S. 45, 25 S.Ct. 539, 49 L.Ed. 937 (1905). For a discussion of this case see § 11.3, supra.

10. 381 U.S. at 482, 85 S.Ct. at 1680.

11. Pierce v. Society of Sisters, 268 U.S. 510, 45 S.Ct. 571, 69 L.Ed. 1070 (1925).

12. Meyer v. Nebraska, 262 U.S. 390, 43 S.Ct. 625, 67 L.Ed. 1042 (1923).

13. 381 U.S. at 493, 85 S.Ct. at 1686 (Goldberg, J., concurring).

Justice Goldberg noted, if a law required husband and wives to be sterilized after having two children, any Justice would have held it unconstitutional absent the most compelling justification regardless of the "implied" nature of the guarantee.

Justice Harlan concurred in the decision, also finding that the due process clause protected fundamental liberties which were not expressed in the Bill of Rights. Just as in his dissent in *Poe v. Ullman,*[14] he found that marital privacy was a basic part of the liberty "protected by the Fourteenth Amendment." In Harlan's opinion it was the role of the Justices to decide when legislation violated "basic values 'implicit in the concept of ordered liberty.' "[15]

Justice White's concurrence followed through on this due process theory; he found no legitimate end of government which could support this law. The state claimed that the statute was to deter illicit sexual relationships but there was no likelihood that a ban on contraceptives for married persons would promote that end. Thus the statute restricted a fundamental constitutional value arbitrarily.

Justices Black and Stewart dissented in *Griswold*. They could find no basis for judicial protection of a right to privacy, and they were committed to the view that the Justices should not follow in the steps of the substantive due process decisions by enforcing values which had no textual basis in the Constitution. It is interesting to note that by the time of the decision on abortion regulations in 1973, Justice Stewart had come to accept this decision as a permissible use of substantive due process theories.

The Court has restricted the ability of states to punish the use of contraceptives by adults. In *Griswold* the Court held that the use of contraceptives by married persons could not be prohibited. Seven years later, in *Eisenstadt v. Baird*[16] the Court invalidated a statute which

prohibited distribution of contraceptives to unmarried persons because a majority found that this separate treatment of unmarried persons violated the equal protection clause. In *Eisenstadt* the Court did not explicitly rely on the fundamental rights-strict scrutiny analysis. Instead, the majority opinion simply found no rational or legitimate way to distinguish between use of contraceptives by married or unmarried persons.

While the majority opinion, by Justice Brennan, purported to apply only the traditional equal protection standard of review, the majority clearly employed some form of independent judicial scrutiny. One conceivable purpose of the statute was the prevention of premarital, as opposed to extramarital sex. The opinion conceded that the state, consistent with the equal protection clause, could treat differently the problems of premarital and extramarital sexual relations. The majority found, however, that prevention of premarital sexual relations was not in fact the purpose of the statute because to accept that interest it would have had to impute to the legislature an intent to punish premarital sexual relations by forced pregnancy and birth of an unwanted child—a conclusion the majority was unwilling to reach. Nor could it be demonstrated that the statute significantly furthered that end. The same statute permitted distribution of contraceptives to unmarried persons for prevention of disease, an exception which diminished considerably the statute's potential effectiveness. The state also asserted its interest in regulating medically harmful substances as a basis for the legislation, but this interest could not support the classification for several reasons. First, the Court concluded that the statute was not in fact a health measure, because it was contained in a chapter of the Massachusetts laws dealing with "Crimes Against Chastity, Morality, Decency and Good Order" and was cast only in terms of morals. Second, the statute

14. 367 U.S. 497, 539–55, 81 S.Ct. 1752, 1774–83, 6 L.Ed.2d 989 (1961) (Harlan, J., dissenting).

15. 381 U.S. at 500, 85 S.Ct. at 1690, quoting Palko v. Connecticut, 302 U.S. 319, 325, 58 S.Ct. 149, 152, 82 L.Ed. 288 (1937).

16. 405 U.S. 438, 92 S.Ct. 1029, 31 L.Ed.2d 349 (1972).

was underinclusive because it could not be shown that the health needs of unmarried persons were greater than those of married persons. Finally, the statute was overbroad in restricting distribution of all contraceptives, while only some could be demonstrated to be dangerous.

Following *Griswold* and *Eisenstadt* it was clear that states may not eliminate the use of contraceptives by adults. However, the states should be able to restrict the manufacture and sale of contraceptive devices to insure that the products meet health and safety standards. For such restrictions the state will have to show that the regulations in fact promote health or safety. Mere assertion of police power ends will not justify limitation of the right to privacy.

In *Carey v. Population Services International*,[17] the Court invalidated a law which allowed only pharmacists to sell nonmedical contraceptive devices to persons over 16 years of age and prohibited the sale of such items to those under 16. As to the general restriction, there was a majority opinion that the burden on an adult's freedom of choice could only be justified by a compelling interest and that distribution only through pharmacists did not advance such an end. The Court struck the restriction on children without a majority opinion.

Writing for four members of the Court, Justice Brennan implied that even young persons have some rights to freedom of choice in these matters.[18] The other three Justices voting to strike the law wanted to avoid any implication of a right of minors to engage in sexual activity. They would allow prohibition of sexual activity, including use of the contraceptives by

minors. But, as there has never been any evidence that denial of contraceptives to young persons deterred them from such activities, for the state to require them to assume greater risks of pregnancy and disease if they violated the law was therefore so arbitrary as to violate due process.[19] Thus when these three are combined with the two dissenting Justices, there appears to be a majority that would allow statutes strictly regulating the sexual activity of minors.

In 2003, the Supreme Court would find that the Court's rulings regarding sterilization and contraception supported the Court's ruling that a state law prohibiting sodomy between persons of the same sex violated the due process clause of the Fourteenth Amendment, because it would not further a legitimate interest of government that would justify a severe intrusion into an area of personal privacy.[20]

§ 14.28 Marriage, Family Relationships, and Sexual Activity as a Part of the Right to Privacy

The right to freedom of choice in marriage and family relationships lies at the heart of the right to privacy. The early due process cases regarding the education and rearing of children showed special concern for the values of free choice in such matters. Justice Harlan first described the modern "right to privacy" in terms of the historic values of privacy and freedom of choice in marriage relationships.[1] On this basis, the right to freedom of choice in marriage relationships is itself a fundamental right. Thus, laws which restrict individual choice regarding marriage or divorce will be

17. 431 U.S. 678, 97 S.Ct. 2010, 52 L.Ed.2d 675 (1977).

18. 431 U.S. at 694–95, 97 S.Ct. at 2021 (opinion of Brennan, J., joined by Stewart, Marshall, & Blackmun, JJ.).

19. The three concurrences actually rested on the dual basis: (1) that the prohibition of distribution violated fundamental rights when applied to interfere with family relations in that it included young married females and distribution from a parent to a child; (2) the ban constituted a totally arbitrary infliction of risk and harm upon children who would violate the laws against sexual relationships in any event. 431 U.S. at 702, 97 S.Ct. at 2025 (White, J., concurring); 431 U.S. at 703, 97 S.Ct. at 2025 (Powell, J. concurring); 431 U.S. at 712, 97 S.Ct. at 2030

(Stevens, J., concurring). Only Chief Justice Burger and Justice Rehnquist dissented from the ruling on the invalidity of the law.

20. Lawrence v. Texas, ___ U.S. ___, 123 S.Ct. 2472, 156 L.Ed.2d 508 (2003), overruling Bowers v. Hardwick, 478 U.S. 186, 106 S.Ct. 2841, 92 L.Ed.2d 140 (1986). The *Bowers* and *Lawrence* decisions are examined in § 14.28 of this Treatise.

§ 14.28

1. See his dissenting opinion in Poe v. Ullman, 367 U.S. 497, 522, 81 S.Ct. 1752, 1766, 6 L.Ed.2d 989 (1961) (Harlan, J., dissenting).

subjected to "strict scrutiny" under the due process or equal protection clauses.

A law which generally limits freedom of choice in marriage for all persons will be invalid under the due process test unless the state can show an overriding or compelling interest in the restriction. Similarly, a law which restricts or inhibits the right of a class of persons to marry will be invalid under the equal protection guarantee unless the state can show that the classification in fact promotes a compelling or overriding interest.[2]

A case of special significance in establishing marriage as a fundamental right is *Loving v. Virginia*.[3] In this case the Court held unconstitutional a statute prohibiting interracial marriage. The statute was found violative of equal protection because it rested solely upon distinctions drawn according to race. It was a denial of due process, for it deprived each individual of significant freedom of choosing whom to marry. Since marriage is a fundamental right, the state could not restrict the right to marry for less than compelling reasons.

In *Boddie v. Connecticut*[4] the Supreme Court held invalid a statute making the payment of court costs a prerequisite to obtaining access to state courts, as applied to persons seeking a divorce who were unable to pay such costs. Appellants were welfare recipients who had been unable to bring a divorce action in a state court solely because of their inability to pay the court fees. Because courts were usually not the sole means available for resolving private disputes, the Supreme Court had seldom

been asked to view the access to courts in a civil context as an element of due process. Here, however, divorce was available only through the judicial machinery of the state. The state's refusal to admit these appellants to its courts, the sole means for obtaining a divorce, was the equivalent of denying them the freedom of choice regarding the dissolution of their marriage. Because the State could show no overriding state interest, this barrier to freedom of choice in marriage was a denial of due process.

The Court's decision was predicated upon the fundamental nature of the right to marry or dissolve that relationship, as well as the monopoly held by the states over the means of dissolution. Indeed, the Court pointed out that its holding was extremely narrow; one could not be denied access to the sole means to adjust a fundamental human relation because of inability to pay court costs. The importance of this observation became clear in later years when the Court refused to order that persons be granted access to courts for such nonfundamental claims as welfare rights[5] or bankruptcy discharges.[6]

A quarter century after *Boddie*, the Supreme Court ruled that a state, based solely on the basis that she could not afford to pay for a transcript of the trial court record, could not deny an individual access to appellate review a trial court decision permanently terminating her parental rights. In *M.L.B. v. S.L.J.*,[7] the Supreme Court considered the case of a woman whose right to have a relationship with her two minor children was permanently terminated by a trial court at the request of her ex-

2. Special Rule For Prison Inmate Cases. In Turner v. Safley, 482 U.S. 78, 107 S.Ct. 2254, 96 L.Ed.2d 64 (1987), the Supreme Court found that restrictions on the exercise of fundamental rights by prison inmates should be upheld so long as the prison regulation at issue was reasonably related to a legitimate penological interest. The Court found that prisoners had a fundamental right to establish a marriage relationship with other persons, but that regulations restricting the exercise of this right by prisoners need not be subject to a compelling interest standard. Nevertheless, the Supreme Court in *Turner* invalidated a prison regulation that prohibited prisoners from marrying any inmate or any person outside of the prison without the permission of the prison superintendent, which was given only if there was a "compelling reason" to give the prisoner permission to marry. The Court found that this restriction on a fundamental consti-

tutional right could not be upheld because there were many alternative marriage regulations that would protect legitimate prison security and rehabilitation interests without virtually eliminating the ability of prison inmates to enter a marriage relationship. See § 10.6 for further analysis of "prisoners' rights" cases.

3. 388 U.S. 1, 87 S.Ct. 1817, 18 L.Ed.2d 1010 (1967).

4. 401 U.S. 371, 91 S.Ct. 780, 28 L.Ed.2d 113 (1971).

5. Ortwein v. Schwab, 410 U.S. 656, 93 S.Ct. 1172, 35 L.Ed.2d 572 (1973).

6. United States v. Kras, 409 U.S. 434, 93 S.Ct. 631, 34 L.Ed.2d 626 (1973).

7. 519 U.S. 102, 117 S.Ct. 555, 136 L.Ed.2d 473 (1996).

husband. The ex-husband sought to terminate his former wife's relationship to the children so that those children could be adopted by his new wife. The ex-husband won in the trial court; that court ruled that the mother's relationship to her children should be terminated. The mother of the children was denied an appeal solely on the basis that she could not pay for record preparation fees; there was no question that she did not have the resources to pay the fees.

In *M.L.B.* the Supreme Court found that the use of the state rule to prohibit the mother's appeal violated both due process and equal protection. The majority opinion in *M.L.B.*, written by Justice Ginsburg, noted that the Court has upheld laws requiring filing fees for civil actions by using a "presumption of constitutionality" and reviewing those laws only under the rationality test. Justice Ginsburg referred to *Boddie* when she stated that the Court had also created "a narrow category of civil cases in which the state must provide access to its judicial processes without regard to a party's ability to pay court fees."[8] As Justice Harlan had in *Boddie*, Justice Ginsburg in *M.L.B.* refrained from calling the rights inherent in the parent-child relationship to be "fundamental constitutional rights" in a technical sense. Her majority opinion in *M.L.B.* referred to *Boddie* when ruling that "choices about marriage and family life and the upbringing of children are among associational rights this Court has ranked as of basic importance in our society."[9]

Justice Ginsburg's majority opinion in *M.L.B.* did not set out a technical test for examining the restriction of a fundamental rights under substantive due process or equal protection. The majority opinion stated that, in such cases, the Court would "inspect the

character and identify of the individual interests at stake [the importance of the parent-child relationship in this case], on the one hand and the state's justification for its exaction [of a fee for the appeal] on the other."[10] Because of the special protection given to the parent child relationship in prior cases, the state could not justify termination of this fundamental civil liberty based solely on its legitimate interest in making the judicial process to be, at least in part, self-supporting. For that reason, the majority ruled that denying a woman the ability to appeal from a termination of her parental rights based solely on her inability to pay a filing or record fee violated both due process and equal protection.[11]

Although governmental regulation of the ability to enter or withdraw from a marriage is subject to close judicial scrutiny, the government may employ marital status classifications in welfare systems. In *Califano v. Jobst*[12] the Justices had little problem in upholding the provisions of the Social Security Act which terminated the benefits of a disabled person, who received benefits as a disabled dependent child of a deceased wage earner covered by the Act, when that person married someone who was not receiving Social Security benefits. An exemption from the "marriage termination rule" for those disabled children who married other persons entitled to benefits under the Social Security Act was held not to be so under-inclusive as to violate the equal protection guarantee embodied in the due process clause of the Fifth Amendment.

The opinion by Justice Stevens for a unanimous Court found the traditional rational relationship test applicable because the law could not be characterized as one based on "stereotyped generalization about a traditionally dis-

---

8.   519 U.S. at 113, 117 S.Ct. at 562.

9.   519 U.S. at 116, 117 S.Ct. at 564.

10.   519 U.S. at 120, 117 S.Ct. at 566.

11.   The five Justices joining in the opinion by Justice Ginsburg found that the rule violated both due process and equal protection. Justice Kennedy concurred solely in the judgment of the Court because he believed that the ruling should have been based entirely on principle of procedural fairness that was a part of the due process clause. M.L.B. v. S.L.J., 519 U.S. 102, 128, 117 S.Ct. 555,

570, 136 L.Ed.2d 473 (1996) (Kennedy, J., concurring in the judgment). Chief Justice Rehnquist and Justices Thomas and Scalia dissented, because they believed that nothing in the Constitution, or its amendments gave the woman a right to an appeal if she could not pay the filing fee. 519 U.S. at 128, 117 S.Ct. at 570 (Rehnquist, C.J., dissenting); 519 U.S. at 128, 117 S.Ct. at 570 (Thomas, J., joined by Scalia, J., and, in part, by Rehnquist, C.J., dissenting).

12.   434 U.S. 47, 98 S.Ct. 95, 54 L.Ed.2d 228 (1977).

advantaged group, or as an attempt to interfere with the individual's freedom to make a decision as important as marriage."[13] It was not irrational for Congress to terminate secondary benefits for the disabled children of deceased social security wage earners when those children were married, even if termination created financial hardship for these persons. Congress sought to alleviate the hardship on some persons dependent upon deceased wage earners and social security benefits by exempting those whose spouse was also entitled to benefits under the Social Security Act. The legislative exemption was not irrationally under-inclusive; Congress was entitled to deal with these economic problems and hardships one at a time. The result in *Califano v. Jobst* is justified because the law placed little burden on the right to marry and it was a reasonable means of identifying a group of financially needy persons for special economic benefits.[14]

In a ruling similar to *Jobst,* the Supreme Court in *Lyng v. Castillo* [15] upheld provisions of the Federal Food Stamp Act that gave lesser food stamp benefits to nuclear families than to nonrelated persons or extended families living together. Under the Amendment to the Food Stamp Act at issue in the case, lesser food stamp benefits were given to a "household"

composed of a group of individuals who customarily purchased food and prepared meals together than to unrelated persons who might share living accommodations but who did not customarily purchase food and prepare meals together. A portion of the Act provided that parents and children, or siblings, would be treated as a single household—a group of individuals who purchased and prepared meals together—so that they would receive lesser benefits.[16]

Justice Stevens' majority opinion in *Lyng* found that this classification should be upheld under the rational relationship standard.[17] The classification was used to define groups of persons who might need a particular type of economic subsidy and did not directly regulate marriage or family living arrangements. Thus, it did not burden a fundamental right so as to· require heightened judicial scrutiny. The Court recognized that a welfare benefit classification might be totally arbitrary if it disadvantaged certain living groups for no reason that rationally related to any intelligible economic or social goal. However, in this case, the classification was rationally related to a theoretical goal of giving lesser food stamp benefits to groups that should achieve savings through the group purchase and preparation of meals.[18] Since no fundamental right was

13. 434 U.S. at 54, 98 S.Ct. at 99–100 (footnotes omitted).

14. A provision of the Social Security Act that was in effect between 1979 and 1983 provided survivor benefits to a widowed spouse (of a deceased wage earner covered by the Social Security benefit system) who remarried after age sixty. However, this provision denied survivor benefits to an otherwise similarly situated divorced, widowed spouse. The Supreme Court upheld this provision of the Social Security Act in Bowen v. Owens, 476 U.S. 340, 106 S.Ct. 1881, 90 L.Ed.2d 316 (1986). The Court in *Bowen* ruled that the law was not a restriction on the fundamental right to marry. It found that there was no classification such as race, national origin, gender, or illegitimacy that required an independent judicial review of the legislative decision to use the classification for the distribution of welfare benefits. Therefore, only the rational relationship test, with its presumption of constitutionality and deference to the legislature, was appropriate in this case.

See also, Califano v. Boles, 443 U.S. 282, 99 S.Ct. 2767, 61 L.Ed.2d 541 (1979) (upholding Social Security Act provision giving greater benefits to married, as opposed to divorced, spouse of a retired wage earner); Mathews v. De Castro, 429 U.S. 181, 97 S.Ct. 431, 50 L.Ed.2d 389 (1976) (upholding provision of Social Security Act requiring

spouse or step-child to have established relationship to deceased wage earner at a specific point-in-time prior to the wage earner's death as a qualification for certain Social Security Act benefits).

15. 477 U.S. 635, 106 S.Ct. 2727, 91 L.Ed.2d 527 (1986).

16. The provision of the Act at issue in the case is summarized at 477 U.S. at 636 n. 1, 106 S.Ct. at 2728 n. 1. The Act treated parents, children, and siblings who lived together as a single household even if they did not in fact customarily purchase and prepare meals together "unless one of the parents or siblings, is an elderly or disabled member."

17. The majority opinion recognized, as did all Justices in the case, that the Fifth Amendment due process clause included an equal protection component that limited the federal government's ability to use classifications violating the principles of equal protection analysis. 477 U.S. at 636 n. 2, 106 S.Ct. at 2729 n. 2.

18. The Supreme Court in *Lyng* distinguished United States Department of Agriculture v. Moreno, 413 U.S. 528, 93 S.Ct. 2821, 37 L.Ed.2d 782 (1973) in which the Court had invalidated, under the rational relationship standard, a food stamp provision that arbitrarily burdened house-

involved, and no classification was involved requiring heightened judicial scrutiny, the Court used only the most deferential form of review.[19]

In *Zablocki v. Redhail*[20] the Justices experienced little difficulty in striking a law which restricted the ability of economically poor persons to marry. Yet the Justices had considerable difficulty in deciding why the law violated the equal protection clause. The Wisconsin statute in question prohibited any Wisconsin resident from marrying without court permission if that person had minor issue who were not in his custody and whom he was required to support according to a court order or judgment. A state court could grant such persons permission to marry only if they submitted proof of compliance with the support obligation and demonstrated that the children covered by the court order were not likely to become "public charges."

Justice Marshall wrote a majority opinion for five members of the Court which was somewhat unclear as to the nature of the right to marriage and the standard of review used in the decision. Justice Marshall described the right to marry as one of "fundamental importance" and a "part of the fundamental right to privacy implicit in the Fourteenth Amendment's due process clause." Thus, the majority opinion seems to continue to recognize marriage as a fundamental right although the language used is weaker than that of previous

majority opinions. Justice Marshall also stated that all regulations of the incidents of marriage need not be subjected to "rigorous scrutiny." The majority opinion referred to the *Califano v. Jobst* decision and observed that "reasonable regulations that do not significantly interfere with decisions to enter into the marital relationship may be legitimately imposed."[21] The opinion did not specify the types of regulations that need not to be tested by "rigorous scrutiny."

The opinion by Justice Marshall found that the permission to marry statute was invalid, the statute prevented a person's marriage but it did not insure support for the children from that person's prior marriage.

The majority opinion in *Zablocki* left the exact nature of the standard of review employed in this case unclear, but that has been true in many of the "fundamental rights" cases.[22] The concurring opinion of Justice Stevens helped to clarify this point by noting that the classification based on marital status in *Califano v. Jobst* simply was not as significant a burden on the right to marriage as was the law reviewed in this case. Justice Stevens indicated that the fact the ability to marry was limited by a law precluded reviewing that law under the most minimal rational relationship test even though such a law need not be subjected to a "level of scrutiny so strict that a holding of unconstitutionality is virtually fore-

holds containing one or more members who were unrelated to the rest. The provision disadvantaging unusual households in *Moreno* did not relate to any arguably legitimate purpose concerning welfare distribution but seemed to constitute only the arbitrary punishment of household units which the federal government disfavored. Lyng v. Castillo, 477 U.S. 635, 640 n. 3, 106 S.Ct. 2727, 2730 n. 3, 91 L.Ed.2d 527 (1986).

19. Justice Marshall's dissent attacked this all or nothing, formal approach to equal protection analysis. 477 U.S. at 643, 106 S.Ct. at 2732 (Marshall, J., dissenting). Justices Brennan and White dissented because they found that the law failed the rational basis test. 477 U.S. at 643, 106 S.Ct. at 2732 (Brennan, J., dissenting); 477 U.S. at 643, 106 S.Ct. at 2732 (White, J., dissenting). The Supreme Court followed the rational basis standard of review, used in *Lyng*, when it upheld a statutory modification of the Aid to Families With Dependent Children program that effectively reduced the payments to certain families.

In Bowen v. Gilliard, 483 U.S. 587, 107 S.Ct. 3008, 97 L.Ed.2d 485 (1987) the Court examined a congressional Amendment to the AFDC program that required a family to take into account the income of all parents, brothers, and sisters living in the same home (in determining the family's eligibility for AFDC benefits). The Court found that the inclusion of the income of the child from a noncustodial parent, which had the effect of reducing benefits to the family unit, did not impair a fundamental right and was subject only to the most deferential standard of review.

20. 434 U.S. 374, 98 S.Ct. 673, 54 L.Ed.2d 618 (1978).

21. 434 U.S. at 386, 98 S.Ct. at 680.

22. Chief Justice Burger concurred in the opinion on the understanding that this ruling would not require the Court to impose some form of "strict scrutiny" when reviewing classifications such as those in *Jobst*. 434 U.S. at 391, 98 S.Ct. at 683 (Burger, C.J., concurring).

ordained."[23] Indeed, the majority opinion by Justice Marshall stated that "when a statutory classification significantly interferes with the exercise of a fundamental right, it cannot be upheld unless it is supported by sufficiently important state interests and is closely tailored to effectuate only those interests."[24] These statements indicate that the Court used a standard of review that approximates one or more of the middle level standards of review that have been previously advocated by Justice Marshall and several legal scholars.[25]

Justice Powell concurred in the judgment in *Zablocki* although he felt the majority opinion swept too broadly by indicating that there might be strict scrutiny of a variety of traditional marriage regulations. He noted that laws prohibiting marriages that would involve incest, bigamy, and homosexuality had been assumed to be within the constitutional scope of state powers.[26] Justice Powell based his decision on the fact that the state had been unable to establish any reasonable basis for foreclosing marriage to citizens who were willing but unable to make payments to meet their previous child support obligations; this was not a reasonable manner of providing for the support of those children.

Justice Stewart would have abandoned the equal protection rationale because he did not feel that this law created any testable classification. He viewed the decision as one based on the concept of substantive due process. Justice Stewart found that marriage was not a constitutional right but only a "privilege" that was protected to some extent by the concept of liberty in the due process clauses. For him, this explains why a state may legitimately create regulations of the marriage relationship so long as the Justices agree that the regulations are reasonable means of promoting important concerns of the state.

Justice Stewart voted to strike the law examined in *Zablocki* because it contained no exception for those who were truly indigent and could not afford to pay their child support obligations. Like Justice Powell, he found that the law was not a reasonable means of furthering important state interests. But Justice Stewart found no purpose in using equal protection language when "the doctrine is no more than substantive due process by another name." Justice Stewart believed that recognition of the use of substantive due process demonstrates why the Supreme Court should be hesitant to reject the decisions of the democratic process concerning important social questions.[27]

Only Justice Rehnquist would have upheld the law in *Zablocki*. In rejecting substantive due process and equal protection strict scrutiny, apart from racial classification cases, the Justice consistently has taken the position that the Court should only determine whether laws which do not touch upon explicit constitutional guarantees bear some rational relationship to legitimate governmental interest. Under the traditional test, of course, the law would have to be upheld; the law was an arguably, though not demonstrably, rational means of preventing an increase in the number of children for whom the state would bear financial responsibility. However, Justice Rehnquist recognized the possibility that the law could not be applied to persons who were truly indigent; under those circumstances the prohibition of marriage might not be even arguably a rational way of enforcing support obligations. He did not have to reach this question for, in his opinion, the litigant did not have standing to raise this issue. It is interesting to note that at the start of Justice Rehnquist's dissent he explicitly rejected the use in this case of either "the strictest judicial scrutiny" or any "intermediate standard of review."[28]

---

23. 434 U.S. at 406–07 n. 10, 98 S.Ct. at 692 n. 10 (Stevens, J., concurring).

24. 434 U.S. at 388, 98 S.Ct. at 682.

25. See § 14.3, supra.

26. Zablocki v. Redhail, 434 U.S. 374, 98 S.Ct. 673, 54 L.Ed.2d 618 (1978) (Powell, J., concurring).

27. 434 U.S. at 395, 98 S.Ct. at 686 (Stewart, J., concurring).

28. 434 U.S. at 407, 98 S.Ct. at 692 (Rehnquist, J., dissenting).

The right to marry should be seen as a part of a broader constitutional right in family relationships.[29] More than a half century ago the Supreme Court recognized that the government must respect the autonomy of the family unit as it held that states could not dictate to parents the conditions under which their child would be educated unless the government regulations were reasonably designed to prevent intellectual or physical harm to the child.[30] The Court has also recognized that there is a fundamental right in the parent-child relationship when it has declared that states must guarantee a parent significant procedural safeguards against improper termination of the parent-child relationship, including a requirement that the parental unfitness be proven by "clear and convincing" evidence.[31] Similarly, the Court's review of laws which establish classifications regarding the custody of children under the equal protection guarantees also reflects judicial concern that the state not allocate or regulate such rights without an overriding interest, such as the promotion of the health or welfare of a child.[32] While the Court has not described the exact parameters

29. The Supreme Court, to date, has not extended the rights discussed in this paragraph to nontraditional families. In Village of Belle Terre v. Boraas, 416 U.S. 1, 94 S.Ct. 1536, 39 L.Ed.2d 797 (1974), the Court upheld a zoning ordinance prohibiting three or more persons from living together unless they were related by blood or lawful marriage, whereas in Moore v. City of East Cleveland, 431 U.S. 494, 97 S.Ct. 1932, 52 L.Ed.2d 531 (1977) (plurality opinion), the Court invalidated a law that would have prohibited members of a traditional family from living together. See § 14.30(a), infra.

30. In Meyer v. Nebraska, 262 U.S. 390, 43 S.Ct. 625, 67 L.Ed. 1042 (1923), the Supreme Court held that a state could not prohibit the teaching of any language other than English in private schools because that statute improperly infringed upon the liberty of both parents and teachers to make educational decisions.

In Pierce v. Society of Sisters, 268 U.S. 510, 45 S.Ct. 571, 69 L.Ed. 1070 (1925), the Court held that a state could not prohibit private schools and require parents to send their children to government operated schools.

Thus, a state should be able to require that private schools meet secular educational and safety standards, but should not be able to dictate the precise terms of a child's education by his or her parents. States should be able to require parents to send their children to a government licensed school; however, some limited exception to this requirement may be made for children and their parents who withdraw from the public educational systems for religious reasons after the child has received a significant public education. See Wisconsin v. Yoder, 406 U.S. 205, 92 S.Ct. 1526, 32 L.Ed.2d 15 (1972), in which the Court declared a very limited exception from a mandatory school attendance law for children who withdrew from the system for religious reasons. See § 17.8, infra.

31. Santosky v. Kramer, 455 U.S. 745, 102 S.Ct. 1388, 71 L.Ed.2d 599 (1982). See also Stanley v. Illinois, 405 U.S. 645, 92 S.Ct. 1208, 31 L.Ed.2d 551 (1972) (due process requires that the child and parent be granted a hearing; equal protection guarantee prohibits discrimination against illegitimates); Smith v. Organization of Foster Families for Equality and Reform, 431 U.S. 816, 97 S.Ct. 2094, 53 L.Ed.2d 14 (1977) (upholding system for removing children from foster homes but assuming arguendo that the foster parent-foster child interest was protected by due process, a point disputed in a concurring opinion by Justices Stewart and Rehnquist and Chief Justice Burger).

In Rivera v. Minnich, 483 U.S. 574, 107 S.Ct. 3001, 97 L.Ed.2d 473 (1987), the Supreme Court found that a state, consistent with the due process guarantee, could allow a mother or child seeking support from a putative father to prove the paternity by a preponderance of evidence. Because the preponderance of evidence standard would allow for a fair determination of paternity, and because these proceedings did not involve the possibility of impairing or terminating the fundamental right in a parent-child relationship, there was no need for a state to adopt a clear and convincing proof standard in these proceedings.

The Supreme Court has not yet examined the substantive due process and equal protection questions concerning a state's ability to define the basis upon which parents are deemed unfit and their parental rights terminated.

32. See, e.g., Caban v. Mohammed, 441 U.S. 380, 99 S.Ct. 1760, 60 L.Ed.2d 297 (1979) (invalidating law which requires consent of mother of an illegitimate child prior to adoption but did not give equal consent rights to the father of the child at any time throughout the life of the child). See also Stanley v. Illinois, 405 U.S. 645, 92 S.Ct. 1208, 31 L.Ed.2d 551 (1972) (due process prohibits taking illegitimate child from the custody of the father who lived with the child upon the death of the mother without a hearing). See generally § 14.17, supra.

A "best interest of the child" standard? The cases referred to in footnotes 25–28 of this section do not address the question of whether the government must act in the best interest of a child. The Supreme Court decisions indicate that the government must be acting in a manner that is narrowly tailored to promote a compelling or overriding interest (such as the best interest of the child) if it seeks to limit a fundamental right, such as the right of parents to retain custody of their children. None of these cases involved a conflict between the biological parents of a child and persons who have adopted the child following some type of state approved adoption procedure.

To say that the government may act in the best interest of children is not to say that it always must act in their best interest. The Supreme Court discussed the best interest of the child standard in a case concerning the detention of alien children by the Immigration and Naturalization Service [INS], although the case did not involve any issue of family rights. In Reno v. Flores, 507 U.S. 292, 113 S.Ct. 1439, 123 L.Ed.2d 1 (1993), on remand 992 F.2d 243 (9th Cir.1993) the Court upheld INS regulations regarding the detention of alien children awaiting deporta-

of the right to maintain family relationships, it clearly has indicated that regulation of these relationships must be justified by an over-riding state interest.[33]

Such regulations are not entitled to a strong presumption of constitutionality because they interfere with a form of liberty with strong roots in the history and traditions of our society. In another context, the Court has reviewed the cases regarding marriage, childbirth, and child rearing and concluded that:

> The Court has long recognized that, because the Bill of Rights is designed to secure individual liberty, it must afford the formation and preservation of certain kinds of highly personal relationships a substantial measure of sanctuary from unjustified interference by the State.... The personal affiliations that exemplify these considerations, and that therefore suggest some relevant limitations on the relationships that might be entitled to this sort of constitutional protection, are those that attend the creation and sustenance of a family—marriage ... childbirth ... the raising and education of children ... and cohabitation with one's relatives.... Family relationships, by their nature involve deep attachments and commitments to the necessarily few other individuals with whom one shares not only a special community of

thoughts, experiences, and beliefs but also distinctly personal aspects of one's life.[34]

It seems clear that the relationship between parent and child is a fundamental aspect of liberty. The government may terminate, or significantly impair, such an interest, if it is acting pursuant to a law that is narrowly tailored to promote a compelling or overriding interest. For example, a law authorizing a government agency to terminate a parent-child relationship on the basis that the parent is unfit, because the parent is placing the child in harm's way or hurting the child, the law might well be narrowly tailored to the compelling or overriding interest in the protection of the child. In such a case, the law would withstand substantive review under due process and equal protection. Nevertheless, when the state sought to severe the parent-child relationship, the parent has a due process right to some type of fair proceeding, under the procedural aspect of the due process clause.

The Court has not defined the nature of family relationships that constitute fundamental aspects of liberty nor has it defined with preciseness the relationships between a child and other relatives of the child such as grandparents.

In *Troxel v. Granville*[35] the Justices, by a 6 to 3 vote, found that a state statute granting

---

tion proceedings. Under the INS regulations, such children would be released to their parents, close relatives, or guardians in the United States. If a child did not have a parent, close relative, or guardian in the United States, the child would remain in federal custody. Under the terms of the regulation a child would be released to a nonrelative who could provide for his care and well-being pending the deportation proceedings only in the most "compelling" circumstances.

In discussing the arguments of the detained juveniles, Justice Scalia examined the argument that the government needed to act in the best interest of the child. Justice Scalia's majority opinion stated:

"The best interest of the child, the venerable phrase familiar from divorce proceedings, is a proper and feasible criterion for making the decision as to which of two parents will be accorded custody. But it is not traditionally the sole criteria-much less the sole *constitutional* criterion—for other, less narrowly channeled judgments involving children, where their interests conflict in varying degrees with the interests of others."

It is hard to predict what, if any, influence this dicta concerning the best interest standard might have in future cases that may involve contests between competing parents for the custody of a child.

33. The Supreme Court has not resolved the issue of what types of procedures, if any, need to be given to a male who asserts that he is the biological father of an illegitimate child. See § 14.17, supra.

34. Roberts v. United States Jaycees, 468 U.S. 609, 619, 104 S.Ct. 3244, 3250, 82 L.Ed.2d 462 (1984). The Court made these statements in order to establish a distinction between the type of relationships that have a clear claim to this type of constitutional protection and those that did not merit this type of Bill of Rights' protection from governmental regulation. In this case, the Court found that a national organization that primarily engaged in commercial activity was properly subject to a state law requiring it to cease discrimination against women applicants for members. The primary focus of the Court was on whether the regulation restricted the First Amendment rights of the organization. See § 16.41, infra, regarding the freedom of association.

35. 530 U.S. 57, 120 S.Ct. 2054, 147 L.Ed.2d 49 (2000) (judgment of the Court announced in an opinion by O'Connor, J., that was joined by Rehnquist, C.J., and Ginsburg and Breyer, JJ.).

visitation rights to grandparents and other persons was so broad that it could not be used, due to the circumstances of the case, to override a mother's decision to limit paternal grandparent visits to her children. However, there was no majority opinion for the Court in Troxel, in part because the Justices could not agree on how to define the nature of the family relationships that were fundamental constitutional liberties.

In *Troxel* the courts had to deal with a situation in which there was a conflict between the mother and paternal grandparents of children. The mother and the father of the children had not been married. The father of the children had committed suicide. The mother of the child sought to limit, but not terminate, the visits of the paternal grandparents to the children. Then the grandparents sought, and received, visitation rights under a Washington state statute that allowed a state court to grant visitation rights to any person whenever "visitation may best serve the interests of the child."

Justice O'Connor announced the judgement of the Supreme Court in *Troxel*, in a plurality opinion that was joined by Chief Justice Rehnquist and Justices Ginsburg and Breyer. The plurality opinion began by noting that the parent-child relationship was the most long recognized fundamental aspect of liberty, by Supreme Court cases going back to the 1920s.[36] There was no problem in justifying independent judicial review of laws that restricted the right.[37]

Justice O'Connor questioned the breadth of the statute, in light of its broad intrusion into the parent-child relationship, but the plurality only voted to invalidate the application of the statute in the particular case. Justice O'Connor's opinion did not find that the statute was totally invalid. Nevertheless, the plurality opinion appears to point out flaws in the stat-

ute that would make it invalid on it's face unless it received a narrowing construction from the state courts. Justice O'Connor noted that there was no requirement that the parent be deemed unfit before the parent's right to control visitation from other persons was limited. She also noted that, in this case, the trial court had taken approach that provided no deference to parental decisions and had not demonstrated why the mother's decision to limit, but not end the visitation from the paternal grandparents was necessary for the well being of the children. For these reasons, the plurality found that limitation of the parent's decision in this case "was an unconstitutional infringement on [the mother's] fundamental right to make decisions concerning the care, custody and control of her two daughters."[38] However, the plurality was careful to emphasize the narrowness of its holding. Justice O'Connor stated: "We do not consider the primary constitutional issue passed on by the Washington Supreme Court–whether the due process clause requires all non-parental visitation statutes to include a showing of harm or potential harm to the child as a condition precedent to granting visitation. We do not and need not define the precise scope of the parental due process rights in the visitation context."[39]

Justice Souter concurred in the judgment of the Court, but he would have preferred an opinion even more narrow than the plurality opinion.[40] He believed United States Supreme Court should simply reaffirm earlier cases in which the Court had held that right was protected by the due process clause, and say that the state supreme court decision to invalidate the statute under the due process clause was constitutionally permissible. Justice Souter saw no reason for any extended analysis of parental rights.

---

36. 530 U.S. at 65, 120 S.Ct. at 2060.

37. For an excellent analysis of how *Troxel* fits with other family privacy, and abortion, cases see: David Meyer, *Lochner* Redeemed: Family Privacy After *Troxel* and *Carhart*, 48 U.C.L.A. L. Rev. (June, 2001).

38. Troxel v. Granville, 530 U.S. 57, 68–73, 120 S.Ct. 2054, 2062–64, 147 L.Ed.2d 49 (2000) (judgment of the Court announced in an opinion by O'Connor, J., that was

joined by Rehnquist, C.J., and Ginsburg and Breyer, JJ.) 530 U.S. at 76, 120 S.Ct. at 2066.

39. 530 U.S. at 72, 120 S.Ct. at 2064.

40. Troxel v. Granville, 530 U.S. 57, 74, 120 S.Ct. 2054, 2065, 147 L.Ed.2d 49 (2000) (Souter, J., concurring in the judgment).

Justice Thomas concurred in the judgment with a brief opinion that assumed for purposes of the case that substantive due process was a legitimate tool of analysis, because the issue of whether the Supreme Court should reject substantive due process had not been presented by the parties to the case.[41] Assuming the substantive due process was a permissible basis for a judicial ruling, Justice Thomas stated that he would "apply strict scrutiny to infringement of fundamental rights," and, on that basis, invalidate the statute.

There were three dissenting Justices in *Troxel,* none of whom joined the opinion of any of the other dissenters. Justice Stevens thought that the case should not have been reviewed at all but that, if he had to reach the merits, he would rule that the statute was not invalid on its face.[42] He believed that the statute was capable of a narrowing construction that would have allowed the state to act to limit a parent's control over visitation rights whenever it was within the best interests of the child and that such a standard would comply with earlier Supreme Court due process rulings.

Justice Scalia dissented in an opinion that recognized the right of parents to control the upbringing of their children as one of the "unalienable rights" which was referred to in the Declaration of Independence.[43] However, he believed that the federal judiciary had no authority under the Fourteenth Amendment due process clause to protect that unalienable right.

Justice Kennedy believed that the plurality opinion was mistaken because it "seems to proceed from the assumption that the parent or parents who resist visitation have always been the child's primary care givers and the third parties who seek visitation rights have no legitimate and established relationship with the child."[44] He believed that courts could grant visitation rights contrary to a parent's desires if the court believed that the visitation would be in the best interest of the child. The state supreme court had invalidated the statute on its face. Justice Kennedy thought that the state supreme court ruling should be overturned without addressing specific constitutional questions or the application of the statute in the particular case.

In the latter part of the twentieth century the Court issued rulings that seemed to be, at least partially, inconsistent regarding state punishing of homosexual conduct, and state legal classifications that disadvantaged persons on the basis of their sexual orientation. At the start of the twenty-first century, in 2003, the Supreme Court ruled that the government could not punish some types of sexual activity done in private by two consenting adults. However, in the Court's 2003 decision ruling left open many questions regarding the nature of the right of privacy.

In 1986, in *Bowers v. Hardwick,*[45] the Supreme Court, by a 5 to 4 vote of the Justices, upheld a state sodomy law that criminalized private homosexual activity between consenting adults.[46] The majority opinion in *Bowers,*

41. 530 U.S. at 78–80, 120 S.Ct. at 2057, 2067–68 (Thomas, J., concurring in the judgment).

42. Troxel v. Granville, 530 U.S. 57, 80–91, 120 S.Ct. 2054, 2068–2074, 147 L.Ed.2d 49 (2000) (Stevens, J., dissenting).

43. 530 U.S. at 91, 120 S.Ct. at 2074 (Scalia, J., dissenting).

44. 530 U.S. at 93, 120 S.Ct. at 2075 (Kennedy, J., dissenting).

45. Bowers v. Hardwick, 478 U.S. 186, 106 S.Ct. 2841, 92 L.Ed.2d 140 (1986).

46. The individual who initiated the litigation in *Bowers* had been charged initially with a violation of Georgia statutes that banned sodomy, but the state prosecutor had decided not to prosecute that individual. The individual then brought suit in federal court. As indicated in the text,

the individual's claim under the Fourteenth Amendment was rejected by the United States Supreme Court.

In 1998, the Georgia Supreme Court ruled that the Georgia sodomy statute could not be applied to noncommercial, voluntary sexual acts between adults that were done in private, because the Constitution of the State of Georgia, in the view of the Georgia Supreme Court, had always protected a right of privacy for consenting adults to engage in sexual activity in private. Powell v. State, 270 Ga. 327, 510 S.E.2d 18 (1998). The Georgia Supreme Court, in *Powell,* cited this Treatise as authority for the proposition that "A state court is free to interpret its state constitution in a way that does not violate principles of federal law, and thereby grant individuals more rights than most provided by the U.S.Constitution." 270 Ga. at 331 n. 3, 510 S.E.2d at 22 n. 3. This ruling by the Georgia Supreme Court shows the wisdom of litigators who realize that state courts may be able to protect their client's civil

written by Justice White, stated that the fundamental right to privacy in the Court's earlier decisions did not have "any resemblance to the claimed constitutional right of homosexuals to engage in acts of sodomy." The *Bowers* majority found that the right to engage in homosexual activity could not be considered a fundamental right because it was not a part of our nation's history and traditions,[47] and it was not form of individual liberty that must be defended from the democratic process.[48] The four dissenting Justices in *Bowers* believed that the right of mentally competent adults, in private, to engage in voluntary sexual conduct that did not result in any physical harm to either party was an essential part of personal autonomy that should be protected by the judiciary from majoritarian decision making and public prosecution.[49]

The majority in *Bowers* ruled that, because no fundamental right was involved in the case, the Court should only determine whether the statute punishing private sexual activity between unmarried persons was rationally related to a legitimate interest. The *Bowers* majority opinion, found that the interest in defining public morality was a legitimate one and that the law might be said to be rationally related to it. The *Bowers* decision left open a variety of questions, such as whether a particular criminal punishment for homosexual activity would

violate the cruel and unusual punishment clause, and whether a state's decision to punish sexual activity outside of marriage only if it were homosexual, rather than heterosexual, activity would violate equal protection.[50]

In 1996, without referring to *Bowers*, the Court in *Romer v. Evans*[51] employed the rationality test to invalidate a state constitutional amendment prohibiting state and local legislatures from passing laws that prohibited discrimination against persons on the basis of their sexual orientation. The majority opinion in *Romer*, written by Justice Kennedy, found that the Court did not have to revisit the question of whether homosexual activity was a fundamental right, or to decide whether classifications based on sexual orientation should be subject to some form of review more strict than the rationality test.

Justice Kennedy, writing for six Justices in *Roemer*, ruled that the classification that prohibited state or local legislatures from passing laws that would stop discrimination against persons on the basis of their sexual orientation did not have a rational relationship to any legitimate interest. The state constitutional amendment that prohibited legislation stopping discrimination based on sexual orientation, in the view of the majority, was not related to any legitimate interest because

---

liberties to an extent beyond those that could be protected by local federal judges, who are restricted to following the rulings of the United States Supreme Court concerning the scope of individual liberties. Surprisingly, the Court in Lawrence v. Texas, ___ U.S. ___, 123 S.Ct. 2472, 156 L.Ed.2d 508 (2003), in overruling *Bowers*, did not refer to the fact that the majority in *Bowers* did not correctly assess the history and traditions of the State of Georgia, much less the history and traditions of the United States.

47. Bowers v. Hardwick, 478 U.S. 186, 190, 195, 106 S.Ct. 2841, 2844, 2846, 92 L.Ed.2d 140 (1986).

48. 478 U.S. at 190, 106 S.Ct. at 2844. In this portion of Justice White's majority opinion he rejected the argument that the ability to engage in homosexual activity was a type of fundamental liberty that was "implicit in the concept of ordered liberty." That phrase was taken from Palko v. Connecticut, 302 U.S. 319, 325–26, 58 S.Ct. 149, 151–52, 82 L.Ed. 288 (1937) in which the Court used this concept to determine which provisions of the Bill of Rights were sufficiently fundamental to be incorporated in the concept of liberty protected by the Fourteenth Amendment due process clause. See § 11.6 of this Treatise regarding the incorporation of the Bill of Rights.

49. Bowers v. Hardwick, 478 U.S. 186, 199, 106 S.Ct. 2841, 2848, 92 L.Ed.2d 140 (1986) (Blackmun, J., joined by Brennan, Marshall, and Stevens, JJ., dissenting); 478 U.S. at 214, 106 S.Ct. at 2856 (Stevens, J., joined by Brennan and Marshall, JJ., dissenting).

50. Justice Powell, whose vote was crucial to the five Justice majority, emphasized that the Court had left open the question of whether homosexual conduct in private could be subject to criminal penalties, particularly if similar heterosexual conduct were not punished. Bowers v. Hardwick, 478 U.S. 186, 197–98, 106 S.Ct. 2841, 2847–48, 92 L.Ed.2d 140 (1986) (Powell, J., concurring). The majority in *Bowers* noted that married persons had originally been plaintiffs in the action challenging the anti-sodomy statute, but that the district court had dismissed their action because they were not in immediate danger of prosecution and that ruling was affirmed by the court of appeals. The Supreme Court majority opinion stated: "We express no opinion on the constitutionality of the Georgia statute as applied to other acts of sodomy." 478 U.S. at 188 n. 2, 106 S.Ct. at 2842 n. 2.

51. Romer v. Evans, 517 U.S. 620, 116 S.Ct. 1620, 134 L.Ed.2d 855 (1996).

there could not be a legitimate interest in denying some persons the ability to lobby the legislature for laws that would protect their interests. The majority opinion in *Romer* made it clear that the state and local legislatures did not have any obligation to pass laws that protected homosexual persons from private sector discrimination. Nevertheless, the state had no legitimate interest in denying homosexual persons the ability to lobby legislatures for laws that would protect them from discrimination. Justice Kennedy stated: "A law declaring that in general it shall be more difficult for one group of citizens than for all others to seek aid from the government is itself a denial of equal protection of the laws in the most literal sense."[52]

The three dissenting Justices in *Romer*, in an opinion written by Justice Scalia, found that the majority failed to give adequate deference to the state's interest in making homosexual conduct illegal.[53] The government had argued that landlords, employers and other persons who dealt with the public and chose not to deal with persons who were homosexuals had a "freedom of association" interest that the state could protect. In response to that argument, Justice Kennedy noted that "the breadth of the Amendment [the state constitutional amendment that prohibited legislatures from passing anti-discrimination laws] is so far removed from [this justification] that we find it impossible to credit the state's argument."[54]

The majority opinion in *Roemer* did not address the issue of whether homosexual activity came within the right of privacy because the majority's rationale for striking down the state amendment that prohibited anti-discrimina-

tion legislation was easily justified by two earlier decisions of the Supreme Court. In those decisions, the Supreme Court had ruled that it was impermissible for a state or local government to identify a group of persons by some type of personal characteristic and then make it more difficult for that group of persons to lobby legislators than for other groups of citizens within the state.[55]

In *Lawrence v. Texas*[56] the Justices, by a 6 to 3 vote, invalidated a state statute that prohibited persons from engaging in sodomy with a person of the same sex. Justice Kennedy, the author of the *Roemer* decision, wrote a majority opinion for five Justices in *Lawrence*. Justice Kennedy's opinion ruled that the state law violated the due process clause of the Fourteenth Amendment. Justice O'Connor concurred only in the judgment of the Court in *Lawrence*; she would have preferred to invalidate the law based on the equal protection clause.[57]

Three Justices dissented in *Lawrence* because they believed that the Court's ruling could not be justified in terms of the Supreme Court's prior cases, or the Court's role in the definition of fundamental rights based on history and traditions of the country. They believed that the Court's invalidation of the law under the rationality test, regardless of the intentions of the Justices who joined the majority opinion, could form the basis for future judicial actions that would invalidate any laws that judges thought were unreasonable and result in the judicial usurpation of legislative functions, such occurred early in the twentieth century.[58]

Justice O'Connor's opinion concurring in the judgment in *Lawrence*, if it had been a

---

52. 517 U.S. at 633, 116 S.Ct. at 1628.

53. 517 U.S. at 635, 116 S.Ct. at 1629–37 (Scalia, J., joined by Rehnquist, C.J., and Thomas, J., dissenting).

54. 517 U.S. at 635, 116 S.Ct. at 1629.

55. This analysis is contained in Parts I and II of Justice Kennedy's majority opinion. Romer v. Evans, 517 U.S. 620, 625–35, 116 S.Ct. 1620, 1624–29, 134 L.Ed.2d 855 (1996).Earlier cases using this type of analysis of classifications that restricted the ability of a specific group of persons to lobby legislatures for assistance include Reitman v. Mulkey, 387 U.S. 369, 87 S.Ct. 1627, 18 L.Ed.2d 830 (1967); and Washington v. Seattle School

District No. 1, 458 U.S. 457, 102 S.Ct. 3187, 73 L.Ed.2d 896 (1982) See §§ 12.4, 14.8, 14.9 of this Treatise.

56. ___ U.S. ___, 123 S.Ct. 2472, 156 L.Ed.2d 508 (2003)

57. Lawrence v. Texas, ___ U.S. ___, ___, 123 S.Ct. 2472, 2484, 156 L.Ed.2d 508 (2003) (O'Connor, J., concurring in the judgment).

58. Lawrence v. Texas, ___ U.S. ___, ___, 123 S.Ct. 2472, 2488, 156 L.Ed.2d 508 (2003) (Scalia, J., joined by Rehnquist, C.J., and Thomas, J., dissenting); ___ U.S. at ___, 123 S.Ct. at 2498 (Thomas, J., dissenting).

majority opinion, would have resulted in a much narrower ruling than Justice Kennedy's majority opinion in *Lawrence*. Justice O'Connor found that there was no need to overrule the Supreme Court's earlier decision in *Bowers*, because the Justices did not have to address the question of whether there was a substantive right to engage in sexual activity outside of marriage.[59] The Texas law at issue in *Lawrence* did not prohibit all sexual activity outside of marriage; the state law did not even ban all sodomy. The state law banned only same-sex sodomy. Thus, the Texas law squarely presented an issue left open by *Bowers*: whether the state could punish sexual activity outside of marriage only by a group of persons defined by some trait that was disliked by a majority of persons in the political process. In Justice O'Connor's view, earlier Supreme Court cases had demonstrated that: "When a law exhibits [a legislative intention to harm a politically unpopular group, we have applied a more searching form of rational basis review] under the equal protection clause of the Fourteenth Amendment."[60] Justice O'Connor did not believe that the Court would have been justified in invalidating this law under the rationality test, if the law could be viewed by the judiciary as a law that dealt with economic and social welfare matters (even matters that involved judgments based on moral principles) in such a way that the political process could be expected to work in the normal fashion.[61] The Justice sought to limit the use of a true reasonableness test (as opposed to a rationality test) to cases involving classifications that were obviously designed to harm persons whose voices would not be heard in the normal political process. Justice O'Connor's opinion

would not have opened the question of whether marriages could be limited to persons of differing sexes, because laws regarding marriages might be regarded as "preserving the traditional institution of marriage," rather than as laws designed to hurt an insular minority.[62]

The five member majority in *Lawrence* chose to disregard Justice O'Connor's admonition to use the equal protection clause, precisely because her approach to the issues in *Lawrence* would have resulted in a narrow ruling. Justice Kennedy's majority opinion in *Lawrence* stated that the argument for invalidating the statute banning same-sex sodomy invalid under the equal protection clause was "a tenable argument." The majority chose to base its ruling on the due process clause because an equal protection clause ruling might lead some persons to question "whether a prohibition would be valid if drawn differently [than the state statute before the Court]."[63]

In three ways, Justice Kennedy's majority opinion in *Lawrence* justified the use of independent judicial review, which would involve virtually no deference to the legislature, to determine whether the statute banning same-sex sodomy was related to a legitimate interest. Justice Kennedy's majority opinion found that the Court's invalidation of a ban on same-sex private conduct was justified by: prior rulings of the Supreme Court; our nation's history and tradition of non-interference with private sexual decisions made by consenting adults concerning truly private activity; and a belief that personal autonomy to define one's own life in terms of the relationship with

---

59. ___ U.S. at ___, 123 S.Ct. at 2484–88 (O'Connor, J., concurring in the judgment).

60. ___ U.S. at ___, 123 S.Ct. at 2484, 2485 (O'Connor, J., concurring in the judgment). Although Justice O'Connor did not refer to them, her view concerning the relationship of the standard of judicial review to the suitability of the democratic process to protect certain groups of persons might be seen as an outgrowth of what was known as the process-oriented approach to constitutional law that had been advocated by scholars such as the late Professor John Hart Ely. See, e.g., J. H. Ely, Democracy and Distrust; J. Choper, Judicial Review and the National Political Process: A Functional Reconsideration of the Role of the Supreme Court (1980) H. Monaghan, *Book Review*,

94 HAR. L. REV. 296 (1980); J. Nowak, *Book Review*, 68 CALIF. L. REV. 1223 (1980). See generally, H. Wechsler, Principles, Politics, and Fundamental Law (1961).

61. ___ U.S. at ___, 123 S.Ct. at 2484–88 (O'Connor, J., concurring in the judgment). In Lawrence v. Texas, ___ U.S. ___, ___, 123 S.Ct. 2472, 2480, 156 L.Ed.2d 508 (2003) the majority opinion referred to Eskridge, Hardwick and Historiography, 1999 U.Ill. L. Rev. 631.

62. Lawrence v. Texas, ___ U.S. ___, ___, 123 S.Ct. 2472, 2484–88, 156 L.Ed.2d 508 (2003) (O'Connor, J., concurring in the judgment).

63. Lawrence v. Texas, ___ U.S. ___, ___, 123 S.Ct. 2472, 2482, 156 L.Ed.2d 508 (2003).

another consenting adult was a part of the ordered liberty or jurisprudential philosophy that had to be protected in any just society. Justice Kennedy's justification of his rulings on each of these points came in terms of statements as to why the majority believed that the *Bowers* case had been incorrectly decided.

First, Justice Kennedy found that the Court's holding, and opinion, in *Bowers* ran contrary to statements regarding personal autonomy that had been made in a series of Supreme Court cases concerning contraception and abortion.[64] Second, Justice Kennedy found that, contrary to the majority opinion in *Bowers*, there was "no long-standing history in this country of laws directed at homosexual conduct as a distinct matter." According to the majority opinion, the anti-sodomy laws that had existed in earlier parts of American history primarily had been directed at "non-procreative sexual activity more generally" than they had been directed against "consenting adults acting in private."[65] Third, Justice Kennedy attempted to demonstrate that there was a jurisprudential basis for protecting the liberty of adults to engage in private sexual activity as "an integral part of human freedom" that should be recognized in any just society.[66] As a part of justifying the judicial protection of private sexual activity between consenting adults, Justice Kennedy referred to both the small number of states in the United States that prohibited homosexual conduct, and the fact that the European Court of Human Rights had found that such conduct could not be punished.

Because the majority opinion found that the Court's earlier decision in *Bowers* was inconsistent with earlier case law, the history and traditions of the nation, and basic jurisprudential principles, the *Lawrence* majority overruled *Bowers*.[67]

In the concluding portion of the majority opinion in *Lawrence,* Justice Kennedy attempted to narrow the Court's ruling, so that the opinion could not be used as justification for future sets of Justices who might wish to second guess all legislative judgments regarding economic and social welfare matters. Justice Kennedy stated: "The [statute before the Court] furthers no legitimate state interest which can justify its intrusion into the personal and private life of the individual."[68] That sentence may be an important one in the future. That sentence indicates that the majority in *Lawrence* employed an ad-hoc balancing test, and ruled that a popular view of morality could not justify an intrusion into private decision making by adults concerning intimate activities in private (even though the Court majority might find that the popular view of morality would justify other limitations on private personal activity).

If the five Justices in the majority in *Lawrence*, in the future, would find that not all private activity had the value of private sexual activity (in terms of defining one's personality) those Justices might rule that the interest in morality was significant enough to justify the limitation of private conduct that was contrary to popular morality. Thus, for example, a law that banned torturing animals in private might be seen as rationally related to a legitimate interest by the majority. The law banning animal cruelty in private could not be justified by a tangible interest in the protection of the economy or of the safety of human beings. But the anti-cruelty law could rationally relate to a legitimate interest in the moral standards for society as a whole.

The majority opinion in *Lawrence* indicated that the Judges would uphold the punishment of sexual activities in which one person was injured or coerced; and that the majority would uphold laws banning sexual conduct by

---

64. ___ U.S. at ___, 123 S.Ct. at 2477, 2481. See §§ 14.27, 14.29 of this Treatise regarding the contraception and abortion cases relied on by the majority in *Lawrence*.

65. Lawrence v. Texas, ___ U.S. at ___, 123 S.Ct. at 2478.

66. ___ U.S. at ___, 123 S.Ct. at 2475, 2483.

67. ___ U.S. at ___, 123 S.Ct. at 2483–84.

68. ___ U.S. at ___, 123 S.Ct. at 2484.

minors.[69] Justice Kennedy avoided ruling on whether government was required to give any type of legal recognition to private relationships between homosexual persons that would be the equivalent to the formal recognition given to heterosexual couples who engaged in a traditional marriage.

The question of whether state governments must give legal protection to monogamous relationships between homosexual persons that is equivalent to the legal recognition given to heterosexuals who enter a traditional marriage is an open question. As we have seen in this section of the Treatise, the Supreme Court has considered marriage to be a part of the fundamental right to privacy; but the Court has only done so in cases that have involved issues regarding the formation of traditional marriages (in the sense that they were legal unions between a male and a female).[70]

The argument that a state must give recognition to homosexual unions equivalent to that of heterosexual unions would have at least two basis. First, after *Lawrence*, those arguing for such a result would claim that the same-sex couple was engaging in the exact type of constitutionally protected activity that a heterosexual couple engaged in after a traditional marriage ceremony. Second, a state denial of legal recognition to a monogamous relationship of two homosexual persons, while the granting of such recognition to a union of two heterosexual persons, could be held to violate equal protection. The denial of legal recognition of homosexual unions might be deemed a sex classification that should be subject to an intermediate form of judicial scrutiny (the substantial relationship to an important interest test).[71] The state would argue that the law did not constitute a gender classification because it treated all males and all females equally. However, the Supreme Court has ruled that a law that banned interracial marriages constituted a racial classification even though the state, in that case, argued that a ban on interracial marriage burdened all races equally (because no person of one race could marry a person of another race).[72] A reasonable argument can also be made that classifications based on sexual orientation should receive at least mid-level judicial judicial scrutiny [so that the government would have to show that such classifications were significantly related to an important interest], because those classifications, [like classifications based on illegitimacy or sex, which receive mid-level scrutiny] are likely to be based on stereotypes, rather than on fair considerations, in the current political process.[73] Those claiming that the state denial of legal recognition to a homosexual union violated equal protection, even if the classification is subject only to minimal judicial scrutiny [the rationality test] could use dicta from as the majority opinion, in *Lawrence* to argue that, despite statements in the opinions concerning the limited nature of the Court's ruling, a denial of equal treatment to a class of persons to an inferior position in our legal system for no legitimate reason[74] Thus, they

---

69. ___ U.S. at ___, 123 S.Ct. at 2484.

70. See the start of this section of the Treatise [§ 14.28].

71. See §§ 14.20–14.24 regarding classifications based on gender.

72. Loving v. Virginia 388 U.S. 1, 87 S.Ct. 1817, 18 L.Ed.2d 1010 (1967).

73. See generally, Note, The Constitutional Status of Sexual Orientation, 98 Harv. L. Rev 1285 (1985). For citations to additional secondary works on this topic see our multi-volume Treatise: R. Rotunda & J. Nowak, Treatise on Constitutional Law: Substance and Procedure (3rd ed. 1999, with annual supplements).

74. Lawrence v. Texas, ___ U.S. ___, ___, 123 S.Ct. 2472, 2484, 156 L.Ed.2d 508 (2003): "[this case] does not involve [questions of] whether the government must give formal recognition to any relationship that homosexual persons seek to enter. The case does involve two adults who, with free and mutual consent from each other, engaged in sexual practices common to a homosexual lifestyle. The petitioners are entitled to respect for their private lives."

In addition to the right to privacy issues left open by *Lawrence*, a variety of First Amendment issues might arise from government actions seeking to harm associations of persons because of their sexual orientation or their viewpoints regarding sexual orientation. See generally, National Gay Task Force v. Board of Education, 729 F.2d 1270 (10th Cir.1984) (per curiam) affirmed by an evenly divided United States Supreme Court, Board of Education v. National Gay Task Force, 470 U.S. 903, 105 S.Ct. 1858, 84 L.Ed.2d 776 (1985). As is customary when the Supreme Court affirms a lower court decision by an evenly divided vote of the Justices, there was no opinion issued either by the Court or individual Justices regarding the affirmance of the 10th Circuit in the National Gay Task Force case (restricting the ability of the government

would argue that the sexual orientation based classification regarding marriage could not withstand even rational basis review.

In responding to claims for legal recognition of homosexual unions, states no doubt, would rely on Supreme Courts cases regarding zoning some areas of residential communities for occupation by only traditional families. Almost thirty years before *Lawrence*, the Court had upheld a law excluding from the residential area of a suburban community persons who wished to share housing together if those persons were not related by blood or marriage. In *Village of Belle Terre v. Boraas*,[75] the Supreme Court stated that a zoning law which effectively zoned-out non-traditional families should be subject only to the rationality test; and that the law was rationally related to the government interest in reserving the residential area for traditional family living.

In *Cleburne v. Cleburne Living Center*[76] the Court invalidated a city's refusal to grant a permit for a group home for a group of mentally retarded persons when the city zoning law would have allowed a similar number of per-

sons (who were not mentally retarded) from living together. The majority opinion found that this zoning law violated the rationality test, because the law excluded mentally retarded persons from living together, even though group homes for mentally retarded persons were not demonstrated to harm to societal interests, while the law allowed other groups of unrelated persons to live together. The majority opinion in *Cleburne* noted that a city zoning law that prohibited persons from living together unless they were related by blood or marriage would not have to have an exemption for a group home for mentally retarded persons.[77]

In one case the Supreme Court invalidated a zoning regulation that was based on a legal definition of family relationships. In *Moore v. City of East Cleveland*,[78] the Supreme Court, without a majority opinion, invalidated a zoning law that restricted the abilities of members of a traditional family to live together when the family unit did not seek to exceed the number of persons who could live in a house under zoning laws regulating the size of

---

to suspend or dismiss teachers for advocating or encouraging homosexual activity). See also Gay Lib v. University of Missouri, 558 F.2d 848 (8th Cir.1977), certiorari denied sub nom. Ratchford v. Gay Lib, 434 U.S. 1080, 98 S.Ct. 1276, 55 L.Ed.2d 789 (1978), re-hearing denied, 435 U.S. 981, 98 S.Ct. 1632, 56 L.Ed.2d 74 (1978).

In Dallas v. Stanglin, 490 U.S. 19, 109 S.Ct. 1591, 104 L.Ed.2d 18 (1989) the Supreme Court upheld a city ordinance restricting certain dance halls to patrons between the ages of 14 and 18. The ordinance was challenged on the basis of the First Amendment, as well as equal protection. The Justices were unanimous in voting to uphold the ordinance. Chief Justice Rehnquist wrote for seven members of the Court when he stated: "It is clear beyond cavil that dance-hall patrons who may number 1,000 on any given night, are not engaged in the sort of intimate human relationships referred to in [prior cases]." 490 U.S. at 19, 109 S.Ct. at 1592 (internal citation and internal quotation marks omitted). See also, FW/PBS, Inc. v. Dallas, 493 U.S. 215, 110 S.Ct. 596, 107 L.Ed.2d 603 (1990) (a city ordinance classifying motels that letted rooms for periods shorter than 10 hours as "sexually oriented businesses," and subjecting those businesses to special regulations, held not to burden the freedom of association or right of privacy).

When a private association excludes persons on the basis of race, religion, sex or sexual orientation it is not subject to the First and Fourteenth Amendments unless it has state action. See Chapter 12 §§ 12.1, 12.4. When a state law prohibits the discrimination the organization may claim that its First Amendment right of freedom of association was violated. In two cases the Supreme Court

has found that an application of an anti-discrimination law that would have required a private organization to admit or accommodate persons with a different sexual orientation so intruded on the expressive abilities of the group that it violated the First Amendment. For example, in Boy Scouts of America v. Dale, 530 U.S. 640, 120 S.Ct. 2446, 147 L.Ed.2d 554 (2000) the Court held that a state's public accommodation, anti-discrimination law could not be applied to the policy of the Boy Scouts that prohibited persons with a homosexual orientation from becoming Scout leaders. The Court found that requiring the Scouts to accept such leaders would have interfered with the Boy Scout's First Amendment freedom to associate for the promotion of certain ideas, which included positions opposed to homosexual conduct. See also, Hurley v. Irish–American Gay, Lesbian and Bisexual Group of Boston, 515 U.S. 557, 115 S.Ct. 2338, 132 L.Ed.2d 487 (1995).

75. 416 U.S. 1, 94 S.Ct. 1536, 39 L.Ed.2d 797 (1974).

76. 473 U.S. 432, 105 S.Ct. 3249, 87 L.Ed.2d 313 (1985).

77. 473 U.S. at 439 n. 8, 105 S.Ct. at 3254 n. 8.

78. 431 U.S. 494, 503–04, 97 S.Ct. 1932, 1937–38, 52 L.Ed.2d 531, 539–44 (1977) (plurality opinion). In this case four Justices thought that the law should be subject to meaningful judicial scrutiny because it interfered with family relationships. Justice Stevens, concurring in the judgment, believed that the law violated due process because of its restrictions on a property owner's ability to use her property in a manner that did not create any social harm.

housing. After *Lawrence,* can a city zone a residential area in a way that allows occupation of a single dwelling only by persons who are related by blood or marriage so that it would exclude from the area persons (whether homosexual or heterosexual) who wish to live together but who are not related to each other by biological ties or marriage? That question is an open one, following the *Lawrence* decision.

The *Lawrence* decision may also lead to litigation regarding the definition of persons eligible to adopt children. The Supreme Court of the United States has not ruled on whether a state can prohibit persons from being eligible to adopt children because the persons are unmarried. More than twenty years before *Lawrence,* the Court had refused to review a state court decision taking away the custody of children from a divorced mother based on the presumption that her cohabitation with an adult male to whom she was not married adversely affected the well-being of her children.[79] But a denial of certiorari does not establish any precedent; we have no ruling from the Supreme Court as to whether unmarried adults can be excluded from the category of persons being considered for adoptions from state agencies or excluded from the group of persons who might legally adopt a child with the approval of the child's parents.

The Court has told us that a state may not find a parent unfit to retain custody of her children merely because she marries a person of another race, but that ruling was an easy one, which involved the application of long-established principles regarding racial classifications.[80] The Supreme Court has also ruled that a state may not simply presume that the father of a child born out of wedlock, who had lived with the mother of the child, should lose

custody of the child following the death of the child's mother.[81] However, that case involved relatively simple principles regarding the use of illegitimacy classification and the need to grant fair process to a parent before the termination of parental rights.[82]

Perhaps the most important question left open by *Lawrence* is whether, in 2003, there was a majority of the Justices on the Supreme Court who would be willing to consider all forms of economic and social welfare legislation under a true reasonableness test. If the Court were to make independent judgments as to whether any and every law limiting individual autonomy was reasonably related to a legitimate interest, we would have a complete return to the form of judicial review that was used by the Court during the period from the mid–1890's until 1937.[83]

§ 14.29 Abortion

(a) An Introductory Note

In this section, we will examine the Supreme Court rulings regarding the right of a woman to have an abortion. In the next subsection, we will examine the basic constitutional principles established by the Supreme Court for the judicial review of laws that proscribe or regulate abortions. In the following subsections, we will examine Supreme Court rulings concerning specific types of abortion regulations, limits on the ability of minor females to have an abortion without notice to, or the consent of, a parent and the ability of states to provide funding for abortion services.

The formal tests that should be employed by a court that is reviewing the constitutionality of any type of abortion regulation are not very

---

79. Jarrett v. Jarrett, 78 Ill.2d 337, 36 Ill.Dec. 1, 400 N.E.2d 421 (1979) cert. denied 449 U.S. 927, 101 S.Ct. 329, 66 L.Ed.2d 155 (1980), rehearing denied 449 U.S. 1067, 101 S.Ct. 797, 66 L.Ed.2d 612 (1980). Justice Brennan filed an opinion dissenting to the denial of certiorari that was joined by Justice Marshall. Justice Blackmun voted to set the case for oral argument; he dissented without opinion.

80. Palmore v. Sidoti, 466 U.S. 429, 104 S.Ct. 1879, 80 L.Ed.2d 421 (1984). See § 14.8 of this Treatise.

81. Stanley v. Illinois, 405 U.S. 645, 92 S.Ct. 1208, 31 L.Ed.2d 551 (1972).

82. Regarding procedural due process principles see §§ 13.4, 13.8 of this Treatise. Regarding the combined gender and illegitimacy classifications involved in these decisions see §§ 14.14, 14.17. Regarding custody of children see note 32, *supra* and Troxel v. Granville, 530 U.S. 57, 120 S.Ct. 2054, 147 L.Ed.2d 49 (2000) (judgment of the Court announced in an opinion by O'Connor, J., joined by Rehnquist, C.J. and Ginsburg and Breyer, JJ.), which is discussed in the previous paragraphs in this section of the Treatise.

83. See §§ 11.1–11.3, 14.3(a), 14.3(b).

clear. In *Roe v. Wade*[1] the Supreme Court found that a woman's right to choose to have an abortion was a part of the fundamental constitutional right of privacy. After establishing that fundamental constitutional principle, the majority opinion in *Roe* ruled that a government regulation of abortion practices could be upheld only if it was narrowly tailored to promote a compelling interest. The *Roe* majority opinion found that the government had a compelling interest in protecting the health of the woman who was having the abortion after the first three months of the pregnancy, and that the government had a compelling interest that would justify prohibiting all abortions (except those that were necessary to protect the life or health of the woman) after the fetus became viable.

In *Roe* the Court only found that a fetus was not a person for purposes of the Fourteenth Amendment. Had the *Roe* Court ruled otherwise, and found that a fetus was a person, states might have been required to have laws that prohibited abortions so as to avoid denying these persons life without due process of law; there might have been a host of equal protection problems raised by medical regulations that allowed for the abortion of some fetuses, but not others.

The Supreme Court has never ruled that a state cannot treat a fetus as if it were a child for purposes unrelated to preventing a woman from exercising her freedom of choice to terminate her pregnancy. None of the abortion regulation cases would resolve the question of whether the government could make it a crime for an individual to beat a woman without her consent for the purpose of causing her to have a miscarriage, and terminate the existence of a fetus within her body. Similarly, none of these cases resolve the question of whether a pregnant woman who ingests substances that are unhealthy for a fetus that she will eventually carry to term could be charged with a crime similar to child abuse or child neglect crimes.[2]

The *Roe* majority opinion has often been described as establishing a rigid "trimester" analysis for determining what types of government regulations of abortion would be constitutional. Although there is no majority opinion that formally changed the *Roe* "tests", the Supreme Court seemed to abandon a strict trimester analysis within a few years after *Roe*. By the 1980s, the Court appeared to be using a reasonableness test for determining the regulation in abortion cases. The Court would uphold the regulation if a majority of the Justices believed that it was a reasonable means of protecting the woman's health; the Court would invalidate the regulation if the Justices found that the law was intended not to protect the health of the woman but only to deter abortions. The Court appeared to use a similar approach for reviewing laws that regulated or prohibited the abortion of viable fetuses. The regulation or prohibition would be upheld if it was reasonably related to the protection of a possibly viable fetus. The Court would invalidate laws designed to protect a viable fetus that did not provide a reasonable exception for protecting the life or health of the woman. The Court never adopted any formal test for the constitutionality of abortion regulating other than the compelling interest test set forth in *Roe*.

In *Webster v. Reproductive Health Services*,[3] it appeared that a majority of the Justices rejected the trimester analytical structure but they did not do so in a majority opinion. The Justices did not replace the *Roe* trimester analysis with any new test for the judicial review of abortion regulations under the due process clauses.

All of the post-*Roe* cases, including *Webster*, might be rationalized by the following princi-

---

§ 14.29

1. 410 U.S. 113, 93 S.Ct. 705, 35 L.Ed.2d 147 (1973).

2. See generally, Ferguson v. Charleston, 532 U.S. 67, 121 S.Ct. 1281, 149 L.Ed.2d 205 (2001). (Supreme Court rules that a government hospital program of screening the urine of some pregnant women to provide prosecutors with evidence to prosecute some women for putting drugs in the blood of the fetus violated the Fourth Amendment; the Court did not rule on whether a woman could be prosecuted for taking drugs and thereby having a fetus that would later be born).

3. 492 U.S. 490, 109 S.Ct. 3040, 106 L.Ed.2d 410 (1989).

ple even though this principle was never adopted by any Justice.

"A state abortion regulation will be upheld if it is a reasonable effort to (1) protect the woman's health, (2) ensure that minors make responsible decisions, or (3) protect a viable or possibly viable fetus. A health regulation may not unduly burden the right to abortion. Statutes protecting possibly viable fetuses must not be so vague as to deter abortions of nonviable fetuses and must allow abortions when a physician finds a significant threat to the life or health of the woman. So long as it does not impose a significant barrier to, or penalty for, abortions, the state may take other steps to discourage women from choosing to have an abortion." [4]

This reasonableness test appears to have been used by lower courts in the 1980s when deciding how to apply the Supreme Court's abortion decisions, many of which were decided without majority opinion. However, the Supreme Court has never adopted, in a majority opinion, a formal test for examining the constitutionality of abortion regulations other than the compelling interest test used in *Roe*. The reasonableness principle described above summarized the position taken in earlier editions of this Treatise and lower court rulings. It is only an aid to understanding the Court's rules.

If one were asked to describe the formal test used by the Court in abortion cases, following all of the Supreme Court decisions of the 1970s and 1980s, the formal answer might be the following. The Supreme Court will only uphold abortion regulations that are supported by a compelling interest; the states have compelling interests in protecting the health of the woman and protecting a viable fetus. A state regulation of an abortion that is to be performed within the first three months of pregnancy must be judicially determined to be narrowly tailored to protect the health of the woman. A state regulation that applies to

abortions after the first three months of pregnancy only has to be reasonably necessary for the health of the woman. A state law that is designed to protect a viable fetus will be upheld if it is narrowly tailored to the promotion of that interest. A law designed to protect a possibly viable fetus must allow an exception for a woman who needs an abortion to protect her life or health. Some special restrictions will be upheld on abortions for minors, due to the societal state interest in the protection of minors. A state may refuse to fund abortions, because the right to privacy includes only a right to choose to have an abortion without governmental interference and not a right to have abortion services provided by the government.

In 1992, the Supreme Court came very close to adopting the reasonableness test that had been used by lower courts in the 1970s and the 1980s (and that has been previously referred to in this introduction). In *Planned Parenthood v. Casey*,[5] the Supreme Court examined a variety of state regulations of abortions. Justice O'Connor wrote an opinion in *Casey* that was, in part, a majority opinion for the Court and, in part, a plurality opinion that reflected only the views of herself and Justices Kennedy and Souter. In the portion of her opinion that was a majority opinion (which was joined by Justices Blackmun and Stevens as well as Justices Kennedy and Souter), Justice O'Connor reaffirmed *Roe's* "essential holding" that the concept of liberty in the due process clause gave rise to a "right of the woman to choose to have an abortion before viability and to obtain it without undue interference from the State." [6] This portion of the majority opinion also recognized the state's ability to restrict abortions after a fetus was viable so long as there was an exception allowing for abortions that were needed to terminate pregnancies that would endanger a woman's life or health. The majority also recognized a state interest in protecting the health of the woman and the

---

4. Farber & Nowak, Beyond the Roe Debate: Judicial Experience With the 1980s "Reasonableness" Test, 76 U.Va.L.Rev., 519, 520 (1990).

5. 505 U.S. 833, 112 S.Ct. 2791, 120 L.Ed.2d 674 (1992), on remand 978 F.2d 74 (3d Cir.1992).

6. 505 U.S. at 845, 112 S.Ct. at 2804.

life of the fetus that might support some restrictions on abortions.

In *Casey*, five Justices reaffirmed the role of the judiciary in protecting the right of a woman to choose to abort a nonviable fetus by independent judicial review of government regulations regarding abortions. Four Justices voted to overrule *Roe* and to find that a woman did not have a fundamental right of freedom of choice regarding the abortion of a nonviable fetus.[7] It appears that there is virtually no likelihood that the basic principles of *Roe* will be overturned in the foreseeable future.

The majority that reaffirmed *Roe* in the *Casey* decision divided when it came to the question of how the Court should formulate a test to implement the basic principles of *Roe*. Justices Stevens and Blackmun wished to adhere to the compelling interest language of *Roe*.[8] The swing votes in the case belonged to Justices O'Connor, Kennedy, and Souter. Justice O'Connor wrote a plurality opinion in which these three Justices found that the basic principles of *Roe* were best implemented by a test that would invalidate only those laws that placed an "undue burden" on a woman's ability to decide to have an abortion.[9] Justice O'Connor stated that: "A finding of an undue burden is a shorthand for the conclusion that a state regulation has the purpose or effect of placing a substantial obstacle in the path of a woman seeking an abortion of a nonviable fetus." [10]

We will examine the *Casey* decision, and Justice O'Connor's plurality opinion, in detail following an examination of the *Roe* and *Webster* decisions. It should be noted from the outset that the plurality opinion in *Casey*, as well as the outcome of the case, seems to continue what has been the position of the Court (albeit without majority opinions) for most of the past two decades. There will be independent judicial review of abortion regulations; a majority of the Justices will strike down abortion regulations that are not designed to protect the pregnant woman, to protect pregnant minors, to promote informed decisions by pregnant women, or to protect a viable or possibly viable fetus.

Stenberg v. Carhart[11] drew great media attention, in 2000, as the first case invalidating a restriction on so-called partial-birth abortion. However, the primary importance *Stenberg*, in the long term, may be the fact that there was a majority opinion adopting the undue burden analysis that had been put forward in a plurality opinion in *Casey*. Additionally, the Court reaffirmed the requirement that otherwise proper regulations of abortion practices must have an exception so that medical personnel can disregard the regulation if it was necessary to protect the life or health of the pregnant woman.

The fact that the majority opinion in *Stenberg* adopted position of the plurality in *Casey* means that the "undue burden" standard set forth in *Casey* must now be used to evaluate all abortion regulations.

We will now turn to an examination of four major Supreme Court cases in this area—*Roe*, *Webster*, *Casey*, and *Stenberg*. We will follow our examination of those cases with an analysis of the Court's rulings on specific types of abortion regulations.

(b) The Cases

(1)(a) *Roe v. Wade*. In *Roe v. Wade*[12] the Supreme Court overturned a Texas statute

---

7. Planned Parenthood v. Casey, 505 U.S. 833, 963, 112 S.Ct. 2791, 2885, 120 L.Ed.2d 674 (1992) (Rehnquist, C.J., joined by White, Scalia, and Thomas, JJ., concurring in the judgment in part and dissenting in part), on remand 978 F.2d 74 (3d Cir.1992); 505 U.S. at 978, 112 S.Ct. at 2873 (Scalia, J., joined by Rehnquist, C.J., and White and Thomas, JJ., concurring in the judgment in part and dissenting in part).

8. Planned Parenthood v. Casey, 505 U.S. 833, 911, 112 S.Ct. 2791, 2838, 120 L.Ed.2d 674 (1992) (Stevens, J., concurring in part and dissenting in part), on remand 978 F.2d 74 (3d Cir.1992); 505 U.S. at 920, 112 S.Ct. at 2843

(Blackmun, J., concurring in part, concurring in the judgment in part, and dissenting in part).

9. Planned Parenthood v. Casey, 505 U.S. 833, 868–78 112 S.Ct. 2791, 2816–21, 120 L.Ed.2d 674 (1992) (opinion of O'Connor, J., joined by Kennedy and Souter, JJ.), on remand 978 F.2d 74 (3d Cir.1992).

10. 505 U.S. at 876, 112 S.Ct. at 2820 (opinion of O'Connor, J., joined by Kennedy and Souter, JJ.).

11. 530 U.S. 914, 120 S.Ct. 2597, 147 L.Ed.2d 743 (2000). This case is examined in § 14.29(b)(2).

12. 410 U.S. 113, 93 S.Ct. 705, 35 L.Ed.2d 147 (1973).

which proscribed procuring or attempting the abortion of a human fetus except when necessary to save the life of the mother. The Court held that the statute violated the due process clause of the Fourteenth Amendment as an unjustified deprivation of liberty in that it unnecessarily infringed on a woman's right to privacy.

The majority opinion, by Justice Blackmun, noted the broad range of decisions involving the right to privacy. With virtually no further explanation of the privacy value, the opinion found that the right of privacy, regardless of exactly what constitutional provision it was ascribed to, "is broad enough to encompass a woman's decision whether or not to terminate her pregnancy."[13] As this was now a part of the liberty protected by the Fourteenth Amendment, the right could not be restricted without due process of law.

Normally the legislature may regulate activities so long as the legislation has some rational relationship to a legitimate state interest. However, where the legislation restricts the exercise of fundamental constitutional rights it will only be upheld if it is necessary to promote a compelling state interest. In this case the Court found that the right to an abortion was not absolute and so it could be limited in some circumstances. But the majority found the right to privacy which included the woman's right to an abortion was "fundamental." Thus, the Court held that limitations on the woman's right to have an abortion would only be upheld where they furthered a "compelling state interest."

There were two state interests which the Court found might support some limitations on the right to an abortion—the interest in the health of the mother and in the life of the fetus. The only interest which might have supported a total ban on abortion was the protection of the fetus as a human life. But the majority found no basis, apart from certain philosophies or religions, for calling the fetus a person. While this argument did not establish the invalidity of the Act, the refusal of the

Court to recognize this interest required the states to demonstrate some independent interest in the life of the mother or the fetus. There would be a "compelling interest" in the mother's life where restriction on the right was needed to protect her life or safety. There would be a "compelling interest" in the fetus when the state could show a viable life which it had an interest to protect.

Through approximately the first third of a pregnancy, abortion performed under a doctor's care was as safe, if not safer, for a woman's health as was completion of the pregnancy. Thus the opinion held there could be no significant restriction on the right of the woman to have an abortion during the first trimester of the pregnancy. The woman was free to have an abortion during this time subject only to her ability to find a licensed physician who would perform the operation. The state could require a few minimal medical safeguards during this period such as requiring that the abortionist be a licensed medical doctor.

The risk to the pregnant woman's health increased after the first trimester. Thus the Court found a "compelling interest" in establishing further medical regulations on abortions performed after that stage of the pregnancy. Later decisions made it clear that the reasonableness of these restrictions would be subjected to independent judicial review and that only those regulations of abortion procedures which the Justices would find to be reasonable and narrowly tailored to protect the health of the woman during a second trimester abortion would be upheld.[14]

With respect to the state's interest in the existence of the fetus, the majority found that the state had a "compelling interest" when the fetus became viable—normally considered to be the beginning of the third trimester (end of the sixth month) of the pregnancy. At this point the fetus could have "meaningful life" outside the mother and the state could demonstrate an important interest in its existence apart from moral philosophy concerning the beginning of life. The Court held that after

---

13. 410 U.S. at 153, 93 S.Ct. at 727.

14. See generally, Farber & Nowak, supra note 3.

the time of viability the legislature could prohibit abortions except where necessary to protect the life or health of the mother. It should be noted that all of the opinions have assumed that an exception would be made to such a proscription to secure the mother's life or prevent serious injury to her health.

The separate opinions of individual Justices foreshadowed the debate over the legitimacy of these decisions. In concurring opinions, Justice Stewart accepted this ruling as a permissible use of the substantive due process theory and Justice Douglas elaborated on the concept of unwritten fundamental values recognized by the Ninth and Fourteenth Amendments.

There were only two dissents but they touched on the points that would lead to later criticism of the decisions. Justice White explained that there was no basis for finding that the judiciary should make decisions concerning the competing values of the mother and the potential life of the fetus. He saw the decision as the "exercise of raw judicial power" rather than the protection of clear constitutional values. Justice Rehnquist noted the similarity in the use of substantive due process between these decisions and the formally repudiated position of the Court in *Lochner v. New York*.[15]

(1)(b) *Webster v. Reproductive Health Services*—Limiting the *Roe v. Wade* Analytical Structure.

The *Roe v. Wade*[16] majority opinion appeared to establish a rigid "trimester" structure for the judicial examination of abortion regulations. Virtually no regulations would be upheld that related to first trimester abortions; any regulation of abortions performed between the end of the first trimester and the time when the fetus was viable (as determined by an attending physician) would be upheld only if the regulation was narrowly tailored to protect the health of the woman. Abortions could be outlawed after the fetus was viable, although the ban on post-viability abortions,

and all other abortion regulations, would have to include an exception for abortions performed to protect the life or health of the woman. In the late 1970s and throughout the 1980s the Supreme Court's rulings, though not its opinions, appeared to adopt a "reasonableness" test for abortion regulations.[17] State abortion regulations that were reasonably related to protecting the pregnant woman, or were reasonably related to protecting the health or existence of a viable fetus, would be upheld. An abortion regulation would be invalidated if a majority of Justices believed that the regulation merely deterred abortions and was not a reasonable means of protecting a pregnant woman or a viable fetus. In 1989, in *Webster v. Reproductive Health Services*,[18] a majority of Justices on the Supreme Court appeared to reject the *Roe v. Wade* formal "trimester" analytical structure although they did not at that time replace the *Roe* analysis with any new test for the judicial review of abortion regulations.

In *Webster,* the Supreme Court examined the constitutionality of four provisions of Missouri state law: (1) a statutory preamble stating that "the life of each human being begins at conception"; (2) a prohibition against public employees performing abortions or public facilities being used for abortions; (3) a prohibition of public funding of abortion counseling; (4) a set of requirements regarding physician's use of certain medical tests to determine whether a fetus was viable. The first three portions of the statute that were easily upheld on the basis of earlier decisions of the Supreme Court. Only the last of the statutory provisions, relating to viability testing, brought into question whether any prior decision of the Supreme Court should be overruled. Chief Justice Rehnquist wrote a majority opinion for the Court regarding the first three provisions; he could not gain a majority for his opinion regarding the viability testing portion of the statute.

---

15. 198 U.S. 45, 25 S.Ct. 539, 49 L.Ed. 937 (1905).

16. 410 U.S. 113, 93 S.Ct. 705, 35 L.Ed.2d 147 (1973).

17. These cases are examined in the next subsection, § 14.29(b)(2).

18. 492 U.S. 490, 109 S.Ct. 3040, 106 L.Ed.2d 410 (1989).

First, the statutory preamble, which included the legislative determination of when life begins, did not present a ripe constitutional question.[19] There was no indication that this legislative preamble would in any way limit a woman's ability to have an abortion in the state. Rather, this legislative statement might only be used to interpret state statutes or regulations unrelated to abortion, such as determining the extent of tort law or probate law protections for unborn children. The Supreme Court majority refused to rule on the constitutionality of the preamble prior to the time when it was interpreted by state courts in such a way as to limit the ability of women to have an abortion.

The second provision at issue, the prohibition of abortions being performed on public facilities or being performed by public employees, was upheld on the basis of earlier Supreme Court cases, which had held that the state's refusal to subsidize abortions did not restrict a woman's right to privacy.[20] In those cases the Supreme Court had found that the right to privacy included a woman's decision to have an abortion without interference by the state but did not include a right of a woman to receive abortion services or funds for such services.[21]

In *Webster* the majority opinion by Chief Justice Rehnquist noted that the state law restrictions on public employees performing abortions did not appear to impose restrictions on the performance of abortions by persons employed by the state if the person was acting on his own time (not during the time when he was employed by the state) and at private hospitals.[22] If a state attempted to prohibit doctors who performed abortions on their own time at privately owned medical facilities from using public medical facilities for any purpose, that prohibition might violate women's right to privacy because it would constitute restriction of women's ability to have an abortion, rather than a mere refusal to subsidize abortions.

The third portion of the statute at issue in *Webster* was a prohibition of public funding of abortion counseling. The statute could have been read to restrict abortion counseling by public employees acting at their own expense and at times at which they were not employed by the state. If the statute had restricted abortion counseling in such a broad manner, the provisions would have presented serious free speech, as well as right to privacy, issues. However, six Justices of the Supreme Court accepted the state's assertion that the statute did nothing other than prohibit the use of public funds for abortion counseling and regulated only those persons responsible for spending public money.[23] The parties attacking the statute admitted that they would not be adversely affected by a statutory prohibition of expending public money for abortion counseling, so long as it did not restrict public employees from speech or associational activities outside of the scope of their employment. For that reason, six Justices found that any previous controversy regarding the abortion counseling provision of this statute was moot.

The final provision of the Missouri statute at issue in *Webster v. Reproductive Health Services* required a physician, before performing an abortion on a woman whom the physician had "reason to believe is carrying an unborn child of twenty or more weeks of gestational age," to determine if the fetus was viable by using the degree of care that would normally

---

19. Webster v. Reproductive Health Services, 492 U.S. 490, 503–06, 109 S.Ct. 3040, 3049–50, 106 L.Ed.2d 410 (1989) (this portion of the opinion is a majority opinion written by Rehnquist, C.J., and joined by White, Kennedy, O'Connor, and Scalia, JJ.).

20. 492 U.S. at 506–11, 109 S.Ct. at 3050–53 (this portion of the opinion written by Rehnquist, C.J. was joined by White, Kennedy, O'Connor, and Scalia, JJ.).

21. See, e.g., Maher v. Roe, 432 U.S. 464, 97 S.Ct. 2376, 53 L.Ed.2d 484 (1977); Poelker v. Doe, 432 U.S. 519, 97 S.Ct. 2391, 53 L.Ed.2d 528 (1977); Harris v. McRae, 448 U.S. 297, 100 S.Ct. 2671, 65 L.Ed.2d 784

(1980). The funding cases are examined in § 14.29(b)(4), infra.

22. Webster v. Reproductive Health Services, 492 U.S. 490, 510 n. 8, 109 S.Ct. 3040, 3052 n. 8, 106 L.Ed.2d 410 (1989).

23. Webster v. Reproductive Health Services, 492 U.S. 490, 511–13, 109 S.Ct. 3040, 3053–54, 106 L.Ed.2d 410 (1989) (this portion of Chief Justice Rehnquist's opinion was joined by Justices White, Kennedy, O'Connor, Scalia, and Stevens).

be exercised by a "prudent physician." [24] The statute went on to say that, in making the viability determination, "the physician shall perform or cause to be performed such medical examination and tests as are necessary to make a finding of the gestational age, weight, and lung maturity of the unborn child." If the statute had been read to create a presumption that every fetus of twenty or more weeks was viable, the statute would have directly conflicted with the analytical structure established by *Roe v. Wade.* However, the parties attacking the statute did not appeal the portion of a lower court decision upholding the statutory provision and finding that the presumption did not restrict abortion rights.[25] Therefore, the Supreme Court in *Webster* made no ruling on whether a state could establish statutory criteria that would bind individual physicians in the viability determination.

The portion of the statute regarding viability determination tests was upheld by five Justices of the Court, though without majority opinion. Chief Justice Rehnquist, joined by Justices White and Kennedy, found that the statute did not require a physician to perform the tests in all circumstances. The statute only required a physician to exercise reasonable professional judgment in determining whether to use those tests to make a finding regarding viability.[26] Even with this reading of the statute, the Rehnquist plurality believed that the statute was in conflict with the trimester framework created by *Roe* and with dicta in earlier cases indicating that legislatures had no role in establishing standards for a determination of viability.[27] Chief Justice Rehnquist's plurality opinion found that the state's interest in the potential life of the

fetus, like the state's interest in the health of a pregnant woman, would support abortion regulations that were tailored to promote that interest throughout the time of a pregnancy.[28]

Though the Rehnquist plurality did not use a compelling interest test, the Chief Justice's opinion appears to reaffirm the *Roe* holding that the potential life of the fetus and the health of the woman were both compelling interests that would justify abortion regulations. The plurality opinion stated that the Missouri statute should be upheld as "reasonably designed to ensure that abortions are not performed where the fetus is viable—an end which all concede is legitimate—and that is sufficient to sustain its constitutionality." [29]

The Chief Justice's opinion did not explicitly challenge the principal holding of *Roe*, that judges should independently review abortion regulations to ensure that they were designed to protect the health of the woman, or to protect a viable fetus, rather than merely to deter or punish abortions. Indeed, the Chief Justice's plurality opinion stated that the dissent's suggestion that plurality opinion would lead to legislative actions regarding abortions "reminiscent of the Dark Ages" was erroneous both as to the likelihood of actions that legislatures would take such actions regarding abortions and "misreads our [the plurality's] views." [30]

Justice O'Connor concurred in the Court's ruling that the viability testing provision was constitutional.[31] Unlike the other Justices in the majority, she did not believe that the viability provision conflicted with earlier decisions of the United States Supreme Court.

24. The Supreme Court reprinted the statutory provision, 492 U.S. at 513, 109 S.Ct. at 3054.

25. This point was emphasized by Justice O'Connor, Webster v. Reproductive Health Services, 492 U.S. 490, 526, 109 S.Ct. 3040, 3061, 106 L.Ed.2d 410 (1989) (O'Connor, J., concurring in part and concurring in the judgment).

26. Webster v. Reproductive Health Services, 492 U.S. 490, 513–16, 109 S.Ct. 3040, 3054–55, 106 L.Ed.2d 410 (1989) (this portion of Chief Justice Rehnquist's opinion was joined only by Justices White and Kennedy).

27. That dicta is contained in Colautti v. Franklin, 439 U.S. 379, 99 S.Ct. 675, 58 L.Ed.2d 596 (1979). The

Colautti decision is examined in the next subsection, § 14.29(b)(2) "Regulations of Abortion Procedures."

28. Webster v. Reproductive Health Services, 492 U.S. 490, 518, 109 S.Ct. 3040, 3057, 106 L.Ed.2d 410 (1989) (Rehnquist, C.J., joined by White and Kennedy, JJ.).

29. 492 U.S. at 520, 109 S.Ct. at 3058 (Rehnquist, C.J., joined by White and Kennedy, JJ.).

30. Id.

31. Webster v. Reproductive Health Services, 492 U.S. 490, 520, 109 S.Ct. 3040, 3058, 106 L.Ed.2d 410 (1989) (O'Connor, J., concurring in part and concurring in the judgment).

Therefore, even though she continued "to consider problematic" the *Roe v. Wade* "trimester framework," she did not address the question of whether any element of *Roe v. Wade* should be modified. Justice O'Connor succinctly stated the basis for her decision: "It is clear to me that requiring the performance of examinations and tests useful to determining whether a fetus is viable, when viability is possible, and when it would not be medically imprudent to do so, does not impose an undue burden on a woman's abortion decision."[32]

Of the five Justices in the majority, only Justice Scalia expressly favored overruling *Roe v. Wade;* Justice Scalia would eliminate any independent judicial scrutiny of laws regulating or prohibiting abortions.[33]

The dissenting Justices believed that the ruling in *Webster v. Reproductive Health Services* impaired the fundamental constitutional right of privacy.[34] The dissent written by Justice Blackmun, who had authored the majority opinion in *Roe,* recognized that both the health of the woman and the protection of viable fetuses would be a compelling interest. Justice Blackmun would not grant significant deference to legislative decisions regarding whether a particular abortion regulation was a narrowing tailored means of promoting those interests.

(1)(c) *Planned Parenthood v. Casey*— Reaffirming and Modifying *Roe v. Wade.*

Roe v. Wade[35] established the constitutional principle that a woman's right to choose to have an abortion was a part of the fundamental right to privacy and that the government could only impair this liberty interest if it was promoting an interest of compelling importance. As we have seen, the Court's initial use of a trimester analysis for the review of specific abortion regulations failed to command the support of a majority of Justices during the 1980s, even though the Court never rejected the ruling that a woman had a fundamental right to choose to have an abortion or the principle that the judiciary had to independently review government acts that regulated or limited a woman's ability to exercise that right.

In 1992, a majority of the Justices, in a majority opinion, reaffirmed the ruling of *Roe* that recognized a woman's fundamental right to choose to abort a nonviable fetus. But seven Justices, though not in a majority opinion, rejected the *Roe* trimester analysis. In *Planned Parenthood v. Casey*[36] the Supreme Court upheld most, but not all, provisions of a Pennsylvania abortion statute. Justice O'Connor, in *Casey,* announced the judgment of the Court in an opinion that was, in part, a majority opinion, and in part a plurality opinion. Justice O'Connor wrote for a majority of the Court in finding that a woman's right to choose to have an abortion of a nonviable fetus was grounded in the concept of liberty protected by the due process clause of the Fourteenth Amendment. This portion of Justice O'Connor's opinion was joined by Justices Blackmun and Stevens as well as by Justices Kennedy and Souter.[37] The "essential holding" of *Roe* was reaffirmed on the basis of an independent analysis of the concept of "liberty" and on the

---

32. 492 U.S. at 530, 109 S.Ct. at 3063 (O'Connor, J., concurring in part and concurring in the judgment).

33. Webster v. Reproductive Health Services, 492 U.S. 490, 531, 109 S.Ct. 3040, 3064, 106 L.Ed.2d 410 (1989) (Scalia, J., concurring in part and concurring in the judgment).

34. 492 U.S. 490, 537, 109 S.Ct. 3040, 3067, 106 L.Ed.2d 410 (1989) (Blackmun, J., joined by Brennan and Marshall, JJ., concurring in part and dissenting in part). Justice Stevens dissented on the basis that the state statute, as he interpreted it, prohibited certain types of contraception as well as limiting abortions; he believed that the statute impaired the right to privacy. He also believed that the statute violated the establishment clause of the First Amendment because it could only have been the result of a legislative decision to adopt and prefer

certain theological doctrines. 492 U.S. at 559, 109 S.Ct. at 3079–85 (Stevens, J., concurring in part and dissenting in part).

35. 410 U.S. 113, 93 S.Ct. 705, 35 L.Ed.2d 147 (1973).

36. 505 U.S. 833, 112 S.Ct. 2791, 120 L.Ed.2d 674 (1992), on remand 978 F.2d 74 (3d Cir.1992).

37. Parts I–III of Justice O'Connor's opinion in *Casey,* which reaffirmed the principle that a woman's right to terminate her pregnancy prior to viability is a fundamental aspect of liberty protected by the due process clause of the Fourteenth Amendment was joined by Justices Blackmun, Stevens, Souter, and Kennedy. Planned Parenthood v. Casey, 505 U.S. 833, 842–68, 112 S.Ct. 2791, 2803–16, 120 L.Ed.2d 674 (1992).

basis of stare decisis. Early in her majority opinion, Justice O'Connor wrote:

"It must be stated at the outset and with clarity that Roe's essential holding, the holding we reaffirm, has three parts. First is a recognition of the right of the woman to choose to have an abortion before viability and to obtain it without undue interference from the State ... Second is a confirmation of the State's power to restrict abortions after fetal viability, if the law contains exceptions for pregnancies which endanger a woman's life or health. And third is the principle that the State has legitimate interest from the outset of the pregnancy in protecting the health of the woman and the life of the fetus ... these principles do not contradict one another...."[38]

Although four Justices dissented from the majority's position concerning a woman's right to an abortion,[39] it seems unlikely that the basic principle established by Roe will be overturned in the near future, if ever.

In addition to the reaffirmation of a woman's constitutional right to choose an abortion the Court reaffirmed the state's power to prohibit abortions of a viable fetus, so long as the prohibition allowed an abortion to be performed when the continuation of the pregnancy would "endanger a woman's life or health." The Casey decision did not involve statutes that defined viability and, therefore, the Court did not have occasion to clarify the concept of viability or to explain the types of dangers to a woman's life or health that might require exceptions from a prohibition on the abortion of viable fetuses.[40]

Justice Blackmun, the author of the majority opinion in Roe, was the only Justice in Casey who wished to reaffirm not only the basic holdings of Roe (set forth in the above quotation from Justice O'Connor's majority opinion) but also the use of a compelling interest test that would be tied to trimester analysis.[41] Justice Stevens favored using a case-by-case test that focused on whether particular abortion regulations promoted societal interests that were so compelling as to outweigh the woman's liberty interest.[42]

With four Justices wishing to reject Roe in its entirety, and two Justices wishing to uphold both Roe's basic principle and some elements of the compelling interest test, the outcome of the Court's decision in Casey rested with Justices O'Connor, Kennedy, and Souter. If Justices O'Connor, Kennedy, and Souter believed that a particular regulation was invalid they would vote with Justices Blackmun and Stevens (who appeared to be using a stricter test) to invalidate the abortion regulation. If these three "swing vote" Justices believed that a particular abortion regulation was constitutional, they would vote with the four Justices who rejected Roe to form a seven member majority to uphold the particular regulation. Thus, special attention must be paid to the views expressed in the three Justice plurality opinion.

Justice O'Connor wrote for herself and Justices Kennedy and Souter in finding that a state regulation of abortions of nonviable fetuses would be permissible only so long as it did not impose an "undue burden" on the woman's freedom to choose to have an abortion.[43] This undue burden test had its roots in

---

38. 505 U.S. at 845, 112 S.Ct. at 2804.

39. Planned Parenthood v. Casey, 505 U.S. 833, 944, 112 S.Ct. 2791, 2855, 120 L.Ed.2d 674 (1992) (Rehnquist, C.J., joined by White, Scalia, and Thomas, JJ., concurring in the judgment in part and dissenting in part), on remand 978 F.2d 74 (3d Cir.1992); 505 U.S. at 978, 112 S.Ct. at 2873 (Scalia, J., joined by Rehnquist, C.J., and White and Thomas, JJ., concurring in the judgment in part and dissenting in part).

40. See the introduction to this section [§ 14.29(a)] regarding how the Casey decision can be viewed as a logical progression of the Court's rulings from 1973 (the date of Roe) to 1992. Later subsections of this section of the Treatise will examine how the Casey decision fits in

with specific Supreme Court rulings regarding various types of state abortion regulations.

41. Planned Parenthood v. Casey, 505 U.S. 833, 921, 112 S.Ct. 2791, 2843, 120 L.Ed.2d 674 (1992) (Blackmun, J., concurring in part, concurring in the judgment in part and dissenting in part).

42. 505 U.S. at 911, 112 S.Ct. at 2838 (Stevens, J., concurring in part and dissenting in part).

43. Planned Parenthood v. Casey, 505 U.S. 833, 868–77, 112 S.Ct. 2791, 2816–21, 120 L.Ed.2d 674 (1992) (part V of the opinion of O'Connor, J., joined by Kennedy and Souter, JJ.).

Justice O'Connor's separate opinion in *Webster v. Reproductive Health Services*.[44] Justice O'Connor's plurality opinion in *Casey* clarifies the undue burden test. After finding that the right to choose to abort a nonviable fetus, like other fundamental aspects of liberty, was not an absolute right and that this right could be subject to state regulations that promoted constitutionally valid ends that had only incidental effects of making it more difficult or expensive to exercise the right, the plurality rejected the "rigid trimester framework of *Roe v. Wade*". Justice O'Connor then explained the meaning of the undue burden test:

"A finding of an undue burden is a shorthand for the conclusion that a state regulation has the purpose or effect of placing a substantial obstacle in the path of a woman seeking an abortion of a nonviable fetus. A statute with this purpose is invalid because the means chosen by the State to further the interest in potential life must be calculated to inform the woman's free choice, not hinder it. And a statute which, while furthering the interest in potential life or some other valid state interest, has the effect of placing a substantial obstacle in the path of a woman's choice cannot be considered a permissible means of serving its legitimate ends.... Some guiding principles should emerge. What is at stake is the woman's right to make the ultimate decision, not a right to be insulated from all others in doing so. Regulations which do no more than create a structural mechanism by which the State, or the parent or guardian of a minor, may express profound respect for the life of the unborn are permitted, if they are not a substantial obstacle to the woman's exercise of the right to choose ... Unless it has that effect [the effect of creating a substantial obstacle] on her right of choice, a state mea-

sure designed to persuade her to choose childbirth over abortion will be upheld if reasonably related to that goal. Regulations designed to foster the health of a woman seeking an abortion are valid if they do not constitute an undue burden.... unnecessary health regulations that have the purpose or effect of presenting a substantial obstacle to a woman seeking an abortion impose an undue burden on the right." [45]

The most important part of the plurality's undue burden test may be the "purpose or effect" aspect of the test. As we noted in the introduction to this section of the Treatise, all of the Supreme Court's 1980s decisions concerning abortion regulations could be understood in terms of a judicial test designed to ensure that regulations of abortions of nonviable fetuses were reasonably designed to protect the health of the woman or to protect the interests of minor pregnant females. There was no clear indication in the previous cases that a law that was tailored to protecting a woman's health or welfare (and had only that effect) might be invalidated on the basis of an improper legislative purpose.

Because the plurality in *Casey* endorsed the purpose branch of undue burden analysis, lower court judges reviewing abortion regulations may not be able to uphold an abortion regulation merely by finding that it is a reasonable health law. But perhaps the purpose branch of undue burden analysis will not be very difficult for judges to apply. It may be that any law that is demonstrably related to protecting the health of the female patient would be found to have a legitimate purpose that would withstand constitutional scrutiny, even though some legislators might have voted for the law for a variety of purposes (including the purpose of making it more difficult for a woman to obtain abortions).[46]

---

44. 492 U.S. 490, 520, 109 S.Ct. 3040, 3058, 106 L.Ed.2d 410 (1989) (O'Connor, J., concurring in part and concurring in the judgment).

45. Planned Parenthood v. Casey, 505 U.S. 833, 876–77, 112 S.Ct. 2791, 2820–21, 120 L.Ed.2d 674 (1992) (O'Connor, J., joined by Kennedy and Souter, JJ.).

46. While *Casey* does not explain the ways in which the Court might look for unconstitutional purpose in an abortion case, the Court has examined the difficulties of

using legislative motive or purpose as a basis for invalidating the law in equal protection cases. See § 14.4 of this Treatise regarding the difficulty of attacking a law on the basis of allegedly discriminatory purpose. In Mazurek v. Armstrong, 520 U.S. 968, 117 S.Ct. 1865, 138 L.Ed.2d 162 (1997) (per curiam) the Court summarily ruled that a law requiring abortions to be performed by licensed physicians did not violate the due process standards established in *Casey*. Although the Court in *Mazurek* noted that there

It is the effect branch of the undue burden test that is most likely to have meaning for future cases and lower court rulings on new types of abortion regulations. According to the plurality opinion, if an abortion regulation has the effect of placing a "substantial obstacle in the path of a woman seeking an abortion of a nonviable fetus" it will be invalid. However, if regulations are designed to protect the health of a woman, to give the woman complete information concerning abortion choices, or to protect the variety of interests in children that might be present when a minor pregnant female seeks an abortion, the law will be seen as only an incidental burden on women who seek abortions rather than an impermissible substantial obstacle.

The meaning of the undue burden test may be clarified by looking at the specific types of abortion regulations that were before the Court in *Casey*. The Pennsylvania statute at issue in *Casey* defined "medical emergency" as a condition that the physician in good judgment could determine "so complicates the medical condition of a pregnant woman as to necessitate the immediate abortion of her pregnancy to avert her death or for which a delay will create serious risk of substantial and irreversible impairment of a major bodily function." The lower courts had interpreted the statute to include a variety of circumstances so

that "compliance with [the state's] abortion regulations would not in any way pose a significant threat to the life or health of the woman." With that understanding of the statute, a majority had no difficulty in approving the definition of a medical emergency.[47] This ruling did not clarify the meaning of the undue burden test, because the statute had been interpreted to fit precisely within the language of earlier cases concerning the need for states to waive abortion regulations whenever necessary to protect the life or health of a pregnant woman. The ruling sheds no light on questions concerning medical conditions that might justify a physician performing an abortion on a viable fetus.[48]

Several types of consent and recordkeeping provisions were before the Court in *Casey*. Justice O'Connor wrote for a majority of the Court in striking down a provision of the Pennsylvania law that required, except in emergency cases, a physician to refrain from performing an abortion on a married woman absent a statement that the woman had notified her spouse about her decision to have the abortion. Justice O'Connor's majority opinion found that Supreme Court decisions had invalidated father-husband consent requirements and that because these requirements placed a substantial obstacle in the path of women choosing to have an abortion that could not be

was no clear proof of improper legislative motivation in this case, the Court's opinion stated: "even assuming the correctness of the Court of Appeals implicit premise—that a legislative *purpose* to interfere with the constitutionally protected right to abortion without the *effect* of interfering with that right (here it is uncontested that there was insufficient evidence of a substantial obstacle to abortion) could render the Montana law invalid—there is no basis for finding a vitiating legislative purpose here." 520 U.S. at 972, 117 S.Ct. at 1867 (emphasis in original). The Court seemed to question whether the type of purpose analysis used to establish racial or gender classifications that did not appear on the face of the statute could be used to invalidate an abortion regulation. The dissenting Justices in *Mazurek*, did not assert that the state requirement that abortions be performed by physicians was invalid. Nevertheless, the dissenting Justices desired to have the case briefed and argued in full, in part to examine the role that determinations of legislative purpose should play in an analysis of abortion regulations. 520 U.S. at 977, 117 S.Ct. at 1869 (Stevens, J., joined by Ginsburg and Breyer, JJ., dissenting). The Supreme Court, prior to *Mazurek*, had upheld statutes requiring all abortions, including first trimester abortions, to be performed by a licensed physi-

cian under the *Roe* trimester analysis. See, Connecticut v. Menillo, 423 U.S. 9, 96 S.Ct. 170, 46 L.Ed.2d 152 (1975) (per curiam) (the Court upholds state prosecution of a nonphysician for performing an abortion).

47. Planned Parenthood v. Casey, 505 U.S. 833, 880, 112 S.Ct. 2791, 2822, 120 L.Ed.2d 674 (1992) (Part V-A of Justice O'Connor's opinion, examining the statutes and lower court's definition of medical emergency, was a majority opinion).

48. The difficulty of determining when, if ever, a state may have restrictions on viability determinations made by doctors is a subject that is examined later in this section in terms of the Court's ruling in Webster v. Reproductive Health Services, 492 U.S. 490, 109 S.Ct. 3040, 106 L.Ed.2d 410 (1989). *Webster* is also examined in the immediately preceding subsection of this section of the Treatise, § 14.29(b)(1)(b).

Further examination of the difficulty of state attempts to define viability, and the danger that such regulations will be unconstitutionally vague, are examined in the next subsection of this Treatise regarding "Regulations of Abortion Procedures", § 14.29(b)(2).

justified now that society had rejected the "common law" view of the status of married women as being subservient to their husbands.[49]

The state's recordkeeping requirements applied to both state funded institutions and privately funded institutions that performed abortions. Records were kept regarding the number of abortions, the specific circumstances surrounding each abortion, and the types of procedures used. Although information from state funded institutions became public, Justice O'Connor found that, as to both public sector and private sector reporting, "the identity of each woman who has had an abortion remains confidential." In accordance with earlier Supreme Court rulings, the plurality found that these record keeping requirements, with their provisions for confidentiality, did not constitute an undue burden on a woman's right to choose to have an abortion of a nonviable fetus. However, the Justices did vote to strike down the part of the state recordkeeping regulation that required reports on whether a married woman had given notice to her husband; the failure of the husband consent requirement meant that this recordkeeping requirement placed an undue burden on the woman's choice.[50]

In *Casey,* the Court upheld a portion of the Pennsylvania statute that prohibited a doctor from performing an abortion on an unemancipated pregnant female under the age of 18 years unless she and one of her parents, or her guardian, had consented to the abortion 24 hours before the procedure was performed unless (1) there was a medical emergency that required the abortion or (2) the minor pregnant female had received court authorization to have the abortion.[51] The plurality found that this parental consent provision had the type of "judicial bypass procedure" that protected the well-being of the pregnant minor so that the requirement did not impose an undue burden on that minor's freedom of choice. Similar parental consent laws had been upheld in earlier Supreme Court cases.[52]

The only pre–1992 rulings of the Supreme Court that were overturned in *Casey* related to (1) formalities imposed by the state for the demonstration of a female patient's consent to an abortion and (2) the imposition of a 24 hour waiting period between the time when a woman consented to have an abortion and the time when the abortion was performed. The State of Pennsylvania required a physician or a

---

49. Planned Parenthood v. Casey, 505 U.S. 833, 887–97, 112 S.Ct. 2791, 2826–2831, 120 L.Ed.2d 674 (1992). The Supreme Court had previously invalidated husband or father consent requirements in Planned Parenthood of Central Missouri v. Danforth, 428 U.S. 52, 96 S.Ct. 2831, 49 L.Ed.2d 788 (1976).

50. Planned Parenthood v. Casey, 505 U.S. 833, 899–901, 112 S.Ct. 2791, 2832–33, 120 L.Ed.2d 674 (1992) (judgment of the Court announced as to this issue in an opinion of O'Connor, J., joined by Kennedy and Souter, JJ.), on remand 978 F.2d 74 (3d Cir.1992). Other issues regarding record keeping requirements are examined in the next subsection of this Treatise, § 14.29(b)(2) "Regulations of Abortion Procedures."

51. The Court in *Casey* upheld a requirement that the minor or her parents or guardian give "informed consent," which was defined by the statute to be a type of consent given only after specific information regarding the abortion, the fetus, and abortion alternatives were provided by a physician or health care professional; the statute also required a 24–hour waiting period between the time the consent was received and the abortion procedure was performed.

The plurality opinion by Justice O'Connor first found that the portion of the statute that required doctors or health care professionals to provide all women (adults as

well as minors) with information concerning the abortion and abortion alternatives was not, on the basis of the record provided by the lower courts, a regulation whose purpose or effect was to place a substantial obstacle in the path of the woman's ability to exercise her right to choose to have an abortion. It was on that basis that Justice O'Connor found that the additional parental consent requirement was not an undue burden on the minor's right to choose to have an abortion and was consistent with earlier Supreme Court decisions upholding parental consent provisions when the requirement included a so-called "judicial bypass" procedure. Planned Parenthood v. Casey, 505 U.S. 833, 899, 112 S.Ct. 2791, 2832, 120 L.Ed.2d 674 (1992) (judgment of the Court as to this issue announced in an opinion by O'Connor, J., joined by Kennedy and Souter, JJ.).

52. Issues regarding parental notification and parental consent requirements are examined in § 14.29(B)(3). In 1990, the Supreme Court approved parental consent requirements so long as the minor was given the opportunity to bypass the requirement through a judicial or administrative procedure that did not present an unjustified barrier to her ability to exercise her right to choose to have an abortion. Hodgson v. Minnesota, 497 U.S. 417, 110 S.Ct. 2926, 111 L.Ed.2d 344 (1990); Ohio v. Akron Center for Reproductive Health, 497 U.S. 502, 110 S.Ct. 2972, 111 L.Ed.2d 405 (1990).

trained physician's assistant, health care worker, or social worker to provide the woman patient with information regarding the nature and risks of the proposed medical treatment, the probable gestational age of fetus, medical risks associated with carrying the child to childbirth, printed material describing abortion alternatives, information regarding medical assistance benefits for childbirth and child care. Some of this information had to be provided to the woman by the physician. A woman's consent would not be valid unless these informational provisions had been complied with 24 hours prior to the time the abortion was performed. Under state law both the information component of the consent requirement and the 24 hour waiting period could be disregarded when there was a "medical emergency".[53]

In earlier cases the Supreme Court had invalidated the requirement that a medical doctor personally provide the woman with the information prior to an abortion and requirements that kept an adult female from having an abortion for a set time period after she gave consent.[54] Justices Stevens and Blackmun thought that those cases should be followed; they believe that there was no interest of sufficient constitutional importance to interfere with the doctor-patient relationship concerning abortion or to deter a woman's ability to have an abortion.[55] The four Justices who voted to overrule *Roe* also voted to uphold the entirety of the Pennsylvania statute, including the consent provisions.[56] Thus, the three Justices who used the undue burden test were left

to decide the constitutional fate of the informed consent provisions.

Justice O'Connor, writing for herself and Justices Kennedy and Souter, found that the informed consent provisions should be upheld because these provisions did not place an undue burden on a woman's ability to choose to have an abortion.[57] Critical to the plurality's decision was a provision of the Pennsylvania law that allowed doctors to disregard the requirements when in good faith they believed it was necessary to do so to protect the life or health of the woman. With that medical emergency exception, the regulation, in the view of the plurality, provided complete information to the woman that might be of assistance to her in making the abortion-childbirth choice. The plurality believed that the informed consent provision was "a reasonable measure to insure an informed choice.... this requirement cannot be considered a substantial obstacle to obtaining an abortion, and, it follows there is no undue burden."[58]

The 24 hour waiting period presented a more difficult issue according to the plurality. On the one hand, the 24 hour waiting period promoted and informed deliberative choice by the woman medical patient. On the other hand, it was possible that the 24 hour waiting period might be very onerous to women who had to travel a great distance to receive abortion services or to women who were in a geographic and social situation where multiple visits to the doctor who would perform an abortion might involve multiple public encounters with persons who sought to block or stop

---

53. The statutory terms are set out in an appendix to the opinion of Justice O'Connor. Planned Parenthood v. Casey, 505 U.S. 833, 901–11, 112 S.Ct. 2791, 2833–38, 120 L.Ed.2d 674 (1992) (appendix to the opinion of O'Connor, J.).

54. Thornburgh v. American College of Obstetricians and Gynecologists, 476 U.S. 747, 106 S.Ct. 2169, 90 L.Ed.2d 779 (1986) and Akron v. Akron Center for Reproductive Health, Inc., 462 U.S. 416, 103 S.Ct. 2481, 76 L.Ed.2d 687 (1983), overruled in part, Planned Parenthood v. Casey, 505 U.S. 833, 881, 112 S.Ct. 2791, 2823, 120 L.Ed.2d 674 (1992) (judgement of the Court as to this issue announced in an opinion by O'Connor, J., joined by Kennedy and Souter, JJ.).

55. Planned Parenthood v. Casey, 505 U.S. 833, 911, 112 S.Ct. 2791, 2838, 120 L.Ed.2d 674 (1992) (Stevens, J., concurring in part and dissenting in part); 505 U.S. at 920,

112 S.Ct. at 2843 (Blackmun, concurring in part, concurring in the judgment in part, and dissenting in part).

56. 505 U.S. at 944, 112 S.Ct. at 2855 (Rehnquist, C.J., joined by White, Scalia, and Thomas, JJ., concurring in the judgment in part and dissenting in part); 505 U.S. at 978, 112 S.Ct. at 2873 (Scalia, J., joined by Rehnquist, C.J., and White and Thomas, JJ., concurring in the judgment in part and dissenting in part).

57. Planned Parenthood v. Casey, 505 U.S. 833, 880–87, 112 S.Ct. 2791, 2822–26, 120 L.Ed.2d 674 (1992) (judgment of the Court as to this issue announced in an opinion by O'Connor, J., joined by Kennedy and Souter, JJ.).

58. 505 U.S. at 884, 112 S.Ct. at 2824 (opinion of O'Connor, J., joined by Kennedy and Souter, JJ.).

legal abortion services. The plurality found that there was nothing about a 24 hour waiting period that inherently imposed an undue burden on a woman's right to an abortion because on its face the regulation was designed to promote an informed choice by the woman. However, Justice O'Connor's plurality opinion left open the possibility that, in the future, in a case where there was proof that a 24 hour waiting period did create real obstacles to a woman's right to choose to abort a nonviable fetus, the Court might find that the purpose or effect of the regulation violated the undue burden standard. At least Justice O'Connor implied as much when she stated that "a particular burden is not of necessity a substantial obstacle ... the District Court did not conclude that the waiting period is such an obstacle even for the women who are most burdened by it. Hence, on the record before us, and in the context of this facial challenge, we are not convinced that the 24–hour waiting period constitutes an undue burden." [59]

The *Casey* decision, and the plurality's undue burden analysis, is the logical outcome of the Court's gradual, but meaningful, shift concerning a woman's right to an abortion between the early 1970s and the early 1990s. The Court has consistently protected the basic right of a woman to choose to abort a nonviable fetus but it has also consistently upheld regulations of a woman's freedom of choice that the Court believed were tailored to promote state interest in the health of the woman or the protection of the viable fetus. Over two decades the Court has come to do less "second guessing" of medical regulations or regulations designed to express a state's preference for childbirth over abortion. But the Court has invalidated those regulations of abortions that the majority sees as being road blocks to a woman's exercise of her constitutional right.[60] The plurality's adoption of an undue burden analysis, and its recognition of the general state interest in the potential life of the fetus, does very little to change the outcome of the previous Supreme Court cases. The ad hoc nature of the Court's rulings requires a separate analysis of Court decisions examining each type of abortion regulation. It is to those cases that we now turn.

(1)(d) *Stenberg v. Carhart*—"Partial Birth Abortion"

The Court's first encounter with a law restricting what many people call "partial birth abortions" was *Stenberg v. Carhart*.[61] The law at issue in *Stenberg* did not prohibit abortions. Rather, the law was addressed to the manner in which a woman could have an abortion, assuming that she was having the abortion in compliance with other state laws. The statute, which applied to pre-viability as well as post-viability abortions stated that "no partial-birth abortion shall be performed in this state unless such procedure is necessary to save the life of the mother whose life in endangered by a physical disorder, physical illness, or physical injury including a life endangering physical condition caused by or arising from the pregnancy itself." The statute then defined partial-

---

59. 505 U.S. at 885–87, 112 S.Ct. at 2825–26 (opinion of O'Connor, J., joined by Kennedy and Souter, JJ.).

60. In the portion of Justice O'Connor's opinion that was a majority opinion for the Court, Justice O'Connor found that plaintiffs could attack an abortion regulation on its face without having to show that every application of the abortion regulation would be unconstitutional. Persons attacking the regulation need only show that "in a large fraction of the cases [involving a contested abortion regulation], it will operate as a substantial obstacle to a woman's choice to undergo an abortion." 505 U.S. at 895, 112 S.Ct. at 2830. There is still uncertainty regarding the ability of plaintiffs to challenge an abortion regulation on its face if the regulation in theory might be applied constitutionally to even one woman under some hypothetical set of circumstances.

In Ada v. Guam Society of Obstetricians and Gynecologists, 506 U.S. 1011, 113 S.Ct. 633, 121 L.Ed.2d 564 (1992) (denying writ of certiorari without opinion by the Court) three Justices dissented from a denial of certiorari on the basis that the lower courts had invalidated abortion regulations due to the alleged overbreadth of the regulations. These three Justices believed that an abortion regulation should be upheld so long as it could constitutionally be applied to some women. 506 U.S. at 1011, 113 S.Ct. at 633–64 (Scalia, J., joined by Rehnquist, C.J., and White, J., dissenting). See also, Leavitt v. Jane L., 518 U.S. 137, 116 S.Ct. 2068, 135 L.Ed.2d 443 (1996) (per curiam). In *Leavitt*, the Court made a summary ruling that unconstitutional provisions of a state statute were severable from, and did not require the invalidation of, the part of the state statute that regulated abortions in a manner consistent with an earlier Supreme Court decision.

61. Stenberg v. Carhart, 530 U.S. 914, 120 S.Ct. 2597, 147 L.Ed.2d 743 (2000).

birth abortions as "an abortion procedure in which the person performing the abortion partially delivers vaginally a living unborn child before killing the unborn child and completing the delivery."[62]

Writing for five members of the Court, Justice Breyer stated that, the majority was using the undue burden standard set forth in the *Casey* plurality opinion.[63] Under this standard, any law that imposes an undue burden on the woman's decision before fetal viability should be ruled unconstitutional. Subsequent to viability a state could proscribe or regulate abortions, assuming that there was an exception for the preservation of the life or health of the mother.

The Court's opinions concerning abortion regulations, including *Stenberg*, accept both that the protection of the viable fetus and the protection of the pregnant woman's health as compelling governmental interests. An abortion regulation that is narrowly tailored to protect those interests should be upheld. On the other hand, any law that is not narrowly tailored to protect those interests constitutes an undue burden on a woman's choice to have a pre-viability abortion will be ruled unconstitutional. Further, all abortion regulations must have an exception that would allow medical personnel judgment to disregard the regulation when necessary to preserve the life or health of the pregnant woman.[64]

For the majority, the statute at issue in *Stenberg* was unconstitutional because of its failure to allow an exception to protect the health (rather than merely the life) of the pregnant woman. Justice Breyer explained that the procedure that was prohibited by the statute was less safe for pregnant women under a variety of circumstances. The statute could not, in the opinion of the majority, force doctors to use a procedure that was less safe for the pregnant woman. The fact that the law applied to pre-viability abortions, as well as

post-viability abortions presented a significant problem for the Court. Justice Breyer's majority opinion stated that "the state's interest in regulating abortion pre-viability is considerably weaker than post-viability."[65]

The *Stenberg* majority opinion clarified, to a slight extent, the nature of the exception that states must have to protect pregnant women. Justice Breyer noted that the state could not limit the protection of the woman exception to circumstances in which it was absolutely necessary to disregard a regulation to save the life of the mother. Although the majority opinion said "by no means must a state grant physicians unfettered discretion in their selection of abortion methods,"[66] it did not explain how a state might limit a physician's authority to disregard the abortion regulation whenever the physician might claim that following the law might impair the health of the woman patient.

Among the questions unanswered in *Stenberg* are whether states must grant an exception from abortion regulations if the doctor believes that following the regulation would harm the psychological, as opposed to physical, health of the woman. Also unanswered are questions concerning whether a physician must be allowed to perform an abortion, and disregard regulations, for health risks that might not be generally considered either to be life-threatening or to cause a permanent impairment of the woman's physical health.

Three concurring Justices sought to emphasize the point that the Court was only following a quarter-century of rulings requiring abortion prohibitions or abortion regulations to have an exception to protect the health or life of the fetus and that the application of the statute to pre-viability abortions was inconsistent with all of the previous rulings of the Supreme Court over the past quarter-century.[67]

62.   530 U.S. at 918–26, 120 S.Ct. at 2604–07.

63.   530 U.S. at 918, 120 S.Ct. at 2604.

64.   530 U.S. at 930, 120 S.Ct. at 2609.

65.   530 U.S. at 930, 120 S.Ct. at 2609.

66.   530 U.S. at 937, 120 S.Ct. at 2613.

67.   Stenberg v. Carhart, 530 U.S. 914, 945, 120 S.Ct. 2597, 2617, 147 L.Ed.2d 743 (2000) (Stevens, J., joined by Ginsburg, J., concurring); 530 U.S. at 945, 120 S.Ct. at 2617 (O'Connor, J., concurring); 530 U.S. at 950, 120 S.Ct. at 2620 (Ginsburg, J., joined by Stevens, J., concurring).

Four Justices dissented in *Stenberg*. Three of the Justices, who had dissented in earlier abortion rulings, believed that the Court did not have a legitimate basis for invalidating regulations of abortions under the due process clause.[68] Justice Kennedy, who had joined plurality opinions striking other types of abortion[69] regulations dissented in *Stenberg* because he believed that the Court was unjustified in striking a law that allowed women to have abortions consistent with earlier cases when the state was only restricting one particular method of abortion that ran contrary to basic societal values.

(2) Regulations of Abortion Procedures.

Since *Roe v. Wade*[70] government regulations of abortions have been subject to independent judicial review. Since *Roe,* the Court has regarded a woman's right to choose to abort a nonviable fetus as a fundamental constitutional right that cannot be abrogated by the state. This right can only be regulated if the regulation is tailored to promote some societal interest that outweighs the incidental impairment of the woman's ability to choose to have the abortion.

At various times the Court has used different language to express the standard of review it uses to determine the constitutionality of abortion regulations. The *Roe* majority opinion, discussed earlier in this section, required abortion regulations to be narrowly tailored to the "compelling interest" in protecting the health of the pregnant woman or the "compelling interest" in the health and existence of a viable fetus. Thereafter, the Court issued rulings without any clear standard of review. But the Court followed *Roe* by upholding only regulations designed to protect the woman or a

viable fetus. Those cases struck down regulations of abortions that impaired a woman's ability to choose to have an abortion that were not closely related to the ends of protecting pregnant women or viable fetuses.

In 1992, a plurality of the Justices found that state laws that regulated abortions of nonviable fetuses should be upheld only if the regulation did not create an "undue burden" on the woman's freedom of choice and that a law that presented a "substantial obstacle" to the woman's choice would be an unconstitutional undue burden. This undue burden analysis came from Justice O'Connor's plurality opinion in *Planned Parenthood v. Casey,*[71] which was discussed previously in this section of the Treatise. As we have noted previously, the *Casey* decision, and the plurality's undue burden analysis, did not significantly alter the Supreme Court's rulings on abortion regulations that were rendered between 1973 and 1992.

The plurality in *Casey* rejected the trimester analysis of *Roe,* but it is not clear that the Court ever used a strict trimester analysis. For example, although the Court in *Roe* discussed first trimester abortions in terms that would make the reader of the opinion believe that no government regulation of an abortion in the first trimester would be valid, the Supreme Court in the 1970s upheld first trimester abortion regulations that were tailored to protect the health of the woman. The Court upheld regulations requiring the abortionist to be a licensed medical doctor and regulations requiring a hospital to keep accurate records of all abortions performed in the hospital, even though those laws applied to first trimester abortions.[72]

68. Stenberg v. Carhart, 530 U.S. 914, 950, 120 S.Ct. 2597, 2620, 147 L.Ed.2d 743 (2000) (Rehnquist, C.J., dissenting); 530 U.S. at 952, 120 S.Ct. at 2621 (Scalia, J., dissenting); 530 U.S. at 978, 120 S.Ct. at 2635 (Thomas, J., joined by Rehnquist, C.J., and Scalia, J., dissenting).

69. Stenberg v. Carhart, 530 U.S. 914, 956, 120 S.Ct. 2597, 2623, 147 L.Ed.2d 743 (2000) (Kennedy, J., joined by Rehnquist, C.J., dissenting).

70. 410 U.S. 113, 93 S.Ct. 705, 35 L.Ed.2d 147 (1973).

71. 505 U.S. 833, 112 S.Ct. 2791, 120 L.Ed.2d 674 (1992). The case is analyzed in detail in the immediately preceding subsection of this Treatise, § 14.29(b)(1)(c).

72. See Connecticut v. Menillo, 423 U.S. 9, 96 S.Ct. 170, 46 L.Ed.2d 152 (1975) (per curiam) (it is constitutional for a state to prosecute a nonphysician for performing an abortion); Planned Parenthood of Central Missouri v. Danforth, 428 U.S. 52, 96 S.Ct. 2831, 49 L.Ed.2d 788 (1976) (record-keeping requirements upheld even though they applied to first trimester abortions).

Any otherwise valid regulation of medical practices that is not designed to have a special impact on abortion procedures (such as requiring surgical procedures to be performed only by a licensed physician) should be constitutional as applied to abortion procedures. Laws that specifically regulate abortion procedures are subject to independent judicial review but there should be no significant distinction in the review of medical regulations regarding abortions performed in the first three months of a pregnancy and abortions performed after the first three months but before viability. If a state asserts that an abortion regulation is designed to protect the health of the woman, a court must make a determination of whether the regulation is a narrowly tailored means of that interest. Regulations of later term abortions are more likely to be upheld because the risks to a woman's health from abortion (and from childbirth) increase as the length of the pregnancy increases. Thus, one would expect to see fewer regulations of early term rather than late term abortions upheld because the state will have a more difficult time of showing that the regulation of an early term abortion is narrowly tailored to protecting the health of the woman.

As mentioned in the previous subsection, the Supreme Court, in the year 2000, was considering whether states could regulate so-called "partial-birth abortions." The Court's ruling in that case might clarify the definition of viability, or the nature of threats to the life or health of a woman that require exemptions from otherwise valid regulations of abortion procedures.[73]

As indicated in *Roe*, and all cases subsequent to it, the state may prohibit post-viability abortions except where there is a threat to the life or health of the woman. The state may have regulations of abortion procedures that are designed to protect the existence of a viable fetus if, but only if, the judiciary determines that the regulation is narrowly tailored

to that end and does not create any significant health risk to the woman.

Because the Court has decided to make each regulation of abortion procedures subject to this type of active judicial review, these rulings have an *ad hoc* quality. The nature of principles enforced by the Court can best be understood by a brief overview of the major decisions of the Supreme Court regarding abortion regulations.

The *Roe* majority opinion stated that it was to be read in conjunction with *Doe v. Bolton*,[74] where the Justices examined procedural requirements of abortion statutes. In *Doe* the Court invalidated a number of procedural restrictions on the woman's ability to secure an abortion. These provisions were invalid as they unnecessarily restricted the woman's right to privacy and, therefore, violated due process.

One requirement was that the abortion be performed in a hospital accredited by a special committee although no such requirement was imposed for nonabortion surgery. The Court held the requirement could not withstand constitutional scrutiny; the State could not show that this distinction was based on differences reasonably related to the purpose of the Act. The State failed to show why the abortion should have to be performed in a licensed hospital rather than some other appropriately licensed institution. The statute also required the approval of two other physicians, despite the fact the performing physician had already been required to exercise his "best clinical judgment" in determining that an abortion was necessary. This requirement was also stricken, for if the physician is licensed and recognized as competent, the required acquiescence has no rational connection with the patient's needs. For almost identical reasons, the Court struck the requirement that the physician's decision to abort be approved by a committee of at least three hospital staff members.

---

73. Stenberg v. Carhart, Supreme Court Docket No. 99–830. Carhart v. Stenberg, 192 F.3d 1142 (8th Cir.1999), cert. granted in part 528 U.S. 1110, 120 S.Ct. 865, 145 L.Ed.2d 725 (2000).

74. 410 U.S. 179, 93 S.Ct. 739, 35 L.Ed.2d 201 (1973).

Other medical and procedural restrictions on the woman's right to receive an abortion were considered in *Planned Parenthood of Central Missouri v. Danforth*.[75] The statute in *Planned Parenthood* was challenged on the basis of its definition of viability and its prohibition of the use of saline amniocentesis as a means of abortion after the first twelve weeks. The statute defined viability as "that stage of fetal development when the life of the unborn child may be continued indefinitely outside the womb by natural or artificial life support systems."[76] The Court upheld this definition, finding it consistent with *Roe v. Wade*. Viability is basically a medical term, and as such it need not be defined as occurring at a specific point in the gestation period but may be left to the judgment of the attending physician.

The ban on saline amniocentesis was stricken because it could not be shown, as required by *Roe*, to be a restriction reasonably related to the preservation and protection of maternal health, though it was related to fetal health. The state general assembly had stated in its statute that the saline amniocentesis type of abortion "for the purpose of killing the fetus and artificially inducing labor is deleterious to maternal health and is hereby prohibited after the first twelve weeks of pregnancy." But saline amniocentesis was the method most commonly used nationwide after the first twelve weeks of pregnancy and was safer than most other methods used to terminate a pregnancy, none of which were banned, and in fact saline amniocentesis was safer than childbirth. Therefore, the majority found that the state law forced women who wished to exercise their right to terminate a pregnancy to use methods more dangerous to maternal health. The law could not withstand the strict judicial scrutiny mandated by *Roe*.

The Court, in *Planned Parenthood of Central Missouri v. Danforth*, upheld a statutory requirement that a woman give written consent to the abortion and a requirement that the hospital keep records of abortions performed because these regulations were reasonably narrow means of protecting the health of the woman patient.[77] The valid regulations were similar to state regulations of a wide variety of surgical procedures.

The *ad hoc* nature of the strict scrutiny test used to examine governmental regulations of abortion procedures was well demonstrated on a single day in 1983 when the Supreme Court decided three separate cases involving several different types of abortion regulations.[78] Six Justices (Chief Justice Burger and Justices Blackmun, Brennan, Marshall, Powell and Stevens) required that government regulations of pre-viability abortions comply with the principles set forth in *Roe*; these regulations must be reasonably related to the "compelling" interest in protecting the health of the woman. These Justices wish to use this approach to protect the *Roe v. Wade* principle that a woman has a fundamental right to choose to have an abortion free from interference by the state with her decision or the professional judgment of her attending physician. In contrast three Justices (Justices O'Connor, Rehnquist, and White) called into question the legitimacy of judicial control of abortion regulations (al-

---

75. 428 U.S. 52, 96 S.Ct. 2831, 49 L.Ed.2d 788 (1976).

76. 428 U.S. at 63, 96 S.Ct. at 2838.

The Supreme Court in Colautti v. Franklin, 439 U.S. 379, 99 S.Ct. 675, 58 L.Ed.2d 596 (1979) rejected a state attempt to be more specific in the definition of viability and distinguished *Danforth* as a case that approved a definition of viability which simply mirrored the language of Supreme Court opinions concerning viability. This issue is discussed in later paragraphs of this subsection.

77. 428 U.S. at 65–67, 79–81, 96 S.Ct. at 2839–40, 2845–47.

The Supreme Court would later reject abortion patient consent requirements that appeared to be designed to deter women from having abortions or that required a physician, rather than another employee of the hospital, to

obtain the woman's consent. The Court in those cases distinguished *Danforth* as involving a requirement that is of such a basic nature that it related to the health of the woman. The consent form at issue in *Danforth*, in the Court's view, was not intended to influence a woman's decisions regarding an abortion but only to insure that she consented to this medical procedure. These cases are discussed in the following paragraphs of this section of the treatise.

78. Akron v. Akron Center for Reproductive Health, Inc., 462 U.S. 416, 103 S.Ct. 2481, 76 L.Ed.2d 687 (1983), on remand 604 F.Supp. 1268 (N.D.Ohio 1984); Planned Parenthood v. Ashcroft, 462 U.S. 476, 103 S.Ct. 2517, 76 L.Ed.2d 733 (1983); Simopoulos v. Virginia, 462 U.S. 506, 103 S.Ct. 2532, 76 L.Ed.2d 755 (1983).

though they did not advocate, at this time, a direct overruling of *Roe*) because they believed that courts should uphold any government regulation of abortions which was not totally arbitrary.

Because the six Justices who exercise strict judicial scrutiny when reviewing abortion regulations sometimes split over the constitutionality of a specific regulation, some of the decisions in the cases turned on the fact that two or more of those six Justices joined with Justices O'Connor, Rehnquist and White to uphold specific regulations.

It is important to note that in each case the Court was ruling on the validity of a law designed to apply only to abortion procedures; these types of laws were subject to strict scrutiny. Doctors should not receive immunity from otherwise valid regulations of all medical procedures when they perform abortions. Thus, the ability to perform abortions may be limited to properly licensed medical doctors; the state may require the patient to consent to the operation in writing, and the doctor or hospital may be required to maintain records of the abortions.[79]

In two cases the Court invalidated laws that required all abortions after the first trimester to be performed in a full service hospital, because a majority of the Justices found that this law was not reasonably designed to protect the health of the woman.[80] In contrast, the Court in another case upheld a law requir-

ing that the abortion be performed in a "hospital" when, under state law, that term included "out-patient clinics" which met certain criteria designed to protect the health of women patients, because this law did not unreasonably deter abortions.[81]

In 1983, the Supreme Court had a majority of Justices who believed that a law requiring an adult female to wait 24 hours after giving her consent to an abortion was inconsistent with her fundamental right to choose to abort a nonviable fetus. In *Akron v. Akron Center for Reproductive Health*[82] the Supreme Court found that a medical consent law that included a 24–hour waiting period was not narrowly tailored to protect the health of the woman patient and that it intruded on the decision of the patient and physician to have the abortion performed in a manner, and at a time best suited to the well-being of the patient. Therefore, a majority of the Justices invalidated the waiting period requirement.

Nine years later, in *Planned Parenthood v. Casey*[83] a majority of the Supreme Court, though not in a majority opinion, upheld a law that prohibited doctors from performing an abortion on an adult woman until 24 hours after the doctor had received the woman's "informed consent" to the abortion procedure except in those cases where a "medical emergency" justified the doctor in disregarding the waiting period requirement. The outcome of the case was determined by Justices O'Connor, Kennedy, and Souter.[84] Justice O'Connor

79. See Planned Parenthood of Central Missouri v. Danforth, 428 U.S. 52, 65–67, 79–81, 96 S.Ct. 2831, 2839–40, 2845–47, 49 L.Ed.2d 788 (1976).

80. Akron v. Akron Center for Reproductive Health, Inc., 462 U.S. 416, 103 S.Ct. 2481, 76 L.Ed.2d 687 (1983), on remand 604 F.Supp. 1268 (N.D.Ohio 1984). See also Planned Parenthood Association of Kansas City, Missouri, Inc. v. Ashcroft, 462 U.S. 476, 103 S.Ct. 2517, 76 L.Ed.2d 733 (1983) (invalidation of similar requirement on the basis of *Akron* case analysis).

81. Simopoulos v. Virginia, 462 U.S. 506, 103 S.Ct. 2532, 76 L.Ed.2d 755 (1983).

82. 462 U.S. 416, 103 S.Ct. 2481, 76 L.Ed.2d 687 (1983), on remand 604 F.Supp. 1268 (N.D.Ohio 1984). Even at this time the Court would have upheld a law requiring a woman to give consent to an abortion procedure if the consent requirement was similar to requirements states have for patients to give consent to many types of medical procedures (requirements that are not designed to deter abortions). See Planned Parenthood of

Central Missouri v. Danforth, 428 U.S. 52, 65–67, 96 S.Ct. 2831, 2839–40, 49 L.Ed.2d 788 (1976).

83. 505 U.S. 833, 112 S.Ct. 2791, 120 L.Ed.2d 674 (1992). This case was examined in detail in the immediately preceding subsection of this section of the Treatise.

84. Justice O'Connor wrote an opinion in *Casey* that was in part a majority opinion and part a plurality opinion; she wrote for three Justices in upholding the informed consent requirements of the Pennsylvania law that was before the Court, including the 24–hour waiting period. Planned Parenthood v. Casey, 505 U.S. 833, 880–87, 112 S.Ct. 2791, 2822–26, 120 L.Ed.2d 674 (1992) (opinion of O'Connor, J., announcing the judgment of the Court as to this issue, joined by Kennedy and Souter, JJ.). The informed consent requirements were upheld because the three Justices who joined in the plurality opinion voted to uphold the law, as did four Justices who believed that a woman had no fundamental constitutional right to choose to abort a nonviable fetus. The four Justices who would vote to uphold virtually any restriction on abortions are

wrote a plurality opinion in *Casey* in which she used an "undue burden" test to determine the constitutionality of the regulations of abortion procedures.

The plurality found that, on its face, a law requiring a 24–hour waiting period between the woman's "informed consent" and the abortion was tailored to the interest in ensuring that each woman made an informed, reflective decision concerning abortion. Because Justices O'Connor, Kennedy and Souter believed that neither the purpose nor effect of the law was the creation of a substantial obstacle to a woman's ability to choose to have the abortion, they voted to uphold the waiting period. The plurality noted that the mere fact that the law might make it inconvenient, and somewhat more expensive, for women to have an abortion was not in itself reason to find that the law was a substantial obstacle to those women's ability to exercise their fundamental right.

However, the plurality opinion noted that it was only ruling on a challenge to the statute on its face. There was no evidence in the record before the Court that the law had placed a substantial obstacle to women's constitutional rights, and an undue burden on their freedom of choice, by subjecting them to serious costs or personal burdens.[85] Thus, it is possible that, in a future case involving a state law requiring a waiting period, the waiting period requirement will be invalidated upon a showing that women have very great difficulty in receiving abortion services in the state because the law imposes serious financial burdens on them (more than merely a slight increase in costs of an abortion caused by two office visits rather than one) or serious personal burdens (by subjecting women to having to cross privately erected picket lines or barriers to abortion clinics).

The Court, by a five to four vote and without majority opinion, upheld a law requiring that a pathology report be filed following each abortion[86] because Justice Powell and Chief Justice Burger agreed that this law mirrored a law requiring tissue from other surgeries to be submitted to a pathologist so as to protect the health of persons who had undergone a variety of surgical procedures. These two Justices voted with the three Justices who would show great deference to the legislature regarding abortion regulations to uphold this statute.

Similarly, the Court, by the same five to four vote, upheld a statutory provision requiring the presence of a second physician during abortions performed after viability, because a majority of the Justices concluded that this law was reasonably related to the compelling state interest in preserving life in post-viability abortions.[87]

Thornburgh v. American College of Obstetricians and Gynecologists[88] provides a good summary of the position of a majority of the Justices concerning the judicial role in reviewing abortion regulations. At issue in *Thornburgh* were six Pennsylvania statutes regulating abortions. When reviewing each of the regulations, the majority opinion by Justice Blackmun found that the law would be invalid unless the state demonstrated that the regulation was narrowly tailored to promote the state's compelling interests in the health of the woman or the protection of a viable fetus. A law not meeting this test would be invalid as an attempt to deter women from exercising

---

Chief Justice Rehnquist and Justices White, Scalia, and Thomas. 505 U.S. at 944, 112 S.Ct. at 2855 (Rehnquist, C.J., joined by White, Scalia, and Thomas, JJ., concurring in the judgment in part and dissenting in part); 505 U.S. at 978, 112 S.Ct. at 2873 (Scalia, J., joined by Rehnquist, C.J., and White and Thomas, JJ., concurring in the judgment in part and dissenting in part).

85. Planned Parenthood v. Casey, 505 U.S. 833, 885–887, 112 S.Ct. 2791, 2825–26, 120 L.Ed.2d 674 (1992) (O'Connor, J., announcing the judgment of the Court in a portion of the opinion joined by Kennedy and Souter, JJ.). The *Casey* opinion is examined at length in the previous subsection of the Treatise, § 14.29(b)(1)(c).

86. Planned Parenthood Association of Kansas City, Missouri, Inc. v. Ashcroft, 462 U.S. 476, 103 S.Ct. 2517, 76 L.Ed.2d 733 (1983). This issue is examined in a portion of Justice Powell's opinion that was joined only by Chief Justice Burger. Justice O'Connor filed a concurring opinion regarding this issue that was joined by Justices White and Rehnquist. On this issue Justices Blackmun, Brennan, Marshall and Stevens dissented.

87. Id.

88. 476 U.S. 747, 106 S.Ct. 2169, 90 L.Ed.2d 779 (1986).

their fundamental right to choose to have an abortion without state interference.

In *Thornburgh* the Supreme Court invalidated statutes that required a woman to give "informed consent" as a condition to receiving abortion services. The Court found that these statutes did not merely require a woman to sign a consent form similar to the consent forms that would be required for other medical procedures. The Pennsylvania statutes at issue in *Thornburgh* required that the physician give the woman printed material concerning abortion procedures and fetus development; the woman was also required to wait 24 hours after a physician gave her the information before her consent would be valid. The Court in *Thornburgh* found the informed consent requirements invalid for two basic reasons: the consent requirements were seen as no more than an attempt to deter women from deciding to have an abortion; the statutes intruded into the physician-patient relationship by requiring a physician personally to provide information that a physician might not deem to be in the woman's best interest.[89] In 1992, this aspect of the *Thornburgh* decision was overruled by the United States Supreme Court. In *Planned Parenthood v. Casey*,[90] a majority of the Supreme Court Justices, although not in a majority opinion, voted to uphold Pennsylvania informed consent statutes.

Justices Stevens and Blackmun were the only two members of the *Thornburgh* majority that were still on the Court at the time of the *Casey* decision. Justices Blackmun and Stevens were the only two Justices who voted in *Casey* to strike Pennsylvania's informed consent requirements.[91] Four Justices in *Casey* believed that a woman did not have a fundamental right to choose to have an abortion; they voted to uphold the informed consent provisions along with all other aspects of the Pennsylvania regulations.[92] Thus, as previously noted in this section, the decision in *Casey* turned on the votes of Justices O'Connor, Kennedy, and Souter. Those three Justices, in a plurality opinion written by Justice O'Connor, adopted an "undue burden" test under which a state regulation of abortions of nonviable fetuses would be invalidated if the purpose or effect of the regulation was to place a "substantial obstacle in the path of the woman" who was choosing to have the abortion.[93]

The informed consent statutes reviewed by the Court in *Casey* required a doctor or other health care professional to provide the woman with information regarding the abortion procedures, the risks from the abortion procedures, the probable gestational age of the fetus, abortion alternatives, the risks of carrying a child to full term (child birth) and the types of medical and financial assistance that might be available for the woman if she chose child birth rather than abortion. Some of the information had to be given to the woman by the physician personally. The plurality believed that these regulations were designed to allow a woman to make a truly informed decision. The regulations allowed physicians to disre-

---

89. Thornburgh v. American College of Obstetricians and Gynecologists, 476 U.S. 747, 106 S.Ct. 2169, 90 L.Ed.2d 779 (1986). Similar laws imposing special restrictions on a woman's consent to an abortion had been invalidated in Akron v. Akron Center for Reproductive Health, Inc., 462 U.S. 416, 103 S.Ct. 2481, 76 L.Ed.2d 687 (1983), on remand 604 F.Supp. 1268 (N.D.Ohio 1984). The Court in the 1970s and 1980s would uphold statutes requiring a woman to consent to an abortion procedure when the consent requirement was not designed to deter abortions and was merely the type of consent requirement imposed by law as a condition for many medical procedures. See, Planned Parenthood of Central Missouri v. Danforth, 428 U.S. 52, 63, 96 S.Ct. 2831, 2838, 49 L.Ed.2d 788 (1976).

90. 505 U.S. 833, 112 S.Ct. 2791, 120 L.Ed.2d 674 (1992).

91. Planned Parenthood v. Casey, 505 U.S. 833, 911, 112 S.Ct. 2791, 2838, 120 L.Ed.2d 674 (1992) (Stevens, J.,

concurring in part and dissenting in part); 505 U.S. at 920, 112 S.Ct. at 2843 (Blackmun, J., concurring in part, concurring in the judgment in part, and dissenting in part).

92. Planned Parenthood v. Casey, 505 U.S. 833, 944, 112 S.Ct. 2791, 2855, 120 L.Ed.2d 674 (1992) (Rehnquist, C.J., joined by White, Scalia, and Thomas, JJ., concurring in the judgment in part and dissenting in part); 505 U.S. at 978, 112 S.Ct. at 2873 (Scalia, J., joined by Rehnquist, C.J., and White and Thomas, JJ., concurring in the judgment in part and dissenting in part).

93. Justice O'Connor explained the undue burden test in part IV of her opinion in *Casey*. 505 U.S. at 868–77, 112 S.Ct. at 2816–21 (opinion of O'Connor, J., joined by Kennedy and Souter, JJ.). The *Casey* decision is examined in detail in the previous subsection of this Treatise, § 14.29(b)(1)(c).

gard the information and waiting period requirements whenever necessary to avoid serious risks to the life or health of the woman patient. Without that exception, the plurality would have voted to invalidate the law. The plurality found that there was no physician-patient right that derived from the first or Fourteenth Amendments that would prevent a state from having consent requirements that were designed to give the woman complete information about her abortion and childbirth options or to express the state's preference for childbirth. Therefore, the plurality Justices voted with the four Justices who believed there was no right to an abortion to uphold the particular Pennsylvania laws before the Court in *Casey* and to overrule the previous Supreme Court decisions that had invalidated similar informed consent requirements.[94]

The portions of the Court's opinion and judgment in *Thornburgh v. American College of Obstetricians and Gynecologists*[95] that did not involve the Pennsylvania informed consent provisions were not overruled by the *Casey* decision.

The Court in *Thornburgh* also invalidated two provisions of the Pennsylvania statutes requiring a doctor to report the basis upon which he or she determined that the fetus to be aborted was not viable. The Court did not find that the state had improperly attempted to dictate to the doctor the criteria by which she or he would determine that the fetus was viable. Any attempt to do so might have been held invalid as a legislative restriction on a woman's fundamental right to have an abortion or an attempt to deter doctors from performing abortions in situations where a wom-

an had a right to have the fetus aborted.[96] The statutes in *Thornburgh* required a report regarding the abortion and the viability determination. The Court found that these statutes were invalid because they created a record system open to the public that included detailed information that could be used to identify women having abortions. A limited record keeping requirement that related to the state interest in monitoring medical practices within the state might be upheld.[97] The statute allowing public disclosure of detailed information might lead to harassment of women who had abortions or doctors who performed abortions. Such a statutory system was not narrowly tailored to serve a compelling interest.[98]

The final set of statutes at issue in *Thornburgh* involved restrictions on post-viability abortions. These statutes required that, in post-viability abortions, the doctor exercise the degree of care necessary and reasonable to preserve the life and health of the unborn child. The statutes also required that there be a second physician present at an abortion when viability is possible, to take control of and provide care for the child if the fetus proved to be viable. The Supreme Court found that in demanding that the doctor attempt to save the fetus, the statute did not allow doctors a reasonable opportunity to protect the health of the woman in a post-viability abortion. The *Roe* decision had allowed states to prohibit post-viability abortions only if there was no serious threat to the life or health of the woman. The Court found that these statutes required a "trade-off" between

94. Planned Parenthood v. Casey, 505 U.S. 833, 880–887, 112 S.Ct. 2791, 2822–26, 120 L.Ed.2d 674 (1992) (judgment of the Court as to this issue announced in opinion by O'Connor, J., joined by Kennedy and Souter, JJ.), on remand 978 F.2d 74 (3d Cir.1992), overruling in part, Thornburgh v. American College of Obstetricians and Gynecologists, 476 U.S. 747, 106 S.Ct. 2169, 90 L.Ed.2d 779 (1986) and Akron v. Akron Center for Reproductive Health, Inc., 462 U.S. 416, 103 S.Ct. 2481, 76 L.Ed.2d 687 (1983).

95. 476 U.S. 747, 106 S.Ct. 2169, 90 L.Ed.2d 779 (1986).

96. See Colautti v. Franklin, 439 U.S. 379, 99 S.Ct. 675, 58 L.Ed.2d 596 (1979).

97. See Planned Parenthood of Central Missouri v. Danforth, 428 U.S. 52, 80, 96 S.Ct. 2831, 2846, 49 L.Ed.2d 788 (1976).

98. The Court noted that the lower courts had found that record keeping requirements, when coupled with the public disclosure of the records, might increase a previous pattern of violence directed against patients and staff of abortion clinics. Thornburgh v. American College of Obstetricians and Gynecologists, 476 U.S. 747, 767 n. 12, 106 S.Ct. 2169, 2182 n. 12, 90 L.Ed.2d 779 (1986). The questions surrounding a judicial definition of the right to privacy that would restrict the government collection and disclosure of data about individuals and their life styles is examined in § 14.30(b) of the treatise.

the women's health and fetus survival; the statutes were invalid because they failed to provide that maternal health should be the physician's paramount consideration. The second physician requirement was found invalid because, as written or interpreted, it did not contain an exception allowing a single doctor to perform a post-viability abortion when the life or health of the mother was at stake. The *Thornburgh* Court distinguished earlier cases where the Supreme Court had upheld second doctor requirements in post-viability abortions and mandatory care for a fetus that might be saved in a post-viability abortion on the basis that the earlier decisions had involved statutes with an emergency exception to the second physician requirement.[99]

The four dissenting Justices in *Thornburgh* attacked the Court's rigorous review of abortion practices. The dissenters did not believe that judges were not competent to second guess legislators or other state agencies regarding medical regulations.[100] However, much of the dissenting opinions appear to be an attack on the Court's original decision in *Roe v. Wade* because the dissenters believe that there was no principled means of defining a judicially enforceable fundamental right of women to have an abortion.

In *Webster v. Reproductive Health Services*,[101] which was examined earlier in his section,[102] the Supreme Court upheld a state law that required a physician to use prudent judgment when deciding whether certain medical tests should be used to determine if a fetus is viable. There was no majority opinion regarding the constitutionality of this legislative attempt to protect a viable fetus. However, the plurality opinion written by Chief Justice Rehnquist,[103] and the concurring opinion written by Justice O'Connor,[104] indicated that the statute was interpreted by the majority of Justices as protecting a viable fetus in a manner that did not present any significant health risk to the pregnant woman. Thus, the holding of this case is not necessarily inconsistent with the Court's earlier decisions regarding abortion regulations.[105]

Vagueness of Abortion Regulations— Definitions of Viability. Prior to the 1978–79 Term the Supreme Court's rulings, if not its opinions, in the area of abortion rights at least had the virtue of clarity. But in 1979 the Court decided an abortion case in which it left the scope of state powers concerning abortion regulations undefined and confused.

In *Colautti v. Franklin*,[106] the Court held void for vagueness a Pennsylvania abortion regulation which required a doctor to make a determination of viability prior to performing an abortion. If the doctor determined that the

---

99. Such a limited requirement of a post-viability second physician in medical care had been upheld in Planned Parenthood Association of Kansas City, Missouri, Inc. v. Ashcroft, 462 U.S. 476, 103 S.Ct. 2517, 76 L.Ed.2d 733 (1983). The provision had been upheld in a portion of Justice Powell's opinion joined only by Chief Justice Burger; Justices O'Connor, White, and Rehnquist had voted with Justice Powell on that limited provision. In the *Thornburgh* decision, Justice Powell voted to hold the regulation unconstitutional.

100. Thornburgh v. American College of Obstetricians and Gynecologists, 476 U.S. 747, 782, 106 S.Ct. 2169, 2190, 90 L.Ed.2d 779 (1986) (Burger, C.J., dissenting); 476 U.S. at 785, 106 S.Ct. at 2192 (White, J., joined by Rehnquist, J., dissenting); 476 U.S. at 814, 106 S.Ct. at 2206 (O'Connor, J., joined by Rehnquist, J., dissenting).

101. 492 U.S. 490, 109 S.Ct. 3040, 106 L.Ed.2d 410 (1989).

102. See § 14.29(1)(b), supra.

103. 492 U.S. at 513–20, 109 S.Ct. at 3054–58 (this portion of Chief Justice Rehnquist's opinion was joined only by Justices White and Kennedy).

104. 492 U.S. at 524, 109 S.Ct. at 3060 (O'Connor, J., concurring in part and concurring in the judgment).

105. In Planned Parenthood v. Casey, 505 U.S. 833, 112 S.Ct. 2791, 120 L.Ed.2d 674 (1992). Justice O'Connor issued an opinion that was, in part, a majority opinion for the Court and, in part, a plurality opinion. In a part of her opinion that was joined only by Justices Kennedy and Souter, Justice O'Connor employed an undue burden test to determine the validity of regulations of abortions of nonviable fetuses. In portions of her opinion that constituted an opinion for the Court (joined by Justices Stevens and Blackmun as well as Justices Kennedy and Souter), and in portions of her plurality opinion, Justice O'Connor reaffirmed the state's ability to ban the abortion of a viable fetus except when an abortion of the viable fetus was necessary to protect the life or health of the pregnant woman. The *Casey* decision is examined in detail in the previous subsection of this section of the Treatise, § 14.19(b)(1)(c). The *Casey* decision does not shed light on how a state might determine when a fetus is viable or the steps that a physician can be required to take in order to make a viability determination.

106. 439 U.S. 379, 99 S.Ct. 675, 58 L.Ed.2d 596 (1979).

fetus was "viable", or if there was "sufficient reason to believe that the fetus may be viable," the doctor was required to "exercise that degree of professional skill, care and diligence to preserve the life and health of the fetus which such person would be required to exercise in order to preserve the life and health of a fetus intended to be born." The statute required that the doctor aborting such a fetus use the abortion technique which "would provide the best opportunity for the fetus to be aborted alive so long as a different technique would not be necessary in order to preserve the life or health of the mother."[107] The statute also stated that a doctor who failed to make the viability determination, or to exercise a required degree of care, would be subject to the same criminal or civil liability as would apply if the fetus had been intended to be born alive.

Justice Blackmun's majority opinion in *Colautti* found that this statute was unconstitutionally vague in two distinct aspects: first, the requirement that the doctor determine if there was sufficient reason to believe the fetus may be viable was vague and, second, the standard of care that the doctor must use, including the guidelines for choosing between a technique to save the fetus and one to protect the health of the mother, also was unconstitutionally vague. Unfortunately, the majority opinion itself was less than a model of clarity and it is difficult, if not impossible, to decide what, if any, principles are established by this opinion.

Before examining the particularities of the Pennsylvania Act, the *Colautti* majority discussed the earlier decisions in the abortion area in order to provide "essential background" and, in so doing, seems to have established a significant new principle in this area. The majority opinion by Justice Blackmun focused on the language in *Roe v. Wade* that discussed the difficulty of predicting an exact

point for viability and which referred to the 24–28 week period as a likely time for viability. The opinion then indicated that the Court had upheld the statutory prohibitions of abortions of viable fetuses in *Doe v. Bolton* and *Planned Parenthood of Central Missouri v. Danforth* because each statute left the determination of viability to the judgment of the physician attending the pregnant woman. Justice Blackmun's opinion concluded that these cases meant that the woman's attending physician has unlimited discretion to determine when viability was attained; the opinion excluded any possibility of a legislative or judicial definition of viability based on objective factors:

> Viability is reached when, in the judgment of the attending physician on the particular facts of the case before him, there is a reasonable likelihood of the fetus' sustained survival outside the womb, with or without artificial support. Because this point may differ with each pregnancy, neither the legislature nor the courts may proclaim one of the elements entering into the ascertainment of viability—be it weeks of gestation or fetal weight or any other single factor—as the determinant of when the State has a compelling interest in the life or health of the fetus. Viability is the critical point. And we have recognized no attempt to stretch the point of viability one way or the other.[108]

This portion of *Colautti* would appear to work a dramatic change in the constitutional principles regarding abortion. It indicates that a state can do no more than write a general statute prohibiting abortions after viability and hope that physicians will not be willing to perform an abortion of a viable fetus. Although the Court left open the question of how the state might establish criteria for prosecution of physicians who act in "bad faith,"[109] its discussion of the Pennsylvania

---

107. The relevant portions of the statute, as reprinted in 439 U.S. at 380 n. 1, 99 S.Ct. at 678 n. 1. The Pennsylvania Abortion Control Act also contained a number of other provisions that presented a variety of issues resolved in the lower court and which were not before the Supreme Court. These issues and the history of the lower

court proceeding are referred to at 439 U.S. at 383–88, 99 S.Ct. at 679–82.

108. 439 U.S. at 388, 389, 99 S.Ct. at 682.

109. 439 U.S. at 396, 99 S.Ct. at 686. The Pennsylvania Abortion Control Act itself prohibited all abortions after the term of viability and punished as second degree

statute showed that it will be difficult for a legislature to establish criteria to prove the intent of such doctors.

The majority began its analysis of the vagueness issue by noting that due process required that criminal statutes give fair notice of what conduct is forbidden and that this principle was particularly important where the vagueness of the statute might inhibit the exercise of important constitutional rights. As a woman's right to abortion, like the rights to speech and association, is one to which the Court has afforded significant constitutional protection, the principles of vagueness and adequate notice had to be applied with particularity to this statute.

Colautti found that the requirement that a physician performing an abortion make a judgment that the fetus is viable or if there is "sufficient reason to believe that the fetus may be viable" was unconstitutionally vague for three reasons. First, it was unclear whether the statute imposed a subjective or a "mixed subjective and objective standard." That is, it was unclear whether the physician was to make the determination based only on his best judgment or on the objective facts that other physicians might think of particular relevance to a viability determination.

Second, the phrase "may be viable" might refer either to viability (the point at which abortions could be prohibited) or to a "grey" area immediately prior to the viability of the fetus. This uncertainty might inhibit physicians from performing abortions when they did not believe that the fetus was viable but where there were indications that it "may be" viable.

Third, the vagueness regarding the standards was exacerbated by the fact that the statute did not punish only those physicians who knowingly or intentionally aborted a viable fetus; the majority opinion described this failure as "the absence of a scienter requirement." The Pennsylvania homicide statute, which was made applicable to physicians by Section 5d of the Abortion Act, required a mental state of "intentionally, knowingly, recklessly, or negligently" taking a human life. Justice Blackmun noted this fact and stated that it was "different from a requirement that the physician be culpable or blameworthy."[110] The majority appears to indicate that a statute with a required mental element of only recklessness or negligence would always be invalid; but the majority stated that, "we need not now decide whether, under a properly drafted statute, a finding of bad faith or some other type of scienter would be required before a physician could be held criminally responsible for an erroneous determination of viability."[111]

The Court also determined that the standard of care provision was unconstitutionally vague, although the majority did not reach the question of whether or not it would be overbroad if it also applied to abortions prior to the time of viability.[112] The Court examined the testimony taken at the lower court that indicated that many physicians appeared to be unclear as to the types of abortion techniques that were required by the act and when a physician could use a procedure that was slightly more safe for a woman even though it increased the likelihood of destroying a fetus that might be viable. Not only was the standard of care requirement unclear, it might

---

murder the killing of a child born alive after an attempted abortion. Neither of these provisions was challenged before the Supreme Court.

In Anders v. Floyd, 440 U.S. 445, 99 S.Ct. 1200, 59 L.Ed.2d 442 (1979), the Court, in a brief per curiam opinion, vacated a ruling of a district court that enjoined prosecution of a doctor for an abortion of a 25 week old fetus. The district court had held that the doctor could not be punished for criminal abortion or murder. The Supreme Court indicated the district court might have based its ruling on an erroneous concept of viability, "which refers to potential, rather than actual, survival of the fetus outside the womb." The Court only remanded the case for reconsideration in light of *Colautti.*

When a state establishes a valid regulation of abortion procedures, it may provide an exception to the procedures based upon medical necessity. The state may write its statutes so that the concept of medical necessity is an affirmative defense for doctors prosecuted under the statute; it need not initially plead or prove a lack of necessity in such prosecutions. See Simopoulos v. Virginia, 462 U.S. 506, 103 S.Ct. 2532, 76 L.Ed.2d 755 (1983).

110. 439 U.S. at 395, n. 12, 99 S.Ct. at 685 n. 12.

111. 439 U.S. at 396, 99 S.Ct. at 686.

112. 439 U.S. at 397, n. 17, 99 S.Ct. at 686–87.

inhibit abortions by making them more expensive or by imposing serious burdens on the physical well being of the woman because of its effect on the physician's choice of abortion techniques. The majority refused to reach the question of whether the state could ever impose regulations on the precise type of abortion technique in order to protect a fetus; the opinion stated, "we hold only that where conflicting duties of this magnitude are involved, the State, at the least, must proceed with greater precision before it may subject a physician to possible criminal sanctions."[113]

Little can be gained, in the terms of definite rules, from this opinion. It would appear that the state may not define the point of viability other than by stating that a fetus is viable when it has the potential to live outside of the mother's womb in the judgment of the attending physician. Perhaps a state might be able to define more clearly what abortion techniques might be used after the time of viability, as determined by the attending physician. However, given the Court's prior invalidation of a ban of saline abortions in *Planned Parenthood* and the analysis used in *Colautti*, it would seem virtually impossible for a state to eliminate any form of abortion that was safe for the woman prior to the time of viability.

Whether states will be able to effectively enforce a prohibition of abortions of viable fetuses is not at all clear; the majority refused to indicate what type of statute might be used to punish the abortion of a viable fetus or what factors might be used to prove bad faith on the part of the attending physician. The dissent by Justice White[114] noted that a requirement that physicians know that the fetus is viable when they abort it, in order to make their actions criminal, will mean that it will be practically impossible to convict many physicians who commit criminal abortions by

aborting viable fetuses. There may be many instances when most doctors would have determined that the fetus was viable but where a particular physician will assert that he believed that the fetus was not viable when he performed the abortion.

Because "strict" judicial scrutiny of abortion regulations involves *ad hoc* decisionmaking, the determination of whether any specific regulation of abortion procedures is constitutional will depend on whether a majority of the Justices believe that the regulation is reasonably designed to protect the health of women or only intended to deter abortions. As a part of this strict judicial scrutiny, a majority of the Justices will require that statutes regulating abortion procedures, particularly those statutes which involve criminal penalties, give a physician very clear notice of the permissible scope of physician activities so that the physicians will not be deterred from performing constitutionally protected abortions by vague statutes. For this reason, the Court has invalidated as unconstitutionally vague a statute requiring physicians, after performing an abortion, to dispose of the fetal remains in a "humane and sanitary manner."[115]

In *Webster v. Reproductive Health Services*[116] the Supreme Court, without a majority opinion as to this point, upheld a state law that required a physician to exercise reasonable judgment in determining whether a fetus that was 20 or more weeks of gestational age was viable and to use a variety of age, fetal weight, and lung capacity tests for determining the viability of such a fetus. Both Chief Justice Rehnquist's plurality opinion as to this point[117] and Justice O'Connor's concurring opinion[118] found that the statute did not require the use of the viability tests in circumstances where the physician did not believe that the tests were necessary for a viability determination.

---

113. 439 U.S. at 400, 401, 99 S.Ct. at 688, 689.

114. Colautti v. Franklin, 439 U.S. 379, 402, 99 S.Ct. 675, 688, 58 L.Ed.2d 596 (1979) (White, J., dissenting). This dissent was joined by Chief Justice Burger and Justice Rehnquist.

115. Akron v. Akron Center for Reproductive Health, Inc., 462 U.S. 416, 103 S.Ct. 2481, 76 L.Ed.2d 687 (1983).

116. 492 U.S. 490, 109 S.Ct. 3040, 106 L.Ed.2d 410 (1989). For a more detailed examination of this decision see § 14.29(1)(b), supra.

117. 492 U.S. at 513–20, 109 S.Ct. at 3054–58 (this part of Chief Justice Rehnquist's opinion was joined only by Justices White and Kennedy).

118. 492 U.S. at 524, 109 S.Ct. at 3060 (O'Connor, J., concurring in part and concurring in the judgment).

Because of the history of this litigation, the issue of whether a state could establish a presumption of viability for all fetuses after a certain number of weeks of gestation was not before the Supreme Court.[119] A majority of Justices believed that the statute was tailored to protect a viable fetus and, therefore, was not unconstitutional. Chief Justice Rehnquist stated that the testing requirement was "reasonably designed to ensure that abortions are not performed where the fetus is viable—an end which all concede is legitimate—and that is sufficient to sustain its constitutionality."[120] Justice O'Connor stated: "the performance of examinations and tests useful to determining whether a fetus is viable, when viability is possible, and when it would not be medically imprudent to do so, does not impose an undue burden on a woman's abortion decision."[121]

Chief Justice Rehnquist and Justice O'Connor differed on whether the ruling in this case undercut the Supreme Court's decision in *Colautti v. Franklin.*[122] The Chief Justice believed that the majority opinion in *Colautti* had attempted to remove completely the ability of a state legislature to limit a physician's viability determination.[123] Justice O'Connor believed that *Colautti* had only prohibited states from legislatively determining that every fetus becomes viable at a certain time in the gestational period without regard for the circumstances in any individual pregnancy.[124] The debate between the plurality and concurrence regarding the *Colautti* decision may not

be of major significance. Both opinions appear to reject interpreting the Constitution to grant physicians total freedom to make viability determinations. The Supreme Court will uphold a government regulation designed to preclude post-viability abortions, so long as the regulation is reasonably designed to promote that end and does not present significant medical risks to the pregnant woman.[125]

(3) Spouse or Parent Requirements.

Husband–Father Consent Requirements. The Supreme Court has found unconstitutional state laws that require a woman to secure the consent of the father of the fetus that is to be aborted. In *Planned Parenthood of Central Missouri v. Danforth,*[126] the Court found that a spouse-father consent requirement would violate the woman's right to privacy that had been recognized in *Roe.* The state did not have the power to prohibit women from having abortions, prior to the time when the fetus might be viable, and it could not delegate or give such a power to an individual other than the woman. The state argued that the decision to abort a fetus should be made mutually by spouses, and that the biological father of the fetus has an interest in its existence. However, the woman's right to control her reproductive functions is a fundamental constitutional right. The Supreme Court found that the state had no interest sufficient to restrict that fundamental right

---

119. This point was emphasized by Justice O'Connor. Webster v. Reproductive Health Services, 492 U.S. 490, 526, 109 S.Ct. 3040, 3061, 106 L.Ed.2d 410 (1989) (O'Connor, J., concurring in part and concurring in judgment).

120. Webster v. Reproductive Health Services, 492 U.S. 490, 520, 109 S.Ct. 3040, 3058, 106 L.Ed.2d 410 (1989) (Rehnquist, C.J., joined by White and Kennedy, JJ.).

121. 492 U.S. at 530, 109 S.Ct. at 3063 (O'Connor, J., concurring in part and concurring in the judgment).

122. 439 U.S. 379, 99 S.Ct. 675, 58 L.Ed.2d 596 (1979).

123. Webster v. Reproductive Health Services, 492 U.S. 490, 517, 109 S.Ct. 3040, 3056, 106 L.Ed.2d 410 (1989) (Rehnquist, C.J., joined by White and Kennedy, JJ.).

124. 492 U.S. at 528, 109 S.Ct. at 3062 (O'Connor, J., concurring in part and concurring in the judgment).

125. In Planned Parenthood v. Casey, 505 U.S. 833, 112 S.Ct. 2791, 120 L.Ed.2d 674 (1992), three Justices—O'Connor, Kennedy, and Souter—used an "undue bur-

den" test to determine whether state regulations of abortions of nonviable fetuses were constitutional. There was no statutory or regulatory definition of viability at issue in *Casey.* Therefore, we cannot be sure that the Justices using undue burden analysis would join with Justices who believe there is no constitutional right of women to have freedom of choice regarding abortion matters to uphold viability definitions that are designed to prevent post-viability abortions. Justices using undue burden analysis might vote to uphold such regulations because the viability definition might not be seen as having the effect of presenting significant medical risks to a pregnant woman or deterring abortions. But the Justices using undue burden analysis might vote to invalidate the viability definition on the basis that it had the purpose of deterring women from having abortions of nonviable fetuses. Thus, the question of whether a state may set standards for a physician's viability determination remains uncertain.

126. 428 U.S. 52, 96 S.Ct. 2831, 49 L.Ed.2d 788 (1976).

through the granting of pre-birth parental rights to a father.[127]

Parent Notification or Consent Requirements. States may place some limitations on the ability of an unemancipated pregnant minor to consent to an abortion. The Supreme Court has not explained, in a majority opinion, the precise extent to which a minor female's abortion choices can be subject to a requirement of parental notification or parental consent. However, the rulings of the Supreme Court provide some guidance as to the types of parental notification or parental consent laws that will be upheld or invalidated.

Before examining the rulings of the Supreme Court, we should explain the terminology used for describing state laws regarding abortions for minor females. A "consent requirement" is a law that requires one or both parents give actual consent to the minor's decision to have an abortion. A "notification requirement" statute does not require the consent of the parents but it does require the physician, or in some statutes another health care provider, to notify one or both of the parents of the minor female at some time prior to the abortion. Notification requirement statutes often require the minor female to wait for 24 or 48 hours after the notification before she can have the abortion.

When courts refer to a "judicial bypass procedure", they are referring to a process by which the minor female may avoid the consent or notification requirement by seeking a ruling from an adjudicatory tribunal. The tribunal may be a judge of a general jurisdiction trial court, a juvenile court judge, or an administrative panel delegated authority by state law to make decisions concerning abortions for minor females. The judicial bypass procedures that have survived Supreme Court review will allow a minor female to have the abortion without notification to, or consent of, either of her

parents if the judge or tribunal finds either (1) that the minor is sufficiently mature to make her own decision regarding the abortion, or (2) that the best interests of the minor are served by her receiving abortion services without notification to her parent(s), even though she is not sufficiently mature to make her own decision regarding the abortion.

Parent Consent or Notification Laws—Overview of the Supreme Court's Cases and Standards. The rulings of the Supreme Court allow the state to require a minor to receive the consent of one parent prior to having the abortion if, but only if, the state has established a judicial bypass procedure.

The judge in the bypass procedure must decide whether the minor should receive the abortion without notification to her parent because she is mature enough to make the decision herself or because the abortion is in her interests. The bypass procedure must operate in a timely manner (so as to avoid an undue burden on the minor's rights due to delay). The bypass procedure must guard against disclosure of the minor's identity (although there is no requirement that the state guarantee complete anonymity).

It appears that a state may also require a minor to receive the consent of both parents prior to an abortion if it has established a judicial bypass procedure that meets the foregoing standards, although the constitutionality of this type of law is not entirely clear. A state may not require that both of a minor's parents receive notification prior to the minor having an abortion, unless the state has provided a constitutionally adequate judicial bypass procedure. A two-parent notification requirement without a judicial bypass procedure is unconstitutional.

It is not clear whether a state may require that one of a minor's parents be notified of her intent to have an abortion, if the state does

---

127. In Planned Parenthood v. Casey, 505 U.S. 833, 112 S.Ct. 2791, 120 L.Ed.2d 674 (1992), O'Connor, J. announced the judgment of the Court in an opinion that was, in part, a majority opinion for the Court and, in part, a plurality opinion. In a part of her opinion that was a majority opinion, O'Connor reaffirmed the Court's earlier rulings and found that a state could not require a woman

to notify her spouse prior to obtaining an abortion. 505 U.S. at 887–97, 112 S.Ct. at 2826–31. *Casey,* also ruled that a regulation requiring doctors to keep records regarding whether a woman who desired to have an abortion had notified her spouse was invalid. 505 U.S. at 901, 112 S.Ct. at 2871.

not provide a judicial bypass procedure. It is arguable that a state may require a doctor to give notice to one of the minor's parents, without a bypass procedure, if the doctor is only required to make a reasonable effort to notify one parent and if the doctor is allowed to perform the abortion without notification when waiting for actual notification to the parent would endanger the health or safety of the minor.

If a state law establishes a parental consent or notification requirement that meets constitutional standards (because it has a judicial bypass procedure) then the state may require the minor to wait for 48 hours after her parents have been notified before the abortion is performed. It is unclear whether a waiting period (following a constitutional notification procedure) that is greater than 48 hours would be permissible.

In the cases that established the foregoing guidelines, a majority of Justices, although without majority opinions, have found that the government can take reasonable steps to protect minors and family units without impairing any fundamental constitutional value. Legal systems often require notification to, or consent of, a parent or guardian before a child

receives significant medical treatment, as a means of protecting an immature child from making a choice that will be physically or psychologically harmful to the child. An abortion notification statute may also protect a legitimate societal interest in promoting a family unit (though not necessarily a "traditional" or "nuclear" family) as a basic component of the social structure. It should be emphasized that the Supreme Court has not issued a majority opinion that identifies these interests as the justification for statutory limitations on a minor female's ability to have an abortion. In each of the cases in which the Supreme Court has examined a parental notification or consent requirement, the Justices have divided into three groups. One set of Justices would invalidate almost any restriction on a minor female's ability to choose to have an abortion; one group of Justices would be so deferential to this state that they would appear to uphold a parental "veto" over the choices of their minor children. The third group of Justices provided the "swing votes".[128]

Parental Consent or Notification—Supreme Court Cases. The Court first confronted the parental consent requirement in *Planned Parenthood of Central Missouri v.*

---

128. This division of the Justices continued in Planned Parenthood v. Casey, 505 U.S. 833, 112 S.Ct. 2791, 120 L.Ed.2d 674 (1992). In *Casey*, Justice O'Connor wrote an opinion that was, in part, a majority opinion and, in part, a plurality opinion. She wrote for a majority of the Court in finding that a woman's right to choose to have an abortion of a nonviable fetus was a fundamental aspect of liberty that would receive judicial protection. She wrote for three Justices in using an "undue burden" test to review specific abortion regulations. Eight Justices voted to uphold the specific parental consent requirements that were before the Court in *Casey*, but there was no majority opinion on this point. Justice O'Connor wrote for three Justices in finding that the statute's requirement of parental consent, following the provision of information to the parent concerning abortions and abortion choices, met standards set out in earlier Supreme Court decisions and did not constitute an undue burden on the minor female's right to choose to have an abortion. 505 U.S. at 899, 112 S.Ct. at 2832 (part V–D of Justice O'Connor's opinion, which was joined by Justices Kennedy and Souter). Justice Stevens believed that a woman's right to have an abortion is a fundamental aspect of liberty that merits independent judicial review; he believed that the parental consent provision at issue met the standards set out in earlier cases, even though he did not agree with the plurality's undue burden test. 505 U.S. at 920 n. 8, 112 S.Ct. at 2838, 2843 n. 8. (Stevens, J., concurring in part and dissenting in part). Four Justices thought that there

was no proper judicial role in reviewing abortion regulations under any meaningful standard of review; because they would vote to uphold virtually all restrictions on abortions, they voted to uphold the parental consent restrictions. 505 U.S. at 944, 112 S.Ct. at 2855 (Rehnquist, C.J., joined by White, Scalia, and Thomas, JJ., concurring in the judgment in part and dissenting in part); 505 U.S. at 978, 112 S.Ct. at 2873 (Scalia, joined by Rehnquist, C.J., and White and Thomas, JJ., concurring in the judgment in part and dissenting in part). Only Justice Blackmun voted to strike down the parental consent law in *Casey*, 505 U.S. at 920, 938, 112 S.Ct. at 2843, 2852.

See also, Janklow v. Planned Parenthood, 517 U.S. 1174, 116 S.Ct. 1582, 134 L.Ed.2d 679 (1996) (Supreme Court summarily denies certiorari to a case involving a question of whether lower federal courts had properly declared unconstitutional on its face a state abortion law that required parental notification and waiting periods). Justice Stevens wrote a memorandum in *Janklow* supporting the denial of certiorari. 517 U.S. at 1174, 116 S.Ct. at 1583. Three Justices dissented from the denial of certiorari in *Janklow*; they wrote an opinion expressing the view that the lower courts had acted unjustifiably in invalidating the abortion regulation on its face. 517 U.S. at 1174, 116 S.Ct. at 1584 (Scalia, J., joined by Rehnquist, C.J., and Thomas, J., dissenting).

Danforth.[129] The statute at issue gave a minor female's parent an absolute veto over her decision to have an abortion. Justice Blackmun wrote a majority opinion for the Court that found that the veto power given to the parents was unconstitutional, because "any independent interest the parents [might] have in the termination of the minor daughter's pregnancy [was] no more weighty than the right of privacy of the competent minor mature enough to have become pregnant." [130] However, the majority opinion recognized that the state had greater authority in regulating abortion procedures for juveniles than it had when it regulated abortions for adult females.[131]

Two of the five Justices who joined the majority opinion in *Danforth,* Justices Stewart and Powell, wrote separately to indicate that the constitutional flaw in the statute was the absolute veto given to the minor's parents. They would have voted to uphold a law that required parental consent or parental consultation if the law provided some alternative (such as a judicial bypass procedure) to protect the interests of the pregnant minor.[132]

In *Bellotti v. Baird (Bellotti I)* [133] the Court examined a parental consent statute that was unclear regarding both the authority of parents to veto the decision of their minor child to have an abortion and the availability of a judicial bypass procedure. Because of the lack of clarity in the statute, the Supreme Court remanded the case to the lower courts.[134] The statute returned to the Supreme Court in *Bel-*

lotti v. Baird (Bellotti II).[135] As clarified by the state court, the statute at issue in *Bellotti II* required a minor to receive the consent of her parents or, in the alternative, to receive judicial approval for an abortion in a proceeding in which a court determined whether an abortion was in the best interests of the minor (without regard to whether the minor was sufficiently mature to make an informed decision regarding the abortion). The Supreme Court of the United States, without a majority opinion, invalidated the statute.

Justice Powell's plurality opinion in *Bellotti II* found that a state could restrict the ability of a minor female to obtain an abortion by requiring notification to, or the consent of, a parent if, but only if, the state established a procedure whereby the female could bypass the consent or notification requirement.[136] The Powell plurality opinion in *Bellotti II* found that there were three reasons for finding that some constitutional rights of children, including the right to have an abortion, were not coextensive with the constitutional rights of adults: "The peculiar vulnerability of children; their inability to make critical decisions in an informed, mature manner; and the importance of the parental role in child rearing." The Powell plurality opinion attempted to craft guidelines for a judicial bypass procedure whereby states could promote these interests.

Justice Powell set several criteria for the procedure. The minor must have the opportunity to go directly to a court, or perhaps an

---

129. 428 U.S. 52, 96 S.Ct. 2831, 49 L.Ed.2d 788 (1976).

130. 428 U.S. at 75, 96 S.Ct. at 2844.

131. 428 U.S. at 72, 74–75, 96 S.Ct. at 2842, 2843–44.

132. 428 U.S. at 89, 96 S.Ct. at 2850 (Stewart, J., joined by Powell, J., concurring).

133. 428 U.S. 132, 96 S.Ct. 2857, 49 L.Ed.2d 844 (1976), mandate conformed to 371 Mass. 741, 360 N.E.2d 288 (1977).

134. Following the Supreme Court decision in *Bellotti I* the federal district court certified questions to the Supreme Judicial Court of Massachusetts pursuant to a state procedure whereby the Supreme Judicial Court will answer questions concerning the meaning of state laws that are at issue in federal litigation. The Massachusetts Supreme Court authoritatively construed the statute, and the federal district court then invalidated the statute based upon its understanding of the principles established by the earlier abortion decisions of the Supreme Court of

the United States. The history of the litigation is set out at the beginning of the *Bellotti II* opinion.

135. 443 U.S. 622, 99 S.Ct. 3035, 61 L.Ed.2d 797 (1979), rehearing denied 444 U.S. 887, 100 S.Ct. 185, 62 L.Ed.2d 121 (1979).

136. The plurality opinion of Justice Powell was joined by Chief Justice Burger, and Justices Stewart and Rehnquist.

Justice Rehnquist indicated in a separate opinion that he would be willing to reconsider the entire question of a minor's right to an abortion but that he would join the opinion of Justice Powell rather than the dissent of Justice White because he believed that, until a majority of the Justices were willing to reconsider their basic abortion rights decisions, the states and lower court judges needed guidance from less fragmented holdings of the Supreme Court 443 U.S. at 651, 99 S.Ct. at 3053 (Rehnquist, J., concurring).

administrative tribunal, to attempt to bypass the consent or notification requirement. The procedures must not be so unwieldy or cumbersome that they effectively cut off the minor's ability to have a safe abortion through delay. The judicial bypass procedure must allow the minor to have an abortion if the court found either that the minor is mature enough to make the abortion decision for herself, or, if she is not mature, that the abortion is in her best interest. The bypass procedure must not be such that the minor's identity would be divulged to her parents, or others, in a way that would deter the use of the procedure and, thereby, effectively give a veto power to parents. The state law in *Bellotti II* failed to meet these guidelines because it did not require the judge to determine whether the minor was sufficiently mature to make her own decision and to honor her decision if she was a mature minor (even if the judge disagreed with her decision).

H.L. v. Matheson [137] provides little insight into the constitutional right of a minor female to have an abortion, even though the case was decided with a majority opinion. In *Matheson*, an unemancipated minor female challenged the constitutionality of a state statute that required a physician to give notice to the parents of a minor whenever possible before performing an abortion on her. The statute was upheld by a six to three vote of the Justices, but the facts of the case resulted in the ruling being a narrow one. Chief Justice Burger

wrote a majority opinion for five of the six Justices who found the statute to be constitutional.[138] Chief Justice Burger ruled that the unemancipated minor female in the case who was living with, and dependent upon, her parents lacked standing to challenge the statute as overbroad.[139] In other words, the majority refused to consider whether the statute would be invalid insofar as it might apply to an emancipated minor female who was not living with, and dependent upon, her parents.

Chief Justice Burger's majority opinion in *Matheson* found that a state could require notification to the parents of the unemancipated child because the notification "furthers a constitutionally permissible end by encouraging an unmarried pregnant minor to seek the help and advice of her parents in making the very important decision whether or not to bear a child." Additionally, the majority opinion found that the state had an interest in promoting and decisionmaking within a family unit that would support some types of notification statutes.

Two factors limited the importance of the *Matheson* decision. First, the Court did not rule on the question of whether a statute requiring the consent of both of a minor's parents would be upheld. Second, the majority opinion did not indicate whether the statute before the Court would be upheld if it was later interpreted by state courts in a manner that did not allow the minor the chance to use

137. 450 U.S. 398, 101 S.Ct. 1164, 67 L.Ed.2d 388 (1981).

138. Justice Stevens wrote a concurring opinion. H.L. v. Matheson, 450 U.S. 398, 420, 101 S.Ct. 1164, 1177, 67 L.Ed.2d 388 (1981) (Stevens, J., concurring in the judgment).

139. The appellant sought to represent a class of unmarried, minor pregnant women who wished to have an abortion but who were prohibited from doing so without notice to and the effective consent of their parents. The United States District Court had held that the Utah notice provision would be unconstitutional if it were applicable to emancipated minors. 450 U.S. at 405, 101 S.Ct. at 1169 citing L.R. v. Hansen (D.Utah) (1980) (unpublished opinion).

Chief Justice Burger's majority opinion supported a strict application of standing rules in this case because the United States District Court had decided that the statute did not apply to emancipated minors, although that court

was of the opinion that the statute would be unconstitutional if it were applicable to such women. The United States Supreme Court found no reason to believe that the statute would not be properly construed only to apply to unemancipated and immature minors. "Since there was no appeal from that ruling, it is controlling on the State. We cannot assume that the statute, when challenged in a proper case, will not be construed also to exempt demonstrably mature minors." H.L. v. Matheson, 450 U.S. at 405, 101 S.Ct. at 1169 (1981) (footnote omitted).

According to the dissent, the narrowness of the majority opinion meant merely that a more "carefully drafted" complaint, specifically asserting a minor's emancipation or maturity and that it was in her best interest not to have her parents notified prior to the abortion, would provide another plaintiff with standing to challenge the statute on the basis of overbreadth. 450 U.S. at 425, 101 S.Ct. at 1179 (Marshall, J., joined by Brennan and Blackmun, JJ., dissenting).

a judicial bypass procedure to avoid the notification requirement.

Two of the six Justices who voted to uphold the statute, and who joined the majority opinion in *Matheson,* wrote a concurring opinion in which they stated that the notification statute could not be constitutionally applied to any minor if the state courts did not provide a judicial bypass procedure that followed the guidelines set out in Justice Powell's opinion in *Bellotti II.*[140] Thus, on the day that *Matheson* was decided, there were five Justices who would have voted to invalidate a state law requiring notice to a parent of a minor female if the state law, as interpreted by the state courts, did not provide an adequate judicial bypass procedure.

Matheson did provide two limited rulings regarding abortions for minors. First, the Court upheld the statutory requirement that a physician, rather than some other person on a medical staff, provide the notice to the parent. The Court rejected the argument that requiring the physician to provide the notification interfered with the physician-patient relationship, or the rights of the minor, in a manner that violated the Constitution. Second, the Court upheld the law even though the law required a minor to delay the time when she had an abortion.

By 1983, it became clear that the Powell plurality opinion in *Bellotti II* had become the *de facto* constitutional standard for parental consent and notification laws. In *Planned Parenthood Association of Kansas City, Missouri, Inc. v. Ashcroft,*[141] the Court upheld a state law requiring a minor to receive the consent of one of her parents for an abortion or, in the alternative, to obtain the consent of a juvenile court judge. Although there was no majority opinion in this case, the case was significant because it marked the first time in which the Court upheld a parental consent requirement.

In *Ashcroft,* Justices Blackmun, Brennan, Marshall, and Stevens voted to invalidate the law even though it had a judicial bypass requirement.[142] Justices O'Connor, White, and Rehnquist voted to uphold the statute and indicated that they would have voted to uphold a statute that gave parents even greater control over the decision of a minor female to have an abortion.[143]

Justice Powell wrote only for himself and Chief Justice Burger in *Ashcroft,*[144] but the standards used by Justice Powell would determine the type of statute that would be upheld or invalidated by the Court. Justice Powell, joined by Chief Justice Burger, found that the interests in the protection of minors and the promotion of family decisionmaking, which had been examined in *Bellotti II* and *Matheson,* justified a parental consent statute that provided for a judicial bypass procedure. Justice Powell indicated that a constitutionally sufficient bypass procedure must have three features. First, the procedure must allow the minor to bypass the consent or notification requirement through a process that did not involve unnecessary delay and an undue burden on the minor's ability to have a safe abortion. Second, the minor would have to be given permission to have the abortion (1) if the minor demonstrated that she was sufficiently mature to make her own decision or, (2) if the judge found that the abortion was in the minor's best interest. Third, the anonymity of the minor needs to be protected, at least insofar as disclosure of her identity would undercut her ability to use the bypass procedure.

By 1990 both Chief Justice Burger and Justice Powell had left the Court. Nevertheless, the views that they had expressed in *Bellotti II* and *Ashcroft* continued to provide the guide-

---

140. H.L. v. Matheson, 450 U.S. 398, 413, 101 S.Ct. 1164, 1173, 67 L.Ed.2d 388 (1981) (Powell, J., joined by Stewart, J., concurring).

141. 462 U.S. 476, 103 S.Ct. 2517, 76 L.Ed.2d 733 (1983).

142. 462 U.S. at 494, 503, 103 S.Ct. at 2526, 2531 (Blackmun, J., joined by Brennan, Marshall, Stevens, JJ., concurring in part and dissenting in part).

143. 462 U.S. at 505, 103 S.Ct. at 2532 (O'Connor, J., joined by White and Rehnquist, JJ., concurring in the judgment in part and dissenting in part).

144. Planned Parenthood Association of Kansas City, Missouri, Inc. v. Ashcroft, 462 U.S. 476, 103 S.Ct. 2517, 76 L.Ed.2d 733 (1983).

lines for determining which types of parental consent or notification statutes would be upheld or invalidated by a majority of the Justices.

In *Ohio v. Akron Center for Reproductive Health* [145] the Court upheld, by a seven to three vote, a statute that required a doctor to give notice to one of the minor's parents or, under some circumstances, to another relative of the minor, before performing an abortion on the minor. The statute allowed the physician and the minor female to avoid the notification requirement through the use of a judicial bypass procedure. Justice Kennedy wrote the majority opinion in *Akron Center*; he explained the criteria for a constitutional bypass procedure. [146] According to Justice Kennedy, the bypass procedure in the *Akron Center* case met the basic standards that had been used by Justice Powell in earlier cases. The bypass procedure allowed the minor to show that she possessed the maturity to make her own abortion decision, after consulting with her physician. The trial court was required to make a decision as to whether the minor should have an abortion without notification to her parents, because the abortion was in the best interest of the minor (in cases where the minor was unable to show that she was sufficiently mature to make her own decision).

Justice Kennedy's majority opinion in *Akron Center* ruled that the state could require the minor to prove that she should have the abortion (either because she was mature or because the abortion was in her best interest) by "clear and convincing" evidence. The majority found that the state did not have to bear the burden of proof on these issues. Due process principles did not give a minor a right to avoid parental notification if she could only demonstrate by a preponderance of the evi-

dence that she was mature, or that her best interests would be served by the abortion. The Court found that the government "may require a heightened standard of proof when, as here, the bypass procedure contemplates an *ex parte* proceeding at which no one opposes the minor's testimony." [147]

Justice Kennedy's majority opinion in *Akron Center* found that a bypass procedure would be upheld so long as the statutory procedure "takes reasonable steps to prevent the public from learning of the minor's identity." The minor might be required to provide identifying information for administrative and judicial purposes as a part of the bypass procedure. A statute would not be declared invalid on its face merely because such information had to be provided, so long as the statute did not provide for public disclosure of the information. This ruling leaves open the question of whether a particular statute, valid on its face, would be invalidated if the state administrative or judicial procedures, in practice, made identifying information available to members of the public.

Justice Kennedy held that the Ohio notification bypass procedure did not unconstitutionally impair a minor's rights by the creation of unnecessary delay. The Ohio statute required the trial court to make a decision within five business days after the minor filed her request; it required a court of appeals to use an expedited process for review of the trial court's decision. In theory, it was possible that the entire bypass procedure could take up to 22 calendar days from the time of filing until the time the minor had final permission to have the abortion without notification to, or the consent of, a parent. The majority opinion in *Akron Center* ruled that the mere possibility of a 22 day delay was an insufficient basis for

145. 497 U.S. 502, 110 S.Ct. 2972, 111 L.Ed.2d 405 (1990).

146. Justice Kennedy did not find that a bypass procedure was required for all parental consent or notification statutes. Because Ohio had created a bypass procedure, the only question presented by the case was whether the bypass procedure provided was constitutional. Justice Kennedy's opinion for the Court explained that, even if due process required a bypass procedure for a parental notification statute, the procedures established by the

Ohio statute met all constitutional standards. Justice Blackmun filed a dissenting opinion in this case, which was joined by Justices Brennan and Marshall. Ohio v. Akron Center for Reproductive Health, 497 U.S. 502, 523, 110 S.Ct. 2972, 2984, 111 L.Ed.2d 405 (1990) (Blackmun, J., joined by Brennan and Marshall, JJ., dissenting).

147. Ohio v. Akron Center for Reproductive Health, 497 U.S. 502, 515, 110 S.Ct. 2972, 2981, 111 L.Ed.2d 405 (1990).

invalidating the statute, absent a showing that the procedure would impose an undue burden on minors who sought to avoid a notification or consent requirement. In other words, procedures established by a state for a bypass system will not be invalidated if they seem to be reasonably designed to provide the minor with an expedited process. A challenge to a statute that is based on the complexity or length of the procedures must be based on facts that show that the constitutional interests of minors (in actual cases) have been impaired by the state's bypass procedure.

Akron Center also found that the a bypass procedure should not be invalidated merely because the state required the filing of pleading forms, and the presentation of oral or written testimony, in a bypass proceeding. Limitations on the minor's ability to have an abortion that promoted the state's interests in protecting minors and fostering family decisionmaking justified a procedure in which the judge was able to make an accurate decision regarding the maturity of the minor or the minor's best interests. The minor was provided with a fair hearing, even though she did not have state paid counsel at the hearing, and even though she had to make a showing of maturity by "clear and convincing" evidence.[148]

Akron Center ruled that a state law requiring a physician to personally notify the minor's parents did not infringe the constitutional rights of either the minor seeking the abortion or her physician (at least, when the state provided a judicial bypass procedure).[149] The Supreme Court, in prior cases, had found that the government could not require a physician, rather than another health care professional, to provide information and counseling to adult women, because that requirement was not narrowly tailored to protecting the best interest of the adult female considering the abortion.[150] The requirement that a physician personally give information to the minor's parents was designed to protect the interests of the minors. The physician would be in the best position to provide full medical information to the parents, so that the parents could provide good advice to their child.[151]

The only part of the opinion by Justice Kennedy in *Ohio v. Akron Center for Reproductive Health* that was not joined by a majority of the Justices was the concluding paragraph of the opinion, in which Justice Kennedy stated that the parental notification statute was permissible because it was a "rational way" to further the state's interest in protection of children and promotion of family decisionmaking.[152] The Justices could not agree on a formal standard of review, but a majority of the Justices were able to agree on the standards for the judicial bypass procedure.

In *Hodgson v. Minnesota*,[153] the Court invalidated a state statute that required notification of both of a minor's parents prior to her having an abortion. In the same case, the Court upheld the requirement that both parents be notified of the abortion, and that there be a 48 hour waiting period between notification and the performance of the abortion, if the notification requirement was accompanied by a judicial bypass procedure that met constitutional standards.

In *Hodgson*, Justice Stevens wrote an opinion that was in part a majority opinion, in part a plurality opinion, and in part a dissent. Justice Stevens' opinion was a majority opinion in the part wherein he found that a state requirement that both parents be notified prior to the abortion, which did not provide a

---

148. 497 U.S. at 516, 517, 110 S.Ct. at 2982. The majority used the standards for determining whether an administrative process complied with procedural due process principles that had been established in Mathews v. Eldridge, 424 U.S. 319, 96 S.Ct. 893, 47 L.Ed.2d 18 (1976). See Chapter 13 of this Treatise regarding procedural due process principles.

149. Ohio v. Akron Center for Reproductive Health, 497 U.S. 502, 518–519, 110 S.Ct. 2972, 2983, 111 L.Ed.2d 405 (1990).

150. City of Akron v. Akron Center for Reproductive Health, Inc., 462 U.S. 416, 446–49, 103 S.Ct. 2481, 2501–2503, 76 L.Ed.2d 687 (1983).

151. Ohio v. Akron Center for Reproductive Health, 497 U.S. 502, 518–519, 110 S.Ct. 2972, 2983, 111 L.Ed.2d 405 (1990).

152. 497 U.S. at 520, 110 S.Ct. at 2983–84.

153. 497 U.S. 417, 110 S.Ct. 2926, 111 L.Ed.2d 344 (1990).

judicial bypass procedure, was unconstitutional.[154] The majority opinion found that requiring two parents to be notified was not a reasonable means of protecting the interests of minors. In a functional and functioning family unit, notification of one parent would be sufficient to initiate family discussion and the protection of the minor. The added requirement of notifying a second parent would pose a significant deterrent to any minor if one of her parents was unlikely to make decisions in her best interest. For example, if the family was disfunctional because of spouse abuse or child abuse, notification of both parents would harm the minor's interests; the mere requirement of notification would deter her from seeking an abortion, even if the abortion was in her best interests. The majority opinion found that the Court's earlier decisions regarding parental notification statutes had not indicated that a state could require notification to both parents.[155]

In *Hodgson* there were six Justices who voted to uphold a 48 hour waiting requirement for abortions for minors, although there was no majority opinion on this point.[156] In a part

of his *Hodgson* opinion that was joined only by Justice O'Connor, Justice Stevens found that if a state had a valid notification requirement (which included a judicial bypass procedure) the state could require the minor to wait 48 hours after notification to her parent before the abortion was performed. These two Justices believed that the waiting period requirement was tailored to serve the best interests of the minor by allowing the parents time to counsel her. The statute did not require any delay after a parent (or a court, in a bypass procedure) had given consent for the minor's abortion. The 48 hour delay after notification was constitutional in the view of these two Justices because it "would reasonably further the legitimate state interest in ensuring that the minor's decision is knowing and intelligent."[157]

Justice Stevens, and three other Justices, dissented to a ruling of the Court in *Hodgson v. Minnesota* that upheld a two-parent notification requirement that was accompanied by a judicial bypass procedure.[158] Justice Kennedy wrote a separate opinion in *Hodgson* that was joined by Chief Justice Rehnquist and Justices

---

154. Hodgson v. Minnesota, 497 U.S. 417, 444, 110 S.Ct. 2926, 2937–2941, 2945–2947, 111 L.Ed.2d 344 (1990). This portion of Justice Stevens' opinion was joined by Justices O'Connor, Marshall, Brennan, and Blackmun. 497 U.S. at 458, 110 S.Ct. at 2949 (O'Connor, J., concurring in part and concurring in the judgment in part). 497 U.S. at 461, 110 S.Ct. at 2951 (Marshall, J., joined by Brennan and Blackmun, JJ., concurring in part, concurring in the judgment in part, and dissenting in part).

155. Hodgson v. Minnesota, 497 U.S. 417, 110 S.Ct. 2926, 2944, 111 L.Ed.2d 344 (1990) (plurality opinion announcing judgment of the Court written by Stevens, J., and joined only by O'Connor, J.).

156. Chief Justice Rehnquist and Justices White, Scalia, and Kennedy would uphold a greater degree of parental authority than would other Justices on the Court. They joined together with Justices O'Connor and Stevens to form the six Justice majority upholding the waiting period requirement for minors. 497 U.S. at 480, 110 S.Ct. at 2961 (Kennedy, J., joined by Rehnquist, C.J., and White and Scalia, JJ., concurring in the judgment in part and dissenting in part).

The decision in this case would seem to put to rest any argument for the validity of the ruling of the United States Court of Appeals in Zbaraz v. Hartigan, 763 F.2d 1532 (7th Cir.1985). The Court of Appeals in this case invalidated a requirement that a minor wait 24 hours after the notification of her parents in order to have an

abortion. The United States Supreme Court considered this case when there were only eight members of the Court and the Supreme Court affirmed the seventh circuit by an equally divided vote and without opinion. Hartigan v. Zbaraz, 484 U.S. 171, 108 S.Ct. 479, 98 L.Ed.2d 478 (1987) (per curiam), affirming by an equally divided vote, Zbaraz v. Hartigan, 763 F.2d 1532 (7th Cir.1985). The Supreme Court has now upheld a waiting requirement of 48 hours after notification to a minor's parents (with a parental notification statute that had a judicial bypass procedure). Justices Stevens and O'Connor cited the dissenting opinion of Judge Coffey to the Seventh Circuit ruling that had taken a contrary position. Hodgson v. Minnesota, 497 U.S. 417, 448–449, 110 S.Ct. 2926, 2944, 111 L.Ed.2d 344 (1990) (opinion of Stevens, J., joined by O'Connor, J.) citing Zbaraz v. Hartigan, 763 F.2d 1532, 1552 (7th Cir.1985) (Coffey, J., dissenting).

157. 497 U.S. at 448, 110 S.Ct. at 2944 (opinion of Stevens, J., joined by O'Connor, J.).

158. 497 U.S. 417, 455–57, 110 S.Ct. 2926, 2947–49, 111 L.Ed.2d 344 (1990) (opinion of Stevens, J., announcing the judgment of the Court; this portion of the Stevens opinion is a dissenting opinion regarding the Court's ruling on the constitutionality of a two-parent notice requirement accompanied by a judicial bypass procedure). 497 U.S. at 461, 110 S.Ct. at 2951 (Marshall, J., joined by Brennan, and Blackmun, JJ., concurring in part, concurring in the judgment in part, and dissenting in part).

White and Scalia.[159] These four Justices would have upheld the notification requirement even without a judicial bypass procedure. They found that a bypass procedure that allowed the minor female a fair opportunity to prove to a court that she was sufficiently mature to make her own decision, or that an abortion without notification to her parents was in her best interests, should remove any doubt regarding any constitutionality of the notification requirement.

Justice O'Connor provided the fifth vote for upholding a two parent notification requirement that included a judicial bypass procedure.[160] She found that the dangers posed to the best interests of a minor from the two parent notification requirement were removed by a judicial bypass procedure. Justice O'Connor believes a state regulation of abortions should be upheld so long as the regulation does not "unduly burden" the woman. A notification requirement might harm the interests of minors who were the victims of neglect or abuse or who were a part of a dysfunctional family. The judicial bypass procedure would allow such a child to avoid the danger posed to her by notification to her parents.

In the 1990 cases, the Court did not have before it a statute that required notification to one, but not both, of a minor's parents prior to her having an abortion that did not provide for a judicial bypass procedure. There is an open question regarding whether there must be a judicial bypass procedure for a one-parent notification requirement. If the statute does not give the parent a veto power over the decision of the minor, and if the statute allows the physician to protect the health of the minor when the delay caused by notification might pose a significant threat to the health of the

minor, a one parent notification requirement right be upheld. The 1990 cases do make clear that a state may require the consent of, or notification to, one or both of a minor's parents if the state provides a judicial bypass procedure for the minor that meets the standards set out in *Ohio v. Akron Center for Reproductive Health,*[161] which seems to have adopted the position taken by Justice Powell in earlier cases.

In 1992, the Supreme Court upheld a statute that required a physician to refrain from performing an abortion on a woman who was less than 18 years old unless he obtained the "informed consent" of the pregnant young woman and of one of her parents, or her guardian, except when there was a medical emergency or when the minor made use of a judicial bypass procedure.[162] The statute required the physician, a qualified physician assistant, health care practitioner, or social worker to provide the woman, and the parent with material regarding fetal development, alternatives to abortions, and possible assistance for child birth and child care. The information and consent had to be given at least 24 hours before the abortion, although all of these restrictions could be disregarded in the case of a medical emergency. In *Planned Parenthood v. Casey,*[163] the Court upheld this parental consent requirement by an eight to one vote of the Justices. Only Justice Blackmun believed that the law placed too great a burden on the right of young women that choose to have an abortion.[164] However, there was no majority opinion on this point. Justice O'Connor wrote for three Justices in finding that the statute did not impose an "undue burden" on a minor female's ability to have the abortion because it included a judicial bypass provision of the type that had been upheld in earlier

---

159. Hodgson v. Minnesota, 497 U.S. 417, 480, 110 S.Ct. 2926, 2961, 111 L.Ed.2d 344 (1990) (Kennedy, J., joined by Rehnquist, C.J., and White and Scalia, JJ., concurring in the judgment in part and dissenting in part).

160. Hodgson v. Minnesota, 497 U.S. 417, 458, 110 S.Ct. 2926, 2949–51, 111 L.Ed.2d 344 (1990) (O'Connor, J., concurring in part and concurring in the judgment in part).

161. 497 U.S. 502, 110 S.Ct. 2972, 111 L.Ed.2d 405 (1990).

162. The statute is set out in the appendix to Planned Parenthood v. Casey, 505 U.S. 833, 901, 112 S.Ct. 2791, 2833, 120 L.Ed.2d 674 (1992).

163. 505 U.S. 833, 112 S.Ct. 2791, 120 L.Ed.2d 674 (1992).

164. 505 U.S. at 920, 938, 112 S.Ct. at 2843, 2852 (Blackmun, J., concurring in part, concurring in the judgment in part, and dissenting in part).

cases.[165] Justice Stevens believed that the parental consent requirement should be upheld on the basis of the Court's earlier decisions, even though he did not agree with the undue burden test as a standard for reviewing abortion regulations.[166] Four Justices voted to uphold these parental consent requirements, because they did not believe that a woman of any age had a constitutional right to choose to have a fetus aborted.[167]

In the 1990s, the Court continued to uphold parental notification laws, and parental consent laws, if, but only if, such laws offered a pregnant minor female the opportunity for a "bypass procedure" at which she would present her request to a judge (or some other type of impartial decision-maker) for permission to have an abortion without notification to her parents.[168] In accordance with the Court's 1990 decision in *Akron II*, the government may impose the burden of proof on the minor in a bypass procedure so that she will be denied the ability to have an abortion without notification to, or the consent of, her parents unless she can demonstrate (1) that she is sufficiently mature to make the decision, or (2) that the abortion, without parental notification, is in her best interest.

The Supreme Court, in the cases referred to in this Section, has ruled that the burden of proof can be placed on the pregnant minor in a bypass procedure.[169] However, the Court has not explained precisely what the government may require the minor to prove in order to receive an abortion without parental notification or parental consent. *Bellotti II* and *Ashcroft* appear to establish the principle that the minor should be allowed to have the abortion if she can demonstrate that she is sufficiently mature to make her own decision regarding her best interests and the choice to have an abortion.

If the pregnant minor cannot prove that she is sufficiently mature to make decisions regarding abortion, can a state require the minor to demonstrate *both* (1) that the abortion in is her best interest, *and* (2) that the abortion without notification to her parents is in her best interest? Alternatively, is the state limited to requiring the minor to show *only* that the abortion is in her best interest? The Supreme Court did not rule on these questions in *Lambert v. Wicklund*.[170] Nevertheless, the Court's ruling in *Lambert* indicates that a state law requiring a minor to prove *both* that the abortion would be in her best interest, *and* that avoiding parental notification would be in her best interest, would be valid. The Court, in *Lambert,* upheld a statute that required an unemancipated minor either to notify one of her parents or to prove that the abortion was in her best interest. The opinion of the Court, stated that: "Underlying our statement [in *Akron II*] was an assumption that a judicial bypass procedure requiring a minor to show that *parental notification is not* in her best interests is equivalent to a judicial bypass procedure requiring a minor to show that *abortion without notification* is in her best interests."[171] Three concurring Justices in *Lambert* believed

---

165. Justice O'Connor announced the judgment of the Court in *Casey;* her opinion was, in part, a majority opinion for the Court and, in part, a plurality opinion. The portion of her opinion in which the parental consent statute was upheld was a plurality opinion that was joined by Justices Kennedy and Souter. Planned Parenthood v. Casey, 505 U.S. 833, 899, 112 S.Ct. 2791, 2832, 120 L.Ed.2d 674 (1992) (judgment of the Court as to this issue announced in an opinion by O'Connor, J., joined by Kennedy and Souter, JJ.), on remand 978 F.2d 74 (3d Cir. 1992).

166. 505 U.S. at 920, 911, n. 8, 112 S.Ct. at 2838, 2843 n. 8 (Stevens, J., concurring in part and dissenting in part).

167. Planned Parenthood v. Casey, 505 U.S. 833, 944, 112 S.Ct. 2791, 2855, 120 L.Ed.2d 674 (1992) (Rehnquist, C.J., joined by White, Scalia, and Thomas, JJ., concurring in the judgment in part and dissenting in part), 505 U.S.

at 979, 112 S.Ct. at 2873 (Scalia, J., joined by Rehnquist, C.J., and White and Thomas, JJ., concurring in the judgment in part and dissenting in part).

168. Ohio v. Akron Center for Reproductive Health (Akron II), 497 U.S. 502, 110 S.Ct. 2972, 111 L.Ed.2d 405 (1990); Bellotti v. Baird (Bellotti II), 443 U.S. 622, 99 S.Ct. 3035, 61 L.Ed.2d 797 (1979), rehearing denied 444 U.S. 887 100 S.Ct. 185, 62 L.Ed.2d 121 (1979); Planned Parenthood Association of Kansas City, Missouri, Inc. v. Ashcroft, 462 U.S. 476, 103 S.Ct. 2517, 76 L.Ed.2d 733 (1983).

169. Hodgson v. Minnesota, 497 U.S. 417, 110 S.Ct. 2926, 111 L.Ed.2d 344 (1990).

170. 520 U.S. 292, 117 S.Ct. 1169, 137 L.Ed.2d 464 (1997) (per curiam).

171. 520 U.S. at 297, 117 S.Ct. at 1172 (emphasis in original).

that the state statute before the Court did not require a minor to prove both that the abortion was in her best interest and that notification was not in her best interest.[172] The concurring Justices asserted that the Supreme Court had not resolved the question of what the minor must prove regarding the abortion, parental notification, and her best interest.

(4) Public Funding of Abortions. The Court defines a woman's right to an abortion in terms of her freedom to make a decision free of governmental restraints. Indeed, a majority of the Justices refuse to accept governmental attempts to demonstrate a societal interest in preservation of the fetus that would limit this freedom of choice by the woman. Yet the Court has found that indigent women have no claim of right to public funding for abortions. The woman's right includes only her own decision to attempt to secure an abortion in the private sector; the Court will not issue a ruling here which might have wealth reallocation effects even though it will leave many women without a realistic chance to secure the abortion which they have a fundamental right to choose.

In 1977 the Court had upheld the refusal of federal and local governmental entities to fund abortions that were not necessary to preserve the health of a pregnant woman. In *Maher v. Roe,*[173] the Court held that neither the state nor federal governments were required to subsidize non-therapeutic abortions. Indeed, the Court upheld a variety of systems granting payments for maternity and childbirth costs but not abortions.[174] The majority saw these programs as merely the encouragement of childbirth rather than the penalizing of those who sought abortion but could not afford to pay for them. The three dissenting Justices viewed this case as a retreat from the recognition of the right as truly fundamental.[175] But the majority was unconvinced that the right to privacy included a right to government benefits in order to procure an abortion.

Three years later, in *Harris v. McRae,*[176] the Court upheld the federal government's exclusion from federal medical benefits programs of funding for abortion for indigent women even when a woman's attending physician had determined that an abortion was necessary to safeguard her health. The Court found that the "Hyde Amendment" not only eliminated federal funding for almost all abortions,[177] but also freed the states of any duty to fund abortions that were not funded by the federal Medicaid program.[178]

The majority opinion, written by Justice Stewart, found that the Court's previous decisions in the area of abortion established only a fundamental right of a woman to be able to choose to have an abortion without direct gov-

---

172. 520 U.S. at 299–301, 117 S.Ct. at 1173–74 (Stevens, J., joined by Ginsburg and Breyer, JJ., concurring in the judgement).

173. 432 U.S. 464, 97 S.Ct. 2376, 53 L.Ed.2d 484 (1977).

174. Id.; Beal v. Doe, 432 U.S. 438, 97 S.Ct. 2366, 53 L.Ed.2d 464 (1977) (Social Security Act does not require abortion payments); Poelker v. Doe, 432 U.S. 519, 97 S.Ct. 2391, 53 L.Ed.2d 528 (1977) (city hospital may provide childbirth procedures and refuse abortions).

175. Maher v. Roe, 432 U.S. 464, 482, 97 S.Ct. 2376, 2386, 53 L.Ed.2d 484 (1977) (Brennan, Marshall & Blackmun, JJ., dissenting).

176. 448 U.S. 297, 100 S.Ct. 2671, 65 L.Ed.2d 784 (1980).

177. There were three versions of the Hyde Amendment. As originally passed for the 1977 Fiscal Year, the Amendment prohibited federal funding for abortions except where "the life of the mother would be in danger if the fetus were carried to term."

For the majority of the 1978 and all of the 1979 Fiscal Year, the Hyde Amendment additionally provided for funds in cases where "such medical procedures [are] nec-

essary for the victims of rape or incest when such rape or incest has been reported promptly to a law enforcement agency or public health service" and in "instances where severe and long-lasting physical health damage to the mother would result if the pregnancy were carried to term when so determined by two physicians."

For the 1980 Fiscal Year, Congress amended the previous version of the Hyde Amendment to exclude federal funding for the last described category of abortions. Harris v. McRae, 448 U.S. 297, 100 S.Ct. 2671, 65 L.Ed.2d 784 (1980).

178. In Williams v. Zbaraz, 448 U.S. 358, 100 S.Ct. 2694, 65 L.Ed.2d 831 (1980), decided the same day as McRae, the Court relied on its ruling in McRae that state governments were not required to fund abortions not covered by the federal Medicaid plan and that the refusal of the state to fund such abortions did not violate the due process or equal protection clauses of the Fourteenth Amendment. The Court in Williams relied entirely on the McRae opinion to establish the constitutionality of the state refusal to fund medically necessary abortions.

ernment interference. The government could not attempt to limit a woman's right to an abortion with an artificial definition of the time at which a fetus became viable, or medical regulations which were designed to inhibit a woman's access to abortion services, because such laws interfered with a fundamental right of the woman and were not supported by a compelling government interest. Justice Stewart reasoned that the Hyde Amendment "places no governmental obstacle in the path of a woman who chooses to terminate her pregnancy, but rather, by means of unequal subsidization of abortion and other medical services, encourages alternative activity deemed in the public interest." [179] The fact that a woman could not exercise her fundamental right to secure an abortion in the private sector was of no concern to the Justices, for her inability to exercise her freedom of choice was the result of her own lack of resources rather than government action. The government was not required to reallocate resources so as to enable persons to exercise their rights, according to the majority. [180]

Having thus dispensed of the claim that failure to provide a woman with resources for exercising her right to choose to have an abortion violated the fundamental right of privacy, the Court had little problem in dismissing the indigent women's equal protection claim. Because the failure to provide funds for such women did not deprive them of a fundamental right, the law was not to be tested by the compelling interest test. Rather, the majority found that it need only determine whether the Hyde Amendment "bears a rational relationship to [the government's] legitimate interest in protecting the potential life of the fetus." [181]

The Court had no problem in upholding the statute against the equal protection attack under the deferential rational basis standard. Unless a law allocates the ability to exercise a fundamental right by economic status, the Court refuses to scrutinize rigorously the validity of wealth classifications. [182]

The Court quickly dispensed with the claim that the Hyde Amendment violated the religion clauses of the First Amendment. The fact that the Hyde Amendment coincided with the doctrines of certain religious sects did not provide a basis for its invalidation because the Amendment could be seen as having a secular purpose in encouraging childbirth. To use the establishment clause to prohibit laws which have an ethical basis in some religion would be to deprive the government of an ability to act in many areas traditionally recognized as being within the police power of the state. [183] No plaintiff attacking the validity of the Hyde Amendment in these cases had standing to claim that the law violated the free exercise clause of the First Amendment as, not unexpectedly, none were able to demonstrate that they must procure an abortion under compulsion of their religious beliefs. [184]

Four Justices dissented from these rulings denying indigent women funding for therapeutic abortions. [185] Although Justice Stewart, a member of the five person majority and author of the *Harris* opinion, later resigned from the Court, it seems unlikely that the Court in the near future will find that the government must provide resources for the funding of an abortion, for such a position seems contrary to the libertarian philosophy which currently

---

179. Harris v. McRae, 448 U.S. 297, 314, 100 S.Ct. 2671, 2687, 65 L.Ed.2d 784 (1980) quoting Maher v. Roe, 432 U.S. 464, 474, 97 S.Ct. 2376, 2382, 53 L.Ed.2d 484 (1977).

180. 448 U.S. at 316–320, 100 S.Ct. at 2687–90.

181. 448 U.S. at 324, 100 S.Ct. at 2692.

182. The Court's refusal to find wealth classifications to be deserving of meaningful judicial review is examined in Section VI of this chapter.

183. Harris v. McRae, 448 U.S. 297, 320, 100 S.Ct. 2671, 2689–90, 65 L.Ed.2d 784 (1980).

184. 448 U.S. at 320, 100 S.Ct. at 2689–90.

185. Justices Brennan, Marshall, and Blackmun focused their dissents on the Hyde Amendment's effective interference with an indigent pregnant woman's freedom of choice to have an abortion, which they found to be a fundamental constitutional right. Justice Stevens would have employed a reasonableness standard to find that there was no basis for exclusion from a government "pool of benefits" of individuals who had a medical need for an abortion. Harris v. McRae, 448 U.S. 297, 329, 100 S.Ct. 2671, 2694, 65 L.Ed.2d 784 (1980) (Brennan, J., joined by Marshall and Blackmun, JJ., dissenting); 448 U.S. at 337, 100 S.Ct. at 2706 (Marshall, J., dissenting); 448 U.S. at 348, 100 S.Ct. at 2711 (Blackmun, J., dissenting); 448 U.S. at 349, 100 S.Ct. at 2712 (Stevens, J., dissenting).

holds sway on the Supreme Court.[186] Were the Court to find that the government must use reasonable classifications in its allocation of "welfare" benefits in order to avoid effectively denying a woman her fundamental right to an abortion, it would be only a short philosophic step away from justifying judicial review of the reasonableness of welfare classifications and a wide variety of laws which have a disparate impact on economically disadvantaged persons.

A majority of the Justices on the Supreme Court, throughout the 1980s, believed that the right of privacy only protected a woman's ability to choose to have an abortion without certain types of government interference and did not give women a right to have an abortion at government expense. Thus, in *Webster v. Reproductive Health Services* [187] the Supreme Court upheld a state law prohibition against the use of public facilities or public funds for abortion services. The Court's rulings regarding the state's ability to refuse to subsidize abortions should not be taken as indicating that the state may attempt to use its economic power to restrict private sector abortions. The majority opinion in *Webster,* written by Chief Justice Rehnquist, noted: "A different analysis might apply if a particular State had socialized medicine and all of its hospitals and physicians were publicly funded. This case might also be different if the State barred doctors who performed abortions in private facilities from the use of public facilities for

any purpose." [188] Each of those hypothetical statutes might be ruled to be an unconstitutional attempt to restrict the availability of private sector abortions.

But when the government has not monopolized the provision of abortion services, it is not required to fund abortions. In *Rust v. Sullivan,*[189] the Court upheld the Department of Health and Human Services' regulations which prohibited private doctors who received federal funds for "family planning services" from giving abortion information to a woman client of the federally funded family planning service except when an individual woman might need an abortion to prevent a serious threat to her life. Chief Justice Rehnquist wrote the majority opinion in this five to four decision. Most of the Chief Justice's opinion explained the nature of the restrictions on persons or organizations receiving family planning funds and why those restrictions did not violate the First Amendment.[190] The majority opinion also ruled that the restrictions on providing abortion information in federally funded family planning services did not violate the Fifth Amendment due process clause. The regulations, according to the majority, did not impair a woman's right to choose whether to terminate a pregnancy. Chief Justice Rehnquist relied on the Supreme Court's earlier decisions in *Maher, McRae,* and *Webster* for the principle that "the government has no

---

186. For citations to secondary sources on this topic, see R. Rotunda & J. Nowak, Treatise on Constitutional Law: Substance and Procedure, vol. 3, § 18.29 (3rd ed. 1999, with annual supplements).

187. 492 U.S. 490, 109 S.Ct. 3040, 106 L.Ed.2d 410 (1989).

188. 492 U.S. at 510 n. 8, 109 S.Ct. at 3052 n. 8 (citing Harris v. McRae, 448 U.S. 297, 317 n. 19, 100 S.Ct. 2671, 2688 n. 19, 65 L.Ed.2d 784 (1980).). Chief Justice Rehnquist's opinion regarding the funding issue was joined by Justices Kennedy, O'Connor, Scalia, and White.

189. 500 U.S. 173, 111 S.Ct. 1759, 114 L.Ed.2d 233 (1991). This case was decided by a five to four vote of the Justices. Three Justices dissented on both constitutional and statutory interpretation grounds. 500 U.S. at 203, 111 S.Ct. at 1778 (Blackmun, joined by Marshall and Stevens, JJ., dissenting and joined in part by O'Connor, J.). Justice O'Connor dissented only on statutory grounds; she would have found that the statute did not authorize the executive branch to have regulations of the type at issue in this case. Therefore, she joined Justice Blackmun's dissenting opinion only as to the statutory

interpretation issues; and she would have avoided ruling on constitutional issues. 500 U.S. at 222, 111 S.Ct. at 1788 (O'Connor, J., dissenting). Although Justice Stevens joined Justice Blackmun's dissent, Justice Stevens wrote a separate dissenting opinion that emphasized his reasons for finding that the Court should have found that the regulations issued by the Secretary of Health and Human Services were not authorized by any federal statute. 500 U.S. at 219, 111 S.Ct. at 1786 (Stevens, J., dissenting). See also, Dalton v. Little Rock Family Planning Services, 516 U.S. 474, 116 S.Ct. 1063, 134 L.Ed.2d 115 (1996) (per curiam). In *Dalton* the Court ruled that a lower federal court injunction against state constitutional provision prohibiting public funding of abortions, except when necessary to save the woman's life, was overbroad. The lower court injunction in *Dalton* was upheld to the extent that the state constitutional provision violated federal law controlling jointly funded federal-state medical benefits.

190. See Chapter 16 of this Treatise regarding the First Amendment issues in this case.

constitutional duty to subsidize an activity merely because the activity is constitutionally protected and [the government] may validly choose to fund child birth over abortion." In the view of the majority, a pregnant woman who visited a federally funded family planning clinic, and who could not be provided with information concerning abortions by that family planning clinic, was "in no worse position than if Congress had never enacted Title X [the act that provided family planning services grants]." [191]

§ 14.30　Emerging Issues Regarding the Right to Privacy

(a) Accumulation and Distribution of Data Concerning Individual Citizens

The Supreme Court has not yet held that the right to privacy limits governmental powers relating to the collection of data concerning private individuals. In *Whalen v. Roe*[1] the Court unanimously upheld a New York law that required physicians and pharmacists to forward to state authorities copies of prescriptions for medicines containing certain narcotics. The majority opinion by Justice Stevens held that the statute was valid even if the right to privacy places some restriction on the ability of government to collect data concerning individual citizens. The New York law was found to be related to the legitimate goal of controlling illegal drug distribution and reasonable in its limitations on the use and distribution of the collected data. The mere possibility that the data would be used improperly did not void the law. Justice Stevens noted, however, that government data collection did threaten individual privacy, and, for that rea-

son, that the right to collect such data normally would be limited by a duty to avoid unwarranted disclosure of the information collected. The majority opinion stated that this duty "arguably has its roots in the Constitution," but did not rule on this issue.

In a concurring opinion, Justice Brennan stated his belief that governmental data collection practices that were not carefully limited as to the use of information concerning private persons would deprive those persons of a constitutionally protected privacy interest.[2]

In a separate concurring opinion, Justice Stewart noted that the majority had not adopted Justice Brennan's views. Justice Stewart was of the opinion that the Constitution, apart from the Fourth Amendment, did not create a general right to privacy that would restrict governmental activities of this nature.[3]

The Supreme Court's decision in *Thornburgh v. American College of Obstetricians and Gynecologists*[4] may support Justice Brennan's theory in *Whalen* that the due process right to privacy places restrictions on government collection and use of data on individual citizens. In *Thornburgh*, the Court invalidated a variety of state regulations that restricted a woman's right to have an abortion, a majority believed that those restrictions were not reasonably related to the state's compelling interests in the protection of a viable fetus or the protection of the health of the woman.[5] One of the regulations that the Court invalidated in *Thornburgh* required that a physician report the basis for the determination that the fetus was not viable. The required medical reports

---

191. It is interesting to note that Chief Justice Rehnquist's majority opinion found that the regulations did not expressly bar abortion counseling, or abortion referrals, when a patient at a Title X project was pregnant and her pregnancy placed her life in peril. The Chief Justice found that the regulations were designed to promote a congressional end in preventing federal funds from being used to promote abortion as a means of family planning and that the regulations would allow "otherwise prohibited abortion-related activities in such circumstances [when a pregnancy placed a woman's life in imminent peril]." 500 U.S. at 195, 111 S.Ct. at 1773. The majority opinion did not indicate whether a restriction on abortion counseling in those circumstances would violate either the First Amendment or the Fifth Amendment.

§ 14.30

1. 429 U.S. 589, 97 S.Ct. 869, 51 L.Ed.2d 64 (1977).

2. Whalen v. Roe, 429 U.S. 589, 606–07, 97 S.Ct. 869, 880, 51 L.Ed.2d 64 (1977) (Brennan, J., concurring).

3. 429 U.S. at 607–09, 97 S.Ct. at 880–81 (Stewart, J., concurring).

4. 476 U.S. 747, 106 S.Ct. 2169, 90 L.Ed.2d 779 (1986).

5. For a review of the Court's decisions regarding the extent to which the government may regulate abortion medical practices, see § 14.29(b)(2).

included a great amount of detail about the physician's actions and the condition of the woman in the individual abortion. The Court found that this law was not reasonably tailored to protecting the health of pregnant women; it was, therefore, an unconstitutional means of deterring abortions. In so ruling, the Court in *Thornburgh* distinguished its earlier decision in *Planned Parenthood of Central Missouri v. Danforth*,[6] which had upheld a requirement that doctors keep records regarding abortions. In the *Danforth* case, the state's use of the information did not result in the identity of women who were having abortions being made public or otherwise result in deterring women from exercising the right to have an abortion.

Although the statute at issue in *Thornburgh* did not require that the abortion patient's name be identified in the medical reports, those reports included information that would make it possible to identify women who had abortions. Moreover, the reports were open to public inspection.[7] The majority opinion in *Thornburgh*, written by Justice Blackmun, did not discuss a general privacy limitation on the government collection or use of data regarding private citizens. The majority invalidated the law because it restricted a woman's fundamental right to an abortion by creating a system

that might deter women from exercising that right.[8] In so ruling, Justice Blackmun relied on the Court's First Amendment decisions which had found that government laws or regulations requiring authors of handbills to identify themselves[9] or associations to disclose their membership[10] were unconstitutional, except in those instances where the requirements were narrowly tailored to promote a compelling or overriding interest of government.[11] The Court in *Thornburgh* did not cite *Whalen* for the proposition that a due process right of privacy generally limited government data collection and data use practices; the Court only cited *Whalen* with a "see also" citation at the end of its opinion regarding the general duty of courts to enforce a constitutional principle "that a certain private sphere of individual liberty will be kept largely beyond the reach of government."[12]

The Supreme Court has confronted the question of the propriety of government collection of data only in terms of the Fourth Amendment right to be free from unreasonable searches and seizures, and the Fifth Amendment prohibition against compelling persons to incriminate themselves.[13] Indeed, in its determination of this application and meaning of the Fourth and Fifth Amend-

---

6. 428 U.S. 52, 80, 96 S.Ct. 2831, 2846, 49 L.Ed.2d 788 (1976).

7. Thornburgh v. American College of Obstetricians and Gynecologists, 476 U.S. 747, 764–768, 106 S.Ct. 2169, 2181–82, 90 L.Ed.2d 779 (1986).

8. 476 U.S. at 767 n. 12, 106 S.Ct. at 2182 n. 12 (noting that parties to the litigation asserted in the lower courts that there had been "a continuous pattern of violence and harassment directed against the patients and staff of abortion clinics" and that the district court had concluded that these practices "would be increased" by the required disclosures).

9. See, Talley v. California, 362 U.S. 60, 80 S.Ct. 536, 4 L.Ed.2d 559 (1960) (invalidating a city ban on unsigned handbills).

10. See, e.g., NAACP v. Alabama ex rel. Patterson, 357 U.S. 449, 78 S.Ct. 1163, 2 L.Ed.2d 1488 (1958) (finding invalid a compelled disclosure of NAACP membership list because the disclosure was not narrowly tailored to an overriding interest of the state), on remand 268 Ala. 531, 109 So.2d 138 (1959) judgment of Alabama Supreme Court reversed 360 U.S. 240, 79 S.Ct. 1001, 3 L.Ed.2d 1205 (1959) (per curiam), rehearing denied 361 U.S. 856, 80 S.Ct. 43, 4 L.Ed.2d 96 (1959).

11. The Court also relied on Lamont v. Postmaster General, 381 U.S. 301, 85 S.Ct. 1493, 14 L.Ed.2d 398

(1965), in which the Court had invalidated a Post Office requirement that a recipient addressee affirmatively request that "communist" materials be delivered to him before the Post Office would make such a delivery.

12. Thornburgh v. American College of Obstetricians and Gynecologists, 476 U.S. 747, 770–772, 106 S.Ct. 2169, 2184–85, 90 L.Ed.2d 779 (1986).

13. See, e.g., Winston v. Lee, 470 U.S. 753, 105 S.Ct. 1611, 84 L.Ed.2d 662 (1985) (Fourth Amendment prohibits court from ordering serious surgical procedure to obtain bullet from a criminal defendant on the facts in this case). In several cases the Court has noted the existence of issues relating to a possible right of privacy regarding personal data without ruling on these issues.

In Nixon v. Administrator of General Services, 433 U.S. 425, 97 S.Ct. 2777, 53 L.Ed.2d 867 (1977), the Court upheld the Presidential Recordings and Materials Act and the requirement that former President Nixon leave certain papers and tapes in control of the government. Because of the overriding interest of the nation in these records, the Court upheld the Act, even assuming that Mr. Nixon had a constitutionally protected privacy interest as to some portion of these items.

ments, the Court has failed to acknowledge the possibility of other "privacy" limitations on governmental data collection practices. The Supreme Court has held that neither Amendment was violated by a federal law requiring banks to obtain and record information concerning their customers and their customer's financial transactions.[14]

Thereafter, in *United States v. Miller*,[15] the Court held that the government could subpoena bank records of specific persons in an investigation of criminal activity. The majority opinion in *Miller* found that individuals had no expectation of privacy in the records, checks, or deposit slips which were kept by their bank. Unless the Court would begin to recognize some general right of privacy limitation on government data collection, *Miller* would allow the government to engage in the wholesale collection and examination of data concerning the financial transactions of persons not connected to criminal activity.[16]

The Court has also held that a search of newspaper offices, pursuant to warrant, for photographic evidence of the identity of demonstrators who had severely beaten police officers was not unconstitutional. In *Zurcher v. Stanford Daily*,[17] a majority of the Court found that a search pursuant to a valid warrant is constitutionally sound even when the owner or possessor of the premises searched is not suspected of any crime. The Court then went on to hold that the First and Fourth Amendments permit searches of press offices pursuant to warrant and do not require use of the less intrusive subpoena *duces tecum* where practicable. The Court reasoned that the reasonableness, specificity, and probable cause requirements of the warrant procedure provided sufficient protection to First Amendment interests, and noted that, where such requirements were properly applied, there would be no occasion for police to "rummage at large in newspaper files."[18]

Zurcher makes plain the fact that, in the context of a criminal investigation, privacy interests endangered by government actions will be tested and protected almost exclusively under the Fourth Amendment. The majority opinion, however, did emphasize that where "the materials sought to be seized may be protected by the First Amendment, the requirements of the Fourth Amendment must be applied with scrupulous exactitude."[19]

In dissent, Justice Stewart, with whom Justice Marshall joined, observed that the majori-

---

14. California Bankers Association v. Shultz, 416 U.S. 21, 94 S.Ct. 1494, 39 L.Ed.2d 812 (1974). This decision upheld the general record keeping requirements because the majority saw that as reasonable regulation of financial institutions and related to the preservation of information that might be used for legitimate governmental purposes. For citations to additional Supreme Court cases on this point, see R. Rotunda & J. Nowak, Treatise on Constitutional Law: Substance and Procedure, vol. 3, § 18.30 (3rd ed.1999, with annual supplements).

15. 425 U.S. 435, 96 S.Ct. 1619, 48 L.Ed.2d 71 (1976).

16. Similarly, the Court has held that telephone companies could be directed to assist federal law enforcement officials in the installation of pen register devices on telephone lines, so long as the federal authorities had secured a search warrant authorizing the installation of such devices. United States v. New York Telephone Co., 434 U.S. 159, 98 S.Ct. 364, 54 L.Ed.2d 376 (1977).

The Supreme Court held that the Fourth Amendment did not restrict the use of pen register devices, which record the telephone numbers dialed from a particular telephone, at telephone company offices because the person using the telephone does not have a "legitimate expectation of privacy" in the dialed phone numbers. Smith v. Maryland, 442 U.S. 735, 99 S.Ct. 2577, 61 L.Ed.2d 220 (1979).

For further analysis, see 3 R. Rotunda & J. Nowak, Treatise on Constitutional Law: Substance and Procedure

§ 18.30 (3d ed. 1999, with annual supplements). For an examination of all Fourth Amendment issues, see Wayne LaFave, Treatise on Search and Seizure (3rd Edition, 1999, with annual supplements).

17. 436 U.S. 547, 98 S.Ct. 1970, 56 L.Ed.2d 525 (1978).

18. 436 U.S. at 566, 98 S.Ct. at 1982.

19. 436 U.S. at 564, 98 S.Ct. at 1981. Justice Powell, in a concurring opinion, noted that, as the Court's opinion makes clear, newspapers might receive added protection because magistrates considering warrants for searches of press facilities "can and should take cognizance of the independent values protected by the First Amendment." 436 U.S. at 570, 98 S.Ct. at 1983 (Powell, J., concurring). The First Amendment grants the press the right to disclose some information given to the press by persons who obtained the information through means that violated statutes designed to protect the privacy of individuals. See, Bartnicki v. Vopper, 532 U.S. 514 121 S.Ct. 1753, 149 L.Ed.2d 787 (2001) (statutory prohibition against disclosing communications that were illegally intercepted could not be applied to the disclosure of information about a cellular telephone call that was broadcast by a news media entity, so long as the news media entity did not have any connection to the illegal activity that intercepted the telephone conversation).

ty holding would allow police to "ransack the files of a newspaper," and would ultimately result in a chilling of confidential sources and a suppression of news.[20] But this dissent did not challenge the general ability of government agents to search for evidence of a crime in the possession of innocent persons.

Only Justice Stevens noted the relationship between *Zurcher* and the danger posed to the privacy interests of private, non-media persons. He would have required the police to use the subpoena procedure in order to limit the number and scope of searches of persons not suspected of committing a crime.[21]

For many years it had been the law that the Fourth Amendment allowed searches only for instrumentalities or fruits of a crime, or other contraband items. However, in *Warden v. Hayden*[22] the Court ruled that a search for evidence of a crime based upon probable cause and, in most instances, a procedurally proper warrant would comply with the Fourth Amendment. This ruling opened two new privacy issues: (1) whether government agents could search for a defendant's records or other written evidence of his criminal activity, and (2) whether searches for "mere evidence" of a crime believed to be possessed by persons not suspected of criminal activity required special justification. In *Andresen v. Maryland*[23] the Court resolved the first issue by finding that the police could search for records of criminal

activity even though the records were "testimonial" in nature. In *Zurcher* the Court resolved the second issue by finding that third person searches were allowed upon a basic finding of probable cause to believe that the person possessed evidence of a crime, even though he had not been involved in the criminal activity. Whether these decisions foreclose the use of a more generalized right to privacy analysis to limit probable cause searches by the police remains unclear.

The Justices appear to be willing to limit governmental activity relating to the collection and distribution of data only when that activity impairs First Amendment rights[24] or constitutional restrictions on the criminal justice process. Yet the concept of a "right to privacy" should impose some requirement of reasonableness on government officials who engage in such activity.[25]

In considering the extent to which the right to privacy may limit the government collection and use of data concerning private individuals, it is important to remember that the Supreme Court has held that the press could not be prohibited, consistently with the First Amendment, from reporting information which was lawfully obtained from public records.[26] Nor can persons who are not participants in confidential judicial proceeding be subject to criminal sanctions for publishing accurate reports of such proceedings.[27] Because individuals

20. Zurcher v. Stanford Daily, 436 U.S. 547, 571–574, 98 S.Ct. 1970, 1984–86, 56 L.Ed.2d 525 (1978) (Stewart & Marshall, JJ., dissenting.)

21. Zurcher v. Stanford Daily, 436 U.S. 547, 582–583, 98 S.Ct. 1970, 1990–91, 56 L.Ed.2d 525 (1978) (Stevens, J., dissenting).

22. 387 U.S. 294, 87 S.Ct. 1642, 18 L.Ed.2d 782 (1967).

23. 427 U.S. 463, 96 S.Ct. 2737, 49 L.Ed.2d 627 (1976).

24. The ability of a government official to disclose information regarding an individual citizen or organization may be limited by statute or court rule in such a way that constitutional issues may be avoided. Cf. Illinois v. Abbott & Associates, Inc., 460 U.S. 557, 103 S.Ct. 1356, 75 L.Ed.2d 281 (1983) (federal statute authorizing attorney general of the United States to make available federal antitrust grand jury materials to a state attorney general does not dispense with requirement for a showing of a particularized need for the grand jury material by the state).

25. Laws requiring disclosure of information regarding political candidates, political parties or campaign contribu-

tors are subject to independent judicial review to determine if they comply with the principles of the First Amendment. The campaign disclosure law which requires every political party to disclose the names of members of the party or campaign contributors may not be applied to a minor political party which has demonstrated that it is subject to private or governmental hostility and that disclosures will impair the rights of the freedom of speech and association of members of the party. See, Brown v. Socialist Workers '74 Campaign Committee, 459 U.S. 87, 103 S.Ct. 416, 74 L.Ed.2d 250 (1982).

26. Cox Broadcasting Corp. v. Cohn, 420 U.S. 469, 95 S.Ct. 1029, 43 L.Ed.2d 328 (1975).

27. Landmark Communications, Inc. v. Virginia, 435 U.S. 829, 98 S.Ct. 1535, 56 L.Ed.2d 1 (1978). See also Smith v. Daily Mail Publishing Co., 443 U.S. 97, 99 S.Ct. 2667, 61 L.Ed.2d 399 (1979) (state may not punish a newspaper's truthful publication of an alleged juvenile delinquent's name lawfully obtained by a newspaper).

Parties to a proceeding, however, may be restricted in their use of information gained through the litigation

cannot be punished for reporting information lawfully obtained from government records, the government might be under some duty to exclude public access to records concerning private individuals. The extent to which the government will be able to keep such records secret depends upon what, if any, right of access to government records is granted to members of the press or public under the First Amendment.[28]

Even if the Supreme Court were to define a right to privacy that would limit government data collection practices, it might be quite difficult for anyone to maintain a lawsuit that would vindicate that right. The Court has held that an injury to an individual's reputation through the release of even false data about him does not establish a constitutional violation, although this decision may be only a limitation of procedural due process principles.[29] In any event, unless an individual could show identifiable harm from government investigation or data collection practices that individual would not have standing to maintain a suit to limit such practices.[30]

(b) The Right to Die

As Professor Yale Kamisar has noted, there is no "right to die" issue presented in a case unless the case involves a decision to reject life sustaining medical treatment that was made by a mentally competent adult who has made a decision to refuse medical treatment for himself based on the most complete information that he can receive.[31] When the case involves an individual who is not competent to make a decision regarding her own medical treatment

(perhaps because she is in a coma) there is no right to die issue. Whenever a case involves the question of whether a patient's doctor, family, or a designated "surrogate" should determine whether life support systems should be employed for a comatose individual, the case could be considered a "right to kill" case, according to Professor Kamisar.

If a state allows persons other than the individual patient to make a decision to refuse or terminate life sustaining treatment for that individual, the state should create some procedure to protect the life, liberty, and property interests of the patient whose medical treatment will be terminated. The due process clause of the Fourteenth Amendment (applicable to state and local government actions) or the due process clause of the Fifth Amendment (applicable to actions of the federal government) should be considered when determining whether the government may create a system in which the life of one person is terminated by the decision of another person. A decision to terminate life support for a comatose individual will involve "state action" if the decision is made pursuant to a court order or if the individual is being treated at a government hospital.[32] The due process clause should require a process that fairly determines whether the interests of the individual who is to die (after the termination of the life sustaining treatment) have been fairly appraised. If a doctor at a state hospital withdraws life sustaining treatment or nutrition from a comatose patient, the government has taken the life of the individual. There should have been

---

process. Seattle Times Co. v. Rhinehart, 467 U.S. 20, 104 S.Ct. 2199, 81 L.Ed.2d 17 (1984) (upholding trial court protective order restricting use of information gained through pretrial discovery process).

28. See § 16.19. For references to cases, and secondary authorities, on this point see the multi-volume edition of this Treatise: R. Rotunda & J. Nowak, Treatise on Constitutional law: Substance and Procedure §§ 18.30, 20.19 (3rd ed. 1999, with annual supplements).

29. Paul v. Davis, 424 U.S. 693, 96 S.Ct. 1155, 47 L.Ed.2d 405 (1976). See § 13.5, supra.

30. Laird v. Tatum, 408 U.S. 1, 92 S.Ct. 2318, 33 L.Ed.2d 154 (1972), rehearing denied 409 U.S. 901, 93 S.Ct. 94, 34 L.Ed.2d 165 (1972).

31. Yale Kamisar, On the Meaning and Impact of the Physician–Assisted Suicide Cases, 82 Minn. L. Rev. 895 (1998); Yale Kamisar, The Reasons So Many People Sup-

port Physician–Assisted Suicide–And Why These Reasons Are Not Convincing, 12 Issues in Law & Medicine, 113 (1996); Yale Kamisar, The "Right to Die": On Drawing (and Erasing) Lines, 35 Duquesne L. Rev. 481, (1996). See also, Wright, J., dissenting, quoting Treatise in, Compassion In Dying v. State of Wash., 49 F.3d 586, 595–96 (9th Cir.1995), rehearing en banc granted 62 F.3d 299 (9th Cir.1995). For references to additional secondary authorities on this point see the multi-volume edition of this Treatise: R. Rotunda & J. Nowak, Treatise on Constitutional Law: Substance and Procedure § 18.30 (3rd ed. 1999, with annual supplements).

32. For an analysis of the concept of state action see Chapter 12 of this Treatise.

some fair process to determine that the decision to withdraw life support was not made arbitrarily or for malevolent purpose (such as a decision by a family member who desired to inherit the property of the comatose individual).[33]

The question of whether the Constitution of the United States limits the government's ability to require doctors and hospitals to take all means to sustain the life of an individual, when that individual or his family objected to the medical treatment, is of recent origin. Some Supreme Court rulings on the free exercise of religion might be interpreted to give support to the argument that the government could not force an individual to accept medical treatment that violated the principles of his religion.[34] Before 1990, there was no indication that there was any substantive constitutional right, apart from the religion clauses, to refuse life sustaining medical treatment.

Cruzan v. Director, Missouri Department of Health[35] upheld a state's ability to require family members to prove by clear and convincing evidence that an incompetent person would desire to order the withdrawal of life sustaining treatment. There was a 5 to 4 division in *Cruzan* and the ruling in the case was a narrow one. The concurring opinion of Justice O'Connor in *Cruzan,* and dicta in the majority opinion, resulted in the states being left with little guidance regarding whether they were required to recognize any type of right to refuse life sustaining medical treatment.

The *Cruzan* decision involved a review of Missouri law. The Missouri Supreme Court had found that state law required a hospital to give life sustaining treatment to an individual (at least when the individual was under the control of the government) unless: (1) the individual was a mentally competent adult who refused the medical treatment on the basis of adequate information[36] or, (2) the guardian (or close family members) of a patient who was not competent could prove by "clear and convincing evidence" that the incompetent patient would have rejected life sustaining treatment under the circumstances present in the case.

In *Cruzan,* the Supreme Court of the United States held that the state supreme court ruling requiring parents or guardians to prove that the individual would have rejected the treatment by clear and convincing evidence did not violate any principle established by the Fourteenth Amendment to the Constitution of the United States. The majority opinion, written by Chief Justice Rehnquist, assumed for the purposes of the case (but did not decide) that the "liberty" protected by the due process clauses of the Fifth and Fourteenth Amendments included a right of mentally competent individuals to refuse life saving or life sustaining medical treatment.[37] Even assuming that such a right existed, the majority found that the state could limit the ability to refuse such medical treatment to the person herself or to a guardian who established the intent of the comatose individual by clear and convincing evidence. The importance of the individual interest at stake (the termination of the individual's life) justified the state's decision to use a standard of proof that reduced the chance for error. The state could refuse to make an independent judgment about the quality of a life. The state was not required to accept decisions of family members that the

---

33. For an analysis of the procedural fairness requirements established by the due process clause see Chapter 13 of this Treatise.

34. There is no Supreme Court decision holding that an individual has a right to reject medical treatment that was inconsistent with his religious beliefs. However, the free exercise clause decisions of the Supreme Court could be used to argue for the recognition of a mentally competent adult to reject medical treatment inconsistent with his sincerely held religious beliefs. See, e.g., Application of the President and Directors of Georgetown College, Inc., 331 F.2d 1010, 1015 (D.C.Cir.1964) (petition for rehearing en banc—Burger, J., dissenting). Regarding

free exercise clause analysis, see §§ 13.6, 13.9 of this Treatise.

35. 497 U.S. 261, 110 S.Ct. 2841, 111 L.Ed.2d 224 (1990).

36. The Missouri Supreme Court had based the right of a competent adult to refuse medical treatment on state law and not on the basis of a federal constitutional right. Cruzan v. Harmon, 760 S.W.2d 408 (Mo.1988).

37. Cruzan v. Director, Missouri Department of Health, 497 U.S. 261, 279, 110 S.Ct. 2841, 2852, 111 L.Ed.2d 224 (1990).

best interest of the patient would be saved by terminating medical treatment. The state could prefer the preservation of life over other interests asserted on behalf of the individual, at least in a situation where the patient herself had not made the decision to reject life sustaining treatment.

A Return to the *Lochner* Era? The majority opinion in *Cruzan* found it unnecessary to determine whether an individual right to refuse medical treatment could be based on the fundamental right of privacy. Chief Justice Rehnquist found that the history of state law rulings regarding an individual's right to refuse medical treatment showed societal recognition of the right. The Chief Justice also referred to prior Supreme Court cases concerning the ability of states to force an individual to be vaccinated [38] and prior Supreme Court cases regarding government ordered mental health care treatment for persons in its custody.[39] The majority opinion only assumed "for purposes of this case" that a mentally competent adult had a right to refuse medical treatment, the majority opinion stated: "we think the logic of the cases discussed above [vaccination cases and mental health care cases] would embrace such a liberty interest."[40]

In cases decided since 1937, the Supreme Court has found that judges should not make an independent assessment as to whether a law is an impermissible restriction of liberty unless the law restricts a fundamental right. Substantive restrictions on liberty are upheld so long as there is a rational relationship between the law at issue and any arguably legitimate interest of government.[41] In procedural

due process cases, wherein an individual is being restrained or having a constitutional right taken from him, the Court will determine the fairness of procedures used to determine that the individual's liberty interest should be taken.[42] In the modern era, substantive restrictions on liberty (the rules that limit individual choices in life) are only subjected to independent judicial review if the right restricted was a fundamental right.

The *Cruzan* majority opinion might support the argument that the judiciary is free to invalidate any restriction on individual liberty unless the government can prove that law at issue only limited individual liberty in order to prevent harm to societal interests. That was the argument used to justify substantive due process between 1900 and 1937. In the so-called "*Lochner* Era," the Supreme Court invalidated a variety of worker protection laws on the theory that each worker had the liberty to agree to work for extremely low wages or for extremely long hours. State laws prohibiting such an exercise of "liberty" were invalid because the state had been unable to prove to the Supreme Court's satisfaction that those employment practices harmed legitimate societal interests.[43]

In *Cruzan* the Court only assumed, and did not decide, that an individual had a right to refuse life saving treatment. It seems unlikely that Chief Justice Rehnquist meant to use this case as a step toward "*Lochner*–Era" judicial review of state and federal regulatory actions under the concept of substantive due process. Nevertheless, if the *Cruzan* majority opinion had focused on the question of whether the

---

38. "In Jacobson v. Massachusetts, 197 U.S. 11, 24–30, 25 S.Ct. 358, 360–361, 49 L.Ed. 643 (1905), for instance, the Court balanced an individual's liberty interest in declining an unwanted smallpox vaccine against the state's interest in preventing disease." Cruzan v. Director, Missouri Department of Health, 497 U.S. 261, 278, 110 S.Ct. 2841, 2851, 111 L.Ed.2d 224 (1990). In *Jacobson*, the Court had upheld the vaccination requirement although the individual objected to the vaccination on the basis of religious beliefs.

39. 497 U.S. at 278, 110 S.Ct. at 2851. The Chief Justice referred to cases regarding: the commitment to a mental health care facility of persons who had not been convicted of crimes; the due process rights of prisoners who were being transferred to a mental health care facili-

ty. These cases involve procedural due process principles limiting the ability of government to deprive a person of liberty without a fair procedure. The Supreme Court's decisions concerning the process that is required before committing someone (whether or not they are an inmate in a prison) to a mental health care facility are examined in §§ 13.4, 13.9 of this Treatise.

40. 497 U.S. at 279, 110 S.Ct. at 2852.

41. See § 11.4 "Substantive Due Process Since 1937."

42. See §§ 13.4, 13.9 for an analysis of procedural due process cases.

43. See § 11.3 "Substantive Due Process from 1900 to 1936."

constitutional right at issue was a fundamental right that justified independent judicial review, the opinion would have been easier to understand in terms of post–1937 substantive due process and equal protection decisions of the Supreme Court.[44]

A Right to Die? The majority opinion in *Cruzan* left open the question of whether the due process clauses establish a right to refuse lifesaving medical treatment. Chief Justice Rehnquist only assumed that such a right existed for the purpose of deciding the case. The opinions of the four dissenting Justices,[45] and the concurring opinion of Justice O'Connor,[46] indicate that at least five Justices, on the date the *Cruzan* case was decided, believed that there was a right of a mentally competent adult to refuse lifesaving medical treatment or lifesaving nutrition. However, there was no majority opinion or ruling regarding the issue of whether there is a "right to die."

The Court did not determine, in *Cruzan*, whether a competent adult could designate another person to make decisions regarding life sustaining or lifesaving medical treatment for her, if she was in a condition that made her incompetent to make that decision herself.[47] Of course, if there were no right to reject lifesaving treatment, there would be no right to appoint a "surrogate" decisionmaker. The four dissenters in *Cruzan* believed that an individual had a right to control the decision to reject life sustaining treatment through the appointment of a surrogate. Justice O'Connor's concurring opinion indicated that she might vote to require states to honor both medical decisions made by the patient while she was competent, and the decisions of a surrogate who had been given the power to make such decisions by the now comatose patient at a point in time when the patient was competent to make that decision.[48]

As pointed out in Justice Scalia's concurring opinion in *Cruzan*,[49] if an individual has a constitutionally protected right to refuse life-saving medical treatment and life sustaining nutrition, it would seem to be unconstitutional for a state to make it a crime for that person to take active steps to terminate his life. If an individual has a right to refuse life sustaining nutrition, and, thereby, starve to death, then it is hard to understand why the decision to commit suicide could be a basis for committing the person to a mental health care facility.

One answer to the questions raised by Justice Scalia is that only a mentally competent adult would have a constitutional right to refuse medical treatment. Some state laws allow for involuntary commitment of an adult to a mental health care facility if the government, or other persons, can prove that the individual represents a danger to himself. Are these commitment statutes constitutional? But, if there is a "right to die" how could a court order mental health care for a person whose only "abnormal behavior" is his stated desire to kill himself? A court would be unable to determine whether such a person was a "competent adult" or an "incompetent adult" unless the court decided whether the individual had correctly decided that the continuation of his life was not worthwhile. In other words, if there were a constitutional right to die, it would seem difficult for courts to avoid making quality of life decisions when determining whether an individual could be held in a mental health care facility solely because he might kill himself.

In 1997 the Supreme Court refused to extend the *Cruzan* ruling, as the Court held that

44. See: § 14.3 "An Introduction to Standards of Review Under the Equal Protection Guarantee"; § 11.4 "Substantive Due Process Since 1937"; § 11.7 "Fundamental Rights."

45. Cruzan v. Director, Missouri Department of Health, 497 U.S. 261, 301, 110 S.Ct. 2841, 2863, 111 L.Ed.2d 224 (1990) (Brennan, J., joined by Marshall and Blackmun, JJ., dissenting). 497 U.S. at 330, 110 S.Ct. at 2878 (Stevens, J., dissenting).

46. 497 U.S. at 287, 110 S.Ct. at 2856 (O'Connor, J., concurring).

47. Cruzan v. Director, Missouri Department of Health, 497 U.S. 261, 287 n. 12, 110 S.Ct. 2841, 2856 n. 12, 111 L.Ed.2d 224 (1990).

48. 497 U.S. at 290–92, 110 S.Ct. at 2857–58 (O'Connor, J., concurring).

49. Cruzan v. Director, Missouri Department of Health, 497 U.S. 261, 292–301, 110 S.Ct. 2841, 2859–63, 111 L.Ed.2d 224 (1990) (Scalia, J., concurring). The various questions raised in the remaining paragraphs of this section are based upon Justice Scalia's concurring opinion.

state statutes prohibiting a person from assisting another person to commit suicide did not violate substantive due process or equal protection principles. While the Justices were unanimous in upholding the statutes on their face, the decisions left open significant questions concerning the extent of a terminally ill patient's constitutional right to choose, and a physician's right to provide, medical treatment that would relieve the patient's pain, but hasten the patient's death.

In *Washington v. Glucksberg*[50] the Supreme Court considered a substantive due process challenge to a state law prohibiting anyone from aiding another person to commit suicide. The United States Court of Appeals for the Ninth Circuit had found that the plaintiffs, who had alleged that they were in terminal phases of painful illnesses, were denied liberty without due process by a statute that prohibited them from receiving assistance in terminating their life as they wished.[51] The Justices of the United States Supreme Court unanimously overruled the Ninth Circuit; the Justices ruled that the statute, on its face, did not violate due process.

In *Vacco v. Quill*[52] the Court considered a claim by physicians in New York that state statutes that made it a crime for them to assist persons in the commission of suicide during a terminal illness violated the equal protection clause of the Fourteenth Amendment. New York statutes allowed mentally competent terminally ill persons to refuse, or direct the removal of, life support systems but did not allow terminally ill persons to receive medical assistance to hasten their death by other means (such as a lethal dose of medication). The United States Court of Appeals for the Second Circuit believed that the statutory classifications violated equal protection.[53] The Jus-

tices were unanimous in overturning the Court of Appeals decision; the Supreme Court ruled that the distinction between suicide and refusing lifesaving medical support did not violate equal protection.

Chief Justice Rehnquist wrote the majority opinions in both *Glucksberg* and *Vacco*. The Chief Justice's opinions involved straight-forward applications of the substantive due process and equal protection analysis used by the Supreme Court since 1937. In both cases, the Chief Justice first considered whether the ability to commit suicide was a fundamental right. If there was a fundamental constitutional right to commit suicide, then the Court would have to engage in independent scrutiny of the legislative ends, to determine if those ends were sufficiently compelling, and the relationship between each law and those ends.[54] However, if the ability to commit suicide was not a fundamental right (and the right was not allocated on a suspect basis, such as through the use of a racial classification) the statutes prohibiting assistance to persons who wanted to commit suicide would have a presumption of constitutionality. With the presumption of constitutionality, such laws would be upheld unless the persons attacking those laws could show that there was no conceivable state of facts under which the statutes might be rationally related to any legitimate interest of government.[55] Because the Supreme Court in *Glucksberg* and *Vacco* found that there was no fundamental right to commit suicide, it used the rational basis standard to find that: (1) the prohibition on assisted suicides did not violate substantive due process; and (2) the distinction between allowing individuals to refuse life

50. 521 U.S. 702, 117 S.Ct. 2258, 138 L.Ed.2d 772 (1997).

51. Compassion in Dying v. Washington, 49 F.3d 586 (9th Cir.1995), rev'd, Washington v. Glucksberg, 521 U.S. 702, 117 S.Ct. 2258, 138 L.Ed.2d 772 (1997).

52. 521 U.S. 793, 117 S.Ct. 2293, 138 L.Ed.2d 834 (1997).

53. Quill v. Vacco, 80 F.3d 716 (2d Cir.1996), rev'd, Vacco v. Quill, 521 U.S. 793, 117 S.Ct. 2293, 138 L.Ed.2d 834 (1997).

54. Washington v. Glucksberg 521 U.S. 702, 772, 117 S.Ct. 2258, 2268, 138 L.Ed.2d 772 (1997); See also, Vacco v. Quill, 521 U.S. 793, 799–800, 117 S.Ct. 2293, 2297–98, 138 L.Ed.2d 834 (1997).

55. Washington v. Glucksberg 521 U.S. 702, 726–28, 117 S.Ct. 2258, 2271, 138 L.Ed.2d 772 (1997); Vacco v. Quill, 521 U.S. 793, 800, 117 S.Ct. 2293, 2298, 138 L.Ed.2d 834 (1997).

support and the prohibition of suicide did not violate equal protection.[56]

The Court's primary consideration whether an individual has a fundamental constitutional right to commit suicide was set forth in *Washington v. Glucksberg*.[57] Chief Justice Rehnquist wrote for five Justices in ruling that an individual did not have a fundamental constitutional right to terminate his or her life. The Chief Justice noted that the Court would begin its consideration of the substantive due process claim "as we do in all due process cases, by examining our nation's history, legal traditions, and practices."[58] With a method of analysis similar to that set forth in Professor Kamisar's articles concerning assisted suicides, Chief Justice Rehnquist found that the history of legal treatment of society in the United States, and the difficulty of precisely defining a "right" to commit suicide, led to the conclusion that "the asserted right to assistance in committing suicide is not a fundamental liberty interest."[59]

Chief Justice Rehnquist noted that, when determining whether a right was fundamental, the Court would examine whether the asserted right was "deeply rooted in this nation's history and tradition" and whether it was possible for the judiciary to establish a "careful description of the asserted fundamental interest."[60] The Chief Justice acknowledged that government infringement of a fundamental right would have to be "narrowly tailored to serve a compelling state interest."[61] However, because the right to engage in suicide was not a fundamental constitutional interest, the prohibition on assisted suicide only had to be "rationally related to legitimate government interest."[62] The majority had no difficulty in upholding the ban on assisted suicides under the rationality test, because the Chief Justice

found that the states had legitimate interests in the preservation of human life, the integrity of the medical profession, and the protection of vulnerable groups of persons who might feel pressured in to terminating their lives.[63]

The majority opinion in *Vacco v. Quill*[64] tracked the reasoning of *Glucksberg*. The State of New York allowed mentally competent adults, under certain circumstances, to refuse life sustaining medical treatment although the state prohibited anyone from aiding another person to commit suicide. Physicians asserted that the statutes prohibiting a terminally ill patient from receiving assistance in suicide while allowing other patients to refuse life sustaining medical treatment created an arbitrary classification that violated the equal protection clause. Because the New York statute did not employ traits such as race, gender, or legitimacy which would have justified independent judicial review of the classification, the classification would not be subjected to independent judicial review, and so-called strict scrutiny, unless the asserted right (to commit suicide) was a fundamental constitutional right.[65] The majority in *Vacco* ruled that there was no fundamental right to commit suicide, and, therefore, that the distinction between allowing a patient to refuse medical treatment and prohibiting a patient from receiving assistance in committing suicide was subject only to the rational basis test. The classification, according to the majority, had to be upheld so long as there was any possible relationship between the classification and any legitimate state interest.[66] In *Vacco* the Chief Justice found that the distinction in the statutes was rationally related to the state's interests in the health and welfare of individuals and the ethics of the medical profession. Indeed, according

56. Washington v. Glucksberg 521 U.S. 702, 726–35, 117 S.Ct. 2258, 2271–75, 138 L.Ed.2d 772 (1997); Vacco v. Quill, 521 U.S. 793, 807–09, 117 S.Ct. 2293, 2301–2, 138 L.Ed.2d 834 (1997).

57. 521 U.S. 702, 117 S.Ct. 2258, 138 L.Ed.2d 772 (1997).

58. 521 U.S. at 710, 117 S.Ct. at 2262.

59. 521 U.S. at 727–28, 117 S.Ct. at 2271. References to Professor Kamisar's articles are referred to at several places in this section of the Treatise. Chief Justice Rehnquist's majority opinion referred to some of Professor Kamisar's writing on this subject. Washington v. Glucks-

berg, 521 U.S. 702, 733 n. 23, 117 S.Ct. 2258, 2274 n. 23, 138 L.Ed.2d 772 (1997).

60. 521 U.S. at 721, 117 S.Ct. at 2268.

61. 521 U.S. at 721, 117 S.Ct. at 2268.

62. 521 U.S. at 728, 117 S.Ct. at 2271.

63. 521 U.S. at 727–36, 117 S.Ct. at 2271–75.

64. 521 U.S. 793, 117 S.Ct. 2293, 138 L.Ed.2d 834 (1997).

65. 521 U.S. at 799–800, 117 S.Ct. at 2297.

66. 521 U.S. at 799–801, 117 S.Ct. at 2297–98.

to the majority opinion, each person in New York was treated in an identical manner in the sense that every person had the right under state law to refuse unwanted life saving medical treatment and no person was allowed to assist in the commission of a suicide.[67] The distinction between suicide and refusal of life support, in the statutes, followed longstanding "legal principles of causation and intent" that had been used in the law.[68] Thus, the statutory classifications were rationally related to legitimate state interests.

The Justices were unanimous in upholding the Washington and New York statutes prohibiting assisted suicide on their face. Nevertheless, the concurring opinions in *Glucksberg* and *Vacco* demonstrated that there were at least four Justices in 1997 who believed that, in a future case, the Supreme Court might rule that a person facing imminent death has a fundamental right to receive medical treatment that would ease his pain even though the treatment would invariably hasten his death.

Justice O'Connor concurred in the majority opinions written by Chief Justice Rehnquist, but she also wrote a concurring opinion in *Glucksberg* and *Vacco*.[69] She asserted that the majority had not addressed, and there was no need to reach, "the question of whether suffering patients have a constitutionally cognizable interest in obtaining relief from suffering" that might hasten their deaths.[70] Justices Ginsburg and Breyer were willing to join Justice O'Connor only to the extent that she was

explaining the questions left open by the Court.[71] Neither Justice Ginsburg nor Breyer was willing to join any part of the Chief Justice's majority opinion.

Justice Stevens concurred in the judgments in *Glucksberg* and *Vacco* only to the extent that the Court had refused to overturn each statutory ban on assisting suicides in its entirety.[72] Justice Stevens asserted that significant constitutional questions might be raised, on a case by case basis, as to whether a ban on assisted suicide could be used to prohibit individuals from receiving, and doctors from administering, drugs that would hasten an otherwise certain death and reduce the extent of pain that an individual had to endure before.

In *Washington v. Glucksberg*, Justice Souter, concurred only in the judgment of the Court with a lengthy opinion that was not joined by any other Justice.[73] Justice Souter tracked the reasoning that had been used by Justice Harlan in his dissent in *Poe v. Ullman* to determine whether an asserted right was of such "constitutional significance" that the judiciary should independently review whether the asserted ends of government were important enough to restrict the right and whether the means used by the government were narrowly tailored to promote the asserted important interest.[74] After an extensive review of the Supreme Court's substantive due process cases, Justice Souter concluded that at this point in our history, the legislatures as opposed to the judiciary, "have superior opportunities to ob-

---

67. 521 U.S. at 801–02, 117 S.Ct. at 2298.

68. 521 U.S. at 801–02, 117 S.Ct. at 2298.

69. Justice O'Connor's single concurring opinion, for the two cases, appears as:

Washington v. Glucksberg 521 U.S. 702, 736, 117 S.Ct. 2302, 2303, 138 L.Ed.2d 772 (1997) (O'Connor, J., joined, in part, by Ginsburg and Breyer, JJ., concurring); Vacco v. Quill, 521 U.S. 793, 736, 117 S.Ct. 2293, 2303, 138 L.Ed.2d 834 (1997) (O'Connor, J., joined, in part, by Ginsburg and Breyer, JJ., concurring).

70. 521 U.S. at 736, 117 S.Ct. at 2303 (O'Connor, J., joined, in part, by Ginsburg and Breyer, JJ. concurring).

71. Justice Ginsburg's one paragraph opinion for the two cases appears as: Washington v. Glucksberg 521 U.S. 702, 789, 117 S.Ct. 2302, 2310, 138 L.Ed.2d 772 (1997) (Ginsburg, J., concurring); Vacco v. Quill, 521 U.S. 793, 789, 117 S.Ct. 2293, 2310, 138 L.Ed.2d 834 (1997) (Ginsburg, J., concurring in the judgments).

Justice Breyer's brief concurring opinion in the two cases appears as: Washington v. Glucksberg 521 U.S. 702, 789, 117 S.Ct. 2302, 2310, 138 L.Ed.2d 772 (1997) (Breyer, J., concurring in the judgments); Vacco v. Quill, 521 U.S. 793, 789, 117 S.Ct. 2293, 2310, 138 L.Ed.2d 830 (1997) (Breyer, J., concurring in the judgments).

72. The opinion of Justice Stevens appears as: Washington v. Glucksberg 521 U.S. 702, 738, 117 S.Ct. 2302, 2304, 138 L.Ed.2d 772 (1997) (Stevens, J., concurring in the judgments).

73. Washington v. Glucksberg, 521 U.S. 702, 752–89, 117 S.Ct. 2258, 2275–93, 138 L.Ed.2d 772 (1997) (Souter, J., concurring in the judgment).

74. Justice Souter's discussion of Justice Harlan's views, as set forth in Poe v. Ullman, 367 U.S. 497, 543, 81 S.Ct. 1752, 1777, 6 L.Ed.2d 989 (1961) (Harlan, J., dissenting) appears, in part at Washington v. Glucksberg, 521 U.S. 702, 752, 117 S.Ct. 2258, 2275, 2284, 138 L.Ed.2d 772 (1997) (Souter, J., concurring in the judgment).

tain the facts necessary for a judgment about the present controversy."[75] Thus, he concluded that "while I do not decide for all time that respondents claim [to assistance in terminating their life] should not be recognized, I acknowledge that the legislative institutional competence as the better one to deal with that claim at this time."[76]

In *Vacco*, Justice Souter explained that his review of substantive due process claims led him to believe that, at this time, the judiciary should not be second guessing legislative classifications concerning life support and medications that might relieve pain while hastening death.[77] Justice Souter claimed to be following the method of analysis used in marital privacy cases by the second Justice Harlan. Nevertheless, Justice Souter, appears ready to return to the type of reasonable review advocated by the first Justice Harlan in the "Lochner Era" and to second guess legislative judgments concerning a right to die in future years.[78]

§ 14.31 The Right to Vote: The Electoral Franchise as a Fundamental Right

(a)(1) Introduction

The Constitution initially contained two provisions that related to the exercise of the elec-

toral franchise. Article I, section two of the Constitution mandates that electors for members of the House of Representatives shall meet the same qualifications as "Electors for the most numerous Branch of the State Legislature."[1] Article II, section one and the Twelfth and Twentieth Amendments, establish the procedure whereby members of the Electoral College select the President and Vice-President.[2] Article II, section one grants the states discretion in the manner of selecting the members of the Electoral College. The Supreme Court has used these provisions to support the proposition that the states, because of this inherent constitutional authority to control the electoral process, can require persons to meet certain reasonable requirements before they vote in state or national elections.[3]

Later Amendments to the Constitution, however, have placed restrictions on the ability of states to impose franchise requirements. The Fifteenth Amendment, for example, prohibits the states from impairing the franchise on the basis "of race, color, or previous condition of servitude".[4] The Nineteenth Amendment forbids discrimination in voting by sex. The Twenty-Fourth Amendment prevents the states from imposing "any poll tax or other tax" on a person before that person can vote

---

75. Washington v. Glucksberg, 521 U.S. 702, 788–89, 117 S.Ct. 2258, 2293, 138 L.Ed.2d 772 (1997) (Souter, J., concurring in the judgment).

76. 521 U.S. at 788–89, 117 S.Ct. at 2293 (Souter, J., concurring in the judgment).

77. Vacco v. Quill, 521 U.S. 793, 809, 117 S.Ct. 2293, 2302, 138 L.Ed.2d 834 (1997) (Souter, J., concurring in the judgment). In 1998, Justice Souter wrote a majority opinion that employed a form of substantive due process analysis similar to the method of analysis employed in his concurring opinion in *Vacco*. Sacramento v. Lewis, 523 U.S. 833, 118 S.Ct. 1708, 140 L.Ed.2d 1043 (1998). The *Lewis* case is examined in § 10.6.

78. See § 11.3.

§ 14.31

1. "The House of Representatives shall be composed of Members chosen every second year by the People of the Several States, and the Electors in each State shall have the Qualifications requisite for Electors of the most numerous Branch of the State Legislature." U.S.Const. art. I, § 2, cl. 1.

2. "Each State shall appoint, in such Manner as the Legislature thereof may direct, a Number of Electors, equal to the whole Number of Senators and Representa-

tives to which the State may be entitled in the Congress; but no Senator or Representative, or Person holding an Office of Trust or Profit under the United States, shall be appointed an Elector." U.S.Const. art. II, § 1, cl. 2. See U.S.Const. amends. 12 and 20 for current procedures.

3. See, e.g., Kramer v. Union Free School District, 395 U.S. 621, 625, 89 S.Ct. 1886, 1888–89, 23 L.Ed.2d 583 (1969). The Court sustained residency and citizenship requirements in Marston v. Lewis, 410 U.S. 679, 93 S.Ct. 1211, 35 L.Ed.2d 627 (1973); Burns v. Fortson, 410 U.S. 686, 93 S.Ct. 1209, 35 L.Ed.2d 633 (1973). The Court discussed age requirements in Oregon v. Mitchell, 400 U.S. 112, 91 S.Ct. 260, 27 L.Ed.2d 272 (1970).

4. "The right of citizens of the United States to vote shall not be denied or abridged by the United States or by any State on account of race, color, or previous condition of servitude." U.S.Const. amend. 15, § 1. If any division of the federal or state governments were to use an explicit racial or ethnic classification to deny persons the right to vote in an election, that governmental action would violate the Fifteenth Amendment. See, Rice v. Cayetano, 528 U.S. 495, 120 S.Ct. 1044, 145 L.Ed.2d 1007 (2000) (the Court, by a 7 to 2 vote, invalidates a state constitutional provision limiting the ballot for trustees of a state agency managing a fund for two subclasses of state residents who

for a candidate for a federal office.[5] The Twenty-Sixth Amendment grants the right to vote to all citizens of the United States who are eighteen years of age or older.

Besides the explicit constitutional provisions that pertain to the election process, the Supreme Court has held that the Fourteenth Amendment restricts the power of the states to place qualifications on the exercise of the franchise in several ways. The Court has used the Amendment to fashion a fundamental right to vote.[6] It has recognized that the right to vote is one of those rights that "is preservative of other basic civil and political rights."[7] Therefore, any alleged impairment of the right should be subjected to "strict scrutiny" by the Court.[8] Because the right to vote is a fundamental right, any classification defining the ability to exercise the right must meet, under a strict scrutiny review, the dictates of the equal protection guarantee before the Court can sustain the measure as constitutional.[9] Additionally because the Fourteenth Amendment does apply to state laws that regulate the election process, the Court has recognized that Congress has some power to legislatively override the states' authority to govern the exercise of the franchise.[10]

Although the Supreme Court has restricted the authority of the states over the electoral process, at the same time, it has acknowledged the states' right to impose some restrictions on the right to vote. The right to vote is a fundamental right and restrictions on it are subject to "strict scrutiny" but in this context "strict scrutiny" means only that judges must independently review the voting regulation or restriction. If restriction is in fact related to important or overriding state interests, the Court will sustain that regulation or restriction. For example, the Court has upheld reasonable age, citizenship, and residency requirements.[11] The determination, however, of what is a reasonable restriction or impairment on the voting right often is difficult to make.

A government regulation restricting the ability of citizens to nominate or vote for the candidate of their choice restricts their First Amendment right of political association and also raises equal protection problems concerning any classifications contained in, or created by, the regulation. Voting regulations regarding the ability of an individual voter to participate in an election most often are examined under the equal protection guarantee because a regulation of this type usually involves a classification that separates persons who may or may not vote in an election or that dilutes the voting power of a particular classification of persons. Although the First Amendment right of political association might be raised in most, if not all, voting rights cases, the right of political association tends to be the primary focus of the Supreme Court in cases involving the ability of independent candidates or minor political parties to gain a place on a general

---

were of Hawaiian ancestry to persons who were Native Hawaiians and Hawaiians under the Fifteenth Amendment). The extent to which the government may employ race conscious districting to assist minority race voters is considered in § 14.10(b)(4).

5. "The right of citizens of the United States to vote in any primary or other election for President or Vice President, for electors for President or Vice President, or for Senator or Representative in Congress, shall not be denied or abridged by the United States or any State by reason of failure to pay any poll tax or other tax." U.S.Const. amend. 24, § 1.

6. See Reynolds v. Sims, 377 U.S. 533, 84 S.Ct. 1362, 12 L.Ed.2d 506 (1964).

7. 377 U.S. at 562, 84 S.Ct. at 1381.

8. See Kramer v. Union Free School District, 395 U.S. 621, 626, 89 S.Ct. 1886, 1889, 23 L.Ed.2d 583 (1969).

9. See Harper v. Virginia State Bd. of Elections, 383 U.S. 663, 666, 86 S.Ct. 1079, 1081, 16 L.Ed.2d 169 (1966).

10. See Katzenbach v. Morgan, 384 U.S. 641, 86 S.Ct. 1717, 16 L.Ed.2d 828 (1966). See §§ 15.2, 15.5, infra.

11. The Court has upheld 50 day residency requirements for voting in local elections. Marston v. Lewis, 410 U.S. 679, 93 S.Ct. 1211, 35 L.Ed.2d 627 (1973); Burns v. Fortson, 410 U.S. 686, 93 S.Ct. 1209, 35 L.Ed.2d 633 (1973).

The Court has also held that only resident citizens of a municipality need be given a vote in local elections and upheld the denial of voting privileges to persons in unincorporated residential areas adjacent to a city. Holt Civic Club v. Tuscaloosa, 439 U.S. 60, 99 S.Ct. 383, 58 L.Ed.2d 292 (1978).

The Court discussed the validity of age requirements in Oregon v. Mitchell, 400 U.S. 112, 91 S.Ct. 260, 27 L.Ed.2d 272 (1970). Much of that discussion was made irrelevant by the Twenty-sixth Amendment.

ballot or the ability of a political party to define and control its membership.[12]

Under either equal protection or First Amendment analysis, a restriction on the right to vote should be subject to "strict scrutiny." However, strict scrutiny analysis in this area may only require the state to demonstrate that its regulation is narrowly tailored to promote an interest that is significant enough to outweigh any incidental restriction on the right to vote or the right of political association. Laws that totally prohibit a class of persons from voting in a general election or laws that are designed to restrict the voting power of a particular class of persons in a general election are unlikely to survive such a standard. Laws that regulate the electoral system to promote substantial state interests in the conduct of efficient and honest elections need to be examined on a case-by-case basis.

In *Burdick v. Takushi* [13] the Supreme Court openly adopted this case-by-case balancing approach to voting rights issues and upheld the State of Hawaii's prohibition on write-in voting. Justice White wrote for a majority of the Court in finding that: "The rigorousness of our inquiry into the propriety of a state election law depends on the extent to which a challenged regulation burdens First and Fourteenth Amendment rights.... when those rights are subjected to 'severe' restrictions the regulation must be narrowly drawn to advance a state interest of compelling importance ... but when a state election law provision imposes only 'reasonable, nondiscriminatory restrictions' upon First and Fourteenth Amendment rights of voters the state's important regulato-

ry interests are generally sufficient to justify the restrictions." [14]

Burdick found that the Hawaii laws regarding the ability of persons to become candidates in primaries, including the ability to be a candidate on nonpartisan primary ballots, complied with the previous rulings of the Court. The prohibition of write-in voting limited the ballot to persons with some demonstrated political support so as to avoid "unrestrained factionalism" and to facilitate the workings of the democratic process.[15] These state interests outweighed the desire of the voter to add a name to the ballot, when the person for whom he wished to write-in a vote had not gone through the primary system and, therefore, had no demonstrated public support.

The case by case balancing approach used in *Burdick* was reaffirmed by the Supreme Court in *Timmons* v. *Twin Cities Area New Party*.[16] The Court, in *Timmons*, upheld a state law prohibiting candidates from appearing on a ballot as a candidate for more than one political party. Chief Justice Rehnquist, writing for the majority in *Timmons*, stated that, in election law cases, the Court would "weigh the character and magnitude of the burden, the state's ruling imposes on those rights [First and Fourteenth Amendment association rights] against the interest the State contends justify that burden ... severe burdens on plaintiffs' rights must be narrowly tailored and advance a compelling state interest. Lesser burdens, however, trigger less exacting scrutiny and a state's important regulatory

---

12. For examples of Supreme Court analysis of ballot access and political party regulations, see §§ 14.31(g), 14.32(e), 14.33.

13. 504 U.S. 428, 434, 112 S.Ct. 2059, 119 L.Ed.2d 245 (1992).

14. 504 U.S. at 433–35, 112 S.Ct. at 2063–64. The dissenting Justices in *Burdick* agreed that there was no First Amendment issue in this case because there was no restriction on the right of political association. The dissent also appeared to endorse the majority's general approach to voting rights issues by endorsing a type of balancing test. However, the dissenting Justices believed that the prohibition on write-in voting was such a severe deprivation of each voter's voice to select candidates that it could not survive any type of realistic judicial review.

Burdick v. Takushi, 504 U.S. 428, 442, 112 S.Ct. 2059, 2068, 119 L.Ed.2d 245 (1992) (Kennedy, joined by Blackmun and Stevens, JJ., dissenting).

15. See § 14.32 of this Treatise regarding "The Right to Be a Candidate" for cases examining ballot access restrictions.

16. 520 U.S. 351 117 S.Ct. 1364, 137 L.Ed.2d 589 (1997). Chief Justice Rehnquist wrote a majority opinion for six Justices in *Timmons*. Justice Stevens filed a dissenting opinion that was joined by Justice Ginsburg, and, in part, by Justice Souter. 520 U.S. at 370, 117 S.Ct. at 1375 (Stevens, J., dissenting joined by Ginsburg, J., and, in part, Souter, J.).; 520 U.S. at 382, 117 S.Ct. at 1381 (Souter, J., dissenting).

interest will usually be enough to justify reasonable, nondiscriminatory restrictions."[17]

The Court has used mathematical criteria to determine whether a state's legislative apportionment has diluted the right to vote. This subject is discussed in later sections.[18] In this section we will focus on the Court's determination of constitutionality of other laws that either impair or dilute the right to vote.

In *Richardson v. Ramirez*[19] the Court found that section two of the Fourteenth Amendment justified a state's denial of the right to vote to those persons who had been convicted of felonies, even though they had completed serving their sentences. Section two of the Fourteenth Amendment protected the right to vote of persons within the states from improper discrimination through a reduction in congressional representation for states who improperly denied the vote to male inhabitants except for those who had engaged in "participation and rebellion, or other crime." The wording and history of the Fourteenth Amendment justified the denial of the vote to connected felons. However, the Court in this decision did not indicate that states had any authority to violate the fundamental principles of equal protection when classifying persons for voting privileges.

In *Hunter v. Underwood*[20] the Justices unanimously invalidated a provision of the Alabama Constitution, adopted in 1901, which denied the vote to persons convicted of "any crime . . . involving moral turpitude". The Justices found that the persons attacking the classification had proved in the lower court proceedings that this provision was adopted for the purpose of disproportionately disenfranchising black persons and that the law continued to have that effect into modern times. The Court ruled that section two of the Fourteenth Amendment "was not designed to permit the purposeful racial discrimination" that the motivating force for this type of disenfranchisement provided. In response to the state's

argument that the Tenth Amendment should protect state autonomy in regulating voting privileges, Justice Rehnquist's opinion for the Court stated: "The Tenth Amendment can not save legislation prohibited by the subsequently enacted Fourteenth Amendment."

It is important to remember that the Court's rulings concerning the right to vote have come in terms of equal protection. The decision to find the right to vote to be constitutionally "fundamental" and subject to a meaningful form of judicial review may best be described as a substantive due process decision because it is based on an analysis of the importance of that right and it restricts the substance of legislation regulating the exercise of the electoral franchise. However, the Court has never held that all important governmental positions must be elective, rather than appointive, or that all restrictions on voting activities will be subject to some virtually insurmountable test such as the traditional strict scrutiny-compelling interest test.

Thus, in *Rodriguez v. Popular Democratic Party*,[21] the Court upheld a statute of Puerto Rico that provided that vacancies in the Puerto Rican legislature caused by the death, resignation or removal of a legislator would be filled until the next regularly scheduled election by the political party with which the previous incumbent was affiliated. The Court noted that the Seventeenth Amendment permitted a vacancy in the United States Senate to be filled by appointment by the state's governor and found that "no provision of the federal constitution" mandated the procedures by which a state or Puerto Rico must follow in filling vacancies in its legislature. Similarly, the Court has rejected challenges to "super-majority" requirements that subject the decision on some public issues, such as tax increases, to a voter referendum and require that more than 50 percent of the voters approve the referendum issue.[22]

---

17.   520 U.S. at 358, 117 S.Ct. at 1370.

18.   See §§ 14.34–14.36, infra. See, e.g., Gaffney v. Cummings, 412 U.S. 735, 93 S.Ct. 2321, 37 L.Ed.2d 298 (1973); White v. Weiser, 412 U.S. 783, 93 S.Ct. 2348, 37 L.Ed.2d 335 (1973).

19.   418 U.S. 24, 94 S.Ct. 2655, 41 L.Ed.2d 551 (1974).

20.   471 U.S. 222, 105 S.Ct. 1916, 85 L.Ed.2d 222 (1985).

21.   457 U.S. 1, 102 S.Ct. 2194, 72 L.Ed.2d 628 (1982).

The Supreme Court has required that judges exercise independent judicial review when examining classifications that allocate voting rights. It is important that the judiciary not simply defer to legislative decisions in this area but, instead, insure that voting classifications promote important societal interests and are not simply attempts by persons in power to impair or dilute the right to vote of disfavored classes.

If any division of the federal or state governments were to use an explicit racial or ethnic classification to deny persons the right to vote in an election, that governmental action would violate the Fifteenth Amendment.[23]

(a)(2) The 2000 Presidential Election and the Right to Vote

Introduction. The actions of the United States Supreme Court that effectively decided the 2000 presidential election undoubtedly will be the subject of debate for many years. While reasonable (or unreasonable, for that matter) persons may debate the wisdom and, indeed, legitimacy of the Court's rulings in *Bush v. Gore*,[24] the legal issues addressed by the Court in that case were fairly straightforward ones. In order to understand those rulings one must review the constitutional provisions that might be at issue in voting cases, in general, and the controversy concerning the naming of the State of Florida's presidential and vice presidential electors, in particular.

Article II of the Constitution, and several Amendments, govern the election and terms of the President and Vice President of the United States. Section 1, Clause 2, of Article II gives each state the power to appoint "in such manner as the Legislature thereof may direct," a certain number of electors, equivalent to the state's congressional delegation and sets the terms for electors. Although states are given a plenary power in the naming of electors, Article II Section 1, Clause 4, gives Congress power to determine the time when states choose electors and the date when electors should submit their votes for President and Vice President. The Twelfth Amendment superceded Article II Section 1, Clause 3 regarding the procedures by which electors cast their ballots, and the role of the Congress in choosing a President and Vice President when no individual receives a majority of the electoral votes for those positions. The Twelfth Amendment was modified by Amendment Twenty, which establishes the starting date for the terms of the President and Vice President (as well as Congress), and established a provision for dealing with a situation in which a President-elect shall have died at the time for the beginning for his or her term of office. Amendment Twenty–Two establishes a two-term limit on the Presidency. Amendment Twenty–Five provides rules concerning succession of the President and Vice President. Amendment Twenty–Three gives residents of the seat of government of the United States [the District of Columbia] the power to name electors for President and Vice President.

No single provision of the Constitution or its Amendments establishes a right of individuals to vote, except for Article I, § 2, which gives the people of each state the right to vote for members of the House of Representatives, and Amendment Seventeen, which transferred the election of Senators from state legislatures to individual voters. Nevertheless, it has been easy for the Court to rule that, once a state creates a system whereby individuals can vote in elections, the courts must treat the right to vote as a fundamental right whose abridgement requires close judicial scrutiny. Several amendments support the position that this type of "right to vote" has been a fundamental

---

22. Gordon v. Lance, 403 U.S. 1, 91 S.Ct. 1889, 29 L.Ed.2d 273 (1971) (sixty percent voter approval requirement for bond issue upheld).

23. Rice v. Cayetano, 528 U.S. 495, 120 S.Ct. 1044, 145 L.Ed.2d 1007 (2000) (The Court, by a 7 to 2 vote, invalidates a state constitutional provision limiting the ballot for trustees of a state agency managing a fund for two subclasses of state residents who were of Hawaiian ances-

try to persons who were Native Hawaiians and Hawaiians under the Fifteenth Amendment). The extent to which the government may employ race conscious districting to assist minority race voters is considered in § 14.10(c) of this Treatise.

24. 531 U.S. 98, 121 S.Ct. 525, 148 L.Ed.2d 388 (2000) (per curiam).

aspect of our constitutional history and tradition. Amendment Fifteen prohibits allocating the right to vote on the basis of race; the Nineteenth Amendment prohibits allocating the vote on the basis of sex. The Twenty–Fourth Amendment prohibits denying the vote in federal elections to those persons who refuse to pay a poll tax, by making such taxes unconstitutional. The Twenty–Sixth Amendment prohibits discrimination based on age, so long as the person who seeks to vote is at least 18 years of age. The Twenty–Third Amendment gave the residents of the District of Columbia representation in the election of the President and the Vice President, even though residents of the District do not have true representation in Congress.[25] The equal protection clause of the Fourteenth Amendment has been the basis for a wide variety of Court rulings prohibiting discrimination concerning the right to vote, although the equal protection clause, contained in the first section of Article I, must sometimes be interpreted in light of Section 2 of the Fourteenth Amendments, which allows states to disenfranchise persons who have committed certain crimes.[26]

Regulations of voting that are considered to be a substantial impairment of the voting powers of an individual or a class of individuals will be subject to close judicial scrutiny, although regulations of voting practices that do not impose a substantial burden on the right to vote will be reviewed on a more lenient standard.[27] One particular aspect of equality in voting is the so-called one person-one vote rule that requires mathematical similarity between districts that are created for the purpose of electing individuals to a body with rule making power over persons in those districts.[28] The requirement of mathematical similarity between the population of districts for congresspersons is derived from Article I, § 2, rather than the equal protection clause.

The First Round of Litigation: The _Bush I_ Decision. The public voting for the 2000 presidential election was held on November 7, 2000. The candidates of the Republican Party were then Governor George W. Bush of Texas, for President, and Richard Cheney, for Vice President. The candidates of the Democratic Party were then-Vice President Albert Gore, and United States Senator Joseph Lieberman. Ultimately, the presidential election was won by George W. Bush, then-Governor of Texas and, as Vice President, Richard Cheney. The Democratic Party candidates received a majority of the popular vote on a nation-wide basis, but they lost the electoral vote to the Republican nominees. It may be that the Republican nominees would have received the greatest number of votes in the Electoral College if the United States Supreme Court had not entered into the controversy concerning the vote in Florida.[29] Nevertheless, in fact, litigation would provide the final answer as to which set of candidates would receive the electoral votes of the State of Florida, and, ultimately, the Presidency and Vice Presidency of the United States.

---

25. U.S. Const. Amend XXIII. See generally Kamins v. Board of Elections for District of Columbia, 324 A.2d 187 (D.C.1974), referring to D.C. Code 1973, § 1–1110(a)(2) provides in pertinent part: "Each vote cast for a candidate ... whose name appears on the general election ballot shall be counted as a vote cast for the candidates for presidential electors of the party supporting such presidential and vice-presidential candidate...."

26. Section II of the Fourteenth Amendment indirectly limited state authority regarding the granting of ballot access by penalizing states in terms of their representation in Congress if the state denied the right to vote to any male citizen over 21 years of age, "except for participation in rebellion, or other crime...." The Court has ruled that states, pursuant to this provision of Section II of the Fourteenth Amendment, can't deny the vote to persons who have been convicted of felonies. Richardson v. Ramirez, 418 U.S. 24, 94 S.Ct. 2655, 41 L.Ed.2d 551 (1974).

27. See notes 7–17, and accompanying text, at the start of § 14.31.

28. Gray v. Sanders, 372 U.S. 368, 83 S.Ct. 801, 9 L.Ed.2d 821 (1963). The one-person, one-vote principle is examined in §§ 14.34–14.36.

29. Several studies done after the election was decided indicated that George W. Bush would have won the Florida popular vote by a slim margin under most methods that might have been used for a full recount, if the United States Supreme Court had allowed one to go on. See, Dennis Cauchon, _Special Report: Newspapers' Recount Shows Bush Prevailed in Florida Vote_, USA TODAY, April 4, 2001, 2001 WL 545902, 4–4–01 USA TD A.01; John Podhoretz, _Bush Still Wins: The Supreme Court Answer Right_, NEW YORK POST, 4–6–01, 2001 W.L. 9390495; Joel Englehardt, _Newspapers Failed to Find Clear Victor_, THE MILWAUKEE JOURNAL SENTINEL, April 8, 2001.

Although there would be some recounts in other states, the election turned on the final tabulations of the votes in Florida.[30] Whichever set of candidates received the electoral votes of the State of Florida would win the presidency and vice-presidency. Immediately following the popular vote, the State of Florida Division of Elections determined that Governor Bush had received fewer than 2,000 more votes than Vice President Gore. Florida statutes provided for an automatic recount whenever the first tally of votes yielded a difference between candidates of less than one-half of one percent of the total votes cast in the state. This initial recount was conducted primarily by machine processing of ballots. The first recount again tallied the greatest number of votes for Governor Bush, although the margin was even smaller than that which had been reported on November 8. Following the initial recount, the Democratic candidates, pursuant to Florida statutes, requested manual recounts in four counties.

The electoral vote of a state that was submitted to Congress could be challenged in the Congress itself; Congress would have the power to make the final determination of whether and how a state had cast its electoral votes. However, a federal statute [referred to as a "safe harbor" provision] protected a state's electoral votes from being challenged if the state, in selecting its electors, had followed state "laws enacted prior to the day fixed for the appointment of electors."[31]

Florida election statutes contained provisions that appeared to be conflicting. There appeared to be a conflict between the time the statute set for manual recounts and the times when counties had to submit final returns. There also appeared to be a conflict between a statutory provision that might be read to require the Florida's Secretary of State to refuse to recognize late election returns, and a provision which might be read as giving the Florida Secretary of State some discretion to accepting

returns were submitted by counties after statutory deadlines.

Following litigation in the state trial court, the Florida Supreme Court ruled that the Secretary of State had the power and duty to ignore some of the statutory deadlines, and accept some county manual recounts that took longer than normally allowed under Florida statutes.[32]

The Florida Supreme Court's interpretation of the Florida statutes, allowing the Secretary of State to accept late recount totals, was challenged in the United States Supreme Court, by the Republican nominees, on two basis. First, they alleged that the Florida Supreme Court had changed the law that had existed prior to the time fixed for the appointment of the state electors in violation of federal statutes and Article II. Second, they alleged that the Florida Supreme Court violated the equal protection clause of the Fourteenth Amendment by creating a system that would treat similarly situated voters in a disparate and arbitrary manner.

In its first ruling on the Florida election, *Bush v. Palm Beach County Canvassing Board*, [*Bush I*],[33] the Justices of the United States Supreme Court unanimously vacated the judgment of the Florida Supreme Court. In a per curiam opinion, the United States Supreme Court required the Florida Supreme Court to clarify its decision, because "We [the United States Supreme Court Justices] are unclear as to the extent to which the Florida Supreme Court saw the Florida Constitution as circumscribing the legislature's authority under Article II, § 1, clause 2 [the provision of the U.S. Constitution granting the legislature of the state the authority to appoint electors in presidential and vice-presidential elections]. We are also unclear as to the consideration the Florida Supreme Court accorded to 3 U.S.C. § 5 [the statute providing a safe-harbor for the

---

30. See newspaper articles cited in note 29, supra. See generally, Samuel Issacharoff, Pamela S. Karlan, and Richard H. Pildes, When Elections Go Bad: The Law of Democracy and the Presidential Election of 2000 (revised edition, 2001).

31. 3 U.S.C.A. § 5.

32. Palm Beach County Canvassing Board v. Harris, 772 So.2d 1220 (Fla.2000).

33. 531 U.S. 70, 121 S.Ct. 471, 148 L.Ed.2d 366 (2000) (per curiam).

slate of state electors so long as the contests were decided by a law enacted prior to the time when the electors were chosen]."[34]

In coming to its conclusion, the per curiam opinion in *Bush I* relied on language from *McPherson v. Blacker*[35] in finding that the Justices of the United States Supreme Court could review a state court determination regarding state law for the purpose of determining whether the a state court ruling resulted in a violation of Article II, § 1 clause 2, which gives the power to appoint electors to the state legislature rather than the "state" generally, or to state judges.[36]

It is worth noting how the course of the litigation might have changed if the Florida Supreme Court's initial opinion, or the arguments of those who sought to sustain the Florida Supreme Court's initial decision, had convinced a majority of the United States Supreme Court Justices that the state supreme court had merely applied Florida statutes in a manner consistent with the traditional role of state courts, and Article II of the United States Constitution.

Let us assume that the United States Supreme Court accepted the following two points. First, the Florida Supreme Court was simply applying state legislative mandates, established prior to the time for appointment of electors, so that its electors would be appointed consistently with Article II and come within the safe harbor provision of 3 U.S.C. § 5. Second, the Florida Supreme Court, applying traditional principles of statutory interpretation, properly ruled that the Florida election code had always given the Secretary of State power to accept late returns and provide for manual recounts beyond the seven day period specified in one portion of the statute, so long as the delay would not endanger the state electors from having their votes counted in the presidential election.

If the state law basis of the Florida court's ruling had been clear in the first instance [or if the United States Supreme Court had accepted such arguments in the first instance] the United States Supreme Court would have had to address the question of whether recount procedures established by the Florida Supreme Court violated Article II, or the equal protection clause and due process clauses of the Fourteenth Amendment. If the United States Supreme Court had been presented with a clear state court ruling on December 4, the Justices might have made a ruling regarding equal protection or due process standards that would have allowed a manual state-wide recount to go forward.

Interestingly, in *Bush I*, not a single Justice of the United States Supreme Court found that the state law or the state court ruling was clear enough for the Court to address federal constitutional issues on December 4, 2002. The Florida Supreme Court would not clarify its decision concerning the Secretary of State's powers until December 11.[37]

The Second Round of Litigation: The *Bush II* & *Bush III* Decisions. On November 26, the Florida Election Canvassing Commission certified the Florida election results so that Governor Bush would receive Florida's 25 electoral votes. The next day, Vice President Gore contested that certification in a Florida trial court. This litigation was technically separate from the litigation that had led to the Palm Beach County decision by the United States Supreme Court on December 4.

In the second round of litigation, the state trial court found that the Democratic candidates had failed to provide a sufficient basis for rejecting the certification of the vote issued by the Florida Elections Canvassing Commission. That decision was appealed directly to the Florida Supreme Court, which modified the trial court's ruling. The Florida State Supreme Court found that the trial court had

34. 531 U.S. at 77, 121 S.Ct. at 475.

35. 146 U.S. 1, 13 S.Ct. 3, 36 L.Ed. 869 (1892).

36. Bush v. Palm Beach County Canvassing Board, 531 U.S. 70, 76, 121 S.Ct. 471, 474, 148 L.Ed.2d 366 (2000) (per curiam).

37. Palm Beach County Canvassing Board v. Harris, 772 So.2d 1273 (Fla.2000).

properly rejected the Vice President's challenge to certified results in one county and his allegation that certain votes cast in Palm Beach County were not "legal votes."[38] The Florida Supreme Court ruled, however, that the Democratic candidates had met the burden of proof in challenging Miami–Dade County's failure to include in a recount 9,000 ballots which had not registered a vote when they were put through the election machines [so-called "undervotes"]. The Florida Supreme Court ordered a hand recount of the 9,000 ballots, and, additionally, ruled that the trial court could order a manual recount of undervotes in all counties that had not conducted a manual recount. The Florida Supreme Court also ruled that the trial court had to accept votes that had been tabulated after a November 26 deadline in two counties [Palm Beach County and Miami–Dade County], even though the manual vote recounting teams in those counties had used different standards to recount the ballots, with some teams counting (and other not counting) both under-votes and over-votes. An over-vote was the term used for a ballot on which the voter punches through two chads, or marked two spots on a card ballot, indicating that the voter may have bee attempting to vote for two candidates for the same office.

The Florida Supreme Court's ruling effectively required a state-wide manual recount of ballots that had not been counted by the machines [because the voter had failed to entirely punch through a portion, or chad, of the ballot next to the presidential candidate's name or had made a mark or punched the place next to more than one presidential candidate's name]. The Florida Supreme Court ruled that the persons conducting the manual recount were to examine each ballot that had been legally cast [though not counted by a machine] to determine the intent of the voter who cast the ballot, if possible.

In *Bush v. Gore,* [*Bush II*][39] on December 9, the United States Supreme Court, by a 5 to 4 vote of the Justices, stayed Florida Supreme Court ruling requiring the manual recount of legally cast undervotes, and set oral arguments for the next day, which was Sunday, December 10. Justice Stevens, joined by Justices Souter, Ginsburg and Breyer dissented from the Court's ordering a stay of the Florida Supreme Court's ruling.

The dissenting Justices in *Bush II* believed that the Republican candidates, who challenged the state court decision, had not made a "substantial showing of the likelihood of irreparable harm" from allowing the state court ruling to take effect until such time as it could be reviewed by the United States Supreme Court.[40]

Justice Scalia, who concurred in the order of the Court that stayed the Florida Supreme Court ruling and the recount, noted that allowing a recount that would be unconstitutional or unlawful would cause substantial harm to the election process in two ways: "degradation of the ballots, which renders a subsequent recount inaccurate," and the mere fact of the recounting might cast a "cloud" on the legitimacy of the outcome of the election.[41]

On December 12, in *Bush v. Gore* [*Bush III*],[42] the United States Supreme Court made two rulings. First, the Court ruled that the system for the recounting of ballots established by the Florida Supreme Court violated the equal protection clause of the Fourteenth Amendment. Second, the Court ruled that all recounting of Florida ballots had to be stopped, so that the state's electoral vote could be certified and cast in a manner that would grant Florida the benefit of the safe harbor provision of 3 U.S.C. § 5. The per curiam opinion for the Court in *Bush v. Gore* was joined by five Justices: Chief Justice Rehnquist, and Justices O'Connor, Scalia, Kennedy, and Thomas.

38. Gore v. Harris, 772 So.2d 1243 (Fla.2000).

39. Bush v. Gore, 531 U.S. 1046, 121 S.Ct. 512, 148 L.Ed.2d 553 (per curiam order).

40. 531 U.S. at 1047, 121 S.Ct. at 512–13 (Stevens, J., joined by Souter, Ginsburg and Breyer, JJ., dissenting).

41. 531 U.S. at 1046, 121 S.Ct. at 512 (Scalia, J., concurring).

42. Bush v. Gore, 531 U.S. 98, 121 S.Ct. 525, 148 L.Ed.2d 388 (2000).

There were three basic issues that faced the Court in *Bush v. Gore*, two concerning substantive provisions of the Constitution, and one concerning any further proceedings in the case.

The first issue, which was never ruled on by the United States Supreme Court, was whether the Florida Supreme Court's interpretation of state statutes violated Article II, § 1, clause 2 of the United States Constitution insofar as the state court was preventing the state legislature from effectively exercising control over the system for the appointment of electors and the casting of electoral votes for the President and Vice President of the United States. A related issue was whether the state court ruling was in conflict with 3 U.S.C. § 5 insofar as it deprived the state of making use of the safe harbor provision by altering the state law that had existed prior to the time for the casting of the popular vote and the determination of the electors for the state. Because the majority ruled that the state supreme court recount system violated the equal protection clause, the majority opinion in *Bush v. Gore* never ruled on the Article II issue or the related statutory issue.[43]

Three of the Justices who joined the per curiam opinion in *Bush v. Gore*, Chief Justice Rehnquist and Justices Scalia and Thomas, wrote separately to explain their belief that the Florida court ruling also violated the provision of the United States Constitution granting the legislature, rather than the courts, of a state authority over the appointment of electors.[44] Four Justices in *Bush v. Gore* believed that the Florida court's interpretation and application of state law did not violate Article II of the United States Constitution.[45] This debate between the concurring and dis-

senting Justices on this point, which was irrelevant to the outcome of the case, is examined at the end of this subsection.

The second issue before the United States Supreme Court was whether the system adopted by the Florida Supreme Court for the recounting of ballots, which allowed canvassing boards to determine voter intent without any objective guidelines to limit their determinations, violated the due process or equal protection clauses by giving unequal treatment to similarly cast ballots by similarly situated voters. The per curiam opinion, for five Justices, ruled that the state could not have a system for counting votes that did not have any objective standards without violating the equal protection clause's requirement that similarly situated voters (and their votes) be treated in a similar manner.[46]

Two additional Justices, Justices Souter and Breyer, agreed with majority's conclusion that the recount system established by the Florida Supreme Court violated equal protection clause, although they dissented from the portion of the United States Supreme Court ruling that prohibited the state court from attempting to fashion a different recount system that would not violate equal protection and that could be concluded in time for Florida's electoral vote to be counted in the final determination of who would be the President of the United States.[47] However, these two justices did not label their opinions as "concurring in part and dissenting in the judgment." They simply dissented.

Only Justices Stevens and Ginsburg believed that the system established by the Florida Supreme Court for the manual recounting of ballots did not violate the equal protection

---

43. This issue is examined in footnotes 68–82 and accompanying text in this section.

44. Bush v. Gore, 531 U.S. 98, 110, 114, 121 S.Ct. 525, 533, 535, 148 L.Ed.2d 388 (2000) (Rehnquist, C.J., joined by Scalia and Thomas, JJ., concurring).

45. The dissenting Justices were Justices Stevens, Souter, Ginsburg, and Breyer.

46. Bush v. Gore, 531 U.S. 98, 108, 121 S.Ct. 525, 532–33, 148 L.Ed.2d 388 (2000) (per curiam).

47. Justices Souter and Breyer agreed that the standardless recount system raised serious equal protection

issues and that a truly standardless recount would violate the equal protection guarantee. Justices Stevens and Ginsburg did not join the portions of the opinions written by Justice Souter and Justice Breyer that discussed equal protection. Bush v. Gore, 531 U.S. 98, 127, 121 S.Ct. 525, 542, 148 L.Ed.2d 388 (2000). (Souter, J., joined by Breyer, J., and in part by Stevens and Ginsburg, JJ., dissenting); 531 U.S. at 143, 121 S.Ct. at 550 (Breyer, J., joined in part by Stevens and Ginsburg, JJ. and in part by Souter, J., dissenting).

clause.[48] Justice Stevens did not address the equal protection issue in his opinion; he joined Justice Ginsburg's opinion, which stated that there was no substantial equal protection issue in the case.

The third issue was whether the United States Supreme Court should remand the case to the state court for further action or whether the United States Supreme Court should simply end the litigation by ruling that the state court lacked any power to alter the results that had been certified by the state board and the Florida Secretary of State. Of course, if the Court had ruled that the Florida Supreme Court's recount mandate did not violate the Constitution of the United States, or the Amendments thereto, the United States Supreme Court would never have reached this issue.

The United States Supreme Court was not confronted with the question of whether it should rule that all electoral college issues and the counting of electoral votes was a political question.[49] The Court's ruling effectively would reject any argument that electoral college issues are entirely political questions to be resolved by the Congress of the United States in the vote counting process set out in Article II and Amendments Twelve and Twenty. However, all of the Justices of the United States Supreme Court recognized that regardless of the United States Supreme Court ruling, the ultimate determination of the legitimacy of each state's votes for the President and Vice President of the United States would rest in the hands of the United States House of Representatives and the United States Senate.[50] Because the Florida Supreme Court ruling might have determined the appointment of electors in a manner that could have come under the terms of the "safe harbor" provision of the federal statute, it is arguable that the United States Supreme Court had to intervene in order to make clear that Congress had the final authority over electoral college issues.

The Republican nominees contended that the Florida Court's establishment of a system of a manual recount of votes that had not registered on machines violated both the due process and equal protection clauses insofar as the Florida Supreme Court had refused to adopt any objective standards and empowered the officials doing the recounts to create their own standards for determining voter intent. The per curiam opinion in *Bush III* ruled that the Florida Supreme Court system violated the equal protection clause, although the majority also made a passing reference to the due process clause.[51] The majority's analysis was entirely based on the equal protection clause, rather than due process.

48. Bush v. Gore, 531 U.S. 98, 136, 121 S.Ct. 525, 546, 148 L.Ed.2d 388 (2000) (Ginsburg, J., joined by Stevens, J., and in part by Souter and Breyer, JJ., dissenting). Only Justice Stevens joined the portion of Justice Ginsburg's opinion that dealt with equal protection. Justice Stevens issued a separate dissenting opinion in which he discussed his view that it was inappropriate for the Court to review the state court ruling in this case, but his opinion did not expand upon the equal protection position taken by Justice Ginsburg. 531 U.S. at 122, 121 S.Ct. at 539 (Stevens, J., joined by Ginsburg and Breyer, JJ., dissenting).

49. The political question topic is examined in § 2.16 of this Treatise. The opinion of Justice Breyer came close to taking a position that courts should not rule on the issues in this case and should leave the matter for Congress, but he did not take the position that all issues regarding the Florida recount, including equal protection, should be declared to be political questions. Bush v. Gore, 531 U.S. 98, 143, 121 S.Ct. 525, 550, 148 L.Ed.2d 388 (Breyer, J., joined in part by Stevens and Ginsburg, JJ., and in part by Souter, J., dissenting).

50. The majority opinion in *Bush III* ended the recount in Florida in a manner that allowed the state to come under the "safe harbor" provision of 3 U.S.C.A. § 5, which would have prevented a challenge in Congress but the Court did not rule that Congress was precluded from considering the validity of the electoral vote in Florida or any other state. The portion of Justice Breyer's dissent that discussed the role of Congress in reviewing the electoral ballots cast by states was joined by Justices Stevens and Ginsburg. Bush v. Gore, 531 U.S. 98, 152–58, 121 S.Ct. 525, 550, 555–58, 148 L.Ed.2d 388 (2000) (Breyer, J., joined as to this portion of the opinion by Stevens and Ginsburg, JJ., dissenting). Part A of Justice Souter's dissenting opinion consisted of one paragraph which in part recognized the authority of Congress to make the final determination regarding the electoral ballots cast by states; this portion of the Souter dissent was joined by the three other dissenting Justices. 531 U.S. at 126, 128, 121 S.Ct. at 542, 543 (Souter, J., joined by Breyer, J., and as to all except Part C, by Stevens and Ginsburg, JJ., dissenting.).

51. Bush v. Gore, 531 U.S. 98, 103, 121 S.Ct. 525, 529, 148 L.Ed.2d 388 (2000) (end of part I of the per curiam opinion).

The per curiam opinion in *Bush III* noted that, under Article II, "the individual citizen has no federal constitutional right to vote for electors" until the state legislature adopted a statewide election system as the means of exercising and implementing the state legislator's power to appoint members to the Electoral College.[52] This position merely reflected the long established position, endorsed in 1892 by the Court, that a state had plenary power over the appointment of electors.[53]

The *Bush III* opinion found that once a state legislature gave individuals the right to vote for a government office, in general, or for electors for the presidency, in particular, "the right to vote as the legislature has prescribed is fundamental; and one source of its fundamental nature lies in the equal weight accorded to each vote and the equal dignity owed to each voter."[54] The Court cited both access to ballot and one person-one vote cases as precedent establishing the principle that the judiciary would review voting systems to determine that the state did not violate equal protection clause principles in allocating voting power among voters within the state.[55]

Although the majority opinion in *Bush III* described the right to vote as being a fundamental constitutional right, that opinion did not set out a specific standard of review to be employed when judging legislative classifications that related to voting rights. The reason for the Court's failure to state a specific standard of review may be a simple one. The five Justices who joined the per curiam opinion, and two concurring Justices, believed that a system for manually recounting votes that had no objective standards to guide the search for voter intent by different vote counters was totally arbitrary and that the disparate treatment of similarly cast votes was not related to any legitimate governmental interest. Because the Court was reviewing a government action

that could severely impair a fundamental right (the right to vote) the Court would not grant a presumption of constitutionality to the system established by the Florida court. Rather, seven Justices chose to independently examine the standardless recount procedure to determine if it would create arbitrary classifications and disparate treatment of similarly situated voters. Prior to examining the specific reasons set forth by the majority opinion, our reader might be well advised to review the basic command of equal protection, which requires that similarly situated persons be dealt with in a similar manner by the government.[56]

After setting forth basic principles regarding equal protection and the nature of voting rights, the per curiam opinion pointed out several ways in which similarly cast votes would be treated in a disparate manner. The basic ruling in *Bush III* was that similarly situated voters could have their votes treated in a different manner by different vote counters or vote canvassing boards (under the Florida Court's ruling) and that such disparate treatment of voters was so arbitrary as to violate equal protection.

First, the Court noted that "the standards for accepting or rejecting contested ballots might vary not only from county to county but indeed within a single county from one recount team to another."[57] In other words, with no objective guidelines, one recounting team might count a ballot in which the area to be punched out next to a candidate's name [a "chad"] was only partially indented but not punched through could be counted in one county but not another. In this way, two similarly situated voters [both of whom had cast ballots with the chad partially punched or indented in an identical manner] might be treated differently, with one vote counting and one not counting, solely because of the views of individual counting teams. This unrestrained

---

52. 531 U.S. at 103, 121 S.Ct. at 529 (Part II D of the per curiam opinion).

53. McPherson v. Blacker, 146 U.S. 1, 13 S.Ct. 3, 36 L.Ed. 869 (1892).

54. Bush v. Gore, 531 U.S. 98, 103, 121 S.Ct. 525, 529, 148 L.Ed.2d 388 (2000) (per curiam).

55. 531 U.S. at 104, 121 S.Ct. at 530. Ballot access cases are examined throughout this section [§ 14.31] of this Treatise; the one-person, one-vote principle is examined in §§ 14.34–14.36.

56. See § 14.2 of this Treatise.

57. Bush v. Gore, 531 U.S. 98, 106, 121 S.Ct. 525, 531, 148 L.Ed.2d 388 (2000) (per curiam).

discretion on the part of counting teams was not related to any legitimate end of government. The Court cited cases related to the one person one vote principle [*Gray* and *Moore*] for the principle that a state could not accord "arbitrary and disparate treatment to voters in its different counties."[58]

The United States Supreme Court majority noted that the state supreme court ruling exacerbated the equal protection problem by requiring early recount totals from two counties to be considered in the new certified vote and allowing for the recount totals from a third county even though none of the counties had been ones in which Vice President Gore had contested the election totals. Those three counties had used differing standards when recounting all of the ballots in their districts, not just those that had failed to record a vote on the voting machines on November 7 or 8. This resulted in a great number of ballots being subject to the open-ended discretionary recount system. Additionally, the state supreme court order included a partial recount in a county even though the total recount could not be done within the time limits established by the state supreme court.

In discussing the ways in which similarly cast votes could be treated in a dissimilar manner, the majority in *Bush III* concluded that the system adopted by the Florida Supreme Court was "inconsistent with the minimum procedures necessary to protect the fundamental right of each voter in the special instance of a statewide recount under the authority of a single state judicial officer."[59] The Court, in *Bush III* did not establish a general rule for the standards that a state would have to adopt when conducting manual recounts of votes, but stated that its consideration was

limited only to the particular standardless system adopted by the Florida Supreme Court.

Only Justices Stevens and Ginsburg believed that the recount system adopted by the Florida Supreme Court did not present a substantial question under the equal protection clause. Justice Stevens noted that many states followed the "intent of the voter standard" in recounts of contested election votes. Justice Stevens stated that any problems created by recounting teams using differing standards would be "alleviated–if not eliminated–by the fact that a single impartial magistrate will ultimately adjudicate all objections arising from the recount procedure."[60] Justice Ginsburg did not believe that there was a significant equal protection problem in this case because she believed that the recount procedure adopted by the Florida court would not count the ballots in any way that was "any less fair or precise than the certification that had preceded the recount [and that had been admittedly conducted in accordance with Florida statutes]."[61]

Justices Souter and Breyer agreed with the majority's conclusion, but not its opinion, concerning the equal protection flaws in the recount system adopted by the Florida Supreme Court. Nevertheless Justices Breyer and Souter dissented from the majority's decision to block any further recounting of the ballots cast in Florida. Justice Souter, in a part of his dissenting opinion that was joined only by Justice Breyer, noted the ways in which similarly cast votes might be treated in different manners by different counting teams in the recount system established by the Florida Supreme Court. Justice Souter concluded that there was "no legitimate interest served by these differing treatments of the expression of

---

58. Id. The Court relied on Gray v. Sanders, 372 U.S. 368, 83 S.Ct. 801, 9 L.Ed.2d 821 (1963). See §§ 14.34—14.36 regarding the one-person, one-vote principle.

59. Bush v. Gore, 531 U.S. 98, 108, 121 S.Ct. 525, 532, 148 L.Ed.2d 388 (2000) (per curiam).

60. Bush v. Gore, 531 U.S. 98, 122, 121 S.Ct. 525, 539, 541, 148 L.Ed.2d 388 (2000) (Stevens, J., joined by Ginsburg and Breyer, JJ., dissenting). In his dissent, Justice Stevens addressed only questions regarding the Court's approach to reviewing state laws under Article II of the

Constitution. Nevertheless, Justice Stevens' statements concerning the determination of voter intent appear to reflect his support for Justice Ginsburg's conclusion that the case did not present any substantial equal protection problems.

61. 531 U.S. at 135, 121 S.Ct. at 546, 550 (Ginsburg, J., joined by Stevens, J., and in part by Souter and Breyer, JJ., dissenting). Only Justice Stevens joined part II of Justice O'Connor's opinion, which addressed the equal protection issue.

voters' fundamental rights."[62] Justice Breyer, in a portion of his dissenting opinion that was joined by Justice Souter, concluded that "basic principles of fairness may well have counseled the adoption of a uniform standard to address the problem [of recounting votes]."[63]

Justices Souter and Breyer dissented from the Court's ruling, despite their apparent agreement with much of the Court's equal protection analysis, because they disagreed with the five member majority on the disposition of the case. Justices Souter and Breyer believed that the case should have been remanded to the Florida Supreme Court to give that Court an opportunity to create a recount system that had objective standards that might limit the discretion of voting recount teams so as to eliminate the arbitrary treatment of similarly situated votes. They would have allowed the recount to continue at a time that would have gone past the time established for the state to make use of the so-called safe harbor provision of federal law so long as the state could complete its recount prior to the time when its electors had to be named and their electoral votes cast for the presidency and vice presidency.[64]

The five Justice majority in *Bush III* concluded that the case should not be remanded to the state courts, which would have given the state courts another opportunity to attempt to establish a recount system that might not violate equal protection.[65] The reason for the majority's ruling rested on the prior Florida Supreme Court decisions concerning the election, both of which had indicated that existing Florida statutes evidenced a legislative desire to have the Florida presidential votes, and all contest to vote totals, concluded in

time to have the electoral votes cast in a manner that would comply with 3 U.S.C. § 5 and come under the federal safe harbor standard.[66] In other words, according to the per curiam opinion in *Bush III*, the Florida Supreme Court had identified a clear legislative intent to protect the Florida electoral vote from being challenged in Congress by coming within the safe harbor provision of the federal statute. The five Justice majority in *Bush III* believed that it would be impossible for the state courts to establish a uniform system for the recount, and complete that recount by December 12, the date which would be the final time for making use of the federal safe harbor provision. Therefore, the *Bush III* per curiam opinion ruled that implementation of any recounts under state court authority should end, so that the Florida Secretary of State could certify the vote totals and the electors be appointed in a manner that came within the time frame established by the federal safe harbor provision and Florida legislation.[67]

Bush III and the Role of the U.S. Supreme Court in Reviewing State Court Determinations of the Meaning of State Law When Those Decisions Affect Federal Rights. The majority opinion in *Bush v. Gore* [*Bush III*][68] did not discuss the role of the United States Supreme Court in reviewing state court determinations of the meaning of state law. The majority opinion simply accepted the Florida Supreme Court's determination that the state legislature intended to make use of the safe harbor provisions of 3 U.S.C. § 5. Because the majority found an equal protection violation the majority opinion did not

---

62. Bush v. Gore, 531 U.S. 98, 129, 133, 121 S.Ct. 525, 542, 545, 148 L.Ed.2d 388 (2000) Souter, J., joined by Breyer, J. and, in part, by Stevens and Ginsburg, JJ., dissenting. Justices Stevens and Ginsburg did not join Part C of Justice Souter's opinion, which addressed the equal protection issue.

63. 531 U.S. at 143, 145, 121 S.Ct. at 550, 551 (Breyer, J., joined in part by Stevens and Ginsburg, JJ., and in part by Souter, J., dissenting). Justices Stevens and Ginsburg did not join part I–A–1 of Justice Breyer's opinion, which addressed the equal protection issue.

64. All four dissenting Justices agreed that the case should have been remanded to the Florida Supreme Court for further proceedings. Bush v. Gore, 531 U.S. 98, 135,

121 S.Ct. 525, 546, 148 L.Ed.2d 388 (2000) (Souter, J., joined by Breyer, J., and in part by Stevens and Ginsburg, JJ., dissenting); 531 U.S. at 143, 121 S.Ct. at 550 (Breyer, J., joined in part by Stevens and Ginsburg, JJ., and in part by Souter, J., dissenting).

65. Bush v. Gore, 531 U.S. 98, 108–110, 121 S.Ct. 525, 532–33, 148 L.Ed.2d 388 (2000) (per curiam).

66. 531 U.S. at 110, 121 S.Ct. at 533.

67. Id.

68. Bush v. Gore, 531 U.S. 98, 121 S.Ct. 525, 148 L.Ed.2d 388 (2000) (per curiam).

consider either whether the Florida court had erred in any way regarding its interpretation of state statutes or whether the Florida court's interpretation of state statutes violated Article II by improperly taking away power over the nomination of the electors from the state legislature.

Seven Justices, in separate opinions, addressed the question of whether the Florida Supreme Court had the authority to interpret state law concerning the selection of presidential electors as it had done and whether that Florida Supreme Court ruling violated the grant of authority to state legislature set out in Article II, § 1, clause 2. Justices O'Connor and Kennedy, whose votes were crucial to forming the five Justice per curiam opinion in *Bush III* refused to address this issue. Four Justices believed that the Supreme Court should not review the meaning of Florida statutes for the purposes of determining whether the Florida Supreme Court action conflicted with Article II § 1 clause 2, or federal statutes.

The opinions of the three concurring Justices, and the four dissenting Justices, concerning the role of the Supreme Court in reviewing state court interpretations of state law, and Article II were irrelevant to the outcome of the case. The majority opinion did not address the Article II issue or the role of the United States Supreme Court in reviewing a state court interpretation of state law. In other words, the *Bush v. Gore* decision did not, in any sense turn on the United States Supreme Court review of the state supreme court's interpretation of state statutes; the United States Supreme Court majority made no ruling on whether the rulings of the Florida Supreme Court had undercut legislative authority in a manner that violated Article II of the United States Constitution.

Chief Justice Rehnquist wrote an opinion concurring in both the opinion and the judgment of the Court.[69] The Chief Justice's concurrence was opinion joined by Justices Scalia and Thomas, joined the per curiam opinion entirely. These three Justices wrote separately

to discuss the role of the Court in reviewing state court decisions concerning presidential elections as a basis for the conclusion of these three Justices that the ruling of the Florida Supreme Court improperly removed legislative authority in violation of Article II, § 1, clause 2 and that it was inconsistent with Florida statutes and the safe harbor provision of 3 U.S.C. § 5.

Chief Justice Rehnquist found that "in most cases, comity and respect for federalism compel us to defer to the decisions of state court on issues of state law. That practice reflects our understanding that decisions of state courts are definitive pronouncements of the will of states as sovereigns."[70] The second quoted sentence, at first glance, might seem inconsistent with the first. The first part of the quoted statement indicates that the United States Supreme Court only chooses to defer to state courts on state law; the second sentence indicates that the United States Supreme Court must accept state courts as the final interpreters of state law. These statements may be seen as consistent if one interprets them in the following manner. First (as reflected in the second quoted sentence) state supreme courts are indeed the final authority on the meaning of state law so long as there is no federal issue that turns on the meaning of state law. Thus, for example, a state court interpretation of a rule of contracts law would be absolutely final as to the meaning of contracts in the state so long as there was no federal issue involved. Second, the United States Supreme Court makes the final determination of all issues of federal law so that state courts may not dictate the outcome of a federal issue.

Two hypothetical contract cases should serve as examples of the Chief Justice's position. In the first case, a state court decides that in a contract between two private parties a promise to deliver goods or services in exchange only for a peppercorn does not constitute a valid contract so that if the seller of the property refuses to deliver it to the buyer

69. 531 U.S. at 110, 121 S.Ct. at 533 (Rehnquist, C.J., joined by Scalia and Thomas, JJ., concurring).

70. 531 U.S. at 112, 121 S.Ct. at 534 (Rehnquist, C.J., joined by Scalia and Thomas, JJ., concurring).

there is no breach of contract. This case would present no federal questions; no matter how bad the state court decision might seem in terms of the common law of contracts the United States Supreme Court would not review the state court decision concerning the formation of contracts in that state.

In the second case, the state supreme court rules that a state agreement to grant a charter to have a university to a specific group of people, which would bring them specific benefits under state tax law and property law did not constitute a contract so that it could be repealed by the state legislature, and the educational group deprived of the property and benefits, at the mere whim of the legislature. The state legislature then passes a law rescinding the charter to the educational group, thus depriving them of the tax and property benefits that were a part of the charter. The party that had received the charter challenges the legislative action under the contracts clause of Article I § 10, and the Fourteenth Amendment to the Constitution of the United States. In determining whether there had been a contract for contract clause purposes, or whether the individuals had been deprived of property without just compensation in violation of the Fourteenth Amendment, the United States Supreme Court should make an independent determination of whether the educational charter granted constituted a contract, or property, for federal law purposes.[71]

The Chief Justice, together with Justices Scalia and Thomas, stated that the Court was required to make an independent judgment as to whether the Florida Supreme Court had significantly deviated from the intent of the Florida Legislature when interpreting Florida statutes regarding challenges to elections for members of the Electoral College. The Chief Justice majority believed that Supreme Court review of state court decision on this topic was "Our responsibility to enforce the specific requirements of Article II [which gave the power over the appointing of electors to the state legislature rather than the state judiciary]."[72]

After justifying the review of the state court's interpretation of state statutes, the Chief Justice found that there was no basis in Florida's statutes for the state court ruling that required the counting of improperly marked ballots, and its disregard of the limits established for the certification of the electoral vote. The Chief Justice concluded that, in light of the Florida legislature's desire to take advantage of the safe harbor provision of 3 U.S.C. § 5, as well as the statutes governing challenges to votes in the outcomes of elections under Florida statutes, the ruling of the Supreme Court of Florida was not appropriate in light of the Article II delegation of a plenary power to appoint presidential and vice presidential electors to state legislatures.[73]

Justice Breyer's concurring opinion came the close to stating that the Article II question was a political question issue, although he did not explicitly take that position.[74] Justice Breyer, in a portion of his opinion that was joined by Justices Stevens and Ginsburg, in response to the concurring opinion of Chief Justice Rehnquist stated that: "The Twelfth Amendment commits to Congress the authority and responsibility to count electoral votes. A federal statute, the Electoral Act, enacted after the close 1876 Hayes–Tilden Presidential election, specifies that, after states have tried to resolve disputes (through 'judicial' or other means),

---

71. The university charter hypothetical is similar to the facts in Dartmouth College v. Woodward, 17 U.S. (4 Wheat.) 518, 4 L.Ed. 629 (1819). The contracts clause is examined in §§ 11.8, 11.9 of this Treatise.

In Indiana ex rel. Anderson v. Brand, 303 U.S. 95, 100, 58 S.Ct. 443, 446, 82 L.Ed. 685 (1938), the Court in *Anderson* decided that it had to determine for itself if the state court decision claiming that a teacher's tenure was really a contract or just a right that existed so long as the statute granting it existed. The Court decided that it had to "independently" look at the state law to make this decision.

72. Bush v. Gore, 531 U.S. 98, 110, 121 S.Ct. 525, 533, 535, 148 L.Ed.2d 388 (2000) (Rehnquist, C.J., joined by Scalia and Thomas, JJ., concurring).

73. 531 U.S. at 111–12, 121 S.Ct. at 538–39 (Rehnquist, C.J., joined by Scalia and Thomas, JJ., concurring).

74. Bush v. Gore, 531 U.S. 98, 144, 152, 121 S.Ct. 525, 550, 555, 148 L.Ed.2d 388 (2000) (Breyer, J., joined in part by, Stevens and Ginsburg, JJ., and in part by Souter, J., dissenting). Only Justices Stevens and Ginsburg joined part II of Justice Breyer's opinion which emphasized the role of Congress in resolving presidential election disputes.

Congress is the body primarily authorized to resolve remaining disputes.''

Justice Souter, like Justice Breyer, filed a concurring opinion in which he found that there might be equal protection problems with the way in which the Florida recount was being conducted.[75] Like Justice Breyer, he preferred to remand the case to the Florida courts so that they might develop standards for guiding the persons conducting the manual recount so as to avoid totally arbitrary and disparate treatment of similarly situated voters' ballots. Also like Justice Breyer, he was unclear as to whether he would have reviewed the final recount by Florida, which he would have allowed, or whether he would have left he entire determination to Congress.

Justice Souter wrote for four Justices in finding that there was no substantial question concerning the compatibility of the actions of the Florida Supreme Court with either federal statutes or Article II.[76] Justice Souter, in part A of his opinion, noted that the only federal statute on point was the safe harbor provision, which allowed but did not require states to finish their final vote tabulations for elections prior to a certain date. He noted that federal statutes also allowed for the resolution of all disputes regarding elections of presidential electors to be settled by the Congress under 3 U.S.C. § 15. Justice Souter, and the three Justices who joined him, found that there was no possibility that the Florida Court's action violated Article II. He noted: "The Republican nominee [George W. Bush] does not, of course, claim that any judicial act interpreting a statute of uncertain meaning is enough to displace the legislative provision and violate Article II; statutes require interpretation, which does not without more effect the legislative character of a statute within the meaning of the Constitution ... what Bush does argue, as I understand the contention, is that the interpretation of [a section of the Florida election code

by the Florida Supreme Court] was so unreasonable as to transcend the excepted bounds of statutory interpretation, to the point of being a non-judicial act and producing a new law untethered to the legislative act in question."[77] Justice Souter's opinion for four Justices found that, regardless of whether one agreed with the Florida Supreme Court majority, there was no basis in the United States Constitution for finding that the state court interpretation of its own statutes, and its own constitution, violated the United States Constitution.

Justice Stevens, in an opinion joined by Justice Ginsburg and Breyer and Justice Ginsburg, in a portion of her opinion that was joined by Justices Stevens, Souter and Breyer, took issue with the Chief Justice's concurring opinion regarding the propriety and legitimacy of reviewing the Florida Supreme Court's decision concerning the meaning of Florida statutes and the Florida constitution. In his dissenting opinion, Justice Stevens, joined by Justices Ginsburg and Breyer, found that prior United States Supreme Court decisions recognized that the power given to state legislatures under Article II was the ability to exercise power that was given to the state legislature by the constitution of the state. The nature and scope of the state legislature's power depended on the state's constitution, which would have to be interpreted by state courts.[78] Justice Stevens believed that the Florida Court had simply interpreted state law, as was within the authority of any state supreme court. In his view the majority of the United States Supreme Court had to have, perhaps without explicitly saying so, based their entire decision on "an unstated lack of confidence in the impartiality and capacity of the state judges." In his view such an approach was literally contrary to the rule of law and

75. 531 U.S. at 529, 121 S.Ct. at 542 (Souter, J., joined by Breyer, J., and in part by Stevens and Ginsburg, JJ., dissenting).

76. 531 U.S. at 129–33, 121 S.Ct. at 543–45 (Souter, J., joined by Breyer, J., and in part by Stevens and Ginsburg, JJ., dissenting).

77. 531 U.S. at 129, 121 S.Ct. at 543 (Souter, J., joined by Breyer, J., and in part by Stevens and Ginsburg, JJ., dissenting).

78. 531 U.S. at 122, 121 S.Ct. at 539 (Stevens, J., joined by Ginsburg and Breyer, JJ., dissenting).

would undermine faith in the judiciary.[79]

Justice Ginsburg, writing for four Justices, noted that the United States Supreme Court had only in rare instances "rejected an outright interpretation of state law by a state high court," and that those few instances were situations where interpretation of the state law was crucial to deciding a federal issue.[80] Justice Ginsburg wrote: "the extraordinary setting of this case has obscured the ordinary principle that dictates its proper resolution: federal courts defer to state high courts' interpretation of their states' own law. This principle reflects the core of federalism, on which we all agree."[81] The Ginsburg dissenting opinion, however, unlike the Stevens opinion, allows some room for compromise with the concurring opinion. Justice Ginsburg recognized that there were at least some circumstances where federal interpretation of state law, in a manner contrary to a decision of a state supreme court, might be necessary in order to decide a federal issue.[82]

(b) Restricting the Ballot to Interested Voters

In *Kramer v. Union Free School District*[83] the Court examined a New York state law that provided that residents of a school district either had to own or lease taxable property or had to have children enrolled in the district's schools before they could vote in school district elections. The appellant in *Kramer*, a resident of the school district, was a bachelor who neither owned or leased any property and was prevented from voting in school elections. He lived with his parents. He argued that, as a resident of the district, any decisions made by the local school board would affect him, and, consequently, he and the class he represented

suffered discrimination that violated equal protection. The state, on the other hand, contended that it had an interest in limiting the election to interested persons because they would have a better understanding of the complexity of school affairs. The state argued that the classification achieved this purpose.

The Supreme Court reviewed the New York classification scheme under the strict scrutiny standard, because the law denied persons the fundamental right to vote.[84] It was willing to assume arguendo that a state constitutionally could limit the election to interested voters. Nevertheless, this particular New York method for restricting the vote was unconstitutional because it failed to achieve the purpose for which it was designed "with sufficient precision to justify denying appellant the franchise."[85] The statute was both underinclusive and overinclusive as the lines it drew excluded interested persons and included persons who only had "a remote and indirect interest in school affairs."[86] Therefore, the law violated the equal protection clause.

The Court in *Kramer* suggested that in some situations a state legitimately could limit an election to interested voters. Such a law would have to restrict the election precisely to those voters that would be primarily affected by the election. In *Salyer Land Co. v. Tulare Lake Basin Water Storage District*[87] the Court encountered such a law. Certain landowners, lessees, and residents of a water storage district in California attacked the constitutionality of the voter qualification provision of the district. They contended the statute violated the equal protection clause because it allowed only landowners to vote in the water storage district elections.

79. 531 U.S. at 127, 121 S.Ct. at 542 (Stevens, J., joined by Ginsburg and Breyer, JJ., dissenting).

80. 531 U.S. at 135, 139, 121 S.Ct. at 546, 548 (Ginsburg, J., joined by Stevens, J., and in part by Souter and Breyer, JJ., dissenting). All of the dissenting Justices joined this portion of Justice Ginsburg's opinion.

81. 531 U.S. at 141, 121 S.Ct. at 549 (Ginsburg, J., dissenting joined by Stevens, J., and in part by Souter and Breyer, JJ., dissenting).

82. 531 U.S. at 137, 121 S.Ct. at 547 (Ginsburg, J., joined by Stevens, J., and in part by Souter and Breyer, JJ., dissenting).

83. 395 U.S. 621, 89 S.Ct. 1886, 23 L.Ed.2d 583 (1969).

84. 395 U.S. at 626–28, 89 S.Ct. at 1889–90.

85. 395 U.S. at 632, 89 S.Ct. at 1892.

86. 395 U.S. at 632, 89 S.Ct. at 1892. Accord Phoenix v. Kolodziejski, 399 U.S. 204, 90 S.Ct. 1990, 26 L.Ed.2d 523 (1970); Cipriano v. City of Houma, 395 U.S. 701, 89 S.Ct. 1897, 23 L.Ed.2d 647 (1969).

87. 410 U.S. 719, 93 S.Ct. 1224, 35 L.Ed.2d 659 (1973).

The Court, however, believed that the *Kramer* analysis was inappropriate for this case. It observed that the water storage district possessed only limited authority and did not provide general public services like schools or housing. Moreover, the district's operations affect primarily the land within the district, and not residents as residents. Therefore, because the district served a special purpose that had a disproportionate effect on landowners the state could legitimately impose a landownership restriction as a means to establish a demonstrated interest in the election.[88]

It is difficult to reconcile *Kramer* with *Tulare Lake Basin Water Storage District*. But the functions of the water storage district were more specialized than those of a school board and the Court in *Hill v. Stone*[89] found this distinction would reconcile the cases.

In *Hill*, the Court examined the Texas "dual box" voting technique for bond elections. Property owners would place their ballots in one ballot box, and voters who did not own property would place their ballots in another. Before a bond issue could pass, it must receive not only a majority of the total votes cast but also a majority of the votes cast by property owners. The Court declared this scheme unconstitutional.

The Court first noted that any restriction on the vote must promote a compelling state interest unless it is an age, citizenship, or residence requirement. The Court then stated that, if the election is of special interest, the state can limit the election to those who will be primarily affected. The election in *Kramer* was not a special interest election, unlike the election in *Tulare Lake Basin Water Storage District* in the view of the Court. Therefore, the Court reasoned that "as long as the election in question is not one of special interest, any classification restricting the franchise on grounds other than residence, age, and citizenship cannot stand unless the district or State

can demonstrate that the classification serves a compelling state interest."[90] In a previous case the Court had declared that a general obligation bond issue is of general interest.[91] Therefore, because the election scheme at issue in *Hill* failed to serve a compelling state interest, the dual box voting device violated the equal protection clause.

As a result of these decisions a state can impose a "demonstrated interest" requirement on the exercise of the franchise only for special interest elections. Although the Court has failed to define exactly the nature of a special interest election, it has stated that it will sustain a "demonstrated interest" restriction for such elections as long as a reasonable basis exists for the limitation. On the other hand, the Court will review strictly any "demonstrated interest" requirement for general interest elections.

The Court has not allowed state or local governments to limit referenda or elections for representation on governmental bodies with generalized powers to a subclass of registered voters. However, the Court appears to have become lenient in its determination of what governmental entities qualify as ones exercising "general governmental power" requiring an unrestricted grant of the franchise to all otherwise eligible voters in compliance with the one person, one vote rule.

In *Ball v. James*[92] the Supreme Court allowed the State of Arizona to create a system for electing directors of a water reclamation district which limited voting eligibility to land owners who were otherwise eligible to vote and which apportioned voting power according to the amount of land owned by each voter. The Arizona system was in essence a one acre, one vote system. Fractional votes were given to those persons who owned less than an acre of land within the district and no vote to tenant farmers.

---

88. 410 U.S. at 729, 93 S.Ct. at 1230. Accord, Associated Enterprises, Inc. v. Toltec Watershed Imp. District, 410 U.S. 743, 93 S.Ct. 1237, 35 L.Ed.2d 675 (1973).

89. 421 U.S. 289, 95 S.Ct. 1637, 44 L.Ed.2d 172 (1975).

90. 421 U.S. at 297, 95 S.Ct. at 1643.

91. Phoenix v. Kolodziejski, 399 U.S. 204, 90 S.Ct. 1990, 26 L.Ed.2d 523 (1970).

92. 451 U.S. 355, 101 S.Ct. 1811, 68 L.Ed.2d 150 (1981).

The majority opinion by Justice Stewart had little trouble in upholding this system even though the water district whose voting system was at issue in *Ball* was authorized to and, in fact, did generate and sell electric power to a large portion of the state and distribute water to urban areas as well as farming areas, and issued tax exempt bonds. The majority opinion found that the district's absence of a general taxing power or other typical "governmental powers" exempted it from the one person, one vote rule. While its control over the allocation of water, the regulation of flood control, and the sale of electricity might have economic repercussions throughout the state or district, it was only a "limited purpose" governmental entity whose actions had a "disproportionate relationship . . . to the specific class of people whom the system makes eligible to vote."[93]

The majority upheld the restriction of the right to vote because it found that everyone affected by the operations of a government entity need not be enfranchised and that "the question was whether the effect of the entity's operations on them [the persons allowed to vote] was disproportionately greater than the effect on those seeking the vote."[94] If a state government cannot convince the Court that it has created only a limited purpose governmental entity, or that one group of citizens is distinctly affected by the action of a governmental entity, it will be able to limit the vote to a group of interested voters only if a majority of the Justices find that the law bears a

reasonable relationship to important statutory objectives.

(c) Voting Taxes

The Twenty-fourth Amendment prohibits the states from imposing a poll tax as a prerequisite for voting in presidential and congressional elections.[95] The Amendment does not apply to local or state elections.[96] Nevertheless, the Supreme Court has declared poll taxes for state and local elections unconstitutional under the Fourteenth Amendment.

In *Harper v. Virginia State Board of Elections*[97] the Court entertained a direct challenge to the Virginia poll tax for state elections. Although the Court recognized that the Constitution did not grant an expressed right to vote in state elections, the opinion stated that once the state granted the franchise the state must follow the dictates of the equal protection clause. The Court reasoned that because the ability to vote has no relationship to wealth, any impairment of the voting right based on wealth would violate the Fourteenth Amendment. In short, "a state violates the equal protection clause of the Fourteenth Amendment whenever it makes affluence of the voter or payment of any fee an electoral standard."[98]

(d) Literacy Tests

Traditionally, the most common restriction on the franchise based on "ability" was the literacy test. The Court considered the constitutionality of literacy tests in *Lassiter v.*

---

93. Ball v. James, 451 U.S. 355, 369, 101 S.Ct. 1811, 1820, 68 L.Ed.2d 150 (1981).

94. 451 U.S. at 369–71, 101 S.Ct. at 1820–21. Four Justices did dissent to the Court's lenient approach to defining limited versus general purpose elections. Ball v. James, 451 U.S. 355, 101 S.Ct. 1811, 68 L.Ed.2d 150 (1981) (White, J., joined by Brennan, Marshall, and Blackmun, JJ., dissenting). With a slight change in the membership of the Court the approach to such decisions could change in the future.

The Supreme Court has not upheld any type of limitation of the right to vote, or the right to be a candidate, that is based on the ownership of property except in the "water storage district" cases examined in this section. Normally, any requirement of land ownership for voting or candidacy rights should be considered so arbitrary as to be without a rational relationship to a legitimate government interest. See, Quinn v. Millsap, 491 U.S. 95, 109

S.Ct. 2324, 105 L.Ed.2d 74 (1989) (requirement of property ownership for appointment to a "board of freeholders," which recommends city and county reorganization plans to voters, violates the equal protection clause); Turner v. Fouche, 396 U.S. 346, 90 S.Ct. 532, 24 L.Ed.2d 567 (1970) (property ownership requirement for membership on an elected school board violates the equal protection clause).

See also Holt Civic Club v. City of Tuscaloosa, 439 U.S. 60, 99 S.Ct. 383, 58 L.Ed.2d 292 (1978) (upholding residency requirement for voting in municipal election although municipality exercises some powers over bordering, unincorporated community).

95. U.S.Const. amend. 24.

96. See, e.g., Harman v. Forssenius, 380 U.S. 528, 85 S.Ct. 1177, 14 L.Ed.2d 50 (1965).

97. 383 U.S. 663, 86 S.Ct. 1079, 16 L.Ed.2d 169 (1966).

98. 383 U.S. at 666, 86 S.Ct. at 1081.

Northampton County Board of Elections.[99] The appellants, black citizens from North Carolina, asked the Court to declare unconstitutional on its face a state statute that required a person to pass a literacy test before he could vote in state elections. The Court previously had held literacy tests constitutional in *Guinn v. United States*[100] and it refused to overrule *Guinn.* The *Lassiter* Court believed that the states have broad power to establish requirements that a person must meet before exercising the franchise. As long as the states do not use literacy tests to promote discrimination, the Court will refuse to declare the use of literacy tests unconstitutional.[101] The Court added that the ability to read and write has a direct relationship to the intelligent use of the voting right, and, therefore, classifications based on literacy are neutral.

Although the Court sustained the use of literacy tests, Congress later declared that the states cannot use these tests as a voting requirement. Congress began the process of outlawing literacy tests with the 1965 Voting Rights Act.[102] In a series of cases the Court sustained the Act against several challenges to its constitutionality. The Act gave the Attorney General the authority to prohibit the states from using literacy tests whenever less than half of the state's eligible voters were registered to vote.[103] The Court held that the Fifteenth Amendment gave Congress the power to prohibit racial discrimination in voting and it deferred to the congressional judgment on the most appropriate means to eliminate any discrimination that existed. Using the same reasoning the Court sustained an extension of the Voting Rights Act that prohibited voting literacy tests anywhere within the nation.[104]

(e) Physical Access to Polling Places—Inmates of Correctional Facilities

A state's authority to restrict the franchise based on a physical ability to go to the polls was challenged in *McDonald v. Board of Election Commissioners.*[105] The appellants were inmates confined in the Cook County Jail while awaiting trial. They were qualified voters but were unable to get to the polls to vote. A state statute only allowed Illinois election officials to give absentee ballots to the physically handicapped and to those who would be outside of the county on election day. The appellant failed to qualify for absentee ballots and they contended that the state's refusal to provide them with such ballots violated their fundamental right to vote.

A unanimous Court disagreed, but on narrow grounds. The Court first noted that the statute's classifications as to who could receive absentee ballots were not based on race or wealth. The burden, the Court said, speaking through Chief Justice Warren, was on securing an absentee ballot, not on voting. "It is thus not a right to vote that is at stake here but a claimed right to receive absentee ballots."[106] Moreover, the record was too sparse:

> Appellants agree that the record is barren of any indication that the State might not, for instance, possibly furnish the jails with special polling booth or facilities on election day, or provide guarded transportation to the polls themselves for certain inmates, or entertain motions for temporary reductions in bail to allow some inmates to get to the polls on their own.[107]

The statute denying the appellants absentee ballots was then judged constitutional under traditional, deferential equal protection standards and the state law was upheld.

---

99.   360 U.S. 45, 79 S.Ct. 985, 3 L.Ed.2d 1072 (1959).

100.   238 U.S. 347, 35 S.Ct. 926, 59 L.Ed. 1340 (1915).

101.   Louisiana v. United States, 380 U.S. 145, 85 S.Ct. 817, 13 L.Ed.2d 709 (1965); Alabama v. United States, 371 U.S. 37, 83 S.Ct. 145, 9 L.Ed.2d 112 (1962).

102.   See Katzenbach v. Morgan, 384 U.S. 641, 86 S.Ct. 1717, 16 L.Ed.2d 828 (1966).

103.   See South Carolina v. Katzenbach, 383 U.S. 301, 317, 86 S.Ct. 803, 813, 15 L.Ed.2d 769 (1966).

104.   See Oregon v. Mitchell, 400 U.S. 112, 131–34, 91 S.Ct. 260, 268–69, 27 L.Ed.2d 272 (1970).

105.   394 U.S. 802, 89 S.Ct. 1404, 22 L.Ed.2d 739 (1969).

106.   394 U.S. at 807, 89 S.Ct. at 1408.

107.   394 U.S. at 808, n. 6, 89 S.Ct. at 1408 n. 6.

In *Goosby v. Osser*[108] the Court emphasized that *McDonald* was concerned with a barren record and that a different record, in which it was shown that a statutory scheme absolutely prohibited otherwise confined inmates from voting, might result in a different decision. In *O'Brien v. Skinner*[109] the Court was faced with a sufficient record in a case brought by imprisoned persons who were either awaiting trial or convicted of misdemeanors. None was subject to any voting disability under state law.

Chief Justice Burger, who delivered the opinion of the Court in *O'Brien*, distinguished *McDonald* as a case disposed of only on failure of proof.[110] The New York election and correctional officials refused either to issue ballots, to establish registration or voting facilities within the jail, or to transport the appellants to the polls. The decision as to who would receive absentee ballots, as the state's election statutes were construed by its highest courts, was found to be "wholly arbitrary." For example, those held in jail awaiting trial in a county other than their residence were permitted to register by mail and vote by absentee ballot, but if a person were confined for the same reason in the county of their own residence, he would be completely denied the ballot. The state cannot, the Court concluded, deny voters "any alternative means of casting their vote although they are legally qualified to vote." [111]

It is unclear how broadly one should read *O'Brien*. The basis of the Court's decision was not that absentee ballots are constitutionally required but that if the state has this absentee procedure it cannot be "wholly arbitrary" in deciding what classes of voters may use it. But the majority's broad concluding dictum supports a view that a state cannot refuse to provide means for qualified citizens to exercise the franchise who are physically unable to get to the polls. In any event, this line of cases should be distinguished from the power of the state to deny completely the ballot (absentee or otherwise) from certain classes of voters, for example, convicted felons.[112]

(f) Residency Requirements

The Supreme Court has recognized that the state may qualify the voting right with reasonable residency restrictions. Several Court decisions have given some insight into what the Court considers reasonable. In *Carrington v. Rash*,[113] for example, the Court declared unconstitutional a Texas statute that prevented members of the armed services who moved to Texas from voting in state elections regardless of the length of time they had lived in Texas or their status as property-owners.[114] The Court held that the law violated the equal protection clause of the Fourteenth Amendment, and that Texas must develop a more precise means to determine the validity of a claim of residency than the challenged statute's classification scheme.[115]

Another residency limitation the states may use to restrict the voting right is to impose a durational residency requirement. The Congress, however, abolished residency requirements for presidential elections with the 1970 Voting Rights Act, and the Court sustained this provision of the Act.[116] Nevertheless, the Voting Rights Act allowed the states to place a durational residency restriction on the right to vote in state elections.

In *Dunn v. Blumstein*[117] the Court considered the constitutionality of Tennessee's durational residency requirement. Tennessee law provided that before a person could vote in

---

108. 409 U.S. 512, 93 S.Ct. 854, 35 L.Ed.2d 36 (1973).

109. 414 U.S. 524, 94 S.Ct. 740, 38 L.Ed.2d 702 (1974).

110. 414 U.S. at 529, 94 S.Ct. at 743.

111. 414 U.S. at 530, 94 S.Ct. at 743.

112. The Court, however, has sustained the states' authority to deny the vote to those convicted of felonies even though the convicted individual has completed serving his sentence. The Court found support for the prohibition in section two of the Fourteenth Amendment. Richardson v. Ramirez, 418 U.S. 24, 94 S.Ct. 2655, 41

L.Ed.2d 551 (1974), certiorari denied 418 U.S. 904, 94 S.Ct. 3194, 41 L.Ed.2d 1152 (1974).

113. 380 U.S. 89, 85 S.Ct. 775, 13 L.Ed.2d 675 (1965).

114. 380 U.S. at 89–90 n. 1, 85 S.Ct. at 776–77 n. 1.

115. 380 U.S. at 75–76, 85 S.Ct. at 779–80.

116. See Oregon v. Mitchell, 400 U.S. 112, 118–19, 91 S.Ct. 260, 261–62, 27 L.Ed.2d 272 (1970), (opinion of Black, J.).

117. 405 U.S. 330, 92 S.Ct. 995, 31 L.Ed.2d 274 (1972).

state elections that person not only had to meet age and citizenship requirements but also had to be a resident of the state for one year and of the county for three months. Although the *Dunn* Court acknowledged that the states can require their voters to be residents, this particular durational requirement was unwarranted and violated the Fourteenth Amendment. Tennessee's durational residency restriction on the right to vote impaired both voting rights and the right to travel. The Court reasoned that other means were available to determine bona fide residence and that with the prevalence of mass communications, citizens who have moved into an area can learn about local affairs quickly.[118] Consequently, Tennessee's one year requirement was invalid.

The test appears to be one of reasonableness. The Court has upheld a fifty-day durational restriction.[119] A restriction of less than two months may be necessary to verify voter lists or records and prevent fraud.

The exercise of extra-territorial jurisdiction by a municipality over nonresidents who could not vote in municipal elections was approved in *Holt Civic Club v. Tuscaloosa*.[120] Holt, an unincorporated community, was within three miles of Tuscaloosa, Alabama; under relevant Alabama statutes Holt residents were subject to the police and sanitary regulations of Tuscaloosa, a major municipal entity. Under these statutes, Tuscaloosa also had the power to license certain businesses, trades, and professions in Holt; however, license fees collected by a city from businesses in an unincorporated community could not exceed one-half the fee charged similar businesses in the city. Holt residents sought a ruling that the extension of Tuscaloosa's jurisdiction over them was unconstitutional because they were not given the opportunity to participate in elections for city

officials; they sought invalidation of the extraterritorial powers of the city or, in the alternative, extension of the right to vote in municipal elections to all those subject to the municipality's jurisdiction.

In *Holt*, the Supreme Court, in a majority opinion by Justice Rehnquist, rejected the equal protection and due process claims of the Holt residents. In so doing the majority opinion went through three analytical steps relevant to determination of similar extraterritorial jurisdiction cases. First, the majority concluded that this case involved no denial of the right to vote that was cognizable under the equal protection clause or previous rulings of the Court. The opinion noted that the previous decisions of the Court concerning the exclusion of some persons from the voting process because of residency or special interest requirements had invalidated only unreasonable durational residency requirements and impermissible definitions of the special interest that could be solely represented in an election.[121] The Court found that the use of residency as a requirement for voting was permissible because the use of a governmental "impact analysis" to determine who should vote in city elections was unworkable. Municipal actions often may affect many persons living immediately outside city boundaries in a variety of ways. The Court therefore concluded that "the line heretofore marked by this Court's voting qualification decision coincides with the geographical boundary of the governmental unit at issue."[122]

The second step was to determine if there was another equal protection problem with the classification. If there was no voting rights issue involved in the analysis then the equal protection test to be applied to this economic and social welfare legislation was the tradi-

---

118. 405 U.S. at 349–60, 92 S.Ct. at 1006–12.

119. See Marston v. Lewis, 410 U.S. 679, 93 S.Ct. 1211, 35 L.Ed.2d 627 (1973); Burns v. Fortson, 410 U.S. 686, 93 S.Ct. 1209, 35 L.Ed.2d 633 (1973).

120. 439 U.S. 60, 99 S.Ct. 383, 58 L.Ed.2d 292 (1978).

121. See also Evans v. Cornman, 398 U.S. 419, 90 S.Ct. 1752, 26 L.Ed.2d 370 (1970) (persons living on the grounds of the National Institute of Health, a federal enclave located within Maryland's boundaries, cannot be

denied the right to vote in Maryland elections; the state treats such persons as residents in its census and in determining congressional apportionment and the fiction that the enclave is not part of Maryland is rejected). *Evans* was specifically distinguished in *Holt* because the NIH inhabitants were, under a federal law, residents of Maryland.

122. 439 U.S. at 70, 99 S.Ct. at 390.

tional rational basis test. This test required only a determination of "whether any state of facts reasonably may be conceived to justify Alabama's system of police jurisdiction." [123] The majority concluded that the Alabama legislature might have conceived that the extension of city jurisdiction was a reasonable means of facilitating possible future annexation of territory to cities, helping to insure that the population outside of its cities do not go without basic municipal services, and insuring that businesses were regulated without the extraction of onerous license fees.

In the third phase of its analysis in *Holt*, the Court found no basis for a due process claim to participate in the election. The opinion noted that the Court has never declared any generalized right to vote under the due process clause and upheld the law since the classification was not totally arbitrary. Justice Brennan, joined by Justices White and Marshall in dissent, would have found that the Alabama system violated the equal protection clause. [124] Because the residents of Holt were directly affected by Tuscaloosa's police jurisdiction and governed in a substantial manner by the officials of Tuscaloosa, the dissenters would have required the city and state to demonstrate a "compelling interest" in denying the franchise to the residents of the unincorporated area. Indeed, Justice Brennan found that the distinction between city residents and unincorporated community residents to be "irrational"; the city was not merely affecting people in the surrounding area, it was governing them as it did city residents. However, this view was rejected by the majority and it would appear

that most statutes of this type will be approved if they are arguably reasonable and not in fact based on an invidious classification such as race. [125]

(g) Restrictions Based on Party Affiliation

States often conduct primary elections before the final general election. The primary election will provide political parties with a means to select their candidates for the next at-large election the state will conduct. To prohibit voters who belong to one political party from voting for a weak candidate in another party's primary, the states may restrict a person's ability to vote in party primary elections. [126] In *Rosario v. Rockefeller* [127] the State of New York required its voters to register with the state and to select their party thirty days before the November election; otherwise they could not vote in the next primary. The registration deadline generally occurred eight to eleven months before the primary. The primary registration statute was challenged as unconstitutional because it placed a limitation on the right to vote. The Court, however, sustained the law because it furthered the legitimate state goal of preventing party raiding. [128] The time limit the statute imposed bore a reasonable relationship to that goal because a voter probably would not register in one party when he intended to vote the other party's ticket in the November election. [129] If the relationship between the means and the end had not been so direct, the Court would have declared the law void.

The party affiliation statute challenged in

---

123. 439 U.S. at 73, 99 S.Ct. at 392.

124. 439 U.S. at 79, 99 S.Ct. at 394. (Brennan, J. dissenting, joined by White & Marshall, JJ.).

125. If the voting classification or boundary was drawn on the basis of race it would be invalid, see Gomillion v. Lightfoot, 364 U.S. 339, 81 S.Ct. 125, 5 L.Ed.2d 110 (1960).

Justice Stevens, in a concurring opinion, appeared to use a more realistic test, approaching one of the middle level standards of review. Yet he concluded that the residents of Holt were not denied equal protection because he found that their ability to vote for county, state, and federal officials allowed them to participate in the governance process and that residents had not been subjected to clearly unreasonable burdens or cost for municipal ser-

vices. However, Justice Stevens left open the possibility that he would vote against the extension of extraterritorial jurisdiction in particular cases wherein the exercise of jurisdiction, or the denial of the vote, could be demonstrated to be truly arbitrary or invidious. Holt Civic Club v. City of Tuscaloosa, 439 U.S. at 76–79, 99 S.Ct. at 393–95 (1978) (Stevens, J., concurring).

126. See, Note, Developments in the Law—Elections, 88 Harv.L.Rev. 1111, 1164 (1975).

127. 410 U.S. 752, 93 S.Ct. 1245, 36 L.Ed.2d 1 (1973).

128. 410 U.S. at 760–62, 93 S.Ct. at 1251–52.

129. 410 U.S. at 762, 93 S.Ct. at 1252.

Kusper v. Pontikes[130] was related directly to the legitimate state purpose of preventing voting raids in party primaries, but the Court declared it unconstitutional. The Court held that the law placed unnecessary restrictions on the voting right. Illinois prohibited a person from voting in the primary election of one political party if that person had voted in another party's primary election anytime within the previous twenty-three months.[131] The Court reasoned that the Illinois provision "locked-in" a voter into a particular party affiliation and the only way a person could break free was to forego voting in primaries for almost two years.[132] The Court believed that less drastic alternatives were available to Illinois to prevent party raiding.

Justice Blackmun dissented in *Kusper*.[133] He believed Illinois' scheme had a more rational relationship to its goal than New York's. New York used a flat time limit that would affect not only "primary raiders" but also persons who simply failed to register through an oversight. Illinois, "on the other hand, affects only party switchers,"[134] because those who regularly vote in party primaries usually will belong to "the group most amenable to organized raiding."[135] Moreover, the Justice reasoned that the twenty-three month limitation in practice amounted only to a one year limitation and in this context the state legislators

had drawn the classification scheme as narrowly as possible.

A state statute that restricts the ability of an individual to vote in a party primary election may impair First Amendment interests of the members of the political party. The First Amendment protects the freedom of association; this implied First Amendment right, as all First Amendment rights, applies to the states through the Fourteenth Amendment. When a political party's internal regulations enable an individual to vote in the party's primary and a state law denies that individual the right to vote in the primary, the state has prohibited the members of the party from being able to define the nature of their political association. This restriction of the right to vote and the freedom of association should only be upheld if the voting regulation is narrowly tailored to promote a clearly legitimate state interest, such as the interest in running efficient and honest elections. The Supreme Court sometimes has indicated that such laws must be narrowly tailored to promote a "compelling interest" of the state, but the Court has not clearly required that all such laws should be formally subjected to a compelling interest standard.[136]

In *Burdick v. Takushi*[137] the Court upheld a Hawaii statute that banned write-in voting in both the primary and general elections. Jus-

---

130. 414 U.S. 51, 94 S.Ct. 303, 38 L.Ed.2d 260 (1973).

131. 414 U.S. at 57, 94 S.Ct. at 307–08.

132. 414 U.S. at 57, 94 S.Ct. at 307–08.

133. Kusper v. Pontikes, 414 U.S. 51, 61, 94 S.Ct. 303, 310, 38 L.Ed.2d 260 (1973) (dissenting opinion, Blackmun, J.).

134. 414 U.S. at 65, 94 S.Ct. at 311.

135. 414 U.S. at 65, 94 S.Ct. at 311.

136. When the Supreme Court examines restrictions on freedom of association and freedom of speech that result from restrictions on the activities of political parties or persons campaigning for political office it normally states that a statute that has a significant restriction of those First Amendment rights must be narrowly tailored to promote a compelling interest. See, e.g., Eu v. San Francisco County Democratic Central Committee, 489 U.S. 214, 230, 109 S.Ct. 1013, 1024, 103 L.Ed.2d 271 (1989) (the Supreme Court invalidates laws that prohibit political party committees from making endorsement of candidates in a party primary and invalidates laws mandating a particular structure for political party committees; the Court uses the compelling state interest test to

determine whether the state may restrict the activities of the political party with the laws at issue in this case).

This First Amendment interest can be impaired in a variety of ways by state laws. State laws that restrict the ability of an individual to be a candidate in a party primary or a general election restrict the associational interests of those persons who would wish to vote for the candidate. Candidate regulations are examined in § 18.32 of this Treatise. The legislative or judicial control of political parties will directly raise freedom of association issues. These issues are examined in § 14.33(c) and § 17.41 of this Treatise.

The Supreme Court has not held that "closed" political primaries (wherein only registered members of the party are allowed to vote in that party's primary) are unconstitutional. The *Rosario* opinion, discussed in the preceding paragraphs of this section, appears to uphold the validity of such systems. See also *Nader v. Schaffer*, 417 F.Supp. 837 (D.Conn.1976), summarily affirmed 429 U.S. 989, 97 S.Ct. 516, 50 L.Ed.2d 602 (1976).

137. 504 U.S. 428, 112 S.Ct. 2059, 119 L.Ed.2d 245 (1992).

tice White's majority opinion found that this restriction did not involve any First Amendment issues because it was not a restriction on political associations or political expression in any way.[138] The majority ruled that the ban on write-in voting was not a severe restriction on the electoral franchise because, in light of the ease with which would-be candidates could be placed on primary ballots in Hawaii, there was no significant deprivation of the voter's right to make free choices in the election process. Hawaii allowed persons to participate in open primaries. The primary election system included established party candidates, persons named by primary petitions filed by new parties who could obtain signatures of one percent of the voters, or independent candidates who filed for positions on the nonpartisan primary ballot (by filing nominating papers containing 15 to 25 signatures).

The majority in *Burdick* concluded that "in light of the adequate ballot access" afforded by the state, the state's "ban on write-in voting imposes only a limited burden on voters' rights." Because there was no severe burden on the right to vote, the state law did not have to be justified by a compelling interest. The important state interest in avoiding "unrestrained factionalism" at the general election was determined to "outweigh petitioners' limited interest in waiting until the eleventh hour to choose his preferred candidate."[139]

The Court relied on *Burdick* in *Timmons v. Twin Cities Area New Party*,[140] when it upheld a state "antifusion law" that prohibited any person from appearing on a ballot as a candidate for more than one political party. Chief Justice Rehnquist's majority opinion in *Timmons* found that the antifusion law made it more difficult for minor parties to nominate a candidate who had a realistic possibility of being elected. Nevertheless, the Chief Justice said that the burdens the law imposed on new and minor political parties, "though not trivial," were not severe. For that reason, the majority in *Timmons,* did not require Minnesota to justify its law with a compelling interest; the law only had to be related to an important state interest. Chief Justice Rehnquist ruled that the antifusion law was related to, and justified by, the state's interest in "protecting the integrity, fairness, and efficiency" of their election process and the "stability of [the state's] political systems."[141]

In *Tashjian v. Republican Party of Connecticut,*[142] the Court invalidated a state statute which required voters in any political party primary to be registered members of that political party, insofar as the law conflicted with a Republican party regulation that permitted independent voters (registered voters who had not affiliated with any political party) to vote in the Republican primary elections for federal and statewide offices. Because this law restricted the First Amendment freedom of association, the Court gave little deference to the state when it examined whether any asserted state interest would be sufficient to justify the state regulation. The Supreme Court noted

138. The dissenting Justices agreed with the majority's conclusion that their laws involved no restriction on First Amendment activity and with the Court's use of a balancing test in this case. However, the dissenting Justices believed that the restrictions on voter's ability to choose a candidate of his choice that resulted from the total ban on write-in voting was severe, that no real state interest was advanced by the law, and that the ban should not survive any meaningful form of judicial review. Burdick v. Takushi, 504 U.S. 428, 442, 112 S.Ct. 2059, 2068, 119 L.Ed.2d 245 (1992) (Kennedy, J., joined by Blackmun and Stevens, JJ., dissenting). See § 14.32 of this Treatise regarding "The Right to Be a Candidate". Many of the cases discussed in § 14.32 of this Treatise were relied upon by the majority in finding that the state ban on write-in voting did not restrict political associations or political expression similar to state laws regulating candidate qualifications for ballot access that had been invalidated in earlier Supreme Court cases.

139. Burdick v. Takushi, 504 U.S. 428, 438-39, 112 S.Ct. 2059, 2066–67, 119 L.Ed.2d 245 (1992).

140. 520 U.S. 351, 117 S.Ct. 1364, 137 L.Ed.2d 589 (1997).

141. 520 U.S. at 1368, 117 S.Ct. at 1373, 1374. Justices Stevens, Ginsburg, and Souter dissented in *Timmons*. The dissenting Justices did not believe that the state's interest could justify this prohibition on minority parties being able to nominate the candidate of their choice and to link their interest with candidates and political parties that were likely to win elections. 520 U.S. at 370, 117 S.Ct. at 1375 (Stevens, J., joined by Ginsburg, J., and, in part, by Souter, J., dissenting); 520 U.S. at 382, 117 S.Ct. at 1381 (Souter, J., dissenting).

142. 479 U.S. 208, 107 S.Ct. 544, 93 L.Ed.2d 514 (1986).

that the state argued that the law promoted "compelling interests", but the Court found that the promotion of any legitimate interest of the state was, in fact, "insubstantial". Thus, it is not clear whether the Court was applying the compelling interest standard in this case.

In *Tashjian*, Connecticut asserted that excluding independent voters from party primaries, despite a conflicting rule by the political party, aided the administration of the primary system, prevented inter-party raiding, avoided voter confusion in primary and general elections, and protected the "two-party" system. Five members of the Supreme Court rejected the state's argument in a majority opinion written by Justice Marshall. The majority found that a state might take administrative and financial considerations into account "in choosing whether or not to have a primary system at all", but that it could not restrain the political party member's freedom of association based merely on the need for administrative convenience. Justice Marshall did not question the validity of the *Kusper* decision; he found that the state law did not curtail inter-party raiding in this case. The Republican party regulation that conflicted with this state law did not require the state to allow persons who were registered members of the Democratic party (or other political parties) to vote in the Republican election. Instead, the Republican regulation would only allow voters to participate in the Republican primary if they were either registered Republicans or persons who had not registered as members of any political party.

There was no demonstration by the state that the statute avoided voter confusion or otherwise protected the integrity of the voting system itself. The state's assertion that members of the general public would find it difficult to understand what a candidate stood for, if the candidate was nominated through a primary other than one that restricted primary votes to registered members of the party, was unsupported by substantial evidence. The Court found that the state had a legitimate interest in preventing voter confusion but that the slight promotion of that interest by this statute was insufficient to offset the burden imposed on the associational rights of the members of the Republican party.

Finally, the Court recognized that the state had a legitimate interest in protecting the integrity of a political party. The Republican party in Connecticut did not seek to open its primary to all voters, including members of other parties. If it had done so, it would have raised the question of whether it was attempting to impair the integrity of other political parties by inviting inter-party raiding on behalf of certain candidates in the Republican party. However, a Republican primary that allowed independent voters to take part in the party's nomination system did not threaten the integrity of other political parties or impair any other substantial interest of the state.[143]

If a state voting regulation places a significant burden on a political party's ability to control its membership and to select candi-

---

143. In Tashjian v. Republican Party of Connecticut, 479 U.S. 208, 224–29, 107 S.Ct. 544, 554–56, 93 L.Ed.2d 514 (1986). The Supreme Court also held that the qualifications clauses of Article I, § 2 of the Constitution and the Seventeenth Amendment applied to primary elections "in precisely the same fashion that they applied to general congressional elections." Article I, § 2, cl. 1 (regarding elections for the House of Representatives) and the Seventeenth Amendment (regarding the election of Senators) state, in relevant part, that the voters in each state who elect persons to Congress "shall have the qualifications requisite for electors" of representatives to the most numerous branch of the state's legislature. The party primary rule at issue in *Tashjian* would have allowed independent voters (who were not registered members of the Republican party) to vote in the party primary for the purpose of electing the party nominees for the United States Senate, the House of Representatives, and state-

wide offices but not for nominations for members of the state legislature.

The Supreme Court found that the qualifications clauses of Article I and the Seventeenth Amendment did not require precise symmetry between the definition of voters for state and federal elections. The Court found that the purposes of both Article I and the Seventeenth Amendment would be satisfied "if all those qualified to participate in the selection of members of the more numerous branch of the state legislature are also qualified to participate in the election of Senators and members of the House of Representatives." The primary rule was permissible "because it does not disenfranchise any voter in a federal election who is qualified to vote in a primary or general election for the more numerous house of the state legislature."

dates that reflect the interests of the members, the state regulation must be narrowly tailored to a compelling interest. This requirement is based on the First Amendment right of persons to associate to promote political ideas.[144]

In *California Democratic Party v. Jones*,[145] by a 7 to 2 vote, found that California's adoption of a primary system that allowed a "blanket vote" violated the First Amendment. The California law at issue in *Jones* created a single ballot on which all of the candidates for nomination for every office from all of the political office were listed. Thus, for example, all of the candidates for the Democratic, Republican, Libertarian, and Peace Parties for Governor would be listed on the same ballot, as would the names of all of the candidates for those party's nominations for other state and local offices. Under this system, a voter might cast a vote for a Democratic Party candidate for Governor, while simultaneously voting for a Republican nominee for some other state-wide position. Four political parties had rules that limited voting in their primaries to members of their primary. The California law was in complete conflict with those rules. The California law was not like the laws in so-called "open primary" states, where a voter may on primary election day choose the ballot of one political party without having previously being registered as a member of that party. In an open primary state the voter in essence declares herself to be a member of the party for which she is asking the ballot; she cannot vote in the party nomination system for more than one party. Thus a voter in an open primary state who selected a democratic ballot could only choose among the Democratic Party nominees for Governor, Attorney General, and state legislative positions. The four parties

who desired their nomination process to be limited to members of their party, challenged the law as a violation of the First Amendment.

Justice Scalia wrote the majority opinion for seven Justices in *Jones*; he found that there was a severe burden on the interests of the parties in defining and promoting their political ideas. Justice Scalia then examined the interest that the states asserted were compelling. The majority found that three state claims that related to producing nominees who generally reflected the views of the voters rather than a limited view of the party were not compelling interests because they were simply statements that the government wished to disregard the desire of political parties to define themselves and the types of candidates which they wish to put forward in the general election. The state asserted that in it was "promoting fairness, affording voters greater choice, increasing voter participation, and protecting privacy" but the Supreme Court found that "in the circumstances of the case" these interests were not compelling.[146] The majority did not have to rule on whether or not the interest might be compelling under other circumstances, because the majority ruled that "even if all these state interests were compelling [the California blanket primary proposition] is not a narrowly tailored means of furthering them."[147] Other alternatives, according to Justice Scalia's opinion, would be to allow political parties to initially choose their candidates for a first round of primary balloting which would choose the finalists who would then go on to the general election. Such a system would result in non–partisan voting but it would not involve persons outside of a political party choosing that political party's nominee.[148]

---

144. See Chapter 16 § 16.41, infra.

145. California Democratic Party v. Jones, 530 U.S. 567, 120 S.Ct. 2402, 147 L.Ed.2d 502 (2000), on remand 242 F.3d 1201 (9th Cir.2001).

146. 530 U.S. at 583, 120 S.Ct. at 2413.

147. 530 U.S. at 585, 120 S.Ct. at 2414.

148. 530 U.S. at 585, 120 S.Ct. at 2414. Justice Kennedy filed an opinion concurring in the opinion in judgement of the Court to emphasize his view that the law at issue in the case when combined with state controlled political parties spending place unjustifiable burdens on the ability

of individuals to form political parties and advance political ideas. 530 U.S. at 585, 120 S.Ct. at 2414 (Kennedy, J., concurring). Justice Stevens believed that when the political party used the state primary election system it no longer had a right to exclusive expressive association within that system, a point on which he was joined by Justice Ginsburg. Justice Stevens questioned whether the proposition that had been added to the Constitution of California by popular initiative might violate the elections clause of the United States Constitution, Article I, Section 4, Clause 1, which gave state legislatures control of the means of defining the systems for the elections of members to the

(h) Racial Restrictions

The Supreme Court has invalidated laws regulating the right to vote whenever the Court has found the law is designed to deny the right to vote to persons because of their race or to dilute the voting strength of a racial minority. A governmental action that excludes persons from receiving a ballot because they are members of a certain racial or ethnic group will violate the Fifteenth Amendment; certain government actions designed to harm minority race voters will violate the equal protection guarantee.[149]

A series of cases commonly called the *White Primary Cases*[150] clearly established that a state could not exclude a minority race from the franchise. In the first of the *White Primary Cases, Nixon v. Herndon*,[151] the Court declared unconstitutional a Texas law that expressly excluded blacks from voting in the Democratic primary. The law violated the Fourteenth Amendment because it impaired the right to vote on account of race or color. Later primary cases declared unconstitutional other schemes that states adopted in attempts to circumvent *Nixon v. Herndon*.[152]

Not only does the Constitution prohibit the states from expressly infringing the right to vote on the basis of race, but it also prohibits the states from applying facially neutral laws to disenfranchise racial minorities. In *Gomillion v. Lightfoot*[153] an Alabama statute altered

the city limits of Tuskegee. It changed the shape of the city from a square to a twenty-eight sided figure. The record also indicated that the modification of the city boundaries removed nearly 400 black voters but no white voters from the city.[154] The opinion stated that the Constitution limits the states' regulatory powers over their political subdivisions. The Court held that this affirmative legislative action deprived citizens of the vote on the basis of race and thus Alabama had violated the Fifteenth Amendment. The Court recognized the racial purpose of the state's action and declared the law unconstitutional.[155]

In *Mobile v. Bolden*[156] the Supreme Court refused to invalidate a city commission system whereby all three members of the city's governing body were elected at-large. The system was challenged by black voters who claimed that the city's refusal to elect commission members by district ensured that no black person could ever be elected to city government. In accordance with the Court's rulings concerning the proof of racial discrimination through statistical evidence, the challenge to the city's election system had to be dismissed because of the plaintiff's failure to prove that the at-large voting system was created or maintained for a "racially discriminatory purpose." Statistical proof of the racially discriminatory impact of a voting regulation is relevant but not determinative proof in cases wherein a governmental act is challenged on

United States Congress, although he did not express a conclusion on this point, which was not raised by the parties in the case. Justice Ginsburg did not join this part of the Stevens dissent. 530 U.S. at 589–602, 120 S.Ct. at 2416–2423 (Stevens, J., joined in part by Ginsburg, J., dissenting).

149. See §§ 14.4 regarding establishing whether a law that is racially neutral on its face in fact constitutes a racial classification. See § 14.10 (c) regarding the ability of government to employ race conscious legislative districting to help strengthen the voting power of minority race voters. Prohibiting some voters from receiving a ballot on the basis of their race or ancestry will violate the Fifteenth Amendment. See, e.g., Rice v. Cayetano, 528 U.S. 495, 120 S.Ct. 1044, 145 L.Ed.2d 1007 (2000) (Hawaii constitutional provision limiting the right to vote for a state agency to persons whose ancestry qualified them to be designated "Hawaiians" or "Native Hawaiians" violates Fifteenth Amendment).

150. Terry v. Adams, 345 U.S. 461, 73 S.Ct. 809, 97 L.Ed. 1152 (1953), rehearing denied 345 U.S. 1003, 73

S.Ct. 1128, 97 L.Ed. 1408 (1953); Smith v. Allwright, 321 U.S. 649, 64 S.Ct. 757, 88 L.Ed. 987 (1944); Nixon v. Condon, 286 U.S. 73, 52 S.Ct. 484, 76 L.Ed. 984 (1932); Nixon v. Herndon, 273 U.S. 536, 47 S.Ct. 446, 71 L.Ed. 759 (1927). Regarding the White Primary Cases, see § 14.33 infra.

151. 273 U.S. 536, 47 S.Ct. 446, 71 L.Ed. 759 (1927).

152. Terry v. Adams, 345 U.S. 461, 73 S.Ct. 809, 97 L.Ed. 1152 (1953), rehearing denied 345 U.S. 1003, 73 S.Ct. 1128, 97 L.Ed. 1408 (1953); cf. Georgia v. United States, 411 U.S. 526, 93 S.Ct. 1702, 36 L.Ed.2d 472 (1973); Tancil v. Woolls, 379 U.S. 19, 85 S.Ct. 157, 13 L.Ed.2d 91 (1964). See § 14.33.

153. 364 U.S. 339, 81 S.Ct. 125, 5 L.Ed.2d 110 (1960).

154. 364 U.S. at 341, 81 S.Ct. at 127.

155. 364 U.S. at 342, 81 S.Ct. at 127–28. For a detailed discussion of this case, see § 14.4, supra.

156. 446 U.S. 55, 100 S.Ct. 1490, 64 L.Ed.2d 47 (1980).

the basis of the Fourteenth or Fifteenth Amendment.

In contrast to *Mobile v. Bolden*, the Supreme Court in *Rogers v. Lodge*[157] upheld federal district court and court of appeals rulings finding that an at-large election system for the commissioners of a rural county violated the equal protection clause. In *Rogers*, the majority opinion found that the lower courts had properly required plaintiffs to prove that the voting system was maintained for a racially discriminatory purpose and that there was sufficient evidence that that standard had been met in this case. It was not only the fact that no black person had ever been elected to the county board of commissioners in *Rogers* that supported the lower federal courts' rulings. Those courts had also found evidence that the system was maintained by persons holding political power in the county so that they could consistently disregard the interests and concerns of members of racial minorities within the county. The Supreme Court found that this issue of intent was primarily a factual matter and it would not disturb the finding of the two lower federal courts.

In *Hunter v. Underwood*[158] the Justices were unanimous in invalidating a state constitutional provision that denied voting privileges to persons convicted of "any crime ... involving moral turpitude." Justice Rehnquist, writing for the Court, found that the records of the state constitutional convention, and the testimony of historians analyzing the facts surrounding the adoption of this constitutional provision by that convention, established "beyond peradventure" that this constitutional provision would not have been adopted "but for" the purpose of disenfranchising black persons. Because of the motivation of the delegates at the 1901 convention and the fact that

the provision "continues to this day" to have the effect of disproportionately denying the vote to black persons, Justice Rehnquist's majority opinion found that the disqualification provision "violates equal protection."

Election regulations that have a disparate impact on minority races will not be invalidated on that basis alone; only those laws which are enacted or maintained for the purpose of diluting or impairing the votes of members of a racial minority will be held to violate the equal protection guarantee or the Fifteenth Amendment. However, Congress, by statute, may invalidate state or local laws which have a discriminatory impact on the voting power of minority racial groups.[159]

(i) Adjusting the Majority Requirement

The Court has recognized that the states legitimately may require more than a simple majority of the vote cast before the government can adopt certain programs. In *Gordon v. Lance*,[160] for example, voters challenged the constitutionality of a provision in the West Virginia Constitution that prevented political subdivisions of the state from incurring bonded indebtedness unless sixty percent of the voters approved the bond issue in a referendum. They contended that the provision violated the Fourteenth Amendment; the Court rejected the contention. The state constitutional scheme did not single out any discrete or insular minority. Moreover, the Court realized that although "any departure from strict majority rule gives disproportionate power to the minority,"[161] the Constitution fails to contain any requirement that a simple majority must always prevail.

The Court in *Town of Lockport v. Citizens for Community Action*[162] confronted another challenge to a state law that required more

---

157. 458 U.S. 613, 102 S.Ct. 3272, 73 L.Ed.2d 1012 (1982).

158. 471 U.S. 222, 105 S.Ct. 1916, 85 L.Ed.2d 222 (1985).

159. The subject of race conscious districting is examined in § 14.10(c). Congress may regulate or prohibit state election regulations which have the effect of diluting the voting rights of members of racial minorities. Rome v. United States, 446 U.S. 156, 100 S.Ct. 1548, 64 L.Ed.2d 119 (1980). For citations to additional Supreme Court

cases on this point, see 3 R. Rotunda & J. Nowak, Treatise on Constitutional Law: Substance and Procedure § 18.4 (3rd ed. 1999, with annual supplements).

160. 403 U.S. 1, 91 S.Ct. 1889, 29 L.Ed.2d 273 (1971). Regarding the requirements of "one man, one vote" and super-majorities, see § 14.36(f), infra.

161. 403 U.S. at 6, 91 S.Ct. at 1892.

162. 430 U.S. 259, 97 S.Ct. 1047, 51 L.Ed.2d 313 (1977).

than a simple majority before a political subdivision of a state could act. A New York statute required that, before a county could adopt a new county charter, a majority of all the voters in the cities of the county must approve the charter and also a majority of all the non-city voters must approve the charter. In this particular case a majority of the city voters had approved the new charter. A majority of the non-city voters, however, had rejected the charter. Even though an overall majority of all the county voters had approved the charter, the measure was defeated. The disappointed city voters contended that this concurrent majority requirement violated the equal protection clause of the Fourteenth Amendment. The federal district court agreed and held that the concurrent majority requirement violated the one person-one vote principle. The Supreme Court, however, reversed.

The Court decided that the one person-one vote analysis was inappropriate. That analysis is applicable for the election of representatives not for referendums.[163] A referendum is an expression of direct voter will. Consequently, the Court concluded that two considerations became important. First, the Court must consider whether a genuine difference in interests exists in the two groups of voters the statute created. Second, if a genuine difference does exist, the Court must determine whether the enhancement of the minority voting strength worked an "invidious discrimination."[164]

The Court found a genuine difference in interests because the cities were more autonomous from county government than were non-city areas. Moreover, the Court failed to find that the statutory scheme invidiously discriminated against city voters. Because such refer-

enda can shift political power from towns to the city, the state can recognize "constituencies with separate and potentially opposing interests."[165] Thus, the Court held that the New York concurrent majority requirement did not violate the equal protection clause.

§ 14.32　The Right to Be a Candidate

(a) Introduction

The Constitution contains no express provision that guarantees the right to become a candidate.[1] The states are free, therefore, to create restrictions on the ability to become a candidate, but the restrictions created must not violate provisions of the Constitution that are of general application.[2] The states have exercised their discretion and have placed conditions on the right to candidacy. They have justified the creation of these conditions with several arguments. First, the restrictions on the right to become a candidate have helped the state to limit the size of the ballot, and thus reduce the potential for voter confusion.[3] Second, limiting the number of potential candidates will help insure that the candidate that eventually wins will have received a majority of the popular vote. Having an elected official who has received a majority of the popular vote will give citizens additional confidence in the ability of the official and faith in the democratic form of government. The state does not have an interest in minimizing the number of candidates who appear on the ballot but it has an interest in political stability.[4] Finally, restricting the right to candidacy will help avoid the potential for frivolous candidacies and thus preserve the integrity of the electoral process.[5] The Supreme Court has recognized these reasons as legitimate inter-

---

163.　430 U.S. at 266, 97 S.Ct. at 1052–53.

164.　430 U.S. at 268, 97 S.Ct. at 1053.

165.　430 U.S. at 271, 97 S.Ct. at 1055.

§ 14.32

1.　For citations to additional cases, and secondary authorities, on this subject see the multi-volume edition of this treatise: R. Rotunda & J. Nowak, Treatise On Constitutional Law: Substance and Procedure §§ 18.31–18.33.

2.　See e.g. Storer v. Brown, 415 U.S. 724, 728, 94 S.Ct. 1274, 1278, 39 L.Ed.2d 714 (1974); Bullock v. Carter, 405

U.S. 134, 142–43, 92 S.Ct. 849, 855–56, 31 L.Ed.2d 92 (1972).

3.　See e.g., Storer v. Brown, 415 U.S. 724, 732, 94 S.Ct. 1274, 1280, 39 L.Ed.2d 714 (1974).

4.　See Anderson v. Celebrezze, 460 U.S. 780, 103 S.Ct. 1564, 75 L.Ed.2d 547 (1983); Williams v. Rhodes, 393 U.S. 23, 32, 89 S.Ct. 5, 11, 21 L.Ed.2d 24 (1968).

5.　See American Party of Texas v. White, 415 U.S. 767, 781–85, 94 S.Ct. 1296, 1306–08, 39 L.Ed.2d 744 (1974).

ests of the states and as acceptable justification for some restrictions on access to the ballot.[6]

The states have used several methods to qualify the right to become a candidate. These methods include: (1) wealth restrictions;[7] (2) residency restrictions;[8] (3) property ownership requirements;[9] (4) party affiliation[10] and demonstrated support limitations;[11] and (5) racial classifications.[12]

Although the Supreme Court has recognized the power of the states to control the electoral process in some ways, it also has held that various constitutional provisions will limit the state's power to regulate access to the ballot. Ballot access restrictions, for example, must follow the dictates of the equal protection clause.[13] Moreover, the individual rights that the Constitution protects may have more weight with the Court than the right of the states to regulate the right to candidacy. The right to vote and the right to associate are the principal individual rights that may restrict the ability of the states to control candidate access to the ballot.[14] Consequently, the Court may use several constitutional provisions to

void state restrictions on the right to become a candidate.

Although the Supreme Court has recognized that basic constitutional rights are intertwined in the electoral process, the Court also has noted that elections are largely political creatures and that the courts should refrain from getting too involved in basically political decisions. Nonetheless, restrictions on candidacy for elective office impair the right of voters to cast a ballot for the candidate of their choice, protected by the Fourteenth Amendment due process and equal protection clauses, and the right of persons to associate in the expression of views in a political campaign, which is protected by the First Amendment. Therefore, the judiciary must independently scrutinize the basis for such legislation to insure that ballot access restrictions are a reasonable, non-discriminatory means of promoting important state interests.[15]

The ability of persons to be candidates for political office is certainly intertwined with the freedom of choice of voters to place persons into electoral office. Nevertheless, it would be misleading to characterize the right to be a

---

6. American Party of Texas v. White, 415 U.S. 767, 781–85, 94 S.Ct. 1296, 1306–08, 39 L.Ed.2d 744 (1974).

7. See Lubin v. Panish, 415 U.S. 709, 94 S.Ct. 1315, 39 L.Ed.2d 702 (1974).

8. See, e.g., Chimento v. Stark, 353 F.Supp. 1211 (D.N.H.1973), affirmed mem. 414 U.S. 802, 94 S.Ct. 125, 38 L.Ed.2d 39 (1973).

9. See Turner v. Fouche, 396 U.S. 346, 90 S.Ct. 532, 24 L.Ed.2d 567 (1970).

10. See McCarthy v. Briscoe, 429 U.S. 1317, 97 S.Ct. 10, 50 L.Ed.2d 49 (1976).

11. See Williams v. Rhodes, 393 U.S. 23, 89 S.Ct. 5, 21 L.Ed.2d 24 (1968).

12. Any law that constitutes a purposeful discrimination against minority race candidates or dilution of minority race voting power will be found to be a violation of equal protection and, perhaps, the Fifteenth Amendment. However, the Court has not set forth clear guidelines concerning the extent to which a governmental unit may consider race in order to create electoral districts in which members of racial minority groups will be able to control the outcomes of elections and to elect minority race persons to legislative bodies. The issue of racial affirmative action in election laws is considered in § 14.10(c) of this Treatise.

13. Bullock v. Carter, 405 U.S. 134, 141, 92 S.Ct. 849, 854–55, 31 L.Ed.2d 92 (1972).

14. See, e.g., Williams v. Rhodes, 393 U.S. 23, 30, 89 S.Ct. 5, 10, 21 L.Ed.2d 24 (1968).

15. See, Anderson v. Celebrezze, 460 U.S. 780, 103 S.Ct. 1564, 75 L.Ed.2d 547 (1983) (invalidating March deadline for filing nominating petition of independent presidential candidate for November election).

The method of judicial review used by the majority in *Anderson* involved the open use of a balancing test. The Justices balanced the degree of impact of the ballot restriction on First and Fourteenth Amendment rights against the interests asserted by the state and the relationship between the restriction and these interests.

Throughout this section of the treatise we examine a variety of cases upholding or invalidating restrictions on an individual's ability to become a candidate whose name appears on a primary or general election ballot. Related topics are considered in §§ 14.31, 14.33. Candidacy restrictions often involve First Amendment issues; restrictions on political parties or organizations often involve freedom of association and freedom of speech issues. See § 16.41 of this Treatise.

In Chandler v. Miller, 520 U.S. 305, 117 S.Ct. 1295, 137 L.Ed.2d 513 (1997) the Supreme Court, by an eight to one vote, ruled that a state law requiring candidates for election to certain government offices to, take, and pass, drug tests violated the Fourth Amendment. The majority opinion in *Chandler*, written by Justice Ginsburg, did not examine any First Amendment or equal protection clause issues.

candidate as a fundamental right which requires the Court to employ "strict scrutiny" and the "compelling interest" test to all laws restricting candidate access to the ballot. Laws which regulate candidacy for elective office certainly should be subject to independent judicial review. While the Justices should not impose unduly strict limitations on states' abilities to promote legitimate goals through regulating the candidacy of persons for elective office, the Justices should not simply defer to legislative judgments in this area.

The difficulty of employing a standard of review, such as a balancing test, which is less than strict, but not merely deferential is demonstrated by the Court's decision in *Clements v. Fashing*.[16] In *Clements* the Court upheld provisions of the Texas constitution that restricted a public official's ability to become a candidate for a public office other than that office which he already held. The Texas constitution prohibited certain state and county officeholders from becoming candidates for another state or federal office. These provisions were upheld by a five to four vote and without a majority opinion.

Four Justices who voted to uphold the law in *Clements* found that candidacy for elective office was not a fundamental right which subjected all candidate regulations to strict judicial scrutiny.[17] Because the law did not allocate the ability to become a candidate based upon wealth nor impose arbitrary burdens on small political parties or independent candidates, these Justices found no reason to independently review the reasonableness of the regulation. Justice Stevens, concurring in the judgment of the Court, found that requiring certain state officers to forego seeking another

elective office until they fulfilled their duties and their term of office did not impinge upon any interest protected by the federal Constitution.[18]

It is unfortunate that there was no majority opinion in this case and that some Justices made it appear as if there should be no independent judicial review of laws regulating candidacy for elective office that do not involve wealth classifications or small political parties. The dissent in *Clements* accused the majority of abdicating the proper judicial role in the review of candidacy classification by failing to require the classification of officeholders prohibited from being candidates for another office to be reasonably related to a legitimate legislative purpose.[19] However, the dissent failed to focus on the question of whether all candidacy regulations should be subjected to strict judicial review or whether the Court should only subject to strict scrutiny those classifications which appeared to disadvantage a disfavored classification of persons such as economically poor persons or independent candidates.[20]

The year after *Clements* was decided, the Court demonstrated that it was not willing to abdicate the judicial role of independently reviewing restrictions on candidate ballot access. In *Anderson v. Celebrezze*,[21] the Court invalidated a state statute which required an independent candidate for President of the United States to file his nominating petition in the month of March prior to the general election. This filing date preceded the time when major political parties had to name their candidates because the statute gave them an exemption due to their demonstrated political support. A

---

16. 457 U.S. 957, 102 S.Ct. 2836, 73 L.Ed.2d 508 (1982). Justice Rehnquist delivered an opinion which was a majority opinion as to certain jurisdictional and First Amendment issues. Those portions of Justice Rehnquist's opinion which addressed the equal protection issue was joined only by Chief Justice Burger and Justices Powell and O'Connor.

17. 457 U.S. at 961–65, 102 S.Ct. at 2843–44 (Rehnquist, J., joined by Burger, C.J., and Powell & O'Connor, JJ.)

18. Clements v. Fashing, 457 U.S. 957, 971–73, 102 S.Ct. 2836, 2848, 73 L.Ed.2d 508 (1982) (Stevens, J., concurring).

19. Clements v. Fashing, 457 U.S. 957, 976, 102 S.Ct. 2836, 2850, 73 L.Ed.2d 508 (1982), (Brennan, J., joined by Marshall, Blackmun & White, JJ., dissenting).

20. 457 U.S. at 982–84, 102 S.Ct. at 2854. The dissent did not address this point because the dissenters believed that the classification could not survive even the minimal rationality test.

21. 460 U.S. 780, 103 S.Ct. 1564, 75 L.Ed.2d 547 (1983). See § 14.32(e), infra.

five-Justice majority ruled that the regulation impaired the First and Fourteenth Amendment rights of voters; the majority did not distinguish between due process, equal protection, or First Amendment analysis in this area. Courts, according to the majority, were required to balance the degree to which the regulation impaired these First and Fourteenth Amendment rights against the degree to which the regulation advanced important state interests. In this case, the state could justify some cut-off for candidate filing but not one so far in advance of the general election. The majority concluded that the early filing date did not sufficiently advance the interest in political stability, voter awareness, or equal treatment of candidates to justify such a significant restriction on voter freedom of choice and freedom of association.

Thus, the Court seems committed to independent judicial review of candidate restrictions through the means of a rather ill-defined balancing test which weighs the restriction on voter First and Fourteenth Amendment freedom against the state interest in helping the populace have sufficient elections for the selection of public officers. The Court will also examine conflicts between state law and politi-

cal party regulations regarding the eligibility of persons to participate in primary elections as voters or candidates to determine whether the state is unconstitutionally interfering with the freedom of association of persons who have joined together to form the political party.[22]

If the law constitutes a severe restriction on the ability of a voter to exercise an electoral choice, or a significant impairment of political association and political expression rights of voters and candidates, the law will only be upheld if it is narrowly tailored to promote a compelling interest.[23] If a state voting regulation does not significantly impair the First Amendment freedom of political association, and does not impose a severe restriction on a voter's ability to make a free choice as to the exercise of the electoral franchise, the state law will be subjected only to a balancing test that recognizes legitimate, politically neutral state interests.[24] In the cases that are examined in this section of the Treatise, the reader will find that those candidate restrictions that appear to interfere with both the First Amendment right of freedom of association and the right to exercise the franchise are likely to be invalidated.[25]

---

22. Democratic Party of the United States v. Wisconsin ex rel. La Follette, 450 U.S. 107, 101 S.Ct. 1010, 67 L.Ed.2d 82 (1981) (state may not bind delegates elected in "open" state primary to vote in a particular way at the national party convention in violation of the political party's rules). See § 14.33(c).

23. Regulations of candidates and political parties access to ballot positions inherently involve First Amendment as well as equal protection issues. These cases are examined in § 14.32(g) of this Treatise. General restrictions on the ability to vote are examined in § 14.31. The one person-one vote rule is examined in §§ 14.35, 14.36. The voting rights cases that most clearly involve First Amendment issues are those in which political gerrymandering is alleged; that subject is examined in § 14.36(e) of this Treatise.

24. In Norman v. Reed, 502 U.S. 279, 112 S.Ct. 698, 116 L.Ed.2d 711 (1992), the Supreme Court applied the compelling interest test to determine the legitimacy of state laws that regulated a new political party's access to the ballot. Because the laws constituted a severe restriction on political association the Court used the compelling interest test. This case is examined in § 14.32(e) of this Treatise.

25. In Burdick v. Takushi, 504 U.S. 428, 112 S.Ct. 2059, 119 L.Ed.2d 245 (1992) the Supreme Court upheld the State of Hawaii's prohibition on write-in voting at primaries, and the general election, without using the compelling interest test because (1) the ease with which

candidates could qualify for Hawaii's open partisan and nonpartisan primary ballots meant there was no significant restriction on First Amendment rights and (2) the ballot access laws provided ample opportunities for all candidates to be on the ballot so that there was no significant restriction of a voter's freedom of choice that required the state law to be justified by a compelling interest. In Timmons v. Twin Cities Area New Party, 520 U.S. 351, 117 S.Ct. 1364, 137 L.Ed.2d 589 (1997) the Court, by a six to three vote, upheld a state law prohibiting any individual from appearing as a candidate for a state political office for more than one political party in part because the law did not prohibit any individual from being a candidate for a political office. Chief Justice Rehnquist, writing for the majority, found that the burden that the law imposed on the associational rights was not severe and, therefore, that the law need not be subject to the compelling interest test. The majority in *Timmons* upheld the law on the basis that it was related to the state interest in protecting the election process and the stability of the political system. Justices Stevens, Ginsburg, and Souter dissented in *Timmons*. 520 U.S. at 368, 117 S.Ct. at 1375 (Stevens, J., joined by Ginsburg, J., and, in part, Souter, J., dissenting); 520 U.S. at 380, 117 S.Ct. at 1381 (Souter, J., dissenting). See §§ 14.31, 14.33 of this Treatise regarding other voter rights issues and the one person-one vote rule.

In *U.S. Term Limits, Inc. v. Thornton*,[26] the Supreme Court, by a five to four vote, ruled that a State could not limit the number of times that a person could be elected to, or the number of years that a person could serve in, the United States Senate or House of Representatives. The Court's ruling was based on federalism concerns and the history of Article I.[27]

(b) Wealth Restrictions

Many states require potential candidates for public office to pay a filing fee before the state will place their names on the ballot. In *Bullock v. Carter*[28] the appellees challenged the constitutionality of the Texas filing fee requirement. The appellees met all the other qualifications necessary to become candidates for public office but could not afford to pay the requisite fee of $1000. These candidates contended that the fee requirement violated the equal protection clause.

As a preliminary issue the *Bullock* Court had to determine the level of review it would use to assess the constitutionality of the Texas wealth restriction. The opinion recognized that the states had broad powers under the Constitution to establish the rules and regulations for elections. Moreover, the state of Texas imposed the fee requirement on candidates and not voters, and the Constitution did not explicitly guarantee any right to candidacy. Nevertheless, the filing fee requirement did affect voters because it limited the choice on the ballot. The size of the fee at issue was "patently exclusionary" and could exclude qualified candidates from the election. Consequently, the effect on qualified voters was direct and obvious; their choice of candidates became limited and the poor voter may not have a qualified representative running for office. Because the filing fee requirement affected the fundamental right to vote, the Court would use strict scrutiny to review the Texas law.

In support of the filing fee requirement the state argued that the fee was necessary to limit the size of the ballot and to frustrate frivolous candidates. Furthermore, the state contended that the filing fee helped finance the election. The Court acknowledged the state's legitimate interest in protecting the integrity of the ballot, but the Court also observed that appellees were not unwilling to pay the fee but simply were unable to pay. Hence, the filing fee requirement excluded legitimate as well as frivolous candidates. As to Texas' financing argument the Court held that the purpose of financing the election served a rational basis for the fee requirement. However, the opinion employed a strict scrutiny level of review and the state failed to show that the fee requirement was necessary to finance the election.[29] Moreover, the force of the financing argument was diluted by the realization that candidates for statewide office paid a lower fee than candidates for local office. Hence, the *Bullock* Court held that the Texas filing fee requirement was unconstitutional because it violated the equal protection clause.

Two years after *Bullock* the Court decided *Lubin v. Panish*[30] in which candidates for local and state offices attacked the constitutionality of the California filing fee requirement. The fee equaled two per cent of the annual salary of the state office sought. The Court decided that the California filing fee violated the equal protection clause of the Fourteenth Amendment insofar as it was applied to indigent candidates. Again the Court recognized the legitimate needs of the state to keep the size of the ballot manageable. To achieve that end, however, the state must adopt means that will not "unreasonably burden either a minority party's or individual candidate's equally important interest in the continued availability of political opportunity."[31] The states must allow voters a reasonable choice of candidates, and an absolute filing fee requirement uncon-

---

26. 514 U.S. 779, 115 S.Ct. 1842, 131 L.Ed.2d 881 (1995)

27. The *Thornton* case is examined § 3.5 of this Treatise. See generally, Ronald D. Rotunda, The Aftermath of *Thornton*, 13 Constitutional Commentary 201 (1996).

28. 405 U.S. 134, 92 S.Ct. 849, 31 L.Ed.2d 92 (1972).

29. 405 U.S. at 147, 92 S.Ct. at 857–58.

30. 415 U.S. 709, 94 S.Ct. 1315, 39 L.Ed.2d 702 (1974).

31. 415 U.S. at 716, 94 S.Ct. at 1320.

stitutionally limited that choice. The opinion reasoned that the state may require a filing fee only if a reasonable alternative to the fee exists to gain access to the ballot. The Court believed that a minimum wealth requirement does not reflect a potential candidate's popular support or the seriousness of the candidacy. Hence, the state must provide alternative means for indigent candidates to qualify for a ballot position.

(c) Residency Restrictions

State election laws often require persons running for elective office to meet durational residency requirements. Lower federal courts and state courts have considered durational residency restrictions on the right to be a candidate on several occasions.[32] The Supreme Court has affirmed by memorandum several three judge district court decisions that have decided the constitutionality of such limitations on the right to access to the ballot.[33] But memorandum affirmances are of limited precedential value,[34] and the constitutionality of durational residency requirements is still an open question.

A three-judge federal district court in *Chimento v. Stark*[35] sustained the constitutionality of New Hampshire's durational residency requirement for elective office. The New Hampshire statute required gubernatorial candidates to have resided within the state for seven years before running for office. Those challenging the statute's constitutionality contended that the law violated the equal protection clause by impairing the right to travel and the right to associate.

Because the *Chimento* court agreed that the statute affected these fundamental rights, it decided that it must use a strict standard of review.[36] The court, however, sustained the

law. It reasoned that the durational residency requirement only delayed the opportunity to become a candidate. Therefore, the court decided that the law only imposed a minimal burden on potential candidates and voters. Moreover, the state imposed the seven year requirement only on candidates for the state's highest elective office. The court suggested it might have reached a different result if the requirement existed for lesser public offices.[37] Finally, the court concluded that the state had a legitimate interest in creating the seven year durational requirement. The restriction helps insure not only that candidates will become familiar with local issues, but also that local voters will become familiar with the candidates. Therefore, the restriction can both promote the integrity of the election process and avoid voter confusion.

Frustrated candidates for elective office face a major constitutional obstacle whenever they challenge durational residency requirements. The Constitution itself requires candidates for federal elective office to meet certain residency standards.[38] Therefore unless the residency requirement is patently unreasonable in length for the particular elective office the courts usually have sustained such qualifications on the right to candidacy. The Supreme Court, however, has not explained what constitutes a reasonable and constitutional residency requirement.

(d) Property Ownership Requirements

The Supreme Court assessed the constitutionality of a property ownership restriction on the access to ballot position in *Turner v. Fouche*,[39] where black citizens brought a class action challenging the constitutionality of Georgia's statutory restriction on school board

---

32. See, e.g., Woodward v. City of Deerfield Beach, 538 F.2d 1081 (5th Cir.1976); Sununu v. Stark, 383 F.Supp. 1287 (D.N.H.1974), affirmed 420 U.S. 958, 95 S.Ct. 1346, 43 L.Ed.2d 435 (1975); Chimento v. Stark, 353 F.Supp. 1211 (D.N.H.1973), affirmed mem. 414 U.S. 802, 94 S.Ct. 125, 38 L.Ed.2d 39 (1973).

33. See, e.g., Chimento v. Stark, 353 F.Supp. 1211 (D.N.H.1973), affirmed mem. 414 U.S. 802, 94 S.Ct. 125, 38 L.Ed.2d 39 (1973).

34. See § 2.5, supra.

35. 353 F.Supp. 1211 (D.N.H.1973), affirmed 414 U.S. 802, 94 S.Ct. 125, 38 L.Ed.2d 39 (1973). Accord, Sununu v. Stark, 383 F.Supp. 1287 (D.N.H.1974), affirmed 420 U.S. 958, 95 S.Ct. 1346, 43 L.Ed.2d 435 (1975) (seven years residence for state senatorial candidate).

36. 353 F.Supp. at 1214.

37. 353 F.Supp. at 1215–16 n. 10.

38. U.S.Const. art. I, §§ 2, 3 and art. II, § 1.

39. 396 U.S. 346, 90 S.Ct. 532, 24 L.Ed.2d 567 (1970); Elections, supra note 1, at 1220–21.

candidates. Georgia limited school board membership to those with an interest in real property. This restriction was found to violate the equal protection clause.

The Court stated that the appellants "have a federal constitutional right to be considered for public service without the burden of invidiously discriminatory qualifications."[40] The Court reasoned that the property ownership restriction failed to serve a valid state purpose. The status of being a non-freeholder did not reflect any lack of attachment to the local community or the local schools. Hence, Georgia's classification scheme for school board candidates was unconstitutional.

The Court relied on *Turner* when it invalidated a property ownership requirement for appointment to a "Board of Freeholders." In *Quinn v. Millsap*[41] the Supreme Court found that it need not make a determination of the appropriate standard of review for all voting and candidacy rights cases in order to invalidate a state law requiring the ownership of real property as a condition for being appointed to a government board that could recommend a plan of governmental reorganization to the electorate of a city and county. Although the Board did not have significant governmental powers, it played a significant function in the governmental process by recommending city-county reorganization to the electorate. The Court found that there was no rational relationship between property ownership and the ability of persons to understand issues in the community; individuals who did not own real property could not be presumed to be persons who lack knowledge about issues or who lacked true attachment to the community and its well-being.

(e) Party Affiliation and Demonstrated Support Requirements

A party affiliation qualification requires persons who want to run for elective office to be a member of certain political parties; this requirement gives candidates who are members of major political parties certain advantages over independent candidates.[42] In *Storer v. Brown*[43] California prohibited independent candidates from running in the general election if the candidates either had voted in an immediately preceding party primary or had registered their party affiliation with a qualified party within one year of the primary. Storer challenged the constitutionality of the prohibition. He had been a registered Democrat and the state had disqualified him from running as an independent candidate. He contended that the provision violated his First Amendment rights and the dictates of the Fourteenth Amendment.

The Supreme Court held that the Constitution did not prevent California from adopting a party affiliation statute. The state, however, must adopt reasonable alternative means for independent candidates and minor political parties to get a ballot position, and the alternative means must not place too heavy a burden on the right to vote and the right to associate.

The Court noted in *Storer* that the state has an interest in imposing some candidate qualifications to avoid voter confusion, to prevent burdening the election process, and to facilitate the election winner receiving a majority.[44] The California party affiliation restriction helped achieve these goals because it kept a loser in the party primary from running in the general election. Therefore, the state reduced

---

40. 396 U.S. at 362, 90 S.Ct. at 541.

The Court has summarily reversed a state court decision that upheld a requirement that appointed members of an airport commission (with some governmental powers) own property in the locality. The Supreme Court merely cited *Turner* and reversed the state decision. Chappelle v. Greater Baton Rouge Airport District, 431 U.S. 159, 97 S.Ct. 2162, 52 L.Ed.2d 223 (1977), rehearing denied 433 U.S. 915, 97 S.Ct. 2990, 53 L.Ed.2d 1102 (1977).

41. 491 U.S. 95, 109 S.Ct. 2324, 105 L.Ed.2d 74 (1989). Justice Blackmun, writing for a unanimous Court, found that there was no need to consider whether a "strict

standard of review" should apply in this case, because the classification could not survive even rationality review. 491 U.S. at 107 n. 10, 109 S.Ct. at 2332 n. 10.

42. See generally, Douglas, J., citing Treatise in State ex rel. Purdy v. Clermont County Board of Elections, 77 Ohio St.3d 338, 673 N.E.2d 1351, 1355 (Ohio 1997); Moyer, J., dissenting and citing Treatise in State ex rel. Purdy v. Clermont County Board of Elections, 77 Ohio St.3d 338, 673 N.E.2d 1351, 1358 (Ohio 1997).

43. 415 U.S. 724, 94 S.Ct. 1274, 39 L.Ed.2d 714 (1974).

44. 415 U.S. at 732, 94 S.Ct. at 1280.

the potential for political factionalism and splintered parties, and prevented the general election ballot from becoming a forum for intra-party feuds. Moreover, the state provided the necessary alternative means for ballot qualification. A party member who intended to run as an independent could disaffiliate himself from the party before the deadline and, by using the alternative methods to a primary election, gain a position on the general election ballot. Consequently, the Court found the California party affiliation provision constitutional.

Justice Powell, sitting as a Circuit Justice, summarized the Court's present position on party affiliation statutes in *McCarthy v. Briscoe*.[45] Supporters of Eugene McCarthy sought a mandatory injunction to force the state of Texas to place his name on the general election ballot as a presidential candidate. Texas required presidential candidates to be members of a major organized political party before they could gain access to the ballot. The only alternative for independent candidates was a "write-in" campaign. Justice Powell granted the injunction. He noted that the Court in *Storer v. Brown* rejected the idea that a state could force an independent candidate to join or organize a political party to gain access to the ballot. The state could require some showing of demonstrated support but it had to provide alternative means to an independent candidate to get a position on the ballot. Therefore, Texas had to place former Senator McCarthy's name on the ballot as a candidate for President.

For many years states have imposed demonstrated support requirements on independent candidates or minor political parties.[46] Typically, the demonstrated support statute requires independent candidates or minor parties to submit petitions containing a certain number of signatures from qualified voters before they can receive access to the ballot. The number of signatures required is often related to the percentage of votes cast in the

last general election. States will relieve a political party of the petition requirement if the party's candidates received a minimum percentage of the votes cast in the previous election. In short, these statutes require independent candidates or minor political parties to demonstrate their popular support before they gain a ballot position.

The Court has considered several challenges to the constitutionality of demonstrated support requirements. One of the first cases was *Williams v. Rhodes*.[47] Members of a minor political party contended that the Ohio demonstrated support statute strongly favored the established political parties, and thus violated the equal protection clause. Ohio required new political parties to submit petitions with signatures of qualified voters equaling in number fifteen percent of the number of votes cast in the last gubernatorial election. Moreover, Ohio had an early filing deadline for the petition. No petition was required if the party received ten percent of the vote in the previous gubernatorial election. The state contended that the law was constitutional because it furthered three state interests. First, the measure promoted the two party system. Second, the law would insure that the voters would elect a candidate with a majority vote. Third, the statute helped prevent voter confusion, the standard state interest argument.

The Court reviewed the requirements under the strict scrutiny standard because it burdened both the right to vote and the right to associate.[48] Consequently, the state had to justify these burdens with a compelling state interest and the Court found the proffered state interests less than compelling. Although the Ohio scheme did support the two party system, it did so by favoring two particular parties—the Democratic and Republican parties. The Court agreed that Ohio's law assured the election of majority candidates but it did so by suppressing the growth of new parties. Finally, the Court acknowledged that the statute helped avoid voter confusion, but the

45. 429 U.S. 1317, 97 S.Ct. 10, 50 L.Ed.2d 49 (1976).

46. Note, Developments in the Law—Elections, 88 Harv.L.Rev. 1111, 1124–25 (1973).

47. 393 U.S. 23, 89 S.Ct. 5, 21 L.Ed.2d 24 (1968).

48. 393 U.S. at 30, 89 S.Ct. at 10.

Court believed that the means Ohio chose to achieve this goal were not necessary to that end. Thus, it could not justify the burden on the fundamental rights to vote and associate.[49] Under this strict level of review the Court found that the Ohio law violated the equal protection clause.

A demonstrated support statute may discriminate against some voters as well as some candidates. In *Moore v. Ogilvie*[50] Illinois required independent candidates for President and Vice President to submit petitions with signatures from 25,000 qualified voters. The Illinois law, however, also required that among these signatures at least 200 signatures had to come from each of fifty different Illinois counties out of the state's 102 counties. The state argued that this additional requirement was necessary to insure that the independent candidate had statewide support. The Supreme Court found that the law discriminated against the more populous counties. Nearly 94% of Illinois voters, who lived in only forty-nine counties, could not form a new party, but 6.6% of the voters in the remaining 53 counties could form a new party.[51] The law violated the principle of equality among voters and was an unreasonable burden on candidates.

After *Moore v. Ogilvie*, the Illinois election code required that new political parties and independent candidates obtain the signatures of 25,000 qualified voters to appear on the ballot for statewide elections; they did not have to receive a specific number of votes from specific counties, the requirement which was invalidated in *Moore*. However, the Illinois election code required that independent candi-

dates, or candidates of new parties, for offices of political subdivisions in Illinois had to receive signatures from at least five percent of the number of people who had voted in the previous election of that particular subdivision. The distinction in the statute, as applied to City of Chicago or Cook County elections, required that these candidates receive substantially more signatures to gain access to the Chicago or Cook County ballots than would similar independent candidates for statewide office. Thus, an independent candidate would need 35,000 signatures for inclusion on the ballot in a Chicago election, while a candidate for statewide office would need only 25,000 signatures.

In *Illinois State Board of Elections v. Socialist Workers Party*,[52] the Supreme Court unanimously held that this political subdivision requirement violated equal protection and that the new political parties or independent candidates could not be required to obtain more signatures than the statewide requirement (25,000) for city or county elections. The majority opinion, by Justice Marshall, found the classification subject to the compelling interest test because it affected the fundamental rights of association and voting. Justice Marshall's opinion seemed to indicate that exclusion of frivolous candidates was an acceptable purpose for the legislation, although he described that goal only as a "legitimate" one. The majority held that the subdivision signature requirement was invalid because it was not the most narrow, or least restrictive, means of excluding frivolous candidates from the ballot.[53]

---

49. 393 U.S. at 30, 89 S.Ct. at 10.

50. 394 U.S. 814, 89 S.Ct. 1493, 23 L.Ed.2d 1 (1969).

51. 393 U.S. at 819, 89 S.Ct. at 1496.

52. 440 U.S. 173, 99 S.Ct. 983, 59 L.Ed.2d 230 (1979).

53. 440 U.S. at 188, 99 S.Ct. at 992. Mr. Justice Blackmun concurred in the result but not in the use of the "compelling interest test." He believed that the law should be subject to "strict scrutiny" but that the phrases "compelling state interest" and "least drastic means" were vague and an open ended invitation to lower court judges to engage in a form of substantive due process analysis similar to that used earlier this century in the economic area. 440 U.S. at 188–189, 99 S.Ct. at 992 (Blackmun, J., concurring).

Justice Stevens also concurred separately in the judgment; he would have preferred to rest the decision on a

due process rationale. Justice Stevens thought that there might sometime be sufficient reasons for distinguishing city and state election requirements but that the 5% requirement was excessive, given the fact that the state did not defend it as other than an historical remnant of an earlier election code. Thus, Justice Stevens believed that this particular requirement deprived the candidates of liberty without due process. 440 U.S. at 189, 99 S.Ct. at 992 (Stevens, J., concurring).

Justice Rehnquist concurred because he found no rational basis for the higher requirement for the city elections, but he noted that the unreasonableness of this requirement stemmed from the Supreme Court action in *Moore* and lower court invalidation of other portions of the election code. Had it not been for these judicial actions, with which Rehnquist apparently did not agree, the elec-

Not all demonstrated support statutes are unconstitutional. The Supreme Court sustained Georgia's demonstrated support requirement in *Jenness v. Fortson*.[54] Georgia law required candidates for elective office who ran without winning a primary election to file petitions with signatures from qualified voters equaling five percent of the vote cast in the last general election for that office. If the candidate belonged to a political party that received more than twenty percent of the votes in the last gubernatorial election, the state relieved the candidate of the petition requirement. The Court distinguished *Williams* by suggesting that the Ohio statute challenged in that case presented an " 'entangling web of election laws.' "[55] Georgia, on the other hand, not only permitted independent candidates but also did not require any unreasonable early filing deadline. Moreover, the five percent Georgia requirement was not a "suffocating" restriction like the fifteen percent Ohio requirement. Finally, the Court noted that, unlike Ohio, Georgia often had independent candidates running for election office. The Court thus concluded that the Georgia election scheme did not violate either the First Amendment or equal protection clause.[56]

A demonstrated support statute may be unconstitutional if it limits too narrowly the pool of available voters who can sign the required petition, or if it limits too severely the time period to submit the petition. Those who challenged the California Election Code in *Storer v. Brown*[57] specifically questioned the constitutionality of the demonstrated support provisions. The provisions allowed non-qualified political parties twenty-four days to gather the necessary signatures on the support peti-

tion. Furthermore, the statute discounted any signature from a qualified voter who had voted in the primary election. The Court found that the record provided insufficient information on whether these requirements excessively burdened the ability of minor political parties to gain access to the ballot. Consequently, the Court remanded this phase of the *Storer* litigation back to the district court with an order to gather the necessary facts and make the determination on the extent of the burden. The Court indicated that if these requirements were too severe on minor political parties they would violate the equal protection clause.[58]

Demonstrated support requirements may impair the ability of minor political parties and independent candidates to run an effective campaign in several ways. The Federal Elections Campaign Act of 1971, for example, granted an amount of federal funds to minor or new political parties that was less than that for the major parties. In *Buckley v. Valeo*[59] the Supreme Court considered constitutional challenges to these restrictions. The Court initially decided that it would review this portion of the Act under a rational relationship standard of review.[60] Although the Court realized that restrictions on access to the electoral process may limit a voter's choice, it reasoned that a denial of public financing did not directly infringe the right to vote.[61] Moreover, the restriction promoted a proper governmental purpose: prohibiting an artificial incentive for splinter parties and avoiding factionalism. Hence, the Court concluded that Congress properly may require " 'some preliminary showing of a significant modicum of support'

tion code would have been reasonable in requiring statewide candidates to have a lesser number of signatures but requiring that set numbers of signatures be obtained in a specific number of counties around the state. 440 U.S. at 189–90, 99 S.Ct. at 992–93 (Rehnquist, J., concurring).

54. 403 U.S. 431, 91 S.Ct. 1970, 29 L.Ed.2d 554 (1971).

55. 403 U.S. at 437, 91 S.Ct. at 1973 (quoting *Williams*).

56. 403 U.S. at 439–40, 91 S.Ct. at 1974–75; see Note, Developments in the Law—Elections, 88 Harv.L.Rev. 1111, 1133–42 (1975).

57. 415 U.S. 724, 94 S.Ct. 1274, 39 L.Ed.2d 714 (1974).

58. 415 U.S. at 746, 94 S.Ct. at 1286–87; but see American Party of Texas v. White, 415 U.S. 767, 94 S.Ct. 1296, 39 L.Ed.2d 744 (1974), where the Court sustained the Texas Election Code that had a fifty-five day time period for filing election petitions, and a restriction on the size of the pool of voters who could sign an election petition. 415 U.S. at 779–88, 94 S.Ct. at 1305–10.

59. 424 U.S. 1, 96 S.Ct. 612, 46 L.Ed.2d 659 (1976), motion granted 424 U.S. 936, 96 S.Ct. 1153, 47 L.Ed.2d 727 (1976).

60. 424 U.S. at 85, 96 S.Ct. at 666.

61. 424 U.S. at 93–97, 96 S.Ct. at 670–72.

... as an eligibility requirement for public funds."[62]

The *Buckley* Court also assessed a provision of the Federal Elections Campaign Act that required political committees and candidates to keep detailed records and to disclose the sources of contributions.[63] It was contended that the government's interest in such information was minimal but the danger of impairing rights of association and free expression was great. The Court rejected the arguments and indicated that an impairment of First Amendment rights was only speculative. Before the Court would order minor parties or independent candidates to be exempted from this provision, it would require evidence of a reasonable probability that harassment or threats to contributors resulted from the compelled disclosures. The Court stated that if such evidence existed, it would review the constitutionality of the disclosure requirement with strict scrutiny.[64] Until the production of such evidence, however, the Court would sustain the provision under the reasonable relationship test because it furthered governmental interests in the deterrence of corruption and the prevention of fraud.[65]

Any restriction on the ability of potential candidates to appear on the general election ballot may implicate the First Amendment associational rights and the Fourteenth Amendment due process and equal protection rights of voters. However, the states must impose some candidate access restrictions in order to run honest, efficient elections in which the populace may choose its government officials. As the Court has stated: "the state's important regulatory interests [in orderly, honest elections] are generally sufficient to justify reasonable, nondiscriminatory restrictions."[66] The judiciary must independently review ballot access regulations to insure that they are justified by such state interests.

In *Anderson v. Celebrezze*[67] the Court, by a five to four vote, invalidated a state statute which required an independent candidate for President to file his nominating petition in March prior to the general election. This March filing date preceded the time when major political parties, which had sufficient demonstrated support to reserve a place on the ballot, named their candidates. The state could justify some date certain cut-off for candidate filing but not one so far in advance of the general election. The majority stated that judges, in reviewing such a restriction, were to balance the degree to which the regulation impaired the first and fourteenth rights of voters against the degree to which the regulation advanced important state interests. The Court concluded the early filing date did not sufficiently advance the interests in political stability, voter awareness, or equal treatment of candidates to justify such a significant restriction on the voter's freedom of choice and freedom of association.

The Supreme Court cases examining demonstrated support requirements for potential candidates for political office do not establish a clear test for determining the constitutionality of such regulations. The Court has indicated that regulations restricting an individual's ability to be a candidate raise concerns under both the equal protection guarantee (because they involve classifications as to which types of persons or parties may appear on the ballot) and the implied First Amendment right of freedom of association (because the laws restrict the ability of persons to associate for political purposes through the nomination of a candidate). In some voting rights cases, the Supreme Court has stated that the state needs a compelling or overriding interest to justify classifications and restrictions on political association.

---

62. 424 U.S. at 96, 96 S.Ct. at 671 (quoting from Jenness v. Fortson, 403 U.S. 431, 442, 91 S.Ct. 1970, 1976, 29 L.Ed.2d 554 (1971)).

63. 424 U.S. at 60, 96 S.Ct. at 654 (1976).

64. 424 U.S. at 73–85, 96 S.Ct. at 660–66. See note 65, infra.

65. First Amendment limitations on political party activities and expenditures are examined in §§ 16.50, 16.51 of this Treatise.

66. Anderson v. Celebrezze, 460 U.S. 780, 788, 103 S.Ct. 1564, 1569–70, 75 L.Ed.2d 547 (1983) (footnote omitted).

67. 460 U.S. 780, 103 S.Ct. 1564, 75 L.Ed.2d 547 (1983).

In the demonstrated support cases, the Court has not rigidly applied a compelling interest standard. Rather, the Court has found that the states have interest in running efficient and honest elections that will justify some candidate regulations. In some of these cases, such as *Anderson,* the Supreme Court seems to have openly balanced the burden imposed on the First and Fourteenth Amendment rights of the candidate and voters against the degree to which the regulation advanced these legitimate and important state interests. In other cases, the Court has indicated that it would uphold demonstrated requirements so long as the requirement was reasonably tailored to promote the state interest in efficient and honest elections and did not create an unreasonable barrier to ballot access for independent candidates and minor political parties.

For example, in *Munro v. Socialist Workers Party* [68] the Supreme Court upheld a state law that required minor-party candidates for partisan political offices to receive at least one percent of all votes cast for that office in the state's primary election as a condition for having the candidate's name placed on the general election ballot. *Munro* did not clearly state the standard of review that was used to determine the constitutionality of this law. Justice White's opinion for the Court stated that there was no "litmus-paper test" for deciding whether a demonstrated support requirement violated the Constitution. Justice White stated: "It is now clear that states may condition access to the general election ballot by a minor-party or independent candidate upon a showing of a modicum of support among the potential voters for the office." A state was not required, according to the majority opinion, to show that there was a danger that voters in the state would be confused by "ballot overcrowding" if it did not have a demonstrated support requirement. The state need only show that the law was reasonably tailored to promote the operation of efficient and honest elections and that it did not constitute an unreasonable burden on, or purposeful discrimination against, minor-party or independent candidates. Unfortunately, the majority opinion gave no standard for determining when a demonstrated support requirement for candidate access to a ballot would be deemed unreasonable or would be deemed to significantly impinge on constitutionally protected rights.

The state election system at issue in *Munro* required minor-party candidates to be initially nominated by a party meeting or convention, which was to be conducted before the filing period for the primary election ballot. The nominee of the minor party for the state office would then be placed on the primary election ballot. The nominee of the minor-party would not receive a place on the general election ballot unless he or she received at least one percent of all votes cast for the particular office in the primary (such as one percent of all the votes cast for the office of governor in the entire primary election). The minor party had argued that the one percent requirement placed an unreasonable burden on it because it had to compete for votes against the major parties, whose voters would almost certainly vote in their own party primary. A majority of the Justices in *Munro* found that the law gave the minor party a reasonable opportunity to demonstrate that there was some significant support from its candidate among the general populace. States are under no obligation to place a candidate on the ballot who could not show some reasonable amount of support among potential voters.

The Supreme Court uses a type of modified balancing test in voting and ballot access cases. A law deemed by the Court to be a severe impairment of voter's freedom of choice, or First Amendment rights must be supported by a compelling interest. A state regulation of voting and election systems that does not involve restriction of First Amendment rights, and does not constitute a severe impairment of the ability of a voter to exercise the franchise in a meaningful way, will be upheld so long as any incidental regulation of

---

68. 479 U.S. 189, 107 S.Ct. 533, 93 L.Ed.2d 499 (1986).

voting freedom is outweighed by a significant or important state interest.

Burdick v. Takushi [69] upheld the State of Hawaii's total ban on write-in votes at primary and general elections by finding that important state interests in stopping unrestrained factionalism at the general election and inter-party raiding outweighed any minor restrictions on a voter's ability to vote for the candidate of his choice. Critical to the *Burdick* decision was the Supreme Court's finding that Hawaii's primary system allowed persons to qualify for partisan and nonpartisan ballots very easily. Persons who wished to be in the nonpartisan primary could qualify with petitions that needed only 15 or 25 signatures from registered voters. Because there was no regulation of political association or political expression, there was no First Amendment issue in the case. Because of the open primary system, the voters' choices were not significantly restricted by the ban on that large voting. Therefore, the state did not need an interest of compelling importance to justify its ban on write-in voting. [70]

In the same term in which the Supreme Court decided *Burdick,* the Court used the compelling interest test to evaluate state restrictions on new political parties that significantly impaired the ability of persons to place the names of a new political party's candidates on the ballot. In *Norman v. Reed* [71] the Supreme Court examined Illinois' statutes that required a new party to obtain 25,000 nominating signatures for at-large offices in a county election. When the county was subdivided into separate districts (for election of district representatives on a county board) a new party had to collect 25,000 signatures from each of the districts in the county (in order to have

candidates for county positions that were allocated to the separate districts within the county).

Norman involved an effort by the Harold Washington Party to field at-large candidates for election to the Cook County Board, candidates from the City of Chicago district, and candidates from the suburban district of Cook County. The Harold Washington Party received in excess of 50,000 signatures on their ballot petition but fewer than 8,000 of these signatures were from the suburban district. The Supreme Court examined the restrictions on the ability of the Harold Washington Party members to express their political preferences to have their candidates on the ballot. The Court concluded that the state law imposed severe restrictions on the First Amendment right of political association and implicated the Fourteenth Amendment equal protection guarantee, which protects the right to vote. Because of the severity of the restriction on these fundamental rights, the Supreme Court found that these laws had to be "narrowly drawn to advance a state interest of compelling importance." [72]

The Court, in *Norman,* found that the state did not have a compelling interest in disqualifying all of the Harold Washington Party's candidates in the Cook County election simply because of the party's failure to obtain 25,000 signatures in each district. The Party would have to be allowed to run candidates from the Chicago district, and for at-large county offices, because the government's interest in ensuring that a candidate or party had demonstrated support was satisfied when the party gathered more than 25,000 signatures. The State of Illinois only required 25,000 signa-

69. 504 U.S. 428, 112 S.Ct. 2059, 119 L.Ed.2d 245 (1992).

70. Burdick v. Takushi, 504 U.S. 428, 112 S.Ct. 2059, 2063–64, 119 L.Ed.2d 245 (1992): "As we have recognized when those rights are subject to severe restrictions, the regulation must be narrowly tailored to advance a state interest of compelling importance.... when a state election law provision imposes only reasonable nondiscriminatory restrictions upon the First and Fourteenth Amendment rights of voters the state's important regulatory interests are generally sufficient to justify the restrictions." (internal quotations and citations deleted).

71. 502 U.S. 279, 112 S.Ct. 698, 116 L.Ed.2d 711 (1992).

72. 503 U.S. at 288, 112 S.Ct. at 705: "For more than two decades, this court has recognized the constitutional right of citizens to create and develop new political parties. The right derives from the First and Fourteenth Amendments and advances the constitutional interest of like-minded voters to gather in pursuit of political ends ... we have accordingly required any severe restriction to be narrowly drawn to advance a state interest of compelling importance." (internal quotations and citations omitted).

tures for placing the name of a candidate for state-wide office on the ballot. The state's argument that it sought a demonstration of county-wide support for candidates running for at-large positions on a county board was undercut by the fact that state laws did not require a demonstration of geographic diversity of support for new parties or independent candidates who sought access to the state-wide ballot in elections for state-wide offices.

The Supreme Court upheld the Illinois law that prohibited the new political party from running candidates for the suburban district positions on the county board because of the failure to obtain 25,000 nominating signatures from the suburban district. Previous Supreme Court decisions ruled that a 25,000 signature requirement for as populous a district as the suburban Cook County district was permissible.[73] In *Norman,* the Supreme Court also examined an Illinois law that in a rather convoluted manner prohibited persons affiliated with the Harold Washington Party in the City of Chicago from running under that party's name for county-wide or suburban elections. The Supreme Court held that this restriction on the First Amendment freedoms of political association and expression was not justified by any compelling interest because

any interest in preventing the fraudulent use of a party's name could be achieved by simply requiring persons running under the Harold Washington Party designation to demonstrate that they had formal permission from the Party to use its name. The severe restriction on First and Fourteenth Amendment rights required the state to demonstrate an interest of compelling importance.[74]

The modified balancing test set out in *Burdick* now seems to be firmly established in the Court's decisions. Six Justices employed by *Burdick* method of analyzing election laws in *Timmons v. Twin Cities Area New Party*[75] to uphold a Minnesota law that prohibited any person from appearing on the ballot as a candidate for a state office for more than one political party. Chief Justice Rehnquist's majority opinion in *Timmons,* stated that, when reviewing a candidate regulation, the Supreme Court would "weigh the character and magnitude of the burden [on First and Fourteenth Amendment associational rights] ... against the interests [asserted by the government] and consider the extent to which the states concerns make the burden necessary.... regulations imposing severe burdens on [candidates and political parties associational rights] must be narrowly tailored and advance a compelling

73. Norman v. Reed, 502 U.S. 279, 294, 112 S.Ct. 698, 708, 116 L.Ed.2d 711 (1992), on remand 154 Ill.2d 77, 180 Ill.Dec. 685, 607 N.E.2d 1198 (1992), cert. denied 509 U.S. 906, 113 S.Ct. 3000, 125 L.Ed.2d 693 (1993), referring to Jenness v. Fortson, 403 U.S. 431, 91 S.Ct. 1970, 29 L.Ed.2d 554 (1971).

74. Illinois law made a distinction between "established" and "new" political parties not only in terms of state wide elections but in terms of local elections. The Harold Washington Party was an established party in the City of Chicago (where it had fielded candidates for office in previous elections) but it was a new party in Cook County (in terms of fielding candidates for county and suburban offices). Illinois laws, as understood and described by the United States Supreme Court, effectively prohibited the persons in the case from using the Harold Washington Party name in the county elections. The Supreme Court found that the law was not narrowly tailored to any compelling end because there were alternative ways that the state might protect against misuse or fraudulent use of the party's name without totally banning the candidates in this case from using the name of the Harold Washington Party in Cook County. Norman v. Reed, 502 U.S. 279, 288–93, 112 S.Ct. 698, 705–707, 116 L.Ed.2d 711 (1992).

In *Norman,* the Supreme Court of the United States avoided ruling on the question of whether the so-called "full slate" requirement (which required parties to have a complete slate of candidates for an election) was invalid on its face or as applied to the new Harold Washington Party in Cook County (the party had not fielded candidates for elected judicial offices). The Supreme Court of Illinois had not addressed the question of whether the party's omission of judicial candidates eliminated the Harold Washington Party's ability to field any candidates for county offices; the United States Supreme Court believed that all issues related to this question should be addressed in the first instance by the state supreme court. Thus, there was no ruling on either the constitutionality of the full slate requirement that might include a requirement that candidates be fielded for judicial office. Norman v. Reed, 502 U.S. 279, 294–97, 112 S.Ct. 698, 708–09, 116 L.Ed.2d 711 (1992). The *Norman* decision was decided by a seven to one vote of the Justices. Justice Souter delivered the majority opinion; Justice Thomas did not take part in the decision. Only Justice Scalia dissented. 502 U.S. at 297, 112 S.Ct. at 709 (Scalia, J., dissenting).

75. 520 U.S. 351, 117 S.Ct. 1364, 137 L.Ed.2d 589 (1997).

state interest. Lesser burdens [might be justified by] important regulatory interest."[76] Although the Chief Justice's opinion noted that the Minnesota "antifusion law" imposed burdens on minor political parties were that "not trivial," the majority ruled those burdens were not severe enough to invoke the compelling interest test. The *Timmons* majority upheld the Minnesota law on the basis that law was related to the important state interests in protecting the integrity of the election process and the stability of the political system.[77]

(f) Racial Classifications

Any state law that impairs a person's ability to become a candidate for elective office because of that person's race is unconstitutional. Such a law would violate the Fourteenth and Fifteenth Amendments.[78] The Constitution prevents the states from directly dictating, casually promoting, or facilitating "a distinction in the treatment of persons solely on the basis of race."[79] Thus, a state could not designate on a ballot which candidates were black and which were white.[80] Such a designation requirement would provide an easy means of discrimination. Moreover, race has no relationship to the determination of a person's capabilities to function in public office.[81]

§ 14.33 Primary Elections & Political Party Candidate Selection Systems

(a) The White Primary Cases

The *White Primary Cases*[1] represented the major effort by the Court prior to the 1960's to prevent racial discrimination in voting. In this sequence of cases the Supreme Court steadily loosened the constitutional requirements of state action in order to protect the effectiveness of the voting franchise. The Supreme Court prohibited states from forbidding black participation in state primaries;[2] struck down an analogous resolution passed by a party executive committee acting pursuant to the authority of a state statute;[3] held that the failure of state officials acting under color of law to count ballots properly in a primary election was a violation of a section in the United States Code prohibiting such "state action;"[4] overruled a prior decision to find that the right to vote free of racial discrimination embodied in the Fifteenth Amendment applied to primaries as well as a general election;[5] and barred racial discrimination in an unofficial primary conducted by a private group.[6] An analysis of the *White Primary Cases* and their progeny suggests that the unarticulated premise and most easily understood reasoning be-

---

76. 520 U.S. at 358, 117 S.Ct. at 1370.

77. 520 U.S. at 362–68, 117 S.Ct. at 1372–1375. Chief Justice Rehnquist's majority opinion was written for six members of the Court; there were no concurring opinions. Justices Stevens, Ginsburg, and Souter dissented. Timmons v. Twin Cities Area New Party, 520 U.S. 351, 368, 117 S.Ct. 1364, 1375, 137 L.Ed.2d 589 (1997) (Stevens, J., joined by Ginsburg, J., and, in part, by Souter, J., dissenting); 520 U.S. at 380, 117 S.Ct. at 1381 (Souter, J., dissenting).

78. Cf. Georgia v. United States, 411 U.S. 526, 93 S.Ct. 1702, 36 L.Ed.2d 472 (1973); Gomillion v. Lightfoot, 364 U.S. 339, 81 S.Ct. 125, 5 L.Ed.2d 110 (1960).

79. Hamm v. Virginia State Bd. of Elections, 230 F.Supp. 156, 157 (E.D.Va.1964), affirmed sub nom. Tancil v. Woolls, 379 U.S. 19, 85 S.Ct. 157, 13 L.Ed.2d 91 (1964).

80. Anderson v. Martin, 375 U.S. 399, 84 S.Ct. 454, 11 L.Ed.2d 430 (1964).

81. See §§ 14.4, 14.10(d), 14.31(h), 14.33. For citations to additional cases, and secondary authorities, see the multi-volume edition of this treatise: R. Rotunda & J. Nowak, Treatise On Constitutional Law: Substance and Procedure Chapters 18, 19 (3rd ed. 1999, with annual supplements).

§ 14.33

1. E.g., Terry v. Adams, 345 U.S. 461, 73 S.Ct. 809, 97 L.Ed. 1152 (1953); Smith v. Allwright, 321 U.S. 649, 64 S.Ct. 757, 88 L.Ed. 987 (1944). United States v. Classic, 313 U.S. 299, 61 S.Ct. 1031, 85 L.Ed. 1368 (1941); Nixon v. Condon, 286 U.S. 73, 52 S.Ct. 484, 76 L.Ed. 984 (1932); Nixon v. Herndon, 273 U.S. 536, 47 S.Ct. 446, 71 L.Ed. 759 (1927). See also, Baskin v. Brown, 174 F.2d 391 (4th Cir.1949); Rice v. Elmore, 165 F.2d 387 (4th Cir.1947), certiorari denied 333 U.S. 875, 68 S.Ct. 905, 92 L.Ed. 1151 (1948).

2. Nixon v. Herndon, 273 U.S. 536, 47 S.Ct. 446, 71 L.Ed. 759 (1927).

3. Nixon v. Condon, 286 U.S. 73, 52 S.Ct. 484, 76 L.Ed. 984 (1932).

4. United States v. Classic, 313 U.S. 299, 61 S.Ct. 1031, 85 L.Ed. 1368 (1941).

5. Smith v. Allwright, 321 U.S. 649, 64 S.Ct. 757, 88 L.Ed. 987 (1944).

6. Terry v. Adams, 345 U.S. 461, 73 S.Ct. 809, 97 L.Ed. 1152 (1953). See § 12.2, supra.

hind the cases is that all integral steps in an election for public office are public functions and therefore state action subject to some constitutional scrutiny, particularly if a complaint is based on racial discrimination. The *White Primary Cases* thus carry the seed of an expansive reading.

The first white primary case was *Nixon v. Herndon*,[7] where a black plaintiff sued the Judges of Elections for refusing to allow him to vote in a Texas state primary for senator and representatives of Congress and for various state offices. A Texas statute provided that "in no event shall a negro be eligible to participate in a Democratic party election held in the State of Texas."[8] Justice Holmes, speaking for a unanimous Court, in a very short opinion, held that the statute violated the Fourteenth Amendment's equal protection clause, finding it "unnecessary to consider the Fifteenth Amendment."[9]

The state of Texas reacted to this case by repealing its statute and enacting another which provided that "every political party in this State through its State Executive Committee shall have the power to prescribe the qualifications of its own members and shall in its own way determine who shall be qualified to vote or otherwise participate in such political party...."[10] The State Executive Committee of the Democratic Party then adopted a resolution providing that only white democrats could vote in the Democratic party. Nixon was again denied participation in the primary because of his color, and once again the Supreme Court decided in his favor in *Nixon v. Condon*,[11] a five to four decision. The respondents argued that it was not the state but a political party, "a voluntary" association, which denied Nixon his ballot; private associations, it was contended, have the inherent power to deter-

mine their own membership. The Court rejected this argument but appeared to decide on narrow grounds: the state delegated power to the executive committee, which then became an agency of the state for this purpose. The executive committee, by virtue of the state statute, became a repository of official power, and therefore became subject to the equal protection clause.[12]

Texas refused to give up. After the *Condon* decision the Texas Democratic Convention itself barred blacks from voting in its primaries. This time, in *Grovey v. Townsend*,[13] the Court upheld the color bar. Since no state statutes authorized any color discrimination or delegated that power to any party organ and since the party convention did have inherent power to set up the qualifications of its members, there was no state action. Less than a decade later *Grovey* was overruled in *Smith v. Allwright*,[14] with Justice Roberts complaining that such prompt reversals of direction by the Court "tends to bring adjudications of this tribunal into the same class as a restricted railroad ticket, good for this day and train only."[15] *Grovey's* speedy rejection was made possible by the leading decision in *United States v. Classic*,[16] which occurred between *Grovey* and *Allwright*.

In *Classic* a federal indictment was upheld charging various state officials, who were conducting a primary election under Louisiana law, with willfully altering and falsely counting the ballots.

The questions for decision are whether the rights of qualified voters to vote in the Louisiana primary and to have their ballots counted is a right "secured by the Constitution" within the meaning of [certain stat-

---

7. 273 U.S. 536, 47 S.Ct. 446, 71 L.Ed. 759 (1927).
8. See 273 U.S. at 540, 47 S.Ct. at 446.
9. 273 U.S. at 540, 47 S.Ct. at 446.
10. Quoted in Nixon v. Condon, 286 U.S. 73, 82, 52 S.Ct. 484, 485, 76 L.Ed. 984 (1932).
11. 286 U.S. 73, 52 S.Ct. 484, 76 L.Ed. 984 (1932).
12. 286 U.S. at 85–88, 52 S.Ct. at 486–87.
13. 295 U.S. 45, 55 S.Ct. 622, 79 L.Ed. 1292 (1935).
14. 321 U.S. 649, 64 S.Ct. 757, 88 L.Ed. 987 (1944).

15. 321 U.S. at 669, 64 S.Ct. at 768 (Roberts, J., dissenting).
16. 313 U.S. 299, 61 S.Ct. 1031, 85 L.Ed. 1368 (1941). Cf. United States v. Saylor, 322 U.S. 385, 64 S.Ct. 1101, 88 L.Ed. 1341 (1944), rehearing denied 323 U.S. 809, 65 S.Ct. 27, 89 L.Ed. 645 (1944). See, Bixby, The Roosevelt Court, Democratic Ideology, and Minority Rights: Another Look at United States v. Classic, 90 Yale L.J. 741 (1981).

utes of the Criminal Code]. . . .[17]

In *Classic*, the Court concluded:

Where the state law has made the primary an integral part of the procedure of choice, or where in fact the primary effectively controls the choice, the right of the elector to have his ballot counted at the primary is likewise included in the right protected by Article 1, § 2. ... Here ... [t]he right to choose a representative is in fact controlled by the primary ... the practical influence of the choice of candidates may be so great as to affect profoundly the choice at the general election, even though there is no effective legal prohibition. ...[18]

The Court was concerned with reality, not merely the formal fact of state regulation and therefore the Court found it essential that congressional power over "elections" extend to primary elections.[19] As if to anticipate the argument that a private primary or party convention would not constitute state action, the Court noted that the Article I, section 2 command "unlike those guaranteed by the Fourteenth and Fifteenth Amendments, is secured against the action of individuals as well as of states."[20] *Grovey* was not discussed.

Smith v. Allwright,[21] relying on the Fifteenth Amendment, expanded *Classic* by finding state action in a party primary election; it explicitly overruled *Grovey*.[22] In *Allwright*[23] the Court struck down a party convention resolution forbidding blacks from voting in a party primary regulated by the state. The Court reasoned that when a state delegated the power to fix voting qualifications to a party which made party membership necessary

for voting in a primary, then the state had made the action of the party action of the state.[24] The constitutional "grant to the people of the opportunity for choice [without regard to race] is not to be nullified by a State casting its electoral process in a form which permits a private organization to practice racial discrimination in the election."[25]

While *Allwright* emphasized the state's close regulation of political parties, such a factor should not be crucial in determining state action for purposes of the Fourteenth or Fifteenth Amendments, since the absence of state regulation of party elections in effect produces a delegation of the state's possible authority to the party. *Terry v. Adams*[26] illustrates this point. There, a racially discriminatory primary was conducted by the Jaybird party, a private organization operating without state aid of any kind. This primary was conducted prior to the Democratic primary. The Court explained that the distinction between the private primary and the Democratic primary it preceded was merely a distinction of form, even though the Jaybird nominees entered their own names as candidates in the Democratic primary.[27] While the plurality opinion noted that the Democratic primary and the general election following it had only been the "perfunctory ratifiers" of the choice made in the prior Jaybird primary, the language of Justice Black's opinion went well beyond relying on the peculiar power of the Jaybird election. The state had violated the Fifteenth Amendment by *permitting* within its borders a private device that would have been forbidden in a public election.[28]

17. 313 U.S. at 307, 61 S.Ct. at 1034.

18. 313 U.S. at 318–19, 61 S.Ct. at 1039.

19. 313 U.S. at 315–16, 61 S.Ct. at 1037–38.

20. 313 U.S. at 315, 61 S.Ct. at 1037–38. Article I, § 2 deals with the states' power to regulate the selection of Representatives. Article II, § 1 deals with the states' power to regulate the election of presidential electors. A comparison of the two sections indicates that if there is no state action requirement limiting the rights secured by art. I, § 2, there must be no state action requirement for art. II, § 1. Similarly, there appears to be no state action requirement limiting the rights secured by the Seventeenth Amendment (election of U.S. Senators).

21. 321 U.S. 649, 64 S.Ct. 757, 88 L.Ed. 987 (1944).

22. 321 U.S. at 666, 64 S.Ct. at 766.

23. Smith v. Allwright, 321 U.S. 649, 64 S.Ct. 757, 88 L.Ed. 987 (1944).

24. 321 U.S. at 664–65, 64 S.Ct. at 765–66.

25. 321 U.S. at 664, 64 S.Ct. at 765.

26. 345 U.S. 461, 73 S.Ct. 809, 97 L.Ed. 1152 (1953).

27. 345 U.S. at 465–66, 73 S.Ct. at 811–12. (Plurality opinion by Black, J., joined by Douglas & Burton, JJ.) There was no opinion by the Court.

28. 345 U.S. at 469, 73 S.Ct. at 813. (Black, J., joined by Douglas & Burton, JJ.).

The rulings in the *White Primary Cases* provided a needed basis for judicial intervention in the voting process to prevent racial discrimination in the allocation of power within the self-governance system. In other sections of this treatise, we have examined in greater detail the requirement that those attacking an electoral system as racially biased must prove that the system was created or maintained for a racially discriminatory purpose.[29] In this section we examine the question of whether these cases provide a basis for judicial intervention in the activities of political parties.

(b) The "Public Function" Analysis of Each Stage of the Election Process

The logic of the *White Primary Cases* supports the conclusion that an election for public office is a public function and that any integral part of that function must conform to the Constitution. In fact, probably only the public function analysis adequately explains the extension of constitutional restrictions against racial discrimination to private groups such as the Jaybirds. The Court has held that constitutional restrictions and limitations apply to those who assume governmental functions. This concept should easily apply to what is in essence the holding of an election for public office. The nomination process may appear to be more a private than a governmental function because it is generally carried on by individuals in their role as private citizens. But

even the process of a final election is carried on only by the individual *qua* private citizen. Conversely, as Dean Pollak has urged, "only a state can conduct elections—especially so where the state is one in which, under the Constitution, a republican form of government is perpetually guaranteed."[30]

If an election is state action, any integral part of that election is also state action. Several circuits have already explicitly adopted the public function rationale with respect to judicial review of political parties.[31] It is this rationale which most naturally explains the *White Primary Cases*. Several state courts have also accepted the principle that state action exists whenever the party performs a public electoral or nominating function.[32] The public function analysis does not even break down if the nominating vehicle is a convention rather than a primary. The Supreme Court in *Classic* adopted for constitutional purposes a definition of "election" that was "no less than the expression by qualified electors of their choice of candidates,"[33] a definition sufficient to include a primary, caucus, or convention.

Delegate Selection to National Nominating Conventions. Decisions subsequent to the *White Primary Cases* have continued to define "election" broadly in order to subject to constitutional scrutiny all state action relevant to the electoral process.[34] For example, even the procedures for selecting delegates to the

---

29. See §§ 14.4, 14.31(h), 14.32(f), supra. See also §§ 12.2–12.4, supra. For an examination of the basis upon which the judiciary may find that a seemingly private entity, such as a political party, has sufficient contacts with the government to subject it to the constitutional limitations on its action.

30. Pollak, Racial Discrimination and Judicial Integrity: A Reply to Professor Wechsler, 108 U.Pa.L.Rev. 1, 23 (1959).

With respect to presidential, senatorial, and congressional elections, it should be noted that the rights secured respectively by Article II, § I; Art. I, § II; and the Seventeenth Amendment are not limited to state action. Cf. New York v. United States, 326 U.S. 572, 582, 66 S.Ct. 310, 314, 90 L.Ed. 326 (1946) (concurring opinion of Frankfurter, J.).

31. Seergy v. Kings County Republican County Committee, 459 F.2d 308, 313 (2d Cir.1972); Lynch v. Torquato, 343 F.2d 370, 373 (3d Cir.1965) (dictum).

32. E.g., Bentman v. Seventh Ward Democratic Executive Committee, 421 Pa. 188, 203, 218 A.2d 261, 269

(1966) (right to select party nominees for public office is state action under the Fourteenth Amendment); Wagner v. Gray, 74 So.2d 89, 91 (Fla.1954).

33. 313 U.S. at 318, 61 S.Ct. at 1039.

34. In Williams v. Rhodes, 393 U.S. 23, 89 S.Ct. 5, 21 L.Ed.2d 24 (1968), the Court held that the state power under the Constitution to appoint presidential electors is subject to the Fourteenth Amendment. A state law that makes it more difficult for third parties to be placed on the ballot violated the voters' right to effectively exercise their franchise. 393 U.S. at 30, 89 S.Ct. at 10. It follows that if this right does not extend to the nominating process, the right to vote effectively will be stripped of its constitutional protection.

In a subsequent Fourteenth Amendment case the Court again maintained that all state procedures that are an integral part of the election process must not discriminate, nor abridge the right to vote, Moore v. Ogilvie, 394 U.S. 814, 818, 89 S.Ct. 1493, 1495–96, 23 L.Ed.2d 1 (1969).

national nominating conventions amount to state action, as a practical matter, because, in virtually all states, selection is either regulated by state statute or explicitly delegated to the state political party.[35] It is difficult to argue persuasively for purposes of prohibiting racial discrimination that even the Democratic or Republican presidential nominating convention is not an integral part of the presidential election or that it is less an integral part than a state primary.

The state's power under article II, section 1 to appoint presidential electors as their legislatures direct is for constitutional purposes not just a power but a nondelegable duty. The state may by statute, as in *Allwright*, authorize the state parties to set up certain procedures. Or, as in *Terry*, the state may remain silent, allowing the parties to enact their own rules and regulations. But for constitutional purposes it is the state that is acting and that must be held responsible. The duty under article II, section 1 should not be immune from review but should be subject to the Fourteenth and Fifteenth Amendments and judged by their standards.[36] Similarly, the state's duties with respect to congressional elections under article I, section 2 and senatorial elections under the Seventeenth Amendment are also subject to the Fourteenth Amendment.

The Supreme Court in *Ray v. Blair*[37] explicitly adopted the view that any integral part of the presidential election process is a nondelegable state duty, subject to constitutional limitations. In that case, a state statute had allowed the party executive committee to determine qualifications for primary candidates,

and pursuant to this delegation of power the Democratic Party required a loyalty pledge from each candidate for presidential elector. While the Court upheld the loyalty pledge as a legitimate party objective, it recognized that both the state and the party were subject to possible constitutional limitations when the former so delegated power to the latter.[38]

The broad *Classic* definition of "election" provides that an election in the constitutional sense occurs regardless of how small the universe of possible electors or candidates. The smallness of the universe is merely a possible constitutional argument for striking the whole procedure, not an argument for immunizing the scheme from constitutional scrutiny. For example, Georgia law formerly allowed the chairman of the party's state executive committee to appoint delegates to the Democratic National Convention.[39] While only one "voter" existed, the procedure still represented an election which was an integral part of the presidential electoral process. Under *Moore v. Ogilvie*[40] the procedure could have been subject to challenge as discriminatory and an abridgment of the right to vote.[41] The *White Primary Cases* as supported by later case law may be read to support some federal judicial intervention to protect the constitutional "right of qualified voters ... to cast their votes effectively."[42]

A Supreme Court decision breaking new ground may not be entirely clear until later cases interpret and better articulate the grounds of the earlier decision.[43] Later lower court and Supreme Court cases appear to have read the *White Primary* decisions broadly,

35. Chambers & Rotunda, Reform of Presidential Nominating Conventions, 56 Va.L.Rev. 179, 195 (1970).

Terry v. Adams, 345 U.S. 461, 469, 73 S.Ct. 809, 813, 97 L.Ed. 1152 (1953), supports the argument that even if the state withdrew from such regulation, the pre-election selection process might still be an integral part of the election. It is immaterial under *Terry* whether or not the state has given a preferred position on the ballot to the nominee of a completely private primary. 345 U.S. at 465 n. 1, 73 S.Ct. at 811 n. 1.

36. See, e.g., Williams v. Rhodes, 393 U.S. 23, 89 S.Ct. 5, 21 L.Ed.2d 24 (1968).

37. 343 U.S. 214, 72 S.Ct. 654, 96 L.Ed. 894 (1952).

38. 343 U.S. at 227, 231, 72 S.Ct. at 660–61, 662–63.

39. See Chambers & Rotunda, Reform of Presidential Nominating Conventions, 56 Va.L.Rev. 179, 185 (1970).

40. 394 U.S. 814, 89 S.Ct. 1493, 23 L.Ed.2d 1 (1969). An Illinois statute required nominating petitions for independent candidates to demonstrate broad geographic support. The Court found the procedure to be an integral part of the electoral process and struck the requirement as discriminatory.

41. 394 U.S. at 818, 89 S.Ct. at 1495–96.

42. Williams v. Rhodes, 393 U.S. 23, 30, 89 S.Ct. 5, 10, 21 L.Ed.2d 24 (1968).

43. See generally Wright, Professor Bickel, The Scholarly Tradition, and the Supreme Court, 84 Harv.L.Rev. 769 (1971).

making clearer their expansive, public function rationale. In *Moore v. Ogilvie*,[44] a Fourteenth Amendment case, the Court cited *United States v. Classic* and *Smith v. Allwright* as authority for the proposition that no procedures used by a state as an integral part of the election process may operate discriminatorily or abridge the right to vote.[45] The Supreme Court's reliance on *Classic* and *Allwright* to create a Fourteenth Amendment right suggests that the cases have Fourteenth Amendment implications. Similarly, in *Hadley v. Junior College District*,[46] a Fourteenth Amendment reapportionment case,[47] the Court relied in part on *Classic* for the proposition that a voter has a constitutional right not to have his vote "wrongfully denied, debased, or diluted."[48] *Classic*, an article I case, involved state election officials charged with altering and falsely counting ballots, and the dilution referred to in *Hadley* was the Fourteenth Amendment dilution that occurs when the one man, one vote standard is not followed. The premise behind *Classic* must, however, also be relevant to an understanding of Fourteenth Amendment rights, or its citation by the Supreme Court was frivolous.[49]

(c) Judicial Control of Political Parties

One of the major issues left unresolved by the *White Primary Cases* and other such election cases decided in their wake is the extent to which the judiciary will exercise review of political parties when the nominating process takes place by convention or caucus rather than by primary. A case which suggests the direction of the Supreme Court is *Cousins v. Wigoda*,[50] arising out of a 1972 credentials challenge to Mayor Daley's Illinois delegation at the Democratic National Convention. In response to the unseating of Mayor Daley and his loyalists by the convention's Credentials Committee, the Court held that the national interest in selecting candidates for *national* office and the party members' freedom of association overcame an admitted *state* interest in the integrity of its election process; thus national party rules on delegate selection might legitimately disqualify delegates selected according to state law.

Arguably *Cousins* may be read to urge, if not to require, courts to stay out of the national nominating convention process at any stage. But *Cousins* really limited the extraterritorial power of the state. *Cousins* does not prohibit, nor does it even reach the question of, state laws regulating state parties or federal law regulating the national party convention. Moreover, the Court was careful to point out that no claim was made that the party delegate selection rules violated the Constitution. If the party rules complained of involved racial discrimination such as that involved in the *White Primary Cases*, then *Cousins* does not preclude the Court from acting:

> [W]hatever the case of actions presenting claims that the Party's delegate selection procedures are not exercised *within the confines of the Constitution—and no such claims are made here*—this is a case where "the convention itself [was] the proper forum for determining intra-party disputes as to which delegates [should] be seated".[51]

Perhaps it should be noted for comparison that a decision by the Court to outlaw racial

---

44. 394 U.S. 814, 89 S.Ct. 1493, 23 L.Ed.2d 1 (1969).

45. 394 U.S. at 818, 89 S.Ct. at 1495–96.

46. 397 U.S. 50, 90 S.Ct. 791, 25 L.Ed.2d 45 (1970), on remand to 460 S.W.2d 1 (Mo.1970).

47. 397 U.S. at 51, 90 S.Ct. at 792–93.

48. 397 U.S. at 52, 90 S.Ct. at 793.

49. Cf. Bullock v. Carter, 405 U.S. 134, 92 S.Ct. 849, 31 L.Ed.2d 92 (1972); Nixon v. Herndon, 273 U.S. 536, 47 S.Ct. 446, 71 L.Ed. 759 (1927). In Ray v. Blair, 343 U.S. 214, 72 S.Ct. 654, 96 L.Ed. 894 (1952), the Court explained that the Fourteenth Amendment forbids a state from excluding voters from any integral part of the general election unless the exclusion "is reasonably related to a legitimate legislative objective." 343 U.S. at 226 n. 14, 72 S.Ct. at 660 n. 14. The legislative objective was measured

in terms of a party objective. Thus, the state statute in *Blair* allowed the party to require candidates for presidential elector to take a party loyalty pledge; the Supreme Court upheld the pledge as constitutional.

50. 419 U.S. 477, 95 S.Ct. 541, 42 L.Ed.2d 595 (1975).

See generally, Gottlieb, Rebuilding the Right of Association: The Right to Hold a Convention as a Test Case, 11 Hofstra L.Rev. 191 (1982) (objecting to legislative regulation or political parties); Weisburd, Candidate-Making and the Constitution: Constitutional Restraints on and Protections of Party Nominating Methods, 57 So.Calif.L.Rev. 213 (1984).

51. 419 U.S. at 491, 95 S.Ct. at 549 (emphasis added).

discrimination by political parties at their conventions or in their primaries would not necessarily require the prohibition of religious parties, if such might be formed, that have religious qualifications. Unlike racial discrimination, religious liberty is explicitly protected by the First Amendment. A different balance of interests may allow a party to discriminate if motivated by religious grounds while that discrimination may not be justified if motivated by racial grounds.[52]

The Court followed the implications of *Cousins* in *Democratic Party v. Wisconsin ex rel. La Follette*.[53] In *LaFollette* the state tried to impose its *state* rules on the *national* party convention. Though National Democratic Party rules provided that only those willing to affiliate publicly with the Democratic Party may participate in the process of selecting delegates to the party's national convention, Wisconsin state law allowed anyone to vote in the state primary without requiring a public declaration of party preference. In this "open" primary, Wisconsin voters did not vote for delegates but only expressed their choice among the Democratic Party presidential candidates. Later, the Democratic Party caucuses, made up of people who had publicly stated their affiliation with the Democratic Party, selected the delegates to the National Convention. Wisconsin law then purported to bind these delegates to vote at the National Convention in accord with the results of the open presidential preference primary.

Although Wisconsin's open presidential preference primary did not itself violate national party rules, the state's mandate that the results of the primary must determine the allocation of votes cast by the state's delegates at the national convention did violate the Democratic Party rule that the procedure by which delegates to the convention are bound to vote must be limited to those who have publicly declared the Democratic Party preference. The majority found that any issue as to the validity of this type of state law, with its extraterritorial effects, was foreclosed by *Cousins*. The Court broadly stated in dictum: "[T]he freedom to associate for 'the common advancement of political beliefs' necessarily presupposes the freedom to identify the people who comprise the association, and to limit the association to those people only."[54]

The *LaFollette* decision places some limits on the extraterritorial power of the states to regulate national political party conventions. A different question—not considered in that case—is raised by federal regulations of national political party conventions. A related question—also not decided by *LaFollette*—is raised by state regulation of state political party conventions.[55] Whether the Court approves of such regulations should be a function of the extent to which they interfere with the freedom of association. There is certainly no absolute right of the political party to control its membership in all circumstances;[56] the *White Primary Cases* and open primary cases are proof of that.[57]

§ 14.34 The Reapportionment Cases and the Rule of One Person, One Vote: The Creation of Justiciability

The first major case to reach the Supreme Court claiming that Congressional election dis-

52. In a similar manner, the Court has held that the state could give text books to students attending religious schools, Board of Education v. Allen, 392 U.S. 236, 88 S.Ct. 1923, 20 L.Ed.2d 1060 (1968), but not to those attending racially discriminatory schools, Norwood v. Harrison, 413 U.S. 455, 93 S.Ct. 2804, 37 L.Ed.2d 723 (1973). The Court has also held that the Internal Revenue Service acted within its authority and did not violate the religion clauses of the First Amendment when the Service denied tax exempt status to religiously affiliated schools that discriminated on the basis of race. Bob Jones University v. United States, 461 U.S. 574, 103 S.Ct. 2017, 76 L.Ed.2d 157 (1983).

53. 450 U.S. 107, 101 S.Ct. 1010, 67 L.Ed.2d 82 (1981).

54. 450 U.S. at 122, 101 S.Ct. at 1018 (internal citation and footnote omitted). For citations to additional

cases, including lower court cases, and secondary works on this topic see our multi-volume Treatise: R. Rotunda & J. Nowak, Treatise on Constitutional Law: Substance and Procedure (3rd ed. 1999, with annual supplements).

55. See 450 U.S. at 120, 123–24, 101 S.Ct. at 1018, 1019–20 (Court emphasizes that the narrow question, the only question, before it is whether the state can bind the *national* party; and that, like *Cousins*, that is the issue which this case raises).

56. See Roberts v. United States Jaycees, 468 U.S. 609, 104 S.Ct. 3244, 82 L.Ed.2d 462 (1984). See note 54 supra, and § 16.41, infra. See also §§ 14.31(g), 14.32.

57. See §§ 14.31(g), 14.33(a), supra.

tricts for the House of Representatives were malapportioned because they lacked compactness of territory and approximate equality of population was *Colegrove v. Green*.[1] A majority of the voting Justices dismissed the suit, but there was no majority for treating reapportionment as a political question. Justice Frankfurter in an opinion concurred in by only Justices Reed and Burton argued that "due regard for the effective working of our Government revealed this issue to be of a peculiarly political nature and therefore not meet for judicial determination."[2] He strongly urged that "Courts ought not to enter this political thicket."[3] Three Justices found jurisdiction and one concurred on nonjurisdictional grounds.[4]

The next major case to reach the Supreme Court was *Gomillion v. Lightfoot*.[5] Here the Court acted, but purportedly on a narrow ground, in the majority opinion for the Court, written by Justice Frankfurter. In this case black voters, who had been residents of the City of Tuskegee, complained after the Alabama legislature enacted a statute redefining the City of Tuskegee by altering its shape from a square to a strangely shaped twenty-eight-sided figure.[6] Plaintiffs relied on the equal protection guarantees of the Fourteenth Amendment and the right to vote under the Fifteenth Amendment, and claimed that the gerrymandered boundaries were created solely for the purpose of fencing out black voters from the town to deprive them of the pre-existing right to vote in the municipal election.

The Court agreed that the claim was justiciable, relying only on the Fifteenth Amendment.[7] By placing the case on such grounds, Frankfurter perhaps hoped to isolate it from a more general precedent. Justice Whittaker's concurrence was analytically more satisfying; he relied on equal protection:

> It seems to me that the "right ... to vote" that is guaranteed by the Fifteenth Amendment is but the same right to vote as is enjoyed by all others within the same ... political division. ... But ... "fencing Negro citizens out of" Division A and into Division B is an unlawful segregation of races of citizens, in violation of the Equal Protection Clause of the Fourteenth Amendment. ...[8]

Finally, in *Baker v. Carr*,[9] two years after *Gomillion*, the Court found reapportionment cases to be justiciable based on the more general equal protection clause of the Fourteenth Amendment. *Colegrove* was distinguished and the Court held that debasement of a person's vote by malapportionment is a violation of the equal protection guaranty of the Fourteenth Amendment. This claim was significantly different from those based on the nonjusticiable republican form of government clause.[10]

> The question here is the consistency of state action with the Federal Constitution. We have no question decided, or to be decided, by a political branch of government coequal with this Court. Nor do we risk embarrassment of our government abroad, or grave disturbance at home if we take issue with Tennessee as to the constitutionality of her action here challenged. Nor need the appellants, in order to succeed in this action, ask the Court to enter upon policy determinations for which judicially manageable standards are lacking.[11]

Malapportionment claims were now before the Court. But the nature of the constitution-

§ 14.34

1. 328 U.S. 549, 66 S.Ct. 1198, 90 L.Ed. 1432 (1946).

2. 328 U.S. at 552, 66 S.Ct. at 1199.

3. 328 U.S. at 556, 66 S.Ct. at 1201.

4. Justice Rutledge assumed jurisdiction but declined to exercise it for other reasons, including the shortness of time remaining before the election. 328 U.S. at 564, 565, 66 S.Ct. at 1208 (Rutledge, J., concurring). Justices Black, joined by Douglas and Murphy, dissented. 328 U.S. at 566, 66 S.Ct. at 1209. Justice Jackson took no part in the consideration of the case. 328 U.S. at 556, 66 S.Ct. at 1209.

5. 364 U.S. 339, 81 S.Ct. 125, 5 L.Ed.2d 110 (1960).

6. 364 U.S. at 340, 81 S.Ct. at 126.

7. 364 U.S. at 341–43, 81 S.Ct. at 127–28.

8. 364 U.S. at 349, 81 S.Ct. at 132.

9. 369 U.S. 186, 82 S.Ct. 691, 7 L.Ed.2d 663 (1962).

10. U.S.Const. art. IV, § 4.

11. 369 U.S. at 226, 82 S.Ct. at 715.

al right had yet to be decided.[12]

§ 14.35 The Origins of One Person, One Vote

The value of the right recognized in *Baker* was explained in *Reynolds v. Sims*,[1] which created the one person, one vote principle grounded in the equal protection clause. But before that case the Supreme Court laid the groundwork in two others, *Gray v. Sanders*,[2] and *Wesberry v. Sanders*.[3] In *Gray* the Court invalidated the county unit system of nominating the Governor and other officials of Georgia. Under the Georgia law challenged in *Gray*, each candidate in the primary election who won a plurality of the popular vote in any county was entitled to all of the county's electoral "units." A majority of the county unit votes nominated the Governor and the United States Senator; the other nominees needed only a plurality of unit votes.[4] Although the units were not assigned among counties according to population, the Court suggested that apportionment of units on a one person, one vote basis could not cure the constitutional flaws of the unit system because the winner of a county won all of its unit votes.

Using the entire state as the appropriate geographic unit, the Court interpreted the Constitution to require the addition of a minority candidate's votes in one county to the

---

12. The Court may review the method by which Congress divides representation in the House of Representatives between the states. The congressional allocation of representatives is not a political question. However, the Supreme Court will grant Congress much more latitude in determining the appropriate manner of allocating state representation in the House of Representatives than it would give to states when reviewing state laws that create districts for the elections of representatives to Congress. United States Department of Commerce v. Montana, 503 U.S. 442, 112 S.Ct. 1415, 118 L.Ed.2d 87 (1992) (the congressional apportionment of representation among the states is a justiciable political question; the federal statute before the Court allocating representation to the states was within the scope of congressional power and did not violate Article 1, § 2 of the Constitution, which requires apportionment of representatives among the states "according to their respective numbers").

In Wisconsin v. City of New York, 517 U.S. 1, 116 S.Ct. 1091, 134 L.Ed.2d 167 (1996) the Supreme Court upheld the decision of the Secretary of Commerce not to make adjustments to the 1990 census. Chief Justice Rehnquist, writing for a unanimous Court, ruled that the one-person one-vote standard established for judicial review of state created legislative districts does not apply to the federal allocation of positions in the House of Representatives. Therefore, the decision of the Secretary regarding the validity of the census was not subject to independent judicial review, or so-called "heightened scrutiny." The Supreme Court found that there was no basis for finding that the Secretary's decision constituted invidious discrimination against any group of individuals.

See also, Franklin v. Massachusetts, 505 U.S. 788, 112 S.Ct. 2767, 120 L.Ed.2d 636 (1992). The Supreme Court, with an opinion that was in part a majority opinion, upheld a decision of the executive branch (the Secretary of Commerce) that counted the votes of federal employees temporarily stationed outside the United States as applicable to the state of their previous residence. Other rulings in the case, besides rulings regarding the standing of states as plaintiffs, were that (1) a Secretary of Commerce report was not final and reviewable under the Administrative Procedure Act, (2) the decision of the President of the United States in calculating numbers representative to which each state was entitled was not an agency action reviewable under the Administrative Procedure Act, (3) the constitutional challenge to the federal apportionment of congressional representatives was a justiciable question and not a political question, and (4) the allocation of overseas federal employees to their home states and the decennial census for reapportionment did not violate constitutional provisions or the constitutional goal of representation in Congress that reflected population of the states.

In Utah v. Evans, 536 U.S. 452, 122 S.Ct. 2191, 153 L.Ed.2d 453 (2002) The Supreme Court refused to invalidate a statistical method, known as "hot-deck imputation" used by the Census Bureau to supply missing information about certain addresses or housing units from similarly situated units. Five Justices found that the Census Bureau's use of this methodology violated neither federal statutes nor the census clause. Justice O'Connor disagreed with the majority regarding its ruling that the Census Bureau's use of this statistical methodology did not violate federal statutes, although she did not discuss whether she believed the methodology violated the Constitution. 536 U.S. at 478, 122 S.Ct. at 2207 (O'Connor, J., concurring in part and dissenting in part). Two Justices believed that the statistical methodology did not violate federal statutes, but they believed that the use of statistical sampling violated the census clause contained in Article I, Section II, Clause III. 536 U.S. at 488, 122 S.Ct. at 2212 (Thomas, J., joined by Kennedy, J., concurring in part and dissenting in part). Justice Scalia believed that the case should have been dismissed on the basis that the state did not have standing under Article III to challenge an executive branch decision regarding the census counts. 536 U.S. at 509, 122 S.Ct. at 2223 (Scalia, J., dissenting).

§ 14.35

1. 377 U.S. 533, 84 S.Ct. 1362, 12 L.Ed.2d 506 (1964).

2. 372 U.S. 368, 83 S.Ct. 801, 9 L.Ed.2d 821 (1963).

3. 376 U.S. 1, 84 S.Ct. 526, 11 L.Ed.2d 481 (1964).

4. 372 U.S. at 371–72, 83 S.Ct. at 803–04.

votes he received in the other counties.[5] Thus:

> Once the geographic unit for which a representative is to be chosen is designated, all who participate in the election are to have an equal vote—whatever their race, whatever their sex, whatever their occupation, whatever their income, and wherever their home may be in the geographic unit. This is required by the Equal Protection Clause of the Fourteenth Amendment.[6]

In *Wesberry* the Court required that congressional districts be apportioned equally, but the Court did not base its holding on the equal protection clause but rather the command of Article I, section 2, that the Representatives be chosen "by the People of the several States." That clause, said Justice Black speaking for the Court, "means that as nearly as practicable one man's vote in a congressional election is to be worth as much as another's. ... To say that a vote is worth more in one district than in another would not only run counter to our fundamental ideas of democratic government; it would cast aside the principle of a House of Representatives elected 'by the People'. ..."[7]

In *Reynolds v. Sims* the Court was faced with a challenge to the malapportionment of the Alabama state legislature. This time, relying on the equal protection clause, Chief Justice Warren formulated the broad one person, one vote rule:

> Legislators represent people, not trees or acres. ... And, if a State should provide that the votes of citizens in one part of the State should be given two times, or five times, or 10 times the weight of votes of citizens in another part of the State, it could hardly be contended that the right to vote of those residing in the disfavored areas had not been effectively diluted ... the Equal Protection Clause requires that the seats in both houses of a bicameral state legislature must be apportioned on a population basis.[8]

In one of the companion cases[9] the Court struck down an election apportionment scheme in which one house was malapportioned by use of an area representation system analogous to the U.S. Senate.[10] While it was contended that the state voters in every county of the State had approved of their malapportioned State Senate, the malapportionment was still flawed: "An individual's constitutionally protected right to cast an equally weighted vote cannot be denied even by a vote of a majority of a State's electorate. ..."[11] The majority cannot waive the rights of the minority, nor should the majority be able to waive the rights of future generations of voters.

Although the Supreme Court made the issue of malapportionment subject to judicial review, it did not authorize federal courts to create new legislative districts merely because the federal court disagreed with the legislative apportionment scheme established by the state legislature or the state courts. A federal court

---

5. 372 U.S. at 381 n. 12, 83 S.Ct. at 809 n. 12.

6. 372 U.S. at 379, 83 S.Ct. at 808. *Gray* explicitly declined to address the situation in which a convention instead of a primary election nominates the candidates. 372 U.S. at 378 n. 10, 83 S.Ct. at 807 n. 10. See Chambers & Rotunda, Reform of Presidential Nominating Conventions, 56 Va.L.Rev. 179, 199–203 (1970).

7. 376 U.S. at 7–8, 84 S.Ct. at 530 (footnote omitted). The method by which Congress divides representation in the House of Representatives between the states is a justiciable and not a political question. However, the Supreme Court will grant Congress much more latitude in determining the appropriate manner of allocating state representation in the House of Representatives than it would give to states when reviewing state laws that create districts for the election of representatives to Congress. See note 12 in § 14.34, supra.

8. 377 U.S. at 562, 568, 84 S.Ct. at 1382, 1385.

9. The companion cases were Lucas v. Forty-Fourth General Assembly, 377 U.S. 713, 84 S.Ct. 1459, 12 L.Ed.2d 632 (1964), on remand to 232 F.Supp. 797 (D.Colo.1964), affirmed 379 U.S. 693, 85 S.Ct. 715, 13 L.Ed.2d 699 (1965) (Colorado); WMCA, Inc. v. Lomenzo, 377 U.S. 633, 84 S.Ct. 1418, 12 L.Ed.2d 568 (1964) (New York); Maryland Committee for Fair Representation v. Tawes, 377 U.S. 656, 84 S.Ct. 1429, 12 L.Ed.2d 595 (1964) (Maryland); Davis v. Mann, 377 U.S. 678, 84 S.Ct. 1441, 12 L.Ed.2d 609 (1964), on remand to 238 F.Supp. 458 (E.D.Va.1964), affirmed 379 U.S. 694, 85 S.Ct. 713, 13 L.Ed.2d 698 (1965) (Virginia); Roman v. Sincock, 377 U.S. 695, 84 S.Ct. 1449, 12 L.Ed.2d 620 (1964) (Delaware).

10. Lucas v. Forty–Fourth General Assembly, 377 U.S. 713, 84 S.Ct. 1459, 12 L.Ed.2d 632 (1964), on remand to 232 F.Supp. 797 (D.Colo.1964), affirmed 379 U.S. 693, 85 S.Ct. 715, 13 L.Ed.2d 699 (1965).

11. 377 U.S. at 736, 84 S.Ct. at 1473.

should only intervene in the state legislative districting process if the court finds that the legislative districts drawn by the local or state governmental units do not meet the constitutional standards established by the Supreme Court. Additionally, the Supreme Court has required federal courts to abstain from imposing a judicially mandated legislative districting map on a local or state governmental unit if the state legislature, or state courts, are considering the creation of new legislative districts that might be adopted in time to be used in the next election and within a time frame that allows for judicial review of the new districting system.[12]

§ 14.36 The Application of the One Person, One Vote Principle

(a) To the Appointment of the State Governor and Other Such Officials

In *Fortson v. Morris*[1] the Supreme Court upheld the election of Georgia's Governor by the state legislature. When no candidate had received a majority of the votes cast in the state's general election, the state constitution allowed the General Assembly to elect the Governor from the two front runners.[2] The voters of each legislative district elected the state representatives who in turn elected the Governor. One major procedural defect struck down in *Gray v. Sanders*[3]—not adding a minority candidate's votes in one part of the

state to the votes he receives in other parts— was approved in *Fortson* as it applied to the "delegates" who elect another person. The case indicates that the equal protection principle underlying *Gray* and other reapportionment cases should be inapplicable to voting by bodies which, like party conventions, perform a deliberative, but non-legislative function.

Gray and *Fortson* are in one sense difficult to reconcile with one another. On one level they appear directly contradictory. *Gray*, on the one hand, seems to hold that where the voters are asked or required to participate, equal protection mandates that each vote be counted equally. *Fortson*, on the other hand, upholds the selection of a state official by what had earlier been ruled to be a malapportioned legislature.[4] On another level, however, *Fortson* sanctions a representative process in the performance of a nonlegislative task, after the voters have exercised untrammeled their right to choose first-tier spokesmen. *Fortson* and *Gray* together thus appear to permit selection of an officer through indirect "election"—i.e., appointment—by a state legislature, but not by a mechanical unit system.

The *Fortson-Gray* theory developed above would permit multi-stage representative selection of delegates to the national conventions. A majority of the registered voters in a particular area—a county, for example—could con-

---

12. Federal courts are prohibited from obstructing the state reapportionment process (in either the state legislative or judicial branches) unless it appears that the state government will not create new districts within a time frame that would allow the new districts to be used in the next election. A federal court might, under some circumstances, require the state redistricting process to be completed in time for federal district court review. The federal courts cannot require states to complete their legislative redistricting at a date that would allow for federal district court and federal appellate court review prior to the next general election. Growe v. Emison, 507 U.S. 25, 113 S.Ct. 1075, 122 L.Ed.2d 388 (1993); Scott v. Germano, 381 U.S. 407, 85 S.Ct. 1525, 14 L.Ed.2d 477 (1965) (per curiam). See also, Chapman v. Meier, 420 U.S. 1, 27, 95 S.Ct. 751, 766, 42 L.Ed.2d 766 (1975).

§ 14.36

1. 385 U.S. 231, 87 S.Ct. 446, 17 L.Ed.2d 330 (1966).

2. Ga.Const. art. V, § 1, para. IV (1945). The Court noted that this provision had been in the Georgia Constitution since 1824 and had been readopted by Georgia

voters in the 1945 constitution, 385 U.S. at 233, 87 S.Ct. at 448. In 1968 the voters ratified an amendment which repealed this procedure and substituted a provision which calls for a run-off election between the two candidates with the highest number of votes. Ga.Const. art. V, § 1, para. IV (1945), as amended, 1968 Ga.Laws 1562–63, ratified Nov. 5, 1968 (codified in Ga.Code Ann. § 2–2704 (1977).)

3. 372 U.S. 368, 83 S.Ct. 801, 9 L.Ed.2d 821 (1963).

4. The Court relied on its ruling in Toombs v. Fortson, 384 U.S. 210, 86 S.Ct. 1464, 16 L.Ed.2d 482 (1966), affirming per curiam 241 F.Supp. 65 (N.D.Ga.1965), that the Georgia Assembly as then constituted could function until May 1, 1968, to hold that the Assembly was not disqualified to elect the Governor.

But see Fortson v. Morris, 385 U.S. 231, 245, 87 S.Ct. 446, 454, 17 L.Ed.2d 330 (1966), (Fortas, J., dissenting) ("We have declined to deprive a malapportioned legislature of its de facto status as a legislature. But not until today has this Court allowed a malapportioned legislature to be the device for doing indirectly what a State may not do directly.")

stitutionally elect a delegate to a state convention, which in turn chooses the national delegates. The minority voters in the county are not disenfranchised, as they would be under a unit system, because they will be represented at higher levels by a delegate who, though committed to a differing point of view, can think, compromise and change in the deliberative process, the purpose of which is to select the "best man" for the Presidency.[5]

Pragmatic reasons may also explain *Fortson:* Georgia already had two primaries, one general election, and still failed to choose a governor. Justice Black argued that "Statewide elections cost time and money and it is not strange that Georgia's people decided to avoid repeated elections".[6]

In any event, *Fortson*, at the least, shows that the Constitution does not require that the governor of a state be popularly elected. The state can choose to appoint members to an official position rather than elect them. If there is no popular election, the one person, one vote rule does not apply.

Thus, for example, a state or commonwealth statute may provide that if an interim vacancy in the state legislature is created, then the political party with which the previous incumbent was a member may fill that vacancy.[7] Such a statute does not restrict access to the electoral process because the interim appointment is not an election. Nor is such a statute defective because the appointment power is given to a political party rather than to an elected official: the legislature "could reasonably conclude that appointment by the previous incumbent's political party would more fairly reflect the will of the voters than appointment by the Governor or some other elected official."[8]

(b) To Local Government Elections

In *Sailors v. Board of Education*,[9] the Supreme Court approved the choice of county school board members by a method whereby each local school board appointed only one delegate and was allowed only one vote at the caucus convened to elect the county school board, even though the districts represented by the local school boards were of disproportionate population. The Supreme Court held that the state has discretion to decide whether or not such a board shall be appointed by a representative process, or popularly elected, and that if the board is appointed, the districts its members represent need not be equal in population. The Court stated that "we see nothing in the Constitution to prevent experimentation."[10] In *Sailors* the school board was not found to exercise legislative powers but only administrative powers. This purported distinction between administrative and legislative powers was continued in a case decided

5. Cf. Burke's Politics 115–16 (R. Hoffman & P. Levack eds. 1949) (Speech of Edmund Burke to the Electors of Bristol, Nov. 3, 1774). Consider also the historical reasons for the electoral college. See, e.g. The Federalist No. 68 (A. Hamilton). The concept of the national party convention as a deliberative body searching to select the "best man" appears to be fictional. The same is true of the Georgia legislature when it elected the Governor after *Fortson* was decided, for the ballots followed straight party lines.

6. 385 U.S. at 234, 87 S.Ct. at 449. The speed with which *Fortson* was heard on both district and Supreme Court levels bespeaks the simple need for Georgia to have a Governor: the general election took place on November 8, a three-judge federal court gave its decisions on November 17, the Supreme Court heard arguments on December 5 and rendered its decision on December 12.

7. Rodriguez v. Popular Democratic Party, 457 U.S. 1, 102 S.Ct. 2194, 72 L.Ed.2d 628 (1982). See also Valenti v. Rockefeller, 393 U.S. 405, 89 S.Ct. 689, 21 L.Ed.2d 635 (1969), (per curiam), affirming 292 F.Supp. 851 (S.D.N.Y.

1968) (three judge court) (Governor may fill vacancy in U.S. Senate by appointment pending next regularly scheduled congressional election, even though the wait in that case was over 29 months; the court relied on the Seventeenth Amendment).

8. Rodriguez v. Popular Democratic Party, 457 U.S. 1, 11–13, 102 S.Ct. 2194, 2200–02, 72 L.Ed.2d 628 (1982) (footnote omitted).

9. 387 U.S. 105, 87 S.Ct. 1549, 18 L.Ed.2d 650 (1967).

10. 387 U.S. at 111, 87 S.Ct. at 1553. In *Fortson* it was clear that the Georgia legislature was malapportioned and had been ordered to reapportion itself. Toombs v. Fortson, 241 F.Supp. 65 (N.D.Ga.1965), affirmed mem. 384 U.S. 210, 86 S.Ct. 1464, 16 L.Ed.2d 482 (1966). But in *Sailors* the Board was not required to reapportion itself though it was clearly malapportioned. One district with a population of over 200,000 could send one delegate to the caucus selecting the county school board; another district, with fewer than 100 people, also had one delegate. Brief for Appellants at 4, Sailors v. Board of Education, 387 U.S. 105, 87 S.Ct. 1549, 18 L.Ed.2d 650 (1967).

a year later. In *Avery v. Midland County*[11] the Court required that county commissioners who exercised "general governmental powers over the entire geographic area served by the body"[12] and who are popularly elected be districted according to population.

In *Hadley v. Junior College District*,[13] the Court seemed to abandon the distinction between administrative and legislative powers and fashion a new test. The trustees in *Hadley* could levy and collect taxes, issue some bonds, hire and fire teachers, perform other activities and in general manage the junior college. While the powers were less than those in *Avery*, where the commissioners maintained the county jail, set the county tax rate, built and ran hospitals, airports, and libraries and had similar duties, the Court found the governmental powers general enough and of sufficient impact to justify the one person, one vote rule. But the decision appeared to find crucial another factor:

> [While] the case now before us ... differs in certain respects from those offices considered in prior cases, it is exactly the same in one crucial factor—*these officials are elected by popular vote.* ... If there is any way of determining the importance of choosing a particular governmental official, we think the decision of the State to select that official by popular vote is a strong enough indication that the choice is an important one.[14]

The Court then refused to distinguish for purposes of the apportionment rule between elections for "legislative" officials and those for "administrative" officials.[15] And it held that:

> [A]s a general rule, whenever a state or local government decides to select persons by popular election to perform governmental functions, [equal protection] requires that each

qualified voter must be given an equal opportunity to participate in that election, and when members of an elected body are chosen from separate districts, each district must be established on a basis which will insure, as far as is practicable, that equal numbers of voters can vote for proportionally equal numbers of officials. It is of course possible that there might be some case in which a State elects certain functionaries whose duties are so far removed from normal governmental activities and so disproportionately affect different groups that a popular election in compliance with [one man, one vote] might not be required.[16]

Sailors and *Fortson v. Morris*[17] were distinguished as cases where the State chose to appoint members to an official body rather than elect them.[18] But once a popular election mechanism is chosen one person, one vote must apply. If an official is appointed to a position, then one person, one vote need not apply.

However, the Court has found, in conformity with the *Hadley* principle, that some elected entities are so specialized that the one person, one vote rule need not be applied to them. In several cases the Court upheld the restriction of votes to elected members of a water storage district which gave the franchise only to local owners and weighted the votes according to the amount of property the individuals held. While not a classic districting case, these franchise restrictions did allow for differing degrees of voter participation. The activities of the water storage district fell disproportionally on the landowners as a group. The Court upheld this deviation from the one person, one vote principle because in these cases the restrictions furthered the interest of insuring that land owners controlled the limited water supply in these areas.[19]

---

11. 390 U.S. 474, 88 S.Ct. 1114, 20 L.Ed.2d 45 (1968).

12. 390 U.S. at 485, 88 S.Ct. at 1120.

13. 397 U.S. 50, 90 S.Ct. 791, 25 L.Ed.2d 45 (1970).

14. 397 U.S. at 54, 55, 90 S.Ct. at 794–95 (emphasis added).

15. 397 U.S. at 55, 90 S.Ct. at 794–95.

16. 397 U.S. at 56, 90 S.Ct. at 795.

17. 385 U.S. 231, 87 S.Ct. 446, 17 L.Ed.2d 330 (1966).

18. 397 U.S. at 58, 90 S.Ct. at 796.

19. Salyer Land Co. v. Tulare Lake Basin Water Storage District, 410 U.S. 719, 93 S.Ct. 1224, 35 L.Ed.2d 659 (1973); Associated Enterprises, Inc. v. Toltec Watershed Improvement District, 410 U.S. 743, 93 S.Ct. 1237, 35 L.Ed.2d 675 (1973).

Over the strong dissents of four Justices the Court applied the principle of these cases in Ball v. James, 451 U.S. 355, 101 S.Ct. 1811, 68 L.Ed.2d 150 (1981), where it

The Supreme Court has not subjected the election of judges to the one person, one vote principle.[20] A local government should not be able to insulate a system for the election of officials with general governmental powers merely by describing those officials as "judges". If so-called "judges" have some type of general governmental powers, beyond those normally associated with the judiciary, the election of those "judges" should be subject to the one person, one vote principle but, like all other types of elections, are subject to other Fourteenth Amendment principles and other constitutional limitations on elections such as the Fifteenth Amendment, the Nineteenth Amendment and the Twenty-sixth Amendment. Additionally, Congress may regulate judicial elections or other election systems to protect civil rights (such as those protected by the Fourteenth, Fifteenth, Nineteenth, and Twenty-sixth Amendments).[21]

In *Town of Lockport v. Citizens for Community Action at the Local Level, Inc.*,[22] a unanimous Court upheld a provision of New York law which provided that a new county charter could go into effect only if it is approved by a referendum election by separate majorities of the voters who live in the cities within the county and those who live in the county but

outside of the cities. The Court noted that in order to determine whether a concurrent majority requirement violates the principle of one person, one vote, the Court will focus on two inquiries: first, is there a genuine difference in the relevant interests of the groups that the state electoral classification has created; second, if there is such a difference, does the enhancement of minority votes nonetheless amount to invidious discrimination. The Court analyzed the purposes of the New York law; noted that in some counties the city voters outnumbered the town voters and in other counties the situation was the reverse; and recognized that a new or amended county charter will frequently operate to transfer functions from cities to county. Just as in annexation proceedings the residents of the annexing city and the area to be annexed have sufficiently different constituencies and interests, the decision to restructure county government is similar in impact and justifies the concurrent majorities requirement.

In the *Town of Lockport* case, the Court ruled that the one person, one vote principle was not violated by the referendum approval voting system.[23] In the water storage district cases the Court held that this unique form of governmental entity was so specialized as to

---

upheld the constitutionality of the system for electing the directors of a large Arizona water reclamation district which limited voter eligibility to landowners and apportioned voting power according to the amount of land a voter owns. The Court concluded that the "peculiarly narrow function of this local governmental body and the special relationship of one class of citizens to that body release[d] it from the strict demands of the one-person-one-vote principle. ..." 451 U.S. at 357, 101 S.Ct. at 1814.

20. The Supreme Court has not issued an opinion explaining why judicial elections are not subject to the one person, one vote principle, it has summarily affirmed lower federal court rulings in which the court refused to apply the one person, one vote concept to a judicial election. Wells v. Edwards, 409 U.S. 1095, 93 S.Ct. 904, 34 L.Ed.2d 679 (1973), affirming 347 F.Supp. 453, 454 (M.D.La.1972). In upholding the congressional power to prevent racial discrimination in judicial elections, the majority opinion referred to the *Wells* decision as if it had settled the question of whether the one person, one vote rule could apply to judicial elections. Chisom v. Roemer, 501 U.S. 380, 403, 111 S.Ct. 2354, 2368, 115 L.Ed.2d 348 (1991).

21. The Supreme Court has held that the Voting Rights Act applies to judicial elections. Chisom v. Roemer, 501 U.S. 380, 111 S.Ct. 2354, 115 L.Ed.2d 348 (1991);

Houston Lawyers' Association v. Attorney General, 501 U.S. 419, 111 S.Ct. 2376, 115 L.Ed.2d 379 (1991). In the *Chisom* and *Houston Lawyers' Association* cases, the Supreme Court did not rule on any constitutional issues or on questions concerning the type of proof that would be required to establish a violation of the act in a judicial districting case.

22. 430 U.S. 259, 97 S.Ct. 1047, 51 L.Ed.2d 313 (1977). Cf. Hill v. Stone, 421 U.S. 289, 95 S.Ct. 1637, 44 L.Ed.2d 172 (1975); Phoenix v. Kolodziejski, 399 U.S. 204, 90 S.Ct. 1990, 26 L.Ed.2d 523 (1970); Cipriano v. City of Houma, 395 U.S. 701, 89 S.Ct. 1897, 23 L.Ed.2d 647 (1969).

23. Town of Lockport v. Citizens for Community Action at the Local Level, Inc., 430 U.S. 259, 97 S.Ct. 1047, 51 L.Ed.2d 313 (1977) is discussed in the previous paragraph of this section. The Supreme Court had held prior to Town of Lockport that the one person, one vote principle did not require that a simple majority of the voters be able to approve a referendum. Gordon v. Lance, 403 U.S. 1, 91 S.Ct. 1889, 29 L.Ed.2d 273 (1971) (Supreme Court upholds a state rule prohibiting political subdivision from incurring any bonded indebtedness or raising tax rates beyond specified limits unless the actions receive a 60% approval in a referendum).

allow for the disenfranchisement of persons in the voting district who were not property owners due to the special impact of the water district activity on property owners.[24] In none of these cases did the Court rule that the one person, one vote principle was inapplicable to an elected governmental entity that exercised significant governmental powers.

Board of Estimate v. Morris[25] unanimously ruled that New York City's Board of Estimate was subject to the one person, one vote principle. The Board of Estimate was composed of the elected presidents of each of the city's five boroughs, each of whom cast one vote on the Board, and three officials who were elected by city-wide ballot (the city's mayor, comptroller, and city council president). There was a wide disparity in the populations of each of the boroughs, so that the citizens living in the least populous boroughs had a greater impact on the election of the Board than did persons living in the most populous boroughs. The Board did not have general legislative authority over the city but it did perform a variety of functions similar to those performed by municipal governments, including the calculations of certain utility and property taxes, zoning authority, fixing the salaries of city officers, and

a sharing of legislative function with the city council regarding capital and expense budgets. The Court found that the array of powers possessed by the Board were sufficient to bring it within the requirements of the equal protection clause one person, one vote principle.[26]

It should be remembered that the one person, one vote principle applies where the representative is elected by district and not where the area serves not as a voting district but only as a basis for residence. For example, where the residents of a city are allowed to vote to elect all the representatives but these representatives are required to live in certain areas, the one person, one vote rules do not apply to these areas. Since each person votes for all the representatives, even though each representative must live in a given area, there is no districting of voters. The areas where the representatives live need not be equal in population.[27]

(c) Mathematical Precision

(1) In Federal Elections. In *Wesberry v. Sanders*[28] the Supreme Court required states to draw their congressional districts so that *"as nearly as is practicable* one man's vote in a

---

24. The water district cases were discussed previously in this subsection of the treatise. See, Salyer Land Co. v. Tulare Lake Basin Water Storage District, 410 U.S. 719, 93 S.Ct. 1224, 35 L.Ed.2d 659 (1973); Associated Enterprises, Inc. v. Toltec Watershed Improvement District, 410 U.S. 743, 93 S.Ct. 1237, 35 L.Ed.2d 675 (1973); Ball v. James, 451 U.S. 355, 101 S.Ct. 1811, 68 L.Ed.2d 150 (1981). Apart from these water district cases, the Supreme Court has consistently invalidated property ownership requirements for voting or candidacies. See §§ 14.31(b), 14.32(b), (d).

25. 489 U.S. 688, 109 S.Ct. 1433, 103 L.Ed.2d 717 (1989).

26. Although the Justices were unanimous ruling that this system violated the one person, one vote principle and the equal protection clause because of the disparate populations of the boroughs, they were divided as to the correct method for calculating the relationships between the voters of the various boroughs. The majority opinion, written by Justice White rejected the use of a mathematical formula for determining each voter's likely influence on the decisions of the governmental entity, called the "Banzhaf Index", which would have resulted in a finding that the maximum deviation in voting power between citizens in the least and most populous districts was 30.8% on nonbudget matters and "a higher deviation on budget issues." Board of Estimate v. Morris, 489 U.S. 688, 697–98, 109 S.Ct. 1433, 1440, 103 L.Ed.2d 717 (1989). The

majority found that the Court should take into account the presence of the at-large members of the Board; that calculation indicated that there was a 78% difference in the least and most populous voting districts, rather than a difference of over 100% which would have been the number arrived at without regard to the presence of the city-wide members. The 78% deviation was held to be unjustified and a violation of the equal protection clause. Justice Brennan, joined by Justice Stevens, would have held that the at-large members of the Board should not have been taken into account in calculating the differences in the deviation from the one person, one vote principle. 489 U.S. at 703, 109 S.Ct. at 1443 (Brennan, J., joined by Stevens, J., concurring in part and concurring in the judgment). Justice Blackmun agreed with the Court's method of calculations but would have found that even if the mathematical index were used, so that the deviation from true voter equality was 30.8%, that the deviation from the one person, one vote principle was "too large to be constitutional." 489 U.S. at 703, 109 S.Ct. at 1443 (Blackmun, J., concurring in part and concurring in the judgment).

27. Dallas County v. Reese, 421 U.S. 477, 95 S.Ct. 1706, 44 L.Ed.2d 312 (1975), (per curiam). See Wymbs v. Republican State Exec. Committee, 719 F.2d 1072, 1078 (11th Cir.1983), certiorari denied 465 U.S. 1103, 104 S.Ct. 1600, 80 L.Ed.2d 131 (1984).

28. 376 U.S. 1, 84 S.Ct. 526, 11 L.Ed.2d 481 (1964).

congressional election is to be worth as much as another's."[29] In subsequent litigation the Court has had occasion to explain what it meant, and the Court's explanation has shown it to be literally minded.

In *Kirkpatrick v. Preisler*,[30] for example, a decision rendered when Earl Warren was Chief Justice, the Court struck down a congressional districting plan where "the most populous district was 3.13% above the mathematical ideal, and the least populous was 2.84% below."[31] The Court found no justification for even this small deviation and explicitly rejected any argument that there is any variance small enough to be considered de minimis. Moreover, it was no justification that the State attempted to avoid fragmenting political subdivisions by drawing the Congressional districts along existing county lines or other political subdivisions. In districting for the House of Representatives, the State must "make a good-faith effort to achieve precise mathematical equality."[32] That same day the Court invalidated a New York plan with slightly larger variations.[33]

The Court has continued to follow this principle. Thus in *White v. Weiser*[34] the Court invalidated a reapportionment plan where the differences were even smaller than *Kirkpatrick*. In *White* the average deviation of all districts from the ideal was .745%; the largest district exceeded the ideal by 2.43% and the smallest district under the ideal by only 1.7%. The plan was rejected in favor of one where the largest district exceeded the ideal by .086% and the smallest was under the ideal by .063%.[35] Again it should be remembered that

the one person, one vote requirement in federal elections is based on Article I rather than the equal protection clause of the Fourteenth Amendment.

Although the Supreme Court formally bases congressional redistricting principles on article I, § 2 of the Constitution, the underlying principle that justifies judicial scrutiny of such state activity is one of guaranteeing equality in the power of voters within a state. The Court has not ruled out all deviations from mathematical equality between congressional districts within a state, even though it has found that no deviation in this area is so small that it may be considered *de minimis* and permissible under Article I, section 2 without any justification.[36] The Court, in reviewing congressional district maps, first requires those attacking the districting plan to demonstrate that the population differences between congressional districts could have been reduced or eliminated by a good faith effort to draw districts of equal population. If a plaintiff can demonstrate that the population differences are not a product of a good faith effort to achieve equality, the state will be required to prove that each significant variance between districts was necessary to achieve some legitimate goal.[37]

There will be fewer legitimate reasons for population variances between congressional districts than for variations in state or local legislative districts. States may have more legitimate reasons for wishing to keep voter groups in county or other political subdivisions when voting for state legislative positions. Such political divisions often have political

---

29. 376 U.S. at 7–8, 84 S.Ct. at 530 (emphasis added).

30. 394 U.S. 526, 89 S.Ct. 1225, 22 L.Ed.2d 519 (1969).

31. 394 U.S. at 528–29, 89 S.Ct. at 1227–28 (footnote omitted).

32. 394 U.S. at 530–31, 89 S.Ct. at 1228–29.

33. Wells v. Rockefeller, 394 U.S. 542, 89 S.Ct. 1234, 22 L.Ed.2d 535 (1969) (most populous district 6.488% above the mean; smallest district 6.608% below the mean).

34. 412 U.S. 783, 93 S.Ct. 2348, 37 L.Ed.2d 335 (1973).

35. 412 U.S. at 786, 796–97, 93 S.Ct. at 2350, 2355–56. See also, Karcher v. Daggett, 462 U.S. 725, 103 S.Ct. 2653, 77 L.Ed.2d 133 (1983), on remand 580 F.Supp. 1259

(D.N.J.1984), judgment affirmed 467 U.S. 1222, 104 S.Ct. 2672, 81 L.Ed.2d 869 (1984) (disparity between largest district and smallest district of 0.6984%; plan invalidated).

36. Karcher v. Daggett, 462 U.S. 725, 731, 103 S.Ct. 2653, 2660, 77 L.Ed.2d 133, 143 (1983), on remand 580 F.Supp. 1259 (D.N.J.1984), judgment affirmed 467 U.S. 1222, 104 S.Ct. 2672, 81 L.Ed.2d 869 (1984).

37. This test for determining whether a deviation from mathematical equality in congressional districting will be permitted is derived from the earlier cases discussed in this subsection and was phrased as a two part test in Karcher v. Daggett, 462 U.S. 725, 730, 103 S.Ct. 2653, 2658, 77 L.Ed.2d 133, 104–41 (1983), on remand 580 F.Supp. 1259 (D.N.J.1984), judgment affirmed 467 U.S. 1222, 104 S.Ct. 2672, 81 L.Ed.2d 869 (1984).

powers as units of local government. States may also wish to guarantee representation to small counties because the state legislative system may act on matters which clearly effect different counties in different ways and in which legislative input from all counties or political subdivisions is important.

However, there are fewer reasons to distinguish between voters when they are being divided for the purpose of creating congressional districts. County and other political subdivision lines may be considered less relevant to the determination of congressional districts because persons in Congress are not primarily concerned with legislation which effects specific counties within a state.[38] On the other hand, the state may have some legitimate reasons for creating congressional districts somewhat unequal in size. It is possible that providing for compact and contiguous districts is a goal that would allow some minimal population deviations so as to group voters with similar interests and avoid political gerrymandering.[39] While the reasons that would support any population deviation must not discriminate on the basis of race, it is possible that the districting map could be designed to guarantee that the voting strength of identifiable minorities, such as racial minorities, is not diluted.[40]

If a court finds a significant population difference between congressional districts that was not incidental to a good faith effort to achieve population equality, the state will have the burden of demonstrating that the districting plan is necessary to promote a significant interest which justifies the population deviations.[41] Legislative districts that are equal in population may still be attacked as a violation of equal protection if the districting lines were drawn for the purpose of diluting the voting strength of an identifiable racial or ethnic minority and, perhaps, if they were designed for the purpose of diluting the voting strength of a particular political association.[42]

(2) In State Elections. As we have seen, the one man, one vote mandate with respect to Congressional districting is based on Article I, section 2 of the Constitution, but the apportionment in elections for state or local offices is justified by the Equal Protection Clause of the Fourteenth Amendment. Thus the strict application of the one man, one vote standard for Congressional districting does not require a similar rule for other elections, where the Court has been more flexible. In *Abate v. Mundt*,[43] the Court allowed deviations in a County Board of Supervisors election where the most underrepresented town deviated from the ideal by 7.1% and the most overrepresent-

---

38. See Brown v. Thomson, 462 U.S. 835, 848, 103 S.Ct. 2690, 2699, 77 L.Ed.2d 214, 225 (1983) (O'Connor, J., concurring opinion).

39. See West Virginia Civil Liberties Union v. Rockefeller, 336 F.Supp. 395, 398–400 (S.D.W.Va.1972) (approving congressional district plan with under one percent maximum deviation as being justified by compactness requirement and state constitution), cited with approval in Karcher v. Daggett, 462 U.S. 725, 740–41, 103 S.Ct. 2653, 2663, 77 L.Ed.2d 133, 147 (1983), on remand 580 F.Supp. 1259 (D.N.J.1984), judgment affirmed 467 U.S. 1222, 104 S.Ct. 2672, 81 L.Ed.2d 869 (1984).

40. Any use of racial classifications that is designed to deny a person the right to vote because of the person's race will violate the Fifteenth Amendment and the Fourteenth Amendment equal protection clause. Any law that constitutes a purposeful discrimination against minority race candidates or dilution of minority race voting power will be found to be a violation of equal protection and, perhaps, the Fifteenth Amendment. However, the Court has not set forth clear guidelines concerning the extent to which a governmental unit may consider race in order to create electoral districts in which members of racial minority groups will be able to control the outcomes of

elections and elect minority race persons to legislative bodies. The issue of racial "affirmative action" in election laws is considered in § 14.10(c).

41. See Karcher v. Daggett, 462 U.S. 725, 103 S.Ct. 2653, 77 L.Ed.2d 133 (1983), on remand to 580 F.Supp. 1259 (D.N.J.1984), judgment affirmed 467 U.S. 1222, 104 S.Ct. 2672, 81 L.Ed.2d 869 (1984), in which the Court found invalid a congressional districting map in which the disparity between the largest and smallest districts was less than 0.7 percent because the state was unable to produce evidence showing that the deviation was necessary to promote a legitimate end, such as preserving minority voting strength. The method by which Congress divides representation in the House of Representatives between the states is reviewable by the Court and not a political question. However, the Supreme Court will grant Congress much more latitude in determining the appropriate manner of allocating state representation in the House of Representatives than it would give to states when reviewing state laws that create districts for the elections of representatives to Congress. See note 12 in § 14.34, supra.

42. See § 14.36(e), infra.

43. 403 U.S. 182, 91 S.Ct. 1904, 29 L.Ed.2d 399 (1971).

ed deviated 4.8%. The Court found justification on the "long tradition of overlapping functions and dual personnel in Rockland County government and on the fact that the plan before us does not contain a built-in bias tending to favor particular political interests or geographic areas."[44]

In *Mahan v. Howell*[45] the Court formally recognized that while population alone is the primary criterion to judge a congressional districting scheme, "broader latitude has been afforded the States under the Equal Protection Clause in state legislative redistricting . . ."[46] In *Mahan* the most overrepresented district exceeded the ideal by 6.8%, the most underrepresented exceeded the ideal by 9.6%, these variations were found justified by the state policy of respecting political subdivision boundaries.

Subsequently, de minimis variations were found to require no justifications at all: in a case where the most overrepresented district exceeded the ideal by 5.8% and the most underrepresented was under by 4.1%, for a total variation of 9.9%, the Court held that 9.9% total variation does not make out a prima facie case and does not require any special justification.[47] However, deviations of up to 16.5% for state senate districts and 19.3% for state house of representative districts have been held to violate the one person, one vote principle.[48]

While the Court has not created a special test for local governmental units, it seems clear that deviations in the one person, one vote principle will be held to, at most, no higher a standard than that imposed on state governments. The Court has upheld a deviation of 11.9% for a local government unit at a

time before it recognized the reasonableness test for state governments.[49]

The Supreme Court allows greater deviations from mathematical equality between districts for districting plans for state or local legislative bodies, as opposed to congressional districts. This difference is not based solely on the technical distinction that congressional districting is reviewed under article I while local apportionment is reviewed under the Fourteenth Amendment equal protection clause. The substantive policy justification for allowing greater leeway in local legislative maps is that the government has a wider range of legitimate reasons for deviating from population equality when it creates local or state wide legislative maps. State or city legislative entities often have the power to pass laws that have a particular effect on a limited number of counties or other political subdivisions within the jurisdiction; ensuring that persons within each county or political subdivision are grouped together to elect representatives to the legislative body is a legitimate concern. Because of the regional nature of much state or local legislation, keeping state or local legislative districts compact so that persons are grouped in small geographic districts is also a legitimate concern. Many state constitutions require legislative districts be both contiguous and compact. A state may even go so far as to guarantee every county, or relevant political subdivision, at least one representative in the legislature in order to ensure that persons from that political subdivision have some voice in legislation that affects counties in different ways throughout the state.[50]

When the Supreme Court examines population differences in voter districts, the Court

---

44. 403 U.S. at 187, 91 S.Ct. at 1908.

45. 410 U.S. 315, 93 S.Ct. 979, 35 L.Ed.2d 320 (1973), rehearing denied and opinion modified 411 U.S. 922, 93 S.Ct. 1475, 36 L.Ed.2d 316 (1973).

46. 410 U.S. at 322, 93 S.Ct. at 984.

47. White v. Regester, 412 U.S. 755, 763, 93 S.Ct. 2332, 2338, 37 L.Ed.2d 314 (1973) accord, Gaffney v. Cummings, 412 U.S. 735, 93 S.Ct. 2321, 37 L.Ed.2d 298 (1973).

48. Connor v. Finch, 431 U.S. 407, 97 S.Ct. 1828, 52 L.Ed.2d 465 (1977). Contrast Brown v. Thomson, 462 U.S. 835, 103 S.Ct. 2690, 77 L.Ed.2d 214 (1983) (maxi-

mum deviation of 89% allowed under peculiar circumstances: plaintiffs asked for relief which would not really solve the malapportionment; state plan followed a neutral principle).

49. Abate v. Mundt, 403 U.S. 182, 185, 91 S.Ct. 1904, 1907, 29 L.Ed.2d 399 (1971) (Court notes that local government needs "considerable flexibility" to meet "changing societal" needs).

50. See Brown v. Thomson, 462 U.S. 835, 103 S.Ct. 2690, 77 L.Ed.2d 214 (1983).

will compare the size of the most and least populous districts with the theoretically "ideal" district.   For example, if a city has 5 million people and a city council composed of 5 city council persons, each of whom is elected from a separate geographic area of the city, the ideal population of each district would be 1 million persons.   Let us assume that in our hypothetical city the 5 voting districts have populations of: 600,000; 800,000; 1,000,000; 1,200,000; 1,400,000.   It would be common for courts (though not mathematicians) to describe the most and least populous districts as each having a 40% variance from the ideal district and the city as a whole having a total variation of 80%.   As we have seen in this subsection, the Court has found that a state or local legislative map that has a total deviation of 10% or less does not require special justification by the government.   The Court has upheld state and local legislative maps with total deviations of almost 20%, and it allowed one state to provide a guarantee of at least one representative in the legislature for each county.[51]   Applying this mathematical approach to determining voter equality, the Supreme Court Justices unanimously invalidated a mu-

nicipal governmental election system in *Board of Estimate v. Morris*.[52]   In this case, the Supreme Court found New York City's Board of Estimate, which performed a variety of governmental functions, including the calculation of certain utility tax rates and control over land use regulations, was subject to the one person, one vote principle.[53]   The Board was composed of eight officials, all of whom had been elected to some other governmental office.   Five of the Board members were the presidents of the five boroughs of New York City, each of whom was elected in a separate borough election.   Three members of the Board were elected on a city wide basis (the mayor, comptroller, and president of the city council).   The majority found that, even allowing for the presence of the city wide members, that the difference in population between the least populous and most populous boroughs totalled 78%.   The majority noted "that no case of ours has indicated that a deviation of some 78% could ever be justified" and found that the interest in having persons elected to the Board through elections of its subdivisions, the boroughs, was insufficient to support this great a deviation from voter equality.[54]

---

51.   Compare Mahan v. Howell, 410 U.S. 315, 93 S.Ct. 979, 35 L.Ed.2d 320 (1973) (upholding state legislative apportionment plan with a total percentage deviation of 16.4%, with one district being over-represented by 6.8% and another being under-represented by 9.6%) with Connor v. Finch, 431 U.S. 407, 97 S.Ct. 1828, 52 L.Ed.2d 465 (1977) (state legislative map with maximum deviations of 16.5% for the state's Senate districts and 19.3% for the House of Representative districts are invalid in part because the federal court had failed to identify any unique features of the state political or governmental structure that would have justified this great a deviation from voter equality).

   In Brown v. Thomson, 462 U.S. 835, 103 S.Ct. 2690, 77 L.Ed.2d 214 (1983), the Court upheld Wyoming's system for allocating seats in its house of representatives insofar as it guaranteed a representative to all counties, including the least populous county in the state.   Representation for the least populous county, assessed in a normal mathematical way by the Court, could have been said to result in a deviation of 89% from the ideal voter district.   However, the Court upheld the system because there had been no challenge to the overall voting plan for the house of representatives in Wyoming; the legal challenge was only to the guarantee of a Representative for a county.   Concurring Justices expressed doubts that a state wide plan with such a great deviation could ever be upheld; the dissenting Justices noted that the decision was very narrow and unlikely to affect decisions regarding the permissibility of a legislative districting plan with a significant

deviation from voter equality.   462 U.S. at 848, 103 S.Ct. at 2699 (O'Connor, J., joined by Stevens, J.); 462 U.S. at 850, 103 S.Ct. at 2700 (Brennan, J., joined by White, Marshall, and Blackmun, JJ., dissenting).

52.   489 U.S. 688, 109 S.Ct. 1433, 103 L.Ed.2d 717 (1989).

53.   489 U.S. at 703, 109 S.Ct. at 1438–39.   For an examination of the Court's rulings regarding the type of governmental units to which the one person, one vote principle applies see § 14.36(b) of this chapter.

54.   Board of Estimate v. Morris, 489 U.S. 688, 701, 109 S.Ct. 1433, 1442, 103 L.Ed.2d 717 (1989).   The majority opinion rejected, as had the lower federal courts, the city's attempt to describe the mathematical deviation of the districts from true voter equality in terms of a mathematical formula, a method called the "Banzhaf Index", which would have compared each voter's possible influence on the outcome of various types of votes in the election on the basis of the likelihood of the voter making a difference in who was elected and the possible combinations of board members voting on specific issues.   This computation would have reduced the deviation in the voting power of persons in the various districts to 30.8% on non-budget votes and a slightly higher deviation for votes on budgetary issues.   The Court found that the index should not be used but that the presence of the at-large members of the Board should be factored in to a determination of the deviation in district populations,

(3) Who Counts? The Court has not created a rule which sets a fixed requirement of who must be counted to determine the equality of representation.[55] In general the cases have required that the apportionment be made on the basis of total population even though the actual voters may be apportioned differently because of peculiar distribution of persons of certain ages or other characteristics which may properly preclude them from voting.[56] Thus, the Court has not required the states to "include aliens, transients, short-term or temporary residents, or persons denied the vote for conviction of crime, in the apportionment base by which their legislators are distributed . . . ."[57] However the state cannot reduce the voting strength of an area because it contains military personnel.[58] "The difference between exclusion of all military and military-related personnel and exclusion of those not meeting a State's residence requirements is a difference between an arbitrary and constitutionally permissible classification"[59] because the former discriminates on the basis of employment while the latter does not offer voting strength to those who validly do not have the vote.

The Court has also upheld a state plan which used registered voters as the population basis when the state has a large transient

population and the use of the registered voter figure was not substantially different than a result based on state citizen population.[60]

(d) Multimember Districts

The Court early held that the equal protection clause does not require that even one house of a bicameral state legislature consist of single-member election districts.[61] But multimember districts will be invalidated if they are designed to, and in fact do, "to minimize or cancel out the voting strength of racial or political elements of the voting population."[62] Multimember districts are not per se unconstitutional, even if a group with distinctive interests is found numerous enough to command at least one seat and represents a majority in an area sufficiently compact enough to constitute a single-member district. Also, the State may use such multimember districts in one part of the state and single member districts in other parts.[63]

However, in *White v. Regester*,[64] the Court upheld a judgment of a District Court which invalidated two multimember districts, one found to discriminate against blacks, the other against Mexican-Americans. The Court found that plaintiffs had proven that "the political processes leading to nomination and election were not equally open to participation by the

---

which the majority concluded to be 78% on the basis of documents submitted by the parties. Board of Estimate v. Morris, 489 U.S. 688, 703–04, 109 S.Ct. 1433, 1439–42, 103 L.Ed.2d 717 (1989).

55. For an examination of how the Court computes the extent to which a challenged legislative apportionment system deviates from ideal voter equality (a theoretical division where the ratio of persons in a district to elected representatives is exactly equal in all districts) see the previous subsection of this Chapter, § 14.36(c)(2). Even if a legislative districting map does not violate equal protection due to the number of persons or voters in each district, the legislative map will violate equal protection if it is found that the district lines were drawn for an invidious discriminatory purpose, such as diluting the voting power of racial minorities or a political group. See § 14.36(e), infra, regarding political gerrymandering; see §§ 14.3, 14.31(h), 14.36(e) for discussion of Supreme Court cases examining the proof of a racially discriminatory purpose in the creation of election districts.

56. Burns v. Richardson, 384 U.S. 73, 91–92, 86 S.Ct. 1286, 1296–97, 16 L.Ed.2d 376 (1966); see WMCA, Inc. v. Lomenzo, 377 U.S. 633, 84 S.Ct. 1418, 12 L.Ed.2d 568 (1964) (apportionment based on United States citizenship population).

57. Burns v. Richardson, 384 U.S. 73, 92, 86 S.Ct. 1286, 1296–97, 16 L.Ed.2d 376 (1966).

58. Davis v. Mann, 377 U.S. 678, 691, 84 S.Ct. 1441, 1448, 12 L.Ed.2d 609 (1964), on remand to 238 F.Supp. 458 (E.D.Va.1964), affirmed 379 U.S. 694, 85 S.Ct. 713, 13 L.Ed.2d 698 (1965).

59. Burns v. Richardson, 384 U.S. 73, 92 n. 21, 86 S.Ct. 1286, 1297 n. 21, 16 L.Ed.2d 376 (1966); see Hadley v. Junior College District, 397 U.S. 50, 57 n. 9, 90 S.Ct. 791, 796 n. 9, 25 L.Ed.2d 45 (1970), on remand to 460 S.W.2d 1 (Mo.1970).

60. Burns v. Richardson, 384 U.S. 73, 91–97, 86 S.Ct. 1286, 1296–99, 16 L.Ed.2d 376 (1966).

61. Fortson v. Dorsey, 379 U.S. 433, 85 S.Ct. 498, 13 L.Ed.2d 401 (1965); Burns v. Richardson, 384 U.S. 73, 86 S.Ct. 1286, 16 L.Ed.2d 376 (1966).

62. , 379 U.S. at 439, 85 S.Ct. at 501; 384 U.S. at 88, 86 S.Ct. at 1294. See §§ 14.4, 14.10(c), supra.

63. Whitcomb v. Chavis, 403 U.S. 124, 127–28, 156, 91 S.Ct. 1858, 1861, 1876, 29 L.Ed.2d 363 (1971).

64. 412 U.S. 755, 93 S.Ct. 2332, 37 L.Ed.2d 314 (1973).

group in question—that its members had less opportunity than did other residents in the district to participate in the political processes and to elect legislators of their choice."[65]

In order to establish that an electoral districting system (whether or not it includes a multimember district) creates an unconstitutional racial classification, it must be demonstrated that the legislative or administrative entity creating the district did so for the purpose of diluting the voting power of a racial or ethnic minority. Statistical proof showing lack of representation of members of a particular electoral district's minority population will be admissible evidence of whether the districting authority acted with a racially discriminatory motive. Such statistical proof, however, would rarely be enough in itself to establish racially discriminatory purpose.[66]

When a federal court is forced to fashion a reapportionment plan, "single-member districts are preferable to large multi-member districts as a general matter."[67]

(e) Political Gerrymandering

The one person, one vote principle is not the only criteria for challenging or evaluating the district lines drawn for municipal, state, or federal elections. Even though a legislative districting map complies with the one person, one vote principle, it will be invalid if drawn upon the basis of constitutionally improper criteria.

If the district lines were drawn for the purpose of diluting the voting strength of minority racial or ethnic groups, the law would violate the equal protection clause.[68] A district map which meets the one person, one vote principle and has the effect of diluting the voting strength of identifiable racial minorities will be upheld when the district lines were drawn on the basis of some neutral criteria rather than for the purpose of maintaining or creating a racially discriminatory voting system.[69]

Whether a districting authority may take cognizance of the racial make-up of the population in drawing district lines if it does so for the purpose of ensuring that the voting power of identifiable racial minorities is not diluted is not clear.[70]

The equal protection principle that prohibits purposeful dilution of the voting strength of racial minorities should also prohibit legislative districting or apportionment maps that are created for the purpose of diluting the voting power of a religious group. Indeed, this principle should prohibit the legislature, or other districting authority, from singling out any group of persons, whether or not they constitute a "suspect classification," for disenfranchisement through the creation of electoral districts that would dilute their voting strength and eliminate their representation in a legislative body.

In 1986, the Supreme Court for the first time held that a claim that a legislative dis-

---

65. 412 U.S. at 766, 93 S.Ct. at 2339.

66. For an examination of the need to prove discriminatory purpose to establish a racial classification when none appears on the face of a statute or administrative ruling, see § 14.4. Compare Mobile v. Bolden, 446 U.S. 55, 100 S.Ct. 1490, 64 L.Ed.2d 47 (1980), with Rogers v. Lodge, 458 U.S. 613, 102 S.Ct. 3272, 73 L.Ed.2d 1012 (1982), rehearing denied 459 U.S. 899, 103 S.Ct. 198, 74 L.Ed.2d 160 (1982). For citations to additional Supreme Court cases on this point, see R. Rotunda & J. Nowak, Treatise on Constitutional Law: Substance and Procedure, vol. 3 § 18.4 (3rd ed. 1999, with annual supplements).

67. Connor v. Johnson, 402 U.S. 690, 692, 91 S.Ct. 1760, 1762, 29 L.Ed.2d 268 (1971), rehearing denied 403 U.S. 924, 91 S.Ct. 2220, 29 L.Ed.2d 702 (1971), on remand to 330 F.Supp. 521 (S.D.Miss.1971), district court judgment vacated 404 U.S. 549, 92 S.Ct. 656, 30 L.Ed.2d 704 (1972). For citations to additional Supreme Court cases on this point, see R. Rotunda & J. Nowak, Treatise on

Constitutional Law: Substance and Procedure, vol. 3, §§ 18.35, 18.36 (3rd ed. 1999, with annual supplements).

68. See Gomillion v. Lightfoot, 364 U.S. 339, 81 S.Ct. 125, 5 L.Ed.2d 110 (1960). See § 14.31(h), supra.

69. See §§ 14.4, 14.10(c), 14.31(h), supra. See Mobile v. Bolden, 446 U.S. 55, 100 S.Ct. 1490, 64 L.Ed.2d 47 (1980); Rogers v. Lodge, 458 U.S. 613, 102 S.Ct. 3272, 73 L.Ed.2d 1012 (1982).

70. Any use of racial classifications that is designed to deny a person the right to vote because of the person's race will violate the Fifteenth Amendment and the Fourteenth Amendment equal protection clause. Any law that constitutes a purposeful discrimination against minority race candidates or dilution of minority race voting power will be found to be a violation of equal protection and, perhaps, the Fifteenth Amendment. The issue of racial affirmative action in election laws is considered in § 14.10(c) of this Treatise.

tricting map was politically gerrymandered so as to seriously dilute or eliminate the voting power of persons affiliated with a particular party, was an equal protection issue that the courts could resolve. In *Davis v. Bandemer* [71] the Court ruled that claims of unconstitutional political gerrymandering were not political questions. [72] Although six Justices ruled that this equal protection claim could be adjudicated by the courts under the Fourteenth Amendment, there was no majority opinion regarding the standards to be used in determining whether a particular state districting plan was an unconstitutional political gerrymander. Indeed, only two Justices believed that the particular state districting plan at issue in *Davis* so diluted the voting power of an identifiable political group as to violate the equal protection clause. Because of the voting patterns of the Justices in *Davis,* it is easiest to understand the decision by an examination of the constitutional principles endorsed by different groups of Justices.

Davis involved the review of a map of state house of representatives and state senate electoral districts in Indiana. After the 1982 state elections, a three judge district court had invalidated the 1981 reapportionment plan adopted by the Indiana legislature on the basis that it unconstitutionally diluted the votes of persons who believed in or were affiliated with the Democratic political party in Indiana. In the 1982 election, Democratic candidates for the state house of representatives received 51.9% of the vote statewide but were elected to only 43 of the 100 house seats filled in that election. Of the 25 Democratic candidates for the state senate, however, 13 of the candidates were elected; the Democratic senatorial candidates received 53.1% of the statewide vote. In multimember districts examined in this case,

Democrats received 46.6% of the votes but only 3 of 21 Democratic candidates were elected in these multimember districts. Although the Supreme Court would find that the case presented a justiciable controversy, the Supreme Court overruled the district court's decision, which had invalidated the 1981 apportionment plan.

Justice White announced the judgment of the Court and delivered an opinion that was a majority opinion only on the issue of whether political gerrymandering claims presented a justiciable controversy. All of Justice White's opinion was joined by Justices Brennan, Marshall, and Blackmun. [73] However, Justices Powell and Stevens concurred only in the part of Justice White's opinion regarding the political question issue. [74] Justices O'Connor and Rehnquist and Chief Justice Burger dissented from the political question ruling; those three Justices would have upheld all legislative district plans against claims of unconstitutional political gerrymandering because they believed that such claims could not be properly resolved by the judiciary. [75]

The Indiana legislative districting plan, including its creation of multimember districts, survived judicial review because Justice White, and the three Justices who concurred in his opinion, believed that the evidence in the case did not establish a basis for finding an unconstitutional political gerrymander. They voted with the three Justices who would have rejected all political gerrymandering claims. Justice Powell, in an opinion joined by Justice Stevens, asserted that the facts in this case presented a basis for invalidating the state legislative districting plan.

Justice White and Justice Powell appeared to agree on the basic principle in the case but

71. 478 U.S. 109, 106 S.Ct. 2797, 92 L.Ed.2d 85 (1986).

72. The political question issue in this case, and political question issues generally, are examined in § 2.16.

73. 478 U.S. at 113, 106 S.Ct. at 2800 (opinion of Justice White announcing the judgment of the Court and delivering an opinion joined by Justices Brennan, Marshall, and Blackmun).

74. 478 U.S. at 161, 106 S.Ct. at 2825 (Justice Powell, with whom Justice Stevens joins, concurring in part II [of Justice White's opinion], and dissenting).

75. The Justices who did dissent as to the political question ruling concurred in the judgment because they agreed with Justice White, and the three who voted with him, that the Indiana legislative districting plan should not have been overturned by the district court. Davis v. Bandemer, 478 U.S. 109, 143, 106 S.Ct. 2797, 2816, 92 L.Ed.2d 85 (1986) (Burger, C.J., concurring in the judgment); 478 U.S. at 144, 106 S.Ct. at 2816 (O'Connor, J., joined by Burger, C.J., and Rehnquist, J., concurring in the judgment).

they could not agree on how that principle was to be implemented. Justice White's plurality opinion stated that the ultimate issue in political gerrymandering cases was whether the electoral districts had been established in a way that would "consistently degrade a voter's or group of voters' influence on the political process as a whole." Justice White found that, in order to demonstrate unconstitutional vote dilution on the basis of political affiliation, a party challenging a districting system must prove "both intentional discrimination against an identifiable political group and an actual discriminatory effect on that group." [76] At the start of his opinion, Justice Powell stated that, "the plurality expresses the view, with which I agree, that a partisan political gerrymander violates the equal protection clause only on proof of 'both intentional discrimination against an identifiable group and an actual discriminatory effect on that group.'" [77] Because six Justices appear to agree on this basic principle, one might then ask why there was no majority opinion. The answer lies in the fact that they differed over the facts to be considered when determining whether unconstitutional political vote dilution had been demonstrated.

Justice White's plurality opinion found that there should be no judicial inquiry into the legislative purpose in drawing district lines unless there had first been a finding that "a particular group has been unconstitutionally denied its chance to effectively influence the political process." In examining a boundary for an individual district, Justice White stated that the inquiry would focus on "the opportunities of members of the group [the political party whose votes were allegedly being diluted] to participate in party deliberations in the slating and nomination of candidates, their opportunity to register and vote, and hence their chance to directly influence the election returns and to secure the attention of winning candidates." In a judicial examination of alleged statewide gerrymandering, the inquiry would focus on "the voter's direct or indirect influence on the elections of the state legislature as a whole."

In order to meet what Justice White called a "threshold" requirement in proving unconstitutional vote discrimination, there must be "evidence of continued frustration of the will of the majority of voters or effective denial to a minority of voters of a fair chance to influence the political process." White's plurality opinion then went on to find that continued frustration of the majority's will, or suppression of a minority, could not be established on the basis of the returns from a single election, such as the 1982 Indiana election. The fact that the party receiving a majority of votes did not receive a majority of the seats in an election did not establish the existence of unconstitutional gerrymandering, since members of identifiable subclasses in society did not have a constitutional right to proportional representation in the legislature. The state legislature could divide the districts in a manner that did guarantee some safe seats for members of each political party without violating the Constitution. [78] The fact that some districts were safe seats for a particular party did not establish unconstitutional vote dilution. In the portion of the plurality opinion that most clearly differed from Justice Powell's separate opinion, Justice White found that the intentional drawing of electoral districts for partisan ends would not violate the Constitution unless, in fact, the districting plan had succeeded in degrading the votes of members of an identifiable political party or frustrating the will of the majority on a continual basis. [79]

Justice Powell, joined by Justice Stevens, agreed with the principle that political gerrymandering violates equal protection only when

---

76. Davis v. Bandemer, 478 U.S. 109, 127, 106 S.Ct. 2797, 2808, 92 L.Ed.2d 85 (1986) (plurality opinion by White, J.).

77. 478 U.S. at 161, 106 S.Ct. at 2825 (opinion of Powell, J., joined by Stevens, J.).

78. In Gaffney v. Cummings, 412 U.S. 735, 93 S.Ct. 2321, 37 L.Ed.2d 298 (1973), the Supreme Court upheld a

legislative redistricting plan that complied with the one person, one vote principle although it appeared that some district lines were drawn to achieve "political fairness" and a balance between the major political parties.

79. 478 U.S. at 138–39, 106 S.Ct. at 2813–14 (opinion of White, J.).

there was proof of both an improper legislative intention to dilute the votes of a specific class of voters and an actual discriminatory effect on that group. However, Powell would allow an initial judicial inquiry into legislative intent. He would not allow a legislative plan to withstand judicial review merely because the number of members of a political party elected to a legislature was not consistently out of proportion to the number of voters in the state who were affiliated with that political party.[80] Justice Powell believed that a judicial inquiry into unconstitutional gerrymandering "properly focuses on whether the boundaries of the voting districts have been distorted deliberately and arbitrarily to achieve illegitimate ends." In making this determination, he would allow the judiciary to consider not only the numerical evidence regarding elections under a particular plan but also the shapes of voting districts, whether the voting districts seem to adhere to established political subdivision boundaries, the nature of the legislative procedures by which the apportionment plan was adopted, and any legislative history that reflected the actual goals of the legislative redistricting. Justice Powell concluded that, "to make out a case of unconstitutional partisan gerrymandering, the plaintiff should be required to offer proof concerning these factors, which bear directly on the fairness of redistricting plan, as well as evidence concerning population disparities and statistics tending to show vote dilution. No one factor should be dispositive."[81]

Because there was no majority opinion in *Davis* on any issue other than the political question issue, the case leaves lower courts with some problems. When plaintiffs allege that an electoral districting plan (either in the setting of electoral districts statewide or the creation of a specific single member or multi-member district) the courts will have to examine that claim because it has now been ruled to be justiciable. Unless, however, the plaintiff can make some clear statistical showing that there has been the continued frustration of the will of the majority of voters or the effective denial to a minority of voters of a fair chance to influence the political process, there may be no need for an inquiry into the actual intention of the legislature that adopted the districting plan. If one follows the White plurality, the failure to offer that type of proof would mean that there was a failure to demonstrate the type of effect that would allow a court to invalidate the districting plan as a violation of the equal protection clause. There would be no judicial inquiry into legislature's intent so long as that threshold requirement was not met.

Perhaps the only thing clear about *Davis v. Bandemer* is that a majority of the Justices did not rule that all forms of political gerrymandering were unconstitutional. Consideration of political factors in drawing boundaries for legislative districts to create so-called "safe seats" for a political party is not a *per se* unconstitutional act. In contrast, a legislative district that was created primarily for the purpose of establishing a district containing a majority of persons of one race would constitute a race-based classification, which would be invalid unless it were narrowly tailored to a compelling interest.[82]

The Supreme Court has considered cases in which a legislative district was alleged to be an

---

80. Justice Powell attacked the plurality opinion on the basis that it allowed mathematical evidence (which he likened to a one-person, one-vote approach) to satisfy the state's duty to show that there was some neutral, legitimate rationale for drawing the district lines. He believed that this mathematical approach avoided the proper inquiry into whether the districting plan in fact served no purpose other than to favor one segment of the community at the expense of the voting power of others. Davis v. Bandemer, 478 U.S. 109, 169–73, 106 S.Ct. 2797, 2829–31, 92 L.Ed.2d 85 (1986) (opinion of Powell, J.).

81. 478 U.S. at 173, 106 S.Ct. at 2832 (opinion of Powell, J.) (footnote omitted). Justice Powell relied on the description of unconstitutional districting given by former Justice Fortas. There is an unconstitutional drawing of district lines when the districting plan constitutes "the deliberate and arbitrary distortion of district boundaries and populations for partisan or personal political purposes." Davis v. Bandemer, 478 U.S. 109, 164, 106 S.Ct. 2797, 2827, 92 L.Ed.2d 85 (1986) (opinion of Powell, J.) quoting in part Kirkpatrick v. Preisler, 394 U.S. 526, 538, 89 S.Ct. 1225, 1232, 22 L.Ed.2d 519 (1969), rehearing denied 395 U.S. 917, 89 S.Ct. 1737, 23 L.Ed.2d 231 (1969) (Fortas, J., concurring).

82. See §§ 14.4, 14.10(b)(4) of this Treatise for an examination of those cases.

invalid race-based district, and in which the state government has asserted that district boundaries were created for political, rather than racial considerations. In one case, *Hunt v. Cromartie* [*Hunt II*],[83] the Supreme Court found that a district court should have upheld a legislative district because the persons challenging the district had failed to prove that race, rather than political factors was the predominating motive in the creation of the boundaries for the challenged legislative district. Both the majority and dissenting opinions, in *Hunt II* were based on the assumption that some forms of political gerrymandering would be constitutional.

The Court's decisions in cases involving allegations that a legislative district was created for racial rather than political reasons have not explained the extent to which a legislature may use political party affiliation (political gerrymandering) as the basis for drawing legislative district boundaries.[84]

(f) Departures From Strict Majority Rule

In *Gordon v. Lance*[85] the Court upheld a West Virginia law requiring a 60% vote requirement before political subdivisions of the State incurred bonded indebtedness or increased tax notes above a certain amount. The 60% vote requirement constituted no geographic discrimination unlike the typical reapportionment case. The Court also appeared

not to disapprove a requirement that more than a majority vote be assembled for some issues in a state legislature or that a given issue be approved by a majority of all registered voters.[86] "[T]here is nothing in the language of the Constitution, our history, or our cases that requires that a majority always prevail on every issue."[87]

Explicitly not considered in *Gordon* was whether a provision requiring unanimity or giving a veto to a "very small group" would be constitutional, or whether it was proper to require "extraordinary majorities" to elect public officers.[88]

§ 14.37 The Right to Travel Abroad

The right to travel abroad pits the constitutional right of travel against the broad power of the government in the international area. Just as the equal protection rights of illegitimates are significantly lessened in the context of the government's foreign affairs power over immigration,[1] so also when the right to travel is exercised in the context of international travel, governmental power frequently overcomes this right.

The Court's rulings upholding government restrictions on the ability to engage in international travel, except in those cases when the government action is totally arbitrary or endangers a specific constitutional right, indicate that there is no fundamental right to engage in international travel.[2]

---

83. Hunt v. Cromartie [*Hunt II*], 532 U.S. 234, 121 S.Ct. 1452, 149 L.Ed.2d 430 (2001). The *Hunt II* decision is examined in § 14.4 of this Treatise.

84. See §§ 14.4, 14.10(b)(4).

85. 403 U.S. 1, 91 S.Ct. 1889, 29 L.Ed.2d 273 (1971).

86. 403 U.S. at 7, 91 S.Ct. at 1892–93.

87. 403 U.S. at 6, 91 S.Ct. at 1892.

88. 403 U.S. at 8 n. 6, 91 S.Ct. at 1893 n. 6. Cf. Town of Lockport v. Citizens for Community Action, 430 U.S. 259, 97 S.Ct. 1047, 51 L.Ed.2d 313 (1977) (concurrent majority requirements upheld for local government units under special circumstances). For citations to additional cases, including lower court cases, and secondary works on this topic see our multi-volume Treatise: R. Rotunda & J. Nowak, Treatise on Constitutional Law: Substance and Procedure (3rd ed. 1999, with annual supplements).

§ 14.37

1. Compare Fiallo v. Bell, 430 U.S. 787, 97 S.Ct. 1473, 52 L.Ed.2d 50 (1977), with Trimble v. Gordon, 430 U.S.

762, 97 S.Ct. 1459, 52 L.Ed.2d 31 (1977). See also Miller v. Albright, 523 U.S. 420, 118 S.Ct. 1428, 140 L.Ed.2d 575 (1998) (without a majority opinion, the Court refuses to invalidate gender based and legitimacy based classifications in a naturalization law). The cases involving immigration restrictions that disadvantage illegitimate children are examined in § 14.18.

2. A person who is a citizen of the United States, and who has left the country, would have a right to reenter the country. However if the person's international travel, or other activities, violated federal law, the federal government would be free to punish the individual for those actions, even though he could not take away his citizenship or banish him from the territory of the United States on the basis of his illegal acts. See the multi-volume edition of this Treatise regarding citizenship and immigration issues: R. Rotunda & J. Nowak, Treatise on Constitutional Law: Substance and Procedure, Chapter 22 (3rd ed. 1999, with annual supplements).

The Supreme Court decisions concerning the right of interstate travel frequently do not make any reference to a

In *Kent v. Dulles*[3] the Court ruled that the Secretary of State had improperly denied passports to two persons on the basis of their alleged association with the Communist Party. The ruling in *Kent* was based on an interpretation of federal statutes.[4] Justice Douglas's majority opinion in *Kent* included *dicta* concerning a right to travel, even though the majority opinion based the Court's ruling on statutory grounds.

Justice Douglas first discussed the history of passports in this country. Except for certain intervals in our history, particularly in wartime, for "most of our history a passport was not a condition to entry or exit."[5] It was a document addressed to foreign powers, requesting that the bearer be allowed to pass safely and freely as an American citizen;[6] and it established citizenship to enable the bearer to reenter the United States.[7]

Justice Douglas noted that it had often been said that the issuance of passports is a discretionary act, but the Justice was unwilling to accept this earlier dictum. The majority opinion stated: "The right to travel is part of the 'liberty' of which the citizen cannot be deprived without due process of law under the Fifth Amendment."[8] Moreover, while the dictum of discretion as to the issuance of passports is broad, in fact the power over issuance has been exercised quite narrowly. Thus, the Court hesitated to impute to Congress, "when in 1952 it made a passport necessary for foreign travel and left its issuance to the discretion of the Secretary of State, a purpose to give him unbridled discretion to grant or withhold a passport from a citizen for any substantive reason he may choose."[9] The Court did not decide that the reasons relied on by the Secretary of State could not be enacted by Congress nor did it decide that such broad delegation

could not occur; it simply said that such broad delegation had not occurred. But within this context the dictum supporting the right to travel abroad seemed quite broad.

In *Aptheker v. Secretary of State*[10] the Court appeared to follow the broad language of *Kent*, but again its decision rested on narrower grounds. In this case several ranking officials of the Communist Party of the United States had their passports revoked. This time there was no question of whether Congress had delegated such power to the Secretary of State; it had. Section 6 of the Subversive Activities Control Act of 1950 provided that it was unlawful for any member of a Communist organization which was registered or under a final order to register, to use, apply for, renew a passport if the applicant had knowledge or notice that the organization is registered or that an order to register was final.

Justice Goldberg's opinion for the Court quoted with approval the language in *Kent* as to the right to travel abroad.[11] But Goldberg's opinion actually decided the case on another ground. Given the importance of the right to travel, the degree of the legislative abridgement must be restricted to the least drastic means of achieving the same purpose.[12] In this case, Section 6 was overbroad on its face. The section applied whether or not the member actually knew or believed he was associated with what was deemed to be a communist-action or communist-front organization. The section also included both knowing and unknowing members. For these and similar reasons the section was held unconstitutional on its face. But the Court did not hold that Congress could not enact a more narrowly drawn statute.

---

possible right to engage in international travel. For example, in Saenz v. Roe, 526 U.S. 489, 119 S.Ct. 1518, 143 L.Ed.2d 689 (1999) the Supreme Court discussed several aspects of the "right to travel" but did not make any reference to international travel. The *Saenz* decision is examined in § 14.38.

3. 357 U.S. 116, 78 S.Ct. 1113, 2 L.Ed.2d 1204 (1958).

4. 357 U.S. at 123, 78 S.Ct. at 1117.

5. Kent v. Dulles, 357 U.S. 116, 123, 78 S.Ct. 1113, 1117, 2 L.Ed.2d 1204 (1958).

6. Urtetiqui v. D'Arcy, 34 U.S. (9 Pet.) 692, 699, 9 L.Ed. 276 (1835).

7. Browder v. United States, 312 U.S. 335, 339, 61 S.Ct. 599, 602, 85 L.Ed. 862 (1941).

8. 357 U.S. at 125, 78 S.Ct. at 1118.

9. 357 U.S. at 128, 78 S.Ct. at 1119.

10. 378 U.S. 500, 84 S.Ct. 1659, 12 L.Ed.2d 992 (1964).

11. 378 U.S. at 505–06, 84 S.Ct. at 1663.

12. 378 U.S. at 508, 84 S.Ct. at 1664–65.

In *Zemel v. Rusk*[13] the Court was faced with an explicit, narrow Congressional prohibition of travel to Cuba. This prohibition was upheld, with Chief Justice Warren writing the opinion of the Court. The opinion found, first, that Congress had authorized the Secretary of State to refuse to validate American passports for travel to Cuba—where the United States had broken diplomatic and consular relations—and second, that the exercise of that authority is constitutional. The Court admitted that the legislative history of the basic passport act does not affirmatively indicate an intention to authorize area restrictions on travel abroad, but "its language is surely broad enough to authorize area restrictions...."[14]

This reading of Congressional delegation illustrates an approach not displayed in *Kent v. Dulles*.[15] *Kent* was distinguished first, because the history of administrative practice in *Kent* was different than that shown in *Zemel*, and second, because the issue involved in *Kent* was whether a citizen could be denied a passport because of his political beliefs or associations, while in *Zemel* the Secretary of State refused to validate the passport "not because of any characteristic peculiar to appellant, but rather because of foreign policy considerations affecting all citizens."[16]

The constitutionality of the Secretary's decision was then upheld basically by relying on the foreign policy context of the case. "That the restriction which is challenged in this case is supported by the weightiest considerations of national security is perhaps best pointed up by recalling that the Cuban missile crisis of October 1962 preceded filing of appellant's complaint by less than two months."[17] The majority again cited with approval the *Kent* dictum that the right of travel is a part of the liberty of which a citizen cannot be deprived without due process, but it pointedly noted that the fact "a liberty cannot be inhibited without due process of law does not mean it can under no circumstances be inhibited."[18] In this case, the inhibition was proper.[19]

Following these three cases the Court was asked to rule on the constitutionality of congressional restrictions on the payment of certain Social Security benefits; these restrictions limited payments to those who, in certain circumstances, exercised their right to engage in international travel. In *Califano v. Aznavorian*[20] a unanimous Supreme Court upheld a provision of the Social Security Act which provided that benefits would not be paid to a recipient residing outside of the United States for 30 days until that person once again had been a resident of this country for 30 days.

The Court first found that the constitutionality of welfare legislation should be upheld if a *rational basis* existed for the classification; scrutiny of the law would be intensified only if the classification related to a fundamental right or employed a suspect classification. The right to travel *abroad*, however, is not judged by the same standards applied to laws which directly burden the right of *interstate* travel by use of durational residence requirements.[21] Moreover, this law had a lesser impact on international travel than those examined in *Kent, Aptheker*, or *Zemel* because here the statutory provision did not limit the availability of passports nor burden the exercise of

13.   381 U.S. 1, 85 S.Ct. 1271, 14 L.Ed.2d 179 (1965).

14.   381 U.S. at 8, 85 S.Ct. at 1276.

15.   357 U.S. 116, 78 S.Ct. 1113, 2 L.Ed.2d 1204 (1958).

16.   381 U.S. at 13, 85 S.Ct. at 1279.

17.   381 U.S. at 16, 85 S.Ct. at 1280.

18.   381 U.S. at 14, 85 S.Ct. at 1279 (footnote omitted).
As to the test to govern federal burdens on travel between the states of the United States and the District of Columbia on the one hand, and Puerto Rico on the other, see Harris v. Rosario, 446 U.S. 651, 100 S.Ct. 1929, 64 L.Ed.2d 587 (1980), rehearing denied 448 U.S. 912, 101 S.Ct. 27, 65 L.Ed.2d 1173 (1980), holding that Congress may treat Puerto Rico differently so long as there is a rational basis for its actions. In that case Congress could provide less federal welfare benefits to Puerto Rican residents, who do not pay U.S. income taxes. See also, Califano v. Gautier Torres, 435 U.S. 1, 98 S.Ct. 906, 55 L.Ed.2d 65 (1978) (per curiam) (unique status of Puerto Rico justified federal limitations on payment of supplemental social security).

19.   Justices Black, Douglas, and Goldberg all dissented. 381 U.S. at 20, 85 S.Ct. at 1282 (Black, J.); 381 U.S. at 23, 85 S.Ct. at 1284 (Douglas J., joined by Goldberg, J.); 381 U.S. at 27, 85 S.Ct. at 1286 (Goldberg, J.).

20.   439 U.S. 170, 99 S.Ct. 471, 58 L.Ed.2d 435 (1978).

21.   Cf. § 14.38, infra.

First Amendment rights. "It merely withdraws a governmental benefit during and shortly after an extended absence from the country. Unless the limitation imposed by Congress is wholly irrational, it is constitutional in spite of its incidental effect on international travel."[22]

In *Haig v. Agee*,[23] the Court, relying on *Zemel v. Rusk*,[24] upheld the powers of the Secretary of State to revoke the passport of one Philip Agee, an American residing abroad, on the grounds that his activities caused or were likely to cause serious damage to American national security or foreign policy. In *Agee*, however, unlike *Zemel* the Court did not rely on prior administrative *practice* but rather on administrative *policy*.

Agee was a former employee of the Central Intelligence Agency who had been trained in clandestine operations. In 1974 he publicly announced his intention to expose CIA officers and agents. To carry out his program he would travel to a given country and consult with people within the local diplomatic service he knew based on his prior CIA experience. "He recruit[ed] collaborators and train[ed] them in clandestine techniques designed to expose the 'cover' of CIA employees and sources."[25]

In 1979 the Secretary of State revoked Agee's passport, pursuant to departmental regulations and based on a determination that his activities "are causing or are likely to cause serious damage to the national security

of the United States."[26] Agee sued claiming that Congress had not authorized the regulation and that it was unconstitutional. He moved for summary judgment and for "purposes of that motion, Agee conceded the Government's factual averments and its claim that his activities were causing or were likely to cause serious damage to the national security or foreign policy of the United States."[27]

The Court first concluded that although the Passport Act of 1926 "does not in so many words confer upon the Secretary a power to revoke a passport,"[28] the fact that there was no evidence that Congress intended to repudiate the prior administrative construction led the Court to find that Congress, in 1926, adopted the previous assertions of executive power. An "unbroken line of Executive Orders, regulations, instructions to consular officials, and notices to passport holders"[29] evidenced the prior interpretation.

Agee responded that in order for the Executive to establish implicit congressional approval it must show "longstanding and consistent *enforcement* of the claimed power: that is, by showing that many passports were revoked on national security and foreign policy grounds."[30] The Court rejected that argument. "[I]f there were no occasions—or few— to call the Secretary's authority into play, the absence of frequent instances of enforcement is wholly irrelevant."[31] It is enough that the Executive's announcement of policy was " 'sufficiently substantial and consistent' to compel

---

22. 439 U.S. at 177, 99 S.Ct. at 475. Justices Marshall and Brennan concurred in the result but objected to the "wholly irrational" test if that standard implied a lesser standard of review than the traditional rational basis test. 439 U.S. at 178, 99 S.Ct. at 476. Congress may pass separate legislation for territories and may treat a territory, such as Puerto Rico, differently than the states in terms of federal assistance. This disparate treatment will be upheld "so long as there is a rational basis for its [the Congress'] actions." Harris v. Rosario, 446 U.S. 651, 100 S.Ct. 1929, 64 L.Ed.2d 587 (1980), (per curiam) (upholding lower level of federal reimbursement to Aid to Families with Dependent Children program in Puerto Rico).

23. 453 U.S. 280, 101 S.Ct. 2766, 69 L.Ed.2d 640 (1981).

24. 381 U.S. 1, 85 S.Ct. 1271, 14 L.Ed.2d 179 (1965).

25. Haig v. Agee, 453 U.S. at 284, 101 S.Ct. at 2770. See also, 453 U.S. at 283 & n. 2, 101 S.Ct. at 2770 & n. 2.

See P. Agee & L. Wolf, eds., Dirty Work: The CIA in Western Europe (1978).

26. 453 U.S. at 286, 101 S.Ct. at 2771.

27. 453 U.S. at 287, 101 S.Ct. at 2772 (footnotes omitted).

28. 453 U.S. at 290, 101 S.Ct. at 2773.

29. 453 U.S. at 298, 101 S.Ct. at 2777.

30. 453 U.S. at 301–02, 101 S.Ct. at 2779 (emphasis in original). Agee relied on Kent v. Dulles, 357 U.S. 116, 127–28, 78 S.Ct. 1113, 1118–19, 2 L.Ed.2d 1204 (1958).

31. 453 U.S. at 302, 101 S.Ct. at 2779. The Court contended that *Kent* was "not contrary" to its ruling in *Agee*. 423 U.S. at 303, 101 S.Ct. at 2780. However, the Court of Appeals had ruled that *Kent* required a ruling in Agee's favor. 629 F.2d 80, 87 (D.C.Cir.1980), reversed 453 U.S. 280, 101 S.Ct. 2766, 69 L.Ed.2d 640 (1981).

the conclusion that Congress has approved it."[32]

Justice Blackmun, in his concurrence, correctly recognized that the majority opinion, although purporting to rely upon *Zemel v. Rusk*[33] and *Kent v. Dulles*,[34] was actually cutting back on their reasoning because those cases required not merely the announcement of administrative *policy* but also substantial and consistent administrative *practice* in order to establish that Congress had implicitly approved the administrative interpretation.[35] Justice Brennan, joined by Justice Marshall, agreed with that analysis, but supported the original reasoning of *Zemel* and *Kent* and therefore dissented in a forceful opinion.[36]

The majority also rejected the other grounds which Agee raised. Relying on *Califano v. Aznavorian*[37] the Court majority found no violation of the freedom to travel abroad because the restriction on travel served a reasonable, indeed compelling, governmental interest: protecting the security of the nation.[38]

The Court then quickly turned to and rejected without any substantial discussion Agee's other constitutional arguments that the passport violated his free speech and constituted a taking of his liberty interests without procedural due process.[39] Agee responded by securing a new passport from Grenada; he announced that he would continue his activities against the CIA.[40]

The Supreme Court's decisions since *Zemel* may be categorized as showing a high degree of deference to the executive branch both in

terms of finding statutory authority for executive branch actions regarding foreign affairs and in imposing only minimal constitutional restraints on executive actions taken with Congressional authority.[41] This reluctance to interfere with executive decisions regarding foreign policy, absent an express Congressional restriction on executive power, provided the basis for the Court's decision in *Regan v. Wald*.[42]

At issue in *Regan v. Wald* was a Treasury Department regulation that effectively eliminated travel from America to Cuba except for certain types of travel, such as official visits, news gatherings, professional research, and visits to relatives located in Cuba.[43] The lower federal courts found that the Executive Department was not authorized to restrict travel in a way that did not exist at the time of the passage of a Congressional statute limiting executive authority to restrict economic trade with foreign nations without Congressional authorization. However, the Supreme Court ruled that Congress had established a grandfather clause which allowed the President to continue regulations which had existed in 1977. The Court found that, given the existence of some Treasury Department regulations regarding travel to Cuba, the Court should interpret a grandfather clause to exclude from new Congressional control, areas where the President had been exercising authority in 1977, regardless of whether such areas were modified by later Executive Department regulations.[44] Having found that the

---

32.   453 U.S. at 306, 101 S.Ct. at 2781.

33.   381 U.S. 1, 85 S.Ct. 1271, 14 L.Ed.2d 179 (1965).

34.   357 U.S. 116, 78 S.Ct. 1113, 2 L.Ed.2d 1204 (1958).

35.   453 U.S. at 310, 101 S.Ct. at 2783 (Blackmun, J., concurring).

36.   453 U.S. at 310–21, 101 S.Ct. at 2784–88 (Brennan, J., joined by Marshall, J., dissenting).

37.   439 U.S. 170, 99 S.Ct. 471, 58 L.Ed.2d 435 (1978).

38.   453 U.S. at 308, 101 S.Ct. at 2782–83.

39.   453 U.S. at 308–09, 101 S.Ct. at 2782–83.

40.   Newsweek, Aug. 10, 1981, at 15 ("Philip Agee's Grenadian Passport").

41.   See generally, Farber, National Security, The Right to Travel, And The Court, 1981 Sup.Ct.Rev. 263; Nowak and Rotunda, A Comment on The Creation and Resolution of a "NonProblem": Dames and Moore v.

Regan, The Foreign Affairs Power, and The Role of The Court, 29 U.C.L.A.L.Rev. 1129 (1982) for a discussion on judicial deference to both the Executive and Legislative Branches in the foreign affairs area.

42.   468 U.S. 222, 104 S.Ct. 3026, 82 L.Ed.2d 171 (1984), rehearing denied 469 U.S. 912, 105 S.Ct. 285, 83 L.Ed.2d 222 (1984).

43.   The regulations also allowed travel sponsored by Cuba because no economic benefits would be provided to Cuba by such travel.

44.   468 U.S. at 238, 104 S.Ct. at 3035, 82 L.Ed.2d at 183: "In our opinion, a full examination of the legislative history—the subcommittee hearings, markup sessions, floor debates, and House and Senate reports—does not support the view that only those restrictions actually in place on July 1, 1977 were to be grandfathered." (footnote omitted).

Treasury Department was acting within its scope of Congressionally delegated authority, the Court found no constitutional issue here that was not already settled by *Zemel v. Rusk.*

The Court in *Regan v. Wald* held that there was no reason to require the Executive or Legislative Departments to demonstrate that there was some danger to national or foreign policy interests presented by travel to Cuba in the 1980's that was similar to the basis for the government actions following the Cuban missile crisis in the 1960's. *Zemel*, in the Court's view, did not rest upon an analysis of the foreign policy interest that supported the restriction on travel but was, rather, "merely an example of this classical deference to the political branches in matters of foreign policy." The decision of the State Department and the Treasury Department that it was contrary to the national interest for American travelers to provide hard currency to Cuba was sufficient to restrict whatever travel rights might be created by the due process clause of the Fifth Amendment "given the traditional deference to executive judgment" regarding foreign policy.

Thus, while it would seem that the Fifth Amendment does grant some protection to arbitrary restrictions on the ability of American citizens to travel to other countries, the Court will uphold those restrictions whenever the Executive Department can reasonably argue that the restrictions are related to our foreign policy interest and there is no clear basis for finding that Congress has restricted Executive authority.

§ 14.38   The Right to Interstate Travel

Introduction–Summary. A "right to travel" has been established by the Supreme Court, but the scope of that right is less than clear. Defining the right to travel is difficult because state or local laws may interfere with several aspects of an individual's ability to travel; the Supreme Court has used several provisions of the Constitution, and its Amend-

ments, in cases that might be described as right to travel cases. State or local laws that restrict travel by restricting transportation between and among the states might be challenged under the commerce clause of Article I, the privileges and immunities clause of Article IV, or all three clauses of the second sentence of the Fourteenth Amendment [the privileges or immunities clause, the due process clause, and the equal protection clause].

When a law is challenged under the due process clause or the equal protection clause, the judiciary will uphold the law so long as it is rationally related to any legitimate end, unless the law substantially impairs a fundamental right or employs a classifying trait (such as race, ancestry, gender or illegitimacy) that justifies independent judicial review.[1] A law that restricts the movement of persons between states will not be subjected to independent judicial review under the due process or equal protection clause unless the law regulates the "right to travel" that the Supreme Court has found to be a fundamental constitutional right. A law that substantially impairs the ability of all persons to engage in the right to travel would be tested under the due process guarantee; a law that restricts the right to travel of one class of persons will be subject to review under the equal protection guarantee.

Separating the types of laws that relate to the fundamental constitutional right to travel from the types of laws that restrict transportation or travel of persons is not easy. A state law that restricts interstate movement of individuals or products, but neither restricts the ability of individuals to establish residency in the state nor treats newly arrived residents less favorably than long time residents, should not be seen as an impairment of the fundamental right to travel. For example, a state license fee for trucks that travel through a state certainly restricts travel (in the sense of reducing the amount of transportation through a state), but it does not impair the

1. See §§ 11.4, 14.3 regarding the standards of review used in substantive due process and equal protection cases.

right to travel. The Court has not subjected truck license fees to strict judicial scrutiny under the due process or equal protection clauses. If the state's truck license fee discriminates against interstate commerce, the licensing fee would be invalidated under commerce clause principles.[2]

The privileges and immunities clause of Article IV protects citizens as they travel to states other than the state in which they reside. That clause prohibits state and local governments from restricting certain basic rights, such as the ability to engage in private sector commercial activity or the ability to exercise a constitutionally protected liberty, to permanent residents of the state or local jurisdiction. Thus, for example, a state cannot require a person to be a resident of the state in order to engage in private sector activities, including being an attorney, in the state.[3] However, because it protects only citizens, this clause cannot be invoked by persons who are not citizens of the United States.[4]

When we look to the Supreme Court's Fourteenth Amendment decisions for a definition of the right to travel, we find that the Court has focused on the protection of the right of individuals, particularly United States citizens, to establish residency in a state and to be treated in the same manner as persons who have been long time residents of the state. The Court has not engaged in independent judicial review of laws that are designed to encourage a person to establish residency within a state or that discourage a person from traveling out of the state after becoming a resident.

The Supreme Court has ruled that states do not have to give a welfare benefit (any type of property, money or service that goes directly from the government to the individual) to persons who are not bona fide residents of the state. A person who is receiving subsistence welfare benefits from a state may lose those benefits if he changes his residency to another state, because states are not required to provide benefits to persons in other jurisdictions. Based on that principle, a state can refuse to employ a person in a government job if the person does not reside within the state boundaries.[5] Similarly, a city or state can refuse to provide a public school education to a child who is merely a temporary resident in the jurisdiction.[6] The Court also upheld a law making the abandonment of a child by a parent a more serious crime if the parent leaves the state after abandoning the child.[7] None of these laws were subjected to strict judicial scrutiny, because these laws had the effect of encouraging people to remain within the state, rather than deterring migration into the state.

Although the Supreme Court has held that a state can require an individual to be a bona fide resident in order to receive government benefits, the Court has invalidated a variety of durational residency requirements. A simple residency requirement in a state law would allow an individual to have the government benefit as soon as the individual entered the state, so long as the individual could in good faith assert that he was now a resident of the state for the indefinite future and for all purposes. On the other hand, a durational resi-

---

2. See Chapter 8 of this Treatise regarding commerce clause restrictions on state laws. See Chapter 13 of the multi-volume edition of this treatise: R. Rotunda & J. Nowak, Treatise On Constitutional Law: Substance and Procedure (1999, with annual supplements) regarding the constitutionality of state taxation laws challenged under commerce clause principles. In one of the earliest right to travel cases the Supreme Court struck down a California law barring anyone from bringing "an indigent person" into the state under the commerce clause. Edwards v. California, 314 U.S. 160, 62 S.Ct. 164, 86 L.Ed. 119 (1941). Justice Jackson concurred in *Edwards* on the basis of his belief that this restriction on travel by indigent persons violated the privileges or immunities clause of the Fourteenth Amendment. 314 U.S. at 183–86, 62 S.Ct. at 171–72 (Jackson, J., concurring). In 1999 the Supreme Court cited Justice Jackson's separate opinion as authority for

the principle that the states "do not have any right to select their citizens." Saenz v. Roe, 526 U.S. 489, 509–11, 119 S.Ct. 1518, 1530, 143 L.Ed.2d 689 (1999).

3. Supreme Court of New Hampshire v. Piper, 470 U.S. 274, 105 S.Ct. 1272, 84 L.Ed.2d 205 (1985). See § 9.6.

4. See § 9.6 regarding the privileges and immunities clause of Article IV.

5. See generally, McCarthy v. Philadelphia Civil Service Commission, 424 U.S. 645, 96 S.Ct. 1154, 47 L.Ed.2d 366 (1976).

6. Martinez v. Bynum, 461 U.S. 321, 103 S.Ct. 1838, 75 L.Ed.2d 879 (1983).

7. Jones v. Helms, 452 U.S. 412, 101 S.Ct. 2434, 69 L.Ed.2d 118 (1981).

dency requirement that requires an individual to be in the jurisdiction for a certain amount of time before he can receive the government benefit or engage in some activity. The waiting period established by a durational residency requirement has an impact on the fundamental constitutional right to travel.

There are two ways in which a durational residency requirement may impair the right to travel. First, whenever the government requires an individual to be in the state for a period of time prior to being able to exercise a basic constitutional right, or prior to receiving some government distributed benefit, the law may deter migration into the state. If the Court determines that the requirement that an individual be in the state for a certain period of time prior to receiving the benefit would substantially restrict the freedom of all individuals, or a class of individuals, to move into the state, that durational residency requirement will be subjected to strict judicial scrutiny.

The standard used by the Supreme Court to review durational residency requirements is less than clear. The Court has stated that a waiting period for the granting of basic welfare benefits must be narrowly tailored to a compelling government interest.[8] However, the Court has also indicated that waiting periods which do not deter migration into the state might be upheld either on the basis that the law does not impair the constitutionally protected right to travel, or because such a law will survive some type of intermediate scrutiny (such as being related to an important government interest). It is possible that the Court may engage in a type of ad hoc balancing when reviewing durational residency requirements, by balancing the degree to which the law will deter migration into the state against the nature of the interests that are advanced by the waiting period.[9] Most of the Supreme Court's right to travel cases, which are examined in this Section, have involved durational residen-

cy requirements that might deter the right to travel. In those cases, the Court has upheld laws that seemed to be narrowly tailored to ensure that persons claiming benefits are good faith residents of the state. The Court has invalidated durational residency requirements that were not tailored to the state's interest in insuring that it is not giving benefits to persons who are fraudulently claiming state residency.

The second way in which a durational residency requirement can impair the right to travel results from a law that distributes government benefits based on length of residency. Such a law distributes benefits based on the duration that each individual has lived within the state. If a law prospectively granted each individual $100 per year if they reside in the state, the law would not involve a durational residency requirement, because every person who is a bona fide resident of the state would receive the same amount of money in each year. A person who remained in the state for 10 years would ultimately receive more than a person who resided in the state for only a single year, but that result would not be a function of a law distributing benefits based on the length of each person's residency. On the other hand, a law that gave $100 to each resident for every year that they had lived in the state prior to the passage of the law would involve a durational residency classification. The person who arrived in the state only two years ago would receive only $200, whereas the person who had arrived twenty years ago would receive $2,000, even though both persons were bona fide residents of the state at the time the law was passed. Once a state determines that a person is a bona fide resident, the state must treat the new resident the same as long-time residents of the state.[10]

In *Saenz v. Roe*[11] the Supreme Court ruled that the privileges or immunities clause of the Fourteenth Amendment provided the basis for reviewing and striking down laws that gave a

8.   Shapiro v. Thompson, 394 U.S. 618, 89 S.Ct. 1322, 22 L.Ed.2d 600 (1969).

9.   See notes 48–74, and accompanying text, infra.

10.   Zobel v. Williams, 457 U.S. 55, 102 S.Ct. 2309, 72 L.Ed.2d 672 (1982). See notes 77–98, and accompanying text, infra.

11.   Saenz v. Roe, 526 U.S. 489, 119 S.Ct. 1518, 143 L.Ed.2d 689 (1999).

preference to long-time residents of a state over newly arrived citizens. Only five states had higher basic welfare benefits under the Aid to Families with Dependent Children program than had California in the early 1990s. California, in 1992, put a limit on the amount of benefits that would be paid under the Aid to Families with Dependent Children program to new residents of the state. Under the California statute, for the first year in which a person or family lived in the state they would receive AFDC benefits only in the amount that they would have received if they continued to live in the state in which they resided prior to moving to California. By a 7 to 2 vote of the Justices, the Court in *Saenz* ruled that the California limitation on benefits for new citizens violated the privileges or immunities clause of the Fourteenth Amendment.[12]

The Court's action in invalidating the California law was not surprising, given the fact that the Supreme Court, under the equal protection clause, had invalidated one-year residency requirements for subsistence welfare benefits and several laws that scaled government benefits to the length of time that a person had lived in a state.[13] The majority opinion in *Saenz*, written by Justice Stevens, was surprising in two respects. First, the Court invalidated the law under the privileges or immunities clause of the Fourteenth Amendment, which had been virtually unused since its ratification, rather than the equal protection clause.[14] Second, Justice Stevens's description of various aspects of the "right to travel" recast the holdings of earlier Supreme Court decisions, and made the topic area more confusing than ever.

The *Saenz* majority may have chosen to use the privileges or immunities clause because its language could easily be understood to invalidate the type of law that had been passed by California and because use of the clause meant that the majority did not have to explain the appropriate standard of review to be used in fundamental rights cases. In 1872, the Court had limited the privileges or immunities clause by ruling that it protected only rights that were attributes of national, rather than state, citizenship but, in so doing, the Court referred to the ability of a citizen of a state to move to a new state as one of those rights of United States citizens that was protected by the privileges and immunities clause.[15]

Once the *Saenz* majority decided that the privileges or immunities clause guaranteed newly arrived citizens the same rights as long-time citizens of the state, invalidation of the California law required no discussion of standards of review. The majority opinion by Justice Stevens found that the "appropriate standard [for this type of privileges or immunities clause case] may be more categorical than [the compelling interest test used in some equal protection right to travel cases] but it is surely no less strict."[16] The majority opinion went on to explain why the classifications created by the California statute did not relate to any interest that could justify discrimination against newly arrived citizens. It appears that the Court in *Saenz* was creating an absolute bar to the type of law enacted by California.

The Court's use of the privileges or immunities clause has the benefit of clarifying the series of rulings in which the Supreme Court had held that state laws that favored long-time

---

12. The Court in *Saenz* also ruled that Congress had not approved the type of durational residency requirement used by California and that Congress did not have the authority to authorize a violation of Section 1 of the Fourteenth Amendment. 526 U.S. at 506–10, 119 S.Ct. at 1528–30. Only two of the Justices believed that the distribution of benefits based on the length of residency did not violate the privileges or immunities clause of the Fourteenth Amendment. 526 U.S. at 510, 119 S.Ct. at 1530 (Rehnquist, C.J., joined by Thomas, J., dissenting); 526 U.S. at 520, 119 S.Ct. at 1535 (Thomas, J., joined by Rehnquist, C.J., dissenting).

13. See notes 48–62, 77–98, infra, and accompanying text.

14. The Court had restricted the meaning of the clause in the Slaughter–House cases, 83 U.S. (16 Wall.) 36, 21 L.Ed.394 (1872). The Court had used the clause to strike down a law in only one case, which it later overruled. Colgate v. Harvey, 296 U.S. 404, 56 S.Ct. 252, 80 L.Ed. 299 (1935) overruled in Madden v. Kentucky, 309 U.S. 83, 60 S.Ct. 406, 84 L.Ed. 590 (1940).

15. The Slaughter-House cases, 83 U.S.(16 Wall.) 36, 79–81, 21 L.Ed. 394 (1872).

16. Saenz v. Roe, 526 U.S. 489, 504, 119 S.Ct. 1518, 1527, 143 L.Ed.2d 689 (1999).

residents over new residents violated equal protection.[17] But the Court's use of the clause limited the nature of the right that it was protecting, by limiting that right to citizens of the United States. Unlike the due process and equal protection clauses of the Fourteenth Amendment, the privileges or immunities clause protects only citizens. Language used in the Stevens majority opinion in *Saenz* makes it appear that the Court will limit the protection given by that case to United States citizens,[18] just as the Court had previously limited the protections of the Article IV privileges and immunities clause to United States citizens.[19] If a state law imposed a durational residency requirement for welfare benefits only on lawfully resident aliens, the law might still be invalidated under the equal protection clause or by a judicial ruling that the law had been preempted by federal legislation regarding the treatment of foreign nationals who were lawful residents of the United States.[20]

Justice Stevens's majority opinion in *Saenz* may have added confusion to the right to travel area by his subdividing of the right. The majority opinion in *Saenz* first noted that the right to travel had been found by the Court to be constitutionally protected under a variety of provisions of the Constitution. Justice Stevens noted that the Court had held that the creation of a classification that effectively imposed a penalty on establishing residency in the state would violate the equal protection clause unless the classification was necessary to a compelling government interest.[21] In the next portion of the opinion, however, Justice Stevens divided the right to travel into three

parts; he did not make reference to the cases using the compelling interest test in the description of any of his three branches of the right to travel. Justice Stevens divided the right to travel in the following way:

"The 'right to travel' discussed in our cases embraces at least three different components. It protects the right of a citizen of one state to enter and to leave another state, the right to be treated as a welcome visitor rather than an unfriendly alien when temporarily present in the second estate, and, for those travelers who elect to become permanent residents, the right to be treated like other citizens of that state."[22]

In discussing the "second component" Justice Stevens found that the protection of citizens while they went into a state temporarily was provided by the Article IV privileges and immunities clause; his opinion broke no new ground in this area.[23]

The majority opinion in *Saenz* found that the California law involved only the "third aspect of the right to travel–the right of the newly arrived citizen to the same privileges and immunities enjoyed by other citizens of the same state."[24] The majority then created and applied the categorical prohibition on the scaling of benefits for the purpose of rewarding long-time citizens or deterring the entry of new citizens into the state.

Justice Stevens's references to the right to cross state borders, which was the first aspect of the right to travel that he listed in his opinion, was very confusing. In his description

---

17. See notes 48–62, 77–98 and accompanying text, infra.

18. Saenz v. Roe, 526 U.S. 489, 504, 119 S.Ct. 1518, 1526, 143 L.Ed.2d 689 (1999): "That right [to be treated like other citizens of the state] is protected not only by the new arrival's status as a state citizen, but also by her status as a citizen of the United States." See also Id. at 516, 119 S.Ct. at 1530 referring to the right of "citizens of the United States" to choose the state of residence and to be treated equally with other state residents.

19. The protection of the Article IV clause is limited to United States citizens, see Blake v. McClung, 172 U.S. 239, 19 S.Ct. 165, 43 L.Ed. 432 (1898). The Court in 1999 referred to the citizenship clause and privileges and immunities clause of the Fourteenth Amendment as being designed to guarantee "newly freed black citizens" that they

could claim state citizenship and the protections of Article IV and similar provisions of the Constitution. Saenz v. Roe, 526 U.S. 489, 502 n. 15, 119 S.Ct. 1518, 1526 n. 15, 143 L.Ed.2d 689 (1999).

20. See §§ 14.11–14.13 regarding the use of United States citizenship classifications.

21. Saenz v. Roe, 526 U.S. 489, 497–99, 119 S.Ct. 1518, 1524–25, 143 L.Ed.2d 689 (1999) referring to and quoting from Shapiro v. Thompson, 394 U.S. 618, 89 S.Ct. 1322, 22 L.Ed.2d 600 (1969).

22. Saenz v. Roe, 526 U.S. 489, 500, 119 S.Ct. 1518, 1525, 143 L.Ed.2d 689 (1999).

23. 526 U.S. at 500–02, 119 S.Ct. at 1525–26.

24. 526 U.S. at 502, 119 S.Ct. at 1526.

of this aspect of the right to travel, Justice Stevens referred only to commerce clause prohibitions on bringing persons into the state, and to Congress' power to protect travelers from being harmed by private persons or government actors when they used highways or other means of interstate commerce.[25] In this portion of the majority opinion, there was no mention of the cases that invalidated durational residency requirements under the equal protection clause. Nevertheless, in Part V of the majority opinion, where he analyzed the deficiencies in the California law, Justice Stevens focused on the nature of the classifications established by the law. That portion of the majority opinion relied heavily on those cases that had invalidated durational residency requirements under the equal protection clause.[26]

It is possible that the Court, in future years, will build upon *Saenz* and analyze all durational residency requirements under the privileges or immunities clause of the Fourteenth Amendment, rather than the equal protection clause. It appears that the analysis used in the equal protection right to travel cases will still be used by the Supreme Court, even if that analysis will be given the label of privileges or immunities clause analysis.

The only durational residency requirements that have been upheld by the Supreme Court were tailored to establishing that the individual claiming the benefit was, in fact, a good faith resident of the state. In *Saenz*, Justice Stevens noted that the persons attacking the California law were admitted to be honestly claiming that they were permanent residents of California, so that the Court had "no occasion to consider what weight might be given to a citizen's length of residence if the bona fides claim to state citizenship were questioned."[27]

In earlier cases, the Supreme Court had upheld a one-year waiting requirement for an individual to get a divorce[28], and had indicated that a one-year waiting period to obtain in-state residency for in-state college tuition would be upheld.[29] Those decisions had not had a clear rationale, because the Court had refused to state any clear equal protection standard in those cases. Its possible that those cases were instances in which the Court believed that the state needed a one-year residency requirement to ensure the good faith of the person who sought a divorce or the benefit of in-state tuition at a government owned university. The Court in *Saenz* avoided analyzing those cases, although the majority opinion stated that those cases had involved situations where the elimination of a waiting period might have resulted in encouraging persons from other states "to establish residency for just long enough to acquire some readily portable benefit, such as a divorce or a college education, that will be enjoyed after they return to their original domicile."[30]

Because the Court in *Saenz* did not overturn any prior ruling concerning the right to travel, each of the Court's earlier rulings concerning the right to travel currently stands for the principle that there is a fundamental constitutional right to travel protected by the Fourteenth Amendment. A law that constitutes a substantial impairment of that right will be subject to independent judicial review and is unlikely to be upheld unless the Court finds that it is narrowly tailored to a compelling interest. However, it may be that all of the cases involving durational residency requirements will, in the future, be referred to as privileges or immunities clause cases. Regardless of whether the Court uses equal protection clause or privileges or immunities clause

---

25. 526 U.S. at 500, 119 S.Ct. at 1525.

26. 526 U.S. at 504–06, 119 S.Ct. at 1527–28.

27. 526 U.S. at 504, 119 S.Ct. at 1527.

28. Sosna v. Iowa, 419 U.S. 393, 95 S.Ct. 553, 42 L.Ed.2d 532 (1975).

29. The Court in Vlandis v. Kline, 412 U.S. 441, 93 S.Ct. 2230, 37 L.Ed.2d 63(1973) invalidated state regulations that prohibited an individual from ever receiving in-state tuition if he or she had not been a state resident prior to the time they applied for admission to the state

university but indicated that durational residency requirement for in-state tuition would be upheld. In Starns v. Malkerson, 401 U.S. 985, 91 S.Ct. 1231, 28 L.Ed.2d 527 (1971), affirming 326 F.Supp. 234 (D.Minn.1970), summarily affirmed a lower federal court ruling upholding a one-year residency requirement for an individual to receive a lower, in-state tuition at a state university.

30. Saenz v. Roe, 526 U.S. 489, 504, 119 S.Ct. 1518, 1527, 143 L.Ed.2d 689 (1999).

terminology, a durational residency requirement should not be upheld if it constitutes a significant deterrence to persons migrating into a state, unless the waiting period established by the law is narrowly tailored to ensure the good faith of persons claiming a state provided benefit.

Early Decisions of the Court. The right to travel has been recognized in one form or another throughout the history of the Republic. The Articles of Confederation explicitly recognized the right of the people of each state to "have free ingress and regress to and from any other State".[31] This provision was not included in the text of the Constitution or the proposed Bill of Rights and the reason for its exclusion is not clear. It has been suggested that it was believed to be so basic a right that it need not be expressed in the text.[32] Another possibility is that the framers of the original Constitution believed that the guarantee was subsumed in the other protections given the citizens of each state by the privileges and immunities clause of Article IV and by the granting of the national commercial power to Congress.[33] This explanation has a textual basis in that these provisions of the Constitution are similar to those which were joined with the mobility provision in the Articles of Confederation;[34] the concept of interstate travel may have been considered to be a subset of these other rights.

Prior to the Civil War the Court did not directly consider the scope of the right to travel between the states. The Court in 1837 did approve a law which required the registration of passengers entering a state and in so doing

indicated that the individual states had some inherent power to limit the terms upon which people entered the state.[35] However, the case did not involve a direct burden or prohibition and the language was limited only a few years later in *The Passenger Cases*[36] when the Justices invalidated state legislation that imposed a tax upon alien passengers arriving from foreign ports.

Following the Civil War the Supreme Court held that there was an inherent right to individual travel between the states. In *Crandall v. Nevada*,[37] the Court held unconstitutional a statute which imposed a tax on railroads for every passenger carried out of the state. The majority opinion held the matter to be an unconstitutional interference with the inherent right of a citizen to travel. When the Court limited the scope of the privileges or immunities clause of the Fourteenth Amendment in *The Slaughter-House Cases* the opinion still recognized that one of the attributes of national citizenship was the freedom to travel through individual states.[38]

The Court did not expand this concept in terms of an independent national right for some years, although it would occasionally mention the right as one pertaining to national citizenship. The laws relating to travel which were reviewed by the Supreme Court during this period related to the entrance of interstate commerce into a state. However, during this period the Court did uphold a two year residence requirement to become an insurance broker within a state.[39] This comported with the Court's view that the insur-

31. Articles of Confederation, art. IV (1778). The Articles of Confederation are reprinted in 4 R. Rotunda & J. Nowak, Treatise on Constitutional Law: Substance and Procedure Appendix B (2d ed. 1992).

32. United States v. Guest, 383 U.S. 745, 758, 86 S.Ct. 1170, 1178, 16 L.Ed.2d 239 (1966) (majority opinion by Stewart, J.); Z. Chafee, Three Human Rights 185 (1956).

33. The basis for the right to personal mobility is examined in connection with the Commerce Clause restrictions on the states and the Interstate Privileges and Immunities Clause in §§ 8.10, 9.6, supra.

34. The Articles of Confederation, art. IV in part read:

"[T]he free inhabitants of each of these States, paupers, vagabonds and fugitives from Justice excepted, shall be entitled to all privileges and immunities of free citizens in the several States; and the people of each

State shall have free ingress and regress to and from any other State, and shall enjoy therein all the privileges of trade and commerce, subject to the same duties, impositions and restrictions as the inhabitants thereof respectively ...."

35. Mayor and City of New York v. Miln, 36 U.S. (11 Pet.) 102, 9 L.Ed. 648 (1837).

36. 48 U.S. (7 How.) 283, 12 L.Ed. 702 (1849).

37. 73 U.S. (6 Wall.) 35, 18 L.Ed. 745 (1867).

38. The Slaughter-House Cases, 83 U.S. (16 Wall.) 36, 79, 21 L.Ed. 394 (1872).

39. La Tourette v. McMaster, 248 U.S. 465, 39 S.Ct. 160, 63 L.Ed. 362 (1919).

ance industry was a matter for local regulation and that laws which burdened the entry of new insurance businesses into the state did not violate the commerce clause.[40]

The Court's next opportunity to confront the issue of a personal right to travel came in *Edwards v. California.*[41] In an effort to keep out indigents fleeing the economic depression in other parts of the country, the State of California passed the statute which penalized the bringing into the state of any non-resident person by anyone knowing the individual to be "an indigent person." The majority opinion held that this statute violated the commerce clause. Even accepting the state's argument that the migration of poor persons had brought grave problems of health and finance to the state, the majority opinion found that the state's attempt to lock out the transportation of persons across its borders was a classic trade barrier which fell within the prohibition of the commerce clause.[42] Four of the Justices, in concurring opinions, would have held that the statute violated the Constitution because the right to interstate travel was one of the privileges or immunities protected by the Fourteenth Amendment.[43]

Justice Jackson's concurring opinion in that case has become not only the best exposition of the inherent right to travel but also a classic statement regarding the principle that fundamental constitutional rights should not be allocated by wealth. He stated:

> That choice of residence was subject to local approval is contrary to the inescapable implication of the westward movement of our civilization.... We should say now, and in no uncertain terms, that a man's mere property status, without more, cannot be used by a state to test, qualify, or limit

his rights as a citizen of the United States. "Indigence" itself is neither a source of rights nor a basis for denying them.... If I doubted whether his federal citizenship alone were enough to open the gates of California to Duncan, my doubt would disappear on consideration of the obligations of such citizenship.... Rich or penniless, Duncan's citizenship under the Constitution pledges his strength to the defense of California as a part of the United States, and his right to migrate to any part of the land he must defend is something she must respect under the same instrument. Unless this Court is willing to say that citizenship of the United States means at least this much to the citizen, then our heritage of constitutional privileges and immunities is only a promise to the ear to be broken to the hope, a teasing illusion like a munificent bequest in a pauper's will.[44]

The Court next examined the right to interstate travel in connection with the review of a federal statute designed to protect that right. In *United States v. Guest*[45] the Supreme Court upheld the application of the criminal conspiracy provision of the Civil Rights Acts to private individuals who attempted to deprive black persons of the right to enjoy public facilities connected with interstate travel. The majority opinion did not state that Congress could prohibit the actions of private persons that interfere with any rights that might be protected by the Fourteenth Amendment although a majority appeared to accept this position.[46] Justice Stewart had the clear support of more than a majority of the Justices when he held that the right to interstate travel was a fundamental incident of federal citizenship which the Congress was free to protect to its

---

40. Paul v. Virginia, 75 U.S. (8 Wall.) 168, 19 L.Ed. 357 (1868).

41. 314 U.S. 160, 62 S.Ct. 164, 86 L.Ed. 119 (1941).

42. 314 U.S. at 173–74, 62 S.Ct. at 166–67.

43. 314 U.S. at 177, 62 S.Ct. at 168 (Douglas, J., concurring, joined by Black and Murphy, JJ.); 314 U.S. at 181, 62 S.Ct. at 170 (Jackson, J., concurring).

44. Edwards v. California, 314 U.S. 160, 183–86, 62 S.Ct. 164, 171–72, 86 L.Ed. 119 (1941) (Jackson, J., concurring).

45. 383 U.S. 745, 86 S.Ct. 1170, 16 L.Ed.2d 239 (1966).

46. 383 U.S. at 762, 86 S.Ct. at 1180 (Clark, J., concurring, joined by Black and Fortas, JJ.). 383 U.S. at 782 & n. 6, 86 S.Ct. at 1191 & n. 6 (Brennan J., concurring, joined by Warren, C.J., and Douglas, J.). Justice Harlan found it "to say the least, extraordinary" that some of the Justices would "cursorily pronounc[e] themselves" on "far-reaching constitutional questions...." 383 U.S. at 762 n. 1, 86 S.Ct. at 1180 n. 1 (Harlan, J., concurring in part and dissenting in part).

fullest extent. Justice Stewart noted the history of the right which dated back to the Articles of Confederation and had continual, if implicit, recognition in the cases of the Court throughout history.[47] This ruling set the stage for full recognition of the right a few years later when the Court was confronted by state actions which inhibited the right to travel.

The Era of Strict Scrutiny. The landmark decision concerning the right to travel and the permissible scope of the burdens on that right which result from residency requirements came in *Shapiro v. Thompson*.[48] In this case the Justices reviewed the permissibility of two state statutes and a District of Columbia statute which denied welfare benefits to persons who had not resided within the jurisdiction for at least one year. The Court found that the state statutes violated the equal protection clause of the Fourteenth Amendment and the District act violated the equal protection guarantee of the due process clause of the Fifth Amendment.

The basis for this equal protection ruling was that a residency requirement has the effect of deterring the entry of indigent persons into these jurisdictions, thereby limiting their rights to engage in interstate travel. The majority opinion held that, because the right limited was a fundamental constitutional right, the classification had to be invalidated unless it was "shown to be necessary to promote a *compelling* governmental interest."[49] The state's argument that it was attempting to deter indigents who entered the state solely to obtain larger benefits would not be permissible as the states had no right to exclude poor persons from their borders.[50] And the majority found that it was impermissible for the state to try to distinguish between old and new residents when that burdened fundamental rights. While the state might have some requirement that the persons be residents at the

time they applied, they could not create subclasses of citizens based on the duration of time that persons had been residents of the state. There was also no proof that the system significantly promoted the budgeting process of the state and the Court found that administrative efficiency was not such a compelling interest as to support the limitation of a fundamental right.

The primary dissent in *Shapiro* was that of Justice Harlan who attacked not only the Court's strict protection of the right to travel but the entire fundamental rights branch of equal protection analysis.[51] He found no basis for elevating the right to travel to a status under which the Court could review governmental policy in so strict a manner and he believed that protecting rights in this way because of their importance to daily life allowed the Court to sit as a super legislature.

The *Shapiro* analysis has been followed in a series of cases dealing with durational residence requirements. These statutes require not only that persons declare themselves to be residents of the state but that they maintain that residency status for a set duration of time prior to being eligible to receive some benefit or exercise some right. The right involved need not be a fundamental right in order to require the strict scrutiny analysis, for a durational residency requirement burdens the right to travel which is itself a fundamental right. Thus, any classification which burdens the right will be subject to strict judicial scrutiny to determine its legitimacy.

In many of these cases the Court has invoked the language of the "compelling interest" test to indicate that these laws must meet a high standard before the Justices will uphold them. However, in other cases the Court has issued rulings both upholding and striking residency requirements which indicate that the

---

47. 383 U.S. at 758, 86 S.Ct. at 1178.

48. 394 U.S. 618, 89 S.Ct. 1322, 22 L.Ed.2d 600 (1969).

49. 394 U.S. at 634, 89 S.Ct. at 1331 (emphasis in original).

50. The Court later summarily affirmed the invalidation on a similar basis of a statute which was intended to bar only those persons who came into a state for the sole

purpose of obtaining welfare benefits. Gaddis v. Wyman, 304 F.Supp. 717 (N.D.N.Y.1969), affirmed sub nom. Wyman v. Bowens, 397 U.S. 49, 90 S.Ct. 813, 25 L.Ed.2d 38 (1970).

51. Shapiro v. Thompson, 394 U.S. 618, 655, 89 S.Ct. 1322, 1342, 22 L.Ed.2d 600 (1969) (Harlan, J., dissenting). Justice Black and Chief Justice Warren also dissented.

Court may only be employing some form of true "reasonableness" test or an *ad hoc* balancing test when deciding whether these laws serve legitimate governmental purposes which justify a limitation of the right to travel.

The Supreme Court has never held that a state or local government is prohibited from requiring persons to be residents of that location in order to receive government benefits. The state may restrict some welfare benefits to *bona fide* residents.[52] The *Shapiro* rationale only requires close judicial scrutiny of durational residency requirements, a distinction between new and old residents. Each jurisdiction has a right to limit voting to residents of that jurisdiction,[53] and the Court has held that residence within a specific area can be a requirement for public employment.[54] The Court has never foreclosed the possibility that some residence requirement for securing benefits may violate the right to travel, but neither has it indicated that a resident would be enti-

tled to keep any form of state dispensed benefit upon leaving the state.[55]

The Supreme Court has dealt with the right to travel in terms of restrictions on voting eligibility in several cases. In these cases it has stricken the residency requirement whenever it was a period beyond that which was truly reasonable or necessary to protect the electoral process from fraudulent practices or administrative breakdowns.

In *Dunn v. Blumstein*[56] the Court struck down a state law which required a voter to be a resident of the state for one year and the county for three months before he could vote. The Court found that this law had to be reviewed under the compelling interest test, for it touched upon the right to travel as well as the right to vote. Since there was no dispute that the person was a resident, the state could not deny the individual the vote simply be-

---

52. The Supreme Court upheld a state statute which permitted a school district to deny tuition free education to a child who lived apart from his parent or lawful guardian if the child's presence in the school district was "for the primary purpose" of attending school in the district. Martinez v. Bynum, 461 U.S. 321, 103 S.Ct. 1838, 75 L.Ed.2d 879 (1983). "A bona fide residence requirement, appropriately defined and uniformly applied, furthers the substantial state interest in assuring that services provided for its residents are enjoyed only by residents." 461 U.S. at 328, 103 S.Ct. at 1842. The majority opinion found that this residence requirement did not violate the equal protection clause because it was not based on a suspect classification and it did not limit the exercise of a fundamental right. The Court noted that public education was not such a right. 461 U.S. at 328 n. 7, 103 S.Ct. at 1842–43 n. 7. *Martinez* held that the statute at issue was a bona fide residence requirement because it provided free education for all children who resided in the school district with the intent to remain in the district indefinitely. The Court did not pass upon the residency claim of the child in this case, a United States citizen whose parents were non-resident aliens living in Mexico. See 461 U.S. at 333, 103 S.Ct. at 1845 (Brennan, J., concurring). Only Justice Marshall would have invalidated the residency requirement on its face. 461 U.S. at 334, 103 S.Ct. at 1845 (Marshall, J., dissenting).

The Supreme Court has found that some types of preferential treatment for state residents violate neither the commerce clause nor the interstate privileges and immunities clause. See e.g., Reeves, Inc. v. Stake, 447 U.S. 429, 100 S.Ct. 2271, 65 L.Ed.2d 244 (1980) (state may limit sales from state owned cement plant to instate residents); Baldwin v. Fish and Game Commission of Montana, 436 U.S. 371, 98 S.Ct. 1852, 56 L.Ed.2d 354 (1978) (upholding disparity between fees for recreational hunting for resi-

dent and nonresident hunters). These cases, however, did not involve "right to travel" claims.

The Supreme Court also uses the privileges and immunities clause of Article IV to review state or local laws that establish a state or municipality residency or citizenship requirement as a prerequisite to the granting of important benefits or the ability to exercise basic rights. See § 9.6, supra for analysis of these cases.

53. See Rosario v. Rockefeller, 410 U.S. 752, 93 S.Ct. 1245, 36 L.Ed.2d 1 (1973).

54. McCarthy v. Philadelphia Civil Service Com'n, 424 U.S. 645, 96 S.Ct. 1154, 47 L.Ed.2d 366 (1976).

55. The Court noted that this problem might arise in the future but that it did not have to resolve the issue at this time. In Califano v. Torres, 435 U.S. 1, 98 S.Ct. 906, 55 L.Ed.2d 65 (1978) (per curiam), the Supreme Court, in a brief per curiam opinion, held that neither the right to travel, nor the equal protection guarantee of the Fifth Amendment due process clause prohibited the limitation of Social Security Act supplemental security income payments to aged, blind, or disabled persons who are residents of the United States, which was defined by statutes as the fifty states and the District of Columbia. The Court held that the exclusion of Puerto Rico residents from the program did not create a significant equal protection problem because of the unique status of Puerto Rico. 435 U.S. at 3 n. 4, 98 S.Ct. at 907 n. 4.

See also Harris v. Rosario, 446 U.S. 651, 100 S.Ct. 1929, 64 L.Ed.2d 587 (1980), (per curiam). (Congress may treat Puerto Rico differently so long as there is a rational basis for its actions; it is proper for Congress to provide less welfare benefits to Puerto Rican residents, who do not pay U.S. taxes; also increased benefits would disrupt the Puerto Rican economy and greatly burden the treasury).

56. 405 U.S. 330, 92 S.Ct. 995, 31 L.Ed.2d 274 (1972).

cause he had not been present within the state for this duration of time. The opinion found that there was no sufficient connection between a person's ability to intelligently exercise the electoral franchise and the time spent within the state. The small chance of greater familiarity with local issues could not justify this burdening the right to travel. States could limit the right to vote to residents, and take reasonable measures to protect the integrity of their system, but they could not allocate fundamental rights in this manner.

In later cases the Court, in per curiam decisions, upheld statutes which required voters to be resident in a jurisdiction for close to two months prior to the time of an election. Registration requirements up to fifty days were upheld upon the basis that the state needed a reasonable period of time in which to finalize its voter registration list before an election in order to prevent fraud and allow for efficient administration of the system.[57]

The Court in *Rosario v. Rockefeller*[58] upheld a statute which required voters to enroll in the party of their choice thirty days before a general election as a prerequisite to voting in the following primary. This requirement has the effect of requiring persons to register almost a year before the primary, thus requiring their presence and residency in the state at that time. Although this had the effect of a durational residency requirement which served as a limitation on both the right to vote and the right to travel, the law was upheld. The majority opinion found that the state interest in avoiding inter-party rating in primary elections was sufficient to uphold this classification.

But in *Kusper v. Pontikes*[59] the Court struck down a state statute which prohibited a person from voting in a primary election of a particular party if he had voted in the primary of another party within the preceding twenty-three months. While this law was not strictly

a durational residency requirement the Court, in striking the classification indicated, that a requirement of registration twenty-three months before a primary simply was not legitimate means of protecting state interests in the election.

On this basis, it can be expected that any residency requirement for primary elections which exceeds a year would be found to be an illegitimate manner of protecting the party system and that any requirement of residency or registration for more than two months prior to a general election would be found to be an impermissible way of protecting the integrity of the balloting on election day. However, the Court has not decided whether candidates may be subjected to a durational residency requirement that exceeds that of voters, although the basis for such laws appears to be undercut by the Court's conclusion in *Dunn* that residency could not be equated with knowledge of electoral issues. But the extent to which the Court will move to allow states to prohibit "carpetbagger" candidates remains to be seen.[60]

That the right to travel will be protected even when no other fundamental right is involved became clear when the Court decided *Memorial Hospital v. Maricopa County*.[61] In this case an Arizona statute required one year residence in a county as a condition to receiving nonemergency hospitalization or medical care at public expense. The Court found that this classification impinged upon interstate travel and, in so doing, found that it was irrelevant that classification also burdened travel by persons within their own state. This fact could not protect the discrimination against the interstate traveller any more than discrimination against some in-state businesses could justify discrimination against interstate commerce.[62]

---

57. Marston v. Lewis, 410 U.S. 679, 93 S.Ct. 1211, 35 L.Ed.2d 627 (1973); Burns v. Fortson, 410 U.S. 686, 93 S.Ct. 1209, 35 L.Ed.2d 633 (1973).

58. 410 U.S. 752, 93 S.Ct. 1245, 36 L.Ed.2d 1 (1973).

59. 414 U.S. 51, 94 S.Ct. 303, 38 L.Ed.2d 260 (1973).

60. See Note, Durational Residency Requirements for Candidates, 40 U.Chi.L.Rev. 357 (1973).

61. 415 U.S. 250, 94 S.Ct. 1076, 39 L.Ed.2d 306 (1974).

62. As to the invalidity of local burdens on interstate commerce, see Dean Milk Co. v. City of Madison, 340 U.S. 349, 71 S.Ct. 295, 95 L.Ed. 329 (1951).

The Court has never found medical care to be a fundamental right just as it has never found that any form of necessary welfare assistance payment or general government benefit constitutes such a right. But the majority found it was required to use the compelling interest test to protect the right to interstate travel in this setting. With an analysis quite similar to that employed in *Shapiro* the opinion found that the denial of medical services to indigents from other states constituted a severe penalty on their right to engage in interstate travel. The majority opinion found that the denial of this "basic necessity of life" to be such a severe burden on the right to travel that it could not be justified by the state's interest in administrative efficiency or general pursuit of economic policies. The opinion noted that the Court's review of residency requirements for all government benefits might not be scrutinized with such a strict analysis, but that where the state burdened the right to travel by denial of benefits which were essential to the daily life of the new indigent in the state, the Court would require that the state meet his "heavy burden of justification."[63]

As indicated in the *Memorial Hospital* opinion, the Court may not be ready to apply the strict scrutiny analysis of *Shapiro* to every durational residency requirement. Where the requirement relates to activities which are not directly related to the exercise of other rights or the individual's ability to function in a meaningful manner as a new resident of the state, these laws may be upheld on a test which comes close to the rational basis standard.

It should be noted that Justice Douglas indicated that he shared the doubts about the usefulness of the strict scrutiny analysis of residency requirements because it offered little basis for deciding complex questions of the allocation of state resources and wealth. However, he concurred in *Memorial Hospital* because the line drawn on medical aid was so

arbitrary, and the importance of the interest so great, that the requirement could only be described as "invidious discrimination against the poor."[64] Thus, there are significant questions as to whether the Court will require that there be only very short durational residency requirements for other governmental benefits.

State Education Benefits. The Supreme Court has not prohibited states from charging lower tuition at state universities for persons who have been residents for some significant period. In *Vlandis v. Kline*[65] the Court invalidated a Connecticut statute which permanently barred a non-resident student from becoming an in-state resident for the purposes of lower tuition rates in the state university system of higher education. The opinion characterized the statute as creating a permanent and "irrebuttable presumption" of non-residency. However, the only issue in the case was the statutory definition of residency rather than the legitimacy of any durational residency requirement. Under the statute an unmarried student was classified as a non-resident if his address for any part of one year prior to his application for admission had been outside of the state of Connecticut. A married student would be classified as a resident so long as he had an in-state address at the time of his application. These classifications were permanent and the student could do nothing to change his residency status throughout his career at the university.

The Supreme Court in *Vlandis* found that the classification was an irrebuttable presumption against those who might be able to prove residency at some later time. However, the Court did cite with approval its decision in *Starns v. Malkerson*[66] which summarily affirmed a decision upholding Minnesota's requirement that students be residents of the state for one year prior to qualifying for lower tuition. One may conclude that there will be a reasonableness test for durational residency requirements in the area of education which

63. Memorial Hosp. v. Maricopa County, 415 U.S. 250, 263, 94 S.Ct. 1076, 1084, 39 L.Ed.2d 306 (1974).

64. 415 U.S. at 270, 273, 94 S.Ct. at 1088, 1089–90 (Douglas, J., concurring).

65. 412 U.S. 441, 93 S.Ct. 2230, 37 L.Ed.2d 63 (1973).

66. 401 U.S. 985, 91 S.Ct. 1231, 28 L.Ed.2d 527 (1971), affirming 326 F.Supp. 234 (D.Minn.1970), cited in 412 U.S. at 452–53 n. 9, 93 S.Ct. at 2237 n. 9.

will be similar to the test which the Court has used in the primary election cases.

Martinez v. Bynum,[67] upheld a state statute which permitted a school district to deny tuition-free education to a child who lived apart from his parent or lawful guardian if the child's presence in the school district was "for the primary purpose" of attending school in the district. Justice Powell wrote for eight Justices when he stated: "A bona fide residence requirement, appropriately defined and uniformly applied, furthers the substantial state interest in assuring that services provided for its residents are enjoyed only by residents." Powell found that this residence requirement did not violate the equal protection clause because it was not based on a suspect classification and it did not limit the exercise of a fundamental right, because public education was not such a right.[68] The statute at issue in *Martinez* was a bona fide residence requirement because it provided free education for all children who resided in the school district with the intent to remain in the district indefinitely. The Court did not pass upon the residency claim of the child in this case, a United States citizen whose parents were nonresident aliens living in Mexico.[69]

Residency Requirements for Divorce. The Supreme Court has indicated that some burdens on the right to travel will be upheld so long as the Court finds them not to be arbitrary in fact. In *Sosna v. Iowa*[70] the Court upheld a one year residency requirement for parties seeking a divorce from state courts. The Court found that there was no due process violation here because there was no deprivation of access to the state courts but only a delay before they could be used by the parties. This delay was justified by the state's interest in ensuring that it had a real interest in those who sought to use its courts to alter fundamental family relationships and by a desire to insulate state divorce decrees from successful collateral attacks. The opinion distinguished *Shapiro, Dunn*, and *Memorial Hospital* on the basis that this classification did not prevent the woman who sought the divorce from receiving support or functioning as a citizen of the state during this period.

The dissent accused the majority of making a significant departure from *Shapiro* and its progeny.[71] However several factors demonstrate the compatibility between *Sosna* and the earlier decisions. The residency requirement here related to an interest which, while it was of great importance to the individual, was not such that it would usually deter travel. Additionally, the delay was for one year—a length similar to that which the Court had upheld as a residency requirement for such interests as voting in primary elections and receiving lower college tuition. Finally, the opinion in *Sosna* was careful to note that the law was justified by ends which were of greater significance than administrative efficiency or mere dollar savings.[72]

Burdens on Crossing State Lines. The Supreme Court in recent years has endorsed strict judicial review of those state laws which serve as impediments to interstate relocation but it has not been ready to endorse strict judicial supervision of all laws that might serve as some type of barrier to interstate travel. Strict judicial scrutiny of state laws which serve as an impediment to immigration into a state is necessary to preserve our national cohesion as a single economic unit and to avoid states giving preferential treatment to in-state residents in the dispensation of state resources and erecting barriers to immigration from less wealthy states. But not all laws are of that character. An example of judicial review of a right to travel claim on somewhat less than the strictest standard of judicial re-

67. 461 U.S. 321, 103 S.Ct. 1838, 75 L.Ed.2d 879 (1983).

68. 461 U.S. at 328 n. 7, 103 S.Ct. at 1842–43 n. 7.

69. Martinez v. Bynum, 461 U.S. 321, 333, 103 S.Ct. 1838, 1845, 75 L.Ed.2d 879 (1983) (Brennan, J., concurring). Only Justice Marshall voted to invalidate the stat-

ute on its face. 461 U.S. at 334, 103 S.Ct. at 1845 (Marshall, J., dissenting).

70. 419 U.S. 393, 95 S.Ct. 553, 42 L.Ed.2d 532 (1975).

71. Sosna v. Iowa, 419 U.S. 393, 418, 95 S.Ct. 553, 567, 42 L.Ed.2d 532 (1975) (Marshall, J., dissenting).

72. 419 U.S. at 406, 95 S.Ct. at 560–61.

view is *Jones v. Helms*[73] in which the Supreme Court upheld a Georgia statute making willful abandonment of a child by a parent a misdemeanor if the parent remained in the state and a felony if the parent left the state after the abandonment.

The majority opinion, by Justice Stevens, found that the statute did not violate the equal protection clause because a parent who abandoned his child had "qualified his right to travel interstate before he sought to exercise that right."[74] The restriction on the interstate travel of such persons promoted the state interest in ascertaining the guilt of persons who abandoned their child and facilitating remedies which the state might otherwise lawfully seek against the parents who had abandoned their child. The Court found that, "although a simple penalty for leaving a State is simply impermissible," the restriction of travel on the part of those who had engaged in otherwise punishable conduct was permissible.[75] Having found that the fundamental right to interstate travel was not restricted by the Georgia statute, the Court had no trouble in finding that placing a burden on parents who left the state following an abandonment of their child did not violate equal protection but was a nondiscriminatory law applying to all parents residing in Georgia.[76]

Distributing Benefits Based on Length of Residency. In *Zobel v. Williams*[77] the Court was confronted with a case wherein the decision on the merits was easy but the rationalization of the Court's role in reviewing travel restrictions was quite difficult for the Justices. By an eight to one vote, the Court invalidated a statute which distributed state money to residents based upon the length of their residency in the state. The Court did not in this case attempt to define the appropriate standard of review for state laws which impose economic barriers to interstate migration.

In *Zobel*, the Court examined an Alaska statute which distributed money from a state fund which had been enriched by the state's share of oil exploration revenues. Under the state statutes, each citizen of the age of 18 years or more received one "dividend unit" for each year of residency after 1959, which was the first year of Alaska's statehood. The statute fixed the value of each unit at $50 so that a one-year resident would receive $50 while a resident of Alaska since 1959 would receive $1,050. The Court had little trouble invalidating this program; only Justice Rehnquist believed that the Court should defer to the legislative judgment to prefer old residents over new residents in this case.

The *Zobel* majority opinion, by Chief Justice Burger, asserted that the Court would not in this case define the appropriate standard of review for right to travel cases. The Chief Justice correctly noted that "if the statutory scheme could not pass even the minimal proposed by the state [the rationality standard], we need not decide whether any enhanced scrutiny is called for."[78] The majority then found that the law could not withstand even the minimal "rational relationship to a legitimate state interest" test.

The state had argued that the law served three purposes. First, the state claimed that the law created a financial incentive for individuals to establish and maintain their residence in Alaska. But the Court found that the law did not rationally promote that interest because the statute gave benefits retroactively rather than awarding benefits to those who remained in the state after the passage of the act.

---

73. 452 U.S. 412, 101 S.Ct. 2434, 69 L.Ed.2d 118 (1981).

74. 452 U.S. at 419, 101 S.Ct. at 2440.

75. 452 U.S. at 422, 101 S.Ct. at 2442.

76. 452 U.S. at 423–26, 101 S.Ct. at 2442–44. Justice White's concurring opinion was much clearer in terms of his equal protection analysis of the fundamental rights problem than was the majority opinion by Justice Stevens. Justice White employed the compelling interest test analysis used in Shapiro v. Thompson, 394 U.S. 618, 89 S.Ct.

1322, 22 L.Ed.2d 600 (1969) but concluded that the state's interests were significant enough to justify the burden on the right to travel of parents who had abandoned their child in the state. Jones v. Helms, 452 U.S. 412, 426, 101 S.Ct. 2434, 2444, 69 L.Ed.2d 118 (1981) (White, J., concurring).

77. 457 U.S. 55, 102 S.Ct. 2309, 72 L.Ed.2d 672 (1982).

78. 457 U.S. at 60–62, 102 S.Ct. at 2313–14.

Second, the state claimed that the law related to the prudent management of its oil revenue fund. However, the Court found that the law did not rationally promote that end by retroactively granting greater dividends to those who resided in Alaska during the 21 years prior to the enactment of the statute.

Finally, the state claimed that the apportionment of benefits by length of residency was done in recognition of "contributions of various kinds, both tangible and intangible, which residents have made during their years of residency."[79] The law certainly furthered this end. Indeed, the end was defined in terms of the discrimination between new and old residents which the state wished to maintain. The Court found that the state's goal of awarding citizens for past contributions to the state standing on its own was "not a legitimate state purpose ... the equal protection clause prohibits such an apportionment of state services."[80]

It is difficult to conceive of situations in which the state would have a legitimate interest in granting benefits to citizens based solely upon their length of residency in the state. While new residents are, by definition, different from old residents, that difference must relate to some legitimate purpose of the government if it is to be used as a basis for distinguishing between groups of persons for the dispensation of governmental benefits or burdens.[81] When a state grants benefits to citizens based solely on their length of residency in a state, a court may avoid the difficult problem of analyzing a judicial role in protecting the right to travel by finding that the law would fail any standard of review, including the rationality test.

For example, in *Hooper v. Bernalillo County Assessor,*[82] the Court invalidated a state statute that granted a property tax exemption to honorably discharged veterans of the armed forces who had served in the military during the Vietnam War era and who had become residents of the state before May 8, 1976. Chief Justice Burger wrote the majority opinion in this case; he found that the Court need not address the proper standard of review to be applied in right to travel cases generally because "if the statutory scheme cannot even pass the minimum rationality test, our inquiry ends." The majority opinion ruled that this tax statute allocated a tax benefit solely on the basis of length of residency and, therefore, was invalid. The majority opinion found that the state could give a tax benefit to all of its bona fide resident veterans because that action would constitute the dispensation of economic benefits, which do not involve fundamental rights, on a nonsuspect basis.[83]

The Court in *Hooper* was not required to address the question of whether the state had a special interest in granting benefits to persons who had been residents of the state during the time when they were called away for military service. The tax classification at issue in *Hooper* would have granted a tax benefit to a person who resided in the state as an infant before May 8, 1976, then moved to another and served in the armed forces, but recently returned to the state after 1976, whereas it would have denied a tax exemption to a person who had served in the military service for the same period of time but who had never resided in the state until a date after May 8, 1976. The Chief Justice found that: "[the statute] by singling out previous residents for the tax exemption, rewards only

---

79. 457 U.S. at 60–62, 102 S.Ct. at 2313–14.

80. 457 U.S. at 62–64, 102 S.Ct. at 2313–15, in part quoting Shapiro v. Thompson, 394 U.S. 618, 632–33, 89 S.Ct. 1322, 1330, 22 L.Ed.2d 600 (1969).

81. See also Williams v. Vermont, 472 U.S. 14, 105 S.Ct. 2465, 86 L.Ed.2d 11 (1985) (invalidating a state use tax provision that gave credit for sales taxes paid on the purchase of an automobile in another state to persons who were residents of the taxing state at the time that they paid the sales tax in the second state but denying a similar exemption from the use tax to persons who had not been residents of the state when they made the initial purchase of the automobile).

82. 472 U.S. 612, 105 S.Ct. 2862, 86 L.Ed.2d 487 (1985).

83. The Supreme Court previously had upheld the granting of state benefits to residents of the armed services. Personnel Administrator of Massachusetts v. Feeney, 442 U.S. 256, 99 S.Ct. 2282, 60 L.Ed.2d 870 (1979), on remand 475 F.Supp. 109 (D.Mass.1979), affirmed 445 U.S. 901, 100 S.Ct. 1075, 63 L.Ed.2d 317 (1980) (upholding state employment preference for veterans). The federal granting of benefits to veterans is also legitimate, see Johnson v. Robison, 415 U.S. 361, 94 S.Ct. 1160, 39 L.Ed.2d 389 (1974).

those citizens for their 'past contributions' toward our nation's military effort in Vietnam. *Zobel* teaches that such an objective is not a legitimate state purpose."[84]

While claiming not to establish any important principles regarding the judicial review of laws that burden the right to travel, Chief Justice Burger's majority opinions in *Zobel* and *Hooper* offer an insight into the judicial role in this area. In *Zobel* he noted that "right to travel analysis refers to little more than a particular application of equal protection analysis."[85] The Justices must independently examine state laws which seriously restrict the ability of persons to migrate from one state to another or laws which make distinctions between new and long-term residents. In *Hooper* Chief Justice Burger, writing for the Court, stated: "The State may not favor established residents over new residents based on the view that the state may take care of 'its own' if such is defined by prior residence. Newcomers, by establishing bona fide residence in the state, become the state's 'own'

and may not be discriminated against solely on the basis of their arrival in the state after [a specific date]."[86] As was pointed out in Justice Brennan's concurring opinion in *Zobel*, the Court has long recognized that the structure of the federal union requires Justices to actively review laws which burden the right to interstate migration; the basic concept of equality between citizens requires that the state not define citizens as deserving of more or less favorable treatment merely because of the length of their residence in the state.[87]

States may be able to limit the dispensation of benefits to those who are *bona fide* residents.[88] However, it may be difficult for states to "rebate" a specific portion of residents' taxes for past years after *Zobel*.[89]

In *Attorney General of New York v. Soto–Lopez*,[90] the Court invalidated state constitutional and statutory provisions that gave a preference in civil service employment to residents of the state who were veterans of the armed services and who had lived in the state

---

84. Hooper v. Bernalillo County Assessor, 472 U.S. 612, 624, 105 S.Ct. 2862, 2869, 86 L.Ed.2d 487 (1985).

85. 457 U.S. at 60 n. 6, 102 S.Ct. at 2313 n. 6.

86. Hooper v. Bernalillo County Assessor, 472 U.S. 612, 623, 105 S.Ct. 2862, 2869, 86 L.Ed.2d 487 (1985).

87. Zobel v. Williams, 457 U.S. 55, 65, 102 S.Ct. 2309, 2315, 72 L.Ed.2d 672 (1982) (Brennan, J., dissenting, joined by Marshall, Blackmun & Powell, JJ.).

88. In Attorney General of New York v. Soto–Lopez, 476 U.S. 898, 106 S.Ct. 2317, 90 L.Ed.2d 899 (1986), appeal after remand 840 F.2d 162 (2d Cir.1988), the Court invalidated a state statute and state constitutional provision that provided a preference in civil service employment to veterans who lived in the state at the time that they entered military service but denied a similar preference to resident veterans who lived outside the state on the date they entered military service. There was no majority opinion in this case. The plurality opinion, written by Justice Brennan, took the most strict view of the Court's role regarding independent review of classifications that directly impeded the ability to engage in interstate travel and to change one's residence from one state to another. Justice Brennan noted, however, that the Justices "have always carefully distinguished between bona fide residence requirements, which seek to differentiate between residents and nonresidents, and residence requirements, such as durational, fixed date, and fixed point residence requirements, which treat established residents differently based on the time they migrated into the State." 476 U.S. at 903 n. 3, 106 S.Ct. at 2321 n. 3 (plurality opinion by Brennan, J.).

89. The majority opinion by Chief Justice Burger in Zobel v. Williams, 457 U.S. 55, 64 n. 13, 102 S.Ct. 2309,

2315 n. 13, 72 L.Ed.2d 672 (1982) found that Starns v. Malkerson, 401 U.S. 985, 91 S.Ct. 1231, 28 L.Ed.2d 527 (1971), should not be read as contradicting the Court's position in Zobel that the state could not dispense benefits based solely upon a person's length of residency in the state. The Chief Justice, in that footnote, noted that *Starns* was only a "summary affirmance" and that the one-year residency requirement for in-state tuition status examined in *Starns* was reviewed as a "test of bona fide residence, not a return on prior contributions to the state."

Chief Justice Burger may have meant to indicate that the state could limit education benefits to those persons who were in-state residents but that the state could not make distinctions in the education benefits it gave to persons based upon their length of residency within the state. The tuition law must be reasonably related to determining that a person was a *bona fide* resident.

Justice O'Connor, in a concurring opinion joined by no other Justice, found Alaska's distribution scheme invalid under privileges and immunities clause of Article IV. Zobel v. Williams, 457 U.S. 55, 71–73, 102 S.Ct. 2309, 2318–20, 72 L.Ed.2d 672 (1982) (O'Connor, J., concurring). Justice O'Connor focused on the privileges and immunities clause as a means for justifying independent judicial review of laws which make distinctions between persons on the basis of the length of their residence in a state.

Regarding the privileges and immunities clause of Article IV see § 9.6, supra.

90. 476 U.S. 898, 106 S.Ct. 2317, 90 L.Ed.2d 899 (1986), appeal after remand 840 F.2d 162 (2d Cir.1988).

when they entered the military service. These state laws denied a similar preference to veterans who were current residents of the state and in all respects similar to the preferred veterans but for the fact that they did not live in the state when they entered military service. Because a majority of the Justices could not agree on a standard of review in this case, there was no majority opinion delivered for the Court.[91]

Writing for four Justices in *Soto–Lopez,* Justice Brennan announced the judgment of the Court. His plurality opinion stated that a fundamental right of interstate migration and travel had been established in prior decisions of the Court, although the Court had never thought it necessary to identify a precise source for that right.[92] Justice Brennan found that a state law implicates this fundamental right when impeding such travel is a primary objective of the law or when the law employs a classification to penalize persons exercising that right. In discussing the Court's equal protection decisions, Justice Brennan attempted to show that, "[w]henever a state law infringes a constitutionally protected right, we undertake intensified equal protection scrutiny of that law." [93] Justice Brennan believed that the Court must determine the appropriate standard of review for the judiciary to examine such laws before the Justices could turn to a ruling on the individual law.[94] When a fundamental right is restricted by a law, that law should be invalidated unless it is supported by a compelling governmental interest. He found

that the law at issue in *Soto–Lopez* established a penalty on interstate migration and that the law should be invalidated, "unless New York can demonstrate that its classification is necessary to accomplish a compelling state interest."

The plurality opinion in *Soto–Lopez* analyzed the interests asserted by the state of New York to justify its preference for veterans who had been residents of the state at the time that they joined the services. New York's asserted ends of encouraging residents to join the armed services, compensating residents for service at time of war, inducing veterans to return to New York, and providing a valuable class of public servants for New York might arguably be important or even compelling interests. The plurality found, however, that any of these goals could be achieved with a "lesser burden" on constitutionally protected activity by restructuring the preference without a distinction based purely upon whether a person had been a resident of the state at the time that he or she entered the military. The plurality concluded that the policy of compensating veterans with benefits from the state government, "even if deemed compelling, does not support a distinction between resident veterans based on their residence when they joined the military."

Chief Justice Burger, concurring in *Soto–Lopez,* asserted that the Court need not and should not determine the judicial review standard that should be employed when examining

91. The published report of this case as first issued by the United States Supreme Court stated that "Justice Brennan delivered the opinion of the Court." See, 476 U.S. at 899, 106 S.Ct. at 2319. However, Justice Brennan in fact did not deliver an opinion for the Court; his opinion was joined only by Justices Marshall, Blackmun, and Powell. Chief Justice Burger and Justice White filed concurring opinions that differed with Justice Brennan on whether the Court should resolve what standard of review was to be used in right to travel cases. Those two Justices only concurred in the judgment, not in Brennan's opinion. Justices O'Connor, Rehnquist, and Stevens dissented.

92. Attorney General of New York v. Soto–Lopez, 476 U.S. 898, 901–904, 106 S.Ct. 2317, 2320–21, 90 L.Ed.2d 899 (1986) (plurality opinion by Brennan, J.), appeal after remand 840 F.2d 162 (2d Cir.1988). Justice Brennan cited many of the cases examined in this section of the treatise for the principle that the Supreme Court had consistently recognized an implied constitutional right to interstate travel.

93. 476 U.S. at 903–904, 106 S.Ct. at 2321. Interestingly, Justice Brennan cited several opinions of the Supreme Court wherein the majority appeared to have employed only a rationality standard of review, such as City of Cleburne v. Cleburne Living Center, 473 U.S. 432, 105 S.Ct. 3249, 87 L.Ed.2d 313 (1985); Martinez v. Bynum, 461 U.S. 321, 103 S.Ct. 1838, 75 L.Ed.2d 879 (1983); San Antonio Independent School District v. Rodriguez, 411 U.S. 1, 93 S.Ct. 1278, 36 L.Ed.2d 16 (1973), rehearing denied 411 U.S. 959, 93 S.Ct. 1919, 36 L.Ed.2d 418 (1973). Justice Brennan cited specific language in each of these cases which could be read to show that the Court was engaging in some independent form of judicial review, although it was according very significant deference to the legislative authority in each case. Justice Brennan dissented in several of those cases, and he had accused the majority in some of them of not engaging in a sufficiently independent review of the classifications at issue.

94. 476 U.S. at 904–907 nn. 4, 6, 106 S.Ct. at 2322–23 nn. 4, 6 (plurality opinion by Brennan, J.).

laws that arguably restrict a right to engage in interstate travel or migration.[95] He believed that the law could not withstand scrutiny under even the most deferential equal protection test because it did not bear a rational relationship to any legitimate interest of the state. Justice White [96] also believed that the Court's previous decisions prohibiting a state from dispensing benefits purely on the basis of the length of time that a citizen had been a resident of the state [97] required invalidation of this law under the rational relationship standard. The opinions of Chief Justice Burger and Justice White echoed the principle that had been established in prior cases that a state could not merely define new residents as different and then use that asserted difference as a basis for disfavoring new residents.[98]

All of the decisions in which the Supreme Court found that state distribution of benefits based upon the length of a person's residency violated the equal protection clause appeared to involve rather straightforward forms of equal protection analysis even though the Court was not clear about the standard of review being used in those cases. The basic guarantee of equal protection is that similar people will be dealt with in a similar manner. Once the Court took the position that a state did not have a legitimate interest in rewarding long time residents simply because they were long time residents the Court removed any

legitimate interest the State might have asserted in distributing benefits based on a person's length of residency. In other words, these laws had no rational relationship to a legitimate interest because there was no legitimate reason for the state to give lower benefits to some persons simply because they were new residents in the state. However, had been difficult for the Court to describe the standard of review used in the earlier length of residency cases that had been decided under the equal protection clause.[99]

In *Saenz v. Roe*[100] struck down a law that accorded benefits based on the length of residency as a violation of the privileges or immunities clause of the Fourteenth Amendment.[101] Basing the ruling on the privileges or immunities clause allowed the *Saenz* Court to avoid any discussion of equal protection standards of review. In the future, the Court may determine that the length of residency cases that were decided on equal protection grounds were, in fact, cases that enforced the basic principles of the privileges or immunities clause of the Fourteenth Amendment.

§ 14.39 The Guarantees of the Bill of Rights as Fundamental Rights for Equal Protection Analysis: Introduction

The Court has applied most of the provisions of the Bill of Rights to the states because

---

95. Attorney General of New York v. Soto–Lopez, 476 U.S. 898, 912, 106 S.Ct. 2317, 2326, 90 L.Ed.2d 899 (1986) (Burger, C.J., concurring in the judgment), appeal after remand 840 F.2d 162 (2d Cir.1988).

96. 476 U.S. at 916, 106 S.Ct. at 2328 (White, J., concurring in the judgment). Justice White's entire concurrence consisted of the following statement:

"I agree with Justice O'Connor [who dissented in this case] that the right to travel is not sufficiently implicated in this case to require heightened scrutiny. Hence, I differ with Justice Brennan in this respect. But I agree with the Chief Justice that the New York statute at issue denies equal protection of the laws because the classification it employs is irrational. I therefore concur in the judgment."

97. The earlier decisions of the Court striking such classifications under the rational relationship standards of review are Zobel v. Williams, 457 U.S. 55, 102 S.Ct. 2309, 72 L.Ed.2d 672 (1982) and Hooper v. Bernalillo County Assessor, 472 U.S. 612, 105 S.Ct. 2862, 86 L.Ed.2d 487 (1985). Both cases are discussed in this section of the treatise.

98. Justices O'Connor, Rehnquist, and Stevens dissented because they believed that the law had only the most minimal effect on the constitutional right to travel or migrate. They asserted that the Court should defer to a legislature granting this type of benefit to a limited group of persons who had been residents of the state at the time that they made a special contribution to the nation. Attorney General of New York v. Soto–Lopez, 476 U.S. 898, 106 S.Ct. 2317, 2328, 90 L.Ed.2d 899 (1986) (Stevens, J., dissenting), appeal after remand 840 F.2d 162 (2d Cir. 1988); 476 U.S. at 918, 106 S.Ct. at 2329 (O'Connor, J., joined by Rehnquist and Stevens, JJ., dissenting).

99. See § 14.3 for a description of basic equal protection analysis and an overview of the standards of review used in equal protection cases.

100. 526 U.S. 489, 119 S.Ct. 1518, 143 L.Ed.2d 689 (1999).

101. The *Saenz* decision and its relationship to the nature of a constitutional right to travel were examined at the start of this section of the Treatise [§ 14.38], see notes 2–30, and accompanying text, supra.

it found them to be fundamental to the American system of government and inherent in the concept of liberty under the due process clause.[1] These rights also are to be considered as fundamental rights for the purposes of equal protection analysis.

However, laws which classify persons in terms of their abilities to exercise rights which have specific recognition in the first eight Amendments do not generally arise as equal protection issues. In these instances the denial of the right to one class of persons is likely to be held a violation of the specific guarantee without any need to resort to equal protection analysis. Thus, if the state or federal government were to deny to a specific class of persons the right to bail upon certain criminal charges, the classification should be analyzed to determine the compatibility of the law with the substantive guarantees of the Eighth Amendment prohibition of excessive bail, although it could just as easily be analyzed as an equal protection issue.

There are two areas of rights which deserve some specific mention because they have been the subject of particular interest in terms of the government's ability to establish laws which burden particular classes of persons in the exercise of these rights. The areas involve the exercise of rights protected by the First Amendment and the concept of fairness in the criminal justice system, which is derived from the various restraints placed upon the criminal process by the Bill of Rights.

§ 14.40   First Amendment Guarantees

Each of the guarantees of the First Amendment has been held to be a fundamental right and made applicable to the states through the due process clause of the Fourteenth Amendment. Thus whenever a state burdens the freedom of religion,[1] speech,[2] press,[3] assembly,[4] or petition[5] the law must be analyzed under the strict scrutiny required by the First Amendment as well as the general guarantees of the due process and equal protection provisions. The right of freedom of association is not mentioned in the First Amendment but is implied by its provisions and analyzed in the same manner as those specific guarantees.[6]

Whenever a state law impermissibly burdens the exercise of one of these rights there is actually a violation of the due process guarantee. Since the provisions are made applicable to the states by the due process clause, state laws which burden these rights constitute a denial of liberty as protected by that clause. Because the interpretation of the substantive guarantees of the First Amendment are the same regardless of whether the provisions are being applied to state or federal actions, there is little need to discuss substantive due process guarantees in these cases. This same analysis applies in equal protection cases.

It is generally unnecessary to analyze laws which burden the exercise of First Amendment rights by a class of persons under the equal protection guarantee, because the substantive guarantees of the Amendment serve as the strongest protection against the limitation of

§ 14.39

1. See §§ 11.5–11.7, supra. Contrast, e.g., Farber & Muench, The Ideological Origins of the Fourteenth Amendment, 1 Constitutional Commentary 235 (1984), with R. Berger, Government by Judiciary (1977). For additional references to materials regarding the history of the Fourteenth Amendment see our multi-volume treatise, 3 R. Rotunda & J. Nowak, Treatise on Constitutional Law: Substance and Procedure § 18.39 (3rd ed. 1999, with annual supplements).

§ 14.40

1. Cantwell v. Connecticut, 310 U.S. 296, 60 S.Ct. 900, 84 L.Ed. 1213 (1940) (free exercise clause); Everson v. Board of Education, 330 U.S. 1, 67 S.Ct. 504, 91 L.Ed. 711 (1947), (establishment clause).

2. Gitlow v. New York, 268 U.S. 652, 666, 45 S.Ct. 625, 629–30, 69 L.Ed. 1138 (1925); Fiske v. Kansas, 274 U.S.

380, 47 S.Ct. 655, 71 L.Ed. 1108 (1927); Stromberg v. California, 283 U.S. 359, 51 S.Ct. 532, 75 L.Ed. 1117 (1931).

3. Near v. Minnesota, 283 U.S. 697, 701, 51 S.Ct. 625, 626, 75 L.Ed. 1357 (1931).

4. De Jonge v. Oregon, 299 U.S. 353, 57 S.Ct. 255, 81 L.Ed. 278 (1937).

5. De Jonge v. Oregon, 299 U.S. 353, 364, 365, 57 S.Ct. 255, 260, 81 L.Ed. 278 (1937); Hague v. CIO, 307 U.S. 496, 59 S.Ct. 954, 83 L.Ed. 1423 (1939); Bridges v. California, 314 U.S. 252, 62 S.Ct. 190, 86 L.Ed. 192 (1941).

6. NAACP v. Alabama ex rel. Patterson, 357 U.S. 449, 460–61, 78 S.Ct. 1163, 1170–71, 2 L.Ed.2d 1488 (1958); Bates v. City of Little Rock, 361 U.S. 516, 522–3, 80 S.Ct. 412, 416–17, 4 L.Ed.2d 480 (1960).

these rights. Laws which classify persons in their exercise of these rights will have to meet strict tests for constitutionality without need to resort to the equal protection clause. Should the laws survive substantive review under the specific guarantees they are also likely to be upheld under an equal protection analysis, for they have already been found to represent the promotion of government values which override the individual interest in exercising the specific right.

For example, a law which requires public employees to refrain from partisan political activities creates a classification in terms of First Amendment rights. But the Court has decided that this restriction promotes an overriding governmental interest and is valid under the First Amendment. Therefore it is a permissible classification in terms of the equal protection guarantee.[7] Similarly if a law favors or burdens a religious group it will undergo strict scrutiny under the establishment and free exercise clauses of the First Amendment, so that we do not tend to see such laws analyzed as equal protection issues.[8]

Although the analysis of First Amendment classification under the equal protection guarantee is not common, it is important to remember that it is always permissible to review such laws under the guarantee. The First Amendment rights have been held to be fundamental and, therefore, the classifications in terms of the ability to exercise those rights are subject to strict judicial scrutiny.

For example in *Police Department of Chicago v. Mosley*[9] the Court invalidated a statute which prohibited pickets and demonstrations within 150 feet of local schools during school hours, but which exempted "peaceful picketing" caused by a labor dispute within the school. The Court found that the classification regarding permissible picketing was a violation of the equal protection guarantee for there was no overriding state interest to support a distinction between labor pickets and other forms of speech. While local governments might create laws to protect schools from disruption that were compatible with both the First and Fourteenth Amendments they could not classify the ability to speak in a manner that was not supported by overriding interest. In this case the Court specifically found that where statutory classifications affected conduct within the protection of First Amendment rights, it would be inappropriate to review them under traditional rational basis standards of the equal protection guarantee.[10]

This form of analysis may offer some benefits in decisions where the Court feels that the classification in terms of the fundamental right is not permissible but, for some reason, is unwilling to interpret the substantive guarantee of the First Amendment in terms of the state activity involved in the case.[11]

---

7. Broadrick v. Oklahoma, 413 U.S. 601, 607 n. 5, 93 S.Ct. 2908, 2913 n. 5, 37 L.Ed.2d 830 (1973).

See also California Medical Ass'n v. Federal Election Com'n, 453 U.S. 182, 101 S.Ct. 2712, 69 L.Ed.2d 567 (1981) (holding that limitations on contributions to multicandidate political committees which differed from the limitation placed on union and corporate contributions do not violate either the First Amendment or the equal protection component of the Fifth Amendment).

8. See, e.g., McGowan v. Maryland, 366 U.S. 420, 81 S.Ct. 1101, 6 L.Ed.2d 393 (1961) (Sunday closing law upheld against both claims); Sherbert v. Verner, 374 U.S. 398, 83 S.Ct. 1790, 10 L.Ed.2d 965 (1963) (law refusing unemployment benefits to those who will not work on Saturday violates free exercise clause; no need to examine equal protection).

9. 408 U.S. 92, 92 S.Ct. 2286, 33 L.Ed.2d 212 (1972).

10. 408 U.S. at 98–99, 102, 92 S.Ct. at 2291–92, 2293–94.

In Carey v. Brown, 447 U.S. 455, 100 S.Ct. 2286, 65 L.Ed.2d 263 (1980), the Supreme Court invalidated a state statute which prohibited the picketing of residences or dwellings but exempted from its prohibition the peaceful picketing of a residence which was also a place of employment involved in a labor dispute. The statute was found to violate the equal protection clause because it discriminated among picketers on the basis of the subject matter of their speech. As was true in *Mosley*, the Court chose to rest its decision on an equal protection rather than First Amendment rationale.

11. Taxation of the Press. Prior to 1991, it appeared that the Supreme Court had established a rule requiring strict judicial scrutiny of any tax that applied only to the press or to any subclass of the press. Then, in Leathers v. Medlock, 499 U.S. 439, 111 S.Ct. 1438, 113 L.Ed.2d 494 (1991), on remand 305 Ark. 610, 808 S.W.2d 785 (1991), the Supreme Court upheld the application of a general sales tax to the sale of cable television services or satellite subscription television services even though the sales tax exempted the print media. Justice O'Connor's majority opinion in *Leathers* stated that "taxation of speakers, even members of the press, does not implicate the First Amendment unless the tax is directed at, or

When the Supreme Court examines a classification that relates to First Amendment rights, it is possible that the Court will engage in only First Amendment, rather than equal protection, analysis. If the Court examines the classification under the First Amendment and finds that the classification does not violate any First Amendment right, the Court is unlikely to invalidate that classification under equal protection principles. When the Court is willing to directly examine a government classification regarding speech, assembly, or association under First Amendment principles, it has no need to engage in independent equal protection analysis. Thus, if the Supreme Court finds that a classification regarding speech or associational rights does not infringe First Amendment freedoms, it is likely to find that the classification does not violate equal protection because it has determined that the law does not constitute the improper allocation of a fundamental right. Such an equal protection ruling follows from the decision that the classification is consistent with the values of the First Amendment.[12]

§ 14.41   Right to Fairness in the Criminal Justice System

There is no single decision of the Court in which a majority of the Justices specifically recognize a "fundamental right" to fair treatment in the criminal justice system for purposes of equal protection analysis. However, the Court has established this right through a series of related decisions.[1] Most of the guar-

---

presents the danger of suppressing, particular ideas." Justice O'Connor found that differential taxation of First Amendment speakers is constitutionally suspect only when it "threatens to suppress the expression of particular ideas or viewpoints." In earlier cases, the Supreme Court had invalidated special taxes on the press on the basis of the equal protection clause or the First Amendment; the *Leathers* decision did not overrule any earlier decision of the Supreme Court. After *Leathers* it appears that a tax on members of the press will be subject to strict judicial scrutiny if: the tax is based on the content of publications; the tax is limited solely to the press; or if the tax is targeted at a small group of the press, or, other speakers, in a way that raises concerns about censorship or reprisal against particular viewpoints. *Leathers* found that the application of the general sales and use tax to cable and subscription television services was not based on the content of the programs carried by such services and that the tax did not raise concerns about censorship. Therefore, the tax at issue in *Leathers* was not subject to strict judicial scrutiny. A law that subjects the press, or a subcategory of the press, to special taxation should be subject to analysis under both First Amendment and equal protection principles, even though some of these taxes will be valid. See § 16.22.

12. See, e.g., Boos v. Barry, 485 U.S. 312, 108 S.Ct. 1157, 99 L.Ed.2d 333 (1988) (statute prohibiting certain congregations within 500 feet of an embassy in the District of Columbia is consistent with the First Amendment freedom of assembly and does not violate the equal protection component of the Fifth Amendment due process clause); Lyng v. International Union, 485 U.S. 360, 108 S.Ct. 1184, 99 L.Ed.2d 380 (1988) (Amendment to Food Stamp Act that restricted eligibility of a household for food stamps when a member of the household became unemployed due to a labor strike does not violate either the First Amendment right of association or the equal protection component of the Fifth Amendment due process clause); New York State Club Association, Inc. v. City of New York, 487 U.S. 1, 108 S.Ct. 2225, 101 L.Ed.2d 1 (1988) (statute prohibiting discrimination of various types by clubs that provide certain benefits to business entities

and members does not violate the freedom of association protected by the First and Fourteenth Amendments; the exemption of certain benevolent and religious organizations from the statute's restriction on discrimination does not violate equal protection); Dallas v. Stanglin, 490 U.S. 19, 109 S.Ct. 1591, 104 L.Ed.2d 18 (1989) (Supreme Court upholds a statute limiting the use of certain dance halls in the city to persons between the ages of 14 and 18; after finding that the statute did not infringe the implied First Amendment right of association the majority opinion finds that the statute should be upheld under the "rational basis" standard because it involved no suspect classification and no limitation of a fundamental constitutional right).

See generally, Strom, Senior Dist. J., quoting Treatise, in Richenberg v. Perry, 909 F.Supp. 1303, 1309 (D.Neb. 1995), affirmed 73 F.3d 172 (8th Cir.1995); Lozano, J., citing Treatise in TJ's South, Inc. v. Town of Lowell, 895 F.Supp. 1124, 1134 (N.D.Ind.1995);Economus, District Judge, citing Treatise in Angeline v. Mahoning County Agr. Soc., 993 F.Supp. 627 (N.D.Ohio 1998).

§ 14.41

1. In Cooper v. Oklahoma, 517 U.S. 348, 116 S.Ct. 1373, 134 L.Ed.2d 498 (1996) the Supreme Court ruled that a state law presuming that a defendant in a criminal case is competent to stand trial unless the defense could prove incompetence by clear and convincing evidence violated due process. Justice Stevens' majority opinion in *Cooper* referred to the basic fairness principles established by the due process clause as "guaranteeing a fundamental constitutional right." 517 U.S. at 366, 116 S.Ct. at 1383, in part relying on and quoting from, Patterson v. New York, 432 U.S. 197, 201–202, 97 S.Ct. 2319, 2322, 53 L.Ed.2d 281 (1977). This conclusion seems unassailable. Nevertheless, there is no decision of the Supreme Court with a majority opinion explaining the extent to which fundamental rights analysis justifies strict judicial scrutiny of legislative regulations of criminal trials that are challenged as being violations of substantive due process or equal protection principles.

antees of the Bill of Rights concern fairness in the investigation and adjudication of criminal charges against individuals. All of these provisions except for the grand jury clause of the Fifth Amendment have been found to be fundamental and made applicable to the states through the due process clause of the Fourteenth Amendment.[2] The Court has also found that the concept of due process itself requires the establishment of procedures which will result in the fair treatment of individuals when the state seeks to prosecute them on criminal charges.[3] In cases dealing with required filing fees or other practices which hamper the review of criminal convictions, the Supreme Court has established a right of access to courts to vindicate claims of mistreatment of individuals within the criminal justice system.[4] Taken together these cases recognize fairness in the criminal justice system as a fundamental right of each individual.

When a state takes actions which treat an individual unfairly in terms of the adjudication of his individual case, those actions may be reviewed under the due process guarantee as well as under specific Amendments.[5] When the government takes actions that burden the rights of a classification of persons in terms of their treatment in a criminal justice system it is proper to review these laws under the strict scrutiny standard for equal protection. However, it is often unnecessary to resort to equal protection analysis because the legitimacy of the law may be determined by the substantive interpretation of a specific guarantee of the Bill of Rights.

For example, if a state refuses to provide the assistance of counsel to indigent defendants at any "critical stage" of the proceedings prior to appeal it will have violated the Sixth Amendment guarantee of a right to counsel.[6] In these cases it is unnecessary to rely on an equal protection analysis since the Sixth Amendment itself requires equal opportunities for indigents. However, following conviction at trial the right to counsel has been analyzed

---

This section of the Treatise deals only with criminal cases. The Supreme Court has ruled that states must waive court filing fees, or transcript fees, in cases wherein the denial of access to the court would deny the ability to exercise a fundamental right to indigent persons. In Boddie v. Connecticut, 401 U.S. 371, 91 S.Ct. 780, 28 L.Ed.2d 113 (1971) the Court ruled that a state could not deny a divorce to a married couple solely because they did not have the financial resources to pay the required court fees. In M.L.B. v. S.L.J., 519 U.S. 102, 117 S.Ct. 555, 136 L.Ed.2d 473 (1996), the Court held that a state violated both due process and equal protection by denying an indigent woman the ability to appeal from a trial court determination permanently terminating her parental rights (permanently terminating her relationship to and her ability to visit her children) solely because she could not afford to pay for a transcript of the trial proceedings. See §§ 13.8, 13.9, 14.28 regarding required filing fees and the constitutional protection for family relationships. The Court has also required that filing fees be waived for candidates for political office who lack the financial resources to pay such a fee, because of the fundamental nature of the right to vote and the fundamental associational interest that are involved when political parties seek to place a candidate on the ballot. See § 14.32(b).

2. Hurtado v. California, 110 U.S. 516, 4 S.Ct. 111, 28 L.Ed. 232 (1884). See §§ 11.5–11.7, supra.

3. In re Winship, 397 U.S. 358, 90 S.Ct. 1068, 25 L.Ed.2d 368 (1970) (beyond a reasonable doubt standard—juvenile cases); Bounds v. Smith, 430 U.S. 817, 97 S.Ct. 1491, 52 L.Ed.2d 72 (1977) (prison law libraries).

4. See, e.g., Burns v. Ohio, 360 U.S. 252, 79 S.Ct. 1164, 3 L.Ed.2d 1209 (1959) (appellate filing fees); Bounds v.

Smith, 430 U.S. 817, 97 S.Ct. 1491, 52 L.Ed.2d 72 (1977) (prison libraries necessary for access).

Treatment of Children in the Criminal Process. When children are charged with crimes under "adult standards" they should receive the same procedural and substantive safeguards as adults. However, there may be limited circumstances under which the detention of a child in the criminal justice process might be permitted, even though an adult might not be kept in detention under similar circumstances. In Schall v. Martin, 467 U.S. 253, 104 S.Ct. 2403, 81 L.Ed.2d 207 (1984) the Supreme Court upheld a limited form of pretrial detention for juveniles who were accused of a serious crime. See also, Reno v. Flores, 507 U.S. 292, 113 S.Ct. 1439, 123 L.Ed.2d 1 (1993), on remand 992 F.2d 243 (9th Cir.1993) (upholding Immigration Naturalization Service regulations limiting, in almost all circumstances, the release from government custody of alien juveniles being held prior to a deportation proceeding to those juveniles who have a close relative or guardian in the United States). See § 10.6.

5. Rochin v. California, 342 U.S. 165, 72 S.Ct. 205, 96 L.Ed. 183 (1952); Mullaney v. Wilbur, 421 U.S. 684, 95 S.Ct. 1881, 44 L.Ed.2d 508 (1975). See generally, Brown, J., quoting Treatise in, State v. Martin, 191 Wis.2d 646, 530 N.W.2d 420, 423 (App.1995).

6. Gideon v. Wainwright, 372 U.S. 335, 83 S.Ct. 792, 9 L.Ed.2d 799 (1963). An indigent criminal defendant only has right to appointed counsel in those cases wherein the defendant receives a punishment of imprisonment. Scott v. Illinois, 440 U.S. 367, 99 S.Ct. 1158, 59 L.Ed.2d 383 (1979). For citations to additional cases, and secondary authorities, see the multi-volume edition of this treatise: R. Rotunda & J. Nowak, Treatise On Constitutional Law:

under an equal protection analysis.[7] The Court has held that counsel need only be provided in the first appeal.[8]

It was not until 1956 that the Court used equal protection analysis to require the government to provide a guaranteed minimum form of fairness to all defendants, regardless of whether the claim related to a right with specific recognition in the first eight Amendments. In *Griffin v. Illinois*[9] the Supreme Court held that the state had to provide a defendant with a stenographic transcript of criminal trial proceedings where that was necessary to his appeal. The state could not provide these transcripts to only a small class of defendants or those who offered to pay for them; the Court found that all defendants were entitled to some form of "equal justice." Although the state might not be required to provide an appellate system, once it did so, it was required to grant access to the system in ways designed to ensure fair treatment of individuals. This principle has been continually upheld by the Court. In the years since *Griffin* it has ruled that indigents must be provided with transcripts, or their functional equivalent, for appeal and post conviction proceedings.

The type of charge involved in the case does not alter the indigent's right to equal treatment as the Court has held that the state must waive transcript fees required for appeal even in cases which do not involve incarceration of the defendant. In *Mayer v. Chicago*[10] a unanimous Court held that the state must provide transcripts in all cases. The state's fiscal and other interests could not be promoted by eliminating access to basic review procedures for indigent defendants. The Court stated, "*Griffin* does not represent a balance between the need of the accused and the inter-

est of society; its principle is a flat prohibition against pricing indigent defendants out of as effective an appeal as would be available to others able to pay their own way."[11]

The Court has recognized through a series of decisions that part of the right to fair treatment in the criminal justice system is a right of access to review procedures. The state may not impose burdens on the indigent's right to access to courts unless it can demonstrate some truly compelling interest in the limitation. The Court has held that defendants may not be required to pay filing fees in order to have access to appellate courts[12] or even as a requirement for post conviction proceedings following appeals.[13]

Even after the defendant's right to counsel has expired, states may not take other actions to limit his access to the court. Thus the Court has held that where counsel is not provided to defendants for collateral attack proceedings, the state cannot prohibit prisoners from assisting each other with the preparation of papers seeking further review of their criminal convictions.[14] The Supreme Court has also extended this principle to include a right of access to the courts to contest deprivations of rights while in prison. Thus it held that the states could not prohibit inmates from providing assistance to each other in the filing of civil rights actions while they were in prison.[15] This right of access to courts includes a right to the materials that are necessary to prepare and file documents seeking review of criminal convictions or civil rights actions. States must also provide prisoners with adequate legal research materials for these purposes.[16]

The Court has not guaranteed that all defendants will be able to present their defense or prosecute their appeals with equal re-

Substance and Procedure Chapter 17 (3rd ed. 1999, with annual supplements).

7. Douglas v. California, 372 U.S. 353, 83 S.Ct. 814, 9 L.Ed.2d 811 (1963).

8. Ross v. Moffitt, 417 U.S. 600, 94 S.Ct. 2437, 41 L.Ed.2d 341 (1974).

9. 351 U.S. 12, 76 S.Ct. 585, 100 L.Ed. 891 (1956).

10. 404 U.S. 189, 92 S.Ct. 410, 30 L.Ed.2d 372 (1971).

11. 404 U.S. at 196–97, 92 S.Ct. at 416.

12. Burns v. Ohio, 360 U.S. 252, 79 S.Ct. 1164, 3 L.Ed.2d 1209 (1959).

13. Smith v. Bennett, 365 U.S. 708, 81 S.Ct. 895, 6 L.Ed.2d 39 (1961).

14. Johnson v. Avery, 393 U.S. 483, 89 S.Ct. 747, 21 L.Ed.2d 718 (1969).

15. Wolff v. McDonnell, 418 U.S. 539, 94 S.Ct. 2963, 41 L.Ed.2d 935 (1974).

16. Bounds v. Smith, 430 U.S. 817, 97 S.Ct. 1491, 52 L.Ed.2d 72 (1977).

sources, for it is incapable of leveling the economic ability of some defendants to pay for superior legal or investigative services that may be of some assistance to them. However, the Court has sought to guarantee a basic level of fair treatment as a fundamental constitutional right.[17] This distinction between insuring required fair treatment and leveling economic distinctions is the basis for the Court's rulings concerning the scope of counsel following a criminal conviction.

In *Douglas v. California*[18] the Court held that a state could not dismiss the appeals of indigent criminal defendants with a separate system which did not include representation by counsel for the defendant. While the state might not be required to establish an appellate system, it could not grant appellate review on the basis of the wealth of the individual defendants. Thus it was required to provide counsel for indigent defendants in their first appeal as of right in order to grant them a meaningful form of judicial review.

A decade later, however, the Supreme Court held that this principle did not require states to provide attorneys for indigent defendants in discretionary appeals or collateral attack proceedings following their first appeal as of right. In *Ross v. Moffitt*,[19] the Court held that these proceedings were not so essential to a fair determination of the individual criminal defendant's claims regarding his trial that they required the assistance of counsel. Furnishing the individual defendant with counsel and transcripts during his first appeal as of right sufficiently enabled him to receive fair treatment in the process of applying for discretionary appeals or collateral review of his conviction.

The Supreme Court has not yet fully considered the extent to which the right to fairness in the criminal process requires states to provide indigent defendants with access to other forms of assistance, or aid to present a defense or to prosecute an appeal. In *Ake v. Oklahoma*[20] the Court held that under the due process clause an indigent defendant, who makes a preliminary showing that his sanity at the time of the alleged offense is likely to be a significant factor at his trial, is entitled to access to a state-provided psychiatrist. This psychiatrist will examine him and assist in the evaluation, preparation, and the presentation of his defense. In addition, at the sentencing phase of a capital case, if the state introduces evidence of the future dangerousness of the indigent defendant that defendant is entitled to similar state-supported assistance. The issue has not often arisen in a manner which has received extensive judicial review, because many jurisdictions already provide for some form of investigative services or expert assistance, either through a public defender's office or direct payment for services in a limited group of cases.[21]

In addition to the unresolved equal protection issues there are also questions as to whether the Sixth Amendment right to compulsory process of witnesses might include some right to state assistance to secure expert testimony to aid in the presentation of a defense. If analysis in this area follows that used in the right to counsel decisions, one could expect the Court to find a right, under either the Sixth Amendment or the equal protection guarantee, to those forms of assistance which are necessary to a fair presentation of a particular defense but not to every form of

17. United States v. Chavez, 627 F.2d 953, 958 (9th Cir.1980) (Kilkenny, C.J., quoting an earlier edition of this treatise), certiorari denied 450 U.S. 924, 101 S.Ct. 1376, 67 L.Ed.2d 353 (1981).

18. 372 U.S. 353, 83 S.Ct. 814, 9 L.Ed.2d 811 (1963).

19. 417 U.S. 600, 94 S.Ct. 2437, 41 L.Ed.2d 341 (1974). For citations to additional Supreme Court cases, and secondary authorities, on this point, see 2 R. Rotunda & J. Nowak, Treatise on Constitutional Law: Substance and Procedure, ch. 17 (3rd ed. 1999, with annual supplements).

20. 470 U.S. 68, 105 S.Ct. 1087, 84 L.Ed.2d 53 (1985).

21. See also, Tuggle v. Netherland, 516 U.S. 10, 116 S.Ct. 283, 133 L.Ed.2d 251 (1995) (per curiam) (failure to provide indigent defendant in capital murder case with an independent psychiatrist, in violation of the principles established in *Ake*, does not in all circumstances require that the defendant's death sentence must be set aside; under some circumstances, reviewing courts might find the existence of a valid aggravating factor that was not affected by the constitutional error in the case). For an examination of criminal procedure issues, see W. LaFave, J. Israel & N. King, Criminal Procedure (1999).

assistance that a person of greater resources might secure in the private sector.

The right to equality in the criminal justice system also includes the right to fair treatment in sentencing. Most sentencing decisions are dealt with through the use of standards governing the discretion of the trial court and a determination of whether an individual sentence violates the cruel and unusual punishment clause of the Eighth Amendment.[22]

The equal protection issue arises where indigent defendants are incarcerated because they cannot pay a fine. The Court has used equal protection analysis rather than the Eighth Amendment prohibition of excessive fines to determine the constitutionality of these procedures.[23] The Court has held that the inability to pay a fine could not be used as a basis for extending the prison term of a defendant beyond the maximum period fixed by statute or imposing any incarceration on the individual when there was only a system of fines for punishment of those who were able to pay them.[24]

The rights in the criminal justice system relate either to specific guarantees or to fairness in the system of investigating and adjudicating individual claims. The Court has not held that the government is required to grant

any permanent form of economic benefits to persons in the criminal process because they are without funds to pay for them. Thus, the Court has upheld statutory provisions that require convicted indigent defendants to repay the state for the services of counsel that were provided them at trial or on appeal,[25] but those statutes which subjected these persons to arbitrary classifications in the enforcement of debts will be held to violate equal protection.[26]

§ 14.42 Interests That Do Not Constitute Fundamental Rights: Introduction

In this Chapter we have outlined those rights which the Supreme Court has held to be fundamental for purposes of reviewing classifications under the equal protection guarantee. When combined with the sections on the incorporation of the Bill of Rights,[1] we have a complete listing of all interests which the Supreme Court has found to be fundamental constitutional rights. While laws limiting these rights will be subjected to strict review under the due process and equal protection guarantees, laws limiting other rights will be subjected only to the rationality test because the Court finds them to be matters of "economics or social welfare." Under the due process guarantee of fair adjudicative proce-

---

22. See Solem v. Helm, 463 U.S. 277, 103 S.Ct. 3001, 77 L.Ed.2d 637 (1983) (life sentence without possibility of parole for repeated minor offenses held invalid).

23. Revocation of a defendant's probation for failure to pay a fine absent a determination that the defendant was responsible for the failure and that alternative forms of punishment are inadequate will violate the principle of fundamental fairness protected by the due process and equal protection clauses. Bearden v. Georgia, 461 U.S. 660, 103 S.Ct. 2064, 76 L.Ed.2d 221 (1983).

See also Black v. Romano, 471 U.S. 606, 105 S.Ct. 2254, 85 L.Ed.2d 636 (1985) (neither substantive due process nor procedural of due process principles require a court to consider alternatives to incarceration before revoking probation; due process guarantees fair treatment in determining whether the basis for the parole or probation revocation occurred but due process did not place a limit on the automatic probation revocation in this case). The concept of fundamental fairness protected by the due process and equal protection clauses restricts the ability of courts to incarcerate indigent defendants who have no control over the basis for their probation revocation, because they cannot afford to pay the fine. Neither due

process nor equal protection limits the ability of states to have automatic incarceration for probation revocation cases such as *Black* where the revocation is based upon a second criminal action undertaken by the defendant while on probationary status. The Court in *Black* did state: "we need not decide today whether concerns for fundamental fairness would preclude the automatic revocation of probation in circumstances other than those involved in *Bearden*." Black v. Romano, 471 U.S. at 615, 105 S.Ct. at 2259.

24. Williams v. Illinois, 399 U.S. 235, 90 S.Ct. 2018, 26 L.Ed.2d 586 (1970) (exceeding maximum sentence invalid); Tate v. Short, 401 U.S. 395, 91 S.Ct. 668, 28 L.Ed.2d 130 (1971), (incarceration in lieu of fine invalid).

25. Fuller v. Oregon, 417 U.S. 40, 94 S.Ct. 2116, 40 L.Ed.2d 642 (1974).

26. Rinaldi v. Yeager, 384 U.S. 305, 86 S.Ct. 1497, 16 L.Ed.2d 577 (1966); James v. Strange, 407 U.S. 128, 92 S.Ct. 2027, 32 L.Ed.2d 600 (1972).

§ 14.42

1. See §§ 11.5–11.7, supra.

dures,[2] the Court has granted some protection against the termination of individual interests which do not qualify as fundamental constitutional rights. Yet such procedural rights have not increased the substantive protection of those interests.

It would be fruitless to try to list all of the interests that the Court has held not to be fundamental, for it is composed of the entire universe of individual interests other than those which we have detailed in previously mentioned sections.[3] However, it is worth noting four particular interests that have been the subject of great debate as to their constitutional significance. The Court has refused to declare these to be of fundamental constitutional value. Even as to these interests we will list only the most recent, or major, decisions of the Court since the findings of "nonfundamentality" are part of every case in which the Court has considered a law burdening these interests. The four interests are: (1) governmental subsistence payments or welfare; (2) housing; (3) education; and (4) government employment.

When considering these rights one should also reflect upon the Supreme Court's refusal to find that classifications based on wealth are "suspect" or otherwise deserving of significant protection under the equal protection guarantee.[4] The rights which have been the subject of the most debate concerning whether they should be accorded fundamental constitutional recognition are those which relate to the allocation of resources to provide basic subsistence benefits. The argument that these rights

should be recognized as fundamental involves the concept that individuals are entitled to a minimum quantum of the items or benefits necessary to be a productive member of society and to enjoy other rights.

This concept relates in large measure to the philosophy expounded by John Rawls in *A Theory of Justice*,[5] and transformed into equal protection arguments by Professor Frank Michelman.[6] Professor Michelman has argued that the rights for the poor should be thought of not as requiring equal protection but as a constitutionally guaranteed "minimum protection." Under this theory of the equal protection guarantee the Court would have to decide upon the basic quantum of these items which was necessary for an individual to be a functioning member of modern American society who might enjoy a significant degree of liberty and the ability to exercise other fundamental rights. However, any such determination, no matter how strong the philosophy behind it, clearly does involve the reallocation of wealth through the means of judicial decisions.

Decisions which distribute benefits by striking wealth classifications may be attacked on an economic basis, in that these decisions may decrease the total "efficiency" or "product" of society and, thereby, injure all of society despite the original good motives of those making the reallocation of wealth. This argument against the Rawls-Michelman position was most ably expounded by Professor (now Judge) Ralph Winter, who took the position that the Court is institutionally incapable of making

---

2. See §§ 13.7–13.9, supra.

3. Thus in § 14.30(a), supra, we noted that the Court had not created a right to engage in consensual conduct or to live a particular "life style." For an in-depth analysis of these issues, see Wilkinson & White, Constitutional Protection for Personal Lifestyles, 62 Cornell L.Rev. 563 (1977).

4. See § 14.25, supra.

5. J. Rawls, A Theory of Justice (1971).

6. Michelman, On Protecting the Poor Through the Fourteenth Amendment, 83 Harv.L.Rev. 7 (1969). Professor Michelman has examined the theoretical basis for a constitutional right to welfare benefits and concluded that such rights may be better protected through the political process rather than the judicial process. However, Michelman believes that courts might play a significant role in protecting the ability of all groups to participate in the

democratic process; this function might include the judicial protection of certain minimum wants that are necessary for anyone's meaningful participation in society. See Michelman, Welfare Rights In A Constitutional Democracy, 1979 Washington U.L.Q. 659 (1979). Professor Appleton has analyzed Professor Michelman's theories in terms of the current debate between various schools of constitutional jurisprudence and, in so doing, has clarified the positions of those jurisprudential schools in the debate concerning welfare rights. See Appleton, Commentary: Professor Michelman's Quest for a Constitutional Welfare Right, 3 Washington U.L.Q. 715 (1979); Appleton, Beyond the Limits of Reproductive Choice: The Contributions of the Abortion-Funding Cases to Fundamental-Rights Analysis and to the Welfare-Rights Thesis, 81 Columbia L.Rev. 721 (1981).

wealth reallocation decisions.[7] Thus, he argued the Court should withdraw from reviewing legislative decisions on the allocation of basic benefits since there is no clear textual basis for such a judicial role. Indeed, he uses economic analysis to demonstrate that the Justices cannot be sure whether they are helping or hurting any specific class of individuals in making such economic impact decisions. Professor Winter's position may also be supported by a libertarian philosophy which advocates great freedom of individual action and a correspondingly limited role for government. Robert Nozick has advanced this type of political philosophy as a jurisprudential answer to the theory of Rawls.[8]

As we have noted in our discussion of wealth classifications, the Court has taken a middle road between these two positions. The Justices have held that fundamental rights may not be allocated by an individual's ability to pay for them; where no fundamental rights are involved the Court will not engage in active review of wealth classifications. Let us now briefly consider the major decisions of the Supreme Court by which it has refused to hold that basic economic benefits should be the subject of active judicial review.

§ 14.43   Welfare Payments

There is no opinion of the Supreme Court in which a majority of Justices have held that there is any right to receive subsistence payments or welfare benefits of any kind. Instead the Justices have considered such programs as general economic and social welfare measures which are to be reviewed under the basic ra-

tionality standard of the due process and equal protection guarantees.[1] These laws will be subjected to strict scrutiny if they dispense the benefits upon suspect criterion or exclude classes of persons upon a status which deserves active protection by the judiciary.[2] Similarly, these laws will be subject to the strict scrutiny test if the welfare system has limitations which burden other fundamental constitutional values such as the right to travel.[3] Where the state has declared that someone is "entitled" to receive these benefits, the individual has a right to a hearing, in accordance with the procedural due process guarantee, prior to their termination.[4] But even in the area of procedural due process the Court has left the states free to determine the basis upon which they will grant these benefits and the definition of those persons who are entitled to receive or retain them.[5]

The most vivid example of this type of analysis is contained in *Dandridge v. Williams*.[6] In this case the Court upheld a state law for the administration of Aid to Families with Dependent Children (AFDC) which in effect put an upper limit on the number of children for which any family could receive subsistence payments. The majority opinion by Justice Stewart not only upheld the law but found that it was one concerning only "economics and social welfare".[7] Thus, the majority subjected the classification and allocation of benefits to only the rational relationship-invidious discrimination test. The Court stated that although the classification "involved the most basic needs of impoverished human beings . . . we can find no basis for applying a different

7. Winter, Poverty, Economic Equality and the Equal Protection Clause, 1972 Sup.Ct.Rev. 41.

8. R. Nozick, Anarchy, State and Utopia (1974).

§ 14.43

1. See generally §§ 14.3, 14.25, 14.42. For analysis of Supreme Court decisions in a variety of areas relating to wealth classifications and an argument that the "antinobility clauses" [art. I, § 9 and art. I, § 10] justify a judicial role in the review of wealth transfer decisions of the government, see Delgado, Inequality "From the Top": Applying an Ancient Prohibition to an Emerging Problem of Distributive Justice, 32 U.C.L.A. L.Rev. 100 (1984).

2. See, e.g., Graham v. Richardson, 403 U.S. 365, 91 S.Ct. 1848, 29 L.Ed.2d 534 (1971) (aliens); see also New

Jersey Welfare Rights Organization v. Cahill, 411 U.S. 619, 93 S.Ct. 1700, 36 L.Ed.2d 543 (1973) (illegitimates).

3. Shapiro v. Thompson, 394 U.S. 618, 89 S.Ct. 1322, 22 L.Ed.2d 600 (1969).

4. Goldberg v. Kelly, 397 U.S. 254, 90 S.Ct. 1011, 25 L.Ed.2d 287 (1970).

5. This includes some ability to define the scope of even procedural guarantees, see Mathews v. Eldridge, 424 U.S. 319, 96 S.Ct. 893, 47 L.Ed.2d 18 (1976); see also Bishop v. Wood, 426 U.S. 341, 96 S.Ct. 2074, 48 L.Ed.2d 684 (1976). For an examination of these issues see §§ 13.7–13.9, supra.

6. 397 U.S. 471, 90 S.Ct. 1153, 25 L.Ed.2d 491 (1970).

7. 397 U.S. at 485, 90 S.Ct. at 1161.

constitutional standard."[8] This case also gave rise to the first exposition of a theoretical basis for a middle level standard of review between the strict scrutiny-compelling interest test and the minimal protection-rationality test.

In a dissenting opinion, which was joined by Justice Brennan, Justice Marshall took the position that the "mere rationality test," while well suited for testing economic and business regulations, should not be applied to the interests of the poor in basic subsistence. While these interests might not qualify as ones which deserved a form of strict review under which almost any legislative classification would be invalid, they did merit some meaningful form of judicial review. To Justice Marshall it made no sense to have equal protection or due process standards be an all or nothing dichotomy.[9] Instead, the Court should realize that there was a wide range of interests which required an independent determination of whether people were being treated in a nonarbitrary manner in terms of permissible governmental goals and the importance of the interested individual freedom in society. Although the Court has never adopted such an approach to welfare classifications Justice Marshall's views have given rise to a variety of academic justifications for a third standard of review under the equal protection guarantee.[10]

Following *Dandridge* the Court continued to uphold classifications relating to welfare benefits under the rationality test. Thus the Court has upheld classifications for the payment of

different forms of welfare which left families with dependent children in a much worse position, in terms of the percentage of their need that was met, than to other forms of welfare.[11] The Court's use of the rationality test to review welfare classifications has not been limited to those systems dispensing only cash subsistence payments. The Court has also upheld classifications relating to public housing[12] and public education[13] under this standard because it found no basis to strictly review any welfare distribution system which does not allocate fundamental constitutional rights or employ suspect criteria.[14]

It should be noted, however, that in two cases the Court did invalidate provisions of the Food Stamp Act under what seemed to be a more meaningful standard of review than the basic rationality test. In *United States Department of Agriculture v. Moreno*[15] the Court invalidated a section of the Food Stamp Act which made any household comprised of unrelated individuals ineligible to receive food stamps. Writing for six members of the Court, Justice Brennan indicated that the traditional rationality test was being employed,[16] although both the concurring and dissenting Justices could not agree to this position.[17] The majority opinion found that the disqualification of these households could further no legitimate governmental interests and that it seemed only to be the arbitrary and invidious exclusion of household units for which there was some public animosity.

8. 397 U.S. at 485, 90 S.Ct. at 1161.

9. Dandridge v. Williams, 397 U.S. 471, 517–22, 90 S.Ct. 1153, 1177–80, 25 L.Ed.2d 491 (1970), (Marshall, J., dissenting).

10. See, e.g., Gunther, In Search of Evolving Doctrine on a Changing Court: A Model for a Newer Equal Protection, 86 Harv.L.Rev. 1 (1972); Nowak, Realizing the Standards of Review Under the Equal Protection Guarantee—Prohibited, Neutral and Permissive Classifications, 62 Georgetown L.J. 1071 (1974). See § 14.3, supra.

11. Jefferson v. Hackney, 406 U.S. 535, 92 S.Ct. 1724, 32 L.Ed.2d 285 (1972).

12. James v. Valtierra, 402 U.S. 137, 91 S.Ct. 1331, 28 L.Ed.2d 678 (1971).

13. San Antonio Independent School District v. Rodriguez, 411 U.S. 1, 93 S.Ct. 1278, 36 L.Ed.2d 16 (1973).

14. The Supreme Court recently reaffirmed the principle that classifications relating to welfare benefits are to be upheld under the rational basis test so long as they

conceivably might relate to a legitimate governmental purpose, when the Justices unanimously upheld a federal law denying social security benefits to recipients who left the United States for 30 days. Califano v. Aznavorian, 439 U.S. 170, 99 S.Ct. 471, 58 L.Ed.2d 435 (1978).

See also United States R.R. Retirement Bd. v. Fritz, 449 U.S. 166, 101 S.Ct. 453, 66 L.Ed.2d 368 (1980) (Congress may eliminate payment of dual retirement benefits to some employees who had engaged in both railroad and non-railroad employment on any basis that is not "patently arbitrary or irrational"). For a more complete listing of decisions on this issue see § 14.3, supra.

15. 413 U.S. 528, 93 S.Ct. 2821, 37 L.Ed.2d 782 (1973).

16. 413 U.S. at 533, 93 S.Ct. at 2825.

17. 413 U.S. at 542–3, 93 S.Ct. at 2829–30. (Douglas, J., concurring); 413 U.S. at 546–7, 93 S.Ct. at 2831–32 (Rehnquist, J., dissenting).

In a companion decision, *United States Department of Agriculture v. Murry*[18] the Court invalidated a section of the act which disqualified any household that included a member who was over 18 years of age and who had been claimed as a tax dependent by a nonmember of the household in the previous year. The majority opinion invalidated this classification as an "irrebuttable presumption" due to the failure to make an individualized determination of need. However, Justice Marshall, in a concurring opinion, seems correct in noting that the due process and equal protection guarantees seem to merge in this situation.[19]

Unfortunately the Court did not in either instance explain why it was employing an increased standard of review, if indeed the Justices even appreciated that they were going beyond the rationality test. It may be that the Justices were less hesitant to strike a classification which separated very similar groups of claimants. It is also possible that a few Justices felt that this was so arbitrary that the classification violated the rationality test and that these Justices, when combined with the votes of Justices who would use an increased standard to review all classifications within welfare systems, formed a majority. In any event, these two decisions stand out as atypical findings that a law fails to meet the rationality test.

In *Lyng v. Castillo*[20] the Court upheld a provision of the Food Stamp Act that effectively disadvantaged members of traditional, nuclear families living together by declaring them to be a "household" and giving them fewer food stamp benefits than would be given to a group of unrelated individuals living together.[21] The majority opinion by Justice Stevens ruled that the law did not directly and substantially interfere with "family living arrangements," and therefore, did not "burden a fundamental right."

The majority in *Lyng* thus would review the classification only under the rational relationship standard.[22] It was not irrational for the federal government to assume that certain types of families were a group capable of achieving economic savings in the group purchasing of food and preparation of meals, even though many of these traditional families might not realize such savings. Thus, the law did not treat arbitrarily a type of household disfavored by the legislature.[23] The Supreme Court continues to endorse the use of the rational relationship test only, with its strong presumption of constitutionality and required deference to legislative authority, in cases involving classifications relating to welfare benefits.[24]

18. 413 U.S. 508, 93 S.Ct. 2832, 37 L.Ed.2d 767 (1973).

19. 413 U.S. at 517–19, 93 S.Ct. at 2837–38 (Marshall, J., concurring).

20. 477 U.S. 635, 106 S.Ct. 2727, 91 L.Ed.2d 527 (1986).

21. The portion of the Act at issue was set out at 477 U.S. at 636 n. 1, 106 S.Ct. at 2728 n. 1. The Amendments to the Act gave lesser food stamp benefits to groups of individuals who live together and customarily purchase food and meals together for home consumption than to unrelated individuals who might live together and purchase their food and prepare meals separately. The Act required that parents and children, or siblings, be treated as a single household even if they did not generally prepare meals together for home consumption, unless one of the parents or siblings was an elderly or disabled member of the household.

22. 477 U.S. at 638–39, 106 S.Ct. at 2729–30. The majority opinion recognized that the federal government's classifications were restricted by the implied equal protection component of the Fifth Amendment due process clause. 477 U.S. at 636 n. 2, 106 S.Ct. at 2729 n. 2.

23. The Supreme Court in *Lyng* distinguished *United States Department of Agriculture v. Moreno* as a case

where households of unrelated persons were excluded from food stamp benefits on a totally arbitrary basis that had no relationship to any legitimate interest of government. Lyng v. Castillo, 477 U.S. 635, 639 n. 3, 106 S.Ct. 2727, 2731 n. 3, 91 L.Ed.2d 527 (1986).

24. Justices Brennan and White dissented on the basis that the classification failed even the rationality test. Lyng v. Castillo, 477 U.S. 635, 643, 106 S.Ct. 2727, 2732, 91 L.Ed.2d 527 (1986) (Brennan, J., dissenting); 477 U.S. at 643, 106 S.Ct. at 2732 (White, J., dissenting). Justice Marshall dissented in an opinion that challenged the Court's continued adherence to two or three formal standards of review and argued that judicial use of any realistic standard of review would result in invalidation of the classification at issue. 477 U.S. 635 at 643, 106 S.Ct. at 2732, 91 L.Ed.2d 527 (Marshall, J., dissenting).

The Supreme Court applied this deferential standard of review in Bowen v. Gilliard, 483 U.S. 587, 107 S.Ct. 3008, 97 L.Ed.2d 485 (1987) when it upheld a statutory Amendment to the Aid to Families with Dependent Children program that effectively reduced the benefits for certain families by requiring these families to include within the family-unit (for determining the eligibility for benefits and the level of benefits) the income of all parents and chil-

Although a particular classification defining eligibility for welfare payments may have significant impact on a group composed primarily of women or illegitimates, that fact alone will not render the classification gender-based or illegitimacy-based for purposes of equal protection analysis.[25] Thus, the Court has upheld laws which required a spouse or a stepchild to have established their relationship to a deceased wage earner several months prior to the wage earner's death as a qualification for Social Security Act death benefits[26] and which gave greater benefits to a married, as opposed to divorced, spouse of a retired wage earner.[27]

The Supreme Court also upheld the Social Security Act restriction which makes "mother's insurance benefits" available to widows and divorced wives of a deceased wage earner if that spouse supports the children of the wage earner; the provision denied benefits to the mother of the wage earner's children if she was never married to the wage earner.[28] The provision was no longer gender based because the Supreme Court previously had invalidated the mother-father distinction in this program.[29] It was not a law discriminating on the basis of legitimacy or illegitimacy because the benefits were for the surviving parent and the qualification was a reasonable means of identifying surviving parents who were dependent upon a deceased wage earner at the time of the wage earner's death.[30] Because the law did not employ a suspect classification or discriminate between claimants based upon the immutable characteristics of gender or illegitima-

cy it was to be upheld under the rational basis test.

§ 14.44 Housing

The Supreme Court has never found that there is any right to government assistance to secure adequate housing or other forms of shelter. Indeed, the Court has not subjected governmental actions which might burden persons' abilities to find adequate private housing to any standard of review above the rationality test of the due process and equal protection guarantees. Of course, if these laws involve the use of suspect classifications or burden fundamental rights they will be subjected to the strict scrutiny standard of review. This dichotomy has been brought out in a series of decisions by the Court.

The Court has held that a city charter which required a referendum to implement a fair housing ordinance was invalid because the Court found it to effectively constitute a classification designed to exclude members of minority races from the locality.[1] However, when there was no proof that a referendum system was used to exclude minority members, the Court upheld a state constitutional provision that prohibited the development of low-rent public housing projects unless approved by a vote of the residents of the locality in which the housing unit was to be placed.[2] Although this voter approval clearly imposed a significant barrier to the establishment and

dren living in the same household (including the income of children who were receiving support payments from non-custodial parents).

25. See § 13.4, supra.

26. Weinberger v. Salfi, 422 U.S. 749, 95 S.Ct. 2457, 45 L.Ed.2d 522 (1975).

27. Mathews v. De Castro, 429 U.S. 181, 97 S.Ct. 431, 50 L.Ed.2d 389 (1976).

28. Califano v. Boles, 443 U.S. 282, 99 S.Ct. 2767, 61 L.Ed.2d 541 (1979).

See also, Bowen v. Owens, 476 U.S. 340, 106 S.Ct. 1881, 90 L.Ed.2d 316 (1986) (Court upholds now superseded provision of Social Security Act that granted survivors' benefits to wage earner's widowed spouse who remarried after age sixty but denied benefits to an otherwise similarly situated divorced widowed spouse who remarried after age sixty. The provision was reviewed only under the rational relationship standard).

29. Weinberger v. Wiesenfeld, 420 U.S. 636, 95 S.Ct. 1225, 43 L.Ed.2d 514 (1975).

30. Four Justices would have found that the primary purpose of the Social Security Act program in question related to providing support for children of the deceased wage earners through the surviving parent; these Justices would have invalidated the program as being impermissible based on a distinction between legitimate and illegitimate children. Califano v. Boles, 443 U.S. 282, 99 S.Ct. 2767, 61 L.Ed.2d 541 (1979) (Marshall, J., dissenting joined by Brennan, White, and Blackmun, JJ.)

§ 14.44

1. Hunter v. Erickson, 393 U.S. 385, 89 S.Ct. 557, 21 L.Ed.2d 616 (1969); see also Reitman v. Mulkey, 387 U.S. 369, 87 S.Ct. 1627, 18 L.Ed.2d 830 (1967).

2. James v. Valtierra, 402 U.S. 137, 91 S.Ct. 1331, 28 L.Ed.2d 678 (1971).

dispensation of public housing, it did not constitute the limitation of a fundamental constitutional right such as would require a meaningful form of review in the opinion of the majority. Similarly, the Justices have held that statistical disparities between racial representation in a locality will not prove that its exclusion of multi-family housing units constitutes a racial classification, absent proof that the zoning system is designed to purposely exclude racial minorities.[3] Thus, the Court has indicated that there is no right to the development of either multi-family or low income housing which justifies overturning a municipality's decision to exclude these uses from its zoning plan.

A similar refusal to recognize a right to housing in the private sector was evidenced in the Court's decision that states were free to enact summary eviction statutes which gave landlords a right to repossession of premises while excluding defenses based on the landlord's failure to meet his obligations under a building code.[4]

The Supreme Court's rulings regarding zoning ordinances appear to undercut an argument for a fundamental constitutional right to adequate housing or a freedom of choice regarding housing.[5]

In *Cuyahoga Falls v. Buckeye Community Hope Foundation*[6] the Justices unanimously rejected both equal protection and due process challenges to a city's refusal to grant building permits for a low-income housing project pending a voter referendum and a judicial review of the legality of that referendum. The city in this case had initially passed an ordinance that allowed the building of a housing complex for low-income persons. Pursuant to city law, the city administrators refused to issue building permits to begin the construction project after some voters had initiated a referendum process that might overturn the ordinance that allowed the construction of the low-income housing units. The referendum that would have prohibited the low-income housing was approved by a majority of the voters. However, the referendum ultimately had no effect because the state supreme court ruled that the city ordinance authorizing construction of housing was not subject to repeal through a referendum process. Following the state supreme court's decision, the not-for-profit corporation that was responsible for creation of the low-income housing, received the building permits and was able to begin construction of the project.

The not-for-profit corporation, in the *Cuyahoga Falls* case, sought damages for the delay in the building of the project, based on allegations that the city's refusal to issue permits to the not-for-profit corporation, violated both equal protection and due process. Justice O'Connor, writing for a unanimous Court, found that the corporation was unable to sustain an equal protection clause challenge against the city officials because there was no proof that city officials' refusal to grant the building permits pending the referendum process was based on racially discriminatory intent.[7] While there was some proof that the voters who sought to repeal the ordinance that had allowed the housing project were motivated by racial bias, there was no proof that would have allowed the Court to find that any government officials, or anyone who might be considered to be a state actor, had taken actions based on racially discriminatory motives.[8]

---

3. Arlington Heights v. Metropolitan Housing Development Corp., 429 U.S. 252, 97 S.Ct. 555, 50 L.Ed.2d 450 (1977).

4. Lindsey v. Normet, 405 U.S. 56, 92 S.Ct. 862, 31 L.Ed.2d 36 (1972).

5. Regarding the taking of property issue and zoning laws see § 11.12 of this treatise.

6. 538 U.S. 188, 123 S.Ct. 1389, 155 L.Ed.2d 349 (2003).

7. 538 U.S. at 194–98, 123 U.S. at 1394–96 (Part II of majority opinion). In the lower federal courts, the not-for-profit corporation had alleged that the delay in the grant-

ing of the building permits violated the Federal Fair Housing Act, 42 U.S.C.A. § 3601 at et seq., because the city's action had a disparate impact on racial minorities. At the United States Supreme Court, the corporation abandoned the Fair Housing Act claim; and the Supreme Court did not have to rule on whether the impact of the city's actions were such that they would have violated the federal statute. 538 U.S. at 200, 123 S.Ct. at 1397.

8. Supreme Court's decision in the *Cuyahoga Falls* case did not modify any previous decisions finding that actions taken jointly by government officials and private persons would constitute state action subject to constitutional restraints, nor did the Court's decision alter any of

There was neither a fundamental right nor a suspect classification involved in the case; the Court reviewed the law under a rationality standard. Justice O'Connor ruled that the actions of the administrators in this case, which followed city law, could not be considered so arbitrary as to violate substantive due process principles.[9]

§ 14.45 Education

The Supreme Court has not held that publicly financed primary or secondary education is a fundamental right. It has avoided the ultimate issue, but it has refused to impose upon the states the requirement that they provide equal access to high quality forms of education.[1] However, the Court has held that once educational rights are granted a student, they cannot be terminated without procedural due process safeguards,[2] although these safeguards will not protect the individual student against certain actions, such as physical punishment, within the school system.[3] Under the guarantees of due process and freedom of religion the Court has recognized that individuals have the right to withdraw their children from the public school system and send them to private schools.[4] These private schools may be made to meet certain educational standards, but the state may not control all facets of their curriculum.[5]

The most important decision of the Court concerning a "right" to education is *San Antonio Independent School District v. Rodriguez.*[6] In this case the Supreme Court, by a five to four vote, upheld the use of local property taxes to finance primary and secondary education, although the system allowed areas within a single school district to have great disparities in the amount of money spent per student on educational programs and resources.

The majority opinion, by Justice Powell, applied the standard of minimal scrutiny; it found it arguably reasonable for the legislature to use local property taxation to advance goals of local control over schools. The Court accepted these interests at face value and never inquired whether the system in fact bore a rational relationship to a state interest of a quality sufficient to justify the lower standard of education for children in the least wealthy districts. The majority opinion never found it

the standards regarding the basis upon which racially discriminatory purpose in the administration of laws can be proven. See § 12.3 of this Treatise regarding the finding of state action in conspiracies, or other joint activities, involving both private persons and government officials. See § 14.4 of this Treatise regarding the basis upon which a law that is racially neutral in its language may be found to constitute a racial classification based on the intent of persons who enacted the law or the intent of persons who administered the law.

9. Justice O'Connor's opinion cited both cases finding that executive action could not be overturned under substantive due process principles unless it was arbitrary and capricious, and cases employing a rationality standard to review legislative actions under the due process and equal protection clauses. Cuyahoga Falls v. Buckeye Community Hope Foundation, 538 U.S. 188, 123 S.Ct. 1389, 1396, 155 L.Ed.2d 349 (2003) (Part III of majority opinion). Justices Scalia and Thomas wrote an opinion concurring in both the opinion and the judgment of the Court; they restated their view that an arbitrary executive action by a government official would not violate substantive due process principles. 538 U.S. at 200, 123 S.Ct. at 1397 (Scalia, J., joined by Thomas, J., concurring). The not-for-profit corporation, which challenged the temporary denial of the building permit, had not alleged violations of procedural due process principles; and the majority did not examine procedural due process principles. Justice Scalia's concurring opinion noted that the outcome of a popular referendum had never been found to violate procedural due

process principles in past cases. See § 13.8 regarding the general principles the Court uses to determine whether a governmental process meets procedural due process standards. In its brief to the United States Supreme Court, the not-for-profit corporation whose building permits had been delayed alleged that city officials acted jointly with private persons to block the housing project because of the race of persons who were likely to be residents of that project. However, that claim had not been reviewed by the lower courts and, it was abandoned at oral argument before the United States Supreme Court. Cuyahoga Falls v. Buckeye Community of Hope Foundation, 538 U.S. 188, 197, 123 S.Ct. 1389, 1395, 155 L.Ed.2d 349 (2003).

§ 14.45

1. San Antonio Independent School District v. Rodriguez, 411 U.S. 1, 93 S.Ct. 1278, 36 L.Ed.2d 16 (1973).

2. Goss v. Lopez, 419 U.S. 565, 95 S.Ct. 729, 42 L.Ed.2d 725 (1975).

3. Ingraham v. Wright, 430 U.S. 651, 97 S.Ct. 1401, 51 L.Ed.2d 711 (1977).

4. Pierce v. Society of Sisters, 268 U.S. 510, 45 S.Ct. 571, 69 L.Ed. 1070 (1925); see also, Wisconsin v. Yoder, 406 U.S. 205, 92 S.Ct. 1526, 32 L.Ed.2d 15 (1972).

5. Meyer v. Nebraska, 262 U.S. 390, 43 S.Ct. 625, 67 L.Ed. 1042 (1923).

6. 411 U.S. 1, 93 S.Ct. 1278, 36 L.Ed.2d 16 (1973).

necessary to inquire as to whether the state's legitimate goals would still be met if an equal amount of money was expended on the education of each child in the state. The Court found that no suspect classification was involved since there was no correlation in this case between district wealth and race.

It had been argued that the relationship between education and fundamental freedoms of speech and voting should establish education as a fundamental right, but the opinion found no authority to guarantee the citizenry the most effective participation in the public process. The majority opinion did not exclude the possibility that some level of educational opportunity might be a fundamental right but it stated that—

> [e]ven if it were conceded that some identifiable quantum of education is a constitutionally protected prerequisite to the meaningful exercise of either right we have no indication that the [low taxation] system fails to provide each child with an opportunity to acquire the basic minimal skills.[7]

Thus, there appears to be no fundamental right to receive publicly funded education above the possibility of some amount so minimal that it could be provided by a very small, and unequal, expenditure of public funds.

Because education has not been deemed to be a "fundamental right," most laws which regulate access to education or allocate differ-

ing amounts of educational benefits to different classes of persons will not be subject to strict judicial scrutiny. However, if a state singles out a class of children and denies them all educational opportunity, that classification should be subject to some form of independent judicial review.[8] The basis upon which the class is defined need not be suspect because the singling out of an identified class of children for complete denial of this important governmental benefit would seem to be arbitrary on its face.

For example, if a state denied all state funded education to left-handed children or red-haired children, one would assume that the law would be subject to some meaningful form of judicial review and that the Justices would not simply presume that the legislature was acting within its constitutional authority by refusing to grant any educational benefits to these children. Thus, the Court invalidated a state statute which denied public education to the children of illegally resident aliens, even though the Court refused to find that education was a fundamental right or that illegal aliens constituted a class of persons who merited close judicial scrutiny of laws which disadvantaged them.[9]

Because education is not a fundamental right, the Supreme Court has allowed states to restrict the provision of tuition-free education to children who are bona fide residents of the state or local school district.[10] Of course, a

---

7. 411 U.S. at 36–67, 93 S.Ct. at 1298–99.

8. In Papasan v. Allain, 478 U.S. 265, 106 S.Ct. 2932, 92 L.Ed.2d 209 (1986), the Supreme Court held that the Eleventh Amendment barred federal court resolution of a claim seeking to require state officials to provide appropriate "trust income" (from the sale of land that originally belonged to the Chickasaw Indian nation) for certain school districts. In that decision, the Court also found that a claim alleging that the disparity in distribution of school funds violated the equal protection clause was not barred by the Eleventh Amendment. Justice White noted that the Court had used only the rational relationship standard to review disparities in the funding of educational school districts, but that "this Court has not yet definitively settled the questions whether a minimally adequate education is a fundamental right and whether a statute alleged to discriminatorily infringe that right should be accorded heightened equal protection review." 478 U.S. at 285, 106 S.Ct. at 2944.

Thus, in cases involving an alleged deprivation of a minimally adequate education to a classification of stu-

dents, a plaintiff should be allowed to place into evidence facts demonstrating that a state's or city's funding of education fails to provide children with a minimally adequate education. The issues regarding whether there is a right to minimally adequate education and whether all state and local laws regarding education should be upheld so long as they are merely "rational" remain open.

For an examination of the theoretical basis for independent judicial review of laws denying children the opportunity for a meaningful education see Levin, Education as a Constitutional Entitlement: A Proposed Judicial Standard for Determining How Much is Enough, 3 Washington U.L.Q. 703 (1979).

9. Plyler v. Doe, 457 U.S. 202, 102 S.Ct. 2382, 72 L.Ed.2d 786 (1982), rehearing denied 458 U.S. 1131, 103 S.Ct. 14, 73 L.Ed.2d 1401 (1982). This case is analyzed in § 14.13, supra.

10. The Supreme Court, by an eight to one vote, upheld a state statute which permitted a school district to deny tuition free education to a child who lived apart from

state may not deny educational benefits or even limit educational opportunities to persons because of constitutionally suspect criteria. Laws that allocate educational benefits on the basis of race, national origin, or United States citizenship should be subject to strict judicial scrutiny.[11] The Court has not yet prohibited states from offering "separate but equal" educational opportunities to males and females on the basis of their gender. However, any law allocating educational benefits on the basis of gender should be held invalid unless the state can demonstrate that the classification is substantially related to an important state interest.[12]

Applying the foregoing principles, the Supreme Court found that a school district fee for transportation to a public grade school or high school did not violate the equal protection clause. In *Kadrmas v. Dickinson Public Schools*[13] the Court upheld interrelated state and local legislation that resulted in some school districts in North Dakota providing transportation to their local public school at

no cost for students, while other districts in the state imposed a fee for such transportation and denied school bus transportation to those families who could not or would not pay the fee. Justice O'Connor wrote the majority opinion in *Kadrmas;* she found that the bus fee classification was subject only to the most lenient standard of review and would be upheld so long as it was rationally related to a legitimate government purpose. The majority opinion noted that education had never been found to be a fundamental right and, therefore, that the nature of the right being allocated in this case did not justify strict judicial review. Justice O'Connor's majority opinion found that the Court's earlier decision striking a state statute that denied all publicly funded education to children who could not prove that they were in the United States lawfully should be limited to its own facts, because it represented a unique situation involving the total denial of education to a group of children resident in the state and a penalty on children for the illegal conduct of their parents.[14] The

---

his parent or lawful guardian if the child's presence in the school district was "for the primary purpose" of attending school in the district. Martinez v. Bynum, 461 U.S. 321, 103 S.Ct. 1838, 75 L.Ed.2d 879 (1983). "A bona fide residence requirement, appropriately defined and uniformly applied, furthers the substantial state interest in assuring that services provided for its residents are enjoyed only by residents." 461 U.S. at 328, 103 S.Ct. at 1842.

The majority opinion found that this residence requirement did not violate the equal protection clause because it was not based on a suspect classification and it did not limit the exercise of a fundamental right. 461 U.S. at 328, 103 S.Ct. at 1842–43 n. 7. *Martinez* held that the statute at issue was a bona fide residence requirement because it provided free education for all children who resided in the school district with the intent to remain in the district indefinitely. The Court did not pass upon the residency claim of the child in this case, a United States citizen whose parents were non-resident aliens living in Mexico. See 461 U.S. at 333, 103 S.Ct. at 1845 (Brennan, J., concurring). Only Justice Marshall would have invalidated the residency requirement on its face. 461 U.S. at 334, 103 S.Ct. at 1845 (Marshall, J., dissenting).

Residency Requirements for Higher Education Benefits. The Supreme Court has upheld the granting of lower tuition benefits at state universities to students who are bona fide residents of the state, although it has subjected the state system for determination of residency to independent judicial review under the due process clause. Starns v. Malkerson, 401 U.S. 985, 91 S.Ct. 1231, 28 L.Ed.2d 527 (1971), summarily affirming 326 F.Supp. 234 (D.Minn.1970); Vlandis v. Kline, 412 U.S. 441, 93 S.Ct. 2230, 37 L.Ed.2d 63 (1973). See § 14.38 regarding edu-

cation benefits and the right to travel. See generally, Strickman, The Tuition-Poor, the Public University, and Equal Protection, 29 U.Fla.L.Rev. 595 (1977).

11. See §§ 14.5–14.13, supra. In order to demonstrate that a school system is allocating benefits on a constitutionally and permissible criteria such as race or national origin, the person attacking the system must show that the law on its face allocates educational benefits on that basis or that the law which has a disadvantageous impact on a racial or ethnic minority was enacted or maintained for a racially discriminatory purpose, see § 14.4, supra.

12. See, Mississippi University for Women v. Hogan, 458 U.S. 718, 102 S.Ct. 3331, 73 L.Ed.2d 1090 (1982) (invalidating state exclusion of men from state operated nursing schools under the substantial relationship test but refusing to address the question of whether states can provide separate but equal educational benefits for persons based upon their gender). See United States v. Virginia, 518 U.S. 515, 116 S.Ct. 2264, 135 L.Ed.2d 735 (1996) (finding that a state university that used a military education type of teaching program violated the equal protection clause by totally excluding women from the program and the college). This case is examined in §§ 14.20, 14.23 of this Treatise.

13. 487 U.S. 450, 108 S.Ct. 2481, 101 L.Ed.2d 399 (1988).

14. Justice O'Connor's majority opinion seemed to limit the decision in Plyler v. Doe, 457 U.S. 202, 102 S.Ct. 2382, 72 L.Ed.2d 786 (1982) to its facts. Kadrmas v. Dickinson Public Schools, 487 U.S. 450, 457–60, 108 S.Ct. 2481, 2487–88, 101 L.Ed.2d 399 (1988). See § 14.13 for an analysis of the problem involved in *Plyler*.

classification at issue in *Kadrmas* denied benefits to persons who could not afford to pay for access to the school bus transportation, but classifications based on wealth, or the lack thereof, have not been subjected to strict judicial scrutiny when those classifications did not relate the fundamental rights. Under the rational relationship to a legitimate government objective test, Justice O'Connor, in her majority opinion, stated that it was "quite clear that a state's decision to allow local school boards the option of charging patrons a user fee for bus service is constitutionally permissible." Encouraging the development of school bus service without using general revenues to subsidize that service was a legitimate end; the Court found that the state and local system of legislation was rationally related to that end. Thus, the denial of bus service to those children who could not or would not pay the fee was not so arbitrary or invidious as to violate the equal protection guarantee.

While the Court has not authorized judicial intervention in school regulations generally, the judiciary should protect students in the exercise of their fundamental rights even though they seek to exercise those rights in an educational setting. Thus, the Court has required that school systems respect students' rights to speak and present ideas in a manner compatible with the orderly operation of the school.[15]

While the Court has not granted strict review over the substantive limitations on access to public education it has applied the procedural due process requirements to the denial of educational benefits. In *Goss v. Lopez*[16] the Court held that fair procedures had to be established for determining the basis of the suspension of students from public school systems. Since state law appeared to allow students to continue with their education, absent dismissal for cause, they had a property right

or "entitlement" to continued access to the educational system. When the suspension or termination of their educational benefits may affect their employment or associational opportunities in the future, they may also be deprived of a constitutionally significant interest in liberty by such a suspension.

However, the Court has refused to extend the rationale of *Goss* to protect the student's interests against the arbitrary imposition of disciplinary actions which do not involve the termination or suspension of the educational benefits. Thus, in *Ingraham v. Wright*[17] the Court refused to impose any meaningful federal limitations on the imposition of corporal punishment on students in public school systems. The majority held that the Eighth Amendment prohibition of cruel and unusual punishment did not apply outside of the criminal setting.

As the dissent in *Ingraham* pointed out, this reading of history makes the safeguard apply only to areas in which punishments are least likely to offend the principles of society.[18] The majority opinion did recognize that the taking of physical discipline against the student did constitute a deprivation of his or her liberty[19] but it found that the possibility of later tort suits against the teachers was a sufficient process to safeguard this interest under the due process clause.

§ 14.46   Government Employment

So long as the government does not employ suspect criteria or burden fundamental rights, the Court defers to legislative and executive judgments concerning the terms of public employment in the same way it treats other forms of economic and social welfare legislation. Thus, the Court has upheld mandatory retirement from government service at age 50 since classifications by age are not "suspect" or of special constitutional significance.[1]

---

15. See, Tinker v. Des Moines Independent Community School District, 393 U.S. 503, 89 S.Ct. 733, 21 L.Ed.2d 731 (1969).

16. 419 U.S. 565, 95 S.Ct. 729, 42 L.Ed.2d 725 (1975).

17. 430 U.S. 651, 97 S.Ct. 1401, 51 L.Ed.2d 711 (1977).

18. 430 U.S. at 692, 97 S.Ct. at 1423 (White, J., dissenting).

19. 430 U.S. at 674, 97 S.Ct. at 1414.

§ 14.46

1. Massachusetts Board of Retirement v. Murgia, 427 U.S. 307, 96 S.Ct. 2562, 49 L.Ed.2d 520 (1976). It should be noticed that the mandatory retirement policy did not constitute an invalid "irrebuttable presumption" of inability to fasten in a position.

In *Vance v. Bradley*[2] the Supreme Court, with only one dissent, upheld a requirement that participants in the foreign service retirement system[3] retire from their government positions at age 60. The plaintiff employees had alleged that the distinction between the mandatory retirement at age 60 for their job classifications and the general federal requirement of retirement at age 70 for the federal Civil Service Retirement System personnel violated the equal protection component of the Fifth Amendment.

The Court, in an opinion by Justice White, found that the retirement classification should be tested by general equal protection principles,[4] but that it did not violate the equal protection guarantee. Although the parties agreed that the law should be tested under the traditional rational basis standard, Justice White's opinion stressed that the federal judiciary is not to review seriously those classifications that do not involve fundamental rights or suspect classifications:

> The Constitution presumes that, absent some reason to infer antipathy, even improvident decisions will eventually be rectified by

the democratic process and that judicial intervention is generally unwarranted no matter how unwisely we may think a political branch has acted. Thus, we will not overturn such a statute unless the varying treatment of different groups or persons is so unrelated to the achievement of any combination of legitimate purposes that we can only conclude that the legislature's actions were irrational.[5]

The majority then applied the rational basis test, which had been employed in *Massachusetts Board of Retirement v. Murgia*[6] to uphold a mandatory retirement of state police officers at age 50, to the retirement classification. Although it appeared that the plaintiffs had abandoned their claim that the classification between those over and under age 60 was irrational, and only pressed the claim of discrimination between foreign service employees and civil service employees, the majority opinion made it clear that the rational relationship test was the only form of review justified for reviewing any aspect of this mandatory retirement program.[7]

Congress in the Age Discrimination in Employment Act of 1967, 29 U.S.C.A. § 621 et seq. as amended by the Age Discrimination in Employment Act Amendments of 1978, Pub.L. No. 95–256 (April 6, 1978), has made it unlawful for covered employers to discriminate against or discharge individuals between the ages of 40 and 70 due to their ages.

The congressional extension of the Age Discrimination Act, which applies the Act to state and local governments, is within the federal commerce power and does not violate any right of state and local governments that is protected by the Tenth Amendment. E.E.O.C. v. Wyoming, 460 U.S. 226, 103 S.Ct. 1054, 75 L.Ed.2d 18 (1983). Congress has excluded some federal employees from the provisions of the Age Discrimination Act. A federal statute requiring certain federal employees to retire at a specified age, such as requiring federal fire fighters to retire at age 55, does not in itself establish that a similar age is a bona fide occupational qualification for similar private sector employees or employees of other governmental units. Johnson v. Mayor and City Council of Baltimore, 472 U.S. 353, 105 S.Ct. 2717, 86 L.Ed.2d 286 (1985). For examinations of the Age Discrimination Act, and its interpretation by the courts, see generally, 3 A. Larson, Employment Discrimination, Chapter 21, §§ 98.00–108.20 (1984). For citations to additional Supreme Court cases, and secondary authorities, on this point, see 3 R. Rotunda & J. Nowak, Treatise on Constitutional Law: Substance and Procedure §§ 18.3, 18.45 (2d ed. 1992, with annual supplements).

2. 440 U.S. 93, 99 S.Ct. 939, 59 L.Ed.2d 171 (1979).

3. This retirement system and requirement applied to career foreign service officers, foreign service information officers and certain other career staff in the International Communications Agency.

4. 440 U.S. at 94 n. 1, 99 S.Ct. at 941 n. 1. This point corresponds with the well established principle that the equal protection guarantee of the due process clause of the Fifth Amendment mirrors that of equal protection clause of the Fourteenth Amendment. See § 14.3, supra.

5. 440 U.S. at 97, 99 S.Ct. at 942–43 (footnote omitted).

6. 427 U.S. 307, 96 S.Ct. 2562, 49 L.Ed.2d 520 (1976).

7. Justice Marshall, the only dissenter, argued that the court should consider the age distinction, as well as the retirement system distinction, as a basis for engaging in some meaningful form of review of the classifications. Vance v. Bradley, 440 U.S. 93, 113, 99 S.Ct. 939, 950–51, 59 L.Ed.2d 171 (1979) (Marshall, J., dissenting).

Justice Marshall was also the only dissenter when the Court upheld the 50 year old retirement provision for a state police force. Massachusetts Bd. of Retirement v. Murgia, 427 U.S. 307, 317, 96 S.Ct. 2562, 2569, 49 L.Ed.2d 520 (1976).

Chapter 15

CONGRESSIONAL ENFORCEMENT
OF CIVIL RIGHTS

§ 15.1 Introduction

Following the Civil War, Congress enacted a series of civil rights statutes to counter the Southern Black Codes. Various states enacted these Codes in order to take away from the ex-slaves those rights thought to be associated with the Thirteenth Amendment outlawing both slavery and its badges and incidents.[1] The Civil Rights Act of 1866, which passed over President Andrew Johnson's veto, gave all citizens the same right "as is enjoyed by white citizens" to give evidence in court, sue and be sued, to make and enforce contracts, and to buy, sell, inherit, and lease property.[2]

Because of questions as to whether the Thirteenth Amendment offered sufficient constitutional power to justify Congressional inroads on matters that previously had been entrusted to the states, Congress proposed the Fourteenth Amendment, the last section of which gave Congress explicit power to "enforce by appropriate legislation the provisions of this article."[3] Several years later, the ratification of the Fifteenth Amendment gave added support to civil rights legislation. In 1870, Congress then reenacted the Civil Rights Act of 1866,[4] along with other civil rights laws.[5] In subsequent years, Congress enacted further protective laws.[6]

This Chapter focuses on the interpretations of the various civil rights statutes to the extent that these interpretations significantly illuminate congressional power under the Thirteenth, Fourteenth, and Fifteenth Amendments. Rather than discussing these Amendments in the order in which they became part of the Constitution, the development of the case law makes it easier to discuss, first, Congress' power under section 5 of the Fourteenth Amendment. Then we shall turn to the scope of Congress' power under the Thirteenth Amendment, and under the Fifteenth Amendment.

---

§ 15.1

1. See 4 Ronald D. Rotunda & John E. Nowak, Treatise on Constitutional Law: Substance and Procedure §§ 19.1–19.39 (West Group, 3d ed.1999).

2. Civil Rights Act of 1866, 14 Stat. 27.

3. Some lower courts found the 1866 Act to be unconstitutional. E.g., People v. Brady, 40 Cal. 198 (1870). Contra, In re Turner, 24 F.Cas. 337 (C.C.Md.1867); People v. Washington, 36 Cal. 658 (1869).

4. 16 Stat. 114. See In re Slaughter–House Cases, 83 U.S. (16 Wall.) 36, 96–97, 21 L.Ed. 394 (1872) (Field, J., dissenting).

5. E.g., § 6 of the Civil Rights Act of 1870, 16 Stat. 190, now codified at 42 U.S.C.A. § 241. See generally United States v. Williams, 341 U.S. 70, 73–82, 71 S.Ct. 581, 582–87, 95 L.Ed. 758 (1951). (Opinion of Frankfurter, J.) See also 341 U.S. at 83–84, 71 S.Ct. at 588–89 (Appendix to Opinion of Frankfurter, J.).

6. E.g. the Ku Klux Klan Act, 17 Stat. 13, now codified in 42 U.S.C.A. §§ 1983, 1985(3). See also the Civil Rights Act of 1875, 18 Stat. 335.

The main civil rights statutes of the Reconstruction legislation are now codified in 42 U.S.C.A. §§ 1981 (Equal Rights Under the Law); 1982 (Property Rights of Citizens); 1983 (Civil Action for Deprivation of Rights); 1985(3) (Depriving Persons of Rights or Privileges); 18 U.S.C.A. §§ 241 (Conspiracy Against Rights of Citizens); 242 (Deprivation of Rights Under Color of Law); and 28 U.S.C.A. § 1443 (Jurisdiction of Civil Rights Cases).

On section 1983 of title 42, see 4 Ronald D. Rotunda & John E. Nowak, Treatise on Constitutional Law: Substance and Procedure §§ 19.13–19.39 (West Group, 3d ed.1999). The major treatise focusing on this area is, Sheldon H. Nahmod, Civil Rights & Civil Liberties Litigation: The Law of Section 1983 (West Group, 4th ed.1999) (2 vols.).

§ 15.2 Congressional Power Under Section 5 of the Fourteenth Amendment: The Historical Background

The congressional framers of the Civil War Amendments intended that they serve "as a basis for a positive, comprehensive federal program—a program defining fundamental civil rights protected by federal machinery against both state and private encroachment."[1] The hearings on the Fourteenth Amendment indicated that—

> most of the abuses still being suffered by the Negro were at the hands of individual white persons rather than state governments or those acting under color of state law. [T]he Negro was not alone in his tribulations; white persons who had supported the Union cause or who were bold enough to advocate civil rights for the Negro were also the victims of terrorism in the South. ...The demonstrated fact that violations of civil rights were primarily the product of individual rather than state action made it unreasonable for the committee to limit the scope of the Amendment to state action.[2]

Yet the early case law under section 5 was not conducive to such a broad reading. In the *Civil Rights Cases*,[3] Justice Bradley speaking for the Court read much of the power out of section 5:

> [T]he last section of the [Fourteenth] Amendment invests Congress with power to enforce it by appropriate legislation. To enforce what? ... It does not invest Congress with power to legislate upon subjects which are within the domain of state legislation; but to provide modes of relief against state

legislation, or state action.... It does not authorize Congress to create a code of municipal law for the regulation of private rights; but to provide modes of redress against the operation of state laws, and the action of state officers. [C]ivil rights, such as are guaranteed by the Constitution against state aggression, cannot be impaired by the wrongful acts of individuals, unsupported by state authority in the shape of laws, customs, or judicial or executive proceedings.[4]

Because of this case law requiring state action, when Congress, nearly a century later, enacted the Civil Rights Act of 1964 providing for injunctive relief against private discrimination in places of public accommodation,[5] it relied on Congress' interstate commerce power as well as on section 5 of the Fourteenth Amendment.[6]

The *Guest* Dictum. In 1966, dictum in *United States v. Guest*[7] invited a wide power in Congress to enforce the Fourteenth Amendment. The government indicted defendants under a law passed in 1870 outlawing, inter alia, two or more persons going "in disguise on the highway, or on the premises of another, with intent to prevent or hinder his free exercise or enjoyment of any right or privilege so secured...."[8] The fourth count of the *Guest* indictment is of particular interest. It charged the defendants, private individuals, with conspiring to intimidate some black citizens to prevent them from exercising the right to use the facilities of interstate commerce within the State of Georgia. The Court held that the indictment should not have been dismissed as to this paragraph because a conspiracy against

---

§ 15.2

1. R. Carr, Federal Protection of Civil Rights: Quest for a Sword 36 (1947).

2. Gressman, The Unhappy History of Civil Rights Legislation, 50 Mich.L.Rev. 1323, 1329–30 (1952).

3. 109 U.S. 3, 3 S.Ct. 18, 27 L.Ed. 835 (1883).

4. In re Civil Rights Cases, 109 U.S. 3, 11, 17, 3 S.Ct. 18, 21, 25, 27 L.Ed. 835 (1883).

5. Now codified as 42 U.S.C.A. §§ 2000a–2000a–6.

6. See 42 U.S.C.A. § 2000a–1(b); Hearings before the Senate Commerce Committee on S. 1732, 88th Cong., 1st Sess., Parts 1 & 2 (1963). The Supreme Court affirmed the

constitutionality of the law on the basis of the commerce although it noted that Congress had also relied on section 5 of the Fourteenth Amendment. Heart of Atlanta Motel, Inc. v. United States, 379 U.S. 241, 249, 85 S.Ct. 348, 353, 13 L.Ed.2d 258 (1964); Katzenbach v. McClung, 379 U.S. 294, 85 S.Ct. 377, 13 L.Ed.2d 290 (1964).

However, there was evidence in the lower courts that supported a much broader reading of section 5 of the Fourteenth Amendment. Brewer v. Hoxie School District No. 46, 238 F.2d 91 (8th Cir.1956) held that a federal court had power to enjoin private individuals from interfering with a state's duty to desegregate.

7. 383 U.S. 745, 86 S.Ct. 1170, 16 L.Ed.2d 239 (1966).

8. Now codified in 42 U.S.C.A. § 241.

the constitutional right to use the facilities of interstate commerce, "whether or not motivated by racial discrimination [is] a proper object of the federal law."[9]

The Court specifically disavowed any intent to consider "the question of what kinds of other and broader legislation Congress might constitutionally enact under § 5 of the Fourteenth Amendment...."[10] Separate opinions, however, did reach that question. Justice Clark, concurring, and joined by Black and Fortas, argued that "the specific language of section 5 empowers the Congress to enact laws punishing all conspiracies—with or without state action—that interfere with Fourteenth Amendment rights."[11] Justice Brennan concurring and dissenting in part, and joined by Warren and Douglas, contended that under section 5 Congress could reach private discrimination and that Congress in fact had exercised that power in the statute construed by the Court.

Although these comments were not holding, it still was the case that six Justices were now on record as approving Congressional legislation that reached private discriminatory actions. As we shall see, the Court has never adopted the position of these six Justices as a holding in a majority opinion,[12] but the way was now clear for a test of Congressional power under section 5. The test came very soon.

The *Morgan* Case. *Katzenbach v. Morgan*[13] upheld the constitutionality of section 4(e) of the Voting Rights Act of 1965. That section provided that no person who has completed the sixth grade in a Puerto Rican school (where the predominant classroom language

was not English) may be denied the right to vote in any election because of his or her inability to read or write English. The statute *pro tanto* prohibited enforcement of New York law requiring an ability to read and write English as a condition of voting.[14] The question in *Morgan* was whether Congress could prohibit enforcement of the state law by legislating under section 5 of the Fourteenth Amendment, regardless of whether the Court would find that the equal protection clause itself nullified New York's literacy requirement.[15]

The Court utilized a two-part analysis to uphold the federal statute. It first construed section 5 as granting Congress, when enforcing the Fourteenth Amendment, the same broad powers it has in the necessary and proper clause.[16] The Court held Congress has the power to determine that the Puerto Rican minority needed the vote to gain nondiscriminatory treatment in public services and that this need warranted federal intrusion on the states.[17] The Court reached the same result in the second part of its analysis. Because it "perceived a basis" on which Congress might reasonably predicate its judgment that the New York literacy requirement was invidiously discriminatory, the Court was willing to uphold the law.

Congress Need Not Explicitly Refer to Section 5. Congress, in the statute upheld in *Katzenbach*, explicitly relied on section 5, but years later the Court made it clear that, when Congress legislates under section 5, it need not do so explicitly as long as that is what it

---

9. 383 U.S. at 760, 86 S.Ct. at 1179. The Government must prove a specific intent to interfere with an individual's right to free interstate passage.

10. 383 U.S. at 755, 86 S.Ct. at 1176.

11. 383 U.S. at 762, 86 S.Ct. at 1180 (Clark, J., concurring).

12. Eventually, the Court specifically rejected the *Guest* dictum in United States v. Morrison, 529 U.S. 598, 120 S.Ct. 1740, 146 L.Ed.2d 658 (2000), although earlier cases portended this result.

13. 384 U.S. 641, 86 S.Ct. 1717, 16 L.Ed.2d 828 (1966).

14. 384 U.S. at 643–44, 86 S.Ct. at 1719–20.

15. 384 U.S. at 649, 86 S.Ct. at 1722–23. In *Lassiter v. Northampton County Board of Elections* the Court refused

to strike down state literacy requirements for voting as a violation of the equal protection clause in the absence of any showing of discriminatory use of the test. 360 U.S. 45, 53–54, 79 S.Ct. 985, 991, 3 L.Ed.2d 1072 (1959). The *Morgan* Court acknowledged *Lassiter* and refused to disturb its earlier ruling. See 384 U.S. at 649–50, 86 S.Ct. at 1722–23.

16. 384 U.S. at 650, 86 S.Ct. at 1723.

17. 384 U.S. at 652–53, 86 S.Ct. at 1724–25. See generally Hawkins v. Town of Shaw, 437 F.2d 1286 (5th Cir. 1971), judgment reaffirmed on rehearing 461 F.2d 1171 (5th Cir.1972).

intends.[18]

Harlan's Dissent. *Morgan*'s first rationale, that Congress may extend the vote to a class of persons injured by discriminatory allocation of government services by a state, offers no support for the argument that legislation could *restrict* the reach of the equal protection guarantee. A court still retains authority to determine whether discrimination exists and whether the legislative remedy is reasonably related to the proper goal.

But *Morgan* offered a second rationale. It said that it might "perceive a basis" for a Congressional judgment that the New York English literacy requirement was discriminatory (even though the Court had not held that a literacy requirement is discriminatory). This explanation, or alternative holding, suggested that Congress can legislate to address specific violations of the equal protection clause. Justice Harlan, in dissent, was concerned that this portion of *Morgan* may have conferred on Congress the power to *define* the reach of equal protection.[19] Harlan specifically attacked this portion of the majority's opinion as allowing Congress to define constitutional rights "so as in effect to dilute [the] equal protection and due process decisions of this Court."[20]

Justice Harlan's concern is a real one. That various Justices of the Supreme Court have explicitly acknowledged and relied on *Morgan* as the reason to respect congressional accommodations of conflicting rights and powers

gives additional support to Harlan's admonition.[21]

In an influential article Professor Archibald Cox contended that Congress does have broad power to determine what constitutes a violation of equal protection. He argued that section 5 makes it irrelevant whether congressional relief for violations of the Fourteenth Amendment granted is greater or lesser than the courts would order.[22] Cox concluded that the *Morgan* rationale requires judicial deference to congressional judgments that limit rights as well as to those that extend them.[23]

Reliance on *Morgan* to support the position that Congress has the power to *dilute* Fourteenth Amendment rights or restrict court-ordered remedies that enforce such rights rests on three questionable predicates: that congressional power to override state law under the Fourteenth Amendment is as broad as an expansive reading of *Morgan* would suggest; that *Morgan* authorizes Congress to override not only state actions, but also federal court constructions of the Fourteenth Amendment that are too restrictive; and that section 5 permits Congress to interpret the equal protection clause not only more broadly than the federal courts, but also more narrowly. Congress can rely on a broad reading of *Morgan* to dilute rights under section 5 of the Fourteenth Amendment only if each of these premises is correct.

---

18. The Court must determine what is the intent of Congress, but Congress need not "recite the words 'section 5' or 'Fourteenth Amendment' or 'equal protection'. . . ." EEOC v. Wyoming, 460 U.S. 226, 243 n. 18, 103 S.Ct. 1054, 1064 n. 18, 75 L.Ed.2d 18, 33 (1983). Cf. Katzenbach v. Morgan, 384 U.S. 641, 643 n. 1, 86 S.Ct. 1717, 1719 n. 1, 16 L.Ed.2d 828 (1966), quoting § 4(e).

19. See 384 U.S. at 653, 86 S.Ct. at 1724–25.

Burt, Miranda and Title II: A Morganatic Marriage, 1969 Sup.Ct.Rev. 81, 133: "*Morgan* allows a restrained Court, intent perhaps on undoing the work of its active predecessors, [to] permit a graceful and selective retreat limited to those areas where the political branch gives an explicit and contrary judgment."

20. 384 U.S. at 668, 86 S.Ct. at 1736 (Harlan, J., dissenting).

21. See Trafficante v. Metropolitan Life Insurance Co., 409 U.S. 205, 212, 93 S.Ct. 364, 368, 34 L.Ed.2d 415 (1972) (White, with Blackmun & Powell, JJ., concurring) (white tenants given standing under section 8(10)(a) of

Civil Rights Act of 1968 despite doubts of case or controversy under article III of Constitution); Welsh v. United States, 398 U.S. 333, 371, 90 S.Ct. 1792, 1813, 26 L.Ed.2d 308 (1970) (White, J., with Burger, C.J., & Stewart, J., dissenting) (argument for respecting congressional judgment accommodating right to free exercise of religion with statute for raising armies). See also, Fullilove v. Klutznick, 448 U.S. 448, 476–78, 100 S.Ct. 2758, 2773–75, 65 L.Ed.2d 902 (1980) (Opinion of Burger, C.J., joined by White & Powell, JJ.) (relying on § 5 of Fourteenth Amendment to justify Congressional decision to set aside 10% of funds for federal work projects for minority group members).

22. Cox, The Role of Congress in Constitutional Determinations, 40 U.Cinn.L.Rev. 199, 259 (1971). See also Cox, Constitutional Adjudication and the Promotion of Human Rights, 80 Harv.L.Rev. 91 (1966).

23. Cox, The Role of Congress in Constitutional Determinations, 40 U.Cinn.L.Rev. 199, at 259–60.

§ 15.3 *Morgan* as Restricted by *Oregon v. Mitchell*, *City of Boerne* and Cases Within their Wake

The broad language in *Morgan*, purporting to give Congress power to define equal protection, was unnecessary to the decision of the case. Moreover, subsequent decisions show that the Court has retreated from the far reaching implications of *Morgan*.

In *Oregon v. Mitchell*,[1] the Court evaluated the constitutionality of provisions of the Voting Rights Act Amendments of 1970,[2] which lowered the minimum voting age in state, local, and federal elections from 21 to 18, barred the use of literacy tests under certain circumstances, and forbade state imposition of residency requirements for presidential and vice-presidential elections. If *Morgan* granted Congress *carte blanche* to enact legislation remedying what Congress regards as denials of equal protection, the Court would have upheld the federal statute on that basis. Instead, the Court, in five separate opinions, struck down the section of the Act that authorized 18 year-olds to vote in state and local elections.[3]

Four Justices,—Douglas, Brennan, White, and Marshall—maintained that Congress had the power under section 5 to determine what are the equal protection requirements as applied to the voting rights of 18 to 21 year-olds in state, local, and federal elections. Brennan argued that because Congress had sufficient evidence to conclude that exclusion of such citizens from the franchise was unnecessary to promote any legitimate state interest, it could properly extend the franchise, regardless of the Court's view of the matter.[4] None of the other Justices of the fragmented Court saw Congress' role as that extensive.

Justice Stewart, joined by Chief Justice Burger and Justice Blackmun, found that Congress could not usurp the role of the courts by determining the boundaries of the equal protection clause.[5] Rather than reading *Morgan* as granting Congress power to define the reach of the equal protection clause, Stewart argued that the Court in *Morgan* only accepted an undoubtedly correct congressional conclusion, that a state statute denying a racial group the right to vote amounts to invidious discrimination under the equal protection clause.[6]

Justice Harlan agreed that Congress could not define the reach of equal protection. He contended that Congress' interpretation of what equal protection means conflicts with the procedures for amending the Constitution, particularly because courts are normally supposed to defer to legislative determinations.[7]

Justices Black and Douglas disagreed on the validity of the Voting Rights Act Amendments of 1970 because of their differing views of the reach of the equal protection clause, but each assumed that the legal question was for the courts, not Congress, to decide.[8]

Although the Court was splintered, a majority of the Justices did reject the contention that section 5 authorizes Congress to define the substantive boundaries of the equal protection clause by invalidating state legislation.[9] *Oregon v. Mitchell* laid the groundwork. Then came the *Boerne* decision.

City of Boerne v. Flores. The Court expanded on what *Oregon v. Mitchell* had portended in *City of Boerne v. Flores*,[10] when it

---

§ 15.3

1. 400 U.S. 112, 91 S.Ct. 260, 27 L.Ed.2d 272 (1970), rehearing denied 401 U.S. 903, 91 S.Ct. 862, 27 L.Ed.2d 802 (1971).

2. Pub.L. No. 91–285, 84 Stat. 314, amending 42 U.S.C.A. § 1973.

3. Oregon v. Mitchell, 400 U.S. 112, 118, 124–31, 91 S.Ct. 260, 261–62, 264–68, 27 L.Ed.2d 272 (1970).

4. 400 U.S. at 240, 280–81, 91 S.Ct. at 322–23, 342–43 (Brennan, J., with White & Marshall, JJ., concurring and dissenting); 400 U.S. at 135, 141–42, 91 S.Ct. at 270, 273–74 (Douglas, J., concurring and dissenting).

5. 400 U.S. at 296, 91 S.Ct. at 350 (Stewart, J., with Burger, C.J., & Blackmun, J., concurring and dissenting).

6. 400 U.S. at 295–96, 91 S.Ct. at 349–50.

7. 400 U.S. at 205, 91 S.Ct. at 305–06 (Harlan, J., concurring and dissenting).

8. 440 U.S. at 117–35, 91 S.Ct. at 261–70 (Black, J., announcing judgments of the Court); 400 U.S. at 135–52, 91 S.Ct. at 270–79 (Douglas J., separate opinion).

9. Little Rock School District v. Mauney, 183 F.3d 816, 824 (8th Cir.1998), quoting Treatise.

10. 521 U.S. 507, 117 S.Ct. 2157, 138 L.Ed.2d 624 (1997). Stevens, J., filed a concurring opinion. Scalia, J., field an opinion concurring part, in which Stevens, J., joined. O'Connor, J., filed a dissenting opinion, in which Breyer, J., joined in part. Souter, J., and Breyer, J., each

ruled that Congress exceed its powers under section 5 of the Fourteenth Amendment when it enacted the Religious Freedom Restoration Act ("RFRA").[11] Congress enacted RFRA to overturn *Employment Division, Department of Human Resources of Oregon v. Smith.*[12]

In *Smith*, the Court had upheld state power to enforce generally applicable neutral laws (in that case, a law banning the use of peyote, an illegal drug) even if the law was applied to deny unemployment benefits to individuals who lost their job because of the illegal peyote use, where the users were members of a Native American Church, and they claimed that they used peyote as a sacrament and the law interfered with their free exercise of religion. RFRA, in contrast to *Smith*, provided that both the state and the federal government cannot "substantially burden" a person's exercise of religion, even under a rule of general applicability, unless the government demonstrates that the burden (1) furthers a "compelling governmental interest;" and, (2) is the "least restrictive means of furthering" that interest. RFRA, in short, sought to overrule *Smith*.

In *Boerne*, local zoning authorities denied a church a building permit to enlarge a church because the enlargement, in the view of the Historical Landmark Commission, conflicted with an historical preservation plan. Archbishop Flores then sued under RFRA. Justice Kennedy, for the Court, held that RFRA was unconstitutional and not justified by section 5 of the Fourteenth Amendment. While Congress has section 5 power to enforce the Free Exercise Clause, its power is the power only to "enforce." Its power is preventive, remedial. Relying on *Oregon v. Mitchell*, the Court said that this section does not give Congress the right to decree the substance of what the First Amendment means. "Legislation which alters the meaning of the Free Exercise Clause cannot be said to be enforcing the Clause."[13]

Congruence. The line between remedial legislation and legislation that makes a substantive change in the law may not always be clear. The Court will give Congress "wide latitude" to decide where to draw the line. However, there must be "congruence and proportionality between the injury to be prevented or remedied and the means adopted to that end."[14]

For example, when Congress enacted (and the Supreme Court in *Katzenbach* later upheld various provisions of) the Voting Rights Act of 1965, there was a long and widespread record before Congress and in the case law documenting racial discrimination in voting. But when one turns to RFRA, there is no evidence of any generally applicable law enacted because of religious bigotry in the last 40 years. There was only evidence of laws that placed incidental burdens on religion, and these laws were not enacted or enforced because of animus or hostility to religion nor did they indicate that there was any widespread pattern of religious discrimination in this country. RFRA, in short, was a major federal intrusion "into the States' traditional prerogative and general authority to regulate for the health and welfare of their citizens."[15]

---

filed dissenting opinions. See William Van Alstyne, The Failure of the Religious Freedom Restoration Act under Section 5 of the Fourteenth Amendment, 46 Duke L. J. 291, 292–303 (1996). The Supreme Court relied on the analysis of this article in its decision in *Boerne*.

See also Ronald D. Rotunda, The Americans with Disabilities Act, Bar Examinations, and the Constitution: A Balancing Act, 66 The Bar Examiner 6 (No. 3, August, 1997); Ronald D. Rotunda, Resurrecting Federalism Under the New Tenth and Fourteenth Amendments, 29 Texas Tech L. Rev. 953 (1998); Ronald D. Rotunda, The Power of Congress Under Section 5 of the Fourteenth Amendment after *City of Boerne v. Flores*, 32 Indiana L. Rev. 163 (1998).

11. 107 Stat. at Large 1488 (1993).

12. 494 U.S. 872, 110 S.Ct. 1595, 108 L.Ed.2d 876 (1990).

13. 521 U.S. at 519, 117 S.Ct. at 2164.

14. 521 U.S. at 520, 117 S.Ct. at 2164.

15. 521 U.S. at 534, 117 S.Ct. at 2171. One of the interesting lower court cases applying RFRA to invalidate a state policy was Cheema v. Thompson, 67 F.3d 883 (9th Cir. 1995). The Ninth Circuit ruled that RFRA required a state elementary school to make exceptions to its "no weapons" policy, so that all Sikh children (7 years old and older) could carry knives to school. This knife (or "Kirpan") has a 7-inch blade. The knives could not be made immovable for that would conflict with Sikh beliefs that require the children to carry and to use the knives to "propagate God's justice."

The "congruence and proportionality" standard does not apply outside the § 5 context. For example, "it does not hold sway for judicial review of legislation enacted, as copyright laws are, pursuant to Article I authorization."[16]

Reaffirming *Boerne*. In a trio of cases decided the same day during the 1998–1999 Supreme Court term, the Court reaffirmed *City of Boerne*, agreed that section 5 of the Fourteenth Amendment gives Congress the power to create causes of action against the state to enforce the Fourteenth Amendment, but then held that this power had not been properly exercised. A different Justice wrote the majority in each of these opinions (all decided by the same five to four vote).

In *Florida Prepaid Postsecondary Education Expense Board v. College Savings Bank*,[17] Chief Justice Rehnquist spoke of the Court. Congress enacted a statute expressly abrogating the states' sovereign immunity from lawsuits for patent violations. Then College Savings Bank sued the Florida State Board for patent infringement, arguing that Congress has properly exercised its powers under section 5 of the Fourteenth Amendment to protect the due process property guarantees of a patent holder. The Court found that section 5 did not authorize this abrogation of Florida's sovereign immunity from suit in federal court.

The Court agreed that Congress—by using its power under section 5 to enforce section 1 of the Fourteenth Amendment—can abrogate a state's sovereign immunity rights and its Eleventh Amendment immunity. The Court also readily agreed that patents are property,

that section 1 does protect the right to property, and that the state cannot take this private property without paying just compensation.[18]

However, because Congress' enforcement power is remedial, Congress must carefully tailor its legislative scheme to remedying or preventing the particular conduct that violates the Fourteenth Amendment. That was not done in this case because this legislation did not enforce the just compensation clause. First, neither the language of the statute nor the legislative history indicated that Congress was trying to enforce the Just Compensation Clause;[19] second, the United States specifically declined to defend the law as based on the Just Compensation Clause.[20]

The law was also not justified on the basis that it protected *procedural* due process, because the state had already provided a fair judicial remedy for a takings or conversion claim.[21] The federal statute merely offered a different procedure, but the state already offered a procedure was adequate for Constitutional purposes.

The federal statute's aim was to provide a uniform procedural remedy for patent infringement and to place states on the same footing as private parties. These are proper Article I concerns, the Court agreed, but Article I does not authorize Congress to abrogate state immunity from suit, and Article I cannot justify action under the Fourteenth Amendment.[22] Hence, the legislation was not "appropriate" under section 5, and was therefore unconstitutional.

In *College Savings Bank v. Florida Prepaid*

---

16. Eldred v. Ashcroft, 537 U.S. 186, 218, 123 S.Ct. 769, 788, 154 L.Ed.2d 683 (2003).

17. 527 U.S. 627, 119 S.Ct. 2199, 144 L.Ed.2d 575 (1999) (5 to 4). Stevens, J., joined by Souter, Ginsburg, & Breyer, JJ., dissented, arguing that the law was an appropriate exercise of Congress' power under § 5 of the Fourteenth Amendment to prevent state deprivations of property without due process of law.

18. Patents are property. E.g., Brown v. Duchesne, 60 U.S. (19 How.) 183, 197, 15 L.Ed. 595 (1856): "For, by the laws of the United States, the rights of a party under a patent are his private property; and by the Constitution of the United States, private property cannot be taken for public use without just compensation."

19. 119 S.Ct. at 2208 n. 7.

20. 119 S.Ct. at 2208.

21. 119 S.Ct. at 2209 n. 9.

22. Justice Stevens, in his dissent, believed that the *Boerne* case "amply supports congressional authority to enact the Patent Remedy Act, whether one assumes that States seldom infringe patents, or that patent infringements potentially permeate an 'unlimited range of state conduct.' "He emphasized "the principle that undergirds all aspects of our patent system: national uniformity." 527 U.S. at 649, 119 S.Ct. at 2211.

Postsecondary Education Expense Board,[23] a companion case, plaintiff sued Florida for false and misleading advertising under the Federal Trademark Act of 1946 (the Lanham Act). The Trademark Remedy Clarification Act ("TRCA") subjected states to suit in federal court. The plaintiff argued that Congress' abrogation of sovereign immunity in the TRCA was constitutional on the grounds that it enforced the guarantee found in section 1 of the Fourteenth Amendment that a state will not deprive anyone of property without due process. Justice Scalia, for the Court, rejected that argument.

The Court explained that laws enacted pursuant to § 5 must be for the purpose of remedying or preventing constitutional violations. But the TRCA did not enforce property rights.

First, there is no "property" because the hallmark of a constitutionally protected property interest is the right to exclude others. The Lanham Act's false-advertising provisions bear no relationship to any right to exclude. The Lanham Act's provisions dealing with infringement of trademarks may well be "property" because the owner can exclude others from using them, but the Lanham Act's false-advertising provisions are not "property" because they bear no relationship to any right to exclude. "Florida Prepaid's alleged misrepresentations concerning its own products intruded upon no interest over which petitioner had exclusive dominion."[24] There is no decision of this Court or any other that recognizes "a property right in freedom from a competitor's false advertising about its own products."[25]

Second, a business's assets, including its good will, are property, and any state taking of those assets is a "deprivation" of property. However, the state action in this case did not take the petitioner's "property." Business, "in the sense of *the activity of doing business*, or *the activity of making a profit* is not property in the ordinary sense—and it is only *that*, and not any business asset, which is impinged upon by a competitor's false advertising."[26]

The third case of this trinity of cases during the 1998–1999 term was *Alden v. Maine.*[27] In that case, the Court held that Congress, using its Article I powers, could not subject a state to suit in *state* court by private parties without the state's consent, just as Congress could not subject a state to suit in *federal* court in similar circumstances. However, the Court expressly declared that this prohibition did not apply when Congress properly exercises its power under § 1 of the Fourteenth Amendment: "Congress may authorize private suits against nonconsenting States pursuant to its § 5 enforcement powers."[28]

The following term the Court invalidated another federal effort to revoke the Eleventh Amendment rights of the states. The Age Discrimination in Employment Act (ADEA) clearly stated that it was subjecting the states to the ADEA and taking away their Eleventh Amendment immunity. However, *Kimel v. Florida Board of Regents*[29] held that Congress could not constitutionally use section 5 in this manner because the abrogation exceeded federal power under section 5.[30] Age is not a suspect class under the equal protection clause and therefore an age classification is constitutional if it is rational.[31] Congress cannot annul

23. 527 U.S. 666, 119 S.Ct. 2219, 144 L.Ed.2d 605 (1999) (5 to 4) (Scalia, J., for the Court).

24. 527 U.S. at 673, 119 S.Ct. at 2225.

25. 527 U.S. at 666, 119 S.Ct. at 2225.

26. 527 U.S. at 675, 119 S.Ct. at 2225 (emphasis in original).

The Court then held that Florida did not impliedly waive its sovereign immunity simply because it engaged in interstate commerce knowing that Congress had regulated that conduct. To reach this result, the Court overruled *Parden v. Terminal Ry. Co. of Alabama State Docks Dept.*, 377 U.S. 184, 84 S.Ct. 1207, 12 L.Ed.2d 233 (1964), which had found an implied or constructive waiver by the state of its sovereign immunity. Breyer, J., joined by Stevens,

Souter, & Ginsburg, JJ., dissented and would follow *Parden.*

27. 527 U.S. 706, 119 S.Ct. 2240, 144 L.Ed.2d 636 (1999). Souter, J., filed a dissenting opinion, joined by Stevens, Ginsburg, & Breyer, JJ.

28. 527 U.S. at 756, 119 S.Ct. at 2267.

29. 528 U.S. 62, 120 S.Ct. 631, 145 L.Ed.2d 522 (2000).

30. This result was forecasted in, Ronald D. Rotunda, The Americans with Disabilities Act, Bar Examinations, and the Constitution: A Balancing Act, 66 The Bar Examiner 6 (No. 3, August, 1997).

31. Gregory v. Ashcroft, 501 U.S. 452, 473, 111 S.Ct. 2395, 115 L.Ed.2d 410 (1991); Vance v. Bradley, 440 U.S. 93, 102–03 n. 20, 108–112, 99 S.Ct. 939, 59 L.Ed.2d 171

the states' Eleventh Amendment immunity merely by stating that it is enforcing the Fourteenth Amendment; the law must actually enforce (not redefine) section 1.

Contrast these cases to *Nevada Department of Human Resources v. Hibbs*.[32] The Court applied the methodology of the prior cases and, this time, upheld the law, which it found to cover a protected class (sex-based discrimination) and it was congruent and proportional to the constitutional injury that the law sought to prevent.

In this case, Hibbs, an employee of the Nevada Department of Human Resources, sought leave to care for his ailing wife under the Family and Medical Leave Act of 1993 (FMLA), which entitles an eligible employee to take up to 12 work weeks of unpaid leave annually for the onset of a "serious health condition" in the employee's spouse and for other reasons. The FMLA creates a private right of action to seek both equitable relief and money damages "against any employer (including a public agency) in any Federal or State court of competent jurisdiction," if that employer interferes with, restrains, or denies the exercise of FMLA rights. Chief Justice Rehnquist, for the Court, held that employees of the State of Nevada may recover money damages in the event of the state's failure to comply with the family-care provision of the Act.

Quoting *City of Boerne*, the Court said that laws passed under § 5 "reaching beyond the scope of § 1's actual guarantees must be an appropriate remedy for identified constitutional violations, not 'an attempt to substantively redefine the States' legal obligations.' "[33] Congress, in the exercise of its § 5 powers, may "do more than simply proscribe conduct that we have held unconstitutional."[34]

The Court summarized the evidence on which Congress based its law. For example, parental leave for fathers is rare, and even where it exists, "men, *both in the public and private sectors*, receive notoriously discriminatory treatment in their requests for such leave."[35] These differential leave policies were based on the "pervasive sex-role stereotype that caring for family members is women's work."

Discrimination in the case of age-or disability-based classifications is not judged under a heightened review standard, and passes muster if there is "a rational basis for doing so at a class-based level." In contrast, a sex-based classification must do more than meet than the rational-basis test—it must "serve important governmental objectives" and be "substantially related to the achievement of those objectives." Hence, it is "easier for Congress to show a pattern of state constitutional violations."[36]

By creating an across-the-board, routine employment benefit for all eligible employees, Congress sought to ensure that family-care leave would no longer be stigmatized as an inordinate drain on the workplace caused by female employees, and that employers could not evade leave obligations simply by hiring men. By setting a minimum standard of family leave for all eligible employees, irrespective of gender, the FMLA attacks the formerly state-sanctioned stereotype that only women are responsible for family caregiving, thereby reducing employers' incentives to engage in discrimination by basing hiring and promotion decisions on stereotypes.[37]

§ 15.4   Application of Section 5 to Federal Court Determinations

Whatever the reach of section 5 as a vehicle for augmenting the power of Congress to regu-

(1979); Massachusetts Board of Retirement v. Murgia, 427 U.S. 307, 317, 96 S.Ct. 2562, 49 L.Ed.2d 520 (1976) (per curiam).

32. 538 U.S. 721, 123 S.Ct. 1972, 155 L.Ed.2d 953 (2003). Souter, J., joined by Ginsburg & Breyer, JJ. filed a concurring opinion. Stevens, J., filed an opinion concurring in the judgment. Scalia, J., filed a dissenting opinion, and Kennedy, J., also filed a dissenting opinion joined by Scalia & Thomas, JJ.

33. 538 U.S. at ___, 123 S.Ct. at 1978.

34. 538 U.S. at ___, 123 S.Ct. at 1977.

35. 538 U.S. at ___, 123 S.Ct. at 1979 (emphasis in original).

36. 538 U.S. at ___, 123 S.Ct. at 1974–75.

37. 538 U.S. at ___, 123 S.Ct. at 1982–83.

late matters otherwise left to the states, it does not provide in itself authority for Congress to interfere with the execution or enforcement of federal court judgments or to overturn federal judicial determinations of the requirements of the Fourteenth Amendment. The history of the Amendment and its perceived purpose as an enduring principle to govern the country mandate this conclusion. To that issue we now turn.

The framers of section 5 considered it a tool to enable "Congress, in case the States shall enact laws in conflict with the principles of the Amendment, to correct that legislation by a formal congressional enactment".[1] Senator Trumbull of Illinois viewed section 5 as the means of "destroy[ing] all these discriminations in civil rights [by the states] against the black man...."[2] Other participants in the debates added that the purpose of the proposed section was to give Congress a means to enforce the Fourteenth Amendment[3] to see that it "was carried out in good faith, and for [no] other [purpose]...."[4]

An original draft of section 1 of the Fourteenth Amendment provided that "Congress shall have power to make all laws ... to secure ... to all persons ... equal protection ...,"[5] but the framers of the Amendment rejected that formulation because they wanted to secure the articulated Fourteenth Amendment guarantees against a future Congress (or Court) that might be unsympathetic.[6] This history will never be completely clear, for the drafters had no reason to anticipate a time when the Court might be more active in granting and enforcing Fourteenth Amendment rights than Congress.

We must remember that the Radical Republicans, who viewed themselves as the principal protectors of the recently freed slaves, dominated Congress at this time. The only Supreme Court that the members of Congress knew was a Court that had not applied the Bill of Rights to the states; had not assisted in giving the protection of the law to the abolitionists in the South prior to the War; had enforced the fugitive slave laws; and had invalidated congressional legislation limiting the expansion of slavery into new territories. There was simply no reason for the framers to anticipate a Court that would recognize individual rights more expansively than Congress, and therefore there is no evidence that they considered this issue. But some limit on the congressional restriction of judicial power did exist, in the first section of the Fourteenth Amendment, for that section established blacks as citizens, overturning *Dred Scott* and protecting these newly acquired citizenship rights of the blacks against a future Congress.

The early judicial interpretations of the scope of the section 5 power support this view. These cases focused initially on the new relationship between Congress and the states and later on the role of the courts in determining violations of equal protection. In 1879 the Supreme Court in *Ex parte Virginia*[7] described the new federalism:

> The prohibitions of the Fourteenth Amendment are directed to the States, and they are to a degree restrictions of State power. It is these which Congress is empowered to enforce, and to enforce against State action,.... Such enforcement is not invasion of State sovereignty.... [T]he constitutional Amendment was ordained for a purpose.[8]

In 1976 the Supreme Court cited *Virginia* for the proposition that the Fourteenth Amendment was intended to be a "limitation of the power of the State and [an]

---

§ 15.4

1. Cong. Globe, 39th Cong., 1st Sess. 2768 (1866) (remarks of Senator Howard, who reported the Amendment to the Senate from the Joint Committee on Reconstruction).

2. Cong. Globe, 39th Cong., 1st Sess. 322 (1865) (debate on Freedman's Bureau bill).

3. See Cong. Globe, 39th Cong., 1st Sess. 41 (1865) (remarks of Senator Wilson).

4. See Cong. Globe, 39th Cong., 1st Sess. 43 (1865) (remarks of Senator Trumbull).

5. Cong. Globe, 39th Cong., 1st Sess. 1033–34 (1866).

6. See Burt, Miranda and Title II: A Morganatic Marriage, 1969 Sup.Ct.Rev. 81, 92–93.

7. 100 U.S. (10 Otto) 339, 25 L.Ed. 676 (1879).

8. 100 U.S. at 346–47.

enlargement of the power of Congress." Thus the Tenth Amendment does not limit section 5.[9]

Other early decisions suggest that section 5 empowers Congress to enforce the guarantees of the Amendment only when Congress and the courts agree that the states have abridged them.[10] Indeed, the Court twice rejected the judgment of Congress expressed in federal legislation that actions of a state government violated the Fourteenth Amendment.[11]

Although *Morgan* may permit Congress to find a state law invalid even if a court would not, neither the legislative history of section 5 nor the subsequent case law authorizes Congress to invalidate federal court action enforcing the Fourteenth Amendment. *Morgan* allows congressional intrusion into state sovereignty where necessary to secure Fourteenth Amendment guarantees. *Morgan* does not relax any other limitations on congressional power, such as those inherent in the Fifth Amendment.[12]

Congress intended section 5 of the Fourteenth Amendment to increase federal power at the expense of the states. Neither the language nor the reasoning behind section 5 supports the view that it increased federal congressional power at the expense of federal judicial power. A brief look at Justice Douglas's comments in *Morgan* should make that clear.

Douglas joined *Morgan*, but only he reserved judgment on whether the federal law (which eliminated English literacy tests as a requirement for voting, as applied to anyone who successfully completed the sixth grade in school accredited by Puerto Rico) was constitutional in all respects. Justice Douglas would reserve "judgment until such time as [the issue] is presented by a member of the class against which that particular discrimination is directed."[13] Should a person literate in a language other than English (e.g., French) be able to challenge the law on equal protection or other constitutional grounds? If a person learned Spanish not in a Puerto Rican school but in a school in Spain, or in Mexico, should he be able to challenge the law on equal protection or other constitutional grounds?

No one but Justice Douglas thought that the answer to this question was difficult. The majority of the *Morgan* Court must have reasoned as follows: if New York decided to drop its literacy requirement entirely, no court accept a challenge of an English-literate voter claiming that his vote was somehow "diluted." It would also be rational for New York to eliminate its English language requirement in part, by relying on the educational system of other American-flag schools (i.e., schools located within the jurisdiction of the United States). Because a state could constitutionally decide to eliminate its literacy requirement entirely (or eliminate it as to people educated in American-flag schools), Congress could similarly eliminate the literacy requirement. If the state could eliminate the literacy requirement directly, Congress could do it by virtue of section 5. A state voter could not successfully complain that Congress had engaged in unconstitutional vote dilution, because such a state voter would have no successful claim if the state itself had decided to eliminate or limit its literacy requirement. The state also cannot complain because section 5 expanded federal legislative power at the expense of the states, and that is *all* section 5 did. It neither gave Congress the right to restrict the meaning of

---

9. Fitzpatrick v. Bitzer, 427 U.S. 445, 454, 96 S.Ct. 2666, 2670, 49 L.Ed.2d 614 (1976). Thus it is quite clear that Congress' powers under section 5 are not limited by the Tenth Amendment.

10. See Virginia v. Rives, 100 U.S. (10 Otto) 313, 317–19, 25 L.Ed. 667 (1879) (under section 5 mode of enforcement of prohibition against discriminatory state action left to discretion of Congress; one means of enforcement is removal from state to federal court); Strauder v. West Virginia, 100 U.S. (10 Otto) 303, 307–09, 25 L.Ed. 664 (1879) (same).

11. See In re Civil Rights Cases, 109 U.S. 3, 18–19, 3 S.Ct. 18, 26–27, 27 L.Ed. 835 (1883) (law preventing private citizens from depriving individuals of equal protection); United States v. Harris, 106 U.S. (16 Otto) 629, 639, 1 S.Ct. 601, 609, 27 L.Ed. 290 (1883) (same).

12. See Cohen, Congressional Power to Interpret Due Process and Equal Protection, 28 Stan.L.Rev. 603, 614 (1975).

13. Katzenbach v. Morgan, 384 U.S. 641, 658–59, 86 S.Ct. 1717, 1728, 16 L.Ed.2d 828 (1966) (separate opinion of Douglas, J.).

equal protection nor did it otherwise expand legislative power at the expense of the federal judiciary.

§ 15.5 Section 5 Power to Narrow Federal Judicial Interpretations of Equal Protection or Other Constitutional Guarantees

Although *Morgan* found broad congressional power under section 5 to determine that state practice interferes with Fourteenth Amendment rights, it also examined the federal statute for consistency with constitutional requirements.[1] The Court's analysis confirms that federal courts will scrutinize congressional action under section 5 to assure that it meets the equal protection requirements embodied in the Fifth Amendment.[2] If the legislation includes a suspect classification or affects a fundamental right, then, under traditional equal protection analysis, only a compelling state interest will support its constitutionality.[3]

The Voting Rights Act of 1965 at issue in *Morgan*, the 1970 Amendments to that Act reviewed in *Mitchell*, and the reconstruction laws involved in earlier cases were attempts by Congress to expand the power of the federal government over the states and to extend protection to a group whose rights had been denied in violation of the Fourteenth Amendment. The Court upheld the statutes in these cases using the rational relationship test. If Congress were to limit federal courts' power to extend to racial minorities constitutionally protected rights, such statutes would place special burdens on those minorities seeking to implement their constitutional rights and would dilute their equal protection rights. A court must strictly scrutinize such a legislative scheme and uphold it only if a compelling state interest supported it.[4] The decision in *Morgan*, upholding the requirement of a more liberal voting eligibility standard than the judicially defined constitutional requirement, does not support the argument that Congress may restrict a court's power to interpret the requirements of the Fourteenth Amendment or that Congress may limit the available remedies for violations of those rights.[5]

A caveat to the Court's opinion in *Morgan* emphasizes the distinction between the power to expand and the power to restrict the reach of equal protection:

> Section 5 does not grant Congress power to exercise discretion in the other direction and to enact "statutes so as in effect to dilute equal protection and due process decisions of this Court." We emphasize that Congress' power under section 5 is limited to adopting measures to enforce the guarantees of the Amendment; section 5 grants Congress no power to restrict, abrogate, or dilute these guarantees. Thus, for example, an enactment authorizing the States to establish racially segregated systems of education would not be—as required by section 5—a measure "to enforce" the Equal Protection Clause since that clause of its own force prohibits such state laws.[6]

§ 15.5

1. See Katzenbach v. Morgan, 384 U.S. 641, 656, 86 S.Ct. 1717, 1726–27, 16 L.Ed.2d 828 (1966).

2. See Bolling v. Sharpe, 347 U.S. 497, 499–500, 74 S.Ct. 693, 694–95, 98 L.Ed. 884 (1954), opinion supplemented 349 U.S. 294, 75 S.Ct. 753, 99 L.Ed. 1083 (1955) (racial discrimination so unjustifiable as to be also a denial of due process; racial segregation in District of Columbia schools such a denial under Fifth Amendment).

3. See e.g. San Antonio Independent School District v. Rodriguez, 411 U.S. 1, 17, 93 S.Ct. 1278, 1288, 36 L.Ed.2d 16 (1973), rehearing denied 411 U.S. 959, 93 S.Ct. 1919, 36 L.Ed.2d 418 (1973). In *Morgan*, however, Congress did not restrict the franchise, but extended it.

4. Cf. Hunter v. Erickson, 393 U.S. 385, 89 S.Ct. 557, 21 L.Ed.2d 616 (1969). *Hunter* held that a provision in a city charter prohibiting the city council from implementing any ordinance dealing with racial, religious, or ancestral discrimination in housing without the approval of the majority of the city's voters was unconstitutional. Although the statute did not discriminate on its face, its effect was to place a burden on a protected minority. 393 U.S. at 391, 89 S.Ct. at 560–61. The state may not make it more difficult to enact legislation to benefit racial minorities. 393 U.S. at 392–93, 89 S.Ct. at 561–62. See also Reitman v. Mulkey, 387 U.S. 369, 380–81, 87 S.Ct. 1627, 1633–34, 18 L.Ed.2d 830 (1967).

5. See Shapiro v. Thompson, 394 U.S. 618, 641, 89 S.Ct. 1322, 1335, 22 L.Ed.2d 600 (1969) (rejecting argument that Congress approved a one year residence).

6. 384 U.S. at 651–52 n. 10, 86 S.Ct. at 1724 n. 10. See also Oregon v. Mitchell, 400 U.S. 112, 128–29, 91 S.Ct. 260, 266–67, 27 L.Ed.2d 272 (1970), rehearing denied 401 U.S. 903, 91 S.Ct. 862, 27 L.Ed.2d 802 (1971) (opinion of Black, J.).

The Court's statement was conclusory, and Justice Harlan's concern may not be that easy to dismiss. It should not be too difficult for a creative legislator to recast a "dilution" of a right as really an "expansion" of another right. For example, someone who intends to prohibit school busing necessary to desegregation will argue that he is expanding freedom of association (implied in due process) in choosing schools, or one who intends to restrict abortion rights will argue that he is expanding the right to life guaranteed in the Fourteenth Amendment.

Although the *Morgan* majority may not have explained it conclusory statement or articulated precisely why the power to enforce does not include the power to dilute, it did recognize that section 5 power to dilute would conflict with a primary purpose of the equal protection clause, to protect citizens' rights under the Fourteenth Amendment against a hostile Congress.[7] The command of the equal protection guarantee of section 1 should control the section 5 power: if section 1 is to be meaningful, neither the states nor Congress should have the power to violate the equal protection clause, as defined by the courts.[8]

Reading section 5 as authorizing only extensions of Fourteenth Amendment guarantees accords with both *Morgan* and the general scheme of the Constitution:

> There is no *a priori* reason for linking power to expand constitutional safeguards with power to dilute them. One can assert without logical fallacy that, since the chief function of the Supreme Court is to protect human rights, it should never defer to any legislative determination which restricts those rights without making its own investigation and characterization of the interest affected, even though it welcomes any legislative determination that extends human

rights and is subject to challenge only as an unconstitutional extension of federal power at the expense of the States.[9]

Morgan provides strong support that section 5 of the Fourteenth Amendment does give Congress broad power to ban state laws authorizing discriminatory acts. But as the Court later recognized in *Mississippi University for Women v. Hogan*,[10] this power should not be considered a power to dilute.

Affirmative Action. Some Justices have sought to rely on section 5 of the Fourteenth Amendment to justify federal statutes that distribute benefits or burdens on the basis of race, for the purpose of affirmative action. After a series of cases, it now appears that a majority of the Justices reject the notion that Congress can use section 5 to justify action that would violate section 1 of the Fourteenth Amendment if a state had engaged in similar action. While the Court has approved of affirmative action in certain cases, it has not relied on section 5 to reach that conclusion.[11] Initially, however, the Court suggested otherwise and the path that led to the present law started with *Fullilove*.

In *Fullilove v. Klutznick*[12] a fragmented Court rejected a challenge on its face to the minority business enterprise (MBE) section of a federal public works act which required that, unless there was an administrative waiver, at least 10% of the federal funds granted for local public works projects must be used by the state or local grantees to purchase services or supplies from businesses owned and controlled by minority group members, defined by statute as American citizens who are "Negroes, Spanish-speaking, Orientals, Indians, Eskimos, and Aleuts."

Chief Justice Burger's plurality opinion specifically relied on Congress' power under sec-

---

7. See 384 U.S. at 651–52 n. 10, 86 S.Ct. at 1724 n. 10.

8. Bolling v. Sharpe, 347 U.S. 497, 499, 74 S.Ct. 693, 694, 98 L.Ed. 884 (1954), opinion supplemented 349 U.S. 294, 75 S.Ct. 753, 99 L.Ed. 1083 (1955).

9. Cox, The Role of Congress in Constitutional Determination, 40 U.Cinn.L.Rev. 199, 253 (1971).

10. 458 U.S. 718, 102 S.Ct. 3331, 73 L.Ed.2d 1090 (1982). *Hogan* held that the state, under the Fourteenth

Amendment, could not have a female-only nursing school; no congressional statute could excuse the state from such sex discrimination.

11. Gratz v. Bollinger, 539 U.S. 244, 123 S.Ct. 2411, 156 L.Ed.2d 257 (2003); Grutter v. Bollinger, 539 U.S. 306, 123 S.Ct. 2325, 156 L.Ed.2d 304 (2003).

12. 448 U.S. 448, 100 S.Ct. 2758, 65 L.Ed.2d 902 (1980).

tion 5 of the Fourteenth Amendment. He was satisfied that Congress, although it made no factual findings, had before it abundant historical evidence "from which it could conclude that traditional procurement practices, when applied to minority businesses, could perpetuate the effects of prior discrimination."[13] This opinion explicitly did not adopt any of the tests advanced in *Bakke*.[14]

The Burger plurality was narrowly drafted, and found it "significant that the administrative scheme provides for waiver and exemption."[15] It only rejected a *facial* attack on the statute, and emphasized that the law provided for administrative scrutiny to remove from the program non-bona-fide, spurious minority front entities. A waiver procedure also dealt with the case of an MBE attempting to exploit the program by charging a price not justified by the present effects of past discrimination. "That the use of racial and ethnic criteria is premised on assumptions rebuttable in the administrative process gives reasonable assurance that application of the MBE program will be limited to accomplishing the remedial objectives contemplated by Congress and that misapplications of the racial and ethnic criteria can be remedied.... The MBE provision may be viewed as a pilot project, appropriately limited in extent and duration, and subject to reassessment and reevaluation by the Congress prior to any extension or reenactment."[16]

Later, *Adarand Constructors, Inc. v. Pena*[17] severely undercut *Fullilove*. The five to four majority held that federal affirmative action programs, like state programs, must comply with strict scrutiny, that is, must be narrowly tailored to further compelling government interests. *Adarand Constructors, Inc.*, like *Fullilove*, involved minority set-asides. The majority explicitly said that, to the extent that *Fullilove* held federal racial classifications to a less rigorous standard, it is no longer controlling.[18]

---

13. 448 U.S. at 481, 100 S.Ct. at 2776. White & Powell, JJ. joined Burger, C.J.

14. 448 U.S. at 491, 100 S.Ct. at 2781, citing Regents of University of California v. Bakke, 438 U.S. 265, 98 S.Ct. 2733, 57 L.Ed.2d 750 (1978).

15. 448 U.S. at 485, 100 S.Ct. at 2778.

16. 448 U.S. at 489, 100 S.Ct. at 2780. The plurality also said that under section 5, "congressional authority extends beyond the prohibition of purposeful discrimination to encompass state action that has discriminatory impact perpetuating the effects of past discrimination." 448 U.S. at 477, 100 S.Ct. at 2744.

Justice Powell's separate concurrence did not really apply the analysis he had advocated in *Bakke*; In *Fullilove* no special freedom of association or academic freedom was applicable to federal public works projects, though Powell had relied on that point in *Bakke*. Also, Powell in *Fullilove* approved of a 10% set aside even though Powell in *Bakke* had strongly objected to the medical school setting aside a minimum number of places reserved for blacks and other minorities. Powell in *Fullilove* did rely on section 5. 448 U.S. at 500, 100 S.Ct. at 2786.

Marshall concurring, joined by Brennan and Blackmun, relied on the Marshall analysis earlier promulgated in *Bakke* and therefore did not find it necessary to rely on section 5. The other three Justices dissented, objecting strongly to the use of racial criteria for the purposes of distributing government benefits. Rehnquist and Stewart, believed that the Constitution absolutely prohibited the use of racial criteria, and Stevens objected because the statute was not narrowly tailored, was not adequately preceded by a consideration of less drastic alternatives, and was not adequately explained by a statement of legislative purpose.

17. 515 U.S. 200, 115 S.Ct. 2097, 132 L.Ed.2d 158 (1995). The *Adarand* Court also overruled Metro Broadcasting, Inc. v. F.C.C., 497 U.S. 547, 110 S.Ct. 2997, 111 L.Ed.2d 445 (1990), which did not apply strict scrutiny to a federal affirmative action program.

18. Between *Fullilove* and *Adarand*, various members of the Court referred to Congressional power under section 5 in opinions supporting Congressional affirmative action programs or invalidating affirmative action programs of states or subdivisions of states. See, e.g., Wygant v. Jackson Board of Education, 476 U.S. 267, 281, 106 S.Ct. 1842, 1850–51, 90 L.Ed.2d 260 (1986), Powell, J., joined by Burger, C.J. & Rehnquist, J., invalidating a Jackson Board of Education affirmative action plan and distinguishing the plan approved in *Fullilove* as "within the remedial power of Congress in part because the 'actual burden shouldered by the nonminority firms is relatively light.' "See also, Richmond v. J.A. Croson Co., 488 U.S. 469, 490, 109 S.Ct. 706, 719, 102 L.Ed.2d 854 (1989), invalidating city affirmative action construction program patterned somewhat after the *Fullilove* program; the plurality opinion of O'Connor, J., joined by Rehnquist, C.J. and White J., noted, in distinguishing *Fullilove*, "What appellant ignores is that Congress, unlike any State or political subdivision, has a specific constitutional mandate to enforce the dictates of the Fourteenth Amendment. The power to 'enforce' may at times also include the power to define situations which *Congress* determines threatens principles of equality and to adopt prophylactic rules to deal with those situations." (emphasis in original).

***Metro Broadcasting* overruled.** Metro Broadcasting Inc. v. F.C.C., 497 U.S. 547, 563, 110 S.Ct. 2997, 3008, 111 L.Ed.2d 445 (1990), Brennan, J., for the Court, upheld an affirmative action program of the Federal Communications Commission, citing *Fullilove* and stating: "It is of

Congress should not, by enacting creative legislation, recast a simple dilution of one right as an expansion of another right. A Congress bent on restricting desegregation might enact a law that purports to provide—in an effort to expand freedom of choice—that states should establish a variety of schools and allow people to transfer to their preferred schools, even if the result of such transfers is that some schools became disproportionately white or black. While a court should not accept a subterfuge, it was not enough for the Court to announce, like an ipse dixit, that section 5 does not authorize Congress to dilute constitutional rights, because legislation can be redrafted so that dilution of some rights is caused by expansion of other rights. While the *Morgan* Court was correct that section 5 could not have been intended to authorize Congress to limit Fourteenth Amendment rights, the Court's opinion would not have suffered if it had offered more explanation.[19]

As a logical matter, section 5 of the Fourteenth Amendment does not grant or fortify any special congressional power to do something that would violate section 1 of the Fourteenth Amendment if a state did it. Recall that in *Morgan*, Congress used section 5 to eliminate state literacy obstacles to the right to exercise the franchise without regard to race. The New York legislature could itself have enacted these reforms without raising any constitutional questions. Section 5 was intended to expand Congressional power at the expense of the states, not at the expense of the Court;

section 5 only allowed Congress to do that which New York could have already done. Section 5 simply allowed Congress to enact these reforms without New York being able to raise successfully a Tenth Amendment defense or any other federalism argument. Thus, if an affirmative action plan violates the Constitution, section 5 should not give Congress any special power to engage in validating such a violation.[20] Otherwise, the caveat in footnote 10 of *Morgan* is wrong.[21]

Private Conduct and Section Five. The present case law does not allow section 5 to be used to reach private conduct. No majority opinion thus far has accepted the invitation of the dictum by the Justices in *Guest*.[22] While *Morgan* and its progeny confirm Congressional power to override state *laws* that interfere with Fourteenth Amendment rights, there is no Supreme Court case holding that Congress, by statute, may reach purely private actions, though some lower courts have so held.[23] The Supreme Court cases dealing with Congressional power to enforce civil rights against purely private acts have justified these laws by a Thirteenth Amendment analysis. It is to those cases that we now turn.

§ 15.6   Congressional Enforcement of the Thirteenth Amendment and State Action

The Thirteenth Amendment is fairly unique in two respects. First, it contains an absolute bar to the existence of slavery or involuntary

---

overriding significance in these cases that the FCC's minority ownership programs have been specifically approved—indeed, mandated—by Congress." The Court overruled *Metro Broadcasting* in Adarand Constructors, Inc. v. Pena, 515 U.S. 200, 115 S.Ct. 2097, 132 L.Ed.2d 158 (1995).

19. Ronald D. Rotunda, The Americans with Disabilities Act, Bar Examinations, and the Constitution: A Balancing Act, 66 The Bar Examiner 6 (No. 3, August, 1997).

20. No Congressional Power to Dilute § 1. Mississippi University for Women v. Hogan, 458 U.S. 718, 102 S.Ct. 3331, 73 L.Ed.2d 1090 (1982). *Hogan* held that the state, under the Fourteenth Amendment, could not have a female-only nursing school, and that no federal statute could excuse the state from such sex discrimination.

Later, the Court reemphasized that—

"Congress has no affirmative power to authorize the States to violate the Fourteenth Amendment and is

implicitly prohibited from passing legislation that purports to validate any such violation."

Saenz v. Roe, 526 U.S. 489, 119 S.Ct. 1518, 1529, 143 L.Ed.2d 689 (1999). Following this statement, the Court extensively quoted language from *Mississippi University for Women* making this same point.

21. 384 U.S. at 651–52 n. 10, 86 S.Ct. at 1724 n. 10.

22. United States v. Guest, 383 U.S. 745, 86 S.Ct. 1170, 16 L.Ed.2d 239 (1966).

23. E.g., Westberry v. Gilman Paper Co., 507 F.2d 206 (5th Cir.1975) (42 U.S.C.A. § 1985(3) applicable to private discriminatory acts; here private persons allegedly conspired to kill plaintiff in violation of 14th Amendment equal protection and due process guarantees); but see, Bellamy v. Mason's Stores, Inc., 508 F.2d 504 (4th Cir. 1974) (while 42 U.S.C.A. § 1985(3) does not apply to private acts, perhaps Congress could enact such a statute).

servitude; there is no requirement of "state action." Thus it is applicable to individuals as well as states. "By its own unaided force and effect it abolished slavery, and established universal freedom."[1] Secondly, like the Fourteenth and Fifteenth Amendments, it contains an enforcement clause, enabling Congress to pass all necessary legislation.

§ 15.7 The Civil Rights Cases and the Thirteenth Amendment

The Supreme Court first examined comprehensively the scope of the Thirteenth Amendment in the *Civil Rights Cases*[1] in 1883. Five cases were joined, all arising from criminal prosecutions against private citizens who denied blacks the privileges and accommodations of hotels or theaters. The issue was the constitutionality of the Civil Rights Act of 1875, which provided that all persons were entitled to equal access to inns, public conveyances and places of amusement regardless of race and that any person denying another such access was subject to suit. The government contended that the Thirteenth Amendment justified the statute.

The Court agreed that the Thirteenth Amendment abolished slavery and that its prohibition applied to individual citizens, as well as the states. The Court also found that "the power vested in Congress to enforce the article by appropriate legislation, clothes Congress with power to pass all laws necessary and proper for abolishing all badges and incidents of slavery in the United States...."[2]

The question then became whether "the denial to any person of admission to the accommodations and privileges of an inn, a public conveyance, or a theatre [subjected] that person to any form of servitude or [tended] to fasten upon him any badge of slavery."[3] The Court ruled it did not and that the Thirteenth

Amendment did not authorize Congress to enact such a law. The purpose of the Thirteenth Amendment is to vindicate "those fundamental rights which appertain to the essence of citizenship"[4] not to adjust "social rights."[5] The Court said it would be carrying the slavery concept too far if it were applied to actions denying blacks access to inns or theaters. "Mere discriminations on account of race or color were not regarded as badges of slavery."[6] The Court held that the Thirteenth Amendment did not justify the first two sections of the Civil Rights Act of 1875 (because they did not involve the badges of slavery), and the Fourteenth Amendment did not justify them either (because they did not involve state action).[7] The Court then invalidated these sections of the Civil Rights Act of 1875.

However, the Court did go on and carefully distinguish Congress' enforcement powers under the Thirteenth and Fourteenth Amendments:

Under the Thirteenth Amendment, the legislation, so far as necessary or proper to eradicate all forms and incidents of slavery and involuntary servitude, may be direct and primary, operating upon the acts of individuals, whether sanctioned by State legislation or not; under the Fourteenth as we have already shown, it must necessarily be, and can only be, corrective in its character, addressed to counteract and afford relief against state regulations or proceedings.[8]

Justice Harlan dissented vigorously. He did not believe the Court should place a limitation on the Congress' power to define and prohibit badges of slavery. He stated further that discrimination on the basis of race could constitute a badge of slavery. The rights involved here are fundamental rights. No class of people should be in practical subjection to another

---

§ 15.6

1. In re Civil Rights Cases, 109 U.S. 3, 20, 3 S.Ct. 18, 28, 27 L.Ed. 835 (1883).

§ 15.7

1. 109 U.S. 3, 3 S.Ct. 18, 27 L.Ed. 835 (1883).
2. 109 U.S. at 20, 3 S.Ct. at 28.
3. 109 U.S. at 21, 3 S.Ct. at 28.

4. 109 U.S. at 22, 3 S.Ct. at 30.
5. 109 U.S. at 23, 3 S.Ct. at 30.
6. 109 U.S. at 25, 3 S.Ct. at 32.
7. 109 U.S. at 24, 3 S.Ct. at 30–31.
8. 109 U.S. at 23, 3 S.Ct. at 30.

class.[9]

For the most part, after the *Civil Rights* decision the Thirteenth Amendment lay dormant for nearly a century.[10]

§ 15.8   Section 1982 and the Modern Thirteenth Amendment

The Supreme Court finally gave the anti-slavery Amendment new force in *Jones v. Alfred H. Mayer Co.*[1] The controversy in *Jones* arose when defendants, a subdivision developer, builder, and realtor, refused to sell housing or land to blacks. Mr. Joseph Lee Jones and his wife then sued; they were not allowed to buy property because the husband was black.[2] There was no state action; in fact, the private developer even provided all facilities such as sewer, garbage collection and sidewalks. No federal aid was involved that might have subjected the defendants to executive orders or federal statutes prohibiting discrimination in publicly financed projects. The principal issue

was, then, one of private racial discrimination in refusing to sell housing. To decide this case, the Court resurrected a provision of the 1866 Civil Rights Act.[3]

Notwithstanding some arguable ambiguities,[4] the Court read the legislative history of Section 1982, along with its language and judicial history,[5] as proof that the drafters intended the act to apply to private as well as public acts of discrimination. The Court ruled that legislation *rationally* connected with eradicating slavery or its badges or incidents is valid under the Thirteenth Amendment, and that private discrimination may constitute such a badge or incident.[6] It then concluded that Section 1982 should be construed as reaching private discrimination in the sale of property. As so construed, it is a valid enactment under the Thirteenth Amendment.[7]

Thus, the primary basis of this decision became the Thirteenth Amendment. What had

---

9.   109 U.S. at 27–62, 3 S.Ct. at 33–57.

10.   Conscripted Labor for the State. An important case during this period is Butler v. Perry, 240 U.S. 328, 36 S.Ct. 258, 60 L.Ed. 672 (1916). The Supreme Court there stated:

> "[The Thirteenth Amendment] certainly was not intended to interdict enforcement of those duties which individuals owe to the State, such as services to the army, militia, on the jury, etc."

240 U.S. at 333, 36 S.Ct. at 259.

In *Butler* the court upheld a state statute requiring able-bodied males between 21 and 45 years of age to work on public roads for a certain time, or to provide in lieu of the work the sum of $3 or an able-bodied substitute.

The Military Draft. The military draft laws forcing labor out of soldiers and conscientious objectors have also been upheld. Arver v. United States, 245 U.S. 366, 390, 38 S.Ct. 159, 165, 62 L.Ed. 349 (1918).

Labor Disputes. Injunctions in labor disputes do not involve involuntary servitude. International Union v. Wisconsin Employment Relations Bd., 336 U.S. 245, 69 S.Ct. 516, 93 L.Ed. 651 (1949), rehearing denied 336 U.S. 970, 69 S.Ct. 935, 93 L.Ed. 1121 (1949).

Peonage. The state may not engage a person in forced labor in order to liquidate a civil debt or obligation. Peonage Cases, 123 Fed. 671 (M.D.Ala.1903). "The state may impose involuntary servitude as a punishment for crime, but it may not compel one man to labor for another in payment of a debt, by punishing him as a criminal if he does not perform the service or pay the debt:" Bailey v. Alabama, 219 U.S. 219, 244, 31 S.Ct. 145, 152, 55 L.Ed. 191 (1911).

§ 15.8

1.   392 U.S. 409, 88 S.Ct. 2186, 20 L.Ed.2d 1189 (1968).

2.   See the lower court decision, 379 F.2d 33, 35 (8th Cir.1967). Judge (later Justice) Blackmun wrote this decision, which the Supreme Court reversed.

Mr. Jones' wife was white.

3.   Ch. 31, § 1, 14 Stat. 27, codified at 42 U.S.C.A. § 1982.

4.   Section 1982, guaranteeing to all citizens "the same right, in every State and Territory, as is enjoyed by white citizens thereof to inherit, purchase, lease, sell, hold and convey real and personal property", had been interpreted to have an enforcement provision (now codified as 18 U.S.C.A. § 242), which applied to only acts committed under color of state law. See In re Civil Rights Cases, 109 U.S. 3, 16–17, 3 S.Ct. 18, 24–25, 27 L.Ed. 835 (1883). The state action requirement, though an arguable limitation on the substance of § 1982, was neither clearly applicable nor clearly inapplicable to the provision.

5.   See Section IV of Justice Stewart's opinion, 392 U.S. at 422, 88 S.Ct. at 2194 (legislative history); Section III, 392 U.S. at 420, 88 S.Ct. at 2193 (plain meaning); Section II, 392 U.S. at 417, 88 S.Ct. at 2191–92 (judicial history).

6.   392 U.S. at 437–44, 88 S.Ct. at 2202–06. See also 392 U.S. at 440–41, 88 S.Ct. at 2203–04: "Nor can we say that the determination Congress has made is an irrational one."

7.   In re Civil Rights Cases, 109 U.S. 3, 3 S.Ct. 18, 27 L.Ed. 835 (1883) avoided the question of the constitutionality of § 1982 by noting that it was limited in its scope by the enforcement provision, now 18 U.S.C.A. § 242, which applies only to state action. 109 U.S. at 16–17, 3 S.Ct. at 24–25.

been described as "an unserviceable antique"[8] now became the basis for a broad Congressional protection of civil rights without a "state action" limitation. The enabling clause of the Amendment, the Court held, is a grant of power to Congress not only to outlaw forced labor but also to identify "badges of slavery" and pass legislation "necessary and proper" to eliminate them.[9] If the Thirteenth Amendment does not give Congress the power to insure minorities at least the "freedom to buy whatever a white man can buy, the right to live wherever a white man can live," then its promise of freedom would be a hollow one, a "mere paper guarantee."[10]

The Court found it necessary to make several incidental holdings in order to reach this conclusion. The Court interpreted section 1982 to provide an equitable remedy despite the fact that it may be read to be declaratory in nature.[11] The Court also overruled *Hodges v. United States*,[12] a case that had ruled that the Thirteenth Amendment did not affect individual rights unconnected with the institution of slavery.[13]

Lower courts applied the principles enunciated in *Jones* to the sale of used homes,[14] and the leasing of housing and apartments.[15] In *Sullivan v. Little Hunting Park, Inc.*,[16] the Supreme Court extended *Jones* to hold that discrimination in certain community facilities in connection with the rental of property entitles the injured party to a private right of action for damages under section 1982.

Petitioner Sullivan was a white member of Little Hunting Park, Inc., a corporation organized for the benefit of residents in a subdivision of Fairfax County, Virginia. Membership entitled a resident and his family to use various recreational facilities. The share in the corporation designating membership could be assigned by the shareholder to the lessee of his residence, subject to approval by the board of directors. Sullivan attempted an assignment to his black lessee, T. R. Freeman, but Little Rock Park, Inc. refused him admittance to the nonstock corporation and denied him use of its facilities.[17] In addition, Little Rock Park expelled Sullivan after he began a campaign to convince the board to reverse its decision.

Petitioners brought action for monetary and injunctive relief under the Civil Rights Act of 1866.[18] In reversing the trial court's judgment[19] the Supreme Court held that Little Rock Park could not refuse to approve an assignment on the basis of the lessee's race. *Sullivan* logically extended the reach of § 1982 beyond the interpretation in *Jones* by holding that distinctions between real and personal property in characterizing the membership share are immaterial, because section 1982 covers both types of property.[20] The Supreme Court also rejected the Virginia trial court's finding that the Little Hunting Park was a truly private social club:

There was no plan or purpose of exclusiveness. It is open to every white person within

8. Note, The "New" Thirteenth Amendment: A Preliminary Analysis, 82 Harvard Law Review 1294 (1969).

9. 392 U.S. at 439–40, 88 S.Ct. at 2203.

10. 392 U.S. at 443, 88 S.Ct. at 2205.

11. 392 U.S. at 414, n. 13, 88 S.Ct. at 2189–90 n. 13.

12. 203 U.S. 1, 27 S.Ct. 6, 51 L.Ed. 65 (1906).

13. 392 U.S. at 441–43, n. 78, 88 S.Ct. at 2204–05 n. 78.

14. Contract Buyers League v. F & F Investment, 300 F.Supp. 210 (N.D.Ill.1969), judgment affirmed 420 F.2d 1191 (7th Cir.1970), certiorari denied 400 U.S. 821, 91 S.Ct. 40, 27 L.Ed.2d 49 (1970).

15. Vaughn v. Ting Su, 1 Race Rel.L.Survey 45 (N.D.Cal. July 19, 1968); Bush v. Kaim, 17 Ohio Misc. 259, 297 F.Supp. 151 (N.D.Ohio 1969); Pina v. Homsi, 1 Race Rel.L.Survey 183 (D.Mass. July 10, 1969).

16. 396 U.S. 229, 90 S.Ct. 400, 24 L.Ed.2d 386 (1969).

17. After Sullivan's assignment of the membership share to the lessee, the board of directors for the corporation refused to approve petitioner Freeman's membership. Sullivan had third party standing to maintain this action. "[T]he white owner is at times 'the only effective adversary' . . ." 396 U.S. at 237, 90 S.Ct. at 404.

18. Ch. 31, § 1, 94 Stat. 27, now U.S.C.A. § 1982, which reads as follows:

"All citizens of the United States shall have the same right in every State and Territory, as is enjoyed by white citizens thereof to inherit, purchase, lease, sell, hold and convey real and personal property."

19. The trial court had upheld the board's action and the Supreme Court of Appeals of Virginia refused to review the decision.

20. 396 U.S. at 236, 90 S.Ct. at 404.

the geographic area, there being no selective element other than race.[21]

Section 1982 Used by Whites

Section 1982 is aimed at protecting people from racially based discrimination. It is not essential that the plaintiff in a section 1982 action be black; it is only necessary that the defendants' actions be motivated by racial animus and that such animus was directed towards the kind of animus that Congress—in the middle of the Nineteenth Century—intended to protect when it passed section 1982. It is true that section 1982 uses the phrase, "the same right ... as is enjoyed by white citizens ..." but the purpose of this phrase is merely to emphasize the racial character of the rights being protected and does not preclude the use of this law by non-blacks.[22]

Indeed, section 1982 can be used not only by whites claiming racial discrimination in favor of blacks,[23] but also encompasses claims of discrimination by one Caucasian group against another, because the Nineteenth Century Congress, which enacted section 1982, understood race in terms of ethnic groups. The legislative history makes that clear. For example, the Congressmen of that time referred to the law as protecting blacks, Anglo–Saxons, Jews, Spanish, Latinos, Scandinavians, and so on.[24] As Representative Shellabarger said in 1866:

> Who will say that Ohio can pass a law enacting that no man of the *German race* ... shall ever own any property in Ohio....

If Ohio may pass such a law, and exclude a German citizen ... because he is of the German *nationality or race*, then may every other State do so.[25]

Thus, *Shaare Tefila Congregation v. Cobb*,[26] ruled that Jews could use section 1982 to sue other *white* defendants who had allegedly desecrated their synagogue. At the time section 1982 was adopted, "Jews and Arabs were among the peoples then considered to be distinct races and hence within the protection of the statute."[27]

Statutes of Limitations

Section 1982 does not contain a statute of limitations. Because claims under that section are in essence claims of personal injury—the personal right to engage in certain activities (to inherit, lease, sell, and convey real and personal property) without regard to racial discrimination—the courts should, as a matter of federal law, borrow the state statute of limitations applicable to claims for personal injury.[28]

§ 15.9   Sections 1985 and 1986

Griffin and § 1985.

The Supreme Court built on its earlier cases and further expanded the range of federal civil remedies available to victims of private racial discrimination when it determined, in *Griffin v. Breckenridge*,[1] that actions for damages under section 1985(3) of title 42[2] do not have to

---

21.   396 U.S. at 236, 90 S.Ct. at 404.

22.   See, McDonald v. Santa Fe Trail Transportation, 427 U.S. 273, 96 S.Ct. 2574, 49 L.Ed.2d 493 (1976), on remand 540 F.2d 219 (5th Cir.1976) (construing a parallel law, § 1981).

23.   McDonald v. Santa Fe Trail Transportation Co., 427 U.S. 273, 96 S.Ct. 2574, 49 L.Ed.2d 493 (1976).

24.   See, e.g., Cong.Globe, 39th Cong., 1st Sess., 499 (1866) (Scandinavians); id. at 238 (Latinos); id. at 251 (Spanish); id. at 542 (Anglo–Saxons, Jews, and Mexicans); id. at 498 (Gypsies).

25.   Cong.Globe, 39th Cong., 1st Sess., 1294 (1866) (emphasis added).

26.   481 U.S. 615, 107 S.Ct. 2019, 95 L.Ed.2d 594 (1987). See also, Saint Francis College v. Al–Khazraji, 481 U.S. 604, 107 S.Ct. 2022, 95 L.Ed.2d 582 (1987), where the Court held that § 1981 protected Arabs who claimed discrimination solely because of their ancestry or ethnic

characteristics; if the plaintiff must prove that he was subjected to intentional discrimination based on the fact that he was born an Arab, rather than solely on the place or nation of his origin, or his religion, then he has a cause of action under § 1981.

27.   481 U.S. at 617, 107 S.Ct. at 2020.

28.   Cf. Goodman v. Lukens Steel Co., 482 U.S. 656, 107 S.Ct. 2617, 96 L.Ed.2d 572 (1987) (discussing § 1981).

§ 15.9

1.   403 U.S. 88, 91 S.Ct. 1790, 29 L.Ed.2d 338 (1971).

2.   42 U.S.C.A. § 1985(3) provides in part:

"If two or more persons ... conspire or go in disguise on the highway ... for the purpose of depriving, either directly or indirectly, any person or class of persons of the equal protection of the laws, or of equal privileges and immunities under the laws; ... whereby another is injured in his person or property, or deprived of having and exercising any right or privilege of a citizen of the

allege state action. Prior to *Griffin*, federal civil remedies against purely private conduct protected only racially motivated denials of a few specific rights.[3] Although 42 U.S.C.A. § 1983 protects civil rights in general, it requires action under color of law. *Griffin* established § 1985(3) as a major federal remedy giving broad protection against private racial discrimination.

Griffin was based on events that occurred in the summer of 1966, when the civil rights movement was at its peak and racial tensions were high, particularly in the South. Plaintiffs, four black residents of Mississippi, were passengers in a car being driven on a public highway in Mississippi by a black resident of Tennessee. Two local white residents, mistaking the driver of the car for a civil rights worker, blocked the car on the highway, forced the occupants out, and then severely beat them with clubs.

The four black passengers, sustaining severe physical injuries and emotional damage, sued under section 1985(3) seeking damages for the alleged racially motivated assault and conspiracy to interfere with the right of a citizen to travel. The district court dismissed the complaint because there was no allegation that the defendants were acting under color of state law. The Fifth Circuit affirmed, relying on an earlier case that had held that section 1985(3) applied only to conspiracies involving state action.[4] The Supreme Court reversed and remanded for trial on the merits holding that actions can be brought under section 1985(3) against private conspiracies that interfere with the right of interstate travel.

The Court thus eliminated the "color of law" requirement that it had read into section 1985(3) earlier,[5] at least for plaintiffs alleging racial motivation. *Griffin* looked at the equal protection language of section 1985(3) and found "nothing inherent in the phrase that requires the action working the deprivation to come from the State."[6] The Court interpreted the terms "equal protection" and "equal privileges", at least as applied to private action in section 1985(3), to mean the "equal enjoyment of legal rights" free from all interference.[7] Writing for a unanimous Court, Justice Stewart stated that, as applied to the complaint in *Griffin*, section 1985(3) is constitutional under the enforcement clause of the Thirteenth Amendment. Alternatively, the Court held, by a vote of eight to one, that the statute as applied was constitutional as an exercise of congressional power to protect the fundamental right of interstate travel.[8]

The statute's requirement of a purpose to deprive of equal rights means that in a section 1985(3) case, plaintiff must show some "racial, or perhaps otherwise class-based, invidiously discriminatory animus behind the conspirators' action."[9] The Court wanted to make sure that this statute does not become a general federal tort law. However, the Court explicitly stated that proof of specific intent was not necessary to establish a cause of action under the statute.[10]

Thus, as interpreted in *Griffin*, plaintiffs' complaint stated a cause of action because it alleged the four necessary elements: 1) there was a conspiracy; 2) "for the purpose of depriving, either directly or indirectly, any person or class of persons of the equal protection

---

United States, the party so injured or deprived may have an action for the recovery of damages...."

3. See, e.g., 42 U.S.C.A. § 1982 (the right to purchase or rent property); 42 U.S.C.A. § 2000a–3.

4. See Collins v. Hardyman, 341 U.S. 651, 71 S.Ct. 937, 95 L.Ed. 1253 (1951).

5. Collins v. Hardyman, 341 U.S. 651, 71 S.Ct. 937, 95 L.Ed. 1253 (1951). *Collins* was not a constitutional decision, only one of statutory interpretation.

6. 403 U.S. at 97, 91 S.Ct. at 1796.

7. 403 U.S. at 102–03, 91 S.Ct. at 1798.

8. The Court did not reach the Fourteenth Amendment question.

Justice Harlan declined to rely on the right to interstate travel as a constitutional basis for the statute as applied. 403 U.S. at 107, 91 S.Ct. at 1801. His vote was not necessary to the opinion of the Court, which all the other Justices joined in its entirety.

9. 403 U.S. at 102, 91 S.Ct. at 1798. Cf. General Building Contractors Ass'n, Inc. v. Pennsylvania, 458 U.S. 375, 102 S.Ct. 3141, 73 L.Ed.2d 835 (1982) holding that proof of racially discriminatory intent is necessary to make out a violation of 42 U.S.C.A. § 1981.

10. 403 U.S. at 102 n. 10, 91 S.Ct. at 1798 n. 10. This test differs from 18 U.S.C.A. § 241, the criminal analogue to § 1985(3), which requires proof of specific intent to deprive the victims of the conspiracy of a constitutional right.

of the laws, or of equal privileges and immunities under the laws;" 3) there was an act in furtherance of the conspiracy; 4) whereby someone was injured in his person or property or deprived of any right or privilege of a citizen of the United States.[11]

Free Speech. *Griffin* involved racial animus. The application of section 1985(3) is different if the purpose of the alleged conspiracy is to infringe First Amendment rights. "[A]n alleged conspiracy to infringe First Amendment rights is not a violation of § 1985(3) unless it is proved that the state is involved in the conspiracy or that the aim of the conspiracy is to influence the activity of the state."[12] The conspiracy in *Griffin* involved rights protected by the Thirteenth Amendment and the right to travel.[13] Violation of these rights do not require proof of state action.

However, conspiracies aimed at violations of the right to speech are different. Because the First Amendment "only restrains official conduct," section 1985(3) plaintiffs must "prove that the state was somehow involved in or affected by the conspiracy."[14] Even if section 1985(3) might reach conspiracies against organizations because of their political views, that section does not apply to conspiracies motivated by the economic views of others, or their economic status, or their economic activities. Thus, section 1985(3) does not apply to

conspiracies against workers who refuse to join a union.[15]

Free Speech and Abortion Clinics. *Bray v. Alexandria Women's Health Clinic*[16] held that the first clause of section 1985(3) does not provide a federal cause of action against persons obstructing access to abortion clinics. The lower court had enjoined Operation Rescue, an antiabortion group, claiming that the group and its members conspired to deprive women seeking abortions of their right to interstate travel. The Supreme Court rejected that conclusion, holding that opposition to abortion does not reflect an animus to women as a class. Opponents of abortion include women, and their opposition to abortion does not focus on women "by reason of their sex." Moreover, it was irrelevant to the opponents of abortion that many of the women seeking abortion engaged in interstate travel prior to the abortion.[17]

Section 1985(1), (2), & (3), Compared.

The first part of § 1985(2), which prohibits intimidation of witnesses in federal court, requires no allegation of class based animus because of its plain language, its legislative history, the federal government's unquestioned and inherent authority to protect the processes of its own courts, and the absence of any need to limit this section in order to avoid creating any general federal law of torts.[18]

---

11. 403 U.S. at 102–03, 91 S.Ct. at 1798, 29 L.Ed.2d at 348. See also, United Brotherhood of Carpenters and Joiners of America v. Scott, 463 U.S. 825, 829, 103 S.Ct. 3352, 3356, 77 L.Ed.2d 1049 (1983), on remand 715 F.2d 161 (5th Cir.1983), rehearing denied 464 U.S. 875, 104 S.Ct. 211, 78 L.Ed.2d 186 (1983).

12. United Brotherhood of Carpenters and Joiners of America v. Scott, 463 U.S. 825, 830, 103 S.Ct. 3352, 3357–58, 77 L.Ed.2d 1049 (1983), on remand 715 F.2d 161 (5th Cir.1983), rehearing denied 464 U.S. 875, 104 S.Ct. 211, 78 L.Ed.2d 186 (1983).

13. 403 U.S. at 105–07, 91 S.Ct. at 1799–1801, 29 L.Ed.2d at 350–51.

14. 463 U.S. at 833, 103 S.Ct. at 3358, 77 L.Ed.2d at 1057.

15. 463 U.S. at 836–38, 103 S.Ct. at 3359–60, 77 L.Ed.2d at 1059–60.

16. 506 U.S. 263, 113 S.Ct. 753, 122 L.Ed.2d 34 (1993). Scalia, J., wrote the opinion for the Court, joined by Rehnquist, C.J. & White, Kennedy, & Thomas, JJ. Stevens, J. & O'Connor, J., each filed dissenting opinions, both of which Blackmun, J., joined.

17. The Hindrance Clause. The Court also rejected the position of the dissenters, who argued that there was any violation of the second clause of § 1985(3), which covers conspiracies to prevent or hinder any state securing equal protection to all persons. The majority said that if any party had raised it below, it would likely fail because the hindrance clause also contains requirement of "class-based animus." Also, the trial court had found that Operation Rescue and its members did not intend to hinder official law enforcement.

18. Kush v. Rutledge, 460 U.S. 719, 103 S.Ct. 1483, 75 L.Ed.2d 413 (1983) (Stevens, J., for a unanimous Court). The Court said that a similar result would be reached with respect to 42 U.S.C.A. § 1985(1) (federal officers); the first part of § 1985(2) (federal judicial proceedings); and the second part of § 1985(3) (federal elections). In contrast, the second part of § 1985(2) (conspiracies to obstruct justice in state courts) and the first part of § 1985(3) (conspiracy to go in disguise on the highway) are not institutionally linked to federal interests and do require that the conspirators' actions be motivated by intent to deprive victims of equal protection.

Similarly, the conspirators need not be motivated by an intent to deprive their victims of equal protection in order to find a violation of § 1985(1) (federal officers); the first part of § 1985(2) (federal judicial proceedings); and the second part of § 1985(3) (federal elections). In contrast, the second part of § 1985(2) (conspiracies to obstruct justice in state courts) and the first part of § 1985(3) (conspiracy to go in disguise on the highway) are not institutionally linked to federal interests and do require that the conspirators' actions be motivated by intent to deprive victims of equal protection.[19]

The purpose of § 1985(2) is to protect persons against conspiracies to intimidate them or retaliate against them because they are witnesses in federal court proceedings. A litigant suing under this section need not show that he or she has suffered a constitutionally protected property interest in order to state a claim because neither the language nor the purpose of the first clause of § 1985(2) impose such a requirement. Hence, a terminated at-will employee states a cause of action for damages under this section when he alleges that the defendants conspired to have him fired from his job in retaliation for obeying a federal grand jury subpoena and to deter him from testifying at a federal criminal trial.[20]

Section 1986.

Supplementing the principal civil rights remedies of section 1985, is section 1986, which imposes an affirmative duty on those persons with knowledge[21] of a planned section 1985 violation and the power to prevent it (e.g., city police).[22] Any person[23] who neglects or refuses to exercise his preventive power is liable to a section 1985 plaintiff for the damages he reasonably could have prevented. Implicit in the damages provision of section 1986 is the necessity of a successful section 1985 claim.[24] Thus, a section 1986 claim incorporates each element of the section 1985 cause of action on which it is based.

§ 15.10 Section 1981 in the Modern Era

While section 1982 prohibits racial discrimination in property, section 1981 regulates the making and enforcing of contracts and other rights.[1] The question whether federal law prohibits a private school denying admission to

---

19. Kush v. Rutledge, 460 U.S. 719, 724–25, 103 S.Ct. 1483, 1487, 75 L.Ed.2d 413 (1983)

20. Haddle v. Garrison, 525 U.S. 121, 119 S.Ct. 489, 142 L.Ed.2d 502 (1998).

21. "Liability under § 1986 ... is dependent on proof of actual knowledge by a defendant of the wrongful conduct of his subordinates." Hampton v. City of Chicago, 484 F.2d 602 (7th Cir.1973), certiorari denied 415 U.S. 917, 94 S.Ct. 1413, 39 L.Ed.2d 471 (1974).

22. In Hampton v. Hanrahan, 600 F.2d 600 (7th Cir. 1979), reversal of award of attorneys' fees 446 U.S. 754, 100 S.Ct. 1987, 64 L.Ed.2d 670 (1980), plaintiffs alleged claims under §§ 1985(3) and 1983 against Chicago police and attorneys in the Cook County State's Attorney's Office.

23. "Person" does not include a municipal corporation. A plaintiff may not maintain a § 1986 cause of action against a city, though he may proceed against city officials individually. Bosely v. City of Euclid, 496 F.2d 193, 195 (6th Cir.1974). See also Arunga v. Weldon, 469 F.2d 675, 675–76 (9th Cir.1972).

24. Creative Environments, Inc. v. Estabrook, 680 F.2d 822 (1st Cir.1982), certiorari denied 459 U.S. 989, 103 S.Ct. 345, 74 L.Ed.2d 385 (1982) (§ 1986 claim fails with no § 1985 claim to support it).

§ 15.10

1. 42 U.S.C.A. § 1981 provides, as amended in 1991, which added subsections (b) and (c):

"(a) All persons within the jurisdiction of the United States shall have the same right in every State and Territory to make and enforce contracts, to sue, be parties, give evidence, and to the full and equal benefit of all laws and proceedings for the security of persons and property as is enjoyed by white citizens, and shall be subject to like punishment, pains, penalties, taxes, licenses, and exactions of every kind, and to no other.

"(b) For purposes of this section, the term 'make and enforce contracts' includes the making, performance, modification, and termination of contracts, and the enjoyment of all benefits, privileges, terms, and conditions of the contractual relationship.

"(c) The rights protected by this section are protected against impairment by nongovernmental discrimination and impairment under color of State law."

Congress enacted the 1991 Amendments to overrule part of Patterson v. McLean Credit Union, 491 U.S. 164, 109 S.Ct. 2363, 105 L.Ed.2d 132 (1989), which had interpreted § 1981 not to apply to racial harassment that occurs *after* the formation of the contract. Rotunda, The Civil Rights Act of 1991: A Brief Introductory Analysis of the Congressional Response to Judicial Interpretation, 68 Notre Dame L.Rev. 923 (1993).

qualified applicants solely because of their race (a contract right) came before the Supreme Court in *Runyon v. McCrary*.[2] Michael C. McCrary and Colin M. Gonzales, two black children, brought suit through their parents alleging that they had been denied entrance to the petitioner schools because of their race in violation of section 1981 of title 42.

The *Runyon* Case. Bobbe's Private School in Arlington, Virginia, and Fairfax–Brewster School, Inc., of Fairfax County, Virginia, were privately owned schools that regularly and widely advertised for applicants. Neither school had ever accepted a black applicant. In response to a mailed brochure addressed to "resident," and to an advertisement in the "Yellow Pages" of the telephone directory, Mr. & Mrs. Gonzales visited the Fairfax–Brewster School and submitted an application on behalf of their son Colin. The school refused his admission for the stated reason that the school was not integrated. Mr. Gonzales then telephoned the Bobbe's School, which had also sent the family a brochure mailed to "occupant." Once again, the school refused to admit Colin because he was not white. In August, 1972, Mrs. McCrary phoned the same school in response to an advertisement in the telephone book. When she inquired about nursery school facilities for her son, the school told that it was not integrated. The families then sued the schools under section 1981,[3] seeking declaratory, injunctive relief, and damages. The lower courts found for the children and petitioners appealed.

The Court held that section 1981 prohibits racial discrimination in the making and enforcement of private contracts. Hence, it prohibits private, commercially operated, non-sectarian schools from denying admission to prospective students because of their race.

The private schools had violated the respondent's contractual rights by not offering services on an equal basis to white and nonwhite students.

Later, *Jones v. Alfred H. Mayer Co.*[4] had held that section 1982 reached purely private acts of racial discrimination:

> Just as in *Jones*, a Negro's [§ 1982] right to purchase property on equal terms with whites was violated when a private person refused to sell to the prospective purchaser solely because he was a Negro, so also a Negro's [§ 1981] right to "make and enforce contracts" is violated if a private offeror refuses to extend to a Negro, solely because he is a Negro, the same opportunity to enter into contracts as he extends to white offerees.[5]

The schools had advertised and offered their services to the members of the general public in what was clearly an offering of a contractual relationship. The schools were to have performed educational services for the plaintiffs and in return would receive payments for the instructions. The children had been refused solely because they were black. This racial exclusion amounted to a "classic violation" of § 1981.[6]

Racial Discrimination by Religious Schools. *Runyon* specifically left open the question whether section 1981 would apply to a school that discriminated on the basis of race for religious reasons. Unlike pure racial discrimination, which has no constitutional protection, religiously based discrimination may possibly find some protection in the First Amendment.[7]

***Moose Lodge* Compared.** Unlike the facts

---

2. 427 U.S. 160, 96 S.Ct. 2586, 49 L.Ed.2d 415 (1976), appeal after remand 569 F.2d 1294 (4th Cir.1978), certiorari denied 439 U.S. 927, 99 S.Ct. 311, 58 L.Ed.2d 320 (1978). See, Rotunda, *Runyon v. McCrary* and the Mosaic of State Action, 67 Wash.U.L.Q. 47 (1989).

3. Suit was also brought under Title II of the Civil Rights Act of 1964, 42 U.S.C.A. § 2000a et seq., but the Title II claim was withdrawn before trial.

4. 392 U.S. 409, 441–43, 88 S.Ct. 2186, 2204–05, 20 L.Ed.2d 1189 (1968).

5. Runyon v. McCrary, 427 U.S. 160, 170–71, 96 S.Ct. 2586, 2594, 49 L.Ed.2d 415 (1976) (footnote omitted).

6. Runyon v. McCrary, 427 U.S. 160, 96 S.Ct. 2586, 49 L.Ed.2d 415 (1976), appeal after remand 569 F.2d 1294 (4th Cir.1978), certiorari denied 439 U.S. 927, 99 S.Ct. 311, 58 L.Ed.2d 320 (1978).

7. See, e.g., Bagni, Discrimination in the Name of the Lord: A Critical Evaluation of Discrimination by Religious Organizations, 79 Colum.L.Rev. 1514 (1979).

in *Moose Lodge No. 107 v. Irvis*,[8] the Court in *Runyon* did not have before it any question of the right of a private social organization to limit membership on the basis of race. *Moose Lodge* had held that the grant of a state liquor license to a private club that refused to serve blacks, and the continuing regulation of the liquor served in the club by the state liquor control board, did not constitute sufficient state action to invoke the equal protection clause of the Fourteenth Amendment.

Although the Court allowed private discrimination in *Moose Lodge* and barred it in *Runyon*, the distinction between the cases did not rely on the fact that the first involved liquor and the second education, nor in the fact that *Moose Lodge* did not purport to resolve the section 1981 issue. Both involved private contracts, but the key to distinguishing these cases lies in the nature of the facility itself.

Runyon involved educational facilities that were open to any white who could pay the set fees. The schools only refused applicants who were black. *Moose Lodge*, on the other hand, was not open to the general public. One could become a member only by invitation and the Lodge denied membership to some whites as well as all blacks. The key between the cases lies in the public nature of these schools and the private nature of the Lodge. The schools avidly solicited applications from all parents in the area and then denied contracts only to blacks. Although plaintiff in *Moose Lodge* did not attempt to rely on section 1981, that law would not have helped him because *Moose Lodge* did not solicit applications from the general public. Therefore section 1981 did not apply.

8. 407 U.S. 163, 92 S.Ct. 1965, 32 L.Ed.2d 627 (1972).

9. See Karst, The Freedom of Intimate Association, 89 Yale L.J. 624 (1980) (defines the freedom and explores its constitutional origins).

10. Hishon v. King & Spalding, 467 U.S. 69, 104 S.Ct. 2229, 81 L.Ed.2d 59 (1984).

11. Roberts v. United States Jaycees, 468 U.S. 609, 104 S.Ct. 3244, 82 L.Ed.2d 462 (1984) upheld a state law and administrative action that prohibited discrimination on the basis of sex in the membership practices of a large organization that engaged in both commercial and expressive activity. However, in so doing, the Court discussed the fact that various types of association, because of the na-

***Runyon* and Freedom of Association.** In *Runyon* the private schools solicited applications from the general public, while the private club in *Moose Lodge* did not. The Court found this distinction important in determining the application of section 1981, and therefore one would expect that section 1981 would not apply to truly private matters such as marriage contracts or similar contractual arrangements where the parties discriminate for various reasons, not merely because of race. Such contracts are not solicited from the general public. In addition, the application of section 1981 to such contracts would raise freedom of association issues.[9]

The Supreme Court has found that the governmental interest in ending "invidious private discrimination" allows some government-imposed restrictions of freedom of association through the use of laws prohibiting discrimination on the basis of sex or race.[10] However, the nature and purposes of an association may some provide constitutional protection from governmental intrusion.[11] For example, it is not clear to what extent the government may require religious groups or small political parties to alter their membership practices or other practices essential to their existence and purpose by prohibiting the groups from making certain decisions on the basis of race or sex. The Constitution may prohibit the government from providing aid to organizations that engage in invidious racial or sexual discrimination, even if the government may not prohibit some small constitutionally protected associations from engaging in discriminatory practices, if these practices do not have sufficient adverse public effects to justify government regulation.[12]

ture of their purposes, might receive greater protection from governmental regulations. Other organizations might receive less protection, where governmental regulations would not destroy the organization's very purpose or its members' ability to engage in First Amendment activity. The Court did not rule that any organization might be immune from antidiscrimination laws, but the Court did not address that question either in this case or in the *Runyon* case discussed in the previous paragraphs of this chapter.

12. States are constitutionally prohibited from giving aid to schools that discriminate in admissions decisions on the basis of race even though similar aid could be given to

Section 1981 Used by Whites. *Johnson v. Railway Express Agency, Inc.*[13] held that section 1981 provided blacks with a federal remedy against racial discrimination in private employment contracts. One year later the Court extended that ruling to protect whites. The Court ruled that the same remedy is available to any victim of racial discrimination in employment, white as well as black. In *McDonald v. Santa Fe Trail Transportation Co.*[14] two white employees, discharged for misappropriating cargo from one of the company's shipments, challenged their dismissal as racially discriminatory because the company did not fire a black accused of the same theft.

Relying on the language and legislative history of the act,[15] *McDonald* held that the law applies to protect whites despite the description in the statute of the protected rights being those "enjoyed by white citizens."[16] This phrase, in the Court's view, merely "emphasiz[ed]" the racial character of rights being protected and did not preclude use of the section by non-blacks. If the Court had held that the law only applied to protect blacks (or any racial group other than whites), the Court would have had to decide if such a law constituted unconstitutional reverse discrimination. *McDonald*'s interpretation of section 1981 avoided this question.

Not only may whites use section 1981 when claiming racial discrimination that favors blacks, but one Caucasian group may sue this law to bring claims of discrimination against another Caucasian group. The mid-nineteenth century Congress that enacted section 1981 intended to protect a person subject to discrimination "because he or she is genetically part of an ethnically and physiognomically distinctive sub-grouping of homo sapiens." However, a distinctive physiognomy is "not essential" under section 1981.[17]

Thus, *Saint Francis College v. Al–Khazraji*[18] held that an American citizen born in Iraq, who was denied tenure, could sue under section 1981 claiming discrimination: if the plaintiff "can prove that he was subjected to intentional discrimination based on the fact that he was *born an Arab*, rather than solely on the place or nation of his origin, or his religion, he will have made out a case under § 1981."[19]

Proving Racially Discriminatory Intent. One of the most important issues in this area of civil rights litigation involves the question of the inferences to be drawn from undisputed evidence. *Memphis v. Greene*[20] illustrates this issue. The Court upheld a city's closing of one end of a street traversing a white residential community. The street led to a neighbor-

---

nondiscriminatory private schools, including religious schools. See Norwood v. Harrison, 413 U.S. 455, 93 S.Ct. 2804, 37 L.Ed.2d 723 (1973). The Court has also upheld a governmental decision to refuse to aid racially discriminatory schools, including a school that discriminated in admissions on the basis of race because of the school's religious doctrine, by upholding the authority of the Internal Revenue Service to deny tax exempt status to such schools. Bob Jones University v. United States, 461 U.S. 574, 103 S.Ct. 2017, 76 L.Ed.2d 157 (1983).

13. 421 U.S. 454, 95 S.Ct. 1716, 44 L.Ed.2d 295 (1975).

14. 427 U.S. 273, 96 S.Ct. 2574, 49 L.Ed.2d 493 (1976), on remand 540 F.2d 219 (5th Cir.1976).

15. Section 1981, now codified under 42 U.S.C.A., was derived from the Civil Rights Act of 1866.

16. Section 1981 gives "[a]ll persons ... the same right ... to make and enforce contracts ... as is enjoyed by white citizens." 42 U.S.C.A. § 1981. But cf. United Steelworkers v. Weber, 443 U.S. 193, 99 S.Ct. 2721, 61 L.Ed.2d 480 (1979), on remand 611 F.2d 132 (5th Cir. 1980) (as a matter of statutory construction, Title VII and *McDonald* do not apply to affirmative action plans voluntarily adopted by private parties to eliminate traditional patterns of racial segregation).

17. Saint Francis College v. Al–Khazraji, 481 U.S. 604, 611, 107 S.Ct. 2022, 2027, 95 L.Ed.2d 582 (1987), rehearing denied 483 U.S. 1011, 107 S.Ct. 3244, 97 L.Ed.2d 749 (1987).

18. 481 U.S. at 613, 107 S.Ct. at 2028.

19. 481 U.S. at 613, 107 S.Ct. at 2028 (emphasis added).

Brennan, J., concurring, opined that he read the Court's opinion "to state only that discrimination based on *birthplace alone* is insufficient to state a claim under § 1981." 481 U.S. at 614, 107 S.Ct. at 2029 (emphasis in original).

20. 451 U.S. 100, 101 S.Ct. 1584, 67 L.Ed.2d 769 (1981), rehearing denied 452 U.S. 955, 101 S.Ct. 3100, 69 L.Ed.2d 965 (1981). See also, Reno v. Bossier Parish School Board, 520 U.S. 471, 117 S.Ct. 1491, 1503, 137 L.Ed.2d 730 (1997), noting that the important starting point for proving discriminatory intent is whether the impact of the official action bears more heavily on one race than another. One should also look to: the historical background of the decision; the specific sequence of events leading to the challenged action; departures from any normal procedures; and the legislative or administrative history, particularly contemporary statements made by members of the decision-making body.

hood with a predominantly black population. The closing of the street forced residents of the adjoining black neighborhood to use alternative routes for certain trips within the city.

The majority found that legitimate, nonracial reasons existed to justify the street closing and that the impact on the black citizens and neighborhood could not be characterized as a badge or incident of slavery violative of either the Thirteenth Amendment or section 1982: "[T]he inconvenience of the drivers is a function of where they live and where they regularly drive—not a function of their race. . . ."[21] And "it does not involve any impairment to the kind of property interests that we have identified as being within the reach of § 1982."[22]

The *Greene* majority[23] did not reach the issue of whether a violation of section 1982 could be established without proof of purposeful discrimination. But the Court did reach that issue—at least as to section 1981—in *General Building Contractors Association, Inc. v. Pennsylvania.*[24] The Court there held that to make out a violation of section 1981 it is not enough to prove disproportionate impact; there must be proof of a racially discriminatory intent. Without such proof, a court may not impose vicarious liability in the form of a detailed and burdensome injunction on employers and trade associations.[25]

In *General Building* the employers and trade associations, pursuant to collective bargaining agreements, used union hiring halls to select workers. The unions had intentionally discriminated on the basis of race, but the contractors and trade associations had not. There was not even evidence that they were

aware of the union's discrimination. The Court therefore held that the employers and trade associations did not violate section 1981. Nor were they liable under a theory of *respondeat superior* or similar theory: the union is not the fiduciary and agent of the employer, which has no right to control the union. The requirement of purposeful discrimination necessary to make out a violation of section 1981 also exists with respect to section 1982, which the Court specifically noted was a companion statute with similar origins and scope.[26]

Statute of Limitations

Claims under section 1981 are, in essence, claims for personal injury. Because section 1981 does not contain its own statute of limitations, the courts should, as a matter of federal law, borrow the state statute of limitations applicable to such claims.[27]

§ 15.11 Congressional Enforcement of the Fifteenth Amendment: The Early Law

With the enactment of the Fifteenth Amendment in 1870, the Reconstruction Congress did not sit on its haunches. It was not content to rely on its self-executing section 1, but passed implementing legislation pursuant to section 2. The Enforcement Act of 1870[1] made it a criminal offense for either public officials or private persons to obstruct the right to vote. The next year Congress tightened that law by careful federal supervision of registration through the certification of election returns.[2] But as the "years passed and fervor for racial equality waned, enforcement of the laws became spotty and ineffective, and most of their provisions were repealed in 1894."[3]

---

21. 451 U.S. at 128, 101 S.Ct. at 1600–01.

22. 451 U.S. at 124, 101 S.Ct. at 1598.

23. Justice White, concurring in the judgment, objected to the majority acting as a fact-finder and "rehash[ing]" the evidence. 451 U.S. at 130, 101 S.Ct. at 1601–02. Only Marshall, joined by Brennan and Blackmun, JJ., dissented.

24. 458 U.S. 375, 102 S.Ct. 3141, 73 L.Ed.2d 835 (1982).

25. 458 U.S. at 397–401, 102 S.Ct. at 3154–55. Cf. Hacker & Rotunda, The Reliance of Counsel Defense in Securities Cases: Damage Actions vs. Injunctive Actions, 1 Corp.L.Rev. 159, 161–62 (1978) (discussing relevance of good faith in decision to grant injunctive relief).

26. 458 U.S. at 382–84, 102 S.Ct. at 3146. Marshall, J., joined by Brennan, J., filed a dissenting opinion; O'Connor, J., joined by Blackmun, J., filed a concurring opinion.

27. Goodman v. Lukens Steel Co., 482 U.S. 656, 107 S.Ct. 2617, 96 L.Ed.2d 572 (1987).

§ 15.11

1. 16 Stat. 170.

2. 16 Stat. 433.

3. South Carolina v. Katzenbach, 383 U.S. 301, 310, 86 S.Ct. 803, 809, 15 L.Ed.2d 769 (1966), footnote omitted, citing the repealing legislation, 28 Stat. 36.

Portions of the country responded by vigorous efforts to disenfranchise blacks through the use of grandfather clauses, procedural hurdles, primary elections open only to whites, improper voting challenges, racial gerrymandering, and discriminatory application of voting tests, all struck down in a long series of Supreme Court opinions.[4] In 1965, Congress again entered the battle in a major way with a new weapon, the Voting Rights Act of 1965.[5]

§ 15.12 Congressional Enforcement of the Fifteenth Amendment: The Modern Era

South Carolina v. Katzenbach[1] is the leading modern case interpreting Congress' power under section 2 of the Fifteenth Amendment to enforce its guarantee that no state or the United States may deny American citizens the right to vote on account of race, color, or previous condition of servitude. *Katzenbach* upheld various challenged portions of the Voting Rights Act of 1965. South Carolina brought this original case in the Supreme Court pursuant to Article III, section 2. All states were invited to submit amicus briefs and a majority did so, some supporting South Carolina and others supporting the Attorney General.[2]

Chief Justice Warren, writing the opinion for the Court, observed that Congress, prior to passage of the Voting Rights Act, "explored with great care the problem of racial discrimination in voting."[3] This Congressional investigation showed, first, that certain parts of the country had long used various means to defy the command of the Fifteenth Amendment, and that, second, stronger federal legislative remedies were in order. For example, in spite of previous court actions and earlier federal

legislation,[4] the registration of voting age blacks in Mississippi rose from only 4.9% to 6.4% between 1954 and 1964.[5]

One of the sections attacked was the Act's coverage formula. This formula provides coverage as to any state, county, parish, or similar political subdivision, that the Attorney General has determined that on November 1, 1964, maintained a "test or device" to qualify voting rights and, that the Director of the Census has determined that less than 50% of its voting age residents were registered on November 1, 1964, or voted in that year's presidential election. The term "test or device" is defined as any requirement that the registrant be able to read or interpret any matter, or demonstrate any educational achievement or knowledge of any particular subject, or possess good moral character, or prove his voting qualifications by the voucher of registered voters or others. No court may review the findings of the Attorney General or the Census Director under these sections. Such statutory coverage is terminated if the area persuades a court to grant it a declaratory judgment that tests and devices have not been used within the last five years to abridge the vote on racial grounds. This declaratory judgment must be obtained from a particular court, a three judge court of the District Court for the District of Columbia, with a direct appeal to the Supreme Court.

As long as the statutory coverage is effective, the state or political subdivision is barred from enforcing its tests or devices. Also, before the state or political subdivision may change its election qualifications or procedures, it must submit its changes to the Attorney General for approval or obtain a declaratory judgment from a three-judge court of the District

---

4. See, 383 U.S. at 310–12, 86 S.Ct. at 809–10 and cases cited therein.

5. 79 Stat. 437, 42 U.S.C.A. § 1973.

§ 15.12

1. 383 U.S. 301, 86 S.Ct. 803, 15 L.Ed.2d 769 (1966).

2. 383 U.S. at 307 & n. 2, 86 S.Ct. at 807–08 & n. 2.

3. 383 U.S. at 308, 86 S.Ct. at 808.

4. Previous legislative remedies included the Civil Rights Act of 1957, 71 Stat. 634, which authorized the Attorney General to sue to enjoin public and private racial

interference with the right to vote; Amendments to the Civil Rights Act of 1960, 74 Stat. 86, which allowed states to be joined as defendants, gave the Attorney General access to local voting records, and authorized courts to register voters in areas of systematic voting discriminations; and the Civil Rights Act of 1964, title I, 78 Stat. 241, 42 U.S.C.A. § 1971, which expedited voting cases heard by three-judge courts, and outlawed various tactics used to disenfranchise blacks.

5. 383 U.S. at 313, 86 S.Ct. at 811.

Court for the District of Columbia, with direct appeal to the Supreme Court.

If the Attorney General certifies certain facts to the Civil Service Commission, it must appoint voting examiners. The Attorney General's certification is either that he or she has received meritorious written complaints alleging racial discrimination in voting from at least twenty residents or that the appointment of the examiners is otherwise necessary to implement the guarantees of the Fifteenth Amendment. These certifications are also not reviewable in any court. These examiners test the voting qualifications of applicants; any applicant meeting the nonsuspended portions of state law is to be promptly placed on the list of eligible voters.

The Court quickly rejected the argument that the Act violated the due process rights of the states by employing an invalid presumption: the word "person" in the due process clause of the Fifth Amendment does not include the states of the Union.[6] The Court also dismissed the objection that the statutory bar to judicial review of administrative findings constituted an unconstitutional bill of attainder and violated the separation of powers by adjudicating guilt through legislation, because these principles apply only to protect individual persons and private groups, not the state. Nor does a state have standing to invoke these provisions on behalf of its citizens.[7]

The Supreme Court next rejected the argument that only the judiciary may strike down state statutes and procedures. Section 2 of the Fifteenth Amendment contemplates a role for Congress.[8] "As against the reserved powers of the States, Congress may use any rational means to effectuate the constitutional prohibi-

tions of racial discrimination in voting."[9] To determine if this Congressional legislation is valid, the basic test is to apply Chief Justice Marshall's test for the validity of legislation under the necessary and proper clause.

> Let the end be legitimate, let it be within the scope of the constitution, and all means which are appropriate, which are plainly adapted to that end, and which are not prohibited, but consist with the letter and spirit of the constitution, are constitutional.[10]

Thus, Congress under section 2 may do more than to forbid violations of the Fifteenth Amendment in general terms.[11]

The Court said that it was a legitimate response for Congress to prescribe voting discrimination remedies without going into prior adjudication given the ample evidence showing that case-by-case litigation was inadequate to combat the persistent discrimination.[12] It was no flaw in the statute that the remedies were confined to certain locations because Congress had learned that the problem was localized and in these areas immediate action seemed necessary. "The doctrine of the equality of States, invoked by South Carolina, does not bar this approach, for that doctrine applies only to the terms on which States are admitted to the Union and not to the remedies for local evils which have subsequently appeared."[13]

The coverage formula Congress devised to determine the applicability of the Act was proper because it was "rational" in both theory and practice.[14] The rules relating to statutory presumptions in criminal cases does not bind Congress when it is prescribing civil remedies against other organs of government pur-

6.   383 U.S. at 323, 86 S.Ct. at 816.

7.   383 U.S. at 324, 86 S.Ct. at 816.

8.   383 U.S. at 325–26, 86 S.Ct. at 816–18.

9.   383 U.S. at 324, 86 S.Ct. at 816. See also, Briscoe v. Bell, 432 U.S. 404, 97 S.Ct. 2428, 53 L.Ed.2d 439 (1977) (no judicial review of determination of coverage); cf. Morris v. Gressette, 432 U.S. 491, 97 S.Ct. 2411, 53 L.Ed.2d 506 (1977).

10.   383 U.S. at 326, 86 S.Ct. at 818, quoting M'Culloch v. Maryland, 17 U.S. (4 Wheat.) 316, 421, 4 L.Ed. 579 (1819). See also 17 U.S. at 327, 86 S.Ct. at 818, quoting Ex

parte Virginia, 100 U.S. (10 Otto) 339, 345–46, 25 L.Ed. 676 (1879) and citing James Everard's Breweries v. Day, 265 U.S. 545, 558–59, 44 S.Ct. 628, 631, 68 L.Ed. 1174 (1924).

11.   383 U.S. at 327, 86 S.Ct. at 818.

12.   383 U.S. at 328, 86 S.Ct. at 818–19.

13.   383 U.S. at 328–29, 86 S.Ct. at 819, citing Coyle v. Smith, 221 U.S. 559, 31 S.Ct. 688, 55 L.Ed. 853 (1911) and cases cited therein.

14.   383 U.S. at 330, 86 S.Ct. at 820.

suant to section 2 of the Fifteenth Amendment.[15]

It was also proper for Congress to limit litigation under challenged provisions of the Act to a single court in the District of Columbia. And, when this litigation does occur, the burden of proof of nondiscrimination that the state must shoulder is bearable, particularly since the relevant facts are peculiarly within the knowledge of the states and political subdivisions involved. The bar to judicial review of certain findings is not invalid because these findings consist of objective statistical determinations and routine analysis of state statutes. Moreover, the state can always go to the district court to seek termination of its statutory coverage provided that it has not been guilty of voting discrimination in recent years.[16]

The provisions of the Act suspending literacy tests and devices for a period of five years from the last occurrence of substantial voting discrimination were a proper Congressional response under section 2 of the Fifteenth Amendment.[17] These provisions may be "an uncommon exercise of congressional power,"[18] but the exceptional circumstances justify it.[19]

The Court also concluded that the District Court's opinions issued under the Act are not advisory, because the state seeking to change its voting laws has a concrete controversy with the federal government. The appointment of federal examiners and the expeditious challenge procedure of those whom the examiners list as qualified to vote are also an appropriate response to the problem. Thus, the majority upheld all of the provisions of the Voting Rights Act challenged in that case.[20]

Cases since *South Carolina v. Katzenbach*[21] have illustrated the effectiveness of the new Voting Rights Act. For example, *Allen v. State Board of Elections*[22] held that private litigants may invoke the jurisdiction of the district court to assure that their political subdivision complies with the requirement of section 5 of the Act, which provides that no person shall be denied the right to vote for failure to comply with an unapproved new enactment subject to section 5.[23] "Congress intended to reach any

---

15. 383 U.S. at 330, 86 S.Ct. at 820.

16. 383 U.S. at 331–33, 86 S.Ct. at 820–21.

17. 383 U.S. at 334, 86 S.Ct. at 821–22.

18. 383 U.S. at 334, 86 S.Ct. at 821–22.

19. 383 U.S. at 335, 86 S.Ct. at 822.

20. Justice Black concurred and dissented in part. First, he objected to the part of the Act providing that in no way may a state covered by the Act amend its constitution or laws relating to voting without first trying to persuade the Attorney General or a federal district court that the changes do not have the purpose or effect of denying citizens the right to vote on the basis of color. This provision was unconstitutional, he thought, because it required the district court to issue an advisory opinion. 383 U.S. at 357, 86 S.Ct. at 833 (Black, J., dissenting).

Secondly, Black argued, if the dispute can be brought in a court, the appropriate court, given the dignity of a state and the fact that it is a party to the litigation, is the Supreme Court. If the Voting Rights Act, by seeking to limit litigation to the District Court for the District of Columbia, is an attempt to limit the constitutionally created original jurisdiction of the Supreme Court, then that section, Black argued, was also unconstitutional. 383 U.S. at 357 n. 1, 86 S.Ct. at 833 n. 1 (Black, J., dissenting). However, § 14(b) should not be interpreted to limit what Justice Black referred to as "the constitutionally created original jurisdiction of this Court. . . ." Id. The majority, after all, accepted South Carolina's bill of complaint filed in the Supreme Court. "Original jurisdiction," held the Court, "is founded on the presence of a controversy be-

tween a State and a citizen of another State under Art. III, § 2, of the Constitution." 383 U.S. at 307, 86 S.Ct. at 807.

Finally, the provision giving federal officials the power to veto state laws, Justice Black thought, violated the obligation of the United States to guarantee to every state a republican form of government. 383 U.S. at 359 & n. 2, 86 S.Ct. at 834, & n. 2.

21. 383 U.S. 301, 86 S.Ct. 803, 15 L.Ed.2d 769 (1966).

22. 393 U.S. 544, 89 S.Ct. 817, 22 L.Ed.2d 1 (1969).

23. 393 U.S. at 557, 89 S.Ct. at 827. Private litigants may bring their suit in any federal district court and, unlike the state, are not limited to the District Court for the District of Columbia. 393 U.S. at 560, 89 S.Ct. at 828–29.

When Poll Tax Is Exacted by Political Party Convention. Morse v. Republican Party of Virginia, 517 U.S. 186, 116 S.Ct. 1186, 134 L.Ed.2d 347 (1996). All registered voters in Virginia who declared their intent to support Republican Party nominees could become delegates to the Party's state convention to nominate candidates on payment of what was called a "registration fee." Stevens, J., in his plurality opinion, ruled that § 5 of the Voting Rights Act of 1965 required preclearance of the Party's decision to exact the fee, and that the appellants were permitted to challenge the fee as a poll tax prohibited by § 10 of the Act. The Stevens' plurality opinion [517 U.S. at 199, 116 S.Ct. at 1196] cited and relied on, Ronald D. Rotunda, Constitutional and Statutory Restrictions on Political Parties in the Wake of *Cousins v. Wigoda*, 53 Texas L.Rev. 935, 953–54 (1975). The fragmented Court remanded the case.

state enactment which altered the election law of a covered State in even a minor way."[24]

Georgia v. United States[25] squarely held that reapportionment plans come within section 5 of the Voting Rights Act. *Beer v. United States*[26] held that the Voting Rights Act does not permit implementation of a reapportionment plan that "would lead to a retrogression in the position of racial minorities with respect to their effective exercise of the electoral franchise."[27]

In *United Jewish Organizations of Williamsburgh, Inc. v. Carey*[28] a very fragmented Court even approved the use of racial criteria by the State of New York in its attempt to comply with section 5 of the Voting Rights Act and secure the approval of the Attorney General. While there was no opinion of the Court, a majority found that—in the particular circumstances of that case—use of racial criteria did not violate either the Fourteenth or Fifteenth Amendments. These changes did not change the number of districts with nonwhite majorities but did change the size of the nonwhite

majorities in most of those districts. To create substantial nonwhite majorities in these districts, the changes split an Hasidic Jewish Community between two senate and two assembly districts.[29]

Later, *Shaw v. Reno*[30] narrowly interpreted *United Jewish Organizations* and rejected the notion that there is "benign" racial gerrymandering.[31] In *Shaw*, white citizens of North Carolina challenged redistricting on the grounds that the state engaged in unconstitutional racist gerrymandering. The plaintiffs alleged that the state legislature created two districts concentrating a majority of black voters "arbitrarily—without regard to any other consideration, such as compactness, contiguousness, geographical boundaries, or political subdivisions." Justice O'Connor, for the Court, held that plaintiffs stated a cause of action under the equal protection clause when they claimed that the redistricting legislation is "so extremely irregular on its face that it rationally can be viewed only as an effort to segregate

24. 393 U.S. at 566, 89 S.Ct. at 832. The Court held that the Voting Rights provisions did apply to the enactments at issue in this case. 393 U.S. at 569, 89 S.Ct. at 833–34. The Court left "to another case" any consideration of possible conflict between "our interpretation of the statute and the principles involved in the reapportionment cases." Id. See also, Perkins v. Matthews, 400 U.S. 379, 91 S.Ct. 431, 27 L.Ed.2d 476 (1971); Holt v. City of Richmond, 406 U.S. 903, 92 S.Ct. 1602, 31 L.Ed.2d 814 (1972).

See City of Rome v. United States, 446 U.S. 156, 100 S.Ct. 1548, 64 L.Ed.2d 119 (1980), rehearing denied 447 U.S. 916, 100 S.Ct. 3003, 64 L.Ed.2d 865 (1980). upheld the constitutionality of broad federal power under section 5 of the Voting Rights Act of 1965. The Attorney General declined to approve certain city annexations and other electoral changes after concluding Rome, Georgia (where whites were in the majority, and where there was racial bloc voting) had not met its burden of showing that the disapproved changes would not dilute the black vote. The disapproved changes were not made for any discriminatory *purpose* but did have a discriminatory *effect*. The Court ruled that the Attorney General acted properly because the statute required that the electoral change must have neither the purpose nor effect of abridging the right to vote on the basis of color. This interpretation, the Court held, was constitutional even if section 1 of the Fifteenth Amendment prohibits only purposeful discrimination, because of broad Congressional broad power under section 2 of that Amendment.

25. 411 U.S. 526, 93 S.Ct. 1702, 36 L.Ed.2d 472 (1973). White, Powell, and Rehnquist, JJ., dissented. 411 U.S. at 542, 93 S.Ct. at 1711.

26. 425 U.S. 130, 96 S.Ct. 1357, 47 L.Ed.2d 629 (1976).

27. 425 U.S. at 141, 96 S.Ct. at 1364. See City of Richmond v. United States, 422 U.S. 358, 95 S.Ct. 2296, 45 L.Ed.2d 245 (1975); City of Lockhart v. United States, 460 U.S. 125, 103 S.Ct. 998, 74 L.Ed.2d 863 (1983).

28. 430 U.S. 144, 97 S.Ct. 996, 51 L.Ed.2d 229 (1977).

29. Notwithstanding this benign racial gerrymandering, "four out of the five 'safe' (65%+) nonwhite districts established by the 1974 plan have since elected white representatives." Burger, C.J., dissenting, 430 U.S. at 185, 97 S.Ct. at 1020.

Cf. Gomillion v. Lightfoot, 364 U.S. 339, 81 S.Ct. 125, 5 L.Ed.2d 110 (1960), where the Court invalidated racial gerrymandering. In that case, however, the power of Congress under section 2 of the Fifteenth Amendment was not involved. Also, in *Gomillion* there was a fencing out of the black population from the political process and their voting strength was invidiously minimized; in the New York plan, in contrast, "there was no fencing out of the white population from participation in the political process of the county, and the plan did not minimize or unfairly cancel out white voting strength." 430 U.S. at 165, 97 S.Ct. at 1010 (opinion of White, J.).

30. 509 U.S. 630, 113 S.Ct. 2816, 125 L.Ed.2d 511 (1993). White, J., joined by Blackmun & Stevens JJ., filed a dissenting opinion. Blackmun, J., Stevens, J. & Souter, J., each filed dissenting opinions.

31. 509 U.S. at 653, 113 S.Ct. at 2830.

the races for the purposes of voting, without regard for traditional districting principles and without sufficient compelling justification."[32] The Court remanded for further proceedings, and emphasized that a reapportionment plan that satisfies section 5 of the Voting Rights Act "still may enjoined as unconstitutional."[33]

The Court further undermined *United Jewish Organizations* in *Miller v. Johnson.*[34] This case extended *Shaw* and invalidated a Georgia congressional redistricting plan that involved racial gerrymandering that favored racial minorities. In *Miller*, the proof showed that race was the "predominate factor" in drawing the lines for the Eleventh District. The shape of the district was particularly bizarre, and there was considerable other evidence that the district was "unexplainable other than by race."

The state argued that it had to draw the district that way in order to comply with pre-

clearance mandates issued by the Department of Justice, but the Court rejected that justification because Georgia's earlier enacted plans did not violate § 5 of the Voting Rights Act and hence Georgia's redrawing of the Eleventh District was not necessary.[35]

The following term, *Shaw v. Hunt*[36] further elaborated on the principle of *Miller.* First, the Court agreed with the unanimous lower court finding that the "serpentine" districting was deliberately drawn to produce one or more districts of a certain racial composition. Then the Court turned to the second major issue: the trial court had also held (2 to 1) that the redistricting plan was narrowly tailored to further the state's compelling interests in complying with §§ 2 and 5 of the Voting Rights Act. On this issue, the Court reversed and held that the "bizarre-looking" majority-black district violated the equal protection clause.[37]

---

32. 509 U.S. at 642, 113 S.Ct. at 2824.

33. 509 U.S. at 654, 113 S.Ct. at 2831.

34. 515 U.S. 900, 115 S.Ct. 2475, 132 L.Ed.2d 762 (1995). On remand, the district court adopted a redistricting plan with only one majority-black district, and the U.S. Supreme Court affirmed. Abrams v. Johnson, 521 U.S. 74, 117 S.Ct. 1925, 138 L.Ed.2d 285 (1997). The Court ruled, 5 to 4, that the district court was not required to defer to unconstitutional plans previously adopted by the Georgia legislature and that the lower court acted within its discretion in concluding that it could not draw two majority-black districts without engaging in racial gerrymandering. The district court plan also did not result in dilution of black voting strength or retrogression in the position of racial minorities in violation of the Voting Rights Act, and did not violate the Constitutional requirement of one person, one vote.

"Clearly Erroneous" Test. Lawyer v. Department of Justice, 521 U.S. 567, 117 S.Ct. 2186, 138 L.Ed.2d 669 (1997), upheld a state redistricting plan and ruled that the district court's finding that the settlement agreement did not subordinate traditional districting principles to race in violation of *Miller v. Johnson*, 515 U.S. 900, 915–___, 115 S.Ct. 2475, 2488–89, 132 L.Ed.2d 762 (1995), was not clearly erroneous.

35. Cf. Rice v. Cayetano, 528 U.S. 495, 120 S.Ct. 1044, 145 L.Ed.2d 1007 (2000). A provision in the Hawaiian Constitution limits the rights to vote for nine trustees chosen in a statewide election to "Hawaiians" and "Native Hawaiians." The trustees compose the governing authority of a state agency known as the Office of Hawaiian Affairs. The Court (7 to 2) held that this racial limitation on voting violated the Fifteenth Amendment. The Fifteenth Amendment protects "all person," said the Court, not just members of a particular race. Moreover, Congress

could not authorize Hawaii to engage in this type of racial discrimination in voting.

36. 517 U.S. 899, 116 S.Ct. 1894, 135 L.Ed.2d 207 (1996), which was on remand from Shaw v. Reno, 509 U.S. 630, 113 S.Ct. 2816, 125 L.Ed.2d 511 (1993), on remand 861 F.Supp. 408 (E.D.N.C.1994).

See also Bush v. Vera, 517 U.S. 952, 116 S.Ct. 1941, 135 L.Ed.2d 248 (1996). A Texas redistricting plan created two majority-black districts and one majority-Hispanic district. The Department of Justice precleared the redistricting as complying with the Voting Rights Act. Voters challenged the redistricting as racially gerrymandered in violation of the Fourteenth Amendment, a three-judge district court agreed, and the Supreme Court, with no majority opinion, affirmed.

37. Distinguishing Unconstitutional *Racial* Gerrymandering from Constitutional *Political* Gerrymandering. Hunt v. Cromartie, 526 U.S. 541, 119 S.Ct. 1545, 143 L.Ed.2d 731 (1999), holding that fact issues regarding the state legislature's allegedly racial motive in drawing a redistricting plan precluded summary judgment. Because making a judgment as to the legislature's motive in drawing district lines is a complex endeavor, the court should inquire into all available circumstantial and direct evidence.

The appellants claimed that the state legislature intended to make a strong Democratic district, not to engage in racial gerrymandering. Justice Thomas, for the Court, distinguished between unconstitutional racial gerrymandering and constitutional political gerrymandering:

"Our prior decisions have made clear that a jurisdiction may engage in constitutional political gerrymandering, even if it so happens that the most loyal Democrats happen to be black Democrats and even if the State were *conscious* of that fact."

First, the Court found that the asserted state interest in eliminating the effects of past discrimination was not a compelling interest because that claimed interest did not actually precipitate the use of race in this redistricting plan. Second, creating an additional majority-black district was not required under a correct reading of § 5.[38] Third, the Court concluded that racial gerrymandering was not a narrowly tailored remedy to comply with § 2 of the Act because the minority group was not geographically compact.

Distinguishing Unconstitutional *Racial* Gerrymandering from Constitutional *Political* Gerrymandering. After *Shaw v. Hunt*, the state redrew the boundaries (it was now 47% African–American), a three-judge district court ruled on summary judgment that the state still had racial considerations dominating. The Supreme Court reversed and remanded in *Hunt v. Cromartie*,[39] holding that there was a genuine issue of material fact as to whether the evidence showed that the state had an unconstitutional race-based objective. *Hunt* also held that fact issues regarding the state legislature's allegedly racial motive in drawing a redistricting plan precluded summary judgment. Because making a judgment as to the legislature's motive in drawing district lines is a complex endeavor, the court should inquire into all available circumstantial and direct evidence.

The appellants claimed that the state legislature intended to make a strong Democratic district, not to engage in racial gerrymandering. Justice Thomas, for the Court, distinguished between unconstitutional racial

gerrymandering and constitutional political gerrymandering:

"Our prior decisions have made clear that a jurisdiction may engage in constitutional political gerrymandering, even if it so happens that the most loyal Democrats happen to be black Democrats and even if the State were *conscious* of that fact."[40]

On remand, the lower court held a three-day trial, and reached the same conclusion that racial considerations dominated. The Court reversed again, in *Easley v. Cromartie*,[41] which was the fourth time this case went to the Supreme Court. Again, the Court reversed, and held that the lower court was "clearly erroneous," because the evidence before the lower court "also was consistent with a constitutional political objective, namely the creation of a safe Democratic seat."[42] Justice Breyer spoke for the Court,[43] arguing that the challengers did not meet the burden of showing that a facially neutral law is unexplainable on grounds other than race. Because a legislature trying to secure a safe Democratic seat is interested in voting behavior, "a legislature may, by placing reliable Democratic precincts within a district without regard to race, end up with a district containing more heavily African–American precincts, but the reasons would be political rather than racial."[44]

Justice Breyer, in arguing for what looks like political gerrymandering, did not distinguish or even cite *Davis v. Bandemer*,[45] where a majority of the justices (with no majority opinion) concluded that political gerrymandering [dividing voters based on their politics] may be unconstitutional. In *Davis*, Justices Powell and Stevens would have held that political gerrymandering violates the Equal Protec-

---

526 U.S. at 551, 119 S.Ct. at 1551 (emphasis in original).

38. However, the Court did not reach the question whether compliance with the Voting Rights Act, § 5 was, on its own, a compelling state interest.

39. 526 U.S. 541, 119 S.Ct. 1545, 143 L.Ed.2d 731 (1999).

40. Hunt v. Cromartie, 526 U.S. 541, 551, 119 S.Ct. 1545, 1551.

41. 532 U.S. 234, 121 S.Ct. 1452, 149 L.Ed.2d 430 (2001).

42. Neither Justice Breyer nor any other Justice cited Davis v. Bandemer, 478 U.S. 109, 106 S.Ct. 2797, 92 L.Ed.2d 85 (1986), where a majority of the justices (with

no majority opinion) concluded that political gerrymandering [dividing voters based on their politics] may be unconstitutional. Justices Powell and Stevens would have held that political gerrymandering violates the Equal Protection Clause if its only purpose is to favor a political segment, such as Democrats. The White plurality would have found an Equal Protection violation if it "consistently degrades a voter's or a group of voter's influence on the political process as a whole."

43. He was joined by Stevens, O'Connor, Souter, & Ginsburg, JJ.

44. Easley v. Cromartie, 532 U.S. 234, 235, 121 S.Ct. 1452, 1455.

45. 478 U.S. 109, 106 S.Ct. 2797, 92 L.Ed.2d 85 (1986).

tion Clause if its only purpose is to favor a political segment, such as Democrats. The White plurality would have found an Equal Protection violation if it "consistently degrades a voter's or a group of voter's influence on the political process as a whole."

Justice Thomas, joined by Rehnquist, C.J., Scalia & Kennedy, JJ., dissented, arguing that

the appellate court is not the trier of fact and should not "weigh evidence in the first instance."[46] Looking a the direct evidence of racial motive and the reasonable inferences that can be drawn, the dissent was satisfied that the trial court's finding "was permissible, even if not compelled by the record."[47]

46. 532 U.S. 234, 267, 121 S.Ct. 1452, 1475.

47. 532 U.S. 234, 267, 121 S.Ct. 1452, 1475.

Chapter 16

FREEDOM OF SPEECH

§ 16.1 Introduction and Chapter Summary

We begin this Chapter by examining the historical and philosophical background of the English and American experiences with laws restricting speech, especially political speech. Then we explore the techniques that the Court has used and attitudes or viewpoints that it is has embraced in reviewing laws affecting speech.

This introductory section summarizes most of the major topics that later sections of this Chapter analyze and examine in much greater detail. One should turn to the specific sections to understand the issues of this Chapter, which focuses on the First Amendment freedoms,[1] with the exception of the Religion Clauses, which are examined in the next Chapter.[2]

The Court has used the Fourteenth Amendment to incorporate all of the First Amendment freedoms to be applicable to states and local governments.[3] Thus, the scope of First Amendment freedoms protect individuals from actions by local and state governments, as well as from actions by the federal government.[4]

The modern complexity into which the First Amendment has developed was not even a gleam in the Framers eyes when the people ratified the First Amendment in 1791.[5] Indeed, the Supreme Court did not actively protect the freedom of speech until the end of the first quarter of the Twentieth Century.[6] For much of the Twentieth Century, the Court was unclear regarding the standards to use to review governmental restrictions on speech. In the last third of the twentieth century, the Court developed a basic framework for analysis of the government's ability to restrict expressive activity, which the Court continues to use.[7]

Government punishment or restriction of expressive activities has been the focus of almost all of the Court's free speech jurisprudence. For that reason, this Chapter focuses on various types of government restraints on expressive activities. In a few instances, the government has attempted to influence expressive activities by granting and denying monetary benefits, which is the focus of a separate section in this Chapter.[8] In the future, government speech, especially through means such as the Internet generally, or the World Wide Web specifically, may have a dramatic impact on

§ 16.1

1. See §§ 16.2–16.4 (the background and drafting of the First Amendment). The text of the Constitution and all ratified Amendments appear in the appendix.

2. Chapter 17.

3. See § 11.6

4. In some circumstances, private persons or private legal entities, such as corporations, may have sufficient "state action" so that the First and Fourteenth Amendments limit their actions. See, Chapter 12, State Action.

5. Ronald D. Rotunda, Bicentennial Lessons from the Constitutional Convention of 1787, 21 Suffolk U. L. Rev. 589 (1987) (the Twentieth Donahue Lecture).

6. See John Nowak, The "Sixty Something" Anniversary of the Bill of Rights, 1992 U. Ill. L. Rev.445. For further references, see our multi-volume Treatise: Ronald D. Rotunda & John E. Nowak, Treatise on Constitutional Law: Substance and Procedure, Chapter 21 (3rd ed. 1999), with annual supplements.

7. Ronald D. Rotunda, Original Intent, The View of the Framers, and the Role of the Ratifiers, 41 Vanderbilt L. Rev. 507 (1988).

8. See § 16.11.

the political beliefs of the public, but the Court has not yet restricted government speech under the First Amendment, apart from some rulings regarding the establishment clause.[9]

The bulk of this Chapter considers how the Court deals with specific types or categories of speech in concrete situations, such as subversive speech; obscene speech; the speech of the broadcast media and of the traditional print media; libelous speech; speech affecting associational rights; speech before hostile audiences; symbolic speech; speech that affects the right to a fair trial; and speech associated with rights of assembly and petition.

These categories are neither exhaustive nor airtight, but they are useful, because the Supreme Court often develops different tests when it evaluates the permissible scope of restrictions on the various categories of speech. This difference in treatment is expected because the relevant interests of one type of speech, e.g., political speech, may vary from those of another, e.g., obscene speech. Moreover, the Court applies the techniques of reviewing alleged restrictions on speech (overbreadth, vagueness, and so on) differently to each category, either consciously or unconsciously.

Content–Based and Viewpoint–Based Laws. In examining government restrictions on expressive activities, an initial question is whether the government regulation is based on the content of the expression or the idea being promoted by an association. The Court often says that content-based restrictions on speech are subject to strict scrutiny, whereas non-content based restrictions are subject to a more lenient form of judicial review. However,

that simple distinction between content-based restrictions and content-neutral restrictions on speech is probably too simplistic. We need to subdivide content-based restrictions on speech in order to understand the Court's approach to various types of government restraints on expressive activity.

There are two types of content-based restrictions. First, the government may be totally banning some type of speech for content. Second, the government may be requiring individuals who wish to put forth certain types of speech to certain times or places so that the type of speech does not adversely affect its environment.

A government action that totally bans a certain type of expressive activity due to its content will be subject to strict judicial scrutiny. By strict judicial scrutiny the Court means that it will not uphold a true ban on a certain type of expression (based on the language used or the idea conveyed in the expression) unless the government can bear the burden of proving that its action is narrowly tailored to a compelling interest.

The government only rarely meets this strict scrutiny test for punishing certain types of categories of speech. The Supreme Court has allowed the punishment of speech based on content if the content is being punished through a clear and narrow regulation that is limited to the proscription of: (1) speech that incites to imminent lawless action, such as a speaker who urges the lynch mob to act;[10] (2) speech that triggers an automatic violent response (so-called "fighting words") or "true threats;"[11] (3) obscenity,[12] (which the Court narrowly defines to exclude much material

---

9. See, John E. Nowak, Using the Press Clause to limit Government Speech, 30 Ariz. L. Rev. 1 (1988); John E. Nowak, First Amendment Values and Government Participation in the Marketplace, Fifty years after the Hutchins Report, 3 Communications Law and Policy 275 (1998); Ronald D. Rotunda, Let Nothing You Display: Making Room for Religion in Public Forums, Legal Times (of Washington, D.C.), Jan. 3, 2000, at pp. 43, 45; John E. Nowak, Jury Trials and First Amendment Values in "Cyber World," 34 U. Richmond L. Rev. 1313 (2001); Ronald D. Rotunda & John E. Nowak, Treatise on Constitutional Law: Substance and Procedure, Chapter 21 (3rd ed. 1999), with annual supplements.

10. See §§ 16.12–16.15. See, Ronald D. Rotunda, The Warren Court and Freedom of the Press, in The Warren Court: A 25 Year Retrospective 85 (Bernard Schwartz, ed., Oxford University Press 1996); Ronald D. Rotunda, *Pravo na svobody slova v voennoe vremiz v knostitutsii SShA: istoki i evoliutsiia*, Pravo I Zakonodatel'stvo, 2003, No. 2, c. 63–65; *The Right of Freedom of Speech in Wartime In the Constitution of the USA: Sources And Evolution*, Law and Legislation, 2003, No. 2, pp. 63–65.

11. See §§ 16.37–16.40. See, Ronald D. Rotunda, A Brief Comment on Politically Incorrect Speech in the Wake of R.A.V., 47 So. Methodist U. L. Rev. 9 (1993).

12. See §§ 16.56–16.61

that the popular press often describes as pornography); (4) child pornography, a limited category of speech involving photographs and films of young children;[13] (5) certain types of defamatory speech;[14] and (6) certain types of commercial speech, primarily false or misleading speech connected to the sale of a service or product, or offers to engage in illegal activity, such as an advertisement for a male-only employee when the law forbids sex discrimination.[15]

If the government wants to punish speech based on its content apart from these categories, the government bears a heavy burden of proving that its regulation is one that is narrowly drawn to promote a what the Court concludes is compelling government interest.[16] The government has met this strict scrutiny test (apart from the punishment of speech that fits within one of the previously mentioned categories) only in a few instances and to a limited extent, such as the circumstances where the Court has allowed some limits on campaign financing, including limitation of some types of monetary contributions to political candidates.[17]

Content-based government restrictions are different than viewpoint-based government restrictions. The fact that the Court has allowed the government to punish certain categories of speech does not mean that the Court will allow the government to punish individuals because they hold points of view that differ from those of the government. All of the clauses of the First Amendment are tied together by the concept of a freedom of belief. Although the freedom of belief, or freedom of thought, is not explicitly mentioned in the First Amendment, it is the core value of all of the clauses of the First Amendment.

In the middle of the last century, Justice Jackson explained that the freedom of belief was inviolate.[18] Today we would say that the government may not punish an individual for holding a viewpoint opposed to any view or theoretical position taken by government officials, The modern Court seems to leave open a situation where the government could restrict viewpoint if the government action was truly necessary to promote what the Court calls "a compelling interest." However, the Court has never openly approved a government action punishing an individual merely on the basis that the government's views of a particular issue differed from those of the individual.

Not all content-based punishment involves viewpoint-based punishment. Yet all viewpoint-based punishment involves content-based punishment. For example, a law that bans all obscene movies is content-based, but a law that bans obscene movies that make fun of the President is both content-based and viewpoint-based. Similarly, if an obscenity law banned only against movies with graphic sexual scenes that were critical of the government's war activities it would constitute viewpoint discrimination. In other words, the law as written or applied would not be the punishment of the category of obscenity but, rather, the punishment of a viewpoint (an anti-war message) that was contrary to that of the government.

Content–Neutral Regulations. The Court often says that the government can place reasonable time, place and manner restrictions on speech without regard to content. For example, the government can place reasonable restrictions on parades—there cannot be two parades on the same street at the same time.

---

13. See § 16.61(b).

14. See §§ 16.32–16.36.

15. See §§ 16.26–16.31. See, Ronald D. Rotunda, The Constitutional Future of the Bill of Rights: A Closer Look at Commercial Speech and State Aid to Religiously Affiliated Schools, 65 N. Car. L. Rev. 917 (1987); Ronald D. Rotunda, Lawyer Advertising and the Philosophical Origins of the Commercial Speech Doctrine, 36 U. Richmond L. Rev. 91 (2002) (Allen Chair Symposium of 2001).

16. See, e.g., Simon & Schuester, Inc. v. Members of the New York State Crime Victims Board, 502 U.S. 112

S.Ct. 501, 116 L.Ed.2d 476 (1991); see § 16.22; Cohen v. California, 403 U.S. 15, 91 S.Ct. 1780, 29 L.Ed.2d 284 (1971); see § 16.39.

17. See § 16.51 regarding restrictions on campaign contributions.

18. See, West Virginia State Board of Education v. Barnette, 319 U.S. 624, 63 S.Ct. 1178, 87 L.Ed. 1628 (1943) (ruling that the government could not require a child to pledge allegiance to the flag). See §§ 16.11, 16.13, 16.48, 17.6, 17.7.

But the government cannot ban an anti-war parade because that is a restriction on the content or message of the parade.

Determining if a restriction is content-based is not always obvious. If we were told that an individual was arrested because he was giving a speech criticizing the city mayor, our initial reaction to that information might be to assume that the government had violated the First Amendment. Details regarding that arrest might change our position. Assume that the person making the speech was doing so at 2:00 a.m., while trespassing on someone else's privately-owned parking lot next to a private hospital, and using a bullhorn to amplify his speech. The First Amendment does not prevent the government from controlling speech at that time (2:00 a.m.), place (the private property next to a hospital), or manner (the use of the bullhorn in a way that disturbed the hospital patients).

Time, place, and manner regulations have the incidental effect of limiting the amount of speech in our society. However, some time, place, or manner regulations must exist if we are to have any semblance of order in our society. Because regulations of this type are not designed to suppress any particular message they are not subject to the strictest form of judicial scrutiny. In other words, time, place, and manner regulations do not have to be narrowly tailored to a compelling interest.

While time, place, and manner regulations of speech are not subject to the compelling interest test, the Court will not merely rubber-stamp the validity of any law that the government asserts to be a time, place, or manner regulation. In due process and equal protection cases, when no fundamental right or special classification is involved in a case, the Court upholds a law so long as it is rationally related to any legitimate interest.[19] If the Court were to approve all time, place, or manner regulations under a rationality standard the government might be able to greatly suppress the

amount of speech in our society. For that reason, the Court has adopted an intermediate approach (between the mere rationality and compelling interest standards) to time, place, or manner regulations. This approach involves greater scrutiny of the law than would the Court's approach under the mere rationality test, but this approach does not involve the strict judicial scrutiny that is used to examine laws subject to the compelling interest standard.

The intermediate approach (or intermediate judicial scrutiny) that the Court uses in a time, place, or manner case involves a three-part test. To be upheld as a time, place, or manner regulation of speech, the regulation must be narrowly tailored to promote an important or significant government interest that is unrelated to the suppression of expression. This principle, which was first developed in so-called symbolic speech cases,[20] becomes a three-part test when it is used to examine a specific time, place, or manner regulation. To be upheld, a time, place, or manner regulation of speech or other First Amendment activity (such as assembling or gathering to protest) must: (1) be content-neutral; (2) be narrowly tailored to an important or significant government interest; and (3) leave open adequate alternative channels of communication.[21]

The most important part of the time, place, or manner standard is the requirement that the law be content-neutral both as written and applied. A law that is not neutral regarding content cannot be upheld as a time, place, or manner regulation. A law that is not content-neutral will only be valid if it can survive strict judicial scrutiny.

Several related examples demonstrate this point. Let us assume that a city law bans all signs on front lawns of single family homes that are larger than four square feet. Such a law might or might not be a valid time, place, or manner law, depending on whether it is content-neutral, and narrowly tailored to serve

---

19. See § 18.3 regarding standards of review under the equal protection clause.

20. See §§ 16.48, 16.49; United States v. O'Brien 391 U.S. 367, 88 S.Ct. 1673, 20 L.Ed.2d 672 (1968).

21. See § 16.47. See, e.g., Ward v. Rock Against Racism, 491 U.S. 781, 109 S.Ct. 2746, 105 L.Ed.2d 661 (1989).

an important or significant government interest that left open alternative channels of communication. In other words, because the law is content-neutral it would only have to survive the intermediate form of judicial review. The Court usually states that such a law is upheld if it is narrowly tailored to promote a significant interest unrelated to the suppression of expression.

Now, let us assume that the city law banned all signs on the front lawns of privately owned homes if the sign included material that is "obscene." If the city's law as written and applied only prohibited signs with words or pictures that met the Supreme Court definition of obscenity the law is valid even though it is not content-neutral. The Court has held that "obscenity" is not speech and the state can ban it. This law, by definition, is narrowly tailored to a compelling interest if it punishes only the category of speech that the Supreme Court has determined to be "obscene."

Now, let us turn to a third example, a city law that bans "for sale" signs. The Supreme Court has invalidated a city law that banned all for sale signs on private homes.[22] This law was content-based, not content-neutral, because it banned signs based on the content of the message displayed on the sign. For this content-based law to have been valid, the government would have had to establish either that the law fell within the narrow lists of proscribable categories of speech (e.g., it is obscene, or incites imminent lawless behavior) or that the law was narrowly tailored to a compelling interest. But when a homeowner truthfully states that her house is for sale, that is not misleading and so is not the type of commercial speech that the government can prohibit. The prohibition of truthful information about houses being sold is not narrowly tailored to promote a compelling government interest.[23]

A law that is content-neutral on its face will be treated as a law that is content-based if the individual whom the government wants to

punish can show that the government only enforces the law so as to prohibit one type of content or viewpoint. Consider laws that are enforced in a discriminatory way.

Let us return to our example of a city that bans all signs on private property that are larger than four square feet. Assume that an individual is charged with a violation of the law after he places a sign that exceeds the limit on his property that states: "Vote for Jane Jones for Mayor." If the individual charged with violation of the law can demonstrate that the police had not enforced the size restriction against persons who put up signs that exceeded four square feet so long as those signs promoted the mayoral candidacy of Sam Smith (the incumbent Mayor), the person charged with the violation of the law will have shown that the law, as applied, is both content-based and viewpoint-based. The Court will invalidate this type of viewpoint discrimination under the strict scrutiny standard. After the defendant showed that the seemingly content-neutral law was being used to punish a particular content or viewpoint, the government could not win unless it demonstrated that the selective use of the law against certain content or certain viewpoints was narrowly tailored to a compelling government interest—and one cannot expect the government to meet that strict test.

If the Court finds that a law is content-neutral, as written and as applied, the Court is likely to uphold the law as a valid time, place, or manner regulation. The basic principle employed by the Court in such cases requires that all such regulations must be narrowly tailored to promote an important or significant interest *unrelated to the suppression of the content of the speech*. If a law is found to be truly content-neutral, the law is unrelated to the suppression of expression. The Court will still determine whether the content-neutral law is narrowly tailored to promote an important or significant interest.

---

22. Ladue v. Gilleo, 512 U.S. 43, 114 S.Ct. 2038, 129 L.Ed.2d 36 (1994). See § 16.31.

23. Ronald D. Rotunda, The Commercial Speech Doctrine in the Supreme Court, 1976 U. Ill. L. Forum 1080 (1976).

The Court breaks down this part of the time, place, or manner standard into two formal inquiries, though those inquiries seem to be closely linked. First, the Court requires that the content-neutral law be narrowly tailored to promote an important or significant interest. Second, the Court requires that the law be one that leaves open adequate channels for communication.

The Court employs the concept of narrow tailoring into both of the last two branches of the test for the validity of time, place or manner laws. If a content-neutral law does not leave open adequate or ample alternative channels of communication, then the Court will strike the law as not being narrowly tailored to a significant interest. Conversely, if the Court rules that the law is narrowly tailored to promote an important or significant interest, the Court will rule that the law leaves open adequate alternative channels of communication.

When the Court employs the narrow tailoring requirement in time, place, or manner cases, the Court is not requiring the government to use the least restrictive means of advancing the asserted significant or important government interest. Rather, the Court is merely exercising a form of ad-hoc independent judicial review, sometimes termed "intermediate scrutiny," to determine whether the law is a reasonable means of advancing an important societal interest.

The manner in which the Court decides whether the asserted interests of the government constitute important or significant interests is uncertain. The Court has never yet found that any interest asserted by government to justify a time, place, or manner regulation of expressive activity was so insignificant that it did not qualify as an "important" or "significant" interest. However, the Court has invalidated a number of laws on the basis that these laws were not narrowly tailored to the interest that the government asserted.

It may well be that the Court is employing an ad-hoc balancing test in time, place, and manner regulation cases.[24] If the Court engages in an ad-hoc balancing, then the Court, in each case, would determine whether the extent to which the time, place, or manner law lessened the amount of expressive activity in society was justified by the degree to which the law promoted a significant societal interest. If the Justices believed that the promotion of societal interests outweigh any incidental burden on speech caused by the content-neutral law, they would find that the time, place, or manner regulation is narrowly tailored to a significant or important government interest and that it leaves open adequate alternative channels of communication. If they believed to the contrary, they would invalidate the law.

The problem with ad hoc judgements, or weighing the interests, is that, unless the Court tells us how to calibrate the scales and actually weigh different interests, we (and the lower courts) do not know how cases will come out until the Court bothers to tell us. Granted, the open use of a balancing test for the judicial review of truly content-neutral laws explains easily the results in some cases, because one can always decide that the balance should tilt one way or the other. For example, the interest in the esthetic quality of a city may justify some limited restrictions on handing out leaflets for the size or type of signs on privately owned property. However, those same interests are not sufficient to justify a total prohibition in handing out leaflets within an entire town or the total prohibition of all signs on residential property. When the burden on speech is small, the government interest in the esthetic quality of the city is sufficient to justify the law. But the interest in esthetic quality is not sufficiently important to justify the banning of all leaflets or signs.

Symbolic Speech. Non-verbal activity can

---

24. Some great scholars have advanced this theory, e.g., Professors Ely and Emerson. John Hart Ely, Flag Desecration: a Case Study in the Roles of Categorization and Balancing in First Amendment Analysis, 88 Harv. L. Rev 1482 (1975); Thomas Emerson, The System of Free- dom of Expression (1970); Ronald D. Rotunda & John E. Nowak, Treatise on Constitutional Law: Substance and Procedure, Chapter 21 (3rd ed. 1999), with annual supplements.

be speech.[25] Symbolic speech is simply a phrase used to describe non-verbal activity that is treated as if the activity were speech. If people understand that waving a red flag is a call to action, then waving a red flag is a form of speech, such as Paul Revere's ride was prompted by signals ("one if by land, two if by see"). The question is when the state can ban or regulate symbolic speech.

The problem of symbolic speech is intertwined with the problems presented by time, place, or manner regulations of expression. Indeed, the only difference between a symbolic speech case and a time, place, or manner regulation case is the need to determine (in a so-called symbolic speech case) whether non-verbal activity should be treated as if it is speech.

The general rule is that the government may restrict speech if it meets a four-part test: [1] if it is within the constitutional power of the Government; [2] if it furthers an important or substantial governmental interest; [3] if the governmental interest is unrelated to the suppression of free expression; and [4] if the incidental restriction on alleged First Amendment freedoms is no greater than is essential to the furtherance of that interest. The crucial fact, in symbolic speech cases is part 3: *if the governmental interest is unrelated to the suppression of free expression.*

For example, the government can prohibit burning draft cards because its rationale is unrelated to the content of the act. The government will argue that the draft cards are useful as a backup copy of each person's status under the draft laws. That purpose is *unrelated to the suppression of free expression.*[26] However, if the government banned *public* draft card burning, or burning a draft card "with contempt," that ban does not fit within the rationale proffered, to have a backup copy of each person's status under the draft laws. The government is seeking to ban an symbolic act because it communicates a particular message, opposition to war.

Assume that Mr. Adam Adams lives in a small town that has recently made it illegal to burn leaves, or any other items, outside of enclosed furnaces. Adams is very upset with the law because he previously had burned his leaves on his driveway every Autumn. Adams in private, tells his spouse that he is going to burn leaves on the sidewalk "as a means of demonstrating my protest against this unjust limitation of my liberty." Or Adams announces to the world that he is burning leaves as a form of protest. Adam then burns leaves on the sidewalk and the police charge him with a criminal violation of the anti-leaf burning ordinance.

Adams's actions are not "speech" for First Amendment purposes any more than John Wilkes Booth's assassination of Lincoln was symbolic speech, although Booth shouted "Sic Semper Tyrannis" as he killed the President. The law against leaf-burning, like the law against murder, is unrelated to the message that the perpetrator seeks to communicate.

The intention of the actor who engages in the non-verbal conduct cannot in itself determine whether the conduct is the equivalent of speech. In other words, the fact that we know that Adam intended to convey a message by his leaf burning does not, in itself, mean that the judiciary would have to treat his leaf-burning as speech. There is some indication in the cases that, to be considered as speech, non-verbal activity must be of a type that a reasonable onlooker would understand as conveying some type of message. However, in cases involving restrictions on nude dancing, the Court has assumed that nudity and nude dancing constitutes some form of expression, even though it is not clear exactly what message one conveys by dancing naked (as opposed to dancing with some minimal clothing).[27] An easier case to understand the symbolic impact of dancing would be a law prohibiting only nude dancing that is alluring; that law only prohib-

---

25. Ronald D. Rotunda, The Politics of Language: Liberalism as Word and Symbol (U. of Iowa Press, 1986).

26. United States v. O'Brien, 391 U.S. 367, 376, 88 S.Ct. 1673, 1678, 20 L.Ed.2d 672 (1968). See §§ 16.48, 16.49.

27. See § 16.61(*l*).

its some conduct, and that conduct relates to the content of the message.

What is significant is the intention of the government—a law prohibiting only *public* draft card burning in conclusive evidence that the government is concerned with the message of the burning, not the need to have every draft-eligible person keep a copy of his draft status. A law prohibiting leaf-burning, even on private property, is a law unrelated to the freedom of expression because its purpose relates to the pollution from the act and not the motive of the speaker when he performs the act.

The Court has described the time, place, or manner principle as involving intermediate judicial scrutiny because, once the Court determines that the non-verbal activity constitutes expression, it will not merely approve the law and the prosecution with the mere rationality standard. So long as the Court finds that the law is not content-based, the law will apply to time, place or manner standard rather than engaging in strict judicial scrutiny. In other words, if a law restricting the symbolic speech is neutral, that is, not content-based, the Court will not require the government to demonstrate that the law is narrowly tailored to promote a compelling interest.

The Court has often been able to avoid deciding whether particular non-verbal action involved in a case constitutes speech by looking at the nature of the government regulation involved in the case. Many times the government regulation that is being applied to the non-verbal activity is clearly designed to suppress a certain type of expressive message. In such a situation, the non-verbal activity must be considered to be speech, because the only possible interest in the government regulation would be to suppress content of expression. The cases involving flag burning have been ones in which nonverbal activity are treated as speech, because the purpose of the law is to punish the flag-burner because of his or her

motive when burning the flag. The typical statute banning flag-burning makes it a crime to desecrate the flag, such as burning it out of disrespect. The correct way to handle a flag that has become too worn is, according to flag etiquette manners, to burn the flag out of respect.[28]

The government could not defend these laws as being content-neutral. These laws did not ban the destruction of all red, white and blue cloth, and if it did, one wonders what rational justification the government had to create such a law. The law did not ban burning of any cloth item either. Indeed, these laws did not ban all burning of flags; these laws allowed a flag to be burned in a respectful manner as a means of disposing of a used flag. Because laws banning desecration of the flag are symbolic speech and content related, the Court invalidated them. The government could not show that such laws were narrowly tailored to a compelling interest. The Court refused to add flag destruction to the limited types of speech, such as obscenity, that the government could prohibit.[29]

In *Virginia v. Black*[30], a majority of the Justices upheld a Virginia statute that banned burning a cross with the intent to intimidate another person. The statute banning cross burning with intent to intimidate could not be defended as a content-neutral law, because the statute was aimed at banning a certain type of expression: a threat designed to intimidate another person. The cross-burning had to be treated as a law restricting speech because the only reason for banning the cross burning was to suppress a true threat.

The Court upheld this law, although it was content-related, because a majority of the Justices found that it was narrowly tailored to serve a compelling interest—true threats against specific individuals. This threat or specific intimidation was a form of "fighting words" that presented a danger that can be

28. See § 16.48. See also Peter Maggs & Ronald D. Rotunda, Meanwhile, Back in Mother Russia, Legal Times (of Washington, D.C.), Oct. 2, 1989, at 35.

29. Texas v. Johnson, 491 U.S. 397, 109 S.Ct. 2533, 105 L.Ed.2d 342 (1989); United States v. Eichman, 496

U.S. 310, 110 S.Ct. 2404, 110 L.Ed.2d 287 (1990). See § 16.48.

30. 538 U.S. 343, 123 S.Ct. 1536, 155 L.Ed.2d 535 (2003).

totally banned without undercutting the basic values of the First Amendment.

Symbolic speech or non-verbal activity is speech, but, like other speech, the state can impose reasonable regulation of time, place, or manner regulation *without* regard to content. Let us assume that an individual wishes to burn the American flag in protest of an American foreign policy decision. This person burns the flag in the street while proclaiming that she is doing so as a sign that she is no longer proud of being a United States citizen. If she is arrested for desecrating the flag, she could not be punished because flag-burning is constitutionally protected symbolic speech. However, she could be punished under a content-neutral environmental law that banned the burning of any item in the public streets. In other words, an individual has no right to disregard the anti-air pollution ordinance merely because she chooses to burn the flag rather than trees leaves. Because flag burning is speech, the Court would ask whether the environmental regulation was narrowly tailored to promote an important or significant government interest *unrelated to the suppression of expression*. The Court would uphold the environmental regulation, and the conviction for air pollution by the flag burner, if the Court found that: (1) the law as written and applied was truly content-neutral; (2) the law banning the burning of all items in the public streets was narrowly tailored to promote a significant or important interest (in health or environmental matters); and (3) people had ample alternative means to express anti-government viewpoints and messages without having to violate smoke reduction ordinances.

Hybrid Problems Involving Aspects of Content and Non–Content Based Programs. The Court sometimes indicates that all laws regulating speech must be either be either reasonable time, place, or manner regulations that are content-neutral, or laws that are content-based but are narrowly tailored to pro-

mote a compelling government interest. However, at various points in this Chapter, we will see the Court uphold a law that appears to be content-based, but does not totally proscribe a message, or the law deals only with the effects of a certain type of content on a specific environment.[31]

For example, the Court has allowed the prohibition of certain types of speech related to sexual activity broadcast over radio and television channels at times when children might be watching or listening to the broadcast. These cases can best be understood by recognizing that the technical aspects of broadcasting make it difficult, if not impossible, for the government to keep minors from seeing or hearing material that it may declare unfit for minors over the broadcast airwaves, whereas the government has means other than content prohibition for protecting children from adult material that is transmitted via cable or satellite systems. The government interest in protection of children is like an interest in protecting an environment. The unfiltered speech over broadcast airwaves at times when children will be watching and listening has a specific impact on the environment. The government will not be able to totally outlaw such speech, but it will be able to restrict the speech so as to further the societal interest in the protection of children.

The Court has upheld laws that establish separate areas in a city or town for adult entertainment.[32] In these cases, the Court claims that laws creating separate zoning requirements for adult entertainment are content-neutral. But the determination that entertainment is "adult entertainment" means that the government has to look at the content. The concept of content-neutrality in a zoning law that regulates the places for certain types of entertainment based on whether the entertainment involves sexual material is a complete legal fiction. If a movie theater owner in a town with such zoning wishes to know

---

31. This approach to explaining the cases was advanced two decades ago in Daniel A. Farber and John E. Nowak, The Misleading Nature of public Forum Analysis: Content and Context in First Amendment Adjudication, 70 U. Va. L. Rev. 1219 (1984). See also, Ronald D. Rotunda &

John E. Nowak, Treatise on Constitutional Law: Substance and Procedure, Chapter 21 (3rd ed. 1999), with annual supplements.

32. See § 16.61(d).

where he can place his theater he will have to first determine the content of the movies he is going to show in order to understand whether he is restricted to those areas zoned for adult entertainment or whether he can build his theater in areas zoned for general business and general entertainment purposes.

In these zoning cases, the Court has emphasized that the adult content of the speech has a different effect on government interests unrelated to the suppression of expression, namely, the property values of parcels of property near the entertainment establishment. Any type of activity will have a secondary economic effect of influencing prices on real estate surrounding the site of the economic activity. Placing an adult theater in a neighborhood demonstrably has a more serious effect on real estate values of nearby residential property than would placing a theater for showing only movies that are fit for children. In these zoning cases, the laws did not completely prohibit the message conveyed in the adult entertainment.

When analyzing a First Amendment problem, one should ask whether the law in the specific case is truly content-neutral as written and applied. If so, the law might be upheld as a time, place, or manner regulation. If the law is designed truly to proscribe a message or viewpoint, the law will be upheld only if it is proscribing a category of speech that the Court has held can be totally banned (e.g., obscenity, as the Court has defined it) or, in the alternative, if the government can demonstrate that the prohibition is narrowly tailored to serve a compelling interest.

In a few situations, the Court has allowed the government to restrict speech in a particular environment because the content of the speech has a special effect on that environment, even though the Court has not clearly established any guidelines for deciding when content can be regulated because of its impact on interests unrelated to the suppression of

expression. The Court will use some form of judicial review more lenient that strict judicial scrutiny where a government action is content-based, but is designed to deal with the impact of the content on a certain type of environment and does not involve a true government proscription of some type of speech or message.

For example, the Court has allowed the government to ban speech near a court house with the intent of interfering with, obstructing, or impeding the administration of justice,[33] even though it has not allowed the government to ban all speech from the sidewalks near the Supreme Court of the United States.[34] Unfortunately, the Supreme Court opinions did not carefully explain the difference between speech near normal courthouses and speech near the United States Supreme Court.

The rulings might be tied together by finding that speech advocating that juries or lower courts might change their verdicts to accord with public opinion, whereas messages regarding the public's view of United States Supreme Court rulings are not at all likely to influence the outcome of Supreme Court decisions. In the first case the Court did say, "There can be no question that a State has a legitimate interest in protecting its judicial system from the pressures which picketing near a courthouse might create. Since we are committed to a government of laws and not of men, it is of the utmost importance that the administration of justice be absolutely fair and orderly."[35]

Distinguishing Different Types of Forums or Fora. When government restricts speech on property that it owns (the streets, public buildings), or in a medium of communication owned by the government (such as a public school newspaper or a public school campus mail system), the Court will analyze the restrictions on speech in terms of the type of forum that is involved in the problem. Forum analysis applies only to government-

---

33. Cox v. Louisiana, 379 U.S. 559, 85 S.Ct. 476, 13 L.Ed.2d 487 (1965) (Court reverses convictions because of due process violation that related to the specific facts involved in arrest and prosecution of demonstrators, but all the Justices indicate that the law was valid on its face).

34. See, United States v. Grace, 461 U.S. 171, 103 S.Ct. 1702, 75 L.Ed.2d 736 (1983).

35. Cox v. Louisiana, 379 U.S. 559, 562–62, 85 S.Ct. 476, 479.

owned property, not to privately owned property or privately owned channels of communication. If the government wishes to control speech in privately owned schools or in privately owned homes, the analysis of the problem does not relate to whether the government may restrict speech in any particular type of forum.

The Court has divided all types of government owned property into three types of fora (or forums). Government owned property may be described as a public forum, a limited public forum, or a nonpublic forum.

A public forum is a type of government property that has traditionally been open to public discourse, such as public sidewalks and public parks. When controlling speech in a public forum, the general rule is that the government may impose content-neutral time, place, or manner regulations.

In addition, the government may restrict speech in these public forums if the speech (like other categories of speech) falls into one of the categories of speech that the Court has held that the government may prohibit even if the prohibition is content-based. In other words, (1) the speech falls within one of the categories of speech that the Court has held the state can totally prohibited (e.g., obscene displays on the streets) or (2) the content-based prohibition the Court finds is necessary to promote a compelling interest.

The phrases "limited public forum," "designated public forum," and "part-time public forum" are really interchangeable. Courts and commentators may use any of these terms to refer to a government-owned channel of communication, or government-owned property, that is not traditionally open to public discourse but a governmental entity has chosen to throw open this channel or property to public discourse for a time.

This type of public forum is usually not as difficult to identify as the previous sentence might indicate. A limited public forum is simply a place or channel of communication that

the government owns and that (given our history and traditions) you would not expect to be open to public discourse. Nevertheless, the government entity that owns and controls that property has chosen to open it to public speech. For example, when the classrooms in a government-owned school are not in use for class purposes, the government might keep those classrooms closed and the public would have no right to use those classrooms. However, if the government entity that controls the public school chooses to allow the public to use those classrooms when school is not in session, then the government has turned those classrooms into a limited public forum.

The government cannot close traditional public forums: it could not say that no one may walk on the public sidewalks carrying a sign opposing the government's policy on medicare. But the government can simply close a limited public forum so long as it does so in a way that does not discriminate based on content.

If the government does discriminate on content, it can do so for the same reason it can prohibit any speech based on content, that is, the speech is in a category that the Court has ruled the government may prohibit, such as the speech is obscene, or the regulation is narrowly tailored to promote a compelling government interest. These are the same basic tests that apply to all speech that government seeks to regulate based on content. The categories are not voluminous, as we will see later in the chapter, which goes over all of these issues in a more detailed way.

For example, the government cannot exclude religious groups from using the public school classrooms for after-hours meetings *if* the government has opened these classrooms to general public discourse.[36] If the government opens up the public school classroom for use by the registered student groups after school hours (e.g., the chess club), then it cannot ban the speech of a registered student religious group because that would be based on

36. See e.g., Widmar v. Vincent, 454 U.S. 263, 102 S.Ct. 269, 70 L.Ed.2d 440 (1981). See §§ 16.45–16.47, 17.5(e).

the content of the speech (religious oriented speech). The state cannot prohibit religious student groups from using property on an equal basis with other student groups.

The last type of government owned property where government owned channel of communication is a non-public forum, that is, government property, or a government-owned channel of communication that has not traditionally been open to public discourse and that the government has chosen not to throw open to public discourse. Examples of a non-public forum would include a public school classroom when class is in session or a courtroom.

There are three ways that the government may control speech in a nonpublic forum, two of which mirror the government's powers over a public forum. First, as with a public forum or limited public forum, the government may employ content-neutral time, place, or manner regulations. Second, as with the public forum and limited public forum, the government may prohibit speech that falls within a proscribed category of speech or that is subject to a regulation that is narrowly tailored to a compelling interest.

The third reason is a little different. The government may regulate speech in a nonpublic forum if the regulation is (a) reasonable (in light of the uses and purpose of the nonpublic forum) and (b) viewpoint-neutral (in the sense of not being a regulation designed to punish or suppress a viewpoint with which the government disagrees). It is common for courts and commentators to simply say that the government may control speech in a nonpublic forum with a regulation that is reasonable and viewpoint-neutral.[37] That statement is correct, although one should remember that the government's power to enact reasonable, viewpoint-neutral regulations of expressive activity in a non-public forum is in addition to the powers the government would have over speech in a public forum or a limited public forum.

The government is not allowed to engage in viewpoint punishment in a nonpublic forum (or anywhere else). For example, the government could choose to close all public school classrooms when classes are not in session. When a class is in session, it can limit the speech in ways that are content-based but not viewpoint-based; for example, the government can reserve the American history classroom for the teaching of American history when the American history class is in session (the content is American history, not mathematics). But the government cannot engage in viewpoint-based discrimination (the government cannot prohibit the teacher or students from saying something critical of American history).

Or, let us assume that a public school teacher dismisses two students from mathematics class because they were talking about baseball during class. This restriction of speech is content-based because it separates baseball speech from mathematics speech. Although the government cannot to ban speech regarding baseball from the public streets, it can ban it from the mathematics classroom because of its impact on the teaching environment. But the government could not engage in viewpoint-based punishment: if the two students were having their baseball discussion because one of them was a Chicago Cubs fan, and one was a St. Louis Cardinals fan, the public school teacher and school would be violating the First Amendment if they chose only to punish one student (the student whose team the school favored).

"Facial" and "as Applied" First Amendment Challenges.

In several topic areas, you will see cases in which Justices struggle over the question of whether they should invalidate a law "on its face" or merely leave the law subject to "as applied" challenges. If the Court invalidates a law "on its face," it will totally invalidate a law. When a defendant challenges a law on its face the defendant is, in effect, saying: "The law I have been charged with is totally invalid,

---

37. See § 16.47(c). See, e.g., Perry Education Association v. Perry Local Educators' Association., 460 U.S. 37, 46, 103 S.Ct. 948, 955, 74 L.Ed.2d 794 (1983); Cornelius v.

NAACP Legal defense and Educational Fund, Inc., 473 U.S. 788, 806, 105 S.Ct. 3439, 3451, 87 L.Ed.2d 567 (1985).

so that it cannot be used to punish anyone, under any circumstances. You should rule that I cannot be punished because the statute is totally invalid, even though my words might have been punished consistently with the First Amendment, if the State had a better drafted statute."

When the Court determines whether a law is invalid on its face, it looks at not only the statutory language but also the way the courts and enforcement authorities have interpreted the language. The Court will strike a law on its face if it is vague (a concept that may meld due process and First Amendment concerns) or substantially overbroad (because the law punishes speech that cannot be punished consistently with the First Amendment, even though the law make criminal some speech that could be punished consistently with the First Amendment).[38]

If a law is not invalid on its face, the litigant can still argue that it invalid as applied in a specific case. In an "as applied" challenge to a law, a defendant charged with violating the law is, in effect, saying "Even if the law is constitutional on its face, I cannot be convicted under this law for what I did."

Let us assume that the Illinois has a law that states: "Dirty movies are illegal; Any theater owner who shows a dirty movie to the public will be subject to a $1,000 fine and 3 months in jail." The state convicts a theater owner for showing a movie with explicit nudity in it, even though he presented evidence that the movie was critically acclaimed and even won the Academy Award. The state supreme court affirmed the conviction and the U.S. Supreme has accepted certiorari.

At the trial and appellate levels, the movie theater owner would challenge the law both on its face and as applied. If the Illinois Supreme Court had not clarified the law to explain that "dirty movies" meant "obscene movies" as the Supreme Court has defined the term, the law

will be invalid on its face, as either vague (because the law did not give clear notice to persons regarding what types of movies are illegal) or overbroad (because it punished sexually related movies that are not "obscene"), or both.

If the law is invalid on its face, the state cannot use it to convict anyone for showing a movie, even if the movie is really "obscene." However if the state court had interpreted the "dirty movies" to mean precisely what the U.S. Supreme Court means by "obscene," then the law is not invalid on its face. As construed by the state court, the law would not be vague or overbroad because the law would be clear (when understood in light of the state court cases) and narrowly tailored to punish only material that was truly obscene under Supreme Court rulings (because of the state court interpretations of the statute).[39]

Even if the law is constitutional on its face, the theater owner would still have an "as applied" challenge, arguing that the movie displayed in his theater won an Academy Award for Best Picture of the Year and cannot be so lacking in value as to come within the Supreme Court's definition of "obscenity." The Illinois Dirty Movies Law would be valid on its face, but invalid insofar in so far as it was applied to the movie that won the Academy Award, a movie that clearly, when taken as a whole, had serious artistic value.[40]

A Final Word Regarding Prior Restraints. Government will encounter special problems if it seeks to use a "prior restraint" which is a formal government mechanism to prevent speech from being distributed, published, spoken, or otherwise put into the marketplace of ideas and given to persons other than the speaker.

A large penalty for speech that is deemed illegal may deter people from speaking, but subsequent punishment for speech is different

---

38. See §§ 16.8–16.10.

39. In Ward v. Illinois, 431 U.S. 767, 97 S.Ct. 2085, 52 L.Ed.2d 738 (1977), an Illinois anti-obscenity statute survived a United States Supreme Court challenge, based on an Illinois State Supreme Court clarification of the law,

40. State are prohibited from punishing, as obscene, movies that a reasonable person would find, when viewed as a whole, has serious value (regardless of local standards). See, Pope v. Illinois, 481 U.S. 497, 107 S.Ct. 1918, 95 L.Ed.2d 439 (1987); Jenkins v. Georgia, 418 U.S. 153, 94 S.Ct. 2750, 41 L.Ed.2d 642 (1974).

from a prior restraint that prevents the speech from ever being uttered. Prior restraints are a more significant power and so the Court imposes greater safeguards on its use.

Let us suppose that a state imposes a fifty-year sentence on any movie theater owner who shows an obscene movie. The possibility of being subject to a half-century of incarceration will deter movie theater owners from showing any movies other than those that they are sure are not obscene under the terms of Supreme Court rulings. That law, nevertheless, would not be a prior restraint in legal terminology.

A prior restraint would occur if the law prohibited the theater from showing the movie until it was first approved by a government administrative panel. A court injunction prohibiting someone from showing the movie is another form of prior restraint.

Prior restraints, more than subsequent punishment, to a greater extent effectively prevent ideas from being sent to the public. Some discussion of prior restraint occur at various points in this Chapter.[41]

§ 16.2   An Introduction to the Historical Background

Freedom of speech is one of the preeminent rights of Western democratic theory, the touchstone of individual liberty.[1] Justice Cardozo characterized it as "the matrix, the indispensable condition of nearly every other form of freedom."[2] Most people may love free speech in theory, but in application it has often provoked bitter public controversy. As Justice Holmes has observed, it is "not free thought for those who agree with us, but freedom for the thought that we hate"[3] that gives the theory its most enduring value.

The First Amendment envisions a system of freedom of expression that is difficult, sophisticated, and complex, because it reflects life. Understanding this theory "does not come naturally to the ordinary citizen but needs to be learned," and it must be "restated and reiterated not only for each generation, but for each new situation."[4] Consequently, it is necessary to examine the historical and philosophical context out of which the concept of free speech emerged.

§ 16.3   The English Background

(a) Introduction

The intransigence of the developing nation-states toward the idea that speech, regardless of its content, is protected, was a natural outgrowth of the authoritarian nature of those societies following the Middle Ages. Political authority derived its legitimacy from religious authority, where truth is determined by divine revelation. Under this theory, controversies are to be resolved by God, through his infallible human agents in the government and churches. Dissent from this authority meant not only to be wrong, but to be damned.

Governments did not become more tolerant of dissent when they became responsive to political, rather than spiritual needs. It was essential, if divine authority were removed, that the government maintain popular opinion so that the people would continue to support it, pay taxes, and submit to military conscription. The government frankly admitted that it could not survive unless "the people should have a good opinion of it," and to maintain that opinion, it was essential that the govern-

41. See §§ 16.16, 16.17, 16.46, 16.47(c).

§ 16.2

1. Keady, D.J., quoting Treatise, in Dunagin v. City of Oxford, 489 F.Supp. 763, 769 (N.D.Miss.1980), reversed on other grounds 701 F.2d 335 (5th Cir.1983) (per curiam); Waters, C.J., citing Treatise in, Knights of the Ku Klux Klan v. Arkansas State Highway & Transportation Dept., 807 F.Supp. 1427, 1433 (W.D.Ark.1992); Davis v. Yovella, 110 F.3d 63 (6th Cir.1997) (per curiam), citing Treatise.

See, 4 Ronald D. Rotunda & John E. Nowak, Treatise on Constitutional Law: Substance and Procedure §§ 20.1–

20.61 (West Group, 3d ed. 1999) for a more thorough analysis of the issues in this Chapter.

2. Palko v. Connecticut, 302 U.S. 319, 327, 58 S.Ct. 149, 152, 82 L.Ed. 288 (1937).

3. United States v. Schwimmer, 279 U.S. 644, 654–55, 49 S.Ct. 448, 451, 73 L.Ed. 889 (1929) (dissenting opinion).

4. Thomas Emerson, Toward A General Theory of the First Amendment, 72 Yale L.J. 877, 894 (1963). For an excellent introduction to, and analysis of, the free speech clause, see Van Alstyne, A Graphic Review of the Free Speech Clause, 70 Calif.L.Rev. 107 (1982).

ment punish those who criticize the government.[1]

In England, the schism between the English and Roman Catholic Church as well as the protracted struggle for supremacy between King and Parliament exacerbated this situation. Thus, in the three centuries prior to the Declaration of Independence, the King repeatedly sought to contain ideas antagonistic to the Crown. The two primary methods to effectuate suppression were the punishment of seditious libel and the licensing and regulation of the press.[2]

(b) Seditious Libel

The English Court of the Star Chamber developed the theory that the King, as the originator of Justice, was above popular criticism. Therefore, publication of statements critical of the sovereign or his agents was considered seditious libel. Publication of opinions critical of the government were a criminal assault. Truth was not a defense, for "the greater the truth, the greater the libel" against the government.[3] There was no need to prove intent to incite insurrection, for if one intended to publish criticism, he acted unlawfully merely by finding "fault with his masters and betters."[4] Prosecution was vigorous.

Eventually Parliament enacted Fox's Libel Act,[5] in 1792, which turned the issue of guilt to the jury, who could bring in a general verdict of guilty or not guilty. No longer could the judge direct the jury to find the defendant guilty merely on proof of the publication. After Fox's Libel Act, seditious prosecutions in England continued with "shameful severity" but the new Act was still a safeguard.[6] This Act was silent as to whether truth should be allowed as a defense.

(c) Prior Restraints

Until 1694, English authors also had to contend with an elaborate system of licensing. All writing that was to be published had to be licensed prior to publication. Without the license, there could be no lawful publication. "The struggle for the freedom of the press was primarily directed against the power of the licensor."[7]

Justice Story, in his Commentaries on the Constitution, concisely summarizes the history of this censorship:

> The art of printing soon after its introduction, we are told, was looked upon, as well in England as in other countries, as merely a matter of state, and subject to the coercion of the crown. It was, therefore, regulated in England by the King's proclamations, prohibitions, charters of privilege, and licenses, and finally by the decrees of the Court of Star–Chamber, which limited the number of printers and of presses which each should employ, and prohibited new publications, unless previously approved by proper licensors. On the demolition of this odious jurisdiction, in 1641, the Long Parliament of

---

§ 16.3

1. Thus, Lord Holt in Rex v. Tuchin, Holt 424 (1704) reasoned:

"If men should not be called to account for possessing the people with an ill opinion of the government, no government can subsist; for it is very necessary for every government, that the people should have a good opinion of it. And nothing can be worse to any government, than to endeavor to produce animosities as to the management of it. This has always been looked upon as a crime, and no government can be safe unless it be punished."

2. Constructive Treason. A third, but less used, method of suppression was that of conviction for constructive treason. See 1 H. Taylor, The Origin and Growth of the English Constitution 511 (1898); 3 H. Taylor, The Origin and Growth of the English Constitution 250–51 (1911); C. D. Bowen, The Lion and the Throne: The Life and Times of Sir Edward Coke: 1552–1634 (1956), at 200–203.

3. Prosser and Keeton, Handbook of the Law of Torts 771–73 (5th ed. 1984); 2 J. S. Stephen, A History of the Criminal Law of England 381 (London 1883); L. Levy, Judgments: Essays on American Constitutional History 119 (1972); Z. Chafee, Free Speech in the United States 500 (1941).

4. Z. Chafee, Free Speech in the United States 19 (1941). William Mayton, Seditious Libel and the Lost Guarantee of a Freedom of Expression, 84 Colum.L.Rev. 91 (1984).

5. 32 Geo. 3, c. 60 (1792). J. S. Stephen, A History of the Criminal Law of England 340–49 (1882).

6. Z. Chafee, Free Speech in the United States 23, 35 (1941).

7. Lovell v. Griffin, 303 U.S. 444, 451, 58 S.Ct. 666, 669, 82 L.Ed. 949 (1938), opinion conformed 57 Ga.App. 901, 197 S.E. 347 (1938).

Charles the First, after their rupture with that prince, assumed the same powers which the Star–Chamber exercised with respect to licensing books; and during the Commonwealth (such is human frailty and the love of power even in republics!) they issued their ordinances for that purpose, founded principally upon a Star–Chamber decree in 1637. After the restoration of Charles the Second, a statute on the same subject was passed, copied, with some few alterations, from the parliamentary ordinances. The act expired in 1679, and was revived and continued for a few years after the revolution of 1688. Many attempts were made by the government to keep it in force; but it was so strongly resisted by Parliament that it expired in 1694, and has never since been revived.[8]

§ 16.4 The Colonial Background

Although much of the initial emigration to the New World is credited to the repressive religious policies prevalent in Europe, the colonies exhibited no tendencies to liberalize free communication within their own communities. "Colonial America was an open society dotted with closed enclaves, and one could generally settle with his co-believers in safety and comfort and exercise the right of oppression."[1]

The Trial of John Peter Zenger. The decline in the use of censorship in England no doubt contributed to its relative absence in pre-Revolutionary America. However, the doctrine of seditious libel was in full force on both sides of the Atlantic. Although the last prosecution for seditious libel in the colonies, that of New York printer John Peter Zenger, occurred in 1735, the threat of prosecution in the following years did not cease.[2]

The trial of Zenger was the first cause célèbre in the name of free speech in America.

Zenger had published articles critical of the policies of New York's Governor Cosby. The royal governor then instituted suit, over the reluctance of the colonial legislature. The defense, organized and argued by a prominent attorney, Andrew Hamilton, centered on the novel assertion that truth should be a proper defense to the crime. Hamilton recognized that truth, if determined by the jury, would exculpate his client, for the intrusion of the King into colonial affairs was already deeply resented. The Court rejected Hamilton's argument, but he prevailed by persuading the jury to ignore the law and return a general verdict of acquittal.[3]

Colonial Legislative Practice. At the same time that the people criticized the King and his royal governors, their popularly elected legislatures were imposing rather draconian punishments, through summary contempt procedures, on printers who criticized their policies.[4] Many people, then as now, cherished liberty to speak critically of the government in the abstract, but, in practice, acted differently.

Blackstone, in his influential *Commentaries*, first published in 1765, articulated the general common law view at the time the Constitution was drafted. At that time, the practice of censorship had withered away, but the law of seditious libel was still viable.[5] Blackstone explained that the main focus of free speech was the objection to prior restraint. "The liberty of the press is indeed essential to the nature of a free state; but this consists in laying no *previous* restraint upon publications, and not in freedom from censure for criminal matter when published. Every freeman has an undoubted right to lay what sentiments he pleases before the public; to forbid this, is to destroy the freedom of the press; but if he publishes what is improper, mischievous, or il-

---

8. 2 J. Story, Commentaries on the Constitution of the United States, § 1882 (5th ed. 1891) (footnote omitted).

§ 16.4

1. J. Roche, American Liberty: An Examination of the "Tradition" of Freedom, in Shadow and Substance: Essays on the Theory and Structure of Politics 11 (1964).

2. Z. Chafee, Free Speech in the United States 21 (1941).

3. In England, it was not until 1843 that there was a defense of truth, if publication was for the public benefit. See Lord Campbell's Act, 6 & 7 Vict. (1843), c. 96.

4. See, L. Levy, Judgments: Essays on American Constitutional History 125–34 (1972).

5. There were 70 prosecutions and 50 convictions for seditious libel by the English authorities from 1760 to 1776. 2 T. S. May, Constitutional History of England 9n (2d ed. 1912).

legal, he must take the consequences of his own temerity. . . ."[6]

§ 16.5   Enactment of the First Amendment

The framers of the Constitution felt no need to include in the original document a provision expressly upholding a general theory of freedom of speech, because of their belief that the government they envisioned, limited to the enumerated powers, could not constitutionally enact a law restricting free speech because that was not among the government's enumerated powers. Popular pressure, however, demanded a more articulate expression of the freedom of individuals from governmental interference. This pressure culminated in the adoption of the Bill of Rights in 1791. Thus, the First Amendment states:

> Congress shall make no law respecting an establishment of religion, or prohibiting the free exercise thereof; or abridging the freedom of speech, or of the press; or the right of the people peaceably to assemble, and to petition the Government for a redress of grievances.

Little can be drawn from the debates within the House concerning the meaning of the First Amendment, and there are no records of debates in the Senate or the states on its ratification.[1] Perhaps the members were following Madison's dictum that they should avoid discussing with particularity "abstract propositions, of which judgment may not be convinced. . . . If we confine ourselves to an enumeration of simple, acknowledged principles, the ratification will meet with but little difficulty."[2]

When interpreting the First Amendment, courts and commentators often refer to the intent of the framers. This reference to intent continues, even following the expansion of the

constitutional guarantee in recent years. Intent is often not clear, but that simply means that the search for it is never-ending.

Professor Zachariah Chafee believed that Blackstone's limited, legalistic view of free speech was supplemented in the New World by a tangible popular meaning: the right of unrestricted discussion of public affairs. Thus, the framers intended free speech to serve the dual purpose of eliminating all vestiges of censorship in America and destroying the viability of the doctrine of seditious libel. Because the government abandoned the practice of censorship well before the drafting of the First Amendment, Chafee contends that it could not have been intended solely as a prohibition against a non-existent practice. The Zenger trial, in Chafee's view, is not only a repudiation of the legitimacy of seditious libel in the colonies but also an expression of the colonists' cherished belief in the principle of free speech.[3]

In contrast, the influential historian, Leonard Levy, maintained that a careful historical study showed that it was merely "sentimental hallucination" to believe that a broad libertarian approach to freedom of speech was a cherished principle. There was nothing in the tradition of the colonists to influence them to overthrow seditious libel, and their activities would indicate that free speech in the revolutionary period was accorded only to those who had favorable opinions of the struggle for independence.[4]

The Alien and Sedition Acts. Whatever the view of the framers at the time of the drafting of the First Amendment, a broader interpretation of that language was ensured by the controversy surrounding the Alien and Sedition Acts of 1798.[5] Under the Alien Act, the President could order to leave the country all aliens "as he shall judge dangerous to the

---

6. Commentaries on the Laws of England, Book IV pp. *151–152 (T. Cooley ed., Chicago: 2d ed., rev. ed. 1872) (emphasis in original).

§ 16.5

1. Constitution of the United States: Analysis & Interpretation, 92d Cong., 2d Sess., Senate Document 92–82 (1973), at p. 936.

2. 1 Annals of Congress, 738 (August 15, 1789).

3. Z. Chafee, Free Speech in the United States (1941) at 19–21.

4. L. Levy, Legacy of Suppression: Freedom of Speech and Press in Early American History, ch. 2 (1960).

5. J. Smith, Freedom's Fetters—The Alien and Sedition Laws and American Civil Liberties (1956).

peace and safety of the United States...."[6] The law was never formally invoked, and expired after two years, but its existence did result in some aliens leaving the country or going into hiding.

The Sedition Act prohibited "publishing any false, scandalous and malicious writing or writings against the government of the United States, or either house of Congress ... or the President ... with intent to defame ... or to bring them ... into contempt or disrepute...."[7] Truth was a defense and the jury had a right to determine the law and facts under the direction of the court. In this respect the Act was actually a fairly liberal one for its time. England did not establish a defense of truth until 1843[8] (though it did allow a general verdict of the jury in the 1790's[9]).

President Adams' Federalist administration employed the Sedition Act against members of Jefferson's Democratic–Republican party because of their criticism of his administration. Despite the Republicans' subsequent retaliation after Jefferson's election,[10] the Jeffersonian criticism of the Federalists' politically motivated prosecutions and their resulting restriction upon free expression provided the foundation for the modern theory of the First Amendment.

The Supreme Court never reviewed the constitutionality of the Alien and Sedition Acts, but they remain the epitome of an unconstitutional abridgement of free speech. Justice Brennan later wrote that the Sedition Act first crystallized a national awareness of the central meaning of the First Amendment.[11] He added:

Although the Sedition Act was never tested in this Court, the attack upon its validity has carried the day in the court of history. Fines levied in its prosecution were repaid by Act of Congress on the ground that it was unconstitutional.... Calhoun, reporting to the Senate on February 4, 1836, assumed that its invalidity was a matter "which no one now doubts." ... Jefferson, as President, pardoned those who had been convicted and sentenced under the Act.... The invalidity of the Act has also been assumed by Justices of this Court.... These views reflect a broad consensus that the Act, because of the restraint it imposed upon criticism of government and public officials, was inconsistent with the First Amendment.[12]

§ 16.6   The Value of Speech and the Function of the First Amendment

Looking at the history of the First Amendment does not end the search for its true meaning. The tools available to calibrate the framers' intent are imprecise and capable of divergent interpretations. We must also look to the policies behind the guarantee. To the extent that we understand the value of free speech and the function of the First Amendment, we will better understand how to interpret the guarantee. The purposes of free speech necessarily animates its coverage and protection.

Understanding the policies that support free speech also avoids the error of using history to impose a narrow view of the First Amendment and to ignore the dynamic nature of its provisions.[1] The fact that the framers intended the First Amendment to protect speech and press did not mean that they intended to exclude movies, digital recordings, or the electronic

---

6. 1 Stat. at Large 570.

7. 1 Stat. at Large 596.

8. 6 & 7 Vic. c. 96 (1843) (Lord Campbell's Act); 2 J. S. Stephen, A History of the Criminal Law of England 383 (London, 1883).

9. Fox's Libel Act, 32 Geo. 3, c. 60 (1792).

10. L. Levy, Jefferson & Civil Liberties—The Darker Side 58–59 (1963). Once Jefferson, in a letter to the Governor of Pennsylvania, noted that the Federalists, having failed to destroy the press by their gag law, now appeared to be doing so by encouraging its licentiousness, and that a few well-placed prosecutions might be necessary to restore the integrity of the press.

11. New York Times Co. v. Sullivan, 376 U.S. 254, 273, 84 S.Ct. 710, 722, 11 L.Ed.2d 686 (1964), motion denied 376 U.S. 967, 84 S.Ct. 1130, 12 L.Ed.2d 83 (1964).

12. New York Times Co. v. Sullivan, 376 U.S. 254, 276, 84 S.Ct. 710, 723–24, 11 L.Ed.2d 686 (1964), motion denied 376 U.S. 967, 84 S.Ct. 1130, 12 L.Ed.2d 83 (1964) (footnote omitted).

§ 16.6

1. E.g., Paul Brest, Process of Constitutional Decisionmaking, ch. 2 (1975).

highway. We know that the policies behind the First Amendment support coverage. If the framers had foreseen modern methods of communication, there is no reason to believe that they would have excluded them from the First Amendment, because that would not promote its policies.

Justice Holmes thought that the main purpose of the free speech guarantee of the First Amendment "is 'to prevent all such *previous restraints* upon publications as had been practiced by other governments', and they do not prevent the subsequent punishment of such as may be deemed contrary to the public welfare."[2] Yet he also admitted: "There is no constitutional right to have all general propositions of law once adopted remain unchanged."[3] It is appropriate to appreciate the underlying values of free speech in order to ascertain the proper degree of judicial solicitude.

John Milton. A prime justification for a system of free speech is its value in preventing human error through ignorance. John Milton's battle with the English censorship laws led to one of the most eloquent defenses of free speech. In *Areopagitica*, Milton said:

> [T]hough all the winds of doctrine were let loose to play upon the earth, so truth be in the field, we do injuriously, by licensing and prohibiting, to misdoubt her strength. Let her and falsehood grapple; whoever knew truth put to the worse in a free and open encounter?[4]

Make speech free, make the search for knowledge uninhibited, and eventually the truth will prevail.

John Stuart Mill. John Stuart Mill expanded Milton's arguments two centuries later

in his 1859 essay, *On Liberty*, by his recognition of the public good—the public enlightenment—that results from the free exchange of ideas.

> First, if any opinion is compelled to silence, that opinion for aught we can certainly know, be true. To deny this is to assume our own infallibility. Secondly, though this silenced opinion be in error, it may, and very commonly does, contain a portion of the truth; and since the generally prevailing opinion on any subject is rarely or never the whole truth, it is only by the collision of adverse opinions that the remainder of the truth had any chance being supplied. Thirdly, even if the received opinion be not only true but the whole truth; unless it is suffered to be, and actually is, vigorously and earnestly contested, it will, by most of those who receive it, be held in the manner of a prejudice, with little comprehension of feeling of its rational grounds. And not only this, but fourthly, the meaning of the doctrine itself will be in danger of being lost or enfeebled. . . .[5]

Holmes and the Marketplace of Ideas. Justice Oliver Wendell Holmes offered another influential view of free speech based on an economic metaphor. He saw it as a "marketplace of ideas."[6] This theory is built on the premise that the First Amendment prohibits government suppression of ideas because the truth of any idea can only be determined in the "marketplace" of competing ideas.

Individual Self–Fulfillment. An important function of free speech is to enhance the potential of individual contribution to the social welfare, thus enlarging the prospects for individual self-fulfillment.[7] Another function, a

---

2. Patterson v. Colorado, 205 U.S. 454, 462, 27 S.Ct. 556, 558, 51 L.Ed. 879 (1907) (emphasis in original).

3. Patterson v. Colorado, 205 U.S. 454, 461, 27 S.Ct. 556, 557, 51 L.Ed. 879 (1907).

4. J. Milton, Areopagitica, A Speech for the Liberty of Unlicensed Printing to the Parliament of England (1644). Milton was not as assured of the strength of truth as it appeared, however, for he disavowed any legitimacy for popery, open superstition, impiety, or evil.

5. J. S. Mill, On Liberty (1859), Ch. II.

6. Abrams v. United States, 250 U.S. 616, 630, 40 S.Ct. 17, 22, 63 L.Ed. 1173 (1919) (dissenting opinion).

7. See Redish, The Value of Free Speech, 130 U.Penn. L.Rev. 591, 593 (1982).

Free Speech and the Nature of Language. Professor Chevigny has argued that a right to free expression may also be derived from and rooted in, the nature of language itself; the necessity of a dialogue in order to understand words at all means that society should allow the dialogue to proceed. Chevigny, Philosophy of Language and Free Expression, 55 N.Y.U.L.Rev. 157 (1980). See

corollary of the first, is that the health of a society of self-government is nurtured by the contributions of individuals to its functioning.[8]

Curbing Government Abuse. Once we allow the government any power to restrict the freedom of speech, we may have taken a one-way slippery slope. A central value of free press, speech, and assembly lies in checking the abuse of power by public officials.[9] Line drawing in such an abstract area is always difficult and especially so when a government's natural inclination is moving the line more towards suppression of unpopular ideas and any criticism of the government. Thus, even if one could distinguish between illegitimate and legitimate speech, it may still be necessary to protect all speech in order to afford real protection for legitimate speech.[10]

A Safety Valve for Society. One of the reasons that Government should not suppress speech is that free speech is a safety valve. Just as the ancient Romans eventually learned that executing Christians did not suppress Christianity, modern Governments should realize that forbidding people to talk about certain topics does not encourage public stability. It only creates martyrs. Punishing people for speech does not discourage the speech; it only drives it underground, and encourages conspiracy. In the battle for public order, free speech is the ally, not the enemy.

Justice Brandeis, in his forceful concurring opinion in *Whitney v. California*,[11] warned that, those who won our independence—

knew that order cannot be secured merely through fear of punishment for its infraction; that it is hazardous to discourage thought, hope and imagination; that fear

breeds repression; that repression breeds hate; that hate menaces stable government; that the path of safety lies in the opportunity to discuss freely supposed grievances and proposed remedies; and that the fitting remedy for evil counsels is good ones.... Fear of serious injury cannot alone justify suppression of free speech and assembly. Men feared witches and burned women.[12]

§ 16.7 Balancing versus Absolutism

(a) A Preferred Position for Free Speech?

United States v. Carolene Products Co.[1] upheld the power of Congress to regulate "filled milk" as it endorsed the post–1937 concept of judicial deference to acts of other branches of government in their regulation of economic activities. In the course of the now famous footnote 4 of the opinion, Chief Justice Stone said that the Court should not always be so deferential. He argued that certain rights might properly receive more active judicial protection against the democratic process:

There may be narrower scope for operation of the presumption of constitutionality when legislation appears on its face to be within a specific prohibition of the Constitution, such as those of the first ten Amendments which are deemed equally specific when held to be embraced within the Fourteenth....

It is unnecessary to consider now whether legislation which restricts those political processes which can ordinarily be expected to bring about repeal of undesirable legislation, is to be subjected to more exacting

also, Martin, On a New Argument for Freedom of Speech, 57 N.Y.U.L.Rev. 906 (1982); Chevigny, A Dialogic Right of Free Expression: A Reply to Michael Martin, 57 N.Y.U.L.Rev. 920 (1982); R. Rotunda, The Politics of Language: Liberalism as Word and Symbol (U. of Iowa Press, 1986).

8. See T. Emerson, The System of Freedom of Expression (1970); Bollinger, Free Speech and Intellectual Values, 92 Yale L.J. 438 (1983).

9. Blasi, The Checking Value in First Amendment Theory, 1977 A.B. Foundation Res.J. 521; Wellington, On Freedom of Expression, 88 Yale L.J. 1105 (1979); Coleman, A Free Press: The Need to Ensure an Unfettered

Check on Democratic Government Between Elections, 59 Tulane L.Rev. 243 (1984).

10. On the other hand, some argue that protection should only be for explicitly political speech, and not to scientific, literary or obscene speech. Robert Bork, Neutral Principles and Some First Amendment Problems, 47 Ind. L.J. 1 (1971).

11. 274 U.S. 357, 47 S.Ct. 641, 71 L.Ed. 1095 (1927) (Brandeis, J., concurring).

12. 274 U.S. at 375–76, 47 S.Ct. at 648, 71 L.Ed. at 1106 (Brandeis, J., concurring).

§ 16.7
1. 304 U.S. 144, 58 S.Ct. 778, 82 L.Ed. 1234 (1938).

judicial scrutiny under the general prohibitions of the Fourteenth Amendment than are most other types of legislation. . . .[2]

A few years later the Court was even more explicit: "Freedom of press, freedom of speech, freedom of religion are in a preferred position."[3]

Footnote 4 is not merely an assertion; it has a strong rationale. Unlike economic legislation, which is only a product of the political process, and therefore may to some extent be subject to an inner political check, speech is part of the legislative process itself. Restriction of speech alters the democratic process and undercuts the basis for deferring to the legislation that emerges. The restraint of speech is often a short range aid to societal programs because it insulates the current government from criticism caused by debate. This natural tendency of government conflicts with the First Amendment value of open debate. Thus the judiciary should be more active to protect this value against the will of a temporary majority.

Justice Frankfurter and the Preferred Position of Free Speech. Justice Frankfurter strongly criticized the use of the "preferred position" terminology, because its use might imply that any law touching communication has a "presumptive invalidity," radiating "a constitutional doctrine without avowing it."[4] His criticism is a warning against unwarranted extension of judicial principle, rather than an attack on established judicial dogma. In fact, in the same opinion criticizing the preferred position for speech, Frankfurter wrote eloquently of the importance of freedom of speech.

[W]ithout freedom of expression, thought becomes checked and atrophied. Therefore, in considering what interests are so funda-mental as to be enshrined in the Due Process Clause, those liberties of the individual which history has attested as the indispensable conditions of an open as against a closed society come to this Court with a momentum for respect lacking when appeal is made to liberties which derive merely from shifting economic arrangements. Accordingly, Mr. Justice Holmes was far more ready to find legislative invasion where free inquiry was involved than in the debatable area of economics.[5]

Since Frankfurter's sharp attack on the language of "preferred position," the words may be avoided but the substance remains. The preferential treatment of the First Amendment is exemplified by the variety of judicial tools utilized by the Court in its review of challenged legislation. As we shall see, the Court has applied a narrowed presumption of constitutionality, strictly construed statutes to avoid limiting First Amendment freedoms, restricted prior restraint and subsequent punishment, relaxed general requirements of standing to sue and generally set higher standards of procedural due process in order to give vitality to those freedoms over ordinary governmental functions.[6]

(b) Is Free Speech an Absolute?

The First Amendment appears to speak in absolutist terms: "Congress shall make *no* law . . . abridging the freedom of speech. . . ." A comparison with the Fourth Amendment's prohibition against "*unreasonable* searches and seizures" emphasizes the strictness of this language.

If free speech is an absolute right it is certainly in a preferred position compared the majority of rights in the Constitution, which

---

2. 304 U.S. at 152–53 n. 4, 58 S.Ct. at 783–84 n. 4 (1938). See, 4 Ronald D. Rotunda & John E. Nowak, Treatise on Constitutional Law: Substance and Procedure § 23.5(a)(West Group, 3d ed.1999).

3. Murdock v. Pennsylvania, 319 U.S. 105, 115, 63 S.Ct. 870, 876, 87 L.Ed. 1292 (1943).

Chief Justice Stone first made the attempt to recognize First Amendment freedoms as being in a "preferred position," in his dissent in Jones v. Opelika, 316 U.S. 584, 600, 608, 62 S.Ct. 1231, 1240–41, 1244, 86 L.Ed. 1691 (1942), judgment vacated and judgments of the state courts re-versed 319 U.S. 103, 63 S.Ct. 890, 87 L.Ed. 1290 (1943) (per curiam).

4. Kovacs v. Cooper, 336 U.S. 77, 90, 69 S.Ct. 448, 455, 93 L.Ed. 513 (1949), rehearing denied 336 U.S. 921, 69 S.Ct. 638, 93 L.Ed. 1083 (1949) (concurring opinion).

5. Kovacs v. Cooper, 336 U.S. 77, 95, 69 S.Ct. 448, 458, 93 L.Ed. 513 (1949), rehearing denied 336 U.S. 921, 69 S.Ct. 638, 93 L.Ed. 1083 (1949) (concurring opinion).

6. McKay, The Preference for Freedom, 34 N.Y.U.L.Rev. 1182, 1184 (1959).

like the Fourth Amendment, are not expressed in absolute terms. An absolute right, by definition, is not subject to balancing. Even freedom of religion is on a slightly different plane, for the religion clauses of the First Amendment may be read to require some balancing of interests—laws must neither establish a religion nor prohibit its free exercise.

Justices Black and Douglas[7] championed an absolutist view of free speech, and they are most closely associated with this position, but a majority of the Court has never adopted it. Black himself summarized his views in *Konigsberg v. State Bar of California:*[8]

> The recognition [that a State] has subjected "speech and association to the deterrence of subsequent disclosure" is, under the First Amendment, sufficient in itself to render the action of the State unconstitutional unless one subscribes to the doctrine that permits constitutionally protected rights to be "balanced" away whenever a majority of this Court thinks that a State might have interest sufficient to justify abridgement of those freedoms.... I do not subscribe to that doctrine for I believe that the First Amendment's unequivocal command that there shall be no abridgement of the rights of free speech and assembly shows that the men who drafted our Bill of Rights did all the "balancing" that was to be done in this field.... [T]he Court's "absolute" statement that there are no "absolutes" under the First Amendment must be an exaggeration of its own views.[9]

Justice Harlan has often been associated with the "balancing view." In *Konigsberg*, where Black wrote his defense of the absolutist position, Harlan wrote for the Court, and presented his justification for judicial balancing.

> [W]e reject the view that freedom of speech and association ... as protected by the First and Fourteenth Amendments, are "absolutes," not only in the undoubted sense that where the constitutional protection exists it must prevail, but also in the sense that the scope of that protection must be gathered solely from a literal reading of the First Amendment. Throughout its history this Court has consistently recognized at least two ways in which constitutionally protected freedom of speech is narrower than an unlimited license to talk. On the one hand, certain forms of speech, or speech in certain contexts, has been considered outside the scope of constitutional protection.... On the other hand, general regulatory statutes, not intended to control the content of speech but incidentally limiting its unfettered exercise, have not been regarded as the type of law the First or Fourteenth Amendment forbade Congress or the States to pass, when they have been found justified by subordinating valid governmental interests, a prerequisite to constitutionality which has necessarily involved a weighing of the governmental interest involved....[10]

Harlan never advocated an *ad hoc* balancing. The result of his balancing was a rule of law and a holding that had precedential effect.

Harlan's balancing approach is not necessarily inconsistent with the language of the First Amendment. It does not forbid abridging speech, but abridging the *freedom* of speech.[11] How does the Court decide what speech should be free? Must it balance? "The First Amendment is not the guardian of unregulated talk-

7. Konigsberg v. State Bar of California, 366 U.S. 36, 56, 81 S.Ct. 997, 1010, 6 L.Ed.2d 105 (1961), rehearing denied 368 U.S. 869, 82 S.Ct. 21, 7 L.Ed.2d 69 (1961) (dissenting opinion). See, Frank, Hugo L. Black: Free Speech and the Declaration of Independence, in R. Rotunda, ed., Six Justices on Civil Rights, 11, 31–37 (Oceana Publications, Inc. 1983); Countryman, Justice Douglas and Freedom of Expression, in, id., at 107.

8. 366 U.S. 36, 81 S.Ct. 997, 6 L.Ed.2d 105 (1961), rehearing denied 368 U.S. 869, 82 S.Ct. 21, 7 L.Ed.2d 69 (1961).

9. Konigsberg v. State Bar of California, 366 U.S. 36, 60–61, 63, 68, 81 S.Ct. 997, 1012, 1014, 1016, 6 L.Ed.2d 105 (1961) (Black, J., dissenting, joined by Douglas, J., and Chief Justice Warren) (footnote omitted), rehearing denied 368 U.S. 869, 82 S.Ct. 21, 7 L.Ed.2d 69 (1961).

10. 366 U.S. 36, 49–51, 81 S.Ct. 997, 1005–07, 6 L.Ed.2d 105 (1961), rehearing denied 368 U.S. 869, 82 S.Ct. 21, 7 L.Ed.2d 69 (1961) (footnote omitted). See Farber & Nowak, Justice Harlan and the First Amendment, 2 Const. Commentary 425 (1985).

11. A. Meiklejohn, Free Speech and Its Relation to Self Government (1948) p. 19.

ativeness."[12] The values perceived in a system of free expression determine whether there exists an inhibition on that freedom.

Harlan and Black Compared. Harlan's balancing view should not be regarded as necessarily more subservient to state authority than Black's approach. Thus in *Street v. New York*,[13] a flag burning case, Harlan wrote the majority opinion sustaining the First Amendment challenge on the facts of that case, while Black dissented. Black believed the prosecution permissible because it did not rest on spoken words; there was talking, but it took place "as an integral part of conduct."[14] Black also did not believe that the right of free speech broadly granted "a constitutional right to engage in the conduct of picketing or patrolling, whether on publicly owned streets or on privately owned property."[15]

One may criticize Black's view because, contrary to his assertion, he may really be using a balancing test to decide what is speech and what is only expressive conduct. This balancing is more covert and intuitive than Harlan's frank balancing of interests.[16] On the other hand, Harlan's balancing may invite, if not justify, legislative attempts to encroach on the guarantees of free speech.[17]

§ 16.8 The Overbreadth Doctrine

Two closely related doctrines particularly important in dealing with free speech issues are the prohibitions against overbreadth and vagueness. Because of the importance of the free speech guarantee, even when the state does have the power to regulate an area, it must exercise that power very carefully, so as not, in accomplishing a permissible end, unduly infringe on a protected freedom.[1] This section considers the overbreadth doctrine, and then turns to the vagueness doctrine.

An overbroad statute—a statute that is written too broadly, or more broadly than necessary—is one that is designed to burden or punish activities that are not constitutionally protected, but its flaw is that, as drafted, it also includes activities protected by the First Amendment.[2] In the case of a statute that is overbroad on its face, a carefully drawn statute could have reached the conduct. Nevertheless the Court will strike the overbroad statute

12. A. Meiklejohn, Free Speech and Its Relation to Self Government (1948) at 26.

13. 394 U.S. 576, 89 S.Ct. 1354, 22 L.Ed.2d 572 (1969), on remand 24 N.Y.2d 1026, 302 N.Y.S.2d 848, 250 N.E.2d 250 (1969).

14. Street v. New York, 394 U.S. 576, 610, 89 S.Ct. 1354, 1374, 22 L.Ed.2d 572 (1969) (Black, J. dissenting), on remand 24 N.Y.2d 1026, 302 N.Y.S.2d 848, 250 N.E.2d 250 (1969).

Black emphasized: "I would not balance away the First Amendment mandate that speech not be abridged in any fashion whatsoever ... [But it] is immaterial to me that words are spoken in connection with the burning [of an American flag.]" 394 U.S. at 610, 89 S.Ct. at 1374.

15. Cox v. Louisiana, 379 U.S. 559, 578, 85 S.Ct. 476, 13 L.Ed.2d 487 (1965) (Black, J. dissenting), rehearing denied 380 U.S. 926, 85 S.Ct. 879, 13 L.Ed.2d 814 (1965).

16. McCurn, J., citing Treatise in, Fox v. Board of Trustees, 649 F.Supp. 1393, 1397 (N.D.N.Y.1986); Mendelson, The First Amendment and the Judicial Process: A Reply to Mr. Frantz, 17 Vand.L.Rev. 479, 482 (1964).

17. See Coyne, J., citing Treatise in, State v. Casino Marketing Group, 491 N.W.2d 882, 887 (Minn.1992), cert. denied sub. nom., Hall v. Minnesota, 507 U.S. 1006, 113 S.Ct. 1648, 123 L.Ed.2d 269 (1993).

§ 16.8

1. Cantwell v. Connecticut, 310 U.S. 296, 304, 60 S.Ct. 900, 903, 84 L.Ed. 1213 (1940); Local 189 International Union of Police Associations v. Barrett, 524 F.Supp. 760, 765 (N.D.Ga.1981) (overbreadth and vagueness are two separate concepts that often go hand in hand), citing Treatise; Coffey, J., dissenting, citing Treatise in, City of Watseka v. Illinois Public Action Council and American Civil Liberties Union, 796 F.2d 1547, 1563, n. 1 (7th Cir.1986); Gerber, J., quoting Treatise in, Arizona v. Jones, 177 Ariz. 94, 98, 865 P.2d 138, 143 (App.1993); In re Advisory From Governor, 633 A.2d 664, 674 (R.I.1993), quoting Treatise; Jesson, C.J., citing Treatise, in McDougal v. State of Arkansas, 324 Ark. 354, 359, 922 S.W.2d 323, 326 (1996).

2. Rubin, J., quoting Treatise, in Hill v. City of Houston, 764 F.2d 1156, 1161 & n. 16 (5th Cir.1985); Fidel, P.J., quoting Treatise, in State v. Baldwin, 184 Ariz. 267, 269, 908 P.2d 483, 485 (App.1995); Arnold, J., citing Treatise, in Arkansas Game and Fish Commission v. Murders, 327 Ark. 426, 98, 938 S.W.2d 854, 855 (1997). Crabb, J., citing Treatise, in Gaylor v. Thompson, 939 F.Supp. 1363, 1373 (W.D.Wisc.1996). Jesson, C.J., citing Treatise in, McDougal v. State, 324 Ark. 354, 359–360, 361, 922 S.W.2d 323, 326, 327 (1996). H. Franklin Waters, District Judge, citing Treatise, in Arkansas Right to Life State Political Action Comm. v. Butler, 983 F.Supp. 1209 (W.D.Ark.1997). Arnold, Chief J., citing Treatise, in Bailey v. State, 334 Ark. 43, 52, 972 S.W.2d 239, 244 (1998).

because it might apply to others, not before the Court, who may engage in *protected* speech or activity that the statute appears to outlaw.[3]

An overbroad statute chills the protected speech of others. As Justice Brennan explained for the Court in *NAACP v. Button:*[4]

> [T]he instant decree may be invalid if it prohibits privileged exercises of First Amendment rights *whether or not* the record discloses that the petitioner has engaged in privileged conduct. For in appraising a statute's inhibitory effect upon such rights, this Court has not hesitated to take into account possible applications of the statute in other factual contexts besides that at bar.

On the other hand, in non First Amendment areas, "one to whom application of a statute is constitutional will not be heard to attack the statute on the ground that impliedly it might also be taken as applying to other persons or other situations in which its application might be unconstitutional."[5] *Kunz* illustrates the power of the overbreadth doctrine as a First Amendment test; to that case we now turn.

Kunz v. New York. Karl Kunz, a Baptist Minister, was convicted of violating an ordinance that prohibited holding a religious meeting on streets without a permit. The New York Court of Appeals,[6] affirmed the conviction but the Supreme Court reversed, in *Kunz v. New York.*[7] Under the city ordinance those desiring to conduct religious worship meetings on the street had to first obtain a permit from the city police commissioner. Kunz received a one year permit in 1946, later revoked, in November 1946, on the basis of evidence that Kunz had "ridiculed and denounced other religious beliefs in his meeting." Kunz denounced the Pope as "the anti-Christ," and Jews as "Christ-killers" who "should have been burnt in incinerators." The ordinance, however,

made no mention of the grounds for revoking or refusing permits. Kunz reapplied for a permit in 1947 and 1948; his application was rejected in both years. In 1948 he was arrested and convicted for speaking without a permit.

Writing for the Court, Chief Justice Vinson was only concerned with the propriety of the police commissioner's action in refusing to issue that permit. The ordinance authorized an administrative official, the police commissioner, to deny a permit application for conduct that the police commissioner determined, in his discretion, to be condemned by the ordinance. The Court held that ordinances giving discretionary power to administrative officials over a citizen's right to speak about religion on the city streets were an invalid prior restraint on a First Amendment right. "New York can not vest restraining control over the right to speak on religious subjects in an administrative official when there are *no appropriate standards* to guide his action."[8]

While a narrowly drawn statute, with appropriate standards, might validly have been used to deny Kunz's permit, the overbroad statute must fail under the First Amendment standards. Jackson, in dissent, argued that one must consider the statute only as applied. While this argument was acceptable in a non First Amendment context, the majority found it unacceptable here, because the statute affected free speech.[9]

The Doctrine of Substantial Overbreadth. It is difficult to determine how creative a challenging party must be in conceiving of situations where the language of a statute might be applied to protected speech that is not before the Court. In First Amendment overbreadth cases, a statute should fall only if it is "substantially overbroad" and not readily interpreted to avoid privileged activity, be-

---

3. People v. Holder, 103 Ill.App.3d 353, 356, 59 Ill.Dec. 142, 145, 431 N.E.2d 427, 430 (1982) (Hopf, J.) (holding intimidation statute not unconstitutionally overbroad), quoting this portion of an earlier edition of this treatise, judgment reversed 96 Ill.2d 444, 71 Ill.Dec. 677, 451 N.E.2d 831 (1983).

4. 371 U.S. 415, 432, 83 S.Ct. 328, 338–39, 9 L.Ed.2d 405 (1963) (emphasis added).

5. United States v. Raines, 362 U.S. 17, 21, 80 S.Ct. 519, 522, 4 L.Ed.2d 524 (1960).

6. People v. Kunz, 300 N.Y. 273, 90 N.E.2d 455 (1949), motion denied 302 N.Y. 704, 98 N.E.2d 493 (1951).

7. 340 U.S. 290, 71 S.Ct. 312, 95 L.Ed. 280 (1951).

8. 340 U.S. at 295, 71 S.Ct. at 315 (emphasis added).

9. 340 U.S. at 304–305, 71 S.Ct. at 320 (Jackson, J., dissenting).

cause if it is not substantially overbroad, it is unlikely to have a substantial inhibitory effect.

Broadrick v. Oklahoma[10] warned that the overbreadth doctrine is "strong medicine."[11] Therefore it required that substantial overbreadth should exist before invoking the doctrine, particularly when the speech is joined with conduct:

[The function of the overbreadth doctrine is] a limited one at the outset, [and] attenuates as the otherwise unprotected behavior that it forbids the State to sanction moves from "pure speech" toward conduct and that conduct—even if expressive—falls within the scope of otherwise valid criminal laws that reflect legitimate state interests in maintaining comprehensive controls over harmful, constitutionally unprotected conduct.... To put the matter another way, particularly where conduct and not merely speech is involved, we believe that the overbreadth of a statute must not only be real, but substantial as well, judged in relation to the statute's plainly legitimate sweep.[12]

Such a test is hardly a mechanical one and, perhaps, is most important in showing an attitude of hesitancy to employ the doctrine. Elsewhere in *Broadrick v. Oklahoma*, the Court offered a more specific test when it stated that it would invalidate statutes for overbreadth "only when the flaw is a substantial concern in the context of the statute as a whole."[13]

Censorial Laws, Inhibitory Laws, and Remedial Laws Compared. For purposes of the overbreadth doctrine, there are three types of overbreadth statutes: censorial laws, inhibitory laws, and remedial laws. The first type, *censorial laws* (such as criminal syndicalism laws), seek to burden the advocacy of matters of public concern.[14] The Court is less tolerant of overbreadth statutes in this area than it is of *inhibitory laws*, such as libel laws. Inhibitory laws impinge on expressive and associational conduct, but their "impact tends to be neutral as to viewpoints sought to be advocated."[15] The Court is less tolerant of overbreadth of inhibitory laws than it is of *remedial laws*. Remedial laws include, for example, laws regulating lobbying, campaign contributions, and union elections.[16] Remedial laws hamper First Amendment activities for the purpose of promoting values that are within the concern of the First Amendment. The law upheld in *Broadrick* fits under this analysis, for it was a remedial law: it regulated partisan political activity of state employees.[17]

Overbreadth and Commercial Speech. Within this framework, it is not entirely clear to what extent the overbreadth doctrine applies to so-called commercial speech.[18] In *Ohralik v. Ohio State Bar*,[19] the Supreme Court upheld the Ohio state bar's discipline of an attorney for in-person solicitation under the circumstances of that case. In the course of the opinion the majority opinion stated that such in-person solicitation was commercial speech and such speech "is not as likely to be deterred as noncommercial speech, and therefore does not require the added protection afforded by the overbreadth doctrine".[20] But the majority immediately went on to say that "[e]ven if

10. 413 U.S. 601, 93 S.Ct. 2908, 37 L.Ed.2d 830 (1973).

11. Broadrick v. Oklahoma, 413 U.S. 601, 613, 93 S.Ct. 2908, 2916, 37 L.Ed.2d 830 (1973).

12. Broadrick v. Oklahoma, 413 U.S. 601, 615, 93 S.Ct. 2908, 2917–18, 37 L.Ed.2d 830 (1973). See Haden, C.J., citing Treatise in, West Virginia Pride, Inc. v. Wood County, West Virginia, 811 F.Supp. 1142, 1148 (S.D.W.Va. 1993).

13. 413 U.S. 601, 616 n. 14, 93 S.Ct. 2908, 2918, n. 14, 37 L.Ed.2d 830 (1973). See Village of Schaumburg v. Citizens for a Better Environment, 444 U.S. 620, 636–38, 100 S.Ct. 826, 835–37, 63 L.Ed.2d 73 (1980), rehearing denied 445 U.S. 972, 100 S.Ct. 1668, 64 L.Ed.2d 250 (1980).

14. E.g., Brandenburg v. Ohio, 395 U.S. 444, 89 S.Ct. 1827, 23 L.Ed.2d 430 (1969) (per curiam); Herndon v. Lowry, 301 U.S. 242, 57 S.Ct. 732, 81 L.Ed. 1066 (1937);

De Jonge v. Oregon, 299 U.S. 353, 57 S.Ct. 255, 81 L.Ed. 278 (1937).

15. Note, The First Amendment Overbreadth Doctrine, 83 Harv.L.Rev. 844, 918 (1970).

16. Note, The First Amendment Overbreadth Doctrine, 83 Harv.L.Rev. 844, 920 (1970).

17. Broadrick v. Oklahoma, 413 U.S. at 603, n. 1, 93 S.Ct. at 2911–12, n. 1 (1973).

18. See §§ 16.26–16.31 infra.

19. 436 U.S. 447, 98 S.Ct. 1912, 56 L.Ed.2d 444 (1978), rehearing denied 439 U.S. 883, 99 S.Ct. 226, 58 L.Ed.2d 198 (1978).

20. 436 U.S. at 462–63, 98 S.Ct. at 1921–22.

the commercial speaker could mount an over-breadth attack," then the requirements of *Broadrick v. Oklahoma*[21] must be met. The Court decided *In re Primus*[22] the same day as *Ohralik*. In that companion case, the Court did in fact apply the overbreadth doctrine,[23] however it did not find the attorney solicitation to be "commercial" speech.

Thus, if speech is deemed to be commercial speech, then the overbreadth analysis is probably inapplicable. "Because of the special character of commercial speech and the relative novelty of First Amendment protection for such speech, we act with caution in confronting First Amendment challenges to economic legislation that serves legitimate regulatory interests."[24]

Although the Court will not employ overbreadth analysis to invalidate a regulation of commercial speech that is designed to stop false or misleading commercial practices, the Court will require the government to regulate commercial speech in a manner that is "not more extensive than necessary" to serve a substantial government interest.[25]

Overbreadth and Standing Compared.
When the Court examines a claim that a statute should be invalidated as being an unconstitutionally overbroad regulation of speech, it is

easy to confuse standing and First Amendment issues.

Justices who argue against use of the overbreadth doctrine to strike a statute on its face have often asserted that the individuals before the Court lacked standing to raise the rights of hypothetical persons to whom the statute could not be applied without violating the First Amendment. However, it is not precise to think of the overbreadth problem as a form of standing or as a justiciability issue.

Rather, one should recognize that when the Court is asked to strike a law on its face as being overbroad, the individual is asserting that no one—including persons whose speech is unprotected by the First Amendment—can be subjected to punishment under a statute so sweeping that it could include both protected and unprotected speech within its scope.[26] If the Court believes that the statute is so sweeping that it would deter persons from engaging in protected speech, or that the statute may be used on an arbitrary basis against political dissenters, the Court will strike the law as overbroad. If the Court believes that there is little chance that the statute will deter constitutionally protected speech, or will be used in a selective manner to punish dissenters, it will uphold the law and allow it to be applied on a case-by-case basis.[27]

---

21. 413 U.S. 601, 615, 93 S.Ct. 2908, 2917–18, 37 L.Ed.2d 830 (1973).

22. 436 U.S. 412, 98 S.Ct. 1893, 56 L.Ed.2d 417 (1978).

23. 436 U.S. at 433, 438–39, 98 S.Ct. at 1905–06.

24. Friedman v. Rogers, 440 U.S. 1, 11 n. 9, 99 S.Ct. 887, 894 n. 9, 59 L.Ed.2d 100 (1979), rehearing denied 441 U.S. 917, 99 S.Ct. 2018, 60 L.Ed.2d 389 (1979). The Court also noted: "Our decisions dealing with more traditional First Amendment problems do not extend automatically to this as yet uncharted area." 440 U.S. at 11 n. 9, 99 S.Ct. at 894, n. 9.

In deferring to commercial regulation, however, the Court should recognize that when this regulation takes the form of restrictions on truthful speech, the First Amendment interests should be considered compelling. Rotunda, The First Amendment Now Protects Commercial Speech, 10 The Center Magazine: A Publication of the Center for the Study of Democratic Institutions 32, 33 (May/June 1977).

25. Central Hudson Gas & Elec. Corp. v. Public Serv. Commission, 447 U.S. 557, 571, 100 S.Ct. 2343, 65 L.Ed.2d 341 (1980).

26. See, Judge Barker, citing Treatise in, Indiana Voluntary Firemen's Association, Inc. v. Pearson, 700 F.Supp. 421, 434 (S.D.Ind.1988).

27. As Applied. A statute that is valid on its face because it does not, by its terms, unconstitutionally restrict free speech, may still be examined as applied to a specific case. Ehrlich, J., citing Treatise, in State v. McLamb, 188 Ariz. 1, 932 P.2d 266 (App.1996).

Standing in "As Applied" Cases. If a statute (or injunction) may be unconstitutional as applied, the litigant objecting, must have standing to object. Madsen v. Women's Health Center, Inc., 512 U.S. 753, 775, 114 S.Ct. 2516, 2530, 129 L.Ed.2d 593 (1994) held that petitioners did not have standing to challenge a court order as vague and overbroad because it applied to those "acting in concern" with the parties named in the injunction. The injunction did not apply to pure speech but to conduct (interfering with an abortion clinic). The people "acting in concert" with the petitioners were not parties to this case. The petitioners have no standing to attack a portion of the order that does not apply to them. Nor can they claim that the order interferes with their freedom of association because it does not prohibit them from associating with others and expressing their view. The order only banned them from acting in concert with others to deprive third parties of their lawful rights.

Los Angeles Police Dept. v. United Reporting Publishing Corp., 528 U.S. 32 120 S.Ct. 483, 145 L.Ed.2d 451 (1999)

One must be able to separate true jurisdictional or standing issues from substantive First Amendment rulings on the overbreadth of statutes in order to understand many Supreme Court decisions. This problem is illustrated in *Secretary of State v. Joseph H. Munson Co., Inc.*,[28] a case that illustrates some important distinctions.

Secretary of State v. Joseph H. Munson, Inc. The Court reviewed a statute that imposed a twenty-five percent limit on fund raising expenses of charities. A professional profit-making fund raiser (that is, one who entered into contracts with not-for-profit organizations to raise funds for them) challenged the statute. This fund raiser regularly charged an amount in excess of twenty-five percent of the gross amount of funds raised through the promotion. The governmental administrator charged with enforcing the statute informed the fund raiser that it would be subject to prosecution under the statute by contracting for, and accepting more than, twenty-five percent of the proceeds from such promotions.

Munson invalidated the statute based on earlier decisions finding that restrictions on the amount of money spent by charitable organizations for fund raising directly limited their First Amendment rights to spend money on the dissemination of information. Fund raising is a promotional activity. It can educate prospective donors about the charity. The Court held that the statute was not narrowly tailored to promote the governmental interest in protecting the public from fraudulent solicitations by noncharitable organizations.[29]

The majority opinion (by Justice Blackmun) and the dissent (by Justice Rehnquist, joined by three other members of the Court) disagreed both as to whether the fund raiser should have been allowed to assert the First Amendment rights of the charitable organizations, and whether the statute was overbroad.[30] To have a clear picture of the disagreement between the majority and the dissent in this case, it is important to separate standing issues from substantive First Amendment issues.

First, the Court had to decide whether there was a case or controversy that was ripe for adjudication. Because the fund raising company had been threatened with suit and the case

---

offers an interesting example of an "as applied" case. United Reporting, a private publishing service, provided the names and addresses of recently arrested persons to its customers, who included lawyers, insurance companies, drug and alcohol counselors, and driving schools. United Reporting obtained this information from California state and local law enforcement agencies until a state law required the person requesting the information to affirm that the request was for one of five official purposes (scholarly, journalistic, political, governmental purpose, or investigatory purposes by a licensed private investigator). The affirmation must also state: "Address information obtained pursuant to this paragraph shall not be used directly or indirectly to sell a produce or service" to anyone. The lower court held that the statute was facially because it burdened commercial speech.

The Supreme Court reversed (7 to 2), holding that the statute was not subject to a facial challenge in these circumstances. The law, for purposes of a *facial* challenge, does not abridge anyone's right to engage in speech, commercial or otherwise. It simply regulated access to information in the government's hands. It did not prevent United Reporting from using information that it already possesses. California could decide not to give out the arrestee information at all. The statute does not prevent speech, it only restricts access to government information. United Reporting's facial challenge relied on the statute's effect on parties not before the court (United's potential customers), but United's claims do not fall within the case law allowing courts to entertain such facial challenges.

E.g., no one threatened the private publishing service with prosecution or a cutoff of funds. Hence, the statute does not "chill" any third party's speech.

28. 467 U.S. 947, 104 S.Ct. 2839, 81 L.Ed.2d 786 (1984).

29. The Court struck a similar statute in Village of Schaumburg v. Citizens for a Better Environment, 444 U.S. 620, 100 S.Ct. 826, 63 L.Ed.2d 73 (1980), rehearing denied 445 U.S. 972, 100 S.Ct. 1668, 64 L.Ed.2d 250 (1980). In *Village of Schaumburg*, however, the challenged statute had not allowed for any waiver of the limitation on funds raised through charitable solicitation that could be spent for administrative expenses. The state in *Joseph H. Munson Co.* sought to distinguish its statute on the basis of its provision allowing for an administrative waiver of the limitation by a showing of economic hardship to specific charities. The state argued that this waiver provision mitigated the statute's impact on First Amendment activity.

30. Secretary of State v. Joseph H. Munson Co., Inc., 467 U.S. 947, 975, 104 S.Ct. 2839, 2857, 81 L.Ed.2d 786 (1984) (Rehnquist, J., dissenting, joined by Burger, C.J., and Powell and O'Connor, JJ.). Justice Stevens' concurring opinion made clear the disagreement and the difference between Article III case or controversy issues, Article III standing issues, and the First Amendment overbreadth determination. Secretary of State v. Joseph H. Munson Co., Inc., 467 U.S. 947, 970, 104 S.Ct. 2839, 2854, 81 L.Ed.2d 786 (1984) (Stevens, J., concurring).

had been fully adjudicated by the state courts, there was no doubt that an actual controversy was presented.

Second, the Court had to decide whether the fund raising company had standing to raise the First Amendment claims of the charity that wished to spend more than twenty-five percent of its charitable receipts on expenses. This was not a First Amendment overbreadth issue but really a third party standing issue.[31] The majority allowed third party standing. The Court noted that, where First Amendment rights were at issue, third party standing should be granted to allow persons to challenge the restriction on speech of others "not primarily for the benefit of the litigant but for the benefit of society—to prevent the statute from chilling the First Amendment rights of other parties not before the court." The Court referred to this issue as part of the overbreadth problem, although it recognized the need to separate the standing issue from the question of whether the statute was overbroad.

Even though a case or controversy was present, and even though the Court allowed the fund raiser to assert the constitutional rights of the charities, the Court could still have found that the statute did not violate the First Amendment and was valid on its face. The decision to grant standing does not decide the substantive First Amendment determination of whether the statute is unconstitutionally overbroad.[32]

The third issue in *Joseph H. Munson Co.* was whether the statute limiting fund raising expenses was valid on its face. If the statute was upheld on its face, courts would have to determine if the statute was valid as applied. The court would determine, in each case, whether the restriction on fund raising expenses limited the ability of a charitable organization to disseminate its views. The majority found that the statute was invalid on its face, even though it included an escape valve,

a provision allowing a charity to obtain a waiver from the twenty-five percent limitation if that limitation would impose economic hardship on the charity. The majority, nonetheless, found that the limitation was not precisely tailored to prevent fraud because high solicitation costs or expenses in the dissemination of information are not necessarily correlated to fraudulent activity.

Munson recognized that it normally does not strike a statute on its face but only decides whether a statute may constitutionally be applied to the conduct of a specific case before the Court. However, in the majority's view, there was no question that the statute was substantially overbroad because "there is no core of easily identifiable and constitutionally proscribable conduct that the statute prohibits." Although some organizations might have high fund raising costs totally unconnected with First Amendment activity, the statute operated directly to restrict the expenses of all charitable solicitations, including the dissemination of information, a protected First Amendment activity. The waiver provision did not save the law because it did not exempt the charitable organization's dissemination of information from the spending ceiling. The charity had a free speech right to spend as much of its donations as it wished to disseminate information.

The dissent saw the statute as only a restriction on the percentage of the receipts of the fund raising events that could be paid to professional fund raisers or spent on other administrative expenses unrelated to true advocacy. The dissent would have upheld the statute on its face, while recognizing that the Court, in specific cases, would invalidate the statute as applied to charities that kept their administrative expenses below the twenty-five percent level, but who spend an additional percentage of their donations on First Amendment activity, such as the dissemination of information about their charity.

31. See, 1 Ronald D. Rotunda & John E. Nowak, Treatise on Constitutional Law: Substance and Procedure § 2.13(f)(3) (West Group, 3d ed.1999).

32. Murphy, Circuit J., citing Treatise in National Council for Improved Health v. Shalala, 122 F.3d 878

(10th Cir.1997). Murphy, J., quoting Treatise in National Council for Improved Health v. Shalala, 122 F.3d 878 (10th Cir.1997).

§ 16.9 The Void–for–Vagueness Doctrine

Closely related to the overbreadth doctrine is the void for vagueness doctrine. The problem of vagueness in statutes regulating speech activities is based on the same rationale as the overbreadth doctrine and the Supreme Court often speaks of them together.[1]

Vagueness and Criminal Laws Generally. The void for vagueness doctrine applies to all criminal laws, not merely those that regulate speech or other fundamental constitutional rights. All such laws must provide fair notice to persons before making their activity criminal and also to restrict the authority of police officers to arrest persons for a violation of the law.[2] To the extent that a threat is greater and its prohibition or regulation cannot be expressed more concretely, the Court will tolerate comparatively more vagueness.

For example, a statute forbidding reckless *walking* would be unconstitutionally vague, while a statute forbidding reckless *driving* is not void for vagueness.[3] Firs, people, in their ordinary experience, have a good sense of what constitutes reckless driving; second, it is hard to make such a law more clear; and third, the dangers of reckless driving include the loss of life. None of that applies to reckless walking.

Vagueness and the First Amendment. When a law criminalizes conduct that relates to speech, to the normal concerns of every criminal law, we have to add the value of free speech.

Several rationales justify special judicial strictness to insure that laws that regulate speech, a fundamental constitutional right, are not vague. First, the requirement that a law place persons on notice as to precisely what activity is made criminal is particularly important when the activity relates to a speech. To the extent that the law is vague, it might have an *in terrorem* effect and deter persons from engaging in protected activities. An unclear law, a law that does not draw bright lines, might regulate (or appear to regulate) more than is necessary, and thus deter or chill persons from engaging in protected speech.[4]

In contrast, an unclear law relating to many economic matters, such as an unclear negligence law, would chill activity that does not have special First Amendment significance. The lessened risk to the Constitution makes more palatable the wait until such time as the statute is clarified by the appropriate courts. Indeed, the vagueness, in the non-speech area, may be both necessary and advantageous. For example, if a law that forbids reckless driving causes people to be more cautious than absolutely necessary while driving, that is a good thing, not a bad thing. We are not concerned that the law will "chill" people's ability to drive as recklessly as possible without crossing the line from legal to illegal.

Another rationale for the void for vagueness doctrine is to require that there be clear guidelines to govern law enforcement. Without

---

§ 16.9

1. E.g. Dombrowski v. Pfister, 380 U.S. 479, 486, 85 S.Ct. 1116, 1120–21, 14 L.Ed.2d 22 (1965).

Judge Barker, citing Treatise in Indiana Voluntary Fireman's Ass'n, Inc. v. Pearson, 700 F.Supp. 421, 434 (S.D.Ind.1988); Ridgely, J., citing Treatise in, United Video Concepts, Inc. v. City of Dover, 1994 WL 682321, *3 (Del.Super.1994); Crabb, J., citing Treatise in Gaylor v. Thompson, 939 F.Supp. 1363, 1374 (W.D.Wisc.1996); Magill, J., citing Treatise in Families Achieving Independence and Respect v. Nebraska Department of Social Services, 111 F.3d 1408, 1425 n. 23 (8th Cir.1997); Rosen, District J., citing Treatise in Kevorkian v. Thompson, 947 F.Supp. 1152, 1172 n. 19 (E.D.Mich.1997).

2. The reasons for striking laws for vagueness apply whenever the lack of notice in a law might deter the exercise of a fundamental constitutional right, including rights that are not protected by the First Amendment. See, e.g., Colautti v. Franklin, 439 U.S. 379, 99 S.Ct. 675,

58 L.Ed.2d 596 (1979) (holding void for vagueness a state regulation of abortions requiring a doctor to determine if there was "sufficient reason to believe that a fetus may be viable" before determining whether the doctor was permitted to perform the abortion procedure).

3. When there is no danger that the law will deter lawful speech, the Court is less strict in enforcing the vagueness requirement. See, e.g., Village of Hoffman Estates v. Flipside, 455 U.S. 489, 102 S.Ct. 1186, 71 L.Ed.2d 362 (1982), rehearing denied 456 U.S. 950, 102 S.Ct. 2023, 72 L.Ed.2d 476 (1982), on remand 688 F.2d 842 (7th Cir.1982) (upholding statutes requiring a business to obtain a special license if it sells items "designed or marketed for use with illegal drugs" where the Court did not believe the statute deterred constitutionally protected speech).

4. Munson, J., citing Treatise in United States v. Lamb, 945 F.Supp. 441, 447 (N.D.N.Y.1996).

these guidelines, law enforcement officers have too much discretion to enforce the statute on a selective basis. This discretion is most dangerous when the law regulates a fundamental right, such as speech, so that the officers might be subjecting persons to arrest and prosecution because they disagree with the message that the person wishes to convey, or for some other constitutionally suspect reason.[5]

Because the First Amendment needs breathing space, the governmental regulation that is tolerated must be drawn with "narrow specificity."[6] Narrow, clear statutes are more likely to reflect the considered judgment of the legislature that certain speech activities must be regulated.[7] The vagueness doctrine requires the legislature to make clear what it really intends, so Courts are less likely to interpret the law in a way that unnecessarily infringes on free speech.

In the First Amendment area, there is a special danger of tolerating penal statutes susceptible of sweeping and improper application. Freedom of speech is "delicate and vulnerable, as well as supremely precious in our society," so the "threat of sanctions may deter their exercise almost as potently as the actual application of sanctions."[8] Thus, the vagueness doc-

trine prohibits statutes that burden speech in terms that are so vague that they either include protected speech, or leave an individual without clear guidance as to the nature of speech for which she can be punished.[9]

§ 16.10   The Least Restrictive Means Test

Even if the legislative purpose is legitimate, and one of substantial governmental interest, the government cannot pursue it by means that broadly stifle personal liberties if the end can be more narrowly achieved. "The breadth of legislative abridgement must be viewed in the light of less drastic means for achieving the same basic purpose."[1] The Court requires that legislation use means that are the "least restrictive" of free speech. This least restrictive means test is also been applied in some nonspeech areas, such as state regulation affecting interstate commerce,[2] but it is particularly important to the free speech area.

Shelton v. Tucker[3] is an important case illustrating the doctrine of least restrictive means. In *Shelton*, a state law required each Arkansas teacher to file an annual affidavit listing all organizations to which he or she belonged or contributed in the last five years. Shelton and

---

5. Kolender v. Lawson, 461 U.S. 352, 103 S.Ct. 1855, 75 L.Ed.2d 903 (1983). *Kolender* invalidated a state statute requiring persons who loitered or wandered on streets to provide "credible and reliable" identification and to account for their presence when requested to do so by a police officer. The most important aspect of the vagueness doctrine is that it imposes guidelines that prohibit arbitrary, selective enforcement on a constitutionally suspect. This rationale is of special concern if there is the potential for arbitrary suppression of First Amendment liberties and restrictions on the freedom of movement. 461 U.S. at 357, 103 S.Ct. at 1858–59, 75 L.Ed.2d at 908.

6. NAACP v. Button, 371 U.S. 415, 433, 83 S.Ct. 328, 338, 9 L.Ed.2d 405 (1963), citing Cantwell v. Connecticut, 310 U.S. 296, 311, 60 S.Ct. 900, 906, 84 L.Ed. 1213 (1940).

7. But cf. NAACP v. Button, 371 U.S. 415, 432–33, 83 S.Ct. 328, 337–38, 9 L.Ed.2d 405 (1963): "The objectionable quality of vagueness and overbreadth does not depend upon absence of fair notice to a criminally accused or upon unchanneled delegation of legislative powers...."

8. NAACP v. Button, 371 U.S. 415, 433, 83 S.Ct. 328, 338, 9 L.Ed.2d 405 (1963) (footnote omitted).

9. State v. Princess Cinema of Milwaukee, Inc., 96 Wis.2d 646, 292 N.W.2d 807, 813 (1980) (Day, J., citing this Treatise); Levine v. United States District Court, 764 F.2d 590, 599 (9th Cir.1985) (Beezer, J., for plurality, citing Treatise).

Investigatory Power and Vagueness. City of Mesquite v. Aladdin's Castle, Inc., 455 U.S. 283, 291, 102 S.Ct. 1070, 1075–76, 71 L.Ed.2d 152 (1982), motion to recall judgment denied 464 U.S. 927, 104 S.Ct. 329, 78 L.Ed.2d 300 (1983). A city ordinance directing the police chief to consider whether an applicant for a license to operate coin-operated amusement establishment has any "connections with criminal elements" is not unconstitutionally vague because the applicant's possible connection with criminal elements is merely a subject that the ordinance directs the Police Chief to investigate before he makes his recommendation to the City Manager. The test—"connections with criminal elements"—is not used as the standard by the City Manager for approval or disapproval of the application: "The Federal Constitution does not preclude a city from giving vague or ambiguous directions to officials who are authorized to make investigations and recommendations."

§ 16.10

1. Shelton v. Tucker, 364 U.S. 479, 488, 81 S.Ct. 247, 252, 5 L.Ed.2d 231 (1960) (footnotes omitted). See also, Judge Coffey, dissenting, citing Treatise in City of Watseka v. Illinois Public Action Council and American Civil Liberties Union, 796 F.2d 1547, 1563, n. 1 (7th Cir.1986).

2. See, e.g., Dean Milk Co. v. Madison, 340 U.S. 349, 71 S.Ct. 295, 95 L.Ed. 329 (1951).

3. 364 U.S. 479, 81 S.Ct. 247, 5 L.Ed.2d 231 (1960).

others refused to file an affidavit and his teaching contract was not renewed. The trial showed that he was not a member of the Communist Party or any organization advocating the overthrow by force of the Government, but he was a member of the NAACP. The trial court found the information requested in the affidavit relevant.

The Supreme Court readily agreed that the state had an interest in investigating the competence and fitness of its teachers, but the Arkansas statute went well beyond its legitimate purposes. The information filed under the law was not kept confidential, allowing public exposure. That, in turn, meant that teachers risked offending superiors if they belonged to an unpopular group.

Moreover the state disclosure requirement was "completely unlimited." The teacher was required to list any associational tie—social, professional, religious, avocational—and his financial support, even though many such relationships had no possible bearing on the teacher's occupational fitness. The "unlimited and indiscriminate sweep of the statute" went "far beyond what might be justified in the exercise of the State's legitimate inquiry into the fitness and competence of its teachers"[4] and thus it was invalid.

§ 16.11 Government Prescribed Speech, Government Subsidies for Speech, Unconstitutional Conditions, and Equal Protection Analysis

Almost all First Amendment cases that have reached the United States Supreme Court in-

volve governmental attempts to regulate speech. In this section we discuss the more rare situation, where a government enters the First Amendment marketplace to advance messages favorable to the government.

Government Speech and Propaganda. The most direct way for government to enter the political marketplace is to have government officials or agencies issue messages or reports designed to convince the public to support governmental positions on domestic or foreign policy. Supreme Court decisions do not directly and clearly define the limitations that are placed on such activity.[1] This absence of case law may be considered a strength rather than a weakness of the democratic system, for there has not been a clear need for the Court to intervene to establish precise limits on propaganda efforts by government agencies in the United States. However, with the growing number of reports that are issued by the government and the increasing potential for the governmental use of electronic media, the future may see the need to define more carefully the limits on government speech.[2]

Undoubtedly there is a valid public interest, and First Amendment value, in the government conveying to the public information regarding government programs. Governmental activities—from Congressional reports to presidential news conferences, or reports of executive agencies—provide the basis for the discussion and debate of self-governance issues that has been a touchstone value in First Amend-

---

4. Shelton v. Tucker, 364 U.S. 479, 490, 81 S.Ct. 247, 253, 5 L.Ed.2d 231 (1960). Another example of a case employing the least restrictive means test is Virginia State Board of Pharmacy v. Virginia Citizens Consumer Council, Inc., 425 U.S. 748, 96 S.Ct. 1817, 48 L.Ed.2d 346 (1976).

§ 16.11

1. Other courts have often considered these issues. See Anderson v. City of Boston, 376 Mass. 178, 380 N.E.2d 628 (1978), appeal dismissed 439 U.S. 1060, 99 S.Ct. 822, 59 L.Ed.2d 26 (1979). The Massachusetts Supreme Judicial Court enjoined the city of Boston from using appropriated funds to influence voters to vote for passage of a state constitutional Amendment. The city had sought to counteract the corporate expenditures that the United States Supreme Court had allowed in First National Bank v. Bellotti, 435 U.S. 765, 98 S.Ct. 1407, 55 L.Ed.2d 707 (1978), rehearing denied 438 U.S. 907, 98 S.Ct. 3126, 57

L.Ed.2d 1150 (1978). See Boyce, J., citing Treatise in Federal Trade Commission v. Freecom Communications, 966 F.Supp. 1066, 1070 (D.Utah 1997).

See, Nowak, Using the Press Clause to Limit Government Speech, 30 Ariz.L.Rev. 1 (1988); Rotunda, Subsidized Speech for the Rich, Chicago Tribune, Dec. 12, 1999, at § 1, p. 23.

2. See, Van Alstyne, The First Amendment and the Suppression of Warmongering Propaganda in the United States: Comments and Footnotes, 31 Law & Contemp.Prob. 530, 531–36 (1966); Shriffin, Government Speech, 27 U.C.L.A.L.Rev. 565 (1980); Ziegler, Government Speech and the Constitution: The Limits of Official Partisanship, 21 Bos.College L.Rev. 578 (1980); Delgado, The Language of the Arms Race: Should the People Limit Government Speech?, 69 Bos.U.L.Rev. 961 (1984).

ment analysis.[3] However, if the government were to create publicly funded television stations whose purpose was to present programs favorable to government policies without the possibility of reply, the governmental attempt to foreclose opposing views may be seen as a violation of the First Amendment.[4]

Federal Communications Commission v. League of Women Voters[5] invalidated a section of the Public Broadcasting Act that prohibited any noncommercial educational broadcasting station receiving a grant from the Corporation for Public Broadcasting from engaging in editorializing or the endorsement of candidates. The four dissenting Justices believed that the prohibition on editorializing protected the public from having stations writing editorials favorable to the government so as to increase their prospects for receipt of public funding.[6] The majority believed that the ban was not narrowly tailored to providing a balanced presentation of issues to the public, but only suppressed the role of such stations in bringing matters of public concern to the attention of the public. All nine Justices, however, recognized that the government was not free to subsidize speech that favored governmental policy on publicly owned stations while refusing to fund speech adverse to governmental interests.

Government Required Speech. The government may not enter the political marketplace by forcing private persons to subscribe to or advance messages favorable to the government. Such activity is inconsistent with the fundamental freedom of belief that lies at the core of all First Amendment guarantees. The government should not be able to force a person who objects to a position to endorse that position absent the most unusual and compelling circumstances, none of which have appeared in the cases to date.

For example, in *West Virginia State Board of Education v. Barnette*[7] the Court prohibited states from requiring children to pledge allegiance to the country at the start of the school day. The children who objected to taking the oath were members of a religious sect that objected to such practices, but the majority opinion by Justice Jackson was careful not to limit the decision by basing it on the religion clauses of the First Amendment alone. School children are not government employees, and the opinion made available to all private persons a First Amendment right to refuse to pledge allegiance to the country or its symbols because of the freedom of thought and belief that is central to all First Amendment freedoms.[8]

Similarly, *Wooley v. Maynard*[9] prohibited a state from punishing a person for making ille-

---

3. Keller v. State Bar of California, 496 U.S. 1, 110 S.Ct. 2228, 110 L.Ed.2d 1 (1990) unanimously held that the State Bar of California may not constitutionally use compulsory dues to finance political and ideological causes (e.g., a nuclear freeze initiative) that the petitioners oppose. State law created the State Bar and requires all lawyers to belong to it and pay dues as a condition of practicing law. The State Bar may only use compulsory due to finance regulation of the legal profession or improve the quality of legal services (for example, bar dues may be used to finance an attorney discipline system). *Keller* distinguished the State Bar from the State Government: while government officials may use tax dollars to espouse their views, the State Bar of California is not part of the general government of California. Although state law creates the bar, it is more analogous to labor unions representing public and private employees, and therefore it should be subject to the same constitutional rule in order to protect free speech and free association interests.

4. See Douglas, J., dissenting in Public Utilities Commission v. Pollak, 343 U.S. 451, 467–69, 72 S.Ct. 813, 823–24, 96 L.Ed. 1068, 1080–81 (1952); Douglas, J., concurring, in Lehman v. City of Shaker Heights, 418 U.S. 298, 305–08, 94 S.Ct. 2714, 2718–20, 41 L.Ed.2d 770, 778–80 (1974).

5. 468 U.S. 364, 104 S.Ct. 3106, 82 L.Ed.2d 278 (1984) (five to four).

6. The dissenters believed that an effective way to avoid governmental speech being favored over speech adverse to the government interest is to prevent a subsidized station from all on-the-air editorializing. They viewed the statute as a valid means to prevent this occurrence. 468 U.S. at 402, 104 S.Ct. at 3129 (Rehnquist, J., dissenting, joined by Burger, C.J., & White, J.); 468 U.S. at 410, 104 S.Ct. at 3133 (Stevens, J., dissenting).

7. 319 U.S. 624, 63 S.Ct. 1178, 87 L.Ed. 1628 (1943).

8. Lynch v. Donnelly, 465 U.S. 668, 104 S.Ct. 1355, 79 L.Ed.2d 604 (1984), rehearing denied 466 U.S. 994, 104 S.Ct. 2376, 80 L.Ed.2d 848 (1984) found that the government subsidy for a Christmas display of a creche provided only remote and incidental benefits to any religion and was not an advancement or endorsement of religion. 465 U.S. at 683, 104 S.Ct. at 1364, 79 L.Ed.2d at 616.

9. 430 U.S. 705, 97 S.Ct. 1428, 51 L.Ed.2d 752 (1977).

The Pledge of Allegiance Led by Public School Teachers. While the state may not require students to recite the pledge, the state may continue to start the

gible a portion of his automobile license plate that the state required him to put on his car. This portion made illegible was the state motto "Live Free or Die." A Jehovah's Witness objected to carrying this message based on his religious belief. However, the Court based its decision on the free speech clause, not the free exercise clause. *Wooley* held that no private person could be required to broadcast governmental symbols or to endorse governmental positions absent the most compelling circumstances. A person will not have the right to deface the numbers on his license plate that identify his vehicle, or the right to mutilate American currency that has the motto, "In God We Trust." *Wooley* recognized that some government regulations are necessary to advance societal interests that have nothing to do with censorship or propaganda, such as the identification of vehicles in traffic accidents and the need for a uniform monetary system.[10]

Compelled Subsidization of Advertising Generic Goods. *Glickman v. Wileman Brothers & Elliott, Inc.*[11] upheld a federal statutory scheme that required certain farm producers to pay for advertising promoting generic goods. The Secretary of Agriculture, pursuant to statute, issued various orders that imposed assessments to cover the cost of generic advertising of California nectarines, plums, and peaches. Growers, handlers, and processors of California tree fruits challenged the validity of these

orders, claiming that their forced subsidization of such generic advertising violated their rights of free speech.

The Court (5 to 4) rejected these challenges, noting that these marketing orders are a form of economic regulation that has displaced competition in certain markets. The marketing orders must be approved by affected producers who market at least at least two-thirds of the volume of the commodity. Among the collective activities that Congress authorized is any form of marketing promotion including paid advertising. This advertising serves the producers' and handlers' common interest in selling particular products. Various regulations seek to minimize the risk that the generic advertising might adversely affect the interests of any individual producer. The central message of this generic advertising is that "California Summer Fruits" are "wholesome, delicious, and attractive to discerning shoppers."

The Court neither accepted nor rejected the factual assumption that generic advertising may not be the most effective method of promoting the sale of these commodities. But it concluded that compelling the respondents to fund this advertising was an economic question for Congress, rather than a First Amendment issue for the Court.

Glickman acknowledged that there is a free speech right not to be compelled to contribute

---

school day with the pledge so long as no student is forced to participate. School teachers may constitutionally continue to lead the students in the Pledge. Sherman v. Community Consolidated School District, 980 F.2d 437 (7th Cir. 1992), cert. denied, 508 U.S. 950, 113 S.Ct. 2439, 124 L.Ed.2d 658 (1993).

The reason for this distinction is that *Barnette* was really based on the First Amendment principle that the state may not compel *students* to recite the Pledge of Allegiance. The government has more power over the teachers because they are government employees, the school children are not. *Barnette* did not preclude the state from starting the school day with the Pledge; it merely prohibited the state from requiring the students to recite or participate in the Pledge. *Barnette* does not preclude state loyalty oaths of state *employees*. The constitutionality of loyalty oaths and other restrictions on state employees are judged by other standards. See §§ 16.42(a).

10. *Wooley*, indicated that carrying money with the motto "In God We Trust" is not an endorsement of that message and distinguished this motto from the license plate motto on two grounds. First, currency is transferred among people and thus the message is not associated with

any one person; second, the person carrying the money is not displaying it to the public. 430 U.S. at 715 n. 15, 97 S.Ct. at 1436 n. 15 (1977).

11. 521 U.S. 457, 117 S.Ct. 2130, 138 L.Ed.2d 585 (1997). Stevens, J., joined by O'Connor, Kennedy, Ginsburg, & Breyer, JJ., wrote the opinion for the Court. Souter, J. (joined by Rehnquist, C.J., & Scalia, J., (& Thomas, J., in part)) filed a lengthy dissent, arguing that compelled subsidization of speech should only be lawful if the government can prove that it has a substantial interest, the regulation directly advances that interest, and it is narrowly tailored. The program challenged here fails all three prongs.

Thomas, J., joined by Scalia, J., in part, also dissented. He argued that it is incongruous for the majority to suggest that the forced subsidization of this advertising does not really involve speech while a law that forbade voluntary contributions would violate the First Amendment. Thomas also noted his continued disagreement with the balancing test of Central Hudson Gas & Electric Corp. v. Public Service Commission of New York, 447 U.S. 557, 100 S.Ct. 2343, 65 L.Ed.2d 341 (1980), and the discounted weight that the Court has given to commercial speech.

to an organization whose expressive activities conflict with one's freedom of belief. For example, the state can compel union members to pay dues to support activities related to collective bargaining, because those costs are germane to an otherwise lawful regulatory program, but the state cannot compel union members to make contributions for political purposes unrelated to collective bargaining.[12] However, the Court distinguished such cases because these assessments are germane to the regulatory program and requiring respondents to pay them cannot be said "to engender any crisis of conscience."[13]

The Court limited *Glickman*, in *United States v. United Foods, Inc.*[14] The Mushroom Promotion, Research, and Consumer Information Act, required fresh mushroom handlers to pay assessments that were used primarily to fund generic advertisements promoting mushroom sales. United Foods claimed that its branded mushrooms are better, and argued that the First Amendment prohibited this assessment.

In *United Foods*, unlike *Glickman*, almost all of the funds collected under the mandatory mushroom assessments had but one purpose: generic advertising. "Beyond the collection and disbursement of advertising funds, there are no marketing orders that regulate how mushrooms may be produced and sold, no exemption from the antitrust laws, and nothing preventing individual producers from making their own marketing decisions."[15] The expression that the statute requires United Foods to support is not germane to a purpose related to an association *independent from* the speech itself. Hence, it is unconstitutional.

Subsidization and Unconstitutional Conditions. Another way that the govern-

ment participates in political expression is to subsidize persons on the condition that they engage in, or refrain from engaging in, a certain type of speech or association. This type of governmental activity is often said to be subject to the principle of no "unconstitutional conditions." Some discussions make it appear that any conditions on the granting of government benefits are invalid but that is not the case. In each instance, courts must examine the substance of the condition to determine whether it violates constitutional principles.[16]

For example, it would be permissible for the federal government to condition a grant to a farmer on a requirement that the farmer not plant more than a specific acreage of a commodity because, under its commerce power, Congress could directly limit agricultural production.[17] On the other hand, an agricultural grant conditioned on a farmer's promise not to criticize government farm policy would be invalid, a penalty on speech protected by the First Amendment.

Similarly, the government cannot grant money to a research scientist on the condition that the scientist refrain from criticizing the government. But the government should be able to fund advocacy research. For example, it could grant money to the scientist to investigate only the harmful (or only the beneficial) effects of marijuana. If the scientist took the grant on the condition that he investigate the benefits of marijuana, the government should be able to discipline the grantee if he used the money to explore the harmful effects of marijuana, just as it ought to be able to discipline the grantee if he took the money and used it to investigate wine.

The difficulty in assessing the constitutionality of a condition to receiving a government

---

12. Abood v. Detroit Board of Education, 431 U.S. 209, 97 S.Ct. 1782, 52 L.Ed.2d 261 (1977).

13. 521 U.S. at 472, 117 S.Ct. at 2139.

14. 533 U.S. 405, 121 S.Ct. 2334, 150 L.Ed.2d 438 (2001). Kennedy, J., spoke for the Court, joined by Rehnquist, C.J., and Stevens, Scalia, Souter, & Thomas, JJ. Stevens, J., and Thomas, J., filed concurring opinions. Breyer, J., dissenting, argued that the Court "converts 'a question of economic policy for Congress and the Executive' into a 'First Amendment issue.'"

15. 533 U.S. at 411, 121 S.Ct. at 2339.

16. Westen, Incredible Dilemmas: Conditioning One Constitutional Right on the Forfeiture of Another, 66 Iowa L.Rev. 741 (1981); Mark Yudof, When Government Speaks: Politics, Law, and Government Expression in America 234–45 (U.Calif.Press, 1983).

17. When the Court believed that the Tenth Amendment restricted federal power over agriculture, it invalidated such a condition. United States v. Butler, 297 U.S. 1, 56 S.Ct. 312, 80 L.Ed. 477 (1936).

grant that is related to speech may be seen by contrasting several cases. *Regan v. Taxation with Representation of Washington*[18] unanimously upheld a portion of the Internal Revenue Code that granted a special tax exempt status to organizations that did not use tax deductible contributions for lobbying activity. A pivotal factor in this decision was that a companion section of the Internal Revenue Code granted a slightly different type of tax exempt status to organizations that did use nondeductible contributions for lobbying activities.

If an organization qualifies as a not-for-profit organization that does not use deductible contributions for lobbying activities, it is entitled to status as a Section 501(C)(3) organization; in that case, persons who contribute to it may deduct those contributions on their federal income tax returns. A similar not-for-profit organization that desires to use contributions for lobbying activities may receive tax exempt status under Section 501(C)(4). While the 501(C)(4) organization is exempt from taxes, contributions to it are not deductible from individual income tax returns. An organization is allowed to have separate branches, one of which qualifies for deductible contributions and one of which does not. In other words, a single organization, such as the Taxpayers with Representation of Washington, may use a section 501(C)(3) organization for nonlobbying activities and receive tax deductible contributions to that branch of its operations while it simultaneously operates a Section 501(C)(4) affiliate to lobby. Although the Section 501(C)(4) affiliate would be exempt from taxation itself, it would not be eligible to receive tax deductible contributions.

The law did not penalize persons for engaging in speech, the lobbying of governmental organization. Rather, Congress only refused to subsidize lobbying activities. There is no un-constitutional condition when Congress refuses to subsidize certain political activities.

Rust v. Sullivan[19] upheld federal regulations that prohibited recipients of Title X grants from engaging in abortion related activities where abortion is a method of family planning. Nothing in the Title X program provided for post-conception care, including abortion (which obviously occurs after conception). Title X required that its funds could only be used to support pre-conception family planning, population research, infertility services, and related services. The regulations expressly prohibited a Title X project from referring a pregnant woman to an abortion provider as a method of family planning. Federal funds could not be used to "promote or advocate" abortion as a "method of family planning."[20]

Rust emphasized that the government was simply refusing to fund activities (including speech that promoted those activities) when the scope of the project excluded such activities. Petitioners argued that the regulations prohibited a Title X project from referring a woman to an abortion service even if her pregnancy placed her life in imminent danger, but the Court specifically rejected that interpretation of the regulations. The regulations only prohibit abortion as a "method of family planning." Referring a woman who needs an abortion for medical reasons is not equivalent to referral for purposes of family planning.

The Court also emphasized that employees in a Title X project remain free to pursue abortion related activities on their own time, when they are not acting under the auspices of the Title X project. If there are any inquiries regarding abortion, the regulations provided that a permissible response is: "the project does not consider abortion as an appropriate method of family planning and therefore does not counsel or refer for abortion."[21] However, nothing in the regulations require the doctor or any other employee to mislead any patient

---

18. 461 U.S. 540, 103 S.Ct. 1997, 76 L.Ed.2d 129 (1983).

19. 500 U.S. 173, 111 S.Ct. 1759, 114 L.Ed.2d 233 (1991). O'Connor, J., dissented, arguing that the statute did not authorize the challenged regulations. Blackmun, J., joined by Marshall & Stevens, JJ., dissented, made the

same point (O'Connor, J., joined this portion of the dissent), and argued that the regulations were unconstitutional. Stevens, J., also filed a dissenting opinion.

20. 500 U.S. at 193 n. 4, 111 S.Ct. at 1773 n. 4.

21. 500 U.S. at 179, 111 S.Ct. at 1765.

or to "represent as his own any opinion that he does not in fact hold."[22] The Court recognized that while employees were actually working on the Title X project, their freedom of expression is limited, but "this limitation is a consequence of their decision to accept employment in a project, the scope of which is permissibly restricted by the funding authority."[23]

In contrast, *Federal Communications Commission v. League of Women Voters*[24] held that Congress was creating an unconstitutional condition to the receipt of federal money when it banned editorials by any noncommercial educational broadcast station that received a grant from the Corporation for Public Broadcasting. The condition violated the First Amendment because it was not narrowly tailored to further the substantial government interest in insuring adequate and balanced coverage of public issues but was, instead, a penalty on those stations who sought to engage in constitutionally protected analysis of issues of public concern.

The four dissenting Justices pointed out that the ban on editorial activity or endorsement of candidates by groups receiving federal money constituted only a refusal to subsidize those activities. This restriction insured that publicly funded stations would not subtly tailor their editorializing so as to please the government agencies that funded them.

Justice Brennan, for the majority, rejected this rationale and argued that the ban was not precisely tailored to eliminating government influence over editorials. For example, the statutory ban was "leveled solely" at the expression of editorial opinion by local station management, but those editorials are more likely to be aimed at a local audience, to have less national impact, and to be confined to local issues. Moreover, the ban also applied to

private, noncommercial community organizations that own and operate stations but are not controlled in any way by state or local government.

The majority stated that, if Congress were to amend the statutes so as to prohibit noncommercial educational broadcasting stations from using federal funds to subsidize their editorial or candidate endorsement activities, this restriction would be valid under *Taxation with Representation*. Congress could require stations to segregate their funds and use only nonfederal funds for activities that Congress did not wish to subsidize. However, Congress could not withdraw *all* public funding from a station that engaged in editorializing.

Another decision that stands in stark contrast to *Rust v. Sullivan*[25] is *Legal Services Corporation v. Velazquez*.[26] Clients and others challenged the constitutionality of federal funding restrictions on the Legal Services Corporation (LSC). The Supreme Court invalidated the federal restriction, which prohibited local recipients of LSC funds from engaging in representation involving efforts to amend or otherwise challenge validity of existing welfare laws.

The situation in *LSC v. Velazquez* is different than the facts of *Rust* because the Government in *Velazquez* was hiring people, such as lawyers, to represent other people's interests, not its interests. When the Government spends money to facilitate private speech it does not have the same latitude to engage in viewpoint discrimination because it is not promoting the *Government's* speech. For example, even though the Government pays the salaries of public defenders, they represent their clients, not the Government, which is represented by its own prosecutors. The purpose of the public defender program is not to transmit

22. 500 U.S. at 200, 111 S.Ct. at 1776.

23. 500 U.S. at 198, 111 S.Ct. at 1775.

24. 468 U.S. 364, 104 S.Ct. 3106, 82 L.Ed.2d 278 (1984).

25. 500 U.S. 173, 111 S.Ct. 1759, 114 L.Ed.2d 233 (1991). O'Connor, J., dissented, arguing that the statute did not authorize the challenged regulations. Blackmun, J., joined by Marshall & Stevens, JJ., dissented, made the

same point (O'Connor, J., joined this portion of the dissent), and argued that the regulations were unconstitutional. Stevens, J., also filed a dissenting opinion.

26. 531 U.S. 533, 121 S.Ct. 1043, 149 L.Ed.2d 63 (2001). Kennedy, J., wrote the opinion for the Court, joined by Stevens, Souter, Ginsburg, & Breyer, JJ. Scalia, J., dissented, in an opinion joined by Rehnquist. C.J. and O'Connor & Thomas, JJ.

information about Government programs. The public defender does not speak on behalf of the Government.

The issue before the Court involved a portion of the statute providing that, if an LSC client is seeking specific relief from a welfare agency, that relief may "not involve an effort to amend or otherwise challenge existing law in effect on the date of the initiation of the representation." The Court invalidated that specific restriction. The Court agreed that Congress was not required to fund an LSC lawyer to represent indigents, and, when it did so, it was not required to fund the whole range of legal representations or relationships. But, Congress may not define the scope of the litigation it funds to exclude certain vital theories and ideas. Where private speech is involved, even Congress' antecedent funding decision cannot be aimed at the suppression of ideas thought inimical to the Government's own interest.

Government Subsidization of the Arts. *National Endowment for the Arts v. Finley*[27] upheld as facially constitutional the "decency and respect" standard that Congress imposed for NEA grants. In this case various artists' organizations and performance artists sued the NEA claiming that the denials of their applications for NEA grants violated their First Amendment rights. The statute in question required the NEA, in distributing grants, to take into consideration general standards of "decency and respect" for diverse beliefs and values. The language is "advisory" and it "admonishes the NEA merely to take 'decency and respect' into consideration. . . ."[28] Justice

O'Connor, for the Court, avoided deciding the case on broad grounds and only held this statute did not so inherently interfere with First Amendment so as to be facially invalid.[29] The government does not discriminate on the basis of viewpoint if it merely chooses to fund one activity instead of another.

In addition, the statute was not constitutionally vague. The statute merely added some imprecise considerations to an already subjective selection process. When the Government is acting as a patron of the arts rather than acting as a sovereign, the consequences of statutory impression are not constitutionally severe.

Equal Protection. Whenever a statute allows some persons to speak or assemble, but not others, or grants a subsidy for some types of speech activities to a limited group of persons or entities, the statute at issue can be analyzed under equal protection as well as First Amendment principles.[30] Generally, the government may classify persons for the receipt of benefits or burdens so long as there is a rational relationship between the classification and a legitimate end of government. However, if the law employs suspect criteria, such as race, to establish the classification, or if the law creates a classification that allocates the ability to exercise a fundamental constitutional right, then the Court will strictly scrutinize the basis for that classification.

It is difficult to describe the exact standard of review in these cases, but it is often said that when a law regulates the ability to engage in a fundamental constitutional right, the

---

27. 524 U.S. 569, 118 S.Ct. 2168, 141 L.Ed.2d 500 (1998). Only Justice Souter dissented.

Scalia, J., joined by Thomas, J., filed an opinion concurring in the judgment. Justice Scalia argued that the majority "sustains the constitutionality of 20 U.S.C. § 954(d)(1) by gutting it." 524 U.S. at 590, 118 S.Ct. at 2180. He argued that the statute should be evaluated as it was written, and that it is still constitutional. The statute, he said, "established content and viewpoint-based criteria upon which grant applications are to be evaluated. And this is perfectly constitutional." 524 U.S. at 590, 118 S.Ct. at 2180.

28. 524 U.S. at 582, 118 S.Ct. at 2176.

29. 524 U.S. at 587–89, 118 S.Ct. at 2179. See also, John E. Nowak, Using the Press Clause to Limit Govern-

ment Speech, 30 Ariz. L. Rev. 1 (1988); Ronald D. Rotunda, Returning Art to the People: No Subsidies and No Strings, 17 Legal Times (of Washington, D.C.) 43 (Mar. 6, 1995). John E. Nowak, First Amendment Values and Government Participation in the Marketplace Fifty Years after the Hutchins Report, 3 Communication Law & Policy 275 (1998); Ronald D. Rotunda, Subsidized Speech for the Rich, Chicago Tribune, Dec. 12, 1999, at § 1, p. 23; Ronald D. Rotunda, Let Nothing You Display: Making Room for Religion in Public Forums, Legal Times (of Washington, D.C.), Jan. 3, 2000, at pp. 43, 45.

30. Briscoe, Circuit J., citing Treatise in American Constitutional Law Foundation, Inc. v. Meyer, 120 F.3d 1092, 1100 (10th Cir.1997).

courts must determine whether the classification is narrowly tailored to promote a compelling or overriding governmental interest. All First Amendment rights are fundamental rights and, therefore, classifications relating to them are subjected to this compelling interest standard.

Whenever the Court finds that a classification violates the First Amendment, it alternatively could rule that the classification violated equal protection.[31] For example, if a city ordinance allowed distribution of leaflets by persons who favor the policies of the mayor, but prohibited distribution of leaflets on public streets by persons who opposed the mayor, the law could be stricken under First Amendment principles as the suppression of content that did not create an imminent danger of inciting lawless action. Alternatively, the statute could be held invalid under equal protection because the classification regarding who could use the sidewalks to engage in a fundamental constitutional right was not narrowly tailored to promote a compelling governmental interest.[32] The equal protection argument does not make the analysis any easier, because the Court is really applying First Amendment principles, dressed up in equal protection garb.

§ 16.12　The Advocacy of Violence or Other Illegal Conduct

The Court has not treated First Amendment guarantees prohibiting Congress from passing laws abridging speech, press, or peaceful assembly as an absolute. It has preferred the view that, in certain special situations, an individual's rights to freely express his or her beliefs must be subordinated to other interests of society.[1] Yet a willingness to balance First Amendment rights against other interests has not diminished the importance of free speech, because the Court has developed tests to limit

governmental power. One of the standards the Supreme Court first considered to justify abridgement of speech that advocates violence or other illegal conduct is the "clear and present danger" test. Although the Court, during the early part of the twentieth century, did not use this test to overturn a conviction, its evolution explains why we got where we are today.

There are three phases in the development of the "clear and present danger" doctrine. First, its genesis, which was in the early part of the twentieth century. The test originated in a number of opinions written by Justices Holmes and Brandeis dealing primarily with the Espionage and Sedition Acts of World War I. This test competed with the "bad tendency" test, which was even less protective of free speech.

In the second phase, when the Cold War was at its height, a later generation of Supreme Court Justices and federal judges, including Chief Justice Vinson and Judge Learned Hand, applied the "clear and present danger" doctrine in a manner restricting First Amendment freedoms. This restrictive approach influenced the Court to develop a "balancing test" for protecting freedom of expression.[2]

Finally, in the 1960's the Supreme Court attempted to breathe new life into the doctrine and, as we shall see in the following sections, formulated a new, more strict test. This most recent test learns from the mistakes of the past, and is more protective of free speech than the old clear and present danger test.

§ 16.13　The Holmes–Brandeis "Clear and Present Danger" Test

(a) The Origins and Development

From the time the First Amendment was ratified until just prior to World War I the

---

31. Phillips, Chief J., citing Treatise, in Commission for Lawyer Discipline v. Benton, 980 S.W.2d 425 (Tex. 1998).

32. Police Department of City of Chicago v. Mosley, 408 U.S. 92, 92 S.Ct. 2286, 33 L.Ed.2d 212 (1972); Carey v. Brown, 447 U.S. 455, 100 S.Ct. 2286, 65 L.Ed.2d 263 (1980).

§ 16.12

1. Whitney v. California, 274 U.S. 357, 375–76, 47 S.Ct. 641, 648, 71 L.Ed. 1095 (1927) (Brandeis, J., concur-

ring). See, Cardine, J., citing Treatise in, McCone v. Wyoming, 866 P.2d 740, 745 (Wyo.1993); Borden, J., citing Treatise in, Connecticut v. Indrisano, 228 Conn. 795, 833, 640 A.2d 986, 1005 (1994).

2. For discussions of the balancing test, see Dennis v. United States, 341 U.S. 494, 517, 71 S.Ct. 857, 871, 95 L.Ed. 1137 (1951), rehearing denied 342 U.S. 842, 72 S.Ct. 20, 96 L.Ed. 636 (1951) (J. Frankfurter concurring); Emerson, Toward a General Theory of the First Amendment, 72 Yale L.J. 877, at 912–14 (1963).

Supreme Court had little exposure to freedom of expression issues. Except for the passage of the 1798 Alien and Sedition Acts[1] Congress generally followed the First Amendment directive that "Congress shall make no law" restricting free speech, assembly or press,[2] but abandoned a hands off approach when the United States involvement in World War I met with vocal resistance. During this period there was the "Red Scare," a general concern about Socialists, Bolshevists, anarchists, and revolutionaries.

During time of war, one of the first casualties is free speech. Yet in ancient Athens, the cradle of democracy, the Greeks widely believed that freedom of speech made their armies more brave. They practiced a lesson we often forget. Herodotus writes that the Athenians could win victories over the more numerous Persians, in the first part of the fifth century, B.C., because the Athenians fought as free people, not as slaves. "Thus grew the power of Athens, and it is proved not by one but by many instances that equality is a good thing; seeing that while they were under despotic rulers the Athenians were no better in war than any of their neighbors, yet once they got rid of despots they were far and away the first of all," because once "they were freed each man was zealous to achieve for himself."[3]

Often we forget this ancient truth. People who are free work more intensely because they work for themselves, not for a master. It is for the same reason that it takes many hunting dogs to catch one fox. The fox works harder because he is self-employed. America is strong because of, not in spite of, free speech.[4]

Nevertheless, Congress, in response to domestic political unrest, passed the Espionage Act of 1917[5] and the Sedition Act of 1918.[6] This legislation provided the Supreme Court with the opportunity to develop standards for approaching First Amendment questions at a time when the climate was not conducive to an expansive reading of the free speech guarantee.

In 1919, the year that first saw the Palmer raids (named after Attorney General A. Mitchell Palmer) directed against Communists and radicals,[7] the Supreme Court handed down two important decisions involving free speech issues, *Schenck v. United States*[8] and *Abrams v. United States*,[9] where the Court first discussed "clear and present danger" theory.

The *Schenck* Case. In *Schenck* the Court affirmed appellants' conviction for conspiracy to violate the Espionage Act of 1917. Appellants had mailed leaflets to men eligible for military service asserting that the draft violated the Thirteenth Amendment.[10] These leaflets, the government argued, were prohibited by provisions in the Espionage Act forbidding obstruction of military recruiting.

Justice Holmes, writing for the Court, upheld the convictions and the restraint on free-

---

§ 16.13

1. Alien Act of June 25, 1798, ch. 58, 1 Stat. 570. Sedition Act of July 14, 1798, ch. 74, 1 Stat. 596.

2. Pre World War I History. For the early history, see Anderson, The Formative Period of First Amendment Theory, 1870–1915, 24 Am.J.Legal Hist. 56 (1980); Leonard Levy, Legacy of Suppression (1960); William Mayton, Seditious Libel and the Lost Guarantee of a Freedom of Expression, 84 Colum.L.Rev. 91 (1984); David Rabban, The Emergence of Modern First Amendment Doctrine, 50 U.Chi.L.Rev. 1205 (1983).

3. Herodotus, 4 vols. (Loeb Classical Library, 1922–1931), 5:78 (3:87), quoted in I.F. Stone, The Trial of Socrates 50 (1988).

4. Rotunda, Pravo na svobody slova v voennoe vremiz v knostitutsii SShA: istoki I evoliutsiia, Pravo I zakonoda-tel'stvo, 2003, No. 2, c. 63–65; The Right of Freedom of Speech in Wartime In the Constitution of the USA: Sources And Evolution, Law and Legislation, 2003, No. 2, pp. 63–65.

5. Espionage Act of June 15, 1917, ch. 30, 40 Stat. 217.

6. Sedition Act of May 16, 1918, ch. 75, 40 Stat. 553.

7. See, e.g., A. Kelly & W. Harbison, The American Constitution: Its Origins and Development 690 (1970):

"In 1919 a great Red scare began, inspired by Communist successes in Russia and central Europe. This fear was aggravated by the activities of a few bomb-throwing anarchists and of the Industrial Workers of the World.... In January 1919, Attorney–General A. Mitchell Palmer launched a gigantic two-year Red hunt, highlighted by mass arrests without benefit of habeas corpus, by hasty prosecutions, and by mass deportation of Communists and other radicals."

8. 249 U.S. 47, 39 S.Ct. 247, 63 L.Ed. 470 (1919).

9. 250 U.S. 616, 40 S.Ct. 17, 63 L.Ed. 1173 (1919).

10. 249 U.S. at 49–51, 39 S.Ct. at 247–49.

dom of expression as necessary to prevent grave and immediate threats to national security. Ordinarily, Holmes, believed, the leaflets would have been constitutionally protected but:

> The most stringent protection of free speech would not protect a man in falsely shouting fire in a theater and causing a panic. It does not even protect a man from an injunction against uttering words that may have all the effect of force.... The question in every case is whether the words used are used in such circumstances and are of such a nature as to create a clear and present danger that they will bring about the substantive evils that Congress has a right to prevent. It is a question of proximity and degree.[11]

Holmes concluded that First Amendment protection should not be extended during wartime to protect speech hindering the war effort.[12]

Holmes, dissenting in *Abrams v. United States*,[13] further explained his "clear and present danger" test. The Government had convicted the appellants of conspiracy to violate the Espionage Acts amendments, which prohibited speech encouraging resistance to the war effort and curtailment of production "with intent to cripple or hinder the United States in the prosecution of the war."[14] They had dis-

tributed pamphlets criticizing the United States' involvement in the effort to crush Russia's new Communist Government.

The majority in *Abrams* was unimpressed with Holmes' clear and present danger test as outlined in *Schenck*.[15] Because of the "bad tendency" of the defendants' speech, the majority affirmed, even though the defendants' sentences were twenty years.[16] Under the bad tendency test, speech could be prohibited if it was of a type that would tend to bring about harmful results.

Holmes criticized the Court's decision to uphold the conviction, arguing that it was ridiculous to assume these pamphlets would actually hinder the government's war efforts in Germany. As a matter of statutory construction Holmes would have reversed the convictions. But he also quickly moved to consider the constitutional issues.

He contended that the government could only restrict freedom of expression when there was "present danger of immediate evil or an intent to bring it about.... Congress certainly cannot forbid all effort to change the mind of the country."[17] Laws regulating free speech, Holmes conceded, would be an effective way for the government to stifle opposition, but—

---

11. 249 U.S. at 52, 39 S.Ct. at 249.

In Debs v. United States, 249 U.S. 211, 39 S.Ct. 252, 63 L.Ed. 566 (1919) Holmes affirmed the conviction of Eugene Debs, a prominent Socialist of the time, for allegedly encouraging listeners to obstruct the recruiting service. Holmes in this case spoke more in common law speech terms, which were adopted later by the Court (but not by Holmes) in the *Abrams* and *Gitlow* cases discussed below.

12. One week after writing *Schenck* Holmes wrote two other opinions for the Court affirming convictions in similar cases. In Frohwerk v. United States, 249 U.S. 204, 39 S.Ct. 249, 63 L.Ed. 561 (1919) he stated: "[T]he First Amendment while prohibiting legislation against free speech as such cannot have been, and obviously was not, intended to give immunity for every possible use of language.... [W]e have decided in Schenck v. United States, that a person may be convicted of a conspiracy to obstruct recruiting by words of persuasion." 249 U.S. at 206, 39 S.Ct. at 250.

13. 250 U.S. 616, 624, 40 S.Ct. 17, 20, 63 L.Ed. 1173 (1919).

14. Espionage Act of June 15, 1917, ch. 30, 40 Stat. 217, as amended May 16, 1918, 40 Stat. 553.

15. The United States at this time was at war with Germany, not Russia. The theory of the trial court and the Supreme Court majority was that to reduce arms produc-

tion for the Russian fight might aid Germany (with whom the United States was at war) because the United States would have less total arms. The Court did not require any specific intent by defendants.

16. 250 U.S. at 629, 40 S.Ct. at 21–22.

Disquieting echoes of the majority's bad tendency test are found in Haig v. Agee, 453 U.S. 280, 101 S.Ct. 2766, 69 L.Ed.2d 640 (1981). There the majority upheld the power of the Secretary of State to revoke the passport of Agee, a former CIA agent engaged in a policy of exposing clandestine CIA agents abroad. In rejecting Agee's First Amendment claims the majority said: "Agee's disclosures, among other things, have the declared purpose of obstructing intelligence operations and the recruiting of intelligence personnel." 453 U.S. at 308–09, 101 S.Ct. at 2783. Note the similarities with Abrams v. United States, 250 U.S. 616, 620–21, 40 S.Ct. 17, 19, 63 L.Ed. 1173 (1919): "The purpose of this [published article] was to persuade the persons to whom it was addressed to turn a deaf ear to patriotic appeals in behalf of the Government of the United States, and to cease to render it assistance in the prosecution of the war."

17. 250 U.S. at 628, 40 S.Ct. at 21.

the ultimate good desired is better reached by free trade in ideas—that the best test of truth is the power of thought to get itself accepted in the competition of the market.[18]

Holmes warned against overzealous repression of unpopular ideas:

> [W]e should be eternally vigilant against attempts to check the expression of opinions that we loathe and believe to be fraught with death, unless they so imminently threaten immediate interference with the lawful and pressing purposes of the law that an immediate check is required to save the country.[19]

Hence he concluded that the appellants had been unjustly convicted for exercising their First Amendment rights.

The *Gitlow* Decision. The Court continued to use the bad tendency test and remained reluctant to apply the clear and present danger test to protect defendants. The defendants in *Gitlow v. New York*[20] were convicted of violating New York's "criminal anarchy statute," which prohibited advocating violent overthrow of the government. They had printed and circulated a radical manifesto encouraging political strikes. There was no evidence that the manifesto had any effect on the individuals who received copies.

Gitlow upheld the conviction under the statute, finding the "clear and present danger test" inapplicable. The Court argued that only when a statute prohibits particular acts without including any restrictions on language should the "clear and present danger" standard be employed. In such a case the government must prove the defendants' language brought about the statutorily prohibited result. But, in *Gitlow*, the Court noted, the legislature had already determined what utterances would violate the statute. The government's decision that certain words are likely to cause the substantive evil "is not open for consideration." The government must then show only

that there is a reasonable basis for the statute. It is irrelevant that the particular words do or do not create a "clear and present danger."[21]

Holmes and Brandeis dissented. Holmes wrote that if the "clear and present danger" test was properly applied it would be obvious there was no real danger that the appellants' boring pamphlets would instigate political revolution. If the manifesto presented an immediate threat to the stability of the government then, Holmes admitted, there would be a need for suppression. But in the absence of immediate danger, Holmes concluded, the appellants were entitled to exercise their First Amendment rights.

The majority was unpersuaded. Why wait until the manifesto presents an immediate threat? If the state may prevent speech that advocates revolution, why not nip it in the bud. Why wait until the eleventh hour, when it may be too late. Even if the defendants' pamphlets were boring, why should that matter? If the state can punish exciting pamphlets, why should it not be able to punish boring ones as well?

The *Whitney* Decision. Two years later, in 1927, the "clear and present danger" test made its appearance once again, but this time, at least, it was in a concurrence. *Whitney v. California*[22] affirmed the conviction of Mrs. Whitney for violating the California Criminal Syndicalism Act by assisting in the organization of the Communist Labor Party of California. The statute defined criminal syndicalism as any doctrine "advocating teaching or aiding and abetting ... crime, sabotage ... or unlawful acts of force and violence" to effect political or economic change.

Whitney maintained that, at the organizing convention, she only advocated political reform through the democratic process. The majority of the convention, however, supported change through violence and terrorism. She said that she had not assisted the Communist Party with knowledge of its illegal purpose. The

---

18. 250 U.S. at 630, 40 S.Ct. at 22.

19. 250 U.S. at 630, 40 S.Ct. at 22.

20. 268 U.S. 652, 45 S.Ct. 625, 69 L.Ed. 1138 (1925).

21. 268 U.S. at 671, 45 S.Ct. at 632.

Bork, Neutral Principles and Some First Amendment Problems, 47 Ind.L.J. 1, 23 (1971).

22. 274 U.S. 357, 47 S.Ct. 641, 71 L.Ed. 1095 (1927).

state convicted her because of her mere presence at the convention and, consequently, she alleged deprivation of liberty without due process.[23] But the Court affirmed the conviction, holding that the jury had resolved the question of facts regarding her participation at the convention, that the united action of the Communist Party threatened the welfare of the state, and that Mrs. Whitney was a part of that organization.

Brandeis' Concurring Opinion in *Whitney*. This time, Justice Brandeis, rather than Holmes wrote a concurring opinion (which Holmes joined). While the opinion was labeled a "concurrence" it read like a dissent. Brandeis specifically objected to any notion, first presented in *Gitlow*, that the enactment of a statute foreclosed the application of the clear and present danger test by the Court. "[T]he enactment of the statute cannot alone establish the facts which are essential to its validity."[24]

Brandeis then proceeded to justify and elaborate on the clear and present danger test. He argued that the "state is, *ordinarily*, denied the power to prohibit dissemination of social, economic and political doctrine which a vast majority of its citizens believe to be false and fraught with evil consequence."[25] He eloquently explained that the framers "valued liberty both as an end and as a means. They believed liberty to be the secret of happiness and courage to be the secret of liberty."[26] Free speech is not merely useful. More than the metaphor of a market place supports it. Free speech is a good in and of itself.

Brandeis also argued that public order was secured by free speech. "[R]epression breeds hate; ... hate menaces stable government; ... the path of safety lies in the opportunity to discuss freely supposed grievances and proposed remedies...."[27]

Brandeis placed strong emphasis on the state's need to show *incitement*:

> But even advocacy of [law] violation however reprehensible morally, is not a justification for denying free speech where the advocacy falls short of incitement and there is nothing to indicate that the advocacy would be immediately acted on.... [N]o danger flowing from speech can be deemed clear and present, unless the incidence of the evil apprehended is so imminent that it may befall before there is opportunity for full discussion.[28]

Only when speech causes unthinking, immediate reaction is the protection of the First Amendment withdrawn. The real question is not whether the pamphlet or the speaker is eloquent or boring, exciting or monotonous. Instead, it is important if the context of the speech breeds incitement. There is no time for the market place of ideas to debate when the context provokes immediate reaction, as when the demagogue incites the lynch mob.

Brandeis then argued that, in situations where the rights of free speech and assembly were infringed, the defendant may contest this suppression by alleging that no "clear and present danger" actually existed. He said that Mrs. Whitney should have argued her conviction was void because no "clear and present danger" of a serious evil resulted from the convention activities. However, she had not challenged her conviction on that basis, so Brandeis said that he was unable to pass on the "clear and present danger" issue.[29]

Because of this procedural technicality, Brandeis concurred. His concurrence was a dissent in all but name, upholding the conviction only on this narrow procedural ground. In later years, he could cite it as a concurring opinion. Calling the opinion a concurrence gave to it a little more authority.

23.　274 U.S. at 363–67, 47 S.Ct. at 644–45.

24.　274 U.S. at 374, 47 S.Ct. at 648 (Brandeis, J., concurring). See, Nathanson, "The Philosophy of Mr. Justice Brandeis and Civil Liberties Today", in R. Rotunda, ed., Six Justices on Civil Rights 161–71 (Oceana Publications, Inc. 1983).

25.　274 U.S. at 374, 47 S.Ct. at 648 (emphasis added).

26.　274 U.S. at 375, 47 S.Ct. at 648.

27.　274 U.S. at 375, 47 S.Ct. at 648.

28.　274 U.S. at 376–77, 47 S.Ct. at 648–49.

29.　274 U.S. at 379, 47 S.Ct. at 649.

The *Herndon* Case. In a few cases during this period, the Court did reverse convictions of speech advocacy, but it did not do so under the clear and present danger rationale.[30] Finally, in *Herndon v. Lowry*,[31] a five to four decision, the Court reversed a conviction for violating a statute prohibiting attempts to incite insurrection, in effect rejecting the *Gitlow* test. The Court held that a state could not restrict words that only had a "tendency" to be dangerous. Power to abridge people's rights to freely express themselves "even of utterances of a defined character must find its justification in a reasonable apprehension of danger to organized government."[32]

Almost immediately after using the doctrine, the Court began to expand its application. For a few years, the "clear and present danger" test was employed in a number of cases, but these did not involve sedition.[33] Perhaps the most important of these cases—and the type of speech to which the "clear and present danger" language is applied to this day—involved a series of contempt-of-court decisions. Outside of these contempt of court cases the Court has developed different tests to determine when governmental restraints may be placed on different types of speech.[34]

(b) Present Application in the Contempt of Court Cases

Originally, in contempt of court cases, the Court had held that any spoken or printed criticism of courts obstructed the administration of justice and therefore was not constitutionally protected.[35] In *Bridges v. California*,[36] however, a contempt case, Justice Black writing for the majority applied the "clear and present danger" test stating "the substantive evil must be extremely serious and the degree of imminence extremely high before utterances can be punished."[37] The petitioners' statements criticizing pending court proceedings were not likely, Black reasoned, to bring about a "substantive evil" requiring abridgement of free expression.[38] In *Nebraska Press Association v. Stuart*[39] used the language of "clear and present danger" and reversed a court order restraining reporters from publishing allegedly prejudicial pretrial material.

Outside of the contempt of court cases, the Court turned to different tests to evaluate the competing interests where the government re-

---

30. In Fiske v. Kansas, 274 U.S. 380, 47 S.Ct. 655, 71 L.Ed. 1108 (1927), decided immediately after *Whitney*, the Court—in a decision written not by Justice Holmes but by Justice Sanford—reversed a conviction of a member of the Industrial Workers of the World under the Kansas Criminal Syndicalism Act. The Court applied the *Whitney* test; the State simply did not meet it. The simple reference in the I.W.W.'s Constitution to a class struggle was insufficient.

Several years later, Stromberg v. California, 283 U.S. 359, 51 S.Ct. 532, 75 L.Ed. 1117 (1931), reversed, on vagueness grounds, a conviction under California's statute forbidding the display of the red flag "as a sign, symbol and emblem of opposition to organized government...." 283 U.S. at 361, 51 S.Ct. at 533.

31. 301 U.S. 242, 57 S.Ct. 732, 81 L.Ed. 1066 (1937). Cf. De Jonge v. Oregon, 299 U.S. 353, 57 S.Ct. 255, 81 L.Ed. 278 (1937), holding that peaceable assembly for lawful discussion cannot be made a crime; the Court spoke of the need to show incitement. 299 U.S. at 359–65, 57 S.Ct. at 739–42.

32. 301 U.S. at 258, 57 S.Ct. at 257.

33. Thornhill v. Alabama, 310 U.S. 88, 60 S.Ct. 736, 84 L.Ed. 1093 (1940) (peaceful picketing); Cantwell v. Connecticut, 310 U.S. 296, 308, 60 S.Ct. 900, 905, 84 L.Ed. 1213 (1940) (power of state to punish clear and present danger of riot); West Virginia State Board of Education v. Barnette, 319 U.S. 624, 63 S.Ct. 1178, 87 L.Ed. 1628 (1943) (flag salutes); Terminiello v. Chicago, 337 U.S. 1, 4–

5, 69 S.Ct. 894, 895–96, 93 L.Ed. 1131 (1949), rehearing denied 337 U.S. 934, 69 S.Ct. 1490, 93 L.Ed. 1740 (1949) (breach of the peace).

34. Cf. Redish, Advocacy of Unlawful Conduct and the First Amendment: In Defense of Clear and Present Danger, 70 Calif.L.Rev. 1159 (1982).

35. Toledo Newspaper Co. v. United States, 247 U.S. 402, 38 S.Ct. 560, 62 L.Ed. 1186 (1918).

36. 314 U.S. 252, 62 S.Ct. 190, 86 L.Ed. 192 (1941).

37. 314 U.S. at 263, 62 S.Ct. at 194.

38. 314 U.S. at 270, 278, 62 S.Ct. at 197.

See also, Pennekamp v. Florida, 328 U.S. 331, 350, 66 S.Ct. 1029, 1039, 90 L.Ed. 1295 (1946); Craig v. Harney, 331 U.S. 367, 67 S.Ct. 1249, 91 L.Ed. 1546 (1947), mandate conformed 150 Tex.Crim. 598, 204 S.W.2d 842 (1947).

39. 427 U.S. 539, 562–63, 96 S.Ct. 2791, 2804–05, 49 L.Ed.2d 683 (1976), citing United States v. Dennis, 183 F.2d 201, 212 (2d Cir.1950) (L. Hand, J.), affirmed 341 U.S. 494, 71 S.Ct. 857, 95 L.Ed. 1137 (1951). Cf. 427 U.S. at 569, 96 S.Ct. at 2807–08 (1976).

See Landmark Communications, Inc. v. Virginia, 435 U.S. 829, 844, 98 S.Ct. 1535, 1544, 56 L.Ed.2d 1 (1978), noting that older cases have shown that out of court comments concerning pending cases or grand jury investigations do not constitute a clear and present danger to the administration of justice and cannot be punished by contempt.

strains different types of speech, such as obscenity or defamation. Even in cases involving the advocacy of violence, breach of the peace, or criminal syndicalism, the "clear and present danger" test underwent considerable revision before the Court considered it serviceable.

§ 16.14 Revision of the "Clear and Present Danger" Test in the 1950's

In the early 1950's the Supreme Court decided to reexamine the validity of the Holmes–Brandeis "clear and present danger" doctrine. With the advent of the cold war and the McCarthy paranoia, freedom of expression, especially speech criticizing the government or threatening national security, was severely restricted. The tone of the times was reflected in the Court's opinions, as it managed to avoid direct confrontation with the other branches of government over these issues.

The federal government convicted the defendants in *Dennis v. United States*[1] of violating the Smith Act by conspiring to organize the Communist Party of the United States. The party's goal allegedly was to overthrow the existing government by force and violence.

The Court affirmed, but with no majority opinion. Chief Justice Vinson, writing for himself and three other Justices, indicated Congress possessed the power to promulgate laws restricting speech. The issue the Court had to decide, thought Vinson, was whether the means Congress employed in suppressing free expression conflicted with First Amendment guarantees. He believed the questions would most effectively be resolved by applying the "clear and present danger" test.[2] But that test, as he construed it, meant much less than the original Holmes–Brandeis theory.

The Vinson reformulation of the clear and present danger test contained two steps. First, the Government had to show a substantial interest in limiting the speech. Congress, the Court held, did have a substantial interest in

preventing violent overthrow of the government. Second, the words or actions restricted in the legislation must be shown to constitute a "clear and present danger:"

[T]he words cannot mean that before the Government may act, it must wait until the *putsch* is about to be executed.... If Government is aware that a group aiming at its overthrow is attempting to indoctrinate its members ... action by the Government is required.... Certainly an attempt to overthrow the Government by force, even though doomed from the outset because of inadequate numbers or power of the revolutionists, is a sufficient evil for Congress to prevent.[3]

Speech that advocates more extreme dangers, such as overthrow of the Government, may be prohibited even though the danger is more remote. Vinson contended it was no longer realistic to assert that probability of success should be the basis of determining whether the danger is clear and present.

The Court adopted the lower court's interpretation of the rule, quoting Chief Judge Learned Hand:

In each case [courts] must ask whether the gravity of the "evil," discounted by its improbability, justifies such invasion of free speech as is necessary to avoid danger.[4]

In other words, the greater the gravity of the act advocated, the less clear and present danger is needed to justify governmental intrusion. Advocacy of revolution is fairly grave, so the danger need not be that clear or that present. So rephrased, the clear and present danger test became a disguised balancing test that weighed the seriousness of the danger against competing interest in free speech.

Petitioners' conspiracy to advocate revolution, even though it was merely in a preparatory stage, was a "clear and present" danger.

§ 16.14

1. 341 U.S. 494, 71 S.Ct. 857, 95 L.Ed. 1137 (1951), rehearing denied 342 U.S. 842, 72 S.Ct. 20, 96 L.Ed. 636 (1951).

2. 341 U.S. at 501–05, 71 S.Ct. at 863–65.

3. 341 U.S. at 509, 71 S.Ct. at 867.

4. 341 U.S. at 510, 71 S.Ct. at 868, quoting from, 183 F.2d 201, 212 (2d Cir.1950).

It is the existence of conspiracy which creates the danger.... If the ingredients of the reaction are present, we cannot bind the Government to wait until the catalyst is added.[5]

The Vinson–Hand reformulation of clear and present danger meant that in practice any radical political doctrine would receive little protection, because it would always appear as a threat to the nation and thus the most serious of all possible evils. "This is simply the remote bad tendency test dressed in modern style."[6]

Under traditional criminal conspiracy law the Government could always prosecute a criminal agreement coupled with some overt act. The indictment only places on the Government the burden of proving the elements of a traditional conspiracy. It does not require that the "putsch is about to be executed."[7] But conspiracy based on advocacy is not the typical conspiracy case, because advocacy implicates free speech. The strategy of the Government, approved by *Dennis*, was to assume only the relatively light burden of showing tendencies and probabilities.

Justice Frankfurter concurred in the affirmance but he was also unsympathetic to the defense. He criticized the clear and present danger test as too inflexible:

> The demands of free speech in a democratic society as well as the interest in national security are better served by candid and informal weighing of the competing interests, within the confines of the judicial process.[8]

He said that would have not affirmed the convictions in the *Gitlow* case because the circumstances then did not justify serious concern, but he thought that the conspiracy the Government faced in 1951 justified the legislative judgment that there was a substantial threat to national order and security. Frankfurter advocated acceptance of a "balancing" test to determine the constitutionality of speech restrictions as a replacement for the now vague clear and present danger theory. He did not appreciate that every generation perceives the evil attacking it as serious, while it views the (unsuccessful) evils attacking prior generations as imagined.

Yates v. United States[9] retreated from the broad doctrine of the *Dennis*. Yates and other Communist party officials were convicted for conspiring to "advocate and teach the necessity of overthrowing the federal government by violence" and organizing the Communist party to carry out this revolution in violation of the Smith Act.[10] The Supreme Court held that the trial court had incorrectly interpreted the *Dennis* precedent.

In the Court's opinion, Justice Harlan observed that the District Court had "apparently thought that *Dennis* obliterated the traditional dividing line between advocacy of abstract doctrine and advocacy of action."[11] Relying on the *Dennis* decision, the trial court had refused to instruct the jury that the statute prohibited advocacy actually inciting violent revolution and actions but not a mere abstract doctrine of forcible overthrow.[12] It was apparent from legislative history that Congress intended the Smith Act to be "aimed at the advocacy and teaching of concrete action for forcible overthrow of the Government, and not at principles divorced from action," the Supreme Court

---

5.   341 U.S. at 511, 71 S.Ct. at 868.

6.   Shapiro, Freedom of Speech: The Supreme Court and Judicial Review 65 (1966). The *Dennis* test is even less hospitable to free speech than the bad tendency test because it "considers the gravity of the evil discounted by *its* improbability—not the improbability that the speech in question will bring the evil about, but that it will occur from any cause." Id. (emphasis in original).

7.   Nathanson, The Communist Trial and the Clear–and–Present–Danger Test, 63 Harv.L.Rev. 1167, 1172–73 (1950).

8.   341 U.S. at 524–25, 71 S.Ct. at 875 (Frankfurter, J., concurring).

9.   354 U.S. 298, 77 S.Ct. 1064, 1 L.Ed.2d 1356 (1957).

10.   18 U.S.C.A. §§ 371, 2385.

11.   354 U.S. at 315–18, 77 S.Ct. at 1075–77.

12.   354 U.S. at 312–13, 77 S.Ct. at 1073–74.

ruled.[13]

The essence of the *Dennis* holding, Harlan stated, was that teaching and preparing a group for immediate or future violent action are not constitutionally protected, if it is reasonable to believe based on the circumstances, size, and commitment of the group that the action or revolution will occur:

> *Dennis* was ... not concerned with a conspiracy to engage at some future time in seditious advocacy, but rather with a conspiracy to advocate presently the taking of forcible action in the future. It was action not advocacy, that was to be postponed until "circumstances" would "permit."[14]

Harlan concluded that the petitioners' statements advocated a philosophy and did not incite action. Without evidence of any actual action or possibility of action, the Court would not affirm the convictions.[15]

Yates did not spell the end to Communist membership prosecutions. In *Scales v. United States*[16] the Court affirmed the petitioners' conviction for violating the membership clause of the Smith Act.[17] The trial court found the petitioners were active members of the Communist Party who were aware of the illegality of their teachings and advocated violent revolution and overthrow of the government "as speedily as circumstances would permit."

Justice Harlan, again writing the Court's opinion, upheld the lower court's findings, indicating that its interpretation of the membership clause did not impute "guilt to an individual merely on the basis of his associations and sympathies."[18] Said Harlan:

[T]he statute [as interpreted] is found to reach only "active" members having also a guilty knowledge and intent, and which therefore prevents a conviction on what otherwise might be regarded as merely an expression of sympathy with the alleged criminal enterprise, unaccompanied by any significant action in its support or any commitment to undertake such action.[19]

Though the record in *Scales* did not show advocacy of immediate violence, it did show present advocacy of future action for violent overthrow, which satisfied the limited requirements of *Dennis* and *Yates*:

> *Dennis* and *Yates* have definitely laid at rest any doubt that present advocacy of *future* action for violent overthrow satisfies statutory and constitutional requirements equally with advocacy of *immediate* action to that end.... [T]his record cannot be considered deficient because it contains no evidence of advocacy for immediate overthrow.[20]

Appellant's advocacy of violent revolution was intended to be a guide for future revolutionary action and consequently violated the Smith Act. If the record did not evidence support for at least advocacy of future action, the Court would dismiss the prosecution for Communist Party membership.[21]

Justice Douglas dissented to this whole theory. He did not see a red scare. He argued that "the essence of the crime ... is merely belief," and the conviction was a "sharp break with traditional concepts of First Amendment rights."[22]

After the *Dennis* and *Yates*, the Court rejected the "clear and present danger" doctrine to a great extent.[23] The doctrine, as defined by

---

13.   354 U.S. at 319–20, 77 S.Ct. at 1077.

14.   354 U.S. at 324, 77 S.Ct. at 1079–80.

15.   *Yates* reversed the conviction of five defendants and remanded for retrial as to the remaining nine; the charges against these nine were dismissed at the request of the Government, which found that it could not meet the tougher evidentiary requirements set out in *Yates*. Mollan, Smith Act Prosecutions: The Effect of the Dennis and Yates Decisions, 26 U.Pitt.L.Rev. 705, 732 (1965).

16.   367 U.S. 203, 81 S.Ct. 1469, 6 L.Ed.2d 782 (1961), rehearing denied 366 U.S. 978, 81 S.Ct. 1912, 6 L.Ed.2d 1267 (1961).

17.   18 U.S.C.A. § 2385.

18.   367 U.S. at 220, 81 S.Ct. at 1481–82.

19.   367 U.S. at 228, 81 S.Ct. at 1486.

20.   367 U.S. at 251, 81 S.Ct. at 1497 (emphasis in original).

21.   E.g. Noto v. United States, 367 U.S. 290, 81 S.Ct. 1517, 6 L.Ed.2d 836 (1961) (conviction reversed).

22.   367 U.S. at 262–65, 81 S.Ct. at 1503–04.

23.   Cf. Brennan, The Supreme Court and the Meiklejohn Interpretation of the First Amendment, 79 Harv. L.Rev. 1, 8 (1965).

Holmes, proved to be no viable test for restricting governmental invasion of free expression. To many people at the time, the cold war threat of a communist takeover was a very real possibility. The requirement that the danger resulting from speech must be imminent before First Amendment protection was denied was unsettling to those living in fear of communism,[24] and as a result the "balancing test" replaced the "clear and present danger" doctrine. The case law was ripe for the third phase of the clear and present danger test.

§ 16.15   The *Brandenburg* Test

The Holmes and Brandeis "clear and present danger" theory evolved during the late 1960's, as the Court focused on protecting the advocacy of unpopular ideas. This modification of the Holmes–Brandeis theory was particularly apparent in three cases decided in the late 1960's: *Bond v. Floyd*,[1] *Watts v. United States*,[2] and *Brandenburg v. Ohio*.[3]

The *Julian Bond* Case. Members of the Georgia House, in *Bond v. Floyd*,[4] challenged the right of a duly elected representative, Julian Bond, to be seated. Bond had publicly expressed his support of a statement issued by the Student Nonviolent Coordinating Committee (SNCC) criticizing the United States' involvement in Viet Nam and the operation of the draft laws. The Georgia legislature conducted a special hearing to determine if Bond could in good faith take the mandatory oath to support the Constitution. At the hearing Bond argued that he was willing and able to take his oath of office. He testified that he supported individuals who burned their draft cards, but he had not burned his own nor counseled anyone to burn their card.[5] The Georgia House voted not to administer the oath or seat Bond.

The Supreme Court held that the Georgia House violated Bond's right of free expression. Although the oath of office was constitutionally valid, Chief Justice Warren wrote, this requirement did not empower the majority of the representatives to challenge a duly elected legislator's sincerity in swearing allegiance to the Constitution. Such authority could be used to stifle dissents of legislators who disagreed with majority views.[6]

Warren believed that it would have been unconstitutional to convict Bond under federal law because his statements could not be interpreted as a call to unlawful refusal to be drafted. Bond actually appeared to have been advocating legal alternatives to the draft, not inciting people to violate the law.

The *Watts* Decision. Traces of a modified "clear and present danger" analysis are evident in *Watts v. United States*.[7] In a per curiam opinion the Supreme Court reversed the appellant's conviction for violating a statute prohibiting persons from "knowingly and willfully ... threat[ening] to take the life of or to inflict bodily harm upon the President." Watts, during a public rally in Washington, D.C., stated he would not report for his scheduled draft physical, continuing:

> If they ever make me carry a rifle the first man I want to get in my sights is L.B.J. They are not going to make me kill my black brothers.[8]

On its face the statute was held constitutional. The nation certainly has a valid interest in protecting the President, but a statute criminalizing certain forms of pure speech must be interpreted with the First Amendment in mind. "What is a threat must be

---

24. Emerson, Toward a General Theory of the First Amendment, 72 Yale L.J. 877, 911 (1963).

§ 16.15

1. 385 U.S. 116, 87 S.Ct. 339, 17 L.Ed.2d 235 (1966).

2. 394 U.S. 705, 89 S.Ct. 1399, 22 L.Ed.2d 664 (1969) (per curiam).

3. 395 U.S. 444, 89 S.Ct. 1827, 23 L.Ed.2d 430 (1969) (per curiam).

4. 385 U.S. 116, 87 S.Ct. 339, 17 L.Ed.2d 235 (1966).

5. 385 U.S. at 123–24, 87 S.Ct. at 343–44. The Court later upheld the constitutionality of federal laws punishing draft card burning. United States v. O'Brien, 391 U.S. 367, 88 S.Ct. 1673, 20 L.Ed.2d 672 (1968), rehearing denied 393 U.S. 900, 89 S.Ct. 63, 21 L.Ed.2d 188 (1968).

6. 385 U.S. at 132, 87 S.Ct. at 347–48.

7. 394 U.S. 705, 89 S.Ct. 1399, 22 L.Ed.2d 664 (1969) (per curiam).

8. 394 U.S. at 706, 89 S.Ct. at 1401.

distinguished from what is ... protected speech."[9]

The Court held that Watts' statement was "political hyperbole" and not a true threat. In context, the conditional nature of the remarks and the fact the listeners had laughed at the statement indicated to the Court that the words could only be interpreted as an expression of political belief. Had the circumstances of the speech amounted to a literal *incitement* of violence, the Court's decision would have been different. In context, there was no danger of incitement.

The pivotal determination in *Bond* was the fact that the appellant was merely expressing his grievances with the government, not *inciting* unlawful action. This distinction appeared to be based on the identical distinction that Brandeis advocated in his concurrence in *Whitney v. California*.[10] *Watts* also reversed the petitioner's conviction when the Court concluded the statement did not clearly present an *imminent* threat to the President.

The *Brandenburg* Test. *Brandenburg v. Ohio*[11] was only a per curiam opinion, but that should not mask its significance. The Warren Court may have been influenced by the reasoning of "clear and present danger," but *Brandenburg* has crucial differences in phrasing and emphasis to assure that its free speech protections remain undiluted.

Brandenburg overruled *Whitney*[12] and, significantly, it never explicitly referred to the "clear and present danger" standard. However it rejected the deference to the government that had prevailed in the "bad tendency" and "balancing" years.

Brandenburg reversed the conviction of a Ku Klux Klan leader for violating Ohio's Criminal Syndicalism statute. The appellant had been charged with advocating political reform through violence and for assembling with a group formed to teach criminal syndicalism. A man identified as the appellant arranged for a television news crew to attend a Klan rally. During the news film made at the rally, Klan members, allegedly including Brandenburg, discussed the group's plan to march on Congress.

The Court acknowledged that a similar criminal syndicalism statute had been upheld in *Whitney*, but it recognized that later decisions discredited *Whitney*. The Court then held advocacy of violence protected by the First Amendment as long as the advocacy did not incite people to *imminent* action. The key is "incitement." When a speaker uses speech to cause unthinking, immediate lawless action, one cannot rely on more speech in the market place of ideas to correct the errors of the original speech; there simply is not enough time. The speech provokes, incites, an unthinking reaction, not a debate.

The state has a significant interest in, and no other means of, preventing the resulting lawless conduct. The situation is analogous to someone who falsely shouts fire in a crowded theater. In that case, there is no time for a reasoned debate. Thus, under *Brandenburg* the state must prove that (1) the speaker *subjectively intended* incitement; (2) in context, the words used were *likely to produce* imminent, lawless action; and (3) the words used by the speaker *objectively encouraged* and urged incitement. This third part of the test, with its focus on the objective words used by the speaker, is derived from *Hess v. Indiana*,[13] discussed below.

Brandenburg adopted a new test to judge laws that restrict speech that advocates unlawful conduct: "[The state may not] forbid or proscribe advocacy of the use of force or of law violation except where such advocacy is directed to inciting or producing imminent lawless action and is likely to incite or produce such action."[14] Mere teaching of abstract doctrines

---

9. 394 U.S. at 707, 89 S.Ct. at 1401.

10. 274 U.S. 357, 372–80, 47 S.Ct. 641, 647–50, 71 L.Ed. 1095 (1927) (Brandeis, J., concurring).

11. 395 U.S. 444, 89 S.Ct. 1827, 23 L.Ed.2d 430 (1969) (per curiam).

12. 274 U.S. 357, 47 S.Ct. 641, 71 L.Ed. 1095 (1927).

13. 414 U.S. 105, 94 S.Ct. 326, 38 L.Ed.2d 303 (1973).

14. 395 U.S. at 447, 89 S.Ct. at 1829 (footnote omitted).

is not the same as leading a group in a violent action. Moreover, the statute must be narrowly drawn, and, if it failed to distinguish between advocacy of a theory and advocacy of action, it abridged First Amendment freedoms.

Criminal syndicalism, as defined in the Ohio statute, could not meet the *Brandenburg* test. The statute forbade teaching of violent political revolution with the intent of spreading such doctrine or assembling with a group advocating this doctrine. At the appellant's trial no attempt was made to distinguish between incitement and advocacy. Therefore, the statute violated the First and Fourteenth Amendments. Any law punishing mere advocacy of Ku Klux Klan doctrine and assembly of Klan members to advocate their beliefs was unconstitutional.

Justice Douglas concurred separately, with an important caveat. He said that there is no place for the "clear and present danger" test in any cases involving First Amendment rights. He was distrustful of that test, which he believed could be easily manipulated, as it was in *Dennis* and other cases, to deny constitutional protection to any speech critical of existing government.[15]

Brandenburg's new formulation offers broad new protection for strong advocacy. Its major focus is on the inciting language of the speaker, that is, on the *objective* words, in addition to the need to show not only that the speech is directed to produce *immediate*, unthinking lawless action but that in fact the situation makes this purpose likely to be successful.[16]

The Opinion in *Hess v. Indiana*. A post-Warren Court decision, *Hess v. Indiana*[17] indicates that the Court is serious and literal in its application of the test proposed in *Branden-*

burg. Hess had been arrested and convicted for disorderly conduct when he shouted "we'll take the fucking street later (or again)" during an antiwar demonstration. Two witnesses testified that Hess did not appear to exhort demonstrators to go into the street just cleared by the police, that he was facing the crowd, and that his tone of voice was not louder than any of the other demonstrators, although it was loud.[18] The Indiana Supreme Court upheld the trial court's finding that the remarks were in fact intended to incite further riotous behavior and were likely to produce such a result.

The United States Supreme Court reversed, and in a per curiam opinion stated:

At best ... the statement could be as counsel for present moderation; at worst it amounted to nothing more than advocacy of illegal action at some indefinite future time. This is not sufficient to permit the state to punish Hess' speech. Under our decisions, "the Constitutional guarantees of free speech and free press do not permit a state to forbid or proscribe advocacy of the use of force or of law violation except where such advocacy is directed to inciting or producing *imminent* lawless action and is likely to incite or produce such action."[19]

The Court concluded that because Hess' speech was "not directed to any person or group of persons" Hess had not advocated action that would produce imminent disorder. His statements, therefore, did not violate the disorderly conduct statutes.[20]

The new *Brandenburg* test—a test more vigorously phrased and strictly applied than the older clear and present danger test—now is the proper formula for determining when speech that advocates criminal conduct may

---

15. 395 U.S. at 450–52, 89 S.Ct. at 1831–32. (Douglas, J., concurring). Justice Black also concurred separately, and similarly objected to the clear and present danger test as construed in *Dennis*. 395 U.S. at 449–450, 89 S.Ct. at 1831.

16. Gunther, Learned Hand and the Origins of Modern First Amendment Doctrine: Some Fragments of History, 27 Stan.L.Rev. 719 (1975).

17. 414 U.S. 105, 94 S.Ct. 326, 38 L.Ed.2d 303 (1973).

18. 414 U.S. at 106–07, 94 S.Ct. at 327–28.

19. 414 U.S. at 108, 94 S.Ct. at 328 (emphasis in original), citing Brandenburg v. Ohio, 395 U.S. 444, 447, 89 S.Ct. 1827, 1829, 23 L.Ed.2d 430 (1969).

20. 414 U.S. at 108–09, 94 S.Ct. at 328–29. Rehnquist, J., joined by Burger, C.J. & Blackmun, J., dissented, objected to the per curiam opinion's "somewhat antiseptic description of this massing" of people and preferred to rely on the decision of the trial court, which was free to reject some testimony and accept other testimony. The majority, Rehnquist claimed, was merely interpreting the evidence differently and thus exceeding the proper scope of review. 414 U.S. at 109–12, 94 S.Ct. at 329–30.

constitutionally be punished. With its emphasis on incitement, imminent, unthinking lawless action, and the objective words of the speaker, it should provide a strong measure of First Amendment protection.

Should the Court confront a situation where a speaker advocates violence through the use of a speech that does not literally advocate action, such as Marc Antony's funeral oration for Caesar,[21] the government may urge the Court to abandon the protections of the *Brandenburg* test and, instead, look for proximity to violence rather than to the literal words of incitement. However, if the Court is true to the *Brandenburg* test, it will protect Marc Antony's speech.

§ 16.16   The Distinction Between Prior Restraint and Subsequent Punishment of Speech

The Common Law Background. Since the expiration of the English licensing system in 1695, under which nothing could be published without prior approval of the church or state authorities,[1] prior restraint has been considered a more drastic infringement on free speech than subsequent punishment.

While it is no longer true that the First Amendment means only freedom from prior restraint of speech, prior restraint is still con-

sidered a more serious restriction on free speech than subsequent punishment. Freedom of speech and of the press "has meant, principally although not exclusively, immunity from previous restraints or censorship."[2]

The Special Problem of Obscenity. In modern times prior restraint usually takes the form of court injunctions rather than a system of licensing by a Board of Censors. The only major exception is the case of allegedly obscene speech, where, in practice, there often may be censorship by board review prior to court action.

The courts have generally tolerated more prior restraint in situations involving allegedly obscene movies, because "obscenity" is not protected by the First Amendment guarantee of free speech, but even in such cases restraint is still suspect. Another section of this chapter discusses prior restraint of allegedly obscene speech.[3] Here we are primarily concerned with the prior restraint of other types of speech, which often but not necessarily occur in a political context.[4]

Prior Restraint and Subsequent Punishment Compared. If a given utterance may be punished, is there any real difference if one is enjoined from making the speech or whether one is punished *after* having made the

---

21. The *Brandenburg* test would protect Marc Antony's funeral oration in Shakespeare's *Julius Caesar*, Act III, scene ii. Marc Antony's objective words in his speech did not urge violence, even if that was his subjective intent.

Tort Claims Against the Media, Because of What They Broadcast. In National Broadcasting Co., Inc. v. Niemi, 434 U.S. 1354, 98 S.Ct. 705, 54 L.Ed.2d 742 (1978) (Rehnquist, Circuit Justice), certiorari denied 435 U.S. 1000, 98 S.Ct. 1657, 56 L.Ed.2d 91 (1978), appeal after remand 126 Cal.App.3d 488, 178 Cal.Rptr. 888 (1981), the respondent sought damages from a television network and publisher for injuries allegedly inflicted on her by persons acting under the stimulus of observing a scene of brutality broadcast in a television drama. The petitioners sought a stay of the state court order remanding for a trial. While Circuit Justice Rehnquist denied the stay for procedural reasons, he noted that the trial judge had rendered judgment for petitioners because he found that the film "did not advocate or encourage violent and depraved acts and thus did not constitute an incitement." 434 U.S. at 1356, 98 S.Ct. at 706. The *Brandenburg* test should be applicable to determine the free speech defense to plaintiff's tort claim.

§ 16.16

1. Near v. Minnesota, 283 U.S. 697, 713–14, 51 S.Ct. 625, 630, 75 L.Ed. 1357 (1931).

See 4 Ronald D. Rotunda & John E. Nowak, Treatise on Constitutional Law: Substance and Procedure § 20.2–20.5, 20.16 (West Group, 3d ed.1999).

2. Near v. Minnesota, 283 U.S. 697, 716, 51 S.Ct. 625, 631, 75 L.Ed. 1357 (1931). See also, New York Times Co. v. United States, 403 U.S. 713, 714, 91 S.Ct. 2140, 29 L.Ed.2d 822 (1971); Organization for a Better Austin v. Keefe, 402 U.S. 415, 419, 91 S.Ct. 1575, 1577–78, 29 L.Ed.2d 1 (1971); Bantam Books, Inc. v. Sullivan, 372 U.S. 58, 70, 83 S.Ct. 631, 639, 9 L.Ed.2d 584 (1963).

3. See § 16.61(c), infra.

4. E.g., Southeastern Promotions, Ltd. v. Conrad, 420 U.S. 546, 95 S.Ct. 1239, 43 L.Ed.2d 448 (1975) (denial by city of the use of a municipal theater for showing the musical "Hair"); Blount v. Rizzi, 400 U.S. 410, 91 S.Ct. 423, 27 L.Ed.2d 498 (1971) (postal stop orders); Freedman v. Maryland, 380 U.S. 51, 85 S.Ct. 734, 13 L.Ed.2d 649 (1965) (movies allegedly obscene); Nebraska Press Ass'n v. Stuart, 427 U.S. 539, 96 S.Ct. 2791, 49 L.Ed.2d 683 (1976) (judicial gag orders).

speech? Historically, prior restraint has always been viewed as more dangerous to free speech, but why? The marketplace theory of free speech supports this historical distinction between prior restraint and subsequent punishment. While subsequent punishment may deter some speakers, at least the ideas or speech at issue can be placed before the public. But prior restraint limits public debate and knowledge more severely. Punishment of speech, after it has occurred, chills free expression. Prior restraint freezes free speech.[5]

The procedural differences between enjoining speech and punishing speech make subsequent punishment a less onerous alternative. It is to that issue that we now turn.

Procedural Differences. Instead of subsequent punishment, the state is encouraged to use the procedural device of a prior restraint because, procedurally, it is easier to initiate a civil injunction action than to start a criminal prosecution. An application for a temporary restraining order is filed in cases where immediate and expeditious relief is needed. Once the court grants a temporary restraining order it sets a hearing, at the earliest possible date, to determine if a preliminary injunction should be issued.[6] In contrast to the rapid disposition of injunctive actions, a criminal prosecution must proceed through indictment or information,[7] arraignment,[8] pleadings, pretrial motions,[9] and jury selection if there is a possibility of imprisonment of six months or more,[10] before the accused is even brought to trial.

The hearing on an application for an injunction, an historically equitable action, is before a judge sitting without a jury.[11] If the injunctive order is violated there is generally no right to a jury at the contempt proceedings[12] except in some cases of criminal contempt.[13] The standard of proof in injunctive actions, as in most equitable proceedings, is not the strict criminal requirement of "beyond a reasonable doubt"[14] but the more lenient "clear and convincing proof" standard.[15] Unlike an injunctive

---

5. See A. Bickel, The Morality of Consent 61 (1975). See also, Redish, The Proper Role of the Prior Restraint Doctrine in First Amendment Theory, 70 Virginia L.Rev. 53 (1984); Mayton, Toward a Theory of First Amendment Process: Injunctions of Speech, Subsequent Punishment, and the Costs of the Prior Restraint Doctrine, 67 Cornell L.Rev. 245 (1982); Hunter, Toward a Better Understanding of the Prior Restraint Doctrine: A Reply to Professor Mayton, 67 Cornell L.Rev. 283 (1982).

Daniel J., quoting Treatise, in Local Organizing Committee, Denver Chapter, Million Man March v. Cook, 922 F.Supp. 1494, 1497, 109 Ed. Law Rep. 223 (D.Colo.1996); Colins, President Judge, quoting Treatise, in Brighton Management Serv. v. City of Philadelphia Tax Review Board, 667 A.2d 757, 759 (Commonwealth Court 1995), *appeal denied*, 544 Pa. 685, 679 A.2d 230 (1996).

6. See Fed.R.Civ.P. 65; see also United States v. United Mine Workers, 330 U.S. 258, 67 S.Ct. 677, 91 L.Ed. 884 (1947); Houghton v. Meyer, 208 U.S. 149, 28 S.Ct. 234, 52 L.Ed. 432 (1908); Moore, Federal Practice and Procedure, § 65.07.

7. Fed.R.Crim.P. 7. Cf. Nebraska Press Ass'n v. Stuart, 427 U.S. 539, 559, 96 S.Ct. 2791, 2802–03, 49 L.Ed.2d 683 (1976).

8. Fed.R.Crim.P. 10.

9. Fed.R.Crim.P. 11.

10. Baldwin v. New York, 399 U.S. 66, 69, 90 S.Ct. 1886, 1888, 26 L.Ed.2d 437 (1970), mandate conformed 27 N.Y.2d 731, 314 N.Y.S.2d 539, 262 N.E.2d 678 (1970).

11. See Ross v. Bernhard, 396 U.S. 531, 90 S.Ct. 733, 24 L.Ed.2d 729 (1970); Beacon Theatres, Inc. v. Westover, 359 U.S. 500, 79 S.Ct. 948, 3 L.Ed.2d 988 (1959); Dairy

Queen, Inc. v. Wood, 369 U.S. 469, 82 S.Ct. 894, 8 L.Ed.2d 44 (1962).

12. Shillitani v. United States, 384 U.S. 364, 365, 86 S.Ct. 1531, 1533, 16 L.Ed.2d 622 (1966).

13. See Gompers v. Buck's Stove & Range Co., 221 U.S. 418, 449, 31 S.Ct. 492, 501, 55 L.Ed. 797 (1911); 18 U.S.C.A. § 402.

Jail Time. If the length of the sentence is in the judge's discretion rather than fixed by statute, the Sixth Amendment requires a jury trial in criminal contempt cases if the sentence imposed is in fact more than six months. In contrast, in ordinary criminal cases defendant has a right to a jury trial if the sentence that *could* be imposed is in excess of six months. Codispoti v. Pennsylvania, 418 U.S. 506, 94 S.Ct. 2687, 41 L.Ed.2d 912 (1974); Muniz v. Hoffman, 422 U.S. 454, 476, 95 S.Ct. 2178, 2190, 45 L.Ed.2d 319 (1975).

Fines. As for fines, in criminal contempt cases there is no fixed line that determines when the Constitution requires a jury trial. Muniz v. Hoffman, 422 U.S. 454, 95 S.Ct. 2178, 45 L.Ed.2d 319 (1975) held that the Constitution did not require a jury trial, given the facts of that case, when the fine for criminal contempt was $10,000. If the case had involved an ordinary crime a jury would be required if the fine could exceed $500. 18 U.S.C.A. § 1(3). Subsequently a lower court, in the exercise of its supervisory power, limited fines for criminal contempt to $500. Douglass v. First Nat. Realty Corp., 543 F.2d 894 (D.C.Cir. 1976).

14. In re Winship, 397 U.S. 358, 361, 90 S.Ct. 1068, 1071, 25 L.Ed.2d 368 (1970).

15. McCormick, Evidence, § 340 at 796 (2d ed., E. Clearly, ed.1972); see, e.g., Fisher v. Miceli, 291 S.W.2d

case, in criminal prosecutions the government generally has no right of appeal,[16] a limitation imposed by the double jeopardy provision of the Fifth Amendment.[17] Because injunctive cases are civil proceedings, the Government's right to appeal in civil cases is limited only by the nonconstitutional principle of res judicata.[18]

The injunctive remedy with its speedier procedural framework is thus more subject to abuse and to indiscriminate application, whereas criminal prosecution entails a more thorough self-selection process resulting in fewer applications and successes. The overall chilling effect on speech is consequently less with criminal prosecution. Also, even if a temporary restraining order is ultimately found to have been improperly granted, the Government may have in fact achieved its end by restraining speech at a crucial time.[19] Although the speech may be subsequently allowed, its impact may then be negligible because of the time elapsed. If subsequent punishment chills, prior restraint freezes.

Disobeying Court Orders and Violating Statutes, Compared. Courts usually treat violations of prior restraint orders as a more serious offense than deliberate refusals to abide by a statute. A significant illustration of this principle is found in a comparison of two Supreme Court cases. In one, the High Court reversed the conviction of civil rights demonstrators who had been convicted of violating an ordinance found to be unconstitutionally vague. The ordinance forbade issuance of a license for a protest march if "the public welfare, peace, safety, health, decency, good order,

morals or convenience" require that it be refused.[20] Justice Stewart for the Court said that "a person faced with such an unconstitutional licensing law may ignore it and engage with impunity in the exercise of the right of free expression for which the law purports to require a license."[21]

The Court earlier had upheld the conviction of marchers who violated that same statute *after* the statute had been copied verbatim into an ex parte injunction. While one could violate the statute with impunity, violation of the state court's ex parte injunction was another matter:

> The breadth and vagueness of the injunction itself would also unquestionably be subject to substantial constitutional question. But the way to raise that question was to apply to the Alabama courts to have the injunction modified or dissolved.[22]

In short, while one is free to violate an unconstitutional statute restricting free speech, one is not free to violate the same words when written as a court injunction.

Courts are more adamant in punishing contempt of their orders than in punishing violations of criminal statutes. Because the defendant has violated a specific order of the judge, the judge may interpret a contempt action as an attack on the courts themselves or as a violation of the respect that judges feel is due them; however, this self-interest of the court is not present in criminal cases, where the judge has no personal stake in enforcement of the criminal statute.[23] Because the judge may ob-

---

845, 848 (Mo.1956); Hyder v. Newcomb, 236 Ark. 231, 365 S.W.2d 271, 274 (1963).

16. Ashe v. Swenson, 397 U.S. 436, 445, 90 S.Ct. 1189, 1195, 25 L.Ed.2d 469 (1970); Benton v. Maryland, 395 U.S. 784, 793–795, 89 S.Ct. 2056, 23 L.Ed.2d 707 (1969), on remand 8 Md.App. 388, 260 A.2d 86 (1969).

17. Ball v. United States, 163 U.S. 662, 668–670, 16 S.Ct. 1192, 1194–95, 41 L.Ed. 300 (1896).

18. Cf. 28 U.S.C.A. § 1292.

19. Cf. Walker v. City of Birmingham, 388 U.S. 307, 336, 87 S.Ct. 1824, 1840, 18 L.Ed.2d 1210 (1967), rehearing denied 389 U.S. 894, 88 S.Ct. 12, 19 L.Ed.2d 202 (1967) (Douglas, J., dissenting).

20. Shuttlesworth v. Birmingham, 394 U.S. 147, 150–151, 89 S.Ct. 935, 938–39, 22 L.Ed.2d 162 (1969), on remand 45 Ala.App. 723, 222 So.2d 377 (1969).

21. 394 U.S. at 151, 89 S.Ct. at 938–39.

22. Walker v. Birmingham, 388 U.S. 307, 317, 87 S.Ct. 1824, 1830, 18 L.Ed.2d 1210 (1967), rehearing denied 389 U.S. 894, 88 S.Ct. 12, 19 L.Ed.2d 202 (1967).

23. See Walker v. Birmingham, 388 U.S. 307, 87 S.Ct. 1824, 18 L.Ed.2d 1210 (1967), rehearing denied 389 U.S. 894, 88 S.Ct. 12, 19 L.Ed.2d 202 (1967) where the Court held that, even though a state injunction forbidding a demonstration was unconstitutional, the subjects of it could be prosecuted for violating it rather than appealing it and seeking reversal. Warren, C.J., in dissent noted:

ject more to the violation of his own order than to the violation of a state's statute, he may correspondingly be more severe in enforcing prior restraints relative to subsequent punishments.

The Court has focused on the principle that the individual before the court in a case where the judge is issuing the prior restraint has access to a neutral determination of the issue. If the litigant objects to the trial court's ruling, he or she can always appeal. The litigant does not have to violate the court injunction in order to appeal. (In contrast, often the best or only way to attack the constitutionality of a statute is to violate it.) If there were no reasonable review procedures available in injunction cases there should be a different conclusion. But so long as there is outstanding a judicial order, the legal process cannot tolerate an individual's choice to disregard a court order and then claim a right to attack that order collaterally.

Judicial Predictions Regarding Effects of Speech on National Security. In the case of prior restraint of controversial political speech touching on national security or similar interests, new problems emerge. In such cases the government may argue that an injunction should issue because publication will cause substantial damage to the United States. In ruling on the application, the Court is really asked to predict the future; that is, will publication in fact cause this vague but substantial damage?

Courts are ill-equipped for such a task. If the Court says no damage will occur and allows publication, there are two possible consequences. The damage may actually occur (or some damage may occur and appear to have been linked with earlier publication) and the Court consequently will share the blame for the damage to the United States' security. If,

alternatively, the asserted damage does not occur, the judiciary has still engaged in a risky expenditure of its esteem without noticeable advantage. Thus courts are not encouraged to under-predict the dangers of publication.

On the other hand, if the Court does not allow publication, the public will probably never know if the Court was wrong, because the allegedly damaging papers may never be published or, if they are printed, may be seized prior to distribution. The public then is never able to judge for itself the importance of the suppressed speech. The Court will never lose esteem or share blame in such cases where it over-predicts the danger from publication, and there will be little or no damage to its reputation when the newspapers do not publish information that the court has enjoined. Prior restraint, with its emphasis on predicting an unknowable future, encourages courts to over-predict the potential damage from publication and under-predict the benefits. The dangers of under-prediction and the judicial tendency towards over-prediction make prior restraint a more serious and more effective weapon against free speech.

No Injunctions Against Crimes. For these historical, procedural, and substantive reasons prior restraint—particularly in the context of political speech attacking governmental policies—has long been suspect. Just as the common law forbade equity from enjoining a crime,[24] the over effectiveness of prior restraint and its strong potential for abuse has made it much more chilling on the exercise of First Amendment rights, than subsequent punishments.

Distinguishing Injunctions That Are Prior Restraints from Those that Are Not. Obviously, an injunction against speech is a prior restraint. But if a court enjoins

---

"It has never been thought that violation of a statute indicated such a disrespect for the legislature that the violator always must be punished even if the statute was unconstitutional.... [But an ex parte] injunction [is] such potent magic that it transformed the command of an unconstitutional statute into an impregnable barrier, challengeable only in what likely would have been protracted legal proceedings and entirely superior in the meantime even to the United States Constitution."

388 U.S. 307, 327, 330, 87 S.Ct. 1824, 1835, 1837, 18 L.Ed.2d 1210 (1967), rehearing denied 389 U.S. 894, 88 S.Ct. 12, 19 L.Ed.2d 202 (1967).

24. Milliken v. Stone, 16 F.2d 981, 983 (2d Cir.1927), certiorari denied 274 U.S. 748, 47 S.Ct. 764, 71 L.Ed. 1331 (1927); In re Debs, 158 U.S. 564, 593–94, 15 S.Ct. 900, 909–10, 39 L.Ed. 1092 (1895).

conduct and the injunction also has an incidental and limited effect on speech, the issue is more complicated. *Madsen v. Women's Health Center, Inc.*[25] briefly considered this issue. The divided Court upheld portions of a Florida state court injunction involving an abortion clinic that was the target of protests that made it difficult for patients and staff to enter the clinic. Given the lower court's specific factual findings, the Court upheld an injunction that created a 36 foot buffer zone prohibiting picketing. The purpose of this buffer zone was to allow access to the clinic. The Court invalidated other portions of the injunction.

The majority in *Madsen* rejected the argument that the injunction involved prior restraint of speech. The injunction did not prevent the petitioners from expressing their message in other places, but "they are simply prohibited from expressing it within the 36 foot buffer zone," which the majority called a "speech-free buffer zone." The Court said that the lower court did not issue the injunction "because of the content of petitioners' expression, as was the case in *New York Times Co.* [*v. United States*]," but because of their "prior unlawful conduct."[26] The state court had found that when the petitioners were within the 35 foot buffer zone, "they repeatedly had interfered with the free access of patients and staff."[27] Because the state court did not enjoin the petitioners from demonstrating outside of the speech-free buffer, the Court declined to treat the injunction as a prior restraint.

---

25. 512 U.S. 753, 114 S.Ct. 2516, 129 L.Ed.2d 593 (1994), on remand 644 So.2d 86 (Fla.1994).

26. 512 U.S. at 764 n. 2, 114 S.Ct. at 2524 n. 2. See also Schenck v. Pro–Choice Network of Western New York, 519 U.S. 357, 117 S.Ct. 855, 870 (1997).

27. 512 U.S. at 769, 114 S.Ct. at 2526.

§ 16.17

1. 283 U.S. 697, 51 S.Ct. 625, 75 L.Ed. 1357 (1931).

2. 403 U.S. 713, 91 S.Ct. 2140, 29 L.Ed.2d 822 (1971).

Heavy Presumption Against Prior Restraint. Organization for a Better Austin v. Keefe, 402 U.S. 415, 419, 91 S.Ct. 1575, 1578, 29 L.Ed.2d 1 (1971) reversed a prior restraint on the OBA that, to encourage integrated housing, had peacefully distributed leaflets objecting to block busting and panic peddling. The leaflets specifically criticized Keefe, a real estate broker. The Court emphasized that any prior restraint has a " 'heavy' presumption

§ 16.17 From *Near* to the Pentagon Papers and Beyond

Near v. Minnesota[1] firmly embedded the prior restraint doctrine in modern jurisprudence. Four decades later, *New York Times Co. v. United States*[2] applied those principles to the special problem of national security.

Near involved a state statute that permitted the state courts to enjoin as a nuisance any "malicious, scandalous and defamatory newspaper, magazine or other periodical."[3] Defendant published "The Saturday Press" and had printed articles with strong antisemitic overtones critical of local officials. The trial court issued a permanent injunction against defendant, and the highest state court affirmed.

The Supreme Court reversed the conviction on the grounds that it was an infringement of the liberty of the press as guaranteed in the First and Fourteenth Amendments. In reaching this conclusion, the Court enumerated the gravity of the statute's consequences: (1) In order to obtain an injunction under the statute, one did not need to prove the falsity of the charges made in the publication, as in libel law. The statute only permitted the defense that "truth was published with good motives and for justifiable ends."[4] (2) The statute was directed to publications critical of private citizens and public officers. (3) The object of the statute was not ordinary punishment but suppression. (4) The statute operated not only to

---

against its constitutional validity." CBS, Inc. v. Davis, 510 U.S. 1315, 114 S.Ct. 912, 127 L.Ed.2d 358 (1994) (Blackmun, J., in Chambers, staying preliminary injunction of a CBS broadcast of a videotape that allegedly was procured by trespass, and aiding and abetting a violation of the South Dakota's Trade Secrets Act).

Business Week Prior Restraint. A district court restrained a publisher (Business Week Magazine) from publishing an article containing any disclosure of any documents filed under seal, or the contents thereof. The Sixth Circuit reversed and rebuked the trial court, saying that the prior restraint was "patently invalid," and that it should never have been entered. Procter & Gamble Company v. Bankers Trust Company, 78 F.3d 219 (6th Cir. 1996).

3. 283 U.S. 697, 701–02, 51 S.Ct. 625, 626, 75 L.Ed. 1357 (1931).

4. 283 U.S. at 702, 51 S.Ct. at 626.

suppress the publication but also to effectively place the publisher under censorship.[5]

The Court summarized the working of the statute as "the essence of censorship."[6]

A statute that functioned in this way was inconsistent with the historical conception of the freedom of the press guarantee.[7]

To reach this conclusion, the Court accepted a major initial postulate: the chief purpose of the freedom of the press guarantee is to prevent prior restraints on publication.[8] Thus, there could be very few exceptions to the principle of immunity from previous restraint.

In dictum, the Court listed three "exceptional cases" that *might* justify previous restraint:[9] (1) if it were necessary so that "a government might prevent actual obstruction

to its recruiting service or the publication of the sailing dates of transports or the number and location of troops;"[10] (2) the requirements of decency could justify prior restraint on obscene publications; (3) if it were necessary to avoid "incitements to acts of violence and the overthrow by force of orderly government."[11] Because none of these exceptions was applicable to the statute so far as it authorized the proceedings of this action, prior restraint was not constitutionally justified in *Near*.

The Pentagon Papers Case. Forty years later, the doctrine of prior restraint of political speech received special attention in *New York Times Co. v. United States* (The Pentagon Papers Case).[12] The case involved a massive leak of secret government documents. First, the *New York Times*, then the *Washington*

---

5. 283 U.S. at 710–12, 51 S.Ct. at 629–30.

6. 283 U.S. at 713, 51 S.Ct. at 630.

7. **The Investment Advisers Act and Prior Restraint.** Compare Lowe v. SEC, 472 U.S. 181, 105 S.Ct. 2557, 86 L.Ed.2d 130 (1985). After Christopher Lowe was convicted of misappropriating funds of an investment client, of tampering with evidence to cover up fraud of an investment client, of stealing from a bank, and of other similar activities, the Securities and Exchange Commission ordered Lowe not to associate with any investment adviser. About a year later the SEC filed suit to permanently enjoin Lowe and others who were alleged to be violating the 1940 Investment Advisers Act and the earlier SEC order by publishing investment newsletters and soliciting subscriptions for a stock chart service, without being registered as investment advisers or being exempt under the Investment Advisers Act. "There was no evidence that Lowe's criminal convictions were related to the publications; no evidence that Lowe had engaged in any trading activity in any securities that were the subject of advice or comment in the publications; and no contention that any of the information published in the advisory services had been false or materially misleading." 472 U.S. at 187, 105 S.Ct. at 2561 (footnotes omitted).

The Court, to avoid constitutional problems, interpreted the 1940 Investment Advisers Act to exclude Lowe's newsletters and publications from its definition of "investment adviser." If the communications between petitioners and their subscribers remain entirely impersonal "and do not develop into the kind of fiduciary, person-to-person relationships that were discussed at length in the legislative history of the Act and are characteristic of investment adviser-client relationships, we believe the publications are, at least presumptively, within the exclusion and thus not subject to registration under the Act." 472 U.S. at 210, 105 S.Ct. at 2573 (footnote omitted). Thus an unregistered adviser may publish newsletters containing investment advice not specifically tailored to the needs of individual clients. Cf. Robert C. Hacker & Ronald D. Rotunda, SEC Registration of Private Investment Partnerships after

Abrahamson v. Fleschner, 78 Columbia Law Review 1471 (1978).

White, J., joined by Burger, C.J., and Rehnquist, J., concurred in the result. They interpreted the Act to include Lowe as an investment adviser, but would hold that the Act could not constitutionally be applied in these circumstances.

8. 283 U.S. at 713, 51 S.Ct. at 630.

9. 283 U.S. at 716, 51 S.Ct. at 631.

10. 283 U.S. at 716, 51 S.Ct. at 631.

The majority relied on this dictum in upholding the power of the Secretary of State to revoke the passport of a former CIA agent who was seeking to expose CIA agents abroad. Haig v. Agee, 453 U.S. 280, 101 S.Ct. 2766, 69 L.Ed.2d 640 (1981). The passport revocation, the majority argued, did not violate Agee's First Amendment rights because it only inhibited Agee's *"action"*, not his "speech." 453 U.S. at 309, 101 S.Ct. at 2783 (emphasis in original). Just as the hypothetical disclosures in *Near* obstruct the government's recruiting services, Agee's disclosures "have the declared purpose of obstructing intelligence operations and the recruiting of intelligence personnel." 453 U.S. at 308–09, 101 S.Ct. at 2782–83.

Brennan, J., in dissent, found *Near* to be an irrelevant and unconvincing precedent. Under the majority's speech-action rationale, "a 40 year prison sentence imposed upon a person who criticized the Government's food stamp policy would represent only an 'inhibition of action.' After all, the individual would remain free to criticize the United States Government, albeit from a jail cell." 453 U.S. at 320–21 n. 10, 101 S.Ct. at 2788 n. 10.

11. 283 U.S. at 716, 51 S.Ct. at 631.

12. 403 U.S. 713, 91 S.Ct. 2140, 29 L.Ed.2d 822 (1971). The Court therefore reversed the Second Circuit and affirmed the D.C. Circuit. The Court also lifted its own stay. 403 U.S. 943, 91 S.Ct. 2271, 29 L.Ed.2d 853 (1971). The D.C. Circuit had refused to enjoin but still restrained the *Post* pending Supreme Court review.

Post, and then other newspapers, received volumes of a secret government study of the Viet Nam war, which was still going on while the newspapers published the Pentagon Papers.

The Court dismissed temporary restraining orders and stays against the *New York Times* and the *Washington Post,* and refused to enjoin the newspapers from publishing this classified study on United States policy-making in Viet Nam. The fragmented Court decided the case in nine separate opinions. There was a six to three majority, but all nine Justices agreed on two general themes—any system of prior restraint of expression bears a heavy presumption against its constitutional validity, and the Government carries a heavy burden to justify any system of prior restraint.[13]

The opinions in this case can be grouped in three categories: Justices Black and Douglas maintained that there can never be prior restraint on the press; Justices Brennan, White, Stewart and Marshall maintained that there could be prior restraint on the press in some circumstances but not in this case; and Justices Burger, Harlan, and Blackmun, maintained that the prior restraint was appropriate in this case.

Justices Black and Douglas argued that no system of prior restraint was ever justified. A holding that the publication of news may sometimes be enjoined, according to Justice Black, would "make a shambles of the First Amendment," and the operation of the injunctions was a "flagrant, indefensible, and continuing violation of the First Amendment."[14]

Black characterized the very purpose of the press as exposing the secrets of government and informing the people: "paramount among the responsibilities of a free press is the duty to prevent any part of the government from deceiving the people and sending them off to distant lands to die of foreign fevers and foreign shot and shell."[15] Rather than be enjoined or condemned for publishing the Pentagon Pa-

pers, these newspapers should be "commended for serving the purpose that the Founding Fathers saw so clearly.... The Press was to serve the governed, not the governors."[16]

Justice Douglas deplored governmental restraint on the press and also interpreted the dominant purpose of the First Amendment "to prohibit the widespread practice of governmental suppression of embarrassing information."[17] Although Douglas left unanswered the question whether the war power of Congress might change the doctrine of prior restraint, as the doctrine exists now, even serious impact from disclosures of publication cannot justify prior restraint on the press.

Justice Brennan did leave open the possibility of some constitutional prior restraints, but his test was so strict that none might pass any realistic review. Brennan first pointed out the impropriety of granting injunctive relief in the instant case. The basis of the Government's argument was that publication might damage the national interest but, according to Brennan, "the First Amendment tolerates absolutely no prior judicial restraints of the press predicated upon surmise or conjecture that untoward consequences may result."[18]

Brennan did find one situation that would justify an exception to the First Amendment ban on prior restraint, when the nation is at war. However, Brennan invoked a high standard for imposition of prior restraint even then. The Government must allege and prove that the publication of information must "inevitably, directly, and immediately" cause the happening of an event such as nuclear holocaust.[19] Thus, although Brennan conceptually allowed the possibility of prior restraint, his test is so strict as to be virtually a prohibition.

Justice Stewart argued that prior restraint imposed by the Executive could be justified in order to maintain internal security, because the Executive has a constitutional obligation to preserve the confidentiality required to ef-

---

13.   403 U.S. at 714, 91 S.Ct. at 2141.

14.   403 U.S. at 715, 91 S.Ct. at 2142.

15.   403 U.S. at 717, 91 S.Ct. at 2143.

16.   403 U.S. at 717, 91 S.Ct. at 2143.

17.   403 U.S. at 723–24, 91 S.Ct. at 2146.

18.   403 U.S. at 725–26, 91 S.Ct. at 2147 (footnote omitted).

19.   403 U.S. at 726–27, 91 S.Ct. at 2148.

fectively perform its duties related to national defense and foreign affairs. However, the Executive must show that disclosure of information will result in "direct, immediate, and irreparable damage to our Nation or its people," and the Government did not meet this test for all the documents involved in the instant case.[20]

Even though he was convinced disclosure of the material would do substantial damage to the public interest, Justice White concurred in the Court's judgment because the Government did not satisfy the "very heavy burden" it must meet to justify prior restraint.[21] White implied that Congressional authorization for prior restraint might lessen this "very heavy burden" and emphasized that the Government could still proceed against the newspapers for criminal publication.

Justice Marshall based his concurrence on the absence of Congressional authorization for prior restraint in this situation. He argued that it would be against the separation of powers concept for the Court, through use of the contempt power, to restrain actions Congress has chosen not to prohibit. Although the power of the Executive could constitutionally justify prior restraint, Congress had clearly refused to give the President the power he sought to exercise here by enjoining publication of these materials. Marshall dismissed the injunction because "[w]hen Congress specifically declines to make conduct unlawful it is not for this Court to redecide those issues—to overrule Congress."[22]

The remaining three Justices dissented. Chief Justice Burger did not speak directly to the merits of the case, arguing instead that undue haste in the proceedings removed any possibility of orderly litigation of the proceedings and meant that the Justices "literally do not know what we are acting on."[23] He would have upheld the injunction to allow the Court enough time for an orderly hearing on the merits. However, Burger criticized the New

York Times as being largely responsible for the "frenetic haste" of the proceedings and his sympathies were apparent in that he "agreed generally" with Harlan's dissent.[24]

Harlan did uphold use of the injunction on the merits, albeit "within the severe limitations imposed by the time constraints."[25] Unlike Justice Marshall, Harlan used the theory of the constitutional separation of powers to justify prior restraint of the Pentagon Papers. Harlan argued that the Executive has constitutional primacy in the field of foreign affairs and that the judiciary has only two narrow areas of inquiry over Executive decisions in foreign policy. The Judiciary can (1) insure that the area of dispute actually lies within the scope of the President's foreign relations power; and (2) insure that the decision that disclosure of the subject matter would irreparably impair the national security be made by the head of the executive department concerned, such as the Secretary of State or the Secretary of Defense. But it is not within the power of the Court to redetermine the probable impact of disclosure on national security once this decision has been made by the Executive.

Justice Blackmun argued that there was need for developing proper standards between the "broad right of the press to print and . . . the very narrow right of the Government to prevent."[26] Representing the opposite extreme from Black's praise of the New York Times, Blackmun included a strong attack on the newspapers and concurring Justices who comprised the majority of the Court:

[I]f, with the Court's action today, these newspapers proceed to publish the critical documents and there results therefrom "the death of soldiers, the destruction of alliances, the greatly increased difficulty of negotiation with our enemies, the inability of our diplomats to negotiate," to which list I might add the factors of prolongation of the

20.   403 U.S. at 730, 91 S.Ct. at 2149.
21.   403 U.S. at 731, 91 S.Ct. at 2150.
22.   403 U.S. at 745–46, 91 S.Ct. at 2157.
23.   403 U.S. at 751, 91 S.Ct. at 2160.

24.   403 U.S. at 751–52, 91 S.Ct. at 2161.
25.   403 U.S. at 755, 91 S.Ct. at 2162.
26.   403 U.S. at 761, 91 S.Ct. at 2165.

war and of further delay in the freeing of United States prisoners, then the Nation's people will know where the responsibility for these sad consequences rests.[27]

The Government lost its injunctive suit and the newspaper proceeded to finish publishing the excerpts of the Pentagon Papers that they had secured by an unauthorized leak from a former government employee, Daniel Ellsberg. The Government never showed or claimed that Blackmun's parade of horribles occurred because of the Pentagon Papers publication. Nor did the Government ever prosecute any of the newspapers—an option not foreclosed by the Pentagon Papers case[28]—but it did prosecute Daniel Ellsberg. Ellsberg, however, was never convicted. The trial judge directed a verdict of acquittal for Ellsberg because of various prosecution improprieties.

The *Snepp* Case and the CIA. Following the Pentagon Papers Case, the Court decided *Snepp v. United States.*[29] The brief per curiam opinion held that a former agent of the Central Intelligence Agency breached his fiduciary obligation and his employment contract when he failed to submit for pre-publication review a book concerning the CIA, even though the

Government conceded, for the purposes of the case, that the book divulged no classified information. Therefore, the Court put into constructive trust for the Government all the profits from Snepp's book.

The majority explained that the proper procedure that Snepp should have followed, in light of his explicit employment agreement to submit all material to the CIA for prepublication review, would be to submit the material so that the Agency could determine if it contained harmful disclosures. If Snepp and the CIA failed to agree on this issue, the Agency would have the burden to seek an injunction against publication.[30] Without any further discussion the Court appeared to approve of what amounts to prior restraint in those special cases where former CIA employees have been in a position of trust and have signed employment contracts accepting prepublication review of information dealing with the CIA.

The dissent objected: "the Court seems unaware of the fact that its drastic new remedy [of a constructive trust for failure to abide by prepublication clearance] has been fashioned to enforce a species of prior restraint on a

27. 403 U.S. at 763, 91 S.Ct. at 2166. Over the years, it appears that Justice Blackmun changed his views. In CBS, Inc. v. Davis, 510 U.S. 1315, 114 S.Ct. 912, 914, 127 L.Ed.2d 358 (1994), Blackmun, J., in chambers, stayed a preliminary injunction of a CBS broadcast of a videotape that allegedly was the product of trespass, breach of a fiduciary duty of loyalty, and of aiding and abetting a violation of South Dakota's Trade Secrets Act. Relying on *New York Times,* Blackmun said, "Nor is the prior restraint doctrine inapplicable through the 'calculated misdeeds' of CBS." Also, courts cannot rely on speculative predictions, such as "significant economic harm" to justify a prior restraint.

28. Cf. Landmark Communications, Inc. v. Virginia, 435 U.S. 829, 98 S.Ct. 1535, 56 L.Ed.2d 1 (1978). The holding in *Landmark*—protecting third party publication of confidential judicial disciplinary proceedings—may not be applicable to a situation like the Pentagon Papers case, where a newspaper might be subject to subsequent punishment for publishing allegedly top secret national security data since the interests of the state in protecting such information is much greater. However, a major issue in such a case would still be whether data was properly classified as top secret, since a "legislature appropriately inquires into and may declare the reasons impelling legislative action but the judicial function commands analysis of whether the specific conduct falls within the reach of the statute. . . ." 435 U.S. at 844, 98 S.Ct. at 1544.

See also, Smith v. Daily Mail Publishing Co., 443 U.S. 97, 104, 99 S.Ct. 2667, 2671, 61 L.Ed.2d 399 (1979) (if a newspaper lawfully obtains truthful information about a matter of public significance "then state officials may not constitutionally punish publication of the information, absent a need to further a state interest of the highest order.")

29. 444 U.S. 507, 100 S.Ct. 763, 62 L.Ed.2d 704 (1980), rehearing denied 445 U.S. 972, 100 S.Ct. 1668, 64 L.Ed.2d 250 (1980) (per curiam). Cf. United States v. Marchetti, 466 F.2d 1309 (4th Cir.1972), certiorari denied 409 U.S. 1063, 93 S.Ct. 553, 34 L.Ed.2d 516 (1972).

When Saigon fell on April 30, 1975, Frank W. Snepp III, a senior analyst for the C.I.A., was one of the last Americans evacuated by helicopter from the roof of the American embassy. He was awarded the C.I.A.'s Medal of Merit when he returned to the United States, but he quit the Agency and wrote *Decent Interval* (1977), his version of the final days, which criticized, the C.I.A.'s evacuation planning. See R. Rotunda, Modern Constitutional Law: Cases and Notes 783 (1981); Medow, The First Amendment and the Secrecy State: Snepp v. United States, 130 U.Pa.L.Rev. 775 (1982).

30. 444 U.S. at 515, n. 8, 100 S.Ct. at 767, n. 8.

citizen's right to criticize his government."[31]

Snepp should stand only for the proposition that the government may condition the use of information disclosed to persons who have no constitutional right of access to that information, such as the government's employees: (1) when those persons in fact agree not to discuss or disclose such information; (2) when the governmental interest supporting the condition is significant; (3) when that interest is truly unrelated to the suppression of expression; and (4) when the agreement is a narrow means of promoting governmental interests unrelated to censorship goals.[32] *Snepp* does not give the government the right to condition all government employment on the employee's waiver of free speech rights.

§ 16.18 A Right of Access to the Press

(a) The Fairness Doctrine and the Regulation of the Broadcast Media

The Court, in general, has accepted the argument that the unique nature of electronic media and the present state of the art mean that there is no comparable right of everyone to broadcast on radio and television what one could speak, write, or publish elsewhere.[1] Frequencies presently available for wireless broadcast are finite, and when some are given the privilege to use some bands of the airways, others must be denied. No particular licensee has a First Amendment right to broadcast and his existing privilege may be qualified through reasonable regulation. Therefore, the govern-

ment may subject award of a broadcast license to reasonable regulation with goals, *other than the suppression of ideas.* This regulation is permissible because the Court considers the right of the listeners and viewers to be paramount, not the rights of the broadcasters.

National Broadcasting Co. v. United States[2] first recognized that, because no one has a First Amendment right to a radio license or to monopolize a radio frequency, to deny a station a license on the grounds of public interest is not a denial of free speech. In this action challenging the FCC's regulations of multiple station "chain" broadcasting as an unconstitutional restraint on free speech, the opinion of the Court made much of the fact that broadcasting is a limited media and that an absolute First Amendment right of access is not feasible.

Writing for the Court, Justice Frankfurter emphasized that regulation was essential to develop the full potential of radio[3] and that the overriding interest to be served must be "the interest *of the listening public* in 'the larger and more effective use of radio'."[4] To further the public interest in use of this limited resource, government must allocate use of the airways.

The Fairness Doctrine and *Red Lion*. The extent of the right of the government to control the electronic media was not made clear by *NBC*, but it was brought into sharp focus by *Red Lion Broadcasting Co. v. Federal Communication Commission,*[5] which chal-

---

31. 444 U.S. at 527, 100 S.Ct. at 774 (footnote omitted) (Stevens, J., dissenting, joined by Brennan and Marshall, JJ.).

32. This interpretation is consistent with the approach that the Court took in Seattle Times Co. v. Rhinehart, 467 U.S. 20, 104 S.Ct. 2199, 81 L.Ed.2d 17 (1984), which found that a court order restricting the disclosure of information gained through pretrial discovery should not be examined as a classic prior restraint because it did not constitute government censorship of ideas but only a narrow restriction on the disclosure of information designed to protect a substantial governmental interest in open pretrial discovery and the privacy rights of individuals.

§ 16.18

1. See, 4 Ronald D. Rotunda & John E. Nowak, Treatise on Constitutional Law: Substance and Procedure § 20.18 (West Group, 3d ed. 1999). While the Supreme Court has often commented on the monopoly nature of

broadcasting, e.g., National Broadcasting Co. v. United States, 319 U.S. 190, 226, 63 S.Ct. 997, 1014, 87 L.Ed. 1344 (1943); Red Lion Broadcasting Co. v. FCC, 395 U.S. 367, 376–77, 89 S.Ct. 1794, 1799–1800, 23 L.Ed.2d 371 (1969), commentators have attacked this premise. E.g., Fowler and Brenner, A Marketplace Approach to Broadcast Regulation, 60 Tex.L.Rev. 207 (1982).

2. 319 U.S. 190, 63 S.Ct. 997, 87 L.Ed. 1344 (1943).

3. 319 U.S. at 217–27, 63 S.Ct. at 1009–14.

4. 319 U.S. at 216, 63 S.Ct. at 1009 (emphasis added).

5. 395 U.S. 367, 89 S.Ct. 1794, 23 L.Ed.2d 371 (1969).

See William Van Alstyne, The Möbius Strip of the First Amendment: Perspectives on Red Lion, 29 So.Car.L.Rev. 539 (1978); Krattenmaker & Powe, The Fairness Doctrine Today: A Constitutional Curiosity and an Impossible Dream, 1985 Duke L.J. 151.

lenged the right of the FCC to require broadcasters to follow a "fairness doctrine." The fairness doctrine required broadcasters to allow reply time to the public in cases involving personal attacks or political editorials. The case was the first time that the Supreme Court ruled on a challenge made to the FCC's fairness doctrine on constitutional grounds.

In *Red Lion*, the petitioner operated a radio station under FCC license. During a broadcast on the station the Reverend Billy James Hargis verbally attacked author Fred J. Cook.[6] Cook demanded free reply time and, when the station refused, he filed a formal letter of complaint with the Federal Communications Commission. The Commission deemed the incident a "personal attack" and ordered the station to grant Cook the time requested.

The broadcasters challenged the fairness doctrine and its specific manifestations in the personal attack and political editorial rules on conventional First Amendment grounds. Their argument was based on the contention that the First Amendment protected their desire to use their allotted frequency continuously to broadcast whatever they choose, and to exclude whomever they choose from using that frequency; if no man could be prevented from publishing or saying what he thinks, or from refusing in his speech to give equal weight to the views of his opponents, then broadcasters must have a similar First Amendment right, it was argued.

Red Lion unanimously rejected this argument that broadcasters have a free speech right that is identical to published or spoken speech.[7] The "differences in the characteristics of news media justify differences in the First Amendment standards applied to them;"[8] a limited media does not have an absolute right of free speech:

Where there are substantially more individuals who want to broadcast than there are frequencies to allocate, it is idle to posit an unabridgeable First Amendment right to broadcast comparable to the right of every individual to speak, write, or publish.[9]

The Court reasoned that the fiduciary nature of the relationship between the licensee and the general public put those who hold a license in no more favored position than those to whom licenses are refused. Where the public interest requires, the government could demand that a licensee fulfill his obligation "to present those views and voices which are representative of his community and which would otherwise, by necessity, be barred from the airwaves."[10] Because of this fiduciary role, the rights of the broadcasters must be subordinate to the right of viewers and listeners to suitable access to ideas and information.

It is important to note that while the *Red Lion* case only upheld a Federal Communication Commission rule, parts of the Court's opinion appeared to go much farther and were written as if the fairness doctrine is constitutionally required:

It is the right of the public to receive suitable access to social, political, esthetic, moral, and other ideas and experiences which is crucial here. That right may not constitutionally be abridged either by Congress or by the [Federal Communication Commission].[11]

Yet other portions were more narrow:

[W]e do hold that the Congress and the Commission do not violate the First Amendment when they require a radio or television station to give reply time to answer personal attacks and political editorials.[12]

While the fairness doctrine regulations do not constitute a prior restraint in the classic

---

6. During part of a "Christian Crusade" broadcast series, Hargis discussed Cook's book, Goldwater—Extremist on the Right. Hargis claimed that Cook had been fired from a newspaper for leveling false charges at a city official and had subsequently worked for "one of the most scurrilous publications of the left (The Nation)." 395 U.S. at 371–372, n. 2, 89 S.Ct. at 1797 n. 2.

7. Justice Douglas was not present at oral argument and abstained from taking part in the decision.

8. 395 U.S. at 386–87, 89 S.Ct. at 1805, citing Joseph Burstyn, Inc. v. Wilson, 343 U.S. 495, 503, 72 S.Ct. 777, 781, 96 L.Ed. 1098 (1952).

9. 395 U.S. at 388, 89 S.Ct. at 1806.

10. 395 U.S. at 389, 89 S.Ct. at 1806.

11. 395 U.S. at 390, 89 S.Ct. at 1807.

12. 395 U.S. at 396, 89 S.Ct. at 1810.

sense,[13] they do place a recognizable burden on broadcaster programming discretion. *Red Lion* Court spent little time discussing the competing considerations involved in placing this additional burden. The broadcasters' claims that they would be forced into self-censorship and would substantially curtail coverage of controversial issues under a right-to-reply rule was summarily dismissed as "at best speculative."[14]

The Court did admit that if the rules should result in such a reduction of coverage, then "there will be time enough to reconsider the constitutional implications".[15] While as a practical matter, it should be hard to measure a drop in the amount of free speech caused by the fairness doctrine, the Court's acknowledgment of a reconsideration of the fairness rule in such circumstances supports the position that, in spite of the Court's earlier strong language, the fairness doctrine is not constitutionally required.[16]

No General Right of Access. Notwithstanding the Court's suggestion, the generally broad language of *Red Lion* led some commentators to argued that there is a constitutional right of individual access to the airwaves beyond the scope of the fairness doctrine. They saw this right both in the decision's qualifications on the broadcaster's First Amendment rights and in the FCC's power to compel presentation of individual responses to personal attacks and political editorials.[17] The Demo-

cratic National Committee (DNC) and an anti-war group called the Business Executive's Movement for Vietnam Peace (BEM) tried to establish the existence of a constitutional right of access in *Columbia Broadcasting System v. Democratic National Committee.*[18]

The issue in *CBS* was whether "responsible" groups have a constitutional right under the First Amendment to purchase air time for the presentation of advertisements and programs in order to make known their views about controversial issues of public importance. The two groups claiming such a right, DNC and BEM, were challenging separate decisions of the FCC. In the case of BEM, the FCC had held that a radio station acted within its authority in refusing to air BEM's spot advertisement opposed to the Vietnam conflict; in the case of DNC the FCC had held that as a general matter the DNC did not have a right to purchase time to air its views on controversial public issues.[19]

The Supreme Court upheld the FCC ruling in both cases and said that there is no such right of access under the Constitution. Though the Court divided on several issues, six Justices agreed that the First Amendment would not require the sale of time to responsible groups even if state action was involved.[20] The Court of Appeals below had held that "a flat ban on paid public issue announcements is in violation of the First Amendment, at least when other sorts of paid announcements are

---

13. See, e.g., Near v. Minnesota, 283 U.S. 697, 51 S.Ct. 625, 75 L.Ed. 1357 (1931).

14. 395 U.S. at 393, 89 S.Ct. at 1808.

15. 395 U.S. at 393, 89 S.Ct. at 1808. Assuming that the broadcaster does indeed have a monopoly, the fairness doctrine might not increase the publication of ideas. It penalizes the broadcaster for presenting controversial ideas by requiring him to present all sides of a controversy. Richard Posner, Economic Analysis of Law § 22.3 at 313 (1972).

16. FCC v. WNCN Listeners Guild, 450 U.S. 582, 101 S.Ct. 1266, 67 L.Ed.2d 521 (1981) held that neither federal statutes nor the U.S. Constitution require the Commission to review past or anticipated changes in a station's entertainment programming when it rules on an application for renewal or transfer of a radio broadcast license. The Commission may rely on market forces to promote diversity and serve the public interest in entertainment programming.

17. See, e.g., Marks, Broadcasting and Censorship: First Amendment Theory After Red Lion, 38 Geo. Wash.L.Rev. 974 (1970); J. Barron, Freedom of the Press for Whom? The Right of Access to Mass Media (1973). But see, Jaffe, The Editorial Responsibility of the Broadcaster: Reflections on Fairness and Access, 85 Harv.L.Rev. 768 (1972).

18. 412 U.S. 94, 93 S.Ct. 2080, 36 L.Ed.2d 772 (1973).

19. Business Executive's Movement for Vietnam Peace, 25 F.C.C.2d 242 (1970); Democratic National Committee, 25 F.C.C.2d 216 (1970).

20. The majority opinion consisted of Parts I, II, and IV of Burger, C.J.'s opinion, which Rehnquist, White, Blackmun, and Powell, JJ., joined. The latter three emphasized in their concurring opinion, 412 U.S. at 146–48, 93 S.Ct. at 2108–09, that the state action question had not been decided.

accepted."[21]

The opinion of the Court emphasized that a balancing of the First Amendment interests involved must be carried out within the framework of the regulatory scheme already imposed by Congress on the broadcast media. It noted that Congress had dealt with, and firmly rejected, the argument "that the broadcast facilities should be open on a nonselective basis to all persons wishing to talk about public issues."[22]

Although a Congressional decision cannot be deemed decisive in an issue of constitutional interpretation, the Court was persuaded that the rationale behind this legislative decision was based on sound principles. The *CBS* decision made it clear that any right of access to the electronic media is very limited and that in balancing the competing interests involved "[o]nly when the interests of the public are found to outweigh the private journalistic interests of the broadcasters will government power be asserted within the framework of the [Federal Communications] Act."[23]

The Court concluded that an unlimited right of access would not best serve the public interest. The views of the affluent could still prevail because they could purchase more time to air their views. Valuable broadcast time might be wasted by groups concerned with trivialities. The Court was reluctant to allow full access by individuals who had no responsibilities or accountability to act in the public interest; complete access rights might exchange "public trustee" broadcasting for "a system of self-appointed editorial commentators."[24] The fairness doctrine was not thought to be applicable

to editorial advertisements and the BEM and DNC's argument on this basis was inappropriate.[25]

In a later case the Court held that the Communications Act not only does not mandate any claimed right of access,[26] but also that neither that Act nor the Constitution authorizes or permits the FCC to require broadcasters to extend a range of public access. The majority relied on the fact that section 3(h) of the Act stipulates that broadcasters shall not be treated as common carriers; and it distinguished the fairness doctrine because that rule contemplates a wide range of licensee discretion and does not mandate access to anyone.

The State Action Question. The Court in *CBS* strongly split on the question of whether state action was involved but the decision is of little precedential value on this issue. Chief Justice Burger, joined by Stewart and Rehnquist, emphasized that the government was not a "partner" nor in a "symbiotic relationship" with the licensee;[27] they saw no governmental action involved here that would invoke the proscriptions of the First Amendment. Justices White, Blackmun and Powell, on the other hand, emphasized in their concurring opinions that the case had been decided on other grounds and that the Court did not reach the state action issue.[28] Justice Douglas, in his concurrence, argued that "the activities of licensees of the government operating in the public domain are governmental actions, so far as constitutional duties and responsibilities are concerned,"[29] but admitted that this view "has not been accepted."[30] Justice Brennan, joined by Marshall, dissented and argued that

---

21. BEM v. FCC, 450 F.2d 642 (D.C.Cir.1971).

22. 412 U.S. at 105, 93 S.Ct. at 2088.

23. 412 U.S. at 110, 93 S.Ct. at 2090.

24. 412 U.S. at 125, 93 S.Ct. at 2098.

25. 412 U.S. at 124–26, 93 S.Ct. at 2097–98. The Court did not clearly discuss this issue, although some lower courts had already developed a theory that commercial advertising is subject to the fairness doctrine. See, e.g., Friends of Earth v. FCC, 449 F.2d 1164 (D.C.Cir.1971); Retail Store Employees Union v. FCC, 436 F.2d 248 (D.C.Cir.1970).

26. FCC v. Midwest Video Corp., 440 U.S. 689, 705 n. 14, 99 S.Ct. 1435, 1444 n. 14, 59 L.Ed.2d 692 (1979). The

Court reserved the question whether it would be constitutional for Congress to give the FCC the power to treat broadcasters as common carriers. Cf. FCC v. WNCN Listeners Guild, 450 U.S. 582, 603–04, 101 S.Ct. 1266, 1279, 67 L.Ed.2d 521 (1981) (FCC may rely on market forces to promote diversity in radio entertainment formats).

27. 412 U.S. at 119, 93 S.Ct. at 2094.

28. 412 U.S. at 146–148, 93 S.Ct. at 2108–09.

29. 412 U.S. at 150, 93 S.Ct. at 2110.

30. 412 U.S. at 150, 93 S.Ct. at 2110. Because of this admission, Douglas argued that broadcasters are like newspapers and should be treated no differently. Stewart said that Douglas' views "closely approach" his own. 412 U.S. at 132, 93 S.Ct. at 2101.

there was governmental action and that it was improper to rely on the fairness doctrine as the sole means of presenting controversial ideas; rather citizens should be permitted some opportunity to speak directly for themselves.[31]

Antitrust Considerations, Divestiture, and Free Speech. In *FCC v. National Citizens Committee for Broadcasting*,[32] the Court held that the FCC, consistent with the First Amendment, may enact a rule prospectively barring the common ownership of a radio or television station and a daily newspaper located in the same community, and retroactively requiring divestiture of such co-located newspaper-broadcast combinations in the "most egregious" cases. Such regulations further both antitrust and First Amendment goals and do not violate the First Amendment rights of newspapers because—given the physical limitations of the broadcast spectrum—there is no unabridgeable First Amendment right to broadcast comparable to the right of persons to speak, write, or publish.

The Court acknowledged that the government may not restrict the speech of some in order to enhance the relative voice of others, but argued that this general rule does not apply to the broadcasting media, which poses unique problems justifying special regulations. These FCC regulations are not content related, nor do they unfairly single out newspaper owners, since owners of radio stations, television stations, and newspapers are, by the new rule, treated alike in their ability to acquire licenses for co-located broadcast stations.

The Right of Access of Political Candidates. In *CBS, Inc. v. FCC*[33] the Court upheld, as consistent with the First Amendment, the power granted to the FCC under 47

U.S.C.A. § 312(a)(7). This law offered legally qualified candidates for federal elective office an affirmative, promptly enforceable right of reasonable access, to purchase broadcast time without reference to whether an opponent has secured time. Violation of this section authorizes the FCC to revoke a broadcaster's license. The Court emphasized that it was not approving any "*general* right of access to the media."[34] But section 312(a)(7) is constitutional and properly balances the First Amendment rights of the public, the broadcasters, and the candidates because it "creates a *limited* right to 'reasonable' access that pertains only to legally qualified federal candidates and may be invoked by them only for the purpose of advancing their candidacies once a campaign has commenced."[35]

Note that in *CBS, Inc. v. Democratic National Committee*[36] the Court refused to create a right of access. In *CBS, Inc. v. FCC*, on the other hand, the Court upheld the constitutionality of a carefully drawn statute providing for limited access. In both cases the Court was deferring to the judgment of Congress and the FCC in their regulation of the broadcast media. Given the complexity of this area it is not unusual that the Court relies so heavily on congressional judgment and administrative expertise.[37]

That was the case in *Arkansas Educational Television Commission v. Forbes*.[38] This case involved a state-owned public television broadcaster (AETC), which sponsored a debate between the two major party candidates for the 1992 election in the Third Congressional District in Arkansas. AETC denied Ralph P. Forbes, a third-party candidate with little popular support, permission to participate in the televised debate. Forbes filed suit claiming that the First Amendment gave him a right to

---

31. 412 U.S. at 180, 189–90, 93 S.Ct. at 2130 (Brennan, J., dissenting).

32. 436 U.S. 775, 98 S.Ct. 2096, 56 L.Ed.2d 697 (1978).

33. 453 U.S. 367, 101 S.Ct. 2813, 69 L.Ed.2d 706 (1981).

34. 453 U.S. at 396, 101 S.Ct. at 2830 (emphasis in original).

35. 453 U.S. at 396, 101 S.Ct. at 2830 (emphasis in original).

36. 412 U.S. 94, 93 S.Ct. 2080, 36 L.Ed.2d 772 (1973).

37. Cf. Radio Corp. of America v. United States, 341 U.S. 412, 420, 71 S.Ct. 806, 810, 95 L.Ed. 1062 (1951): "[C]ourts should not overrule an administrative decision merely because they disagree with its wisdom."

38. 523 U.S. 666, 118 S.Ct. 1633, 140 L.Ed.2d 875 (1998). See John E. Nowak, First Amendment Values and Government Participation in the Marketplace Fifty Years after the Hutchins Report, 3 Communication Law & Policy 275 (1998).

participate in the debate. Kennedy, J., for the Court, held (six to three) that the televised debate was a nonpublic forum from which the broadcaster could exclude a candidate in the reasonable, viewpoint-neutral exercise of its journalistic discretion. The jury made express findings that AETC's decision to exclude Forbes had not been influenced by political pressure or by disagreement with his views.

In general, Kennedy explained, the public forum doctrine[39] should not be transplanted to public television broadcasting because any broad right of access is antithetical to the discretion that stations must exercise to fulfill their journalistic and statutory obligations. "As a general rule, the nature of editorial discretion counsels against subjecting broadcasters to claims of viewpoint discrimination. [E]ven principled exclusions rooted in sound journalistic judgment can often be characterized as viewpoint-based."[40] Just like universities select one commencement speaker, a broadcaster will, by nature, choose some viewpoints over others. If the judiciary required, defined, and approved, pre-established criteria for access, it would risk implicating the courts in judgments that should be left to the exercise of journalistic discretion.[41]

The Court said that the First Amendment does not, of its own force, impose neutral rules for access to public broadcasting. However, this "is not to say that the First Amendment would bar the legislative imposition of neutral rules for access to public broadcasting."[42] The Court, perhaps suggesting that the legislature take the initiative, explained that, as a general matter, public broadcasting should not be scrutinized under the public forum doctrine for two reasons. First, unlike a political talk show (where the host can express partisan ideas and limit discussion to them), a debate is designed to be a forum for the political speech

of the candidates. Second, candidate debates are "of exceptional significance in the electoral process."

The candidate debate was a nonpublic forum, from which AETC could exclude Forbes in the reasonable, viewpoint-neutral exercise of its journalistic discretion. Here, the debate was not an "open-microphone" format. The AETC reserved eligibility for participation to candidates in the Third Congressional District, and then "made candidate-by-candidate determinations" as to which candidates could participate. Under the First Amendment, "the exclusion of a speaker from a nonpublic forum must not be based on the speaker's viewpoint and must otherwise be reasonable in light of the purpose of the property." AETC met these requirements.

Constitutional issues in the area of electronic media such as radio and television have presented special problems to the courts because of the unique influence of the form of communication. While *Red Lion* emphasized that the monopoly nature arises from "inherent" technological restraints on these media, later developments have undercut both the factual assumption of a necessary monopoly, and the assumption that regulation, rather than more competition, is the best method to regulate the electronic media.

Censorship and "Adult" Language. The First Amendment rights of free speech in a broadcasting context raise questions not only of access but also of censorship. In *FCC v. Pacifica Foundation*[43] a sharply divided Court upheld the power of the FCC to regulate "adult speech" over the radio air waves, at least in some limited circumstances. The Court held that the FCC does have statutory and constitutional power to regulate a radio broadcast that is "indecent" but not "obscene" in

---

39. On the question of the Public Forum, see § 20.45 to 20.47, infra.

40. 523 U.S. at 673, 118 S.Ct. at 1639.

41. Stevens, J., joined by Souter & Ginsburg, JJ., dissented. These justices agreed that a state-owned television network does not have the obligation to allow every candidate access to the political debates that it sponsors, but that AETC acted unconstitutionally because this particular decision was ad hoc, and—whether it was based on

"newsworthiness," as argued in the Supreme Court, or "political viability," as argued in the Court of Appeals—it was made by the staff without "pre-established, objective criteria."

42. 523 U.S. at 675, 118 S.Ct. at 1640.

43. 438 U.S. 726, 98 S.Ct. 3026, 57 L.Ed.2d 1073 (1978), rehearing denied 439 U.S. 883, 99 S.Ct. 227, 58 L.Ed.2d 198 (1978).

the constitutional sense and also does not constitute "fighting words" in the constitutional sense.[44]

In the particular case a radio station broadcast for nearly 12 minutes a record of a George Carlin humorous monologue. This broadcast occurred in the early afternoon when the Court assumed that children were likely to be in the audience. (The Court did not explain why it did not assume that children old enough to understand the Carlin monologue were more likely to be in school in the early afternoon.). During this monologue Carlin repeatedly used various words[45] referring to sexual and excretory activities and organs, and mocked middle class attitudes toward them.

The FCC, after having received one complaint, from a man who had heard the broadcast with his son on the car radio, issued a "Declaratory Order" against Pacifica. While the FCC did not impose formal sanctions it did add the complaint to the station's license file and noted that, if subsequent complaints were received, the FCC would then decide whether to utilize any of the sanctions it has, ranging from issuing a cease and desist order or imposing a fine, to revoking the station's license.

First, the Justices considered the statutory authority of the FCC to take such actions. One statutory provision forbids the FCC from en-

gaging in "censorship;"[46] another prohibits "obscene, indecent, or profane" broadcasts.[47] Five members of the Court held that the censorship language only prohibits the Commission from engaging in prior censorship. While the Commission cannot excise material in advance, it can review the content of completed broadcasts in fulfilling its regulatory duties.[48] Second, the majority held that the second statutory provision prohibits not only constitutionally "obscene" language but also "indecent" language, defined as "nonconformance with accepted standards of morality."[49]

Next the Court had to decide if the statute as construed by the majority was constitutional. Five members agreed that broadcasting receives "the most limited" free speech protections of all forms of communication because it is "a uniquely pervasive presence in the lives of all Americans" and "is uniquely accessible to children, even those too young to read."[50] But they could not agree any further on the constitutional rationale for their holding.

Justice Stevens, joined by Chief Justice Burger and Justice Rehnquist, thought that "indecency is largely a function of context ..." and that "a broadcast of patently offensive words dealing with sex and excretion may be regulated because of its content."[51]

---

44. Dial–a–Porn. Sable Communications of California, Inc. v. FCC, 492 U.S. 115, 109 S.Ct. 2829, 106 L.Ed.2d 93 (1989) held that Congress can constitutionally impose an outright ban on "obscene" interstate, pre-recorded, commercial telephone messages ("dial-a-porn"). The First Amendment does not protect obscenity. However, the Court invalidated the portion of the statute at issue that imposed an outright ban, regardless of age, on "indecent" dial-a-porn messages. Sexual expression that is not obscene is entitled to First Amendment protection even though it is indecent. The Government does have a compelling interest in protecting minors, but the law at issue was not narrowly tailored for that purpose. Congress could have used credit card, access code, and scrambling rules to keep indecent dial-a-porn out of the reach of minors. The Court carefully distinguished *Pacifica* as "an emphatically narrow holding" that relied on the "unique" aspects of broadcasting not involved in this case, and further relied on the "captive" or unwilling audience, a fact pattern also inapplicable here.

45. The seven words "that you can't say" were: "shit, piss, fuck, cunt, cocksucker, motherfucker, and tits." Later Carlin added "three more words ... you could never say on television, and they were fart, turd and twat...." 438 U.S. at 751, 755, 98 S.Ct. at 3041, 3043 (appendix).

The entire monologue is reprinted in an appendix to the opinion.

46. 47 U.S.C.A. § 326.

47. 18 U.S.C.A. § 1464.

48. 438 U.S. at 735, 98 S.Ct. at 3033. This five person majority also said: "Respect for that [congressional] intent requires that the censorship language be read as inapplicable to the prohibition on broadcasting obscene, indecent, or profane language." 438 U.S. at 738, 98 S.Ct. at 3034. This language, however, would appear to allow even prior censorship of indecent language. Since the rationale of the opinion does not support this broad language, the majority should not be considered to have embraced it.

49. 438 U.S. at 439–40, 98 S.Ct. at 3035 (footnote omitted).

50. 438 U.S. at 749, 98 S.Ct. at 3040.

51. 438 U.S. at 743, 98 S.Ct. at 3037. (Separate Opinion of Stevens, J., joined by Burger, C.J., and Rehnquist, J.). Another case where Justice Stevens has propounded his viewpoint (also not accepted by a majority of the Court) that there can be valid regulations on speech based on the *content* of the communication in his separate opinion in Young v. American Mini Theatres, 427 U.S. 50, 52,

Justice Powell, joined by Blackmun, wrote a separate opinion. They specifically rejected Stevens' view that the Court is free to decide "on the basis of its content which speech protected by the First Amendment is most valuable.... The result turns instead on the unique characteristics of the broadcast media, combined with society's right to protect its children from speech generally agreed to be inappropriate for their years, and with the interest of unwilling adults in not being assaulted by such offensive speech in their homes."[52]

Justices Stewart and White dissented on statutory grounds and did not read the constitutional issues.[53] Justice Brennan, joined by Justice Marshall, did reach the constitutional issues and strongly dissented. They argued that when an individual turns to a radio station or any transmission broadcast to the public at large, there is no fundamental privacy interest implicated. The listener has, by tuning in, decided to take part in an on-going public discussion. Neither, they believed, is the FCC regulation justified by the need to protect children. While parents have the right to make certain decisions for their children, it is the parents and not the Government who are to make these decisions: "As surprising as it may be to individual members of the Court, some parents may actually find Mr. Carlin's unabashed attitude towards the seven 'dirty words' healthy, and deem it desirable to expose their children to the manner in which Mr. Carlin defuses the taboo surrounding the

words."[54] Moreover, the Government, in its efforts to protect children, was denying to adults the right to listen to language that was not constitutionally obscene even as to children. Justice Brennan accused the majority of attempting "to unstitch the warp and woof of First Amendment law...."; and he added, the majority's "fragile sensibilities" were the result of "an acute ethnocentric myopia."[55]

The five member majority emphasized that their decision was very narrow, not involving a two-way radio conversation, an Elizabethan comedy, a closed-circuit transmission, or an occasional expletive. The time of day and the content of the program in which the language is used may also be relevant, as well as the type and amount of punishment imposed.[56] Yet the three member plurality's willingness to allow government regulation of content, so long as the regulation appears to these Justices to promote reasonable ends—in this case, the end of prohibiting "nonconformance" with accepted standards of morality—is a disquieting and a significant departure from traditional First Amendment theory, which normally subjects any type of content regulation to very careful and principled judicial review.

In other types of speech, not involving broadcasting, the Court has been much more protective of the First Amendment. When the Court allowed the prohibition of obscenity, it found that such speech when taken as a whole, must lack any serious literary, artistic, political, or scientific value.[57] It did not judge some

96 S.Ct. 2440, 2443–44, 49 L.Ed.2d 310 (1976), rehearing denied 429 U.S. 873, 97 S.Ct. 191, 50 L.Ed.2d 155 (1976).

52. 438 U.S. at 761–762, 98 S.Ct. at 3051 (Powell, J., joined by Blackmun, J., concurring).

53. The four in dissent argued that "indecent" means no more than "obscene" in the constitutional sense. A related federal statute, the dissent noted, forbade the mailing of every "obscene, ... indecent, ... or vile article," and the Court had previously construed that language as only referring to obscenity in the constitutional sense. Since Carlin's monologue was conceded to be not obscene, the dissent argued that the FCC had no statutory grounds to regulate it. See 438 U.S. at 779–780, 98 S.Ct. at 3056 (Stewart, J., dissenting, joined by Brennan, White, & Marshall, JJ.).

54. 438 U.S. at 770, 98 S.Ct. at 3051.

55. 438 U.S. at 775, 98 S.Ct. at 3054. Brennan feared that the majority's various rationales could justify banning

from FCC regulated media the Nixon tapes and important literary works, including the Bible, all of which uses one or more of the indecent words of the Carlin monologue. See 438 U.S. at 770–771, & n. 5, 98 S.Ct. at 3051–52 & n. 5 (footnote 5 of Brennan's dissent quotes passages from the Bible using several of Carlin's indecent words).

The majority thought such examples to be distinguishable: "Even a prime time recitation of Chaucer's Miller's Tale would not be likely to command the attention of many children who are both old enough to understand and young enough to be adversely affected by passages such as, 'And prively he caughte hir by the queynte.' G. Chaucer, The Miller's Tale, 1. 3276 (c. 1386)." 438 U.S. at 750, n. 29, 98 S.Ct. at 3041 n. 29.

56. 438 U.S. at 750, 98 S.Ct. at 3041.

57. Note also that the zoning of adult movies allowed in Young v. American Mini Theatres, 427 U.S. 50, 96 S.Ct. 2440, 49 L.Ed.2d 310 (1976), involved valid goals other

types of obscene speech to be more worthy of protection than other types, nor find that obscenity in an Elizabethan comedy is permissible but obscenity in a modern comedy is not. Rather it attempted to fashion a principled means of distinguishing a certain type of speech. But Justice Stevens would prohibit the use of a word in the Carlin monologue though he would allow the same word to be used in a reading of Chaucer's Miller's Tale,[58] or an Elizabethan comedy,[59] apparently because he feels that the latter types of speech are more valuable than the Carlin satire. Similarly, he would allow the same words to be used if he thought the monologue had political content.[60]

The four member dissent, as well as Justices Powell and Blackmun in their concurring opinion, specifically avoided a theory that the degree of protection of speech varies with the ad hoc view of five members of the Court as to its social value, but the latter two Justices did agree that the FCC action was constitutional. With this decision, then, one is left in doubt as to the strictness with which the Court will review content regulation—at least as regards the electronic media—in the future.

It appears that the permissibility of this type of regulation may depend on the personal notions of at least five Justices concerning the worth of the regulated speech. As Justice Stevens concluded in a portion of his opinion joined by four Justices:

> We simply hold that when the Commission finds that a pig has entered the parlor [instead of the barnyard], the exercise of its regulatory power does not depend on proof that the pig is obscene.[61]

This "pig in the parlor" test will not be too helpful to lower courts.

Censorship and Bans on Editorials by Public Broadcast Stations. The concept of frequency scarcity and the special impact of the electronic media on listeners or viewers have provided the basis for judicial approval of government regulation of electronic media beyond the permissible scope of regulatory control of nonbroadcast media. However, the Supreme Court should not adopt the position of total deference to the Congress or its executive agencies in the regulation of the electronic media lest it allow those branches of government to impair First Amendment values.

In *Federal Communications Commission v. League of Women Voters*[62] the Court (five to four vote) invalidated a section of the Public Broadcasting Act that forbade any nonprofit educational broadcasting station that receives a grant from the Corporation for Public Broadcasting to engage in editorializing or endorsing candidates for political office. Writing for the majority, Justice Brennan concluded that restrictions on the electronic media have been upheld only when the restriction is narrowly tailored to further a substantial governmental interest, "such as ensuring adequate and balanced coverage of public issues."[63] This standard had been developed in earlier cases on the basis of several fundamental principles: that Congress, acting pursuant to its commerce clause power, has the right to regulate the use of this scarce national resource; that in the exercise of this power Congress could assure that the public received a balanced presentation of information; and that the First Amendment interest of listeners and broadcasters in broadcast stations performing independent communicative activity must shape

than the regulation of speech, 427 U.S. at 71 n. 34, 96 S.Ct. at 2453 n. 34 (Stevens, J.) & 427 U.S. at 80, 96 S.Ct. at 2457 (Powell, J.). See also 438 U.S. at 774, 98 S.Ct. at 3053 (Brennan, J., dissenting).

58. See 438 U.S. at 775, 98 S.Ct. at 3054.

59. 438 U.S. at 770–71 & n. 5, 98 S.Ct. at 3051–52 & n. 5.

60. 438 U.S. at 746, 98 S.Ct. at 3038–39.

61. 438 U.S. at 750–51, 98 S.Ct. at 3041.

62. 468 U.S. 364, 104 S.Ct. 3106, 82 L.Ed.2d 278 (1984).

63. 468 U.S. at 380, 104 S.Ct. at 3118. The Court found that even the decision in FCC v. Pacifica Foundation, 438 U.S. 726, 98 S.Ct. 3026, 57 L.Ed.2d 1073 (1978), rehearing denied 439 U.S. 883, 99 S.Ct. 227, 58 L.Ed.2d 198 (1978), discussed above, was consistent with this standard in that the reduction of the risks of unwilling listeners being offended by indecent language and the access to that material by children were of sufficient importance to justify the regulation. 468 U.S. at 379–81 n. 13, 104 S.Ct. at 3117–18 n. 13.

Congress' exercise of its regulatory powers.[64]

The dissenting Justices in *League of Women Voters* pointed out that the statute at issue appeared to further First Amendment values in that the restriction on editorializing was designed to achieve the twin goals of (1) avoiding a station's tailoring of editorials or endorsements to gain favor with the governmental entities that funded them, and (2) reducing the government's role in putting forth or funding messages in the political marketplace.[65] The majority, however, found the restriction to be invalid because it suppressed a form of speech that lies at the heart of First Amendment protection; the restriction banned speech related to self-governance issues solely because of the content of the suppressed speech. Even though the statute banned all editorials or endorsements, rather than merely those that objected to the official views of the government or the views held by incumbent office holders, this statute was still censorial because it prohibited discussion of an entire topic and thereby shaped and reduced the agenda for public debate.[66]

The statute at issue in *League of Women Voters* was invalid under Justice Brennan's test because it was not narrowly tailored to further the substantial interest in presenting balanced information to the public. The interest in providing balanced coverage could be advanced by other less, restrictive means such as the requirement that opposing viewpoints be broadcast free of charge. Indeed, the majority found that the structure of the system for financing public broadcasting already operated to insulate local stations from governmental interference. The majority did agree with the dissenters that Congress could avoid funding that portion of a noncommercial educational broadcasting station's budget that was used for editorials or candidate endorsements. Although Congress could refuse to fund speech activities of this type, it could not punish a station that engaged in editorializing by terminating all federal funding for the station.[67]

THE REGULATION OF CABLE TELEVISION

The Court has been hesitate to make firm rules regarding the intersection between the First Amendment and cable television. This hesitancy is seen in a complex series of decisions, discussed below.

Monopoly Restitution. In *City of Los Angeles v. Preferred Communications, Inc.*[68] the Court rejected a city's claim that its refusal to grant a franchise to a cable television company raised no First Amendment concerns. The applicant had not participated in an auction for a single franchise, but the city did not dispute that there was excess physical capacity that would allow more than one cable television franchise. The Court readily concluded that the cable operator's claims raised valid First Amendment issues but also decided that they could not be resolved solely on the basis of the complaint, so it remanded and directed the trial court to balance the First Amendment values against competing societal interests, after a full development of the disputed issues. Beyond that, *Preferred Communications* offered no hint of the ultimate resolution of the controversy except to emphasize that the city ordinance will not be saved merely because it is rational.

Economic Regulations of Cable. In contrast, *FCC v. Beach Communications, Inc.*[69] the Court applied the rational basis test to a rule that it held a mere economic regulation, even though it affected the cable television

---

64. 468 U.S. at 377, 104 S.Ct. at 3116.

65. 468 U.S. 364, 402, 104 S.Ct. 3106, 3129, 82 L.Ed.2d 278, 306 (1984) (Rehnquist, J., dissenting, joined by Burger, C.J., and White, J.); 468 U.S. at 408, 104 S.Ct. at 3132, 82 L.Ed.2d at 310 (opinion of White, J.); 468 U.S. at 410, 104 S.Ct. at 3133, 82 L.Ed.2d at 310 (Stevens, J., dissenting).

66. 468 U.S. at 385, 104 S.Ct. at 3120, 82 L.Ed.2d at 294. The Court here referred to its opinion in Consolidated Edison Co. v. Public Service Commission, 447 U.S. 530, 100 S.Ct. 2326, 65 L.Ed.2d 319 (1980), prohibiting Public

Service Commission from banning all advertising for certain products or power uses.

67. 468 U.S. at 399, 104 S.Ct. at 3127, 82 L.Ed.2d at 303.

68. 476 U.S. 488, 106 S.Ct. 2034, 90 L.Ed.2d 480 (1986).

69. 508 U.S. 307, 113 S.Ct. 2096, 124 L.Ed.2d 211 (1993). Thomas, J., wrote the opinion for the Court. There were no dissents, but Stevens, J., did file an opinion concurring in the judgment

industry. When Congress regulated the cable television industry, it drew a distinction between facilities that serve separately owned and managed buildings versus those that serve one or more buildings under common ownership or management. The statute exempted from regulations those cable facilities that fell in the latter category, so long as they provided services without using the public rights-of-way. The District of Columbia Circuit held that this distinction was irrational and violated the implied equal protection component of the Fifth Amendment. The Supreme Court, without dissent, reversed.

In this case, it is "plausible," said the Court, for Congress to assume that systems under common ownership would typically be limited in size or would share some other attribute such that regulations were not needed. Second, the statutory distinction may reflect a concern over the potential for effective monopoly power: the first operator of a satellite master antenna television system to gain a foothold by installing a dish on one building in a block of separately owned buildings would have significant cost advantages in competing for the remaining subscribers, because it could connect additional buildings for the cost of a length of cable while its competitors would have to recover the cost of their own satellite facilities. As economic regulation it is entirely irrelevant for constitutional purposes whether the legislature was actually motivated by the conceived reason for the challenged distinction.

The "Must–Carry Provisions" of Cable Regulation. In *Turner Broadcasting System, Inc. v. FCC*,[70] the Court continued its tentative exploration of the free speech rights of cable operators in light of the developing technology.

In 1992, Congress enacted the Cable Television and Consumer Protection and Competition Act. Sections 4 and 5 required cable television systems to devote a portion of their channels to the transmission of local broadcast stations, in an effort, according to the sponsors of the legislation, to aid the competitive viability of broadcast television. In the view of the Court, the law regulated cable speech in two major ways: first, it reduced the number of channels over which the cable operators exercised unfettered control; and, second, it made it more difficult for cable programmers to compete for carriage on the limited number of channels remaining.

Cable operators sued, claiming that these "must-carry" provisions violated the First Amendment. The three–judge district court, over dissent, granted summary judgment for the United States, but Justice Kennedy, for the Court, vacated that judgment and remanded for further proceedings.

First, the *Turner* Court ruled that it should not use the less rigorous standard of review reserved for broadcast regulation because the problems of scarcity of broadcast frequencies and signal interference do not apply in the context of cable; "soon there may be no practical limitation on the number of speakers who may use the cable medium."[71] Second, the Court would not apply strict scrutiny to the must-carry rules because they are content-neutral: the must-carry rules, on their face, impose burdens and confer benefits without reference to the content of speech.

Justice Kennedy conceded that, unlike cable programming, "broadcast programming, is subject to certain limited content restraints

---

70. 512 U.S. 622, 114 S.Ct. 2445, 129 L.Ed.2d 497 (1994).

71. 512 U.S. at 639, 114 S.Ct. at 2457. Contrast Hurley v. Irish–American Gay Lesbian and Bisexual Group of Boston, 515 U.S. 557, 115 S.Ct. 2338, 132 L.Ed.2d 487 (1995). In *Turner*, the Court treated cable television as a conduit for broadcast signals. There was little risk that the cable viewers would assume that the broadcast stations carried on a cable system convey ideas or messages that the cable operator necessarily endorsed. In contrast, people do not assume that parades and demonstrations are neutrally presented by the organizers of the parade or demonstration. Thus, the *Hurley* Court ruled, unanimous-

ly, that a state may not constitutionally require private individuals who organize a parade to include among the marchers a group imparting a message that the parade organizers do not wish to convey. In this particular case, the group advocated gay rights and gay solidarity.

Boy Scouts of America v. Dale, 530 U.S. 640, 120 S.Ct. 2446, 147 L.Ed.2d 554 (2000), came to a similar conclusion, but the Court split 5 to 4. The majority held that applying New Jersey's public accommodations law to require the Boy Scouts to admit plaintiff, a publicly declared homosexual, violated Boy Scouts' First Amendment right of expressive association.

imposed by statute and FCC regulations."[72] But, he rejected the argument that the preference for broadcast stations "*automatically* entails content requirements."[73] In his view, the congressional purpose was to ensure that broadcast television will retain a large enough potential audience to earn necessary advertising revenue, not to control content: "Congress' overriding objective in enacting must-carry was not to favor programming of a particular subject matter, viewpoint, or format, but rather to preserve access to free television programming for the 40 percent of Americans without cable."[74]

The Court then announced that it should use the intermediate level of scrutiny that applies to content-neutral restrictions that impose an incidental burden on speech. The government need not impose the least restrictive means of advancing its interests, but the regulation must promote "a substantial government interest that would be achieved less effectively absent the regulation."[75]

In a portion of Justice Kennedy's opinion that was a plurality opinion and not an opinion of the Court, Justice Kennedy emphasized that on remand the government "must demonstrate that the recited harms are real, not merely conjectural, and that the regulation will in fact alleviate these harms in a direct and material way."[76] The government must show, for example, that the economic health of local broadcasting is in genuine jeopardy and in need of the protection afforded by "must-carry." While Congress' predictive judgments

are entitled to "substantial deference," they are not "insulated from meaningful review altogether."[77] The dissent was more protective of the free speech and would have held the regulations content-based and invalid.[78]

Three years later, in *Turner Broadcasting System, Inc. v. FCC,*[79] Justice Kennedy again spoke for the Court. He upheld the "must-carry" provisions [sections 4 and 5] of the Cable Television Consumer Protection and Competition Act of 1992. Based on the more full factual record that had been developed on remand, the Court affirmed the majority of the three-judge district court. Kennedy concluded that the congressional interests in preserving free, over-the-air television broadcasts, promoting numerous sources to broadcast information, and promoting fair competition in the television broadcasting market justified the congressional decision to impose the must-carry rules. The factual record—in the view of the majority but not the dissent—supported the congressional judgment that cable systems would refuse to carry a significant number of broadcast stations in the absence of the must-carry rules, and that the local broadcast stations that were not carried would be at serious risk of financial difficulty.

The Court concluded that the must-carry provisions, in this context, met the intermediate scrutiny under the First Amendment. That is, the regulations were content-neutral and advanced important governmental interests in a direct and effective way; they where unrelat-

---

72. 512 U.S. at 649, 114 S.Ct. at 2462 (footnote 7 omitted, giving examples, such as the requirement that broadcasters serve "educational and informational needs of children;" offer reasonable access to candidates for federal elective office; restrict "indecent programming;" and air programs that serve "the public interest, convenience or necessity").

73. 512 U.S. at 649, 114 S.Ct. at 2462 (emphasis in original).

74. 512 U.S. at 646, 114 S.Ct. at 2461.

75. 512 U.S. at 662, 114 S.Ct. at 2469.

76. 512 U.S. at 662, 114 S.Ct. at 2470 (plurality opinion).

77. 512 U.S. at 666, 114 S.Ct. at 2471 (plurality opinion).

78. 512 U.S. at 681–83, 114 S.Ct. at 2479 (O'Connor, J., concurring in part and dissenting in part, and joined, as to this part of her opinion, by Scalia, Ginsburg, & Thomas,

JJ.); 512 U.S. at 684, 114 S.Ct. at 2481 (Ginsburg, J., concurring in part and dissenting in part) calling the regulations "an unwarranted content-based preference" that "hypothesizes a risk to local stations that remains imaginary."

79. 520 U.S. 180, 117 S.Ct. 1174, 137 L.Ed.2d 369 (1997). Kennedy, J., delivered an opinion of the Court for all except a portion of Part II–A–1. Justice Breyer did not join Part II–A–1 insofar as it relied on an anticompetitiveness rationale to support the must-carry rules. The Kennedy plurality in this portion of the opinion concluded that the record below supported the Congressional conclusion that the must-carry rules were justified by a real threat to local broadcasting's economic well-being. Stevens, J., concurred and filed an opinion; Breyer, J., concurred in part and filed an opinion; O'Connor, J., joined by Scalia, Thomas, & Ginsburg, JJ., filed a vigorous dissent.

ed to the suppression of free speech, and they did not burden substantially more speech than was necessary to further these governmental interests.

Cable Television and the Regulation of Sexually Oriented Material. The fluidity of this area of the law is illustrated by *Denver Area Educational Telecommunications Consortium, Inc. v. FCC.*[80] In this case, the Court considered challenges to three sections of the 1992 Cable Act designed to regulate cable television broadcasting of "patently offensive" sex-related material. The very fragmented Court invalidated two provisions and upheld one provision. Justice Breyer announced the judgment of the Court and delivered the opinion of the Court with respect to Part III.[81]

First the Justices turned their attention to the regulation of *leased cable channels*. A leased cable channel is a channel that the relevant federal law required a cable system operator to reserve for commercial lease by unaffiliated third parties.

Section 10(b) of the law in question required cable system operators to segregate "patently offensive" sex-related material that appears on leased channels (but not on other channels) to a separate channel, to block that channel, to unblock that channel within 30 days of a subscriber's written request, and to re-block it within 30 days of a subscriber's written request. Justice Breyer, for the Court, invalidated this provision under the First Amendment. The delays of up to 30 days would require subscribers to engage in significant advanced planning, and the writing would adversely affect viewers who would fear for their reputations if the list were inadvertently made public. These restrictions were not the "least restrictive alternative" nor "narrowly tailored" to protect children. Congress used less restrictive means to deal with non-leased cable channels, and the record of-

fered no explanation for the difference in treatment. For example, the Court wondered why blocking alone—without written access-requests—adequately protected children from exposure to regular sex-dedicated channels, but could not adequately protect those same children from programming on similarly sex-dedicated channels that are leased.

Section 10(a) of the law permitted (but did not require) cable system operators to prohibit "patently offensive" or "indecent" programming transmitted over leased channels. Between 1984 and 1992, other laws prohibited cable system operators from exercising editorial control. Breyer (joined only by Stevens, O'Connor, and Souter) upheld this provision, in a ruling described as narrow. This industry is dynamic, and, Breyer argued, the Court should not impose "a rigid single standard, good now and for all future media and purposes," which may "straightjacket" the government's ability to respond to serious problems.

Section 10(c) permitted a cable operator to prevent transmission of "patently offensive" programming on public access channels. The law defined a *public access channel* as channel capacity that cable operators agreed to reserve for public, governmental, and educational access as part of the consideration that municipalities obtained in exchange for awarding a cable franchise. Breyer (joined only by Stevens and Souter) ruled that this section, unlike section 10(a), is unconstitutional. Cable operators did not historically exercise editorial control over these channels, and therefore section 10(c), unlike section 10(a), "does not restore to cable operators editorial rights that they once had, and the countervailing First Amendment interest is nonexistent, or at least diminished." In addition, that section 10(c) was less necessary to protect children because public

---

80. 518 U.S. 727, 116 S.Ct. 2374, 135 L.Ed.2d 888 (1996). Ronald D. Rotunda, Media Accountability In Light of the First Amendment, 21 Social Philosophy & Policy 269 (Cambridge University Press, No. 2, 2004).

81. Justices Stevens, O'Connor, Kennedy, Souter, & Ginsburg joined the Opinion of the Court. Breyer also delivered an Opinion with respect to Parts I, II, & V (which Stevens, O'Connor & Souter, JJ., joined), and an

Opinion with respect to Parts IV & VI (which Stevens & Souter, JJ., joined). Stevens, J., and Souter, J., filed concurring opinions. O'Connor, J., filed an Opinion concurring in part and dissenting in part. Kennedy, J., filed an Opinion concurring in part, concurring in the judgment in part, & dissenting in part (which Ginsburg, J., joined). Thomas, J., filed an Opinion concurring in the judgment in part & dissenting in part (which Rehnquist, C.J., & Scalia, J., joined).

access channels "are normally subject to complex supervisory systems of various sorts, often with both public and private elements." The municipality itself, or a nonprofit body, may be the access channel manager.

Justice Kennedy, joined by Justice Ginsburg, agreed with the opinion of the Court invalidating section 10(b), but they would invalidate the other two sections as well. Sections 10(a) and (c), Kennedy pointed out, disadvantaged nonobscene, indecent programming, which is a protected category of expression. Sections 10(a) and (c) apply to access channels, each of which is a "designated public forum," which the government has opened for expressive activity by the public. Kennedy frankly criticized the plurality's narrow focus and its "evasion of any clear legal standard in deciding this case."[82] He argued that, at a minimum, the proper standard for reviewing the law is strict scrutiny. He elaborated:

> The plurality opinion, insofar as it upholds § 10(a) of the 1992 Cable Act, is adrift. When confronted with a threat to free speech in the context of an emerging technology, we ought to have the discipline to analyze the case by reference to existing elaborations of constant First Amendment principles. This is the essence of the case-by-case approach to ensuring protection of speech under the First Amendment, even in novel settings. Rather than undertake this task, however, the plurality just declares that, all things considered, § 10(a) seems fine.[83]

Justice Thomas, joined by Rehnquist and Scalia, concurred in the judgment in part and dissented in part. Thomas would uphold all three sections, based on *Turner Broadcasting System v. FCC*. While the Justices in *Turner* disagreed whether the "must-carry" rules

were content-based, Thomas pointed out that "there was agreement that cable operators should enjoy the same First Amendment rights as the nonbroadcast media."[84] Like a free-lance writer seeking a paper in which to publish newspaper editorials, a television programmer is protected in searching for an outlet to publish cable programming, but the programmer has no free-standing First Amendment right to force the cable company to transmit.[85] While viewers have a general right to see what a willing operator transmits, they have no right to force an unwilling operator to transmit, any more than a print author can force a bookstore to carry his or her books.

Thomas argued that the law should recognize the general primacy of the cable operator's editorial rights over the rights of programmers and viewers. None of the petitioners in these cases were cable operators; they were cable viewers or access programmers or their representative organizations. Thomas questioned whether the First Amendment protects the interests that these particular petitioners asserted, and neither petitioners nor the plurality adequately explained the source or justification of those asserted rights in his view.[86] Under this analysis, leased channels and public access channels are a type of "forced speech." Government rules that force access—rules that tell the cable operators what they must broadcast may be justified, if at all, only under some form of heightened scrutiny. In other words, the government could constitutionally impose content-neutral restrictions on the cable operators' editorial discretion only if those rules furthered an important governmental interest unrelated to the suppression of free speech and were no greater than is essential to further that interest.[87]

---

82. 518 U.S. at 784, 116 S.Ct. at 2405.

83. 518 U.S. at 780–81, 116 S.Ct. at 2404.

84. 518 U.S. at 814, 116 S.Ct. at 2420.(Thomas, J., concurring in the judgment and dissenting in part).

85. Justice Thomas would give to the cable operators the same free speech rights that the First Amendment gives to operators of newspapers. See, Miami Herald Publishing Co. v. Tornillo, 418 U.S. 241, 94 S.Ct. 2831, 41 L.Ed.2d 730 (1974), on remand, 303 So.2d 21 (Fla.1974).

86. 518 U.S. at 817–18, 116 S.Ct. at 2421–22.

87. 116 S.Ct. at 2423 (Thomas, J.). Justice O'Connor's analysis in Turner Broadcasting System, Inc. v. FCC, 512 U.S. 622, 680–83, 114 S.Ct. 2445, 2477–79, 129 L.Ed.2d 497 (1994) (O'Connor, J., concurring in part and dissenting in part, joined by Scalia, Ginsburg, & Thomas, J.J.), required strict scrutiny.

(b) The Fairness Doctrine and the Regulation of Traditional Print Media

Traditional media, particularly newspapers, have come under pressure from those advocating a right of access to make their views on public issues known, similar to the restrictions placed on the electronic media.[88] Some commentators argued that the right of free speech guaranteed by the Constitution is meaningless if the speakers are not also given access to the media necessary to present these views to the general public[89] because of the monopolistic nature of modern newspapers.

No Right of Access to Newspapers. The Supreme Court has strongly rejected the notion that a government guaranteed right of access or a fairness doctrine can apply to the press. In *Miami Herald Publishing Co. v. Tornillo*,[90] a unanimous Court struck down a Florida statute that required newspapers to give free reply space to political candidates whom they had attacked in their columns. A statute that told a newspaper what it must print was, in fact, exacting a penalty on the basis of the content of the newspaper. That is unconstitutional censorship.[91]

Although not subject to the same finite limitations of the broadcast media that were deemed so important in the electronic media cases[92] the opinion of the Court recognizes that newspapers are also subject to space limitations that must be considered in balancing the public interest in access against the rights of the publishers.[93] But such physical limitations are not the primary concern in denying reply space in newspapers, an issue the Court only briefly discussed.[94] Even if a compulsory law did not create economic problems or cause the newspaper to have to forego printing something else to give space to a reply, the reply law's great evil was that it intruded on the rights and functions of the newspaper and its editors and reporters.

Miami Herald firmly established that the right of newspaper editors to choose what they wish to print or not to print cannot be abridged to allow the public access to the newspaper media. There is a "virtually insurmountable barrier"[95] that the freedom of the press erects between governmental regulation and the print media.

An important distinction between the fairness doctrine as applied to electronic media and the fairness doctrine that cannot be applied to the print media is that the former enjoys a legal monopoly, which serves to justify FCC regulations requiring "fairness."[96] There is no *legal* monopoly of—and no technological justification for a legal monopoly of—newspapers. Laws may not require people to get a license or a certificate of public convenience and necessity before starting up a new newspaper.

While some local towns may be served by only one paper, yet there is competition in the form of other print media—nationwide news-

---

88. Cf. Red Lion Broadcasting Co. v. FCC, 395 U.S. 367, 89 S.Ct. 1794, 23 L.Ed.2d 371 (1969) (fairness doctrine upheld); CBS, Inc. v. Democratic National Committee, 412 U.S. 94, 93 S.Ct. 2080, 36 L.Ed.2d 772 (1973) (no right of access to broadcast media is constitutionally required for groups seeking to place editorial advertisements).

89. E.g., Barron, Access to the Press—A New First Amendment Right, 80 Harv.L.Rev. 1641 (1967).

90. 418 U.S. 241, 94 S.Ct. 2831, 41 L.Ed.2d 730 (1974), on remand 303 So.2d 21 (Fla.1974).

91. In discussing precedent, the Court noted that its clear implication has been that any compulsion to publish that which reason tells the newspaper publishers should not be published is unconstitutional. The vice of the Florida statute is that it exacts a penalty on the basis of the content of a newspaper. 418 U.S. at 256, 94 S.Ct. at 2839.

92. See, e.g., National Broadcasting Co. v. United States, 319 U.S. 190, 63 S.Ct. 997, 87 L.Ed. 1344 (1943);

Red Lion Broadcasting Co. v. FCC, 395 U.S. 367, 89 S.Ct. 1794, 23 L.Ed.2d 371 (1969); Columbia Broadcasting System, Inc. v. Democratic National Committee, 412 U.S. 94, 93 S.Ct. 2080, 36 L.Ed.2d 772 (1973).

93. "It is correct, as appellee contends, that a newspaper is not subject to the finite technological limitations of time that confront a broadcaster but it is not correct to say, that, as an economic reality, a newspaper can proceed to infinite expansion of column space to accommodate the replies that a government agency determines or a statute commands the readers should have available." 418 U.S. at 256–57, 94 S.Ct. at 2839 (footnote omitted).

94. 418 U.S. at 256–57, 94 S.Ct. at 2838–39.

95. 418 U.S. at 259, 94 S.Ct. at 2840 (White, J., concurring opinion).

96. Red Lion Broadcasting Co. v. FCC, 395 U.S. 367, 89 S.Ct. 1794, 23 L.Ed.2d 371 (1969).

papers such as the New York Times, weekly news magazines, or so-called underground newspapers—all of which cannot be legally barred from serving the local town. If someone believes that the local newspaper is printing his views, he may publish his own pamphlets, posters, or leaflets—all without securing a Government license and opening up his channels of communication to others of opposing views. Moreover if a newspaper is sufficiently insensitive to the needs of its readers, the economic system will develop competitors who are.

If we assume that the problem of lack of access is as serious as those arguing for government regulation of the print media assert, the solution of access overestimates its effectiveness:

> How shall we make the *New York Times* "accountable" for its anti-Vietnam policy? Require it to print letters to the editor in support of the war? If the situation is as grave as stated, the remedy is fantastically inadequate. But the situation is not that grave. The *New York Times*, the *Chicago Tribune*, NBC, ABC, and CBS play a role in policy formation, but clearly they were not alone responsible, for example, for Johnson's decision not to run for reelection, Nixon's refusal to withdraw the troops from Vietnam, ... The implication that the people of this country—except the proponents of the theory—are mere unthinking automatons manipulated by the media, without interests, conflicts, or prejudices is an assumption which I find quite maddening. The de-

velopment of constitutional doctrine should not be based on such hysterical overestimation of media power and underestimation of the good sense of the American public.[97]

No Right of Equal Access to City-Owned Billboards. In the same term with *Miami Herald* the Court considered another access case, this time not involving the private press but rather the use of billboard space on a city-owned public transportation system. In *Lehman v. Shaker Heights*,[98] a divided Court[99] held that a city that operates a public rapid transit system does not violate the First or Fourteenth Amendments by selling commercial advertising space for cigarette companies, banks, liquor companies, churches, and public service groups on its vehicles while refusing to accept any political advertising on behalf of candidates for public office or public issue advertising.[100]

The essential problem in *Lehman* was not a pure right to access, but rather a right of equal access. Plaintiffs argued that, by making the advertising space available for some uses, the city had created a public forum and could not now censor the content of speech in that forum by banning political advertisements. The majority of the Court firmly rejected the contention that space on a city transit system is to be deemed a public forum. The city acted properly to minimize chances of abuse, the appearance of favoritism, and the risk of imposing on a captive audience.[101]

Justice Douglas' concurring opinion emphasized the distinctions between this claimed fo-

97. Jaffe, The Editorial Responsibility of the Broadcaster: Reflections on Fairness and Access, 85 Harv.L.Rev. 768, 786–87 (1972).

98. 418 U.S. 298, 94 S.Ct. 2714, 41 L.Ed.2d 770 (1974).

99. Justice Blackmun's opinion was joined in by three other Justices; Justice Douglas, the fifth vote, wrote his own concurrence, relying heavily on the idea that the audience of a bus is captive. 418 U.S. 298, 305–308, 94 S.Ct. 2714, 2718–20, 41 L.Ed.2d 770 (1974).

100. Lehman v. City of Shaker Heights, 418 U.S. 298, 300–301, 94 S.Ct. 2714, 2716, 41 L.Ed.2d 770 (1974). See also, United States Postal Service v. Council of Greenburgh Civic Associations, 453 U.S. 114, 101 S.Ct. 2676, 69 L.Ed.2d 517 (1981) (18 U.S.C.A. § 1725, prohibiting the deposit of unstamped, "mailable matter" in a letter box approved by the U.S. Postal Service is constitutional; mail

boxes are not public forums, and section 1725 does not regulate on the basis of content).

101. 418 U.S. at 304, 94 S.Ct. at 2717–18. "These are reasonable legislative objectives advanced by the city in a proprietary capacity. In these circumstances, there is no First or Fourteenth Amendment violation." 418 U.S. at 304, 94 S.Ct. at 2718.

Contrast Metromedia, Inc. v. San Diego, 453 U.S. 490, 101 S.Ct. 2882, 69 L.Ed.2d 800 (1981), on remand 32 Cal.3d 180, 185 Cal.Rptr. 260, 649 P.2d 902 (1982). There a fragmented Court invalidated laws restricting the display of billboards. The zoning laws drew a distinction between on-site commercial advertising (allowed) and on-site noncommercial advertising (not allowed). The Court found this distinction unconstitutional. In this case, however, the city was not acting in a proprietary capacity.

rum and the situations that had previously given rise to the concept of a "public forum."

But a streetcar or bus is plainly not a park or sidewalk or other meeting place for discussion, any more than is a highway. It is only a way to get to work or back home. The fact that it is owned and operated by the city does not without more make it a forum.... And if we are to turn a bus or streetcar into either a newspaper or a park, we take great liberties with people who because of necessity become commuters and at the same time captive viewers or listeners.[102]

The Court noted that the city, like a newspaper or the electronic media, could exercise its discretion concerning the types of advertising it accepted;[103] however, because of the state action involved, policies governing access by advertisers must not be "arbitrary, capricious, or invidious."[104]

Although cases have extended the public forum concept beyond parks and streets, to include a public auditorium,[105] the Court in *Lehman* refused to expand the doctrine to include public transportation facilities. "If a bus is a forum it is more akin to a newspaper than to a park," and newspapers cannot be forced to include items that outsiders may desire but that the owner abhors.[106]

No Right of Access to Utility Company's Billing Envelopes. In *Pacific Gas & Electric Co. v. Public Utilities Commission,*[107] a fragmented Court, with no majority opinion, held that the California Public Utilities Commission may not require a privately owned utility company to include, in its billing envelopes, the speech of a third party (in this case, a private group called TURN, "Toward Utility Rate Normalization") with which the utility disagreed.[108] Justice Powell's plurality opinion concluded that the utility's newsletter is "no different from a small newspaper." Its stories ranged from energy-savings tips to wildlife conservation to billings to recipes. The Utility Commission may not force the utility to grant TURN access to the utility's newsletter.

Because the Utility Commission believed that the public would benefit "more from exposure to a variety of views," it concluded that TURN should be allowed to use the "extra space" in the billing envelope four times a year. The "extra space" was defined as the space remaining in the billing envelope after the monthly bill and required legal notices up to the total envelope weight so as not to result in any additional postage. Although the Commission ruled that the ratepayers owned this extra space, it expressly declined to hold that, under California law, the utility's customers own the entire billing envelopes and everything that they contained. The "Commission's access order thus clearly requires appellant to use *its* property as a vehicle for spreading a message with which it disagrees."[109]

102. 418 U.S. at 306–07, 94 S.Ct. at 2718–19 (concurring opinion). See also 418 U.S. at 304, 94 S.Ct. at 2717–18 (Blackmun, J.) Cf., Hague v. CIO, 307 U.S. 496, 515–16, 59 S.Ct. 954, 964, 83 L.Ed. 1423 (1939), where Justice Roberts argued parks and streets are public forums whose use "may be regulated in the interest of all ... but it must not, in the guise of regulation, be abridged or denied". While a majority of the Court at that time did not join in this view, the Court later adopted it. E.g., Schneider v. State, 308 U.S. 147, 163, 60 S.Ct. 146, 151–52, 84 L.Ed. 155 (1939); Kunz v. New York, 340 U.S. 290, 293, 71 S.Ct. 312, 314–15, 95 L.Ed. 280 (1951).

103. 418 U.S. at 303, 94 S.Ct. at 2717. Cf. Public Utilities Commission v. Pollak, 343 U.S. 451, 72 S.Ct. 813, 96 L.Ed. 1068 (1952).

104. 418 U.S. at 303, 94 S.Ct. at 2717.

105. See, e.g., Southeastern Promotions, Ltd. v. Conrad, 420 U.S. 546, 95 S.Ct. 1239, 43 L.Ed.2d 448 (1975). Here the Court evidenced willingness to apply public forum analysis whenever use of a public facility is denied those who wish to exercise their free speech rights; held: a municipal auditorium is a public forum.

106. Lehman v. Shaker Heights, 418 U.S. 298, 306, 94 S.Ct. 2714, 2719, 41 L.Ed.2d 770 (1974) (Douglas, J., concurring); Miami Herald Publishing Co. v. Tornillo, 418 U.S. 241, 94 S.Ct. 2831, 41 L.Ed.2d 730 (1974), on remand 303 So.2d 21 (Fla.1974).

107. 475 U.S. 1, 106 S.Ct. 903, 89 L.Ed.2d 1 (1986), rehearing denied 475 U.S. 1133, 106 S.Ct. 1667, 90 L.Ed.2d 208 (1986).

108. Cf. Wooley v. Maynard, 430 U.S. 705, 97 S.Ct. 1428, 51 L.Ed.2d 752 (1977). (New Hampshire may not require persons to display slogan on their license plates and thus use their private property as a mobile billboard for the state). In *Pacific Gas & Electric* the plurality said of *Wooley:* "The 'private property' that was used to spread the unwelcome message was the automobile, not the license plates." 475 U.S. at 17, 106 S.Ct. at 912.

109. 475 U.S. at 17, 106 S.Ct. at 912.

PruneYard Shopping Center v. Robins, 447 U.S. 74, 100 S.Ct. 2035, 64 L.Ed.2d 741 (1980) upheld a provision of the state constitution preventing a shopping center owner from excluding pamphleteers from the area in the shop-

§ 16.19   A Right of Access by the Press—Speech in a Restricted Environment

Speech and Press Clauses Compared. Does the press generally, or the institutional press in particular, have any preferred rights under the First Amendment? Does the press clause guarantee the press any rights of access that is different from, or greater than, the rights that any individual might have under the free speech clause?

Thus far, when the Court has guaranteed a right of access—as the right of access to a criminal trial, the right of a public trial[1]—it has granted this right to all; the right is not limited to the institutional press.[2] (Given the limited seating in a court room, it is a custom—but not a constitutional requirement—to favor the institutional press in handing out passes.) The Court has refused to draw any constitutional distinction between speech and the press, or the "institutional press," or the "organized media." There is no principled way for the Court to do so. Statutes may draw arbitrary lines, but judicial decisions are not supposed to be arbitrary.

Prisons. In *Pell v. Procunier*[3] and *Saxbe v. Washington Post Co.*,[4] the Court rejected claims by prisoners and the press that the First Amendment guaranteed a right of access to newspapers to interview individual prisoners. It upheld California and federal prison regulations that prohibited face-to-face interviews between prisoners and members of the news media.[5]

Saxbe did not explore the constitutional right of inmates to seek individual interviews with members of the press because inmates were not a party to the litigation.[6] *Pell v. Procunier*,[7] however, explored this aspect of the First Amendment in light of the prisoners' unique position in society. Justice Stewart, writing for the majority,[8] noted that while an absolute ban on interviews applied to the public at large would clearly involve a freedom of speech issue, but the right to hold a press conference does not necessarily survive incarceration. Starting from the proposition that "[l]awful incarceration brings about the necessary withdrawal or limitation of many privileges and rights, a retraction justified by the considerations underlying our penal system",[9]

---

ping center open to the public at large. In *PruneYard*, though, the right of access was not content-based, and granting such access would not affect the shopping center owner's own right to speak. See 475 U.S. at 12, 106 S.Ct. at 910. The shopping center in *PruneYard* was not like a newspaper unlike the utility's newsletter in *Pacific Gas & Electric*.

§ 16.19

1. See e.g., Richmond Newspapers, Inc. v. Virginia, 448 U.S. 555, 100 S.Ct. 2814, 65 L.Ed.2d 973 (1980). See also, Roth, J., citing Treatise in United States v. Antar, 38 F.3d 1348, 1360, Fed.Sec.L.Rep. ¶ 98,436, 40 Fed.R.Evid.Serv. 1006, 22 Media L.Rep. 2417 (3d Cir.1994).

2. Burger, C.J., analyzed these issues in his concurring opinion in First National Bank v. Bellotti, 435 U.S. 765, 795, 98 S.Ct. 1407, 1426, 55 L.Ed.2d 707, 730 (1978), rehearing denied 438 U.S. 907, 98 S.Ct. 3126, 57 L.Ed.2d 1150 (1978) and concluded that the Press Clause did not confer special or extraordinary privileges on the "institutional press." See also, Fisher, J., citing Treatise in, Mid–America Mailers, Inc. v. State Board of Tax Commissioners, 639 N.E.2d 380, 383 n. 1 (Ind.Tax Ct.1994).

3. 417 U.S. 817, 94 S.Ct. 2800, 41 L.Ed.2d 495 (1974).

4. 417 U.S. 843, 94 S.Ct. 2811, 41 L.Ed.2d 514 (1974).

5. *Pell* challenged § 415.071 of the California Department of Corrections Manual (Aug. 23, 1971), which read as follows: "Press and other media interviews with specific individual inmates will not be permitted." 417 U.S. at 819, 94 S.Ct. at 2802. In *Saxbe*, the Washington Post and one

of its reporters challenged Policy Statement 1220 1A para. 4b(6) of the Federal Bureau of Prisons (February 11, 1972), which read as follows:

"Press representatives will not be permitted to interview individual inmates. This rule shall apply even where the inmate requests or seeks an interview. However, conversation may be permitted with inmates whose identity is not to be made public, if it is limited to the discussion of institutional facilities, programs and activities." 417 U.S. at 844 n. 1, 94 S.Ct. at 2812 n. 1.

6. Only the newspaper involved, the Washington Post, and one of its reporters brought suit against the Attorney General to challenge the regulation.

7. 417 U.S. 817, 94 S.Ct. 2800, 41 L.Ed.2d 495 (1974).

8. Justice Powell concurred in the majority opinion holding that the prison regulations did not abridge the inmates' freedom of speech but dissented on the issue of the press' right. 417 U.S. at 835–36, 94 S.Ct. at 2810–11 (1974). Justice Douglas, joined by Justices Brennan and Marshall, dissented in both Pell v. Procunier and Saxbe v. Washington Post Co. See 417 U.S. at 836, 94 S.Ct. at 2827. Cf. Jones v. North Carolina Prisoners' Labor Union, Inc., 433 U.S. 119, 97 S.Ct. 2532, 53 L.Ed.2d 629 (1977).

9. 417 U.S. at 822, 94 S.Ct. at 2804, quoting Price v. Johnston, 334 U.S. 266, 285, 68 S.Ct. 1049, 1060, 92 L.Ed. 1356 (1948).

The principle that a convicted prisoner does not possess the full range of freedoms of an unincarcerated person

the Court proceeded to balance the rights of inmates against the state's legitimate interests in security and rehabilitation of prisoners.[10]

The Court placed great emphasis on the fact that the prisoners had alternative means of communication with the press, including uncensored mailing privileges and a visitation policy allowing face-to-face conversation with family, attorneys, the clergy and longstanding friends. These alternative channels are sufficient to ensure that reasonable and effective means of communication with the outside remain open to the prisoner. A restriction of only one manner of communication is not sufficient to violate a prisoner's First Amendment rights.[11]

The Court admitted that the availability of such alternatives are unimpressive as justification for governmental restriction of personal communication among members of the general public. But prisoners are in a different relationship with their wardens than the average person is with the state. So long as reasonable and effective means of communication remain open and there is no discrimination in terms of content, the courts should accord prison offi-

cials latitude in drawing lines and making distinctions.[12]

Both *Pell* and *Saxbe* considered whether this limitation on press interviews violates freedom of the press as guaranteed by the Constitution. The press contended that, irrespective of any First Amendment rights of the prisoners, members of the press have a constitutional right of access to interview any willing inmate. This right, they claimed, could only be abridged if the prison authorities made an individualized determination that interviewing a particular inmate would constitute a clear and present danger to prison security or another substantial interest of the prison system. The press did not claim a violation or restriction of their right to publish, only of their right to gather news.

The Court rejected this argument in both cases, stating in *Pell* that: "[N]ewsmen have no constitutional right of access to prisons or their inmates beyond that afforded the general public."[13] While the Court agreed that a journalist is free to seek out sources of information, this freedom was a far cry from saying that the Constitution places on the State "the

"applies equally" to lawfully incarcerated pretrial detainees, although the detainees have not yet been convicted beyond a reasonable doubt. Bell v. Wolfish, 441 U.S. 520, 545–547, 553, 99 S.Ct. 1861, 1877–78 1881–82, 60 L.Ed.2d 447 (1979).

10. 417 U.S. at 822–24, 94 S.Ct. at 2804–05. At the time that these regulations were adopted, prison officials were very concerned that press attention to individual inmates was fostering a "big wheel" syndrome and causing certain prisoners to gain prestige and undue influence over the other inmates. California, in fact, enacted its regulation two days after one of these "big wheels" had engineered an escape attempt that resulted in the deaths of three staff members and two inmates.

11. 417 U.S. at 824–28, 94 S.Ct. at 2805–07.

Outgoing versus Incoming Mail. Turner v. Safley, 482 U.S. 78, 107 S.Ct. 2254, 96 L.Ed.2d 64 (1987) rejected a strict scrutiny test and upheld prison regulations that prohibited prison inmates from writing to non-family inmates. Later, Thornburgh v. Abbott, 490 U.S. 401, 109 S.Ct. 1874, 104 L.Ed.2d 459 (1989) rejected a facial attack on prison regulations that authorized prison officials to reject outside publications, such as magazines, sent to prisoners if the prison officials find the publications to be "detrimental to security, good order, or discipline of the institution or if it might facilitate criminal activity." The prison warden, under the regulations, had to review each issue of the magazine separately. The Court applied the deferential standard of *Turner*: the regulations are valid if they are reasonably related to legitimate penological inter-

ests. The Court rejected the stricter standard of Procunier v. Martinez, 416 U.S. 396, 94 S.Ct. 1800, 40 L.Ed.2d 224 (1974) and limited that case to the situation where the prison regulations concern *outgoing* correspondence.

Thornburgh v. Abbott explained that there is an important difference between *outgoing* correspondence and *incoming* materials. *Martinez* is limited to outgoing correspondence because the prison security implications for outgoing correspondence are of a categorically lesser magnitude. To the extent that *Martinez* might suggest that more than the *reasonableness* standard of *Turner* should apply to incoming correspondence from nonprisoners, "we today overrule that case; the Court accomplished much of this step when it decided *Turner*." Thornburgh v. Abbott, 490 U.S. 401, 413, 109 S.Ct. 1874, 1881, 104 L.Ed.2d 459 (1989).

Consistent with the First Amendment, prison authorities may prohibit the prisoners from *receiving* hardcover books unless they are mailed directly from publishers, book stores, or book clubs. That restriction is limited and reasonable, because hardback books are especially serviceable for smuggling contraband, and it is difficult and time consuming to search them effectively. Bell v. Wolfish, 441 U.S. 520, 548–51, 99 S.Ct. 1861, 1879–81, 60 L.Ed.2d 447 (1979).

12. 417 U.S. at 826, 94 S.Ct. at 2806, citing Cruz v. Beto, 405 U.S. at 321, 92 S.Ct. at 1081.

13. 417 U.S. at 834, 94 S.Ct. at 2810.

affirmative duty to make available to journalists sources of information not available to members of the public generally."[14]

The majority of the Court found *Saxbe* to be constitutionally indistinguishable from *Pell* on these issues. In *Saxbe*, the record revealed that the press had actually been given more access to the prisoners than the general public had, noting that newsmen could tour, take pictures, and even conduct on-the-spot interviews with inmates they encountered.[15]

Pell and *Saxbe* may not have much precedential value outside the restricted environment of a prison, for they do not apply usual First Amendment standards. However, the cases do firmly reject a right of access by the press greater than that of the general public, a holding that goes beyond prison cases, although *Pell* acknowledged that "news gathering is not without its First Amendment protections."[16]

A few years later, in another prison case, *Houchins v. KQED, Inc.*[17] reversed a lower court injunction ordering prison officials to grant the press access to certain prison facilities. The seven-member, fragmented court could produce no majority opinion. The plurality found that there is no First or Fourteenth Amendment right of access to government information or sources of information within the government's control. Further, the press has no greater right of access than that of the public generally.[18]

Justice Stewart concurred in the judgment, but on much narrower grounds. He agreed the press has no right of access "superior to that of the public generally," but that the concept of equal access must be flexibly applied "to accommodate the practical distinctions between the press and the general public."[19] In the context of this case, he believed that flexibility could require reasonable use of camera and sound equipment to members of the press in the areas open to both press and public, because the fact that "the First Amendment speaks separately of freedom of speech and of the press is no constitutional accident, but an acknowledgment of the critical role played by the press in American society."[20] Because the lower court injunction was overbroad and had granted the press greater access to prison areas than the public generally, he agreed with the reversal, but would not prohibit more carefully tailored relief on remand.

Justice Stevens, joined by Justices Brennan and Powell, dissented. They distinguished *Pell* and *Saxbe*[21] as limited to the case where there already was substantial press and public access to the prison. The dissent would grant a right of public and press access to prisons, while allowing prison officials only a right to regulate reasonably the time and manner of that access. The dissent agreed that the press has "no greater right of access to information than that possessed by the public at large" but would not have reversed the lower court injunction granting a greater access to the press because the public generally had not requested separate relief and it was proper for the lower court to fashion relief to the needs of the litigant before it.

Because there was no majority opinion and two Justices—Marshall and Blackmun—did not participate, the *Houchins* decision proba-

---

14. 417 U.S. at 834, 94 S.Ct. at 2810.

15. Justice Powell, dissenting in *Saxbe*, felt that testimony had shown that personal interviews are crucial to effective reporting and rejected the idea of alternative means of communication as adequate. Powell was joined by Brennan and Marshall, 417 U.S. at 850–54, 94 S.Ct. at 2815–17. Douglas dissented from both *Pell* and *Saxbe* in the same opinion, 417 U.S. at 836, 94 S.Ct. at 2811.

16. 417 U.S. at 833, 94 S.Ct. at 2809, quoting Branzburg v. Hayes, 408 U.S. 665, 707, 92 S.Ct. 2646, 2670, 33 L.Ed.2d 626 (1972).

17. 438 U.S. 1, 98 S.Ct. 2588, 57 L.Ed.2d 553 (1978). The vote was four to three, with two Justices not participating.

18. Burger, C.J., was joined by White and Rehnquist, JJ.

19. 438 U.S. at 16, 98 S.Ct. at 2597–98 (Stewart, J., concurring). Contra, Burger, C.J., concurring in First Nat. Bank v. Bellotti, 435 U.S. 765, 795, 98 S.Ct. 1407, 1426, 55 L.Ed.2d 707 (1978).

20. 438 U.S. at 17, 98 S.Ct. at 2598 (Stewart, J., concurring).

21. Pell v. Procunier, 417 U.S. 817, 94 S.Ct. 2800, 41 L.Ed.2d 495 (1974); Saxbe v. Washington Post Co., 417 U.S. 843, 94 S.Ct. 2811, 41 L.Ed.2d 514 (1974).

bly will not end litigation over public access to prisons in cases where there is only limited access to parts of the jail.[22] However, the seven justices did agree that the press has no greater right of access to prisons than the public generally. The Court, once again, rejected the notion that the institutional press has greater First Amendment rights than the public generally.

Open School Board Meetings. The Supreme Court has invalidated a state employment commission's order requiring a school board to prohibit teachers who are not union representatives from speaking at open meetings that permit public participation, even if the speech is addressed to the subject of pending collective bargaining negotiations,[23] thus giving the press and the public a similar right of access to such speech.

Access to Trials. The press has no constitutional right of access to evidence given at trials greater than that of the general public. *Nixon v. Warner Communications, Inc.*,[24] held that neither the First Amendment guarantee of free speech and press nor the Sixth Amendment guarantee of a public trial gives the press the right to copy evidence given at trial. News organizations sought to copy several Watergate tapes that had been introduced at the trial of several defendants, but the Court held that the opportunity to listen to the tapes at trial and to receive transcripts of them had satisfied both constitutional guarantees. The Court held that within the courtroom, the

press enjoys no greater rights than does the public, but that the press is free, within broad limits, to report what its representatives have seen at the proceeding.[25]

Publication of Rape Victim's Name. While the press has no greater rights than the general public, neither should it have any less. *Florida Star v. B.J.F.*[26] invalidated a Florida statute that made a newspaper civilly liable for publishing the name of a rape victim. The press had obtained this name from publicly released police reports. The Court concluded that if a newspaper publishes information that it has lawfully obtained, the state may impose punishment, if at all, only when the law is narrowly tailored to a state interest of the highest order. The facts of this case did not meet that test.[27] Justice Scalia, concurring in part and in the judgment, astutely noted that Florida limited the press, but it placed no limits at all on gossip by the victim's neighbors. Thus it discriminated against the press. "This law has every appearance of a prohibition that society is prepared to impose upon the press but not upon itself."[28]

§ 16.20 The Press and the Antitrust Laws

The First Amendment does not bestow antitrust immunity on newspapers, broadcasters, and other news media even if enforcement of the antitrust laws might cause them to go bankrupt.[1] Justice Black explained the basic

---

22. Cf. Philadelphia Newspapers, Inc. v. Jerome, 434 U.S. 241, 98 S.Ct. 546, 54 L.Ed.2d 506 (1978), on remand 478 Pa. 484, 387 A.2d 425 (1978), appeal dismissed 443 U.S. 913, 99 S.Ct. 3104, 61 L.Ed.2d 877 (1979) (per curiam) (raising issue of press and public access to pretrial suppression hearings; state court judgment vacated to clarify the record).

23. City of Madison v. Wisconsin Employment Relations Commission, 429 U.S. 167, 97 S.Ct. 421, 50 L.Ed.2d 376 (1976).

24. 435 U.S. 589, 98 S.Ct. 1306, 55 L.Ed.2d 570 (1978).

25. 435 U.S. at 608–609, 98 S.Ct. at 1317–18. The Court also held that the common law right of access to judicial records does not authorize release of the tapes, in light of the Presidential Recordings Act. Marshall and Stevens dissented, each writing a separate opinion, and White dissented in part, joined by Brennan.

26. 491 U.S. 524, 109 S.Ct. 2603, 105 L.Ed.2d 443 (1989).

27. Cox Broadcasting Corp. v. Cohn, 420 U.S. 469, 95 S.Ct. 1029, 43 L.Ed.2d 328 (1975) held that the state, even in a right to privacy action, may not impose sanctions on the accurate publication of a rape victim's name obtained from public records open to public inspection. Cf. Butterworth v. Smith, 494 U.S. 624, 110 S.Ct. 1376, 108 L.Ed.2d 572 (1990), which invalidated a Florida statute that prohibited (with some limited exceptions) a grand jury witness from disclosing testimony that he gave to the grand jury, even after the grand jury term had ended. The unanimous Court held that the state's interest in preserving grand jury secrecy is either not served by, or is insufficient, to warrant prohibiting truthful speech on matters of public concern.

28. 491 U.S. at 542, 109 S.Ct. at 2614. See, § 16.25.

§ 16.20

1. Citizen Publishing Co. v. United States, 394 U.S. 131, 89 S.Ct. 927, 22 L.Ed.2d 148 (1969). See also Lorain Journal Co. v. United States, 342 U.S. 143, 72 S.Ct. 181,

principles in *Associated Press v. United States:*[2]

> Freedom to publish means freedom for all and not for some. Freedom to publish is guaranteed by the Constitution, but freedom to combine to keep others from publishing is not. Freedom of the press from governmental interference under the First Amendment does not sanction repression of that freedom by private interests [through conspiracies in restraint of trade]. The First Amendment affords not the slightest support for the contention that a combination to restrain trade in news and views has any constitutional immunity.[3]

The applicable antitrust laws must be even-handed, nondiscriminatory and neutral on their face and in effect. A discriminatory state antitrust law—written only to apply to the dissemination of news—is unconstitutional.[4]

Thus, *FTC v. Superior Court Trial Lawyers Association*[5] applied the antitrust laws to various self-employed individual lawyers (not employees of any employer) in Washington, D.C. These lawyers agreed among themselves not to represent indigent criminal defendants in the Superior Court unless the District increased their compensation. The District eventually

responded by raising the Criminal Justice Act rates. Later, the Federal Trade Commission ruled that the lawyers' conduct violated § 5 of the FTC Act, and issued a cease-and-desist order against future such boycotts. The lawyers claimed that their concerted action was protected speech, but the Court held that it was a "plain violation" of the antitrust laws. The *per se* rules against price fixing and boycotts are justified by administrative convenience and reflect the long-standing judgment that the prohibited practices adversely affect competition.

§ 16.21   The Press and the Labor Laws

On a theory similar to that used in the antitrust area, *Associated Press v. NLRB*[1] held that the First Amendment does not bar nondiscriminatory application of the National Labor Relations Act to the news media. The law in question did not affect the impartial distribution of news.[2]

§ 16.22   The Press and the Tax Laws

The Government may not impose taxes that serve to burden a privilege guaranteed by the Bill of Rights.[1] Thus, *Follett v. McCormick*[2]

---

96 L.Ed. 162 (1951); United States v. Radio Corp. of America, 358 U.S. 334, 79 S.Ct. 457, 3 L.Ed.2d 354 (1959); Roth, J., citing Treatise in United States v. Antar, 38 F.3d 1348, 1360, Fed.Sec.L.Rep. ¶ 98,436, 40 Fed.R.Evid.Serv. 1006, 22 Media L.Rep. 2417 (3d Cir.1994).

2. 326 U.S. 1, 65 S.Ct. 1416, 89 L.Ed. 2013 (1945), rehearing denied 326 U.S. 802, 66 S.Ct. 6, 90 L.Ed. 489 (1945).

3. 326 U.S. at 20, 65 S.Ct. at 1425 (footnote omitted).

4. Cf. Grosjean v. American Press Co., 297 U.S. 233, 250–51, 56 S.Ct. 444, 449, 80 L.Ed. 660 (1936).

5. 493 U.S. 411, 110 S.Ct. 768, 107 L.Ed.2d 851 (1990). NAACP v. Claiborne Hardware Co., 458 U.S. 886, 102 S.Ct. 3409, 73 L.Ed.2d 1215 (1982), did not immunize this boycott from the antitrust laws. In *Claiborne,* the boycott supporters sought no special advantage for themselves; *Claiborne* does not apply to a boycott conducted by business competitors who "stand to profit financially from a lessening of competition in the boycotted market." The immediate objective of the respondents in this case was to increase the price that they would be paid for their services.

§ 16.21

1. 301 U.S. 103, 57 S.Ct. 650, 81 L.Ed. 953 (1937).

2. Associated Press v. NLRB, 301 U.S. at 132, 57 S.Ct. at 655–56 (1937). See also Oklahoma Press Publishing Co.

v. Walling, 327 U.S. 186, 66 S.Ct. 494, 90 L.Ed. 614 (1946) (Wage and hour laws).

§ 16.22

1. Murdock v. Pennsylvania, 319 U.S. 105, 113, 63 S.Ct. 870, 875, 87 L.Ed. 1292 (1943).

2. Follett v. Town of McCormick, S.C., 321 U.S. 573, 64 S.Ct. 717, 88 L.Ed. 938 (1944).

As to the constitutionality of a license tax in a nonreligious context, see City of Corona v. Corona Daily Independent, 115 Cal.App.2d 382, 252 P.2d 56 (1953), certiorari denied 346 U.S. 833, 74 S.Ct. 2, 98 L.Ed. 356 (1953). Justice Douglas, joined by Justice Black, dissented from the denial of certiorari. He summarized the case as follows:

"Petitioners publish a newspaper in Corona, California. The city has by ordinance imposed a license tax for the privilege of engaging in any business in the city, including the business of publishing a newspaper. Petitioners refused to pay the license fee, and the California courts have held that they may be compelled to do so." (346 U.S. at 833, 74 S.Ct. at 3).

Justice Douglas argued that such a license tax violates the First Amendment because "No government can exact a price for the exercise of a privilege which the Constitution guarantees." 346 U.S. at 834, 74 S.Ct. at 3. Note that the California tax was nondiscriminatory.

struck down a *flat license*[3] tax as applied to one who earns his livelihood as an evangelist or preacher. Those who preach, "like other citizens, may be subject to general taxation [but that] does not mean that they can be required to pay a tax for the exercise of that which the First Amendment has made a high constitutional privilege."[4]

The Court has also invalidated discriminatory taxes on the dissemination of news. *Grosjean v. American Press Co.*[5] struck down a state tax (which was a tax in addition to other taxes of general applicability) on 2% of the gross receipts of advertising in those newspapers with circulation of more than 20,000 copies per week. The tax is invalid because—

in the light of its history and of its present setting, it is seen to be a deliberate and calculated device *in the guise of a tax* to limit the circulation of information to which the public is entitled in virtue of the constitutional guaranties....

The form in which the tax is imposed is in itself suspicious. It is not measured or limited by the volume of advertisements. It is measured alone by the extent of the circulation of the publication in which the advertisements are carried, with the plain purpose of penalizing the publishers and curtailing the circulation of a selected group of newspapers.[6]

Though the state may apply general business taxes without violating the First Amendment, even though some of these business activities relate to free speech,[7] it may not enact laws, in the guise of a tax, designed to limit the circulation of newspapers.

Minneapolis Star and Tribune Co. v. Minnesota Commissioner of Revenue[8] interpreted *Grosjean* as dependent on the legislature having improper censorial goals or motive.[9] However, even without such improper goals, a tax may be invalid. In Minnesota, the state's general sales and use taxes exempted periodic publication, but the state had a special "use" tax on the cost of paper and ink products consumed in the production of periodic publications after the first $100,000 worth of ink and paper consumed in a calendar year.

The economic result of this tax was to discriminate against larger publishers, and to favor smaller ones, and to discriminate against those more likely to use ink and paper (that is, the press). *Minneapolis Star* correctly invalidated this tax, which singled out the press for special tax burdens.

The state's interest in revenue "cannot justify the special treatment of the press" because the state could "raise the revenue by taxing businesses generally...."[10] The Court emphasized this point by noting that a nondiscriminatory sales tax, which also taxed the sale of newspapers, would be constitutional.[11] Fi-

---

3. See, Jimmy Swaggart Ministries v. Board of Equalization, 493 U.S. 378, 110 S.Ct. 688, 107 L.Ed.2d 796 (1990). A unanimous Court held that the religion clauses of the First Amendment do not prevent a state from imposing generally applicable sales and use taxes, with such taxes also applying to sales of books, tapes, and other religious and nonreligious merchandise by religious organizations. Sales and use taxes are to be distinguished from *flat* license taxes: because flat taxes are fixed in amount and unrelated to the scope of the activities or to revenues received, they operate as preconditions or prior restraints on the exercise of religious freedom.

With *Jimmy Swaggart Ministries* compare, Texas Monthly, Inc. v. Bullock, 489 U.S. 1, 109 S.Ct. 890, 103 L.Ed.2d 1 (1989), invalidating a Texas statute that exempted from its sales tax periodicals and books published by a religious faith that consist "wholly of writings" that promulgate the faith. The Court held that the law violated the Establishment Clause. The state would have to make a religious judgment about the content of the books to grant the exemption.

White, J., concurring in the judgement, argued that the law violated the Press Clause because it discriminated against writings based on their content.

4. 321 U.S. at 578, 64 S.Ct. at 719.

5. 297 U.S. 233, 56 S.Ct. 444, 80 L.Ed. 660 (1936).

6. 297 U.S. at 250–51, 56 S.Ct. at 449 (emphasis added).

7. Cf. Cammarano v. United States, 358 U.S. 498, 79 S.Ct. 524, 3 L.Ed.2d 462 (1959) (Government may forbid as a business deduction, money spent on lobbying activities).

8. 460 U.S. 575, 103 S.Ct. 1365, 75 L.Ed.2d 295 (1983), on remand 332 N.W.2d 914 (Minn.1983).

9. 460 U.S. at 580, 103 S.Ct. at 1369.

10. 460 U.S. at 586, 103 S.Ct. at 1372 (footnote omitted).

11. 460 U.S. at 586–87 n. 9, 103 S.Ct. at 1373 n. 9. The Court rejected a rule that would allow the state to single out the press for a different method of taxation so long as

nally, the Court held the Minnesota use tax improper because it targeted a small group within the press, those who would exceed the $100,000 exemption. Singling out only the larger publishers had a strong potential for abuse.[12]

Similarly, a state may not constitutionally levy a sales tax on certain types of magazines based on the content of those magazines—the state sales tax in question applied to general interest magazines but exempted newspapers and certain types of magazines (any religious, professional, trade or sports periodical was exempted, but not a general interest magazine).[13]

Leathers v. Medlock[14] illustrates the Court's analysis in cases where the press complains that a tax discriminates. In that case the Court held that it does not violate free speech for Arkansas to extend its generally applicable sales tax to cable television services alone, or to cable and satellite services while exempting the print media. The tax in question covered *all* tangible personal property and a broad range of services. Thus it did not single out the press and threaten its role as a watchdog of government activity. Furthermore, the tax did not target cable television in a purposeful attempt to interfere with free speech; nor is the tax structured so as to raise suspicion that Arkansas had a bad intent, for the state did

not select a small group of speakers to bear the full tax burden. Finally, the tax was not content based.

The "Son of Sam" Law. *Simon & Schuster, Inc. v. Members of the New York State Crime Victims Board*,[15] relied on *Leathers* to invalidate New York's "Son of Sam" statute, so-called because it was enacted in response to a criminal who called himself the "Son of Sam." This law required that any income of an accused or "convicted" person derived from works describing his crime be deposited in an escrow account, where they were available to victims of the crime and the criminal's creditors. The statute treated as "convicted" any person who admitted to a crime, even if that person had not been prosecuted.

The law was the functional economic equivalent of a tax because it imposed a financial disincentive to create or publish works with a particular content. Justice O'Connor, for the Court, ruled that the statute was overbroad and regulated speech based on content. A statute that imposes a financial burden on speakers because of the content of their speech is "presumptively inconsistent with the First Amendment. . . ." To justify such differential treatment, the regulation must be "necessary to serve a compelling state interest and narrowly drawn to achieve that end."[16]

---

the effective tax burden was no greater, because differential treatment threatens the press and courts are ill-equipped to evaluate with precision the relative burdens of various methods of taxation. 460 U.S. at 589, 103 S.Ct. at 1374 (footnote omitted).

12. 460 U.S. at 591–92, 103 S.Ct. at 1375.

Contrast Matter of Assessment of Additional North Carolina and Orange County Use Taxes Against Village Pub. Corp. for Period from April 1, 1972 through March 31, 1978, 312 N.C. 211, 322 S.E.2d 155 (1984), appeal dismissed for want of a substantial federal question, sub nom., Village Publishing Corp. v. North Carolina Department of Revenue, 472 U.S. 1001, 105 S.Ct. 2693, 86 L.Ed.2d 710 (1985) (constitutionality of North Carolina Sales and Use Tax exemption upheld; the law exempts sales of newspapers "by resident newspaper street vendors and by newsboys making house-to-house deliveries and sales of magazines by resident magazine vendors making house-to-house sales.")

White, J., joined by Brennan, J., dissented, in view of *Minneapolis Star*. The state law offers newspapers using a certain means of delivery a tax benefit denied to other members of the press, thus raising free speech and equal protection problems.

13. Arkansas Writers' Project, Inc. v. Ragland, 481 U.S. 221, 107 S.Ct. 1722, 95 L.Ed.2d 209 (1987), on remand 293 Ark. 395, 738 S.W.2d 402 (1987). The Court did not decide whether a distinction between different types of periodicals—e.g., newspapers versus all magazines—would also be invalid. 481 U.S. at 232, 107 S.Ct. at 1729. Such a distinction is not content-based.

In Texas Monthly, Inc. v. Bullock, 489 U.S. 1, 109 S.Ct. 890, 103 L.Ed.2d 1 (1989), the Court, with no majority opinion, invalidated a Texas statute that exempted from the state sales tax those periodicals "published or distributed by a religious faith and that consist wholly of writings promulgating the teaching of the faith and the books that consist wholly of writings sacred to a religious faith."

14. 499 U.S. 439, 111 S.Ct. 1438, 113 L.Ed.2d 494 (1991). Marshall, J., joined by Blackmun, J., filed a dissenting opinion.

15. 502 U.S. 105, 112 S.Ct. 501, 116 L.Ed.2d 476 (1991). Blackmun, J. and Kennedy, J., each filed separate opinions concurring in the judgment.

16. 502 U.S. at 117, 112 S.Ct. at 509.

The state has a compelling interest to insure that criminals do not profit from their crimes and in compensating victims by using the fruits of the criminal's crime, but the statute was not narrowly tailored to that objective. It was over inclusive because it applies to works on any subject, whenever the author expresses thoughts or recollections about a crime, however tangentially. The law, as written, would even apply to the *Confessions of Saint Augustine*, where Saint Augustine, the author, deplores his "past foulness," including his theft of pears from a neighbor's vineyard. It would cover *The Autobiography of Malcolm X*, which described crimes committed before Malcolm X became a public figure.

The Court explicitly did not comment on the statutes of other jurisdictions designed to serve similar purposes. *Simon & Schuster* does not purport to preclude laws that are narrowly tailored. In reaction to the *Son of Sam* decision, prosecutors have written large fines into plea bargains, in an effort to prevent criminal defendants from profiting from their crimes. Judges have also imposed large fines, even on paupers, to make sure that if they sell their story to the media, they still would not be able to walk away with a net profit, after having paid the fine.[17]

In short, when there is a complaint that the tax discriminates among the media or within a medium, the First Amendment is implicated if the tax is directed at, or presents the danger of, suppressing particular ideas.

§ 16.23 An Introduction to Fair Trial versus Free Press

The press and the government are natural adversaries. Each has functions that sometimes conflicts with the other. Yet they also can supplement each other. As the Supreme Court has observed:

A responsible press has always been regarded as the handmaiden of effective judicial administration, especially in the criminal field. Its function in this regard is documented by an impressive record of service over several centuries. The press does not simply publish information about trials but guards against the miscarriage of justice by subjecting the police, prosecutors, and judicial processes to extensive public scrutiny and criticism.[1]

It is not surprising that this relationship is accompanied by a certain degree of rancor as well as suspicion that each is attempting to stunt the effectiveness of the other by intruding unnecessarily into the other's respective sphere of responsibility.

The central question in this area is whether there exists any order of preeminence among the conflicting rights and duties with constitutional recognition. Courts and commentators have assessed this question in several contexts. First, does the First Amendment provide for the protection of confidential sources when such information is relevant to a criminal investigation or prosecution? Second, does there exist any power in the government to restrain the publication of information that may jeopardize a defendant's rights to a fair trial? It is to those issues that we now turn.

§ 16.24 The Reporter's Privilege

Branzburg v. Hayes **and a Reporter's Privilege.** In *Branzburg v. Hayes*,[1] a bare five to four majority rejected a reporter's claim that the flow of information available to the press would be seriously impeded if reporters are compelled to release the names of confidential sources for use in a government investigation. The Court also rejected the claim that the First Amendment embraced a reporter's

---

17. Junda Woo, Big Fines Are Replacing Son of Sam Laws, Wall Street Journal, April 26, 1994, at B1, col. 3–5 (midwest ed.).

§ 16.23

1. Sheppard v. Maxwell, 384 U.S. 333, 350, 86 S.Ct. 1507, 1515, 16 L.Ed.2d 600 (1966). See Rotunda, Reporting Sensational Trials: Free Press, a Responsible Press,

and Cameras in the Courts, 3 Communications Law and Policy 295 (No. 2, Spring, 1998).

§ 16.24

1. 408 U.S. 665, 92 S.Ct. 2646, 33 L.Ed.2d 626 (1972).

See, Vincent Blasi, Press Subpoenas: An Empirical and Legal Analysis (1972); Murasky The Journalist's Privilege: Branzburg and Its Aftermath, 52 Tex.L.Rev. 829 (1974)

privilege to refuse to divulge confidential sources.

Though the issue before *Branzburg* has far-reaching implications, Justice White, for the Court, phrased the question and holding more narrowly: "The issue in these cases is whether requiring newsmen to appear and testify before state or federal grand juries abridges the freedom of speech and press guaranteed by the First Amendment. We hold that it does not."[2] Left undecided was the scope of a newsman's privilege, if any, in administrative hearings, legislative hearings, and civil suits.

Although the Court agreed that some protection of news sources was necessary unless the information-gathering process was to be totally eviscerated, petitioners had not established that the press needed greater protection than that it traditionally had:

Only where news sources themselves are implicated in crime or possess information relevant to the grand jury's task need they or the reporter be concerned about grand jury subpoenas. Nothing before us indicates that a large number or percentage of *all* confidential news sources falls into either category and would in any way be deterred by our holding that the Constitution does not, as it never has, exempt the newsman from performing the citizen's normal duty of appearing and furnishing information relevant to the grand jury's task.[3]

The public interest in the investigation and prosecution of crimes outweighs any special reporter's privilege, the Court concluded.

Moreover, the difficulties of administering such a privilege would be enormous. It would be necessary to categorize the various individuals and organizations participating in the distribution of information to determine those qualified to exercise the privilege. This would be a most "questionable procedure in light of the traditional doctrine that liberty of the press is the right of the lonely pamphleteer ... as much as of the large metropolitan publisher...."[4] In addition, because the asserted privilege was only conditional, each assertion would require a judicial determination that it was properly invoked: that there existed alternative methods to obtain this information, that it was not relevant to the subject of the investigation, or that such information is not intrinsic to a successful prosecution.[5]

In spite of these arguments, the Court did leave open an avenue of redress for newsmen who feel they are being harassed by government officials:

[G]rand jury investigations if instituted or conducted other than in good faith, would pose wholly different issues for resolution under the First Amendment. Official harassment of the press undertaken not for purposes of law enforcement but to disrupt a reporter's relationship with his news sources would have no justification. Grand juries are subject to judicial control and subpoenas to motions to quash.[6]

Justice Powell, who cast the crucial fifth vote, struck a somewhat problematical note for future litigation relying on *Branzburg*. Because he believed that the "state and federal authorities are not free to 'annex' the news media as 'an investigative arm of government,' " he urged, in his concurrence, a broader test than mere "good faith" for assessing the need to disclose confidential sources. In his view:

[I]f the newsman is called upon to give information bearing only a remote and tenuous relationship to the subject of the investigation, or if he has some other reason to believe that his testimony implicates confidential source relationships without a legitimate need of law enforcement, he will have access to the Court on a motion to quash

---

2. 408 U.S. at 667, 92 S.Ct. at 2649–50.

3. Branzburg v. Hayes, 408 U.S. 665, 691, 92 S.Ct. 2646, 2661–62, 33 L.Ed.2d 626 (1972) (emphasis in original).

4. 408 U.S. at 704, 92 S.Ct. at 2668.

5. 408 U.S. at 705, 92 S.Ct. at 2668–69. Petitioner did not assert an absolute privilege, but one where informa-

tion could be compelled only on a showing of exhaustion of alternative sources and under strict guidelines as to relevance. 408 U.S. at 630, 92 S.Ct. at 2644–45.

6. 408 U.S. at 707–08, 92 S.Ct. at 2670 (footnote omitted).

and an appropriate protective order may be entered.[7]

The ambiguity surrounding "a legitimate need of law enforcement" suggests an approach not too dissimilar to that rejected in the majority opinion due to inherent administrative difficulties.[8] Indeed, Justice Stewart's dissent interpreted this ambiguity as offering "some hope of a more flexible view in the future."[9]

State Shield Laws. Despite intensive lobbying efforts, Congress has enacted no federal bill that would provide a statutory privilege for newsmen. However, several states have enacted "state shield" laws that offer varying protection, depending on the statutory language and state court interpretation.[10] Under the supremacy clause of the Constitution such state shield laws could not apply to limit the power of federal courts exercising jurisdiction over federal questions.

The *Farber* Decision. State shield laws may vary greatly in how they are applied in state cases to prevent a state court from subpoenaing information from a reporter when such information may be helpful to a criminal defendant. For example, the New Jersey Supreme Court decision, *In re Farber*,[11] held that its seemingly strong shield law must yield to the Sixth Amendment rights and state constitutional provisions giving rights to criminal defendants. The state court said: "[W]hen faced with the shield law, [the criminal defendant] invokes the rather elementary but entirely sound proposition that where the Constitution and statute collide, the latter must yield."[12]

Farber then held that the press only would have a right to a preliminary determination (before being required to submit materials to the trial judge for *in camera* inspection) that there was a reasonable likelihood that the information sought was material and relevant, that it could not be secured from any less intrusive source, and that the defendant had a legitimate need to see and use it. Several other state courts have also shown hostility to state shield laws both on federal and state constitutional law grounds.[13]

This hostility is not warranted, and the logic of *Farber* is assailable. *Branzburg v. Hayes*[14] specifically recognized that Congress and states have the freedom to fashion a statutory reporter's privilege "as narrow or broad as deemed necessary...." States are free, "within First Amendment limits, to fashion" their own shield laws, and state courts could construe their state constitutions "so as to recognize a newsman's privilege, either qualified or absolute."[15]

Criminal defendants certainly have rights, but one should recognize that many statutory or judge-made laws create a host of privileges that serve to deprive the accused or the prosecutor of relevant evidence. The attorney-client privilege, the doctor-patient privilege, the husband-wife privilege—all serve certain important social policies and none of them violate the accused's rights. To illustrate, if a client confesses to a particular crime to his attorney, it is the general rule that neither the state nor a criminal defendant may subpoena the attorney to breach the wall of secrecy (without the client's consent). If that "shield" law is constitutional, may one logically treat the reporter-source privilege any differently?

A Reporter's Privilege and Civil Cases. Assertion of a reporter's privilege in civil cases has met with a qualified success, the lower courts distinguishing *Branzburg* on the

---

7. 408 U.S. at 710, 92 S.Ct. at 2671. See Stewart, "Or of the Press," 26 Hast.L.J. 631, 635 (1975).

8. See Note, The Supreme Court, 1971 Term, 86 Harv. L.Rev. 1, 144 (1972).

9. Branzburg v. Hayes, 408 U.S. 665, 725, 92 S.Ct. 2646, 2671, 33 L.Ed.2d 626 (1972).

10. See Marcus, The Reporter's Privilege: An Analysis of the Common Law, Branzburg v. Hayes, and Recent Statutory Developments, 25 Ariz.L.Rev. 815 (1984).

11. 78 N.J. 259, 394 A.2d 330 (1978), certiorari denied 439 U.S. 997, 99 S.Ct. 598, 58 L.Ed.2d 670 (1978).

12. In re Farber, 78 N.J. 259, 394 A.2d 330 (1978), certiorari denied 439 U.S. 997, 99 S.Ct. 598, 58 L.Ed.2d 670 (1978).

13. See Goodale, Courts Begin Limiting Scope of Various State Shield Laws, 1 Nat'l Law Jrl. 28 (Dec. 11, 1978).

14. 408 U.S. 665, 92 S.Ct. 2646, 33 L.Ed.2d 626 (1972).

15. 408 U.S. at 706, 92 S.Ct. at 2669.

grounds that a civil action does not present as significant a countervailing interest as a criminal prosecution, particularly where the plaintiffs seeking access to a reporter's notes are not parties to a pending criminal action, but merely prospective witnesses.

Thus, in one case that accepted the privilege, the court required the party seeking discovery to exhaust alternative sources and to show that the information requested is central to the party's claim.[16] Such a claim may well be present in libel suits brought by public officials and figures against the media, because the plaintiff needs to establish "malice" or *New York Times* scienter in publishing the defamatory information in order to be successful.[17] If the story is purportedly based on the information obtained from a confidential source, scienter can be proven by a showing that the source is non-existent.[18]

Search Warrants of Newsrooms. *Zurcher v. The Stanford Daily*[19] refused to create any special protections for newspapers that might be searched by government authorities pursuant to a search warrant based on probable cause to look for evidence of a crime. The majority quickly dismissed arguments based on the need to protect confidential sources.

In *Zurcher* the police had probable cause to believe that the files of the student newspaper at Stanford University would contain photographs of persons who had assaulted police officers during a sit-in demonstration. On this basis they secured a search warrant to search for and seize such photographs in the newspaper office. Though locked drawers and rooms were not opened, the police did have an opportunity to read the newspaper's notes and correspondence, and the police did search the newspaper's photographic laboratories, filing

cabinets, desks and waste paper baskets. No materials were removed from the newspaper offices. The newspaper later sued in federal court seeking, among other things, a declaratory judgment that the search violated the First and Fourth Amendments, as applied to the states through the Fourteenth Amendment. The district granted the declaratory judgment but the Supreme Court reversed.

First, the majority rejected any argument that the Fourth Amendment establishes different requirements for search warrants that are issued to search for material in possession of one not suspected of a crime, such as the student newspaper, which only was thought to have evidence of a crime committed by others. The Court held that the Fourth Amendment is not a barrier to search for property for which there is probable cause to believe that the fruits, instrumentalities, or evidence of a crime is located, whether or not the owner or possessor of the premises covered by the warrant is reasonably suspected of involvement in the crime being investigated.

Secondly, *Zurcher* rejected any rule based on the First Amendment that would require the use of subpoenas, rather than the more intrusive search procedure, when the premises to be searched are a newspaper's offices. The Supreme Court, however, did emphasize that where "the materials sought to be seized may be protected by the First Amendment, the requirements of the Fourth Amendment must be applied with 'scrupulous exactitude.' "[20] Thus the Court has invalidated a search warrant authorizing a search of a private home for all books, records, and other materials relating to the Communist Party. The warrant in that context was the functional equivalent of a general warrant, which was prohibited by the

16. Democratic Nat. Committee v. McCord, 356 F.Supp. 1394 (D.D.C.1973).

17. New York Times Co. v. Sullivan, 376 U.S. 254, 84 S.Ct. 710, 11 L.Ed.2d 686 (1964), motion denied 376 U.S. 967, 84 S.Ct. 1130, 12 L.Ed.2d 83 (1964).

18. See, e.g., Carey v. Hume, 492 F.2d 631 (D.C.Cir. 1974), application denied 417 U.S. 905, 94 S.Ct. 2636, 41 L.Ed.2d 231 (1974), certiorari dismissed 417 U.S. 938, 94 S.Ct. 2654, 41 L.Ed.2d 661 (1974).

Cf. Herbert v. Lando, 441 U.S. 153, 99 S.Ct. 1635, 60 L.Ed.2d 115 (1979).

19. 436 U.S. 547, 98 S.Ct. 1970, 56 L.Ed.2d 525 (1978), rehearing denied 439 U.S. 885, 99 S.Ct. 231, 58 L.Ed.2d 200 (1978).

20. 436 U.S. at 564, 98 S.Ct. at 1981, citing Stanford v. Texas, 379 U.S. 476, 485, 85 S.Ct. 506, 511, 13 L.Ed.2d 431 (1965), rehearing denied 380 U.S. 926, 85 S.Ct. 879, 13 L.Ed.2d 813 (1965).

Fourth Amendment.[21]

Zurcher did not believe that its ruling would result in a rash of incidents of police rummaging through newspaper files. First, there have been only a few instances since 1971 that search warrants have been issued to apply to newspaper premises,[22] and search warrants themselves—which are only issued by the judiciary on proof of probable cause—are more difficult to obtain than subpoenas.[23] The local prosecutor would not likely choose the more difficult procedure unless he or she had a special reason. The prosecutor may wish to utilize the warrant procedure because of fear that the evidence might be destroyed if the less intrusive subpoena method were used. In *Zurcher*, the student newspaper had an announced policy of destroying photographs that could aid in the prosecution of protestors.[24]

Finally, while a subpoena is less intrusive, it is also much less satisfactory for prosecutorial purpose than a search warrant because the Fifth Amendment privilege against self incrimination is not available to one resisting a search warrant.[25] Thus, there are practical reasons supporting the majority's holding and past practices do not suggest that the warrant powers applied to newspaper premises will be abused.

Congressional Response to *Zurcher*. Congress responded to *Zurcher* by enacting the Privacy Protection Act;[26] this law applies to state as well as federal law enforcement personnel. It limits their power to secure evidence from the news media by search warrant, and requires in many circumstances that they prefer a subpoena.

Ironically, if the Privacy Protection Act had been applied to the facts of *Zurcher*, the results of the case would not have been different. That is because the Privacy Protection Act provides that its restrictions do not apply if there is reasonable cause to believe that giving notice would result in destruction or alteration or concealment of the materials. Justice Powell's concurring opinion noted that the Stanford Daily had announced that it would destroy any photographs that might aid the prosecution of protesters.

§ 16.25 Judicial Protective Orders and the Press

The commitment to an "uninhibited, robust, and wide-open" discussion of public issues in a free press[1] may sometimes conflict with the commitment to a criminal process in which the conclusions to be reached in a case are based on only evidence and argument in open court.[2] The problem of rights in conflict is a subject of long standing debate.[3] The problem becomes more acute with the growth of national news coverage and the electronic media. A major question is the extent to which a trial judge may insulate his or her courtroom procedures from the intrusion of outside prejudice caused by publicity surrounding the case. In this area the rights of the press may conflict with the rights of the accused.

The Supreme Court offered an important answer to this problem when it invalidated a

---

21. 436 U.S. at 564, 98 S.Ct. at 1981.

22. 436 U.S. at 566, 98 S.Ct. at 1982. The problem raised by *Zurcher* would not have arisen until after 1967 when the Supreme Court finally rejected the "mere evidence" rule and thus allowed search warrants for mere evidence of a crime. Warden v. Hayden, 387 U.S. 294, 87 S.Ct. 1642, 18 L.Ed.2d 782 (1967). After that case, the focus of a special reporter's privilege was on the question of subpoenas, the issue dealt with in Branzburg v. Hayes, 408 U.S. 665, 92 S.Ct. 2646, 33 L.Ed.2d 626 (1972).

23. 436 U.S. at 562–63, 98 S.Ct. at 1980.

24. 436 U.S. at 568 n. 1, 98 S.Ct. at 1983 n. 1 (Powell, J., concurring).

25. Maness v. Meyers, 419 U.S. 449, 95 S.Ct. 584, 42 L.Ed.2d 574 (1975). Both Justice Stevens' dissent in *Zurcher*, and Justice Stewart's dissent (joined by Justice Marshall) did not answer this point.

26. Pub.L. 96–440, 94 Stat. 1879, codified at 42 U.S.C.A. §§ 2000aa–2000aa–12.

§ 16.25

1. New York Times Co. v. Sullivan, 376 U.S. 254, 84 S.Ct. 710, 11 L.Ed.2d 686 (1964), motion denied 376 U.S. 967, 84 S.Ct. 1130, 12 L.Ed.2d 83 (1964).

2. Patterson v. Colorado, 205 U.S. 454, 27 S.Ct. 556, 51 L.Ed. 879 (1907).

3. See Chief Justice Burger's discussion of the history of this conflict in Nebraska Press Association v. Stuart, 427 U.S. 539, 547–51, 96 S.Ct. 2791, 2797–99, 49 L.Ed.2d 683 (1976). See also, Rotunda, Independent Counsel and the Charges of Leaking: A Brief Case Study, 68 Fordham Law Review 869 (1999).

Nebraska district court "gag order" that prohibited the press from publishing certain evidence pertaining to a murder suspect until the jury selection process was completed.[4] Before focusing on this decision, let us turn to the line of cases that lead to it.

Pre–Trial Publicity, Cameras in the Courts, and Court Orders Against the Press. The first reversal of a state conviction due to prejudicial pre-trial publicity occurred in 1961[5] in *Irvin v. Dowd.*[6] In that case, ninety percent of the venire and eight of the twelve members of the petit jury admitted that they had formed opinions based on the publicity surrounding the murder, and this result was obtained *after* a change of venue to an adjoining county. Justice Clark, for a unanimous Court, stated:

> With his life at stake, it is not requiring too much that petitioner be tried in an atmosphere undisturbed by so huge a wave of public passion and by a jury other than one in which two-thirds of the members admit, before hearing any testimony, to possessing a belief in his guilt.[7]

Justice Frankfurter, concurring in the judgment, portended the future by noting with acerbity the Court's failure to discuss the responsibilities of the press in protecting the fair trial guarantee:

> The Court has not yet decided that, while convictions must be reversed and miscarriages of justice result because the minds of jurors or potential jurors were poisoned, the poisoner is constitutionally protected in plying his trade.[8]

Rideau v. Louisiana[9] found that a denial of a request for change in venue offended due process when a local television had broadcast a film of the defendant confessing to the crimes in response to leading questions by the sheriff. The opinion indicates that the Court's reaction may be attributable to the coercive and pervasive nature of the television medium and the apparent complicity of the state in the broadcast.[10]

This view of the case is buttressed by the result in *Estes v. Texas,*[11] which held that the presence of television cameras recording the trial for rebroadcast over the defendant's objections was so inherently intrusive that a violation of due process was inevitable. As the majority opinion of Justice Clark observed:

> It is true that in most cases involving claims of due process deprivations we require a showing of identifiable prejudice to the accused. Nevertheless, at times a procedure employed by the state involves such a probability that prejudice will result that it is deemed inherently lacking in due process.[12]

The Court found that the incremental value of television reporting over traditional print reporting in serving the press function of providing the public with information on the operation of the criminal justice system was negligible and could justifiably be sacrificed in light of the impact that television cameras had on the judicial process. However Justice Harlan's thoughtful concurring opinion left open the possibility that future experimentation with the television might produce admirable results.[13]

Nearly two decades later, the Court retreated from the broad implications of Justice

---

4. Nebraska Press Association v. Stuart, 427 U.S. 539, 96 S.Ct. 2791, 49 L.Ed.2d 683 (1976).

5. Previously, the Court overturned federal convictions in the exercise of its federal supervisory power, see Marshall v. United States, 360 U.S. 310, 79 S.Ct. 1171, 3 L.Ed.2d 1250 (1959).

6. 366 U.S. 717, 81 S.Ct. 1639, 6 L.Ed.2d 751 (1961).

7. 366 U.S. at 723, 728, 81 S.Ct. at 1642–43.

8. 366 U.S. at 730, 81 S.Ct. at 1646.

9. 373 U.S. 723, 83 S.Ct. 1417, 10 L.Ed.2d 663 (1963), on remand 246 La. 451, 165 So.2d 282 (1964). Clark and Harlan, JJ., dissented.

10. Justice Clark's dissent found this conduct reprehensible, but argued that, as state officials, they violated no constitutional mandate and remedies were properly left to the states. 373 U.S. at 727–33, 83 S.Ct. at 1419–23.

11. 381 U.S. 532, 85 S.Ct. 1628, 14 L.Ed.2d 543 (1965), rehearing denied 382 U.S. 875, 86 S.Ct. 18, 15 L.Ed.2d 118 (1965), on remand 396 S.W.2d 123 (Tex.Cr.App.1965).

12. 381 U.S. at 542–43, 85 S.Ct. at 1632–33.

13. Justice Harlan limited the majority holding to merely stating that no requirement existed that television be allowed in a courtroom over the defendant's objections, particularly on a case of great notoriety, 381 U.S. at 587, 85 S.Ct. at 1662.

Clark's opinion in *Estes* and instead followed the more flexible approach of Justice Harlan's *Estes'* concurring opinion.[14] *Chandler v. Florida*[15] held that there is no per se constitutional prohibition against Florida providing for radio, television, and still photographic coverage of a criminal trial for public broadcast, notwithstanding the objection of the accused.

In *Chandler*, Chief Justice Burger for the Court, first concluded that *Estes* did not establish a per se rule. The Court then noted that many of the negative factors relating to television coverage that existed in 1962, when *Estes* was tried—"cumbersome equipment, cables, distracting lighting, numerous camera technicians—are less substantial factors today than they were at that time."[16]

In addition, the Florida program avoided many of the most egregious problems that had concerned the Justices in *Estes*. The Florida rules admonish the courts to protect certain witnesses—e.g., children, victims of sex crimes, some informants, the very timid—from the tensions of being televised. If the accused objects to broadcast coverage, the trial judge may define the steps necessary to eliminate the risks of prejudice to the accused.[17] The Florida guidelines also provided other safeguards such as the use of only one television camera in a fixed position, only one technician, no artificial lighting, no changing of film, videotape and lenses while court is in session, and no filming of the jury.

The Court held that due process did not require any per se prohibition against broadcasting of criminal trials. Because the defendants did not demonstrate with "specificity that the presence of cameras impaired the ability of jurors to decide the case on only the evidence before them or that the trial was affected adversely by the impact on any of the participants of the presence of cameras and

the prospect of broadcast," the Court affirmed the convictions.[18]

The *Sam Sheppard* Case. In addition to problems related to what is often called "cameras in the courts," the Court has lay guidelines governing judicial power to restrict prejudicial pretrial publicity. *Sheppard v. Maxwell*,[19] the appeal from the celebrated Dr. Sam Sheppard murder trial, found the Court held that the trial judge had failed to properly protect the defendant, jurors, and witnesses from the firestorm of publicity, much of which was erroneous and prejudicial. The Court then reversed the conviction.

Sheppard noted that there were more than adequate procedures at the judge's disposal to prevent a murder trial from being converted into a "carnival." In particular, the Court emphasized stricter control over the activities of the press within the courtroom and provision for the insulation of witnesses.

Initially, the Court said, the judge has the duty of intensive voir dire examination of prospective jurors to assure himself that excessive pre-trial publicity has not clouded the juror's presumed impartiality. Once a jury is selected, sequestration will protect its members from being subjected to the opinions and possible intimidations of an aroused community. Should the judge determine that such procedures have already been rendered inadequate by press accounts of the crime and its investigation, the alternatives of a continuance or a change of venue should be considered.

Sheppard also stressed the responsibilities of the parties to the case, i.e., defense and prosecution counsel, police officers, and witnesses, not to release information to the press. Should they abdicate this responsibility, the judge should impose it by court order.[20]

And, in a highly significant passage, the Court concluded:

---

14. 381 U.S. at 587, 85 S.Ct. at 1662.

15. 449 U.S. 560, 101 S.Ct. 802, 66 L.Ed.2d 740 (1981).

16. 449 U.S. at 575, 101 S.Ct. at 810. See Rotunda, Dealing with the Media: Ethical, Constitutional, and Practical Parameters, 84 Illinois State Bar Journal 614 (December 1996).

17. 449 U.S. at 577, 101 S.Ct. at 811.

18. Rotunda, Reporting Sensational Trials: Free Press, a Responsible Press, and Cameras in the Courts, 3 Communications Law and Policy 295 (No. 2, Spring, 1998).

19. 384 U.S. 333, 86 S.Ct. 1507, 16 L.Ed.2d 600 (1966).

20. Rotunda, Judicial Comments on Pending Cases: The Ethical Restrictions and the Sanctions–A Case Study of the Microsoft Litigation, 2001 U. Ill.L.Rev. 611 (2001).

[T]here is nothing that proscribes the press from reporting events that transpire in the courtroom.... But we must remember that reversals are but palliatives; the cure lies in those remedial measures that will prevent the prejudice at its inception. The courts must take such steps by rule and regulation that will protect their processes from prejudicial outside interferences.[21]

Within those words lay the genesis of future controversy.

Faced with increasing claims of prejudice following *Sheppard*,[22] trial courts began increasing utilization of protective orders to prevent the publication of inflammatory material, at least until a jury was impaneled. The most heinous crimes attracted the greatest publicity, and were the crimes most prone to be prejudicially affected by that publicity.[23] Protective orders provided an all too easy method of controlling this possibility.

The *Nebraska Press* Decision. The Supreme Court focused on the overuse of judicial restraining orders against the press in *Nebraska Press Association v. Stuart*.[24] Members of the state press association challenged a restraining order prohibiting them from publishing confessions by an accused in a murder trial (except those made directly to members of the press) as well as other facts "strongly implicative" of the accused.[25] In this case, the press itself was directly challenging the validity of a judicial order in light of the hostility of the First Amendment toward prior restraints.[26] The Court unanimously held the order invalid, but there were five separate opinions.

The Chief Justice, speaking for the Court,[27] narrated the history of those cases invalidating

prior restraints, and characterized them as follows:

> Prior restraints on speech are the most serious and least tolerable infringement on First Amendment rights.... A prior restraint ... has an immediate and irreversible sanction. If it can be said that a threat of criminal or civil sanctions after publication "chills" speech, prior restraint "freezes" it at least for the time.[28]

By contrast, deprivations of due process do not inevitably result from unregulated publicity surrounding notorious crimes. Rather, it was only in a rare circumstance that publicity could fatally infect the judicial process.[29] The Court was unwilling to assume that the Sixth Amendment overrides the First.[30]

The Court must protect both rights. In this case, despite the fact that pretrial press coverage posed a severe danger to the neutrality of the trial, the trial court in *Nebraska Press* had not made a showing that the entire panoply of procedures outlined in *Sheppard* would be insufficient to forestall this occurrence. Such procedures include, for example, continuance, change of venue, intensive voir dire examination, sequestration of the jurors, instruction on the duty of each juror to decide the issues on the evidence, and restraining orders on the parties involved and their attorneys in discussing issues with the press. In the absence of such a showing, the imposition of a protective order could never overcome the heavy presumption against constitutionality that inevitably attaches to prior restraints.

Further, there existed no assurance that the judge's broad order would even have served to eliminate the offending danger. Equity should not issue fruitless orders, but in context the

21. 384 U.S. at 362–65, 86 S.Ct. at 1522 (emphasis added).

22. E.g., U.S. ex rel. Doggett v. Yeager, 472 F.2d 229 (3d Cir.1973).

23. See Report of the President's Commission on the Assassination of President Kennedy, 94–99 (Assoc. Press ed. 1964) for the publicity of the Lee Harvey Oswald case.

24. 427 U.S. 539, 96 S.Ct. 2791, 49 L.Ed.2d 683 (1976).

25. 427 U.S. at 541, 96 S.Ct. at 2794.

26. See Near v. Minnesota, 283 U.S. 697, 51 S.Ct. 625, 75 L.Ed. 1357 (1931); New York Times Co. v. United States, 403 U.S. 713, 91 S.Ct. 2140, 29 L.Ed.2d 822 (1971).

27. White, Blackmun, Powell, & Rehnquist, JJ., joined in the majority opinion. Brennan, J. (joined by Stewart & Marshall, JJ.), & White, Powell, & Stevens, JJ. all wrote separate concurring opinions.

28. Nebraska Press Ass'n v. Stuart, 427 U.S. 539, 559, 96 S.Ct. 2791, 2803, 49 L.Ed.2d 683 (1976).

29. 427 U.S. at 560–61, 96 S.Ct. at 2803–04.

30. 427 U.S. at 561, 96 S.Ct. at 2803–04.

judge's order was fruitless. The editors of some of the publications might well lie beyond the reach of the *in personam* jurisdiction of the court even though their publications are distributed throughout the country or district from which the jurors are drawn. Moreover, the speculative nature of a protective order created problems in drafting because it appeared to prohibit the publication of material that would not possess a prejudicial effect, while not encompassing seemingly innocent information that would later develop into very damaging evidence.

Finally, the Court emphasized the portion of the order that prohibited the publication of information obtained in open court could not, under any circumstances, prevail. As *Sheppard* warned: "there is nothing which proscribes the press from reporting events that transpire in the courtroom".[31] The judge may in his discretion, if the relevant statutes allow, and subject to constitutional limitations discussed below, close the courtroom during portions of the proceedings, but if that alternative is bypassed, the trial court cannot effectuate that result retroactively by a protective order. If the information is lawfully obtained from an open hearing in court, the court cannot restrain its republication by the press.[32]

Justice Brennan in his separate opinion argued that the only instance where the presumption against prior restraints is rebuttable is in crises affecting national security. In all other situations, the protections of the First Amendment must remain preeminent. The de-

fendant's rights to a fair trial must rest on those procedures that had traditionally been within the province of the trial judge.[33]

However, five of the Justices felt that it was unnecessary to formulate such a broad rule on the basis of the facts. Because the state courts had made no finding as to the efficacy of these alternative procedures, it may, in theory, still be permitted to argue that, in highly unusual circumstances, a fair trial will be impossible to obtain without a limitation on the information that the press can publish.[34] Such a position might possibly be acceptable to only some of the Justices, and then, only as a last resort.

The *Gentile* Case—Controlling Lawyers and the "Substantial Likelihood of Material Prejudice" Test

A practical result of the *Nebraska Press Association* case may be the increasing use of restraining orders on the parties under the trial court's control: the attorneys, the police, and witnesses. These orders may prove more effective than in the past because *Branzburg v. Hayes*[35] supports the power of the courts to compel reporters to reveal the source of their information.

Courts also try to control trial and pretrial publicity by enforcing attorney ethics rules. But such "silence orders" will not be upheld, unless there is a substantial likelihood of material prejudice. The "substantial likelihood" test is the rule after *Gentile v. State Bar of Nevada*.[36] This test is less strict than *Nebraska*

---

31. Sheppard v. Maxwell, 384 U.S. 333, 86 S.Ct. 1507, 16 L.Ed.2d 600 (1966); cf. Cox Broadcasting Corp. v. Cohn, 420 U.S. 469, 95 S.Ct. 1029, 43 L.Ed.2d 328 (1975), on remand 234 Ga. 67, 214 S.E.2d 530 (1975).

32. Cf. Cox Broadcasting Corp. v. Cohn, 420 U.S. 469, 95 S.Ct. 1029, 43 L.Ed.2d 328 (1975), on remand 234 Ga. 67, 214 S.E.2d 530 (1975).

Landmark Communications, Inc. v. Virginia, 435 U.S. 829, 98 S.Ct. 1535, 56 L.Ed.2d 1 (1978) held that a state cannot punish a newspaper or other third party who is neither an employee nor participant of a judicial disciplinary commission for publishing truthful information about a confidential investigation in progress.

Smith v. Daily Mail Publishing Co., 443 U.S. 97, 99 S.Ct. 2667, 61 L.Ed.2d 399 (1979) (state may not punish a newspaper's truthful publication of an alleged juvenile delinquent's name lawfully obtained by a newspaper).

33. 427 U.S. at 572–613, 96 S.Ct. at 2809–2829, Justices Stewart and Marshall joining.

34. See United States v. Abbott Laboratories, 369 F.Supp. 1396 (E.D.N.C.1973), judgment reversed 505 F.2d 565 (4th Cir.1974), certiorari denied 420 U.S. 990, 95 S.Ct. 1424, 43 L.Ed.2d 671 (1975). *Abbott Laboratories* was an unusual case. The trial court dismissed an indictment for introduction of adulterated drugs into interstate commerce on the grounds that alternative procedures were insufficient to ensure a fair trial. This ruling of the trial court is not justified, for its logical conclusion is that if a crime is heinous enough—perhaps even was committed on television—the resulting publicity (created by the crime itself) should be enough to prevent a trial. The appellate court appropriately reversed.

35. 408 U.S. 665, 92 S.Ct. 2646, 33 L.Ed.2d 626 (1972).

36. 501 U.S. 1030, 111 S.Ct. 2720, 115 L.Ed.2d 888 (1991). Several lower courts anticipated that some of the state ethics rules raised First Amendment problems. See, Chicago Council of Lawyers v. Bauer, 522 F.2d 242 (7th

Press Association because the judicial order is not against the press (which is not a party to the proceeding) but against the lawyers, who represent parties to the proceeding.

Attorney Gentile held a press conference a few hours after Nevada had indicted his client. Gentile made a brief statement, and gave a sketch of his client's defense, stating that Nevada sought the conviction of an innocent man as a "scapegoat," and it had not "been honest enough to indict the people who did it; the police department, crooked cops." He declined to answer reporters' questions seeking more detailed comments. Six months later, a jury acquitted Gentile's client of all counts.

Then the Nevada State Bar filed a complaint claiming that Gentile had violated Nevada's Supreme Court Rule 177, governing pretrial publicity. This ethics rule was almost identical to the American Bar Association's Model Rule 3.6, of the ABA Model Rules of Professional Conduct. (The ABA later amended that rule in response to *Gentile.*) Rule 177(1) prohibited a lawyer from making "an extrajudicial statement that a reasonable person would expect to be disseminated by means of public communication" if a reasonable lawyer would know that it "will have a substantial likelihood of materially prejudicing an adjudicative proceeding." Rule 177(3) purported to provide a "safe harbor," listing statements that can be made (e.g., the general nature of the defense, information in a public record) "notwithstanding" previous subsections of the Rule.

In a portion of the opinion of the Court that Justice Kennedy wrote, the Court held that Rule 177, as interpreted by the state court, was unconstitutionally vague. The "notwithstanding" language misled Gentile into thinking that he would give his press conference if complied with Rule 177(3).

Chief Justice Rehnquist authored another portion of the Opinion for the Court. It approved of the Rule 177's general test, prohibiting lawyers from publicly disseminating information that one reasonably knows has "substantial likelihood of materially prejudicing an adjudicative proceeding." This test is neutral as to points of view and does not forbid the lawyer from speaking but only postpones it until after the trial.

It is important to note that the Nevada Rule, like the ABA Model Rule, allows an attorney to say what is in a public record. As a constitutional matter, it should be easy to justify allowing an attorney to reveal what is already in a public record.[37] However, this public records exception—not merely found in the ethics rules but an inherent byproduct of the First Amendment—provided an important exception, because of the tendency of prosecutors and defense counsel to tell a story when they file pleadings. An indictment, for example, need not be limited to the bare bones. The prosecutor may describe the alleged crime in detail, may refer to unindicted alleged co-conspirators and what they may have said or done, and so forth. One defendant claimed that "he had never known that his nickname was 'The Snake' until he saw it stated as an alias in an indictment—and then heard the prosecutor repeatedly calling him that on television."[38] (It should not be too controversial to suggest that "the Snake" has pejorative connotations.) Defense counsel, as well, can file pleadings, such as bail motions or other pretrial motions, that tell a detailed story and make detailed allegations that become part of the public record.

***Gannett* and the Right to a Public Trial.** To cope with problems of pretrial publicity, courts at times have sought to close portions of the proceedings to the public, because where

---

Cir.1975), certiorari denied sub nom. Cunningham v. Chicago Council of Lawyers, 427 U.S. 912, 96 S.Ct. 3201, 49 L.Ed.2d 1204 (1976); Hirschkop v. Snead, 594 F.2d 356 (4th Cir.1979) (per curiam). But see, United States v. Tijerina, 412 F.2d 661 (10th Cir.1969), certiorari denied 396 U.S. 990, 90 S.Ct. 478, 24 L.Ed.2d 452 (1969).

These issues, and the ABA's reaction to Gentile, are discussed in, Rotunda, Can You Say That?, 30 Trial Magazine 18 (December, 1994).

37. Cf. Sheppard v. Maxwell, 384 U.S. 333, 362–63, 86 S.Ct. 1507, 1522, 16 L.Ed.2d 600 (1966): "there is nothing that proscribes the press from reporting events that transpire in the courtroom."

38. See, Monroe Freedman, Muzzling Trial Publicity: New Rule Needed, Legal Times (of Washington, D.C.) April 5, 1993.

the press lawfully obtains information the court cannot thereafter prohibit the press from publishing it.[39] In *Gannett Co., Inc. v. DePasquale*,[40] the Supreme Court upheld this practice under the narrow circumstances of that case. The Court held, by a five to four vote, that neither the public nor the press has an independent constitutional right to insist on access to a *pretrial* suppression hearing, *if* the accused, the prosecutor, and the trial judge all agree that the proceeding should be closed in order to assure a fair trial.

There were various suggestions in *Gannett* that the opinion should be read narrowly. The majority emphasized that any denial of public access was only temporary, because once the danger of prejudice had dissipated the court made available a transcript of the suppression hearing.[41] The majority also discussed the dangers of pretrial publicity in this particular case. In addition, the decision was a five to four opinion, so a shift of even one vote would change the result. Three of the five member majority wrote separate concurrences. Chief Justice Burger emphasized that what was involved in their case was "not a *trial;* it is a *pre* trial hearing."[42] Justice Powell concurring, stated that he would have held that the press, as an agent of the public, does have a First Amendment right to be present at the pretrial suppression hearing but that, on balance, this non-absolute right was adequately respected in the present case.[43]

The *Richmond* Case. A narrow interpretation of *Gannett* limited to pretrial hearings is supported by the decision shortly thereafter in *Richmond Newspapers, Inc. v. Virginia*.[44] The fragmented Court, with only Justice Rehnquist

dissenting (and Justice Powell not participating), rejected the asserted power of a state trial judge to close a criminal trial. The state judge had relied on a state statute granting broad discretion in such matters.

Chief Justice Burger, joined by Justices White and Stevens, relied on the First and Fourteenth Amendments to give the public the right of access to criminal trials. There is a "presumption of openness,"[45] and that "[a]bsent an overriding interest articulated in findings, the trial of a criminal case must be open to the public."[46]

Justice Brennan, joined by Justice Marshall, concurred in the judgment; though they did not appear to disagree with any of the substance of Chief Justice Burger's opinion they did not join it. They noted that mere agreement of the trial judge and parties cannot constitutionally close a trial to the public in light of the First Amendment guarantees. And, because the state statute in this case authorized the trial judge and parties to engage in trial closures with unfettered discretion, "[w]hat countervailing interest might be sufficiently compelling to reverse this presumption of openness need not concern us now. . . ."[47]

The *Globe Newspaper* Ruling. In *Globe Newspaper Co. v. Superior Court*[48] the Court produced a majority opinion, elaborated on the meaning of *Richmond Newspapers*, and invalidated a state statute, unique to Massachusetts, that *required* trial judges to exclude the press and general public from the courtroom during the testimony of the victim in cases involving certain specified sexual offenses. Although the Court invalidated the mandatory state law

---

39. Landmark Communications, Inc. v. Virginia, 435 U.S. 829, 98 S.Ct. 1535, 56 L.Ed.2d 1 (1978); Smith v. Daily Mail Pub. Co., 443 U.S. 97, 99 S.Ct. 2667, 61 L.Ed.2d 399 (1979).

40. 443 U.S. 368, 99 S.Ct. 2898, 61 L.Ed.2d 608 (1979).

41. 443 U.S. at 392, 99 S.Ct. at 2911–12.

42. 443 U.S. at 394, 99 S.Ct. at 2913 (Burger, C. J., concurring) (emphasis in original).

43. 443 U.S. at 403, 99 S.Ct. at 2917.

44. 448 U.S. 555, 100 S.Ct. 2814, 65 L.Ed.2d 973 (1980).

45. 448 U.S. at 576, 100 S.Ct. at 2826–27. This case is the first ever to find constitutional protection for a right of

access, a right to acquire newsworthy information. 448 U.S. at 583, 100 S.Ct. at 2830–31.

46. 448 U.S. at 587, 100 S.Ct. at 2833 (footnote omitted).

47. 448 U.S. at 600, 100 S.Ct. at 2840 (footnote omitted). Justice Stewart, concurring in the judgment, also relied on a First Amendment right of access. Justice Blackmun, concurring in the judgment, relied principally on the Sixth Amendment, but also acknowledged the secondary role of the First Amendment as a source of this right to access.

48. 457 U.S. 596, 102 S.Ct. 2613, 73 L.Ed.2d 248 (1982).

(which required no particularized determinations in individual cases), it left open the possibility that under appropriate circumstances and in individual cases the trial court could exclude the press and public during the testimony of minor victims of sex crimes.

Justice Brennan, for the Court, explained that under *Richmond Newspapers* the First Amendment, as applied to the states, grants to the press and general public "a right of access to *criminal trials*"[49] because historically such trials have been open and such openness aids in the functioning of the judicial process and the government of the whole. Thus states may deny access only if denial serves "a compelling governmental interest, and is narrowly tailored to serve that interest."[50]

The statute was said to serve two basic state interests: first, protecting minor victims of sex crimes from further trauma and embarrassment and, second, encouraging victims to come forward and testify truthfully. Though this first interest was compelling, it did "not justify a *mandatory*-closure rule, for it is clear that the circumstances of the particular case may affect the significance of the interest."[51] The judge should consider the minor victim's wishes regarding disclosure, as well as the victim's age and maturity, the interests of relatives, the nature of the crime, and so on. In the present case the defendant objected to closure, the state made no motion for closure, and the victims may have been willing to testify without closure.

The second interest—to encourage witnesses to come forward—was speculative, and, given the nature of the statute, illogical: the statute did not deny the press access to the transcript or other possible sources that could provide an account of the testimony; the press could still publish the victim's identity and the substance of the testimony. Finally, the state's interest is not compelling. The asserted state interest would justify too many types of closure because "minor victims of sex crimes are [not] the *only* crime victims who, because of publicity attendant to criminal trials, are reluctant to come forward."[52]

Voir Dire Proceedings: The *Press–Enterprise* Test. In *Press–Enterprise Co. v. Superior Court*,[53] the Court held that the First Amendment protected a right of access to voir dire proceedings for the screening of potential jurors. Chief Justice Burger, for the majority opinion, found that the history of open jury selection and First Amendment values justified the conclusion that these pretrial proceedings should come within the presumption of openness that had been established in the *Richmond Newspapers* and *Globe Newspaper* cases. Burger then set out a standard to be followed by lower courts when determining whether a portion of the trial process should be closed: "The presumption of openness may be overcome only by an overriding interest based on findings that closure is essential to preserve higher values and is narrowly tailored to serve that interest. The interest is to be articulated along with findings specific enough that a reviewing court can determine whether the closure order was properly entered."[54]

---

49. 457 U.S. at 604–05, 102 S.Ct. at 2619 (emphasis in original).

50. 457 U.S. at 607, 102 S.Ct. at 2620.

51. 457 U.S. at 608, 102 S.Ct. at 2621.

52. 457 U.S. at 610, 102 S.Ct. at 2622 (emphasis in original).

O'Connor, J., concurred in the judgment and emphasized her view that neither *Richmond Newspapers* nor this case carried implications outside of criminal trials. Burger, C. J., joined by Rehnquist, J., dissented and objected to the paradox that the Court decision "denies the victim the kind of protection routinely given to juveniles who commit crimes." 457 U.S. at 620, 102 S.Ct. at 2627.

53. 464 U.S. 501, 104 S.Ct. 819, 78 L.Ed.2d 629 (1984).

54. 464 U.S. at 510, 104 S.Ct. at 824, 78 L.Ed.2d at 638. There is a two step method of analysis. First, a court

must find that the interest asserted is overriding or compelling and outweighs the First Amendment right of access of the press and the public to attend trial proceedings. Second, the court must make specific findings determining that the closure is essential to preserve those compelling or overriding interests, and that alternative procedures cannot adequately protect those interests.

Sixth Amendment Right to Public Trial. A defendant has a Sixth Amendment right to a trial and this right applies to the states through the Fourteenth Amendment. The right of the defendant to a public trial applies to pretrial proceedings as well as to the trial itself. The Court has found that the *defendant's* Sixth Amendment right is no less protective of a public trial than the *public's* First Amendment right established in these cases.

Waller v. Georgia, 467 U.S. 39, 104 S.Ct. 2210, 81 L.Ed.2d 31 (1984), on remand 253 Ga. 146, 319 S.E.2d 11

In the *Press–Enterprise* case, the Court found that the lower courts were not justified in closing all but a few days of a six week jury selection process. However, Burger's opinion for the Court stated that "the jury selection process may, in some circumstances, give rise to a compelling interest of a prospective juror when interrogation touches upon deeply personal matters...."[55] The lower court had not articulated findings showing that no alternative procedure less intrusive on First Amendment rights would have protected the privacy rights of jurors in this case. Burger indicated that courts should require potential jurors to affirmatively request that some portion of the selection process be closed to protect their privacy interest and that the trial court should determine both that the individual privacy interest asserted outweighed the First Amendment right of access and that no other alternative to closure would adequately protect that interest.

Publication of Rape Victim's Name. In 1975 the Court held that the state, even in a right to privacy action, may not impose sanctions on the accurate publication of a rape victim's name obtained from public records open to public inspection.[56]

Nearly a decade and a half later, the issue came up again in *Florida Star v. B.J.F.*,[57] The respondent sought to distinguish the earlier case on the grounds that a statute could punish publication of a sexual offense victim's name or other identifying information where it had not yet become "part of an open public record" by virtue of being revealed in "open, public judicial proceedings."[58]

The Court did not buy the distinction, and held that a Florida statute could not make a newspaper civilly liable for publishing the name of a rape victim, a name that the newspaper had obtained from a publicly released police report. However, the majority did not hold broadly that the state may never punish truthful publication; rather, its ruling was more narrow. Where a newspaper publishes truthful information lawfully obtained, the state may lawfully impose punishment, if at all, only when the statute is "narrowly tailored to a state interest of the highest order, and that no such interest is satisfactorily served by imposing liability" under the facts of this case.

Justice Scalia, concurring in part and concurring in the judgment, noted various inconsistencies in the Florida law. For example, because it did not prohibit gossip by the rape victim's acquaintances, the law discriminated against the institutional press. The institutional press should enjoy *no fewer rights* than any ordinary individual exercising freedom of speech, but the Florida law gave the press fewer rights.

Juvenile Proceedings. Similarly, it is unconstitutional for a court to issue a pretrial order enjoining the media from publishing the name or photograph of an 11–year-old boy in connection with the child's juvenile proceeding that reporters had attended.[59]

Witnesses' Disclosure of Their Own Testimony Before the Grand Jury. In *Butterworth v. Smith*,[60] the Court invalidated a

---

(1984) found that when a defendant requests pretrial proceedings to be open to the public there can be a closure of the proceedings only if the trial court makes findings sufficient to "meet the tests set out in *Press–Enterprise* and its predecessors." The trial court must make specific findings as to the interest that would justify closure of any portion of the pretrial proceedings.

55. 464 U.S. at 511, 104 S.Ct. at 825, 79 L.Ed.2d at 639.

56. Cox Broadcasting Corp. v. Cohn 420 U.S. 469, 95 S.Ct. 1029, 43 L.Ed.2d 328 (1975).

57. 491 U.S. 524, 109 S.Ct. 2603, 105 L.Ed.2d 443 (1989).

See, Rotunda, Eschewing Bright Lines, 25 Trial Magazine 52, 54–55 (Dec. 1989) (discussing *Florida Star v. B.J.F.*).

58. The Florida Star v. B.J.F., 491 U.S. 524, 529 n. 3, 109 S.Ct. 2603, 2607 n. 3; Brief for Appellee 12, 24, 25. Appellee also argued that the privacy interests at stake were far less profound than in the present case. See, e.g., Brief for Appellee, at 34. At the oral argument, the appellee candidly urged the Court to overrule *Cox Broadcasting* and replace it with a categorical rule that publication of the name of a rape victim never enjoys constitutional protection. Tr. of Oral Arg. 44.

59. Oklahoma Publishing Co. v. Oklahoma County District Court, 430 U.S. 308, 97 S.Ct. 1045, 51 L.Ed.2d 355 (1977).

60. 494 U.S. 624, 110 S.Ct. 1376, 108 L.Ed.2d 572 (1990). Scalia, J., concurring, thought that "there is considerable doubt whether a witness can be prohibited, even while the grand jury is sitting, from making public what he knew before he entered the grand-jury room. Quite a

Florida statute that, with certain limited exceptions, prohibited a grand jury witness from ever disclosing testimony that he gave before the grand jury. A reporter for a Florida newspaper had written a series of articles about alleged improprieties committed by his county's State Attorney's Office and Sheriff's Department, and later testified before a grand jury that was called to investigate the alleged improprieties. After the grand jury had terminated its investigation, he sought a declaration of the statute's invalidity because he wanted to publish a series of articles (or perhaps a book) about the investigation and his experiences in dealing with the grand jury.

A unanimous Court held that insofar as the Florida law prohibits a grand jury witness from disclosing his own testimony after the term of the grand jury has ended, it violates the First Amendment. The state's interest in preserving grand jury secrecy is either not served by, or insufficient to warrant, proscription of truthful speech on matters of public concern.

The Public's Right to Attend Civil Cases. In *Richmond Newspapers* Chief Justice Burger noted that while the question of the public's right to attend trials in *civil* cases was not before it, "we note that historically both civil and criminal trials have been presumptively open."[61]

Notwithstanding this legal fact, empirical evidence shows that some judges claim an inherent power to close civil trials, in order, it is alleged, to protect "privacy." In fact, judges are more likely to close civil trials in order to protect the establishment (and the sons and

daughters of the wealthy) from public scrutiny.[62]

Although the Supreme Court has consistently invalidated judicial protective orders that prohibited newspapers from publishing information about trial proceedings, in *Seattle Times Co. v. Rhinehart*,[63] the Court upheld a protective order restricting the use of information gained through pretrial civil discovery by a newspaper that was a party to the litigation.

Trial courts have the power to order parties to civil litigation to disclose a wide range of information to opposing parties that is of possible relevance to the preparation for trial of the lawsuit. This power to order wide-ranging discovery in virtually every jurisdiction also involves court authority to issue a protective order requiring the parties to whom the information is disclosed not to publish or disclose the information for any purpose other than the limited purposes of preparing for and trying the lawsuit if disclosure of the information would cause demonstrable harm to the disclosing party.[64]

In *Seattle Times*, the Court examined a trial court order restricting a newspaper, which was a defendant in a defamation action, from publishing information gained from the plaintiff. The order allowed the newspaper to publish identical information if it could show that it had received that information from a source independent of the pretrial discovery proceedings. The Supreme Court found that this order constituted neither a true prior restraint of speech nor any other impermissible prohibition of speech or suppression of publications.

---

different question is presented, however, by a witness's disclosure of the grand-jury proceedings, which is knowledge he acquires not 'on his own' but only by virtue of being made a witness."

61. Richmond Newspapers, Inc. v. Virginia, 448 U.S. 555, 581 n. 17, 100 S.Ct. 2814, 2829 n. 17, 65 L.Ed.2d 973 (1980) (plurality opinion of Burger, C.J., joined by White & Stevens, JJ.) See also, e.g., North Jersey Media Group, Inc. v. Ashcroft, 308 F.3d 198, 206–207 (3d Cir.2002).

62. See, Rooney, Sealed Court Files a Growing Concern, 136 Chicago Daily Law Bulletin, at 1, col. 1–3 & 7, col.1–4 (April, 1990), showing that many judges routinely seal court files to protect well-known people. For example, Illinois courts impounded two lawsuits involving a well-known Chicago divorce lawyer accused of improperly coaxing a client into having sexual relations with him. In at

least one of these cases, entitled Suppressed v. Suppressed (Circuit Court), II. 88 L 22434 (Appellate Court) No. 1–89–2950, the plaintiff's lawyer opposed the impoundment order, which the trial judge issued anyway.

63. 467 U.S. 20, 104 S.Ct. 2199, 81 L.Ed.2d 17 (1984).

64. For a description of the scope of modern discovery and the need for protective orders in relation to the discovery process, see Marcus, Myth and Reality in Protective Order Litigation, 69 Cornell L.Rev. 1 (1983). *Seattle Times Co. v. Rhinehart* cited this article for the description of the nature of the process and the need for protective orders, and also for the proposition that pretrial discovery proceedings normally are conducted in private so there could be no analogy to a public right of access to this information similar to that established by the Court in the cases dealing with access to trials.

Nonetheless, the Court was unanimous in finding that the order should be upheld only if it was narrowly tailored to promote an important or substantial governmental interest—an interest that must be unrelated to the suppression of expression. The government's interest in protecting the privacy rights of parties to litigation and operating a system of truly open pretrial discovery that would facilitate the adjudicatory process were both substantial and unrelated to any governmental interest in suppressing or punishing speech. The order allows publication of the information if it were gained from an independent source, so it was not unnecessarily restrictive of the newspaper's rights.[65]

Public Disclosure of Recordings of Private Telephone Calls. *Bartnicki v. Vopper*[66] considered the constitutionality of state and federal wiretap laws applied in an unusual circumstance. An unknown third party intercepted and taped a cellular telephone conversation of the plaintiffs. This third party gave the tapes to media defendants who broadcast the tape. The plaintiff sued the media, asserting claims under federal and Pennsylvania wiretapping acts. In the facts of this case, the Court held the statutes were unconstitutional as applied. The holding is narrow, so it is important to understand the facts.

Bartnicki, in short, held, first, the prohibitions of the wiretap acts against intentional disclosure of illegally intercepted communication that the disclosing party knows or should know was illegally obtained are content-neutral laws of general applicability; and, second,

the application of those provisions against these defendants violated their free speech rights, because the tape concerned matter of public importance and the defendants had played no part in the illegal interception.[67]

This case began when an unidentified person intercepted and recorded a cell phone conversation between a chief union negotiator and a union president engaged in labor negotiations with a local school board The president said: "If they're not gonna move for three percent, we're gonna have to go to their, their homes.... To blow off their front porches, we'll have to do some work on some of those guys." After the union signed a contract, respondent Vopper, a radio commentator, played a tape of this conversation on his public affairs talk show in connection with news reports about the settlement. Petitioners filed this damages suit under both federal and state wiretapping laws, alleging that their conversation had been surreptitiously intercepted by an unknown person; that another respondent (who said he found the tape in his mail box) intentionally disclosed it to media representatives; and that they repeatedly published the conversation even though they knew or had reason to know that it had been illegally intercepted.

Under the relevant statutes, an individual violated the law by intentionally disclosing the contents of an electronic communication when he or she knows or has reason to know that the information was obtained through an illegal interception, even if the individual was not

65. The majority opinion stated that: "A litigant has no First Amendment right of access to information made available only for purposes of trying his suit.... Thus, continued court control over the discovered information does not raise the same specter of government censorship that such control might suggest in other situations." 467 U.S. at 32, 104 S.Ct. at 2207.

This statement should not be taken too broadly. It does not mean that all trial court protective orders, no matter how broad or unnecessary to the promotion of a significant governmental interest unrelated to censorship goals, should be upheld. Rather, the statement only suggests that a limited order, which is reasonably tailored to promote the interest in protecting the personal or commercial privacy of the litigants or in promoting wide-ranging discovery, may be upheld. The court issuing the protective order should make findings as to the nature of interests

that are to be protected, so that the appellate court could determine whether it was necessary or at least reasonably related to the protection of governmental interests unrelated to the suppression of expression.

66. 532 U.S. 514, 121 S.Ct. 1753, 149 L.Ed.2d 787 (2001).

67. Breyer, J., joined by O'Connor, J., concurring, emphasized that he "would not extend that holding beyond these present circumstances." Rehnquist, C.J., joined by Scalia & Thomas, JJ., dissented. "Court's decision diminishes, rather than enhances, the purposes of the First Amendment, chilling the speech of the millions of Americans who rely upon electronic technology to communicate each day," if the conversation is on "a matter of 'public concern,' an amorphous concept that the Court does not even attempt to define."

involved in that interception. The issue before the Court was the constitutionality of these statutes as applied to this case, where the Court assumed that, first, respondents played no part in the illegal interception; second, they lawfully obtained access to the tapes, although someone else had obtained the tapes unlawfully; and third, the subject matter of the conversations "were a matter of public concern," that is, that they were "newsworthy".

Justice Stevens, speaking for the Court, held the statutes unconstitutional on these facts and emphasized the narrowness of the ruling. He began by noting that *New York Times v. United States*[68] had upheld the right of the press to publish information of great public concern obtained from documents stolen by a third party. *New York Times* "focused on the character of the stolen documents's contents and the consequences of public disclosure," rather than the fact that the newspapers published information "obtained from stolen documents."[69]

While the federal law and its state analog are content-neutral laws of general applicability, still, this "naked prohibition against disclosures is fairly characterized as a regulation of pure speech," not conduct, just like the delivery of a handbill is really speech, not conduct.[70] The general rule, said the Court, is that "state action to punish the publication of truthful information seldom can satisfy constitutional standards."[71]

The first interest that the federal and state statutes served is in removing an incentive for parties to intercept private conversations. This interest did not justify the statutes' restrictions as applied to those who were not involved in the initial illegality because the government may still prosecute the person who acted illegally.

The second interest, minimizing harm to persons whose conversations have been illegally intercepted, is considerably stronger, but still does not justify the statute in this case, because "privacy concerns give way when balanced against the interest in publishing matters of public importance." A cost inevitably associated with participation in public affairs is an accompanying loss of privacy. As Warren and Brandeis, in their classic law review article, *The Right to Privacy*, acknowledged: "The right of privacy does not prohibit any publication of matter which is of public or general interest."[72]

The Court did not reach the question whether the law is constitutional as applied to "disclosures of trade secrets or domestic gossip or other information of purely private concern."[73]

§ 16.26 Commercial Speech: An Introduction

Commercial speech, such as advertising, has always been subject to substantial governmental regulation. Until relatively recently the Court has simply excluded all commercial speech, even truthful advertising, from the coverage of the First Amendment. Now commercial speech appears to be vested with extensive First Amendment protection. However, commercial speech still does not have the full First Amendment protection of political speech. The state can issue reasonable time, place, or manner regulations of commercial speech. In addition, the state has a broader power to regulate misleading commercial speech than its power to regulate misleading or libelous speech about public officials or public figures.

Commercial speech may be understood as speech of any form that advertises a product or service for profit or for business purpose. Commercial speech proposes a commercial transaction. This definition is not precise, and

68. 403 U.S. 713, 91 S.Ct. 2140, 29 L.Ed.2d 822 (1971) (per curiam).

69. Bartnicki v. Vopper, 532 U.S. at 528, 121 S.Ct. at 1762.

70. 532 U.S. 514, 526–27, 121 S.Ct. 1753, 1761.

71. Bartnicki v. Vopper 532 U.S. 514, 527–28, 121 S.Ct. 1753, 1761, quoting Smith v. Daily Mail Publishing

Co., 443 U.S. 97, 102, 99 S.Ct. 2667, 61 L.Ed.2d 399 (1979).

72. Warren and Brandeis, The Right to Privacy, 4 Harv.L.Rev. 193, 214 (1890). See also Restatement (Second) of Torts § 652D (1977).

73. Bartnicki v. Vopper, 532 U.S. 514, 533, 121 S.Ct. 1753, 1764.

courts have not consistently applied it. Neither is it self-evident why this category of speech should be treated differently from other types of speech. Keep these points in mind as we consider the free speech rights of commercial speech.

§ 16.27   Origins of the Commercial Speech Doctrine

In *Valentine v. Chrestensen*,[1] an entrepreneur in New York City distributed a leaflet containing on one side an advertisement for a commercial exhibition of a former Navy submarine and on the other side a message protesting the City's denial of wharfage facilities for the exhibition. The entrepreneur was convicted of violating a sanitary code provision forbidding the distribution of advertising matter in the streets.

The Supreme Court upheld the conviction unanimously, even though, three years earlier, the Court had struck down several municipal ordinances applied to severely restrict the distribution of political or religious handbills in the streets or in house-to-house canvassing.[2] The Court earlier had stated that "the public convenience in respect of cleanliness of the streets does not justify an exertion of the police power which invades the free communication of information and opinion secured by the Constitution."[3] But the Court had carefully noted that it had not held "that commercial soliciting and canvassing may not be subjected to such regulation as the ordinance requires."[4]

Chrestensen took this dictum and expanded it into what has become known as the "commercial speech" doctrine:

This court has unequivocally held that the streets are proper places for the exercise of

the freedom of communicating information and disseminating opinion and that, though the states and municipalities may appropriately regulate the privilege in the public interest, they may not unduly burden or proscribe its employment in these public thoroughfares. We are equally clear that the Constitution imposes *no such restraint on government as respects purely commercial advertising.*[5]

For many years cases relied on this simple pronouncement to exclude completely so-called "commercial speech" from any protection of the First Amendment.

In distributing his leaflet, the entrepreneur in *Chrestensen* was, in the Court's view, attempting to "pursue a gainful occupation in the streets,"[6] and his right to do so was purely a matter for "legislative judgment."[7] The state does not need to justify its judgment by an overriding or compelling state interest, or balance its rule against any inherent right to employ advertising as a business technique. The Court said that if speech is "purely commercial," it is subject to regulation to the same extent and for the same reasons as other forms of commercial activity. *Chrestensen*, "without citing precedent, historical evidence, or policy considerations, ... effectively read commercial speech out of the First Amendment."[8] Commercial speech, under this ruling, is not subject to less First Amendment protection; it is subject to no First Amendment protection.

The entrepreneur had placed a political protest message on the back of his advertising leaflet. The Court disposed of that fact with the statement that it was "enough" that the

---

§ 16.27

1. 316 U.S. 52, 62 S.Ct. 920, 86 L.Ed. 1262 (1942).

See generally, 4 Ronald D. Rotunda & John E. Nowak, Treatise on Constitutional Law: Substance and Procedure §§ 20.27–31 (West Group, 3d ed.1999).

2. Schneider v. State (Town of Irvington), 308 U.S. 147, 60 S.Ct. 146, 84 L.Ed. 155 (1939); see also Lovell v. Griffin, 303 U.S. 444, 58 S.Ct. 666, 82 L.Ed. 949 (1938), opinion conformed 57 Ga.App. 901, 197 S.E. 347 (1938). In both cases the ordinances were held unconstitutional, apparently for reasons of overbreadth.

3. Schneider v. State (Town of Irvington), 308 U.S. 147, 163, 60 S.Ct. 146, 151, 84 L.Ed. 155 (1939).

4. 308 U.S. at 165, 60 S.Ct. at 152.

5. 316 U.S. at 54, 62 S.Ct. at 921 (emphasis added).

6. Valentine v. Chrestensen, 316 U.S. 52, 54, 62 S.Ct. 920, 921, 86 L.Ed. 1262 (1942).

7. 316 U.S. 52, 54, 62 S.Ct. 920, 921, 86 L.Ed. 1262 (1942).

8. Redish, The First Amendment in the Marketplace: Commercial Speech and the Values of Free Expression, 39 Geo.Wash.L.Rev. 429, 450 (1971).

message had admittedly been designed "with the intent, and for the purpose, of evading the prohibition of the ordinance."[9] Thus, the Court declined to "indulge nice appraisals based upon subtle distinctions,"[10] and, instead, looked to the primary purpose of the protest message.

Apparently the Court considered the "speech-on-the-handbill" to be "commercial" and thus not within the First Amendment. Even *Chrestensen* did not suggest that it would have allowed a court to enjoin the entrepreneur from simply telling someone about his submarine. If *Chrestensen* would indeed have made a distinction between the "speech" versus the "speech-on-the-handbill," then the difficulty of defining "commercial" speech with any precision is emphasized.

The Court might have issued a narrower ruling, by simply approving the regulation as a reasonable one under the particular circumstances. Instead it fashioned a more general approach for future cases: when the primary purpose of the speech is "commercial," it falls within a category of speech that lacks the protection of the First Amendment.

§ 16.28   Subsequent Development of the Commercial Speech Doctrine

In *Murdock v. Pennsylvania*[1] and *Breard v. Alexandria*[2] the Court elaborated on the reach of *Chrestensen* and its primary purpose test. *Murdock* overturned the convictions of several Jehovah's Witnesses who had violated an ordinance by selling religious books without paying a license tax. The Court stated flatly that a "state may not impose a charge for the enjoyment of a right guaranteed by the Federal Constitution" and equated the power to impose the license tax with "the power of censorship which this Court has repeatedly struck

down."[3] The Court stressed that the fact that the books had been sold did not automatically bring the books within the Commercial Speech doctrine nor diminish the petitioners' First Amendment privileges; the sales had been "merely *incidental* and collateral" to a principal purpose of disseminating religious beliefs.[4]

The petitioners had not attempted to profit from the sales, and indeed there is some suggestion in the Court's opinion that this fact influenced the Court nearly as much as the petitioners' religious motives.[5] At one point the Court stated in dictum that the "constitutional rights of those spreading their religious beliefs through the spoken and printed word are not to be gauged by standards governing retailers or wholesalers of books.'"[6] In its holding, however, *Murdock* is authority for the more limited principle that the exercise of an established First Amendment right cannot be circumscribed merely because it contains an incidental commercial aspect. Apparently, however, if the profit in the sales had been the primary purpose of the speech, *Chrestensen* would have applied.[7]

This view is supported by *Breard*, where the Court faced the profit motive squarely in upholding an ordinance prohibiting unsolicited door-to-door magazine subscription sales. Earlier, *Martin v. Struthers*,[8] pointing to the freedoms of speech and religion, had voided a similar ordinance applied to prevent Jehovah's Witnesses from distributing free religious tracts door-to-door. *Breard* agreed that "the fact that periodicals are sold does not put them beyond" the First Amendment, but it reasoned that in *Martin* "no element of the commercial" had entered into the distribution, and here, the "selling . . . brings into the transac-

---

9. 316 U.S. at 55, 62 S.Ct. at 921–22.

10. 316 U.S. at 55, 62 S.Ct. at 921–22.

§ 16.28

1. 319 U.S. 105, 63 S.Ct. 870, 87 L.Ed. 1292 (1943).

2. 341 U.S. 622, 71 S.Ct. 920, 95 L.Ed. 1233 (1951), rehearing denied 342 U.S. 843, 72 S.Ct. 21, 96 L.Ed. 637 (1951).

3. 319 U.S. at 113, 63 S.Ct. at 875.

4. 319 U.S. at 112, 63 S.Ct. at 874 (emphasis added).

5. The Court noted that the Witnesses' main object was to preach and publicize the doctrines of their order. 319 U.S. at 112, 63 S.Ct. at 874.

6. 319 U.S. at 111, 63 S.Ct. at 874.

7. Although *Murdock* did limit somewhat the reach of *Chrestensen*, it left unclear how a court should determine the "primary purpose" of a communication.

8. 319 U.S. 141, 63 S.Ct. 862, 87 L.Ed. 1313 (1943).

tion a commercial feature.'"[9] The Court found that the appellant's sales pitch was not itself protected speech: "Only the press or oral advocates of ideas could urge this point. It was not open to the solicitors for gadgets or brushes."[10] The Court did not hold that the First Amendment does not extend to any speech possessing a commercial feature,[11] but the *profit motive* underlying magazine sales was sufficient in *Breard* to deprive those sales of at least some First Amendment protection.

The Court reached this result, not by a subjective, factual inquiry into motive, but by "balancing ... the conveniences between some householders' desire for privacy and the publisher's right to distribute publications in the precise way that those soliciting for him think brings the best results."[12] At first glance, the Court's reliance on this balancing process would appear to have been a rather severe departure from the categorizing approach in *Chrestensen.* In *Chrestensen,* once speech fell into the category of commercial speech, it became mere commercial activity, a matter for legislative judgment; suddenly in *Breard* it was a "right" to be balanced against that of privacy.

But the two cases are not really inconsistent. In *Breard* the Court did not directly hold that door-to-door magazine subscription solicitation is "purely commercial" in the sense contemplated by *Chrestensen.* While the Court did not dwell on the extent to which effective competition is necessary to a free press, a factor that the dissent discussed at length,[13] it was undoubtedly aware that if subscription solicitation were deemed purely commercial, logically the state could ban all such solicitation without regard to the inevitable effects of such a ban on the content of magazines.

Viewed conversely, *Breard* might be interpreted to stand for the concept that the First Amendment does not automatically extend to profit-making aspects of otherwise protected activity. As such *Breard* is consistent with the line of decisions upholding the neutral application of the antitrust, labor, and tax laws to newspapers and other communications media.[14]

§ 16.29 What Is "Commercial" Speech?

If speech is labeled "commercial", it loses, under the *Chrestensen* line of cases, all First Amendment protection. But when is speech commercial?

Primary Purpose Test. Shortly after *Breard,* the Court, in rejecting the argument that motion pictures are unprotected because they are made and exhibited for profit, noted that books, newspapers, and magazines are published and sold for profit but does not prevent them from being a form of expression whose liberty is safeguarded by the First Amendment. "We fail to see why operation for profit should have any different effect in the case of motion pictures."[1]

Later, *New York Times v. Sullivan*[2] declined to apply *Chrestensen* to sustain a libel action against a newspaper that had published an allegedly offensive paid political advertisement. The advertisement in *New York Times,* said the Court—

was not a "commercial" advertisement in the sense in which the word was used in *Chrestensen.* It communicated information, expressed opinion, recited grievances, protested claimed abuses, and sought financial support on behalf of a movement whose

---

9. Breard v. Alexandria, 341 U.S. 622, 642–43, 71 S.Ct. 920, 932–33, 95 L.Ed. 1233 (1951), rehearing denied 342 U.S. 843, 72 S.Ct. 21, 96 L.Ed. 637 (1951).

10. 341 U.S. at 641, 71 S.Ct. at 932.

11. 341 U.S. at 642, 71 S.Ct. at 932–33.

12. 341 U.S. at 644, 71 S.Ct. at 933.

13. 341 U.S. at 646–48, 71 S.Ct. at 934–35.

14. Citizen Publishing Co. v. United States, 394 U.S. 131, 89 S.Ct. 927, 22 L.Ed.2d 148 (1969) (antitrust); Associated Press v. NLRB, 301 U.S. 103, 57 S.Ct. 650, 81 L.Ed. 953 (1937) (labor laws); Oklahoma Press Publishing

Co. v. Walling, 327 U.S. 186, 66 S.Ct. 494, 90 L.Ed. 614 (1946) (wage and hour laws).

§ 16.29

1. Joseph Burstyn, Inc. v. Wilson, 343 U.S. 495, 501–502, 72 S.Ct. 777, 780, 96 L.Ed. 1098 (1952) (footnote omitted).

2. 376 U.S. 254, 84 S.Ct. 710, 11 L.Ed.2d 686 (1964), motion denied 376 U.S. 967, 84 S.Ct. 1130, 12 L.Ed.2d 83 (1964).

existence and objectives are matters of the highest public interest and concern.[3]

If nothing else, *New York Times* should have laid to rest the primary purpose test for determining commercial speech. The newspaper's commercial motives in publishing the advertisement were irrelevant; it was the advertisement's content that swayed the Court to apply First Amendment protection.

The "purely commercial advertising" that case law appeared to exclude from First Amendment protection was, following *New York Times*, confused. While financial motive is not enough to make speech "commercial,"[4] where sales are the so-called "primary purpose" of the speech, inclusion of political comment or other material that itself is protected will not suffice to pull the "commercial" speech within the ambit of the First Amendment.[5]

This primary purpose test apparently looks not to the form but to the function of the publication. First, under this primary purpose test, a book or other expression that itself could fall within the guarantee of free speech can be the subject of otherwise prohibited regulation if either the book is promoted by advertising, in which case the advertising may be regulated,[6] or the book itself is used to advertise or promote the sale of another product.[7] Second, statements that might be considered non-commercial if made by persons not materially interested in the affected trade, apparently can take on a different character when one involved in trade makes the statement.[8]

Speech That Proposes a Commercial Transaction. The Court now says that speech is "commercial" if it does no more than propose a commercial transaction.[9] On one level, this definition seems simple enough. A newspaper editorial is not commercial speech, but an advertisement urging consumers to buy the New York Times is commercial speech, because it is urging the recipient of the message to buy a product.

However, this definition could exclude a great deal of modern day advertising, much of which does not propose anything in particular. For example, an advertisement might simply show a celebrity stating: "Pepsi Cola; It's the right one, baby. Uh huh!" Or, "When you drive a Lexus, people will know that you have really arrived." These advertisements simply make statements that are difficult or impossible to verify. They do not advertise a sale, propose a transaction, or directly urge any specific action. Rather, they serve to create a mood, just like some political advertisements try to create a mood.

On the other hand, this definition might include some types of political advertising, those that propose a barter type of transaction. The same agencies that create advertisements to sell soft drinks or soap also hire themselves out to politicians, so it should not be shocking that political advertisements can share some of the attributes of commercial speech. Some political advertisements say something very close to: "Vote for me, and I'll lower your taxes," or, "Vote for me and I'll

---

3. 376 U.S. at 266, 84 S.Ct. at 718.

4. See, e.g., New York Times Co. v. Sullivan, 376 U.S. 254, 84 S.Ct. 710, 11 L.Ed.2d 686 (1964), motion denied 376 U.S. 967, 84 S.Ct. 1130, 12 L.Ed.2d 83 (1964) (protection of publication of public political advertisement is not diminished by the fact that newspaper was paid to carry the ad); Cammarano v. United States, 358 U.S. 498, 514, 79 S.Ct. 524, 534, 3 L.Ed.2d 462 (1959) ("The profit motive should make no difference.").

5. Valentine v. Chrestensen, 316 U.S. 52, 55, 62 S.Ct. 920, 922, 86 L.Ed. 1262 (1942) (advertising handbill not protected where political statement was included "with the intent, and for the purpose, of evading the prohibition" on commercial handbills).

6. See Bantam Books, Inc. v. F.T.C., 275 F.2d 680 (2d Cir.1960), certiorari denied 364 U.S. 819, 81 S.Ct. 51, 5 L.Ed.2d 49 (1960) (F.T.C. regulation of book labeling

upheld without discussion of First Amendment); Witkower Press, Inc., 57 F.T.C. 145 (1960).

7. Compare United States v. 8 Cartons, etc., 103 F.Supp. 626, 628 (W.D.N.Y.1951) ("The seizure relates not to books offered for bona fide sale but to copies of the book claimed to be offending against the Act by being associated with the article ... in such a way as to misbrand the product.") and United States v. Articles of Drug, 32 F.R.D. 32, 35 (S.D.Ill.1963), with Koch v. FTC, 206 F.2d 311, 317–18 (6th Cir.1953).

8. Compare, Scientific Manufacturing Co. v. FTC, 124 F.2d 640, 644 (3d Cir.1941), with Perma–Maid Co. v. FTC, 121 F.2d 282 (6th Cir.1941).

9. E.g., Central Hudson Gas & Electric Corporation v. Public Service Commission, 447 U.S. 557, 566, 100 S.Ct. 2343, 2351, 65 L.Ed.2d 341 (1980).

raise the taxes on the other fellow, not on you."

The Court is not troubled by the definition problem. It offers less protection to commercial speech than to political speech, and claims that the definition of "commercial speech" is a matter of common sense.[10]

§ 16.30 Rationales and Criticisms of the Commercial Speech Doctrine

The validity of *Chrestensen's* Commercial Speech doctrine was controversial, a controversy encouraged by the uncertain and confusing tests used to determine when speech is commercial. In 1959, Justice Douglas stated that the "ruling [in *Chrestensen*] was casual, almost offhand. And it has not survived reflection."[1] But the view was expressed in a concurring opinion and the Court did not embrace it. Other Justices on occasion agreed with Justice Douglas,[2] and commentators also criticized the doctrine as inflexible and insensitive to the informational value of commercial advertising.[3]

One obvious logical problem in distinguishing commercial speech from political expression is the simple fact that inherent in every speech labeled as "commercial" is at least some noncommercial message: the expression of ideas and values such as materialism or capitalism. There is no such thing as "pure" commercial speech.[4] Certainly the First Amendment, and the marketplace of ideas, makes no obvious distinction between commercial and non-commercial speech, and the difficulty of the Court over the years in defining commercial speech at least suggests that the distinction does not really exist.

In an attempt to rationalize the doctrine, some have argued that since "state and federal governments enjoy wide powers of regulation" over "the economic welfare of business enterprises", the "possibly desirable objectives furthered by advertising would not seem to require its protection by the First Amendment...."[5] The state, however, does not use the commercial speech doctrine to protect advertising, but to restrict or forbid it. When the form of the regulation over business is not a direct economic matter (such as taxes, subsidies, minimum wages), but direct control over speech, should there be some role for the Court in reviewing the reasonableness of the restrictions on speech?

Unlike straightforward economic regulation, regulations over speech are more likely to hide what is going on. For example, if the state seeks to subsidy the price of an item, what the state is doing is clear, and the people can debate whether that is good policy. What the state is doing is straight-forward, and its affect on the state budget is clear. When the state forbids companies from advertising the price of a particular good, there is no effect on the state budget, but the state is still affecting the price of the item. If companies cannot advertise the cost of the item, it is more likely to cost more, but it is more difficult to debate the policy because what the state is doing is less clear.

Others justify the doctrine on the grounds that only minimal protection of commercial advertising is necessary because there is little risk that its regulation will exist "for political purposes or even that its regulation will hamper the workings of democracy."[6] This argu-

---

10. Powell, J., in Ohralik v. Ohio State Bar, 436 U.S. 447, 455–66, 98 S.Ct. 1912, 1918, 56 L.Ed.2d 444 (1978).

§ 16.30

1. Cammarano v. United States, 358 U.S. 498, 514, 79 S.Ct. 524, 534, 3 L.Ed.2d 462 (1959) (Douglas, J., concurring).

2. Lehman v. Shaker Heights, 418 U.S. 298, 314–15, 94 S.Ct. 2714, 2722–23, 41 L.Ed.2d 770 (1974) (Brennan, J., dissenting); Pittsburgh Press Co. v. Pittsburgh Commission on Human Relations, 413 U.S. 376, 401 & n. 6, 93 S.Ct. 2553, 2566 & n. 6, 37 L.Ed.2d 669 (1973) (Stewart, J., dissenting), rehearing denied 414 U.S. 881, 94 S.Ct. 30, 38 L.Ed.2d 128 (1973).

3. See Redish, The First Amendment in the Marketplace: Commercial Speech and the Value of Free Expression, 39 Geo.Wash.L.Rev. 429, 432–38 (1971); Rotunda, The Commercial Speech Doctrine in the Supreme Court, 1976 U.Ill.L.Forum 1080.

4. E.g., Black, He Cannot Choose But Hear: The Plight of the Captive Auditor, 53 Colum.L.Rev. 960 (1953).

5. Note, Freedom of Expression in a Commercial Context, 78 Harv.L.Rev. 1191, 1195 (1965).

6. Cooper, The Tax Treatment of Business Grassroots Lobbying: Defining and Attaining the Public Policy Objectives, 68 Colum.L.Rev. 801, 832 (1968).

ment is really an empirical assertion, and its factual validity is not obvious. As a constitutional matter, the Court implicitly has rejected this justification by its refusal to construe the antitrust laws to prohibit anticompetitive activities that the First Amendment shelters.[7]

If a political candidate is selling himself, the First Amendment applies in full force; yet if he sells peanuts, *Chrestensen* asserts that there is *no* First Amendment protection. Rationalizing these results is more than a little difficult. Certainly *Chrestensen* is not based on a realistic belief that the dangers of falsehood are less likely when the speech is political.

Commentators have asserted that the "government is more likely to be impartial in censoring speech influencing commercial decisions than in regulating speech affecting its own policies and composition."[8] Really? Commercial regulation usually is enacted to benefit one economic group (businessmen, a certain class of businessmen, consumers, a certain class of consumers) and impose a burden on other classes. The government merely responds to these pressures. Why we would always expect the result of these conflicting pressures to be impartial is a mystery.

Until more modern times, neither the states nor the federal government had much interest in prohibiting truthful advertising. The older cases usually concerned the power of the state to prohibit false or misleading speech, or regulations affecting the time and manner of the communication.[9] But, as government began to

exercise a broader power to regulate speech affected by a commercial interest, the cases reconsidered the earlier law and decided to grant substantial First Amendment protection to commercial speech. It is to those cases we now turn.

§ 16.31 The Modern Commercial Speech Doctrine

(a) The Road to *Central Hudson*

In *Capital Co. v. Mitchell*[1]—a pre-*Central Hudson* opinion—a three-judge district court gave commercial speech very little protection. The Supreme Court affirmed without opinion. This decision upheld a flat statutory ban on the advertising of cigarettes over any medium of electronic communications subject to FCC jurisdiction. The district court mechanically applied the old case law. It noted that "advertising is less vigorously protected than other forms of speech" and, thus, that "Congress has the power to prohibit the advertising of cigarettes in any media" as an exercise of its power to regulate commerce. The district court's analysis belied any effort to limit its approval of congressional regulation either to cigarettes (on the theory that they are uniquely hazardous) or to electronic media (which are necessarily subject to regulation).

The dissent argued, to no avail, that because cigarette advertising expressed a position on a matter of public controversy,[2] it is not merely commercial speech but comes "within the core protection of the First Amendment." The dis-

---

7. The Noerr–Pennington Cases. In two related cases, Eastern R.R. Presidents Conference v. Noerr Motor Freight, Inc., 365 U.S. 127, 81 S.Ct. 523, 5 L.Ed.2d 464 (1961), rehearing denied 365 U.S. 875, 81 S.Ct. 899, 5 L.Ed.2d 864 (1961) and United Mine Workers of America v. Pennington, 381 U.S. 657, 85 S.Ct. 1585, 14 L.Ed.2d 626 (1965), on remand 257 F.Supp. 815 (D.Tenn.1966), judgment affirmed in part, reversed in part 400 F.2d 806 (6th Cir.1968), certiorari denied 393 U.S. 983, 89 S.Ct. 450, 21 L.Ed.2d 444 (1968), rehearing denied 393 U.S. 1045, 89 S.Ct. 616, 21 L.Ed.2d 599 (1969), the Court held, on First Amendment grounds, that the Sherman and Clayton Acts do not extend to exercises of the right to petition the government in either a legislative or administrative setting, despite anticompetitive effects. Compare, National Society of Professional Engineers v. United States, 435 U.S. 679, 98 S.Ct. 1355, 55 L.Ed.2d 637 (1978).

8. Note, Freedom of Expression in a Commercial Context, 78 Harv.L.Rev. 1191, 1195 (1965).

9. One important exception may be Williamson v. Lee Optical of Oklahoma, Inc., 348 U.S. 483, 489–90, 75 S.Ct. 461, 465–66, 99 L.Ed. 563 (1955), rehearing denied 349 U.S. 925, 75 S.Ct. 657, 99 L.Ed. 1256 (1955), where the Court upheld a state law prohibiting solicitations for the sale of optical appliances. However, the First Amendment issues were not discussed; the Court relied on the state's asserted special interest in the underlying health related conduct.

§ 16.31

1. 333 F.Supp. 582 (D.D.C.1971), affirmed without opinion sub nom. Capital Broadcasting Co. v. Acting Attorney General Kleindienst, 405 U.S. 1000, 92 S.Ct. 1290, 31 L.Ed.2d 472 (1972).

2. Banzhaf v. FCC, 405 F.2d 1082 (D.C.Cir.1968), certiorari denied 396 U.S. 842, 90 S.Ct. 50, 24 L.Ed.2d 93 (1969).

sent may be read to implicitly reject the commercial speech doctrine. The Supreme Court affirmed without opinion.

Capital Broadcasting is a troublesome case. If Congress may forbid truthful advertising urging the purchase of a legal, validly offered item, it is hard to see a way to establish a principled limitation in its power to restrict advertisements for anything it chooses to consider "harmful." May Congress prohibit the advertising of movies that are not obscene,[3] or of political pamphlets that do not constitute advocacy directed "to inciting or producing imminent lawless action and [are] likely to incite or produce such actions?"[4] These were serious questions following *Capital Broadcasting.*

(b) The *Central Hudson* Test

The Four–Part Test of *Central Hudson.* In *Central Hudson Gas & Electric Corporation v. Public Service Commission,*[5] the Court made clear that it was rejecting *Chrestensen* and offering First Amendment protection to commercial speech. *Central Hudson* built on the case law since *Chrestensen* and invalidated a Public Service Commission regulation that completely banned all public utility advertising promoting the use of electricity.

The Commission argued that such promotional advertising discouraged conserving energy. The Court, per Justice Powell, applied a four-part analysis to the question:

At the outset we must determine whether the expression is protected by the First Amendment. For commercial speech to come within that provision, it at least must concern lawful activity and not be misleading. Next we ask whether the asserted governmental interest is substantial. If both inquiries yield positive answers, we must determine whether the regulation directly advances the governmental interest asserted, and whether it is not more extensive than is necessary to serve that interest.[6]

Applying this test the *Central Hudson* Court invalidated the New York regulation. Promotional advertising is lawful commercial speech;[7] the state interests in conservation are substantial; the ban on promotional advertising advances this ban; but the state's complete suppression of speech was more extensive than necessary to further energy conservation. For example, some promotional advertising would cause no net increase in energy use. Also more limited restrictions might promote conservation sufficiently. The state could "require that the advertisements include information about the relative efficiency and expense of the offered service, both under current conditions and for the foreseeable future."[8]

The four-part test of *Central Hudson* is based on a two-step method of analysis synthesized from the modern commercial speech cases. First, a court must determine whether the speech is truthful, nonmisleading speech concerning a lawful commercial activity. Promotion of illegal activity therefore is not protected advertising.[9] If the government is attempting to deter or punish false or misleading advertising it will not be subjected to overbreadth analysis and therefore will not be required to demonstrate that its law is no more extensive than necessary to achieve that goal.[10] Second, after finding that the government regulation restricts nonmisleading commercial communications, a court must determine

3. See Miller v. California, 413 U.S. 15, 93 S.Ct. 2607, 37 L.Ed.2d 419 (1973), rehearing denied 414 U.S. 881, 94 S.Ct. 26, 38 L.Ed.2d 128 (1973).

4. Brandenburg v. Ohio, 395 U.S. 444, 447, 89 S.Ct. 1827, 1829, 23 L.Ed.2d 430 (1969) (footnote omitted) (per curiam).

5. 447 U.S. 557, 100 S.Ct. 2343, 65 L.Ed.2d 341 (1980).

6. 447 U.S. at 566, 100 S.Ct. at 2351.

7. Accord, Consolidated Edison Co. of New York, Inc. v. Public Service Com'n, 447 U.S. 530, 100 S.Ct. 2326, 65 L.Ed.2d 319 (1980). See also Bolger v. Youngs Drug Products Corp., 463 U.S. 60, 103 S.Ct. 2875, 77 L.Ed.2d 469 (1983) (law prohibiting mailing of unsolicited advertisements for contraceptives invalid).

8. 447 U.S. at 571, 100 S.Ct. at 2354.

9. See Pittsburgh Press Co. v. Pittsburgh Commission on Human Relations, 413 U.S. 376, 93 S.Ct. 2553, 37 L.Ed.2d 669 (1973), rehearing denied 414 U.S. 881, 94 S.Ct. 30, 38 L.Ed.2d 128 (1973); National Society of Professional Engineers v. United States, 435 U.S. 679, 697–98 nn. 26, 27, 98 S.Ct. 1355, 1368–69 nn. 26, 27, 55 L.Ed.2d 637, 654 nn. 26, 27 (1978).

10. See Ohralik v. Ohio State Bar, 436 U.S. 447, 462–63, 98 S.Ct. 1912, 1921–22, 56 L.Ed.2d 444, 457–58 (1978).

whether the government regulation directly advances a substantial government interest without unnecessary restrictions on the freedom of speech. The government regulation will fail if the interest is not sufficiently substantial to justify a restriction on speech or if the means used to advance a substantial interest either do not directly advance the government interest or do so with an unnecessary burden on the ability to communicate the commercial message.[11]

The Court has often cited and applied this four-part test, as we shall see in this section. But some Justices have questioned whether it is sufficiently protective of free speech interests. Indeed the seeds of criticism were planted in the very case that gave birth to this four-part test. Justice Blackmun, concurring in *Central Hudson,* and joined by Justice Brennan, objected to applying this test when the State is trying "to manipulate a private economic decision that the State cannot or has not regulated or outlawed directly."[12]

The "Least Restrictive Means" Test. The Court has refined this four-part test by amending the "least restrictive means" test so that, in commercial speech cases, the government need only show that there is a "reasonable" fit—not necessarily perfect—between

the governmental ends and the means chosen to accomplish those ends. The means must be "narrowly tailored."

Board of Trustees of the State University of New York v. Fox[13] ruled that it was error to apply the "least restrictive means" test to commercial speech cases. Cases like *Central Hudson* do not require that government restrictions on commercial speech be "absolutely the least severe that will achieve the desired end." Rather, there must be only a "reasonable" fit—a "fit that is not necessarily perfect"—between the governmental ends and the means chosen to accomplish those ends. So long as the means are "narrowly tailored" to achieve the desired objectives, it is for the government decisionmakers to judge what manner of regulation may best be employed. The government, however, has the burden to show that its goal is "substantial" and that "the cost [has been] carefully calculated." The "least restrictive means" test does not apply to commercial speech cases.[14]

(c) Specific Problem Areas

In a series of three decisions—*Pittsburgh Press Co. v. Pittsburgh Commission on Human Rights,*[15] *Bigelow v. Virginia,*[16] and *Virginia State Board of Pharmacy v. Virginia Citizens*

---

11. In Bolger v. Youngs Drug Products Corp., 463 U.S. 60, 103 S.Ct. 2875, 77 L.Ed.2d 469 (1983), the justices were unanimous in striking down a federal statute prohibiting the unsolicited mailing of contraceptive advertisements. The Court found that the interest in shielding mail recipients from offensive materials was not sufficiently substantial to burden speech, and that the regulation did not directly and narrowly promote a substantial interest in aiding parents' efforts to discuss birth control methods with their children.

12. 447 U.S. at 573–75, 100 S.Ct. at 2355–56, and citing, Rotunda, The Commercial Speech Doctrine in the Supreme Court, 1976 U. Illinois Law Forum 1080, 1080–83 (1976).

13. 492 U.S. 469, 109 S.Ct. 3028, 106 L.Ed.2d 388 (1989), on remand 764 F.Supp. 747 (N.D.N.Y.1991). The State University of New York (SUNY) had a rule (Resolution 66–156) prohibiting private commercial enterprises from operating in SUNY facilities. The Resolution prohibited students in their dormitories from hosting Tupperware-type parties demonstrating and selling housewares of the American Future System, Inc. (AFS). Justice Scalia, for the Court, concluded that the student AFS parties were commercial speech because they " 'propose a commercial transaction,' which is the test for identifying commercial speech." Although these Tupperware-type parties

touch on other subjects, such as how to run an efficient home, that fact does not put them in the category of fully protected speech. It is incorrect to conclude that pure speech and commercial speech are "inextricably intertwined" because: "No law or man or nature makes it impossible to sell housewares without teaching home economics...." 492 U.S. at 473, 109 S.Ct. at 3031.

The Court remanded to consider respondents' other challenges to Resolution 156. The Court noted that the Resolution reaches other conduct that consists of speech for profit (such as private tutoring, legal advice, and medical consultation). The Court then said simply: "While these examples consist of speech for a profit, they do not consist of speech that *proposes* a commercial transaction, which is what defines commercial speech." 492 U.S. at 482, 109 S.Ct. at 3036 (emphasis in original).

14. 492 U.S. at 477–81, 109 S.Ct. at 3033–35. See also San Francisco Arts & Athletics, Inc. v. United States Olympic Committee, 483 U.S. 522, 537 n. 16, 107 S.Ct. 2971, 2981 n. 16, 97 L.Ed.2d 427 (1987).

15. 413 U.S. 376, 93 S.Ct. 2553, 37 L.Ed.2d 669 (1973), rehearing denied 414 U.S. 881, 94 S.Ct. 30, 38 L.Ed.2d 128 (1973).

16. 421 U.S. 809, 95 S.Ct. 2222, 44 L.Ed.2d 600 (1975).

Consumer Council, Inc.[17]—the Supreme Court the law governing the advertising of illegal versus legal activities.

ADVERTISING ILLEGAL ACTIVITIES.

In *Pittsburgh Press*, a newspaper was charged with violating an ordinance prohibiting sex-designated help-wanted advertisements except where the employer or advertiser would be free to make hiring decisions on the basis of sex. The newspaper argued that the advertisements involved the exercise of editorial judgment as to where to place the advertisement. Therefore the advertisements, it was argued, were sufficiently noncommercial to fall within the ambit of the First Amendment. The Supreme Court disagreed.

If *Pittsburgh Press* had stopped here in its analysis, it would have merely given further support to a broad reading of the *Capital Broadcasting* case. But significantly, the Court admitted that "the exchange of information is as important in the commercial realm as in any other,"[18] a view that is a common basis for criticism of the rationale in *Chrestensen*. And, the Court did not reject that argument, but said, in response to the urging of the newspaper that the Justices abrogate the distinction between commercial and other speech—

Whatever the merits of this contention may be in other contexts, it is unpersuasive in this case. Discrimination in employment is not only commercial activity, it is *illegal* commercial activity under the Ordinance. We have no doubt that a newspaper constitutionally could be forbidden to publish a want ad proposing a sale of narcotics or soliciting prostitutes. Nor would the result be different if the nature of the transaction were indicated by placement under columns captioned "Narcotics for Sale" and "Prostitutes Wanted" rather than stated within the four corners of the advertisement.[19]

Even more importantly, after emphasizing the illegal nature of this activity, the opinion cited, with approval, the *dissent* in *Capital Broadcasting*.[20] The Court, while not yet rejecting *Chrestensen*, relied on a much narrower and more concrete test: if an activity is illegal, the state may prohibit advertising or touting that activity. The negative implication of this reasoning is that if the activity is legal, the state may not prohibit advertising the activity. The Court's reasoning follows a traditional balance of interests:

Any First Amendment interest which might be served by advertising an ordinary commercial proposal and which might arguably outweigh the governmental interest supporting the regulation is altogether absent when the commercial activity itself is illegal and the restriction on advertising is incidental to a valid limitation on economic activity.[21]

---

17. 425 U.S. 748, 96 S.Ct. 1817, 48 L.Ed.2d 346 (1976).

18. 413 U.S. at 388, 93 S.Ct. at 2560.

19. 413 U.S. at 388, 93 S.Ct. at 2560 (emphasis in original) (footnote omitted).

Drug Paraphernalia Stores. Village of Hoffman Estates v. Flipside, Hoffman Estates, Inc., 455 U.S. 489, 102 S.Ct. 1186, 71 L.Ed.2d 362 (1982), rehearing denied 456 U.S. 950, 102 S.Ct. 2023, 72 L.Ed.2d 476 (1982), on remand 688 F.2d 842 (7th Cir.1982). In that case a city ordinance required a business to obtain a license if it sells any items "designed or marketed for use with illegal drugs." The Court, in rejecting a preenforcement challenge on its face to the ordinance on the grounds of vagueness and overbreadth, turned to the free speech claims.

The ordinance did not infringe noncommercial speech interests of drug paraphernalia stores, or "head shops" ("head" is slang for frequent user of drugs), even though the city guidelines treated the proximity of drug related literature to paraphernalia as evidence that the paraphernalia was marketed for use with illegal drugs. The ordinance did not prohibit the sale of the literature itself but "simply regulates the commercial marketing of items that

the labels reveal may be used for an illicit purpose." As for commercial speech, the ordinance's restriction on the manner of marketing does not significantly limit the store's communication of information with the exception of commercial activity promoting or encouraging illegal drug use. If that activity is "speech," then it is speech proposing an illegal transaction, which a government may regulate or ban entirely. 455 U.S. at 496, 102 S.Ct. at 1192.

20. Pittsburgh Press Co. v. Pittsburgh Commission on Human Relations, 413 U.S. 376, 388 n. 12, 93 S.Ct. 2553, 2560 n. 12, 37 L.Ed.2d 669 (1973), rehearing denied 414 U.S. 881, 94 S.Ct. 30, 38 L.Ed.2d 128 (1973), citing Wright, J., dissenting, in Capital Broadcasting Co. v. Mitchell, 333 F.Supp. 582, 593 n. 42 (D.D.C.1971), judgment affirmed 405 U.S. 1000, 92 S.Ct. 1289, 31 L.Ed.2d 472 (1972).

21. 413 U.S. at 389, 93 S.Ct. at 2561. See also, National Society of Professional Engineers v. United States, 435 U.S. 679, 697–98, 98 S.Ct. 1355, 1368–69, 55 L.Ed.2d 637(1978). In that case the Court held that the Professional Society's canon of ethics prohibiting competitive bidding violates section 1 of the Sherman Act. Hence, the district

ADVERTISING LEGAL ACTIVITIES.

Advertisements for Abortions. *Bigelow v. Virginia*[22] established a corollary principle that was implicit in *Pittsburgh Press*: If an activity is legal, the state cannot prohibit advertising it. In *Bigelow* a newspaper publisher had been convicted of violating a state statute outlawing advertisements that "encourage or prompt the procuring of abortion."[23] The advertisement in question had been placed by a profit-making organization, located in New York, that had offered to arrange for legal abortions in New York. The Court stated that—

> Viewed in its entirety, the advertisement conveyed information of potential interest and value to a diverse audience—not only to readers possibly in need of the services offered, but also to those with a general curiosity about, or genuine interest in, the subject matter or the law of another State and its development, and to readers seeking reform in Virginia. [Also], the activity advertised pertained to constitutional interests.... Thus, in this case, appellant's First Amendment interests coincided with the constitutional interests of the general public.[24]

However, the Court did not rule that the advertisement was sufficiently editorial or noncommercial in nature to fall outside the ambit of *Chrestensen*. Instead, *Bigelow* reinterpreted *Chrestensen*:

> the holding [in *Chrestensen*] is distinctly a limited one: the ordinance was upheld as a reasonable regulation of the manner in

which commercial advertising could be distributed. The fact that it had the effect of banning a particular handbill does not mean that *Chrestensen* is authority for the proposition that all statutes regulating commercial advertising are immune from constitutional challenge.[25]

This view of *Chrestensen* was a new one, to say the least. *Bigelow*, by reducing *Chrestensen* to an exercise in a generalized balancing process, significantly reinterpreted the commercial speech doctrine.

One might have argued that, in spite of the language of *Bigelow*, its facts allow a very narrow interpretation: the state may not prohibit one from advertising an activity that is a constitutional right. In this case, the right is that very special right created in *Roe v. Wade*,[26] the right to an abortion. Under *Pittsburgh Press*, the state may prohibit advertisements of *illegal* commercial activity; under *Bigelow*, the state may not prohibit advertisements of activity that enjoys special constitutional protection. However, a later decision, *Virginia State Board of Pharmacy v. Virginia Citizens Consumer Council, Inc.*[27] indicated that this narrow view of *Bigelow* is inappropriate and that commercial speech is now within the protection of the First Amendment.

Advertising Prescription Drug Prices: The *Virginia Pharmacy* Case. In *Virginia State Board of Pharmacy*, a consumer group claimed that the First Amendment invalidated a statute making illegal the advertisement of prescription drug prices. The statute was defended on the grounds that it was a permissi-

---

court could enjoin the Society from adopting any official opinion, policy statement, or guideline stating or implying that competitive pricing is unethical, even though the Society can seek to influence governmental action. "While the resulting order may curtail the exercise of liberties that the Society might otherwise enjoy, that is a necessary and, in cases such as this, unavoidable consequence of the violation. Just as an injunction against price fixing abridges the freedom of businessmen to talk to one another about prices, so too the injunction in this case must restrict the Society's range of expression on the ethics of competitive bidding." 435 U.S. at 697, 98 S.Ct. at 1368 (footnote omitted).

On the relationship between professional ethics, the antitrust laws, and free speech, see, Morgan, The Evolving Concept of Professional Responsibility, 90 Harv.L.Rev. 702 (1977); Rotunda, The Word "Profession" Is Only a La-

bel—And Not a Very Useful One, 4 Learning and the Law 16 (No. 2, Summer, 1977); Rotunda, The First Amendment Now Protects Commercial Speech, 10 The Center Magazine: A Publication of the Center for the Study of Democratic Institutions 33 (May–June 1977).

22. 421 U.S. 809, 95 S.Ct. 2222, 44 L.Ed.2d 600 (1975).

23. 421 U.S. at 812–13, 95 S.Ct. at 2228.

24. 421 U.S. at 822, 95 S.Ct. at 2232–33.

25. 421 U.S. at 819–20, 95 S.Ct. at 2231.

26. 410 U.S. 113, 93 S.Ct. 705, 35 L.Ed.2d 147 (1973), rehearing denied 410 U.S. 959, 93 S.Ct. 1409, 35 L.Ed.2d 694 (1973).

27. 425 U.S. 748, 96 S.Ct. 1817, 48 L.Ed.2d 346 (1976).

ble regulation of commercial speech that had the effect of maintaining professional standards of pharmacy. Justice Blackmun, writing for the majority, phrased the issue simply:

> Our pharmacist does not wish to editorialize on any subject, cultural, philosophical, or political. He does not wish to report any particularly newsworthy fact, or to make generalized observations even about commercial matters. The "idea" he wishes to communicate is simply this: "I will sell you the X prescription drug at the Y price." Our question, then, is whether this communication is wholly outside the protection of the First Amendment.[28]

The Court held that the consuming public had a protected First Amendment interest in the free flow of truthful information concerning lawful activity.[29]

At the same time, the *Virginia State Board of Pharmacy* opinion reaffirmed the states' authority to issue regulations of the time, place, and manner of speech, if such restrictions are justified without reference to the content of the speech, serve a significant governmental interest and leave open other channels of communication.[30] Also untruthful speech, "commercial or otherwise, has never been protected for its own sake."[31] Thus the state may continue to regulate so as to prohibit false or even misleading speech.

In disposing of the claim that the advertising prohibition protected professional standards, the Court rejected the rationale that banning advertising was justified by the alleged salutary results—more small pharmacies, less demand for potentially dangerous drug consumption, and high public esteem for the pharmaceutical profession. Conceding the

desirability of those results, the Court rejected the advertising ban as a paternalistic means of securing them. In essence, the state was taking away the consumer's ability to choose among economic decisions (where to shop, what prescription to request, and so on) by depriving him of the information needed to make these decisions intelligently. Such preemption of individual decision-making is objectionable in a free-market economy.

The Court did not use classical, laissez-faire economic thinking to restrict the government's ability to regulate industry, only to show that the government could not accomplish these ends by suppression of First Amendment freedoms. It clearly allowed Virginia to subject its pharmacists to "close regulation", to adopt other professional standards or to "subsidize them or protect them from competition in other ways."[32] What the state cannot do is to completely suppress dissemination of concededly truthful information about entirely lawful activity.

The advertising prohibition in this case was really being used to implement hidden policy decisions that were better left to be decided by free and open debate. For example, the statute allegedly protected the small, high service pharmacy by keeping the consumer uninformed as to the cost she pays for such services. The desired results of the statute may yet be attained in a non-paternalistic fashion by *encouraging* dissemination of information, rather than restricting it.

Presumably, if there is value to individual service from pharmacists, a fully informed consumer (or a sufficient number of them) will choose to bear the cost of such service. Alter-

28. 425 U.S. at 761, 96 S.Ct. at 1825. To emphasize the lack of any nice distinction between commercial and noncommercial speech, the Court noted that "[o]ur pharmacist, for example, could cast himself as a commentator on store-to-store disparities in drug prices, giving his own and those of a competitor as proof. We see little point in requiring him to do so, and little difference if he does not." 425 U.S. at 764–65, 96 S.Ct. at 1827.

29. 425 U.S. at 773, 96 S.Ct. at 1831.

30. 425 U.S. at 771, 96 S.Ct. at 1830.

31. 425 U.S. at 771, 96 S.Ct. at 1830. Unlike libel actions, where the First Amendment offers some protec-

tion even for false factual assertions, the commercial advertiser generally is not under the deadline pressures of the press, generally knows the product or service he seeks to sell, and is in a position to verify the accuracy of his factual assertions. Therefore, there is less danger that state regulation of false or misleading price or product advertising will chill nondeceptive commercial expression. 425 U.S. at 777–78, 96 S.Ct. at 1833–34 (Stewart, J., concurring).

32. 425 U.S. at 770, 96 S.Ct. at 1829. Cf. Parker v. Brown, 317 U.S. 341, 63 S.Ct. 307, 87 L.Ed. 315 (1943).

natively, the government may choose to subsidize low-volume, high-service pharmacies through tax advantages, or outright subsidies, and this decision itself may be the subject of public debate. Similarly, if it is socially desirable to discourage the indiscriminate consumption of drugs, warnings of the hazards of consumption may prevent abuses; if not, an informed public may choose to discourage consumption of prescription drugs by taxing or prohibiting certain drugs.

After *Virginia State Board of Pharmacy* the state may reach the same policy goals as it chose to reach before, but it may not use the means of prohibiting the dissemination of truthful information about lawful activity. The purpose of this holding is not merely to tidy-up the interpretation of the First Amendment; rather it is to encourage more rational majority decision-making and a more open weighing of the advantages and disadvantages of policy alternatives by preventing the use of the "commercial speech" concept to deny entirely First Amendment protection to an important area of speech.

Advertising Compounded Drugs. A provision of the Food and Drug Administration Modernization Act (FDAMA) prohibited advertising and promoting particular compounded drugs. Drug compounding occurs when a pharmacist or doctor combines, mixes, or alters ingredients to create a medication tailored to an individual patient's needs. Licensed pharmacies challenged this section on free speech

grounds. The trial court, the Ninth Circuit, and the Supreme Court all agreed that these advertising and solicitation restrictions violated the First Amendment.[33] Justice O'Connor, speaking for the Court, argued that forbidding the advertisement of compounded drugs would prevent pharmacists with no interest in mass-producing medications, but who serve clienteles with special medical needs, from truthfully informing doctors treating those clients about the alternative drugs available through compounding. A pharmacist serving a children's hospital where many patients are unable to swallow pills could not tell the children's doctors about a new development in compounding that allowed a drug that was previously available only in pill form to be administered another way. The FDAMA's prohibition of such seemingly useful speech, even though doing so does not appear to directly further any asserted governmental objective, confirms that the prohibition is unconstitutional.

Truthful Advertising of Harmful Substances, Such as Cigarettes.

Two additional aspects of *Virginia State Board of Pharmacy* should be noted. First, the decision by implication raises anew the question of the constitutionality of restrictions on the advertising of cigarettes in the electronic media. Despite Justice Blackmun's offhand dismissal of the point as having been based on the "special problem of the electronic broadcast media" not present in this case,[34] the

---

33. Thompson v. Western States Medical Center, 535 U.S. 357, 122 S.Ct. 1497, 152 L.Ed.2d 563 (2002). Breyer, J., joined by Rehnquist, C.J., and Stevens & Ginsburg, JJ., dissented

34. 425 U.S. at 773, 96 S.Ct. at 1831. See Lamar Outdoor Advertising, Inc. v. Mississippi State Tax Com'n, 701 F.2d 314 (5th Cir.1983), on rehearing 718 F.2d 738 (1983), certiorari denied 467 U.S. 1259, 104 S.Ct. 3553, 82 L.Ed.2d 855 (1984) (citing an earlier edition of this treatise). The *Lamar* fifth circuit panel, in an opinion by Judge Gee, invalidated, as a violation of free speech, certain statutes and regulations of Mississippi which effectively banned liquor advertising on billboards and in printed and electronic media originating within the state.

The en banc fifth circuit reversed *Lamar* and affirmed a companion decision in a case entitled Dunagin v. Oxford, 718 F.2d 738 (5th Cir.1983) (en banc), the Supreme Court denied certiorari in 467 U.S. 1259, 104 S.Ct. 3553, 82 L.Ed.2d 855 (1984). The Supreme Court cited *Dunagin*

with approval in Posadas de Puerto Rico v. Tourism Company, 478 U.S. 328, 343, 344 n. 9, 106 S.Ct. 2968, 2978, 2979 n. 9, 92 L.Ed.2d 266 (1986).

The Supreme Court avoided ruling on whether a state law prohibiting cable television systems from retransmitting out-of-state signals containing alcoholic beverage commercials violated the First Amendment because the Court found that the state law conflicted with, and was preempted by, federal regulation of the cable television industry in Capital Cities Cable, Inc. v. Crisp, 467 U.S. 691, 104 S.Ct. 2694, 81 L.Ed.2d 580 (1984). *Capital Cities Cable* held that an invalidation of the state law on this basis was consistent with the twenty-First Amendment because the limited restriction on advertising was not closely related to "exercising control over whether to permit importation or sale of liquor and to structure the liquor distribution system," 467 U.S. at 716, 104 S.Ct. at 2709, 81 L.Ed.2d at 599 (internal quotation and citation omitted). But see, Capital Broadcasting Co. v. Mitchell, 333 F.Supp. 582 (D.D.C.1971), affirmed without opinion sub nom. Capital

Capital Broadcasting decision was not based upon any special aspects of the broadcast media; rather it was squarely based on a view of the commercial speech doctrine promulgated in *Chrestensen,* that so-called commercial speech is completely outside the protections of the First Amendment.

Justice Rehnquist's conclusion in his dissent in *Virginia State Board of Pharmacy* that television cigarette ads may no longer be completely prohibited[35] is probably correct. The state, of course, may tax cigarettes to discourage their use and the federal government may place a nationwide tax on cigarettes, or prohibit their production and sale entirely. To prevent misleading advertisements the FCC may require warnings to be placed in the commercials, as well as require anticigarette ads under the fairness doctrine.[36] But unless Congress outlaws cigarettes, it should not be able to prohibit "concededly truthful information"— e.g., brand X cigarettes offer less tar and nicotine than any other cigarette—about "entirely lawful activity"—the smoking of cigarettes. Any other conclusion would allow Virginia to prohibit the advertising of drug prices on radio or television.

Perhaps the Court may one day fashion some special constitutional rules dealing with this problem in the still formative area of the First Amendment and the broadcast media.[37] But the Court has not yet done so; certainly Justice Blackmun's brief, inaccurate reference to the *Capital Broadcasting* decision banning cigarette advertising on television hardly qualifies as a legal distinction of constitutional proportions. Moreover, Chief Justice Burger's attempt, in his concurrence, to distinguish between advertisements by "true professionals" (doctors and lawyers) and advertisements by pseudo-professionals (pharmacists)[38] creates a distinction as unworkable as that inherent in the *Chrestensen* doctrine itself, and since rejected in *Bates v. State Bar,*[39] discussed below.

Gambling and the *Posadas* Case. In *Posadas de Puerto Rico Associates v. Tourism Company,*[40] Justice Rehnquist, for a bare five-Justice majority, upheld the constitutionality of a Puerto Rican statute that restricted local advertising inviting the residents of Puerto Rico to patronize gambling casinos but that did not restrict local advertising targeted at tourists, even though the local advertising aimed at the tourists may incidentally reach the hands of a resident. In fact, during oral argument before the Supreme Court, counsel for Puerto Rico said that a casino advertising in a Spanish Language Daily, with ninety-nine percent local circulation would be permitted, so long as the advertising "is addressed to tourists and not to residents." The plaintiffs attacked the statute on its face and the court rejected this facial attack.

The Court said that it applied the general principles identified in *Central Hudson.*[41] The commercial speech in *Posadas* "concerns a lawful activity and is not misleading or fraudulent," hence, it met the first prong of the four-part test of *Central Hudson.* The governmen-

Broadcasting Co. v. Acting Attorney General Kleindienst, 405 U.S. 1000, 92 S.Ct. 1290, 31 L.Ed.2d 472 (1972).

35. 425 U.S. at 781, 96 S.Ct. at 1935.

36. This assumes that the fairness doctrine is still constitutional under the later case law.

37. Compare Red Lion Broadcasting Co. v. FCC, 395 U.S. 367, 89 S.Ct. 1794, 23 L.Ed.2d 371 (1969), with Columbia Broadcasting System, Inc. v. Democratic Nat. Committee, 412 U.S. 94, 93 S.Ct. 2080, 36 L.Ed.2d 772 (1973).

38. 425 U.S. at 774, 96 S.Ct. at 1831–32 (Burger, C.J., concurring).

39. 433 U.S. 350, 97 S.Ct. 2691, 53 L.Ed.2d 810 (1977), rehearing denied 434 U.S. 881, 98 S.Ct. 242, 54 L.Ed.2d 164 (1977).

The scope of attorney advertising when restricted by professional association rather than by the state also raises important issues of antitrust law. The Justice Depart-

ment for example sued the American Bar Association claiming its advertising restrictions in the Code of Professional Responsibility violate the antitrust laws. See Bar News, A Special Report on the Justice Department Antitrust Suit Against the ABA (Summer 1976); see generally T. Morgan & R. Rotunda, Problems and Materials on Professional Responsibility 95–132 (1976), and its 1978 Supplement, ch. 4. This suit was later settled.

40. 478 U.S. 328, 106 S.Ct. 2968, 92 L.Ed.2d 266 (1986). Rotunda, The Constitutional Future of the Bill of Rights: A Closer Look at Commercial Speech and State Aid to Religiously Affiliated Schools, 65 No.Car.L.Rev. 917, 921–29 (1987).

41. Central Hudson Gas & Electric Corp. v. Public Service Commission, 447 U.S. 557, 100 S.Ct. 2343, 65 L.Ed.2d 341 (1980).

tal interest in reducing the demand for casino gambling by Puerto Rican residents because of the legislature's apparent belief that excessive casino gambling would seriously harm the health, safety, and welfare of Puerto Rican citizens is "substantial," however, and the majority believed that the challenged restrictions "directly advance" Puerto Rico's asserted interest because "the legislature's belief is a reasonable one."[42]

The majority was unpersuaded that the challenged advertising was underinclusive merely because other kinds of gambling (such as horse racing, cockfighting, and the lottery) may be advertised to residents of Puerto Rico. First, the advertising restrictions " 'directly advance' the legislature's interest in reducing demand for games for chance," and second, the legislative interest "is not necessarily to reduce demand for all games of chance, but to reduce demand for casino gambling." That is, the majority thought that the legislature must have felt that the risks associated with casino gambling are greater because these other forms of gambling " 'have been traditionally part of the Puerto Rican's roots.' "[43] The majority did not otherwise elaborate on why casino gambling may be different in kind from other games of chance. Nonetheless, the law, in the view of the majority, met the second and third prongs of the *Central Hudson* test.

Then, the Court turned to the fourth prong: are the restrictions no more extensive than necessary to serve the state's interest? The Court concluded that the fit between the legislature's ends and its means was close enough. The restriction, limited to advertising aimed at residents of Puerto Rico, was no more extensive than necessary to serve the governmental interest.

The majority cited with approval lower court cases approving of advertising restrictions on smoking and alcohol, and sought to distinguish *Carey v. Population Services International*,[44] (advertising of contraceptives is protected speech), and *Bigelow v. Virginia*[45] (advertising of abortion clinic is protected speech) as cases where underlying conduct that was the subject of the advertising restrictions was constitutionally protected. "Here, on the other hand, the Puerto Rico Legislature surely could have prohibited casino gambling by the residents of Puerto Rico altogether. In our view the greater power to completely ban casino gambling necessarily includes the lesser power to ban advertising of casino gambling, and *Carey* and *Bigelow* are hence inapposite."[46]

Restrictions on Cigarette and Tobacco Advertising Dictum in *Posadas* may (but need not) be read to suggest that legislatures could similarly engage in a limited restriction of advertising of other subjects that the Court views as harmful, even though the activity itself may not be illegal in the particular jurisdiction, such as advertising of cigarettes, alco-

---

42. Does a Ban on Advertising Necessarily Dampen Demand for a Product: the Case of Cigarettes. The Court's easy assumption that a ban on advertising of legal casino gambling will dampen demand by Puerto Rican citizens appears reasonable enough—but the empirical evidence suggests otherwise. Take, for example, the case of tobacco advertising.

It is generally assumed that if tobacco companies could not advertise in the print media, consumption of cigarettes would fall. However, that does not happen. An advertising ban may shift demand from one product to another, but it may also give tobacco the air of forbidden fruit and encourage total consumption. Alcohol was not advertised during Prohibition, but that did not put the bootleggers out of business.

Canada imposed a ban on cigarette advertising in 1989. From then until 1997, the percentage of Canadians who smoke has not decreased, but increased slightly, from 30% to 31%. Finland imposed a partial ban on cigarette advertising in 1978. From that date until 1997 the percentage of

Finish teenagers who smoke increased from 22% to 24%. Portugal, which has one of the highest rates of cigarette smoking in Europe, has banned all cigarette advertising for decades. In 1997, one of the most chic cigarette brands in London was called "Death Head" cigarettes, sold in black-and-white packs with a skull and crossbones on the cover. A cross-national study by London's INFO–TAB and Children's Research Unit showed that 36% of 15–year-old children smoke in Norway, where tobacco advertising is banned! But in Hong Kong, where there are very few restrictions on tobacco advertising, only 11% of 15–year-olds smoke. See, 4 Ronald D. Rotunda & John E. Nowak, Treatise on Constitutional Law: Substance and Procedure § 20.31 (West Group, 3d ed. 1999).

43. 478 U.S. at 343 & n. 8, 106 S.Ct. at 2977–78 & n. 8.

44. 431 U.S. 678, 97 S.Ct. 2010, 52 L.Ed.2d 675 (1977).

45. 421 U.S. 809, 95 S.Ct. 2222, 44 L.Ed.2d 600 (1975).

46. 478 U.S. at 345–46, 106 S.Ct. at 2979.

hol, and legal prostitution.[47] However, the extent to which this dictum is valid is unclear, particularly after the fragmented decision in *Lorillard Tobacco Co. v. Reilly*.[48]

In *Lorillard*, manufacturers and sellers of cigarettes, smokeless tobacco products, and cigars challenged Massachusetts regulations restricting sale, promotion, and labeling of tobacco products. The purpose of these various restrictions on truthful tobacco advertising was to dampen demand for the product, particularly by minors by restricting information about it.

Justice O'Connor, speaking for a fragmented Court,[49] concluded that: (1) the Federal Cigarette Labeling and Advertising Act (FCLAA) preempted state regulations governing outdoor and point-of-sale cigarette advertising; (2) regulations prohibiting outdoor advertising of smokeless tobacco or cigars within 1,000 feet of school or playground violated the First Amendment; (3) regulations prohibiting indoor, point-of-sale advertising of smokeless tobacco and cigars lower than 5 feet from floor of retail establishment located within 1,000 feet of school or playground violated the First Amendment; but (4) regulations requiring retailers to place tobacco products behind counters and requiring customers to have contact with salesperson before they are able to handle such products did not violate First Amendment.

"[T]he greater power ... includes the lesser power...." It is unclear to what extent the Court's statement in *Posadas*—that "the greater power ... includes the lesser power...."—represents any real principle of law. For example, the power to ban casinos does not imply the power to allow casinos and to ban all political discussions within the casinos. Nor does the power to ban casinos in their entirety imply the power to allow casinos, but ban within them, any discussions of the merits of the Puerto Rico restriction of casino advertising inviting the residents of Puerto Rico to patronize the casinos.

In an earlier case, the Court rejected entirely the suggestion that the state's power to directly ban the use of products that waste electricity implies the power to completely ban an electrical utility from engaging in promotional advertising encouraging the use (including the wasteful use) of electricity.[50] In later cases, the Court made clear that whatever this statement means—the greater power includes the lesser—the Court rejects the argument that the power to restrict or prohibit an activity includes the power to restrict speech about that activity.[51]

A few years later the Court went further and specifically rejected the "greater includes the lesser" argument even in the commercial speech context, and even when the government is regulating the advertising of harmful (but lawful) products. In *Rubin v. Coors Brew-*

---

47. 478 U.S. at 350 & n. 10, 106 S.Ct. at 2979–80 & n. 10.

See, e.g., Nevada Revised Statutes §§ 201.430, 201.440 (1986) (prohibiting advertising of houses of prostitution in certain instances even though prostitution legal in counties with less than 250,000 people). Nev.Rev.Stat. §§ 244, 345(1), (8).

48. 533 U.S. 525, 121 S.Ct. 2404, 150 L.Ed.2d 532 (2001).

49. Although Justice O'Connor wrote for the Court, and on several issues she spoke for a unanimous Court, there were still a great many separate opinions.

50. Central Hudson Gas & Elec. Corp. v. Public Service Commission, 447 U.S. 557, 100 S.Ct. 2343, 65 L.Ed.2d 341 (1980). Compare: City of Lakewood v. Plain Dealer Publishing Co., 486 U.S. 750, 763, 108 S.Ct. 2138, 2147, 100 L.Ed.2d 771 (1988): "[The] 'greater-includes-lesser' syllogism ... is blind to the radically different constitutional harms inherent in the 'greater' and 'lesser' restric-

tions. Presumably in the case of an ordinance that completely prohibits a particular manner of expression, the law on its face is both content and viewpoint neutral. In analyzing such a hypothetical ordinance, the Court would apply the well-settled time, place, and manner test. The danger giving rise to the First Amendment inquiry is that the government is silencing a channel of speech.... Therefore, even if the government may constitutionally impose content-neutral prohibitions on a particular manner of speech, it may not *condition* that speech on obtaining a license or permit from a government official in that official's boundless discretion." (footnote and internal citations omitted; emphasis in original).

51. Rubin v. Coors Brewing Co., 514 U.S. 476, 482 n. 2, 115 S.Ct. 1585, 1589 n. 2, 131 L.Ed.2d 532 (1995); 44 Liquormart, Inc. v. Rhode Island, 517 U.S. 484, 513–14, 116 S.Ct. 1495, 1513, 134 L.Ed.2d 711 (1996) (Stevens, J.); Greater New Orleans Broadcasting Association, Inc. v. United States, 527 U.S. 173, 182, 119 S.Ct. 1923, 1929, 144 L.Ed.2d 161 (1999).

ing Co.[52] the Court (with no dissent) invalidated, under the First Amendment, a law that prohibited beer labels from displaying alcohol content. The government argued that the labeling ban was necessary to suppress "strength wars," whereby brewers would brag, in their advertisements, about the alcohol content of their beers. In a footnote that may overshadow the rest of the opinion, the Court acknowledged *Posadas,* found that the "greater includes lesser" argument to be mere dictum, and then specifically rejected the government's claim that "legislatures have broader latitude to regulate speech that promotes socially harmful activities, such as alcohol consumption than they have to regulate other types of speech."[53]

It is often the case that a partial ban—or a ban on speech advertising a product—is not a lesser power but a greater one, for it allows the state to avoid the hard choices that come with a decision to engage in a complete ban. A complete ban has within it an inner political check that restricts the excesses of state power. For example, in *Posadas,* in order for Puerto Rico to engage in a complete ban of casinos, it must give up tax revenue and tourist income associated with legalized casino gambling. The "lesser" power to prohibit speech allows the state to avoid the inner political check that the First Amendment provides.

The *Posadas* Dissent. Justice Brennan, joined by Justices Marshall and Blackmun, dissented. They noted that the justices have "consistently invalidated restrictions designed to deprive consumers of accurate information about products and services legally offered for sale,"[54] citing cases where the underlying conduct was *not* constitutionally protected including *Linmark Associates, Inc. v. Willingboro,*[55]

(ban on for-sale signs in front of houses invalidated); *Virginia Pharmacy Board v. Virginia Citizens Consumer Council,*[56] (ban on advertising of prescription drug prices by pharmacists invalidated); *Bates v. State Bar,*[57] (ban on advertising of lawyer's services invalidated). The Brennan dissent objected to the "relaxed standards" used by the majority, because, when the state "seeks to suppress the dissemination of nonmisleading commercial speech relating to legal activities for fear that recipients will act on the information provided, such regulation should be subject to strict judicial scrutiny."[58] The government should not be allowed "to manipulate private behavior by depriving citizens of truthful information concerning lawful activities."[59]

The dissent also noted that the Puerto Rican legislature had never "actually asserted" that advertising of casino gambling aimed at Puerto Rican residents will cause serious harmful effects.[60] Moreover, Puerto Rico allows its residents to legally patronize casinos, and residents of Puerto Rico are permitted to gamble at horse and dog racing, cockfighting, and the Puerto Rican lottery, "all of which are allowed to advertise freely to residents."[61] Perhaps, suggested Brennan, the state legislature was not really concerned with the evils of casino gambling; it simply wanted the residents to spend their gambling dollars on the government run lottery.[62] Brennan also objected to the new principle which Justice Rehnquist tried to advance, that the state may ban truthful advertising if the state could ban the activity directly. "[A] ban on casino advertising is [not] 'less intrusive' than an outright ban on such activity. [T]he 'constitutional doctrine' which bans Puerto Rico from banning adver-

---

52. 514 U.S. 476, 115 S.Ct. 1585, 131 L.Ed.2d 532 (1995).

53. 517 U.S. at 482 n. 2, 115 S.Ct. at 1589–90, n. 2.

54. 478 U.S. at 350, 106 S.Ct. at 2981 (Brennan, J., dissenting, joined by Marshall & Blackmun, JJ.).

55. 431 U.S. 85, 97 S.Ct. 1614, 52 L.Ed.2d 155 (1977).

56. 425 U.S. 748, 96 S.Ct. 1817, 48 L.Ed.2d 346 (1976).

57. 433 U.S. 350, 97 S.Ct. 2691, 53 L.Ed.2d 810 (1977), rehearing denied 434 U.S. 881, 98 S.Ct. 242, 54 L.Ed.2d 164 (1977). Note that Central Hudson Gas & Elec. Corp. v. Public Service Commission, 447 U.S. 557, 100 S.Ct. 2343,

65 L.Ed.2d 341 (1980) invalidated a state regulation that *completely* banned promotional advertising by an electrical utility, even though the state could have directly banned wasteful use of electricity.

58. 478 U.S. at 351, 106 S.Ct. at 2982.

59. 478 U.S. at 351, 106 S.Ct. at 2982.

60. 478 U.S. at 354, 106 S.Ct. at 2984.

61. 478 U.S. at 353, 106 S.Ct. at 2983 (footnote omitted).

62. 478 U.S. at 354, 106 S.Ct. at 2983.

tisements concerning lawful casino gambling is not so strange a restraint—it is called the First Amendment."[63]

Justice Stevens noted that "Puerto Rico blatantly discriminates in its punishment of speech depending on the publication, audience, and words employed." And the prohibition is based on a "standard that is hopelessly vague and unpredictable."[64]

In *Virginia Pharmacy Board,* Justice Blackmun for the Court had said that the choice "between the dangers of suppressing information and the dangers of its misuse if it is freely available" is a choice "that the First Amendment makes for us."[65] He added:

Virginia is free to require whatever professional standards it wishes of its pharmacists; it may subsidize them or protect them from competition in other ways. But it may not do so by keeping the public in ignorance of the entirely lawful terms that competing pharmacists are offering. In this sense, the justifications Virginia has offered for suppressing the flow of prescription drug price information, far from persuading us that the flow is not protected by the First Amendment, have reinforced our view that it is. We so hold.[66]

Justice Rehnquist was the only dissenter in *Virginia Pharmacy Board.* That case is still good law: indeed, the *Posadas* majority cited it with approval.

Radio and Television Broadcasts of Lottery Results. *United States v. Edge Broadcasting Co.*[67] upheld the constitutionality of federal statutes that prohibit the broadcast of lottery advertising by a broadcaster licensed in a state that does not allow lotteries; however, the federal statutes allowed such broadcasting by a broadcaster licensed in a state that sponsors a lottery, even if that signal reached into a state where lotteries were illegal. Reversing both the federal trial and appellate courts, a divided Supreme Court held that, as

applied to respondent, these statutes do not violate the First Amendment.

Edge Broadcasting is a radio station licensed in North Carolina, which has no state-sponsored lottery. Indeed, participating or advertising any nonexempt raffle or lottery is a crime in that state. However, over 90% of Edge Broadcasting's listeners live in Virginia, which does sponsor a lottery. The Edge radio station, on the border between the two states, wanted to broadcast Virginia lottery advertisements.

Justice White, for the Court, specifically did not consider the government's argument that *Central Hudson* was inapplicable on the theory that the "greater power" to prohibit "vices" such as gambling "necessarily includes the lesser power" to ban advertisements about them.[68] Instead the Court applied the four-part test of *Central Hudson,* and upheld the law.

First, the majority assumed, like the courts below, that Edge, if permitted, would broadcast nonmisleading information about the Virginia lottery, a legal activity. Second, the Court was "quite sure" that the federal government has a substantial interest in supporting the policies of nonlottery states while also not interfering with the policies of lottery states. The third and fourth factors under *Central Hudson* basically require the court to consider the fit between the legislature's ends and the means chosen to accomplish those ends. In this case, the majority said that "[w]e have no doubt that the statutes directly advanced the governmental interest at stake in this case." Indeed, the majority announced, without elaboration, that Congress "might have continued to ban all radio or television lottery advertisements, even by stations in States that have legalized lotteries." The congressional desire to balance the interests of the antigambling policy of states like North Carolina, while not unduly interfering with the lotteries sponsored by states like Virginia, is the substantial governmental interest that sat-

---

63. 478 U.S. at 354–55 n. 4, 106 S.Ct. at 2984 n. 4.

64. 478 U.S. at 359, 106 S.Ct. at 2986 (Stevens, J., dissenting, joined by Blackmun & Marshall, JJ.).

65. 425 U.S. at 77, 96 S.Ct. at 1829.

66. 425 U.S. at 77, 96 S.Ct. at 1829 (internal citation omitted).

67. 509 U.S. 418, 113 S.Ct. 2696, 125 L.Ed.2d 345 (1993), on remand 5 F.3d 63 (4th Cir.1993).

68. 509 U.S. at 426, 113 S.Ct. at 2703.

isfies *Central Hudson,* and is also the interest directly served by applying the statutory restriction to all stations in North Carolina, even if, as applied to respondent, "there were only marginal advancement of that interest."

Applying the fourth prong of *Central Hudson,* the majority concluded that the regulations at issue were not more extensive than necessary to serve the governmental interest because, as in *Posadas,* the fit, while "not necessarily perfect," was "reasonable." If the respondent's broadcast signals reached a portion of the North Carolina audience, then "this would be in derogation of the substantial federal interest in supporting North Carolina's laws making lotteries illegal."

The majority also concluded that the lower courts were in error in concluding that the statutory restrictions, as applied to the respondent, were ineffectual in that 11% of Edge Broadcasting's audience (the North Carolina residents) also listened to Virginia radio and television advertisements and read Virginia newspapers, all of which carried the lottery advertisements: "Even if all of the residents of Edge's North Carolina service area listened to lottery advertisements from Virginia stations, it would still be true that 11% of radio listening time in that area would be free of such material."[69]

Liquor Advertisements. In *Rubin v. Coors Brewing Co.*[70] the Court invalidated a federal law that prohibited beer labels from displaying alcohol content. (This labeling law provided

that it was inapplicable if state law required disclosure of alcohol content.) The trial court, the Tenth Circuit, and the Supreme Court (without dissent) all invalidated that ban under the First Amendment. Justice Thomas, for the Court found that the commercial speech concerns a lawful activity and is not misleading. Next, the government argued that the federal labeling law served a substantial interest—it supported state laws that banned display of alcohol content. The Court rejected that argument as well, because there was no evidence that states were in need of federal assistance. "Unlike the situation in *Edge Broadcasting,* the policies of some States do not prevent neighboring States from pursuing their own alcohol related policies within their respective borders." States could directly ban disclosure of alcohol content, "subject, of course, to the same First Amendment restrictions that apply to the Federal Government."[71]

The Court did agree that the government has a substantial interest in the health, safety, and welfare of citizens by preventing "strength wars," among brewers competing based on the potency of their beers. However, the federal law did not "directly and materially advance" that interest because of its "overall irrationality." For example, the federal law allows disclosure of alcohol content on the labels of wine and hard liquor, and even compels disclosure for wines of more than 14% alcohol. The law also allows brewers to signal high alcohol content by using the term "malt liquor." The government's labeling ban also is

---

69. 509 U.S. at 432, 113 S.Ct. at 2706.

In a portion of the opinion, Part III–D, that was not the opinion of the Court, Justice White also said: "Nor need we be blind to the practical effect of adopting respondent's view of the level of particularity of analysis appropriate to decide its case. [T]he piecemeal approach it advocates would act to vitiate the Government's ability generally to accommodate States with differing policies." 509 U.S. at 435, 113 S.Ct. at 2708. See, Part III–D, where White, J. was joined by Rehnquist, C.J. & Scalia & Thomas, JJ.

Stevens, J., joined by Blackmun, J., dissented, arguing that the fit between the government's ends and means was not good. The means were not in proportion to the proposed end of protecting the antilottery policies of nonlottery states. "I would hold that suppressing truthful advertising regarding a neighboring State's lottery, an activity which is, of course, perfectly legal, is a patently unconstitutional means of effectuating the Government's

asserted interest in protecting the policies of non-lottery States. Indeed, I had thought that we had so held almost two decades ago [in] *Bigelow v. Virginia,*" 509 U.S. at 437, 113 S.Ct. at 2709.

70. 514 U.S. 476, 115 S.Ct. 1585, 131 L.Ed.2d 532 (1995). Stevens, J., concurring in the judgment, argued that the statute's unconstitutionality is "more patent than the Court's opinion indicates." The Government should not be able to suppress truthful speech merely because it happens to appear on the label of a product for sale. Brewers should be able to tell their customers that their beverages "are stronger—or weaker—than competing products." The Government could impose some regulations that "increase consumer awareness," but the law in this case "is nothing more than an attempt to blindfold the public." 514 U.S. at 498, 115 S.Ct. at 1595 (Stevens, J., concurring in the judgment).

71. 514 U.S. at 486, 115 S.Ct. at 1591.

not sufficiently tailored to its goal. Instead of the restriction on speech, the government, e.g., could directly limit the alcohol content of beer. Even a ban on marketing efforts emphasizing high alcohol strength (assuming that is constitutional) would be less intrusive of free speech rights.

In *44 Liquormart, Inc. v. Rhode Island*,[72] the Court invalidated a state law banning advertisements of accurate information about retail liquor prices except at the point of sale. The Court was fragmented as to its reasoning, but no Justice dissented. Part of Justice Stevens' opinion was the opinion of the Court and part was a plurality opinion. Stevens (joined by Kennedy, Souter & Ginsburg) recognized that bans on "truthful, nonmisleading commercial messages rarely protect consumers" from deception or overreaching, but often serve only to obscure an "underlying governmental policy" that could be implemented without regulating speech. For example, in this case, the state could have promoted temperance by imposing higher taxes on liquor or by instituting educational campaigns to promote temperance. Under either alternative, there would have been no need to restrict any speech. Stevens cautioned: "The First Amendment directs us to be especially skeptical of regulations that seek to keep people in the dark for what the government perceives to be their own good."[73]

Justice Thomas, concurring in the judgment and in parts of the Opinion of the Court, warned that when "the government's asserted interest is to keep legal users of a product or service ignorant in order to manipulate their choices in the marketplace, the balancing test" of *Central Hudson Gas* should not be applied. That asserted interest is "*per se* illegitimate" and should not be able to justify regulation of

commercial speech any more than it can justify regulation of noncommercial speech.[74]

For example, if the Government had been able to show that restrictions on advertising of liquor actually did reduce consumption significantly, that showing should not justify the ban. The theory that restrictions on advertising are permissible if they are effective in manipulating people is contrary to the central principle justifying *Virginia Pharmacy Board*—that all attempts to machinate consumers and dissuade them from making legal choice by keeping them in the dark are impermissible under the First Amendment. If the Government admits that the purpose of its prohibition of truthful speech is to keep the public in the dark about the truth, the admission should spell the death knell for the policy, not justify it.

Compelled Subsidization of Generic Advertising. In *Glickman v. Wileman Brothers & Elliott, Inc.*,[75] the Court upheld federal rules that imposed assessments on farmers and others to cover the cost of generic advertising of California nectarines, plums, and peaches. The marketing orders, pursuant to the federal law, had to be approved by affected producers who marketed at least two-thirds of the volume of the commodity. Among the collective activity that Congress authorized is any form of marketing promotion including paid advertising. Congress had concluded that this advertising served the producers' and handlers' common interest in selling particular products. Various regulations minimized the risk that the generic advertising might adversely affect the interests of any individual producer. "The central message of the generic advertising" is that "California Summer

---

72. 517 U.S. 484, 116 S.Ct. 1495, 134 L.Ed.2d 711 (1996).

73. 517 U.S. at 503, 116 S.Ct. at 1508.

The Application of the Twenty–First Amendment. Part VII of the Stevens Opinion in *44 Liquormart* (which was an Opinion of the Court) rejected any notion that the Twenty–First Amendment affects the reach of the First Amendment. 517 U.S. at 514–15, 116 S.Ct. at 1514. The Court specifically disavowed the reasoning (but not the conclusion) of the Court in California v. LaRue, 409 U.S. 109, 93 S.Ct. 390, 34 L.Ed.2d 342 (1972), which used the Twenty–First Amendment to support its conclusion that

the First Amendment did not invalidate California's prohibition of grossly sexual exhibitions in places licensed to serve alcohol. The Court similarly rejected the reasoning of cases that had relied on *LaRue*, such as New York State Liquor Authority v. Bellanca, 452 U.S. 714, 101 S.Ct. 2599, 69 L.Ed.2d 357 (1981)(per curiam); Newport v. Iacobucci, 479 U.S. 92, 107 S.Ct. 383, 93 L.Ed.2d 334 (1986)(per curiam).

74. 517 U.S. at 518, 116 S.Ct. at 1515–16.

75. 521 U.S. 457, 117 S.Ct. 2130, 138 L.Ed.2d 585 (1997).

Fruits" are "wholesome, delicious, and attractive to discerning shoppers." Growers, handlers, and processors of California tree fruits challenged the validity of these orders, claiming that their forced subsidization of such generic advertising violated their rights of free speech.

The Court rejected these challenges, concluding that these marketing orders are a form of economic regulation that has displaced competition in certain markets. It was error, said the majority, to apply *Central Hudson* to this generic advertising. It was irrelevant that the Federal Government had failed to prove that generic advertising was more effective than individual advertising in increasing demand for California nectarines, plums, and peaches.

The Court neither accepted nor rejected the factual assumption that generic advertising may not be the most effective method of promoting the sale of these commodities. Instead, the Court ruled that this case should *not* be decided under *Central Hudson*. It concluded that compelling the respondents to fund this advertising was an economic question for Congress, rather than a First Amendment issue for the Court. The majority acknowledged that there is a free speech right not to be compelled to contribute to an organization whose expressive activities conflict with one's "freedom of belief." For example, the state can compel union members to pay dues to support activities related to collective bargaining, because those costs are germane to an otherwise lawful regulatory program, but the state cannot compel union members to make contributions for political purposes unrelated to collective bargaining.[76] In this case the assessments are germane to the regulatory program and requiring respondents to pay them cannot be said "to engender any crisis of conscience."[77]

Glickman should not be read broadly. Later, *United States v. United Foods, Inc.*,[78] agreed with mushroom producers who challenged an assessment that the Secretary of Agriculture imposed pursuant to the Mush-

room Promotion, Research, and Consumer Information Act. The purpose of the assessment was to fund generic advertisements promoting mushroom sales. The Court held that the assessment requirement violated the First Amendment, where the assessments were not ancillary to a more comprehensive program restricting market autonomy, and the advertising itself was the principal object of the regulatory scheme. United Foods claimed that its branded mushrooms were better, refused to pay the assessment, and argued that the First Amendment prohibited it. The Sixth Circuit and the U.S. Supreme Court agreed, holding that *Glickman* did not control because the mandated payments in this case were not part of a comprehensive statutory agricultural marketing program.

Attempts to Ban For Sale Signs. The Court has continued the principle of *Virginia Board of Pharmacy* in *Linmark Associates, Inc. v. Township of Willingboro*.[79] There the unanimous Court ruled that the First Amendment did not permit a municipality to prohibit by ordinance the posting of "For Sale" or "Sold" signs even though the town acted to stem what it perceived as the flight of white homeowners from a racially integrated community.

The respondent argued that the First Amendment concerns were less because the ordinance only restricted one form of communication. The Court decided, however, that the other forms of advertising—mainly by newspapers and realtor listings—were more costly and less effective. Also, the Court emphasized that the township's ordinance, by its own terms, made clear that it was not concerned with the time, place, or manner of the speech but its content. It did not prohibit all lawn signs, or all lawn signs of a particular size, in order, perhaps, to promote aesthetic values or other goals unrelated to the suppression of free expression. In addition, the "respondents have not demonstrated that the place or man-

76. See, Abood v. Detroit Board of Education, 431 U.S. 209, 97 S.Ct. 1782, 52 L.Ed.2d 261 (1977).

77. 521 U.S. at 472, 117 S.Ct. at 2139

78. 533 U.S. 405, 121 S.Ct. 2334, 150 L.Ed.2d 438 (2001).

79. 431 U.S. 85, 97 S.Ct. 1614, 52 L.Ed.2d 155 (1977).

ner of speech produces a detrimental 'secondary effect' on society.... Rather, Willingboro has proscribed particular types of signs based on their content because it fears their 'primary' effect—that they will cause those receiving the information to act upon it."[80]

Finally, the *Linmark* Court was unwilling to regard the governmental objective of assuring that Willingboro remains an integrated community as sufficient to justify the ordinance. The Court rejected this rationale on two grounds, one very narrow and one much broader. First, the Court concluded that the record before it did not support the township's fears that it was experiencing panic selling by white homeowners because of a belief the township was changing from a white to a black community.[81] More broadly, the Court found the defect in the ordinance "more basic" because if "dissemination of this information can be restricted, then every locality in the country can suppress any facts that reflect poorly on the locality, so long as a plausible claim can be made that disclosure would cause the recipients of the information to act 'irrationally.' "[82]

With *Linmark* one should compare *City of Ladue v. Gilleo*.[83] Justice Stevens, for a unanimous Court, invalidated a city ordinance that banned all residential signs subject to certain exceptions: the law, for example, allowed small residential signs advertising that the property is for sale, signs for churches and schools, commercial signs in commercially zoned districts. The ordinance in question did not allow Margaret Gilleo to display an 8.5 by 11 inch sign in her window, stating: "For Peace in the Gulf." Gilleo opposed the Persian Gulf War of 1990 to 1991. The City justified the ordinance as an effort to prevent "ugliness, visual blight and clutter," because signs "tarnish the natural beauty of the landscape," and so forth.

The Court assumed that the ordinance was viewpoint and content-neutral and that the various exemptions in the ordinance reflected legitimate differences among the side of effects of various kinds of signs. The Court invalidated the law, not because of its various exemptions—that is, not because the law discriminated on the basis of the content of speech—but because the law simply prohibited too much speech. Even content-neutral restrictions are invalid if they unduly limit one's ability to engage in free expression. Unlike *Linmark*—

Ladue has almost completely foreclosed a venerable means of communication that is both unique and important. It has totally foreclosed that medium to political, religious, or personal messages. [R]esidential signs play an important part in political campaigns, during which they are displayed to signal the resident's support for particular candidates, parties, or causes.... Although prohibitions foreclosing entire media may be completely free of content or viewpoint discrimination, the danger they pose to the freedom of speech is readily apparent—by eliminating a common means of speaking, such measures can suppress too much speech. Displaying a sign from one's own residence often carries a message quite distinct from placing the same sign someplace else, or conveying the same text or picture by other means. Precisely because of their location, such signs provide information about the identity of the "speaker."[84]

In a footnote, the Court explained that different considerations might apply "in the case of signs (whether political or otherwise) displayed by residents for a fee, or in the case of off-site commercial advertisements on residential property. We also are not confronted here

---

80. 431 U.S. at 94, 97 S.Ct. at 1619, citing Young v. American Mini Theatres, Inc., 427 U.S. 50, 71 n. 34, 96 S.Ct. 2440, 2452 n. 34, 49 L.Ed.2d 310 (1976), rehearing denied 429 U.S. 873, 97 S.Ct. 191, 50 L.Ed.2d 155 (1976).

81. The Court specifically cast doubt on Barrick Realty, Inc. v. Gary, 491 F.2d 161 (7th Cir.1974) which upheld Gary, Indiana's prohibition of "For Sale" signs on a record which showed that whites were fleeing en masse. "We express no view as to whether *Barrick Realty* can

survive *Bigelow* and *Virginia Pharmacy*." 431 U.S. 85 at 95 n. 9, 97 S.Ct. 1614 at 1620 n. 9, 52 L.Ed.2d 155.

82. 431 U.S. 85 at 96, 97 S.Ct. 1614 at 1620, 52 L.Ed.2d 155.

83. 512 U.S. 43, 114 S.Ct. 2038, 129 L.Ed.2d 36 (1994). O'Connor, J., also filed a concurring opinion.

84. 512 U.S. at 54–56, 114 S.Ct. at 2045–46 (footnotes omitted).

with mere regulations short of a ban."[85] For the Court to invite such distinctions make sense. An individual's on-site residential sign indicating his or her political viewpoints offer a very inexpensive free speech outlet for individuals, while a commercial advertiser of, for example, bacon, has many other outlets in addition to his front porch window. Even a political advertiser who is paying a fee has many choices, because he is paying a fee. In the case of commercial signs, the advertiser may also care less where the sign is located (whether on residential or commercial property) if the expected audience is approximately the same.

Bans on Contraceptives. In *Carey v. Population Services International*,[86] the Court invalidated a prohibition of any advertisement or display of contraceptives, a product which was not only legal but constitutionally protected. The arguments that such a prohibition was necessary because advertisements would be offensive or embarrassing to some or would legitimize sexual activities were rejected as "classically not justifications. . . ."[87]

PROBLEMS RELATED TO LAWYER ADVERTISING.

The *Bates* Case. In 1977, in *Bates v. State Bar*[88] the Court struck down state limitations on attorney advertising. The majority noted that the case did not involve person-to-person solicitation nor advertising as to the quality of legal services, but only the question of whether lawyers may constitutionally advertise the

prices of routine services, such as uncontested divorces, uncontested adoptions, simple personal bankruptcies, and changes of name.[89] Such advertising is constitutionally protected.

At this point in the development of the case law the *Bates* Court left open the extent to which certain types of advertising may be misleading, though it found appellants' particular advertisement not misleading. The Court also raised the question of whether advertising claims as to the quality of services "may be so likely to be misleading as to warrant restriction. . . . And the special problems of advertising on the electronic broadcast media will [also] warrant special consideration."[90]

The *R.M.J.* Case. *In re R.M.J.*,[91] applied *Bates* and invalidated various restrictions on lawyer advertising.[92] Justice Powell spoke for a unanimous Supreme Court. The state supreme court had reprimanded R.M.J. because he had deviated from the precise listing of areas of practice included in the state's Rule 4 governing lawyer advertising; for example, his advertisement listed "real estate" instead of "property," and he listed "contracts," although Rule 4 did not list that latter term at all.

Because the state did not show that R.M.J.'s listing was deceptive and because the state could show no substantial interest which its restriction on advertising promoted, the Court invalidated it. Similarly the Court invalidated a part of Rule 4 prohibiting a lawyer from identifying the jurisdictions in which he is licensed to practice law.[93] The Court also

85. 512 U.S. at 59 n. 17, 114 S.Ct. at 2047 n. 17.

86. 431 U.S. 678, 97 S.Ct. 2010, 52 L.Ed.2d 675 (1977).

87. 431 U.S. at 701, 97 S.Ct. at 2024. See also Bolger v. Youngs Drug Products Corp., 463 U.S. 60, 103 S.Ct. 2875, 77 L.Ed.2d 469 (1983) (law prohibiting mailing of unsolicited advertisements for contraceptives invalid).

88. 433 U.S. 350, 97 S.Ct. 2691, 53 L.Ed.2d 810 (1977), rehearing denied 434 U.S. 881, 98 S.Ct. 242, 54 L.Ed.2d 164 (1977). See, Ronald D. Rotunda, Lawyer Advertising and the Philosophical Origins of the Commercial Speech Doctrine, 36 U. Richmond L. Rev. 91 (2002)(Allen Chair Symposium of 2001).

89. 433 U.S. at 366, 97 S.Ct. at 2700.

90. 433 U.S. at 383–84, 97 S.Ct. at 2709. After this case the American Bar Association amended its Model Code of Professional Responsibility to allow radio and television advertising subject to certain restrictions. See, e.g., D.R. 2–101(D): "If the advertisement is communicat-

ed to the public over television or radio, it shall be prerecorded, approved for broadcast by the lawyer, and a recording of the actual transmission shall be retained by the lawyer." See Ronald D. Rotunda, Legal Ethics: The Lawyer's Deskbook on Professional Responsibility (West Group–ABA, 2nd ed. 2002), at §§ 46–1 to 46–5.

91. 455 U.S. 191, 102 S.Ct. 929, 71 L.Ed.2d 64 (1982).

92. Rotunda, Lawyer Advertising and the Philosophical Origins of the Commercial Speech Doctrine, 36 University of Richmond Law Review 91 (2002)(Allen Chair Symposium of 2001).

93. 455 U.S. at 205, 102 S.Ct. at 938.

R.M.J. also emphasized in large boldface type that he was a member of the U.S. Supreme Court bar, a "relatively uninformative fact" but the record did not show that it was misleading. Rule 4 did not specifically identify this information as misleading, nor place a limitation on the

struck a prohibition against the lawyer widely mailing announcement cards to persons other than lawyers, former clients, personal friends, and relatives. These cards announced the opening of his law office. The state produced no evidence justifying such a restrictive prohibition.

Targeted Direct Mail–Advertising.

Shapero v. Kentucky Bar Association[94] invalidated, as a violation of free speech, state prohibitions against attorneys sending truthful, non-deceptive letters to potential clients known to face particular legal problems (i.e., targeted, direct-mail advertising). The state rule was based on the American Bar Association's Model Rule of Professional Conduct, Rule 7.3. The Court relied primarily on *Zauderer v. Office of Disciplinary Counsel,* and noted that the Supreme Court's lawyer advertising cases have never distinguished among various modes of written advertising to the general public. For example, *In re R.M.J.* treated mailed announcement cards the same as newspaper and telephone directory advertisements.[95]

Mass mailing is a form of advertising and therefore also constitutionally protected. Given that attorneys may engage in mass mailing, it makes little sense for the state to prohibit targeted mailing, which is only a more efficient form of advertising than mass mailing. It is quite reasonable for an attorney to mail a letter only to those who are more likely to find it of interest.

Targeted Direct Mail Within 30 Days of an Accident.

The ethics rules in Florida prohibited personal injury lawyers from sending targeted direct mail soliciting employment to victims and their relatives until 30 days have passed following an accident or disaster. This rule prevented the personal injury *plaintiff's* attorney from contacting the accident victim or a relative, but it imposed no restrictions on the *defense* attorney from contacting either the victim or the relative. In *Florida Bar v. Went for It, Inc.,*[96] the Court did not disturb *Shapero,* but held (5 to 4) that, even though targeted mailing is constitutionally protected, Florida may ban targeted mailing by plaintiffs' attorneys for 30 days after the cause of action has occurred. Justice O'Connor, who dissented in *Shapero,* wrote the majority opinion in *Went for It.*[97]

Justice O'Connor, for the Court, applied the basic test advanced in *Central Hudson,*[98] and claimed that the state bar had substantial interests to protect and that its restrictions were narrowly tailored to directly and substantially advance that interest. She told us that the Florida rule was necessary to protect the privacy of the victims and preventing invasive conduct by lawyers. However, an airline crash or similar misfortune is not a private act. It is widely reported in the newspapers, television, and radio. The recipient of the letter does not have to respond; he or she can just throw it away. The Florida rule does nothing about invasive conduct by defense counsel or insurance adjusters.

type size, nor require any explanation of the significance of admission to the U.S. Supreme Court bar. 455 U.S. at 205–06, 102 S.Ct. at 938–39.

94. 486 U.S. 466, 108 S.Ct. 1916, 100 L.Ed.2d 475 (1988), on remand 763 S.W.2d 126 (Ky.1989).

95. Brennan, J., in a plurality opinion went on to conclude that petitioner's particular letter was not misleading merely because it engaged in the liberal use of underscored, upper case letters, such as, "Call NOW, don't wait"; "it is FREE, there is NO charge for calling." Nor was the letter misleading because it contained assertions that state no objective fact ("It may surprise you what I may be able to do for you"). The plurality said that a "truthful and nondeceptive letter, no matter how big its type and how much it speculates can never 'shou[t] at the recipient' or 'gras[p] him by the lapels,' as can a lawyer engaging in face-to-face solicitation. The letter simply presents no comparable risk of overreaching."

96. 515 U.S. 618, 115 S.Ct. 2371, 132 L.Ed.2d 541 (1995), on remand 66 F.3d 270 (11th Cir.1995). Ronald D. Rotunda, Professionalism, Legal Advertising, and Free Speech In the Wake of *Florida Bar v. Went For It, Inc.,* 49 Ark. L. Rev. 703 (1997).

97. O'Connor's dissent in *Shapero* was joined by Rehnquist, C.J. and Scalia, J. Both of these Justices, along with Thomas & Breyer, JJ., joined the five person majority. The majority in *Shapero* included Kennedy, J. (who joined all of the Brennan plurality) & Stevens, J. (who joined Parts I and II of the Brennan plurality). In *Went For It,* Kennedy, J. filed a dissenting opinion joined by Stevens, Souter, & Ginsburg, JJ.

98. Central Hudson Gas & Electric Corp. v. Public Service Commission, 447 U.S. 557, 100 S.Ct. 2343, 65 L.Ed.2d 341 (1980).

O'Connor also argued that the Florida rule was necessary in order to prevent "the erosion of confidence in the profession that such repeated invasions have engendered."[99] She emphasized that the situation in *Went For It* was unlike the situation in *Shapero,* because *Shapero* only dealt "with a broad ban on *all* direct-mail solicitations, whatever the time frame and whoever the recipient," and, unlike *Shapero,* the Florida State Bar had collected evidence that it was important to have this 30 day ban on plaintiff-lawyers in order to protect the public perception of lawyers.

What was this evidence that is of constitutional significance? The state bar's evidence was both statistical and anecdotal. O'Connor, for example, regarded as particularly "[s]ignificant" a poll showing that "27% of direct-mail recipients reported that their regard for the legal profession and for the judicial process as a whole was 'lower' as a result of receiving the direct mail."[100] One does not have to be a rocket scientist to figure out that if 27% did not like the mailing, then for the remaining 73%, the direct mail did not lower their respect for the profession. But O'Connor says that the state can keep everyone in the dark because 27% of the people might think better of us if they did not know what was going on.

In a significant passage, the Court said:

Florida permits lawyers to advertise on prime-time television and radio as well as in newspapers and other media. They may rent space on billboard. They may send *untargeted letters* to the general population, *or to discrete segments thereof.*[101]

So, it appears that lawyers can still send letters, as long as they also send them to people who are less interested in receiving them. As for the recipients, one wonders how they will know if the letters are targeted or not. With modern computers, one can receive magazines that print the recipient's name on the magazine instead of pasting on a label. Similarly, a mass mailing can begin the letter with the phrase, "Dear Mr. Smith," rather than, "Dear Occupant." Unless the letter refers to a very specific fact (e.g., a particular accident rather than the problem of accidents generally) the recipient will not know from the letter whether it was sent only to him or to others, such as his neighbor.

If people really do not like to receive targeted mailing, then this problem should be self-policing. That is, people who do not like to hire lawyers who send letters seeking employment will not hire such lawyers. If most people do not like these letters, lawyers who send them will learn the hard way not to waste money on them. In fact, these letters must have been useful for the majority of recipients because otherwise the lawyers (who were not sending out the letters for their own health or amusement) would not have sent them.

However, now that the Florida Bar rule is in effect, a client may find out that he or she has hired the type of lawyer who (but for the Florida rule) would have sent a targeted letter. Therefore, by keeping people ignorant of the facts, the Florida rule takes away from clients the right to refuse to hire a lawyer who would send this type of targeted mailing. Meanwhile, under the Florida rule, clients are kept in the dark for 30 days while being fair game for defense lawyers, who can contact them.

The majority justified the Florida prohibition as a means to protect the public perception of lawyers. People might think better of lawyers if only they did not know the type of people that many of the lawyers are. As Justice Kennedy pointed out in his dissent, "for the first time since *Bates v. State Bar of Arizona,*[102] the Court now orders a major retreat from the constitutional guarantees for commercial speech in order to shield its own profession from public criticism."[103]

Advertising That a Lawyer Is a "Specialist" or "Certified." The Illinois Su-

---

99.   515 U.S. at 635, 115 S.Ct. at 2381.

100.   515 U.S. at 627, 115 S.Ct. at 2377.

101.   515 U.S. at 633, 115 S.Ct. at 2380 (emphasis added).

102.   433 U.S. 350, 97 S.Ct. 2691, 53 L.Ed.2d 810 (1977), rehearing denied 434 U.S. 881, 98 S.Ct. 242, 54 L.Ed.2d 164 (1977).

103.   515 U.S. at 644, 115 S.Ct. at 2386 (Kennedy, J., dissenting).

preme Court promulgated ethical rules governing lawyers. These rules did not permit an attorney to hold himself out as "certified" or a "specialist" except for patent, trademark, and admiralty lawyers. Therefore the Illinois Supreme Court publicly censured Peel, an Illinois attorney, because his letterhead stated that he is certified as a civil trial specialist by the National Board of Trial Advocacy (NBTA), a bona fide private group that developed a set of objective and demanding standards and procedures for periodic certification of lawyers with experience and competence in trial work. In *Peel v. Attorney Registration and Disciplinary Commission of Illinois*[104] the U.S. Supreme Court (five to four, with no majority opinion) reversed.

The facts on Peel's letterhead were both verifiable and true. The issue before the Court was whether a lawyer has a constitutional right, under the standards applicable to commercial speech, to advertise his or her certification as a trial specialist by NBTA. Though Peel's claim was facially accurate, Illinois argued that Peel's letterhead implied a higher quality or ability, than noncertified lawyers. Justice Stevens' plurality opinion explained that Illinois had confused "the distinction between statements of opinion or quality and statements of objective facts that may support an inference of quality."[105]

Peel's statement of certification by a private group, the NBTA, has no more potential to mislead than an attorney advertising that he is admitted to practice before the U.S. Supreme Court, a statement the Supreme Court approved in, *In re R.M.J.* Thus, Peel's letterhead was neither actually nor inherently nor potentially misleading. If the state believes that statements of private certification might be potentially misleading, the state might be able to require a disclaimer about the certifying

organization or the standards of a specialty.[106] To require more disclosure is better than a total prohibition.

The Illinois Supreme Court claimed that Peel's statement that he was certified was misleading because, that court said, everyone knows that "certified" means that he was certified by the state, because a certificate is— and here the Illinois Supreme Court, in an effort to gather support for its claim, quoted from *Webster's Dictionary*—

> [A] document issued by ... a state agency, ... certifying that one has satisfactorily ... attained professional standing in a given field and may officially practice or hold a position in that field. Webster's Third New International Dictionary 367 (1986 ed.)[107]

It is ironic, to say the least, that the Illinois Supreme Court criticized Peel for being misleading while the Illinois Supreme Court itself was misleading, for the full quotation to which the Illinois court referred, *without* the ellipses, is quite different. A certificate is—

> [A] document issued by *a school,* a state agency, *or a professional organization* certifying that one has satisfactorily *completed a course of studies, has passed a qualifying examination, or has* attained professional standing in a given field and may officially practice or hold a position in that field. Webster's Third New International Dictionary 367 (1986 ed.)

The portions that the Illinois Supreme Court deleted are in italics.

As the Stevens' plurality noted, the consuming public knows that states routinely issue licenses for a host of activities—such as licenses to sell liquor, or drive a car—all the time. Similarly, private groups issue certificates to

---

104. 496 U.S. 91, 110 S.Ct. 2281, 110 L.Ed.2d 83 (1990).

105. 496 U.S. at 101, 110 S.Ct. at 2288. (Stevens, J., joined by Brennan, Blackmun, & Kennedy, JJ.).

106. 496 U.S. at 110 n. 17, 110 S.Ct. at 2292 n. 17.

107. In re Peel, 126 Ill.2d 397, 405, 128 Ill.Dec. 535, 534 N.E.2d 980, 984 (1989), reversed 496 U.S. 91, 110 S.Ct. 2281, 110 L.Ed.2d 83 (1990). After this case, the Illinois Supreme Court promptly modified its rules and

required lawyers who used the words "certified," "specialist," "expert," or "any other, similar terms", to state, *inter alia,* that "the Supreme Court of Illinois does not recognize certifications of specialists in the practice of law and that the certificate, award or recognition is not a requirement to practice law in Illinois." See, Illinois Amended Rule 7.4 (July 16, 1990), reprinted in, T. Morgan & R. Rotunda, Problems and Materials on Professional Responsibility 446 (Foundation Press, 5th ed. 1991).

commemorate a solo flight or a hole in one. It is hardly uncommon for people to claim that they are foreign car "specialists" or air conditioning "specialists" without the public automatically believing that the state has formally recognized these claims. Justice Stevens rejected the paternalistic assumption that the reader of Peel's stationery was no more discriminating or sophisticated than those who watch children's television. The state's rule was overbroad: one does not burn down the house to roast the pig.[108]

Lawyer's Designation as Certified Public Accountant and Certified Financial Planner. In *Ibanez v. Florida Department of Business and Professional Regulation, Board of Accountancy.*[109] Justice Ginsburg, for the Court, held that it violated free speech when the Florida Board of Accountancy reprimanded Silvia Ibanez, an attorney, because she truthfully stated in her advertising, that she was a Certified Public Accountant (CPA) and a Certified Financial Planner (CFP). The state Board of Accountancy licensed her as a CPA, and a bona fide private organization, not the state, licensed her as a CFP. Attorney Ibanez argued her own case.

Justice Ginsburg, for a unanimous Court, upheld Ibanez's right to use the CPA designation. "[W]e cannot imagine how consumers could be misled by her truthful representation" that she is a CPA.[110]

The Court, seven to two, also rejected sanctions based on the fact that Ms. Ibanez had truthfully stated that she was a CFP. The Board relied on a Florida rule that prohibits the use of "specialist" unless accompanied by a disclaimer "in the immediate proximity of the statement that implies formal recognition as a specialist." It must also state that "the recognizing agency is not affiliated with or

sanctioned by the state or federal government," and must set out the requirements for recognition, "including, but not limited to, education, experience[,] and testing." Justice Ginsburg, for the Court, remarked on the "failure of the Board to point to any harm that is potentially real, not purely hypothetical," and criticized the detail required on the disclaimer, which would effectively rule out use of the designation on a business card, letterhead, or yellow pages listing. She then concluded, "We have never sustained restrictions on constitutionally protected speech based on a record so bare as the one on which the Board relies here."[111]

O'Connor, J., joined by Rehnquist, C.J., dissented on this point, arguing that the CFP designation is both inherently and potentially misleading because a private organization, not the state, confers the designation of Certified Financial Planner.

Disclosure Requirements. In *Zauderer v. Office of Disciplinary Counsel,*[112] Justice White for the Court held that the state may not discipline an attorney who solicits business by running newspaper advertisements containing nondeceptive illustrations and legal advice. The attorney in question placed an advertisement offering to represent women who had suffered injury from the Dalkon Shield Intrauterine Device. This advertisement included a drawing of the Shield and offered legal advice, such as the advice that claims may not yet be time barred. Though the legal advice regarded a specific legal problem, it was neither false not deceptive, and did not involve face-to-face solicitation.

However, the Court held that the state could discipline an attorney for failure to include in his advertisements some information reasonably necessary to make his advertisement not

---

108. 496 U.S. at 105–06, 110 S.Ct. at 2290. Cf. Bolger v. Youngs Drug Products Corp., 463 U.S. 60, 74, 103 S.Ct. 2875, 2884, 77 L.Ed.2d 469 (1983), where the Court invalidated a federal statute prohibiting unsolicited mailings of contraceptive advertisements. *Bolger* rejected the argument that the statute aided parents' efforts to discuss birth control with their parents. To purge all mailboxes of material suitable for adults because some children may see it is more extensive regulation than the First Amendment allows.

109. 512 U.S. 136, 114 S.Ct. 2084, 129 L.Ed.2d 118 (1994).

110. 512 U.S. at 144, 114 S.Ct. at 2089.

111. 512 U.S. at 148, 114 S.Ct. at 2089–91.

112. 471 U.S. 626, 105 S.Ct. 2265, 85 L.Ed.2d 652 (1985).

misleading. The lawyer advertised that he was available to represent clients on a contingent fee basis and that "if there is no recovery, no legal fees are owed by our clients." Thus, the advertisement failed to disclose that the clients might be liable for significant litigation costs even though their lawsuits were unsuccessful.

The Court first carefully distinguished between disclosure requirements and outright prohibitions of speech. A disclosure requirement prohibits no speech and the lawyer's "constitutionally protected interest in *not* providing any particular factual information in his advertising is minimal."[113] As long as the disclosure requirements (1) are reasonably related to the state's interest in preventing deception of consumers, and, (2) there is no problem of vagueness,[114] and, (3) they are not "unjustified or unduly burdensome,"[115] there is no First Amendment violation. This "unduly burdensome" caveat is an important one. The Supreme Court did not give regulatory authorities a blank check to make every advertisement look like a securities prospectus.

But if the disclosure requirements meet this three-part test, it is not necessary for the state to demonstrate that they are the least restrictive means to serve the state's purposes. Nor is a disclosure requirement invalid if it is underinclusive, i.e., if it does not get at all facets of the problem it is designed to ameliorate. As a general matter, governments are entitled to attack problems piecemeal, unless their policies implicate rights that are so fundamental that strict scrutiny must be applied.

Applying these principles the Court concluded that the state may regulate the advertisement to prevent deceptive practices. The advertisement told the public that "if there is no recovery, no legal fees are owed by our clients." But it did not disclose the distinction between "legal fees" and "costs," thus suggesting that representation in a losing cause would come entirely free of charge. The assumption many potential clients would be misled "is hardly a speculative one." "When the possibility of deception is as self-evident as it is in this case, we need not require the State to 'conduct a survey of the ... public before it [may] determine that the [advertisement] had a tendency to mislead.' "[116]

Solicitation of Legal Business and Face-to-Face Encounters. In the year following the *Bates* decision, the Court began to define the limits of state regulation of attorney solicitation of clients in two cases decided the same day, *Ohralik v. Ohio State Bar*[117] and *In re Primus*.[118] In so doing the majority, speaking through Justice Powell, appeared to resurrect some elements of the "commercial" speech distinction that had been discredited by the earlier cases. Justice Powell said in *Ohralik* that the distinction between other types of speech and commercial speech is a "commonsense" one, though later he stated in *Primus* that the line between commercial and noncommercial speech "will not always be easy to draw,"[119] an admission that suggests the distinction is not so commonsensical.

113. 471 U.S. at 651, 105 S.Ct. at 2282 (emphasis in original). Brickley, C.J., citing Treatise, in Michigan State AFL–CIO v. Employment Relations Commission, 453 Mich. 362, 375, 551 N.W.2d 165, 170 (1996).

114. 471 U.S. at 653 n. 15, 105 S.Ct. at 2283 n. 15.

115. 471 U.S. at 651, 105 S.Ct. at 2282.

116. 471 U.S. at 652, 105 S.Ct. at 2282.

117. 436 U.S. 447, 98 S.Ct. 1912, 56 L.Ed.2d 444 (1978).

118. 436 U.S. 412, 98 S.Ct. 1893, 56 L.Ed.2d 417 (1978).

119. 436 U.S. at 455–56, 438 n. 32, 98 S.Ct. at 1918, 1908 n. 32. Justice Powell said that the line is "based in part on the motive of the speaker and the character of the expressive activity...." Id. Justice Rehnquist, dissenting, noted that to the extent this " 'commonsense' distinction

focuses on the content of the speech, it is at least suspect under many of the Court's First Amendment cases ... and to the extent it focuses upon the motive of the speaker, it is subject to manipulation by clever practitioners." 436 U.S. at 441–42, 98 S.Ct. at 1910.

Moreover, Justice Powell's tortured discussion of attorney's fees—in which he sought to demonstrate that there are differences in counsel fees awarded by the court and counsel fees awarded in a "traditional" manner—demonstrates that distinguishing between commercial and noncommercial speech is a fruitless endeavor. Justice Powell said, inter alia, that:

"Counsel fees [here] are awarded in the discretion of the court; awards are not drawn from the plaintiff's recovery, and are usually premised on a successful outcome; and the amounts awarded may not correspond to fees generally obtainable in private litigation." 436 U.S. at 430, 98 S.Ct. at 1903–04.

It is difficult to derive any specific principle of law from *Ohralik* and *Primus* because language in each case suggests both broad and narrow holdings.[120] The decisions in the two cases, taken together, indicate that the state may regulate lawyer solicitation in order to protect the public from false or deceptive commercial practices, so long as the regulations are reasonable and are not applied to speech that does not clearly present such dangers to the public.[121]

The Court recognized in *Ohralik* that the state has an interest in protecting the "unsophisticated, injured, or distressed lay person" from "those aspects of solicitation that involve fraud, undue influence, intimidation, overreaching, and other forms of 'vexatious conduct.'"[122] This rule is justified in part because of the special nature of "in-person" solicitation. In general advertising the recipient may simply turn away, but in-person solicitation may exert pressure and seek an immediate response from the prospective client, who then has less opportunity for reflection. The Bar and supervisory authorities have less opportunity to engage in counter education in such circumstances. And there is less opportunity for public scrutiny because the in-person solicitation often takes place in private, with no witness other than the lawyer and the prospective client.[123]

However, even these distinctions apparently do not justify a broad, per se rule against in-person solicitation, for the *Ohralik* majority seemed careful to limit its holding to the facts before the Court. The opinion emphasized that the issue was whether the antisolicitation rule could constitutionally be applied to the appellant,[124] and that "the appropriate focus is on appellant's conduct."[125]

Justice Powell began the opinion by summarizing in detail the appellant's outrageous in-person solicitation, and concluded by restating the factual context:

[T]he disciplinary rules constitutionally could be applied to appellant. He approached two young accident victims at a time when they were especially incapable of making informed judgments or of assessing and protecting their own interests. He solicited Carol McClintock in a hospital room where she lay in traction and sought out Wanda Lou Holbert on the day she came home from the hospital, knowing from his prior inquiries that she had just been released. Appellant urged his services upon the young women and . . . employed a concealed tape recorder,

All of these characteristics, even the last one supposedly unique to the ACLU litigation, apply to many private securities lawsuits where the attorneys secure a benefit for shareholders but create no res. Similar types of fees may be generated by truth in lending cases. See, e.g., Mills v. Electric Auto–Lite Co., 396 U.S. 375, 389–97, 90 S.Ct. 616, 624–28, 24 L.Ed.2d 593 (1970), appeal after remand 552 F.2d 1239 (7th Cir.1977), certiorari denied 434 U.S. 922, 98 S.Ct. 398, 54 L.Ed.2d 279 (1977), rehearing denied 434 U.S. 1002, 98 S.Ct. 649, 54 L.Ed.2d 499 (1977); Mirabal v. General Motors Acceptance Corp., 576 F.2d 729 (7th Cir. 1978), certiorari denied 439 U.S. 1039, 99 S.Ct. 642, 58 L.Ed.2d 699 (1978).

120. For example, in *Ohralik,* Justice Powell for the majority summarized *Primus* as follows:

"We hold today in *Primus* that a lawyer who engaged in solicitation as a form of protected political association may not be disciplined without proof of actual wrongdoing that the State constitutionally may proscribe." 436 U.S. at 462–63 n. 20, 98 S.Ct. at 1922 n. 20.

Yet in *Primus* itself, Powell for the majority spoke more hesitantly, stating, for example, that "[w]e express no opinion whether an analysis of this case [*Primus*] would be different [if the ACLU had shared court awarded fees between the state chapter and the private attorney cooper-

ating with the ACLU]." 436 U.S. at 430 n. 24, 98 S.Ct. at 1904 n. 24.

121. The distinction between this type of regulation and unjustified prohibition of lawyer advertising is evidenced by the fact that the majority in *Ohralik* accepted reasons for regulating attorney solicitation that would not be sufficient to ban attorney advertising. Thus in *Ohralik* the Court emphasized that law is a "profession," that the transaction in question was commercial in nature, and that a strong prophylactic rule was necessary to protect the unsophisticated, even though there is no explicit proof or finding of harm. Such rationales were rejected in Bates v. State Bar, 433 U.S. 350, 97 S.Ct. 2691, 53 L.Ed.2d 810 (1977), rehearing denied 434 U.S. 881, 98 S.Ct. 242, 54 L.Ed.2d 164 (1977), when they were used to prohibit attorney advertising.

122. 436 U.S. at 462, 98 S.Ct. at 1921 (footnote omitted).

123. 436 U.S. at 466, 98 S.Ct. at 1923–24.

124. 436 U.S. at 462–63 n. 20, 98 S.Ct. at 1922 n. 20.

125. 436 U.S. at 463, 98 S.Ct. at 1922. The attorney who argued the *Ohralik* case on behalf of the state bar also believes that the case should be limited to its facts. (June 13, 1978) (Report of A.B.A. Disciplinary Workshop, in 46 U.S.L.W. 2662).

seemingly to insure that he would have evidence of Wanda's oral assent to the representation. He emphasized that his fee would come out of the recovery, thereby tempting the young women with what sounded like a cost-free and therefore irresistible offer. He refused to withdraw when Mrs. Holbert requested him to do so only a day after the initial meeting between appellant and Wanda Lou and continued to represent himself to the insurance company as Wanda Holbert's lawyer.[126]

Justice Marshall's thoughtful concurring opinion specifically would allow "benign" commercial solicitation, that is "solicitation by advice and information that is truthful and that is presented in a noncoercive, nondeceitful and dignified manner to a potential client who is emotionally and physically capable of making a rational decision either to accept or reject the representation with respect to a legal claim or matter that is not frivolous."[127] Nothing in the majority opinion rejects Justice Marshall's conclusions.

In the companion case, *In re Primus,*[128] a lawyer whose firm was cooperating with the American Civil Liberties Union (ACLU) wrote to a woman who had been sterilized as a condition of receiving public medical assistance. The lawyer offered the ACLU's services to represent her. The state had disciplined the attorney for this action but the Supreme Court of the United States reversed that decision.

The Court distinguished *Ohralik* because of the nature of the interests involved. Solicitation for private gain under the circumstances of *Ohralik* could be proscribed without showing harm in a given case because the circumstances were likely to result in the misleading, deceptive, and overbearing conduct, but solicitation on behalf of nonprofit organiza-

tions which litigate as a form of political expression may be regulated only when actual harm is shown in the particular case.[129] The Court reviewed the record in *Primus* and found nothing indicating fraud, overreaching or other behavior that the state could regulate. Consequently, it held the solicitation within the zone of political speech and association protected in *NAACP v. Button.*[130]

Under *Ohralik,* the states are free to proscribe in-person solicitation for gain in circumstances where it is likely to be fraudulent, misleading, or overreaching, but under *Primus* they may only proscribe solicitation on behalf of nonprofit political organizations if it is in fact misleading, and then regulations must be "carefully tailored" so as not to "abridge unnecessarily the associational freedom of nonprofit organizations, or their members, having characteristics like those of the NAACP or the ACLU."[131]

Justice Powell's opinion for the Court seems to emphasize two factors distinguishing *Primus* from *Ohralik:* the absence of misrepresentation and pressure tactics, and the lack of major pecuniary award. Yet a careful reading of the *Primus* opinion indicates a third, equally important factor: the form of the solicitation. In *Ohralik* the solicitation was "in-person," *face-to-face.*[132] In *Primus,* the attorney first was invited to address a gathering of women and then sent a letter to one of them offering free representation after being advised that the woman wished to sue the doctor who had sterilized her. This "act of solicitation took the form of a letter.... This was not *in-person* solicitation for pecuniary gain."[133]

Later the Court was more specific in recognizing that a letter is not face-to-face solicita-

126. 436 U.S. at 467, 98 S.Ct. at 1924.

127. 436 U.S. at 472 n. 3, 98 S.Ct. 1927 n. 3 (Marshall, J., concurring).

128. 436 U.S. 412, 98 S.Ct. 1893, 56 L.Ed.2d 417 (1978).

129. 436 U.S. at 435, 98 S.Ct. at 1906–07. The Court noted that in *Primus* the lawyer did not attempt to "pressure" the prospective client into filing the suit. 436 U.S. at 417 n. 7, 98 S.Ct. at 1897 n. 7. "[A]ppellant's letter

cannot be characterized as a pressure tactic." 436 U.S. at 435 n. 28, 98 S.Ct. at 1906 n. 28.

130. 371 U.S. 415, 83 S.Ct. 328, 9 L.Ed.2d 405 (1963).

131. 436 U.S. at 439, 98 S.Ct. at 1908.

132. It does not matter whether the face-to-face solicitation was by the lawyer himself or one of his agents or "runners." 436 U.S. at 464 n. 22, 98 S.Ct. at 1923 n. 22.

133. 436 U.S. at 422, 98 S.Ct. at 1899 (emphasis added).

tion but is more like the advertising protected in *Bates:*

> The transmittal of this letter—as contrasted with in-person solicitation—involved no appreciable invasion of privacy; nor did it afford any significant opportunity for overreaching or coercion. Moreover, the fact that there was a written communication lessens substantially the difficulty of policing solicitation practices that do offend valid rules of professional conduct.[134]

As Powell himself had earlier recognized in his separate opinion in *Bates:* "No distinction can be drawn between newspapers and a rather broad spectrum of other means—for example, magazines, signs in buses and subways, posters, handbills, and mail circulations."[135] The letter in *Primus* seems identical to the "mail circulations" referred to in *Bates.*

Later, Powell for a unanimous Court, invalidated a state rule that prohibited mailing cards (which announced the opening of his office) to persons other than "lawyers, former clients, personal friends and relatives." The silent record did not justify the reason for the absolute prohibition. Even if a reason existed, the state could use less restrictive means, such as requiring that a copy of any mailings be filed with the state, if the state wished to supervise mailings. "[A]lthough the states may regulate commercial speech, the First and Fourteenth Amendments require that they do so with care and in a manner no more extensive than reasonably necessary to further substantial interests."[136] Later, the Court approved of targeted, direct mail advertising.[137] Thus, letters and other non-face-to-face solicitation are "in-person" solicitation for purposes of *Ohralik,* even if the lawyer seeks pecuniary gain.

Separate treatment of face-to-face solicitation by the state can be justified by the greater public need to guard against possible deceptive or coercive advertising practices. Of course, actual misrepresentation and overreaching can always be prohibited. As Justice Marshall's concurrence emphasized, "[w]hat is objectionable about Ohralik's behavior here is not so much that he solicited business for himself, but rather the circumstances in which he performed that solicitation and the means by which he accomplished it."[138]

Comparison of Lawyer Solicitation Cases With Accountant Solicitation Cases. The Court's deference to state regulation that limits the power of lawyers to engage in face to face, in-person solicitation of clients should be contrasted with the strict limits the Court has placed on the state powers to limit face to face, in person solicitation by accountants. In *Edenfield v. Fane,*[139] the Court invali-

---

134. 436 U.S. at 435–36, 98 S.Ct. at 1906–07 (footnote omitted) (emphasis added).

135. Bates v. State Bar, 433 U.S. 350, 402 n. 12, 97 S.Ct. 2691, 2718 n. 12, 53 L.Ed.2d 810 (1977), rehearing denied 434 U.S. 881, 98 S.Ct. 242, 54 L.Ed.2d 164 (1977). See also Koffler v. Joint Bar Ass'n, 51 N.Y.2d 140, 432 N.Y.S.2d 872, 412 N.E.2d 927 (1980), certiorari denied 450 U.S. 1026, 101 S.Ct. 1733, 68 L.Ed.2d 221 (1981) (direct mail communications are not "in-person" solicitation within the meaning of *Ohralik* and therefore protected under *Bates*); Kentucky Bar Ass'n v. Stuart, 568 S.W.2d 933 (Ky.1978) (same). Contra, Allison v. Louisiana State Bar Ass'n, 362 So.2d 489 (La.1978).

136. In re R.M.J., 455 U.S. 191, 207, 102 S.Ct. 929, 939, 71 L.Ed.2d 64 (1982).

137. Shapero v. Kentucky Bar Association, 486 U.S. 466, 108 S.Ct. 1916, 100 L.Ed.2d 475 (1988), discussed above.

138. 436 U.S. at 470, 98 S.Ct. at 1926 (Marshall, J., concurring).

At the end of *Primus,* Justice Powell for the majority stated in dictum:

> "And a State may insist that lawyers not solicit on behalf of lay organizations that exert control over the actual conduct of any ensuing litigation."

436 U.S. at 439, 98 S.Ct. at 1908.

The only authority for that assertion was dictum by Justice White concurring and dissenting in NAACP v. Button, 371 U.S. 415, 447, 83 S.Ct. 328, 345, 9 L.Ed.2d 405 (1963). Justice Powell's dictum—at least in its broad form—is not even supported by the American Bar Association. See A.B.A. Formal Opinion 334 (Aug. 10, 1974) (dealing with restrictions on lawyers' activities by legal services offices as they affect independence of professional judgment).

Justice Marshall specifically disassociated himself from Justice Powell's dictum and noted that it "is by no means self-evident, has never been the actual holding of this Court and is not put in issue by the facts presently before us." 436 U.S. at 471, 98 S.Ct. at 1927. See also 436 U.S. at 439, 98 S.Ct. at 1908 (Blackmun, J., concurring).

139. 507 U.S. 761, 113 S.Ct. 1792, 123 L.Ed.2d 543 (1993). Kennedy, J., delivered the opinion of the Court, which voted 8 to 1 to invalidate the state restrictions. Only O'Connor, J., dissented.

dated a Florida ban on in-person, uninvited, direct *face-to-face* or telephone contact by Certified Public Accountants soliciting business in the business context. The Court held that, as applied, the Florida ban on CPA solicitation in the business context violated free speech. The CPA who is soliciting business intends to communicate truthful, nondeceptive information proposing a lawful commercial transaction.

This Florida law need only be reasonably tailored to serve a substantial state interest. Yet even under this intermediate standard of review, the Court found that the law is unconstitutional as applied. Although the state's interest in protecting consumers from fraud and overreaching, in protecting their privacy, and in maintaining the fact and appearance of CPA impartiality is substantial, Florida did not meet its burden to show that the rule is reasonably tailored to meet those interests, that its serves these purposes in a direct and material manner. For example, the state offered no studies or even anecdotal evidence that personal solicitation by CPAs creates dangers of fraud, overreaching, or compromised independence.

Ohralik does not support the CPA restriction. It's "narrow" holding—said the Court in *Edenfield*—depended on "unique" features of in-person solicitation by lawyers. The CPA, unlike a lawyer, is not trained in the art of persuasion. The CPA, in contrast to the lawyer, is trained in "independence and objectivity, not advocacy." In addition, the CPA's prospective clients, unlike the young accident victim in *Ohralik*, are sophisticated experienced business executives. The people whom the CPA wishes to solicit meet the CPA in their own offices, and there is no pressure to retain the CPA on the spot. *Ohralik*, in short, does not relieve the state of the obligation to prove that the preventative measures that it proposes will contribute "in a material way" to relieving a "serious" problem.

The Noncommercial, Political Speech of Corporations

The Supreme Court in *First National Bank v. Bellotti*,[140] held that states cannot prohibit corporations from spending money to express their views on referendum questions even if such issues are not directly related to their business interests.[141] The Court characterized its recent commercial speech decisions as illustrating that the First Amendment prohibits government from limiting the stock of information from which the public may draw, and noted that the state's argument that it could not regulate commercial speech of corporations but could ban their political speech, would reverse the traditional constitutional values attaching to political and commercial speech.[142]

Commercial Speech and Trade Names.

140. 435 U.S. 765, 98 S.Ct. 1407, 55 L.Ed.2d 707 (1978), rehearing denied 438 U.S. 907, 98 S.Ct. 3126, 57 L.Ed.2d 1150 (1978).

141. 435 U.S. at 783–84 & n. 20, 98 S.Ct. at 1419–20 & n. 20. The Court did caution that "our consideration of a corporation's right to speak on issues of general public interest implies no comparable right in the quite different context of participation in a political campaign for election to public office. Congress might well be able to demonstrate the existence of a danger of real or apparent corruption in independent expenditures by corporations to influence candidate elections." 435 U.S. at 788 n. 26, 98 S.Ct. at 1422 n. 26.

Justice Rehnquist, dissenting, argued that corporations as creatures of the state, have only those rights granted them and those necessarily incident to their business purposes. 435 U.S. at 822–28, 98 S.Ct. at 1439–43. Justice White, joined by Justices Brennan and Marshall, also dissented.

Federal Election Commission v. Massachusetts Citizens for Life, Inc., 479 U.S. 238, 107 S.Ct. 616, 93 L.Ed.2d 539 (1986) explained that in First National Bank of Boston v. Bellotti, 435 U.S. 765, 98 S.Ct. 1407, 55 L.Ed.2d 707

(1978), rehearing denied 438 U.S. 907, 98 S.Ct. 3126, 57 L.Ed.2d 1150 (1978) the state law was invalid because it provided for "complete foreclosure of any opportunity for political speech . . . ." 479 U.S. at 259 n. 12, 107 S.Ct. at 628 n. 12. It is different when the state regulates the corporate form of a commercial enterprise because of unfair deployment of wealth for political purposes: "Direct corporate spending on political activity raises the prospect that resources amassed in the economic marketplace may be used to provide an unfair advantage in the political marketplace." 479 U.S. at 257, 107 S.Ct. at 628.

142. In Consolidated Edison Co. of New York, Inc. v. Public Service Commission, 447 U.S. 530, 100 S.Ct. 2326, 65 L.Ed.2d 319 (1980), the Court, applying a similar analysis, invalidated a state public utility commission order which prohibited a utility from inserting in monthly electric bills inserts discussing controversial issues of public policy. In this case the utility advocated nuclear power. See also Central Hudson Gas & Elec. Corp. v. Public Service Commission, 447 U.S. 557, 100 S.Ct. 2343, 65 L.Ed.2d 341 (1980).

Friedman v. Rogers,[143] was a shift, or at least a detour, in the direction of the Supreme Court. In this case the Court held that Texas constitutionally could prohibit the practice of optometry under a trade name, assumed name, or corporate name.

In upholding the ban on trade names the majority refrained from establishing rigid rules for the regulation of commercial speech, but it established some guidelines that tie together the earlier cases and help provide a framework for the future determination of the permissibility of particular regulations of commercial practices involving speech.

Friedman differentiated "commercially motivated" speech, which appears entitled to full First Amendment protection, from "commercial speech," which is subject to the *ad hoc* approach.[144] It is now clear that cases such as *New York Times Co. v. Sullivan*[145] and *First National Bank of Boston v. Bellotti*[146] did not involve "commercial speech" in the sense of speech designed to sell a product or solicit patronage for profit. Instead, as was suggested in each of those decisions, those cases involved

speech concerning non-commercial issues, even though the speech might have been motivated by commercial and monetary desires of the speakers. This commercially motivated speech is not "commercial speech" and it is protected by all First Amendment principles.[147]

The majority opinion in *Friedman* indicated that commercial speech is speech connected to the selling of a product or service. Such speech has more limited First Amendment protection than does non-commercial speech. Justice Powell noted that principles relating to "more traditional First Amendment problems" are not to be applied automatically to commercial speech regulations in a "yet uncharted area."[148]

For example, *Friedman* treated *Bigelow v. Virginia*[149]—which invalidated a law forbidding a profit making organization's advertisement offering to arrange for legal abortions out of state—as "more than" a commercial speech case because it "did more than simply propose a commercial transaction."[150] By way of contrast, *Virginia State Board of Pharmacy v. Virginia Citizens Consumer Council*[151]—invali-

---

143. 440 U.S. 1, 99 S.Ct. 887, 59 L.Ed.2d 100 (1979), rehearing denied 441 U.S. 917, 99 S.Ct. 2018, 60 L.Ed.2d 389 (1979).

The Court also upheld regulations in this case that required four of the six members of an optometrist regulatory board to be members of a specific professional organization. Because this regulation governed general and economic welfare matters, the Court applied only the minimum rationality test to this law. 440 U.S. at 17, 99 S.Ct. at 898. The Court also refused to consider whether or not a board composed of members of a particular trade association could fairly judge disciplinary proceedings brought against a non member. 440 U.S. at 17, 99 S.Ct. at 898.

144. 440 U.S. at 11 n. 10, 99 S.Ct. at 895 n. 10.

145. 376 U.S. 254, 84 S.Ct. 710, 11 L.Ed.2d 686 (1964), motion denied 376 U.S. 967, 84 S.Ct. 1130, 12 L.Ed.2d 83 (1964). See §§ 20.32–20.36, infra.

146. 435 U.S. 765, 98 S.Ct. 1407, 55 L.Ed.2d 707 (1978), rehearing denied 438 U.S. 907, 98 S.Ct. 3126, 57 L.Ed.2d 1150 (1978), discussed above.

147. See also Village of Schaumburg v. Citizens for a Better Environment, 444 U.S. 620, 636, 100 S.Ct. 826, 835–36, 63 L.Ed.2d 73 (1980), rehearing denied 445 U.S. 972, 100 S.Ct. 1668, 64 L.Ed.2d 250 (1980): "[B]ecause charitable solicitation does more than inform private economic decisions and is not primarily concerned with providing information about the characteristics and costs of goods and services, it has not been dealt with in our cases as a variety of purely commercial speech." (footnote omitted). Secretary of State of Maryland v. Joseph H. Munson Co., Inc., 467 U.S. 947, 104 S.Ct. 2839, 81 L.Ed.2d 786

(1984) (statute placing twenty-five percent limit on charitable fund raising expenses invalidated as a violation of the First Amendment right of charities to engage in First Amendment activity in connection with economic solicitation).

148. 440 U.S. at 10 n. 9, 99 S.Ct. at 895 n. 9.

149. 421 U.S. 809, 95 S.Ct. 2222, 44 L.Ed.2d 600 (1975).

150. Friedman v. Rogers, 440 U.S. at 11 n. 10, 99 S.Ct. at 895 n. 10 quoting Bigelow v. Virginia, 421 U.S. at 822, 95 S.Ct. at 2232. In re Von Wiegen, 63 N.Y.2d 163, 481 N.Y.S.2d 40, 470 N.E.2d 838, 842 (1984) (Simons, J.) (citing this treatise), on remand 108 A.D.2d 1012, 485 N.Y.S.2d 399 (1985), certiorari denied 472 U.S. 1007, 105 S.Ct. 2701, 86 L.Ed.2d 717 (1985).

151. 425 U.S. 748, 96 S.Ct. 1817, 48 L.Ed.2d 346 (1976).

The majority's efforts to distinguish commercial from noncommercial speech made no effort to explain why movies exhibited purely for profit and advertisements of such movies—"a mere solicitation of patronage...." 440 U.S. at 11 n. 10, 99 S.Ct. at 895 n. 10 is nonetheless apparently entitled to full First Amendment protection under the prior case law. See, e.g., Joseph Burstyn, Inc. v. Wilson, 343 U.S. 495, 501–02, 72 S.Ct. 777, 780–81, 96 L.Ed. 1098 (1952). Perhaps, under Justice Powell's theories, such advertisements are entitled to lessened First Amendment protection. He has joined in cases offering lessened First Amendment protection for nonobscene but

dating a law forbidding advertisements offering prescription drugs for sale at certain prices—was, in the view of the majority, only commercial speech because the advertisements simply offered to make an economic exchange for profit. Yet the law was still invalidated because of "the other interests in the advertisements...." For example, information about prices at competing pharmacies would enable consumers to enjoy, at a lesser cost, the "basic necessities."[152]

Once the speech is found to be commercial speech, the majority opinion found, first, that the government could place more general restrictions on the time, place, or manner of commercial speech than on noncommercial speech and, second, that the government would be given greater latitude in forming regulations of the content of commercial speech to avoid potentially false, deceptive, or misleading commercial practices.

The government has greater powers in controlling this type of speech for several reasons: commercial speech is more verifiable because it relates to a particular product or service; the communicative value of this speech is less likely to be inhibited or deterred by regulations due to the economic incentive to engage in alternative forms of commercial communication; effective rules to prevent false, deceptive or misleading practices may not be too precise.

Although the Court did not establish rigid categories of commercial speech, the *Friedman* majority indicated that there would be a distinction in the degree of permissible government regulation related to the types of commercial speech. For regulations of commercial speech that contain explicit product, price, or service information the state must demonstrate a clear relationship between the regulation and the avoidance of false, deceptive, or

misleading practices. If it cannot do so, the state must demonstrate that the regulation of this commercial speech is a demonstrably reasonable restriction of the time, place, or physical manner of the commercial expression. However when the "commercial speech" conveys less substantive information the government has greater latitude in regulating the speech because, in the view of the majority, the state need not tolerate practices with little or no communicative content that might be used in a deceptive or misleading manner, even though the possible deception could also be cured by less drastic means, for example, if the state were to require the publication of additional information to clarify or offset the effects of the spurious communication.[153]

Based upon these assumptions, Powell allowed the state to prohibit the use of trade names by optometrists. The opinion noted that the use of these trade names had a purpose which was "strictly business" and was "a form of commercial speech and nothing more."[154] This point differentiated the case from the commercially motivated speech cases in which the speaker desires more than simply an offer to sell goods or solicit patronage.

Justice Powell also sought to distinguish this prohibition from the earlier prohibitions on advertising service and price information that had been overturned in *Virginia Pharmacy* and *Bates*. Those messages, he argued, contained useful information, which inherently has meaning. Trade names, on the other hand, do not have any inherent meaning. The majority did concede that trade names might acquire some meaning over a period of time, and become a valuable property right. But such a property interest in the trade name only meant that such property could not be taken without due process of law. The fact of a

---

"adult" movies. Young v. American Mini Theatres, Inc., 427 U.S. 50, 73, 96 S.Ct. 2440, 2453, 49 L.Ed.2d 310 (1976) (Powell, J., concurring), rehearing denied 429 U.S. 873, 97 S.Ct. 191, 50 L.Ed.2d 155 (1976). Cf. FCC v. Pacifica Foundation, 438 U.S. 726, 759–763, 98 S.Ct. 3026, 3045–3048, 57 L.Ed.2d 1073 (1978) (Powell, J., concurring) (FCC may regulate radio broadcast which is not obscene in a constitutional sense but is "indecent"), rehearing denied 439 U.S. 883, 99 S.Ct. 227, 58 L.Ed.2d 198 (1978).

See also Hospital & Service Employees Union, Local 399 v. N.L.R.B., 743 F.2d 1417, 1428 n. 8 (9th Cir.1984) (Choy, J.) (citing Treatise and recognizing that the Supreme Court's definition of commercial speech is difficult to apply).

152. 440 U.S. at 8, 99 S.Ct. at 893.

153. 440 U.S. at 12 n. 11, 99 S.Ct. at 895 n. 11.

154. 440 U.S. at 11, 99 S.Ct. at 895 (footnote omitted).

property interest neither enlarged nor diminished First Amendment rights.[155]

In both the *Virginia Pharmacy*[156] case, involving pharmacists, and the *Bates*[157] case, involving lawyers, the Court was not moved by the argument that these occupations were "professions," a title which was supposed to justify lessened First Amendment protection. But in *Friedman* the majority, without explanation, found it important to emphasize that the Texas legislature considered optometry to be a profession.[158]

Because this use of trade names, or any commercial speech practice, has the potential of conveying information, the majority indicated that the state had to assert some reasonable basis for the prohibition. But the majority readily accepted the state's assertion that some optometrists in the past had used trade names in a misleading manner and that this history justified the general prohibition of trade names even if the particular plaintiff in this case had never engaged in a misleading practice.

Friedman suggests that the Court will defer to the state when reviewing statutes that regulate speech in circumstances where the speech is found to be commercial speech, *and* that speech does not explicitly convey product, service, or price, or similar information. Yet, the scope of *Friedman* remains unclear. For example, may the state prohibit lawyers from practicing under a trade name even though the state allows lawyers to use the name of one or more deceased or retired partners as the firm

name?[159] May the state consistently contend that trade names are inherently misleading while at the same time maintaining that a firm named after lawyers who died and left the firm years ago is not in reality a trade name?[160]

It appears that the justices will prohibit states from banning the truthful commercial information but they will allow the state a much greater leeway in protecting against false, deceptive or misleading practices. The lower the informational content of the regulated speech, the greater latitude the Court will give the government in drafting such regulations.

News Racks on Sidewalks. In *City of Cincinnati v. Discovery Network, Inc.*,[161] the Court invalidated a Cincinnati ordinance that prohibited the distribution of commercial handbills on public property. The City applied this ordinance to require the removal of those news racks on the city sidewalks that contained so-called "commercial" publications (such as free magazines advertising real estate sales), but the city did not extend the ban to similar news racks containing newspapers. The city called the commercial publications "commercial handbills" and argued that the purpose of its prohibition was to make the sidewalks more attractive and promote safer streets (e.g., people might trip over the news racks). However, while the city sought to remove the 62 news racks distributing these commercial publications, it did not apply its prohibition to news racks (numbering about 1,500 to 2,000) that

---

155. 440 U.S. at 12 n. 11, 99 S.Ct. at 895 n. 11.

156. Virginia State Bd. of Pharmacy v. Virginia Citizens Consumer Council, Inc., 425 U.S. 748, 96 S.Ct. 1817, 48 L.Ed.2d 346 (1976).

157. Bates v. State Bar, 433 U.S. 350, 97 S.Ct. 2691, 53 L.Ed.2d 810 (1977), rehearing denied 434 U.S. 881, 98 S.Ct. 242, 54 L.Ed.2d 164 (1977).

158. 440 U.S. at 5 n. 7, 99 S.Ct. at 892 n. 7.

159. Compare, Police Dept. of Chicago v. Mosley, 408 U.S. 92, 92 S.Ct. 2286, 33 L.Ed.2d 212 (1972); see ABA Model. Code of Professional Responsibility, D.R. 2–102(B). The ABA later rejected this distinction. ABA Model Rules of Professional Conduct, Rule 7.5(a).

160. 440 U.S. at 19, 99 S.Ct. at 899 (Blackmun, J., concurring and dissenting joined by Marshall, J.). Justice Blackmun joined in part III of the Court's opinion which validated the composition of the optometry board. Blackmun noted that the use of trade names would allow for

more efficient advertisement of eye glasses and therefore a lowering in the price of such items, which he described as one of the basic necessities of life. He found, as he had indicated in some of his earlier opinions, that the increase in informational transaction costs was prohibited unless the state could demonstrate an overriding reason for the speech prohibition.

While Justice Powell thought that "because a trade name has no intrinsic meaning it can cause deception," the dissent countered that "[b]ecause a trade name has no intrinsic meaning, it cannot by itself be deceptive. A trade name will deceive only if it is used in a misleading context." 440 U.S. at 24, 99 S.Ct. at 901 (Blackmun, J., joined by Marshall, J., dissenting and concurring in part).

161. 507 U.S. 410, 113 S.Ct. 1505, 123 L.Ed.2d 99 (1993).

sold regular *newspapers,* which the City deemed to be publications published daily or weekly and *primarily* covering or commenting on current events.

Applying *Central Hudson* and *Fox,* the Court invalidated the city's ban. It concluded, first, that the city had the burden to establish a "reasonable fit" between its legitimate interests in safety and esthetics and its choice of a limited and selective prohibition of news racks as the means chosen to serve those legitimate interests. Second, Cincinnati did not meet its burden of establishing a "reasonable fit." Cincinnati's equivocal distinction that it attempted to draw between newspapers and commercial handbills "bears no relationship *whatsoever* to the particular interests that the city has asserted."[162]

The city has a valid concern with the aggregate number of news racks on the streets, but not with their contents, because each news rack, whether it contains "newspapers" or "commercial handbills" is equally unattractive. There is, in short, no basis of distinction between "newspapers" and "handbills" that is relevant to any interest that the city has asserted. Even if it were assumed that the city could ban all news racks on public property, that would not justify the discriminatory ban (based on the content of the news racks) that the city imposed. This content-based restriction is also not a valid time, place, or manner restriction.[163]

§ 16.32 Group Libel Laws

Beauharnais v. Illinois[1] upheld a state law making it a *crime* to libel of a class of citizens. Petitioner had distributed a racist leaflet calling for white unity against further "encroachment ... by the Negro" and urging "the need to prevent the white race from becoming mongrelized by the negro [sic]...."[2] *Beauharnais* could have reached a decision based on the narrow facts of the case, avoiding the issue of the constitutionality of the statute and holding that the particular pamphlet did not violate the terms of the Illinois group libel law.[3] However, Justice Frankfurter, for the Court, preferred to affirm the conviction in a broad holding stating that libelous, insulting, or fighting words are not constitutionally protected speech.[4] State statutes that curtail group libel do not raise a constitutional problem, he proclaimed, unless they are a "wilful and purposeless restriction unrelated to the peace and well being of the state."[5]

The dissenting views in *Beauharnais* were a precursor to the future position of the Court concerning libel. Justice Douglas argued that the expansion of individual and criminal libel to include group libel constituted an invasion of free expression that should occur only in circumstances wherein the "peril of speech must be clear and present ... raising no doubts as to the necessity of curbing speech in order to prevent disaster."[6] Free expression is more important than vindicating reputation, Justice Black argued, because of the "unequiv-

---

162. 507 U.S. at 424, 113 S.Ct. at 1514 (emphasis in original).

163. Blackmun, J., concurring, stated that he believed that "the analysis set forth in *Central Hudson* and refined in *Fox* affords insufficient protection for truthful, noncoercive commercial speech concerning lawful activities." Intermediate scrutiny is appropriate for time, place, or manner restrictions (without regard to content) or when the restraint on commercial speech is designed to protect the consumer from misleading or coercive speech, but not for a regulation that suppresses truthful commercial speech to serve some other government purpose. He concluded by stating that he hoped that the Court "ultimately will come to abandon *Central Hudson's* analysis entirely" in favor of giving "full protection for truthful, noncoercive commercial speech about lawful activities." 507 U.S. at 430–33, 113 S.Ct. at 1517–18 (Blackmun, J., concurring).

Rehnquist, C.J., joined by White & Thomas, JJ., filed a dissenting opinion.

§ 16.32

1. 343 U.S. 250, 72 S.Ct. 725, 96 L.Ed. 919 (1952), rehearing denied 343 U.S. 988, 72 S.Ct. 1070, 96 L.Ed. 1375 (1952). See, Tate, J., dissenting, citing Treatise, in Levine v. CMP Publications, Inc., 738 F.2d 660, 678–79 (5th Cir.1984), rehearing denied 753 F.2d 1341 (1985); Holderman, J., citing Treatise in, Air Line Pilots Association v. Department of Aviation, 1993 WL 462834, *3 (N.D.Ill.1993).

2. 343 U.S. at 252, 72 S.Ct. at 728.

3. The law banned "any lithograph, moving picture, play, drama, or sketch" that was libelous to a class of citizens. The Court called Beauharnais' leaflet, a "lithograph."

4. 343 U.S. at 256–57, 72 S.Ct. at 730–31.

5. 343 U.S. at 258, 72 S.Ct. at 731.

6. 343 U.S. at 285, 72 S.Ct. at 745.

ocal First Amendment command that its defined freedoms shall not be abridged."[7] Black was very concerned that the Illinois statute would allow the state to proceed against a book publisher, newspaper, radio or television station. The danger of stifling thought and speech outweighed any possible danger that might constitute group libel.[8]

As we shall see in this section, the views of Justices Black and Douglas, to a great extent, have prevailed in later cases. And while the Court has never explicitly overruled *Beauharnais*, it should be impossible to reach its results under the modern cases.[9] That is not to say the reputation is unimportant. It is only to say that the dangers of allowing libel laws are great, and that free speech should prevail.

When we think of the value of reputation, we often quote Iago, who says in Shakespeare's *Othello*:

Who steals my purse steals trash—'tis something, nothing;

'Twas mine, 'tis his, and has been slave to thousands;

But he that filches from me my good name

Robs me of that which not enriches him

And makes me poor indeed.[10]

Yes, we quote those lines and we believe in the importance of reputation. But let us put things in perspective; Shakespeare did. The same Iago also says to Cassio (when Cassio complained that he had lost his reputation):

As I am an honest man, I thought you had received some bodily wound. There is more sense in that than in reputation. Reputation is an idle and most false imposition; off' got without merit and lost without deserving. You have lost no reputation at all unless you repute yourself such a loser.[11]

§ 16.33   *New York Times v. Sullivan* and Libel of a Public Official

(a) The Case

Although *Beauharnais v. Illinois* has never been explicitly rejected, it should not represent present law in light of *New York Times Co. v. Sullivan*.[1] The Court held that constitutional protections for speech and press limit state powers to award damages in libel actions brought by public officials against critics of official conduct.

Sullivan, one of three elected commissioners of Montgomery, Alabama, brought the action against four individuals and the *New York Times*, claiming he had been libeled in two paragraphs of a full page advertisement. Even though he was not mentioned by name in the

---

7.   343 U.S. at 269, 72 S.Ct. at 737.

8.   343 U.S. at 275, 72 S.Ct. at 740.

Enjoining Defamation. It has long been established that courts simply cannot enjoin a libel. Such an injunction would be contrary to equitable principles, American Malting Co. v. Keitel, 209 Fed. 351 (2d Cir.1913), and would violate the First Amendment, Parker v. Columbia Broadcasting System, Inc., 320 F.2d 937 (2d Cir.1963); Konigsberg v. Time, Inc., 288 F.Supp. 989 (S.D.N.Y.1968).

9.   No Group Libel. Various lower courts have properly recognized that because the purpose of defamation is to protect *individuals,* a group may be so large that a statement concerning it cannot defame individual group members. Khalid Abdullah Tariq Al Mansour Faissal Fahd Al Talal v. Fanning, 506 F.Supp. 186 (N.D.Cal.1980). See also, Fowler v. Curtis Publishing Co., 182 F.Supp. 377 (D.C.Cir.1950). In Michigan United Conservation Clubs v. CBS News, 485 F.Supp. 893 (W.D.Mich.1980), affirmed 665 F.2d 110 (6th Cir.1981), the court—also prohibiting group libel—noted obvious First Amendment concerns:

"Statements about a religious, ethnic, or political group could invite thousands of lawsuits from disgruntled members of these groups claiming that the portray-

al was inaccurate and thus libelous. Such suits would be especially damaging to the media, and could result in the public receiving less information about topics of general concern."

485 F.Supp. at 900.

The Seventh Circuit invalidated local ordinances designed to prevent a march of a Nazi organization. That court found that the *Beauharnais* rationale would not justify prohibition of a peaceful march based on its implied message of racial animosity or the racial beliefs of the marchers. Collin & National Socialist Party v. Smith, 578 F.2d 1197 (7th Cir.1978), certiorari denied 439 U.S. 916, 99 S.Ct. 291, 58 L.Ed.2d 264 (1978) (Blackmun, J., joined by White, J., dissented).

10.   Othello, Act III, iii, lines 155–62.

11.   Othello, Act II, iii, lines 256–61.

§ 16.33

1.   376 U.S. 254, 84 S.Ct. 710, 11 L.Ed.2d 686 (1964), motion denied 376 U.S. 967, 84 S.Ct. 1130, 12 L.Ed.2d 83 (1964). See 4 Ronald D. Rotunda & John E. Nowak, Treatise on Constitutional Law: Substance and Procedure § 20.33 (West Group, 3d ed.1999).

advertisement, Sullivan recovered $500,000 damages against the *New York Times*, based on a state legal doctrine whereby criticism of the Montgomery Police Department was transmuted to criticism of him as the official in charge. The state court instructed the jury that such criticism was libel per se. Under such instruction Sullivan need only prove that the statement was false and that it referred to him.

The Supreme Court reversed in a holding broader than was strictly necessary given the facts of the case. The Court might have reversed by creating a narrower constitutionally based theory: no defamation on its face existed in the ad because Sullivan was not mentioned; alternatively, it might have held that the amount of damages was constitutionally regulated and that only actual, out of pocket damages would be allowed; or, it could have held that a newspaper that merely republished an advertisement drawn up by others should have some constitutional protection; it also might have created a defense that the statements alleged in the advertisement were substantially true. Instead, the majority opinion by Justice Brennan formulated a much more dramatic change in state libel law.

The Court reasoned that a state must safeguard freedom of speech and press in its libel laws as required by the First Amendment as applied to the states through the Fourteenth Amendment. This First Amendment protection exists against the background of "profound national commitment to the principle that debate on public issues should be uninhibited, robust, and wide-open, and that it may well include vehement, caustic, and sometimes unpleasantly sharp attacks on government and public officials."[2] Neither erroneous statement nor injury to official reputation forfeits the First Amendment protection, which should provide "breathing space" for freedom of expression.

The Test Under *New York Times*. The Court drew an analogy to the Sedition Act of 1798,[3] an early attempt to prohibit criticism of the government. State statutes punishing libel of public officials must likewise be restricted by the First Amendment, for a broad libel law serving to protect public officials from criticism is closely analogous to the Sedition Laws. The Alabama statute did provide for a defense of truth, but given the importance of safeguarding the "breathing space" necessary so as not to discourage valid criticism of public officials, a "defense for erroneous statements honestly made" was essential.[4]

Given this basic policy, the Court laid out the standard for recovery of any alleged defamatory falsehood relating to a public official's conduct. First, the defamatory statement would have to relate to the individual plaintiff-government official;[5] no generalized criticism of government policy could be punished, for that would constitute a sedition action. The plaintiff-government official would also have the burden of proving that the statement was false. Citizens are certainly free to disclose truthful information about their officials. Finally, and most significantly, for there to be a defamation action, the plaintiff must allege and prove that the defendant had made the defamatory statements with "malice."

The Requirement of *New York Times* "Malice." On this point—the question of "malice"—the Court said:

> The constitutional guarantees require, we think, a federal rule that prohibits a *public official* from recovering damages for a defamatory falsehood relating to his official conduct unless he proves that the statement was made with *"actual malice"*....[6]

The Court defined "actual malice" as "knowledge that [the defamation that was published] was false or with reckless disregard of whether

---

2.　376 U.S. at 270, 84 S.Ct. at 721.

3.　376 U.S. at 273–77, 84 S.Ct. at 722–24.

4.　376 U.S. at 278, 84 S.Ct. at 725.

5.　The *New York Times* Court also held unconstitutional the Alabama position that criticism of a government agency is transmuted to criticism of the official in charge,

a practice that strikes at the center of constitutionally protected area of free expression by expanding the law of libel beyond the requirement of scienter.

6.　376 U.S. at 279–80, 84 S.Ct. at 726 (emphasis added).

it was false or not."[7] While the Court used the word "malice," it was not referring to the old, common law libel meaning of "malice" as hatefulness or ill will;[8] rather, from its definition, the Court meant "*scienter*."[9]

(b) *New York Times* Scienter

This scienter requirement was clearly applied in *Garrison v. Louisiana*.[10] There the Supreme Court struck down a Louisiana statute that permitted liability for true statements about public officials made negligently, "not made in the reasonable belief of its truth," or made with "actual malice" in the common law sense. The Court reiterated that only the knowing or reckless falsehood could be subject to civil or criminal sanction.

Defining "Reckless Disregard." Four years after *Garrison*, the Court made clear that "reckless disregard" could not be shown by proof of mere negligence. For "reckless disregard" there must be "serious doubts as to the truth of [the] publication."[11] The standard is that of the knowing lie—at the time of publication defendant must have known that the statement was false, or must have had serious doubts as to the statement's truth and have published it despite these doubts.

Thus, where one defendant had relied solely on a union member's affidavit charging a public official with criminal conduct and did not verify the charges with other union members, the Court would not allow plaintiff to go to the jury with a charge of reckless falsity.[12] There was not enough evidence of New York Times scienter to go to the jury. Similarly, the Court has not found "reckless falsity" when defendant has failed to conduct an affirmative investigation,[13] or where there are omissions that could constitute merely an error of judgment.[14]

"Reckless disregard" means that the defendant has a "high degree of awareness" of probably falsity or has "entertained serious doubts" as to the truth of his or her publication. It is not enough for the plaintiff to show

---

7. 376 U.S. at 280, 84 S.Ct. at 726.

8. W. Prosser, Torts 771–72 (4th ed. 1971). See also, Cantrell v. Forest City Publishing Co., 419 U.S. 245, 251–52, 95 S.Ct. 465, 469–70, 42 L.Ed.2d 419 (1974).

9. Cf. Herbert v. Lando, 441 U.S. 153, 199, 99 S.Ct. 1635, 1660–61, 60 L.Ed.2d 115 (1979) (Stewart, J., dissenting): "Although I joined the Court's opinion in *New York Times*, I have come greatly to regret the use in that opinion of the phrase 'actual malice.' . . . In common understanding, malice means ill will or hostility. . . . [but *New York Times* malice] has nothing to do with hostility or ill will. . . ."

10. 379 U.S. 64, 78, 85 S.Ct. 209, 217–18, 13 L.Ed.2d 125, 135 (1964).

Criminal Libel. *Garrison* applied the *New York Times* scienter rule and invalidated the conviction of Garrison, who was charged with criminal libel under Louisiana law. The Court held that the Louisiana criminal law was unconstitutional as interpreted because it punished true statements made with ill will. 379 U.S. at 77–78, 85 S.Ct. at 217, 13 L.Ed.2d at 134–35. The Court also held that the statute was not narrowly drawn:

"... Louisiana's rejection of the clear-and-present danger standard as irrelevant to the application of its statute, coupled with the absence of any limitation in the statute itself calculated to cause breaches of the peace, leads us to conclude that the Louisiana statute is not this sort of narrowly drawn statute."

379 U.S. 64, 70, 85 S.Ct. 209, 213, 13 L.Ed.2d 125, 130 (1964).

Thus, a statute called a criminal libel statute would be unconstitutional unless it was narrowly drawn and incorporated *both* the *New York Times* scienter requirement

and also was likely to cause a breach of the peace (so called "fighting words"), see Chaplinsky v. New Hampshire, 315 U.S. 568, 62 S.Ct. 766, 86 L.Ed. 1031 (1942), or incited the listeners to violence within the meaning of *Brandenburg v. Ohio*, 395 U.S. 444, 89 S.Ct. 1827, 23 L.Ed.2d 430 (1969) (per curiam). Unless a criminal libel statute met these strict requirements, it would be unconstitutional.

See Emerson, Toward a General Theory of the First Amendment, 72 Yale L.J. 877, 924 (1963): "[I]t can hardly be urged that maintenance of peace requires a criminal prosecution for private defamation."

11. St. Amant v. Thompson, 390 U.S. 727, 730–33, 88 S.Ct. 1323, 1325–27, 20 L.Ed.2d 262 (1968). See, Bryant v. Harris, 985 F.2d 559 n. 3- (6th Cir.1993)(per curiam), citing Treatise.

12. St. Amant v. Thompson, 390 U.S. 727, 730–33, 88 S.Ct. 1323, 1325–27, 20 L.Ed.2d 262 (1968).

13. Beckley Newspapers Corp. v. Hanks, 389 U.S. 81, 88 S.Ct. 197, 19 L.Ed.2d 248 (1967).

14. St. Amant v. Thompson, 390 U.S. 727, 88 S.Ct. 1323, 20 L.Ed.2d 262 (1968).

The Petition Clause. McDonald v. Smith, 472 U.S. 479, 105 S.Ct. 2787, 86 L.Ed.2d 384 (1985) held that the petition clause of the First Amendment does not give a defendant in a libel action absolute immunity. The plaintiff had charged defendant with knowingly sending false and libelous letters to President Reagan and others in order to undermine the chances of his being appointed U.S. Attorney. The petition clause does not require state libel law to expand the qualified privilege already afforded by *New York Times v. Sullivan*.

that the newspaper wished to promote the candidacy of someone opposed to plaintiff, or that the newspaper wished to increase its circulation, or that the newspaper engaged in an "extreme departure from professional standard", or that the newspaper bore ill-will towards the plaintiff.[15]

(c) Burden of Proof

In subsequent cases, the Supreme Court also clarified other issues first raised in *New York Times v. Sullivan*—the burden of proof requirement and the definition of "public official."

Convincing Clarity. According to *New York Times v. Sullivan*, plaintiff bears the burden of proving actual malice with "convincing clarity."[16] This standard is somewhere between "preponderance of the evidence" and "beyond a reasonable doubt," because later the Court uses the term "clear and convincing,"[17] a standard of proof that historically has required plaintiff in a civil case to bear more of a burden than a bare "preponderance."

The "clear and convincing" standard has its origins in the standards that chancellors used in finding facts in equity cases. It now is expanded in many states to include other classes of cases such as charges of fraud. In general, this standard is used if there is a special danger of deception, or if the court considers that a particular type of claim should be disfavored on policy grounds.[18] In libel

cases, the trial court instructs the jury to apply the "clear and convincing" standard, and it is also applied on review to determine if there was a sufficient basis for the verdict.

If the affidavits *after full discovery* show no genuine issue for the jury, the defendant should not be put through the burden of a full trial. Because a summary judgment motion is similar to a directed verdict motion, plaintiff must show more than a mere "scintilla" of evidence: the issue for summary judgment is "whether the evidence presented is such that a reasonable jury might find that actual malice [i.e., scienter] had been shown with convincing clarity."[19] While the defendant has the burden of showing no genuine issue of fact, the plaintiff, in order to survive the summary judgment motion, must present affirmative evidence to support a jury verdict. "This is true even where the evidence is likely to be within the possession of the defendant, as long as the plaintiff has held a full opportunity to conduct discovery."[20] It is not enough for the plaintiff to rest on mere denial of the defendants pleadings.

Appellate Review. Appellate courts must independently review a trial court finding of actual malice to determine whether the finding that the defendant acted with actual malice in publishing a knowing or reckless falsehood was established by clear and convincing evidence.[21] During the 1980's, empirical research

---

15. Harte–Hanks Communications, Inc. v. Connaughton, 491 U.S. 657, 664, 665–69, 109 S.Ct. 2678, 2684, 2685–86, 105 L.Ed.2d 562 (1989). In this case the Court, with no dissents, upheld a $200,000 libel verdict in favor of an unsuccessful candidate for judge against a local newspaper that supported his opponent. This case was the first time in 22 years that the Court upheld a damage award against the news media in a case that a public figure had brought.

16. 376 U.S. 254 at 285–86, 84 S.Ct. 710 at 729, 11 L.Ed.2d 686.

17. Gertz v. Robert Welch, Inc., 418 U.S. 323, 331–32, 94 S.Ct. 2997, 3003, 41 L.Ed.2d 789 (1974); see also Beckley Newspapers Corp. v. Hanks, 389 U.S. 81, 83, 88 S.Ct. 197, 199, 19 L.Ed.2d 248 (1967) (per curiam).

18. E. Cleary, et al., McCormick's Handbook of the Law of Evidence § 340, at 798 (2d ed. 1972); Arnold, J., citing Treatise in, Mueller v. Abdnor, 972 F.2d 931, 936 (8th Cir.1992).

19. Anderson v. Liberty Lobby, Inc., 477 U.S. 242, 257, 106 S.Ct. 2505, 2515, 91 L.Ed.2d 202 (1986). Brennan, J.,

filed a dissenting opinion. Rehnquist, J., joined by Burger, C.J., also filed a dissenting opinion.

20. 477 U.S. at 257, 106 S.Ct. at 2514.

21. Bose Corp. v. Consumers Union of United States, Inc., 466 U.S. 485, 104 S.Ct. 1949, 80 L.Ed.2d 502 (1984), rehearing denied 467 U.S. 1267, 104 S.Ct. 3561, 82 L.Ed.2d 863 (1984). If actual "malice" standard of New York Times v. Sullivan is applicable, "[a]ppellate judges in such a case must exercise independent judgment and determine whether the record establishes actual malice with convincing clarity." 466 U.S. at 514, 104 S.Ct. at 1967.

In a defamation case there might be other questions of fact that are irrelevant to the constitutional standard of New York Times v. Sullivan and to which a "clearly erroneous" standard of appellate review, such as was established by the Federal Rules of Civil Procedure, might be used in reviewing trial court findings. 466 U.S. at 514 n. 31, 104 S.Ct. at 1967 n. 31, 80 L.Ed.2d at 526 n. 31.

showed that less than a third of libel verdicts against media defendants survived after an independent appellate review.[22]

Discovery of Editorial Thought Processes. In meeting his or her burden of proof, plaintiff may directly depose the defendants about their thought processes and state of mind. In *Herbert v. Lando*,[23] the press urged the Supreme Court to create a privilege based on the First Amendment that would bar a plaintiff suing for libel to inquire into the editorial processes of those responsible for the publication. The majority refused. Plaintiffs are not limited to proving intent by inferences from objective circumstances; they may also ask about the ultimate fact directly. Similarly, there is no privilege for collegiate conversations or exchanges with fellow editors or damaging admissions to third persons;[24] nor must plaintiff first prove a prima facie case of falsity making such inquiries.[25]

However, there may be some First Amendment protection from discovery in other circumstances. The case should be different if plaintiff claimed libel for a false statement of opinion rather than a false assertion of fact. The majority specifically stated that: "There is no law that subjects the editorial process to private or official examination merely to satisfy curiosity or to serve some general end such as the public interest; and if there were, it would not survive constitutional scrutiny as the First Amendment is presently construed."[26]

The Single Publication Rule. Both public figures and private persons who suffer injury from the publication of false statements may have a choice of bringing suit against the publisher in any one of several states. Various state statutes of limitations, statutory definitions of damages or privilege, state systems of pretrial discovery and other procedural rules that vary by state may influence a plaintiff's choice of jurisdiction.

A state jurisdictional statute may allow a plaintiff who resides in another state to use the state courts to sue a publisher from a third state because of the damage done to the individual's reputation in the forum state. Such a state may allow the plaintiff to bring action against the publisher not only for the damage done to the plaintiff's reputation in the forum state but also, under a "single publication rule," for the damage done to the plaintiff's reputation throughout the nation. In other words, a plaintiff who resides in state *A* may sue the publisher, editor, or reporter of a magazine published in state *B* in the courts of state *C* if some copies of the magazine were distributed in state *C*. State *C*'s jurisdictional statutes or rules may allow the plaintiff to bring suit in state *C* not only for the damage done by the distribution of the magazine in state *C* but also for the damages caused the plaintiff by the distribution of the magazine in various states throughout the nation.[27]

(d) Public Officials

Candidates for Public Office and Non-elected Public Officials as "Public Officials." A special reason for the constitutional restriction on libel laws is that they might deter criticism of official conduct. The Court later extended the *New York Times* privilege by expanding the definition of "public official" to include those who were candidates for public office and to statements that did not relate

---

22. Milo Geyelin, Libel Defendants Fare Well on Appeal, Research Finds, Wall Street Journal, May 31, 1994, at B10, col. 1 (midwest ed.).

23. 441 U.S. 153, 99 S.Ct. 1635, 60 L.Ed.2d 115 (1979).

24. 441 U.S. at 169–71, 99 S.Ct. at 1645–46.

25. Justice Brennan, dissenting, took that position, 441 U.S. at 180, but the majority specifically rejected such a bifurcated approach. 441 U.S. at 174 n. 23, 99 S.Ct. at 1648 n. 23.

26. 441 U.S. at 174, 99 S.Ct. at 1648 (footnote omitted).

27. Courts are to judge the extension of jurisdiction over magazines in defamation suits solely by due process standards as to whether the defendant magazine has sufficient minimum contacts with the forum state. Courts are not to consider the fact that the plaintiff has virtually no previous contact with the state other than the injury caused by the distribution of the magazine in that state. Keeton v. Hustler Magazine, Inc., 465 U.S. 770, 104 S.Ct. 1473, 79 L.Ed.2d 790 (1984); Calder v. Jones, 465 U.S. 783, 104 S.Ct. 1482, 79 L.Ed.2d 804 (1984).

to official conduct but did relate to fitness for office.[28] The Court also included certain non-elected officials in the expanded definition of "public official."[29]

The Test for Public Official. The breadth of the concept of "public official" is illustrated in *Rosenblatt v. Baer*,[30] where the Court applied the *New York Times* privilege to the discharged supervisor of a county-owned ski resort. The Court held that in order to encourage criticism of government, the "public official" designation must apply "at the very least to those among the hierarchy of government employees who have, or appear to the public to have, substantial responsibility for or control over the conduct of governmental affairs."[31]

The *New York Times* privilege exists for criticism of any government position of such "apparent importance that the public has an independent interest in the qualifications and performance of the person who holds it."[32] Thus, while many persons occupying low level technical positions might not be included in this category, any government employee with discretionary power in matters of public interest should be considered a public official.[33] Even a public employee who is not at the top of the bureaucratic hierarchy may be a public official. Thus, a public grade school teacher should be a "public official" for purposes of *New York Times* malice-scienter, because he or she performs a task going "to the heart of representative government."[34]

(e) Actual Damages, Punitive Damages, and a Right of Retraction

Punitive Damages. If the plaintiff in a libel action is a private individual suing on a matter of public concern—that is, one not a public official within the doctrine of *New York Times v. Sullivan*, nor even a public figure within the meaning of later case law that has extended *New York Times v. Sullivan* to those who assume "roles of especial prominence in the affairs of society"[35]—then that plaintiff (suing on a matter of public concern) can collect punitive damages or damages not supported by the evidence (i.e., presumed damages) *only if* the plaintiff can prove *New York Times* "malice."[36] By analogy, then, if the plaintiff is a public official or public figure, this type of plaintiff could not collect actual damages if there is only proof of negligence, and should not be able to collect punitive damages because such a plaintiff must prove *New York Times* "malice" (i.e., scienter) merely to get actual damages. If the private person must prove more than *New York Times* "malice" to go beyond actual damages, then the public official or public person (who must prove scienter just to get actual damages) should have to prove *more than* scienter to get punitive damages. But there is nothing more than scienter.

Although the Court has not explicitly ruled that a public official or public figure could not collect punitive damages, it has suggested that, and a contrary conclusion would be surprising.[37] The Court has condemned the inhibiting effect of damage awards in excess of any actual injury,[38] so one should expect it to hold that

---

28. Monitor Patriot Co. v. Roy, 401 U.S. 265, 91 S.Ct. 621, 28 L.Ed.2d 35 (1971), on remand to 112 N.H. 80, 290 A.2d 207 (1972).

29. Rosenblatt v. Baer, 383 U.S. 75, 86 S.Ct. 669, 15 L.Ed.2d 597 (1966).

30. 383 U.S. 75, 86 S.Ct. 669, 15 L.Ed.2d 597 (1966).

31. 383 U.S. at 85, 86 S.Ct. at 676 (footnote omitted).

32. 383 U.S. at 86, 86 S.Ct. at 676. See also, Hutchinson v. Proxmire, 443 U.S. 111, 119 n. 8, 99 S.Ct. 2675, 2680 n. 8, 61 L.Ed.2d 411 (1979) ("public official" cannot "be thought to include all public employees....").

33. Mihm, C.J., citing Treatise in, Grossman v. Smart, 807 F.Supp. 1404, 1411 (C.D.Ill.1992).

34. Ambach v. Norwick, 441 U.S. 68, 75–76, 99 S.Ct. 1589, 1593–94, 60 L.Ed.2d 49 (1979). See, Johnston v. Corinthian Television Corp., 583 P.2d 1101 (Okla.1978),

holding that a grade school wrestling coach is a public official. Lower courts have gone all over the lot on this issue.

35. Gertz v. Robert Welch, Inc., 418 U.S. 323, 345, 94 S.Ct. 2997, 3009, 41 L.Ed.2d 789, 811 (1974), appeal after remand 680 F.2d 527 (7th Cir.1982), certiorari denied 459 U.S. 1226, 103 S.Ct. 1233, 75 L.Ed.2d 467 (1983).

36. Gertz v. Robert Welch, Inc., 418 U.S. 323, 350, 94 S.Ct. 2997, 3012, 41 L.Ed.2d 789, 811 (1974), appeal after remand 680 F.2d 527 (7th Cir.1982), certiorari denied 459 U.S. 1226, 103 S.Ct. 1233, 75 L.Ed.2d 467 (1983).

37. Cf. 418 U.S. at 350, 94 S.Ct. at 3012. But see Rodney Smolla, Let the Author Beware: The Rejuvenation of the American Law of Libel, 132 U.Pa.L.Rev. 1, 91 (1983).

38. Gertz v. Robert Welch, Inc., 418 U.S. 323, 94 S.Ct. 2997, 41 L.Ed.2d 789 (1974), appeal after remand 680 F.2d

any punitive damage awards for libels against public officials or public persons interfere with the "breathing space" required in the exercise of robust First Amendment debate.

Actual Damages. A libel plaintiff, whether or not he or she is a public official, can collect "actual damages," which the Court has defined broadly to include not only out-of-pocket losses, but also "impairment of reputation and standing in the community, personal humiliation, and mental anguish and suffering."[39] There is no need for evidence that assigns an actual dollar value to the injury.[40]

Under present law, defamation is an oddity of the law of torts, the only tort that allows substantial recovery without any proof of injury.[41] If the Supreme Court would limit damages in libel actions to out-of-pocket costs, such as provable loss of income, the news media's concern about the risks of libel actions would largely evaporate.

Rights of Reply. The Supreme Court has held that it is unconstitutional for a state to force a newspaper to give a political candidate a right to equal space in order to reply to attacks on his record.[42] But the Supreme Court has never ruled out the possibility that a court could order a retraction statement from a person who is found (under the proper standard for the case) to have defamed another. Members of the Court covering the ideological spectrum from Justices Brennan to Rehnquist have noted that the constitution prohibition

on "right of reply" statutes does not suggest that a right of retraction statute would be forbidden.[43]

§ 16.34 Libel of Public Figures

The *New York Times v. Sullivan* doctrine and its requirement of "actual malice," that is, scienter, applies to alleged defamations against people who do not fit into the definition of "public official" but who are nonetheless "public figures."[1]

In *Curtis Publishing Co. v. Butts* and *Associated Press v. Walker*,[2] Chief Justice Warren's concurring opinion noted that the distinction between government and the private sector was increasingly blurred. He therefore created a new category within the *New York Times* rule, called "public figure" and defined as those who are "intimately involved in the resolution of important public questions or, by reason of their fame, shape events in areas of concern to society at large."[3] Warren reasoned that the *New York Times v. Sullivan* standard should apply to these people precisely because they are not subject to the restraints of the political process—"public opinion may be the only instrument by which society can attempt to influence their conduct."[4]

The broad range of those whom the Court intended to classify as "public figures" is evident in that in *Associated Press*, Walker was a retired army general, and in *Curtis Publish-*

527 (7th Cir.1982), certiorari denied 459 U.S. 1226, 103 S.Ct. 1233, 75 L.Ed.2d 467 (1983).

39. 418 U.S. at 350, 94 S.Ct. at 3012, 41 L.Ed.2d at 811 (1974).

40. 418 U.S. at 350, 94 S.Ct. at 3012, 41 L.Ed.2d at 811.

41. Anderson, Reputation, Compensation, and Proof, 25 Wm. & Mary L.Rev. 747, 748 (1984). Professor Anderson concludes that "compensating individuals for actual harm to reputation is the only legitimate purpose of defamation law today.... By actual harm, I mean provable injury to reputation. Nonpecuniary reputational losses would qualify, but mental anguish alone would not." Id. at 749. Cf. Van Alstyne, First Amendment Limitations on Recovery from the Press—An Extended Comment on "The Anderson Solution," 25 Wm. & Mary L.Rev. 793 (1984); LeBel, Defamation and the First Amendment: The End of the Affair, 25 Wm. & Mary L.Rev. 779 (1984).

42. Miami Herald Pub. Co. v. Tornillo, 418 U.S. 241, 94 S.Ct. 2831, 41 L.Ed.2d 730 (1974), on remand to 303 So.2d 21 (1974).

43. Miami Herald Pub. Co. v. Tornillo, 418 U.S. at 258, 94 S.Ct. at 2839–40, 41 L.Ed.2d at 741–42 (1979) (Brennan, J., joined by Rehnquist, J., concurring).

§ 16.34

1. Levine v. CMP Publications, Inc., 738 F.2d 660, 678–79 (5th Cir.1984) (Tate, J., dissenting) (citing this Treatise), rehearing denied 753 F.2d 1341 (5th Cir.1985); Wood, J., citing Treatise in Pope v. Chronicle Publishing Co., 95 F.3d 607, 613 (7th Cir.1996).

2. 388 U.S. 130, 87 S.Ct. 1975, 18 L.Ed.2d 1094 (1967), mandate conformed 418 S.W.2d 379 (1967), certiorari denied 391 U.S. 966, 88 S.Ct. 2036, 20 L.Ed.2d 880 (1968).

3. 388 U.S. at 164, 87 S.Ct. at 1996 (Warren, C.J., concurring). There was no majority opinion. See Rotunda, The Warren Court and Freedom of the Press, in The Warren Court: A 25 Year Retrospective 85 (Bernard Schwartz, ed., Oxford University Press 1996).

4. 388 U.S. at 164, 87 S.Ct. at 1996.

ing, Butts was athletic director of the University of Georgia.[5] The Court has explained:

> For the most part [public figures are] those who attain this status [by assuming] roles of especial prominence in the affairs of society. Some occupy positions of such persuasive power and influence that they are deemed public figures for all purposes. More commonly, those classed as public figures have thrust themselves to the forefront of particular public controversies in order to influence the resolution of the issues involved.[6]

Thus, the Court has ruled that a research scientist who is the recipient of a government grant, the award of which a U.S. Senator attacked as wasteful in allegedly defamatory statements, is not a "public figure" even for the limited purpose of comment on his receipt of public funds.[7] The mere receipt of public funds did not confer public figure status; nor could it be said in this case that the scientist-libel plaintiff assumed any role of public prominence in the broad question of public expenditures. The scientist's limited access to the media for the purpose of responding to the Senator's charges did not establish the regular and continuing access to the media that is a sign of a public figure.

Emotional Distress Awards

Hustler Magazine v. Falwell[8] held that the First and Fourteenth Amendments forbid a public figure from recovering damages for intentional infliction of emotional distress. The plaintiff, Jerry Falwell, a nationally known televangelist, sued Hustler Magazine because it featured a parody of an advertisement that portrayed him and his mother as drunk and immoral. The parody was labeled as a parody, and the jury found that it could not be reasonably understood as describing any actual facts.

The Court held that public figures—and also public officials—cannot recover damages for intentional infliction of emotional distress without also showing that the publication contains a false statement "of fact" made with actual knowledge that the statement was false or with reckless disregard of whether or not it was true. In this case, the parody was not reasonably believable, so no damages could be awarded.

§ 16.35   Libel of Private Individuals

(a) *Time, Inc. v. Hill*

Because of their general fame and notoriety both Walker and Butts could be considered public figures for all purposes. In *Time, Inc. v. Hill*[1] the Supreme Court faced the issue of a private individual being thrust into the limelight for the purpose of one particular event. In 1952, the Hill family had been the subject of national news coverage when three escaped convicts held them hostage in their home. The incident was fictionalized in a play, and in 1955 Life Magazine published a picture story that showed the play's cast re-enacting scenes from the play in the former Hill house.

---

5. In a nine to zero decision, the Supreme Court reversed a Mississippi jury award of $500,000 compensatory and $300,000 punitive damages for the eyewitness news report that stated that Walker had personally taken command of a violent crowd's charge against federal marshals who were enforcing a court decree ordering the University of Mississippi to enroll a black student. According to the Court, the situation involved reporting "hot" news by a trustworthy and competent reporter. The evidence was insufficient to support even a finding of negligence.

In a five to four decision, however, the Court affirmed Butts' damage award for a Saturday Evening Post article that accused him of conspiring to fix a football game by divulging information on Georgia plays. Four Justices held that the Post had met Harlan's negligence test of "highly unreasonable conduct" and Chief Justice Warren joined them to create a majority by holding that the Post had met the *New York Times v. Sullivan* standard of "reckless disregard" and that the jury had been properly instructed.

6. Gertz v. Robert Welch, Inc., 418 U.S. 323, 345, 94 S.Ct. 2997, 3009, 41 L.Ed.2d 789 (1974), appeal after remand 680 F.2d 527 (7th Cir.1982), certiorari denied 459 U.S. 1226, 103 S.Ct. 1233, 75 L.Ed.2d 467 (1983).

7. Hutchinson v. Proxmire, 443 U.S. 111, 99 S.Ct. 2675, 61 L.Ed.2d 411 (1979). See also Wolston v. Reader's Digest Ass'n, Inc., 443 U.S. 157, 99 S.Ct. 2701, 61 L.Ed.2d 450 (1979) (court rejects the argument that any person who engages in criminal conduct automatically becomes a public figure for purposes of a limited range of issues relating to his conviction).

8. 485 U.S. 46, 108 S.Ct. 876, 99 L.Ed.2d 41 (1988).

§ 16.35

1. 385 U.S. 374, 87 S.Ct. 534, 17 L.Ed.2d 456 (1967). See Levine v. CMP Publications, Inc., 738 F.2d 660, 678–79 (5th Cir.1984) (Tate, J., dissenting) (citing this Treatise), rehearing denied 753 F.2d 1341 (5th Cir.1985).

The Hills sued on the basis of a New York state privacy statute that made truth a complete defense but allowed a privacy action to "newsworthy people" or "events" in case of "[m]aterial and substantial falsification."[2] However, the Supreme Court applied the *New York Times* standard of "knowing or reckless falsity" to alleged defamations concerning false reports of matters of public interest.[3]

In determining the standard of liability for private individuals, the Court looked to whether these individuals were involved in a matter of public interest. If they were so involved, the Court held the more stringent standard of recovery defined in *New York Times v. Sullivan* to be applicable, even in the circumstances like that of the Hills, who were thrust into the limelight by events not of their own doing.

Although the Court applied the *New York Times* standard to the Hill's privacy action, it left open the question of whether the same standard of liability should be applicable in a libel action to persons voluntarily and involuntarily thrust into the public limelight.[4] Four years later the Court offered a tentative answer to this question in *Rosenbloom v. Metromedia*,[5] a fragmented plurality decision containing five separate opinions. The Court ruled, in a decision that did not attract even a bare majority of the Justices, that the *New York Times v. Sullivan* standard must apply to private citizens caught up in events of public interest—whether voluntarily or involuntarily so involved. But this concept ended as abruptly as it appeared.

(b) *Gertz v. Robert Welch, Inc.*

Private Figures Who are Public Figures for Certain Purposes. The *Rosenbloom* issue was still open and three years later the Court, in a five to four decision, rejected the extension of the *New York Times v. Sullivan* doctrine to publication of all matters of public interest. Instead, in *Gertz v. Robert Welch,*

Inc.,[6] the Court created a third category within which the *New York Times v. Sullivan* doctrine applied: private citizens who obviously are not public officials and who are not public enough to be public figures for all purposes, may be public figures with respect to a particular controversy. The Court decided that the important question was not whether the alleged defamation was a matter of public interest but whether the individual defamed was a private citizen for purposes of that activity.

A person is not to be considered a public figure for the purpose of libel actions absent clear evidence of general fame and notoriety in the community or the assumption of roles of special prominence in the affairs of society. But even though one is not a public figure for all purposes, one may be a public figure for a particular incident. An individual's status as "public figure" can be determined by looking specifically to his participation in the "*particular* controversy giving rise to the defamation;"[7] he may be a public figure for some purpose but not for others. According to the Court, private individuals may be "public figures" for purposes of *New York Times* if they have "thrust themselves to the forefront of particular public controversies in order to influence the resolution of the issues involved."[8] The truly involuntary public figure is rare.

Under this newly defined category, Gertz was an example of a private citizen who was not public enough to be a public figure for all purposes and who was not a public figure with respect to the particular controversy giving rise to the defamation. In the facts of that case a Chicago policeman, Richard Nuccio, shot and killed a young man, Nelson. Nuccio was ultimately convicted of murder in the second degree. Gertz filed his libel action after a 1969 article in American Opinion Magazine, a monthly outlet for the views of the John Birch Society, alleged that he had been the architect

---

2. 385 U.S. at 383, 386, 87 S.Ct. at 539, 541.

3. 385 U.S. at 387–88, 87 S.Ct. at 542.

4. 385 U.S. at 390–91, 87 S.Ct. at 543–44.

5. 403 U.S. 29, 91 S.Ct. 1811, 29 L.Ed.2d 296 (1971).

6. 418 U.S. 323, 94 S.Ct. 2997, 41 L.Ed.2d 789 (1974), appeal after remand 680 F.2d 527 (7th Cir.1982), certiora-

ri denied 459 U.S. 1226, 103 S.Ct. 1233, 75 L.Ed.2d 467 (1983).

7. 418 U.S. at 352, 94 S.Ct. at 3013 (emphasis added); see also 418 U.S. at 345, 94 S.Ct. at 3009–10.

8. 418 U.S. at 345, 94 S.Ct. at 3009–10; see also 418 U.S. at 352, 94 S.Ct. at 3013.

of a Communist frame-up that led to Nuccio's murder conviction.

Gertz, a reputable Chicago lawyer, had acted as counsel for the Nelson family in civil litigation and had attended the coroner's inquest, but Gertz did not discuss Nuccio with the press and was not involved in the criminal proceedings against Nuccio.[9] Although Gertz had been active in community affairs, according to the Court he was not a "public figure" for all purposes of libel law. In making this determination, the Court relied on the fact that Gertz seemingly did nothing to thrust himself into the public eye nor did he attempt to engage the public's attention during the period during which the controversy arose.

Because Gertz was neither sufficiently public to be a public figure, nor was he "public" with respect to the particular controversy, the Court had to determine the standard of libel recovery for such private individuals. It held that the standard was a matter for the States to determine: "[S]o long as they do not impose liability without fault, the States may define for themselves the appropriate standard of liability for a publisher or broadcaster of defamatory falsehood injurious to a private individual."[10] The Court found this solution to be an equitable balance for the competing interests. "It recognizes the strength of the legitimate state interest in compensating private individuals for wrongful injury to reputation, yet

shields the press and broadcast media from the rigors of strict liability for defamation."[11]

The Burden of Proof Standard Against Private Persons. If the plaintiff is a truly private person in a libel action, the plaintiff can collect actual money damages on the basis of defendant's negligence, if state law so provides. State law could require a tougher standard for plaintiffs, but *Gertz* provides that a state could not provide a more favorable standard for libel plaintiffs: strict liability for defamatory speech would not be tolerated.[12] Any reward for the plaintiff would have to be supported by competent evidence, "although there need be no evidence which assigns an actual dollar value to the injury."[13] Such plaintiffs would not (as a Constitutional requirement) have to prove *New York Times* "malice" *unless* the plaintiff sought to collect punitive damages or damages not supported by the evidence (i.e., presumed damages).

The Burden of Proof on the Issue of Falsity. In a *Gertz* situation, the plaintiff must not only prove negligence; the plaintiff, in general, has the burden of proving falsity. There can be no common law presumption that defamatory speech is false. Because of the need to encourage debate on public issues, it is unconstitutional for the state to shift the burden of proving falsity to the defendant. As the Court explained in *Philadelphia Newspapers,*

---

9. 418 U.S. at 352, 94 S.Ct. at 3013.

10. 418 U.S. at 347, 94 S.Ct. at 3010.

11. 418 U.S. at 348, 94 S.Ct. at 3011.

Gertz **Applied to The Nonmedia Defendant.** Because of language (such as that quoted in the text) in *Gertz* referring to the broadcast media defendant, some lower courts have tried to draw a distinction between media and non-media defendants, with the protections of *Gertz* being afforded only the media defendant. See, e.g., Denny v. Mertz, 106 Wis.2d 636, 318 N.W.2d 141 (1982), certiorari denied 459 U.S. 883, 103 S.Ct. 179, 74 L.Ed.2d 147 (1982).

Other courts have rejected this unprincipled distinction. Jacron Sales Co. v. Sindorf, 276 Md. 580, 350 A.2d 688 (1976); Antwerp Diamond Exchange v. Better Business Bureau, 130 Ariz. 523, 637 P.2d 733 (1981).

The purported distinction finds no support in the Supreme Court case law, which has routinely applied the protection of *New York Times v. Sullivan* to the nonmedia defendant. See, e.g., New York Times v. Sullivan, 376 U.S.

254, 286, 84 S.Ct. 710, 729, 11 L.Ed.2d 686, 710 (1964) (noting that *New York Times* was decided together with Abernathy et al. v. Sullivan, and the Court applied the *New York Times* rule to protect the "individual petitioners" as well as the Newspaper). See also, Henry v. Collins, 380 U.S. 356, 85 S.Ct. 992, 13 L.Ed.2d 892 (1965); Garrison v. Louisiana, 379 U.S. 64, 85 S.Ct. 209, 13 L.Ed.2d 125 (1964).

The attempted distinction between media and nonmedia defendants is also peculiar policy, for it gives more protection to those who can cause the most damage.

12. 418 U.S. at 350, 94 S.Ct. at 3012.

13. 418 U.S. at 350, 94 S.Ct. at 3012. The appellate courts must independently review findings of "actual malice" in defamation cases. Bose Corp. v. Consumers Union of United States, 466 U.S. 485, 104 S.Ct. 1949, 80 L.Ed.2d 502 (1984), rehearing denied 467 U.S. 1267, 104 S.Ct. 3561, 82 L.Ed.2d 863 (1984). Levine v. CMP Publications, Inc., 738 F.2d 660, 678–79 (5th Cir.1984) (Tate, J., dissenting) (citing this Treatise), rehearing denied 753 F.2d 1341 (5th Cir.1985).

Inc. v. Hepps,[14] "at least where a newspaper publishes speech of public concern, a private-figure plaintiff cannot recover damages without also showing that the statements at issue are false."[15] Thus, in order to tip the balance in favor of protecting speech, the *private-figure plaintiff* must show not only fault on the part of defendant but also that the speech was false. Even if the media defendant relied on a shield law (allowing media employees to refuse to divulge their sources), the plaintiff must still prove falsity.[16]

If the plaintiff is a *public figure or public official,* and the speech is "of public concern," then *New York Times v. Sullivan* applies, and the plaintiff must prove scienter as well as falsity. If the plaintiff *is not a public figure and if the matter is "exclusively private concern,"* then the Court said, enigmatically, "the constitutional requirements do not necessarily force any change in at least some of the features of the common-law landscape."[17]

Actual Damages and Punitive Damages. Although *Gertz* also held that a private individual must prove actual damages in order to recover under a standard requiring less than knowing or reckless falsity in a libel action, the Court defined actual damages quite broadly to include not only out-of-pocket loss but also "impairment of reputation and standing in the community, personal humiliation, and mental anguish and suffering."[18] This broad definition has been subject to well taken scholarly criticism.[19] *Gertz* may be an invitation to convert defamation suits to a new remedy for mental distress.[20]

In order for a private individual who has been libeled to collect punitive damages the

Constitution requires that such a plaintiff prove that the defendant engaged in *New York Times* "malice." Under the First Amendment, states may not permit recovery of presumed or punitive damages, "at least when liability is not based on a showing of knowledge of falsity or reckless disregard for the truth."[21]

While the *Gertz* Court did leave open the possibility that a private person could recover punitive damages if knowing or reckless falsity were proven, it left unresolved the question of whether a *public* figure or *public* official could recover punitive damages at all. *Gertz* in fact condemned the inhibiting effect of damage awards in excess of any actual injury, so it should not be surprising if it were held that any punitive damage awards for libels directed against public figures or officials impinge on the "breathing space" required in the exercise of First Amendment freedoms.

(c) *Time, Inc. v. Firestone*

Two years after its decision in *Gertz v. Robert Welch, Inc.,*[22] the Court re-emphasized the narrow applicability of the *New York Times* scienter test when one moves outside the category of "public official" into the "public figure" domain of *Gertz.* In *Time, Inc. v. Firestone,*[23] a libel action was brought after Time Magazine reported that plaintiff's husband divorced her "on grounds of extreme cruelty and adultery."[24] The state court had actually granted the divorce on the grounds that "neither party is domesticated, within the meaning of that term as used by the Supreme Court of Florida."[25]

The Court decided that *New York Times* scienter should not be the standard of recovery

---

14. 475 U.S. 767, 106 S.Ct. 1558, 89 L.Ed.2d 783 (1986).

15. 475 U.S. at 768, 106 S.Ct. at 1559. Justice O'Connor wrote the opinion for the Court.

16. 475 U.S. at 778, 106 S.Ct. at 1565.

17. 475 U.S. at 775, 106 S.Ct. at 1563.

18. 418 U.S. at 350, 94 S.Ct. at 3012.

19. See, Anderson, Reputation, Compensation, and Proof, 25 Wm. & Mary L.Rev. 747, 749 (1984).

20. Ashdown, *Gertz* and *Firestone*: A Study in Constitutional Policy–Making, 61 Minn.L.Rev. 645, 670–71 (1977): "Any plaintiff who can persuade a jury that defa-

mation caused him anguish apparently can satisfy the [*Gertz*] standard." See also, Anderson, Reputation, Compensation, and Proof, 25 Wm. & Mary L.Rev. 747, 757 (1984).

21. 418 U.S. at 349, 94 S.Ct. at 3011.

22. 418 U.S. 323, 94 S.Ct. 2997, 41 L.Ed.2d 789 (1974), appeal after remand 680 F.2d 527 (7th Cir.1982), certiorari denied 459 U.S. 1226, 103 S.Ct. 1233, 75 L.Ed.2d 467 (1983).

23. 424 U.S. 448, 96 S.Ct. 958, 47 L.Ed.2d 154 (1976), on remand to 332 So.2d 68 (Fla.1976).

24. 424 U.S. at 452, 96 S.Ct. at 964.

25. 424 U.S. at 450–51, 96 S.Ct. at 963–64.

in the case; plaintiff's role in Palm Beach society did not make her a "public figure" for the purpose of the libel action, nor did plaintiff "thrust herself to the forefront of any particular public controversy in order to influence the resolution of the issues involved in it."[26] The Court said that a "public controversy" is not *any* controversy of interest to the public—it had rejected that definition of "public controversy" when it repudiated *Rosenbloom v. Metromedia* in *Gertz*. Firestone had no choice but to go to court in order to dissolve her marriage, the Court reasoned, and by this action she did not freely choose to publicize her marital problems nor did she assume "special prominence in the resolution of public questions."[27]

Significantly the Court also said that Firestone's several press conferences during divorce proceedings did not convert her into a "public figure." The press conferences were not an attempt to influence the outcome of the divorce proceedings nor were they an attempt to influence the outcome of some unrelated controversy, according to the Court.[28]

The Court thus limited the media's ability to make an issue a "public controversy" and then claim the *New York Times* standard of recovery in libel actions arising therefrom. Mere existence or generation of public interest is not sufficient to define someone as a "public figure" for the purpose of libel law. *Firestone* therefore applied the *Gertz* standard.

The rationale of *Firestone* should indicate that *Time v. Hill* no longer governs the standard for "false light" privacy suits, which cause the plaintiff mental anguish and humiliation. Such suits are based on a theory that the disclosure of private facts is made in a way that casts the individual in a false and unflattering light before the public. Unless the Court were to resurrect the *Rosenbloom* plurality

opinion, the *Gertz* standard should apply to these cases where the plaintiff is a private person.[29]

While it is possible that the Court will preserve *Hill* and instead rely on one element of the *Rosenbloom* public issues concept for people caught up in public issues by finding such people to be involuntary public figures, we must remember that the Court in *Firestone* emphasized that Mrs. Firestone had not voluntarily placed herself in the public domain. *Hill*, discussed above, involved the opening of a new play linked to an actual incident that had been a matter of public interest; the Hill family was involuntarily a part of this actual incident, and, like Mrs. Firestone, the Hills did not voluntarily place themselves in the public domain.[30]

(d) *Dun & Bradstreet, Inc. v. Greenmoss Builders, Inc.*

Those who thought that the constitutional law of libel could not be made more complex must be few in number after the fragmented Supreme Court decision in *Dun & Bradstreet, Inc. v. Greenmoss Builders, Inc.*[31] Justice Powell, joined by Justices Rehnquist and O'Connor, wrote a plurality opinion. Chief Justice Burger and Justice White each wrote separate opinions concurring in the judgment, and Justice Brennan, joined by Justices Blackmun, Marshall, and Stevens, dissented.

In this case plaintiff was a construction contractor who discovered that Dun & Bradstreet, a credit reporting agency, had, on July 26, 1976, sent a report to five of its subscribers. This report mistakenly indicated that the contractor had filed a petition for voluntary bankruptcy. The contractor learned of this error on the same day, when the president of the contracting company talked to its bank about financing. The contractor called Dun & Brad-

---

26. 424 U.S. at 453, 96 S.Ct. at 965.

27. 424 U.S. at 454–55, 96 S.Ct. at 965.

28. 424 U.S. at 454–55 n. 3, 96 S.Ct. at 965 n. 3.

29. See Wood v. Hustler Magazine, Inc., 736 F.2d 1084, 1092 (5th Cir.1984), rehearing denied 744 F.2d 94 (1984) (Reavley, J., for a unanimous court, citing treatise), certiorari denied 469 U.S. 1107, 105 S.Ct. 783, 83 L.Ed.2d 777 (1985).

30. See Fitzgerald v. Penthouse International, Ltd., 525 F.Supp. 585, 602 (D.Md.1981) (Miller, D.J.), citing treatise; affirmed in part, reversed in part 691 F.2d 666 (4th Cir.1982), certiorari denied 460 U.S. 1024, 103 S.Ct. 1277, 75 L.Ed.2d 497 (1983).

31. 472 U.S. 749, 105 S.Ct. 2939, 86 L.Ed.2d 593 (1985).

street's regional office, explained the error, asked for a correction, and asked for the names of the firms to whom Dun & Bradstreet sent the false credit report. Dun & Bradstreet promised to look into the matter but refused to divulge the names of the recipients of the credit report. About one week after Dun & Bradstreet released the incorrect credit report to the five subscribers, it issued a corrective notice on or about August 3, 1976. It reported that one of the contractor's former employees, not the contractor, had filed for bankruptcy, and that the contractor "continued in business as usual." The contractor again asked for the list of subscribers and Dun & Bradstreet refused.

The contractor then sued in Vermont state court for defamation. The trial established that Dun & Bradstreet's error occurred when one of its employees (a 17 year old high school student) inadvertently misattributed the bankruptcy filing of the contractor's former employee to the contractor. Dun & Bradstreet did not check the accuracy of this report, though it was routine to do so.

The trial judge gave the jury instructions that failed to define many of the crucial terms. The trial judge did tell the jury that the credit report was libelous per se and that the plaintiff was not required to prove actual damages "since damage and loss [are] conclusively presumed."[32] The trial court also permitted the jury to award presumed and punitive damages without proof of scienter.[33] The jury awarded $50,000 in so-called "compensatory" or presumed damages and $300,000 in punitive damages.[34] The Supreme Court, with no majority opinion, affirmed this award.

The Powell Plurality: Speech Involving Matters of Public Concern. Justice Powell's

opinion, joined only by Justices Rehnquist and O'Connor, concluded that in all of the previous cases where the Court found constitutional limits to state libel laws, the speech involved expression "on a matter of public concern," or "*public speech.*"[35] These Justices believed that because speech on matters of "purely private" concern[36] is of less First Amendment concern, "the state's interest [in reputation] adequately supports awards of presumed and punitive damages—even absent a showing of 'actual malice.'"[37] They reasoned the plaintiff could collect "presumed" damages because proof of actual damage is often impossible and yet plaintiffs reputation has been tarnished. So a jury should be allowed to presume damages.

Justices Powell, Rehnquist and O'Connor clearly concluded that plaintiffs could collect punitive and presumed damages without any showing of "actual malice" or *New York Times* scienter if the alleged defamation did not involve a matter of "public concern." They did not discuss whether a plaintiff in such circumstances could collect presumed or punitive damages in the absence of even negligence on the part of the defendant. *Gertz v. Robert Welch*[38] had required proof of negligence before a private person could collect damages for defamation, but Justices Powell, Rehnquist, and O'Connor explicitly limited *Gertz* as a case that "involved expression on a matter of undoubted public concern."[39] Thus, for these three Justices, it may well be the case that if the speech did not involve a matter of public concern, they would allow plaintiff to collect presumed or punitive damages without proof of any kind of fault on the part of the defendant. Justice White's separate opinion concurring in the judgment so concluded.[40]

Public Officials and Matters Not of Public Concern. There is nothing in the

32.   472 U.S. at 755, 105 S.Ct. at 2943.

33.   472 U.S. at 755, 105 S.Ct. at 2943. These instructions thus did not satisfy the requirements of Gertz v. Robert Welch, Inc., 418 U.S. 323, 94 S.Ct. 2997, 41 L.Ed.2d 789 (1974), appeal after remand 680 F.2d 527 (7th Cir.1982), certiorari denied 459 U.S. 1226, 103 S.Ct. 1233, 75 L.Ed.2d 467 (1983).

34.   472 U.S. at 753, 105 S.Ct. at 2942.

35.   472 U.S. at 757 & n. 4, 105 S.Ct. at 2944 & n. 4 (emphasis on original).

36.   472 U.S. at 761, 105 S.Ct. at 2946.

37.   472 U.S. at 761, 105 S.Ct. at 2946 (footnote omitted). When these Justices use the term "actual malice" they mean "scienter."

38.   418 U.S. 323, 94 S.Ct. 2997, 41 L.Ed.2d 789 (1974).

39.   472 U.S. at 757, 105 S.Ct. at 2944.

40.   472 U.S. at 774, 105 S.Ct. at 2953 (White, J.).

Powell plurality that would limit its application to cases where the plaintiff is a private person. That is, for the three Justices who make up the Powell plurality, it may well be the case that a public official or public figure could also collect presumed or punitive damages without even showing any negligence on the part of the defendant if the alleged defamation does not involve a matter of "public concern."

Defining a Matter of Public Concern. The final question for the Powell plurality was whether the credit report involved a matter of public concern. The Powell plurality argued that it did not.

First, the Powell plurality announced that the credit report concerned "no public issue. It was speech solely in the individual interest of the speaker and its specific business audience."[41] From this statement one might be tempted to conclude that all credit reports or all commercial speech are in the category of reduced free speech protection as involving matters not of "public concern." But the Powell plurality, without discussion, specifically rejected that conclusion. Some credit reports are of public concern; some are not. "The protection to be accorded a particular credit report depends on whether the report's 'content, form, and context' indicate that it concerns a public matter."[42]

Secondly, the Powell plurality relied on the fact that the credit report was made available only to five subscribers who were under contract not to disseminate it further: the confidential nature of the communication is evidence that it does not involve a matter of public concern. The anomaly created by Justice Powell's argument is that to the extent that the defendant's alleged libel is not treated confidentially, it is more likely to be protected by *Gertz* and *New York Times v. Sullivan*; to the extent that the defendant takes care not to spread the alleged defamatory remarks, he is more likely subject to liability.

Finally, the Powell plurality believed that speech involving credit reporting is likely not to be chilled by libel laws because the free market already provides many incentives to be accurate "since false credit reporting is of no use to creditors."[43] However, that free market check would seem to undercut the need for libel protection.

The Burger and White Opinions. Chief Justice Burger concurred in the judgment. He had dissented in *Gertz* and now would overrule it. He also argued that *New York Times* should be reexamined.

Justice White also concurred in the judgment. Like Burger, he had dissented in *Gertz* and still believed that decision is wrong. He had joined the Court in *New York Times v. Sullivan* but he "came to have increasing doubts about the soundness of the Court's approach and about some of the assumptions underlying it."[44] He suggested "that the press would be no worse off financially if the common-law rules were to apply and if the judiciary was careful to insist that damage awards be kept within bounds."[45]

The Dissent. Justice Brennan's dissent would have applied *Gertz* to the facts of this case. And he criticized the five members of the Court who, in three different opinions, affirmed the damage award but "have provided almost no guidance as to what constitutes a protected 'matter of public concern.'"[46]

The Future of the "Public Concern" Doctrine. Nearly a decade and half before the Supreme Court plurality decision in *Dun & Bradstreet* another plurality of the Court in *Rosenbloom v. Metromedia, Inc.*[47] tried to offer *New York Times* protection for defendants who made defamatory statements about private individuals when those statements were related to matters of "public concern." In that

---

41. 472 U.S. at 763, 105 S.Ct. at 2947 (footnote omitted).

42. 472 U.S. at 762 n. 8, 105 S.Ct. at 2947 n. 8.

43. 472 U.S. at 763, 105 S.Ct. at 2947.

44. 472 U.S. at 768, 105 S.Ct. at 2950.

45. 472 U.S. at 774, 105 S.Ct. at 2953.

46. 472 U.S. at 788, 105 S.Ct. at 2960.

47. 403 U.S. 29, 30, 91 S.Ct. 1811, 1813, 29 L.Ed.2d 296 (1971) (plurality opinion of Brennan, J., joined by Burger, C.J., and Blackmun, J.).

case Justices Marshall, Stewart and Harlan in dissent warned that courts are not equipped for such an ill-defined task inevitably involving ad hoc balancing.[48] Courts "will be required to somehow pass on the legitimacy of interest in a particular event or subject; what information is relevant to self-government. The danger such a doctrine portends for freedom of the press seems apparent."[49] Judges are not able to determine what is "public concern" without examining the contents of the speech and then applying their subjective judgments.[50]

It may well be that the road the Powell plurality in *Dun & Bradstreet* seeks to travel will end in a dead end, as it did the last time the Court took that route.[51] What is clear from *Dun & Bradstreet* is that a majority of the Court is unhappy with the constitutional law of libel as formulated in *New York Times* and *Gertz*. And this unhappiness goes well beyond

complaints about the entire system of credit reporting. The future should witness new efforts to modify or even overhaul present doctrine.

Libel for Assertions of Fact versus Statements of Opinion. A plaintiff should not be able to bring a libel action merely when he is complaining that someone defamed him by publicizing an unflattering opinion. Speech often uses epithet, hyperbole, charges and countercharges.[52] Most lower courts have ruled that allegedly defamatory expression of opinion are absolutely protected—the question of whether plaintiff can prove *New York Times* scienter is never reached.[53]

In *Milkovich v. Lorain Journal Co.*,[54] the Court, speaking through Chief Justice Rehnquist, rejected any artificial dichotomy be-

---

48. 403 U.S. at 78–81, 91 S.Ct. at 1836–38, 29 L.Ed.2d at 331–33 (dissent of Marshall, J., joined by Stewart, J.). Justice Harlan's separate dissent agreed with this analysis. 403 U.S. at 62, 91 S.Ct. at 1829, 29 L.Ed.2d at 323.

49. 403 U.S. at 79, 91 S.Ct. at 1837, 29 L.Ed.2d at 332 (Marshall, L., dissenting, joined by Stewart, J.).

50. Mihm, C.J., citing Treatise, in Grossman v. Smart, 807 F.Supp. 1404, 1411 (C.D.Ill.1992).

51. Gertz v. Robert Welch, Inc., 418 U.S. 323, 94 S.Ct. 2997, 41 L.Ed.2d 789 (1974), appeal after remand 680 F.2d 527 (7th Cir.1982), certiorari denied 459 U.S. 1226, 103 S.Ct. 1233, 75 L.Ed.2d 467 (1983) rejected the *Rosenblum* plurality because, inter alia, it forced state and federal judges to decide on "an ad hoc basis" when publications address issues of "general or public interest." 418 U.S. at 346, 94 S.Ct. at 3010, 41 L.Ed.2d at 809.

"Matters of Public Concern" in the Government Employment Area Distinguished. In the government employment area, nontenured (typically low-level) government employees cannot be fired solely because of their political beliefs. See, e.g., Pickering v. Board of Education, 391 U.S. 563, 88 S.Ct. 1731, 20 L.Ed.2d 811 (1968).

The Court has had to create some test to limit the applicability of the First Amendment protection from discharge in order to prevent nontenured public employees from securing de facto tenure by deciding to criticize their superior and disrupt office morale. The public employer need not accept action that he or she reasonably believes disrupts the office, undermines authority, and destroys close working relationships. Connick v. Myers, 461 U.S. 138, 103 S.Ct. 1684, 75 L.Ed.2d 708 (1983). The Court distinguishes between the type of speech that protects the public employee from discharge and the type of speech that does not, and labels the former a "matter of public concern."

It is one thing to decide what is a matter of public concern for the purpose of protecting a government employee from discharge—where the Court must tie in the

type of speech engaged in to the effective functioning of the office—and quite another thing for the Court to engage in the much more open-ended task of trying to decide what is a "matter of public concern" in the *Dun & Bradstreet* sense.

52. Erickson, J., citing Treatise in, Keohane v. Stewart, 882 P.2d 1293, 1296 (Colo.1994) (en banc), cert. denied 513 U.S. 1127, 115 S.Ct. 936, 130 L.Ed.2d 882 (1995).

53. E.g., Ollman v. Evans, 750 F.2d 970 (D.C.Cir. 1984), certiorari denied 471 U.S. 1127, 105 S.Ct. 2662, 86 L.Ed.2d 278 (1985), where the D.C. Circuit held that various statements in an Evans and Novak newspaper column about plaintiff Ollman—including that his principal scholarly work is "a ponderous tone in adoration of [Karl Marx] the master," and that an unnamed source said that "Ollman has no status within the profession, but is a pure and simple activist"—is a nonactionable statement of opinion.

See also National Foundation for Cancer Research, Inc. v. Council of Better Business Bureaus, Inc., 705 F.2d 98 (4th Cir.1983), certiorari denied 464 U.S. 830, 104 S.Ct. 108, 78 L.Ed.2d 110 (1983), finding that statement that charity was not "spending a reasonable percentage of total income on program services" was constitutionally protected opinion based on the authority of Greenbelt Cooperative Publishing Association v. Bresler, 398 U.S. 6, 90 S.Ct. 1537, 26 L.Ed.2d 6 (1970). *Greenbelt* had ruled that a newspaper could not be held liable for reporting statements made by citizens at a city council meeting, which statements described the conduct of a local real estate developer and builder as "blackmail." The Court found that characterizing the bargaining tactics as blackmail could not fairly be understood as charging him with a criminal act and therefore the words could not be punished.

54. 497 U.S. 1, 110 S.Ct. 2695, 111 L.Ed.2d 1 (1990).

tween "opinion" and "fact." There is no "wholesale defamation exemption for anything that might be labeled 'opinion.'" In this case a newspaper columnist wrote an article implying that a local high school wrestling coach lied under oath in a judicial proceeding about an altercation involving his team at a home wrestling match. The article, for example, said that "Anyone who attended the meet ... knows in his heart that Milkovich and Scott lied at the hearing after each having given his solemn oath to tell the truth."

After *Milkovich*, if a statement is [1] of opinion, and [2] relates to matters of public concern, and [3] does not contain a provable false factual connotation, then it will receive full constitutional protection.[55] For example, the statement—"I think that Mayor Jones lied"—is really no different than the statement—"Jones is a liar." Both statements may be proved to be false because the speaker did not really think that Jones lied, but published the statement anyway or, because Jones had not really lied. On the other hand, the statement—"In my opinion Mayor Jones shows his abysmal ignorance by accepting the teachings of Marx and Lenin"—is not actionable because "it is a statement of opinion relating to matters of public concern which does not contain a provable false factual connotation...."[56] The issue of falsity relates to "the *defamatory* facts implied by a statement."[57] Similarly, mere vigorous epithet (to label a real estate developer's negotiating position as "blackmail") is not actionable when the reasonable reader perceived the words as mere rhetorical hyperbole.

The Court summed up the law regarding fact versus opinion with respect to public figures and officials, private individuals, and matters of public concern as follows:

[W]here a statement of "opinion" on a matter of public concern reasonably implies false and defamatory facts regarding public figures or officials, those individuals must

show that such statements were made with knowledge of their false implications or with reckless disregard of their truth. Similarly, where such a statement involves a private figure on a matter of public concern, a plaintiff must show that the false connotations were made with some level of fault as required by *Gertz*. Finally, the enhanced appellate review required [in such cases] provides assurance that the foregoing determinations will be made in a manner so as not to "constitute a forbidden intrusion of the field of free expression."[58]

Justice Brennan, joined by Justice Marshall, filed a dissenting opinion. They agreed with the majority that only defamatory statements that are capable of being proved false are subject to liability under state libel law, and that plaintiff must prove that what is false is not the literal phrase published but what a reasonable reader would have understood the author to have said. But, in the view of the dissent, the statements at issue in this case "cannot reasonably be interpreted as stating or implying defamatory facts about petitioner" because, read in context, the columnist's assumption that the petitioner lied at the court hearing is patently conjecture.[59]

§ 16.36 Rights of Privacy and Rights of Publicity

Publication of "Private" Truthful Details. In addition to the categories of public officials, public figures, and *Gertz*-public figures, we have true privacy cases: the accurate description of private facts. May the state, to protect an individual's privacy, prohibit the publication of information that is true but that admittedly relates to and infringes on private matters? This general issue was raised in *Cox Broadcasting Corp. v. Cohn*[1] but the Court decided the case on narrow grounds.

Cohn, father of a deceased rape victim, brought suit against an Atlanta, Georgia, tele-

---

55. 497 U.S. at 19, 110 S.Ct. at 2706.

56. 497 U.S. at 19, 110 S.Ct. at 2706.

57. 497 U.S. at 19 n. 7, 110 S.Ct. at 2706 n. 7 (emphasis in original).

58. 497 U.S. at 19–22, 110 S.Ct. at 2706–07.

59. 497 U.S. at 24, 110 S.Ct. at 2709.

§ 16.36

1. 420 U.S. 469, 95 S.Ct. 1029, 43 L.Ed.2d 328 (1975), on remand 234 Ga. 67, 214 S.E.2d 530 (1975).

vision station after a news broadcast reported the name of his victim-daughter. The television station obtained the name from judicial records open to public inspection and maintained in connection with public prosecution.

The Supreme Court held that a state may not impose liability for public dissemination of true information derived from official court records open to public inspection. Because the state allowed the court records to be public, it could not forbid the republication of the information by the press. The strong interest of the public to know about governmental operations and the strong interest in a free press not subject to self-censorship outweighed the individual's interest in privacy concerning information already published in public records. The public interest was presumably being served, the Court continued, when the information was placed in the public domain on official court records. Privacy interests must be protected by means that avoid the initial public documentation, concluded the Court, not by limiting the press.

The Supreme Court confined its holding to the narrow facts of the case—accurate republication of information in court records lawfully available to the public. At this point in the development of the law the Court left unresolved the constitutional question of a state policy that denies access to the public and press of certain kinds of official records that are not public information and normally cannot be lawfully obtained by the press, such as juvenile court proceedings.[2]

Cox Broadcasting reserved the question whether truth must be recognized as a defense in a defamation action brought by a truly private person (as distinguished from a public official or public figure). It noted that *Time, Inc. v. Hill*[3] had also reserved this question.

However, in light of later constitutional cases, and given the general rationale articulated by the Supreme Court over the years, the state should always recognize that truth is a defense in a defamation or right of privacy action—*unless* the defendant publishes confidential information that he himself has stolen.[4] In such cases, the right of action is not really based on defamation but on an attempt to prevent the thief from benefitting from the publication of knowingly stolen materials.

Thus, *Landmark Communications, Inc. v. Virginia*[5] answered one of the questions reserved in *Cox Broadcasting Corp.* when it held that the First Amendment prohibits the criminal punishment of persons (including newspapers) who are not participants to a judicial disciplinary inquiry from divulging or publishing truthful information regarding confidential proceedings of the judicial inquiry board. The Court found it unnecessary to hold broadly that truthful reporting about public officials in connection with their official duties is always insulated from criminal punishment by the First Amendment, nor did the Court consider any special right of access to the press or the applicability of the state confidentiality statutes to one who secures the information by illegal means and thereafter divulges it.[6]

---

2. 420 U.S. at 496 n. 26, 95 S.Ct. at 1047 n. 26. See Oklahoma Publishing Co. v. District Court, 430 U.S. 308, 97 S.Ct. 1045, 51 L.Ed.2d 355 (1977) (per curiam).

3. 385 U.S. 374, 87 S.Ct. 534, 17 L.Ed.2d 456 (1967). See 420 U.S. at 490–91, 95 S.Ct. at 1043–44. Justice Powell, concurring in *Cox*, thought that Gertz v. Robert Welch, Inc., 418 U.S. 323, 94 S.Ct. 2997, 41 L.Ed.2d 789 (1974), appeal after remand 680 F.2d 527 (7th Cir.1982), certiorari denied 459 U.S. 1226, 103 S.Ct. 1233, 75 L.Ed.2d 467 (1983) "largely resolves this issue" and makes truth a complete defense. 420 U.S. at 498, 95 S.Ct. at 1047.

4. Kennard, J., concurring and citing Treatise, in Shulman v. Group W Prod., Inc., 18 Cal.4th 200, 74 Cal. Rptr.2d 843, 955 P.2d 469 (Cal.1998).

5. 435 U.S. 829, 98 S.Ct. 1535, 56 L.Ed.2d 1 (1978).

6. 435 U.S. at 837–838, 98 S.Ct. at 1540–41. Smith v. Daily Mail Publishing Co., 443 U.S. 97, 99 S.Ct. 2667, 61

L.Ed.2d 399 (1979) (state may not punish a newspaper's truthful publication of an alleged juvenile delinquent's name lawfully obtained by a newspaper).

Publication of Rape Victim's Name. Florida Star v. B.J.F., 491 U.S. 524, 109 S.Ct. 2603, 105 L.Ed.2d 443 (1989) held that a Florida statute could not make a newspaper civilly liable for publishing the name of a rape victim, a name that the newspaper had obtained from a publicly released police report. The Court, interestingly, distinguished *Cox Broadcasting* because Cox Broadcasting had obtained the name from the courthouse. The press has a special role to play, said the Court, in reporting accurately *judicial* proceedings. However, the Court still reversed, applying *Smith v. Daily Mail.* The majority, once again, did not hold broadly that the state may never punish truthful publication; rather it said: where a newspaper publishes truthful information lawfully obtained, "punishment may lawfully be imposed, if at all, only when

The Right of Publicity. In *Zacchini v. Scripps–Howard Broadcasting Co.*[7] the Court upheld, in a five to four decision, the power of the state to allow a damage action brought by a performer against the operator of a television broadcasting station when it telecast a videotape of the plaintiff's entire 15 second act. The majority stressed that it was the entire act that was telecast. Plaintiff was a "human cannonball" who was shot from a cannon into a net at a county fairgrounds. The videotaping was done after Zacchini had asked the freelance reporter not to do it.

The majority divided privacy into four branches. (1) *Time, Inc. v. Hill* was a "false-light" privacy case; there also are cases involving: (2) an appropriation of a name or likeness for the purposes of trade; or (3) publicizing private details about a non-newsworthy person or event; or (4) a performer with a name having commercial value with a claim to a "right of publicity."[8]

The plaintiff, Zacchini, fell into the fourth category of a person with a right to publicity, and the majority found that the unauthorized telecast of his entire performance (even though accompanied by favorable commentary) injured his propriety interest. Without violating free speech guarantees, the state need not, but may, protect this interest, which the Court found analogous to the goals of the copyright and patent laws.

It is unclear, given the majority's emphasis on the telecast of the "entire" performance, whether *Zacchini* has any application to cases where the videotaping is less than the entire act. Even in Zacchini's case, Justice Powell's dissent noted that the plaintiff-Zacchini might not be able to bring himself within the Court's holding because it is unlikely that the "entire" act took only 15 seconds. Fanfare likely accompanied it.[9]

Zacchini was also unclear about the measure of damages in the case. The majority simply said that Zacchini had to prove his damages. Monetary damages would not exist if the defendant's news broadcast increased the value of Zacchini's performance by stimulating the public's interest in seeing the live act.[10]

Free Speech and Copyright Laws

There is an inevitable tension between copyright protection and free speech. One cannot consider in detail all of this tension, for that would require a careful analysis of the entire statutory law of copyright.[11] Yet the subject demands discussion, even if only broad principles can be outlined.

To some extent, of course, copyright protects free speech, because it protects the value in speech created by authors. Copyright law adds a stick to that bundle of rights we call "property." Copyright law protects "the creations of authors from exploitation by others...."[12] Yet, as the Court has also recognized, to suppress

---

narrowly tailored to a state interest of the highest order, and that no such interest is satisfactorily served by imposing liability" under the facts of this case.

Justice Scalia, concurring in part and concurring in the judgment, noted inconsistencies in the Florida law (the law, for example, did not prohibit gossip by the rape victim's acquaintances) and concluded that the law discriminated against the institutional press. The institutional press, in other words, should enjoy *no fewer rights* than any ordinary individual exercising freedom of speech. See, Rotunda, Eschewing Bright Lines, 25 Trial Magazine 52, 54–55 (Dec. 1989) (discussing *Florida Star v. B.J.F.*).

7. 433 U.S. 562, 97 S.Ct. 2849, 53 L.Ed.2d 965 (1977), on remand 54 Ohio St.2d 286, 376 N.E.2d 582 (1978).

8. 433 U.S. at 571–72 & nn. 7 & 8, 97 S.Ct. at 2855–56 & nn. 7 & 8. The Court relied on distinctions that Dean Prosser had developed.

9. 433 U.S. at 579 n. 1, 97 S.Ct. at 2859 n. 1 (Powell, J., dissenting, joined by Brennan & Marshall, JJ.).

10. 433 U.S. at 575 n. 12, 97 S.Ct. at 2857 n. 12.

11. See, e.g., 1 Ronald D. Rotunda & John E. Nowak, Treatise on Constitutional Law: Substance and Procedure § 3.8 (West Group, 3d ed.1999). Nimmer, Does Copyright Abridge the First Amendment Guarantees of Free Speech and Press, 17 U.C.L.A.L.Rev. 1180 (1970); Breyer, The Uneasy Case for Copyright in Books, Photocopies, and Computer Programs, 84 Harv.L.Rev. 281 (1970); M. Nimmer, Nimmer on Freedom of Speech § 2.05[c][2] (1984).

12. Dallas Cowboys Cheerleaders, Inc. v. Scoreboard Posters, Inc., 600 F.2d 1184, 1187 (5th Cir.1979).

Schnapper v. Foley, 667 F.2d 102, 114 (D.C.Cir.1981), cert. denied 455 U.S. 948, 102 S.Ct. 1448, 71 L.Ed.2d 661 (1982) (the First Amendment interests are based on "the author's freedom to speak or remain silent as an end in itself.").

particular words runs "a substantial risk of suppressing ideas in the process."[13]

As Justice Douglas noted: "Serious First Amendment questions would be raised if Congress' power over copyrights were construed to include the power to grant monopolies over certain ideas."[14] Copyright law thus only protects the form of expression, not the facts or ideas expressed.[15] Nonetheless, tensions still remain between free speech and copyright protection, and the line is not as bright as we might wish.

In one case, for example, a court held photographs of the assassination of President John Kennedy did not have full copyright protection because of the "public interest in having the fullest information available...."[16] In contrast, *Harper & Row, Publishers, Inc. v. Nation Enterprises,*[17] held that *The Nation* Magazine violated the copyright laws when it published, without permission, extensive quotations from a purloined copy of former President Ford's then unpublished memoirs, "A Time to Heal." *The Nation* excerpt—published in an effort to scoop *Time* Magazine's authorized excerpt—focused on Ford's pardon of former President Nixon.

The Court held that *The Nation*'s "generous verbatim excerpts" were, under the circumstances, a copyright infringement that was not sanctioned as a "fair use" under the Copyright Act. *The Nation* Magazine's "*intended purpose*" was to interfere with the copyright holder's valuable right of first publication.[18] The

Court then rejected the argument that the First Amendment required a different standard simply because the information conveyed is of high public concern.[19]

In *San Francisco Arts & Athletics, Inc. v. United States Olympic Committee,*[20] a divided Court offered broad protection for the United States Olympic Committee (USOC) and the International Olympic Committee in their use of the word "Olympics." Section 110 of the Amateur Sports Act of 1978 grants to the USOC the right to prohibit (without its consent) any person from using the word "Olympic" for the "purpose of trade, to induce the sale of any goods or services, or to promote any theatrical exhibition, athletic performance, or competition." San Francisco Arts & Athletics, Inc. (SFAA), a nonprofit corporation, sought to promote the "Gay Olympic Games" in 1982 and every four years thereafter. The Gay Games were touted as opening with a ceremony that "will rival the traditional Olympic Games." The winners of the various contests would receive gold, silver, and bronze medals. The SFAA proposed to sell T-shirts, buttons and other items, all showing the title "Gay Olympic Games."

At the request of the USOC the district court enjoined the use of the word "Olympic" in the description of the planned games (which were then held under the name "Gay Games I," in 1982, and "Gay Games II" in 1986). The Supreme Court, in a divided opinion, af-

---

13. Cohen v. California, 403 U.S. 15, 26, 91 S.Ct. 1780, 1788, 29 L.Ed.2d 284 (1971), rehearing denied 404 U.S. 876, 92 S.Ct. 26, 30 L.Ed.2d 124 (1971) (state cannot punish person for wearing a jacket with the words "Fuck the Draft" written on it).

Some words have acquired meanings and "a life and force of their own. They cannot be replaced with definitions...." J.B. White, When Words Lose Their Meaning 11 (1984); R. Rotunda, The Politics of Language: Liberalism as Word and Symbol (U. Iowa Press, 1986) (certain words "reflect and mold the way we think and act.").

14. Lee v. Runge, 404 U.S. 887, 892, 92 S.Ct. 197, 200, 30 L.Ed.2d 169 (1971) (Douglas, J., dissenting to denial of certiorari).

15. E.g., International News Service v. Associated Press, 248 U.S. 215, 234, 39 S.Ct. 68, 71, 63 L.Ed. 211 (1918); New York Times Co. v. United States, 403 U.S. 713, 726 n.*, 91 S.Ct. 2140, 2147 n.*, 29 L.Ed.2d 822, 832 n.* (1971) (Brennan, J., concurring).

16. Time, Inc. v. Bernard Geis Associates, 293 F.Supp. 130, 146 (S.D.N.Y.1968). Oddly enough, the court then relied on the copyright doctrine of "fair use" to allow the defendant to make and publish a copy of the *Zapruder Film* of the Kennedy assassination.

17. 471 U.S. 539, 105 S.Ct. 2218, 85 L.Ed.2d 588 (1985). Brennan, J., joined by White and Marshall, JJ., dissented.

18. 471 U.S. at 562, 105 S.Ct. at 2232 (emphasis in original).

19. 471 U.S. at 556–60, 105 S.Ct. at 2229–30, citing Zacchini v. Scripps–Howard Broadcasting Co., 433 U.S. 562, 575, 97 S.Ct. 2849, 2857, 53 L.Ed.2d 965 (1977), on remand 54 Ohio St.2d 286, 376 N.E.2d 582 (1978).

20. 483 U.S. 522, 107 S.Ct. 2971, 97 L.Ed.2d 427 (1987).

firmed.[21]

Justice Powell, for the Court, concluded that Congress intended to provide the USOC with protection broader than normal trademark protection in that the USOC has "exclusive control of the use of the word 'Olympic' *without* regard to whether an unauthorized use of the word tends to cause confusion." In addition, an unauthorized user of "Olympic" would not have the normal statutory trademark defenses.[22] Nonetheless, the Court noted, given that the SFAA sought to sell T-shirts, bumper stickers, etc., all emblazoned with "Gay Olympic Games," the "possibility of confusion as to sponsorship is obvious."[23]

The Court said that section 110 "extends to promotional uses of 'Olympic' even if the promotion is not used to induce the sale of goods."[24] The Court then added language that narrowed its holding: under section 110, "the USOC may prohibit purely promotional uses of the word *only* when the promotion relates to an athletic or theatrical event. The USOC created the value of the word by using it in connection with an athletic event."[25]

The Court did not decide whether Congress could ever grant a private entity exclusive use of a generic word, because, the Court said, "Olympic" is not generic. The Court found that it was reasonable for Congress to conclude that the commercial and promotional value of the word "Olympic" was the product of the USOC's own talents and energy.[26] The USOC and the International Olympic Committee have used the word "Olympic" since 1896, when the modern Olympic Games began. Congress could reasonably conclude that the word has acquired a special "secondary meaning." Thus, Congress could grant the USOC a "limited property right" in the word "Olympic."

In addition, the majority argued, Congress acted reasonably when it did not require the USOC to prove that an unauthorized use of "Olympic" is likely to confuse the public. The Congressional prohibition did not prevent the SFAA from holding its athletic event in its planned format. Section 110 may not even restrict purely expressive uses of the word "Olympic."[27] The Congressional restrictions on the use of "Olympic" are incidental to the primary Congressional purpose of encouraging and rewarding the USCC's activities.

Product Disparagement and Defamation. The Supreme Court has not decided whether First Amendment principles should restrict defamation or privacy actions when the plaintiff is complaining that a competitor is defaming a commercial product, or a commercial performance. Invasion of an individual's right of publicity for commercial purposes may be subjected to greater state regulation than publication of information regarding a person's private life or activity when such publication is unrelated to a commercial venture.[28]

---

21. O'Connor, joined by Blackmun, concurring in part and dissenting in part, agreed with the First Amendment issue but would have found that the USOC was a state actor and remand for a determination of discriminatory enforcement.

Brennan, joined by Marshall, dissenting, argued that there was state action and that § 110 violated the First Amendment because it was overbroad, because it is susceptible to substantial amount of noncommercial speech, and because the law discriminates on the basis of content. Brennan noted that there are *over* 200 organizations listed in just the Los Angeles and Manhattan telephone directories whose names start with the word "Olympic."

22. 483 U.S. at 531, 107 S.Ct. at 2978 (emphasis added).

23. 483 U.S. at 539, 107 S.Ct. at 2982. The Court emphasized this point. See, e.g., 483 U.S. at 535 & n. 12, 107 S.Ct. at 2980 & n. 12.

24. 483 U.S. at 540, 107 S.Ct. at 2983.

25. 483 U.S. at 540, 107 S.Ct. at 2983 (emphasis added).

26. 483 U.S. at 533, 107 S.Ct. at 2979.

27. See 483 U.S. at 536 & n. 15, 107 S.Ct. at 2981 & n. 15. At this point the Court cited with approval a lower court decision, Stop the Olympic Prison v. United States Olympic Committee, 489 F.Supp. 1112, 1118–21 (S.D.N.Y. 1980), which upheld the use of the Olympic logo of five interacting rings and the Olympic torch on a poster opposing the planned conversion of the Olympic Village at Lake Placid: the lower court "found that the use of the symbols did not fit the commercial or promotional definition of uses in § 110." 483 U.S. at 537 n. 14, 107 S.Ct. at 2981 n. 14.

28. In Bose Corp. v. Consumers Union of United States, Inc., 466 U.S. 485, 104 S.Ct. 1949, 80 L.Ed.2d 502 (1984), rehearing denied 467 U.S. 1267, 104 S.Ct. 3561, 82 L.Ed.2d 863 (1984), the Supreme Court ruled that appellate courts must independently review findings of actual "malice" in defamation cases. The subject matter of this case was a claim for "product disparagement" by the manufacturer of a product claimed to be falsely described in a derogatory manner by a magazine reviewing the

False Light Privacy Cases. *Cantrell v. Forest City Publishing Co.*[29] upheld a jury verdict for compensatory damages in a "false light" privacy case brought by a mother and son against a newspaper publisher and reporter. The article discussed the impact on the family of the death of the father in a bridge collapse. The story contained several inaccuracies regarding the description of the poverty in which the plaintiffs were living and the dilapidated conditions of their home. The plaintiffs' cause of action was based on the argument that the defendants, by publishing the false feature story, made the plaintiffs the object of pity and ridicule, causing them to suffer outrage, mental distress, shame and humiliation. In this diversity case the *Cantrell* Court implicitly acknowledged that a false light privacy case, where the publication is inaccurate *and* causes mental anguish and humiliation, is constitutional.[30]

Cantrell carefully left open the question of burden of proof. The trial court had instructed the jury that liability could be imposed only if the false statements were made with *New York Times* scienter.[31] The Court affirmed the trial verdict, but made clear that it was not ruling that, as a constitutional matter, the plaintiff in a false light privacy case must prove *New York Times* scienter. No party had made any objection to the jury instruction and the issue was not before the Court.[32] Thus it left open the question of whether a more relaxed standard should apply.

Several years before, in *Time, Inc. v. Hill*,[33] discussed earlier, the Court had held that the plaintiff must prove *New York Times* scienter given the facts of that case. However, subsequent Supreme Court cases indicate that *Time, Inc. v. Hill* should no longer govern the burden of proof standard for false light privacy torts that cause the plaintiff to suffer mental anguish and humiliation. The *Gertz v. Robert Welch*[34] standard should apply in cases where the plaintiff is a private person.

Thus in *Wood v. Hustler Magazine, Inc.*,[35] the Fifth Circuit applied the *Gertz* standard when the plaintiff sued Hustler Magazine because it published a stolen photograph depicting her in the nude. Plaintiff was awarded actual damages of $150,000 for negligence because Hustler Magazine had placed her in an offensive false light. The photographs were submitted by the thief with a forged consent form. This form also included false information regarding plaintiff's sexual fantasies. Hustler Magazine had been negligent in determining the authenticity of the consent form.

§ 16.37 Fighting Words and Hostile Audiences: Introduction

The Court allows government regulation of speech when the purpose of the statute is to prohibit "fighting words."[1] While the definition of this phrase is discussed below, it is important, in understanding this doctrine, to understand the rationale that supports it. The traditional hypothetical situation of the individual shouting "fire" in a crowded theater illustrates the dichotomy between action and speech.

In one sense, a "fighting words" conviction regulates speech because "fighting words" are still just words. Yet fighting words also can be an incitement to unthinking, immediate, vio-

---

product. The lower courts had believed that the *New York Times v. Sullivan* standards should apply in this case because the producer of the product was the equivalent of a public figure. The Supreme Court accepted, for the purpose of this case, the lower court's assumption that the *New York Times* standard should be applied in this situation but noted that it was not ruling on that issue. 466 U.S. at 513, 104 S.Ct. at 1966–67, 80 L.Ed.2d at 525.

29. 419 U.S. 245, 95 S.Ct. 465, 42 L.Ed.2d 419 (1974).

30. Cf. 419 U.S. at 248–50, 95 S.Ct. at 468–69.

31. 419 U.S. at 250, 95 S.Ct. at 469.

32. 419 U.S. at 249–50 & n. 3, 95 S.Ct. at 469 & n. 3.

33. 385 U.S. 374, 87 S.Ct. 534, 17 L.Ed.2d 456 (1967).

34. 418 U.S. 323, 94 S.Ct. 2997, 41 L.Ed.2d 789 (1974), appeal after remand 680 F.2d 527 (7th Cir.1982), certiorari denied 459 U.S. 1226, 103 S.Ct. 1233, 75 L.Ed.2d 467 (1983).

35. 736 F.2d 1084, 1092 (5th Cir.1984) (Reavley, J., for a unanimous court) (citing treatise), rehearing denied 744 F.2d 94 (1984), certiorari denied 469 U.S. 1107, 105 S.Ct. 783, 83 L.Ed.2d 777 (1985).

§ 16.37

1. Taylor, P.J., quoting Treatise, in South v. City of Mountain Brook, 688 So.2d 292, 294 (Ala.Crim.App.1996); McMillan, J., citing Treatise in, Conkle v. State, 677 So.2d 1211, 1220 (Ala.Crim.App.1995).

lent *action*, just like falsely shouting fire in a crowded theater immediately incites action (that is, a riot). The immediate reaction means that there is no time to debate, to trust the free marketplace of ideas. The state's interest in order overshadows the minimal protection to be afforded the "slight social value as a step to truth"[2] of the speech.

The theory of the regulation of "fighting words" is not contrary to the theory of the free marketplace of ideas because this speech triggers an automatic, unthinking reaction, rather than a consideration of an idea. The speaker does not intend the words to convey any intellectual content, but merely to provoke an emotional message intended, and likely to result in, an *immediate*, violent response. A speaker says (or hurls) "fighting words" at a particular individual in order to provoke him or her. "Fighting words" are really a retail version of the kind of speech that, if engaged in on a wholesale level, is within *Brandenburg v. Ohio*.[3]

The prohibition of "fighting words" is not on the thought or idea itself but on the *manner* or mode of expressing it. The fighting words doctrine allows the state to prohibit an intolerable manner of expressing an idea, but does not authorize the state to ban the idea itself.[4]

§ 16.38 Fighting Words and Hostile Audiences: The Doctrine Emerges

In 1942, *Chaplinsky v. New Hampshire*[1] unanimously upheld a statute previously con-

strued by the state court to ban "face-to-face words plainly likely to cause a breach of the peace by the addressee."[2] Chaplinsky's conviction was based on his face-to-face encounter with the City Marshal of Rochester whom he described as a "God damned racketeer and a damned fascist"[3] as a policeman was leading Chaplinsky away from a public sidewalk because of fear that his distribution of religious literature was causing a public disturbance. It is important to remember that Chaplinsky was not convicted for his distribution of religious literature or because of the policeman's fear of a public disturbance, but for his denunciations made directly to the fire marshal.

The Court argued that Chaplinsky's epithet was without communicative value, because these "epithets are likely to provoke the average person to retaliation, and thereby cause a breach of the peace."[4] Justice Murphy stated in dictum that " 'fighting' words—those which by their very utterance inflict injury or *tend to incite* an *immediate* breach of the peace"—are not constitutionally protected because their slight social value as a step to truth is "clearly outweighed by the social interest in order and morality."[5]

The Court spoke broadly and indicated that this breach of the peace conviction was valid even though there was merely a danger the listener will be incited to violence. The state did not need to prove actual violence between the fire marshal and Chaplinsky. The state court also properly refused "to admit evidence of provocation and evidence bearing on the truth or falsity of the utterances...."[6]

2. Chaplinsky v. New Hampshire, 315 U.S. 568, 572, 62 S.Ct. 766, 769, 86 L.Ed. 1031 (1942). On hostile audiences and fighting words, see, 4 R Ronald D. Rotunda & John E. Nowak, Treatise on Constitutional Law: Substance and Procedure §§ 20.37–20.40 (West Group, 3d ed.1999); Rotunda, A Brief Comment on Politically Incorrect Speech in the Wake of R.A.V., 47 So. Methodist U.L.Rev. 9 (1993); Rotunda, Can You Say That?, 30 Trial Magazine 18 (December, 1994).

3. 395 U.S. 444, 89 S.Ct. 1827, 23 L.Ed.2d 430 (1969)(per curiam). See § 16.15.

4. Rotunda, Racist Speech and Attorney Discipline, 6 The Professional Lawyer 1 (A.B.A., No. 6, 1995); Rotunda, What Next? Outlawing Lawyer Jokes?, Wall Street Journal, Aug. 8, 1995, at A12, col. 3–5 (Midwest ed.).

§ 16.38

1. 315 U.S. 568, 62 S.Ct. 766, 86 L.Ed. 1031 (1942). See Parker, J., citing Treatise in, Shell v. Host International Corp., 513 N.W.2d 15, 18 (Minn.App.1994).

2. 315 U.S. at 573, 62 S.Ct. at 770. The state statute forbade a person to address "any offensive, derisive or annoying word to any other person who is lawfully in any street or other public place." 315 U.S. at 569, 62 S.Ct. at 768.

3. 315 U.S. at 569, 62 S.Ct. at 768.

4. 315 U.S. at 574, 62 S.Ct. at 770.

5. 315 U.S. at 572, 62 S.Ct. at 769 (footnotes omitted) (emphasis added).

6. 315 U.S. at 574, 62 S.Ct. at 770.

Chaplinsky's basic test was whether or not men of common intelligence would understand the words as likely to cause the average addressee to fight, words and expressions that by general consent are "fighting words" when said "without a disarming smile."[7] The Court gave no real consideration whether fire marshals or policemen should be expected to resist epithets that would produce violent responses in the average citizen who has not been trained to prevent breaches of the peace. All that would be left to later cases.

§ 16.39   Fighting Words and Hostile Audiences: Subsequent Modifications

Decisions following *Chaplinsky* reflect the Court's desire to limit the broad implications of that doctrine. Later cases also recognize the potential social value in statements that might come under the initial definition of "fighting words." The Court did not overrule *Chaplinsky*, but narrowed its scope.

Terminiello v. Chicago[1] overturned a municipal ordinance prohibiting breaches of the peace. The trial court's instruction to the jury construed the statute as prohibiting conduct that "stirs the public to anger, invites dispute, brings about a condition of unrest or creates a disturbance."[2] Terminiello's address was a denunciation of Jews and blacks. Outside of the auditorium where he spoke, a "howling" crowd gathered in protest and he denounced them as well.

The majority opinion of Justice Douglas analyzed the purpose of free speech:

[A] function of free speech ... is to invite dispute. It may indeed best serve its high purpose when it induces a condition of unrest, creates dissatisfaction with conditions as they are, or even stirs people to anger.

Speech is often provocative and challenging. It may strike at prejudices and preconceptions and have profound unsettling effects as it presses for acceptance of an idea ... the alternative would lead to standardization of ideas either by legislatures, courts, or dominant political or community groups.[3]

Douglas invalidated the statute as vague and overbroad, which allowed the Court to avoid the more difficult question of whether the First Amendment protected the speech. The strong language of the majority opinion did, however, indicate a retreat from the *Chaplinsky* "uncontrollable impulse" test by recognizing that a certain amount of provocative and challenging speech is protected.

Two years later, *Feiner v. New York*[4] upheld the conviction of petitioner under a state disorderly conduct statute. *Feiner* directly raised the question of the hostile audience. Feiner's address included descriptions of President Truman as a "bum", the mayor of Syracuse as a "champagne sipping bum", and the American Legion as a "Nazi Gestapo." The speaker urged blacks to "rise up in arms and fight for equal rights."[5] These racial statements " 'stirred up a little excitement.' Some of the onlookers made remarks to the police about their inability to handle the crowd and at least one threatened violence if the police did not act. There were others who appeared to be favoring petitioner's arguments."[6] The police asked Feiner to stop, but he refused. After their request, the officer arrested Feiner, who had been speaking for over a half hour.

The Chief Justice Vinson's majority opinion stressed that the arrest was not an attempt to censor the content of the speech, but an effort to protect the peace before the threatened violent reaction took place.

---

7. Chaplinsky v. New Hampshire, 315 U.S. at 573, 62 S.Ct. at 770. See also 315 U.S. at 572, 62 S.Ct. at 769.

§ 16.39

1. 337 U.S. 1, 69 S.Ct. 894, 93 L.Ed. 1131 (1949), rehearing denied 337 U.S. 934, 69 S.Ct. 1490, 93 L.Ed. 1740 (1949).

2. 337 U.S. at 3, 69 S.Ct. at 895. Four Justices dissented on the grounds that the instructions issue was not properly preserved for review.

3. Terminiello v. Chicago, 337 U.S. 1, 4, 69 S.Ct. 894, 896, 93 L.Ed. 1131 (1949), rehearing denied 337 U.S. 934, 69 S.Ct. 1490, 93 L.Ed. 1740 (1949).

4. 340 U.S. 315, 71 S.Ct. 303, 95 L.Ed. 295 (1951).

5. 340 U.S. at 330, 71 S.Ct. at 311–12 (Douglas, J. dissenting).

6. 340 U.S. at 317, 71 S.Ct. at 305.

It is one thing to say that the police cannot be used as an instrument for the suppression of unpopular views, and another to say that, when as here the speaker passes the bounds of argument or persuasion and undertakes *incitement to riot*, they are powerless to prevent a breach of the peace.[7]

Feiner's claim differed from Terminiello's in that he did not assert that the statute was unconstitutionally broad or vague, but that the police had abused their discretion and were motivated by a desire to suppress the content of his speech, an assertion that the majority found unsupported by evidence.

In *Feiner,* Justices Douglas and Black dissented vigorously, arguing that the minimal threat of violence was insufficient to justify this suppression. Moreover, both Douglas and Black emphasized that the first duty of the police is to protect the speaker's rights by dissuading those threatening violence, an attempt not evidenced in this case. By immediately acquiescing in the face of a single threat by one individual, the police had acted merely as conduits for the desires of suppression and denied the provocation value attributed to speech in *Terminiello,*[8] regardless of the impetus that motivated the policemen. Thus, the dissent raised the ultimate question in "fighting words" cases: whose rights are pre-eminent in a *Feiner* situation, the audience voluntarily listening, or the speaker?[9]

The authority of *Feiner* has been undercut significantly in subsequent cases where the Court applied the language of *Terminiello* and distinguished *Feiner* on its facts. *Edwards v. South Carolina,*[10] for example, involved a civil rights demonstration on the grounds of the state legislature. Although the state officials and lower courts found that the crowd observing the demonstration was growing increasingly restive, and the demonstrators refused to leave when requested, the Court (in 1963) refused to consider the conduct of the demonstrators—the singing of religious and patriotic hymns and a "religious harangue" urging them to go to segregated lunch counters—to constitute "fighting words." Neither did the "hostile audience" doctrine apply.

Although the situation in *Edwards* might have been potentially more dangerous than that of *Feiner,* the Court appreciated the ability of an expansive *Feiner* doctrine to suppress civil rights demonstrations by persons falsely claiming that their emotions were uncontrollably aroused. As a factual matter the Court found the situation in *Edwards* a "far cry" from the hostile audience problem in *Feiner.*[11] Recall that the Court had found that Mr. Feiner was seeking to incite a riot.

It is important to distinguish *Terminiello, Feiner,* and *Edwards* from *Chaplinsky,* which involved *face-to-face* confrontation where insults were delivered that were likely to provoke violence by the listeners. The harangues delivered in the other cases were not personally directed to particular members of the audience—"fighting words," a *face-to-face* confrontation with particular members of the audience. The audience was not even compelled to listen. While the speech may have offended the listeners' sensibilities, the Court has generally emphasized that regulation of speech needs more compelling justification so that the state will not censor unpopular ideas.

Cohen v. California,[12] decided in 1971, provides important support for this distinction and leaves the authority of *Feiner* in a questionable state. *Cohen* was convicted for breach of the peace based on his presence in a Los

---

7. 340 U.S. at 321, 71 S.Ct. at 306 (emphasis added).

8. 340 U.S. at 326–27, 71 S.Ct. at 309–10 (Black, J., dissenting) and 340 U.S. at 331, 71 S.Ct. at 312 (Douglas, J., dissenting).

9. The better view is that hecklers would be arrested rather than speakers when the former arrived with preconceived intent to commit violence. Sellers v. Johnson, 163 F.2d 877 (8th Cir.1947), certiorari denied 332 U.S. 851, 68 S.Ct. 356, 92 L.Ed. 421 (1948).

10. 372 U.S. 229, 83 S.Ct. 680, 9 L.Ed.2d 697 (1963); see also Cox v. Louisiana, 379 U.S. 536, 85 S.Ct. 453, 13 L.Ed.2d 471 (1965).

11. 372 U.S. at 236, 83 S.Ct. at 684.

12. 403 U.S. 15, 91 S.Ct. 1780, 29 L.Ed.2d 284 (1971), rehearing denied 404 U.S. 876, 92 S.Ct. 26, 30 L.Ed.2d 124 (1971).

Angeles courthouse wearing a jacket bearing the clearly printed words "Fuck the Draft."

The Court recognized that people in public places must be subject to some objectionable speech, but they could simply avert their eyes and ears. The Court, in the majority opinion of Justice Harlan, stated that—

> [T]he ability of government, consonant with the Constitution, to shut off discourse solely to protect others from hearing it is ... dependent on a showing that substantial privacy interests are being invaded in an essentially intolerable manner.[13]

The fact that an offensive expletive was utilized does not detract from the protection afforded the speech, because, in Justice Harlan's phrase, "one man's vulgarity is another's lyric."[14] Moreover, the offensive words were not "a direct personal insult" specifically directed at the hearer; neither was the state exercising its police power (as in *Feiner*) "to prevent a speaker from intentionally provoking a given group to a hostile reaction."[15]

The *Cohen* limitations weakened *Chaplinsky* substantially. *Cohen* requires a critical examination of the audience, the results of the speech, the length of the speech, the actual results of the speech, and the wording of the statute:

> [W]e do not think the fact that some unwilling "listeners" in a public building may have been briefly exposed to [the offensive speech] can serve to justify this breach of the peace conviction where, as here, there was no evidence that persons powerless to

avoid appellant's conduct did in fact object to it, and where that portion of the statute upon which Cohen's conviction rests evinces no concern, either on its face or as construed ... with the special plight of the captive auditor....[16]

The Court has not overruled the "fighting words" doctrine, but any conviction based on it faces careful judicial scrutiny.

Content Based Fighting Words—the Problem of Hate Speech. *R.A.V. v. City of St. Paul*,[17] is a significant decision explaining and limiting the "fighting words" doctrine. The City of St. Paul enacted an ordinance that provided:

> "Whoever places on public or private property a symbol, object, appellation, characterization or graffiti, including, but not limited to, a burning cross or a Nazi swastika, which one knows or has reasonable grounds to know arouses anger, alarm or resentment in others on the basis of race, color, creed, religion or gender commits disorderly conduct and shall be guilty of a misdemeanor."

The City alleged that R.A.V. and several other teenagers burned a cross *inside* the privately owned, *fenced* yard of a black family, who lived across the street from where R.A.V. was staying. R.A.V., of course, intended to terrorize the black family. The only question was the constitutionality of this ordinance.[18]

The state supreme court held that the ordinance only reached expressions that constituted "fighting words," within the meaning of

13. 403 U.S. at 21, 91 S.Ct. at 1786.

14. 403 U.S. at 25, 91 S.Ct. at 1788.

15. 403 U.S. at 20, 91 S.Ct. at 1786.

16. Cohen v. California, 403 U.S. 15, 22, 91 S.Ct. 1780, 1786, 29 L.Ed.2d 284 (1971), rehearing denied 404 U.S. 876, 92 S.Ct. 26, 30 L.Ed.2d 124 (1971).

17. 505 U.S. 377, 112 S.Ct. 2538, 120 L.Ed.2d 305 (1992). Scalia, J., delivered the opinion of the Court, joined by Rehnquist, C.J., and Kennedy, Souter, and Thomas, JJ. White, J., filed an opinion concurring in the judgment, in which Blackmun and O'Connor, JJ., joined, and in which Stevens, J., joined except as to Part I–A. Blackmun, J., filed an opinion concurring in the judgment. Stevens, J., also filed an opinion concurring in the judgment, in Part I of which White and Blackmun, JJ. joined.

See, Robert Sedler, The Unconstitutionality of Campus Bans on "Racist Speech:" The View from Without and Within, 53 U.Pittsburgh L.Rev. 631 (1992); Ronald D. Rotunda, A Brief Comment on Politically Incorrect Speech in the Wake of R.A.V., 47 So. Methodist U.L.Rev. 9 (1993); William Van Alstyne, The University in the Manner of Tiananmen Square, 21 Hastings Const. L. Q.1 (1993).

18. The state also charged R.A.V. with violation of a state law that prohibited racially motivated assault, but there was no Constitutional challenge to that count. Minn. Stat. § 609.2212(4), cited in R.A.V. v. City of St. Paul, 505 U.S. at 381 n. 2, 112 S.Ct. at 2541 n. 2. See also, 505 U.S. at 380 n. 1, 112 S.Ct. at 2541 n. 1, referring to other applicable laws under which R.A.V. could have been charged, such as terroristic threats, arson, and criminal damage to property.

Chaplinsky, and that it was a "narrowly tailored means toward accomplishing the compelling governmental interest in protecting the community against bias-motivated threats to public safety and order." The state court upheld the ordinance, but the U.S. Supreme Court disagreed.

Justice Scalia, for the majority, accepted the state court's interpretation, but ruled that the ordinance is unconstitutional on its face, because it "prohibits otherwise permitted speech solely on the basis of the subject [that] the speech addresses." It has long been the rule that content-based restrictions on speech are presumptively unconstitutional. *R.A.V.* applied this principle to the "fighting words" doctrine: the government may not regulate even fighting words "based on hostility—or favoritism—towards the underlying message expressed."[19]

This case is best understood by turning to a hypothetical that Justice Scalia used to explain the ruling of the Court. The problem with the St. Paul ordinance is that, under its provisions—

> One could hold up a sign saying, for example, that all "anti-Catholic bigots" are misbegotten; but not that all "papists" are, for that would insult and provoke violence "on the basis of religion." St. Paul has no such authority to license one side of a debate to fight freestyle, while requiring the other to follow Marquis of Queensberry Rules.[20]

Justice Stevens' separate opinion concurring in the judgment sought to distinguish this hypothetical, but in order to distinguish it, he first had to change it! He recited exactly the above-indented quotation, and then said the following, including the bracketed language:

> This may be true, but it hardly proves the Court's point. The Court's reasoning is asymmetrical. The response to a sign saying that "all [religious] bigots are misbegotten"

is a sign saying that "all advocates of religious tolerance are misbegotten."[21]

The problem with Justice Stevens' reasoning is that the hypothetical ordinance, in fact, does make it a crime to state that "all papists are misbegotten," but not a crime to state that "all anti-Catholic bigots are misbegotten." The ordinance, by its own terms, only seeks to ban certain types of fighting words: it seeks to ban words that would insult and provoke on the basis of religion, but not similar words that do not fit within that content. In order for Stevens to criticize Scalia's hypothetical, he first had to modify it, and then criticize a hypothetical different than the one that Scalia had advanced.

The Minnesota Supreme Court, in upholding the ordinance, emphasized that the ordinance was directed against "bias-motivated" hatred, and messages "based on virulent notions of racial supremacy."[22] This content-based purpose was the fatal flaw of the statute.

Some speech can be prohibited because of its content, in the sense that we must look at the content of speech to see what category the speech is in. For example, is the speech at issue "fighting words" or "obscene"? But that does not mean that the state has *carte blanche* to do as it wishes merely because speech falls in the category of "fighting words" or "obscene."

Title VII and Sexually Derogatory Fighting Words. *R.A.V.* said that the state "may not prohibit only that commercial advertising that depicts men in a demeaning fashion."[23] That would fail the requirement that there must be "no realistic possibility that official suppression of ideas is afoot."[24] Advertising that depicts men (or women) in a demeaning fashion is not to be admired, but it is still protected by the First Amendment. The

---

19. 505 U.S. at 386, 112 S.Ct. at 2545.

20. 505 U.S. at 392, 112 S.Ct. at 2548.

21. 505 U.S. at 435, 112 S.Ct. at 2571 (Stevens, J., concurring in the judgment). Justice Stevens also stated that it "seems to me" to be "extremely unlikely" that such signs "could be fighting words." However, if Justice Scalia had substituted a more vernacular, vulgar, or colloquial term than the polysyllabic word, "misbegotten"—

often fighting words are monosyllabic—it should not be difficult to conceive of the expression being placed in the category of "fighting words."

22. 464 N.W.2d at 508, 511.

23. 505 U.S. at 389, 112 S.Ct. at 2546.

24. 505 U.S. at 390, 112 S.Ct. at 2547.

Government cannot seek to drive out or disfavor this particular viewpoint.

The state can ban certain discriminatory *conduct,* and one cannot immunize one's self from that ban merely by accompanying it with speech. A murderer does not cloak himself with the First Amendment merely because he shouts, "Death to Tyrants," while pulling the trigger. Pursuant to Title VII, Congress has banned sexual discrimination in employment practices. Such conduct (e.g., a refusal to promote someone to a better job because of sexism) is not immune from prohibition merely because the practitioner accompanies the bad conduct with sexually disparaging statements. Sexually derogatory fighting words, "among other words, may produce a violation of Title VII's general prohibition against sexual discrimination in employment practices," because where "the government does not target conduct on the basis of its expressive content, acts are not shielded from regulation merely because they express a discriminatory idea or philosophy."[25] The words may even amount to admissions of the offensive conduct. Proof that the individual uttered sexist remarks may be useful evidence to impeach his claim that he would never say such a thing.[26] But the power to criminalize conduct is quite a bit different than the power to criminalize speech, even offensive speech.

In contrast to *R.A.V.,* the following year the unanimous Court in *Wisconsin v. Mitchell,*[27] upheld a Wisconsin statute that enhanced a defendant's sentence if he intentionally selected his victim based on the victim's race. The statute in *R.A.V.* was explicitly directed at speech; but the statute in *Mitchell* was aimed at *conduct* (aggravated battery by Mitchell, who selected and beat up his victim on the grounds of color). The First Amendment does not protect this conduct. The trial court only looked at the defendant's motives in determining what sentence to impose.

Although the sentencing judge may not constitutionally take into account the defendant's *abstract* beliefs,[28] the First Amendment does not prevent the court from looking at the defendant's motive in this case. A sentencing judge often looks at motive in determining punishment. A defendant may receive a minimum sentence because he was acting with good motives, or a high sentence because of bad motives. The state may consider, as an aggravating circumstance, the fact that defendant murdered for hire, because a paid hitman is particularly dangerous. The more purposeful the offense, the more severely it may be punished.[29] It is proper, in a murder case, for the trial judge (in deciding to sentence the defendant to death) to take into account the racial hatred of the defendant towards the victim, and the desire of the defendant to provoke a race war.[30] It is constitutional for Wisconsin to single out bias-inspired *conduct* for enhancement of criminal penalty simply because it concluded that this type of conduct inflicted greater individual and societal harm.[31]

Threats, Intimidation, & Cross–Burning. The state may, consistent with the First Amendment, ban "true threats." Thus, the state may prosecute an individual for cross-burning, if the state can prove that he burned the cross with an intent to *intimidate* someone. As O'Connor explained, in *Virginia v.*

---

25. 505 U.S. at 90, 112 S.Ct. at 2546–47

See Kingsley R. Browne, Title VII as Censorship: Hostile–Environment Harassment and the First Amendment, 52 Ohio State L.J. 481 (1991), a thoughtful article analyzing the free speech problems of "hostile work environment" cases.

26. See, Dawson v. Delaware, 503 U.S. 159, 112 S.Ct. 1093, 117 L.Ed.2d 309 (1992).

27. 508 U.S. 476, 113 S.Ct. 2194, 124 L.Ed.2d 436 (1993).

28. Dawson v. Delaware, 503 U.S. 159, 112 S.Ct. 1093, 117 L.Ed.2d 309 (1992), on remand 608 A.2d 1201 (Del. 1992).

29. Tison v. Arizona, 481 U.S. 137, 156, 107 S.Ct. 1676, 1687, 95 L.Ed.2d 127 (1987), rehearing denied 482 U.S. 921, 107 S.Ct. 3201, 96 L.Ed.2d 688 (1987).

30. Barclay v. Florida, 463 U.S. 939, 103 S.Ct. 3418, 77 L.Ed.2d 1134 (1983) (plurality opinion).

31. *Wisconsin v. Mitchell* rejected the argument that a penalty enhancement for some criminal *acts* may somehow chill free speech. It is unlikely that a bigot will suppress his or her bigoted beliefs on the theory that if the bigot commits an admittedly criminal act (such as assault, or murder), then the state might seek to discover and then introduce evidence of that bigotry. The chain of events is too speculative to justify a conclusion that the Wisconsin statute chills free speech.

Black,[32] in a portion of the opinion that was the opinion of the Court:

> Intimidation in the constitutionally proscribable sense of the word is a type of true threat, where a speaker directs a threat to a person or a group of persons with the intent of placing the victim in hear of bodily harm or death.[52]

The Virginia state law in question made it a felony "for any person ..., with the intent of intimidating any person or group ..., to burn ... a cross on the property of another, a highway or other public place." The statute also specified that "[a]ny such burning ... shall be prima facie evidence of an intent to intimidate a person or group." The Virginia Supreme Court held that, based on *R.A.V. v. City of St. Paul*,[33] the cross burning statute was facially unconstitutional under the First Amendment and also overbroad.

Justice O'Connor, for the Court, reversed. She held that Virginia's ban on cross burning with intent to intimidate did not violate the First Amendment. However, as interpreted by the jury instruction given at defendant's trial, a provision of Virginia cross burning statute that stated that burning of a cross in public view "shall be prima facie evidence of an intent to intimidate," was facially unconstitutional under the First Amendment. This state law construction of the statute was, of course, binding on the U.S. Supreme Court.

O'Connor acknowledged that, "whether the message is a political one or whether the message is also meant to intimidate, the burning of a cross is a 'symbol of hate,'" even though sometimes it carries "no intimidating message."[34] Virginia can ban cross-burning with

an intent to intimidate because those threats, like threats against the President, it does not discriminate "on the basis of content by targeting only those individuals who 'provoke violence' on a basis specified in the law."[35]

The Court concluded that this case is different than *R.A.V.*

Virginia's statute does not run afoul of the First Amendment insofar as it bans cross burning with intent to intimidate. Unlike the statute at issue in R.A.V., the Virginia statute does not single out for opprobrium only that speech directed toward "one of the specified disfavored topics." It does not matter whether an individual burns a cross with intent to intimidate because of the victim's race, gender, or religion, or because of the victim's "political affiliation, union membership, or homosexuality."[36]

In fact, the record showed that cross burners do not direct their intimidating conduct solely to racial or religious minorities, but also burn crosses to intimidate union members, or others.[37]

The law at issue in *R.A.V.* was flawed because it allowed the city to impose special prohibitions on speakers who express views on disfavored subjects. But the Virginia law did not share that infirmity. The Virginia law did not single out for opprobrium only that speech directed certain disfavored topics.

In short, Virginia, under the First Amendment, may outlaw cross burnings done with the intent to intimidate because burning a cross is a particularly virulent form of intimi-

---

32. Virginia v. Black, 538 U.S. 343, ___, 123 S.Ct. 1536, 1548, 155 L.Ed.2d 535 (2003).

33. 505 U.S. 377, 112 S.Ct. 2538, 120 L.Ed.2d 305 (1992). Scalia, J., delivered the opinion of the Court, joined by Rehnquist, C.J., and Kennedy, Souter, and Thomas, JJ. White, J., filed an opinion concurring in the judgment, in which Blackmun and O'Connor, JJ., joined, and in which Stevens, J., joined except as to Part I–A. Blackmun, J., filed an opinion concurring in the judgment. Stevens, J., also filed an opinion concurring in the judgment, in Part I of which White and Blackmun, JJ. joined.

See, Robert Sedler, The Unconstitutionality of Campus Bans on "Racist Speech:" The View from Without and Within, 53 U.Pittsburgh L.Rev. 631 (1992); Ronald D.

Rotunda, A Brief Comment on Politically Incorrect Speech in the Wake of R.A.V., 47 So. Methodist U.L.Rev. 9 (1993); William Van Alstyne, The University in the Manner of Tiananmen Square, 21 Hastings Const. L. Q.1 (1993).

34. Virginia v. Black, 538 U.S. 343, 123 S.Ct. 1536, 1546.

35. 538 U.S. at ___, 123 S.Ct. at 1548.

36. 538 U.S. ___, 123 S.Ct. 1536, 1549.

37. E.g., State v. Miller, 6 Kan.App.2d 432, 629 P.2d 748 (1981) (defendant burned a cross in the yard of the lawyer who had previously represented him and who was currently prosecuting him).

dation. Instead of prohibiting all intimidating messages, Virginia may choose to regulate this subset of intimidating messages in light of cross burning's long and pernicious history as a signal of impending violence.[38]

The flaw in the Virginia cross burning statute was the court's interpretation that allowed the state to secure a conviction merely by proving the cross burning. A "burning cross is not always intended to intimidate." It may be "a statement of ideology, a symbol of group solidarity. It is a ritual used at Klan gatherings, and it is used to represent the Klan itself."[39] As Justice White said in *R.A.V.*, a cross burning "at a political rally would almost certainly be protected expression."[40] Cross burnings, when they appear in movies such as *Mississippi Burning*, and in plays, like the stage adaptation of Sir Walter Scott's *The Lady of the Lake*, are not intended to intimidate.[41]

The Court reversed the conviction because the law as interpreted: "does not distinguish between a cross burning at a public rally or a cross burning on a neighbor's lawn. It does not treat the cross burning directed at an individual differently from the cross burning directed at a group of like-minded believers."[42]

This opinion drew several separate opinions. Justice Thomas, for example, concluded that, "A conclusion that the statute prohibiting cross burning with intent to intimidate sweeps beyond a prohibition on certain conduct into the zone of expression overlooks not only the words of the statute but also reality," given the history of the Ku Klux Klan.[43]

§ 16.40 Fighting Words, Hostile Audiences, and the Problem of Vagueness and Overbreadth

In addition to the explicit limitations that *Cohen* and *R.A.V.* placed on *Chaplinsky,* other cases also indicate that the Court does not look with favor on prosecutions for "fighting words."[1] The Court has often employed the vagueness and overbreadth standards to avoid upholding convictions. Thus, in *Gooding v. Wilson,*[2] the defendant addressed a policeman, "you son of a bitch I'll choke you to death." Similarly, in *Lewis v. City of New Orleans,*[3] the defendant said "you goddamn motherfucking police." The Court overturned both convictions because the statutes were vague and overbroad.

Gooding stated that convictions may be upheld under the *Chaplinsky* standard,[4] if the statute is narrowly drawn or construed. The Court then went on to conduct its own examination of state case law. The state decisions did not really limit the statute "to words that 'have a direct tendency to cause acts of violence by the person to whom individually, the remark is addressed.' "[5] And, in *Lewis* the Court made clear that words conveying or intended to convey disgrace are not "fighting words."[6]

Norwell v. City of Cincinnati[7] refused to uphold the conviction of one "verbally and negatively" protesting his arrest. Also, in *Hess v. Indiana*[8] the Court held the speaker's statement during an antiwar protest that "We'll take the fucking street later" was constitutionally protected. Like the situation in *Cohen,* the words were not aimed at anyone in particular. There was no face-to-face, eyeball to eyeball encounter.

---

38. 538 U.S. ___, 123 S.Ct. 1536, 1549.

39. 538 U.S. at ___, 123 S.Ct. at 1551.

40. R.A.V. v. St. Paul, 505 U.S., at 402, n. 4, 112 S.Ct. 2538 (White, J., concurring in judgment).

41. 538 U.S. at ___, 123 S.Ct. at 1551.

42. 538 U.S. at ___, 123 S.Ct. at 1551.

43. Virginia v. Black, 538 U.S. at ___, 123 S.Ct. at 1563 (2003).

§ 16.40

1. Newbern, J., concurring and dissenting in part and citing Treatise, in Bailey v. State, 334 Ark. 43, 972 S.W.2d 239 (Ark.1998).

2. 405 U.S. 518, 92 S.Ct. 1103, 31 L.Ed.2d 408 (1972).

3. 415 U.S. 130, 94 S.Ct. 970, 39 L.Ed.2d 214 (1974).

4. 405 U.S. 518, 523, 92 S.Ct. 1103, 1106–07, 31 L.Ed.2d 408 (1972).

5. Gooding v. Wilson, 405 U.S. 518, 524, 92 S.Ct. 1103, 1107, 31 L.Ed.2d 408 (1972).

6. 415 U.S. 130, 133, 94 S.Ct. 970, 972, 39 L.Ed.2d 214 (1974).

7. 414 U.S. 14, 94 S.Ct. 187, 38 L.Ed.2d 170 (1973).

8. 414 U.S. 105, 94 S.Ct. 326, 38 L.Ed.2d 303 (1973).

Similarly, *Dawson v. Delaware*[9] held that, in a capital sentencing proceeding, the First Amendment prohibits the introduction of evidence that the defendant was a member of an organization called the Aryan Brotherhood, a white racist organization, because the evidence had no relevance to the issues being decided. Both defendant and victim were white, so no element of racial hatred was involved in the murder. The evidence showed nothing more than the defendant's abstract beliefs, where those beliefs had no bearing on the issue being tried.

If the "fighting words" doctrine is still alive, the Court will carefully scrutinize any convictions under it. Justice Blackmun complained in his dissent in *Gooding v. Wilson*,[10] that "the Court, despite its protestations to the contrary, is merely paying lip service to *Chaplinsky*."[11] *R.A.V. v. City of St. Paul*[12] indicates that the Court will not allow content based restrictions on speech even though the state seeks to justify the restrictions by the fighting words doctrine.

Similarly, while the Court has never overruled *Feiner,* it has repeatedly distinguished it[13] and not allowed the state to prosecute speakers for breach of the peace simply because the speech was before a hostile audience. Words are "fighting words" when they are an offer to exchange fisticuffs.[14] But the state should not punish a person because others (who don't like his mental attitude) engage in violence against him. This "breach of the peace theory is peculiarly liable to abuse when applied against unpopular expressions and practices," because it makes a person "a criminal simply because his neighbors have no self-control and cannot refrain from violence."[15]

§ 16.41 Introduction—The Freedom to Associate and Not to Associate

The Right of Association as Derived From Freedom of Speech and Assembly. In *NAACP v. Alabama ex rel. Patterson*,[1] a unanimous Court, speaking through Justice Harlan, enunciated a right of association. The Court held that Alabama could not compel the National Association for the Advancement of Colored People to reveal to the state's Attorney General the names and addresses of all of its Alabama members without regard to their positions and functions in the NAACP. The NAACP showed that compelled disclosure of its rank and file members on past occasions exposed them to economic reprisal, loss of employment, threat of physical coercion, and general public hostility. The NAACP was not an organization with illegal ends,[2] and its nondisclosure interest directly related to the right of the members of pursue their lawful interests privately.

In the course of its opinion, the Court announced in clearest form the right of association:

> Effective advocacy of both public and private points of view, particularly controversial ones, is undeniably enhanced by group asso-

---

9. 503 U.S. 159, 112 S.Ct. 1093, 117 L.Ed.2d 309 (1992), on remand 608 A.2d 1201 (Del.1992). Chief Justice Rehnquist wrote the opinion for the Court. Blackmun, J. filed a concurring opinion. Thomas, J., dissented.

10. 405 U.S. 518, 92 S.Ct. 1103, 31 L.Ed.2d 408 (1972).

11. 405 U.S. at 537, 92 S.Ct. at 1113 (Blackmun, J., dissenting).

12. 505 U.S. 377, 112 S.Ct. 2538, 120 L.Ed.2d 305 (1992), discussed above.

13. E.g., Gregory v. City of Chicago, 394 U.S. 111, 89 S.Ct. 946, 22 L.Ed.2d 134 (1969) (civil rights demonstration); see also, Cox v. Louisiana, 379 U.S. 536, 551, 85 S.Ct. 453, 462, 13 L.Ed.2d 471 (1965) (citing *Feiner* but distinguishing it as a "far cry" from the civil rights demonstration involved in the instant case); Bachellar v. Maryland, 397 U.S. 564, 567, 90 S.Ct. 1312, 1314, 25 L.Ed.2d 570 (1970) (antiwar demonstration); Edwards v. South Carolina, 372 U.S. 229, 236, 83 S.Ct. 680, 684, 9 L.Ed.2d 697 (1963) (civil rights demonstration; a "far cry from the situation . . ." in *Feiner*).

14. Daniel J., quoting Treatise, in Local Organizing Committee, Denver Chapter, Million Man March v. Cook, 922 F.Supp. 1494, 1500, 109 Ed. Law Rep. 223 (D.Colo. 1996).

15. Z. Chaffee, Free Speech in the United States 151–52 (1942).

§ 16.41

1. 357 U.S. 449, 78 S.Ct. 1163, 2 L.Ed.2d 1488 (1958).

2. The Court so distinguished Bryant v. Zimmerman, 278 U.S. 63, 49 S.Ct. 61, 73 L.Ed. 184 (1928) which upheld a New York State requirement of disclosure of the roster of membership of all unincorporated associations that required an oath as a condition to membership, as applied to the Ku Klux Klan, an organization that required an oath of its members. See 357 U.S. at 465, 78 S.Ct. at 1173.

ciation, as this Court has more than once recognized by remarking upon the close nexus between the freedoms of speech and assembly. [F]reedom to engage in association for the advancement of beliefs and ideas is an inseparable aspect of the "liberty" assured by the Due Process Clause of the Fourteenth Amendment, which embraces freedom of speech. Of course, it is immaterial whether the beliefs sought to be advanced by association pertain to political, economic, religious or cultural matters, and state action which may have the effect of curtailing the freedom to associate is subject to the closest scrutiny.[3]

The Three Separate Aspects of the Right of Association. Since *NAACP v. Alabama ex rel. Patterson*,[4] the Supreme Court has examined at least three separate aspects of the right to associate or to refuse to associate, though later case development may reveal a wide variety of other types or variations of associational rights beyond these three categories.

First, individuals might associate to achieve economic or other goals that are unconnected to any fundamental constitutional right. For example, individuals may join together in labor unions or trade associations. This ability to control one's economic associations is a part of the liberty protected by due process, but the Court has refused to substitute its judgment for the legislature's as to the legitimate basis for restricting such types of association. So long as the legislature is rationally promoting an arguably legitimate government goal by restricting the activities of a business association, the Court will not invalidate this legislation.[5]

A second type of freedom to associate is protected by the concept of liberty in the due process clauses and as an implicit part of the Bill of Rights guarantees; this right is connected to the fundamental right to privacy. The type of association declared to be a fundamental right connected to the concept of privacy includes the freedom to choose one's spouse[6] and to maintain a relationship with members of one's family. The rationale for protecting these relationships could provide a basis for active judicial review of laws restricting the ability of persons to enter into other highly personal associations.[7]

Third, the Court has recognized a right to associate for the purpose of engaging in types of activity expressly protected by the First Amendment.[8] For example, the ability to associate for religious purposes clearly cannot be restricted by the state unless the state is pursuing a compelling interest and acting in conformity with the Court's definition of religious freedom. The exercise of other First Amendment rights, such as speech or assembly, of necessity involves association with other persons either physically or in organizations designed to promote expressive activity.

The Court has deduced the right to associate for expressive activity from the express guarantees found in the First Amendment. The government cannot limit this right to associate unless the limitation serves a compelling governmental interest unrelated to the suppression of ideas and this governmental interest cannot be furthered through means that are significantly less restrictive of the associational or expressive freedom. In other words, the regulation of association must be narrowly tailored to promote an end that is unrelated to suppressing the message that will be advanced

---

3. NAACP v. Alabama, 357 U.S. 449, 460–61, 78 S.Ct. 1163, 1171, 2 L.Ed.2d 1488 (1958) (internal citations omitted without indication).

4. 357 U.S. 449, 78 S.Ct. 1163, 2 L.Ed.2d 1488 (1958).

5. Railway Mail Ass'n v. Corsi, 326 U.S. 88, 93–94, 65 S.Ct. 1483, 1487, 89 L.Ed. 2072 (1945) (upholding state law prohibiting labor organization from denying membership to persons because of their race). Brickley, C.J., citing Treatise, in Michigan State AFL–CIO v. Employment Relations Commission, 453 Mich. 362, 375, 551 N.W.2d 165, 171 (1996); Levin, J., concurring, citing Treatise, in Michi-

gan State AFL–CIO v. Employment Relations Commission, 453 Mich. 362, 399, 551 N.W.2d 165, 181 (1996).

6. Loving v. Virginia, 388 U.S. 1, 87 S.Ct. 1817, 18 L.Ed.2d 1010 (1967).

7. Moore v. City of East Cleveland, 431 U.S. 494, 97 S.Ct. 1932, 52 L.Ed.2d 531 (1977) (plurality opinion) (constitutional protection of family relationships extends beyond nuclear family).

8. See Judge Doty, citing Treatise in, Cornerstone Bible Church v. City of Hastings, 740 F.Supp. 654, 663 (D.Minn.1990).

by the association and is unrelated to suppressing the association because of government disapproval of its purposes.

The *Roberts* Decision. In some instances the precise type of associational right that is asserted in a case may not be easily categorized, but the Court must consider the nature of the right in order to determine the validity of governmental restrictions at issue. The Court's diagnosis of the type of associational freedom at issue will dictate the position it should take in determining how much, if any, deference it owes the legislative or executive branches of government in the particular case.

Consider, for example, *Roberts v. United States Jaycees.*[9] The Court reviewed a state law and state administrative action that prohibited a state branch of a national nonprofit corporation from refusing to grant full membership rights to women solely because of their sex. The seven Justices who voted in this case were unanimous in upholding the state's ability to restrict this right of association, but there was some difficulty in identifying the correct standard of review that should be employed in this case. Justice Brennan spoke for the majority. He explained that the cases protect "freedom of association" in two distinct senses.

FIRST, to secure individual liberty, the Bill of Rights "must afford the formation and preservation of certain kinds of highly personal relationships a substantial measure of sanctuary from unjustified interference by the State."[10] This type of freedom of association is related to the fundamental right of privacy that protects family relationships and personal decisions regarding such matters as childbirth and abortion.

This type of association is relatively small, highly selective, and, in its nature, almost exclusive because they concern highly personal relationships. On the other extreme would be a large business enterprise, which seems remote from this constitutional protection of association. The Constitution "undoubtedly imposes constraints on the State's power to control the selection of one's spouse that would not apply to regulations affecting the choice of one's fellow employees."[11] There is a range of relationships between the most intimate, which embrace the fundamental right to privacy, and the non-intimate, economic associations, for which there is very little constitutional protection. The Jaycees were "outside of the category of relationships worthy of this kind of constitutional protection" because the organization was a "large and basically unselective" organization designed to promote commercial activity, community programs, and award ceremonies.[12]

SECOND, there is the freedom of the association to choose its membership. Limitations on the organization's ability to choose its members should be subjected to significant review under the First Amendment because the Jaycees were organized in part for the purpose of expressive activity. The courts could not vigorously protect an individual's freedom to speak, to worship, and to petition the Government for the redress of grievances unless there exists a correlative freedom to engage in group effort toward those ends. Thus, implicit in the right to engage in activities protected by the First Amendment is "a corresponding right to associate with others in pursuit of a wide variety of political, social, economic, educational, religious, and cultural ends."[13]

The Court found that this right of association is not absolute and that infringements may be justified by regulations adopted to serve "compelling state interests, unrelated to the suppression of ideas, that cannot be achieved through means significantly less restrictive of associational freedoms."[14]

The Court upheld the state law requiring the Jaycees to admit women to full membership because the state interest in guaranteeing equal access to publicly available goods and

---

9. 468 U.S. 609, 104 S.Ct. 3244, 82 L.Ed.2d 462 (1984) (Chief Justice Burger and Justice Blackmun did not participate in this decision).

10. 468 U.S. at 619, 104 S.Ct. at 3250.

11. 468 U.S. at 621, 104 S.Ct. at 3251.

12. 468 U.S. at 621, 104 S.Ct. at 3251.

13. 468 U.S. at 623, 104 S.Ct. at 3252.

14. 468 U.S. at 623, 104 S.Ct. at 3252.

services without racial or sex discrimination was among "compelling state" interests of the highest order. In addition to advancing a compelling state interest, the state demonstrated that its regulation was the least restrictive means of achieving its end because it did not impose serious burdens on the male members' freedom of expressive association.[15]

To be sure, the determination of who would be a member in the association was a significant restriction on the Jaycees' associational freedom, but the state law did not affect what the Jaycees must believe or could promote. The law "requires no change in the Jaycees' creed of promoting the interests of young men, and it imposes no restrictions on the organization's ability to exclude individuals with ideologies or philosophies different from those of its existing members."[16] Any incidental abridgement of the speech of the organization was "no greater than is necessary to accomplish the State's legitimate purposes"[17] of eliminating sex or racial discrimination in the distribution of public services.

Justice O'Connor wrote an astute concurring opinion in *Roberts*. She believed that the Court must determine whether the organization was significantly dedicated to First Amendment activity or whether it was primarily a commercial organization that only incidentally exercised First Amendment[18] rights. She realized that "[m]any associations cannot readily be described as purely expressive or purely commercial"; she was more insightful than the majority in realizing that the key decision to be made in such cases is whether the state need have more than a rational basis

for regulating an association's membership practices.

O'Connor was correct in noting that subjecting every regulation of organizational activity to a meaningful form of review under the First Amendment, even under a sliding scale of First Amendment associational interests, presented an unnecessary judicial hurdle for a legislature to clear in order to demand an end to discrimination in the membership practices of commercial organizations. A sliding scale also has a very *ad hoc*, unprincipled quality. The Court, she noted, should establish a strong presumption of validity for regulations of commercial organizations even though the Court also should "give substance to the ideal of complete protection for purely expressive association, even while it readily permits state regulation of commercial affairs." She would allow regulation of the association's membership practices under a due process, rational basis standard "when, and only when, the association's activities are not predominantly of the type protected by the First Amendment."[19]

One who chooses to speak also has the right to decide what not to say. This is a crucial right derived from free speech and the right of association. Nothing in *Roberts* undermines this important principle. The *Roberts* Court made quite clear that application of the state law imposed no restrictions on the right of an organization to exclude members based on their ideology. Thus, the state cannot require the organizers of a parade celebrating the NAACP to admit the KKK with its own float, anymore than the state could require a KKK parade to include a float celebrating the NAACP.[20] The choice of a speaker to pro-

---

15. 468 U.S. at 626, 104 S.Ct. at 3254.

16. 468 U.S. at 626, 104 S.Ct. at 3254.

17. 468 U.S. at 628, 104 S.Ct. at 3255.

18. She admitted: "[M]any associations cannot readily be described as purely expressive or purely commercial." 468 U.S. at 635, 104 S.Ct. at 3259 (O'Connor, J., concurring in part and concurring in the judgment).

19. 468 U.S. at 635, 104 S.Ct. at 3259.

20. **First Amendment Right of Parade Organizers to Select Parade Marchers.** Hurley v. Irish–American Gay, Lesbian and Bisexual Group of Boston, 515 U.S. 557, 115 S.Ct. 2338, 132 L.Ed.2d 487 (1995)(unanimous decision). Private citizens in Boston organized an annual

St. Patrick's Day parade. The Irish–American Gay, Lesbian and Bisexual Group of Boston, called GLIB, wanted to march in the parade in order to express pride in their Irish heritage and in the sexual orientation of GLIB's members. The parade organizers did not want to include GLIB because it wanted to convey a message that the organizers of the parade did not wish to convey.

The facts showed that the parade organizers did not exclude homosexuals from participating in the parade, and they disavowed any intention of doing so. The only question is whether state law could constitutionally require the parade organizers to admit GLIB with its own parade unit carrying its own banner. Every participating unit in a parade affects the message conveyed by the private orga-

pound, or not to propound, a particular point of view is a choice that is beyond the power of government to control.

The Continuum of Associational Rights. Perhaps it is best to think of associational rights as proceeding on a continuum from the least protected form of association in commercial activities to the most protected forms of association to engage in political or religious speech or for highly personal reasons, such as family relationships. The association of persons for law practice may be regulated to prohibit discrimination on the basis of sex or race.[21] Regulations of law practice that relate to the ability of persons to associate for the advancement of social goals, however, may be protected to a greater extent from governmental regulation.[22]

A boycott for political purposes may receive significant First Amendment protection, although a similar boycott for the purposes of maintaining a preferred economic position for one's business or union may receive very little protection.[23] A prohibition of race or sex discrimination in the employment practices of commercial enterprises or in the admissions practices of schools open to a wide segment of the public should not present significant freedom of association problems.[24] A similar restriction on the membership practices of a religious organization that was highly selective in its membership and dedicated to goals totally inconsistent with the acceptance of members of a particular race or sex might present a more significant freedom of associational problem even if the Court were to find that the goal of ending that form of discrimination would override associational rights.[25] This right of association takes many forms, as *Roberts* recognized.

Student Organizations. A state college cannot deny official recognition (and the loss of privilege to distribute literature on campus and other such privileges that such denial entails) to a student organization because of its parent organization's history.[26]

Group Activity to Obtain Counsel. Under the freedom of association the Court has struck down laws that prevented the NAACP from assisting individuals[27] and that prevented a labor union from assisting its members[28] in

---

nizers. The state law, in essence, ordered parade organizers to alter the expressive content of their parade, and this the state cannot do.

Accord, Boy Scouts of America v. Dale, 10 530 U.S. 640, 120 S.Ct. 2446, 147 L.Ed.2d 554 (2000), holding that New Jersey may not constitutionally apply its public accommodations law to require the Boy Scouts to admit a publicly declared homosexual as a scoutmaster because doing so would violate the Boy Scouts' First Amendment right of expressive association.

21. Hishon v. King & Spalding, 467 U.S. 69, 104 S.Ct. 2229, 81 L.Ed.2d 59 (1984).

22. See, e.g., NAACP v. Button, 371 U.S. 415, 83 S.Ct. 328, 9 L.Ed.2d 405 (1963) (holding ban on solicitation of legal business invalid as applied to NAACP activity in financing desegregation litigation).

Group activity regarding commercial litigation is also protected by the freedom of association. See Brotherhood of R. R. Trainmen v. Virginia, 377 U.S. 1, 84 S.Ct. 1113, 12 L.Ed.2d 89 (1964), rehearing denied 377 U.S. 960, 84 S.Ct. 1625, 12 L.Ed.2d 505 (1964), on remand to 207 Va. 182, 149 S.E.2d 265 (1966), certiorari denied 385 U.S. 1027, 87 S.Ct. 754, 17 L.Ed.2d 675 (1967); United Mine Workers, Dist. 12 v. Illinois State Bar Ass'n, 389 U.S. 217, 88 S.Ct. 353, 19 L.Ed.2d 426 (1967); United Transportation Union v. Michigan State Bar, 401 U.S. 576, 91 S.Ct. 1076, 28 L.Ed.2d 339 (1971).

23. Compare NAACP v. Claiborne Hardware Co., 458 U.S. 886, 102 S.Ct. 3409, 73 L.Ed.2d 1215 (1982), rehearing denied 459 U.S. 898, 103 S.Ct. 199, 74 L.Ed.2d 160

(1982) (boycott of stores organized to influence government practices held to be activity protected by the First Amendment), with NLRB v. Retail Store Employees Union, Local 1001, 447 U.S. 607, 100 S.Ct. 2372, 65 L.Ed.2d 377 (1980) (labor union picket line advocating boycott of secondary employer is prohibited).

24. See Runyon v. McCrary, 427 U.S. 160, 96 S.Ct. 2586, 49 L.Ed.2d 415 (1976), appeal after remand 569 F.2d 1294 (4th Cir.1978), certiorari denied 439 U.S. 927, 99 S.Ct. 311, 58 L.Ed.2d 320 (1978).

25. See Runyon v. McCrary, 427 U.S. 160, 188–89, 96 S.Ct. 2586, 2603, 49 L.Ed.2d 415 (1976), appeal after remand 569 F.2d 1294 (4th Cir.1978), certiorari denied 439 U.S. 927, 99 S.Ct. 311, 58 L.Ed.2d 320 (1978) (Powell, J., concurring).

26. Healy v. James, 408 U.S. 169, 92 S.Ct. 2338, 33 L.Ed.2d 266 (1972).

27. NAACP v. Button, 371 U.S. 415, 429–30, 83 S.Ct. 328, 336–37, 9 L.Ed.2d 405 (1963).

28. Brotherhood of R. R. Trainmen v. Virginia, 377 U.S. 1, 84 S.Ct. 1113, 12 L.Ed.2d 89 (1964), rehearing denied 377 U.S. 960, 84 S.Ct. 1625, 12 L.Ed.2d 505 (1964), on remand to 207 Va. 182, 149 S.E.2d 265 (1966), certiorari denied 385 U.S. 1027, 87 S.Ct. 754, 17 L.Ed.2d 675 (1967); United Mine Workers v. Illinois State Bar Ass'n, 389 U.S. 217, 88 S.Ct. 353, 19 L.Ed.2d 426 (1967); United Transportation Union v. State Bar of Michigan, 401 U.S. 576, 91 S.Ct. 1076, 28 L.Ed.2d 339 (1971).

hiring lawyers to assert the legal rights of these individuals.

Political Parties. The freedom of association allows political parties, within certain bounds, to regulate the selection of delegates to their national conventions even when such regulations are contrary to state law[29] because there must be a limit on the extraterritorial effect of *state* laws that seek to impose conflicting delegate selection rules on *national* conventions.

There is a broader power of states to regulate political parties that are entirely within the state's jurisdiction, though even here, the Supreme Court has placed some limits based on the freedom of association. State laws must sweep no broader than necessary.[30] The leading case is *Tashjian v. Republican Party of Connecticut.*[31]

The Court (five to four), invalidated a state law to the extent that it conflicted with a Connecticut Republican Party rule that permitted *independent* voters to vote in Republican primaries for federal and state-wide offices. The state *law* provided for a closed primary; the Republican party *rules* provided for an open primary for federal and state-

wide offices but a closed primary for other offices (e.g., state legislator, mayor). State law provided that any previously unaffiliated voter may become eligible to vote in the Party's primary simply by enrolling as a Party member as late as noon on the last business day preceding the primary. The Court, surprisingly, never cited *Roberts v. United States Jaycees,*[32] but said that the Connecticut law violated freedom of association.

In 1976 a three judge court had upheld the Connecticut law when an independent voter sought a declaratory judgment that he had a right to vote in the Republican primary. The Supreme Court summarily affirmed that decision in *Nader v. Schaffer.*[33] Several years later the Republican state convention adopted new rules allowing independents to vote in the Republican Party so long as their ballots were limited to federal and state-wide offices (but not other offices, such as mayor, or state representative).[34] The State of Connecticut refused to change its primary laws, so the Party sued.

The Supreme Court specifically approved of its 1976 decision upholding the closed primary, but Justice Marshall, speaking for the Court,

29. See, Democratic Party v. Wisconsin ex rel. La Follette, 450 U.S. 107, 101 S.Ct. 1010, 67 L.Ed.2d 82 (1981). See Chambers & Rotunda, Reform of the Presidential Nominating Conventions, 56 Virginia Law Review 179 (1970); Rotunda Constitutional and Statutory Restrictions on Political Parties in the Wake of Cousins v. Wigoda, 53 Texas Law Review 935 (1975).

30. E.g., Norman v. Reed, 502 U.S. 279, 112 S.Ct. 698, 116 L.Ed.2d 711 (1992), on remand 154 Ill.2d 77, 180 Ill.Dec. 685, 607 N.E.2d 1198 (1992), cert. denied 509 U.S. 906, 113 S.Ct. 3000, 125 L.Ed.2d 693 (1993), invalidated an Illinois statute that broadly prohibited a new party from bearing the name of an established party. The established political party in this case was a third party, called the Harold Washington Party (HWP). The state argued that the purpose of the law was to prevent persons not associated with the party to latch on to its name, causing voter confusion and denigrating party cohesiveness. But the state supreme court read this law so rigidly that it was interpreted to bar candidates running in one political subdivision from using the name of a political party established in another, even if the HWP had authorized the use of the HWP name. The state court's inhospitable reading of the statute sweeps broader than necessary to advance electoral order and therefore violates the First Amendment right of political association.

31. 479 U.S. 208, 107 S.Ct. 544, 93 L.Ed.2d 514 (1986). See also, Eu v. San Francisco County Democratic Central Committee, 489 U.S. 214, 109 S.Ct. 1013, 103 L.Ed.2d 271

(1989), where a unanimous Court invalidated provisions of the California election code that prohibited official governing bodies of political parties from endorsing candidates in party primaries, and dictated the organization and composition of political parties. California could not show that the law advanced a compelling state interest and was narrowly tailored to serve that interest.

32. 468 U.S. 609, 104 S.Ct. 3244, 82 L.Ed.2d 462 (1984).

33. 429 U.S. 989, 97 S.Ct. 516, 50 L.Ed.2d 602 (1976), summarily affirming 417 F.Supp. 837 (D.Conn.1976).

34. The motivation behind this change appeared to be grounded in the fact that U.S. Senator Weicker from Connecticut, in a reelection bid, was concerned that he could not win a primary without an influx of non-Republican voters. (Plaintiffs' admissions, in Joint Appendix at 124–127). Other Republican candidates did not want independents voting in their primary, and so a compromise was reached with independents limited to voting for *state-wide* offices. Weicker subsequently won the Republican primary but still lost his reelection bid for the Senate (in an election where many Republicans publicly supported his Democratic opponent). Later, in 1990, Weicker, running as an independent, was elected Governor of Connecticut.

argued that the earlier case was distinguishable because it was brought by independent voters, not by the Republican Party itself. In *Nader*, "the nonmember's desire to participate in the party's affairs is overborne by the countervailing and legitimate right of the party to determine its own membership."[35] The Republican Party itself objects that the state law "impermissibly burdens the rights of the members to determine for themselves with whom they will associate, and whose support they will seek, in their quest for political success. The Party's attempt to broaden the base of public participation in and support for its activities is conduct undeniably central to the exercise of the right of association."[36]

The Court then added a significant narrowing footnote:

> Our holding today does not establish that state regulation of primary voting qualifications may never withstand challenge by a political party or its membership. A party seeking, for example, to open its primary to all voters, including members of other parties, would raise a different combination of considerations. Under such circumstances, the effect of one party's broadening of participation would threaten other parties with the disorganization effects which the statutes were designed to prevent. We have observed on several occasions that a State may adopt a "policy of confining each voter to a single nominating act," a policy decision which is not involved in the present case. The analysis of these situations derives much from the particular facts involved....[37]

35. 479 U.S. at 215 n. 6, 107 S.Ct. at 549 n. 6.

36. 479 U.S. at 215, 107 S.Ct. at 549.

37. 479 U.S. at 225 n. 13, 107 S.Ct. at 554 n. 13.

38. 479 U.S. at 234, 107 S.Ct. at 559 (emphasis in original).

39. 479 U.S. at 236–37, 107 S.Ct. at 560–61 (emphasis in original).

The Qualifications Clause of the Seventeenth Amendment. The majority also held that the implementation of Party rules—which established qualifications for voting for congressional elections that differ from the voting qualifications in elections for the more numerous house of the state legislature—did not violate the Qualifications Clause, art. I, § 2, cl. 1, and the Seventeenth

Justice Scalia, joined by Chief Justice Rehnquist, and Justice O'Connor, dissented and objected to the majority's freedom of association rationale: "Appellees only complaint is that the Party cannot leave the selection of its candidates to persons who are *not* members of the Party, and are unwilling to become members. It seems to me fanciful to refer to this as an interest in freedom of association between the members of the Republican Party and the putative independent voters."[38] This "associational" interest is based on only casual contact between Republican and nonRepublicans. These nonRepublicans do not even wish to be called "Republicans." Moreover—"*even if* it were the fact that the majority of the Party's members wanted its candidates to be determined by outsiders, there is no reason why the State is bound to honor that desire—any more than it would be bound to honor a party's democratically expressed desire that its candidates henceforth be selected by convention rather than by primary, or by the party's executive committee in a smoke-filled room."[39]

Prohibition of Fusion Candidates and Protecting the Two Party System. "Fusion" is the nomination of two or more political parties of one candidate for the same office at the same political parties of one candidate for the same office at the same general election. In 1946, for example, Earl Warren (later Chief Justice of the U.S. Supreme Court) was the nominee for Governor of both the Democratic and Republican Parties. Because he won both primaries, he ran unopposed in the general election. During the end of the nineteenth century, most states banned fusion candidates; the parties in power did not want the competi-

Amendment. Primaries are subject to these clauses, the Court said, but the purpose of those clauses are satisfied "if all those qualified to participate in the selection of members of the more numerous branch of the state legislature are also qualified to participate in the election of Senators and Members of the House of Representatives." There is no need for "perfect symmetry." 479 U.S. at 227–29, 107 S.Ct. at 555–56. Justice Stevens, joined by Scalia, J., dissented: "The Court nevertheless separates the federal qualifications from their state counterparts, inexplicably treating the mandatory 'shall have' language of the clauses as though it means only that the federal voters 'may but need not have' the qualifications of state voters." 479 U.S. at 230, 107 S.Ct. at 557.

tion of third parties that would pose if they could shift support to a major party candidate. New York State is the major jurisdiction that allows fusion candidates.

Timmons v. Twin Cities Area New Party[40] held that it was constitutional for Minnesota to prohibit candidates from appearing on the ballot of more than one political party, even though the candidate in that case agreed to be nominated by the Democratic–Farmer–Labor Party (a major party); in addition, the New Party (a third party) wanted to nominate the same candidate and the Democratic–Farmer–Labor Party (which had already nominated him) did not object to this dual nomination. Chief Justice Rehnquist, for the Court, concluded that the burden on the New Party was not severe (the New Party could endorse the candidate even it could not nominate him), and that therefore the state need not assert any compelling state interest and no need for the state to offer any elaborate empirical justification of the state's asserted justification. The state argued that it needed to restrict ballot access to make sure that the ballot was not too complicated, although a demonstrated-support requirement would also serve to meet this interest.

In addition, the Court relied on another justification: the need to protect the two-party system.—to encourage political stability and help preserve the two-party system in order to "temper the destabilizing effects of party-shattering and excessive factionalism."[41] States

may not prevent third parties from forming, but they "need not remove all of the many hurdles third parties face in the American political arena today."[42] In the past the Court has not accepted this asserted need to preserve a two-party system as a justification for ballot access by third parties.[43] The present rule, therefore, is that it is a legitimate goal of the state to seek to preserve a two-party system, and to do that the state may place some hurdles (but not too many hurdles) in front of third parties. The state, in short, may give the two major parties some assistance but may not give them a de facto monopoly.

The Right Not to Associate. The right of association raises the issue of the right not to associate. If the state requires an individual to join an organization—for example a union, as a requirement to work, or a state bar, as a requirement in some states to practice law— may, that organization, consistent with the freedom of association, use the dues required of its members to advance causes not favored by all of the members?[44]

Abood v. Detroit Board of Education[45] held that the state may require a public worker to pay dues or a service fee equal to dues insofar as the money is used to finance expenditures by the union for the purposes of collective bargaining, contract administration, and grievance adjustment. But, under the First Amendment, the workers may not be compelled to contribute to political candidates, and the

---

40. 520 U.S. 351, 117 S.Ct. 1364, 137 L.Ed.2d 589 (1997). Rehnquist, C.J., wrote the opinion for the Court. Stevens, J., filed a dissenting opinion joined by Ginsburg, J., and, in part, by Souter, J. Souter, J., also filed a separate dissenting opinion.

41. Timmons v. Twin Cities Area New Party, 520 U.S. at 367, 117 S.Ct. at 1374.

42. 520 U.S. at 367, & n. 10, 117 S.Ct. at 1374 & n. 10.

43. Williams v. Rhodes, 393 U.S. 23, 31–32, 89 S.Ct. 5, 10, 21 L.Ed.2d 24 (1968), noting—and not accepting—Ohio's "claims that the State may validly promote a two-party system in order to encourage compromise and political stability." In context, the Court in *Rhodes* found the restrictions on ballot access too severe. "The fact is, however, that the Ohio system does not merely favor a 'two-party system'; it favors two particular parties—the Republicans and the Democrats—and in effect tends to give them a monopoly." Id.

44. International Ass'n of Machinists v. Street, 367 U.S. 740, 81 S.Ct. 1784, 6 L.Ed.2d 1141 (1961), on remand

to 217 Ga. 351, 122 S.E.2d 220 (1961) (statute construed to avoid association issue by holding that union dues money could only be used, under the statute, to support collective bargaining and not to support political causes); Lathrop v. Donohue, 367 U.S. 820, 81 S.Ct. 1826, 6 L.Ed.2d 1191 (1961), rehearing denied 368 U.S. 871, 82 S.Ct. 23, 7 L.Ed.2d 72 (1961) (integrated bar; issue of whether dues money could constitutionally be used to support causes opposed by a member not reached by the Court). In both of these cases Harlan and Frankfurter, JJ., would have reached the issue and *allowed* the compelled dues money to be spent for causes not approved by the involuntary members. Douglas and Black, JJ., also would have reached the issue but they would have found this use of dues unconstitutional.

45. 431 U.S. 209, 97 S.Ct. 1782, 52 L.Ed.2d 261 (1977), rehearing denied 433 U.S. 915, 97 S.Ct. 2989, 53 L.Ed.2d 1102 (1977).

workers may constitutionally prevent the union's spending a part of its required fees to contribute to political candidates and to express political views unrelated to its duties as exclusive bargaining representative.

Similarly, *Keller v. State Bar of California*[46] unanimously held that the State Bar of California may not constitutionally use *compulsory* dues to finance political and ideological causes that the petitioners oppose. The California Bar was an "integrated bar" or a "unified bar," that is, an association created by state law, to which lawyers must join and pay dues as a condition of practicing law.

The State Bar may only use compulsory due to finance regulation of the legal profession or improve the quality of legal services (for example, bar dues may be used to propose ethical codes or discipline Bar members), not to promote political or ideological activities (for example, to endorse gun control or nuclear freeze initiatives). While it is true that government officials are expected, as a part of the democratic process, to represent and to espouse the views of a majority of their constituents, the State Bar of California is not part of the general government of California, even though state law creates it, and requires lawyers to join it. The State Bar is more analogous to a labor union representing public and private employees, and therefore it should be subject to the same constitutional rule in order to protect free speech and free association interests.

In *Board of Regents of the University of Wisconsin System v. Southworth*,[47] the Court did *not* apply *Keller*, because the fact situation involved student speech at a university. Students sued the University claiming that the mandatory student activity fee violated their Constitutional rights of free speech, free association, and free exercise, unless the University would give them the choice *not to fund* organizations (such as, *e.g.*, the International Socialist Organization, the College Democrats and College Republicans) that engaged in political and ideological expression offensive to

their personal beliefs. This time, the Court, speaking through Justice Kennedy, disagreed and ruled that a public university, unlike the State Bar, may charge its students an activity fee to fund a program to facilitate extracurricular speech "if the program is viewpoint neutral."

The University of Wisconsin required registered student organizations (RSO) to obtain a portion of the allocable fees in one of three ways: (1) from the Student Government Activity Fund (SGAF), (2) from the General Student Services Fund (GSSF)(both were administered by the Associated Students of Madison, the student-government), or (3) directly from a student referendum, which could either approve or disapprove an assessment for a particular RSO. The parties stipulated that the SGAF and GSSF funding was viewpoint neutral, but that stipulation did not extend to the referendum process.

The Court distinguished this case from situations where the government itself is the speaker and seeks to advance a particular message. In that case, it is accountable to the electorate and the political process for its advocacy. Here, the University is not responsible for the speech and its content. Instead, it merely distributes the money to facilitate the students' exchange of ideas, which is part of the University's function.

The Court rejected the "germaneness" test found in *Keller*, both as unworkable as applied to student speech at a university, and as giving "insufficient protection" to the objecting students and to the university. The Court should not say what is or is not germane to the ideas to be pursued in an institution of higher learning. Instead the proper test is to require viewpoint neutrality in the allocation of funding support. The Court borrowed the "viewpoint neutrality" test from the public forum cases, although the student activities fund is not a public forum.

The Court remanded the issue dealing with the allocation by student referendum because

---

46. 496 U.S. 1, 110 S.Ct. 2228, 110 L.Ed.2d 1 (1990).

47. 529 U.S. 217, 120 S.Ct. 1346, 146 L.Ed.2d 193 (2000).

it (unlike the other two alternatives) appeared to be inconsistent with the requirement of viewpoint neutrality. The Court added that a university could decide that its students' free speech interests were better protected by some kind of refund system or an optional system, but it declined to impose that as a constitutional requirement.

The following sections examine some of the basic issues of freedom of association by focusing on the major cases dealing with loyalty and security requirements.

§ 16.42 Public Employment Restrictions

(a) Political Affiliation

Over the years, the Court has developed guidelines that affect the legislature's ability to impose restrictions on public employment. As a result, denial of public employment on the basis of political affiliation violates the First Amendment, unless the political organization is legitimately designated as "subversive," (that is, dedicated to the use of illegal means to effectuate its political or social objectives), *and* the prospective employee is aware of those objectives and intends specifically to further them.[1]

Adler v. Board of Education,[2] the first significant venture of the Court into loyalty programs, involved a teacher's dismissal under a New York statute that disqualified from civil service and public school employment any person advocating, advising, or teaching governmental overthrow by force or violence. The Court found no violation of the teacher's freedom of speech and association because, at this point in the development of the law, the Court did not consider employment to be constitutionally a "right," thus removing it from constitutional protection. If the states employees

do not choose to work on the terms that New York requires, they are at liberty to retain their beliefs and associations and go elsewhere.[3] Or, as Justice Holmes said in his famous dictum, " ... petitioner may have a constitutional right to talk politics, but he has no constitutional right to be a policeman."[4]

Subsequently, the doctrine that public employment was as a mere privilege, and the state could condition employment on an employee surrendering constitutional rights, eroded and eventually disappeared.[5] That change in doctrine forced a re-examination of the basic tenets of *Adler* and eventually removed its constitutional underpinnings.

Loyalty Oaths. *Wieman v. Updegraff*,[6] decided the same term as *Adler*, demonstrated that the Court would not allow even a privilege to be withdrawn on the basis of certain broad classifications. Oklahoma required that its state employees take what is often called a negative oath—that is, an oath requiring an individual to swear that he or she had not done something in the past. (An affirmative oath, in contrast, requires the prospective employee to swear support in the future to the constitutional processes of government.)

The Oklahoma oath required state employees to swear that they were not members of the Communist Party, or—

> any agency, party, organization, association or group ... officially determined ... to be a communist front or subversive organization ... that advocated the overthrow of the Government of the United States or of the State of Oklahoma by force or violence or other unlawful means.[7]

The Oklahoma Supreme Court interpreted that language to require an employee to swear that they were not members of the prohibited organizations, regardless whether the employ-

§ 16.42

1. See 4 Ronald D. Rotunda & John E. Nowak, Treatise on Constitutional Law: Substance and Procedure § 20.42 (West Group, 3d ed. 1999).

2. 342 U.S. 485, 72 S.Ct. 380, 96 L.Ed. 517 (1952), affirmed 342 U.S. 951, 72 S.Ct. 624, 96 L.Ed. 707 (1952) (Justices Black, Douglas, & Frankfurter dissented).

3. 342 U.S. at 492, 72 S.Ct. at 385.

4. McAuliffe v. New Bedford, 155 Mass. 216, 220, 29 N.E. 517 (1892).

5. Van Alstyne, The Demise of the Right—Privilege Distinction in Constitutional Law, 81 Harv.L.Rev. 1439 (1968).

6. 344 U.S. 183, 73 S.Ct. 215, 97 L.Ed. 216 (1952).

7. 344 U.S. at 184–85 n. 1, 73 S.Ct. at 215–16 n. 1.

ees had knowledge of the actual activities of the organizations. Therefore, the Court held that the oath violated due process.[8] Denial of public employment for subversive association stigmatizes the individual and is unjustified when the member is innocent of the group's illegal and subversive goals.[9]

Following *Wieman*, the Supreme Court, at first, dealt with loyalty qualifications primarily by the use of the vagueness and overbreadth doctrines. Thus, *Shelton v. Tucker*,[10] invalidated an Arkansas statute requiring teachers to file an affidavit listing all the organizations to which they had belonged or contributed within the past five years. The state's legitimate interest in investigating the loyalty of its teachers did not justify the "unlimited and indiscriminate sweep" of the statute when less restrictive alternatives, offering less impingement on the teachers' freedom of association, were available.

In *Cramp v. Board of Public Instruction*,[11] the Court unanimously invalidated a Florida statute requiring employees to swear, "I have not and will not lend my aid, support, advice, counsel or influence to the Communist Party."[12] The consequences of such vague and ambiguous wording would not only inhibit legitimate activity by those whose "conscientious scruples were the most sensitive," but would increase the likelihood of prosecution for ideas antithetical to those held by the general community.

Employing a similar rationale in *Baggett v. Bullitt*,[13] the Court invalidated two Washington loyalty oath requirements. The first required the affiant to promote, by teaching and example, "respect for the flag and the institutions of the United States of America and the State of Washington" and the second, to swear

that he or she was not a member of a "subversive organization." Once again, the language was susceptible of an interpretation applying to a broad spectrum of behavior with which the State could not interfere. The lack of any criminal sanction for its future violation did not prevent the oath from being stricken, because this oath would not avoid the prohibited deterrent effect on those who will only swear to that which they can obey.

The Leading Case of *Elfbrandt v. Russell*. The Court eventually found that the *Wieman* standard—mere knowledge of illegal aims of the organization—was insufficient to terminate an individual's employment. *Elfbrandt v. Russell*[14] involved a challenge to an Arizona statute imposing an oath on the prospective employee that he had not knowingly and willfully become or remained a member of an organization dedicated to the overthrow by force or violence of the government with knowledge of its illegal aims.

The majority opinion found this oath to prohibit "knowing, but guiltless" behavior because the oath did not require the individual to have participated in, or subscribed to the unlawful activities in order for employment to be terminated and prosecution for perjury to be instituted. The Court relied on previous decisions involving criminal prosecutions under the Smith Act and held that the same standards were applicable to employment discrimination; "knowing membership" coupled with a specific intent to further the illegal aims of the organizations would be required because "quasi-political parties or other groups ... may embrace both legal and illegal aims."[15] Following *Elfbrandt* the Court focused its attention to substantive loyalty-security restrictions on public employment. We shall now

---

8. See Garner v. Board of Public Works, 341 U.S. 716, 71 S.Ct. 909, 95 L.Ed. 1317 (1951), rehearing denied 342 U.S. 843, 72 S.Ct. 21, 96 L.Ed. 637 (1951).

9. 344 U.S. at 191, 73 S.Ct. at 219.

10. 364 U.S. 479, 81 S.Ct. 247, 5 L.Ed.2d 231 (1960) (Frankfurter, Harlan, Clark, & Whittaker, JJ., dissented).

11. 368 U.S. 278, 82 S.Ct. 275, 7 L.Ed.2d 285 (1961), on remand to 137 So.2d 828 (Fla.1962).

12. 368 U.S. at 279 n. 1, and 286–287, 82 S.Ct. at 276 n. 1 and 280–81.

13. 377 U.S. 360, 84 S.Ct. 1316, 12 L.Ed.2d 377 (1964).

14. 384 U.S. 11, 86 S.Ct. 1238, 16 L.Ed.2d 321 (1966).

15. Elfbrandt v. Russell, 384 U.S. at 15, 86 S.Ct. at 1240, quoting Scales v. United States, 367 U.S. 203, 229, 81 S.Ct. 1469, 1486, 6 L.Ed.2d 782 (1961), rehearing denied 366 U.S. 978, 81 S.Ct. 1912, 6 L.Ed.2d 1267 (1961).

See also, Cole v. Richardson, 405 U.S. 676, 92 S.Ct. 1332, 31 L.Ed.2d 593 (1972), discussed below.

consider these decisions, and their contribution to the development of the law, and then revisit the loyalty oath cases when the Court in the next decade turned its sights once again on the loyalty oath.

Substantive Loyalty–Security Employment Restrictions. In *Keyishian v. Board of Regents*,[16] the Court finally came full circle and invalidated the Feinberg Law, which *Adler* had upheld only fifteen years earlier. Noting the pertinent constitutional doctrines that had arisen in the interim, and the absence of any claim of vagueness in *Adler*, the Court decided that *Adler* was no longer controlling. Justice Brennan, speaking for the Court, ruled that the complex law was unconstitutionally vague.

> The very intricacy of the plan and the uncertainty as to the scope of its proscriptions make it a highly efficient *in terrorem* mechanism. It would be a bold teacher who would not stay as far as possible from utterances or acts which might jeopardize his living by enmeshing him in this intricate machinery.[17]

A provision added to the statute since the *Adler* decision stated that mere membership in a prohibited organization created *prima facie* evidence of disqualification for employment, which the appellant could rebut in only one of three ways: denial of membership, denial that the organization advocated overthrow, or denial that appellant had knowledge of such advocacy. The Court invalidated this provision as overbroad relying on *Elfbrandt*, because the New York law did not allow employee to rebut the presumption by denial of specific intent to further the unlawful aims of the organization or denial of active membership.[18]

In the same year, *United States v. Robel*[19] dealt with employment restrictions in federal legislation. The majority opinion of Chief Justice Warren held that § 5(a)(1)(D) of the Subversive Activities Control Act was unconstitutionally overbroad by denying to members of designated "communist-action" groups employment in any defense facility.

The statutory language made irrelevant the active or passive status of the individual's membership, his knowledge of the illegal aims of the organization or lack of it, the degree of his agreement or disagreement with those aims, and the sensitive nature of his position of employment as it affected national security. The Court found that the statute literally established guilt by association and inhibited the exercise of First Amendment rights while less restrictive means of achieving the legislative objective were at hand.

Thus, the constitutional requirements involving loyalty-security qualifications for employment by either federal or state governments parallel each other quite closely. An individual may not be punished or deprived of public employment for political association unless: (1) he is an active member of a subversive organization; (2) such membership is with knowledge of the illegal aims of the organization; *and* (3) the individual has a specific intent to further those illegal ends, as opposed to general support of the objectives of an organization.

Robel does leave an indication that the federal government's interest in national security may, on occasion, override individual rights of association, depending on the sensitivity of the employment. The government may be able to deny an individual a position, if it has a demonstrable relationship to important national security interests, in circumstances where the government can only show that the person's status is nothing more than active, knowing membership in a subversive organization, but the individual may potentially adopt illegal means to achieve the organization's political objectives, and circumstances may reasonably exist that would not offer the government an

---

16. 385 U.S. 589, 87 S.Ct. 675, 17 L.Ed.2d 629 (1967).

17. 385 U.S. at 601, 87 S.Ct. at 683 citing Wieman v. Updegraff, 344 U.S. 183, 195, 73 S.Ct. 215, 221, 97 L.Ed. 216 (1952) (Frankfurter, J. concurring).

18. In light of Speiser v. Randall, 357 U.S. 513, 78 S.Ct. 1332, 2 L.Ed.2d 1460 (1958), it is doubtful that the

addition of those requirements would save the statute because the burden remains on the affiant to establish his innocent connection with the organization.

19. 389 U.S. 258, 88 S.Ct. 419, 19 L.Ed.2d 508 (1967).

adequate opportunity to thwart those illegal means.[20]

Loyalty Oaths Revisited. *Connell v. Higginbotham*,[21] a per curiam opinion, invalidated a section of a Florida loyalty oath requiring the affiant to disclaim belief in the overthrow of the federal or state government by force or violence. The statute's requirement of dismissal without notice or hearing for failure to take the oath violated due process because the appellant had no opportunity to explain his refusal, thus potentially allowing dismissal for possible protected activity.

The Court applied similar standards in unanimously invalidating an Indiana oath requiring that political parties, before they had access to the ballot, must disclaim *any* advocacy of overthrow of the government by force.[22]

Negative Oaths, Affirmative Oaths, and Cole v. Richardson. The Court decision in *Cole v. Richardson*[23] is an opinion of significant impact on statutory oaths as opposed to substantive legislative restrictions. *Cole* indicated a greater willingness to construe arguably overbroad or vague oath requirements so as to comport with constitutional guidelines.

Cole began its analysis by acknowledging that previous decisions had established a distinction between oaths that require individuals to swear to the appropriateness of their past conduct, so-called negative oaths, and oaths that merely require the individual to swear support in the future to the constitutional processes of government, so-called affirmative oaths.[24]

Unlike negative oaths, affirmative oaths have traditionally been viewed as constitutionally permissible despite the inherent vagueness of the terms employed. Indeed, the body

of the Constitution requires such oaths: both the presidential oath[25] and the oath for federal and state officials are affirmative oaths.[26] The purpose behind the enactment of such affirmative oaths is merely to assure that those in positions of public trust are willing to commit themselves to live by the constitutional processes.[27] The effect is that affirmative oaths are substantially equivalent to a vow of allegiance.[28]

The oath in *Cole*, which Massachusetts required of its state employees, read as follows:

> I do solemnly swear (or affirm) that I will uphold and defend the Constitution of the United States ... and the Constitution of the Commonwealth of Massachusetts and that I will oppose the overthrow of the government of the United States of America or of this Commonwealth by force, violence or by any illegal or unconstitutional method.[29]

Chief Justice Burger, writing for a four to three majority, read the first portion of the oath, swearing to "uphold and defend", as a permissible "affirmative oath." This result allowed the Court to conclude that a literal reading of the second part, requiring opposition to attempted overthrow, was unnecessary.

Thus, the second part of this oath was not unduly vague; it did not raise the specter of some undefinable responsibility to actively combat a potential revolution. Rather, it should be read as merely a negative restatement of the affirmative oath, the "support" oath:

> The second clause does not expand the obligation of the first; it simply makes clear the application of the first clause to a particular issue. Such repetition, whether for emphasis

---

20. See 389 U.S. at 266–68, 88 S.Ct. at 424–26.

21. 403 U.S. 207, 91 S.Ct. 1772, 29 L.Ed.2d 418 (1971) (per curiam).

22. Communist Party of Indiana v. Whitcomb, 414 U.S. 441, 94 S.Ct. 656, 38 L.Ed.2d 635 (1974), rehearing denied 415 U.S. 952, 94 S.Ct. 1476, 39 L.Ed.2d 568 (1974).

23. 405 U.S. 676, 92 S.Ct. 1332, 31 L.Ed.2d 593 (1972).

24. See Bond v. Floyd, 385 U.S. 116, 135, 87 S.Ct. 339, 349, 17 L.Ed.2d 235 (1966); Knight v. Board of Regents, 269 F.Supp. 339 (S.D.N.Y.1967), affirmed per curiam 390 U.S. 36, 88 S.Ct. 816, 19 L.Ed.2d 812 (1968).

25. Art. II, § 1, cl. 8.

26. Art. VI, cl. 3.

27. Cole v. Richardson, 405 U.S. at 684, 92 S.Ct. at 1337 (1972).

28. Knight v. Board of Regents, 269 F.Supp. 339, 341 (S.D.N.Y.1967), per curiam 390 U.S. 36, 88 S.Ct. 816, 19 L.Ed.2d 812 (1968). See Ohlson v. Phillips, 397 U.S. 317, 90 S.Ct. 1124, 25 L.Ed.2d 337 (1970).

29. 405 U.S. at 677–78, 92 S.Ct. at 1334 (footnote omitted).

or cadence, seems to be the wont of authors of oaths. That the second clause may be redundant is no ground to strike it down; we are not charged with correcting grammar but with enforcing a constitution.[30]

The dissenters, Justices Douglas, Marshall, and Brennan, ignored the nebulous nature of the positive portion of the oath, but argued that the vagueness of "oppose" left the affiant in a quandary concerning when and by what method he must demonstrate his opposition. As Justice Douglas put the dilemma, the oath "requires that appellee 'oppose' that which she has an indisputable right to advocate."[31]

Thus, after *Cole* and *Elfbrandt v. Russell*[32] it is now clear that oaths must be clear, concise, and narrow in scope. The Court accords a wider ranger of permissibility to affirmative oaths, relating only to allegiance to constitutional processes of government. The Court in likely to construe arguably vague requirements so as to avoid the constitutional issue. However, negative oaths cannot require a disclaimer of past conduct or belief other than that for which the employee may be constitutionally denied employment pursuant to an investigation, i.e. the two step standard of *Elfbrandt*.

Political Patronage Dismissals. *Cole* has not signaled any diluting of the basic proposition that one may not be excluded from public employment on the basis of political affiliation unless the proscribed organization is truly subversive. The Court (with no majority opinion) emphasized this constitutional rule in *Elrod v. Burns*,[33] where it invalidated political patronage dismissals by the Democratic Sheriff of Cook County. Respondents' discharge was unrelated to membership in any subversive organization. They were Republicans discharged

or threatened with discharge because they were Republicans.

While individuals affiliated with subversive organizations may be denied public employment pursuant to the safeguards outlined in *Keyishian* and *Robel*, dismissal merely for membership in an opposing political party that poses no illegal threat to the democratic process falls squarely within the overarching principle of those cases: the imposition of burdens based solely on political association is forbidden. *Elrod* did entertain arguments alleging the existence of a significant state interest in political patronage, primarily the preservation of the two party system and promotion of interest in lower echelon elections, but such interests were unpersuasive when weighed against the restraint such practices placed on the freedoms of belief and association.[34]

The Court reaffirmed *Elrod*'s protection against political patronage dismissals in *Branti v. Finkel*,[35] an opinion that, unlike *Elrod*, attracted a majority. The proper test, said the majority, to determine whether political affiliation is a legitimate factor to consider in government employment is not whether the label "policymakers" or "confidential" fits a particular position. Instead, the question is whether the hiring authority can demonstrate that "party affiliation is an appropriate requirement for the effective performance of the public office involved."[36] *Branti* explained that a state's election laws could require that there be two election judges, each representing one of the two main parties, even though election supervision does not involve policy making or access to confidential information. Similarly, the state could not fire a state university football coach because of his political affiliation, even though his job involves some policy making. In *Branti* the Court prohibited the Demo-

---

30. Cole v. Richardson, 405 U.S. at 684, 92 S.Ct. at 1337.

31. 405 U.S. at 689, 92 S.Ct. at 1339 (dissenting opinion).

32. 384 U.S. 11, 86 S.Ct. 1238, 16 L.Ed.2d 321 (1966), discussed supra.

33. 427 U.S. 347, 96 S.Ct. 2673, 49 L.Ed.2d 547 (1976).

34. Boudin, Circuit J., citing Treatise in Flynn v. City of Boston, 140 F.3d 42 (1st Cir.1998).

35. 445 U.S. 507, 100 S.Ct. 1287, 63 L.Ed.2d 574 (1980). See also, McCormick v. Edwards, 646 F.2d 173 (5th Cir.1981), rehearing denied 651 F.2d 776 (5th Cir.1981), certiorari denied 454 U.S. 1017, 102 S.Ct. 552, 70 L.Ed.2d 415 (1981), rehearing denied 454 U.S. 1165, 102 S.Ct. 1042, 71 L.Ed.2d 323 (1982).

36. 445 U.S. at 521, 100 S.Ct. at 1296.

cratic Public Defender from firing the Republican Assistant Public Defenders solely because of their political beliefs.

Branti ruled that a state official may not terminate the employment of a public defender for purely political grounds because any policy making role he might have should not relate to partisan political interests; his confidential information based on the attorney client relationship has no relation to partisan political concerns; to make his tenure depend on his political affiliation would not advance the effective performance of his duties. However, a public employee cannot secure tenure by the simple expedient of undermining and criticizing her superiors and disrupting office morale. In the usual case it is only when the public employee speaks on "matters of public concern" that the First Amendment prohibits a retaliatory discharge.[37]

Elrod and *Branti* serve to silhouette the basic legislative goals that may serve as a constitutional basis for denial or termination of public employment. The initial focus must be on the character of the organization; unless it is posing a threat to democratic government not only in terms of its advocacy but also its ultimate goals there is little chance that there can be found to be significant state interest in prohibiting its members *qua* members from serving on the public payroll. Moreover, even if the organization is one that may constitutionally be guarded against, only those members who have knowledge of its illegal goals and have a specific intent to further those

goals may be precluded from public employment.[38]

Rutan v. Republican Party of Illinois,[39] extended *Branti*. Justice Brennan, for the Court, held that not only the patronage practice of discharging public employees on the basis of their political affiliation violates the First Amendment, but related patronage practices involving low-level public employees—regarding hiring, promotion, transfer, and recall after layoff—also may not constitutionally be based on party affiliation and support. "Unless these patronage practices are narrowly tailored to further vital government interests, we must conclude that they impermissibly encroach on First Amendment freedoms."[40]

The breadth of *Rutan* is illustrated in a footnote. The Court said that the First Amendment "protects state employees not only from patronage dismissals but 'even an act of retaliation as trivial as failing to hold a birthday party for a public employee ... when intended to punish her for exercising her free speech rights.'"[41] In short, it violates the First Amendment for the government to determine promotions, transfers, recalls after layoffs, or birthday parties, based on the political affiliation of low-level the government employees.

The majority insisted that the First Amendment does not give government workers tenure. The Government has an interest in having effective employees, and it can discharge, demote or transfer staff members who work is deficient.[42] The government, the Court acknowledged, also has an interest in securing employees who will loyally implement its poli-

---

37. Matters of Public Concern. See Connick v. Myers, 461 U.S. 138, 103 S.Ct. 1684, 75 L.Ed.2d 708 (1983), where the Court (5 to 4) upheld the firing of an assistant district attorney for circulating a questionnaire regarding office policies. The questionnaire did not touch on matters of public concern in any real sense. The employer need not tolerate action reasonably believed to disrupt the office, undermine authority, and destroy close working relationships. "We hold only that when a public employee speaks not as a citizen upon matters of public concern, but instead as an employee upon matters of personal interest, absent the most unusual circumstances, a federal court is not the appropriate forum in which to review the wisdom of a personnel decision taken by a public agency allegedly in reaction to the employee's behavior." 461 U.S. at 147, 103 S.Ct. at 1690.

An employee may speak out on a matter of public concern even though she arranges to speak privately. Givhan v. Western Line Consolidated School District, 439 U.S. 410, 415–16, 99 S.Ct. 693, 696–97, 58 L.Ed.2d 619 (1979).

38. *Robel* offers a potential exception for individuals in highly sensitive governmental jobs who are knowing members, as they may adopt, subsequent to their employment, the illegal aims of the organization. See United States v. Robel, 389 U.S. 258, 266–68, 88 S.Ct. 419, 424–26, 19 L.Ed.2d 508 (1967).

39. 497 U.S. 62, 110 S.Ct. 2729, 111 L.Ed.2d 52 (1990).

40. 497 U.S. at 72, 110 S.Ct. at 2736.

41. 497 U.S. at 76 n. 8, 110 S.Ct. at 2738 n. 8.

42. 497 U.S. at 75, 110 S.Ct. at 2737.

cies, but the government can meet this interest by choosing or dismissing "high-level employees" on the basis of their political views.[43]

Independent Contractors of the Government. In *O'Hare Truck Service, Inc. v. City of Northlake,*[44] the Court refused to draw any distinction between government employees and independent contractors for the Government. Once again, the case arose in Illinois. O'Hare Truck Service, on a rotation list of companies available to perform towing services at the request of the city, was removed from the list after its owner (John Gratzianna), allegedly because he refused to contribute to the respondent mayor's reelection campaign. The Seventh Circuit dismissed the claim, arguing that *Branti* and *Elrod* do not apply to independent contractors. Justice Kennedy, for the Court, reversed. If the government retaliates against a contractor or regular provider of services because of its exercise of rights of political association or the expression of political allegiance, there is a violation of the guarantee of free speech.

This is not a case, Kennedy said, where O'Hare Trucking was "part of a constituency that must take its chance of being favored or ignored in the larger political process—for example, by residing or doing business in a region the government rewards or spurns in the construction of public works." Instead, the politicians imposed on Gratzianna a specific demand for political support. When he refused, the city terminated a relationship that, based on his prior longstanding practice, "he had reason to believe would continue."[45]

In a further effort to caution litigants not to read this case too broadly, Kennedy said that it was "inevitable" that there should be case-by-case adjudication so that the courts will allow government appropriate discretion in awarding contracts.[46] Thus, there is no First Amendment violation if the government terminates its affiliation with the contractor for reasons unrelated to free speech (e.g., the provider is unreliable) if either the asserted justification is not a pretext, or if the contractor's affiliation is an appropriate requirement for the effective performance of the job.

A companion case was *Board of County Commissioners v. Umbehr.*[47] Umbehr, was a trash hauler and an outspoken critic of the Board of County Commissioners. Umbehr alleged that the County Commissioners voted to terminate or prevent the automatic renewal of his at-will contract to haul trash because of his criticism of them. Justice O'Connor, for the Court, held that the First Amendment protects independent contractors from termination of at-will government contracts in retaliation for their exercise of free speech.

O'Connor, for the Court, emphasized "the limited nature of our decision today." This case concerned the termination of a *"pre-existing* commercial relationship with the government," so "we need not address the possibility of suits by bidders or applicants for new government contracts who cannot rely on such a relationship."[48] Then she laid out the guidelines for what Umbehr must prove.

---

43. 497 U.S. at 62, 110 S.Ct. at 2737. The Court did not discuss this issue further, but stated that the scope of the exception in *Branti*—where "party affiliation is an appropriate requirement for the effective performance of the public office involved"—"does not concern us here as respondents concede that the five employees who brought this suit are not within it." 497 U.S. at 70 n. 5, 110 S.Ct. at 2735 n. 5. The Court remanded for trial.

Justice Scalia, joined by Rehnquist, C.J., Kennedy, J., and (in part), O'Connor, J., dissented, arguing that *Branti* should be overruled. Stevens, J., filed a concurring opinion.

44. 518 U.S. 712, 116 S.Ct. 2353, 135 L.Ed.2d 874 (1996).

45. 518 U.S. at 721, 116 S.Ct. at 2358.

46. 518 U.S. at 719, 116 S.Ct. at 2358.

47. 518 U.S. 668, 116 S.Ct. 2342, 135 L.Ed.2d 843 (1996).

48. 518 U.S. at 685, 116 S.Ct. at 2352. (emphasis added). Scalia, J., joined by Thomas, J., filed a dissenting opinion to both *Umbehr* and *O'Hare Truck*: "The Democratic mayor gives the city's municipal bond business to what is known to be a solid Democratic law firm—taking it away from the solid Republican law firm that had the business during the previous, Republican, administration. What else is new? Or he declines to give the construction contract for the new municipal stadium to the company that opposed the bond issue for its construction, and that in fact tried to get the stadium built across the river in the next State." Such favoritism is common, and "no one has ever thought it violated—of all things—the First Amendment." 518 U.S. at 711, 116 S.Ct. at 2373.

Umbehr must demonstrate that the termination of his contract was motivated by his speech on a matter of public concern. Initially, he must prove "more than the mere fact that he criticized the Board members before they terminated him." If he shows that, the Board will win if it can show, by a preponderance of the evidence, that, in light of their knowledge at the time of the termination, the Board members would have terminated the contract regardless of the speech, or if the Board proves that "the County's legitimate interests as contractor, *deferentially viewed*, outweigh the free speech interests at stake." In accessing the appropriate remedy, it is relevant to consider evidence that the Board members discovered facts after termination that would have led to a later termination anyway. Umbehr's loss would be mitigated by means of subsequent contracts with the cities.

(b) Exercise of the Fifth Amendment

Questions occasionally arise as to the legitimacy of sanctions applied against a public employee who has asserted the Fifth Amendment privilege against self-incrimination when questioned as to his political associations. *Slochower v. Board of Higher Education of New York City*[49] considered a summary dismissal of a teacher following his refusal to answer such questions. A provision in the New York municipal charter required the dismissal—without any notice or hearing—of any city employee who pled the Fifth Amendment to refuse to answer questions related to his official conduct. The city law treated the failure to answer the questions asked as a confession, which became the basis of the discharge of the

city employee (in this case an associate professor at Brooklyn College).

The dismissal in these circumstances is unconstitutional. Without further evidence that is independent of the assertion of the privilege, it violates due process for the state to dismiss an employee simply for asserting a constitutional right.

Use Immunity. The Fifth Amendment does not serve as an impenetrable barrier that will protect the identity of one's political affiliations. If the government grants "use immunity"[50] to the employee, he or she can no longer assert the privilege, and may be compelled to answer.[51] However, if no immunity is offered, the employee cannot be forced to choose between forfeiture of his public employment or self-incrimination.[52]

Under use immunity, which (unlike transaction immunity) is a limited immunity, the government may use the employees answers against him in a decision to terminate his employment, because use immunity only bars use of the testimony in a criminal case.[53] A termination hearing is a civil proceeding, not a criminal one. For example, if the employee has use immunity and admits to theft from the state agency, the agency can use that admission to fire the employee.

(c) National Security Restrictions

The Court has justified various First Amendment restrictions on the activities of present or former government employees on the basis of the contract of employment. In the leading case the litigant against whom the Court upheld restraints was a former employ-

---

49. 350 U.S. 551, 76 S.Ct. 637, 100 L.Ed. 692 (1956), rehearing denied 351 U.S. 944, 76 S.Ct. 843, 100 L.Ed. 1470 (1956); see also Konigsberg v. State Bar of California, 353 U.S. 252, 77 S.Ct. 722, 1 L.Ed.2d 810 (1957), rehearing denied 354 U.S. 927, 77 S.Ct. 1374, 1 L.Ed.2d 1441 (1957) discussed below.

50. Use immunity, as defined in 18 U.S.C.A. § 6002, provides immunity from the use of the compelled testimony and evidence derived therefrom.

51. Kastigar v. United States, 406 U.S. 441, 92 S.Ct. 1653, 32 L.Ed.2d 212 (1972), rehearing denied 408 U.S. 931, 92 S.Ct. 2478, 33 L.Ed.2d 345 (1972).

52. Garrity v. New Jersey, 385 U.S. 493, 87 S.Ct. 616, 17 L.Ed.2d 562 (1967).

Lefkowitz v. Cunningham, 431 U.S. 801, 97 S.Ct. 2132, 53 L.Ed.2d 1 (1977) (state statute that provided that if an officer of a political party subpoenaed by a grand jury or other authorized tribunal to testify concerning the conduct of his office refuses to testify or refuses to waive immunity from later prosecution from the use of his testimony, then the statute immediately terminates his party office and prohibits him from holding any other party or public office for a period of five years, held unconstitutional as a violation of the self incrimination clause of the Fifth Amendment as applied to the states through the Fourteenth Amendment).

53. Kastigar v. United States, 406 U.S. 441, 453, 92 S.Ct. 1653, 1661, 32 L.Ed.2d 212 (1972), rehearing denied 408 U.S. 931, 92 S.Ct. 2478, 33 L.Ed.2d 345 (1972).

ee of the Central Intelligence Agency. In *Snepp v. United States*,[54] a former CIA agent, Frank W. Snepp, III, published a book concerning CIA involvement in South Vietnam, without seeking or securing the Agency's prepublication approval, in violation of his employment contract. Snepp, in this contract had promised that he would "not ... publish ... any information or material relating to the Agency, its activities or intelligence activities generally, either during or after the term of [his] employment ... without specific prior approval of the Agency."[55] He also agreed not to disclose any classified material without proper authorization.

Because Snepp published his book without submitting it for prepublication review, the CIA sued for an order enjoining him to submit future writings for prepublication review, a declaration that he had breached his contract, and a constructive trust for the Government of all profits earned from the publication of the book. For purposes of this litigation the Government conceded that Snepp's book disclosed *no* classified intelligence.

The Court, in a short per curiam opinion, delivered without benefit of oral arguments or full briefing, granted all of the Government's requested relief. A footnote dismissed Snepp's First Amendment claims: "[E]ven in the absence of an express agreement—the CIA could have acted to protect substantial government interests by imposing reasonable restrictions on employee activities that in other contexts might be protected by the First Amendment. The Government has a compelling interest in protecting both the secrecy of information important to our national security and the appearance of confidentiality so essential to the effective operation of our foreign intelligence service. The agreement that Snepp signed is a reasonable means for protecting this vital interest."[56]

The majority contended that because Snepp's employment involved a high degree of

trust and he explicitly agreed to submit for prepublication review all material, whether classified or not, Snepp's violation impaired the CIA's statutory functions by limiting the CIA's ability to guarantee the security of information and protect intelligence sources. What Snepp should have done, rather than flout his preclearance obligation, said the majority, was to submit the book for prepublication review. This Agency clearance would be subject to judicial review. Thus if the CIA claimed that the book contained harmful classified disclosures and Snepp disagreed, the CIA then would have the burden of seeking an injunction against publication.[57]

The strong dissent of Justice Stevens, joined by Brennan and Marshall argued that because the Government had stipulated that the book contained no classified nonpublic material, the interest in confidentiality that Snepp's employment agreement was designed to protect had not been affected. Moreover there was no precedent to authorize a constructive trust because his book did not use, or profit from, confidential information as the Government stipulated.

§ 16.43 Regulation of Labor Organizations

The Court has on several occasions dealt with federal legislation attempting to limit subversive influence in the labor hierarchy. Because the decisions are quite dissimilar in both approach and result, it is difficult to draw any thread of uniformity. The easy answer may be simply that the difference in the membership of the Court as well as the political climate in each decision best explains the philosophical disparity. Wholly new considerations may apply to any future attempts by Congress to control subversives in the labor movement.

The first case, *American Communications Association v. Douds*,[1] decided in 1950, consid-

---

54. 444 U.S. 507, 100 S.Ct. 763, 62 L.Ed.2d 704 (1980), rehearing denied 445 U.S. 972, 100 S.Ct. 1668, 64 L.Ed.2d 250 (1980) (per curiam).

55. 444 U.S. at 508, 100 S.Ct. at 765.

56. 444 U.S. at 511, n. 3, 100 S.Ct. at 765, n. 3 (citations omitted).

57. 444 U.S. at 513, n. 8, 100 S.Ct. at 767, n. 8.

§ 16.43

1. 339 U.S. 382, 70 S.Ct. 674, 94 L.Ed. 925 (1950), rehearing denied 339 U.S. 990, 70 S.Ct. 1017, 94 L.Ed. 1391 (1950).

ered a challenge to § 9(h), the "non-Communist affidavit" provision of the Taft–Hartley Act of 1947.[2] Pursuant to that provision, any labor organization that desired the benefits of the National Labor Relations Act (N.L.R.A.) was required to have its officers file annually with the National Labor Relations Board affidavits disavowing membership in or support of the Communist Party as well as disclaiming membership, support, or belief in any organization that advocates or believes in the overthrow of the federal government by force or any illegal or unconstitutional means.[3] Legislative findings of fact supporting this statute determined that strikes called to achieve political, rather than economic goals, posed a severe threat to the flow of interstate commerce. The past beliefs and associations of the individuals designated by the provision would serve as a reasonable method to identify them as potential instigators of such strikes.

The Court agreed that there was a reasonable relationship between the evil and the means implemented to avoid that evil, because past beliefs and associations are sufficient criterion to infer future conduct.[4] The Court said that further analysis was required because the means employed discouraged the lawful exercise of First Amendment freedoms. However, the Court still upheld the statute.

The Court rejected appellant's claim that the clear and present danger test is the appropriate one to use whenever rights of free speech and association are impaired. In the Court's view, Congress had focused the thrust of its prohibition at preventing conduct. The subsequent effect on speech was merely inci-

dental. The government's interest was not in preventing the dissemination of Communist doctrine. Instead, Congress feared, and found, that some persons "have the will and power to do so *without* advocacy or persuasion that seeks acceptance in the competition of the market."[5]

Because the effect on the First Amendment was minimal and the public interest in an untrammeled flow of commerce great, the Court felt that it would be absurd to require the government to show imminent national peril before it could invoke prophylactic measures.[6]

In view of the great public interest in protecting the flow of commerce and the relative handful of individuals whose beliefs may actually be restrained by their desire for union office, as well as the fact that those individuals who were affected were not required to forego their beliefs because they could resign their position with the union with their beliefs intact, the Court found that Congress had not violated the First Amendment.[7] The Court also construed the portions of the Act prohibiting mere belief to encompass only those union officials who held the belief in violent overthrow of the Government to be an objective, as opposed to a prophecy.[8]

Following *Douds*, the Government instituted 18 prosecutions for the filing of false affidavits.[9] In only one of these cases did the appeal reach the Supreme Court, and in that case, *Killian v. United States*,[10] the Court reversed petitioner's conviction on procedural grounds. In the course of this decision, it approved a broad interpretation of the requirement of

---

2. Officially known as the Labor–Management Relations Act; 61 Stat. 136, 146, 29 U.S.C.A. §§ 141, 159(h). Section 159(h) was later repealed by the Labor–Management Reporting and Disclosure Act of 1959, 73 Stat. 519, 525, 29 U.S.C.A. § 201(d).

3. 339 U.S. at 385–86, 70 S.Ct. at 677–78.

4. American Communications Ass'n v. Douds, 339 U.S. 382, 391, 70 S.Ct. 674, 680, 94 L.Ed. 925 (1950).

5. 339 U.S. at 396, 70 S.Ct. at 682–83 (emphasis in original; footnote omitted).

6. 339 U.S. at 397, 70 S.Ct. at 683.

7. 339 U.S. at 404, 70 S.Ct. at 686–87.

8. 339 U.S. at 407, 70 S.Ct. at 688. Justice Jackson, although concurring in the decision as it related to the

prohibition on members of the Communist Party, dissented as to the prohibition based on mere belief. 339 U.S. at 437–43, 70 S.Ct. at 703–06; Justice Black dissented, stating that the statute should have outlawed political strikes and avoided the unnecessary impairment of First Amendment freedoms. 339 U.S. at 445, 70 S.Ct. at 707; Justices Douglas, Clark, and Minton did not participate.

9. 1 N. Dorsen, P. Bender, B. Newborne, Emerson, Haber, & Dorsen's Political and Civil Rights in the United States, 111 (4th ed. 1976).

10. 368 U.S. 231, 82 S.Ct. 302, 7 L.Ed.2d 256 (1961), rehearing denied 368 U.S. 979, 82 S.Ct. 476, 7 L.Ed.2d 441 (1962).

"membership or affiliation" as related to the Communist Party. The Court emphasized that no criminal sanctions applied to membership in, or affiliation with, the Communist Party under the terms of the Act. Thus, it rejected petitioner's claim that membership could only be determined by factual phenomena, such as a "specific formal act of joining."[11] The Court approved the jury instruction that allowed membership to be shown by state of mind: "the desire on the part of the individual to belong to the Communist Party and a recognition by that Party that it considers him as a member."[12]

In 1959, Congress repealed § 9(h) and replaced with § 504 of the Landrum–Griffin Act[13], which provided:

> No person who is or has been a member of the Communist Party ... shall serve ... as an officer, director, trustee, member of any executive board or similar governing body, business agent, manager, organizer, or other employee ... of any labor organization.[14]

United States v. Brown,[15] invalidated this provision as a bill of attainder. The Court did not deny the legislative power to prevent political strikes by rationally related means, but a blanket decree against all individuals on the membership rolls of the Communist Party was unjustifiable because it determined guilt by legislative fiat.

In language casting doubt on the reasoning in *Douds*, Chief Justice Warren's majority opinion declared:

> The designation of Communists as those persons likely to cause political strikes ... rests, as the Court in *Douds* explicitly recognized ... upon an empirical investigation by Congress of the acts, characteristics, and propensities of Communist Party members. In a number of decisions, this Court has pointed out the fallacy of the suggestion that membership in the Communist Party, or

any other political organization, can be regarded as an alternative, but equivalent expression for a list of undesirable characteristics.[16]

However, since § 9(h) of the Taft–Hartley Act had permitted Communists to resign their membership in the Party if they wished to remain in their position as union officials, *Douds* was not explicitly overruled. While the decision may have blurred the lines between a bill of attainder and an *ex post facto* law, the Court in *Brown* held that, because former Communists could not serve as union officials for five years after their resignation, the statute served as prohibited legislative punishment,[17] regardless of the argument that the function of the statute was preventive rather than retributive:

> It would be archaic to limit the definition of "punishment" to "retribution." Punishment serves several purposes: retributive, rehabilitative, deterrent—and preventive.[18]

The authority of *Douds*, in the wake of this language, is nebulous, although the Court has not relied on *Brown* as precedent to overturn any further restrictions banning Communists or other political groups.

In the absence of federal regulation, many unions have provided for limitation of subversive influence in their constitutions or have excluded subversives without the benefit of a constitutional provision. The courts have declined to interfere in these intra-union activities.

§ 16.44 Restrictions on Entry Into the Bar

States routinely require that applicants for membership to the bar possess certain attributes of character that are consistent with the practice of law. A significant component of this character, as a prospective member of a "pro-

---

11. 368 U.S. at 247, 82 S.Ct. at 312.

12. 368 U.S. at 247 n. 5, 82 S.Ct. at 312 n. 5.

13. Officially, the Labor–Management Reporting and Disclosure Act, 73 Stat. 536, 29 U.S.C.A. § 504.

14. 368 U.S. at 247 n. 5, 82 S.Ct. at 312 n. 5.

15. 381 U.S. 437, 85 S.Ct. 1707, 14 L.Ed.2d 484 (1965).

16. 381 U.S. at 455, 85 S.Ct. at 1718.

17. The statute must impose punishment to be voided as a bill of attainder; Cummings v. Missouri, 71 U.S. (4 Wall.) 277, 18 L.Ed. 356 (1866).

18. 381 U.S. at 458, 85 S.Ct. at 1720.

fession dedicated to the peaceful and reasoned settlement of disputes between men, and between a man and his government,"[1] is loyalty to that system of government fostered by the Constitution and a devotion to "the law in its broadest sense, including not only its substantive provision, but also its procedures for orderly change."[2]

Not surprisingly, denials of admission to the bar on grounds of disloyalty have produced a spate of litigation alleging that such requirements restrict the applicant's rights of belief and association. Such cases have generally been presented in two basic contexts: the legitimacy of a denial based on inferences of disloyalty due to specific incidents in the applicant's past or the legitimacy of a denial due to a refusal to answer questions delving into the applicant's past political associations.[3]

Ex parte Garland,[4] the initial case dealing with loyalty oaths for attorneys, invalidated as a bill of attainder and an ex post facto law an oath that the individual had never supported or expressed sympathy for the enemies of the United States, foreign or domestic. Although *Garland* did not rest on the First Amendment, which was not applicable to the states at that time, the modern cases make it clear that the statute would be invalid under present First Amendment theory.

Political association cannot be construed as evidence of disloyalty unless the standard for criminally punishable political affiliation delineated in *Scales v. United States*[5] is satisfied. The rationale is also much the same. Disabilities imposed by the legislatures on an organization's ability to attract members cannot be justified unless the goals of such an organization encompass violent overthrow of the con-

stitutionally established governments. Therefore, a member cannot be punished for his political affiliations unless he has knowledge of those illegal goals and has evidenced a specific intent to aid in the implementation of those goals.

Schware v. Board of Bar Examiners[6] raised the question whether the state must show active membership status to infer disloyalty as a character trait. In that case the New Mexico Board of Bar Examiners disqualified the petitioner on the grounds that, fifteen years prior to his application for admission to the bar, he had been a member of the Communist Party. The Supreme Court unanimously reversed. As Justice Black noted in his majority opinion, membership in the Communist Party had not even been illegal at the time of Schware's membership. Moreover, the affirmative evidence produced by the petitioner as to his loyalty during the intervening fifteen years had demonstrated that his past affiliation with the Party was sufficiently attenuated from his present life so as to remove any justification for relying on it as grounds for disloyalty.[7]

The general rule to be gleaned from the cases may be that past membership in a subversive organization cannot create an irrebuttable presumption of unfitness for the bar. But, the First Amendment will not protect an active, knowing member of the Communist Party who has specific intent to aid in its illegal goals.

Following *Schware*, the Court dealt with a series of cases in which there was no claim that past incidents in the applicant's life had revealed characteristics incompatible with the practice of law. Rather, the applicants had asserted a privilege to refuse to answer ques-

---

§ 16.44

1. Law Students Civil Rights Research Council, Inc. v. Wadmond, 401 U.S. 154, 166, 91 S.Ct. 720, 728, 27 L.Ed.2d 749 (1971). See Rotunda, The Case Against Permanent Disbarment, 5 The Professional Lawyer 22 (A.B.A., No. 2, Feb. 1994); Rotunda & Devlin, Permanent Disbarment: A Market Oriented Proposal, 9 The Professional Lawyer 2 (A.B.A., No. 9, 1997).

2. Konigsberg v. State Bar of California, 366 U.S. 36, 52, 81 S.Ct. 997, 1008, 6 L.Ed.2d 105 (1961), rehearing denied 368 U.S. 869, 82 S.Ct. 21, 7 L.Ed.2d 69 (1961) (Konigsberg II).

3. The early cases are collected in Note, 18 A.L.R.2d 268, 283–91, 335–36 (1951).

4. 71 U.S. (4 Wall.) 333, 18 L.Ed. 366 (1866).

5. 367 U.S. 203, 81 S.Ct. 1469, 6 L.Ed.2d 782 (1961), rehearing denied 366 U.S. 978, 81 S.Ct. 1912, 6 L.Ed.2d 1267 (1961).

6. 353 U.S. 232, 77 S.Ct. 752, 1 L.Ed.2d 796 (1957).

7. See also In re Summers, 325 U.S. 561, 65 S.Ct. 1307, 89 L.Ed. 1795 (1945), rehearing denied 326 U.S. 807, 66 S.Ct. 94, 90 L.Ed. 491 (1945).

tions that they believed intruded unnecessarily into their First Amendment freedoms.

The first case, *Konigsberg v. State Bar of California*[8] (*Konigsberg I*), decided the same term as *Schware*, dealt with the range of inferences that could properly be drawn from the applicant's refusal to answer questions relating to his past political affiliations. The California Bar had determined that petitioner's refusal to respond to inquiries into his membership in the Communist Party, coupled with other characteristics, required it to deny admission on the grounds that the petitioner had failed to establish his good moral character as well as his non-advocacy of illegal overthrow of the government.

The Court found this conclusion unjustified. There must exist some authentic, affirmative evidence of disloyalty to deny admission to an applicant, not a conclusion of disloyalty based on suspicions deduced from a refusal to answer questions.

Konigsberg (I) expressed no opinion as to the propriety of denying admission to the bar solely on the basis of an applicant's refusal to answer, because it did not consider that issue before it. Four years later the same parties appeared before the Court to litigate that question.[9] On re-hearing for Konigsberg's application for admission to the bar of California, the applicant introduced further evidence of his good character and reiterated that he did not believe in or advocate violent overthrow of the government. Further he stated that he had never knowingly been a member of any organization with such objectives. Nevertheless, he steadfastly refused to answer questions concerning possible membership in the Communist Party. Relying solely on this refusal as an obstruction to a legitimate investigation, the bar examiners again denied him certification to practice law in that State.

In *Konigsberg (II)* the majority opinion of Justice Harlan rejected the claim that the state had placed on Konigsberg the burden of establishing his loyalty, which would contravene the holding of *Speiser v. Randall*.[10] The denial had not been based on any inference as to Konigsberg's character, but simply on his obstruction of the investigation. Because the state had the burden of producing evidence as to disloyalty, an applicant could not be allowed to frustrate that burden by refusing to submit relevant information.

The majority reasoned that the regulatory statute imposed only an incidental infringement on speech. The state's interest in this regulation is weighed against the appellant's interest in remaining silent, with the balance struck in favor of the state:

> [W]e regard the State's interest in having lawyers who are devoted to the law in its broadest sense, including not only its substantive provisions, but also its procedures for orderly change, as clearly sufficient to outweigh the minimal effect upon free association occasioned by compulsory disclosure in the circumstances here presented.[11]

The petitioner's voluntary disclosure of his general beliefs and associations did not moot the issue or make the question irrelevant, for the Committee is entitled to conduct its investigation in the manner it deems best suited to its purposes. Thus, although a denial of admission to the bar may not be premised on arbitrary or irrelevant information, there is no privilege to refuse to provide legitimate information. The state may deny the application to practice in order to prevent any frustration of its investigation.[12]

Justice Black, in dissent, wrote one of his most celebrated attacks on the theory of "balancing" in the First Amendment area. Although he disagreed with the majority's char-

---

8. 353 U.S. 252, 77 S.Ct. 722, 1 L.Ed.2d 810 (1957), rehearing denied 354 U.S. 927, 77 S.Ct. 1374, 1 L.Ed.2d 1441 (1957) (Frankfurter, Harlan and Clark, JJ., dissented).

9. Konigsberg v. State Bar of California, 366 U.S. 36, 38, 81 S.Ct. 997, 1000, 6 L.Ed.2d 105 (1961), rehearing denied 368 U.S. 869, 82 S.Ct. 21, 7 L.Ed.2d 69 (1961) (Konigsberg II).

10. 357 U.S. 513, 78 S.Ct. 1332, 2 L.Ed.2d 1460 (1958).

11. 366 U.S. at 52, 81 S.Ct. at 1008.

12. See also In re Anastaplo, 366 U.S. 82, 81 S.Ct. 978, 6 L.Ed.2d 135 (1961), rehearing denied 368 U.S. 869, 82 S.Ct. 21, 7 L.Ed.2d 69 (1961).

acterization of this scheme as an "incidental" abridgement of speech,[13] he focused the brunt of his attack on his philosophical antipathy towards balancing.

> I fear that the creation of "tests" by which speech is left unprotected under certain circumstances is a standing invitation to abridge it. . . . The Court suggests that a "literal reading of the First Amendment" would be totally unreasonable because it would invalidate many widely accepted laws . . . it certainly would invalidate all laws that abridge the right of the people to discuss matters of religious or public interest, in the broadest meaning of those terms, for it is clear that a desire to protect this right was the primary purpose of the First Amendment.[14]

Balancing, in Black's view, is inherently dangerous and wholly lacking in judicial integrity because the application of the test is "necessarily tied to the emphasis particular judges give to competing societal values."[15] As if to illustrate this dictum, he stated that the appropriate characterization of these values would give emphasis to the social value of maintaining unimpaired freedoms of association and belief over a bar committee's curiosity concerning the applicant's possible membership in the Communist Party.

The validity of *Konigsberg (II)* was reemphasized by a trio of cases decided in 1971. The primary case, *Law Students Civil Rights Research Council, Inc. v. Wadmond*,[16] involved an attack on the manner in which New York screened its applicants for the bar. The appellants had challenged that the appellees' use of a questionnaire, which had a bifurcated inquiry between knowing membership and membership with intent to further illegal goals. They argued that the questionnaire unnecessarily intruded into rights of association by requiring applicants to divulge knowing mem-

bership although there could be no inference of disloyalty based on such information. The Court, however, held that it was within reasonable legislative boundaries to inquire into knowing membership as a preliminary inquiry on which to base further investigation.

Thus, an applicant to the bar may be required to answer a question concerning his knowing membership on pain of denial of certification. If the applicant responds affirmatively, the examiners may probe more deeply into the nature of that association to determine if it is appropriate to deny admission. Judicial review is available to remedy any abuses resulting from solely an admission of knowing membership. Moreover, *Wadmond* found that there was no constitutional infirmity in inquiring into the applicant's ability to take the oath required of attorneys without any mental reservations,[17] because such inquiry is incorporated into the federal oath for uniformed and civil service personnel.

In the two accompanying decisions also handed down in 1971, *Baird v. State Bar of Arizona*[18] and *Application of Stolar*,[19] the Court reaffirmed the rationale of *Wadmond* by invalidating denials of admission to the bar based on the petitioners' refusal to answer questions that were not limited to ascertaining "knowing" membership. Because the questions were overbroad and beyond the legitimate interest of the state in the affiliations of its attorneys, the denial of admission to the bar was improper.

Thus, the First Amendment does not provide an unlimited sanctuary for a bar applicant who does not desire to disclose his political affiliations. The state has an interest in informing itself about the applicant, particularly since it has the burden of establishing affirmative evidence of disloyalty. Frustration of a legitimate inquiry is subject to a denial of

---

13. 366 U.S. at 71, 81 S.Ct. at 1017 (Black, J., dissenting joined by Warren, C.J., and Douglas, J.).

14. 366 U.S. at 63–64, 81 S.Ct. at 1014 (Black, J., dissenting).

15. 366 U.S. at 75, 81 S.Ct. at 1019.

16. 401 U.S. 154, 91 S.Ct. 720, 27 L.Ed.2d 749 (1971). (Black, Douglas, Brennan and Marshall dissented).

17. See also In re Summers, 325 U.S. 561, 65 S.Ct. 1307, 89 L.Ed. 1795 (1945), rehearing denied 326 U.S. 807, 66 S.Ct. 94, 90 L.Ed. 491 (1945).

18. 401 U.S. 1, 91 S.Ct. 702, 27 L.Ed.2d 639 (1971).

19. 401 U.S. 23, 91 S.Ct. 713, 27 L.Ed.2d 657 (1971).

application for membership in the bar. However, the state's interest does not extend beyond interrogation concerning knowing membership, and a question beyond that permissible spectrum may be refused without penalty.

§ 16.45   The Public Forum: An Introduction

Justice Roberts, in his concurring opinion in *Hague v. CIO*,[1] expressed a narrow view of the Government's power to control speech that takes place on public property: "Wherever the title of streets and parks may rest, they have immemorially been held in trust for the use of the public and, time out of mind, have been used for purposes of assembly, communicating thoughts between citizens, and discussing public questions."[2]

Yet other Justices have inserted language in later opinions treating public property as if it were private property for free speech purposes. Justice Black, who had concurred with Roberts, later stated that he did not think the First and Fourteenth Amendments granted "a constitutional right to engage in the conduct of picketing or patrolling, whether on publicly owned streets or on privately owned property."[3] Justice Black's position, if taken literally, is an echo of Justice Holmes' view when he was a state court judge: "For the Legislature absolutely or conditionally to forbid public speaking in a highway or public park is no more an infringement of the rights of a member of the public than for the owner of a private house to forbid it in his house."[4]

One's judgments between these competing viewpoints is a function of how one weighs the interests at stake, that is, the right to disseminate ideas in public places versus government claims to keep the peace and to protect other interests of a civilized community.[5] To this balance one should add claims of a special right of access by the public to treat public places as a Public Forum.[6] Subsequent sections examine the leading cases in this area in order to illustrate the major rules that have developed.

§ 16.46   Licensing Schemes Implemented by Administrators and Injunctions Issued by the Courts

Often the state seeks to exercise time, place, or manner restrictions on speech in public places by use of licensing schemes. But the administrator's net of control must not be cast too broadly.[1] Thus, a licensing standard that gives an official the authority to censor the content of a speech is quite different from one limited by its terms, or by nondiscriminatory practice, to valid considerations, such as public safety.[2]

---

§ 16.45

1. 307 U.S. 496, 59 S.Ct. 954, 83 L.Ed. 1423 (1939).

2. Hague v. Committee for Industrial Organization, 307 U.S. 496, 515, 59 S.Ct. 954, 964, 83 L.Ed. 1423 (1939) (Roberts, J., concurring, joined by Black, J.). Subsequently Justice Black appeared to retreat from this narrow view. E.g., Cox v. Louisiana, 379 U.S. 559, 575, 85 S.Ct. 476, 486, 13 L.Ed.2d 487 (1965), rehearing denied 380 U.S. 926, 85 S.Ct. 879, 13 L.Ed.2d 814 (1965) (Black, J., concurring and dissenting in part); Adderley v. Florida, 385 U.S. 39, 47–48, 87 S.Ct. 242, 247, 17 L.Ed.2d 149 (1966), rehearing denied 385 U.S. 1020, 87 S.Ct. 698, 17 L.Ed.2d 559 (1967) (Black, J.).

3. Cox v. Louisiana, 379 U.S. 559, 575 85 S.Ct. 476, 486, 13 L.Ed.2d 487 (1965), rehearing denied 380 U.S. 926, 85 S.Ct. 879, 13 L.Ed.2d 814 (1965) (Black, J. concurring and dissenting in part).

4. Commonwealth v. Davis, 162 Mass. 510, 511, 39 N.E. 113, 113 (1895), affirmed sub nom. Davis v. Massachusetts, 167 U.S. 43, 17 S.Ct. 731, 42 L.Ed. 71 (1897).

5. Niemotko v. Maryland, 340 U.S. 268, 273–274, 71 S.Ct. 328, 328–29, 95 L.Ed. 280 (1951) (Frankfurter, J., concurring).

6. See Kalven, The Concept of the Public Forum: Cox v. Louisiana, 1965 S.Ct.Rev. 1.

§ 16.46

1. Niemotko v. Maryland, 340 U.S. 268, 282, 71 S.Ct. 328, 333, 95 L.Ed. 280 (1951) (concurring). See, 4 R. Rotunda & J. Nowak, Treatise on Constitutional Law: Substance and Procedure § 20.46 (West Group, 3d ed.1999).

2. Niemotko v. Maryland, 340 U.S. 268, 282, 71 S.Ct. 325, 333, 95 L.Ed. 267 (1951). Compare Watchtower Bible & Tract Society of New York, Inc. v. Village of Stratton, 536 U.S. 150, 122 S.Ct. 2080, 153 L.Ed.2d 205 (2002). A village ordinance prohibited "canvassers" and others from going on private residential property to promote any cause without first securing a "Solicitation Permit" from the mayor. The Court invalidated the ordinance as it applied to religious proselytizing, anonymous political speech, and the distribution of handbills. The law necessarily prevented anonymous speech and it banned a substantial amount of spontaneous speech. The ordinance was not necessary to protect the privacy of residents who could either refuse to converse with the solicitor or post a "no soliciting" sign. Nor is the ordinance carefully tailored to prevent crime,

In short, a permit scheme, first, may not grant to the government administrator an overly broad amount of discretion. And second, the administrator must not base the decision to grant or to deny the permit on the content of the message.

For example, in *Thomas v. Chicago Park District*,[3] a unanimous Supreme Court rejected a facial challenge to a Chicago Park District ordinance that required a permit in order to conduct a public assembly, parade, picnic, or other event involving more than 50 people, or to engage in any activity emitting any amplified sound. The law simply imposed content-neutral regulations governing the time, place, and manner restrictions designed to coordinate multiple uses of limited space.

The Park District ordinance was narrowly written: it provided that the Park District must grant or deny the permit within 14 days, subject to a 14-day extension; the Park District must process applications in the order of receipt; it could deny the application for any of 13 specified grounds, none of which were content-based (such as, the application contained a material falsehood, or the applicant is legally incompetent, or the applicant damaged Park District property in the past and not paid in full for such damage).

The law was not limited to communicative activity but directed at all activity in a public park, such as picnics or soccer, if the 50-person limit is reached. A unsuccessful applicant could appeal to the Park District's General Superintendent and then to the state court. The grounds to deny a permit were reasonably specific and objective; there was no evidence that the Park District engaged in a pattern of

granting waivers to favored speakers and denying waivers to disfavored ones.[4]

When an Administrator Denies a License. In *Lovell v. Griffin*,[5] a member of the Jehovah's Witnesses[6] was prosecuted for disobeying a city ordinance that forbade the distribution of circulars, advertising matter, and similar material unless one secured a permit from the city manager. The city argued that its sanitary and litter problems made "apparent" the reasons for the ordinance.[7]

In *Lovell* the defendant was convicted for distributing religious tracts. Because she had not secured a license nor even applied for it, the city argued that she was not in the "position of having suffered from the exercise of the arbitrary and unlimited power of which she complains."[8] If she had applied and then been denied, the city argued, then she would have suffered loss of constitutional right; in other words, only then would she have standing to complain.

The city's arguments failed to persuade a unanimous Supreme Court. This ordinance had an unusually broad sweep: it prohibited the distribution of literature of any kind under every sort of circulation, at any time, at any place, and in any manner, without a permit from the City Manager. Its literal language could have been applied to newspapers, although there was no evidence of that. This law "strikes at the very foundation of the freedom of the press by subjecting it to license and censorship."[9] Hence, it was invalid on its face, a prior restraint of free speech.[10] And, because it was void on its face, the defendant did not have to apply for a permit before she could contest ordinance. As the Court had earlier articulated in *Thornhill v. Alabama*:[11] "One

---

because it did not preclude criminals from knocking on doors (e.g., they could pose as people asking for directions).

3. 534 U.S. 316, 122 S.Ct. 775, 151 L.Ed.2d 783 (2002).

4. The Court did not reach the issue whether the requirement of prompt judicial review means a prompt determination or a prompt commencement of the judicial proceedings.

5. 303 U.S. 444, 58 S.Ct. 666, 82 L.Ed. 949 (1938).

6. In the approximately three decades following *Lovell*, more than thirty cases in the Supreme Court raised issues of the regulation of speech in the public forum. A large majority of these cases involved the Jehovah's Witnesses.

Kalven, The Concept of the Public Forum: Cox v. Louisiana, 1965 S.Ct. Rev. 1 n. 2.

7. 303 U.S. at 445, 58 S.Ct. at 667 (argument for appellee).

8. 303 U.S. at 446, 58 S.Ct. at 667.

9. Lovell v. City of Griffin, Ga., 303 U.S. 444, 451, 58 S.Ct. 666, 668.

10. 303 U.S. at 451, 58 S.Ct. at 669.

11. 310 U.S. 88, 60 S.Ct. 736, 84 L.Ed. 1093 (1940). **Peaceful Picketing and the *Thornhill* Doctrine.** *Thornhill* also held that "the dissemination of information concerning the facts of a labor dispute must be regarded

who might have had a license for the asking may therefore call into question the whole scheme of licensing when he is prosecuted for failure to procure it."[12]

To be distinguished from *Lovell* and its progeny is the line of cases represented by *Poulos v. New Hampshire*,[13] another Jehovah's Witness case. In *Poulos* the defendant was convicted for conducting a religious service in a public park without a proper license. Unlike *Lovell*, the defendant did apply for the license. He was denied the license but he did not appeal that denial in the state court system. And, equally important, his defense in the criminal charge was not that the licensing statute was so vague or overbroad as to be void on its face but rather that the City Council arbitrarily and unreasonably refused his application for a license.

The state trial court held that, on its face, the ordinance in question was constitutional, as a reasonable restriction of the time, place, and manner of speech in public places. The court also found that the refusal of the City Council to grant the requested license was arbitrary and unreasonable. Nonetheless the trial court upheld the criminal prosecution, and the state supreme court affirmed. Because, "the ordinance was valid on its face the state court determined the [defendant's] remedy was by certiorari to review the unlawful refusal of the [city] Council to grant the license, not by holding public religious services in the park without a license, and then defending because the refusal of the license was arbitrary."[14]

The Supreme Court affirmed the conviction, with Justice Frankfurter concurring in the result and only Justices Black and Douglas dissenting. First, the licensing statute, as construed by the state court, required uniform, nondiscriminatory, and consistent treatment regarding the granting of licenses for public meetings on public streets and parks. This law was constitutional on its face; it provided only a ministerial role for the police.

Secondly, the defendant could be convicted for holding his religious meeting without a license, even though it had wrongly been denied to him by the city. The defendant, instead of using the public park without a proper license, should have sought judicial review of the license denial:

> It must be admitted that judicial correction of arbitrary refusal by administrators to perform official duties under valid laws is . . . costly. But to allow applicants to proceed without the required permits to . . . hold public meetings without prior safety arrangements or take other unauthorized action is apt to cause breaches of the peace or create public dangers. . . . Delay is unfortunate, but the expense and annoyance of litigation is a price citizens must pay for life in an orderly society where the rights of the First Amendment have a real and abiding meaning.[15]

There are some exceptions to the *Poulos* rule regarding the failure to obtain a license where the relevant licensing statute is not void on its face. A state could choose to allow a defense that the administrator unlawfully refused to grant a permit.[16] But, if the statute is valid on its face, it is constitutional for the state to disallow this defense because of failure

---

as within that area of free discussion that is guaranteed by the Constitution." 310 U.S. at 102, 60 S.Ct. at 744. But the Court does not grant full First Amendment protection to all forms of peaceful labor picketing. Thus, "a State, in enforcing some public policy, whether of its criminal or its civil law, and whether announced by its legislature or its courts, could constitutionally enjoin peaceful picketing aimed at preventing effectuation of that policy." International Brotherhood of Teamsters v. Vogt, Inc., 354 U.S. 284, 293, 77 S.Ct. 1166, 1171, 1 L.Ed.2d 1347 (1957), rehearing denied 354 U.S. 945, 77 S.Ct. 1423, 1 L.Ed.2d 1558 (1957).

12. 310 U.S. at 97, 60 S.Ct. at 742. In Forsyth County v. The Nationalist Movement, 505 U.S. 123, 112 S.Ct.

2395, 120 L.Ed.2d 101 (1992). the Court invalidated, on its face, an ordinance permitting the administrator to vary the permit fee based on the content of the demonstration or parade. Even a nominal fee would be unconstitutional because it was based on content.

13. 345 U.S. 395, 73 S.Ct. 760, 97 L.Ed. 1105 (1953), rehearing denied 345 U.S. 978, 73 S.Ct. 1119, 97 L.Ed. 1392 (1953).

14. 345 U.S. at 400, 73 S.Ct. at 763–64.

15. 345 U.S. at 409, 73 S.Ct. at 768.

16. 345 U.S. at 409 n. 13, 73 S.Ct. at 769 n. 13.

to apply for a license. The state may give the applicant the choice of complying with the regulation, or not engaging in the regulated activity, or, before he or she acts, petitioning the appropriate civil tribunals for a modification of, or exception from, the regulation[17]

Justice Frankfurter's concurrence emphasized that nothing in the record even suggested that the judicial remedy in the state court that Poulos must utilize was a procedural pretense or even would effectively frustrate and delay his right to speech. Poulos did not show the unavailability of a prompt judicial remedy, particularly given the fact that Poulos was denied his license on May 4 for meetings that were not to be held until June 25 and July 2.[18] If there were no prompt judicial remedy in the state court system, *Poulos* should have come out differently.

Note that *Poulos* upheld the statute as construed by the state court. This power of a state court to save the constitutionality of a statute by narrow interpretation has some limits, for it can deprive a litigant of fair warning if a statute that appears void on its face is later upheld in the very case in which the litigant is protesting its application. Therefore, even though the state court may authoritatively construe a statute for its future application, when the interpretation is "a remarkable job of plastic surgery"[19] and it would have taken "extraordinary clairvoyance" to anticipate the decision,[20] a conviction under the statute, when one could not know its limited construction, could not stand.

Differing Permit Fees. *Forsyth County v. The Nationalist Movement*[21] invalidated, on its face, an ordinance that, in effect, allowed the administrator to base the permit fee on the content of the demonstration or parade. The fee was not to exceed $1000 per day of the parade, open air meeting, or procession.

First, the ordinance granted the administrator too much discretion. For example, it was up to the county administrator to decide whether the fee would include any or all of the county's administrative expenses. The administrator could also decide to charge *no fee.*[22]

Second, the ordinance, in effect, required that the fee must depend on the content of the demonstration, parade, or procession. The fee varied, based on administrator's estimate of the cost of maintaining public order. Given this statutory requirement, the administrator must, of necessity, look at the content of the message that is displayed, estimate the response of persons observing that message, and determine the number of police necessary to meet the expected response. To the extent that observers of the parade are likely to throw bottles, the organizers of the parade will have to pay more for their permit, because it is the seekers of the license, not the observers, that must pay the costs. A fee based on the listeners' reaction to speech is not a content-neutral basis for regulation. The fact that the speaker provokes controversy rather than is boring is not a reason to increase the permit fee. Free speech should not become more costly simply because the observers turn themselves into a hostile mob.

The $1000 maximum cap on the fee did not save it from invalidity. In fact, even a nominal fee would be unconstitutional because the amount of the fee is a function of the content of the speech, and imposition of fee lacks procedural safeguards. No fee cap can remedy these constitutional violations.

Rehnquist, C.J., joined by White, Scalia, and Thomas, JJ., filed a dissenting opinion.

17. 345 U.S. at 410 n. 13, 73 S.Ct. at 769 n. 13.

18. 345 U.S. at 420, 73 S.Ct. at 773–74 (Frankfurter, J., concurring).

19. Shuttlesworth v. Birmingham, 394 U.S. 147, 153, 89 S.Ct. 935, 940, 22 L.Ed.2d 162 (1969), on remand to 45 Ala.App. 723, 222 So.2d 377 (1969).

20. Shuttlesworth v. Birmingham, 394 U.S. 147, 156, 89 S.Ct. 935, 941, 22 L.Ed.2d 162 (1969), on remand to 45 Ala.App. 723, 222 So.2d 377 (1969).

21. 505 U.S. 123, 112 S.Ct. 2395, 120 L.Ed.2d 101 (1992). Blackmun, J., delivered the opinion of the Court.

22. Contrast, Cox v. New Hampshire, 312 U.S. 569, 576–77, 61 S.Ct. 762, 765–66, 85 L.Ed. 1049 (1941). While the language of the statute in *Cox* appeared to grant the administrator a great deal of discretion, as the statute was interpreted and applied, the discretion was not unfettered but limited in important ways. In *Forsyth County*, there was no testimony or evidence that indicated any limits on the administrator's unfettered discretion. 505 U.S. at 133 n. 11, 112 S.Ct. at 2403 n. 12.

When a Court Enjoins Speech in the Public Forum. To be distinguished from the *Lovell* and *Poulos* line of cases—where the application for the license is made to an administrator—is the situation when the speaker is prevented from speaking, not by the denial of a license, but by a court injunction or temporary restraining order. Although one may collaterally attack a licensing ordinance that is invalid on its face under the doctrine of *Lovell v. Griffin*,[23] one may not disregard a court injunction or temporary restraining order issued by a court with jurisdiction, even though the court order is equally void on its face. The proper procedure to attack the court order is to appeal it, and therefore the individual may be barred in a collateral proceeding from contesting the validity of the injunction, if he is prosecuted for violating it.[24]

Walker v. Birmingham[25] illustrates this principle. In that case the Court upheld the contempt of court convictions of Martin Luther King Jr. and other black ministers who participated in civil rights marches and parades in violation of an *ex parte* temporary injunction issued by a state circuit court.[26]

The Supreme Court found that the state court had jurisdiction over the petitioners and over the subject matter of the controversy. Moreover the injunction was not "transparently invalid" nor did it have "only a frivolous pretense to validity."[27] The majority did not define those terms, but it should be understood that it would be the most atypical injunctive order that could probably meet this test, for the *Walker* order, as the majority admitted, was written in terms of such "breadth and vagueness" as to "unquestion-

ably" raise a "substantial constitutional question."[28]

Two terms later, the Supreme Court held that marchers in the *same events* involved in *Walker* did not have to comply with the same Birmingham licensing ordinance, because it was invalid on its face and could not be saved even by judicial construction applied to the parties before the state court.[29] Thus, an *ex parte* court order is not "transparently invalid" simply because it "recites the words of the invalid statute."[30] In other words the marchers could ignore an ordinance that was invalid on its face (pursuant to the *Lovell* doctrine) but they had to obey a court order that merely repeated the words of the invalid ordinance. Courts are much more disturbed when litigants disobey a court injunction than they are when litigants disobey a statute.

Walker was concerned that the petitioners did not even attempt to appeal within the Alabama court system the lower court's order. The proper procedure was to apply to the Alabama courts to have the injunction modified or dissolved. If petitioners had done so and had been met with delay or frustration of their constitutional claims, then the case "would arise in quite a different constitutional posture."[31] Finally, the majority concluded:

> This Court cannot hold that the petitioners were constitutionally free to ignore all the procedures of the law and carry their battle to the streets. One may sympathize with the petitioners' impatient commitment to their cause. But respect for judicial process is a small price to pay for the civilizing hand of law, which alone can give abiding meaning

23. 303 U.S. 444, 58 S.Ct. 666, 82 L.Ed. 949 (1938).

24. Compare Walker v. Birmingham, 388 U.S. 307, 87 S.Ct. 1824, 18 L.Ed.2d 1210 (1967), rehearing denied 389 U.S. 894, 88 S.Ct. 12, 19 L.Ed.2d 202 (1967), with Shuttlesworth v. Birmingham, 394 U.S. 147, 89 S.Ct. 935, 22 L.Ed.2d 162 (1969), on remand to 45 Ala.App. 723, 222 So.2d 377 (1969).

25. 388 U.S. 307, 87 S.Ct. 1824, 18 L.Ed.2d 1210 (1967), rehearing denied 389 U.S. 894, 88 S.Ct. 12, 19 L.Ed.2d 202 (1967).

26. Petitioners were each sentenced to five days in jail and $50 fine. 388 U.S. at 312, 87 S.Ct. at 1827.

27. 388 U.S. at 315, 87 S.Ct. at 1829.

28. 388 U.S. at 317, 87 S.Ct. at 1830. The order was reprinted in 388 U.S. at 321–322, 87 S.Ct. at 1832–33.

29. Shuttlesworth v. Birmingham, 394 U.S. 147, 89 S.Ct. 935, 22 L.Ed.2d 162 (1969), on remand to 45 Ala. App. 723, 222 So.2d 377 (1969). The Court also acknowledged that the "petitioner here was one of the petitioners in the *Walker* case . . . ." 394 U.S. at 157, 89 S.Ct. at 942.

30. Walker v. Birmingham, 388 U.S. 307, 346, 87 S.Ct. 1824, 1845, 18 L.Ed.2d 1210 (1967) (Brennan, J., dissenting, joined by Warren, C. J., and Douglas and Fortas, JJ.).

31. 388 U.S. at 318, 87 S.Ct. at 1831.

to constitutional freedom.[32]

Chief Justice Warren, Justices Douglas, Brennan, and Fortas all dissented vigorously.[33] As Chief Justice Warren argued in his dissent, the petitioners should be treated the same as persons who challenge the constitutionality of a statute and then defend themselves on the grounds that the statute is unconstitutional. "It has never been thought that violation of a statute indicated such a disrespect for the legislature that the violator always must be punished even if the statute was unconstitutional."[34]

Several years later the Supreme Court held unconstitutional the *ex parte* procedure in free speech cases such as *Walker*, where officials obtain an *ex parte* court order restraining the holding of meetings or rallies. An order in such cases is defective if it is issued *ex parte*, without notice to the subjects of the order, and without any effort, even an informal one, to invite or permit their participation, unless a showing is made that it is impossible to serve or to notify the opposing parties and give them an opportunity to respond.[35] In the case in which the Court announced this holding, the petitioners *obeyed* the order and then appealed it rather than disobeying it and attacking it collaterally.

§ 16.47 Reasonable Time, Place, and Manner Restrictions on Speech, Without Regard to Content

(a) Introduction

In general, the state may place reasonable time, place, or manner restrictions on speech that takes place in the public forum, but these regulations must be implemented without regard to the content of the speech.[1] Otherwise the state would be able to cloak restrictions on speech in the guise of regulations of the mode of speech or the place—the streets, the parks, public buildings—that is used for the speech. To prevent abuse of the power to make reasonable regulations, and to help assure that the regulations are in fact reasonable, the Court will independently determine if the regulation is a narrow means of protecting important interests unrelated to content.[2]

The Court has phrased its test in two slightly different forms. First, there is a general principle that government regulation is permissible: "if it is within the constitutional power of the Government; if it furthers an important or substantial governmental interest; if the governmental interest is unrelated to the suppression of free expression; and if the incidental restriction on alleged First Amendment freedoms is no greater than is essential to the furtherance of that interest."[3] The second method of analysis elaborates on this general principle by restating it in terms of a three-part test. The Court will uphold time, place, or manner restrictions if they are content-neutral, narrowly tailored to serve a significant government interest, and leave open ample alternative channels of communication.[4]

Whether the Court states its test in terms of a general principle or a three-part test, when the Court reviews time, place, or manner re-

---

32. 388 U.S. at 321, 87 S.Ct. at 1832.

33. 388 U.S. at 324–349, 87 S.Ct. at 1833–47.

34. 388 U.S. at 327, 87 S.Ct. at 1835 (Warren, C.J., dissenting, joined by Brennan and Fortas, JJ.).

35. Carroll v. President and Commissioners of Princess Anne, 393 U.S. 175, 89 S.Ct. 347, 21 L.Ed.2d 325 (1968). Cf. A Quantity of Copies of Books v. Kansas, 378 U.S. 205, 84 S.Ct. 1723, 12 L.Ed.2d 809 (1964).

§ 16.47

1. E.g., Madison, Joint School District v. Wisconsin Employment Relations Commission, 429 U.S. 167, 176, 97 S.Ct. 421, 426, 50 L.Ed.2d 376 (1976) ("when the board sits in public meetings to conduct public business and hear the views of citizens, it may not be required to discriminate between speakers on the basis of their employment, or the content of their speech."); Linmark Associates, Inc. v. Township of Willingboro, 431 U.S. 85, 97 S.Ct. 1614, 52 L.Ed.2d 155 (1977) (ordinance banning "for sale" and "sold" signs for the purpose of stemming the flight of white homeowners from racially integrated town invalidated; ordinance concerned with content of speech); Hoffman, J., citing Treatise in, Borchert v. Indiana, 621 N.E.2d 657, 658 (Ind.App.1993).

2. Blair Arnold, joined by Corbin, J., citing Treatise and dissenting in Hodges v. Gray, 321 Ark. 7, 17, 901 S.W.2d 1, 6 (1995).

3. United States v. O'Brien, 391 U.S. 367, 377, 88 S.Ct. 1673, 1679, 20 L.Ed.2d 672 (1968), rehearing denied 393 U.S. 900, 89 S.Ct. 63, 21 L.Ed.2d 188 (1968).

4. United States v. Grace, 461 U.S. 171, 177, 103 S.Ct. 1702, 1707, 75 L.Ed.2d 736 (1983).

strictions, it really is engaging in a two-step form of analysis. First, it determines whether the regulation is in fact an attempt to suppress speech because of its message. A content-based restriction of is valid only if it fits within a category of speech that the First Amendment does not protect, for example, obscenity.[5] If the First Amendment protects the category of speech, then the state may enforce a content-based restriction on speech only if its regulation is necessary to serve a compelling state interest and is narrowly tailored to achieve that goal.[6]

If the regulation is not an attempt to censor content, the Court will go on to determine whether the incidental restriction on speech is outweighed by the promotion of significant governmental interests. Although this method of analysis is sometimes stated as a least restrictive means test, the analysis also evaluates whether the regulation leaves open ample means for communication of the message and is not an unnecessary or gratuitous suppression of communication.[7]

(b) Regulation of Sound and Noise

Noise Ordinances. *Saia v. New York*[8] invalidated a city ordinance that forbade the use of sound amplification devices such as loudspeakers on trucks, except with permission of the Chief of Police. The ordinance was unconstitutional on its face because the Chief of Police had uncontrolled discretion. The abuses of loudspeakers can be controlled, the majority agreed, if the control is pursuant to a narrowly-drawn statute.[9]

Kovacs v. Cooper[10] upheld such a noise statute, though the fragmented Court could not agree on the reasons.[11] Justice Reed's plurality opinion found the city ordinance in *Kovacs* not overbroad nor vague. It prohibited sound trucks and similar devices from emitting "loud and raucous noises." These words were found not to be too vague. Moreover the New Jersey courts by construction had narrowed the ordinance's applicability only to vehicles containing a sound amplifier or any other instrument emitting loud and raucous noises, when operated or standing in the public streets, alleys or thoroughfares of the city.[12] Justice Reed added that just as unrestrained use of all sound amplifying devices in a city would be intolerable, "[a]bsolute prohibition within municipal limits of all sound amplification, even though reasonably regulated in place, time and volume, is undesirable and probably unconstitutional as an unreasonable interference with normal activities."[13]

---

5. See § 16.56. The Court examines content-based restrictions very strictly. E.g., Regan v. Time, Inc., 468 U.S. 641, 104 S.Ct. 3262, 82 L.Ed.2d 487 (1984). Federal statutes prohibited photographing or reproducing photographs of government currency except it permitted the "printing, publishing or importation ... of illustrations of ... any ... obligation or other security of the United States ... for philatelic, numismatic, educational, historical, or newsworthy purposes in articles, books, journals, newspapers or albums...." Eight Justices of the Court invalidated the exemption portion of the statute because the exemption was content based. However, there was no majority opinion whether the statute could be upheld after striking down the part of the exemption that related to purpose of publication.

6. See § 16.47(c), discussing, e.g., Perry Education Association v. Perry Local Educators' Association, 460 U.S. 37, 44–46, 103 S.Ct. 948, 954–55, 74 L.Ed.2d 794 (1983), on remand 705 F.2d 462 (7th Cir.1983).

7. It may be that once a court has determined that a statute is truly content neutral the court can do nothing except balance the extent to which the regulation promotes a legitimate interest unrelated to the suppression of ideas against the degree to which society is deprived of communications by the regulation. See Farber and Nowak, The Misleading Nature of Public Forum Analysis: Content

and Context in First Amendment Adjudication, 70 Va. L.Rev. 1219 (1984).

8. 334 U.S. 558, 68 S.Ct. 1148, 92 L.Ed. 1574 (1948). See Sharp, J., citing Treatise in, Bovey v. City of Lafayette, 586 F.Supp. 1460, 1468 (N.D.Ind.1984); Conover, J., citing Treatise in, Mesarosh v. State, 459 N.E.2d 426, 427 (Ind.App.1984).

9. 334 U.S. at 562, 68 S.Ct. at 1150–51.

10. 336 U.S. 77, 69 S.Ct. 448, 93 L.Ed. 513 (1949), rehearing denied 336 U.S. 921, 69 S.Ct. 638, 93 L.Ed. 1083 (1949).

11. Justice Reed announced the judgment of the Court, in an opinion by Vinson, C.J., and Burton, J.; Murphy, J. dissented without opinion. Frankfurter, J. concurred. Jackson, J. concurred in a separate opinion. Black, J., dissented in an opinion joined by Douglas and Rutledge, JJ. Rutledge, J., also wrote a separate dissent.

12. 336 U.S. at 83, 69 S.Ct. at 451 (opinion of Reed, J.).

13. 336 U.S. at 81–82, 69 S.Ct. at 450–51 (opinion of Reed, J.). See also Grayned v. Rockford, 408 U.S. 104, 107–121, 92 S.Ct. 2294, 2298–2306, 33 L.Ed.2d 222 (1972) (antinoise ordinance prohibiting a person while on grounds adjacent to a building in which school is in

The Right Not to Hear. Somewhat related is the class of cases where recipients of information claim a right not to hear a message. *Public Utilities Commission v. Pollak*,[14] found no violation of either the First or Fifth Amendment when a city-regulated bus company, in exchange for money, broadcast FM music, news, and commercials on buses and streetcars.[15] The Court deferred to the ruling of the Public Utilities Commission allowing the practice.[16]

Pollak, however, does not forbid the state from deciding to protect those who do not wish to be recipients. Thus, it is constitutional for a statute to provide that any addressee of mail may request the post office to prohibit all future mailings from any particular sender. The law was upheld because the government made no decision on the basis of the content of the speech but only allowed the addressee to act in his sole discretion.[17] Without a request by the addressee, the post office could not impose on the addressee the burden to request certain mail. Such a statute would chill the addressee by requiring him to request mailings that the Government determined that he not receive. Also, less drastic means of protecting recipients are available, for the law could place the burden on the unwilling addressees to

request that certain types of mail not be delivered.[18]

Similarly, a city may protect householders from unwanted solicitors knocking on their doors, but the means selected must not be unreasonably harsh: a city ordinance may prohibit the business practice of soliciting magazine subscriptions door-to-door without prior invitation of the homeowner.[19] This rule merely reverses the common law privilege that did not find a trespass when one who was a stranger knocked on a private person's door without first securing permission. The Court struck the balance of interests differently in *Martin v. Struthers*,[20] where the Court invalidated a far broader ordinance applied to prohibit a person distributing free leaflets that advertised a religious meeting.

Under analogous reasoning, a city cannot forbid all leaflet distribution in order to prevent littering, fraud, or disorder, because the state can less drastically prohibit only the actual littering, fraud, or disorder.[21]

(c) Where the Speech Takes Place— The Degrees of Public Forum

Regulation of Content. *Police Department of Chicago v. Mosley*[22] considered the constitutionality of a city ordinance that prohibited picketing on a public way within 150 feet of a

---

session from making a noise or diversion that disturbs the peace and good order of the school session is not unconstitutionally vague or overbroad); Ward v. Rock Against Racism, 491 U.S. 781, 109 S.Ct. 2746, 105 L.Ed.2d 661 (1989) (Court rejects a facial challenge to New York City regulations designed to regulate the volume of excessively amplified music in a bandshell in Central Park); Madsen v. Women's Health Center, Inc., 512 U.S. 753, 772–73, 114 S.Ct. 2516, 2528–29, 129 L.Ed.2d 593 (1994), upholding portions of an injunction that (1) limited the hours that protesters could use sound amplification equipment in the area of an abortion clinic, where patients undergo surgery and recover, and (2) prohibited sound amplification equipment within 300 feet of the residences of staff of the abortion clinic because the sound overwhelmed the residential neighborhood.

14. 343 U.S. 451, 72 S.Ct. 813, 96 L.Ed. 1068 (1952).

15. The majority was "assuming that the action of Capital Transit in operating the radio service, together with the action of the Commission in permitting such operation, amounts to sufficient Federal Government action to make the First and Fifth Amendments applicable thereto." 343 U.S. at 462–463, 72 S.Ct. at 820–21.

16. Justice Black issued a separate opinion dissenting insofar as the majority allowed the passengers of Capital

Transit to be subjected to news, public speeches, views, or propaganda of any kind. He would only allow musical programs. Douglas also dissented in a separate opinion. Justice Frankfurter disqualified himself for the following reasons:

"My feelings are so strongly engaged as a victim of the practice in controversy that I had better not participate in judicial judgment upon it." (343 U.S. at 467, 72 S.Ct. at 823.)

17. Rowan v. U.S. Post Office Dept., 397 U.S. 728, 90 S.Ct. 1484, 25 L.Ed.2d 736 (1970).

18. Lamont v. Postmaster General, 381 U.S. 301, 85 S.Ct. 1493, 14 L.Ed.2d 398 (1965).

19. Breard v. Alexandria, 341 U.S. 622, 71 S.Ct. 920, 95 L.Ed. 1233 (1951), rehearing denied 342 U.S. 843, 72 S.Ct. 21, 96 L.Ed. 637 (1951). The Court specifically relied on the commercial nature of the transactions in question. One should compare this case with the modern view of the commercial speech doctrine.

20. 319 U.S. 141, 63 S.Ct. 862, 87 L.Ed. 1313 (1943).

21. Schneider v. New Jersey, 308 U.S. 147, 60 S.Ct. 146, 84 L.Ed. 155 (1939).

22. 408 U.S. 92, 92 S.Ct. 2286, 33 L.Ed.2d 212 (1972).

grade or high school from one-half hour before the school was in session until one-half hour after the school session had been concluded. However, the ordinance exempted peaceful labor picketing. The ordinance was invalidated.

While the ordinance purported to regulate the time, place, and manner of speech activities in the public forum, it did so based on the content of the speech. A careful look at the restrictions of the ordinance and its exceptions demonstrated that the law regulated content. That content regulation was the fatal flaw in the ordinance:

> Peaceful picketing on the subject of a school's labor-management dispute is permitted, but all other peaceful picketing is prohibited. The operative distinction is the message on a picket sign. But, above all else, the First Amendment means that government has no power to restrict expression because of its message, its ideas, its subject matter, or its content.... Necessarily, then, under the Equal Protection Clause, not to mention the First Amendment itself, government may not grant the use of a forum to people whose views it finds acceptable, but deny use to those wishing to express less favored or more controversial views.... Once a forum is opened up to assembly or speaking by some groups, government may not prohibit others from assembling or speaking on the basis of what they intend to say.[23]

Carey v. Brown[24] invalidated an Illinois statute that prohibited all picketing of residences or dwellings except for the peaceful picketing of a place of employment involved in a labor dispute. The majority relied on *Mosley.*

The Three Categories of Public Forum: The Analysis in *Perry*. The Supreme Court made the first major effort to recognize and classify the types of public forums in *Perry Education Ass'n v. Perry Local Educators' Ass'n.*[25] In that case a teachers' union, the Perry Education Association (PEA), was the duly elected exclusive bargaining representative of the teachers in a certain school district. A collective bargaining agreement granted this union, and no other union, the right to access to the interschool mail system and teacher mailboxes in that school system. The rival union, the Perry Local Educators' Association (PLEA), sought similar access. In a five to four opinion the Supreme Court, in an opinion by Justice White, found that the school's denial of access to the rival union of the mailboxes and interschool mail system was no violation of free speech.

Of significance is the majority's reasoning. The Court recognized that there were degrees of public forums. Along the spectrum, three major distinctions exist:

> In places which by long tradition or by government fiat have been devoted to assembly and debate, the rights of the state to limit expressive activity are sharply circumscribed. At one end of the spectrum are streets and parks which "have immemorially been held in trust for the use of the public, and, time out of mind, have been used for purposes of assembly, communicating thoughts between citizens, and discussing public questions." In these quintessential public forums, the government may not prohibit all communicative activity. For the state to enforce a content-based exclusion it must show that its regulation is necessary to serve a compelling state interest and that it is narrowly drawn to achieve that end. The state may also enforce regulations of the time, place, and manner of expression which are content-neutral, are narrowly tailored to

---

23. 408 U.S. at 95–96, 92 S.Ct. at 2290. Accord Grayned v. Rockford, 408 U.S. 104, 105–107, 92 S.Ct. 2294, 2297–98, 33 L.Ed.2d 222 (1972). See also, Niemotko v. Maryland, 340 U.S. 268, 71 S.Ct. 328, 95 L.Ed. 280 (1951) (Jehovah's Witnesses cannot be denied permit to use a city park for Bible talks when other religious and political groups had been allowed to use the park for similar purposes); Fowler v. Rhode Island, 345 U.S. 67, 73 S.Ct. 526, 97 L.Ed. 828 (1953) (same).

24. 447 U.S. 455, 100 S.Ct. 2286, 65 L.Ed.2d 263 (1980). Rehnquist, J., joined by Burger, C.J., and Blackmun, J., dissented. Subsequently, the Court upheld a narrowly drawn anti-residential picketing law. See Frisby v. Schultz, 487 U.S. 474, 108 S.Ct. 2495, 101 L.Ed.2d 420 (1988), on remand 857 F.2d 1175 (7th Cir.1988), discussed below, in this section.

25. 460 U.S. 37, 103 S.Ct. 948, 74 L.Ed.2d 794 (1983), on remand 705 F.2d 462 (7th Cir.1983).

serve a significant government interest, and leave open ample alternative channels of communication.[26]

The restrictions on residential picketing on the public streets—which the Court invalidated in *Carey v. Brown*[27]—fall in this first category, where the Court is most likely to invalidate regulation.

The Court then turned to the second category:

> A second category consists of public property which the state has opened for use by the public as a place for expressive activity. The Constitution forbids a state to enforce certain exclusions from a forum generally open to the public even if it was not required to create the forum in the first place. Although a state is not required to indefinitely retain the open character of the facility, as long as it does so it is bound by the same standards as apply in a traditional public forum. Reasonable time, place and manner regulations are permissible, and a content-based prohibition must be narrowly drawn to effectuate a compelling state interest.[28]

Thus in *Widmar v. Vincent*[29] a state university made its facilities generally available for registered student groups. Having done so, it could not discriminate among those groups on the basis of content without a compelling justification. The Court therefore held that the state university could not close its facilities to a registered student group desiring to use its facilities for religious worship and discussion.

Because the university created the forum, it had to justify its discriminations and exclusions.

Notice that *Widmar* involved religious speech. Once the school opened its facilities to registered student groups, it could not discriminate against those groups based on content, even if those students wanted to pray. In various cases the Court has made clear that if there is a public forum, the state cannot discriminate against religious speech in that forum. The fact that speech is religious certainly does not mean that the speech should have *less* First Amendment protection. To have freedom of speech without freedom of religious speech would be like playing *Hamlet* without the prince.[30] The establishment clause prohibits the government from endorsing religion, but the free speech and free exercise clauses protect private speech endorsing religion. "[P]rivate religious speech, far from being a First Amendment orphan, is as fully protected under the Free Speech Clause as secular private expression."[31]

Finally the Court turned to the third category of public forum analysis:

> Public property which is not by tradition or designation a forum for public communication is governed by different standards. We have recognized that the "First Amendment does not guarantee access to property simply because it is owned or controlled by the government." In addition to time, place,

26. 460 U.S. at 44–46, 103 S.Ct. at 954–55 (internal citations omitted without indication).

See, Farber & Nowak, The Misleading Nature of Public Forum Analysis; Content and Context in First Amendment Adjudication, 70 Va.L.Rev. 1219 (1984).

27. 447 U.S. 455, 100 S.Ct. 2286, 65 L.Ed.2d 263 (1980).

28. 460 U.S. at 45–46, 103 S.Ct. at 955 (internal citations omitted without indication).

29. 454 U.S. 263, 102 S.Ct. 269, 70 L.Ed.2d 440 (1981). See also, Flower v. United States, 407 U.S. 197, 198, 92 S.Ct. 1842, 1843, 32 L.Ed.2d 653 (1972) (per curiam), mandate conformed 462 F.2d 1133 (5th Cir.1972) (street technically within the jurisdiction of military fort treated by the military as a public thoroughfare of the city; the military authorities could not then order a person to leave the street because he was distributing leaflets any more than a city policeman could order someone off the streets).

30. Religious Speech and the Public Forum. Capitol Square Review and Advisory Board v. Pinette, 515 U.S. 753, 115 S.Ct. 2440, 132 L.Ed.2d 650 (1995). State law made Capitol Square, an open area next to the state capitol, the seat of government. It was used for public speeches, festivals, and celebrations advocating various causes, both secular and religious. To use the square, the applicant must meet several criteria concerning safety, sanitation, and noninterference with other uses of this public square. However, the state refused to issue a permit to the Ku Klux Klan, which wanted to display a Latin cross, on the grounds that displaying the cross would violate the establishment clause. The Klan sued, the federal court ordered that the permit be issued, and the Supreme Court affirmed. One might compare the display to a parade, except that the display was stationary.

31. 519 U.S. at 760, 115 S.Ct. at 2446 (Scalia, J., for the Court).

and manner regulations, the state *may reserve the forum for its intended purposes, communicative or otherwise, as long as the regulation on speech is reasonable* and *not an effort to suppress expression merely because public officials oppose the speaker's view.* As we have stated on several occasions, "the State, no less than a private owner of property, has power to preserve the property under its control for the use to which it is lawfully dedicated."[32]

A few years earlier the Supreme Court had held that a U.S. mailbox was not a public forum, and that therefore it was constitutional to prohibit the deposit of unstamped, "mailable matter" in a mailbox approved by the U.S. Postal Service.[33] Now the Court ruled that the school mail facilities also fell in this third class.

After *Perry* it is clear that it is very important to determine into which category the alleged public forum falls. What is substantially less clear from *Perry* is what test the courts should use to decide whether—a school classroom, a school mail system, etc.—is in the second category or the third category. The first category—the streets and parks—may be self-defining for most purposes, but the latter two categories are not.

Perry really offered no litmus test to distinguish between the second category (public property opened for use by the public as a place for expressive activity) and the third category (public property not by designation or tradition a forum for public communication).[34] *Perry* merely announced that the school internal mail system is in the third category, even though the mail system was open to nonschool groups like the Cub Scouts. *Widmar* placed the school classroom in the second category, although the school officials in that case probably believed that their classrooms should fall into the third category.

In a later case, the Court tried offer further explanation between the types of fora. It said that *designated* public fora, in contrast to *traditional* public fora (like the streets and parks) are created by purposeful governmental action. The government must intentionally open a nontraditional public forum for public discourse, to make the property "generally available." A designated public forum is not created when the government allows *selective access* for individual speakers rather than general access for a class of speakers. For example, said the Court, if a university were to make its meeting facilities "generally open" to registered student groups, it would create a designated public forum. "General access" indicates that the property is a designated public forum, while "selective access" indicates the property is a nonpublic forum.[35]

This distinction between general and selective access should encourage the government to open its property to some expressive activity in cases where, if faced with an all-or-nothing choice, it might not open the property at all. Yet, it still has a conclusory quality about it. All of the parties in *Perry* agreed that the school board could close its mail system to all but official business. Presumably the board could also simply close down the system entirely. But it had done neither. Although the internal mail system was not open to the public generally, the school sometimes allowed private, nonschool groups to use the mail system. Also, prior to the certification of the PEA, the PLEA and the PEA both had unrestricted access. However, the fact that groups like the Cub Scouts and YMCA had access did not convert the mailboxes to a public forum, because the constitutional right of access would only extend to other entities of similar character.[36]

---

32. 460 U.S. at 46, 103 S.Ct. at 955 (emphasis added) (internal citations omitted without indication). Adderley v. Florida, 385 U.S. 39, 87 S.Ct. 242, 17 L.Ed.2d 149 (1966) (jail grounds not public forum).

33. United States Postal Serv. v. Council of Greenburgh Civic Associations, 453 U.S. 114, 101 S.Ct. 2676, 69 L.Ed.2d 517 (1981).

34. See Highsmith, J., quoting this Treatise in Pritchard v. Carlton, 821 F.Supp. 671, 675 n. 8 (S.D.Fla.1993).

35. Arkansas Educational Television Commission v. Forbes, 523 U.S. 666, 118 S.Ct. 1633, 140 L.Ed.2d 875 (1998).

36. "While the school mail facilities thus might be a forum generally open for use by the Girl Scouts, the local boys' club and other organizations that engage in activities of interest and educational relevance to students, they would not as a consequence be open to an organization such as PLEA, which is concerned with the terms and

When the school did decide to preclude the PLEA, the school did not discriminate against the content of the speech of the PLEA; the PEA Union (the other union), however, did object to the viewpoint expressed by the PLEA Union. The Court did not address that point directly, but concluded: "We believe it more accurate to characterize the access policy as based on the *status* of the respective unions rather than their views. Implicit in the concept of the nonpublic forum is the right to make distinctions in access on the basis of subject matter and speaker identity."[37]

The PLEA, in short, could say what it wanted and communicate with teachers on school property, post notices on school bulletin boards, and make announcements on the public address system. It simply could not use the mailboxes. The Court concluded that the school's policies were consistent with preserving the property for the use to which it was lawfully dedicated. The school allowed the PEA to use the mailboxes, which facilitated its obligations to represent all of the teachers. In contrast, the PLEA had no official responsibility. "[W]hen government property is not dedicated to open communication the government may—without further justification—restrict use to those who participate in the forum's official business."[38]

Applying the *Perry* Analysis

The General Rule. When the government regulates speech in a traditional public forum it may only base its restrictions on the content of the speech being regulated (1) if that content falls within a category of speech that the Supreme Court has held is not protected by the First Amendment (e.g., obscenity), or (2) if the government can demonstrate a compelling interest in suppressing the speech and the

content-based restriction is narrowly drawn to achieve this interest.

The government has greater leeway to impose a time, place, or manner regulation of speech in a public forum. The government regulations may impose *reasonable* time, place, and manner regulations, but the regulations must be *content neutral*; they must be *narrowly tailored* to serve a significant government interest; and they must *leave open ample alternative channels* of communication.[39]

If the government opens public property to the public as a place for expressive activity, even though it is not a traditional public forum, the government is subject to the same restrictions of its actions in this forum as would be applicable to regulations of speech in a traditional public forum. The government will be able to employ only reasonable time, place, or manner regulations. Any content based prohibition of speech in this forum must relate to a compelling governmental interest. However, the government may choose to close the forum to the public and expressive activities. It does not have to keep this type of forum open indefinitely.

Perry's third category is public property not open to the public, either by designation or by tradition. The government may dedicate property to the promotion of a specific governmental purpose. Government may reserve this type of property for its intended purpose, and regulate expressive activity occurring on this type of property as long as the speech regulation is reasonable and not an effort to suppress expression merely because public officials oppose the speaker's view. Let us consider these general statements in light of the specific facts that follow.

---

37. 460 U.S. at 49, 103 S.Ct. at 957 (emphasis in original).

38. 460 U.S. at 53, 103 S.Ct. at 959 (footnote omitted). Brennan, J., joined by Marshall, Powell, and Stevens, JJ., dissented, arguing that the exclusive access provision in the collective bargaining agreement was viewpoint discrimination and violated the First Amendment.

39. E.g., United States v. Grace, 461 U.S. 171, 177, 103 S.Ct. 1702, 1707, 75 L.Ed.2d 736 (1983), remanded 717 F.2d 1480 (D.C.Cir.1983).

conditions of teacher employment." 460 U.S. at 48, 103 S.Ct. at 956. See, Greer v. Spock, 424 U.S. 828, 838 n. 10, 96 S.Ct. 1211, 1217–18 n. 10, 47 L.Ed.2d 505 (1976) (military regulations of Fort Dix, New Jersey upheld; the regulations banned speeches and demonstrations of a partisan political nature; the military authorities did not treat the Fort as a public forum; and there was no viewpoint discrimination in the regulations); Brown v. Glines, 444 U.S. 348, 354 n. 2, 100 S.Ct. 594, 597 n. 2, 62 L.Ed.2d 540 (1980), on remand 618 F.2d 623 (9th Cir.1980).

Public Sidewalks and Parks. Two months after *Perry*, the Court in *United States v. Grace*[40] applied the *Perry* analysis and invalidated a portion of a federal statute prohibiting picketing on the public sidewalks surrounding the United States Supreme Court building. The public sidewalks are in the first category under *Perry* and the Government could not present the strong justification needed to allow such a restriction on the public forum. There was no evidence, for example, that the picketing obstructed access to the Supreme Court building.

The prohibition of all speech of this type in a public forum is a total suppression of the ability to communicate messages in a public place. *Grace* summarized and restated the test for time, place, or manner regulations of speech in a public forum as follows: "[t]he government may enforce reasonable time, place, and manner regulations as long as the restrictions are content neutral, are narrowly tailored to serve a significant government interest, and leave open ample alternative channels of communication."[41]

The Court employed the *Grace* test to uphold a National Park Service refusal to allow an around-the-clock demonstration in a park in Washington, D.C. *Clark v. Community for Creative Non-Violence*,[42] upheld a regulation limiting the time when a public park could be used, even though the limitation restricted the ability of the would be demonstrators to bring their message to the attention of the public by sleeping in symbolic "tent cities" in the park.

The refusal to allow a demonstration was a valid time, place, or manner regulation because it was a content neutral means of promoting the government interest in preserving parks and the regulation allowed adequate alternative channels of communication.[43] People can protest without moving in and living in the park day and night.

In *United States v. Kokinda*,[44] the Court, with no majority opinion, upheld the constitutionality of a federal law prohibiting solicitation on postal property. The respondents in this case were members of a political advocacy group who set up a table on a sidewalk near the entrance to a United States Post Office in order to solicit contributions, sell books and subscriptions, and distribute literature. The sidewalk, which lies entirely on Postal Service property, was the only way that customers could travel from the post office to the parking lot. The solicitors impeded the normal flow of traffic, and it is intrusive for the postal customers to confront people, face-to-face, soliciting contributions.

News Racks on Public Sidewalks. The City of Cincinnati banned the distribution of "commercial" publications (such as free magazines advertising real estate sales) through the use of free-standing news racks on public property, such as city sidewalks. However, the city did not extend the ban to similar news racks containing newspapers. The city argued that the purpose of its prohibition was to make the sidewalks more attractive and promote safer

---

40. 461 U.S. 171, 103 S.Ct. 1702, 75 L.Ed.2d 736 (1983), remanded 717 F.2d 1480 (D.C.Cir.1983). Marshall, J., and Stevens, J., each filed separate opinions concurring in part and dissenting in part. However, neither these Justices nor any other objected to the majority's reliance on the *Perry* analysis.

41. 461 U.S. at 177, 103 S.Ct. at 1707 (internal quotations and citations omitted).

42. 468 U.S. 288, 104 S.Ct. 3065, 82 L.Ed.2d 221 (1984).

43. The review of time, place, or manner regulations is designed to determine whether they are content based or an unnecessary restriction of the ability to communicate. Courts must still accord deference to the other branches of government in determining the reasonableness of regulations. Clark v. Community for Creative Non–Violence, 468 U.S. 288, 300, 104 S.Ct. 3065, 3072, 82 L.Ed.2d 221, 231 (1984).

44. 493 U.S. 807, 110 S.Ct. 47, 107 L.Ed.2d 16 (1989). O'Connor, J., joined by Rehnquist, C.J., and White & Scalia, JJ., concluded that the post office sidewalk was not a traditional public forum open to the public, because it was not a public passageway and was constructed solely to provide for the passage of customers engaged in postal business.

Kennedy, J., concurring in the judgment, argued that the postal regulation was constitutional *even if* the sidewalk is a public forum because it is a reasonable time, place, and manner regulation. Because the rule prohibited in-person solicitation for immediate payments on the premises. He relied on the special nature of in-person solicitation and the Postal Service's past experience.

Brennan, J., joined by Marshall, Stevens, JJ. (and by Blackmun, J., in part), dissented.

streets (e.g., people might trip over the news racks). However, while the city sought to remove the 62 news racks distributing these commercial publications, it did not apply its prohibition to news racks (numbering about 1,500 to 2,000) that sold regular *newspapers*.

City of Cincinnati v. Discovery Network, Inc.,[45] invalidated the ban. Cincinnati's equivocal distinction between newspapers and commercial handbills bore no relationship to the particular interests that the city asserted. After all, if a news rack is an eyesore, that defect does not change merely because the contents of the news rack is a daily newspaper (with real estate advertisements) rather than a listing of real estate advertisements. The likelihood that someone might trip over a news rack is not a function of whether the news rack contains newspapers or handbills.

Residential Picketing. The Court has been quite strict in reviewing laws that purport to regulate residential picketing, even though the purpose of such statutes is to protect residential privacy. Thus, *Carey v. Brown*[46] invalidated a narrowly drawn ordinance restricting residential picketing. It purported to prohibit all picketing of all residences or dwellings, but it did allow peaceful picketing of a place of employment involved in a labor dispute, thus regulating speech based on content. The statute did not forbid picketing, if the message of the picketers related to labor conditions.

In *Frisby v. Schultz*[47] the Court, over several dissents, finally approved a residential picketing statute, but only after interpreting it in an unusually narrow fashion, based on a strained construction. The majority rejected a facial challenge to a statute that it interpreted to ban only "focused" picketing, that is, picketing that would take place solely in front of a particular residence. Such picketing is directed at the household, not the public at large. The statute did not preclude marching through residential neighborhoods or even walking in front of an entire block of houses.[48]

Public Street Posts. Recall that the third category of public forum analysis under *Perry* is public property not open to the public either by designation or by tradition. The government may operate property that is dedicated to the promotion of a specific governmental purpose. As stated in *Perry*, the government may reserve this type of property for its intended purpose, and regulate expressive activity therein, "as long as the regulation on speech is reasonable and not an effort to suppress expression merely because public officials oppose the speaker's view."[49]

Members of the City Council of Los Angeles v. Taxpayers for Vincent[50] illustrates this third category of public forum analysis. The Court upheld a city ordinance that prohibited posting of signs on public property and upheld the application of that ordinance to prohibit placing campaign signs on street light posts in the

---

45. 507 U.S. 410, 113 S.Ct. 1505, 123 L.Ed.2d 99 (1993). Rehnquist, C.J., joined by White & Thomas, JJ., filed a dissenting opinion.

46. 447 U.S. 455, 100 S.Ct. 2286, 65 L.Ed.2d 263 (1980).

47. 487 U.S. 474, 108 S.Ct. 2495, 101 L.Ed.2d 420 (1988), on remand 857 F.2d 1175 (7th Cir.1988). Brennan, J., joined by Marshall, J., dissented and would not allow the government to ban residential picketing, but would allow the government to limit the number of picketers, the their hours, and their noise level. Stevens, J. dissented on the grounds that the statute was overbroad: it forbade picketing even if the recipient accepted its message. It would prevent fifth graders from standing outside of the residence of a classmate with signs saying: "Get well, Charlie; our team needs you." However, if the ordinance were redrafted as Stevens wanted, the new ordinance would run up against the problem of the ordinance invalidated in *Carey*: it would then regulate speech based on content.

Following *Frisby* the demonstrators stopped stationary picketing but continued nonstationary picketing. The doctor, who was the subject of the picketing, moved his practice and later declared bankruptcy, which stemmed in part from a malpractice suit that he claimed was sponsored by his opponents. He also announced that he would no longer perform abortions. Wall Street Journal, April 7, 1993, at B10, col. 1–2 (midwest ed.).

48. Contrast, Madsen v. Women's Health Center, Inc., 512 U.S. 753, 775–76, 114 S.Ct. 2516, 2530, 129 L.Ed.2d 593 (1994), the Court invalidated an injunction against demonstrating within 300 feet of the residences of the staff of an abortion clinic. This ban was larger than necessary and was not limited to focused picketing solely in the front of a particular residence; it also banned general marching.

49. 460 U.S. at 46, 103 S.Ct. at 955.

50. 466 U.S. 789, 104 S.Ct. 2118, 80 L.Ed.2d 772 (1984), on remand 738 F.2d 353 (9th Cir.1984).

city. The majority opinion by Justice Stevens noted that light posts are not a type of government property traditionally designated for public communication and did not constitute a public forum. The prohibition of speech was permissible because it promoted important government interests in aesthetic values and the environment that were unrelated to the suppression of a particular viewpoint.

Private Meetings. *Minnesota State Board for Community Colleges v. Knight*[51] upheld a state law that required academic administrators to "meet and confer" with teachers regarding questions of policy and governance but limited these discussions to representatives of the teachers selected by a union that had been elected to be the exclusive bargaining representative of the teachers. Justice O'Connor, for the Court, found that the meet and confer sessions were not a forum of any type and could be reserved for discussions between administrators and representatives of the exclusive bargaining agent of the teachers even though the issues to be discussed at these meetings were outside of the scope of contract negotiations. The regulation did not significantly restrict the ability of nonunion employees to communicate their views on policy issues to college administrators. Because this meeting was not open to the public, it could be reserved for communication between the administration and union representatives.[52]

Military Bar Letters. *United States v. Albertini*[53] illustrates another application of, and lack of clarity of, the *Perry* public forum categorizing analysis. Section 1382 of title 18 makes it a crime to reenter a military base after having been barred by the commanding officer. In 1972 Albertini received a letter (a "bar letter") from the commanding officer of Hickam Air Force Base ("Hickman") barring him from reentering without the written permission of the Commander or his designee.

Albertini received the bar letter because he and a companion had entered Hickam and destroyed secret Air Force documents by pouring animal blood on them. For these acts he was convicted of conspiracy to destroy Government property.

Nearly a decade later, in 1981, Hickam advertised that while it "is normally a closed base, the gates will be open to the public for this 32nd Annual Armed Forces Day Open House." Radio advertisements stated that "the public is invited and it's all free." Albertini and four friends attended, passed out leaflets, and, in front of a B–52 bomber display, unfurled a banner reading "Carnival of Death." Albertini did not disrupt the Open House activities. After he and his friends were escorted off the base, he was convicted of violating § 1382.

Justice O'Connor, in a six to three decision, upheld the conviction, relying heavily on the bar letter. The original bar order was valid and had not been issued in response to activity protected by the First Amendment. This case was distinguished from *Flower v. United States*,[54] where the defendant had received a bar letter because he tried to distribute unauthorized publications on a military base that was always open to the public. This distribution of publications was protected by the First Amendment, but Albertini's act of vandalism in 1972 was not. He was not prosecuted for his 1981 peaceful demonstration; rather, he was prosecuted for reentering the base in violation of the 1972 bar letter.

Second, even if Hickam was temporarily transformed into a public forum on the day of the open house, Albertini's position was different from that of the general public because he had previously received a valid bar letter. "Where a bar letter is issued on valid grounds,

---

51. 465 U.S. 271, 104 S.Ct. 1058, 79 L.Ed.2d 299 (1984).

52. Although the government can create a special purpose public forum and limit access to it, the government could not use a similar classification to restrict speech in the public forum. Thus, the government could not totally prohibit teacher access to a school board meeting open to the public because that would be a content based restriction on speech in a public forum. See City of Madison

Joint School Dist. No. 8 v. Wisconsin Employment Relations Commission, 429 U.S. 167, 97 S.Ct. 421, 50 L.Ed.2d 376 (1976).

53. 472 U.S. 675, 105 S.Ct. 2897, 86 L.Ed.2d 536 (1985), on remand 783 F.2d 1484 (9th Cir.1986).

54. 407 U.S. 197, 92 S.Ct. 1842, 32 L.Ed.2d 653 (1972) (per curiam).

a person may not claim immunity from its prohibition on entry merely because the military has temporarily opened a military facility to the public. Section 1382 is content-neutral and serves a significant Government interest in barring entry to a military base by persons whose previous conduct demonstrates that they are a threat to security."[55] The majority also rejected as "implausible" Albertini's claim that he lacked notice that his entry was prohibited. "The bar letter in no way indicated that it applied only when public access to Hickam was restricted."[56] If Albertini was uncertain, he should have requested permission to reenter, the majority argued.

Charitable Solicitation on Government Property. Shortly after *Albertini*, the Court, in a four to three opinion, upheld an Executive Order limiting charitable solicitation of federal employees during working hours, in *Cornelius v. NAACP Legal Defense and Educational Fund, Inc.*[57] The federal government participates in the Combined Federal Campaign (CFC), a charity drive directed at federal employees during working hours. An Executive Order limited participation to tax-exempt, nonprofit charitable agencies that provide direct health and welfare services to individuals or their families. The Order specifically excluded legal defense and political advocacy organizations. The Court, applying *Perry*, upheld the constitutionality of the Executive Order.

The Court, again speaking through Justice O'Connor, readily agreed that charitable solicitation is a form of speech protected by the First Amendment, even though the participating organizations did not engage in face to face solicitation but instead submitted 30-word statements that were included in the CFC literature.

Then the Court turned to the question of what was the relevant forum. The relevant forum, said the Court, is the CFC, not the federal workplace, because the respondents only seek access to a particular means of communication, the CFC. Respondents did not claim any general right of access to the federal workplace. In determining what is the relevant forum, the focus should be on the type of access sought, not merely on the physical Government property at issue.

The Court concluded that the CFC is a nonpublic forum. Neither the Government's practice nor policy suggests any intent to convert the CFC into a public forum open to all tax-exempt organizations. The charitable organizations have to seek permission to solicit. Although the record did not show how many organizations have been denied permission throughout the 24-year history of CFC, the Court was satisfied with the fact that there was no evidence suggesting that the granting of the requisite permission was merely ministerial.[58]

The Court concluded that control "over access to a nonpublic forum can be based on subject matter and speaker identity so long as the distinctions drawn are reasonable in light of the purpose served by the forum and are viewpoint neutral."[59] Turning to the first issue, the Court found that it was reasonable for the Government to conclude that money given directly for food and shelter to the needy is more beneficial than money given for litigation. Second, the restrictions on access avoided the appearance of government favoritism or entanglement with particular viewpoints. Also, the record was adequate enough to support an inference that the respondents' participation in the CFC jeopardized its success and the federal workplace. The evidence was only in the form of correspondence and telephone calls

---

55. 472 U.S. at 688, 105 S.Ct. at 2906.

56. 472 U.S. at 684, 105 S.Ct. at 2904. Justice Stevens, joined by Brennan and Marshall, JJ., dissented: "respondent's visit to the open house in this case in response to a general invitation to the public extended nine years after he was removed from the base and ordered not to reenter does not involve the kind of reentry that Congress intended to prohibit when it enacted the 1909 statute." 472 U.S. at 694, 105 S.Ct. at 2909.

57. 473 U.S. 788, 105 S.Ct. 3439, 87 L.Ed.2d 567 (1985). Marshall and Powell, JJ., did not participate. Blackmun, J., joined by Brennan, J., filed a dissenting opinion. Stevens, J., also filed a dissenting opinion.

58. 473 U.S. at 804–06, 105 S.Ct. at 3450–51. Cf. *Perry*, 460 U.S. at 47, 103 S.Ct. at 956.

59. 473 U.S. at 806, 105 S.Ct. at 3451. See also *Perry*, 460 U.S. at 49, 103 S.Ct. at 957.

from federal workers "expressing concern" about the inclusion of political groups in the CFC.

As for the need to avoid workplace disruption, the Court assumed this point and analogized to *Perry,* where exclusion of the rival union was thought necessary to insure labor peace.[60] The First Amendment does not forbid a viewpoint neutral exclusion of speakers who would disrupt a nonpublic forum and hinder its effectiveness for its intended purpose. Because this is a nonpublic forum, there is no requirement that the Government's restrictions on access be "narrowly tailored," or that its interests in exclusion be "compelling." The Court added: "Although the avoidance of controversy is not a valid ground for restricting speech in a public forum, a nonpublic forum by definition is not dedicated to general debate or the free exchange of ideas."[61]

The Court then remanded to determine whether the Government had impermissibly excluded the respondents from the CFC because it disagreed with their viewpoints.[62]

Justice Stevens also filed a dissenting opinion questioning the *Perry* analysis as not "particularly helpful."[63] He emphasized that none of the advocacy organizations would receive any CFC donations unless the employees specifically designated such an organization; thus he believed that the arguments in favor of excluding such organizations from the CFC "are so plainly without merit that they actually lend support to an inference of bias."[64]

School Assemblies. *Bethel School District No. 403 v. Fraser*[65] upheld a broad power of school authorities to discipline a student for delivering, at a school assembly, a speech that promoted another student as a candidate for

student government by the use of "persuasive sexual innuendo." Fraser promoted his candidate in a speech describing him as "a man who is firm—he's firm in his pants, he's firm in his shirt, his character is firm—but most of all, his belief in you, the students of Bethel, is firm." The student added that his candidate was also "a man who takes his point and pounds it in;" "a man who will go to the very end—even to the climax, for each and every one of you." The audience of about 600 students included students 14 years old or older. Some responded to the speech with hooting and yelling. Chief Justice Burger's majority opinion described this speech as "lewd and obscene"[66] and refused to quote it. One must turn to the separate opinion of Justice Brennan to find out exactly what Mr. Fraser said.[67]

Chief Justice Burger said that the speech "was plainly offensive to both teachers and students," "was acutely insulting to teen-age girl students," and "could well be seriously damaging to its less mature audience, many of whom were only 14 years old and on the threshold of awareness of human sexuality." Burger asserted, "The determination of what manner of speech in the classroom or in school assembly is inappropriate properly rests with the school board."[68] Thus, this case is probably limited to its facts, that is, to speech in school or the school assembly.

Justice Brennan, normally a strong proponent of free speech, concurred in the result. He said that the speech was no more obscene or lewd "than the bulk of programs currently on prime-time television or in the local cinema." Nonetheless, he would uphold the school board action because this speech may be punished as "disruptive" in the school environment.[69]

---

60. 473 U.S. at 810, 105 S.Ct. at 3453. Compare *Perry,* 460 U.S. at 52, 103 S.Ct. at 959.

61. 473 U.S. at 812, 105 S.Ct. at 3454.

62. Blackmun, joined by Brennan, dissented. They accepted *Perry* but criticized the Court's reasoning. 473 U.S. at 821, 105 S.Ct. at 3459.

63. 473 U.S. at 835, 105 S.Ct. at 3466.

64. 473 U.S. at 836, 105 S.Ct. at 3467 (footnote omitted).

65. 478 U.S. 675, 106 S.Ct. 3159, 92 L.Ed.2d 549 (1986), on remand 800 F.2d 222 (9th Cir.1986).

66. 478 U.S. at 679, 106 S.Ct. at 3163 (Burger, C.J., for the Court).

67. 478 U.S. at 687, 106 S.Ct. at 3167 (Brennan, J., concurring in the judgment).

68. 478 U.S. at 683, 106 S.Ct. at 3165.

69. 478 U.S. at 688, 106 S.Ct. at 3166 (Brennan, J., concurring in the judgment). Justice Blackmun concurred in the result without opinion.

Justice Marshall, dissenting, said that the speech was not even disruptive. In fact, both lower courts found no evidence of disruption at all. Justice Stevens, also dissenting, focused on what he saw as a procedural problem: the student "should not be disciplined for speaking frankly in a school assembly if he had no reason to anticipate punitive consequences." The student had discussed his proposed speech with three teachers beforehand, but had not been warned that he risked discipline. Moreover, said Stevens, Fraser's contemporaries did not appear upset by his speech: they shortly thereafter elected him to be their graduation speaker. Fraser was in a better position to judge his contemporaries than is "a group of judges who are at least two generations and 3,000 miles away from the scene of the crime."[70]

School Newspapers. *Hazelwood School District v. Kuhlmeier*[71] relying on *Bethel*, affirmed the broad power of a *high school* over expressive activities such as *school-sponsored* publications and school sponsored plays. The school and its newspaper were not traditional public forums, and the evidence indicated that the school did not intend to convert its newspaper to a public forum. The school newspaper was part of a Journalism course, for which the students received academic credit and grades. The Journalism teacher exercised a great deal of control over the newspaper by selecting its editors, setting publication dates, editing stories, etc. The school principal then reviewed every issue prior to publication. Because the high school sponsored this newspaper, it could properly exercise a great deal of control over it.

The high school did not offend the First Amendment by exercising editorial control over the style and content of student speech if its actions are reasonably related to "legitimate pedagogical concerns."[72] Applying this test the Court upheld the high school principal's decision to excise two pages from the student newspaper because he reasonably concluded that the articles unfairly impinged on the privacy rights of pregnant students and others. The Court specifically noted that it need "not now decide whether the same degree of [judicial] deference is appropriate to school-sponsored expressive activities at the college and university level."[73]

School Buildings, After Hours. In *Lamb's Chapel v. Center Moriches Union Free School District*,[74] the Court, without dissent, invalidated New York regulations that were used to deny to a church access to school premises (after the regular school day was completed). The school denied access because the church wished to exhibit, for public viewing and for religious purposes, a film that dealt with family and child-rearing issues. The school rule allowed after-hours use of school property for social, civic, and recreational uses *but not* for religious purposes. While the school created only a limited public forum, it denied access to a nonpublic forum *based on the viewpoint* of the speaker. The rule violated the First Amendment because it permitted school property to be used for the presentation of all views about family planning and child-rearing except those dealing with the subject from a religious viewpoint.[75]

State University Funding of Student Organizations, Including Student Reli-

---

70. 478 U.S. at 692, 106 S.Ct. at 3169 (Stevens, J., dissenting) (footnote omitted).

71. 484 U.S. 260, 108 S.Ct. 562, 98 L.Ed.2d 592 (1988). In contrast to Tinker v. Des Moines Independent Community School District, 393 U.S. 503, 89 S.Ct. 733, 21 L.Ed.2d 731 (1969), the speech in *Hazelwood* was *school-sponsored*. Thus, the strict test in *Tinker* does not apply to determine when the school may refuse to lend its name and resources to further student expression.

Contrast also, Papish v. Board of Curators, 410 U.S. 667, 93 S.Ct. 1197, 35 L.Ed.2d 618 (1973)(per curiam). In *Papish* the Court ordered an expelled graduate student to be readmitted. She had been expelled because she distributed on campus a newspaper that contained, in the view of

the Dean of students, indecent speech. The newspaper was not school-sponsored. It was an underground newspaper that was merely sold on the state university campus.

72. 484 U.S. at 273, 108 S.Ct. at 571 (footnote omitted).

73. 484 U.S. at 273 n. 7, 108 S.Ct. at 571, n. 7.

74. 508 U.S. 384, 113 S.Ct. 2141, 124 L.Ed.2d 352 (1993).

75. The Court also concluded that there was no establishment clause violation under the three-part test of Lemon v. Kurtzman, 403 U.S. 602, 91 S.Ct. 2105, 29 L.Ed.2d 745 (1971).

gious Groups. The University of Virginia, a state school, paid the printing costs of publications of student groups. These student groups were independent of the University and not controlled by it. The Student Activities Fund (SAF) would pay outside contractors for these printing costs. In administering SAF, the University engaged in viewpoint discrimination against a particular student newspaper; the school refused to pay the publication costs of a particular student group because it had a Christian perspective. University regulations gave funds to student groups *except* those that "promot[ed] or manifest[ed] a particular belie[f] in or about a deity or an ultimate reality." These regulations violated the First Amendment.

In *Rosenberger v. Rector and Visitors of the University of Virginia*,[76] Justice Kennedy, for the Court, held that the SAF was a limited public forum, and—in light of *Lamb's Chapel*—the University was unconstitutionally discriminating against the viewpoint advocated by this particular student publication. Providing funds to student publications on a neutral basis is no different than providing access to facilities. Just as the school in *Lamb's Chapel* could not constitutionally deny access to a public forum on the basis of religious belief, so also the University of Virginia could not constitutionally refuse to provide funding for a particular student publication because of the religious advocacy of that publication. The University could not deny funding to the publications of a student group based on the secular views of the group; religious views are deserving of no lesser status under the First Amendment. There was no establishment clause violation because the government was neutral towards religion.

Justice Souter, speaking for a four-person dissent, equated the University of Virginia's

payment to the third party of photo-copying and publication costs to the state's payment of the salary of a clergyman. He claimed that the majority required the University of Virginia to use public funds to subsidize preaching "the word," which is "categorically forbidden by the Establishment Clause."[77] However, state payment of the salary of clergy is different because that payment cannot be neutral. Preaching the gospel is religious. But a school can neutrally give access to student groups, whether those groups advocate religion or politics. And the state can neutrally fund student publications, whether those publications advocate religion, atheism, politics, or hedonism.

Souter did not object to earlier cases where the Court approved of government aid neutrally given to religious and nonreligious groups. But, he argued, in those cases "the aid was indirect."[78] However, if "directness" is so important, the aid in *Rosenberger* was indirect, because it never went directly to the student group; instead the University paid publication costs to a third party. And, if Souter is really insistent that the state cannot aid neutrally, it would, under Souter's view, be antagonistic towards religion. Surely the fire department, in putting out a blaze, should not refuse to help a local church if it were on fire, even though the church never paid property or income taxes to finance the fire department. Souter has no real answer to this problem. In a footnote he acknowledged that police and fire protection should be provided, but he did not explain why his analysis allowed that.[79]

Prisons. *Turner v. Safley*[80] upheld prison regulations that, in effect, prohibited prison inmates from writing to non-family inmates. The Court rejected the argument that the ban on inmate-to-inmate correspondence violated the First Amendment. It also rejected a

---

76. 515 U.S. 819, 115 S.Ct. 2510, 132 L.Ed.2d 700 (1995). See also Board of Education of Westside Community Schools v. Mergens, 496 U.S. 226, 248, 252, 110 S.Ct. 2356, 2370–71, 2373, 110 L.Ed.2d 191 (1990); Board of Education of Kiryas Joel Village School District v. Grumet, 512 U.S. 687, 702–03, 114 S.Ct. 2481, 2491, 129 L.Ed.2d 546 (1994).

77. 515 U.S. at 868, 115 S.Ct. at 2535 (Souter, J., dissenting, joined by Stevens, Ginsburg, & Breyer, JJ.).

78. 515 U.S. at 880, 115 S.Ct. at 2541 (Souter, J., dissenting, joined by Stevens, Ginsburg, & Breyer, JJ.).

79. 515 U.S. at 879 n. 5, 115 S.Ct. at 2541 n. 5 (Souter, J., dissenting, joined by Stevens, Ginsburg, & Breyer, JJ.).

80. 482 U.S. 78, 107 S.Ct. 2254, 96 L.Ed.2d 64 (1987). For analysis of the prison cases where the press or the public seek access to inmates, or where prisoners seek access to the press, see § 16.19.

strict scrutiny test. The evidence showed that the prison adopted the correspondence rule primarily for security reasons. Inmate mail between prisons can compromise protective custody offered to inmates from other institutions; such correspondence facilitates communications between gang members who had been transferred to other prisons in an effort to break up the gang; and such correspondence helps communicate escape plans and assault efforts. The correspondence rule is content-neutral, logically advances the goals of institutional security and safety, and is not an exaggerated response to those objectives.[81]

In *Overton v. Bazzetta*,[82] a unanimous Court emphasized that the test in these cases is whether the prison regulations are rationally related to legitimate penological objectives. Courts must grant "substantial deference" to the professional judgment of prison administrators, because they bear a significant responsibility for defining the legitimate goals of a corrections system and for determining the most appropriate means to accomplish them.[83] In this case, the Court held that various restrictions on prison visitation did not violate any right of association or other constitutional rights.[84]

Airports

Vagueness. The Board of Airport Commissioners of Los Angeles International Airport adopted a Resolution that explicitly provided, in part, that "the Central Terminal Area at Los Angeles International Airport is not open for First Amendment activities by any individual and/or entity." Jews for Jesus, Inc., a nonprofit religious corporation, challenged the Resolution and a unanimous Court invalidated it in, *Board of Airport Commissioners of City of Los Angeles v. Jews for Jesus, Inc.*[85] The Court ruled that, even if the airport were a nonpublic forum, the Resolution is still unconstitutionally overbroad.

Public Forum. Subsequently, *International Society for Krishna Consciousness, Inc. v. Lee*[86] surprised many observers by holding that a government-owned airport open to the public is *not* a public forum. The International Society for Krishna Consciousness challenged the New York Port Authority's restrictions on the distribution of literature and the solicitation of contributions in airport terminals. The New York Port Authority controls three airport terminals in the New York City metropolitan area. They are generally open to the public and contain various stores, snack shops, restaurants, newsstands, etc. Nearly all the people who use the terminals are either terminal employees or visit for reasons related to air travel, such as changing planes, dropping off or picking up passengers, or taking flights. The Krishnas said that their religion required them to go to public places, distribute religious literature, and solicit contributions.

The majority readily agreed that the Krishnas were engaging in a form of speech, but rejected the argument that airport terminals, like the sidewalks and streets, are public fora. First, "given the lateness with which the modern air terminal has made its appearance" on the public scene, it cannot be described as

---

81. 482 U.S. at 93, 107 S.Ct. at 2264. In another portion of this opinion, the Court invalidated an inmate marriage regulation that prohibited inmates from marrying inmates unless the prison superintendent determined that there were compelling reason for marriage. Cf. Thornburgh v. Abbott, 490 U.S. 401, 109 S.Ct. 1874, 104 L.Ed.2d 459 (1989).

82. 539 U.S. 126, 123 S.Ct. 2162, 156 L.Ed.2d 162 (2003).

83. Overton v. Bazzetta, 539 U.S. at ___, 123 S.Ct. 2162, 2167.

84. The prison regulations at issue excluded (from family members with whom inmates were entitled to non-contact visits) any minor nieces and nephews and children as to whom parental rights had been terminated; they also prohibited inmates from visiting with former inmates; they required children to be accompanied by a family member or legal guardian; and they banned inmates with two substance-abuse violations to at least two years on future visitation.

85. 482 U.S. 569, 107 S.Ct. 2568, 96 L.Ed.2d 500 (1987).

86. 505 U.S. 672, 112 S.Ct. 2701, 120 L.Ed.2d 541 (1992). Rehnquist, C.J., delivered the opinion of the Court, joined by White, O'Connor, Scalia, and Thomas, JJ. O'Connor, J., filed a concurring opinion. Kennedy, J., filed an opinion concurring in the judgment, in part I of which Blackmun, Stevens, and Souter, JJ., joined. Souter, J., filed a dissenting opinion, in which Blackmun and Stevens, JJ., joined.

"immemorially" held in the public trust.[87] On the other hand, one could say the same thing about superhighways, or state-owned oases alongside these highways. The airplane, no less than the automobile, is a relatively late invention.

In some respects, state-owned air terminals are like state-owned streets: people use these facilities to go from one place to another; alongside streets are restaurants, newsstands, stores, etc. One need not possess an airline ticket to roam freely in the public area outside the security check-points. Admittedly the main purpose of a terminal is not to promote expressive activity, but the same can be said of a street or sidewalk. An important similarity between the publicly-owned airport terminal and the city sidewalks is that, in both cases, expressive activity is harmonious and compatible with the transportation uses of the facility.

The majority also rejected the comparison of airports with bus or rail terminals, even though all may be regarded as transportation centers. Although bus or train stations historically have allowed expressive activities such as distribution of literature or solicitation of funds, this fact is "irrelevant" because, said the majority, the crucial difference is that "bus and rail terminals traditionally have had *private* ownership."[88] On the other hand, one would think that if, historically, even *private* bus and train terminals have been opened up for general expressive activities, then *a fortiori,* a *public* transportation terminal should be considered a public forum. The majority also argued that when new methods of transportation are developed, there should be new inquiries as to whether the transportation necessities are compatible with various types of expressive activity.

The majority emphasized that state-owned airports are like privately owned airports in that they are *commercial* establishments funded by user fees and designed to make a regulated profit. This purpose may be frustrated if airports are also required to provide for the free exchange of ideas.

Solicitation of Funds. *International Society for Krishna Consciousness, Inc. v. Lee.*[89] also held that prohibiting the solicitation of funds in an airport terminal (a nonpublic forum) is constitutional because it is *"reasonable."* Solicitors might slow down the pace of traffic, affecting passengers in a hurry to catch a flight. Passengers wishing to avoid the solicitor would have to alter their path; the very act of solicitation might slow down the harried passenger, who may already be loaded with luggage and children in tow.

The Court also argued that *face to face* solicitation[90] of funds creates special risks of duress and fraud. The people solicited are often too polite to tell the solicitor to just go away. The unsavory solicitor can target the most vulnerable (the handicapped, or those accompanied by small children) who may be on tight schedules and cannot easily avoid the solicitation. In this environment, the solicitor can more easily commit fraud and short-change the purchaser. For these reasons, the Port Authority limited solicitation to the sidewalk areas outside of the airport terminals. The Court upheld these anti-solicitation regulations, because it was not necessary for the Port Authority to demonstrate that they were the most reasonable, or only reasonable, way of dealing with the problem.

Distribution of Literature. In *Lee v. International Society for Krishna Consciousness, Inc.,*[91] a short per curiam opinion following *Lee,* a different majority of judges (unable to

87.   505 U.S. at 678, 112 S.Ct. at 2706.

88.   505 U.S. at 681, 112 S.Ct. at 2707 (emphasis on original).

89.   505 U.S. 672, 112 S.Ct. 2701, 120 L.Ed.2d 541 (1992).

90. Face-to-Face Solicitation. In prior cases dealing with solicitation of donations, the Court did not really distinguished between face-to-face solicitation and other

types of solicitation. See, Schaumburg v. Citizens for a Better Environment, 444 U.S. 620, 629, 100 S.Ct. 826, 832, 63 L.Ed.2d 73 (1980), rehearing denied 445 U.S. 972, 100 S.Ct. 1668, 64 L.Ed.2d 250 (1980); Riley v. National Federation of the Blind of North Carolina, Inc., 487 U.S. 781, 788–89, 108 S.Ct. 2667, 2673, 101 L.Ed.2d 669 (1988).

91.   505 U.S. 830, 112 S.Ct. 2709, 120 L.Ed.2d 669 (1992) (per curiam).

agree on a rationale)[92] held that the First Amendment does *not* allow the Port Authority to ban the distribution of literature in the airport terminals. Justice O'Connor's separate opinion made clear that only the *free* distribution of literature or leafleting is protected because it does not present the same kinds of problems (other than litter) associated with face-to-face solicitation of funds. That opinion, together with the views of Chief Justice Rehnquist and Justices White, Scalia, and Thomas, added up to a five person majority that allowed the Port Authority to ban the face-to-face *sale* of literature.[93]

Content-Based Restrictions Surrounding Polling Places

Burson v. Freeman[94] is an atypical case. The Court, with no majority opinion, approved content-based restrictions in a public forum. The Court balanced two important rights: the right to engage in political speech, which is at the heart of the First Amendment, and the right to vote, the right that is preservative of all our rights and at the heart of democracy.

A Tennessee law (like the law of many other jurisdictions) prohibited the solicitation of votes and the display or distribution of campaign materials within 100 feet of the entrance to a polling place. The law was clearly content-based. It did not prohibit commercial solicitation in the area immediately surrounding the voting booth, but it banned public discussion of an entire topic within the "campaign free" zone. The Supreme Court, with no majority opinion, upheld the law.

Justice Blackmun's plurality found that the section survived an exacting scrutiny test. The law served a compelling state interest, to prevent voter intimidation and election fraud. "The only way to preserve the secrecy of the ballot is to limit access to the area around the voter." The next question is *how large* a restricted zone is permissible or sufficiently tailored." The plurality rejected the argument that the 100 foot boundary was not narrowly tailored. The Tennessee Supreme Court had required that the boundary be reduced to 25 feet, but it takes only about 15 seconds to walk the 75 additional feet. Whatever the boundary is, the plurality concluded that a 100 foot boundary is on the constitutional side of the line. This is the "rare case" that "survives strict scrutiny."[95]

Justice Scalia, concurring in the judgment, argued that if the category of "traditional public forum" is to be an analytical tool rather than a conclusory label, "it must remain faithful to its name and derive its content from

---

92. Lee v. International Society for Krishna Consciousness, Inc., 505 U.S. 830, 112 S.Ct. 2709, 120 L.Ed.2d 669 (1992) (per curiam). See, O'Connor, J., concurring in No. 91–155 and concurring in the judgment in No. 91–339; Kennedy, J., joined by Blackmun, Stevens, and Souter, JJ. as to Part I, concurring in the judgment; Souter, joined by Blackmun and Stevens, JJ., concurring in the judgment in No. 91–339 and dissenting in No. 91–155.

93. Kennedy, J., (joined by Blackmun, Stevens, and Souter, JJ. on this point) argued that air terminals are public fora. In the remainder of Kennedy's separate opinion (in a portion that no one else joined), he argued that face-to-face solicitation could still be forbidden to the extent that the solicitor asked for the "immediate payment of money." He would allow the distribution of pre-addressed envelopes. Kennedy also concluded (again, with no one agreeing with him on this point) that the Port Authority's "flat ban on the distribution or sale of printed material must, in my view, fall in its entirety." International Society for Krishna Consciousness, Inc. v. Lee, 505 U.S. 672, 708, 112 S.Ct. 2711, 2723, 120 L.Ed.2d 541 (1992) (Kennedy, J., concurring in the judgment). The anomalous result of the Kennedy rule is that the solicitor cannot simply ask you for a donation, but he can ask that you pay him $15 for a one page typed brochure. Note that

Justice Kennedy thinks that this distinction is constitutionally required!

While Kennedy's opinion argued that the face-to-face sale of literature is constitutionally protected in the airport terminals, the separate opinion of Souter, J., joined by Blackmun and Stevens, JJ. argued that all face-to-face solicitation of funds is constitutionally protected free speech. Souter, J., joined by Blackmun and Stevens, JJ., concurring in the judgment in No. 91–339 and dissenting in No. 91–155. 505 U.S. 672, 112 S.Ct. 2711, 2724–26, 120 L.Ed.2d 541.

94. 504 U.S. 191, 112 S.Ct. 1846, 119 L.Ed.2d 5 (1992). Blackmun, J., announced the judgment of the Court, joined by Rehnquist, C.J. & White & Kennedy, JJ. Kennedy, J., filed a concurring opinion; Scalia, J., filed an opinion concurring in the judgment. Stevens, J., joined by O'Connor and Souter, JJ., dissented. Thomas, J., took no part in the consideration or decision of this case.

The National Labor Relations Board also restricts what would otherwise be free speech activities when they are engaged in, at or near polling places in union representation elections. E.g., NLRB v. Carroll Contracting & Ready-Mix, Inc., 636 F.2d 111 (5th Cir.1981).

95. 504 U.S. at 211, 112 S.Ct. at 1857 (Blackmun, J.).

tradition."[96] The area around the polling booth, *"by long tradition,"* was not a public forum. He viewed the law as a reasonable, viewpoint-neutral regulation of a *non*public forum.

Injunctions and Statutory Restrictions of Protests in the Public Forum: Abortion Clinics

Madsen v. Women's Health Center, Inc.[97] considered the constitutionality of a state court injunction entered against protestors at a Florida abortion clinic. The original state court injunction prohibited petitioners from interfering with public access to the abortion clinic and from physically abusing persons entering or leaving the clinic. The injunction applied to protest activities in the traditional public forum, the streets and sidewalks. The state court broadened this injunction after it concluded that protestors were still interfering with clinic access. This broadened injunction applied to petitioners, Operation Rescue and various other named organizations, their agents, and "all persons acting in concert or participation with them, or on their behalf;" it prohibited them from engaging in various acts. Chief Justice Rehnquist, for a divided Court, invalidated parts of this injunction and upheld other parts.

Madsen concluded that, given the particular factual circumstances and the record before the Court, the state court's establishment of a 36 foot buffer zone on a public street from which demonstrators were excluded does not violate the First Amendment because it burdened no more speech than necessary to prevent unlawful conduct. But *Madsen* invalidated other parts of the injunction as violating the First Amendment because they were broader than necessary. The Court invalidated a 36 foot buffer zone applied to private property, a prohibition of "images observable" from the abortion clinic, and a 300 foot buffer zone around residences.

Injunctions and the Requirement of Content Neutral Speech. The majority rejected the argument that the injunction was content based simply because it only applied to restrict the speech of abortion protestors. An injunction, by its very nature, said the Court, applies to particular persons in the context of a specific dispute. The injunction regulates "their activities, and perhaps their speech," because of their past actions in a specific circumstance.[98] Although the amended injunction did not apply to prohibit demonstrations by people supporting abortions, that fact did not make it content based, said the majority, because there were no demonstrations by people favoring abortions and thus no request for relief from such demonstrations.

The trial court injunction imposed "incidental restrictions" on the petitioners' message because they had "repeatedly violated" the original injunction. The fact that the "injunction covered people with a particular viewpoint does not itself render the injunction content or viewpoint based;" it only suggests that "those in the group *whose conduct* violated the court's order happen to share the same opinion regarding abortions being performed at the clinic."[99] Therefore the injunction does not de-

---

96.   504 U.S. at 214, 112 S.Ct. at 1859 (emphasis in original).

97.   512 U.S. 753, 114 S.Ct. 2516, 129 L.Ed.2d 593 (1994). Rehnquist, C.J., delivered the opinion of the Court, joined by Blackmun, O'Connor, Souter, & Ginsburg, JJ., and in part by Stevens, J. Souter, J., also filed a concurring opinion.

Stevens, J., filed an opinion concurring in part and dissenting in part. He would have upheld the 300 foot buffer zone around the clinic.

Scalia, J., joined by Kennedy & Thomas, JJ., filed an opinion concurring in part and dissenting in part. Justice Scalia's vigorous dissent would have invalidated the entire injunction on free speech grounds. He argued that the Court was creating a special rule for abortion cases, which have worked "a major distortion in the Court's constitutional jurisprudence," with the Court's "ad hoc nullifica-

tion machine claim[ing] its greatest, and most surprising victim, the First Amendment." He explained:

> "Because I believe that the judicial creation of a 36–foot zone in which only a particular group, which has broken no law, cannot exercise its rights of speech, assembly, and association, and the judicial enactment of a noise prohibition, applicable to that group and that group alone, are profoundly at odds with out First Amendment precedents and traditions, I dissent." 512 U.S. at 785, 114 S.Ct. at 2535.

Cf. Cheffer v. McGregor, 6 F.3d 705, 711 (11th Cir.1993).

98.   512 U.S. at 762, 114 S.Ct. at 2523.

99.   512 U.S. at 763, 114 S.Ct. at 2524 (emphasis in original).

mand the "heightened scrutiny" of *Perry Educational Association*.

The Test for Content–Neutral Injunctions. *Madsen* evaluated an injunction, not a statute. Though the Court concluded that the injunction was content neutral, it still limited protest activities in the traditional public forum. A statute or ordinance is generally applicable and represents a choice made by the legislative processes. In contrast, an injunction has a greater risk of censorship and discriminatory application because one judge imposes it on certain individuals, without any legislative debate. Unlike a law, an injunction can be specifically tailored.

In light of these considerations, there should be a "somewhat more stringent application of general First Amendment principles" than would be applied in traditional time, place, and manner analysis.[100] The proper test is to determine whether the injunction burdens "no more speech than necessary" to accomplish its objective. The injunction must be narrowly drawn, "couched in the narrowest terms" necessary to accomplish its "pin-pointed objectives."[101]

On the factual record of this case, *Madsen* found that the governmental interests that the Florida Supreme Court had identified were "quite sufficient" to justify an appropriately tailored injunction. The state court wished to protect a woman's right to secure a lawful abortion and receive medical counseling, public safety, the free flow of traffic on the city streets and sidewalks, and property rights and residential privacy.

36 Foot Buffer Zone To Keep Streets Open. *Madsen* upheld the constitutionality of the 36 foot buffer zone around the clinic entrance and driveway. This buffer zone allowed the protesters to be seen and heard from the clinic parking lots. This portion of the injunction, moreover, banned "focused picketing," and did not ban general dissemination of information, such as distributions of handbills and solicitation. The injunction, in these circumstances, burdened no more speech than necessary to protect access to the clinic and to assist an orderly traffic flow on the street.

The Court said that, although the need for a complete buffer may be debatable, it should defer to the state court, which is more familiar with the facts. Also, the petitioners never certified a full record to the U.S. Supreme Court and argued against including the factual record. Significantly, the petitioners "are assuming, *arguendo,* that a factual basis exists to grant injunctive relief." Thus the Court must judge the case "*on the assumption* that the evidence and testimony presented to the state court supported its findings that the protesters standing, marching, and demonstrating near the clinic's entrance interfered with ingress to and egress from the clinic despite the issuance of the earlier injunction."[102]

36 Foot Buffer Zone As Applied to Private Property. *Madsen* invalidated the injunction creating the buffer zone as applied to private property on the north and west sides of the clinic, because it burdened more speech than necessary. The patients and clinic staff did not have to cross the private property to reach the clinic. In addition, the record did not show that the protestors' activities on private property interfered with the clinic operation or access.

Noise Restrictions. The Court upheld the limited noise restrictions because they burdened no more speech than necessary to protect the well-being of the clinic's patients. It is reasonable to have noise control around medi-

100. 512 U.S. at 765, 114 S.Ct. at 2524. Justice Scalia argued that content neutral *injunctions* are "*at least* as deserving of strict scrutiny as a statutory, content-based restriction," 512 U.S. at 792, 114 S.Ct. at 2538 (emphasis in original) (Scalia, J., concurring in the judgment in part and dissenting in part), because injunctions are procedurally harder to challenge than statutes and individual judges should not be trusted in situations where they can suppress particular ideas. Stevens, J., in contrast, argued that the reviewing court should be more deferential to the

court ordering the injunction. 512 U.S. at 777, 114 S.Ct. at 2531 (Stevens, J., concurring in part and dissenting in part).

101. 512 U.S. at 767, 114 S.Ct. at 2526. See also, Carroll v. President and Commissioners of Princess Anne, 393 U.S. 175, 183, 89 S.Ct. 347, 353, 21 L.Ed.2d 325 (1968).

102. 512 U.S. at 771, 114 S.Ct. at 2527–28 (second emphasis added).

cal facilities where patients undergo surgery and have recovery.[103]

Ban on "Images Observable." *Madsen* invalidated the injunction against displaying images observable from the clinic. It is broader than necessary, because the clinic could simply pull the window curtains if a patient is bothered by disagreeable placards. If the goal of the injunction is to reduce patients' anxiety, it could have been limited to signs that could be interpreted as threats or veiled threats.

300 Foot No Approach Zone. *Madsen* invalidated the injunction prohibiting petitioners from physically approaching anyone seeking clinic services within 300 feet of the clinic, unless that person indicated a desire for communication. It is difficult, said the Court, to justify prohibiting "*all* uninvited approaches" no matter how peaceful the contact might be.[104]

The "consent" requirement alone (prohibiting communication unless the person approached indicates a desire for communication) invalidates this part of the injunction because it burdens more speech than necessary to prevent intimidation and provide for access to the clinic.[105]

300 Foot Zone Residential Zone. The injunction prohibited using sound amplification equipment within 300 feet of the residences of the clinic staff. *Madsen* allowed that restriction because it is reasonable for the government to demand that the petitioners turn down the volume if the protests overwhelm the neighborhood.

The injunction also prohibited impeding access to streets that provide the sole access to residences of the clinic staff. The Court upheld this provision, because it was necessary for the clinic staff to return to their residences.

The Court invalidated the prohibition against picketing and demonstrating within 300 feet of the residences of clinic staff. Although the residence is the "last citadel of the tired, the weary, and the sick,"[106] the 300 foot ban is much larger than necessary. Also, it is not limited to focused picketing solely in front of a particular residence, but bans general marching. A narrower ban, limited as to time, duration, and number of pickets outside a smaller zone, could accomplish any legitimate purposes of the state.[107]

Standing and the "in concert" Restriction. Petitioners did not have standing to challenge the court order as vague and overbroad simply because it applied to those "acting in concert" with the parties named in the injunction. Those people "acting in concert" with petitioners are not parties to this dispute. The petitioners cannot attack the portion of the order that does not apply to them.[108]

Freedom of Association. *Madsen* rejected the claim that the "in concert" prohibition restricted the petitioners' freedom of association. The petitioners could associate with others and express their viewpoints. The injunction only banned them from acting in concert with others to deprive third parties of their lawful rights.

Statutory Restrictions on Abortion Protests. *Hill v. Colorado*,[109] upheld (five to four) the constitutionality of a 1993 Colorado statute that regulates speech-related conduct

---

103. 512 U.S. at 772, 114 S.Ct. at 2528. See also, NLRB v. Baptist Hospital, Inc., 442 U.S. 773, 783–84 n. 12, 99 S.Ct. 2598, 2604–05 n. 12, 61 L.Ed.2d 251 (1979).

104. 512 U.S. at 774, 114 S.Ct. at 2529 (emphasis in original).

105. 512 U.S. at 774, 114 S.Ct. at 2529. See also, Boos v. Barry, 485 U.S. 312, 322, 108 S.Ct. 1157, 1164, 99 L.Ed.2d 333 (1988), stating that, as "a general matter, we have indicated that in public debate our own citizens must tolerate insulting and even outrageous speech in order to provide adequate breathing space to the freedoms protected by the First Amendment."

106. 512 U.S. at 775, 114 S.Ct. at 2529.

107. Contrast Frisby v. Schultz, 487 U.S. 474, 484, 108 S.Ct. 2495, 2502, 101 L.Ed.2d 420 (1988). In contrast to the broad injunction in *Madsen*, the *Frisby* Court upheld an ordinance that was limited to "focused picketing taking place solely in font of a particular residence."

108. 512 U.S. at 775–76, 114 S.Ct. at 2530. See Regal Knitwear Co. v. N.L.R.B., 324 U.S. 9, 14–15, 65 S.Ct. 478, 481–82, 89 L.Ed. 661 (1945). In that case, a party had no standing to challenge an injunction applying to "successors and assigns" of the enjoined party, if the challenger was not a successor or assign; thus the challenge was an "abstract controversy over the use of these words."

109. 530 U.S. 703, 120 S.Ct. 2480, 147 L.Ed.2d 597 (2000).

within 100 feet of the entrance to any health care facility. The specific section of the statute challenged, made it unlawful for any person within the regulated areas to "knowingly approach" within eight feet of another person, without that person's consent, "for the purpose of passing a leaflet or handbill to, displaying a sign to, or engaging in oral protest, education, or counseling with such other person. . . ."

The Court was bitterly divided. The majority concluded that the statute was (1) a narrowly-tailored content-neutral time, place and manner regulation; (2) was neither overbroad nor unconstitutionally vague; and (3) did not any impose unconstitutional prior restraint on speech.

The majority acknowledged the petitioners's free speech interests, but argued that the State's police powers may justify a special focus on access to health care facilities and the avoidance of potential trauma to patients associated with confrontational protests. Rules providing specific guidance to law enforcement authorities encourage evenhanded application of the law. The majority contended that the Colorado statute does not restrict a speaker's right to address a willing audience, but does protect listeners from unwanted communications.

The Court claimed that the statute was content-neutral for three reasons. First, the statute regulates the places where some speech may occur, rather than regulate speech itself. Second, the legislature did not adopt the law because of disagreement with the message of any speech, and the state court had held that the restrictions apply to all demonstrators, without regard to viewpoint. The statute, in short, made no reference to the content of speech. Third, the State's interests, said the Court, were unrelated to the content of the demonstrators' speech.

However, the statute applies to persons who "knowingly approach" within eight feet of another to engage in "oral protest, education, or counseling." Hence, the petitioners said that the law was "content-based" because it requires examination of the content of a speaker's comments. The Court, however, responded that state enforcement authorities may look at a statement's content in order to determine whether a rule of law applies to a course of conduct. "it is unlikely that there would often be any need to know exactly what words were spoken in order to determine whether 'sidewalk counselors' are engaging in 'oral protest, education, or counseling' rather than pure social or random conversation."[110]

Thus, the majority said, the Colorado law is "easily distinguishable" from *Carey v. Brown*,[111] where the Court invalidated a law that prohibited all picketing except for picketing of a place of employment in a labor dispute, thereby preferring expression concerning one particular subject.

The dissent was unpersuaded. Justice Scalia's dissent, joined by Justice Thomas, derided the majority's conclusion that a regulation directed to only certain categories of speech (protest, education, and counseling) is not "content-based." It also mocked the majority's conclusion that this law "is narrowly tailored to serve a government interest," the citizens "right to be let alone," because this is a rationale that the state has "explicitly" disclaimed, "probably for the reason that, as a basis for suppressing peaceful private expression, it is patently incompatible with the guarantees of the First Amendment."[112]

Justice Kennedy also penned a strong dissent, concluding that for "the first time, the Court approves a law which bars a private citizen from passing a message, in a peaceful manner and on a profound moral issue, to a fellow citizen on a public sidewalk."[113]

110. 530 U.S. at 720, 120 S.Ct. at 2492.

111. 447 U.S. 455, 462, 100 S.Ct. 2286, 2291, 65 L.Ed.2d 263 (1980).

112. 530 U.S. at 741, 120 S.Ct. at 2503 (Scalia, J., dissenting).

113. 530 U.S. at 765, 120 S.Ct. at 2516 (Kennedy, J., dissenting).

(d) Regulation to Prevent Fraud and Annoyance

Anonymity. An author is generally free to be anonymous. *The Federalist Papers* were published anonymously. Anonymity protects the author who may be motivated by fear of economic, official, or social reprisal, or merely has a desire to preserve her privacy. An author's decision to exclude her name is like other editorial decisions, an aspect of free speech.[114]

Talley v. California[115] invalidated, on its face, a state statute banning anonymous handbills. Throughout history, some persecuted groups have been able to criticize oppressive practices either anonymously or not at all. This right to anonymity is a function of the freedom of association,[116] because identification and the subsequent fear of reprisal could effectively chill legitimate discussions of public interest. *Talley* specifically did not pass on the validity of a more narrowly tailored ordinance, limited to identifying those responsible for fraud, false advertising, or libel.[117]

The Court dealt with that question in *McIntyre v. Ohio Elections Commission*,[118] which invalidated an Ohio statute that prohibited the distribution of anonymous campaign literature. Margaret McIntyre distributed leaflets objecting to a proposed school tax levy. Some of the handbills identified her as expressing the views of "concerned parents and taxpayers." The Ohio Election Commission imposed a $100 fine, and the Ohio Supreme Court rejected her First Amendment challenge, arguing that the law serves to identify those who engage in fraud, libel, and false advertising.

The Ohio law is limited to writings designed to influence an election ("core political speech"), and applies even if there is no hint of falsity or libel. It also regulates the speech based on its content (when the purpose of the speech is to influence an election). Because the law limits "core political expression," it must be subjected to "exacting scrutiny."

In *McIntyre*, the name of the private author would probably be unknown to the recipient of the handbill, and identifying the author added little to the reader's ability to evaluate the document's message. Ohio has other laws that prohibit fraud and libel. Moreover, the present law is overbroad. It applies not only to election of public officers but also to ballot issues although ballot issues present neither a substantial risk of libel nor any potential appearance of corrupt advantage. The Ohio law applies to candidates and also to persons acting independently using only their own modest resources. The Court acknowledged that the State might be able to justify a limited identification requirement, but Ohio's restriction is much too broad.[119]

Anonymous, unidentified pamphleteering is not an evil that the state should stamp out; rather than being "a pernicious, fraudulent practice," it is an honorable tradition of advocacy and of dissent.[120] Ohio's blunderbuss approach violates free speech guarantees. A state may not seek "to punish fraud indirectly, by indiscriminately outlawing a category of speech, based on its content, with no necessary relationship to the danger sought to be prevented."[121]

---

114. 514 U.S. 334, 115 S.Ct. 1511, 131 L.Ed.2d 426 (1995).

115. 362 U.S. 60, 80 S.Ct. 536, 4 L.Ed.2d 559 (1960).

116. See, e.g., Gibson v. Florida Legislative Investigation Committee, 372 U.S. 539, 83 S.Ct. 889, 9 L.Ed.2d 929 (1963); Louisiana ex rel. Gremillion v. NAACP, 366 U.S. 293, 81 S.Ct. 1333, 6 L.Ed.2d 301 (1961); NAACP v. Alabama, 357 U.S. 449, 78 S.Ct. 1163, 2 L.Ed.2d 1488 (1958); Thomas v. Collins, 323 U.S. 516, 65 S.Ct. 315, 89 L.Ed. 430 (1945), rehearing denied 323 U.S. 819, 65 S.Ct. 557, 89 L.Ed. 650 (1945).

117. 362 U.S. at 64, 80 S.Ct. at 538–39.

118. 514 U.S. 334, 115 S.Ct. 1511, 131 L.Ed.2d 426 (1995). Ginsburg, J., filed a concurring opinion. Thomas, J., concurred in the result. Scalia, J., joined by Rehnquist, C.J., dissented.

119. In other contexts, the Court has, at times, approved of narrow restrictions on anonymous speech. In First National Bank of Boston v. Bellotti, 435 U.S. 765, 792 n. 32, 98 S.Ct. 1407, 1424 n. 32, 55 L.Ed.2d 707 (1978), rehearing denied 438 U.S. 907, 98 S.Ct. 3126, 57 L.Ed.2d 1150 (1978), the Court said that "Identification of the source of [corporate] advertising may be required as a means of disclosure so that the people will be able to evaluate the arguments to which they are being subjected." *Bellotti* dealt with corporate expenditures, which the Court has often treated as different from, and less protected than, individual communications.

120. 514 U.S. at 357, 115 S.Ct. at 1524.

121. 514 U.S. at 357, 115 S.Ct. at 1524.

Earlier, in *Buckley v. Valeo*[122] the Court mentioned that "sources of a candidate's financial support also alert the voter to the interests to which a candidate is most likely to be responsive and thus facilitate predictions of future performance in office." This language only referred to financial contributions to a candidate or expenditures authorized by a candidate or his agent. Later in *Buckley* the Court approved of a requirement that "independent expenditures in excess of a threshold level be reported to the Federal Election Commission."[123] However, that comment did not refer to any prohibition of anonymous leafleting. The disclosure rule mentioned in *Buckley* only required identification to the Federal Election Commission of the amount and use of money expended in support of a candidate. The disclosure rule did not require self-identification of all writings related to elections.

In *United States v. Harriss*,[124] the Court upheld limited disclosure requirements for lobbyists. Unlike the situation in *McIntyre*, lobbyists have direct access to elected officials, and the lack of any disclosure may cause the appearance of corruption and improper influence.

Watchtower Bible & Tract Society of New York, Inc. v. Village of Stratton,[125] invalidated a village ordinance that prohibited "canvassers" and others from "going in and upon" private residential property to promote any "cause" without first securing a "Solicitation Permit" from the mayor. There was no charge for the permit, which was issued routinely after an applicant filled out a detailed "Solicitor's Registration Form." The canvasser could then visit premises listed on the registration form, but he must carry the permit and exhibit it if a police officer or resident requests it. The ordinance sets forth grounds for the denial or revocation of a permit (e.g., incomplete information or fraud by the applicants in filling out the form), but the record before the Court did

not show that any application had been denied or that any permit had been revoked. Jehovah's Witnesses (who offered religious literature without cost, but did accept donations) objected to the permit requirement and did not apply for it.

The Court held that this municipal ordinance violates the First Amendment protection accorded to anonymous pamphleteering or discourse. The Court invalidated the ordinance as it applied to religious proselytizing, anonymous political speech, and the distribution of handbills. The ordinance necessarily resulted in surrender of anonymity of individuals supporting causes; it imposed an objective burden on some speech of citizens holding religious or patriotic views; it banned a significant amount of spontaneous speech. The ordinance is not necessary to protect the privacy of residents because they could either refuse to converse with the solicitor or post a "no soliciting" sign. Nor is the ordinance carefully tailored to prevent crime, because it does not preclude criminals from knocking on doors in situations not covered by the ordinance (they could pose as surveyors or people asking for directions). The Court said that, had the ordinance applied only to commercial activities and the solicitation of funds, arguably the ordinance would have been tailored to the Village's interest in protecting the privacy of its residents and preventing fraud.

Fraud. If a city seeks to regulate to prevent fraud, its law must be carefully tailored to achieve this purpose without unduly limiting speech. *Village of Schaumburg v. Citizens for a Better Environment*[126] invalidated, as overbroad, a local ordinance that prohibited the solicitation of contributions by charitable organizations that do not use at least 75% of their receipts directly for "charitable purposes," which the law defined as excluding the expenses of solicitation, salaries, overhead, and other administrative expenses.

122. 424 U.S. 1, 67, 96 S.Ct. 612, 657, 46 L.Ed.2d 659 (1976) (per curiam), motion granted 424 U.S. 936, 96 S.Ct. 1153, 47 L.Ed.2d 727 (1976)

123. 424 U.S. at 157–59, 160, 96 S.Ct. at 699–700, 701.

124. 347 U.S. 612, 74 S.Ct. 808, 98 L.Ed. 989 (1954),

125. 536 U.S. 150, 122 S.Ct. 2080, 153 L.Ed.2d 205 (2002).

126. 444 U.S. 620, 100 S.Ct. 826, 63 L.Ed.2d 73 (1980), rehearing denied 445 U.S. 972, 100 S.Ct. 1668, 64 L.Ed.2d 250 (1980).

The Village justified its regulation as a prevention of fraud. It argued that if an organization spends more than one quarter of its fundraising receipts on overhead, it really is engaged in a profit enterprise benefiting itself. But the Court said that this reasoning cannot apply to those organizations that are primarily engaged in research, advocacy, or public education, and who use paid staff to carry out these functions as well as to solicit financial support.[127]

The Village could protect its antifraud interests by more narrowly drawn regulations that would directly prohibit fraudulent misrepresentations, or require that charitable organizations inform the public how their moneys are spent. The Court also argued that the law did not serve to protect privacy because there is no reason to believe that solicitors covered by the 75 percent rule were somehow more intrusive than solicitors not within the ordinance's prohibition. Because the ordinance did not serve a "strong, subordinating interest that the Village is entitled to protect" and is a "direct and substantial limitation on protected activity" the Court invalidated it under the First and Fourteenth Amendments.[128]

The Court has shown hostility to state laws that regulation the fund raising activities of charities. *Secretary of State v. Joseph H. Munson Co., Inc.*[129] examined a statute that placed a twenty-five percent limitation on charitable fund raising expenses. The statute was slightly different from that examined in *Citizens for a Better Environment* because the statute in *Joseph H. Munson* allowed for an administrative waiver of the limitation based on a demonstration of financial necessity by a charity. The

Court still concluded that a waiver provision did not save the statute from being stricken as unconstitutionally overbroad.

Waiver of the limitation for a charity that faced economic hardship did not significantly decrease the restriction on protected First Amendment activity because the waiver did not exempt from the spending ceiling the money spent on the dissemination of information by the organization. Because this statute involved a direct restriction on speech and the means chosen to prevent the public from being defrauded were "imprecise," the Court found that the statute created an unnecessary risk of chilling free speech and should be validated on its face.[130]

However, the First Amendment does not bar fraud claims asserted under Illinois law against professional fundraisers hired by charitable organization, if the claims are based on allegations that fundraisers made false or misleading representations designed to deceive donors about how their donations would be used.[131] For example, it is misleading for a Telemarketer to affirmatively represented that a significant amount of each dollar donated would be paid over to a veterans' organization to be used for specific charitable purposes if in fact Telemarketers knew that only 15 cents or less of each dollar would be available for those purposes.

Allegedly Pejorative Labeling Requirements and Disclosure of Foreign Origin

The Government may require labeling or disclosure requirements in order to protect (or disclose information) to recipients so long as these requirements do not unduly burden the

---

127. 444 U.S. at 639, 100 S.Ct. at 837. See also, Riley v. National Federation for the Blind of North Carolina, Inc., 487 U.S. 781, 108 S.Ct. 2667, 101 L.Ed.2d 669 (1988), where the Court invalidated various state rules designed to regulate professional fund raising fees and to compel certain disclosures.

128. 444 U.S. at 639, 100 S.Ct. at 837. Justice Rehnquist was the sole dissent.

129. 467 U.S. 947, 104 S.Ct. 2839, 81 L.Ed.2d 786 (1984).

130. Charitable Fund Raising. In some cases, charities are very efficient in raising money. The American Cancer Society, in its fiscal year ending August 31, 1989,

spent 16.1% of its budget on fund raising. But many charities spend about 90 cents of every dollar on the expenses of fund raising. Because of accounting changes, these charities can pass off many of the expenses of fund raising as "public education." Some charities "are selling their names [to professional fund raisers] for 10 cents on the dollar." Crossen, Organized Charities Pass Off Mailing Costs as "Public Education," Wall Street Journal, Oct. 28, 1990, at 1, col. 1. Some charities seem to be primarily in the business of raising money.

131. Illinois, ex rel. Madigan v. Telemarketing Associates, Inc., 538 U.S. 600, 123 S.Ct. 1829, 155 L.Ed.2d 793 (2003).

free speech of the disseminators and are not based on content. For example, it is constitutional for a statute to provide that the addressee of mail may instruct the post office not to deliver all future mailings from any given sender.[132] The government, in such a case, itself places no restrictions on speech on the basis of content. The government merely respects the wishes of the intended recipient.

However a statute cannot authorize the Secretary of the Treasury to prohibit the post office from delivering mail to an address if the Secretary decides it is "communist political propaganda," unless the addressee returns a reply card certifying his desire to receive such mail.[133] That law violates the First Amendment, because neither the Secretary nor the Post Office may regulate the flow of mail based on its content. The government's physical detention of the materials, not the fact that a government official labeled them as "communist political propaganda," offended the First Amendment.[134]

This point is made clear in *Meese v. Keene*.[135] In that case the Court upheld certain provisions of the Foreign Agents Registration Act. That Act defines the term "political propaganda" to include any communication that is reasonably adapted to, or intended to, influence the recipient within the United States with reference to "the policies of a foreign country or foreign political party."[136] When the agent of a foreign principal disseminates this "political propaganda" the law requires that he or she must make a disclosure statement to the recipients; this disclosure includes the agent's identity, the identity of the principle for whom the agent acts, a statement that a report describing the extent of the material is registered

with the Department of Justice, and that such registration "does not indicate approval of the contents of this material by the United States Government."

The term "political propaganda" does *not* appear in the disclosure form that must be filed, but it is used in the Act. This registration requirement "is comprehensive, *applied equally* to agents of friendly, neutral, and unfriendly governments."[137] The Act defines, "propaganda" as all advocacy materials, even those that are completely accurate.[138]

Barry Keene, a member of the California State Senate, wanted to exhibit three Canadian films distributed by the National Film Board of Canada, a registered agent of the Government of Canada. Keene did not want the Department of Justice and the public to regard him as the disseminator of "foreign political propaganda," but wanted to exhibit Canadian motion picture films that were so identified.[139] The films discussed acid rain and nuclear war. The district court ruled that Congress violated the First Amendment by using the term "political propaganda" as the statutory name for the regulated category of expression;[140] the Supreme Court reversed.

The purpose of the statute, as written, and as the district court acknowledged, was to inform recipients of the source of advocacy materials produced by or under the aegis of a foreign government. The statute did not prohibit, edit, or restrain the distribution of the foreign advocacy materials. Congress simply required disclosure—the labeling of information to disclose its foreign origin. The law did not prohibit Keene or others from explaining to prospective viewers (before, during, or after

---

132. Rowan v. United States Post Office Dept., 397 U.S. 728, 90 S.Ct. 1484, 25 L.Ed.2d 736 (1970).

133. Lamont v. Postmaster General of U.S., 381 U.S. 301, 85 S.Ct. 1493, 14 L.Ed.2d 398 (1965).

134. See 381 U.S. at 306, 85 S.Ct. at 1496: "The Act sets administrative officials astride the flow of mail to inspect it, appraise it, write the addressee about it, and await a response before dispatching the mail. . . . [F]ederal agencies regulate the flow of mail."

135. 481 U.S. 465, 107 S.Ct. 1862, 95 L.Ed.2d 415 (1987).

136. 481 U.S. at 471, 107 S.Ct. at 1866.

137. 481 U.S. at 469, 107 S.Ct. at 1865 (emphasis added). See also, 481 U.S. at 483 n. 17, 107 S.Ct. at 1872 n. 17 (the Act's definition of propaganda is "neutrally applied" and includes allies as well as adversaries).

138. See 22 U.S.C.A. § 611(j); 481 U.S. at 477, 107 S.Ct. at 1869.

139. 481 U.S. at 467, 107 S.Ct. at 1864.

140. 481 U.S. at 467, 469, 107 S.Ct. at 1864, 1865. The constitutionality of the underlying registration requirements of the Foreign Agents Registration Act were not at issue. 481 U.S. at 467, 107 S.Ct. at 1864.

the film's viewing, or in a separate context) that Canada's interest in acid rain does not necessarily undermine the integrity or the persuasiveness of its advocacy.[141]

(e) Zoning Regulations

In recent years the Court has scrutinized with particular care state zoning laws that have the effect of restricting speech. In addition to *Carey v. Brown*[142], dealing with state restrictions on residential picketing, other cases include *Heffron v. International Society for Krishna Consciousness, Inc.*,[143] governing state "zoning" restrictions on solicitation of donations at a state fair; *Metromedia, Inc. v. City of San Diego*,[144] and similar cases governing zoning restrictions on billboards; and *Schad v. Mount Ephraim*,[145] governing zoning restrictions on live entertainment.

In *Schad v. Borough of Mount Ephraim*[146] a zoning ordinance banned *all* live entertainment in a commercial zone. An adult bookstore operating in the commercial zone wished to introduce a special type of coin operated machine whereby a customer, having inserted a coin, could watch a live nude dancer performing behind a glass panel. The Court invalidated the ordinance under the First Amendment as overbroad. The Borough argued that it was a reasonable time, place and manner restriction, yet it did not "identify the municipal interests making it reasonable to exclude all commercial live entertainment but to allow a variety of other commercial uses in the Borough."[147] The Borough presented no evidence

that the manner of expression—live entertainment—is basically incompatible with the normal activities allowed in the commercial zone.

Secondly, to be reasonable, time, place and manner restrictions not only must serve significant state interests but also leave open adequate alternative channels of communication. The Borough did not leave open alternative channels because it totally banned live entertainment. Unlike *Young v. American Mini Theatres, Inc.*[148] where the Court had upheld a zoning law that had dispersed but not completely banned theatres showing nonobscene "adult films," the zoning law in *Schad* completely excluded live entertainment.

The Borough argued that live entertainment, including nude dancing, was available in nearby areas. This "position suggests the argument that if there were countywide zoning, it would be quite legal to allow live entertainment in only selected areas of the county and to exclude it from primarily residential communities, such as the Borough of Mount Ephraim." The Court said that this argument "may well be true" but it was of no help to Mount Ephraim.[149] There was no countywide zoning and, the record did not show that such entertainment was available in reasonably nearby areas.

Finally—and somewhat incongruously, in light of its earlier apparent emphasis that the ordinance should have left open alternative channels of speech—the Court stated: " '[O]ne is not to have the exercise of his liberty of expression in appropriate places abridged on the plea that it may be exercised in some other place.' "[150]

141. Justice Blackmun, joined by Brennan and Marshall, JJ., dissented based on their views of Congress' motives: " ... the underlying goal was to control the spread of propaganda by foreign agents." They also believed that it "strains credulity" to believe that the term "propaganda" is neutral. 481 U.S. at 486, 107 S.Ct. at 1874.

142. 447 U.S. 455, 100 S.Ct. 2286, 65 L.Ed.2d 263 (1980).

143. 452 U.S. 640, 101 S.Ct. 2559, 69 L.Ed.2d 298 (1981), on remand 311 N.W.2d 843 (Minn.1981).

144. 453 U.S. 490, 101 S.Ct. 2882, 69 L.Ed.2d 800 (1981), on remand 32 Cal.3d 180, 185 Cal.Rptr. 260, 649 P.2d 902 (1982).

145. 452 U.S. 61, 101 S.Ct. 2176, 68 L.Ed.2d 671 (1981).

146. 452 U.S. 61, 101 S.Ct. 2176, 68 L.Ed.2d 671 (1981).

147. 452 U.S. at 74–75, 101 S.Ct. at 2186 (footnote omitted).

148. 427 U.S. 50, 96 S.Ct. 2440, 49 L.Ed.2d 310 (1976), rehearing denied 429 U.S. 873, 97 S.Ct. 191, 50 L.Ed.2d 155 (1976).

149. 452 U.S. at 76, 101 S.Ct. at 2187.

150. 452 U.S. at 76–77, 101 S.Ct. at 2187 quoting Schneider v. New Jersey, 308 U.S. 147, 163, 60 S.Ct. 146, 151, 84 L.Ed. 155 (1939).

In *Heffron v. International Society for Krishna Consciousness, Inc.*[151] the Court held that a state may require a religious organization that desired to distribute and sell religious literature and to solicit donations at a state fair to do so only at an assigned booth within the fairgrounds. These booths were rented to anyone on a first come, first serve basis. This Minnesota state fair rule applied to all enterprises, whether nonprofit, charitable, or commercial. It also allowed anyone to engage in face to face discussions with fair visitors anywhere on the fairgrounds.

The Krishna Society argued that one of its religious rituals, called "Sankirtan," required its members to distribute and sell religious literature and solicit donations. The Court, however, upheld the rule as a reasonable time, place, and manner regulation, not violative of the First and Fourteenth Amendments. First, the rule was not based on the content or subject matter of the speech. Second, the method of allocating rental space was nondiscriminatory and not open to arbitrary application. Third, the rule served a significant government interest because of the state's special need to maintain the orderly movement of the crowd, given the large number of exhibitors and visitors attending the fair. Unlike a city street, which is "continually open, often congested, and constitutes not only a necessary conduit in the daily affairs of a locality's citizens, but also a place where people may enjoy the open air or the company of friends and neighbors in a relaxed environment," a state fair "is a temporary event attracting great numbers of visitors who come to the event for a short period.... The flow of the crowd and demands of safety are more pressing in the context of the fair."[152]

Finally, less restrictive alternatives, such as directly penalizing disorder and disruption,

would probably not work to meet the state's interests because any exemption applied to the Krishna Society would also have to apply to a large number of other groups. These other groups would include religious, social, political, charitable, and perhaps even commercial organizations.

None of the Court's previous cases suggest that the Krishna Society and the ritual of Sankirtan have any "special claim" to First Amendment protection compared to that of other religions, which also distribute literature and solicit funds, but do not ritualize or label the process. *Heffron* also said that, for present purposes, religious organizations do not enjoy rights to communicate, distribute, and solicit on the fairgrounds that are superior to those of other organizations "having social, political, or other ideological messages to proselytize."[153] A decision favoring the Krishna Society would raise the question whether commercial organizations have a similar right under the First Amendment,[154] a question avoided by the majority's disposition of this case.

Restrictions on Billboards. The question of the constitutionality of zoning laws restricting billboards severely fragmented the Supreme Court in *Metromedia, Inc. v. City of San Diego*,[155] a case producing five separate opinions.[156] San Diego, in an attempt to eliminate the hazards caused by "distracting sign displays" and to "improve the appearance of the City," enacted a comprehensive zoning ordinance prohibiting outdoor display signs, subject to several important restrictions.

These exceptions fell into two main categories. First, the law allowed "on-site signs." On-site signs are those "designating the name of the owner or occupant of the premises upon

---

151. 452 U.S. 640, 101 S.Ct. 2559, 69 L.Ed.2d 298 (1981), on remand 311 N.W.2d 843 (Minn.1981).

152. 452 U.S. at 651, 101 S.Ct. at 2566.

153. 452 U.S. at 652, 101 S.Ct. at 2566.

154. 452 U.S. at 653, 101 S.Ct. at 2566–67: "The question would also inevitably arise as to what extent the First Amendment also gives commercial organizations a right to move among the crowd to distribute information about or to sell their wares as respondents claim they may do."

155. 453 U.S. 490, 101 S.Ct. 2882, 69 L.Ed.2d 800 (1981), on remand 32 Cal.3d 180, 185 Cal.Rptr. 260, 649 P.2d 902 (1982).

156. White, J., announced the judgment of the Court and delivered an opinion joined by Stewart, Marshall, and Powell, JJ. Brennan, J., joined by Blackmun, J., concurred in the judgment. 453 U.S. at 521, 101 S.Ct. at 2900. Stevens, J., Burger, C.J., and Rehnquist, J., each wrote dissenting opinions. 453 U.S. at 540, 555, 569, 101 S.Ct. at 2909, 2917, 2924.

which such signs are placed, or identifying such premises; or signs advertising goods manufactured or produced or services rendered on the premises upon which such signs are placed." The second category of exemptions were really twelve specified exemptions: "government signs; signs located at public bus stops; signs manufactured, transported or stored within the city, if not used for advertising purposes; commemorative historical plaques; religious symbols; signs within shopping malls; for-sale and for-lease signs; signs on public and commercial vehicles; signs depicting time, temperature, and news; approved temporary, off-premises, subdivision directional signs; and 'temporary political campaign signs.' "[157] Companies in the outdoor advertising business sued, claiming a violation of their First Amendment rights in that enforcement of the ordinance would in effect destroy their business.

The plurality opinion of Justice White first turned to the zoning law insofar as it regulated commercial speech and found that portion of the ordinance constitutional.[158] However the plurality was less tolerant of the distinctions the city drew as to noncommercial advertising. Because the city allowed on-site commercial advertising it had to allow on-site *non* commercial advertising so that an occupant could display its own ideas or the ideas of others.

The noncommercial billboard would not be any more distracting or nonaesthetic than a permitted, on-site commercial billboard.[159] Nor was the ordinance a time, place, or manner restriction because it completely banned on-site noncommercial billboards based on content, i.e., that their content was noncommercial. The plurality then concluded that because the ordinance reached "too far into the realm of protected speech," it was "unconstitutional on its face"; on remand the state court could decide if the unconstitutional portions of the ordinance could be severed from the constitutional parts.[160]

Justice Brennan, joined by Justice Blackmun, concurred in the judgment. However they analyzed the case quite differently, gave much less deference to the legislative judgment, and found the entire ordinance unconstitutional. The practical effect of the ordinance was to ban totally all billboards, which was unconstitutional, because the city had not provided "adequate justification" for its assertion that billboards actually impair traffic safety in San Diego.[161] Similarly they believed that the city's interests in aesthetics was not "sufficiently substantial in the commercial and industrial areas of San Diego," which might already be so blighted that the removal of billboards would have a negligible impact and not be worth the trouble.[162]

157. 453 U.S. at 494–95, 101 S.Ct. at 2886. See also, 453 U.S. at 495 n. 3, 101 S.Ct. at 2886 n. 3.

158. Because the outdoor advertising was concerned with lawful activity and was not misleading, it was protected as commercial speech. But the governmental regulations in this case were valid restrictions on commercial speech, meeting the four part test of Central Hudson Gas & Electric Corp. v. Public Service Commission, 447 U.S. 557, 100 S.Ct. 2343, 65 L.Ed.2d 341 (1980). That is, the two goals that the ordinance furthered were substantial: traffic safety and the city's aesthetic interests. The ordinance directly advanced those interests and regulated no further than necessary.

Although the law did permit on-site commercial advertising while prohibiting off-site billboards, it was permissible for the city to conclude that off-site advertising, with "periodically changing content, presents a more acute problem than does on-site advertising." 453 U.S. at 511, 101 S.Ct. at 2894, citing Railway Express Agency, Inc. v. New York, 336 U.S. 106, 110, 69 S.Ct. 463, 465, 93 L.Ed. 533 (1949).

159. 453 U.S. at 513, 101 S.Ct. at 2895. See also, 453 U.S. at 515, 101 S.Ct. at 2896.

160. 453 U.S. at 521 & n. 26, 101 S.Ct. at 2899–2900 & n. 26.

161. 453 U.S. at 528, 101 S.Ct. at 2903. These Justices analogized the case to Schad v. Borough of Mt. Ephraim, 452 U.S. 61, 72, 101 S.Ct. 2176, 2184–85, 68 L.Ed.2d 671 (1981).

162. 453 U.S. at 530–31, 101 S.Ct. at 2904–05. At one point Brennan suggested that "San Diego could demonstrate its interest in creating an aesthetically pleasing environment is genuine and substantial" by "showing a comprehensive commitment to making its physical environment in commercial and industrial areas more attractive and by allowing only narrowly tailored exceptions if any...." 453 U.S. at 532, 101 S.Ct. at 2905–06 (footnotes omitted). Yet at another point Brennan suggested that San Diego might never meet this burden: "I express no view on whether San Diego or other large urban areas will be able to meet the burden." 453 U.S. at 534, 101 S.Ct. at 2906 (footnote omitted). The three dissenters all would have upheld the billboard ordinance in its entirety.

Chief Justice Burger's strong dissent rejected the view of the plurality, which apparently gave the city a choice of banning all signs (a choice that the plurality might not allow if actually faced with deciding that issue) or permitting all noncommercial signs without any restriction. "This is the long arm and voracious appetite of federal power—this time judicial power—with a vengeance, reaching and absorbing traditional concepts of local authority."[163] Burger also believed that the distinctions that the City made are reasonable. For example, on-site signs, by identifying the premises (even if in the process of advertising), could actually promote traffic safety because prohibiting them would require motorists to pay more attention to small street numbers and less to traffic.[164]

Metromedia and its babel of opinions raise more questions than the case settles. It is likely that, if a city enacts a law that restricts billboards only to the extent that they convey commercial speech, a majority of the Court (composed of the White plurality and the three dissenters) would uphold the ordinance. If litigants attacked the constitutionality of the federal Highway Beautification Act of 1965,[165] it is unclear how the Court would respond. The three dissenters would no doubt uphold this law, but the other six Justices specifically refused to reach this question, though the White plurality, at least, hinted that the federal law might be distinguishable.[166]

Members of the City Council of Los Angeles v. Taxpayers for Vincent[167] upheld an ordinance prohibiting posting signs on public property; this ordinance also prohibited posting political signs on light posts. Justice Stevens, for the majority, stated that the proper test in reviewing this type of viewpoint neutral regulation is to determine (1) whether the statute promoted an important or substantial government interest unrelated to the suppression of expression, and (2) whether the "incidental restriction on alleged First Amendment freedoms is no greater than is essential to the furtherance of that interest."[168] The Court found that the city's interest in protecting the aesthetic quality of the community as well as its property justified the prohibition. The Court also said that *Metromedia* justified this conclusion.[169]

The *Vincent* regulation, although it prohibited one form of communication, was narrowly tailored to promote this interest because it did not restrict any individual's freedom to speak or distribute literature in the same place where posting signs on public property was prohibited. The ordinance only eliminated the ability to create visual clutter by posting material on public property that has never been converted into a public forum for speech.[170] The aesthetic interest in the elimination of signs on public property justified this content neutral restriction on the posting of signs on such property. This ordinance was not a content based restriction merely because the gov-

---

163. 453 U.S. at 556, 101 S.Ct. at 2917. He added: "The Court today unleashes a novel principle, unnecessary and, indeed, alien to First Amendment doctrine announced in our earlier cases." 453 U.S. at 569, 101 S.Ct. at 2924.

164. 453 U.S. at 564–65 & n. 6, 101 S.Ct. at 2921–22 & n. 6.

165. 23 U.S.C.A. § 131. That law also regulated billboards and permitted on-site commercial billboards in certain circumstances where it forbade billboards carrying noncommercial messages.

166. 453 U.S. at 515 n. 20, 101 S.Ct. at 2896 n. 20: "[U]nlike the San Diego ordinance, which prohibits billboards conveying noncommercial messages throughout the city, the federal law does not contain a total prohibition of such billboards in areas adjacent to the Interstate and primary highway systems." (White, J.) See also 453 U.S. at 534 n. 11, 101 S.Ct. at 2906 n. 11: "I express no opinion on the constitutionality of the Highway Beautification Act. . . ." (Brennan, J.).

167. 466 U.S. 789, 104 S.Ct. 2118, 80 L.Ed.2d 772 (1984), on remand 738 F.2d 353 (9th Cir.1984).

168. 466 U.S. at 804–05, 104 S.Ct. at 2129, quoting United States v. O'Brien, 391 U.S. 367, 377, 88 S.Ct. 1673, 1679, 20 L.Ed.2d 672 (1968), rehearing denied 393 U.S. 900, 89 S.Ct. 63, 21 L.Ed.2d 188 (1968).

169. 466 U.S. at 806–07, 104 S.Ct. at 2130: "There the Court considered the city's interest in avoiding visual clutter, and seven Justices explicitly concluded that this interest was sufficient to justify a prohibition of billboards. . . . We reaffirm the conclusion of the majority in *Metromedia*."

170. On this basis, the Court distinguished cases such as Schneider v. State, 308 U.S. 147, 60 S.Ct. 146, 84 L.Ed. 155 (1939), which held that the interest in preventing litter in the streets could not justify a total prohibition of the ability to distribute handbills and leaflets in public places.

ernment did not prohibit similar signs on private property.[171]

§ 16.48   The Special Problem of Symbolic Speech

The Supreme Court has recognized the notion that speech may be nonverbal as far back as 1931.[1] *Stromberg v. California*[2] provided First Amendment protection to certain forms of symbolic expression. A state statute that prohibited the displaying of a red flag "as a sign, symbol or emblem of opposition to organized government" was found to be unconstitutional on First Amendment grounds because it was so vague as to allow punishment for the fair use of "the opportunity for free political discussion."[3]

Twelve years later, the Court gave another form of symbolic speech protection, in *West Virginia State Board of Education v. Barnette*.[4] The Court held that the state cannot force public school children to salute the flag. The children refused to salute for religious reasons, but the Court's rationale was grounded in free speech, not free exercise:

> "[N]o official ... can prescribe what shall be orthodox in politics, nationalism, religion or other matters of opinion or force citizens to confess by word or *act* their faith therein."[5]

The Court has not retreated from the position that certain actions are a form of symbolic speech, entitled to First Amendment protec-

tion. Thus, in *Brown v. Louisiana*,[6] a 1966 decision that involved a peaceful sit-in at a segregated public library, the opinion of Justice Fortas (there was no opinion of the Court), reemphasized that First Amendment rights "are not confined to verbal expression," but also embrace action that includes "the right in a peaceable and orderly manner to protest ... unconstitutional segregation of public facilities."[7]

§ 16.49   Fashioning a Test for First Amendment Protection for Symbolic Speech and the Role of Improper Legislative and Administrative Motivation

The Court has long accepted the premise that certain "expressive" acts are entitled to First Amendment protection, but not all activity with an expressive component has full First Amendment protection. The Court began to set boundaries for the extent of First Amendment protection afforded to symbolic speech in 1968, in *United States v. O'Brien*.[1] O'Brien burnt his selective service registration certificate on the steps of the South Boston Courthouse and was convicted for violating section 462(b) of the Universal Military Training and Service Act of 1948. As amended by Congress in 1965, section 462(b) made it an offense for any person who "forges, alters, knowingly destroys, knowingly mutilates ..."[2] or changes such certificate in any manner.

---

171.   466 U.S. at 811, 104 S.Ct. at 2132.

§ 16.48

1.   283 U.S. 359, 51 S.Ct. 532, 75 L.Ed. 1117 (1931). See, 4 R. Rotunda & J. Nowak, Treatise on Constitutional Law: Substance and Procedure §§ 20.48–20.49 (West Group, 3d ed.1999).

2.   283 U.S. 359, 51 S.Ct. 532, 75 L.Ed. 1117 (1931).

3.   283 U.S. at 369, 51 S.Ct. at 535.

On the importance of symbolic speech, see, F. Haiman, Speech and Law in a Free Society 6 (U.Chi.Press 1981): "Symbolic behavior is one of the most fundamental ways in which human beings express and fulfill themselves. Its exercise thus lies at the core of a free society." See, Ronald D. Rotunda, The Politics of Language: Liberalism as Word and Symbol (U. of Iowa Press, 1986); Benjamin Whorf, Language, Thought, and Reality 251 (Carroll, ed. 1956): "Natural man, whether simpleton or scientist, knows no more of the linguistic forces that bear upon him than the savage knows of gravitational forces."

4.   319 U.S. 624, 63 S.Ct. 1178, 87 L.Ed. 1628 (1943). The remedy in this case allowed the Jehovah Witness

children to refuse to salute the flag. This remedy itself indicates that the case is a *free-speech* case and *not an establishment* of religion case, for if it were the latter, the remedy should have been to enjoin all flag salutes, just as the Court later enjoined school prayer. Cf. Engel v. Vitale, 370 U.S. 421, 82 S.Ct. 1261, 8 L.Ed.2d 601 (1962) and, School District of Abington Township v. Schempp, 374 U.S. 203, 83 S.Ct. 1560, 10 L.Ed.2d 844 (1963) (Establishment of Religion clause bars school prayer whether or not the laws establishing prayer operate directly to coerce nonobserving individuals).

5.   319 U.S. at 642, 63 S.Ct. at 1187 (emphasis added).

6.   383 U.S. 131, 86 S.Ct. 719, 15 L.Ed.2d 637 (1966).

7.   383 U.S. at 142, 86 S.Ct. at 724 (footnote omitted).

§ 16.49

1.   391 U.S. 367, 88 S.Ct. 1673, 20 L.Ed.2d 672 (1968).

2.   391 U.S. at 370, 88 S.Ct. at 1675 (emphasis eliminated).

O'Brien argued that the 1965 Amendment was unconstitutional as applied to him because it restricted his freedom of expression. The Court rejected this contention: "We cannot accept the view that an apparently limitless variety of conduct can be labeled 'speech' whenever the person engaging in the conduct intends thereby to express an idea."[3]

The Court likewise rejected the contention that an action with a clearly noncommunicative aspect is outside any First Amendment consideration. Rather, the Court presumed that O'Brien's action had a "communicative element" sufficient to bring the First Amendment into play.[4] However, this presumption does not mean that the conduct automatically receives full First Amendment protection. The government may prohibit such conduct in certain circumstances: When "speech" and "nonspeech" elements are combined in the same course of conduct, "a sufficiently important governmental interest in regulating the nonspeech element can justify incidental limitations on First Amendment freedoms."[5]

O'Brien set out a four-part test for determining when a government interest sufficiently justifies the regulation of expressive conduct. A government regulation is permissible:

[1] if it is within the constitutional power of the Government; [2] if it furthers an important or substantial governmental interest; [3] if the governmental interest is unrelated to the suppression of free expression; and [4] if the incidental restriction on alleged First Amendment freedoms is no greater than is essential to the furtherance of that interest.[6]

O'Brien ruled that the 1965 Amendment of the Universal Military Training and Service Act met the requirements of this test, and consequently it was constitutional to convict O'Brien for violating it.

The 1965 Amendment easily met the requirements of the first part of the test because

it is within the constitutional power of the Government to raise and support armies and to make all laws necessary to that end. This requirement is not grounded in the First Amendment, but is part of the basic Constitutional principle that the federal government is one of enumerated powers, and a government regulation, to be permissible, must find authority in an enumerated power, either express or implied.

Part two of the test was also fulfilled because the Selective Service certificate served a number of purposes in addition to initial notification. These purposes include quick determination of those registrants delinquent in Selective Service obligations; facilitation of quick induction in time of national crisis; facilitation of communication between registrants and local boards; reminders of notification of changes in status; deterrence for deceptive use of certificates.

These important governmental interests met the requirements of part three of the test because they were unrelated to the suppression of free expression. The Court noted a distinction between the case at bar and one where "the communication allegedly integral to the conduct is itself thought to be harmful."[7] For example, the 1965 Amendment did not bar only *contemptuous* destruction, or only bar *public* destruction; if the act had been written in the former terms, it would have indicated that its purpose was to punish the publication of certain opinions, in violation of part three of the *O'Brien* test.

Finally, *O'Brien* concluded that the 1965 Amendment was sufficiently limited to insure the smooth functioning of the Selective Service System towards the purposes enumerated, meeting the requirements of part four of the *O'Brien* test.

At this point in the development of the law the Court, under "settled principles,"[8] refused

---

3. 391 U.S. at 376, 88 S.Ct. at 1678.
4. 391 U.S. at 376, 88 S.Ct. at 1678.
5. 391 U.S. at 376, 88 S.Ct. at 1678.
6. 391 U.S. at 377, 88 S.Ct. at 1679.
7. 391 U.S. at 382, 88 S.Ct. at 1682.

8. 391 U.S. at 383, 88 S.Ct. at 1682. But see the discussion of Board of Education, Island Trees Union Free School District No. 26 v. Pico, 457 U.S. 853, 102 S.Ct. 2799, 73 L.Ed.2d 435 (1982), discussed in this section, infra.

to examine subjective legislative motive in deciding a statute's constitutionality. Thus, after *O'Brien* it seemed that so long as a statute on its face serves one "important governmental interest," unrelated to the regulation or suppression of speech, with only incidental restrictions on free speech no greater than necessary, there is an opportunity for the legislature to regulate symbolic speech without further review by the Court. The Court found that O'Brien was convicted because "he willfully frustrated this governmental interest. For this noncommunicative impact of his conduct, and for nothing else, he was convicted."[9]

School Armbands. One year after *United States v. O'Brien*,[10] the Court decided a case involving a similar form of expressive conduct, the wearing of black armbands to show objection to the Vietnam War. In *Tinker v. Des Moines Independent Community School District*,[11] the school authorities suspended some high school and junior high school students who had refused to remove the armbands in spite of a school policy adopted two days earlier in anticipation of the students' armband protest. The lower federal courts denied the students injunctive relief on the grounds that school authorities acted reasonably in order to prevent disturbance. The Supreme Court upheld the petitioners' right to wear the armbands and characterized the act as one "closely akin" to pure speech.[12]

The Court characterized the wearing of armbands in the circumstances of *Tinker v. Des Moines School District*[13] as an action that involved "direct, primary First Amendment rights,"[14] entitling the participants to comprehensive protection under the First Amendment. Wearing armbands was symbolic speech, and the school regulation that forbade the action clearly failed the third part of the *O'Brien* test: the regulation was *not* unrelated to the suppression of free expression.

Unlike the statute in *O'Brien*, which banned all draft card destruction, the school authorities did not ban all political symbols—students were even allowed to wear the Iron Cross, and some did. Instead, the school singled out a particular symbol—black armbands worn to exhibit opposition to this Nation's involvement in Vietnam—for prohibition. This governmental interest is definitely related to the suppression of free expression. The prohibition of these symbols would relate to the regulation of ideas rather than conduct.

Having failed the *O'Brien* test, the regulation must be analyzed within general First Amendment principles. Thus, the problem in *Tinker* was really one of balancing the students' exercise of First Amendment rights against the conflicting rules of school authorities. To resolve this conflict, *Tinker* adopted the standard that the Fifth Circuit used in *Burnside v. Byars*:[15] the school cannot prohibit conduct unless it "materially and substantially interfere[s] with the requirements of appropriate discipline in the operation of the school."[16] There was no such showing in this case. Petitioners' action was a "silent, passive expression of opinion" and there was "no indication that the work of the schools or any class was disrupted."[17]

Tinker made two further points in concluding that the case did not meet the requirements of *Burnside* for prohibiting expression in schools. First, the school officials' ban of the armbands was not based on disruptive effect on school work or impingement on other students' rights. Rather, the purpose of the prohibition was to avoid legitimate controversy. The "undifferentiated fear" stemming from this silent expression of political opinion was not enough to override the First Amendment.

Second, *Tinker* emphasized that the prohibition of one particular opinion was not constitutionally permissible. The regulation failed the *O'Brien* test for symbolic speech and failed

---

9. 391 U.S. at 382, 88 S.Ct. at 1681–82.

10. 391 U.S. 367, 88 S.Ct. 1673, 20 L.Ed.2d 672 (1968).

11. 393 U.S. 503, 89 S.Ct. 733, 21 L.Ed.2d 731 (1969).

12. 393 U.S. at 505, 89 S.Ct. at 736. See also 393 U.S. at 508, 89 S.Ct. at 737.

13. 393 U.S. 503, 89 S.Ct. 733, 21 L.Ed.2d 731 (1969).

14. 393 U.S. at 508, 89 S.Ct. at 737.

15. 363 F.2d 744, 749 (5th Cir.1966).

16. 393 U.S. at 509, 89 S.Ct. at 738.

17. 393 U.S. at 508, 89 S.Ct. at 737.

the *Burnside* test for prohibiting expression in schools. The wearing of armbands in the instant case was thus permitted under the strong First Amendment protections for speech.

Tinker raised, but does not decide, the issue of whether the protections for symbolic speech encompass other school regulations, such as hair or shirt length or style or types of clothing.[18] The lower courts split on these issues.[19]

Flag Desecration and Flag Burning Statutes. An important area where the Supreme Court has elaborated on *O'Brien* is in litigation surrounding flag desecration statutes. The first case was *Street v. New York.*[20] In response to the slaying of a civil rights leader, Street burned his personally-owned flag on a street corner in New York while talking out loud to a group of approximately thirty people. The arresting officer testified that he heard Street say, "We don't need no damn flag."[21] Street was convicted under a statute making it a misdemeanor "publicly [to] mutilate, deface, defile or defy, trample upon, or cast contempt upon either by *words* or *act* [any flag of the United States]...."[22]

The Court overturned Street's conviction in a narrow holding that avoided the question whether a statute could prohibit flag desecration, not by words, but by *action*. On the basis of the record, the Court said that it was possible that Street's words alone, or his words and actions together, were the basis of his conviction. The Court said that a conviction based on Street's words—totally or in part—would be unconstitutional.

Spence v. Washington[23] held the First Amendment protects an individual's alteration of a flag under specific circumstances. To both surfaces of a personally-owned flag, appellant had affixed peace symbols made from black masking tape. He then displayed the flag upside down in the window of his apartment. He was convicted under the state's "improper use" statute, which prohibited placing a figure, design or mark on a United States flag.

In a narrow holding, the Court overturned appellant's conviction because he had engaged in a form of constitutionally protected First Amendment activity. The Court enumerated several facts important in its decision: the flag was privately owned; the flag was displayed on private property; there was no evidence of any risk of breach of the peace. However, the Court did leave open the possibility that there could be a legitimate state interest in preserving the flag as an "unalloyed symbol of our country."[24]

In *Smith v. Goguen,*[25] the state convicted defendant because he wore a small flag sewn to the seat of his trousers in violation of a Massachusetts flag misuse statute that made it a crime if one "publicly ... treats contemptuously" the United States flag.[26] Justice Powell, for the Court, again avoided symbolic speech analysis and instead overturned defendant's conviction because the statute was void for vagueness. Although the Court did not rely on *O'Brien*, the "treats contemptuously" language would fall within the prohibition of part three: the governmental interest is, as expressed in the statute in *Goguen*, related to the suppression of free expression.

Texas v. Johnson[27] finally decided the symbolic speech question. The case broadly held

18. 393 U.S. at 507–08, 89 S.Ct. at 736–37.

19. New Rider v. Board of Education, 414 U.S. 1097, 94 S.Ct. 733, 38 L.Ed.2d 556 (1973), rehearing denied 415 U.S. 939, 94 S.Ct. 1456, 39 L.Ed.2d 497 (1974) (Douglas, J., joined by Marshall, J., dissenting from denial of certiorari.) Cf. Kelley v. Johnson, 425 U.S. 238, 96 S.Ct. 1440, 47 L.Ed.2d 708 (1976), on remand 543 F.2d 465 (2d Cir.1976) (county regulation of police hair length upheld because policeman is not an ordinary citizen).

20. 394 U.S. 576, 89 S.Ct. 1354, 22 L.Ed.2d 572 (1969), on remand 24 N.Y.2d 1026, 302 N.Y.S.2d 848, 250 N.E.2d 250 (1969).

21. 394 U.S. at 579, 89 S.Ct. at 1359.

22. 394 U.S. at 578, 89 S.Ct. at 1358 (emphasis added).

23. 418 U.S. 405, 94 S.Ct. 2727, 41 L.Ed.2d 842 (1974) (per curiam).

24. 418 U.S. at 412–14, 94 S.Ct. at 2731–32.

25. 415 U.S. 566, 94 S.Ct. 1242, 39 L.Ed.2d 605 (1974).

26. 415 U.S. at 568, 94 S.Ct. at 1245.

27. 491 U.S. 397, 109 S.Ct. 2533, 105 L.Ed.2d 342 (1989). For a thoughtful analysis of the competing issues, see, Roger Pilon, ed., Flag–Burning, Discrimination, and the Right to Do Wrong (Cato Institute, Center for Constitutional Studies 1990).

that a Texas law—making it a crime to "desecrate" or otherwise "mistreat" the American flag in a way that the "actor knows will seriously offend one or more persons likely to observe or discover his actions"—was unconstitutional as applied to one Gregory Lee Johnson, whom the trial court has sentenced to one year in jail and a $2000 fine because he unfurled an American flag, doused it with kerosene, and set it afire while protestors chanted: "America, the red, white, and blue, we spit on you." There were no physical injuries and no threats of injury, but several witnesses testified that they were seriously offended by the flag burning. This flag burning was part of a demonstration that coincided with the Republican National Convention's renomination of President Reagan to a second term.

The state did not charge Mr. Johnson with stealing an American flag, or burning or destroying someone else's property. Nor was he charged with trespass, disorderly conduct, or arson. The state charged him only for flag burning with an improper motive. If Johnson had burned the flag because it was dirty or worn out, he could not have been convicted of flag "desecration" because federal law provides that burning the flag is the preferred means of disposing of it when it is in such a condition that it is no longer a fitting emblem for display.[28] The state prosecuted Johnson

because of what he thought and what he intended to convey while burning the flag. He was prosecuted for his expressive conduct. In fact, at oral argument, counsel for Texas conceded that Johnson's conduct was expressive.[29]

Though this decision did not sail into uncharted waters, it drew four dissenting votes.[30] Public outcry also greeted the decision. President Bush and others proposed a constitutional Amendment, which failed to secure the necessary votes in Congress. Congress did pass a new statute outlawing flag burning. This new statute was purportedly content neutral, but it really had the same fatal flaw as the statute invalidated in *Texas v. Johnson,* for the statute did not prohibit "any conduct consisting of the disposal of a flag when it has become worn or soiled."[31] The next term the Supreme Court, by the same five to four majority, overturned convictions brought under that statute as well, in *United States v. Eichman.*[32]

The *Eichman* majority agreed that Congress has the right to protect the flag (even a privately owned flag) at least as much as it can protect a "trademark" like "Smokey the Bear" or the name "Olympics."[33] Congress and the states can protect the flag from being "diluted" or misused just like it can protect other "trademarks" like Smokey the Bear from dilution.[34]

---

28. 36 U.S.C.A. § 176(k).

29. Transcript of Oral Argument at 4, in Texas v. Johnson.

30. Rehnquist, C.J., joined by White & O'Connor, JJ., filed a blistering dissent that included long excerpts quoted from poems (such as Ralph Waldo Emerson's "Concord Hymn" and John Greenleaf Whittier's "Barbara Frietchie") hailing the flag. Stevens, J. claimed that the majority's opinion would allow vandals to spray graffiti on the Washington Monument. 491 U.S. at 436, 109 S.Ct. at 2556 (Stevens, J., dissenting). However, Congress owns the Washington Monument and can prosecute those who defile it as an ordinary trespass. Texas did not prosecute Johnson for trespass, disorderly conduct, arson, etc.

31. 18 U.S.C.A. § 700(a)(2). Some commentators argued that the new federal law was constitutional. Hearings on Statutory and Constitutional Responses to the Supreme Court Decision in *Texas v. Johnson,* Hearings Before the Subcommittee of the House Committee on the Judiciary, 101st Cong., 1st Sess. (1989), at 48 (testimony of Professor Walter Dellinger); at 99 (testimony of Professor Laurence Tribe); Hearings Before the Committee of the Judiciary, United States Senate, 101st Cong., 1st Sess. (1989) at 140 (testimony of Professor Laurence Tribe,

arguing that it is a "bizarre constitutional theory" that a federal statute could not make flag burning a crime in light of *Texas v. Johnson* is).

32. 496 U.S. 310, 110 S.Ct. 2404, 110 L.Ed.2d 287 (1990). The Court noted that some of the appellees were charged with causing wilful injury to federal property in violation of another statute. Nothing in *Eichman* affects the constitutionality of that prosecution. 496 U.S. at 312 n. 1, 110 S.Ct. at 2406 n. 1. Similarly, the government has an interest in protecting the flags that it owns (its property) and may enact special measures to protect that interest. 496 U.S. at 316 n. 5, 110 S.Ct. at 2408 n. 5.

33. See San Francisco Arts & Athletics, Inc. v. United States Olympic Committee, 483 U.S. 522, 107 S.Ct. 2971, 97 L.Ed.2d 427 (1987), holding that Congress may protect the name "Olympics" from being used, without consent from the United States Olympic Committee, for purpose of trade, to induce sales of goods or services, or to promote any theatrical exhibition, athletic event, or competition.

34. 496 U.S. at 315 n. 4, 110 S.Ct. at 2408 n. 4, citing Halter v. Nebraska, 205 U.S. 34, 27 S.Ct. 419, 51 L.Ed. 696 (1907). In *Halter,* Justice Harlan, for the Court, upheld a Nebraska statute that made it a misdemeanor to

Hate Crimes. The flag-burning cases do not forbid Congress or the states from protecting its property (the tomb of the Unknown Soldier) or other people's property (a house of worship or a graveyard) from "hate-crimes." Congress or the states may also constitutionally punish some crimes more than others. For example, a state may punish some forms of vandalism (spraying a Nazi emblem on a synagogue, or burning a cross in someone's yard) more severely and vigorously than a simple act of vandalism (spray painting a nonsense word on a subway train). The hate or terrorism element of the crime affects both the harm caused by the act and the likelihood of recidivism by the perpetrator. But the state may not punish people merely for belonging to a racist organization or merely engaging in hate speech not connected with a crime.[35]

Eichman did not say that a "political" act of vandalism—vandalism coupled with an intent to broadcast hate or terrorize—cannot be punished (or cannot be punished more severely) than a nonpolitical act of vandalism. Thus, a unanimous Court in *Wisconsin v. Mitchell*,[36] upheld the constitutionality of a Wisconsin statute that provided for enhancement of a defendant's sentence whenever he or she intentionally selects a victim based on the victim's race. The *Mitchell* statute was aimed at *conduct* (battery in the facts of that case, where the defendant beat up his victim on the grounds of color). The trial court looked at the defendant's motives in determining what sentence to impose.

A court often considers motive when sentencing. It is common for a judge to impose a lesser sentence if the defendant was acting with good motives, or a very high sentence if

he was acting for bad motives. Murder for hire is often punished more severely than murder committed in a temporary rage. The First Amendment does not offer protection for criminal acts just because they were committed with a political motive. If that were the law, then Martin Luther King's assassin—who claimed that his murder of King was a political crime—could not have been convicted.[37]

The power of the state to prosecute hate crimes does not give the state *carte blanche* whenever hate is at issue. The state may not punish an individual merely for belonging to an association, even a racist one. Thus, *Dawson v. Delaware*[38] held that the First Amendment prohibited the state from introducing, in a capital sentencing proceeding, the fact that the defendant was a member of a racist organization called the Aryan Brotherhood, where that evidence had no relevance to the issues being decided. The victim, like the defendant, was white, so no elements of racial hatred were involved in the murder. The evidence showed nothing more than the defendant's abstract beliefs, where those beliefs had no bearing on the issue being tried. However, the state could have avoided this result by presenting evidence tying defendant's racist associations to the sentencing question.

The prosecution in *Dawson* claimed that its expert witness (who did not testify) would have demonstrated that the Aryan Brotherhood is a white racist prison gang associated with drugs and violent escape attempts at prisons, and it advocates the murder of fellow inmates. Such specific evidence, the Court explained, might have been relevant in rebutting the defendant's mitigating evidence consisting of testimony about his kindness to family

---

sell merchandise that had printed or placed on it, for purposes of advertisement, a representation of the flag of the United States. The state law expressly excepted from its operation any newspaper, periodical, or book on which there was a representation of a flag "disconnected from any advertisement." The defendants had offered for sale a bottle of beer on which, for purposes of advertisement, there was printed a representation of the American flag. Only Justice Peckham dissented, without opinion.

35. Dawson v. Delaware, 503 U.S. 159, 112 S.Ct. 1093, 117 L.Ed.2d 309 (1992), on remand 608 A.2d 1201 (Del. 1992). The rule was different in the U.S.S.R. Peter Maggs

& Ronald D. Rotunda, Meanwhile, Back in Mother Russia, Legal Times of Washington, D.C., Oct. 2, 1989, at 35.

36. 508 U.S. 476, 113 S.Ct. 2194, 124 L.Ed.2d 436 (1993).

Hate Crimes and Fighting Words. See § 16.39, above, for more extensive discussion of hate crimes.

37. Najam, J., citing Treatise in, Board of Trustees of Hamilton Heights School Corp. v. Landry, 638 N.E.2d 1261 (Ind.App.1st Dist.1994).

38. 503 U.S. 159, 112 S.Ct. 1093, 117 L.Ed.2d 309 (1992), on remand 608 A.2d 1201 (Del.1992).

members and the good time credits he earned by enrolling in various drug and alcohol programs in prison.[39]

License Plate Desecration. In *Wooley v. Maynard*,[40] the Court applied settled symbolic speech principles and held that a motorist has a free speech right not to be prosecuted for obscuring on *his own* license plates the state's motto, "Live Free or Die." The individual (who was a Jehovah's Witness) claimed political, moral, and religious objections to the views expressed by the motto.

The Court held that the state cannot force an individual to be an instrument of an ideological point of view with which he disagrees. The state's claimed interests of facilitating identification of passenger vehicles and promoting state pride and an appreciation of history and individualism were insufficient to justify the restriction on free speech.

Book Banning in Public Schools and the Problem of Motivation. Though *Wooley* raised no difficult problem of the motivation of the legislative or administrative decision-maker, the Court certainly did return to that issue and elaborate on the uses of motivation and the implications of *Tinker v. Des Moines Independent Community School District*[41] in the case of *Board of Education, Island Trees Union Free School District No. 26 v. Pico.*[42] The Court was asked to decide what were the First Amendment restrictions on a decision of a local school board to remove certain books

from high school and junior high school libraries.

The books were not obscene in a constitutional sense but the board had concluded that the books were "anti-American, anti-Christian, anti-Semitic, and just plain filthy."[43] The Court produced no majority opinion and returned the case to the lower courts for a trial on the merits, in order to determine the motivation of the school board.

Justice Brennan, in an opinion joined by Marshall and Stevens, and in part by Blackmun, emphasized that the Court was dealing with a case that did not involve any textbooks or required reading; nor did the case involve judicial intrusion on the Board's discretion to prescribe curricula. "[T]he only books at issue are *library* books, books that by their nature are optional rather than required reading."[44] And even as to these books, Brennan noted, the Court's ruling would not affect the discretion of the local school board to decide which books to add. The only action challenged in this case "is the *removal* from school libraries of books originally placed there by the school authorities, or without objection from them."[45] Because this case is concerned with the suppression of ideas, the holding affects "only the discretion to *remove* books."[46] Brennan then focused heavily on the subjective motivations of the decision-makers.

Students have a right to receive ideas.[47] Although First Amendment rights must be inter-

---

39. 503 U.S. at 167–68, 112 S.Ct. at 1099. Justice Thomas, dissenting, argued that the prison gang membership was relevant because it tended to establish future dangerousness and rebut the defendant's effort to show that he was kind to others. The majority replied that the material that the dissent advanced on the nature of prison gangs "would, if it had been presented to the jury, have made this a different case." But Delaware only presented evidence of Dawson's "mere abstract beliefs...." The jurors should not be able to punish Dawson merely because they find his beliefs to be morally reprehensible.

40. 430 U.S. 705, 97 S.Ct. 1428, 51 L.Ed.2d 752 (1977).

41. 393 U.S. 503, 89 S.Ct. 733, 21 L.Ed.2d 731 (1969).

42. 457 U.S. 853, 102 S.Ct. 2799, 73 L.Ed.2d 435 (1982).

43. 457 U.S. at 857–858, 102 S.Ct. at 2803.

After a parents group raised objections, the Board decided (contrary to the recommendations of a Book Review Committee that it had appointed) that the book, *Black Boy*, by Richard Wright, should be made available in the

high school library, subject to parental approval, and that nine other books should be removed from elementary and secondary libraries and from use in the curriculum—*Slaughter House Five*, by Kurt Vonnegut, Jr.; *The Naked Ape*, by Desmond Morris; *Down These Mean Streets*, by Piri Thomas; *Best Short Stories of Negro Writers*, edited by Langston Hughes; *Go Ask Alice*, of anonymous authorship; *A Hero Ain't Nothin' But a Sandwich*, by Alice Childress; *Soul on Ice*, by Eldridge Cleaver; *A Reader for Writers*, edited by Jerome Archer; and *The Fixer*, by Bernard Malamud.

44. 457 U.S. at 861–62, 102 S.Ct. at 2805 (emphasis in original).

45. 457 U.S. at 865–66, 102 S.Ct. at 2807 (emphasis in original).

46. 457 U.S. at 870–72, 102 S.Ct. at 2810 (emphasis in original).

47. 457 U.S. at 866–68, 102 S.Ct. at 2808, citing, inter alia, Martin v. Struthers, 319 U.S. 141, 143, 63 S.Ct. 862, 863, 87 L.Ed. 1313 (1943); Stanley v. Georgia, 394 U.S.

preted in light of the special characteristics of the school environment, the school library is a special locus of First Amendment freedoms. And, in a in a far cry from *O'Brien*, Brennan focused on the motivation of the school board:

> Petitioners rightly possess significant discretion to determine the content of their school libraries. But that discretion may not be exercised in a narrowly partisan or political manner. If a Democratic school board, motivated by party affiliation, ordered the removal of all books written by or in favor of Republicans, few would doubt that the order violated the constitutional rights of the students denied access to those books. [W]hether petitioners' removal of books from their school libraries denied respondents their First Amendment rights depends upon the motivation behind petitioners' actions. If petitioners *intended* by their removal decision to deny respondents access to ideas with which petitioners disagreed, and if this intent was the decisive factor in petitioners' decision, then petitioners have exercised their discretion in violation of the Constitution. [A]n unconstitutional motivation would *not* be demonstrated if it were shown that petitioners had decided to remove the books at issue because those books were pervasively vulgar. [I]f it were demonstrated that the removal decision was based solely upon the "educational suitability" of the books in question, then their removal would be "perfectly permissible."[48]

Justice Blackmun, concurring in part and in the judgment, emphasized that school officials may not remove books "for the *purpose* of restricting access to the political ideas or social perspectives discussed in them, when that action is motivated simply by the officials' disapproval of the ideas involved."[49] For example, an elementary school library could remove a

learned treatise criticizing American foreign because the students would not understand. That removal is "unrelated to the *purpose* of suppressing ideas." However, to remove the same book "because it is 'anti-American' raises a far more difficult issue."[50]

Blackmun also questioned whether the distinction between removing and failing to acquire a book was analytically sound, but he did recognize that there was a practical and evidentiary distinction because removal of a book (more than a mere failure to acquire it) suggests an impermissible motive. Many justifications, including finite resources, could explain why a book was not purchased, but it is more difficult to explain why it would be removed from a library not filled to capacity.[51]

Chief Justice Burger, joined by Powell, Rehnquist, and O'Connor, dissented. The Board was not really a censor because it placed no restraints of any kind on the students. They could read the books, available from public libraries, bookstores, or elsewhere. The students could discuss the books in class. The school library need not be the conduit; there is no " 'right' to have the government provide continuing access to certain books," to be made "a slavish courier of the materials of third parties."[52] The plurality's test allowing the books to be withdrawn if "educationally unsuitable" is standardless test, argued the dissent. Why must a book be "pervasively vulgar" before it is offensive; would not "random" vulgarity be enough to make the book inappropriate?[53]

The Burger dissent found no justification in the plurality's distinction between *removing* unwanted books and *acquiring* books. Books do not have any constitutional tenure, argued the dissent.

557, 564, 89 S.Ct. 1243, 1247–48, 22 L.Ed.2d 542 (1969); Kleindienst v. Mandel, 408 U.S. 753, 762–63, 92 S.Ct. 2576, 2581–82, 33 L.Ed.2d 683 (1972).

48. 457 U.S. at 870–72, 102 S.Ct. at 2810 (emphasis in original).

49. 457 U.S. at 878–80, 102 S.Ct. at 2814 (emphasis in original).

50. 457 U.S. at 880–82, 102 S.Ct. at 2815 (emphasis in original).

51. 457 U.S. at 879 n. 1, 102 S.Ct. at 2814 n. 1. Justice White, concurring in the judgment, discussing what he called a "dissertation" on the Constitutional issues involved until after a full trial as to why the Board removed the books. 457 U.S. at 882–84, 102 S.Ct. at 2816.

52. 457 U.S. at 888–89, 102 S.Ct. at 2819.

53. 457 U.S. at 890–91, 102 S.Ct. at 2820.

Justice Rehnquist's dissent, joined by Burger, and Powell, stated that it could agree with the plurality that a Democratic school board could not order the removal of all books written by Republicans, but would save for another day such extreme examples because the books here were removed because of their vulgarity and profanity. Moreover, if Justice Brennan "truly has found a 'right to receive ideas,'" his "distinction between acquisition and removal makes little sense."[54]

Selective Enforcement. The decision to violate the law may be considered symbolic speech if the violation is engaged in as a form of protest. Yet it is clear that a person who violates a criminal law as a form of protest does not thereby acquire immunity from prosecution. The Government does not engage in selective prosecution in violation of the First Amendment unless its enforcement policy is discriminatory against the First Amendment on its face, or has a discriminatory effect *and* was motivated by a discriminatory purpose. The Government's mere knowledge of the discriminatory effect does not call into question an otherwise valid enforcement scheme; the Government must actually have a discriminatory intent.

These principles are well illustrated in *Wayte v. United States*,[55] where the Court upheld the constitutionality of the government's passive enforcement policy in cases where individuals refuse to register with the Selective Service System. The government made the decision to prosecute only those who reported themselves as having violated the law or who were reported by others. The government would send these reported violators a letter requesting that the alleged violator either comply with the law or explain why he was not subject to registration. Petitioner Wayte received such a letter but did not respond. Thus his name, along with others, was sent to the Department of Justice, which sent to each of the nonregistrants a letter and an FBI agent who encouraged them to change their minds and register. This procedure was called the "beg policy." Then, the Department of Justice, after its grace period had ended and its beg policy had been ignored, began to prosecute, although it acknowledged, in an internal memorandum, that those prosecuted were "liable to be vocal proponents of nonregistration" or holding "religious or moral objections," and that such prosecutions would "undoubtedly result in allegations that the [case was] brought in retribution for the nonregistrant's exercise of his First Amendment rights."[56]

Wayte claimed that he and other vocal opponents of registration—16 had been indicted out of 674,000 nonregistrants—were targeted because of their First Amendment beliefs. Wayte did not show that the Government intended any discriminatory effect, only that the Government was aware of the likely effect of its program and the claims of vocal protestors. Wayte could not prove that the government "prosecuted *him because of* his protest activities."[57]

The Court applied the four part test of *United States v. O'Brien*,[58] and found that the passive enforcement scheme passed constitutional muster. First, it was undisputed that the registration system is within the constitutional power of the Government. Second, the passive enforcement scheme furthered the important governmental interest in military security. The Government justified this particular enforcement policy because it conserved resources, for an active enforcement scheme would have been very costly. Also, the letters admitting noncompliance were strong evidence of intent not to register. And prosecuting visible nonregistrants would promote general deterrence. Third, it was undisputed—in light of the earlier analysis in this case—that the governmental interest is unrelated to the suppression of free expression. And the fourth prong

---

54. 457 U.S. at 909–11, 102 S.Ct. at 2830. O'Connor and Powell, JJ., each also wrote dissenting opinions. 457 U.S. at 894–95, 102 S.Ct. at 2822 (Powell, J.), 457 U.S. at 919–21, 102 S.Ct. at 2835 (O'Connor, J.).

55. 470 U.S. 598, 105 S.Ct. 1524, 84 L.Ed.2d 547 (1985).

56. 470 U.S. at 605, 105 S.Ct. at 1529.

57. 470 U.S. at 610, 105 S.Ct. at 1532 (emphasis in original).

58. 391 U.S. 367, 376, 88 S.Ct. 1673, 1678, 20 L.Ed.2d 672 (1968).

of the *O'Brien* test was met as well: the incidental restrictions on First Amendment freedoms caused by this interim enforcement system were no greater than necessary to ensure registration for the national defense.[59]

Finally the Court found petitioner's arguments proved too much, and were equally applicable to an active enforcement system as applied to a nonregistrant who reported himself. Such a view "would allow any criminal to obtain immunity from prosecution simply by reporting himself and claiming that he did so in order to 'protest' the law."[60]

Selective Enforcement Defense Unavailable to Illegal Alien Being Deported. In *Reno v. American–Arab Committee*[61] resident aliens sued Attorney General Janet Reno and others, claiming that the defendants targeted them for deportation, in violation of the First and Fifth Amendments, because they were affiliated with an politically unpopular group (in this case, the Popular Front for the Liberation of Palestine). While the plaintiffs' suit was pending, Congress enacted a law restricting judicial review of the Attorney General's "decision or action" to "commence proceedings, adjudicate cases, or execute removal orders against any alien under this Act."[62] The Court held that this new law, deprived the federal courts of jurisdiction to issue injunctive relief, and was constitutional. The Court broadly stated: "Our holding generally deprives deportable aliens of the defense of selective prosecution."[63]

In this case, the Government admitted that "the alleged First Amendment activity was the basis for selecting the individuals for adverse action."[64] Given this admission, the holding may first appear to be a very unusual one. But various reasons justify an opinion that led to only one dissent.[65] The Court was dealing with a matter involving foreign policy. The Executive should not have to disclose to a court or the general public its "real" reasons for deeming nationals of a particular country a special threat. For reasons of foreign policy, the President may simply wish to antagonize a particular foreign country by focusing on that country's nationals. Even if the President did disclose his real rationales, a court would be "ill equipped to determine their authenticity and utterly unable to assess their adequacy." The alien is not be criminally prosecuted for an alleged act, only deported, that is, "being held to the terms under which he was admitted." His visa may have expired. In "all cases, deportation is necessary to bring to an end *an ongoing violation* of United States law."[66]

When an alien's "continuing presence in this country is in violation of the immigration laws, the Government does not offend the Constitution by deporting him for the additional reason that it believes him to be a member of an organization that supports terrorist activity."[67] However, the Court left open the opportunity to distinguish a future case: "To resolve the present controversy, we need not rule out the possibility of a rare case in which the alleged basis of discrimination is so outrageous that the foregoing considerations can be overcome."[68]

Conclusion. Symbolic speech cases really present no issues different from those in other types of speech cases, once the court has determined that the activity being regulated or prohibited should be considered speech. It is this decision—to determine that an activity is speech—that may not always appear easy. In-

---

59. Borman, J., citing Treatise in, Fieger v. Thomas, 872 F.Supp. 377, 387 (E.D.Mich.1994); Conlon, J., citing Treatise in, Gomez v. Comerford, 1995 WL 23527, *10 (N.D.Ill.1995).

60. 470 U.S. at 614, 105 S.Ct. at 1534.

61. 525 U.S. 471, 119 S.Ct. 936, 142 L.Ed.2d 940 (1999).

62. 8 U.S.C.A. § 1252(g). This new law deprived the federal courts of jurisdiction from granting any class-wide injunctive relief, but specified that this ban did not extend to individual cases 525 U.S. at 481–82, 119 S.Ct. at 942.

63. 525 U.S. at 488 n. 10, 119 S.Ct. at 945 n. 10.

64. 525 U.S. at 488 n. 10, 119 S.Ct. at 945 n. 10.

65. Scalia, J., wrote the opinion of the Court. Only Souter, J., dissented. Ginsburg, J., filed an opinion concurring in part and in the judgment, joined by Breyer, J. as to Part I. Stevens, J., filed an opinion concurring in the judgment.

66. 525 U.S. at 491, 119 S.Ct. at 947 (emphasis in original).

67. 525 U.S. at 491–92, 119 S.Ct. at 947.

68. 525 U.S. at 491, 119 S.Ct. at 947.

dividuals may take actions that other persons do not recognize as communicating a message. For example, an individual might wish to make a symbolic statement of his opposition to an ordinance prohibiting the burning of leaves or garbage by burning such materials on the driveway of his residential property. However, a court, in considering whether he may be convicted for violating this ordinance need only apply the *O'Brien* test, without having to decide whether leaf-burning is communicative or not. A city ordinance prohibiting leaf-burning, for example, would easily meet parts one, two, and four of the four-part *O'Brien* test. If the ordinance only prohibits leaf burning by socialists, it would fail part three of the *O'Brien* test because the governmental interest is *not* unrelated to the suppression of free expression. If the city ordinance prohibited leaf burning only if done in a contemptuous manner, or if done for the purpose of protesting the city's environmental policy, it likewise fails part three of *O'Brien*. But if the city ordinance is a typical one, it prohibits all leaf burning. Then, like the statute in *O'Brien* (which prohibited knowing destruction of a draft card—it did not prohibit only contemptuous destruction of a draft card, or destruction with intent to hinder the war effort), the leaf burning ordinance would be constitutional.

In *O'Brien* the Court assumed that draft card burning was a form of speech. However, the Court stated, "[w]e cannot accept the view that an apparently limitless variety of conduct can be labeled 'speech' whenever the person engaging in the conduct intends thereby to express an idea."[69] But the real question is not the motive of the speaker so much as it is the purpose of the governmental regulation: in the words of *O'Brien*, is the governmental interest

"unrelated to the suppression of free expression"?

If conduct is treated as symbolic speech, it can still be regulated, if the pure speech could be regulated. Pure speech or symbolic conduct can be regulated in two distinct ways. First, the expressive activity, whether symbolic or express, may be prohibited because of its message, if that message fits one of the categories of speech, such as obscenity, which the Court has found punishable consistently with the First Amendment. If the content of the speech does not fit within such a category, the content cannot be proscribed unless the Court finds that the government has a compelling interest in prohibiting such messages so as to create a new category of punishable content.[70]

Second, the time, place, or manner aspects of speech, whether express or symbolic, may be regulated through laws or administrative actions narrowly tailored to promote an important or substantial governmental interest unrelated to suppressing the message. Time, place, or manner regulations must be content neutral because if they are related to the content of the speech the Court must determine whether the content fits within a category of punishable speech. These regulations must be narrowly tailored to serve an important or substantial governmental interest and leave open ample alternative channels of communication to assure the Court that channels of communication in society have not been eliminated for insubstantial or content-based reasons.[71]

§ 16.50 Regulating the Electoral Process: An Introduction

There can be little question now that political expression lies at the core of First Amendment values.[1] Nonetheless, in some cases po-

---

69. 391 U.S. at 376, 88 S.Ct. at 1678, 20 L.Ed.2d at 679 (1968).

70. Farber and Nowak, The Misleading Nature of Public Forum Analysis: Content and Context in First Amendment Adjudication, 70 Va.L.Rev. 1219 (1984); Ely, Flag Desecration: A Case Study in the Roles of Categorization and Balancing in First Amendment Analysis, 88 Harv. L.Rev. 1482 (1975).

71. In United States v. Grace, 461 U.S. 171, 177, 103 S.Ct. 1702, 1707, 75 L.Ed.2d 736 (1983), the Court restated the test as a three-part test: "the government may

enforce reasonable time, place, and manner regulations as long as the restrictions are content-neutral, are narrowly tailored to serve a significant government interest, and leave open ample alternative channels of communication." (internal quotations and citation omitted).

§ 16.50

1. Buckley v. Valeo, 424 U.S. 1, 96 S.Ct. 612, 46 L.Ed.2d 659 (1976) (per curiam), mandate conformed to 532 F.2d 187 (D.C.Cir.1976); Williams v. Rhodes, 393 U.S. 23, 89 S.Ct. 5, 21 L.Ed.2d 24 (1968); Cf. United States v.

litical expression is subject to government regulation provided the state can show a substantial interest in such regulation. The legislative objective in this field is the elimination of corruption and the appearance of corruption in order that public participation in the electoral process is not dampened by cynicism or alienation. As a result, the Court will uphold reasonable legislative proscriptions on political activity by government employees,[2] as well as regulation of the conduct of, and contributions to, political campaigns.[3]

On the other hand, the Court always bears in mind that it is the politicians who legislate the laws that regulate campaign financing. One can analogize this situation to the case where the government regulates an industry (the business of getting elected)—but in this case, the industry is regulated by part of the industry, those who are already elected, the incumbents. We should not be surprised if the incumbents, in a purported effort to regulate campaign contributions or other aspects of the race for election, sometimes create rules that tip the scales against challengers.

Regulating the Campaign Promises of Legislative and Executive Branch Candidates. Consider *Brown v. Hartlage.*[4] A political candidate promised the voters that he intended, if elected, to serve at a salary less than that "fixed by law." The state claimed that such statements violated a statute prohibiting candidates from offering material benefits to voters in consideration for their votes. One does not have to be cynical to realize that incumbents did not like it that a challenger promised to not accept a pay raise if elected. So, the state tried to prosecute the candidate for bribery of the voters.

Without a dissent, the Court held that the statute could not constitutionally be applied in such circumstances; the promise hardly fitted into the category of a private, politically corrupt arrangement. The state can prohibit bribes, but it cannot constitutionally prohibit open promises made to voters generally. As a matter of free speech, the candidate has the right to make such promises. The state law, in effect, made it a crime for a politician to make and keep a campaign promise. Under the state's view, incumbents would be protected from challengers who tried to make an issue of salaries that the incumbents had voted themselves.

Regulating the Campaign Promises of Judicial Candidates. The Court has also upheld the political campaign speech of judges running for election, but, unlike *Hartlage*, the Court was not unanimous. The leading case is *Republican Party of Minnesota v. White,*[5] a five to four decision.

Minnesota, like 39 other states, chooses judges through popular elections. Rules of judicial conduct limit the candidates' speech. One rule (which *White* did not challenge) prohibits a judicial candidate or judge from making "pledges or promises" on how he will rule in a particular case. A second rule of judicial ethics prohibits a candidate for judicial office from "announcing" a view on any "disputed legal or political" issue if the issue might come before a court. This cause prohibits a candidate's "mere statement" even if he does not bind himself bind himself to maintain that position after election.

In *Republican Party of Minnesota v. White,* Justice Scalia, writing for the Court, held that this second prohibition on judicial candidates

---

O'Brien, 391 U.S. 367, 88 S.Ct. 1673, 20 L.Ed.2d 672 (1968), rehearing denied 393 U.S. 900, 89 S.Ct. 63, 21 L.Ed.2d 188 (1968).

See, 4 Ronald D. Rotunda & John E. Nowak, Treatise on Constitutional Law: Substance and Procedure §§ 20.50–20.52 (West Group, 3d ed.1999).

2. United Public Workers v. Mitchell, 330 U.S. 75, 67 S.Ct. 556, 91 L.Ed. 754 (1947); United States Civil Service Commission v. National Ass'n of Letter Carriers, 413 U.S. 548, 93 S.Ct. 2880, 37 L.Ed.2d 796 (1973); Broadrick v. Oklahoma, 413 U.S. 601, 93 S.Ct. 2908, 37 L.Ed.2d 830 (1973); Keyishian v. Board of Regents, 385 U.S. 589, 605–

06, 87 S.Ct. 675, 684–85, 17 L.Ed.2d 629 (1967); Pickering v. Board of Education, 391 U.S. 563, 88 S.Ct. 1731, 20 L.Ed.2d 811 (1968).

3. Buckley v. Valeo, 424 U.S. 1, 96 S.Ct. 612, 46 L.Ed.2d 659 (1976) (per curiam), mandate conformed to 532 F.2d 187 (D.C.Cir.1976).

4. 456 U.S. 45, 102 S.Ct. 1523, 71 L.Ed.2d 732 (1982).

5. 536 U.S. 765, 122 S.Ct. 2528, 153 L.Ed.2d 694 (2002). Rotunda, Judicial Campaigns in the Shadow of Republican Party v. White, 14 The Professional Lawyer 2 (ABA, No. 1, 2002).

violates the First Amendment.[6] Citing *Brown v. Hartlage*, the Court said, in order for the announce clause to be narrowly tailored, it must not "unnecessarily circumscribe protected expression". The Minnesota rule did not meet this test. One common view of "impartiality" is no bias for or against any party to the proceeding. But the clause is not tailored to serve that interest because "it does not restrict speech for or against particular parties, but rather speech for or against particular issues." "Impartiality" in the sense of no preconception for or against a particular legal view, is not a compelling state interest, because it is "virtually impossible, and hardly desirable, to find a judge who does not have preconceptions about the law," particularly since the Minnesota Constitution requires judges to be "learned in the law."

Nor does the prohibition promote impartiality in the sense of "openmindedness" because the announce clause is "woefully underinclusive." For example, a judge may confront a legal issue on which he has expressed an opinion while on the bench. Judges often state their views on disputed legal issues outside the context of adjudication, if they teach classes or write books or give speeches. Indeed, the Minnesota Code like the ABA Model Code of Judicial Conduct, not only permits but encourages this.[7] The Minnesota rule prohibits a judicial candidate from saying, "I think it is constitutional for the legislature to prohibit same-sex marriage." Yet he may the very same thing, until "the very day before he declares himself a candidate, and may say it repeatedly (until litigation is pending) after he is elected. As a means of pursuing the objective of openmindedness that respondents now articulate,

the announce clause is so woefully underinclusive as to render belief in that purpose a challenge to the credulous."[8]

What Minnesota may not do "is censor what the people hear as they undertake to decide for themselves which candidate is most likely to be an exemplary judicial officer. Deciding the relevance of candidate speech is the right of the voters, not the State."[9]

Under the Minnesota rule, judges could criticize the opinions of other judges by writing dissents or dictum in their own decisions, but challengers to the sitting judge did not have this option. This restriction on campaign speech is like incumbent protection legislation, for it served to limit criticism of existing judges by the people most likely to engage in such criticism—the people running for office to unseat them.[10]

§ 16.51   Regulation of Campaign Financing

(a) Introduction

Due to scandals in financing elections as well as concern for the possible effects on democratic government of the spiraling costs of election campaigns, Congress enacted the Federal Election Campaign Act of 1971 and added more stringent Amendments with the Federal Election Campaign Act Amendments of 1974.[1] These statutes involved the federal government in the regulation of much of the day-to-day operation of political campaigns for federal office.[2] There are four primary regulations: (1) regulating the amounts contributed to or expended by the candidate or his cam-

---

6. Rotunda, Judicial Elections, Campaign Financing, and Free Speech, 2 Election Law Journal 79 (No.1, 2003).

7. 536 U.S. at 779, 122 S.Ct. at 2537. Rotunda, Judicial Campaigns in the Shadow of Republican Party v. White, 14 The Professional Lawyer 2 (ABA, No. 1, 2002).

8. 536 U.S. 765, 780, 122 S.Ct. 2528, 2537.

9. 536 U.S. 765, 794, 122 S.Ct. 2528, 2545. Rotunda, Judicial Impartiality and Judicial Campaign Contributions: Evaluating the Data, 4 Engage 127 (# 1, 2004).

O'Connor, J., & Kennedy, J., filed concurring opinions. Stevens, J., filed a dissenting opinion, which Souter, Ginsburg, & Breyer, JJ., joined. Ginsburg, J., filed a dissenting opinion, which Stevens, Souter, & Breyer, JJ., joined: "In

view of the magisterial role judges must fill in a system of justice, a role that removes them from the partisan fray, States may limit judicial campaign speech by measures impermissible in elections for political office."

10. Ronald D. Rotunda, Legal Ethics: The Lawyer's Deskbook on Professional Responsibility § 62–2.2 (ABA–West Group, 2nd ed. 2002).

§ 16.51

1. Federal Election Campaign Act of 1971, Pub.L. No. 92–225, 86 Stat. 3, as amended by Federal Election Campaign Act Amendments of 1974, Pub.L. No. 93–443, 88 Stat. 1263.

2. See Rotunda, Yet Another Article on Bush v. Gore, 64 Ohio State Law Journal 283 (2003).

paign committee; (2) forbidding "dirty tricks" by creating penalties for the "fraudulent misrepresentation of campaign authority"; (3) requiring public disclosure of contributions to and expenditures by a candidate, his campaign committee or individual expenditures on behalf of a candidate; (4) providing for public financing of all phases of presidential elections.

The Supreme Court heard a comprehensive challenge to this statute in *Buckley v. Valeo*[3], which raised significant First Amendment issues relating to central provisions of the Act. Distinguishing between the speech interest inherent in campaign contributions and campaign expenditures, the Court, per curiam, upheld the limitations imposed on contributions, but invalidated those related to expenditures. The disclosure and reporting requirements were sustained as necessary for the enforcement of the Act.[4]

Some people see the fight to limit campaign contributions as partisan in nature. However, it is useful to remember that the plaintiffs in *Buckley* included all parts of the political spectrum. James Buckley was a U.S. Senator from New York and a candidate of the Conservative Party. Co-plaintiffs included liberal Senator Eugene McCarthy, whose anti-Vietnam war candidacy caused President Lyndon Johnson to withdraw from his reelection efforts. The New York Civil Liberties Union, the Libertarian Party and the American Conservative Union were also plaintiffs, along with Stewart Mott, who had contributed $200,000 to jump start Senator McCarthy's presidential challenge. Years later, Buckley wrote that he could

not have won as a third-party candidate under the post-*Buckley* law, and Senator McCarthy also could not have launched is challenge to President Johnson. The law upheld in *Buckley*, he said, has had unexpected consequences: "by limiting the size of individual contributions it has made fund raising the central preoccupation of incumbents and challengers alike," and it created the Federal Election Commission, which issues complex, Byzantine regulations.[5]

It is important to note the underlying rationale for the result in *Buckley*. Campaign contributions and expenditures are speech or are so intrinsically related to speech that any regulation of campaign funding must comply with the First Amendment.[6] *Buckley* recognizes that, under the First Amendment, "money talks,"[7] not just figuratively, but literally.

(b) Campaign Contributions and Expenditures

The primary importance of *Buckley* lies in its distinction between campaign contributions and expenditures.[8] The distinction is of constitutional significance.

Contributions. *Buckley* concluded that the speech interests in campaign contributions are marginal, because they convey only an undifferentiated expression of support rather than the specific values that motivate that support.[9] This tangential relationship to First Amendment values cannot outweigh the primary purpose and effect of the limitation on those contributions—a reduction in the probability of corruption and a reduction in the appearance of corruption.[10] Because the limitations im-

---

3. 424 U.S. 1, 96 S.Ct. 612, 46 L.Ed.2d 659 (1976) (per curiam), mandate conformed to 532 F.2d 187 (D.C.Cir. 1976).

4. In holdings unrelated to First Amendment considerations, the Court invalidated the provisions of the Act creating a Federal Election Commission appointed by Congress. The Court upheld public financing of campaigns as a legitimate exercise of the taxing and spending power.

5. James L. Buckley, Campaign Finance: Why I Sued in 1974, Wall St. Jrl., Oct. 11, 1999, at A23.

6. 424 U.S. at 18–23, 96 S.Ct. at 634–37 (per curiam). Cf. United States v. O'Brien, 391 U.S. 367, 88 S.Ct. 1673, 20 L.Ed.2d 672 (1968).

7. 424 U.S. at 262, 96 S.Ct. at 747 (White, J. concurring in part and dissenting in part).

8. Congress had defined contributions to include not only funds given directly to the campaign, but also money spent in support of a candidate when the expenditure was within the candidate's control and coordination.

9. 424 U.S. at 19, 20, 96 S.Ct. at 634–35.

10. The alleged assumption that contributions cause elected officials to change their views is now subject to empirical criticism. Ronald D. Rotunda, A Preliminary Empirical Inquiry into the Connection between Judicial Decision Making and Campaign Contributions to Judicial Candidates, 14 The Professional Lawyer 16 (ABA, No. 2, 2003); Ronald D. Rotunda, Appearances Can Be Deceiving: Should the Law Worry About Campaign Money Looking Dirty When the Facts Show That the System's Clean?, The Legal Times, Sept. 15, 2003, at p. 84.

posed on *contributions* do not have a substantial effect on the ability of a candidate to obtain funding (they require only that a broader base of contributors be drawn upon rather than lessening the total funds used), contribution limitations are within the power of the legislature to control.[11]

The Federal Election Campaign Act of 1971 limited contributions by individuals to any single candidate for federal office to $1,000 per election. The Court upheld these contributions limits, noting that they left persons "free to engage in independent political expression...."[12] Years later the Court (6 to 3) held that this $1000 did not have to be indexed for inflation.[13]

Buckley made clear that Congress cannot imposed limitations on expenditures by third parties ("independent political expression") by treating them as "contributions" to candidates. The government's interest in preventing corruption is inadequate to justify a ceiling on *independent* expenditures. In a significant passage, *Buckley* said:

> So long as persons and groups eschew expenditures that in express terms advocate the election or defeat of a clearly identified candidate, they are free to spend as much as they want to promote the candidate and his views.[14]

This "exacting interpretation of the statutory language" is necessary to avoid unconstitutionality.[15]

Hence, an advertisement that said, "We believe in free trade, and we all know that Jane Doe supports free trade," would not run afoul if it was an independent expenditure because this expenditure for the advertisement does not, "in express terms" clearly advocate the election or defeat of anyone; it does support free trade and indicates that one of the candidates does too.

Expenditures. *Buckley* distinguished *expenditures*, because they are directly related to the expression of political views. They are on a higher plane of constitutional values, so the justification for such legislative intrusion into protected speech requires more exacting scrutiny.[16]

Because there exists little relationship between the campaign expenditures in bulk and the corruptive influence on the electoral process, particularly in light of the limitations on the amount an individual may contribute, *Buckley* held that the amount of money an individual can spend to advocate either his own candidacy or that of another is a matter within his own discretion.

Expenditure limitations cannot be saved by the argument that the government must limit the escalating costs of political campaigns, to help those candidates who are less able to attract massive amounts of capital. This justification necessarily implies that regulation may impinge on the operation of the political marketplace by restricting the effectiveness of a candidate's most salable commodity, his or her appeal to the voters, in order to benefit those whose attraction is less. If money talks, more money talks louder, more effectively. Just as the Government cannot still some voices in order to enhance the persuasiveness of others, it cannot still political expenditures. The Government may not prevent one candidate from renting a bull horn to advocate her views any more than the Government can prevent a candidate from renting a larger auditorium than another candidate.

The Court found nothing "invidious, improper, or unhealthy"[17] in allowing a political campaign to turn on the ability of a candidate to attract a broad base of financial support, because the law limiting the amount of contri-

---

11.   424 U.S. at 21–22, 96 S.Ct. at 635–36.

12.   424 U.S. at 28–29, 96 S.Ct. at 639–40.

13.   Nixon v. Shrink Missouri Government, 528 U.S. 377, 120 S.Ct. 897, 145 L.Ed.2d 886 (2000). The Court, per Souter, J., held that *Buckley* is authority for state limits on campaign contributions and that the $1000 did not have to be inflation-adjusted. Kennedy, J., filed a dissent-

ing opinion; Thomas, J., filed a dissenting opinion that Scalia, J., joined.

14.   424 U.S. at 45, 96 S.Ct. at 647.

15.   424 U.S. at 45, 96 S.Ct. at 647.

16.   424 U.S. at 19, 96 S.Ct. at 634–35 (footnote omitted).

17.   424 U.S. at 44, 96 S.Ct. at 646–47.

butions allowed served to reduce or eliminate the possibility that *quid pro quos* would be offered for large contributions.

The Political Speech of Corporations and Other Entities.

The *Bellotti* Case. *First National Bank v. Bellotti*[18] held unconstitutional a Massachusetts law that prohibited corporate expenditures for the purpose of influencing the vote on any referendum submitted to the voters other than one materially affecting the property, business, or assets of the corporation. The statute was applied to corporations that had sought to spend money to publicize their view in opposition to a proposed progressive income tax on corporations.

Bellotti easily rejected the argument that corporate speech is protected only when it pertains directly to the corporation's business interests. No precedent supported this arbitrary distinction. Then *Bellotti* considered the question of whether the state statute, which restricted corporate speech, could "survive the exacting scrutiny necessitated by a state-imposed restriction on freedom of expression."[19] Measured by this test, the state did not show a compelling, subordinating interest.

The "fact that advocacy may persuade the electorate is hardly a reason to suppress it."[20] The purpose of allegedly protecting corporate shareholders was contradicted by the over-and under-inclusiveness of the statute. Thus, the statute did not prohibit the use of corporate funds for lobbying nor allow the prohibited expenditures if all the shareholders would unanimously authorize the spending.

The dissent noted that the majority holding calls into question federal law barring corporate contributions to political campaigns.[21] However the Court distinguished corporate contributions to referenda from corporate contributions to political candidates on the grounds that the latter raises more clearly problems of corruption through the creation of political debt. The government has an important interest in regulating such corruption.

Massachusetts Citizens for Life. The *Bellotti* Court emphasized that laws prohibiting corporate gifts to candidates were not before the Court, and that "Congress might well be able to demonstrate the existence of a danger of real or apparent corruption in independent expenditures by corporations to influence candidate elections."[22] Nonetheless, *Bellotti*, in connection with *Buckley*,[23] raised questions about the constitutionality of federal limitations on corporate political expenditures. The two situations should be contrasted.

Bellotti involved a complete suppression of corporate political speech, and that speech related to a political *issue*; it did not involve giving a corporate campaign contribution to a political *candidate*. In other cases the Court has distinguished between funds accumulated in the economic marketplace versus funds accumulated in the political marketplace. Congress may protect an individual (who invests in a commercial, corporate enterprise) so that the commercial enterprise does not use those funds (invested for economic gain) for political candidates that the investor does not support.[24]

18. 435 U.S. 765, 98 S.Ct. 1407, 55 L.Ed.2d 707 (1978), rehearing denied 438 U.S. 907, 98 S.Ct. 3126, 57 L.Ed.2d 1150 (1978).

19. 435 U.S. at 786, 98 S.Ct. at 1421.

20. 435 U.S. at 790, 98 S.Ct. at 1423.

21. 435 U.S. at 811, 98 S.Ct. at 1434 (White, J., dissenting, joined by Brennan and Marshall, JJ.). Justice Rehnquist filed a separate dissent.

22. 435 U.S. at 788 n. 26, 98 S.Ct. at 1422 n. 26.

23. Buckley v. Valeo, 424 U.S. 1, 96 S.Ct. 612, 46 L.Ed.2d 659 (1976) mandate conformed in 532 F.2d 187 (D.C.Cir.1976) (per curiam).

24. See, Pipefitters Local Union No. 562 v. United States, 407 U.S. 385, 414–15, 92 S.Ct. 2247, 2264, 33 L.Ed.2d 11 (1972); Federal Election Commission v. National Right to Work Committee, 459 U.S. 197, 208, 103 S.Ct. 552, 559, 74 L.Ed.2d 364 (1982), on remand 716 F.2d 1401 (D.C.Cir.1983).

Congress, historically, has had broad authority to regulate political activities by commercial corporations. See United States v. International Union United Automobile, Aircraft and Agr. Implement Workers of America, 352 U.S. 567, 570–84, 77 S.Ct. 529, 530–37, 1 L.Ed.2d 563 (1957), rehearing denied 353 U.S. 943, 77 S.Ct. 808, 1 L.Ed.2d 763 (1957).

In *Federal Election Commission v. Massachusetts Citizens for Life, Inc.*[25] a fragmented Court considered a different situation, the case of the Massachusetts Citizens for Life, Inc., a nonprofit corporation, that published a newsletter urging readers to vote "prolife" in an upcoming primary election. The Federal Election Commission ruled that the nonprofit corporation violated a section of the Federal Election Campaign Act prohibiting direct expenditures of corporate funds in connection with election to public office. The Supreme Court, speaking through Justice Brennan, held that the section violated the First Amendment, as applied.

The money that a commercial enterprise collects from investors does not reflect the investors' support for the political ideas favored by the corporation's management. "Direct corporate spending on political activity raises the prospect that resources amassed in the economic marketplace may be used to provide an unfair advantage in the political marketplace."[26] Thus, it should be proper for Congress to require *commercial* corporations that make expenditures in connection with any election to any public office to finance those expenditures by "voluntary" contributions to a separate, segregated fund, although such a requirement would be unconstitutional as applied to voluntary political associations that happen to be incorporated but that cannot engage in business activities, have no shareholders or others who have a claim on its assets or earnings, and are not a conduit for a business corporation or a union.[27]

Compare *Federal Election Commission v. Beaumont*,[28] which upheld the federal ban on direct corporate *contributions* to federal candidates as it is applied to nonprofit advocacy corporations. *Beaumont* distinguished *Massachusetts Citizens for Life*, which invalidated a parallel *expenditure* ban as applied to such entities, by concluding that such non-profit advocacy entities pose a potential for corruption if they are allowed to contribute anything without complying with PAC regulations. The Court rejected the argument that a non-profit corporation's supporters (unlike stockholders in a for-profit corporation) know that it exists in part to influence the political process and this purpose is not corrupt. The Court responded that non-profits may well be able to amass substantial political war chests and may be misused as conduits for circumventing the contribution limits imposed on individuals.

Austin. In *Austin v. Michigan Chamber of Commerce*[29] the Court upheld provisions of the Michigan Campaign Finance Act that prohibits corporations—excluding media corporations—from using corporate treasury funds for independent expenditures in support of, or in opposition to, any candidate in elections for state office. The law, however, did allow corporations to make expenditures from segregated funds used solely for political purposes. The law in question did not regulate independent expenditures of unincorporated labor unions.

The Michigan State Chamber of Commerce challenged the law. The Chamber is a nonprofit corporation with both political and nonpolitical purposes, as its bylaws explain. It funds its activities through annual dues from its members, three-quarters of whom are for-profit corporations. The Chamber wanted to run an advertisement, in a local newspaper, in support of a particular candidate for state office. It sought to enjoin the Michigan statute as

25. 479 U.S. 238, 107 S.Ct. 616, 93 L.Ed.2d 539 (1986).

26. Federal Election Commission v. Massachusetts Citizens for Life, Inc., 479 U.S. 238, 259, 107 S.Ct. 616, 628, 93 L.Ed.2d 539 (1986).

27. Though, the Court did say that the particular question is "not before us," its reasoning would allow regulations on commercial enterprises in the corporate form that would be unconstitutional as applied to political organizations that simply happen to be in the corporate form. Federal Election Commission v. Massachusetts Citizens for Life, Inc., 479 U.S. 238, 260, 107 S.Ct. 616, 629, 93 L.Ed.2d 539 (1986). Government regulation of corporate political activity does not reflect concern about the

use of the corporate form *per se*, but rather about the potential for "unfair deployment of wealth for political purposes." 479 U.S. at 259, 107 S.Ct. at 628 (footnote omitted).

28. 539 U.S. 146, 123 S.Ct. 2200, 156 L.Ed.2d 179 (2003).

29. 494 U.S. 652, 110 S.Ct. 1391, 108 L.Ed.2d 652 (1990). Marshall, J., was joined by Rehnquist, C.J., and Brennan, White, Blackmun, & Stevens, JJ. Brennan, J. and Stevens, J. also filed concurring opinions. Scalia, J., filed a dissenting opinion. Kennedy, J., also filed a dissenting opinion in which O'Connor & Scalia, JJ. joined.

unconstitutional but the Court upheld the provision, reversing the Court of Appeals.

The Chamber, said the Court, is not a voluntary political association like *Massachusetts Citizens for Life (MCFL)*. MCFL's narrow focus on promoting particular political ideas assured that its resources reflected its political support. It was formed for an express political purpose and could not engage in any business activities. MCFL had no shareholders or other persons with a claim on its assets or earnings. If any of MCFL's members disagreed with its political activities, they could dissociate themselves without suffering any economic disincentive.

In contrast, many of the Chamber's activities are "politically neutral" and focus on economic and business issues; it provides its members with, for example, group insurance and educational seminars. While the Chamber also has no shareholders, its members have economic disincentives that discourage them from disassociating themselves with the Chamber; the members, for example, might wish to enjoy the Chamber's nonpolitical programs and the contacts with the other members of the business community acquired through membership in the Chamber.

MCFL took no contributions from business corporations, while the Chamber receives three-quarters of its contributions from for-profit corporations, who (by paying dues to the Chamber) would be able to circumvent the state restrictions on campaign contributions and expenditures. *Buckley v. Valeo* allows the state to regulate the campaign contributions and expenditures of these for-profit corporations. Thus for-profit business corporations could use the Chamber as a conduit.

The Court concluded that the state's decision to regulate only corporations—not unincorporated labor unions, and not media corporations, such as broadcasting stations, newspapers, magazines, or other commentary

in the "regular course of publication or broadcasting"—did not violate the equal protection clause of the Fourteenth Amendment. Michigan's decision to regulate only non-media corporations is "precisely tailored to serve the compelling state interest of eliminating from the political process the corrosive effect of political 'war chests' amassed with the aid of the legal advantages given to corporations."[30]

Justice Scalia issued a strong dissent, calling the majority's opinion "Orwellian." What Michigan has done, and what the Court has endorsed, said Scalia, is power of the state to restrict speech on the ground that too much speech is an evil. The state can decide how much speech is enough. It was as if the state had said: "Attention all citizens. To assure the fairness of elections by preventing disproportionate expression of the view of any single powerful group, your Government has decided that the following associations of persons shall be prohibited from speaking in support of any candidate: _____."[31]

Justice Scalia also noted that the Court only concluded that Michigan's exemption for media corporations was constitutional, not that it was constitutionally necessary.[32] But, said Scalia, Michigan might change its mind and forbid newspapers or other media corporations from making candidate endorsements. Michigan might decide that media corporations should be regulated: "Amassed corporate wealth that regularly sits astride the ordinary channels of information is much more likely to produce the New Corruption (too much of one point of view) than amassed corporate wealth that is busy making money elsewhere."[33]

One should not read *Austin* too broadly. The issue was only the constitutionality of the state's ban on corporations making independent expenditures in connection with state candidate elections. The Court upheld the ban.

---

30. 494 U.S. at 666, 110 S.Ct. at 1401.

31. 494 U.S. at 680, 110 S.Ct. at 1408 (Scalia, J., dissenting).

32. See, Marshall, J., for the Court, 494 U.S. at 667, 110 S.Ct. at 1402: "Although the press' unique societal role may not entitle the press to greater protection under

the Constitution, it does provide a compelling reason for the State to exempt media corporations from the scope of political expenditure limitations."

33. 494 U.S. at 690, 110 S.Ct. at 1414 (Scalia, J., dissenting).

The law did not prohibit corporations from endorsing candidates, only from making independent expenditures on their behalf. If a newspaper (that is, a newspaper organized in a corporate form) published an editorial in favor of a candidate, the marginal cost to the newspaper in publishing that editorial would be zero, for if the newspaper did not publish the editorial on one subject, it would publish it on another. Consequently, the fact that the *Austin* majority approved the state law at issue in that case offers no support for a state law that would purport to ban newspapers from writing editorials endorsing or opposing candidates. In other words, *Austin* does not suggest that a state could restrict newspapers from endorsing candidates. Similarly, the Chamber of Commerce, in its regular newsletter, should be able to endorse a candidate. That newsletter endorsement corresponds to the newspaper's editorial. What the Chamber wanted to do in *Austin* was buy an advertisement supporting a particular candidate. The marginal cost of that advertisement is not zero. The Chamber could not do that any more than a newspaper should be able to buy an advertisement in another newspaper supporting a particular candidate.

Justice Kennedy also dissented. He objected to two forms of censorship: first, Michigan's content-based law makes it a crime for a nonprofit corporate speaker to endorse or oppose a candidate for Michigan public office; and second, the "value-laden, content-based" speech suppression allows some nonprofit corporations to engage in political speech but not others.[34]

California Medical Association. In *California Medical Association v. Federal Election Commission*,[35] a fragmented Court rejected new challenges to the Federal Election Campaign Act of 1971. The California Medical Association (CMA), an unincorporated association of doctors, formed a political committee, the California Medical Political Action Com-

mittee (CALPAC), which was registered with the Federal Election Commission. The Federal Election Commission charged CMA with making contributions in excess of $5000 to CALPAC and also charged CALPAC with knowingly accepting such contributions in violation of the Act, which prohibits individuals and unincorporated associations from contributing more than $5000 per year to any multicandidate political committee such as CALPAC. The Act similarly prohibits political committees such as CALPAC from knowingly accepting contributions in excess of this limit.

The Court formed a majority on this issue, and ruled that, although a corporation or labor union's contributions to a segregated political fund are unlimited under the Act, the limitation on the unincorporated association's contributions did not violate the equal protection aspects of the Fifth Amendment. "Appellants' claim of unfair treatment ignores the plain fact that the statute as a whole imposes far *fewer* restrictions on individuals and unincorporated associations than it does on corporations and unions."[36] For example, individuals and unincorporated associations may contribute to candidates, and their committees, and to all other political committees while corporations and unions are absolutely barred from making any such contributions. The different restrictions "reflect a judgment by Congress that these entities have differing structures and purposes, and that they therefore may require different forms of regulations in order to protect the integrity of the electoral process."[37]

Nor did the law violate the First Amendment. Marshall's plurality opinion on this issue found that the statute did not limit the amount that CMA or its members may independently spend to advocate political views. Rather the law only limits the amount that CMA may contribute to CALPAC. The analysis in *Buckley v. Valeo*[38] allows this limitation:

34. 494 U.S. at 694, 110 S.Ct. at 1416 (Kennedy, J., dissenting, joined by O'Connor & Scalia, JJ.)

35. 453 U.S. 182, 101 S.Ct. 2712, 69 L.Ed.2d 567 (1981).

36. 453 U.S. at 200, 101 S.Ct. at 2724 (emphasis in original).

37. 453 U.S. at 201, 101 S.Ct. at 2724.

38. 424 U.S. 1, 96 S.Ct. 612, 46 L.Ed.2d 659 (1976) (per curiam), mandate conformed to 532 F.2d 187 (D.C.Cir.1976).

If the First Amendment rights of a contributor are not infringed by limitations on the amount he may contribute to a campaign organization which advocates the views and candidacy of a particular candidate, the rights of a contributor are similarly not impaired by limits on the amount he may give to a multicandidate political committee, such as CALPAC, which advocates the views and candidacies of a number of candidates.[39]

Independent Expenditures by Political Committees. *Federal Election Commission v. National Conservative Political Action Committee*[40] invalidated a section of the Presidential Election Campaign Fund Act that makes it a criminal offense for an *independent* political committee to spend more than $1,000 to further the election of a presidential candidate who elects public funding. In this case the National Conservative Political Action Committee (NCPAC) and the Fund for a Conservative Majority (FCM), two political action committees or PAC's, solicited funds in support of President Reagan's 1980 presidential campaign. They spent these funds on radio and television advertising. These expenditures were "independent"; that is, these political committees did not make any expenditures at the request of, or in coordination with, the Reagan Election Committee.

The Court—relying on *Buckley v. Valeo* and the distinction it drew between expenditures and contributions—held that the political committee's *independent* expenditures were consti-

tutionally protected, for they "produce speech at the core of the First Amendment."[41] The Court then added:

The PACs in this case, of course, are not lone pamphleteers or street corner orators in the Tom Paine mold; they spend substantial amounts of money in order to communicate their political ideas through sophisticated media advertisements. And of course the criminal sanction in question is applied to the expenditure of money to propagate political views, rather than to the propagation of those views unaccompanied by the expenditure of money. But for purposes of presenting political views in connection with a nationwide Presidential election, allowing the presentation of views while forbidding the expenditure of more than $1,000 to present them is much like allowing a speaker in a public hall to express his views while denying him the use of an amplifying system.[42]

The Court distinguished *California Medical Association v. Federal Election Commission*[43] because that case upheld regulations on *contributions* to political action committees, not regulations on their *expenditures*. However, the Court explicitly did not decide whether it would be constitutional to restrict a *corporation* in making independent expenditures to support or influence elections for public office. The Court invalidated the statute before it because it was not limited in its application just to corporations.[44]

---

39. 453 U.S. at 197, 101 S.Ct. at 2722 (footnote omitted).

40. 470 U.S. 480, 105 S.Ct. 1459, 84 L.Ed.2d 455 (1985).

41. 470 U.S. at 493, 105 S.Ct. at 1467.

42. 470 U.S. at 493, 105 S.Ct. at 1467.

43. 453 U.S. 182, 101 S.Ct. 2712, 69 L.Ed.2d 567 (1981).

44. The Court distinguished Federal Election Committee v. National Right to Work Committee (NRWC), 459 U.S. 197, 103 S.Ct. 552, 74 L.Ed.2d 364 (1982), on remand 716 F.2d 1401 (D.C.Cir.1983). The Court said:

"We upheld *this limitation on solicitation of contributions* as applied to the National Right to Work Committee, a *corporation without capital stock,* in view of the well-established constitutional validity of legislative regulation of corporate contributions to candidates for public office. NRWC is consistent with this Court's earlier

holding that a corporation's *expenditures* to propagate its views on issues of general public interest are of a different constitutional stature than corporate *contributions* to candidates. First National Bank of Boston v. Bellotti, 435 U.S. 765, 789–790, 98 S.Ct. 1407, 1422–1423, 55 L.Ed.2d 707 (1978)."

470 U.S. at 496, 105 S.Ct. at 1468 (emphasis added).

Note that the Court did not emphasize the distinction between the statute in the instant case, which limited expenditures and was invalidated, and the law is the NRWC case, which regulated contributions and was upheld. Rather, the Court seemed to focus on the corporate form, a distinction that appears metaphysical. The Court wished to leave open the question of whether it is constitutional for the Government to restrict a corporation in making independent expenditures to support *particular candidates* for public office. The Court explained:

"In *Bellotti*, of course, we did not reach, nor do we need to reach in this case, the question whether a

In *Federal Election Commission v. Massachusetts Citizens for Life, Inc.*,[45] the Court invalidated, *as applied*, Section 441b of title 2, a provision of the Federal Election Campaign Act that prohibits corporations from using treasury funds to make an expenditure "in connection with any election to any public office."[46] The election law requires that such expenditures must be financed, instead, by voluntary contributions to a separate segregated fund. The Massachusetts Citizens for Life, Inc. (MCFL) is a nonprofit, nonstock corporation dedicated to fostering respect for human life, "born and unborn." It raises money through garage sales, raffles, etc., and receives voluntary donations from interested people but does not accept contributions from business corporations or unions.

The Federal Election Commission claimed that the MCFL violated Section 441b when it used its corporate funds to widely distribute a "Special Election Edition" newsletter prior to the September 1978 primary elections. This newsletter urged people to support pro-life candidates and listed the candidates' views on MCFL legislation.

Justice Brennan, for the Court, acknowledged that direct "corporate spending on political activity raises the prospect that resources amassed in the economic marketplace may be used to provide an unfair advantage in the political marketplace."[47] Relying on *Federal Election Commission v. National Conservative Political Action Committee*,[48] the Court agreed that, normally, Congress could restrict "the influence of political war chests funneled through the corporate form...."[49] While the

relative availability of funds is a rough barometer of support, the resources in the treasury of a *business* corporation "are not an indication of popular support for the corporation's political ideas."[50] Thus, Section 441b requires that the corporation establish political committees in order to engage in campaign spending. But MCFL is not a *business* corporation. "Groups such as MCFL, however, do not pose that danger of corruption. MCFL was formed to disseminate political ideas, not to amass capital."[51]

MCFL has three features that the Courts said are essential to the holding that it may not constitutionally be bound by Section 441b. First, MCFL was formed for the express purpose of promoting political ideas and cannot engage in business activities. Second, it has no shareholders who have a claim to its assets. Third, MCFL was not established by a business corporation or labor union and accepts no contributions from such entities so it will not be their conduit. Thus, section 441b was unconstitutional as applied to MCFL, a non-commercial enterprise. Such noncommercial corporations (which are more like voluntary political associations) should not have to bear the independent spending limitations imposed solely because they happen to be incorporated. The Government may regulate commercial corporations because of concern over unfair deployment of economic wealth for political purposes; but noncommercial enterprises like MCFL, which merely use the corporate form, cannot be so regulated.[52]

(c) Disclosure and Reporting Requirements

corporation can constitutionally be restricted in making independent expenditures to influence elections for public office."

470 U.S. at 496, 105 S.Ct. at 1468.

45. 479 U.S. 238, 107 S.Ct. 616, 93 L.Ed.2d 539 (1986).

46. Fed. Election Campaign Act § 316, 2 U.S.C.A. § 441b.

47. 479 U.S. at 258, 107 S.Ct. at 628.

48. 470 U.S. 480, 105 S.Ct. 1459, 1471, 84 L.Ed.2d 455 (1985).

49. 479 U.S. at 257, 107 S.Ct. at 627.

50. 479 U.S. at 259, 107 S.Ct. at 628.

51. 479 U.S. at 259, 107 S.Ct. at 628. See also, Federal Election Commission v. National Right to Work Committee, 459 U.S. 197, 204, 209–10, 103 S.Ct. 552, 557, 560, 74 L.Ed.2d 364 (1982), on remand 716 F.2d 1401 (D.C.Cir. 1983); Pipefitters Local Union No. 562 v. United States, 407 U.S. 385, 416, 92 S.Ct. 2247, 2264, 33 L.Ed.2d 11 (1972).

52. However, even in the case of commercial corporate political activity, the state cannot impose "complete foreclosure of any opportunity for political speech...." 479 U.S. at 259 n. 12, 107 S.Ct. at 628 n. 12, citing First Nat. Bank of Boston v. Bellotti, 435 U.S. 765, 98 S.Ct. 1407, 55 L.Ed.2d 707 (1978), rehearing denied 438 U.S. 907, 98 S.Ct. 3126, 57 L.Ed.2d 1150 (1978).

The statutes challenged in *Buckley*,[53] also required the campaign committees to disclose a list of their contributors as well as requiring individual contributors to report contributions to a candidate or expenditures in support of a candidate.[54] In the only previous case challenging the disclosure of campaign finances, decided in 1934, the Court had upheld the requirement over claims that such a disclosure impaired the individuals' right of association.[55] Following that decision, the Court recognized that compelled disclosure of membership lists may constitute a restraint on the associational rights of the members, because there may exist an interest in maintaining the privacy of such associations.[56]

NAACP v. Alabama[57] had denied the State the right to compel the disclosure of the NAACP's members for the purpose of ferreting out subversives within the association. The state's interest was only tenuously related to the request and was outweighed by the legitimate fears of the members that they would be subject to harassment and intimidation if their associational ties were made public, regardless of the presence of any subversive connection.

The appellant in *Buckley* relied on this case to argue that disclosure in campaign financing would violate those interests in private political associations. *Buckley* Court distinguished *NAACP v. Alabama*[58] because, unlike that case, the countervailing interests of the state, to be served by such disclosure—providing information in order to allow the voter a more informed judgment as to the candidates' future performance in office; deterring corruption by providing notice that contributions and expenditures would be exposed; and establishing machinery for the enforcement of the Act—were directly related to the purposes in requiring the disclosure.[59]

The Court emphasized that there had been no showing in *Buckley* that potential contributors were deterred by fear of humiliation or public ridicule if their identities were linked to a particular candidate.[60] Although such fears were not unreasonable when related to the funding of minority parties, there also existed no evidence that legitimate associational activity would necessarily be dampened in all minority parties by disclosure. Therefore, only if a party could show a reasonable probability that compelled disclosure of the list of its contributors—or the recipients of campaign disbursements—would subject those contributors or recipients to threats, harassment, or reprisals from either government officials or private parties, will an exemption from the disclosure provisions for that organization be granted.[61] The creation of a blanket exemption, for all minority parties, irrespective of the inherent administrative difficulties, was simply not shown to be necessary to protect the individual member's rights of association.

The Political Party Expenditure Provision of the Federal Election Act of 1971. The Federal Election Campaign Act of 1971 included a provision that imposed dollar limits on a political party's expenditures "in connection with the general election campaign of a [congressional] candidate." In *Colorado Republican Federal Campaign Committee v. Federal Election Commission (Colorado I)*,[62] the

53. Buckley v. Valeo, 424 U.S. 1, 96 S.Ct. 612, 46 L.Ed.2d 659 (1976) (per curiam), mandate conformed to 532 F.2d 187 (D.C.Cir.1976).

54. 2 U.S.C.A. § 431 et seq.

55. Burroughs and Cannon v. United States, 290 U.S. 534, 54 S.Ct. 287, 78 L.Ed. 484 (1934).

56. E.g., United States v. Rumely, 345 U.S. 41, 73 S.Ct. 543, 97 L.Ed. 770 (1953).

57. 357 U.S. 449, 78 S.Ct. 1163, 2 L.Ed.2d 1488 (1958); see also Talley v. California, 362 U.S. 60, 80 S.Ct. 536, 4 L.Ed.2d 559 (1960).

58. 357 U.S. 449, 78 S.Ct. 1163, 2 L.Ed.2d 1488 (1958).

59. 424 U.S. at 66, 67, 96 S.Ct. at 657, 658.

60. 424 U.S. at 72–73, 96 S.Ct. at 660–61.

61. 424 U.S. at 74, 96 S.Ct. at 661. *Buckley* actually referred only to "a party's contributors' names . . ." but in a later case the Court made clear that the *Buckley* dictum sets forth the correct test to determine when the First Amendment protects minor parties from compelled disclosure and that test applies not only to contributors but also to the recipients of campaign disbursements. Brown v. Socialist Workers '74 Campaign Committee, 459 U.S. 87, 103 S.Ct. 416, 74 L.Ed.2d 250 (1982) (holding that an Ohio statute was unconstitutional as applied to the Socialist Workers Party, given the evidence of threats, harassment, and reprisals).

62. 518 U.S. 604, 116 S.Ct. 2309, 135 L.Ed.2d 795 (1996). Breyer, J., announced the judgment of the Court, and delivered an opinion joined by O'Connor & Souter, JJ. They refused to consider the broader question whether, in

Colorado Republican Party (before it had selected its Senate candidate) bought radio advertisements attacking the Democratic Party's likely candidate for Senate. The Federal Election Commission claimed that this "expenditure" exceeded the dollar limits that the Federal Election Campaign Act imposed on a political party's expenditure in connection with the general election campaign. A fragmented Court, with no majority opinion, ruled that the First Amendment prohibited applying that limitation to expenditures that the political party made "independently," that is, without coordination with any candidate. The Court then remanded to consider the Party's broader claim that even coordinated limits on a party's congressional campaign expenditures are unconstitutional on their face. In *Colorado* II,[63] the Court (5 to 4) rejected the facial challenge and held that Congress can restrict a party's coordinated expenditures (unlike expenditures truly independent) to minimize circumvention of contribution limits.

McConnell v. Federal Election Commission,[64] upheld (5 to 4) most of the constitutionality of

The Bipartisan Campaign Reform Act of 2002 (BCRA), often called the McCain–Feingold campaign finance law, after its two main sponsors. This law amended the Federal Election Campaign Act of 1971 (FECA), the Communications Act of 1934, and various other portions of the United States Code, in a far-reaching and elaborate effort to purge national politics of what the sponsors believed to be the pernicious influence of very large campaign contributions. The opinion is both long and complex. The Court's syllabus alone is nearly twenty pages in length. The entire opinion in the U.S. Reports totals 298 pages. The Court itself split a variety of ways, with various justices writing parts of the majority opinion.[65] It delivered its ruling in December, 2003, on an expedited basis after the justices returned early from their summer recess in September. It rejected most of the facial challenges to the law and found that no one had standing to raise certain issues.[66]

BCRA dealt with three important developments in the years since *Buckley v. Valeo*.[67]

---

the special case of political parties, the First Amendment also forbids congressional efforts to limit coordinated expenditures. Kennedy, J., joined by Rehnquist, C.J., & Scalia, J., filed an opinion concurring in the judgment and dissenting in part. They concluded that the FECA, on its face, violates the First Amendment when it restricts spending of a political party in cooperation, consultation, or concert with a candidate. Thomas, J., joined by Rehnquist, C.J. & Scalia, J., also filed an opinion concurring in the judgment and dissenting in part, concluding that § 441a(d)(3) is unconstitutional on its face. Thomas, J., in a portion of his opinion not joined by any other Justice, argued that the Court should reject *Buckley v. Valeo* because there is no constitutionally significant difference between campaign contributions and expenditures. Bribery laws and disclosure laws offer less restrictive means of preventing corruption.

63. FEC v. Colorado Republican Federal Campaign Committee, 533 U.S. 431, 121 S.Ct. 2351, 150 L.Ed.2d 461 (2001) (*Colorado* II).

64. 540 U.S. ___, 124 S.Ct. 619, 157 L. Ed. 2d 491 (2003).

65. Stevens and O'Connor, JJ., delivered the opinion of the Court with respect to BCRA Titles I and II, in which Souter, Ginsburg, and Breyer, JJ., joined. Rehnquist, C. J., delivered the opinion of the Court with respect to BCRA Titles III and IV, in which O'Connor, Scalia, Kennedy, and Souter, JJ., joined, in which Stevens, Ginsburg, and Breyer, JJ., joined except with respect to BCRA 305, and in which Thomas, J., joined with respect to BCRA 30 4, 305, 307, 316, 319, and 403(b). Breyer, J.,

delivered the opinion of the Court with respect to BCRA Title V, in which Stevens, O'Connor, Souter, and Ginsburg, JJ., joined. Scalia, J., filed an opinion concurring with respect to BCRA Titles III and IV, dissenting with respect to BCRA Titles I and V, and concurring in the judgment in part and dissenting in part with respect to BCRA Title II. Thomas, J., filed an opinion concurring with respect to BCRA Titles III and IV, except for BCRA 311 and 318, concurring in the result with respect to BCRA 318, concurring in the judgment in part and dissenting in part with respect to BCRA Title II, and dissenting with respect to BCRA Titles I, V, and 311, in which opinion Scalia, J., joined as to Parts I, IIA, and -IIB. Kennedy, J., filed an opinion concurring in the judgment in part and dissenting in part with respect to BCRA Titles I and II, in which Rehnquist, C. J., joined, in which Scalia, J., joined except to the extent the opinion upholds new FECA 323(e) and BCRA 202, and in which Thomas, J., joined with respect to BCRA 213. Rehnquist , C. J., filed an opinion dissenting with respect to BCRA Titles I and V, in which Scalia and Kennedy, JJ., joined. Stevens, J., filed an opinion dissenting with respect to BCRA 305, in which Ginsburg and Breyer, JJ., joined.

66. For example, a "millionaire's provisions" of the law permits candidates running against wealthy opponents to receive campaign money in larger amounts than otherwise permitted. The validity of that provision will await another day.

67. 424 U.S. 1, 96 S.Ct. 612, 46 L.Ed.2d 659 (per curiam).

FIRST, the enactment of the FECA led to the increased importance of "soft money," The FECA imposed stringent disclosure and reporting requirements on so-called "hard money," that is, contributions made for the purpose of influencing an election for federal office. Political parties and candidates were able to circumvent FECA's limitations by contributing "soft money"—money unregulated under FECA—to be used for activities intended to influence state or local elections; for mixed-purpose activities such as get-out-the-vote drives (GOTV) and generic party advertising; and for legislative advocacy advertisements, even if they mentioned a federal candidate's name, so long as the advertisements did not expressly advocate the candidate's election or defeat.

SECOND, parties and candidates eluded FECA by using "issue ads," which were intended to affect election results, but did not contain explicit words, such as "Vote Against Jane Doe" that would have subjected these advertisements to FECA's restrictions.

THIRD, a Senate Committee, in 1998, investigated the 1996 Presidential Election and concluded that the "soft money loophole" had led to a "meltdown" of the campaign finance system that had been intended "to keep corporate, union and large individual contributions from influencing the electoral process."[68]

Justices Stevens and O'Connor concluded their portion of the lengthy opinion with a caveat:

We abide by that conviction in considering Congress' most recent effort to confine the ill effects of aggregated wealth on our political system. We are under no illusion that BCRA will be the last congressional statement on the matter. Money, like water, will always find an outlet. What problems will arise, and how Congress will respond, are concerns for another day. In the main we uphold BCRA's two principal, complementary features: the control of soft money and the regulation of electioneering communications.[69]

The Court, in brief, held: (1) BCRA may constitutionally ban political parties and candidates from using "soft money" for federal election activities; (2) BCRA's ban on party donations to tax-exempt entities tax-exempt political organizations that make expenditures in connection with federal elections did not violate free speech rights, at least in so far as it prohibited donation of unregulated "soft money"; (3) "soft money" could not be used for issue ads that clearly identified a candidate; (4) the restrictions on the disclosure of persons who fund "electioneering communications"[70] and restrictions on the corporations' and labor unions' funding of electioneering communications are valid;[71] (5) the cost of third-party issue advertisements that are coordinated with federal candidates' campaigns may validly be considered as contributions to those campaigns; (6) it is constitutional to require labor unions and corporations to pay for issue advertisements from separately segregated funds; (7) however, the statutory prohibition on political donations by minors was invalid;[72] and (8) the requirement that broad-

---

68. 540 U.S. at ___, 124 S.Ct. 619, 652.

69. 540 U.S. at ___, 124 S.Ct. 619, 706.

70. The statute defined "electioneering communication" to include, any "broadcast, cable, or satellite communication that

"(I) refers to a clearly identified candidate for Federal office;

"(II) is made within—

"(aa) 60 days before a general, special, or runoff election for the office sought by the candidate; or

"(bb) 30 days before a primary or preference election, or a convention or caucus of a political party that has authority to nominate a candidate, for the office sought by the candidate; and

"(III) in the case of a communication which refers to a candidate other than President or Vice President, is targeted to the relevant electorate."

540 U.S. at ___, 124 S.Ct. 619, 686–87.

71. The law requires that "electioneering communication" may be paid for only with money raised and spent pursuant to federal disclosure rules and limitations on donations. No soft money may pay for these advertisements; proponents of these advertisements must establish federally regulated political action committees and pay for the ads through them.

72. The Court held that BCRA, § 318, which forbids individuals "17 years old or younger" to make contributions to candidates and political parties, violates the First Amendment rights of minors.

casters disclose records of requests for air time for political advertisements is valid.

Justice Scalia, dissenting, warned that what is called campaign financing "reform" is really incumbent protection legislation:

Who could have imagined that the same Court which, within the past four years, has sternly disapproved of restrictions upon such inconsequential forms of expression as virtual child pornography, tobacco advertising, dissemination of illegally intercepted communications, and sexually explicit cable programming, would smile with favor upon a law that cuts to the heart of what the First Amendment is meant to protect: the right to criticize the government. For that is what the most offensive provisions of this legislation are all about. [T]his legislation prohibits the criticism of Members of Congress by those entities most capable of giving such criticism loud voice: national political parties and corporations, both of the commercial and the not-for-profit sort. It forbids pre-election criticism of incumbents by corporations, even not-for-profit corporations, by use of their general funds; and forbids national-party use of "soft" money to fund "issue ads" that incumbents find so offensive.

To be sure, the legislation is evenhanded: It similarly prohibits criticism of the candidates who oppose Members of Congress in their reelection bids. But as everyone knows, this is an area in which evenhandedness is not fairness. If all electioneering were evenhandedly prohibited, incumbents would have an enormous advantage. Likewise, if incumbents and challengers are limited to the same quantity of electioneering, incumbents are favored. In other words, any restriction upon a type of campaign speech that is equally available to challengers and incumbents tends to favor incumbents.

Beyond that, however, the present legislation targets for prohibition certain catego-

ries of campaign speech that are particularly harmful to incumbents. Is it accidental, do you think, that incumbents raise about three times as much "hard money"—the sort of funding generally not restricted by this legislation—as do their challengers? Or that lobbyists (who seek the favor of incumbents) give 92 percent of their money in "hard" contributions?[73]

The majority rejected this argument, as they also rejected the distinction that *Buckley v. Valeo* had earlier made between issue advocacy and express advocacy. Under Buckley, there could be no regulation of advertisements that did not expressly advocate the victory or defeat of a specific candidate. *McConnell v. FEC* dismissed that limitation.

We should expect to see other lawsuits dealing with the intricacies of this very complex law. The system will be in constant flux. In 2004, the spending limits for New Hampshire (the first primary state) were set the same as the spending limit for America Samoa. In 2004, two of the major Democratic presidential challengers, Howard Dean and John Kerry, and Republican incumbent, George W. Bush, all dropped out of the public financing system.[74] In response to the new federal restrictions, people are creating new legal entities, such as "Americans Coming Together," a Democratically-aligned group of activists set up with a $10 million donation from billionaire George Soros, who has vowed to spend much of his wealth to defeat President Bush.[75] We should expect that Republican groups may also be established if these new entities are not covered by the current law.

§ 16.52   Regulation of Political Activity of Government Employees

The governmental interest in fair and effective operation of the federal government justifies regulation of partisan political activities of government employees.[1] Section 9(a) of the

73. 540 U.S. at ___, 124 S.Ct. 619, 720–21 (Scalia, J., concurring and dissenting) (internal citations omitted).

74. Jeanne Cummings, Candidates Play Money Game, Wall Street Journal, Jan. 16, 2004, at A4.

75. Jeanne Cummings, Political–Funding Fight Heads to Election Panel, Wall Street Journal, Jan. 16, 2004, at

A2; Jeanne Cummings, The New Rules of Bankrolling a Candidate, Wall Street Journal, Jan. 21, 2004 at D1.

§ 16.52

1. United Public Workers v. Mitchell, 330 U.S. 75, 67 S.Ct. 556, 91 L.Ed. 754 (1947) and United States Civil

Hatch Act,[2] forbids government employees from taking "an active part in political management or political campaigns. All such persons shall retain the right to vote as they may choose and to express their opinions on all political subjects." In *United States Civil Service Commission v. National Association of Letter Carriers*,[3] the Court reaffirmed its 26 year old holding in *United Public Workers v. Mitchell*[4] that such restrictions on public employment are valid, because they serve an overriding state interest, only restrict certain methods of political expression, and do not deny to governmental employees the right to hold political views or express those views outside the context of a political campaign.

The government's interest in regulating the speech and conduct of its employees differs from its interest in such regulation of general citizens for several reasons.[5] First, government employees, by virtue of their position, exert a great deal of influence as the growth of government increasingly affects the daily life of private citizens. To allow that employee to reap political dividends because of his employment demeans the government and induces disrespect for its functionaries. Second, political participation by public employees may threaten the effective operation of government. It is essential that employees implement the will of Congress, unswayed by the directives of a political party.

The prohibitions on political activity also serve the related concern of insuring that government employees are not required to engage in partisan political support in order to retain their positions, so that governmental employees avoid engaging in "political justice" and also that they "appear to the public to be avoiding it...."[6] Because the interest of the employee in the right to political association is not dampened, but only his right to participate in political campaigns, the overwhelming governmental interest must prevail.

Thus, *Letter Carriers* held that federal employees can be prevented from engaging in "plainly identifiable acts of political management and political campaigning"[7] such as holding a party office, working at the polls, acting as a party paymaster for other party workers, organizing a political party or club, actively participating in fund-raising activities for a partisan candidate, becoming a partisan candidate or campaigning for an elective political office, initiating or circulating a partisan nominating petition, soliciting votes for a partisan candidate for political office, or serving as a delegate to a political party convention.[8]

Union Rules and Public and Private Criticism on Matters of Public Concern by Government Employees. Governmental interests is regulating the controversial speech of its employees are not boundless. Rather, the regulations must be narrowly drawn to serve the objectives of effective government without intruding unnecessarily into the private associations and beliefs of its employees. As the Court noted in *Pickering v. Board of Education*,[9]

> The problem in any case is to arrive at a balance between the interests of the [employee], as a citizen, in commenting upon matters of public concern and the interest of the [government], as an employer in promoting the efficiency of the public services it performs through its employees.[10]

Thus the Board of Education was prohibited from firing a teacher who wrote and published

---

Service Commission v. National Ass'n of Letter Carriers, 413 U.S. 548, 93 S.Ct. 2880, 37 L.Ed.2d 796 (1973). Broadrick v. Oklahoma, 413 U.S. 601, 93 S.Ct. 2908, 37 L.Ed.2d 830 (1973) applied the same principles to a state restriction on political activities of public employees. Batchelder, J., citing Treatise in Carver v. Dennis, 104 F.3d 847, 851 n. 7 (6th Cir.1997).

2. 5 U.S.C.A. § 7324. See United States Civil Service Commission v. National Ass'n of Letter Carriers, 413 U.S. 548, 560–61, 93 S.Ct. 2880, 2887–88, 37 L.Ed.2d 796 (1973).

3. 413 U.S. 548, 93 S.Ct. 2880, 37 L.Ed.2d 796 (1973).

4. 330 U.S. 75, 67 S.Ct. 556, 91 L.Ed. 754 (1947).

5. Pickering v. Board of Education, 391 U.S. 563, 88 S.Ct. 1731, 20 L.Ed.2d 811 (1968).

6. 413 U.S. at 565, 93 S.Ct. at 2890.

7. 413 U.S. at 567, 93 S.Ct. at 2891.

8. Crooks, J., citing Treatise in L.L.N. v. Clauder, 209 Wis.2d 674, 563 N.W.2d 434, 440 (Wisc.1997).

9. 391 U.S. 563, 88 S.Ct. 1731, 20 L.Ed.2d 811 (1968).

10. 391 U.S. at 568, 88 S.Ct. at 1734–35.

in a newspaper a letter criticizing the Board's budgetary policies and public information methods.

As to those charges by the teacher that were substantially correct, they were also matters of "public concern" and presented no issues of faculty discipline or harmony; hence they did not justify dismissal. The charges that were false were also concerned with issues of public concern and similarly were not shown to have interfered with the teacher's job or with the school's general operation. In the absence of the scienter required in *New York Times v. Sullivan*[11] of a knowing or reckless falsehood, the Board could not fire the teacher from his public employment.

Similarly, *Elrod v. Burns*[12] struck down a system of political patronage in determining eligibility for government employment. The program delved into beliefs and associations of the employees without a significant countervailing interest.

Givhan v. Western Line Consolidated School District[13] made clear that the First Amendment protection of public employees is not limited by any requirement that the speech must be public, when the statements involve matters of public concern.[14] The Court explained that no First Amendment freedom "is lost to the public employee who arranges to communicate privately with his employee rather than to spread his views before the public."[15]

Thus, while *Letter Carriers* indicates that certain modes of actively expressing partisan political belief may be banned in the interest of preserving a non-partisan government work force, *Pickering* and *Burns* establish that political beliefs, and their reasonable expression, are not subject to the dictates of the government employer. *Madison School District v. Wisconsin Employment Relations Committee*[16] reaffirmed this principle. It held that the state employment commission could not bar a public school board from allowing a teacher to address it at a public meeting. The employment commission sought to prevent the teacher from addressing the board on pending labor negotiations, because the teacher was not a union representative and in fact was not even a union member. However the meeting was *public*, and *public participation* was generally permitted.

Although the state cannot punish a public employee because of her associations or because she speaks freely, the state has no obligation to listen, to recognize the association, and bargain with it. *Smith v. Arkansas State Highway Employees, Local 1315*[17] held that a state agency can refuse to consider or act upon grievances when filed by the union rather than by the employee directly. The converse is also true. If the state does recognize a union as an exclusive representative, the state has no First Amendment obligation to confer with its public employees who are not members of the bargaining unit.[18]

---

11.   376 U.S. 254, 84 S.Ct. 710, 11 L.Ed.2d 686 (1964), motion denied 376 U.S. 967, 84 S.Ct. 1130, 12 L.Ed.2d 83 (1964).

12.   427 U.S. 347, 96 S.Ct. 2673, 49 L.Ed.2d 547 (1976). Accord, Branti v. Finkel, 445 U.S. 507, 100 S.Ct. 1287, 63 L.Ed.2d 574 (1980).

13.   439 U.S. 410, 99 S.Ct. 693, 58 L.Ed.2d 619 (1979), on remand 592 F.2d 280 (5th Cir.1979), appeal after remand 691 F.2d 766 (1982).

14.   Givhan v. Western Line Consolidated School District, 439 U.S. 410, 99 S.Ct. 693, 58 L.Ed.2d 619 (1979), on remand 592 F.2d 280 (5th Cir.1979), appeal after remand 691 F.2d 766 (1982) unanimously held that the teacher could not be discharged for privately communicating her grievances about allegedly racially discriminatory policies or her opinion concerning other public issues, to her employer.

Contrast Connick v. Myers, 461 U.S. 138, 103 S.Ct. 1684, 75 L.Ed.2d 708 (1983) (5 to 4), which upheld the firing of an assistant district attorney for circulating a questionnaire regarding office policies; the questionnaire did not touch on matters of public concern. The employer need not tolerate action that he reasonably believes would disrupt the office, undermine his authority, and destroy close working relationships.

15.   439 U.S. at 415, 99 S.Ct. at 696–97.

16.   429 U.S. 167, 97 S.Ct. 421, 50 L.Ed.2d 376 (1976).

17.   441 U.S. 463, 99 S.Ct. 1826, 60 L.Ed.2d 360 (1979) (per curiam). Accord, Babbitt v. United Farm Workers Nat. Union, 442 U.S. 289, 99 S.Ct. 2301, 60 L.Ed.2d 895 (1979).

18.   Minnesota State Board for Community Colleges v. Knight, 465 U.S. 271, 104 S.Ct. 1058, 79 L.Ed.2d 299 (1984). See also, Bi–Metallic Investment Co. v. State Board of Equalization, 239 U.S. 441, 445, 36 S.Ct. 141, 142, 60 L.Ed. 372 (1915).

Restrictions on the Compensation Earned by Government Employees for Making Speeches and Writing Articles. In 1989 Congress enacted § 501(b) of the Ethics in Government Act, a section that broadly prohibited federal employees from accepting any compensation for making speeches or writing articles, even if the subject of the speech or article has no connection with the employee's official duties. Executive Branch Employees below the grade of GS–16 sued to invalidate this law in *United States v. National Treasury Employees Union*.[19] In the past these plaintiffs had received compensation for writing or speaking about matters such as religion, history, dance, and the environment. Generally, neither the groups paying the plaintiffs nor the subjects discussed had any connection with their official duties.

The Court held that § 501(b) violated the First Amendment. The employees were speaking on matters of public concern, not on matters of personal interest. Hence, the Government must demonstrate that the recited harms are real, not conjectural, and that the law will alleviate these harms in a direct and substantial way.

While § 501(b) did not restrict speech based on content or viewpoint, the prohibition on compensation did impose a significant economic disincentive on the plaintiffs. The Government offered no evidence of misconduct by the vast number of employees (nearly 1.7 million) below the rank of GS–16. Limited evidence of actual or apparent impropriety by high-level executives or Congressmen does not justify extension of the compensation ban to lower-level rank and file employees who have negligible power to grant favors to those who might pay to read their writings or hear them speak.

In addition, the law was ineptly drafted. For example, "a rather strange" section of the statute allowed compensation for a *"series"* of articles if no nexus existed between the author's employment and either the subject matter of the expression or the identity of the payor. But pay is taboo for an *individual* article or speech even there is no nexus to the author's duties.[20] The law restricted only expressive activities and did not ban other off-duty activities that are nonexpressive ways of collecting compensation, such as payment for services on corporate boards. This "crudely crafted burden" on the plaintiffs' free speech is not "as carefully tailored as it should have been," and hence § 501(b) violated the First Amendment.

The Court then ruled that the relief should be limited to the parties before the Court—Executive Branch employees below GS–16. The Government, in a later case, might be able to advance a different justification of a compensation ban limited to more senior officials. The Court also refused to limit the statute's compensation ban to cases involving an undesirable nexus between the speaker's official duties and the subject matter of the expression or the identity of the payor because Congress should have the responsibility of redrafting the statute.

§ 16.53 The Rights of Assembly and Petition: An Introduction

The Magna Carta. When King John signed the Magna Carta in 1215, he established the base from which comes our modern right of petition for redress of grievances. Originally, both houses of the English Parliament had the right to petition the Crown for redress of grievances, but as Commons became more important than the House of Lords, petitions for redress grievances began to be directed to it, instead of the Crown. The right to petition the House of Commons, as an extension of the

---

19. 513 U.S. 454, 115 S.Ct. 1003, 130 L.Ed.2d 964 (1995). O'Connor, J., concurred in the judgment in part and dissented in part. She would hold the law unconstitutional only to the extent that it bars these lower level federal employees (below GS–16) from receiving compensation for nonwork-related speeches, appearances, and articles. Rehnquist, C.J., joined by Scalia & Thomas, JJ., dissented, arguing that the Court understated the Govern-

ment's justifications, overstated the amount of speech actually deterred, and only discussed the impact of the statute as to a handful of its most appealing individual situations, but then invalidated the entire law as to all employees below GS–16.

20. 513 U.S. at 473–74, 115 S.Ct. at 1016 (emphasis in original).

original Magna Carta provision, was later guaranteed to every commoner.[1]

John Quincy Adams and Petitioning the Government. The last clause of the First Amendment provides: "Congress shall make no law ... abridging ... the right of the people peaceably to assemble and to petition the Government for a redress of grievances." The first clear test under this clause took place in 1836.

In that year, the United States House of Representatives, inundated with abolitionist petitions, adopted a gag rule that had the effect of tabling, without discussion, petitions concerned with slavery or the abolition of slavery. John Quincy Adams of Massachusetts, who had opposed adoption of the gag rule as a direct violation of the Constitution of the United States, was even more strongly opposed to the strengthening of that rule in 1840, to prohibit the receipt of any petition on the subject of slavery. The former President was finally successful in obtaining repeal of the rule in 1844, when the strength of antislavery views in the North intensified.[2]

Incorporation Into the Fourteenth Amendment. It was not until *Hague v. C.I.O.*,[3] that the Supreme Court recognized that states may not abridge the rights of assembly and petition. The justices used two different lines of reasoning in striking down a Jersey City, New Jersey ordinance.

Justice Roberts, with Chief Justice Hughes and Justice Black concurring, found protection for the right of assembly as a privilege and immunity of a United States citizen, within the meaning of the Fourteenth Amendment.[4] The opinion of Justice Stone, with Justice Reed concurring, found protection for the right of assembly in the due process clause of the Fourteenth Amendment.[5] The due process theory has prevailed and it is into that broad clause that the Supreme Court has breathed an expansive interpretation of civil rights.[6]

Schneider v. Smith[7] reaffirmed the importance and central meaning of the rights to peacefully assemble and petition. The Court struck down regulations dealing with the reading habits, political philosophy, beliefs, and attitudes on social and economic issues of prospective seamen on United States merchant vessels. Justice Douglas, explained:

The purpose of the Constitution and Bill of Rights, unlike more recent models promoting a welfare state, was to take government off the backs of the people. The First Amendment's ban against Congress "abridging" freedom of speech, the right peaceably to assemble and to petition, and the "associational freedom" ... that goes with those rights create a preserve where the views of the individual are made inviolate. This is the philosophy of Jefferson, that "the opinions

§ 16.53

1. C. Stephenson & F. Marcham, Sources of English Constitutional History 125 (2d ed. 1972). In the 1790's, Parliament forbade public meetings held in order to petition the King if more than 50 persons were present, unless the meeting was held in the presence of a magistrate with authority to arrest everybody present. 4 Ronald D. Rotunda & John E. Nowak, Treatise on Constitutional Law: Substance and Procedure §§ 20.53–20.55 (West Group, 3d ed.1999).

See Sherrard v. Hull, 53 Md.App. 553, 456 A.2d 59, 64 (1983), affirmed 296 Md. 189, 460 A.2d 601 (1983), citing treatise.

2. A. H. Kelly & W. H. Harbison, The American Constitution: Its Origins and Development, 357–58 (4th ed. 1970).

The Right to Petition and the Law of Libel. McDonald v. Smith, 472 U.S. 479, 105 S.Ct. 2787, 86 L.Ed.2d 384 (1985) held that the petition clause of the First Amendment does not give a defendant in a libel action absolute immunity. The plaintiff had charged defendant with knowingly sending false and libelous letters to President Reagan and others in order to undermine the chances of his being appointed U.S. Attorney. The petition clause does not require state libel law to expand the qualified privilege already afforded by New York Times v. Sullivan, 376 U.S. 254, 84 S.Ct. 710, 11 L.Ed.2d 686 (1964).

See also White v. Nicholls, 44 U.S. (3 How.) 266, 11 L.Ed. 591 (1845).

3. 307 U.S. 496, 59 S.Ct. 954, 83 L.Ed. 1423 (1939).

4. 307 U.S. at 512, 59 S.Ct. at 962–63.

5. 307 U.S. at 525, 59 S.Ct. at 968–69.

6. E.g., De Jonge v. Oregon, 299 U.S. 353, 364, 57 S.Ct. 255, 259–60, 81 L.Ed. 278 (1937); Thomas v. Collins, 323 U.S. 516, 532, 65 S.Ct. 315, 323–24, 89 L.Ed. 430 (1945), rehearing denied 323 U.S. 819, 65 S.Ct. 557, 89 L.Ed. 650 (1945); Douglas v. Jeannette, 319 U.S. 157, 162, 63 S.Ct. 877, 880, 87 L.Ed. 1324 (1943); Shelton v. Tucker, 364 U.S. 479, 493, 81 S.Ct. 247, 254–55, 5 L.Ed.2d 231 (1960).

7. 390 U.S. 17, 88 S.Ct. 682, 19 L.Ed.2d 799 (1968).

of men are not the object of civil government, nor under its jurisdiction...."[8]

It is not significant whether one is engaged in speech, association, assembly, or petition. All four rights are elements of a broad right to freedom of expression.[9] Let us now turn to some specific cases particularly related to assembly and petition.

§ 16.54 The Basic Legal Principles Regarding Assembly and Petition

The First Amendment allows a peaceful gathering of persons for almost any lawful purpose.[1] The Supreme Court early recognized that the state cannot make it a crime to participate in a peaceful assembly.[2] Thus, active participation in a Communist Party political meeting cannot be a crime if no violence is incited.[3] The Court has protected assembly for marches, demonstrations, and picketing as lawful assemblages.[4] Labor organizing meetings are lawful exercises of the First Amendment right of assembly.[5]

Anonymous Membership. Implicit in the right of assembly is the right of association, which is implied from the expressly listed rights concerning free expression in the First Amendment. Association is more than the right to attend a meeting: "it includes the right to express one's attitudes or philosophies by membership in a group, or affiliation with it or by other lawful means."[6] *Bates v. Little Rock*[7] recognized that a corollary of this right is the right of an association to conceal from the state the names of the individual members if it is likely that a deprivation of the personal liberty of the individuals would result, a deprivation not balanced by the state demonstrating a "controlling justification" for the information.[8]

Securing Legal Advice and Suing. The right to petition the government for redress of grievances includes the right to institute non-frivolous lawsuits.[9] One group of these cases involve the efforts of associations to refer their members to lawyers after having first advised their members of their legal rights.[10] The Court upheld that practice based in part on the First Amendment right of every person to petition for redress of grievances.

In many situations, litigation is the only practical method open to redress of one's

---

8. 390 U.S. at 25, 88 S.Ct. at 687. (footnote omitted).

9. E.g., De Jonge v. Oregon, 299 U.S. 353, 364, 57 S.Ct. 255, 259–60, 81 L.Ed. 278 (1937); Thomas v. Collins, 323 U.S. 516, 65 S.Ct. 315, 89 L.Ed. 430 (1945), rehearing denied 323 U.S. 819, 65 S.Ct. 557, 89 L.Ed. 650 (1945); Schneider v. Smith, 390 U.S. 17, 88 S.Ct. 682, 19 L.Ed.2d 799 (1968); United Mine Workers v. Illinois State Bar Ass'n, 389 U.S. 217, 88 S.Ct. 353, 19 L.Ed.2d 426 (1967).

§ 16.54

1. Griswold v. Connecticut, 381 U.S. 479, 482, 85 S.Ct. 1678, 1680–81, 14 L.Ed.2d 510 (1965). Pollock, J., citing Treatise, in Snyder v. American Association of Blood Banks, 144 N.J. 269, 295, 676 A.2d 1036, 1049 (1996).

Prisons and Peaceful Assembly. Jones v. North Carolina Prisoners' Labor Union, Inc., 433 U.S. 119, 97 S.Ct. 2532, 53 L.Ed.2d 629 (1977) upheld prison regulations that made more difficult the organizing efforts of a prisoners' union. The restrictive environment of a penal institution was emphasized. While the prison authorities had forbade union solicitation, the union itself was allowed.

2. De Jonge v. Oregon, 299 U.S. 353, 57 S.Ct. 255, 81 L.Ed. 278 (1937).

3. 299 U.S. at 363–65, 57 S.Ct. at 259–60.

4. Hague v. CIO, 307 U.S. 496, 59 S.Ct. 954, 83 L.Ed. 1423 (1939).

5. Thomas v. Collins, 323 U.S. 516, 65 S.Ct. 315, 89 L.Ed. 430 (1945), rehearing denied 323 U.S. 819, 65 S.Ct. 557, 89 L.Ed. 650 (1945).

6. Griswold v. Connecticut, 381 U.S. 479, 483, 85 S.Ct. 1678, 1681, 14 L.Ed.2d 510 (1965); see also Bates v. Little Rock, 361 U.S. 516, 523, 80 S.Ct. 412, 416–17, 4 L.Ed.2d 480 (1960).

7. 361 U.S. 516, 80 S.Ct. 412, 4 L.Ed.2d 480 (1960); see also, NAACP v. Alabama, 357 U.S. 449, 78 S.Ct. 1163, 2 L.Ed.2d 1488 (1958); Shelton v. Tucker, 364 U.S. 479, 81 S.Ct. 247, 5 L.Ed.2d 231 (1960).

8. 361 U.S. at 527, 80 S.Ct. at 418–19.

9. See discussion in, Ronald D. Rotunda, Legal Ethics: The Lawyer's Deskbook on Professional Responsibility §§ 46–4, 49–1, & 49–3 (ABA–West Group, 2000)

10. United Transportation Union v. State Bar of Michigan, 401 U.S. 576, 91 S.Ct. 1076, 28 L.Ed.2d 339 (1971); United Mine Workers v. Illinois State Bar Ass'n, 389 U.S. 217, 88 S.Ct. 353, 19 L.Ed.2d 426 (1967); Brotherhood of Railroad Trainmen v. Virginia, 377 U.S. 1, 84 S.Ct. 1113, 12 L.Ed.2d 89 (1964), rehearing denied 377 U.S. 960, 84 S.Ct. 1625, 12 L.Ed.2d 505 (1964), on remand 207 Va. 182, 149 S.E.2d 265 (1966), certiorari denied 385 U.S. 1027, 87 S.Ct. 754, 17 L.Ed.2d 675 (1967); NAACP v. Button, 371 U.S. 415, 83 S.Ct. 328, 9 L.Ed.2d 405 (1963); Ohralik v. Ohio State Bar, 436 U.S. 447, 98 S.Ct. 1912, 56 L.Ed.2d 444 (1978); In re Primus, 436 U.S. 412, 98 S.Ct. 1893, 56 L.Ed.2d 417 (1978).

grievances.[11] A common thread of cases in this area is that "collective activity undertaken to obtain meaningful access to the courts is a fundamental right within the protection of the First Amendment."[12]

The right is not limited solely to religious or political causes, but is applicable to any field of human endeavor, including business or other economic activity.[13] A state statute cannot require labor union organizers to register with a state official before urging workers to join a union, for such a statute imposes a prior restraint on free speech and free assembly.[14]

The right to petition for redress of grievances is a defense to criminal actions brought for violation of assembly laws.[15] As long as the assembly to petition for redress of grievances is peaceful, and no violence is advocated, it is protected.[16]

Liability of Member of an Association for the Torts of the Association. Even if violence is advocated, the First Amendment rights require that the state may not impose tort liability for business losses caused by violence or the threat of violence, if such conduct occurs in the context of constitutionally protected activity, unless there is "precision of regulation."[17]

NAACP v. Claiborne Hardware Co.,[18] without a single dissent, overturned a Mississippi state court judgment of over one and one quarter million dollars against the NAACP and certain individuals for business losses suffered by several white merchants because of an economic boycott against them. On October 31, 1969, after black citizens in Claiborne

County failed to achieve their demands for racial equality and integration several hundred blacks at a local NAACP meeting voted to boycott white merchants. Although some boycott supporters engaged in acts of violence, most of the practices used to encourage support for the boycott were peaceful, orderly, and protected by the First Amendment. All of the marches were carefully controlled.

The state can constitutionally impose liability for "the consequences of violent conduct [but] it may not award compensation for the consequences of nonviolent, protected activity. Only those losses proximately caused by unlawful conduct may be recovered."[19] A member of a group cannot be liable simply because another member of the same group proximately caused damage by violence:

> Civil liability may not be imposed merely because an individual belonged to a group, some members of which committed acts of violence. For liability to be imposed by reason of association alone, it is necessary to establish that the group itself possessed unlawful goals and that the individual held a specific intent to further those illegal goals.[20]

Mere association cannot make one liable, but those persons who actually engaged in violence or other illegal activity can be held liable for the injuries that they caused.[21]

Claiborne Hardware Co. then turned to the NAACP and ruled that the lower court findings were also not adequate to support the judgment against it. "To impose liability without a finding that the NAACP authorized—

---

11. 371 U.S. at 429–30, 83 S.Ct. at 335–36.

12. 401 U.S. at 585, 91 S.Ct. at 1082.

13. Thomas v. Collins, 323 U.S. 516, 65 S.Ct. 315, 89 L.Ed. 430 (1945), rehearing denied 323 U.S. 819, 65 S.Ct. 557, 89 L.Ed. 650 (1945).

14. 323 U.S. at 532, 65 S.Ct. at 323–24.

15. De Jonge v. Oregon, 299 U.S. 353, 57 S.Ct. 255, 81 L.Ed. 278 (1937); Thomas v. Collins, 323 U.S. 516, 65 S.Ct. 315, 89 L.Ed. 430 (1945), rehearing denied 323 U.S. 819, 65 S.Ct. 557, 89 L.Ed. 650 (1945); Edwards v. South Carolina, 372 U.S. 229, 83 S.Ct. 680, 9 L.Ed.2d 697 (1963); Bridges v. California, 314 U.S. 252, 62 S.Ct. 190, 86 L.Ed. 192 (1941).

16. De Jonge v. Oregon, 299 U.S. 353, 364, 57 S.Ct. 255, 259–60, 81 L.Ed. 278 (1937); Thomas v. Collins, 323

U.S. 516, 532, 65 S.Ct. 315, 323–24, 89 L.Ed. 430 (1945), rehearing denied 323 U.S. 819, 65 S.Ct. 557, 89 L.Ed. 650 (1945); Douglas v. Jeannette, 319 U.S. 157, 162, 63 S.Ct. 877, 880, 87 L.Ed. 1324 (1943); Shelton v. Tucker, 364 U.S. 479, 493, 81 S.Ct. 247, 254–55, 5 L.Ed.2d 231 (1960); Edwards v. South Carolina, 372 U.S. 229, 83 S.Ct. 680, 9 L.Ed.2d 697 (1963).

17. 371 U.S. at 438, 83 S.Ct. at 340–41.

18. 458 U.S. 886, 102 S.Ct. 3409, 73 L.Ed.2d 1215 (1982), rehearing denied 459 U.S. 898, 103 S.Ct. 199, 74 L.Ed.2d 160 (1982).

19. 458 U.S. at 918, 102 S.Ct. at 3429.

20. 458 U.S. at 920, 102 S.Ct. at 3430 (footnote omitted).

21. 458 U.S. at 926–28, 102 S.Ct. at 3433.

either actually or apparently—or ratified unlawful conduct would impermissibly burden the rights of political association that are protected by the First Amendment."[22]

Conspiracy Laws, Sham Litigation, and the *Noerr–Pennington* Doctrine. Protection for the actions of groups or individuals is not unlimited under the First Amendment rights of assembly and petition. In several instances, courts have justified limitations on those rights. The initial broad limitation on these rights is that they must be enjoyed in a law abiding manner.[23] Rights may not be used as a shield to violate valid statutes,[24] nor may they be used as a pretext for achieving substantive evil.[25]

Thus the antitrust laws may be applied to groups that conspire to bar competitors from meaningful access to the agencies and the courts.[26] Similarly, the antitrust laws may prohibit a conspiracy with a licensing authority to eliminate a competitor.[27] Criminal conspiracy laws deserve no First Amendment protection if the conspiracy is to achieve a criminal end in the immediate future rather than merely a conspiracy to advocate ideas (even violent ideas) to promote future change.[28]

In short, there is no protection for "sham" litigation, that is, baseless litigation designed not to win a favorable judgement but to harass a competitor and deter others by the process of litigation itself, regardless of outcome. The motive or scienter that is important is the intent to harm one's competitors, not by the result of litigation, but by the initiation of the litigation.[29] Litigation that is objectively reasonable cannot be a "sham," even though the plaintiff had bad motives in instituting it. To constitute a "sham," the claim for judicial relief must be so baseless that no reasonable litigation could have expected to secure relief.[30]

Everyone has a right to institute non-baseless litigation. A lawsuit is a form of a petition for the redress of grievances. Under the Noerr–Pennington Doctrine, business interests have the First Amendment right to combine and lobby to influence the legislative, executive, or judicial branches of government or the administrative agencies without violating the antitrust laws,[31] for such activities are protected by the right of petition.[32]

§ 16.55 The Special Case of Assemblies Related to Labor Disputes

Sometimes people question whether the freedoms of speech and assembly apply with equal force to the activities of individuals who engage in picketing, in distributing leaflets, or in other public speech relating to labor organization and labor disputes. Although the Supreme Court has allowed both state and federal courts and legislatures to control such

22. 458 U.S. at 931, 102 S.Ct. at 3435.

23. Cox v. Louisiana, 379 U.S. 559, 85 S.Ct. 476, 13 L.Ed.2d 487 (1965), rehearing denied 380 U.S. 926, 85 S.Ct. 879, 13 L.Ed.2d 814 (1965).

24. California Motor Transport Co. v. Trucking Unlimited, 404 U.S. 508, 92 S.Ct. 609, 30 L.Ed.2d 642 (1972).

25. NAACP v. Button, 371 U.S. 415, 438, 83 S.Ct. 328, 340–41, 9 L.Ed.2d 405 (1963).

26. California Motor Transport Co. v. Trucking Unlimited, 404 U.S. 508, 512, 92 S.Ct. 609, 612–13, 30 L.Ed.2d 642 (1972).

27. Walker Process Equipment, Inc. v. Food Machinery & Chemical Corp., 382 U.S. 172, 175–77, 86 S.Ct. 347, 349–50, 15 L.Ed.2d 247 (1965).

28. Brandenburg v. Ohio, 395 U.S. 444, 89 S.Ct. 1827, 23 L.Ed.2d 430 (1969). See also, NAACP v. Claiborne Hardware Co., 458 U.S. 886, 928–29, 102 S.Ct. 3409, 3434, 73 L.Ed.2d 1215 (1982), rehearing denied 459 U.S. 898, 103 S.Ct. 199, 74 L.Ed.2d 160 (1982).

29. Winterland Concessions Co. v. Trela, 735 F.2d 257, 263–64 (7th Cir.1984).

30. Professional Real Estate Investors, Inc. v. Columbia Pictures, Industries, Inc., 508 U.S. 49, 113 S.Ct. 1920, 123 L.Ed.2d 611 (1993).

31. Eastern R. R. Presidents Conference v. Noerr Motor Freight, Inc., 365 U.S. 127, 81 S.Ct. 523, 5 L.Ed.2d 464 (1961), rehearing denied 365 U.S. 875, 81 S.Ct. 899, 5 L.Ed.2d 864 (1961); United Mine Workers v. Pennington, 381 U.S. 657, 85 S.Ct. 1585, 14 L.Ed.2d 626 (1965), on remand 257 F.Supp. 815 (E.D.Tenn.1966), affirmed in part, reversed in part 400 F.2d 806 (6th Cir.1968), certiorari denied 393 U.S. 983, 89 S.Ct. 450, 21 L.Ed.2d 444 (1968), rehearing denied 393 U.S. 1045, 89 S.Ct. 616, 21 L.Ed.2d 599 (1969); California Motor Transport Co. v. Trucking Unlimited, 404 U.S. 508, 92 S.Ct. 609, 30 L.Ed.2d 642 (1972).

32. California Motor Transport Co. v. Trucking Unlimited, 404 U.S. 508, 92 S.Ct. 609, 30 L.Ed.2d 642 (1972).

Cf. Citizens Against Rent Control/Coalition for Fair Housing v. Berkeley, 454 U.S. 290, 294, 102 S.Ct. 434, 436, 70 L.Ed.2d 492 (1981).

activities, the Court has attempted to fit its rulings within the previously described principles regarding these First Amendment freedoms. Of course, those who picket, distribute literature, or speak in public regarding labor issues are subject to content neutral time, place, and manner restrictions, as would be any other person in a public place.

If a group of workers engage in a strike that is illegal under state or federal law, and they form a picket line or distribute literature outside of an employer's premises with the intent to cause other workers to join in their illegal strike, their activities may be punished or enjoined.[1] The theory in these cases is that such picketing is only a call to illegal action by encouraging others to help the picketers engage in applying coercive pressure on an employer in a manner that violates state or federal law. Therefore, the picketing is enjoinable as an invitation to engage in illegal activity.

In other contexts, the Court has upheld lower courts prohibitions of organizations from engaging in conspiracies and other speech/action that constitute a violation of antitrust laws.[2] In earlier decades the Court was quite lenient in upholding laws or court actions that restrained labor organization activities, such as the distribution of literature or the picketing of businesses, whenever these activities could be said to transgress state or federal policies regarding the proper conduct of labor disputes. But the Court has attempted to define a principle that the government could not prohibit or enjoin labor picketing unless there was some valid government policy regarding the control of labor organizations or labor disputes that was jeopardized by such picketing.

Where a labor organization is engaging in a strike or organizational activities that are clearly illegal under valid state or federal statutes, then laws restricting picketing or the distribution of information regarding such strike, even though the activity is called only "informational," may be compatible with First Amendment theory. The rationale is that the government can force persons in a labor dispute to resolve their grievance through legally established channels rather than seeking to secure the support of others, through illegal strikes or other illegal activities.[3]

Secondary Boycotts. The Supreme Court has upheld prohibitions of union activities that constitute "secondary boycotts" even though those activities might be seen as only the distribution of information. In a secondary boycott case, union members picket or distribute information outside of a business asking persons not to deal with that business because the business uses the products of or otherwise deals with a second business with which the union has a dispute. Federal labor laws, with exceptions, require the union to picket only the primary business with which it has a dispute and not seek to coerce the persons with whom that business deals to side with the union.

The Court has held that such activity may be prohibited or enjoined because it constitutes coercion of persons (the boycotted enterprise) to aid the union in its attempt to violate federal law. However, giving information to the public, whether through picketing or other means, regarding the nature of a labor organization's dispute with a business (business #1)

---

§ 16.55

1. See International Brotherhood of Teamsters v. Vogt, Inc., 354 U.S. 284, 77 S.Ct. 1166, 1 L.Ed.2d 1347 (1957), rehearing denied 354 U.S. 945, 77 S.Ct. 1423, 1 L.Ed.2d 1558 (1957) (state injunction against picketing upheld when picketing was for the purpose of "coercing" employers to induce employees to join union and had caused drivers of several trucks to refuse to transport goods to employer's plant).

2. See National Society of Professional Engineers v. United States, 435 U.S. 679, 697–98 nn. 26, 27, 98 S.Ct. 1355, 1368–69 nn. 26, 27, 55 L.Ed.2d 637 (1978) (prohibition of professional society's use of canon of ethics to restrain competitive bidding).

3. See International Longshoremen's AFL–CIO v. Allied International, Inc., 456 U.S. 212, 102 S.Ct. 1656, 72 L.Ed.2d 21 (1982), on remand 554 F.Supp. 32 (D.Mass. 1982), finding illegal a refusal of a longshoremen's union to load or unload ships engaged in trade with the Soviet Union as a protest against the Soviet Union's invasion of Afghanistan. The Union activity was found to be a "secondary boycott" in that it was a refusal to deal with the shippers on the basis of the actions of another party. The application of the anti-secondary boycott provision did not violate the First Amendment rights of the union or its members.

at the site of a second business (business #2) that engages in trade with business #1 (with whom the organization has a dispute) may be considered only the peaceful conveyance of information and protected by the First Amendment. Although the Court has not defined the exact nature of the informational activity protected by the First Amendment, it appears to be attempting to make some accommodation between proscribable and nonproscribable labor organization speech through its interpretation of federal labor relations laws.[4]

Initially it may appear easy for the Court to justify the punishment of labor picketing that only coerces or "signals" others to aid the union in engaging in activity that violates valid labor statutes.[5] But it is difficult to distinguish the area of informational activity by labor organizations that could be made punishable (because it relates to a labor dispute) from the constitutionally protected activities of persons who organize boycotts of businesses for the purpose of coercing those businesses to help them influence government action.[6]

Thus, there may be some type of speech by labor organizations or employers that cannot be prohibited because it relates to public issues or the need to influence government action. In general, however, the Supreme Court will allow the injunction or punishment of speech by employers or organizations when that speech would undercut the legitimate governmental regulation of the manner in which labor disputes must be resolved.

§ 16.56   The Problem of Obscenity: An Introduction

Edmund Wilson was, without question, one of the most influential literary critics of the twentieth century. A conservative and exacting man, he was to F. Scott Fitzgerald "my artistic conscience,"[1] an admission that in all honesty might well have been made by many of the American novelists of the 1920's and 1930's whose work, taken together, is now an indelible part of the American self-image.

Wilson was also a novelist himself. In 1946, at the peak of his reputation, he published his second novel, *Memoirs of Hecate County*, in which he related two rather spiritless passages describing sexual intercourse. The New York Society for the Suppression of Vice complained, and the state charged the novel's publisher, Doubleday & Co., under a state criminal obscenity statute. Despite the testimony of Columbia University Professor Lionel Trilling, who said that the allegedly-obscene passages were inextricably related to the novel's literary merit, a three-judge trial panel found Doubleday guilty. The Appellate Division and the

---

4. See Edward J. DeBartolo Corp. v. National Labor Relations Board, 463 U.S. 147, 103 S.Ct. 2926, 77 L.Ed.2d 535 (1983) (avoiding constitutional issue regarding "publicity proviso" exemption from secondary boycott provision because it had not been ruled on by the labor relations board although the Court narrowly construed the nature of the exemption for such activities); National Labor Relations Board v. Retail Store Employees Union, Local 1001, 447 U.S. 607, 100 S.Ct. 2372, 65 L.Ed.2d 377 (1980) (in a plurality opinion on this issue, four Justices find that picketing encouraging a secondary boycott is not constitutionally protected); National Labor Relations Board v. Fruit and Vegetable Packers and Warehousemen, 377 U.S. 58, 84 S.Ct. 1063, 12 L.Ed.2d 129 (1964) (National Labor Relations Act held not to prohibit all peaceful consumer picketing at secondary sites).

5. Justice Stevens has based his vote to uphold restrictions on picketing on this basis. See National Labor Relations Board v. Retail Store Employees Union, Local 1001, 447 U.S. 607, 618–19, 100 S.Ct. 2372, 2379–80, 65 L.Ed.2d 377, 387–88 (1980) (Stevens, J., concurring in part and concurring in the result).

On the distinction between illegal signal picketing and picketing that should be protected by the First Amend-

ment, see T. Emerson, The System of Freedom of Expression 445–49 (1971).

6. See NAACP v. Claiborne Hardware Co., 458 U.S. 886, 913, 102 S.Ct. 3409, 3426, 73 L.Ed.2d 1215, 1236 (1982), rehearing denied 459 U.S. 898, 103 S.Ct. 199, 74 L.Ed.2d 160 (1982) (organization could not be punished for organizing boycott to cause economic injury to merchants so as to influence the merchants to aid the organization in changing government policies regarding race discrimination). "The right of states to regulate economic activity could not justify a complete prohibition against a nonviolent, politically-motivated boycott designed to force governmental and economic change and to effectuate rights guaranteed by the Constitution itself." (footnote omitted).

§ 16.56

1. F. S. Fitzgerald, Pasting It Together, in The Fitzgerald Reader 415 (A. Mizener ed. 1963). See, 4 Ronald D. Rotunda & John E. Nowak, Treatise on Constitutional Law: Substance and Procedure §§ 20.56–20.61 (West Group 3d ed.1999).

New York Court of Appeals[2] upheld the verdict, and the United States Supreme Court, in one of the first major obscenity cases to reach it, affirmed without opinion in a four-to-four vote.[3]

The Court's affirmation came down in 1948. A year later, in Philadelphia, several booksellers were charged with violating a Pennsylvania criminal statute that outlawed the sale of "any obscene, lewd, lascivious, filthy, indecent or disgusting book...."[4] Among the books to which the Commonwealth applied these adjectives were James T. Farrell's *Studs Lonigan* trilogy, William Faulkner's *Sanctuary* and *The Wild Palms*, and Erskine Caldwell's *God's Little Acre*, books that are now familiar items on a college English major's required-reading list. In this case, however, the prosecution failed.

In his trial opinion, Judge Curtis Bok granted the "several general dicta by the Supreme Court to the effect that obscenity is indictable just because it is obscenity,"[5] but he reasoned that constitutionally, conviction under a criminal obscenity statute requires a "causal connection"[6] beyond a reasonable doubt between the allegedly-obscene activity—here, the sale of the books—and actual or imminent criminal behavior in individuals exposed to the activity. On this basis, Judge Bok found the booksellers not guilty.

Among the "several general dicta" to which Judge Bok referred was Justice Murphy's statement in *Chaplinsky v. New Hampshire*[7] that the "lewd and obscene" are among "certain well-defined and narrowly limited classes of speech, the prevention and punishment of which have never been thought to raise any Constitutional problem."[8] The dicta continued after Judge Bok's decision.

In *Beauharnais v. Illinois*,[9] decided in 1952, Justice Frankfurter equated obscenity with group libel as being beyond "the area of constitutionally protected speech."[10] Frankfurter did not elaborate his point; neither, for that matter, had Murphy, whose inclusion of obscenity with libel and "fighting words" in a single, undifferentiated constitutional classification seemed offhand, almost peremptory. To Justice Murphy, the "lewd and obscene" were among the utterances about which "[i]t has been well observed that [they] are no essential part of any exposition of ideas, and are of such slight social value as a step to truth that any benefit that may be derived from them is clearly outweighed by the social interest in order and morality."[11]

In making this statement, Justice Murphy cited and paraphrased the work of Professor Zachariah Chafee, Jr. To Chafee, "profanity and indecent talk and pictures" were inherently void of "any exposition of ideas,.... The harm is done as soon as they are communicated, or is liable to follow almost immediately in the form of retaliatory violence. The only sound explanation of the punishment of obscenity and profanity is that the words are criminal, not because of the ideas they commu-

---

2. People v. Doubleday & Co., 272 App.Div. 799, 71 N.Y.S.2d 736 (1947), affirmed 297 N.Y. 687, 77 N.E.2d 6 (1947), affirmed by an equally divided Court, sub nom. 335 U.S. 848, 69 S.Ct. 79, 93 L.Ed. 398 (1948).

3. Doubleday & Co. v. New York, 335 U.S. 848, 69 S.Ct. 79, 93 L.Ed. 398 (1948) (Justice Frankfurter not participating).

A few years later the Court did invalidate a New York statute that banned "sacrilegious" motion pictures. The Court held that motion pictures are not precluded from First Amendment protection even though they are sold for profit. The statute was then struck down as too vague. Joseph Burstyn, Inc. v. Wilson, 343 U.S. 495, 72 S.Ct. 777, 96 L.Ed. 1098 (1952). This case does have important implications for obscenity legislation, although the Court did not specifically decide it on such grounds. See also, Kingsley International Pictures Corp. v. Regents of New York, 360 U.S. 684, 79 S.Ct. 1362, 3 L.Ed.2d 1512 (1959)

(denial of license to show the film "Lady Chatterley's Lover" is reversed; decision not on obscenity grounds).

4. As cited in M. Konvitz, Fundamental Liberties of a Free People 160 (1957).

5. Commonwealth v. Gordon, 66 Pa.D. & C. 101, 146 (1949), affirmed sub nom. Commonwealth v. Feigenbaum, 166 Pa.Super. 120, 70 A.2d 389 (1950) (per curiam).

6. 66 Pa.D. & C. 101 at 156.

7. 315 U.S. 568, 62 S.Ct. 766, 86 L.Ed. 1031 (1942).

8. 315 U.S. at 571–72, 62 S.Ct. at 769.

9. 343 U.S. 250, 72 S.Ct. 725, 96 L.Ed. 919 (1952), rehearing denied 343 U.S. 988, 72 S.Ct. 1070, 96 L.Ed. 1375 (1952).

10. 343 U.S. at 266, 72 S.Ct. at 735.

11. Chaplinsky v. New Hampshire, 315 U.S. 568, 572, 62 S.Ct. 766, 769, 86 L.Ed. 1031 (1942).

nicate, but like acts because of their immediate consequences to the five senses."[12]

So Justice Murphy created a definitional dilemma for the Court. This dilemma was obvious in the prosecutions involving Edmund Wilson, James T. Farrell, and William Faulkner. If Faulkner, whose work brought him a Nobel Prize, played an "essential part" in the "exposition of ideas," if his Snopes trilogy, for example, may be taken as "a step to truth," then under the dictum in *Chaplinsky*, Faulkner's work could not have been obscene to Justice Murphy. But according to Professor Chafee, on whom Justice Murphy so heavily relied, the more enticing passages in some of Faulkner's novels were by definition unrelated to the useful exposition of ideas, and were thus as a matter of law of "such slight social value" as to be beyond the protection of the First Amendment. Yet Faulkner surely addressed himself to matters "of social concern". It may be easy to draw a distinction between labor picketing and 50–cent peep shows, but can the distinction be drawn where the "obscenity" at issue takes the form of a paragraph in *Sanctuary*?

In 1946, Justice Douglas noted in passing in *Hannegan v. Esquire*,[13] that:

[u]nder our system of government there is an accommodation for the widest varieties of tastes and ideas. What is good literature, what has educational value, what is refined public information, what is good art, varies with individuals as it does from one generation to another. There doubtless would be a contrariety of views concerning Cervantes' *Don Quixote*, Shakespeare's *Venus and Adonis*, or Zola's *Nana*. But a requirement that literature or art conform to some norm

prescribed by an official smacks of an ideology foreign to our system.[14]

Nonetheless, when Judge Bok observed in 1949 that to the Supreme Court, "obscenity is indictable just because it is obscenity," he was alluding to an accurate contemporary legal principle. He was also alluding to the core problem of this area of First Amendment law: What is obscenity?

§ 16.57 Obscenity—The *Roth* Case

The dicta on obscenity in *Chaplinsky v. New Hampshire*[1] and *Beauharnais v. Illinois*[2] raised the obvious question of how the Court would treat the issue when it rendered its first decision on the subject. That decision, *Roth v. United States*,[3] was handed down in 1957, and at its core it is still the law of obscenity under the Constitution. In *Roth*, two state criminal statutes were invoked against the publication and sale of obscene matter.

After stating in a footnote that "[n]o issue is presented [here] concerning the obscenity of the material involved,"[4] Justice Brennan, writing for the Court, stated: "The dispositive question is whether obscenity is utterance within the area of protected speech and press."[5] On the basis of a series of earlier cases in which obscenity had been discussed in dictum, including *Chaplinsky* and *Beauharnais*, the Court had always "assumed" that obscenity was not protected by the First Amendment.[6] The Court then discussed several historical elements underlying the phrasing of the First Amendment, and concluded; "All ideas having even the slightest redeeming social importance—unorthodox ideas, controversial ideas, even ideas hateful to the prevailing climate of opinion—have the full protection of the guaranties [of the First Amendment], un-

---

12. Z. Chafee, Free Speech in the United States 150 (1941).

13. 327 U.S. 146, 66 S.Ct. 456, 90 L.Ed. 586 (1946).

14. 327 U.S. at 157–58, 66 S.Ct. at 462.

§ 16.57

1. 315 U.S. 568, 571–72, 62 S.Ct. 766, 768–69, 86 L.Ed. 1031 (1942).

2. 343 U.S. 250, 266, 72 S.Ct. 725, 735, 96 L.Ed. 919 (1952), rehearing denied 343 U.S. 988, 72 S.Ct. 1070, 96 L.Ed. 1375 (1952).

3. 354 U.S. 476, 77 S.Ct. 1304, 1 L.Ed.2d 1498 (1957), rehearing denied 355 U.S. 852, 78 S.Ct. 8, 2 L.Ed.2d 60 (1957). *Roth* was consolidated with Alberts v. California, and all references to *Roth* include *Alberts*.

4. 354 U.S. at 481 n. 8, 77 S.Ct. at 1307 n. 8.

5. 354 U.S. at 481, 77 S.Ct. at 1307 (footnote omitted).

6. 354 U.S. at 481, 77 S.Ct. at 1307.

less excludable because they encroach upon the limited area of more important interests. But implicit in the history of the First Amendment is the rejection of obscenity as utterly without redeeming social importance."[7] Then, after quoting the *Chaplinsky* dictum at some length, the Court converted its traditional assumption into a rule of law, and held that "obscenity is not within the area of constitutionally protected speech or press."[8]

At this point the Court attempted to dispose of two lingering issues. First, it rejected the contention that there is a burden on the state to prove that a given piece of obscene material must be related to antisocial conduct. The Court adopted Justice Frankfurter's comment in *Beauharnais* and held that if obscenity is without constitutional protection, it may be proscribed by statute without further justification.[9]

Second, the Court drew a distinction between sex and obscenity. "Obscene material," said the Court, "is material which deals with sex in a manner appealing to prurient interest," while the mere portrayal of sex in art, literature, scientific works, and similar forums "is not itself sufficient reason to deny material the constitutional protection of freedom of speech and press."[10] In fleshing out this distinction, the Court adopted the standard of whether "to the average person, applying contemporary community standards, the dominant theme of the material taken as a whole appeals to prurient interest."[11]

The Court closed its opinion with the observation that, in accordance with *United States v. Petrillo*,[12] a statute outlawing obscenity will not violate due process by a mere lack of precision. Except in marginal cases, the Court suggested that the language of such a statute will be sufficient if it gives "adequate warning

of the conduct proscribed" and enables the law to be administered fairly.[13]

Thus when reduced to a formula, *Roth* provided that material may be deemed obscene, and therefore wholly without constitutional protection, if it (a) appeals to a prurient interest in sex, (b) has no redeeming literary, artistic, political, or scientific merit, and (c) is on the whole offensive to the average person under contemporary community standards.

There are two elements in *Roth* that deserve special attention. First, there is the problem with the word "prurient." This single word was quite clearly the touchstone of Justice Brennan's analysis of the case. Its application spelled the difference between sex and obscenity, between applicable community standards and mere community prejudice, between material that is sanctioned by the Constitution and material that may be subject to criminal penalty. To the Court, prurient material was that which has "a tendency to excite lustful thoughts."[14] This definition deserved some further explication, and the Court provided it with excerpts from Webster's Second New International Dictionary, i.e., that "prurient" is " ... [i]tching; longing; uneasy with desire or longing; of persons, having itching, morbid, or lascivious longings; of desire, curiosity, or propensity, lewd...."[15]

It is obviously possible that material can be prurient and political; that it can be possessed of a tendency to excite lustful thoughts and contain profound social commentary; or that it can create in an individual morbid and lascivious desires and constitute poetry of the highest order. It was with this in mind, perhaps, that Chief Justice Warren stated in concurrence that the conduct of the defendant, not the obscenity of the book or picture, is the central issue. "The nature of the materials is, of course, relevant as an attribute of the defen-

---

7.   354 U.S. at 484, 77 S.Ct. at 1309.

8.   354 U.S. at 485, 77 S.Ct. at 1309.

9.   354 U.S. at 486–87, 77 S.Ct. at 1309–10.

10.   354 U.S. at 487, 77 S.Ct. at 1310.

11.   354 U.S. at 489, 77 S.Ct. at 1311. The Court explicitly rejected the leading English case holding that obscenity is to be judged merely by the effect of an isolated

passage on particularly susceptible persons. Regina v. Hicklin, [1868] L.R. 3 Q.B. 360.

12.   332 U.S. 1, 7–8, 67 S.Ct. 1538, 1542, 91 L.Ed. 1877 (1947).

13.   *Roth*, 354 U.S. at 491, 77 S.Ct. at 1313.

14.   354 U.S. at 487 n. 20, 77 S.Ct. at 1310 n. 20.

15.   354 U.S. at 487 n. 20, 77 S.Ct. at 1310 n. 20.

dant's conduct, but the materials are thus placed in context from which they draw color and character. A wholly different result might be reached in a different setting."[16]

In a separate opinion, Justice Harlan, concurring and dissenting, carried Chief Justice Warren's observation further. He objected to the very concept of reducing a constitutional question to a "distinct, recognizable and classifiable ... poison ivy" under the term "prurient."[17] To Harlan, obscenity was by its nature an abstraction; and under the Constitution it presents a problem that "cannot be solved in such a generalized fashion."[18] Harlan preferred a case-by-case approach, so that a reviewing court could take into account the fact that "[e]very communication has an individuality and 'value' of its own":[19]

[A] reviewing court must determine for *itself* whether the attacked expression is suppressable within constitutional standards. Since those standards do not readily lend themselves to generalized definitions, the constitutional problem in the last analysis becomes one of particularized judgments which appellate courts must make for themselves.[20]

The second element in *Roth* to which one should pay special attention is the now-famous dissent of Justices Douglas and Black. This short dissent is often cited as evidence of its authors' absolutist approach to speech and press issues under the First Amendment. It contains a direct challenge to Justice Harlan's view that in the last analysis obscenity becomes one of particularized judgments that appellate courts must make for themselves. Justice Harlan assumed these judgments would be made under the applicable constitu-

tional standard; but to Justices Douglas and Black the appropriate standard should not, in any event, give the censor free range over a vast domain. "To allow the State to step in and punish mere speech or publication that the judge or jury thinks has an *undesirable* impact on thoughts but that is not shown to be a part of unlawful action is drastically to curtail the First Amendment...."[21]

They concluded that obscenity, under any definition in any environment, is a form of expression, and as such "can be suppressed if, and to the extent that, it is so closely brigaded with illegal action as to be an inseparable part of it.... As a people, we cannot afford to relax that standard."[22] Thus Justices Douglas and Black adopted Judge Curtis Bok's approach in *Commonwealth v. Gordon*,[23] and argued that there must be a causal connection between the allegedly-obscene expression—which at all times must, for analytical purposes, be deemed to be within the protection of the First Amendment—and illegal conduct, which, under long-established principle, could be sufficient to render the expression unlawful.

§ 16.58 The Implications of *Roth*

There is a small curiosity in the *Roth* opinion that, in some respects, symbolizes the nature and import of the opinion as a whole. As we have noted, Justice Brennan placed this prefatory footnote at the beginning of his majority opinion: "No issue is presented [here] concerning the obscenity of the material involved."[1] Apparently, the purpose of this footnote was to clarify the Court's limited task on review, which was to determine the facial validity of two state criminal obscenity statutes rather than the validity of those statutes in

---

16. 354 U.S. at 495, 77 S.Ct. at 1314–15 (concurring opinion).

17. 354 U.S. at 497, 77 S.Ct. at 1315 (concurring in the result in *Alberts*—the state case—and dissenting in *Roth*—the federal case).

18. 354 U.S. at 497, 77 S.Ct. at 1315.

19. 354 U.S. at 497, 77 S.Ct. at 1315.

20. 354 U.S. at 497, 77 S.Ct. at 1316 (emphasis in original).

21. 354 U.S. at 509, 77 S.Ct. at 1322 (dissenting opinion) (emphasis in original).

22. 354 U.S. at 514, 77 S.Ct. at 1324 (dissenting opinion).

23. 66 Pa.D. & C. 101 (1949), affirmed sub nom. Commonwealth v. Feigenbaum, 166 Pa.Super. 120, 70 A.2d 389 (1950).

§ 16.58

1. Roth v. United States, 354 U.S. 476, 481 n. 8, 77 S.Ct. 1304, 1307 n. 8, 1 L.Ed.2d 1498 (1957), rehearing denied 355 U.S. 852, 78 S.Ct. 8, 2 L.Ed.2d 60 (1957).

light of the circumstances under which they were invoked.

This disclaimer points to a broad problem in the case. Because the Court dealt only with the facial validity of two typically-comprehensive anti-obscenity statutes, the Court was able to treat obscenity as an abstract proposition and to formulate a definitional standard for obscenity in terms of abstract Constitutional principle. While in a limited technical sense, there was nothing "advisory" about *Roth*, and while the *Roth* test was not dictum, the opinion came perilously close to a loose theoretical exercise in Constitutional law. Unburdened by the factual circumstances that triggered the case in the first place, the Court in *Roth* rendered a decision that was framed in terms that would not easily address themselves to the plethora of varying factual circumstances that would burden the Court in obscenity cases in the years to come.

Shortly after *Roth* was handed down, Dean William B. Lockhart and Professor Robert C. McClure of the University of Minnesota Law School wrote two influential law review articles[2] that proposed two alternative approaches to an understanding of *Roth*. First, they suggested that the case settled only two aspects of the obscenity question:[3] (1) that the material in question must be considered as a whole, and cannot be condemned on the basis of isolated passages; and (2) that the material, taken as a whole, must be examined in light of the average person whose attitudes reflect a common community standard, not in terms of the material's impact on the exceptional individual who is particularly susceptible to the material's prurient aspects.

Second, Lockhart and McClure argued that the attention paid by the Court in *Roth* to the possibly redeeming social importance of allegedly-obscene material indicated an implied ac-

ceptance of a concept they termed "variable obscenity." Under this concept the pivotal word "prurient" can be understood only in a relative sense; its meaning and application would vary according to the tastes and sophistication of the audience at which the material is directed.

It was this sort of situation, perhaps, that Chief Justice Warren had in mind when he stated in his concurrence in *Roth* that the central issue in obscenity is the conduct of the defendant himself, and thus the "context from which [the materials] draw color and character." This situation certainly lends support to Justice Harlan's objections to a rigid, undifferentiating approach to obscenity under the term "prurient." In any event the Court did move in the direction of "variable obscenity" in *Ginzburg v. United States*[4] and *Ginsberg v. New York*,[5] which are discussed below.

The value of Lockhart and McClure's scholarship, however, must be balanced against the inherently insoluble enigma of *Roth* that renders virtually any theoretical attempt to "explain" the case into an exercise in apologetics. The enigma was perhaps best described by Justice Stewart in his short concurring opinion in *Jacobellis v. Ohio*,[6] one of a series of cases in which the Court applied *Roth* to an allegedly obscene motion picture. Justice Stewart's concurrence, in its entirety, with only citations omitted, is as follows:

It is possible to read the Court's opinion in *Roth v. United States* and *Alberts v. California* . . . in a variety of ways. In saying this, I imply no criticism of the Court, which in those cases was faced with the task of trying to define what may be indefinable. I have reached the conclusion, which I think is confirmed at least by negative implication in the Court's decisions since *Roth* and *Alberts*, that under the First and Fourteenth Amend-

---

2. Lockhart and McClure, Censorship of Obscenity: The Developing Constitutional Standards, 45 Minn.L.Rev. 5 (1960); Lockhart and McClure, Obscenity Censorship: The Core Constitutional Issue—What is Obscene?, 7 Utah L.Rev. 289 (1961).

3. W. Lockhart & R. McClure, Censorship of Obscenity: The Developing Constitutional Standards, 45 Minn. L.Rev. 5, 53 (1960).

4. 383 U.S. 463, 86 S.Ct. 942, 16 L.Ed.2d 31 (1966), rehearing denied 384 U.S. 934, 86 S.Ct. 1440, 16 L.Ed.2d 536 (1966).

5. 390 U.S. 629, 88 S.Ct. 1274, 20 L.Ed.2d 195 (1968), rehearing denied 391 U.S. 971, 88 S.Ct. 2029, 20 L.Ed.2d 887 (1968).

6. 378 U.S. 184, 84 S.Ct. 1676, 12 L.Ed.2d 793 (1964).

ments criminal laws in this area are constitutionally limited to hard-core pornography. I shall not today attempt further to define the kinds of material I understand to be embraced within that shorthand description; and perhaps I could never succeed in intelligibly doing so. But I know it when I see it, and the motion picture involved in this case is not that.[7]

Perhaps, when all else is said, that is the best that any judge can do; he cannot define obscenity, but he can admit that "I know it when I see it."

It is worth noting that Edmund Wilson, whose novel *Memoirs of Hecate County* was the subject of the Court's first decision of record on obscenity, somewhat accidentally stumbled into an "art" movie house in Utica, New York in the summer of 1968. He found himself watching a movie consisting largely of an actress manipulating her genitals, which, he said, "close up and magnified, had the thoroughly repellant appearance of the pieces of raw meat in a butcher's shop."[8] The great critic concluded with little explanation that "I do not think that such films should be allowed."[9] Perhaps he thought that the subject did not deserve detailed discussion, that his judgment required no justification. He, too, knew it when he saw it; and for him that was the beginning and the end of the matter.

§ 16.59 The Development of the Case Law Under *Roth*

Two years after *Roth* the Court held that the state could not eliminate the need to prove *scienter* in an obscenity prosecution, in a case where a bookseller was convicted under a statute that dispensed with the state proving any requirement of knowledge of the contents of the books on the part of the seller.[1]

Then, in *Jacobellis v. Ohio*,[2] the Court held, *inter alia*, "that, in 'obscenity' cases as in all others involving rights derived from the First Amendment guarantees of free expression, this Court cannot avoid making an independent constitutional judgment on the facts of the case as to whether the material involved is constitutionally protected." In short, a trial court's findings as to the obscenity of the material at issue is not binding on review—if the appellate court takes the case, it will have to watch the movie or read the book itself.

Thus, the import of *Roth* would unfold as the Supreme Court was forced to reconsider the implications of the *Roth* test in terms of the problems of specific areas. As one might expect, the applications of *Roth* eventually subverted some of the major analytical elements of the opinion itself; it also revealed the failure of the Supreme Court to agree on any real tests to apply in practice to allegedly obscene material.

Fanny Hill. Two examples illustrating this problem may be found in the decisions of the Court's 1966 term. First, a fragmented Supreme Court used the "social value" test to overturn a conviction under the Massachusetts obscenity statute that held the book *Fanny Hill* to be obscene, in *A Book Named "John Cleland's Memoirs of a Woman of Pleasure" v. Attorney General of Massachusetts*.[3] Justice Brennan announced the judgment of the Court reversing the state court's finding of obscenity, but Brennan's opinion was only joined by Chief Justice Warren and Justice Fortas.

Brennan argued that each of the three elements of the *Roth* test must be applied independently,[4] and thus that material cannot be

---

7. 378 U.S. at 197, 84 S.Ct. at 1683 (concurring opinion) (citations omitted).

8. E. Wilson, Upstate: Records and Recollections of Northern New York 311 (1971).

9. E. Wilson, Upstate: Records and Recollections of Northern New York 311 (1971).

§ 16.59

1. Smith v. California, 361 U.S. 147, 80 S.Ct. 215, 4 L.Ed.2d 205 (1959), rehearing denied 361 U.S. 950, 80 S.Ct. 399, 4 L.Ed.2d 383 (1960).

2. 378 U.S. 184, 190, 84 S.Ct. 1676, 1679, 12 L.Ed.2d 793 (1964) (footnote omitted).

3. 383 U.S. 413, 86 S.Ct. 975, 16 L.Ed.2d 1 (1966).

4. 383 U.S. at 419, 86 S.Ct. at 977–78.

adjudged obscene if it passes muster under any of them. Brennan reasoned that **Fanny Hill**, which has long been a classic of ribald literature, could not properly be deemed to be *"utterly* without redeeming social value,"[5] and thus is sheltered by the First Amendment. By applying the elements of the *Roth* test independently, Brennan stepped away from the strict definitional approach employed in *Roth*. *Fanny Hill* may or may not have appealed to prurient interests under any definition or under any set of community standards, but this was now irrelevant; the book contained at least a modicum of literary value, and that was enough to save it from suppression by the Attorney General of Massachusetts. Suddenly "pruriency" was no longer the pivotal element of obscenity under the First Amendment.

Pandering. Far more important, however, was Justice Brennan's opinion for the Court in *Ginzburg v. United States*.[6] In *Ginzburg*, the Court was faced with three professionally produced publications devoted to sex, including EROS, which the Court described as "a hardcover magazine of expensive format."[7] The Court found the publications to be obscene because they represented "commercial exploitation of erotica solely for the sake of their prurient appeal." In reaching this conclusion, the Court stated that the "leer of the sensualist" had "permeate[d]" the manner in which the publications had been distributed and advertised:[8] mailing privileges had been sought from Intercourse and Blue Ball, Pennsylvania, and Middlesex, New Jersey; and the advertising circulars describing the publications "stressed the sexual candor of the respective

publications, and openly boasted that the publishers would take full advantage of what they regarded as an unrestricted license allowed by law in the expression of sex and sexual matters."[9]

The Court argued that the "brazenness"[10] of the defendant's marketing tactics unveiled his intent in distributing the materials, and that this intent was the heart of the matter: "Where the purveyor's sole emphasis is on the sexually provocative aspects of his publications, that fact may be decisive in the determination of obscenity."[11] If the defendant had earlier claimed, even boasted that his publication was obscene, that "testimony" can be used against him.

In the *Memoirs* case, Justice Brennan emphasized that "the social value of the book can neither be weighed against nor canceled by its prurient appeal or patent offensiveness."[12] But in *Ginzburg*, the Court, per Justice Brennan, did not even address the question of the social value of the three publications—its decision rested solely on the defendant's intent, his pandering. Thus an intent to appeal "solely" to prurient interests *can* outweigh the social value of the materials in question while the prurient appeal of the materials, of itself, cannot.

The *Redrup* Approach. In a series of obscenity decisions the rationales of the individual members became more, rather than less, divergent. There was no majority agreement concerning the "contemporary community standards" aspect of the *Memoirs* plurality, with some Justices favoring a national commu-

---

5. 383 U.S. at 419, 86 S.Ct. at 977–78 (emphasis in original). Justice Stewart concurred in the reversal for a different reason: he felt that the material was not hard core pornography. Justice Black in his separate concurrence emphasized that the Court's opinions in this area agreed only on results and not on reasons, offering no useful tests or guidance for lower courts or laymen. Justice Douglas, composing the sixth vote, concurred because he believed that the First Amendment forbade censorship of any expression not intertwined with illegal conduct. And the three remaining Justices (Clark, Harlan, and White) dissented, each writing separate opinions.

6. 383 U.S. 463, 86 S.Ct. 942, 16 L.Ed.2d 31 (1966), rehearing denied 384 U.S. 934, 86 S.Ct. 1440, 16 L.Ed.2d 536 (1966).

7. 383 U.S. at 466, 86 S.Ct. at 945.

8. 383 U.S. at 468, 86 S.Ct. at 946. Later pandering cases include Splawn v. California, 431 U.S. 595, 97 S.Ct. 1987, 52 L.Ed.2d 606 (1977), and Hamling v. United States, 418 U.S. 87, 130, 94 S.Ct. 2887, 2914, 41 L.Ed.2d 590 (1974), rehearing denied 419 U.S. 885, 95 S.Ct. 157, 42 L.Ed.2d 129 (1974).

9. 383 U.S. at 468, 86 S.Ct. at 946.

10. 383 U.S. at 470, 86 S.Ct. at 947.

11. 383 U.S. at 470, 86 S.Ct. at 947.

12. A Book Named "John Cleland's Memoirs of a Woman of Pleasure" v. Attorney General of Massachusetts, 383 U.S. 413, 419, 86 S.Ct. 975, 978, 16 L.Ed.2d 1 (1966).

nity standard;[13] others favoring a national standard for federal prosecutions;[14] still others favoring local community or flexibility for state standards.[15]

As to the "prurient interest" aspect, some Justices held that if the material was designed for and primarily disseminated to a clearly defined deviant sexual group rather than the public at large, the prurient-appeal requirement is satisfied by looking to that group and not to the "average" or "normal" person referred to in *Roth*.[16] Other cases emphasized the element of "pandering" in close cases[17] or defined obscenity in terms of the juvenile audience.[18] And various Justices also had differing views of the tests used to determine the "social value" aspect of the *Memoirs* test.[19]

As Justice Brennan later openly acknowledged:

In the face of this divergence of opinion the Court began the practice in *Redrup v. New York*, 386 U.S. 767, 87 S.Ct. 1414, 18 L.Ed.2d 515 (1967), rehearing denied 388 U.S. 924, 87 S.Ct. 2091, 18 L.Ed.2d 1377 (1967) of *per curiam* reversals of convictions for the dissemination of materials that at least five members of the Court, applying their separate tests, deemed not to be obscene. This approach capped the attempt in *Roth* to separate all forms of sexual oriented

expression into two categories—the one subject to full governmental suppression and the other beyond the reach of governmental regulation to the same extent as any other protected form of speech or press.[20]

No fewer than 31 cases had followed this *Redrup* approach.[21]

§ 16.60   The *Miller* Decision

Finally, *Miller v. California*[1] abandoned the *Memoirs* approach entirely, and for the first time since *Roth* a majority of the Justices agreed to the proper test for obscenity:

While *Roth* presumed "obscenity" to be "utterly without redeeming social importance," *Memoirs* [the *Fanny Hill* case] required that to prove obscenity it must be affirmatively established that the material is "*utterly* without redeeming social value." Thus, even as they repeated the words of *Roth*, the *Memoirs* plurality produced a drastically altered test that called on the prosecution to prove a negative, *i.e.*, that the material was "*utterly* without redeeming social value"—a burden virtually impossible to discharge under our criminal standards of proof. Such considerations caused Mr. Justice Harlan to wonder if the "*utterly* without redeeming social value" test had any meaning at all.[2]

---

13. Jacobellis v. Ohio, 378 U.S. 184, 192–195, 84 S.Ct. 1676, 1680–82, 12 L.Ed.2d 793 (1964) (Brennan, J., joined by Goldberg, J.).

14. Manual Enterprises, Inc. v. Day, 370 U.S. 478, 488, 82 S.Ct. 1432, 1437–38, 8 L.Ed.2d 639 (1962) (Harlan, J., joined by Stewart, J.).

15. Jacobellis v. Ohio, 378 U.S. 184, 200–201, 84 S.Ct. 1676, 1684–85, 12 L.Ed.2d 793 (1964) (Warren, C. J., joined by Clark, J., dissenting) (local community standards); Hoyt v. Minnesota, 399 U.S. 524, 90 S.Ct. 2241, 26 L.Ed.2d 782 (1970) (Blackmun, J., joined by Burger, C. J., and Harlan J., dissenting) (flexibility of state standards).

16. Mishkin v. New York, 383 U.S. 502, 508, 86 S.Ct. 958, 963, 16 L.Ed.2d 56 (1966), rehearing denied 384 U.S. 934, 86 S.Ct. 1440, 16 L.Ed.2d 535 (1966) (Brennan, J., for the Court, with Douglas, Black, and Stewart, JJ., dissenting, and Harlan, J., concurring).

17. Ginzburg v. United States, 383 U.S. 463, 86 S.Ct. 942, 16 L.Ed.2d 31 (1966), rehearing denied 384 U.S. 934, 86 S.Ct. 1440, 16 L.Ed.2d 536 (1966) (Brennan, J., for the Court, with Black, Douglas, Stewart, and Harlan, JJ., each dissenting separately).

18. Ginsberg v. New York, 390 U.S. 629, 88 S.Ct. 1274, 20 L.Ed.2d 195 (1968), rehearing denied 391 U.S. 971, 88

S.Ct. 2029, 20 L.Ed.2d 887 (1968) (Brennan, J., for the Court, with Stewart, J., concurring in the result; Fortas, J., dissenting; and Harlan, J., concurring).

19. E.g., A Book Named "John Cleland's Memoirs of a Woman of Pleasure" v. Attorney General of Massachusetts, 383 U.S. 413, 445, 86 S.Ct. 975, 991, 16 L.Ed.2d 1 (1966) (Clark, J., dissenting) (consider "social importance" together with evidence that the material in question "appeals to prurient interest and is patently offensive"); Id. at 462 (social importance not an independent test of obscenity but "relevant only to determin[e] the predominant prurient interest of the material . . .").

20. Paris Adult Theatre I v. Slaton, 413 U.S. 49, 82–83, 93 S.Ct. 2628, 2646–47, 37 L.Ed.2d 446 (1973) (Brennan, J., dissenting) (footnote omitted).

21. 413 U.S. at 82 n. 8, 93 S.Ct. at 2647 n. 8.

§ 16.60

1. 413 U.S. 15, 93 S.Ct. 2607, 37 L.Ed.2d 419 (1973), rehearing denied 414 U.S. 881, 94 S.Ct. 26, 38 L.Ed.2d 128 (1973).

2. 413 U.S. at 21–22, 93 S.Ct. at 2613. (emphasis in original).

Miller might well have been correct in pointing to the difficulties that the *Memoirs* approach imposed on the practicalities of meeting the burden of proof where the state is asked, in effect, to prove a negative. But in *Memoirs* the Brennan plurality emphasized the adjective "utterly" in order to give the word an independent significance, not to give it an overriding meaning as suggested in *Miller.*

In any event, in rejecting the *Memoirs* approach, *Miller* had to return to the problems that the *Memoirs* plurality had tried to resolve. *Miller* noted that "in the area of freedom of speech and press the courts must always remain sensitive to any infringement on genuinely serious literary, artistic, political, or scientific expression. This is an area in which there are few eternal verities."[3] On this basis the Court stated that "State statutes designed to regulate obscene materials must be carefully limited";[4] thus the Court held that "we now confine the permissible scope of [state] regulation [of obscenity] to works which depict or describe sexual conduct."

The actual test for obscenity set forth in *Miller* is as follows:

The basic guidelines for the trier of fact must be: (a) whether "the average person, applying contemporary community standards" would find that the work, taken as a whole, appeals to the prurient interest, (b) whether the work depicts or describes, in a patently offensive way, sexual conduct specifically defined by the applicable state law, and (c) whether the work, taken as a whole, lacks serious literary, artistic, political, or scientific value.[5]

For pedagogical reasons it makes sense to consider these three elements out of order.

First, we shall look at the third element, then the second element, and then the first element of the *Miller* test.

The Third Element of the *Miller* Test. The third element of the *Miller* test—"whether the work, taken as a whole, lacks serious literary, artistic, political, or scientific value"—appears on its face less restrictive than the "utterly without redeeming social value" test in *Roth* given independent significance in *Memoirs* through the emphasis on the word "utterly." The shift from "utterly" to "serious" indicates that juries may be given greater leeway under this standard. In addition, the Court eliminated the concept of "social value" and replaced it with "literary, artistic, political, or scientific value"—a distinction without a difference, perhaps, unless one believes that material can contain "social" value without being literary, artistic, political, or scientific. However, to the extent that the Court requires judicial supervision of these issues and the directing of verdicts when the evidence shows the speech to be "serious" in nature, there may be little practical difference.[6]

In deciding this "value" question, the third prong of the *Miller* test, is *not* to be determined by reference to community standards. The first two prongs of *Miller* (patent offensiveness and prurient appeal) are discussed in terms of "contemporary community standards" but the third element is not.[7] The value of the work does not vary from community to community based on the degree of local acceptance it has won.[8] The test is whether a reasonable person (not an ordinary member of any given community) would find value in the material taken as a whole.[9] The fact that only a minority of people in the relevant community may believe that the work has serious value

---

3. 413 U.S. at 22–23, 93 S.Ct. at 2614.

4. 413 U.S. at 23–24, 93 S.Ct. at 2614.

5. 413 U.S. at 24, 93 S.Ct. at 2615.

6. See Jenkins v. Georgia, 418 U.S. 153, 94 S.Ct. 2750, 41 L.Ed.2d 642 (1974).

Brockett v. Spokane Arcades, Inc., 472 U.S. 491, 497 n. 7, 105 S.Ct. 2794, 2798 n. 7, 86 L.Ed.2d 394 (1985) noted:

"The basic difference between the *Memoirs* test and the *Miller* test was the *Memoirs* requirement that in

order to be judged obscene, a work must be 'utterly without redeeming social value.' . . ."

7. Smith v. United States, 431 U.S. 291, 301, 97 S.Ct. 1756, 1763, 52 L.Ed.2d 324 (1977).

8. Pope v. Illinois, 481 U.S. 497, 501, 107 S.Ct. 1918, 1921, 95 L.Ed.2d 439 (1987), on remand 162 Ill.App.3d 299, 113 Ill.Dec. 547, 515 N.E.2d 356 (1987).

9. 481 U.S. at 501 & n. 3, 107 S.Ct. at 1921 & n. 3.

does not mean that the "reasonable person" standard is not met.

The Second Element of the *Miller* Test. With respect to the second part of the *Miller* test, the Court offered "a few plain examples of what a state statute could define for regulation under part (b) of the standard announced in this opinion. . . ." These examples were:

(a) Patently offensive representations or descriptions of ultimate sexual acts, normal or perverted, actual or simulated.

(b) Patently offensive representations or descriptions of masturbation, excretory functions, and lewd exhibition of the genitals.[10]

The Court explicitly acknowledged that under *Miller*, "no one [may] be subject to prosecution for the sale or exposure of obscene materials unless these materials depict or describe patently offensive 'hard core' sexual conduct specifically defined by the regulating state law, as written or construed."[11]

This portion of the test might have served as a basis for improving the ability of individuals to engage in publishing or film-making by offering them clear notice of what is prohibited by statute. But the Court has allowed state courts to save their statutes by construction and in so doing expand the Court's list of examples. Thus sadomasochistic materials may be constitutionally prohibited even though not listed in *Miller*: the *Miller* specifics "were offered merely as 'examples' . . ., they 'were not intended to be exhaustive.' "[12]

The First Element of the *Miller* Test. The most controversial aspect of the *Miller* decision may be the first part of its test with its rejection of national standards. The nation-

al standards concept had never been adopted by a majority of the Court.[13] It was only the most restrictive concept that could get a working majority of Justices to suppress an item as obscene. Now a majority finally agreed on the national standards test—and they rejected it.

In *Miller*, the Court decided to give the "community standards" aspect of the *Roth* test a more literal meaning, and it held that trial courts may draw on actual community standards in determining whether the material at issue is factually obscene. As *Miller* explicitly stated: "In resolving the inevitable sensitive questions of fact and law, we must continue to rely on the jury system, accompanied by the safeguards that judges, rules of evidence, presumption of innocence, and other protective features provide. . . ."[14]

Curiously, *Miller* reiterated the notion that had provided the basis for the plurality *Jacobellis* national-standards test in the first place, that "fundamental First Amendment limitations on the powers of the States do not vary from community to community."[15] Thus the Constitutional source for the *Miller* "community standards" test is difficult to locate. Any implication in *Miller* of a broader role for the jury, as we shall see in the next section below, has not proven correct. It may be that the Court only meant that the trier of fact should not be required to guess at some hypothetical "median" standard.

Justice Brennan, in a dissent in another case filed the same day as *Miller*, expressed deep concern with the vagueness of the obscenity tests as developed from *Roth* to *Miller*. He felt that the differences between *Miller* and his plurality opinion in *Memoirs* "are, for the most part, academic,"[16] but he nonetheless felt

10. 413 U.S. at 25, 93 S.Ct. at 2615.

11. 413 U.S. at 27, 93 S.Ct. at 2616.

Material that provokes only normal, healthy sexual desires cannot be characterized as obscene. Brockett v. Spokane Arcades, Inc., 472 U.S. 491, 105 S.Ct. 2794, 86 L.Ed.2d 394 (1985).

12. Ward v. Illinois, 431 U.S. 767, 773, 97 S.Ct. 2085, 2089, 52 L.Ed.2d 738 (1977), quoting Hamling v. United States, 418 U.S. 87, 114, 94 S.Ct. 2887, 2906, 41 L.Ed.2d 590 (1974), rehearing denied 419 U.S. 885, 95 S.Ct. 157, 42 L.Ed.2d 129 (1974). Cf. Mishkin v. New York, 383 U.S.

502, 86 S.Ct. 958, 16 L.Ed.2d 56 (1966), rehearing denied 384 U.S. 934, 86 S.Ct. 1440, 16 L.Ed.2d 535 (1966).

13. See Jacobellis v. Ohio, 378 U.S. 184, 84 S.Ct. 1676, 12 L.Ed.2d 793 (1964) (no opinion of the Court).

14. 413 U.S. at 26, 93 S.Ct. at 2616.

15. 413 U.S. at 30, 93 S.Ct. at 2618.

16. Paris Adult Theatre I v. Slaton, 413 U.S. 49, 95, 93 S.Ct. 2628, 2653, 37 L.Ed.2d 446 (1973), rehearing denied 414 U.S. 881, 94 S.Ct. 27, 38 L.Ed.2d 128 (1973), on remand 231 Ga. 312, 201 S.E.2d 456 (1973), certiorari denied 418 U.S. 939, 94 S.Ct. 3227, 41 L.Ed.2d 1173

compelled to reject it as well as his earlier *Roth* opinion.[17] After considering and rejecting a wide variety of tests for the validity of obscenity legislation he offered his own bright line approach:

> In short, while I cannot say that the interests of the State—apart from the question of juveniles and unconsenting adults—are trivial or nonexistent, I am compelled to conclude that these interests cannot justify the substantial damage to constitutional rights and to this Nation's judicial machinery that inevitably results from state efforts to bar the distribution even of unprotected material to consenting adults.... I would hold, therefore, that at least in the absence of distribution to juveniles or obtrusive exposure to unconsenting adults, ... the First and Fourteenth Amendments prohibit the State and Federal Governments from attempting wholly to suppress sexually oriented materials on the basis of their allegedly "obscene" contents. Nothing in this approach precludes those governments from taking action to serve what may be strong and legitimate interests through regulation of the manner of distribution of sexually oriented material.[18]

Justice Brennan's position has not persuaded his colleagues, who have followed *Miller*. But then a majority has always held that some speech known as "hard core" pornography can be banned. Indeed for fifteen years Justice Brennan had espoused this view.

§ 16.61　Special Considerations in Light of the *Miller* Case

(a) Private Possession

Stanley v. Georgia,[1] relying on the First and Fourteenth Amendments, held that "mere private possession of obscene matter"[2] is not a crime. *Stanley*, however, must be read quite narrowly. The crucial fifth vote in *Stanley* was Justice Harlan's; in spite of the broad language of the opinion, the *Stanley* Court's own summary of its decision emphasized that "the States retain broad power to regulate obscenity; that power simply does not extend to mere possession by the individual in the privacy of his own home."[3] The Court itself had previously emphasized, in other contexts, the privacy of the home[4] and Justice Harlan in particular had been concerned with the sanctity of the home,[5] although he repeatedly has emphasized the broad power of the state over obscenity outside of the home.[6]

While the Court has refused to expand *Stanley* it has also not explained why a seller of obscenity may not raise the third-party right of persons to keep the obscenity in the home. In other contexts the Supreme Court has allowed such derivative rights.[7] Under *Stanley* one may enjoy obscene material in one's own home, but the state may prohibit an individual from transporting the material for private use,[8] and may also prohibit the individual from receiving the materials through the mails,[9] or from importing them from foreign countries.[10]

(1974), rehearing denied 419 U.S. 887, 95 S.Ct. 163, 42 L.Ed.2d 133 (1974) (Brennan, J., dissenting) (footnote omitted).

17.　413 U.S. at 98, 93 S.Ct. at 2655.

18.　413 U.S. at 112–13, 93 S.Ct. at 2662.

§ 16.61

1.　394 U.S. 557, 89 S.Ct. 1243, 22 L.Ed.2d 542 (1969), on remand 225 Ga. 273, 167 S.E.2d 756 (1969).

2.　394 U.S. at 568, 89 S.Ct. at 1249.

3.　394 U.S. at 568, 89 S.Ct. at 1250.

4.　E.g., Griswold v. Connecticut, 381 U.S. 479, 85 S.Ct. 1678, 14 L.Ed.2d 510 (1965).

5.　E.g., Griswold v. Connecticut, 381 U.S. 479, 499, 85 S.Ct. 1678, 1689–90, 14 L.Ed.2d 510 (1965) (concurring opinion); Poe v. Ullman, 367 U.S. 497, 550, 81 S.Ct. 1752,

1781, 6 L.Ed.2d 989 (1961), rehearing denied 368 U.S. 869, 82 S.Ct. 21, 7 L.Ed.2d 69 (1961) (dissenting opinion).

6.　E.g., Smith v. California, 361 U.S. 147, 169, 80 S.Ct. 215, 227, 4 L.Ed.2d 205 (1959), rehearing denied 361 U.S. 950, 80 S.Ct. 399, 4 L.Ed.2d 383 (1960) (concurring opinion).

7.　Griswold v. Connecticut, 381 U.S. 479, 85 S.Ct. 1678, 14 L.Ed.2d 510 (1965); Carey v. Population Services International, 431 U.S. 678, 97 S.Ct. 2010, 52 L.Ed.2d 675 (1977) (third party standing and right to distribute contraceptives).

8.　United States v. Orito, 413 U.S. 139, 93 S.Ct. 2674, 37 L.Ed.2d 513 (1973).

9.　United States v. Reidel, 402 U.S. 351, 91 S.Ct. 1410, 28 L.Ed.2d 813 (1971).

10.　United States v. 12 200–Foot Reels of Super 8MM. Film, 413 U.S. 123, 93 S.Ct. 2665, 37 L.Ed.2d 500 (1973);

The state may regulate obscene materials even if those using them voluntarily sought them out.[11] Though the private possession of obscene materials in the home is protected activity, virtually any process that leads to such possession may be declared illegal.

As the Court later admitted: *"Stanley* should not be read too broadly."[12]

(b) Protection of Minors

Ginsberg v. New York,[13] adopted the "variable obscenity" approach suggested by Professors Lockhart and McClure and held that a statute defining obscenity in terms of an appeal to the prurient interest of minors was constitutional. As such, *Ginsberg* represents a departure from a pure or neutral concept of "pruriency" as explicated in *Roth*; it is also a departure from the "average man" standard. In light of the Court's revision of the *Roth* test in *Miller*, however, *Ginsberg* may be theoretically reconcilable within the "community standards" test currently in operation.

Statutes for the protection of children must be narrowly drawn in two respects. First, the statute must not be overbroad; the state cannot prevent the general public from reading or having access to materials on the grounds that the materials would be objectionable if read or seen by children. Second, the statute must not be vague.

Butler v. Michigan[14] reversed a conviction under a statute that made it an offense to make available to the general public materials found to have a potentially deleterious influence on minors. The state argued that by "quarantining the general reading public against books not too rugged for grown men and women in order to shield juvenile innocence, it is exercising its power to promote the general welfare."[15] The unanimous Court answered: "Surely, this is to burn the house to roast the pig."[16] This law was overbroad.

Second, the statute in *Butler* was too vague. The problem of vagueness is not reduced simply because the regulation is one of classification rather than direct suppression. In addition, the fact that the legislature adopted the statute for the salutary purpose of protecting children of protecting children does not reduce the fatal flaw of vagueness.[17]

Later, in *United States v. Playboy Entertainment Group, Inc.*,[18] invalidated "signal bleed" provision of the Telecommunications Act. This section required cable television operators providing channels "primarily dedicated to sexually-oriented programming" to "fully scramble or otherwise fully block" those channels. Al-

---

see also United States v. 37 Photographs, 402 U.S. 363, 91 S.Ct. 1400, 28 L.Ed.2d 822 (1971).

11. Paris Adult Theatre I v. Slaton, 413 U.S. 49, 93 S.Ct. 2628, 37 L.Ed.2d 446 (1973), rehearing denied 414 U.S. 881, 94 S.Ct. 27, 38 L.Ed.2d 128 (1973), on remand 231 Ga. 312, 201 S.E.2d 456 (1973), certiorari denied 418 U.S. 939, 94 S.Ct. 3227, 41 L.Ed.2d 1173 (1974), rehearing denied 419 U.S. 887, 95 S.Ct. 163, 42 L.Ed.2d 133 (1974).

12. Osborne v. Ohio, 495 U.S. 103, 107, 110 S.Ct. 1691, 1695, 109 L.Ed.2d 98 (1990). *Osborne* held that the state may constitutionally proscribe the possession and viewing of child pornography, even in one's home.

13. 390 U.S. 629, 88 S.Ct. 1274, 20 L.Ed.2d 195 (1968), rehearing denied 391 U.S. 971, 88 S.Ct. 2029, 20 L.Ed.2d 887 (1968). See, Ronald D. Rotunda, Media Accountability In Light of the First Amendment, 21 Social Philosophy & Policy 269 (Cambridge University Press, No. 2, 2004).

14. 352 U.S. 380, 77 S.Ct. 524, 1 L.Ed.2d 412 (1957). Cf. FCC v. Pacifica Foundation, 438 U.S. 726, 98 S.Ct. 3026, 57 L.Ed.2d 1073 (1978), rehearing denied 439 U.S. 883, 99 S.Ct. 227, 58 L.Ed.2d 198 (1978) (FCC has power to regulate radio broadcast that is "indecent" but not "obscene" because, in part, of the presence of children in the early afternoon audience).

15. 352 U.S. at 383, 77 S.Ct. at 526.

16. 352 U.S. at 383, 77 S.Ct. at 526.

17. Interstate Circuit, Inc. v. Dallas, 390 U.S. 676, 688–89, 88 S.Ct. 1298, 1306, 20 L.Ed.2d 225 (1968) (footnote omitted); see also, Erznoznik v. Jacksonville, 422 U.S. 205, 95 S.Ct. 2268, 45 L.Ed.2d 125 (1975) (ordinance prohibiting drive-in movie theater from showing nudity invalid on its face; the broad nudity ban exceeds the permissible restraints on obscenity and thus applies to protected speech; assuming that the law is aimed at youths, it is still not sufficiently limited—the law would seek to bar even a baby's buttocks from being shown on the drive-in movie screen).

Dial–a–Porn. In Sable Communications of California, Inc. v. F.C.C., 492 U.S. 115, 109 S.Ct. 2829, 106 L.Ed.2d 93 (1989) the Court held that Congress can constitutionally impose an outright ban of "obscene" interstate, pre-recorded commercial telephone messages ("Dial–A–Porn"), because obscenity is not protected speech. But Congress cannot impose a *total* ban on non-obscene, "indecent" dial-a-porn because such speech is not obscene as to adults. A total legislative ban is not narrowly tailored to serve the compelling interest in protecting minors. A narrowly tailored rule might use credit cards, access codes, and scrambling devices.

18. 529 U.S. 803, 120 S.Ct. 1878, 146 L.Ed.2d 865 (2000).

ternatively, they could limit their transmission to hours when children are unlikely to be viewing, set by administrative regulation as between 10 p.m. and 6 a.m.

Because scrambling can be imprecise (either or both audio and visual portions of the scrambled programs might still be heard or seen) (what is called "signal bleed"), the majority of cable operators adopted the "time channeling" approach. So, for two-thirds of the day, no household in those service areas could receive the programming, whether or not the household or the viewer wanted to do so. The Court, citing *Butler*, invalidated this requirement because there was a less restrictive alternative: the cable operator could fully scramble any channel the subscriber does not wish to receive, on a household-by-household basis ("targeted blocking").

Child Abuse. *New York v. Ferber*,[19] without a dissent, upheld a law that passed both the vagueness and overbreadth requirements. The legislature had designed this statute to prevent the abuse of children. New York made it a crime for a person knowingly to promote sexual performances by children under the age of 16 by distributing material that depicts such performances even though the materials themselves were not necessarily "obscene" in a constitutional sense.[20]

Ferber articulated five basic premises. First, the state's interests in protecting the physical and psychological well being of minors is compelling. Second, prohibiting the distribution of films and photos depicting such activities are closely related to this compelling governmental interest in two ways: the permanent record of the child's activity and its circulation exacerbates the harm to the minor, and the distribution encourages the sexual exploitation of the children and the production of the material. Third, advertising and selling the material en-

courages the evil by supplying an economic motive. Fourth, the value of allowing live performances and photographic reproduction of children engaged in lewd sexual conduct is *de minimis*. After all, the person who put together the material depicting the sexual performance could always use a model over the statutory age who looked younger. And, fifth, the classification of child pornography as outside of First Amendment protection is consistent with earlier precedent and justified by the need to protect the welfare of the children.

Ferber cautioned that there were limits to the extent to which child pornography is unprotected speech. The statute prohibiting the conduct must adequately define and describe it. And, the circumstances of this case require that the crime "be limited to works that *visually* depict conduct by children below a specified age."[21]

The Court then explained how the *Miller*[22] test must be modified when dealing with child pornography:

The *Miller* formulation is adjusted in the following respects: A trier of fact need not find that the material appeals to the prurient interest of the average person; it is not required that sexual conduct portrayed be done so in a patently offensive manner; and the material at issue need not be considered as a whole. We note that the distribution of descriptions or other depictions of sexual conduct, not otherwise obscene, which do not involve live performance or photographic or other visual reproduction of live performances, retains First Amendment protection. As with obscenity laws, criminal responsibility may not be imposed without some element of scienter on the part of the defendant.[23]

---

19. 458 U.S. 747, 102 S.Ct. 3348, 73 L.Ed.2d 1113 (1982), on remand 57 N.Y.2d 256, 455 N.Y.S.2d 582, 441 N.E.2d 1100 (1982). Blackmun, J. concurred in the result without opinion. O'Connor, J., filed a concurring opinion. Brennan, J., joined by Marshall, J., filed an opinion and concurred in the judgment. Stevens, J., wrote a separate opinion also concurring in the judgment. White, J., wrote the opinion of the Court.

20. The films in this case primarily depicted young boys masturbating. 458 U.S. at 752, 102 S.Ct. at 3352.
21. 458 U.S. at 764, 102 S.Ct. at 3358 (emphasis in original) (footnote omitted).
22. Miller v. California, 413 U.S. 15, 93 S.Ct. 2607, 37 L.Ed.2d 419 (1973), rehearing denied 414 U.S. 881, 94 S.Ct. 26, 38 L.Ed.2d 128 (1973).
23. 458 U.S. at 764–65, 102 S.Ct. at 3358.

Ferber dealt with the New York law as if it were a type of obscenity legislation. However, it is easier to understand the case if one realizes that the *Ferber* statute was really quite different. The purpose of obscenity legislation is to protect the minds and well being of the consumers or viewers of obscenity, by preventing them from watching the obscene movie, or reading the obscene magazine, etc. The purpose of the New York law is *not* to protect the consumers who watch a child's sexual performance; it is *to protect the young children* from being used and abused as performers in a sexual performance. Because the New York law focuses on protecting the juvenile performers it should be easy to uphold.

Osborne v. Ohio[24] supports this distinction when it held that the state may constitutionally prohibit the possession and viewing of child pornography at home. The distinction with *Stanley v. Georgia*[25] the Court concluded was "obvious." Unlike *Stanley* the state here does not rely on a paternalistic interest in regulating Osborne's mind. Rather, the purpose of the law is to protect the children, victims of child pornography. The state hopes to destroy a market for the exploitative use of children.

Osborne went on to conclude that the statute was not overbroad. The law prohibited any person from possessing or viewing any material or performance showing a minor who is not his child or ward in a state of nudity unless (a), the material or performance is presented for a bona fide purpose by or to a person having a proper interest therein, or (b) the possessor knows that the minor's parents or guardian has consented in writing to such photographing or use of the minor. As construed by the Ohio Supreme Court the law requires proof of scienter and is limited to depictions of nudity that involve *lewd* exhibi-

tion or involve graphic focus of the minor's genitals.[26]

In *Ashcroft v. Free Speech Coalition*,[27] the Court relied on *Ferber* and invalidated part of the Child Pornography Prevention Act of 1996 (CPPA), which expanded the federal prohibition of child pornography to include "virtual pornography," that is, sexually explicit images that appear to depict minors but are produced without using any real children. The images could be created by using adults who look like minors or by using computer imaging. The new technology makes it possible to create realistic images of children who do not exist. The CPPA is not directed at obscene speech, which a different statute prohibits. The Court found CPPA unconstitutional to the extent that it prohibited speech that is not obscene under *Miller* and also to the extent it prohibited virtual child pornography because, under *Ferber*, the materials were not produced by the exploitation of real children.

(c) Prior Restraint

The Court has often stated that "Any system of prior restraints of expression comes to this Court bearing a heavy presumption against its constitutional validity."[28] Prior Restraint means that the court or another body, such as an administrator, issues an order that prevents communications (that are the subject of the prior restraint) prior to the time that the communications would occur but for the order. The point of a prior restraint is to freeze (restrain) speech before (prior to the time) it occurs.[29] If a speaker must secure the prior approval of an agency or a court *before* speaking, that requirement is a classic prior restraint.

Obscenity is one of a few areas where the Court has upheld prior restraint. However,

24. 495 U.S. 103, 110 S.Ct. 1691, 109 L.Ed.2d 98 (1990).

25. 394 U.S. 557, 89 S.Ct. 1243, 22 L.Ed.2d 542 (1969).

26. However the Court remanded for a new trial because of the trial court's failure to instruct the jury on the state's obligation to prove lewdness. Brennan, J., joined by Marshall & Stevens, JJ., dissented, arguing that "our decision in *Stanley v. Georgia* prevents the State from criminalizing appellant's possession of the photographs at

issue in this case." 495 U.S. at 125, 110 S.Ct. at 1705 (Brennan, J., dissenting).

27. 535 U.S. 234, 122 S.Ct. 1389, 152 L.Ed.2d 403 (2002).

28. Bantam Books, Inc. v. Sullivan, 372 U.S. 58, 70, 83 S.Ct. 631, 639, 9 L.Ed.2d 584 (1963).

29. Alexander v. United States, 509 U.S. 544, 550, 113 S.Ct. 2766, 2771, 125 L.Ed.2d 441 (1993), rehearing denied 510 U.S. 909, 114 S.Ct. 295, 126 L.Ed.2d 244 (1993).

even in this area, the Court has imposed constitutional safeguards on the procedures employed in the prior restraint of allegedly-obscene materials.

The leading case is *Freedman v. Maryland*.[30] The Court held that before a local censorship board could revoke a book or motion-picture distributor's license for the sale or display of obscene materials, or otherwise engage in the prior restraint of allegedly-obscene materials, it must: (1) afford the accused party a prompt hearing; (2) assume the burden of showing that the material is, in fact, obscene; (3) defer to a judicial proceeding for the imposition of a valid final restraint on the material; and (4) either refrain from making a finding of obscen-

ity or, as a requirement of law under the board's enabling statute or clear judicial mandate, take action on its own behalf in a court of law to seek an affirmation of its initial finding of obscenity.

In the court proceeding, the distributor or retailer may contest the issue of obscenity even though the book or film has been found to be obscene in other cases to which he was not a party.[31] Even if a judge rather than an administrative tribunal initially issues the prior restraint, the procedural safeguards of *Freedman* must be followed, in order to mitigate the unconstitutional consequences if the restraint were erroneously entered.[32]

---

30. 380 U.S. 51, 85 S.Ct. 734, 13 L.Ed.2d 649 (1965); see also, e.g., Carroll v. President and Commissioners of Princess Anne, 393 U.S. 175, 89 S.Ct. 347, 21 L.Ed.2d 325 (1968).

Prior Restraint of Books. It is unlikely that the *Freedman* rule of prior restraints would apply if the allegedly obscene material were not films but only books. Cf. Bantam Books, Inc. v. Sullivan, 372 U.S. 58, 83 S.Ct. 631, 9 L.Ed.2d 584 (1963); Lowe v. SEC, 472 U.S. 181, 105 S.Ct. 2557, 86 L.Ed.2d 130 (1985).

Burden of Proof. In an injunctive proceeding, which is civil, there is no federal constitutional requirement that proof be beyond a reasonable doubt, Cooper v. Mitchell Bros.' Santa Ana Theater, 454 U.S. 90, 102 S.Ct. 172, 70 L.Ed.2d 262 (1981) (per curiam), on remand 128 Cal. App.3d 937, 180 Cal.Rptr. 728 (1982), certiorari denied 459 U.S. 944, 103 S.Ct. 259, 74 L.Ed.2d 202 (1982), rehearing denied 459 U.S. 1093, 103 S.Ct. 581, 74 L.Ed.2d 940 (1982).

Jury. Nor is there a federal constitutional requirement of a jury. Alexander v. Virginia, 413 U.S. 836, 93 S.Ct. 2803, 37 L.Ed.2d 993 (1973) (per curiam), rehearing denied 414 U.S. 881, 94 S.Ct. 29, 38 L.Ed.2d 128 (1973), mandate conformed 214 Va. 539, 203 S.E.2d 441 (1974).

31. McKinney v. Alabama, 424 U.S. 669, 96 S.Ct. 1189, 47 L.Ed.2d 387 (1976) (in rem proceeding not bar to litigation of the obscenity issue of the material as to a distributor not party to the in rem proceeding).

32. Vance v. Universal Amusement Co., Inc., 445 U.S. 308, 100 S.Ct. 1156, 63 L.Ed.2d 413 (1980), rehearing denied 446 U.S. 947, 100 S.Ct. 2177, 64 L.Ed.2d 804 (1980) (per curiam).

Licensing of Sexually Oriented Businesses. In FW/PBS v. City of Dallas, 493 U.S. 215, 110 S.Ct. 596, 107 L.Ed.2d 603 (1990), a fragmented Court affirmed in part, reversed in part, vacated in part, and remanded a case where the Fifth Circuit had upheld an ordinance that licensed sexually oriented businesses, such as adult book stores, adult cabarets, and escort agencies. There was no issue whether the entertainment, books, videos, etc. were obscene. O'Connor, J., joined by Stevens & Kennedy, JJ., invalidated the licensing scheme as an invalid prior re-

straint under *Freedman*. The city licensing system required that premises to be used for "sexually oriented businesses" must be first approved by the health and fire departments and the building official before the chief of police issued a license. Because the ordinance did not provide for an effective limitation on the time within which the licensor's decision must be made, and, because it also failed to provide for prompt judicial review, it was invalid as to those businesses engaged in First Amendment activity (as determined by the court on remand).

However, O'Connor did not require the ordinance meet the third requirement of *Freedman*—that is, the First Amendment does not require that the city bear the burden of going to court to effect the denial of the license; nor must the city bear the burden of proof once in court. O'Connor reasoned that the city does not judge the content of any protected speech. Rather, it reviews the general qualifications of each license applicant, a ministerial action that is not presumptively invalid. Then she argued that the movie distributor in *Freedman* might be deterred from challenging the licensing decision of a particular movie. In this case, the license applicants have much more at stake, because the license is the key to the applicant's obtaining a business, so "there is every incentive" to pursue a license denial through the courts. Apparently, the fact that the license denial was so damaging was a factor that helped its constitutionality!

Brennan, J., joined by Marshall, & Blackmun, JJ., concurring in the judgment, would have applied all three of the *Freedman* procedural safeguards.

Forfeiture of Defendant's Assets in RICO Prosecution. Alexander v. United States, 509 U.S. 544, 113 S.Ct. 2766, 125 L.Ed.2d 441 (1993), rehearing denied 510 U.S. 909, 114 S.Ct. 295, 126 L.Ed.2d 244 (1993) held that it was no violation of free speech when the government provided for the forfeiture of defendant's assets, used in the adult entertainment business, following defendant's conviction for participating in racketeering activities in violation of the Racketeer Influenced and Corrupt Organizations Act (RICO). The forfeiture is not a prior restraint on speech—there was no court or agency that prevented defendant from engaging in expressive activities in the future. The courts imposed no legal restraint on defen-

Search Warrants. If materials that are the subject of a search warrant may be protected by the First Amendment—when the "things" seized are books or films, and the basis for their seizure is the ideas that they contain— then the requirements of the Fourth Amendment must be applied with "most scrupulous exactitude."[33] The search warrant must be particularized and should not be issued only on the police officer's conclusory assertion in order that there be an opportunity for the judicial officer to "focus searchingly on the question of obscenity."[34]

However, there is no higher Fourth Amendment standard of probable cause. The court should use the same standard of probable cause used to review warrant applications generally, but the police cannot rely on the "exigency" exception to the Fourth Amendment warrant requirement.[35] In addition, the police may not seize allegedly obscene material without a warrant even though the seizure is contemporaneous with, and an incident to, an arrest.[36]

Where the censorship board or other state body confiscates a single piece of allegedly obscene material (while others are available for exhibition) for the purpose of preserving it as evidence, the board need not provide a hearing so long as the confiscation is made pursuant to a warrant issued upon a showing of probable cause. Then, the Constitution requires a prompt judicial hearing to determine whether the material is obscene. If the trial court determines that other copies of the film are not available for exhibition, it should permit the seized film to be copied so that the exhibition can be continued until the obscenity issue is resolved in an adversary hearing. Otherwise the film must be returned.[37]

Before a search warrant may be issued for the seizure of allegedly obscene material, there must be an opportunity for a neutral and detached judicial officer to focus searchingly on the question of obscenity. That neutrality and detachment do not exist when the Town Justice signed an open-ended warrant and then joined the law enforcement officials in conducting a search of the book store lasting nearly six hours and examining and seizing numerous films and magazines. The judicial officer in effect conducted a prohibited generalized search and seizure and became "a member, if not, the leader of the search party, which was essentially a police operation."[38]

(d) Zoning Laws and Public Exhibition of "Adult" Non–Obscene Material

Paris Adult Theatre I v. Slaton,[39] decided on the same day as *Miller*, held that the state may prohibit public exhibitions or displays of

---

dant's ability to engage in any expressive activity. The forfeiture only prevents him from *financing* his expressive activities with assets derived from *prior* racketeering offenses found to be criminal.

33. Stanford v. Texas, 379 U.S. 476, 485, 85 S.Ct. 506, 511–12, 13 L.Ed.2d 431 (1965) (5 hour search and seizure of 2000 books, pamphlets, and papers invalidated).

See also, Wilkey v. Wood, 19 How.St.Tr. 1153 (1763); Entick v. Carrington, 19 How.St.Tr. 1029 (1765).

34. Marcus v. Search Warrants, 367 U.S. 717, 732, 81 S.Ct. 1708, 1716, 6 L.Ed.2d 1127 (1961).

See also, A Quantity of Copies of Books v. Kansas, 378 U.S. 205, 210, 84 S.Ct. 1723, 1725–26, 12 L.Ed.2d 809 (1964); Lee Art Theatre, Inc. v. Virginia, 392 U.S. 636, 637, 88 S.Ct. 2103, 2104, 20 L.Ed.2d 1313 (1968) (per curiam); Roaden v. Kentucky, 413 U.S. 496, 502, 93 S.Ct. 2796, 2800, 37 L.Ed.2d 757 (1973); Heller v. New York, 413 U.S. 483, 489, 93 S.Ct. 2789, 2793, 37 L.Ed.2d 745 (1973).

35. New York v. P.J. Video, Inc., 475 U.S. 868, 875 & n. 6, 106 S.Ct. 1610, 1615 & n. 6, 89 L.Ed.2d 871 (1986), on remand 68 N.Y.2d 296, 508 N.Y.S.2d 907, 501 N.E.2d 556 (1986), cert. denied 479 U.S. 1091, 107 S.Ct. 1301, 94 L.Ed.2d 156 (1987).

36. Roaden v. Kentucky, 413 U.S. 496, 497–98, 504, 93 S.Ct. 2796, 2798–2801, 37 L.Ed.2d 757 (1973).

However, there is no "search" when a police officer enters a store open to the public and buys materials offered for sale. Maryland v. Macon, 472 U.S. 463, 471, 105 S.Ct. 2778, 2783, 86 L.Ed.2d 370 (1985).

37. Heller v. New York, 413 U.S. 483, 93 S.Ct. 2789, 37 L.Ed.2d 745 (1973), on remand 33 N.Y.2d 314, 352 N.Y.S.2d 601, 307 N.E.2d 805, (1973), certiorari denied 418 U.S. 944, 94 S.Ct. 3231, 41 L.Ed.2d 1175 (1974).

38. Lo–Ji Sales, Inc. v. New York, 442 U.S. 319, 325–27, 99 S.Ct. 2319, 2323–25, 60 L.Ed.2d 920 (1979), distinguishing Heller v. New York, 413 U.S. 483, 93 S.Ct. 2789, 37 L.Ed.2d 745 (1973), on remand 33 N.Y.2d 314, 352 N.Y.S.2d 601, 307 N.E.2d 805 (1973).

39. 413 U.S. 49, 93 S.Ct. 2628, 37 L.Ed.2d 446 (1973), rehearing denied 414 U.S. 881, 94 S.Ct. 27, 38 L.Ed.2d 128 (1973), on remand 231 Ga. 312, 201 S.E.2d 456 (1973), certiorari denied 418 U.S. 939, 94 S.Ct. 3227, 41 L.Ed.2d 1173 (1974), rehearing denied 419 U.S. 887, 95 S.Ct. 163, 42 L.Ed.2d 133 (1974). The Court thus restricted Stanley

obscenity even if access to the exhibitions is limited to consenting adults. The Court carried *Paris Adult Theatre* a step further in *Young v. American Mini Theatres, Inc.*,[40] in which it held that an appropriately definite zoning ordinance prohibiting the location of an "adult movie theatre" within 1000 feet of any two other "regulated uses," including 10 different kinds of establishments in addition to adult theatres, is constitutionally permissible *even* if the theatre is not displaying obscene material.

While the ordinance in question characterized an adult theatre as one presenting certain specified "sexual activities" or "anatomical areas," the Court reasoned that the ordinance did not constitute an exercise in prior restraint, but rather a valid use of the city's zoning power to regulate the location of commercial establishments. The Court specifically held that this zoning power overrides the First Amendment element in the display of the material at any locality the distributor chooses. However the Court placed great emphasis on the continual availability of these movies and the fact that the restrictions were unrelated to the suppression of ideas.

It was true that a concentration of these theatres brought certain physical changes to the neighborhoods where they were located. These changes were due not only to the advertisements and posters associated with the theatres but also to the size and type of crowd they attracted. The zoning of a reasonable amount of space between such theatres avoided the concentration of this physical effect on a neighborhood. Nevertheless the regulation describes the theatres in terms of the content of their films.

The language of Justice Stevens' plurality opinion in *American Mini Theatres* supports

confining the doctrine and not expanding it to other types of speech:

> Since what is ultimately at stake is nothing more than a limitation on the place where adult films may be exhibited, even though the determination of whether a particular film fits that characterization turns on the nature of its content, we conclude that the city's interest in the present and future character of its neighborhoods adequately supports its classification of motion pictures.[41]

Schad v. Borough of Mount Ephraim[42] distinguished *American Mini Theatres* and invalidated a zoning ordinance that, as construed by the state courts, forbade *all* "live entertainment," including nonobscene nude dancing, in a commercial zone. "[N]o property in the Borough may be principally used for the commercial production of plays, concerts, musicals, dance, or any other form of live entertainment."[43] An adult book store, operating in a commercial zone in the Borough of Mount Ephraim, introduced a coin operated device: a customer, after inserting a coin, would be able to watch a live dancer, usually nude, perform behind a glass panel. The store was therefore found guilty of violating the ordinance.

Before the Supreme Court, counsel for Mount Ephraim presented some justifications, but none of these were persuasive and none had been articulated by the state courts. The Borough argued that it could allow a broad range of commercial uses but nonetheless exclude live entertainment because that use led to special problems such as increased need for parking, trash pick-up, police protection, and medical facilities. However the Borough presented no evidence to support this assertion, and the Court did not find it "self-evident that a theatre, for example, would create greater

---

v. Georgia, 394 U.S. 557, 89 S.Ct. 1243, 22 L.Ed.2d 542 (1969), on remand 225 Ga. 273, 167 S.E.2d 756 (1969).

40. 427 U.S. 50, 96 S.Ct. 2440, 49 L.Ed.2d 310 (1976), rehearing denied 429 U.S. 873, 97 S.Ct. 191, 50 L.Ed.2d 155 (1976). See also, Bellanca v. New York State Liquor Authority, 54 N.Y.2d 228, 241, 445 N.Y.S.2d 87, 93, 429 N.E.2d 765, 771 (1981), (Gabrielli, J., dissenting), citing treatise, certiorari denied 456 U.S. 1006, 102 S.Ct. 2296, 73 L.Ed.2d 1300 (1982).

41. 427 U.S. at 70–72, 96 S.Ct. at 2452–53 (footnote omitted) (opinion of Stevens, J., joined by Burger, C. J., and White & Rehnquist, JJ.). Justice Stevens has been the prime force in encouraging the Court to allow restrictions (in some circumstances) to be placed on speech because of its content.

42. 452 U.S. 61, 101 S.Ct. 2176, 68 L.Ed.2d 671 (1981).

43. 452 U.S. at 66, 101 S.Ct. at 2181 (footnote omitted).

parking problems than would a restaurant."[44] Assuming that live entertainment would create special problems not associated with other commercial uses, the Borough had not narrowly tailored a zoning law to address any unique problems. The Borough's claim that its zoning restriction was an attempt to create a commercial area catering only to the residents' "immediate needs" also did not survive scrutiny. The Borough introduced no evidence to support this assertion and the face of the ordinance contradicted it, for the ordinance permitted car showrooms, hardware stores, offices, etc.

The *American Mini Theatres* analysis did not support the constitutionality of the ordinance, for the restriction in *American Mini Theatres* did not ban all adult theatres or even affect the number of adult movie theatres in the city. It just dispersed them.[45] And in *American Mini Theatres* the city had presented evidence that a concentration of adult theatres led to a deterioration of surrounding neighborhoods.

While *American Mini Theatres* allowed a city to disperse adult theatres, *City of Renton v. Playtime Theatres, Inc.*[46] allowed a city to concentrate them. Justice Rehnquist for the Court (with only Brennan and Marshall dissenting) upheld a zoning ordinance that prohibited "adult" motion picture theatres from locating within 1,000 feet of any residential zone, single or multiple-family dwelling, church, park, or school. The district court

found that the city council's "*predominate concerns*" were with the secondary effects of adult theatres—e.g., to prevent crime, protect the city's retail trade, maintain property values, and preserve the quality—of life and not with the content of adult films themselves.[47] This finding was "more than adequate to establish that the city's pursuit of its zoning interests here was unrelated to the suppression of free expression." The ordinance was a "content-neutral" speech regulation because it was "*justified* without reference to the content of the regulated speech."[48]

The Court then upheld the ordinance because it served a substantial governmental interest (preserving the quality of life), and allowed reasonable alternative avenues of communication, for more than five percent of the entire land area of Renton was allowed to be used by adult theatres. And unlike *Schad*, the Renton ordinance was "narrowly tailored" to those theatres producing the unwanted secondary effects.[49]

(e) Obscenity and the Twenty–First Amendment

For a brief time, the Court ruled that the state had special power, under the Twenty–First Amendment, to regulate "adult" speech in establishments licensed by the state to serve liquor. As stated in *New York State Liquor Authority v. Bellanca*:[50] "The State's power to ban the sale of alcoholic beverages entirely includes the lesser power to ban the sale of

---

44. 452 U.S. at 74, 101 S.Ct. at 2185 (footnote omitted).

45. 452 U.S. at 71, 101 S.Ct. at 2184.

46. 475 U.S. 41, 106 S.Ct. 925, 89 L.Ed.2d 29 (1986), rehearing denied 475 U.S. 1132, 106 S.Ct. 1663, 90 L.Ed.2d 205 (1986).

47. 475 U.S. at 47, 106 S.Ct. at 929 (emphasis in original).

48. 475 U.S. at 48, 106 S.Ct. at 929 (emphasis in original).

49. 475 U.S. at 52, 106 S.Ct. at 931, contrasting Schad v. Mount Ephraim, 452 U.S. 61, 101 S.Ct. 2176, 68 L.Ed.2d 671 (1981). Compare Erznoznik v. Jacksonville, 422 U.S. 205, 95 S.Ct. 2268, 45 L.Ed.2d 125 (1975) (law too vague).

50. 452 U.S. 714, 101 S.Ct. 2599, 69 L.Ed.2d 357 (1981), on remand 54 N.Y.2d 228, 445 N.Y.S.2d 87, 429 N.E.2d 765 (1981), certiorari denied 456 U.S. 1006, 102 S.Ct. 2296, 73 L.Ed.2d 1300 (1982) (per curiam). Accord,

California v. LaRue, 409 U.S. 109, 93 S.Ct. 390, 34 L.Ed.2d 342 (1972), rehearing denied 410 U.S. 948, 93 S.Ct. 1351, 35 L.Ed.2d 615 (1973). *LaRue*, the first case that raised this issue, discussed the facts in some detail. In the licensed liquor establishments, there were both topless and bottomless dancers. "Customers were found engaging in oral copulation with women entertainers; customers engaged in public masturbation; and customers placed rolled currency either directly into the vagina of a female entertainer, or on the bar in order that she might pick it up herself. Numerous other forms of contact between the mouths of male customers and the vaginal areas of female performers were reported to have occurred." Some of the female dancers were involved in prostitution in and around the licensed premises and both rape and attempted rape took place "on or immediately adjacent to such premises." 409 U.S. 109, 111, 93 S.Ct. 390, 393, 34 L.Ed.2d 342 (1972), rehearing denied 410 U.S. 948, 93 S.Ct. 1351, 35 L.Ed.2d 615 (1973).

liquor on premises where topless dancing occurs."[51] The legislature judged that "mixing alcohol and nude dancing" causes disturbances that the state sought to avoid by placing restrictions on places that sell liquor for consumption on the premises. The Court said it should respect this judgment, to which the Twenty–First Amendment gave an "added presumption."[52]

The argument that the Twenty–First Amendment modifies the First Amendment is, frankly, a little strange. Should the state be able to forbid speech about politics in bars, on the ground that the state's power to ban all alcoholic beverages includes the "lesser power" to ban the sale of liquor on premises where political arguments occur? May the state take away the liquor license of a bar that allows religious debates on the premises, based on the claim that mixing alcohol and religious controversies cause disturbances?

The Twenty–First Amendment has long been used to grant the states extensive authority over liquor, and to some extent immunize state regulation from commerce clause challenge.[53] However, the Twenty–First Amendment has never been read to immunize state regulation over liquor from the civil liberties guarantees of the Constitution.[54]

The Court bowed to these logical arguments in *44 Liquormart, Inc. v. Rhode Island*.[55] The Court invalidated a state law that banned accurate retail liquor advertisements except at the point of sale, and rejected the state's argument that it could limit truthful information in an effort to manipulate consumers and promote temperance. In a portion of the decision that was an opinion of the Court, the Court emphatically disavowed the reasoning of cases like *Bellanca*. Justice Stevens, for the Court, announced that the result in the earlier cases would have been "precisely the same" even if there had been no reliance on the 21st Amendment. The Twenty-first Amendment "does not qualify the constitutional prohibition against laws abridging the freedom of speech embodied in the First Amendment."[56]

(f) Non–pictorial Obscenity

On the same day that *Miller v. California*[57] was decided, the Court ruled in *Kaplan v. California*[58] that books alone, containing only words and no pictures, may be obscene.[59] The

---

51. 452 U.S. at 717, 101 S.Ct. at 2601.

52. 452 U.S. at 718, 101 S.Ct. at 2602, quoting California v. LaRue, 409 U.S. 109, 118, 93 S.Ct. 390, 397, 34 L.Ed.2d 342 (1972), rehearing denied 410 U.S. 948, 93 S.Ct. 1351, 35 L.Ed.2d 615 (1973). Only Stevens, J., dissented. Marshall J., concurred in the judgment but filed no written opinion. Brennan, J., dissented from the summary disposition of the case and would have set it for oral argument.

On remand the New York State Court of Appeals held that the state statute violated the free speech provisions of the state constitution, because the Twenty–First Amendment does not confer a power on the states that is superior to, or free from, state constitutional restraints. 54 N.Y.2d 228, 445 N.Y.S.2d 87, 429 N.E.2d 765 (1981), certiorari denied 456 U.S. 1006, 102 S.Ct. 2296, 73 L.Ed.2d 1300 (1982). See also, 54 N.Y.2d at 241, 445 N.Y.S.2d at 93, 429 N.E.2d at 771 (Gabrielli, J., dissenting), citing Treatise.

53. See, e.g., State Bd. of Equalization v. Young's Market Co., 299 U.S. 59, 57 S.Ct. 77, 81 L.Ed. 38 (1936) (California may impose $500 fee for privilege of importing into that state beer from a sister state even though such a fee would have violated the commerce clause prior to the Twenty–First Amendment).

54. See, e.g., Craig v. Boren, 429 U.S. 190, 97 S.Ct. 451, 50 L.Ed.2d 397 (1976), rehearing denied 429 U.S. 1124, 97 S.Ct. 1161, 51 L.Ed.2d 574 (1977), where the Court invalidated a state statute prohibiting the sale of

3.2% beer to males under 21 and females under 18; the discrimination based on sex violated the equal protection guarantees of the Fourteenth Amendment.

55. 517 U.S. 484, 116 S.Ct. 1495, 134 L.Ed.2d 711 (1996).

56. 517 U.S. at 516, 116 S.Ct. at 1514. The Court similarly rejected the reasoning of cases that had relied on *LaRue*, such as New York State Liquor Authority v. Bellanca, 452 U.S. 714, 101 S.Ct. 2599, 69 L.Ed.2d 357 (1981)(per curiam); Newport v. Iacobucci, 479 U.S. 92, 107 S.Ct. 383, 93 L.Ed.2d 334 (1986)(per curiam). *LaRue* "did not involve commercial speech about alcohol, but instead concerned the regulation of nude dancing in places where alcohol was served." Rubin v. Coors Brewing Co., 514 U.S. 476, 482, 115 S.Ct. 1585, 1589, 131 L.Ed.2d 532 (1995).

57. 413 U.S. 15, 93 S.Ct. 2607, 37 L.Ed.2d 419 (1973), rehearing denied 414 U.S. 881, 94 S.Ct. 26, 38 L.Ed.2d 128 (1973).

58. 413 U.S. 115, 116, 93 S.Ct. 2680, 2682–83, 37 L.Ed.2d 492 (1973), rehearing denied 414 U.S. 883, 94 S.Ct. 28, 38 L.Ed.2d 131 (1973).

59. Only once between *Roth* and *Miller*, in Mishkin v. New York, 383 U.S. 502, 86 S.Ct. 958, 16 L.Ed.2d 56 (1966), rehearing denied 384 U.S. 934, 86 S.Ct. 1440, 16 L.Ed.2d 535 (1966), did the high Court hold books to be obscene, and in that case most if not all of the books were illustrated. 383 U.S. at 505, 86 S.Ct. at 961–62. See also Kaplan v. California, 413 U.S. 115, 118 n. 3, 93 S.Ct. 2680,

Court recognized that books "have a different and preferred place in our hierarchy of values.... "[60] But they nonetheless may be found to be obscene.

(g) Use of Experts

Once the allegedly obscene material is actually placed into evidence the state need not present expert testimony that the material is obscene, lacks serious artistic value, or any other ancillary evidence of obscenity.[61] The defense, however, is free to introduce appropriate expert testimony.[62]

(h) National Versus Local Standards

Part of *Miller v. California*[63] held that a state court may decide the obscenity question by applying contemporary community standards, not national standards. In that case, the state trial court instructed the jury to consider state community standards.

The following year the Court extended the *Miller* holding to apply to a federal prosecution.[64]

The Court has since made clear that *Miller* did not mandate use of a statewide standard. *Miller* permits the trial court to use a national standard, and the trial court may instruct the jury to apply "community standards" without instructing it what community was specified.[65] It is unclear if such holdings mean that a trial court may instruct the jury to apply national standards even if it could be shown that na-

tional standards apply a stricter definition of obscenity than local standards.

In *Smith v. United States*[66] the Court placed some limits on the power of the state to attempt to define legislatively the contemporary community standard of appeal to prurient interest or patent offensiveness. First, in *state* obscenity proceedings:

[The state could, if it wished] impose a geographic limit on the determination of community standards by defining the area from which the jury could be selected in an obscenity case, or by legislating with respect to the instructions that must be given to the jurors in such cases. [However] the question of the community standard to apply, when appeal to prurient interest and patent offensiveness are considered, is not one that can be defined legislatively.[67]

No state law can regulate distribution of obscene materials and define contemporary standards in *federal* obscenity proceedings. In a federal prosecution for mailing allegedly obscene material, it is irrelevant that the state in which the mailings took place did not even regulate obscenity aimed at adults, and that the mailings were wholly intrastate. A state's laissez-faire attitude towards obscenity cannot nullify federal efforts to regulate it. In federal obscenity prosecutions the federal courts should give federal jury instructions (not state jury instructions) as to community standards.[68]

2683 n. 3, 37 L.Ed.2d 492 (1973), rehearing denied 414 U.S. 883, 94 S.Ct. 28, 38 L.Ed.2d 131 (1973).

60. 413 U.S. at 119, 93 S.Ct. at 2684.

61. 413 U.S. at 121, 93 S.Ct. at 2685; Paris Adult Theatre I v. Slaton, 413 U.S. 49, 56, 93 S.Ct. 2628, 2634–35, 37 L.Ed.2d 446 (1973), rehearing denied 414 U.S. 881, 94 S.Ct. 27, 38 L.Ed.2d 128 (1973), on remand 231 Ga. 312, 201 S.E.2d 456 (1973), certiorari denied 418 U.S. 939, 94 S.Ct. 3227, 41 L.Ed.2d 1173 (1974).

There might be a case where the allegedly obscene material is directed at such a bizarre deviant group that the experience of the jurors would be inadequate to judge if the material appeals to the particular prurient interest. In such a case, the government may have to use expert testimony. Pinkus v. United States, 436 U.S. 293, 303, 98 S.Ct. 1808, 1814–15, 56 L.Ed.2d 293 (1978), on remand 579 F.2d 1174 (9th Cir.1978), certiorari dismissed 439 U.S. 999, 99 S.Ct. 605, 58 L.Ed.2d 674 (1978).

62. 413 U.S. at 121, 93 S.Ct. at 2685; Smith v. California, 361 U.S. 147, 164–65, 80 S.Ct. 215, 224–25, 4 L.Ed.2d 205 (1959) (Frankfurter, J., concurring).

63. 413 U.S. 15, 93 S.Ct. 2607, 37 L.Ed.2d 419 (1973), rehearing denied 414 U.S. 881, 94 S.Ct. 26, 38 L.Ed.2d 128 (1973).

64. Hamling v. United States, 418 U.S. 87, 105–06, 94 S.Ct. 2887, 2901–02, 41 L.Ed.2d 590 (1974), rehearing denied 419 U.S. 885, 95 S.Ct. 157, 42 L.Ed.2d 129 (1974).

65. Jenkins v. Georgia, 418 U.S. 153, 94 S.Ct. 2750, 41 L.Ed.2d 642 (1974), on remand 232 Ga. 797, 209 S.E.2d 151 (1974).

66. 431 U.S. 291, 97 S.Ct. 1756, 52 L.Ed.2d 324 (1977).

67. 431 U.S. at 303, 97 S.Ct. at 1765 (dictum).

68. 431 U.S. at 304, 97 S.Ct. at 1765–66.

Retroactive Application of *Miller* Test. The standards of Miller v. California, 413 U.S. 15, 93 S.Ct. 2607, 37 L.Ed.2d 419 (1973), rehearing denied 414 U.S. 881, 94 S.Ct. 26, 38 L.Ed.2d 128 (1973) are not applied retroactively to the extent that they burden criminal defendants but they are applied retroactively to the extent they benefit criminal defendants. Marks v. United States, 430 U.S. 188, 97 S.Ct. 990, 51 L.Ed.2d 260 (1977).

In *Pinkus v. United States*,[69] the Court clarified several requirements concerning jury instructions in federal obscenity prosecutions governed by the standards of *Roth v. United States*.[70] While *Pinkus* was decided under the *Roth* test of obscenity, the instructions approved of as to which people are in the community still should be law under *Miller v. California*.[71] because—as to that issue—*Miller* only rejected a national standards test in favor of a smaller geographic area: the actual local community.

The Court overturned Pinkus' conviction for mailing obscene materials based on its statutory interpretation that the court should not include children in determining what are the community standards.[72] *Pinkus* went on to state that under the Constitution, it was permissible to include "particularly sensitive persons" when considering community standards, because the "community includes all adults who comprise it." The jury may not be instructed to focus on the most susceptible and sensitive members of the community, but the jury need not exclude such people from the community as a whole for purposes of judging the material's obscenity.[73] Finally, the Constitution allows an instruction on prurient appeal to deviant sexual groups as part of the instruction concerning the appeal of the materials to the average person when the evidence supports such a charge.

In *Pope v. Illinois*,[74] the Court made clear that the "value" of an allegedly obscene work (the third prong of the *Miller* test) is not to be determined by the jury applying local "contemporary community standards" but by the jury being instructed to decide whether a reasonable person would find serious literary, artistic, political, or scientific value in the material taken as a whole.[75] The value of a work, unlike its prurient appeal or patent offensiveness (the first two elements of *Miller*) does not vary from community to community based on the degree of local acceptance it has won.

(i) Role of the Jury After *Miller*

While *Miller v. California*[76] talked of the necessity of relying on the jury system and suggested that there might be a lesser role for appellate courts in reviewing obscenity convictions, that has not come to pass. In *Jenkins v. Georgia*[77] the Court held that even though "questions of appeal to the 'prurient interest' or of patent offensiveness are 'essentially questions of fact'; it would be a serious misreading of *Miller* to conclude that juries have unbridled discretion in determining what is 'patently offensive.' "[78] The appellate courts can conduct an "independent review" of the constitutional claims where necessary.[79]

In *Jenkins* itself the Court concluded that "Our *own viewing of the film* satisfies us that . . ." it is not obscene.[80] In spite of *Miller*, the Court was still left with the burden of watching every movie in every obscenity case that it took. Justice Brennan commented that *Miller* and *Jenkins* seem to have brought the Court back to the case-by-case approach.[81]

69. 436 U.S. 293, 98 S.Ct. 1808, 56 L.Ed.2d 293 (1978), on remand 579 F.2d 1174 (9th Cir.1978), certiorari dismissed 439 U.S. 999, 99 S.Ct. 605, 58 L.Ed.2d 674 (1978).

70. 354 U.S. 476, 77 S.Ct. 1304, 1 L.Ed.2d 1498 (1957), rehearing denied 355 U.S. 852, 78 S.Ct. 8, 2 L.Ed.2d 60 (1957).

71. 413 U.S. 15, 93 S.Ct. 2607, 37 L.Ed.2d 419 (1973), rehearing denied 414 U.S. 881, 94 S.Ct. 26, 38 L.Ed.2d 128 (1973).

72. "[C]hildren are not to be included . . . as part of the 'community' as that term relates to the 'obscene materials' proscribed by 18 U.S.C.A. § 1461." 436 U.S. at 297, 98 S.Ct. at 1812. It appears that the decision is based on an interpretation of the federal statute. Whether the states, as a matter of constitutional law, must follow this ruling, was not an issue in the case.

73. 436 U.S. at 299–300, 98 S.Ct. at 1812–13.

74. 481 U.S. 497, 107 S.Ct. 1918, 95 L.Ed.2d 439 (1987), on remand 162 Ill.App.3d 299, 113 Ill.Dec. 547, 515 N.E.2d 356 (1987).

75. 481 U.S. at 501, 107 S.Ct. at 1921.

76. 413 U.S. 15, 93 S.Ct. 2607, 37 L.Ed.2d 419 (1973), rehearing denied 414 U.S. 881, 94 S.Ct. 26, 38 L.Ed.2d 128 (1973).

77. 418 U.S. 153, 94 S.Ct. 2750, 41 L.Ed.2d 642 (1974), on remand 232 Ga. 797, 209 S.E.2d 151 (1974).

78. 418 U.S. at 160, 94 S.Ct. at 2755.

79. 418 U.S. at 160, 94 S.Ct. at 2755.

80. 418 U.S. at 161, 94 S.Ct. at 2755 (emphasis added).

81. 418 U.S. at 162–165, 94 S.Ct. at 2755 (Brennan, J., concurring in the result, joined by Stevens & Marshall, JJ.).

If the state does not prosecute criminally, and brings a civil obscenity case, such as a proceeding to abate a public nuisance, or a case of prior restraint, there is no federal constitutional mandate requiring the state to use a jury.[82]

(j) Burden of Proof

If the government brings a *criminal* prosecution in an obscenity case, then it must prove its charges "beyond a reasonable doubt" because this burden of proof requirement is an element of due process binding on both the state and federal governments.[83] But an obscenity case may be a *civil* proceeding as well, such as a proceeding to abate a public nuisance. In such instances, there is no federal constitutional requirement of proof beyond a reasonable doubt.[84]

(k) Feminism and Pornography

The state can criminalize anything that is constitutionally "obscene." Many people also object to speech that is not constitutionally obscene, but is often called "adult" entertainment, or pornography, or simply dirty books. In this section of the treatise, let us here label such nonobscene speech as "pornography."[85]

Historically, support of laws to ban such pornography was based on the ground that the state should regulate to protect morality. By the late 1970's and the 1980's some people— using a new argument—objected to this type of speech. Some feminists focused their support of various types of anti-pornography legislation on the ground that the state should regulate because pornography degrades women.[86]

Thus, some feminists have proposed various antipornography ordinances. Supreme Court doctrine requires us to test these laws by the same legal principles that govern other obscenity legislation, whether the supporters of the laws base their arguments on the theory that pornography is immoral or that it is a form of sex discrimination. Good motives, or different motives, cannot validate an otherwise invalid law. Therefore, the federal court invalidated an Indianapolis ordinance that sought to limit the availability of materials that depict the "sexually explicit subordination of women, graphically depicted, whether in pictures or in words...."[87] The court found that this definition—and its use of the term "subordination of women"—was unconstitutionally vague.[88]

82. Melancon v. McKeithen, 345 F.Supp. 1025, 1035–45, 1048 (E.D.La.1972), affirmed sub nom. Mayes v. Ellis, 409 U.S. 943, 93 S.Ct. 289, 34 L.Ed.2d 214 (1972); Alexander v. Virginia, 413 U.S. 836, 93 S.Ct. 2803, 37 L.Ed.2d 993 (1973), rehearing denied 414 U.S. 881, 94 S.Ct. 29, 38 L.Ed.2d 128 (1973), mandate conformed 214 Va. 539, 203 S.E.2d 441 (1974) (per curiam). Brennan, J., joined by Marshall, J., dissented for the reasons stated in his separate opinion, concurring in part, in McKinney v. Alabama, 424 U.S. 669, 687–89, 96 S.Ct. 1189, 1199–1200, 47 L.Ed.2d 387 (1976).

83. In re Winship, 397 U.S. 358, 364, 90 S.Ct. 1068, 1072–73, 25 L.Ed.2d 368 (1970), mandate conformed 27 N.Y.2d 728, 314 N.Y.S.2d 536, 262 N.E.2d 675 (1970).

84. Cooper v. Mitchell Bros.' Santa Ana Theater, 454 U.S. 90, 102 S.Ct. 172, 70 L.Ed.2d 262 (1981), on remand 128 Cal.App.3d 937, 180 Cal.Rptr. 728 (1982), certiorari denied 459 U.S. 944, 103 S.Ct. 259, 74 L.Ed.2d 202 (1982), rehearing denied 459 U.S. 1093, 103 S.Ct. 581, 74 L.Ed.2d 940 (1982) (per curiam). The Court noted that in some civil areas of great importance it has required the "clear and convincing" standard of proof in civil cases, rather than the "preponderance of the evidence" test normally used. 454 U.S. at 93, 102 S.Ct. at 173. See, e.g., Addington v. Texas, 441 U.S. 418, 431, 99 S.Ct. 1804, 1812, 60 L.Ed.2d 323 (1979), on remand 588 S.W.2d 569 (Tex.1979) (clear and convincing standard in civil commitment); Rosenbloom v. Metromedia, 403 U.S. 29, 52, 91 S.Ct. 1811, 1824, 29 L.Ed.2d 296 (1971) (clear and convincing standard in libel cases) (opinion of Brennan, J.); Woodby v.

INS, 385 U.S. 276, 285–86, 87 S.Ct. 483, 487–88, 17 L.Ed.2d 362 (1966) (deportation); Chaunt v. United States, 364 U.S. 350, 353, 81 S.Ct. 147, 149–50, 5 L.Ed.2d 120 (1960) (deportation); Schneiderman v. United States, 320 U.S. 118, 159, 63 S.Ct. 1333, 1353, 87 L.Ed. 1796 (1943) (denaturalization). But see Vance v. Terrazas, 444 U.S. 252, 100 S.Ct. 540, 62 L.Ed.2d 461 (1980), rehearing denied 445 U.S. 920, 100 S.Ct. 1285, 63 L.Ed.2d 606 (1980), on remand 494 F.Supp. 1017 (N.D.Ill.1980), judgment affirmed 653 F.2d 285 (7th Cir.1981) (constitutional for Congress to establish preponderance of evidence standard in expatriation cases).

85. "Adult" entertainment is really a misnomer; it probably should be called callow entertainment, because it appeals to puerile or juvenile tastes.

86. The literature on this topic is growing. E.g., L. Lederer, ed., Take Back the Night: Women on Pornography (1980); S. Griffin, Pornography and Silence (1981); A. Dworkin, Pornography: Men Possessing Women (1981).

87. American Booksellers Ass'n, Inc. v. Hudnut, 598 F.Supp. 1316, 1329 (S.D.Ind.1984), affirmed 771 F.2d 323 (7th Cir.1985), rehearing denied 475 U.S. 1132, 106 S.Ct. 1664, 90 L.Ed.2d 206 (1986).

88. 598 F.Supp. at 1338. The court added:

"Many, if not all of the other words and phrases challenged by the plaintiff in this lawsuit on the grounds of vagueness are as difficult, indeed mystifying, as is 'the subordination of women.'"

While the court noted that the state has a strong interest in prohibiting sex discrimination and in protecting the physical and psychological well-being of women, this interest was not compelling enough to override the First Amendment.

It would be a mistake to conclude that all feminists support censorship of speech that is demeaning to women. Many feminists oppose such censorship and conclude that regulating "pornography" would undermine women's rights and interests by perpetuating patronizing stereotypes about women and their alleged innate sexual vulnerability.[89]

Moreover, there is no reason to believe that the censorship would be no broader than necessary. In fact, if the censorship were narrowly and carefully implemented, it would be the first time in history that the censor continually exercised self-restraint and did not eventually use the heavy hand of suppression.[90] Like the boy who said that he knew how to spell "banana," but did not know when to stop, censors do not know when to stop.

(l) Nude Dancing

For years the Court intimated that the First Amendment might protect nonobscene, public nude dancing as expressive conduct. It never elaborated on the degree of First Amendment protection that exists until *Barnes v. Glen Theatre, Inc.*[91] No opinion attracted a majority, but a majority of the Court did uphold an Indiana law that prohibited "knowingly or intentionally" appearing nude in "a public place."

Chief Justice Rehnquist's plurality opinion accepted the notion that nonobscene nude dancing has some free speech protection, but

he also acknowledged the substantial governmental interest in protecting societal order and morality. He treated the Indiana law as a question of symbolic speech and upheld the law because its restrictions were unrelated content and hence unrelated to the suppression of free speech. The law prohibited nudity, whether or not that nudity is combined with any expressive activity. The law does not single out and ban only nudity that conveys an erotic message. It bans all nudity. Nor does the law ban erotic dancing. Dancers can present erotic dances so long, as they are not nude. They must wear at least a scant amount of clothing.

Justice Scalia concurred in the judgment on the grounds that the statute was a general law regulating conduct and thus was entitled to no First Amendment scrutiny. It was not specifically directed against expression and did not target nude expression. Instead, it targeted public nudity and would apply to nude beaches as well as nude dancing. He also objected to the dissent's argument that the Indiana law cannot be applied to consenting adults. "The purpose of Indiana's nudity law would be violated, I think, if 60,000 consenting adults crowded into the Hoosier Dome to display their genitals to one another, even it there were not an offended innocent in the crowd."[92] The state often bans activities such as sadomasochism, bestiality, obscenity, and prostitution, even among consenting adults.

Justice Souter also concurred in the judgment, and would uphold the law because he claimed that it is similar to a zoning law intended to deal with harmful secondary effects and reduced property values associated

---

598 F.Supp. at 1339.

89. Nadine Strossen, A Feminist Critique of "the" Feminist Critique of Pornography, 79 Va.L.Rev. 1099 (1993). Nadine Strossen, The Convergence of Feminist and Civil Liberties Principles in the Pornography Debate, 62 N.Y.U.L.Rev. 201 (1987).

90. The Canadian Experience. The Supreme Court of Canada, in the case of Butler v. Her Majesty, 1 S.C.R. 452 (1992), adopted the theories of Catharine MacKinnon and Andrea Dworkin, who have argued that the government should ban sexually explicit or erotic words or images, on the grounds that they "degrade" women. The

Canadian authorities have used this power to ban lesbian, gay, and feminist materials. Canada even seized (as pornographic) two of Andrea Dworkin's books arguing that pornography should be banned! After a public outcry the authorities finally released the books. See Leanne Katz, Censors' Helpers, New York Times, Dec. 4, 1993, at 15, col. 3–6.

91. 501 U.S. 560, 111 S.Ct. 2456, 115 L.Ed.2d 504 (1991). See, Gardebring, J., citing Treatise in, Knudtson v. City of Coates, 519 N.W.2d 166, 170 (Minn.1994).

92. 501 U.S. at 575, 111 S.Ct. at 2465.

with adult entertainment.[93] He did not appear to be concerned that Indiana did not justify the law on those grounds and introduced no factual findings to support his hypothesis of reduced property values. No other Justice agreed with Souter's rationale.

Justice White, joined by Marshall, Blackmun, and Stevens, dissented. They argued that the Indiana law was not really a general prohibition of nudity because the law did not prohibit nudity in the home. (They also noted that Indiana could not constitutionally prohibit nudity in the home.) Hence, they would invalidate the law and could find no way that the legislature could write a statute that would be constitutional.

(m) Sexually Oriented Material on Broadcast or Cable Channels

Whatever the definition of "obscenity," if materials are found to be constitutionally "obscene," the Government can ban them from broadcast or cable channels, because the Government can ban completely any obscene materials. However, the Court has not always agreed on the power of the Government to ban or restrict materials that are not "obscene" in the constitutional sense but are sexually oriented—often called "adult material"[94]—when that material is broadcast over the airwaves or by cable.

In *FCC v. Pacifica Foundation*,[95] a majority of the Court, but without a majority opinion,

concluded that the FCC constitutionally could regulate "indecent" or "adult speech" that was broadcast over the radio air waves in the early afternoon, when the Court assumed that children were more likely to be in the listening audience. (Oddly enough, the Court did not weigh the possibility that children are more likely in school during the early afternoon.) The five Justices who upheld the power of the FCC to sanction the radio station emphasized that their rule was very narrow[96] and did not involve other means of broadcast, such as two-way radio or closed circuit transmission. Nor did the ruling, the Justices emphasized, cover broadcasts that had only an occasional expletive.

Denver Area Educational Telecommunications Consortium, Inc. v. FCC[97] considered challenges to three sections of the 1992 Cable Act designed to regulate cable television broadcasting of "patently offensive" sex-related material. The very fragmented Court invalidated two provisions of the Cable Television Consumer Protection and Competition Act of 1992 and upheld one provision.

A majority of the Justices decided that a provision of the Act that *permitted* the cable operator to prohibit patently offensive or indecent programming on public access channels violated the First Amendment. "PUBLIC ACCESS CHANNELS" are channel capacity that cable operators agreed to reserve for public, govern-

---

93. Cf. Renton v. Playtime Theatres, Inc., 475 U.S. 41, 106 S.Ct. 925, 89 L.Ed.2d 29 (1986), rehearing denied 475 U.S. 1132, 106 S.Ct. 1663, 90 L.Ed.2d 205 (1986).

94. The speech in question is often called "adult," although it is adolescent, callow, puerile speech and it might be more correct to call it "infantile" or "juvenile."

95. 438 U.S. 726, 98 S.Ct. 3026, 57 L.Ed.2d 1073 (1978), rehearing denied, 439 U.S. 883, 99 S.Ct. 227, 58 L.Ed.2d 198 (1978). Compare, Sable Communications of California, Inc. v. FCC, 492 U.S. 115, 109 S.Ct. 2829, 106 L.Ed.2d 93 (1989), which upheld the Communications Act outright ban on constitutionally obscene pre-recorded commercial telephone messages (so-called "dial-a-porn"), but invalidated the portion of the Act that banned "indecent" (but not constitutionally obscene) messages, regardless of age. The Government, in that instance, could have protected minors by a much more narrowly drafted statute. The FCC's own investigation showed that access codes and scrambling rules would be sufficient to keep indecent messages out of the reach of minors.

96. Later, Sable Communications of California, Inc. v. FCC, 492 U.S. 115, 109 S.Ct. 2829, 106 L.Ed.2d 93 (1989) described *Pacifica* was "an emphatically narrow holding." Ronald D. Rotunda, Current Proposals for Media Accountability in Light of the First Amendment, 21 Social Philosophy & Policy 269 (No. 2 Cambridge University Press, 2004).

97. 518 U.S. 727, 116 S.Ct. 2374, 135 L.Ed.2d 888 (1996). Justice Breyer wrote the plurality Opinion and the Opinion of the Court. Stevens, O'Connor, Kennedy, Souter, & Ginsburg, JJ., joined the Opinion of the Court. Breyer also delivered an Opinion with respect to Parts I, II, & V (which Stevens, O'Connor & Souter, JJ., joined), and an Opinion with respect to Parts IV & VI (which Stevens & Souter, JJ., joined). Stevens, J., and Souter, J., filed concurring opinions. O'Connor, J., filed an Opinion concurring in part and dissenting in part. Kennedy, J., filed an Opinion concurring in part, concurring in the judgment in part, & dissenting in part (which Ginsburg, J., joined). Thomas, J., filed an Opinion concurring in the judgment in part & dissenting in part (which Rehnquist, C.J., & Scalia, JJ., joined).

mental, and educational access as part of the consideration that municipalities obtained in exchange for awarding a cable franchise.

On the other hand, a majority of the Justices concluded that a provision *permitting* the operator to prohibit patently offensive or indecent programming on leased access channels was found to be constitutional. A "LEASED CABLE CHANNEL" is a channel that the relevant federal law required a cable system operator to reserve for commercial lease by unaffiliated third parties. Finally, the fragmented Court invalidated a third provision, that *required* leased channel operators to segregate "patently offensive" programming on a single channel and to block that channel from viewer access, and then to un-block it (or re-block it) within 30 days of a subscriber's written request.

Justice Kennedy's separate opinion concurring in the judgment would have invalidated all of the provisions of the law. Kennedy criticized the narrowness of the Breyer plurality. "When confronted with a threat to free speech in the context of an emerging technology, we ought to have the discipline to analyze the case by reference to existing elaborations of constant First Amendment principles."[98] Justice Breyer, in contrast, was unwilling to embrace any definite standard.

(n) Sexually Oriented Material on the Internet

Reno v. ACLU[99] invalidated various provisions of the Communications Decency Act of 1996 ("CDC"),[100] which were designed to protect minors from allegedly "indecent" and "patently offensive" material on the Internet. Cyberspace, like the physical world, is entitled to the protections of the First Amendment. The Court has granted the Government great-

er power to regulation the broadcast media on the grounds that there is a scarcity of broadcast channels and it is invasive in nature. These considerations simply do not apply to cyberspace.[101]

First, the Court concluded that the provisions of the CDC prohibiting transmission of obscene or indecent communications by means of a telecommunications to persons under the age of 18, or sending patently offensive communications to persons under the age of 18, were content-based restrictions on speech, not time, place or manner regulations. Because they were content-based, there they were overbroad on their face in violation of the First Amendment.

The CDC s prohibition of indecent transmission and patently offensive" communications abridge freedom of speech. These terms are vague and ambiguous, and the statute does not require that the patently offensive material lack socially redeeming value. It does not allow parents to consent to their children's use of the restricted materials. The law suppresses materials that adults have a constitutional right to send and receive. The law does not allow less restrictive alternatives, such as currently available user-based software that parents can use to limit what their children can access.

Pursuant to the severability clause in the statute, the Court severed the word "indecent" from § 223(a) of the CDC, and allowed the Government to prohibit the transmission of material that is constitutionally "obscene." The Government can ban "obscene" speech in its entirety, so it can ban such speech from cyberspace as well.[102]

---

98. 518 U.S. at 781, 116 S.Ct. at 2404.

99. 521 U.S. 844, 117 S.Ct. 2329, 138 L.Ed.2d 874 (1997). O'Connor, J., joined by Rehnquist, C.J., filed an opinion concurring in the judgment in part and dissenting in part.

100. See Title V of the Telecommunications Act of 1996, Pub. L. 104–104.

101. E.g. FCC v. Pacifica Foundation, 438 U.S. 726, 98 S.Ct. 3026, 57 L.Ed.2d 1073 (1978), rehearing denied, 439 U.S. 883, 99 S.Ct. 227, 58 L.Ed.2d 198 (1978).

102. Congress responded to *Reno v. ACLU* by enacting the Child Online Protection Act ("COPA"). Respondents promptly filed a facial challenge to COPA on First Amendment grounds, the Third Circuit affirmed a preliminary injunction, but the Supreme Court reversed, holding that COPA's reliance on community standards to identify material harmful to minors "does not by itself render the statute substantially overbroad for purposes of the First Amendment." The Court then remanded for further proceedings. The Third Circuit again invalidated the act, ACLU v. Ashcroft, 322 F.3d 240 (3d Cir.2003), cert. granted, 540 U.S. ___, 124 S.Ct. 399, 157 L.Ed.2d 274 (2003).

Chapter 17

FREEDOM OF RELIGION

§ 17.1 Introduction—The Natural Antagonism Between the Two Clauses

There are two clauses of the First Amendment which deal with the subject of religion.[1] The Amendment mandates that "Congress shall make no law respecting an establishment of religion, or prohibiting the free exercise thereof. . . ." The first clause is referred to as the establishment clause; the second is the free exercise clause. The Supreme Court has held that both of these clauses are made applicable to the states by the due process clause of the Fourteenth Amendment.[2]

There is a natural antagonism between a command not to establish religion and a command not to inhibit its practice. This tension between the clauses often leaves the Court with having to choose between competing values in religion cases. The general guide here is the concept of "neutrality." The opposing values require that the government act to achieve only secular goals and that it achieve them in a religiously neutral manner. Unfortunately, situations arise where government may have no choice but to incidentally help or hinder religious groups or practices.

In the middle of the twentieth century, Professor Philip Kurland advanced the theory that government can only remain neutral by prohibiting the use of religion as a standard for government action.[3] So long as a law avoids "classification in terms of religion either to confer a benefit or to impose a burden"[4] he would find it in conformity with both clauses. This position has much to recommend it, for insistence on avoiding incidental aid to religion is likely to inhibit its free exercise. Similarly, requiring a great degree of government accommodation of religious practices might result in impermissible aid to religion. However, despite the great theoretical appeal of the Kurland position,[5] the Court has never adopted such a theory. Instead the Court has reviewed the claims under the different clauses on independent bases and has developed separate tests for determining whether a law violates either clause. While "neutrality" is still a central principle of both clauses, we have no single standard for determining what is a religiously neutral act. Instead, we must examine the neutrality or permissibility of a law in terms of the challenge to it.

As we will see in other sections in this chapter, the Supreme Court has been sensitive to the concept of neutrality as a central principle of the religion clauses in its refusal to define the nature of the types of beliefs constituting religious beliefs and in its circumscrip-

§ 17.1

1. It should also be noted that art. VI, cl. 3, of the Constitution provides that "no religious Test shall ever be required as a Qualification to any Office of Public Trust under the United States."

2. The free exercise clause was first held applicable to the states in Cantwell v. Connecticut, 310 U.S. 296, 60 S.Ct. 900, 84 L.Ed. 1213 (1940). The establishment clause was held applicable to the states in Everson v. Board of Education, 330 U.S. 1, 67 S.Ct. 504, 91 L.Ed. 711 (1947),

rehearing denied 330 U.S. 855, 67 S.Ct. 962, 91 L.Ed. 1297 (1947).

3. P. Kurland, Religion and Law (1962).

4. Kurland, supra note 3, at 112.

5. For additional citations to secondary sources on this topic see, R. Rotunda & J. Nowak, Treatise on Constitutional Law: Substance and Procedure, § 17.1 (3rd ed. 1999, with annual supplements).

tion of governmental authority to either define religion or inquire into the sincerity of religious beliefs in some circumstances.[6]

In at least one respect, the neutrality concept has given rise to a principle that applies in both establishment clause and free exercise clause cases. Both clauses will prevent the government from singling out specific religious sects for special benefits or burdens. If the government were to give benefits to a group of persons defined by their religious beliefs, it would have created a sect preference that would violate the establishment clause unless it was necessary to promote a compelling interest.[7] If the government were to impose burdens on a group of persons solely because of their religious beliefs, its action would violate the free exercise clause unless the action was necessary to promote a compelling interest.[8]

A law that is alleged to violate the establishment clause will not be insulated from judicial review by a presumption of constitutionality. When examining a law that provides incidental aid to religion, the Supreme Court will question whether the law could have a non-religious purpose, whether its primary effect is one that advances or inhibits religion, and whether the law creates an impermissible entanglement between government and religion.[9] In contrast with its review of laws under the establishment clause, the Court will give great deference to religiously neutral government actions that are challenged under the free exercise clause. The Supreme Court has found

that the free exercise clause does not give an individual a right to be exempted from a religiously neutral criminal law based solely on the fact that the individual cannot comply with both the law and her religious beliefs.[10]

The Supreme Court's adoption of separate tests for establishment clause and free exercise clause cases may seem to bring the values embodied in those two clauses into conflict. Perhaps the Court's creation of independent tests has put American governmental entities in a position in neutrality towards religion that accommodates the values of both clauses, but that is a value judgment that each reader must make for himself or herself. In the last sections of this chapter a series of problems, under the general title of "Other Establishment—Free Exercise Problems",[11] we examine a series of problems in which the Supreme Court has directly confronted the apparent tension between its establishment clause and free exercise clause rulings. The case descriptions in the sections of this Chapter titled "The Establishment Clause,"[12] and "The Free Exercise Clause,"[13] will also include some examination of whether the Supreme Court's rulings on a specific area created some tension between the establishment clause and free exercise clause values.

When the Supreme Court examines a legislative attempt to accommodate religious activities or organizations, the judicial examination of that legislative action will involve a determination of whether the legislature's promotion of free exercise values aided religion in a man-

---

6. See §§ 17.8, 17.9(a), 17.11, 17.12, infra.

The Supreme Court has upheld government programs providing aid to students at all schools, including students attending religiously affiliated schools, when the criteria used for the distribution of the aid was religiously neutral. These cases are discussed in §§ 17.3, 17.4 of this Treatise.

7. See, e.g., Board of Education of Kiryas Joel Village School District v. Grumet, 512 U.S. 687, 114 S.Ct. 2481, 129 L.Ed.2d 546 (1994); Larson v. Valente, 456 U.S. 228, 102 S.Ct. 1673, 72 L.Ed.2d 33 (1982), rehearing denied 457 U.S. 1111, 102 S.Ct. 2916, 73 L.Ed.2d 1323 (1982). See § 17.3 of this Treatise.

8. See, e.g., Church of the Lukumi Babalu Aye, Inc. v. Hialeah, 508 U.S. 520, 113 S.Ct. 2217, 124 L.Ed.2d 472 (1993), on remand 2 F.3d 369 (11th Cir.1993). See §§ 17.6, 17.8 of this Treatise.

9. We will examine the Supreme Court's establishment clause rulings in §§ 17.3–17.5

10. The Court will invalidate any law that it deems to be a direct punishment of religious beliefs, even though it will not require the government to grant individuals religiously based exemptions from neutral laws. We will examine the free exercise clause rulings of the Supreme Court in §§ 17.6–17.9.

11. See §§ 17.10–17.16

12. See part II of this Chapter, §§ 17.3–17.5. The tension between accommodating and advancing religion is brought out in the variety of problems that the Court has faced regarding "religion and the public schools," see §§ 17.5(a), 17.5(e).

13. See § 17.6–17.9.

ner that violated the establishment clause.[14]

An example of the way in which the judicial definition of values under the religion clauses has created a tension between those two clauses is *Texas Monthly, Inc. v. Bullock.*[15] In this decision, the Supreme Court by a vote of six to three, invalidated a Texas statute that exempted from the state sales tax those "periodicals that are published or distributed by a religious faith and that consists wholly of writings promulgating the teaching of the faith and books that consist wholly of writings sacred to a religious faith." Justice White believed that this statute violated the press clause of the First Amendment, and did not reach the problem of whether the statute also violated the establishment clause.[16] Five Justices believed that this legislative attempt to accommodate religious activities violated the establishment clause, but there was no majority opinion explaining why the statute was invalid. Justice Brennan, joined by Justices Marshall and Stevens, found that laws that aid religion, whether or not they are designed to "accommodate" religion, must be reviewed under the standards that the Court has developed in its establishment clause cases.[17] In the view of the Brennan plurality, the Supreme Court's earlier decisions approving exemptions from taxes

for religious organizations involve statutes that exempted religious organizations together with other organizations that provided nonsectarian public services (such as a tax exemption given to all nonprofit private schools, both religious and nonreligious).[18] In the view of these Justices, a legislative accommodation of religion is permissible only if the statute aids a large group of activities defined in nonreligious terms (of which religious activity could be a part).[19] The Brennan plurality opinion found that the Supreme Court cases from the 1940s that prohibited the imposition of a flat fee license tax on persons who came into a state to engage in preaching and selling of religious books or pamphlets only meant that the free exercise clause would prevent the government from establishing a special tax on religious activities, or from applying a flat fee license tax to religious preachers if the structure of the tax was such that it would effectively prevent persons from engaging in the religious activity.[20]

Justices Blackmun and O'Connor, in the *Texas Monthly* decision, believed that the Texas statute violated the establishment clause, although they found it "difficult to reconcile in this case the Free Exercise and Establishment

---

14. In addition to the case discussed in the closing paragraphs of this section, the Court has examined legislative attempts to accommodate religion when it has reviewed laws regulating employment practices of both nonreligious and religious entities. See §§ 17.3, 17.5, 17.6, 17.15.

15. 489 U.S. 1, 109 S.Ct. 890, 103 L.Ed.2d 1 (1989).

16. 489 U.S. at 25, 109 S.Ct. at 905 (White, J., concurring).

17. Texas Monthly, Inc. v. Bullock, 489 U.S. 1, 109 S.Ct. 890, 103 L.Ed.2d 1 (1989) (Brennan, J., announces the judgment of the Court in an opinion joined by Marshall and Stevens, JJ.).

18. The tax exemption case that was the subject of dispute between the Justices was Walz v. Tax Commission, 397 U.S. 664, 90 S.Ct. 1409, 25 L.Ed.2d 697 (1970) (sustaining a property tax exemption that applied to property owned by religious organizations; the real estate tax also provided the tax exemption to a variety of nonprofit organizations).

19. The Supreme Court has upheld the exemption of religious organizations from laws prohibiting employment discrimination on the basis of religion, so that a religious organization could make membership in the religion an

employment qualification. Corporation of Presiding Bishop of Church of Jesus Christ of Latter–day Saints v. Amos, 483 U.S. 327, 107 S.Ct. 2862, 97 L.Ed.2d 273 (1987). The Supreme Court has invalidated a statute that required employers to give every employee a release from work on the employee's Sabbath. Estate of Thornton v. Caldor, Inc., 472 U.S. 703, 105 S.Ct. 2914, 86 L.Ed.2d 557 (1985). See §§ 17.13, 17.15.

20. See Murdock v. Pennsylvania, 319 U.S. 105, 117, 63 S.Ct. 870, 876–77, 87 L.Ed. 1292 (1943); Follett v. Town of McCormick, 321 U.S. 573, 64 S.Ct. 717, 88 L.Ed. 938 (1944). In a case decided one year after the *Texas Monthly* decision, the Justices unanimously found that these decisions from the 1940s did not give religious organizations a right to be exempt from taxes of general applicability. Jimmy Swaggart Ministries v. Board of Equalization, 493 U.S. 378, 110 S.Ct. 688, 107 L.Ed.2d 796 (1990) (religious organization has no constitutional right to an exemption from a general sales and use tax law that would require the religious organization to collect and pay such taxes for the sales of goods and literature in a state). The taxes invalidated in the 1940s decisions were flat-fee license taxes that the Supreme Court found to be an invalid means of restricting the ability to engage in First Amendment activities in a manner similar to an invalid prior restraint on speech.

Clause values." [21] These two Justices believed that a state could draft a tax exemption statute that would preserve both free exercise and establishment clause values by defining the class of literature that was exempt from the tax laws to include both religious literature and "philosophical literature distributed by nonreligious organizations devoted to such matters of conscience as life and death, good and evil, being and nonbeing, right and wrong." [22] Such a tax exemption might not survive the establishment clause tests espoused by Justice Brennan, because it would involve tax exempt class of activities that were either religious activities or activities that were clearly analogous to religious activities.

Justice Scalia was joined by Chief Justice Rehnquist and Justice Kennedy in dissent. [23] These Justices believed that the Supreme Court holding in the *Texas Monthly* case, and the opinions of both Justice Brennan and Justice Blackmun, subordinated free exercise clause values to values that the majority read into the establishment clause. In the view of the dissent, the accommodation of religion that was required by the free exercise clause meant that a law that was designed to accommodate religion did not endanger the values of the establishment clause.

In *Santa Fe Independent School District v. Doe*[24] the Justices, by a 6 to 3 vote, invalidated a school district policy that permitted students to elect a student to give a non-denominational prayer before public school football games. Justice Stevens wrote for six members of the Court in finding that such a program was not a neutral accommodation of religion. [25] Rather,

the majority opinion ruled that the football game prayer program involved: an impermissible religious based purpose in its adoption; government endorsement of religion; and to some extent, the coercion of persons who did not believe in religion who attended the football games. Chief Justice Rehnquist, joined by Justices Scalia and Thomas, dissented in *Santa Fe Independent School District*. The dissenters believed that the school program should not have been invalidated on its face, because they believed the program was capable of being applied in a religiously neutral manner. [26]

§ 17.2   The Appeal to History

There is a seemingly irresistible impulse to appeal to history when analyzing issues under the religion clauses. This tendency is unfortunate because there is no clear history as to the meaning of the clauses. It is of course true that many of the colonists fled religious persecution, but in this country the experience differed widely throughout the colonies. It is common to refer to the Virginia experience when arguing for a complete separation of religious matters from secular government. In Virginia, Jefferson and Madison led a continuing battle for total religious freedom and an end of government aid to religion. Their position was most clearly stated by Madison in his "Memorial and Remonstrance" against an assessment bill to aid religion. [1] The First Amendment was a product of Madison and the Virginia influence in the first Congress. However, this is not the only history that is relevant to these issues. The clauses were ratified as a part of the Bill of Rights, and the inten-

---

21. Texas Monthly, Inc. v. Bullock, 489 U.S. 1, 25, 109 S.Ct. 890, 905, 103 L.Ed.2d 1 (1989) (Blackmun, J., joined by O'Connor, J., concurring in the judgment).

22. 489 U.S. at 26, 109 S.Ct. at 906.

23. Texas Monthly, Inc. v. Bullock, 489 U.S. 1, 28, 109 S.Ct. 890, 907, 103 L.Ed.2d 1 (1989) (Scalia, J., joined by Rehnquist, C.J., and Kennedy, J., dissenting).

24. Santa Fe Independent School District v. Doe, 530 U.S. 290, 120 S.Ct. 2266, 147 L.Ed.2d 295 (2000).

25. The Court in the Santa Fe Independent School District Case relied heavily on *Lee v. Weisman*, 505 U.S. 577, 112 S.Ct. 2649, 120 L.Ed.2d 467 (1992) (finding that a public school graduation ceremony involving nonsectarian prayer by a member of the clergy violated the establishment clause).

26. Santa Fe Independent School District v. Doe, 530 U.S. 290, 316, 120 S.Ct. 2266, 2283, 147 L.Ed.2d 295 (2000) (Rehnquist, C.J., joined by Scalia and Thomas, JJ., dissenting).

§ 17.2

1. This Madison "Remonstrance" was reprinted in Walz v. Tax Com'n, 397 U.S. 664, 719–27, 90 S.Ct. 1409, 1437–41, 25 L.Ed.2d 697 (1970) (Douglas, J., dissenting, app. II). For citations to secondary sources on this topic see, R. Rotunda & J. Nowak, Treatise on Constitutional Law: Substance and Procedure, § 17.2 (3rd ed. 1999, with annual supplements).

tion of those in the ratifying states should be as important as that of the Virginia representatives. Moreover, because the First Amendment was only a limitation on the actions of the federal government,[2] one could read this history as an affirmance of state sovereignty over this subject.

In other states close ties existed between church and state, with a number of states having established churches until well after the time of the revolution.[3] For these states the Amendment insured that the federal government could not interfere with their state preferences for certain religions. It also would forbid the federal government from benefiting one religion over another. The close ties between religion and state governments indicate that many states would not have opposed federal government aid to all religions on an equal basis. Indeed, Justice Story was certain that the federal government was barred only from punishing or benefiting specific religions.[4] He thought the Amendment allowed for aid to all religions on an equal basis. However, beyond this unclear history, little can be said with any certainty. Even after the established churches had ended in the states, aid to religious entities continued. For example, religious teachers often made use of public schools, and the tax exempt status of churches was guaranteed in many states.[5]

The religion clauses were among the first portions of the Bill of Rights incorporated into the Fourteenth Amendment and made applicable to the states by the Supreme Court. Although the original understanding of the drafters of the First and Fourteenth Amendments may be unclear, a majority of the Justices on the Supreme Court during the past 50 years consistently has held that the values protected by the religion clauses are funda-

mental aspects of liberty in our society and must be protected from both state and federal interference.

Since assessing history to determine the exact meaning of the religious freedom that was to be guaranteed by the First Amendment will not produce clear answers to current issues, we must plunge ahead and study the development of the separate doctrines in the case law. Here we will find that the Court has both found and created certain "historic" principles which are suited to protecting religious freedom—past and present. As almost all of the important Supreme Court decisions in this area have come after 1940, we have only the modern Court's view of history and the Justices' current tests to guide us.[6]

§ 17.3 The Establishment Clause—Introduction

The establishment clause applies to both the federal and local governments. It is a prohibition of government sponsorship of religion which requires that government neither aid nor formally establish a religion. While at its inception the clause might not have been intended to prohibit governmental aid to all religions, the accepted view today is that it also prohibits a preference for religion over nonreligion. However, the government simply cannot avoid aiding religion in some manner unless it actively opposes religion—something that it is forbidden to do by the free exercise clause. For example, the granting of police or fire protection to churches clearly aids the practice of religion, but the withholding of such services would single out religious activities for a special burden. Thus it is clear that some test is required to determine when such

---

2. In Barron v. Mayor and City Council of City of Baltimore, 32 U.S. (7 Pet.) 243, 8 L.Ed. 672 (1833) the Court, per Chief Justice Marshall, held that the Bill of Rights was not applicable to the activities of state or local governments.

3. For an examination of early history of church-state relationship and theories, see C. Antieau, A. Downey, & E. Roberts, Freedom From Federal Establishment (1964).

4. J. Story, Commentaries on the Constitution of the United States 627–34 (5th ed. 1891).

5. See, Choper, The Establishment Clause and Aid to Parochial Schools, 56 Calif.L.Rev. 260, 263 (1969); C. Antieau, P. Carroll, C. Antieau, P. Carroll, & T. Burke, Religion under the State Constitutions (1965).

6. The Supreme Court did decide several important cases under the free exercise clause between 1878 and 1940. These are discussed in § 17.7, infra.

incidental aid is permissible and when it is prohibited.[1]

Since 1970, the Supreme Court has considered three factors when determining whether a government action that does not include a "sect preference" violates the establishment clause. When determining whether a law that is religiously neutral on its face violates the establishment clause, the Court will consider: (1) whether the law has a secular purpose; (2) whether the primary effect of the law advances or inhibits religion; (3) whether the law creates an excessive entanglement between government and religion.

From 1970 to 1997, the Supreme Court ruled that a three part test would be used in establishment clause cases. The three part test is often referred to as "the *Lemon* test," or "the *Lemon* tests," because the Court in *Lemon v. Kurtzman*[2] ruled that a law would violate the establishment clause unless it had a secular purpose, a primary effect that neither advanced nor inhibited religion, and avoided creating an "excessive entanglement" between government and religion. The Court

in *Lemon* also found that, when in determining whether a statute that provided financial aid to an institution involved an "excessive entanglement" between government and religion, the judiciary must consider the nature of the institution that received the benefit from the government, the nature of the aid that the government gave to the religiously affiliated institution, and the resulting relationship between the government and religious authorities.[3]

In 1997, in *Agostini v. Felton*,[4] a majority of the Justices found that the judiciary must consider the purpose and effect of a law to determine whether a law that provides government aid to a religious institution violated the establishment clause. The majority opinion in *Agostini*, written by Justice O'Connor, described the inquiry into whether the government aid program gave rise to excessive entanglement between the government and religion as a part of the judicial inquiry into whether the challenged governmental program had the impermissible primary effect of aiding or inhibiting religion.[5] The Court in *Agostini* "re-

§ 17.3

1. A legislative accommodation of religion may or may not survive review under the establishment clause, depending on the particular statute. For example, the Supreme Court in Corporation of the Presiding Bishop of the Church of Jesus Christ of Latter–day Saints v. Amos, 483 U.S. 327, 107 S.Ct. 2862, 97 L.Ed.2d 273 (1987) upheld a statutory exemption for religious organizations from the statutory prohibition against discrimination in employment on the basis of religion. The exemption allowed a religious organization to make employment decisions based on the religious beliefs of job applicants or employees, although a nonreligious organization could not distinguish between its employees on the basis of religion. The majority opinion found that a legislative purpose of avoiding "governmental interference" with the religious organization's activities was a permissible purpose. The Supreme Court also found that the exemption did not aid religion or did not create an entanglement between government and religion. Conversely, in Estate of Thornton v. Caldor, Inc., 472 U.S. 703, 105 S.Ct. 2914, 86 L.Ed.2d 557 (1985) the Supreme Court invalidated a state statute that gave every employee a right to be released from work on the employee's Sabbath. Writing for a majority in *Estate of Thornton,* Chief Justice Burger found that the law had a primary effect that advanced religion because it subjected employers and coworkers of the religious employee to significant costs in order to accommodate the desire of an employee to take actions based upon his religion. These cases are examined in §§ 17.13, 17.15.

2. Lemon v. Kurtzman, 403 U.S. 602, 91 S.Ct. 2105, 29 L.Ed.2d, 745 (1971). In 1970 the Court had indicated that

it would adopt a three part test for analyzing whether religiously neutral laws involved a form of impermissible aid to religious entities in Walz v. Tax Commission, 397 U.S. 664, 90 S.Ct. 1409, 25 L.Ed.2d 697 (1970). The cases preceding and establishing the three part test for establishment clause issues are examined in § 17.4. In some establishment clause cases in the 1980's and 1990's, the Supreme Court ruled that government actions violated the establishment clause without expressly relying on, or rejecting, the purpose—effect–entanglement test. See, e.g., County of Allegheny v. American Civil Liberties Union, 492 U.S. 573, 109 S.Ct. 3086, 106 L.Ed.2d 472 (1989) (invalidating the government's display of religious symbols on government property under the facts of the case); Lee v. Weisman, 505 U.S. 577, 112 S.Ct. 2649, 120 L.Ed.2d 467 (1992) (religious invocation at the start of a public high school graduation violates the establishment clause).

3. Lemon v. Kurtzman, 403 U.S. 602, 615, 91 S.Ct. 2105, 2122, 29 L.Ed.2d 745 (1971).

4. 521 U.S. 203, 117 S.Ct. 1997, 138 L.Ed.2d 391 (1997) overruling Aguilar v. Felton, 473 U.S. 402, 105 S.Ct. 3232, 87 L.Ed.2d 290 (1985).

5. Agostini v. Felton, 521 U.S. 203, 234, 117 S.Ct. 1997, 2015, 138 L.Ed.2d 391 (1997).

Justice O'Connor, writing for the majority in *Agostini,* endorsed an inquiry into the purpose, effect, and excessive entanglement factors for determining the compatibility of a government aid program with the establishment clause. In other cases, Justice O'Connor has advanced the idea that the establishment clause creates a "non-endorsement

packaged" the three part purpose–effect–entanglement test that had been used from 1971 to 1997. Nevertheless, the Justices in *Agostini* indicated that they would continue to examine the purpose, effect, and entanglement factors when determining whether a facially neutral law provided aid to religious persons, or religious institutions, in a way that would violate the establishment clause.

The Supreme Court will not make an inquiry into the purpose or effect of a law that creates a "denominational preference" or a "sect preference" for religious entities. The Court will not inquire into whether denominational preference or sect preference gives rise to an excessive entanglement between government and religion. Rather, the Court will rule that any law that employs a denominational preference violates the establishment clause unless the government can demonstrate that the law is necessary to promote a compelling interest. If a law creates a denominational preference it will violate the establishment clause unless its distinction between different religious denominations is necessary to promote a compelling interest. It is difficult to imagine the circumstances under which the government would have a compelling need to prefer some religions over others.

Because of the stringency of the test used to examine denominational preferences, some cases involve disputes concerning whether a denominational preference was created by a statute. For example, in *Larson v. Valente*[6] the Supreme Court invalidated a state statute that regulated the solicitation of donations by charitable organizations if, but only if, the

organization solicited more than 50% of its funds from nonmembers. This law was viewed as creating a denominational preference because the burdens of the regulation, in the view of the Court, clearly discriminated against religious organizations that were significantly involved in fund raising activities aimed at nonmembers. The majority opinion in *Larson* was written by Justice Brennan; he found that the imposition of regulatory burdens only on certain types of charitable and religious fund raising was not "closely fitted" to any compelling interest. Therefore, the law violated the establishment clause, and no further examination of the statute under other types of establishment clause tests was necessary.

The Court in *Larson* chose to base its decision on the establishment clause. The law at issue in *Larson* also could have been invalidated under the free exercise clause, if the majority had chosen to categorize the law as being an attempt to suppress the activity of identifiable religious groups with a law that was not a religiously neutral law of general applicability.[7]

In the 1990s, the Supreme Court slightly modified the three part purpose-effect-entanglement test. Nevertheless, the Justices remained committed to enforcing the concept of religious neutrality in establishment clause rulings; neither denominational preferences nor delegations of government authority to religious sects would survive establishment clause review.

In *Agostini v. Felton*[8] the Supreme Court, in a majority opinion written by Justice O'Con-

---

principle" that prohibits the government from taking actions that constitute the endorsement of religion or particular religious sects. See, e.g., Capitol Square Review and Advisory Board v. Pinette, 515 U.S. 753, 771, 115 S.Ct. 2440, 2451, 132 L.Ed.2d 650 (1995) O'Connor, J., (joined by Souter and Breyer, J.J., concurring in part and concurring in the judgment); Lynch v. Donnelly, 465 U.S. 668, 690, 104 S.Ct. 1355, 1366, 79 L.Ed.2d 604 (1984) (O'Connor, J., concurring); Witters v. Washington Department of Services for the Blind, 474 U.S. 481, 493, 106 S.Ct. 748, 755, 88 L.Ed.2d 846 (1986) (O'Connor, J., concurring); County of Allegheny v. American Civil Liberties Union, 492 U.S. 573, 623, 109 S.Ct. 3086, 3117, 106 L.Ed.2d 472 (1989) (O'Connor, J., concurring in part and concurring in the judgment).

6. 456 U.S. 228, 102 S.Ct. 1673, 72 L.Ed.2d 33 (1982), rehearing denied 457 U.S. 1111, 102 S.Ct. 2916, 73 L.Ed.2d 1323 (1982).

7. The Supreme Court relied on *Larson* in Church of the Lukumi Babalu Aye, Inc. v. Hialeah, 508 U.S. 520, 533, 535, 113 S.Ct. 2217, 2227, 2228, 124 L.Ed.2d 472 (1993), on remand 2 F.3d 369 (11th Cir.1993) when the Court held that a city law prohibiting the sacrifice of animals violated the free exercise clause because the law was designed to suppress a particular religion.

8. Agostini v. Felton, 521 U.S. 203, 234, 117 S.Ct. 1997, 2016, 138 L.Ed.2d 391 (1997) overruling Aguilar v. Felton, 473 U.S. 402, 105 S.Ct. 3232, 87 L.Ed.2d 290 (1985). In some establishment clause cases in the 1980s and 90s, the Supreme Court ruled against government

nor, described the inquiry into whether government aid to religious institutions created an excessive entanglement between government and religion as a part of the analytical method for determining whether a government program had an effect of favoring, or disfavoring, religion that would violate the establishment clause. In the future, the Court might formally adopt a two part purpose and effect test for establishment clause cases. The two part test would require courts to determine that any government program that provides incidental aid to religion has both a primary secular purpose and a primary effect that neither advances nor inhibits religion. The degree to which a challenged government program entangles the government and religion would then be merely one of the factors the judiciary would consider when determining whether a government program has an effect that violates the establishment clause.

In *Board of Education of Kiryas Joel Village School District v. Grumet* [9] the Supreme Court invalidated a state law that created a separate school district for a small village that was inhabited entirely by members of one religious sect. Two decades before this Supreme Court case, members of the Satmar Hasidim, who are believers in a form of Judaism, moved to an undeveloped subdivision in New York. In 1977, employing a state law of general applicability, the Satmars separated from the town with which they had been associated and established the Village of Kiryas Joel.

The residents of the Village of Kiryas Joel educated their children at two religious schools, one for male students and one for female students. These schools were admittedly sectarian in nature, although they provided the students with instruction in general secular subjects (e.g., reading and mathematics) as well as religious courses. The Village of Kiryas Joel was in a general public school district. Parents who resided in the Village could have sent their children to public schools

that were located outside the Village, but within the public school district.

The religious schools in the Village of Kiryas Joel did not offer any special services for handicapped children. At one time, the public school district which included the territory of the Village provided services for handicapped children who attended the two religious schools in the Village. These services were provided by the public school district at an annex to one of the religious schools. In 1985, the government services for the handicapped children in the religious schools were ended in response to United States Supreme Court decisions concerning the provision of services to children who attended religiously affiliated schools in other communities.[10]

Between 1985 and 1989, handicapped children from the Village of Kiryas Joel could only receive special educational services if they attended the public schools. But the Satmar children found that leaving their Village, with its distinctive life style, and attending the public schools was difficult to the point of being traumatic. In 1989, only one child from the Village still attended the public schools. All of the other handicapped children from the Village either received limited, privately funded services or they did not receive any special educational services.

The New York legislature, in 1989, passed a statute creating a separate school district that had boundaries identical to the Village of Kiryas Joel. The new Kiryas Joel Village School District had all of the powers and duties of any other school district; the state statute provided for a locally elected board to operate the school district. The Village School District was composed solely of persons who were a member of one religion. The persons elected to the school board were members of that religion. The Village School District then operated only a special education program for handicapped children; the District also accept-

9. 512 U.S. 687, 114 S.Ct. 2481, 129 L.Ed.2d 546 (1994).

10. Grand Rapids School District v. Ball, 473 U.S. 373, 105 S.Ct. 3216, 87 L.Ed.2d 267 (1985); Aguilar v. Felton, 473 U.S. 402, 105 S.Ct. 3232, 87 L.Ed.2d 290 (1985).

actions without expressly relying on the purpose, effect, and entanglement test. See, e.g., County of Allegheny v. American Civil Liberties Union, 492 U.S. 573, 109 S.Ct. 3086, 106 L.Ed.2d 472 (1989); Lee v. Weisman, 505 U.S. 577, 112 S.Ct. 2649, 120 L.Ed.2d 467 (1992).

ed handicapped students from neighboring school districts. All of the children in the Village who were not handicapped continued to attend the religiously affiliated schools. The Kiryas Joel Village School District offered to send any child in the Village who was not handicapped, and who wanted to attend a public school, to a public school in the neighboring school district. The Village would pay the tuition and expenses for such a nonhandicapped child.[11]

Justice Souter wrote an opinion in the *Grumet* case that was, in part, a majority opinion and, in part, a plurality opinion. Writing for a majority of the Court, Justice Souter ruled that the New York law creating the Village School District was a sect preference that violated the neutrality principle, which is a core value of the establishment clause.[12] If the Village had been able to establish a school district by following laws of general applicability, the majority might have ruled that the mere existence of a public school district that primarily served children of one religion, in a local geographical area, did not violate the First Amendment. The flaw in the New York law, according to the majority, was that the law creating the Village School District constituted a clear preference for one religious sect. New York had defended its law as a secular way of accommodating the desire of children and parents in the village to keep their children close to home and their religious way of life. The state believed that the law should be upheld because the public school operated by

the Kiryas Joel Village School District did not have any religious characteristics. Justice Souter found that categorizing the law as an accommodation of religion would not save the state law from invalidation if the law gave preferential treatment to a religious sect. Justice Souter stated: "The fundamental source of constitutional concern here is that the legislature itself may fail to exercise governmental authority in a religiously neutral way." [13]

The state believed that the creation of the Village School District should be seen as a permissible accommodation for a small, unique group of children. The majority in *Grumet* refused to allow even this seemingly minor deviation from the neutrality principle. Justice Souter found that a sect preference given to a "small religious group causes no less a constitutional problem than would follow from aiding a sect with more members or religion as a whole." [14] The state could pursue other forms of accommodations for the children from the Village who needed special educational services. Justice Souter noted that earlier Supreme Court cases allowed for the provision of special education services "at a neutral site" near religiously affiliated schools.[15]

Justice Souter wrote a majority opinion in *Grumet* concerning New York's violation of the neutrality principle. But he wrote for only four Justices when he found that the New York law violated the establishment clause due to an improper delegation of governmental authority to a religious entity.[16] Justice Souter

---

11. The facts regarding the history of the Village of Kiryas Joel, and the local public school district, and the creation of the new school district are set forth in Board of Education of Kiryas Joel Village School District v. Grumet, 512 U.S. 687, 690–95, 114 S.Ct. 2481, 2485–87, 129 L.Ed.2d 546 (1994) (Part I of the opinion by Justice Souter).

12. Board of Education of Kiryas Joel Village School District v. Grumet, 512 U.S. 687, 702–06, 114 S.Ct. 2481, 2491–2493, 129 L.Ed.2d 546 (1994). This portion of Justice Souter's opinion was joined by Justices Blackmun, Stevens, O'Connor, and Ginsburg.

13. 512 U.S. at 703, 114 S.Ct. at 2491.

14. 512 U.S. at 704, 114 S.Ct. at 2492.

15. 512 U.S. at 706, 114 S.Ct. at 2493. For an examination of the aid that can be provided to students at religiously affiliated primary and secondary schools see § 17.4(a).

16. Board of Education of Kiryas Joel Village School District v. Grumet, 512 U.S. 687, 697–700, 114 S.Ct. 2481, 2487–2490, 129 L.Ed.2d 546 (1994). This portion of Justice Souter's opinion was joined by Justices Blackmun, Stevens, and Ginsburg. Justice Blackmun wrote an opinion concurring in both the judgment and opinion of the Court in which he found that the Court's ruling in this case was consistent with the principles that formed the basis of the three part purpose-effect-entanglement test which had been used in most of the establishment clause cases of the Supreme Court after 1971. 512 U.S. at 710, 114 S.Ct. at 2494 (Blackmun, J., concurring). Justice Stevens was joined by Justices Blackmun and Ginsburg in stating the view that the special aid given to the children of the Village could not be characterized as an accommodation of religion in any way because it was designed to provide special aid to members of one particular religious faith. 512 U.S. at 710, 114 S.Ct. at 2495 (Stevens, J., joined by Blackmun and Ginsburg, JJ., concurring).

was joined by Justices Blackmun, Ginsburg and Stevens in finding that the state law could only be understood as delegating governmental power to a group of people defined by their membership in a religious sect. The Court had previously held that the establishment clause would prevent the government from delegating governmental authority to a religious organization, such as a church or the authorities who governed a religious community.[17]

The state had argued that there was no delegation of authority to a religious organization in this case because the new Village School District operated in presumably the same way any other school district in the State. Justice Souter, in the portion of his opinion that did not represent the views of a majority of the Justices, found that there was no realistic difference between the granting of governmental power to "a group of religious individuals united by common doctrine" and a delegating governmental power to a religious group's official leadership or to a formal religious organization.[18] The plurality believed that the creation of the school district was "substantially equivalent to defining a political subdivision" in which the relevant governmental power was given to a religious sect. In their view, the state law created an unconstitutional "fusion of governmental and religious functions." [19]

Justice O'Connor concurred in the portion of Justice Souter's opinion that was a majority opinion, because she agreed that the New York law was an impermissible denominational preference.[20] However, Justice O'Connor did not join the portion of Justice Souter's opinion concerning whether the New York law constituted an improper delegation of governmental power to a religion. In her concurring opinion

in *Grumet,* Justice O'Connor indicated that the Village of Kiryas Joel School District could have been created if the state had a generally applicable state law allowing local communities (regardless of any religious connection) to create a school district. She also reiterated her belief that the government should be able to provide special education services at private schools, including religious schools, so long as the services provided at the site of a religiously affiliated private school were nonreligious in character. Justice O'Connor believed that it might be impossible to create a "unitary test" for the wide range of cases that involved incidental government aid to religion, but she would find that laws which were not religiously neutral in character must be held to violate the establishment clause.

Justice Kennedy voted to invalidate the New York law creating the Kiryas Joel Village School District, but he did not join any portion of Justice Souter's opinion in *Grumet.*[21] He believed that a legislature might respond to the need of a group of persons who would not follow a generally applicable law because of their religious beliefs, so long as the legislature did not create a sect preference. But Justice Kennedy rejected the majority's position that the establishment clause should prohibit a legislature from passing a law to accommodate the needs of a particular religious group simply because, at some future date, the legislature might fail to provide a similar accommodation, if requested to do so, for members of another religion. Nevertheless, Justice Kennedy took the position that "a religious accommodation demands careful scrutiny" and that the New York law in *Grumet* was a sect preference that violated the establishment clause.

---

17. 512 U.S. at 696–70, 114 S.Ct. at 2487–90. The plurality likened the case before it to Larkin v. Grendel's Den, Inc., 459 U.S. 116, 103 S.Ct. 505, 74 L.Ed.2d 297 (1982) in which the Court had invalidated a law giving religious entities a power to veto applications for liquor licenses in areas near the operations of those religious organizations. The *Larkin* case is examined in this section of the Treatise.

18. Board of Education of Kiryas Joel Village School District v. Grumet, 512 U.S. 687, 696, 114 S.Ct. 2481,

2488, 129 L.Ed.2d 546 (1994) (opinion of Souter, J., joined by Blackmun, Stevens, and Ginsburg, JJ.).

19. 512 U.S. at 700, 114 S.Ct. at 2490 (internal citations and quotation marks omitted).

20. Board of Education of Kiryas Joel Village School District v. Grumet, 512 U.S. 687, 710, 114 S.Ct. 2481, 2495, 129 L.Ed.2d 546 (1994) (O'Connor, J., concurring in part and concurring in the judgment).

21. 512 U.S. at 720, 114 S.Ct. at 2500 (Kennedy, J., concurring in the judgment).

Justice Scalia, joined only by Chief Justice Rehnquist and Justice Thomas, dissented in *Grumet*.[22] These three Justices believed that the Supreme Court's rulings during the previous quarter century had improperly prevented government entities from engaging in religious accommodation. Chief Justice Rehnquist, and Justices Scalia and Thomas, might be joined by Justices O'Connor and Kennedy, in a future case, to give the government more power to accommodate the needs of members of a religious group to educate their children outside of the public school system, so long as the government did not employ a sect preference. There may be a new majority of Justices who will vote to uphold more types of government aid to religiously affiliated schools than would have been tolerated by a majority of the Justices during the Warren Court and Burger Court eras.[23]

In 1985, the Supreme Court, in *Aguilar v. Felton*[24] and *School District of Grand Rapids v. Ball*[25] had held that school districts could not use public employees to provide remedial classes at religiously affiliated schools even if the classes were provided in portions of the private school property that did not have any religious symbols and were not used for religion instruction. In 1997, a majority of Justices interpreted the establishment clause in a manner that allowed more religiously neutral aid to go to students of sectarian schools, without dramatically altering the establishment clause test used in prior cases. In *Agosti-*

ni v. Felton,[26] the Supreme Court ruled that a public school board, with its own money or with federal funds, could provide educational assistance, such as remedial reading courses or tutorials, to religious school students.

In *Agostini*, Justice O'Connor wrote a majority opinion in which she stated that the Court would continue to determine whether government programs that aided religion had a nonreligious purpose and a primary effect that neither advanced nor inhibited religion.[27] The majority in *Agostini* found that the intent of the government in providing educational assistance in remedial programs was to provide aid to all students in a jurisdiction, a purpose that was not sectarian and did not violate the establishment clause.[28]

Rather than describing excessive entanglement analysis to be an entirely separate establishment clause standard, Justice O'Connor stated that the determination of whether a government program created an excessive entanglement between government and religion was an aspect of determining whether a government program had an impermissible religious effect.[29] According to the *Agostini* majority, the Court in the 1980s had simply assumed that any provision of aid to students at religious schools would either be a form of aid to the religious instruction at the school or result in an excessive entanglement between government and religion, if government attempted to avoid having its aid go to the religious mission of the school. The majority found that these

---

22. 512 U.S. at 730, 114 S.Ct. at 2505 (Scalia, J., joined by Rehnquist, C.J., and Thomas, J., dissenting).

23. The permissible scope of government aid to religiously affiliated schools is examined in § 17.4.

24. Aguilar v. Felton, 473 U.S. 402, 105 S.Ct. 3232, 87 L.Ed.2d 290 (1985), overruled by Agostini v. Felton, 521 U.S. 203, 117 S.Ct. 1997, 138 L.Ed.2d 391 (1997).

25. Grand Rapids School District v. Ball, 473 U.S. 373, 105 S.Ct. 3216, 87 L.Ed.2d 267 (1985).

26. Agostini v. Felton, 521 U.S. 203, 117 S.Ct. 1997, 138 L.Ed.2d 391 (1997), overruling Aguilar v. Felton, 473 U.S. 402, 105 S.Ct. 3232, 87 L.Ed.2d 290 (1985).

27. Agostini v. Felton, 521 U.S. 203, 222–223, 117 S.Ct. 1997, 2010, 138 L.Ed.2d 391 (1997): "To be sure, the general principles we use to evaluate whether government aid violates the establishment clause have not changed since Aguilar was decided. For example, we continue to ask whether the government acted with the purpose of

advancing or inhibiting religion, and the nature of that inquiry has remained largely unchanged ... likewise, we continue to explore whether the aid has the effect of advancing or inhibiting religion." (Internal quotations and citations omitted).

28. The Court in 1997, as it had in 1985, found that the educational assistance program had a secular purpose. Agostini v. Felton, 521 U.S. 203, 219, 117 S.Ct. 1997, 2008, 138 L.Ed.2d 391 (1997).

29. Agostini v. Felton, 521 U.S. 203, 232, 117 S.Ct. 1997, 2015, 138 L.Ed.2d 391 (1997): "Whether a government aid program results in such a [excessive entanglement] has consistently been an aspect of our establishment clause analysis ... the factors we use to assess whether an entanglement is excessive are similar to the factors we use to examine effect ... it is simplest to recognize excessive entanglement ... as an aspect of the inquiry into a statute's effect." (Internal quotations and citations omitted).

assumptions were simply unwarranted and that there was not reason to believe that aid that was provided by religiously neutral criteria, such as the criteria used to determine disadvantaged students who needed remedial educational assistance did not violate the establishment clause. In examining whether or not the government aid had an impermissible effect, the majority examined the nature of the criteria used to select the students who receive government aid, whether the government action involved aid to religious indoctrination of students, or whether it created an excessive entanglement between government administrators and religious entities. The Court found that the provision of remedial aid to disadvantaged students by public employees on the grounds of religious schools that were not pervasively sectarian did not have any effect that was prohibited by the establishment clause. The Court used purpose, effect, and entanglement analysis to decide that this government program should be upheld.[30]

In *Agostini* a majority of the Justices agreed that, when looking at the permissibility of incidental aid to religious organizations under the establishment clause, the Court would determine: (1) whether the government had a permissible non-sectarian purpose; and (2) whether the law had a non-religious primary effect. In determining whether the effect of the law made it permissible, or impermissible under the establishment clause, the Court would look to three factors: (1) whether the aid was used in or resulted in governmental "indoctrination;" (2) whether the aid program defined recipients by some reference to religion; and

(3) whether there was an excessive entanglement between government and religion as a result of the aid program.[31]

In the year 2000, the Court could not produce a majority opinion regarding the real meaning of the *Agostini* tests and how they should be applied. In *Mitchell v. Helms*[32] the Court upheld a government program that gave non-religious educational materials to private schools, including religiously affiliated schools. Though six Justices voted to uphold the program in *Mitchell* there was no majority opinion.

In *Mitchell*, four Justices interpreted *Agostini* to allow any form of aid to religious institutions that was religiously neutral in itself, even if the recipient had diverted the government aid so as to support religious activities.[33] Two Justices rejected the approach of the plurality; they found that religiously neutral aid could be upheld so long as persons challenging the program had not proven that an aid recipient had diverted the government assistance into support for religious indoctrination[34] Three dissenting Justices believed that there should be a strict separation of church and state, and that the government should not be allowed to grant aid to religiously affiliated institutions if that aid was capable of being diverted for religious activities.[35]

In *Zelman v. Simmons–Harris*[36] the Supreme Court, by a 5 to 4 vote of the Justices, held that the establishment clause did not prevent a state from providing tuition vouchers, which could be used at private as well as public schools, to parents of inner-city chil-

---

30. *Agostini* was decided by a five to four vote of the Justices. The dissenters believed that the use of government employees to provide educational assistance on property owned by, and used for, a sectarian school violated the establishment clause. Agostini v. Felton, 521 U.S. 203, 240, 117 S.Ct. 1997, 2019, 138 L.Ed.2d 391 (1997) (Souter, J., joined by Stevens and Ginsburg, JJ., and, in part, by Breyer, J., dissenting). Justice Ginsburg's dissent focused on the majority's decision to reopen the 1985 ruling. 521 U.S. at 254, 117 S.Ct. at 2026 (Ginsburg, J., joined by Stevens, Souter, and Breyer, JJ.,dissenting)

31. Agostini v. Felton, 521 U.S. 203, 234, 117 S.Ct. 1997, 2015, 138 L.Ed.2d 391 (1997).

32. Mitchell v. Helms, 530 U.S. 793, 120 S.Ct. 2530, 147 L.Ed.2d 660 (2000). Cases concerning aid to religious institutions are examined in § 24.1.

33. The judgment of the Court was announced in a plurality opinion written by Justice Thomas, which was joined by Chief Justice Rehnquist and Justices Scalia and Kennedy. Mitchell v. Helms, 530 U.S. 793, 120 S.Ct. 2530, 147 L.Ed.2d 660 (2000).

34. Mitchell v. Helms, 530 U.S. 793, 836, 120 S.Ct. 2530, 2556, 147 L.Ed.2d 660 (2000) (O'Connor, J., joined by Breyer, J., concurring in the judgment).

35. 530 U.S. at 866, 120 S.Ct. at 2572 (Souter, J., joined by Stevens and Ginsburg, JJ., dissenting).

36. Zelman v. Simmons–Harris, 536 U.S. 639, 122 S.Ct. 2460, 153 L.Ed.2d 604 (2002).

dren. The majority opinion, by Chief Justice Rehnquist, found that the purpose and effect tests that protected establishment clause values were not offended by a program that was designed to give parents a true choice of alternatives between a variety of public school offerings and private schools.[37] Justice O'Connor, concurring in *Zelman*, stated that the approach to religious aid that the Court had adopted in *Agostini* embodied the basic established clause tests used in the Supreme Court's decisions during the prior 30 years.[38] Justice O'Connor found that *Agostini* merely "folded the entanglement inquiry into the primary effect inquiry."[39] In her view, the Court's ruling in *Zelman* was consistent with earlier cases, including *Lemon v. Kurtzman.*[40]

Taxes and the Religion Clauses. The Supreme Court, in *Hernandez v. Commissioner of Internal Revenue*,[41] upheld the denial of a tax deduction to a taxpayer for a contribution to a church that was a "fixed donation" for religious services provided by the church. In *Hernandez*, a member of the Church of Scientology wanted to deduct from his gross income the amount of money he paid for "auditing" and "training" services provided by the Church. The Church had a system of mandatory fixed charges for these religious services; no member would receive the service without paying the fixed price. The Internal Revenue Code was interpreted by both the Internal Revenue Service and the Supreme Court to preclude a deduction for a payment made to a charity that constituted an exchange for a product or service. The Supreme Court ruled that the Internal Revenue Code prohibition of a charitable deduction under such circumstances did not violate the establishment or free exercise

clauses of the First Amendment. The Court found that the tax classification was not subject to the compelling interest test because the Internal Revenue Code did not on its face create any distinction between different types of religious entities. Because the statute, and the interpretation of it by the Internal Revenue Service, contained no denominational preference, the tax code provision was subject only to the three part establishment clause test (the purpose-effect-entanglement test). First, the Court found that there was no evidence of animus to any religion, or to religion in general, in the purpose of the statute. Second, the Court ruled that the statute's effect of encouraging general gifts to charitable entities that were not in exchange for goods or services neither advanced or inhibited religion. Third, the Court held that the Internal Revenue Code did not create any entanglement between the government and religion, because the minimal regulatory interaction between taxpayers, churches, and the Internal Revenue Service was not the kind of administrative entanglement that endangered religion clause values.[42]

The Court in *Hernandez* also ruled that the denial of the deduction did not violate the free exercise clause for two reasons. First, the Internal Revenue Code did not place a substantial burden on any person who was carrying out a tenet of a religious belief. Second, the public interest in maintaining a tax system free of exemptions tailored to accommodate a wide variety of religions outweighed any burden on persons who were denied deductions under these circumstances.[43]

In *Jimmy Swaggart Ministries v. Board of Equalization*,[44] the Justices unanimously found

---

37. The *Zelman* case is examined more fully at § 17.4, infra.

38. Zelman v. Simmons–Harris, 536 U.S. 639, 668, 122 S.Ct. 2460, 2473, 153 L.Ed.2d 604 (2002) (O'Connor, J., concurring).

39. 536 U.S. at 668, 122 S.Ct. at 2476 (O'Connor, J., concurring).

40. Lemon v. Kurtzman, 403 U.S. 602, 91 S.Ct. 2105, 29 L.Ed.2d 745 (1971).

41. 490 U.S. 680, 109 S.Ct. 2136, 104 L.Ed.2d 766 (1989).

42. For an examination of a variety of cases involving regulations of religious organizations or their members

that are asserted to violate both the free exercise and establishment clauses. See §§ 17.13, 17.15, 17.16.

43. The Supreme Court's ruling on the free exercise claim was consistent with its earlier decision in United States v. Lee, 455 U.S. 252, 102 S.Ct. 1051, 71 L.Ed.2d 127 (1982) in which the Court found that Amish employers of Amish individuals did not have a constitutional right to an exemption from compulsory participation in the Social Security System. See § 17.8.

44. 493 U.S. 378, 110 S.Ct. 688, 107 L.Ed.2d 796 (1990).

that a religious organization, and the members of the organization, had no right to refuse to pay general sales and use taxes for the sales of religious goods and literature. Justice O'Connor's opinion for the unanimous Court tracked the reasoning of the *Hernandez* decision. Because sales and use taxes were designed to tax solely at religious activities, the taxes did not have to be justified by a compelling state interest. If a "flat tax" operates as a license fee (a fixed fee) that restricts the ability of persons to engage in religious activities that tax would be analogous to a prior restraint on speech activities. The Court would find that the flat-tax license fee, as applied to religious activity, violated the establishment and free exercise clauses.[45] However, a tax applying to all sales and uses of tangible personal property, like a tax on individual or corporate income, did not raise the concern of whether the tax was a "flat license tax that would act as a precondition to the free exercise of religious beliefs."[46] Thus, it appears that the Supreme Court would be highly unlikely to find that any tax on its face, or as applied to religious organizations, violates the establishment clause or the free exercise clause unless the tax singled out religious activity for a special tax or created a flat fee that was a precondition to the exercise of religious beliefs.[47]

An outline of the history of the establishment clause tests may give some added perspective. There were only two significant decisions under the establishment clause prior to 1947. In that year, the Court held the clause applicable to the states, while approving the reimbursement of bus fees for all students, including those attending parochial schools. It did so without a clear standard, for a majori-

ty simply found that no prohibited form of aid was involved in that program. In the cases dealing with prayers and Bible reading in the public schools the Court enunciated a "secular purpose and primary effect" test. This two part test was the sole standard for a time and was used in reviewing the permissibility of loaning textbooks to parochial school students. In 1970, the Court upheld property tax exemptions for churches while using for the first time the present purpose-effect-entanglement test.

To withstand analysis under the establishment clause a government act must have not only a secular purpose and a primary effect which neither advances nor inhibits religion, it also must avoid creating the type of entanglement between government and religion which might lead to an erosion of the principle of government neutrality in religious decision-making. The government may take action for secular purposes which aid all persons in a religiously neutral manner even though there is some incidental aid to religious organizations. Additionally, the Supreme Court in limited circumstances has allowed the government to recognize the historic role of religion in American society.

Direct Entanglement with Religion—Delegation of Legislative Power. In some instances it is relatively easy to determine that a governmental action violates the establishment clause because it either delegates governmental power to a religious group in a manner that allows for excessive entanglement between the government and religion or it constitutes a preference for certain religions. For

45. Murdock v. Pennsylvania, 319 U.S. 105, 63 S.Ct. 870, 87 L.Ed. 1292 (1943) (invalidating an ordinance requiring persons canvassing or soliciting within a city to pay a flat fee for a license tax as applied to a person distributing religious literature); Follett v. McCormick, 321 U.S. 573, 64 S.Ct. 717, 88 L.Ed. 938 (1944) (invalidating a flat fee tax as applied to a religious minister selling religious literature). These decisions involved rulings regarding the free exercise clause, but the decisions seem to provide constitutional protection of a variety of First Amendment activities (such as the activities of sellers of nonreligious books) as well as the specific protection of religiously motivated actions. See §§ 17.6–17.8.

46. Jimmy Swaggart Ministries v. Board of Equalization, 493 U.S. 378, 110 S.Ct. 688, 107 L.Ed.2d 796 (1990). "Our concern in *Murdock* and *Follett*—that a flat license tax would act as a *precondition* to the free exercise of religious beliefs—is simply not present where a tax applies to all sales and uses of tangible personal property in the state." 493 U.S. at 387, 110 S.Ct. at 694 (emphasis in original).

47. Id. For an examination of the instances in which the free exercise clause may require a state to grant an exemption from laws of general applicability, see §§ 17.6–17.8.

example, in *Larkin v. Grendel's Den, Inc.*[48] the Supreme Court found that a zoning law violated the establishment clause by granting to all churches or schools a veto power over the issuance of a liquor license for any premises within a five hundred foot radius of the church or school.

Although the law might have had a secular purpose (the promotion of a quiet atmosphere around certain cultural and educational centers) that purpose alone could not establish the statute's constitutionality. The statute was clearly susceptible to being used for the promotion of religious rather than secular ends. Under the statute each church exercised a governmental power which was subject to no clear secular standard; that power could be used to promote primarily religious goals. Even if one assumed that the statute had both a secular purpose and primary effect, the law clearly failed the excessive entanglement test. The law vested governmental authority in churches; in the words of the Court, the law "enmeshes churches in the exercise of substantial government powers contrary to our consistent interpretation of the establishment clause."[49] The excessive entanglement test was meant to avoid the danger to both secular government and religious autonomy that accompanies a sharing of power between religious and governmental agencies.

The government may regulate the actions of all persons, including actions undertaken by some persons for religiously motivated reasons, without violating the establishment clause or free exercise clause if the regulation is religiously neutral and promotes significant societal interests. A law which regulates the activities of religious organizations or private persons will be invalid if it distinguishes between various types of activities on the basis of the religious belief, or the religious affiliation, of the persons or organizations that engage in the activity.[50] If a law regulating private sector activity favors persons with religious beliefs over other persons it may have the primary effect of advancing religion; such a law would violate the establishment clause.[51]

A law which is religiously neutral may have to give way to a claim for exemption from the regulation by persons whose religious beliefs prevent them from complying with the law. The government will not have to grant an exemption from a religiously neutral regulation of activities of all persons if the regulation does not impose a significant burden on the ability of persons seeking the exemption to maintain their religious beliefs. If the regulation does impose such a burden, the government will have to grant the exemption unless the regulation promotes a societal interest which outweighs the burden imposed on those who must follow it despite their religious beliefs.[52]

The Use of Historical Evidence to Determine Establishment Clause Violations. In several instances the Court has based a finding that a governmental practice did not violate the establishment clause on a history of that practice which the Court believed showed that the governmental practice involved no significant danger of eroding governmental neutrality regarding religious matters.

In *Walz v. Tax Commission*[53] the Supreme Court upheld a state law exempting from state

---

48. 459 U.S. 116, 103 S.Ct. 505, 74 L.Ed.2d 297 (1982).

49. 459 U.S. at 127, 103 S.Ct. at 512.

50. See, e.g., Larson v. Valente, 456 U.S. 228, 102 S.Ct. 1673, 72 L.Ed.2d 33 (1982), rehearing denied 457 U.S. 1111, 102 S.Ct. 2916, 73 L.Ed.2d 1323 (1982) finding a violation of the establishment clause when a state statute regarding solicitation of charitable contributions imposed regulations and reporting requirements only on those religious organizations which solicited more than fifty percent of their funds from nonmembers. This law was considered a "denominational preference" that was a clear violation of the establishment clause. For further examination of this case, see § 17.16, infra.

51. Estate of Thornton v. Caldor, Inc., 472 U.S. 703, 105 S.Ct. 2914, 86 L.Ed.2d 557 (1985) (state legislation which gives workers an absolute right to refuse to engage in employment activities on their sabbath day violates the establishment clause because it has the primary effect of advancing religion through an "unyielding" and inflexible system of giving preferences in employment practice to employees with religious beliefs). This case is examined further in § 17.13.

52. Regarding the free exercise clause basis upon which courts may find that the government must exempt from its regulations persons who seek to take actions, or refrain from taking actions, based on sincerely held religious beliefs see §§ 17.8, 17.9, 17.15, 17.16.

53. 397 U.S. 664, 90 S.Ct. 1409, 25 L.Ed.2d 697 (1970).

taxation property and income of religious organizations. The tax exemption survived the three-part purpose-effect-entanglement test primarily because of historical evidence that the federal and state governments since the time of the American Revolution had granted tax exemptions to such property and income as a part of general tax exemptions for nonprofit or socially beneficial organizations. The majority opinion by Chief Justice Burger found that this history established that the legislature's purpose in creating the exemption was not one that contravened the principle of separation of church and state; history showed no significant danger that such exemptions would give rise to either a religious effect or an entanglement of government and religion.

In *Marsh v. Chambers* [54] the Court, again in an opinion by Chief Justice Burger, upheld a legislature's practice of employing a religious chaplain whose primary duty was to open each legislative day with a prayer. The Court based its finding that there was no establishment clause violation on the "unambiguous and unbroken history of more than two hundred years" of legislative prayer, although the majority opinion also stated that history "could not justify contemporary violations" of the First Amendment. In the majority's view, legislative prayer was a recognition of a belief widely held among the people of the country; its history demonstrated that such activity did not constitute the type of religious purpose, religious effect, or entanglement between government and religion that threatened the First Amendment value of religious neutrality on the part of government.

Chief Justice Burger also wrote for the Court in *Lynch v. Donnelly.* [55] In *Lynch* the Court upheld a municipal policy under which a city park was decorated with displays celebrating the Christmas holiday season, including a Christian nativity scene. The majority opinion found that the use of the nativity scene, at least in the context of a Christmas display

which included nonreligious as well as religious symbols of the holiday, was not done for any purpose which threatened establishment clause values because there was no governmental purpose to aid religion in general or to aid a particular faith. The Chief Justice found that the history of Christmas celebrations in this country was such that it was unlikely that members of the public, when viewing the scene, would find the practice to be an endorsement of religion; there was no other primary effect of the city's action that would constitute a substantial or impermissible benefit to religion. For these reasons, the majority also found that there was no entanglement between government and religion.

Although Chief Justice Burger wrote for the Court in *Walz, Marsh* and *Lynch*, it is not clear whether the Chief Justice, and a majority of the Justices in these cases, was taking the position that certain practices which have existed throughout our history should be exempted from the three-part test. The Chief Justice appears to have found that the three-part test was met in each case because in each case there was historic proof that there had been no entanglement which had threatened the religious neutrality of government; in addition, there had been no effect of granting a benefit to religion (or any particular religion) flowing from any of these practices, and the legislature's purpose in each case must not have been one which contravened the policies of the First Amendment because none of the practices had ever led to any impermissible erosion of religious neutrality on the part of government.

In *County of Allegheny v. American Civil Liberties Union* [56] there was significant disagreement between the Justices concerning both the constitutionality of holiday displays on public property and the method by which the judiciary should determine whether holiday displays with religious connotations violate establishment clause principles. At issue

---

54. 463 U.S. 783, 103 S.Ct. 3330, 77 L.Ed.2d 1019 (1983).

55. 465 U.S. 668, 104 S.Ct. 1355, 79 L.Ed.2d 604 (1984), rehearing denied 466 U.S. 994, 104 S.Ct. 2376, 80 L.Ed.2d 848 (1984).

56. 492 U.S. 573, 109 S.Ct. 3086, 106 L.Ed.2d 472 (1989).

in *County of Allegheny* were two holiday displays located on public property. The first display was a creche on the staircase of a county courthouse which had been set up by a Roman Catholic organization. The creche was accompanied by flowers and a sign stating the display had been donated by the Holy Name Society. There was a fence around the creche display; there were no other holiday decorations on the county courthouse staircase area. The second display was approximately one city block away from the first; the second display was at the entrance to the main office building for the city and county. The dispute regarding the second display related to an 18 foot menorah, which was owned by a Jewish organization but stored, maintained, and erected by the city. The menorah was next to a large (over 40 foot tall) decorated evergreen (Christmas) tree. The second display also included a sign referring to the display as a "Salute to Liberty."

In *County of Allegheny*, a majority of Justices found that the first display (the creche display), violated the establishment clause but that the second display (the menorah-tree-sign display), did not violate the establishment clause. Justice Kennedy, joined by Chief Justice Rehnquist and Justices White and Scalia, would have found that both displays were consistent with the establishment clause. Those Justices believe that government accommodation of, and acknowledgment of public support for, religion were permissible so long as the government was not providing direct benefits to religion or coercing of religious beliefs.[57]

Justices Brennan, Marshall, and Stevens believed that the three-part (purpose-effect-en-

tanglement) test that had been used for two decades in cases examining incidental aid to religion should be used to review holiday displays. They believed that both displays were unconstitutional forms of aid to religion.[58]

In *County of Allegheny*, only Justices Blackmun and O'Connor believed that there was a constitutional difference between the two displays but, as they were the "swing votes" in the case, their view dictated the outcome of the case. In earlier cases, Justice O'Connor had stated her belief that establishment clause should prohibit government aid to religion if the government action effectively endorsed religion in a way that would send a message to the populace that the government favored certain types of religions and that those persons who were not a part of the religions being aided were disfavored.[59] In her view the display that included only the creche involved a type of government endorsement of religion that was prohibited by the establishment clause. However, the menorah-tree-sign display included a variety of holiday symbols and did not constitute an impermissible endorsement of religion.[60]

Justice Blackmun wrote an opinion that was in part a majority opinion, in part a plurality opinion, and in part an opinion expressing only his own views.[61] Justice Blackmun believed that the three-part (purpose-effect-entanglement) test used in establishment clause cases since the early 1970s was the proper test to use in this case. However, Justice Blackmun also believed that Justice O'Connor's endorsement test was consistent with earlier cases applying the three part establishment

---

57. County of Allegheny v. American Civil Liberties Union, 492 U.S. 573, 655, 109 S.Ct. 3086, 3134, 106 L.Ed.2d 472 (1989) (Kennedy, J., joined by Rehnquist, C.J., and White and Scalia, JJ., concurring in the judgment in part and dissenting in part).

58. County of Allegheny v. American Civil Liberties Union, 492 U.S. 573, 646, 109 S.Ct. 3086, 3129, 106 L.Ed.2d 472 (1989) (Stevens, J., joined by Brennan and Marshall, JJ., concurring in part and dissenting in part).

59. See, e.g., Lynch v. Donnelly, 465 U.S. 668, 690, 104 S.Ct. 1355, 1366, 79 L.Ed.2d 604 (1984) (O'Connor, J., concurring); Witters v. Washington Department of Services for the Blind, 474 U.S. 481, 493, 106 S.Ct. 748, 755, 88 L.Ed.2d 846 (1986) (O'Connor, J., concurring).

60. County of Allegheny v. American Civil Liberties Union, 492 U.S. 573, 624, 109 S.Ct. 3086, 3117, 106 L.Ed.2d 472 (1989) (O'Connor concurring in part and concurring in the judgment; Justice O'Connor's opinion is joined in part by Justices Brennan and Stevens).

61. County of Allegheny v. American Civil Liberties Union, 492 U.S. 573, 109 S.Ct. 3086, 106 L.Ed.2d 472 (1989) (judgment of the Court announced by Justice Blackmun in an opinion that is in part a majority opinion, in part an opinion joined by Justices O'Connor and Stevens, in part an opinion joined only by Justice Stevens, in part an opinion (in respect to part VI) that is not joined by any other Justice).

clause test.[62] Justice Blackmun found that the display that included the menorah, tree, and liberty sign did not violate the three-part test because the symbols had both secular and religious aspects; the message conveyed by the display was a basically secular one that endorsed the values of liberty. The menorah-sign-tree display, in Justice Blackmun's view, had a permissible purpose, did not aid religion, and did not create an excessive entanglement between government and religion. Justice Blackmun believed that the creche display violated the establishment clause because it conveyed a religious message that could not be defended as a secular government display.

In *Lee v. Weisman*,[63] the Court was presented with a challenge to a government practice of having a prayer at a public middle school graduation ceremony. School principals were permitted by state and local law to invite members of the clergy to offer invocation and benediction prayers at the start of formal graduation ceremonies for high schools and middle schools. Clergy who gave the prayers were provided with a document titled "Guidelines for Civic Occasions", which was prepared by the National Conference of Christians and Jews, and which recommended that prayers at nonsectarian ceremonies be designed so as to avoid offending the sensibilities of any persons at the proceedings. In the particular case before the Court, a middle school graduation had included an invocation and benediction given by a Rabbi. The Supreme Court found that the school policy permitting the prayer at a school graduation violated the establishment clause.

The *Lee* decision helped to clarify the Supreme Court's view of the establishment clause in the early 1990s but it left open the question of what specific test should be used in examining government actions that are alleged to violate the establishment clause. The case was decided by a five to four vote; the four dissenting Justices were unsuccessful in their attempt to get the Court to approve incidental aid to religion that did not favor a particular sect.[64] The majority opinion by Justice Kennedy found that the government's use of prayers at school graduations violated the "central principles" of the establishment clause so that the case did not require the Justices to "revisit the difficult question dividing us in recent cases, questions of the definition and full scope of the principles governing the extent or permitted accommodation by the state for the religious beliefs and practices of many of its citizens ... we do not accept the invitation ... to reconsider our decision in *Lemon v. Kurtzman*." [65]

The majority ruled that state sponsored and directed religious exercise constituted an involvement of government and religion that literally constituted the establishment of religion. Justice Kennedy found that the principle of government neutrality was central to the establishment and free exercise clauses and that this principle was violated by the state directed prayer.[66] The majority opinion did not hold that only government actions that posed a danger of coercion of people's beliefs in religious matters would violate the establishment clause. But Justice Kennedy's majority opinion stated government practices that coerced people to support, or participate in, religious activities would be violations of the establishment clause.[67]

---

62. 492 U.S. at 590–93, 109 S.Ct. at 3099–3101 (this language appears in part III A of the Blackmun opinion, which was joined by a majority of the Justices).

63. 505 U.S. 577, 112 S.Ct. 2649, 120 L.Ed.2d 467 (1992).

64. 505 U.S. at 630, 112 S.Ct. at 2678 (Scalia, J., joined by Rehnquist, C.J., and White and Thomas, JJ., dissenting).

65. Lee v. Weisman, 505 U.S. 577, 586, 112 S.Ct. 2649, 2655, 120 L.Ed.2d 467 (1992) citing Lemon v. Kurtzman, 403 U.S. 602, 91 S.Ct. 2105, 29 L.Ed.2d 745 (1971), rehearing denied 404 U.S. 876, 92 S.Ct. 24, 30 L.Ed.2d 123 (1971). The *Lemon* case created the three part (purpose,

effect, entanglement) test that is examined at the start of this section of the Treatise and in § 17.4(a) of this Treatise.

66. Lee v. Weisman, 505 U.S. 577, 588, 112 S.Ct. 2649, 2656, 120 L.Ed.2d 467 (1992): "The First Amendment's Religion Clauses mean that religious beliefs and religious expression are too precious to be either proscribed or prescribed by the state."

67. The majority opinion stated: "It is beyond dispute that, at a minimum, the Constitution guarantees that the government may not coerce anyone to support or participate in religion or its exercise...." 505 U.S. at 587, 112 S.Ct. at 2655. "If citizens are subjected to state-spon-

The majority opinion in *Lee* did not give lower courts specific tests for reviewing every type of possible fact situation in which the government might be alleged to violate the establishment clause. The *Lee* majority opinion noted that the Court's concerns about coercion were "most pronounced" when reviewing the practices of public schools because the government subjecting children to the choice of participating in religious activities or missing classes, or graduation ceremonies, puts the young people in a real "conflict of conscience".[68] But the meaning of *Lee* outside the school setting is unclear. The majority concluded by noting: "We do not hold that every state action implicating religion is invalid if one or a few citizens find it offensive."[69]

The *Lee* decision demonstrated that the Court at the start of the 1990s was committed to defending establishment clause principles. A majority of the Justices were concerned about government neutrality in matters that would involve the religious beliefs of persons in our society. Those Justices rejected the argument that all nonsectarian or nonpreferential aid to religion generally was compatible with the establishment clause.[70] The *Lee* court did not reject the three part purpose, effect, and entanglement test used in earlier cases; it did not make "coercion" the touchstone of establishment clause analysis.[71]

In the year 2000, the Supreme Court reaffirmed *Lee*, but the Justices, in another case, showed that they could not agree on the proper test to use in establishment clause cases.

In *Santa Fe Independent School District v. Doe*[72] The Court, by a 6 to 3 vote, invalidated a public school district policy that allowed public high school students to elect one of their fellow students to give a "non-sectarian, non-proselytizing prayer" before football games. Justice Stevens wrote for six Justices in finding that the result in this case involved a simple application of the *Lee* decision. Involvement of the government in the election system, the provision of a forum for the prayer, and the involvement with a school function were all factors in establishing that the policy violated the establishment clause. Justice Stevens' majority opinion found that the law: constituted an endorsement of religion; had a coercive effect, on non-believers who attended the football games; and was enacted for a religious purpose.[73]

Only nine days after the *Santa Fe* decision, the Justices, again by a 6 to 3 vote, upheld a government program that provided non-religious materials and equipment to public and private schools including religiously affiliated schools. The Court made this ruling in *Mitchell v. Helms*,[74] without a majority opinion. Four of the Justices in *Mitchell* believed that virtually any form of religiously neutral aid could

sored religious exercises, the state disavows its own duty to guard and respect that sphere of inviolable conscience and belief which is the mark of a free people." 505 U.S. at 592, 112 S.Ct. at 2658.

68. Lee v. Weisman, 505 U.S. 577, 592–95, 112 S.Ct. 2649, 2658–60, 120 L.Ed.2d 467 (1992).

69. 505 U.S. at 597, 112 S.Ct. at 2661.

70. The rejection of the nonpreferentialist argument was stressed in Justice Souter's concurring opinion, which was joined by Justices Stevens and O'Connor. Lee v. Weisman, 505 U.S. 577, 609, 112 S.Ct. 2649, 2667, 120 L.Ed.2d 467 (1992) (Souter, J., joined by Stevens and O'Connor, JJ., concurring).

71. Justice Blackmun wrote an opinion concurring in the judgment and in the majority opinion that was joined by Justices Stevens and O'Connor. Justice Blackmun pointed out that in every establishment clause case decided after 1971 the Court had used the three part test known as the *Lemon* test because it came from the decision in Lemon v. Kurtzman, 403 U.S. 602, 91 S.Ct. 2105, 29 L.Ed.2d 745 (1971), rehearing denied 404 U.S. 876, 92

S.Ct. 24, 30 L.Ed.2d 123 (1971) except for the decision in Marsh v. Chambers, 463 U.S. 783, 103 S.Ct. 3330, 77 L.Ed.2d 1019 (1983) (which upheld a legislature's employment of a religious chaplain). Lee v. Weisman, 505 U.S. 577, 597, 603 n. 4, 112 S.Ct. 2649, 2661, 2663 n. 4, 120 L.Ed.2d 467 (1992) (Blackmun, J., joined by Stevens and O'Connor, JJ., concurring).

72. Santa Fe Independent School District v. Doe, 530 U.S. 290, 120 S.Ct. 2266, 147 L.Ed.2d 295 (2000).

73. 530 U.S. at 316, 120 S.Ct. at 2283 (Rehnquist, C.J., joined by Scalia and Thomas, JJ., dissenting). The dissent believed that the policy met establishment clause principles even though it was possible that a particular school might violate the establishment clause under certain circumstances. For more discussion of the relationship of the establishment clause to public school activities, see § 17.5.

74. Mitchell v. Helms, 530 U.S. 793, 120 S.Ct. 2530, 147 L.Ed.2d 660 (2000) (judgment of the Court announced in an opinion by Thomas, J., joined by Rehnquist, C.J., and Scalia and Kennedy, JJ.). For further examination of cases involving aid to religiously affiliated institutions, see § 17.4.

be given to religiously affiliated schools. Three Justices believed that there had to be a strict separation of church and state that would prohibit any aid to religious organizations that had the potential for being diverted to subsidizing religious activities or religious indoctrination[75] Justices O'Connor and Breyer cast the votes that decided the *Mitchell* case; they believed that a government program of non-religious aid to private schools should be upheld, although they also believed that a specific grant to a private school would violate the establishment clause if that school was proven to have used that government aid to subsidize its religious activities.[76]

Two years after the *Santa Fe* and *Mitchell* decisions, a majority of the Justices agreed that they should apply the purpose and effect tests to determine the constitutionality of financial aid to religiously affiliated organizations. In *Zelman v. Simmons–Harris*[77] the Justices, by a 5 to 4 vote, upheld an Ohio program that provided parents the option of sending their children to a variety of public schools or to use tuition vouchers at private schools, including religiously affiliated schools.[78] Justices O'Connor and Breyer, who had voted to uphold the program at issue in *Mitchell,* took different views of the Ohio tuition voucher program. Justice O'Connor joined the majority opinion in *Zelman.* She also wrote a concurring opinion in which she stated that the Court's use of the purpose and effect test to uphold the program included an analysis of the possible entanglement between church and state.[79] Justice Breyer believed that the tuition voucher program should be invalidated because it entangled government with religion in a way that would give rise to divisions in society along religious lines.[80]

Religious Expression and the Free Speech Clause.

In a series of cases, the Supreme Court has prohibited government entities from suppressing, or discriminating against, speech of religious organizations.[81] In each of these cases, a government entity attempted to deny access to government property to a religious group on the basis that, in the view of the government, the religious group's use of the public property would constitute a violation of the establishment clause. The Supreme Court, in these cases, ruled that allowing a religious organization to use a public forum for religiously oriented speech activities did not constitute a violation of the establishment clause, so long as the religious group was not given preferential treatment. However, in these cases, the Supreme Court was unable to identify a specific standard for determining if, or when, speech by private persons on government property would constitute a violation of the establishment clause. These cases did not formally reject the three-part *Lemon* Test, although several Justices believed that the Court should employ an "endorsement test" for determining when government aid to religious activities or government connection to religious speech violated the First Amendment.

In *Lamb's Chapel v. Center Moriches Union Free School District,*[82] the Supreme Court ruled that a government school board violated the First Amendment freedom of speech when it denied a religious organization the right to conduct a meeting in a school building after school hours, at a time when the board allowed nonreligious groups to use the school premises for their meetings. Regardless of whether the school building was viewed as a "limited public forum" or a "nonpublic forum," the government's discrimination against religious speech

75. 530 U.S. at 866, 120 S.Ct. at 2572 (Souter, J., joined by Stevens and Ginsburg, JJ., dissenting).

76. 530 U.S. at 836, 120 S.Ct. at 2556 (O'Connor, J., joined by Breyer, J., concurring in the judgment).

77. Zelman v. Simmons–Harris, 536 U.S. 639, 122 S.Ct. 2460, 153 L.Ed.2d 604 (2002).

78. This case is examined more fully in § 17.4, infra.

79. Zelman v. Simmons–Harris, 536 U.S. 639, 668, 122 S.Ct. 2460, 2473, 153 L.Ed.2d 604 (2002) (O'Connor, J., concurring).

80. 536 U.S. at 716, 122 S.Ct. at 2502 (Breyer, J., dissenting); 536 U.S. at 685, 122 S.Ct. at 2485 (Souter, J., joined by Stevens, Ginsburg, and Breyer, JJ., dissenting).

81. See the cases discussed in § 17.5(e), such as Widmar v. Vincent, 454 U.S. 263, 102 S.Ct. 269, 70 L.Ed.2d 440 (1981), as well as the cases discussed in this section of the Treatise.

82. 508 U.S. 384, 113 S.Ct. 2141, 124 L.Ed.2d 352 (1993).

constituted a form of viewpoint discrimination that violated the First Amendment.

The school board had attempted to justify its action by arguing that allowing the religious group to use the school property would violate the establishment clause. Justice White, writing for a majority in *Lamb's Chapel,* found that granting the religious organization equal access to the school would promote free speech values and would not violate the establishment clause. Justice White noted that the three-part *Lemon* test had never been overruled and that the *Lemon* test served, at that time, as the standard for determining if a government action violated the establishment clause.[83] Three concurring Justices in *Lamb's Chapel* agreed with the majority that the school board's discrimination against religious organizations violated the free speech clause, but these Justices objected to the majority opinion's reference to the *Lemon* tests.[84] Although the concurring Justices believed that the *Lemon* tests were not the proper basis for determining the compatibility of a government action with the establishment clause, these Justices were not clear regarding the establishment clause standards they would use in place of the *Lemon* tests.

The Supreme Court relied on *Lamb's Chapel* when the Justices, by a seven to two vote, ruled that allowing a private organization to place a religious symbol (a cross) in a public square, which was part of the state capitol grounds, would not violate the establishment clause. In *Capitol Square Review and Advisory Board v. Pinette*[85] the Court held that a state government would not violate the establishment clause if it permitted the Ku Klux Klan to place an unattended cross on public property that had been opened to private persons and organizations for the placement of signs and symbols. The government had denied the

Klan's request on the basis that placing an unattended cross on the square would violate the establishment clause. The lower federal courts ruled that the government had violated the free speech rights of the Klan, because (1) the capitol grounds had become a "limited public forum" or "public forum," and (2) the display of a religious symbol in that setting would not violate the establishment clause.

Justice Scalia wrote an opinion in the *Capitol Square Review* case that was, in part, a majority opinion, and in part, a plurality opinion. Justice Scalia wrote for a majority when he held that the only question that had been properly presented to the Court in the *Capitol Square Review* case was the question of whether a cross being placed in a public forum by a private group violated the establishment clause. Justice Scalia wrote only for himself, Chief Justice Rehnquist, and Justices Kennedy and Thomas when he found that the Court had not adopted an "endorsement test" for resolving all establishment clause issues and refused to use an endorsement test to determine if the placement of the cross in the square would violate the establishment clause. According to the plurality opinion, if the endorsement test were to be used by the judiciary at all, its use should be limited to determining when the government's speech, or government grants of financial aid to religious organizations, linked the government with religious activity in a way that violated the establishment clause. Justice Scalia stated that the religious expression of private persons could not violate the First Amendment when the expression took place in a public forum that was open to all persons and speakers on equal terms.[86]

Justices O'Connor, Souter, and Breyer concurred in the part of Justice Scalia's opinion

83. 508 U.S. at 394 n. 7, 113 S.Ct. at 2148 n. 7.

84. Lamb's Chapel v. Center Moriches Union Free School District, 508 U.S. 384, 396, 113 S.Ct. 2141, 2149, 124 L.Ed.2d 352 (1993) (Kennedy, J., concurring in part and concurring in the judgment); 508 U.S. at 396, 113 S.Ct. at 2149 (Scalia, J., joined by Thomas, J., concurring in the judgment).

85. 515 U.S. 753, 115 S.Ct. 2440, 132 L.Ed.2d 650 (1995). Justice Thomas joined all of Justice Scalia's major-

ity opinion, but he also wrote a concurring opinion. 515 U.S. at 768, 115 S.Ct. at 2450 (Thomas, J., concurring). Only Justices Stevens and Ginsburg dissented in *Capitol Square.* 515 U.S. at 796, 115 S.Ct. at 2464 (Stevens, J., dissenting); 515 U.S. at 816, 115 S.Ct. at 2474 (Ginsburg, J., dissenting).

86. 515 U.S. at 768, 115 S.Ct. at 2450 (opinion of Scalia, J., joined by Rehnquist, C.J., and Kennedy and Thomas, JJ.).

that framed the issues in the *Capitol Square* case.[87] However, they did not concur in the part of the plurality opinion in which Justice Scalia had discussed the establishment clause standards. These three Justices favored adopting the endorsement test that had been used in separate opinions by Justice O'Connor in earlier Supreme Court cases.[88] The three concurring Justices believed that the endorsement test was the proper test to use when determining whether there was a link between the government and religious activity by private persons that violated the establishment clause. The concurring Justices relied on the *Lamb's Chapel* decision because, in their view, it could be best understood as using the endorsement test, even though Justice White's majority opinion in *Lamb's Chapel* had specifically made use of the *Lemon* tests for determining whether granting a religious organization access to a public forum might violate the establishment clause.[89]

A majority of Justices appear to be using the concept of religious neutrality as the principle component of establishment clause analysis, even though the *Lemon* tests have never been completely rejected. In cases based on the analysis set forth in *Lamb's Chapel*, the Court has found that giving money to a university student publication that was religiously oriented, and allowing religious groups to use school facilities for meetings under religiously neutral criteria, did not violate the establishment clause.[90] The Court has also ruled that denial of government resources to groups solely be-

cause of their religious orientation, and the religious topics that would be discussed at their meetings, would violate the free speech clause.[91] The Court upheld a tuition voucher program because a majority of the Justices found that it was a religiously neutral means of offering the parents of inner-city students the ability to freely choose between a variety of public school options and the opportunity to send their children to private schools.[92]

§ 17.4   The Establishment Clause— Aid to Religious Institutions

(a) Primary and Secondary Schools

The fact that most of the Supreme Court's decisions concerning the meaning of the establishment clause in the second half of the twentieth century involved governmental aid to religiously affiliated primary and secondary schools may explain why the Supreme Court was not clear in describing establishment clause principles.

In establishment clause cases concerning aid to religious schools prior to 1970, the Supreme Court considered only whether the challenged government aid program evidenced a purpose on the part of government to aid religion and whether the challenged program had the primary effect of advancing or inhibiting religious activity. Between 1970 and 1997, the Supreme Court adopted a three part test for evaluating whether government programs that aided religious schools violated the establishment

---

87. Capitol Square Review and Advisory Board v. Pinette, 515 U.S. 753, 771, 115 S.Ct. 2440, 2451, 132 L.Ed.2d 650 (1995) (O'Connor, J., joined by Souter and Breyer, JJ., concurring in part and concurring in the judgment); 515 U.S. at 783, 115 S.Ct. at 2457 (Souter, J., joined by O'Connor and Breyer, JJ., concurring in part and concurring in the judgment).

88. See, e.g., Lynch v. Donnelly, 465 U.S. 668, 690, 104 S.Ct. 1355, 1366, 79 L.Ed.2d 604 (1984) (O'Connor, J., concurring), rehearing denied 466 U.S. 994, 104 S.Ct. 2376, 80 L.Ed.2d 848 (1984); Witters v. Washington Department of Services for the Blind, 474 U.S. 481, 493, 106 S.Ct. 748, 755, 88 L.Ed.2d 846 (1986) (O'Connor, J., concurring), rehearing denied 475 U.S. 1091, 106 S.Ct. 1485, 89 L.Ed.2d 737 (1986); County of Allegheny v. American Civil Liberties Union, 492 U.S. 573, 623, 109 S.Ct. 3086, 3117, 106 L.Ed.2d 472 (1989) (O'Connor, J., concurring in part and concurring in the judgment).

89. Capitol Square Review and Advisory Board v. Pinette, 515 U.S. 753, 770–75, 115 S.Ct. 2440, 2451–53, 132 L.Ed.2d 650 (1995) (O'Connor, J., joined by Souter and Breyer, JJ., concurring in part and concurring in the judgment); 515 U.S. at 789, 115 S.Ct. at 2460 (Souter, J., joined by O'Connor and Breyer, JJ., concurring in part and concurring in the judgment). See footnote 40, and accompanying text, supra.

90. Rosenberger v. Rector and Visitors of the University of Virginia, 515 U.S. 819, 115 S.Ct. 2510, 132 L.Ed.2d 700 (1995) (religiously neutral funding of student organizations); Good News Club v. Milford Central School, 533 U.S. 98, 121 S.Ct. 2093, 150 L.Ed.2d 151 (2001).

91. See § 17.5(e).

92. Zelman v. Simmons–Harris, 536 U.S. 639, 122 S.Ct. 2460, 153 L.Ed.2d 604 (2002). This case is examined in § 17.4, infra.

clause.[1] During this time, the Court held that any program that provided direct to religiously affiliated schools, or their students, would be invalid unless the government program: (1) had a secular purpose; (2) did not have a primary effect of advancing or inhibiting religion; and (3) avoided the creation of an "excessive entanglement" between government and religion. In the 1970's and early 1980's, very few government programs that provided aid to religious schools or religious school students survived the three part test.

In the late 1980's and early 1990's, the Justices appeared to apply the establishment clause tests less strictly than they had during the previous decades. In 1997, the Justices slightly modified the establishment clause tests that would be used to review aid to students at religiously affiliated schools. In *Agostini v. Felton*,[2] the Court upheld a government program that provided remedial services, including remedial educational services, to students at both religious and nonreligious schools, by ruling that this government program had a secular purpose and that it did not have a primary effect that advanced religion. The Court in *Agostini*, however, did not reject the use of the three part test that had been used by the Court during previous decades. Rather, the majority opinion in *Agostini* found that consideration of whether a government program created an excessive entanglement between government and religion was a part of the Court's consideration of whether the challenged government program had the impermissible effect of advancing or inhibiting religion.

In *Agostini*, the majority opinion found that a law providing aid to religious institutions would be invalid if it: (1) was enacted for the purpose of advancing or inculcating religious beliefs; or (2) if the law had a primary effect that advanced religion. In determining whether the law had an impermissible effect, the Court would look at three factors: (1) whether the governmental aid involved in religious indoctrination of students (2) whether the aid program defined recipients in religious terms; (3) whether the aid program created an excessive entanglement between government and religion.[3] Unfortunately, these standards were easier to state than apply. A few years after *Agostini*, the Court seemed hopelessly fragmented concerning how these standards should be applied.[4] For that reason, one must go through the history of Supreme Court cases concerning aid to religion in general, and aid to religiously affiliated schools in particular, if one is to attempt to determine what standards the Justices are actually using in establishment clause cases.

The Court has not established a separate test for the analysis of whether aid that goes to private individuals and then is passed on to religiously affiliated organizations violates the establishment clause. Rather, the Court has applied the purpose and effect test (including an analysis of whether the program creates an excessive entanglement between government and religion) when examining all types of aid to religiously affiliated institutions. Nevertheless, the fact that a government program involves only aid to students or their parents (which allows those persons to make a totally

---

§ 17.4

1. Lemon v. Kurtzman, 403 U.S. 602, 91 S.Ct. 2105, 29 L.Ed.2d 745 (1971). In 1970 the Court had indicated that it would adopt a three part test for analyzing whether religiously neutral laws involved a form of impermissible aid to religious entities in Walz v. Tax Commission, 397 U.S. 664, 90 S.Ct. 1409, 25 L.Ed.2d 697 (1970). The cases establishing the three part test for establishment clause issues are examined in § 17.4.

2. Agostini v. Felton, 521 U.S. 203, 117 S.Ct. 1997, 138 L.Ed.2d 391 (1997) overruling Aguilar v. Felton, 473 U.S. 402, 105 S.Ct. 3232, 87 L.Ed.2d 290 (1985).

3. Agostini v. Felton, 521 U.S. 203, 234, 117 S.Ct. 1997, 2015, 138 L.Ed.2d 391 (1997).

4. An example of the difficulty in discerning Supreme Court standards was the overruling of Meek v. Pittenger, 421 U.S. 349, 95 S.Ct. 1753, 44 L.Ed.2d 217 (1975) and Wolman v. Walter, 433 U.S. 229, 97 S.Ct. 2593, 53 L.Ed.2d 714 (1977) in Mitchell v. Helms, 530 U.S. 793, 120 S.Ct. 2530, 147 L.Ed.2d 660 (2000) even though there was no majority opinion in *Mitchell*. In *Mitchell*, six Justices voted to uphold the government program that provided religiously neutral teaching materials and equipment to religiously affiliated schools; but there was no majority opinion in this case, because the six Justices in the majority could not agree on the meaning or application of the establishment clause standard set out in previous majority opinions. These cases are discussed in a later portion of this section of the Treatise.

free choice as to whether to use the aid in secular or religiously related schools) will be likely to influence the Justices to rule that the program has neither a religious purpose nor primary religious effect that would violate the establishment clause.

In *Zelman v. Simmons–Harris*,[5] the Court distinguished true private choice programs from aid that went directly to religiously affiliated institutions. The five Justices who voted to uphold the tuition voucher program at issue in *Zelman* found that it had neither a primary purpose of advancing religion nor a primary effect that advanced religion in a manner inconsistent with establishment clause values.[6] Justice O'Connor, concurring in *Zelman*, stated that the *Agostini* decision had merely made a formal change in the *Lemon* tests by including the entanglement factor as part of effect analysis[7] The majority opinion in *Zelman* noted that "while our jurisprudence with respect to the constitutionality of direct aid [to religious institution] programs has changed significantly over the past two decades, [citing *Agostini*], our jurisprudence with respect to true private choice programs has remained consistent and unbroken."[8] The dissenting Justices in *Zelman* believed that the majority had not correctly analyzed the way in which the tuition voucher program constituted a direct form of aid to religious activity and had disregarded the extent to which this type of entanglement between government and religion would give rise to social divisions based along religious lines that violated establishment clause values.[9]

Student Transportation. In *Everson v. Board of Education*[10] the Court, by a five to four vote, upheld a program which in effect paid the transportation costs of parochial school students. Pursuant to a state statute, a local school board established a program which reimbursed the parents of students at public and nonprofit private schools for the amounts they spent for bus transportation.[11] The only private nonprofit school in the district was a Catholic school.

A majority of the Justices upheld this program even though they took the position that no aid could be given to a religion in accordance with the establishment clause. The majority was of the view that the provision of free bus transportation to all school children on an equal basis constituted only a general service to benefit and safeguard children rather than an aid to religion. The opinion noted that basic governmental services, such as fire and police protection, could be extended to religious institutions along with the rest of the public without aiding religion. Because the majority saw the general provision of free transportation to be akin to such a service, the program was approved.

At a later time one member of the majority in *Everson* indicated that he felt the case was wrongly decided.[12] However, *Everson* remains the law today and the Court has shown no inclination to reverse its position on basic bus fare reimbursement programs, even though, as discussed later in this section, the state cannot pay for parochial school "field trips."

---

5. Zelman v. Simmons–Harris, 536 U.S. 639, 122 S.Ct. 2460, 153 L.Ed.2d 604 (2002).

6. The case is examined more fully in later paragraphs in this subsection of the Treatise.

7. 536 U.S. at 662, 122 S.Ct. at 2473 (O'Connor, J., concurring).

8. Zelman v. Simmons–Harris, 536 U.S. 639, 647, 122 S.Ct. 2460, 2465–66, 153 L.Ed.2d 604 (2002) (internal citation omitted).

9. 536 U.S. at 683, 122 S.Ct. at 2484 (Stevens, J., dissenting); 536 U.S. at 685, 122 S.Ct. at 2485 (Souter, J., joined by Stevens, Ginsburg, and Breyer, JJ., dissenting); 536 U.S. at 716, 122 S.Ct. at 2502 (Breyer, J., dissenting).

10. 330 U.S. 1, 67 S.Ct. 504, 91 L.Ed. 711 (1947). The dissent of Justice Rutledge is worth noting for it contains a history of many of the circumstances that led to the

drafting of the Amendment. 330 U.S. 1, 33–43, 67 S.Ct. 504, 520–25, 91 L.Ed. 711 (1947) (Rutledge, J., dissenting).

11. There should be no serious problem presented by the exclusion of students at private profit-making or proprietary schools. To date the legislature is free to classify on the basis of wealth or financial characteristics so long as the classification is not irrational or clearly invidious. Cf., San Antonio Independent School District v. Rodriguez, 411 U.S. 1, 28, 93 S.Ct. 1278, 1293–94, 36 L.Ed.2d 16 (1973).

12. Engel v. Vitale, 370 U.S. 421, 443–44, 82 S.Ct. 1261, 1273–74, 8 L.Ed.2d 601 (1962) (Douglas, J., concurring).

If a similar aid program was limited by statute to public and parochial school students the Court would come to a different conclusion because of the exclusion of children in private nonprofit schools. Such a statute would have the effect of preferring religious school students over students at other nonprofit schools and this preference should be held to violate the establishment clause.

By the time that the Court was next confronted with a program of aid to parochial school students, it was employing the "purpose and effect" test to resolve establishment clause claims.[13] Under this test the purpose of a state program must be secular in nature. Additionally, the program may not have a primary effect of either advancing or inhibiting religion or religious practices to withstand review under this test.

Textbooks. In *Board of Education v. Allen* [14] the Court upheld a program of providing textbooks to parochial school students under the purpose and effect test. The New York textbook law under review required school boards to loan textbooks to students in all public or private schools. This resulted in books being given to parochial school students for their studies in the religious schools. However, only books for secular studies could be loaned to students and the books had to be either ones used in public schools or approved by the school board as being secular in nature. The opinion found no religious purpose in this law because it accepted the position that the program was designed to aid the secular education of students. This secular purpose—the improvement of the educational opportunities for all children—has sufficed in every case relating to aid for religious schools.[15]

The *Allen* majority also found that the program did not have a primary effect of advancing religion. At this time a majority of the Justices refused to assume that the religious schools—including Catholic primary and secondary schools—were so permeated by religion that even classes in secular subjects advanced religion. Thus the majority could find that the books were used only for the secular teaching component of such schools. The local board's insuring that only secular books were loaned, and the absence of proof that secular classes were used to advance religion, were the mainstays of the majority position.[16] It must be noted that such textbook programs would be invalid if they aided schools that discriminated on the basis of race.[17]

Tax Exempt Status for Religious Organizations. In *Walz v. Tax Commission* [18] the Court expanded the establishment clause tests while upholding another form of aid to religious entities. In this case the Court upheld the granting of exemptions from property taxes to churches as a part of a general exception for a wide variety of nonprofit institutions.[19] Presumably this ruling validates the granting of tax exemptions to religious schools so long as the exemption is granted to all nonprofit schools.

The majority opinion by Chief Justice Burger required that the program withstand a

---

13. This test was developed in the "school prayer" cases, see § 17.5(c), infra.

14. 392 U.S. 236, 88 S.Ct. 1923, 20 L.Ed.2d 1060 (1968).

15. The only cases which center on a finding of religious purpose are Epperson v. Arkansas, 393 U.S. 97, 89 S.Ct. 266, 21 L.Ed.2d 228 (1968) which is discussed in § 17.5, infra, and Stone v. Graham, 449 U.S. 39, 101 S.Ct. 192, 66 L.Ed.2d 199 (1980), which is examined in § 17.5(c), infra.

16. Board of Education v. Allen, 392 U.S. 236, 245–48, 88 S.Ct. 1923, 1927–29, 20 L.Ed.2d 1060 (1968).

17. In Bob Jones University v. United States, 461 U.S. 574, 103 S.Ct. 2017, 76 L.Ed.2d 157 (1983), the Supreme Court upheld the authority of the Internal Revenue Service to deny tax exempt status to private schools which practice racial discrimination in their admission standards or educational policy on the basis of the religious doctrine

of the school's administration. Because the Internal Revenue Service had chosen to follow earlier lower federal court rulings prohibiting such tax exempt status for racially discriminatory private schools, the Supreme Court was not required to determine whether a Congressional or administrative decision to grant such status to discriminatory organizations would violate the equal protection component of the Fifth Amendment due process clause. See §§ 12.4(c), 14.9(a)(2)(b), supra.

18. 397 U.S. 664, 90 S.Ct. 1409, 25 L.Ed.2d 697 (1970).

19. It should be noted that the opinion did not approve granting exemptions for church property where no similar exemption existed for other social service or nonprofit activities. Such a preferential exemption would almost certainly constitute a prohibited direct aid to certain religious entities.

three-part test to avoid invalidation under the establishment clause. The program would be invalid unless it: (1) had a secular purpose, (2) had no primary effect of advancing or inhibiting religion, and (3) avoided causing an "excessive entanglement" between government and religion.[20] The general tax exemption was found to have a secular purpose and provide only incidental aid to religion. The majority opinion also found that the taxation of church property would cause at least as much administrative entanglement between government and religious authorities as did the exemption. The Court was clearly persuaded by the long history of such exemptions: more than 200 years of a virtually uniform practice in the states without any further "establishment" effects.[21]

Other Forms of Aid to Religiously Affiliated Schools or Their Students. The Court invalidated two state attempts to subsidize the costs of parochial school education in *Lemon v. Kurtzman*.[22] Rhode Island provided a fifteen percent salary supplement to teachers of secular subjects in private schools where the per-pupil expenditure was below that of the public schools. In the second program, Pennsylvania authorized the reimbursement of nonpublic schools for a fraction of teacher salaries and instructional materials in secular subjects. Under both state systems, Catholic schools were the main beneficiaries of the programs.[23]

Once again, the Court accepted the legislatures' position that they were pursuing the secular end of promoting the nonreligious education of young children. The Court did not come to an exact ruling on whether the programs had a primary effect of advancing religion.[24] However, the Court's discussion of the

need for avoiding administrative entanglement indicated that such programs could have a prohibited effect. Because the majority assumed that religious elementary and secondary schools were likely to advance religion even in their secular subjects, it would seem that these subsidies would constitute direct aid to religion.

Instead of basing the ruling on the effect of these programs, the opinion in *Lemon* struck down these statutes because it found that they fostered an excessive entanglement between church and state. Chief Justice Burger, writing for the majority, held that, in assessing the degree of entanglement, three factors were to be considered: (1) the character and purpose of the institution benefited; (2) the nature of the aid; (3) the resulting relationship between government and religious authorities.[25]

In applying this three part test the majority opinion first found that Catholic elementary and secondary schools were an integral part of the religious program of that church. The religious atmosphere and control of this type of school showed that religious teaching might be advanced, even inadvertently, in secular courses. Second, the aid here was a subsidy for teacher salaries. The Court noted that, unlike textbooks, teachers could not be checked in advance to insure that they would not teach religion. Though the teachers could in good faith promise to remain neutral, they might inadvertently advance religion in the classroom. Finally, the majority found that in order to insure that religious activities or teaching were not aided by the program, the state would have to place a great number of restrictions on the schools and engage in a monitoring program which would be little

---

20. 397 U.S. at 664, 90 S.Ct. at 1409.

21. 397 U.S. at 676–80, 90 S.Ct. at 1115–17.

22. 403 U.S. 602, 91 S.Ct. 2105, 29 L.Ed.2d 745 (1971). At this time the Court also decided Tilton v. Richardson, 403 U.S. 672, 91 S.Ct. 2091, 29 L.Ed.2d 790 (1971) involving aid to religious colleges.

23. While the majority has noted this fact in several cases it is difficult to see its relevance. It might be used in an attempt to show a religious "purpose" but the Court has never looked into the motives of the legislature in such a manner. The religious effect of administrative entanglements might be quantitatively (but not qualitatively) greater if a large number of parochial schools were

aided. This would not relate to the number or names of the religions involved. The Justices may feel that Catholic primary schools are uniquely permeated with religion, but that raises questions as to the basis for such a judicial ruling and why other parochial schools are treated in the same manner by the Court. Finally, the Justices might feel that Catholic schools generate greater political division. One might question both the propriety and usefulness of such judicial assumptions.

24. 403 U.S. at 613–14, 91 S.Ct. at 2111–12.

25. 403 U.S. at 615, 91 S.Ct. at 2112.

short of ongoing surveillance. Thus, the character of the school and the aid required complex ongoing relationships between secular and religious authorities. This three part analysis showed that the program would result in an excessive entanglement violative of the establishment clause.

The Chief Justice also stressed the fact that these types of programs were politically divisive. The provision of significant ongoing aid to parochial elementary and secondary schools injected an explosive political issue which caused division along religious lines. These programs virtually guarantee that there will be yearly public debate and political conflict between religious factions. The majority opinion stated that this division was to be eliminated by the establishment clause.[26] However, the opinion was not clear as to whether this was merely the reason for strict application of the purpose-effect-entanglement test, a branch of the entanglement test, or a fourth test. Thus, we can only say that where the majority views an aid program as causing an undue amount of political division along religious lines the program is likely to be invalidated.

Since the *Lemon* decision in 1970 the Supreme Court has reviewed a wide variety of government programs of aid to religiously affiliated schools, the students of those schools, or the parents of those students. The Court has used the purpose, primary effect, and excessive entanglement tests for reviewing the validity of those laws. The Court also has used the *Lemon* three part approach to assessing the excessive entanglement issue as it has in each case looked at the character of the institution benefited, the nature of the aid, and the resulting relationship between government and religious authorities. Because many of the Supreme Court cases involve the review of several types of aid to religious schools or students we will review those decisions chronologically rather than in terms of specific

types of government aid programs. In most of these cases the Court invalidated the government attempt to aid parochial schools or students. Near the end of this section we will review the cases that have approved forms of aid to religious schools beyond the granting of basic student transportation, textbook programs, and tax-exempt status which we have examined previously in this section.[27]

The Court held invalid a law granting all private schools a payment for services mandated by state law in *Levitt v. Committee for Public Education.*[28] The lump sum per pupil payment was to cover the cost of keeping certain records, preparation of various reports to the state, and the testing of students on required subjects. The largest amount was for required tests, some of which were prepared by the private school teachers and some by the state. A majority of the Justices easily concluded that these grants constituted a prohibited form of aid to religion. Given the nature of religious primary and secondary schools these unrestricted lump sum grants might go to advance the sectarian activities as well as the secular functions of these schools. The fact that these services were required by the state could not furnish a way to avoid the prohibition against subsidizing religious activities.

The Court examined the constitutionality of tuition reimbursement and tax credit programs in *Committee for Public Education v. Nyquist*[29] and *Sloan v. Lemon.*[30] In these cases New York and Pennsylvania had attempted to reimburse the parents of students attending nonpublic schools for a portion of the tuition which they paid to those schools. Once again, the greatest number of these schools were Catholic schools, and both programs were invalidated by the Court. The *Nyquist* case gave rise to the more significant opinion because New York had attempted to insure the secular effect of its program by

---

26. 403 U.S. at 622, 91 S.Ct. at 2115–16.

27. In the years in which the Court ruled on these forms of aid to grade schools and high schools the Court also examined, and upheld in some cases, aid to religiously affiliated colleges. See, e.g., Hunt v. McNair, 413 U.S.

734, 93 S.Ct. 2868, 37 L.Ed.2d 923 (1973). See § 17.4(b), infra.

28. 413 U.S. 472, 93 S.Ct. 2814, 37 L.Ed.2d 736 (1973).

29. 413 U.S. 756, 93 S.Ct. 2955, 37 L.Ed.2d 948 (1973).

30. 413 U.S. 825, 93 S.Ct. 2982, 37 L.Ed.2d 939 (1973).

making the payments and granting the tax credits directly to the parents, limiting the amounts to no more than one-half of the tuition paid, and excluding high income families.[31]

The Court invalidated both programs when it found that the programs had the effect of advancing religion. The state had to insure that these funds did not advance religion and the majority was unwilling to accept statistical guarantees that only the secular function could benefit from this aid. In *Nyquist* and *Sloan*, the Court invalidated statutory grants, tax credits, and tax deductions that reimbursed only private school students for educational costs.

A statute which granted tax deductions to *all* students or parents based upon actual expenditures for attending public *or* private schools would appear to have a religiously neutral purpose and effect. Such a statute might not require an excessive entanglement between government and religion in order to limit deductions to secular expenses. Therefore, the Court will uphold a statute granting a tax deduction for educational expenses that is truly neutral in its treatment of public and private school students and their expenses.[32]

Two cases decided during the 1970s, *Meek v. Pittenger*[33] and *Wolman v. Walter*[34], involved

highly technical applications of the *Lemon* test; those decisions appeared to be inconsistent with the *Allen* decision. In 2000, both the *Meek* and *Wolman* decisions would be overruled.[35]

In *Meek v. Pittenger*[36] the Court invalidated several new forms of aid to nonpublic schools. Following the rejection of its earlier program, Pennsylvania had adopted three new forms of aid for students at nonpublic schools: (1) a textbook-loan program similar to the one approved in *Allen;* (2) the loaning to nonpublic schools of instructional materials of a secular nature; (3) the provision of auxiliary guidance, testing, remedial, and therapeutic services by public school employees who would provide services at the private schools. The Court upheld the textbook program but invalidated the other two forms of aid. The textbook program was upheld on the basis of the *Allen* decision. But, due to the view of parochial schools taken in later cases and the new entanglement test, some Justices would even have reconsidered the validity of such programs.[37]

The loan of instructional materials, such as recording equipment, laboratory materials or maps was held invalid in *Meek* because such loans had the impermissible effect of aiding religion. Although the majority accepted the

---

31. The law provided for payments to parents with an annual taxable income of under $15,000 and tax credits to those with an adjusted gross income of under $25,000. In no event could the payment exceed the lesser of the statutory limits (set between $50 and $100) or 50 percent of the tuition actually paid. The law, complete with tax tables, is reprinted at 413 U.S. at 761–67, 93 S.Ct. at 2959–63.

32. The Supreme Court later upheld a state statute allowing taxpayers to deduct, when computing their income tax liability, the cost of "tuition, textbooks, and transportation" expenses incurred to send their children to either a public or private school. Because the deduction was available to all students or parents, not just those who attended private or religious schools, five Justices found that the law had a nonreligious purpose and effect. Because only neutral, incidental aid was given to students attending religious schools, the majority ruled that the government involvement in audits of deductions to insure proper tax computations, and disallowance of deductions for textbooks used to teach religious doctrines, did not constitute an excessive entanglement between government and religion. Mueller v. Allen, 463 U.S. 388, 103 S.Ct. 3062, 77 L.Ed.2d 721 (1983).

33. 421 U.S. 349, 95 S.Ct. 1753, 44 L.Ed.2d 217 (1975).

34. 433 U.S. 229, 97 S.Ct. 2593, 53 L.Ed.2d 714 (1977), overruled 530 U.S. 793, 120 S.Ct. 2530, 147 L.Ed.2d 660 (2000).

35. These decisions were overruled, without a majority opinion, in Mitchell v. Helms, 530 U.S. 793, 120 S.Ct. 2530, 147 L.Ed.2d 660 (2000). By a 6 to 3 vote, the Justices approved the use of federal funds by local school districts to provide aid in the form of non-religious teaching equipment as well as textbooks to public and private schools, including religiously affiliated primary and secondary schools. In so doing, both the plurality and concurring opinions took the position that the *Meek* and *Wolman* cases were inconsistent with other Supreme Court decisions and should be overruled. 530 U.S. at 834, 120 S.Ct. at 2555 (Part IV of the opinion of Thomas, J., joined by Rehnquist, C.J., and Scalia and Kennedy, JJ., announcing the judgment of the Court); 530 U.S. at 836, 120 S.Ct. at 2556 (O'Connor, J., joined by Breyer, J., concurring in the judgment).

36. 421 U.S. 349, 95 S.Ct. 1753, 44 L.Ed.2d 217 (1975).

37. 421 U.S. at 378–79, 95 S.Ct. at 1769–70 (Brennan, J., concurring in part, dissenting in part).

lower court characterization of these materials as so secular that they were "self-policing," [38] the opinion found an impermissible degree of aid to religion in this program. The grant of materials to the schools aided their operation and made the entire religious enterprise a more viable institution. As the function of parochial primary and secondary schools was inherently religious, this constituted impermissible aid to religion in the majority's view. This "aid-to-the-enterprise" theory is the culmination of the view of parochial schools taken in earlier cases and it eliminates most forms of aid which might help these schools.

The provision of auxiliary services also was invalidated in *Meek*. The state sought to avoid a religious effect by using its own employees to provide assistance in developing purely secular educational skills. In this way the state hoped to also avoid the necessity for a surveillance of the teachers and programs which might constitute an excessive entanglement. Justice Stewart, writing for the majority, found the use of state employees insufficient to guarantee a purely secular program. In the majority's view there remained the possibility that even a public school employee might advance religious ends in such a situation. Consequently, the Court held that it is impossible to avoid all possible religious effects, even in secular programs for remedial students, without supervision of the programs on a scale that would result in a prohibited form of entanglement.

In *Meek* the majority indicated that certain diagnostic health or speech services might be compatible with the establishment clause. Thus, if a state used its own employees to go into public schools to make diagnosis of illness or educational disabilities and, perhaps, offer some basic treatment the program should withstand constitutional challenge.

In *Wolman v. Walter*[39] the Court examined a variety of school and student aid programs. In a complicated statutory program, Ohio attempted to aid private schools, which were primarily Catholic schools. This program consisted of six types of aid for all nonpublic elementary and secondary schools: (1) a textbook program like the ones approved in earlier Supreme Court cases; (2) the provision of funds to distribute and score standardized educational tests; (3) diagnostic services with state personnel testing individual children for specified health and educational problems; (4) therapeutic services for health and educational disabilities provided by state personnel at sites outside of the parochial school; (5) loans to students of instructional materials and equipment; (6) funds for commercial transportation or the use of state school buses for field trips.

The textbook program (#1) in *Wolman* was upheld by a vote of six to three on the basis of *Allen*. The testing and test scoring provision (#2), was upheld by a six to three vote, because, unlike *Levitt*, these were standard educational tests prepared by state employees and designed to insure that private school students are in fact being properly educated. The diagnostic services (#3) were upheld by a vote of eight to one, because there was an important secular goal in caring for children and no possible religious effect. The therapeutic services (#4) were upheld by a vote of seven to two, because the removal of the services from the school eliminated the danger of religious permeation of the program. The instructional materials program (#5) was held invalid, by a six to three vote, on precisely the same basis as was the similar program in *Meek*. The provision of transportation aid (#6) was held invalid, by a five to four vote.

The *Wolman* opinion by Justice Blackmun was a majority opinion in part and a plurality opinion in part.

The reason for the differing votes in *Wolman* was that the Justices were evenly split between three positions. Chief Justice Burger and Justices White and Rehnquist would have allowed the state to help the education of all children so long as there is no clear aid to religion. Justices Stewart, Blackmun, and

---

38. Meek v. Pittenger, 421 U.S. 349, 365, 95 S.Ct. 1753, 1763, 44 L.Ed.2d 217 (1975), quoting Meek v. Pittinger, 374 F.Supp. 639, 660 (E.D.Pa.1974).

39. 433 U.S. 229, 97 S.Ct. 2593, 53 L.Ed.2d 714 (1977).

Powell believed that an independent application of the three part test would allow the state to promote secular education without impermissibly fostering religion. Justices Brennan, Marshall, and Stevens were committed to the position that the First Amendment was designed to prohibit any aid to religion.

Reimbursement of Parochial Schools for Grading State Tests and Reporting Data to the State. In *Committee for Public Education and Religious Liberty v. Regan*,[40] the Supreme Court upheld, by a five to four vote, a state statute which reimbursed non-public schools for expenses incurred in administering and scoring standardized educational achievement tests; recording and reporting data concerning student attendance; and compiling and reporting statistical information about the students, staff, and facilities of each institution.

Writing for the majority, Justice White found that the program had a secular purpose, that its principal or primary effect neither advanced nor inhibited religion, and that it did not foster an excessive government entanglement with religion. The promotion of quality nonreligious education of students in private schools was once again found sufficient to pass the first prong of the three part test.

The Court found that the program did not have a religious effect because, unlike the state law stricken in *Levitt v. Committee for Public Education*,[41] this program involved repayment for administrative costs connected to specific state-required functions and, therefore, had virtually no potential for aiding the propagation of religious beliefs. The Court already had approved the use of state standardized educational achievement tests in private schools in *Wolman v. Walter*. In *Committee for Public Education and Religious Liberty*, the Court held that direct cash reimbursement to nonpublic schools for administering and grading the examinations did not promote sectarian beliefs because the content of the tests was controlled by public authorities and the grad-

ing of the objective and essay questions did not provide any realistic opportunity to advance religious beliefs. The other administrative and record-keeping expenses reimbursed by the state involved the collection and reporting of attendance records and information concerning the personnel, facilities, and curriculum of each school. The majority found that state payment of such costs created no appreciable risk of aiding the religious function of the school even though the reimbursement might free other funds within the school's budget for unspecified purposes.

Finally, in *Committee for Public Education and Religious Liberty* the majority concluded that there was no excessive entanglement fostered by this program even though the program required the schools to maintain separate accounts for the reimbursable expenses and to submit the accounts for audits by public authorities. Since the services were "discrete and clearly identifiable" the Court held that the review process did not pose a danger to either government neutrality or religious freedom. In this case Justices Stewart and Powell, who had often voted to apply the three part test very strictly in order to invalidate state programs aiding religious schools, joined with Chief Justice Burger and Justices White and Rehnquist in voting to uphold the reimbursement program.

The *Wolman* and *Meek* decisions would be rejected in the year 2000, by a United States Supreme Court that was still split between three positions on how to analyze aid to religiously affiliated schools. As a precursor to the 2000 decision, in 1997, the Supreme Court's majority opinion in *Agostini v. Felton*[42] set forth a basic approach for analyzing aid to religious institution problems. A majority of the Justices agreed that the concept of excessive entanglement should be only one of the factors examined in determining whether a law had an impermissible primary effect that advanced or inhibited religion in violation of

---

40. 444 U.S. 646, 100 S.Ct. 840, 63 L.Ed.2d 94 (1980).

41. 413 U.S. 472, 93 S.Ct. 2814, 37 L.Ed.2d 736 (1973).

42. 521 U.S. 203, 117 S.Ct. 1997, 138 L.Ed.2d 391 (1997). See notes 62–68, and accompanying text, in this section of the Treatise.

the establishment clause.[43]

In 2000, the Justices split concerning the meaning of *Agostini* and approach to be taken to school aid cases. In Mitchell v. Helms[44] the Court by a 6 to 3 vote, but without a majority opinion, held that local school districts could use federal funds for providing educational equipment and materials to both public and private schools, including non-religious schools. In the *Mitchell* case, the school board had used part of its federal funds to provide "library books, computers, and computer software, and also slide and movie projectors, overhead projectors, television sets, tape recorders, VCRs, projection screens, laboratory equipment, maps, globes, film strips, slides and cassette recordings" to public and private schools, including 41 religiously affiliated schools.[45] The persons challenging the program had not alleged that the law had a religious purpose, so that the Court's focus was solely on whether the granting of this type of aid to religiously affiliated schools and their students had an impermissible effect under the establishment clause.

In *Mitchell*, both the plurality opinion, written by Justice Thomas for four Justices, and the concurring opinion, by Justices O'Connor and Breyer, agreed that the effect of the law should be analyzed in terms of whether it: (1) involved governmental indoctrination of students; (2) defined recipients with religious references; or (3) created an excessive entanglement between government and religion. The plurality and concurring opinions also agreed that the program at issue in *Mitchell* was valid, and that the *Meek* and *Wolman* decisions should be overruled. However, the plurality and concurring opinions took very different approaches to this result. Justice Thomas, who

was joined by Chief Justice Rehnquist and Justices Scalia and Kennedy, found that religiously neutral aid could be given to schools consistently with the establishment clause even if recipient schools were pervasively sectarian and, in fact, used the aid in their religious education classes and for religious activities.[46]

Justice O'Connor, joined by Justice Breyer, concurred only in the judgment of the Court in *Mitchell*.[47] The two concurring Justices believed that a program of religiously neutral aid should be upheld but they also believed that a particular grant to a school would be invalid if the persons challenging the grant could show that the particular religious school in fact had diverted the religiously neutral materials given to the school by the government into religious education and religious indoctrination.

Three Justices dissented in *Mitchell*, because they believed that any form of aid to religious schools that had the theoretical potential for being misused and diverted to religious indoctrination or religious education ran afoul of establishment clause principles.[48]

Tuition Tax Credits or Deductions. In *Mueller v. Allen*,[49] the Court, by five to four vote, upheld a state tax statute which allowed taxpayers to deduct from their state income tax the expenses incurred in providing "tuition, textbooks and transportation" for their children attending any public or private elementary or secondary school in the state. Justice Rehnquist, who wrote the majority opinion, found that the law was valid under the purpose-effect-entanglement test. The state's secular purpose was to improve the education of all young persons within the state. The majority could rely on earlier Supreme Court

---

43. Agostini v. Felton, 521 U.S. 203, 234, 117 S.Ct. 1997, 2015, 138 L.Ed.2d 391 (1997).

44. Mitchell v. Helms, 530 U.S. 793, 120 S.Ct. 2530, 147 L.Ed.2d 660 (2000) judgment of the Court announced by Thomas, J., in an opinion joined by Rehnquist, C.J., and Scalia and Kennedy, JJ.). 530 U.S. at 836, 120 S.Ct. at 2556 (O'Connor, J., joined by Breyer, J., concurring in the judgment). 530 U.S. at 866, 120 S.Ct. at 2572 (Souter, J., joined by Stevens and Ginsburg, JJ., dissenting.

45. 530 U.S. at 803–05, 120 S.Ct. at 2538–39. (Plurality opinion).

46. 530 U.S. at 820–28, 120 S.Ct. at 2547–52 (plurality opinion).

47. 530 U.S. at 836, 856, 120 S.Ct. at 2556, 2567 (O'Connor, J., joined by Breyer, J., concurring in the judgment).

48. 530 U.S. at 866, 120 S.Ct. at 2572 (Souter, J., joined by Stevens and Ginsburg, JJ., dissenting).

49. 463 U.S. 388, 103 S.Ct. 3062, 77 L.Ed.2d 721 (1983). The basic portion of the Minnesota statute at issue was reprinted in footnote 1 of the Court's opinion.

recognition that legislators have a nonreligious purpose in aiding the secular education of children regardless of where they attend school.

Justice Rehnquist differentiated this tuition and expense deduction from those which had been stricken down in earlier cases.[50] In the earlier cases states had given tax credits or deductions only to those parents who sent their children to nonpublic schools; this created a governmentally established preference for nonpublic and religious schools. In *Mueller,* Justice Rehnquist stressed that the legislature had attempted to equalize the tax burden of all of its citizens by allowing all parents, whether their children attended public or private schools, to deduct their children's educational expenses. This was religiously neutral help to the students which conferred only the most "attenuated financial benefit" on religious schools.[51] The fact that parents sending their children to nonpublic schools might receive greater tax deductions because they had greater expenses would not constitute an impermissible form of aid to religion since those attending public schools received a direct subsidy. This provision was on its face a neutral attempt by the state to award financial and tax benefits to students and their parents. Similarly, the fact that most private school students in the state attended religiously affiliated schools would not affect the Court's analysis. A law which neutrally helped children would not be upheld or stricken solely upon the fact that in a given year persons who claimed the otherwise nonobjec-

tionable benefit sent their children to a school affiliated with a particular religion.

Finally, these Justices found no violation of the entanglement test even though the deduction could not be allowed for "instructional books and materials used in the teaching of religious tenets, doctrines or worship, the purpose of which is to inculcate such tenets, doctrines or worship." The majority found that this determination of the legitimacy of any individual's deduction required no more entanglement between government and religion than would a determination of whether textbooks given or loaned to parents or children attending nonpublic schools were truly secular in nature, a type of administrative entanglement that had been upheld in previous cases.[52] The Justices were concerned here only with whether there was such administrative entanglement between the government and religion as to jeopardize the concept of neutrality and the principles that underlie the establishment clause rather than with a concern with whether such programs created political divisiveness.[53]

Secular Instruction and Secular Services for Religious School Students: the 1997 Rejection of the "Assumptions" used by the Court in 1985. In 1985, the Justices believed that the religious and secular educational functions of religiously affiliated primary and secondary schools were so intertwined that it was impossible for the government to provide educational assistance to stu-

---

50. See Committee for Public Education v. Nyquist, 413 U.S. 756, 93 S.Ct. 2955, 37 L.Ed.2d 948 (1973); Sloan v. Lemon, 413 U.S. 825, 93 S.Ct. 2982, 37 L.Ed.2d 939 (1973). See notes 24–28 supra and accompanying text.

51. In his *Mueller* majority opinion, Justice Rehnquist compared the aid in this case to the religiously neutral activity of government in providing a forum open to religious as well as nonreligious speech that was endorsed in Widmar v. Vincent, 454 U.S. 263, 102 S.Ct. 269, 70 L.Ed.2d 440 (1981). *Widmar* is noted in § 17.5(e), infra. See Mueller v. Allen, 463 U.S. 388, 397, 103 S.Ct. 3062, 3068–69, 77 L.Ed.2d 721, 730–31 (1983).

52. See Board of Education v. Allen, 392 U.S. 236, 88 S.Ct. 1923, 20 L.Ed.2d 1060 (1968).

53. Although political divisiveness was not at issue in the *Mueller* case, the Court noted that the language of the Supreme Court regarding such a concern "must be regarded as confined to cases where direct financial subsidies are

paid to parochial schools or to teachers in parochial schools." Mueller v. Allen, 463 U.S. 388, 403–04 n. 11, 103 S.Ct. 3062, 3071 n. 11, 77 L.Ed.2d 721, 733 n. 11 (1983).

The dissenting Justices in *Mueller* would have invalidated the law because the tax benefit that flowed to students and parents made it possible for them to increase their financial support for and payments to the school. These Justices believed that this type of aid to the general educational functions of such schools resulted in aid to the sectarian enterprise as a whole. The result of this aid to the enterprise theory was to view the provision of such aid as prohibited by earlier cases as "at odds with the fundamental principle that a State may provide no financial support whatsoever to promote religion." Mueller v. Allen, 463 U.S. 388, 417, 103 S.Ct. 3062, 3078, 77 L.Ed.2d 721, 742 (1983) (Marshall, J., joined by Brennan, Blackmun and Stevens, JJ., dissenting).

dents on the property of a religiously affiliated school without either aiding the religion function of the school, or creating an excessive entanglement between government and religion. In 1997, the Supreme Court would reject the assumptions that meant that any form of aid to students at religious schools would either have an impermissible effect of aiding religious indoctrination or, in the alternative, give rise to an excessive entanglement between government and religion. After examining the approach the Supreme Court used in 1985 to analyze the constitutionality of government assistance to students at religiously affiliated schools, we will explain how the Court, in 1997, was able to overturn the 1985 decisions without altering any establishment clause principles.

In *Grand Rapids School District v. Ball* [54] the Court invalidated two programs which it found to have a primary religious effect. The Grand Rapids City School District had adopted two programs to provide nonreligious classes for private school students that were taught by teachers who were hired by the school system and conducted in "leased" classrooms in the private schools, virtually all of which were sectarian schools. The classroom space for both programs was leased at a rate of six dollars per classroom per week; the regulations stated that these rooms were to be considered public school classrooms and had to be free of any religious symbols.

One of the Grand Rapids programs was titled a "community education program"; the second program was titled a "shared time program." The community education program offered classes for both adults and children at private elementary schools at the close of the regular school day. None of the classes offered was available at the regular day sessions of the private schools and the classes were not considered part of the basic curriculum. Similar courses, however, were a regular part of the more extensive curriculum of the Grand Rapids public schools. The community edu-

cation program teachers were private school teachers who were considered part time public school employees.

Under the shared time program, the Grand Rapids school board financed a program in which full time public employees went into the private schools and moved from classroom to classroom during the course of a school day teaching nonreligious courses. These courses supplemented the core curriculum courses required by the state of Michigan as a part of an accredited school's program. These subjects were labeled "remedial" and "enrichment" courses; they involved subjects such as art, mathematics, and reading. Approximately ten percent of each private school student's time, according to the findings of the lower court, was spent in the shared time program.

Justice Brennan wrote the majority opinion in *Grand Rapids School District* and held that the community education program and the shared time program were both invalid because each had a primary effect of advancing religion. Justice Brennan's majority opinion stated that the establishment clause would absolutely prohibit government financed or government sponsored indoctrination into the beliefs of a particular religious faith. Both programs involved a significant risk of state sponsored indoctrination of religious beliefs. In arriving at this conclusion Justice Brennan employed the approach adopted in *Lemon v. Kurtzman* [55] and previously used in *Wolman v. Walter* [56] to invalidate the use of state paid professional staff to provide remedial and accelerated instruction to nonpublic school students on religious school premises.

The community education program was easily invalidated in *Grand Rapids School District*, as seven Justices found that the attempt to use religious school teachers to teach secular subjects on religious school premises had a significant potential for inadvertent, as well as conscious, communication of religious beliefs and attitudes during the secular course. [57] The

---

54. 473 U.S. 373, 105 S.Ct. 3216, 87 L.Ed.2d 267 (1985).

55. 403 U.S. 602, 91 S.Ct. 2105, 29 L.Ed.2d 745 (1971).

56. 433 U.S. 229, 97 S.Ct. 2593, 53 L.Ed.2d 714 (1977).

57. In Grand Rapids School District v. Ball, 473 U.S. 373, 105 S.Ct. 3216, 87 L.Ed.2d 267 (1985), Justice Bren-

shared time program, which involved government employees teaching nonreligious subjects in the religious schools, was invalidated by a five to four vote of the Justices in *Grand Rapids School District.* A majority of the Justices found that religiously affiliated grade schools and high schools are pervasively sectarian and that any government aid to the educational function of such schools might advance religion.

As to both of the programs in *Grand Rapids School District,* Justice Brennan found an impermissible advancement of religion in three ways. First, the teachers participating in the programs might intentionally or inadvertently advance particular religious tenets or beliefs. Second, the programs provided a crucial symbolic link between government and religion, thereby enlisting—at least in the eyes of impressionable youngsters—the power of government to support the religious denomination operating the school. Third, the programs could have the effect of directly promoting religion by impermissibly providing a subsidy to the primary religious mission of the institutions affected. The shared time program, as well as the community education program, involved aid to the basic educational function of religious schools and thereby freed religious school resources for other purposes, including the teaching of religion classes.

In *Aguilar v. Felton,*[58] the Court, by a five to four vote of the Justices, invalidated a program under which New York City used federal funds it received under Title I of the Elementary and Secondary Education Act to pay the salaries of public school district employees who provided nonreligious instruction and services at private schools, including religiously affiliated schools. Justice Brennan again wrote the majority opinion; he found that the New York program violated the excessive entanglement

test. The federal law provided funds for local school districts to provide services for both public and private school students. The Supreme Court in *Aguilar* did not invalidate the federal law but prohibited the use of funds for programs wherein the services or courses were provided for students on the grounds of a religiously affiliated school. The majority opinion in *Aguilar* did not overturn the ruling of *Wolman v. Walter*[59] that allowed state-supported testing for health or learning problems on parochial school premises and remedial education and health services for religious school students if those services were offered away from religious school premises.

The New York program at issue in *Aguilar* involved public employees providing courses or programs for remedial reading skills, remedial mathematics, English as a second language, and a variety of guidance services. All the services were provided by public school teachers, counselors, psychologists, psychiatrists or social workers as the particular service or program required. Unlike the programs that the Court had invalidated in *Grand Rapids School District,* the New York program appeared to involve administrative regulations designed to insure that the services offered by the public school teachers at the parochial schools could not involve religious content or the advancement of religious beliefs. The majority opinion in *Aguilar* dispensed with primary effect analysis and invalidated the program because it created an excessive entanglement between church and state. Justice Brennan's majority opinion approached the analysis of the excessive entanglement issue as the Court had in the cases in the 1970's. The majority opinion found that the schools were pervasively sectarian and that the type of aid involved a significant potential for the advancement of religion. Justice Brennan also found that pervasive monitoring would be required to avoid a pri-

---

nan's majority opinion, which invalidated both the community education program and shared time program was joined by Justices Blackmun, Marshall, Powell, and Stevens. Chief Justice Burger and Justice O'Connor concurred in the judgment in *Grand Rapids School District* insofar as the Court invalidated the community education program; they dissented from the invalidation of the shared time program. 473 U.S. at 400, 105 S.Ct. at 3231 (Burger, C.J., concurring in the judgment in part and

dissenting in part); id. (O'Connor, J., concurring in the judgment in part and dissenting in part). Justices White and Rehnquist dissented; they would have upheld both programs.

58. 473 U.S. 402, 105 S.Ct. 3232, 87 L.Ed.2d 290 (1985).

59. 433 U.S. 229, 97 S.Ct. 2593, 53 L.Ed.2d 714 (1977).

mary religious effect. The degree of administrative involvement between government and religion required to avoid the advancement of religion as an effect of the program created an excessive entanglement between governmental and religious authorities. That type of entanglement potentially could lead to the exercise of improper governmental authority over a religious organization and an improper influence in government decisionmaking by members of the denomination which the government was regulating. The majority opinion in *Aguilar* also noted, though it did not emphasize this point, that the danger of political divisiveness along religious lines increases as the degree of involvement between government decisionmakers and religious authorities increases.

The *Grand Rapids School District,* and *Aguilar* decisions appeared to make it virtually impossible for the government to provide even religiously neutral educational aid to students with special needs (such as physically handicapped children) on religious school property. However, in the 1990s, the Supreme Court would take a new approach to evaluating such programs.

In *Board of Education of Kiryas Joel Village School District v. Grumet,*[60] the Supreme Court invalidated a state law which created a separate school district for a Village composed of entirely of members of one religion. Justice Souter wrote an opinion that was, in part, a majority opinion and, in part, a plurality opinion in which he ruled that the state law constituted an improper sect preference that violated the establishment clause.[61] But the division of the Justices in *Grumet* made it appear that a majority of Justices were ready to depart from the view that any provision of on-site remedial services beyond educational

testing, and some health related services, at religious schools would violate the establishment clause.

Justice O'Connor only joined part of Justice Souter's opinion in *Grumet.*[62] She believed the state statute creating the special school district for members of a particular religion violated the establishment clause. But in her concurring opinion, Justice O'Connor stated that, she would vote to uphold the provision of religiously neutral educational services "onsite" at religiously affiliated schools.[63]

Justice Kennedy concurred only in the judgment of the Court in *Grumet.*[64] Unlike Justice O'Connor, he did not clearly indicate that he would vote to overrule the *Grand Rapids* and *Aguilar* cases. But Justice Kennedy stated that those decisions "may have been erroneous" and that "it may be necessary for us to reconsider them." According to Justice Kennedy, the provision of religiously neutral aid to handicapped children who attended religious schools was the "preferable way" to address the problem of the students in *Grumet.*[65]

Justice Scalia, joined by Chief Justice Rehnquist and Justice Thomas, dissented in *Grumet.*[66] These three Justices voted to allow the government to accommodate the needs of children for special educational services on the premises of a religiously affiliated school.

In 1997, the Supreme Court overruled the approach to establishment clause analysis used by the Court in the *Aguilar* and *Ball* cases without formally changing any of the basic establishment clause standards that are used for evaluating government programs that provided aid to religiously affiliated organizations or persons between 1971 and 1997.

---

60. 512 U.S. 687, 114 S.Ct. 2481, 129 L.Ed.2d 546 (1994).

61. Justice Souter's opinion was joined in its entirety by Justices Blackmun, Stevens, and Ginsburg. Justice O'Connor joined only part of Justice Souter's opinion. The Court's ruling in *Grumet,* and the various opinions issued by the Justices in that case, are examined in § 17.3 of this Treatise.

62. 512 U.S. at 710, 114 S.Ct. at 2495 (O'Connor, J., concurring in part and concurring in the judgment).

63. 512 U.S. at 716, 114 S.Ct. at 2498 (O'Connor, J., concurring in part and concurring in the judgment).

64. 512 U.S. at 716, 114 S.Ct. at 2500 (Kennedy, J., concurring in the judgment).

65. 512 U.S. at 730, 114 S.Ct. at 2505 (Kennedy, J., concurring in the judgment).

66. Board of Education of Kiryas Joel Village School District v. Grumet, 512 U.S. 687, 730, 114 S.Ct. 2481, 2505, 129 L.Ed.2d 546 (1994) (Scalia, J., joined by Rehnquist, C.J., and Thomas, J., dissenting).

Agostini v. Felton[67] involved the same litigation that had resulted in the *Aguilar* ruling in 1985. Following the indication of a new approach to establishment clause questions raised by the concurring and dissenting opinions in *Grumet*, the New York City Board of Education that had been subject to the permanent injunction in *Aguilar* sought to have that case reopened. The Board of Education wanted to have the injunction overturned so that the Board could use federal money and government employees to provide remedial education and counseling to students eligible for aid under the Federal Elementary and Secondary Education Act.

In *Agostini,* Justice O'Connor wrote for five members of the Court in finding that the approach to establishment clause problems taken by the *Aguilar* majority had been undermined during the intervening twelve years and that New York Board of Education could seek relief under Federal Rules of Civil Procedure, that allowed a party to seek to have a permanent order overturned on the basis of change, conditions, or legal principles.[68]

At issue in *Agostini* were the same programs that had been challenged in *Aguilar*; the majority opinion in *Agostini* found that the ap-

proach taken to analyzing the provision of remedial services at the property of religiously affiliated schools in both the *Aguilar* and *Ball* decisions had been improper. Thus, the Court effectively overruled *Ball*, while technically overturning only the permanent injunction that had been issued in 1985 in Aguilar.[69]

Justice O'Connor, writing for the majority in *Agostini*, did not reject the Lemon three-part purpose, effect, entanglement test. Rather, the majority expressly approved analyzing the purpose and the effect and the entanglement factors. In finding that the Court had not changed its approach to these issues Justice O'Connor stated:

"The general principles we use to evaluate whether government aid violates the Establishment Clause have not changed since *Aguilar* was decided. For example, we continue to ask whether the government acted with the purpose of advancing or inhibiting religion, and the nature of that inquiry has remained largely unchanged . . . likewise, we continue to explore whether the aid has the effect of advancing or inhibiting religion. What had changed since we decided *Ball* and *Aguilar* is our understanding of the criteria

---

67. 521 U.S. 203, 117 S.Ct. 1997, 138 L.Ed.2d 391 (1997).

68. Agostini v. Felton, 521 U.S. 203, 214–16, 117 S.Ct. 1997, 2006–7, 138 L.Ed.2d 391 (1997). In Part II of the opinion Justice O'Connor examined Federal Rule of Civil Procedure 60(b)(5) and concluded that whether the school board had established a sufficient change in conditions so as to justify reopening the question of the validity of the injunction depended on "whether our later establishment clause cases have so undermined Aguilar that it is no longer good law." 521 U.S. at 216, 117 S.Ct. at 2007. In Part IV of her opinion, which was the concluding portion of the majority opinion, Justice O'Connor found that lower federal courts, or other courts, did not have authority to rule that recent decisions of the Supreme Court have overruled by implication earlier decisions of the United States Supreme Court. Nevertheless, in this portion of the opinion, the majority found that the opinions of the Court since 1985 had so undermined the basis for the ruling in Aguilar that there was no reason for the Court to wait for a later case in which it would revise the approached analyzing the provision of religiously neutral aid to students at religiously affiliated schools. 521 U.S. at 236–40 117 S.Ct. at 2017–2019.

Justice O'Connor's majority opinion was joined by Chief Justice Rehnquist and Justices Scalia, Kennedy, and Thomas. There were no concurring opinions in *Agostini*.

Justices Stevens, Souter, Ginsburg, and Breyer dissented in *Agostini*. Justice Ginsburg wrote a dissenting opinion focusing on the lack of a principled basis for reopening a final injunction under the conditions that were presented in the case. 521 U.S. at 254, 117 S.Ct. at 2026 (Ginsburg, J., joined by Stevens, Souter, and Breyer, JJ., dissenting).

Justice Souter wrote a dissenting opinion that focused on why the dissenters believed that the majority had misconstrued establishment clause decisions of the Court between 1985 and 1987. The dissent asserted that providing direct aid to students on the premises of religious schools violated neutrality principles at the heart of the establishment clause cases. Justice Breyer did not join the part of the dissenting opinion that defended the 1985 rulings, though he did not file a separate dissenting opinion. Agostini v. Felton, 521 U.S. 203, 240, 117 S.Ct. 1997, 2019 138 L.Ed.2d 391 (1997) Souter, J., joined by Stevens and Ginsburg, JJ., and, in part, by Breyer, J., dissenting.

69. Agostini v. Felton, 521 U.S. 203, 224, 117 S.Ct. 1997, 2011, 138 L.Ed.2d 391 (1997): "We have departed from the rule relied on in *Ball* that all government aid that directly aids the educational functions of religious schools is invalid." Thus, although the *Agostini* litigation only involved the injunction in *Aguilar*, it appears that the majority was also overruling Grand Rapids School District v. Ball, 473 U.S. 373 105 S.Ct. 3216, 87 L.Ed.2d 267 (1985).

used to assess whether aid to religion has an impermissible effect."[70]

Justice O'Connor's majority opinion found that the inquiry into whether a government program gave rise to an excessive entanglement between government and religion was "an aspect of the inquiry into a statute's effect."[71] Thus the majority in *Agostini* examined the purpose and effect of the aid program invalidated in Aguilar and the extent to which the provision of educational assistance to students in religious schools might give rise to an excessive entanglement between government and religion.

In *Agostini*, the majority asserted that it was still examining the purpose, effect, and entanglement factors, as had the Justices in the 1985 cases. Nevertheless, in 1997, a majority of the Justices reach an opposite conclusion than the Court had reached in 1985. Justice O'Connor's majority opinion in *Agostini* ruled that the majority in the 1985 decisions had used assumptions that were at best questionable in 1985, and that those assumptions had to be rejected in light of later Court rulings. According to Justice O'Connor, the Court in *Aguilar* and *Ball* had assumed that "the placement of public employees on parochial school grounds inevitably results in the impermissible effect of state-sponsored indoctrination or constitutes a symbolic union between government and religion" and that the government would need such complex procedures to avoid that effect that the monitoring of such programs would inevitably give rise to an excessive between government and religion.[72] Without those assumptions, there was no reason for the Court to find that the provision of purely secular services (such as remedial reading classes or counseling) would result in helping the religious mission of the school. Absent those assumptions, there was no reason to find that complex monitoring would be necessary to prevent the public employees sent to the school to provide nonreligious services to students from assisting the religious mission of

the schools. A key element in analyzing the validity of a program that provided aid to students at religious schools was the analysis of whether the criteria used to select the students and distribute the aid was in any way religious. Justice O'Connor found that the federal and city programs identified disadvantaged students and the nature of aid that would be provided to them without use of any criteria that could be even arguably called religious in nature.

The *Agostini* majority, like the *Aguilar* Court had found that there was no religious purpose that would invalidate the law providing aid to disadvantaged students. In ruling that there was no impermissible effect of advancing religion from the law, the Court summarized its rulings with somewhat new terminology. Justice O'Connor concluded that the analysis of New York educational assistance program "does not run afoul of any of the three primary criteria we currently use to evaluate whether the government aid has the effect of advancing religion: it does not result in government indoctrination; define its recipients by reference to religion; or create an excessive entanglement."[73]

Because the aid to students was consistent with the principle of government neutrality in religious matters, the Court upheld the provision of secular services to students at all schools, including schools that were religiously affiliated. Following the *Agostini* decision, the government would no longer have to provide remedial programs, or other secular services, only at public schools or at mobile units that were brought to, or near, religiously affiliated schools. Government employees could provide services, as well as basic testing, to students at the religious schools so long as the government educational assistance program used religiously neutral criteria, and did not in fact result in an excessive entanglement between the government and religious entities.

---

70. Agostini v. Felton, 521 U.S. 203, 222, 117 S.Ct. 1997, 2010, 138 L.Ed.2d 391 (1997).

71. 521 U.S. at 232, 117 S.Ct. at 2015.

72. 521 U.S. at 222, 232, 117 S.Ct. at 2010, 2015.

73. 521 U.S. at 234, 236–40, 117 S.Ct. at 2016, 2017–19.

Educational Aid Payments to Handicapped Students. *Witters v. Washington Department of Services for the Blind* [74] unanimously upheld a state program providing physically handicapped students with "vocational rehabilitation assistance" payments which allowed those students to obtain "special education and/or training in the professions, businesses or trades." The state courts had ruled that payment of aid to a blind student attending a Christian college and preparing himself for a career as a religious pastor, missionary, or youth director violated the First Amendment establishment clause. Justice Marshall's majority opinion ruled that the aid program, including payment to the blind student engaged in religious studies at a religiously affiliated school, had both a sufficient nonreligious purpose and nonreligious primary effect to withstand scrutiny under the Court's prior decisions. [75] The state courts had not sufficiently analyzed the question of whether there was improper administrative entanglement between government administrators and religious schools under this program. The Supreme Court, for this reason, did not rule on that issue.

None of the Justices in *Witters* found that the state had any purpose to endorse religion. Even those persons who attacked the law admitted that it had a nonreligious purpose. The aid program did not have an impermissible primary religious effect because it was a payment made directly to visually handicapped students to provide them with sufficient finan-

cial resources for vocational training. Justice Marshall reasoned that a student's decision to use the money at a religious school or for religious vocational studies was "only as a result of the genuinely independent and private choices of the aid recipient." In this sense, the aid did not differ from generalized aid to segments of society or payments to government employees. Persons who receive any type of monetary payment from the government could always make an independent decision to donate some of their money to a religious organization or to attend a religious school. Interestingly, the majority opinion stated that "nothing in the record indicates that, if petitioner [the blind student and the state] succeeds, any significant portion of the aid expended under the Washington program as a whole will end up flowing to religious education." It is difficult to understand the significance of this statement, since Justice Marshall did not state that the program would become invalid if a higher percent of students receiving the aid attended religious schools. [76]

In *Zobrest v. Catalina Foothills School District*, [77] the Supreme Court relied heavily on *Mueller* and *Witters* and ruled that the establishment clause did not prevent a public school district from providing a sign language interpreter to a deaf student who was attending a religiously affiliated school within the district's boundaries. This student had attended a school for the deaf during his early years of education; he had attended public schools op-

74. 474 U.S. 481, 106 S.Ct. 748, 88 L.Ed.2d 846 (1986), rehearing denied 475 U.S. 1091, 106 S.Ct. 1485, 89 L.Ed.2d 737 (1986).

75. The *Witters* decision involved a curious alignment of the Justices, which might indicate that the case would have a more sweeping impact than the majority opinion indicates. Although Justice Marshall wrote for a majority of the Court, five Justices wrote separate opinions. Justice White joined the majority opinion but wrote separately to indicate that he remained in disagreement with the Court's earlier, strict restrictions on aid to religious schools. 474 U.S. at 490, 106 S.Ct. at 753 (White, J., concurring).

Justice O'Connor concurred in the judgment in *Witters* and wrote an opinion concurring in part to indicate her belief that the law should be upheld because it could not be reasonably construed by anyone to constitute an endorsement of religious beliefs or practices. She continues to hold the belief set forth in her concurring opinion in

Lynch v. Donnelly, 465 U.S. 668, 690, 104 S.Ct. 1355, 1366, 79 L.Ed.2d 604 (1984), rehearing denied 466 U.S. 994, 104 S.Ct. 2376, 80 L.Ed.2d 848 (1984) (O'Connor, J., concurring) that the primary test under the establishment clause is whether a government program constitutes endorsement of religion. Witters v. Washington Department of Services for the Blind, 474 U.S. 481, 493, 106 S.Ct. 748, 755, 88 L.Ed.2d 846 (1986), rehearing denied 475 U.S. 1091, 106 S.Ct. 1485, 89 L.Ed.2d 737 (1986) (O'Connor, J., concurring).

76. Justice Powell, joined by Chief Justice Burger and Justice Rehnquist wrote a concurring opinion in *Witters* indicating that the law should be upheld on the basis of the Court's decision regarding the permissibility of tax credits or deductions for students and parents. 474 U.S. at 490–92, 106 S.Ct. at 753–55 (Powell, J., joined by Burger, C.J., and Rehnquist, J., concurring).

77. 509 U.S. 1, 113 S.Ct. 2462, 125 L.Ed.2d 1 (1993).

erated by this school district for grades 6 through 8. While he was in the public schools, the district furnished him with a sign language interpreter. When the student entered a Catholic high school he claimed that the federal Individuals with Disabilities Education Act required the school district to provide him with a sign language interpreter. The school district refused to provide him with a sign language interpreter because, it claimed, that the provision of such aid to a religious school student would violate the establishment clause.

A majority of the Supreme Court Justices believed that they should assume that federal law would require the school district to provide a sign language interpreter to the student so long as this form of aid did not violate the establishment clause.[78] Two of the Justices refused to reach any constitutional issues because of their belief that the constitutional issue should be avoided and that the case should be remanded for an exploration of statutory issues.[79] Of the seven Justices who reached the constitutional issue in *Zobrest*, five Justices rejected the school district's claim that the provision of a sign language interpreter for the religious school student would violate the establishment clause.

Chief Justice Rehnquist wrote for the majority in *Zobrest;* he cited and relied upon the *Mueller* and *Witters* cases. The Chief Justice found that the Supreme Court "[has] consistently held that government programs that neutrally provide benefits to a broad class of

citizens defined without reference to religion are not readily subject to an establishment clause challenge because sectarian institutions may also receive an attenuated financial benefit."[80] The school district alleged that the provision of sign language interpreter services to the religious school student would be similar to the provision of teaching equipment (such as maps, charts, and tape recorders) or publicly paid teachers to teach the nonreligious subjects in religious schools. Those types of school aid programs had been invalidated in earlier Supreme Court cases. The Chief Justice, in *Zobrest*, distinguished the provision of goods or services to religious schools on the basis that those invalidated government programs had "relieved sectarian schools of costs they otherwise would have borne in educating their students ... handicapped children, not sectarian schools, are the primary beneficiaries of the [federal statute under which the child claimed a right to a sign language interpreter]; to the extent sectarian schools receive a benefit at all from [the statute and the sign language interpreter], they are only incidental beneficiaries."[81]

The dissenting Justices asserted that there should be an absolute prohibition against public employees providing services in religious schools,[82] but the majority in *Zobrest* rejected that position. Chief Justice Rehnquist stated: "The establishment clause lays down no absolute bar to the placing of a public employee in a sectarian school."[83] Because the majority viewed the program as "a neutral government

---

78. The majority in *Zobrest* found that the failure of the school board to press its statutory and regulatory issues before the Court of Appeals meant that "the prudential rule of avoiding constitutional questions has no application." 509 U.S. at 7, 113 S.Ct. at 2466.

79. Justices O'Connor and Stevens believed that the *Zobrest* case should be remanded to the lower courts for determination of whether federal statutes and regulations precluded the provision of aid to this student because, if the statute and regulations did so, there would be no need to reach a constitutional question. These two Justices joined only the portion of Justice Blackmun's dissent that dealt with the need to avoid constitutional issues and the need to have the statutory questions addressed in this case. 509 U.S. at 24, 113 S.Ct. at 2475 (O'Connor, J., joined by Stevens, J., dissenting). Justices Blackmun dissented from both the majority's decision to consider the constitutional issues and the majority's ruling on the

establishment clause issue. 509 U.S. at 12, 113 S.Ct. at 2469 (Blackmun, J., joined by Souter, J., dissenting; this dissenting opinion was joined in part by O'Connor and Stevens, JJ.).

80. Zobrest v. Catalina Foothills School District, 509 U.S. 1, 7, 113 S.Ct. 2462, 2466, 125 L.Ed.2d 1 (1993).

81. Zobrest v. Catalina Foothills School District, 509 U.S. 1, 10–12, 113 S.Ct. 2462, 2468–69, 125 L.Ed.2d 1 (1993).

82. 509 U.S. at 16–24, 113 S.Ct. at 2471–75 (Blackmun, joined by Souter, J., dissenting). Justices O'Connor and Stevens did not join a portion of Justice Blackmun's dissent that involved an analysis of the establishment clause issue in this case.

83. Zobrest v. Catalina Foothills School District, 509 U.S. 1, 2, 113 S.Ct. 2462, 2469, 125 L.Ed.2d 1 (1993).

program dispensing aid not to schools but to individual handicapped children," the majority found that the establishment clause would not prevent the government from providing a sign language interpreter to the deaf student at the Catholic high school. The Chief Justice's opinion reached this result by finding that the nature of the aid to the deaf child should not be considered aid to the religious school or to religious activities.

Conclusion. Since the early 1970's, the Supreme Court has examined three factors in determining whether a government program that aids religiously affiliated schools, or their students, violates the establishment clause. Those factors are: the purpose of the law; the primary effect of the law; and the "entanglement" between government and religion that would result from the challenged law.

The Supreme Court continues to rule that a government program of aid to religious schools or their students, must survive both a purpose and effect test. The governmental program must have a secular purpose. Additionally, the government aid program must have a primary effect that neither advances nor inhibits religion.

A majority of the Justices continue to consider whether a challenged governmental program creates an excessive entanglement between government and religion. Some of these Justices believe that the excessive entanglement consideration should be deemed a separate establishment clause standard. Some of these Justices believe that the concept of excessive entanglement is only a factor to be considered when determining whether a government program has the impermissible effect of abandoning or inhibiting religion. When any of these Justices consider the excessive entanglement factor, they are likely to examine the character and purposes of the institution that has benefitted, the nature of the aid that is being distributed by the government, and the resulting relationship between government and religious authorities. It is possible that a

Justice's view of the potential of the challenged program to be politically divisive may influence how strictly the Justice will apply the excessive entanglement concept. However, political divisiveness has never been a clearly identified test for determining whether a government program is compatible with the establishment clause.

Tuition Voucher Programs. The *Mueller*, *Witters*, and *Zoebrest* decisions provided the basis for the Court upholding an Ohio tuition voucher system in *Zelman v. Simmons–Harris*.[84] The *Zelman* case involved an Ohio statutory program designed to help students in the worst performing schools in that state.[85] In the mid–1990's a federal court had placed the entire Cleveland School District under the control of the State of Ohio, rather than local control, due to the conditions of the Cleveland schools, which were among the worst academically performing schools in the United States. The State of Ohio passed its Pilot Project Scholarship Program [the program] which took several paths in the road towards improving Cleveland's schools. The program provided tutorial aid for those students who chose to remain enrolled in their public schools. The program also provided tuition aid (tuition vouchers) for students in elementary school who chose to attend a public or private school that participated in the program. In addition to the tuition aid provided by the program to children in the Cleveland schools, Ohio also established community and magnet schools. A community school would be run by its own school board rather than a local school district. For each student attending a community school, that school would receive over $4,500.00 in state funding (more than twice for that of the voucher program students). The Ohio magnet schools would be public schools operated by a local school board and that would emphasize one aspect of teaching or learning. Students at magnet schools would receive over $4,000.00 of state aid and the school district would receive almost $8,000.00

---

84. 536 U.S. 639, 122 S.Ct. 2460, 153 L.Ed.2d 604 (2002).

85. The facts regarding lower court litigation and the working of the Ohio Pilot Program are set forth in the

Chief Justice's majority opinion in *Zelman*. 536 U.S. at 640–47, 122 S.Ct. at 2462–2465.

of government money for each student at a magnet school.

The tuition aid portion of the Ohio program [which we will refer to as the voucher program] provided families with vouchers that could be used at participating public and private schools. Religious and non-religious private schools could participate in the program and accept students, together with their vouchers, so long as the school was located within the district and met certain educational standards. To be part of the program, a private school receiving student tuition vouchers would be required to agree not to discriminate on the basis of race, religious or ethnic background. Additionally, a participating private school was required to agree that it would not to advocate, promote or teach hatred of individuals on the basis of their race or religion.

The Ohio program provided tuition aid to students in kindergarten through third grade; the program would expand each year so that students through the eighth grade would eventually be able to participate in the program. The program provided aid to students, and the families of students, in all districts that had been subject to federal court control due to the poor academic performance of the school district. Realistically, only Cleveland students would be receiving benefits through the pilot program.

Under the Ohio program, tuition assistance was given to families of students in the eligible district based upon financial need. Families with incomes very significantly below a poverty line set forth in the statute would receive assistance with up to ninety percent of private school tuition. The maximum amount that could be paid to a private school through the voucher for the poorest families was $2,250.00. Schools that participated in the program were prohibited from charging the lowest income families more than $250.00 in excess of the voucher amount they received from the State of Ohio. For all other students, and their families, the Ohio program would pay seventy-five percent of the cost of tuition at a participating

private school, up to a limit of $1,875.00. For families that did not meet the statutory definition of low-income families, participating private schools were free to have additional charges that were not subject to state limitation. Under the Ohio program, vouchers (checks) were made payable to the parents who chose a private school for their child. The parents were then able to endorse the voucher over to the participating private school.

Chief Justice Rehnquist's majority opinion in *Zelman*, stated that the program would be invalid if it had the purpose or effect of advancing or inhibiting religion.[86] There was no contention at any point in the litigation that the program had been enacted for a religious, rather than a secular, purpose. For that reason, the Court considered only whether the program had an impermissible effect of advancing or inhibiting religion in violation of the establishment clause.

The majority opinion stated that the Court's "decisions have drawn a consistent distinction between programs that provide a direct aid to religious schools ... and programs of true private choice, in which government aid reaches religious schools only as a result of the genuine and independent choices of private individuals...."[87] According to the Chief Justice's opinion, the *Mueller*, *Witters* and *Zobrest* decisions "make clear that where a government aid program is neutral with respect to religion, and provides assistance directly to a broad class of citizens, who, in turn, direct government aid to religious schools wholly as a result of their own genuine and independent private choice, the program is not readily subject to challenge under the establishment clause."[88]

The majority found that the program was religiously neutral in that it did not provide any financial incentive so parents could choose religious, rather than non-religious, education. The *Zelman* majority rejected the position taken by dissenting Justices that the Ohio program should be invalidated on the basis that

---

86. Zelman v. Simmons–Harris, 536 U.S. 639, 649, 122 S.Ct. 2460, 2465, 153 L.Ed.2d 604 (2002).

87. 536 U.S. at 469, 122 S.Ct. at 2465.

88. 536 U.S. at 652, 122 S.Ct. at 2467.

most of the participating private schools had religious affiliations. The majority noted that making a program invalid merely because many students chose to use their vouchers at religiously affiliated schools, as suggested by the dissent, would lead to "the absurd result" that a school choice program that was religiously neutral would be valid in parts of a state that happen to have a lower percentage of religiously affiliated private schools than parts of a state where the percentage of religiously affiliated private schools was higher.[89]

Because no aid went directly to the schools, the majority in *Zelman* was able to distinguish *Committee for Public Education and Religious Liberty v. Nyquist*[90] in which the Court invalidated a New York program that gave benefits only to students attending private schools. In *Zelman*, the Court found that the Ohio tuition voucher program was simply part of a package of alternatives presented to parents, and that the program was entirely neutral with respect to religion.[91]

Justice O'Connor wrote a concurring opinion in *Zelman*, even though she joined with the Chief Justice's majority opinion. Her concurring opinion emphasized the importance of considering all of the choices that the State of Ohio presented to parents in terms of receiving state aid for their children's education. She also explained how, in her view, the *Zelman* decision did not distort or depart from earlier cases regarding establishment clause limits on aid to religiously affiliated institutions or persons who attended such institutions.[92] Justice O'Connor had written the majority opinion in *Agostini*.[93] In *Zelman*, Justice O'Connor explained that *Agostini* had not freed the courts

from considering whether government aid program created impermissible entanglement between government and religion. Rather, the *Agostini* decision had simply "folded the entanglement inquiry into the primary effect inquiry."[94] She found that the fact that the program was neutral in its operation meant that there would be no impermissible effect as a result of Ohio's tuition voucher program. Justice Thomas also wrote a concurring opinion explaining the importance of providing all children with a wide variety of educational choices and why the provision of free choice did not violate establishment clause values.[95]

Justice Souter wrote a dissent for four Justices in *Zelman*[96] Justice Souter believed that the majority had created a new stage in establishment clause analysis in which merely formal neutrality would save a government aid program that in fact directly supported religious activities and resulted in an impermissible entanglement of government and religion. In the view of the dissenting Justices, the Ohio program should not be considered neutral because the aid, in fact, went only to students who attended schools other than public schools in the district, and because the aid went primarily to students attending religious schools. Dissenters found excessive entanglement between government and religion that would endanger the exercise clause values by making the religiously affiliated private schools conform to a wide variety of state regulations in a way that would undermine the religious schools' freedom of belief.

Justice Breyer wrote a separate dissenting opinion that was joined by Justices Stevens and Souter, but not Justice Ginsburg. Justice

---

89. 536 U.S. at 655–59, 122 S.Ct. at 2469–71. This point was also emphasized by Justice Thomas in his concurring opinion. 536 U.S. at 676, 122 S.Ct. at 2480 (Thomas, J., concurring).

90. 413 U.S. 756, 93 S.Ct. 2955, 37 L.Ed.2d 948 (1973).

91. Zelman v. Simmons–Harris, 536 U.S. 639, 649, 655–59, 122 S.Ct. 2460, 2466, 2469–71, 153 L.Ed.2d 604 (2002).

92. 536 U.S. at 668, 122 S.Ct. at 2473 (O'Connor, J., concurring).

93. Agostini v. Felton, 521 U.S. 203, 117 S.Ct. 1997, 138 L.Ed.2d 391 (1997). The *Agostini* decision is examined in earlier paragraphs in this subsection of the Treatise.

94. Zelman v. Simmons–Harris, 536 U.S. 639, 668, 122 S.Ct. 2460, 2476, 153 L.Ed.2d 604 (2002) (O'Connor, J., concurring).

95. 536 U.S. at 676, 122 S.Ct. at 2480 (Thomas, J., concurring). In his concurring opinion, Justice Thomas also suggested that the establishment clause might not apply, in his view, with the same strictness to state programs as to federal programs that aided religion.

96. Zelman v. Simmons–Harris, 536 U.S. 639, 686, 122 S.Ct. 2460, 2485, 153 L.Ed.2d 604 (2002) (Souter, J., joined by Stevens, Ginsburg, and Breyer, JJ., dissenting).

Breyer's dissent focused almost exclusively on political divisiveness caused by government aid to religiously affiliated institutions.[97] These three dissenting Justices believed that prevention of social divisions along religious lines was a value that the drafters and ratifiers of the First Amendment had meant to protect.[98]

Justice Stevens also wrote a separate dissenting opinion in which he stated that the Court should focus on the fact that the tuition voucher program only helped children attending private schools, and that almost all of these students were attending religiously affiliated schools.[99] Justice Ginsburg joined the Souter dissent but she did not join the dissents written by either Justices Breyer or Stevens.

A law providing aid to parents and students on a religiously neutral basis should not constitute prohibited aid to religion so long as the amount of aid provided to a particular student who attends a religiously affiliated private school is not greater than the aid given to students at public schools and is not established in a way that encourages students to attend religiously affiliated schools rather than public schools or non-sectarian private schools. In the 1920's the Court had ruled that parents have a right to send their children to private schools so long as those schools meet reasonable accreditation standards.[100] For the parents of many children that choice exists only in theory, because the parents cannot afford to send their children to a private school. If the state provides aid only in the form of public school opportunities the state effectively keeps low-income parents from exercising their constitutional right to send their child to a private school. Providing parents with a wide variety of choices as to how they will receive state aid

for their children, including the choice of taking a cash benefit in the form of a voucher, should be permissible so long as it is not slanted towards encouraging students to attend religious schools.[101] The majority in *Zelman* found that such a tuition voucher program did not impermissibly advance religion.[102]

(b) Aid to Colleges and Universities

Although aid to nonpublic institutions of higher education has been the subject of only a few Supreme Court decisions, it is clear that government programs aiding these schools must be tested under the same tests that have been employed in the primary school cases. The aid must have a secular purpose, its primary effect cannot advance or inhibit religion, and it must avoid creating an excessive entanglement between government and religion.

In determining whether excessive entanglement exists, three factors are examined: (1) the character of the institutions benefited; (2) the nature of the aid provided; (3) the resulting relationship between government and church authorities. Additionally, the program must not be of a type which will cause political division along religious lines. Once again, the Court will accept the legislative purpose of the aid programs as secular in nature. The announced intention of the legislature to assist the secular portion of all students' education has never been challenged by the Court in any school aid case.

These programs also have been held not to have a primary effect of aiding religion where there was at least some formal guarantee by the college authorities that the funds would not be used for religious instruction or other sectarian activities. The Court has refused to

---

97. 536 U.S. at 717, 122 S.Ct. at 2502 (Breyer, J., joined by Stevens and Souter, JJ., dissenting).

98. See § 17.4(d) regarding the meanings that different Justices have ascribed to the excessive entanglement concept, including the views of Justices who believe that the establishment clause should prohibit programs that give rise to political divisiveness based along religious lines.

99. 536 U.S. at 684, 122 S.Ct. at 2484 (Stevens, J., dissenting).

100. Pierce v. Society of the Sisters of the Holy Names of Jesus and Mary, 268 U.S. 510, 45 S.Ct. 571, 69 L.Ed.

1070 (1925). See §§ 18.26, 18.30, 2041, and 17.7 of this Treatise.

101. John Nowak, The Supreme Court, The Religion Clauses and the Nationalization of Education, 70 Northwestern University Law Review 883 (1976).

102. The Chief Justice also rejected the suggestion of Justice Breyer that the Court should find that there was improper entanglement between government and religion because of the possibility that a tuition voucher program might lead to divisiveness in society along religious lines. Zelman v. Simmons–Harris, 536 U.S. 639, 662 n. 7, 122 S.Ct. 2460, 2472 n. 7, 153 L.Ed.2d 604 (2002).

assume that religious colleges are so permeated with religion that their secular functions cannot be separated from their religious mission. Thus, a program which is tied to only secular instruction will not have an effect of advancing religion.

However, if the institution to be aided is sectarian to the extent that the advancing of religious beliefs permeated its entire program then this analysis could not apply. Such an institution would be similar to the parochial elementary and secondary schools which the majority of Justices have deemed to have a primary function of propagating religious doctrine. In such a situation the secular teaching function could not be sufficiently separated from the religious mission of the school. Thus any significant aid to the school would have the prohibited effect of advancing religion.

Thus, there is a two part test to determine whether a specific aid program for religiously affiliated colleges and universities has a "primary effect" of advancing religion. To avoid such an effect: (1) the institution's secular function must not be permeated with a religious atmosphere, and (2) there must be assurances by the college and the government authority that the aid will not be used for religious teaching or other religious activities.

It is relatively easy for these programs aiding higher education to pass the three factor test for determining the presence of excessive entanglement. First, since the institutions are not "permeated" with religion, there is little need for extensive controls to insure against advancing religion.

Second, the aid is usually granted for a specific secular purpose. If so, it is likely to be only a one-time grant which is easily monitored. However, the Court has also upheld annual general grants to colleges where the college and government authorities would give assurances of their use for secular purposes.

Third, the administrative contacts between government and religious authorities can easily be kept to a minimum in such programs. Because the nature of the institution and aid

do not have a high potential for advancing religion, the state need not engage in a program of constant surveillance. As long as the Court is of the impression that the program invokes little more contact between the religious authorities and the state than the normal accreditation procedures, no excessive administrative entanglement will be found.

Finally, these programs have not been found to be politically divisive by the Court. The one-time grants for specific purposes rarely stir emotion concerning government subsidies to religion. Even annual grant programs are not the subject of debate along religious lines. The largely secular atmosphere of these institutions, and the public evaluation of higher education, helps to keep debate on such subjects focused on educational and fiscal policy rather than religion. Additionally, the high percentage of nonsectarian private colleges prevents these programs from becoming religious issues.

Government aid to religiously affiliated institutions of higher education has been the subject of several Supreme Court decisions. In *Tilton v. Richardson* [103] the Court, by a five to four vote, upheld the federal Higher Education Facilities Act. Under this act federal grants were made for the construction of college facilities for other than religious activities or religious instruction.

In accordance with the analysis outlined above, the program was found to be permissible under the purpose-effect-entanglement test. First, the purpose of the program was to aid secular education. Second, the court found that aid to these religious colleges did not have a primary religious effect. Their dedication to secular educational goals, the policy of academic freedom and the nature of higher education were such that these colleges were not found to be permeated with religion; the program did not have the effect of advancing religion so long as the government was given assurances that the buildings were not to be used for a sectarian purpose. Third, no excessive entanglement was created by these programs. This conclusion followed from

103. 403 U.S. 672, 91 S.Ct. 2091, 29 L.Ed.2d 790   (1971).

three factors: (1) the institution was not permeated with religion, (2) the aid was a one-time grant for specific buildings, and (3) the resulting contact between church and state could be kept to a minimum. Finally, the majority found that this program was not likely to result in political division.

One section of the federal law was held invalid in *Tilton*. Under the act the government gave up any ability to demand a return of funds after twenty years even if the buildings then were used for religious purposes. A majority of the Justices concluded that the limitation of the government's enforcement powers after twenty years would be the equivalent of an unrestricted gift to the college after that time. Since this delayed grant could have the effect of advancing religion, the Court held that both the assurance of secular use and the government power to demand return of money used for religious purposes must continue so long as the facility was of any value.

In *Hunt v. McNair* [104] the Court upheld a state program of issuing revenue bonds for the benefit of private colleges, including religiously affiliated schools. An "Educational Facilities Authority" issued bonds to finance construction of facilities which did not involve sectarian uses and the schools repaid these bonds from their own revenues. Although the state incurred no financial obligation under the program, the state authority issued the bonds, financed the construction with the bond revenues and leased the facilities to the institution. The use of the state bonding system allowed these schools to sell bonds at a reduced interest rate; this saved the schools significant interest payments. The Authority also was authorized to establish regulations and conduct inspections to insure secular use of the buildings which were conveyed to it.

This program easily withstood review under the three part purpose-effect-entanglement

test. The Court found no impermissible effect in this case. There would be a primary effect of advancing religion if either (1) the institution was so religious in character that its function was subsumed in the religious mission, or (2) the funded activity was religious in nature. Under this program the institutions aided were not subsumed in their religious mission and only secular facilities were financed by the bonds. The Court also found the act permissible under the excessive entanglement test. The three factor entanglement analysis required this result: (1) the institution was not permeated with religion, (2) the aid was not of a general character, and (3) the state authority would not be involved in detailed relationship with the college. While it was possible that the state authority might be involved in such a relationship if it had to help a program which was becoming financially insolvent, no such case was before the Court. [105]

In *Roemer v. Board of Public Works*, [106] the Justices approved an annual grant program which benefited religious colleges. Maryland established a program of annual grants which provided for each full time student (excluding those enrolled in seminary or theological programs) a grant of 15% of the per-pupil amount that the state spent in the public college system. Originally this program was subject to virtually no restrictions on the use of the grant money. However, Maryland had amended the act to provide that the Maryland Council of Higher Education screen the institution application to insure that the institution was not pervasively religious and that the institution had given adequate assurance that the funds would be used for a secular purpose. The Court, by a five to four vote, upheld this amended program. [107]

Justice Blackmun, in *Roemer*, wrote an opinion (joined by Chief Justice Burger and Justice Powell) which found that the amended pro-

104. 413 U.S. 734, 93 S.Ct. 2868, 37 L.Ed.2d 923 (1973).

105. For this reason the majority specifically refused to consider the degree to which the state could become involved in such a situation. 413 U.S. at 748–49, 93 S.Ct. at 2876–77.

106. 426 U.S. 736, 96 S.Ct. 2337, 49 L.Ed.2d 179 (1976) (plurality opinion by Blackmun, J.).

107. The invalidity of the first program was in effect conceded by the state and the Court did not consider it. The status of the payments under programs which are later held invalid is considered in the next section of this chapter.

gram passed the three part purpose-effect-entanglement test. Justices White and Rehnquist agreed that the program had a secular purpose and effect, but they did not apply an entanglement test because they believe that no such test is mandated by the establishment clause.[108] The plurality opinion of Justice Blackmun accepted the purpose of the act as secular. He found that it did not have a primary effect of aiding religion because it neither aided an institution subsumed in religion nor in a specific religious activity. As these institutions were not "pervasively sectarian," the requirement of assurance of secular use and review by the Council on Higher Education was sufficient guarantee to avoid an effect of advancing religion.

The Blackmun plurality opinion found that using the three factor assessment did not result in a finding of excessive entanglement. First, the character of the institution was not pervasively sectarian so as to require constant surveillance of the aid. Second, the nature of a specific program was not before the Court and so the Justices could only consider the character of an annual grant program in the last part of the test. Third, the resulting relationship was not materially distinguishable from earlier cases. While the aid consisted of annual grants, the Justices were of the opinion that this would not involve significantly greater contact between the state and the colleges than did normal accreditation procedures.

Finally, Justice Blackmun noted what may be the key factor that has caused the Court to uphold these programs—the absence of political division resulting from the enactment of such aid programs. Debate on aid to institu-

tions of higher education, Justice Blackmun found, does not involve lobbying by churches and intense divisions among religious sects. Instead, those programs tend to be evaluated on their educational and fiscal merits. A majority of the Justices has not been disposed to overturn such programs without a very clear showing of an impermissible purpose, effect or excessive administrative entanglement.[109]

(c) Other Issues in Aid to Religious Institutions

(1) Payments Under Programs Later Held Invalid. Even though a program of aid to religious schools has been held invalid under the establishment clause, payments may have been made to schools under the law prior to its invalidation. The question then arises as to whether the recipient institutions should be ordered to return the funds. This is precisely the situation that was present in *Lemon v. Kurtzman (Lemon II).*[110] Prior to the Supreme Court's decision in *Lemon I,*[111] Pennsylvania had made substantial payments to parochial schools under the challenged act. The Court held that two factors were relevant in determining whether to grant a retroactive remedy: (1) the reasonableness and degree of reliance by the institution on the payments, and (2) the necessity of refunds to protect the constitutional right involved.

In *Lemon II* the Court found that reimbursement was not required because reliance had been reasonable. Additionally, the return of funds would not be necessary to guard against impermissibly aiding religion as the money had been spent on secular purposes under the supervision of secular authorities.[112]

---

108. Roemer v. Board of Public Works, 426 U.S. 736, 767, 96 S.Ct. 2337, 2354–55, 49 L.Ed.2d 179 (1976) (White, J., concurring).

109. During the 1977–1978 Term, the Supreme Court summarily affirmed two cases that upheld state programs which provided scholarships, tuition assistance, and financial aid to college students, including some students attending religiously affiliated schools. Smith v. Board of Governors, 434 U.S. 803, 98 S.Ct. 39, 54 L.Ed.2d 65 (1977), affirming 429 F.Supp. 871 (W.D.N.C.1977) (three-judge court); Americans United for Separation of Church and State v. Blanton, 434 U.S. 803, 98 S.Ct. 39, 54 L.Ed.2d 65 (1977), affirming 433 F.Supp. 97 (M.D.Tenn.1977) (three-judge court).

110. 411 U.S. 192, 93 S.Ct. 1463, 36 L.Ed.2d 151 (1973).

111. Lemon v. Kurtzman, 403 U.S. 602, 91 S.Ct. 2105, 29 L.Ed.2d 745 (1971). In this case the Court invalidated a Pennsylvania program involving payments to religious primary schools. The case is discussed in § 17.4(a), supra.

112. This reasoning was reaffirmed in Roemer v. Board of Public Works, 426 U.S. 736, 745 n. 11, 767 n. 23, 96 S.Ct. 2337, 2344 n. 11, 2354 n. 23, 49 L.Ed.2d 179 (1976) (plurality opinion by Blackmun, J.). Here the Court did not have to consider the constitutionality of payments made under a superceded statute which was admittedly unconstitutional. However, the opinion indicated that the earlier payments to religious colleges under

In *New York v. Cathedral Academy*,[113] the Court invalidated a state statute that would have granted reimbursement to private schools for state mandated record keeping and testing services under a program that previously had been held to violate the First and Fourteenth Amendments. A federal district court had found the original state act regarding payments for record keeping and testing to be unconstitutional; this had been upheld by the Supreme Court.[114] The district court had enjoined the distribution of funds for this program including distribution of funds for the last half of the 1971–72 school year. In June 1972, the state legislature attempted to limit the impact of the district court injunction by passing a new state statute granting reimbursement for expenses incurred prior to July, 1972, by schools that had attempted to follow the previous record keeping and testing requirements.

In *Cathedral Academy*, the Supreme Court held that this reimbursement act was invalid, and distinguished it from the situation in *Lemon II*. In *Lemon I* the state program violated the First Amendment because it created an excessive entanglement between government and religion. The lower court's refusal to grant retroactive injunctive relief in that case was justified because allowing payments for the prior period did not do any further damage to constitutional values; those payments involved no further entanglement between government and religion, and the payments did not serve a religious purpose. In *Cathedral Academy*, the district court had enjoined all payments in the original action; the Supreme Court indicated that it could not allow state legislators to modify the impact of such injunctions.

However, the opinion recognized that the primary issue was whether the new act itself violated the religion clauses of the First

Amendment, as applied to the states by the Fourteenth Amendment. The Court found that the reimbursement statute failed the three part establishment test on two bases: (1) the reimbursement payments would have a religious effect because the grant program itself had been a prohibited form of aid to religion; (2) the procedures required by the Act to insure the secular nature of the reimbursement payments would involve an excessive entanglement between state and religious authorities. Thus, there could be no reimbursement payments under the statute even though some religious schools might have relied on the original statute, prior to the first federal court action, when they incurred these expenses. The differences in the original trial court actions in *Lemon I* and *Levitt*,[115] as well as the nature of the aid programs, resulted in the different holdings in *Lemon II* and in *Cathedral Academy*.

(2) Aid to Schools That Discriminate on the Basis of Race. Although a program of state aid to a private school may not violate the establishment clause, it cannot aid a school that discriminates on the basis of race. In *Norwood v. Harrison*[116] the Supreme Court held that textbooks could not be loaned to students of a school which discriminated on the basis of race. Such a textbook program may aid religious schools as they represent a value in the free exercise of religion which offsets any slight aid to religion. However, there is no countervailing constitutional value which could justify state aid to a racially discriminatory system. Thus, the aid to these students would violate the equal protection clause of the Fourteenth Amendment.

A related issue is the question of whether Congress can prohibit a private school from discriminating on the basis of race because it is affiliated with a religion which requires seg-

---

the invalid program need not be returned to the state as the state's actions were reasonable. It was also noted that the separation of church and state would not be promoted by making the state a judgment creditor of these religious institutions.

113.   434 U.S. 125, 98 S.Ct. 340, 54 L.Ed.2d 346 (1977).

114.   Levitt v. Committee for Public Education, 413 U.S. 472, 93 S.Ct. 2814, 37 L.Ed.2d 736 (1973).

115.   Levitt v. Committee for Public Education, 413 U.S. 472, 93 S.Ct. 2814, 37 L.Ed.2d 736 (1973).

116.   413 U.S. 455, 93 S.Ct. 2804, 37 L.Ed.2d 723 (1973).

regation as a tenet of the religious belief.[117] It may well be that the free exercise clause requires only that such religious-segregated schools be accommodated in that their existence is not made illegal. Indeed, it is not clear whether the mere existence of such schools is prohibited by the Thirteenth Amendment or legislation passed pursuant to it.[118] The Civil War Amendments might be found to establish racial equality as a preeminent goal which overrides the interests of religiously affiliated schools.

At a minimum, the Thirteenth and Fourteenth Amendments represent values that should prevent the government from actively aiding these schools. Because those schools represent values opposed to constitutional rights of racial minorities, only accommodation of their existence and the provision of such general governmental services as police and fire protection might be required.

In *Bob Jones University v. United States*,[119] the Court upheld the authority of the Internal Revenue Service to deny tax exempt status to private schools which practice racially discriminatory admissions standards on the basis of their religious doctrine. The Court noted that the denial "of tax benefits will inevitably have a substantial impact on the operation of private religious schools, but will not prevent

those schools from observing their religious tenets." Moreover, "the Government has a fundamental, overriding interest in eradicating racial discrimination in education" and this interest "substantially outweighs whatever burden denial of tax benefits places on petitioners' exercise of their religious beliefs."

The Court found that the compelling governmental interest in avoiding aid to racially discriminatory schools could not be equally served by "less restrictive means," through an accommodation of an exemption for schools that practice such discrimination on the basis of religious doctrines, thus there was no free exercise clause violation.[120] The establishment clause was not violated even though the effect of the requirement that schools not discriminate on the basis of race was to allow some religious schools to receive tax exempt status while those religiously affiliated schools that could not comply with the requirement would fail to receive the exemption. This rule was not a preference of one religion over another but merely the carrying out of a policy founded on a "neutral, secular basis" which was uniformly applied to all schools.

In addition to the nonreligious purpose and primary effect of the Internal Revenue Service position, the denial of exemptions to all

---

117. In Runyon v. McCrary, 427 U.S. 160, 96 S.Ct. 2586, 49 L.Ed.2d 415 (1976), the Supreme Court ruled that federal statute 42 U.S.C.A. § 1981 prohibited racial discrimination in private schools but explicitly reserved the question of whether the statute did or could apply to prohibit racial discrimination by religiously affiliated schools where the discrimination was required by religious doctrine. 427 U.S. at 167 n. 6, 96 S.Ct. at 2593 n. 6. See generally § 14.9(a)(2)(b), supra. The Supreme Court declined to review a decision that might have resolved the issue of whether a religious school could exclude racial minorities. Brown v. Dade Christian Schools, Inc., 556 F.2d 310 (5th Cir.1977) (en banc), certiorari denied 434 U.S. 1063, 98 S.Ct. 1235, 55 L.Ed.2d 763 (1978). The lower court in *Brown* had found that the school in question was secular and that the school could not base a claim on the religious principles of some of its students. For this reason, the application of 42 U.S.C.A. § 1981 to this school presented no significant free exercise clause problem.

In Bob Jones University v. United States, 461 U.S. 574, 103 S.Ct. 2017, 76 L.Ed.2d 157 (1983), the Supreme Court ruled that a denial of tax exempt status to religiously affiliated racially discriminatory schools violated neither the establishment clause nor the free exercise clause of the

First Amendment. However, in that case the Internal Revenue Service had chosen to follow lower court opinions finding that the granting of tax exempt status to such schools would be a violation of the equal protection component of the Fifth Amendment. For that reason the Supreme Court did not have to address the question of whether the granting of tax exempt status to racially discriminatory schools or organizations, whether or not religiously affiliated, would violate the equal protection component of the Fifth Amendment or the equal protection clause of the Fourteenth Amendment, if such tax exempt status were granted by a state or local government.

118. The Supreme Court has held that legislation passed pursuant to the Thirteenth Amendment prohibits the racial discrimination by private schools. Runyon v. McCrary, 427 U.S. 160, 96 S.Ct. 2586, 49 L.Ed.2d 415 (1976). The Court specifically left open the case where a school discriminated by race due to religious beliefs, 427 U.S. at 167 n. 6, 96 S.Ct. at 2593 n. 6.

119. 461 U.S. 574, 103 S.Ct. 2017, 76 L.Ed.2d 157 (1983).

120. 461 U.S. at 604, 103 S.Ct. at 2035, 76 L.Ed.2d at 181.

schools that practice racial discrimination avoided a potential for excessive entanglement between government and religion by avoiding the necessity of inquiring into the sincerity of those asserting a religious basis for their discriminatory practices.[121]

(3) State Constitutional Restrictions. A number of states have constitutional provisions that specifically protect the free exercise of religion, or restrict aid to religious institutions.[122] In some states even such forms of aid as bus fees, textbooks, and tax exemptions might be denied to religious institutions by the state constitution. Because the Supreme Court of the United States has only indicated that such forms of aid are permissible if the state desires to furnish them, there is no violation of the First Amendment if a state refuses to aid religious schools.

If a state went so far as to deny basic governmental services such as police and fire protection to religious institutions, there would be a significant issue as to whether the denial of services so inhibited the practice of religion as to amount to a violation of the free exercise clause. However, no state has done this.

(4) Government Payments of Money "Owned" by Private Individuals. The government may pay the tuition of students at religious schools if the tuition payment is made with money owned or earned by the students. *Reuben Quick Bear v. Leupp*[123] upheld a federal government payment to religious organizations on Indian reservations since the money used was owned by the Indian tribes and only held in trust by the federal government. A similar analysis might support the use of tuition payments for veterans of the armed services to religious colleges, or the government loaning money at reduced interest rates to all students regardless of whether they attend religiously affiliated schools.[124]

(5) Financial Aid to Religiously Affiliated Institutions Other Than Schools. If the government is granting financial aid to a religiously affiliated institution of any type, the program must be tested under the establishment clause in the same manner as are programs which aid schools. Thus, the program must have a secular purpose, no primary effect which either advances or inhibits religion and no excessive entanglement between government and religious authority. Again, excessive entanglement will be looked at in terms of: (1) the character of the institution, (2) the type of aid, and (3) the resulting administrative relationships. Additionally, the potential of the program for causing political division along religious lines will be an important factor in determining its validity.

The key to analysis of any such program is the determination of the degree of the independent secular function in the institution to be aided. If the institution is pervasively reli-

---

121. 461 U.S. at 604 n. 30, 103 S.Ct. at 2035 n. 30, 76 L.Ed.2d at 181 n. 30.

122. For a review of such provisions see, C. Antieau, P. Carroll & T. Burke, Religion Under the State Constitutions (1965); Note, Beyond the Establishment Clause: Enforcing Separation of Church and State through State Constitutional Powers, 71 U.Va.L.Rev. 625 (1985).

123. 210 U.S. 50, 28 S.Ct. 690, 52 L.Ed. 954 (1908).

124. The Court unanimously upheld a program of state aid to visually handicapped students in Witters v. Washington Department of Services for the Blind, 474 U.S. 481, 106 S.Ct. 748, 88 L.Ed.2d 846 (1986), rehearing denied 475 U.S. 1091, 106 S.Ct. 1485, 89 L.Ed.2d 737 (1986). The program was upheld although the student involved in the individual case had used the aid to attend a religiously affiliated school for the purpose of pursuing a religious vocation. The Court found that the aid to handicapped students had a secular purpose, as the program did not have a religious effect because it merely increased the economic resources of all visually handicapped persons

who wished to obtain special education or vocational training. The majority opinion by Justice Marshall stated that any aid that flowed to religious schools from the program "does so only as a result of the genuinely independent and private choices of the aid recipients." Justice Marshall analogized these payments to the payment of government employees' salaries. Government employees could use their economic resources to pursue a religious education or make donations to a religious entity. The case, therefore, seems to support the statement made in this paragraph that the payment of money to persons who are employees or wards of the government does not constitute a violation of the establishment clause even though those persons independently choose to use that money for religious purposes.

In Zobrest v. Catalina Foothills School District, 509 U.S. 1, 113 S.Ct. 2462, 125 L.Ed.2d 1 (1993) the Court ruled that the establishment clause would not prevent the government from providing a sign language-speech interpreter for a deaf student even though the deaf student was attending a religiously affiliated high school.

gious, it will be practically impossible to aid the institution without either having the impermissible effect of aiding religion or else having to establish so many procedural safeguards that an excessive entanglement results. However, if the institution has a clearly independent secular function the state should be able to design a program which aids only the secular activities. This type of institution can then be aided with a minimum of administrative entanglement, as the lesser potential for aiding the religious function requires fewer safeguards.

During the last century the Supreme Court upheld grants to church affiliated hospitals in *Bradfield v. Roberts*,[125] cited in modern times with approval by the Court.[126] As religious hospitals seem to have an independent secular function, the analysis should be the same as that for religious colleges—the state need only avoid aiding pervasively religious institutions or clearly religious activities. So long as the hospital aided is not so "pervasively sectarian" as to subsume its role as a hospital in its religious mission, its secular medical function may receive state aid.

The Supreme Court relied on *Bradfield* when it upheld a federal statute that granted funds to public and nonprofit organizations to provide services, other than family planning or abortion related services, to pregnant adolescents and to conduct programs to prevent adolescent sexual relations.[127] In *Bowen v. Kendrick*[128] the Supreme Court upheld the constitutionality of the Adolescent Family Life Act [AFLA] against the claim that the AFLA on its face violated the establishment clause of the First Amendment. Under the AFLA grants are given to various organizations to give care or counselling to pregnant adolescents and their parents or to counsel adolescents (through prevention services and programs). The AFLA specifically states that religious and charitable organizations, as well as other public and nonprofit organizations, are eligible for these grants; the AFLA requires grant applicants to show how they will involve families of adolescents, and religious and charitable organizations and other associations and groups in the private sector, in the services that the grantee would provide to adolescents and their parents. The AFLA prohibits the use of any grant money for family planning services, abortions, abortion counselling, or the promotion of abortion.

In *Kendrick* the Court, in a majority opinion written by Chief Justice Rehnquist, ruled that the AFLA on its face did not violate the establishment clause, although the Court also found that individual grants made under the AFLA might be invalid under the establishment clause. The AFLA on its face survived the purpose, effect, and entanglement tests that had been developed for determining whether any type of government support for religion violated the establishment clause.[129] Congress had asserted the nonreligious purpose of addressing problems associated with adolescent sexuality; Chief Justice Rehnquist found that the AFLA did not have a religious purpose. Congress could not be found to have endorsed religion merely because its views on the subject of abortion coincided with those of religious organizations.[130]

Chief Justice Rehnquist, writing for the majority, ruled that the AFLA on its face did not have an effect that either advanced or inhibited religion in a manner that would violate the establishment clause. The establishment clause did not prevent religious organizations from participating in government funded programs to promote social welfare goals. So long as the government program and the use of government aid did not advance religion,

---

125. 175 U.S. 291, 20 S.Ct. 121, 44 L.Ed. 168 (1899).

126. Roemer v. Board of Public Works, 426 U.S. 736, 746, 96 S.Ct. 2337, 2344–45, 49 L.Ed.2d 179 (1976) (plurality opinion by Blackmun, J.).

127. Bradfield v. Roberts, 175 U.S. 291, 20 S.Ct. 121, 44 L.Ed. 168 (1899), cited by the Supreme Court with approval in Bowen v. Kendrick, 487 U.S. 589, 609, 108 S.Ct. 2562, 2574, 101 L.Ed.2d 520 (1988).

128. 487 U.S. 589, 108 S.Ct. 2562, 101 L.Ed.2d 520 (1988).

129. See, §§ 17.3–17.5 regarding the development and application of these establishment clause tests in other areas.

130. Bowen v. Kendrick, 487 U.S. 589, 604, 108 S.Ct. 2562, 2571, 101 L.Ed.2d 520 (1988).

the primary effect test would not be violated. Chief Justice Rehnquist found that the AFLA on its face did not have the effect of advancing religion for four reasons. First, the statute did not indicate that a large proportion of the funds would go to "pervasively sectarian" organizations. Second, the funding of programs under the AFLA did not necessarily result in religious organizations using the funds for religious purposes; nothing in the statute or prior cases justified a presumption that religious organizations could not carry out these grant programs in a secular manner. Third, the statute did not advance religion merely because many religious organizations agreed with the message that Congress intended to promote with AFLA grants. Fourth, the AFLA was designed to promote the social welfare through nonreligious means and it would not be invalidated on the theory that any participation of religious organizations in government programs created a "symbolic link" between government and religion.

The Court in *Kendrick* also ruled that the AFLA did not, on its face, give rise to an excessive government entanglement with religion. The majority opinion found no reason to assume that the religious organizations that were receiving grants were so "pervasively sectarian" that the government would need to engage in such extensive monitoring of their programs, in order to ensure that the grant money was not used for religious purposes, that it would become enmeshed in an excessive entanglement with those religious organizations.[131]

When the Court upholds a statute granting money to religiously affiliated organizations,

such as it did in *Kendrick*, it is not ruling that every possible grant given under the authority of the statute will be valid. In *Kendrick* the Supreme Court only upheld the AFLA on its face; the Court did not rule on the question of whether individual grants to religious organizations to provide counselling or services to adolescents violated the establishment clause. The majority opinion by Chief Justice Rehnquist found that taxpayers had standing to challenge specific grants under the AFLA. Taxpayers could attempt to show that a specific grant violated the establishment clause because it had the effect of advancing religion or because it would give rise to an excessive entanglement between government and religion.[132] Chief Justice Rehnquist's opinion is not clear regarding whether a grant to a "pervasively sectarian" institution is per se unconstitutional, or whether a grant to a pervasively sectarian institution was only presumptively unconstitutional, due to the fact that a grant to a pervasively sectarian organization might need extensive monitoring to ensure that the government funds were not used for religious teaching or other religious activities.[133]

§ 17.5 The Establishment Clause— Religion and the Public Schools

(a) Introduction

Questions concerning the introduction of religion into the governmentally operated school system may arise in several ways. Many of the cases examining particular ways in which public schools had become involved with religious activities or beliefs were decided before the emergence of the three-part purpose-effect-entanglement test.[1] We will divide this

---

131. 487 U.S. at 616 n. 14, 108 S.Ct. at 2578 n. 14.

132. Bowen v. Kendrick, 487 U.S. 589, 617–21, 108 S.Ct. 2562, 2579–81, 101 L.Ed.2d 520 (1988).

133. Id. At least two Justices believe that not all grants to pervasively sectarian religious organizations are per se unconstitutional. Bowen v. Kendrick, 487 U.S. 589, 624, 108 S.Ct. 2562, 2582, 101 L.Ed.2d 520 (1988) (Kennedy, J., joined by Scalia, J., concurring).

§ 17.5

1. See, e.g., Stone v. Graham, 449 U.S. 39, 101 S.Ct. 192, 66 L.Ed.2d 199 (1980); Widmar v. Vincent, 454 U.S. 263, 102 S.Ct. 269, 70 L.Ed.2d 440 (1981). See §§ 17.5(c), 17.5(e), infra.

In a limited group of cases the Court has found a historical basis for ruling that an involvement between government and religion did not constitute an establishment of religion and has not employed with any strictness the three part purpose-effect-entanglement test. See Marsh v. Chambers, 463 U.S. 783, 103 S.Ct. 3330, 77 L.Ed.2d 1019 (1983) (upholding legislature's practice of opening of each day of legislature with a prayer by a chaplain); Lynch v. Donnelly, 465 U.S. 668, 104 S.Ct. 1355, 79 L.Ed.2d 604 (1984), rehearing denied 466 U.S. 994, 104 S.Ct. 2376, 80 L.Ed.2d 848 (1984) (upholding city action of erecting a Christmas display on public property which included a nativity scene). See § 17.3, supra.

section of the treatise into various subsections based on the problem areas—the particular types of involvement between religion and public schools—that have been the subject of Supreme Court opinions. The reader can then evaluate the Court's use of establishment clause tests in terms of specific problem areas.

The cases examined in this section involve issues concerning religious activities in government schools or other connections between government schools and religious beliefs. The situations in these cases differ from the situation confronted by the Court in *Board of Education of Kiryas Joel Village School District v. Grumet.*[2] The Supreme Court, in *Grumet,* invalidated a state law that created a separate public school district for a Village composed entirely of members of one religion. The only public school in the new Village School District was operated in a completely nonreligious manner for handicapped children within the district. The government school had no involvement with religion that would have violated the establishment clause. A majority of the Justices in *Grumet* found that the state law creating the Village School District was a preference for members of one religious sect that violated the establishment clause's neutrality principle.[3]

(b) Released or Shared Time

The Supreme Court has considered public school programs involving the exemption of public school students from class so that they could receive religious instruction. The Court has held that the students could not be given religious instruction on the public school premises because such a program has the direct effect of aiding the establishment of religious beliefs. However, the state may release students from school so that they may attend religious instruction away from the public

school. This early release of students is viewed as only an accommodation of individual religious preferences rather than an aid to the religions.

In *Illinois ex rel. McCollum v. Board of Education*[4] the Court held invalid a system whereby religious teachers came into the public school to give instruction to students. The program allowed members of any religious organization to instruct those students who had requested the instruction. Students who did not request instruction remained in the school, as the programs took place during a time when the compulsory attendance laws required all students below the age of 17 to be in school.

The Court found a direct aid to religion as government facilities were being used for the propagation of religious beliefs. While no formal test was employed, the opinion noted that this policy removed any "wall" between church and state as it had the government giving direct help to the advancing of religion. It was irrelevant that all religions might be helped by the program as the First Amendment was held to forbid the advancement of religious beliefs over nonreligious ones as well as the advancement of a particular sect.

Only four years later, in *Zorach v. Clauson,*[5] the Court upheld a program where students were released from public schools so that they could receive religious instruction at other locations. Although all children were required to be either in school or at religious classes during this period, a majority of the Justices found that the program did not constitute government aid to religion. Because no government funds or other support went to the advancement of religious ends, this was considered to be only the accommodation of the desires of individual students and their families to be free of the public school system so

---

In Lee v. Weisman, 505 U.S. 577, 112 S.Ct. 2649, 120 L.Ed.2d 467 (1992) the Court, by a five to four vote of the Justices, found that school sponsored invocations and benediction prayers at graduation ceremonies violated the establishment clause. The majority opinion in *Lee,* found that this practice violated the "central principles" of the establishment clause, so that the Court would not "revisit the difficult questions dividing us in recent cases" concerning whether the three part (purpose, effect, entanglement) test should be used in all, or even some, establish-

ment clause cases. 505 U.S. at 586, 112 S.Ct. at 2655. The *Lee* decision is examined in §§ 17.3, 17.5(c).

2. 512 U.S. 687, 114 S.Ct. 2481, 129 L.Ed.2d 546 (1994).

3. The *Grumet* decision is analyzed in § 17.3.

4. 333 U.S. 203, 68 S.Ct. 461, 92 L.Ed. 649 (1948).

5. 343 U.S. 306, 72 S.Ct. 679, 96 L.Ed. 954 (1952).

that they could receive their religious education. Moreover, there was no religious doctrine taught on public property, in the public schools.

The key concept here is the neutral principle of "accommodation." If there had been proof that the program coerced students into attending religious classes, the state support of those programs would violate both the free exercise and the establishment clauses.[6] However, there was no such proof in this case and, on this basis, the majority found the program to be a mere accommodation of the desires of individual students to exercise rights whose values are reflected in the free exercise clause.[7]

(c) Prayers or Bible Reading

The use of officially authorized prayers or Bible readings for motivational purposes constitutes a direct violation of the establishment clause. Even though a practice may not be coercive, active support of a particular belief raises the danger of eventual establishment of state approved religious views. Although a given prayer or practice may not favor any one sect, the principle of neutrality in religious matters is violated by any program which places tacit government approval on "religious" views or practices. Under the basic purpose-and-effect test these programs must be found to violate the First Amendment. The purpose of the program might be a neutral or secular one of state accommodation of student desires. However, the effect of any such practice is to give government aid and support to the advancement of religious beliefs. Thus the programs were held invalid even prior to the use of the additional entanglement test.

Not all religious references must be banned from the public schools. Religion and religious literature, including the Bible, may be studied in a purely academic manner. So long as the study does not amount to prayer or the advancement of religious beliefs, a teacher may discuss such materials in the secular course of study.[8] Religious references in official ceremonies, including some school exercises, will also be allowed as a part of our secularized traditions and not an advancement of religion similar to state approved prayer.[9]

In *Engel v. Vitale* [10] the Supreme Court held that the use of a "nondenominational prayer" written by government authorities violated the establishment clause. The decision was easily reached because the government writing of a prayer was sponsorship of religious views similar to the official establishment of religion, which many of the framers of the First Amendment had fled from and feared. Moreover, like the program in *Illinois ex rel. McCollum v. Board of Education*, discussed above, the religious exercise was performed on school property.

In a second case, *School District v. Schempp*,[11] the Court examined school programs of voluntary Bible reading or the use of the "Lord's Prayer." Unlike *Engel*, it was not part of the job of any public official to compose a prayer: the prayer came from the Bible. Yet this difference did not save the program from constitutional attack. In *Schempp* the Court used the purpose and effect test to review the programs under the establishment clause. Although the program was voluntary and did not favor any sect, the effect was to aid the advancement of religion; it constituted a generalized religious ceremony. Thus, it violated

---

6. 343 U.S. at 311, 72 S.Ct. at 682.

7. In Board of Education of Westside Community Schools v. Mergens, 496 U.S. 226, 110 S.Ct. 2356, 110 L.Ed.2d 191 (1990) the Supreme Court upheld a federal statute that gave "equal access" to student groups (including religious student groups) to the premises of high schools that received federal financial assistance. See § 17.5(e) infra for an examination of equal access issues and cases.

8. School District v. Schempp, 374 U.S. 203, 225, 83 S.Ct. 1560, 1573, 10 L.Ed.2d 844 (1963).

9. Engel v. Vitale, 370 U.S. 421, 435 n. 21, 82 S.Ct. 1261, 1269 n. 21, 8 L.Ed.2d 601 (1962). The Court has upheld a state legislature's employment of a chaplain and use of an opening prayer. These practices were upheld on the basis of the history of legislative prayer, which dated back to the Congress which drafted the First Amendment. The ruling does not modify the principles regarding religious activity in public schools. Marsh v. Chambers, 463 U.S. 783, 103 S.Ct. 3330, 77 L.Ed.2d 1019 (1983); see note 16, infra.

10. 370 U.S. 421, 82 S.Ct. 1261, 8 L.Ed.2d 601 (1962).

11. 374 U.S. 203, 83 S.Ct. 1560, 10 L.Ed.2d 844 (1963).

the concepts of separation and neutrality between government and religion and there was but one dissent to the invalidation of these practices.[12]

An important part of the *Schempp* decision was the majority's answer to the argument that elimination of voluntary prayers would amount to government sponsorship of an antireligious position. The Court found that neutrality in religious matters did not constitute the implied teaching of a "religion of secularism."[13] This viewpoint is important to the decisions involving aid to religious schools for it rejects the argument that providing publicly funded education only in secular schools inhibits the free exercise of religion by those who want their children trained in a religious manner. So long as the state does not legally prohibit private, religious schools, its offering of public education in this manner is not a violation of the religion clauses.[14]

In *Stone v. Graham*,[15] the Supreme Court held that a Kentucky statute requiring the posting of the Ten Commandments on the wall of each public classroom in the state violated the establishment clause. Any use of prayers or Bible passages in school must be reviewed under the three part test for compatibility with the establishment clause. First, the statute must have a secular legislative purpose. Second, its primary effect must neither advance nor inhibit religion. Third, the statute must not create an excessive entanglement between government and religion.[16] Any use of prayers or religious literature for inspirational purposes would violate the purpose and effect tests for validity.

The Supreme Court's opinion in *Stone* stated that the preeminent purpose of the Ken-

tucky statute was "plainly religious in nature" and had no secular legislative purpose, even though the legislation included a statement of avowed secular purpose.[17] The fact that the Bible verses were to be posted rather than read aloud, and the fact that they were to be financed by voluntary private contributions, had no bearing on the validity of the statute because it had a plainly religious purpose, and "it is no defense to urge that the religious practices here may be relatively minor encroachments on the First Amendment."

In a different context, the Supreme Court has upheld governmental involvement with prayer services. In *Marsh v. Chambers*[18] the Court upheld a state legislature's action in employing a chaplain for the primary purpose of opening each legislative day with a prayer. The majority opinion by Chief Justice Burger relied heavily on the history of American legislatures (including the Continental Congress and the first United States Congress) employing legislative chaplains and prayer in the legislative day. The majority opinion stated that history alone "could not justify contemporary violations" of the establishment clause. Yet the Chief Justice found that historical evidence indicated that the Court should not apply the three-part test so strictly as to find that this practice was a violation of the establishment clause because such activity, in fact, never had resulted in an establishment of religion or encroachment on the separation of religious beliefs from governmental functions. Nothing in the *Marsh v. Chambers* majority opinion, however, shed any light on whether the Court would uphold practices in public schools which might have some incidental religious effect but which do not involve the type of prayers or inspirational use of the Bible

---

12. Justice Stewart was the sole dissenter. 374 U.S. at 308, 83 S.Ct. at 1616.

13. 374 U.S. at 225–26, 83 S.Ct. at 1573–74.

14. The Court's rulings on aid to parochial schools and the refusals to recognize a state interest in enabling students to attend those schools are the subject of § 17.4(a), supra.

15. 449 U.S. 39, 101 S.Ct. 192, 66 L.Ed.2d 199 (1980).

16. 449 U.S. at 40, 101 S.Ct. at 193, citing Lemon v. Kurtzman, 403 U.S. 602, 612–13, 91 S.Ct. 2105, 2111, 29 L.Ed.2d 745 (1971).

17. The Kentucky legislation required the following notation in small print at the bottom of each posted copy of the Ten Commandments: "The secular application of the Ten Commandments is clearly seen in its adoption as the fundamental legal code of Western Civilization and the Common Law of the United States." K.R.S. 158.178 (1980). Stone v. Graham, 449 U.S. 39, 40 n. 1, 101 S.Ct. 192, 193 n. 1, 66 L.Ed.2d 199 (1980).

18. 463 U.S. 783, 103 S.Ct. 3330, 77 L.Ed.2d 1019 (1983).

which have been found to violate the establishment clause in earlier cases.[19]

Some state governments and school boards, following the school prayer decisions, passed statutes either requiring or allowing a period of silence in each public school day, during which time students would be free to think, meditate, or pray silently. In *Wallace v. Jaffree*,[20] the Court did not have to rule on a true moment of silence statute. The litigation that resulted in the Supreme Court case initially involved constitutional challenges to three Alabama statutes. The first statute, enacted in 1978 by the Alabama legislature, established a "period of silence not to exceed one minute in duration, that should be observed for meditation." The Supreme Court did not have to rule on this statute because the persons who attacked the statute in the lower court, "abandoned any claim" that the statute was unconstitutional in their argument before the Supreme Court of the United States.[21]

The second statute passed by Alabama, in 1981, authorized a period of silence "for meditation or voluntary prayer". The third statute was enacted in 1982; it stated that any teacher "in any educational institution within the state of Alabama, recognizing that the Lord God is one, at the beginning of any homeroom or any class" could lead a legislatively prescribed prayer.[22] There was no significant issue regarding the constitutionality of the third statute which was clearly invalid on the basis of the Court's previous rulings regarding government prescribed prayer.[23] Thus, the only significant issue facing the Court in *Wallace* was the constitutionality of the period of silence for "meditation or voluntary prayer" statute.

The Court found in *Wallace* one of the rare cases in which a piece of legislation passed by a legislative body was unconstitutional because the legislature was motivated only by a religious purpose in enacting the statute. The

---

19. See also, Lynch v. Donnelly, 465 U.S. 668, 104 S.Ct. 1355, 79 L.Ed.2d 604 (1984), rehearing denied 466 U.S. 994, 104 S.Ct. 2376, 80 L.Ed.2d 848 (1984), in which the Supreme Court upheld a city policy which called for the erection of a Christmas display in a public park that included a Christian nativity scene in part on the basis that such displays of the nativity scene, through historic use in the country, had come to constitute observance of a general holiday season and not the endorsement of a religious faith or the granting of a benefit to a particular faith. In this case, as in *Marsh*, Chief Justice Burger wrote a majority opinion that focused on the history of this particular practice as he found that there was no violation of the three-part purpose-effect-entanglement test. The opinion did not indicate that the Court would modify its strict view against the government's use of prayer or inspirational Bible readings in public schools.

20. 472 U.S. 38, 105 S.Ct. 2479, 86 L.Ed.2d 29 (1985).

21. 472 U.S. at 40 n. 1, 105 S.Ct. at 2481, n. 1.

22. The statute and prayer are set out at 472 U.S. at 40 n. 3, 105 S.Ct. at 2481 n. 3.

23. The district court upheld the government prescribed prayer and all three of the statutes on the theory that the Supreme Court rulings regarding religious activities were not binding precedent on the states because, according to the district court, the First Amendment religion clauses should never have been made applicable to the states. This ruling of the district court had been reversed by the court of appeals. The Supreme Court, in fact, had earlier summarily affirmed the Court of Appeals ruling overturning the district court. Jaffree v. Board of School Commissioners, 554 F.Supp. 1104 (S.D.Ala.1983), reversed Jaffree v. Wallace, 705 F.2d 1526, 1535 (11th Cir.1983), court of appeals affirmed Wallace v. Jaffree, 466 U.S. 924, 104 S.Ct. 1704, 80 L.Ed.2d 178 (1984) (summary

affirmance and notation of probable jurisdiction as to one question in the case). The Supreme Court now took time to explain why it should reverse what the majority opinion kindly referred to only as the "remarkable" ruling of the district court regarding the applicability of the First Amendment to the states. The majority opinion by Justice Stevens found, as the Court has in all cases since the 1940's, that the values of the First Amendment are a fundamental part of the liberty protected by the Fourteenth Amendment. The federal government and local governments are prohibited from interfering with principles which the Supreme Court has delineated under the establishment and free exercise clauses of the First Amendment. Wallace v. Jaffree, 472 U.S. 38, 50–55, 105 S.Ct. 2479, 2486–89, 86 L.Ed.2d 29 (1985).

Justice O'Connor's concurring opinion in *Wallace*, 472 U.S. at 69, 105 S.Ct. at 2496, and the dissenting opinions of Chief Justice Burger, 472 U.S. at 86, 105 S.Ct. at 2505, and Justice White, 472 U.S. at 92, 105 S.Ct. at 2508 questioned the strictness of the court's ruling. These separate opinions were based in part on Justices' desire to reassess some earlier decisions of the Court, and in part on a belief that the history of the First and Fourteenth Amendments did not justify judicial exclusion of all religious activity or aid to religion from state school systems.

Justice Rehnquist was alone in voting to approve the district court's ruling based on his reexamination of the history of the First Amendment. This reexamination led Justice Rehnquist to believe that the First Amendment had limited applicability to state and local governmental activities which have an incidental effect of advancing religion through what he described as a "generalized endorsement of prayer." Wallace v. Jaffree, 472 U.S. 38, 92, 105 S.Ct. 2479, 2508, 86 L.Ed.2d 29 (1985) (Rehnquist, J., dissenting).

Court ruled that the "meditation or voluntary prayer" statute violated the establishment clause due to the religious purpose of the legislature. This ruling made it unnecessary to consider whether a similarly worded statute enacted for religiously neutral reasons by another legislature might be upheld or whether such a moment of silence statute could be upheld, if at all, only if it referred to meditation rather than prayer.

Six Justices found that the legislative history of the Alabama statute made it clear that the law at issue was passed only for a religious purpose and that this improper motivation required the Court to invalidate the law. Justice Stevens, in a majority opinion for five members of the Court, stated that the legislation would have to be invalidated under the First Amendment if it was motivated entirely by a purpose to advance religion.[24] Statements of legislators inserted into the legislative record, and testimony of the bill's sponsor before the district court, made it clear that the persons who drafted and passed the Amendment had not attempted to justify the statute in terms of any nonreligious purpose. The majority opinion concluded that "the legislative intent to return prayer to the public schools is, of course, quite different from merely protecting every student's right to engage in voluntary prayer during an appropriate moment of silence during the school day." Although the Court did not rule on a true moment of silence statute, it appears that such a statute may be upheld if it was not passed for

entirely religious purposes and if it was not used as a means for governmental encouragement of religious beliefs or religious activities on public school property.[25]

Even if the Court in the future abandons the "*Lemon* tests"[26] (the formal three part tests: purpose-effect-entanglement), the Court might not overrule its decisions finding that officially authorized prayers, or readings from religious texts, in government grade schools and high schools violate the establishment clause. This point was clearly made by the Court in *Lee v. Weisman*,[27] as the Court found that religious invocations at public school graduations violated the establishment clause.

Lee involved a school district policy that allowed high school and middle principals to have members of the clergy give invocations or benedictions at formal graduation ceremonies. Though the invocations or benedictions might be written with guidelines that were designed to avoid offending anyone, the practice could not withstand establishment clause analysis.[28] *Lee v. Weisman* was decided by a five to four vote of the Justices. But the strong support for basic establishment clause principles by a majority of the Justices is more important than the closeness of the vote. The four dissenting Justices would approve government involvement with religion that arguably is supported by historical practices in our country, at least so long as the government action at issue did not involve a preference for one

---

24. Wallace v. Jaffree, 472 U.S. 38, 57, 105 S.Ct. 2479, 2490, 86 L.Ed.2d 29 (1985).

25. Justice Powell concurring in the opinion of the Court, and Justice O'Connor concurring only in the judgment, both stated that they believed that a true moment of silence statute should be upheld. Wallace v. Jaffree, 472 U.S. 38, 63, 105 S.Ct. 2479, 2493, 86 L.Ed.2d 29 (1985) (Powell, J., concurring); 472 U.S. at 69, 105 S.Ct. at 2496 (O'Connor, J., concurring in the judgment). Chief Justice Burger and Justices White and Rehnquist dissented in *Wallace*. Thus, five Justices appeared to be willing to uphold such a statute in a future case.

In Karcher v. May, 484 U.S. 72, 108 S.Ct. 388, 98 L.Ed.2d 327 (1987) the Supreme Court avoided ruling on the constitutionality of a statute providing for a minute of silence at the beginning of a school day. The Court in *Karcher* ruled that the appellants, who were former members of the state legislature, could not appeal from an adverse judgment regarding the minute of silence statute

once these individuals had lost their status as officers of the state legislature.

26. Lemon v. Kurtzman, 403 U.S. 602, 91 S.Ct. 2105, 29 L.Ed.2d 745 (1971), rehearing denied 404 U.S. 876, 92 S.Ct. 24, 30 L.Ed.2d 123 (1971).

27. 505 U.S. 577, 112 S.Ct. 2649, 120 L.Ed.2d 467 (1992).

28. The majority opinion in *Lee* noted that guidelines were used by the school district for members of the clergy who gave invocations at school graduation ceremonies. Members of the clergy who were to give such invocations or benedictions were given a copy of a document entitled "Guidelines for Civic Occasions" that had been prepared by the National Conference of Christians and Jews for persons who were requested to give public prayers at nonsectarian civic ceremonies. Lee v. Weisman, 505 U.S. 577, 579, 112 S.Ct. 2649, 2652, 120 L.Ed.2d 467 (1992).

religious sect over another.[29] Justice Kennedy wrote a majority opinion in *Lee*, even though he had dissented in cases in which the Court had invalidated government actions that aided religion, such as the government creation or toleration of religious symbols in holiday displays on government property.[30] Justice Kennedy, in *Lee*, found that the government practice of religious prayers at school graduations could not withstand any meaningful form of judicial review under basic establishment clause principles.

Justice Kennedy's majority opinion in *Lee v. Weisman* did not make use of the purpose, effect, or entanglement tests. The majority opinion stated:

"The case does not require us to revisit the difficult cases dividing us in recent cases, questions of the definition in full scope of the principles governing the extent of permitted accommodation by the state for religious beliefs and practices ... for without reference to those principles and other contexts, the controlling precedence as they relate to prayer and religious exercise in primary and secondary public schools compel the holding here ... the State's involvement in the school prayers challenged today

violates [the establishment clause] central principles." [31]

This majority opinion is a very strong endorsement of the concept that government neutrality in religious matters is a touchstone of establishment clause analysis; the concept of neutrality was clearly violated by government authorized prayers in public grade schools and high schools. Justice Kennedy's opinion did not find that coercion of individuals to give up or modify their religious beliefs, or to act inconsistently with their religious beliefs, was a prerequisite for an establishment clause violation.

The majority opinion stated that "it is beyond dispute that, at a minimum, the Constitution guarantees that the government may not coerce anyone to support or participate in religion or its exercise." [32] Justice Kennedy noted that "there are heightened concerns with protecting freedom of conscience from subtle coercive pressure in the elementary and secondary public schools." [33] Absent a significant change in the membership of the Court, the Justices will not accept the argument that government may authorize or endorse religious prayers, readings, or teachings in the

29. 505 U.S. 577, 629, 112 S.Ct. 2649, 2678, 120 L.Ed.2d 467 (1992) (Scalia, J., joined by Rehnquist, C.J., and White and Thomas, JJ., dissenting).

30. Justice Kennedy had dissented when the Court ruled that a county violated the establishment clause by having a creche display at a county courthouse that was set up by a Roman Catholic organization. County of Allegheny v. American Civil Liberties Union, 492 U.S. 573, 655, 109 S.Ct. 3086, 3134, 106 L.Ed.2d 472 (1989) (Kennedy, J., joined by Rehnquist, C.J., and White and Scalia, JJ., concurring in the judgment in part and dissenting in part), on remand 887 F.2d 260 (3d Cir.1989).

31. Lee v. Weisman, 505 U.S. 577, 586, 112 S.Ct. 2649, 2655, 120 L.Ed.2d 467 (1992). In a concurring opinion Justice Blackmun noted that the Court in *Lee* had taken a position that was consistent with the three part purpose-effect-entanglement test that the Supreme Court had used in every establishment clause case since 1971 (with the exception of the Court's decision upholding the use of a chaplain by a state legislature). 505 U.S. at 597, 603 n. 4, 112 S.Ct. at 2661, 2663 n. 4. The one post–1971 case in which the Court had not used the three part test was Marsh v. Chambers, 463 U.S. 783, 103 S.Ct. 3330, 77 L.Ed.2d 1019 (1983). The majority opinion in *Lee* found that the "inherent differences between the public school system and a session of the state legislature" made the Court's decision in *Marsh* irrelevant to the question of

whether the government could have religious benedictions at school graduations that put students and their parents who disagreed with the religious prayers to the choice of either acting inconsistently with their beliefs or foregoing the graduation ceremony. Lee v. Weisman, 505 U.S. 577, 595–97, 112 S.Ct. 2649, 2660–61, 120 L.Ed.2d 467 (1992).

32. Lee v. Weisman, 505 U.S. 577, 586, 112 S.Ct. 2649, 2655, 120 L.Ed.2d 467 (1992).

33. 505 U.S. at 592, 112 S.Ct. at 2658. The Supreme Court in *Lee* did not rule that there would be a violation of the establishment clause whenever there was any involvement of government and religion. The majority opinion appears to endorse a case-by-case approach to protect the establishment clause values without establishing any clear tests. "We do not hold that every state action implicating religion is invalid if one or a few citizens find it offensive ... our jurisprudence in this area is of necessity one of line-drawing, of determining at what point a dissenter's rights of religious freedom are infringed." Lee v. Weisman, 505 U.S. 577, 597–98, 112 S.Ct. 2649, 2661, 120 L.Ed.2d 467 (1992).

Lee did not examine the issues or standards used in cases involving accommodation of religious beliefs of persons who wish to use government property and whose inability to use the property might inhibit their ability to carry out their beliefs. Statutes allowing for "equal access" to school facilities are examined in § 17.5(e).

public schools as a part of the official school day or school ceremonies.

At the start of the twenty-first century, the Supreme Court reaffirmed the *Lee* analysis. In *Santa Fe Independent School District v. Doe,*[34] the Supreme Court, by a 6 to 3 vote of the Justices, ruled that a public school district policy that permitted public high school students to select one of their fellow students to give a non-sectarian prayer at high school football games violated the establishment clause. The school district that adopted the football game prayer program attempted to distinguish *Lee,* and other public school prayer cases, on the basis that: (1) under their program students voted both for the adoption of the rule and selection of the student: (2) and that football games, unlike classes or graduation ceremonies, did not require student attendance.

Justice Stevens wrote the majority opinion in *Santa Fe Independent School District*; he found that the case was indistinguishable from *Lee.* The government's establishment of the policy, and provision of the forum for the activities, directly involved the government in the religious activity. Some students, such as those on a football team or in a band, were required to attend the football game. Justice Stevens also stated that there would be an element of coercion in the program, even if the Court assumed that every student's decision to attend the football game was truly voluntary, because the prayer had "the improper effect of coercing those present to participate in an act of religious worship."[35] Justice Stevens pointed out that no Supreme Court ruling prohibited "any public school student from voluntarily

praying at any time before, during, or after the school day."[36]

Three dissenting Justices in *Santa Fe Independent School District* wanted to uphold the program on its face, although they admitted that the program could be implemented in an unconstitutional manner under certain circumstances.[37] Justice Stevens' majority opinion ruled that the statute had to be invalidated on its face, because the program had been adopted for the unconstitutional purpose of having the government endorsement of school prayer.[38]

The *Santa Fe* decision, like the *Lee* decision before it, did not establish any specific standard for determining the extent to which government involvement with religion would violate the establishment clause.[39]

(d) Modification of the Curriculum for Religious Purposes

The Supreme Court has ruled that a state may not eliminate the teaching of certain ideas related to normal classroom subjects because they conflict with religious beliefs. In *Epperson v. Arkansas*[40] the Court reviewed a statute which made it unlawful for teachers in state schools to teach a theory of human biological evolution. The Court held that the statute violated the establishment clause because it had a religious purpose—thus failing the secular purpose test. It was an impermissible breach of the principle of government neutrality for the state to eliminate a particular piece of information from a course merely because it conflicted with some religious beliefs.

It should be noted that this case does not, by itself, eliminate the ability of the state to ad-

---

34. 530 U.S. 290, 120 S.Ct. 2266, 147 L.Ed.2d 295 (2000).

35. 530 U.S. at 311, 120 S.Ct. at 2280.

36. 530 U.S. at 312, 120 S.Ct. at 2281.

37. Santa Fe Independent School District v. Doe, 530 U.S. 290, 318, 120 S.Ct. 2266, 2283, 147 L.Ed.2d 295 (2000) (Rehnquist, C.J., joined by Scalia and Thomas, JJ., dissenting).

38. Santa Fe Independent School District v. Doe, 530 U.S. 290, 314–317, 120 S.Ct. 2266, 2281–83, 147 L.Ed.2d 295 (2000).

39. Only nine days after the *Santa Fe* decision, the Supreme Court Justices were unable to produce a majority

opinion when they upheld a government program that provided non-religious teaching materials and teaching equipment to religiously affiliated schools, together with public and non-religious private schools. Mitchell v. Helms, 530 U.S. 793, 120 S.Ct. 2530, 147 L.Ed.2d 660 (2000) (judgment of the Court announced in an opinion by Thomas, J., joined by Rehnquist, C.J., and Scalia and Kennedy, JJ.); 530 U.S. at 836, 120 S.Ct. at 2556 (O'Connor, J., joined by Breyer, J., concurring in the judgment); 530 U.S. at 866, 120 S.Ct. at 2572 (Souter, J., joined by Stevens and Ginsburg, JJ., dissenting).

40. 393 U.S. 97, 89 S.Ct. 266, 21 L.Ed.2d 228 (1968).

just or eliminate the subjects that are taught in its school system. Justice Black, in a concurring opinion, noted that a state should be able to eliminate any given subject matter from its school system without raising a First Amendment issue.[41] This principle would seem to be true, for if the state is under no obligation to teach a specific subject there should be nothing wrong with eliminating a given course.

However, there are two bases for making an exception to this deference to state educational authority. First, where the state has eliminated only one element from a course of study for religious reasons it has attempted to help the religious point of view by eliminating ideas which would challenge that view. In *Epperson*, the Court focused extensively on the evidence that the state's motivation for excluding the teaching of evolution was improper. Second, where the state can offer no secular educational reason for altering the curriculum there is no reason to defer to the state's educational policy. It was this unusual case of an open attempt to aid certain religious views that was presented to the Court in *Epperson*. This official attempt to aid a specific religious view openly breached the principle of neutrality, which is the core of the religion clauses.

In *Edwards v. Aguillard*,[42] the Supreme Court, by a seven to two vote of the Justices, invalidated another legislative attempt to modify the curriculum of the public schools for religious purposes.[43] At issue in *Edwards* was the Louisiana "balanced treatment for creation-science and evolution-science in public school instruction" legislation. Under the legislation, any public school that taught the theory of human biological evolution was required to give equal treatment to "creation science." The majority opinion by Justice Brennan found that the legislative history of the statute, and the language of the statute itself, demonstrated that the legislation was designed to promote religion and, therefore, that it violated the establishment clause.[44]

The state had attempted to show that the law promoted academic freedom and the comprehensiveness of science instruction; but the statute itself, in the majority's view, undercut these arguments by removing the teachers' authority to examine only theories of human biological evolution and discouraging rather than encouraging the teaching of all scientific theories about the origins of the human race (by requiring the teaching of creation science when other theories of evolution were taught).

The Court did not attempt to restrict the authority of the legislatures or the school boards to design a curriculum for non-religious reasons. It would appear that all references to religion need not be excised from a public school curriculum. References to religion may be a part of public school instruction in history or literature, or any other subject, so long as the references to religion or a religious text do not have the purpose or effect of advancing religious goals.[45]

41. 393 U.S. at 113–14, 89 S.Ct. at 275–76 (Black, J., concurring).

42. 482 U.S. 578, 107 S.Ct. 2573, 96 L.Ed.2d 510 (1987).

43. Justice Scalia, joined by Chief Justice Rehnquist, found that the statute had a non-religious purpose; they also challenged the validity of the secular purpose test. 482 U.S. at 609, 107 S.Ct. at 2591 (Scalia, J., dissenting, joined by Rehnquist, C.J.). Justice White concurred only in the judgment of the court, 482 U.S. at 608, 107 S.Ct. at 2590 (White, J., concurring in the judgment). Justices Powell and O'Connor wrote a concurring opinion to emphasize that legislative actions with some religious purpose were not invalid unless the religious purpose predominated the legislative decision and that public school instruction could include references to religion so long as the references did not have the purpose of advancing religious beliefs. 482 U.S. at 596, 107 S.Ct. at 2584 (Powell, J., joined by O'Connor, J., concurring).

44. Since 1971 the Supreme Court, in most establishment clause cases, has required that government actions which have the effect of advancing religion meet a three-part test: (1) the governmental entity adopting the law or regulation must have a secular purpose; (2) the statute's primary effect must neither advance nor inhibit religion; (3) the statute must not create an excessive entanglement between government and religion. The three-part test is examined in §§ 17.3, 17.4.

45. The majority opinion by Justice Brennan noted that the potential for influencing college students' thinking about religion through the introduction of or references to religious documents was less than the potential for influencing the beliefs of grade school and high school students in public school courses. For this reason, state supported colleges and universities had greater authority than state grade schools or high schools to offer courses regarding religion or theology. Edwards v. Aguillard, 482 U.S. 578, 584 n. 5, 107 S.Ct. 2573, 2577 n. 5, 96 L.Ed.2d 510 (1987).

(e) Equal Access to School Facilities

In *Widmar v. Vincent*[46] the Supreme Court invalidated a state university regulation which denied access to school facilities to religious student organizations as a violation of the freedom of speech.[47] In so doing the Court provided some insight into the related problem of defining the scope of university involvement with religious organizations.

In 1977 the University of Missouri at Kansas City began to enforce a policy prohibiting the use of university buildings or grounds "for purposes of religious worship or religious teaching." University officials informed a registered student religious group that the University was discontinuing what had been a four-year practice of permitting the group to conduct its meetings in university facilities. The majority opinion in *Widmar* by Justice Powell found that once it had opened its facilities for use by student groups the university had created a public forum. It was then required to justify any content-based exclusions under the applicable standard of review and the regulation would be upheld only if it was necessary to serve a compelling state interest and if it was narrowly drawn to achieve that end.

Justice Powell's opinion stated that the university's interest in maintaining a strict separation of church and state, as mandated by the establishment clauses of the federal and Missouri constitutions was compelling. However, Justice Powell, applying the three pronged purpose-effect-entanglement test, did not agree that a policy allowing equal access to university facilities to religious groups would violate the establishment clause.

He found that the first and last parts of the test—purpose and entanglement—were clearly met: a policy fostering an open university forum for all registered student groups has a secular purpose. Opening facilities to all students would not involve excessive entanglement between government and religion. In addition, the Court was satisfied that the "primary effect" of allowing student religious groups to share the limited public forum, open to all forms of discourse, was not to benefit religion. Any religious benefits would be merely incidental for two reasons. First, the creation of a limited public forum at the university, and allowing religious groups access to that forum, does not confer state approval on any religious sect or practice. Second, the forum was available to a broad class of non-religious, as well as religious, groups. In the absence of concrete evidence that campus religious groups would dominate the open forum, the Court was unwilling to find that the benefits to religion were to any degree greater than the general benefits such as police and fire protection which were clearly compatible with the establishment clause.

Justice Powell also held that, despite the fact that the Missouri constitution required stricter separation of church and state than the federal Constitution, the State's interest in achieving complete separation of church and state was limited by the free exercise and free speech clauses of the First Amendment and was not sufficiently compelling to justify the content-based discrimination against these students' speech activities.

It should be noted that in *Widmar* the Court ruled only that a state university could not engage in content-based discrimination against religious speech. If the university had not

---

Justices Powell and O'Connor noted that: "As a matter of history, school children can and should properly be informed of all aspects of this Nation's religious heritage. I would see no constitutional problem if school children were taught the nature of the Founding Fathers' religious beliefs and how these beliefs affected the attitudes of the times and the structure of our government. Courses in comparative religion are, of course, customary and constitutionally appropriate." 482 U.S. at 605–09, 107 S.Ct. at 2589–90 (Powell, J., joined by O'Connor, J., concurring).

In a case that was decided before the Supreme Court's adoption of the three-part purpose-effect-entanglement

test, Justice Brennan, the author of the majority opinion in *Edwards,* stated his belief that a state school would be allowed to make references to the Bible and other religious literature so long as the courses did not constitute governmental aid to or promotion of religion. School District of Abington Tp., Pa. v. Schempp, 374 U.S. 203, 300–302, 83 S.Ct. 1560, 1612–13, 10 L.Ed.2d 844 (1963) (Brennan, J., concurring).

46. 454 U.S. 263, 102 S.Ct. 269, 70 L.Ed.2d 440 (1981).

47. Id. See §§ 16.45–16.47, supra.

created the "public forum" it would not have been required to furnish facilities for use by religious groups. Thus, the case may be of little relevance to determining if high school student religious organizations must be allowed access to some high school facilities, where there may be no "public forum." [48]

In *Board of Education of Westside Community Schools v. Mergens* [49] the Supreme Court upheld a federal statute that requires any secondary school receiving federal financial assistance to provide "equal access" to student groups. The statute achieved this result by prohibiting a secondary school from denying equal access to student groups on the basis of the group's religious, political or philosophical beliefs (or the content of their speech) if (1) the school received federal financial assistance and (2) if the school had created a "limited open forum" by providing access to any "non-curriculum related student group." The *Mergens* case presented only the issue of whether the statutory access granted to religiously oriented student groups violated the establishment clause. The Court did not reach the question of whether the free speech principles that it had examined in *Widmar,* would require a high school to provide access to school facilities in a situation where the federal statute did not apply.

Justice O'Connor wrote an opinion in *Mergens* that was, in part, a majority opinion and, in part, a plurality opinion. In the portions of her opinion that were joined by a majority of Justices, Justice O'Connor interpreted and explained the meaning and coverage of the feder-

al statute. The majority concluded that the statutory term "limited open forum" was different from the Supreme Court's definition, in First Amendment cases, of a "limited public forum." The statute applied whenever a "noncurriculum related" student group was given access to school facilities. A "noncurriculum related" student group, according to the majority, was any student group whose activities and purpose did not directly relate to courses offered by the school. Thus, both a chess club and a student organization that provided social services for needy persons in the community were not curriculum related groups, even though math professors and social science professors at the school might strongly encourage participation in those clubs. The equal access requirement of the statute only prohibited the denial of access to school premises at noninstructional times to a group, if the denial was based on the religious or political content of the group's speech or beliefs. The Act allowed a faculty member to monitor the student group's activities, but the Act limited participation by school officials at any meeting of religious groups. Persons who were not a part of the faculty, staff, or student body would not be able to direct or regularly attend the activities of student groups at the public school premises.

Although the constitutionality of the Equal Access Act was upheld by an eight to one vote of the Justices, there was no majority opinion explaining why the statute was consistent with the establishment clause. [50] Justice O'Connor

---

48. The Supreme Court faced a related problem in McCreary v. Stone, 739 F.2d 716 (2d Cir.1984), judgment affirmed sub nom. by an evenly divided Court, Board of Trustees v. McCreary, 471 U.S. 83, 105 S.Ct. 1859, 85 L.Ed.2d 63 (1985) (per curiam). In this case, two groups sought to place a Nativity scene in a public park in a business district during the December holiday season. The village had no content-neutral regulations that precluded the display; the village allowed other types of decorations, displays and speech-related activities in the park. The village denied consent to groups wishing to place a Nativity scene on the park although no content-neutral regulation required the denial. The court of appeals held that the village could not rely on the establishment clause principles set forth in supreme court cases to deny these groups permission to place the Nativity scene in the park. The court of appeals ruled that a content-based denial of access appeared to violate Widmar v.

Vincent, 454 U.S. 263, 102 S.Ct. 269, 70 L.Ed.2d 440 (1981), but that the placing of the Nativity scene, or any other speech activities in the park, could be subject to time, place, or manner restrictions. Justice Powell did not take part in the Supreme Court review of the court of appeals decision and the other eight Justices divided evenly in this case. The court of appeals was affirmed by an evenly divided Court and without an opinion issuing from the United States Supreme Court.

49. 496 U.S. 226, 110 S.Ct. 2356, 110 L.Ed.2d 191 (1990).

50. Board of Education of Westside Community Schools v. Mergens, 496 U.S. 226, 246–53, 110 S.Ct. 2356, 2370–73, 110 L.Ed.2d 191 (1990) (Part III of Justice O'Connor's opinion, in which she examined the constitutionality of the statute, was joined by Chief Justice Rehnquist and Justices White and Blackmun). There were two

wrote an opinion, which was joined by Chief Justice Rehnquist and Justices White and Blackmun, in which she found that the statute complied with the three part test—the purpose, primary effect, excessive entanglement tests—used most commonly by the Supreme Court in establishment clause cases.[51] First, Justice O'Connor found that the legislative purpose of prohibiting discrimination on the basis of political, philosophical or religious views was not a legislative purpose that violated the establishment clause.[52] Second, Justice O'Connor found that the law did not have a primary effect of advancing religion, because the law did not involve a subsidy to the teaching of religion that might be seen as the government endorsement of religious beliefs.[53] The law did not involve meetings of religious groups during instructional time, the participation of school officials in the meetings, or any direct or indirect coercion of student participation in such groups.[54] Finally, the plurality found that the law did not create an "excessive entanglement" between government and religion, because any faculty sponsor

for the group would be unable to participate actively in the religious group's meetings.

Justices Marshall and Brennan concurred only in the judgment of the Court, even though they did not challenge the use of the three-part test to evaluate the constitutionality of the statute.[55] These Justices wrote separately to state their belief that any school that allowed a religiously oriented student group to meet on its premises would have to take very clear steps to avoid giving any appearance that it was endorsing the views of the religious group. Justice O'Connor's plurality did not explain how an individual school might violate the establishment clause by appearing to endorse a particular religious group's beliefs. Justice Marshall's concurring opinion appears to establish standards requiring school authorities to distance themselves from the religious group that would not be endorsed by a majority of the Justices.

Justices Kennedy and Scalia voted to uphold the Act, but they refused to join Justice

concurring opinions. 496 U.S. at 258, 110 S.Ct. at 2376 (Kennedy, J., joined by Scalia, J., concurring in part and concurring in the judgment); 496 U.S. at 262, 110 S.Ct. at 2378 (Marshall, J., joined by Brennan, J., concurring in the judgment). Justice Stevens was the sole dissenter, his dissent focused on the interpretation of the statute. 496 U.S. at 270, 110 S.Ct. at 2356 (Stevens, J., dissenting).

51. The three pronged test is referred to as the "Lemon test" because it was first clearly stated by the Court in Lemon v. Kurtzman, 403 U.S. 602, 91 S.Ct. 2105, 29 L.Ed.2d 745 (1971). Under this three-part test a law is invalid unless: (1) the law has a secular purpose; (2) the primary effect of the law is neither the advancement or inhibition of religion; (3) the law does not give rise to an excessive entanglement between government and religion. This test is examined in §§ 17.3, 17.4 of this Treatise. Justice O'Connor has at times advocated replacement of the three-part test with a test which would determine whether the government action at issue involved an unconstitutional "endorsement" of religion. See, e.g., Lynch v. Donnelly, 465 U.S. 668, 690, 104 S.Ct. 1355, 1366, 79 L.Ed.2d 604 (1984) (O'Connor, J., concurring). The endorsement test used by Justice O'Connor may be blending with the three-part Lemon test; the endorsement test may be the way in which the Court determines whether a particular government law or program has a primary effect of advancing or inhibiting religion. See, County of Allegheny v. American Civil Liberties Union, 492 U.S. 573, 590–93, 109 S.Ct. 3086, 3099–3101, 106 L.Ed.2d 472 (1989).

52. Board of Education of Westside Community Schools v. Mergens, 496 U.S. 226, 248–49, 110 S.Ct. 2356, 2371, 110 L.Ed.2d 191 (1990) (O'Connor, J., joined by

Rehnquist, C.J., and White and Blackmun, JJ.). The Supreme Court has found in other cases that the legislative "accommodation" of persons with religious beliefs is not a purpose that violates the establishment clause. See, Corporation of Presiding Bishop of Church of Jesus Christ of Latter–day Saints v. Amos, 483 U.S. 327, 107 S.Ct. 2862, 97 L.Ed.2d 273 (1987), which is examined in § 17.15 of this Treatise.

53. Board of Education of Westside Community Schools v. Mergens, 496 U.S. 226, 249–53, 110 S.Ct. 2356, 2371–73, 110 L.Ed.2d 191 (1990) (O'Connor, J., joined by Rehnquist, C.J., and White and Blackmun, JJ.). The plurality therefore found that this program did not suffer from the constitutional defect in the "release time" programs whereby students were released from regular class sessions, at a portion of the day in which they were otherwise required to be in school, in order to attend meetings of religious organizations conducted on school premises. Such a program had been invalidated in Illinois ex rel. McCollum v. Board of Education, 333 U.S. 203, 68 S.Ct. 461, 92 L.Ed. 649 (1948). The "release time" decisions of the Supreme Court are examined at the beginning of this section of the Treatise.

54. Board of Education of Westside Community Schools v. Mergens, 496 U.S. 226, 251–52, 110 S.Ct. 2356, 2373, 110 L.Ed.2d 191 (1990) (O'Connor, J., joined by Rehnquist, C.J., and White and Blackmun, JJ.).

55. Board of Education of Westside Community Schools v. Mergens, 496 U.S. 226, 262, 110 S.Ct. 2356, 2378, 110 L.Ed.2d 191 (1990) (Marshall, J., joined by Brennan, J., concurring in the judgment).

O'Connor's use of the three-part establishment clause test.[56] These two Justices believed that only two questions should be asked in determining whether the equal access law was consistent with the establishment clause. First, did the law give direct benefits to religion in such a way as to establish a state religion or to have a clear tendency to establish a state religion? Second, did the government act coerce student participation in religious activities? These two Justices found that both questions should be answered in the negative and, therefore, that the Act was constitutional. They did not believe that the establishment clause requires the Court to determine whether the law could be described as government endorsement of religion. They would not use the purpose, effect, and entanglement tests to place significant restrictions on government accommodation of religion.

The government may not disfavor a speaker by punishing his speech, or denying him the ability to speak, based upon the religious viewpoint expressed by that speaker. This principle, which was established in the *Widmar* and *Mergens* cases, was unanimously reaffirmed in *Lamb's Chapel v. Center Moriches Union Free School District.*[57]

A New York law allowed local school boards to adopt regulation for the use of school property, at times when schools were not in session, for specified purposes, including "social, civic, and recreational meetings and entertainments and other uses pertaining to the welfare of the community." The state law stated that the uses should be: "non-exclusive and open to the public" but it left the implementation of the law and the definition of permitted uses

largely to the local school boards in the state. In the *Lamb's Chapel* case, the school board for the Center Moriches Union Free School District authorized the use of school property, when it was not otherwise being used for school purposes, for social, civic, or recreational uses and for uses by political organizations. However, this school board denied a religious congregation the ability to use the school property at a time when classes were not in session and the school was not being used for previously scheduled activities.

In *Lamb's Chapel*, the Justices unanimously ruled that this school board regulation, as applied in this case, violated the free speech clause of the First Amendment. Justice White wrote for seven members of the Court in finding that the board's action constituted viewpoint discrimination because the school board would have allowed groups to use the school property for discussions about childrearing and family values that were not connected to the views of a religious organization. Such viewpoint discrimination violates the First Amendment freedom of speech even when the government is regulating access to a nonpublic forum.

The school board in the *Lamb's Chapel* case attempted to justify its action by alleging that it had a compelling interest in denying access to the religious organization in order to avoid violating the establishment clause of the First Amendment. Justice White found that granting equal access to government property would not constitute a violation of the establishment clause tests adopted by the Supreme Court in earlier cases.[58] The school board also claimed

---

56. 496 U.S. at 258, 110 S.Ct. at 2376 (Kennedy, J., joined by Scalia, J., concurring in part and concurring in the judgment).

57. 508 U.S. 384, 113 S.Ct. 2141, 124 L.Ed.2d 352 (1993).

58. Justice White's majority opinion found that the intended use of the property "would not have been an establishment of religion under the three-part test articulated in Lemon v. Kurtzman, 403 U.S. 602, 91 S.Ct. 2105, 29 L.Ed.2d 745 (1971). The challenged governmental action has a secular purpose, does not have the principal or primary effect of advancing or inhibiting religion, and does not foster an excessive entanglement with religion." After this passage in his majority opinion, Justice White

noted that, despite the statements in the concurring opinion, the *Lemon* tests had not been overruled. 508 U.S. at 394 n. 7, 113 S.Ct. at 2148 n. 7.

Three Justices joined the Court's unanimous ruling concerning the school district's violation of the free speech clause differed with the majority opinion insofar as the majority continued to use the three-part *Lemon* tests. These three Justices believe that those tests unjustifiably restrict the actions of government that might assist religion. Lamb's Chapel v. Center Moriches Union Free School District, 508 U.S. 384, 396, 113 S.Ct. 2141, 2149, 124 L.Ed.2d 352 (1993) (Kennedy, J., concurring in part and concurring in the judgment). 508 U.S. at 396, 113 S.Ct. at 2149 (Scalia, J., joined by Thomas, J., concurring in the judgment).

that the particular church that wanted access to the property would be engaging in such highly sectarian proselytizing that the church's use of public property would lead to "threats of public unrest and even violence." However, the majority opinion found that there was "nothing in the record to support such a justification, which in any event would be difficult to defend as a reason to deny the presentation of a religious point of view about a subject that the [school district board] otherwise makes open to discussion on [school district] property." [59]

In *Good News Club v. Milford Central School*[60] the Supreme Court examined a public school's refusal to allow a religious organization for children between the ages of 6 and 12 to use the school facilities at times when the school was not in session. This public school district had adopted a policy allowing local residents to use school facilities at times when school was not in session for virtually any type of educational, artistic, entertainment or community event.

When two adult sponsors of the Christian Organization for Young Children sought permission to use the school cafeteria, at a time when the school was not in session, for weekly meetings involving "singing songs, hearing a bible lesson and memorizing scripture," their request was turned down. The majority opinion in *Good News Club*, written by Justice Thomas, found that the denial of the facilities to this group violated the free speech clause, because the government's decision was based on viewpoint discrimination.[61]

A government might be able to discriminate against a particular message or viewpoint if its action was narrowly tailored to a compelling interest. The school's action in this case was not supported by any compelling interest. The school (as had the school districts in *Weidmar* and *Lamb's Chapel*) claimed that allowing the use of the religious school by the group would violate the establishment clause. Justice Thomas's majority opinion ruled that allowing the group to use the school cafeteria on a religiously neutral basis would not violate the establishment clause. Justice Thomas pointed out that unlike cases where use of school facilities had violated the establishment clause, there would be no involvement of school officials with these club meetings. The school had been under no obligation to open its facilities to public groups, but, once it had done so, it could not discriminate against certain groups because of their religious beliefs.

The majority in *Good News Club* did not employ, or reject, the *Lemon* test. Justice Thomas pointed out that the guarantee of religious neutrality would be endangered by discriminating against the group's use of the school, rather than by allowing the students to meet on school facilities. He explained that no establishment clause value would be threatened by allowing the group to use the school facilities on a religiously neutral basis. Justice Thomas also noted that there would be no coercive pressure on the students because it would be the parents, rather than the elementary school children themselves, who would be deciding whether their young children would attend the meeting. In a footnote, Justice Thomas noted that the club's activities did not constitute mere religious worship divorced from any teaching of moral values.[62]

Justice Scalia concurred in both the judgment and opinion of the Court in *Good News Club*, he also wrote an opinion noting that the Court had not adopted a specific test when it rejected the school's establishment clause argument.[63] In another concurring opinion, Justice Breyer noted that the focus on government neutrality would be only one of the considerations in deciding establishment clause cases and that some uses of pub-

---

59. Lamb's Chapel v. Center Moriches Union Free School District, 508 U.S. 384, 394, 113 S.Ct. 2141, 2148, 124 L.Ed.2d 352 (1993).

60. 533 U.S. 98, 121 S.Ct. 2093, 150 L.Ed.2d 151 (2001).

61. 533 U.S. at 98–119, 121 S.Ct. at 2093–2107 (part IV of the majority opinion).

62. 533 U.S. at 112 n. 5, 115 n. 6, 121 S.Ct. at 2103–4 n. 5, 2105 n. 6.

63. 533 U.S. at 119, 121 S.Ct. at 2107 (Scalia, J., concurring).

lic facilities by religious organizations would violate the establishment clause.[64]

The Court in *Good News Club* did not resolve the question of whether the government had to allow access to a public forum, or a limited public forum, to a religious group that was going to conduct religious worship services on public property.

The three dissenting Justices in *Good News Club* believed that the government was not required to allow a religious group to have religious worship services on government property merely because the government had thrown open the property to use by community groups.[65]

In *Rosenberger v. Rector and Visitors of the University of Virginia,*[66] the Justices, by a five to four vote, ruled that a university violated the free speech clause when it refused to pay for a religious student organization's publication costs under a program that funded other student organization publications.

Under University of Virginia regulations, student groups were eligible to request for payment of bills from outside contractors that printed their newsletters. a group of students formed an organization named "Wide Awake Productions," which they registered as a student organization with the University. Because their registration met University standards, they qualified as a "contracted independent organization" that would be eligible for payment of its publication bills. However, the University refused this student organization's request for the University to pay for the publication of its newsletter, titled "Wide Awake: a Christian Perspective at the University of Virginia." The University asserted that the publication

constituted religious literature that could not be funded because of the religious nature of the organization's expression in their newsletter. In the view of the University, government funding for a religious publication would violate the establishment clause. a majority of the Justices in *Rosenberger* relied on the principles established in the *Widmar, Mergens,* and *Lamb's Chapel* cases in ruling that the University's refusal to fund the student publication solely on the basis of the religious content of its speech constituted viewpoint discrimination that violated the free speech clause.[67]

The University had engaged in viewpoint discrimination when it refused to pay for the student organization's publication costs because of the religious nature of the organization's expression. This viewpoint discrimination could only be upheld if the University had a compelling interest in disfavoring the viewpoint. If a University payment for the religious organization's publication costs would violate the establishment clause, the University would have a compelling interest (the need to follow the Constitution) in refusing to subsidize the publication. The majority opinion in *Rosenberger,* written by Justice Kennedy, ruled that the University funding for the publication would not violate the establishment clause and that the refusal to fund the publication violated the free speech guarantee. The majority opinion did not specify a clear test to be used for determining whether a government action violated the establishment clause. Justice Kennedy stated that, in establishment clause cases, the Court "must in each case inquire first into the purpose and object of the government action in question and then into the practical details of the program's operation ... [a] cen-

---

64. Justice Breyer concurred in the Court's conclusion and much of its First Amendment free speech analysis, although the Justice did not think that it was necessary to decide whether the activities at the school in this case might violate the establishment clause. Good News Club v. Milford Central School, 533 U.S. 98, 127, 121 S.Ct. 2093, 2111, 150 L.Ed.2d 151 (2001) (Breyer, J., concurring in part).

65. Good News Club v. Milford Central School, 533 U.S. 98, 128, 121 S.Ct. 2093, 2112, 150 L.Ed.2d 151 (2001) (Stevens, J., dissenting). Justices Souter and Stevens did not believe that the Court did not have to decide the

establishment clause issue at this stage in the litigation concerning the use of the public school, although they indicated that they would find it a remarkable decision for the Court to take if it meant that "any public school open for civics meetings must be open for use as a church, synagogue, or mosque." 533 U.S. at 134, 138, 121 S.Ct. at 2115, 2117 (Souter, J., joined by Ginsburg, J., dissenting).

66. 515 U.S. 819, 115 S.Ct. 2510, 132 L.Ed.2d 700 (1995).

67. 515 U.S. at 829, 115 S.Ct. at 2517.

tral lesson of our decisions is that significant factor in upholding government programs in the face of establishment clause attack is their neutrality towards religion.''[68] The majority found that the University program for funding students organizations was religiously neutral, and that "the neutrality of the program distinguishes the student fees from a tax levied for the direct support of a church or group of churches.''[69]

In earlier cases, the Supreme Court had held that the establishment clause did not prohibit a government university from granting equal access to its facilities to a religious organization and that viewpoint discrimination against such organizations by a government university would violate the First Amendment free speech clause. The dissenters in *Rosenberger* believed that the establishment clause should be interpreted to prohibit all direct payments to religious organizations, or direct subsidies for the operational costs of religious organizations.[70] However, the majority ruled that: "there is no difference in logic or principle, and no difference of constitutional significance, between a school using its funds to operate a facility to which students have access, and a school paying a third-party contractor to operate the facility on its behalf.''[71] Under the University regulations at issue in *Rosenberger,* the University would not make

monetary payments to the religious organization. The University would pay the third party (the printer) who provided the printing services for student organizations. In the majority's opinion this payment system involved more separation between the University and the religious organization than would school policies that granted the religious organizations equal access to the university physical facilities. Therefore, in *Rosenberger,* the majority ruled that the First Amendment free speech clause prohibited the University from examining the content of publications for the purpose of denying funding to, and discriminating against, religious viewpoints and that there would be "no establishment clause violation in the University's honoring its duties under the free speech clause.''[72]

§ 17.6 The Free Exercise Clause—Introduction and Overview

The text of the Constitution contains one specific provision regarding religious freedom. Article VI prohibits the use of any religious test as a condition or qualification for holding any office or position in the federal government.[1]

The First Amendment provides, in part, that Congress shall make no law "prohibiting the free exercise" of religion.[2] The free exercise clause, like all of the guarantees of the First

---

68.   515 U.S. at 837, 115 S.Ct. at 2521.

69.   515 U.S. at 839, 115 S.Ct. at 2522.

70.   Rosenberger v. Rector and Visitors of the University of Virginia, 515 U.S. 819, 862, 115 S.Ct. 2510, 2533, 132 L.Ed.2d 700 (1995) (Souter, J., joined by Stevens, Ginsburg, and Breyer, JJ., dissenting). Justice Thomas, who joined the majority opinion, also filed a concurring opinion in which he directly challenged the historical analysis used by the dissenting Justices. 515 U.S. at 851, 115 S.Ct. at 2528 (Thomas, J., concurring).

71.   Rosenberger v. Rector and Visitors of the University of Virginia, 515 U.S. 819, 843, 115 S.Ct. 2510, 2524, 132 L.Ed.2d 700 (1995).

72.   Rosenberger v. Rector and Visitors of the University of Virginia, 515 U.S. 819, 845, 115 S.Ct. 2510, 2525, 132 L.Ed.2d 700 (1995). Justice Kennedy's majority opinion in *Rosenberger* assumed that individual students did not have a right to a refund of their student activity fees, which were required to be paid by all students and which were used to fund the publication costs of student organizations including the religious student publication at issue in this case. "The fee is mandatory, and we do not have before us the question whether an objecting student has the First Amendment right to demand a pro rata return to

the extent the fee is expended for speech to which he or she does not describe." 515 U.S. at 839, 115 S.Ct. at 2522. Justice O'Connor joined the majority opinion and wrote a concurring opinion in which she stated that an objecting student might have a free speech right to refuse to be compelled to pay for the speech of student organizations with which the student disagreed and that "while the Court does not resolve the question ... the existence of such an opt-out possibility ... provides a potential basis for distinguishing proceeds of student fees in this case from proceeds of the general assessments in support of religion that lie at the core of the prohibition against religious funding." 515 U.S. at 845–49, 115 S.Ct. at 2525, 2527 (O'Connor, J., concurring).

§ 17.6

1.   "[N]o Religious test shall ever be required as a qualification to any office of public trust under the United States." U.S. Const. art. VI.

2.   "Congress shall make no law respecting an establishment of religion or prohibiting the free exercise thereof. . . ." U.S. Const. amend. 1.

Amendment, applies to state and local governments through the Fourteenth Amendment.[3]

The Supreme Court has invalidated very few government actions on the basis of the free exercise clause. The Court has consistently held that the government may not punish religious beliefs. The government may not impose burdens on, or give benefits to, people solely because of their religious beliefs. Because federal, state and local governmental entities have not engaged in many activities that could be described as the punishment of religious beliefs, there are very few Supreme Court decisions explaining the meaning of that constitutional restriction.

A law would be invalid if the legislature passed the law prohibiting some type of activity only because of the religious belief displayed by the activity or only because the government wished to burden a particular religion. In order to show that a law banning a certain type of activity (such as the killing of a certain animal) violated this prohibition a person would have to prove that the legislative purpose was the promotion of religious beliefs or the suppression of the religious practices of a religious sect.

In *Church of the Lukumi Babalu Aye, Inc. v. Hialeah*[4] the Supreme Court invalidated a city's ordinances prohibiting animal slaughter, insofar as they were applied to a particular religious sect, because the Justices unanimously found that these ordinances were passed for the sole purpose of excluding the religious sect from the city. The Justices avoided ruling on the issue of whether members of a religious sect that used animal slaughter in their rituals would be entitled by the free exercise clause to an exemption from a law prohibiting the slaughter of animals that was a religiously neutral law of general applicability. Instead, the Justices found that the city's ordinances (when all of the classifications and exemptions in the ordinances were combined) prohibited only the type of animal slaughter that was used in the ritual of the Santeria religion; the

timing of the ordinances, and other facts in the record, demonstrated that the city had adopted these ordinances only after learning that members of the Santeria religion were going to establish a place of worship in the city.

Justice Kennedy wrote the majority opinion in *Church of the Lukumi Babalu Aye.* He began the opinion by noting that the Court was using a well established constitutional principle.

"The principle that government may not enact laws that suppress religious belief or practice is so well understood that few violations are recorded in our opinions.... Our review confirms that the laws in question were enacted by officials who did not understand, failed to perceive, or chose to ignore the fact that their official actions violated the Nation's essential commitment to religious freedom. The challenged laws had an impermissible object; and in all events the principle of general applicability was violated because the secular ends asserted in defense of the law, were pursued only with respect to conduct motivated by religious beliefs."[5]

The majority opinion in *Church of the Lukumi Babalu Aye,* found that the judiciary must examine laws regulating conduct of significance to persons because of their religious beliefs to ensure both that the conduct regulation was religiously neutral and that it was of general applicability. A law that failed the neutrality or general applicability standards would be subject to strict judicial scrutiny; it is doubtful that any such law would be truly necessary to a compelling government interest. Justice Kennedy's opinion summarized the Court's ruling as follows:

"[A] law that is neutral and of general applicability need not be justified by a compelling government interest even if the law has the incidental effect of burdening a particular religious practice.... A law failing to satis-

---

3. The free exercise clause was first held applicable to the states in Cantwell v. Connecticut, 310 U.S. 296, 60 S.Ct. 900, 84 L.Ed. 1213 (1940).

4. 508 U.S. 520, 113 S.Ct. 2217, 124 L.Ed.2d 472 (1993), on remand 2 F.3d 369 (11th Cir.1993).

5. 508 U.S. at 524, 113 S.Ct. at 2222.

fy these requirements [the neutrality and general applicability requirements] must be justified by a compelling governmental interest and must be narrowly tailored to advance that interest." [6]

The Supreme Court has wavered in deciding whether the free exercise clause protects religiously motivated actions from a law of general applicability. The Court has usually indicated that a religiously neutral law must be followed by all persons, including persons whose religious beliefs command them to disobey the law. However, in a few cases regarding the granting of unemployment compensation benefits, the Court required an exemption from a requirement for unemployment compensation to be granted to religious persons whose religious beliefs prevented them from meeting the eligibility requirement.

Religious Beliefs. Just as the establishment clause prohibits the government from providing benefits to one religious sect or denomination, the free exercise clause prohibits the government from denying benefits to, or imposing burdens on, persons because of their religious beliefs. The use of religious beliefs as any type of standard for the granting of government benefits and burdens might violate both the establishment and free exercise clauses by violating a religious neutrality principle that is central to both. As a technical matter, it is not clear whether the free exercise clause involves a total prohibition of the government use of religious beliefs as a means of allocating burdens and benefits or whether a government regulation that used religious beliefs in that manner could be justified by a "compelling" government interest. That technical distinction is probably unimportant because the Court has given us no reason to believe that a government law or regulation that denied a benefit to persons because of

their religious beliefs would be upheld by a compelling interest.

There are Supreme Court cases that have invalidated a law on its face because it punished religious beliefs. Just as the federal government is prohibited from using religion as a test for government office, the state and local governments are prohibited from using such tests by the free exercise clause.[7] The Supreme Court, by a unanimous vote but without a majority opinion, invalidated a law that prohibited ministers or members of religious orders from being members of the state legislature.[8] Several of the Justices believed that the exclusion of ministers and clerics from the legislature constituted the imposition of a special disability on someone because of the strength or nature of his religious views.

While the free exercise clause gives no one the right to disregard criminal laws of general applicability, the government may not create a criminal law that is based upon the falsity of a particular religious belief. Such a law would violate the free exercise clause.[9]

When different groups of a religious organization have a dispute over property, the state and federal courts are prohibited from deciding those controversies in any way that would involve a judicial ruling that was based upon the religious beliefs or religious doctrine. The government's use of religious doctrine to solve such a dispute should be held to violate both the establishment clause and the free exercise clause.[10]

Regulations of Actions—Exemptions for Religiously Motivated Actions? A person may be unable to comply with a law because his religious beliefs prohibit him from taking an action that is required by law (such as paying a certain type of tax) or because his religious beliefs require him to do something that is prohibited by the law (such as ingesting

---

6. 508 U.S. at 531, 113 S.Ct. at 2226.

7. Torcaso v. Watkins, 367 U.S. 488, 81 S.Ct. 1680, 6 L.Ed.2d 982 (1961) (invalidating under the free exercise clause a state constitutional provision requiring a declaration of a belief in God as a prerequisite to taking public office). See footnote 1, supra, for the Article VI restriction on the federal government.

8. McDaniel v. Paty, 435 U.S. 618, 98 S.Ct. 1322, 55 L.Ed.2d 593 (1978). This case is examined in § 17.14.

9. The subject of "government inquiries into religious frauds" is examined in § 17.14.

10. The First Amendment problems that arise from "state involvement in ecclesiastical disputes" are examined in § 17.12.

a drug that is banned by law). These types of situations raise the question of whether the free exercise clause requires the government to grant an exemption from a law of general applicability to a person who cannot conform his actions to the law due to his religious beliefs.

It is important to keep in mind the type of fact situation and the type of law, that is at issue in the cases regarding religiously motivated actions. The law at issue in such a case will not be a law that includes religious criteria for determining who is benefitted or burdened by the law. If the law made use of religious criteria as a standard for determining the legality of actions, or for the allocation of benefits or burdens from the government, the law would be invalid as the direct punishment of religious beliefs. The law at issue in the case will not be a law that was enacted only for the purpose of harming people of one religion (who could not comply with the law) because proof of such a purpose on the part of the legislative entity would make the law invalid.

The law that will be at issue in a religiously motivated action case will be a law of general applicability that requires all persons (or a class of persons defined by criteria that do not include religious criteria) to take an action or refrain from taking an action. The claim of the individual in the case is that she cannot comply with the law and remain faithful to her religious beliefs. The person alleges that she should receive an exemption from the law because of the burden placed upon her religious beliefs by the need to conform her actions to a law that conflicts with her beliefs.

There would be no free exercise issue in a case if the individual seeking the exemption could not demonstrate that complying with the law constituted a burden on her religious beliefs. In some Supreme Court cases, there is dicta describing the burden placed upon the person who cannot comply with a law of general applicability as a "direct" or "indirect"

burden. A law would directly burden a religion by making illegal a religious practice. An example of a law that created a direct burden would be a law prohibiting the use of a drug that was a part of the religious ceremony. A law that creates an indirect burden is one that does not regulate a religiously motivated practice as such but which makes the practice of a person's religion more difficult, usually by having the effect of imposing additional economic costs. An example of a law that creates an indirect burden is a law that requires that shops close on Sunday; this law has the effect of imposing a burden on Sabbatarians whose religion requires them to refrain from work on Saturdays. If the Sabbatarians follow both their religious beliefs and the government law, they will have to close their shops on two days a week rather than one. Despite dicta in some cases indicating that a law imposing an indirect burden might be easier to uphold than a law which directly burdens religious activities, it seems clear today that the distinction between direct and indirect burdens does not have any legal significance.

The basic free exercise principle regarding requested exemptions from laws of general applicability is easy to state: the free exercise clause does not require that an exemption be created from laws of general applicability to protect persons with religiously motivated actions. In 1990, a Supreme Court majority opinion stated: "We have never held that an individual's religious beliefs excuse him from compliance with an otherwise valid law prohibiting conduct that the state is free to regulate." [11]

In 1993, the Supreme Court invalidated a city's statutes prohibiting animal slaughter insofar as those laws banned the ritual slaughter of animals by a specific religious sect.[12] The Justices unanimously concluded that the statutes were not religiously neutral laws of general applicability and that the laws were only designed to suppress a particular sect. The Justices did not reach the issue of whether a religiously neutral law that banned all animal

---

11. Employment Division v. Smith, 494 U.S. 872, 878–79, 110 S.Ct. 1595, 1602, 108 L.Ed.2d 876 (1990).

12. Church of the Lukumi Babalu Aye, Inc. v. Hialeah, 508 U.S. 520, 113 S.Ct. 2217, 124 L.Ed.2d 472 (1993), on remand 2 F.3d 369 (11th Cir.1993).

slaughter would have to allow exemptions from the slaughter of animals in religious rituals. A majority of the Justices found no reason to question the principle that a religiously neutral law of general applicability could be applied to persons whose religious beliefs prevented them from complying with the law.[13]

No exemptions from criminal laws of general applicability are required by the free exercise clause. It may also be true that the free exercise clause will not require exemptions from laws regulating conduct of all persons, even if the law is not part of the general criminal law. For example, if an individual was granted a license to have a radio station that broadcast at a certain frequency with a power level that would allow the radio station to be received by persons within a 100 mile radius, the individual would not be free to increase the power in his station so that he could be heard throughout the United States, even if he is a religious minister who claims that God has commanded him to disregard the Federal Communications Commission regulations and to send the word of God to all people across the United States. If the radio station license holder violated federal regulations concerning the amount of power used in his station (regulations that are designed to prevent stations from having the effect of "jamming" each other) then the individual would be subject to punishment, which might involve a criminal punishment or simply the revocation of the license to broadcast.

Between 1963 and 1989, the Supreme Court used a two-step balancing process in determining whether an individual had a free exercise right to be exempted from a law of general applicability. First, the person claiming the exemption had to show that the law at issue interfered with the practice of his religion by requiring him to engage in a practice (or to refrain from engaging in a practice) in violation of his religion. The mere fact that the government had adopted a law or policy that was inconsistent with a person's religious beliefs would not create the type of burden that would trigger the balancing test. In the first step, it was the duty of the individual to show the burden imposed on her by the law. In the second step of the test, the Court required the government to demonstrate that granting an exemption to the person whose religious beliefs prevented compliance with the law would interfere with a governmental interest that could be described as "compelling". The government would be able to meet the second part of the test if the Court determined that the regulation at issue was tailored to promote an end that has enough importance to override the burden on the free exercise of religion by persons who could not comply with the law.

Prior to 1963, the Court had found that the First Amendment required an exemption to be granted from certain types of laws for anyone who was engaging in First Amendment activity such as speech or assembly (regardless of whether the First Amendment activity involved religious or nonreligious speech). For example, the Court prohibited the government from punishing children who refused to pledge allegiance to the United States Flag at the start of the school day regardless of whether the child's refusal was based upon a religious belief or a nonreligious opposition to the Pledge of Allegiance.[14] Similarly, the Court

---

13. The Justices were unanimous in ruling that the City of Hialeah violated the free exercise clause by enacting ordinances designed solely to suppress a particular religious sect. But three of the Justices did not want to endorse the position that religiously neutral laws of general applicability need not provide exemptions for persons whose religious beliefs prevented their compliance. Justices Blackmun and O'Connor thought that the Court should return to using the compelling interest test that had been used in free exercise clause cases decided between 1963 and 1989. Justice Souter wished to reconsider this question in future cases. The majority reaffirmed the Court's earlier ruling, in Employment Division v. Smith, 494 U.S. 872, 110 S.Ct. 1595, 108 L.Ed.2d 876 (1990), denying religiously based exemptions from religiously neu-

tral, generally applicable laws. Compare, Church of the Lukumi Babalu Aye, Inc. v. Hialeah, 508 U.S. 520, 531, 113 S.Ct. 2217, 2226, 124 L.Ed.2d 472 (1993), on remand 2 F.3d 369 (11th Cir.1993) (majority opinion by Justice Kennedy) and 508 U.S. at 557, 113 S.Ct. at 2239 (Scalia, J., joined by Rehnquist, C.J., concurring in part and concurring in the judgment), with 508 U.S. at 558, 113 S.Ct. at 2240 (Souter, J., concurring in part and concurring in the judgment) and, 508 U.S. at 577, 113 S.Ct. at 2250 (Blackmun, J., joined by O'Connor, J., concurring in the judgment).

14. West Virginia State Board of Education v. Barnette, 319 U.S. 624, 63 S.Ct. 1178, 87 L.Ed. 1628 (1943),

exempted both religious and nonreligious speakers from certain types of licensing systems that would have been validly applied to business that did not involve First Amendment activity.[15] But the Supreme Court did not give special protection to religiously motivated activity prior to 1963.

Between 1963 and 1989, the Supreme Court did not require significant governmental accommodation of religion. Although Court opinions used a balancing test read as if the Supreme Court would give significant protection to religiously motivated actions, the Court, in fact ruled, against persons seeking a religiously based exemption from any law of general applicability in every area except two: unemployment eligibility requirements and compulsory school attendance for Amish children of high school age.

First, the Supreme Court held that the government had to waive some types of conditions for the receipt of unemployment compensation by persons who could not comply with the condition because of their religious beliefs. For example, unemployment compensation statutes often make a person ineligible for benefits if the person left his job voluntarily. The rationale for an involuntary unemployment requirement is the need to avoid having persons use the unemployment benefit system as a type of paid vacation by working the minimum number of weeks to qualify for unemployment compensation and then resigning in order to receive a paid vacation through receipt of unemployment benefits. The Supreme Court found that the requirement of involuntary termination from a job had to be waived for a person who resigned from his employment at a factory due to his religious beliefs when his required duties were changed so as to include making parts for tanks and other weapons.[16] Unemployment compensa-

tion statutes in many states require a person to demonstrate that he is looking for, and willing to accept, work by being willing to accept jobs that are referred to him by the unemployment compensation administration. Some of these unemployment compensation statutes require that a person be available for jobs that would require work from Monday through Saturday of each week. The Supreme Court found that this type of six-day a week job availability requirement had to be waived for a person who was prohibited from working on Saturday because of his religious beliefs.[17] In these unemployment compensation cases, the Court found that the condition for unemployment benefits imposed a significant burden on an individual, in the sense of imposing a monetary deterrent to the exercise of the individual's religious beliefs. The Court found that the government interest in these unemployment compensation qualifications would not be impaired by a limited exemption being granted to persons whose sincerely held religious beliefs prevented them from complying with the eligibility condition.

The Supreme Court held that an individual could be made ineligible for unemployment compensation if the basis for ineligibility was the fact that the individual was fired for job related misconduct that involved violation of a criminal law. When a drug counsellor at a privately owned drug rehabilitation facility was found to have violated criminal laws banning the use of peyote, the Supreme Court found that the individual could be fired for misconduct and denied unemployment compensation benefits. The individual's violation of a criminal law was not excused by the fact that his religious beliefs required him to use peyote for sacramental purposes.[18]

---

overruling Minersville School District v. Gobitis, 310 U.S. 586, 60 S.Ct. 1010, 84 L.Ed. 1375 (1940).

15. See, e.g., Cantwell v. Connecticut, 310 U.S. 296, 60 S.Ct. 900, 84 L.Ed. 1213 (1940). These cases, which rested on the free speech and free exercise clauses, are noted in § 17.7, infra.

16. Thomas v. Review Board, 450 U.S. 707, 101 S.Ct. 1425, 67 L.Ed.2d 624 (1981). The unemployment compensation cases are examined in greater detail in § 17.8.

17. Sherbert v. Verner, 374 U.S. 398, 83 S.Ct. 1790, 10 L.Ed.2d 965 (1963); Hobbie v. Unemployment Appeals Commission of Florida, 480 U.S. 136, 107 S.Ct. 1046, 94 L.Ed.2d 190 (1987).

18. Employment Division v. Smith, 494 U.S. 872, 110 S.Ct. 1595, 108 L.Ed.2d 876 (1990).

Why did the Supreme Court require the government to grant exemptions from unemployment compensation requirements (other than requirements that were tied in to criminal laws)? Two reasons may explain the results in these cases. First, the government benefit system required individual decision-making about whether a claimant for unemployment compensation benefits had met criteria that were designed to stop the system from being misused (as a form of government paid vacation time).[19] The government, in a sense, was testing the good faith of persons who applied for unemployment compensation and the system seemed easily suited to determining whether an individual was sincerely asserting a religious belief for failure to comply with a condition for the receipt of the benefits. Second, the government interest in protecting the unemployment system from being misused did not appear to be impaired to any significant degree by accommodating persons who could not comply with one of the technical requirements due to their religious beliefs.[20]

The second area in which the Court, during the 1963–89 balancing era, protected religiously motivated actions involved compulsory education laws. In *Wisconsin v. Yoder*[21] the Court held that state law could not require members of the Amish Church to send their children to school after the eighth grade. *Yoder* stands out as the one instance in which the Court required the government to grant to persons who could not comply with the law due to their religious beliefs an exemption

from a law regulating the conduct of all persons (all parents and all children below a certain age).

In 1990, the Supreme Court described *Yoder* as a case that involved not only the freedom to exercise religion but also the liberty interest of parents to direct the education of their children that was protected by the due process clauses.[22] If we accept the Supreme Court's 1990 characterization of that 1972 decision, the *Yoder* decision can be seen as a variation of the "flag salute" and "speech licensing" cases in which the Supreme Court found that certain types of government regulations had to allow exceptions for both religious and nonreligious activity that was protected by a specific provision of the Constitution such as the free speech clause or the due process clause.[23]

Except for these two areas (unemployment compensation and the Yoder decision) the Supreme Court during the 1963–1990 balancing era ruled in favor of the government in every case in which an individual sought a free exercise clause exemption from a government regulation of the actions of persons within its jurisdiction. In some cases, the Court found that the government had not imposed any burden on an individual, so that the government was not required to justify its law. For example, the Court found that the federal government's destruction of trees in a federally owned national forest did not have to be justified by a compelling interest even though the

---

19. This aspect of the unemployment compensation cases was cited as a key to their validity in the 1990 decision of the Supreme Court that refused to require an exemption to laws prohibiting all use of peyote for persons whose religious beliefs required them to use that substance. Employment Division v. Smith, 494 U.S. 872, 884, 110 S.Ct. 1595, 1603, 108 L.Ed.2d 876 (1990); "The *Sherbert* test [the test used to create the rulings in the unemployment compensation cases], it must be recalled, was developed in a context that lent itself to individualized governmental assessment of the reasons for the relevant conduct."

In Church of the Lukumi Babalu Aye, Inc. v. Hialeah, 508 U.S. 520, 113 S.Ct. 2217, 124 L.Ed.2d 472 (1993), on remand 2 F.3d 369 (11th Cir.1993) the Court invalidated city laws prohibiting some forms of animal slaughter, insofar as the laws applied to a particular religious sect, because these laws were designed to suppress a particular religious sect by prohibiting the type of animal slaughter

used in its religious rituals. In the course of making that ruling, the majority opinion noted that if the government chooses to grant exemptions from a regulation it cannot establish a rule that denies exemptions solely on the basis that the requested exemption is religiously motivated. The majority stated: "[I]n circumstances in which individualized exemptions from a general requirement are available, the government may not refuse to extend that system to cases of religious hardship without compelling reason." 508 U.S. at 536, 113 S.Ct. at 2229 (internal quotation marks and citations omitted).

20. Sherbert v. Verner, 374 U.S. 398, 410, 83 S.Ct. 1790, 1797, 10 L.Ed.2d 965 (1963).

21. 406 U.S. 205, 92 S.Ct. 1526, 32 L.Ed.2d 15 (1972). This case is examined in greater detail in § 17.8.

22. Employment Division v. Smith, 494 U.S. 872, 881 n. 1, 110 S.Ct. 1595, 1601 n. 1, 108 L.Ed.2d 876 (1990).

23. See note 15, supra.

forested area was sacred to the religion of American Indian tribes who were located near to the forest.[24] In some cases, the Court found that the government law at issue imposed a burden on the ability of some persons to exercise their sincerely held religious beliefs but found that the government interest was compelling and justified the denial of any exemption from the law. For example, the Court found that the free exercise clause did not require the military to allow a service person, to wear a religious symbol together with his military uniform while on duty.[25]

Taxation Issues. The cases involving taxation issues indicate that, even during the balancing era, the government would be able to win any free exercise case, so long as the government did not punish religious beliefs or use religious criteria in its laws. The Supreme Court in the 1940s had found that a state or city could not make the payment of a license fee a condition to distributing religious literature, even though that type of license fee could be a condition for allowing a person to sell merchandise in a state.[26] This restriction on license fees was viewed by the Court as a part of the First Amendment prohibition of prior restraints on the exercise of First Amendment freedoms (including both religiously motivated

speech and nonreligious speech activities).[27] In the 1970s and 1980s the Supreme Court ruled that religious groups had no right to a tax deduction or tax exemption that had not been granted by statute so long as the tax was not designed to burden religious beliefs and it was not a license fee. Thus, the Court found that an Amish employer of Amish workmen had to pay Social Security taxes even though compulsory participation in the Social Security system violated their religious beliefs.[28] The Court ruled that a sales and use tax that applied to the sales of all goods and services could be constitutionally applied to the sales and use of religious literature.[29] The Court found that the Internal Revenue Service was justified in refusing to allow members of a church to deduct (as payments to a charitable organization) a payment to the church that was a payment for specific products or services.[30] In each of these cases, the Court found that the burden that was placed on the members of the religion by the tax law at issue was not significant. But the Court also found that, even if the burden were considered substantial, the taxes at issue were justified by the societal interest in a fiscally sound tax system.

---

24. Lyng v. Northwest Indian Cemetery Protective Association, 485 U.S. 439, 108 S.Ct. 1319, 99 L.Ed.2d 534 (1988).

25. Goldman v. Weinberger, 475 U.S. 503, 106 S.Ct. 1310, 89 L.Ed.2d 478 (1986).

Prisoners' Rights Cases. The balancing test was never used in cases in which the judiciary examined legislation, or a prison regulation, that restricts the ability of prison inmates to take actions based on their religious beliefs. In O'Lone v. Estate of Shabazz, 482 U.S. 342, 107 S.Ct. 2400, 96 L.Ed.2d 282 (1987), on remand 829 F.2d 32 (3d Cir.1987), the Court found that a prison regulation restricting the free exercise rights of prisoners should be upheld if the regulation was reasonably related to a legitimate penological interest. Applying this standard, the Court upheld a regulation regarding prisoner work duties outside of the prison that precluded Muslim prisoners from attending religious services on Friday afternoons, as was required by their faith. The Court in O'Lone was applying the standard enunciated in Turner v. Safley, 482 U.S. 78, 107 S.Ct. 2254, 96 L.Ed.2d 64 (1987). In Turner, the Court found that a restriction on the fundamental rights of prison inmates should be upheld so long as the restriction was reasonably related to legitimate penological interests. This standard seems to require a case-by-case approach to determining the reasonableness of all prison

regulations that restrict fundamental rights. In Turner, for example, the Court upheld restrictions on the ability of prison inmates to send mail to each other, but invalidated a prison regulation that virtually prohibited all marriages between prisoners or between a prisoner and a person outside of the prison facility. See § 10.6(c) regarding prisoner rights issues.

26. Murdock v. Pennsylvania, 319 U.S. 105, 63 S.Ct. 870, 87 L.Ed. 1292 (1943); Follett v. McCormick, 321 U.S. 573, 64 S.Ct. 717, 88 L.Ed. 938 (1944).

27. In Jimmy Swaggart Ministries v. Board of Equalization, 493 U.S. 378, 110 S.Ct. 688, 107 L.Ed.2d 796 (1990), the Justices unanimously upheld the application of a sales and use tax to the sales of religious goods and literature in a state. The Court's opinion, written by Justice O'Connor found that the 1940s decisions had invalidated the license fees (which are also described as flat taxes) "that operated as a prior restraint on the exercise of religious liberty".

28. United States v. Lee, 455 U.S. 252, 102 S.Ct. 1051, 71 L.Ed.2d 127 (1982).

29. Jimmy Swaggart Ministries v. Board of Equalization, 493 U.S. 378, 110 S.Ct. 688, 107 L.Ed.2d 796 (1990).

30. Hernandez v. Commissioner of Internal Revenue, 490 U.S. 680, 109 S.Ct. 2136, 104 L.Ed.2d 766 (1989).

In the next sections of this chapter, we will examine in greater detail the cases that have been referred to in this overview of the principles used by the Supreme Court in free exercise cases. There are two questions that the reader should consider when reviewing specific decisions of the Supreme Court. First, does the difficulty of defining religion or testing sincerity play a part in the Court's refusal to create free exercise clause exemptions to law of general applicability? Second, can a legislature provide an accommodation of religion, through statutory exemptions for religiously motivated actions, in situations where the free exercise clause would not require an exemption from the regulatory legislation?

Defining Religion—Testing Sincerity. Assume that the Supreme Court ruled that the free exercise clause required the government to create an exemption to a criminal law for persons whose sincerely held religious beliefs made it impossible for them to comply with the law. That ruling would require the judiciary to define religion or to test the sincerity of individuals who claimed that their religious beliefs allowed them to disregard the law. If the Court did not narrow the potential group of persons who could claim the exemption, a ruling finding that the government must create a religious exemption from the criminal law would make compliance with the law optional for every person. For example, let us assume (contrary to the Court's rulings) that the Supreme Court ruled that the government could not penalize a person for using a banned substance (e.g., peyote) if that substance was used for religious reasons.[31] Every person who was arrested for using the banned substance might claim that he was using the substance because he was commanded to do so by the tenants of his religion. If the Supreme Court did not define religion or allow lower courts to test the sincerity of a person seeking immunity from the drug law, it would allow the individual to grant himself a religious exemption.

Any attempt to define religion, or to test sincerity, raises concerns under both the establishment and free exercise clauses of the First Amendment. It is difficult to see how the Supreme Court could define religion in a manner that would not involve the governmental punishment of beliefs or the granting of a denominational preference. The Supreme Court has not attempted to define religion although it has noted that any exemptions that the judiciary created under the free exercise clause would be limited to persons asserting a religious belief.[32] The Court has never ruled on whether the beliefs must be theocratic (God centered) to be religious beliefs or whether a system of belief could be religious even though it was not based upon the concept of an almighty being.[33] The determination of which beliefs constituted religious beliefs would have to avoid any government declaration (even by the courts) that some beliefs are religious because they are true or reasonable or that some beliefs do not qualify as religious beliefs because the beliefs are ones that no reasonable person would accept, although the Supreme Court has not been clear on this point.[34]

---

31. In fact, the Supreme Court made the opposite ruling and, by denying any right to an exemption from a law banning the use of a specific drug, the Court avoided problems concerning the definition of religion. Employment Division v. Smith, 494 U.S. 872, 110 S.Ct. 1595, 108 L.Ed.2d 876 (1990).

32. "[A]lthough a determination of what is a 'religious' belief or practice entitled to constitutional protection may present a most delicate question, the very concept of ordered liberty precludes allowing every person to make his own standards on matters of conduct in which society as a whole has important interest." Wisconsin v. Yoder, 406 U.S. 205, 215–16, 92 S.Ct. 1526, 1533, 32 L.Ed.2d 15 (1972) (majority opinion by Chief Justice Burger).

33. The Supreme Court interpreted the statutory exemption of conscientious objectors from military service in

a manner that allowed persons with nontheocratic beliefs to qualify for the exemption in some circumstances. The Court did not make a determination of the nature of religious beliefs that would qualify for protection by the free exercise clause in these military service cases. See § 17.9(a) Exemptions From Military Service.

34. In Thomas v. Review Board, 450 U.S. 707, 715, 101 S.Ct. 1425, 1430, 67 L.Ed.2d 624 (1981), (finding that a person could not be disqualified from unemployment compensation benefits for the sole reason that he had left his employment on the basis of his sincerely held religious beliefs) the majority opinion stated that some beliefs asserted by individuals as the basis for a religious exemption from a law might be: "so bizarre, so clearly nonreligious in motivation, as not to be entitled to protection under the free exercise clause." This statement would appear to relate to testing of an individual's sincerity. The state-

The Court has held that a state court may not limit a group of persons who would be receiving a religiously based exemption from an unemployment compensation law to those persons who were members of an organized church.[35] Religious beliefs are not limited to the beliefs asserted by persons who have joined a formal religious organization.

It is possible that the Supreme Court might adopt different definitions of religion under the establishment and free exercise clauses, even though the word religion is mentioned only once in the First Amendment.[36] It is possible to argue that the Court should use a very narrow definition of religion in establishment clause cases because no significant danger to religious freedom would arise from government aid to persons or institutions that promoted a philosophy that is not God centered and not a part of an organized religion. The Supreme Court made a limited ruling concerning the definition of religion for establishment clause purposes by finding that a

public school curriculum that could not include prayer or Bible reading was not teaching a "religion of secularism." [37]

In the free exercise clause cases, one could argue that the Supreme Court should be more lenient in defining religion because the exemption of persons from a law may not raise significant establishment clause concerns. In free exercise cases, the judiciary might be able to find that any asserted belief was religious in nature but that an individual would only have a claim for exemption from a law if he could show that he was sincere in asserting that his religious beliefs prevented him from complying with the law at issue. If the Supreme Court had granted a free exercise clause right to be exempted from laws prohibiting the use of peyote, a person who was charged with the criminal use of peyote then would be unchallenged regarding the question of whether his asserted beliefs were "religious," but the government could challenge the person as to whether he was "sincere" in asserting those

ment does not create or recognize a government power to determine that some beliefs are not "religious" simply because the beliefs are held only by a very small number of people. In *Thomas*, the majority opinion also stated that "courts should not undertake to dissect religious beliefs because the believer admits that he is struggling with his position" and that "the guarantee of free exercise is not limited to beliefs which are shared by all members of a religious sect . . . courts are not arbiters of scriptural interpretation" 450 U.S. at 715–16, 101 S.Ct. at 430–31.

In Frazee v. Illinois Department of Employment Security, 489 U.S. 829, 109 S.Ct. 1514, 103 L.Ed.2d 914 (1989) the Court held that a state could not make membership in an organized church, religious sect, or religious denomination a condition of being able to claim a religious exemption to an unemployment insurance statute requirement that claimants be able to work on all seven days of the week. The Court in *Frazee*, as in *Thomas*, noted that the government did not claim that the individual's beliefs were not religious in nature or that the individual was not sincere. In *Frazee* the Court referred to the passages from the *Thomas* opinion quoted in the previous paragraph and concluded that "claims by Christians that their religion forbids Sunday work cannot be deemed bizarre or incredible." 489 U.S. at 834 n. 2, 109 S.Ct. at 1518 n. 2. This footnote in *Frazee* reinforces the view that the statements in *Thomas* concerning "bizarre" beliefs related to the credibility and sincerity of the claimant, rather than to the definition of religion.

35. Frazee v. Illinois Department of Employment Security, 489 U.S. 829, 109 S.Ct. 1514, 103 L.Ed.2d 914 (1989).

36. For an analysis of the difficulty of attempting to arrive at a legal definition of religion or religious beliefs,

see generally, Bowser, Delimiting Religion in the Constitution: A Classification Problem, 11 Val.U.L.Rev. 163 (1977); Boyan, Defining Religion in Operational and Institutional Terms, 116 U.Pa.L.Rev. 479 (1968); Choper, Defining Religion in the First Amendment, 1982 U.Ill.L.Rev. 579; Freeman, The Misguided Search for the Constitutional Definition of "Religion" 71 Geo.L.J. 1519 (1983).

37. School District v. Schempp, 374 U.S. 203, 225, 83 S.Ct. 1560, 1573–74, 10 L.Ed.2d 844 (1963) (finding that prayers or Bible reading conducted by school officials violates the establishment clause).

In Lee v. Weisman, 505 U.S. 577, 112 S.Ct. 2649, 120 L.Ed.2d 467 (1992) the Supreme Court held that a public school graduation ceremony that included a "nonsectarian" prayer by a member of the clergy (in the particular case, by a Rabbi) violated the establishment clause. The case was decided by a five to four vote of the Justices; Justice Kennedy wrote the majority opinion. Justice Souter wrote an opinion concurring in both the judgment and the majority opinion that was joined by Justices Stevens and O'Connor. Justice Souter found that one of the principal reasons for rejecting the arguments of "nonpreferentialists" (who would allow aid to all religion over nonreligion so long as the government aid did not include a sect preference) was the inability of courts to make decisions concerning the types of competing beliefs that would qualify as religions or theologies. 505 U.S. at 609, 617, 112 S.Ct. at 2667, 2671 (Souter, J., joined by Stevens and O'Connor, JJ., concurring). Justice Blackmun also wrote a concurring opinion in this case. 505 U.S. at 597, 112 S.Ct. at 2261 (Blackmun, J., joined by Stevens and O'Connor, JJ.)

beliefs. The Supreme Court has indicated that the mere testing of a person's sincerity is not a *per se* violation of the religion clauses. However, in testing the sincerity of an individual, a government agency or a court could not use a definition of religion or a test for sincerity that would be based upon religious principles. Courts are precluded from ruling on the truth of religious beliefs.[38]

The difficulty of defining religion or testing sincerity may be a reason why the Supreme Court has not created free exercise clause exemptions from laws of general applicability. In other words, the Court might consider the danger to establishment clause and free exercise clause values that would be part of the process by which courts or government agencies would determine who was eligible for a free exercise clause exemption. When the Court found that there was no free exercise clause right to use peyote,[39] it avoided the problems inherent in judicial definitions of religion or the testimony of sincerity.

Although the Supreme Court's free exercise standards do not require the government to grant exemptions from neutral laws of general applicability, those standards prohibit government actions designed to suppress or burden a group of persons because of their religious beliefs. A law that bans certain actions only because they are of religious significance, and only to suppress a particular religious group, will violate the free exercise clause.[40] Cases

wherein the Court invalidates a law because the Justices find that the law is designed to suppress religious beliefs or a religious sect are not likely to raise problems regarding the definition of religion or testing of sincerity.[41]

Legislative Accommodation of Religion. In several cases in which the Supreme Court found that the Constitution did not require a religiously based exemption from laws of general applicability, the Court has indicated that the legislature could take steps to accommodate the views of persons whose religious beliefs would not allow them to comply with the law. For example, in *Employment Division v. Smith (Smith II)*,[42] the Supreme Court found that a state criminal law that totally prohibited the use of peyote could be applied to someone who used peyote because of a sincerely held religious belief that the drug had to be used in a religious ceremony. Justice Scalia's majority opinion in *Smith II* indicated that a state or federal legislature might create an exemption to drug laws that would accommodate the religious need of some persons to use a banned substance. Justice Scalia said: "Values that are protected against government interference through enshrinement in the Bill of Rights are not thereby banished from the political process.... But to say that a nondiscriminatory religious-practice exemption is permitted, or even that it is desirable, is not to say that it is constitutionally required ... it may fairly be said that leaving accommo-

---

38. The problem of examining the sincerity of a person's assertion of a religious belief is also examined in § 17.11. See also § 17.12.

For additional citations to secondary sources on this topic see, R. Rotunda & J. Nowak, Treatise on Constitutional Law: Substance and Procedure, § 21.6 (3rd ed. 1999, with annual supplements).

39. Employment Division v. Smith, 494 U.S. 872, 110 S.Ct. 1595, 108 L.Ed.2d 876 (1990).

40. "The principle that government may not enact laws that suppress religious belief or practice is so well understood that few violations are recorded in our opinions." Church of the Lukumi Babalu Aye, Inc. v. Hialeah, 508 U.S. 520, 523, 113 S.Ct. 2217, 2222, 124 L.Ed.2d 472 (1993), on remand 2 F.3d 369 (11th Cir.1993). "[A] law that is neutral and of general applicability need not be justified by a compelling governmental interest even if the law has the incidental effect of burdening a particular religious practice.... A law failing to satisfy these requirements must be justified by a compelling governmen-

tal interest and must be narrowly tailored to advance that interest." 508 U.S. at 531, 113 S.Ct. at 2226.

41. For example, in Church of the Lukumi Babalu Aye, Inc. v. Hialeah, 508 U.S. 520, 113 S.Ct. 2217, 124 L.Ed.2d 472 (1993), on remand 2 F.3d 369 (11th Cir.1993) the Justices unanimously invalidated a city law prohibiting the slaughter of animals as it was applied to a particular religious sect because the law was designed only to prevent the practice of that religion within the city. In the course of making that ruling, the majority opinion noted: "The city does not argue that Santeria [the religious sect involved in this case] is not a 'religion' ... [n]or could it ... petitioners' assertion that animal sacrifice is an integral part of their religion 'cannot be deemed bizarre or incredible'.... Neither the city nor the courts below, moreover, have questioned the sincerity of petitioners' professed desire to conduct animal sacrifices." 508 U.S. at 530–31, 113 S.Ct. at 2225–26 (internal citation omitted).

42. 494 U.S. 872, 110 S.Ct. 1595, 108 L.Ed.2d 876 (1990).

dation to the political process will place at a relative disadvantage those religious practices that are not widely engaged in; but that unavoidable consequence of democratic government must be preferred to a system in which each conscience is a law unto itself or in which judges weigh the social importance of all laws against the centrality of religious beliefs." [43]

The Supreme Court has never explained the precise limits that the establishment clause may place on the ability of government to accommodate religion. An exemption from law of general applicability (such as a criminal law or a tax law) that only provided an exemption to members of a specific religion, or an exemption only for persons who held religious beliefs, would establish a denominational preference that would violate the establishment clause. For example, a legislature cannot create a tax exemption from the sales tax solely for sales of religious literature, because that preference for religious activity violates the establishment clause. [44]

Exemptions to taxes and regulatory laws must not involve a denominational preference or the endorsement of religious beliefs. At several points in this Chapter, we will examine the problem of legislative accommodation of religious practices. [45]

In response to the Supreme Court's decision in *Smith II,* Congress passed, and the Presi-

dent signed into law, the "Religious Freedom Restoration Act of 1993." [46] Section 7 of the Act stated that this law is not intended to modify establishment clause principles. The Act did not use language that would provide benefits only to a particular religious denomination under the guise of providing an accommodation of religion. [47] However, the Act might have raised establishment clause problems, if the Act had been interpreted as a grant of special advantages to believers of religious doctrines generally over nonbelievers. [48]

In *Boerne v. Flores,* [49] the Supreme Court, by a six to three vote, invalidated the Religious Freedom Restoration Act. The majority opinion, written by Justice Kennedy, ruled that Section 5 of the Fourteenth Amendment did not give Congress the power to expand the civil liberties that had been established through judicial interpretation of Section 1 of that Amendment. Thus, Congress had no power under the Fourteenth Amendment to expand the scope of rights created by the free exercise clause of the First Amendment, which applies to the states through Section 1 of the Fourteenth Amendment. Of the six Justices in the majority in *Boerne,* only Justice Stevens expressed the view that the Religious Freedom Restoration Act violated the establishment clause, by granting a benefit to some persons that was based on their religious beliefs. [50]

---

43. Employment Division v. Smith, 494 U.S. 872, 890, 110 S.Ct. 1595, 1606, 108 L.Ed.2d 876 (1990).

44. Texas Monthly, Inc. v. Bullock, 489 U.S. 1, 109 S.Ct. 890, 103 L.Ed.2d 1 (1989).

45. This problem is examined in §§ 17.1, 17.9(a), 17.13, 17.15, 17.16.

In Board of Education of Kiryas Joel Village School District v. Grumet, 512 U.S. 687, 114 S.Ct. 2481, 129 L.Ed.2d 546 (1994), the Supreme Court invalidated a state law creating a special school district for a Village that was composed entirely of members of one religion. The Court found this to be an impermissible preference for members of a particular religious sect, rather than a permissible accommodation for persons confronted with special problems. The *Grumet* case is examined in § 17.3 of this Treatise.

See §§ 17.13, 17.15 regarding the accommodation of religious beliefs in statutes regulating the terms and conditions of private employment.

46. Pub.L. 103–141, H.R. 1038, S. 578, 103 Cong. 1st Sess. (1993), 42 U.S.C.A. § 2000bb.

47. A denominational preference or a so-called sect preference would violate the establishment clause. See note 45, supra.

48. A law that does not include a sect preference may, under some circumstances, violate the establishment clause by providing aid to all persons who hold religious beliefs while denying similar aid to nonreligious persons. Compare, Estate of Thornton v. Caldor, Inc., 472 U.S. 703, 105 S.Ct. 2914, 86 L.Ed.2d 557 (1985) (invalidating a state law requiring all employers to honor every employee's desire to refuse work on "his Sabbath") with Corporation of Presiding Bishop of Church of Jesus Christ of Latter-day Saints v. Amos, 483 U.S. 327, 107 S.Ct. 2862, 97 L.Ed.2d 273 (1987) (upholding the exemption of religious organizations from a statutory prohibition against religious discrimination) these cases are examined in §§ 17.13, 17.15.

49. 521 U.S. 507, 117 S.Ct. 2157, 138 L.Ed.2d 624 (1997). The scope of Congress's power to enforce the Fourteenth Amendment is examined in Chapter 15.

50. Justice Stevens wrote an opinion in which he asserted that the Religious Freedom Restoration Act could have been invalidated as a violation of the establishment

Justice Scalia, joined by Justice Stevens, defended the principles set forth in *Smith II*, although the majority in *Boerne* did not consider the free exercise clause or establishment clause issues.[51] Three dissenting Justices in *Boerne* would have been willing to reconsider whether *Smith II* established the correct free exercise clause standards.[52]

§ 17.7   The Free Exercise Clause— The Early Decisions

The claims of religious minorities received little serious attention from the Supreme Court until the middle of the twentieth century.

In *Reynolds v. United States*[1] the Supreme Court upheld the application of a federal law prohibiting polygamy to a Mormon whose religion required him to engage in that practice.[2]

The majority opinion indicated that Congress was free to prohibit any action regardless of its religious implications so long as it did not formally prohibit a belief.[3] The Court upheld other laws which burdened the practice of the Mormon religion by imposing various penalties on polygamy.[4] Similarly, the Court upheld a government system of compulsory vaccinations as applied to those who objected to vaccinations on a religious basis.[5]

Prior to the application of the religion clauses to the states the Supreme Court decided two cases under the due process clause of the Fourteenth Amendment which have significant free exercise implications. In *Hamilton v. Regents of the University of California*,[6] the Court held that requiring male students at a state university to take courses in military training was not a denial of liberty which violated due process. This decision is suspect

---

clause of the First Amendment. Boerne v. Flores, 521 U.S. 507, 117 S.Ct. 2157, 138 L.Ed.2d 624 (1997) (Stevens, J., concurring).

51. Justices Scalia and Stevens joined in the majority opinion in *Boerne*, but they concurred for the purpose of defending the Court's limited rulings concerning the nature of the free exercise clause. 521 U.S. at 537, 117 S.Ct. at 2172 (Scalia, J., joined by Stevens, J., concurring in part).

52. 521 U.S. at 544, 117 S.Ct. at 2176 (O'Connor, J., joined in part by Breyer, J., dissenting); 521 U.S. at 565, 117 S.Ct. at 2185 (Souter, J., dissenting); 521 U.S. at 566, 117 S.Ct. at 2186 (Breyer, J., dissenting).

§ 17.7

1. 98 U.S. (8 Otto) 145, 25 L.Ed. 244 (1878).

2. Actually the church required polygamy by male members only "when circumstances would admit," but it was conceded that Mr. Reynolds' second marriage was sanctioned by the church as being within the requirement. 98 U.S. (8 Otto) at 161.

3. The majority opinion by Chief Justice Waite stated: "Congress was deprived of all legislative power over mere opinion, but was left free to reach actions which were in violation of social duties or subversive of good order." 98 U.S. (8 Otto) at 164. For an argument that the societal interest in prohibiting polygamy should not have been held to outweigh a claim for an exemption from this law, see Miller, A Critique of the Reynolds Decision, 11 Western State U.L.Rev. 165 (1984).

4. Davis v. Beason, 133 U.S. 333, 10 S.Ct. 299, 33 L.Ed. 637 (1890); Late Corporation of the Church of Jesus Christ of Latter-Day Saints v. United States, 136 U.S. 1, 10 S.Ct. 792, 34 L.Ed. 478 (1890), see also State v. Barlow, 107 Utah 292, 153 P.2d 647 (1944), appeal dismissed 324 U.S. 829, 65 S.Ct. 916, 89 L.Ed. 1396 (1945), rehearing denied 324 U.S. 891, 65 S.Ct. 1026, 89 L.Ed. 1438 (1945) (state bigamy law upheld).

The laws at issue in these cases prohibited polygamy without banning the advocacy of polygamy. If a law punished the advocacy of polygamy, the law should be held to violate the freedom of speech. These laws did not punish only those persons who entered polygamous marriages on the basis of their religious beliefs. If an anti-polygamy law, on its face, imposed penalties only on members of a specific religion, that law would violate the free exercise clause.

In Romer v. Evans, 517 U.S. 620, 116 S.Ct. 1620, 134 L.Ed.2d 855 (1996) the Supreme Court invalidated a state constitutional amendment that prohibited any local or state legislative body from passing laws that protected people from discrimination on the basis of sexual orientation. The state, as well as dissenting Justices, argued that *Davis v. Beason* should allow the state to punish any group that engaged in practices deemed immoral by the state. The majority opinion in *Romer* stated: "To the extent that *Davis* held that persons advocating a certain religious practice may be denied the right to vote, it is no longer good law. Brandenburg v. Ohio, 395 U.S. 444, 89 S.Ct. 1827, 23 L.Ed.2d 430 (1969) (per curiam). To the extent that it held that groups designated in the statute may be deprived of the right to vote because of their status, its ruling could not stand without surviving strict scrutiny, a most doubtful outcome." 517 U.S. at 633, 116 S.Ct. at 1628.

See generally, Church of Lukumi Babalu Aye, Inc. v. Hialeah, 508 U.S. 520, 113 S.Ct. 2217, 124 L.Ed.2d 472 (1993), (the Court invalidates a law regarding the treatment of animals that was designed to force a religious sect to leave the community). This case is examined in § 17.8 of this Treatise.

5. Jacobson v. Massachusetts, 197 U.S. 11, 25 S.Ct. 358, 49 L.Ed. 643 (1905); Zucht v. King, 260 U.S. 174, 43 S.Ct. 24, 67 L.Ed. 194 (1922).

6. 293 U.S. 245, 55 S.Ct. 197, 79 L.Ed. 343 (1934).

in light of the Court's decisions regarding the conscientious objector laws but it serves to emphasize the absence of judicial protection for religious minorities during this period.[7]

The second major due process case in this area was *Pierce v. Society of Sisters*.[8] In this case the Court struck down a statute which required that children attend only public schools as an undue restriction on the freedom of both parents and students. Today *Pierce* stands for the right of children to attend private (including religious) schools so long as they meet basic educational standards. In this regard it should be noted that the state apparently cannot control the subjects taught in those schools beyond its assurance that children are given competent instruction in specified secular subjects and that they are in a safe and healthy environment; further restrictions on the educational process would have to be necessary to promote important secular interests.[9]

During the 1940's and 1950's, the Supreme Court invalidated a number of laws which restricted religious practices primarily on the basis that they interfered with the free speech protection of the First Amendment. The most important of these cases was *Cantwell v. Connecticut*,[10] where the Court struck down the conviction of several Jehovah's Witnesses for soliciting funds without a license because they were engaged in the distribution of religious materials. It was in this decision that the Court held the free exercise clause applicable to the states.

The majority in *Cantwell* noted that while the freedom to believe was absolute, the freedom to act was not. A general regulation of solicitation which left no room for official discretion and did not unduly obstruct religious practices would have been permissible. Because this statute allowed a licensing officer discretion to determine whether the solicitation was for a religious cause it was invalid. This law would allow the officer to determine who would be allowed to engage in solicitation based on his view of the religious content of their message. Such a statute would violate both the freedoms of speech and religion.

Cantwell was followed by a number of decisions which overturned statutes regulating the dissemination of religious views because they interfered with both the freedom of speech and religion. In each case, however, it appeared that the free speech claim was central to the decision.

In a series of decisions the Court struck down licensing systems for demonstrations or meetings which gave government officials discretion to deny licenses on the basis of the content of the speech, while upholding ones which had permit requirements based on non-discriminatory "time, place or manner" factors.[11] In these cases the fact that religious meetings were suppressed under discretionary statutes indicated a violation of free exercise rights, but the statutes were held invalid because they conflicted with the free speech clause. Similarly, the Court invalidated laws prohibiting the distribution of handbills on city streets or in residential neighborhoods as applied to those who sought to distribute religious literature.[12] In a decision which focused on religious freedom, the Court held that a license tax on all persons soliciting orders for

---

7. The Supreme Court might today approve such a law, see §§ 17.6, 17.7. The conscientious objector cases are discussed in § 17.9(a), infra.

8. 268 U.S. 510, 45 S.Ct. 571, 69 L.Ed. 1070 (1925).

9. Even prior to the *Pierce* decision the Court held that a state violated the due process clause when it prohibited the teaching of any language other than English in private (and parochial) schools. Meyer v. Nebraska, 262 U.S. 390, 43 S.Ct. 625, 67 L.Ed. 1042 (1923). See generally, Torruella, C.J., citing Treatise in, Brown v. Hot, Sexy And Safer Productions, Inc., 68 F.3d 525, 533 n. 5 (1st Cir.1995), cert. denied 516 U.S. 1159, 116 S.Ct. 1044, 134 L.Ed.2d 191 (1996).

10. 310 U.S. 296, 60 S.Ct. 900, 84 L.Ed. 1213 (1940).

11. See, e.g., Schneider v. New Jersey, 308 U.S. 147, 60 S.Ct. 146, 84 L.Ed. 155 (1939); Largent v. Texas, 318 U.S. 418, 63 S.Ct. 667, 87 L.Ed. 873 (1943) (discretionary sales license system invalid); Kunz v. New York, 340 U.S. 290, 71 S.Ct. 312, 95 L.Ed. 280 (1951) (discretionary public meeting licensing system invalid); Cox v. New Hampshire, 312 U.S. 569, 61 S.Ct. 762, 85 L.Ed. 1049 (1941) (non-discriminatory parade licensing system upheld); Poulos v. New Hampshire, 345 U.S. 395, 73 S.Ct. 760, 97 L.Ed. 1105 (1953) (non-discriminatory system upheld).

12. Jamison v. Texas, 318 U.S. 413, 63 S.Ct. 669, 87 L.Ed. 869 (1943); see also Martin v. Struthers, 319 U.S. 141, 63 S.Ct. 862, 87 L.Ed. 1313 (1943).

goods could not be applied to a Jehovah's Witness who went door to door distributing religious literature and asking for contributions.[13]

Cantwell and the other solicitation and licensing cases were decided on the basis of freedom of speech principles. Laws that impose time, place, or manner limitations on literature distribution or funds solicitation can be validly applied to activities conducted by members of religious sects if the laws are compatible with the freedom of speech.[14]

The Flag Salute Cases. One of the most interesting problems concerned the requiring of school children to take part in a flag salute ceremony. The Court overruled a decision rendered only three years earlier and held that students could not be compelled to salute the flag against their beliefs.[15] Once again basing the decision on the right of free speech, a majority of the Justices found that the requirement invaded the sphere of free intellect and belief that was the core of these First Amendment principles.

In these cases it was the limitation of freedoms essentially protected by the free speech clause which made the requirements unconstitutional. Although the Jehovah Witnesses brought these cases because of their religious objections to the honoring of "idols," the infringement of religious beliefs was not crucial to the decision. Anyone opposed to saluting the flag had to be excused from the requirement without regard to whether their refusal was based on religious or nonreligious grounds.

Despite these seemingly liberal free speech-free exercise decisions, the Supreme Court did not give significant independent protection to the free exercise of religion against police power regulations during this period. Thus, in *Prince v. Massachusetts*,[16] the Court upheld the application of a law prohibiting the sale of merchandise in public places by minors to a nine year old child who was distributing religious literature with her guardian. The majority found that the state's interest in the

---

13. Murdock v. Pennsylvania, 319 U.S. 105, 117, 63 S.Ct. 870, 876–77, 87 L.Ed. 1292 (1943), overruling Jones v. Opelika, 316 U.S. 584, 62 S.Ct. 1231, 86 L.Ed. 1691 (1942); see, also, Jones v. Opelika, 319 U.S. 103, 63 S.Ct. 890, 87 L.Ed. 1290 (1943) (per curiam), vacating Jones v. Opelika, 316 U.S. 584, 62 S.Ct. 1231, 86 L.Ed. 1691 (1942); Follett v. Town of McCormick, 321 U.S. 573, 64 S.Ct. 717, 88 L.Ed. 938 (1944).

The *Murdock* and *Follett* decisions focused on religious freedom; these decisions appear to be based upon the establishment and free exercise clauses. However, these cases may best be understood as a part of the series of decisions in which the Supreme Court protected all First Amendment activities (activities involving assemblies, association, speech, newspaper distribution, and religious activities) from certain types of licensing systems. The latter view of *Murdock* and *Follett* is supported by the Supreme Court decision in Jimmy Swaggart Ministries v. Board of Equalization, 493 U.S. 378, 110 S.Ct. 688, 107 L.Ed.2d 796 (1990) in which the Supreme Court ruled that a religious organization had no right to refuse to pay general sales and use taxes on the sales and use of religious goods and literature in a state. Justice O'Connor wrote for a unanimous Court in *Jimmy Swaggart Ministries*. Justice O'Connor found that a tax of general applicability on the proceeds of sales of goods and services did not violate the establishment clause when it was applied to the sales of religious literature. The free exercise clause did not require an exemption from such a general tax for religious activities. Justice O'Connor's opinion found that each of the taxes invalidated in *Murdock* and *Follett* was a flat tax (license fee) "that operated as a prior restraint on the exercise of religious liberty."

The sales and use taxes could be applied to religious organizations and religious literature because "our concern in *Murdock* and *Follett*—that a flat license tax would act as a *precondition* to the free exercise of religious beliefs—is simply not present where a tax applies to all sales and uses of tangible personal property in the state." 493 U.S. at 386, 110 S.Ct. at 694 (emphasis in original).

14. In Heffron v. International Society for Krishna Consciousness, Inc., 452 U.S. 640, 101 S.Ct. 2559, 69 L.Ed.2d 298 (1981), the Court upheld a state fair rule whereby a non-discretionary licensing system forced all persons to confine distribution or sales of literature and solicitation activities to a fixed location. The rule was upheld on its face and as applied to members of a religious sect. The majority opinion stated:

"None of our cases suggest that the inclusion of peripatetic solicitation as part of a church ritual entitles church members to solicitation rights in a public forum superior to those of members of other religious groups that raise money but do not purport to ritualize the process. Nor for present purposes do religious organizations enjoy rights to communicate, distribute, and solicit on the fairgrounds superior to those of other organizations having social, political, or other ideological messages to proselytize."

452 U.S. at 652, 101 S.Ct. at 2566.

15. West Virginia State Bd. of Education v. Barnette, 319 U.S. 624, 63 S.Ct. 1178, 87 L.Ed. 1628 (1943), overruling Minersville School District v. Gobitis, 310 U.S. 586, 60 S.Ct. 1010, 84 L.Ed. 1375 (1940).

16. 321 U.S. 158, 64 S.Ct. 438, 88 L.Ed. 645 (1944).

health and well-being of young people was a significant secular end which justified the incidental burden on religion.

As of 1960, no case in the Supreme Court had resulted in the overturning of police power regulations solely on the basis that they had a coercive effect on the free exercise of religion. If the end pursued by the government was a significant secular goal, the Court would uphold incidental restrictions on religiously motivated activity. Only when the law proscribed beliefs, or interfered with free speech as well as the exercise of religion, would the Court overturn the law.

§ 17.8 The Free Exercise Clause— The Modern Cases

Overview. Between 1960 and 1990, Justices of the Supreme Court were sharply divided over the extent to which the free exercise clause allowed the judiciary to determine whether a law of general applicability, which included no explicitly religious criteria, could be applied to persons whose sincerely held religious beliefs prevented them from complying with the law. In the cases decided by the Court during this period, as in earlier Supreme Court decisions, the Justices clearly endorsed the principle that the government could not punish a person solely because of his religious belief or allocate benefits or burdens on the basis of people's religious beliefs.

In *Torcaso v. Watkins*,[1] the Court invalidated a state constitutional provision that required a declaration of a belief in God as a prerequisite to taking public office. The majority noted that the original Constitution prohibited the use of religious tests for federal government offices.[2] The Court found that the free exercise clause prohibited the government from awarding benefits to, or imposing burdens on, a person due to his religious beliefs or his lack of religious faith.

The division between the Justices arose in cases concerning whether the Court should declare that a law of general applicability could not be applied to a person whose religious beliefs required him to take actions that were contrary to the law. Between 1963 and 1989, it appeared that the Court would balance the importance of the government interest that was furthered by such a law against the burden on persons who could not follow their religious beliefs if they complied with the law. However, even during the era of the balancing test the government won virtually every case which did not involve the punishment of religious beliefs. The government was only required to grant religious exemptions in (1) a few cases involving technical requirements for unemployment compensation and (2) one case involving an exemption from a compulsory school attendance law for Amish children.

The 1990 Supreme Court decision in *Employment Division v. Smith (Smith II)*[3] summarized a century of the Court's rulings concerning the free exercise clause. *Smith II* involved two individuals who were disqualified from receiving unemployment compensation benefits under a state law that disqualified anyone who had been fired from his job for job related misconduct. These persons had been fired from their positions as drug and alcohol abuse rehabilitation counsellors at a private clinic after it was found out that they had ingested peyote, which was banned by state law. The former drug counselors claimed that the free exercise clause protected their use of peyote in connection with a religious ceremony.

The Supreme Court of the United States, in *Employment Division v. Smith (Smith I)*,[4] had remanded the case to the state court for a determination of whether state law prohibited all use of peyote, including the use of peyote in a religious ceremony. If the state law had provided an exemption for the sacramental use

§ 17.8

1. 367 U.S. 488, 81 S.Ct. 1680, 6 L.Ed.2d 982 (1961).

2. "[No] religious Test shall ever be required as a Qualification to any Office of public Trust under the United States." U.S. Const. art. VI. cl. 3.

3. 494 U.S. 872, 110 S.Ct. 1595, 108 L.Ed.2d 876 (1990).

4. 485 U.S. 660, 108 S.Ct. 1444, 99 L.Ed.2d 753 (1988).

of peyote, the Supreme Court might have avoided the free exercise clause question. The denial of unemployment compensation to individuals who had used the peyote in a lawful manner might have been totally arbitrary. The state supreme court, after the remand of the case, found that state law prohibited any use of peyote, including any religiously motivated or sacramental use. The state court also held that the state's total prohibition of peyote use violated the free exercise clause of the First Amendment to the Constitution of the United States and, for that reason, the state court found that the state could not deny unemployment compensation to the former drug counselors.

In *Smith II,* the Supreme Court of the United States ruled: (1) that the free exercise clause did not require an exemption from criminal laws banning the use of peyote; and (2) that unemployment compensation could be denied to persons whose discharge from employment had been based upon their violation of a valid criminal statute.[5]

In *Smith II,* Justice Scalia wrote the majority opinion which ruled that the free exercise clause did not require the government to justify its refusal to exempt religiously motivated drug use from its general prohibition of drug use. The majority believed that the judiciary was not authorized by the free exercise clause to balance the societal interest in the drug proscription against the degree to which compliance with the law burdened the sincerely held religious beliefs of the individuals in the case.

Justice Scalia, writing for the majority, recognized two basic free exercise clause principles. First, the government is prohibited from regulating religious beliefs. This principle prohibits the government from compelling the affirmation of religious beliefs, punishing religious expression thought to be false, or using of religious doctrine as a basis for judicial decisions.[6]

Second, the free exercise clause would invalidate a law that appeared to be religiously neutral on its face, if it could be shown that the purpose of the legislature that passed the law had been the prohibition or regulation of an act only because of its religious significance. Justice Scalia stated: "It would be true, we think (though no case of ours has involved the point), that a state would be 'prohibiting the free exercise [of religion]' if it sought to ban such acts or abstentions only when they are engaged in for religious reasons, or only because of the religious belief that they display. It would doubtless be unconstitutional, for example, to ban the casting of 'statutes that are to be used for worship purposes,' or to prohibit bowing down before a golden calf."[7]

The free exercise clause does not require exemptions from religiously neutral laws for religious persons who cannot comply with the law. Justice Scalia's majority opinion stated: "The only decisions in which we have held the First Amendment bars application of a neutral, generally applicable law to religiously motivated action have involved not the free exercise clause alone, but the free exercise clause in conjunction with other constitutional protections."[8]

---

5. Employment Division v. Smith, 494 U.S. 872, 110 S.Ct. 1595, 108 L.Ed.2d 876 (1990). The denial of the exemption was upheld by a six to three vote of the Justices. Justice Scalia wrote the majority opinion, his opinion was joined by Chief Justice Rehnquist and Justices White, Stevens, and Kennedy. Justice O'Connor believed that a balancing test should be used in this case, but she found that the government interest was sufficiently compelling to justify a denial of an exemption for persons whose religious beliefs required them to use peyote. 494 U.S. at 891, 110 S.Ct. at 1606 (O'Connor, J., concurring in the judgment). Justices Brennan, Marshall, and Blackmun, joined the portion of Justice O'Connor's opinion in which she explained why the government would need a compelling interest to override the request for an exemption by persons whose religious beliefs prevented them from complying with the law. However, these three

Justices did not agree with Justice O'Connor's use of that test in this case; these three Justices dissented from the ruling in the case. 494 U.S. at 907, 110 S.Ct. at 1615 (1990).

6. Employment Division v. Smith, 494 U.S. 872, 877, 110 S.Ct. 1595, 1599, 108 L.Ed.2d 876 (1990). The problem of punishing false religious statements in fraud prosecutions is examined in § 17.11 of this Treatise. The problems faced by courts in making decisions concerning ecclesiastical disputes is examined in § 17.12 of this Treatise.

7. 494 U.S. at 877–78, 110 S.Ct. at 1595.

8. 494 U.S. at 881, 110 S.Ct. at 1600. The cases in which the Supreme Court found that the free speech and free exercise clauses together prohibited the government

According to the majority opinion in *Smith II*, the only cases that were inconsistent with the principle that religiously neutral, generally applicable laws did not have to provide a religious exemption were a few cases in which the Court had found that the government was required to waive a condition for unemployment compensation benefits (for persons who could not meet the condition due to their sincerely held religious beliefs).[9] In those unemployment compensation cases, the Court had used a two-step balancing test. First, the individual was required to show that complying with the eligibility condition (such as a condition that the individual be available for work on Saturday) imposed a substantial burden on the person's ability to carry out his religious beliefs. If the person made that demonstration, the government, in the second part of the test, was required to demonstrate that granting an exemption from the law at issue would interfere with a compelling or overriding government interest. In *Smith II*, Justice Scalia's majority opinion found that the balancing test had never been used by the Court except to examine conditions for unemployment compensation that were unrelated to a general criminal law.

The *Smith II* decision was reminiscent of the Court's decision in *Braunfeld v. Brown*[10] in 1961. The Court in *Braunfeld* upheld the constitutionality of applying laws that required businesses to be closed on Sundays to persons who were required to observe another day as the Sabbath. A majority of the Justices in *Braunfeld*, although without a majority opinion, held that the additional economic burdens placed on a Sabbatarian (who would be required to be closed more days a week than his competitors) did not violate the free exer-

cise clause. Chief Justice Warren, writing for four members of the Court in *Braunfeld*, found that the law placed a real burden on Sabbatarian retailers. The plurality opinion by Chief Justice Warren found that the state had an overriding nonreligious interest in setting aside a single day for "rest, recreation, and tranquility." Some portions of Chief Justice Warren's plurality opinion appear to involve a balancing of the societal interest in the Sunday closing laws against the burdens placed on Sabbatarians, but the plurality did not require any real justification for the refusal to grant an exemption from the Sunday closing laws to Sabbatarians.

Justices Frankfurter and Harlan, in a concurring opinion in *Braunfeld*,[11] balanced the societal interest in the preservation of the "traditional institution" of a day of rest against the economic disadvantage to the retailer who had to be closed an extra day due to his religious beliefs. Despite the language in the concurring opinion regarding the need to balance the individual retailer's interests against societal interests, Justices Frankfurter and Harlan appeared to uphold the law simply because it imposed only an incidental burden on religious practices. Justices Frankfurter and Harlan found that even if there were no Sunday closing laws, the Sabbatarian retailer would still lose a day of sales opportunities that was available to his nonreligious competitors, due to his religious need to refrain from working on a certain day of the week.

In 1963, the Court for the first time used a balancing test to require the government to grant unemployment compensation benefits to a person who, due to her religious beliefs,

---

from subjecting both religious and nonreligious speakers to certain types of licensing statutes or to other regulations of speech (of both nonreligious and religious content) are examined in § 17.7.

9. Id. The first important case concerning unemployment compensation was Sherbert v. Verner, 374 U.S. 398, 83 S.Ct. 1790, 10 L.Ed.2d 965 (1963).

In Employment Division v. Smith, 494 U.S. 872, 881 n. 1, 110 S.Ct. 1595, 1601 n. 1, 108 L.Ed.2d 876 (1990), Justice Scalia found that the Supreme Court's decision in Wisconsin v. Yoder, 406 U.S. 205, 92 S.Ct. 1526, 32 L.Ed.2d 15 (1972), in which the Court held that Amish parents could not be required to send their children to

school after the eighth grade, was not based solely on the free exercise clause but on a combination of the free exercise clause and the liberty of parents to control the education of their children that was protected by the due process clause of the Fourteenth Amendment. However, the Yoder opinion appears to be based upon the free exercise clause alone. The case is examined in later paragraphs in this chapter and in § 17.6.

10. 366 U.S. 599, 81 S.Ct. 1144, 6 L.Ed.2d 563 (1961).

11. 366 U.S. at 521–22, 81 S.Ct. at 1186–87 (Frankfurter, J., concurring, joined by Harlan, J.).

could not meet all of the requirements for those benefits.[12] That decision was applied in several later cases, which required state to waive conditions for unemployment compensation relating to availability for work.[13]

In 1972, the Court appeared to use a balancing test to find that a state could not require the Amish to send their children to public schools after the eighth grade.[14]

The balancing test used in the unemployment benefits and Amish school cases was quoted in many decisions during the 1963–1990 era. However, other than in the unemployment compensation or school attendance cases, the Court did not rule in favor of any free exercise clause claims during this era that did not involve a regulation of religious beliefs.[15]

Although none of the 1963–1990 free exercise clause decisions of the Supreme Court has been overruled, it is important to remember that the Supreme Court has disavowed the balancing test used in those decisions. In 1993, in *Church of Lukumi Babalu Aye, Inc. v. Hialeah*,[16] the majority opinion by Justice Kennedy summarized the current free exercise clause standards as follows:

"[A] law that is neutral and of general applicability need not be justified by a compelling government interest even if the law has the incidental effect of burdening a particular religious practice. . . . A law failing to satisfy these requirements [the neutrality and general applicability requirements] must be justified by a compelling governmental interest and must be narrowly tailored to advance that interest."[17]

The first part of this summary was an endorsement of *Smith II*, in which the Court refused to require religiously based exemptions for a religiously neutral, generally applicable law prohibiting the use of certain drugs.[18]

The second part of the summary was an endorsement of the principle, recognized in the *Smith II* decision, that a law that is designed to burden or suppress religious beliefs, or a law that prohibits an action solely because of its religious significance, violates the free exercise clause.[19] A law that is not a religiously neutral law of general applicability will be subject to strict judicial scrutiny and the compelling interest test. It is difficult to conceive of circumstances where a compelling interest of government would require the creation of a law designed to burden religious beliefs or to punish actions only because those actions were religiously motivated.

In *Church of the Lukumi Babalu Aye* the Court invalidated a city's ordinances prohibiting certain types of animal slaughter because the Justices unanimously found that the laws were solely designed to suppress a particular

---

12. Sherbert v. Verner, 374 U.S. 398, 83 S.Ct. 1790, 10 L.Ed.2d 965 (1963) (the Court finds that a state cannot deny unemployment benefits to a woman who refused to work on Saturday due to her religious beliefs).

13. Thomas v. Review Board, 450 U.S. 707, 101 S.Ct. 1425, 67 L.Ed.2d 624 (1981); Hobbie v. Unemployment Appeals Commission of Florida, 480 U.S. 136, 107 S.Ct. 1046, 94 L.Ed.2d 190 (1987). These cases are examined in later paragraphs of this section.

14. Wisconsin v. Yoder, 406 U.S. 205, 92 S.Ct. 1526, 32 L.Ed.2d 15 (1972). In Employment Division v. Smith, 494 U.S. 872, 881 n. 1, 110 S.Ct. 1595, 1601 n. 1, 108 L.Ed.2d 876 (1990) the majority found that *Yoder* was not based solely on the free exercise clause. This case is examined in later paragraphs of this section and in § 17.6.

15. Supreme Court decisions finding that laws were invalid because of their punishment of religious beliefs are examined in § 17.11. Inquiries into Religious "Frauds", § 17.12 State Involvement of Ecclesiastical Disputes, § 17.14 Prohibiting "Ministers" from Holding Public Office, § 17.16 Direct Regulation of Religious Organizations.

16. 508 U.S. 520, 113 S.Ct. 2217, 124 L.Ed.2d 472 (1993), on remand 2 F.3d 369 (11th Cir.1993).

17. 508 U.S. at 531, 113 S.Ct. at 2226.

18. Employment Division v. Smith, 494 U.S. 872, 110 S.Ct. 1595, 108 L.Ed.2d 876 (1990). See notes 3–9, supra, and accompanying text.

19. In Church of the Lukumi Babalu Aye, Inc. v. Hialeah, 508 U.S. 520, 523, 113 S.Ct. 2217, 2222, 124 L.Ed.2d 472 (1993) the majority opinion stated:

"The principle that government may not enact laws that suppress religious belief or practice is so well understood that few violations are recorded in our opinions. . . . Our review confirms that the laws in question were enacted by officials who did not understand, failed to perceive, or chose to ignore the fact that their official actions violated the Nation's essential commitment to religious freedom. The challenged laws had an impermissible object; and in all events the principle of general applicability was violated because the secular ends asserted in defense of the law, were pursued only with respect to conduct motivated by religious beliefs."

religious sect. The laws prohibited virtually no other types of animal slaughter except that used by the religious sect; the city did not adopt the laws until the religious sect planned to conduct its religious rituals in a building within the city. Because these city laws were obviously designed to suppress a particular religion, the Court did not need to explain in detail the difference between the requirement that a law be religiously "neutral" or that the law be one of "general applicability." [20] These city laws were invalidated by the Court, insofar as they were applied to the religious sect, because the city could not identify any compelling interest that would require banning only the type of animal slaughter used in the religion's rituals.

Let us assume that a jurisdiction had a religiously neutral law, which was uniformly applied to all persons, that forbid the slaughtering of animals. The law was not designed to suppress religiously motivated acts; the law was designed to promote both public health interests and to prevent the "cruel" treatment of animals. If members of a religious sect in religious rituals slaughtered animals in a manner that violated the law, could they be punished under that law? The Court in the

Church of the Lukumi Babalu Aye case did not reach this question. The Court's ruling in *Smith II* would indicate that the religious sect would not have a constitutional right to an exemption from the law. [21]

The remainder of this section will be divided into the topics that came before the Supreme Court during the 1963–1990 time period.

Unemployment Compensation. In *Sherbert v. Verner* [22] a majority of the Justices held that state unemployment benefits could not be denied to a Seventh Day Adventist because she refused to work on Saturday due to her religious beliefs. Justice Brennan, writing for a seven member majority, stated that for the denial of benefits to withstand scrutiny under the free exercise clause "it must be either because her disqualification as a beneficiary represents no infringement by the state of her constitutional right of free exercise, or because any incidental burden on the free exercise of appellant's religion may be justified by a compelling state interest in the regulation. . . ." [23] The majority employed a two-part balancing test. First, plaintiff had to show a substantial burden on the exercise of her religion from the

---

20. Perhaps the inquiry into "religious neutrality" would involve an inquiry into legislative motive or purpose, whereas an inquiry into general applicability might focus only on the scope of the statute. However, this point is not clear. Justice Kennedy wrote for five Justices in finding that the law was not religiously neutral because the ordinances exempted virtually all forms of animal sacrifice except those used by the Santeria religion. The object of the ordinances could only be understood as the symposium of religion. Church of the Lukumi Babalu Aye, Inc. v. Hialeah, 508 U.S. 520, 533, 113 S.Ct. 2217, 2227–30, 124 L.Ed.2d 472 (1993), on remand 2 F.3d 369 (11th Cir.1993). However, Justice Kennedy wrote only for himself and Justice Stevens when he stated that courts could determine religious neutrality, or the lack thereof, in the same manner in that courts would determine the existence of alleged discriminatory purpose in equal protection cases. 508 U.S. at 539–40, 113 S.Ct. at 2230–31 (opinion of Kennedy, J., joined by Stevens, J., as to part II–A–2). Justice Kennedy wrote for five Justices in finding that the Hialeah animal slaughter laws were not laws of general applicability, 508 U.S. at 540–44, 113 S.Ct. at 2231–33.

Two concurring Justices noted that there might be no clear distinction between an inquiry into whether a law was religiously neutral and an inquiry into whether a law was one of general applicability. Church of the Lukumi Babalu Aye, Inc. v. Hialeah, 508 U.S. 520, 557, 113 S.Ct. 2217, 2239, 124 L.Ed.2d 472 (1993), on remand 2 F.3d 369

(11th Cir.1993) (Scalia, J., joined by Rehnquist, C.J., concurring in part and concurring in the judgment).

21. Justices Blackmun and O'Connor agreed that the Hialeah ordinances violated the free exercise clause because these ordinances were designed to suppress religion. These two Justices wrote separately to restate their disagreement with the approach to free exercise issues adopted by the Court in *Smith II*. However, these two Justices did not reach the issue of whether a religious group must receive an exemption from a religiously neutral law prohibiting certain types of animal slaughter. It is possible that they would vote to deny such an exemption to religious sects even under the combined balancing test and compelling interest test. Church of the Lukumi Babalu Aye, Inc. v. Hialeah, 508 U.S. 520, 577–80, 113 S.Ct. 2217, 2250–52, 124 L.Ed.2d 472 (1993), on remand 2 F.3d 369 (11th Cir.1993) (Blackmun, J., joined by O'Connor, J., concurring in the judgment). Justice Souter wrote a concurring opinion to express his views that the Hialeah ordinances could be invalidated without reaffirming *Smith II*; he would consider reexamining the position the Court took in *Smith II* in a more appropriate case, such as a case involving a religiously neutral, generally applicable law. 508 U.S. at 558, 113 S.Ct. at 2240 (Souter, J., concurring in part and concurring in the judgment).

22. 374 U.S. 398, 83 S.Ct. 1790, 10 L.Ed.2d 965 (1963).

23. 374 U.S. at 403, 83 S.Ct. at 1793.

law under review. Second, such a burden would only be valid if the Court found it necessary to a "compelling state interest" which outweighed the degree of impairment of free exercise rights. This majority opinion implied that the degree of burden on religious activity was balanced against the importance of the state interest and the degree to which it would be impaired by an accommodation for the religious practice. Relevant to such an inquiry is the importance of the state's interest [is it a "compelling" one?] and the degree to which there are alternative means to achieve it which do not burden religious practices [least restrictive means are required].

In *Sherbert* the majority found that the denial of unemployment benefits was invalid under its two part test. First, there was a significant coercive effect on the practice of religion because the Sabbatarian was forced to make a choice between receiving state benefits or following her beliefs. Second, no compelling or overriding interest in the regulation was shown by the state. The state claimed only that this restriction avoided fraudulent claims, but this contention had not been raised in the state courts and was not sustained by the record.[24] Additionally, even if the avoidance of false claims were assumed *arguendo* to be a compelling interest there had been no demonstration that alternative means of avoiding fraud were not available. Thus there was no demonstration by the state that the denial of benefits was necessary to promote a compelling interest and, therefore, the state was required to exempt workers with religious objections to Saturday work from its requirement that they be available for work on Saturdays.

It is interesting that the majority opinion noted that the case was not one where "an employee's religious connections made her a nonproductive member of society."[25] This language indicates that the state would not have to give benefits to those who were permanently unemployable because of their religious beliefs since that would interfere with the state's goal of providing benefits to those in-

voluntarily unemployed but available for work. While the state might have to accommodate certain religious practices which it had no real need to burden, it would not be required to abandon the goal of its program in order to accommodate everyone who might be unemployed for religious reasons.

In *Thomas v. Review Board*[26] the Court was required to determine the validity of an individual's claim that he was acting on the basis of a religious belief when a state asserted that the motivation for his action was nonreligious. Mr. Thomas, a Jehovah's Witness, quit his job when his employer transferred him from a metal foundry to a factory department that produced parts for military tanks and gave him no opportunity to transfer to another job. Thomas testified that he believed his religion prohibited him from working on war materials although he had been advised by at least one fellow employee who was a friend and a Jehovah's Witness that such work did not violate the principles of the religion. Thomas was denied unemployment compensation because state law precluded the granting of benefits to a person who voluntarily terminated his employment for reasons other than "good cause [arising] in connection with [his] work." The unemployment compensation hearing officer and state review board found that Thomas had left his job for religious reasons but that he did not qualify for benefits under the statute.

The state supreme court found that the denial of benefits for voluntary termination of employment did not violate the free exercise clause for three reasons: (1) Thomas's belief was more a "personal philosophical choice" than a religious belief; (2) the burden on Thomas's religious belief was only "indirect"; and (3) the granting of benefits only to persons who voluntarily left employment for religious reasons would violate the establishment clause. The United States Supreme Court had little difficulty finding that the denial of benefits to Thomas violated the free exercise clause; only Justice Rehnquist would have up-

---

24. 374 U.S. at 407, 83 S.Ct. at 1795–96.

25. 374 U.S. at 410, 83 S.Ct. at 1797.

26. 450 U.S. 707, 101 S.Ct. 1425, 67 L.Ed.2d 624 (1981).

held the state supreme court and denied the claim.[27]

The majority opinion in *Thomas* was written by Chief Justice Burger. The Chief Justice avoided ruling on what type of beliefs were "religious," although the majority opinion indicated that judges had to accept an individual's assertion that his belief or motivation for his actions was religious so long as the person asserts the claim in good faith and so long as the belief could arguably be termed religious:

> Courts should not undertake to dissect religious beliefs because the believer admits that he is "struggling" with his position or because his beliefs are not articulated with the clarity and precision that a more sophisticated person might employ ... one can, of course, imagine an asserted claim so bizarre, so clearly nonreligious in motivation, as not to be entitled to protection under the Free Exercise Clause; but that is not the case here, and the guarantee of free exercise is not limited to beliefs which are shared by all members of a religious sect. ... Courts are not arbiters of scriptural interpretation.

The narrow function of a reviewing court in this context is to determine whether there was an appropriate finding that petitioner terminated his work because of an honest conviction that such work was forbidden by his religion....

On this record, it is clear that Thomas terminated his employment for religious reasons.[28]

Once Thomas' reasons were found to be religious, the case was easily disposed of under the First Amendment. Conditioning a significant benefit upon conduct prohibited by a religious belief places a substantial burden on the individual regardless of whether the burden can be labeled direct or indirect.[29] The state's asserted interests in denying benefits to those leaving employment for religious reasons were the avoidance of large scale unemployment and the avoidance of employer inquiries into religious beliefs. However, the state was unable to prove that granting benefits to such persons would lead to either widespread unemployment or detailed questioning of beliefs by employers. Thus, the Court held that "[n]either of the interests advanced is sufficiently compelling to justify the burden upon Thomas' religious liberty."[30] On the basis of *Sherbert v. Verner* the majority opinion by Chief Justice Burger found that the granting of an exception to the conditions for unemployment compensation based upon religious objectives did not promote the establishment of religion but only moved the government to a position of neutrality toward religious beliefs.[31]

The *Sherbert* and *Thomas* decisions were reaffirmed and applied in *Hobbie v. Unemployment Appeals Commission of Florida*.[32] Ms. Hobbie had worked for an employer for over two years before she became a member of a religion that prohibited work from sundown on Friday until sundown on Saturday. Because of her newly formed religious belief, she informed her employer that she could no longer work on Friday evenings or during the day on Saturday. She was then discharged from her employment because of her refusal to work at those times. State law granted full unem-

---

27. 450 U.S. at 720, 101 S.Ct. at 1433 (Rehnquist, J., dissenting). Justice Blackmun joined parts of the majority opinion by Chief Justice Burger and concurred in the result but not the Court's opinion holding that the granting of benefits to religious persons under these circumstances did not constitute an aid to religion. 450 U.S. at 720, 101 S.Ct. at 1433 (Blackmun, J., concurring).

28. 450 U.S. at 715–716, 101 S.Ct. at 1430–31.

In Frazee v. Illinois Department of Employment Security, 489 U.S. 829, 109 S.Ct. 1514, 103 L.Ed.2d 914 (1989) the Justices unanimously held that a state violated the free exercise clause by refusing to grant an exemption from an unemployment compensation system requirement regarding availability for work on all days of the week to an individual who sincerely claimed that his religious

beliefs prohibited him from working on Sunday solely because the individual was not a member of an organized church, sect, or denomination. The Court in *Frazee* noted that, in this case, the sincerity and religious nature of the individual's claim for an exemption was admitted by the government. 489 U.S. at 833, 109 S.Ct. at 1517.

29. 450 U.S. at 717–18, 101 S.Ct. at 1431–32.

30. 450 U.S. at 719, 101 S.Ct. at 1432.

31. Thomas v. Review Bd., 450 U.S. 707, 719, 101 S.Ct. 1425, 1432–33, 67 L.Ed.2d 624 (1981), on remand 421 N.E.2d 642 (Ind.1981).

32. 480 U.S. 136, 107 S.Ct. 1046, 94 L.Ed.2d 190 (1987).

ployment compensation benefits only to persons who became "unemployed through no fault of their own." Ms. Hobbie was found by the state to be ineligible for full unemployment compensation benefits because she had been discharged for her refusal to work her scheduled shifts.

The Supreme Court, by an eight to one vote, found that the *Thomas* and *Sherbert* decisions were indistinguishable from this case, even though the woman formed her religious beliefs following her acceptance of the employment and her previous acceptance of work on Fridays and Saturdays. Justice Brennan, writing for six members of the Court, applied the balancing test that had been used in the *Thomas* and *Sherbert* cases. According to the majority opinion by Justice Brennan, a state law which denied a benefit to an individual because of her sincerely held religious belief imposed a significant burden on the individual's right to free exercise of religion and must be subjected to "strict scrutiny". Once the individual had shown that her free exercise rights were burdened, it was the state's obligation to demonstrate that it had a "compelling interest" that outweighed the burden on the individual's free exercise clause rights.

As in *Sherbert* and *Thomas*, the majority in *Hobbie* found that the state did not have a compelling interest in denying unemployment compensation benefits to persons who had to leave their employment because of religious beliefs. The awarding of unemployment com-

pensation benefits to persons who voluntarily left their jobs for religious reasons, or to persons who were terminated from their employment due to their inability to comply with employment regulations because of their religious beliefs,[33] did not violate establishment clause principles because the granting of benefits merely accommodated religious practices and did not have the primary effect of promoting religion or entangling the state with religious activities or principles.[34]

It should be noted that in *Sherbert*, *Thomas*, and *Hobbie* the unemployment compensation claimant had not violated any criminal law of general applicability; the claimant in each case was only asking for an exemption from a condition to the receipt of unemployment compensation. If a state had a law that denied a person unemployment compensation if he had lost his employment due to his commission of a crime, the government interest in deterring the criminal activity would justify denying unemployment compensation to that person.[35]

Compulsory Education—The *Yoder* Decision. In *Wisconsin v. Yoder*[36] the Court held Wisconsin could not require members of the Amish Church to send their children to public school after the eighth grade. In 1990, the Supreme Court described *Yoder* as a case that was not based upon the free exercise clause alone, but, rather, upon the free exercise clause and the constitutional "right of parents ... to direct the education of their children."[37]

---

33. Justice Brennan's majority opinion found that the government could not inquire into whether the religious beliefs were true or reasonable, but he did not explain whether the government could inquire into whether the beliefs were sincerely held. Hobbie v. Unemployment Appeals Commission of Florida, 480 U.S. 136, 144 n. 9, 107 S.Ct. 1046, 1051 n. 9, 94 L.Ed.2d 190 (1987). The problem of determining whether an individual is sincerely asserting religious beliefs is examined in § 17.11 of this Treatise.

34. Justice Brennan's majority opinion in *Hobbie* found that this decision was not inconsistent with Estate of Thornton v. Caldor, Inc., 472 U.S. 703, 105 S.Ct. 2914, 86 L.Ed.2d 557 (1985) in which the Supreme Court invalidated a state statute that gave employees an absolute right to refuse to work on their Sabbath. Justice Brennan found that granting the unemployment compensation benefits did not result in an impermissible shifting of burdens to employers and coworkers to enable an individual to

exercise her religion. Hobbie v. Unemployment Appeals Commission of Florida, 480 U.S. 136, 145 n. 11, 107 S.Ct. 1046, 1051 n. 11, 94 L.Ed.2d 190 (1987). For an analysis of the establishment clause and free exercise clause problems inherent in regulating employment practices (other than the rulings regarding qualifications for unemployment benefits) see §§ 17.13, 17.15.

35. Employment Division v. Smith, 494 U.S. 872, 110 S.Ct. 1595, 108 L.Ed.2d 876 (1990) (this case is examined at the beginning of this section and in § 17.6).

36. 406 U.S. 205, 92 S.Ct. 1526, 32 L.Ed.2d 15 (1972). The Court was unanimous as to the result in this case, but three Justices filed separate opinions. 406 U.S. at 237, 92 S.Ct. at 1544 (Stewart and Brennan, JJ., concurring), 406 U.S. at 241, 92 S.Ct. at 1546 (Douglas, J., concurring). Two Justices (Powell & Rehnquist) did not participate.

37. Employment Division v. Smith, 494 U.S. 872, 881 n. 1, 110 S.Ct. 1595, 1601 n. 1, 108 L.Ed.2d 876 (1990).

Although Chief Justice Burger's majority opinion cited due process rulings concerning parental rights,[38] the majority opinion in *Yoder* focused on the free exercise clause and the two part balancing test. First, a significant burden on the free exercise of religion would have to be shown. Second, this burden would be balanced against the importance of the state's interest and the degree to which it would be impaired by a religious exemption.

In finding that there was a significant burden on the free exercise of religion, the Court had to determine whether the parents' refusal to send their children to school was based on religious beliefs. As the Court noted, a claim based on a personal or philosophical rejection of secular values would not be protected by the free exercise clause. Thus, if the Amish refused to send their children to school merely to preserve a "traditional way of life", their claim would be denied. Chief Justice Burger stated for the majority in *Yoder*: "although a determination of what is a 'religious' belief or practice entitled to constitutional protection may present a most delicate question, the very concept of ordered liberty precludes allowing every person to make his own standards on matters of conduct in which society as a whole has important interests."[39] In *Yoder* the Court found that the Amish lifestyle, educational practices and refusal to submit their children to further secular education were religious. Central to this determination were the following facts: (1) this was a shared belief by an organized group rather than a personal preference, (2) the belief related to certain theocratic principles and interpretation of religious literature, (3) the system of beliefs pervaded and regulated their daily lives, (4) the system of beliefs and lifestyle resulting therefrom had been in existence for a substantial period of time.[40] It is not clear which, if any, of these factors mentioned in the *Yoder* opinion determined the presence of a "religion" or a "religious belief" as the basis for the parents' claim and the Court's ruling.

Because the Amish had shown their refusal to send children to school after the eighth grade was religiously based, the Court in *Yoder* determined the permissibility of applying the compulsory education laws to them under the two part balancing test. The Court did not use the "compelling interest" test, thus suggesting the use of a more open balancing test.[41] The compulsory attendance laws could be applied to the Amish if "the State does not deny the free exercise of religious belief by its requirement, or that there is a state interest of sufficient magnitude to override the interest claiming protection under the Free Exercise Clause."[42]

The first part of the test—the demonstration of a burden on the exercise of religion—was met by the Amish. The education of their children in the public schools beyond the eighth grade was in conflict with their religious principles and threatened the entire religious training of their children. Because there was a burden on the exercise of religion incident to a state regulation of general activity, the Court had to balance the interests of the state against those of the Amish. Here the state would have to show both that it was promoting an interest which was superior to these free exercise rights and that this goal would be unduly impaired by granting an exemption to the Amish.

The state asserted that the attendance of these children at school between the ages of 14 and 16 was necessary to their development as citizens and members of society. However, the Court found that these goals would not be impaired by an exemption for the Amish. The first eight years of formal education and the home training of young people by the Amish parents made the children both able citizens and productive members of society.

---

38. Wisconsin v. Yoder, 406 U.S. 205, 233–34, 92 S.Ct. 1526, 1542 32 L.Ed.2d 15 (1972) citing and discussing Pierce v. Society of Sisters, 268 U.S. 510, 45 S.Ct. 571, 69 L.Ed. 1070 (1925).

39. Wisconsin v. Yoder, 406 U.S. 205, 215–16, 92 S.Ct. 1526, 1533, 32 L.Ed.2d 15 (1972).

40. 406 U.S. at 215–17, 92 S.Ct. at 1533–34.

41. While the word "compelling" appears at several points in the majority opinion, it was not used as part of the statement of the test to be employed in reviewing claims under the free exercise clause.

42. 406 U.S. at 214, 92 S.Ct. at 1532.

The state also argued that its interest in the children's health and well being justified an absolute rule to grant secondary education to all children. The Court recognized that this interest would overcome a claim for religious freedom where the practice was detrimental to the health, training or well being of a child.[43] But since the record showed that the Amish children were well cared for and well trained in their community, the state's goals would not be impaired by an exemption for the Amish children.

The majority did not find it necessary to discuss the interest of Amish children who wished to attend school after the eighth grade against the wishes of their parents. Absent an actual case involving such a parent-child conflict, the Court refused to decide if the state's interest in the child would allow the government to require a parent to send a child to school at the child's request over the religious objections of the parent. In 1990, the Court ruled that the free exercise clause did not require a religious use exception from law prohibiting the use of peyote and, in dicta, described *Yoder* as a decision that was based on both the free exercise clause and the parental interest in directing the education of their

children that was protected by the due process clause of the Fourteenth Amendment.[44] Thus viewed, *Yoder* appears to create only a very limited exemption from compulsory attendance laws for families who can base their claim for an exemption on shared religious beliefs as well as on a due process-liberty argument.

Taxation. In the 1940s the Supreme Court held that persons who wished to distribute religious literature could not be prohibited from doing so on the basis that they had failed to pay a license fee.[45] Such a fee is often called a "flat tax" because the fee or tax is for a specified amount. These license fees, or flat taxes, had to be paid prior to engaging in the business activity. The 1940s decisions exempting distributors of religious literature from license fees focused on the free exercise clause. However, it appears that those rulings would protect a distributor of any type of literature from a flat tax or license fee because that type of fee-tax may be an unconstitutional prior restraint on First Amendment activity.[46]

If a tax employs a religious classification, or provides a denominational preference, the tax will violate the establishment clause.[47] To the

---

43. 406 U.S. at 229–30, 92 S.Ct. at 1540–41. In this way the Court distinguished the earlier cases relating to child labor or the protection of their health. See Jacobson v. Massachusetts, 197 U.S. 11, 25 S.Ct. 358, 49 L.Ed. 643 (1905) (vaccinations required); Prince v. Massachusetts, 321 U.S. 158, 64 S.Ct. 438, 88 L.Ed. 645 (1944), rehearing denied 321 U.S. 804, 64 S.Ct. 784, 88 L.Ed. 1090 (1944) (child labor law upheld as applied to child distributing religious materials).

44. Employment Division v. Smith, 494 U.S. 872, 881 n. 1, 110 S.Ct. 1595, 1601 n. 1, 108 L.Ed.2d 876 (1990) (discussed at the start of this section and in § 17.6 of this chapter).

45. Murdock v. Pennsylvania, 319 U.S. 105, 63 S.Ct. 870, 87 L.Ed. 1292 (1943); Follett v. McCormick, 321 U.S. 573, 64 S.Ct. 717, 88 L.Ed. 938 (1944).

46. In Jimmy Swaggart Ministries v. Board of Equalization, 493 U.S. 378, 110 S.Ct. 688, 107 L.Ed.2d 796 (1990) the Supreme Court ruled that a religious organization had no right to refuse to pay general sales or use taxes on the sales and use of religious goods and literature in a state. Justice O'Connor wrote for a unanimous Court in *Jimmy Swaggart Ministries.* Justice O'Connor found that a tax of general applicability on the proceeds of sales of goods and services did not violate the establishment clause when it was applied to the sales of religious literature. The free exercise clause did not require an exemption from such a general tax for religious activities. Justice O'Connor's opinion found that each of the taxes

invalidated in *Murdock* and *Follett* was a flat tax or (license fee) "that operated as a prior restraint on the exercise of religious liberty." The sales and use taxes could be applied to religious organizations and religious literature because "our concern in *Murdock* and *Follett*— that a flat license tax would act as a *precondition* to the free exercise of religious beliefs—is simply not present where a tax applies to all sales and uses of tangible personal property in the state." 493 U.S. at 386, 110 S.Ct. at 694 (emphasis in original).

47. See, e.g., Texas Monthly, Inc. v. Bullock, 489 U.S. 1, 109 S.Ct. 890, 103 L.Ed.2d 1 (1989) (statutory exemption from the state sales tax only for religious literature violates the establishment clause); Larson v. Valente, 456 U.S. 228, 102 S.Ct. 1673, 72 L.Ed.2d 33 (1982) (regulation of solicitations by charitable organizations interpreted to provide a denominational preference and, on that basis, to violate the establishment clause).

In Employment Division v. Smith, 494 U.S. 872, 881, 110 S.Ct. 1595, 1599, 108 L.Ed.2d 876 (1990) Justice Scalia's majority opinion cited *Larson* as authority for the proposition that the free exercise clause would invalidate a government action that attempted to "impose special disabilities on the basis of religious views or religious status."

Taxes that provide a benefit to religious and nonreligious organizations of a certain type (such as nonprofit charitable organizations) do not violate the free exercise or establishment clause. Walz v. Tax Commission, 397 U.S. 664, 90 S.Ct. 1409, 25 L.Ed.2d 697 (1970).

extent that such a tax constitutes a burden on some persons due to their religious affiliation the law would also violate the free exercise clause.[48]

The Supreme Court has never ruled that the free exercise clause requires the government to grant any person or organization an exemption from a generally applicable, religiously neutral tax that was not a prior restraint on religious activity.

In *United States v. Lee*,[49] the Court denied an Amish employer of Amish workmen an exemption from compulsory participation in the social security system. The majority opinion, written by Chief Justice Burger, first held that the employer could not claim the statutory exemption allowed self-employed individuals who had religious objections to payment of the tax. The Chief Justice first considered whether the payment of social security taxes by an Amish employer or the receipt of benefits by Amish employees from the system interfered with the free exercise of their religious beliefs. The Chief Justice accepted Lee's claim that both payment of taxes and receipt of benefits were forbidden by the Amish faith. Therefore, because compulsory participation in the social security system violated Lee's and his employee's beliefs, such compulsion constituted a burden on the free exercise of their religion.

In the second part of the opinion, the Chief Justice asked if this burden on the free exercise of religion was justified by an overriding governmental interest and, if so, whether the religious belief could be accommodated without unduly interfering with the achievement of that interest. Chief Justice Burger found that the governmental interest in the social security system was compelling. This was a nationwide system of comprehensive insurance providing a variety of benefits and contributed to by both employers and employees. The government viewed compulsory payments as necessary for the vitality of the system because voluntary participation would undermine its soundness and would be difficult to administer.

The Court in *Lee* did not seriously question whether alternative means were available to achieve the government's interest which would not burden the Amish beliefs. Chief Justice Burger stated that this taxing system was organized in such a way that it would be difficult to accommodate exceptions which might arise from a large spectrum of religious beliefs, except to the extent such accommodation had already been made by Congress in the statutes. The category of persons exempted by statute was narrow (self-employed members of a religious group which made sufficient provision for its dependent members) and readily identifiable.

The Court in *Lee* seemed to be concerned, as Justice Stevens recognized in his concurrence,[50] that granting the exemption in this case would result in numerous other claims for exemptions. Thus, the government's interest in an efficient social security system justified forcing Lee to comply with the law in violation of his faith.

In *Hernandez v. Commissioner of Internal Revenue*,[51] the Supreme Court held that denial of a deduction from gross income for payments made to the Church of Scientology as a "fixed donation" or "price" for certain religious services did not violate the free exercise clause. The Internal Revenue Code gives a taxpayer the right to take a deduction from gross income for contributions that are charitable in nature. However, the Code, as interpreted by the Internal Revenue Service, does not allow a taxpayer to deduct a payment to a charitable organization if that payment was a quid pro quo exchange for services or products. The IRS admitted, for purposes of the litigation, that Scientology should be considered a religion. The Church of Scientology required members to take "training" and "auditing"

---

48. Id. For further examination of these establishment clause and free exercise clause principles, see §§ 17.1, 17.3, 17.6.

49. 455 U.S. 252, 102 S.Ct. 1051, 71 L.Ed.2d 127 (1982).

50. 455 U.S. at 262–64, 102 S.Ct. at 1057–58 (1982) (Stevens, J., concurring).

51. 490 U.S. 680, 109 S.Ct. 2136, 104 L.Ed.2d 766 (1989).

sessions, but the Church would not provide those sessions to any member of the Church who did not pay the fixed price for the training and auditing sessions. The mandatory fixed price system was asserted to be a central tenet of Scientology.

Although the Court in *Hernandez* upheld the denial of the deduction for these payments to the Church, it used a two-step balancing approach to resolve the free exercise clause problem.[52] The majority opinion by Justice Marshall stated: "The free exercise inquiry asks whether government has placed a substantial burden on the observation of a central religious belief or practice and, if so, whether a compelling governmental interest justifies the burden." In other words, the government was required to show that it has an interest that is sufficiently compelling to outweigh the burden which it has placed on the individual if, but only if, the individual first shows that compliance with the government regulation places a substantial burden on the fulfillment of the individual's religious beliefs.

In determining whether the denial of the tax deduction constituted a substantial burden on the ability of members of the Church of Scientology to practice their religion, the majority opinion stated: "it is not within the judicial ken to question the centrality of particular beliefs or practices to a faith or the validity of a particular litigant's interpretation of those creeds." Nevertheless, the majority in *Hernandez* found that the burden on the taxpayer was not very substantial. The denial of a deduction for payments to the Church imposed no greater a burden on an individual than any income tax code provision that imposed a tax burden on individuals. All taxes paid to the government lessen the amount of disposable income that the individual has to give to a church.

The majority opinion, after minimizing the burden on the members of the Church, stated that the Court would not determine whether the burden was a substantial one. The Court found that, even if the burden were considered substantial, the burden on free exercise of religion in this case was "justified by the broad public interest in maintaining a sound tax system free of myriad exceptions flowing from a variety of religious beliefs."[53]

In *Jimmy Swaggart Ministries v. Board of Equalization,*[54] the Supreme Court ruled that a religious organization, and its members, had no right to refuse to pay a state's general sales and use taxes on the sales and use of religious products and religious literature. Justice O'Connor's opinion for a unanimous Court in *Jimmy Swaggart Ministries* tracked the reasoning used in the *Hernandez* decision. The general sales and use taxes did not employ religious criteria and they did not constitute a special tax on religious goods or activities. Because the taxes were not denominational or religious preferences they did not have to be justified by a compelling interest. The taxes did not violate the establishment clause because the general sales and use taxes had a nonreligious purpose, a primary nonreligious effect, and the collection of taxes from a religious person or organization does not constitute an excessive entanglement between government and religion.

Justice O'Connor's opinion found that the general sales and use taxes did not constitute a prior restraint in the sale of religious literature or the ability to engage in religious activity. For that reason these taxes did not violate the free exercise clause principle, established in the 1940s decisions of the Court, that required an exemption from certain occupational license fees for persons who wanted to distribute religious literature.[55]

52. The Court also ruled that the interpretation of the tax code, which disallowed deductions that were made in exchange for services or products, did not constitute a preference for some religious denominations and did not violate the establishment clause. Hernandez v. Commissioner of Internal Revenue, 490 U.S. 680, 109 S.Ct. 2136, 2146–48, 104 L.Ed.2d 766 (1989). See § 17.3.

53. Hernandez v. Commissioner of Internal Revenue, 490 U.S. 680, 699, 109 S.Ct. 2136, 2149, 104 L.Ed.2d 766

(1989) (internal quotation marks omitted) in part quoting United States v. Lee, 455 U.S. 252, 260, 102 S.Ct. 1051, 1057, 71 L.Ed.2d 127 (1982).

54. 493 U.S. 378, 110 S.Ct. 688, 107 L.Ed.2d 796 (1990).

55. 493 U.S. at 391–97, 110 S.Ct. at 697–99. See footnote 39, supra. These cases are also examined in §§ 17.6, 17.7.

In *Jimmy Swaggart Ministries* the individuals and the religious organization did not contend that their religious beliefs prohibited them from paying taxes. Justice O'Connor's opinion dismissed their free exercise clause claim but, in so doing, she appeared to endorse the use of a balancing test for free exercise clause cases. The Court's opinion stated:

"Our cases have established that '[t]he free exercise inquiry asks whether government has placed a substantial burden on the observation of a central religious belief or practice and, if so, whether a compelling governmental interest justifies the burden.'" *Hernandez v. Commissioner,* 490 U.S. 680, 698, 109 S.Ct. 2136, 2148, 104 L.Ed.2d 766 (1989) (citations omitted). ...

Appellant [the religious group in this case] has never alleged that the mere act of paying the tax, by itself, violates its sincere religious beliefs.

"We therefore conclude that the collection and payment of the generally applicable tax in this case imposes no constitutionally significant burden on appellant's religious practices or beliefs. The Free Exercise Clause accordingly does not *require* the State to grant appellant an exemption from its generally applicable sales and use tax. Although it is of course possible to imagine that a more onerous tax rate, even if generally applicable, might effectively choke off an adherent's religious practices, cf. *Murdock* [Murdock v. Pennsylvania], 319 U.S., at 115, 63 S.Ct., at 876 (the burden of a flat tax could render itinerant evangelism 'crushed and closed out by the sheer weight of the toll or tribute which is exacted town by town'), we face no such situation in this case. Accordingly, we

intimate no views as to whether such a generally applicable tax might violate the Free Exercise Clause." [56]

Three months after the decision in *Jimmy Swaggart Ministries,* the Supreme Court issued its decision in *Employment Division v. Smith (Smith II).*[57] Justice Scalia wrote a majority opinion in *Smith II* which ruled that the free exercise clause did not require exemptions from generally applicable criminal laws for persons whose religious beliefs prevented them from complying with the law. Justice Scalia's majority opinion in *Smith II* rejected any judicial role in balancing societal interests in a general regulatory law against the burdens the law placed on persons whose religious beliefs prevented their compliance. Justice O'Connor concurred in the result in *Smith II,* but she wrote a separate opener to express her belief that the free exercise clause required the judiciary to use the balancing approach that was rejected in the majority opinion.[58]

After the rejection of a balancing test in *Smith II* it appears that the Supreme Court will not require the government to grant tax exemptions to religious organizations or persons who refuse to pay a generally applicable, religiously neutral tax that does not operate as a prior restraint on activity protected by the First Amendment. However, if the Supreme Court were to use a "balancing test" in free exercise clause cases it might reverse its position in these tax cases.

Military Regulations. In *Goldman v. Weinberger,*[59] the Court held that the free exercise clause did not require the Air Force to allow a serviceman, an orthodox Jew and ordained rabbi, to wear his yarmulke while on duty and in uniform. The Air Force had a regulation which prohibited on-duty and in-uniform personnel from wearing any non-regulation items of clothing. For some years, this

---

56. 493 U.S. at 384, 391, 110 S.Ct. at 693, 697.

57. 494 U.S. 872, 110 S.Ct. 1595, 108 L.Ed.2d 876 (1990). This decision is examined at the start of this section of the Treatise.

58. Employment Division v. Smith, 494 U.S. 872, 891, 110 S.Ct. 1595, 1606, 108 L.Ed.2d 876 (O'Connor, J., concurring in the judgment). Justices Brennan, Marshall and Blackmun joined the parties of Justice O'Connor's

opinion in which she advocated the use of the balancing test, but they did not agree with her conclusion regarding the outcome of the case. 494 U.S. at 907, 110 S.Ct. at 1615 (Blackmun, J., joined by Brennan & Marshall, JJ., dissenting).

59. 475 U.S. 503, 106 S.Ct. 1310, 89 L.Ed.2d 478 (1986).

officer had worn his yarmulke while on duty and in uniform, without objection from Air Force authorities. Eventually, he was informed that he could not continue to wear the yarmulke while on duty. The majority opinion by Justice Rehnquist appeared to employ a two-step balancing analysis, although Justice Rehnquist's opinion was clouded by a variety of statements concerning the need for the judiciary to defer to military authorities concerning matters of military deportment.

The first step of the inquiry in *Goldman* presented no problem, because the regulation clearly imposed a burden on the officer's ability to conform his actions to his sincerely held religious belief. The second stage of the traditional balancing test would have required a determination of whether the government had a sufficiently important or compelling interest that justified denying the requested exemption from the dress code. Justice Rehnquist's majority opinion in part appears to apply this test and to find the interest in military discipline is a sufficiently important reason to outweigh the incidental burden on an individual's religious belief. In part, Justice Rehnquist's opinion appears to require such deference to military authorities that one might question whether there was any meaningful judicial review of the nature of the government interest in this case.

Three concurring Justices in *Goldman* noted their belief that the government's interest in requiring uniformity in military dress did outweigh the burden on the individual.[60] The uniform dress requirement avoided the need for the government to engage in a case-by-case and religion-by-religion determination of whether specific types of religious symbols or apparel could be worn by individual members of the military without undermining the military's interest in uniformity and discipline. This fact strengthened the concurring Justices' assessment of the military's interest in this case. The four dissenting Justices believed that the government had failed to show any overriding or significant interest that would be undercut by allowing the officer in this case to wear his religious apparel.[61]

In *Johnson v. Robison*,[62] the Supreme Court upheld the granting of educational benefits to veterans who served active duty but denied them to conscientious objectors who performed alternate service. In finding that there was no violation of the free exercise clause, the majority first noted that there was little, if any, real burden on religious practices which resulted from these programs. Second, the government interest in the raising and supporting of armies was of a "kind and weight" sufficient to overcome the alleged burden on the free

---

60. Goldman v. Weinberger, 475 U.S. 503, 510, 106 S.Ct. 1310, 1314, 89 L.Ed.2d 478 (1986) (Stevens, J., joined by White and Powell, JJ., concurring).

61. Goldman v. Weinberger, 475 U.S. 503, 513, 106 S.Ct. 1310, 1316, 89 L.Ed.2d 478 (1986) (Brennan, J., joined by Marshall, J., dissenting); 475 U.S. at 524, 106 S.Ct. at 1322 (Blackmun, J., dissenting); 475 U.S. at 528, 106 S.Ct. at 1324 (O'Connor, J., joined by Marshall, J., dissenting).

Congressional Response to *Goldman*. Congress responded to the *Goldman* decision by enacting legislation governing the wearing of religious apparel while in uniform. The statute, in general, allows members of the armed forces to wear items of religious apparel while in uniform unless the Secretary of Defense, pursuant to regulations, determines that wearing the item "would interfere with the performance of the member's military duties," or the item of apparel is "not neat and conservative." 10 U.S.C.A. § 774. The Supreme Court has not ruled on the constitutionality of this statute. The federal "Religious Freedom Restoration Act of 1993," which was invalidated in Boerne v. Flores, 521 U.S. 507, 117 S.Ct. 2157, 138 L.Ed.2d 624 (1997), is examined in § 17.6, and Chapter 15.

Government accommodation of the needs of religious groups or persons affiliated with the religion must be done in a manner that does not violate the neutrality principle of the establishment clause. In Board of Education of Kiryas Joel Village School District v. Grumet, 512 U.S. 687, 114 S.Ct. 2481, 129 L.Ed.2d 546 (1994), the Supreme Court invalidated a state law creating a special school district for a Village that was composed of entirely of members of one religion. The Court found this to be an impermissible preference for members of a particular religious sect, rather than a permissible accommodation for persons confronted with special problems. Three years after *Grumet,* in Agostini v. Felton, 521 U.S. 203, 117 S.Ct. 1997, 138 L.Ed.2d 391 (1997), the Supreme Court upheld the use of government employees to provide religiously neutral assistance to children at religiously affiliated schools. See §§ 17.3, 17.4, supra.

See §§ 17.13, 17.15 regarding the accommodation of religious beliefs in statutes regulating the terms and conditions of private employment.

62. 415 U.S. 361, 94 S.Ct. 1160, 39 L.Ed.2d 389 (1974).

exercise right of those who did not receive the educational benefits.

Government Administrative Systems— Use of Social Security Numbers. In *Bowen v. Roy* [63] the Supreme Court held that an individual child and her parent did not have a free exercise right to preclude a state agency from using a Social Security number to identify the child. This case involved a challenge to use of Social Security numbers in federal Food Stamp and Aid to Families with Dependent Children programs. Federal statutes require state agencies administering these programs to employ Social Security numbers in identifying the recipients of aid. Initially, the parents of the child contended that obtaining a Social Security number violated their Native American religious beliefs. Because the obtaining and submission of a Social Security number was a condition to the receipt of such benefits, the state refused to pay benefits on the child's behalf. At trial, it was learned that a Social Security number for the child (whose name was Little Bird of the Snow) had been issued very near the time of her birth. At that point in the litigation, the child's father sought an injunction to prohibit the government from making any use of her Social Security number. The Supreme Court rejected the father's attempt to prohibit the state agency from using the child's Social Security number in administering aid programs.

Chief Justice Burger announced the judgment of the Court in *Roy* and delivered an opinion which was, in part, an opinion of the Court and, in part, an opinion expressing only the views of himself and Justices Powell and Rehnquist. In the portion of the opinion by Chief Justice Burger that was a majority opin-

ion, the Court held that the government's use of a Social Security number submitted to it, or the assignment of some type of identifying number to an individual's case file in order to efficiently operate a government program, did not violate the free exercise clause. Government administrative practices do not impose a clear burden on an individual's religious belief if the government is not forcing the person to take an action contrary to her religious belief. Additionally, the government's use of the previously submitted number, or the use of a newly assigned number to the case file, promoted a government interest in operating a welfare program in an efficient and honest manner that outweighs the incidental burden on the objecting individual. [64]

The Court in *Roy* did not rule on the question of whether a federal requirement that a person obtain and provide a Social Security number as a condition for receiving aid violated the First Amendment free exercise clause insofar as no exemption was granted for persons whose sincerely held religious beliefs prevented them from meeting that condition. If a case arises where persons cannot provide an identifying number to the government because of their sincerely held religious beliefs, the government requirement would be upheld if the Supreme Court refused to use a balancing test. [65] However, in such a case the Supreme Court might use the two-step balancing test in determining whether those individuals should be granted an exemption from the condition. [66] In the first step of the analysis, the Court would determine whether there was a significant burden on the person's sincerely held religious belief. Assuming that such a burden existed, the Court would go on to examine

---

63. 476 U.S. 693, 106 S.Ct. 2147, 90 L.Ed.2d 735 (1986).

64. Most of the Chief Justice's analysis of this point was summarized in his assertion that "[n]ever to our knowledge has the Court interpreted the First Amendment to require the Government *itself* to behave in ways that the individual believes will further his or her spiritual development or that of his or her family. The Free Exercise Clause simply cannot be understood to require the Government to conduct its own internal affairs in ways that comport with the religious beliefs of particular citizens." 476 U.S. at 699, 106 S.Ct. at 2152 (emphasis in original).

65. The Supreme Court refused to use a balancing test, when it determined that the government did not have to give an exemption from a law banning the use of peyote to persons who used peyote due to their religious beliefs. Employment Division v. Smith, 494 U.S. 872, 110 S.Ct. 1595, 108 L.Ed.2d 876 (1990). However, in that case the Court did not overrule the cases in which it used a balancing test to determine whether the government had to waive a condition for unemployment compensation cases. These cases were examined in earlier paragraphs of this section of the Treatise.

66. Id.

whether the government had a compelling or sufficiently important interest to justify denying the requested religious exemption. In analyzing the government's interest, and the extent to which it would be undercut by the exemption, the Court might consider possible administrative alternatives. It also might consider whether the danger of persons falsely making a religious claim to be free from identification by number might undercut the government's ability to efficiently operate the aid program.[67] Four of the Justices voting in *Roy* indicated that they would apply a balancing test to determine whether an individual would have to submit an identifying number to the government as a condition to receiving welfare benefits if such a case were clearly presented to the Court.[68] Justice White dissented in *Roy* because he believed that prior decisions of the Supreme Court which established and applied the balancing test required granting this family an exemption to the Social Security number requirement.[69]

Government Administrative Systems—Governmental Use or Destruction of Government Property. The government does not have to justify its administrative practices under the free exercise clause, even if its actions are inconsistent with the sincerely held religious beliefs of persons in our society. In

Bowen v. Roy[70] the Court found that the government would not have to justify its practice of assigning numbers, including social security numbers, to identify the recipients of certain welfare benefits. Although the assigning of numbers to case files might burden the sincerely held religious beliefs of persons who objected to the use of numbers to identify themselves, the government was not requiring those persons to act, or to refrain from acting, in a manner inconsistent with their religion. The government did not have to justify its own practices under the free exercise clause merely because those practices were inconsistent with the religious beliefs of persons that the government regulated.

Similarly, in *Lyng v. Northwest Indian Cemetery Protective Association*[71] the Supreme Court found that the free exercise clause did not restrict the ability of the Federal government to permit timber harvesting, and to engage in road construction, in an area of a federally owned national forest, even though this forested area was sacred to members of American Indian tribes and even though the destruction of the forested area imposed a significant burden on the sincerely held religious beliefs of those persons. The majority opinion in *Lyng*, written by Justice O'Connor,

67. For an explanation of an analytical system that would assess the danger of persons insincerely claiming exemptions as a part of the determination whether the government must grant any exemption from a regulatory statute, see Freed & Polsby, Race, Religion, and Public Policy: Bob Jones University v. United States, 1983 Sup. Ct.Rev. 1.

See Quaring v. Peterson, 728 F.2d 1121 (8th Cir.1984) judgment affirmed by an evenly divided court, Jensen v. Quaring, 472 U.S. 478, 105 S.Ct. 3492, 86 L.Ed.2d 383 (1985) (per curiam). The court of appeals in *Quaring* found that a woman's sincerely held belief that the Second Commandment prohibited her from possessing a photograph was a religious belief though the woman was not a member of an organized church. The government's requirement that all automobile drivers obtain a driver's license with the individual's photograph on it was a burden on her ability to carry out her sincerely held religious belief. The court of appeals concluded that the state interest was not sufficient to deny the woman a driver's license without her photograph if she otherwise was qualified for the license. Justice Powell did not participate in the Supreme Court review of this decision. The other eight Justices split four to four in this case and, therefore, the court of appeals decision was affirmed without opinion by the Supreme Court.

68. Bowen v. Roy, 476 U.S. 693, 712–716, 106 S.Ct. 2147, 2158–60, 90 L.Ed.2d 735 (1986) (Blackmun, J., concurring in part); 476 U.S. at 724–732, 106 S.Ct. at 2164–69 (O'Connor, J., joined by Brennan and Marshall, JJ., concurring in part and dissenting in part). Justice Stevens concurred in part in the majority opinion and did not explain whether he would apply the balancing test to determine whether there should be an exemption from the requirement of obtaining and submitting a social security number. 476 U.S. at 716–723, 106 S.Ct. at 2160–64 (Stevens, J., concurring in part and concurring in the result).

69. Justice White's dissenting opinion consisted entirely of the following statement: "Being of the view that Thomas v. Review Board [citation omitted] and Sherbert v. Verner [citation omitted] control this case, I cannot join the Court's opinion and judgment." Bowen v. Roy, 476 U.S. 693, 733, 106 S.Ct. 2147, 2169, 90 L.Ed.2d 735 (1986) (White, J., dissenting).

70. 476 U.S. 693, 106 S.Ct. 2147, 90 L.Ed.2d 735 (1986).

71. 485 U.S. 439, 108 S.Ct. 1319, 99 L.Ed.2d 534 (1988).

found that *Bowen v. Roy* established the principle that the incidental burden on persons' religious beliefs caused by the government's conduct of its own internal affairs was not subject to free exercise clause restrictions.[72]

Aid to Racially Discriminatory Schools. In *Bob Jones University v. United States*,[73] the Court evidenced little difficulty in finding no violation of the free exercise clause in the denial of tax exempt status under the Internal Revenue Code to all schools that discriminated on the basis of race, including religiously affiliated schools that discriminated because of sincerely held religious beliefs.[74] Because the Court found that the schools which claimed the exemption on the basis of religious beliefs did so sincerely and that the denial of the exemption would have substantial impact on the operation of their schools, the Supreme Court weighed the governmental interest in avoiding aid to racially discriminatory practices against the burden on the free exercise rights of those schools, their students, and the parents of those students.

The governmental interest in ending racial discrimination in education was labeled both a "compelling" and "fundamental, overriding interest." The Court found that the interest of the government did not have to be achieved through "less restrictive means" because the interest asserted by the schools and their students "cannot be accommodated" with the compelling governmental interest in ending racial discrimination in education.

It should be noted, however, that the Court did not rule on the question of whether the government could outlaw the existence of religious schools that discriminated in their admissions or educational policy on the basis of race.[75] The Court ruled only that the governmental interest outweighed "whatever burden denial of tax benefits places on petitioners' exercise of their religious belief" and noted that the denial "will not prevent those schools from observing their religious tenets."

§ 17.9   Recurrent Free Exercise Problems

(a) Exemptions From Military Service

The Supreme Court has never held that the religion clauses require the government to grant an exemption from military service to persons who object to such service on a religious basis. However, it is at least arguable that such an exemption should be required if the interests of those who object to military service were balanced against the government's need for universal conscription in the same manner as other interests are balanced under the modern free exercise clause cases.[1]

---

72. Id. Justice O'Connor, in her opinion for the Court, stated: "whatever may be the exact line between unconstitutional prohibitions on the free exercise of religion and the legitimate conduct by government of its own affairs, the location of the line cannot depend on measuring the effects of a governmental action on a religious objector's spiritual development. The government does not dispute, and we have no reason to doubt, that the logging and road-building projects at issue in this case could have devastating effects on traditional Indian Religious Practices." Lyng v. Northwest Indian Cemetery Protective Association, 485 U.S. 439, 452, 108 S.Ct. 1319, 1327, 99 L.Ed.2d 534 (1988). Thus, the severe impact of the government's use of its property on the religious beliefs of the members of the Indian Tribe did not establish a basis for using the free exercise clause to test the government action.

73. 461 U.S. 574, 103 S.Ct. 2017, 76 L.Ed.2d 157 (1983).

74. Justice Rehnquist, the only dissenter in this case, dissented on the basis that Congress had not authorized the Internal Revenue Service to make such a decision, even though he agreed that Congress could make such an authorization. Bob Jones University v. United States, 461

U.S. 574, 612, 103 S.Ct. 2017, 2039, 76 L.Ed.2d 157, 186 (1983) (Rehnquist, J., dissenting). Justice Powell, concurring, agreed with the Court's constitutional rulings but attempted to limit the Court's ability to allow the Internal Revenue Service to promote "public policy" without clear authorization by Congress. 461 U.S. at 606, 103 S.Ct. at 2036, 76 L.Ed.2d at 182 (Powell, J., concurring in part and concurring in the judgment).

75. The Supreme Court has held that legislation passed pursuant to the Thirteenth Amendment prohibits racial discrimination by private schools. Runyon v. McCrary, 427 U.S. 160, 96 S.Ct. 2586, 49 L.Ed.2d 415 (1976), appeal after remand 569 F.2d 1294 (4th Cir.1978), certiorari denied 439 U.S. 927, 99 S.Ct. 311, 58 L.Ed.2d 320 (1978). The Court specifically left open the question of whether a school that discriminated by race due to religious beliefs would be governed by this statute. 427 U.S. at 167 n. 6, 96 S.Ct. at 2593 n. 6, 49 L.Ed.2d at 423 n. 6.

§ 17.9

1. In assessing the need for a religious exemption from state regulation, the court employs a two part balancing test. First, the claimant must show that the regulation

While there are early decisions which state that the war powers of the government should not be required to yield for the accommodation of individual beliefs,[2] strong considerations weigh in favor of requiring such an exemption under modern free exercise clause analysis.[3] The individual interest in adhering to religious beliefs which prohibit the use of violence would seem strong and the burden imposed on those beliefs by universal conscription is severe. Additionally, the government's interest in raising armies might be adequately met without the conscription of these persons. The possible lack of suitability for armed combat on the part of these persons and the social problems created by the forced conscription of religious objectors also indicates that no important government interest would in reality be furthered by the drafting of these persons into the armed services.

Yet the government interest in defense, especially in time of war, has been historically deferred to by the Supreme Court.[4] Thus, the Court could find that it was not the proper branch of government to weigh these individual interests against the national interest in defense. Indeed, the Court in 1971 approved the government's refusal to exempt those who objected only to particular wars and indicated that even today no exemption might be required.[5] In short, there are good arguments on both sides of this issue. Absent congressional authorization for universal conscription and a case concerning the need for a religious exemption, the question will remain unresolved.

Despite the lack of certainty regarding the need for any religious exemption, the history of statutory exemptions and their interpretation gives us insights into this clash between religious beliefs and the military powers. Even if no exemption need be granted, if the government grants an exemption to any persons who object to war on a religious basis it must do so in a way which violates neither religion clause.

Any exemption must be so broad in nature that it does not benefit particular religions and thereby violate the establishment clause.[6] Thus, any exemption must have a secular purpose, a secular effect and avoid giving rise to an excessive entanglement between government and religion. Establishment clause considerations favor broad exemption from military service for conscientious objectors as narrow definitions are likely to favor a given religion or, at a minimum, common religious beliefs which are theistic (God-centered).

In refusing anyone an exemption under a statute, the government must not violate the free exercise clause. This will require the government to grant the exemption to all whose conscription into military service would not aid the defense effort because their beliefs make them similarly unsuited for service. The government remains free to draft those whose objections to war could be differentiated on a secular basis from those it exempted from service.

The Supreme Court has refused to declare a First Amendment right to avoid military service. However, the Court has read the statutory exemption from service to apply to all persons who are opposed to war in any form on the basis of beliefs which are the functional

substantially burdens the practice of his religion. Second, the government interest in the regulation is weighed against the burden on free exercise rights. For a more complete discussion of the modern cases see § 17.8, supra.

2. See, The Selective Draft Law Cases, 245 U.S. 366, 389–90, 38 S.Ct. 159, 165, 62 L.Ed. 349 (1918); United States v. Macintosh, 283 U.S. 605, 51 S.Ct. 570, 75 L.Ed. 1302 (1931); Dickinson v. United States, 346 U.S. 389, 74 S.Ct. 152, 98 L.Ed. 132 (1953).

3. For a discussion of this and other issues raised by conscientious objectors, see Greenawalt, All or Nothing at All; The Defeat of Selective Conscientious Objection, 1971 Supreme Court Rev. 31.

4. See, e.g., United States v. O'Brien, 391 U.S. 367, 88 S.Ct. 1673, 20 L.Ed.2d 672 (1968), (prohibition of destroying draft cards upheld); Korematsu v. United States, 323 U.S. 214, 65 S.Ct. 193, 89 L.Ed. 194 (1944) (domestic detention of Japanese persons in World War II upheld).

5. Gillette v. United States, 401 U.S. 437, 461 n. 23, 91 S.Ct. 828, 842 n. 23, 28 L.Ed.2d 168 (1971).

6. Welsh v. United States, 398 U.S. 333, 356, 90 S.Ct. 1792, 1804–05, 26 L.Ed.2d 308 (1970) (Harlan, J., concurring).

equivalent of a theistic religious belief.[7] Thus, any persons who objected to all wars on the basis of sincerely held personal principles which occupied a place in their lives similar to religion would receive an exemption. Problems under the religion clauses were avoided by interpreting the exemption so that all those who objected to participation in any war received an exemption. The only ones who failed to qualify for an exemption were those whose objections to all war were not sincere or whose objections were based "solely upon considerations of policy, pragmatism or expediency."[8]

Near the middle of the nineteenth century, some states began to allow those who opposed service on a religious basis to do alternative noncombatant work in lieu of joining the army.[9] By 1864, after the federal government had taken over the administration of the armed services, the first federal statute considering conscientious objectors was passed, providing for alternate service in military hospitals. The Selective Service Law of 1917 provided an exemption from compulsory combatant service to anyone belonging to a "well-recognized" religious sect or organization whose creed forbade members to participate in war in any form and whose religious convictions were against war or participation in it. This provision was upheld by the Supreme Court in 1918.[10]

The Selective Training and Service Act of 1940 broadened the classification by exempting those who by "religious training and belief" were opposed to participation in war in any form. Eight years later, in the Selective Service Act of 1948, the exemption section was narrowed with the addition of a clarification of

"religious training and belief" as "belief in relation to a Supreme Being" and not "essentially political, sociological, or philosophical views or a merely personal moral code."[11]

The "Supreme Being Clause" of the 1948 Act was interpreted by the Selective Service System, and the Department of Justice, as excluding those whose objections to service were not based on theistic beliefs. In *United States v. Seeger*[12] the Supreme Court interpreted the statute as granting an exemption to all those whose nontheistic beliefs occupied in their lives the place of a religion.

The Military Service Act of 1967 reflected the *Seeger* decision and deleted the reference to the "Supreme Being." The exemption clause is now phrased thusly:

> [Nothing] contained in this Act shall be construed to require any person to be subject to combatant training and service in the land or naval forces of the United States who, by reason of religious training and belief, is conscientiously opposed to participation in war in any form. As used in this subsection, the term religious training and belief does not include essentially political, sociological, or philosophical views, or a merely personal code.[13]

In 1970 the Court interpreted this language to include all those whose sincere beliefs required them to refuse to participate in any war for other than purely pragmatic reasons.[14] Justice Harlan concurred in this result because he was of the opinion that the statute's restriction to only religious beliefs violated the establishment clause.[15] But there was no ruling of the Court on this issue because the new statutory interpretation avoided the question. The stat-

---

7. United States v. Seeger, 380 U.S. 163, 85 S.Ct. 850, 13 L.Ed.2d 733 (1965).

8. Welsh v. United States, 398 U.S. 333, 342–43, 90 S.Ct. 1792, 1798, 26 L.Ed.2d 308 (1970) (Plurality opinion by Black, J.).

The scope of court authority to inquire into the sincerity of religious beliefs is examined in § 17.11, infra.

9. E. N. Wright, Conscientious Objectors in the Civil War (1931).

10. The Selective Service Draft Law Cases, 245 U.S. 366, 389–90, 38 S.Ct. 159, 165, 62 L.Ed. 349 (1918). For a

discussion of the Court's position on religious issues during this period see § 17.7, supra.

11. 50 U.S.C.A. § 301.

12. 380 U.S. 163, 85 S.Ct. 850, 13 L.Ed.2d 733 (1965).

13. P.L. No. 90–40, June 30, 1967, 81 Stat. 100, 50 U.S.C.A. § 451 et seq.

14. Welsh v. United States, 398 U.S. 333, 90 S.Ct. 1792, 26 L.Ed.2d 308 (1970) (Plurality opinion by Black, J.).

15. 398 U.S. at 344, 90 S.Ct. at 1798 (Harlan, J., concurring).

utory exemption is granted only to those who oppose participation in any war and denied to those who object only to some wars.

In *Gillette v. United States*[16] a majority of the Justices found that the narrow definition of the statute was compatible with both religion clauses. The Court held that the granting of exemption only to those whose beliefs opposed all war did not violate the establishment clause. The majority found that the limitation was based on secular reasons relating to the persons involved rather than adherence to accepted beliefs. The Court found a secular purpose in defining the exemption so as to exclude in the most fair way those persons not readily available or suitable for service due to their beliefs. The effect of the statute was not religious because it served only to insure a fair process by avoiding a definition which would complicate the determination of those with such claims. The definition did not have the effect of aiding religion because it did not encourage any belief. Finally, the narrow definition avoided further entanglement between government and religion as there was less need to examine the sincerity and character of individual beliefs.

The claimants in *Gillette* also argued that failure to grant an exemption to those who opposed only unjust wars on a religious basis violated the free exercise clause. The majority opinion found that the burden on these persons was justified by substantial government interests in defense and the power to raise armies. The Justices did not view the law as a penalty against any belief or religion.[17]

The persons who were granted a conscientious objector exemption but required to do alternative service did not receive the same benefits as those who served in normal military operations. In *Johnson v. Robison*,[18] the Court found that this differing treatment did

not violate the First Amendment. Since the majority found both a secular distinction between the types of service and a minimal burden on the practice of religion resulting from that distinction, the Justices had little trouble in ruling that the secular governmental interest was sufficient to overrule the conscientious objector's claim for further benefits.

(b) Health and Medical Regulations

The decisions noted in this subsection involve claims by individuals that the free exercise clause entitled them to an exemption from a health or medical regulation. Today, the Supreme Court uses a free exercise clause test that would make it difficult, if not impossible, for an individual to prevail in such a case. The Court's free exercise clause standards were summarized by the Court as follows:

"[A] law that is neutral and of general applicability need not be justified by a compelling government interest even if the law has the incidental effect of burdening a particular religious practice.... A law failing to satisfy [the neutrality and general applicability] requirements must be justified by a compelling governmental interest and must be narrowly tailored to advance that interest." [19]

So long as the health regulation at issue in a free exercise clause case is a generally applicable law that is religiously neutral, the Court would not require the government to grant religiously based exemptions for the law.

Some Justices believe that the Court should apply a balancing test or a compelling interest test in all free exercise cases.[20] If a majority of the Justices, in the future were to adopt any type of case-by-case approach to free exercise clause claims, the Court might find that in some circumstances the social benefit of a particular health law are so slight that the government must grant exemption for persons

---

16. 401 U.S. 437, 91 S.Ct. 828, 28 L.Ed.2d 168 (1971).

17. 401 U.S. at 461–62, 91 S.Ct. at 842–43.

18. 415 U.S. 361, 94 S.Ct. 1160, 39 L.Ed.2d 389 (1974).

19. Church of the Lukumi Babalu Aye, Inc. v. Hialeah, 508 U.S. 520, 531, 113 S.Ct. 2217, 2226, 124 L.Ed.2d 472 (1993), on remand 2 F.3d 369 (11th Cir.1993).

20. See Church of the Lukumi Babalu Aye, Inc. v. Hialeah, 508 U.S. 520, 577, 113 S.Ct. 2217, 2250, 124

L.Ed.2d 472 (1993) (Blackmun, J., joined by O'Connor, J., concurring). Between 1963 and 1989 the Supreme Court Justices, in majority opinions, used a free exercise clause test involving both a balancing of governmental interests against individual claims of religious suppression, and a search for "compelling interests" that might justify restrictions on religious activity. See §§ 17.6, 17.8.

whose religious beliefs prevent them from complying with the law. However, such an approach to these cases would represent a major departure from the Supreme Court's most recent free exercise clause rulings.[21]

(1) Vaccinations. The Supreme Court very early in this century held that an individual could be required to receive a vaccination against disease.[22] Although the submission to such a program might violate the individual's religious beliefs, a compulsory vaccination program is a direct method of effectuating the secular interest in public health. Even when the chance of epidemics has been small, the courts have continually upheld vaccination requirements as a precondition to a child's attendance at public school.[23]

(2) Treatment of Children. American courts have upheld the right of the state to protect the health and safety of minor children over the religiously based objections of the child or his parent. Thus, courts have appointed guardians to consent to necessary medical treatment (such as blood transfusions) for children even though the treatment violates the child's or parent's religion.[24]

Similarly appropriate action may be taken against parents for the neglect of the health or safety of their children regardless of whether the parent acted on the basis of religious principles.[25]

(3) Blood Transfusions and the "Right to Die". Current developments in medicine have permitted the continuation of a person's life for extended periods of time after it is apparent that the person will never recover from some eventually terminal illness or injury. This scientific advance has raised serious questions as to whether an individual can be required to undergo such treatment or whether that person has a "right to die." This problem, in terms of modern life support techniques, has not yet been finally resolved by the Supreme Court.

There is no issue under the religion clauses unless the individual's desire to forego medical treatment and die a "natural" death is based on religious beliefs.[26] If the individual's preference is not religious in nature, there is only a conflict between personal choice relating to health and state medical regulations. Such a conflict would be resolved under the due process clauses. The Supreme Court, in one case, has assumed arguendo that the due process clause would give a competent adult the right to reject medical treatment but the court avoided ruling on this issue.[27]

---

21. In this Chapter we are only concerned with cases in which a individual seeks exemption from health or medical regulations on the basis of the free exercise clause. In limited circumstances an individual might claim that the due process clause of the Fourteenth Amendment gives him a right to refuse life sustaining medical treatment. See § 14.30 of this Treatise regarding the "right to die."

22. Jacobson v. Massachusetts, 197 U.S. 11, 25 S.Ct. 358, 49 L.Ed. 643 (1905).

23. See, e.g., Wright v. DeWitt School District, 238 Ark. 906, 385 S.W.2d 644 (1965); Vonnegut v. Baun, 206 Ind. 172, 188 N.E. 677 (1934); McCartney v. Austin, 57 Misc.2d 525, 293 N.Y.S.2d 188 (1968), judgment affirmed 31 A.D.2d 370, 298 N.Y.S.2d 26 (1969).

24. See, e.g., In re Sampson, 29 N.Y.2d 900, 328 N.Y.S.2d 686, 278 N.E.2d 918 (1972); People ex rel. Wallace v. Labrenz, 411 Ill. 618, 104 N.E.2d 769 (1952), certiorari denied 344 U.S. 824, 73 S.Ct. 24, 97 L.Ed. 642 (1952); Jehovah's Witnesses v. King County Hosp., 278 F.Supp. 488 (W.D.Wash.1967), affirmed 390 U.S. 598, 88 S.Ct. 1260, 20 L.Ed.2d 158 (1968), rehearing denied 391 U.S. 961, 88 S.Ct. 1844, 20 L.Ed.2d 874 (1968).

In a few cases a court has refused to order medical treatment which was beneficial but not related to the preservation of the child's life. See, In re Green, 448 Pa.

338, 292 A.2d 387 (1972), appeal after remand 452 Pa. 373, 307 A.2d 279 (1973).

25. See State v. Perricone, 37 N.J. 463, 181 A.2d 751 (1962), cert. denied 371 U.S. 890, 83 S.Ct. 189, 9 L.Ed.2d 124 (1962).

26. In Wisconsin v. Yoder, 406 U.S. 205, 92 S.Ct. 1526, 32 L.Ed.2d 15 (1972) the Court made it clear that exemption from regulations on the basis of the free exercise clause required a showing that the regulation interfered with religious beliefs and practices. This decision is noted in § 17.8, supra.

27. In Cruzan v. Director, Missouri Department of Health, 497 U.S. 261, 110 S.Ct. 2841, 111 L.Ed.2d 224 (1990) the Court upheld a state requirement that the parents or guardian of a comatose individual prove by "clear and convincing" evidence that the comatose patient would reject life sustaining medical treatment or nutrition if she were competent to make such a decision for herself. The majority opinion, by Chief Justice Rehnquist, assumed, but did not decide, that a mentally competent adult had a right to reject medical treatment that was protected by the due process clause. The *Cruzan* decision is examined in § 14.30(c). The *Cruzan* case did not involve any claims or issues under the free exercise clause.

Although the Supreme Court in *Cruzan* assumed that a mentally competent adult had a right to refuse lifesaving

When the objection to medical treatment is based on religious principles, however, a serious free exercise clause problem is presented. While the modern life support issue has not been resolved, courts have been confronted with cases in which a person has refused medical treatment (usually a blood transfusion) on the basis of religious beliefs. Where the person who needed treatment was a minor[28] or mentally incompetent,[29] the courts have ordered the treatment, but where the person is a mentally competent adult, there is a split among the cases as to whether the life saving treatment may be ordered.

Those courts who view the state as having an identifiable interest in the life of each person will order the treatment, for this state interest will outweigh the individual's right to freedom of conscience.[30] Some courts have taken the position that the state has no interest in protecting a person's life against his own wishes. These courts have approached the problem in a manner similar to that of John Stuart Mill, whose philosophy mandated the primacy of an individual decision to die unless a contrary state decision could be justified by a very narrow and important social interest.[31] Such an approach has led these courts to take the position that life saving procedures cannot be ordered for a competent adult who refuses treatment on a religious basis.[32] Yet it should be noted that even judges who are philosophically disposed to such a view may in fact order treatment when the patient indicates that he wants to live but that he simply will not sign the required consent forms.[33]

The Supreme Court has not resolved this issue, no final opinion can be given regarding the propriety of such orders.

§ 17.10   Sunday Closing Laws

In four companion decisions the Supreme Court upheld "Sunday closing laws" over objections based on the establishment clause, the free exercise clause, and the due process and equal protection clauses.[1] These laws prohibited most forms of commercial activity on Sundays. Several forms of retail commercial activities were allowed to operate on Sunday but these classifications were easily upheld.

Absent consideration under the religion clauses, the goal of providing a uniform day of rest must be held to be a legitimate government goal for the purposes of the due process and equal protection clauses. To rule otherwise would involve a return to the position that it is not a lawful end of government to regulate the hours and conditions of labor. The issue under the equal protection clause was whether the exemptions were reasonable in view of the legislative goal. Because the state laws involved purely economic legislation the classification had to be upheld as long as it

---

medical treatment, the Supreme Court later upheld, against both due process and equal protection attacks, laws that prohibited physicians or other persons from assisting an individual to commit suicide. Washington v. Glucksberg, 521 U.S. 702, 117 S.Ct. 2258, 138 L.Ed.2d 772 (1997) (prohibition of assisted suicide does not violate due process clause); Vacco v. Quill, 521 U.S. 793, 117 S.Ct. 2293, 138 L.Ed.2d 834 (1997) (statutory provisions allowing individuals, under certain circumstances, to refuse lifesaving medical treatment, but prohibiting assisted suicide, do not violate the equal protection clause).

28. See notes 24, 25 of this section, supra.

29. See, e.g., Application of the President and Directors of Georgetown College, 331 F.2d 1000 (D.C.Cir. 1964), rehearing denied 331 F.2d 1010 (D.C.Cir.1964), certiorari denied 377 U.S. 978, 84 S.Ct. 1883, 12 L.Ed.2d 746 (1964); see also Winters v. Miller, 446 F.2d 65 (2d Cir.1971), certiorari denied 404 U.S. 985, 92 S.Ct. 450, 30 L.Ed.2d 369 (1971).

30. See, e.g., John F. Kennedy Memorial Hosp. v. Heston, 58 N.J. 576, 279 A.2d 670 (1971); United States v. George, 239 F.Supp. 752 (D.Conn.1965).

31. J. S. Mill, On Liberty 9–10 (Crofts Classics ed.).

32. See In re Brooks' Estate, 32 Ill.2d 361, 205 N.E.2d 435 (1965); see also the opinion of Judge (now Chief Justice) Burger in Application of the President and Directors of Georgetown College, 331 F.2d 1010, 1015 (D.C.Cir.1964) (Petition for rehearing en banc—Burger, J., dissenting). State court decisions regarding a "right to die" are cited in § 14.30(c).

33. Application of the President and Directors of Georgetown College, 331 F.2d 1000, 1010 (D.C.Cir.1964) (Wright, J.), certiorari denied 377 U.S. 978, 84 S.Ct. 1883, 12 L.Ed.2d 746 (1964).

§ 17.10

1. McGowan v. Maryland, 366 U.S. 420, 81 S.Ct. 1101, 6 L.Ed.2d 393 (1961); Two Guys from Harrison-Allentown, Inc. v. McGinley, 366 U.S. 582, 81 S.Ct. 1135, 6 L.Ed.2d 551 (1961); Braunfeld v. Brown, 366 U.S. 599, 81 S.Ct. 1144, 6 L.Ed.2d 563 (1961); Gallagher v. Crown Kosher Super Market, 366 U.S. 617, 81 S.Ct. 1122, 6 L.Ed.2d 536 (1961).

was arguable that it related to the legitimate state end.[2]

The question of whether these laws violated the establishment clause received the most comprehensive analysis in *McGowan v. Maryland*.[3] Writing for the majority, Chief Justice Warren found that the present "purpose and effect" of these laws was not religious, even though the laws originally had a religious character. Crucial to the majority determination of this question was the history of these laws. Despite their religious origin, such laws had existed in Virginia following the passage of the act for religious freedom that embodied the views of Jefferson and Madison. The existence of such legislation in virtually every one of the original states, including Virginia, detracted from the view that the Amendment was necessarily incompatible with all Sunday closing laws.

If those laws had retained their religious character, the majority would nevertheless have found them invalid as an attempt to advance religion, but the history of these laws showed that they had become non-religious over the years. Sunday closing laws now appeared in some form in every state and these laws had the support of labor and trade associations as measures for the health and welfare of commercial workers. Modern statutory programs appeared to be designed to insure a uniform day of rest and noncommercial activity.

Undoubtedly Sunday closing laws made attendance at religious services easier for workers of majority Christian sects. However, given the secular purpose of the law, this was seen only as an effect which happened to coincide with certain religious beliefs and not a real aid to those religions. To hold otherwise would be to require the state to pursue its goal of establishing a uniform day of rest by choosing a day when the least number of people might use the time to attend religious services. In the Court's view such a result would be hostile to the public welfare without promoting the separation of church and state.

While a majority of the Justices had little trouble in upholding these laws against a general establishment clause challenge,[4] a much more difficult problem was presented by the application of these laws to Sabbatarians. But, as we have seen, the Court held that the state's interest in promoting a uniform day of rest justified the incidental economic burden on these people.[5]

§ 17.11 Inquiries Into Religious Frauds

A question may arise in some cases as to whether an individual is seeking to perpetrate a fraud on others through the false representation of religious beliefs. It is clear that the religion clauses forbid an inquiry by any branch of government, including the courts, into the truth or falsity of asserted religious beliefs. However, it is not clear when an inquiry may be made as to whether an individual is sincerely advocating a religious doctrine (regardless of the truth or falsity of that doctrine) or falsely professing such a belief for fraudulent purposes.

In *United States v. Ballard*[1] the defendants were charged with using the mail to obtain money by fraud. The two defendants, Edna and Donald Ballard, claimed that they had been made divine messengers by "Saint Germain" who was Gary Ballard when he (Gary Ballard) was alive. They represented themselves as the divine messengers and teachers of the "I am" movement with powers to heal many diseases, including some classified medically as incurable. The indictment charged that they "well knew" that these representations were false and that they made the representations to fraudulently collect donations

---

2. McGowan v. Maryland, 366 U.S. 420, 425–28, 81 S.Ct. 1101, 1104–06, 6 L.Ed.2d 393 (1961).

3. Id.

4. Justice Douglas was the only one who would have held that the laws were invalid under the establishment clause, 366 U.S. at 561, 81 S.Ct. at 1218 (Douglas, J., dissenting).

5. Free exercise clause claims are examined in § 17.8, supra.

§ 17.11

1. 322 U.S. 78, 64 S.Ct. 882, 88 L.Ed. 1148 (1944).

from their followers for themselves. The district court had submitted to the jury the question of whether the defendants in good faith believed the representations. The trial judge, however, did not submit to the jury any issue as to the truth or falsity of the representations. The Court of Appeals reversed the defendants' convictions on the basis that it was necessary to prove that the representations were in fact false. The Supreme Court in turn reversed the Court of Appeals decision.

In an opinion by Justice Douglas, a majority of the Justices held that the guarantees against the establishment of any creed and the assurance of the free exercise of any religion constituted a prohibition of inquiries into the truth or falsity of an asserted religious belief. To hold otherwise would allow a trial for heresy. The majority noted that any religion could be made the subject of such a trial, but that we are free to believe what we cannot prove. The "falsity" may rest only in the views of more common faiths rather than in any absolute definition of true religion. But while holding that a court could never inquire into the falsity of a religious belief, the Supreme Court did not rule on whether a court could inquire into whether the defendant honestly held the belief. This issue was never ruled on by the Court, for when the case was returned to it a majority of the Justices reversed the indictment because of the exclusion of women from the jury.[2]

Justice Jackson dissented from the remanding of the case to the circuit court because he found that any inquiry into religious "fraud" was prohibited by the First Amendment.[3] He argued that to allow inquiry into a defendant's good faith in asserting a belief was not materially different from a testing of the belief itself. Unless one proves that the asserted religion is not worthy of belief it is not likely that anyone will be convinced of a defendant's bad faith. Additionally, the possibility that government might begin testing when "preachers" lack

true belief is in itself dangerous to religious freedom.

Justice Jackson noted that a purely secular fraud such as using, for private purposes, money solicited for building a church could be prosecuted since the prosecution would not involve the testing of beliefs. But to find that a would-be religious leader was getting money for his general support through fraud because he did not really believe what he preached could endanger, or "chill", every religious teacher of any faith. That people may give their money or, more importantly, their minds and hopes to religions of dubious merit preached by persons with questionable faith is the price we pay for religious freedom.

It is not at all clear whether a majority of the Justices would accept the Jackson position that the sincerity of one asserting a religious belief may not be put in issue in a prosecution for fraud. However, two points must be noted in relation to both the *Ballard* opinion and Justice Jackson's dissent. First, the inability to inquire into religious beliefs does not prevent the outlawing of actions based on those beliefs. Thus, the issue of whether the government may ban the taking of money for curing cancer by any means other than accepted medical procedure has no relation to an inquiry into religious beliefs. If the government prohibits the act (regardless of whether it is done on a religious basis) there is no inquiry into the merit of any religious belief. The only issue is whether the prohibition of this activity violates the free exercise rights of those who believe in faith healing.[4]

Second, even if the Court were to adopt the Jackson view, the sincerity of one who requested a religious exemption from some general regulation might still be tested by government agencies or the courts. Justice Jackson only took the position that the government could not prosecute a person for his failure to truly believe in some religious principle. He did not examine the question of whether any-

---

2. Ballard v. United States, 329 U.S. 187, 67 S.Ct. 261, 91 L.Ed. 181 (1946).

3. United States v. Ballard, 322 U.S. 78, 92, 64 S.Ct. 882, 889, 88 L.Ed. 1148 (1944) (Jackson, J., dissenting).

4. This is a basic issue in all claims raised under the free exercise clause, see §§ 17.6–17.9, supra.

one who seeks a benefit from government because of his religious beliefs must be taken at his word.

For example, if a person claims the right to be exempted from work on Saturday because he is a Sabbatarian, may the unemployment compensation agency inquire as to whether he honestly holds the belief? This question was not answered in *Sherbert v. Verner*[5] where Sabbatarians were exempted from the six-day work requirement as the issue had not been raised in the case. However, in the draft exemption cases the Court assumed that the sincerity of one seeking a conscientious objection exemption could be tested both by the draft boards and the courts.[6] There would seem to be merit in allowing these tests of sincerity when the person seeks to use his religious beliefs in this manner—as a sword rather than a shield.

In this situation the law allows for a special treatment of some individuals in order to accommodate their religious beliefs. This promotion of the values of the free exercise clause is only applicable where the person in fact does want to practice a religion. There is little or no danger of persecuting unorthodox beliefs here as the individual has requested the exemption. Thus, it is possible that the Court might adopt the Jackson view and prohibit inquiries into the sincerity of one asserting a religious belief where the action is one relating to misrepresentation of religious teaching to others, while requiring those seeking a religious exemption from secular regulatory statutes to demonstrate their sincerity in the asserted religious belief.[7] Of course, in neither case could the agency or the court inquire into the truth or falsity of the belief itself—that is clearly barred by the decision in *Ballard*.

The Court's decisions concerning unemployment compensation appear to assume the va-lidity of testing the sincerity of claimants for religious exemptions from laws of general applicability. In *Thomas v. Review Board*[8] the Supreme Court held that a state could not deny unemployment compensation to an individual who quit his job when his employer transferred him to a department that produced military equipment and gave him no opportunity to transfer to another job. The condition for unemployment compensation that required a claimant not to have voluntarily left his employment could not be applied to this individual, because his resignation was mandated by his religious beliefs. The state court had denied Thomas an exemption (from the statutory denial of benefits to persons who resigned from a job) because it found that his belief was no more than a personal choice. Thomas was a Jehovah's Witness who admitted that he was "struggling" with his beliefs; he admitted that other members of the religion to which he belonged did not believe that working on the production of military equipment was barred by their religion. The Supreme Court, in an opinion by Chief Justice Burger, stated that the Court would assume that the claimant's beliefs were sincere, because the record showed no basis for disputing the individual's sincerity. Although the Chief Justice's majority opinion did not define the types of beliefs that would be "religious," the majority opinion stated that: "one can, of course, imagine an asserted claim so bizarre, so clearly nonreligious in motivation, as not to be entitled to protection under the Free Exercise Clause; but that is not the case here, and the guarantee of free exercise is not limited to beliefs which are shared by all members of a sect.... The narrow function of a review court in this context is to determine whether there was an appropriate finding that petitioner terminated his work because of an honest conviction that such work was forbidden by his religion."[9]

---

5. 374 U.S. 398, 83 S.Ct. 1790, 10 L.Ed.2d 965 (1963). The majority opinion noted that it was not necessary to decide this issue. 374 U.S. at 407–08, 83 S.Ct. at 1795–96.

6. These cases are examined in § 17.9(a), supra.

7. For citations to secondary authorities on this point, see the multi-volume edition of this treatise: R. Rotunda & J. Nowak, Treatise On Constitutional Law: Substance and Procedure § 21.11 (3rd ed. 1999, with annual supplements).

8. 450 U.S. 707, 101 S.Ct. 1425, 67 L.Ed.2d 624 (1981).

9. 450 U.S. at 715–716, 101 S.Ct. at 1430–31. This case, and other cases regarding unemployment compensation statutes and the need to grant exceptions to persons who cannot comply with the conditions in such statutes on the basis of their religious beliefs are examined in § 17.8.

In *Frazee v. Illinois Department of Employment Security* [10] the Supreme Court examined a state court's refusal to grant an exemption to an unemployment compensation requirement that a claimant be available for work on seven days a week to a person who sincerely asserted that he could not work on Sunday due to his beliefs "as a Christian", but who was not a member of an organized church, sect, or denomination. The state courts had ruled that a religious exemption to the work availability requirement would only be given to a person who was a member of an organized church, sect, or denomination. The Justices of the United States Supreme Court unanimously held that requiring membership in a recognized church or sect (as a condition for receiving the exemption) violated the free exercise clause. Justice White's opinion for the Court in *Frazee* stated: "there is no doubt that the only beliefs rooted in religion are protected by the Equal Protection Clause ... purely secular views do not suffice." [11] The Court in *Frazee* did not rule on whether the government could test the sincerity of a person who was claiming a religious exemption to a law of general applicability. However, Justice White's opinion appears to assume that testing the sincerity of persons who are claiming government benefits is permissible. After noting the fact that only religious beliefs were protected by the free exercise clause, Justice White's opinion stated: "nor do we underestimate the difficulty of distinguishing between religious and secular convictions and in determining whether a professed belief is sincerely held. States are clearly entitled to assure themselves that there is an ample predicate for invoking the free exercise clause. We do not face problems

about sincerity or about the religious nature of Frazee's conviction, however. The courts below did not question his sincerity, and the state concedes it." [12]

Some testing of sincerity may be compatible with the restrictions of the establishment and free exercise clause. It appears that the Justices believe that it is possible to test the sincerity of an individual who claims a religious exemption in a manner that avoids endangering the values of the free exercise and establishment clauses. [13]

§ 17.12   State Involvement in Ecclesiastical Disputes

When there is a dispute between factions of a religious organization, one or more of the parties may seek resolution of the dispute by a state court. Of course, the government cannot declare which party is correct in matters of religion, for that would violate the principles of both religion clauses. A judicial declaration of such matters would simultaneously establish one religious view as correct for the organization while inhibiting the free exercise of the opposing belief. Yet when the opposing groups both claim the church property the state will have to make some judgment as to who is entitled to possession. This must be done under carefully circumscribed rules which guarantee the avoidance of civil court rulings on matters of religious belief.

Where the disputed property is subject to some express condition in a deed, a court can rule on the occurrence of the condition if that does not involve a ruling on religious matters. Thus, if a building was deeded to a church for

---

10. 489 U.S. 829, 109 S.Ct. 1514, 103 L.Ed.2d 914 (1989).

11. 489 U.S. at 833, 109 S.Ct. at 1517 (internal quotations omitted), in part quoting Thomas v. Review Board, 450 U.S. 707, 713, 101 S.Ct. 1425, 1430, 67 L.Ed.2d 624 (1981).

12. Frazee v. Illinois Department of Employment Security, 489 U.S. 829, 833, 109 S.Ct. 1514, 1517, 103 L.Ed.2d 914 (1989).

13. Justice White's opinion for a unanimous Court in *Frazee* quoted the language from *Thomas* that some asserted religious beliefs might be "so bizarre, so clearly nonreligious" as to not receive the protection of the free exercise clause. Justice White noted that "claims by

Christians that their religion forbids Sunday work cannot be deemed bizarre or incredible." 489 U.S. at 834 n. 2, 109 S.Ct. at 1518 n. 2. This footnote in *Frazee* would appear to give credence to the view that the reference in *Thomas* to "bizarre" beliefs only reflected a view that the assertion of such beliefs might reflect adversely on the credibility of the persons asserting them. There might be a finding that the individual who asserted "bizarre" beliefs was not sincerely asserting a religious belief. The establishment clause might prohibit a state agency or court from determining that a belief was not religious merely because it was held by very few people or was considered to be "bizarre" by a majority of the populace.

so long as it is used as a place of religious worship, a court could order the return of the property if it were used as a retail sales establishment. But if the condition in the deed was that the general church could keep the property so long as it was true to its doctrine, that condition could not be enforced. Any ruling requiring the return of such property would involve a state ruling on religious beliefs.

Most disputes center around property which is not subject to such a specific condition. In these situations two or more groups present themselves to a court and claim the right to possess and control church property. The permissible basis for court rulings in these situations varies with the type of church involved in the dispute.

Where the church group is an independent congregation, not subject to a general or higher church authority, the will of a majority of the members must control the decision. Because this church group is a self-governing unit, the only secular basis for a ruling between competing groups is based on the preferences of a majority of the members. There might be a separate secular way to determine ownership if the deed or incorporation documents specified some other form of resolving disputes which did not require the court to review religious doctrine. As it is highly unlikely that such a neutral, secular rule for dispute resolution could be found, it is only safe to assume that the majority rule principle must prevail in these cases.

Most commonly, disputes arise between a local congregation and a general church with which it has been affiliated in the past. Where the dispute involves a hierarchical church, or organized body of churches of a similar faith and subject to a common ecclesiastical authority, different principles apply. Here there are only two questions for state court resolution: (1) whether this is a hierarchical church, (2) whether the local group in the past affiliated itself and its property with the hierarchical church. If either of these

questions were answered in the negative, the local group would be an independent congregation. However, when these questions are answered affirmatively the courts must defer to the hierarchical authority. The rulings of the highest ecclesiastical authority must be enforced by the civil courts. Only in the case of clear fraud by persons in that authority could the court question the judgment of ecclesiastical authority—and even this possible exception is subject to dispute. The highest ecclesiastical authority—an assembly in some religions or a clerical superior in others—is the final arbiter of the church doctrine and authority.

Because the few decisions in this area deal with widely varying fact situations, it is important to review the individual rulings of the Supreme Court.

Watson v. Jones,[1] the first case involving internal ecclesiastical dissension,[2] was decided on common law principles rather than a constitutional basis. With jurisdiction based on diversity of citizenship, the federal courts were required to determine which of two contesting groups would be deemed to lawfully control the property of the Walnut Street Presbyterian Church of Louisville. In this case the local elders and trustees had been decreed by a state court to control the church property, even though they had been replaced by the edict of the highest council of the "Presbyterian Church in the United States of America."

The Supreme Court held that in this situation the state courts were required to follow the edicts of the highest ecclesiastical tribunal. Although the First Amendment had not yet been made applicable to the States, the decision is now recognized as reflecting the values of the religion clauses.

The majority in *Watson* found three general rules applicable to civil court resolution of internal ecclesiastical disputes. First, if property is given to a congregation with an express condition in the terms of the grant that it shall be used only to support a specific purpose, the

§ 17.12

1. 80 U.S. (13 Wall.) 679, 20 L.Ed. 666 (1871).

2. There was an earlier decision concerning property held by religious organizations but it did not examine the issues discussed in this section. Terrett v. Taylor, 13 U.S. (9 Cranch) 43, 3 L.Ed. 650 (1815).

civil courts could order a return of the property if the property is no longer used for that purpose. Second, where property has been given to the general use of an independent religious group the property must be used as determined by a majority of the society or by another manner that the group has previously established for this purpose. Third, where property has been acquired by a society or group which constitutes a part of a general religious organization, the established tribunals of that organization must be deferred to by civil courts. The right to church property insofar as it is dependent on questions of religious doctrine or ecclesiastical law must be settled by the highest tribunal or authority of the religious organization.

Two other decisions relating to church disputes were rendered by the Supreme Court prior to the application of the First Amendment to the states. In *Bouldin v. Alexander*[3] the Court held that a civil court could declare who was entitled to control the property of an independent congregational church. In this case a minority of the congregation had met and expelled the majority of the members and the trustees in whom the title to the church property was formally vested. The Court found that civil courts must follow the will of the majority of this congregational church to decide the question of legal title. While it is not clear that this decision was based on First Amendment principles, it is the only case in which the Supreme Court has been presented with a dispute over the property of a clearly independent local congregation and it follows the principle stated in *Watson*.

In *Gonzalez v. Roman Catholic Archbishop of Manila*,[4] the Court refused to allow a civil court to determine the qualification of a chaplain of the Roman Catholic Church. A testatrix had given funds to the Church to establish a "chaplaincy" to which her nearest male relative was to be appointed whenever possible. One of her descendants sought the post, and the income from the fund, but was refused

appointment by the church authorities due to his failure to qualify under ecclesiastical law.

The Supreme Court held that a civil court could not award the fund or the position to the heir as it could not disturb the judgment of the church authorities. Because the chaplaincy was a part of a hierarchical church, the rulings on ecclesiastical matters by the church organization could not be reviewed. However, the Court noted that this conclusion was true in the absence of "fraud, collusion or arbitrariness."[5] In later years this statement has been regarded as dicta. There is no clear ruling of the Supreme Court that would allow courts to review church decisions to determine if they are arbitrary.

Following the application of the religion clauses to the states, the Supreme Court was confronted with legislative and judicial attempts to grant sole control of the property held by the Russian Orthodox Church to American members of that Church. New York passed legislation which would have placed control of the church property of the Russian Orthodox Church in an autonomous part of that church in New York. This was challenged by an archbishop of the church who had been appointed by the ecclesiastical authority of the central church in Moscow. The Russian Orthodox Church was admittedly a hierarchical church to which the American groups had been joined in the past. However, formal title was in a corporation with officers who were citizens of the United States. At issue was whether the American churches could renounce their affiliation to the central church and retain the church property.

Kedroff v. St. Nicholas Cathedral[6] invalidated the New York legislation which would have given control to the American controlled sect. In the majority's view, this legislation violated the principles of the free exercise clause by interfering with the control and decisions of the ecclesiastical authority. A hierarchical church is one which is "organized as a body with other churches having a similar faith and

3.   82 U.S. (15 Wall.) 131, 21 L.Ed. 69 (1872).

4.   280 U.S. 1, 50 S.Ct. 5, 74 L.Ed. 131 (1929).

5.   280 U.S. at 16, 50 S.Ct. at 7.

6.   344 U.S. 94, 73 S.Ct. 143, 97 L.Ed. 120 (1952).

doctrine with a common ruling convocation or ecclesiastical head."[7] If state law allowed one group to take control of the property of such a church against the will of the formal ecclesiastical authority, the state would be determining the status of one faction as the "true" church. As a contrary ruling would prevent the free operation of the hierarchical church, the state must accept the decisions of the highest formal authority in the church when it resolves such disputes. This principle remains true even in the absence of legislation, for civil courts have no more power to review the decisions of a church than does the legislature.[8]

Civil courts may not make any inquiry into the correctness of decisions concerning religious doctrine. In *Presbyterian Church v. Mary Elizabeth Blue Hull Memorial Presbyterian Church*[9] the state courts were confronted with a withdrawal of two local churches from the general Presbyterian Church. The state courts applied a rule of law which granted a trust of church property to a general church on the sole condition that it adhere to the faith and doctrine which existed when the local churches affiliated with it. The Supreme Court of the United States ruled that no inquiry could be made into whether the general church had deviated from its doctrine. This question involved a decision that belonged to the hierarchical church authority, because only that authority could decide the true faith of the church. Thus, the local churches could not retain their property as they had subjected themselves and their property to church control and there was no basis for granting them the property without an inquiry into religious matters.

The state courts can resolve these conflicting claims for property so long as they do not rule on religious matters. For example, a do-

nor might grant property to a church with the provision that the property will revert to the donor on the happening of a specific condition. This condition could be enforced so long as the happening of the event could be determined without a court ruling on religious doctrine. Similarly, state law could establish a purely secular or nonreligious basis for finding title in a local church unless title had been formally granted to the general church. This law would be proper as long as the question of whether control over the property had been given to the general church could be determined without a judicial inquiry into religious doctrine. Thus, even though a local group belonged to a hierarchical church, they could withdraw from the church and retain their property when the state property law, and the deeds for the property, made it clear that the property had never been given over to the control of the general church.[10]

Courts can never question a church's rulings on matters of religious doctrine. When a church is truly local or congregational the will of a majority controls the decision. Once it is found that a group has submitted itself and its property to the control of a hierarchical church, the rulings of the highest formal authority in that church must be accepted by the civil courts.

There is the possibility that the Supreme Court may allow a further inquiry into whether the general church has replaced local authority over the property for reasons of "fraud or collusiveness." However, if such an inquiry can be made at all, the civil court could only prevent a clear theft of local church property for the personal benefit of members of the hierarchical organization.

The hierarchical authority of a religion cannot have its decisions overturned because they

---

7. 344 U.S. at 110, 73 S.Ct. at 151.

8. After this decision, the New York courts held that the American controlled faction of the Russian Church was entitled to the property even though the statute had been held invalid. In Kreshik v. St. Nicholas Cathedral, 363 U.S. 190, 80 S.Ct. 1037, 4 L.Ed.2d 1140 (1960), the Supreme Court overruled the decision of the New York court. The Supreme Court held that civil courts had to defer to the ecclesiastical authorities and that there could be no judicial review of those decisions—regardless of

whether the review was based on statute or "common law."

9. 393 U.S. 440, 89 S.Ct. 601, 21 L.Ed.2d 658 (1969).

10. Such a situation was presented in Maryland & Virginia Eldership of the Churches of God v. Church of God, 396 U.S. 367, 90 S.Ct. 499, 24 L.Ed.2d 582 (1970). A discussion of the secular basis for ruling on such conditions is contained in the concurring opinion of Justice Brennan. 396 U.S. at 368, 90 S.Ct. at 500.

are "arbitrary" or contrary to the church's own rules. In a case concerning this issue, a hierarchical church replaced one of its higher clerics and granted control of the church property to a new officer seemingly in violation of its own rules of procedure. In *Serbian Eastern Orthodox Diocese v. Milivojevich*,[11] the Court ruled that any review of the jurisdiction of the general church authorities or whether they acted in conformity with the church laws would result in undue interference with the freedom of religion. Therefore, state courts must refrain from ruling contrary to such authorities unless their decision is clearly based on principles which have no reference to religious doctrines or rulings.

The Justices were closely divided by the application of these principles to the resolution of a complex dispute between some members of a local religious group and the church with which they had been affiliated in *Jones v. Wolf*[12]. In that case the Court examined a dispute between members of the Vineville Presbyterian Church of Macon, Georgia and between some members of that local church group and the Augusta-Macon Presbytery of the Presbyterian Church in the United States. Approximately 40 years earlier, a local group in Macon, Georgia had founded a congregation and property had been acquired in the name of the trustees of the Vineville Presbyterian Church. When it was organized the Vineville Church group became a member church of the Presbyterian Church in the United States (PCUS). PCUS has a higher hierarchical form of government, as contrasted with a congregational form, but the local church property was never formally deeded over to the general church or subjected to the control of the general church according to any identifiable document.

In 1973 a congregational meeting of the local Vineville Church, at which a quorum of its members were present, voted to separate from PCUS and to unite with another Presbyterian denomination, the Presbyterian Church in America (PCA). A minority of the local

church wished to stay with PCUS and in response to the schism in the local congregation PCUS appointed a commission to resolve the dispute and found that the minority faction was the "true congregation" of the Vineville Church. There then ensued a dispute brought to state court over whether the PCUS and the local minority controlled title to the property or whether the majority, which had disaffiliated itself from PCUS, controlled title.

By a five to four vote the Supreme Court found that the Georgia courts could apply "neutral principles" of property law to determine that title remained in the local congregation and was to be controlled by a majority vote of that congregation. The majority opinion appears to be consistent with earlier Court decisions. The majority held only that state courts may examine the language of real and personal property deeds, the terms of church charters or state statutes relating to the control of property, and documents affiliating the local group with the general church and the constitution of the general church in order to determine technically if the local group had become a member of an hierarchical church and subjected its property to control of that church.

The majority opinion noted that the "neutral principles approach" was to rely only on "objective, well established concepts of trust and property law" and that any examination of the instruments of ownership that were religious documents must be conducted in a strictly secular manner to determine whether those documents technically place property ownership in the local group or the general church. The majority refused to adopt a rule of compulsory deference to the higher church authority in all instances because it felt that the neutral principles approach would involve less entanglement with religious doctrine by requiring judges to abstain from a determination as to what authority is the highest in a church organization and simply to examine the documents in a secular manner to determine

---

11.   426 U.S. 696, 96 S.Ct. 2372, 49 L.Ed.2d 151 (1976).

12.   443 U.S. 595, 99 S.Ct. 3020, 61 L.Ed.2d 775 (1979). The majority opinion in this case was written by Justice

Blackmun and joined by Justices Brennan, Marshall, Rehnquist and Stevens.

where title to the property had been formally placed.

Applying this rule to the specific case before it, the majority found that the Georgia courts could have found that the deeds, contracts of conveyance and trust, and church charters left title to the property in the local church. However, the Georgia courts had not explained how they had determined that the local church was represented by the majority rather than the minority. In determining which group would control the use of property by the local congregation the state was still required to adopt rules that did not involve an examination of religious doctrine. The state could adopt a presumptive rule of majority representation, which could be changed by a showing that the local church group had chosen another means for property control through contract or deed terms. In fact the state could adopt any method of overcoming the majoritarian presumption so long as the civil courts did not entangle themselves in religious controversy or impair free exercise rights.

It was unclear whether the Georgia courts had applied a truly neutral rule of majority ownership or a neutral examination of property and contract terms to determine if majority rule was to control under the terms of the property contracts and deeds of the Vineville Church. Thus, the Supreme Court remanded the case to the Georgia courts to determine if Georgia had a rule requiring deference to a majority of the local congregation or whether state law provided that the identity of the controlling local group was to be determined on the basis of religious principles. The latter position would require a granting of automatic deference to the general church (PCUS) because otherwise the civil court would be involved in questions of religious doctrine rather

than the following of neutral principles of contract and property law.

The dissenting Justices would have required automatic deference to the general church councils (PCUS) because they believed that only such deference could avoid impermissible entanglement between the state and religious authorities.[13] Whenever a local group affiliates technically with a hierarchical church, the dissent would subject the local group to the control of the higher church authorities with no recourse to civil courts. These Justices felt that it would be impossible to apply the Court's neutral principles approach without examining religious documents and effectively making decisions on questions of religious doctrine.

If the majority in *Jones* is correct, and the state courts can be kept to a purely secular examination of documents relating to formal control of property, then its neutral principles approach does not deviate from the analysis employed in earlier Supreme Court decisions. But if ruling on these property disputes involves government agents or judges in examining religious charters in a manner that calls for some evaluation of religious principles or doctrine, the neutral principles approach will lead to what should be deemed an unconstitutional entanglement between government and religion.

§ 17.13   Legislative Action to End Religious Discrimination in Private Employment

Although a governmental unit may attempt to prohibit discrimination against employees based upon an employee's religious beliefs, the establishment clause places limitations on the extent to which the government may force an employer to make accommodations for the religious views and practices of employees.[1] In

---

13. Jones v. Wolf, 443 U.S. 595, 610, 99 S.Ct. 3020, 3029, 61 L.Ed.2d 775 (1979) (Powell, J., dissenting, joined by Burger, C.J., and Stewart and White, JJ.).

§ 17.13

1. In this section we will examine the problem of requiring private employers to accommodate the religious practices of their employees. The regulation, or the absence of regulation, of the employment practices of religious organizations is examined in § 17.15.

Legislative accommodations of religion that do not involve employment practices, and the direct regulation of religious organizations, are discussed in §§ 17.1, 17.3.

Issues regarding the accommodation of student religious organizations that seek "equal access" to school facilities are examined in § 17.5.

Estate of Thornton v. Caldor, Inc.[2] the Court, by an eight to one vote of the Justices, invalidated a state statute which required private employers to honor every employee's desire to refuse to work on "his Sabbath."[3] The majority opinion, by Chief Justice Burger, found that, although the law was an attempt to accommodate the free exercise of religion, the law was subject to the establishment clause tests. Such legislation must have a secular purpose and a primary effect that does not advance or inhibit religion; it must not give rise to an excessive entanglement between government and religion. The Court was not required to focus on the purpose or entanglement tests, as the Chief Justice found that the law was invalid because it had a primary effect that advanced religion.

The law at issue in *Estate of Thornton* gave every employee an absolute right to refrain from work on her or his sabbath. It thus subjected employers and other workers to significant costs in order to accommodate the desire of an employee to take actions based upon religious beliefs. The statute did not require only reasonable accommodation of an employee's religious activities, or a mere prohibition of discrimination on the basis of religious beliefs; the statute did not provide any

exception for employers who were subject to special circumstances or who were presented by employee's claims that would impose a significant shifting of costs and burdens to other employees. The majority opinion, quoting Judge Learned Hand, held that a "fundamental principle of the religion clauses" was that no individual had "the right to insist that in pursuit of their own interests others must conform their conduct to his own religious necessities."[4]

Title VII of the Civil Rights Act of 1964[5] prohibits employers covered by the Act from discriminating against persons because of their religion. This statute has a great impact on the employment market because it applies to most forms of private, as well as governmental, employment and the activities of labor unions.[6]

The Act itself is fairly straightforward in its approach to this problem. It prohibits an employer from discriminating in the hiring, payment or treatment of employees on the basis of their religion.[7] Similarly, the statute makes it unlawful for a labor organization to exclude or burden a worker on the basis of their religion.[8]

---

2. 472 U.S. 703, 105 S.Ct. 2914, 86 L.Ed.2d 557 (1985).

3. The Connecticut statute at issue read as follows: "No person who states that a particular day of the week is observed as his Sabbath may be required by his employer to work on such day. And employee's refusal to work on his Sabbath shall not constitute grounds for his dismissal." Conn.Gen.Stat. §53–303e(b) (Supp. 1962–1984) quoted in 472 U.S. at 707, 105 S.Ct. at 2916. Only Justice Rehnquist dissented in this case, and he did so without opinion. 472 U.S. at 710, 105 S.Ct. at 2918 (Rehnquist, J., dissenting). Justices O'Connor and Marshall concurred in the Court's judgment and opinion but wrote separately to state their belief that the opinion in *Estate of Thornton* would not require invalidation of the accommodation of employee's religious beliefs and practices mandated by Title VII of the federal Civil Rights Act, which is discussed later in this section. 472 U.S. at 711, 105 S.Ct. at 2918 (O'Connor, J., joined by Marshall, J., concurring).

4. Estate of Thornton v. Caldor, Inc., 472 U.S. 703, 710, 105 S.Ct. 2914, 2918, 86 L.Ed.2d 557 (1985) in part quoting Otten v. Baltimore and Ohio R. Co., 205 F.2d 58, 61 (2d Cir.1953).

5. 42 U.S.C.A. § 2000e et seq. (Civil Rights Act of 1964, Pub.L. No. 88–352, title VII, § 701 et seq., 78 Stat. 253).

6. Employers with over 15 employees, most forms of government employment and most labor unions are cov-

ered by the Act. For the exact coverage see 42 U.S.C.A. §§ 2000e & 2000e–1 (as amended).

7. 42 U.S.C.A. § 2000e–2(a) provides in part:

"It shall be an unlawful employment practice for an employer—(1) to fail or refuse to hire or to discharge any individual or otherwise to discriminate against any individual with respect to his compensation, terms, conditions, or privileges of employment, because of such individual's race, color, religion, sex, or national origin; . . . ."

8. 42 U.S.C.A. § 2000e–2(c) provides:

"It shall be an unlawful employment practice of a labor organization—(1) to exclude or to expel from its membership, or otherwise to discriminate against, any individual because of his race, color, religion, sex, or national origin; (2) to limit, segregate, or classify its membership or applicants for membership, or to classify or fail or refuse to refer for employment any individual, in any way which would deprive or tend to deprive any individual of employment opportunities, or would limit such employment opportunities or otherwise adversely affect his status as an employee or as an applicant for employment, because of such individual's race, color, religion, sex, or national origin; or (3) to cause or attempt to cause an employer to discriminate against an individual in violation of this section."

In 1972, the Act was amended to include a definition of religion which also defines an employer's duties in this area. The Act now reads:

The term "religion" includes all aspects of religious observance and practice, as well as belief, unless an employer demonstrates that he is unable to reasonably accommodate to an employee's or prospective employee's religious observance or practice without undue hardship on the conduct of the employer's business.[9]

This Amendment to the Act confirmed some of the previous rulings of the Equal Employment Opportunity Commission (EEOC), which is the agency empowered to promulgate regulations to implement Title VII.[10] Employers now are required not only to refrain from discriminating against persons because of their religion but also to accommodate a wide variety of religious practices.[11]

Whether this statute, as it had been applied by the EEOC and lower courts, would withstand attack under the First Amendment remains an open question. Twice the Justices of the Supreme Court have split four to four in cases which presented this issue.[12] In its third attempt at resolving the issue the Court interpreted the statute in a manner that avoided a constitutional ruling.

In *Trans World Airlines, Inc. v. Hardison*,[13] the Court held that the statute did not require the employer to alter Saturday work schedules in violation of a seniority system established by collective bargaining. By a vote of seven to two the Court held that requiring the employer to bear more than *de minimis* costs was not required by the act. Thus the Court recognized that further congressional action of this type raises most serious issues under the religion clauses.[14]

If an employer claims that it cannot offer any reasonable accommodation to an employee who must deviate from employment rules due to the employee's religious belief, the court must determine whether requiring the employer to provide some accommodation to the employee would result in undue hardship on the employer or on other employees. When an employer offers a plan to an employee that would reasonably accommodate the employee's religious beliefs and practices, the employer has met its obligation under Title VII; the employer is not required to adopt a specific method of accommodation that is preferred by the employee.[15] This interpretation of the employer's statutory obligation to accommodate the religious beliefs and practices of its employees has allowed the Supreme Court to

---

9. Act of March 24, 1972, Pub.L. No. 92–261, § 2, 86 Stat. 103, codified at 42 U.S.C.A. § 2000e, amending 42 U.S.C.A. § 2000e.

10. At first the EEOC interpreted the statute as only prohibiting discriminatory practices and allowing the application of a uniform work week even though it burdened some religions. 29 C.F.R. § 1605.1(a)(3), 31 Fed.Reg. 8370. In 1967 the EEOC required reasonable accommodation such as granting Sabbatarians exemptions from Saturday work requirements. 29 C.F.R. § 1605.1(b), 32 Fed.Reg. 10298.

11. By far the most common issue is the exemption of employees from work on their Sabbath. However, there may be claims for exemption from religious services at business meetings, Young v. Southwestern Savings & Loan Ass'n, 509 F.2d 140 (5th Cir.1975), or exemption from dress or hair style regulations, EEOC Dec. No. 71–2620, 1973 C.C.H. EEOC Dec. 4500 (June 25, 1971).

12. In each of these cases one Justice did not participate in the decision or the remaining eight Justices were evenly divided. In such instances the lower court ruling is affirmed, normally without opinion. Dewey v. Reynolds Metals Co., 402 U.S. 689, 91 S.Ct. 2186, 29 L.Ed.2d 267 (1971), affirming Dewey v. Reynolds Metals, 429 F.2d 324

(6th Cir.1970); Parker Seal Co. v. Cummins, 429 U.S. 65, 97 S.Ct. 342, 50 L.Ed.2d 223 (1976), affirming Cummins v. Parker Seal Co., 516 F.2d 544 (6th Cir.1975).

13. 432 U.S. 63, 97 S.Ct. 2264, 53 L.Ed.2d 113 (1977).

14. In the case in which the Court invalidated a state statute because it gave an absolute right to employees to observe their Sabbath and thereby always shift certain cause to fellow employees, Justices O'Connor and Marshall wrote a concurring opinion to express their view that Title VII could be interpreted to require reasonable accommodation of religious beliefs without involving an endorsement of religion or advancement of religious practices in a way that would violate the First Amendment. Estate of Thornton v. Caldor, Inc., 472 U.S. 703, 710, 105 S.Ct. 2914, 2918, 86 L.Ed.2d 557 (1985) (O'Connor, J., joined by Marshall, J., concurring). Justice Marshall had previously expressed the view that Title VII could be interpreted to mandate a wide degree of accommodation of employee religious beliefs without violating the Establishment Clause. See Trans World Airlines, Inc. v. Hardison, 432 U.S. 63, 90 n. 4, 97 S.Ct. 2264, 2280 n. 4, 53 L.Ed.2d 113 (1977) (Marshall, J., dissenting).

15. Ansonia Board of Education v. Philbrook, 479 U.S. 60, 107 S.Ct. 367, 93 L.Ed.2d 305 (1986).

avoid the question of whether a federal statute requiring a wide degree of accommodation of employee religious beliefs would violate the establishment clause.[16]

§ 17.14 Prohibiting "Ministers" From Holding Public Office

Early in the country's history, several states by statute or constitutional provision, had prohibited members of religious orders or ministers from holding public office. By the turn of this century it was generally recognized that these laws conflict with the free exercise and establishment clauses, and—although the Court had not held them to be *per se* invalid— these laws were repealed or annulled in almost every state that had adopted them. Tennessee had, by statute, barred "ministers of the gospel, or priest[s] of any denomination whatever," from serving as delegates to the state's constitutional convention; this statute mirrored a provision of the state constitution barring such persons from membership in the state legislature. The Supreme Court unanimously found that the statute was unconstitutional in *McDaniel v. Paty*.[1] There was no majority opinion in *McDaniel*, however, because the Justices could not agree on exactly why the statute was unconstitutional. The Court had previously held, in *Torcaso v. Watkins*,[2] that the states could not require persons to take a religious oath before accepting public employment or office. This holding was based on the principle that no individual can be punished for his religious beliefs. The relevance of *Torcaso* to the Tennessee disqualification laws divided the Court.

In *McDaniel*, Chief Justice Burger wrote an opinion, joined by Justices Powell, Rehnquist

and Stevens. Burger concluded that the disqualification statute violated the free exercise clause. The opinion by the Chief Justice found that the law was not one that infringed the "freedom to believe," and, therefore, was not automatically invalid under *Torcaso*.[3] The Chief Justice noted that the history of such disqualification clauses in the original states indicated that such laws had been aimed merely at restricting acts of religious groups that would have further entangled the states with religion. The Tennessee law, however, regulated actions that related to the individual's religion, and, therefore, it was to be tested by the free exercise clause balancing test. Under this test, the state's failure to demonstrate that participation by clergy in the political process would bring about further "establishment" problems indicated that this law in fact did not promote a strong state interest. Thus, the law was invalid because it burdened religious practices without advancing overriding state interests. Burger found no reason to examine whether the state's asserted interest in furthering separation of church and state under other circumstances might constitute a permissible legislative goal.

Justice Brennan, joined by Justice Marshall, found that the statute violated both the free exercise and establishment clauses of the First Amendment, which applied to the states through the Fourteenth Amendment. Unlike the Chief Justice, Justice Brennan found that this law disadvantaged the person because of his religious belief. So construed, the law was a *per se* violation of the free exercise clause; there was no reason to employ the balancing test in such a case. Brennan noted that re-

---

16. In Boerne v. Flores, 521 U.S. 507, 117 S.Ct. 2157, 138 L.Ed.2d 624 (1997), the Supreme Court, by a six to three vote, invalidated the Religious Freedom Restoration Act, which had required federal, state, and local governments, under certain circumstances, to grant exemptions from their laws of general applicability to persons who could not comply with the law due to their sincerely held religious beliefs. The majority opinion, by Justice Kennedy, found that the Act was beyond the power granted to Congress by Section 1 of the Fourteenth Amendment. The majority opinion in *Boerne* did not address the issue of whether the Act violated the First Amendment Establishment Clause by providing preferences to believers in reli-

gions. See § 17.6, and Chapter 15, for further explanation of the Freedom of Restoration Act provisions.

§ 17.14

1. 435 U.S. 618, 98 S.Ct. 1322, 55 L.Ed.2d 593 (1978) (Justice Blackmun did not participate in the decision). A history of the use and repeal of disqualification statutes appears in the plurality opinion written by the Chief Justice. 435 U.S. at 622–625, 98 S.Ct. at 1325–27 (Burger, C.J.).

2. 367 U.S. 488, 81 S.Ct. 1680, 6 L.Ed.2d 982 (1961).

3. McDaniel v. Paty, 435 U.S. 618, 98 S.Ct. 1322, 55 L.Ed.2d 593 (1978) (Burger, C.J., plurality opinion).

quiring a minister to forego either his ministry or public office constituted a sufficient burden to invoke the free exercise prohibition against burdening religious beliefs.[4]

Justice Brennan also found that the law violated the establishment clause. He agreed that a purpose of the establishment clause was to eliminate religious divisiveness, but believed that the state could not pursue that goal through the use of religious classifications. Justice Brennan noted that this law might fail the secular purpose test, because it was at least possible that it was based on the religious beliefs of a dominant sect within the jurisdiction; but he found it unnecessary to resolve this issue.[5] The statute was invalid in Justice Brennan's view because it failed the primary secular effect test. He believed that a primary effect of this statute was the inhibition of the practice of religion.

Justice Stewart concurred in the judgment because he believed, as did Justice Brennan, that the law constituted a restriction on religious beliefs. In his opinion, such restrictions were prohibited by *Torcaso*.[6]

Justice White was the only Justice who did not believe that the disqualification law was invalid under the free exercise clause; he did not believe that the law, in any meaningful way, compelled a person to abandon the ministry. However, he found that it was a significant limitation on the right to seek elective office; many ministers would be deterred from running for office by the law, even though they would not feel compelled to aban-

don their ministries. For this reason, he found the law to be unconstitutional as a violation of the equal protection clause of the Fourteenth Amendment. In support of his position, Justice White noted that the Court had held that the right to vote and the right to be a candidate were of sufficient constitutional magnitude to require the states "to provide substantial justification for any requirement that prevents a class of citizens" from exercising these rights. He found that, while the state's interest in separating church and state might be legitimate, "close scrutiny reveals that the challenged law is not 'reasonably necessary to the accomplishment of ...' that objective."[7]

§ 17.15 Regulation of the Employment Practices of Religious Organizations

When the members of a religious organization take any action in society, they may be subject to religiously neutral regulations. When they claim that religiously neutral regulations of their commercial or noncommercial activities impose a burden on their ability to carry out the religious beliefs, the claim for an exemption from those regulations will be tested under the free exercise clause principles we have examined earlier in this chapter.[1] If employees or employers can show that a governmental employment regulation imposes a burden on their religious faith, a court must determine whether the government has an overriding interest in denying the employee or

---

4. 435 U.S. at 632, 98 S.Ct. at 1330–31 (Brennan, J., concurring in the judgment). The dispute between Justice Brennan and Chief Justice Burger regarding the proper basis for the Court's ruling in *McDaniel* may have been due to the fact that the Supreme Court rarely is called upon to review laws that are clearly intended to burden, punish or disfavor persons because of their religious beliefs. In Church of the Lukumi Babalu Aye, Inc. v. Hialeah, 508 U.S. 520, 113 S.Ct. 2217, 124 L.Ed.2d 472 (1993), on remand 2 F.3d 369 (11th Cir.1993) the Court unanimously invalidated a city law that was designed to suppress a particular religion by outlawing its animal sacrifice ritual. The majority opinion begins with the following statement: "The principle that government may not enact laws that suppress religious belief or practice is so well understood that few violations are recorded in our opinion. Cf. *McDaniel v. Paty*...." 508 U.S. at 523, 113 S.Ct. at 2222.

5. 435 U.S. at 636 n. 9, 98 S.Ct. at 1333 n. 9 (Brennan, J., concurring in the judgment).

6. 435 U.S. at 642–643, 98 S.Ct. at 1336 (Stewart, J., concurring in the judgment).

7. 435 U.S. at 645, 98 S.Ct. at 1337–38 (White, J., concurring in the judgment), quoting from Bullock v. Carter, 405 U.S. 134, 92 S.Ct. 849, 31 L.Ed.2d 92 (1972).

§ 17.15

1. The free exercise clause principles that restrict governmental actions are examined in §§ 17.6, 17.8. When considering the regulation of the employment practices of religious organizations, a court must be cognizant of the limitations that the establishment clause may place on the ability of government to accommodate religion. Government accommodation of religion is examined at several points in this chapter. See §§ 17.1, 17.3, 17.13.

employer an exemption from the regulation. When a religious organization employs persons in commercial activities that duplicate and compete with nonreligious businesses, it should not be surprising if the organization is subjected to religiously neutral business, labor, and taxation statutes.

In *Tony and Susan Alamo Foundation v. Secretary of Labor*,[2] the Justices unanimously upheld the application of the federal Fair Labor Standards Act minimum wage, overtime, and record-keeping requirements to commercial businesses operated by a nonprofit religious organization even though it was claimed that those businesses were "churches in disguise" that were means of "spreading the gospel" and used, in lieu of employees, only members of the religious group who did not wish to receive cash wages or overtime payments. This case presented no significant free exercise clause problem because the "employees" suffered no burden whatsoever from having to receive the minimum wage. The Court found that the employees, under the federal statutes, were free to accept the minimum wage in living arrangements and services and that they were free to return voluntarily any payments that they received from the religious employer back to that employer.

In *United States v. Lee*,[3] an Amish employer and his employees were required to pay social security taxes. Congress had granted a statutory exemption to self-employed individuals who objected on religious grounds to making payments for government-operated retirement and welfare systems. The Court found that the requirement that the employer pay the social security tax on the work of the employees operated as a burden on the employer's Amish faith but found that that burden was outweighed by the government interest in the efficient operation of the Social Security system. The Court in *Lee* stated a principle that is likely to be a guide for the Court in many of the free exercise clause cases:

Congress and the courts have been sensitive to the needs flowing from the free exercise clause, but every person cannot be shielded from all the burdens incident to exercising every aspect of the right to practice religious beliefs. When followers of a particular sect enter into commercial activity as a matter of choice, the limits they accept on their own conduct as a matter of conscience and faith are not to be superimposed on the statutory schemes which are binding on others in that activity.[4]

When the government regulates the practices of a religious organization, including commercial practices, questions may arise as to whether the regulation violates the establishment clause of the First Amendment. A court, in such cases, should apply the establishment clause tests which we examined earlier in this chapter.[5] Such a regulation must have a secular purpose and a primary effect which neither advances nor inhibits religion. In addition, the regulation must not create an excessive entanglement between government and religion. When a religious organization is engaging in a business activity that mirrors nonreligious commercial enterprises, one can expect that the three-part purpose-effect-entanglement test may be easily met and the government regulation upheld. Business regulations are virtually certain to have a secular purpose; it is difficult to imagine what types of general business regulatory actions would not have a primary effect that was religiously neutral. The excessive entanglement test also should not present a significant barrier to most types of regulations of commercial enterprises owned and operated by religious organizations. The involvement between the government and religiously operated business incident to the enforcement of religiously neutral commercial regulations should not endanger governmental neutrality or religious organizational autonomy.

Tony and Susan Alamo Foundation v. Secretary of Labor[6] upheld the application of the

---

2. 471 U.S. 290, 105 S.Ct. 1953, 85 L.Ed.2d 278 (1985).

3. 455 U.S. 252, 102 S.Ct. 1051, 71 L.Ed.2d 127 (1982).

4. 455 U.S. at 261, 102 S.Ct. at 1057.

5. See §§ 17.3–17.5.

6. 471 U.S. 290, 105 S.Ct. 1953, 85 L.Ed.2d 278 (1985).

Fair Labor Standards Act wage requirements to the commercial activities of a religious organization, which alleged that the seemingly commercial enterprises were an integral part of its religious mission and that the record-keeping provisions of the Act led to an excessive entanglement between government and religion. Justice White, writing for a unanimous Court, found that the regulations applied only to "commercial activities undertaken with a 'business purpose' and would therefore have no impact on [the religious organization's] own evangelical activities or on individuals engaged in volunteer work for other religious organizations." The Court ruled that the recordkeeping, and government monitoring, required by the Act did not give rise to an excessive entanglement between government and religion because the law did not give rise to governmental intrusion into religious activities. Justice White's opinion stated: "The establishment clause does not exempt religious organizations from such secular government activity as fire inspections and building and zoning regulations ... the record-keeping requirements of the Fair Labor Standards Act, while perhaps more burdensome in terms of paperwork, are not significantly more intrusive into religious affairs."

If the government sought to regulate the evangelical activities of religious organizations, or activities that involved a combination of religious and secular activities, there would be a question as to whether the law violated the establishment clause. If the law was designed to interfere with the operation of specific religions, it might be held invalid as giving a preference to some religious organizations or sects over others.[7] A religiously neutral regulation of either commercial or noncommercial activity is likely to have a secular purpose.

However, if such a law involves extensive monitoring of religious activities, it is possible that a particular law, or its application to religious organizations through a particular administrative system, might be held invalid under the establishment clause because it had a primary effect that inhibited religion or it created an excessive entanglement between government administrators and religious authorities.

The Supreme Court faced a difficult question regarding the constitutionality of the actions of the National Labor Relations Board in attempting to regulate the relationship between faculty members at religiously affiliated schools and the churches that operated those schools. However, the Court managed to avoid ruling on this issue through its interpretation of federal statutes.

In *National Labor Relations Bd. v. Catholic Bishop of Chicago*[8] the Supreme Court, by a five to four vote, held that the National Labor Relations Board (N.L.R.B.) was not authorized by the National Labor Relations Act to regulate the unionization of lay faculty members at schools affiliated with the Roman Catholic Church. In so doing, the majority opinion by Chief Justice Burger indicated that it was unlikely that the Court would allow secular authorities to engage in detailed regulation of the conditions of labor or the employer-employee relationship at church affiliated schools.

The N.L.R.B. had asserted jurisdiction to resolve questions regarding elections for union representation and union representatives at Catholic schools in Chicago and Indiana.[9] The majority stated that it would have to determine if this extension of jurisdiction gave rise to "serious constitutional questions" and, if so, whether those questions could be avoided by construing the statute to avoid jurisdiction.[10]

7. See § 17.16 regarding the invalidity of direct regulations of religious organization activities that grant a preference to some religions over others.

8. 440 U.S. 490, 99 S.Ct. 1313, 59 L.Ed.2d 533 (1979).

9. The Chicago parochial schools involved in the case were related to the training of young men for the Roman Catholic priesthood; the Indiana schools were more traditional high schools. This distinction, however, played no part in the decision. Both sets of schools were certified by

their respective states as meeting the basic requirements for private educational institutions.

10. 440 U.S. at 501, 99 S.Ct. at 1319. See also St. Martin Evangelical Lutheran Church v. South Dakota, 451 U.S. 772, 101 S.Ct. 2142, 68 L.Ed.2d 612 (1981) in which the Supreme Court construed the Federal Unemployment Tax Act (FUTA) and the Unemployment Compensation Amendments of 1976 so that non-profit church-related schools were not subject to FUTA's unemployment tax on

Chief Justice Burger noted that the Court had stressed in past decisions the important role of a teacher in a church affiliated school. Indeed, this fact has formed the basis for the invalidation of some state laws that would have allowed for government subsidies to parochial schools to offset the cost of teachers for subjects that were not sectarian in nature.[11] The N.L.R.B. claimed that its jurisdiction would only require it to resolve factual issues in disputes between union groups and the church employer and that it could avoid religious issues when ruling on teacher disputes. But the majority opinion found that a significant risk of greater and unconstitutional entanglement between the government agency and church authority would be created if the Board were to regulate this important component of religious education. The Court noted that the resolution of many disputes concerning "terms and conditions of employment" might involve inquiries into the good faith of positions asserted on a religious basis by administrators of these school systems. Indeed, the majority added an appendix to its opinion which was an excerpt of an inquiry by the Board's hearing officer regarding prayers at Catholic schools that involved the questioning of a member of the Catholic clergy concerning the nature of Catholic liturgy and its use at such schools; the majority opinion noted that this type of involvement between secular and religious authorities presented significant dangers to the values protected by the First Amendment.[12]

The majority opinion then went on to examine whether there was a clear congressional authorization of N.L.R.B. jurisdiction over parochial schools, so as to require the Court to face the issue of whether the asserted jurisdiction violated the First Amendment. The majority found the statutes might have been interpreted to allow for such jurisdiction and the necessary conflict with church operated schools, but that Congress had not clearly demonstrated an intent to bring teachers at such schools within the jurisdiction of the N.L.R.B. Therefore, the congressional act would be construed so as to avoid the constitutional question.

The dissenting Justices found that the history of the National Labor Relations Act demonstrated a clear intent to allow the Board to assert jurisdiction over all nonprofit institutions that affected commerce, including private schools affiliated with religious organizations.[13] But the dissent did not express a view on the ultimate constitutional issue because the majority opinion had avoided the issue.

Title VII of the Civil Rights Act of 1964, as amended, exempts religious organizations from the statutory prohibition against discrimination in employment on the basis of religion. Under the statute a religious entity is allowed to make employment determinations based

school personnel. The Court thus avoided ruling on the First Amendment objections to the tax and related regulations raised by the Church.

In Ohio Civil Rights Commission v. Dayton Christian Schools, Inc., 477 U.S. 619, 106 S.Ct. 2718, 91 L.Ed.2d 512 (1986), on remand 802 F.2d 457 (6th Cir.1986), the Supreme Court avoided ruling on the government's power to subject religious entities to laws prohibiting sex discrimination in employment. In this case, the Court held that the district court should have abstained from ruling on whether a charge of illegal sex discrimination by a religious school, then pending before a state's civil rights commission, violated the free exercise and establishment clauses of the First Amendment.

In Roberts v. United States Jaycees, 468 U.S. 609, 104 S.Ct. 3244, 82 L.Ed.2d 462 (1984), the Court held that a state antidiscrimination law could prohibit a commercially-oriented association from discriminating in its membership practices on the basis of gender. However, in *Roberts* the Court did not explain the extent to which the rights of

more intimate associations or religious associations could be restricted in order to end gender or race discrimination.

The Court in Bob Jones University v. United States, 461 U.S. 574, 103 S.Ct. 2017, 76 L.Ed.2d 157 (1983) upheld the denial of tax exempt status to schools discriminating on the basis of race, but the Court did not rule on whether schools not receiving government aid or tax exemptions could be prohibited from engaging in forms of race or gender discrimination that were based upon sincerely held religious beliefs.

11. 440 U.S. at 501–02, 99 S.Ct. at 1319–20.

12. Chief Justice Burger, during his tenure on the Court, provided the leadership in defining the concept of excessive entanglement so as to protect both the autonomy of religious organizations and to avoid providing aid to religious entities.

13. National Labor Relations Bd. v. Catholic Bishop of Chicago, 440 U.S. 490, 508, 99 S.Ct. 1313, 1323, 59 L.Ed.2d 533 (1979) (Brennan, J., dissenting, joined by White, Marshall & Blackmun, JJ.).

upon religious affiliation in its nonprofit activities.

Although regulation of the employment practices of religious organizations may present significant establishment clause and free exercise clause problems, the Supreme Court had little difficulty in finding that the absence of regulation regarding such practices did not violate the establishment clause. In *Corporation of Presiding Bishop of Church of Jesus Christ of Latter–day Saints v. Amos*[14] the Court found that this exemption of religious organizations from the prohibition against religious discrimination did not violate the establishment clause. The Court applied the three-part purpose-effect-entanglement test to determine the validity of this law.[15]

Justice White, who wrote the majority opinion, first found that a legislative purpose to "alleviate significant governmental interference" with the actions of religious organizations was a permissible purpose. Although the purpose might be related to religion, there was no legislative intent to promote a particular religion or religious activity in general. Second, Justice White's opinion ruled that the law did not have a primary effect which advanced or inhibited religion, even though the statute allowed the religious organizations to act upon their religious beliefs. The law did not require a private employer to favor religious employees; it did not provide a special benefit for employees with certain religious beliefs or impose a burden on nonreligious persons.[16] The Court found that "the government itself" had not advanced religion

through this statute. Finally, Justice White's majority opinion found that the law could not create an excessive entanglement between government and religion because exemption reduced the administrative entanglement between government and religion.

§ 17.16 Direct Regulation of Religious Organizations

The activities of religious organizations and their members are subject to religiously neutral regulation. Members of a religious organization who seek to take actions that are prohibited by regulatory statutes, or who claim an inability to conform their conduct to regulatory statutes because of religious beliefs, must show that the government regulations impose some burden on their ability to carry out their faith. If the regulatory statute at issue does impose a burden on the members of the religious organization, those individuals may have a right to an exemption from the statute under the free exercise clause unless the judiciary finds that the government has an overriding interest in denying an exemption from the regulatory system to the members of the religious group.[1]

Additionally, a law which directly regulates religious organizations may be susceptible to attack under the establishment clause. Government interference in the internal organization of a religious group may be held invalid if it has a primary effect of inhibiting religious activity or if it creates an excessive entanglement between government and religion.[2] A

---

14. 483 U.S. 327, 107 S.Ct. 2862, 97 L.Ed.2d 273 (1987).

15. This three-part test has been applied by the Supreme Court in almost all establishment cases since 1971. The three-part test is usually traced to the Supreme Court's decision in Lemon v. Kurtzman, 403 U.S. 602, 91 S.Ct. 2105, 29 L.Ed.2d 745 (1971), rehearing denied 404 U.S. 876, 92 S.Ct. 24, 30 L.Ed.2d 123 (1971). The test was developed in cases regarding aid to religious institutions; it is examined in §§ 17.1, 17.3, 17.5.

16. Corporation of Presiding Bishop of Church of Jesus Christ of Latter–day Saints v. Amos, 483 U.S. 327, 337 n. 15, 107 S.Ct. 2862, 2869 n. 15, 97 L.Ed.2d 273 (1987). In this way the Court distinguished Estate of Thornton v. Caldor, Inc., 472 U.S. 703, 105 S.Ct. 2914, 86 L.Ed.2d 557 (1985) in which the Supreme Court invalidated a state statute that required employers to give every employee

release from work time on the employee's Sabbath. The *Estate of Thornton* decision is examined in § 17.13 of this Treatise.

§ 17.16

1. See § 17.8 regarding the free exercise clause standards used by the Court. Religiously neutral regulations of the time, place, or manner of speech that are consistent with the free speech principles may be applied to the speech and evangelical activities of religious organizations. See Heffron v. International Society For Krishna Consciousness, Inc., 452 U.S. 640, 652–53, 101 S.Ct. 2559, 2566, 69 L.Ed.2d 298 (1981).

2. No branch of the government, including the judiciary, may undertake a direct inquiry into the truth or falsity of religious beliefs although a governmental entity, including the judiciary, may settle disputes between the government and members of religious organizations, or disputes

religiously neutral law may be applied to religious organizations without violation of the establishment clause in most instances. Such a law must have a secular purpose and a primary effect that neither advances nor inhibits religion. Additionally, the type of interaction between government administrators and religious organizations that results from religiously neutral regulation must not constitute an excessive entanglement of government and religion.[3]

When a religious organization receives funds from the government, a court must determine whether the governmental monitoring of the religious organization, which will be necessary to ensure that the religious organization does not use the aid to advance religion, constitutes an excessive entanglement of government and religion.[4]

Although it may be expected that religious organizations can be subject to many forms of religiously neutral regulation, the judiciary should invalidate under the establishment clause any regulation of religious organizations that is found to include on its face or in its purpose a preference for some religious organizations over others. In *Larson v. Valente*,[5] the Court held that a section of the Minnesota Charitable Solicitation Act, which imposed registration and reporting require-

ments upon only those religious organizations which solicit more than 50% of their funds from nonmembers, discriminated against those organizations in violation of the establishment clause of the First Amendment. The Unification Church, a religious organization heavily involved in fund-raising activities aimed at nonmembers, sought a declaration that statute denied its members free exercise of their religion and that it favored some religious organizations over others, contrary to the establishment clause.

Before addressing the establishment clause issue, the Supreme Court, in an opinion by Justice Brennan, noted that the Unification Church was a religious organization within the meaning of the statutory section in question. The State of Minnesota had attempted to force the Church to comply with a rule which applied only to religious organizations and so the state could not now claim that the Church was not a religion. The Court then went on to hold that the denominational preference inherent in the "fifty percent" classification, the statute must be invalidated unless it was justified by a compelling government interest, and unless it was "closely fitted" to further that interest: "The clearest command of the establishment clause is that one religious denomi-

---

between persons within a religious organization, on a religiously neutral basis. See § 17.12 regarding state involvement in ecclesiastical disputes.

3. Regulations of business activities that conflict with the religious beliefs of members of religious organizations which engage in those activities are examined in §§ 17.8, 17.15.

4. The tests for determining whether government aid to religion constitutes a violation of the establishment clause are examined in §§ 17.3, 17.4 of this Treatise. The governmental monitoring of the use of government funds by a religious organization, at least if the organization is not pervasively sectarian, does not constitute a per se violation of the establishment clause. Each government program that involves granting funds to, and monitoring the use of funds by, a religious organization must be examined under the three-pronged purpose-effect-excessive entanglement test used by the judiciary to determine whether such aid violates the establishment clause. See generally, Bowen v. Kendrick, 487 U.S. 589, 108 S.Ct. 2562, 101 L.Ed.2d 520 (1988) (finding that the establishment clause did not prohibit religious organizations from participating in programs giving grants to nonprofit organizations to promote social welfare goals; the monitoring of the use of government funds by such organizations,

at least if they are not pervasively sectarian, does not automatically give rise to an excessive entanglement between government and religion); Hernandez v. Commissioner of Internal Revenue, 490 U.S. 680, 696–97, 109 S.Ct. 2136, 2147–48, 104 L.Ed.2d 766 (1989) (Internal Revenue Code provision that denies charitable deduction for money given to a charitable organization, including a religious organization, in a quid pro quo transaction does not violate the establishment clause; the routine regulatory interaction between the Internal Revenue Service and taxpayers in determining whether an asserted contribution involved a quid pro quo transaction does not constitute excessive entanglement).

In Jimmy Swaggart Ministries v. Board of Equalization, 493 U.S. 378, 110 S.Ct. 688, 107 L.Ed.2d 796 (1990), the Justices unanimously upheld the application of general sales and use taxes to the sales and use of religious goods and literature. Justice O'Connor's opinion for a unanimous Court followed the reasoning used in the majority opinion used in *Hernandez*. Justice O'Connor found that these general taxes, which involved no use of religious criteria to define the transactions or persons subject to the tax, violated neither the establishment clause nor the free exercise clause.

5. 456 U.S. 228, 102 S.Ct. 1673, 72 L.Ed.2d 33 (1982).

nation cannot be officially preferred over another."[6]

Justice Brennan acknowledged Minnesota's significant interest in protecting its citizens from abusive practices in the solicitation of funds for religious organizations. However, the majority found that the fifty percent classification was not tailored to advance this purpose. There was no factual support for the state's claim that members can and will effectively control an organization if they contribute more than half of its solicited income or that religious organizations are any less able to regulate themselves than other charitable organizations. The Court also found it more plausible that the need for public disclosure rose in proportion to the absolute amount, as

opposed to the percentage, of non-member contributions.

Although he deemed it "unnecessary" (because the classification was invalid under the compelling interest test that must be applied to denominational classifications), Justice Brennan also applied the three-pronged purpose-effect-entanglement test. Brennan found that the law violated all three parts of the test. This type of law created a danger of "politicizing religion," because it imposed selective legislative burdens and advantages on particular denominations. This risk was made clear by this law's legislative history, which indicated that the legislature's intention was to include certain religious groups within the regulatory requirements and to exclude others.[7]

---

6. 456 U.S. at 244–45, 102 S.Ct. at 1683.

7. Strict judicial scrutiny of laws regulating religious organizations is only required when there is an apparent interference with the religious freedom of such organizations or an apparent preference for some religious organizations under the legislation or regulation at issue. If the government chooses to refrain from regulating all religious organizations, it need not justify its decision under a compelling interest test.

In Corporation of Presiding Bishop of Church of Jesus Christ of Latter–day Saints v. Amos, 483 U.S. 327, 337–41, 107 S.Ct. 2862, 2869–70, 97 L.Ed.2d 273 (1987) the Supreme Court upheld federal legislation which exempted religious organizations from federal civil rights statutes prohibiting employment discrimination on the basis of religion insofar as the religious organization was making religiously-based employment decisions regarding its non-profit activity. In Amos, the majority opinion by Justice White found that the Larson decision discussed in this paragraph "indicates that laws discriminating among religions are subject to strict scrutiny ... and that laws affording a uniform benefit to all religions should be analyzed under Lemon [the case establishing the commonly used-purpose effect-entanglement tests under the establishment clause]" 483 U.S. at 337–41, 107 S.Ct. at 2869–70 (internal quotations omitted).

In Hernandez v. Commissioner of Internal Revenue, 490 U.S. 680, 109 S.Ct. 2136, 104 L.Ed.2d 766 (1989) the Supreme Court upheld a provision of the Internal Revenue Code that, as interpreted by the Internal Revenue Service, denied a charitable deduction for any payment to a charitable organization, including a religious organization, that was a quid pro quo exchange for goods or services. The Supreme Court ruled that this tax code provision violated neither the establishment clause nor the free exercise clause. The majority opinion by Justice Marshall found

that the law did not on its face involve a preference for some denominations or sects and, therefore, it need not be subject to the strict scrutiny test that had been employed in Larson v. Valente, 456 U.S. 228, 102 S.Ct. 1673, 72 L.Ed.2d 33 (1982). Because the statute did not make a distinction between different types of religions, it was only subject to the three part (purpose-effect-entanglement) test to determine whether it complied with the establishment clause. See §§ 17.1, 17.3. After finding that the law did not violate the establishment clause, the Court found that any incidental interference with the free exercise of religion that resulted from denying a tax deduction for payments to a religious organization that were a part of a quid pro quo transaction was justified by the government interests in the tax system; the denial of the deduction did not violate the free exercise clause. See §§ 17.6, 17.8.

In Jimmy Swaggart Ministries v. Board of Equalization, 493 U.S. 378, 110 S.Ct. 688, 107 L.Ed.2d 796 (1990), the Justices unanimously upheld the application of general sales and use taxes to the sales and use of religious goods and literature. Justice O'Connor's opinion for a unanimous Court followed the reasoning used in the majority opinion used in Hernandez. Justice O'Connor found that these general taxes, which involved no use of religious criteria to define the transactions or persons subject to the tax, violated neither the establishment clause nor the free exercise clause.

In United States Catholic Conference v. Abortion Rights Mobilization, Inc., 487 U.S. 72, 108 S.Ct. 2268, 101 L.Ed.2d 69 (1988), the Supreme Court avoided ruling on whether a federal court could require a church to submit its records to the court when another organization sought, through judicial action, to have the tax exempt status of the church revoked.

Appendix A

THE CONSTITUTION OF THE UNITED STATES*

1787[1]

Preamble

We the People of the United States, in Order to form a more perfect Union, establish Justice, insure domestic Tranquility, provide for the common defence, promote the general Welfare, and secure the Blessings of Liberty to ourselves and our Posterity, do ordain and establish this Constitution for the United States of America.

Article I

Section 1. All legislative Powers herein granted shall be vested in a Congress of the

---

* Adapted, with permission, from United States Code Annotated, Constitution of the United States, Annotated (West Publishing Co. 1968).

1. In May, 1785, a committee of Congress made a report recommending an alteration in the Articles of Confederation, but no action was taken on it, and it was left to the State Legislatures to proceed in the matter. In January, 1786, the Legislature of Virginia passed a resolution providing for the appointment of five commissioners, who, or any three of them, should meet such commissioners as might be appointed to the other States of the Union, at a time and place to be agreed upon, to take into consideration the trade of the United States; to consider how far a uniform system in their commercial regulations may be necessary to their common interest and their permanent harmony; and to report to the several States such an act, relative to this great object, as, when ratified by them, will enable the United States in Congress effectually to provide for the same. The Virginia commissioners, after some correspondence, fixed the first Monday in September as the time, and the city of Annapolis as the place for the meeting, but only four other States were represented, viz.: Delaware, New York, New Jersey, and Pennsylvania; the commissioners appointed by Massachusetts, New Hampshire, North Carolina, and Rhode Island failed to attend. Under the circumstances of so partial a representation, the commissioners present agreed upon a report, (drawn by Mr. Hamilton of New York,) expressing their unanimous conviction that it might essentially tend to advance the interests of the Union if the States by which they were respectively delegated would concur, and use their endeavors to procure the concurrence of the other States, in the appointment of commissioners to meet at Philadelphia on the second Monday of May following, to take into consideration the situation of the United States; to devise such further provisions as should appear to them necessary to render the Constitution of the Federal Government adequate to the exigencies of the Union; and to report such an action for that purpose to the United States in Congress assembled as, when agreed to by them, and afterwards confirmed by the Legislatures of every State, would effectually provide for the same.

Congress, on the 21st of February, 1787, adopted a resolution in favor of a convention, and the Legislatures of those States which had not already done so (with the exception of Rhode Island) promptly appointed delegates. On the 25th of May, seven States having convened, George Washington, of Virginia, was unanimously elected President, and the consideration of the proposed constitution was commenced. On the 17th of September, 1787, the Constitution as engrossed and agreed upon was signed by all the members present, except Mr. Gerry, of Massachusetts, and Messrs. Mason and Randolph, of Virginia. The president of the convention transmitted it to Congress, with a resolution stating how the proposed Federal Government should be put in operation, and an explanatory letter. Congress, on the 28th of September, 1787, directed the Constitution so framed, with the resolutions and letter concerning the same, to "be transmitted to the several Legislatures in order to be submitted to a convention of delegates chosen in each State by the people thereof, in conformity to the resolves of the convention."

On the 4th of March, 1789, the day which had been fixed for commencing the operations of Government under the new Constitution, it had been ratified by the conventions chosen in each State to consider it, as follows: Delaware, December 7, 1787; Pennsylvania, December 12, 1787; New Jersey, December 18, 1787; Georgia, January 2, 1788; Connecticut, January 9, 1788; Massachusetts, February 6, 1788; Maryland, April 28, 1788; South Carolina, May 23, 1788; New Hampshire, June 21, 1788; Virginia, June 26, 1788; and New York, July 26, 1788.

The President informed Congress, on the 28th of January, 1790, that North Carolina had ratified the Constitution November 21, 1789; and he informed Congress on the 1st of June, 1790, that Rhode Island had ratified the Constitution May 29, 1790. Vermont, in convention, ratified the Constitution January 10, 1791, and was on March 4, 1791, by an act of Congress approved February 18, 1791, "received and admitted into this Union as a new and entire member of the United States".

United States, which shall consist of a Senate and House of Representatives.

Section 2. [1] The House of Representatives shall be composed of Members chosen every second Year by the People of the several States, and the Electors in each State shall have the Qualifications requisite for Electors of the most numerous Branch of the State Legislature.

[2] No Person shall be a Representative who shall not have attained to the Age of twenty five Years, and been seven Years a Citizen of the United States, and who shall not, when elected, be an Inhabitant of that State in which he shall be chosen.

[3] [Representatives and direct Taxes shall be apportioned among the several States which may be included within this Union, according to their respective Numbers, which shall be determined by adding to the whole Number of free Persons, including those bound to Service for a Term of Years, and excluding Indians not taxed, three fifths of all other Persons.] The actual Enumeration shall be made within three Years after the first Meeting of the Congress of the United States, and within every subsequent Term of ten Years, in such Manner as they shall by Law direct. The Number of Representatives shall not exceed one for every thirty Thousand, but each State shall have at Least one Representative; and until such enumeration shall be made, the State of New Hampshire shall be entitled to choose three, Massachusetts eight, Rhode Island and Providence Plantations one, Connecticut five, New York six, New Jersey four, Pennsylvania eight, Delaware one, Maryland six, Virginia ten, North Carolina five, South Carolina five, and Georgia three.

The clause of this paragraph inclosed in brackets was amended, as to the mode of apportionment of representatives among the several states, by the Fourteenth Amendment, § 2, and as to taxes on incomes without apportionment, by the Sixteenth Amendment.

[4] When vacancies happen in the Representation from any State, the Executive Au-

thority thereof shall issue Writs of Election to fill such Vacancies.

[5] The House of Representatives shall chuse their Speaker and other Officers; and shall have the sole Power of Impeachment.

Section 3. [1] [The Senate of the United States shall be composed of two Senators from each State, chosen by the Legislature thereof, for six Years; and each Senator shall have one Vote.]

This paragraph and the clause of following paragraph inclosed in brackets were superseded by the Seventeenth Amendment.

[2] Immediately after they shall be assembled in Consequence of the first Election, they shall be divided as equally as may be into three Classes. The Seats of the Senators of the first Class shall be vacated at the Expiration of the Second Year, of the second Class at the Expiration of the fourth Year, and of the third Class at the Expiration of the sixth Year, so that one third may be chosen every second Year; [and if Vacancies happen by Resignation, or otherwise, during the Recess of the Legislature of any State, the Executive thereof may make temporary Appointments until the next Meeting of the Legislature, which shall then fill such Vacancies.]

See note to preceding paragraph of this section.

[3] No Person shall be a Senator who shall not have attained to the Age of thirty Years, and been nine Years a Citizen of the United States, and who shall not, when elected, be an Inhabitant of that State for which he shall be chosen.

[4] The Vice President of the United States shall be President of the Senate, but shall have no Vote, unless they be equally divided.

[5] The Senate shall chuse their other Officers, and also a President pro tempore, in the Absence of the Vice President, or when he shall exercise the Office of President of the United States.

[6] The Senate shall have the sole Power to try all Impeachments. When sitting for that

Purpose, they shall be on Oath or Affirmation. When the President of the United States is tried, the Chief Justice shall preside: And no Person shall be convicted without the Concurrence of two thirds of the Members present.

[7] Judgment in Cases of Impeachment shall not extend further than to removal from Office, and disqualification to hold and enjoy any Office of honor, Trust, or Profit under the United States: but the Party convicted shall nevertheless be liable and subject to Indictment, Trial, Judgment, and Punishment, according to Law.

Section 4. [1] The Times, Places and Manner of holding Elections for Senators and Representatives, shall be prescribed in each State by the Legislature thereof; but the Congress may at any time by Law make or alter such Regulations, except as to the Places of chusing Senators.

[2] The Congress shall assemble at least once in every Year, and such Meeting shall be on the first Monday in December, unless they shall be Law appoint a different Day.

Section 5. [1] Each House shall be the Judge of the Elections, Returns, and Qualifications of its own Members, and a Majority of each shall constitute a Quorum to do Business; but a smaller Number may adjourn from day to day, and may be authorized to compel the Attendance of absent Members, in such Manner, and under such Penalties as each House may provide.

[2] Each House may determine the Rules of its Proceedings, punish its Members for disorderly Behavior, and, with the Concurrence of two thirds, expel a Member.

[3] Each House shall keep a Journal of its Proceedings, and from time to time publish the same, excepting such Parts as may in their Judgment require Secrecy; and the Yeas and Nays of the Members of either House on any question shall, at the Desire of one fifth of those Present, be entered on the Journal.

[4] Neither House, during the Session of Congress, shall, without the Consent of the other, adjourn for more than three days, nor to any other Place than that in which the two Houses shall be sitting.

Section 6. [1] The Senators and Representatives shall receive a Compensation for their Services, to be ascertained by Law, and paid out of the Treasury of the United States. They shall in all Cases, except Treason, Felony and Breach of the Peace, be privileged from Arrest during their Attendance at the Session of their respective Houses, and in going to and returning from the same; and for any Speech or Debate in either House, they shall not be questioned in any other Place.

[2] No Senator or Representative shall, during the Time for which he was elected, be appointed to any civil Office under the Authority of the United States, which shall have been created, or the Emoluments whereof shall have been increased during such time; and no Person holding any Office under the United States, shall be a Member of either House during his Continuance in Office.

Section 7. [1] All Bills for raising Revenue shall originate in the House of Representatives; but the Senate may propose or concur with Amendments as on other Bills.

[2] Every Bill which shall have passed the House of Representatives and the Senate, shall, before it become a Law, be presented to the President of the United States; If he approve he shall sign it, but if not he shall return it, with his Objections to the House in which it shall have originated, who shall enter the Objections at large on their Journal, and proceed to reconsider it. If after such Reconsideration two thirds of that House shall agree to pass the Bill, it shall be sent together with the Objections, to the other House, by which it shall likewise be reconsidered, and if approved by two thirds of that House, it shall become a Law. But in all such Cases the Votes of both Houses shall be determined by Yeas and Nays, and the Names of the Persons voting for and against the Bill shall be entered on the Journal of each House respectively. If any Bill shall not be returned by the President within ten Days (Sundays excepted) after it shall have been presented to him, the Same shall be a Law, in like Manner as if he had signed it,

unless the Congress by their Adjournment prevent its Return in which Case it shall not be a Law.

[3] Every Order, Resolution, or Vote, to Which the Concurrence of the Senate and House of Representatives may be necessary (except on a question of Adjournment) shall be presented to the President of the United States; and before the Same shall take Effect, shall be approved by him, or being disapproved by him, shall be repassed by two thirds of the Senate and House of Representatives, according to the Rules and Limitations prescribed in the Case of a Bill.

Section 8. [1] The Congress shall have Power to lay and collect Taxes, Duties, Imposts and Excises, to pay the Debts and provide for the common Defence and general Welfare of the United States; but all Duties, Imposts and Excises shall be uniform throughout the United States;

[2] To borrow money on the credit of the United States;

[3] To regulate Commerce with foreign Nations, and among the several States, and with the Indian Tribes;

[4] To establish an uniform Rule of Naturalization, and uniform Laws on the subject of Bankruptcies throughout the United States;

[5] To coin Money, regulate the Value thereof, and of foreign Coin, and fix the Standard of Weights and Measures;

[6] To provide for the Punishment of counterfeiting the Securities and current Coin of the United States;

[7] To Establish Post Offices and Post Roads;

[8] To promote the Progress of Science and useful Arts, by securing for limited Times to Authors and Inventors the exclusive Right to their respective Writings and Discoveries;

[9] To constitute Tribunals inferior to the supreme Court;

[10] To define and punish Piracies and Felonies committed on the high Seas, and Offenses against the Law of Nations;

[11] To declare War, grant Letters of marque and Reprisal, and make Rules concerning Captures on Land and Water;

[12] To raise and support Armies, but no Appropriation of Money to that Use shall be for a longer Term then two Years;

[13] To provide and maintain a Navy;

[14] To make Rules for the Government and Regulation of the land and naval Forces;

[15] To provide for calling forth the Militia to execute the Laws of the Union, suppress Insurrections and repel Invasions;

[16] To provide for organizing, arming, and disciplining, the Militia, and for governing such Part of them as may be employed in the Service of the United States, reserving to the States respectively, the Appointment of the Officers, and the Authority of training the Militia according to the discipline prescribed by Congress;

[17] To exercise exclusive Legislation in all Cases whatsoever, over such District (not exceeding ten Miles square) as may, by Cession of particular States and the Acceptance of Congress, become the Seat of the Government of the United States, and to exercise like Authority over all Places purchased by the Consent of the Legislature of the State in which the Same shall be, for the Erection of Forts, Magazines, Arsenals, dock-Yards, and other needful Buildings;—And

[18] To make all Laws which shall be necessary and proper for carrying into Execution the foregoing Powers, and all other Powers vested by this Constitution in the Government of the United States, or in any Department or Officer thereof.

Section 9. [1] The Migration or Importation of Such Persons as any of the States now existing shall think proper to admit, shall not be prohibited by the Congress prior to the Year one thousand eight hundred and eight, but a Tax or duty may be imposed on such Importation, not exceeding ten dollars for each Person.

[2] The privilege of the Writ of Habeas Corpus shall not be suspended, unless when in

Cases of Rebellion or Invasion the public Safety may require it.

[3] No Bill of Attainder or ex post facto Law shall be passed.

[4] No Capitation, or other direct, Tax shall be laid, unless in Proportion to the Census or Enumeration herein before directed to be taken.

[5] No Tax or Duty shall be laid on Articles exported from any State.

[6] No Preference shall be given by any Regulation of Commerce or Revenue to the Ports of one State over those of another: nor shall Vessels bound to, or from, one State be obliged to enter, clear, or pay Duties in another.

[7] No money shall be drawn from the Treasury, but in Consequence of Appropriations made by Law; and a regular Statement and Account of the Receipts and Expenditures of all public Money shall be published from time to time.

[8] No Title of Nobility shall be granted by the United States: And no Person holding any Office of Profit or Trust under them, shall, without the Consent of the Congress, accept of any present, Emolument, Office, or Title, of any kind whatever, from any King, Prince, or foreign State.

Section 10. [1] No State shall enter into any Treaty, Alliance, or Confederation; grant Letters of Marque and Reprisal; coin Money; emit Bills of Credit; make any Thing but gold and silver Coin a Tender in Payment of Debts; pass any Bill of Attainder, ex post facto Law, or law impairing the Obligation of Contracts, or grant any Title of Nobility.

[2] No State shall, without the Consent of the Congress, lay any Imposts or Duties on Imports or Exports, except what may be absolutely necessary for executing it's inspection Laws: and the net Produce of all Duties and Imposts, laid by any State on Imports or Exports, shall be for the Use of the Treasury of the United States; and all such Laws shall be subject to the Revision and Controul of the Congress.

[3] No State shall, without the Consent of Congress, law any Duty of Tonnage, keep Troops, or Ships of War in time of Peace, enter into any Agreement or Compact with another State, or with a foreign power or engage in War, unless actually invaded, or in such imminent Danger as will not admit of delay.

Article II

Section 1. [1] The executive Power shall be vested in a President of the United States of America. He shall hold his Office during the Term of four Years, and, together with the Vice President, chosen for the same Term, be elected, as follows:

[2] Each State shall appoint, in such Manner as the Legislature thereof may direct, a Number of Electors, equal to the whole Number of Senators and Representatives to which the State may be entitled in the Congress; but no Senator or Representative, or Person holding an Office of Trust or Profit under the United States, shall be appointed an Elector.

[3] [The Electors shall meet in their respective States, and vote by Ballot for two Persons, of whom one at least shall not be an Inhabitant of the same State with themselves. And they shall make a List of all the Persons voted for, and of the Number of Votes for each; which List they shall sign and certify, and transmit sealed to the Seat of the Government of the United States, directed to the President of the Senate. The President of the Senate shall, in the Presence of the Senate and House of Representatives, open all the Certificates, and the Votes shall then be counted. The Person having the greatest Number of Votes shall be the President, if such Number be a Majority of the whole Number of Electors appointed; and if there be more than one who have such Majority, and have an equal Number of Votes, then the House of Representatives shall immediately chuse by Ballot one of them for President; and if no Person have a Majority, then from the five highest on the List the said House shall in like Manner chuse the President. But in chusing the President, the Votes shall be taken by States the Representation from each State having one Vote; A quorum for this Purpose shall consist of a

Member or Members from two thirds of the States, and a Majority of all the States shall be necessary to a Choice. In every Case, after the Choice of the President, the Person having the greater Number of Votes of the Electors shall be the Vice President. But if there should remain two or more who have equal Votes, the Senate shall choose from them by Ballot the Vice President.]

This paragraph, inclosed in brackets, was superseded by the Twelfth Amendment, post.

[4] The Congress may determine the Time of chusing the Electors, and the Day on which they shall give their Votes; which Day shall be the same throughout the United States.

[5] No person except a natural born Citizen, or a Citizen of the United States, at the time of the Adoption of this Constitution, shall be eligible to the Office of President; neither shall any Person be eligible to that Office who shall not have attained to the Age of thirty five Years, and been fourteen Years a Resident within the United States.

[6] In case of the removal of the President from Office, or of his Death, Resignation or Inability to discharge the Powers and Duties of the said Office, the Same shall devolve on the Vice President and the Congress may by Law provide for the Case of Removal, Death, Resignation or Inability, both of the President and Vice President, declaring what Officer shall then act as President, and such Officer shall act accordingly, until the Disability be removed, or a President shall be elected.

[7] The President shall, at stated Times, receive for his Services, a Compensation, which shall neither be increased nor diminished during the Period for which he shall have been elected, and he shall not receive within that Period any other Emolument from the United States, or any of them.

[8] Before he enter on the Execution of his Office, he shall take the following Oath or Affirmation: "I do solemnly swear (or affirm) that I will faithfully execute the Office of President of the United States, and will to the best of my Ability, preserve, protect and defend the Constitution of the United States."

Section 2. [1] The President shall be Commander in Chief of the Army and Navy of the United States, and of the militia of the several States, when called into the actual Service of the United States; he may require the Opinion, in writing, of the principal Officer in each of the Executive Departments, upon any Subject relating to the Duties of their respective Offices and he shall have Power to grant Reprieves and Pardons for Offenses against the United States, except in Cases of Impeachment.

[2] He shall have Power, by and with the Advice and Consent of the Senate to make Treaties, provided two thirds of the Senators present concur; and he shall nominate, and by and with the Advice and Consent of the Senate, shall appoint Ambassadors, other public Ministers and Consuls, judges of the supreme Court, and all other Officers of the United States, whose Appointments are not herein otherwise provided for, and which shall be established by Law; but the Congress may by Law vest the Appointment of such inferior Officers, as they think proper, in the President alone, in the Courts of Law, or in the Heads of Departments.

[3] The President shall have Power to fill up all Vacancies that may happen during the Recess of the Senate, by granting Commissions which shall expire at the End of their next Session.

Section 3. He shall from time to time give to the Congress Information of the State of the Union, and recommend to their Consideration such Measures as he shall judge necessary and expedient; he may, on extraordinary Occasions, convene both Houses, or either of them, and in Case of Disagreement between them, with Respect to the Time of Adjournment, he may adjourn them to such Time as he shall think proper; he shall receive Ambassadors and other public Ministers; he shall take Care that the Laws be faithfully executed, and shall Commission all the Officers of the United States.

Section 4. The President, Vice President and all civil Officers of the United States, shall be removed from Office on Impeachment for, and Conviction of, Treason, Bribery, or other high Crimes and Misdemeanors.

Article III

Section 1. The judicial Power of the United States, shall be vested in one supreme Court, and in such inferior Courts as the Congress may from time to time ordain and establish. The Judges, both of the supreme and inferior Courts, shall hold their Offices during good Behaviour, and shall, at stated Times, receive for their Services a Compensation, which shall not be diminished during their Continuance in Office.

Section 2. [1] The judicial Power shall extend to all Cases, in Law and Equity, arising under this Constitution, the Laws of the United States, and Treaties made, or which shall be made, under their Authority;—to all Cases affecting Ambassadors, other public Ministers and Consuls;—to all Cases of admiralty and maritime Jurisdiction;—to Controversies to which the United States shall be a Party;—to Controversies between two or more States;—between a State and Citizens of another State;—between Citizens of different States;—between Citizens of the same State claiming Lands under the Grants of different States, and between a State, or the Citizens thereof, and foreign States, Citizens or Subjects.

[2] In all Cases affecting Ambassadors, other public Ministers and Consuls, and those in which a State shall be a Party, the supreme Court shall have original Jurisdiction. In all the other Cases before mentioned, the supreme Court shall have appellate Jurisdiction, both as to Law and Fact, with such Exceptions, and under such Regulations as the Congress shall make.

[3] The trial of all Crimes, except in Cases of Impeachment, shall be by Jury; and such Trial shall be held in the State where the said Crimes shall have been committed; but when not committed within any State, the Trial shall be at such Place or Places as the Congress may by Law have directed.

Section 3. [1] Treason against the United States, shall consist only in levying War against them, or, in adhering to their Enemies, giving them Aid and Comfort. No Person shall be convicted of Treason unless on the Testimony of two Witnesses to the same overt Act, or on Confession in open Court.

[2] The Congress shall have Power to declare the Punishment of Treason, but no Attainder of Treason shall work Corruption of Blood, or Forfeiture except during the Life of the Person attainted.

Article IV

Section 1. Full Faith and Credit shall be given in each State to the public Acts, Records, and judicial Proceedings of every other State. And the Congress may be general Laws prescribe the Manner in which such Acts, Records and Proceedings shall be proved, and the Effect thereof.

Section 2. [1] The Citizens of each State shall be entitled to all Privileges and Immunities of Citizens in the several States.

[2] A Person charged in any State with Treason, Felony, or other Crime, who shall flee from Justice, and be found in another State, shall on demand of the executive Authority of the State from which he fled, be delivered up, to be removed to the State having Jurisdiction of the Crime.

[3] No Person held to Service or Labour in one State, under the Laws thereof, escaping into another, shall, in Consequence of any Law or Regulation therein, be discharged from such Service or Labour, but shall be delivered up on Claim of the Party to whom such Service or Labour may be due.

Section 3. [1] New States may be admitted by the Congress into this Union; but no new State shall be formed or erected within the Jurisdiction of any other State; nor any State be formed by the Junction of two or more States, or parts of States, without the Consent of the Legislatures of the States concerned as well as the Congress.

[2] The Congress shall have Power to dispose of and make all needful Rules and Regulations respecting the Territory or other Property belonging to the United States; and

nothing in this Constitution shall be so construed as to Prejudice any Claims of the United States, or of any particular State.

Section 4. The United States shall guarantee to every State in this Union a Republican Form of Government, and shall protect each of them against Invasion; and on Application of the Legislature, or of the Executive (when the Legislature cannot be convened) against domestic Violence.

Article V

The Congress, whenever two-thirds of both Houses shall deem it necessary, shall propose Amendments to this Constitution, or, on the Application of the Legislatures of two-thirds of the several States, shall call a Convention for proposing Amendments, which, in either Case, shall be valid to all Intents and Purposes, as part of this Constitution, when ratified by the Legislatures of three-fourths of the several States, or by Conventions in three-fourths thereof, as the one or the other Mode of Ratification may be proposed by the Congress; Provided that no Amendment which may be made prior to the Year One thousand eight hundred and eight shall in any Manner affect the first and fourth Clauses in the Ninth Section of the first Article; and that no State, without its Consent, shall be deprived of its equal Suffrage in the Senate.

Article VI

[1] All Debts contracted and Engagements entered into, before the Adoption of this Constitution shall be as valid against the United States under this Constitution, as under the Confederation.

[2] This Constitution, and the Laws of the United States which shall be made in Pursuance thereof; and all Treaties made, or which shall be made, under the Authority of the United States, shall be the supreme Law of the Land; and the Judges in every State shall be bound thereby, any Thing in the Constitution or Laws of any State to the Contrary notwithstanding.

[3] The Senators and Representatives before mentioned, and the Members of the several State Legislatures, and all executive and judicial Officers, both of the United States and of the several States, shall be bound by Oath or Affirmation, to support this Constitution; but no religious Test shall ever be required as a Qualification to any Office or public Trust under the United States.

Article VII

The Ratification of the Conventions of nine States shall be sufficient for the Establishment of this Constitution between the States so ratifying the Same.

DONE in Convention by the Unanimous Consent of the States present the Seventeenth Day of September in the Year of Our Lord one thousand seven hundred and Eighty seven and of the Independence of the United States of America the Twelfth. IN WITNESS whereof We have hereunto subscribed our Names,

Go. WASHINGTON—
Presidt. and deputy from Virginia

New Hampshire

JOHN LANGDON	NICHOLAS GILMAN

Massachusetts

NATHANIEL GORHAM	RUFUS KING

Connecticut

WM. SAML. JOHNSON	ROGER SHERMAN

New York

ALEXANDER HAMILTON

New Jersey

WIL: LIVINGSTON	WM. PATERSON
DAVID BREARLEY	JONA: DAYTON

Pennsylvania

B. FRANKLIN	THOS. FITZSIMONS
THOMAS MIFFLIN	JARED INGERSOLL
ROBT. MORRIS	JAMES WILSON
GEO. CLYMER	GOUV MORRIS

Delaware

GEO: READ	RICHARD BASSETT
GUNNING BEDFORDJUM	JACO: BROOM
JOHN DICKINSON	

Maryland

JAMES MCHENRY	DANL. CARROLL
DAN OF ST THOS. JENIFER	

Virginia

JOHN BLAIR	JAMES MADISON, JR.

North Carolina

WM. BLOUNT	HU WILLIAMSON
RICHD. DOBBS SPAIGHT	

South Carolina

J. RUTLEDGE	CHARLES PINCKNEY
CHARLES COTESWORTH PINCKNEY	PIERCE BUTLER

Georgia

WILLIAM FEW	ABR BALDWIN

Attest	WILLIAM JACKSON *Secretary*

———————

ARTICLES IN ADDITION TO, AND AMEND-
MENT OF, THE CONSTITUTION OF
THE UNITED STATES OF AMERICA,
PROPOSED BY CONGRESS, AND RATI-
FIED BY THE LEGISLATURES OF THE
SEVERAL STATES PURSUANT TO
THE FIFTH ARTICLE OF THE ORIGI-
NAL CONSTITUTION.[1]

Amendment [I] [1791][2]

Congress shall make no law respecting an
establishment of religion, or prohibiting the
free exercise thereof; or abridging the freedom
of speech, or of the press; or the right of the
people peaceably to assemble, and to petition
the Government for a redress of grievances.

Amendment [II] [1791]

A well regulated Militia, being necessary to
the security of a free State, the right of the
people to keep and bear Arms, shall not be
infringed.

Amendment [III] [1791]

No Soldier shall, in time of peace be quartered in any house, without the consent of the
Owner, nor in time of war, but in a manner to
be prescribed by law.

Amendment [IV] [1791]

The right of the people to be secure in their
persons, houses, papers, and effects, against
unreasonable searches and seizures, shall not
be violated, and no Warrants shall issue, but
upon probable cause, supported by Oath or
affirmation, and particularly describing the
place to be searched, and the persons or things
to be seized.

Amendment [V] [1791]

No person shall be held to answer for a
capital, or otherwise infamous crime, unless on
a presentment or indictment of a Grand Jury,
except in cases arising in the land or naval
forces, or in the Militia, when in actual service
in time of War or public danger; nor shall any
person be subject for the same offence to be
twice put in jeopardy of life or limb; nor shall
be compelled in any criminal case to be a
witness against himself, nor be deprived of life,
liberty, or property, without due process of
law; nor shall private property be taken for
public use, without just compensation.

Amendment [VI] [1791]

In all criminal prosecutions, the accused
shall enjoy the right to a speedy and public
trial, by an impartial jury of the State and
district wherein the crime shall have been
committed, which district shall have been previously ascertained by law, and to be informed
of the nature and cause of the accusation; to
be confronted with the witnesses against him;
to have compulsory process for obtaining witnesses in his favor, and to have the Assistance
of Counsel for his defence.

Amendment [VII] [1791]

In Suits at common law, where the value in
controversy shall exceed twenty dollars, the
right of trial by jury shall be preserved, and no
fact tried by jury, shall be otherwise reexamined in any Court of the United States, than
according to the rules of the common law.

---

1. All of the Amendments except the 13th, 14th, 15th, and 16th, were not specifically assigned a number in the resolution proposing the Amendment. Brackets enclose the number for such Amendments. The 13th, 14th, 15th, and 16th Amendments were ratified by number and thus no brackets enclose such Amendment numbers.

2. The first ten Amendments to the Constitution of the United States were proposed to the legislatures of the several States by the First Congress, on the 25th of September 1789. They were ratified by the following States, and the notifications of ratification by the governors thereof were successively communicated by the President to Congress: New Jersey, November 20, 1789; Mary-

land, December 19, 1789; North Carolina, December 22, 1789; South Carolina, January 19, 1790; New Hampshire, January 25, 1790; Delaware, January 28, 1790; Pennsylvania, March 10, 1790; New York, March 27, 1790; Rhode Island, June 15, 1790; Vermont, November 3, 1791, and Virginia, December 15, 1791. The legislatures of Connecticut, Georgia, and Massachusetts ratified them on April 19, 1939, March 24, 1939, and March 2, 1939, respectively.

Note: other Amendments have also been ratified by states *after* the Amendment has been announced as ratified; these other, after-the-fact ratifications are not usually noted in this appendix.

Amendment [VIII] [1791]

Excessive bail shall not be required, nor excessive fines imposed, nor cruel and unusual punishments inflicted.

Amendment [IX] [1791]

The enumeration in the Constitution of certain rights, shall not be construed to deny or disparage others retained by the people.

Amendment [X] [1791]

The powers not delegated to the United States by the Constitution, nor prohibited by it to the States, are reserved to the States respectively, or to the people.

Amendment [XI] [1798]

The Judicial power of the United States shall not be construed to extend to any suit in law or equity, commenced or prosecuted against one of the United States by Citizens of another State, or by Citizens or Subjects of any Foreign State.

Historical Note

This Amendment was proposed to the legislatures of the several States by the Third Congress, on the 5th September, 1794, and was declared in a message from the President to Congress, dated the 8th of January, 1798, to have been ratified by the legislatures of three-fourths of the States.

Amendment [XII] [1804]

The Electors shall meet in their respective states and vote by ballot for President and Vice–President, one of whom, at least, shall not be an inhabitant of the same state with themselves; they shall name in their ballots the person voted for as President, and in distinct ballots the person voted for as Vice–President, and they shall make distinct lists of all persons voted for as President, and of all persons voted for as Vice–President, and of the number of votes for each, which lists they shall sign and certify, and transmit sealed to the seat of the government of the United States, directed to the President of the Senate;—The President of the Senate shall, in the presence of the Senate and House of Representatives, open all the certificates and the votes shall then be counted;—The person having the greatest number of votes for President, shall be the President, if such number be a majority of the whole number of Electors appointed; and if no person have such majority, then from the persons having the highest numbers not exceeding three on the list of those voted for as President, the House of Representatives shall choose immediately, by ballot, the President, but in choosing the President, the votes shall be taken by states, the representation from each state having one vote; a quorum for this purpose shall consist of a member or members from two-thirds of the states and a majority of all the states shall be necessary to a choice. And if the House of Representatives shall not choose a President whenever the right of choice shall devolve upon them before the fourth day of March next following, then the Vice–President shall act as President, as in the case of the death or other constitutional disability of the President.—The person having the greatest number of votes as Vice–President, shall be the Vice–President, if such number be a majority of the whole number of Electors appointed, and if no person have a majority, then from the two highest numbers on the list, the Senate shall choose the Vice–President; a quorum for the purpose shall consist of two-thirds of the whole number of Senators, and a majority of the whole number shall be necessary to a choice. But no person constitutionally ineligible to the office of President shall be eligible to that of Vice–President of the United States.

Historical Note

This Amendment was proposed to the legislatures of the several States by the Eighth Congress, on the 12th of December, 1803, in lieu of the original third paragraph of the first section of the second article, and was declared in a proclamation of the Secretary of State, dated the 25th of September, 1804, to have been rati-

fied by the legislatures of three-fourths of the States.

Amendment XIII [1865]*

Section 1. Neither slavery nor involuntary servitude, except as a punishment for crime whereof the party shall have been duly convicted, shall exist within the United States, or any place subject to their jurisdiction.

Section 2. Congress shall have power to enforce this article by appropriate legislation.

Historical Note

This Amendment was proposed to the legislatures of the several States by the Thirty-eighth Congress, on the 1st of February, 1865, and was declared, in a proclamation of the Secretary of State, dated the 18th of December, 1865, to have been ratified by the legislatures of twenty-seven of the thirty-six States, viz.: Illinois, Rhode Island, Michigan, Maryland, New York, West Virginia, Maine, Kansas, Massachusetts, Pennsylvania, Virginia, Ohio, Missouri, Nevada, Indiana, Louisiana, Minnesota, Wisconsin, Vermont, Tennessee, Arkansas, Connecticut, New Hampshire, South Carolina, Alabama, North Carolina, and Georgia.

Amendment XIV [1868] *

Section 1. All persons born or naturalized in the United States, and subject to the jurisdiction thereof, are citizens of the United States and of the State wherein they reside. No State shall make or enforce any law which shall abridge the privileges or immunities of citizens of the United States; nor shall any State deprive any person of life, liberty, or property, without due process of law; nor deny to any person within its jurisdiction the equal protection of the laws.

Section 2. Representatives shall be apportioned among the several States according to their respective numbers, counting the whole number of persons in each State, excluding Indians not taxed. But when the right to vote at any election for the choice of electors for President and Vice President of the United States, Representatives in Congress, the Executive and Judicial officers of a State, or the members of the Legislature thereof, is denied to any of the male inhabitants of such State, being twenty-one years of age, and citizens of the United States, or in any way abridged, except for participation in rebellion, or other crime, the basis of representation therein shall be reduced in the proportion which the number of such male citizens shall bear to the whole number of male citizens twenty-one years of age in such State.

Section 3. No person shall be a Senator or Representative in Congress, or elector of President and Vice President, or hold any office, civil or military, under the United States, or under any State, who having previously taken an oath, as a member of Congress, or as an officer of the United States, or as a member of any State legislature, or as an executive or judicial officer of any State, to support the Constitution of the United States, shall have engaged in insurrection or rebellion against the same, or given aid or comfort to the enemies thereof. But Congress may by a vote of two-thirds of each House, remove such disability.

Section 4. The validity of the public debt of the United States, authorized by law, including debts incurred for payment of pensions and bounties for services in suppressing insurrection or rebellion, shall not be questioned. But neither the United States nor any State shall assume or pay any debt or obligation incurred in aid of insurrection or rebellion against the United States, or any claim for the loss or emancipation of any slave; but all such debts, obligations and claims shall be held illegal and void.

Section 5. The Congress shall have power to enforce, by appropriate legislation, the provisions of this article.

* See note 1, supra.

* See note 1, supra.

Historical Note

This Amendment was proposed to the legislatures of the several States by the Thirty-ninth Congress, on the 16th of June, 1866. On the 21st of July, 1868, Congress adopted and transmitted to the Department of State a concurrent resolution, declaring that "the legislatures of the States of Connecticut, Tennessee, New Jersey, Oregon, Vermont, New York, Ohio, Illinois, West Virginia, Kansas, Maine, Nevada, Missouri, Indiana, Minnesota, New Hampshire, Massachusetts, Nebraska, Iowa, Arkansas, Florida, North Carolina, Alabama, South Carolina, and Louisiana, being three-fourths and more of the several States of the Union, have ratified the fourteen article of Amendment to the Constitution of the United States, duly proposed by two-thirds of each House of the Thirty-ninth Congress; therefore, Resolved, That said fourteenth article is hereby declared to be a part of the Constitution of the United States, and it shall be duly promulgated as such by the Secretary of the State." The Secretary of State accordingly issued a proclamation, dated the 28th of July, 1868, declaring that the proposed Fourteen Amendment had been ratified, in the manner hereafter mentioned by the legislatures of thirty of the thirty-six States, viz.: Connecticut, June 30, 1866; New Hampshire, July 7, 1866; Tennessee, July 19, 1866; New Jersey, September 11, 1866, (and the legislature of the same State passed a resolution in April, 1868, to withdraw its consent to it); Oregon, September 19, 1866; Vermont, November 9, 1866; Georgia rejected it November 13, 1866, and ratified it July 21, 1868; North Carolina rejected it December 4, 1866, and ratified it July 4, 1868; South Carolina rejected it December 20, 1866, and ratified it July 9, 1868; New York ratified it January 10, 1867; Ohio ratified it January 11, 1867, (and the legislature of the same State passed a resolution in January, 1868, to withdraw its consent to it); Illinois ratified it January 15, 1867; West Virginia, January 16, 1867; Kansas, January 18, 1867; Maine, January 19, 1867; Nevada, January 22, 1867; Missouri, January 26, 1867; Indiana, January 29, 1867; Minnesota, February 1, 1867; Rhode Island, February 7, 1867; Wisconsin, February 13, 1867; Pennsylvania, February 13, 1867; Michigan, February 15, 1867; Massachusetts, March 20, 1867; Nebraska, June 15, 1867; Iowa, April 3, 1868; Arkansas, April 6, 1868; Florida, June 9, 1868; Louisiana, July 9, 1868; and Alabama, July 13, 1868. Georgia again ratified the Amendment February 2, 1870. Texas rejected it November 1, 1866, and ratified it February 18, 1870. Virginia rejected it January 19, 1867, and ratified October 8, 1869. The amendment was rejected by Kentucky January 10, 1867; by Delaware February 8, 1867; by Maryland March 23, 1867.

Amendment XV [1870]*

Section 1. The right of citizens of the United States to vote shall not be denied or abridged by the United States or by any State on account of race, color, or previous condition of servitude.

Section 2. The Congress shall have power to enforce this article by appropriate legislation.

Historical Note

This Amendment was proposed to the legislatures of the several States by the Fortieth Congress, on the 27th of February, 1869, and was declared, in a proclamation of the Secretary of

---

* See note 1, supra.

State, dated March 30, 1870, to have been ratified by the legislatures of the twenty-nine of the thirty-seven States. The dates of these ratifications (arranged in the order of their reception at the Department of State) were: from North Carolina, March 5, 1869; West Virginia, March 3, 1869; Massachusetts, March 9–12, 1869; Wisconsin, March 9, 1869; Maine, March 12, 1869; Louisiana, March 5, 1869; Michigan, March 8, 1869; South Carolina, March 16, 1869; Pennsylvania, March 26, 1869; Arkansas, March 30, 1869; Connecticut, May 19, 1869; Florida, June 15, 1869; Illinois, March 5, 1869; Indiana, May 13–14, 1869; New York, March 17–April 14, 1869, (and the legislature of the same State passed a resolution January 5, 1870, to withdraw its consent to it); New Hampshire, July 7, 1869; Nevada, March 1, 1869; Vermont, October 21, 1869; Virginia, October 8, 1869; Missouri, January 10, 1870; Mississippi, January 15–17, 1870; Ohio, January 27, 1870; Iowa, February 3, 1870; Kansas, January 18–19, 1870; Minnesota, February 19, 1870; Rhode Island, January 18, 1870; Nebraska, February 17, 1870; Texas, February 18, 1870. The State of Georgia also ratified the Amendment February 2, 1870.

Amendment XVI [1913]*

The Congress shall have power to lay and collect taxes on incomes, from whatever source derived, without apportionment among the several States, and without regard to any census or enumeration.

Historical Note

This Amendment was proposed to the legislatures of the several states by the Sixty–First Congress, on the 31st of July, 1909, and was declared, in a proclamation by the Secretary of

State, dated the 25th of February, 1913, to have been ratified by the legislatures of the states of Alabama, Kentucky, South Carolina, Illinois, Mississippi, Oklahoma, Maryland, Georgia, Texas, Ohio, Idaho, Oregon, Washington, California, Montana, Indiana, Nevada, North Carolina, Nebraska, Kansas, Colorado, North Dakota, Michigan, Iowa, Missouri, Maine, Tennessee, Arkansas, Wisconsin, New York, South Dakota, Arizona, Minnesota, Louisiana, Delaware, and Wyoming, in all, thirty-six. The legislatures of New Jersey and New Mexico also passed resolutions ratifying the said proposed Amendment.

Amendment [XVII] [1913]

[1] The Senate of the United States shall be composed of two Senators from each State, elected by the people thereof, for six years; and each Senator shall have one vote. The electors in each State shall have the qualifications requisite for electors of the most numerous branch of the State legislatures.

[2] When vacancies happen in the representation of any State in the Senate, the executive authority of such State shall issue writs of election to fill such vacancies: *Provided*, that the legislature of any State may empower the executive thereof to make temporary appointments until the people fill the vacancies by election as the legislature may direct.

[3] This Amendment shall not be so construed as to affect the election or term of any Senator chosen before it becomes valid as part of the Constitution.

Historical Note

This Amendment was proposed to the legislatures of the several states by the Sixty–Second Congress, on the 16th of May, 1912, in lieu of the original first paragraph of section 3 of article I, and in lieu of so much of

* See note 1, supra.

paragraph 2 of the same section as related to the filling of vacancies, and was declared, in a proclamation by the Secretary of State, dated the 31st of May, 1913, to have been ratified by the legislatures of the states of Massachusetts, Arizona, Minnesota, New York, Kansas, Oregon, North Carolina, California, Michigan, Idaho, West Virginia, Nebraska, Iowa, Montana, Texas, Washington, Wyoming, Colorado, Illinois, North Dakota, Nevada, Vermont, Maine, New Hampshire, Oklahoma, Ohio, South Dakota, Indiana, Missouri, New Mexico, New Jersey, Tennessee, Arkansas, Connecticut, Pennsylvania, and Wisconsin, said states constituting three-fourths of the whole number of states.

Amendment [XVIII] [1919]

Section 1. After one year from the ratification of this article the manufacture, sale, or transportation of intoxicating liquors within, the importation thereof into, or the exportation thereof from the United States and all territory subject to the jurisdiction thereof for beverage purposes is hereby prohibited.

Section 2. The Congress and the several States shall have concurrent power to enforce this article by appropriate legislation.

Section 3. This article shall be inoperative unless it shall have been ratified as an Amendment to the Constitution by the legislatures of the several States, as provided in the Constitution, within seven years from the date of the submission hereof to the States by the Congress.

Historical Note

This Amendment was proposed to the legislatures of the several states by the Sixty–Fifth Congress, on the 19th day of December, 1917, and was declared, in a proclamation by the Acting Secretary of State, dated on the 29th day of January, 1919, to have been ratified by the legislatures of the states of Alabama, Arizona, California, Colorado, Delaware, Flor-

ida, Georgia, Idaho, Illinois, Indiana, Kansas, Kentucky, Louisiana, Maine, Maryland, Massachusetts, Michigan, Minnesota, Mississippi, Montana, Nebraska, New Hampshire, North Carolina, North Dakota, Ohio, Oklahoma, Oregon, South Dakota, South Carolina, Texas, Utah, Virginia, Washington, West Virginia, Wisconsin, and Wyoming.

Amendment [XIX] [1920]

[1] The right of citizens of the United States to vote shall not be denied or abridged by the United States or by any State on account of sex.

[2] Congress shall have power to enforce this article by appropriate legislation.

Historical Note

This Amendment was proposed to the legislatures of the several states by the Sixty–Sixth Congress, on the 5th day of June, 1919, and was declared, in a proclamation by the Secretary of State, dated on the 26th day of August, 1920, to have been ratified by the legislatures of the states of Arizona, Arkansas, California, Colorado, Idaho, Illinois, Indiana, Iowa, Kansas, Kentucky, Maine, Massachusetts, Michigan, Minnesota, Missouri, Montana, Nebraska, Nevada, New Hampshire, New Jersey, New Mexico, North Dakota, New York, Ohio, Oklahoma, Oregon, Pennsylvania, Rhode Island, South Dakota, Tennessee, Texas, Utah, Washington, West Virginia, Wisconsin and Wyoming.

Amendment [XX] [1933]

Section 1. The terms of the President and Vice President shall end at noon on the 20th day of January, and the terms of Senators and Representatives at noon on the 3d day of January, of the years in which such terms would have ended if this article had not been ratified; and the terms of their successors shall then begin.

Section 2. The Congress shall assemble at least once in every year, and such meeting shall begin at noon on the 3d day of January, unless they shall by law appoint a different day.

Section 3. If, at the time fixed for the beginning of the term of the President, the President elect shall have died, the Vice President elect shall become President. If the President shall not have been chosen before the time fixed for the beginning of his term, or if the President elect shall have failed to qualify, then the Vice President elect shall act as President until a President shall have qualified; and the Congress may by law provide for the case wherein neither a President elect nor a Vice President elect shall have qualified, declaring who shall then act as President, or the manner in which one who is to act shall be selected, and such person shall act accordingly until a President or Vice President shall have qualified.

Section 4. The Congress may by law provide for the case of the death of any of the persons from whom the House of Representatives may choose a President whenever the right of choice shall have devolved upon them, and for the case of the death of any of the persons from whom the Senate may choose a Vice President whenever the right of choice shall have devolved upon them.

Section 5. Sections 1 and 2 shall take effect on the 15th day of October following the ratification of this article.

Section 6. This article shall be inoperative unless it shall have been ratified as an Amendment to the Constitution by the legislatures of three-fourths of the several States within seven years from the date of its submission.

Historical Note

This Amendment was proposed to the legislatures of the several states by the Seventy–Second Congress, on March 3, 1932, and was declared, in a proclamation by the Secretary of State, dated Feb. 6, 1933, to have been ratified by the legislatures of the states of Alabama, Arizona, Ar- kansas, California, Colorado, Connecticut, Delaware, Georgia, Idaho, Illinois, Indiana, Kansas, Kentucky, Louisiana, Maine, Massachusetts, Michigan, Minnesota, Mississippi, Missouri, Montana, Nebraska, New Jersey, New York, North Carolina, North Dakota, Ohio, Oklahoma, Pennsylvania, Rhode Island, South Carolina, South Dakota, Texas, Utah, Virginia, Washington, West Virginia, Wisconsin, and Wyoming.

Amendment [XXI] [1933]

Section 1. The eighteenth article of Amendment to the Constitution of the United States is hereby repealed.

Section 2. The transportation or importation into any State, Territory, or possession of the United States for delivery or use therein of intoxicating liquors, in violation of the laws thereof, is hereby prohibited.

Section 3. This article shall be inoperative unless it shall have been ratified as an Amendment to the Constitution by conventions in the several States, as provided in the Constitution, within seven years from the date of the submission hereof to the States by the Congress.

Historical Note

This Amendment was proposed to the several states by the Seventy–Second Congress, on Feb. 20, 1933, and was declared, in a proclamation by the Secretary of State, dated Dec. 5, 1933, to have been ratified by conventions in the States of Arizona, Alabama, Arkansas, California, Colorado, Connecticut, Delaware, Florida, Idaho, Illinois, Indiana, Iowa, Kentucky, Maryland, Massachusetts, Michigan, Minnesota, Missouri, Nevada, New Hampshire, New Jersey, New Mexico, New York, Ohio, Oregon, Pennsylvania, Rhode Island, Tennessee, Texas, Utah, Vermont, Virginia, Washington, West Virginia, Wisconsin and Wyoming.

Amendment [XXII] [1951]

Section 1. No person shall be elected to the office of the President more than twice, and no person who has held the office of President, or acted as President, for more than two years of a term to which some other person was elected President shall be elected to the office of President more than once. But this Article shall not apply to any person holding the office of President when this Article was proposed by the Congress, and shall not prevent any person who may be holding the office of President, or acting as President, during the term within which this Article becomes operative from holding the office of President or acting as President during the remainder of such term.

Section 2. This article shall be inoperative unless it shall have been ratified as an Amendment to the Constitution by the legislatures of three-fourths of the several States within seven years from the date of its submission to the States by the Congress.

Historical Note

Proposal and Ratification. This Amendment was proposed to the legislatures of the several States by the Eightieth Congress on Mar. 24, 1947 by House Joint Res. No. 27, and was declared by the Administrator of General Services on Mar. 1, 1951, to have been ratified. The legislatures ratified this Amendment on the following dates: Maine, Mar. 31, 1947; Michigan, Mar. 31, 1947; Iowa, Apr. 1, 1947; Kansas, Apr. 1, 1947; New Hampshire, Apr. 1, 1947; Delaware, Apr. 2, 1947; Illinois, Apr. 3, 1947; Oregon, Apr. 3, 1947; Colorado, Apr. 12, 1947; California, Apr. 15, 1947; New Jersey, Apr. 15, 1947; Vermont, Apr. 15, 1947; Ohio, Apr. 16, 1947; Wisconsin, Apr. 16, 1947; Pennsylvania, Apr. 29, 1947; Connecticut, May 21, 1947; Missouri, May 22, 1947; Nebraska, May 23, 1947; Virginia, Jan. 28, 1948; Mississippi, Feb. 12, 1948; New York, Mar. 9, 1948; South Dakota, Jan. 21, 1949; North Dakota, Feb. 25, 1949; Louisiana, May 17, 1950; Montana, Jan. 25, 1951; Indiana, Jan. 29, 1951; Idaho, Jan. 30, 1951; New Mexico, Feb. 12, 1951; Wyoming, Feb. 12, 1951; Arkansas, Feb. 15, 1951; Georgia, Feb. 17, 1951; Tennessee, Feb. 20, 1951; Texas, Feb. 22, 1951; Utah, Feb. 26, 1951; Nevada, Feb. 26, 1951; Minnesota, Feb. 27, 1951, and North Carolina, Feb. 28, 1951.

Subsequent to the proclamation, Amendment XXII was ratified by South Carolina on Mar. 13, 1951; Maryland, Mar. 14, 1951; Florida, Apr. 16, 1951, and Alabama, May 4, 1951.

Certification of Validity. Publication of the certifying statement of the Administrator of General Services that the Amendment had become valid was made on Mar. 1, 1951, F.R.Doc. 51–2940, 16 F.R. 2019.

Amendment [XXIII] [1961]

Section 1. The District constituting the seat of Government of the United States shall appoint in such manner as the Congress may direct:

A number of electors of President and Vice President equal to the whole number of Senators and Representatives in Congress to which the District would be entitled if it were a State, but in no event more than the least populous state; they shall be in addition to those appointed by the states, but they shall be considered, for the purposes of the election of President and Vice President, to be electors appointed by a state; and they shall meet in the District and perform such duties as provided by the twelfth article of Amendment.

Section 2. The Congress shall have power to enforce this article by appropriate legislation.

Historical Note

Proposal and Ratification. This Amendment was proposed by the Eighty-sixth Congress on June 16, 1960 and was declared by the Admin-

istrator of General Services on Apr. 3, 1961, to have been ratified.

The Amendment was ratified by the following States: Hawaii, June 23, 1960; Massachusetts, Aug. 22, 1960; New Jersey, Dec. 19, 1960; New York, Jan. 17, 1961; California, Jan. 19, 1961; Oregon, Jan. 27, 1961; Maryland, Jan. 30, 1961; Idaho, Jan. 31, 1961; Maine, Jan. 31, 1961; Minnesota, Jan. 31, 1961; New Mexico, Feb. 1, 1961; Nevada, Feb. 2, 1961; Montana, Feb. 6, 1961; Colorado, Feb. 8, 1961; Washington, Feb. 9, 1961; West Virginia, Feb. 9, 1961; Alaska, Feb. 10, 1961; Wyoming, Feb. 13, 1961; South Dakota, Feb. 14, 1961; Delaware, Feb. 20, 1961; Utah, Feb. 21, 1961; Wisconsin, Feb. 21, 1961; Pennsylvania, Feb. 28, 1961; Indiana, Mar. 3, 1961; North Dakota, Mar. 3, 1961; Tennessee, Mar. 6, 1961; Michigan, Mar. 8, 1961; Connecticut, Mar. 9, 1961; Arizona, Mar. 10, 1961; Illinois, Mar. 14, 1961; Nebraska, Mar. 15, 1961; Vermont, Mar. 15, 1961; Iowa, Mar. 16, 1961; Missouri, Mar. 20, 1961; Oklahoma, Mar. 21, 1961; Rhode Island, Mar. 22, 1961; Kansas, Mar. 29, 1961; Ohio, Mar. 29, 1961, and New Hampshire, Mar. 30, 1961.

Certification of Validity. Publication of the certifying statement of the Administrator of General Services that the Amendment had become valid was made on Apr. 3, 1961, F.R.Doc. 61–3017, 26 F.R. 2808.

Amendment [XXIV] [1964]

Section 1. The right of citizens of the United States to vote in any primary or other election for President or Vice President, for electors for President or Vice President, or for Senator or Representative in Congress, shall not be denied or abridged by the United States or any State by reason of failure to pay any poll tax or other tax.

Section 2. The Congress shall have power to enforce this article by appropriate legislation.

Historical Note

Proposal and Ratification. This Amendment was proposed by the Eighty-seventh Congress by Senate Joint Resolution No. 29, which was approved by the Senate on Mar. 27, 1962, and by the House of Representatives on Aug. 27, 1962. It was declared by the Administrator of General Services on Feb. 4, 1964, to have been ratified.

This Amendment was ratified by the following States: Illinois, Nov. 14, 1962; New Jersey, Dec. 3, 1962; Oregon, Jan. 25, 1963; Montana, Jan. 28, 1963; West Virginia, Feb. 1, 1963; New York, Feb. 4, 1963; Maryland, Feb. 6, 1963; California, Feb. 7, 1963; Alaska, Feb. 11, 1963; Rhode Island, Feb. 14, 1963; Indiana, Feb. 19, 1963; Utah, Feb. 20, 1963; Michigan, Feb. 20, 1963; Colorado, Feb. 21, 1963; Ohio, Feb. 27, 1963; Minnesota, Feb. 27, 1963; New Mexico, Mar. 5, 1963; Hawaii, Mar. 6, 1963; North Dakota, Mar. 7, 1963; Idaho, Mar. 8, 1963; Washington, Mar. 14, 1963; Vermont, Mar. 15, 1963; Nevada, Mar. 19, 1963; Connecticut, Mar. 20, 1963; Tennessee, Mar. 21, 1963; Pennsylvania, Mar. 25, 1963; Wisconsin, Mar. 26, 1963; Kansas, Mar. 28, 1963; Massachusetts, Mar. 28, 1963; Nebraska, Apr. 4, 1963; Florida, Apr. 18, 1963; Iowa, Apr. 24, 1963; Delaware, May 1, 1963; Missouri, May 13, 1963; New Hampshire, June 12, 1963; Kentucky, June 27, 1963; Maine, Jan. 16, 1964; South Dakota, Jan. 23, 1964.

Certification of Validity. Publication of the certifying statement of the Administrator of General Services that the Amendment had become valid was made on Feb. 5, 1964, F.R.Doc. 64–1229, 29 F.R. 1715. President Johnson and the Administrator signed this certificate on Feb. 4, 1964.

Amendment [XXV] [1967]

Section 1. In the case of the removal of the President from office or of his death or resignation, the Vice President shall become President.

Section 2. Whenever there is a vacancy in the office of the Vice President, the President shall nominate a Vice President who shall take office upon confirmation by a majority vote of both Houses of Congress.

Section 3. Whenever the President transmits to the President pro tempore of the Senate and the Speaker of the House of Representatives his written declaration that he is unable to discharge the powers and duties of his office, and until he transmits to them a written declaration to the contrary, such powers and duties shall be discharged by the Vice President as Acting President.

Section 4. Whenever the Vice President and a majority of either the principal officers of the executive departments or of such other body as Congress may by law provide, transmit to the President pro tempore of the Senate and the Speaker of the House of Representatives, their written declaration that the President is unable to discharge the powers and duties of his office, the Vice President shall immediately assume the powers and duties of the office as Acting President.

Thereafter, when the President transmits to the President pro tempore of the Senate and the Speaker of the House of Representatives his written declaration that no inability exists, he shall resume the powers and duties of his office unless the Vice President and a majority of either the principal officers of the executive department or of such other body as Congress may by law provide, transmit within four days to the President pro tempore of the Senate and the Speaker of the House of Representatives their written declaration and the President is unable to discharge the powers and duties of his office. Thereupon Congress shall decide the issue, assembling within forty-eight hours for that purpose if not in session. If the Congress, within twenty-one days after receipt of the latter written declaration, or, if Congress is not in session, within twenty-one days after Congress is required to assemble, determines by two-thirds vote of both Houses that the President is unable to discharge the powers and duties of his office, the Vice President shall continue to discharge the same as Acting President; otherwise, the President shall resume the powers and duties of his office.

Historical Note

Proposal and Ratification. This Amendment was proposed by the Eighty-ninth Congress by Senate Joint Resolution No. 1, which was approved by the Senate on Feb. 19, 1965, and by the House of Representatives, in amended form, on Apr. 13, 1965. The House of Representatives agreed to a Conference Report on June 30, 1965, and the Senate agreed to the Conference Report on July 6, 1965. It was declared by the Administrator of General Services, on Feb. 23, 1967, to have been ratified.

This Amendment was ratified by the following States: Nebraska, July 12, 1965; Wisconsin, July 13, 1965; Oklahoma, July 16, 1965; Massachusetts, Aug. 9, 1965; Pennsylvania, Aug. 18, 1965; Kentucky, Sept. 15, 1965; Arizona, Sept. 22, 1965; Michigan, Oct. 5, 1965; Indiana, Oct. 20, 1965; California, Oct. 21, 1965; Arkansas, Nov. 4, 1965; New Jersey, Nov. 29, 1965; Delaware, Dec. 7, 1965; Utah, Jan. 17, 1966; West Virginia, Jan. 20, 1966; Maine, Jan. 24, 1966; Rhode Island, Jan. 28, 1966; Colorado, Feb. 3, 1966; New Mexico, Feb. 3, 1966; Kansas, Feb. 8, 1966; Vermont, Feb. 10, 1966; Alaska, Feb. 18, 1966; Idaho, Mar. 2, 1966; Hawaii, Mar. 3, 1966; Virginia, Mar. 8, 1966; Mississippi, Mar. 10, 1966; New York, Mar. 14, 1966; Maryland, Mar. 23, 1966; Missouri, Mar. 30, 1966; New Hampshire, June 13, 1966; Louisiana, July 5, 1966; Tennessee, Jan. 12, 1967; Wyoming, Jan. 25, 1967; Washington, Jan. 26, 1967; Iowa, Jan. 26, 1967; Oregon, Feb. 2, 1967; Minnesota, Feb.

10, 1967; Nevada, Feb. 10, 1967; Connecticut, Feb. 14, 1967; Montana, Feb. 15, 1967; South Dakota, Mar. 6, 1967; Ohio, Mar. 7, 1967; Alabama, Mar. 14, 1967; North Carolina, Mar. 22, 1967; Illinois, Mar. 22, 1967; Texas, Apr. 25, 1967; Florida, May 25, 1967.

Certification of Validity. Publication of the certifying statement of the Administrator of General Services that the Amendment had become valid was made on Feb. 25, 1967, F.R.Doc. 67–2208, 32 F.R. 3287, and signed on July 23, 1967.

Amendment [XXVI] [1971]

Section 1. The right of citizens of the United States, who are eighteen years of age or older, to vote shall not be denied or abridged by the United States or by any State on account of age.

Section 2. The Congress shall have power to enforce this article by appropriate legislation.

Historical Note

Proposal and Ratification. This Amendment was proposed by the Ninety-second Congress by Senate Joint Resolution No. 7, which was approved by the Senate on Mar. 10, 1971, and by the House of Representatives on Mar. 23, 1971. It was declared by the Administrator of General Services on July 5, 1971, to have been ratified.

This Amendment was ratified by the following States: Connecticut, Mar. 23, 1971; Delaware, Mar. 23, 1971; Minnesota, Mar. 23, 1971; Tennessee, Mar. 23, 1971; Washington, Mar. 23, 1971; Hawaii, Mar. 24, 1971; Massachusetts, Mar. 24, 1971; Idaho, Mar. 30, 1971; Montana, Mar. 31, 1971; Arkansas, Apr. 1, 1971; Iowa, Apr. 1, 1971; Nebraska, Apr. 2, 1971; Kansas, Apr. 7, 1971; Michigan, Apr. 7, 1971; Indiana, Apr. 8, 1971; Maine,

Apr. 9, 1971; Vermont, Apr. 16, 1971; California, Apr. 19, 1971; South Carolina, Apr. 28, 1971; West Virginia, Apr. 28, 1971; Pennsylvania, May 3, 1971; New Jersey, May 4, 1971; Texas, May 5, 1971; Maryland, May 6, 1971; New Hampshire, May 13, 1971; Arizona, May 17, 1971; Colorado, May 24, 1971; Louisiana, May 27, 1971; Rhode Island, May 27, 1971; New York, June 2, 1971; Oregon, June 5, 1971; Missouri, June 14, 1971; Wisconsin, June 18, 1971; Illinois, June 29, 1971; Alabama, June 30, 1971; Ohio, June 30, 1971; North Carolina, July 1, 1971; Oklahoma, July 1, 1971.

Certification of Validity. Publication of the certifying statement of the Administrator of General Services that the Amendment had become valid was made on July 7, 1971, F.R.Doc. 71–9691, 36 F.R. 12725, and signed on July 5, 1971.

Amendment [XXVII] [1992]

No law, varying the compensation for the services of the Senators and Representatives, shall take effect, until an election of Representatives shall have intervened.

Historical Note

Proposal and Ratification. The Twenty-seventh Amendment was proposed on September 25, 1789. The State legislatures ratified this Amendment on the following dates: Maryland, North Carolina, South Carolina, Delaware, Vermont, Virginia, 1789–1791; Ohio, May 6, 1873; Wyoming, March 6, 1978; Maine, April 27, 1983; Colorado, April 22, 1984; South Dakota, February 1985; New Hampshire, March 7, 1985; Arizona, April 3, 1985; Tennessee, May 28, 1985; Oklahoma, July 10, 1985; New Mexico, February 14, 1986; Indiana, February 24, 1986; Utah, February 25, 1986; Arkansas, March 13, 1987; Montana, March 17, 1987; Connecticut, May 13, 1987; Wisconsin, July 15, 1987; Georgia, February 2, 1988; West Virginia, March 10, 1988; Louisiana, July 7, 1988; Iowa, February 9, 1989; Idaho, March 23, 1989; Nevada, April 26, 1989; Alaska, May 6, 1989; Oregon, May 19, 1989; Minnesota, May 22, 1989; Texas, May 25, 1989; Kansas, April 5, 1990; Florida, May 31, 1990; North Dakota, March 25, 1991; Alabama, May 5, 1992; Missouri, May 5, 1992; Michigan, May 7, 1992. The State of New Jersey later ratified this Amendment on May 7, 1992.

Certification of Validity. Publication of the certifying statement of the Archivist of the United States, pursuant to 1 U.S.C.A. § 106b, that the Amendment has become valid was made on May 19, 1992, F.R. Doc. 92–11951, 57 F.R. 21187.

*

Appendix B

RESEARCHING CONSTITUTIONAL LAW

Analysis

Section 1. Introduction

Constitutional Law provides a strong base for analyzing even the most complex problem involving constitutional law. Whether your research requires examination of case law, statutes, expert commentary, or other materials, West books and Westlaw are excellent sources of information.

To keep you informed of current developments, Westlaw provides frequently updated databases. With Westlaw, you have unparalleled legal research resources at your fingertips.

Additional Resources

If you have not previously used Westlaw or if you have questions not covered in this appendix, call the West Reference Attorneys at 1–800–REF–ATTY (1–

800–733–2889). The West Reference Attorneys are trained, licensed attorneys, available 24 hours a day to assist you with your Westlaw search questions. To subscribe to Westlaw, call 1–800–344–5008 or visit westlaw.com at **www.westlaw.com**.

Section 2. Westlaw Databases

Each database on Westlaw is assigned an abbreviation called an *identifier*, which you can use to access the database. You can find identifiers for Westlaw databases in the online Westlaw Directory and in the printed *Westlaw Database Directory*. When you need to know more detailed information about a database, use Scope. Scope contains coverage information, lists of related databases, and valuable search tips.

The following chart lists selected Westlaw databases that contain information pertaining to constitutional law. For a complete list of constitutional law databases, see the online Westlaw Directory or the printed *Westlaw Database Directory*. Because new information is continually being added to Westlaw, you should also check the tabbed Westlaw page and the online Westlaw Directory for new database information.

Selected Constitutional Law Databases on Westlaw

Database	Identifier	Coverage
Federal Case Law		
Federal Case Law	ALLFEDS	Begins with 1945
Federal Case Law–Before 1945	ALLFEDS–OLD	1789–1944
U.S. Supreme Court Cases	SCT	Begins with 1945
U.S. Supreme Court Cases–Before 1945	SCT–OLD	1790–1944
U.S. Courts of Appeals Cases	CTA	Begins with 1945
U.S. Courts of Appeals Cases–Before 1945	CTA–OLD	1891–1944
U.S. District Courts Cases	DCT	Begins with 1945
U.S. District Courts Cases–Before 1945	DCT–OLD	1789–1944
Death Penalty–Federal Cases	FDP–CS	Begins with 1789
Federal Civil Rights–Cases	FCIV–CS	Begins with 1789
Federal Civil Rights–Supreme Court Cases	FCIV–SCT	Begins with 1790
Federal Civil Rights–Courts of Appeals Cases	FCIV–CTA	Begins with 1891
Federal Civil Rights–District Courts Cases	FCIV–DCT	Begins with 1789
Federal Criminal Justice–Cases	FCJ–CS	Begins with 1789
Federal Criminal Justice–Supreme Court Cases	FCJ–SCT	Begins with 1790
Federal Criminal Justice–Courts of Appeals Cases	FCJ–CTA	Begins with 1891
Federal Criminal Justice–District Courts Cases	FCJ–DCT	Begins with 1789
Federal Criminal Justice–Briefs	FCJ–BRIEF	Begins with 1870
Federal First Amendment–Cases	FCFA–CS	Begins with 1789

Database	Identifier	Coverage
Federal First Amendment–Supreme Court Cases	FCFA–SCT	Begins with 1790
Federal First Amendment–Courts of Appeals Cases	FCFA–CTA	Begins with 1891
Federal First Amendment–District Courts Cases	FCFA–DCT	Begins with 1789
Transcripts of U.S. Supreme Court Oral Arguments	SCT–ORALARG	Begins with 1990–91 Term
U.S. Supreme Court Briefs	SCT–BRIEF	Merits briefs: begins with 1990–91 Term; amicus briefs: begins with 1995–96 Term
United States Supreme Court Briefs Extension (1976–1990)	SCT–BRIEF–EXT	1976–1990; selected coverage 1870–1975
United States Supreme Court Briefs Multibase	SCT–BRIEF–ALL	Begins with 1870
Doe v. Bush Trial Transcripts and Documents	DOEVBUSH	Begins with February 2003
U.S. Supreme Court Justice Materials		
Retired Supreme Court Justice Harry Blackmun Opinions and Papers	BLACKMUN	Legal career
Supreme Court Justice Anthony Kennedy Opinions and Papers	KENNEDY	Legal career
Supreme Court Justice Antonin Scalia Opinions and Papers	SCALIA	Legal career
Supreme Court Justice Clarence Thomas Opinions and Papers	THOMAS	Legal career
Supreme Court Justice David Souter Opinions and Papers	SOUTER	Legal career
Supreme Court Justice John Paul Stevens Opinions and Papers	STEVENS	Legal career
Supreme Court Justice Ruth Bader Ginsburg Opinions and Papers	GINSBURG	Legal career
Supreme Court Justice Sandra Day O'Connor Opinions and Papers	OCONNOR	Legal career
Supreme Court Justice Stephen Breyer Opinions and Papers	BREYER	Legal career
Supreme Court Justice William Rehnquist Opinions and Papers	REHNQUIST	Legal career
Federal Statutes and Regulations		
United States Code Annotated®	USCA	Current data
United States Public Laws	US–PL	Current data
Code of Federal Regulations	CFR	Current data
Federal Register	FR	Begins with July 1980
Death Penalty–Federal Statutes	FDP–USCA	Current data
Federal Civil Rights–U.S. Code Annotated	FCIV–USCA	Current data
Federal Civil Rights–Code of Federal Regulations	FCIV–CFR	Current data
Federal Civil Rights–Federal Register	FCIV–FR	Begins with July 1980
Federal Criminal Justice–U.S. Code Annotated	FCJ–USCA	Current data

Database	Identifier	Coverage
Federal Criminal Justice–Code of Federal Regulations	FCJ–CFR	Current data
Federal Criminal Justice–Federal Register	FCJ–FR	Begins with July 1980
Legislative History–U.S. Code, 1948 to Present	LH	Begins with 1948
Legislative History–1776	LH–1776	Begins with 1774
Federal Rules and Orders		
Federal Rules	US–RULES	Current data
Federal Orders	US–ORDERS	Current data
Federal Rules Decisions Rules	FRD–RULES	Begins with 1938
Federal Rules of Practice and Procedure Advisory Committee Minutes	US–RULESCOMM	Varies by committee
Federal Criminal Justice–Rules	FCJ–RULES	Current data
Journals and Law Reviews		
Jurisprudence and Constitutional Theory–Law Reviews, Texts, and Bar Journals	JCT–TP	Varies by publication
Civil Rights–Law Reviews, Texts, and Bar Journals	CIV–TP	Varies by publication
Death Penalty–Texts and Periodicals	DP–TP	Varies by publication
First Amendment–Law Reviews, Texts, and Bar Journals	CFA–TP	Varies by publication
American University Journal of Gender, Social Policy, and the Law	AMUJGSPL	Full coverage begins with 1993 (vol. 1)
Buffalo Human Rights Law Review	BFHRLR	Full coverage begins with 1994 (vol. 1)
Chicano–Latino Law Review	CHLLR	Selected coverage begins with 1990 (vol. 10); full coverage begins with 1993 (vol. 13)
Columbia Human Rights Law Review	CLMHRLR	Selected coverage begins with 1984 (vol. 15); full coverage begins with 1993 (vol. 25)
Columbia Journal of Gender and Law	CLMJGL	Selected coverage begins with 1991 (vol. 1); full coverage begins with 1993 (vol. 3, no. 2)
Constitutional Commentary	CONSTCOM	Selected coverage begins with 1985 (vol. 2); full coverage begins with 1993 (vol. 10, no. 2)
Duke Journal of Gender Law and Policy	DUKEJGLP	Full coverage begins with 1994 (vol. 1)
Emerging Issues in State Constitutional Law	EISCL	Selected coverage is from 1988 (vol. 1)–1991 (vol. 4)
Federal Lawyer	FEDRLAW	Selected coverage begins with 1983 (vol. 30)
George Mason University Civil Rights Law Journal	GMUCRLJ	Selected coverage begins with 1990 (vol. 1); full coverage begins with 1993 (vol. 4)
Harvard Civil Rights–Civil Liberties Law Review	HVCRCLLR	Full coverage begins with 1981 (vol. 16)

Database	Identifier	Coverage
Hastings Constitutional Law Quarterly	HSTCLQ	Selected coverage begins with 1983 (vol. 10); full coverage begins with 1993 (vol. 20, no. 3)
National Journal of Constitutional Law	NJCL	Full coverage begins with 1998 (vol. 9)
Seton Hall Constitutional Law Journal	SHCLJ	Selected coverage begins with 1990 (vol. 1); full coverage begins with 1992 (vol. 2, no. 2)
Temple Political and Civil Rights Law Review	TMPPCRLR	Selected coverage begins with 1992 (vol. 1); full coverage begins with 1993 (vol. 2, no. 2)
Texas Journal on Civil Liberties and Civil Rights	TXJCLCR	Full coverage begins with 1996 (vol. 2)
University of Pennsylvania Journal of Constitutional Law	UPAJCL	Full coverage begins with 1998 (vol. 1)
Legal Texts and Practice Materials		
Jurisprudence and Constitutional Theory–Law Reviews, Texts, and Bar Journals	JCT–TP	Varies by publication
Civil Rights–Law Reviews, Texts, and Bar Journals	CIV–TP	Varies by publication
Death Penalty–Texts and Periodicals	DP–TP	Varies by publication
First Amendment–Law Reviews, Texts, and Bar Journals	CFA–TP	Varies by publication
Criminal Procedure Checklists, Fifth Amendment and Sixth Amendment	CPLIST	Current data
Federal Habeas Practitioner Guide	FEDHABPRAC	Current data
Police Misconduct: Law and Litigation	POLICEMISC	2003 edition
Search and Seizure Checklists	SSLIST	Current data
Search Warrant Law Deskbook	SRCHWARLAW	Current data
Searches and Seizures, Arrests and Confessions 2d	SSAC	Current data
Smolla and Nimmer on Freedom of Speech	FREESPEECH	Current data
Treatise on Constitutional Law: Substance and Procedure	CONLAW	Third edition
Legal Newsletters, Current Awareness Materials, and Directories		
Almanac of the Federal Judiciary	AFJ	Current through 2002
BNA's United States Law Week (USLW)	BNA–USLW	Begins with January 1986
BNA's U.S. Law Week–Supreme Court Reports	BNA–USLWSCT	*U.S. Law Week–Supreme Court Today*: begins with September 2003; *U.S. Law Week Daily Edition*: March 1987–September 2003
Discrimination Law Update	DISCRIMLU	Begins with January 1997
NAAG State Constitutional Law Bulletin	NAAGSCLB	Begins with January 1995
United States Supreme Court Actions	USSCACT	Begins with April 2003

Database	Identifier	Coverage
Westlaw Bulletin–U.S. Supreme Court	WLB–SCT	Current data
West Legal Directory®–Civil Rights	WLD–CIV	Current data
West Legal Directory–Constitutional Law	WLD–CON	Current data
West Legal Directory–Judges	WLD–JUDGE	Current data

Section 3.   Retrieving a Document with a Citation: Find and Hypertext Links

3.1   Find

Find is a Westlaw service that allows you to retrieve a document by entering its citation. Find allows you to retrieve documents from any page in westlaw.com without accessing or changing databases. Find is available for many documents, including case law (state and federal), the *United States Code Annotated*, state statutes, administrative materials, and texts and periodicals.

To use Find, simply type the citation in the *Find this document by citation* text box at the tabbed Westlaw page and click **GO**. The following list provides some examples:

To retrieve this document:	Access Find and type:
Atkins v. Virginia 122 S. Ct. 2242 (2002)	**122 sct 2242**
Graves v. Barnes 343 F. Supp. 704 (W.D. Tex. 1972)	**343 fsupp 704**
42 U.S.C.A. § 1971	**42 usca 1971**

For a complete list of publications that can be retrieved with Find and their abbreviations, click **Find** on the toolbar and then click **Publications List**.

3.2   Hypertext Links

Use hypertext links to move from one location to another on Westlaw. For example, use hypertext links to go directly from the statute, case, or law review article you are viewing to a cited statute, case, or article; from a headnote to the corresponding text in the opinion; or from an entry in a statutes index to the full text of the statute.

Section 4. Searching with Natural Language

Overview: With Natural Language, you can retrieve documents by simply describing your issue in plain English. If you are a relatively new Westlaw user, Natural Language searching can make it easier for you to retrieve cases that are on point. If you are an experienced Westlaw user, Natural Language gives you a valuable alternative search method to the Terms and Connectors search method described in Section 5.

When you enter a Natural Language description, Westlaw automatically identifies legal phrases, removes common words, and generates variations of terms in your description. Westlaw then searches for the concepts in your description. Concepts may include significant terms, phrases, legal citations, or topic and key numbers. Westlaw retrieves the documents that most closely match the concepts in your description, beginning with the document most likely to match.

4.1 Natural Language Search

Access a database, such as the Federal First Amendment–Cases database (FCFA–CS). Click **Natural Language** and type the following description in the text box:

constitutionality of pledge of allegiance

4.2 Browsing Search Results

Citations List: The citations list lists the documents retrieved by the search. Click a document's title to display the full text of the document in the right frame.

Best Mode: To display the best portion (the portion that most closely matches your description) of each document in a Natural Language search result, click the **Best** arrows at the bottom of the right frame.

Term Mode: Click the **Term** arrows at the bottom of the right frame to display portions of the document that contain your search terms.

Previous/Next Document: Click the left or right **Doc** arrow at the bottom of the right frame to view the previous or next document in the search result.

4.3 Next 20 Documents

Westlaw displays the 20 documents that most closely match the concepts in your Natural Language description, beginning with the document most likely to match. If you want to view an additional 20 documents, click the right arrow at the bottom of the Result List tab in the left frame.

Section 5.   Searching with Terms and Connectors

Overview: With Terms and Connectors searching, you enter a query consisting of key terms from your issue and connectors specifying the relationship between these terms.

Terms and Connectors searching is useful when you want to retrieve a document for which you know specific details, such as the title or the fact situation. Terms and Connectors searching is also useful when you want to retrieve all documents containing specific terms.

5.1 Terms

Plurals and Possessives: Plurals are automatically retrieved when you enter the singular form of a term. This is true for both regular and irregular plurals (e.g., **child** retrieves *children*). If you enter the plural form of a term, you will not retrieve the singular form.

If you enter the nonpossessive form of a term, Westlaw automatically retrieves the possessive form as well. However, if you enter the possessive form, only the possessive form is retrieved.

Compound Words and Abbreviations: When a compound word is one of your search terms, use a hyphen to retrieve all forms of the word. For example, the term **non-hearsay** retrieves *non-hearsay, nonhearsay,* and *non hearsay.*

When using an abbreviation as a search term, place a period after each of the letters to retrieve any of its forms. For example, the term **a.c.l.u.** retrieves *ACLU, A.C.L.U., A C L U,* and, *A. C. L. U.* The abbreviation does not retrieve the phrase *American Civil Liberties Union,* so remember to add additional alternative terms such as **"american civil liberties union"** to your query.

The Root Expander and the Universal Character: When you use the Terms and Connectors search method, placing the root expander (!) at the end of a root term generates all other terms with that root. For example, adding the ! to the root *discriminat* in the query

discriminat! /s race

instructs Westlaw to retrieve such terms as *discriminate, discriminated, discriminating,* and *discrimination.*

The universal character (*) stands for one character and can be inserted in the middle or at the end of a term. For example, the term

withdr*w

will retrieve *withdraw* and *withdrew.* Adding three asterisks to the root *elect*

elect* * *

instructs Westlaw to retrieve all forms of the root with up to three additional characters. Terms such as *elected* or *election* are retrieved by this query. However, terms with more than three letters following the root, such as *electronic,* are not retrieved. Plurals are always retrieved, even if the plural form of the term has more than three letters following the root.

Phrase Searching: To search for an exact phrase, place it within quotation marks. For example, to search for references to *equal protection,* type **"equal protection"**. When you are using the Terms and Connectors search method, you should use phrase searching only if you are certain that the terms in the phrase will not appear in any other order.

5.2 Alternative Terms

After selecting the terms for your query, consider which alternative terms are necessary. For example, if you are searching for the term *constitutional,* you might also want to search for the term *unconstitutional.* You should consider both synonyms and antonyms as alternative terms. You can also use the Westlaw thesaurus to add alternative terms to your query.

5.3 Connectors

After selecting terms and alternative terms for your query, use connectors to specify the relationship that must exist between search terms in your retrieved documents. The connectors are described below:

Type:	To retrieve documents with:	Example:
& (and)	both search terms	**"first amendment" & terrorism**
or (space)	either search term or both search terms	**constitutional unconstitutional**

Type:	To retrieve documents with:	Example:
/p	search terms in the same paragraph	**execut! /p retarded**
/s	search terms in the same sentence	**right /s counsel**
+s	the first search term preceding the second within the same sentence	**burden +s prov! proof**
/n	search terms within *n* terms of each other (where *n* is a number)	**same-sex! /5 marriage**
+n	the first search term preceding the second by *n* terms (where *n* is a number)	**free! +3 speech**
" "	search terms appearing in the same order as in the quotation marks	**"commerce clause"**

Type:	To exclude documents with:	Example:
% (but not)	search terms following the % symbol	**due /p process % criminal**

5.4 Field Restrictions

Overview: Documents in each Westlaw database consist of several segments, or *fields*. One field may contain the citation, another the title, another the synopsis, and so forth. Not all databases contain the same fields. Also depending on the database, fields with the same name may contain different types of information.

To view a list of fields and their contents for a specific database, see Scope for that database. Note that in some databases not every field is available for every document.

To retrieve only those documents containing your search terms in a specific field, restrict your search to that field. To restrict your search to a specific field, type the field name or abbreviation followed by your search terms enclosed in parentheses. For example, to retrieve the U.S. Supreme Court case titled *New York Times v. Sullivan,* access the U.S. Supreme Court Cases database (SCT) and search for your terms in the title field (ti):

ti("new york times" & sullivan)

The fields discussed below are available in Westlaw case law databases you might use for researching issues related to constitutional law.

Digest and Synopsis Fields: The digest (di) and synopsis (sy) fields summarize the main points of a case. The synopsis field contains a brief description of a case. The digest field contains the topic and headnote fields and includes the complete hierarchy of concepts used by West editors to classify the headnotes to specific West digest topic and key numbers. Restricting your search to the synopsis and digest fields limits your result to cases in which your terms are related to a major issue in the case.

Consider restricting your search to one or both of these fields if

- you are searching for common terms or terms with more than one meaning, and you need to narrow your search; or

- you cannot narrow your search by using a smaller database.

For example, to retrieve federal cases that discuss Internet access in libraries, access the Federal First Amendment–Cases database (FCFA–CS) and type the following query:

sy,di(internet /p library)

Headnote Field: The headnote field (he) is part of the digest field but does not contain topic numbers, hierarchical classification information, or key numbers. The headnote field contains a one-sentence summary for each point of law in a case and any supporting citations given by the author of the opinion. A headnote field restriction is useful when you are searching for specific statutory sections or rule numbers. For example, to retrieve headnotes from federal district court civil rights cases that cite 42 U.S.C.A. § 1981, access the Federal Civil Rights–U.S. District Courts Cases database (FCIV–DCT) and type the following query:

he(42 +5 1981)

Topic Field: The topic field (to) is also part of the digest field. It contains hierarchical classification information, including the West digest topic names and numbers and the key numbers. You should restrict your search to the topic field in a case law database if

- a digest field search retrieves too many documents; or

- you want to retrieve cases with digest paragraphs classified under more than one topic.

For example, the topic Constitutional Law has the topic number 92. To retrieve U.S. Supreme Court cases that discuss ex post facto laws, access the U.S. Supreme Court Cases database (SCT) and type a query like the following:

to(92) /p "ex post facto"

To retrieve cases classified under more than one topic and key number, search for your terms in the topic field. For example, to retrieve recent federal cases discussing peremptory challenges in jury selection, which may contain headnotes classified to either Constitutional Law (92) or Jury (230), access the Federal Case Law database (ALLFEDS) and type a query like the following:

to(peremptory /s challenge /s jury) & da(aft 2002)

For a complete list of West digest topics and their corresponding topic numbers, access the Custom Digest by choosing **Key Numbers and Digest** from the *More* drop-down list on the toolbar.

> *Note*: Slip opinions and cases from topical services do not contain the West digest, headnote, and topic fields.

Prelim and Caption Fields: When searching in a database containing statutes, rules, or regulations, restrict your search to the prelim (pr) and caption (ca) fields to retrieve documents in which your terms are important enough to appear in a section name or heading. For example, to retrieve federal statutes regarding counsel in capital case, access the Federal Criminal Justice–U.S. Code Annotated database (FCJ–USCA) and type the following:

pr,ca(counsel /s capital)

5.5 Date Restrictions

You can use Westlaw to retrieve documents *decided* or *issued* before, after, or on a specified date, as well as within a range of dates. The following sample queries contain date restrictions:

da(2003) & sy,di("equal protection")

da(aft 1998) & sy,di("equal protection")

da(12/20/1995) & sy,di("equal protection")

You can also search for documents *added to a database* on or after a specified date, as well as within a range of dates, which is useful for updating your research. The following sample queries contain added-date restrictions:

ad(aft 1999) & sy,di("equal protection")

ad(aft 11/9/2001 & bef 6/23/2002) & sy,di("equal protection")

Section 6. Searching with Topic and Key Numbers

To retrieve cases that address a specific point of law, use topic and key numbers as your search terms. If you have an on-point case, run a search using the topic and key number from the relevant headnote in an appropriate database to find other cases containing headnotes classified to that topic and key number. For example, to search for federal courts of appeals cases containing headnotes classified under topic 78 (Civil Rights) and key number 1054 (Public Facilities), access the Federal Civil Rights–Courts of Appeals Cases database (FCIV–CTA) and enter the following query:

78k1054

For a complete list of West digest topics and their corresponding topic numbers, access the Custom Digest by choosing **Key Numbers and Digest** from the *More* drop-down list on the toolbar.

> *Note*: Slip opinions and cases from topical services do not contain West topic and key numbers.

6.1 Custom Digest

The Custom Digest contains the complete topic and key number outline used by West editors to classify headnotes. You can use the Custom Digest to obtain a single document containing all case law headnotes from a specific jurisdiction that are classified under a particular topic and key number.

Access the Custom Digest by choosing **Key Numbers and Digest** from the *More* drop-down list on the toolbar. Select up to 10 topics and key numbers from the easy-to-browse outline and click **Search**. Then follow the displayed instructions.

For example, to research issues involving constitutional law, scroll down the Custom Digest page until topic 92, *Constitutional Law*, is displayed. Click the plus symbols (+) to display key number information. Select the check box next to each key number you want to include in your search, then click **Search**. Select the jurisdiction from which you want to retrieve headnotes and, if desired, type additional search terms and select a date restriction. Click the **Search** button.

6.2 KeySearch

KeySearch is a research tool that helps you find cases and secondary sources in a specific area of the law. KeySearch guides you through the selection of terms from a classification system based on the West Key Number System® and then uses the key numbers and their underlying concepts to automatically formulate a query for you.

To access KeySearch, click **KeySearch** on the toolbar. Then browse the list of topics and subtopics and select a topic or subtopic to search by clicking the hypertext links. For example, to search for sources that discuss equal protection in the context of racial discrimination, click **Equal Protection** below *Constitutional Law* at the first KeySearch page. Then click **Racial Discrimination** on the next page. Select the source from which you want to retrieve documents and, if desired, type additional search terms. Click **Search**.

Section 7. Verifying Your Research with Citation Research Services

Overview: A citation research service, such as KeyCite, is a tool that helps you ensure that your cases, statutes, regulations, and administrative decisions are good law; helps you retrieve cases, legislation, articles, or other documents that cite them; and helps you verify the spelling and format of your citations.

7.1 KeyCite for Cases

KeyCite for cases covers case law on Westlaw, including unpublished opinions. KeyCite for cases provides the following:

- direct appellate history of a case, including related references, which are opinions involving the same parties and facts but resolving different issues

- negative indirect history of a case, which consists of cases outside the direct appellate line that may have a negative impact on its precedential value

- the title, parallel citations, court of decision, docket number, and filing date of a case

- citations to cases, administrative materials, secondary sources, and briefs on Westlaw that have cited a case

- complete integration with the West Key Number System so you can track legal issues discussed in a case

7.2 KeyCite for Statutes and Regulations

KeyCite for statutes and regulations covers the *United States Code Annotated* (USCA®), the *Code of Federal Regulations* (CFR), statutes from all

50 states, and regulations from selected states. KeyCite for statutes and regulations provides the following:

- links to session laws or rules amending or repealing a statute or regulation

- statutory credits and historical notes

- citations to pending legislation affecting a federal statute or a statute from selected states

- citations to cases, administrative materials, secondary sources, and briefs that have cited a statute or regulation

7.3 KeyCite for Administrative Decisions

KeyCite for administrative decisions includes the following:

- National Labor Relations Board decisions beginning with 1935

- Board of Contract Appeals decisions (varies by agency)

- Board of Immigration Appeals decisions beginning with 1940

- Comptroller General decisions beginning with 1921

- Environmental Protection Agency decisions beginning with 1974

- Federal Communications Commission decisions beginning with 1960

- Federal Energy Regulatory Commission (Federal Power Commission) decisions beginning with 1931

- Internal Revenue Service revenue rulings beginning with 1954

- Internal Revenue Service revenue procedures beginning with 1954

- Internal Revenue Service private letter rulings beginning with 1954

- Internal Revenue Service technical advice memoranda beginning with 1954

- Decisions from *Public Utilities Reports* beginning with 1974

- U.S. Merit Systems Protection Board decisions beginning with 1979

- U.S. Patent and Trademark Office decisions beginning with 1987

- U.S. Tax Court (Board of Tax Appeals) decisions beginning with 1924

- U.S. patents beginning with 1976

7.4 KeyCite Alert

KeyCite Alert monitors the status of your cases, statutes, regulations, and administrative decisions and automatically sends you updates at the frequency you specify when their KeyCite information changes. To access KeyCite Alert, choose **KeyCite Alert** from the *More* drop-down list on the toolbar.

Section 8. Researching with Westlaw: Examples

8.1 Retrieving Law Review Articles

Law review articles are often a good place to begin researching a legal issue. Law review articles serve as an excellent introduction to a new topic or review for an old one, providing terminology to help you formulate a query; as a finding tool for pertinent primary authority, such as rules, statutes, and cases; and in some instances, as persuasive secondary authority.

Suppose you need to gain background information on freedom of speech in public schools.

Solution

- To retrieve law review articles relevant to your issue, access the First Amendment–Law Reviews, Texts, and Bar Journals database (CFA–TP). Using the Natural Language search method, enter a description like the following:

freedom of speech in public schools

- If you have a citation to an article in a specific publication, use Find to retrieve it. For more information on Find, see Section 3.1 of this appendix. For example, to retrieve the article found at 21 Capital University Law Review 1183, access Find and type the following:

21 cap u l rev 1183

If you know the title of an article but not the journal in which it was published, access CFA–TP and search for key terms in the title field. For example, to retrieve the article "Protecting the Freedom of Speech Rights of Students: The Special Status of the High School Library," type the following Terms and Connectors query:

ti(protecting & status & library)

8.2   Retrieving Cases

Suppose you need to retrieve recent federal case law discussing the three prongs of the Lemon test, which is used to determine whether a government action violates the Establishment Clause.

Solution

- Access the Federal Case Law database (ALLFEDS). Type a Terms and Connectors query such as the following:

three /3 prong! /s lemon & da(aft 2001)

- When you know the citation for a specific case, use Find to retrieve it. For more information on Find, see Section 3.1 of this appendix. For example, to retrieve *Newdow v. U.S. Congress*, 292 F.3d 597 (9th Cir. 2002), access Find and type the following:

292 f3d 597

- If you find a topic and key number that is on point, run a search using that topic and key number to retrieve additional cases discussing that point of law. For example, to retrieve cases from other federal jurisdictions containing headnotes classified under topic 92 (Constitutional Law) and key number 42.1(4) (Education), access ALLFEDS and type the following query:

92k42.1(4)

- To retrieve cases written by a particular judge, add a judge field (ju) restriction to your query. For example, to retrieve opinions written by Judge Wilkinson of the U.S. Court of Appeals for the Fourth Circuit that contain headnotes classified under topic 92 (Constitutional Law), access the U.S. Courts of Appeals Cases database (CTA) and type the following query:

ju(wilkinson) & to(92)

- You can also use KeySearch and the Custom Digest to retrieve cases and headnotes that discuss the issue you are researching.

8.3 Retrieving Statutes and Regulations

Suppose you need to retrieve federal statutes dealing with the proper display of the U.S. flag.

Solution

- Access the United States Code Annotated database (USCA). Search for your terms in the prelim and caption fields using the Terms and Connectors search method:

pr,ca(display! use respect! /s flag)

- When you know the citation for a specific statute or regulation, use Find to retrieve it. For example, to retrieve 4 U.S.C.A. § 8, access Find and type the following:

4 usca 8

- To look at surrounding sections, use the Table of Contents service. Click **Table of Contents** on the Links tab in the left frame. To display a section listed in the Table of Contents, click its hypertext link. You can also use Documents in Sequence to retrieve the section following 4 U.S.C.A. § 8 even if that subsequent section was not retrieved with your search or Find request. Choose **Documents in Sequence** from the *Tools* menu at the bottom of the right frame.

8.4 Using KeyCite

Suppose one of the cases you retrieve in your case law research is *Hamdi v. Rumsfeld*, 296 F.3d 278 (4th Cir. 2002). You want to determine whether this case is good law and to find other cases or sources that have cited this case.

Solution

- Use KeyCite to retrieve direct and negative indirect history for *Hamdi v. Rumsfeld*. Access KeyCite and type **296 f3d 278**.

- Use KeyCite to display citing references for *Hamdi v. Rumsfeld*. Click **Citing References** on the Links tab in the left frame.

*

Table of Cases

A

C

D

F

I

L

N

P

T

V

*

Index

References are to Sections

A

C

†